Dear Customer,

To assist the tourist, the traveler, or those motoring for business or commerce, we are pleased to present the **First Edition of the Pacific Northwest Road Atlas & Driver's Guide**.

Its original geographic coverage of Oregon, Washington, and British Columbia, links a historical travel route between the west coast of California and Canada with coverage spanning over 200,000 square miles.

In addition to large scale maps and colorful graphics, it uniquely includes detailed street map coverage of urban centers along the way, to ease traveling from major freeways and highways into cities in which one wishes to enter.

It bears a natural linkage with our famous **California Road Atlas**, used by millions, that originated the concept of connecting major freeways and highways with urban centers containing detailed street information.

The street detail is taken from our famous **Thomas Guides** of the urban centers in Oregon and Seattle, which are available on CD-ROM and GeoFinder software, and can be viewed on your PC, and include special demographic features.

We extend you our best wishes for pleasure and enjoyment in the use of this new publication.

Sincerely,

Warren Wilson
Chief Executive Officer

Thomas Bros. Maps®
MAP PUBLISHERS SINCE 1915

17731 COWAN, IRVINE, CALIFORNIA 92614 (949) 863-1984 FAX: (949) 757-1564

The Thomas Guide®

PACIFIC NORTHWEST

ROAD ATLAS & DRIVER'S GUIDE

Table of Contents

Section	Contents	Pages	Tab
Introduction	How To Use This Road Atlas & Driver's Guide	B-C	INTRO
	Key Map & City Listings	D-E	
	Legend of Map Symbols	F	
	Cities & Communities Index	G-M	
	General Information	N	
	Distance Map & Mileage Chart	P-Q	
Highway Maps		92-155	HWY
Metro Maps		156-253	METRO
Detail Maps		254-355	DETAIL
Indexes	National & State Parks Information	356-357	INDEX
	List of Abbreviations	358	
	Street Index	359-420	
	Points of Interest Index	421-455	

Thomas Bros. Maps®
SINCE 1915
Call Toll Free:
1-800-899-MAPS
1-800-899-6277

Corporate Office & Showroom
17731 Cowan, Irvine, CA 92614 (949) 863-1984 or 1-888-826-6277

Thomas Bros. Maps® & Books
521 W. 6th St., Los Angeles, CA 90014 (213) 627-4018 or 1-888-277-6277
550 Jackson St., San Francisco, CA 94133 (415) 981-7520 or 1-800-969-3072
Customer Service: 1-800-899-6277
www.thomas.com
e-mail: comments@thomas.com

How To Use this Road Atlas & Driver's Guide

To Find a City or Community:

If you know the general area in which the city or community is located, start with the ***Key Map*** on page "D", then turn to the ***Highway Map*** indicated.

You can also look up major cities in the ***City Listings*** on page "E".

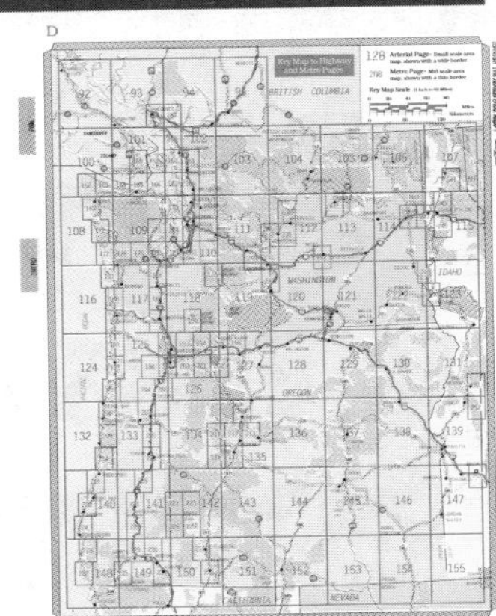

— OR —

Look up the city or community name in the ***Cities and Communities Index*** on pages "G - M". Turn to the page number indicated.

Community	STATE	PAGE	GRID
❖ BEAVERTON	OR	199	B2
❖ BELLEVUE	WA	175	C2
❖ BONNEY LAKE	WA	182	C4
Cabell City	OR	129	C3
❖ CAMAS	WA	193	B7
Cornelius Pass	OR	192	A6
❖ EVERETT	WA	267	G3
❖ GIG HARBOR	WA	181	C1
❖ GRESHAM	OR	200	B1
❖ HOOD RIVER	OR	195	D5
❖ ISLAND CITY	OR	130	A2
Kenton	OR	308	D4
Kingston	WA	170	D5
❖ KOOTENAI	ID	244	A1
❖ MERIDIAN	ID	253	A3
Murphy	ID	147	C2
❖ PORTLAND	OR	316	C3
❖ SEATAC	WA	288	C3
❖ SEATTLE	WA	273	G3
Starlake	WA	175	B7
❖ TACOMA	WA	292	D5
❖ TROY	ID	123	A1
❖ WALLA WALLA	WA	344	E6

Map Pages and Indexes

This Road Atlas & Driver's Guide is divided into three types of map pages: Highway, Metro, and Detail. The Highway map pages cover the entire Pacific Northwest area in this guide. These map pages can be used for trip planning. Highway Map pages can be found on pages 92-155 in this guide.

The Metro Map pages cover major cities and points of interest areas with more map detail. The Metro Map pages provide greater detail and many points of interest within the area shown. Metro Maps pages can be found on pages 156-253.

The Detail Map pages provide full street detail and points of interest in areas covered. Detail Maps can be found on pages 254-355. Some Detail Map pages have two sets of page numbers. The large number represents the page number in this Road Atlas. The smaller number labeled with a "TBM" (Thomas Bros. Maps) corresponds to a map page in a full county Thomas Guide.

You will find major streets and points of interest in the single Street and Points of Interest indexes in the back of this guide. The Street Index can be found on pages 359-420 and the Points of Interest Index can be found on pages 421-455.

For full street detail beyond the areas shown in this Road Atlas & Driver's Guide, Thomas Bros. Maps publishes County Street Guides of the major counties in Oregon and Washington. See the Product List printed on the inside of the back cover for details.

To Find a Location:

① 

Look up the street name in the ***Street Index***. If there are multiple listings, choose the proper city.

Also, major points of interest can be located by category and are listed alphabetically in the ***Points of Interest Index*** in the back of this guide.

② 

The index entry will include a ***Thomas Bros. Maps® Page and Grid*** where the street or point of interest is located.

③ 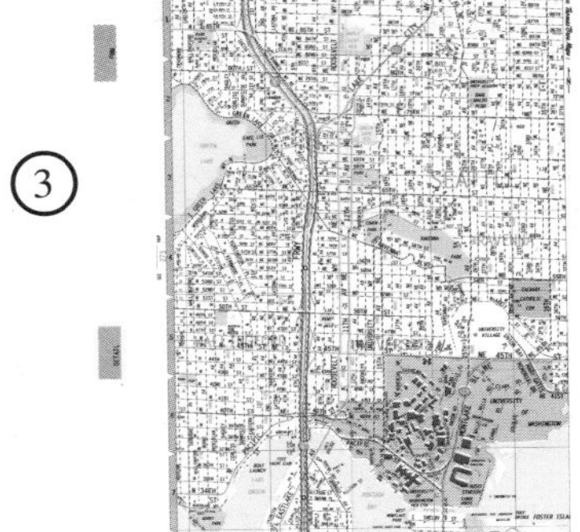

Turn to the page indicated.

④ 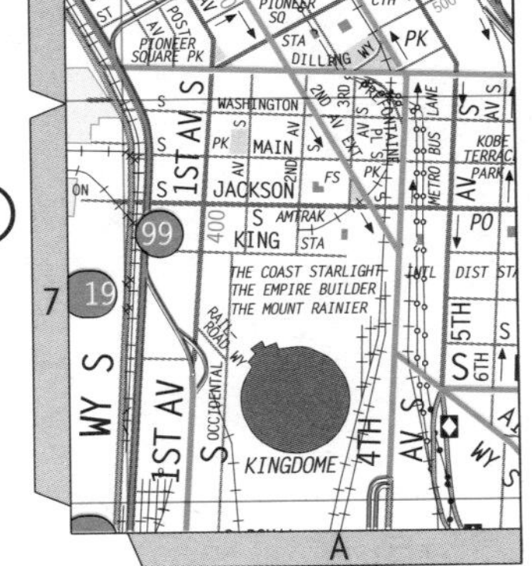

Locate the street or point of interest by following the indicated ***Letter Column and Number Row*** until the two intersect. The street name or point of interest is in this grid.

We Welcome Your Suggestions

Thomas Bros. Maps is proud to provide you with superior mapping products to meet your special needs.

Since 1915, Thomas Bros. Maps has been publishing mapping products, and is recognized as an industry leader. We believe that our best products and enhancements come from your suggestions. We also appreciate your corrections to the map or index. We welcome your suggestions and look forward to providing you with many fine mapping products in the future.

How to Use the Map Pages

Key to Map Pages: 1 inch = 62 Miles

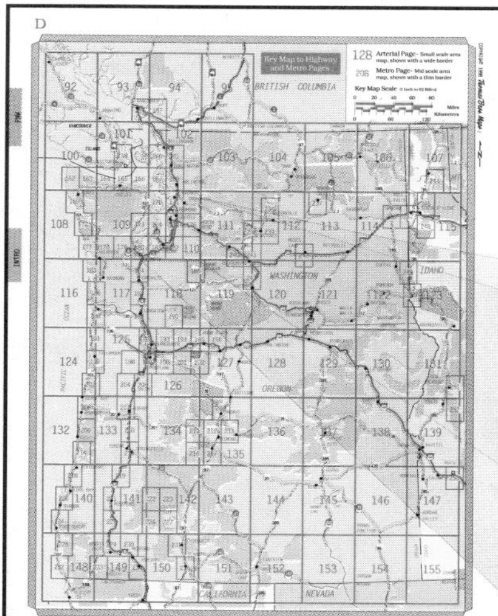

The ***Key Map*** page shows the entire Pacific Northwest area covered in this guide. If you know the general area in which the city, community, or your destination is located, start with the ***Key Map*** located on page "D". Find the general area, then turn to the ***Highway Map*** indicated.

Highway Map: 1 inch = 7.5 Miles

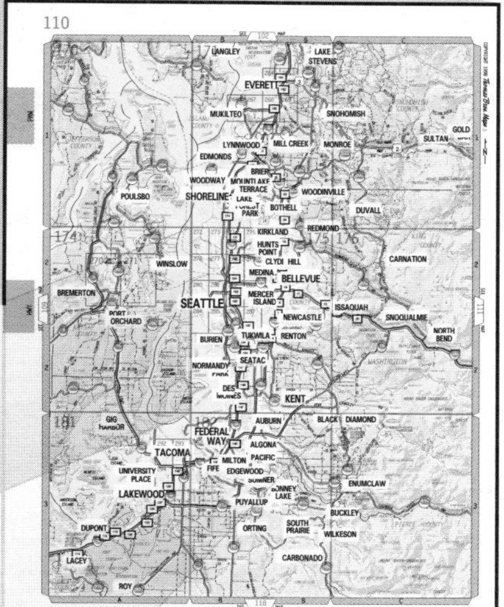

The ***Highway Map*** can be used as a guide for long distance driving. Once on the ***Highway Map***, find the area in which the city, community, or your destination is located, then turn to the ***Metro Map*** indicated.

Metro Map: 1 inch = 2.5 Miles

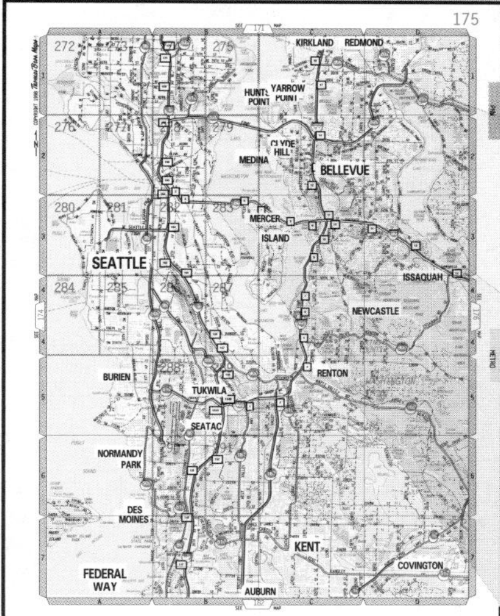

The ***Metro Map*** covers major cities, recreation areas, and areas of special interest. The ***Metro Maps*** provide greater detail and many Points of Interest within the area shown. Once on the ***Metro Map***, find the area in which the city, community, or your destination is located, then turn to the ***Detail Map*** indicated.

Detail Map: 1 inch = 1900 Feet / 1 inch = 3800 Feet

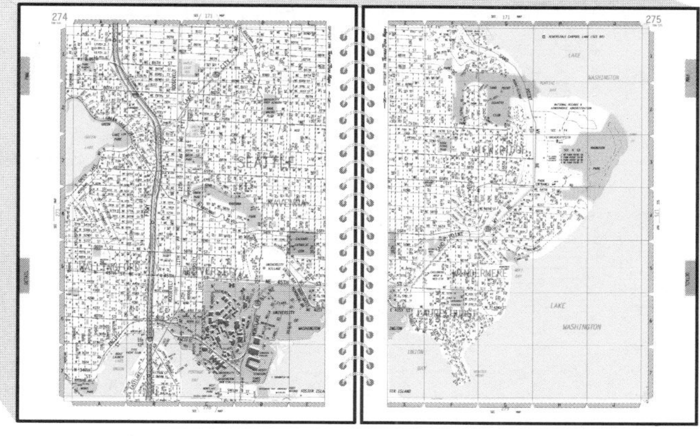

The ***Detail Map*** provides street detail and extensive Points of Interest information for selected areas. Over 100 pages of ***Detail Maps*** are included in this atlas.

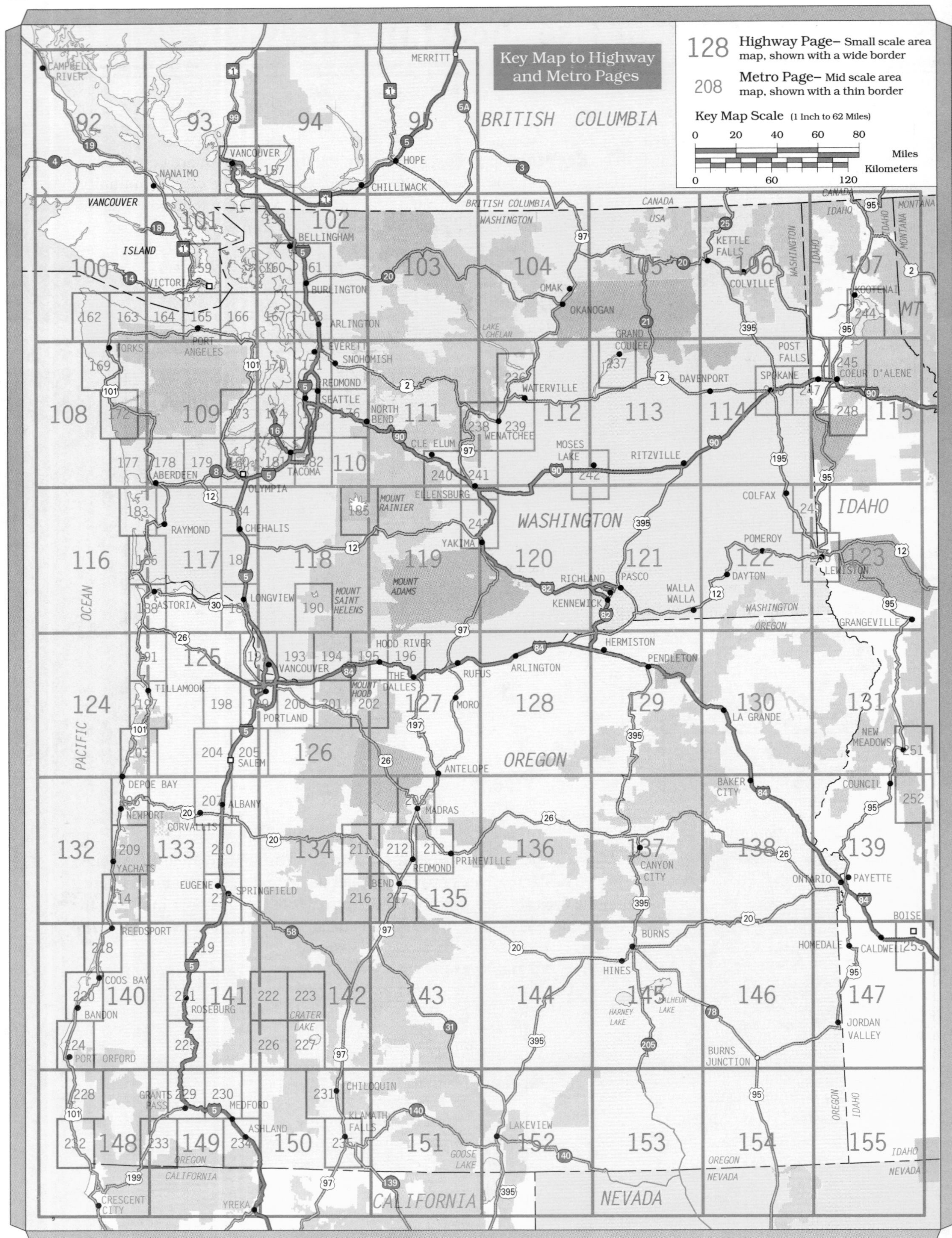
Key Map to Highway and Metro Pages
128 Highway Page– Small scale area map, shown with a wide border
208 Metro Page– Mid scale area map, shown with a thin border
Key Map Scale (1 Inch to 62 Miles)
0 20 40 60 80
Miles
Kilometers
0 60 120
BRITISH COLUMBIA
WASHINGTON
OREGON
IDAHO
MONTANA
CALIFORNIA
NEVADA
PACIFIC
OCEAN
VANCOUVER
ISLAND
CANADA
USA
CAMPBELL RIVER
NANAIMO
VANCOUVER
MERRITT
HOPE
CHILLIWACK
VICTORIA
BELLINGHAM
BURLINGTON
ARLINGTON
EVERETT
SNOHOMISH
REDMOND
SEATTLE
NORTH BEND
TACOMA
OLYMPIA
ABERDEEN
PORT ANGELES
FORKS
RAYMOND
CHEHALIS
LONGVIEW
ASTORIA
CLE ELUM
ELLENSBURG
WENATCHEE
WATERVILLE
LAKE CHELAN
OMAK
OKANOGAN
GRAND COULEE
MOSES LAKE
RITZVILLE
DAVENPORT
SPOKANE
POST FALLS
COEUR D'ALENE
KETTLE FALLS
COLVILLE
KOOTENAI
MT
COLFAX
POMEROY
DAYTON
LEWISTON
WALLA WALLA
PASCO
RICHLAND
KENNEWICK
YAKIMA
MOUNT RAINIER
MOUNT ADAMS
MOUNT SAINT HELENS
GRANGEVILLE
HERMISTON
PENDLETON
HOOD RIVER
THE DALLES
RUFUS
ARLINGTON
MORO
VANCOUVER
PORTLAND
MOUNT HOOD
TILLAMOOK
SALEM
ANTELOPE
LA GRANDE
NEW MEADOWS
BAKER CITY
COUNCIL
DEPOE BAY
NEWPORT
CORVALLIS
ALBANY
MADRAS
YACHATS
EUGENE
SPRINGFIELD
REDMOND
PRINEVILLE
BEND
CANYON CITY
ONTARIO
PAYETTE
BOISE
CALDWELL
HOMEDALE
REEDSPORT
COOS BAY
BANDON
ROSEBURG
CRATER LAKE
BURNS
HINES
HARNEY LAKE
MALHEUR LAKE
JORDAN VALLEY
BURNS JUNCTION
PORT ORFORD
CHILOQUIN
GRANTS PASS
MEDFORD
ASHLAND
KLAMATH FALLS
GOOSE LAKE
LAKEVIEW
CRESCENT CITY
YREKA
92 93 94 95 100 101 102 103 104 105 106 107 108 109 110 111 112 113 114 115 116 117 118 119 120 121 122 123 124 125 126 127 128 129 130 131 132 133 134 135 136 137 138 139 140 141 142 143 144 145 146 147 148 149 150 151 152 153 154 155

Listing of Cities and Map Pages

British Columbia

CITY NAME	DETAIL PAGE	METRO PAGE	HIGHWAY PAGE
City of North Vancouver	254	156	93
City of Vancouver	254	156	93
City of Victoria	256	159	101
District of Burnaby	255	156	93
District of North Vancouver	254	156	93
District of Oak Bay	257	159	101
District of Saanich	256	159	101
District of West Vancouver	254	156	93
Town of Esquimalt	256	159	101
Town of View Royal	256	159	101

Washington

CITY NAME	DETAIL PAGE	METRO PAGE	HIGHWAY PAGE
Anacortes	259	160	102
Bellingham	258	161	102
Bremerton	270	174	110
Burien	285	175	110
Burlington	260	161	102
Centralia	299	184	117
College Place	344	–	121
Des Moines	290	175	110
Everett	264	171	110
Fircrest	294	181	110
Kelso	303	189	117
Kennewick	342	–	121
Kent	291	175	110
Lakewood	294	181	110
Longview	303	189	117
Mercer Island	283	174	110
Millwood	350	246	114
Mount Vernon	260	161	102
Mukilteo	266	171	110
Ocean Shores	298	177	108
Olympia	296	180	109
Pasco	343	–	121
Port Angeles	261	165	101
Port Orchard	270	174	110
Port Townsend	263	167	102
Renton	289	175	110
Richland	341	–	121
Seatac	288	175	110
Seattle	278	175	110
Sequim	262	166	101
Spokane	348	246	114
Tacoma	295	181	110

Washington cont...

CITY NAME	DETAIL PAGE	METRO PAGE	HIGHWAY PAGE
Tukwilla	289	175	110
Tumwater	296	180	109
University Place	294	181	110
Vancouver	305	192	126
Veradale (community)	351	247	114
Walla Walla	345	–	121
West Richland	340	–	121
Westport	298	183	116

Oregon

CITY NAME	DETAIL PAGE	METRO PAGE	HIGHWAY PAGE
Albany	326	207	133
Ashland	337	234	149
Astoria	300	188	116
Bend	332	217	135
Central Point	336	230	149
Coos Bay	333	218	140
Corvallis	327	207	133
Eugene	330	215	133
Gearhart	301	188	116
Grant Pass	335	229	149
Klamath Falls	338	235	150
Lake Oswego	320	199	126
Maywood Park	315	199	126
Medford	336	234	149
Millersburg	326	207	125
Milwaukie	321	199	126
North Bend	333	218	140
Portland	309	199	126
Roseburg	334	221	141
Salem	323	204	125
Seaside	301	188	116
Springfield	331	215	133
Turner	325	205	125
Waldport	328	209	132

Idaho

CITY NAME	DETAIL PAGE	METRO PAGE	HIGHWAY PAGE
Coeur D'Alene	355	245	115
Dalton Gardens	355	245	115
Hauser	353	247	115
Hayden	355	255	115
Huetter	354	247	115
Post Falls	353	247	115

F

PNW

INTRO

- Freeway
- Interchange/Ramp
- Highway
- Scenic Route
- Primary Road
- Secondary Road
- Minor Road
- Restricted Road
- Alley
- Unclassified Road
- Tunnel
- Toll Road
- High Occupancy Veh. Lane
- Stacked Multiple Roadways
- Proposed Road
- Proposed Freeway
- Freeway Under Construction
- One-Way Road
- Two-Way Road
- Trail, Walkway
- Stairs
- Railroad
- Rapid Transit
- Rapid Transit, Underground
- City Boundary
- County Boundary
- State Boundary
- International Boundary
- Military Base, Indian Resv.
- River, Creek, Shoreline
- Ferry

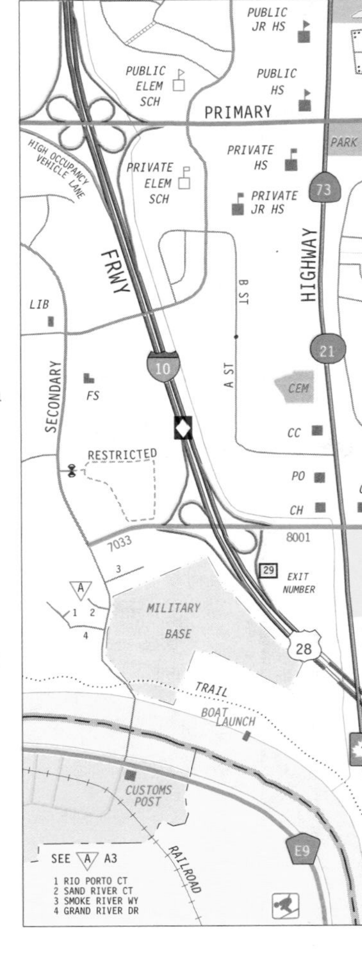

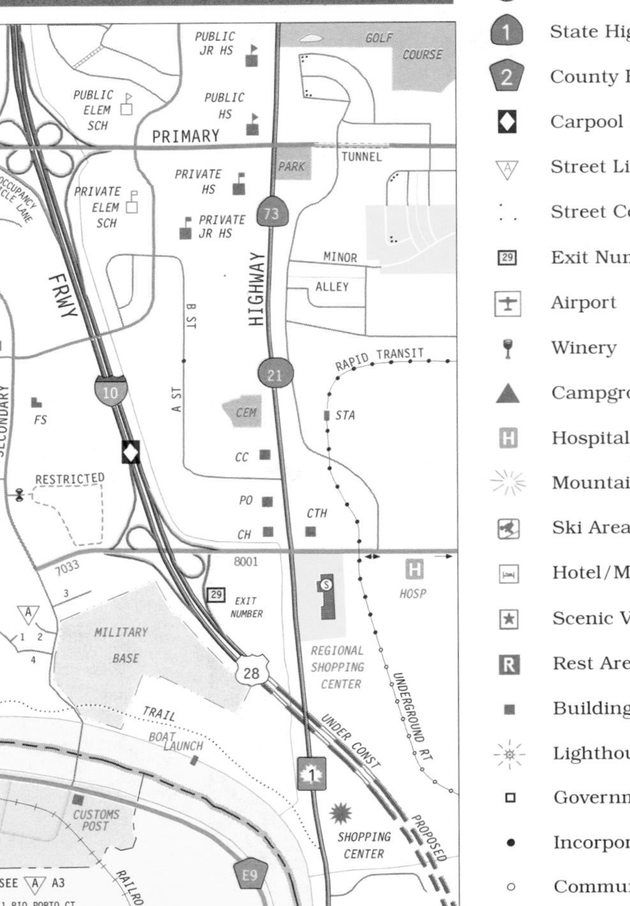

- Interstate
- Interstate (Business)
- U.S. Highway
- Trans Canada Highway
- State, Provincial Highway
- State Highway
- County Highway
- Carpool Lane
- Street List Marker
- Street Continuation
- Exit Number
- Airport
- Winery
- Campground
- Hospital
- Mountain
- Ski Area
- Hotel/Motel
- Scenic Viewpoint
- Rest Area
- Building (See List of Abbreviations Page
- Lighthouse
- Government Seat
- Incorporated City
- Community

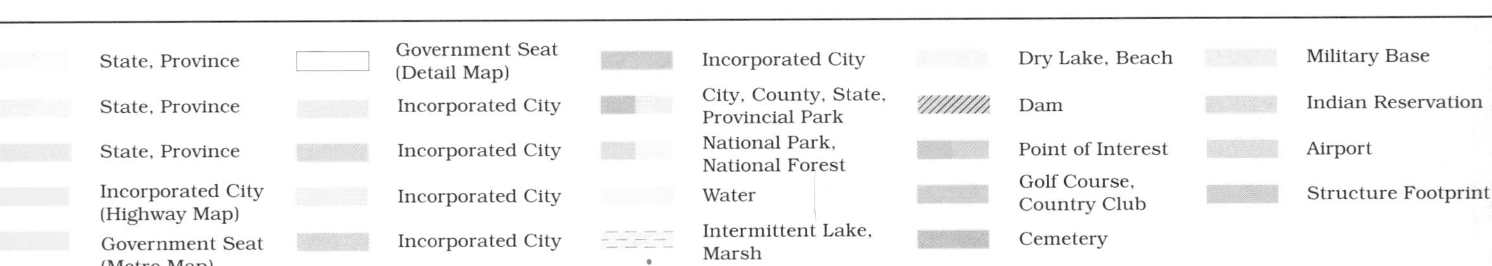

- State, Province
- State, Province
- State, Province
- Incorporated City (Highway Map)
- Government Seat (Metro Map)
- Government Seat (Detail Map)
- Incorporated City
- Incorporated City
- Incorporated City
- Incorporated City
- Incorporated City
- City, County, State, Provincial Park
- National Park, National Forest
- Water
- Intermittent Lake, Marsh
- Dry Lake, Beach
- Dam
- Point of Interest
- Golf Course, Country Club
- Cemetery
- Military Base
- Indian Reservation
- Airport
- Structure Footprint

Highway Map Scale

Pages 92-155

1 Inch to 7.5 Miles

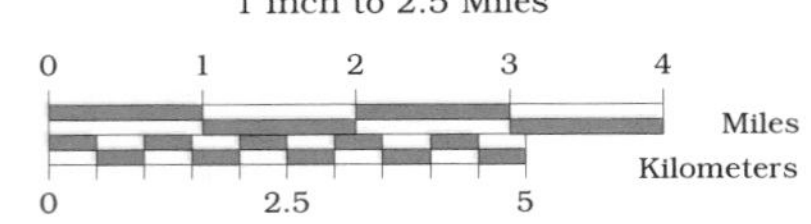

Highway Grid Equivalents
18 x 24.5 Miles
1 Grid Equals:
1 Metro Page

Detail Map Scale

Pages 264-269, 272-295, 304-321

1 Inch to 1900 Feet

0 .25 .5 .75 Miles

0 .5 1.0 Kilometers

Detail Grid Equivalents
2640 x 2640 Feet
1 Grid Equals:
.5 x .5 Miles

Metro Map Scale

Pages 156-253

1 Inch to 2.5 Miles

0 1 2 3 4 Miles

0 2.5 5 Kilometers

Metro Grid Equivalents
4.5 x 3.5 Miles

Detail Map Scale

Pages 254-263, 270-271, 296-303, 322-355

1 Inch to 3800 Feet

0 .25 .5 .75 1.0 Miles

0 .5 1.0 Kilometers

Detail Grid Equivalents
2640 x 2640 Feet
1 Grid Equals:
.5 x .5 Miles

Cities & Communities Index

COMMUNITY	ST.	PG.	GD.
A			
Abbotsford	BC	102	B1
Aberdeen	BC	102	B1
❖ ABERDEEN	WA	178	A7
Aberdeen Gardens	WA	178	B5
Abernethy	OR	317	H1
Abrams	OR	141	C1
Acme	WA	161	C2
Acton	WA	120	C2
Ada	OR	214	B5
❖ ADAMS	OR	129	C1
Addy	WA	106	A3
Adel	WA	152	B2
Adelaide	WA	175	D1
Adelaide	WA	182	A1
Adna	WA	184	A7
❖ ADRIAN	OR	147	A1
Advance	OR	199	C5
Agassiz	BC	94	C3
Agate Beach	OR	206	B3
Agness	OR	148	B1
Agnew	WA	165	D6
Ahsahka	ID	123	C2
Ahtanum	WA	243	A7
Ainsworth Corner	CA	150	C3
Ainsworth Corner	OR	151	A2
Airlie	OR	207	A2
❖ AIRWAY HEIGHTS	WA	246	A4
Ajlune	OR	118	A2
Alameda	OR	314	A1
❖ ALBANY	OR	326	A12
Albee	OR	129	B2
❖ ALBION	WA	249	A4
Alder	OR	130	C2
Alder	OR	133	A1
Alder	WA	118	B1
Alder Creek	OR	201	A4
Aldergate	WA	128	B1
Alderton	WA	182	C4
Alderwood Manor	WA	171	B5
Alexander Beach	WA	259	D6
Alfalfa	OR	135	B3
Alger	WA	161	B3
Algoma	OR	235	C1
❖ ALGONA	WA	182	B2
Alicel	OR	130	A2
Alkali Lake	OR	144	B3
Alki	WA	280	B3
Allegany	OR	218	D7
Allentown	WA	286	D7
Allison	WA	182	A4
Allyn	WA	173	D6
Allyn-Grapeview	WA	173	D7
❖ ALMIRA	WA	237	D7
Almota	WA	122	B1
Aloha	OR	199	A2
Aloha	WA	177	B2
Alpha	WA	118	A2
Alpine	OR	128	C1
Alpine	OR	133	B2
Alsea	OR	133	A2
Alston	OR	189	A4
Altamont	OR	338	H11
Alta Vista	WA	118	B2
Alto	WA	122	A2
Altoona	WA	117	A2
Alvadore	OR	133	B2
Amanda Park	WA	109	A2
Amber	WA	114	B2
Amboy	WA	193	B1
American	OR	210	A3
American	WA	181	C4
❖ AMITY	OR	204	B2
❖ ANACORTES	WA	259	D4
Anatone	WA	122	C3
Anderson	OR	200	B3
Andrews	OR	153	C1
Angle Lake	WA	290	D2
Anlauf	OR	219	B2
❖ ANMORE	BC	157	A3
Annapolis	WA	271	A13
Annex	OR	139	A2
Annieville	BC	156	D6
❖ ANTELOPE	OR	127	C3
Antone	OR	136	B2
Apex	OR	129	B1
Apiary	OR	189	B5
Applegate	OR	149	B2
Appleton	WA	196	B3
Appleyard	WA	239	A5
Arago	OR	220	D6
Arbor Heights	WA	284	D4
Arbor Lodge	OR	308	D5
Arbutus	BC	254	D14
Arcadia	WA	180	C3
Archabal	ID	251	C6
Arch Cape	OR	191	A2
Arden	WA	171	A6
Ardenvoir	WA	112	A1
Ardenwald	OR	318	A6
Argay	OR	193	A7
Ariel	OR	118	A3
Arletta	WA	181	B1
❖ ARLINGTON	OR	128	A1
❖ ARLINGTON	WA	168	D5
Arlington Heights	OR	312	B7
Arlington Heights	WA	102	C3
Arnold Creek	OR	320	C2
Arock	OR	146	C3
Arrow Head Beach	WA	167	D3
Artondale	WA	181	B1
Asert	OR	200	B1
Ashdale	OR	199	D4
Ashford	WA	118	B1
❖ ASHLAND	OR	337	D9
Ashwood	OR	135	C1
❖ ASOTIN	WA	250	B6

COMMUNITY	ST.	PG.	GD.
Aspen Grove	BC	95	C1
❖ ASTORIA	OR	300	F5
❖ ATHENA	OR	129	C1
❖ ATHO	ID	245	B2
Atkinson	WA	176	A6
❖ AUBURN	WA	182	C2
❖ AUMSVILLE	OR	205	B7
❖ AURORA	OR	199	B7
Aurora Village	WA	171	A6
Austa	OR	133	A2
Austin	OR	137	C1
Austin	WA	170	D2
Austin Junction	OR	137	C1
Avon	WA	161	A7
Avondale	WA	171	D7
Ayer	WA	121	C2
Azalea	OR	225	C6
Azwell	WA	112	B1
B			
Baby Island Heights	WA	167	D7
Bade	OR	129	C1
Badger Corner	OR	323	E12
Bagdad Junction	WA	237	D4
Bagley Jct	WA	176	C6
Bainbridge Island	WA	174	D2
❖ BAKER CITY	OR	138	B1
Baker-Langdon	WA	345	E13
Balch	WA	117	B1
Balder	WA	114	C3
Ballard	WA	272	D4
Ballston	OR	204	A3
Bamberton	BC	159	B3
Bamfield	BC	100	A1
Bancroft	OR	140	C3
❖ BANDON	OR	220	B6
Bangor	WA	170	A7
Barber	ID	253	D3
Barberton	WA	192	D5
Baring	WA	111	A1
Barnesdale	OR	191	B5
Barneston	WA	176	B7
Barnett	OR	128	A2
Barnhart	OR	129	B1
Barton	OR	200	B4
Barton Heights	OR	131	B2
Barview	OR	191	A7
Barview	OR	220	C1
Basin City	WA	121	A2
Basque	OR	154	B1
Bassett Junction	WA	113	A3
Bates	OR	137	C1
Batterson	OR	191	D4
Battin	OR	319	G7
❖ BATTLE GROUND	WA	192	D3
Bay Center	WA	183	C7
❖ BAY CITY	OR	191	B7
Bay City	WA	183	B2
Bayne	WA	110	C3
Bayocean	OR	191	A7
Bay Park	OR	333	J13
Bayshore	WA	180	B2
Bayside Gardens	OR	191	B4
Bayview	ID	245	C1
Bayview	OR	328	C2
Bay View	WA	160	D6
Bayview	WA	170	D1
Bay View	WA	181	C2
Bazan Bay	BC	159	B3
Beach Grove	BC	101	C1
Beach Haven	BC	101	C2
Beacon Hill	WA	282	C2
Beacon Hill	WA	303	C3
Bear	ID	131	B3
Beatty	OR	151	A1
Beaumont Wilshire	OR	314	B1
Beaver	OR	197	C5
Beaver	WA	163	A6
Beavercreek	OR	200	A6
Beaver Homes	OR	189	C6
Beaver Marsh	OR	142	C2
Beaver Springs	OR	189	B5
❖ BEAVERTON	OR	199	B2
Bedford	WA	117	B1
Beebe	WA	236	D3
Beech Creek	OR	137	A1
Bel Air	OR	199	B2
❖ BELCARRA	BC	157	A3
Belfair	WA	173	D5
Belknap Springs	OR	134	B2
Bellevue	OR	204	C2
❖ BELLEVUE	WA	175	C2
Bellfountain	OR	133	B2
❖ BELLINGHAM	WA	258	G4
Bells Beach	WA	167	D7
❖ BEND	OR	332	E7
Bendemeer	OR	192	A7
Benewah	ID	115	A3
Benge	WA	122	A1
❖ BENTON CITY	WA	120	C3
Berkeley	WA	182	A6
Berne	WA	111	B1
Berrydale	WA	182	D1
Berteleda	CA	148	B3
Bertsche Terrace	CA	148	B3
Bethany	OR	192	A7
Bethel	OR	329	F4
Bethel	WA	174	B4
Bethel Gospel Park	OR	205	A3
Beulah	OR	138	A3
Beverly	WA	120	B1
Beverly Beach	OR	206	B2
Beverly Beach	WA	167	D7
Beverly Park	WA	268	D4
Bickleton	WA	120	A3
Biggam	WA	120	C3
Biggs	OR	127	C1
Biggs Junction	OR	127	C1

COMMUNITY	ST.	PG.	GD.
Biloxi	WA	174	D4
❖ BINGEN	WA	195	D5
Bingham Springs	OR	130	A1
Birch	WA	110	C3
Birch Bay	WA	158	B4
Birkenfeld	OR	117	B3
Bissell	OR	200	D6
Bitter Lake	WA	171	A7
Blachly	OR	133	A2
Black Butte Ranch	OR	211	C3
Black Creek	BC	92	A1
❖ BLACK DIAMOND	WA	110	C3
Black River Junction	WA	289	H2
Blaine	OR	197	D6
❖ BLAINE	WA	158	A3
Blakeley	OR	129	C1
Blalock	OR	128	A1
Blanchard	ID	107	A3
Blanchard	WA	161	A4
Blewett	WA	238	A5
Bliss Landing	BC	92	B1
Blitzen	OR	153	B1
Blockhouse	WA	127	B1
Blodgett	OR	133	A1
Blooming	OR	198	C2
Blubber Bay	BC	92	B1
Bluecreek	WA	106	A3
Blue Mountain	OR	129	C1
Blue Ridge	WA	171	A7
Blue River	OR	134	A2
Bluestem	WA	114	A2
Bly	OR	151	B1
Blyn	WA	109	C1
❖ BOARDMAN	OR	128	C1
Boardman Junction	OR	128	C1
Bodie	OR	129	C2
Bogachiel	WA	169	D3
Boise	OR	313	F1
Boise	WA	110	C3
❖ BOISE	ID	253	D3
Boise Hills Village	ID	253	D2
Boistfort	WA	187	A2
Bolton	OR	199	D4
❖ BONANZA	OR	151	A2
Bonifer	OR	129	C1
Bonita	OR	199	B3
Bonlow	WA	243	A4
❖ BONNERS FERRY	ID	107	B2
Bonnerville	OR	194	B7
❖ BONNEY LAKE	WA	182	C4
Bonny Slope	OR	199	B1
Bordeaux	WA	184	A2
Boring	OR	200	B3
Boston Bar	BC	95	A1
Boston Harbor	WA	180	C4
❖ BOTHELL	WA	171	C6
Boulevard Park	WA	285	J6
Boundary	WA	106	B1
Bourne	OR	138	A1
❖ BOVILL	ID	123	B1
Bow	WA	161	A4
Bowen Island	BC	93	B3
Bowers Junction	OR	192	A7
Bowmont	OR	147	C1
Bowser	BC	92	B2
Boyd	OR	127	B2
Brackendale	BC	93	C1
Bradwood	OR	117	B3
Brady	WA	179	A7
Brandstrom	WA	168	B3
Braymill	OR	150	C1
Breakers	WA	186	A5
Breidablick	WA	170	B5
Breitenbush Hot Springs	OR	134	B1
❖ BREMERTON	WA	270	G10
Bremerton Junction	WA	174	A4
Brentwood Bay	BC	159	C4
Brentwood-Darlington	OR	318	D6
❖ BREWSTER	WA	104	B3
Briarwood	OR	321	G4
Brickerville	OR	214	D1
Bridal Veil	OR	201	A1
Bridesville	BC	105	A1
Bridge	OR	140	C3
Bridgeport	OR	138	B1
❖ BRIDGEPORT	WA	112	C1
Bridgeton	OR	309	G2
Bridgeview	OR	233	B5
Bridlemile	OR	316	A2
❖ BRIER	WA	171	B6
Brighouse	BC	156	B6
Brighton	OR	191	B5
Brightwood	OR	201	B4
Bristol	WA	196	A4
Britannia Beach	BC	93	C2
Broadacres	OR	205	B1
Broadbent	OR	140	B3
Broadmoor	BC	156	B7
Brogan	OR	138	C2
Bromart	WA	171	D3
Brookdale	WA	182	A5
Brookfield	WA	117	A2
❖ BROOKINGS	OR	232	C6
Brooklyn	OR	317	H2
Brooks	OR	205	A3
Brookwild	OR	318	D7
Brothers	OR	135	C3
Brownsboro	OR	149	C1
Brownsmead	OR	117	A3
Browns Point	WA	181	D1
Brownstown	WA	119	C2
❖ BROWNSVILLE	OR	210	C2
Brush Prairie	WA	193	A4
Bryant	WA	168	D4
Bryn Mawr	WA	175	C4
Buchanan	OR	145	C1
Buck Fork	OR	141	B2

COMMUNITY	ST.	PG.	GD.
❖ BUCKLEY	WA	182	D4
Buckman	OR	313	H6
Bucks Corners	OR	129	A1
❖ BUCODA	WA	184	D4
Buell	OR	125	B3
Buena	WA	120	A2
Buena Vista	OR	207	C2
Buenna	WA	175	A7
Bull Run	OR	200	D3
Bunker Hill	OR	333	J11
Burbank	WA	121	B3
Burbank Heights	WA	121	A3
❖ BURIEN	WA	285	F7
Burley	WA	174	B6
Burlington	OR	192	A6
❖ BURLINGTON	WA	260	D7
Burnett	WA	182	D5
❖ BURNS	OR	145	A1
Burns Junction	OR	146	B3
Burnt Woods	OR	133	A1
Buroker	WA	122	A3
Burop	WA	111	A3
Burr Canyon	WA	121	B2
Burrows	WA	177	C5
Burton	WA	174	D6
Busby	WA	249	B6
❖ BUTTE FALLS	OR	150	A1
Butter Creek Junction	OR	128	C1
Butterfield	OR	301	H1
Butteville	OR	199	A6
Buxton	OR	125	B1
B Z Corner	WA	195	D2
C			
Cabell City	OR	129	C3
Cadboro Bay	BC	257	E4
Calder	ID	115	C2
❖ CALDWELL	ID	147	B1
Calhounville	WA	121	C3
Callahan	OR	141	A2
Cama Beach	WA	167	D6
Camano	WA	167	D5
❖ CAMAS	WA	193	B7
Camas Valley	OR	141	A3
❖ CAMBRIDGE	ID	139	B1
Cameron	ID	123	B1
❖ CAMPBELL RIVER	BC	92	A1
Camp Discovery	WA	170	A5
Camp Elkanah	OR	129	C2
Camp Grande	WA	167	D4
Camp Lagoon	WA	167	D4
Camp Sealth	WA	174	C7
Camp Sherman	OR	211	C1
Camp Twelve	OR	206	C3
Camp Union	WA	173	D2
Canaan	OR	189	C7
Canary	OR	214	B4
❖ CANBY	OR	199	C6
Canby	WA	114	A2
Canemah	OR	199	D5
❖ CANNON BEACH	OR	188	A7
Cannon Beach Junction	OR	188	B6
❖ CANYON CITY	OR	137	B2
Canyon Park	WA	171	C6
❖ CANYONVILLE	OR	225	C3
Cape Meares	OR	197	A1
Capitol Hill	WA	278	C3
❖ CARBONADO	WA	182	D6
Carders	WA	351	B6
Carlsborg	WA	166	A6
Carlson	WA	118	B1
❖ CARLTON	OR	198	B5
Carlton	WA	104	A3
Carnahan	OR	188	B3
Carnation	OR	198	B1
❖ CARNATION	WA	176	B1
Carpenterville	OR	232	C2
Carrolls	WA	189	C4
Carson	OR	131	A3
Carson	WA	194	D4
Carson River Valley	WA	194	D4
Carus	OR	199	D6
Carver	OR	200	A4
Cascade	BC	105	C1
❖ CASCADE	ID	252	D6
Cascade Gorge	OR	150	A1
Cascade Heights	BC	156	C5
❖ CASCADE LOCKS	OR	194	D5
Cascade Summit	OR	142	B1
Cascade Valley	WA	242	C3
Cascadia	OR	134	A2
❖ CASHMERE	WA	238	C2
Casino	BC	106	B1
Casino Corner	WA	268	B5
Casland	WA	111	C3
❖ CASTLE ROCK	WA	187	C7
Cataldo	ID	115	B2
Cathcart	WA	171	D5
Cathedral Park	OR	192	B6
❖ CATHLAMET	WA	117	B3
Caufield	BC	156	A3
Cavalero Corner	WA	171	D1
❖ CAVE JUNCTION	OR	233	A5
Cavelero Beach	WA	167	D5
Caycuse	BC	100	C1
Cayuse	OR	129	C1
Cecil	OR	128	B1
Cecil	WA	106	C2
Cedar	BC	93	A3
Cedardale	BC	254	G4
Cedardale	OR	126	A3
Cedar Falls	WA	176	C6
Cedar Hills	OR	199	B1
Cedarhome	WA	168	B3
Cedarhurst	WA	174	D5
Cedar Mill	OR	199	B1
Cedar Mountain	WA	175	D6
Cedar Point	OR	220	D4

COMMUNITY	ST.	PG.	GD.
Cedar Valley	WA	171	B5
Cedarville	WA	117	B1
Celilo Village	OR	127	B1
Centennial	OR	200	A1
Center	OR	314	D5
Center	WA	170	A2
Centerville	WA	127	B1
Central Area	WA	278	C5
Central Ferry	WA	122	B1
❖ CENTRALIA	WA	299	E4
Central Park	WA	178	C7
Central Point	OR	199	C6
❖ CENTRAL POINT	OR	336	A6
Central Valley	WA	174	B1
Ceres	WA	117	B2
Chaffee	WA	120	C3
Chain Hill	WA	184	D2
Chamber	WA	249	B7
Chapman	OR	125	C1
Chard	WA	122	B2
Charleston	OR	220	C1
Charleston	WA	270	G11
Charlestown	OR	129	A1
Chattaroy	WA	114	C1
❖ CHATCOLET	ID	248	A6
❖ CHEHALIS	WA	299	C10
Chehalis Junction	WA	299	B14
Chehalis Village	WA	117	B1
❖ CHELAN	WA	236	D3
Chelan Falls	WA	236	D4
Chelatchie	WA	118	A3
Chemainus	BC	101	A1
Chemawa	OR	323	D5
Chemult	OR	142	C2
❖ CHENEY	WA	246	A7
Chenois Creek	WA	177	D6
Chenoweth	OR	196	C6
Cherry Grove	OR	198	A2
Cherry Heights	OR	196	C7
Cherry Valley	WA	110	C1
Cherryville	OR	201	A4
Chesaw	WA	105	A1
Cheshire	OR	133	B2
Chester	WA	350	H14
❖ CHEWELAH	WA	106	B3
Chico	WA	270	B4
Chilco	ID	245	A3
❖ CHILOQUIN	OR	231	D4
Chimacum	WA	170	A1
Chinook	WA	186	B7
Chiwaukum	WA	111	C2
❖ CHRISTINA LAKE	BC	105	C1
Christmas Valley	OR	143	C2
Christopher	WA	182	C1
Chrome	OR	220	D4
Chuckanut Village	WA	258	B13
Chumstick	WA	111	C2
Cicero	WA	102	C3
Cinebar	WA	118	A2
❖ CITY OF COLWOOD	BC	159	B7
❖ CITY OF N VANCOUVER	BC	254	J4
❖ CITY OF VICTORIA	BC	256	H7
❖ CITY OF WHITE ROCK	BC	158	A2
Clackamas	OR	199	D3
Clackamas Heights	OR	199	D4
Clallam Bay	WA	163	B3
Claquato	WA	184	B6
Clarkes	OR	200	A7
❖ CLARK FORK	ID	107	C3
Clarkia	ID	115	C3
❖ CLARKSTON	WA	250	B4
Clarkston Heights	WA	250	B4
Clarksville	ID	245	B5
Clarno	OR	128	A3
❖ CLATSKANIE	OR	117	B3
Clatsop Station	OR	188	B3
Clay City	WA	118	B1
Clayton	WA	114	B1
Clearbrook	BC	102	B1
Clear Creek	CA	149	A3
Clear Creek	OR	125	B1
Clear Lake	OR	204	D4
Clear Lake	WA	161	C6
Clearview	WA	171	D5
Clearwater	OR	222	D4
❖ CLE ELUM	WA	240	B2
Clem	OR	128	A2
Cleo	OR	220	D2
Cleveland	OR	221	A3
Clevland	WA	120	A3
Clifton	OR	117	B3
Clifton	OR	195	C5
Clinton	WA	171	A2
Clo-oose	BC	100	B2
Cloquallum	WA	179	C4
Cloverdale	BC	158	B1
Cloverdale	ID	253	B3
Cloverdale	OR	197	B7
Cloverdale	OR	212	D4
Cloverdale	WA	189	D6
Cloverland	WA	122	C2
Clow Corner	OR	204	B6
Clyde	WA	121	C2
❖ CLYDE HILL	WA	175	C2
Coal Canyon	WA	118	B2
Coal Creek	WA	175	D4
Coal Creek	WA	189	B2
Coaledo	OR	220	D3
Coalfield	WA	175	D4
Coalmont	BC	95	C2
Cobble Hill	BC	159	A1
❖ COBURG	OR	210	B7
Cocolalla	ID	107	A3
❖ COEUR D'ALENE	ID	355	E11
Cohassett	WA	183	B2
Colbert	WA	114	C1
Colburn	ID	107	B2

❖ - Indicates City, District or Township

Cities & Communities Index

COMMUNITY	ST.	PG.	GD.
Colby	WA	271	H13
Colchester	WA	271	H14
Cold Springs	OR	129	A1
Cold Springs Junction	OR	129	A1
Coles Corner	WA	111	C1
Colestin	OR	234	D7
❖ COLFAX	WA	122	C1
College Hill	OR	329	J9
❖ COLLEGE PLACE	WA	344	G11
Collins	WA	195	A5
Collins View	OR	320	D2
Colton	OR	126	A3
❖ COLTON	WA	250	A1
Columbia	WA	283	E5
Columbia Beach	WA	171	A2
❖ COLUMBIA CITY	OR	192	B1
Columbia Gardens	BC	106	B1
Columbia Heights	WA	302	G2
Columbia Valley Gardens	WA	302	G6
❖ COLVILLE	WA	106	A2
Colvos	WA	174	D5
❖ COMOX	BC	92	A2
Comstock	OR	219	C1
Concomly	OR	205	A2
❖ CONCONULLY	WA	104	B2
Concord	OR	321	J7
Concordia	OR	310	A6
❖ CONCRETE	WA	102	C2
❖ CONDON	OR	128	A2
Conkling Park	ID	248	A5
Conley	OR	130	A2
❖ CONNELL	WA	121	B1
Conway	WA	168	B2
Cook	WA	195	B5
Coolin	ID	107	A2
Coombs	BC	92	C3
❖ COOS BAY	OR	333	D10
Cooston	OR	218	B7
Copalis Beach	WA	177	B4
Copalis Crossing	WA	177	C4
Copco	CA	150	A3
Copeland	ID	107	B1
Coppei	WA	122	A3
Copperfield	OR	131	A3
Copperville	ID	131	C1
❖ COQUILLE	OR	220	D4
❖ COQUITLAM	BC	157	A3
Corbett	OR	200	C1
Corbett-Terwilliger-Lair Hill	OR	317	F4
Cordova Bay	BC	159	C5
❖ CORNELIUS	OR	198	C1
Cornelius Pass	OR	192	A6
Cornell	WA	168	A6
Cornell Place	OR	129	A1
Corner	WA	168	B3
Cornucopia	OR	130	C3
Coronado Shores	OR	203	A6
Cortes Bay	BC	92	B1
❖ CORVALLIS	OR	327	F7
❖ COSMOPOLIS	WA	178	B7
❖ COTTAGE GROVE	OR	215	B7
❖ COTTONWOOD	ID	123	C3
Cottonwood Bay	WA	158	B4
Cottrell	OR	200	C3
Cougar	WA	190	A5
❖ COULEE CITY	WA	113	A2
❖ COULEE DAM	WA	237	C2
❖ COUNCIL	ID	139	C1
Country Homes	WA	347	B11
County Line	BC	158	D1
❖ COUPEVILLE	WA	167	B4
❖ COURTENAY	BC	92	A2
Courtrock	OR	137	A1
❖ COVE	OR	130	B2
Cove	WA	174	D5
Covello	WA	122	B2
Cove Orchard	OR	198	B4
Covington	WA	175	D7
Cowichan Bay	BC	101	B1
Cowiche	WA	119	C1
Cowlitz	WA	118	A2
Crabtree	OR	133	C1
Crab Tree	WA	114	C3
❖ CRAIGMONT	ID	123	B2
Crane	OR	145	C2
Crates	WA	196	C6
Crawfordville	OR	133	C2
Creosote	WA	174	D2
Crescent	OR	142	C1
Crescent Beach	BC	158	A1
❖ CRESCENT CITY	CA	148	B3
Crescent Lake	OR	142	B1
Crescent Lake Junction	OR	142	B1
❖ CRESTON	WA	113	C1
Creston Kenilworth	OR	318	B2
Crestwood	OR	316	A7
❖ CRESWELL	OR	215	C5
Creswell Heights	WA	193	C5
Criterion	OR	127	B3
Crocker	WA	182	C5
Crofton	BC	101	B1
Cromwell	WA	181	B2
Crosby	WA	173	D3
Cross	WA	174	C6
Crossing	WA	168	C6
Crow	OR	133	B3
Crowfoot	OR	133	C1
Crown Hill	WA	273	E1
Crown Point	OR	220	C2
Cruzatt	WA	194	A7
Crystal Springs	WA	271	D5
❖ CULDESAC	ID	123	B2
Cully	OR	310	D7
Culp Creek	OR	141	C1
Cultus Lake	BC	102	C1
❖ CULVER	OR	208	B7
Cumberland	BC	92	A2

COMMUNITY	ST.	PG.	GD.
Cumberland	WA	110	C3
Cunningham	WA	121	B1
Cuprum	ID	131	B3
Curlew	WA	105	B1
Currinsville	OR	200	C5
Curtin	OR	219	B1
Curtis	WA	187	A1
Cushman	OR	214	B3
❖ CUSICK	WA	106	C3
Custer	WA	158	C4
Cutler City	OR	203	A5
D			
Dabob	WA	170	A4
Dahl Pine	OR	127	A3
Dahua	WA	117	A2
Dairy	OR	151	A2
Dale	OR	129	B3
❖ DALLAS	OR	204	A6
Dallesport	WA	196	C7
❖ DALTON GARDENS	ID	355	E3
Damascus	OR	200	A3
Danner	OR	146	C3
Dant	OR	127	B3
Danville	WA	105	C1
Danville	WA	175	D7
Darknell	WA	114	C2
Darlington	WA	267	J1
Darlingtonia	CA	148	C3
❖ DARRINGTON	WA	103	A3
Dartford	WA	346	H5
Dash Point	WA	181	D1
Dash Point	WA	182	A1
❖ DAVENPORT	WA	114	A2
Davidson	ID	131	B1
Davis	WA	117	B1
Davis Creek	CA	152	A3
Davis Terrace	WA	303	F10
Dawson	OR	133	B2
Day Island	WA	181	C2
Days Creek	OR	225	D2
❖ DAYTON	OR	198	C7
❖ DAYTON	WA	122	A2
Dayton	WA	179	D2
❖ DAYVILLE	OR	136	C2
Deadwood	OR	132	C3
Deady	OR	221	C2
❖ DEARY	ID	123	B1
Deckerville	WA	179	A2
Deep Cove	BC	156	D3
Deep Cove	BC	159	B2
Deep Creek	ID	107	B2
Deep Creek	WA	114	B2
Deep Harbor	WA	101	C2
Deerhorn	OR	133	C3
Deer Island	OR	189	C7
❖ DEER PARK	WA	114	B1
Dehlinger	OR	235	D6
Delake	OR	203	A5
Delaney	WA	122	A2
Delano Heights	WA	237	C3
Delena	OR	189	A4
Delkena	WA	106	C3
Dellwood	OR	140	C2
Dellwood	OR	198	B3
Delphi	WA	184	B1
Delta	ID	115	C2
Deming	WA	102	B1
Denio	NV	153	C3
Denison	WA	114	B1
Denman Island	BC	92	B2
Denmark	OR	224	B3
Denneux	OR	199	B2
❖ DEPOE BAY	OR	203	A7
Deroche	BC	94	C3
De Smet	ID	115	A3
❖ DES MOINES	WA	290	B5
Deschutes River Woods	OR	217	B4
Detour	OR	198	B1
❖ DETROIT	OR	134	B1
Dewatto	WA	173	B5
Dewdney	BC	94	B3
Dewey	OR	198	C4
Dewey	WA	259	J14
Dexter	OR	133	C3
Dexter By The Sea	WA	183	B5
Diablo	WA	103	B2
Diamond	OR	145	C3
Diamond	WA	122	B1
Diamond Lake	OR	223	C6
Diamond Lake	WA	106	C3
Diamond Lake Junction	OR	142	C3
Dickey Prairie	OR	126	A3
Dieringer	WA	182	C2
Dillard	OR	221	B7
Dilley	OR	198	B2
Dilworth	WA	174	D5
Disautel	WA	105	A3
Dishman	WA	350	A9
Disque	WA	164	C5
Disston	OR	141	C1
❖ DIST OF ABBOTSFORD	BC	102	B1
❖ DISTRICT OF BURNABY	BC	255	H10
❖ DIST OF CENTRAL SAANICH	BC	159	C3
❖ DISTRICT OF CHILLIWACK	BC	94	C3
❖ DISTRICT OF DELTA	BC	101	C1
❖ DISTRICT OF KENT	BC	94	C3
❖ DISTRICT OF LANGFORD	BC	159	B6
❖ DISTRICT OF MATSQUI	BC	94	B3
❖ DISTRICT OF METCHOSIN	BC	159	A7
❖ DISTRICT OF MISSION	BC	94	B3
❖ DIST OF NORTH SAANICH	BC	159	C2
❖ DIST OF N VANCOUVER	BC	254	H2
❖ DISTRICT OF OAK BAY	BC	257	C7
❖ DISTRICT OF SAANICH	BC	256	B1
❖ DISTRICT OF SURREY	BC	157	B7
❖ DIST OF WEST VANCOUVER	BC	254	C1
Divide	OR	219	C1

COMMUNITY	ST.	PG.	GD.
Divide	WA	118	B1
Dixie	WA	122	A3
Dixonville	OR	221	D5
Dockton	WA	174	D7
Dodge	WA	122	B2
Dodson	OR	194	B7
Dole	WA	193	C3
Dollarton	BC	156	D3
Dollers Corner	WA	192	D3
Dolomite	WA	106	A1
❖ DONALD	OR	199	A7
Donald	WA	120	A2
❖ DONNELLY	ID	252	D1
Dora	OR	140	C2
Dorena	OR	141	C1
Dorris	CA	150	B3
Dot	WA	128	A1
Doty	WA	117	B1
Douglas	WA	236	D7
Douglas Ridge	OR	200	C5
❖ DOVER	ID	244	A1
Dover	OR	200	D5
Downing	OR	189	A3
Downs	OR	205	C4
Downtown	OR	313	F6
❖ DRAIN	OR	219	A3
Drakes Crossing	OR	205	D6
Draperville	OR	207	D4
Drew	OR	141	C3
Drewsey	OR	137	C3
Drift Creek	OR	209	B1
Dryad	WA	117	B1
Dry Creek	WA	121	C3
Dryden	OR	233	C2
Dryden	WA	238	B2
Dryland	OR	205	D1
Duckabush	WA	173	C1
Dudley	ID	115	B2
Dudley	WA	240	D3
❖ DUFUR	OR	127	B2
Dukes Valley	OR	195	C7
❖ DUNCAN	BC	101	A1
Duncan	WA	246	C7
Duncan Bay	BC	92	A1
Dundarave	BC	254	B2
❖ DUNDEE	OR	198	C6
Dune	OR	127	B1
❖ DUNE CITY	OR	214	B4
Dungeness	WA	262	D2
Dunnean	OR	146	A2
Dunthorpe	OR	321	G4
❖ DUPONT	WA	181	B5
Durham	WA	110	C3
Durkee	OR	138	C1
Duroc	OR	129	C1
Dusty	WA	122	B1
❖ DUVALL	WA	110	C1
Dynamite	WA	246	B7
E			
Eagle	ID	115	C1
❖ EAGLE	ID	253	B1
Eagle Creek	OR	200	B4
Eagledale	WA	174	D2
Eagle Harbour	BC	156	A2
❖ EAGLE POINT	OR	230	D5
Eakin	OR	127	C2
Earlington	WA	289	H3
Earlmont	WA	175	C1
Earls Cove	BC	93	A2
East Aberdeen	WA	178	B7
East Bremerton	WA	270	H6
East Columbia	OR	309	H3
East Farms	WA	352	G7
East Gardener	OR	218	D1
Eastgate	WA	175	D3
❖ EAST HOPE	ID	244	D2
East Hoquiam	WA	178	A7
East Kamiah	ID	123	C2
East Kittitas	WA	241	D6
East Lind	WA	121	C1
Eastman	WA	122	A3
East Maupin	OR	127	B3
Eastmoreland	OR	318	A5
East Olympia	WA	184	D1
Easton	WA	111	B3
Eastport	ID	107	B1
East Port Orchard	WA	174	C4
Eastside	OR	220	D1
East Sooke	BC	164	D1
Eastsound	WA	101	C2
East Spokane	WA	350	A9
❖ EAST WENATCHEE	WA	239	A4
East Wenatchee Bench	WA	239	A4
❖ EATONVILLE	WA	118	B1
Eby	OR	126	A3
❖ ECHO	OR	129	A1
Echo Beach	ID	115	A1
Echo Dell	OR	200	A5
Eckman Lake	OR	328	G7
Eddyville	ID	248	B1
Eddyville	OR	133	A1
Edgecomb	WA	168	D6
Edgewater	WA	171	B2
Edgewick	WA	176	C6
❖ EDGEWOOD	WA	182	B3
Edison	WA	161	A4
Edison Station	WA	161	A4
❖ EDMONDS	WA	171	A5
Edwall	WA	114	A2
Eglon	WA	170	D4
Eightmile	OR	128	B2
❖ ELBE	WA	118	B1
Elberton	WA	114	C3
Eldon	WA	173	B3
❖ ELECTRIC CITY	WA	237	C3
Elgarose	OR	221	A3
❖ ELGIN	OR	130	A1

COMMUNITY	ST.	PG.	GD.
Elgin	WA	174	B7
Eliot	OR	313	G2
Elk	WA	114	C1
Elk City	OR	206	D4
Elkhead	OR	219	C5
Elkhorn	OR	134	A1
Elk Lake	OR	216	A4
❖ ELK RIVER	ID	123	C1
❖ ELKTON	OR	141	A1
Elk Valley	CA	233	A7
Ella	OR	128	B1
Ellendale	OR	125	B3
❖ ELLENSBURG	WA	241	B6
Elliott Avenue	WA	243	A6
Ellisford	WA	104	C1
Ellisport	WA	174	D6
Ellsworth	WA	311	G2
❖ ELMA	WA	179	B7
❖ ELMER CITY	WA	237	C2
Elmira	ID	107	B2
Elmira	OR	133	B2
Elmonica	OR	199	A1
Elsie	OR	125	A1
Eltopia	WA	121	A2
Elwood	OR	200	B7
Embro	WA	111	B1
Emerald Heights	OR	300	H4
Emerson	OR	127	B2
Emida	ID	115	B3
❖ EMMETT	ID	139	C3
Empire	OR	333	C6
Enaville	ID	115	C2
❖ ENDICOTT	WA	122	B1
Enetai	WA	271	C9
Englewood	OR	333	F12
❖ ENTERPRISE	OR	130	C2
❖ ENTIAT	WA	236	A6
❖ ENUMCLAW	WA	110	C3
Eola Village	OR	204	C1
❖ EPHRATA	WA	112	C3
Erlands Point	WA	270	D6
Ernies Grove	WA	176	D4
Espanola	WA	114	B2
❖ ESTACADA	OR	200	C6
Eufaula	WA	189	A2
❖ EUGENE	OR	330	B6
Eureka	WA	121	C3
Evaline	WA	187	C2
❖ EVERETT	WA	267	G3
Evergreen	ID	131	C3
Evergreen	OR	321	F6
❖ EVERSON	WA	102	B1
Ewan	WA	114	B3
Excelsior Beach	ID	115	A1
F			
Factoria	WA	175	C3
Fairbanks	OR	127	B1
Fairchild	WA	114	B2
Fairfax	WA	110	C3
Fairfield	OR	204	D2
❖ FAIRFIELD	WA	114	C2
Fairholm	WA	164	A6
Fairmont	WA	109	C1
Fairmount	WA	171	C4
Fairoaks	OR	221	D1
Fair Oaks	OR	321	H5
Fairview	OR	128	B2
Fairview	OR	140	B2
Fairview	OR	197	C2
❖ FAIRVIEW	OR	200	B1
Fairview	WA	270	E3
Fairview Sumach	WA	243	C7
Fairwood	WA	175	D5
Fairwood	WA	346	H7
Falcon Heights	OR	235	C5
Fall City	WA	176	B3
Fall Creek	OR	133	C3
❖ FALLS CITY	OR	125	A3
Falls View	OR	200	A7
Fanny Bay	BC	92	B2
Fargher Lake	WA	193	A1
Farmington	OR	198	D3
❖ FARMINGTON	WA	115	A3
Farron	WA	119	C2
Faubion	OR	201	C5
Fauntleroy	WA	284	D3
Fawn	OR	134	A1
Fayetteville	OR	210	A1
❖ FEDERAL WAY	WA	182	A1
Felida	WA	192	C5
Fenn	ID	123	C3
❖ FERDINAND	ID	123	B3
❖ FERNAN LAKE VILLAGE	ID	355	J11
Ferncliff	WA	174	D1
Ferndale	WA	121	C3
❖ FERNDALE	WA	158	C6
Fern Heath	WA	175	A6
Fern Hill	OR	188	D2
Fernwood	ID	115	B3
Fernwood	WA	173	A7
Fernwood	WA	174	B4
Fields	OR	153	C2
❖ FIFE	WA	182	A3
Finley	WA	121	A3
Finn Rock	OR	134	A3
❖ FIRCREST	WA	294	A1
Firdale	WA	117	A1
Firdale	WA	171	A6
Fir Grove	OR	200	A5
Fir Grove	OR	215	A1
First Hill	WA	278	C5
Fir Villa	OR	204	A6
Firwood	OR	200	D4
Fischers Mill	OR	200	B5
Fisher	OR	209	D4
Fisher	WA	193	A7
Fishers Corner	OR	199	D6

COMMUNITY	ST.	PG.	GD.
Five Corners	OR	152	A2
Five Corners	WA	192	D5
Fletcher Bay	WA	174	C1
Flett	WA	181	C3
Flora	OR	122	C3
❖ FLORENCE	OR	214	B3
Florence	WA	168	B4
Flynn	OR	133	B1
Foley Springs	OR	134	B2
Folkenberg	OR	192	A6
Foothills	WA	247	A7
Fordair	WA	113	A2
Fords Prairie	WA	299	A2
Forest	ID	123	B3
Forest	WA	187	D1
Forest Beach	WA	173	C6
Forest Beach	WA	181	B1
Forest Glade	WA	110	C1
❖ FOREST GROVE	OR	198	B1
Forest Knolls	BC	157	D7
Forest Park	OR	192	B7
Forfar	OR	206	B6
❖ FORKS	WA	169	D1
Fort Bidwell	CA	152	B3
Fort Dick	CA	148	B3
Fort Hill	OR	125	A3
Fort Klamath	OR	231	C1
Fort Klamath Junction	OR	231	C1
Fort Langley	BC	157	D6
Fort Nisqually	WA	181	C1
Fort Rains	WA	194	C6
Fort Rock	OR	143	B2
Fort Steilacoom	WA	181	C4
Fort Stevens	OR	188	B2
Fortune Branch	OR	225	C6
Foss	OR	191	C4
❖ FOSSIL	OR	128	A3
Foster	OR	134	A2
Foster	WA	289	E2
Foster-Powell	OR	319	E3
Four Corners	OR	200	B6
Four Corners	OR	234	C7
Four Corners	OR	323	F14
Four Corners	OR	336	E4
Four Corners	WA	110	C1
Four Corners	WA	118	A1
Four Corners	WA	170	B5
Four Corners	WA	263	B13
Four Lakes	WA	176	A5
Four Lakes	WA	246	A6
Fourmile	OR	224	B1
Fox	OR	137	A1
Fox Valley	OR	134	A1
Fragaria	WA	174	C5
Frances	WA	117	B2
Franklin	OR	133	B2
Franklin Camp	BC	100	B1
Fraser	BC	156	B5
Fraserview	BC	156	C5
Fredrickson	WA	182	A5
Freedom	WA	114	C2
Freeland	WA	170	D1
Freeman	WA	247	A6
Fremont	WA	273	J7
Frenchglen	OR	145	B3
❖ FRIDAY HARBOR	WA	101	C2
Friend	OR	127	A2
Frisken Wye	WA	179	A2
❖ FRUITLAND	ID	139	A3
Fruitland	OR	205	A6
Fruitvale	ID	131	C3
Fruitvale	WA	243	B6
Fryelands	WA	110	C1
Fulford Harbour	BC	101	B1
Fulton	OR	129	B1
G			
Gabriola	BC	93	A3
Galena	OR	137	B1
Galena	WA	111	A1
Gales Creek	OR	125	B1
Galiano	BC	101	B1
Galice	OR	149	A1
Galvin	WA	184	B5
Ganges	BC	101	B1
❖ GAP	OR	219	D1
❖ GARDEN CITY	ID	253	B2
Garden City	WA	179	C6
Garden Home	OR	199	B2
Garden Village	BC	156	C5
Gardiner	OR	218	C1
Gardiner	WA	166	D7
Garfield	OR	200	C6
❖ GARFIELD	WA	114	C3
Garibaldi	BC	93	C1
❖ GARIBALDI	OR	191	B7
Garibaldi Highlands	BC	93	C2
Garrett	WA	344	E8
Gasquet	CA	148	C3
❖ GASTON	OR	198	B3
Gas Works	OR	234	B2
Gate	WA	184	A3
❖ GATES	OR	134	A1
Gateway	OR	208	C2
Gaylord	OR	140	B3
Gazley	OR	225	D3
❖ GEARHART	OR	301	G4
Geiger Heights	WA	246	B5
Gem	OR	235	D5
❖ GENESEE	ID	250	C1
Geneva	WA	161	A1
George	OR	200	D6
❖ GEORGE	WA	112	B3
Georgetown	WA	176	A7
Georgetown	WA	282	A7
❖ GERVAIS	OR	205	B2
Getchell	WA	168	D7
Getchell Hill	WA	168	D7

❖ - Indicates City, District or Township

Cities & Communities Index

COMMUNITY	ST.	PG.	GD.
Gibbon	OR	129	C1
Gibbon	WA	120	C3
Gibson	BC	93	B3
Gifford	ID	123	B2
❖ GIG HARBOR	WA	181	C1
Gilbert	OR	200	A1
Gilberton	WA	271	C1
Gilchrist	OR	142	C1
Gillespie Corners	OR	133	B3
Gillies Bay	BC	92	C2
Gilmer	WA	195	D2
Givens Hot Springs	ID	147	B1
Glacier	WA	102	C1
❖ GLADSTONE	OR	199	D4
Gladtidings	OR	205	D2
Glasgow	OR	333	H1
Gleed	WA	243	A5
Glen Acres	WA	174	D5
Glenada	OR	214	B3
Glen Avon	OR	126	A3
Glenbrook	OR	133	B2
Glencoe	OR	125	C1
Glen Cove	WA	263	A8
Glendale	ID	131	C3
❖ GLENDALE	OR	225	A7
Glendale	WA	171	A3
Glendale Junction	OR	225	B6
Glen Echo	OR	199	D4
Gleneden Beach	OR	203	B6
Glenfair	OR	200	A1
Glengary	OR	221	B6
Glenoma	WA	118	B2
Glen Valley	BC	94	B3
Glenwood	OR	125	B1
Glenwood	OR	188	B3
Glenwood	OR	330	H8
Glenwood	WA	119	A3
Glide	OR	141	B2
Globe	WA	117	A1
Goble	OR	189	C5
❖ GOLD BAR	WA	110	C1
❖ GOLD BEACH	OR	228	A5
❖ GOLDENDALE	WA	127	C1
❖ GOLD HILL	OR	230	A6
Goldstream	BC	159	A6
Goodnoe Hills	WA	128	A1
Goodrich	ID	139	B1
Gooseberry	OR	128	B2
Goose Hollow	OR	312	D6
Goose Prairie	WA	119	A1
Gordon River	BC	100	C1
Gorst	WA	174	B4
Goshen	OR	330	H14
Gottville	CA	149	C3
Gould City	WA	122	B2
Government Camp	OR	202	A6
Grace	WA	171	D6
Graham	WA	182	B6
Graham Point	WA	180	C2
❖ GRAND COULEE	WA	237	C3
❖ GRAND FORKS	BC	105	C1
Grand Mound	WA	184	B4
Grand Ronde	OR	125	A3
Grand Ronde Agency	OR	125	A3
❖ GRANDVIEW	WA	120	B3
❖ GRANGER	WA	120	A2
❖ GRANGEVILLE	ID	123	C3
❖ GRANITE	OR	137	C1
❖ GRANITE FALLS	WA	102	C3
Grant Park	OR	314	A2
❖ GRANTS PASS	OR	335	D6
❖ GRASS VALLEY	OR	127	C2
Gravelford	OR	140	B2
Gray Gables	WA	177	D6
Grayland	WA	183	B3
Grays Harbor City	WA	177	D7
Grays River	WA	117	A2
Green	OR	221	B6
Green Acres	OR	220	D3
Greenacres	WA	351	E6
Greenbank	WA	167	C6
Greenberry	OR	133	B2
Green Bluff	WA	114	C1
Greenburg	OR	199	B3
Greencreek	ID	123	C3
Green Horn	OR	137	C1
❖ GREENLEAF	ID	147	B1
Greenleaf	OR	133	A2
Greenwater	WA	110	A3
❖ GREENWOOD	BC	105	B1
Greenwood	WA	178	B4
Greenwood	WA	273	G1
Greer	ID	123	C2
Gregory	WA	175	A5
❖ GRESHAM	OR	200	B1
Gresham Butte	OR	200	B1
Grisdale	WA	109	A2
Grizzly	OR	213	C1
Gromore	WA	119	C2
Groners Corner	OR	199	A3
Grosscup	WA	120	C2
Grotto	WA	111	A1
Guerrier	WA	187	D1
Guler	WA	119	A3
Gurdane	OR	129	A2
Gwendolen	OR	128	A2
H			
Hadlock	WA	170	A1
Haig	BC	95	A3
❖ HAINES	OR	130	A3
Haley	OR	200	B3
Halfmoon Bay	BC	93	A2
Halford	WA	111	A1
❖ HALFWAY	OR	131	A3
Haller Lake	WA	171	B7
❖ HALSEY	OR	210	B2
Hamburg	CA	149	B3

COMMUNITY	ST.	PG.	GD.
Hamilton	OR	137	A1
❖ HAMILTON	WA	102	C2
Hamlet	OR	188	D7
Hammond	OR	188	B1
Hampton	ID	123	A1
Hampton	OR	134	A3
Hampton	OR	144	A1
Hamricks Corner	OR	205	D1
Haney	BC	157	C5
Hansville	WA	170	C3
Happy Camp	CA	149	A3
Happy Hollow	OR	203	D1
❖ HAPPY VALLEY	OR	199	D3
Happy Valley	WA	258	E11
Harbeck-Fruitdale	OR	335	H12
Harbor	OR	232	C6
Harbor Island	WA	281	H3
Harborton	OR	192	B6
Hardman	OR	128	C3
Harlan	OR	133	A1
Harmony	OR	127	C2
Harmony	OR	199	D3
Harmony	WA	118	A2
Harmony Point	OR	199	D3
Harney	OR	145	B1
Harper	OR	138	C3
Harper	WA	174	D4
Harper Junction	OR	138	C3
❖ HARRAH	WA	119	C2
Harriman	OR	231	A6
❖ HARRINGTON	WA	113	C2
Harris	OR	133	A1
❖ HARRISBURG	OR	210	A5
❖ HARRISON	ID	248	A4
❖ HARRISON HOT SPRINGS	BC	94	C3
Harrison Mills	BC	94	C3
Hartford	WA	110	C1
Hartland	WA	196	D4
❖ HARTLINE	WA	113	A2
Hartstene	WA	180	D2
Harvard	ID	123	A1
Harwood	WA	243	A7
Hatfield	CA	151	A3
Hathaway Mead	OR	197	C2
❖ HATTON	WA	121	B1
Hatwai	ID	250	C4
❖ HAUSER	ID	353	B2
Hauser	OR	218	B5
Havana	OR	129	B1
Hawkinsville	CA	149	C3
Hay	WA	122	A1
Hay Creek Ranch	OR	135	B1
❖ HAYDEN	ID	245	A5
Hayden Island	OR	304	E6
❖ HAYDEN LAKE	ID	245	A5
Hayesville	OR	323	F5
Hayford	WA	246	A5
Hayhurst	OR	316	A4
Hazel	WA	102	C3
Hazeldale	OR	199	A2
Hazel Dell	WA	192	D5
Hazel Green	OR	205	A4
Hazelia	OR	199	C4
Hazelwood	OR	200	A1
Headquarters	WA	189	D1
Healy Heights	OR	316	C3
Heather	OR	142	B1
Heather	WA	183	B4
Hebo	OR	197	B6
Heceta Beach	OR	214	A2
Heceta Junction	OR	214	B2
Hedges	WA	121	A3
Heisson	WA	193	A2
❖ HELIX	OR	129	B2
Helmer	ID	123	B1
Helsing Junction	WA	184	A3
Helvetia	OR	192	A7
Hemlock	OR	142	A1
Hemlock	OR	197	B5
Hemlock Valley	BC	94	C3
Henley	CA	150	A3
Henley	OR	235	D5
Henrici	OR	199	D5
Henrybro	WA	119	C2
❖ HEPPNER	OR	128	C2
Hereford	OR	138	A1
Hermans	OR	126	A3
❖ HERMISTON	OR	129	A1
Heron	MT	107	C3
Herron	WA	180	D2
Hidaway Springs	OR	129	B2
High Bridge	WA	110	C1
Highland	WA	171	A7
Highland	WA	343	C14
Highland Heights	WA	177	B2
Highlands	ID	253	C2
High Point	WA	176	A4
High Rock	WA	110	C1
Hilda	WA	117	B1
Hilgard	OR	130	A2
Hillcrest	WA	113	C3
Hillgrove	WA	179	D6
Hills	OR	215	D4
❖ HILLSBORO	OR	198	D1
Hillsdale	OR	316	C4
Hillsdale	WA	295	J6
Hillside	OR	312	B5
Hillside	WA	243	C3
Hilltop	WA	102	B1
Hillview	OR	200	B3
Hillyard	WA	349	E3
Hilt	CA	149	C3
❖ HINES	OR	145	A1
Hinkle	OR	129	A1
Hiouchi	CA	148	B3
Hite Center	WA	173	D2
Hito	OR	199	B7

COMMUNITY	ST.	PG.	GD.
Hobart	WA	176	A6
Hobsonville	OR	191	B7
Hockinson	WA	193	A4
Hogback	OR	200	A6
Hoko	WA	163	A2
Holbrook	OR	192	A5
Holden Village	WA	103	C3
Holdman	OR	129	B1
Holiday Beach	OR	206	B5
Holland	OR	233	C5
Holland	WA	249	B5
Holley	OR	133	C2
Hollow Hedges	WA	121	A3
Holly	WA	173	C3
Hollybrook	OR	200	A1
Hollyburn	BC	254	E3
Hollywood	OR	314	B3
Hollywood	WA	171	D7
Hollywood Beach	WA	236	A1
Holman	WA	186	A6
Holtzinger	WA	119	C1
Home	WA	181	A2
Home Acres	WA	265	H6
❖ HOMEDALE	ID	147	A1
Homestead	OR	131	A3
Homestead	OR	316	D2
Home Valley	WA	195	A5
Honeymoon Bay	BC	100	C1
❖ HOOD RIVER	OR	195	D5
Hoodsport	WA	173	A6
Hoodview	OR	199	B5
Hooper	WA	122	A1
❖ HOPE	BC	95	A3
❖ HOPE	ID	244	D2
Hope	OR	138	C3
Hopemere	OR	204	D3
Hopewell	OR	204	C2
Hopington	BC	158	D1
❖ HOQUIAM	WA	178	A7
Horlick	WA	240	C3
Hornbrook	CA	150	A3
Hornby Island	BC	92	B2
Horse Creek	CA	149	B3
Horseshoe Bay	BC	156	A2
❖ HORSESHOE BEND	ID	139	C3
Horton	OR	133	A2
Hosford	OR	317	H1
Hoskins	OR	133	A1
Hosley	OR	235	D7
Hot Lake	OR	130	A2
Hot Springs	OR	151	A2
Hoyt	ID	115	C3
❖ HUBBARD	OR	205	C1
Hubner	WA	111	B3
Hugo	OR	229	B3
Humboldt	OR	309	F6
Humptulips	WA	177	D2
Hunter	WA	105	C3
Hunter Creek	OR	228	A6
Huntingdon	BC	102	B1
❖ HUNTINGTON	OR	138	C2
Huntington Junction	OR	138	B2
Huntley	WA	114	B3
❖ HUNTS POINT	WA	175	C1
Huntsville	WA	122	A2
Hurricane Grange	OR	130	C2
Huscroft	BC	107	B1
Huston	ID	147	B1
Husum	WA	195	D3
Hyak	WA	111	A2
Hyland Hills	OR	199	A2
Hylands	WA	110	C1
I			
❖ IDANHA	OR	134	B1
Idaville	OR	197	B1
Idleyld Park	OR	141	B2
Illahee	WA	177	B6
Illahee	WA	271	C4
Illinois Valley	OR	233	A5
❖ ILWACO	WA	186	A6
❖ IMBLER	OR	130	A2
Imnaha	OR	131	A1
Inchelium	WA	105	C3
❖ INDEPENDENCE	OR	204	B7
❖ INDEX	WA	110	A1
Indian Beach	WA	167	D5
Indianola	WA	170	D6
Indian Valley	ID	139	C1
Indian Village	WA	160	C4
Inglewood	WA	171	C7
Inglis	OR	117	B3
Innis	WA	171	A6
Interbay	WA	272	D7
Intercity	WA	268	C6
Interlachen	OR	200	B1
Inverness	WA	171	B7
Ioco	BC	157	A3
❖ IONE	OR	128	B2
❖ IONE	WA	106	B1
Irondale	WA	263	D13
Irondate	WA	170	A1
Ironside	OR	138	B2
Iron Springs	WA	177	B3
❖ IRRIGON	OR	128	C1
Irvines Landing	BC	93	A2
Irving	OR	215	A1
Irvington	OR	313	H3
Isadore	OR	219	A6
❖ ISLAND CITY	OR	130	A2
Island School Crossing	WA	168	C5
Island View	WA	342	C7
❖ ISSAQUAH	WA	175	D3
Izee	OR	137	A3
J			
❖ JACKSONVILLE	OR	234	A2
Jacktown	OR	198	D3
Jamestown	WA	262	F6

COMMUNITY	ST.	PG.	GD.
Jamieson	OR	138	C2
Jamison Corner	WA	110	C1
Jasper	OR	215	D3
Jean	OR	199	B4
Jeffers Garden	OR	300	B10
❖ JEFFERSON	OR	207	D3
Jefferson	WA	114	C2
Jennings Lodge	OR	199	D4
Jerome Prairie	OR	229	A6
Jewell	OR	117	A3
❖ JOHN DAY	OR	137	B2
Johnson	OR	220	D5
Johnson	WA	249	B7
Jordan	OR	128	B2
Jordan	OR	134	A1
Jordan	WA	102	C3
Jordan Creek	OR	125	A1
❖ JORDAN VALLEY	OR	147	A3
Joseph	ID	131	B1
❖ JOSEPH	OR	130	C2
Jovita	WA	182	B2
Joyce	WA	164	C5
❖ JULIAETTA	ID	123	B1
Juanita	WA	171	C7
❖ JUNCTION CITY	OR	210	A6
Junction City	WA	178	B7
Junction Park	WA	178	B1
Juno	OR	197	B1
Juno	WA	114	B3
Juntura	OR	146	A1
K			
❖ KAHLOTUS	WA	121	C1
Kahneeta Hot Springs	OR	208	B1
❖ KALAMA	WA	189	D5
Kamela	OR	129	C2
❖ KAMIAH	ID	123	C2
Kamilche	WA	180	A4
Kanaka	BC	95	A1
Kanaskat	WA	110	C3
Kangley	WA	176	B7
Keating	OR	130	B3
Keats Island	BC	93	B3
Keechelus	WA	111	A2
Keefers	BC	95	A1
Keelers Corner	WA	171	B4
Keith Lynn	BC	255	D5
❖ KELLOGG	ID	115	C2
Kellogg	OR	141	A1
Kelly Creek	OR	200	B1
Kellys Korner	WA	181	A7
Kelso	OR	200	C3
❖ KELSO	WA	303	F10
❖ KENDRICK	ID	123	B1
Kenmore	WA	171	B6
Kennedy	WA	111	A3
❖ KENNEWICK	WA	342	E9
Keno	OR	235	A5
Kent	OR	127	C3
❖ KENT	WA	291	G5
Kenton	OR	308	D4
Keona	OR	198	B4
Kerby	OR	233	B3
Kerns	OR	313	H5
Kernville	OR	203	A6
Kerrisdale	BC	156	B5
Kerry	OR	117	B3
❖ KETTLE FALLS	WA	106	A2
Kettle Valley	BC	105	A1
Keuterville	ID	123	B3
Keymes Beach	WA	263	C14
Keyport	WA	170	C7
Keystone	WA	167	C5
Kildonan	BC	100	A1
Killarney	BC	156	C5
Kimberly	OR	136	C1
Kimwood	OR	219	D1
King	OR	309	H7
King Cole	OR	150	B2
Kingsgate	BC	107	B1
Kingsley	OR	127	B2
Kingston	ID	115	B2
Kingston	WA	170	D5
Kings Valley	OR	133	A1
Kinton	OR	199	A3
Kinzua	OR	128	B3
Kiona	WA	120	C3
❖ KIRKLAND	WA	171	C7
Kishwalks	OR	127	A3
Kitsap Lake	WA	270	A8
Kitson Hot Spring	OR	142	A1
❖ KITTITAS	WA	241	C6
Kitts Corner	WA	182	B1
Klaber	WA	187	A2
Klamath Agency	OR	231	C3
Klamath Agency Junction	OR	231	C5
❖ KLAMATH FALLS	OR	338	C3
Klamath Junction	OR	234	D5
Klamath River	CA	149	C3
Klaus	WA	187	D1
Klickitat	WA	196	D3
Klickitat Springs	WA	196	D3
Klipsan Beach	WA	186	A3
Klondike	OR	127	C1
Knab	WA	118	A2
Knapp	WA	192	C4
Knappa	OR	117	A3
Knappa Junction	OR	117	A3
Kokel Corner	OR	126	A3
Kooskooskie	WA	122	A3
❖ KOOTENAI	ID	244	A1
Kopiah	WA	184	D6
Kopplein	OR	133	A1
Korea	WA	111	B1
Kosmos	WA	118	B2
Kountze	WA	240	D3
Krain	WA	110	C3
Krewson	OR	219	A2

COMMUNITY	ST.	PG.	GD.
❖ KRUPP	WA	113	A2
Kruse	WA	168	C7
❖ KUNA	ID	253	A5
Kyro	WA	181	A7
L			
Labish Village	OR	323	F2
Lacamas	WA	118	A2
❖ LA CENTER	WA	192	C1
❖ LACEY	WA	297	H7
Laclede	ID	107	A3
Lacomb	OR	133	C1
❖ LA CONNER	WA	167	D1
❖ LA CROSSE	WA	122	A1
Ladd Hill	OR	199	A6
Ladner	BC	101	C1
Ladysmith	BC	101	A1
❖ LAFAYETTE	OR	198	B6
La Granda	WA	118	B1
❖ LA GRANDE	OR	130	A2
Laidlaw	BC	95	A3
Lake	OR	231	C4
Lakebay	WA	181	A2
Lake Cowichan	BC	101	A1
Lakecreek	OR	149	C1
Lakedale	WA	111	B3
❖ LAKE FOREST PARK	WA	171	B6
Lake Fork	ID	251	D6
Lake Grove	OR	320	B7
Lakeland Village	WA	114	B2
❖ LAKE OSWEGO	OR	320	B5
Lake Park	WA	181	D5
❖ LAKESIDE	OR	218	C4
Lakeside	WA	236	C3
❖ LAKE STEVENS	WA	171	D1
Lakeview	ID	245	D1
❖ LAKEVIEW	OR	152	A2
Lakeview	WA	181	C4
Lakeview Park	WA	112	C2
Lakewood	OR	321	F6
Lakewood	WA	168	C6
❖ LAKEWOOD	WA	294	A7
Lakewood Center	WA	181	C4
Lakota	WA	182	A1
Lamar	WA	121	C2
❖ LAMONT	WA	114	A3
Lancaster	OR	210	A5
Lancaster	WA	114	B3
Landore	ID	131	B3
Landsburg	WA	176	A7
Lang Bay	BC	92	C1
Langdon	WA	345	B12
Langell Valley	OR	151	A3
❖ LANGLEY	BC	157	C7
❖ LANGLEY	WA	171	A1
Langlois	OR	224	B2
Langrell	OR	131	A3
Lantzville	BC	93	A3
La Pine	OR	143	A1
La Push	WA	169	A2
❖ LAPWAI	ID	123	A2
Larchmont	WA	181	D4
Lardo	ID	251	C5
Larimers Corner	WA	171	D4
Lasqueti	BC	92	C2
❖ LATAH	WA	114	C2
Latham	OR	215	B7
Latourell	OR	200	D1
Laurel	OR	198	D3
Laurel	WA	158	D5
Laurel Grove	OR	220	A7
Laurelhurst	OR	314	B5
Laurelhurst	WA	275	F6
Laurelwood	OR	198	C3
Lavender	WA	111	B3
Lawen	OR	145	B1
Laws Corner	WA	196	A4
Leaburg	OR	133	C3
Leahy	WA	112	C1
❖ LEAVENWORTH	WA	238	A1
Lebam	WA	117	A1
❖ LEBANON	OR	133	C1
Lehman Springs	OR	129	B3
Leland	ID	123	B1
Leland	OR	229	A2
Lemolo	WA	170	B7
Lena	OR	129	A2
Leneve	OR	220	C4
Lenore	ID	123	B2
Lents	OR	319	H4
Lenz	OR	142	C3
Lenz	OR	195	D6
Leona	OR	219	B2
Lester	WA	111	A3
Letha	ID	139	B3
Lewisburg	OR	207	B5
❖ LEWISTON	ID	250	C4
Lewiston Orchards	ID	250	C5
❖ LEXINGTON	OR	128	C2
Lexington	WA	303	C3
Libby	OR	333	F14
Liberty	OR	324	F6
Liberty	WA	240	D1
Liberty Lake	WA	247	B4
Lilliwaup	WA	173	A5
Lime	OR	138	C2
Lincoln	OR	150	A2
Lincoln	WA	113	C1
Lincoln Beach	OR	203	A7
❖ LINCOLN CITY	OR	203	A4
❖ LIND	WA	121	B1
Lindbergh	OR	189	C4
Lindell Beach	BC	102	C1
Linns Mill	OR	200	A4
Linnton	OR	192	B7
Lions Bay	BC	93	C2
Lisabuela	WA	174	D6
Lister	BC	107	B1

❖ - Indicates City, District or Township

Cities & Communities Index

COMMUNITY	ST.	PG.	GD.
Littell	WA	184	B7
Little Albany	OR	209	C2
Little Falls	WA	114	A1
Little Hoquiam	WA	180	C1
Little Oklahoma	WA	165	D7
Little River	BC	92	A2
Littlerock	WA	184	B2
Little Shasta	CA	150	A3
Little Valley	OR	138	C3
Lobert Junction	OR	231	D4
Lochdale	BC	156	D4
Lochsloy	WA	102	C3
Locoda	OR	117	B3
Lofall	WA	170	B5
Logan	OR	200	B5
Logan Hill	WA	184	D7
Logsden	OR	133	A1
London	OR	219	D3
Lone Cemetery	ID	248	D3
Lone Elder	OR	199	C7
Lone Pine	OR	150	C1
Lone Pine	WA	237	C2
❖ LONEROCK	OR	128	B3
Lone Tree	OR	130	A2
❖ LONG BEACH	WA	186	A5
Longbranch	WA	181	A3
❖ LONG CREEK	OR	137	A1
Long Lake	WA	114	A1
Longmire	WA	185	B5
Long Tom Station	OR	133	A2
❖ LONGVIEW	WA	302	F8
Looking Glass	OR	130	B1
Lookingglass	OR	221	A5
Lookout	OR	142	A1
Loomis	WA	104	C1
Loon Lake	WA	106	B3
Lopez	WA	101	C2
Lorane	OR	133	B3
Lorella	OR	151	A2
❖ LOSTINE	OR	130	C2
Loveland	WA	182	A6
Lowden	WA	121	C3
❖ LOWELL	OR	133	C3
Lowell	WA	265	F7
Lower Highland	OR	200	B7
Lower Nicola	BC	95	C1
Loyal Heights	WA	272	D2
Lucerne	WA	103	C3
Lucile	ID	131	C1
Lummi Island	WA	160	B1
Lund	BC	92	B1
Lunnville	OR	198	B4
Lyle	WA	196	B5
❖ LYNDEN	WA	158	D4
Lynn Creek	BC	255	F1
Lynn Valley	BC	255	C1
❖ LYNNWOOD	WA	171	B5
Lynwood Center	WA	271	F6
❖ LYONS	OR	134	A1
M			
Mabel	OR	133	C2
❖ MABTON	WA	120	B3
Macdoel	CA	150	B3
Machias	WA	110	C1
Mack	WA	122	A1
Macksburg	OR	199	C7
Macleay	OR	205	B6
Madison Park	WA	279	F2
Madison South	OR	315	G3
❖ MADRAS	OR	208	C5
Madras Station	OR	208	C5
Madrona Beach	WA	167	D4
Madrona Park	WA	278	D4
Magnolia Beach	WA	174	D7
Magnolia Bluff	WA	276	D1
Mahan	OR	198	D1
Malahat	BC	159	A4
Malaya	WA	239	B5
❖ MALDEN	WA	114	B3
❖ MALIN	OR	151	A3
Malone	WA	179	C7
Malott	WA	104	C3
Maltby	WA	171	D5
Manchester	WA	271	H12
Manette	WA	271	B10
Manhattan	WA	290	A1
Manhattan Beach	OR	191	B5
Manitou Beach	WA	174	D1
Manning	OR	125	B1
Manning	WA	122	C1
❖ MANSFIELD	WA	112	C1
Manson	WA	236	B2
Manson Landing	BC	92	A1
❖ MANZANITA	OR	191	B4
Manzanita	WA	174	C1
Manzanita	WA	174	D7
Maple Bay	BC	101	B1
Maple Grove	WA	164	D6
❖ MAPLE RIDGE	BC	157	D6
Mapleton	OR	214	D2
Maple Valley	WA	176	A6
Maplewood	WA	174	C6
Maplewood	WA	175	C5
Marble Creek	ID	115	C3
Marblemount	WA	103	A2
Marcellus	WA	113	C3
Marcola	OR	210	D7
Marcus	WA	106	A2
Marengo	WA	122	B2
Marial	OR	140	C3
Marietta	WA	158	C7
Marine Drive	WA	270	D8
Marion	OR	133	C1
Marion Forks	OR	134	C1
Markham	OR	320	B1
Marlin	WA	113	A2
Marmot	OR	201	A4

COMMUNITY	ST.	PG.	GD.
Marpole	BC	156	B5
Marquam	OR	205	D3
Marshall	WA	246	B6
Marshall Park	OR	320	C1
Marshland	OR	117	B3
❖ MARSING	ID	147	B1
Martin	WA	111	A3
Martindale	WA	121	B3
Maryhill	WA	127	C1
Marylhurst	OR	199	C4
Marys Corner	WA	187	D2
❖ MARYSVILLE	WA	168	C7
Mason	WA	114	B2
Massinger Corner	OR	200	A7
Matlock	WA	179	B2
Matsqui	BC	102	B1
❖ MATTAWA	WA	120	B1
❖ MAUPIN	OR	127	B3
Maury	WA	175	A6
May Creek	WA	175	C4
Mayfield	WA	118	A2
Mayger	OR	189	A2
Maynard	WA	109	C1
Mayne	BC	101	B1
Maytown	WA	184	C2
Mayview	WA	122	C1
Mayville	OR	128	A3
Maywood	OR	133	B3
❖ MAYWOOD PARK	OR	315	J2
Mazame	OR	142	C3
McBee	OR	129	B1
❖ MCCALL	ID	251	D5
❖ MCCLEARY	WA	179	D6
McCormac	OR	333	J14
McCormick	WA	117	B2
McCormmach	OR	129	B1
McCoy	OR	204	B3
McCoy	WA	114	C3
McCredie Springs	OR	142	B1
McDermitt	NV	154	B2
McDermitt	OR	154	B2
McDonald	WA	242	D4
McEwan	OR	138	A1
McGuire	ID	353	D7
McKay	OR	129	C2
McKee Bridge	OR	149	B2
McKenna	WA	118	A1
McKenzie Bridge	OR	134	B2
McKinley	OR	140	C2
McLeod	OR	149	C1
McLoughlin Heights	WA	306	D6
McMicken Heights	WA	288	D6
McMillin	WA	182	C5
❖ MCMINNVILLE	OR	198	A7
McMurray	WA	168	C2
McNab	OR	128	B2
McNary	OR	129	A1
Meacham	OR	129	C2
Meacham Corner	OR	125	C1
Mead	WA	347	F7
Meadow Creek	WA	111	A3
Meadowdale	WA	171	B4
Meadowdale	WA	270	H2
Meadows	ID	251	B4
Meadows	WA	184	B4
Meaghersville	WA	238	A7
❖ MEDFORD	OR	336	D11
❖ MEDICAL LAKE	WA	114	B2
Medical Springs	OR	130	B3
Medimont	ID	248	C4
❖ MEDINA	WA	279	J4
Mehama	OR	134	A1
❖ MELBA	ID	147	C1
Melbourne	WA	117	A1
Melmont	ID	147	C1
Melrose	OR	221	A4
Melville	OR	188	C4
Mendota	WA	184	D5
Menlo	WA	117	A1
Menlo Park	WA	181	C3
❖ MERCER ISLAND	WA	283	J2
Merideth	WA	175	B7
❖ MERIDIAN	ID	253	A3
Merlin	OR	229	A4
❖ MERRILL	OR	150	C2
Merritt	BC	95	C1
Merritt	WA	111	C1
Merville	BC	92	A1
Mesa	ID	139	C1
❖ MESA	WA	121	A2
Meskill	WA	117	B1
❖ METALINE	WA	106	B1
❖ METALINE FALLS	WA	106	C1
Metchosin	BC	165	A1
Methow	WA	104	B3
❖ METOLIUS	OR	208	C5
Metzger	OR	199	B3
Mica	ID	247	D4
Mica	WA	247	A5
Michigan Hill	WA	184	A4
Middle Grove	OR	323	F9
❖ MIDDLETON	ID	147	B1
Middleton	OR	199	A5
Midland	OR	235	B5
Midland	WA	182	A4
❖ MIDVALE	ID	139	B1
Midway	BC	105	B1
Midway	ID	147	B1
Midway	OR	125	A3
Midway	OR	129	B1
Midway	OR	198	D3
Midway	OR	336	A3
Midway	WA	181	C1
Midway	WA	290	D7
Mikkalo	OR	128	A2
Milan	WA	114	C1
Milburn	WA	184	A7

COMMUNITY	ST.	PG.	GD.
Miles	WA	113	C1
Miles Crossing	OR	300	C10
Mileta Raeco	WA	175	A7
Mill A	WA	195	B4
Mill Bay	BC	159	A2
❖ MILL CITY	OR	134	A1
❖ MILL CREEK	WA	171	C4
Miller	OR	192	B6
Miller River	WA	111	A1
❖ MILLERSBURG	OR	326	G2
Millican	OR	135	B3
Millington	OR	220	D2
Mill Park	OR	200	A1
Mill Plain	WA	193	A6
Millwood	OR	141	A2
❖ MILLWOOD	WA	350	D5
Milner	BC	157	C7
Milnes Landing	BC	101	A2
Milo	OR	141	B3
❖ MILTON	WA	182	B2
❖ MILTON-FREEWATER	WA	121	C3
❖ MILWAUKIE	OR	318	A7
Milwaukie Heights	OR	321	J4
Mima	WA	184	B3
Minam	OR	130	B1
Mineral	ID	139	A1
Mineral	WA	118	B1
Minerva	OR	214	C1
Minnehaha	WA	305	J1
Minnick	WA	122	A3
Mirrormont	WA	176	A5
Mission	OR	129	B1
Mist	OR	117	B3
Mitchell	OR	136	A1
Moclips	WA	177	B2
Modoc Point	OR	231	D6
Mohler	OR	191	B4
Mohrweis	WA	179	D1
❖ MOLALLA	OR	126	A3
Monitor	OR	205	C2
Monitor	WA	238	C3
Monkland	OR	127	C2
❖ MONMOUTH	OR	204	B7
Monohon	WA	175	D3
❖ MONROE	OR	133	B2
❖ MONROE	WA	110	C1
Monson Corner	WA	168	B3
❖ MONTAGUE	CA	150	A3
Montavilla	OR	315	G6
Montborne	WA	168	C1
Monte Cristo	WA	111	A1
❖ MONTESANO	WA	178	D6
Monte Vista	WA	181	D4
Montlake	WA	278	C1
Montour	ID	139	C3
❖ MONTROSE	BC	106	B1
❖ MONUMENT	OR	136	C1
Moody	OR	127	B1
Moores Corner	WA	186	A5
Moreland	OR	317	H6
Morgan	OR	128	B2
Morgan Acres	WA	347	D11
MORO	OR	127	C2
❖ MORTON	WA	118	B2
❖ MOSCOW	ID	249	C5
❖ MOSES LAKE	WA	242	C3
❖ MOSIER	OR	196	A5
❖ MOSSYROCK	WA	118	A2
Mountaindale	OR	125	C1
Mountain Home	OR	198	D4
Mountain Home	WA	238	A6
Mountain Home Park	WA	122	A3
Mountain View	WA	158	C6
Mountain View Beach	WA	168	A6
❖ MOUNT ANGEL	OR	205	C3
Mount Baker	WA	282	E2
Mount Hebron	CA	150	B3
Mount Hood	OR	200	B1
Mount Hood	OR	202	C1
Mount Hope	OR	126	A3
Mount Hope	WA	114	C2
Mount Idaho	ID	123	C3
❖ MOUNTLAKE TERRACE	WA	171	B6
Mount Pleasant	WA	193	D7
Mount Scott-Arleta	OR	318	D3
Mount Tabor	OR	314	D6
❖ MOUNT VERNON	OR	137	A2
❖ MOUNT VERNON	WA	260	H12
Mount View	OR	150	A2
Mowich	OR	142	C2
❖ MOXEE CITY	WA	243	D7
❖ MOYIE SPRINGS	ID	107	B1
Mud Springs	WA	112	B1
❖ MUKILTEO	WA	266	D5
Mulino	OR	199	D7
Mulloy	OR	199	B5
Multnomah	OR	316	B6
Mumby	WA	184	B2
Munra	OR	129	B1
Murdock	WA	196	C6
Murnen	WA	117	B1
Murphy	ID	147	C2
Murphy	OR	229	B7
Murrayhill	OR	199	A3
Murrayville	BC	158	C1
Myrick	OR	129	B1
❖ MYRTLE CREEK	OR	225	C1
❖ MYRTLE POINT	OR	140	B2
N			
❖ NACHES	WA	243	A4
Naef	OR	199	D4
Nahcotta	WA	186	A2
❖ NAMPA	ID	147	B1
❖ NANAIMO	BC	93	A3
Nanoose Bay	BC	92	C3
❖ NAPAVINE	WA	187	C1
Naples	ID	107	B2

COMMUNITY	ST.	PG.	GD.
Napton	OR	147	A1
Narrows	OR	133	C2
Narrows	OR	145	B2
Naselle	WA	186	C5
Nashville	OR	133	A1
Nason Creek	WA	111	C1
Natal	OR	117	B3
National	WA	118	B1
Navy Yard City	WA	270	E11
Naylor	WA	112	C3
Neah Bay	BC	100	B2
Neahkahnie Beach	OR	191	B3
Neawanna Station	OR	301	J6
Necanicum Junction	OR	188	D7
Nedonna Beach	OR	191	B5
Needy	OR	205	D1
❖ NEHALEM	OR	191	B4
Neilton	WA	109	A2
Nelscott	OR	203	A5
Nelson	WA	240	A2
Nelway	BC	106	C1
Nena	OR	127	B3
Neotsu	OR	203	B4
Neptune Beach	WA	158	B6
Nesika Beach	OR	228	A4
Neskowin	OR	203	B2
❖ NESPELEM	WA	105	A3
Netarts	OR	197	A2
Newaukum	WA	184	B7
❖ NEWBERG	OR	198	D5
New Bridge	OR	139	A1
New Brighton	BC	93	B2
❖ NEWCASTLE	WA	175	C4
New Era	OR	199	C5
Newell	CA	151	A3
Newhalem	WA	103	B2
New Hope	OR	229	B7
New Idaho	OR	152	A2
New Idanha	OR	134	B1
New Kamilche	WA	180	A5
New London	WA	178	A5
Newman Lake	WA	352	F6
❖ NEW MEADOWS	ID	251	A4
New Pine Creek	CA	152	A3
New Pine Creek	OR	152	A3
❖ NEW PLYMOUTH	ID	139	B3
❖ NEWPORT	OR	206	B4
❖ NEWPORT	WA	106	C3
Newport Heights	OR	206	B4
Newport Hills	WA	175	C3
New Princeton	OR	145	C2
Newton	BC	157	A7
Newton	OR	198	D1
Newton	WA	177	C5
❖ NEW WESTMINSTER	BC	156	D5
❖ NEZ PERCE	ID	123	C2
Niagara	OR	134	A1
Nicola	BC	95	C1
Nighthawk	WA	104	C1
Nile	WA	119	B1
Nimrod	OR	134	A3
Ninety One	OR	205	C1
Nippon	WA	111	B1
Nisqually	WA	181	A6
Nisson	WA	178	B4
Nitinat	BC	100	B1
Nolin	OR	129	A1
Nonpareil	OR	141	B2
❖ NOOKSACK	WA	102	B1
Nooksack Salmon Hatchery	WA	102	B1
Noon	OR	133	B1
Norgate	BC	254	H5
Norma Beach	WA	171	B4
Norman	WA	168	B4
❖ NORMANDY PARK	WA	175	A6
North Albany	OR	326	B5
North Beach	OR	214	B5
North Beach	WA	171	A7
North Bend	BC	95	A1
❖ NORTH BEND	OR	333	F6
❖ NORTH BEND	WA	176	C4
❖ NORTH BONNEVILLE	WA	194	C6
North Central	OR	200	B1
North City	WA	171	B6
North Cowichan	BC	101	A1
Northeast	OR	200	B1
Northfork	OR	151	B1
North Fork	OR	214	C7
North Gate	WA	171	B7
North Gresham	OR	200	A1
North Howell	OR	205	B4
Northilla	WA	174	D7
North Junction (Davidson)	OR	127	B3
North Lewiston	ID	250	C4
North Olympia	WA	180	D5
❖ NORTH PLAINS	OR	125	C1
❖ NORTHPORT	WA	106	A1
❖ NORTH POWDER	OR	130	B2
North Prosser	WA	120	C3
North Puyallup	WA	182	A3
North Santiam	OR	133	C1
North Scholls	OR	198	D3
North Springfield	OR	330	G2
Northwest	OR	312	C4
Northwest Industrial	OR	312	B2
Norway	OR	220	D6
Norwood	ID	251	C7
Norwood	OR	199	B4
Noti	OR	133	A2
❖ NOTUS	ID	147	B1
Novelty	WA	110	C1
Nulls Crossing	WA	184	D6
Nye	OR	129	B2
Nyland	WA	110	C1
❖ NYSSA	OR	139	A3
O			
Oak Grove	OR	195	C6

COMMUNITY	ST.	PG.	GD.
Oak Grove	OR	321	J6
❖ OAK HARBOR	WA	167	B2
Oak Hills	OR	199	A1
❖ OAKLAND	OR	219	A7
Oakland	WA	180	B2
Oak Park	OR	323	E9
Oak Park	WA	193	B7
Oak Point	WA	117	B3
❖ OAKRIDGE	OR	142	A1
Oaks	OR	334	E11
❖ OAKSDALE	WA	114	C3
Oak Springs	OR	127	B3
❖ OAKVILLE	WA	117	B1
OBrien	OR	233	A6
OBrien	WA	291	J5
Ocasta	WA	183	B2
Ocean City	WA	177	B5
Oceanlake	OR	203	A4
Ocean Park	BC	158	D1
Ocean Park	WA	186	A2
❖ OCEAN SHORES	WA	298	C2
Oceanside	OR	197	A2
Oceanside	WA	186	A4
Odell	OR	195	C7
Odell Lake	OR	142	B1
Odessa	OR	231	B6
❖ ODESSA	WA	113	B3
Ohop	WA	118	B1
❖ OKANOGAN	WA	104	C3
Oklahoma Hill	OR	117	B3
Olalla	OR	141	A2
Olalla	WA	174	C6
Old Colton	OR	126	A3
Old Town	OR	219	A7
Oldtown	WA	106	C3
Oldtown-Chinatown	OR	313	F5
Olene	OR	150	C2
Olex	OR	128	A2
Olga	WA	160	A3
Olney	OR	188	D3
❖ OLYMPIA	WA	297	C7
Olympic View	WA	170	A7
❖ OMAK	WA	104	C2
Ona	OR	206	B7
Onalaska	WA	118	A2
❖ ONAWAY	ID	249	D1
ONeil	OR	213	A4
ONeil Corners	OR	199	C6
❖ ONTARIO	OR	139	A3
Ontario Heights	OR	139	A3
Opal City	OR	212	D2
Ophir	OR	228	A3
Opportunity	WA	350	H12
Orcas	WA	101	C2
Orchard	WA	193	A6
Orchard Avenue	WA	350	B5
Orchard Heights	WA	271	B14
Orchard Park	WA	349	J6
Orchard View	OR	198	A6
Ordnance	OR	128	C1
Oreana	ID	147	C2
❖ OREGON CITY	OR	199	D5
Oregon Trunk Junction	OR	127	B1
Orenco	OR	199	A1
Oretown	OR	203	B1
Orient	OR	200	C1
Orient	WA	105	C1
Orilla	WA	289	J7
❖ OROFINO	ID	123	C2
Orondo	WA	236	A1
❖ OROVILLE	WA	104	C1
Orrs Corner	OR	204	B6
❖ ORTING	WA	182	C5
Osborn Corner	WA	171	C4
❖ OSBURN	ID	115	C2
Osceola	WA	182	D3
Oso	WA	102	C3
❖ OSOYOOS	BC	104	C1
Ostrander	WA	303	F1
❖ OTHELLO	WA	121	A1
Otis	OR	203	B3
Otis Junction	OR	203	B3
Otis Orchards	WA	352	B9
Otter Bay	BC	101	
Otter Point	BC	101	A2
Otter Rock	OR	206	B2
Outlet Bay	ID	107	A2
Outlook	OR	200	A4
Outlook	WA	120	B2
Overland	OR	220	D3
Overlook	OR	308	C6
Owyhee	ID	253	D6
Owyhee	OR	139	A3
Oxman	OR	138	C1
Oxyoke	OR	229	B3
Oyhut	WA	177	B6
Oyster River	BC	92	A1
Oysterville	OR	206	B5
Oysterville	WA	186	A1
P			
❖ PACIFIC	WA	182	B2
Pacific Beach	WA	177	B2
Pacific Beach	WA	186	A4
Pacific City	OR	197	A7
Packard	WA	113	C3
Packwood	WA	118	C2
Page	ID	115	C2
❖ PAISLEY	OR	151	C1
Palmer Junction	OR	130	B1
❖ PALOUSE	WA	249	B1
Panakanic	WA	196	B1
Pandora	WA	114	C3
Park	WA	161	C2
Parkdale	OR	202	C1
Parker	WA	120	A2
Parkersburg	OR	220	B5
Parkers Mill	OR	128	C3

❖ - Indicates City, District or Township

PNW

INTRO

Cities & Communities Index

COMMUNITY	ST.	PG.	GD.
Parkland	WA	181	D4
Park Place	OR	199	D4
Parkrose	OR	315	J1
Parkrose Heights	OR	315	J3
❖ PARKSVILLE	BC	92	C3
Parkwater	WA	349	H6
Parkwood	WA	174	C4
Parliament	OR	131	B1
❖ PARMA	ID	139	A3
Parvin	WA	122	C1
Pasadena Park	WA	350	E3
❖ PASCO	WA	343	E4
Pataha	WA	122	A2
Pataha	WA	122	B2
❖ PATEROS	WA	112	B1
Paterson	WA	120	C3
Patrick Creek	CA	148	C3
Paulina	OR	136	B3
❖ PAYETTE	ID	139	A3
Payette Heights	ID	139	A3
Pearl District	OR	313	E4
Pebble Beach	WA	168	A7
Peck	ID	123	B2
Pedee	OR	133	B1
❖ PE ELL	WA	117	B2
Pelican City	OR	338	A3
Penawawa	WA	122	B1
Pendair Heights	OR	129	B1
Pender Island	BC	101	B1
❖ PENDLETON	OR	129	B2
Pend Oreille Village	WA	106	B1
Penn Cove Park	WA	167	B4
Peola	WA	122	C2
Peoria	OR	210	A1
Perrinville	WA	171	B5
Perry	OR	130	A2
Perrydale	OR	204	B3
Peshastin	WA	238	A1
Petersburg	OR	196	D7
Peterson	BC	106	A1
Peyton	WA	122	B1
❖ PHILOMATH	OR	133	B1
Phoenix	BC	105	B1
❖ PHOENIX	OR	234	B2
Piedmont	OR	309	F6
Piedmont	WA	164	C6
Pigeon Springs	WA	118	A3
Pilchuck	WA	168	D4
Pillar Rock	WA	117	A2
❖ PILOT ROCK	OR	129	B2
Pinckney	OR	322	G11
Pine	OR	131	A3
Pine City	OR	128	C1
Pine City	WA	114	B3
Pine Glen	WA	111	B3
Pine Grove	OR	127	A3
Pine Grove	OR	195	D6
❖ PINEHURST	ID	115	C2
Pinehurst	ID	131	C2
Pinehurst	OR	150	A2
Pinehurst	WA	269	F2
Pine Ridge	ID	131	C3
Pine Ridge	OR	231	D3
Ping	WA	122	B1
Pirtle	OR	207	C5
Pistol River	OR	232	B1
Pitt	WA	196	C3
❖ PITT MEADOWS	BC	157	B5
Pittsburg	OR	125	B1
Placer	OR	229	C2
Plain	WA	111	C1
Plainview	OR	210	C1
Plainview	OR	212	A6
Plaza	WA	114	C2
Pleasantdale	OR	204	D1
Pleasant Hill	OR	215	D4
Pleasant Hill	WA	189	C1
Pleasant Home	OR	200	C1
Pleasant Valley	OR	197	C4
Pleasant Valley	OR	200	A1
Pleasant Valley	OR	229	B3
Pleasant View	WA	121	C2
❖ PLUMMER	ID	115	A2
Plush	OR	152	B1
Pluvius	WA	117	B2
Plymouth	WA	121	A3
Pocahontas	OR	138	A1
Pocahontas Bay	WA	106	C3
Pocono	ID	115	C3
Point Roberts	WA	101	C1
Point Terrace	OR	214	D2
Point White	WA	271	F7
Pollock	ID	131	C2
❖ POMEROY	WA	122	B2
Pomona	WA	243	C4
❖ PONDERAY	ID	244	A1
Ponderosa Estates	WA	182	C4
Ponders Corner	WA	181	C4
Pondosa	OR	130	B3
Portage	WA	174	D6
❖ PORT ALBERNI	BC	92	B3
❖ PORT ANGELES	WA	261	E5
❖ PORT COQUITLAM	BC	157	B4
Porter	WA	117	B1
Port Gamble	WA	170	C4
Port Hammond	BC	157	C6
Porthill	ID	107	B1
Port Kells	BC	157	B6
❖ PORTLAND	OR	316	C3
Port Ludlow	WA	170	B3
Port Madison	WA	170	D7
Port Mellon	BC	93	B2
❖ PORT MOODY	BC	157	A4
❖ PORT ORCHARD	WA	270	J14
❖ PORT ORFORD	OR	224	A6
Port Renfrew	BC	100	C2
Portsmouth	OR	308	A3

COMMUNITY	ST.	PG.	GD.
❖ PORT TOWNSEND	WA	263	C2
Port Washington	BC	101	B1
Port Williams	WA	262	J8
Possession	WA	171	A3
Post	OR	136	A2
❖ POST FALLS	ID	353	F5
❖ POTLATCH	ID	249	D1
Potlatch	WA	173	A6
Potlatch Junction	ID	249	D1
❖ POULSBO	WA	170	B7
Powell Butte	OR	213	B6
Powellhurst	OR	200	A1
❖ POWELL RIVER	BC	92	C1
Powell Valley	OR	200	B1
Power City	OR	129	A1
Power House	WA	243	A4
❖ POWERS	OR	140	B3
Powers	WA	122	A2
Prahl	OR	199	B6
Prairie Center	WA	167	B4
❖ PRAIRIE CITY	OR	137	B2
Prairie Heights	WA	182	D4
Prairie Ridge	WA	182	C4
Pratum	OR	205	B5
Preachers Slough	WA	117	A1
❖ PRESCOTT	OR	189	C5
❖ PRESCOTT	WA	121	C2
Preston	WA	176	B4
Prichard	ID	115	C1
Priest Rapids	WA	120	B2
❖ PRIEST RIVER	ID	107	A3
❖ PRINCETON	BC	95	C3
Princeton	ID	123	A1
Prindle	WA	194	A7
❖ PRINEVILLE	OR	213	C4
Prineville Junction	OR	212	D4
Pringle	OR	324	J1
Proebstel	WA	193	A5
Prospect	OR	226	C7
Prosper	OR	220	B5
❖ PROSSER	WA	120	B3
Pryor	OR	142	A1
❖ PULLMAN	WA	249	B5
Purdy	WA	174	C6
Purrington	WA	122	B1
❖ PUYALLUP	WA	182	B4
Q			
Qualicum Beach	BC	92	C3
Quartz Mountain	OR	151	C2
Quatama	OR	199	A1
Quathiaski Cove	BC	92	A1
Queen Anne Hill	WA	277	G2
Queen Borough	BC	156	D6
Queets	WA	172	B3
Quilcen	WA	109	C1
Quilchena	BC	95	C1
Quinaby	OR	204	D4
Quinault	WA	109	A2
Quincy	OR	117	B3
❖ QUINCY	WA	112	B3
Quines Creek	OR	225	C6
R			
Rafton	OR	192	A6
Rahms	WA	114	C2
Rainbow	OR	134	B2
❖ RAINIER	OR	302	F14
❖ RAINIER	WA	118	A1
Rainier Beach	WA	287	G3
Rainier Valley	WA	282	D6
Rainrock	OR	214	D1
Raleigh Hills	OR	199	B2
Ramapo	WA	164	D6
Ramey	ID	139	A3
Ramsey	ID	245	A3
Rand	OR	149	A1
Randle	WA	118	C2
❖ RATHDRUM	ID	115	A1
Ravenna	WA	274	D4
Ravensdale	WA	176	A7
❖ RAYMOND	WA	117	A1
❖ REARDON	WA	114	A2
Redd	WA	121	B2
Redland	OR	200	A5
❖ REDMOND	OR	212	D5
❖ REDMOND	WA	171	D7
Redondo	WA	175	B7
Redwood	OR	229	B6
Reed	OR	318	A3
Reeds Mill	OR	128	C3
❖ REEDSPORT	OR	218	C2
Reedville	OR	199	A2
Rees Corner	WA	171	D4
Relief	WA	122	A2
Remac	BC	106	B1
Remote	OR	140	C3
Renfrew Heights	BC	255	E14
❖ RENTON	WA	289	J4
Renton Junction	WA	289	J6
❖ REPUBLIC	WA	105	B2
Reser	WA	121	C2
Reston	OR	141	A2
❖ REUBENS	ID	123	B2
Rex	OR	198	D5
Rhinehart	OR	130	A2
Rhodesia Beach	WA	183	C7
Rhododendron	OR	201	C5
Rhododendron Park	WA	182	C4
Rice	OR	127	B2
Rice	WA	105	C2
Rice Hill	OR	219	A5
❖ RICHLAND	OR	139	A1
❖ RICHLAND	WA	340	E13
❖ RICHMOND	BC	156	C6
Richmond	OR	136	B1
Richmond	OR	318	B1
Richmond Beach	WA	171	A6
Rickreall	OR	204	B6

COMMUNITY	ST.	PG.	GD.
❖ RIDDLE	OR	225	B3
❖ RIDGEFIELD	WA	192	C3
Rieth	OR	129	B1
Rifton	WA	121	C2
❖ RIGGINS	ID	131	C2
Riley	OR	144	C1
Riparia	WA	122	A2
Ripplebrook	OR	126	B3
Risbeck	WA	122	C1
Ritter	OR	129	A3
❖ RITZVILLE	WA	113	C3
Riverdale	OR	321	G2
River Jordan	BC	100	C2
River Junction	OR	192	B6
Riversdale	OR	221	B3
Riverside	ID	123	C2
Riverside	OR	146	A1
Riverside	OR	207	B5
Riverside	WA	102	C3
Riverside	WA	104	C2
Riverton	OR	220	C5
Riverton	WA	289	F1
Riverton Heights	WA	288	D3
Riverwood	OR	321	G3
Roads End	OR	203	A4
Roanoke	WA	283	J1
Roberts	OR	135	C3
Robinette	OR	139	A1
Robinwood	OR	199	C4
Roche Harbor	WA	101	C2
Rochester	WA	184	A3
Rockaway Beach	ID	245	B5
❖ ROCKAWAY BEACH	OR	191	B6
Rock Creek	BC	105	A1
Rock Creek	OR	128	A2
Rock Creek	OR	130	A3
Rock Creek	OR	192	A7
Rockdale	WA	111	A1
Rockford	OR	195	C5
❖ ROCKFORD	WA	114	C2
Rockford Bay	ID	247	D4
❖ ROCK ISLAND	WA	239	B5
Rockport	WA	103	A2
Rockwood	OR	200	A1
Rocky Point	ID	248	B6
Rocky Point	OR	231	B5
Rocky Point	WA	270	E7
Rocky Point	WA	303	E4
Rodena Beach	WA	167	C4
❖ ROGUE RIVER	OR	229	D6
Rollingbay	WA	174	D1
Rollins	WA	114	C2
Rome	OR	146	C3
Ronald	WA	240	A1
Rony	WA	117	B1
Roosevelt	WA	110	C1
Roosevelt	WA	128	A1
❖ ROSALIA	WA	114	C3
Rosario	WA	101	C2
Rosario Beach	WA	259	C14
Roseberry	ID	252	D1
❖ ROSEBURG	OR	334	H4
Rosebush	OR	127	C2
Rose City Park	OR	314	C4
Rosedale	BC	94	C3
Rosedale	OR	324	F11
Rosedale	WA	174	B7
Rosehilla	WA	174	D7
Rose Lake	ID	248	D2
Rose Lodge	OR	203	C4
Rosemont	OR	199	C4
Rose Springs	WA	122	B2
Roseway	OR	315	E2
Rosewood	OR	199	C4
❖ ROSLYN	WA	240	A1
❖ ROSSLAND	BC	106	A1
Roswell	ID	139	A3
Rothe	OR	199	D4
Round Prairie	OR	221	B7
Rowena	OR	196	B6
❖ ROY	WA	181	C7
❖ ROYAL CITY	WA	120	C1
Royal Oak	BC	159	C5
Royston	BC	92	A2
Roy Vadis	OR	125	C1
Roza	WA	243	C3
Rubicon	ID	131	C3
Ruch	OR	149	B2
Ruff	WA	113	A3
❖ RUFUS	OR	127	C1
Ruggs	OR	128	C2
Rupple	WA	119	C2
Rural Dell	OR	205	D2
Russell	OR	133	A1
Russell Landing	WA	311	F1
❖ RUSTON	WA	181	D1
Rutledge	OR	127	C2
Ryderwood	WA	187	B5
Rye Valley	OR	138	C2
Rykerts	BC	107	B1
S			
Saanichton	BC	159	C3
Sabin	OR	313	H1
Safley	OR	219	B2
Sagehill	WA	121	A1
Saginaw	OR	215	B6
Sagle	ID	244	A3
Sago	OR	130	B3
Sahalee	WA	175	D2
Saint Andrews	WA	112	C2
❖ SAINT HELENS	OR	192	B2
Saint Jose	ID	115	B2
❖ SAINT JOHN	WA	114	B3
Saint Johns	OR	192	B6
Saint Joseph	OR	198	B7
Saint Louis	OR	205	A2
❖ SAINT MARIES	ID	248	D7

COMMUNITY	ST.	PG.	GD.
Saint Martins Hot Springs	WA	195	A4
❖ SAINT PAUL	OR	198	D7
Saint Urbans	WA	187	C2
❖ SALEM	OR	325	D5
Salishan	WA	182	A3
Salkum	WA	118	A2
Salmon	OR	201	B4
Salmon Beach	WA	181	C1
Salmonberry	OR	125	A1
Salmon Creek	WA	192	C5
Saltery Bay	BC	92	C1
Samish Island	WA	160	D4
Sams Valley	OR	230	B5
San de Fuca	WA	167	B4
Sanders	ID	115	A3
Sand Hollow	ID	139	B3
Sand Hollow	OR	128	C1
Sandlake	OR	197	B5
❖ SANDPOINT	ID	244	A1
Sandwick	BC	92	A2
❖ SANDY	OR	200	C4
San Marine	OR	328	B14
Santa	ID	115	B3
Santa Clara	OR	215	A1
Santa Cruz	OR	200	C7
Santiam Junction	OR	134	C2
Sappho	WA	163	B6
Saratoga	WA	167	D7
Sardis	BC	94	C3
Satsop	WA	179	A7
Saturna	BC	101	C1
Saunders Lake	OR	218	B5
Savary Island	BC	92	B1
Saxby	WA	247	B7
❖ SCAPPOOSE	OR	192	A3
Scenic	WA	111	B1
Schaefer	WA	113	C3
Schefflin Corner	OR	125	C1
Schneiders Prairie	WA	180	B5
Scholls	OR	198	D4
Schoonover	WA	113	C3
Schrag	WA	113	B3
Schwana	WA	120	B1
Schwarder	WA	243	B7
❖ SCIO	OR	133	C1
Scofield	OR	125	B1
Scott Bar	CA	149	B3
❖ SCOTTS MILL	OR	205	D4
Scottsburg	OR	140	C1
Scribner	WA	246	B6
Seabeck	WA	173	D1
Seabold	WA	170	C7
Seahurst	WA	175	A5
Seal Rock	OR	206	A7
Seal Rock	WA	109	C1
Searose Beach	OR	209	A5
❖ SEASIDE	OR	301	E9
❖ SEATAC	WA	288	C3
❖ SEATTLE	WA	273	G3
Seattle Heights	WA	171	A5
Seaview	WA	186	A6
Sechelt	BC	93	A2
❖ SEDRO-WOOLLEY	WA	260	J2
Seekseequa Junction	OR	208	A4
Seiad Valley	CA	149	B3
Sekiu	WA	163	B2
❖ SELAH	WA	243	B5
Selleck	WA	176	B7
Sellwood	OR	317	H5
Selma	OR	233	B2
❖ SENECA	OR	137	B3
❖ SEQUIM	WA	262	D13
Service Creek	OR	136	B1
Seven Oaks	OR	230	C7
Sexton Mountain	OR	199	A2
Seymour	BC	255	J5
Shadowood	OR	199	C4
Shady	OR	334	E13
Shady Brook	OR	125	C1
❖ SHADY COVE	OR	230	D2
Shady Pine	OR	235	C1
❖ SHANIKO	OR	127	C3
Shale City	OR	150	A2
Shangri-la Mill	OR	141	C3
Sharps Corner	OR	129	A1
Shawnee	WA	122	C1
Shawnigan Lake	BC	159	A2
Sheaville	OR	147	A2
Shedd	OR	210	B1
Shelburn	OR	133	C1
Shelfler	WA	121	B2
❖ SHELTON	WA	180	A3
Sherar	OR	127	B2
❖ SHERIDAN	OR	125	B3
Sheridan Park	WA	270	H8
❖ SHERWOOD	OR	199	A4
Sherwood Beach	ID	107	A2
Shine	WA	170	B4
Shirley	BC	101	A2
Shore Acres	WA	181	C1
❖ SHORELINE	WA	171	A6
Shorewood	OR	218	B6
Shorewood	WA	285	G7
Shorewood Beach	WA	181	B2
Shortys Corner	OR	200	D4
Shrine Beach	WA	236	A1
Shutler	OR	128	A1
Sidley	BC	105	A1
Sidney	OR	207	C2
Sifton	WA	193	A5
Sightly	WA	118	A2
Silcott	WA	250	A4
❖ SILETZ	OR	206	C2
Silica	BC	106	A1
Siltcoos	OR	214	B5
Silvana	WA	168	C5
Silver Beach	WA	102	B1

COMMUNITY	ST.	PG.	GD.
Silver Brook	WA	118	C2
Silver City	ID	147	B3
Silver Creek	WA	118	A2
Silverdale	WA	174	B1
Silver Falls City	OR	205	D7
Silver Lake	BC	95	A3
Silver Lake	OR	143	B2
Silverlake	WA	187	D7
Silver Sands Beach	ID	115	A1
Silverton	ID	115	C2
❖ SILVERTON	OR	205	C4
Silvies	OR	137	B3
Similk Beach	WA	160	C7
Simnasho	OR	127	A3
Sims Corner	WA	112	C1
Sisco	WA	168	D6
Sisco Heights	WA	168	D6
Siskiyou	OR	234	D6
❖ SISTERS	OR	211	D5
Sitkum	OR	140	C2
Siuslaw	OR	132	C3
Six Corners	OR	199	A4
Sixes	OR	224	B4
Six Prong	WA	128	B1
Skamania	WA	194	B7
Skamokawa	WA	117	B2
Skelley	OR	219	A4
Skull Spring	OR	146	B1
❖ SKYKOMISH	OR	111	A1
Skyway	WA	287	J7
Slate Creek	ID	131	C1
Sliammon	BC	92	B1
Smelter Heights	ID	115	C2
❖ SMELTERVILLE	ID	115	C2
Smeltz	OR	129	B1
Smith Prairie	WA	167	C4
Smith River	CA	148	B3
Smithville	WA	196	C6
Smokey Point	WA	168	C6
Snake River	WA	121	B2
Snake River Junction	WA	121	B2
Snee Oosh	WA	160	D7
❖ SNOHOMISH	WA	171	D3
❖ SNOQUALMIE	WA	176	B4
Snowden	WA	196	A2
Snug Harbor	WA	164	D6
❖ SOAP LAKE	WA	112	C2
Soda Springs	WA	119	B2
❖ SODAVILLE	OR	133	C2
Sokulk	WA	114	C3
Somerset West	OR	199	A1
Sooke	BC	101	A2
Sorrento Ridge	OR	199	B3
South Aberdeen	WA	178	B7
South Arm	BC	156	B6
South Bay	WA	180	D5
South Beach	OR	206	B4
South Beach	WA	101	C1
South Beach	WA	174	D3
South Bellingham	WA	258	C10
❖ SOUTH BEND	WA	183	D6
❖ SOUTH BROADWAY	WA	243	B7
South Burlingame	OR	316	D6
South Cheney	WA	114	B2
❖ SOUTH CLE ELUM	WA	240	B2
South Colby	WA	174	C4
South Elma	WA	179	B7
South Highlands	WA	343	C12
South Junction	OR	208	C1
South Lake Oswego	OR	320	E7
❖ SOUTH PRAIRIE	WA	182	D5
South Slope	BC	156	C5
South Tabor	OR	318	E1
South Tacoma	WA	294	D5
South Union	WA	184	C1
South Wellington	BC	93	A3
Southwest	OR	200	A1
Southwest Hills	OR	316	B1
South Westminster	BC	156	D6
Southwick	ID	123	B1
Southworth	WA	174	D4
Spanaway	WA	181	D5
❖ SPANGLE	WA	114	C2
Sparks	OR	129	B1
Sparta	OR	130	C3
Spee-bi-dah	WA	168	B7
❖ SPIRIT LAKE	ID	115	A1
Spitzenberg	OR	125	C1
❖ SPOKANE	WA	346	B13
Spokane Bridge	WA	352	G10
❖ SPRAGUE	WA	114	A3
Sprague River	OR	151	A1
❖ SPRAY	OR	136	B1
Spring Beach	WA	174	C7
Springbrook	OR	198	D5
Springdale	OR	200	C1
❖ SPRINGDALE	WA	106	B3
❖ SPRINGFIELD	OR	331	E6
Springfield Junction	OR	330	F7
Spring Lake	OR	235	C5
Springston	ID	248	B4
Spring Valley	WA	114	C2
Spuzzum	BC	95	A2
❖ SQUAMISH	BC	93	C2
Squaw Canyon	WA	114	C3
Stabler	WA	194	C3
Stafford	OR	199	C4
Staley	WA	249	B6
Stampede	WA	111	A3
❖ STANFIELD	OR	129	A1
Stanfield Junction	OR	129	A1
❖ STANWOOD	WA	168	B4
Star	ID	147	C1
❖ STARBUCK	WA	122	A2
Starkey	ID	131	C3
Starkey	OR	125	C1
Starkey	OR	129	C2

❖ - Indicates City, District or Township

Cities & Communities Index

COMMUNITY	ST.	PG.	GD.
Starlake	WA	175	B7
Startup	WA	110	C1
Starvation Heights	OR	229	D5
State Line Village	ID	352	H9
Stave Falls	BC	94	B3
❖ STAYTON	OR	133	C1
Steelhead	BC	94	B3
Stehekin	WA	103	C3
❖ STEILACOOM	WA	181	B4
Stephens	OR	221	B1
Steptoe	WA	114	C3
Stevens	ID	131	C3
❖ STEVENSON	WA	194	C5
Steveston	BC	156	B7
Stillwater	BC	92	C2
Stillwater	WA	176	B1
Stimson Mill	OR	198	B2
Stoddard	ID	147	C2
Stratford	WA	113	A2
Strawberry	OR	128	C2
Striebels Corner	WA	170	C5
Stronghold	CA	151	A3
Stuck	WA	182	C2
Sturdies Bay	BC	101	B1
Sturgeon	ID	115	A1
❖ SUBLIMITY	OR	133	C1
Sudden Valley	WA	161	B1
Sullivans Gulch	OR	313	J4
Sulphur Springs	OR	214	D7
❖ SULTAN	WA	110	C1
❖ SUMAS	WA	102	B1
Summer Lake	OR	143	C3
❖ SUMMERVILLE	OR	130	A2
Summit	OR	195	C6
Summit	WA	176	A7
Summit	WA	182	A4
Summits	OR	133	A1
Sumner	OR	140	B2
❖ SUMNER	WA	182	B3
❖ SUMPTER	OR	138	A1
Suncrest	BC	156	C5
Sundale	WA	128	A1
Sunderland	OR	310	B4
Sunlight Beach	WA	170	D2
Sunnycrest	OR	198	C5
Sunnydale	WA	175	A5
Sunnydale	WA	184	C3
Sunny Shores	WA	168	B6
Sunny Shores Acres	WA	168	A6
Sunnyside	OR	200	A2
Sunnyside	OR	314	A7
Sunnyside	OR	324	J12
❖ SUNNYSIDE	WA	120	B2
Sunnyside	WA	121	C3
Sunnyslope	WA	174	A4
Sunnyslope	WA	238	D3
Sunny Valley	OR	229	B2
Sunriver	OR	217	A6
Sunset	BC	156	B5
Sunset	OR	131	A3
Sunset	OR	199	D4
Sunset	WA	114	B3
Sunset Beach	OR	188	B3
Sunset Beach	WA	167	D4
Sunset Beach	WA	173	D6
Sunset Beach	WA	174	D6
Sunset Beach	WA	177	B2
Sunset Beach	WA	181	C3
Suplee	OR	136	C3
Suquamish	WA	170	C7
Surrey Centre	BC	157	B7
Susanville	OR	137	B1
❖ SUTHERLIN	OR	221	C1
Sutico	WA	117	B1
Sutton	WA	122	A1
Suver Junction	OR	207	B2
Svensen	OR	117	A3
Svensen Junction	OR	117	A3
Swansonville	WA	170	B3
Swedetown	OR	189	A5
Sweeney	ID	115	C2
Sweet	ID	139	C3
❖ SWEET HOME	OR	134	A2
Sweetwater	ID	123	A2
Swem	WA	117	B1
Swift	WA	122	B1
Swinomish Village	WA	160	D7
Swisshome	OR	132	C3
Sylvan	WA	181	B2
Sylvan Beach	WA	174	D5
Sylvan Highlands	OR	312	A7
Sylvanite	MT	107	C1
T			
Table Rock	OR	230	C6
❖ TACOMA	WA	292	D5
Taft	OR	203	A5
Tahlequah	WA	181	D1
Taholah	WA	172	B6
Tahuya	WA	173	B7
Takilma	OR	233	B6
Talache	ID	244	B5
Talbot	OR	207	C2
❖ TALENT	OR	234	B3
Tamarack	ID	131	C3
Tampico	WA	119	C2
❖ TANGENT	OR	207	C6
Tanner	WA	176	C5
Tasker	WA	119	C1
Taylorville	OR	117	B3
Teanaway	WA	240	C2
❖ TEKOA	WA	114	C3
Telford	WA	113	C1
Telma	WA	111	C1
Telocaset	OR	130	B3
Templeton	OR	218	C4
❖ TENINO	WA	184	D3
Tenino Junction	WA	184	D3
Tenmile	OR	141	A2
Tenmile	OR	218	B4
❖ TENSED	ID	115	A3
Terrace Heights	WA	243	C6
Terrebone	OR	212	D4
Terrys Corner	WA	167	D4
❖ THE DALLES	OR	196	C7
Thomas	WA	175	B7
Thompson	BC	156	A6
Thompson Place	WA	181	A6
Thorndyke	WA	289	E4
Thorn Hollow	OR	129	C1
Thornton	WA	114	C3
Thorp	WA	241	A4
Thrall	WA	241	B7
Thrashers Corner	WA	171	C5
Three Lakes	WA	110	C1
Three Lynx	OR	126	B3
Three Pines	OR	229	B3
Three Rivers	OR	217	A7
Three Rocks	OR	203	A3
Three Tree Point	WA	175	A5
Thrift	WA	182	B6
Thurston	OR	331	J6
Tide	OR	132	C3
Tidewater	OR	209	C1
Tiernan	OR	214	C2
Tierra Del Mar	OR	197	A6
❖ TIETON	WA	119	C1
Tietonview Grange	WA	119	C2
❖ TIGARD	OR	199	B3
❖ TILLAMOOK	OR	197	B2
Tillamook Junction	OR	125	C1
Tiller	OR	141	C3
Tillicum	BC	256	E5
Tillicum	WA	181	C5
Timber Grove	OR	126	A3
Timberlane	WA	175	D7
Tokeland	WA	183	C5
Toketee Falls	OR	222	D4
Tokio	WA	113	C3
Tokul	WA	176	C4
❖ TOLEDO	CA	206	C4
❖ TOLEDO	WA	187	D4
Tolovana Park	OR	191	B1
❖ TONASKET	WA	104	C1
Tongue Point Village	OR	188	D1
Tono	WA	184	D4
Top Hat	WA	285	J5
❖ TOPPENISH	WA	120	A2
Torga	WA	111	A2
Touchet	WA	121	B3
Toutle	WA	118	A2
Town & Country	WA	346	J14
❖ TOWN OF ESQUIMALT	BC	256	C8
❖ TOWN OF SIDNEY	BC	159	C2
❖ TOWN OF VIEW ROYAL	BC	256	A4
❖ TOWNSHIP OF LANGLEY	BC	157	D7
Tracy	OR	200	C6
Tracyton	WA	270	G4
Trail	OR	230	D2
Treharne	OR	125	B1
Trenholm	OR	125	C1
Trent	OR	215	D4
Trentwood	WA	351	A3
Trestle Creek	ID	244	C2
Tri-City	OR	225	C2
Trinity	WA	103	C3
❖ TROUTDALE	OR	200	B1
Trout Lake	WA	119	A3
❖ TROY	ID	123	A1
❖ TROY	MT	107	C2
Troy	OR	122	C3
Trude	WA	176	B7
Tsawwassen	BC	101	C1
❖ TUALATIN	OR	199	B4
Tucannon	WA	122	A2
❖ TUKWILA	WA	289	F3
Tulalip	WA	168	B7
Tulalip Shores	WA	168	B7
Tulameen	BC	95	C2
Tulare Beach	WA	168	B6
Tulelake	CA	151	A3
Tulips	WA	177	C5
Tumalo	OR	217	B1
❖ TUMWATER	WA	296	F9
Tumtum	WA	114	B1
Turkey	WA	166	D7
Turner	WA	122	B2
Turner Corner	WA	171	C5
Twickenham	OR	136	A1
Twin Beaches	ID	248	A1
Twin Lakes	WA	182	A1
Twinlow	ID	115	A1
Twin Rocks	OR	191	A6
❖ TWISP	WA	104	A3
Twomile	OR	220	B7
Tye	WA	111	B1
Tyee	OR	141	A1
Tyee Beach	WA	168	A7
Tygh Valley	OR	127	B2
Tyler	WA	114	B2
Tynehead	BC	157	B6
U			
❖ UKIAH	OR	129	B3
Umapine	WA	121	C3
❖ UMATILLA	OR	129	A1
Umli	OR	142	B1
Umpqua	OR	221	A1
Umtanum	WA	243	C1
Uncas	WA	109	C1
Underwood	WA	195	C4
Underwood Heights	WA	195	C4
❖ UNION	OR	130	B2
Union	WA	173	A7
Union Bay	BC	92	B2
Union Creek	OR	141	A3
Union Creek	OR	226	D4
Union Gap	OR	221	C1
❖ UNION GAP	WA	243	C7
Union Junction	OR	130	B2
Union Mills	OR	126	A3
Union Mills	WA	181	A6
❖ UNIONTOWN	WA	250	B2
Unionville	OR	204	C2
United Junction	OR	192	B6
❖ UNITY	OR	138	A2
University	WA	274	C5
❖ UNIV ENDOWMENT LANDS	BC	156	A4
University Park	OR	308	A5
❖ UNIVERSITY PLACE	WA	294	A4
Upper Farm	OR	206	D2
Upper Highland	OR	200	B7
Upper Mill	WA	110	C3
Upper Preston	WA	176	B4
Upper Soda	OR	134	B2
Usk	WA	106	C3
Ustick	ID	253	B2
Utsalady	WA	167	D3
V			
❖ VADER	WA	187	C4
Vadis	OR	125	C1
Vail	WA	118	A1
Valby	OR	128	B2
❖ VALE	OR	138	C3
Valle Vista	OR	192	A7
Valley	WA	106	B3
Valleycliffe	BC	93	C2
Valley Falls	OR	152	A1
Valleyford	WA	246	D6
Valley Junction	OR	125	A3
Van	OR	137	B3
Vananda	BC	92	B2
Van Asselt	WA	286	D1
❖ VANCOUVER	BC	254	G13
❖ VANCOUVER	WA	305	F3
Vancouver Junction	WA	192	C5
Van Horn	OR	195	D6
Vantage	WA	120	B1
Van Zandt	WA	102	B1
Vasa Park	WA	175	D3
Vashon	WA	174	D5
Vashon Center	WA	174	D6
Vashon Heights	WA	174	D4
Vaughn	OR	133	A2
Vaughn	WA	174	A7
Vega	WA	181	A4
Venator	OR	146	A2
Venersborg	WA	193	B3
❖ VENETA	OR	133	B3
Venice	WA	174	C1
Veradale	WA	351	C8
Verboort	OR	125	B1
Vermon	OR	309	J6
Vesuvius	BC	101	B1
Victoria	BC	156	C5
Vida	OR	134	A2
View Ridge	WA	275	G3
Village Bay	BC	101	B1
Vineland	WA	250	B4
Vinemaple	OR	125	A1
Vinland	WA	170	B6
Vinson	OR	129	A2
Viola	ID	249	C3
Viola	OR	200	B6
Virden	WA	240	D1
Virginia	WA	170	B7
Vision Acres	WA	189	C4
Voltage	OR	145	B2
Voorhies	OR	234	B2
W			
Wabash	WA	182	D2
Waconda	OR	205	A3
Wagner	WA	110	C1
Wagnersburg	WA	239	A1
Wagontire	OR	144	B2
Wahkiacus	WA	196	D3
❖ WAITSBURG	WA	122	A2
Waitsburg Junction	WA	122	A2
Wakonda Beach	OR	328	B10
Waldale	WA	241	B5
❖ WALDPORT	OR	328	C7
Walker	OR	215	B6
❖ WALLACE	ID	115	C2
Wallace	OR	199	B6
❖ WALLA WALLA	WA	344	E6
Walla Walla East	WA	345	E9
Wallingford	WA	274	A5
❖ WALLOWA	OR	130	B1
Wallula	WA	121	B3
Walnut Grove	BC	157	C6
Walnut Grove	WA	192	D5
Walters	WA	114	C3
Walters Ferry	ID	147	B2
Walterville	OR	133	C3
Walton	OR	133	A2
Walville	WA	117	B2
Wamic	OR	127	A2
Wanapum Village	WA	120	B1
Waneta	BC	106	B1
Wankers Corner	OR	199	C4
Wapato	OR	198	B3
❖ WAPATO	WA	120	A2
Wapinitia	OR	127	A3
❖ WARDEN	WA	121	A1
❖ WARDNER	ID	115	C2
Warm Beach	WA	168	A5
Warm Springs	OR	208	A3
Warner	OR	140	B3
Warren	OR	192	A2
Warren	WA	181	B1
❖ WARRENTON	OR	188	B2
Warwick	WA	127	B1
❖ WASCO	OR	127	C1
Washington Harbor	WA	166	B7
❖ WASHOUGAL	WA	193	B7
❖ WASHTUCNA	WA	121	C1
❖ WATERLOO	OR	133	C1
Waterman	OR	129	C1
Waterman	OR	136	B1
Waterman	WA	271	E9
Waterman Point	WA	271	F8
❖ WATERVILLE	WA	236	C7
Watseco	OR	191	A6
Wauna	OR	117	B3
Wauna	WA	174	B6
Wautauga Beach	WA	271	G8
❖ WAVERLY	WA	114	C2
Wawawai	WA	122	C1
Wayland	OR	129	C1
Wayside	WA	114	B1
Weaver	OR	225	C1
Webster Corners	BC	157	D5
Wecoma Beach	OR	203	A4
Wedderburn	OR	228	A5
Weikel	WA	243	A6
❖ WEISER	ID	139	A2
Welches	OR	201	C5
Wellington	BC	93	A3
Wellpinit	WA	114	A1
Wells	WA	114	A3
Wemme	OR	201	C5
❖ WENATCHEE	WA	238	D4
Wenatchee Heights	WA	239	A6
Wendling	OR	133	C2
Wendson	OR	214	C3
West Beach	WA	101	C2
West Blakely	WA	271	H7
West Fairfield	WA	114	C2
❖ WESTFIR	OR	142	A1
West Fork	WA	105	B2
West Haven	OR	199	B1
Westhaven	WA	298	F11
West Highlands	WA	342	H10
West Kelso	WA	303	B7
West Klamath	OR	235	B4
West Lake	OR	188	B4
Westlake	OR	214	A5
Westlake	WA	242	C3
Westland	OR	129	A1
❖ WEST LINN	OR	199	C4
Westma	ID	147	C1
Westmond	ID	244	A5
❖ WESTON	OR	129	C1
Weston	WA	111	A3
West Park	WA	270	D11
West Pastco	WA	342	E5
Westport	OR	117	B3
❖ WESTPORT	WA	298	G13
West Portland Park	OR	320	A2
❖ WEST RICHLAND	WA	120	C2
West Salem	OR	322	F12
West Seattle	WA	280	D4
West Side	OR	152	A2
West Slope	OR	199	B2
Westsound	WA	101	C2
West Spokane	WA	348	F8
West Stayton	OR	133	C1
West Union	OR	192	A7
West Valley	WA	243	A6
West Wenatchee	WA	238	D4
Westwood	WA	285	G2
West Woodbury	OR	205	B1
Wetico	WA	118	A1
Wetmore	OR	128	B3
Wetzels Corner	OR	200	B3
Wheatland	OR	204	D3
❖ WHEELER	OR	191	B3
Wheeler Heights	OR	191	B4
Whelan	WA	249	B4
Whetstone	WA	122	A2
Whiskey Hill	OR	205	C1
❖ WHISTLER	BC	93	C1
Whiststran	WA	120	C3
White	WA	171	D7
❖ WHITE BIRD	ID	131	C1
White Center	WA	285	G4
White City	OR	230	D6
Whites	WA	179	C6
❖ WHITE SALMON	WA	195	D4
Whiteson	OR	204	B1
White Swan	WA	119	C2
Whitewater	OR	126	B3
Whitlow	WA	249	B5
Whitman	WA	121	A3
Whitney	OR	138	A1
Whitney	WA	344	J12
Whittier	WA	111	A3
Whonnock	BC	94	B3
Wickersham	WA	161	C3
Wilbur	OR	221	C2
❖ WILBUR	WA	113	B1
Wilburton	WA	175	C2
Wilcox	OR	127	C3
Wildcat Lake	WA	174	A2
❖ WILDER	ID	147	A1
Wilderness	WA	176	A7
Wilderville	OR	229	A7
Wildwood	WA	187	A4
Wildwood Heights	BC	92	B1
Wiley City	WA	243	A7
Wilhoit Springs	OR	126	A3
Wilkes	OR	200	A1
Wilkes East	OR	200	A1
❖ WILKESON	WA	182	D5
Wilkins	OR	210	B6
Willada	WA	114	B3
Willamette	OR	199	C5
Willamette City	OR	142	A1
❖ WILLAMINA	OR	125	A3
Willapa	WA	117	A1
Willard	WA	195	B3
Williams	OR	149	B2
Willow Creek	OR	138	C2
Willow Ranch	CA	152	A3
Willows	WA	263	A8
Wilson	OR	316	D5
Wilson	WA	118	A2
Wilson Corner	OR	200	B3
❖ WILSON CREEK	WA	113	A2
❖ WILSONVILLE	OR	199	B5
Wimer	OR	229	D4
Winant	OR	206	B5
Winberry	OR	133	C3
Winchester	ID	123	B2
Winchester	OR	221	C3
Winchester	WA	112	C3
Winchester Bay	OR	218	C2
Windermere	WA	275	F5
Windmaster Corner	OR	195	C5
Winema Beach	OR	203	B1
Wingville	OR	130	B3
Winlock	OR	128	B3
❖ WINLOCK	WA	187	C3
Winona	OR	229	C3
Winona	OR	322	E13
Winona	WA	122	B1
Winslow	WA	271	H2
❖ WINSTON	OR	221	B6
Winston	WA	118	A2
Winterville	OR	220	B6
❖ WINTHROP	WA	104	A2
Winton	WA	111	C1
Wishkah	WA	178	B6
Wishram	WA	127	B1
Wishram Heights	WA	127	B1
Witch Hazel	OR	198	D2
Withrow	WA	112	B2
Wocus	OR	338	B1
Wolf Creek	OR	229	B1
Wolf Lodge	ID	248	C1
Wollochet	WA	181	C3
Wonder	OR	149	A1
❖ WOODBURN	OR	205	B1
Woodfibre	BC	93	C2
❖ WOODINVILLE	WA	171	D6
Woodland	ID	131	C3
❖ WOODLAND	WA	189	D7
Woodland Beach	WA	167	D4
Woodland Park	OR	200	A1
Woodland Park	OR	315	J4
Woodland Park	WA	118	A3
Woodlawn	OR	309	H5
Woodmans	WA	170	A1
Woodmont	WA	175	B7
Woodruff	WA	110	C1
Woodruff Mill	WA	196	D2
Woods	OR	197	A7
Woodson	OR	117	B3
Woodstock	OR	318	B4
❖ WOOD VILLAGE	OR	200	B1
❖ WOODWAY	WA	171	A6
Worden	OR	235	B7
❖ WORLEY	ID	115	A2
Wren	OR	133	A1
Wrentham	OR	127	B2
Wye	BC	256	F4
Wyeth	OR	195	A5
Wymer	WA	243	C2
Wynaco	WA	182	C1
Y			
❖ YACHATS	OR	209	A3
❖ YACOLT	WA	193	B1
Yaculta	BC	92	A1
❖ YAKIMA	WA	243	B6
Yale	BC	95	A2
Yale	WA	118	A3
❖ YAMHILL	OR	198	B5
Yamsay	OR	142	C3
Yankton	OR	192	A1
Yaquina	OR	206	B5
❖ YARROW POINT	WA	175	C1
❖ YELM	WA	118	A1
Yennadon	BC	157	D5
Yeomalt	WA	174	D2
Yoakum	OR	129	A1
Yoder	OR	205	D2
Yokeko Point	WA	160	C7
Yoman	WA	181	A3
Yoman Dock	WA	181	B4
❖ YONCALLA	OR	219	A4
Youbou	BC	100	C1
Young	OR	133	C1
❖ YREKA	CA	149	C3
Z			
Zena	OR	204	C4
Zenith	WA	290	A7
Zigzag	OR	201	C5
❖ ZILLAH	WA	120	A2
Zumwalt	OR	131	A1
Zumwalt	WA	122	B2

❖ - Indicates City, District or Township

Pacific Northwest General Information

Highway Patrol

British Columbia **Washington State** **Oregon State** **Idaho State**	In case of emergency, call 911

Road Conditions

British Columbia	British Columbia Ministry of Transportation and Highways: (205) 387-7788 www.th.gov.bc.ca/bchighways/
Washington State	Washington State Department of Transportation: (888) 766-4636 http://traffic.wsdot.wa.gov/
Oregon State	Salem Online: (503) 976-7277 www.oregonlink.com/weather/index.html
Idaho State	Weather Net: (208) 336-6600 www.state.id.us/itd/rdreport.htm

Department of Transportation

British Columbia	BC Ministry of Transportation & Highways: (250) 387-7788 www.th.gov.bc.ca/bchighways/
Washington State	Washington State Department of Transportation: (360) 709-5520 www.wsdot.wa.gov/
Oregon State	Oregon Department of Transportation: (888) ASK-ODOT www.odot.state.or.us
Idaho State	Idaho State Department of Transportation: (208) 334-8000 www.state.id.us/itd/itdhmpg.htm

Ferry Crossing

British Columbia	BC Ferries' Corporate Marketing Group: (250) 381-1401 www.bcferries.bc.ca/ferries
Washington State	Washington State Department of Transportation: (360) 709-5520 www.wsdot.wa.gov/ferries

Crossing the Border

British Columbia	Revenue Canada: (604) 666-0545 http://www.rc.gc.ca/
Washington State	U.S. Customs: (206) 553-0770 www.customs.ustreas.gov/

Weather Conditions

British Columbia	www.weather.com/weather/int/regions/north_america.html#Canada
Washington State	www.weather.com/weather/us/states/Washington.html
Oregon State	www.weather.com/weather/us/states/Oregon.html
Idaho State	www.weather.com/weather/us/states/Idaho.html

Visitor's Information

British Columbia	British Columbia Visitor's Information: (888) 475-3396 www.th.gov.bc.ca/tourismhome.html
Washington State	Washington State Tourism Division Info Package: (800) 544-1800 www.tourism.wa.gov/011.htm
Oregon State	Oregon Association of Convention & Visitors Bureau: (541) 994-2164 www.oregonlink.com/scva/staff.html
Idaho State	Idaho Department of Commerce: (208) 334-2631 www.idoc.state.id.us/

DISTANCE MAP

Distance between points given in miles and/or kilometers. Mileage determined by most direct driving route.

BRITISH COLUMBIA
VANCOUVER
VANCOUVER ISLAND
VICTORIA
BRITISH COLUMBIA / WASHINGTON
CANADA / USA
BRITISH COLUMBIA / IDAHO
MONTANA / IDAHO
WASHINGTON / IDAHO
54 MI
89 KM
BELLINGHAM
61 MI
340 MI
EVERETT
279 MI
PORT ANGELES
110 MI
27 MI
SEATTLE
WASHINGTON
SPOKANE
31 MI
COEUR D'ALENE
144 MI
121 MI
32 MI
TACOMA
110 MI
174 MI
121 MI
ABERDEEN
50 MI
30 MI
OLYMPIA
137 MI
ELLENSBURG
145 MI
102 MI
IDAHO
36 MI
99 MI
76 MI
YAKIMA
76 MI
LEWISTON
114 MI
101 MI
RICHLAND
WALLA WALLA
56 MI
98 MI
ASTORIA
WASHINGTON / OREGON
OCEAN
42 MI
66 MI
83 MI
TILLAMOOK
PORTLAND
THE DALLES
125 MI
PENDLETON
74 MI
252 MI
74 MI
47 MI
PACIFIC
131 MI
167 MI
SALEM
OREGON
167 MI
131 MI
64 MI
EUGENE
128 MI
BEND
260 MI
ONTARIO
54 MI
BOISE
116 MI
71 MI
85 MI
COOS BAY
ROSEBURG
212 MI
137 MI
365 MI
96 MI
IDAHO / OREGON
MEDFORD
76 MI
KLAMATH FALLS
OREGON / CALIFORNIA
OREGON / NEVADA
IDAHO / NEVADA
CALIFORNIA
NEVADA

Pacific Northwest Mileage Chart

	Astoria, Or	Bellingham, Wa	Bend, Or	Boise, Id	Coos Bay, Or	Corvallis, Or	Ellensburg, Wa	Eugene, Or	Grants Pass, Or	Hood River, Or	Medford, Or	Moses Lake, Wa	Newport, Or	Oak Harbor, Wa	Olympia, Wa	Pasco, Wa	Port Angeles, Wa	Portland, Or	Prosser, Wa	Salem, Or	Sea-Tac Airport, Wa	Seattle, Wa	Spokane, Wa	The Dalles, Or	Vancouver, BC	Victoria, BC	Yakima, Wa
Aberdeen, Wa	76	198	303	573	309	224	198	253	388	205	416	266	211	142	50	290	144	143	253	190	94	107	368	226	248	146	203
Albany, Or	158	330	123	437	147	11	293	44	179	131	207	349	65	330	183	287	300	69	268	24	227	241	420	152	382	302	257
Anacortes, Wa	251	39	410	559	462	331	179	360	495	312	523	239	364	21	137	286	87	250	261	297	90	78	329	333	92	25	211
Ashland, Or	374	546	200	483	182	222	468	178	41	346	12	534	252	546	399	461	516	285	447	240	443	457	597	331	598	518	432
Astoria, Or		262	255	518	233	151	266	199	334	154	362	338	135	220	114	305	212	95	267	136	163	176	413	175	319	214	217
Baker City, Or	396	451	247	126	466	356	270	356	488	242	459	230	393	469	408	159	454	304	197	350	383	389	296	221	521	456	247
Bellingham, Wa	262		421	570	473	342	189	371	506	323	534	249	375	50	148	297	116	261	272	308	101	89	340	344	54	64	222
Bend, Or	255	421		314	237	127	281	128	241	152	212	323	183	421	274	252	391	160	276	131	318	332	423	131	473	393	245
Boise, Id	518	570	314		552	442	384	442	524	366	496	350	478	570	521	279	643	430	313	446	492	491	379	347	623	645	361
Bremerton, Wa	150	116	329	533	381	250	110	279	414	231	442	179	283	73	59	218	79	169	193	216	13	1	280	252	142	81	143
Burns, Or	385	547	130	184	367	257	370	259	339	282	311	330	310	551	404	259	554	290	297	261	448	462	395	260	603	556	347
Chehalis, Wa	102	175	247	507	299	168	176	197	332	149	360	245	201	171	29	234	145	87	197	154	73	87	343	170	228	147	147
Cheney, Wa	396	341	406	370	541	415	161	447	647	279	618	92	448	341	307	123	342	338	158	381	268	267	17	249	395	269	183
Coeur d'Alene, Id	444	371	454	427	589	463	205	495	695	327	667	136	496	371	351	167	385	382	202	429	312	311	31	297	423	313	227
Coos Bay, Or	233	473	237	552		135	431	116	142	273	170	488	98	473	326	444	443	212	407	177	370	384	558	294	558	445	396
Corvallis, Or	151	342	127	442	135		305	40	182	142	210	361	54	342	195	299	312	81	280	35	239	254	432	163	394	314	269
Crater Lake, Or	332	504	98	412	177	173	379	133	86	250	71	421	225	504	357	350	474	243	374	197	401	415	521	229	556	476	343
Ellensburg, Wa	266	189	281	384	431	305		330	522	153	493	72	338	188	149	111	187	224	86	271	111	110	174	137	242	112	36
Eugene, Or	199	371	128	442	116	40	330		138	172	166	387	92	371	224	328	341	110	306	64	268	282	464	193	423	343	295
Everett, Wa	204	61	360	509	412	281	128	310	445	262	473	188	314	61	87	236	80	200	211	247	40	27	279	283	114	29	161
Florence, Or	184	425	190	504	48	83	391	61	162	224	190	448	50	432	285	389	402	164	367	118	329	343	525	245	484	404	356
Forks, Wa	185	93	411	681	418	332	241	361	496	313	524	310	320	122	158	406	56	251	368	298	144	132	408	334	226	58	319
Gold Beach, Or	311	551	316	630	78	213	597	194	134	468	162	639	179	551	404	568	521	290	592	555	448	462	739	373	603	523	561
Grand Coulee, Wa	366	262	384	424	547	416	123	446	580	274	596	75	449	265	269	145	286	340	166	382	230	226	87	253	315	228	153
Grants Pass, Or	334	506	241	524	142	182	522	138		307	29	564	212	506	359	493	476	245	517	199	403	417	664	327	558	478	486
Hillsboro, Or	87	278	176	445	206	78	241	117	252	79	280	297	106	278	131	235	248	17	216	50	175	189	368	101	330	250	205
Hood River, Or	154	323	152	366	273	142	153	172	307		335	209	174	323	176	165	293	62	128	108	220	234	296	21	375	295	117
Kennewick, Wa	301	295	248	275	440	295	109	324	489	161	460	77	328	293	246	4	293	212	36	261	217	216	142	141	348	295	86
Klamath Falls, Or	364	540	137	419	245	213	418	173	104	289	76	460	265	540	393	389	510	279	413	234	437	451	560	268	592	512	382
La Grande, Or	352	401	271	169	471	340	226	369	504	198	484	186	372	412	363	115	410	259	153	306	334	333	252	177	465	412	203
Lake Oswego, Or	102	269	169	435	216	78	232	108	239	70	271	288	110	269	122	226	239	8	207	41	166	180	359	89	321	241	196
Lewiston, Id	437	391	379	277	557	425	202	455	590	289	591	159	226	390	377	128	389	362	176	492	313	312	102	263	444	314	216
Long Beach, Wa	17	260	272	534	250	168	260	216	351	171	379	329	152	214	112	323	206	126	294	153	157	170	431	192	313	208	244
Long View, Wa	50	214	210	478	260	131	200	160	295	112	323	265	162	214	67	246	184	48	217	97	112	126	362	133	267	186	167
McMinnville, Or	105	299	158	465	174	46	262	86	224	99	252	318	76	299	152	256	269	38	237	26	196	210	389	120	351	271	226
Medford, Or	362	534	212	496	170	210	493	166	29	335		535	240	534	387	464	504	273	488	227	431	445	635	343	586	506	457
Milton-Freewater, Or	329	350	271	242	449	317	164	347	482	181	483	123	118	350	301	55	350	237	90	284	271	270	166	155	402	352	140
Moses Lake, Wa	338	249	323	350	488	361	72	387	564	209	535		394	250	218	71	255	280	106	327	179	178	105	194	302	180	102
Mt. Rainier, Wa	142	156	302	431	352	188	106	252	38	187	415	172	254	156	66	158	164	140	120	189	55	68	266	171	209	166	70
Mount St. Helens, Wa	107	235	267	535	317	188	222	217	352	169	380	288	219	231	89	274	205	105	236	154	133	147	382	190	288	207	186
Mount Vernon, Wa	237	28	392	542	44	313	161	342	477	294	505	221	346	29	120	269	94	232	243	279	73	60	311	315	81	46	193
Newport, Or	135	375	183	478	98	54	338	92	212	174	240	394		375	228	332	345	114	313	83	272	286	465	196	427	347	302
Newport, Wa	482	387	435	436	627	482	221	511	676	348	647	153	515	387	367	183	401	439	218	448	328	327	47	313	439	329	243
Oak Harbor, Wa	220	50	421	570	473	342	188	371	506	323	534	250	375		148	297	66	261	272	308	101	89	340	324	104	46	222
Okanogan, Wa	386	204	445	461	596	469	158	495	686	317	657	112	502	207	271	182	272	377	203	435	231	221	145	301	256	221	190
Olympia, Wa	114	148	274	521	326	195	149	224	359	176	387	218	228	148		248	121	114	211	161	46	60	320	195	201	123	161
Ontario, Or	464	508	260	54	498	388	322	388	470	312	442	288	424	508	459	217	581	374	251	392	430	429	317	293	561	583	299
Pasco, Wa	305	297	252	279	444	299	111	328	493	165	464	71	332	297	248		295	218	38	265	219	218	136	130	350	297	88
Pendleton, Or	300	349	241	221	419	288	174	318	452	146	454	134	321	360	311	63	358	208	101	254	282	281	200	125	413	360	151
Port Angeles, Wa	212	116	391	643	443	312	187	341	476	293	504	255	345	66	121	295		231	257	278	90	77	354	311	168	2	282
Portland, Or	95	261	160	430	212	81	224	110	245	62	273	280	114	261	114	218	231		199	47	158	172	351	83	313	233	188
Portland Airport, Or	98	261	160	430	223	92	213	121	256	51	284	269	125	261	114	207	220	11	188	58	158	172	340	72	313	222	177
Prosser, Wa	267	272	276	313	407	280	86	306	517	128	488	106	313	272	211	38	257	199		246	186	182	171	116	324	259	50
Richland, Wa	323	285	255	285	447	302	99	331	496	168	467	80	335	285	236	9	286	219	28	268	207	206	145	136	338	288	76
Roseburg, Or	266	438	192	507	85	111	473	71	68	239	96	515	144	438	291	444	408	177	468	132	335	349	615	260	490	410	437
St. Helens, Or	66	236	189	453	240	109	222	139	274	91	302	287	143	236	89	268	206	29	239	76	134	148	384	108	289	208	189
Salem, Or	136	308	131	446	177	35	271	64	199	108	227	327	83	308	161	265	278	47	246		205	219	398	129	360	280	235
Sea-Tac Airport, Wa	163	101	318	492	370	239	111	268	403	220	431	179	272	101	46	219	90	158	186	205		13	281	238	154	15	136
Seattle, Wa	176	89	332	491	384	254	110	282	417	234	445	178	286	89	60	218	77	172	192	219	13		280	244	141	2	142
Shelton, Wa	112	167	292	543	344	113	174	242	377	194	405	240	246	170	22	269	98	132	232	179	68	82	342	215	223	100	182
Spokane, Wa	413	340	423	379	558	432	174	464	664	296	635	105	465	340	320	136	354	351	171	398	281	280		266	392	282	196
Tacoma, Wa	145	121	303	422	355	224	122	253	388	205	416	190	257	121	30	224	110	143	187	190	18	32	292	226	173	112	137
The Dalles, Or	175	344	131	347	294	163	137	193	327	21	343	194	196	324	195	130	311	83	116	129	238	244	266		376	313	101
Tillamook, Or	66	335	206	502	167	90	502	130	269	136	297	354	69	235	188	292	305	74	273	74	232	246	425	157	387	307	262
Vancouver, BC	319	54	473	623	558	394	242	423	558	375	586	302	427	104	210	350	168	313	324	360	154	141	392	376		69	274
Vancouver, Wa	90	253	168	438	220	89	216	118	253	70	281	272	122	253	106	210	222	8	191	55	150	164	343	91	305	224	180
Victoria, BC	214	64	393	645	445	314	112	343	478	295	506	180	347	46	123	297	2	233	259	280	15	2	282	313	43		290
Walla Walla, Wa	337	342	279	250	457	325	156	355	490	189	491	115	126	342	293	47	342	262	82	392	263	262	158	163	394	344	132
Wenatchee, Wa	304	184	353	407	504	377	75	403	594	225	565	66	410	184	188	134	198	296	126	343	148	138	164	209	236	140	108
Yakima, Wa	217	222	245	361	396	269	36	295	486	117	457	102	302	222	161	88	282	188	50	235	136	142	196	101	180	290	

Mileage requires Ferry use and does not include Ferry miles

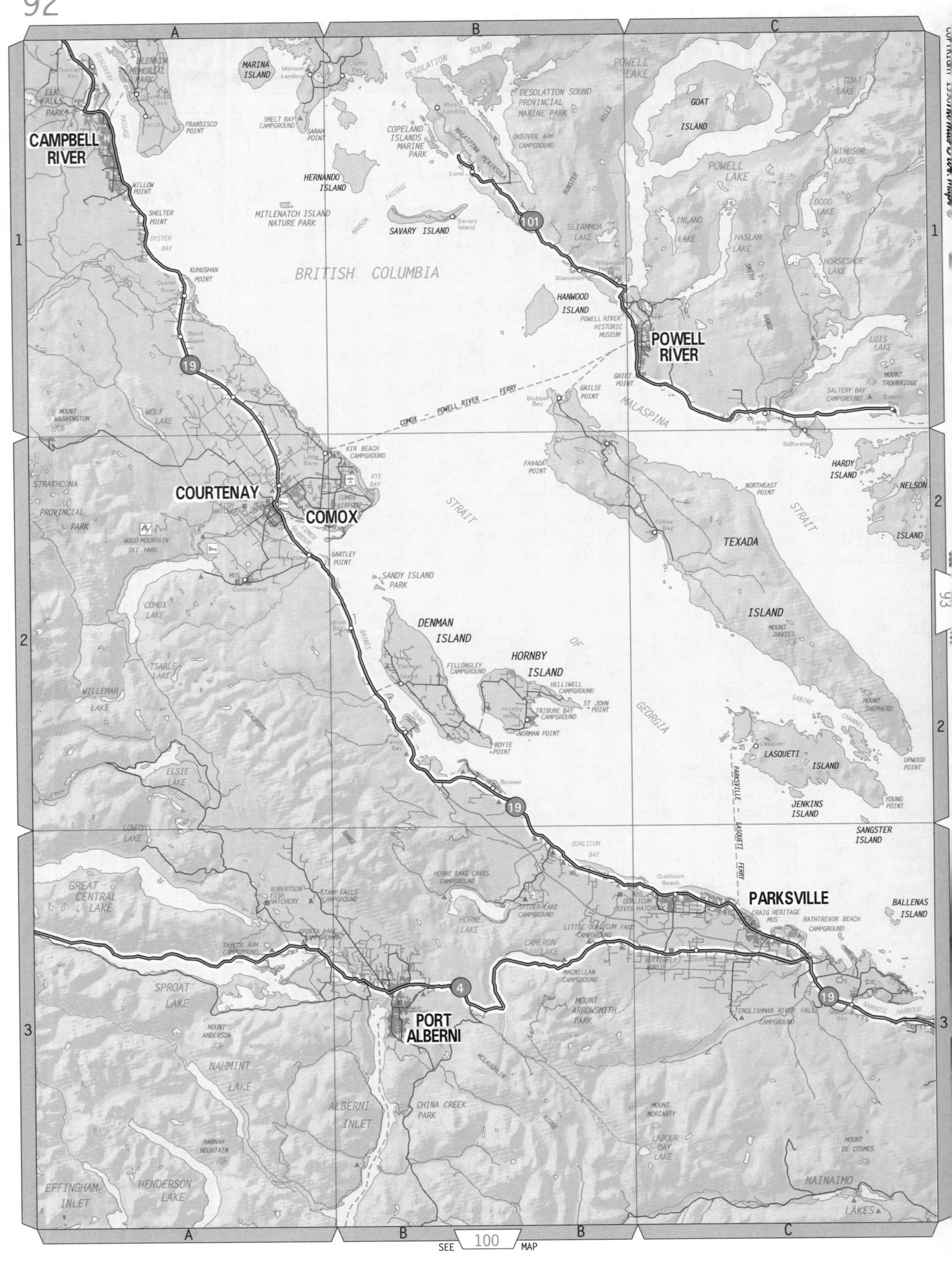

SEE 100 MAP
93

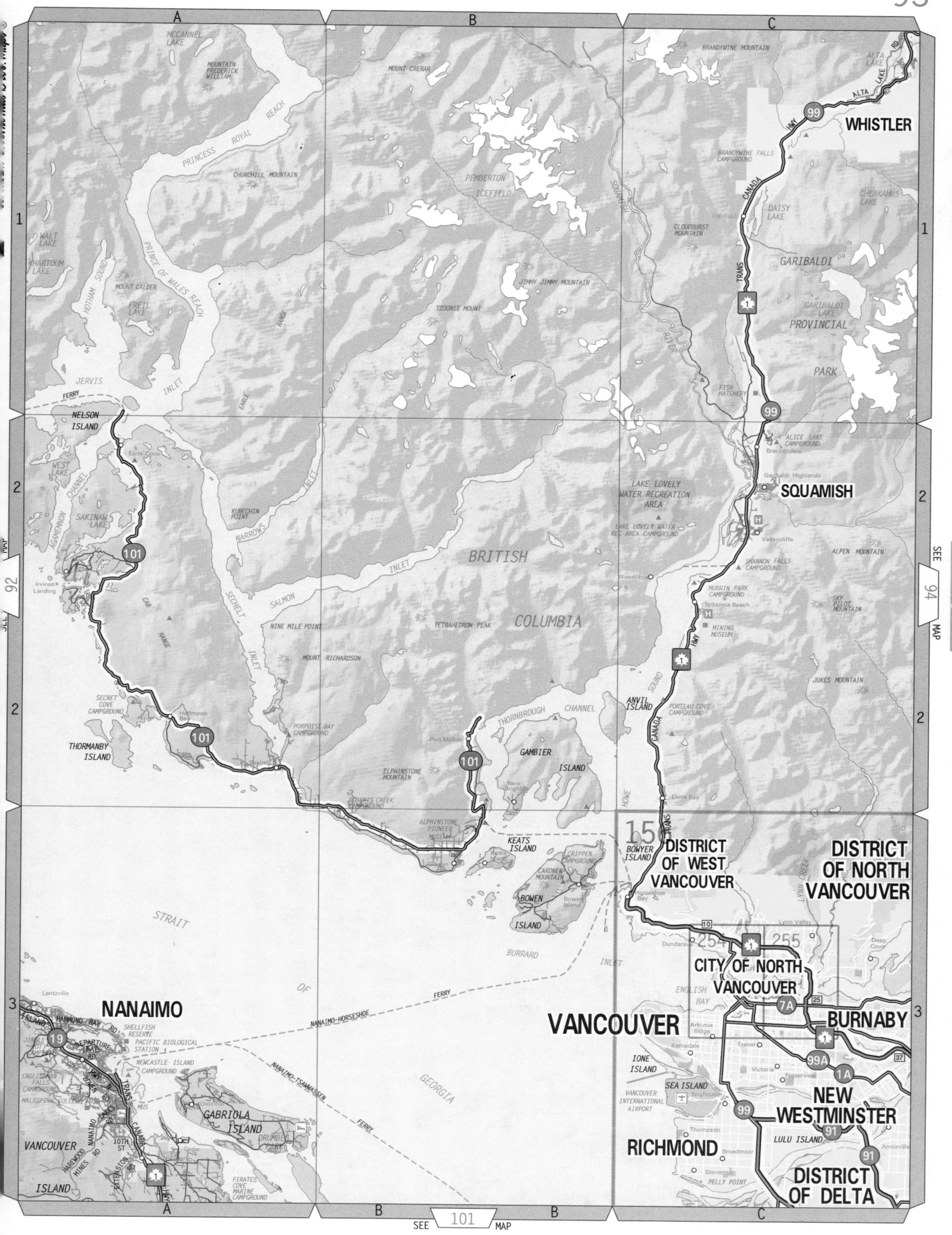
WHISTLER
SQUAMISH
BRITISH
COLUMBIA
DISTRICT OF WEST VANCOUVER
DISTRICT OF NORTH VANCOUVER
CITY OF NORTH VANCOUVER
VANCOUVER
BURNABY
NEW WESTMINSTER
RICHMOND
DISTRICT OF DELTA
NANAIMO
GABRIOLA ISLAND
VANCOUVER ISLAND
NELSON ISLAND
THORMANBY ISLAND
GAMBIER ISLAND
KEATS ISLAND
BOWEN ISLAND
ANVIL ISLAND
BOWYER ISLAND
IONE ISLAND
SEA ISLAND
LULU ISLAND
STRAIT OF GEORGIA
BURRARD INLET
ENGLISH BAY
HOWE SOUND
JERVIS INLET
PRINCESS ROYAL REACH
PRINCE OF WALES REACH
HOTHAM SOUND
AGAMEMNON CHANNEL
SECHELT INLET
SALMON INLET
NARROWS INLET
THORNBROUGH CHANNEL
GARIBALDI PROVINCIAL PARK
LAKE LOVELY WATER RECREATION AREA
PEMBERTON ICEFIELD
CAPE RANGE
EARLE RANGE
SQUAMISH RIVER
TRANS CANADA HWY
ALTA LAKE RD
NANAIMO-HORSESHOE FERRY
NANAIMO-TSAWWASSEN FERRY
VANCOUVER INTERNATIONAL AIRPORT
PACIFIC BIOLOGICAL STATION
SHELLFISH RESERVE
MINING MUSEUM
FISH HATCHERY
ELPHINSTONE PIONEER MUSEUM
PNW
HWY
SEE 92 MAP
SEE 94 MAP

SEE 101 MAP

A
B
C
1
2
3
SEE 93 MAP
SEE 95 MAP
SUMMER LAKE
WEDGE MOUNTAIN
LILLOOET
LAKE
CHEAKAMUS MOUNTAIN
CHEAKAMUS LAKE
MOUNT SIR RICHARD
GARIBALDI
COAST
MOUNTAINS
LILLOOET
RIVER
MOUNT PITT
PROVINCIAL
MAMQUAM MOUNTAIN
MOUNT BREAKENRIDGE
PARK
HARRISON
BRITISH COLUMBIA
MESLILLOET MOUNTAIN
MOUNT BONNYCASTLE
GOLDEN
THOMAS LAKE
EARS
OSPREY MOUNTAIN
PITT
LAKE
LAKE
LONG
ISLAND
PENEPLAIN PEAK
MOUNT BREIER
WIDGEON LAKE
COQUITLAM
LAKE
CROKER ISLAND
INDIAN
ARM
PROVINCIAL
CHEHALIS LAKE
GOOSE ISLAND
RAVEN LAKE
MOUNT JASPER
COQUITLAM ISLAND
WIDGEON PEAK
STAVE LAKE
PARK
MOUNT BLANSHARD
BUNTZEN LAKE
BELCARRA PARK
SIWASH ISLAND
BURKE MOUNTAIN REGIONAL PARK
EUNICE LAKE
ALOUETTE MOUNTAIN
ALOUETTE LAKE
MOUNT CATHERWOOD
ECHO ISLAND
Hemlock Valley
HEMLOCK VALLEY RD
WEAVER CREEK PROV PARK
HEMLOCK SKI AREA
SASQUATCH PROV PARK
BELCARRA
ANMORE
COQUITLAM
LOON LAKE
GOLDCREEK CAMPGROUND
ALOUETTE CAMPGROUND
MOUNT CRICKMER
SAYRES LAKE
DICKSON LAKE
DAVIS LAKE PROVINCIAL PARK
CHEHALIS HATCHERY
MORRIS VALLEY RD
RIVER
PORT MOODY
PITT RIVER
PITT MEADOWS
MAPLE RIDGE
DISTRICT OF MISSION
WINDY POINT
ROLLEY LAKE
CANNELL LAKE
MOUNT AGASSIZ
HARRISON HOT SPRINGS
PORT COQUITLAM
ROLLEY LAKE PROVINCIAL PARK
HARTLEY RD
DISTRICT OF KENT
MCCALLUM RD
Agassiz
Harrison Mills
KIMBERLEY RD
FRASER
Port Hammond
Haney
DEWDNEY
Yennadon
Webster Corners
TRUNK
BELL ST
Stave Falls
HAYWARD LAKE
Steelhead
FARMS STAVE LAKE RD
SYLVESTER RD
HARRISON
SKUMALASPH ISLAND
Deroche
CASTLEMAN RD
YALE RD
NEVIN RD
HWY 1
Walnut Grove
Port Kells
Fort Langley
DISTRICT OF SURREY
1A
TOWNSHIP OF LANGLEY
Forest Knolls
WILSON ST
KEYSTONE AV
CLAY ST
CEDAR ST
FERNDALE
7TH AV
LOUGHEED HWY
Dewdney
NICOMEN ISLAND
SLOUGH
DISTRICT OF MISSION
RIVER
FRASER
SUMAS MOUNTAIN PROV PARK
TRANS CANADA HWY
DISTRICT OF
CHILLIWACK
BRIDAL VEIL FALLS PROV PARK
MCGUIRE RD
BAILEY RD
SOUTH SUMAS RD
LICKMAN RD
VEDDER RD
DISTRICT OF MATSQUI
MATSQUI ISLAND
PAGE RD
CHADSEY LAKE
Glen Valley
Newton
OF SURREY
Surrey Centre
Milner
LANGLEY
7A
7
48
1
15
99A
10
58
11
9
157

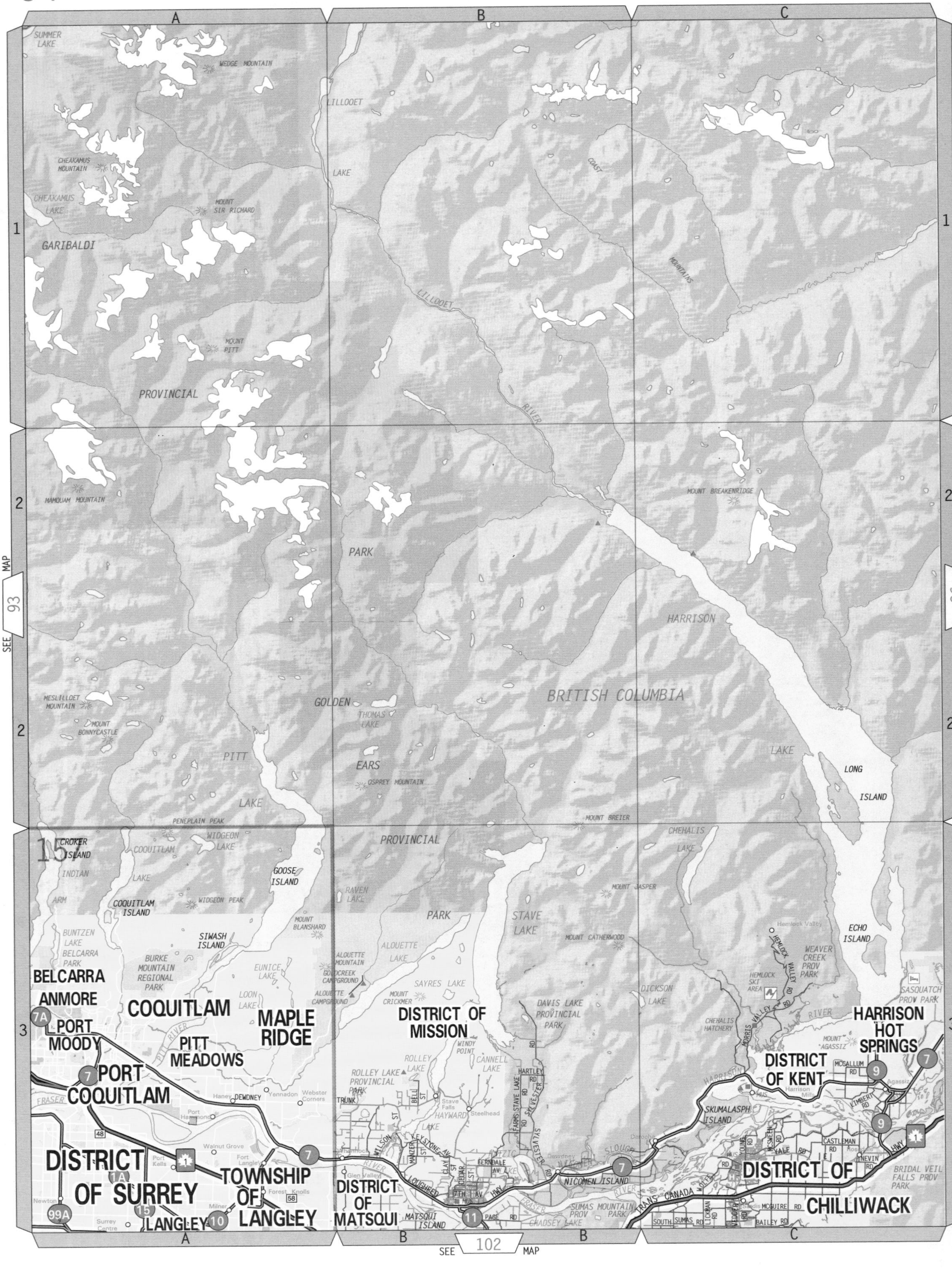

SEE 102 MAP

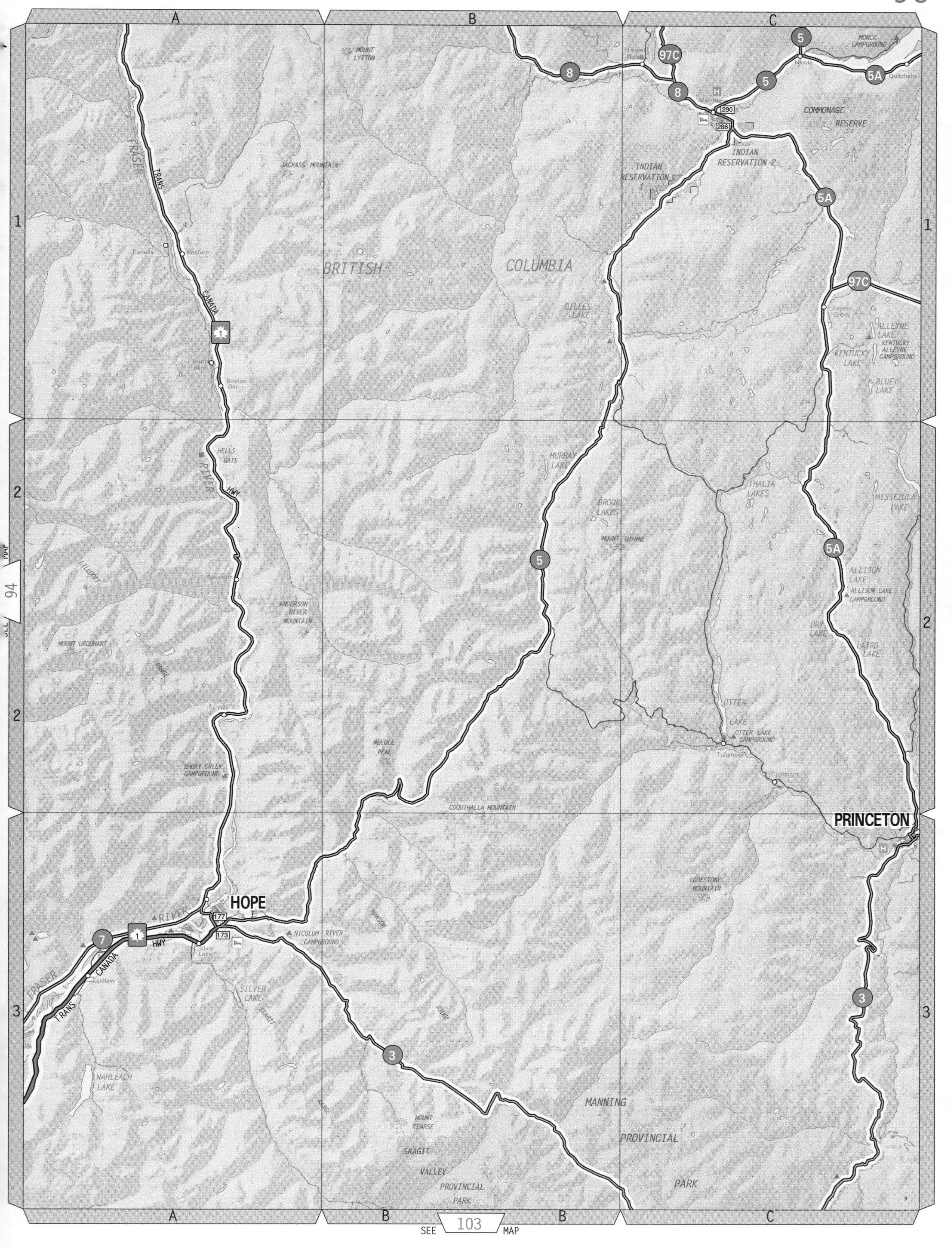
BRITISH COLUMBIA
HOPE
PRINCETON
FRASER RIVER
TRANS CANADA HWY
Kanaka
Keefers
North Bend
Boston Bar
HELLS GATE
Spuzzum
Yale
Haig
Silver Lake
Laidlaw
LILLOOET RANGE
MOUNT URQUHART
MOUNT LYTTON
JACKASS MOUNTAIN
ANDERSON RIVER MOUNTAIN
NEEDLE PEAK
COQUIHALLA MOUNTAIN
EMORY CREEK CAMPGROUND
NICOLUM RIVER CAMPGROUND
SILVER LAKE
SKAGIT RANGE
WAHLEACH LAKE
MANSON RIDGE
MOUNT TEARSE
SKAGIT VALLEY PROVINCIAL PARK
MANNING PROVINCIAL PARK
LODESTONE MOUNTAIN
GILLES LAKE
MURRAY LAKE
BROOK LAKES
MOUNT THYNNE
ITHALIA LAKES
OTTER LAKE
OTTER LAKE CAMPGROUND
Tulameen
Coalmont
Lower Nicola
Merritt
Nicola
Quilchena
MONCK CAMPGROUND
COMMONAGE RESERVE
INDIAN RESERVATION 1
INDIAN RESERVATION 2
Aspen Grove
ALLEYNE LAKE
KENTUCKY ALLEYNE CAMPGROUND
KENTUCKY LAKE
BLUEY LAKE
MISSEZULA LAKE
ALLISON LAKE
ALLISON LAKE CAMPGROUND
DRY LAKE
LAIRD LAKE
PNW
HWY
94
1
3
5
5A
7
8
97C
173
177
286
290

SEE 103 MAP

SEE 92 MAP

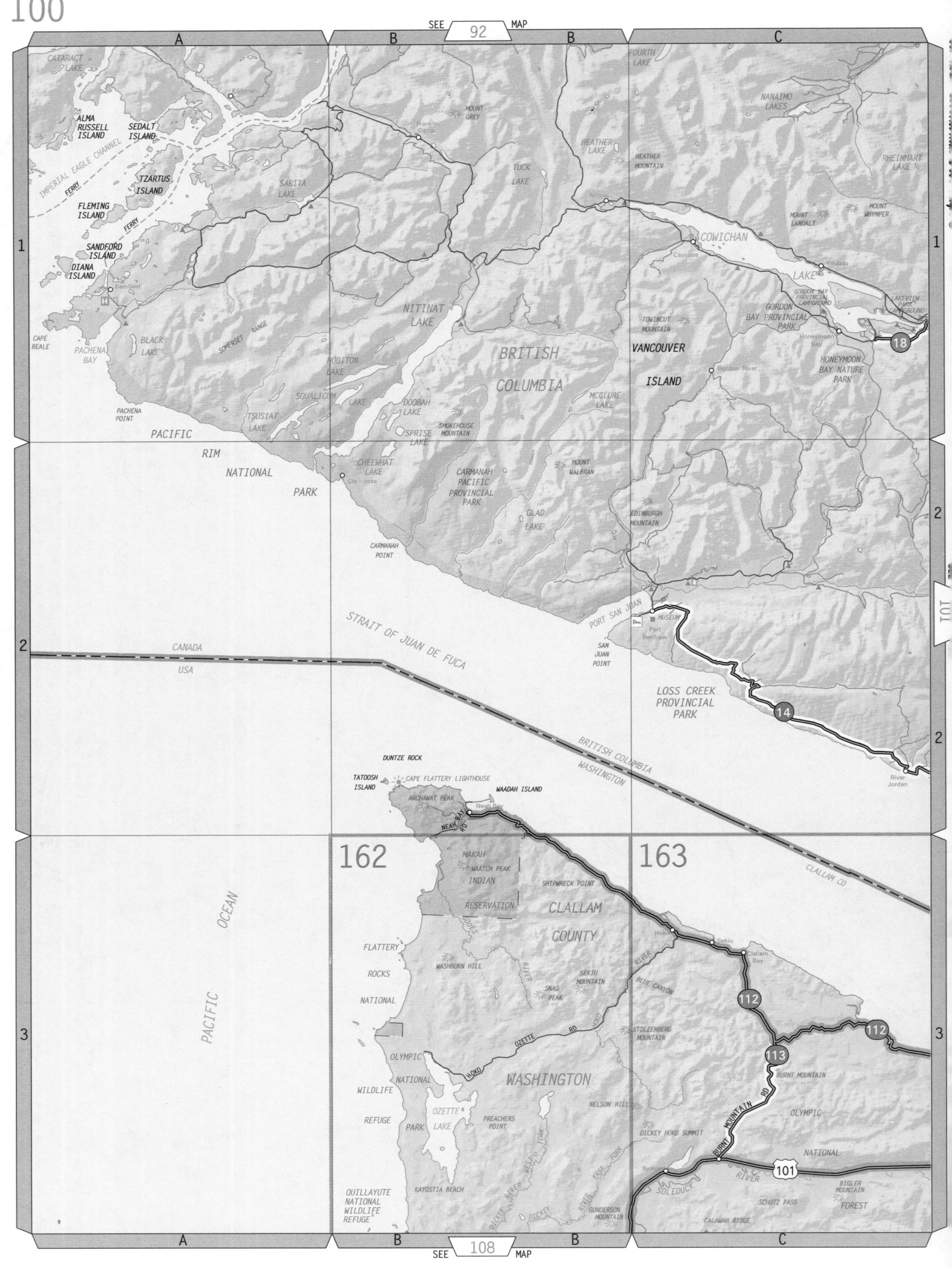

SEE 108 MAP

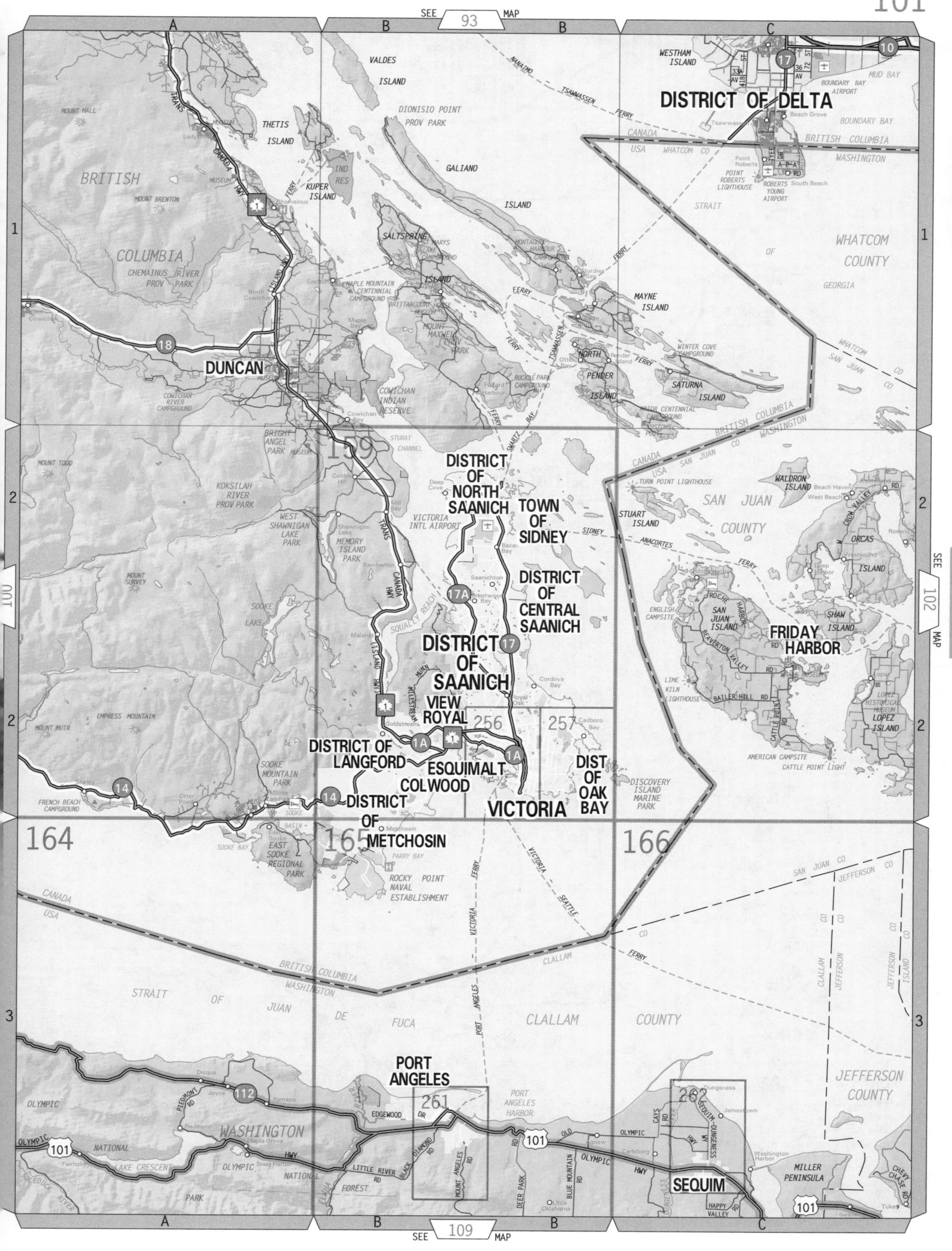
SEE 93 MAP
SEE 109 MAP
SEE 102 MAP
PNW
HWY
DISTRICT OF DELTA
BRITISH COLUMBIA
DUNCAN
VALDES ISLAND
THETIS ISLAND
KUPER ISLAND
GALIANO ISLAND
SALTSPRING ISLAND
MAYNE ISLAND
NORTH PENDER ISLAND
SATURNA ISLAND
DISTRICT OF NORTH SAANICH
TOWN OF SIDNEY
DISTRICT OF CENTRAL SAANICH
DISTRICT OF SAANICH
VIEW ROYAL
DISTRICT OF LANGFORD
ESQUIMALT
COLWOOD
DISTRICT OF METCHOSIN
VICTORIA
DIST OF OAK BAY
WHATCOM COUNTY
STRAIT OF GEORGIA
SAN JUAN COUNTY
WALDRON ISLAND
STUART ISLAND
ORCAS ISLAND
SAN JUAN ISLAND
SHAW ISLAND
FRIDAY HARBOR
LOPEZ ISLAND
STRAIT OF JUAN DE FUCA
CLALLAM COUNTY
JEFFERSON COUNTY
PORT ANGELES
SEQUIM
MILLER PENINSULA
OLYMPIC NATIONAL FOREST
WASHINGTON
OLYMPIC NATIONAL PARK
LAKE CRESCENT
EAST SOOKE REGIONAL PARK
ROCKY POINT NAVAL ESTABLISHMENT
DISCOVERY ISLAND MARINE PARK
159
164
165
166
256
257
261
262

SEE 94 MAP

SEE 101 HWY MAP

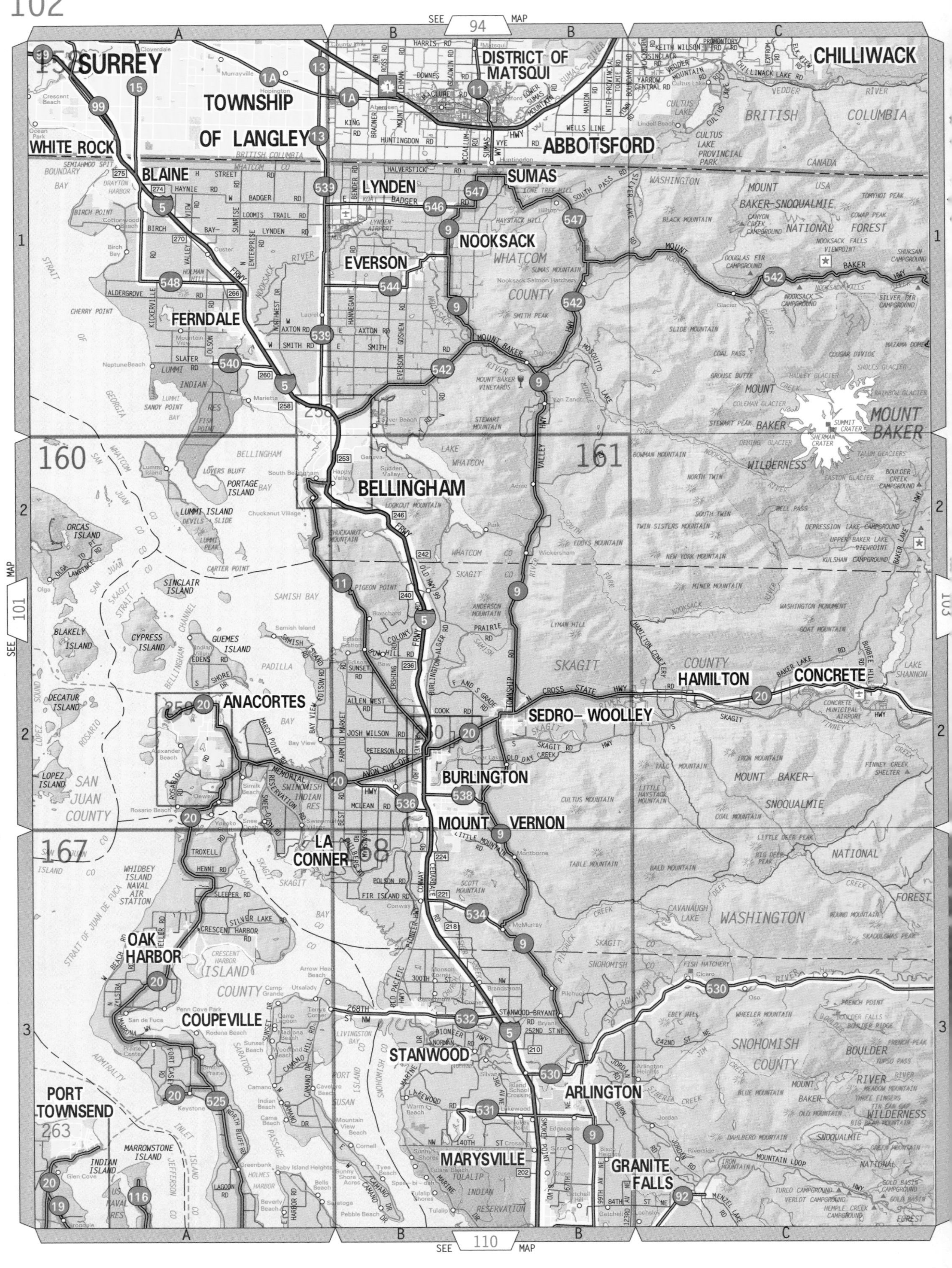

SEE 103 MAP

SEE 110 MAP

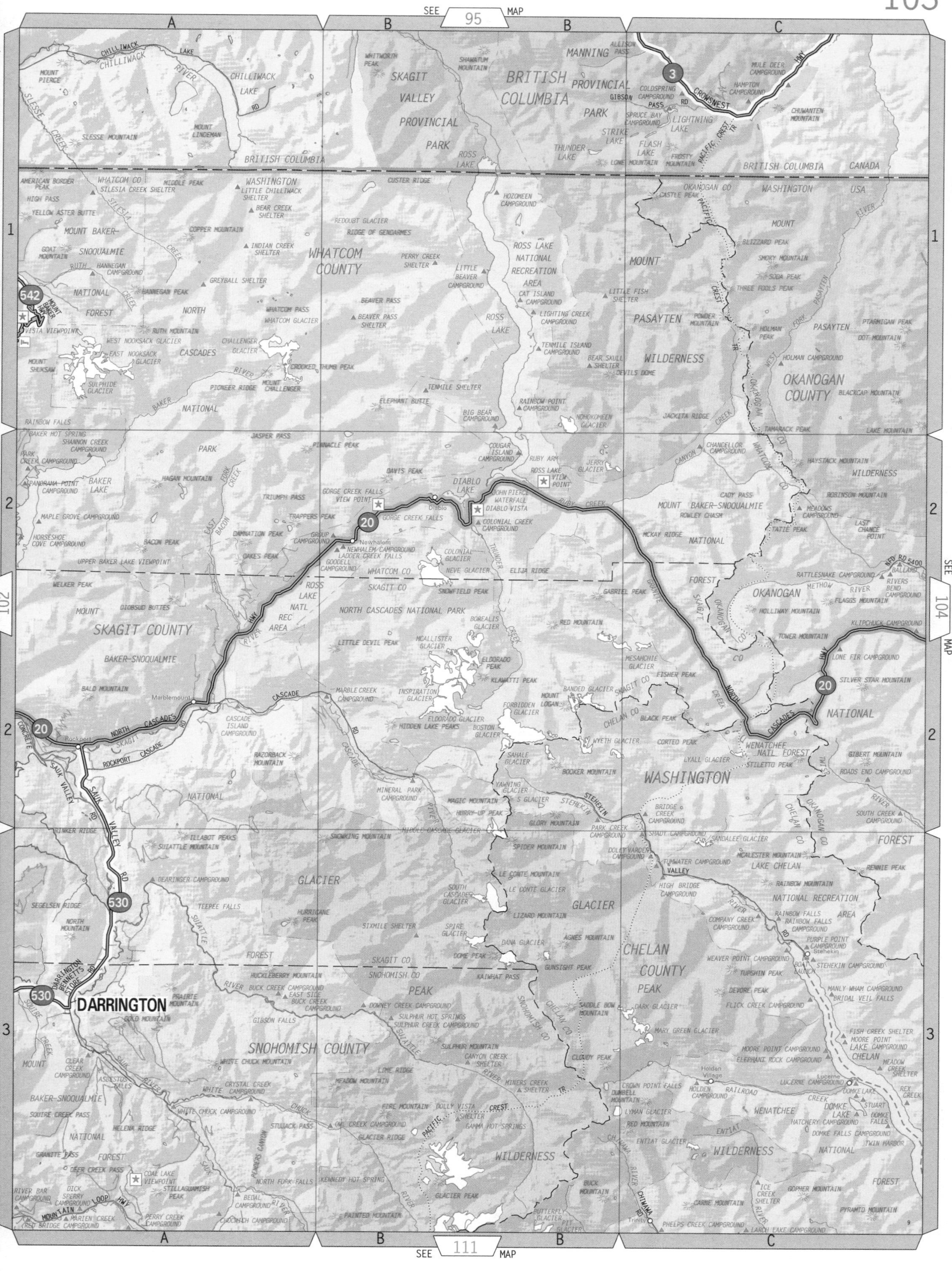

SEE 95 MAP
SEE 111 MAP
SEE 104 MAP
102
PNW
HWY
BRITISH COLUMBIA
WASHINGTON
CANADA
USA
WHATCOM COUNTY
SKAGIT COUNTY
OKANOGAN COUNTY
CHELAN COUNTY
SNOHOMISH COUNTY
SKAGIT VALLEY PROVINCIAL PARK
MANNING PROVINCIAL PARK
ROSS LAKE NATIONAL RECREATION AREA
NORTH CASCADES NATIONAL PARK
LAKE CHELAN NATIONAL RECREATION AREA
PASAYTEN WILDERNESS
GLACIER PEAK WILDERNESS
DARRINGTON
ROSS LAKE
DIABLO LAKE
LAKE CHELAN
CHILLIWACK LAKE

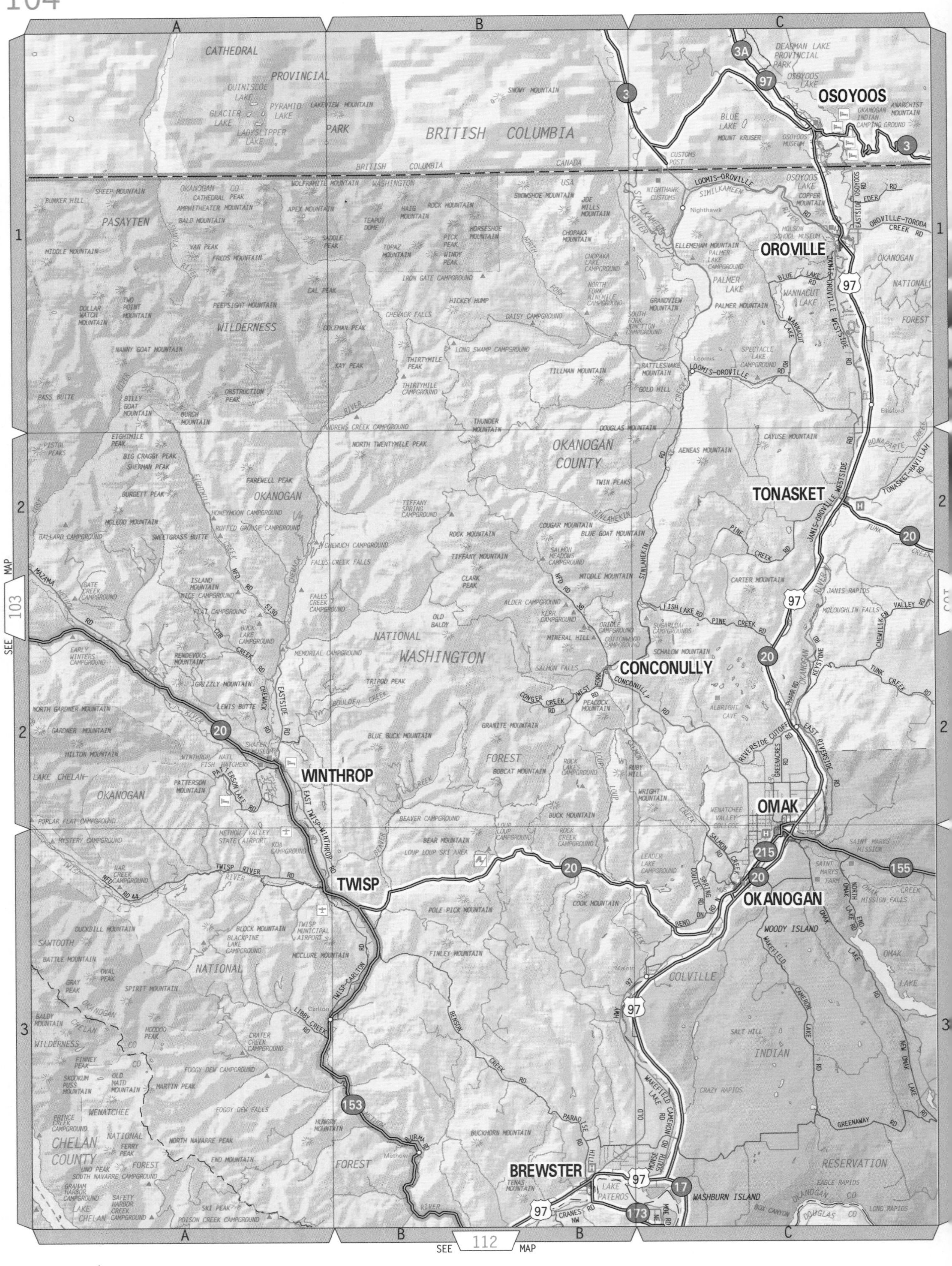
A
B
C
1
2
3
CATHEDRAL
PROVINCIAL
PARK
BRITISH COLUMBIA
OSOYOOS
OROVILLE
TONASKET
CONCONULLY
WINTHROP
OMAK
TWISP
OKANOGAN
BREWSTER
PATEROS
PASAYTEN
WILDERNESS
OKANOGAN
NATIONAL
WASHINGTON
FOREST
OKANOGAN COUNTY
CHELAN COUNTY
WENATCHEE
COLVILLE
INDIAN
RESERVATION
CANADA
USA
3A
3
97
20
215
155
153
17
173
SEE 103 MAP
SEE 112 MAP

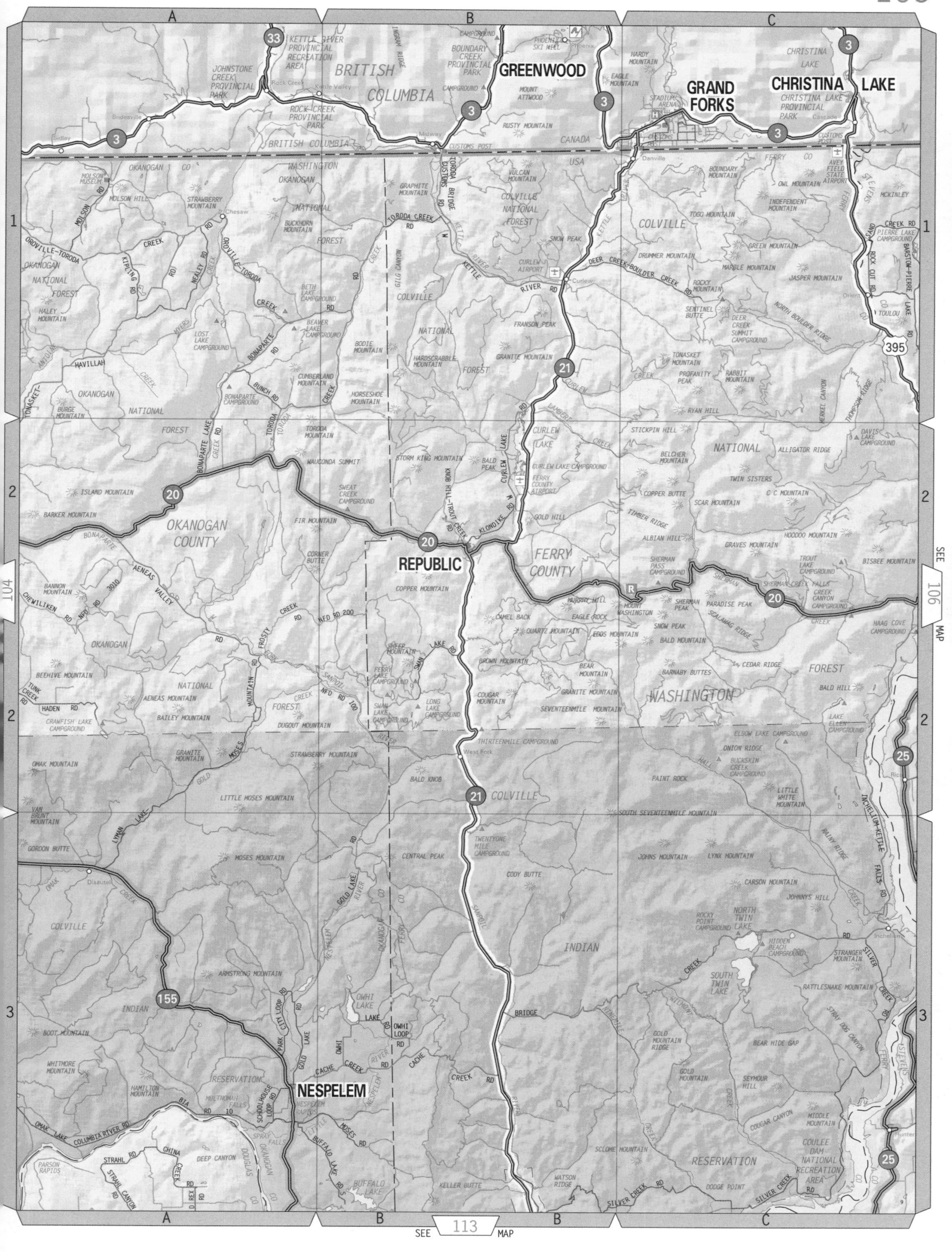

A
B
C
1
2
3
BRITISH COLUMBIA
GREENWOOD
GRAND FORKS
CHRISTINA LAKE
WASHINGTON
OKANOGAN COUNTY
FERRY COUNTY
REPUBLIC
NESPELEM
COLVILLE NATIONAL FOREST
OKANOGAN NATIONAL FOREST
COLVILLE INDIAN RESERVATION
COULEE DAM NATIONAL RECREATION AREA
CUSTOMS POST
CANADA
USA
SEE 104 MAP
SEE 106 MAP
SEE 113 MAP
PNW
HWY

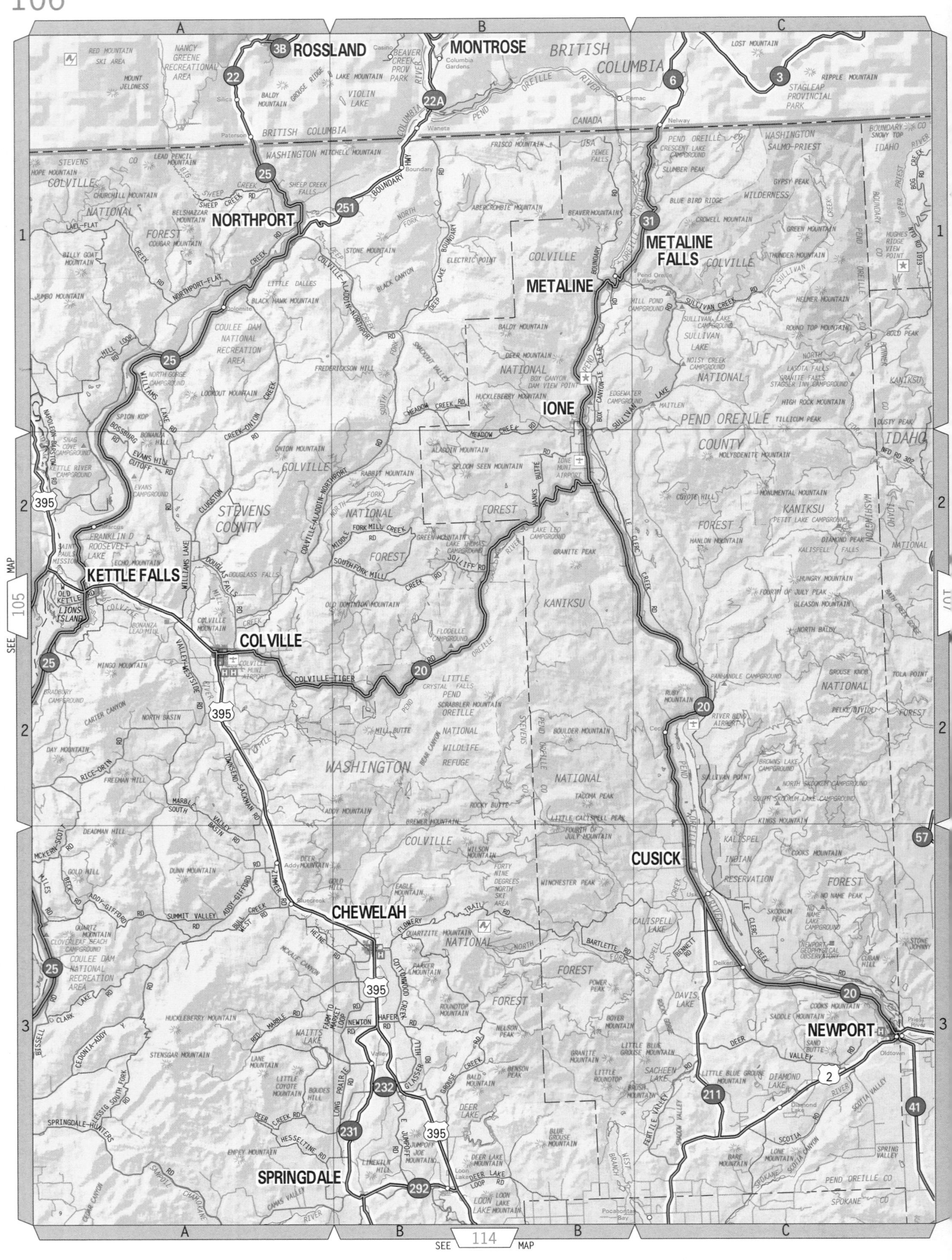

ROSSLAND
MONTROSE
BRITISH COLUMBIA
CANADA
USA
NORTHPORT
METALINE FALLS
METALINE
IONE
KETTLE FALLS
COLVILLE
CUSICK
CHEWELAH
NEWPORT
SPRINGDALE
COLVILLE NATIONAL FOREST
COULEE DAM NATIONAL RECREATION AREA
STEVENS COUNTY
PEND OREILLE COUNTY
KANIKSU NATIONAL FOREST
LITTLE PEND OREILLE NATIONAL WILDLIFE REFUGE
WASHINGTON
IDAHO
KALISPEL INDIAN RESERVATION
SALMO-PRIEST WILDERNESS
FRANKLIN D ROOSEVELT LAKE
STAGLEAP PROVINCIAL PARK
SULLIVAN LAKE
SEE 105 MAP
SEE 107 MAP
SEE 114 MAP

SEE 114 MAP

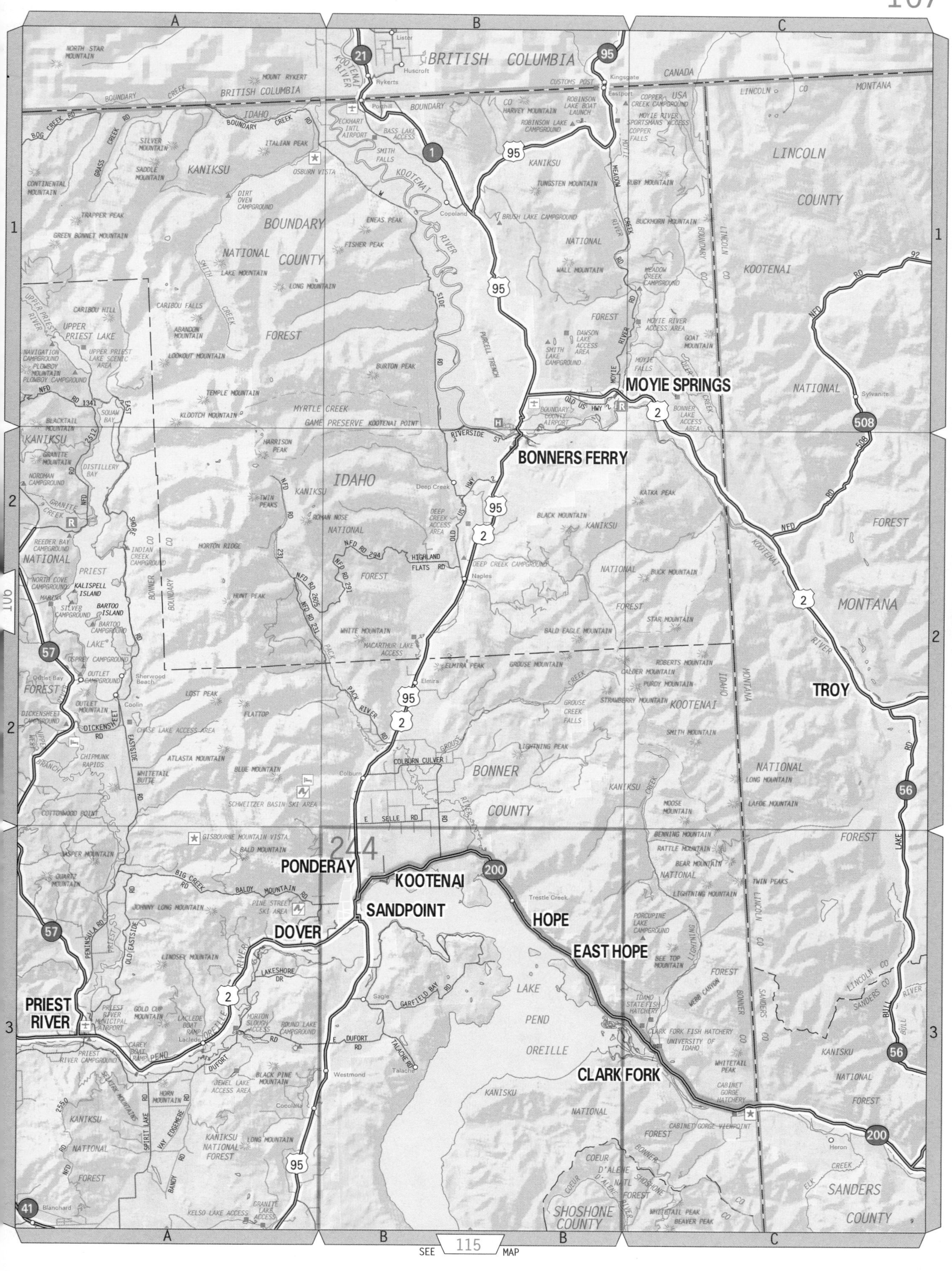
BRITISH COLUMBIA
CANADA
USA
IDAHO
MONTANA
BOUNDARY COUNTY
BONNER COUNTY
LINCOLN COUNTY
SANDERS COUNTY
SHOSHONE COUNTY
KANIKSU NATIONAL FOREST
KOOTENAI NATIONAL FOREST
COEUR D'ALENE NATL FOREST
MOYIE SPRINGS
BONNERS FERRY
TROY
PONDERAY
KOOTENAI
SANDPOINT
DOVER
HOPE
EAST HOPE
PRIEST RIVER
CLARK FORK
LAKE PEND OREILLE
UPPER PRIEST LAKE
PRIEST LAKE
KOOTENAI RIVER
PACK RIVER
Lister
Huscroft
Rykerts
Porthill
Kingsgate
Eastport
Copeland
Deep Creek
Naples
Elmira
Colburn
Sylvanite
Trestle Creek
Sagle
Westmond
Talache
Cocolalla
Laclede
Coolin
Sherwood Beach
Outlet Bay
Blanchard
Heron
MYRTLE CREEK GAME PRESERVE
SCHWEITZER BASIN SKI AREA
PINE STREET SKI AREA
GISBOURNE MOUNTAIN VISTA
CABINET GORGE VIEWPOINT
244
95
2
1
21
200
56
57
41
508
92
A
B
C
1
2
3

SEE 115 MAP

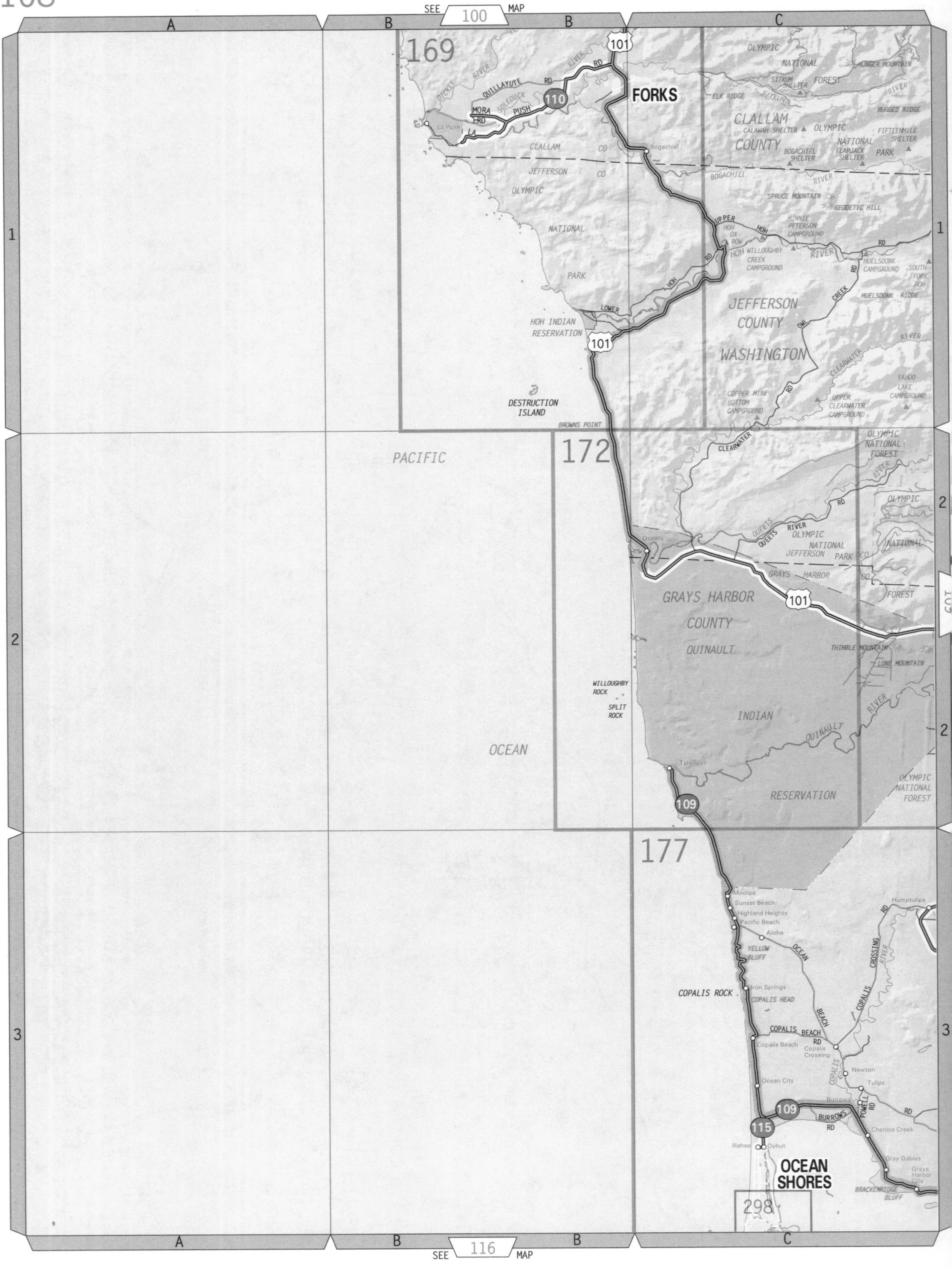

SEE 100 MAP

A B B C

169

101

FORKS

QUILLAYUTE RD

RIVER

DICKEY RIVER

SOLEDUCK

MORA RD

LA PUSH RD

110

La Push

CLALLAM CO

JEFFERSON CO

OLYMPIC

NATIONAL

PARK

HOH INDIAN RESERVATION

LOWER HOH RD

DESTRUCTION ISLAND

BROWNS POINT

Bogachiel

OLYMPIC NATIONAL FOREST

SITKUM SHELTER

ELK RIDGE

HUNGER MOUNTAIN

RUGGED RIDGE

CLALLAM COUNTY

CALAWAH SHELTER

OLYMPIC NATIONAL PARK

FIFTEENMILE SHELTER

BOGACHIEL SHELTER

FLAPJACK SHELTER

BOGACHIEL RIVER

SPRUCE MOUNTAIN

GEODETIC HILL

UPPER HOH RD

HOH OX BOW

MINNIE PETERSON CAMPGROUND

WILLOUGHBY CREEK CAMPGROUND

HOH RIVER

HUELSDONK CAMPGROUND

SOUTH FORK HOH

HUELSDONK RIDGE

JEFFERSON COUNTY

WASHINGTON

OWL CREEK

CLEARWATER RD

COPPER MINE BOTTOM CAMPGROUND

UPPER CLEARWATER CAMPGROUND

YAHOO LAKE CAMPGROUND

PACIFIC

OCEAN

172

CLEARWATER

OLYMPIC NATIONAL FOREST

QUEETS RIVER RD

OLYMPIC NATIONAL PARK

JEFFERSON CO

GRAYS HARBOR CO

Queets

101

GRAYS HARBOR COUNTY

QUINAULT INDIAN RESERVATION

QUINAULT RIVER

THIMBLE MOUNTAIN

LONE MOUNTAIN

WILLOUGHBY ROCK

SPLIT ROCK

Taholah

109

OLYMPIC NATIONAL FOREST

177

Moclips

Sunset Beach

Highland Heights

Pacific Beach

Aloha

YELLOW BLUFF

OCEAN BEACH RD

Iron Springs

COPALIS ROCK

COPALIS HEAD

COPALIS BEACH RD

Copalis Beach

Copalis Crossing

COPALIS CROSSING RD

COPALIS RIVER

Humptulips

Newton

Tulips

Ocean City

Burrows

POWELL RD

BURROWS RD

109

115

Chenois Creek

Illahee

Oyhut

OCEAN SHORES

Gray Gables

Grays Harbor City

BRACKENRIDGE BLUFF

298

1 2 3

SEE 116 MAP

SEE 101 MAP
OLYMPIC NATIONAL PARK
CLALLAM COUNTY
MOUNT OLYMPUS
WASHINGTON
JEFFERSON COUNTY
OLYMPIC NATIONAL FOREST
GRAYS HARBOR CO
MASON CO
KITSAP COUNTY
MASON COUNTY
GRAYS HARBOR COUNTY
THURSTON COUNTY
QUINAULT INDIAN RES
SKOKOMISH INDIAN RES
PNW
SEE 110 MAP
HWY
SEE 117 MAP
HURRICANE RIDGE SKI LODGE
HURRICANE RIDGE VISITORS CENTER
HEART OF THE HILLS RD
OLYMPIC HOT SPRINGS RD
SOL DUC FALLS
CARRIE GLACIER
BLUE GLACIER
HOH GLACIER
HUMES GLACIER
JEFFERS GLACIER
QUEETS GLACIER
HUBERT GLACIER
WHITE GLACIER
ANDERSON GLACIER
HANGING GLACIER
CAMERON GLACIERS
DOSEWALLIPS
DABOB BAY
HOOD CANAL
LAKE CUSHMAN
QUINAULT LAKE
WYNOOCHEE LAKE
NAHWATZEL LAKE
HARTSTENE ISLAND
173
178
179
180
296
297
HOQUIAM
ABERDEEN
COSMOPOLIS
MONTESANO
ELMA
MCCLEARY
SHELTON
OLYMPIA
TUMWATER
LACEY
Quilcene
Brinnon
Hoodsport
Potlatch
Union
Belfair
Allyn
Grapeview
Hoodsport
Lilliwaup
Eldon
Dewatto
Tahuya
Seabeck
Holly
Crosby
Matlock
Dayton
Kamilche
Cloquallum
Neilton
Amanda Park
Quinault
Satsop
Brady
Porter
Malone
Oakville
East Hoquiam
New London
Wishkah
Aberdeen Gardens
Central Park
Grisdale
Little Hoquiam
Bayshore
Arcadia
101
20
104
300
302
106
119
3
102
108
8
12
5

SEE 102 MAP

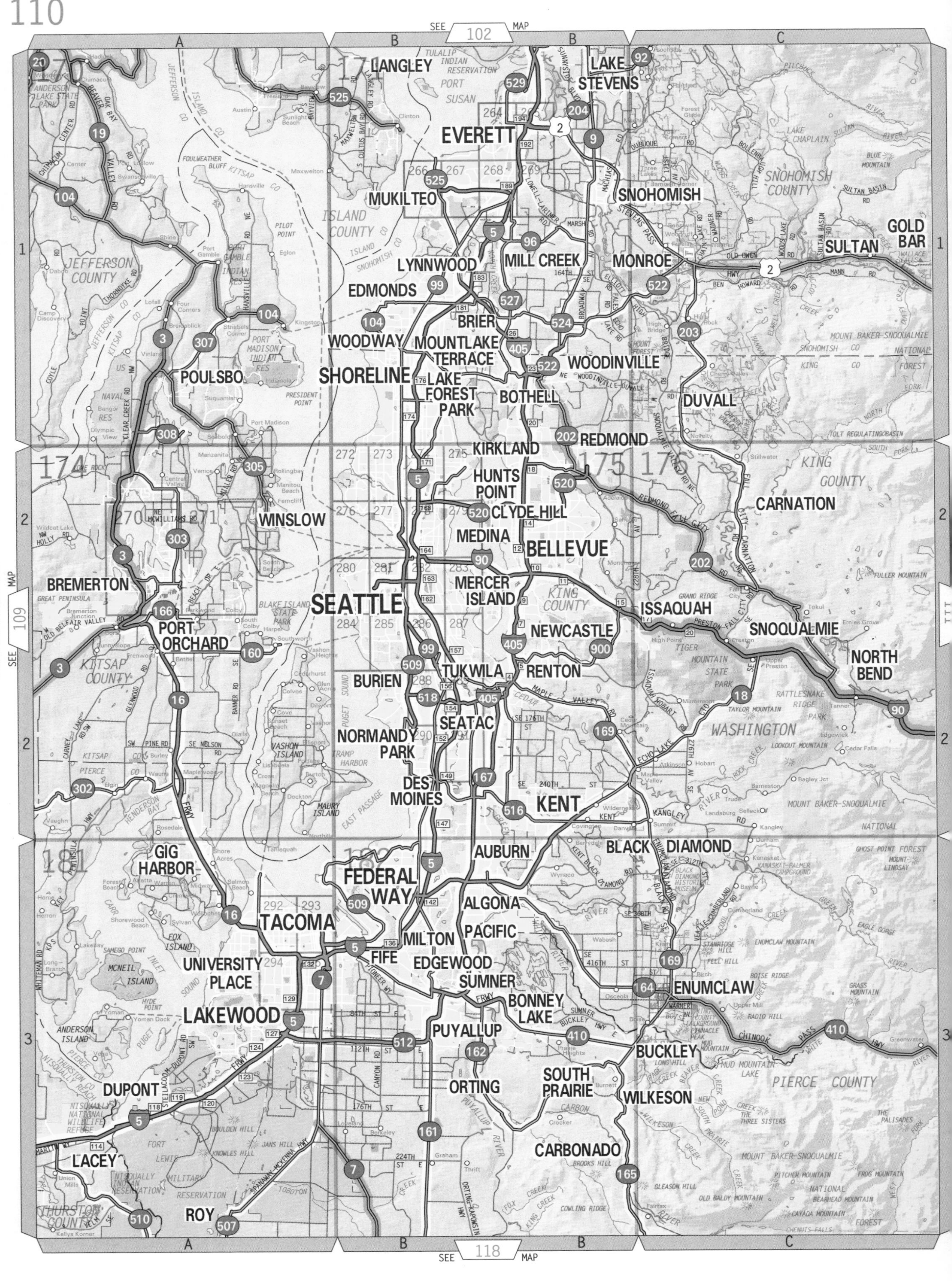

SEE 109 MAP

111

SEE 118 MAP

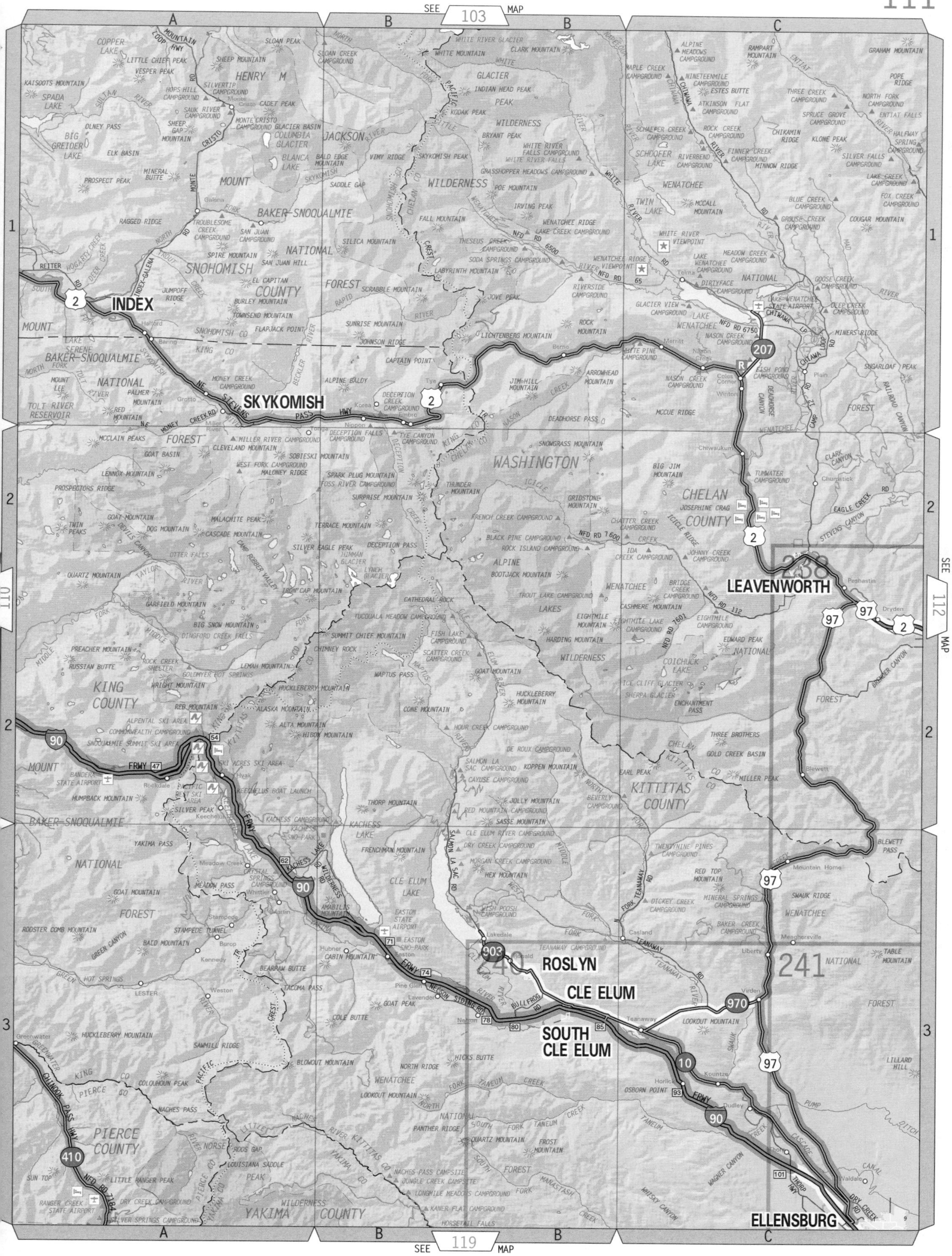
SEE 103 MAP
A
B
C
1
2
3
SEE 112 MAP
SEE 119 MAP
INDEX
SKYKOMISH
LEAVENWORTH
ROSLYN
CLE ELUM
SOUTH CLE ELUM
ELLENSBURG
2
207
97
90
903
970
10
410
238
240
241
HENRY M JACKSON WILDERNESS
GLACIER PEAK WILDERNESS
MOUNT BAKER-SNOQUALMIE NATIONAL FOREST
WENATCHEE NATIONAL FOREST
ALPINE LAKES WILDERNESS
SNOHOMISH COUNTY
KING COUNTY
CHELAN COUNTY
KITTITAS COUNTY
PIERCE COUNTY
YAKIMA COUNTY
WASHINGTON
STEVENS PASS HWY
CHINOOK PASS HWY
LAKE WENATCHEE
CLE ELUM LAKE
KACHESS LAKE
KEECHELUS LAKE
TWIN LAKE
SCHOOFER LAKE
SNOQUALMIE SUMMIT SKI AREA
ALPENTAL SKI AREA
SKI ACRES SKI AREA
BLEWETT PASS
DECEPTION PASS
YAKIMA PASS
NACHES PASS
STAMPEDE TUNNEL
WHITE RIVER VIEWPOINT
WENATCHEE RIDGE VIEWPOINT
LAKE WENATCHEE STATE AIRPORT
BANDERA STATE AIRPORT
EASTON STATE AIRPORT
RANGER CREEK STATE AIRPORT
FRWY
PNW
HWY

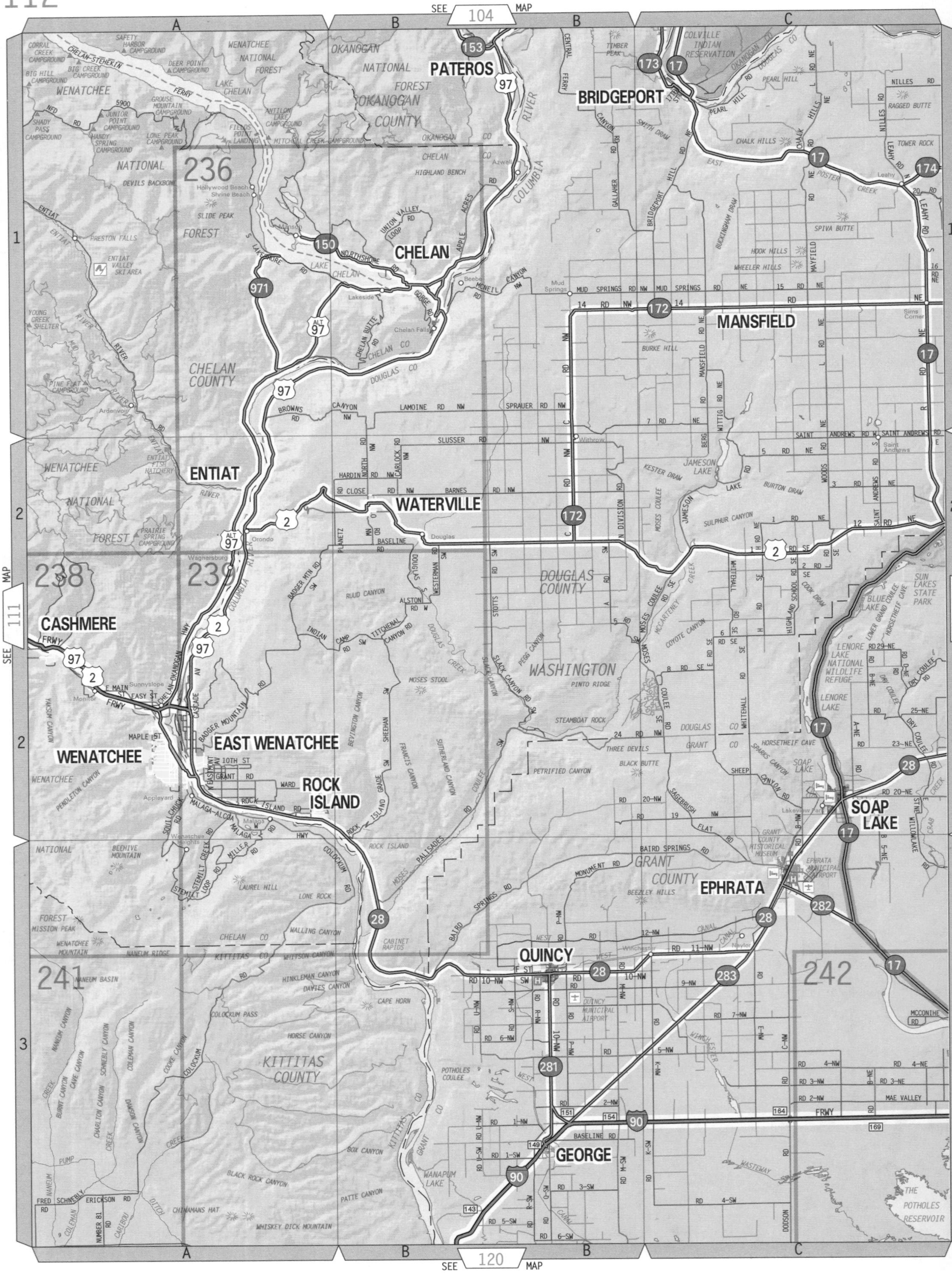

SEE 104 MAP

SEE 111 MAP

SEE 120 MAP

A B C

1 2 3

236 238 239 241 242

PATEROS
BRIDGEPORT
CHELAN
MANSFIELD
ENTIAT
WATERVILLE
CASHMERE
WENATCHEE
EAST WENATCHEE
ROCK ISLAND
SOAP LAKE
EPHRATA
QUINCY
GEORGE

WENATCHEE NATIONAL FOREST
OKANOGAN NATIONAL FOREST
OKANOGAN COUNTY
CHELAN COUNTY
DOUGLAS COUNTY
GRANT COUNTY
KITTITAS COUNTY
WASHINGTON
COLVILLE INDIAN RESERVATION
LAKE CHELAN
COLUMBIA RIVER
ENTIAT RIVER
LENORE LAKE NATIONAL WILDLIFE REFUGE
SUN LAKES STATE PARK
QUINCY MUNICIPAL AIRPORT
EPHRATA MUNICIPAL AIRPORT
GRANT COUNTY HISTORICAL MUSEUM
THE POTHOLES RESERVOIR
WANAPUM LAKE
JAMESON LAKE
BLUE LAKE
LENORE LAKE
ENTIAT VALLEY SKI AREA
ENTIAT FISH HATCHERY

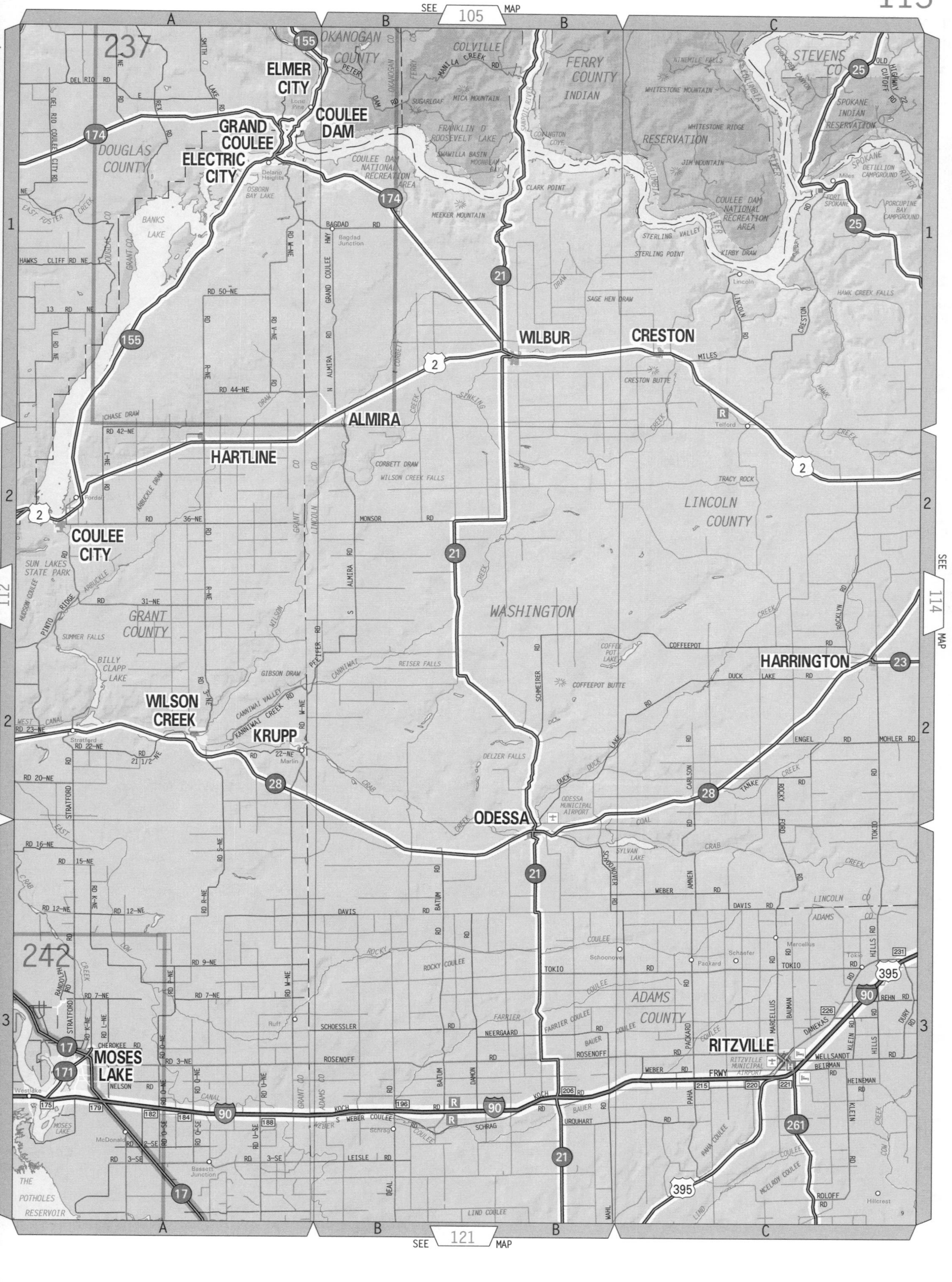

SEE 105 MAP
A
B
C
1
2
3
237
242
ELMER CITY
GRAND COULEE
COULEE DAM
ELECTRIC CITY
OKANOGAN COUNTY
DOUGLAS COUNTY
FERRY COUNTY
INDIAN RESERVATION
STEVENS CO
SPOKANE INDIAN RESERVATION
COLVILLE
MANILA CREEK RD
MICA MOUNTAIN
SUGARLOAF
FRANKLIN D ROOSEVELT LAKE
COVINGTON COVE
SWAWILLA BASIN
COULEE DAM NATIONAL RECREATION AREA
NINEMILE FALLS
WHITESTONE MOUNTAIN
WHITESTONE RIDGE
JIM MOUNTAIN
COLUMBIA RIVER
SPOKANE RIVER
DETILLION CAMPGROUND
PORCUPINE BAY CAMPGROUND
FORT SPOKANE
Miles
CLARK POINT
MEEKER MOUNTAIN
STERLING VALLEY
STERLING POINT
KIRBY DRAW
Lincoln
HAWK CREEK FALLS
SAGE HEN DRAW
BANKS LAKE
OSBORN BAY LAKE
Delano Heights
DEL RIO RD
HAWKS CLIFF RD NE
BAGDAD RD
Bagdad Junction
GRAND COULEE HWY
RD 50-NE
13 RD NE
RD 44-NE
CHASE DRAW
WILBUR
CRESTON
MILES
CRESTON BUTTE
Telford
ALMIRA
HARTLINE
RD 42-NE
CORBETT DRAW
WILSON CREEK FALLS
SINKING CREEK
TRACY ROCK
LINCOLN COUNTY
Fordair
COULEE CITY
SUN LAKES STATE PARK
MONSOR RD
36-NE
WASHINGTON
GRANT COUNTY
SUMMER FALLS
BILLY CLAPP LAKE
PINTO RIDGE
HUDSON COULEE
31-NE
COFFEEPOT
COFFEE POT LAKE
COFFEEPOT BUTTE
HARRINGTON
DUCK LAKE RD
REISER FALLS
GIBSON DRAW
CANNIWAI VALLEY
WILSON CREEK
KRUPP
Marlin
Stratford
WEST CANAL
RD 23-NE
RD 22-NE
RD 20-NE
DELZER FALLS
ENGEL RD
MOHLER RD
TANKE
ODESSA
ODESSA MUNICIPAL AIRPORT
CRAB CREEK
COAL CREEK
SYLVAN LAKE
RD 16-NE
RD 15-NE
RD 12-NE
DAVIS
WEBER RD
DAVIS RD
LINCOLN CO
ADAMS CO
ROCKY COULEE
Schoonover
Packard
Schaefer
Marcellus
Tokio
TOKIO RD
RD 9-NE
RD 7-NE
ADAMS COUNTY
FARRIER COULEE
NEERGAARD
SCHOESSLER
Ruff
CHEROKEE RD
MOSES LAKE
ROSENOFF
BAUER
RITZVILLE
RITZVILLE MUNICIPAL AIRPORT
WELLSANDT
BEIRMAN
HEINEMAN
DANEKAS
REHN RD
NELSON RD
Westlake
KOCH RD
WEBER
FRWY
S WEBER COULEE
Schrag
SCHRAG
URQUHART
McDonald
Bassett Junction
LEISLE RD
MOSES LAKE
THE POTHOLES RESERVOIR
PAHA COULEE
MCELROY COULEE
LIND COULEE
ROLOFF RD
Hillcrest
2
17
21
23
25
28
90
155
171
174
261
395
SEE 121 MAP
SEE 112 MAP
SEE 114 MAP

PNW

HWY

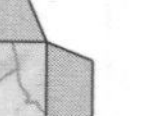

SEE 106 MAP

SEE 113 MAP

SEE 122 MAP

PNW

HWY

CTT

A B B C

1 2 2 3

STEVENS COUNTY

SPOKANE INDIAN RESERVATION

COULEE DAM NATIONAL RECREATION AREA

LINCOLN COUNTY

SPOKANE COUNTY

WASHINGTON

IDAHO

KOOTENAI CO

ADAMS COUNTY

WHITMAN COUNTY

MOUNT SPOKANE STATE PARK

RIVERSIDE STATE PARK

FAIRCHILD AIRFORCE BASE

TURNBULL NATIONAL WILDLIFE REFUGE

DEER PARK

MILLWOOD

SPOKANE

AIRWAY HEIGHTS

DAVENPORT

REARDAN

MEDICAL LAKE

CHENEY

ROCKFORD

SPANGLE

FAIRFIELD

WAVERLY

LATAH

SPRAGUE

ROSALIA

TEKOA

MALDEN

LAMONT

OAKESDALE

SAINT JOHN

GARFIELD

Elk, Milan, Clayton, Chattaroy, Colbert, Green Bluff, Dartford, Fairwood, Mead, Country Homes, Town & Country, Morgan Acres, Foothills, Newman Lake, East Farms, State Line Village, Otis Orchards, Spokane Bridge, Pasadena Park, Hillyard, Parkwater, Trentwood, Carvers, Greenacres, Dishman, East Spokane, Veradale, Liberty Lake, Chester, Mica, Freeman, Saxby, West Spokane, Deep Creek, Fairchild, Hayford, Espanola, Olson Hill, Four Lakes, Geiger Heights, Marshall, Scribner, Lakeland Village, Duncan, Dynamite, Valleyford, Mount Hope, Darknell, South Cheney, Tyler, Amber, Mason, Freedom, Plaza, West Fairfield, Jefferson, Spring Valley, Rollins, Pandora, Squaw Canyon, Balder, McCoy, Pine City, Juno, Huntley, Sunset, Thornton, Ewan, Sokulk, Crab Tree, Waters, Steptoe, Elberton, Willada, Lancaster, Wells, Edwall, Canby, Bluestem, Little Falls, Long Lake, Wellpinit, Tumtum, Fords

LINCOLN COUNTY HISTORICAL MUSEUM

ROSALIA MUNICIPAL AIRPORT

DEER PARK MUNICIPAL AIRPORT

2, 395, 195, 90, 25, 28, 231, 23, 27, 290, 291, 206, 902, 904, 278, 271, 245, 257, 264, 270, 272, 276

246, 247, 346, 347, 348, 349, 352

SEE 107 MAP

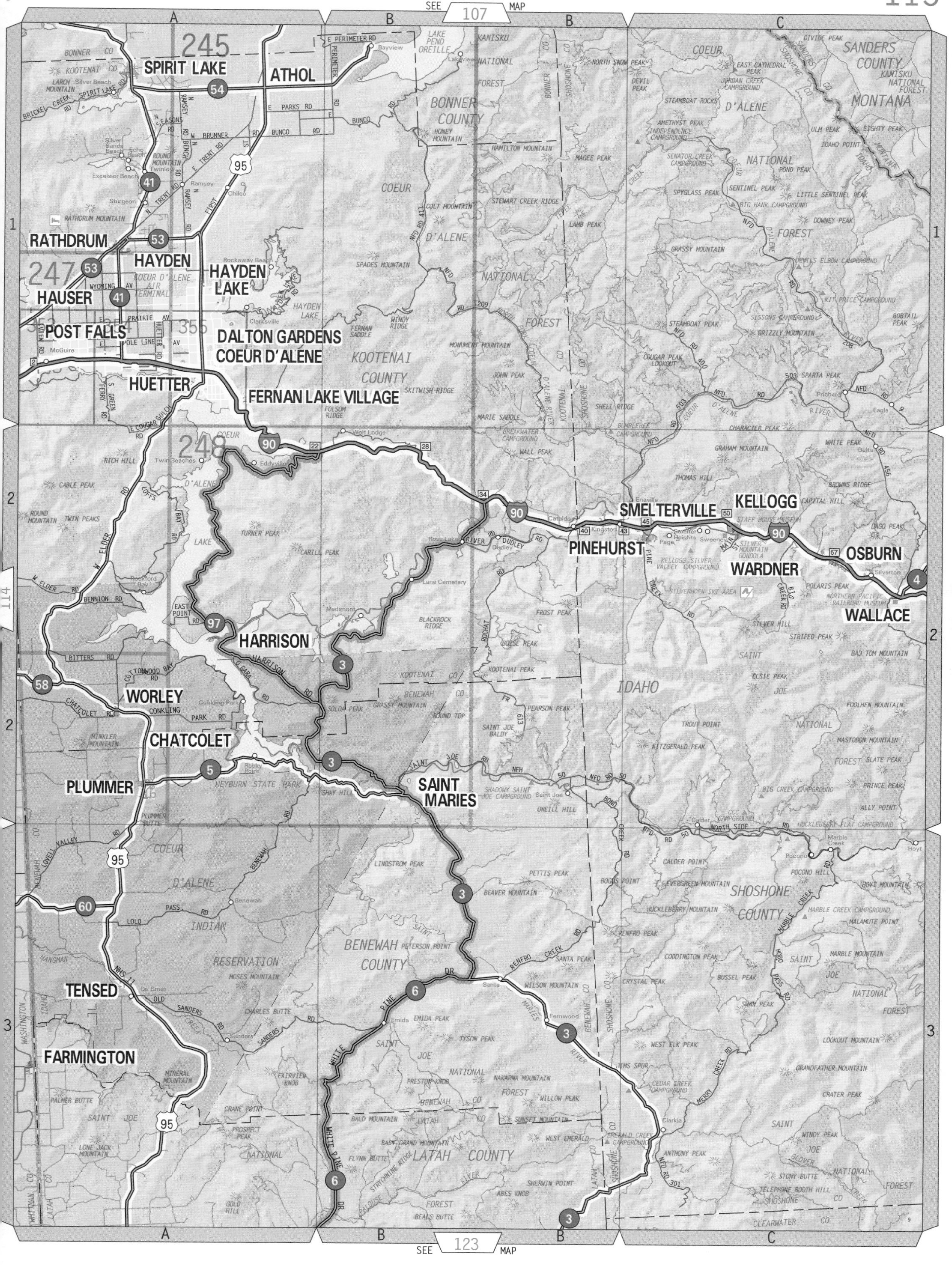

SEE 123 MAP

SEE 108 MAP

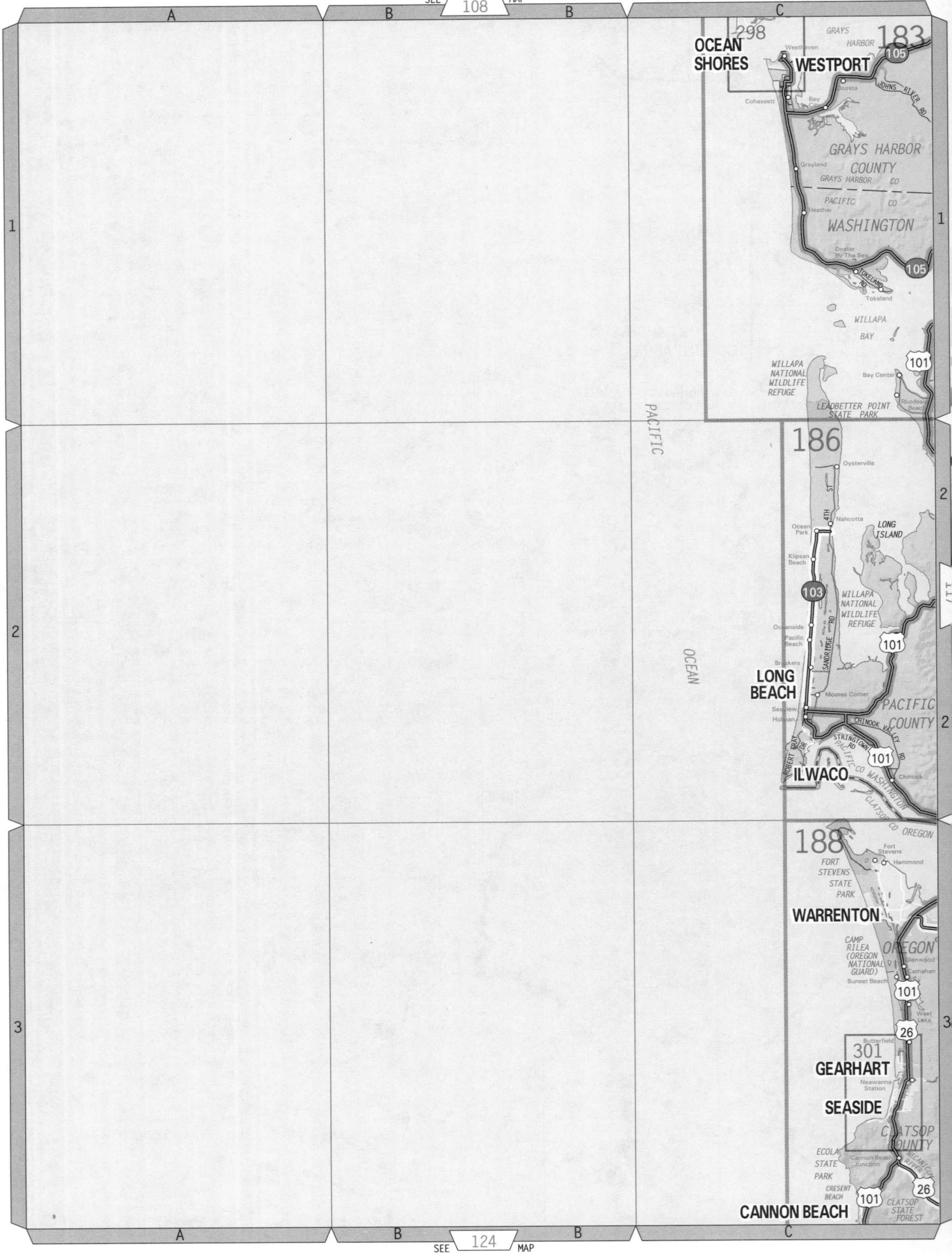

A B B C

183
OCEAN SHORES
WESTPORT
GRAYS HARBOR
105
JOHNS RIVER RD
Westhaven
Cohassett
Bay City
Ocosta
298
GRAYS HARBOR COUNTY
Grayland
GRAYS HARBOR CO
PACIFIC CO
Heather
WASHINGTON
Dexter By The Sea
TOKELAND RD
Tokeland
WILLAPA BAY
WILLAPA NATIONAL WILDLIFE REFUGE
101
Bay Center
Rhodesia Beach
LEADBETTER POINT STATE PARK

PACIFIC OCEAN

186
Oysterville
ST
4TH
Nahcotta
LONG ISLAND
Ocean Park
Klipsan Beach
103
WILLAPA NATIONAL WILDLIFE REFUGE
Oceanside
Pacific Beach
SANDRIDGE RD
Breakers
LONG BEACH
Moores Corner
Seaview
Holman
PACIFIC COUNTY
CHINOOK VALLEY RD
STRINGTOWN RD
ROBERT GRAY DR
PACIFIC CO WASHINGTON
ILWACO
Chinook
CLATSOP CO OREGON

188
Fort Stevens
Hammond
FORT STEVENS STATE PARK
WARRENTON
CAMP RILEA (OREGON NATIONAL GUARD)
OREGON
Glenwood
Carnahan
Sunset Beach
West Lake
26
Butterfield
301
GEARHART
Neawanna Station
SEASIDE
CLATSOP COUNTY
ECOLA STATE PARK
Cannon Beach Junction
NECANICUM RIVER
CRESENT BEACH
CANNON BEACH
CLATSOP STATE FOREST

1 2 3

117

A B B C

SEE 124 MAP

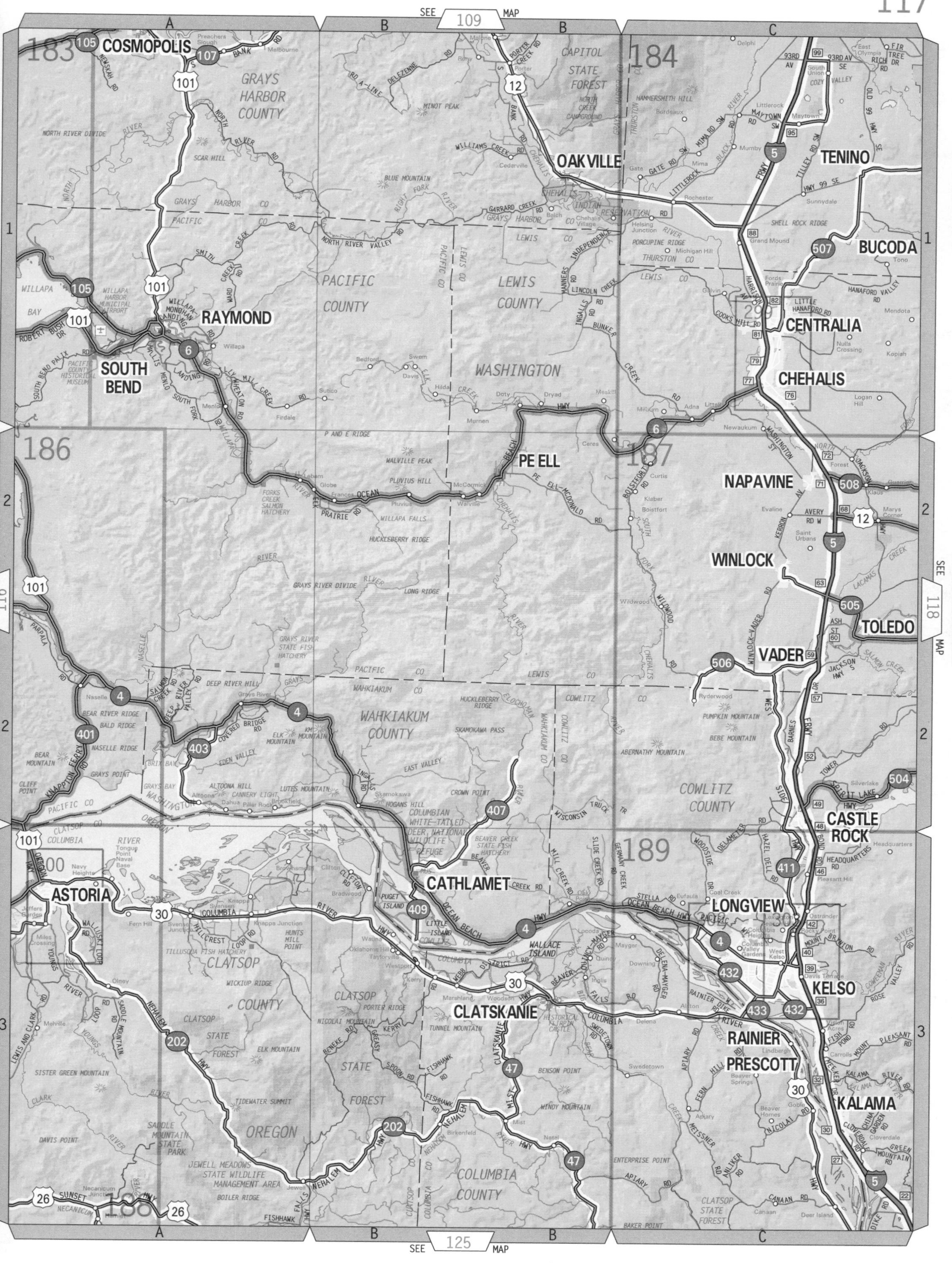
SEE 109 MAP
SEE 125 MAP
SEE 118 MAP
HWY
PNW
183
184
186
187
189
COSMOPOLIS
GRAYS HARBOR COUNTY
CAPITOL STATE FOREST
OAKVILLE
TENINO
BUCODA
RAYMOND
SOUTH BEND
PACIFIC COUNTY
LEWIS COUNTY
WASHINGTON
CENTRALIA
CHEHALIS
PE ELL
NAPAVINE
WINLOCK
TOLEDO
VADER
WAHKIAKUM COUNTY
COWLITZ COUNTY
CASTLE ROCK
CATHLAMET
ASTORIA
LONGVIEW
KELSO
CLATSKANIE
CLATSOP COUNTY
CLATSOP STATE FOREST
RAINIER
PRESCOTT
KALAMA
OREGON
COLUMBIA COUNTY
WILLAPA BAY
CHEHALIS INDIAN RESERVATION
COLUMBIAN WHITE-TAILED DEER NATIONAL WILDLIFE REFUGE
JEWELL MEADOWS STATE WILDLIFE MANAGEMENT AREA
SADDLE MOUNTAIN STATE PARK

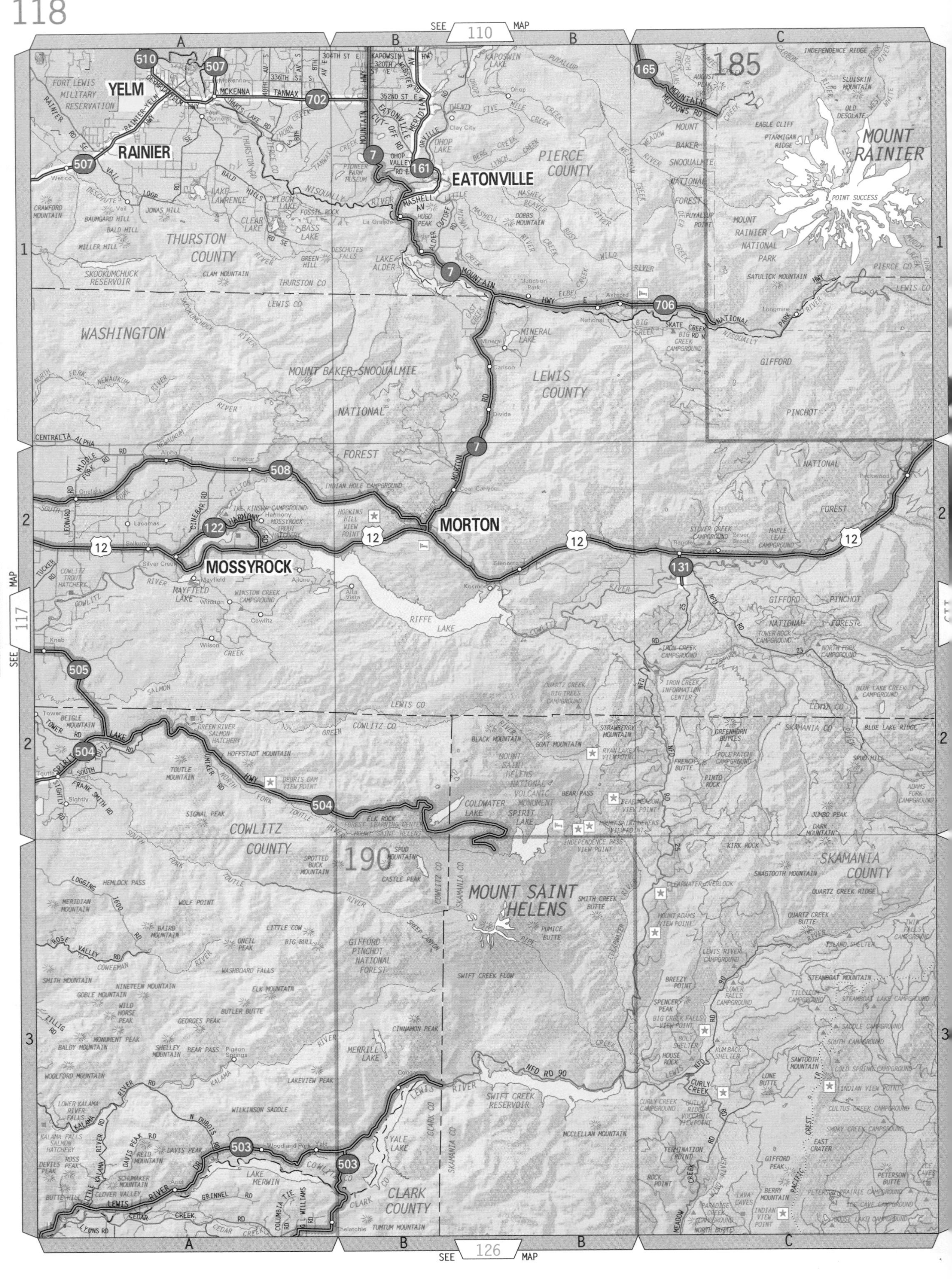
SEE 110 MAP
SEE 117 MAP
SEE 126 MAP
PNW
HWY
A
B
C
1
2
3
185
190
YELM
RAINIER
EATONVILLE
MORTON
MOSSYROCK
FORT LEWIS MILITARY RESERVATION
THURSTON COUNTY
PIERCE COUNTY
LEWIS COUNTY
COWLITZ COUNTY
CLARK COUNTY
SKAMANIA COUNTY
WASHINGTON
MOUNT RAINIER
MOUNT RAINIER NATIONAL PARK
POINT SUCCESS
MOUNT BAKER-SNOQUALMIE NATIONAL FOREST
GIFFORD PINCHOT NATIONAL FOREST
MOUNT SAINT HELENS
MOUNT SAINT HELENS NATIONAL VOLCANIC MONUMENT
RIFFE LAKE
MAYFIELD LAKE
SPIRIT LAKE
COLDWATER LAKE
SWIFT CREEK RESERVOIR
LAKE MERWIN
YALE LAKE
MERRILL LAKE
LAKE ALDER
LAKE LAWRENCE
CLEAR LAKE
BASS LAKE
ELBOW LAKE
OHOP LAKE
KAPOSWIN LAKE
MINERAL LAKE
SKOOKUMCHUCK RESERVOIR
NISQUALLY RIVER
COWLITZ RIVER
TOUTLE RIVER
KALAMA RIVER
LEWIS RIVER
CENTRALIA ALPHA RD
MOSSYROCK
Morton
Mineral
Ashford
Elbe
National
Packwood
Randle
Glenoma
Cougar
Yale
Ariel
Toutle
Silver Creek
Salkum
Onalaska
Cinebar
Alpha
Mayfield
Kosmo
SKATE CREEK
BIG CREEK CAMPGROUND
IRON CREEK CAMPGROUND
NORTH FORK CAMPGROUND
TOWER ROCK CAMPGROUND
MAPLE LEAF CAMPGROUND
SILVER CREEK CAMPGROUND
LEWIS RIVER CAMPGROUND
LOWER FALLS CAMPGROUND
INDEPENDENCE PASS VIEW POINT
WINDY RIDGE
HOFFSTADT MOUNTAIN
SIGNAL PEAK
ELK ROCK
CASTLE PEAK
SPUD MOUNTAIN
SWIFT CREEK FLOW
PUMICE BUTTE
SMITH CREEK BUTTE
STRAWBERRY MOUNTAIN
BLACK MOUNTAIN
GOAT MOUNTAIN
SPOTTED BUCK MOUNTAIN
GREENHORN BUTTES
SPUD HILL
JUMBO PEAK
DARK MOUNTAIN
KIRK ROCK
SNAGTOOTH MOUNTAIN
QUARTZ CREEK RIDGE
QUARTZ CREEK BUTTE
STEAMBOAT MOUNTAIN
SAWTOOTH MOUNTAIN
LONE BUTTE
GIFFORD PEAK
EAST CRATER
PETERSON BUTTE
LAVA CAVES
PACIFIC CREST TR
NFD RD 90
NFD 25
12
7
161
165
122
131
503
504
505
507
508
510
702
706

SEE 111 MAP

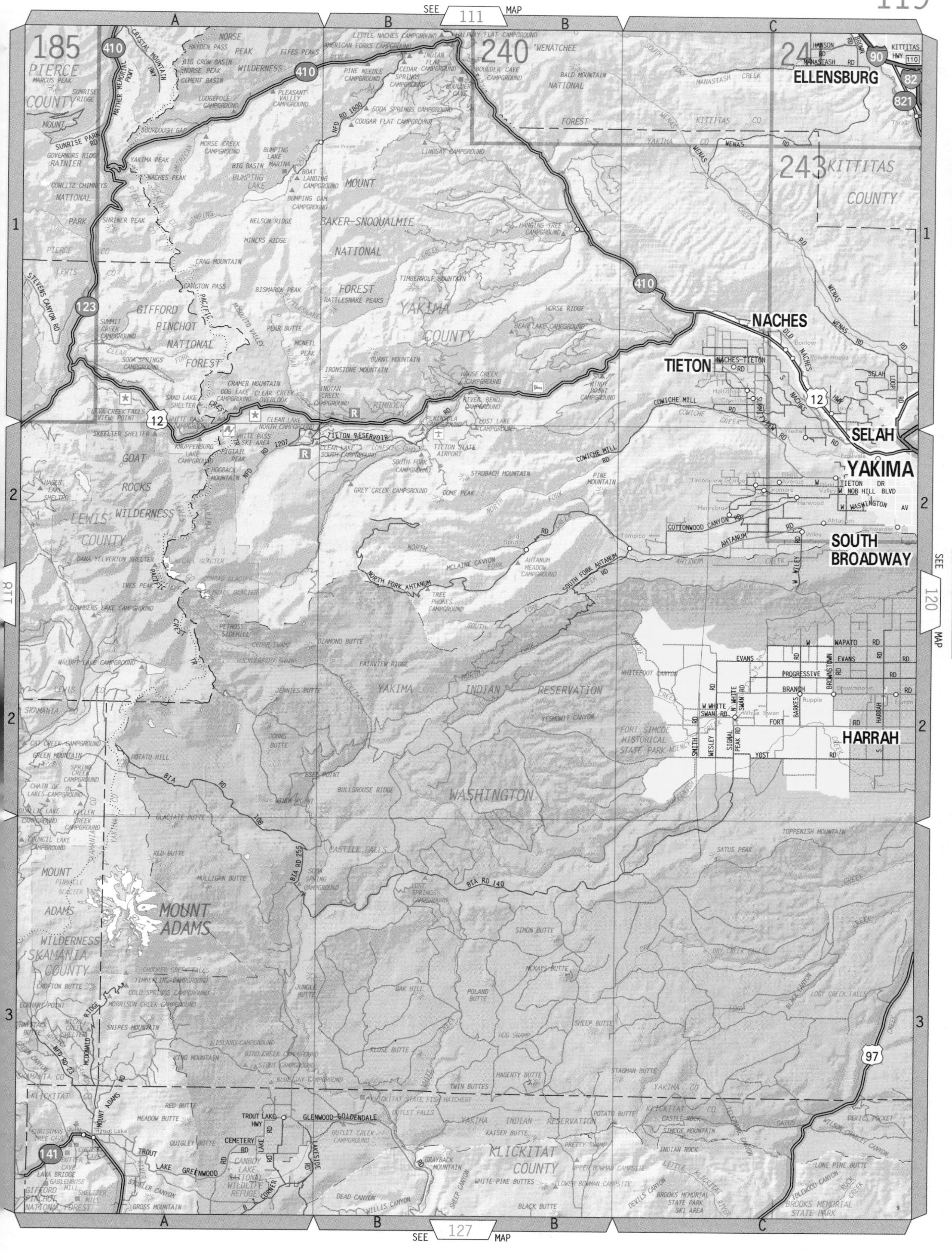

SEE 120 MAP

SEE 118 MAP

SEE 127 MAP

SEE 112 MAP

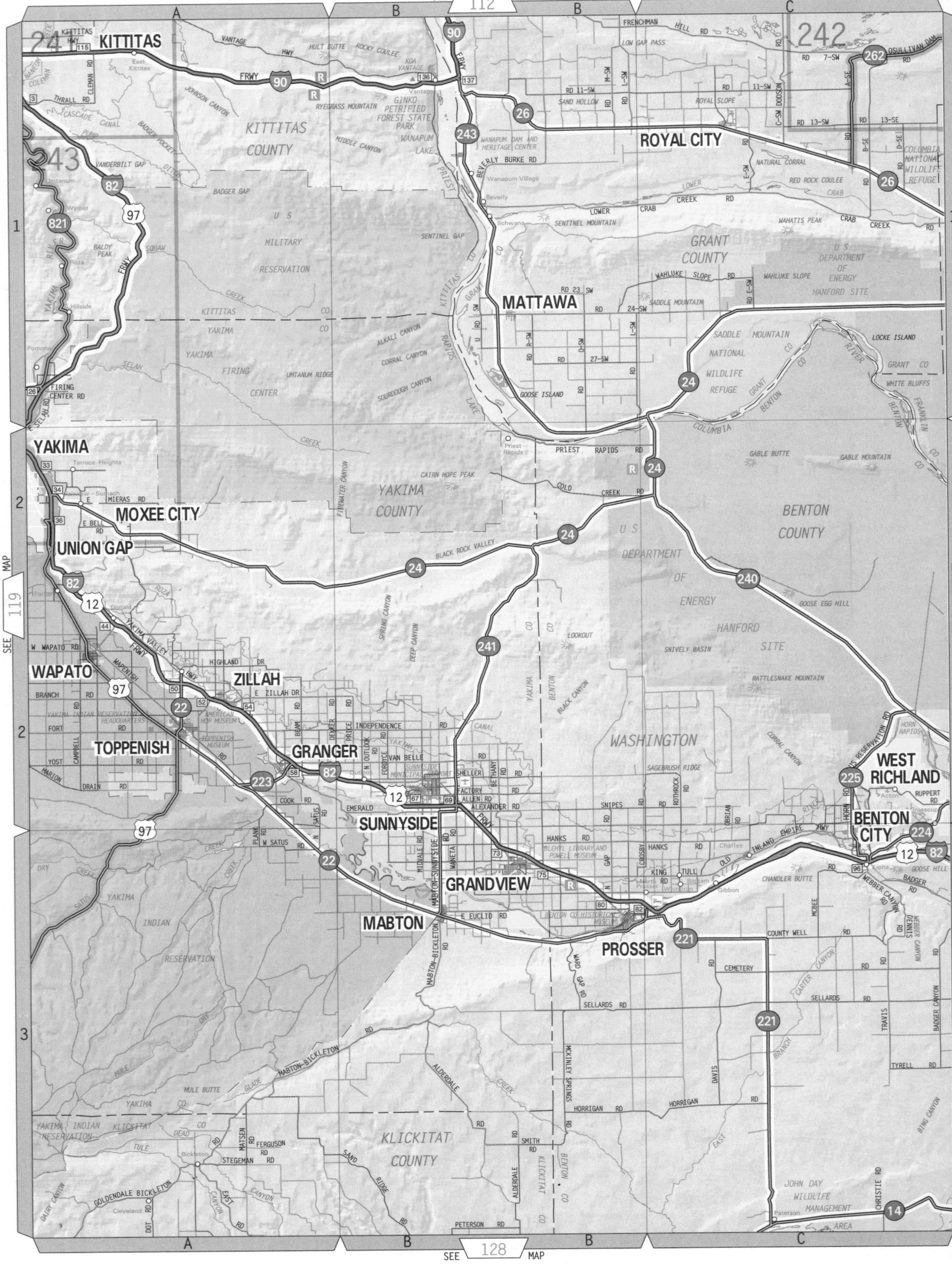

KITTITAS
ROYAL CITY
MATTAWA
YAKIMA
MOXEE CITY
UNION GAP
WAPATO
ZILLAH
TOPPENISH
GRANGER
SUNNYSIDE
GRANDVIEW
MABTON
PROSSER
WEST RICHLAND
BENTON CITY

KITTITAS COUNTY
GRANT COUNTY
YAKIMA COUNTY
BENTON COUNTY
KLICKITAT COUNTY
WASHINGTON

US MILITARY RESERVATION
YAKIMA FIRING CENTER
US DEPARTMENT OF ENERGY HANFORD SITE
SADDLE MOUNTAIN NATIONAL WILDLIFE REFUGE
COLUMBIA NATIONAL WILDLIFE REFUGE
YAKIMA INDIAN RESERVATION
JOHN DAY WILDLIFE MANAGEMENT AREA
GINKO PETRIFIED FOREST STATE PARK

VANTAGE HWY
FRENCHMAN HILL RD
YAKIMA VALLEY FRWY
INLAND EMPIRE HWY
MABTON-BICKLETON RD
GOLDENDALE BICKLETON RD
BLACK ROCK VALLEY
PRIEST RAPIDS RD
COUNTY WELL RD
SELLARDS RD
HORRIGAN RD

SEE 119 MAP
SEE 121 MAP
SEE 128 MAP

SEE 113 MAP
A
B
C
1
2
3
WARDEN
WARDEN MUNICIPAL AIRPORT
LIND
LIND AIRPORT
OTHELLO
OTHELLO MUNICIPAL AIRPORT
COLUMBIA NATIONAL WILDLIFE REFUGE
THE POTHOLES
OSULLIVAN DAM
JACKASS MOUNTAIN
SADDLE MOUNTAINS
ADAMS COUNTY
HATTON
WASHTUCNA
PROVIDENCE
RALSTON-BENGE
HERMAN
SUTTON
CUNNINGHAM RD
CALLOWAY
LIND-WARDEN
MCELROY COULEE
PAHA COULEE
SAND HILLS COULEE
LIND-HATTON
CUNNINGHAM COULEE
PROVIDENCE COULEE
HATTON COULEE
LIND-KAHLOTUS
BENGE-WASHTUCNA
HAMPTON
ROSS FARM
HOLLIDAY COULEE
ADAMS CO
FRANKLIN CO
SCOOTENEY RESERVOIR
Sagehill
CONNELL
CONNELL CITY AIRPORT
HAVLINA
WASHTUCNA COULEE
RATTLESNAKE CANYON
HARDESTY COULEE
KAHLOTUS
MARMES ROCK SHELTER
LYONS FERRY
DEVILS CANYON
Basin City
SHEFFIELD RD
PEPIOT
MESA
MESA KAHLOTUS
OLD MAID COULEE
DUNNIGAN COULEE
LARGENT
REYNOLDS
DE LANEY
PASCO-KAHLOTUS
BURR CANYON
FRANKLIN COUNTY
ESQUATZEL COULEE
SMITH CANYON
HAVERLAND KOONTZ
RINGOLD
US DEPARTMENT OF ENERGY HANFORD SITE
COLUMBIA RIVER
ELTOPIA WEST
Eltopia
RYE GRASS COULEE
WASHINGTON
JUNIPER DUNES WILDERNESS
SACAJAWEA
Snake River Junction
MCCOY CANYON
MCCLENNY
MURPHY
FISH HOOK
RICE HILL
WALLA WALLA COUNTY
Pleasant View
WALKER CANYON
MONUMENTAL
BABCOCK
Clyde
Reser
SMITH
SPRINGS
BADGER HOLLOW
DRY HOLLOW
WINNETT CANYON
PIPER CANYON
SMITH SPRINGS
PRESCOTT
Eureka
Lamar
LAMAR RD
RICHLAND
WEST RICHLAND
KENNEWICK
PASCO
West Pasco
Island View
West Highlands
South Highlands
Finley
Highland
ICE HARBOR DR
Burbank Heights
HUMORIST
Burbank
Martindale
SELPH LANDING
SAGEMOOR
E DOGWOOD
PASCO-KAHLOTUS
LUCKENBILL
TOUCHET
NINE MILE CANYON
ASH HOLLOW
SUDBURY
HARVEY
SHAW
VALLEY GROVE RD
SPRING VALLEY
LOWER WAITSBURG
WAITSBURG
Dry Creek
WALLA WALLA
COLLEGE PLACE
Garrett
Whitman
Lowden
LOWER DRY CREEK
IRELAND
BORGEN
SAND PIT RD
GARDENA
RIGGS RD
FROG HOLLOW
BYRNES
Touchet
Wallula
CLOVER HILL
BENTON COUNTY
LOCUST GROVE
CLODFELTER
BADGER CANYON
SCOUTEN CANYON
C WILLIAMS
STRAUB CANYON
TAYLOR CANYON
BECK
KIRK
FOURMILE CANYON
PLYMOUTH
Plymouth
SILLUSI BUTTE
MCNARY DAM FISH LADDER
COLUMBIA RIVER HWY
UMATILLA COUNTY
OREGON
BUTLER GRADE
N JUNIPER CANYON
Umapine
Ferndale
SUNNYSIDE-UMAPINE HWY
FREEWATER HWY
BIRCH CREEK
SPOFFORD
POWER LINE
MILTON-FREEWATER
MILTON CEMETERY RD
Calbounville
COTTONWOOD
340
341
342
343
344
345
SEE 122 MAP
SEE 129 MAP

SEE 114 MAP
A
B
C
1
2
3
ENDICOTT
PALOUSE
COLFAX
LA CROSSE
ALBION
PULLMAN
COLTON
STARBUCK
POMEROY
DAYTON
WAITSBURG
ADAMS COUNTY
WHITMAN COUNTY
GARFIELD COUNTY
COLUMBIA COUNTY
ASOTIN COUNTY
WALLA WALLA COUNTY
WALLOWA COUNTY
UMATILLA COUNTY
WASHINGTON
OREGON
LYONS FERRY STATE PARK
LAKE HERBERT
LAKE BRYAN
LOWER GRANITE LAKE
PALOUSE FALLS
FRYXELL OVERLOOK
MARMES ROCK SHELTER
COYOTE BUTTE
BLACK BUTTE
MAGEE HILL
WILD HORSE HILL
SNAKE RIVER
UMATILLA NATIONAL FOREST
WENAHA-TUCANNON WILDERNESS
WENAHA-TUCANNON WILDERNESS AREA
TUCANNON GAME RESERVE
WOOTEN GAME RESERVE
BLUEWOOD SKI AREA
TOUCHET SNO-PARK
DIAMOND PEAK
OREGON BUTTE
JASPER MOUNTAIN
ROBINETTE MOUNTAIN
CHASE MOUNTAIN
NEWBY MOUNTAIN
CAHILL MOUNTAIN
GRIFFIN PEAK
DEADMAN PEAK
GREEN PEAK
SQUAW PEAK
PIKES PEAK
SADDLE MOUNTAIN
GOVERNMENT MOUNTAIN
LEWIS PEAK
TWIN BUTTES
WELLER BUTTE
SMOOTH RIDGE
GRANDE RONDE RIVER
ENTERPRISE-LEWISTON HWY
SEE 121 HWY MAP
SEE 130 MAP
PNW
26
27
127
194
195
12
261
124
126
128
129
193
272
3

SEE 115 MAP

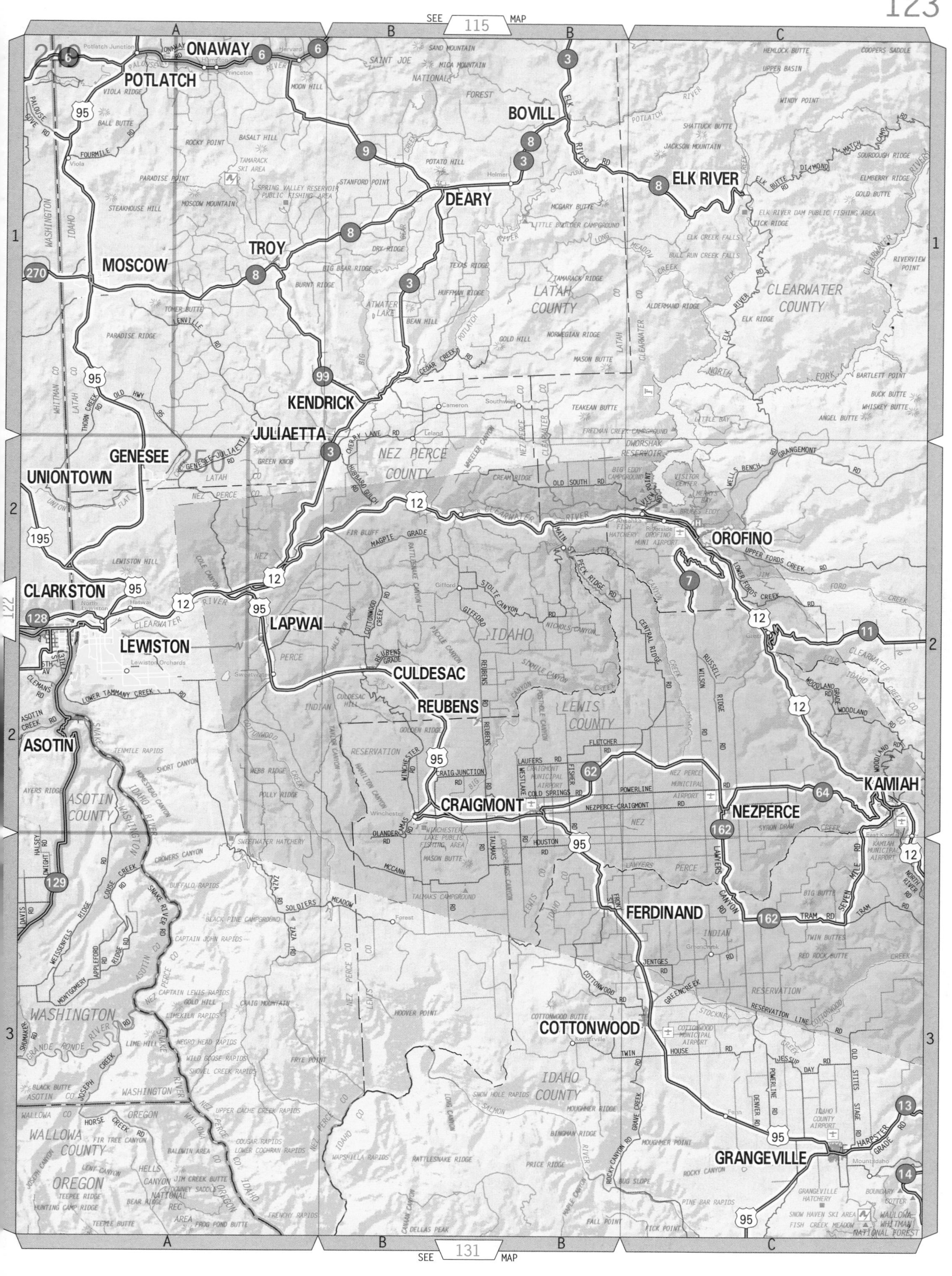

SEE 131 MAP

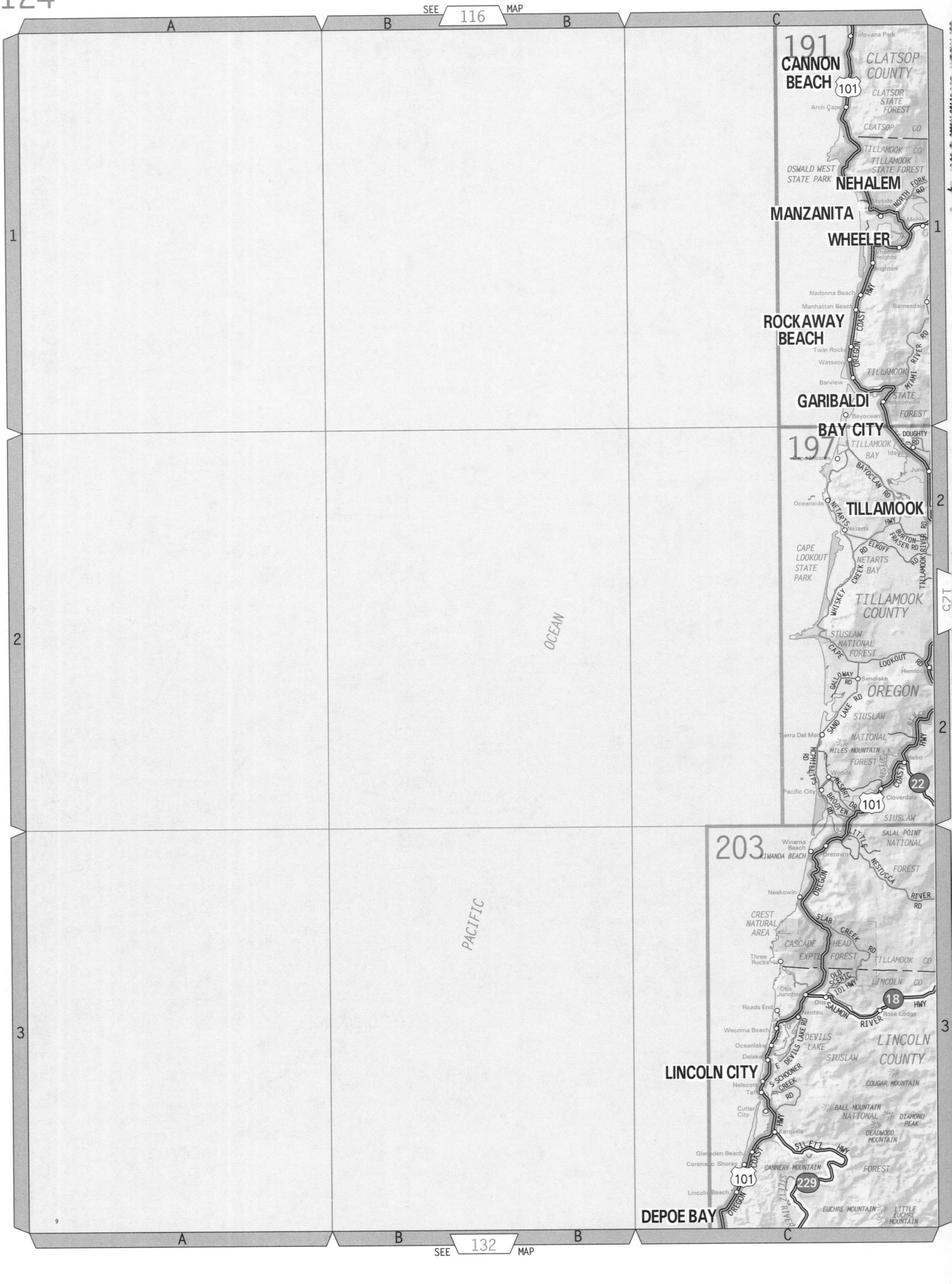

SEE 116 MAP

A B B C

191 CANNON BEACH 101 CLATSOP COUNTY CLATSOP STATE FOREST Tolovana Park Arch Cape CLATSOP CO TILLAMOOK CO TILLAMOOK STATE FOREST OSWALD WEST STATE PARK NEHALEM NORTH FORK RD MANZANITA Mohler WHEELER Wheeler Heights Brighton Nedonna Beach Manhattan Beach Barnesdale ROCKAWAY BEACH OREGON COAST HWY Twin Rocks Watseco MIAMI RIVER RD TILLAMOOK STATE FOREST Barview GARIBALDI Hobsonville Bayocean BAY CITY

197 TILLAMOOK BAY DOUGHTY RD Idaville BAYOCEAN RD Oceanside NETARTS TILLAMOOK HWY Netarts BURTON-FRASER RD ELKOFF RD CAPE LOOKOUT STATE PARK NETARTS BAY WHISKEY CREEK RD TILLAMOOK RIVER RD TILLAMOOK COUNTY SIUSLAW NATIONAL FOREST CAPE LOOKOUT RD Hemlock GALLOWAY RD Sandlake OREGON SAND LAKE RD SIUSLAW NATIONAL FOREST Tierra Del Mar MILES MOUNTAIN McPHILLIPS RD Hebo Woods RESORT DR Pacific City BROOTEN RD 22 101 Cloverdale SIUSLAW

203 Winema Beach NESKOWIN BEACH Oretown LITTLE NESTUCCA RIVER RD SALAL POINT NATIONAL FOREST Neskowin OREGON CREST NATURAL AREA SLAB CREEK RD CASCADE HEAD EXPTL FOREST Three Rocks TILLAMOOK CO OLD SCENIC 101 HWY LINCOLN CO Otis Junction Otis SALMON RIVER 18 HWY Rose Lodge Roads End Neotsu Wecoma Beach DEVILS LAKE RD DEVILS LAKE Oceanlake Delake E DEVILS LAKE SIUSLAW LINCOLN COUNTY LINCOLN CITY S SCHOONER CREEK RD Nelscott Taft COUGAR MOUNTAIN Cutler City BALL MOUNTAIN NATIONAL DIAMOND PEAK HWY Kernville DEADWOOD MOUNTAIN SILETZ HWY Gleneden Beach Coronado Shores COAST 101 CANNERY MOUNTAIN 229 FOREST Lincoln Beach OREGON SILETZ RIVER EUCHRE MOUNTAIN LITTLE EUCHRE MOUNTAIN DEPOE BAY

PACIFIC OCEAN

1 2 3

A B B C

SEE 132 MAP

C7T

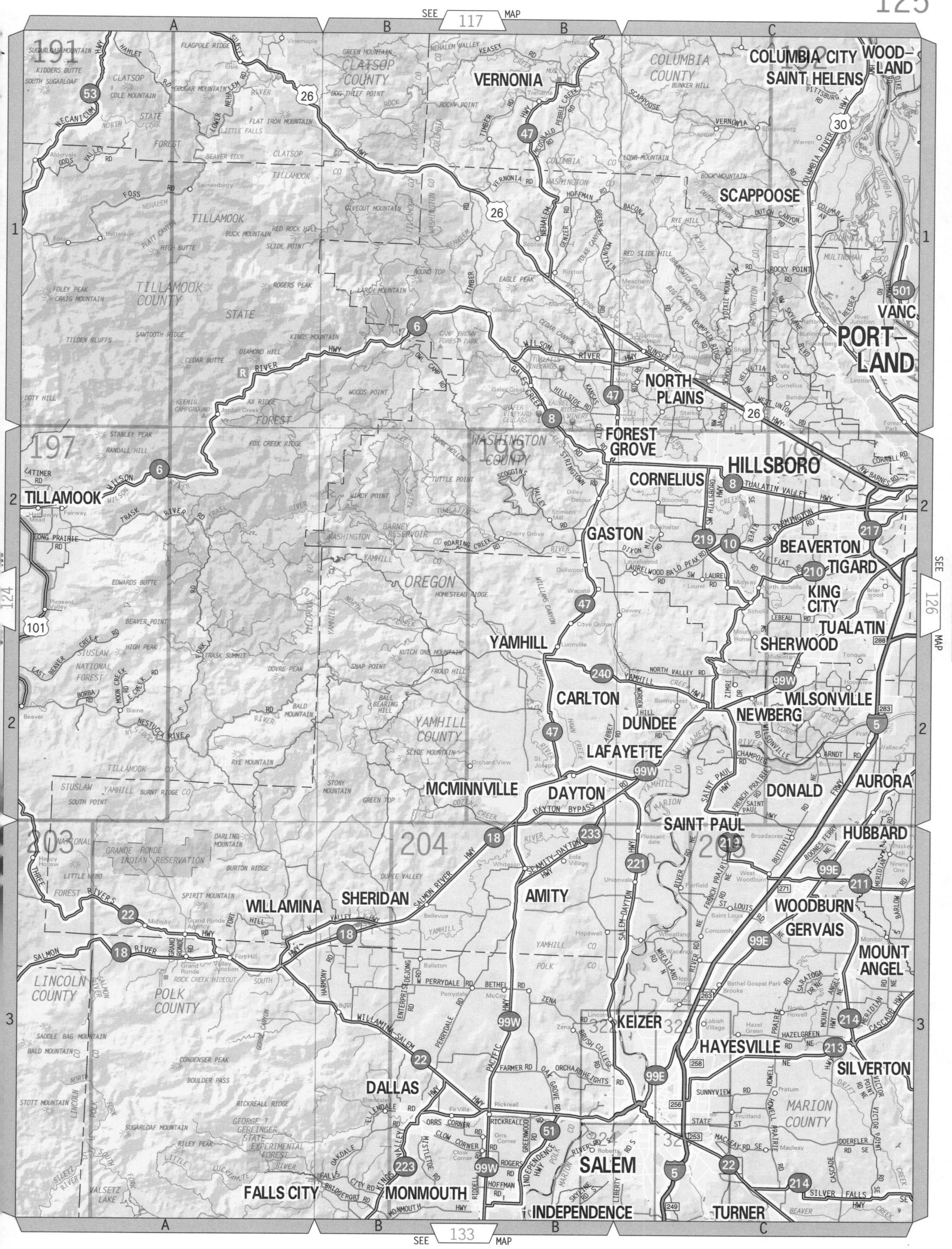

SEE 117 MAP
SEE 133 MAP
SEE 126 MAP
124
PNW
HWY
VERNONIA
COLUMBIA CITY
SAINT HELENS
WOODLAND
SCAPPOOSE
PORTLAND
VANC
NORTH PLAINS
FOREST GROVE
HILLSBORO
CORNELIUS
GASTON
BEAVERTON
TIGARD
KING CITY
TUALATIN
SHERWOOD
WILSONVILLE
NEWBERG
YAMHILL
CARLTON
DUNDEE
LAFAYETTE
DAYTON
MCMINNVILLE
DONALD
AURORA
SAINT PAUL
HUBBARD
WOODBURN
GERVAIS
MOUNT ANGEL
AMITY
SHERIDAN
WILLAMINA
TILLAMOOK
KEIZER
HAYESVILLE
SILVERTON
DALLAS
SALEM
MONMOUTH
FALLS CITY
INDEPENDENCE
TURNER
TILLAMOOK COUNTY
CLATSOP COUNTY
COLUMBIA COUNTY
WASHINGTON COUNTY
YAMHILL COUNTY
LINCOLN COUNTY
POLK COUNTY
MARION COUNTY
GRANDE RONDE INDIAN RESERVATION
SIUSLAW NATIONAL FOREST
GEORGE T GERLINGER STATE EXPERIMENTAL FOREST

SEE 118 MAP

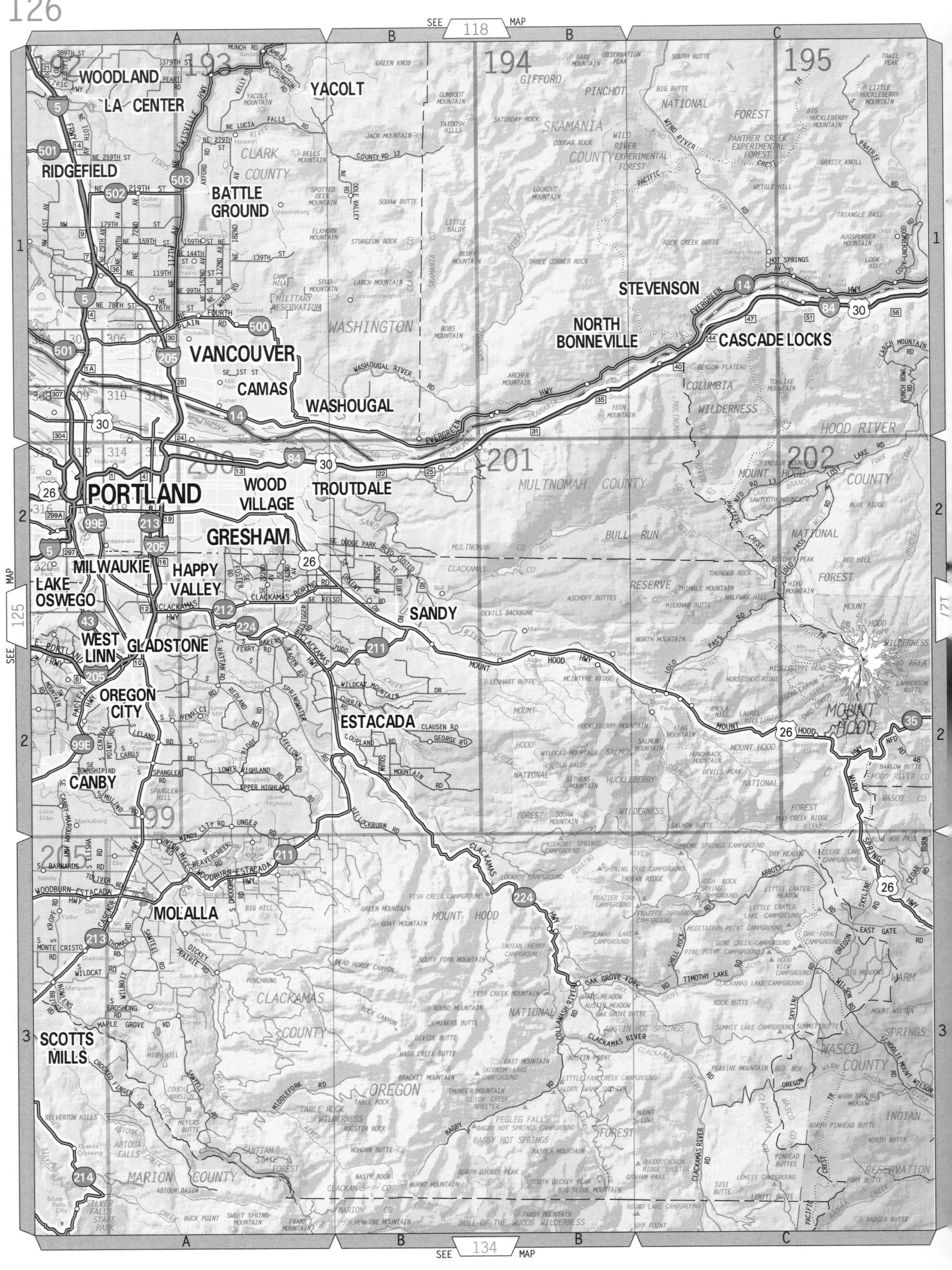

SEE 125 MAP

SEE 127 MAP

SEE 134 MAP

SEE 119 MAP

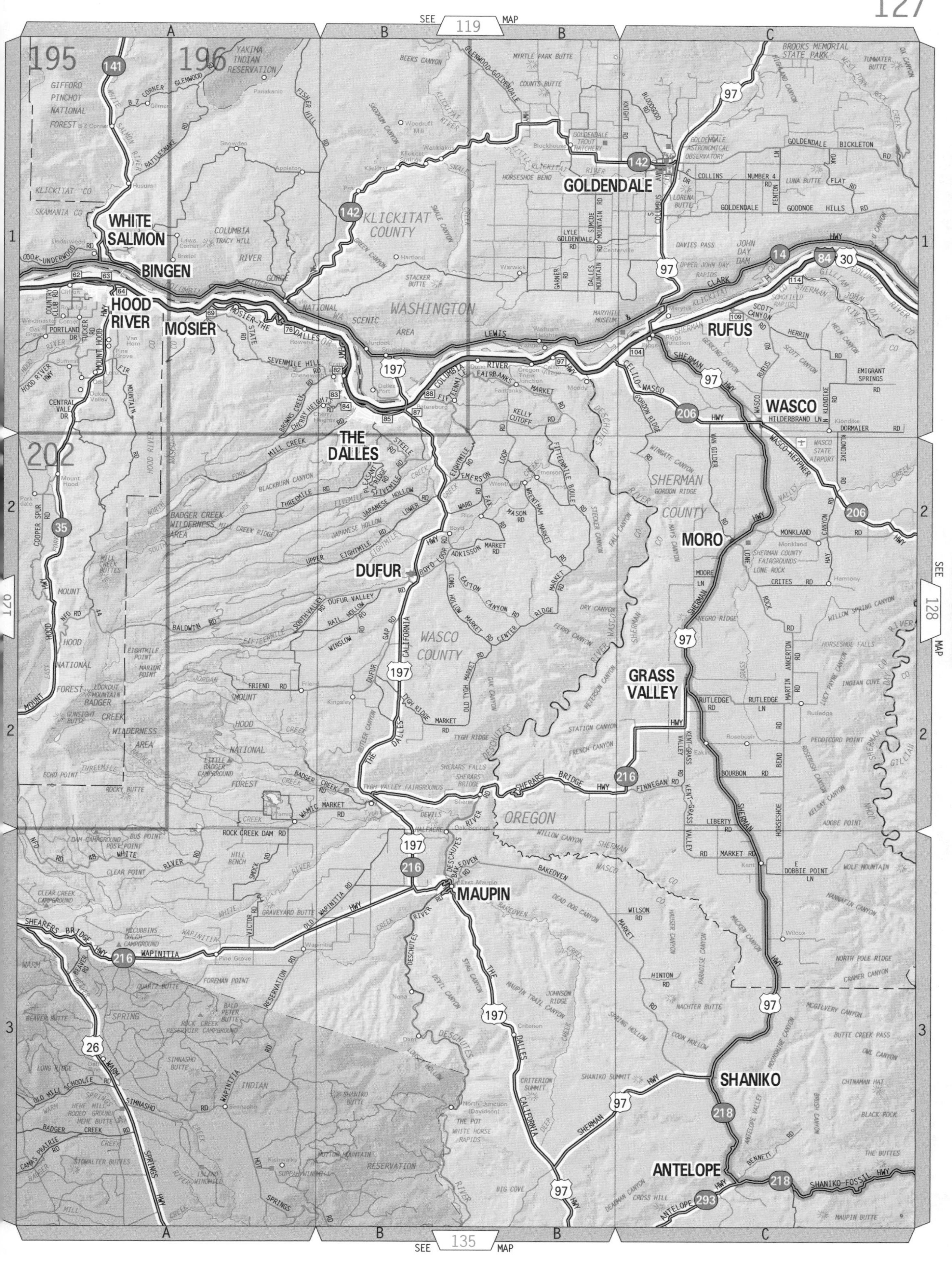

SEE 128 MAP

SEE 135 MAP

SEE 120 MAP

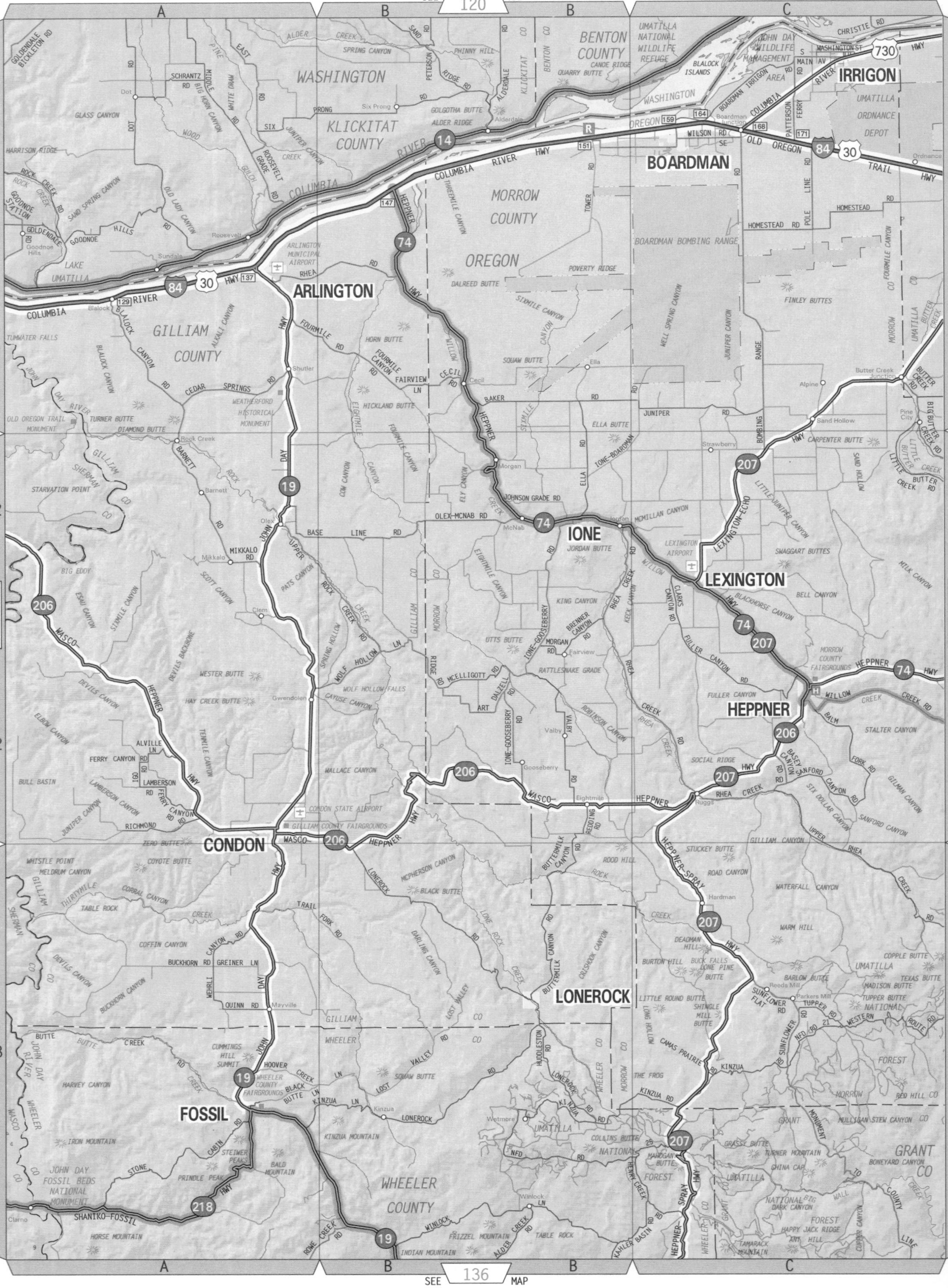

PNW

HWY SEE 127 MAP

A B B C

1 2 2 3

ARLINGTON
BOARDMAN
IRRIGON
IONE
LEXINGTON
HEPPNER
CONDON
LONEROCK
FOSSIL

WASHINGTON
KLICKITAT COUNTY
BENTON COUNTY
UMATILLA NATIONAL WILDLIFE REFUGE
JOHN DAY WILDLIFE MANAGEMENT AREA
UMATILLA ORDNANCE DEPOT
OREGON
MORROW COUNTY
GILLIAM COUNTY
WHEELER COUNTY
GRANT CO
UMATILLA NATIONAL FOREST
JOHN DAY FOSSIL BEDS NATIONAL MONUMENT
BOARDMAN BOMBING RANGE

COLUMBIA RIVER
JOHN DAY RIVER
LAKE UMATILLA
WILLOW CREEK
RHEA CREEK

COLUMBIA RIVER HWY
OLD OREGON TRAIL HWY
HEPPNER HWY
WASCO–HEPPNER HWY
HEPPNER–SPRAY HWY
SHANIKO–FOSSIL HWY
JOHN DAY HWY
LEXINGTON–ECHO HWY

14 84 30 730 74 19 206 207 218

ARLINGTON MUNICIPAL AIRPORT
CONDON STATE AIRPORT
GILLIAM COUNTY FAIRGROUNDS
MORROW COUNTY FAIRGROUNDS
WHEELER COUNTY FAIRGROUNDS
LEXINGTON AIRPORT
OLD OREGON TRAIL MONUMENT
WEATHERFORD HISTORICAL MONUMENT

A B B C

SEE 136 MAP

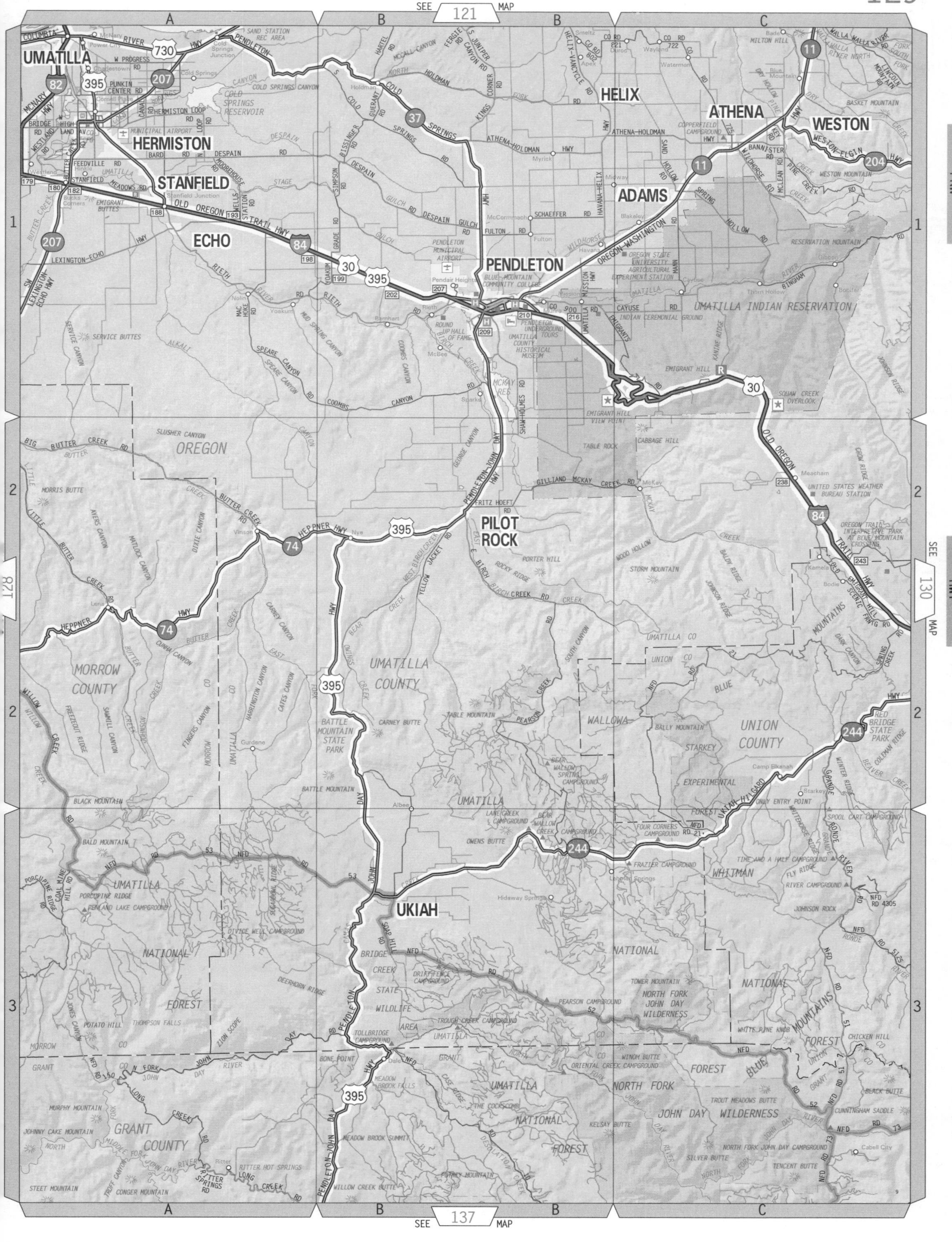

SEE 121 MAP
UMATILLA
HERMISTON
STANFIELD
ECHO
HELIX
ATHENA
WESTON
ADAMS
PENDLETON
PILOT ROCK
UKIAH
UMATILLA INDIAN RESERVATION
OREGON
MORROW COUNTY
UMATILLA COUNTY
UNION COUNTY
GRANT COUNTY
UMATILLA NATIONAL FOREST
NORTH FORK JOHN DAY WILDERNESS
BLUE MOUNTAINS
BATTLE MOUNTAIN STATE PARK
RED BRIDGE STATE PARK
SEE 130 MAP
SEE 128 MAP
SEE 137 MAP

SEE 122 MAP

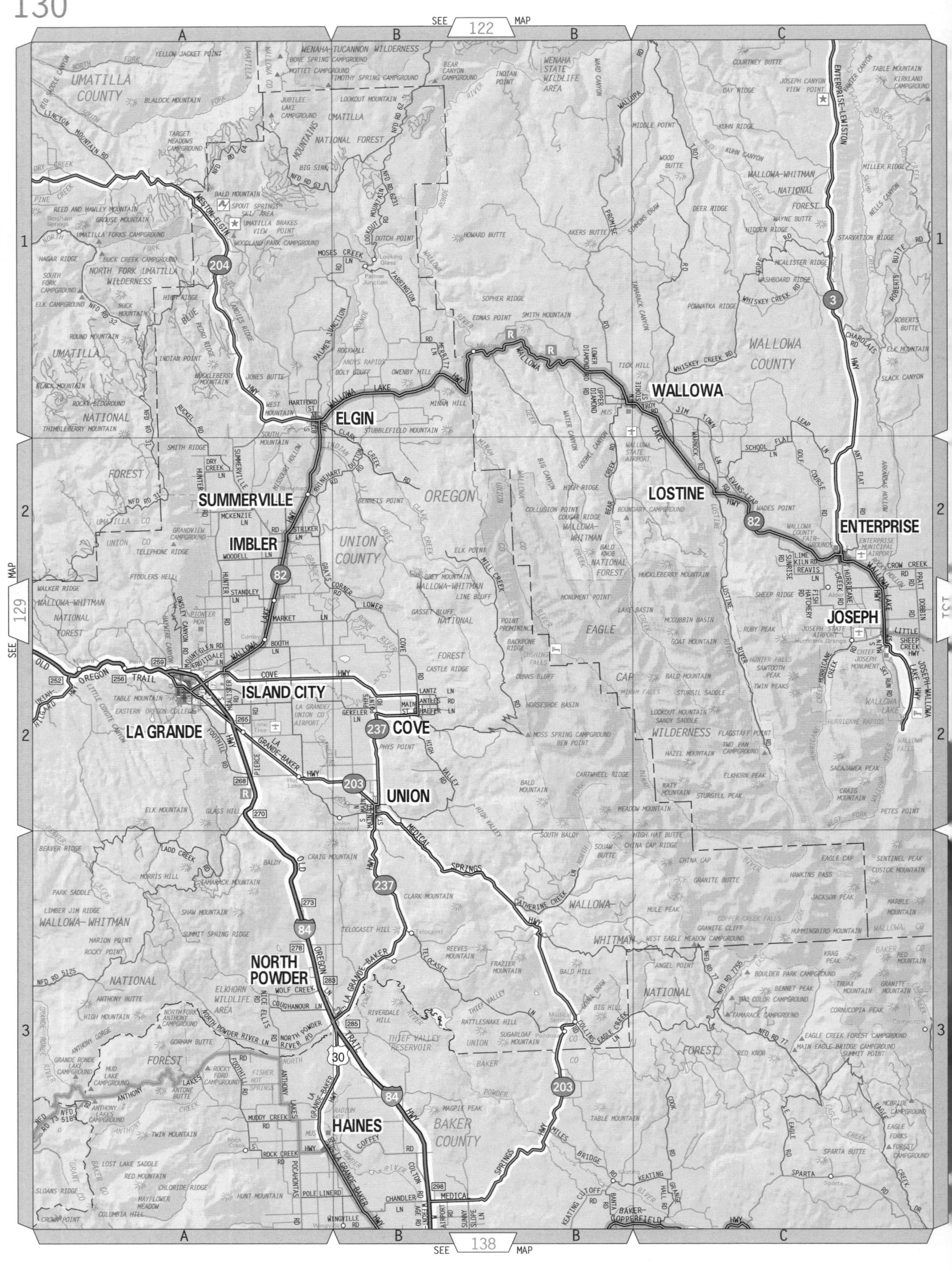

SEE 129 MAP

SEE 138 MAP

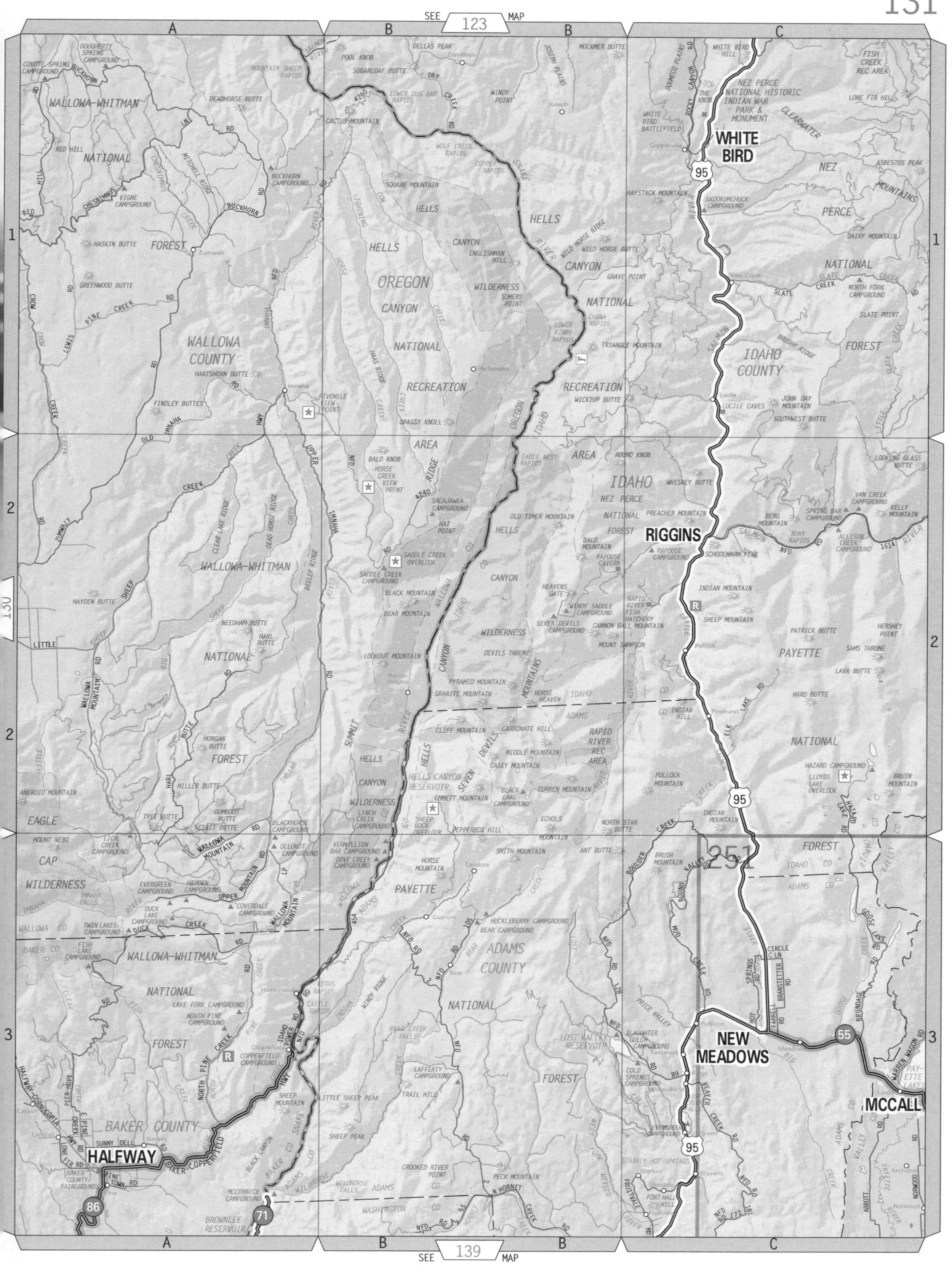
SEE 123 MAP
SEE 139 MAP
WHITE BIRD
RIGGINS
NEW MEADOWS
MCCALL
HALFWAY
WALLOWA COUNTY
IDAHO COUNTY
ADAMS COUNTY
BAKER COUNTY
HELLS CANYON NATIONAL RECREATION AREA
HELLS CANYON WILDERNESS
WALLOWA-WHITMAN NATIONAL FOREST
NEZ PERCE NATIONAL FOREST
PAYETTE NATIONAL FOREST
EAGLE CAP WILDERNESS
NEZ PERCE NATIONAL HISTORIC INDIAN WAR PARK & MONUMENT
RAPID RIVER REC AREA
HELLS CANYON RESERVOIR
BROWNLEE RESERVOIR
SNAKE RIVER
SALMON RIVER
IMNAHA RIVER
PNW
HWY

SEE 124 MAP

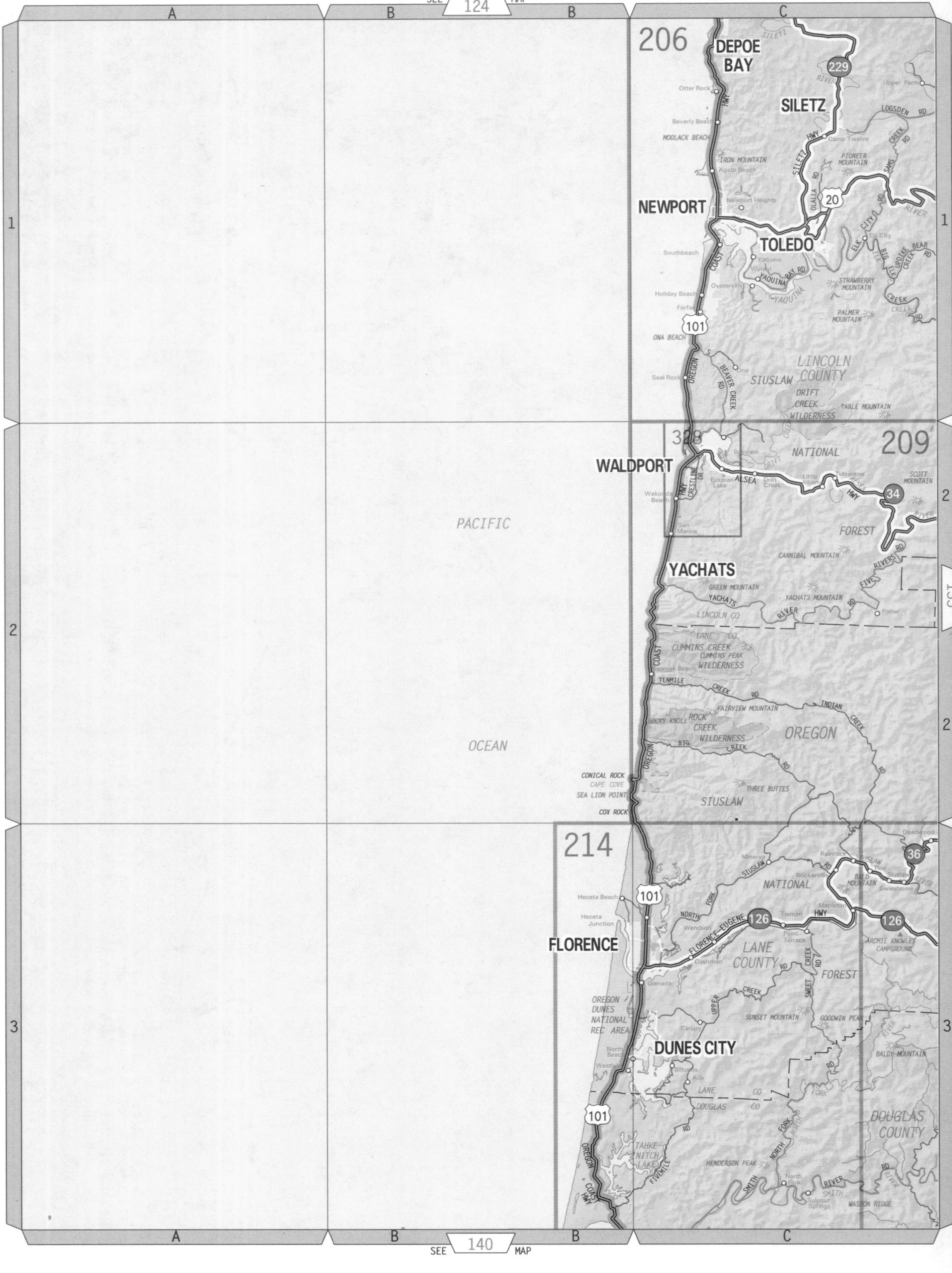

SEE 140 MAP

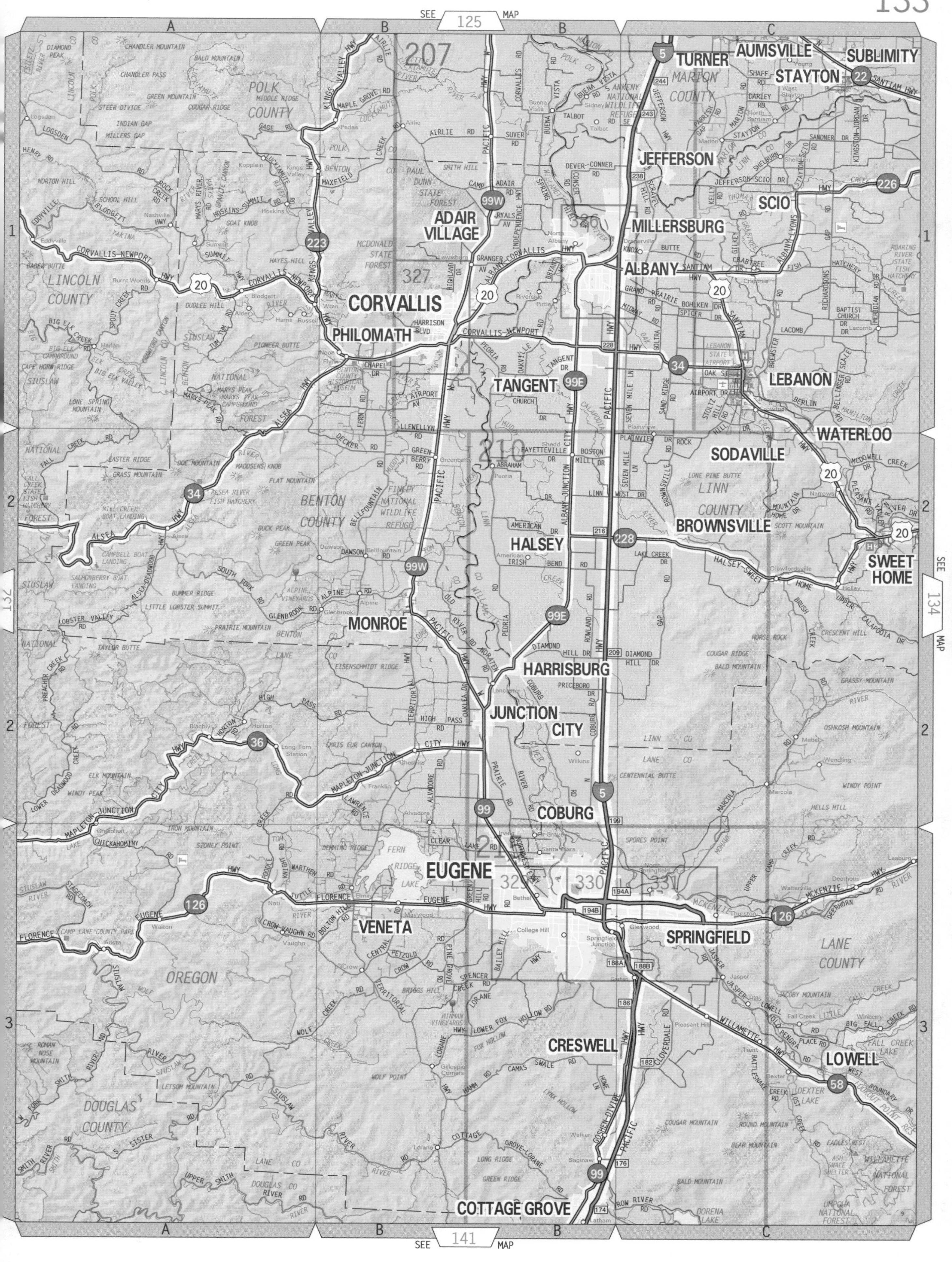
SEE 125 MAP
SEE 141 MAP
SEE 134 MAP
132
PNW
HWY
A
B
C
1
2
3
TURNER
AUMSVILLE
SUBLIMITY
STAYTON
JEFFERSON
SCIO
MILLERSBURG
ALBANY
ADAIR VILLAGE
CORVALLIS
PHILOMATH
TANGENT
LEBANON
WATERLOO
SODAVILLE
BROWNSVILLE
HALSEY
SWEET HOME
MONROE
HARRISBURG
JUNCTION CITY
COBURG
EUGENE
VENETA
SPRINGFIELD
CRESWELL
LOWELL
COTTAGE GROVE
POLK COUNTY
MARION COUNTY
LINCOLN COUNTY
BENTON COUNTY
LINN COUNTY
LANE COUNTY
DOUGLAS COUNTY
OREGON
MCDONALD STATE FOREST
PAUL DUNN STATE FOREST
SIUSLAW NATIONAL FOREST
FINLEY NATIONAL WILDLIFE REFUGE
ANKENY NATIONAL WILDLIFE REFUGE
WILLAMETTE NATIONAL FOREST
UMPQUA NATIONAL FOREST
FERN RIDGE LAKE
DEXTER LAKE
DORENA LAKE
FALL CREEK LAKE
MARYS PEAK
CORVALLIS-NEWPORT HWY
MAPLETON-JUNCTION CITY HWY
207
327
210
326
329
330
331
5
20
22
34
36
58
99
99E
99W
126
223
226
228

SEE 126 MAP

PNW

A B B C

1

SILVER FALLS STATE PARK
HOUSE MOUNTAIN
LOOKOUT MOUNTAIN RD
MILL CREEK
SHELLBURG FALLS
LOWER SHELLBURG FALLS
FERN RIDGE RD
STOUT CREEK FALLS
STASEL FALLS
NORTH FORK
LITTLE NORTH SANTIAM
Elkhorn
NFD RD 2207
LITTLE NORTH SANTIAM RIVER
SHADY COVE CAMPGROUND
SALMON FALLS CAMPGROUND
BUCK MOUNTAIN
MOUNT HOREB RD SE
ROCKY TOP
BULL OF THE WOODS WILDERNESS
BATTLE AX
BATTLE CREEK SHELTER
HAWK MOUNTAIN
SCORPION MOUNTAIN
ELK LAKE CAMPGROUND
GOLD BUTTE
SHORT MOUNTAIN
BOULDER PEAK
BYARS PEAK
BREITENBUSH CAMPGROUND
WILLAMETTE
MOUNT HOOD NATIONAL FOREST
NFD RD 46
CORNPATCH MEADOW
TWIN PEAKS
OLALLIE LAKE SCENIC AREA
DOUBLE PEAKS
CEDAR BUTTE
CINDER CONE
MILL CREEK
WASCO CO
OLALLIE BUTTE
OLALLIE LAKE CAMPGROUND
JEFFERSON CO
TROUT LAKE CAMPGROUND
BOULDER
BIA RD 33
NORTH BUTTE
WARM SPRINGS
ROCK CONE
SHITIKE BUTTE
JEFFERSON COUNTY
INDIAN RESERVATION
LIONSHEAD
CAMP CREEK BUTTE
226
LYONS
MILL CITY
GATES
SANTIAM HWY
NORTH SANTIAM
Fox Valley
LYONS-MILL CITY DR
KINGWOOD AV
DAVIS AIRPORT
MCCULLY MOUNTAIN
ALBANY-LYONS HWY
THOMAS CREEK
ROCKY TOP SHELTER
NATIONAL
BREITENBUSH RD
RIVER
Breitenbush Hot Springs
HUMBUG CAMPGROUND
UPPER ARM CAMPGROUND
DETROIT LAKE STATE PARK
22
DETROIT
IDANHA
HOOVER RIDGE
BOULDER RIDGE
MARION COUNTY
MOUNT JEFFERSON WILDERNESS AREA
BOCA CAVE
PARK BUTTE
FOREST
LITTLE PIGEON PRAIRIE
WHISPERING FALLS CAMPGROUND
BIG SPRINGS CAMPGROUND
MARION CO
LINN CO
CAMP
Jordan
BILYEU CREEK
MORRISON DR
JORDAN VALLEY
SANTIAM STATE FOREST
MONUMENT PEAK
STAHLMAN POINT
New Idanha
DETROIT LAKE
COOPERS RIDGE
WHITEWATER CAMPGROUND
SANTIAM
MILK CREEK GLACIER
WHITEWATER GLACIER
WALDO GLACIER
BALD PETER
BEAR BUTTE
THOMAS CAIRN
SNOW PEAK
CREEK
SLATE ROCK
LUCKY BUTTE
WILLAMETTE
LINN COUNTY
RIVERSIDE CAMPGROUND
MOUNT JEFFERSON
HARRY MOUNTAIN
GREEN MOUNTAIN
BUCK MOUNTAIN
Marion Forks
MARION FORKS CAMPGROUND
BINGHAM RIDGE
FORKED BUTTE
CRABTREE
CRABTREE MOUNTAIN
PINNACLE PEAK
WHITE BULL MOUNTAIN
QUARTZVILLE DR
YELLOWSTONE MOUNTAIN
ROUND MOUNTAIN
GREEN MOUNTAIN
HAMILTON CREEK
SCAR MOUNTAIN
PINE RIDGE
MARION FALLS
MAZAMA CREEK CAMPGROUND
RANGE
CANDLE CREEK CAMPGROUND
LOWER BRIDGE CAMPGROUND
ABBOT CREEK CAMPGROUND
KEEL MOUNTAIN
CASCADE FALLS
MCQUADE CREEK SHELTER
MIDDLE SANTIAM WILDERNESS AREA
MCNABB FALLS
NATIONAL
OREGON
MARION MOUNTAIN
WILDERNESS
SADDLE MOUNTAIN
NFD 12
PIONEER FORD CAMPGROUND
ALLAN SPRINGS CAMPGROUND
WIZARD FALLS
BEAR VALLEY
ROCKY TOP
MIDDLE
WILLAMETTE VALLEY
QUARTZVILLE
BALD PETER
THREE PYRAMIDS
RED BUTTE

2

MCDOWELL CREEK
GREEN PETER
HOGBACK RIDGE
SUNNYSIDE
QUARTZVILLE DR
GREEN PETER LAKE
COUGAR ROCK
SOUTH PYRAMID
BIG MEADOWS CAMPGROUND
DUFFY BUTTE
211
DESCHUTES AREA
CAMPGROUND
METOLIUS RIVER
FOREST
BOAT LAUNCH
NORTH RIVER
MOOSE MOUNTAIN
MENAGERIE WILDERNESS AREA
HARTER MOUNTAIN
CRESCENT MOUNTAIN
MAXWELL BUTTE
SUTTLE-SHERMAN
Camp Sherman
HIGH DECK
FOSTER LAKE
MENEARS BEND CAMPGROUND
Foster
CASCADIA CAVE
Cascadia
SOUTH SANTIAM
SANTIAM HWY
Upper Soda
CONE PEAK
SAWYERS CAVE
Santiam Junction
LOST LAKE CAMPGROUND
SANTIAM
20
HWY
SANTIAM JUNCTION STATE AIRPORT
HOODOO SKI BOWL SNO-PARK
CLAYPOOL BUTTE
JEFFERSON CO
126
BLACK BUTTE
BLACK BUTTE
WILEY CREEK
SWEET HOME
SANTIAM
CASCADIA STATE PARK
NFD RD
MOSS BUTTE
WHISKEY BUTTE
DOE MOUNTAIN
TOMBSTONE PRAIRIE CAMPGROUND
BELKNAP
SAND MOUNTAIN
BIG LAKE CAMPGROUND
BIG LAKE
DESCHUTES CO
LITTLE CACHE MOUNTAIN
NATIONAL
Black Butte Ranch
SANTIAM HWY
WILLAMETTE NATIONAL FOREST
SOAPGRASS MOUNTAIN
WILDCAT MOUNTAIN RESEARCH NATURAL AREA
WILDCAT MOUNTAIN
RABBIT CAMP RD
MOUNT WASHINGTON WILDERNESS AREA
SPRINGS HWY
CHIMNEY ROCK
GREEN BUTTE
SWAMP MOUNTAIN
TWIN BUTTES
SMITH RESERVOIR
TAMOLITCH FALLS
GRAHAM BUTTE
FARMERS BUTTE
NFD RD 2026
WOLF ROCK
UPPER CALAPOOIA
GREEN MOUNTAIN RIDGE
TIDBITS MOUNTAIN
GATE CREEK
RIVER
2654
126
242
HWY
CALAPOOIA DR
NFD RD
HJ
ANDREWS EXPERIMENTAL FOREST
SCOTT MOUNTAIN
TROUT CREEK BUTTE
MOHAWK RIVER
LINN CO
LANE CO
GOLD HILL
MONA CAMPGROUND
H J MONUMENT
LOOKOUT MOUNTAIN
BELKNAP SPRINGS HWY
HAND LAKE SHELTER
SCOTT LAKE CAMPGROUND
SCOTT PASS
FOREST
BLUE RIVER LAKE
Belknap Springs
TWO BUTTES
CASCADE
CREST
ELK MOUNTAIN
Rainbow
McKenzie Bridge
MCKENZIE
SIMS BUTTE
MCKENZIE BRIDGE STATE AIRPORT
MCKENZIE TROUT HATCHERY
Vida
Blue River
DELTA CAMPGROUND
MCKENZIE BRIDGE CAMPGROUND
HORSE
Foley Springs
THREE CREEKS
SQUAW

3

126
Finn Rock
MCKENZIE HWY
GREENWOOD LANDING
MCKENZIE SALMON HATCHERY
SILVER CREEK LANDING
Nimrod
ECHO CAMPGROUND
COUGAR RESERVOIR
MACDUFF MOUNTAIN
RAINBOW FALLS
PROXY POINT
216
(AUFDERHEIDE)
HARVEY MOUNTAIN
LANE
THREE SISTERS
SLIDE CREEK CAMPGROUND
SPHINX BUTTE
BROKEN TOP
PERNOT MOUNTAIN
SCENIC SOUTH BYWY
YANKEE MOUNTAIN
COUNTY
WILDERNESS
BURNT TOP
HAPPY VALLEY
HEHE MOUNTAIN
OLALLIE MOUNTAIN
LITTLE FALL CREEK RD
WILLAMETTE
DEER MOUNTAIN
PYRAMID MOUNTAIN
HORSE MOUNTAIN
SPARKS LAKE
TUMALO MOUNTAIN
CASCADE LAKES HWY
CENTURY DRIVE
BIG FALL CREEK
DELP CREEK SHELTER
BEDROCK CAMPGROUND
TWIN SPRINGS CAMPGROUND
PACIFIC
Elk Lake
DESCHUTES
372
HWY
UPPER END CAMPGROUND
BIG POOL CAMPGROUND
CHICHESTER FALLS
LOWELL MOUNTAIN
FORK RD
SOUTH FORK
AREA
ELK LAKE
HOSMER LAKE
TOT MOUNTAIN
COLLY VARDEN CAMPGROUND
SINKER MOUNTAIN
ROARING RIVER CAMPGROUND
CLIFF LAKE SHELTER
DESCHUTES COUNTY
BEAR MOUNTAIN
NATIONAL
WINBERRY CAMPGROUND
PACKSADDLE MOUNTAIN
MINK LAKE SHELTER
LAVA LAKE
NATIONAL
EDISON ICE CAVE RD
WINBERRY CREEK
LITTLE BLANKET SHELTER
WINBERRY
GRASSHOPPER MOUNTAIN
SHERIDAN MOUNTAIN
WILLAMETTE BYWY
KIAHANIE CAMPGROUND
LUCKY BUTTE
LITTLE ROUNDTOP MOUNTAIN
CANYON RD
CASCADE
SOUTH FORK SHELTER
58
LOOKOUT POINT RESERVOIR
Hampton
SCENIC RD
MOOLACK MOUNTAIN
FISHER
RIVER
HUCKLEBERRY MOUNTAIN
SIAH BUTTE
IRISH MOUNTAIN
WEST CULTUS LAKE CAMPGROUND
WAKE BUTTE
CENTURY DR
LOOKOUT MOUNTAIN RD
FOREST
BOUNDARY
BEAR LAKE CAMPGROUND
WALDO LAKE WILDERNESS AREA
CULTUS LAKE
LAVA LAKE RD
CRANE PRAIRIE RES
PRINGLE FALLS EXPERIMENTAL FOREST ADDITION
WILLAMETTE HWY
HAMPTON CAMPGROUND
ROCK KNOB
NORTH FORK
(AUFDERHEIDE)
PRAIRIE
FOREST
STAG SHELTER
IRISH AND TAYLOR CAMPGROUND
PILLAR PEAK
LITTLE CULTUS CAMPGROUND
HIGH

A B B C

SEE 142 MAP

SEE 133 HWY MAP

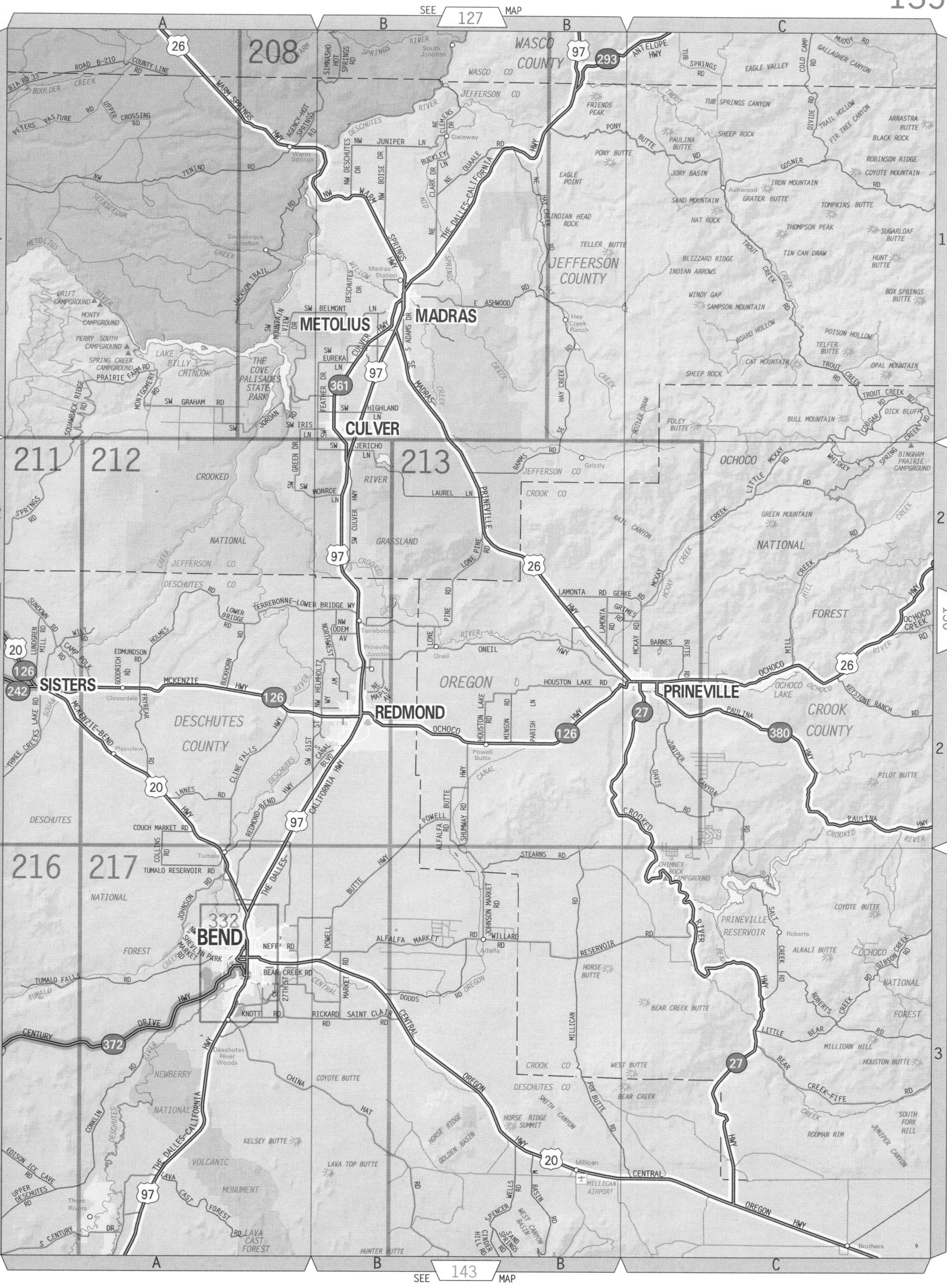
SEE 127 MAP
SEE 143 MAP
SEE 136 MAP
A
B
C
1
2
3
208
211
212
213
216
217
332
WASCO COUNTY
WASCO CO
JEFFERSON CO
JEFFERSON COUNTY
CROOK CO
CROOK COUNTY
DESCHUTES CO
DESCHUTES COUNTY
MADRAS
METOLIUS
CULVER
REDMOND
PRINEVILLE
SISTERS
BEND
Warm Springs
Gateway
Madras Station
Seekseequa Junction
South Junction
Ashwood
Hay Creek Ranch
Grizzly
Terrebonne
Prineville Junction
Cloverdale
Plainview
Powell Butte
Tumalo
Alfalfa
Roberts
Millican
Brothers
Deschutes River Woods
Three Rivers
CROOKED RIVER NATIONAL GRASSLAND
OCHOCO NATIONAL FOREST
DESCHUTES NATIONAL FOREST
NEWBERRY NATIONAL VOLCANIC MONUMENT
LAVA CAST FOREST
THE COVE PALISADES STATE PARK
LAKE BILLY CHINOOK
PRINEVILLE RESERVOIR
OCHOCO LAKE
MILLICAN AIRPORT
HORSE RIDGE SUMMIT
DRIFT CAMPGROUND
MONTY CAMPGROUND
PERRY SOUTH CAMPGROUND
SPRING CREEK CAMPGROUND
BINGHAM PRAIRIE CAMPGROUND
CHIMNEY ROCK CAMPGROUND
THE DALLES-CALIFORNIA HWY
WARM SPRINGS HWY
MCKENZIE HWY
OCHOCO HWY
PAULINA HWY
CENTURY DRIVE
OREGON CENTRAL HWY
ANTELOPE HWY
CAMP POLK RD
MCKENZIE-BEND HWY
TUMALO FALLS RD
ALFALFA MARKET RD
BEAR CREEK RD
KNOTT RD
DODDS RD
RICKARD RD
SAINT CLAIR RD
STEARNS RD
HOUSTON LAKE RD
TERREBONNE-LOWER BRIDGE WY
LAMONTA RD
GERKE RD
EAGLE VALLEY
GRIZZLY
FRIENDS PEAK
PONY BUTTE
EAGLE POINT
INDIAN HEAD ROCK
TELLER BUTTE
PAULINA BUTTE
SHEEP ROCK
JORY BASIN
SAND MOUNTAIN
HAT ROCK
IRON MOUNTAIN
GRATER BUTTE
TOMPKINS BUTTE
THOMPSON PEAK
SUGARLOAF BUTTE
TIN CAN DRAW
BLIZZARD RIDGE
INDIAN ARROWS
WINDY GAP
SAMPSON MOUNTAIN
HUNT BUTTE
BOX SPRINGS BUTTE
POISON HOLLOW
TELFER BUTTE
OPAL MOUNTAIN
CAT MOUNTAIN
BULL MOUNTAIN
DICK BLUFF
FOLEY BUTTE
ARRASTRA BUTTE
BLACK ROCK
ROBINSON RIDGE
COYOTE MOUNTAIN
GREEN MOUNTAIN
PILOT BUTTE
COYOTE BUTTE
ALKALI BUTTE
BEAR CREEK BUTTE
WEST BUTTE
HORSE BUTTE
HOUSTON BUTTE
MILLIORN HILL
RODMAN RIM
SOUTH FORK HILL
KELSEY BUTTE
LAVA TOP BUTTE
HUNTER BUTTE
EDISON ICE CAVE
26
97
20
126
242
293
361
27
380
372

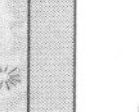

SEE 128 MAP

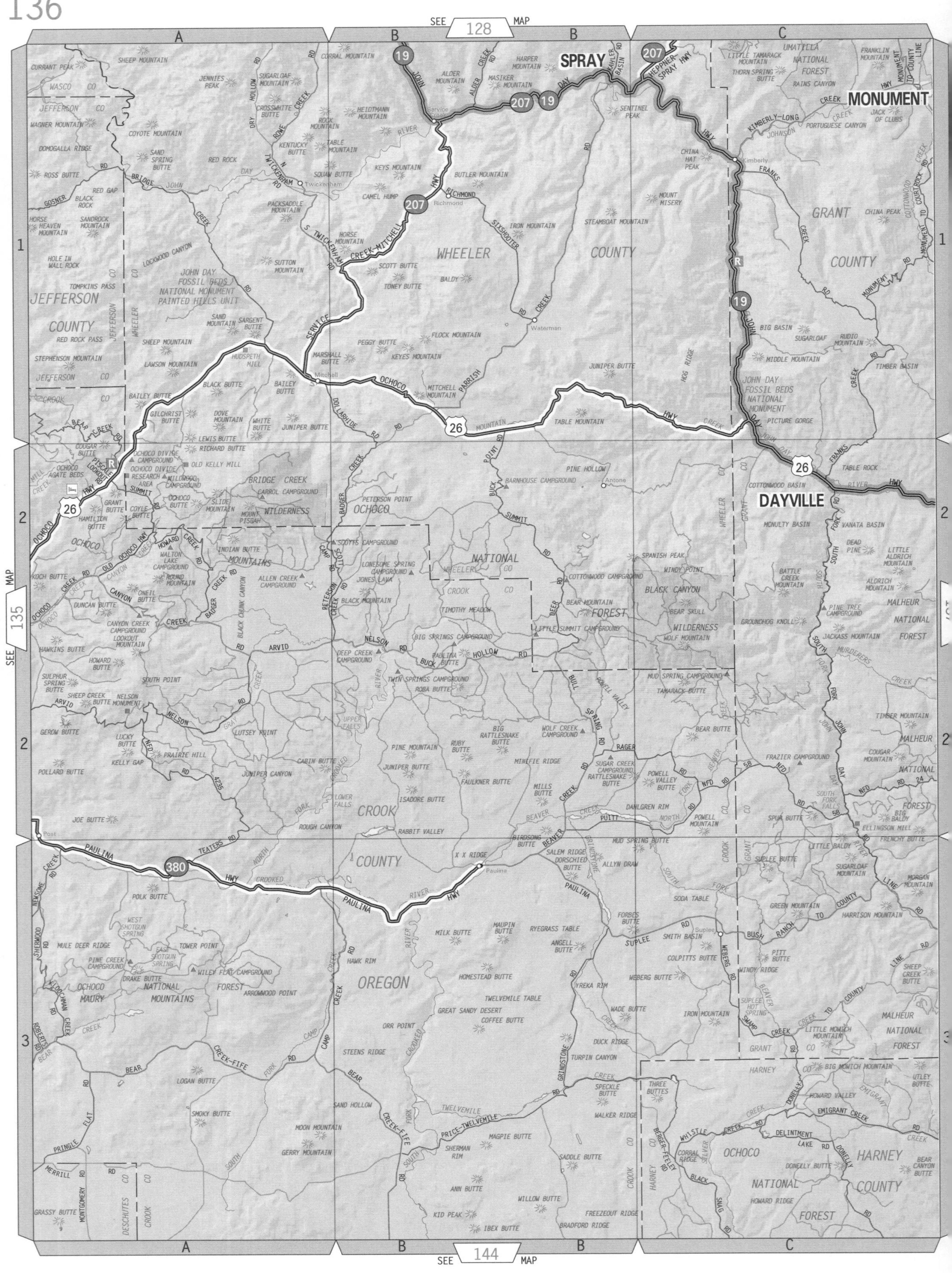

SEE 135 MAP

SEE 144 MAP

SEE 129 MAP

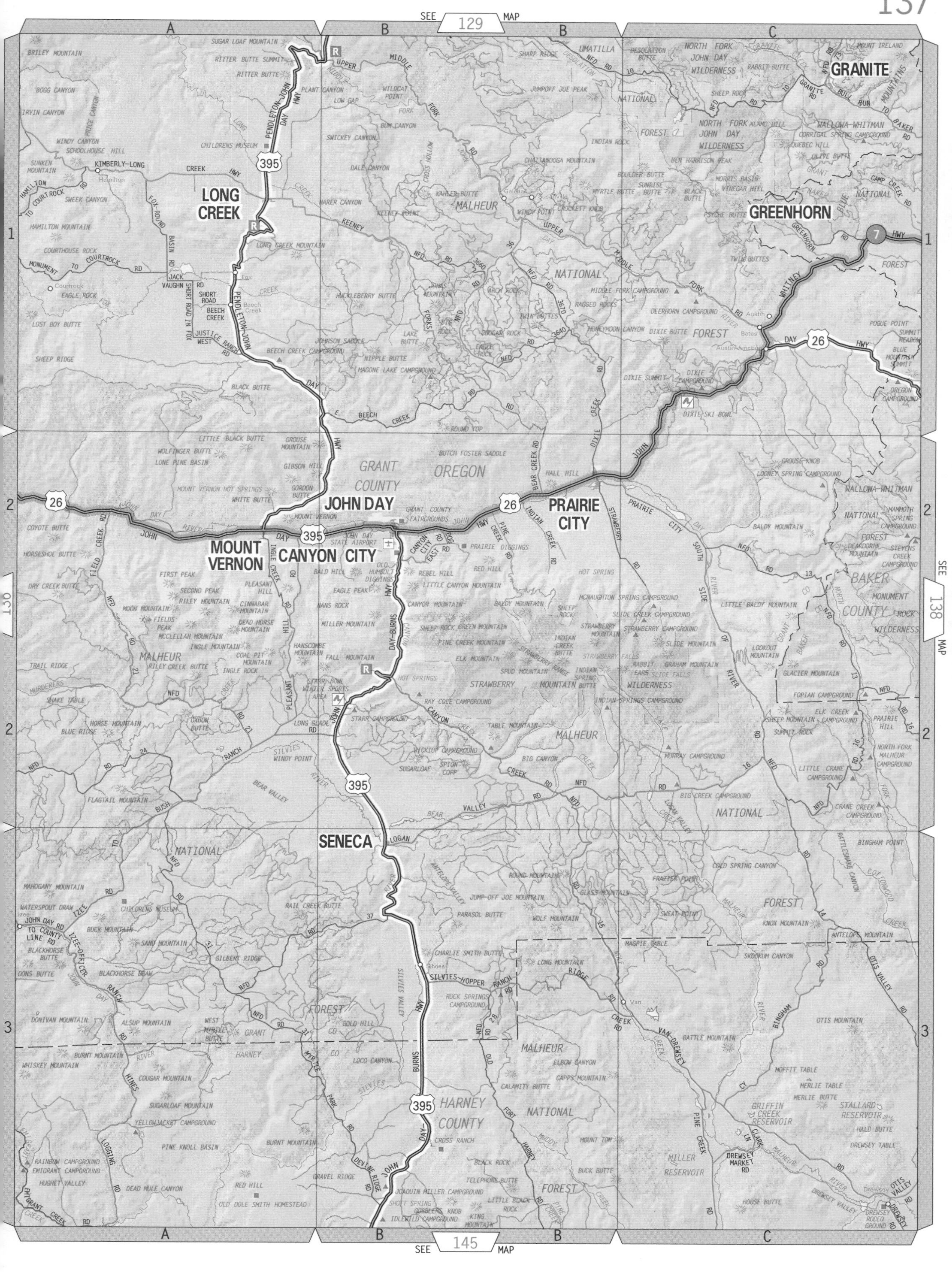

SEE 138 MAP

SEE 145 MAP

PNW

HWY

SEE 130 MAP

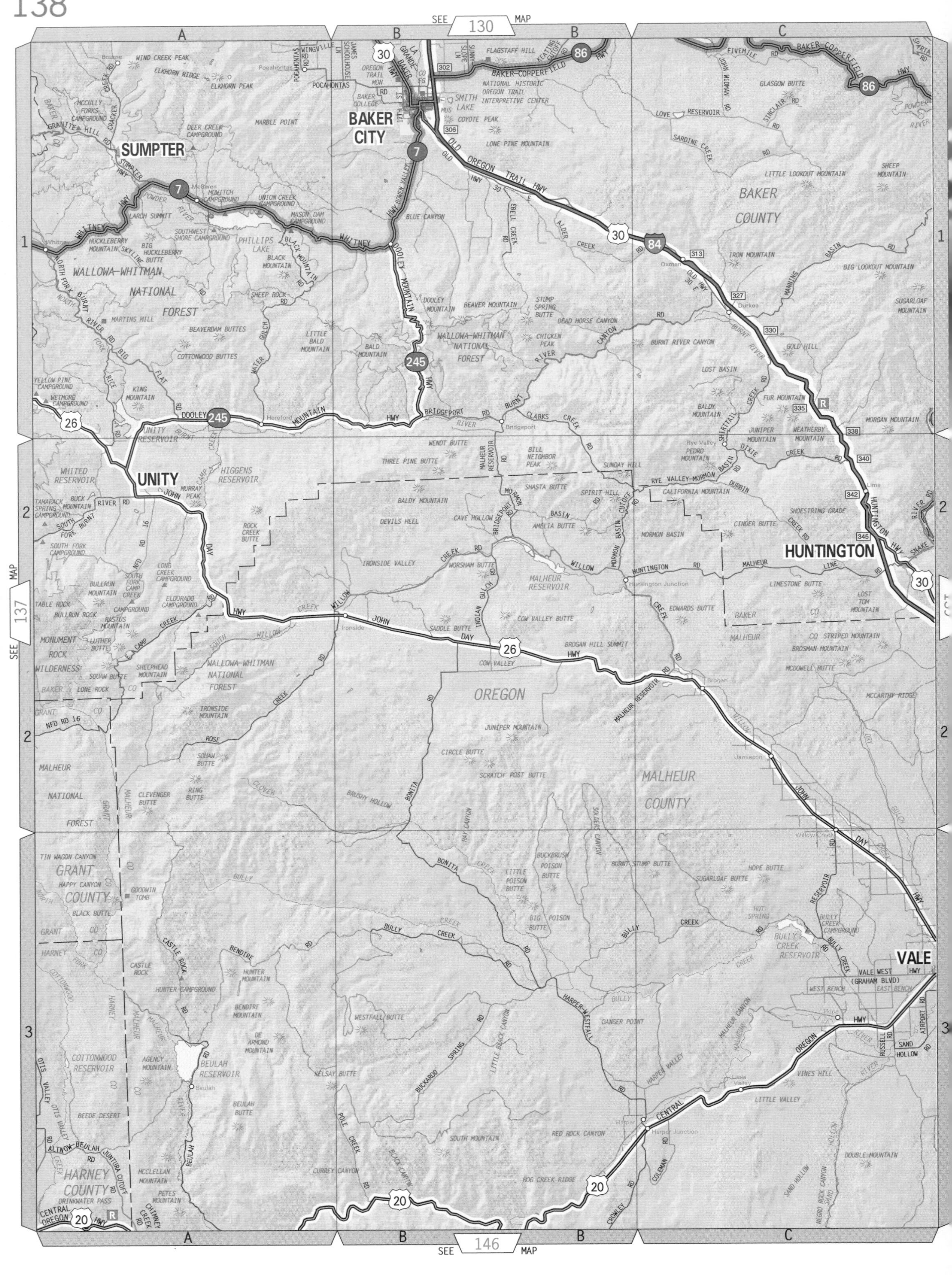

SEE 137 MAP

SEE 146 MAP

SEE 131 MAP

SEE 147 MAP

SEE 132 MAP

PNW

HWY

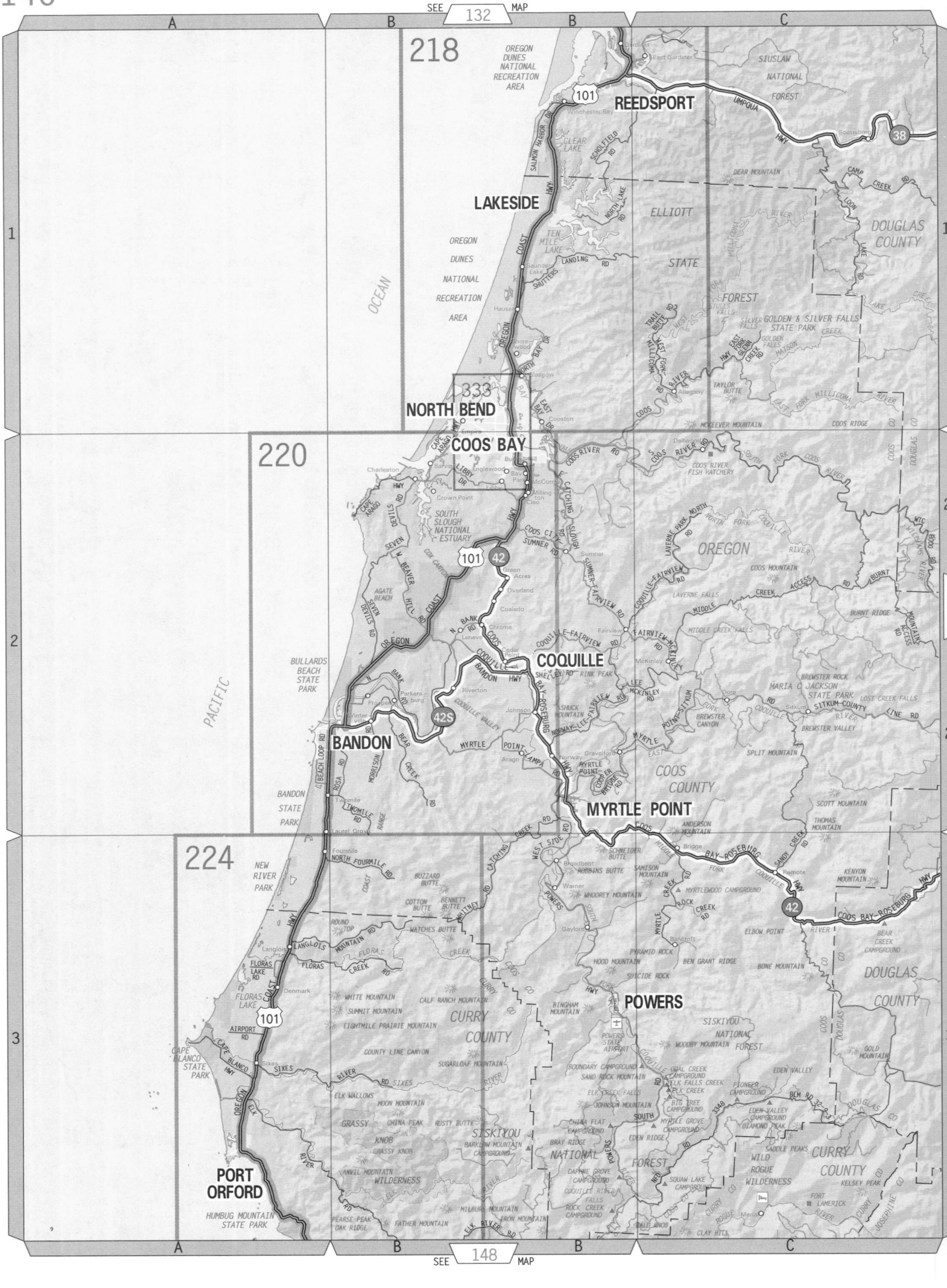

218
OREGON DUNES NATIONAL RECREATION AREA
REEDSPORT
Gardiner
East Gardiner
Winchester Bay
101
UMPQUA HWY
SIUSLAW NATIONAL FOREST
Scottsburg
38
SALMON HARBOR DR
CLEAR LAKE
SCHOLFIELD RD
DEAN MOUNTAIN
CAMP CREEK RD
LAKESIDE
NORTH LAKE RD
ELLIOTT STATE FOREST
LOON LAKE RD
DOUGLAS COUNTY
OREGON DUNES NATIONAL RECREATION AREA
TEN MILE LAKE
Saunders Lake
SHUTTERS
LANDING RD
OCEAN
COAST HWY
Hauser
OREGON
TRAIL BUTTE RD
MILLICOMA
WEST FORK MILLICOMA
STULLS FALLS
SILVER FALLS
GOLDEN & SILVER FALLS STATE PARK
GOLDEN FALLS
MAISON CREEK
EAST FORK GLENN CREEK RD
Shorewood
NORTH BAY DR
Glasgow
TAYLOR BUTTE
Allegany
MILLICOMA RIVER
EAST FORK MILLICOMA RIVER
333
NORTH BEND
EAST BAY DR
Cooston
COOS RIVER
MCKEEVER MOUNTAIN
COOS RIDGE
Empire
COOS BAY
220
CAPE ARAGO HWY
COOS RIVER RD
Dellwood
S COOS RIVER RD
COOS RIVER FISH HATCHERY
SOUTH FORK COOS RIVER
Charleston
Barview
LIBBY DR
Englewood
Bunker Hill
Bay Park
McCormac
Libby
Millington
Cleo
Crown Point
CAPE ARAGO HWY
SOUTH SLOUGH NATIONAL ESTUARY
CATCHING SLOUGH
SEVEN DEVILS
W BEAVER HILL RD
COX CANYON
COOS CITY SUMNER RD
Sumner
LAVERNE PARK
NORTH FORK COQUILLE RIVER
OREGON
WTC 8000 RD
WILLIAMS RIVER
101
42
Green Acres
Overland
SUMNER-FAIRVIEW RD
COQUILLE-FAIRVIEW RD
COOS MOUNTAIN
BURNT RD
ACCESS RD
MIDDLE CREEK
LAVERNE FALLS
BURNT RIDGE
MOUNTAIN ACCESS
AGATE BEACH
SEVEN DEVILS RD
COAST HWY
Coaledo
N BANK RD
Chrome
Leneve
Fairview
FAIRVIEW MCKINLEY
MIDDLE CREEK FALLS
OREGON
BULLARDS BEACH STATE PARK
Cedar Point
COOS
COQUILLE
COQUILLE
SHELLEY RD
RINK PEAK
McKinley
BANDON HWY
N BANK RD
Riverton
Parkersburg
Prosper
LEE MCKINLEY
BREWSTER ROCK
MARIA C JACKSON STATE PARK
LOST CREEK FALLS
PACIFIC
COQUILLE VALLEY
SHUCK MOUNTAIN
NORWAY-LEE-FAIRVIEW
POINT-SITKUM
Dora
Sitkum
SITKUM-COUNTY LINE RD
BREWSTER CANYON
BREWSTER VALLEY
Winterville
42S
Johnson
BAY-ROSEBURG
BANDON
BEAR CREEK
MYRTLE
POINT
Arago
Norway
Gravelford
MYRTLE POINT
SPLIT MOUNTAIN
EAST FORK
COOS COUNTY
BEACH LOOP RD
ROSA RD
MORRISON
CAMPA
COOPER BRIDGE
BANDON STATE PARK
Twomile
TWOMILE RD
RANGE
SCOTT MOUNTAIN
THOMAS MOUNTAIN
MYRTLE POINT
ANDERSON MOUNTAIN
Laurel Grove
224
CATCHING CREEK RD
WEST SIDE RD
COOS
Bridge
SANDY CREEK
SCHNEIDER BUTTE
MIDDLE FORK COQUILLE
BAY-ROSEBURG
Remote
KENYON MOUNTAIN
NEW RIVER PARK
Fourmile
NORTH FOURMILE RD
Broadbent
ROBBINS BUTTE
SAMISON MOUNTAIN
BUZZARD BUTTE
COTTON BUTTE
BENNETT BUTTE
WHITNEY RD
Warner
WHOOREY MOUNTAIN
MYRTLEWOOD CAMPGROUND
ROCK CREEK RD
42
COOS BAY-ROSEBURG HWY
ROUND TOP
WATCHES BUTTE
POWERS
SOUTH
Gaylord
MYRTLE CREEK
ELBOW POINT
RIVER
BEAR CREEK CAMPGROUND
Langlois
LANGLOIS MOUNTAIN RD
FLORAS CREEK
Bancroft
PYRAMID ROCK
BEN GRANT RIDGE
FLORAS LAKE RD
FLORAS CREEK RD
HOOD MOUNTAIN
SUICIDE ROCK
BONE MOUNTAIN
DOUGLAS COUNTY
COOS CO
CURRY CO
Denmark
FLORAS LAKE
WHITE MOUNTAIN
SUMMIT MOUNTAIN
CALF RANCH MOUNTAIN
BINGHAM MOUNTAIN
POWERS
101
EIGHTMILE PRAIRIE MOUNTAIN
CURRY COUNTY
SISKIYOU NATIONAL FOREST
AIRPORT RD
POWERS STATE AIRPORT
COUNTY LINE CANYON
WOODBY MOUNTAIN
GOLD MOUNTAIN
CAPE BLANCO STATE PARK
CAPE BLANCO HWY
Sixes
SIXES RIVER RD
SUGARLOAF MOUNTAIN
BOUNDARY CAMPGROUND
SAND ROCK MOUNTAIN
COAL CREEK CAMPGROUND
ELK FALLS CREEK
ELK CREEK
EDEN VALLEY
ELK CREEK FALLS
PIONEER CAMPGROUND
BLM RD 32-9-1
JOHNSON MOUNTAIN
BIG TREE CAMPGROUND
ELK WALLOWS
MOON MOUNTAIN
OREGON
ELK
3348
EDEN VALLEY CAMPGROUND
DIAMOND PEAK
DOUGLAS
GRASSY KNOB
CHINA PEAK
RUSTY BUTTE
CHINA FLAT CAMPGROUND
SOUTH
MYRTLE GROVE CAMPGROUND
GRASSY KNOB
SISKIYOU
BARKLOW MOUNTAIN CAMPGROUND
BRAY RIDGE
NATIONAL
EDEN RIDGE
SADDLE PEAKS
CURRY COUNTY
WILD ROGUE WILDERNESS
ELK RIVER
PORT ORFORD
ANVIL MOUNTAIN
WILDERNESS
DAPHNE GROVE CAMPGROUND
COQUILLE RIVER FALLS
FOREST
SQUAW LAKE CAMPGROUND
KELSEY PEAK
FORT LAMERICK
JOSEPHINE CO
ROCK CREEK CAMPGROUND
HUMBUG MOUNTAIN STATE PARK
PEARSE PEAK
OAK RIDGE
FATHER MOUNTAIN
MILBURY MOUNTAIN
IRON MOUNTAIN
ELK RIVER RD
EAGLE KNOB
Marial
CLAY HILL
ROGUE RIVER

A B B C
1 2 3

SEE 148 MAP

141

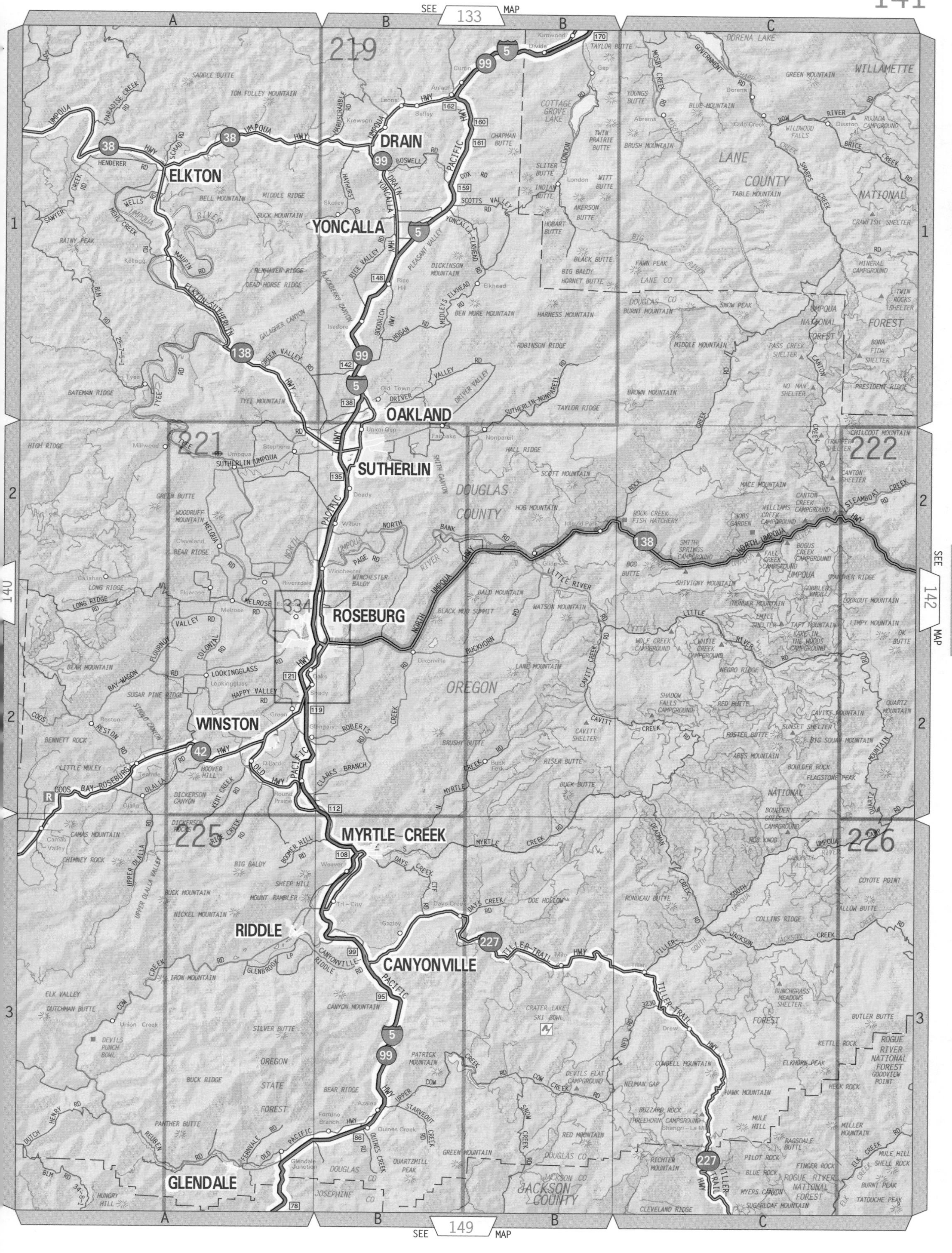
SEE 133 MAP
SEE 149 MAP
SEE 142 MAP
140
PNW
HWY
219
221
222
225
226
334
ELKTON
DRAIN
YONCALLA
OAKLAND
SUTHERLIN
ROSEBURG
WINSTON
MYRTLE CREEK
RIDDLE
CANYONVILLE
GLENDALE
DOUGLAS COUNTY
LANE COUNTY
JACKSON COUNTY
OREGON
WILLAMETTE NATIONAL FOREST
UMPQUA NATIONAL FOREST
OREGON STATE FOREST
ROGUE RIVER NATIONAL FOREST
COTTAGE GROVE LAKE
DORENA LAKE
UMPQUA HWY
NORTH UMPQUA HWY
TILLER-TRAIL HWY
COOS BAY-ROSEBURG
ROCK CREEK FISH HATCHERY
CRATER LAKE SKI BOWL

SEE 134 MAP

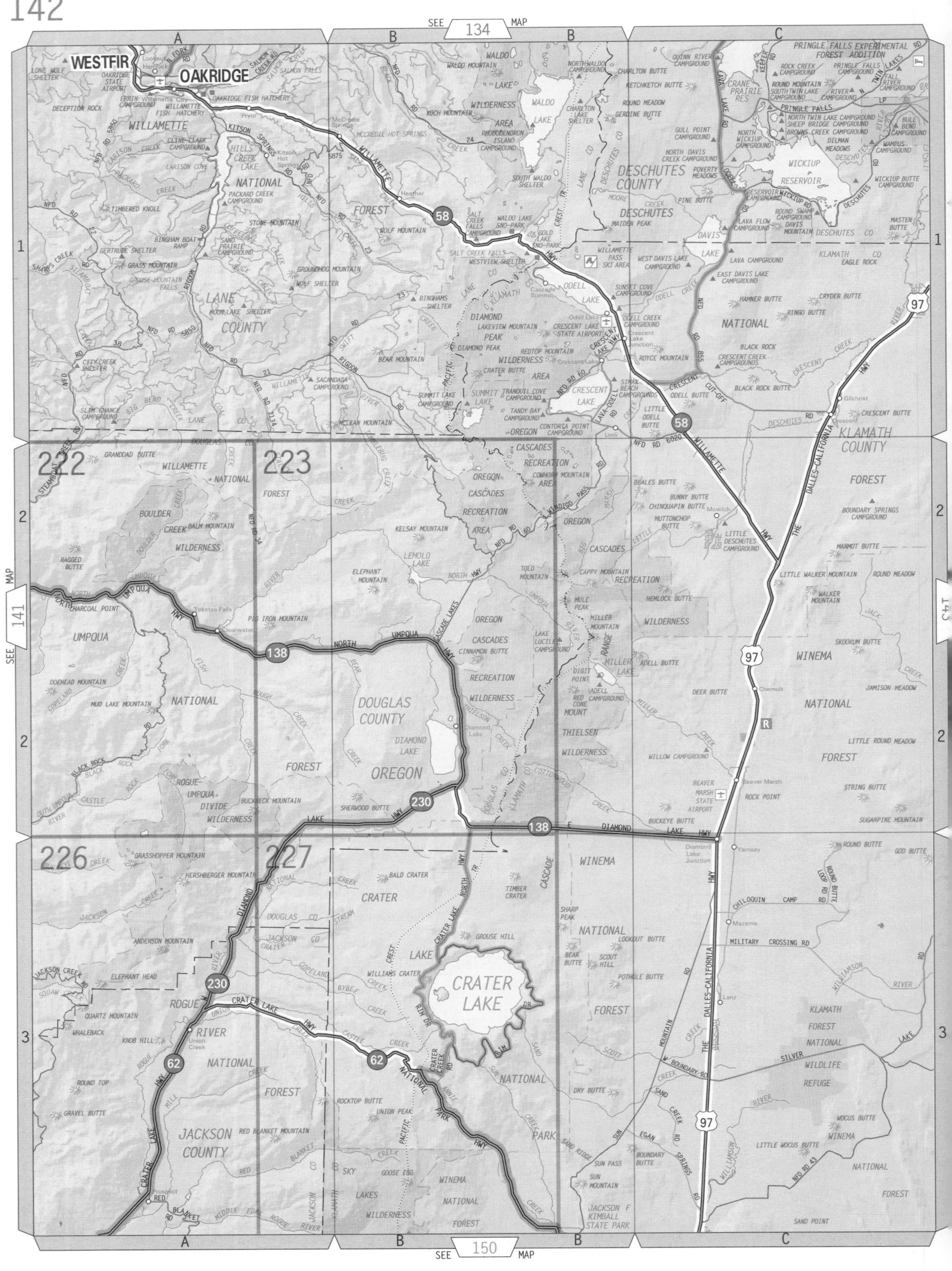

SEE 150 MAP
SEE 141 MAP

SEE 135 MAP

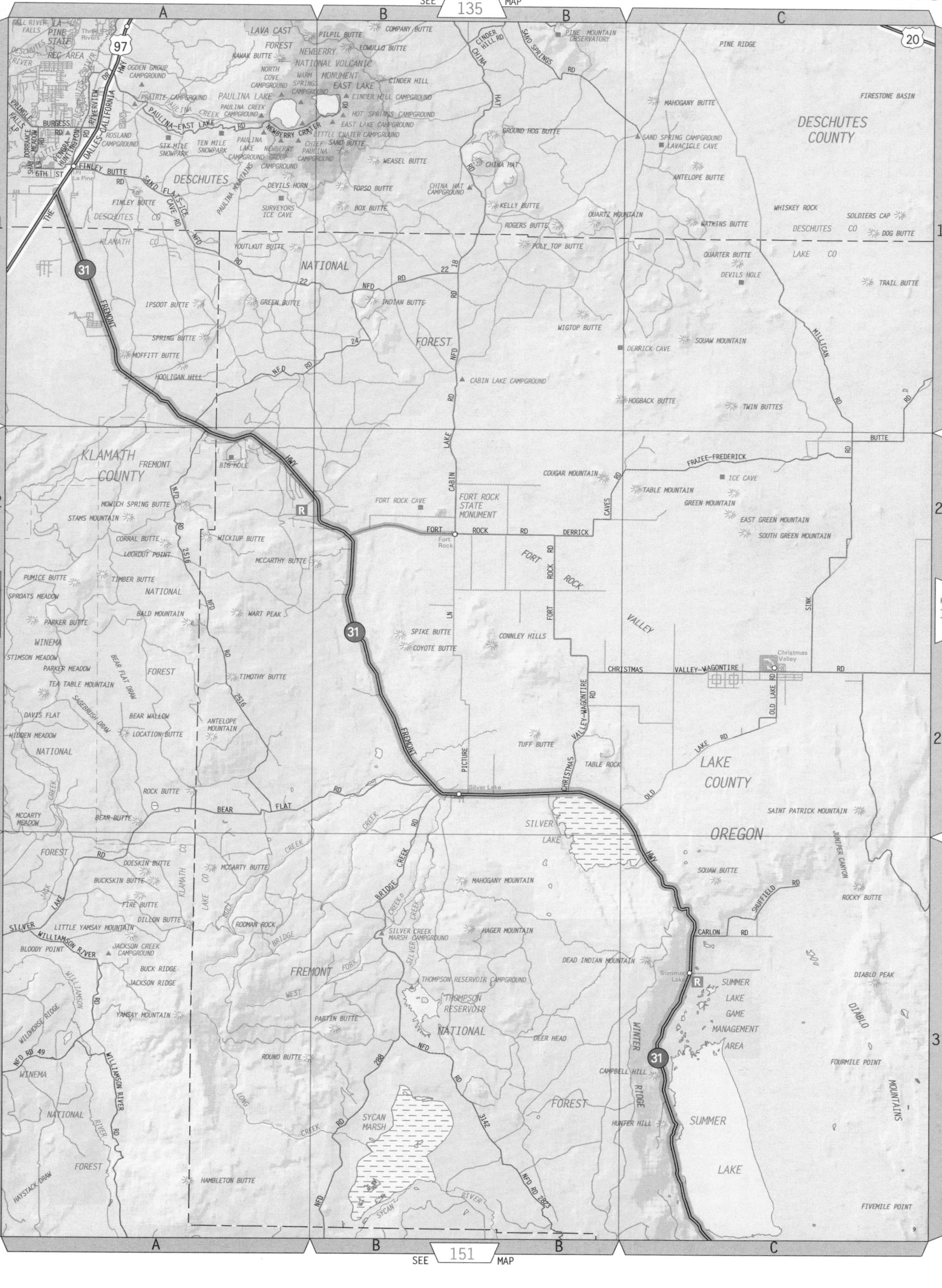

SEE 142 MAP

SEE 144 MAP

SEE 151 MAP

A B B C

DESCHUTES COUNTY

KLAMATH COUNTY

LAKE COUNTY

OREGON

FREMONT NATIONAL FOREST

WINEMA NATIONAL FOREST

DESCHUTES NATIONAL FOREST

NEWBERRY NATIONAL VOLCANIC MONUMENT

FORT ROCK STATE MONUMENT

PAULINA LAKE

EAST LAKE

SILVER LAKE

SUMMER LAKE

THOMPSON RESERVOIR

SYCAN MARSH

SUMMER LAKE GAME MANAGEMENT AREA

FORT ROCK VALLEY

DIABLO MOUNTAINS

WINTER RIDGE

La Pine

Fort Rock

Silver Lake

Christmas Valley

Summer Lake

SEE MAP 136

SEE MAP 143

SEE MAP 145

PNW

HWY

CROOK COUNTY

DESCHUTES COUNTY

LAKE COUNTY

HARNEY COUNTY

OREGON

OCHOCO NATIONAL FOREST

HAMPTON BUTTE

MACKEY BUTTE

BUCK SPRING CAMPGROUND

CHAPIN TABLE

MINERAL CANYON

COYOTE ROCK

BRONCO BUTTE

HAMPTON STATE AIRPORT

Hampton

CORRAL BUTTE

FREDERICK BUTTE

YREKA BUTTE

INDIAN BUTTE

HAT BUTTE

GIBBONS MILL CANYON

DRY MOUNTAIN

GUM BOOT CANYON

CHICKAHOMINY RESERVOIR

ROCK QUARRY CANYON RESERVOIR

Riley

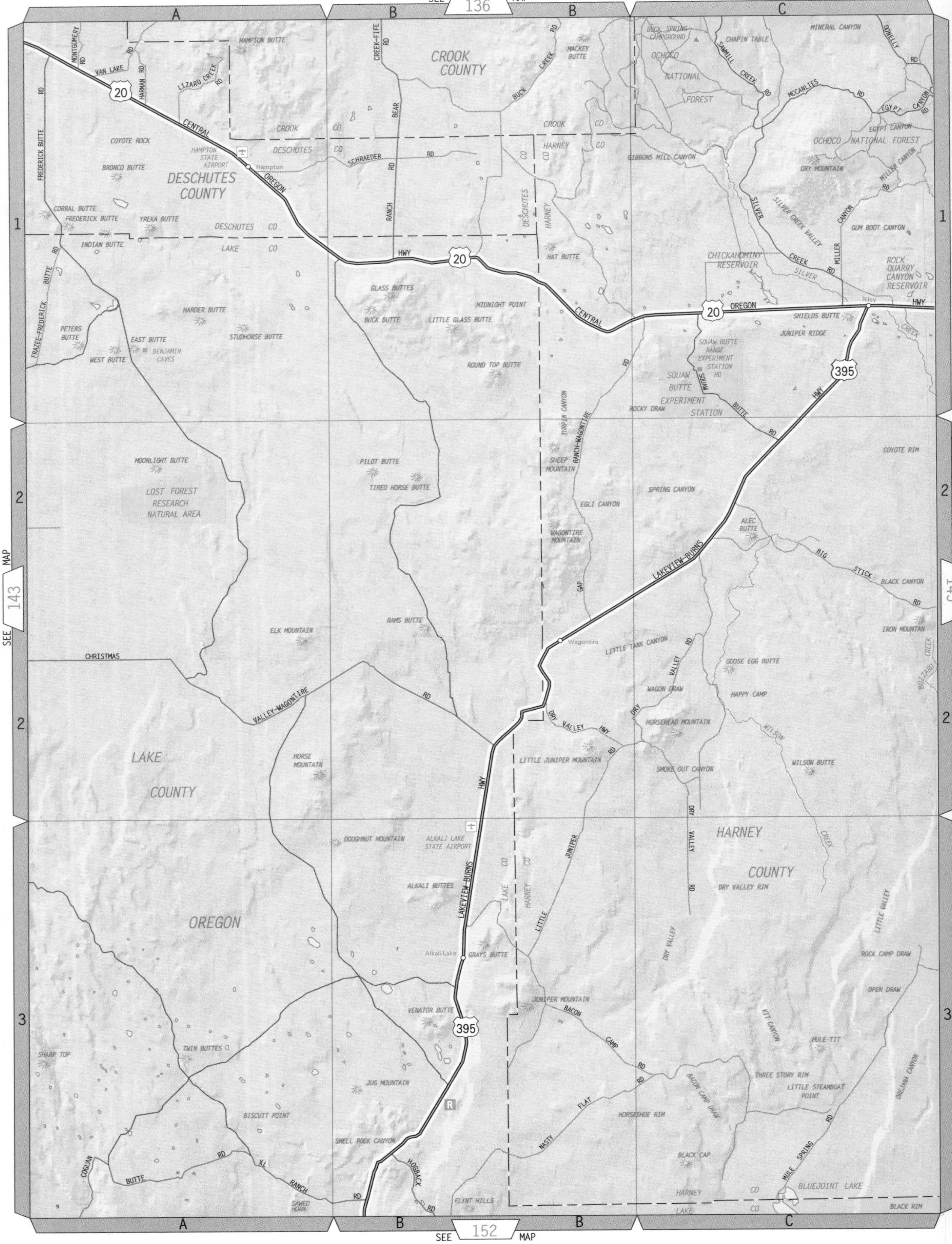

GLASS BUTTES

BUCK BUTTE

LITTLE GLASS BUTTE

MIDNIGHT POINT

HARDER BUTTE

STUDHORSE BUTTE

EAST BUTTE

BENJAMIN CAVES

PETERS BUTTE

WEST BUTTE

ROUND TOP BUTTE

SHIELDS BUTTE

JUNIPER RIDGE

SQUAW BUTTE RANGE EXPERIMENT STATION HQ

SQUAW BUTTE EXPERIMENT STATION

ROCKY DRAW

TURPIN CANYON

SHEEP MOUNTAIN

MOONLIGHT BUTTE

PILOT BUTTE

TIRED HORSE BUTTE

LOST FOREST RESEARCH NATURAL AREA

COYOTE RIM

SPRING CANYON

EGLI CANYON

WAGONTIRE MOUNTAIN

ALEC BUTTE

BLACK CANYON

IRON MOUNTAIN

ELK MOUNTAIN

RAMS BUTTE

Wagontire

LITTLE TANK CANYON

GOOSE EGG BUTTE

HAPPY CAMP

WAGON DRAW

HORSEHEAD MOUNTAIN

LITTLE JUNIPER MOUNTAIN

SMOKE OUT CANYON

WILSON BUTTE

HORSE MOUNTAIN

DOUGHNUT MOUNTAIN

ALKALI LAKE STATE AIRPORT

ALKALI BUTTES

DRY VALLEY RIM

Alkali Lake

GRAYS BUTTE

ROCK CAMP DRAW

OPEN DRAW

JUNIPER MOUNTAIN

VENATOR BUTTE

KIT CANYON

MULE TIT

SHARP TOP

TWIN BUTTES

THREE STORY RIM

LITTLE STEAMBOAT POINT

JUG MOUNTAIN

BISCUIT POINT

HORSESHOE RIM

SHELL ROCK CANYON

BLACK CAP

BLUEJOINT LAKE

SAWED HORN

FLINT HILLS

BLACK RIM

SEE MAP 152

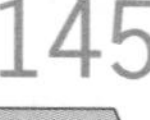

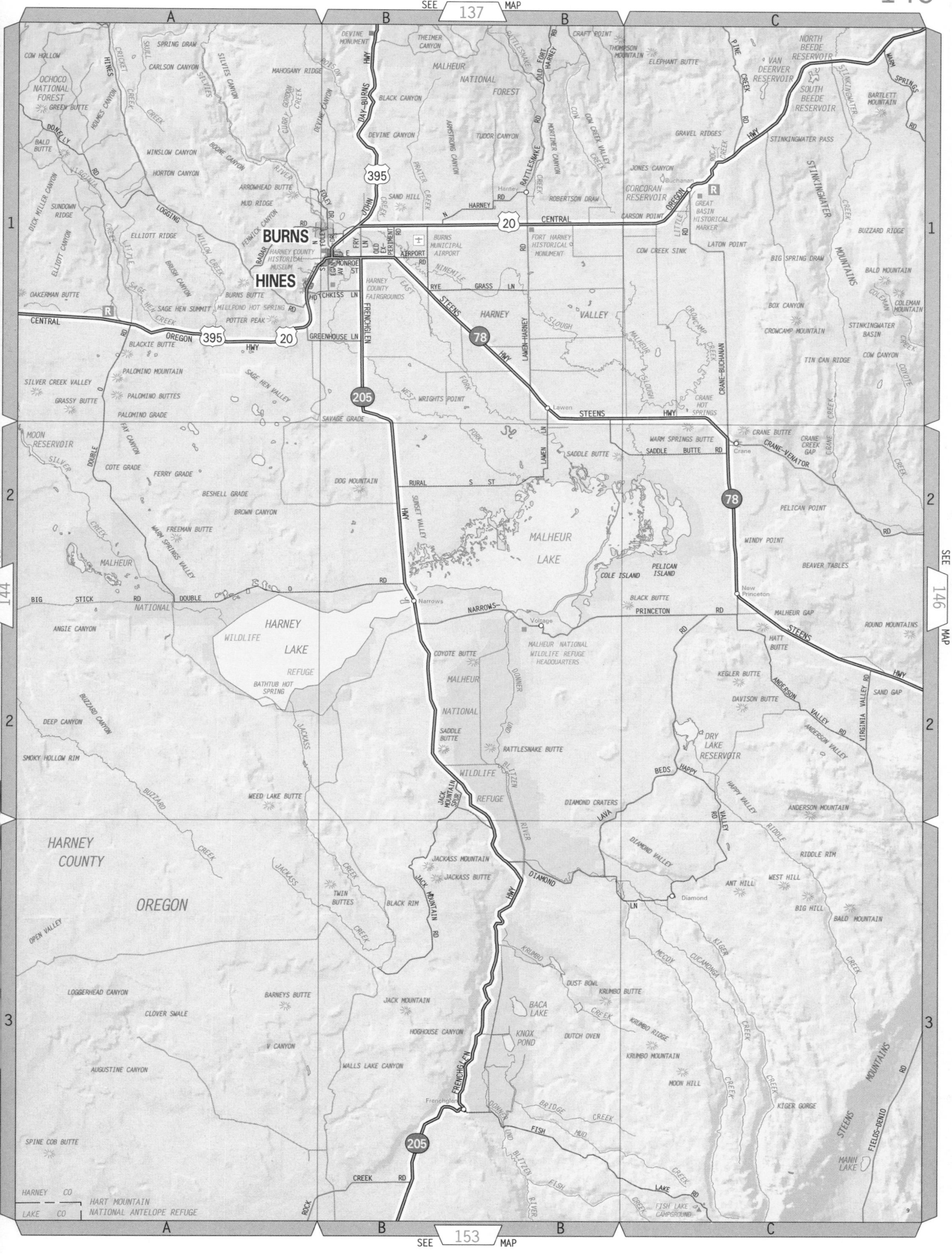
SEE 137 MAP
SEE 153 MAP
SEE 144 MAP
SEE 146 MAP
A
B
C
1
2
3
BURNS
HINES
HARNEY COUNTY
OREGON
OCHOCO NATIONAL FOREST
MALHEUR NATIONAL FOREST
MALHEUR NATIONAL WILDLIFE REFUGE
MALHEUR LAKE
HARNEY LAKE
HARNEY VALLEY
STEENS MOUNTAINS
STINKINGWATER MOUNTAINS
CENTRAL OREGON HWY
STEENS HWY
FRENCHGLEN HWY
DAY-BURNS HWY
CRANE-VENATOR
CRANE-BUCHANAN
LAWEN-HARNEY
NARROWS-PRINCETON RD
DIAMOND LN
FIELDS-DENIO RD
395
20
78
205
HARNEY COUNTY HISTORICAL MUSEUM
BURNS MUNICIPAL AIRPORT
HARNEY COUNTY FAIRGROUNDS
FORT HARNEY HISTORICAL MONUMENT
DEVINE MONUMENT
GREAT BASIN HISTORICAL MARKER
MALHEUR NATIONAL WILDLIFE REFUGE HEADQUARTERS
NORTH BEEDE RESERVOIR
SOUTH BEEDE RESERVOIR
VAN DEERVER RESERVOIR
CORCORAN RESERVOIR
MOON RESERVOIR
DRY LAKE RESERVOIR
BACA LAKE
KNOX POND
COLE ISLAND
PELICAN ISLAND
Harney
Buchanan
Lawen
Crane
New Princeton
Narrows
Voltage
Diamond
Frenchglen
DIAMOND CRATERS
DIAMOND VALLEY
JACKASS MOUNTAIN
JACK MOUNTAIN
KRUMBO RIDGE
KRUMBO MOUNTAIN
KIGER GORGE
MANN LAKE
FISH LAKE CAMPGROUND
SPINE COB BUTTE
HARNEY CO
LAKE CO
HART MOUNTAIN NATIONAL ANTELOPE REFUGE

SEE 138 MAP

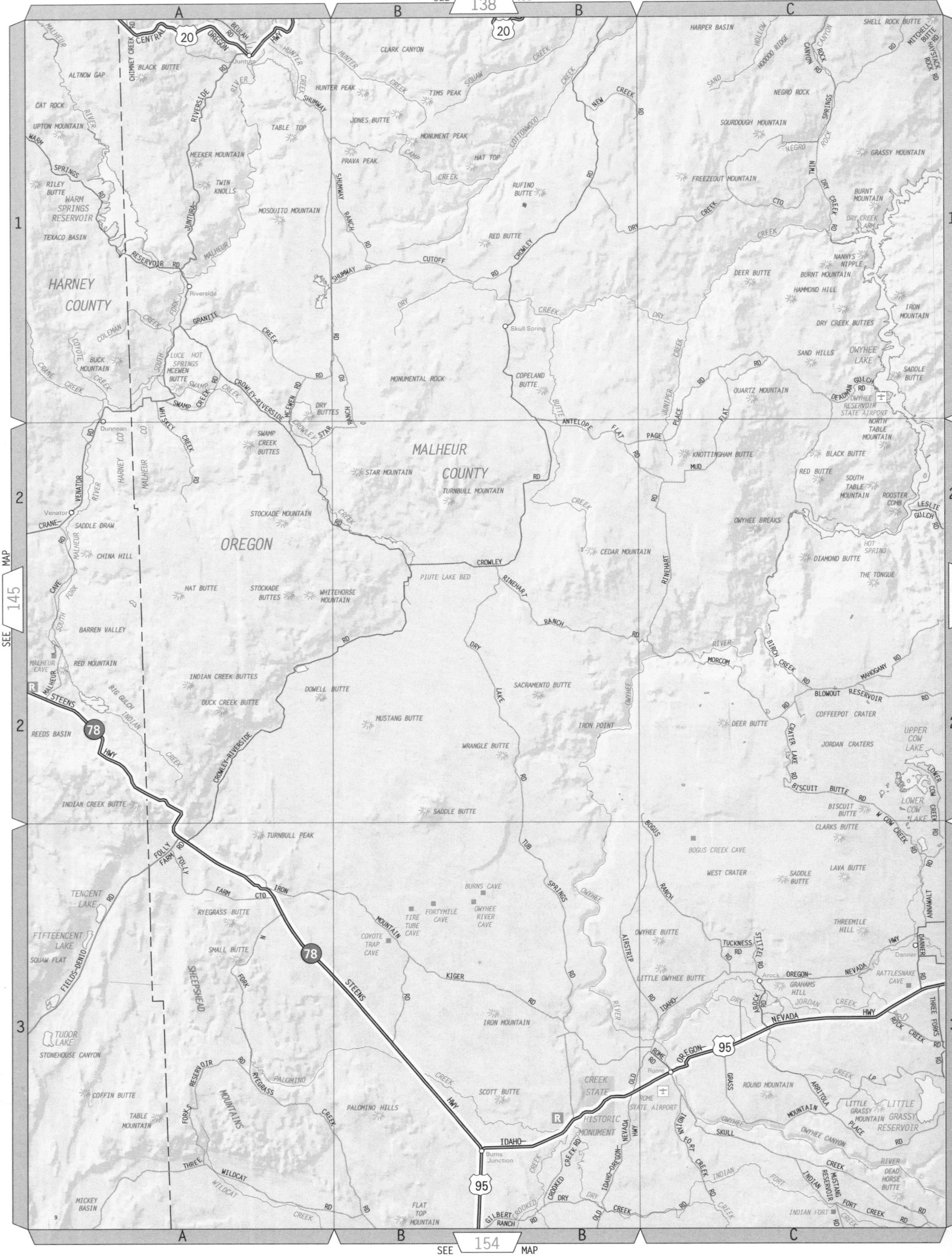
A
B
C
1
2
3
HARNEY COUNTY
MALHEUR COUNTY
OREGON
HARNEY CO
MALHEUR CO
CENTRAL OREGON HWY
BEULAH
Juntura
CHIMNEY CREEK
BLACK BUTTE
ALTNOW GAP
CAT ROCK
UPTON MOUNTAIN
WARM SPRINGS RD
RILEY BUTTE
WARM SPRINGS RESERVOIR
TEXACO BASIN
RIVERSIDE
MEEKER MOUNTAIN
TWIN KNOLLS
JUNTURA-RIVERSIDE
MOSQUITO MOUNTAIN
TABLE TOP
HUNTER CREEK
SHUMWAY
RESERVOIR RD
Riverside
GRANITE CREEK RD
COLEMAN
COYOTE
BUCK MOUNTAIN
CRANE CREEK
LUCE HOT SPRINGS
MCEWEN BUTTE
SWAMP CREEK
CROWLEY-RIVERSIDE
MCEWEN RD
DRY BUTTES
STAR RANCH
Dunnean
WHISKEY CREEK
SWAMP CREEK BUTTES
VENATOR
Venator
CRANE-VENATOR
SADDLE DRAW
CHINA HILL
CAVE
SOUTH FORK
HAT BUTTE
STOCKADE MOUNTAIN
STOCKADE BUTTES
WHITEHORSE MOUNTAIN
BARREN VALLEY
MALHEUR CAVE
RED MOUNTAIN
INDIAN CREEK BUTTES
BIG GULCH
DUCK CREEK BUTTE
STEENS HWY
78
REEDS BASIN
INDIAN CREEK BUTTE
TURNBULL PEAK
FOLLY FARM
FARM CTO
IRON
TENCENT LAKE
RYEGRASS BUTTE
FIFTEENCENT LAKE
SQUAW FLAT
FIELDS-DENIO
SMALL BUTTE
SHEEPSHEAD
TUDOR LAKE
STONEHOUSE CANYON
COFFIN BUTTE
TABLE MOUNTAIN
RESERVOIR RD
RYEGRASS
PALOMINO
MOUNTAINS
FORKS
THREE
WILDCAT
MICKEY BASIN
CLARK CANYON
HUNTER PEAK
JONES BUTTE
TIMS PEAK
MONUMENT PEAK
PRAVA PEAK
HAT TOP
COTTONWOOD
CAMP CREEK
RUFINO BUTTE
RED BUTTE
CUTOFF
CROWLEY RD
DRY CREEK
Skull Spring
MONUMENTAL ROCK
COPELAND BUTTE
STAR MOUNTAIN
TURNBULL MOUNTAIN
CROWLEY
PIUTE LAKE BED
RINEHART RANCH RD
CEDAR MOUNTAIN
DOWELL BUTTE
MUSTANG BUTTE
DRY LAKE RD
SACRAMENTO BUTTE
WRANGLE BUTTE
IRON POINT
SADDLE BUTTE
TUB SPRINGS RD
BURNS CAVE
FORTYMILE CAVE
OWYHEE RIVER CAVE
TIRE TUBE CAVE
COYOTE TRAP CAVE
MOUNTAIN
KIGER RD
IRON MOUNTAIN
SCOTT BUTTE
PALOMINO HILLS
CREEK STATE
HISTORIC MONUMENT
IDAHO-
Burns Junction
95
FLAT TOP MOUNTAIN
GILBERT RANCH
CROOKED CREEK RD
DRY
OLD
IDAHO-OREGON-NEVADA HWY
HARPER BASIN
SHELL ROCK BUTTE
MITCHELL BUTTE
HAYSTACK ROCK
HOLLOW
HOODOO RIDGE
CANYON
ROCK CANYON
SAND
NEW CREEK RD
NEGRO ROCK
SOURDOUGH MOUNTAIN
TWIN SPRINGS
GRASSY MOUNTAIN
FREEZEOUT MOUNTAIN
CTO
DRY CREEK
BURNT MOUNTAIN
DRY CREEK ARM
NANNYS NIPPLE
DEER BUTTE
BURNT MOUNTAIN
HAMMOND HILL
IRON MOUNTAIN
DRY CREEK BUTTES
SAND HILLS
OWYHEE LAKE
SADDLE BUTTE
QUARTZ MOUNTAIN
JUNIPER
DEADMAN GULCH
OWYHEE RESERVOIR STATE AIRPORT
NORTH TABLE MOUNTAIN
ANTELOPE FLAT
PAGE
PLACE
FLAT
KNOTTINGHAM BUTTE
MUD
BLACK BUTTE
RED BUTTE
SOUTH TABLE MOUNTAIN
ROOSTER COMB
LESLIE GULCH
OWYHEE BREAKS
HOT SPRING
DIAMOND BUTTE
THE TONGUE
RINEHART
RIVER
MORCOM
BIRCH CREEK RD
MAHOGANY RD
BLOWOUT RESERVOIR RD
COFFEEPOT CRATER
DEER BUTTE
CRATER LAKE RD
JORDAN CRATERS
UPPER COW LAKE
LOWER COW CREEK
BISCUIT BUTTE RD
BISCUIT BUTTE
LOWER COW LAKE
W COW CREEK
CLARKS BUTTE
BOGUS
BOGUS CREEK CAVE
WEST CRATER
SADDLE BUTTE
LAVA BUTTE
RANCH
OWYHEE
OWYHEE BUTTE
AIRSTRIP
THREEMILE HILL
ANNAWALT
TUCKNESS RD
STITZEL RD
Danner
DANNER
HWY
LITTLE OWYHEE BUTTE
Arock
AROCK RD
OREGON-NEVADA
GRAHAMS HILL
RATTLESNAKE CAVE
JORDAN CREEK
NEVADA HWY
THREE FORKS
ROCK CREEK
ROME RD
Rome
OREGON-
ROME STATE AIRPORT
GRASS
ROUND MOUNTAIN
ARRITOLA
LP
LITTLE GRASSY MOUNTAIN
LITTLE GRASSY RESERVOIR
PLACE
MOUNTAIN
OWYHEE CANYON
SKULL
FORT CREEK RD
INDIAN CREEK
MUSTANG RESERVOIR
DEAD HORSE BUTTE
INDIAN FORT CREEK RD
INDIAN FORT

SEE 145 MAP

147

SEE 154 MAP

PNW

HWY

SEE 139 MAP

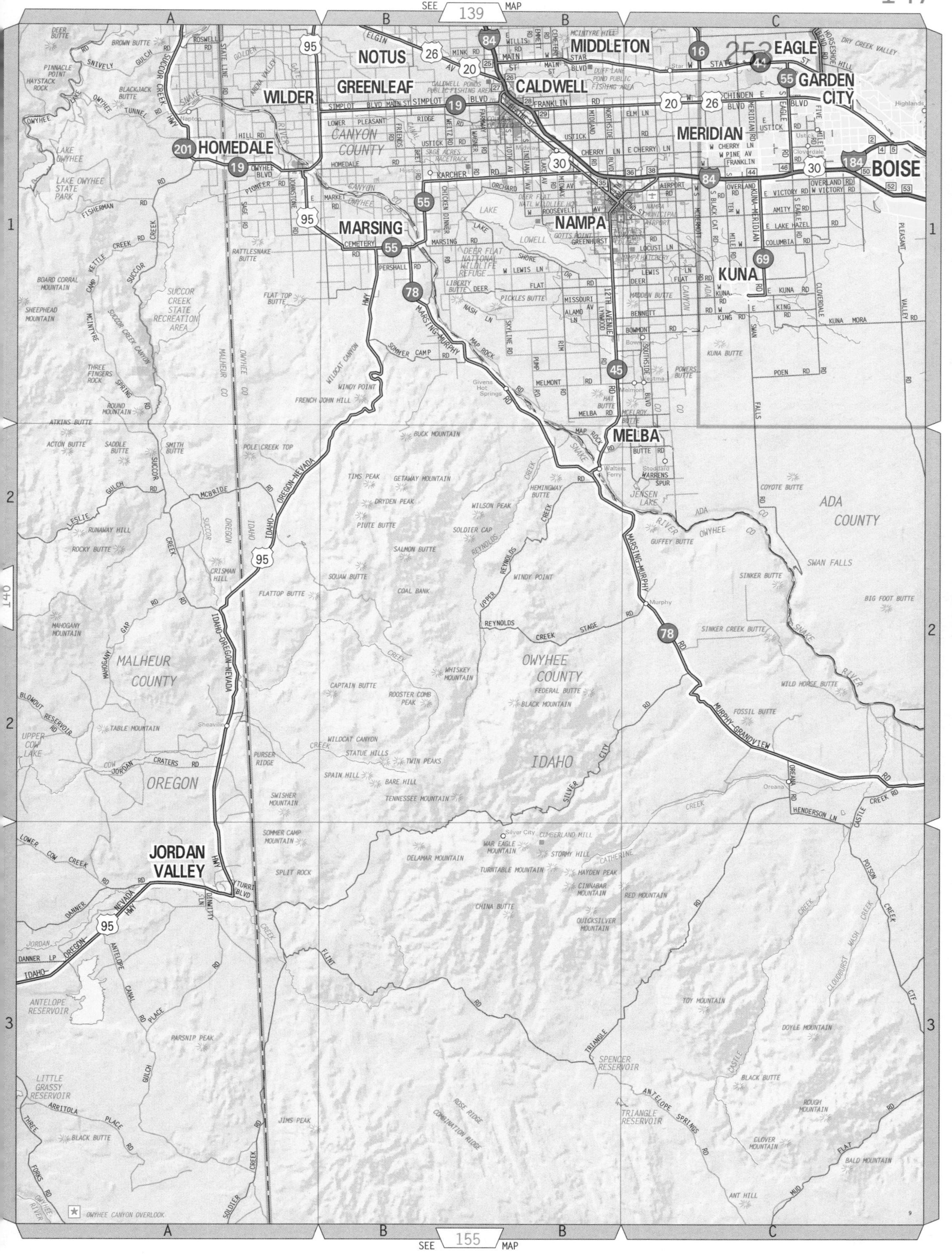

SEE 155 MAP

SEE 140 MAP

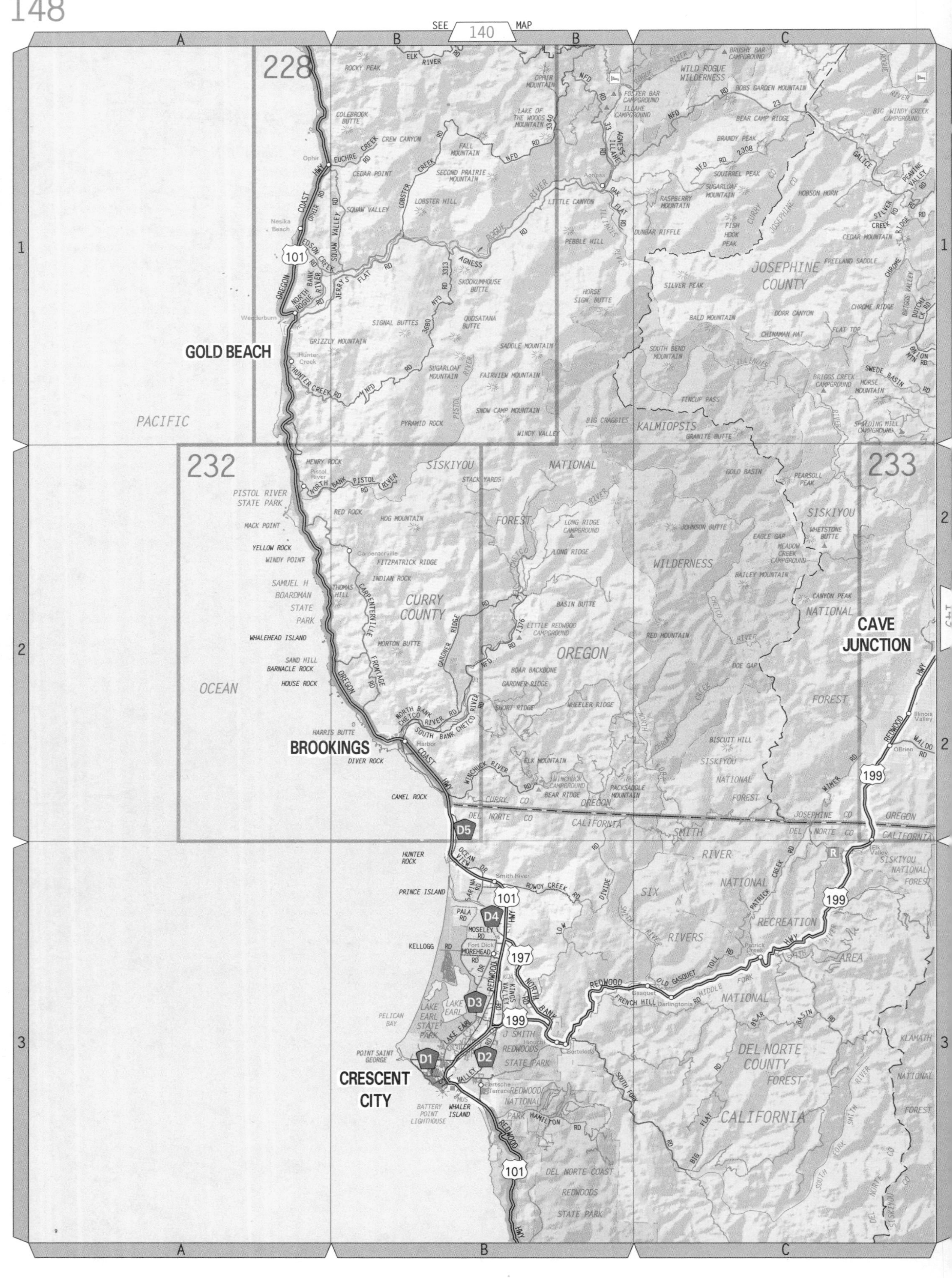
A
B
C
1
2
3
228
232
233
GOLD BEACH
BROOKINGS
CRESCENT CITY
CAVE JUNCTION
PACIFIC
OCEAN
JOSEPHINE COUNTY
CURRY COUNTY
DEL NORTE COUNTY
OREGON
CALIFORNIA
WILD ROGUE WILDERNESS
KALMIOPSIS
SISKIYOU
NATIONAL
FOREST
WILDERNESS
SMITH RIVER NATIONAL RECREATION AREA
SIX RIVERS NATIONAL FOREST
PISTOL RIVER STATE PARK
SAMUEL H BOARDMAN STATE PARK
LAKE EARL STATE PARK
J SMITH REDWOODS STATE PARK
REDWOOD NATIONAL PARK
DEL NORTE COAST REDWOODS STATE PARK
ROCKY PEAK
OPHIR MOUNTAIN
LAKE OF THE WOODS MOUNTAIN
COLEBROOK BUTTE
CEDAR POINT
SECOND PRAIRIE MOUNTAIN
FALL MOUNTAIN
LOBSTER HILL
SQUAW VALLEY
PEBBLE HILL
DUNBAR RIFFLE
SKOOKUMHOUSE BUTTE
SIGNAL BUTTES
GRIZZLY MOUNTAIN
QUOSATANA BUTTE
SADDLE MOUNTAIN
SUGARLOAF MOUNTAIN
FAIRVIEW MOUNTAIN
SNOW CAMP MOUNTAIN
PYRAMID ROCK
WINDY VALLEY
BIG CRAGGIES
GRANITE BUTTE
HENRY ROCK
RED ROCK
HOG MOUNTAIN
STACK YARDS
MACK POINT
YELLOW ROCK
WINDY POINT
FITZPATRICK RIDGE
INDIAN ROCK
THOMAS HILL
MORTON BUTTE
WHALEHEAD ISLAND
SAND HILL
BARNACLE ROCK
HOUSE ROCK
HARRIS BUTTE
DIVER ROCK
CAMEL ROCK
HUNTER ROCK
PRINCE ISLAND
KELLOGG
PELICAN BAY
POINT SAINT GEORGE
BATTERY POINT LIGHTHOUSE
WHALER ISLAND
LONG RIDGE CAMPGROUND
LONG RIDGE
BASIN BUTTE
LITTLE REDWOOD CAMPGROUND
BOAR BACKBONE
GARDNER RIDGE
SHORT RIDGE
WHEELER RIDGE
ELK MOUNTAIN
WINCHUCK CAMPGROUND
BEAR RIDGE
PACKSADDLE MOUNTAIN
GOLD BASIN
JOHNSON BUTTE
RED MOUNTAIN
BISCUIT HILL
PEARSOLL PEAK
WHETSTONE BUTTE
EAGLE GAP
MEADOW CREEK CAMPGROUND
BAILEY MOUNTAIN
CANYON PEAK
DOE GAP
BRUSHY BAR CAMPGROUND
FOSTER BAR CAMPGROUND
ILLAHE CAMPGROUND
BOBS GARDEN MOUNTAIN
BEAR CAMP RIDGE
BRANDY PEAK
SQUIRREL PEAK
SUGARLOAF MOUNTAIN
RASPBERRY MOUNTAIN
FISH HOOK PEAK
HOBSON HORN
CEDAR MOUNTAIN
FREELAND SADDLE
BIG WINDY CREEK CAMPGROUND
SILVER PEAK
HORSE SIGN BUTTE
BALD MOUNTAIN
SOUTH BEND MOUNTAIN
TINCUP PASS
DORR CANYON
CHINAMAN HAT
FLAT TOP
CHROME RIDGE
BRIGGS CREEK CAMPGROUND
HORSE MOUNTAIN
SPALDING MILL CAMPGROUND
Ophir
Nesika Beach
Wedderburn
Hunter Creek
Agness
Pistol River
Carpenterville
Harbor
Smith River
Fort Dick
Hiouchi
Gasquet
Darlingtonia
Patrick Creek
Elk Valley
Illinois Valley
OBrien
101
199
197
D1
D2
D3
D4
D5

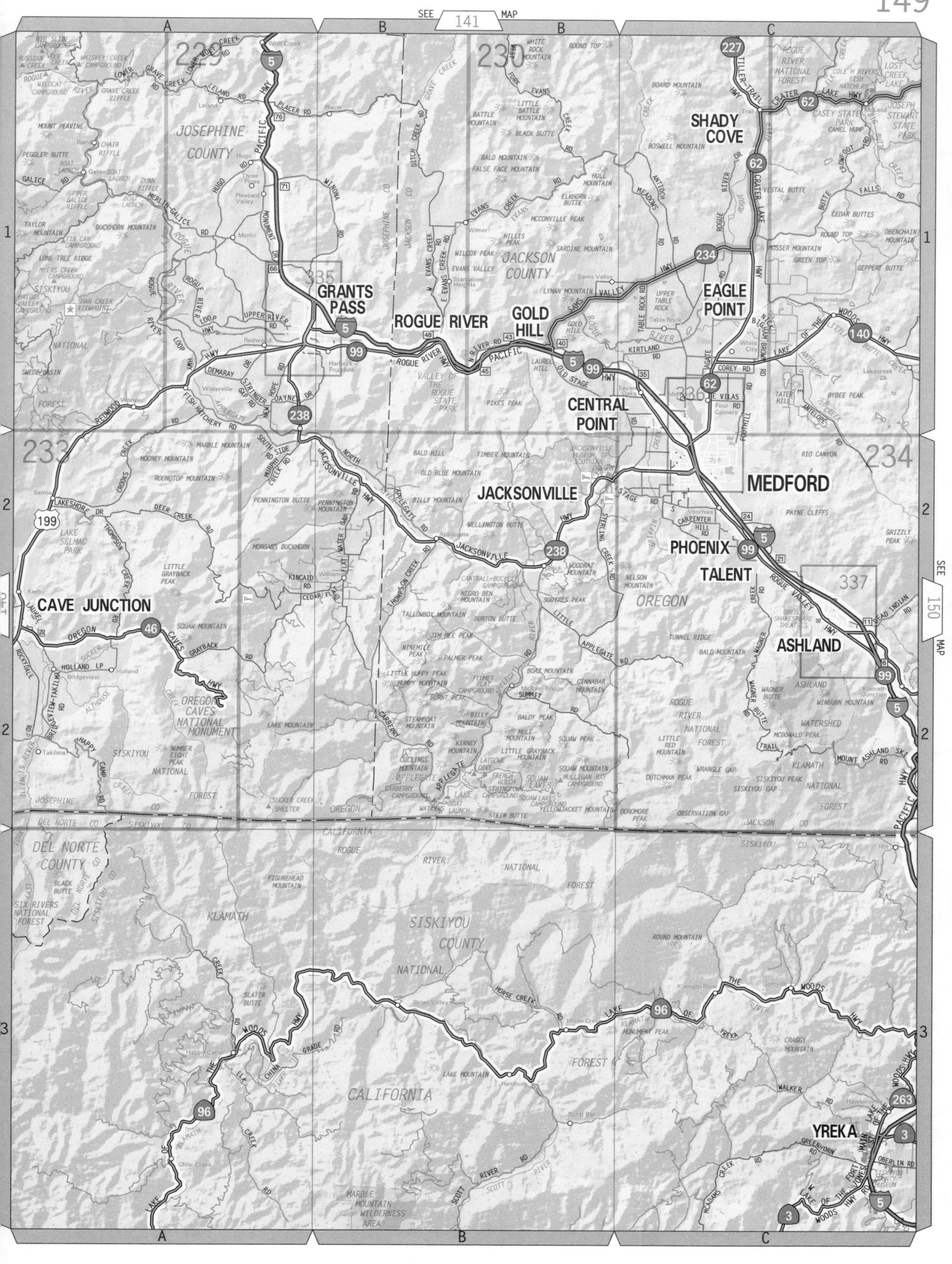
SEE 141 MAP
SEE 150 MAP
GRANTS PASS
ROGUE RIVER
GOLD HILL
SHADY COVE
EAGLE POINT
CENTRAL POINT
MEDFORD
JACKSONVILLE
PHOENIX
TALENT
ASHLAND
CAVE JUNCTION
YREKA
JOSEPHINE COUNTY
JACKSON COUNTY
DEL NORTE COUNTY
SISKIYOU COUNTY
OREGON
CALIFORNIA
ROGUE RIVER NATIONAL FOREST
SISKIYOU NATIONAL FOREST
KLAMATH NATIONAL FOREST
SIX RIVERS NATIONAL FOREST
OREGON CAVES NATIONAL MONUMENT
MARBLE MOUNTAIN WILDERNESS AREA
LAKE SELMAC PARK
VALLEY OF THE ROGUE STATE PARK
CASEY STATE PARK
JOSEPH STEWART STATE PARK

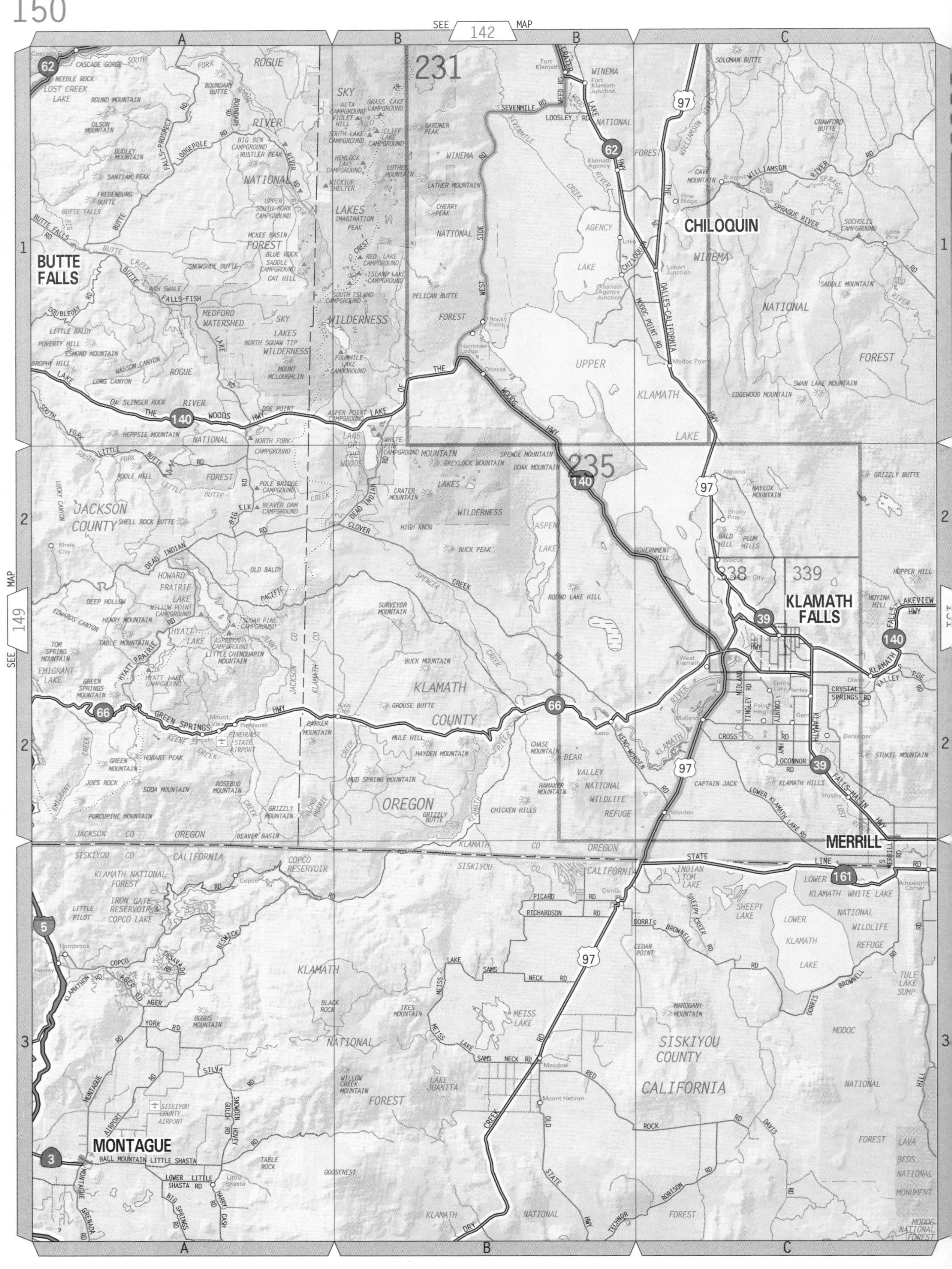
SEE 142 MAP
BUTTE FALLS
CHILOQUIN
KLAMATH FALLS
MERRILL
MONTAGUE
JACKSON COUNTY
KLAMATH COUNTY
OREGON
CALIFORNIA
SISKIYOU COUNTY
ROGUE RIVER NATIONAL FOREST
WINEMA NATIONAL FOREST
KLAMATH NATIONAL FOREST
MODOC NATIONAL FOREST
SKY LAKES WILDERNESS
MOUNTAIN LAKES WILDERNESS
UPPER KLAMATH LAKE
LOWER KLAMATH NATIONAL WILDLIFE REFUGE
BEAR VALLEY NATIONAL WILDLIFE REFUGE
LAVA BEDS NATIONAL MONUMENT
TULE LAKE SUMP
LAKE OF THE WOODS
HOWARD PRAIRIE LAKE
HYATT LAKE
EMIGRANT LAKE
COPCO RESERVOIR
IRON GATE RESERVOIR
MEISS LAKE
LAKE JUANITA
SHEEPY LAKE
LOWER KLAMATH LAKE
WHITE LAKE
SEE 149 MAP
HWY
PNW

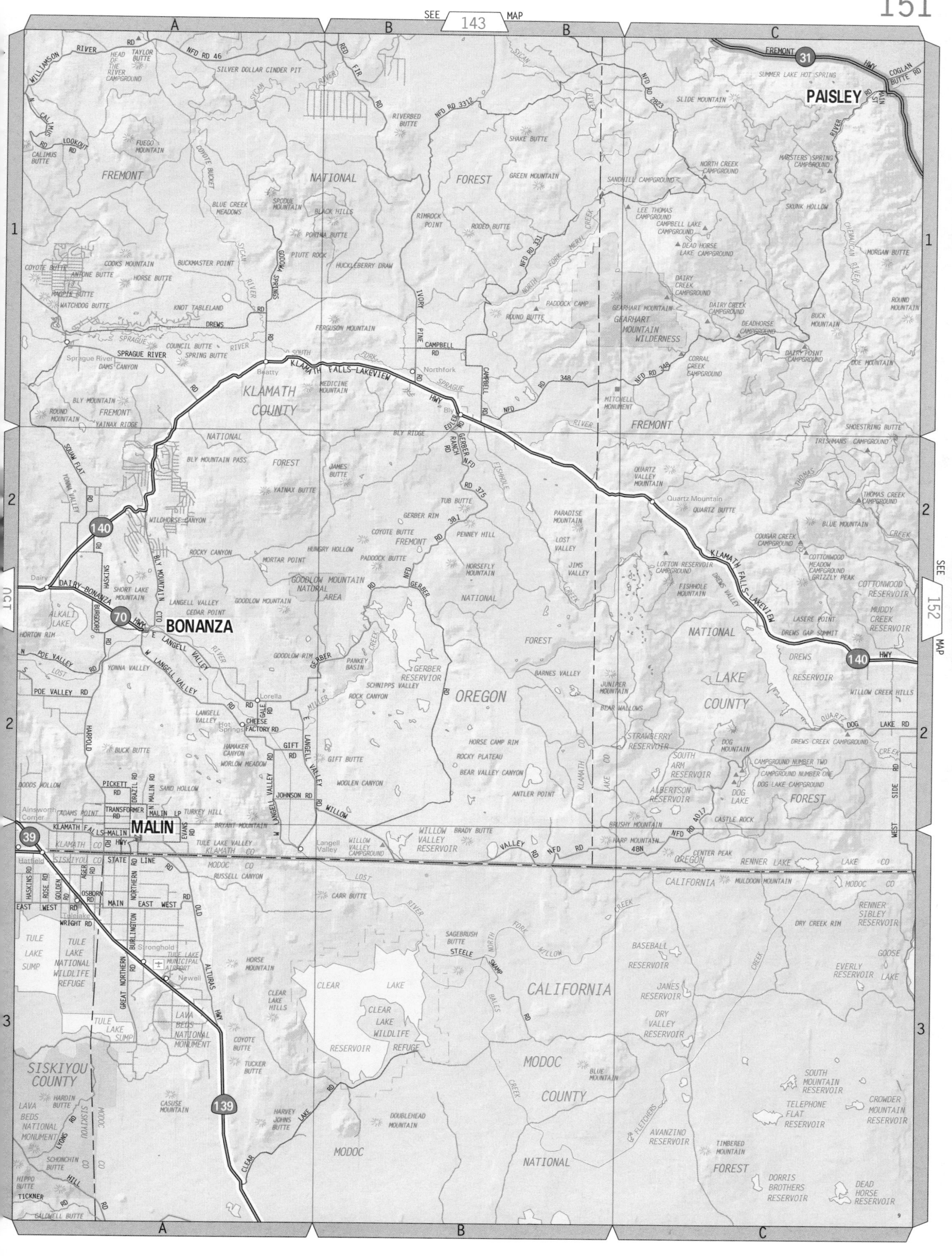
SEE 143 MAP
SEE 152 MAP
PNW
HWY
PAISLEY
BONANZA
MALIN
KLAMATH COUNTY
LAKE COUNTY
MODOC COUNTY
SISKIYOU COUNTY
FREMONT NATIONAL FOREST
OREGON
CALIFORNIA
MODOC NATIONAL FOREST
GEARHART MOUNTAIN WILDERNESS
KLAMATH FALLS-LAKEVIEW HWY
CLEAR LAKE RESERVOIR
CLEAR LAKE WILDLIFE REFUGE
TULE LAKE NATIONAL WILDLIFE REFUGE
LAVA BEDS NATIONAL MONUMENT
GERBER RESERVOIR
WILLOW VALLEY RESERVOIR
DREWS RESERVOIR
SPRAGUE RIVER
Beatty
Bly
Lorella
Langell Valley
Quartz Mountain
Dairy
Hot Springs
Tulelake
Newell
Stronghold

SEE 144 MAP

SEE 151 MAP

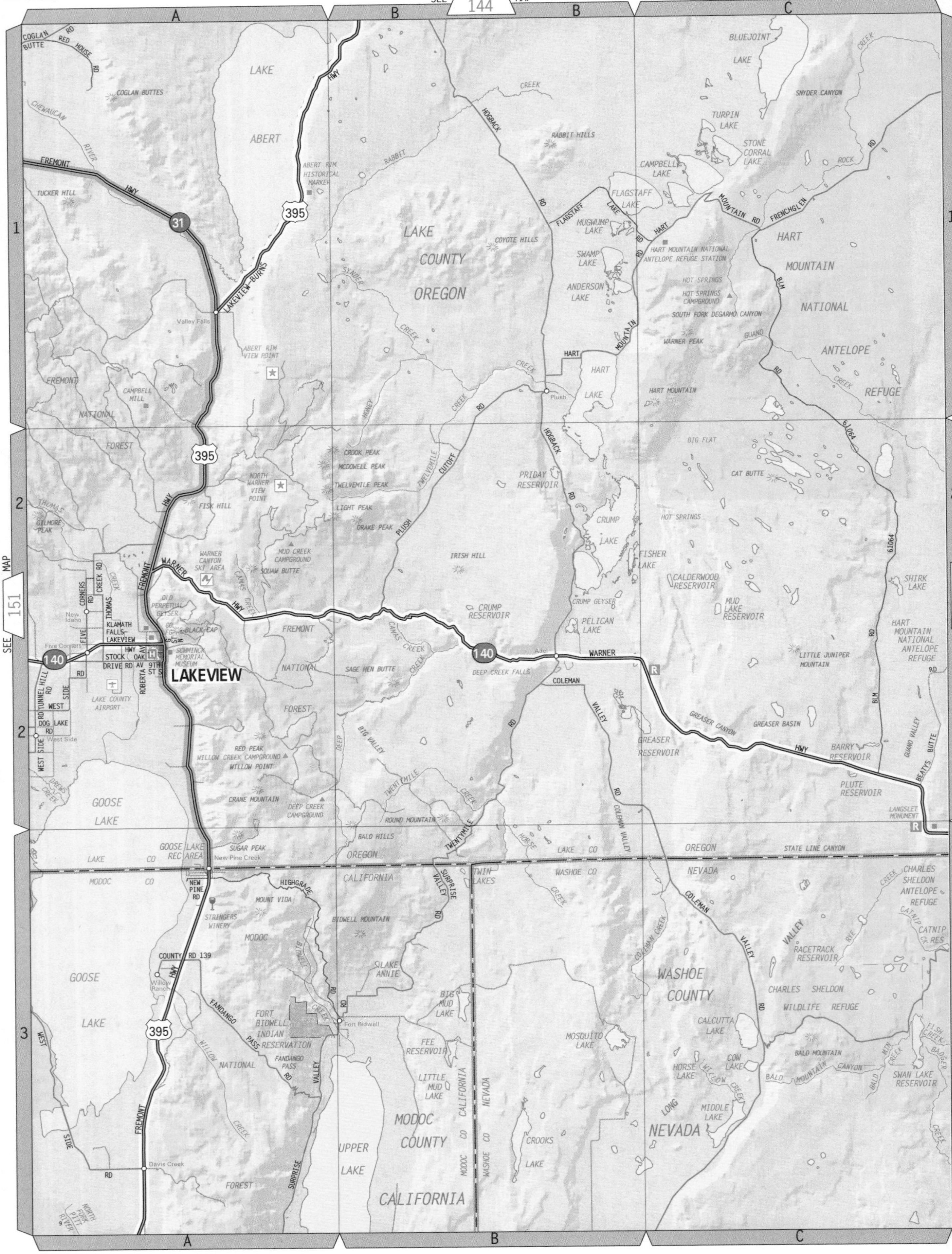

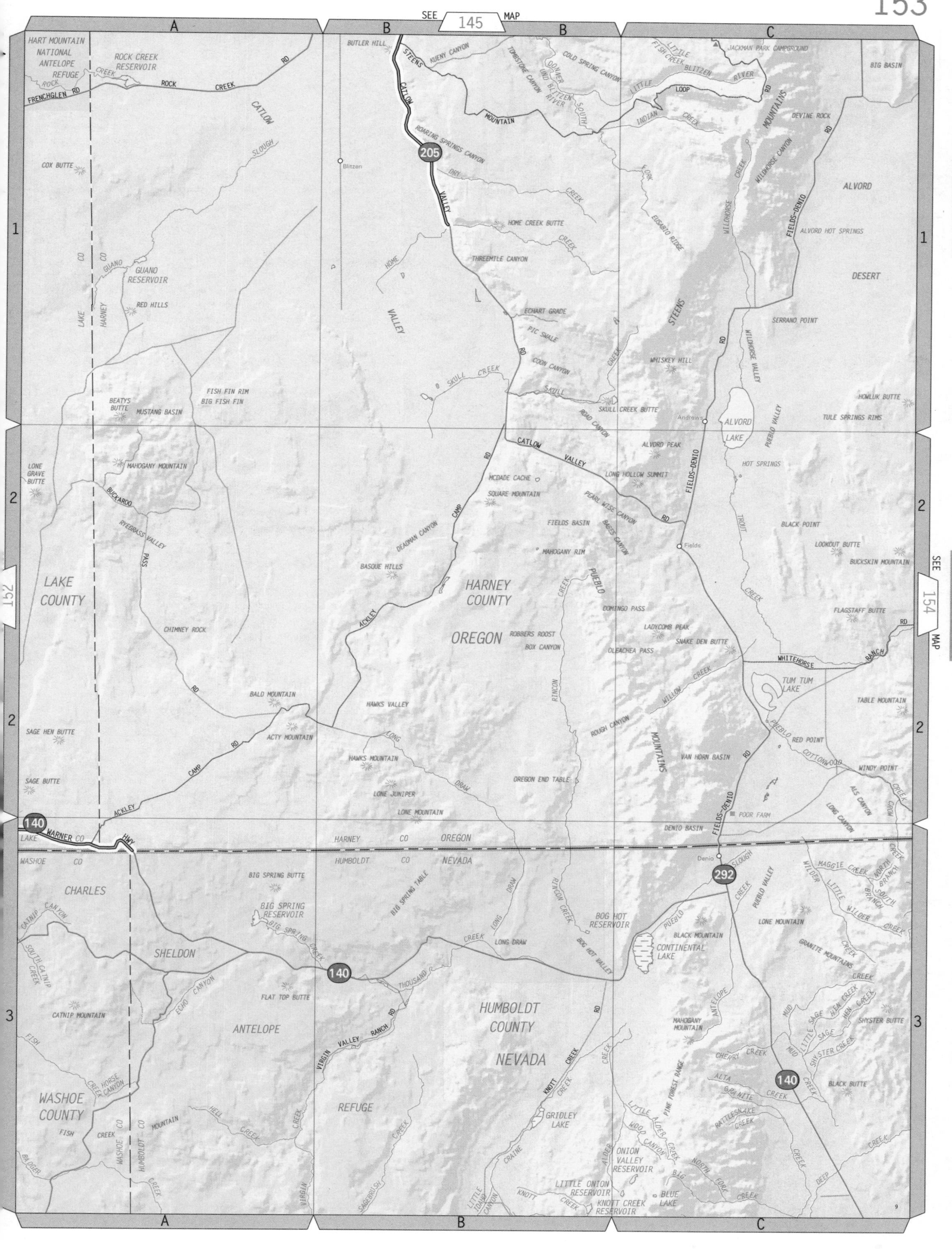
SEE 145 MAP
SEE 154 MAP
152
PNW
HWY
HART MOUNTAIN NATIONAL ANTELOPE REFUGE
ROCK CREEK RESERVOIR
FRENCHGLEN RD
ROCK CREEK RD
CATLOW SLOUGH
COX BUTTE
GUANO RESERVOIR
RED HILLS
LAKE CO
HARNEY CO
FISH FIN RIM
BIG FISH FIN
BEATYS BUTTE
MUSTANG BASIN
MAHOGANY MOUNTAIN
LONE GRAVE BUTTE
BUCKAROO
RYEBRASS VALLEY PASS
LAKE COUNTY
CHIMNEY ROCK
BALD MOUNTAIN
SAGE HEN BUTTE
ACTY MOUNTAIN
SAGE BUTTE
ACKLEY CAMP RD
WARNER
BUTLER HILL
STEENS
KUENY CANYON
CATLOW
ROARING SPRINGS CANYON
Blitzen
DRY CREEK
VALLEY
HOME CREEK BUTTE
THREEMILE CANYON
HOME
VALLEY
ECHART GRADE
PIC SWALE
COON CANYON
SKULL CREEK
SKULL CREEK BUTTE
ROAD CANYON
CATLOW VALLEY RD
MCDADE CACHE
SQUARE MOUNTAIN
DEADMAN CANYON
BASQUE HILLS
HARNEY COUNTY
OREGON
HAWKS VALLEY
HAWKS MOUNTAIN
LONG DRAW
LONE JUNIPER
LONE MOUNTAIN
TOMBSTONE CANYON
DONNER UND BLITZEN RIVER
SOUTH
COLD SPRING CANYON
MOUNTAIN
LITTLE FISH CREEK
BLITZEN RIVER
LITTLE LOOP RD
INDIAN CREEK
JACKMAN PARK CAMPGROUND
BIG BASIN
STEENS MOUNTAINS
DEVINE ROCK
FORK
EUSABIO RIDGE
WILDHORSE CREEK
WILDHORSE CANYON
FIELDS-DENIO RD
ALVORD
ALVORD HOT SPRINGS
DESERT
SERRANO POINT
WHISKEY HILL
WILDHORSE VALLEY
Andrews
ALVORD LAKE
PUEBLO VALLEY
HOWLUK BUTTE
TULE SPRINGS RIMS
ALVORD PEAK
LONG HOLLOW SUMMIT
HOT SPRINGS
PEARL WISE CANYON
FIELDS BASIN
BAGES CANYON
MAHOGANY RIM
Fields
TROUT CREEK
BLACK POINT
LOOKOUT BUTTE
BUCKSKIN MOUNTAIN
PUEBLO
CREEK
DOMINGO PASS
LADYCOMB PEAK
SNAKE DEN BUTTE
FLAGSTAFF BUTTE
ROBBERS ROOST
BOX CANYON
OLEACHEA PASS
WHITEHORSE RANCH RD
TUM TUM LAKE
WILLOW CREEK
RINCON
TABLE MOUNTAIN
ROUGH CANYON
MOUNTAINS
PUEBLO
RED POINT
COTTONWOOD
WINDY POINT
VAN HORN BASIN
OREGON END TABLE
ALS CANYON
LONG CANYON
CROW CREEK
POOR FARM
DENIO BASIN
HARNEY CO OREGON
HUMBOLDT CO NEVADA
WASHOE CO
Denio
SLOUGH
CHARLES
CATNIP CANYON
SOUTH CATNIP CREEK
SHELDON
BIG SPRING BUTTE
BIG SPRING RESERVOIR
BIG SPRING CREEK
BIG SPRING TABLE
LONG DRAW
CREEK
RINCON CREEK
BOG HOT RESERVOIR
BOG HOT VALLEY
PUEBLO
BLACK MOUNTAIN
CONTINENTAL LAKE
PUEBLO VALLEY
LONE MOUNTAIN
WILDER
MAGGIE CREEK
NORTH BRANCH
LITTLE
SOUTH BRANCH
WILDER CREEK
GRANITE MOUNTAINS
CATNIP MOUNTAIN
ECHO CANYON
FLAT TOP BUTTE
THOUSAND
ANTELOPE
VIRGIN VALLEY RANCH RD
HUMBOLDT COUNTY
NEVADA
MAHOGANY MOUNTAIN
ANTELOPE
MUD
LITTLE SAGE HEN CREEK
SAGE HEN CREEK
SHYSTER BUTTE
SHYSTER CREEK
CHERRY CREEK
FISH
HORSE CANYON
WASHOE COUNTY
REFUGE
KNOTT CREEK
PINE FOREST RANGE
ALTA
GRANITE CREEK
BLACK BUTTE
MOUNTAIN
HELL CREEK
GRIDLEY LAKE
LITTLE ALDER CREEK
WOOD CANYON
RATTLESNAKE CREEK
FISH CREEK
WASHOE CO
HUMBOLDT CO
SAGEBRUSH CREEK
CRAINE
ALDER
ONION VALLEY RESERVOIR
NORTH FORK
BIG
BLUE LAKE
LITTLE ONION RESERVOIR
KNOTT CREEK RESERVOIR
LITTLE IDAHO CANYON
VIRGIN
BADGER
CREEK
DEEP CREEK
A
B
C
1
2
3

SEE 146 MAP

SEE HWY 153 MAP

155

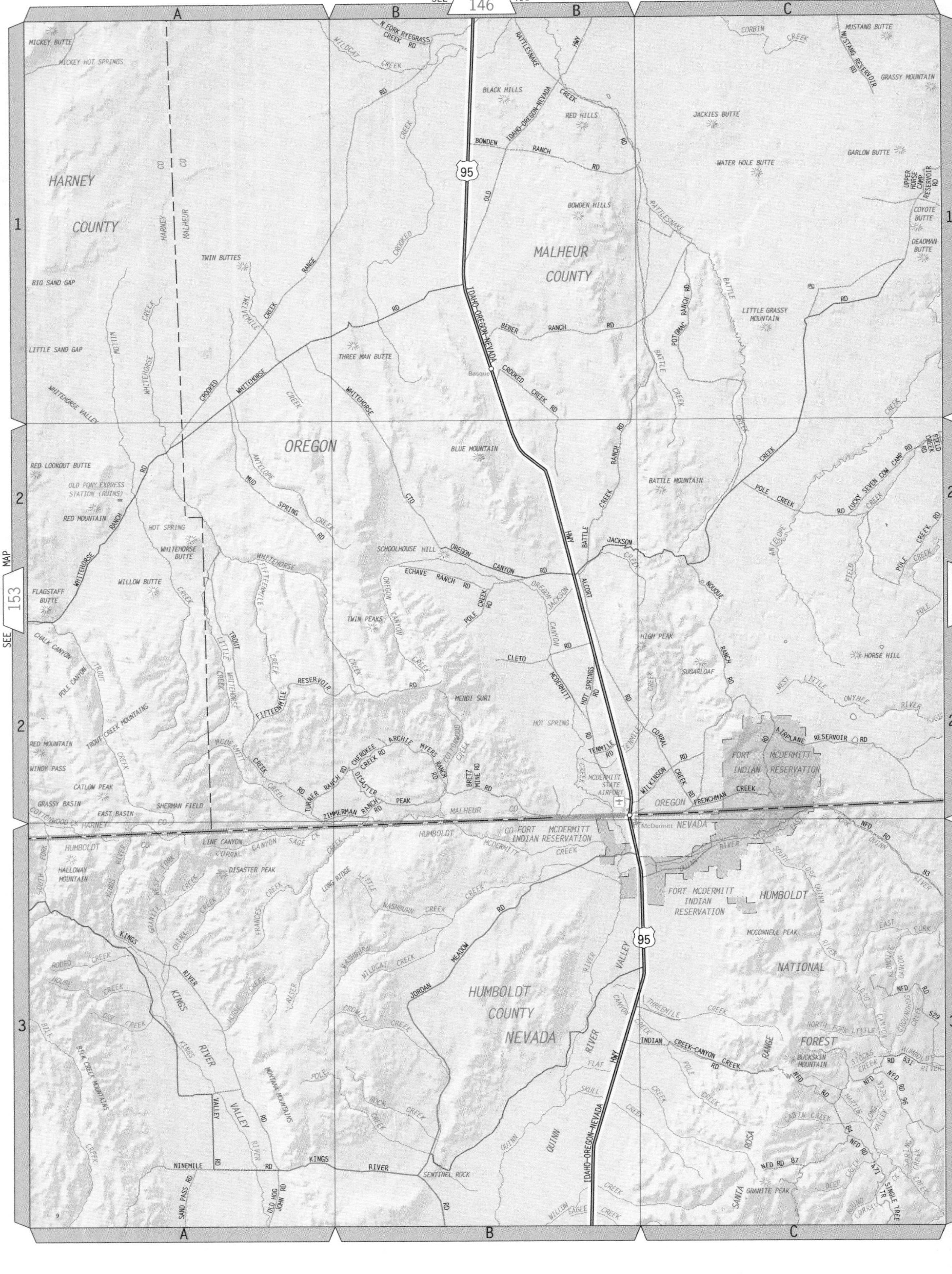

SEE 147 MAP

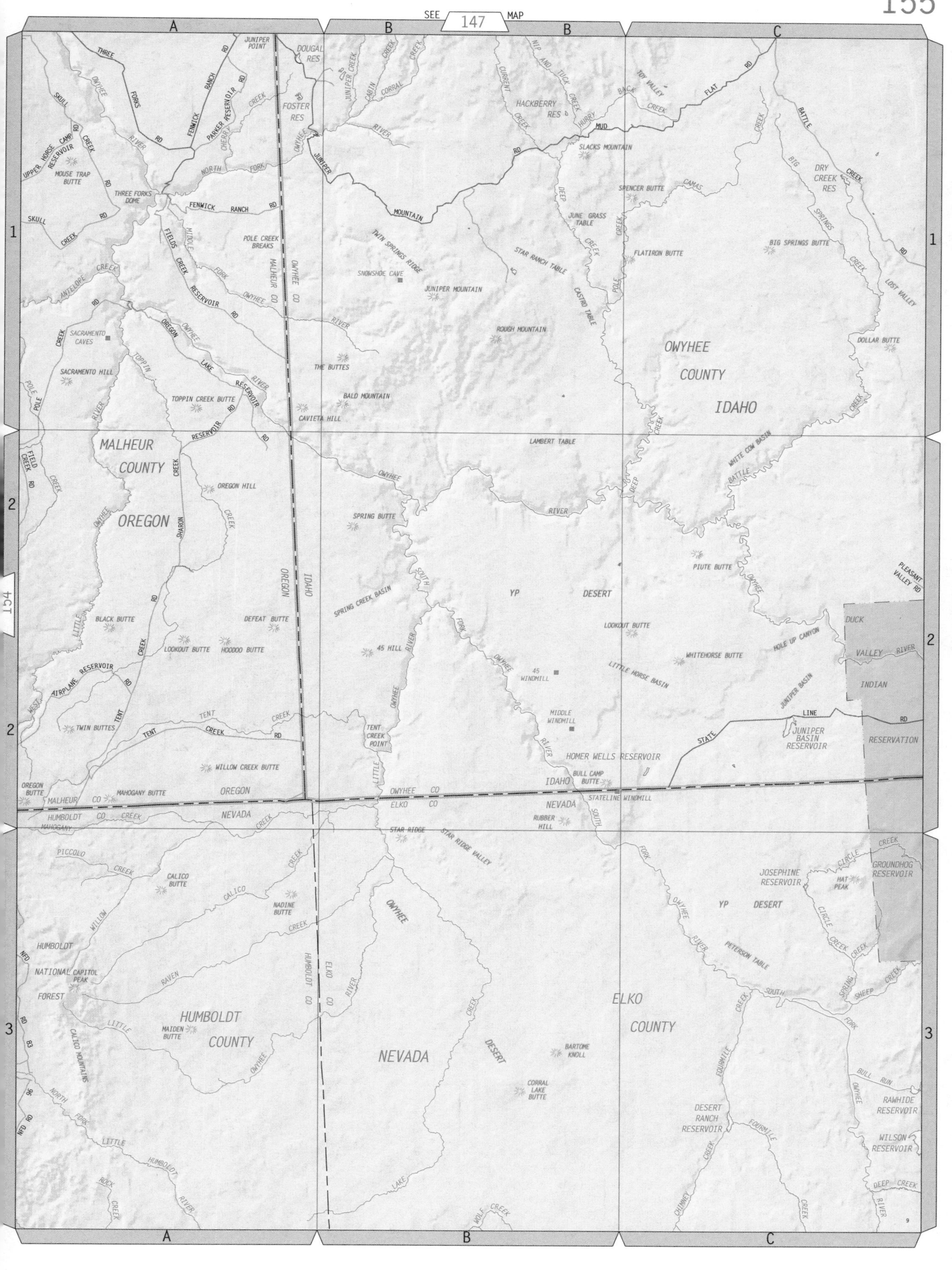
A
B
C
1
2
3
OWYHEE COUNTY
IDAHO
MALHEUR COUNTY
OREGON
HUMBOLDT COUNTY
NEVADA
ELKO COUNTY
YP DESERT
DUCK VALLEY INDIAN RESERVATION
THREE FORKS DOME
MOUSE TRAP BUTTE
UPPER HORSE CAMP RESERVOIR
JUNIPER POINT
DOUGAL RES
FOSTER RES
HACKBERRY RES
SLACKS MOUNTAIN
SPENCER BUTTE
JUNE GRASS TABLE
FLATIRON BUTTE
DRY CREEK RES
BIG SPRINGS BUTTE
POLE CREEK BREAKS
SNOWSHOE CAVE
JUNIPER MOUNTAIN
TWIN SPRINGS RIDGE
STAR RANCH TABLE
CASTRO TABLE
ROUGH MOUNTAIN
SACRAMENTO CAVES
SACRAMENTO HILL
TOPPIN CREEK BUTTE
THE BUTTES
BALD MOUNTAIN
CAVIETA HILL
DOLLAR BUTTE
LAMBERT TABLE
OREGON HILL
SPRING BUTTE
PIUTE BUTTE
SPRING CREEK BASIN
BLACK BUTTE
DEFEAT BUTTE
LOOKOUT BUTTE
HOODOO BUTTE
45 HILL
45 WINDMILL
LITTLE HORSE BASIN
WHITEHORSE BUTTE
HOLE UP CANYON
JUNIPER BASIN
JUNIPER BASIN RESERVOIR
MIDDLE WINDMILL
TWIN BUTTES
TENT CREEK POINT
HOMER WELLS RESERVOIR
WILLOW CREEK BUTTE
BULL CAMP BUTTE
STATELINE WINDMILL
OREGON BUTTE
MAHOGANY BUTTE
RUBBER HILL
STAR RIDGE
STAR RIDGE VALLEY
CALICO BUTTE
NADINE BUTTE
JOSEPHINE RESERVOIR
GROUNDHOG RESERVOIR
HAT PEAK
PETERSON TABLE
HUMBOLDT NATIONAL FOREST
CAPITOL PEAK
CALICO MOUNTAINS
MAIDEN BUTTE
BARTOME KNOLL
CORRAL LAKE BUTTE
DESERT RANCH RESERVOIR
RAWHIDE RESERVOIR
WILSON RESERVOIR
OWYHEE RIVER
MUD FLAT RD
MOUNTAIN RD
PLEASANT VALLEY RD
STATE LINE RD
FENWICK RANCH RD
PARKER RESERVOIR RD
THREE FORKS RD
SKULL CREEK
ANTELOPE CREEK
TOPPIN CREEK
RESERVOIR RD
AIRPLANE RESERVOIR RD
TENT CREEK RD
SHARON CREEK
LITTLE RIVER
DEEP CREEK
BATTLE CREEK
BIG SPRINGS CREEK
LOST VALLEY RD
WHITE COW BASIN
SOUTH FORK OWYHEE RIVER
LITTLE OWYHEE RIVER
CIRCLE CREEK
SPRING CREEK
SHEEP CREEK
BULL RUN
DEEP CREEK
FOURMILE CREEK
CHIMNEY CREEK
LITTLE HUMBOLDT RIVER
ROCK CREEK
WOLF CREEK
PICCOLO CREEK
CALICO CREEK
RAVEN CREEK
WILLOW CREEK
MALHEUR CO
OWYHEE CO
HUMBOLDT CO
ELKO CO
NFD RD 83
NFD RD 96
PNW
HWY
154

SEE 93 MAP

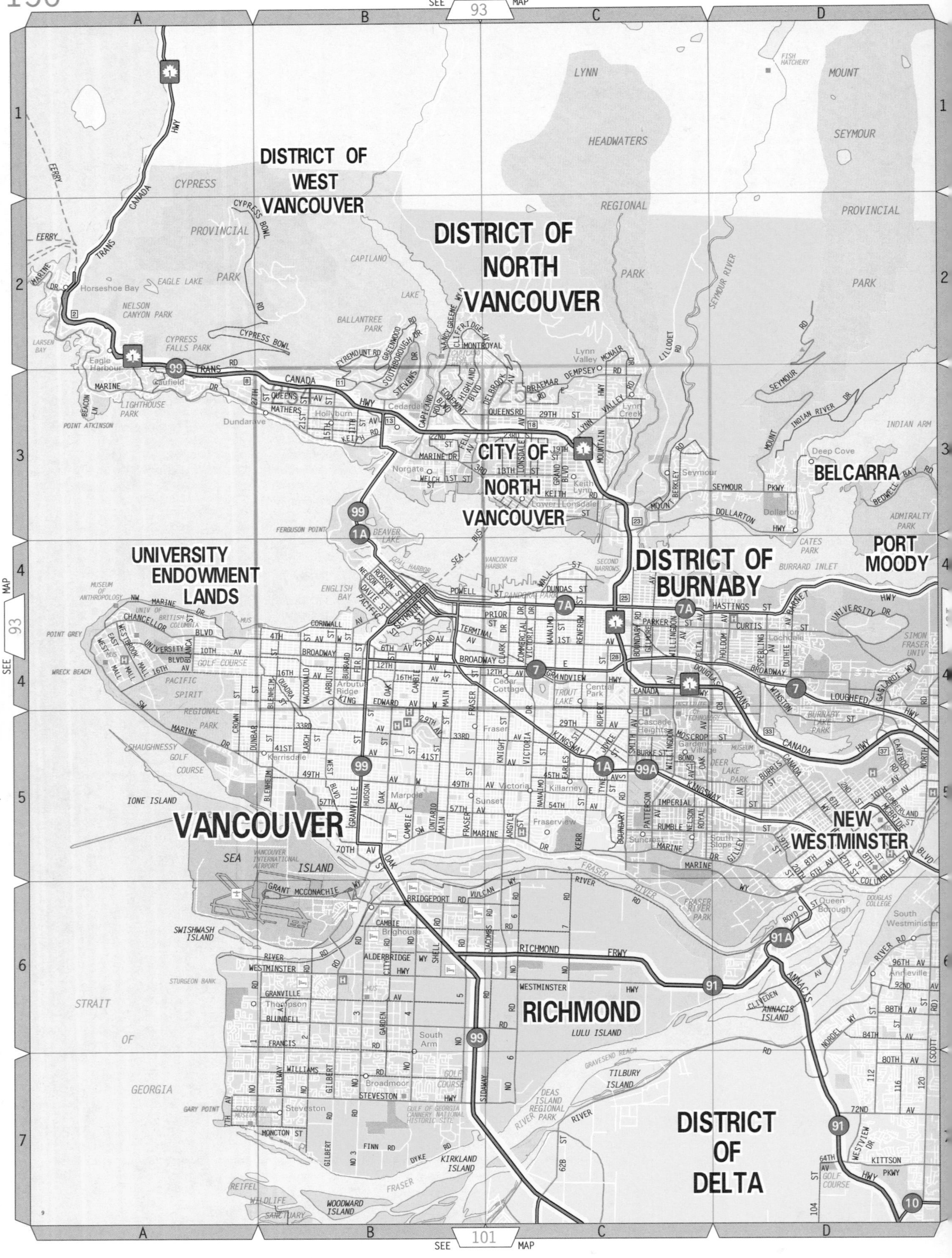

PNW

METRO

SEE 93 MAP

SEE 101 MAP

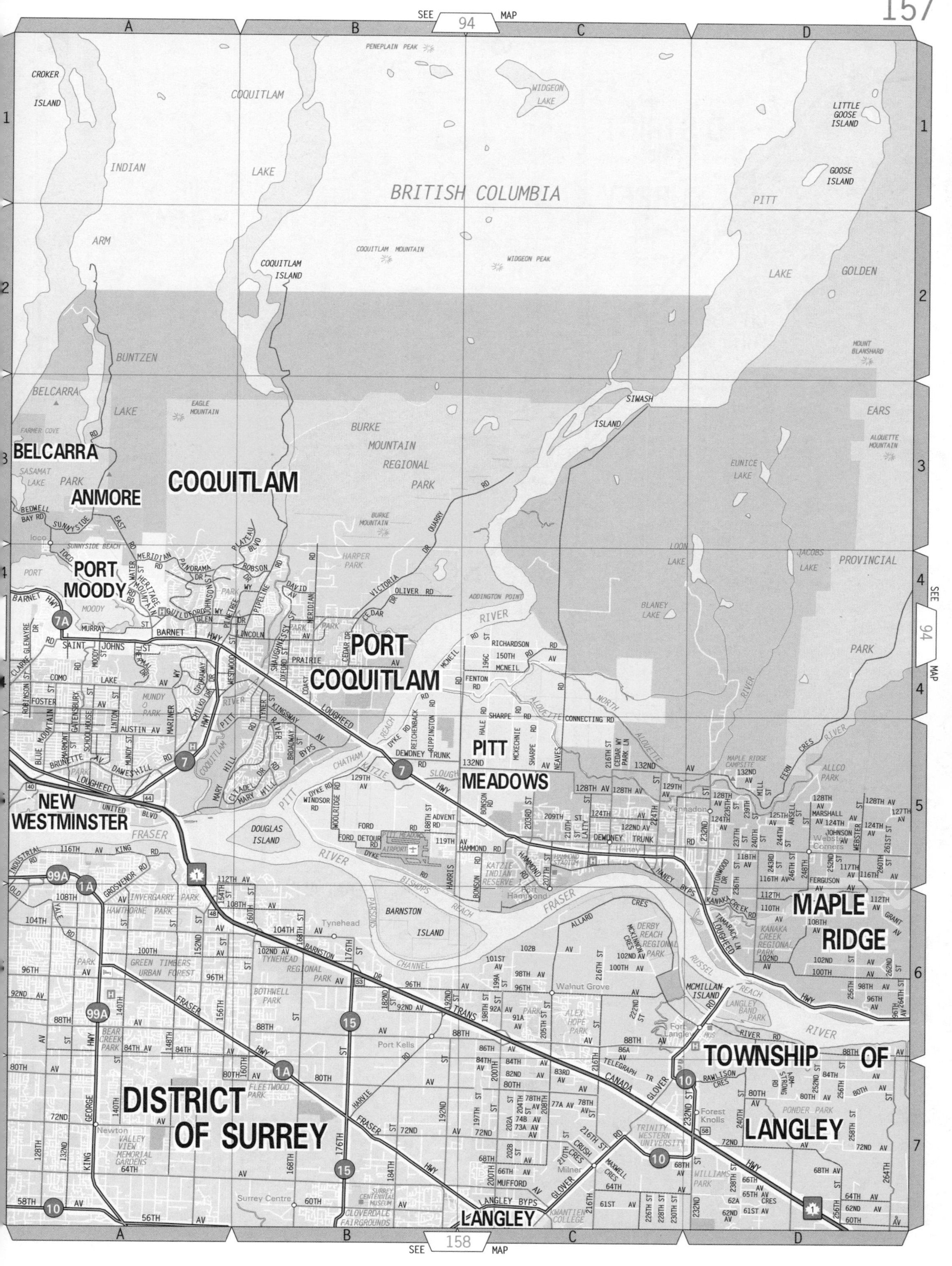

SEE 94 MAP
BRITISH COLUMBIA
COQUITLAM LAKE
INDIAN ARM
CROKER ISLAND
WIDGEON LAKE
PENEPLAIN PEAK
LITTLE GOOSE ISLAND
GOOSE ISLAND
PITT LAKE
GOLDEN EARS PROVINCIAL PARK
COQUITLAM MOUNTAIN
WIDGEON PEAK
COQUITLAM ISLAND
BUNTZEN LAKE
BELCARRA
EAGLE MOUNTAIN
BURKE MOUNTAIN REGIONAL PARK
SIWASH ISLAND
MOUNT BLANSHARD
ALOUETTE MOUNTAIN
EUNICE LAKE
BELCARRA
SASAMAT LAKE
ANMORE
COQUITLAM
LOON LAKE
JACOBS LAKE
BLANEY LAKE
PORT MOODY
PORT COQUITLAM
PITT MEADOWS
NEW WESTMINSTER
DOUGLAS ISLAND
FRASER RIVER
BARNSTON ISLAND
MAPLE RIDGE
DERBY REACH REGIONAL PARK
MCMILLAN ISLAND
TOWNSHIP OF LANGLEY
DISTRICT OF SURREY
LANGLEY
TRINITY WESTERN UNIVERSITY
Port Kells
Walnut Grove
Fort Langley
Surrey Centre
Newton
Milner
Forest Knolls
Haney
Yennadon
Websters Corners
Port Hammond
Tynehead
Ioco
SEE 158 MAP
PNW
METRO

SEE 157 MAP

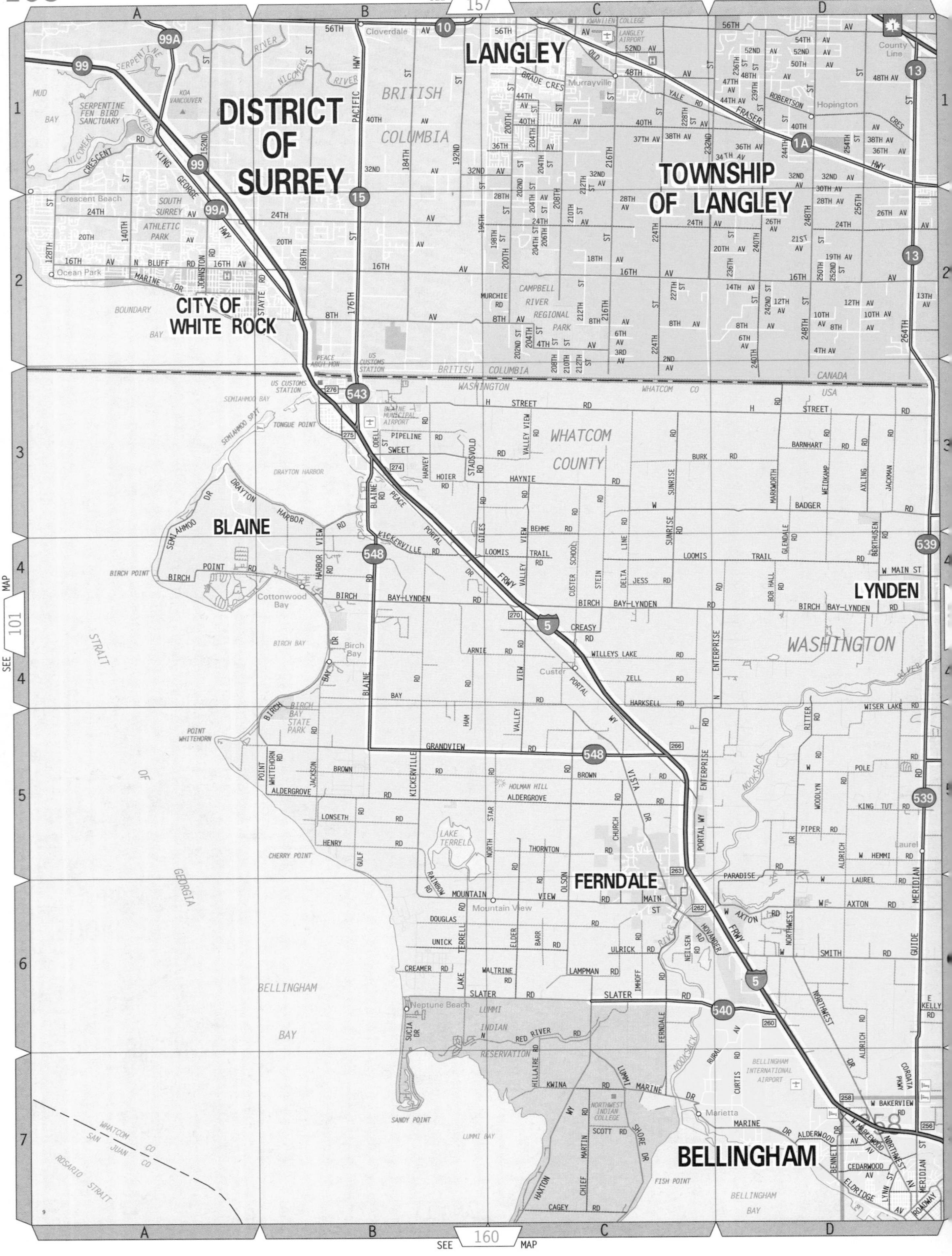

SEE 101 MAP

PNW

METRO

A B C D

1 2 3 4 5 6 7

LANGLEY

DISTRICT OF SURREY

TOWNSHIP OF LANGLEY

CITY OF WHITE ROCK

BRITISH COLUMBIA

WASHINGTON

USA

CANADA

WHATCOM COUNTY

BLAINE

LYNDEN

FERNDALE

BELLINGHAM

Cloverdale

Murrayville

Hopington

County Line

Crescent Beach

Ocean Park

SERPENTINE FEN BIRD SANCTUARY

MUD BAY

BOUNDARY BAY

SEMIAHMOO BAY

DRAYTON HARBOR

TONGUE POINT

BIRCH POINT

Cottonwood Bay

Birch Bay

BIRCH BAY STATE PARK

POINT WHITEHORN

STRAIT OF GEORGIA

CHERRY POINT

LAKE TERRELL

HOLMAN HILL

Custer

Mountain View

Neptune Beach

LUMMI INDIAN RESERVATION

NORTHWEST INDIAN COLLEGE

SANDY POINT

LUMMI BAY

BELLINGHAM BAY

FISH POINT

Marietta

BELLINGHAM INTERNATIONAL AIRPORT

Laurel

ROSARIO STRAIT

WHATCOM CO

SAN JUAN CO

CAMPBELL RIVER REGIONAL PARK

KWANTLEN COLLEGE

LANGLEY AIRPORT

BLAINE MUNICIPAL AIRPORT

PEACE ARCH MON

US CUSTOMS STATION

KOA VANCOUVER

SEE 160 MAP

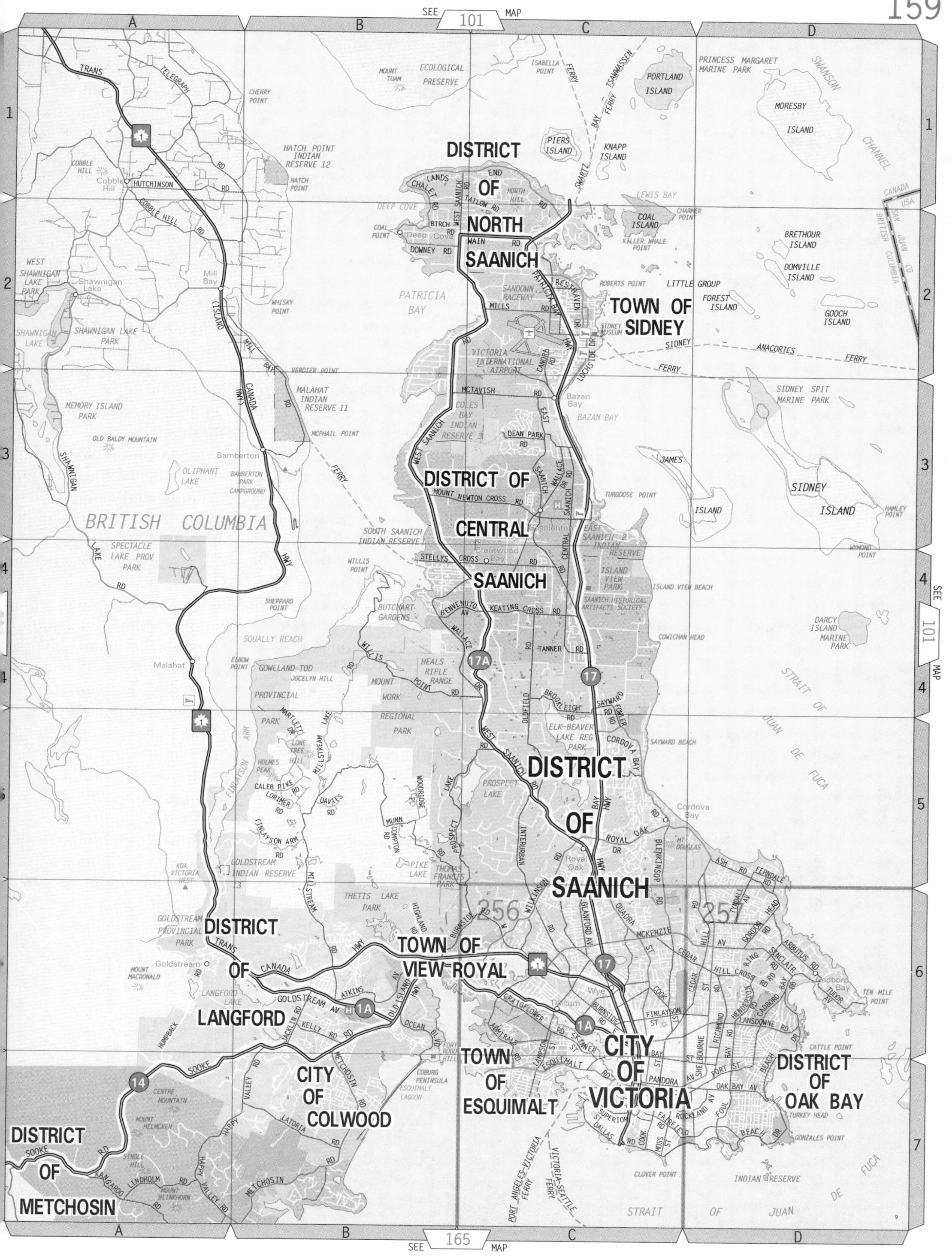

SEE 101 MAP
DISTRICT OF NORTH SAANICH
TOWN OF SIDNEY
DISTRICT OF CENTRAL SAANICH
DISTRICT OF SAANICH
DISTRICT OF LANGFORD
TOWN OF VIEW ROYAL
CITY OF COLWOOD
TOWN OF ESQUIMALT
CITY OF VICTORIA
DISTRICT OF OAK BAY
DISTRICT OF METCHOSIN
BRITISH COLUMBIA
PATRICIA BAY
VICTORIA INTERNATIONAL AIRPORT
PORTLAND ISLAND
PRINCESS MARGARET MARINE PARK
MORESBY ISLAND
SWANSON CHANNEL
PIERS ISLAND
KNAPP ISLAND
COAL ISLAND
BRETHOUR ISLAND
DOMVILLE ISLAND
LITTLE GROUP
FOREST ISLAND
GOOCH ISLAND
SIDNEY SPIT MARINE PARK
JAMES ISLAND
SIDNEY ISLAND
DARCY ISLAND MARINE PARK
HAREN STRAIT
STRAIT OF JUAN DE FUCA
CANADA
USA
SAN JUAN CO
BRITISH COLUMBIA
SIDNEY ANACORTES FERRY
SWARTZ BAY TSAWWASSEN FERRY
PORT ANGELES-VICTORIA FERRY
VICTORIA-SEATTLE FERRY
MALAHAT INDIAN RESERVE 11
HATCH POINT INDIAN RESERVE 12
SHAWNIGAN LAKE PARK
SPECTACLE LAKE PROV PARK
GOWLAND-TOD PROVINCIAL PARK
MOUNT WORK REGIONAL PARK
THETIS LAKE PARK
GOLDSTREAM PROVINCIAL PARK
GOLDSTREAM INDIAN RESERVE
ELK-BEAVER LAKE REG PARK
ISLAND VIEW PARK
BUTCHART GARDENS
HEALS RIFLE RANGE
TRANS CANADA HWY
PATRICIA BAY HWY
WEST SAANICH RD
EAST SAANICH RD
SOOKE RD
METCHOSIN RD
OLD ISLAND HWY
CORDOVA BAY RD
BEACH DR
Mill Bay
Shawnigan Lake
Cobble Hill
Bamberton
Malahat
Goldstream
Brentwood Bay
Saanichton
Royal Oak
Cordova Bay
Bazan Bay
Deep Cove
256
257
1
1A
14
17
17A
SEE 165 MAP
PNW
METRO

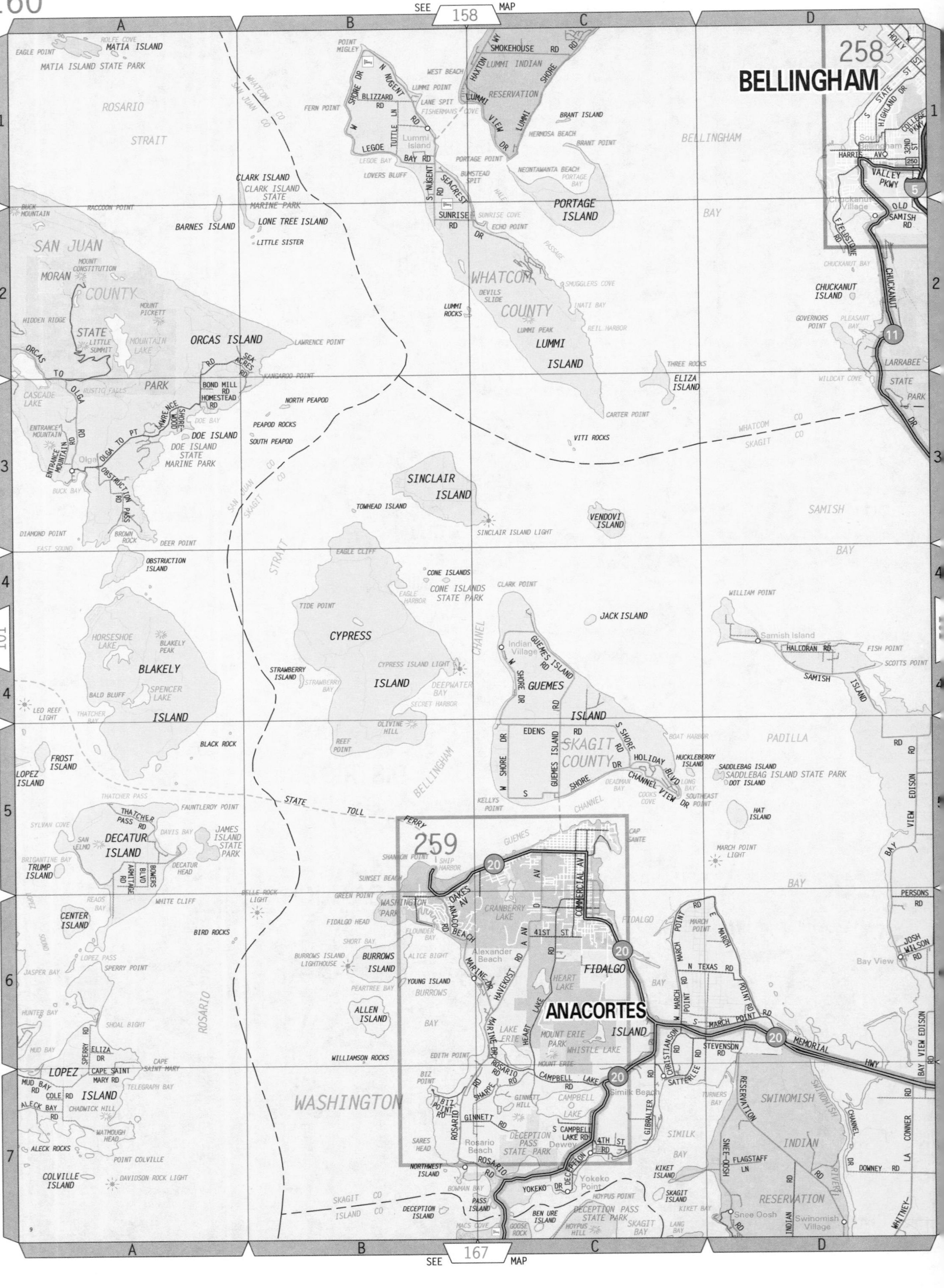
SEE 158 MAP
SEE 167 MAP
SEE 101 MAP
258
259
BELLINGHAM
ANACORTES
PNW
METRO
MATIA ISLAND
MATIA ISLAND STATE PARK
EAGLE POINT
ROLFE COVE
ROSARIO STRAIT
SAN JUAN COUNTY
MORAN STATE PARK
MOUNT CONSTITUTION
MOUNT PICKETT
MOUNTAIN LAKE
LITTLE SUMMIT
HIDDEN RIDGE
ORCAS ISLAND
ORCAS TO OLGA RD
CASCADE LAKE
RUSTIC FALLS
ENTRANCE MOUNTAIN
OLGA TO PT LAWRENCE
OBSTRUCTION PASS RD
BOND MILL RD
HOMESTEAD RD
SEA ACRES RD
LAWRENCE POINT
KANGAROO POINT
DOE ISLAND
DOE ISLAND STATE MARINE PARK
DOE BAY
BUCK BAY
DIAMOND POINT
EAST SOUND
BROWN ROCK
DEER POINT
OBSTRUCTION ISLAND
NORTH PEAPOD
PEAPOD ROCKS
SOUTH PEAPOD
CLARK ISLAND
CLARK ISLAND STATE MARINE PARK
BARNES ISLAND
LONE TREE ISLAND
LITTLE SISTER
BUCK MOUNTAIN
RACCOON POINT
POINT MIGLEY
FERN POINT
W SHORE DR
N NUGENT
BLIZZARD RD
TUTTLE LN
LEGOE BAY RD
Lummi Island
LEGOE BAY
LOVERS BLUFF
LUMMI POINT
LANE SPIT
FISHERMANS COVE
WEST BEACH
SMOKEHOUSE RD
HAXTON WY
LUMMI INDIAN RESERVATION
LUMMI VIEW DR
LUMMI SHORE
BRANT ISLAND
HERMOSA BEACH
BRANT POINT
PORTAGE POINT
BUMSTEAD SPIT
NEONTAWANTA BEACH
PORTAGE BAY
PORTAGE ISLAND
S NUGENT
SEACREST DR
SUNRISE RD
SUNRISE COVE
ECHO POINT
HALE PASSAGE
WHATCOM COUNTY
DEVILS SLIDE
LUMMI ROCKS
SMUGGLERS COVE
INATI BAY
REIL HARBOR
LUMMI PEAK
LUMMI ISLAND
THREE ROCKS
ELIZA ISLAND
CARTER POINT
VITI ROCKS
BELLINGHAM BAY
WHATCOM CO
SKAGIT CO
SAN JUAN CO
HOLLY
STATE ST
HIGHLAND DR
COLLEGE PKWY
32ND ST
South Bellingham
HARRIS AV
VALLEY PKWY
Chuckanut Village
OLD SAMISH RD
FIELDSTONE
CHUCKANUT BAY
CHUCKANUT DR
CHUCKANUT ISLAND
GOVERNORS POINT
PLEASANT BAY
LARRABEE STATE PARK
WILDCAT COVE
SINCLAIR ISLAND
TOWHEAD ISLAND
SINCLAIR ISLAND LIGHT
VENDOVI ISLAND
SAMISH BAY
EAGLE CLIFF
CONE ISLANDS
CONE ISLANDS STATE PARK
EAGLE HARBOR
CLARK POINT
TIDE POINT
CYPRESS ISLAND
CYPRESS ISLAND LIGHT
STRAWBERRY ISLAND
STRAWBERRY BAY
DEEPWATER BAY
SECRET HARBOR
OLIVINE HILL
REEF POINT
GUEMES CHANNEL
JACK ISLAND
WILLIAM POINT
Samish Island
HALLORAN RD
FISH POINT
SCOTTS POINT
SAMISH ISLAND
Indian Village
GUEMES ISLAND RD
W SHORE DR
GUEMES ISLAND
EDENS RD
SKAGIT COUNTY
S SHORE DR
HOLIDAY BLVD
CHANNEL VIEW DR
SHORE
BOAT HARBOR
HUCKLEBERRY ISLAND
SADDLEBAG ISLAND
SADDLEBAG ISLAND STATE PARK
DOT ISLAND
LONG BAY
DEADMAN BAY
COOKS COVE
SOUTHEAST POINT
HAT ISLAND
PADILLA BAY
BAY VIEW EDISON RD
KELLYS POINT
CAP SANTE
MARCH POINT LIGHT
BLAKELY ISLAND
HORSESHOE LAKE
BLAKELY PEAK
SPENCER LAKE
BALD BLUFF
THATCHER BAY
LEO REEF LIGHT
BLACK ROCK
FROST ISLAND
LOPEZ ISLAND
THATCHER PASS
FAUNTLEROY POINT
STATE TOLL FERRY
BELLINGHAM CHANNEL
SYLVAN COVE
SAN ELMO
DECATUR ISLAND
THATCHER PASS RD
DAVIS BAY
JAMES ISLAND STATE PARK
BRIGANTINE BAY
TRUMP ISLAND
ARMITAGE RD
BOWERS BLVD
DECATUR HEAD
REALS BAY
WHITE CLIFF
BELLE ROCK LIGHT
CENTER ISLAND
BIRD ROCKS
SHANNON POINT
SHIP HARBOR
SUNSET BEACH
GREEN POINT
WASHINGTON PARK
OAKES AV
ANACO BEACH RD
CRANBERRY LAKE
COMMERCIAL AV
D AV
41ST ST
FIDALGO BAY
FIDALGO HEAD
FLOUNDER BAY
SHORT BAY
ALICE BIGHT
Alexander Beach
MARINE DR
HAVEKOST RD
A AV
BURROWS ISLAND LIGHTHOUSE
BURROWS ISLAND
YOUNG ISLAND
PEARTREE BAY
BURROWS BAY
ALLEN ISLAND
HEART LAKE
HEART LAKE RD
FIDALGO ISLAND
MARCH POINT RD
E MARCH POINT RD
N TEXAS RD
W MARCH POINT RD
S MARCH POINT RD
PERSONS RD
JOSH WILSON RD
Bay View
LAKE ERIE
MOUNT ERIE PARK
WHISTLE LAKE
MOUNT ERIE
CHRISTIANSON
STEVENSON RD
SATTERLEE
MEMORIAL HWY
EDITH POINT
WILLIAMSON ROCKS
BIZ POINT
ROSARIO RD
SHARPE RD
CAMPBELL LAKE RD
CAMPBELL LAKE
GINNETT HILL
GINNETT RD
S CAMPBELL LAKE RD
Simik Beach
GIBRALTER RD
TURNERS BAY
SIMILK BAY
RESERVATION RD
SWINOMISH INDIAN RESERVATION
SWINOMISH CHANNEL
LA CONNER WHITNEY RD
DOWNEY RD
SNEE-OOSH RD
FLAGSTAFF LN
Snee Oosh
Swinomish Village
INDIAN RD
SARES HEAD
Rosario Beach
DECEPTION PASS STATE PARK
Dewey
4TH ST
DECEPTION RD
YOKEKO DR
Yokeko Point
HOYPUS POINT
KIKET ISLAND
SKAGIT ISLAND
KIKET BAY
NORTHWEST ISLAND
BOWMAN BAY
PASS ISLAND
DECEPTION ISLAND
BEN URE ISLAND
DECEPTION PASS STATE PARK
HOYPUS HILL
SKAGIT BAY
LANG BAY
MACS COVE
GOOSE ROCK
WASHINGTON
ROSARIO STRAIT
LOPEZ PASS
SPERRY POINT
JASPER BAY
HUNTER BAY
SHOAL BIGHT
MUD BAY
SPERRY RD
ELIZA DR
LOPEZ
CAPE SAINT MARY RD
CAPE SAINT MARY
TELEGRAPH BAY
ISLAND
MUD BAY RD
COLE RD
ALECK BAY
CHADWICK HILL
WATMOUGH HEAD
ALECK ROCKS
POINT COLVILLE
COLVILLE ISLAND
DAVIDSON ROCK LIGHT
SKAGIT CO
ISLAND CO

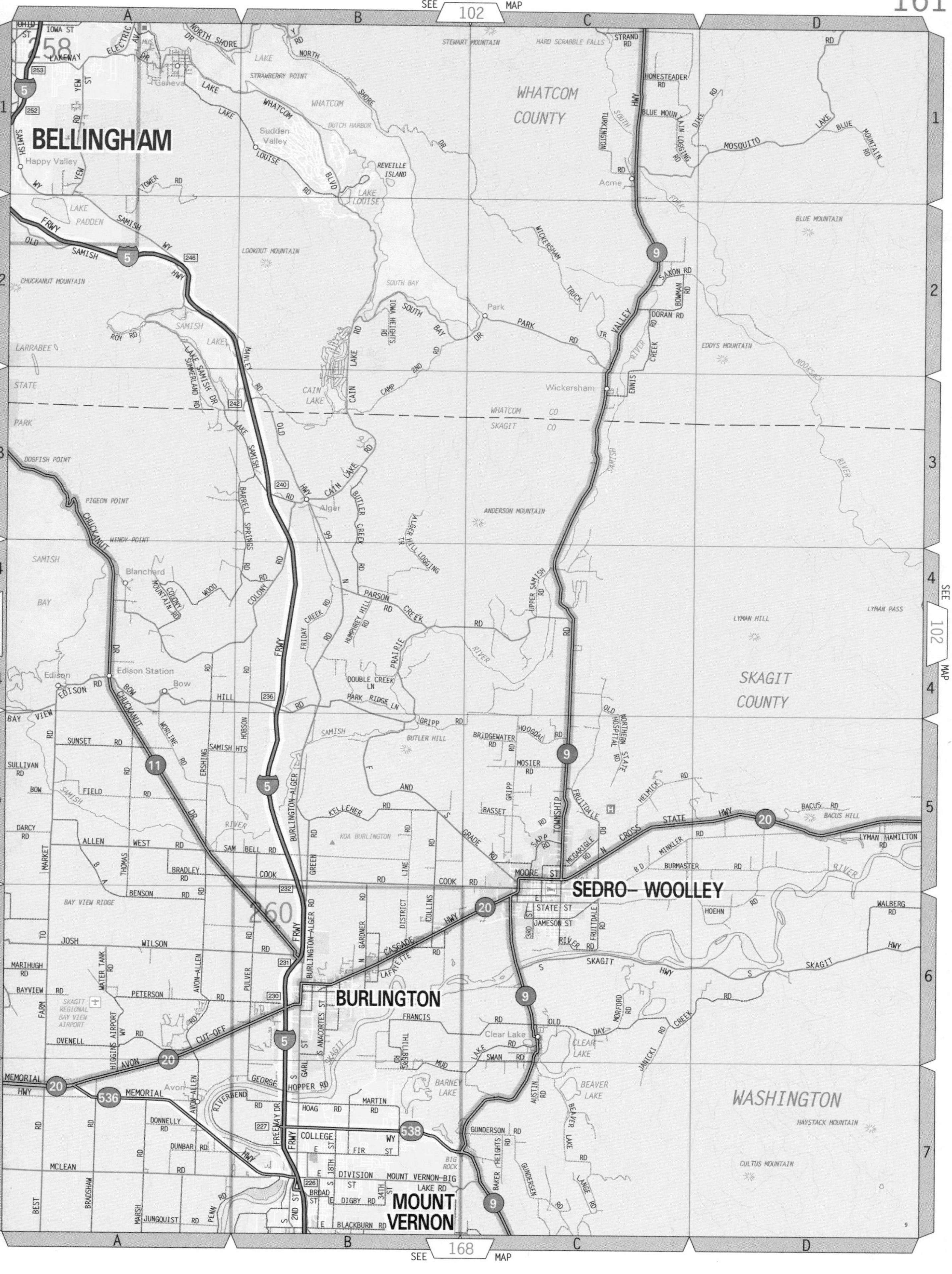

SEE 102 MAP

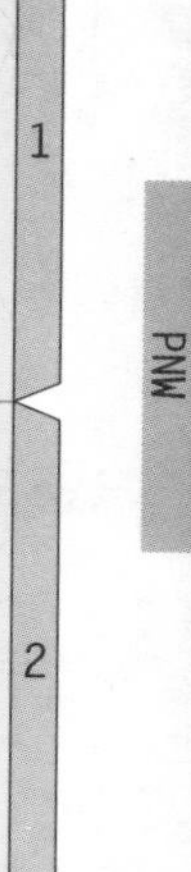

METRO

SEE 102 MAP

BELLINGHAM

Happy Valley

Geneva

Sudden Valley

LAKE WHATCOM

STRAWBERRY POINT

DUTCH HARBOR

REVEILLE ISLAND

LAKE LOUISE

STEWART MOUNTAIN

HARD SCRABBLE FALLS

WHATCOM COUNTY

Acme

LAKE PADDEN

LOOKOUT MOUNTAIN

CHUCKANUT MOUNTAIN

BLUE MOUNTAIN

SOUTH BAY

Park

SAMISH LAKE

LARRABEE STATE PARK

CAIN LAKE

EDDYS MOUNTAIN

Wickersham

WHATCOM CO

SKAGIT CO

DOGFISH POINT

PIGEON POINT

WINDY POINT

Alger

ANDERSON MOUNTAIN

SAMISH BAY

Blanchard

LYMAN HILL

LYMAN PASS

Edison

Edison Station

Bow

SKAGIT COUNTY

BUTLER HILL

KOA BURLINGTON

BACUS HILL

LYMAN

HAMILTON

SEDRO-WOOLLEY

BAY VIEW RIDGE

BURLINGTON

SKAGIT REGIONAL BAY VIEW AIRPORT

Clear Lake

CLEAR LAKE

BARNEY LAKE

BEAVER LAKE

Avon

WASHINGTON

HAYSTACK MOUNTAIN

BIG ROCK

CULTUS MOUNTAIN

MOUNT VERNON

SEE 168 MAP

SEE 100 MAP
A B C D 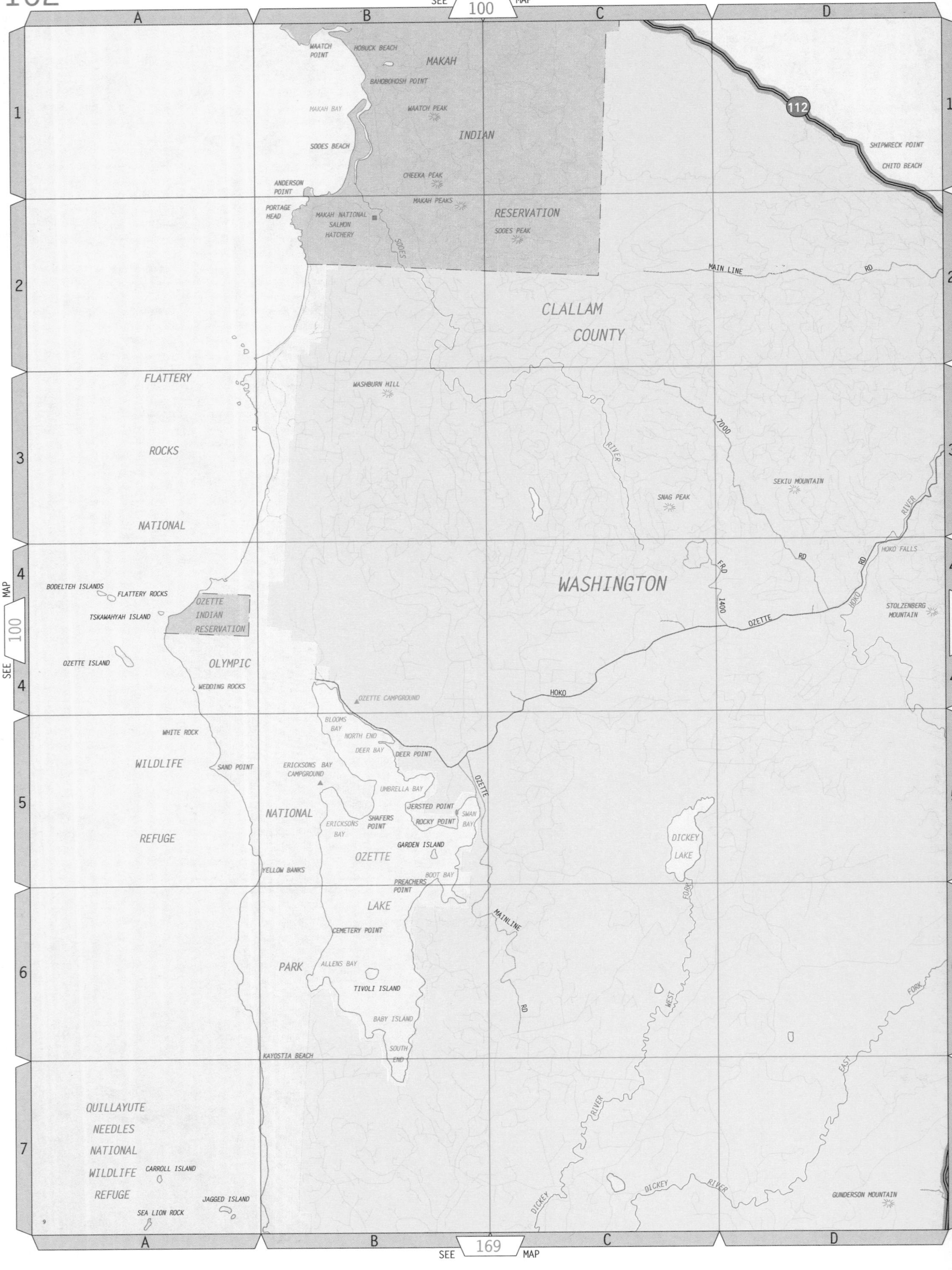
1 2 3 4 5 6 7
PNW
METRO
WAATCH POINT
HOBUCK BEACH
MAKAH INDIAN RESERVATION
BAHOBOHOSH POINT
MAKAH BAY
WAATCH PEAK
SOOES BEACH
ANDERSON POINT
CHEEKA PEAK
MAKAH PEAKS
PORTAGE HEAD
MAKAH NATIONAL SALMON HATCHERY
SOOES PEAK
SOOES
112
SHIPWRECK POINT
CHITO BEACH
MAIN LINE RD
CLALLAM COUNTY
FLATTERY ROCKS NATIONAL WILDLIFE REFUGE
WASHBURN HILL
7000
RIVER
SEKIU MOUNTAIN
SNAG PEAK
RIVER
RD
FRD 1400
HOKO FALLS
RD
WASHINGTON
BODELTEH ISLANDS
FLATTERY ROCKS
OZETTE INDIAN RESERVATION
TSKAWAHYAH ISLAND
OZETTE
HOKO
STOLZENBERG MOUNTAIN
OZETTE ISLAND
OLYMPIC NATIONAL PARK
WEDDING ROCKS
OZETTE CAMPGROUND
HOKO
BLOOMS BAY
NORTH END
WHITE ROCK
DEER BAY
DEER POINT
SAND POINT
ERICKSONS BAY CAMPGROUND
UMBRELLA BAY
OZETTE
JERSTED POINT
SWAN BAY
ROCKY POINT
ERICKSONS BAY
SHAFERS POINT
GARDEN ISLAND
DICKEY LAKE
OZETTE LAKE
YELLOW BANKS
BOOT BAY
PREACHERS POINT
MAINLINE RD
FORK
CEMETERY POINT
ALLENS BAY
TIVOLI ISLAND
WEST
FORK
BABY ISLAND
SOUTH END
KAYOSTIA BEACH
EAST
QUILLAYUTE NEEDLES NATIONAL WILDLIFE REFUGE
RIVER
CARROLL ISLAND
DICKEY
DICKEY RIVER
JAGGED ISLAND
GUNDERSON MOUNTAIN
SEA LION ROCK
9
SEE 169 MAP

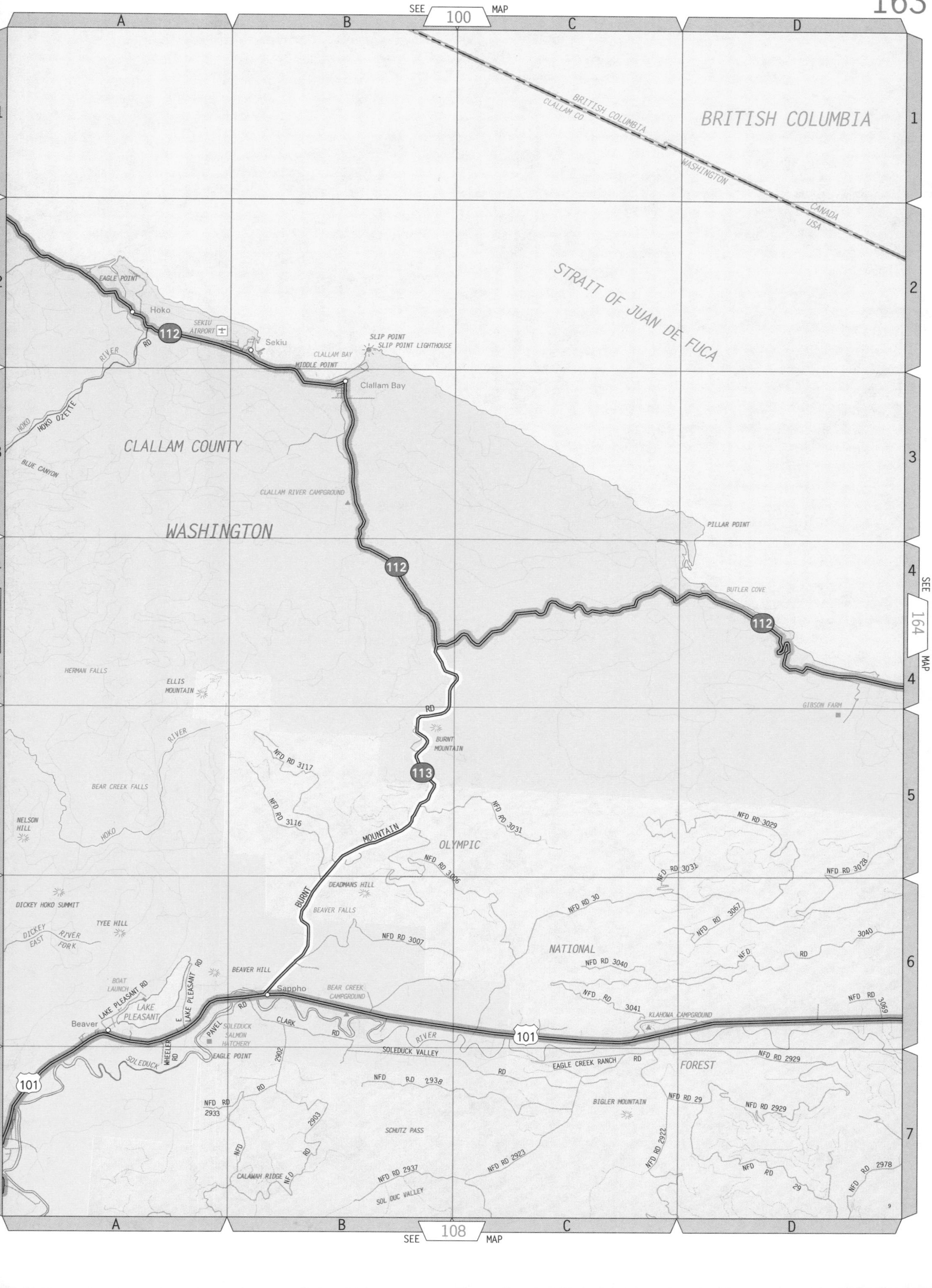
SEE 100 MAP
A
B
C
D
1
2
3
4
5
6
7
BRITISH COLUMBIA
BRITISH COLUMBIA
CLALLAM CO
WASHINGTON
CANADA
USA
STRAIT OF JUAN DE FUCA
EAGLE POINT
Hoko
112
SEKIU AIRPORT
Sekiu
SLIP POINT
SLIP POINT LIGHTHOUSE
CLALLAM BAY
MIDDLE POINT
Clallam Bay
RD
RIVER
HOKO
HOKO OZETTE
CLALLAM COUNTY
BLUE CANYON
CLALLAM RIVER CAMPGROUND
WASHINGTON
PILLAR POINT
BUTLER COVE
SEE 164 MAP
HERMAN FALLS
ELLIS MOUNTAIN
GIBSON FARM
RIVER
NFD RD 3117
BURNT MOUNTAIN
113
BEAR CREEK FALLS
NFD RD 3116
NFD RD 3031
NFD RD 3029
NELSON HILL
HOKO
MOUNTAIN
OLYMPIC
NFD RD 3006
NFD RD 3031
NFD RD 3028
BURNT
DEADMANS HILL
DICKEY HOKO SUMMIT
BEAVER FALLS
NFD RD 30
NFD RD 3067
TYEE HILL
DICKEY
EAST
RIVER
FORK
NFD RD 3007
3040
NATIONAL
NFD
RD
NFD RD 3040
BOAT LAUNCH
LAKE PLEASANT RD
LAKE PLEASANT
E LAKE PLEASANT RD
BEAVER HILL
Sappho
BEAR CREEK CAMPGROUND
NFD RD 3041
NFD RD 3069
KLAHOWA CAMPGROUND
Beaver
RD
PAVEL
SOLEDUCK SALMON HATCHERY
CLARK
RD
RIVER
101
WHEELER RD
SOLEDUCK
EAGLE POINT
2902
SOLEDUCK VALLEY
NFD RD 2929
EAGLE CREEK RANCH
RD
RD
FOREST
101
NFD RD 2938
RD
NFD RD 2933
BIGLER MOUNTAIN
NFD RD 29
NFD RD 2929
2903
SCHUTZ PASS
NFD
RD
NFD RD 2922
NFD RD 2923
NFD RD 2937
CALAWAH RIDGE
NFD
NFD RD 29
NFD RD 2978
SOL DUC VALLEY
SEE 108 MAP

PNW

METRO

SEE 101 MAP

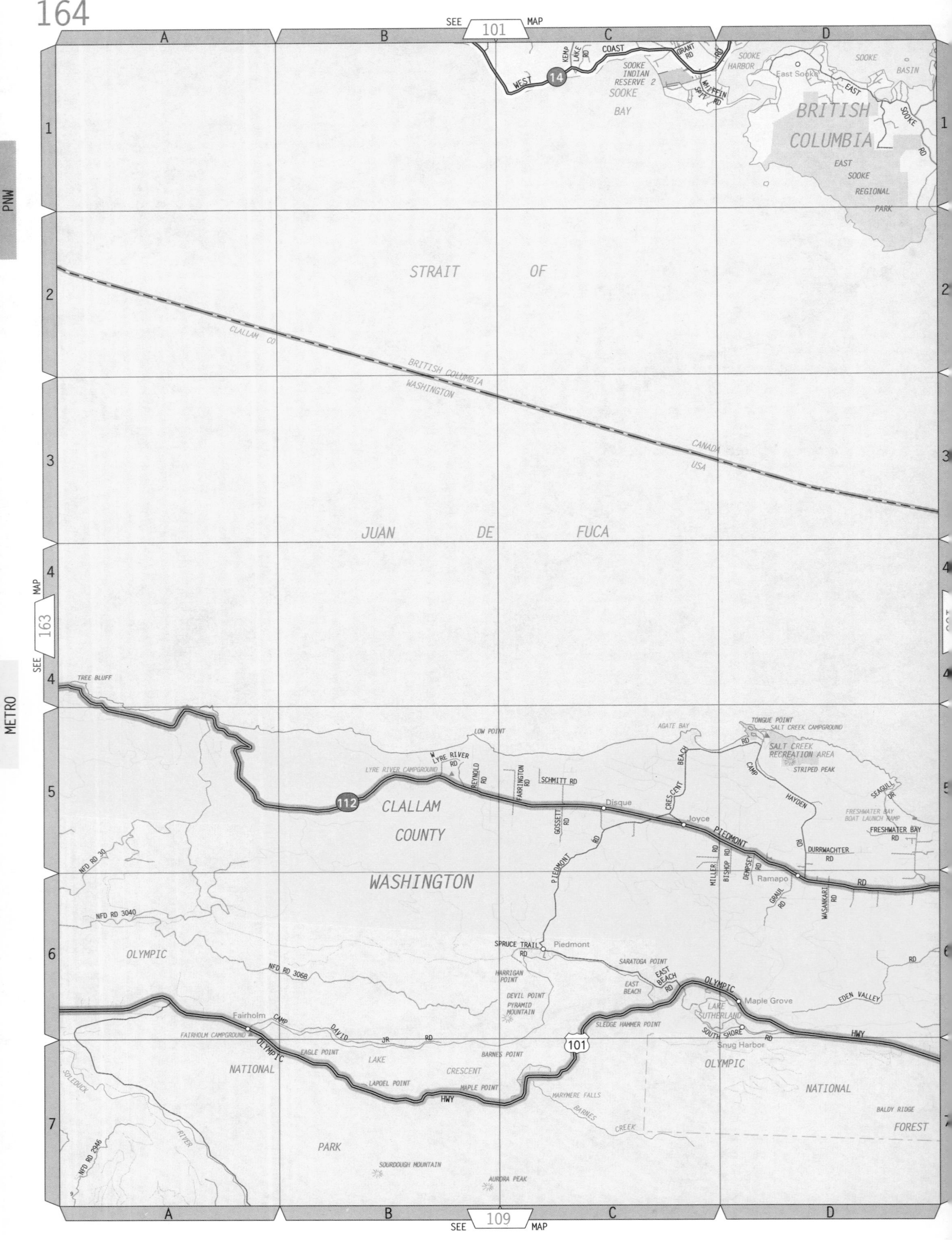

SEE 163 MAP

SEE 109 MAP

PNW

METRO

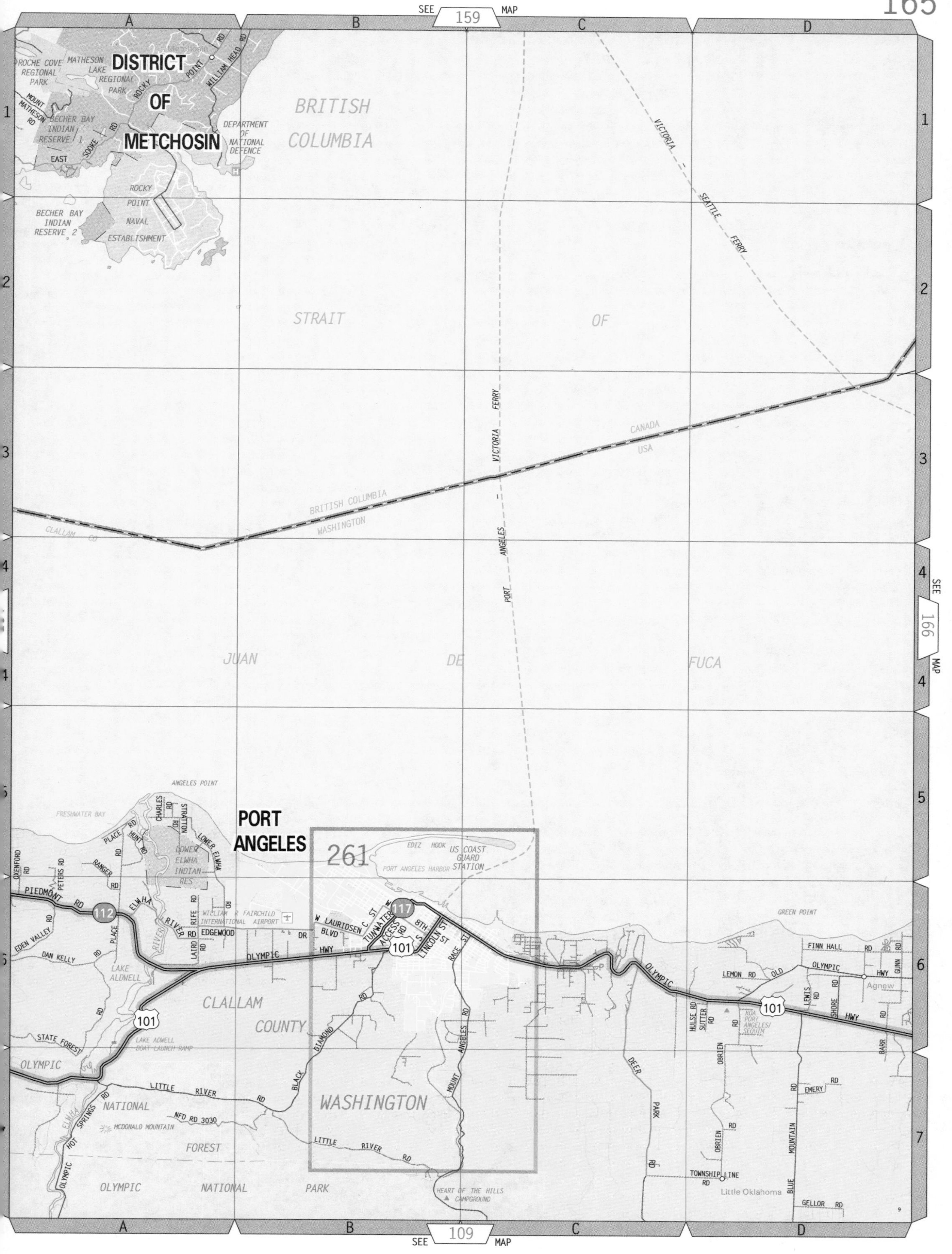

SEE 159 MAP
DISTRICT OF METCHOSIN
ROCHE COVE REGIONAL PARK
MATHESON LAKE REGIONAL PARK
BECHER BAY INDIAN RESERVE 1
DEPARTMENT OF NATIONAL DEFENCE
ROCKY POINT NAVAL ESTABLISHMENT
BECHER BAY INDIAN RESERVE 2
BRITISH COLUMBIA
VICTORIA - SEATTLE FERRY
STRAIT OF JUAN DE FUCA
VICTORIA FERRY - PORT ANGELES
CANADA USA
BRITISH COLUMBIA WASHINGTON
CLALLAM CO
SEE 166 MAP
PNW
METRO
ANGELES POINT
FRESHWATER BAY
PORT ANGELES
LOWER ELWHA INDIAN RES
261
EDIZ HOOK
US COAST GUARD STATION
PORT ANGELES HARBOR
WILLIAM R FAIRCHILD INTERNATIONAL AIRPORT
GREEN POINT
LAKE ALDWELL
CLALLAM COUNTY
LAKE ALDWELL BOAT LAUNCH RAMP
WASHINGTON
OLYMPIC NATIONAL FOREST
MCDONALD MOUNTAIN
OLYMPIC NATIONAL PARK
HEART OF THE HILLS CAMPGROUND
KOA PORT ANGELES/SEQUIM
Agnew
Little Oklahoma
SEE 109 MAP

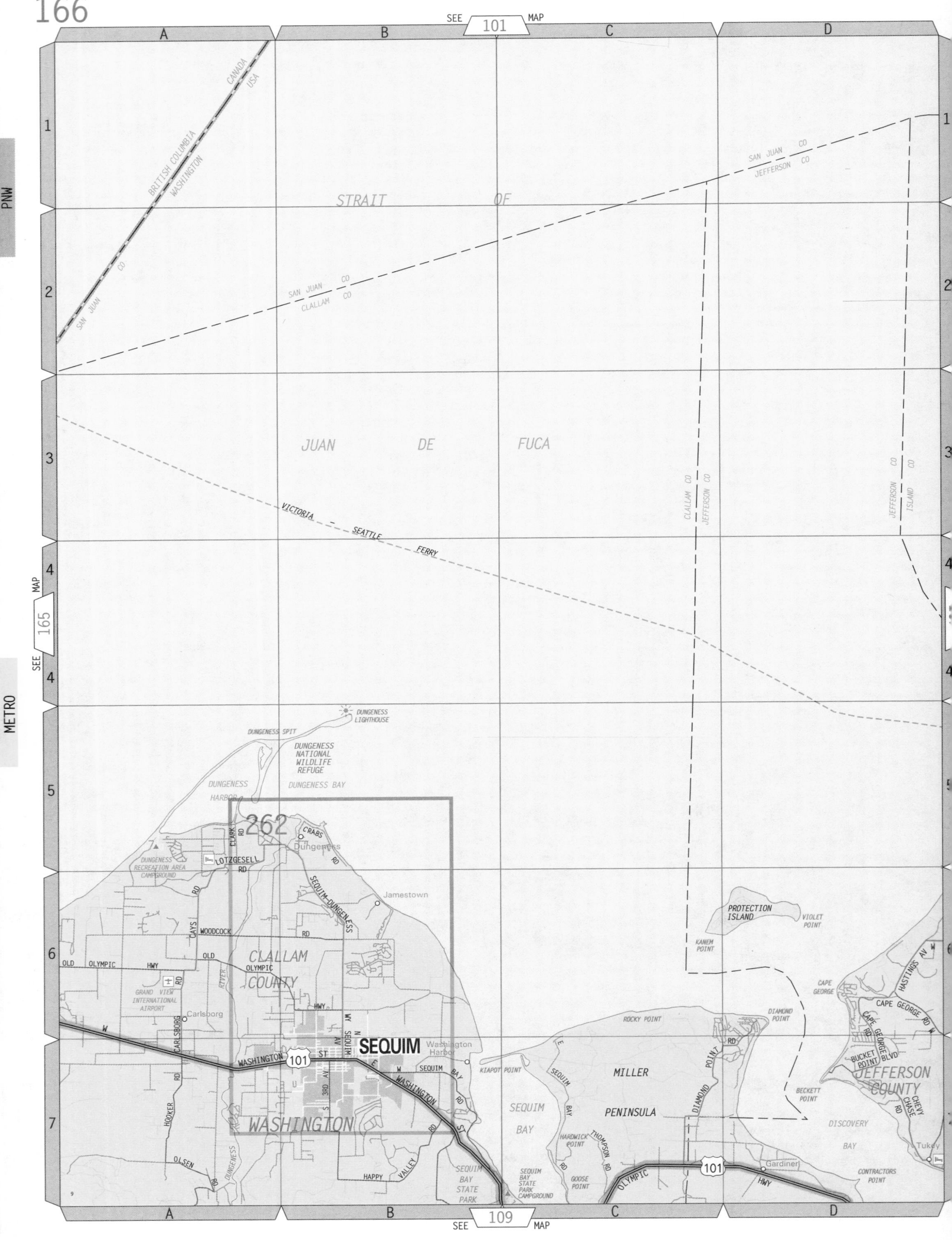
SEE MAP 101
SEE MAP 165
SEE MAP 109
PNW
METRO
A B C D
1 2 3 4 5 6 7
CANADA
USA
BRITISH COLUMBIA
WASHINGTON
SAN JUAN CO
CLALLAM CO
JEFFERSON CO
ISLAND CO
STRAIT OF JUAN DE FUCA
VICTORIA - SEATTLE FERRY
DUNGENESS LIGHTHOUSE
DUNGENESS SPIT
DUNGENESS NATIONAL WILDLIFE REFUGE
DUNGENESS BAY
DUNGENESS HARBOR
262
CRABS RD
Dungeness
CLARK RD
LOTZGESELL RD
DUNGENESS RECREATION AREA CAMPGROUND
SEQUIM-DUNGENESS
Jamestown
CAYS RD
WOODCOCK RD
CLALLAM COUNTY
OLD OLYMPIC HWY
GRAND VIEW INTERNATIONAL AIRPORT
RIVER
Carlsborg
CARLSBORG RD
SEQUIM
N SEQUIM AV
W WASHINGTON ST
101
E WASHINGTON ST
W SEQUIM BAY RD
Washington Harbor
S 3RD AV
WASHINGTON
HOOKER RD
OLSEN RD
DUNGENESS
HAPPY VALLEY RD
SEQUIM BAY STATE PARK
SEQUIM BAY STATE PARK CAMPGROUND
KIAPOT POINT
SEQUIM BAY
E SEQUIM BAY RD
HARDWICK POINT
THOMPSON RD
GOOSE POINT
ROCKY POINT
MILLER PENINSULA
DIAMOND POINT RD
DIAMOND POINT
OLYMPIC HWY
Gardiner
PROTECTION ISLAND
VIOLET POINT
KANEM POINT
CAPE GEORGE
HASTINGS AV W
CAPE GEORGE RD W
CAPE GEORGE BLVD
BUCKET POINT
BECKETT POINT
JEFFERSON COUNTY
CHEVY CHASE RD
DISCOVERY BAY
Tukey
CONTRACTORS POINT

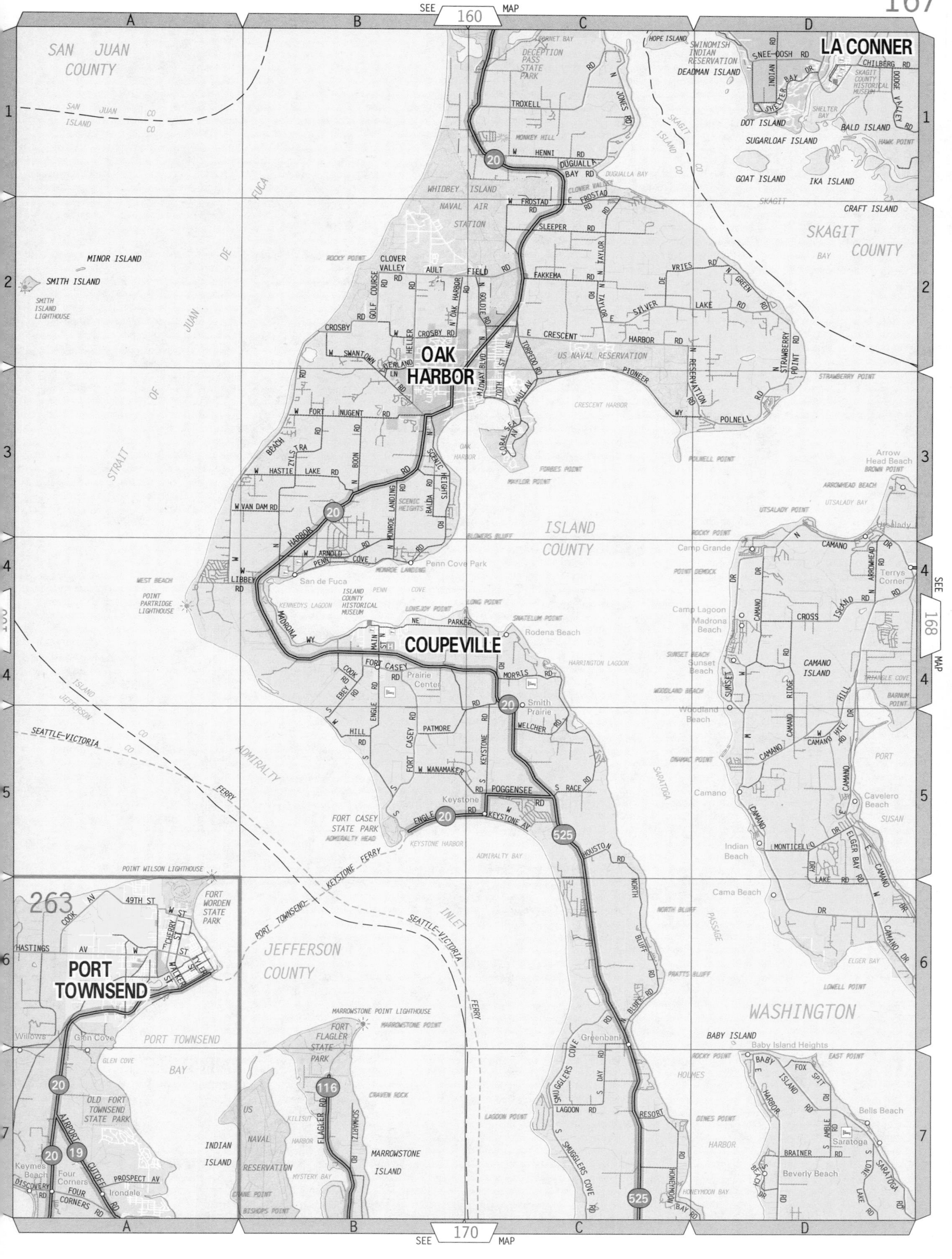
SEE 160 MAP
LA CONNER
OAK HARBOR
COUPEVILLE
PORT TOWNSEND
ISLAND COUNTY
JEFFERSON COUNTY
SKAGIT COUNTY
SAN JUAN COUNTY
WASHINGTON
CAMANO ISLAND
MARROWSTONE ISLAND
INDIAN ISLAND
WHIDBEY ISLAND NAVAL AIR STATION
STRAIT OF JUAN DE FUCA
ADMIRALTY INLET
SARATOGA PASSAGE
PORT SUSAN
263
SEE 168 MAP
SEE 170 MAP
PNW
METRO

SEE 161 MAP

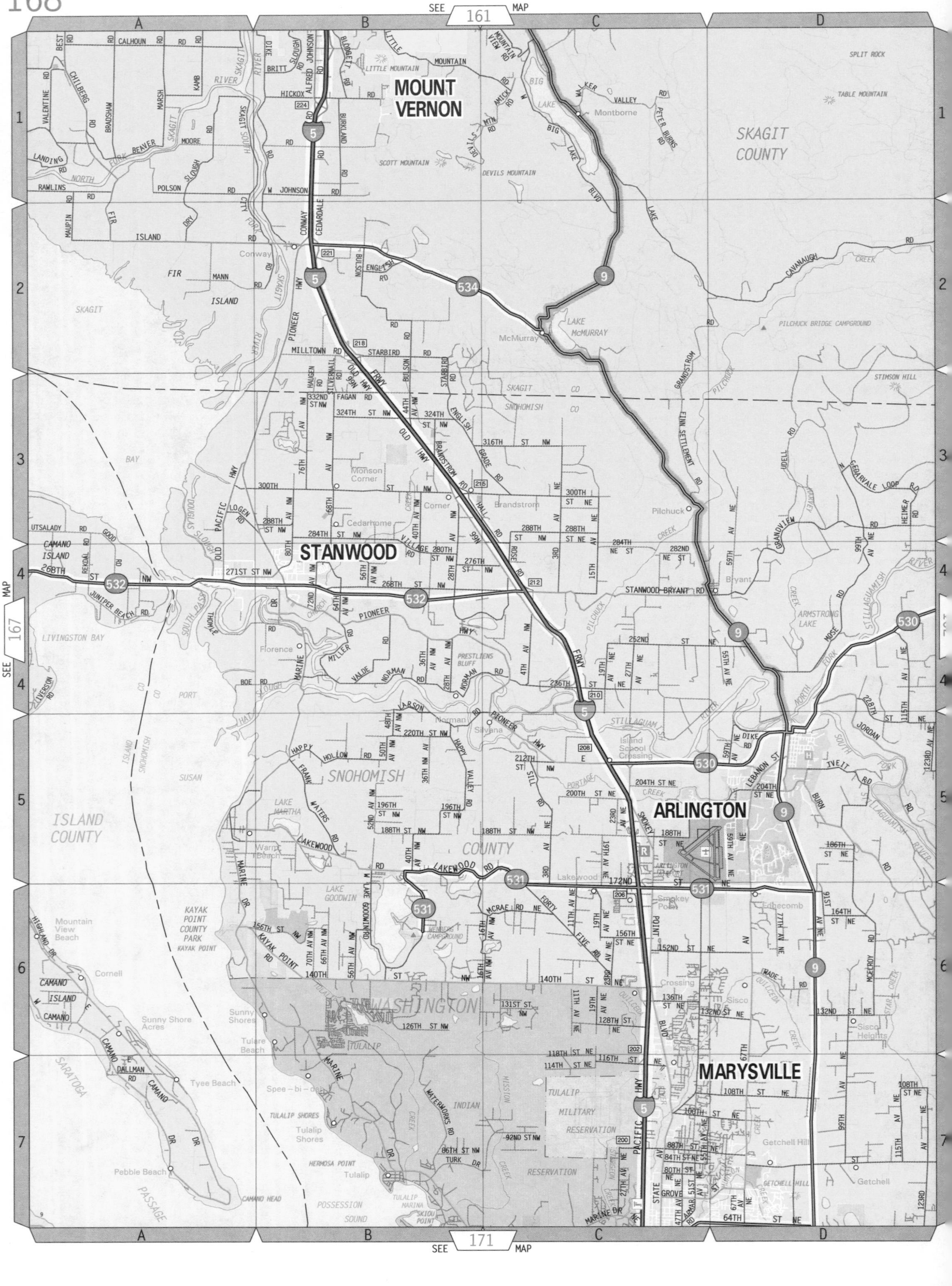

SEE 167 MAP

MOUNT VERNON

STANWOOD

ARLINGTON

MARYSVILLE

SKAGIT COUNTY

ISLAND COUNTY

SNOHOMISH COUNTY

Conway

McMurray

Montborne

Monson Corner

Cedarhome

Brandstrom

Pilchuck

Bryant

Florence

Norman

Silvana

Lake Martha

Warm Beach

Lakewood

Smokey Point

Edgecomb

Crossing

Sisco

Sisco Heights

Getchell Hill

Getchell

Mountain View Beach

Cornell

Sunny Shore Acres

Sunny Shores

Tulare Beach

Tyee Beach

Pebble Beach

Tulalip Shores

Tulalip

KAYAK POINT COUNTY PARK

TULALIP MILITARY RESERVATION

WASHINGTON

TULALIP

INDIAN RESERVATION

LITTLE MOUNTAIN

SCOTT MOUNTAIN

DEVILS MOUNTAIN

SPLIT ROCK

TABLE MOUNTAIN

STIMSON HILL

PILCHUCK BRIDGE CAMPGROUND

LAKE McMURRAY

BIG LAKE

ARMSTRONG LAKE

LAKE GOODWIN

SKAGIT BAY

PORT SUSAN

LIVINGSTON BAY

SARATOGA PASSAGE

POSSESSION SOUND

CAMANO HEAD

HERMOSA POINT

SKIOU POINT

TULALIP MARINA

CAMANO ISLAND

SEE 171 MAP

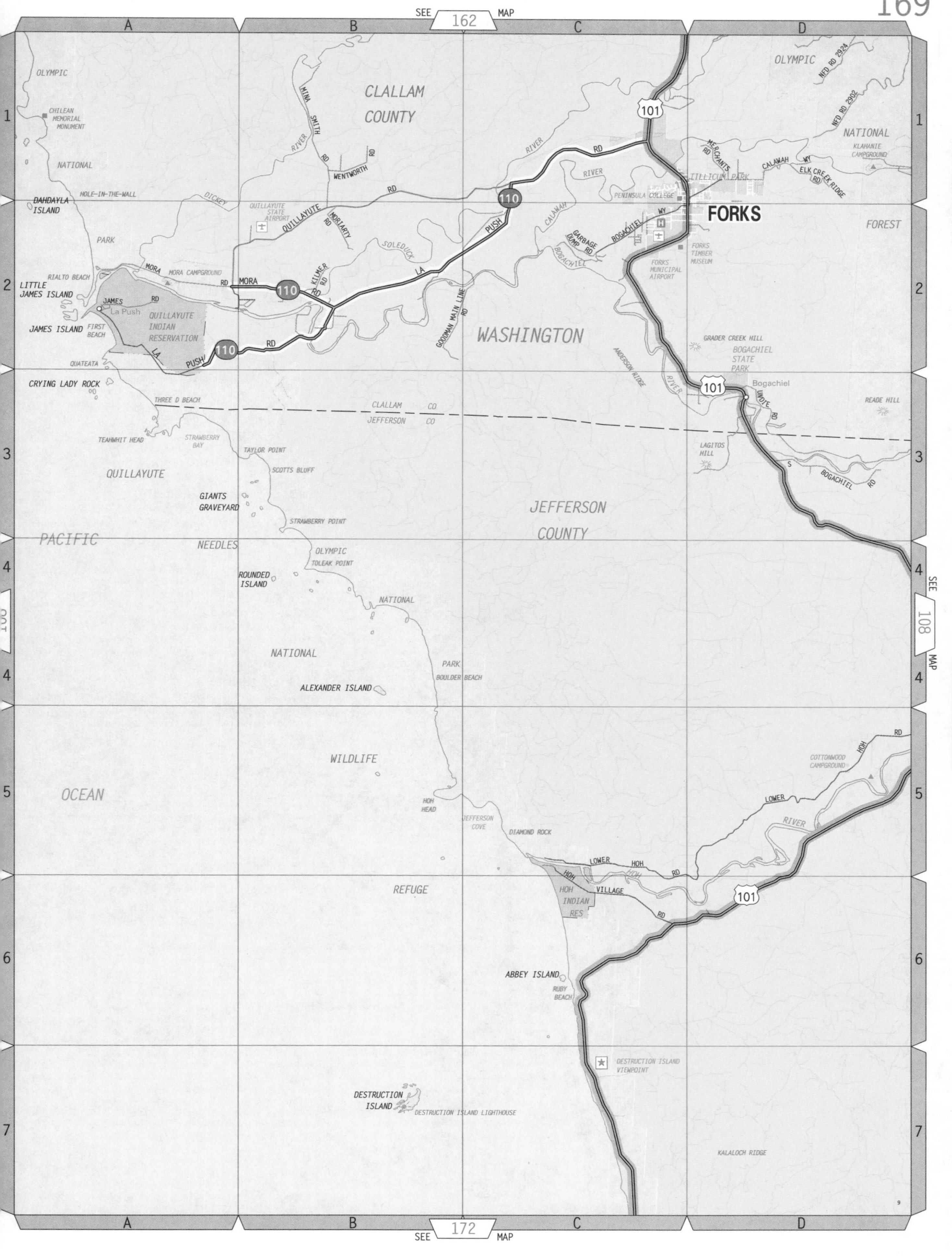
SEE 162 MAP
A
B
C
D
1
2
3
4
5
6
7
OLYMPIC
CHILEAN MEMORIAL MONUMENT
NATIONAL
DAHDAYLA ISLAND
HOLE-IN-THE-WALL
PARK
RIALTO BEACH
LITTLE JAMES ISLAND
JAMES ISLAND
FIRST BEACH
QUATEATA
CRYING LADY ROCK
THREE D BEACH
TEAHWHIT HEAD
STRAWBERRY BAY
QUILLAYUTE
GIANTS GRAVEYARD
PACIFIC
NEEDLES
ROUNDED ISLAND
NATIONAL
ALEXANDER ISLAND
WILDLIFE
OCEAN
REFUGE
DESTRUCTION ISLAND
DESTRUCTION ISLAND LIGHTHOUSE
CLALLAM COUNTY
MINA SMITH RD
WENTWORTH RD
QUILLAYUTE STATE AIRPORT
QUILLAYUTE RD
MORIARTY RD
MORA
MORA CAMPGROUND
MORA RD
JAMES RD
La Push
QUILLAYUTE INDIAN RESERVATION
LA PUSH RD
110
KILMER RD
SOLEDUCK
DICKEY
RIVER
CALAWAH
GOODMAN MAIN LINE RD
WASHINGTON
CLALLAM CO
JEFFERSON CO
TAYLOR POINT
SCOTTS BLUFF
STRAWBERRY POINT
OLYMPIC
TOLEAK POINT
NATIONAL
PARK
BOULDER BEACH
HOH HEAD
JEFFERSON COVE
DIAMOND ROCK
JEFFERSON COUNTY
101
PENINSULA COLLEGE
FORKS
BOGACHIEL WY
GARBAGE DUMP RD
FORKS TIMBER MUSEUM
FORKS MUNICIPAL AIRPORT
MERCHANTS RD
TILLICUM PARK
CALAWAH WY
ELK CREEK RD
ELK CREEK RIDGE
OLYMPIC
NFD RD 2924
NFD RD 2902
NATIONAL
KLAHANIE CAMPGROUND
FOREST
GRADER CREEK HILL
BOGACHIEL STATE PARK
Bogachiel
ANDERSON RIDGE
UNDI RD
READE HILL
LAGITOS HILL
S BOGACHIEL RD
HOH RD
COTTONWOOD CAMPGROUND
LOWER
RIVER
LOWER HOH RD
HOH
HOH INDIAN RES
HOH VILLAGE RD
ABBEY ISLAND
RUBY BEACH
DESTRUCTION ISLAND VIEWPOINT
KALALOCH RIDGE
SEE 108 MAP
PNW
METRO
SEE 172 MAP

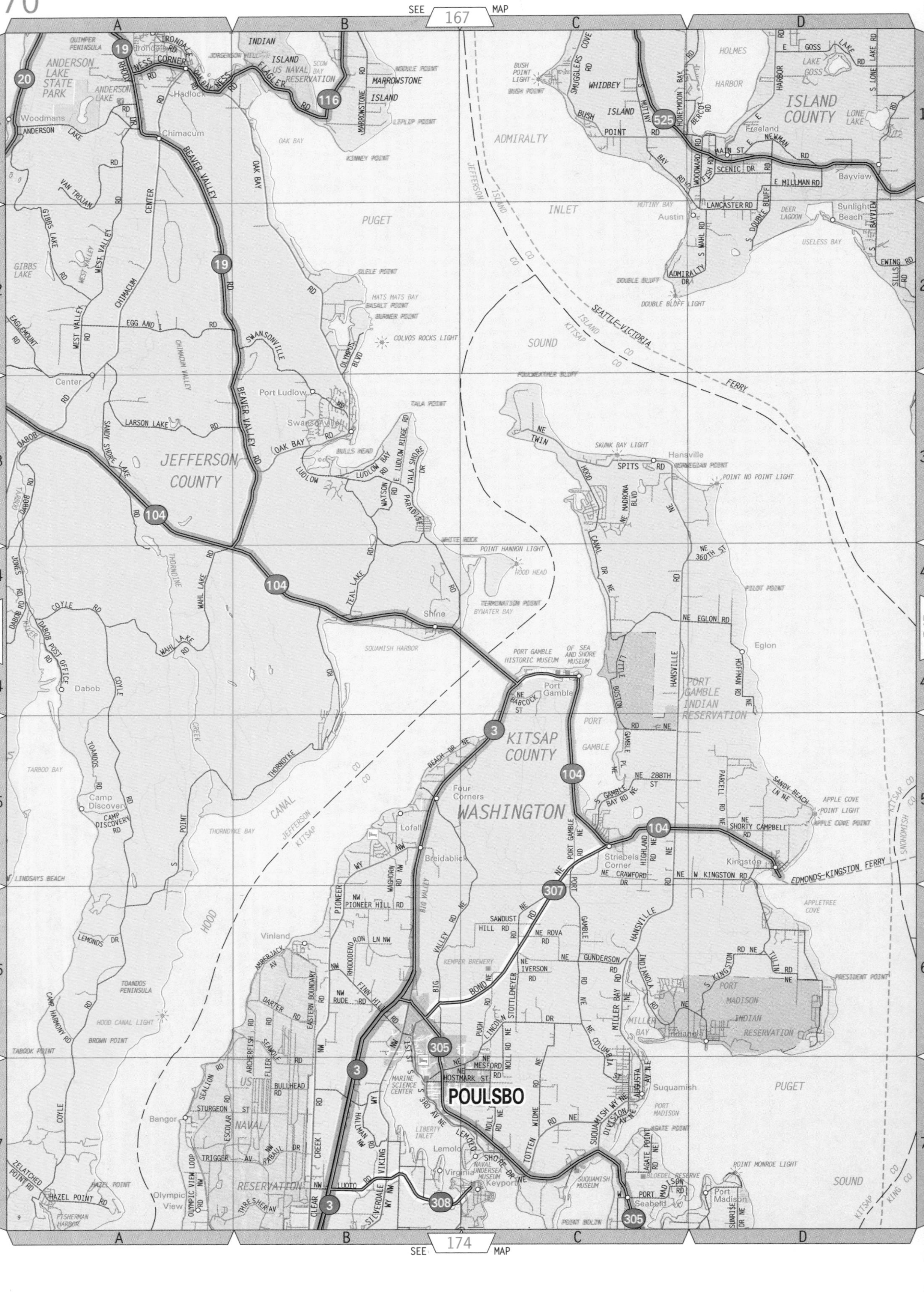
SEE 167 MAP
SEE 174 MAP
SEE 109 MAP
A
B
C
D
1
2
3
4
5
6
7
ANDERSON LAKE STATE PARK
QUIMPER PENINSULA
Irondale
Hadlock
NESS CORNER
INDIAN ISLAND US NAVAL RESERVATION
MARROWSTONE ISLAND
SCOW BAY
NODULE POINT
LIPLIP POINT
OAK BAY
KINNEY POINT
Woodmans
ANDERSON LAKE
Chimacum
BEAVER VALLEY
VAN TROJAN
CENTER
GIBBS LAKE
WEST VALLEY
CHIMACUM
EAGLEMOUNT
EGG AND I RD
SWANSONVILLE
PUGET
OLELE POINT
MATS MATS BAY
BASALT POINT
BURNER POINT
COLVOS ROCKS LIGHT
OLYMPUS BLVD
CHIMACUM VALLEY
Center
Port Ludlow
Swansonville
LARSON LAKE RD
SANDY SHORE LAKE
TALA POINT
BULLS HEAD
LUDLOW BAY
LUDLOW RIDGE
TALA SHORE
PARADISE
WATSON
JEFFERSON COUNTY
DABOB
TARBOO
WHITE ROCK
POINT HANNON LIGHT
HOOD HEAD
THORNDIKE
WAHL LAKE
TEAL LAKE
JONES
COYLE RD
TERMINATION POINT
BYWATER BAY
Shine
SQUAMISH HARBOR
DABOB POST OFFICE
Dabob
TOANDOS
CREEK
THORNDYKE
TARBOO BAY
Camp Discovery
CAMP DISCOVERY RD
THORNDYKE BAY
LINDSAYS BEACH
LEMONDS DR
TOANDOS PENINSULA
HOOD CANAL LIGHT
CAMP HARMONY
BROWN POINT
TABOOK POINT
HOOD CANAL
JEFFERSON CO
KITSAP CO
HAZEL POINT RD
ZELATCHED POINT RD
FISHERMAN HARBOR
Bangor
SEALION
STURGEON
ESCOLAR
TRIGGER AV
ARCHERFISH
FLIER
BULLHEAD
US NAVAL RESERVATION
THRESHER AV
Olympic View
OLYMPIC VIEW LOOP
PABAUL
SEAWOLF
DARTER
AMBERJACK AV
Vinland
EASTERN BOUNDARY
RHODODENDRON LN NW
FINN HILL
NW RUDE
PIONEER HILL RD
PIONEER WY
WAGHORN
Lofall
Breidablick
BIG VALLEY RD NE
Four Corners
WASHINGTON
BEACH DR NE
KITSAP COUNTY
PORT GAMBLE
GAMBLE BAY
BABCOCK ST
Port Gamble
PORT GAMBLE HISTORIC MUSEUM
OF SEA AND SHORE MUSEUM
SAWDUST HILL RD
NE ROVA RD
IVERSON RD
KEMPER BREWERY
BOND NE
STOTTLEMEYER
LINCOLN
PUGH
NOLL RD
POULSBO
MESFORD
HOSTMARK ST
MARINE SCIENCE CENTER
3RD AV NE
1ST ST
LIBERTY INLET
HALLMAN
VIKING
CLEAR CREEK
SILVERDALE WY NW
LUOTO
Lemolo
LEMOLO SHORE DR NE
Virginia
Keyport
NAVAL UNDERSEA MUSEUM
TOTTEN
WIDME
SUQUAMISH WY NE
SUQUAMISH MUSEUM
POINT BOLIN
DIVISION AV NE
AUGUSTA AV NE
Suquamish
PORT MADISON
AGATE POINT
AGATE PASS
BLOEDEL RESERVE
PORT MADISON
Seabold
Port Madison
SUNRISE DR NE
POINT MONROE LIGHT
GUNDERSON
MILLER BAY RD
MILLER BAY
Indianola
INDIANOLA
COLUMBIA
S KINGSTON RD NE
PORT MADISON INDIAN RESERVATION
PRESIDENT POINT
TULIN
APPLETREE COVE
HANSVILLE
W KINGSTON RD
NE CRAWFORD
Striebels Corner
HIGHLAND
Kingston
EDMONDS-KINGSTON FERRY
SHORTY CAMPBELL
APPLE COVE POINT LIGHT
APPLE COVE POINT
SANDY BEACH LN NE
PARCELL RD NE
KITSAP CO
SNOHOMISH CO
KING CO
PUGET SOUND
NE 288TH ST
GAMBLE BAY RD NE
LITTLE BOSTON
PORT GAMBLE INDIAN RESERVATION
HOFFMAN RD
Eglon
NE EGLON RD
PILOT POINT
NE 360TH ST
NE MADRONA BLVD
HOOD CANAL DR NE
TWIN SPITS RD
SKUNK BAY LIGHT
Hansville
NORWEGIAN POINT
POINT NO POINT LIGHT
FOULWEATHER BLUFF
ADMIRALTY INLET
JEFFERSON CO
ISLAND CO
KITSAP CO
SOUND
SEATTLE-VICTORIA FERRY
BUSH POINT LIGHT
BUSH POINT
SMUGGLERS COVE
WHIDBEY ISLAND
BUSH POINT RD
MUTINY BAY RD
MUTINY BAY
HONEYMOON BAY
BERCOT RD
HOLMES HARBOR
GOSS LAKE
LAKE GOSS
S LONE LAKE RD
LONE LAKE
ISLAND COUNTY
Freeland
NEWMAN RD
MAIN ST
SCENIC DR
FISH RD
WOODWARD
E MILLMAN RD
Bayview
LANCASTER RD
Austin
S WAHL RD
S DOUBLE BLUFF
DEER LAGOON
Sunlight Beach
BAYVIEW
USELESS BAY
ADMIRALTY DR
DOUBLE BLUFF
DOUBLE BLUFF LIGHT
EWING RD
SILLS RD
19
20
116
525
104
3
307
305
308

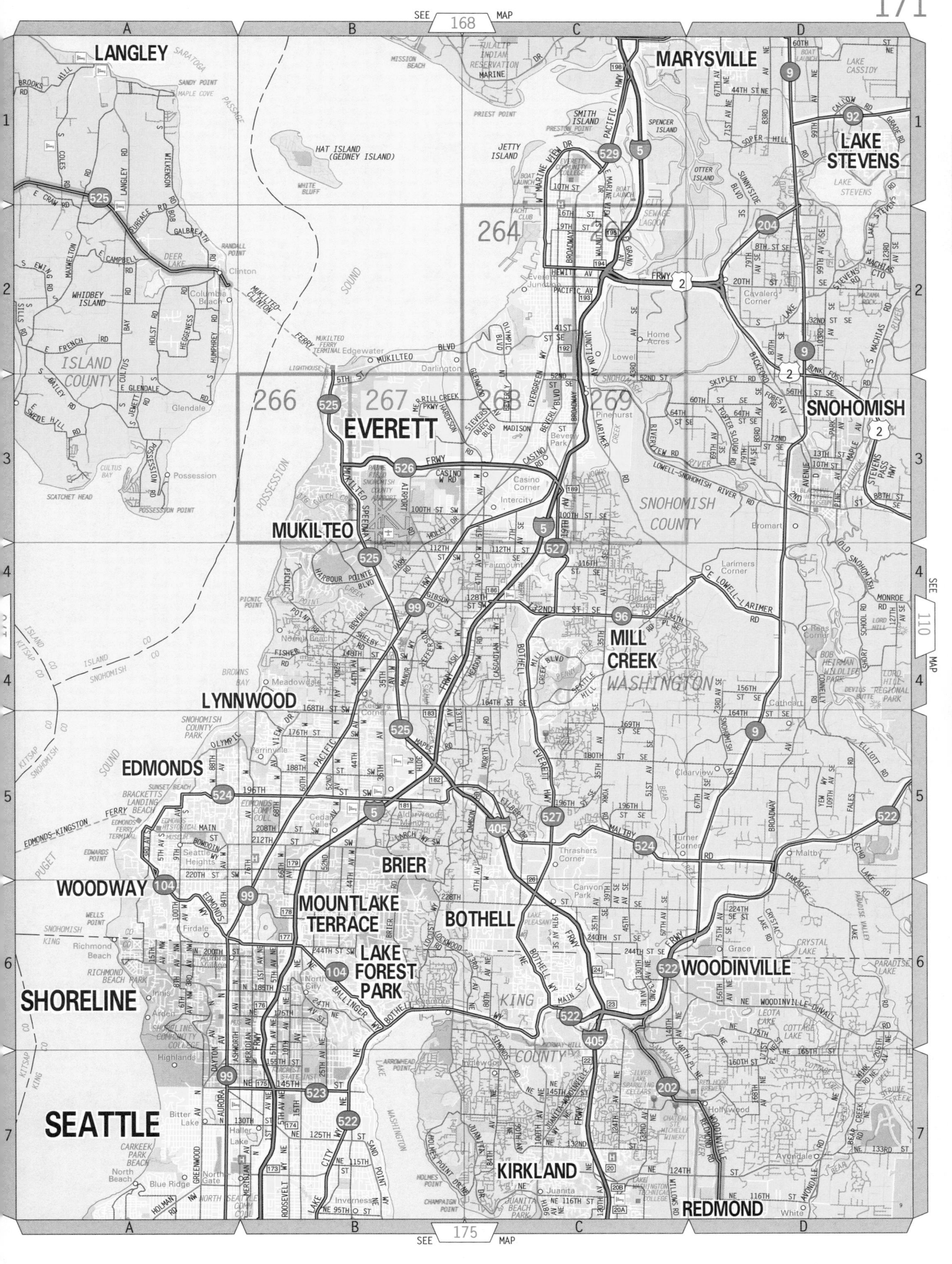
SEE 168 MAP
SEE 175 MAP
SEE 110 MAP
LANGLEY
MARYSVILLE
LAKE STEVENS
EVERETT
SNOHOMISH
MUKILTEO
MILL CREEK
LYNNWOOD
EDMONDS
WOODWAY
BRIER
MOUNTLAKE TERRACE
BOTHELL
LAKE FOREST PARK
WOODINVILLE
SHORELINE
SEATTLE
KIRKLAND
REDMOND
WHIDBEY ISLAND
ISLAND COUNTY
SNOHOMISH COUNTY
KING COUNTY
HAT ISLAND (GEDNEY ISLAND)
JETTY ISLAND
SMITH ISLAND
SPENCER ISLAND
TULALIP INDIAN RESERVATION
POSSESSION SOUND
PUGET SOUND
LAKE WASHINGTON
264
265
266
267
268
269
PNW
METRO

SEE 169 MAP

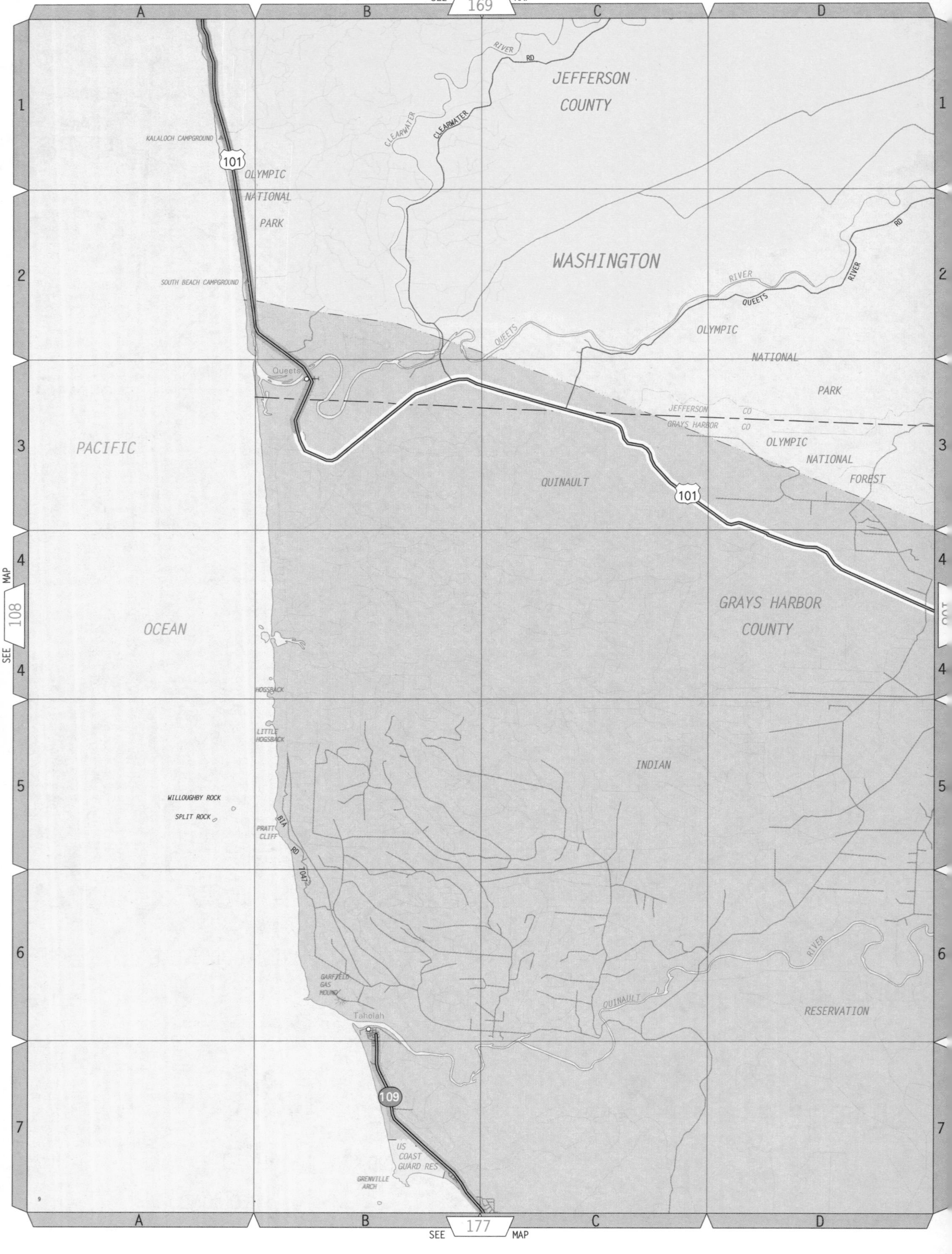

A B C D

1 2 3 4 5 6 7

JEFFERSON COUNTY

WASHINGTON

KALALOCH CAMPGROUND

101

OLYMPIC NATIONAL PARK

CLEARWATER

CLEARWATER RIVER RD

SOUTH BEACH CAMPGROUND

QUEETS RIVER RD

QUEETS

OLYMPIC NATIONAL PARK

Queets

JEFFERSON CO

GRAYS HARBOR CO

PACIFIC

OCEAN

OLYMPIC NATIONAL FOREST

QUINAULT

101

GRAYS HARBOR COUNTY

SEE 108 MAP

HOGSBACK

LITTLE HOGSBACK

INDIAN

WILLOUGHBY ROCK

SPLIT ROCK

BIA RD 7047

PRATT CLIFF

RIVER

GARFIELD GAS MOUND

QUINAULT

Taholah

RESERVATION

109

US COAST GUARD RES

GRENVILLE ARCH

SEE 177 MAP

PNW

METRO

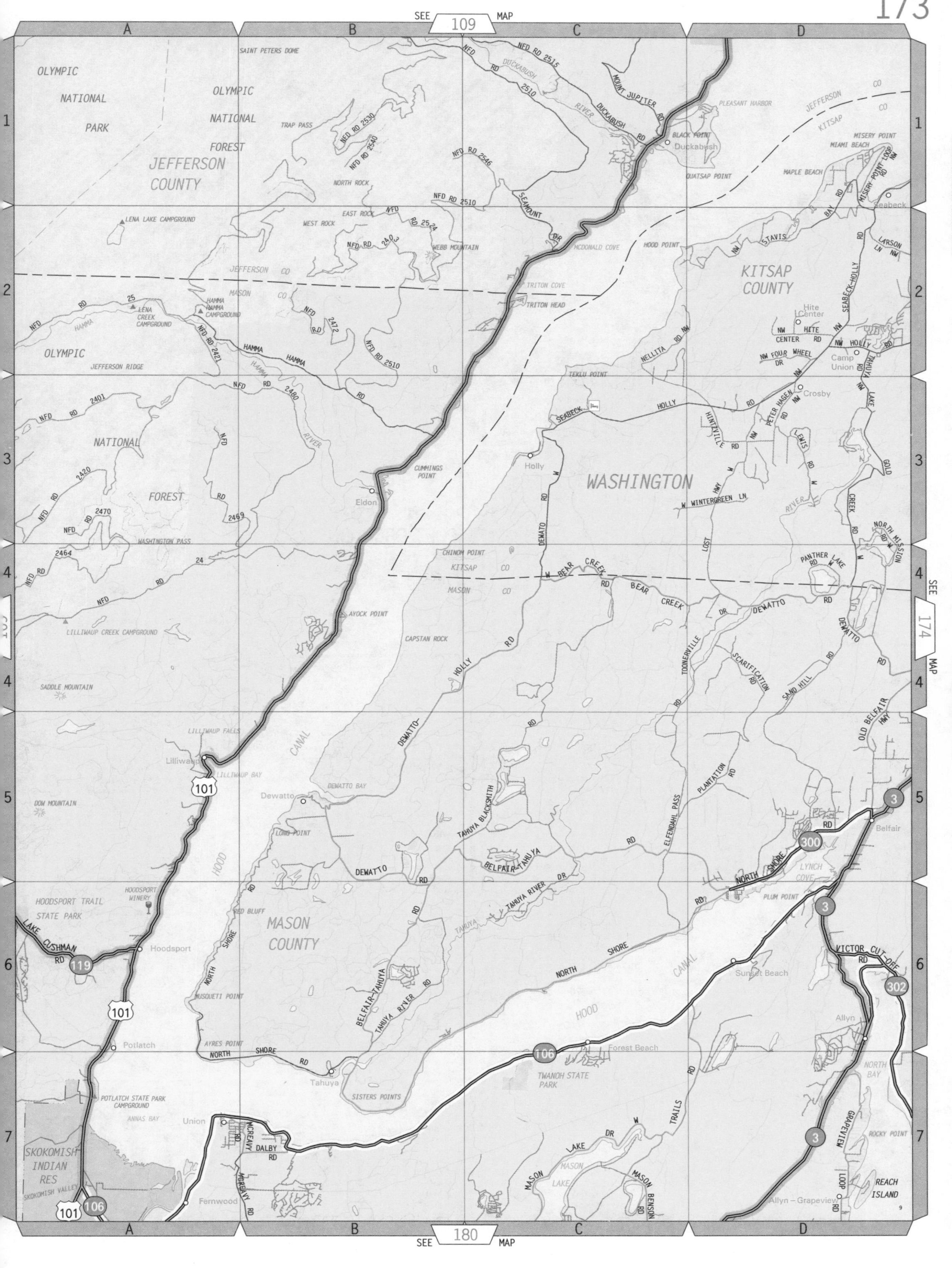
SEE 109 MAP
SEE 180 MAP
SEE 174 MAP
PNW
METRO
JEFFERSON COUNTY
KITSAP COUNTY
MASON COUNTY
WASHINGTON
OLYMPIC NATIONAL PARK
OLYMPIC NATIONAL FOREST
HOOD CANAL
Hoodsport
Lilliwaup
Eldon
Holly
Dewatto
Tahuya
Union
Belfair
Allyn
Seabeck
Brinnon
Duckabush
Potlatch
SKOKOMISH INDIAN RES

SEE 170 MAP

SEE 173 MAP

SEE 181 MAP

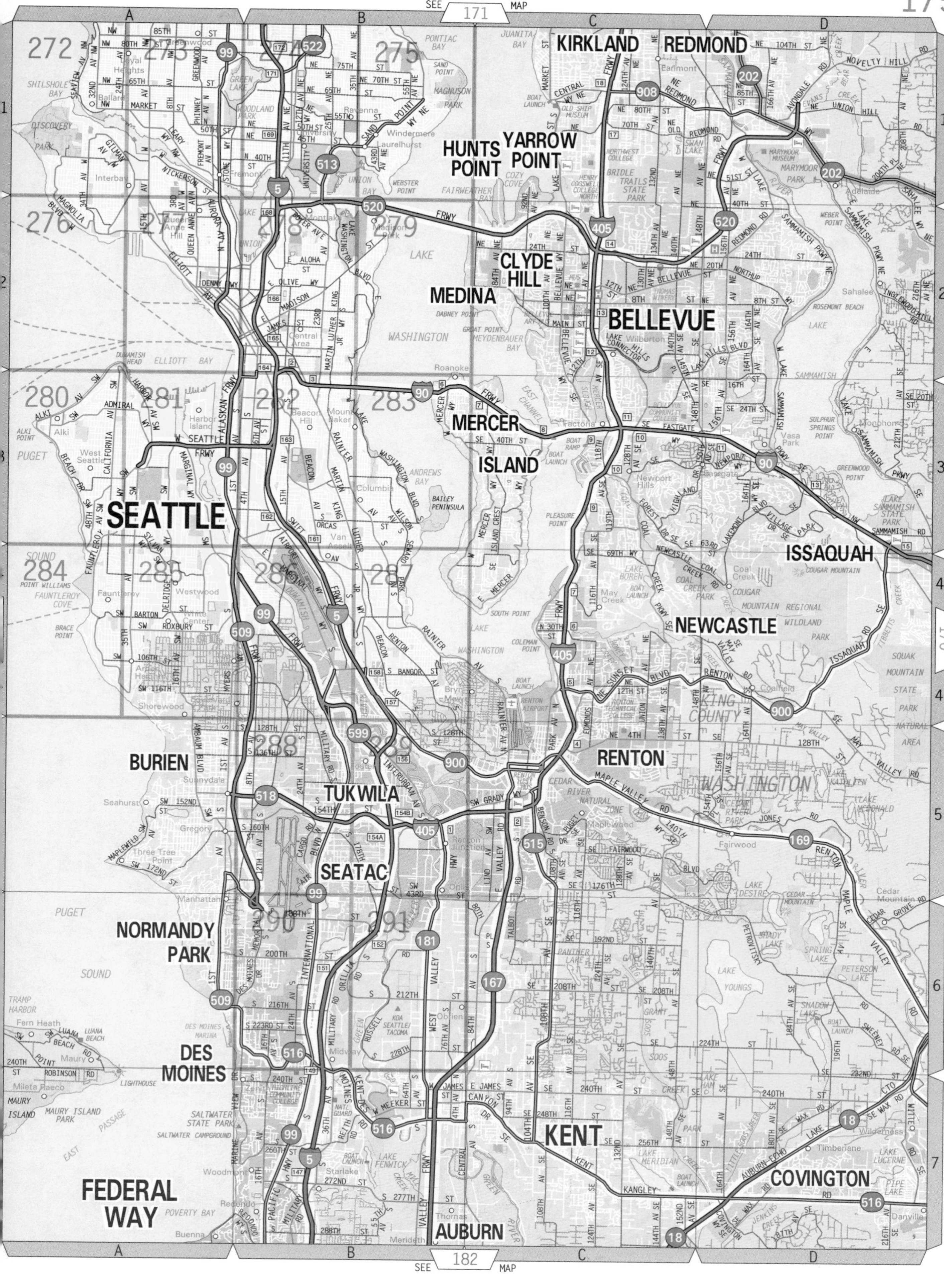

SEE 171 MAP

KIRKLAND
REDMOND
HUNTS POINT
YARROW POINT
CLYDE HILL
MEDINA
BELLEVUE
MERCER ISLAND
SEATTLE
ISSAQUAH
NEWCASTLE
RENTON
BURIEN
TUKWILA
SEATAC
NORMANDY PARK
DES MOINES
KENT
COVINGTON
FEDERAL WAY
AUBURN

SEE 176 MAP

SEE 182 MAP

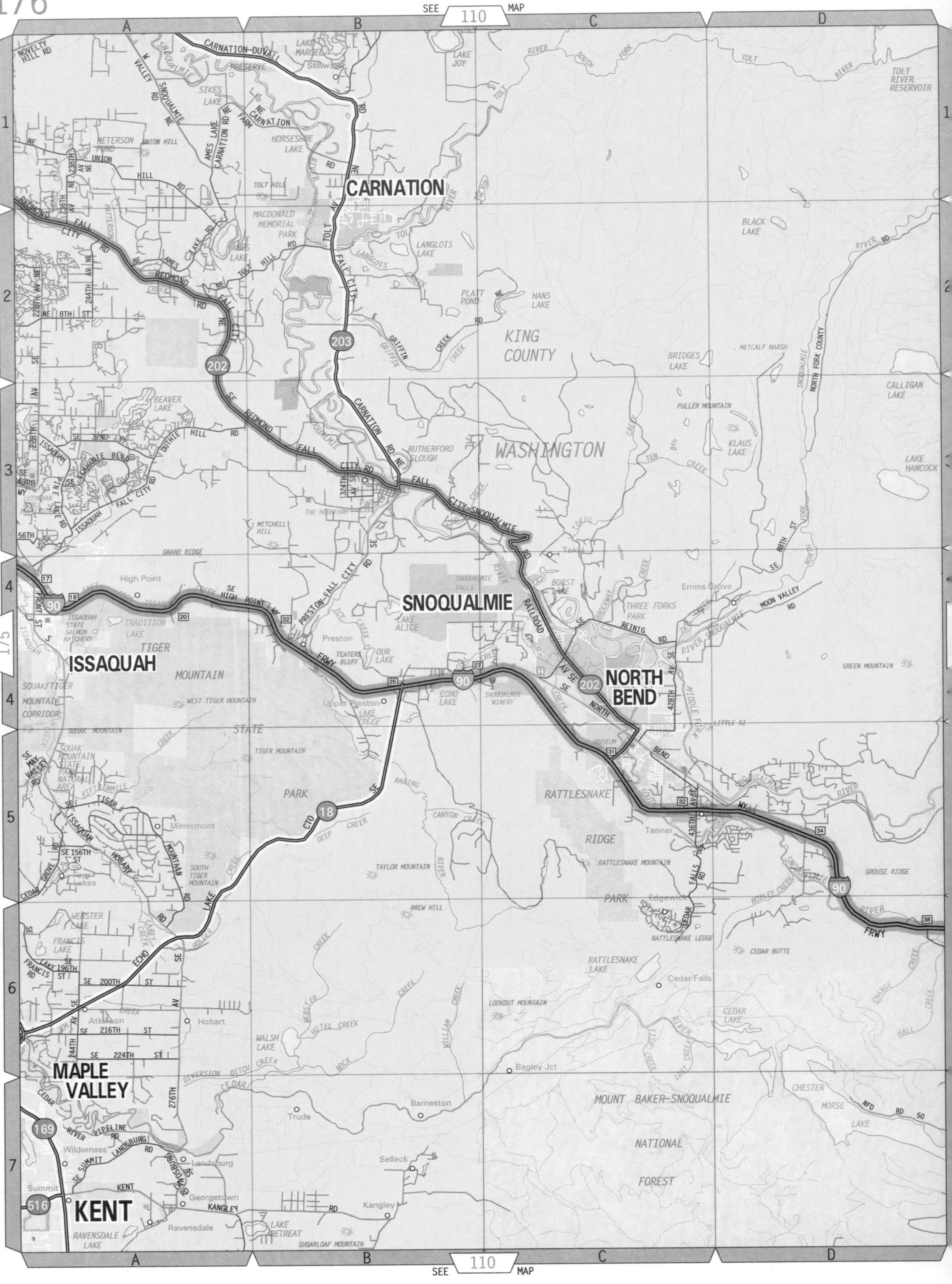

SEE 110 MAP

SEE 175 MAP

PNW

METRO

A B C D

1 2 3 4 5 6 7

CARNATION

SNOQUALMIE

NORTH BEND

ISSAQUAH

MAPLE VALLEY

KENT

KING COUNTY

WASHINGTON

TIGER MOUNTAIN STATE PARK

RATTLESNAKE RIDGE PARK

MOUNT BAKER-SNOQUALMIE NATIONAL FOREST

Stillwater
Tolt Hill
MacDonald Memorial Park
Fall City
Mitchell Hill
Grand Ridge
High Point
Preston
Upper Preston
Lake Alice
Our Lake
Echo Lake
Snoqualmie Falls
Snoqualmie Winery
Tokul
Borst Lake
Three Forks Park
Ernies Grove
Issaquah State Salmon Hatchery
Tradition Lake
West Tiger Mountain
Squak Mountain
Squak Mountain State Park Natural Area
Squak/Tiger Mountain Corridor
Tiger Mountain
South Tiger Mountain
Mirrormont
Taylor Mountain
Brew Hill
Rattlesnake Mountain
Rattlesnake Ledge
Rattlesnake Lake
Cedar Falls
Cedar Lake
Cedar Butte
Edgewick
Tanner
Grouse Ridge
Green Mountain
Little Si
Museum
Lookout Mountain
Bagley Jct
Barneston
Trude
Selleck
Kangley
Walsh Lake
Webster Lake
Francis Lake
Hobart
Atkinson
Wilderness
Summit
Landsburg
Georgetown
Ravensdale
Ravensdale Lake
Lake Retreat
Sugarloaf Mountain
Lake Margaret
Lake Joy
Sikes Lake
Horseshoe Lake
Peterson Pond
Union Hill
Ames Lake
Langlois Lake
Platt Pond
Hans Lake
Beaver Lake
Rutherford Slough
The Herbfarm
Black Lake
Bridges Lake
Metcalf Marsh
Fuller Mountain
Klaus Lake
Calligan Lake
Lake Hancock
Tolt River Reservoir
Chester Morse Lake
Pine Lake
Lutheran Bible Institute

Carnation-Duvall Rd
Redmond-Fall City Rd
Fall City-Snoqualmie Rd
Preston-Fall City Rd
Issaquah-Fall City Rd
Issaquah-Hobart Rd
Maple Valley-Black Diamond Rd
Cedar Falls Rd
SE North Bend Wy
SE Moon Valley Rd
Snoqualmie Valley Rd
Kent-Kangley Rd
Landsburg Rd
SE Summit Landsburg Rd
Cedar River Pipeline Rd
Tolt Hill Rd
Duthie Hill Rd
Union Hill Rd
Ames Lake Carnation Rd NE
SE 200th St
SE 216th St
SE 224th St
SE 156th St
276th Av SE
428th Av SE
436th Av SE
SE 88th St
NFD Rd 50
Snoqualmie River
Tolt River
Middle Fork Snoqualmie River
Cedar River
Raging River

202 203 18 90 169 516

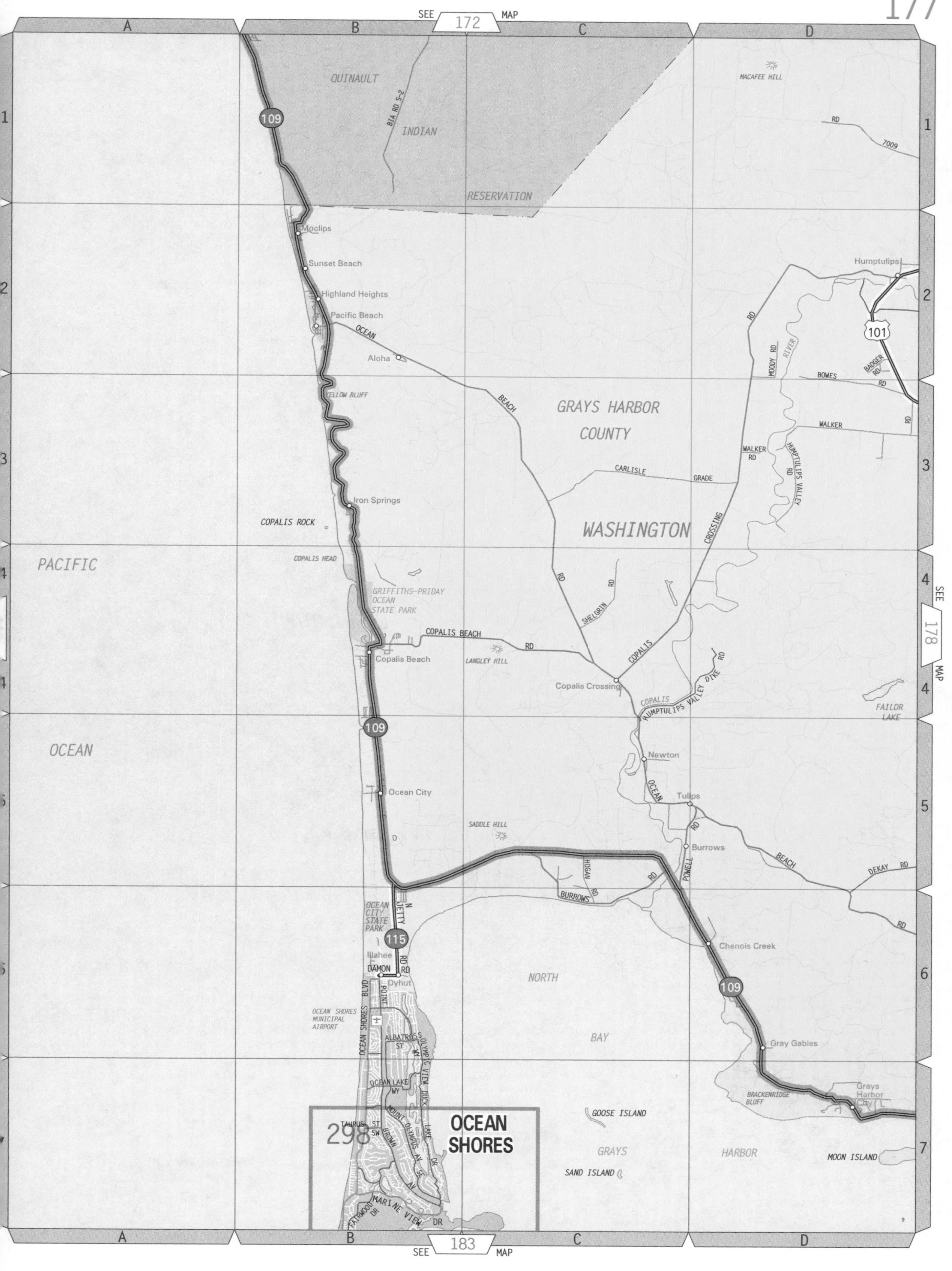
SEE 172 MAP
QUINAULT
INDIAN
RESERVATION
BIA RD S-2
MACAFEE HILL
RD
7009
Moclips
Sunset Beach
Highland Heights
Pacific Beach
OCEAN
Aloha
BEACH
YELLOW BLUFF
GRAYS HARBOR
COUNTY
Humptulips
101
MOODY RD
RIVER
BADGER RD
BOWES RD
WALKER
WALKER RD
HUMPTULIPS VALLEY RD
CARLISLE GRADE
CROSSING
Iron Springs
COPALIS ROCK
WASHINGTON
PACIFIC
COPALIS HEAD
GRIFFITHS-PRIDAY
OCEAN
STATE PARK
COPALIS BEACH RD
SHELGRIN RD
COPALIS
Copalis Beach
LANGLEY HILL
Copalis Crossing
HUMPTULIPS VALLEY DIKE RD
SEE 178 MAP
FAILOR LAKE
109
OCEAN
Newton
OCEAN
Tulips
Ocean City
SADDLE HILL
Burrows
POWELL RD
BEACH
DEKAY RD
HOGAN RD
BURROWS RD
RD
OCEAN CITY STATE PARK
N JETTY RD
115
Illahee
DAMON RD
Dyhut
Chenois Creek
NORTH
BAY
OCEAN SHORES BLVD
POINT
OCEAN SHORES MUNICIPAL AIRPORT
ALBATROSS ST
OLYMPIC VIEW WY
Gray Gables
OCEAN LAKE WY
DUCK LAKE DR
BRACKENRIDGE BLUFF
Grays Harbor City
TAURUS ST SW
MOUNT OLYMPUS AV SE
BROWN AV
298
OCEAN SHORES
GOOSE ISLAND
GRAYS
HARBOR
MOON ISLAND
SAND ISLAND
MARINE VIEW DR
FAIRWOOD DR
SEE 183 MAP
PNW
METRO

SEE 109 MAP

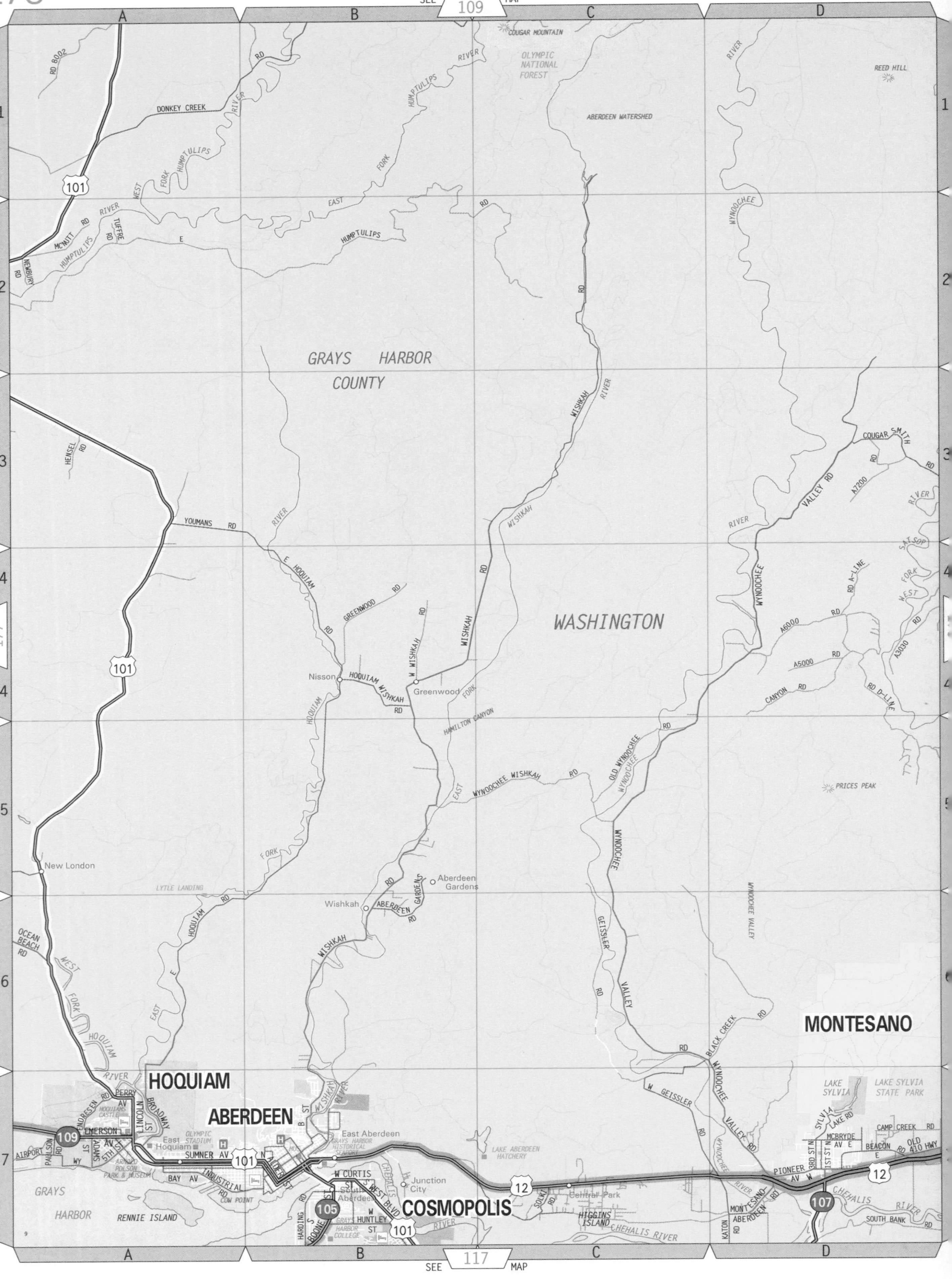

SEE 177 MAP

SEE 117 MAP

PNW

METRO

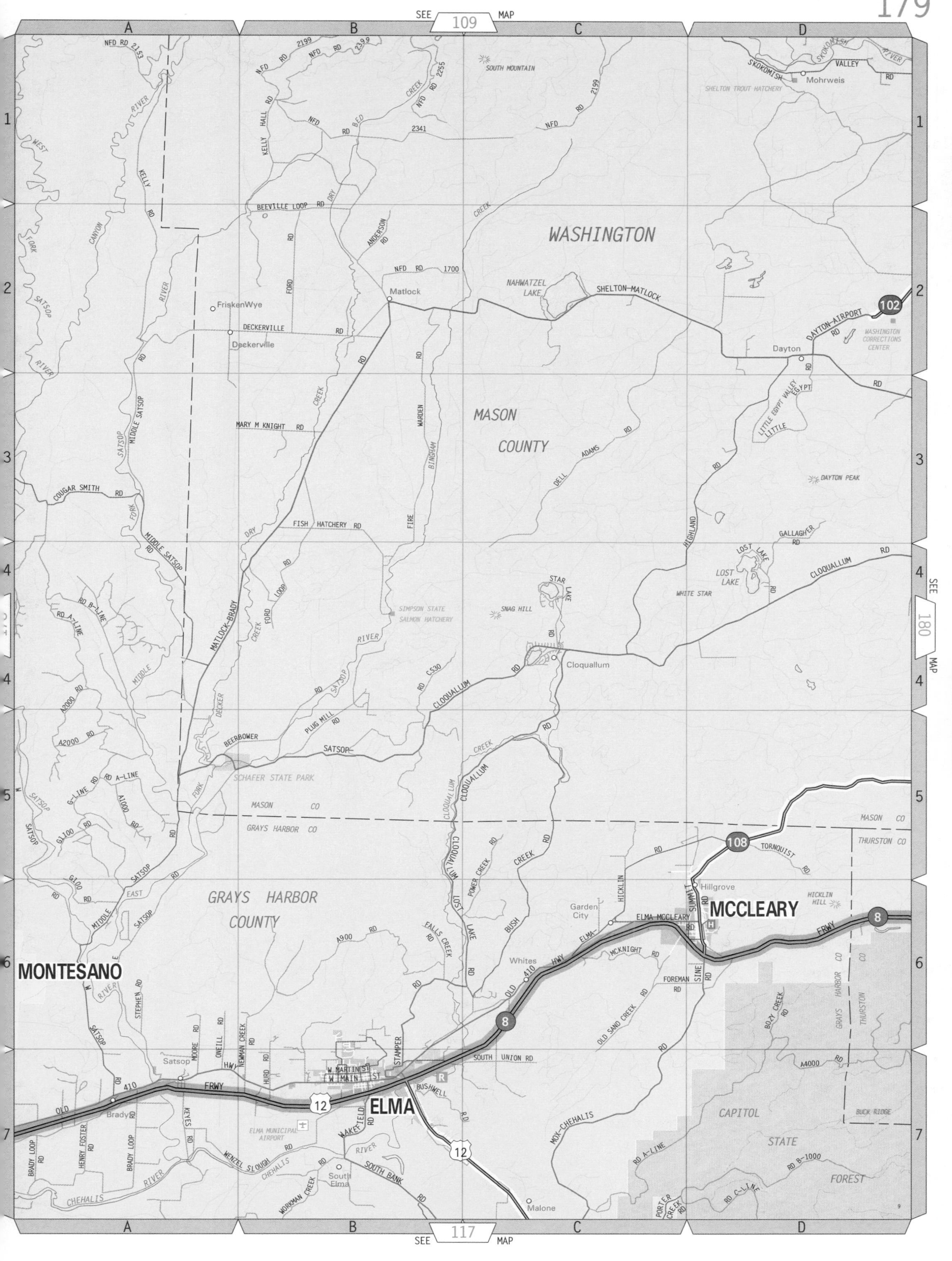
SEE 109 MAP
WASHINGTON
MASON COUNTY
GRAYS HARBOR COUNTY
MONTESANO
ELMA
MCCLEARY
Matlock
FriskenWye
Deckerville
Dayton
Mohrweis
Cloquallum
Hillgrove
Garden City
Whites
Satsop
Brady
South Elma
Malone
SOUTH MOUNTAIN
SHELTON TROUT HATCHERY
NAHWATZEL LAKE
WASHINGTON CORRECTIONS CENTER
DAYTON PEAK
LOST LAKE
STAR LAKE
SNAG HILL
SIMPSON STATE SALMON HATCHERY
WHITE STAR
SCHAFER STATE PARK
HICKLIN HILL
ELMA MUNICIPAL AIRPORT
CAPITOL STATE FOREST
BUCK RIDGE
SHELTON-MATLOCK
DAYTON-AIRPORT RD
CLOQUALLUM RD
MATLOCK-BRADY
ELMA-MCCLEARY RD
OLD 410 HWY
410 FRWY
W MAIN ST
W MARTIN ST
SOUTH UNION RD
MOX-CHEHALIS
CHEHALIS RIVER
SATSOP RIVER
SEE 180 MAP
SEE 117 MAP
PNW
METRO

SEE 173 MAP

SEE 179 MAP

SEE 184 MAP

PNW

METRO

A B C D

1 2 3 4 5 6 7

SHELTON

TUMWATER

OLYMPIA

LACEY

MASON COUNTY

THURSTON COUNTY

PIERCE COUNTY

WASHINGTON

CAPITOL STATE FOREST

SKOKOMISH INDIAN RES

SQUAXIN ISLAND INDIAN RES

HARTSTENE ISLAND

HERRON ISLAND

MCMICKEN ISLAND

STRETCH ISLAND

HOPE ISLAND

THE EVERGREEN STATE COLLEGE

MASON COUNTY MUSEUM

SANDERSON FIELD AIRPORT

GEORGE ADAMS SALMON HATCHERY

Little Hoquiam

Bayshore

Oakland

Hartstene

Herron

Graham Point

Arcadia

Kamilche

New Kamilche

Schneiders Prairie

Boston Harbor

North Olympia

South Bay

MASON LAKE

LAKE LIMERICK

CRANBERRY LAKE

SPENCER LAKE

PHILLIPS LAKE

ISABELLA LAKE

SUMMIT LAKE

BLACK LAKE

WEBB HILL

ROCK CANDY MOUNTAIN

LARCH MOUNTAIN

CAPITOL PEAK

BORDEAUX CAMPGROUND

JOEMMA BEACH CAMPGROUND

HAMMERSLEY INLET

TOTTEN INLET

LITTLE SKOOKUM INLET

ELD INLET

BUDD INLET

HENDERSON INLET

CASE INLET

PICKERING PASSAGE

DANA PASSAGE

OAKLAND BAY

MUD BAY

GRAPEVIEW

PURDY CUTOFF

BROCKDALE RD

DAYTON-AIRPORT RD

MCEWAN PRAIRIE RD

MASON LAKE RD W

PICKERING RD

SPENCER LAKE RD

CRESTVIEW DR

AGATE RD

ARCADIA RD

LYNCH RD

SHELTON-MATLOCK RD

SHELTON VALLEY RD

DEEGAN RD W

CLOQUALLUM RD

MAINLINE

ISABELLA VALLEY

KAMILCHE VALLEY

HURLEY-WALDRIP RD

OLD OLYMPIC HWY

BLOOMFIELD RD

OYSTER BAY RD NW

STEAMBOAT ISLAND RD

SUMMIT LAKE SHORE RD

WILSON RD NW

FIVE FORKS RD SW

CEDAR FLATS RD

BLACK LAKE BLVD

COOPER POINT RD

DIVISION ST

HARRISON AV

MARTIN WY

PACIFIC AV

YELM HWY

BOSTON HARBOR RD NE

PUGET RD

HAWKS PRAIRIE RD NE

101 3 5 8 102 106 108

296 297

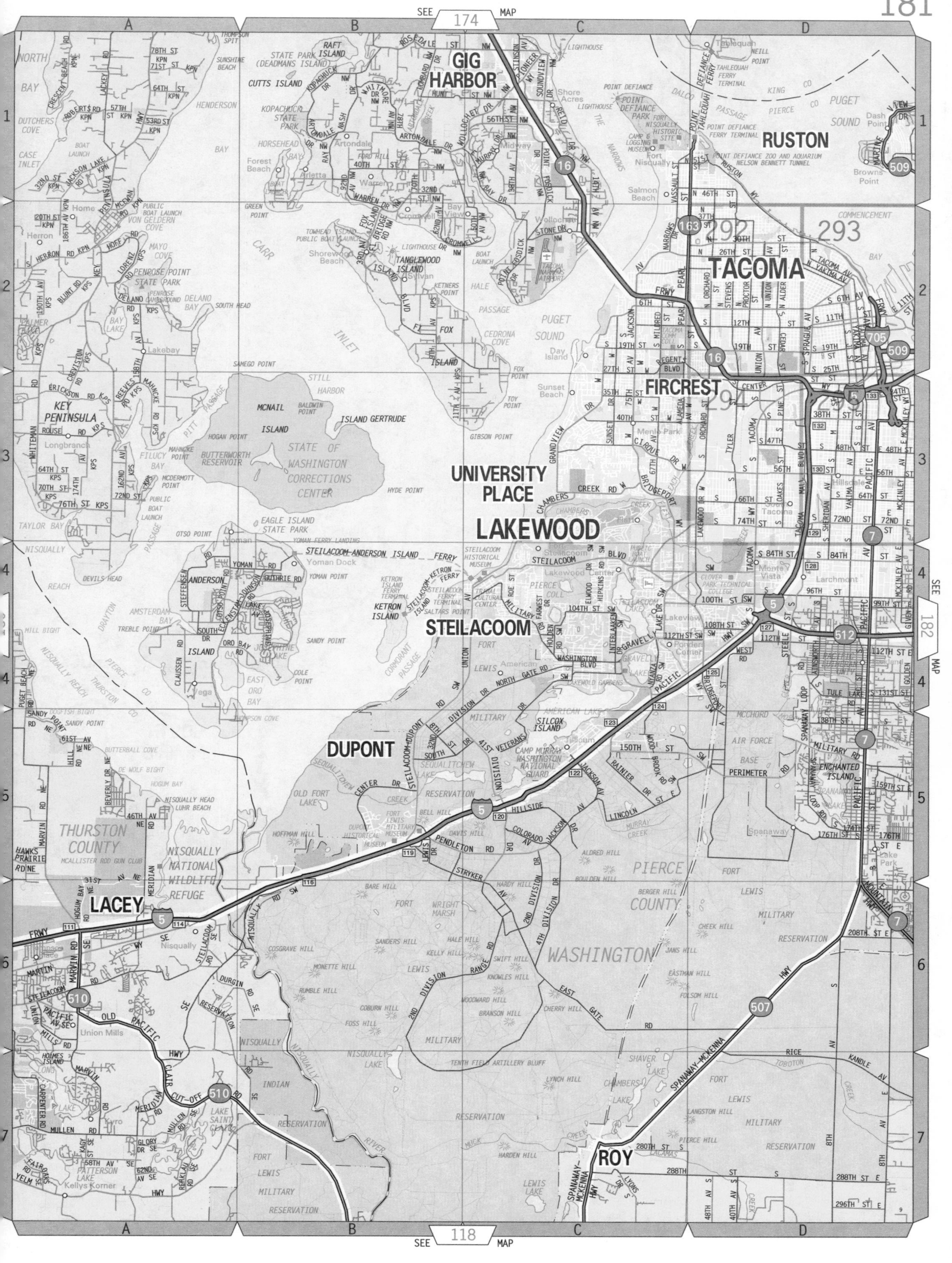
SEE 174 MAP
SEE 118 MAP
SEE 182 MAP
GIG HARBOR
RUSTON
TACOMA
FIRCREST
UNIVERSITY PLACE
LAKEWOOD
STEILACOOM
DUPONT
LACEY
ROY
KEY PENINSULA
ANDERSON ISLAND
MCNAIL ISLAND
STATE OF WASHINGTON CORRECTIONS CENTER
THURSTON COUNTY
PIERCE COUNTY
FORT LEWIS MILITARY RESERVATION
NISQUALLY NATIONAL WILDLIFE REFUGE
NISQUALLY INDIAN RESERVATION
MCCHORD AIR FORCE BASE
CAMP MURRAY WASHINGTON NATIONAL GUARD
PUGET SOUND
CARR INLET
HALE PASSAGE
DALCO PASSAGE
THE NARROWS
POINT DEFIANCE PARK
FOX ISLAND
AMERICAN LAKE
PNW
METRO

SEE 175 MAP

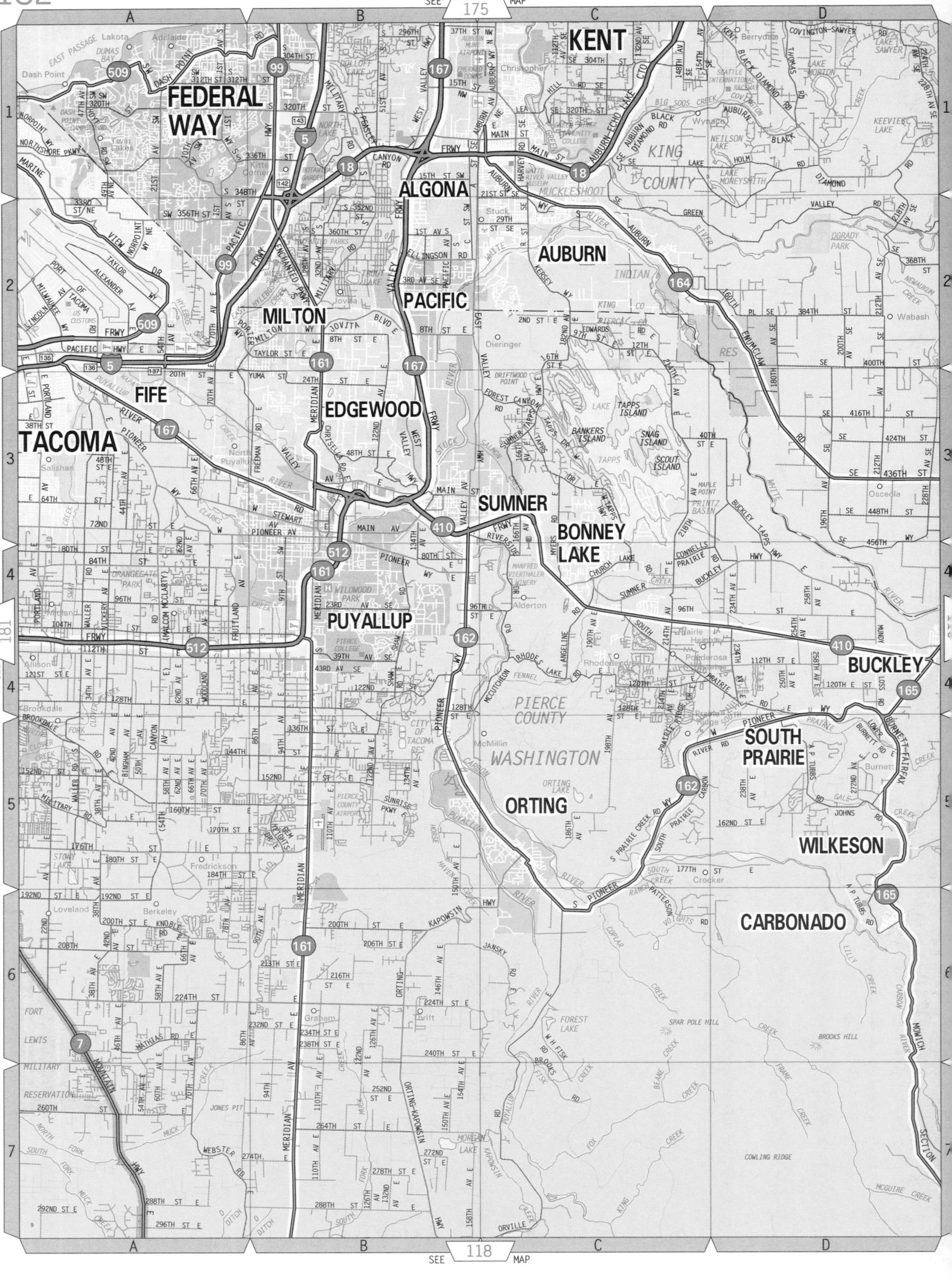

SEE 181 MAP

SEE 118 MAP

A B C D

1 2 3 4 5 6 7

KENT

FEDERAL WAY

ALGONA

AUBURN

PACIFIC

MILTON

FIFE

EDGEWOOD

TACOMA

SUMNER

BONNEY LAKE

PUYALLUP

BUCKLEY

SOUTH PRAIRIE

ORTING

WILKESON

CARBONADO

KING COUNTY

PIERCE COUNTY

WASHINGTON

FORT LEWIS MILITARY RESERVATION

SEE 177 MAP
SEE 117 MAP
SEE 186 MAP
A
B
C
D
1
2
3
4
5
6
7
OCEAN SHORES
WASHINGTON STATE OYHUT GAME RANGE
OCEAN SHORES BLVD SW
WESTPORT
Westhaven
WESTHAVEN
NYHUS ST
MONTESANO
US COAST GUARD RES
FORREST AV
OCEAN AV
FARRAGUT AV
VETERAN AV
BOURNE
ROBERTS RD
CHEHALIS AV
Cohassett
GRASS ISLAND
SOUTH BAY
Bay City
HUNT CLUB RD
SOPUN INLET
ROBERTS FARM
GRAYS
HARBOR
STEARNS BLUFF
BUSTEMEYER RD
TRAITORS INLET
GEORGE CLARK RD
Ocosta
JOHNS RIVER RD
GRAYS HARBOR COUNTY
NEWSKAH RD
NORTH RIVER DIVIDE
AMERICAN MILL RD
BISHOP RD
105
CHESTER AV
WASHINGTON
PACIFIC
OCEAN
BLAKE RD
Grayland
CRANBERRY RD
GRAYS HARBOR CO
PACIFIC CO
EVERGREEN PARK RD
SEASTRAND RIDGE
SEAHURST ACCESS RD
MIDWAY BEACH RD
Heather
LINDGREN RD
UDELL
HANSEN RD
JACOBSON RD
GOULD RD
LARKIN RD
SMITH ANDERSON RD
PACIFIC COUNTY
NORTH RIVER
WILLAPA NATIONAL WILDLIFE REFUGE
SHOALWATER INDIAN RESERVATION
Dexter By The Sea
NORTH COVE
TOKELAND RD
Tokeland
TOKE POINT
HAWKS POINT
RANGE POINT
WILLAPA
BAY
BRUCEPORT PARK
101
ROBERT BUSH DR
STONY POINT
SNAG ISLANDS
SOUTH BEND
PALIX RD
KINGSLEY RD
LEADBETTER POINT
WILSON POINT
WILLAPA NATIONAL WILDLIFE REFUGE
GRASSY ISLAND
BUSH PIONEER COUNTY PARK
GOOSE POINT
Bay Center
KOA BAY CENTER/ WILLAPA BAY
BAY CENTER DIKE RD
BAY CENTER RD
Rhodesia Beach
RHODESIA BEACH RD
SANDY POINT
BEND RD
HAROLD YOUNG RD
RIXON
SOUTH
PALIX RIVER
LEADBETTER POINT STATE PARK
STACKPOLE HARBOR

PNW
METRO

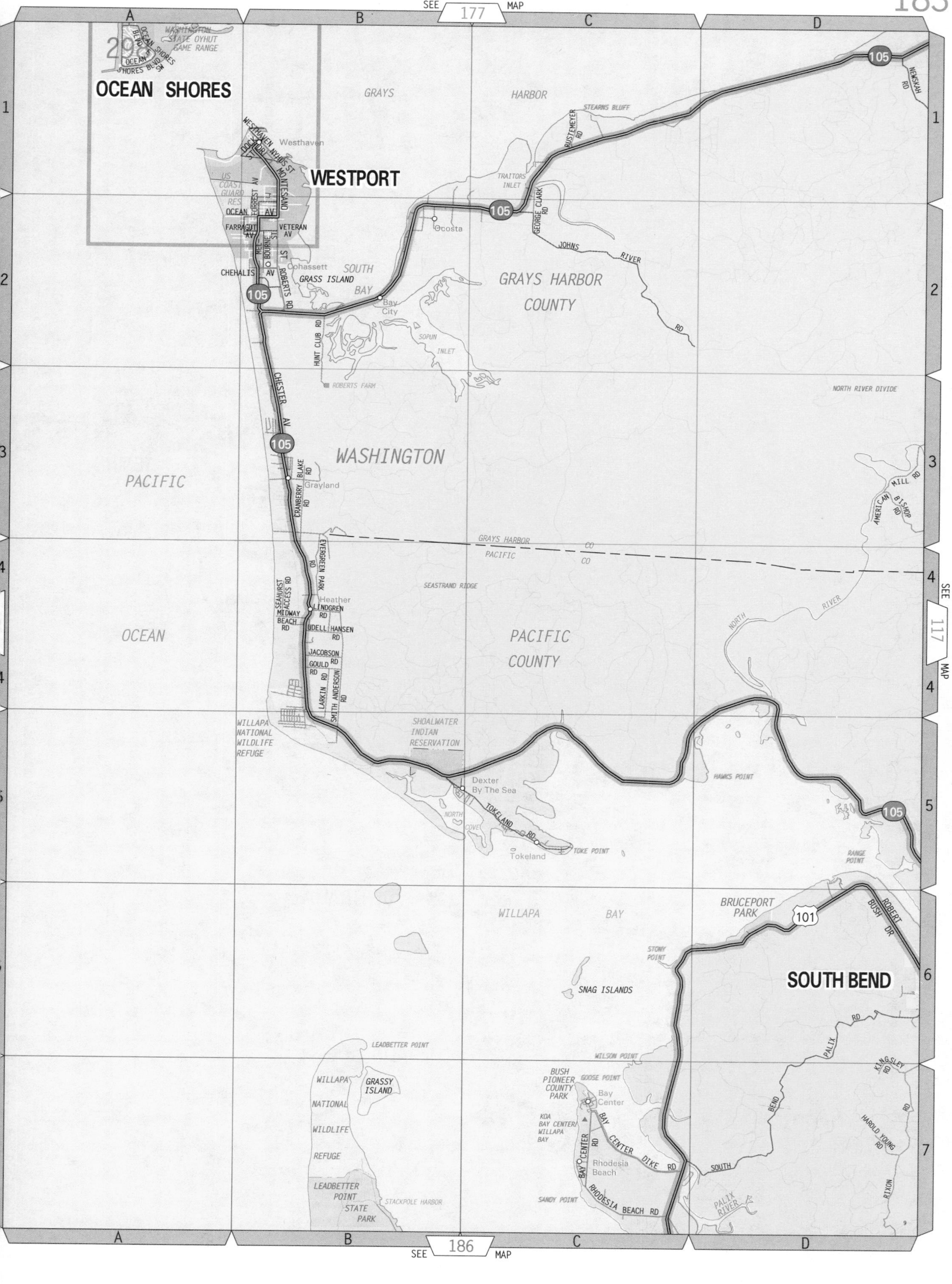

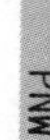

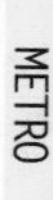

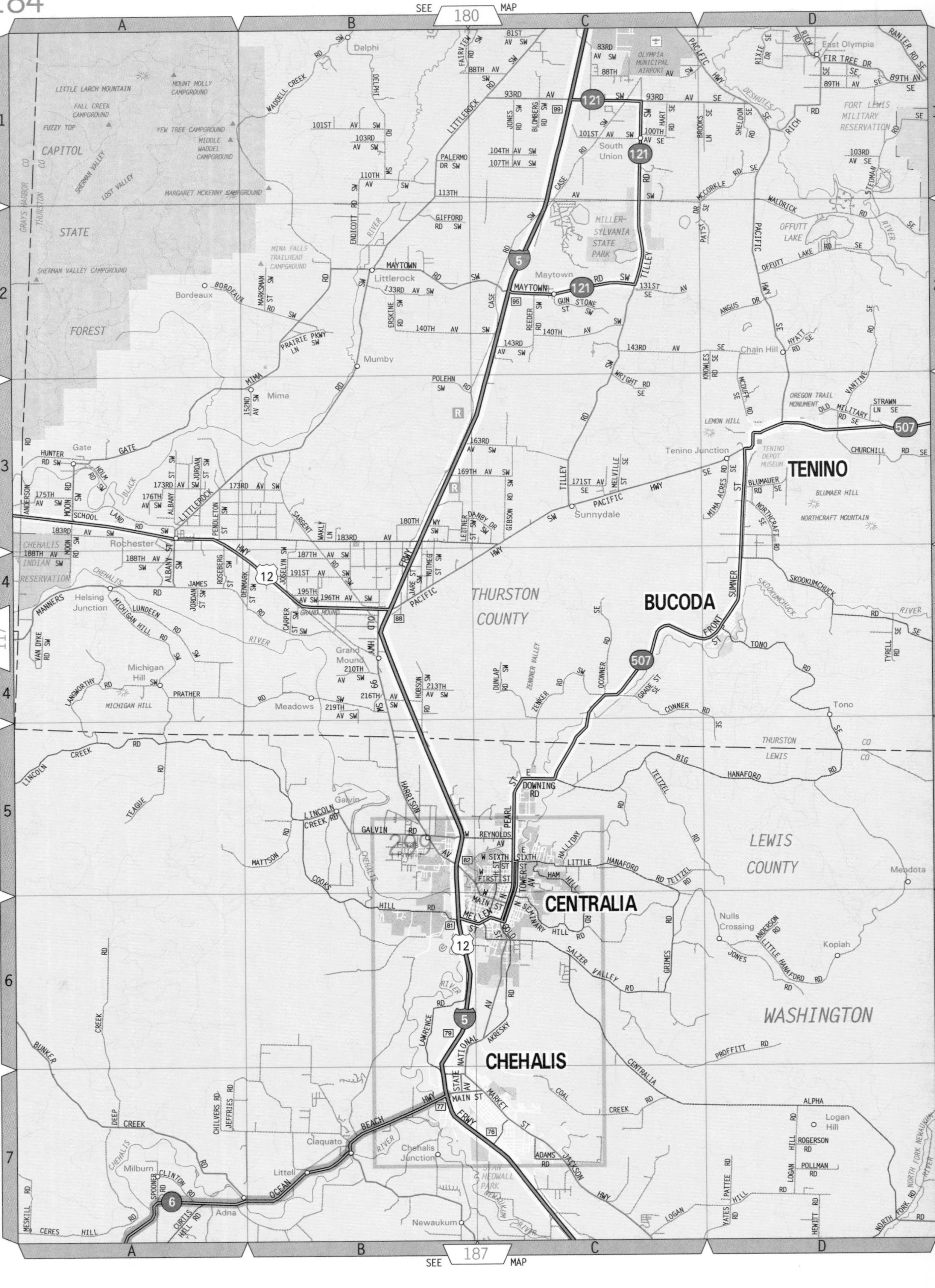

SEE 180 MAP

SEE 117 MAP

PNW

METRO

SEE 187 MAP

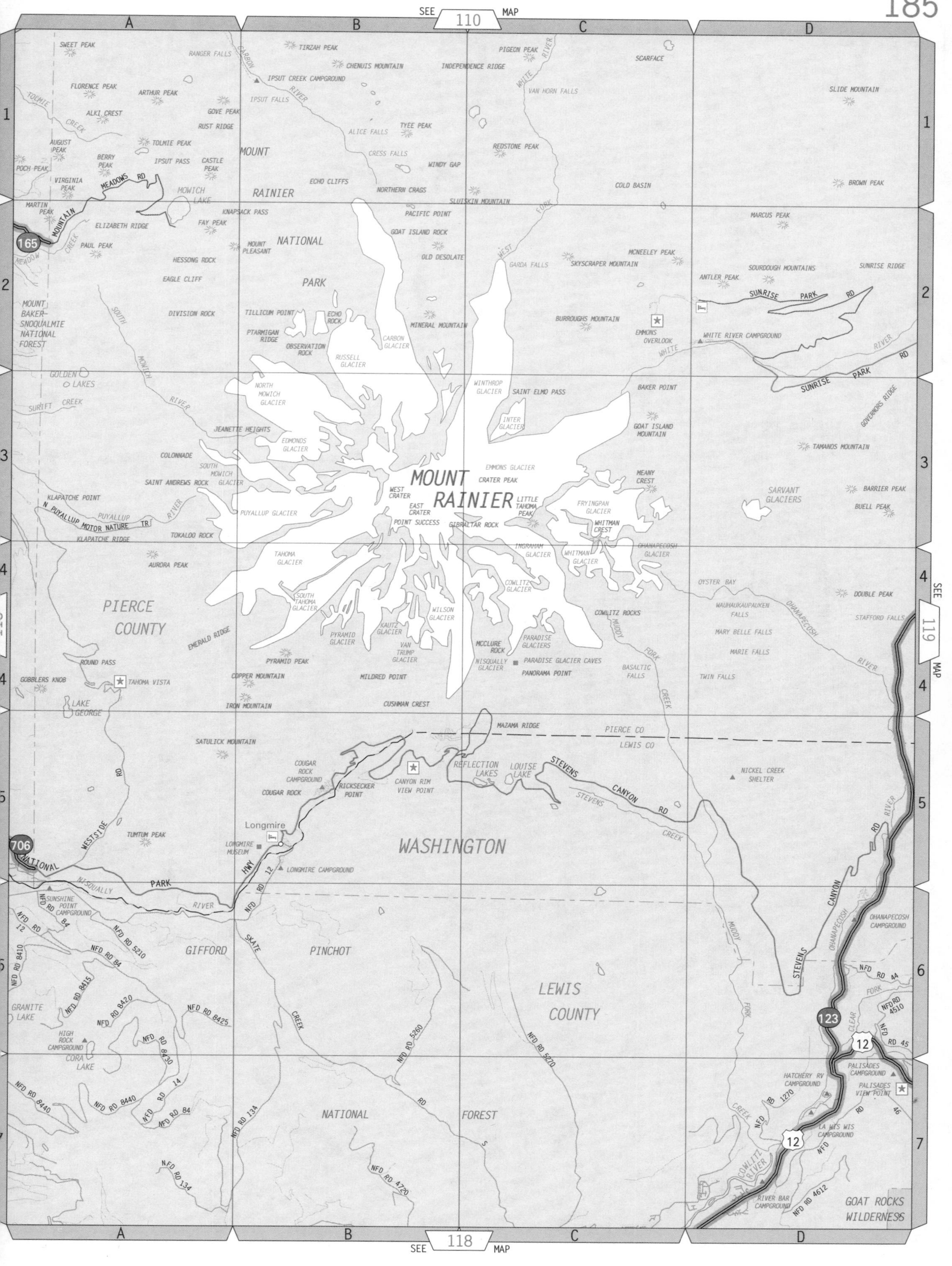

SEE 110 MAP
MOUNT RAINIER NATIONAL PARK
MOUNT RAINIER
PIERCE COUNTY
LEWIS COUNTY
WASHINGTON
GIFFORD PINCHOT NATIONAL FOREST
MOUNT BAKER-SNOQUALMIE NATIONAL FOREST
GOAT ROCKS WILDERNESS
Longmire
LONGMIRE MUSEUM
LONGMIRE CAMPGROUND
EMMONS GLACIER
CRATER PEAK
WEST CRATER
EAST CRATER
POINT SUCCESS
GIBRALTAR ROCK
LITTLE TAHOMA PEAK
CARBON GLACIER
RUSSELL GLACIER
NORTH MOWICH GLACIER
EDMONDS GLACIER
SOUTH MOWICH GLACIER
PUYALLUP GLACIER
TAHOMA GLACIER
SOUTH TAHOMA GLACIER
PYRAMID GLACIER
KAUTZ GLACIER
WILSON GLACIER
VAN TRUMP GLACIER
NISQUALLY GLACIER
PARADISE GLACIERS
COWLITZ GLACIER
INGRAHAM GLACIER
WHITMAN GLACIER
WHITMAN CREST
FRYINGPAN GLACIER
OHANAPECOSH GLACIER
WINTHROP GLACIER
INTER GLACIER
SARVANT GLACIERS
SUNRISE PARK RD
WHITE RIVER CAMPGROUND
EMMONS OVERLOOK
IPSUT CREEK CAMPGROUND
COUGAR ROCK CAMPGROUND
SUNSHINE POINT CAMPGROUND
HIGH ROCK CAMPGROUND
OHANAPECOSH CAMPGROUND
HATCHERY RV CAMPGROUND
PALISADES CAMPGROUND
PALISADES VIEW POINT
LA WIS WIS CAMPGROUND
RIVER BAR CAMPGROUND
CANYON RIM VIEW POINT
TAHOMA VISTA
PARADISE GLACIER CAVES
NICKEL CREEK SHELTER
STEVENS CANYON RD
NATIONAL PARK HWY
WESTSIDE RD
MOUNTAIN MEADOWS RD
N PUYALLUP MOTOR NATURE TR
PIERCE CO
LEWIS CO
165
706
123
12
SEE 119 MAP
SEE 118 MAP

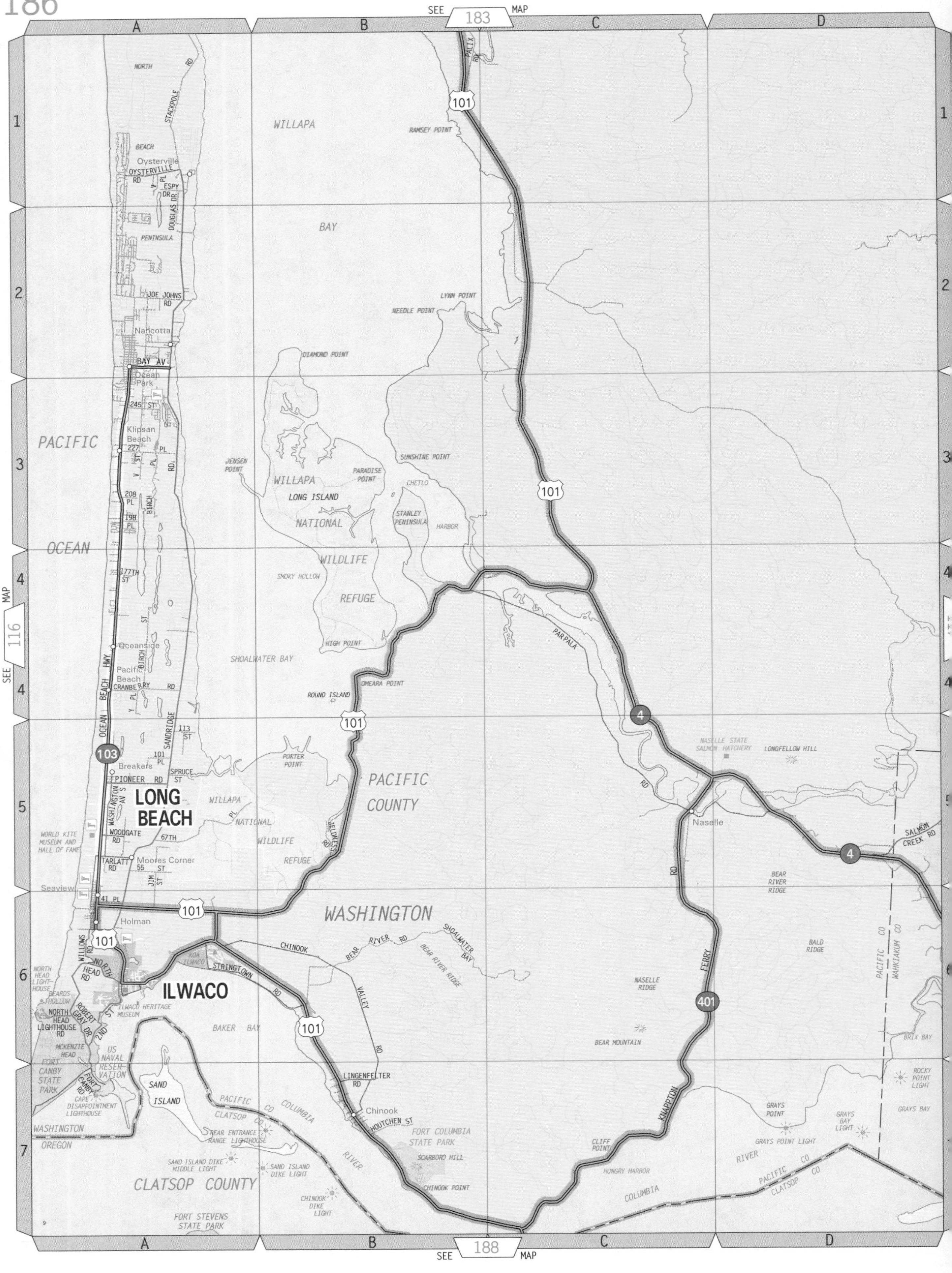
SEE 183 MAP
SEE 188 MAP
SEE 116 MAP
PNW
METRO
A
B
C
D
1
2
3
4
5
6
7
NORTH
BEACH
PENINSULA
STACKPOLE RD
Oysterville
OYSTERVILLE RD
V PL
ESPY
DOUGLAS DR
JOE JOHNS RD
Nahcotta
BAY AV
Ocean Park
245 ST
Klipsan Beach
227 PL
V ST
PL
RD
208 PL
198 PL
BIRCH
177TH ST
ST
Oceanside
BIRCH
Pacific Beach
CRANBERRY RD
Y PL
OCEAN BEACH HWY
103
SANDRIDGE
113 ST
101 PL
Breakers
SPRUCE ST
PIONEER RD
WASHINGTON AV S
LONG BEACH
WOODGATE RD
67TH
WORLD KITE MUSEUM AND HALL OF FAME
TARLATT RD
Moores Corner
55 ST
JIM ST
Seaview
41 PL
101
Holman
WILLOWS RD
NORTH HEAD RD
NORTH HEAD LIGHTHOUSE
BEARDS HOLLOW
NORTH HEAD LIGHTHOUSE RD
ROBERT GRAY DR
2ND ST
ILWACO HERITAGE MUSEUM
ILWACO
KOA ILWACO
STRINGTOWN RD
MCKENZIE HEAD
US NAVAL RESERVATION
FORT CANBY STATE PARK
FORT CANBY RD
CAPE DISAPPOINTMENT LIGHTHOUSE
WASHINGTON
OREGON
PACIFIC
OCEAN
WILLAPA
BAY
RAMSEY POINT
LYNN POINT
NEEDLE POINT
DIAMOND POINT
SUNSHINE POINT
JENSEN POINT
WILLAPA
PARADISE POINT
CHETLO
LONG ISLAND
NATIONAL
STANLEY PENINSULA
HARBOR
WILDLIFE
SMOKY HOLLOW
REFUGE
HIGH POINT
SHOALWATER BAY
OMEARA POINT
ROUND ISLAND
PORTER POINT
PACIFIC COUNTY
WILLAPA PL
NATIONAL
WILDLIFE
REFUGE
JELDNESS RD
WASHINGTON
PALIX RD
PARPALA
4
NASELLE STATE SALMON HATCHERY
LONGFELLOW HILL
RD
Naselle
SALMON CREEK RD
BEAR RIVER RIDGE
RD
FERRY
BALD RIDGE
PACIFIC CO
WAHKIAKUM CO
CHINOOK
BEAR RIVER RD
SHOALWATER BAY
BEAR RIVER RIDGE
NASELLE RIDGE
401
VALLEY
BAKER BAY
RD
BEAR MOUNTAIN
BRIX BAY
LINGENFELTER RD
ROCKY POINT LIGHT
KNAPPTON
SAND ISLAND
PACIFIC CO
CLATSOP CO
COLUMBIA
Chinook
HOUTCHEN ST
GRAYS POINT
GRAYS BAY LIGHT
GRAYS BAY
REAR ENTRANCE RANGE LIGHTHOUSE
FORT COLUMBIA STATE PARK
CLIFF POINT
GRAYS POINT LIGHT
SAND ISLAND DIKE MIDDLE LIGHT
SAND ISLAND DIKE LIGHT
RIVER
SCARBORO HILL
HUNGRY HARBOR
RIVER
PACIFIC CO
CLATSOP CO
CLATSOP COUNTY
CHINOOK POINT
COLUMBIA
CHINOOK DIKE LIGHT
FORT STEVENS STATE PARK

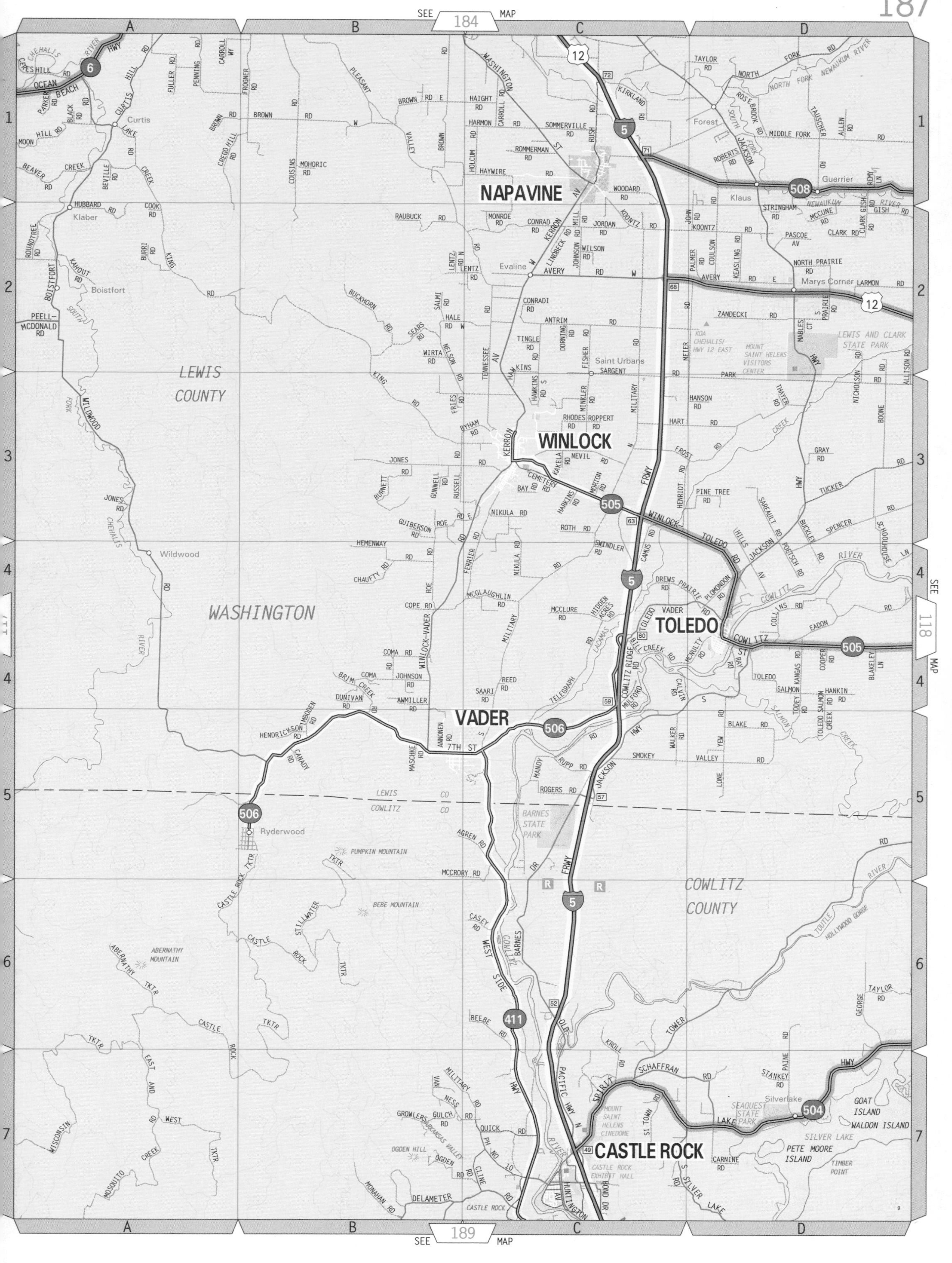
SEE 184 MAP
SEE 189 MAP
SEE 118 MAP
PNW
METRO
A
B
C
D
1
2
3
4
5
6
7
NAPAVINE
WINLOCK
TOLEDO
VADER
CASTLE ROCK
LEWIS COUNTY
WASHINGTON
COWLITZ COUNTY
LEWIS CO
COWLITZ CO
Curtis
Klaber
Boistfort
Wildwood
Ryderwood
Forest
Guerrier
Klaus
Marys Corner
Evaline
Saint Urbans
Silverlake
LEWIS AND CLARK STATE PARK
BARNES STATE PARK
SEAQUEST STATE PARK
KOA CHEHALIS/ HWY 12 EAST
MOUNT SAINT HELENS VISITORS CENTER
MOUNT SAINT HELENS CINEDOME
CASTLE ROCK EXHIBIT HALL
PUMPKIN MOUNTAIN
BEBE MOUNTAIN
ABERNATHY MOUNTAIN
OGDEN HILL
SILVER LAKE
GOAT ISLAND
WALDON ISLAND
PETE MOORE ISLAND
TIMBER POINT
COWLITZ RIVER
TOUTLE RIVER
HOLLYWOOD GORGE
NEWAUKUM RIVER
NORTH FORK NEWAUKUM RIVER
CHEHALIS RIVER
5
6
12
411
504
505
506
508

SEE 186 MAP

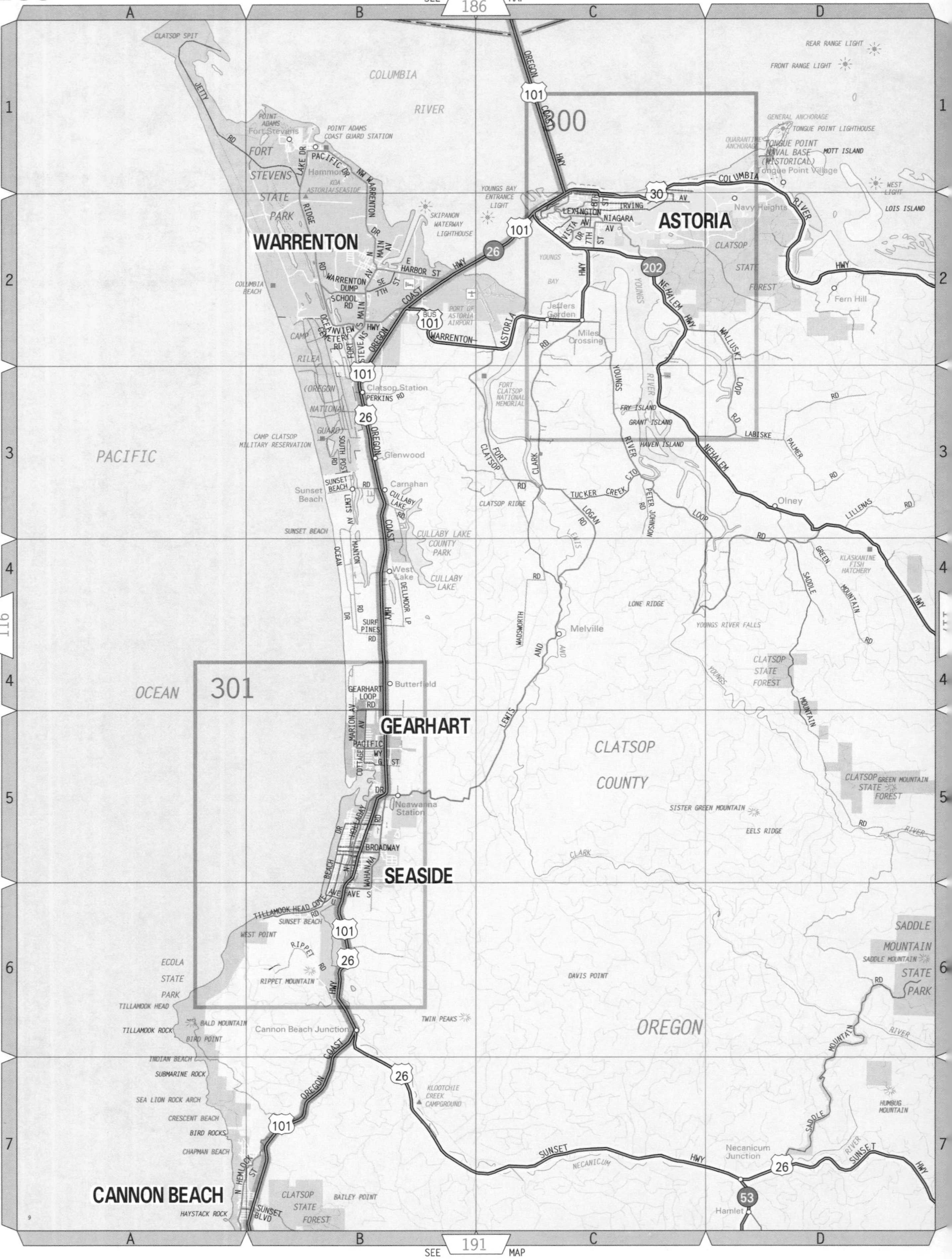

PNW

SEE 116 MAP

METRO

WARRENTON

ASTORIA

GEARHART

SEASIDE

CANNON BEACH

PACIFIC OCEAN

COLUMBIA RIVER

CLATSOP COUNTY

OREGON

300

301

SEE 191 MAP

SEE 187 MAP

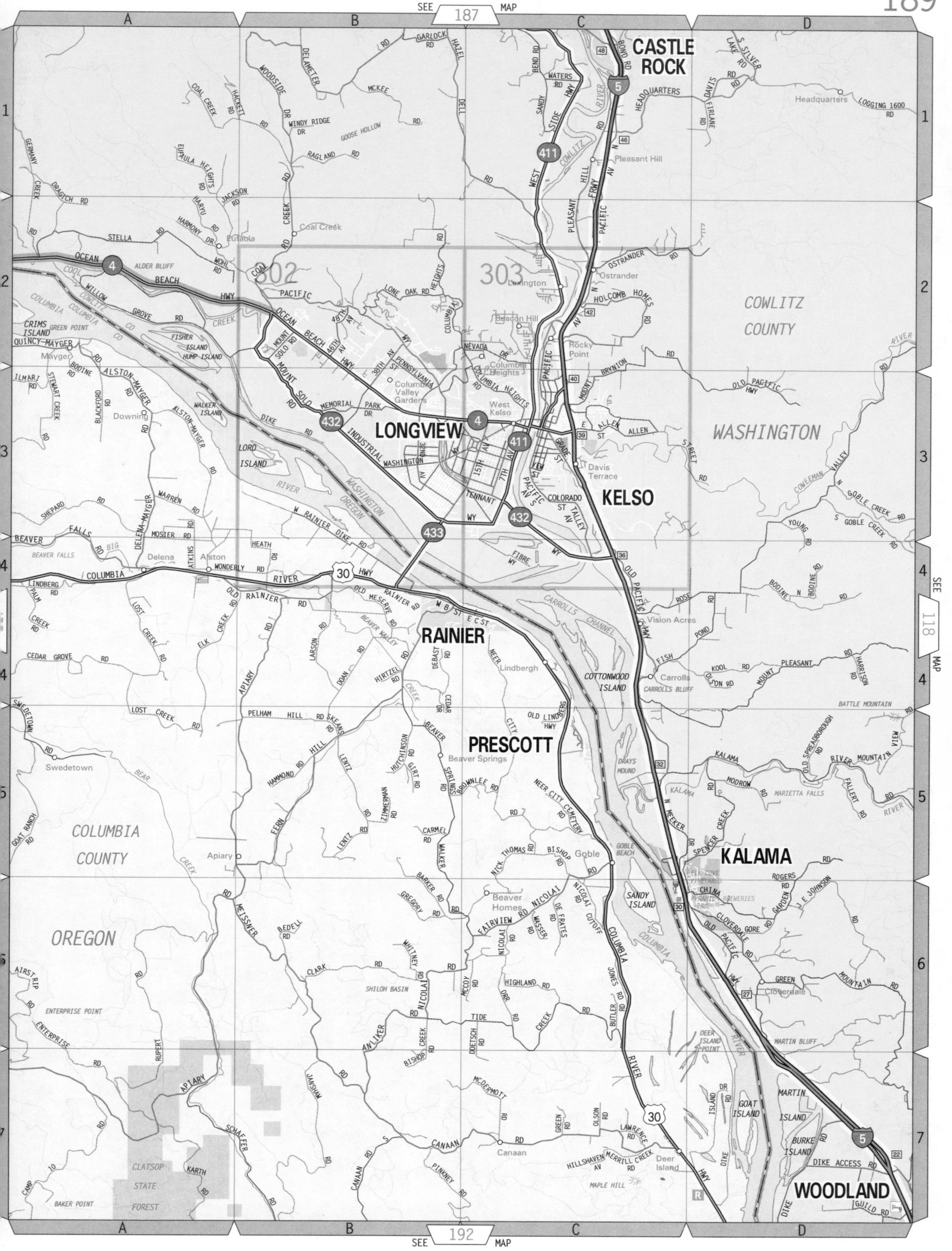

SEE 118 MAP

SEE 192 MAP

PNW

METRO

SEE 118 MAP

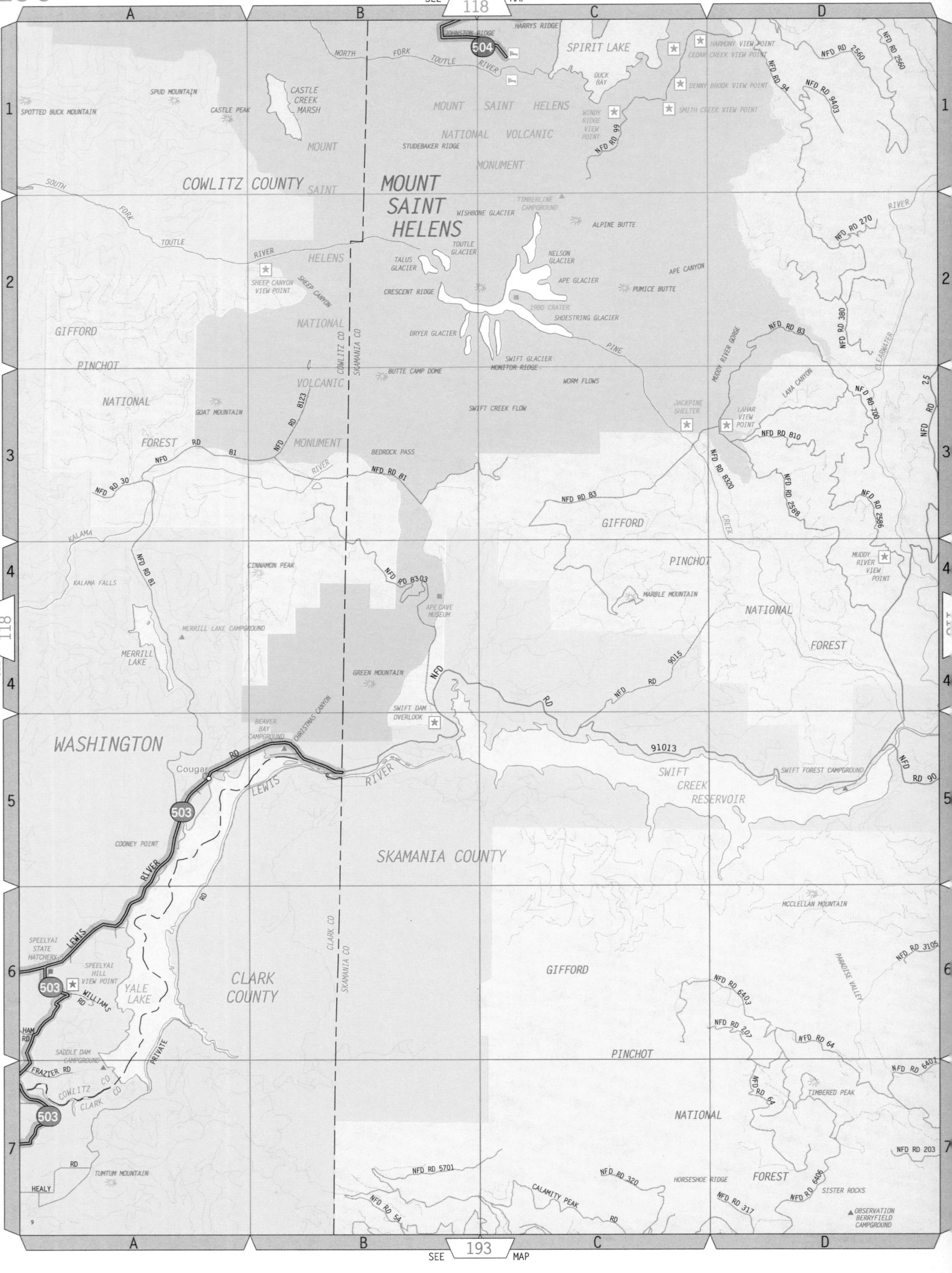

SEE 118 MAP

SEE 193 MAP

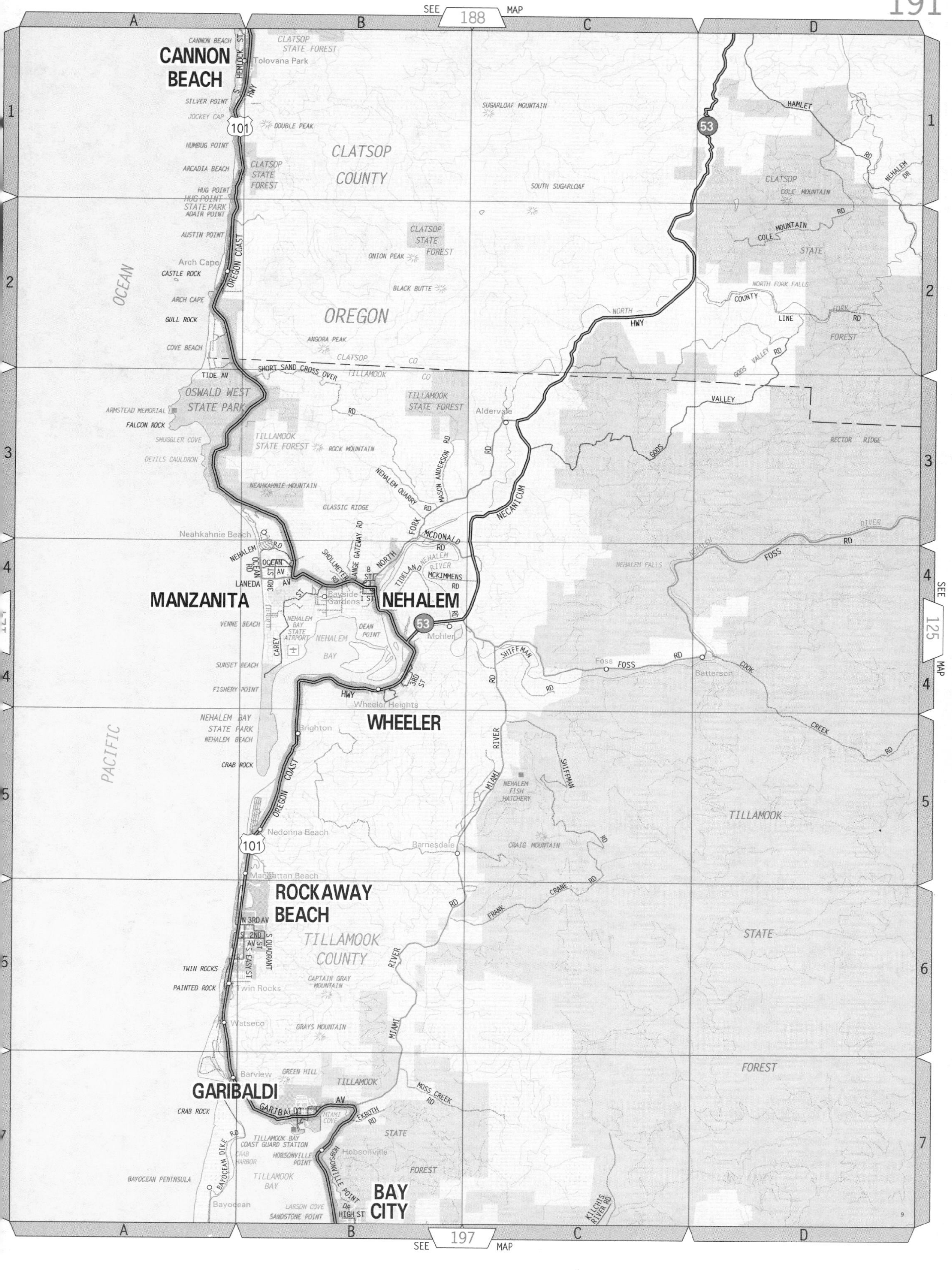

SEE 188 MAP

CANNON BEACH
MANZANITA
NEHALEM
WHEELER
ROCKAWAY BEACH
GARIBALDI
BAY CITY

CLATSOP COUNTY
OREGON
TILLAMOOK COUNTY
PACIFIC OCEAN

Tolovana Park, Arch Cape, Neahkahnie Beach, Bayside Gardens, Mohler, Aldervale, Foss, Batterson, Wheeler Heights, Brighton, Nedonna Beach, Barnesdale, Manhattan Beach, Twin Rocks, Watseco, Barview, Hobsonville, Bayocean

CLATSOP STATE FOREST
TILLAMOOK STATE FOREST
OSWALD WEST STATE PARK
NEHALEM BAY STATE PARK
HUG POINT STATE PARK
TILLAMOOK BAY
NEHALEM BAY

SEE 125 MAP

SEE 197 MAP

SEE 189 MAP

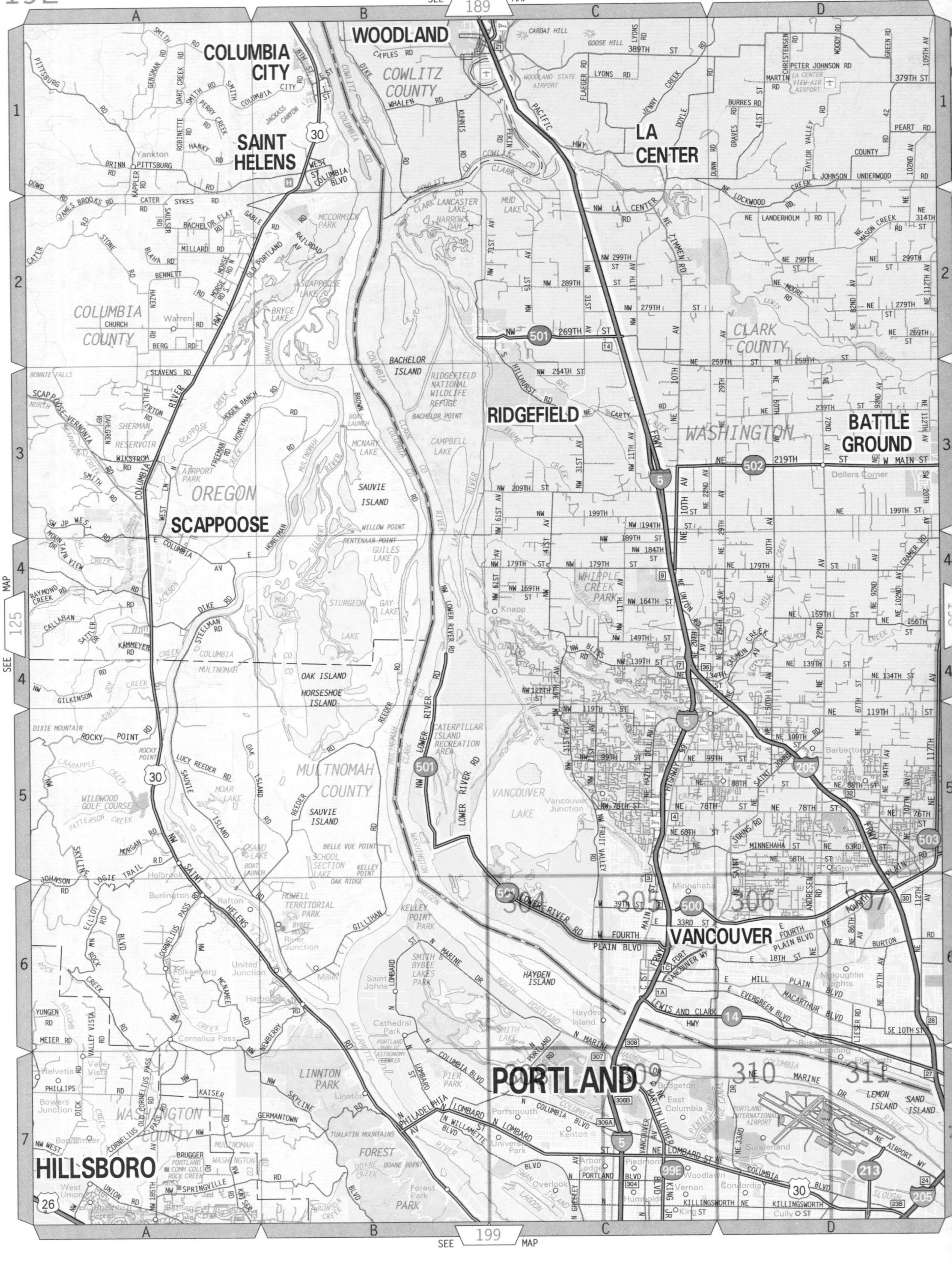

PNW

WOODLAND

COLUMBIA CITY

COWLITZ COUNTY

SAINT HELENS

LA CENTER

COLUMBIA COUNTY

CLARK COUNTY

RIDGEFIELD

WASHINGTON

BATTLE GROUND

OREGON

SCAPPOOSE

SAUVIE ISLAND

RIDGEFIELD NATIONAL WILDLIFE REFUGE

SEE 125 MAP

METRO

MULTNOMAH COUNTY

VANCOUVER LAKE

VANCOUVER

HAYDEN ISLAND

LINNTON PARK

PORTLAND

FOREST PARK

WASHINGTON COUNTY

HILLSBORO

PORTLAND INTERNATIONAL AIRPORT

SEE 199 MAP

SEE 190 MAP

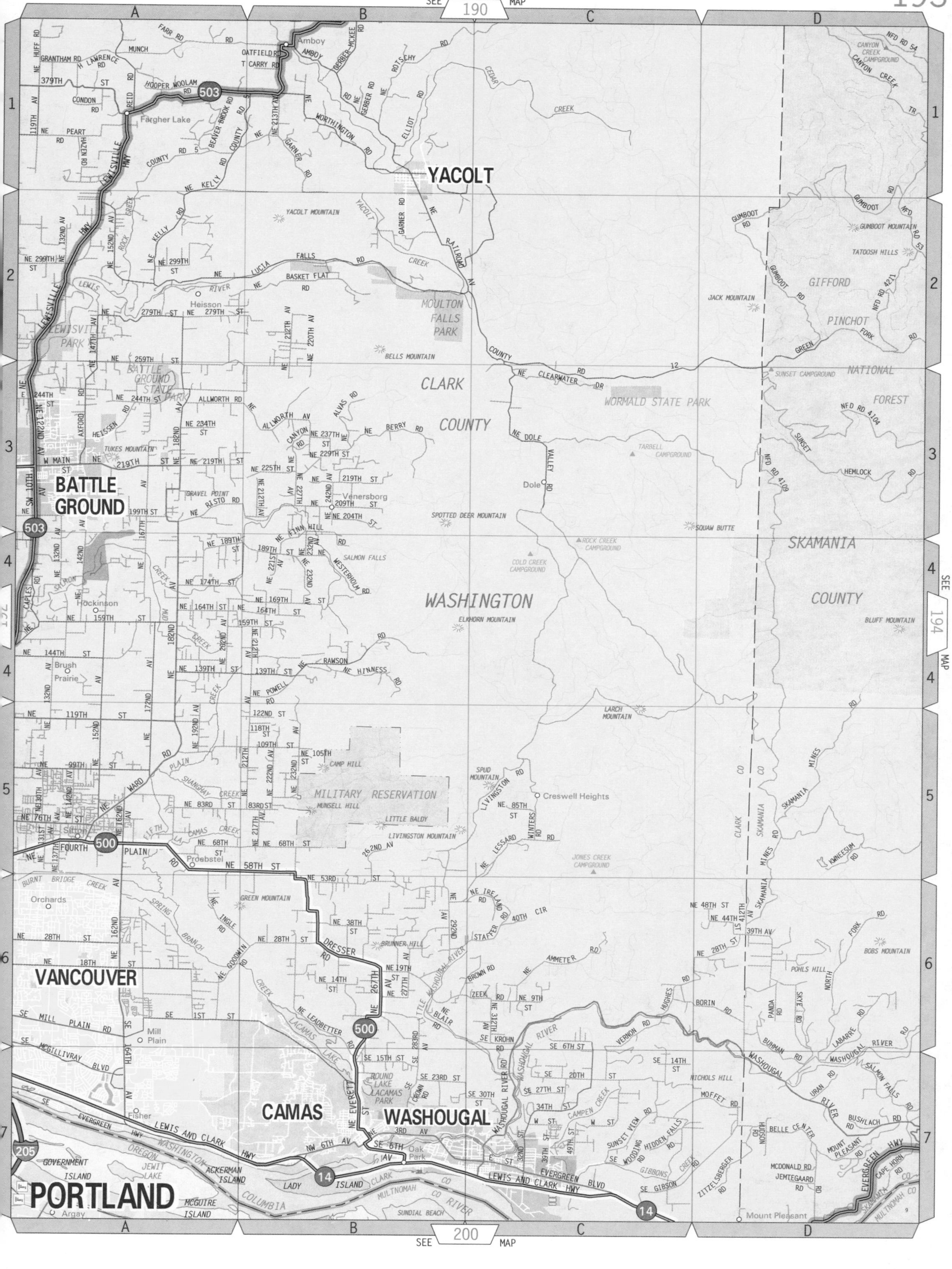

YACOLT

BATTLE GROUND

CLARK COUNTY

WASHINGTON

SKAMANIA COUNTY

GIFFORD PINCHOT NATIONAL FOREST

VANCOUVER

CAMAS

WASHOUGAL

PORTLAND

MILITARY RESERVATION

WORMALD STATE PARK

MOULTON FALLS PARK

LEWISVILLE PARK

BATTLE GROUND STATE PARK

Amboy

Fargher Lake

Heisson

Hockinson

Brush Prairie

Venersborg

Dole

Creswell Heights

Orchards

Mill Plain

Fisher

Proebstel

Sifton

Oak Park

Mount Pleasant

Argay

YACOLT MOUNTAIN

BELLS MOUNTAIN

TUKES MOUNTAIN

SPOTTED DEER MOUNTAIN

ELKHORN MOUNTAIN

LARCH MOUNTAIN

SQUAW BUTTE

JACK MOUNTAIN

GUMBOOT MOUNTAIN

TATOOSH HILLS

BLUFF MOUNTAIN

BOBS MOUNTAIN

POHLS HILL

NICHOLS HILL

SPUD MOUNTAIN

CAMP HILL

MUNSELL HILL

LITTLE BALDY

LIVINGSTON MOUNTAIN

GREEN MOUNTAIN

BRUNNER HILL

SALMON FALLS

TARBELL CAMPGROUND

ROCK CREEK CAMPGROUND

COLD CREEK CAMPGROUND

JONES CREEK CAMPGROUND

SUNSET CAMPGROUND

CANYON CREEK CAMPGROUND

GOVERNMENT ISLAND

JEWIT LAKE

ACKERMAN ISLAND

LADY ISLAND

MCGUIRE ISLAND

SUNDIAL BEACH

ROUND LAKE LACAMAS PARK

COLUMBIA RIVER

OREGON

WASHINGTON

MULTNOMAH CO

CLARK CO

SKAMANIA CO

LEWIS AND CLARK HWY

EVERGREEN HWY

LEWISVILLE HWY

NE LUCIA FALLS RD

NE BASKET FLAT RD

NE CLEARWATER DR

NE DOLE VALLEY RD

NE RAILROAD AV

NE ALLWORTH AV

NE RAWSON RD

NE HINNESS RD

NE POWELL RD

NE WARD RD

NE 58TH ST

NE DRESSER RD

SE MILL PLAIN BLVD

SE MCGILLIVRAY BLVD

WASHOUGAL RIVER RD

SKAMANIA MINES RD

NE 279TH ST

NE 259TH ST

NE 244TH ST

NE 219TH ST

NE 199TH ST

NE 189TH ST

NE 159TH ST

NE 144TH ST

NE 139TH ST

NE 119TH ST

NE 99TH ST

NE 83RD ST

NE 76TH ST

NE 68TH ST

NE 28TH ST

NE 18TH ST

SE 1ST ST

NE 182ND AV

NE 172ND AV

NE 162ND AV

NE 152ND AV

NE 132ND AV

NE 122ND AV

NE 212TH AV

NE 232ND AV

NE 267TH AV

NE 292ND AV

NE 312TH AV

503

500

14

205

12

A B C D

1 2 3 4 5 6 7

SEE 194 MAP

SEE 200 MAP

PNW

METRO

SEE 190 MAP

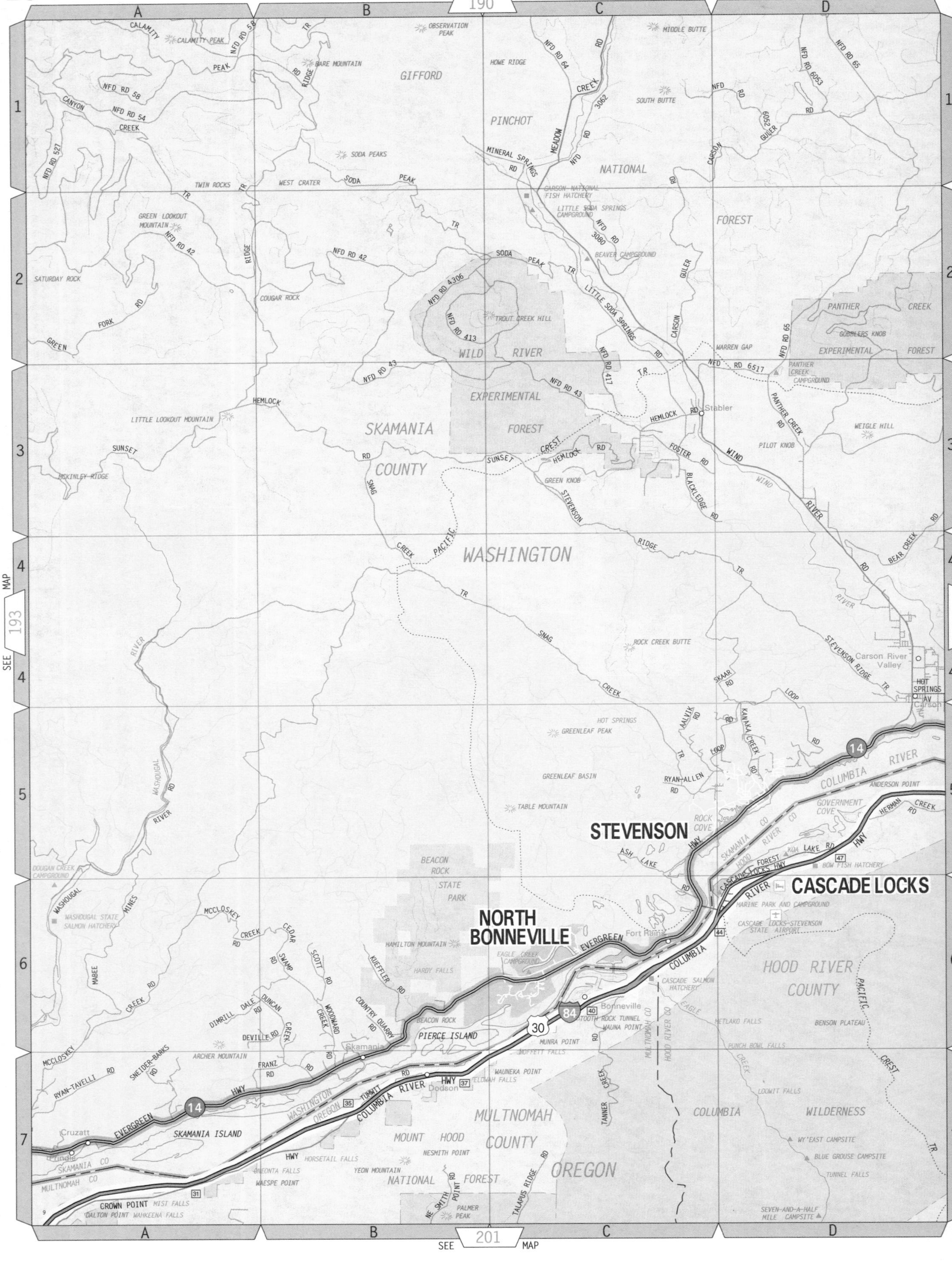

SEE 193 MAP

SEE 201 MAP

SEE 118 MAP

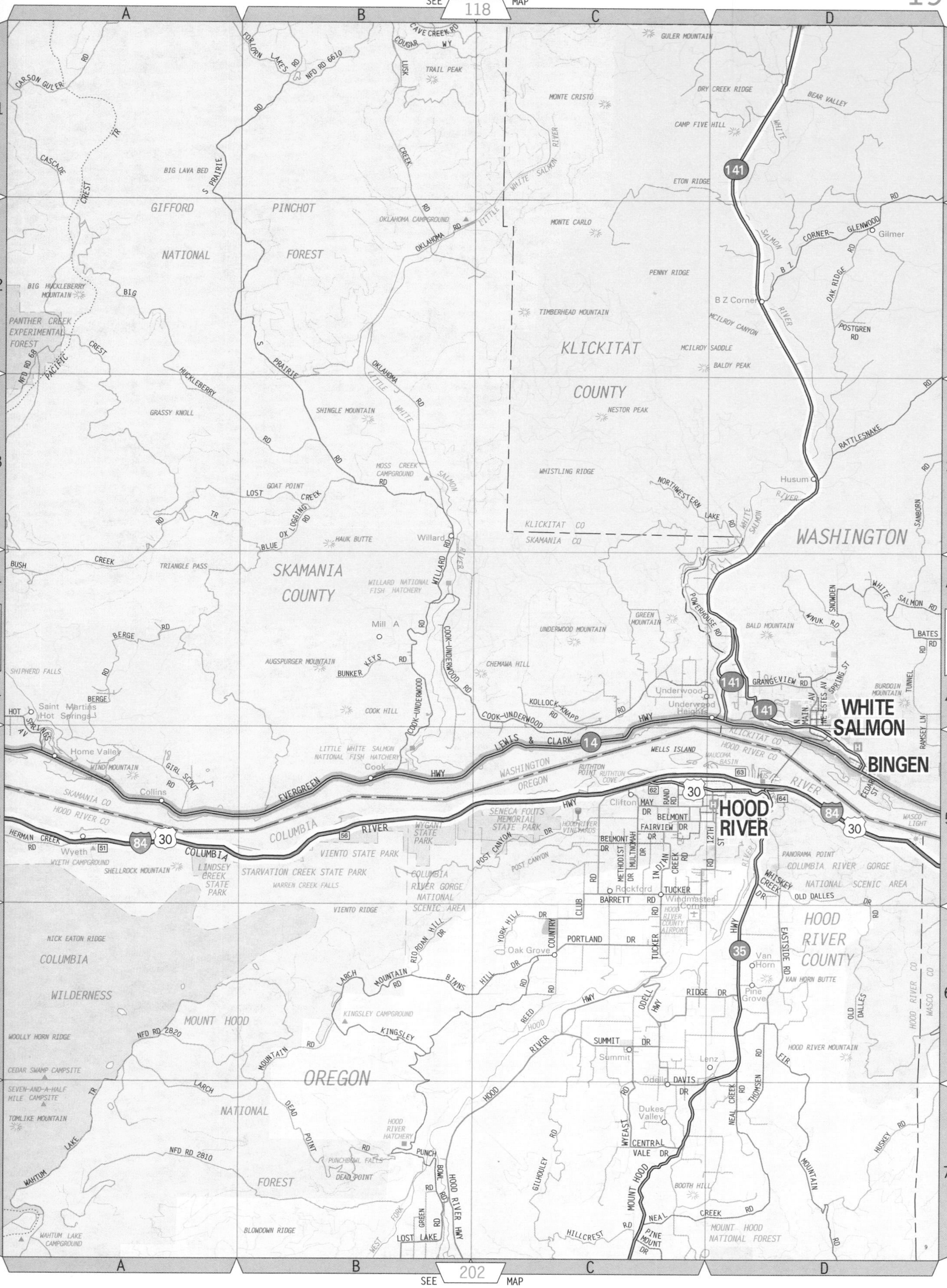

SEE 196 MAP

SEE 202 MAP

SEE MAP 119

KLICKITAT COUNTY

WASHINGTON

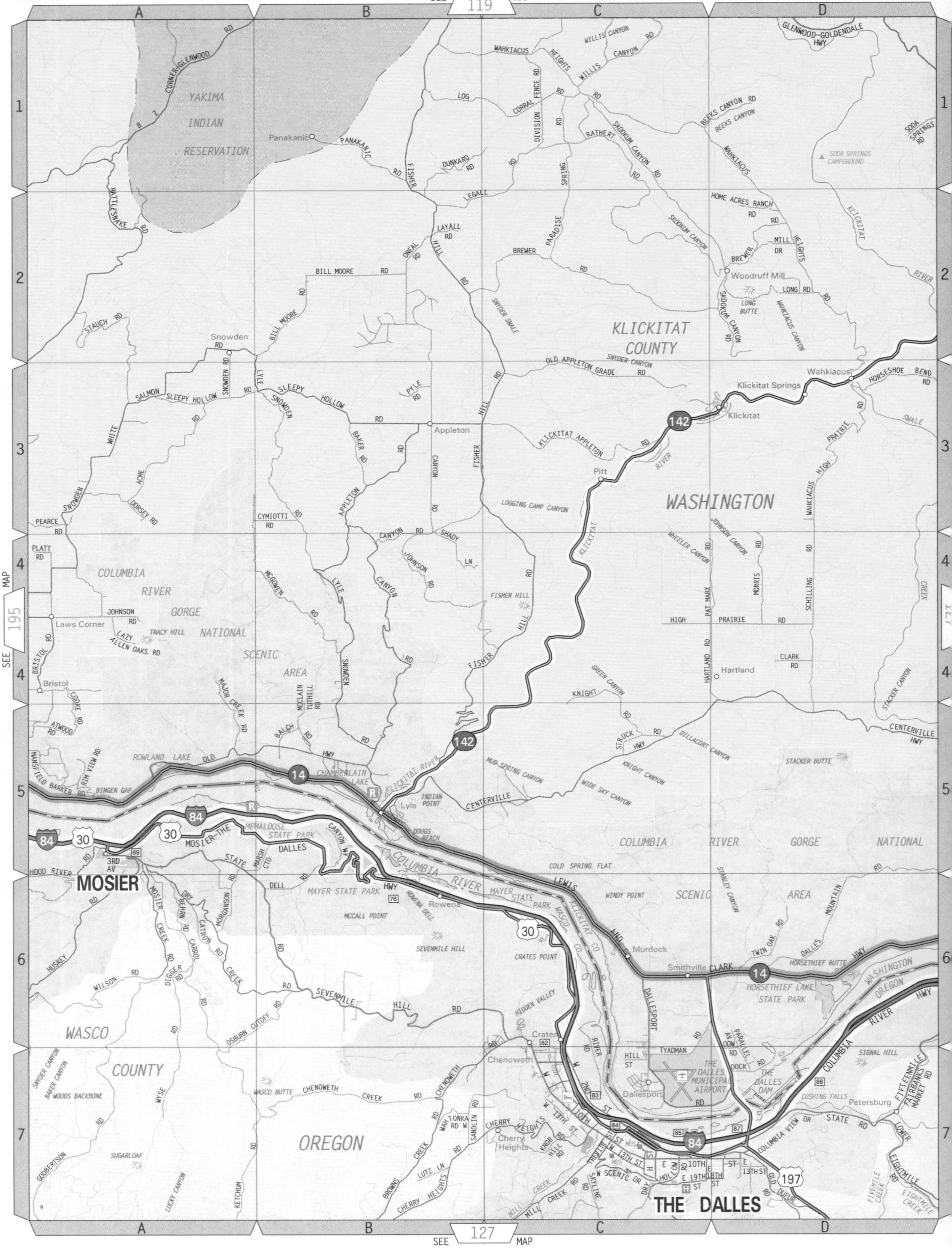

YAKIMA INDIAN RESERVATION

COLUMBIA RIVER GORGE NATIONAL SCENIC AREA

MOSIER

WASCO COUNTY

OREGON

THE DALLES

Panakanic · Snowden · Appleton · Pitt · Klickitat · Klickitat Springs · Wahkiacus · Woodruff Mill · Hartland · Laws Corner · Bristol · Lyle · Rowena · Murdock · Smithville · Dallesport · Crates · Chenoweth · Cherry Heights · Petersburg

SEE MAP 195

SEE MAP 127

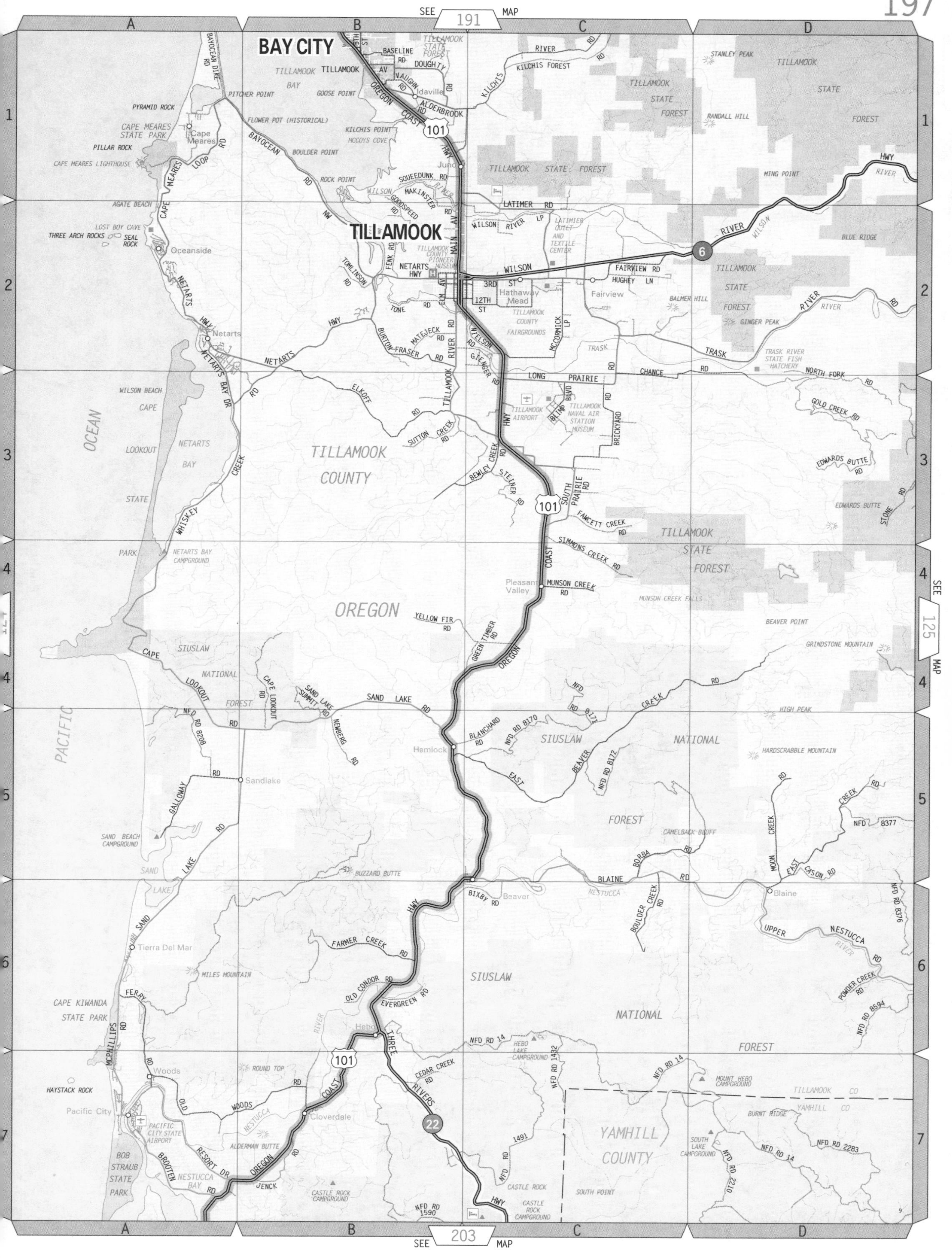
SEE 191 MAP
BAY CITY
TILLAMOOK
TILLAMOOK COUNTY
OREGON
YAMHILL COUNTY
PACIFIC
OCEAN
SIUSLAW NATIONAL FOREST
TILLAMOOK STATE FOREST
Idaville
Cape Meares
Oceanside
Netarts
Fairview
Hathaway Mead
Pleasant Valley
Hemlock
Sandlake
Beaver
Blaine
Tierra Del Mar
Hebo
Woods
Cloverdale
Pacific City
CAPE MEARES STATE PARK
CAPE LOOKOUT STATE PARK
CAPE KIWANDA STATE PARK
BOB STRAUB STATE PARK
NETARTS BAY
TILLAMOOK BAY
NESTUCCA BAY
SEE 203 MAP
SEE 125 MAP
PNW
METRO

SEE 125 MAP

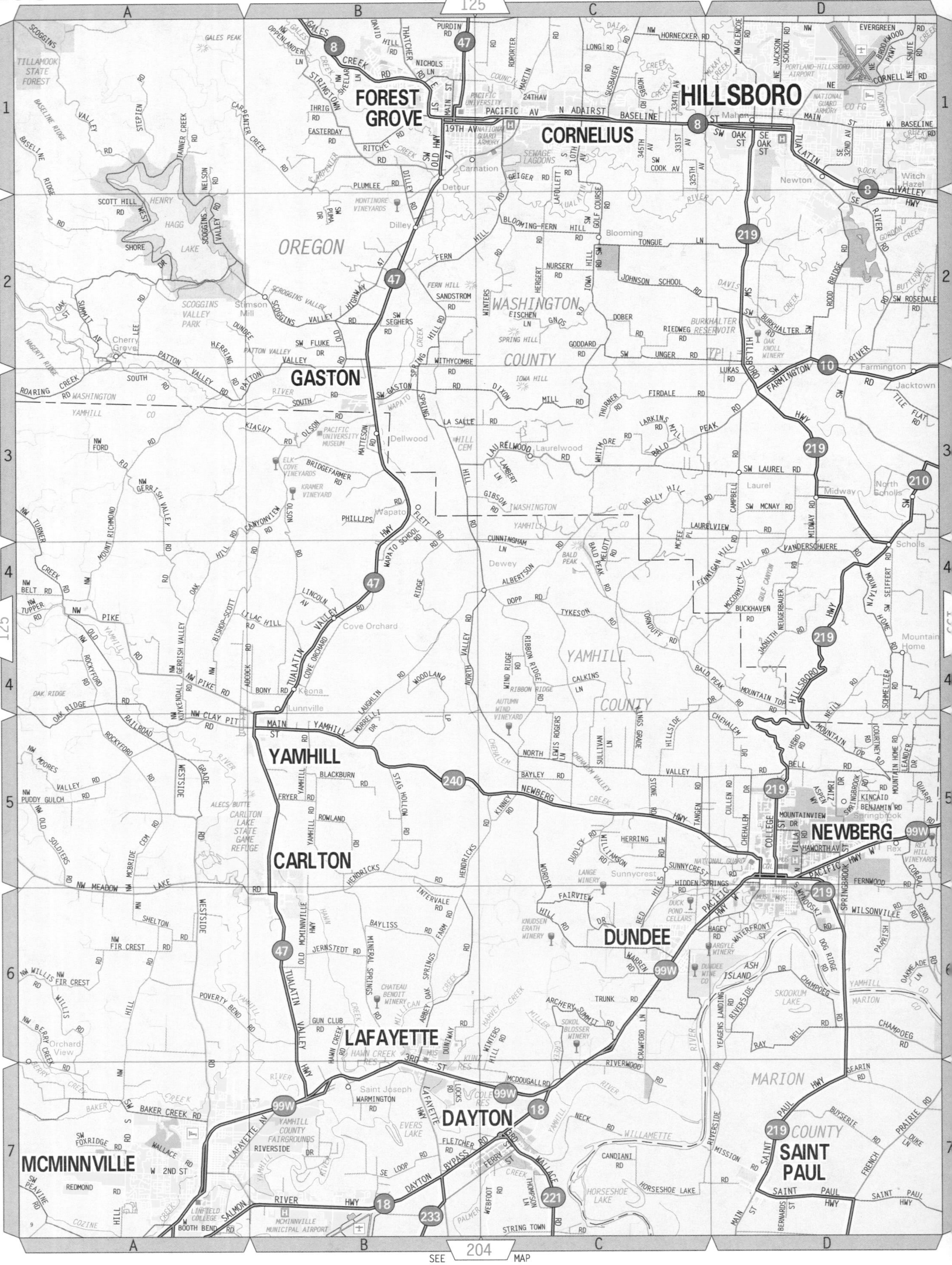

PNW

METRO

A B C D

FOREST GROVE

HILLSBORO

CORNELIUS

OREGON

WASHINGTON COUNTY

GASTON

YAMHILL COUNTY

YAMHILL

CARLTON

NEWBERG

DUNDEE

LAFAYETTE

DAYTON

MCMINNVILLE

MARION COUNTY

SAINT PAUL

SEE 125 MAP

SEE 204 MAP

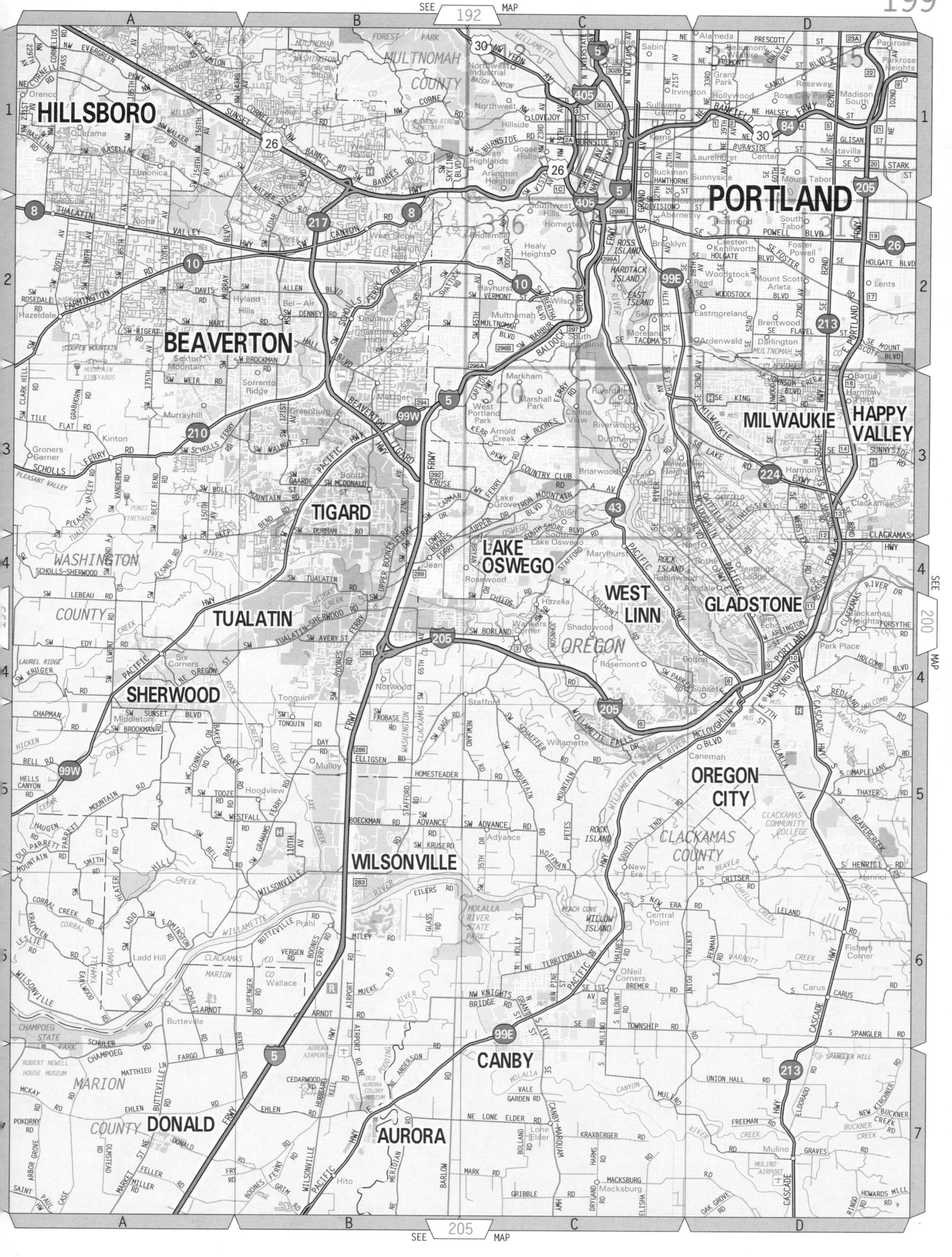
HILLSBORO
BEAVERTON
PORTLAND
TIGARD
LAKE OSWEGO
MILWAUKIE
HAPPY VALLEY
WEST LINN
GLADSTONE
TUALATIN
SHERWOOD
OREGON CITY
WILSONVILLE
CANBY
DONALD
AURORA
MULTNOMAH COUNTY
WASHINGTON COUNTY
CLACKAMAS COUNTY
MARION COUNTY
SEE 192 MAP
SEE 205 MAP
SEE 200 MAP
PNW
METRO

SEE 193 MAP

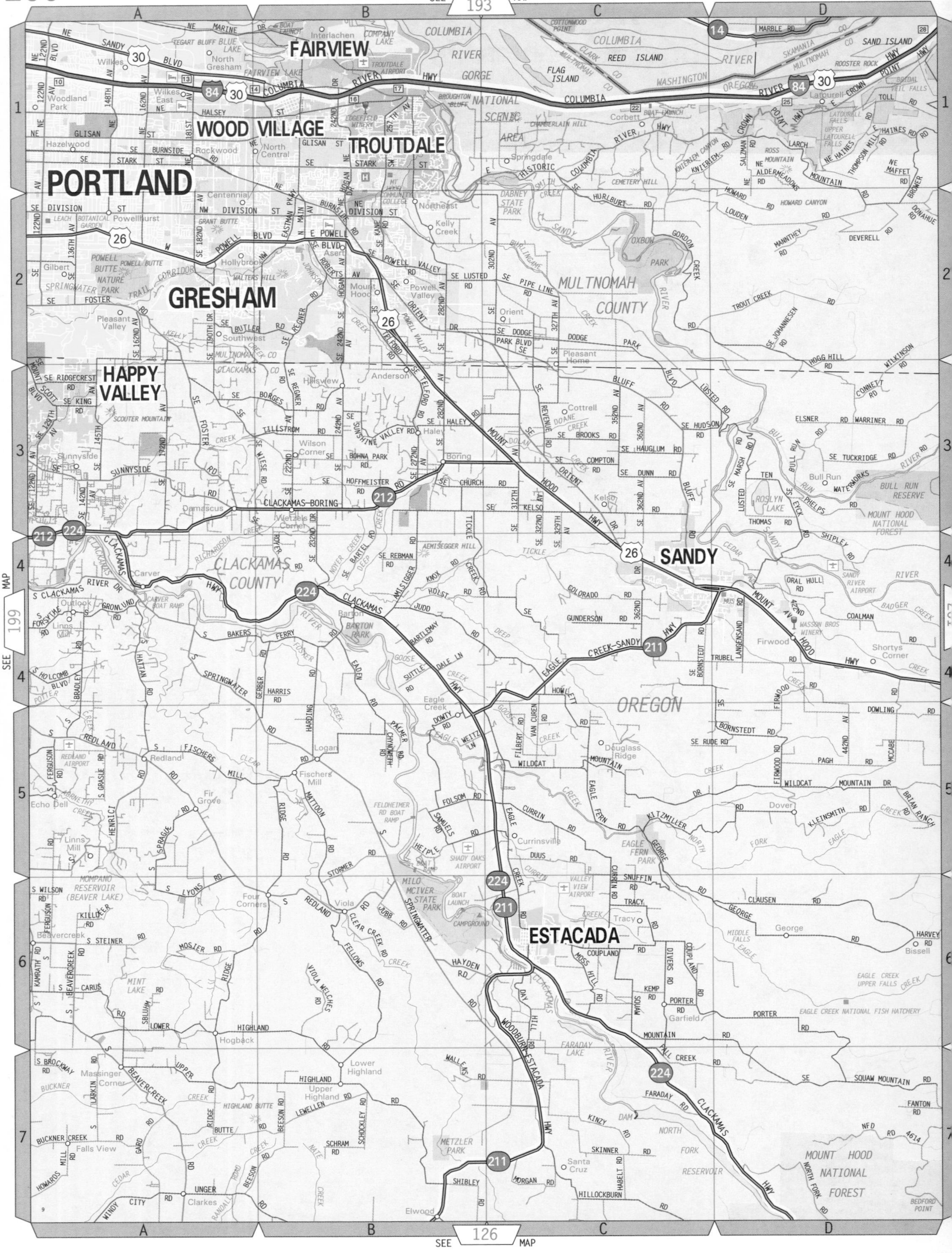

A B C D

1 2 3 4 5 6 7

PNW

METRO

SEE 199 MAP

PORTLAND

FAIRVIEW

WOOD VILLAGE

TROUTDALE

GRESHAM

HAPPY VALLEY

SANDY

ESTACADA

COLUMBIA RIVER GORGE NATIONAL SCENIC AREA

MULTNOMAH COUNTY

CLACKAMAS COUNTY

OREGON

WASHINGTON

MOUNT HOOD NATIONAL FOREST

BULL RUN RESERVE

MILO MCIVER STATE PARK

DABNEY STATE PARK

OXBOW PARK

BARTON PARK

EAGLE FERN PARK

METZLER PARK

POWELL BUTTE NATURE PARK

Hazelwood

Centennial

Powellhurst

Gilbert

Pleasant Valley

Rockwood

North Central

Northeast

Kelly Creek

Powell Valley

Mount Hood

Southwest

Hollybrook

Sunnyside

Damascus

Carver

Boring

Haley

Wilson Corner

Anderson

Hillsview

Pleasant Home

Orient

Cottrell

Kelso

Springdale

Corbett

Latourell

Bull Run

Firwood

Shortys Corner

Eagle Creek

Logan

Fischers Mill

Redland

Fir Grove

Echo Dell

Linns Mill

Outlook

Four Corners

Viola

Currinsville

Tracy

Douglass Ridge

Dover

George

Bissell

Garfield

Beavercreek

Hogback

Lower Highland

Upper Highland

Massinger Corner

Falls View

Clarkes

Elwood

Santa Cruz

SEE 126 MAP

SEE 194 MAP

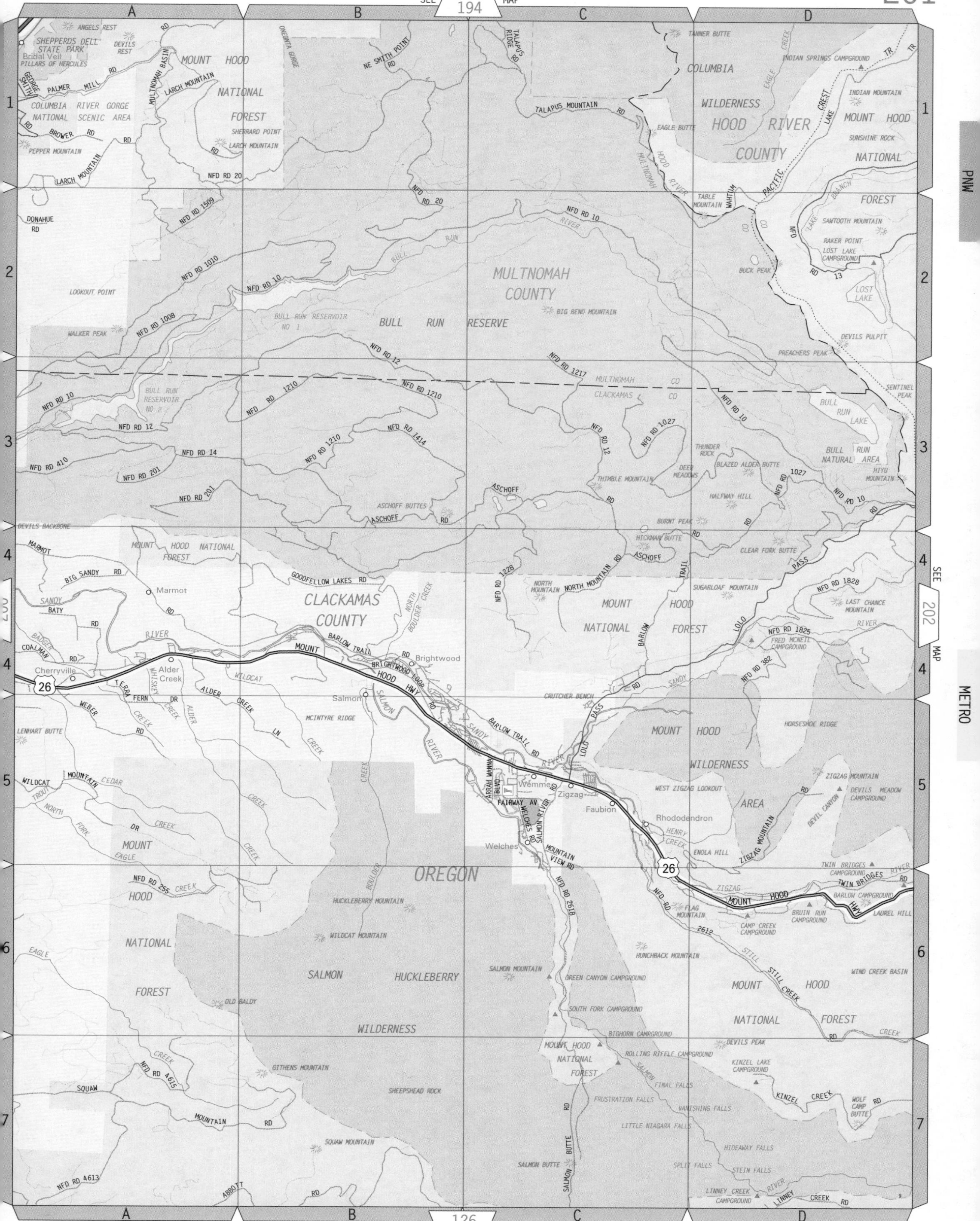

A B C D

1 2 3 4 5 6 7

SHEPPERDS DELL STATE PARK
Bridal Veil
PILLARS OF HERCULES
ANGELS REST
DEVILS REST
GEORGE SMITH
PALMER MILL RD
MULTNOMAH BASIN
LARCH MOUNTAIN
MOUNT HOOD NATIONAL FOREST
COLUMBIA RIVER GORGE NATIONAL SCENIC AREA
BROWER RD
PEPPER MOUNTAIN
LARCH MOUNTAIN RD
SHERRARD POINT
LARCH MOUNTAIN
NFD RD 20
ONEONTA GORGE
NE SMITH POINT RD
TALAPUS RIDGE RD
TALAPUS MOUNTAIN RD
TANNER BUTTE
COLUMBIA WILDERNESS
EAGLE CREEK
INDIAN SPRINGS CAMPGROUND
PACIFIC CREST TR
INDIAN MOUNTAIN
HOOD RIVER COUNTY
MOUNT HOOD NATIONAL FOREST
EAGLE BUTTE
SUNSHINE ROCK
MULTNOMAH CO
HOOD RIVER
TABLE MOUNTAIN
WAHTUM LAKE
LAKE BRANCH
DONAHUE RD
NFD RD 1509
NFD RD 20
NFD RD 10
BULL RUN RIVER
SAWTOOTH MOUNTAIN
RAKER POINT
LOST LAKE CAMPGROUND
NFD LAKE RD 13
BUCK PEAK
LOST LAKE
NFD RD 1010
NFD RD 10
LOOKOUT POINT
MULTNOMAH COUNTY
BIG BEND MOUNTAIN
BULL RUN RESERVOIR NO 1
BULL RUN RESERVE
WALKER PEAK
NFD RD 1008
NFD RD 12
DEVILS PULPIT
PREACHERS PEAK
NFD RD 1217
MULTNOMAH CO
CLACKAMAS CO
SENTINEL PEAK
BULL RUN RESERVOIR NO 2
NFD RD 10
NFD RD 1210
NFD RD 1210
NFD RD 10
BULL RUN LAKE
NFD RD 12
NFD RD 1210
NFD RD 1414
NFD RD 12
NFD RD 1027
THUNDER ROCK
BULL RUN NATURAL AREA
NFD RD 14
NFD RD 410
NFD RD 201
DEER MEADOWS
BLAZED ALDER BUTTE
THIMBLE MOUNTAIN
NFD RD 1027
HIYU MOUNTAIN
NFD RD 201
ASCHOFF
ASCHOFF BUTTES
ASCHOFF RD
HALFWAY HILL
NFD RD 10
BURNT PEAK
DEVILS BACKBONE
HICKMAN BUTTE
RD
ASCHOFF
CLEAR FORK BUTTE
MARMOT
MOUNT HOOD NATIONAL FOREST
NORTH MOUNTAIN RD
LOLO PASS
BIG SANDY RD
GOODFELLOW LAKES RD
NFD RD 1228
NORTH MOUNTAIN
BARLOW TRAIL
SUGARLOAF MOUNTAIN
NFD RD 1828
Marmot
CLACKAMAS COUNTY
NORTH BOULDER CREEK
MOUNT HOOD NATIONAL FOREST
LAST CHANCE MOUNTAIN
SANDY BATY RD
RD
RD
NFD RD 1825
FRED MCNEIL CAMPGROUND
RIVER
BADGER COALMAN RD
RIVER
MOUNT HOOD HWY
BARLOW TRAIL
RD
Brightwood
BRIGHTWOOD LOOP RD
Cherryville
Alder Creek
WILDCAT
NFD RD 382
26
TERRA FERN DR
WHISKEY CREEK
ALDER CREEK LN
Salmon
SALMON RIVER
RD
CRUTCHER BENCH
WEBER RD
CREEK
ALDER
MCINTYRE RIDGE
BARLOW TRAIL RD
SANDY RIVER
HORSESHOE RIDGE
LENHART BUTTE
CREEK
LOLO PASS RD
MOUNT HOOD WILDERNESS AREA
WILDCAT MOUNTAIN RD
CEDAR CREEK
TROUT
ARRAH WANNA BLVD
Wemme
Zigzag
ZIGZAG MOUNTAIN
DEVILS MEADOW CAMPGROUND
WEST ZIGZAG LOOKOUT
RD
NORTH FORK EAGLE CREEK
FAIRWAY AV
WELCHES RD
SALMON RIVER RD
Faubion
DEVIL CANYON
Rhododendron
DR CREEK
MOUNT HOOD
CREEK
HENRY CREEK
Welches
MOUNTAIN VIEW RD
ZIGZAG MOUNTAIN
ENOLA HILL
TWIN BRIDGES CAMPGROUND
OREGON
26
BOULDER CREEK
NFD RD 255 CREEK
HOOD
NFD RD 2618
ZIGZAG
MOUNT HOOD HWY
TWIN BRIDGES RD
BARLOW CAMPGROUND
LAUREL HILL
HUCKLEBERRY MOUNTAIN
NFD RD
FLAG MOUNTAIN
BRUIN RUN CAMPGROUND
CAMP CREEK CAMPGROUND
2612
NATIONAL
WILDCAT MOUNTAIN
EAGLE
SALMON MOUNTAIN
HUNCHBACK MOUNTAIN
STILL CREEK
SALMON
HUCKLEBERRY
GREEN CANYON CAMPGROUND
WIND CREEK BASIN
MOUNT HOOD
FOREST
OLD BALDY
SOUTH FORK CAMPGROUND
NATIONAL FOREST
WILDERNESS
BIGHORN CAMPGROUND
CREEK
RD
DEVILS PEAK
MOUNT HOOD NATIONAL FOREST
ROLLING RIFFLE CAMPGROUND
KINZEL LAKE CAMPGROUND
CREEK
NFD RD A615
GITHENS MOUNTAIN
SALMON
FINAL FALLS
SHEEPSHEAD ROCK
SQUAW
FRUSTRATION FALLS
VANISHING FALLS
KINZEL CREEK
WOLF CAMP BUTTE RD
RD
MOUNTAIN RD
LITTLE NIAGARA FALLS
SQUAW MOUNTAIN
HIDEAWAY FALLS
SALMON BUTTE
SPLIT FALLS
SALMON BUTTE RD
STEIN FALLS
NFD RD A613
ABBOTT
RD
LINNEY CREEK CAMPGROUND
RIVER
LINNEY CREEK RD

SEE 202 MAP

SEE 126 MAP

SEE 195 MAP

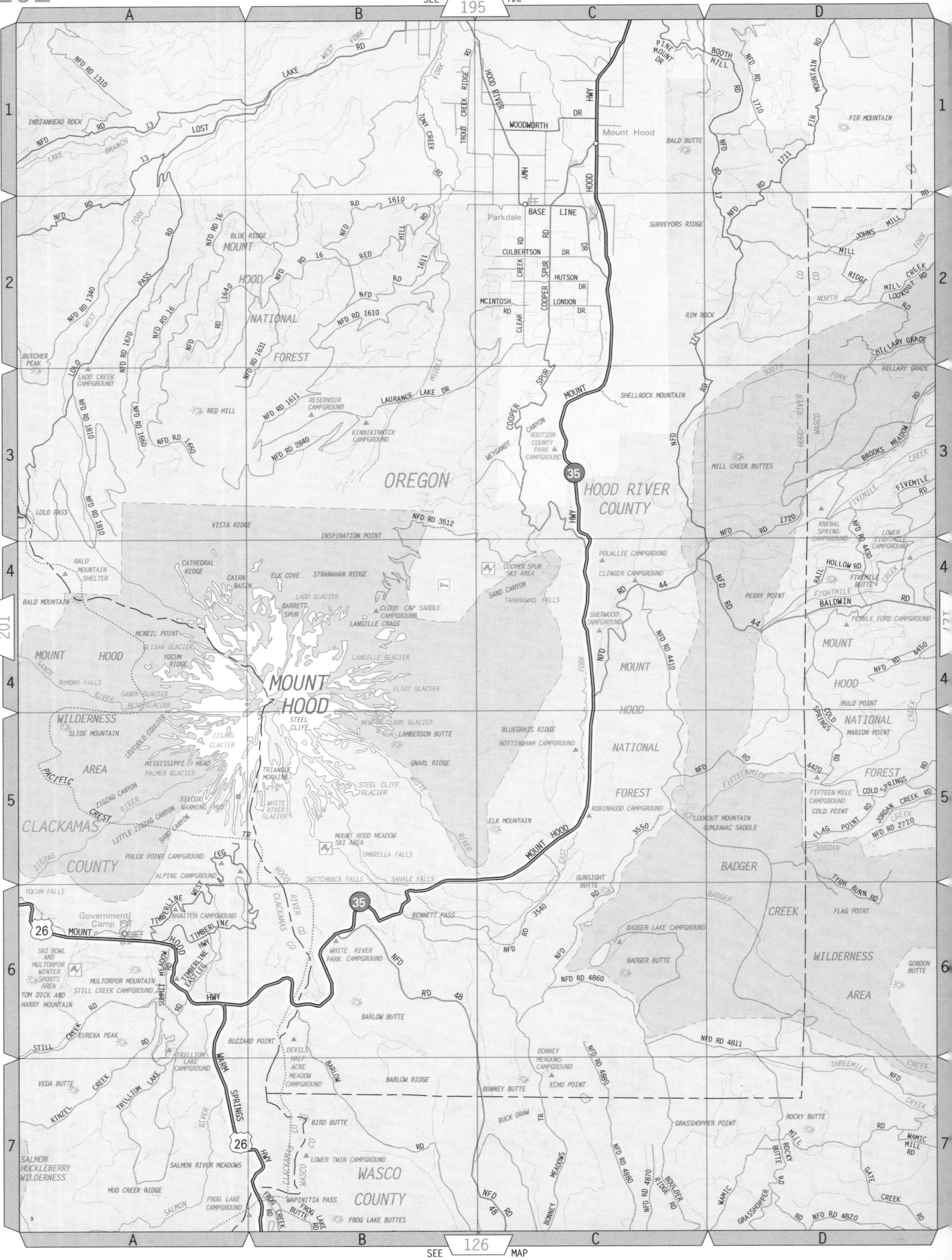

SEE 201 MAP

SEE 126 MAP

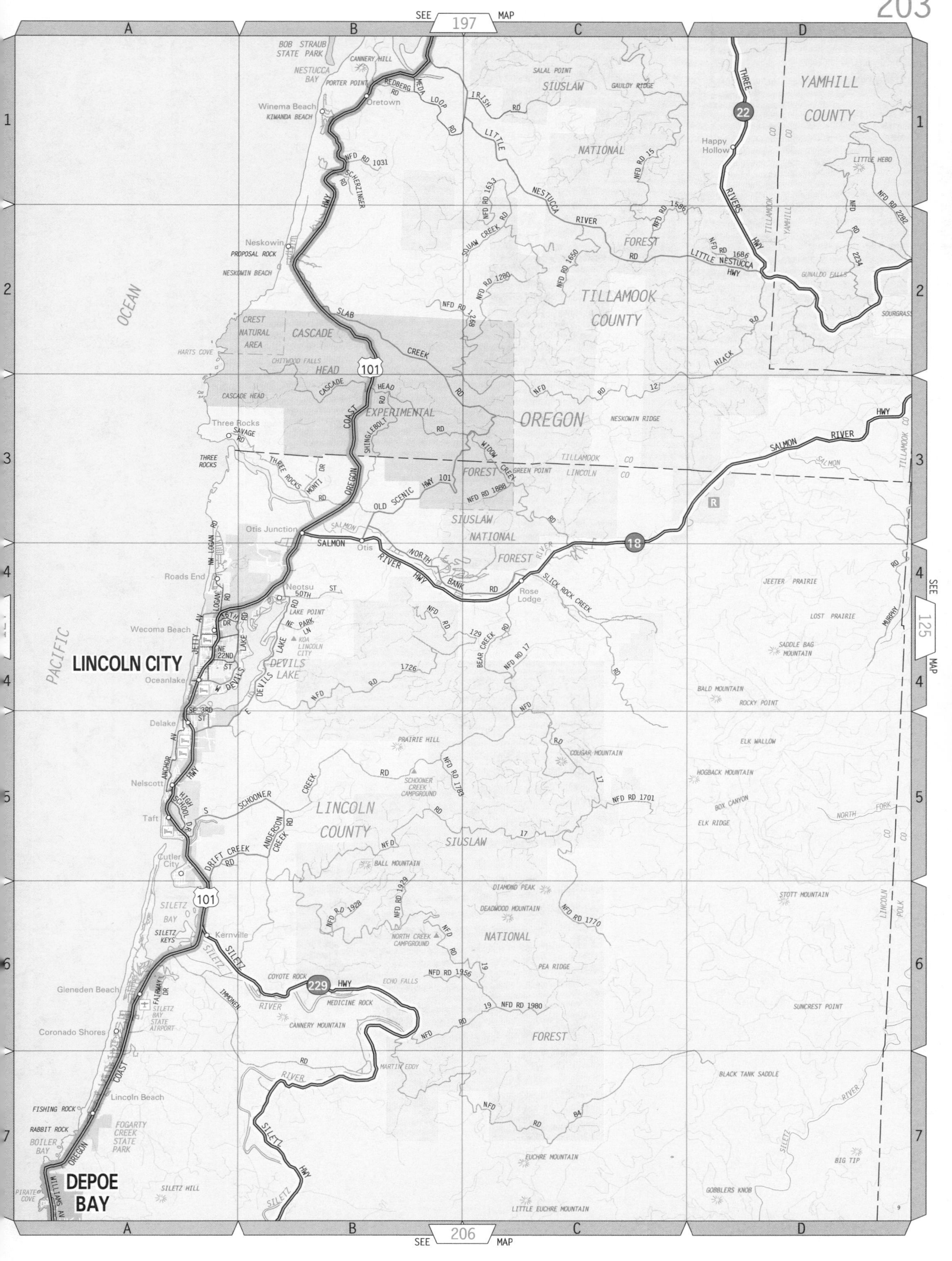

SEE 197 MAP
SEE 206 MAP
SEE 125 MAP
PNW
METRO
LINCOLN CITY
DEPOE BAY
PACIFIC
OCEAN
YAMHILL COUNTY
TILLAMOOK COUNTY
LINCOLN COUNTY
SIUSLAW NATIONAL FOREST
OREGON
BOB STRAUB STATE PARK
NESTUCCA BAY
CANNERY HILL
PORTER POINT
Winema Beach
KIWANDA BEACH
Oretown
Happy Hollow
Neskowin
PROPOSAL ROCK
NESKOWIN BEACH
CASCADE HEAD
CREST NATURAL AREA
HARTS COVE
CHITWOOD FALLS
CASCADE HEAD EXPERIMENTAL FOREST
Three Rocks
THREE ROCKS
Otis Junction
Otis
Rose Lodge
Neotsu
Roads End
Wecoma Beach
Oceanlake
Delake
Nelscott
Taft
Cutler City
SILETZ BAY
SILETZ KEYS
Kernville
Gleneden Beach
SILETZ BAY STATE AIRPORT
Coronado Shores
Lincoln Beach
FISHING ROCK
RABBIT ROCK
BOILER BAY
FOGARTY CREEK STATE PARK
PIRATE COVE
SILETZ HILL
DEVILS LAKE
KOA LINCOLN CITY
SALAL POINT
GAULDY RIDGE
LITTLE HEBO
GUNALDO FALLS
SOURGRASS
NESKOWIN RIDGE
GREEN POINT
JEETER PRAIRIE
LOST PRAIRIE
SADDLE BAG MOUNTAIN
BALD MOUNTAIN
ROCKY POINT
ELK WALLOW
PRAIRIE HILL
COUGAR MOUNTAIN
SCHOONER CREEK CAMPGROUND
HOGBACK MOUNTAIN
BOX CANYON
ELK RIDGE
BALL MOUNTAIN
DIAMOND PEAK
DEADWOOD MOUNTAIN
STOTT MOUNTAIN
NORTH CREEK CAMPGROUND
PEA RIDGE
COYOTE ROCK
ECHO FALLS
MEDICINE ROCK
CANNERY MOUNTAIN
SUNCREST POINT
MARTIN EDDY
BLACK TANK SADDLE
EUCHRE MOUNTAIN
BIG TIP
GOBBLERS KNOB
LITTLE EUCHRE MOUNTAIN
101
22
18
229
THREE RIVERS HWY
LITTLE NESTUCCA HWY
SLAB CREEK RD
SALMON RIVER HWY
NORTH BANK RD
SLICK ROCK CREEK
OLD SCENIC HWY 101
OREGON COAST HWY
SILETZ HWY
SCHOONER CREEK
DRIFT CREEK RD
ANDERSON CREEK RD
IMMONEN
SILETZ RIVER
LITTLE NESTUCCA RIVER
NFD RD 1031
NFD RD 1888
NFD RD 1701
NFD RD 1770
NFD RD 1956
NFD RD 1980
NFD RD 1783
NFD RD 1928
NFD RD 1929

SEE 198 MAP

SEE 125 MAP

SEE 207 MAP

PNW

METRO

SEE 199 MAP

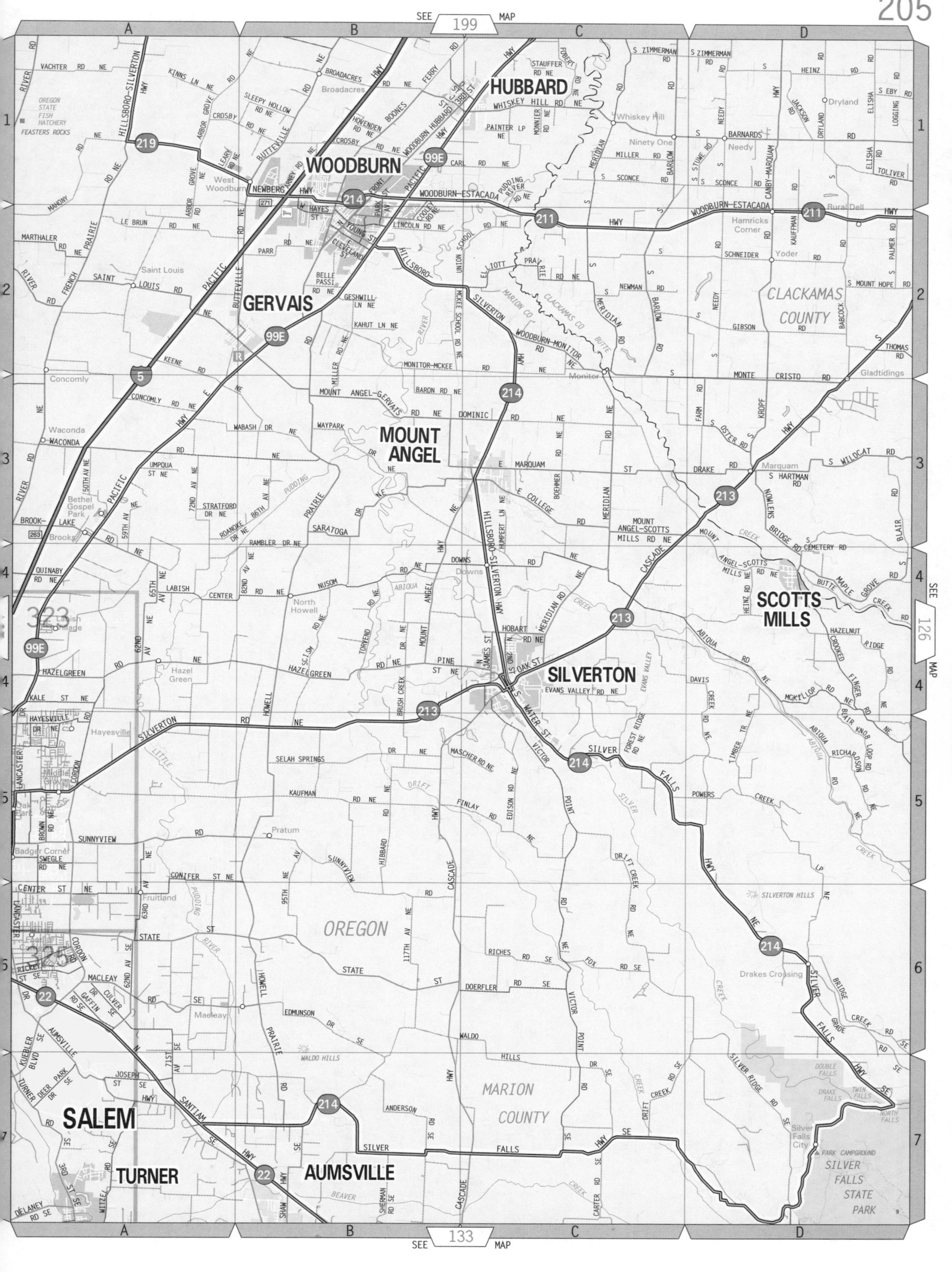

SEE 126 MAP

SEE 133 MAP

SEE 203 MAP

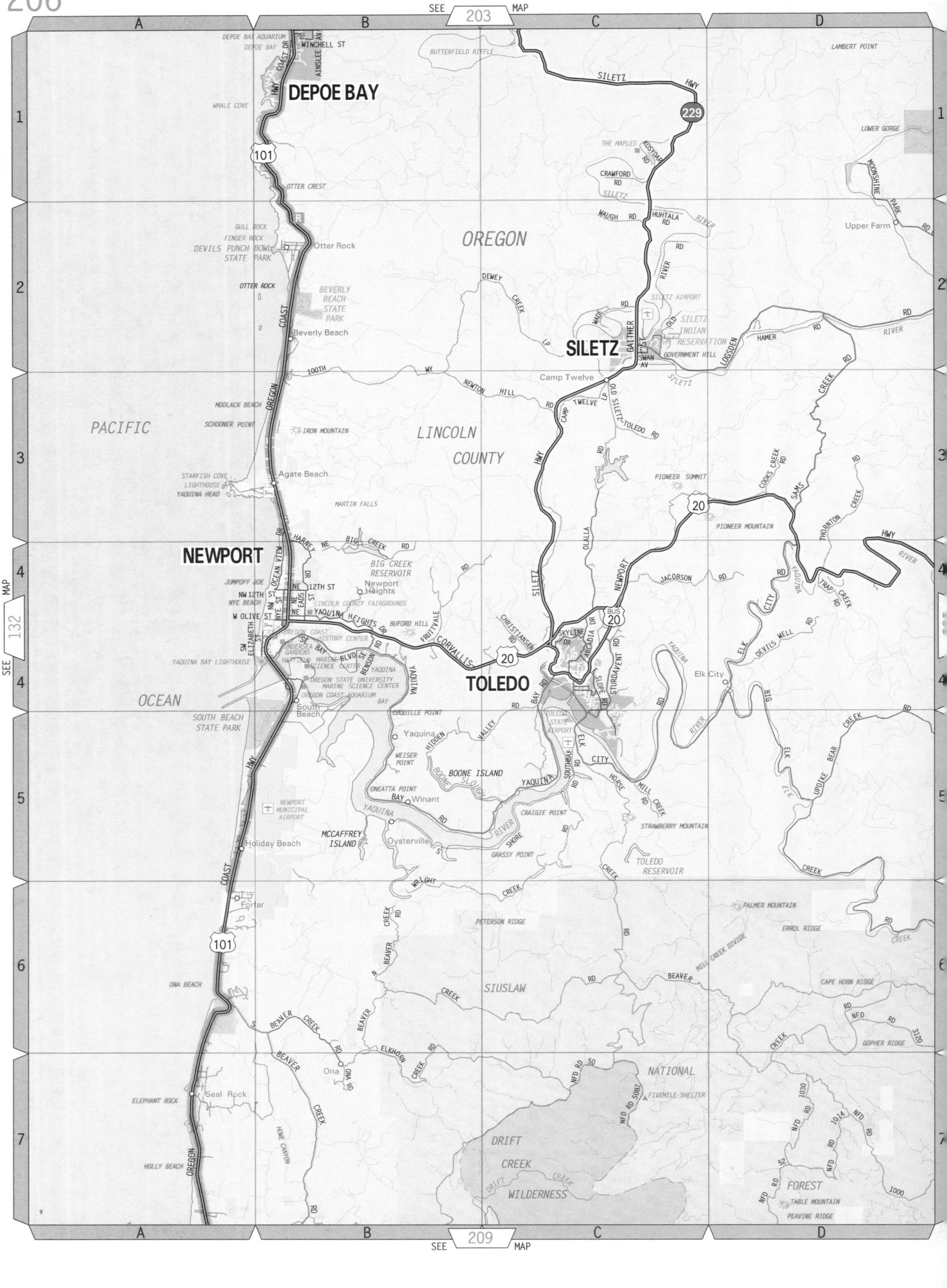

DEPOE BAY
SILETZ
NEWPORT
TOLEDO
OREGON
LINCOLN COUNTY
PACIFIC OCEAN
SIUSLAW NATIONAL FOREST
DRIFT CREEK WILDERNESS

SEE 132 MAP

SEE 209 MAP

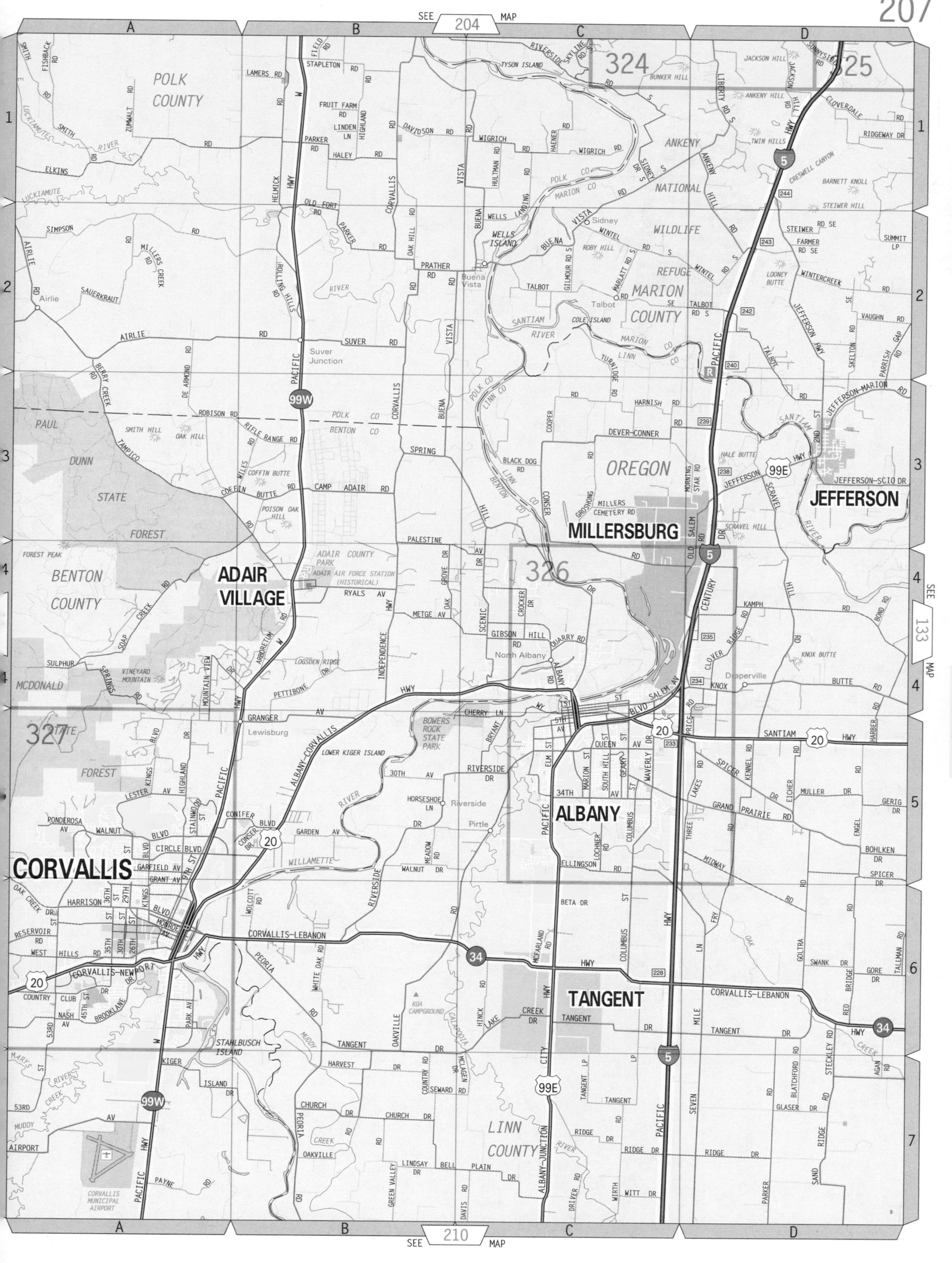

SEE 204 MAP
SEE 210 MAP
SEE 133 MAP
PNW
METRO
POLK COUNTY
BENTON COUNTY
LINN COUNTY
MARION COUNTY
CORVALLIS
ADAIR VILLAGE
MILLERSBURG
JEFFERSON
ALBANY
TANGENT
PAUL DUNN STATE FOREST
MCDONALD STATE FOREST
ANKENY NATIONAL WILDLIFE REFUGE
OREGON
SANTIAM RIVER
WILLAMETTE RIVER
324
325
326
327

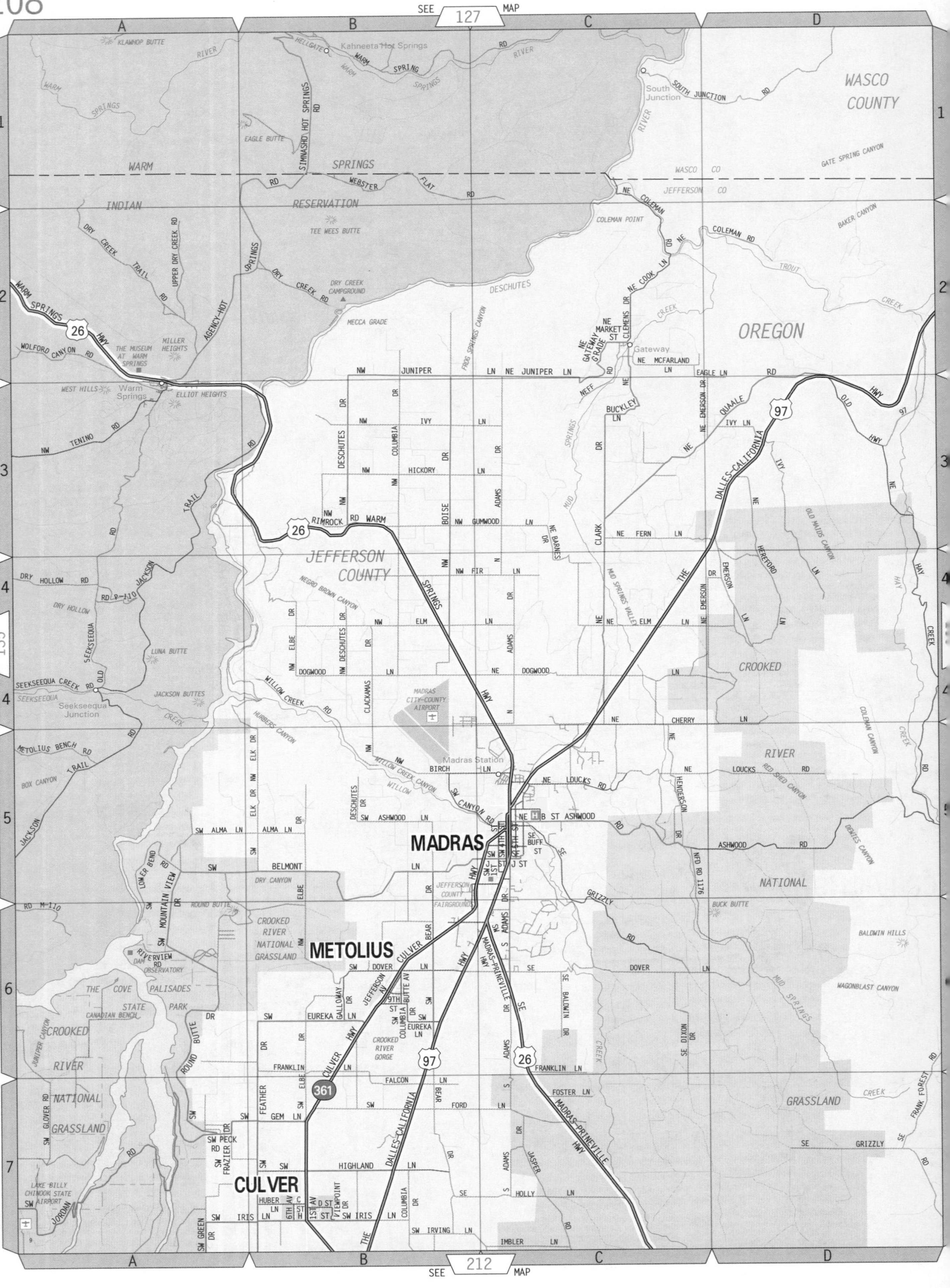
SEE 127 MAP
SEE 135 MAP
SEE 212 MAP
A
B
C
D
1
2
3
4
5
6
7
KLAWHOP BUTTE
Kahneeta Hot Springs
HELLGATE
WARM SPRING RD
RIVER
WARM SPRINGS
SIMNASHO HOT SPRINGS RD
EAGLE BUTTE
South Junction
SOUTH JUNCTION RD
WASCO COUNTY
WARM SPRINGS INDIAN RESERVATION
WEBSTER FLAT RD
WASCO CO
JEFFERSON CO
GATE SPRING CANYON
NE COLEMAN RD
COLEMAN POINT
BAKER CANYON
TEE WEES BUTTE
DRY CREEK TRAIL RD
UPPER DRY CREEK RD
SPRINGS AGENCY-HOT
DRY CREEK RD
DRY CREEK CAMPGROUND
DESCHUTES
TROUT CREEK
NE COOK LN
CLEMENS DR
MECCA GRADE
WARM SPRINGS HWY
26
WOLFORD CANYON RD
THE MUSEUM AT WARM SPRINGS
MILLER HEIGHTS
FROG SPRINGS CANYON
NE MARKET ST
NE GATEWAY GRADE
Gateway
NE MCFARLAND LN
OREGON
NW JUNIPER LN
NE JUNIPER LN
EAGLE LN RD
WEST HILLS
Warm Springs
ELLIOT HEIGHTS
NEFF RD
BUCKLEY LN
NE EMERSON DR
NE QUAALE RD
IVY LN
97
OLD HWY
NW TENINO RD
NW IVY LN
DESCHUTES DR
COLUMBIA DR
DR
MUD SPRINGS
CLARK DR
THE DALLES-CALIFORNIA HWY
IVY
NW HICKORY LN
ADAMS DR
BOISE DR
NE
TRAIL
NW RIMROCK RD
WARM SPRINGS HWY
NW GUMWOOD LN
NE BARNES DR
NE FERN LN
NE HEREFORD
OLD MAIDS CANYON
JEFFERSON COUNTY
NEGRO BROWN CANYON
NW FIR LN
MUD SPRINGS VALLEY
EMERSON LN
HAY CREEK
DRY HOLLOW RD
RD P-110
JACKSON TRAIL
NW ELM LN
NE ELM LN
NE EMERSON
NW ELBE DR
NW DESCHUTES DR
DRY HOLLOW
SEEKSEEQUA
LUNA BUTTE
CROOKED RIVER NATIONAL GRASSLAND
NW DOGWOOD LN
NE DOGWOOD LN
SEEKSEEQUA CREEK RD
OLD
Seekseequa Junction
JACKSON BUTTES
WILLOW CREEK RD
HURBERS CANYON
CLACKAMAS DR
MADRAS CITY-COUNTY AIRPORT
NE CHERRY LN
COLEMAN CANYON
METOLIUS BENCH RD
BOX CANYON TRAIL
ELK DR
NW BIRCH LN
Madras Station
NE LOUCKS RD
NE LOUCKS RD
HENDERSON DR
RED SHED CANYON
WILLOW CREEK CANYON
SW CANYON RD
JACKSON
SW ASHWOOD LN
NE B ST ASHWOOD RD
SW ALMA LN
ALMA LN
MADRAS
SE BUFF ST
ASHWOOD RD
DEWEES CANYON
LOWER BEND RD
SW BELMONT LN
J ST
NFD RD 1176
DRY CANYON
JEFFERSON COUNTY FAIRGROUNDS
RD M-110
MOUNTAIN VIEW DR
ROUND BUTTE
GRIZZLY RD
BUCK BUTTE
BALDWIN HILLS
CROOKED RIVER NATIONAL GRASSLAND
METOLIUS
CULVER HWY
BEAR DR
RIVERVIEW DAM
RD OBSERVATORY
SW DOVER LN
SE DOVER LN
WAGONBLAST CANYON
THE COVE PALISADES STATE PARK
ROUND BUTTE DR
JEFFERSON AV
9TH ST
BUTTE AV
MADRAS-PRINEVILLE HWY
SE BALDWIN DR
CANADIAN BENCH
SW EUREKA LN
GALLOWAY DR
EUREKA LN
COLUMBIA DR
CROOKED RIVER GORGE
SE DIXON DR
JUNIPER CANYON
SW FRANKLIN LN
FRANKLIN LN
CREEK
FALCON LN
361
SW FORD LN
FOSTER LN
FRANK FOREST RD
GLOVER RD
FEATHER DR
ELBE DR
GEM LN
SW PECK RD
SW FRAZIER RD
HIGHLAND LN
SE GRIZZLY RD
LAKE BILLY CHINOOK STATE AIRPORT
JORDAN RD
CULVER
HUBER AV
1ST AV
6TH AV
D ST
VIEWPOINT DR
SW IRIS LN
SW IRVING LN
SE HOLLY LN
JASPER RD
SW GREEN DR
IMBLER LN

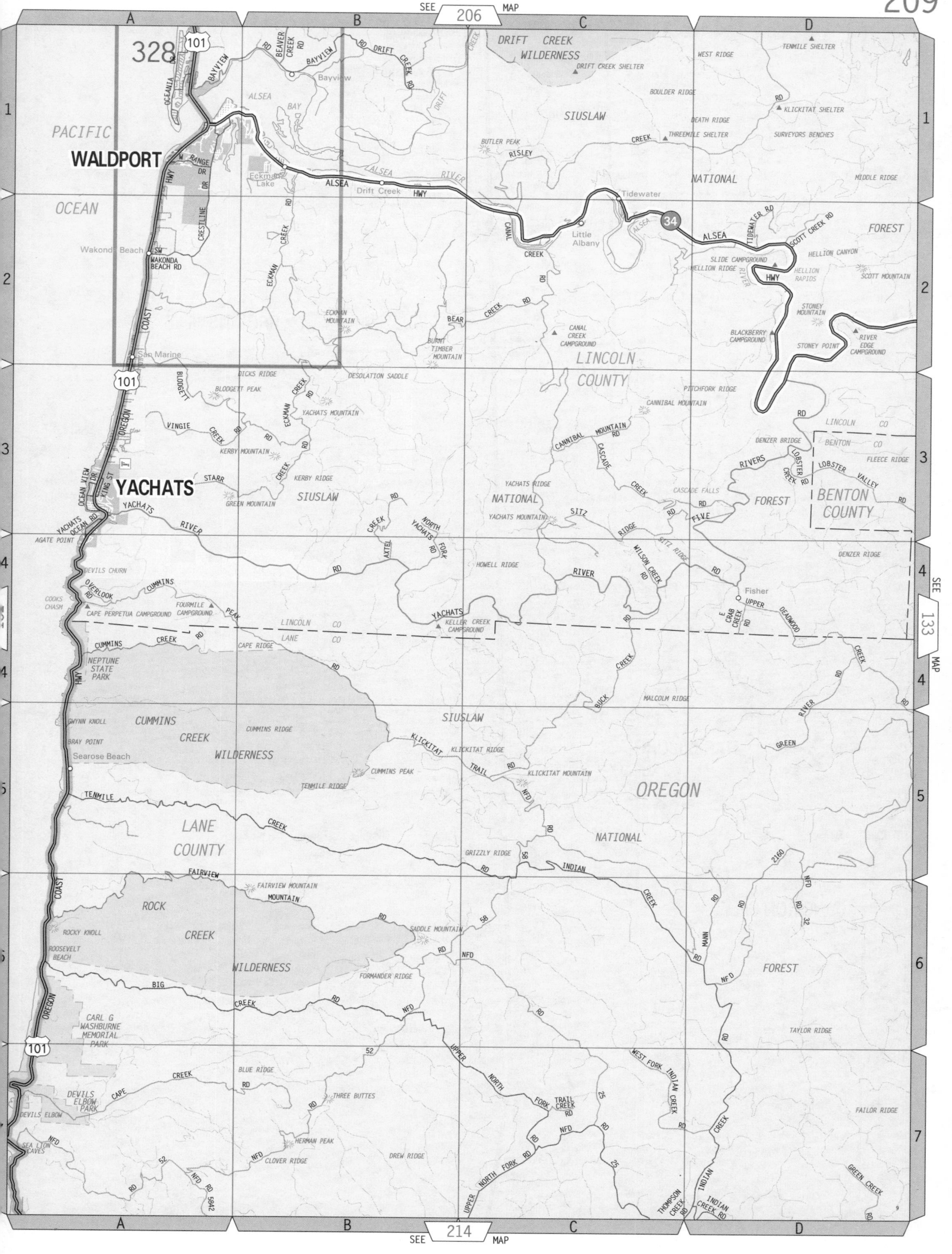

SEE 206 MAP
WALDPORT
YACHATS
PACIFIC OCEAN
ALSEA BAY
DRIFT CREEK WILDERNESS
SIUSLAW NATIONAL FOREST
LINCOLN COUNTY
BENTON COUNTY
LANE COUNTY
CUMMINS CREEK WILDERNESS
ROCK CREEK WILDERNESS
OREGON NATIONAL FOREST
NEPTUNE STATE PARK
CARL G WASHBURNE MEMORIAL PARK
DEVILS ELBOW PARK
Tidewater
Little Albany
Fisher
Bayview
Drift Creek
Eckman Lake
Wakonda Beach
San Marine
Searose Beach
ALSEA HWY
COAST HWY
OREGON COAST HWY
SEE 133 MAP
SEE 214 MAP
328
PNW
METRO

SEE 207 MAP

A B C D

LINN COUNTY

OREGON

BROWNSVILLE

HALSEY

HARRISBURG

JUNCTION CITY

COBURG

LANE COUNTY

BENTON CO
LINN CO
LANE CO

Plainview
Shedd
Fayetteville
Peoria
American
Lancaster
Wilkins
Marcola

HOACUM ISLAND
MARSHALL ISLAND
GREEN ISLAND

THE LIVING ROCK MUSEUM
LINN COUNTY HISTORICAL MUSEUM

ROCK HILL
WARD BUTTE
LONE PINE BUTTE
WASHBURN BUTTE
CEDAR BUTTE
ROBE HILL
SNAKE HILL
POWELL HILLS
TWIN BUTTES
INDIAN HEAD
HORSE ROCK
DIAMOND HILL
COUGAR RIDGE
BALD MOUNTAIN
ROUND MOUNTAIN
TOM MOUNT
WEST POINT HILL
BUCK MOUNTAIN
CENTENNIAL BUTTE
LENON HILL

WILLAMETTE RIVER
CALAPOOIA RIVER
MOHAWK RIVER

SEE 133 MAP

PNW

METRO

SEE 215 MAP

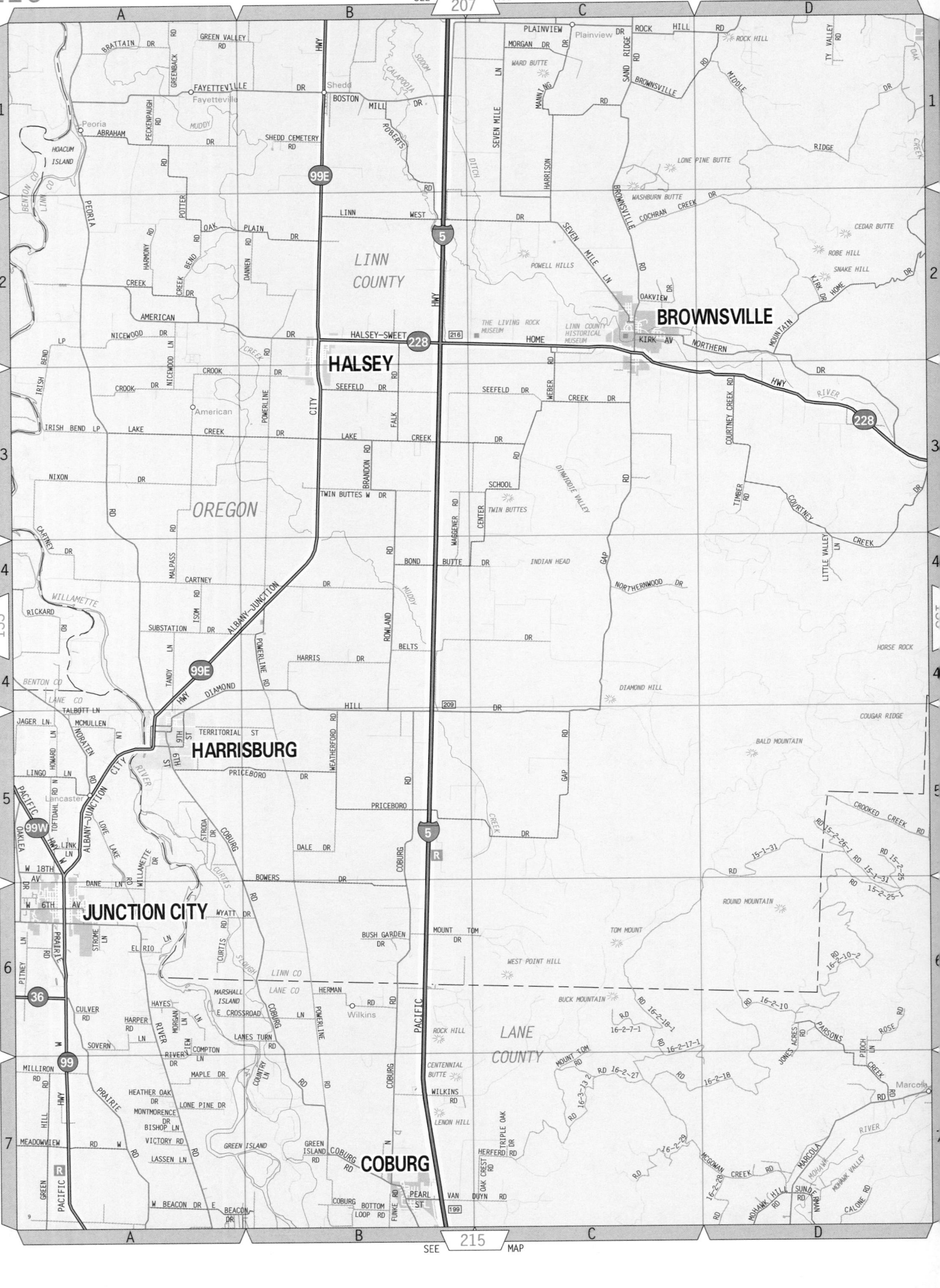

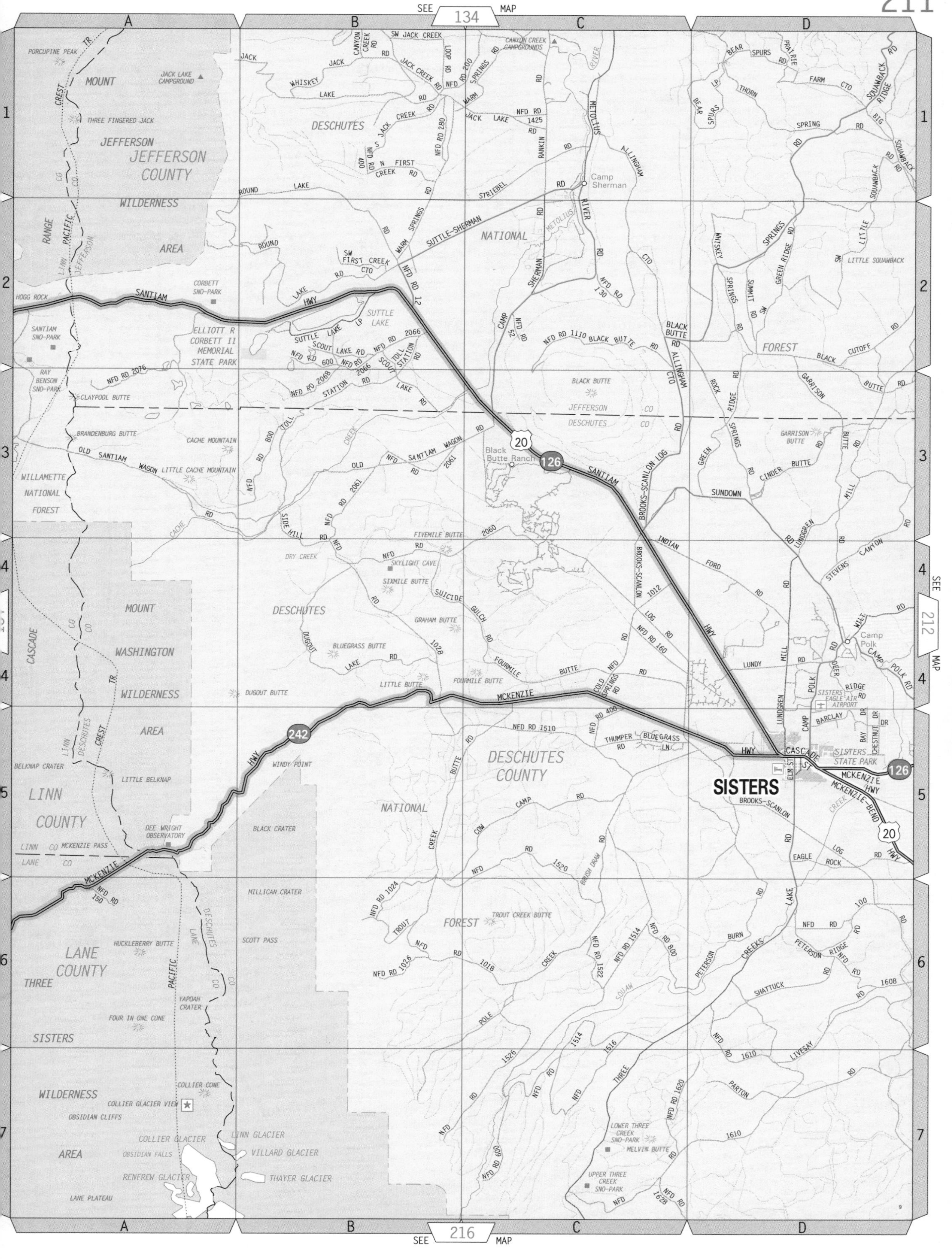

SEE 134 MAP
SEE 216 MAP
SEE 212 MAP
PNW
METRO
JEFFERSON COUNTY
MOUNT JEFFERSON WILDERNESS AREA
DESCHUTES NATIONAL FOREST
DESCHUTES COUNTY
MOUNT WASHINGTON WILDERNESS AREA
LINN COUNTY
LANE COUNTY
THREE SISTERS WILDERNESS AREA
WILLAMETTE NATIONAL FOREST
SISTERS
Camp Sherman
Black Butte Ranch
Camp Polk
SISTERS STATE PARK
SISTERS EAGLE AIR AIRPORT
SANTIAM HWY
MCKENZIE HWY
CASCADE ST
SUTTLE LAKE
SUTTLE-SHERMAN RD
BLACK BUTTE
DEE WRIGHT OBSERVATORY
MCKENZIE PASS
COLLIER GLACIER VIEW

SEE 208 MAP

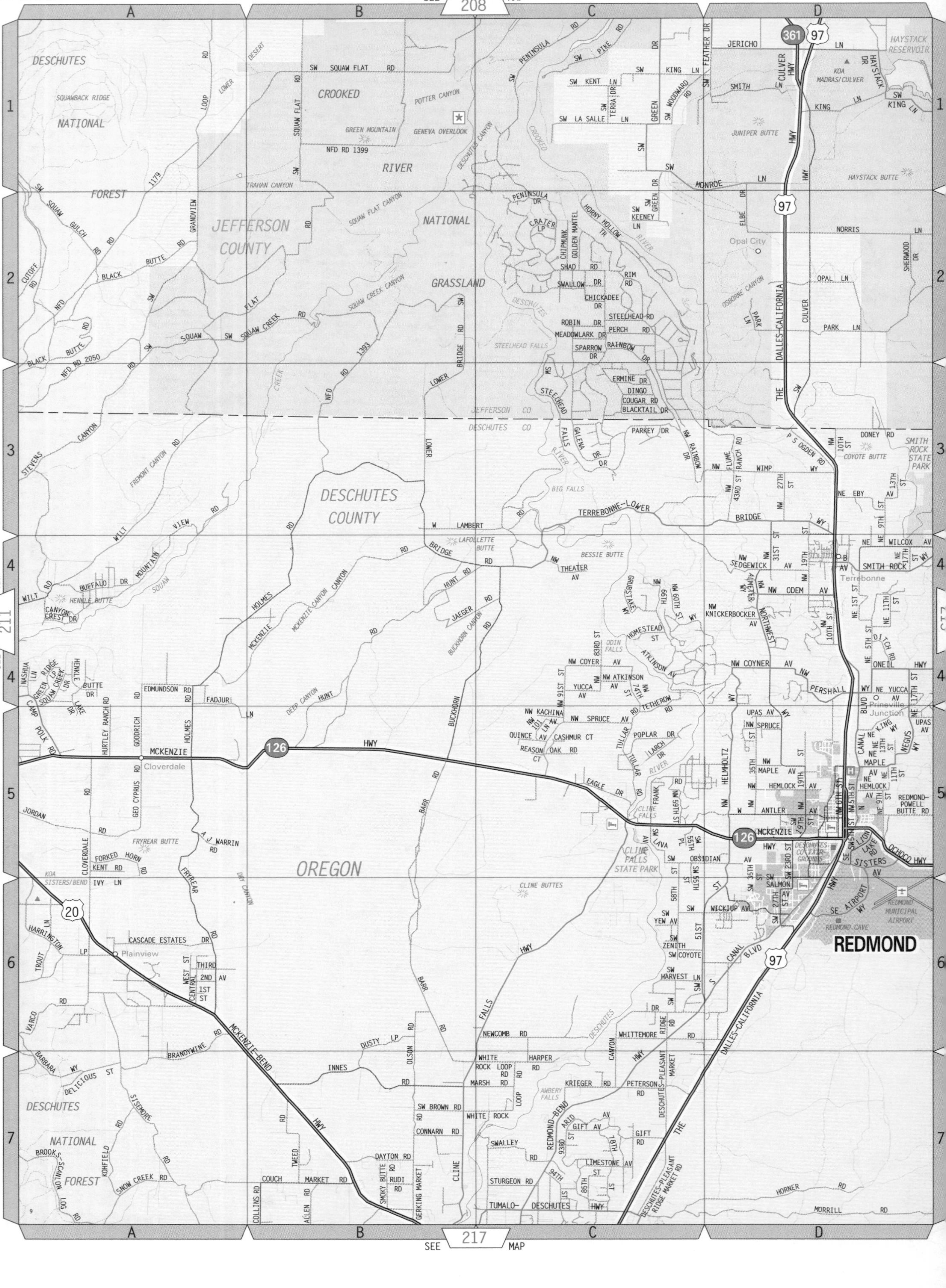
A
B
C
D
1
2
3
4
5
6
7
DESCHUTES
NATIONAL
FOREST
CROOKED
RIVER
NATIONAL
GRASSLAND
JEFFERSON
COUNTY
DESCHUTES
COUNTY
OREGON
JEFFERSON CO
DESCHUTES CO
Opal City
Terrebonne
Prineville Junction
Cloverdale
Plainview
REDMOND
REDMOND MUNICIPAL AIRPORT
DESCHUTES CO FAIR GROUNDS
CLINE FALLS STATE PARK
SMITH ROCK STATE PARK
HAYSTACK RESERVOIR
KOA MADRAS/CULVER
KOA SISTERS/BEND
GREEN MOUNTAIN
GENEVA OVERLOOK
JUNIPER BUTTE
HAYSTACK BUTTE
COYOTE BUTTE
LAFOLLETTE BUTTE
BESSIE BUTTE
HENKLE BUTTE
FRYREAR BUTTE
CLINE BUTTES
STEELHEAD FALLS
BIG FALLS
ODIN FALLS
CLINE FALLS
AWBERY FALLS
REDMOND CAVE
SQUAWBACK RIDGE
POTTER CANYON
TRAHAN CANYON
SQUAW FLAT CANYON
SQUAW CREEK CANYON
OSBORNE CANYON
FREMONT CANYON
DEEP CANYON
MCKENZIE CANYON
BUCKHORN CANYON
DRY CANYON
THE DALLES-CALIFORNIA HWY
MCKENZIE HWY
MCKENZIE-BEND HWY
OCHOCO HWY
97
361
126
20
SEE 211 MAP
SEE 217 MAP

SEE 217 MAP

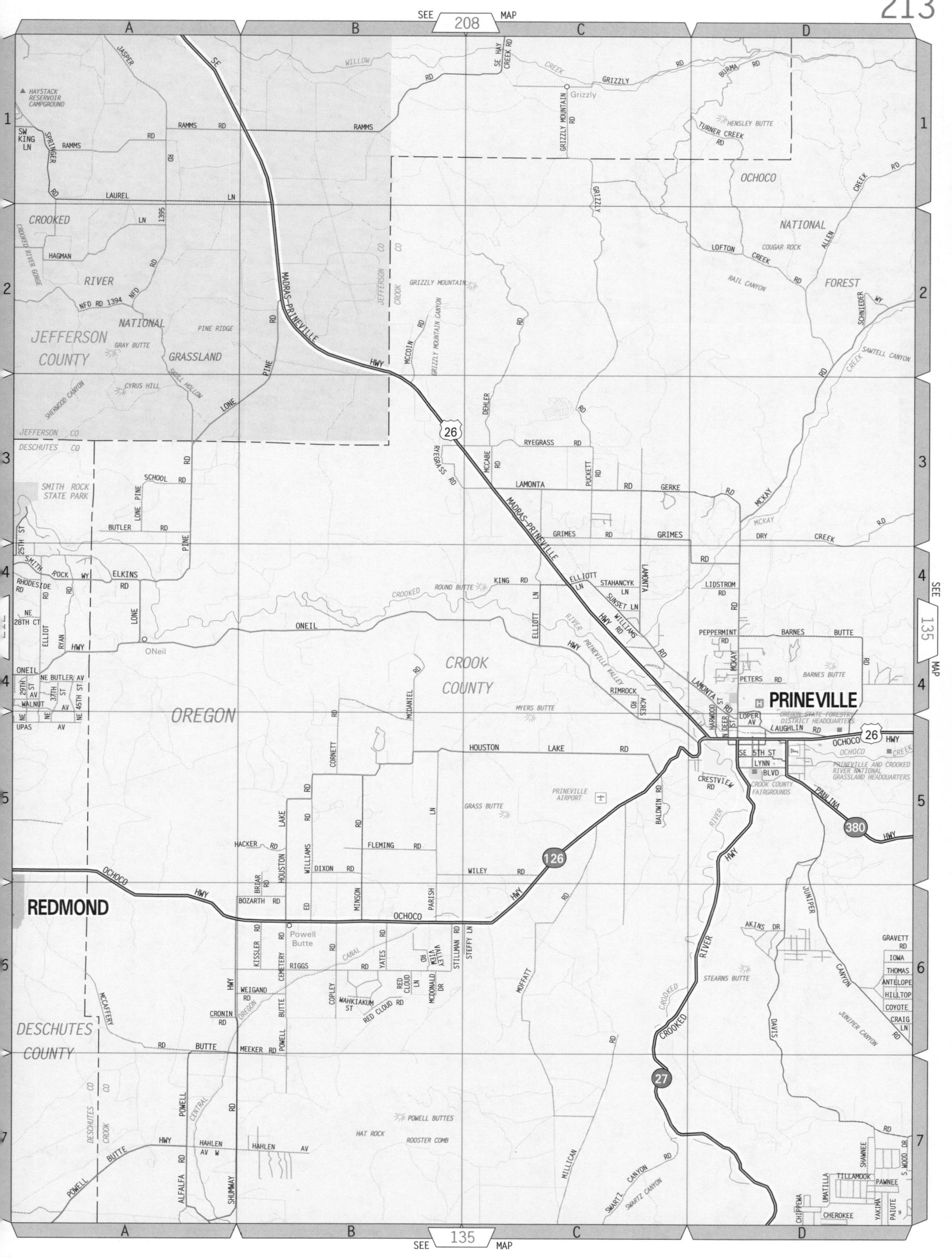

SEE 208 MAP
SEE 135 MAP
PRINEVILLE
REDMOND
JEFFERSON COUNTY
CROOK COUNTY
DESCHUTES COUNTY
OREGON
CROOKED RIVER NATIONAL GRASSLAND
OCHOCO NATIONAL FOREST
SMITH ROCK STATE PARK
HAYSTACK RESERVOIR CAMPGROUND
PRINEVILLE AIRPORT
CROOK COUNTY FAIRGROUNDS
OREGON STATE FORESTRY DISTRICT HEADQUARTERS
PRINEVILLE AND CROOKED RIVER NATIONAL GRASSLAND HEADQUARTERS
MADRAS-PRINEVILLE HWY
OCHOCO HWY
PAULINA HWY
Grizzly
ONeil
Powell Butte
GRIZZLY MOUNTAIN
GRAY BUTTE
CYRUS HILL
ROUND BUTTE
MYERS BUTTE
BARNES BUTTE
GRASS BUTTE
STEARNS BUTTE
POWELL BUTTES
HENSLEY BUTTE
COUGAR ROCK
PNW
METRO

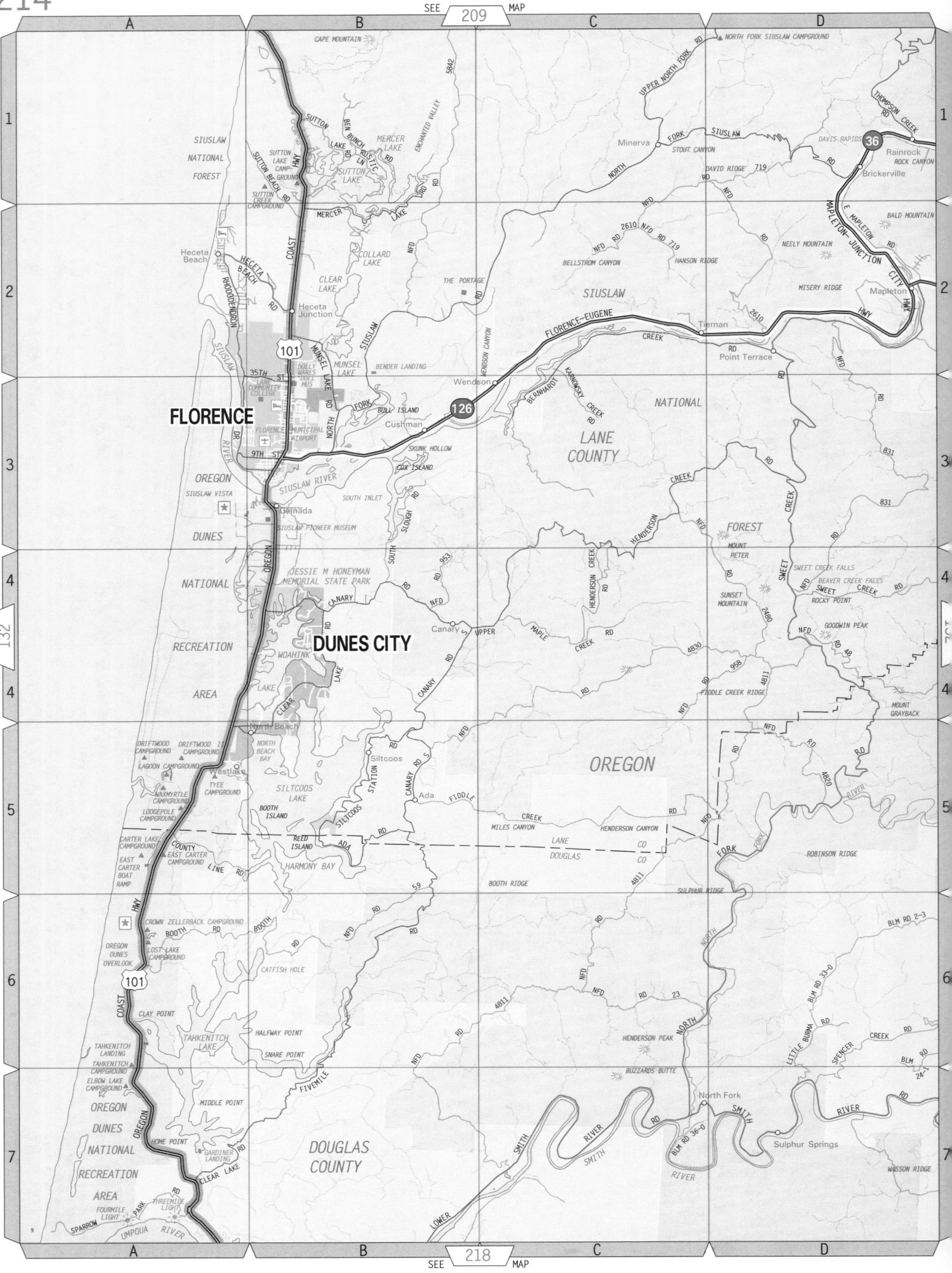
SEE MAP 209
A
B
C
D
1
2
3
4
5
6
7
SEE MAP 218
SEE MAP 132
FLORENCE
DUNES CITY
SIUSLAW NATIONAL FOREST
LANE COUNTY
DOUGLAS COUNTY
OREGON DUNES NATIONAL RECREATION AREA
SIUSLAW NATIONAL FOREST
OREGON
CAPE MOUNTAIN
NORTH FORK SIUSLAW CAMPGROUND
UPPER NORTH FORK RD
THOMPSON CREEK RD
Minerva
NORTH FORK SIUSLAW
STOUT CANYON
DAVIS RAPIDS
Rainrock
ROCK CANYON
Brickerville
DAVID RIDGE
719
SUTTON LAKE RD
BEN BUNCH RD
RUSTIC LN
MERCER LAKE
ENCHANTED VALLEY
SUTTON LAKE CAMPGROUND
SUTTON LAKE
SUTTON BEACH RD
SUTTON CREEK CAMPGROUND
MERCER LAKE RD
5842
COAST HWY
Heceta Beach
HECETA BEACH RD
RHODODENDRON
COLLARD LAKE
CLEAR LAKE
Heceta Junction
THE PORTAGE
2610
NFD RD 719
BELLSTROM CANYON
HANSON RIDGE
NEELY MOUNTAIN
BALD MOUNTAIN
MAPLETON-JUNCTION CITY HWY
E MAPLETON RD
MISERY RIDGE
Mapleton
36
101
MUNSEL LAKE RD
MUNSEL LAKE
SIUSLAW
35TH ST
DOLLY WARES DOLL MUS
LANE COMMUNITY COLLEGE
BENDER LANDING
WENDSON CANYON
FLORENCE-EUGENE
Tiernan
CREEK
Point Terrace
Wendson
BERNHARDT
KARNOWSKY CREEK RD
NORTH FORK
BULL ISLAND
126
Cushman
FLORENCE MUNICIPAL AIRPORT
RIVER DR
9TH ST
SKUNK HOLLOW
COX ISLAND
SIUSLAW RIVER
SIUSLAW VISTA
Glenada
SOUTH INLET
SOUTH SLOUGH RD
SIUSLAW PIONEER MUSEUM
HENDERSON CREEK
FOREST
MOUNT PETER
SWEET CREEK
831
JESSIE M HONEYMAN MEMORIAL STATE PARK
CANARY RD
953
SUNSET MOUNTAIN
2480
SWEET CREEK FALLS
BEAVER CREEK FALLS
ROCKY POINT
Canary
UPPER
MAPLE CREEK RD
4830
GOODWIN PEAK
NFD RD 48
WOAHINK LAKE
CLEAR LAKE
958
4811
FIDDLE CREEK RIDGE
MOUNT GRAYBACK
North Beach
NORTH BEACH BAY
DRIFTWOOD CAMPGROUND
DRIFTWOOD II CAMPGROUND
LAGOON CAMPGROUND
Westlake
TYEE CAMPGROUND
WAXMYRTLE CAMPGROUND
LODGEPOLE CAMPGROUND
Siltcoos
SILTCOOS LAKE
STATION RD
CANARY RD S
Ada
FIDDLE CREEK
4820
BOOTH ISLAND
MILES CANYON
HENDERSON CANYON
CARTER LAKE CAMPGROUND
COUNTY LINE RD
EAST CARTER CAMPGROUND
EAST CARTER BOAT RAMP
REED ISLAND
ADA RD
HARMONY BAY
LANE CO
DOUGLAS CO
ROBINSON RIDGE
SULPHUR RIDGE
BOOTH RIDGE
59
CROWN ZELLERBACK CAMPGROUND
BOOTH RD
OREGON DUNES OVERLOOK
LOST LAKE CAMPGROUND
CATFISH HOLE
BLM RD 2-3
BLM RD 33-0
23
CLAY POINT
TAHKENITCH LAKE
HALFWAY POINT
SNARE POINT
TAHKENITCH LANDING
TAHKENITCH CAMPGROUND
ELBOW LAKE CAMPGROUND
HENDERSON PEAK
LITTLE BURMA RD
SPENCER CREEK RD
BLM RD 24-1
BUZZARDS BUTTE
FIVEMILE
MIDDLE POINT
North Fork
SMITH RIVER
BLM RD 36-0
Sulphur Springs
WASSON RIDGE
HOME POINT
GARDINER LANDING
CLEAR LAKE RD
FOURMILE LIGHT
THREEMILE LIGHT
PARK RD
SPARROW
UMPQUA RIVER
LOWER SMITH RD

PNW
METRO

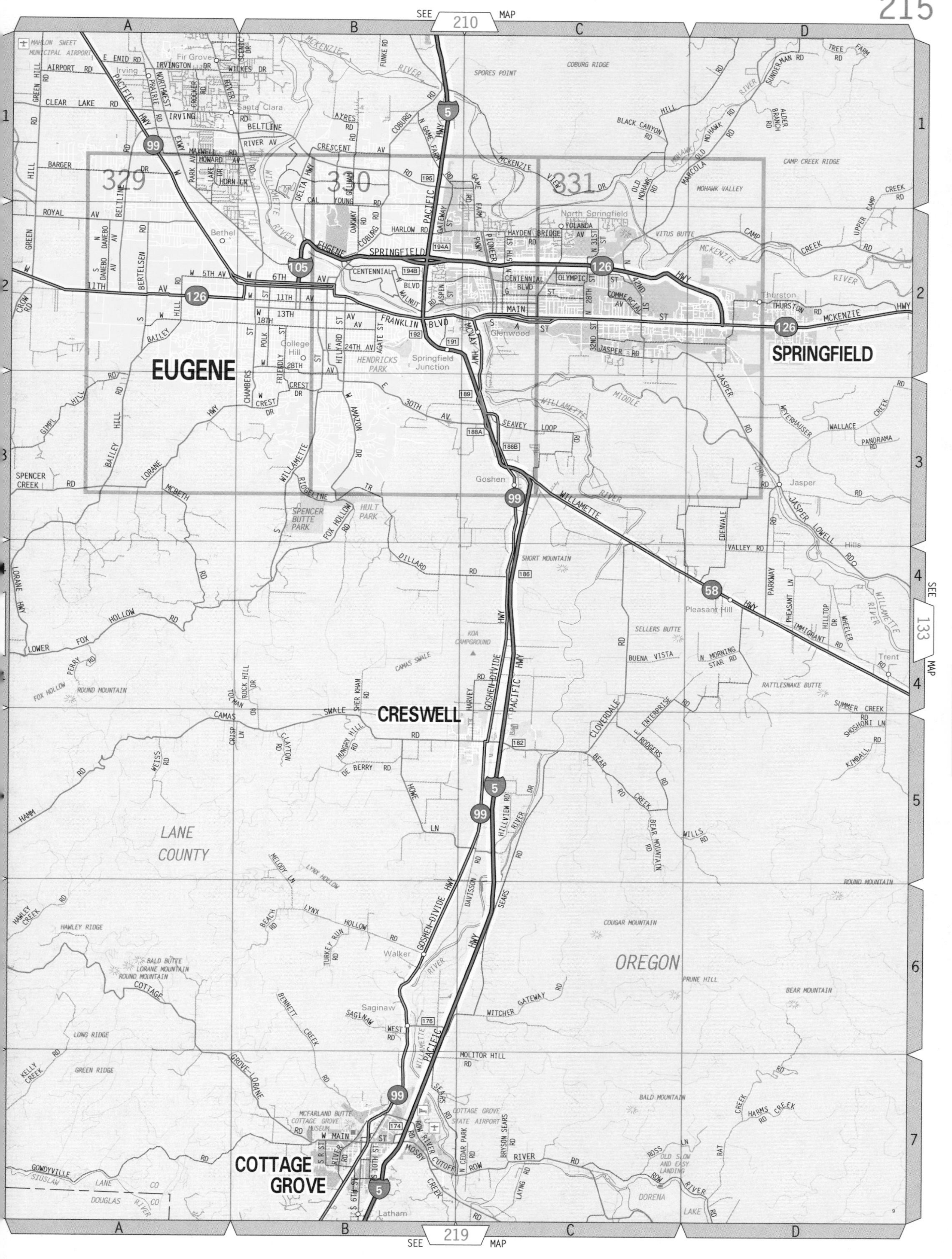
EUGENE
SPRINGFIELD
CRESWELL
COTTAGE GROVE
LANE COUNTY
OREGON
SEE 210 MAP
SEE 219 MAP
SEE 133 MAP
PNW
METRO

SEE 211 MAP

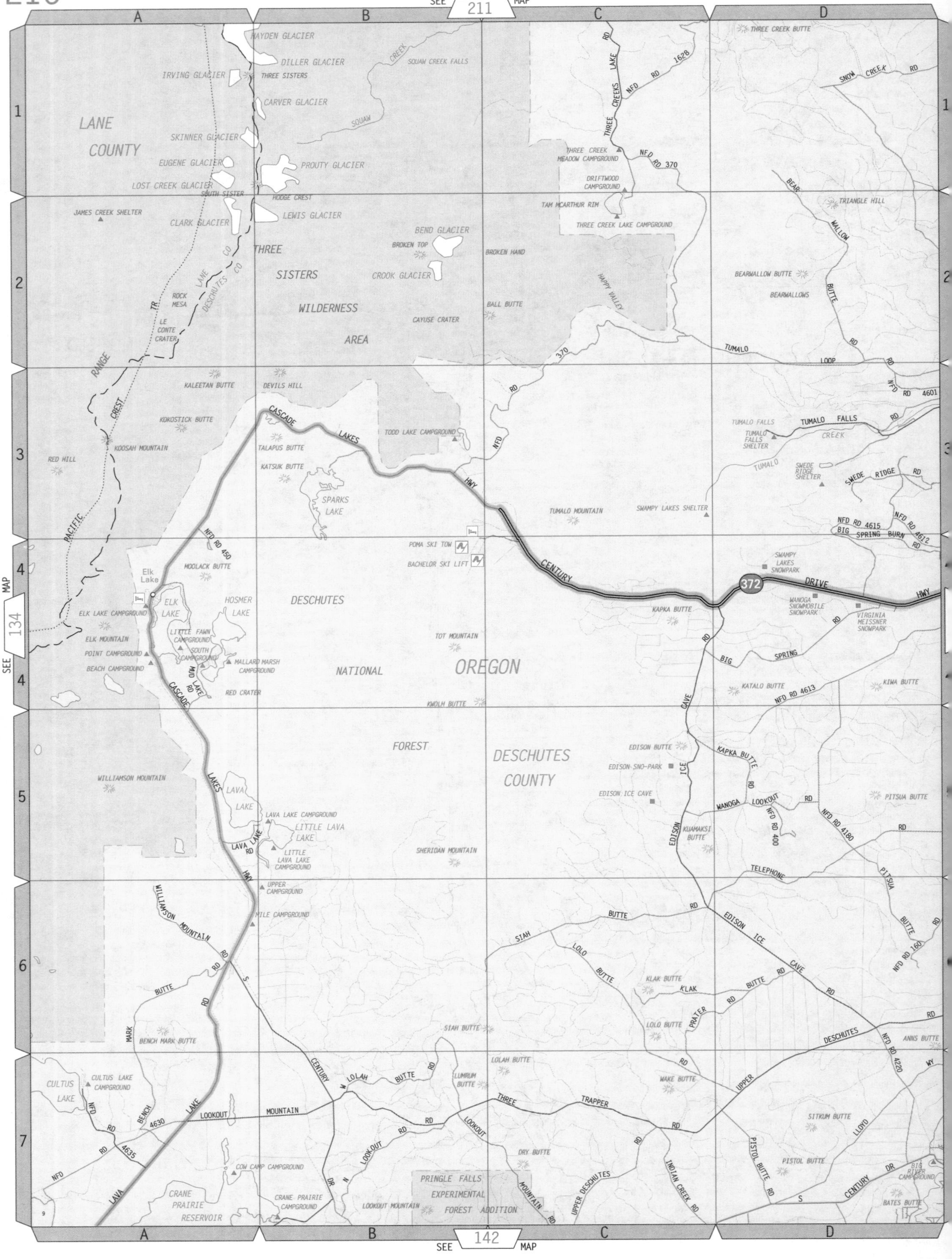

SEE 134 MAP

SEE 142 MAP

PNW

METRO

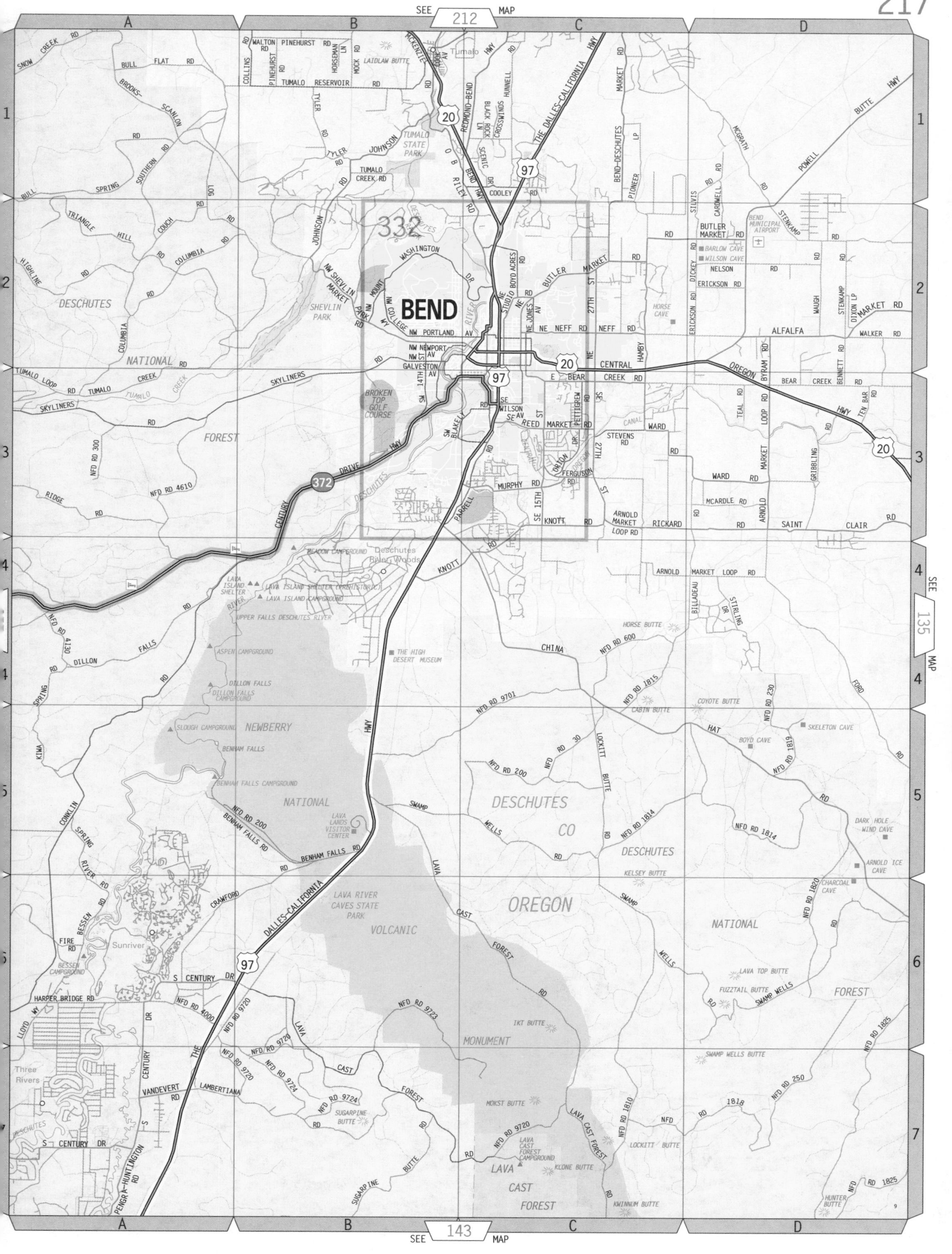
SEE 212 MAP
SEE 143 MAP
SEE 135 MAP
332
BEND
Tumalo
TUMALO STATE PARK
SHEVLIN PARK
BROKEN TOP GOLF COURSE
Deschutes River Woods
Sunriver
Three Rivers
DESCHUTES NATIONAL FOREST
NEWBERRY NATIONAL VOLCANIC MONUMENT
LAVA RIVER CAVES STATE PARK
LAVA LANDS VISITOR CENTER
LAVA CAST FOREST
DESCHUTES CO
OREGON
BEND MUNICIPAL AIRPORT
THE HIGH DESERT MUSEUM
LAVA ISLAND SHELTER (PREHISTORIC)
LAVA ISLAND CAMPGROUND
UPPER FALLS DESCHUTES RIVER
ASPEN CAMPGROUND
DILLON FALLS
DILLON FALLS CAMPGROUND
SLOUGH CAMPGROUND
BENHAM FALLS
BENHAM FALLS CAMPGROUND
BESSEN CAMPGROUND
MEADOW CAMPGROUND
LAVA CAST FOREST CAMPGROUND
HORSE CAVE
BARLOW CAVE
WILSON CAVE
BOYD CAVE
SKELETON CAVE
DARK HOLE WIND CAVE
ARNOLD ICE CAVE
CHARCOAL CAVE
LAIDLAW BUTTE
HORSE BUTTE
COYOTE BUTTE
CABIN BUTTE
KELSEY BUTTE
LAVA TOP BUTTE
FUZZTAIL BUTTE
IKT BUTTE
SWAMP WELLS BUTTE
MOKST BUTTE
SUGARPINE BUTTE
KLONE BUTTE
LOCKITT BUTTE
KWINNUM BUTTE
HUNTER BUTTE
THE DALLES-CALIFORNIA HWY
CENTURY DRIVE HWY
OREGON HWY
BUTTE HWY
NW NEWPORT AV
NW PORTLAND AV
GALVESTON AV
NE NEFF RD
BEAR CREEK RD
REED MARKET RD
MURPHY RD
KNOTT RD
ARNOLD MARKET LOOP RD
CHINA HAT RD
SKYLINERS RD
BENHAM FALLS RD
S CENTURY DR
HARPER BRIDGE RD
VANDEVERT RD
PENGRA-HUNTINGTON RD
LAVA CAST FOREST RD
SWAMP WELLS RD
NFD RD 9720
NFD RD 1814
NFD RD 1825

SEE 214 MAP

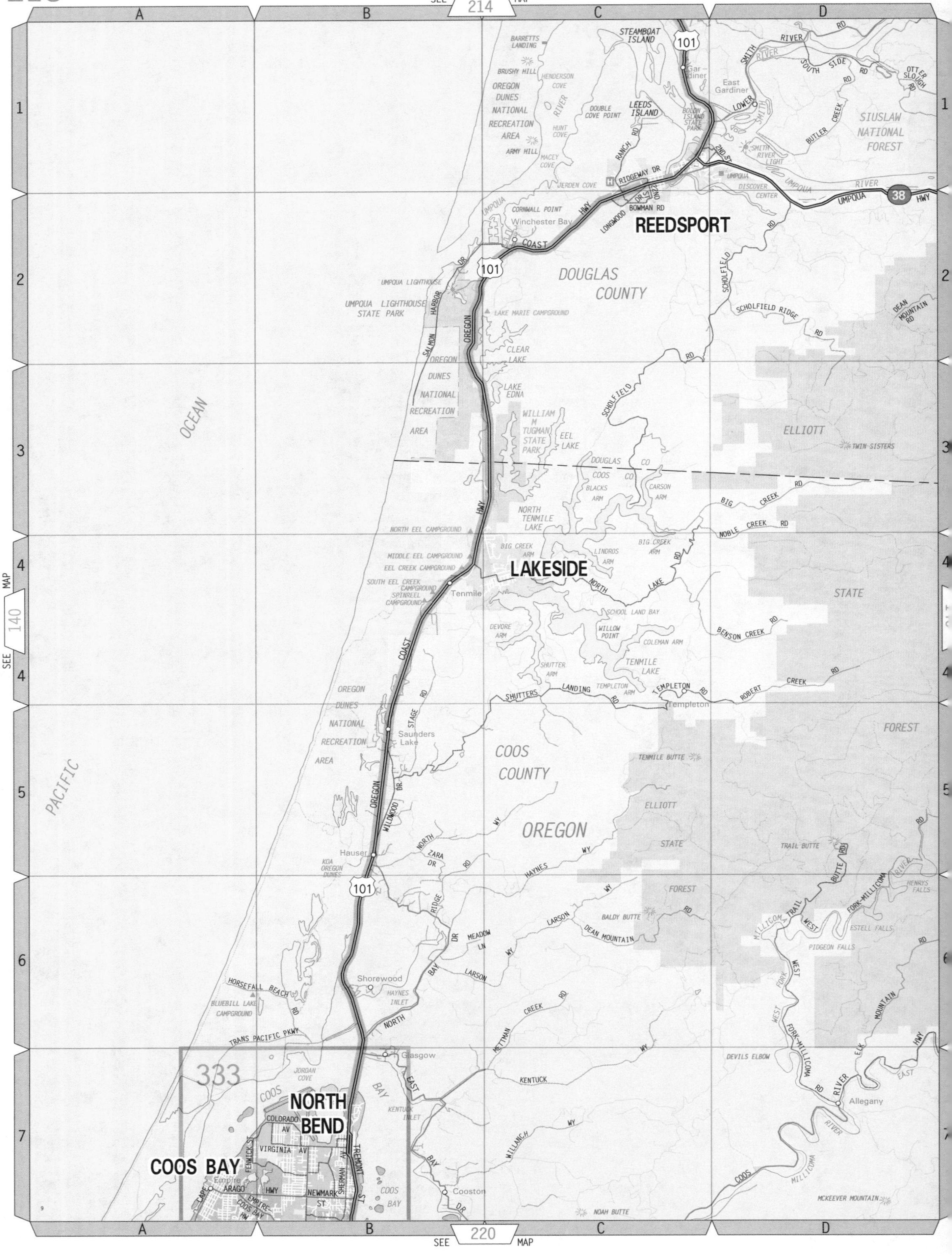
REEDSPORT
LAKESIDE
NORTH BEND
COOS BAY
DOUGLAS COUNTY
COOS COUNTY
OREGON
PACIFIC
OCEAN
OREGON DUNES NATIONAL RECREATION AREA
UMPQUA LIGHTHOUSE STATE PARK
WILLIAM M TUGMAN STATE PARK
SIUSLAW NATIONAL FOREST
ELLIOTT STATE FOREST
STEAMBOAT ISLAND
LEEDS ISLAND
Gardiner
East Gardiner
Winchester Bay
Tenmile
Saunders Lake
Hauser
Shorewood
Glasgow
Templeton
Cooston
Allegany
Empire
CLEAR LAKE
LAKE EDNA
EEL LAKE
NORTH TENMILE LAKE
TENMILE LAKE
UMPQUA RIVER
SMITH RIVER
101
38
333
A
B
C
D
1
2
3
4
5
6
7
PNW
METRO

SEE 140 MAP

SEE 220 MAP

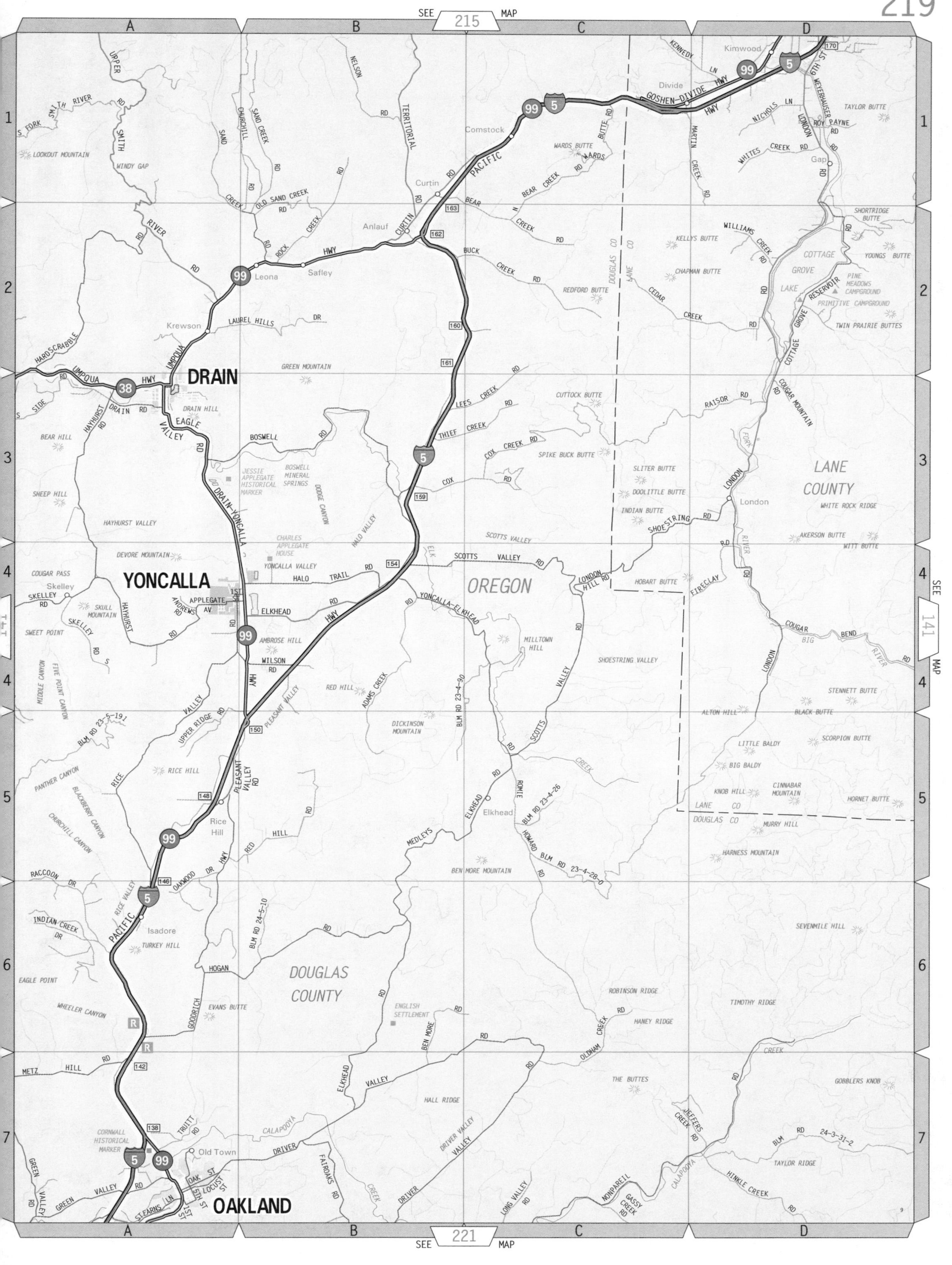

SEE 215 MAP
SEE 221 MAP
SEE 141 MAP
DRAIN
YONCALLA
OAKLAND
OREGON
DOUGLAS COUNTY
LANE COUNTY
Kimwood
Divide
Comstock
Curtin
Anlauf
Leona
Safley
Krewson
Skelley
London
Gap
Rice Hill
Isadore
Elkhead
Old Town
COTTAGE GROVE LAKE
LOOKOUT MOUNTAIN
WINDY GAP
GREEN MOUNTAIN
DRAIN HILL
BEAR HILL
SHEEP HILL
HAYHURST VALLEY
DEVORE MOUNTAIN
COUGAR PASS
SKULL MOUNTAIN
SWEET POINT
JESSIE APPLEGATE HISTORICAL MARKER
BOSWELL MINERAL SPRINGS
CHARLES APPLEGATE HOUSE
YONCALLA VALLEY
AMBROSE HILL
RED HILL
DICKINSON MOUNTAIN
MILLTOWN HILL
SHOESTRING VALLEY
RICE HILL
BEN MORE MOUNTAIN
TURKEY HILL
EAGLE POINT
WHEELER CANYON
EVANS BUTTE
ENGLISH SETTLEMENT
ROBINSON RIDGE
HANEY RIDGE
TIMOTHY RIDGE
THE BUTTES
HALL RIDGE
GOBBLERS KNOB
TAYLOR RIDGE
CORNWALL HISTORICAL MARKER
WARDS BUTTE
KELLYS BUTTE
CHAPMAN BUTTE
REDFORD BUTTE
CUTTOCK BUTTE
SPIKE BUCK BUTTE
SLITER BUTTE
DOOLITTLE BUTTE
INDIAN BUTTE
HOBART BUTTE
TAYLOR BUTTE
SHORTRIDGE BUTTE
YOUNGS BUTTE
PINE MEADOWS CAMPGROUND
PRIMITIVE CAMPGROUND
TWIN PRAIRIE BUTTES
WHITE ROCK RIDGE
AKERSON BUTTE
WITT BUTTE
STENNETT BUTTE
ALTON HILL
BLACK BUTTE
LITTLE BALDY
SCORPION BUTTE
BIG BALDY
KNOB HILL
CINNABAR MOUNTAIN
HORNET BUTTE
MURRY HILL
HARNESS MOUNTAIN
SEVENMILE HILL
SCOTTS VALLEY
PACIFIC HWY
GOSHEN-DIVIDE HWY
UMPQUA HWY
BLM RD 23-5-19.1
BLM RD 23-4-90
BLM RD 23-4-26
BLM RD 23-4-28-0
BLM RD 24-5-10
BLM RD 24-3-31-2

SEE 218 MAP

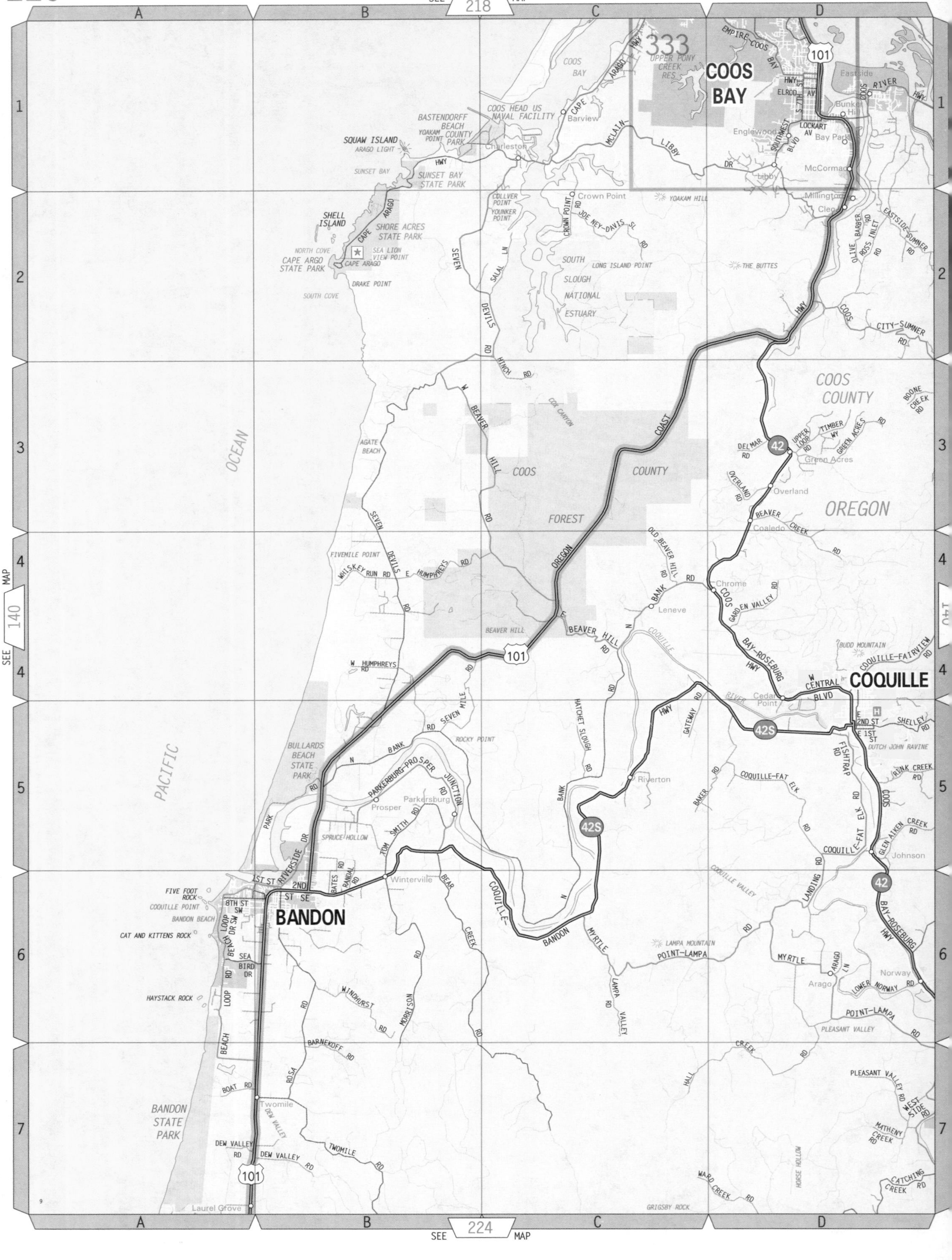

COOS BAY

COQUILLE

BANDON

COOS COUNTY

OREGON

PACIFIC OCEAN

COOS COUNTY FOREST

SOUTH SLOUGH NATIONAL ESTUARY

CAPE ARGO STATE PARK

SHORE ACRES STATE PARK

SUNSET BAY STATE PARK

BASTENDORFF BEACH COUNTY PARK

BULLARDS BEACH STATE PARK

BANDON STATE PARK

SEE 140 MAP

SEE 224 MAP

SEE 219 MAP

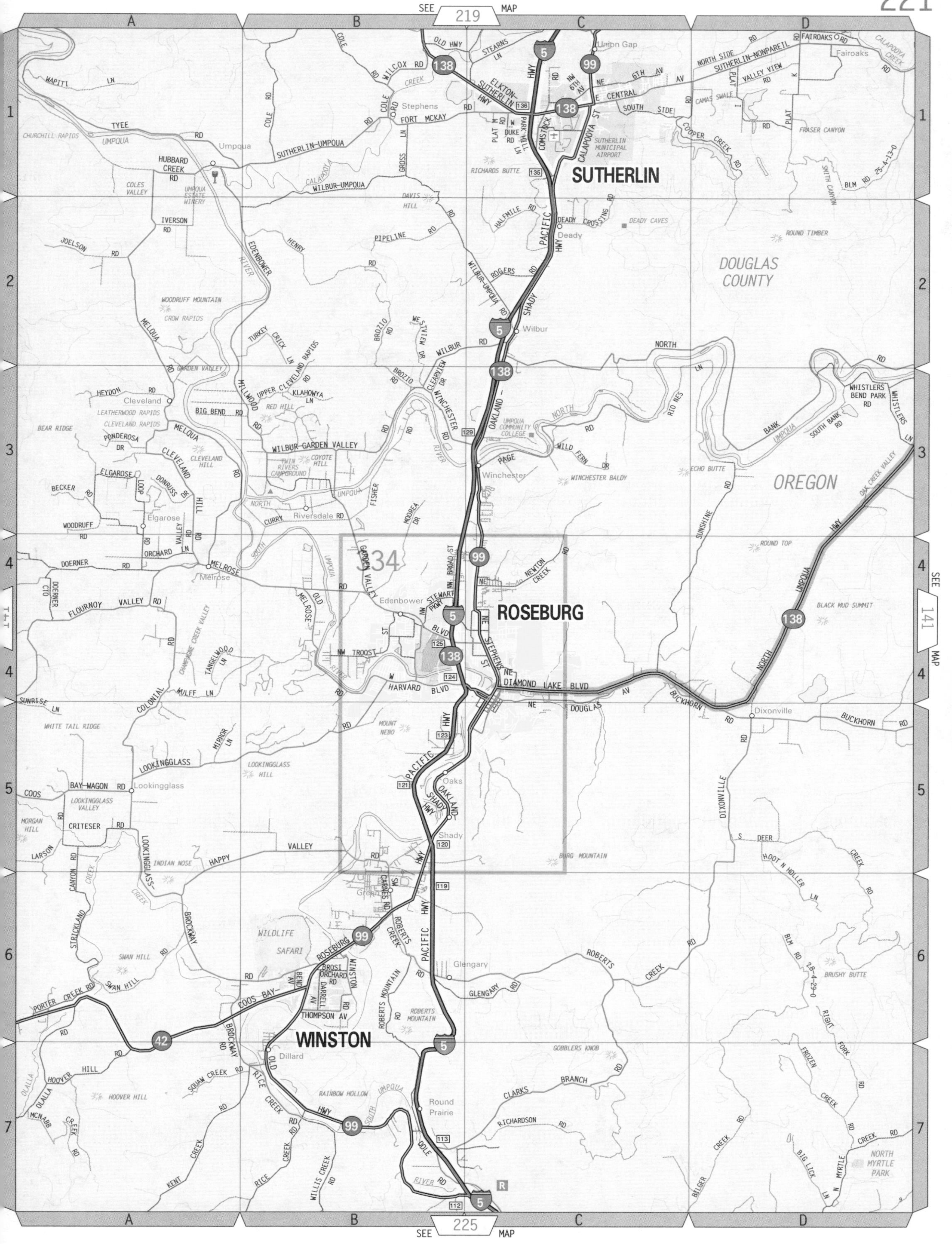

SEE 141 MAP

PNW

METRO

SEE 225 MAP

SEE 142 MAP

SEE 141 MAP

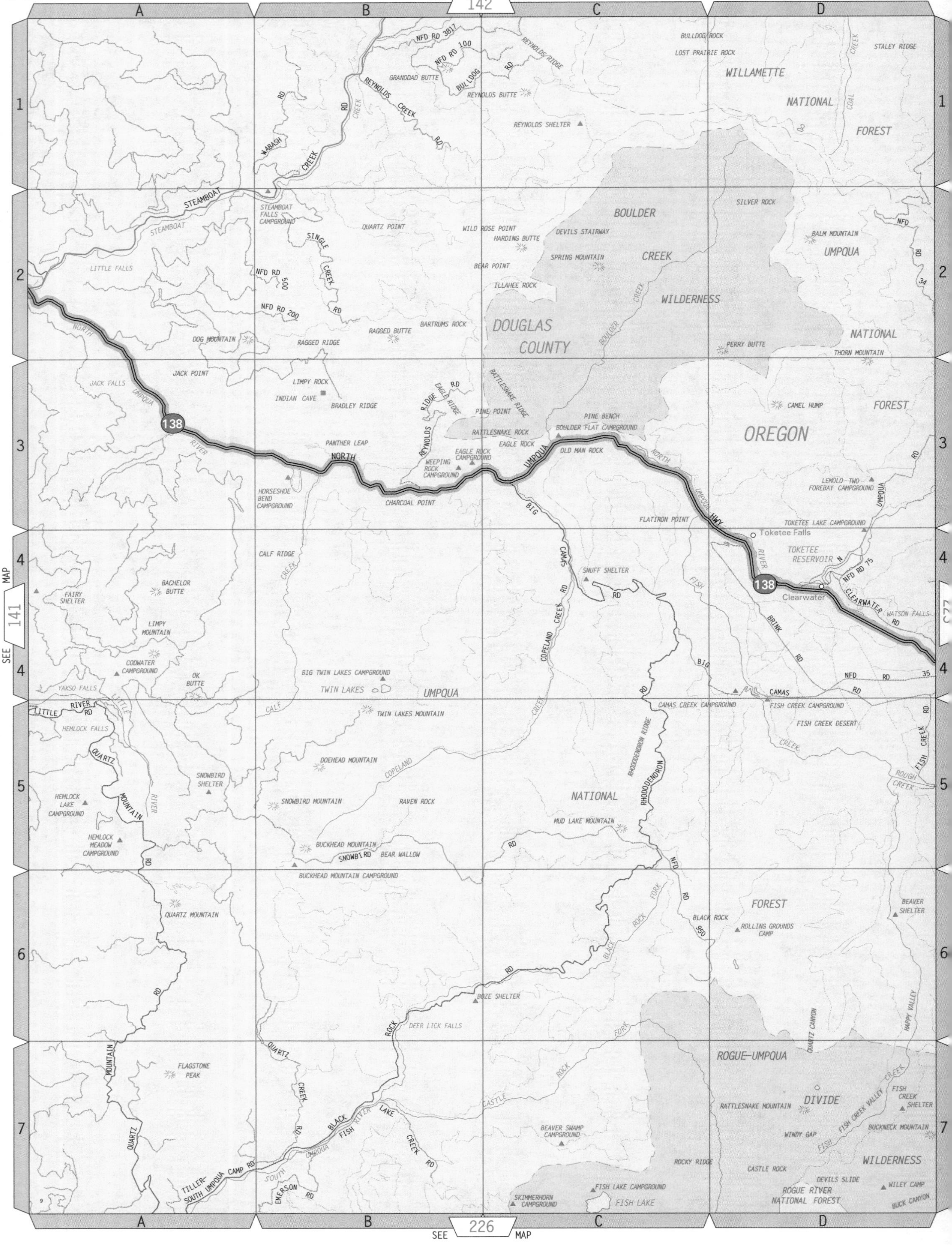

SEE 226 MAP

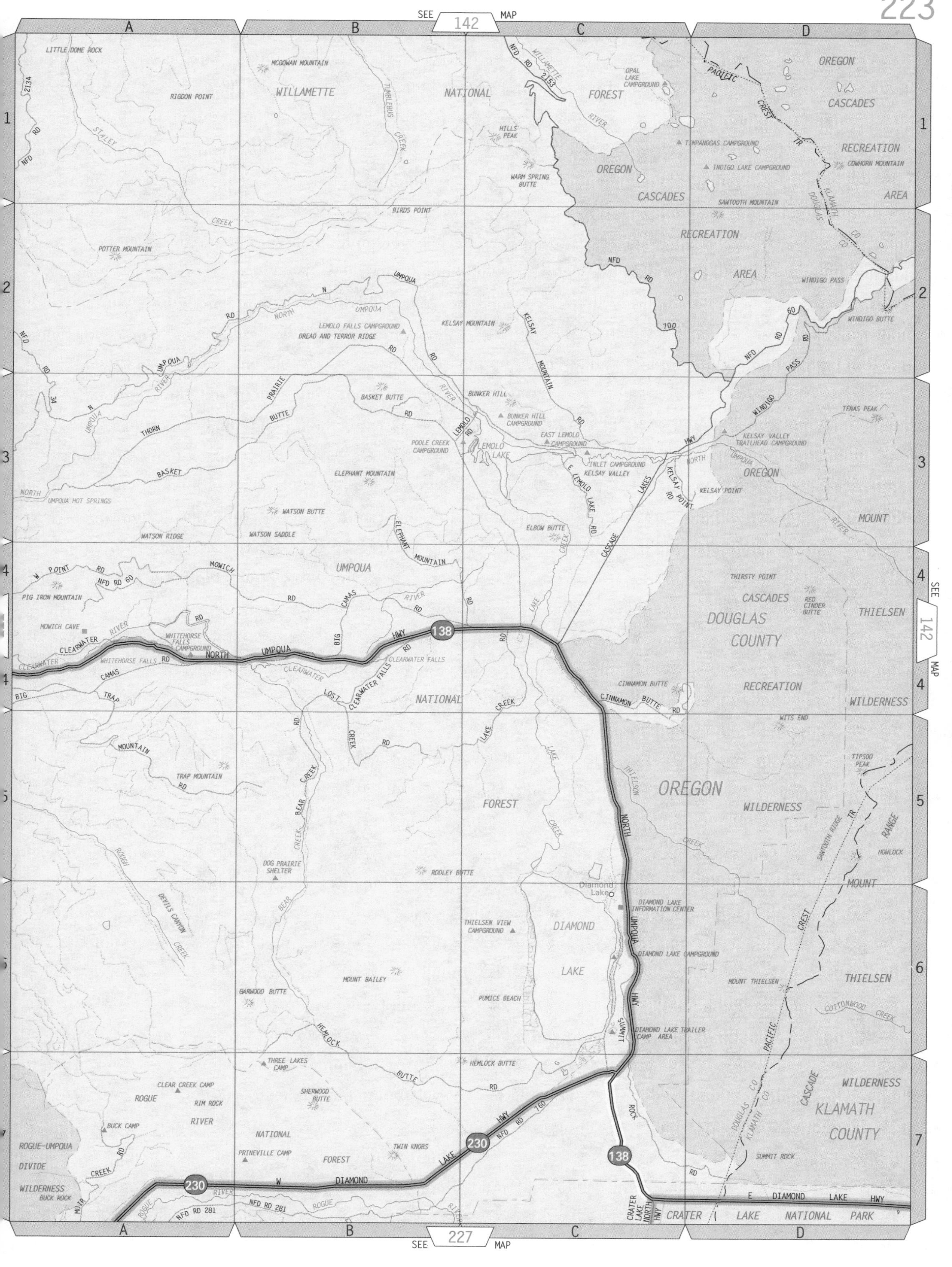
SEE 142 MAP
WILLAMETTE NATIONAL FOREST
OREGON CASCADES RECREATION AREA
UMPQUA NATIONAL FOREST
DOUGLAS COUNTY
MOUNT THIELSEN WILDERNESS
OREGON CASCADES RECREATION AREA
DIAMOND LAKE
ROGUE RIVER NATIONAL FOREST
ROGUE-UMPQUA DIVIDE WILDERNESS
KLAMATH COUNTY
CRATER LAKE NATIONAL PARK
NORTH UMPQUA HWY
CASCADE LAKES HWY
W DIAMOND LAKE HWY
E DIAMOND LAKE HWY
Diamond Lake
DIAMOND LAKE INFORMATION CENTER
LEMOLO LAKE
MOUNT BAILEY
MOUNT THIELSEN
SEE 227 MAP

PNW
METRO

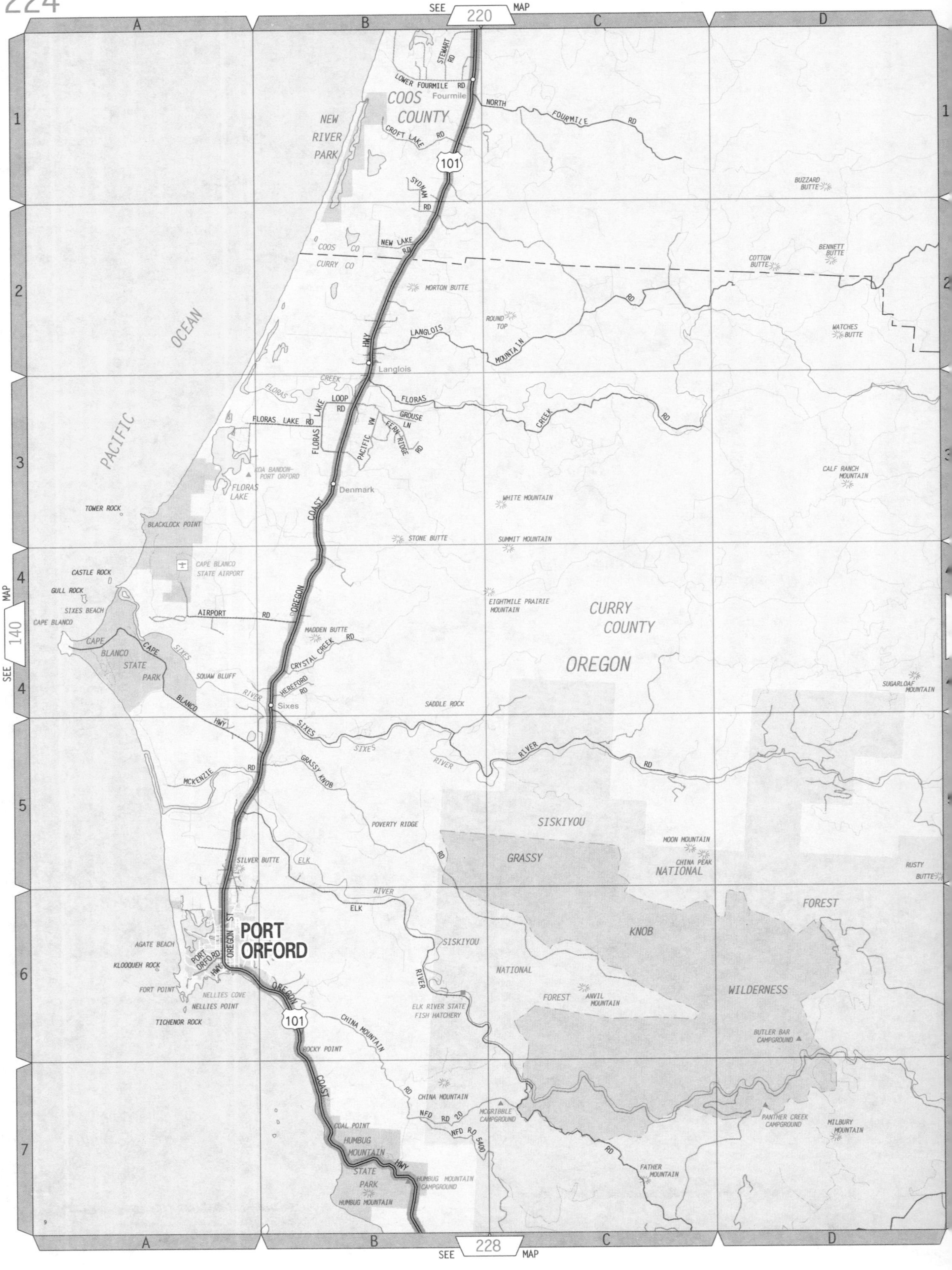
SEE 220 MAP
SEE 228 MAP
SEE 140 MAP
A
B
C
D
1
2
3
4
5
6
7
STEWART RD
LOWER FOURMILE RD
Fourmile
COOS COUNTY
NORTH FOURMILE RD
NEW RIVER PARK
CROFT LAKE RD
101
SYDNAM RD
BUZZARD BUTTE
NEW LAKE RD
COOS CO
CURRY CO
COTTON BUTTE
BENNETT BUTTE
MORTON BUTTE
RD
ROUND TOP
WATCHES BUTTE
OCEAN
LANGLOIS MOUNTAIN
HWY
Langlois
CREEK
FLORAS
LOOP RD
FLORAS LAKE RD
GROUSE LN
FLORAS CREEK RD
FERN RIDGE RD
PACIFIC VW
PACIFIC
KOA BANDON-PORT ORFORD
Denmark
CALF RANCH MOUNTAIN
FLORAS LAKE
WHITE MOUNTAIN
TOWER ROCK
COAST
BLACKLOCK POINT
STONE BUTTE
SUMMIT MOUNTAIN
CAPE BLANCO STATE AIRPORT
CASTLE ROCK
GULL ROCK
EIGHTMILE PRAIRIE MOUNTAIN
SIXES BEACH
OREGON
AIRPORT RD
CURRY COUNTY
CAPE BLANCO
MADDEN BUTTE
CAPE BLANCO STATE PARK
CAPE
SIXES
CRYSTAL CREEK RD
OREGON
SQUAW BLUFF
HEREFORD RD
SUGARLOAF MOUNTAIN
BLANCO HWY
RIVER
Sixes
SADDLE ROCK
SIXES RIVER RD
GRASSY KNOB
MCKENZIE RD
SISKIYOU
POVERTY RIDGE
MOON MOUNTAIN
GRASSY
CHINA PEAK
NATIONAL
RUSTY BUTTE
SILVER BUTTE
ELK RIVER
ELK
FOREST
KNOB
AGATE BEACH
PORT ORFORD
OREGON ST
PORT ORFORD RD
HWY
KLOOQUEH ROCK
SISKIYOU NATIONAL FOREST
RIVER
FORT POINT
NELLIES COVE
NELLIES POINT
ANVIL MOUNTAIN
WILDERNESS
ELK RIVER STATE FISH HATCHERY
TICHENOR ROCK
CHINA MOUNTAIN
BUTLER BAR CAMPGROUND
ROCKY POINT
CHINA MOUNTAIN
MCGRIBBLE CAMPGROUND
NFD RD 20
NFD RD 5400
PANTHER CREEK CAMPGROUND
MILBURY MOUNTAIN
COAL POINT
HUMBUG MOUNTAIN STATE PARK
FATHER MOUNTAIN
HUMBUG MOUNTAIN CAMPGROUND
HUMBUG MOUNTAIN

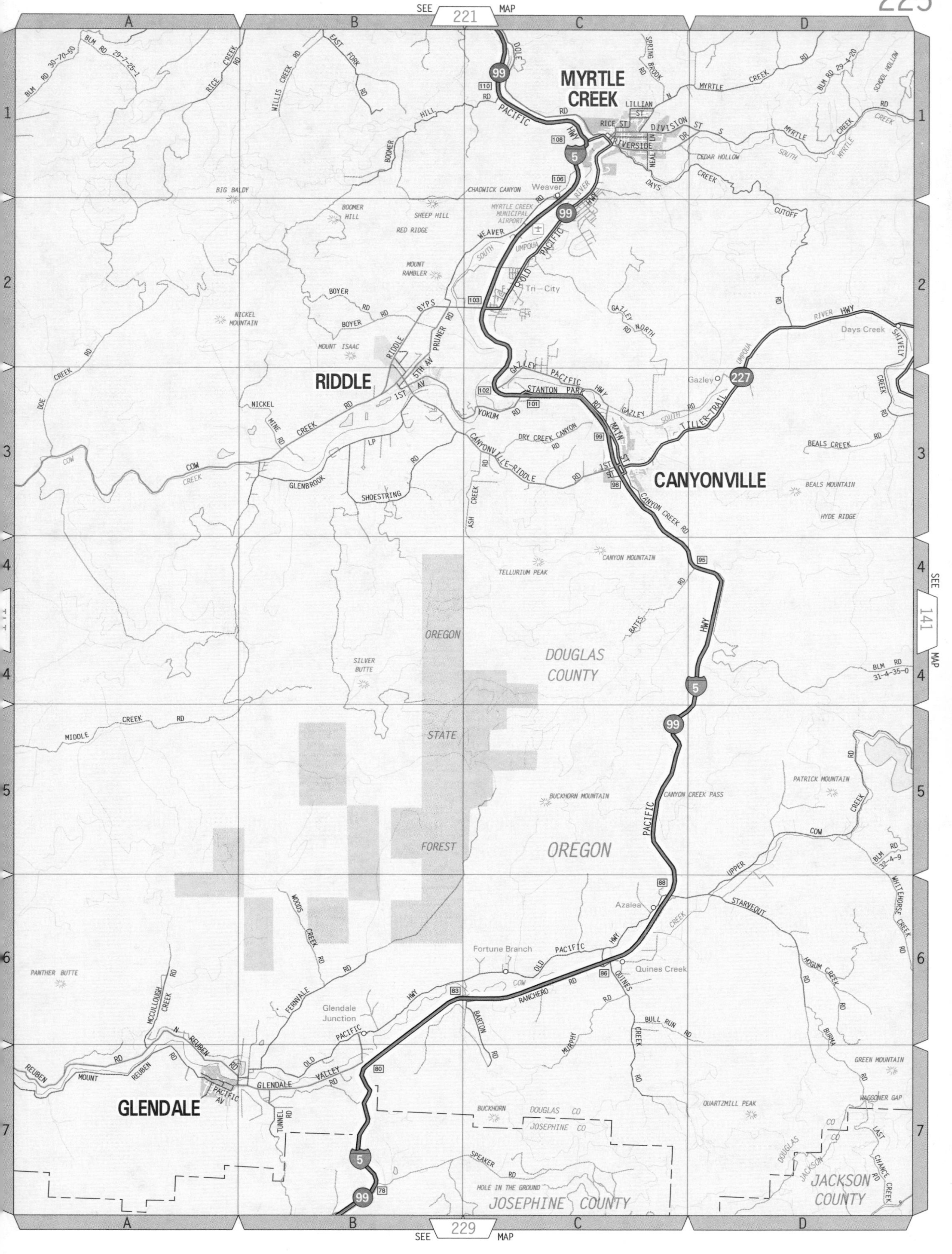
SEE 221 MAP
MYRTLE CREEK
RIDDLE
CANYONVILLE
GLENDALE
Weaver
Tri-City
Days Creek
Gazley
Azalea
Fortune Branch
Quines Creek
Glendale Junction
DOUGLAS COUNTY
OREGON
OREGON STATE FOREST
JOSEPHINE COUNTY
JACKSON COUNTY
SEE 141 MAP
SEE 229 MAP
PNW
METRO

SEE 222 MAP

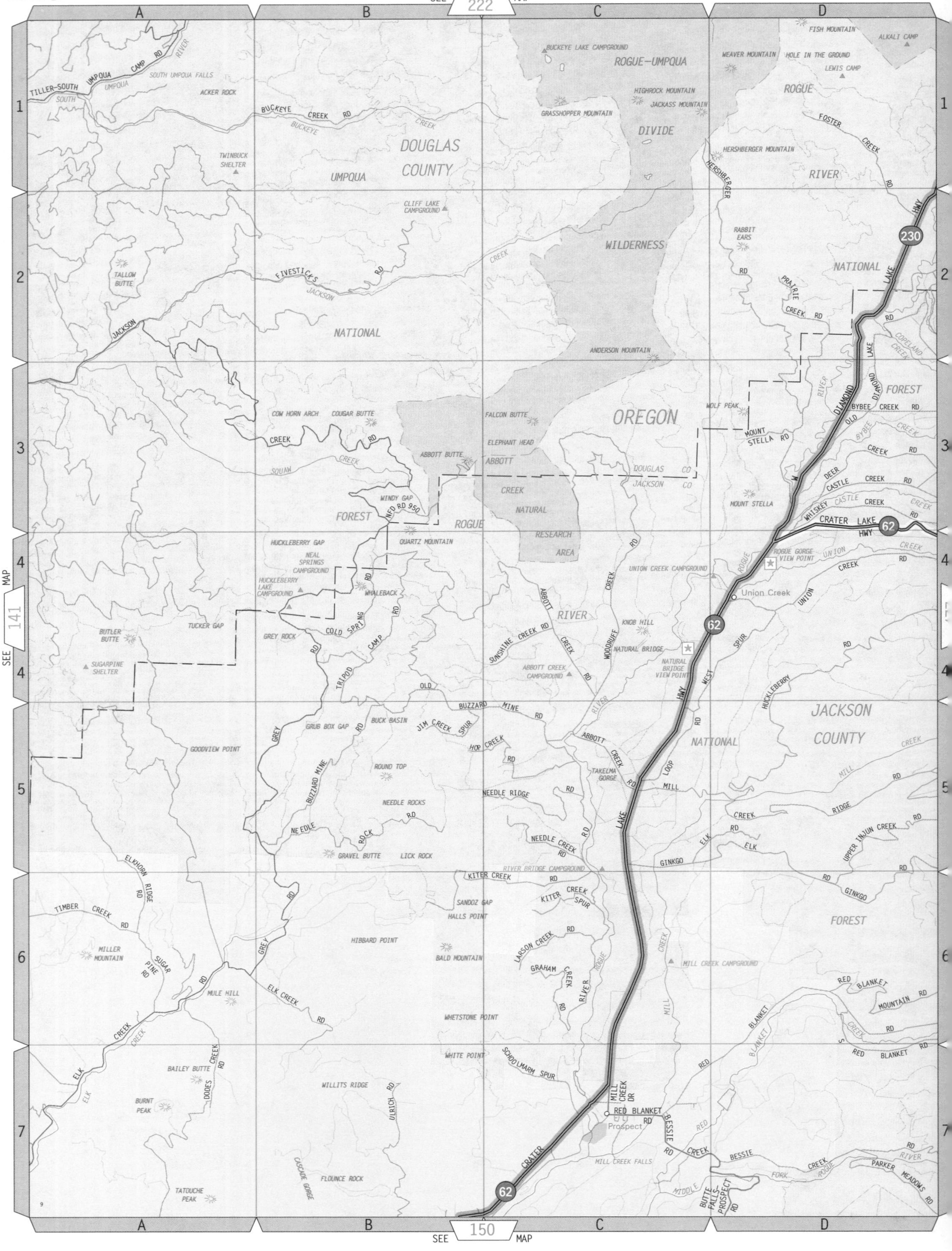

SEE 141 MAP

DOUGLAS COUNTY
UMPQUA NATIONAL FOREST
ROGUE-UMPQUA DIVIDE WILDERNESS
ROGUE RIVER NATIONAL FOREST
OREGON
JACKSON COUNTY
ABBOTT CREEK NATURAL RESEARCH AREA
DOUGLAS CO
JACKSON CO

TILLER-SOUTH UMPQUA CAMP RD
SOUTH UMPQUA FALLS
ACKER ROCK
BUCKEYE CREEK RD
BUCKEYE LAKE CAMPGROUND
GRASSHOPPER MOUNTAIN
HIGHROCK MOUNTAIN
JACKASS MOUNTAIN
FISH MOUNTAIN
ALKALI CAMP
WEAVER MOUNTAIN
HOLE IN THE GROUND
LEWIS CAMP
FOSTER CREEK RD
HERSHBERGER MOUNTAIN
HERSHBERGER RD
TWINBUCK SHELTER
CLIFF LAKE CAMPGROUND
RABBIT EARS
TALLOW BUTTE
FIVESTICKS RD
JACKSON CREEK
PRAIRIE CREEK RD
ANDERSON MOUNTAIN
COPELAND CREEK
DIAMOND LAKE HWY
OLD DIAMOND LAKE HWY
230
WOLF PEAK
MOUNT STELLA RD
MOUNT STELLA
BYBEE CREEK RD
CREEK RD
DEER CREEK
CASTLE CREEK RD
WHISKEY
CRATER LAKE HWY
62
COW HORN ARCH
COUGAR BUTTE
CREEK RD
SQUAW CREEK
FALCON BUTTE
ELEPHANT HEAD
ABBOTT BUTTE
WINDY GAP
NFD RD 950
QUARTZ MOUNTAIN
HUCKLEBERRY GAP
NEAL SPRINGS CAMPGROUND
HUCKLEBERRY LAKE CAMPGROUND
WHALEBACK
TUCKER GAP
BUTLER BUTTE
GREY ROCK
COLD SPRING
CAMP RD
TRIPOD
SUGARPINE SHELTER
UNION CREEK CAMPGROUND
ROGUE GORGE VIEW POINT
Union Creek
UNION CREEK
WEST UNION SPUR RD
ABBOTT CREEK RD
WOODRUFF CREEK RD
KNOB HILL
NATURAL BRIDGE
NATURAL BRIDGE VIEW POINT
SUNSHINE CREEK RD
ABBOTT CREEK CAMPGROUND
HUCKLEBERRY
OLD BUZZARD MINE RD
GRUB BOX GAP
BUCK BASIN
JIM CREEK SPUR
HOP CREEK RD
GREY RD
GOODVIEW POINT
BUZZARD MINE
ROUND TOP
TAKELMA GORGE
LOOP RD
MILL CREEK
RIDGE RD
NEEDLE RIDGE RD
NEEDLE ROCKS
NEEDLE ROCK RD
NEEDLE CREEK RD
ELK CREEK
UPPER INJUN CREEK RD
GRAVEL BUTTE
LICK ROCK
RIVER BRIDGE CAMPGROUND
GINKGO RD
ELKHORN RIDGE RD
TIMBER CREEK RD
KITER CREEK RD
KITER CREEK SPUR
SANDOZ GAP
HALLS POINT
HIBBARD POINT
BALD MOUNTAIN
LARSON CREEK RD
GRAHAM CREEK RD
ROGUE RIVER
MILL CREEK CAMPGROUND
MILLER MOUNTAIN
SUGAR PINE RD
MULE HILL
ELK CREEK RD
RED BLANKET MOUNTAIN RD
WHETSTONE POINT
BLANKET RD
S RED BLANKET RD
ELK CREEK
WHITE POINT
SCHOOLMARM SPUR
BAILEY BUTTE
DODES CREEK RD
WILLITS RIDGE
ULRICH RD
MILL CREEK DR
RED BLANKET RD
BESSIE RD
BESSIE CREEK
Prospect
BURNT PEAK
CRATER LAKE HWY
MILL CREEK FALLS
MIDDLE FORK ROGUE RIVER
BUTTE FALLS PROSPECT RD
PARKER MEADOWS RD
CASCADE GORGE
FLOUNCE ROCK
TATOUCHE PEAK

SEE 150 MAP

SEE 223 MAP

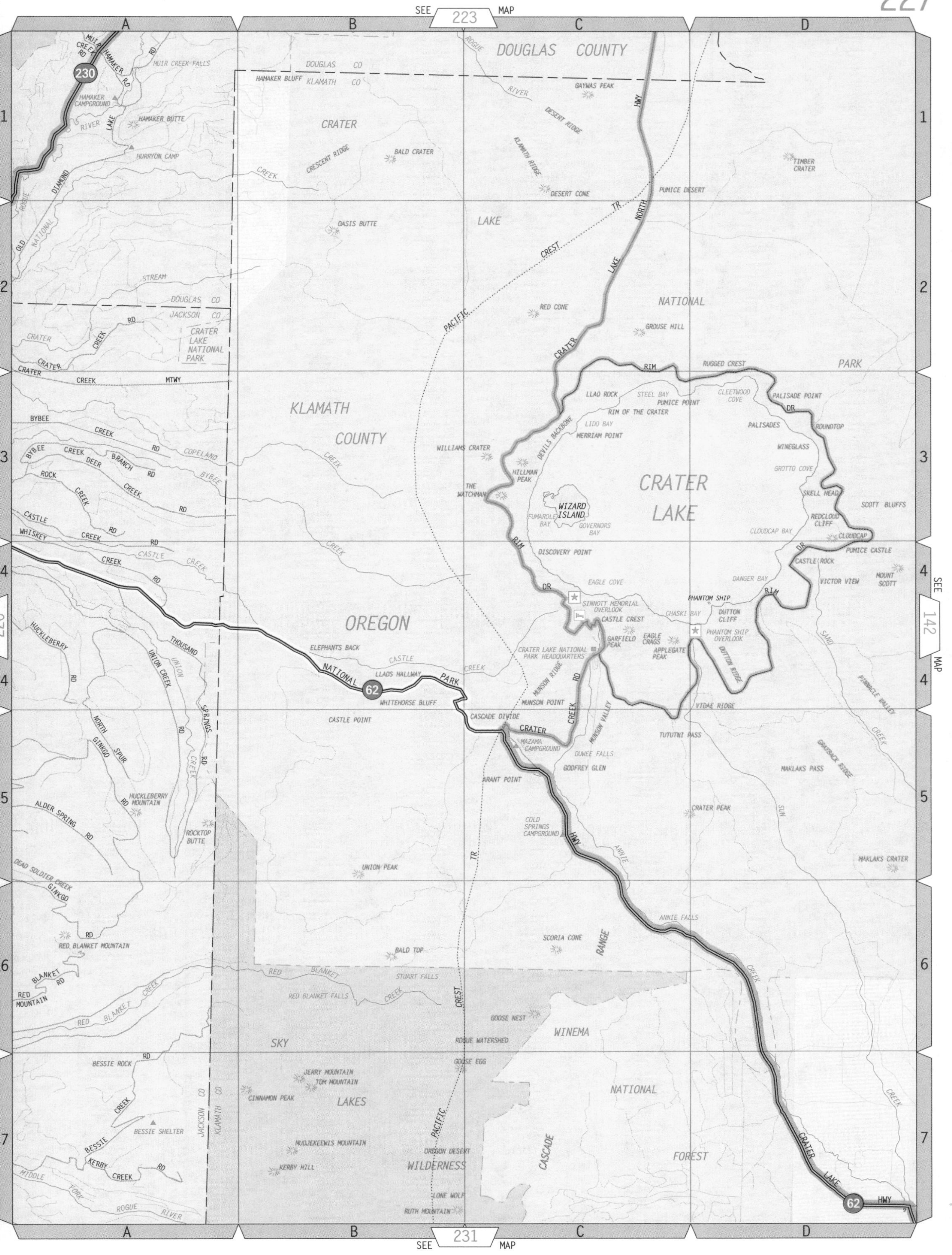

SEE 142 MAP
SEE 231 MAP

PNW

METRO

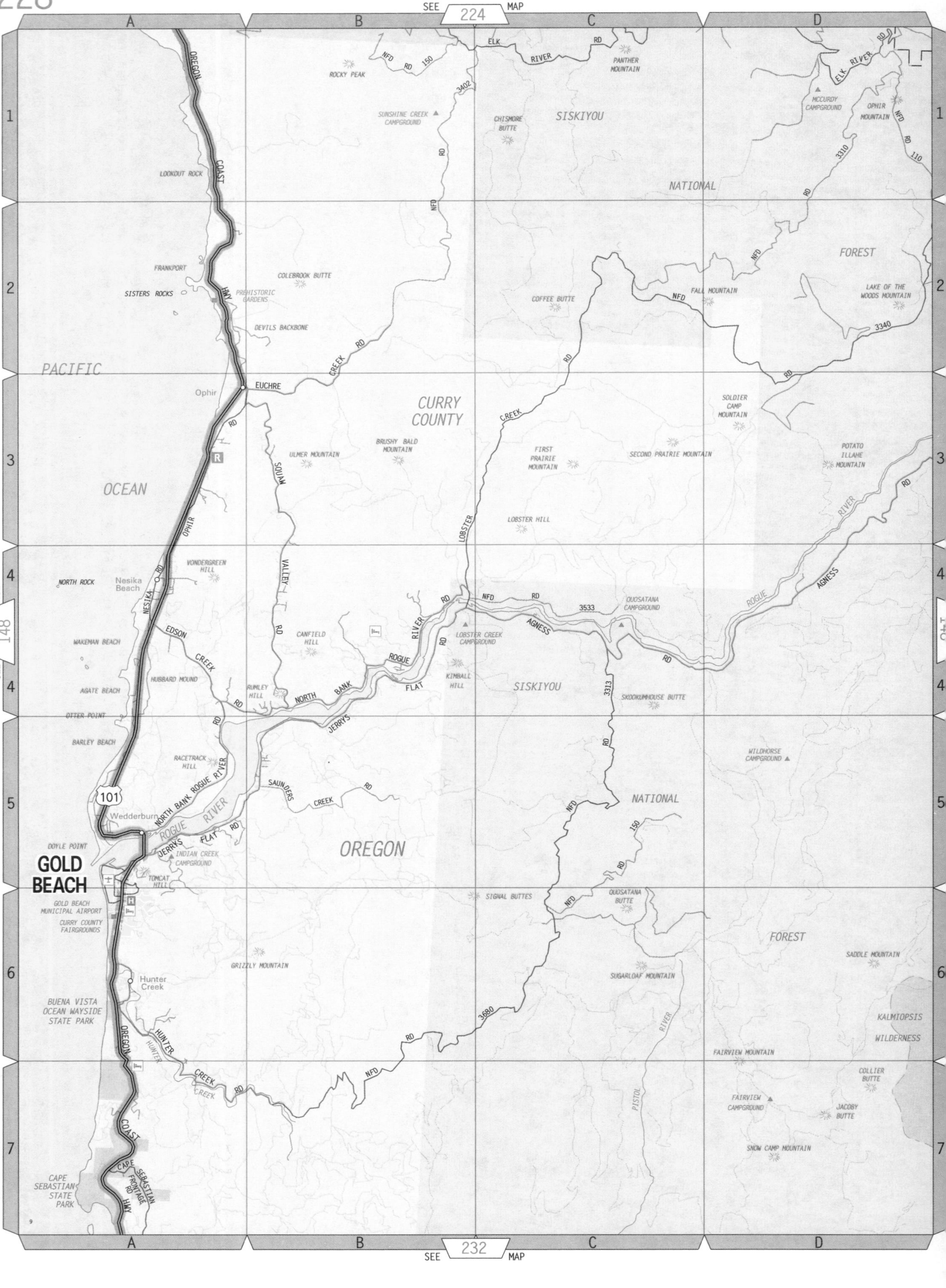

SEE 224 MAP

A B C D

1 2 3 4 5 6 7

PACIFIC OCEAN

CURRY COUNTY

OREGON

SISKIYOU NATIONAL FOREST

GOLD BEACH

Ophir
Euchre
Nesika Beach
Wedderburn
Hunter Creek

LOOKOUT ROCK
FRANKPORT
SISTERS ROCKS
PREHISTORIC GARDENS
COLEBROOK BUTTE
DEVILS BACKBONE
ROCKY PEAK
SUNSHINE CREEK CAMPGROUND
CHISMORE BUTTE
PANTHER MOUNTAIN
MCCURDY CAMPGROUND
OPHIR MOUNTAIN
COFFEE BUTTE
FALL MOUNTAIN
LAKE OF THE WOODS MOUNTAIN
SOLDIER CAMP MOUNTAIN
BRUSHY BALD MOUNTAIN
ULMER MOUNTAIN
FIRST PRAIRIE MOUNTAIN
SECOND PRAIRIE MOUNTAIN
POTATO ILLAHE MOUNTAIN
LOBSTER HILL
NORTH ROCK
VONDERGREEN HILL
WAKEMAN BEACH
CANFIELD HILL
LOBSTER CREEK CAMPGROUND
QUOSATANA CAMPGROUND
KIMBALL HILL
AGATE BEACH
HUBBARD MOUND
RUMLEY HILL
SKOOKUMHOUSE BUTTE
OTTER POINT
BARLEY BEACH
RACETRACK HILL
WILDHORSE CAMPGROUND
DOYLE POINT
INDIAN CREEK CAMPGROUND
TOMCAT HILL
GOLD BEACH MUNICIPAL AIRPORT
CURRY COUNTY FAIRGROUNDS
SIGNAL BUTTES
QUOSATANA BUTTE
GRIZZLY MOUNTAIN
SUGARLOAF MOUNTAIN
SADDLE MOUNTAIN
BUENA VISTA OCEAN WAYSIDE STATE PARK
KALMIOPSIS WILDERNESS
FAIRVIEW MOUNTAIN
COLLIER BUTTE
FAIRVIEW CAMPGROUND
JACOBY BUTTE
SNOW CAMP MOUNTAIN
CAPE SEBASTIAN STATE PARK

OREGON COAST HWY
101
ELK RIVER RD
NFD RD 150
NFD RD 3402
NFD RD 110
NFD RD 3310
NFD RD 3340
EUCHRE CREEK RD
OPHIR RD
SQUAW VALLEY RD
LOBSTER CREEK RD
NESIKA RD
EDSON CREEK RD
NORTH BANK ROGUE RIVER RD
NORTH BANK RD
JERRYS FLAT RD
ROGUE RIVER RD
NFD RD 3533
AGNESS RD
ROGUE RIVER
NFD RD 3313
SAUNDERS CREEK RD
NFD RD 150
NFD RD 3680
HUNTER CREEK RD
PISTOL RIVER
CAPE SEBASTIAN FRONTAGE RD

SEE 148 MAP

SEE 232 MAP

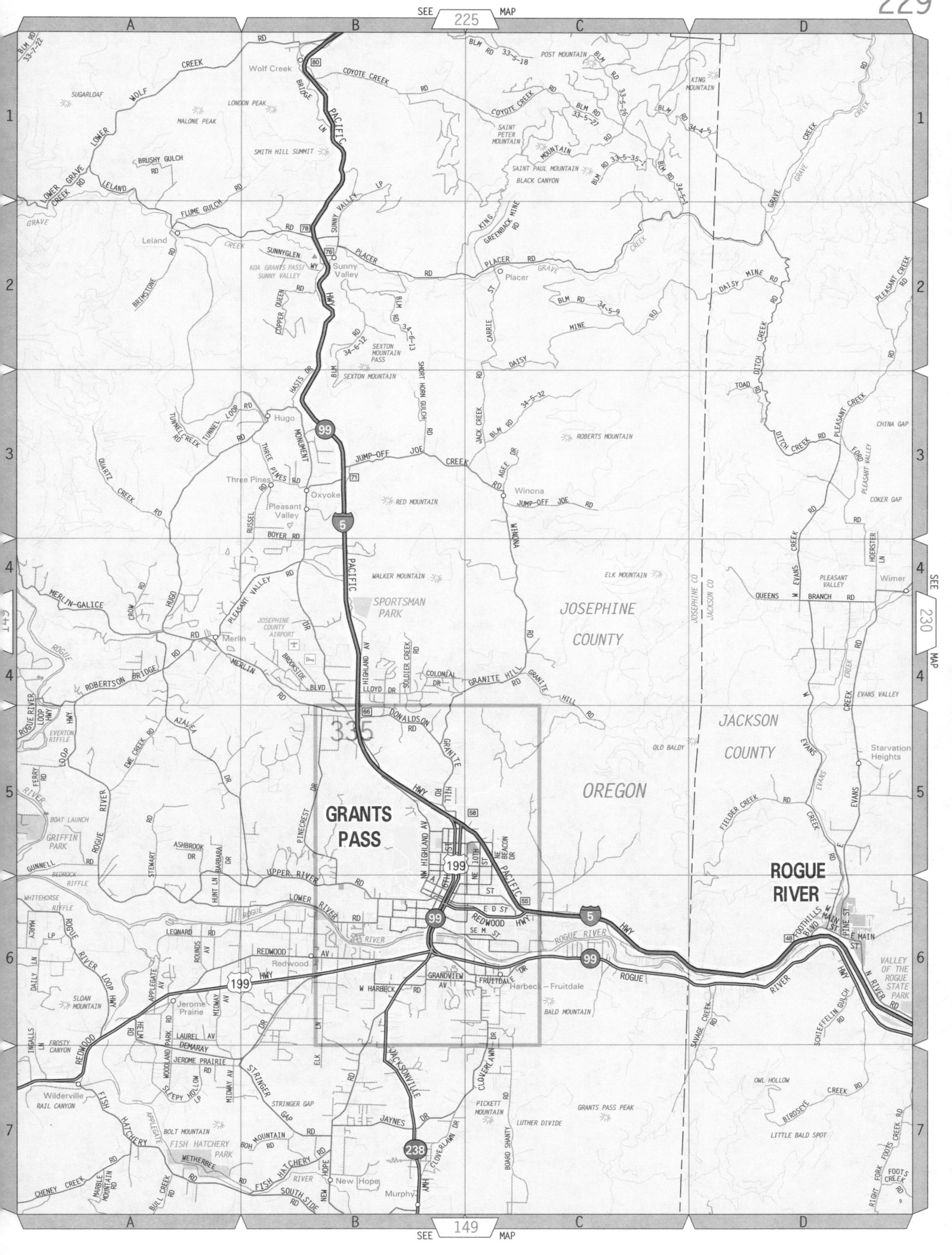
SEE 225 MAP
SEE 149 MAP
SEE 230 MAP
GRANTS PASS
ROGUE RIVER
JOSEPHINE COUNTY
JACKSON COUNTY
OREGON
Wolf Creek
Leland
Sunny Valley
Placer
Hugo
Three Pines
Oxyoke
Pleasant Valley
Winona
Merlin
Wimer
Starvation Heights
Redwood
Jerome Prairie
Harbeck - Fruitdale
Wilderville
New Hope
Murphy
SPORTSMAN PARK
GRIFFIN PARK
FISH HATCHERY PARK
VALLEY OF THE ROGUE STATE PARK
JOSEPHINE COUNTY AIRPORT
335
PNW
METRO

SEE 141 MAP

SEE 229 MAP

SHADY COVE

JACKSON COUNTY

OREGON

GOLD HILL

EAGLE POINT

CENTRAL POINT

MEDFORD

White City

Sams Valley

Table Rock

Seven Oaks

Midway

Four Corners

Trail

336

ROGUE RIVER NATIONAL FOREST

WHITE ROCK MOUNTAIN

PEAVINE RIDGE

HORSE MOUNTAIN

ROUND TOP

BATTLE MOUNTAIN

LITTLE BATTLE MOUNTAIN

FRY PEAK

BEAR WALLOW

SPIGNET BUTTE

BLACK BUTTE

MILL HOLLOW

BOSWELL MOUNTAIN

BOARD MOUNTAIN

WILLY ROCK

WILLY MOUNTAIN

LUCKY HOLLOW

BALD MOUNTAIN

HULL MOUNTAIN

RAMSEY CANYON

FALSE FACE MOUNTAIN

CINNABAR MOUNTAIN

LOVER PEAK

BRATON HOLLOW

ELKHORN BUTTE

CHIMNEY ROCK BUTTE

TURTLE ROCK

NEIL ROCK

MCCONVILLE PEAK

SARDINE MOUNTAIN

HILLIS PEAK

WILCOX PEAK

DEBENGER GAP

MOSSER MOUNTAIN

THE OREGON VORTEX & HOUSE OF MYSTERY

RATTLESNAKE RAPIDS

LONG MOUNTAIN

UPPER TABLE ROCK

LOWER TABLE ROCK

LYMAN MOUNTAIN

DILLON FALLS

HARDY RIFFLE

BLACKWELL HILL

KOA MEDFORD/GOLD HILL

TOU VELLE STATE PARK

AGATE DESERT

CRATER ROCK MUSEUM

MILLPOND CAMPGROUND

COKER BUTTE

TILLER-TRAIL HWY

CRATER LAKE HWY

SAMS VALLEY HWY

LAKE OF THE WOODS HWY

PACIFIC HWY

EVANS CREEK RD

ROGUE RIVER

WARDS CREEK

FOOTS CREEK

LEFT FORK FOOTS CREEK RD

MIDDLE FORK FOOTS CREEK RD

A B C D

1 2 3 4 5 6 7

SEE 234 MAP

SEE 227 MAP

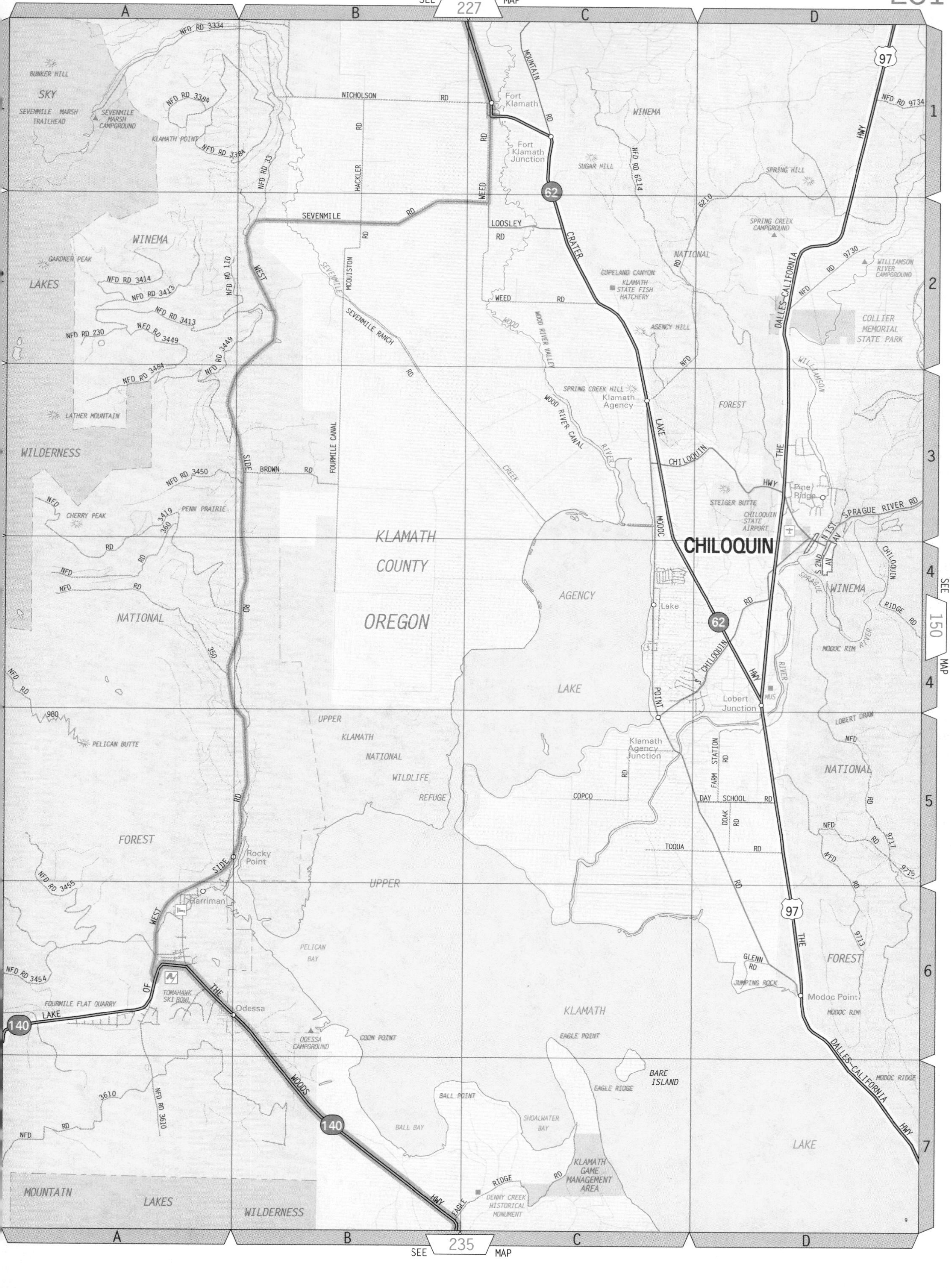

A B C D

CHILOQUIN

KLAMATH COUNTY

OREGON

WINEMA NATIONAL FOREST

SKY LAKES WILDERNESS

MOUNTAIN LAKES WILDERNESS

UPPER KLAMATH NATIONAL WILDLIFE REFUGE

AGENCY LAKE

UPPER KLAMATH LAKE

Fort Klamath

Fort Klamath Junction

Klamath Agency

Lobert Junction

Klamath Agency Junction

Rocky Point

Harriman

Odessa

Modoc Point

Pine Ridge

Lake

COLLIER MEMORIAL STATE PARK

KLAMATH GAME MANAGEMENT AREA

BARE ISLAND

SEE 150 MAP

PNW

METRO

SEE 235 MAP

SEE 228 MAP

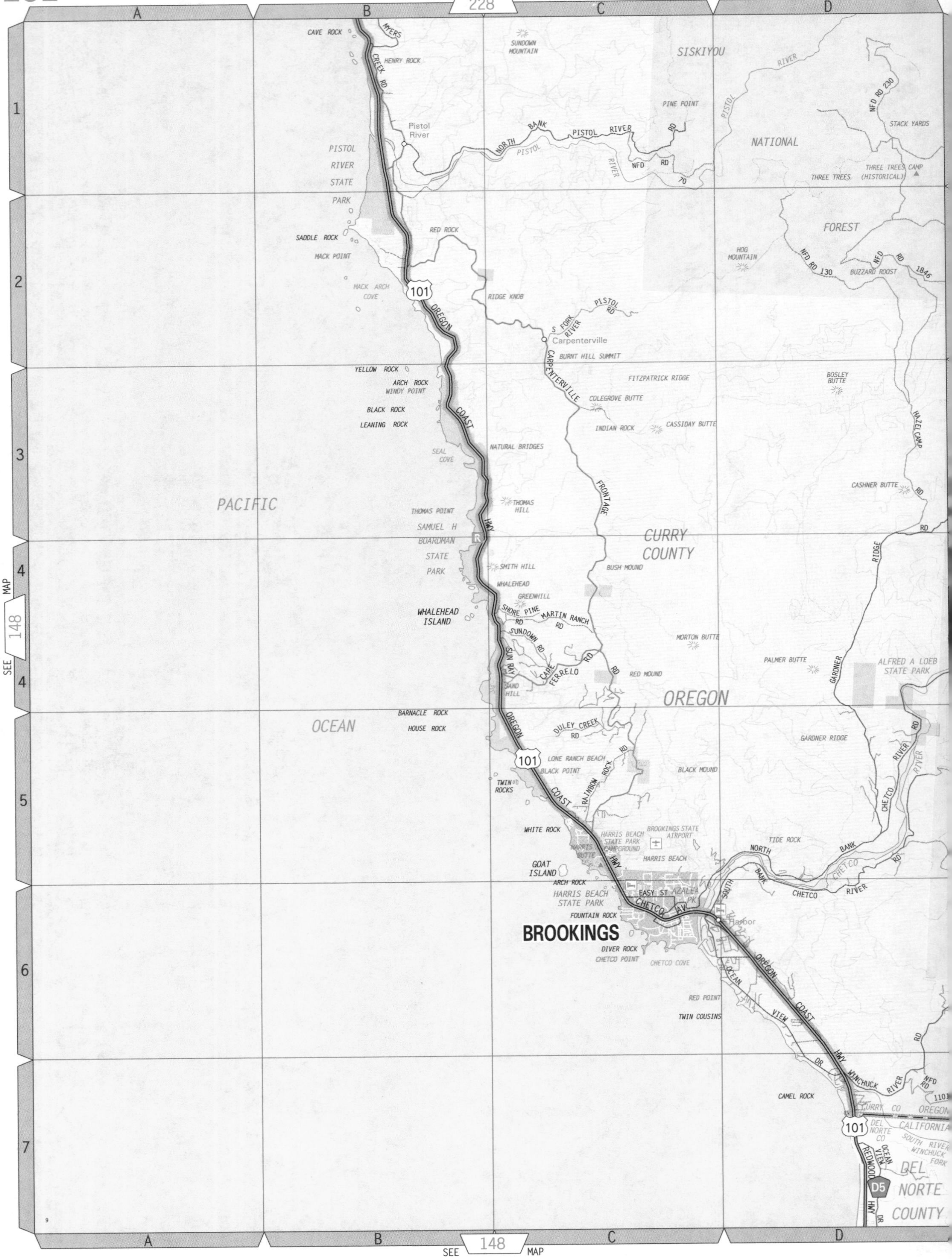

A B C D

PNW

PISTOL RIVER STATE PARK

CAVE ROCK

MYERS CREEK RD

HENRY ROCK

SUNDOWN MOUNTAIN

SISKIYOU NATIONAL FOREST

Pistol River

NORTH BANK PISTOL RIVER RD

NFD RD 70

PINE POINT

NFD RD 230

STACK YARDS

THREE TREES

THREE TREES CAMP (HISTORICAL)

RED ROCK

SADDLE ROCK

MACK POINT

MACK ARCH COVE

HOG MOUNTAIN

NFD RD 130

BUZZARD ROOST

NFD RD 1846

101

RIDGE KNOB

S FORK PISTOL RIVER RD

Carpenterville

BURNT HILL SUMMIT

YELLOW ROCK

ARCH ROCK

WINDY POINT

BLACK ROCK

LEANING ROCK

FITZPATRICK RIDGE

BOSLEY BUTTE

CARPENTERVILLE

COLEGROVE BUTTE

INDIAN ROCK

CASSIDAY BUTTE

HAZELCAMP RD

OREGON COAST HWY

NATURAL BRIDGES

SEAL COVE

PACIFIC OCEAN

FRONTAGE

THOMAS HILL

CASHNER BUTTE

THOMAS POINT

SAMUEL H BOARDMAN STATE PARK

CURRY COUNTY

RIDGE RD

SMITH HILL

BUSH MOUND

WHALEHEAD

GREENHILL

SEE 148 MAP

WHALEHEAD ISLAND

SHORE PINE RD

MARTIN RANCH RD

SUNDOWN RD

MORTON BUTTE

SUN RAY

CAPE FERRELO RD

RED MOUND

PALMER BUTTE

GARDNER

ALFRED A LOEB STATE PARK

SAND HILL

OREGON

METRO

BARNACLE ROCK

HOUSE ROCK

DULEY CREEK RD

GARDNER RIDGE

LONE RANCH BEACH

BLACK POINT

RAINBOW ROCK RD

BLACK MOUND

CHETCO RIVER

TWIN ROCKS

WHITE ROCK

HARRIS BEACH STATE PARK CAMPGROUND

BROOKINGS STATE AIRPORT

TIDE ROCK

HARRIS BUTTE

HARRIS BEACH

NORTH BANK CHETCO RIVER RD

GOAT ISLAND

ARCH ROCK

EASY ST

AZALEA PK

HARRIS BEACH STATE PARK

CHETCO AV

SOUTH

FOUNTAIN ROCK

Harbor

BROOKINGS

DIVER ROCK

CHETCO POINT

CHETCO COVE

OCEAN VIEW DR

RED POINT

TWIN COUSINS

WINCHUCK RIVER

NFD RD 1101

CAMEL ROCK

CURRY CO OREGON

DEL NORTE CO CALIFORNIA

SOUTH RIVER WINCHUCK FORK

OCEAN VIEW DR

REDWOOD HWY

D5

DEL NORTE COUNTY

1 2 3 4 5 6 7

SEE 148 MAP

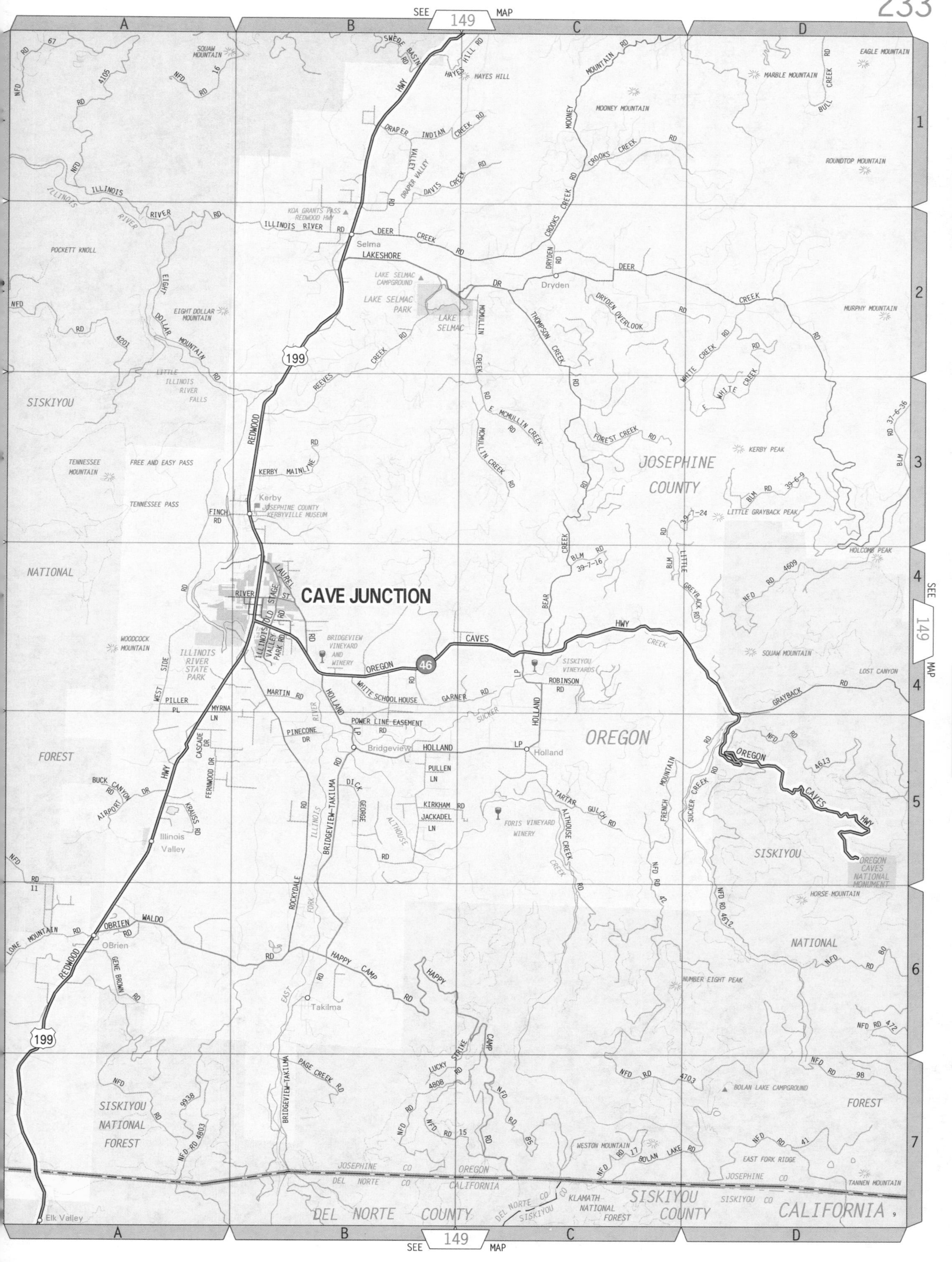
SEE 149 MAP
A
B
C
D
1
2
3
4
5
6
7
CAVE JUNCTION
JOSEPHINE COUNTY
OREGON
SISKIYOU NATIONAL FOREST
SIKIYOU
NATIONAL
FOREST
DEL NORTE COUNTY
SISKIYOU COUNTY
CALIFORNIA
KLAMATH NATIONAL FOREST
JOSEPHINE CO
DEL NORTE CO
OREGON
CALIFORNIA
SISKIYOU CO
199
46
REDWOOD HWY
OREGON CAVES HWY
Selma
Kerby
Dryden
Bridgeview
Holland
Illinois Valley
OBrien
Takilma
Elk Valley
SQUAW MOUNTAIN
HAYES HILL
MOONEY MOUNTAIN
MARBLE MOUNTAIN
EAGLE MOUNTAIN
ROUNDTOP MOUNTAIN
POCKETT KNOLL
EIGHT DOLLAR MOUNTAIN
MURPHY MOUNTAIN
KERBY PEAK
TENNESSEE MOUNTAIN
FREE AND EASY PASS
TENNESSEE PASS
LITTLE GRAYBACK PEAK
HOLCOMB PEAK
WOODCOCK MOUNTAIN
SQUAW MOUNTAIN
LOST CANYON
HORSE MOUNTAIN
NUMBER EIGHT PEAK
BOLAN LAKE CAMPGROUND
WESTON MOUNTAIN
EAST FORK RIDGE
TANNEN MOUNTAIN
KOA GRANTS PASS REDWOOD HWY
LAKE SELMAC CAMPGROUND
LAKE SELMAC PARK
LAKE SELMAC
LITTLE ILLINOIS RIVER FALLS
JOSEPHINE COUNTY KERBYVILLE MUSEUM
BRIDGEVIEW VINEYARD AND WINERY
SISKIYOU VINEYARDS
FORIS VINEYARD WINERY
ILLINOIS RIVER STATE PARK
OREGON CAVES NATIONAL MONUMENT
ILLINOIS RIVER RD
DEER CREEK RD
LAKESHORE DR
DRAPER VALLEY RD
INDIAN CREEK RD
DAVIS CREEK RD
CROOKS CREEK RD
MOONEY MOUNTAIN RD
DRYDEN RD
DRYDEN OVERLOOK RD
THOMPSON CREEK RD
MCMULLIN CREEK RD
E MCMULLIN CREEK RD
WHITE CREEK RD
E WHITE CREEK
FOREST CREEK RD
REEVES CREEK RD
EIGHT DOLLAR MOUNTAIN RD
KERBY MAINLINE
FINCH RD
LAUREL ST
OLD STAGE RD
RIVER ST
ILLINOIS VALLEY PARK RD
WHITE SCHOOL HOUSE
GARNER RD
ROBINSON RD
MARTIN RD
HOLLAND LP
WEST SIDE RD
PILLER PL
MYRNA LN
PINECONE DR
POWER LINE EASEMENT RD
CASCADE DR
FERNWOOD DR
KRAUSS RD
AIRPORT DR
BUCK CANYON RD
PULLEN LN
KIRKHAM RD
JACKADEL LN
DICK GEORGE RD
BRIDGEVIEW-TAKILMA RD
ROCKYDALE RD
TARTAR GULCH RD
ALTHOUSE CREEK RD
FRENCH MOUNTAIN
SUCKER CREEK RD
BEAR CREEK RD
LITTLE GREYBACK RD
GRAYBACK RD
BLM RD 39-7-16
BLM RD 39-6-9
39-7-24
BLM RD 37-6-36
NFD RD 4609
NFD RD 4613
NFD RD 4612
NFD RD 42
NFD RD 80
NFD RD 472
NFD RD 98
NFD RD 4703
NFD RD 41
NFD RD 17
BOLAN LAKE RD
NFD RD 4808
NFD RD 15
NFD RD 85
LUCKY STRIKE RD
CAMP RD
PAGE CREEK RD
HAPPY CAMP RD
WALDO RD
OBRIEN RD
LONE MOUNTAIN RD
GENE BROWN RD
NFD 9938 RD
NFD RD 4803
NFD 4201 RD
NFD 4105 RD
NFD 16 RD
NFD 67 RD
NFD RD 11
SWEDE BASIN
HAYES HILL RD
ILLINOIS RIVER
EAST FORK ILLINOIS RIVER
ALTHOUSE CREEK
SUCKER CREEK
SEE 149 MAP

SEE 230 MAP

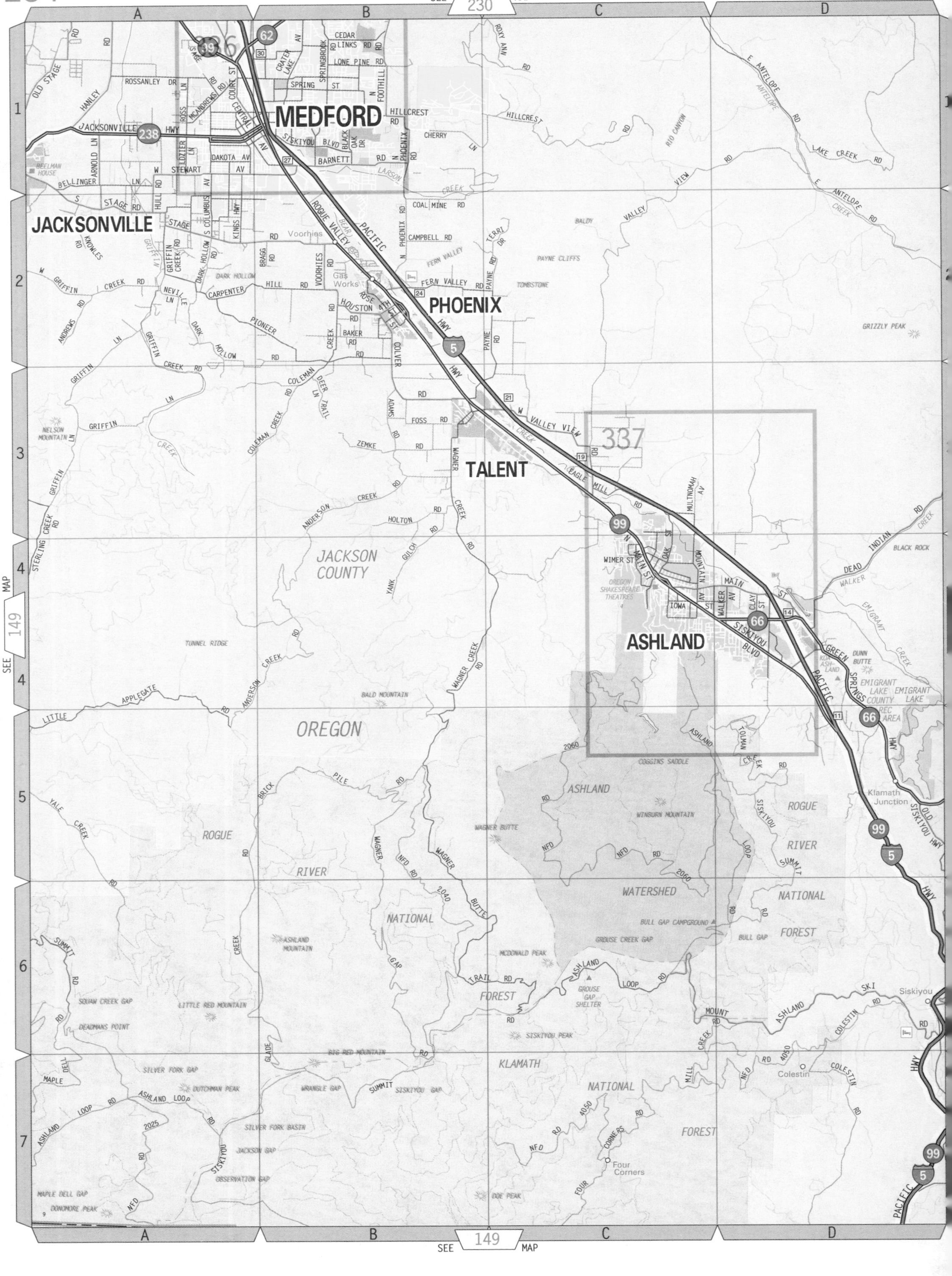

MEDFORD

JACKSONVILLE

PHOENIX

TALENT

ASHLAND

JACKSON COUNTY

OREGON

ROGUE RIVER NATIONAL FOREST

KLAMATH NATIONAL FOREST

ASHLAND WATERSHED

Klamath Junction

Siskiyou

Colestin

Four Corners

GRIZZLY PEAK

BALD MOUNTAIN

WAGNER BUTTE

SISKIYOU PEAK

EMIGRANT LAKE COUNTY REC AREA

EMIGRANT LAKE

OREGON SHAKESPEARE THEATRES

SEE 149 MAP

SEE 149 MAP

PNW

METRO

SEE 231 MAP

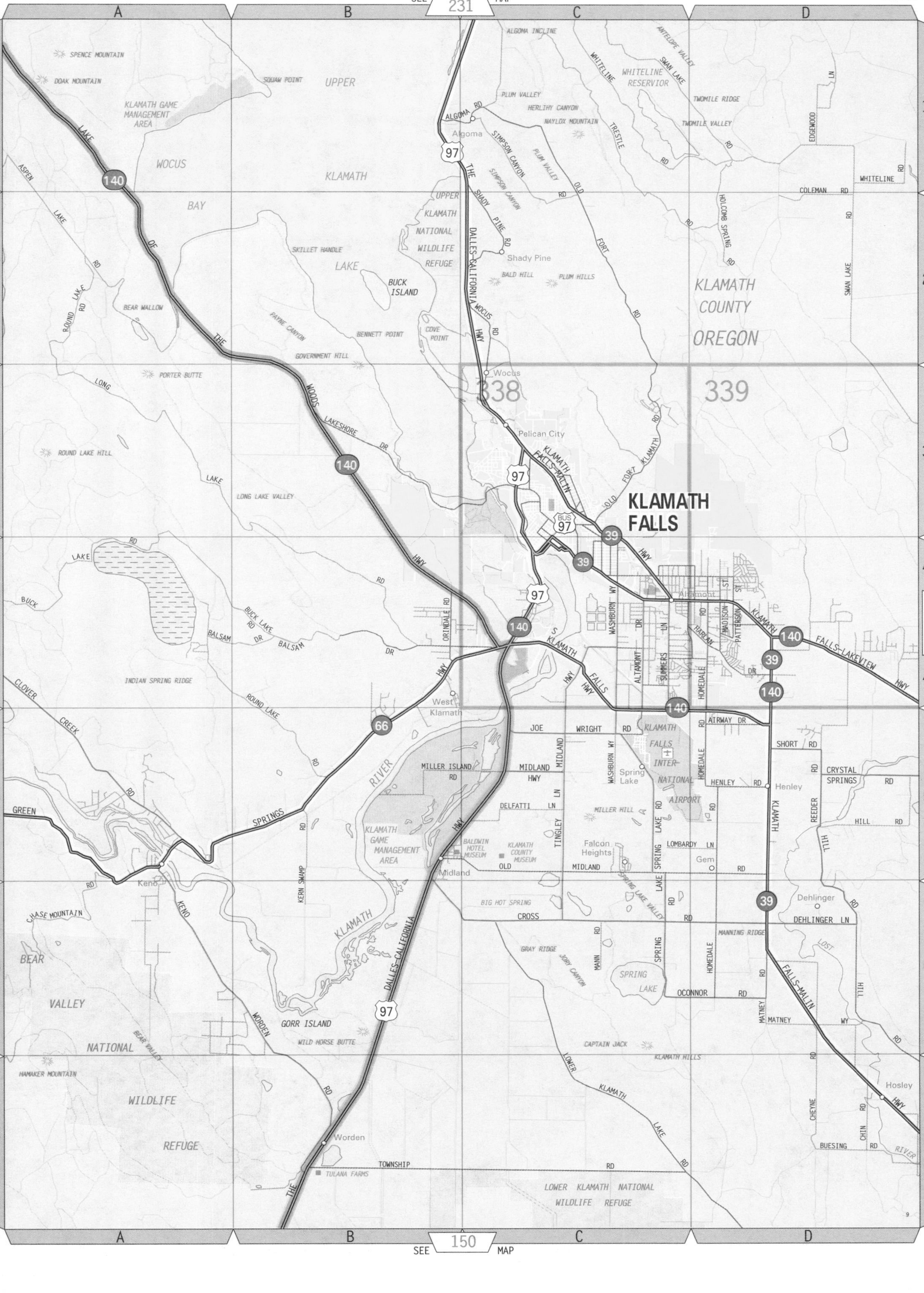

SEE 150 MAP

KLAMATH FALLS

KLAMATH COUNTY
OREGON

338
339

UPPER KLAMATH LAKE
WOCUS BAY
UPPER KLAMATH NATIONAL WILDLIFE REFUGE
KLAMATH GAME MANAGEMENT AREA
BEAR VALLEY NATIONAL WILDLIFE REFUGE
LOWER KLAMATH NATIONAL WILDLIFE REFUGE
KLAMATH FALLS INTERNATIONAL AIRPORT
KLAMATH RIVER
LOST RIVER
SPRING LAKE

Algoma
Shady Pine
Wocus
Pelican City
Altamont
West Klamath
Spring Lake
Henley
Falcon Heights
Gem
Midland
Keno
Dehlinger
Hosley
Worden

PNW

METRO

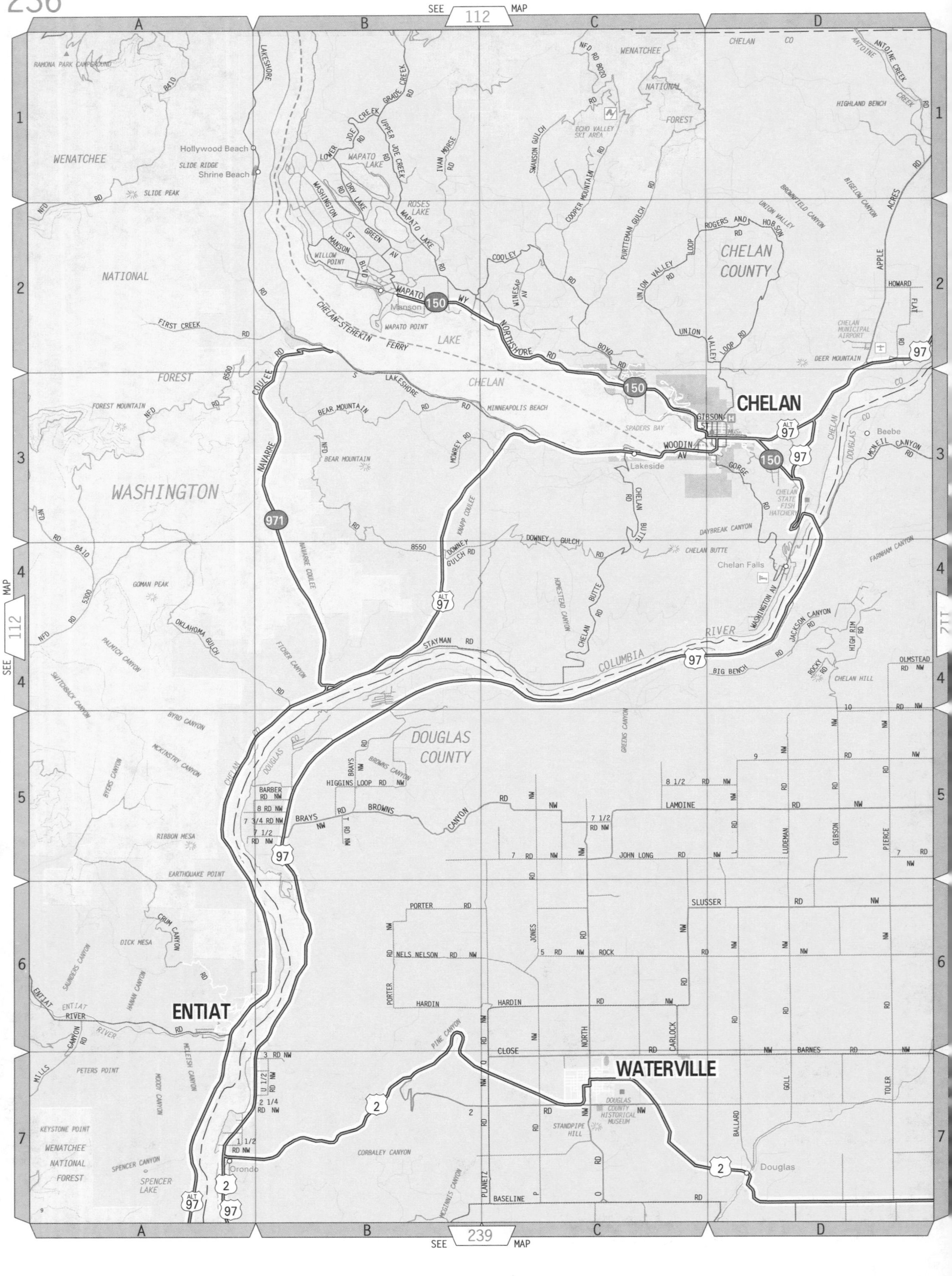
SEE 112 MAP
SEE 239 MAP
SEE MAP 112
A
B
C
D
1
2
3
4
5
6
7
CHELAN
WATERVILLE
ENTIAT
CHELAN COUNTY
DOUGLAS COUNTY
WENATCHEE
NATIONAL
FOREST
WASHINGTON
WENATCHEE NATIONAL FOREST
LAKE
CHELAN
COLUMBIA
RIVER
Manson
Hollywood Beach
Shrine Beach
SLIDE RIDGE
SLIDE PEAK
RAMONA PARK CAMPGROUND
ECHO VALLEY SKI AREA
ROSES LAKE
WAPATO LAKE
WAPATO POINT
WILLOW POINT
CHELAN-STEHEKIN FERRY
MINNEAPOLIS BEACH
SPADERS BAY
Lakeside
CHELAN MUNICIPAL AIRPORT
DEER MOUNTAIN
Beebe
CHELAN STATE FISH HATCHERY
Chelan Falls
CHELAN BUTTE
DAYBREAK CANYON
BEAR MOUNTAIN
FOREST MOUNTAIN
GOMAN PEAK
RIBBON MESA
EARTHQUAKE POINT
DICK MESA
PETERS POINT
KEYSTONE POINT
SPENCER LAKE
SPENCER CANYON
CORBALEY CANYON
PINE CANYON
STANDPIPE HILL
DOUGLAS COUNTY HISTORICAL MUSEUM
Orondo
Douglas
CHELAN HILL
JACKSON CANYON
FARNHAM CANYON
BIG BENCH
HIGHLAND BENCH
UNION VALLEY
BROWNFIELD CANYON
BIGELOW CANYON
NAVARRE COULEE
KNAPP COULEE
HOMESTEAD CANYON
GREENS CANYON
WOODIN AV
GIBSON ST
WAPATO WY
NORTHSHORE RD
S LAKESHORE RD
LAKESHORE RD
DOWNEY GULCH RD
STAYMAN RD
BRAYS NW
BROWNS CANYON RD
HIGGINS LOOP RD NW
JOHN LONG RD NW
SLUSSER RD NW
PORTER RD
NELS NELSON RD NW
HARDIN RD NW
CLOSE RD NW
BARNES RD NW
BASELINE RD
LAMOINE RD NW
ROCK RD NW
JONES RD
NORTH RD
CARLOCK RD
BALLARD
GOLL
TOLER
LUDEMAN
GIBSON
PIERCE
PLANETZ
OLMSTEAD RD NW
150
971
97
ALT 97
2

SEE 105 MAP

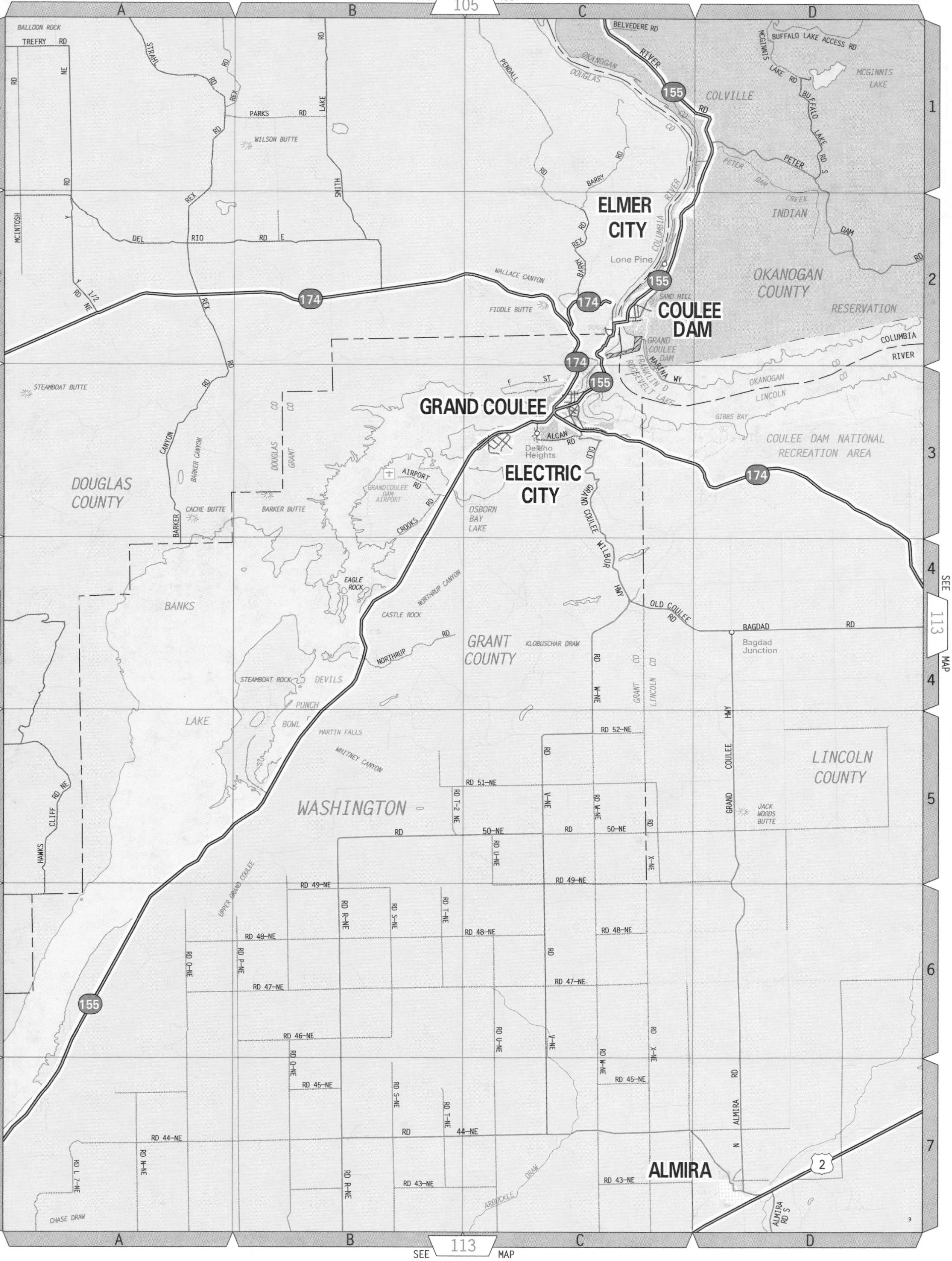

A B C D

1 2 3 4 5 6 7

ELMER CITY

COULEE DAM

GRAND COULEE

ELECTRIC CITY

ALMIRA

Lone Pine

Delano Heights

Bagdad Junction

DOUGLAS COUNTY

GRANT COUNTY

LINCOLN COUNTY

OKANOGAN COUNTY

COLVILLE INDIAN RESERVATION

COULEE DAM NATIONAL RECREATION AREA

BANKS LAKE

WASHINGTON

DEVILS PUNCH BOWL

FRANKLIN D ROOSEVELT LAKE

COLUMBIA RIVER

OKANOGAN RIVER

MCGINNIS LAKE

OSBORN BAY LAKE

GRAND COULEE DAM

GRANDCOULEE DAM AIRPORT

BALLOON ROCK, WILSON BUTTE, STEAMBOAT BUTTE, CACHE BUTTE, BARKER BUTTE, FIDDLE BUTTE, EAGLE ROCK, CASTLE ROCK, STEAMBOAT ROCK, JACK WOODS BUTTE, SAND HILL, GIBBS BAY

WALLACE CANYON, BARKER CANYON, NORTHRUP CANYON, WHITNEY CANYON, KLOBUSCHAR DRAW, ARBUCKLE DRAW, CHASE DRAW, MARTIN FALLS, UPPER GRAND COULEE

TREFRY RD, MCINTOSH RD, Y NE RD, Y 1/2 RD NE, STRAHL RD, REX RD, PARKS RD, LAKE RD, SMITH RD, DEL RIO RD E, BARRY RD, PENDALL RD, BELVEDERE RD, RIVER RD, BUFFALO LAKE ACCESS RD, MCGINNIS LAKE RD, BUFFALO LAKE RD S, PETER DAM CREEK RD, INDIAN DAM RD, CANYON RD, BARKER RD, F ST, AIRPORT RD, CROOKS RD, ALCAN RD, MARINA WY, OLD GRAND COULEE WILBUR HWY, OLD COULEE RD, BAGDAD RD, NORTHRUP RD, HAWKS CLIFF RD NE, GRAND COULEE HWY, N ALMIRA RD, ALMIRA RD S

RD 52-NE, RD 51-NE, RD 50-NE, RD 49-NE, RD 48-NE, RD 47-NE, RD 46-NE, RD 45-NE, RD 44-NE, RD 43-NE

RD L 7-NE, RD N-NE, RD O-NE, RD P-NE, RD Q-NE, RD R-NE, RD S-NE, RD T-NE, RD T-2 NE, RD U-NE, RD V-NE, RD W-NE, RD X-NE

155, 174, 2

SEE 113 MAP

SEE 113 MAP

9

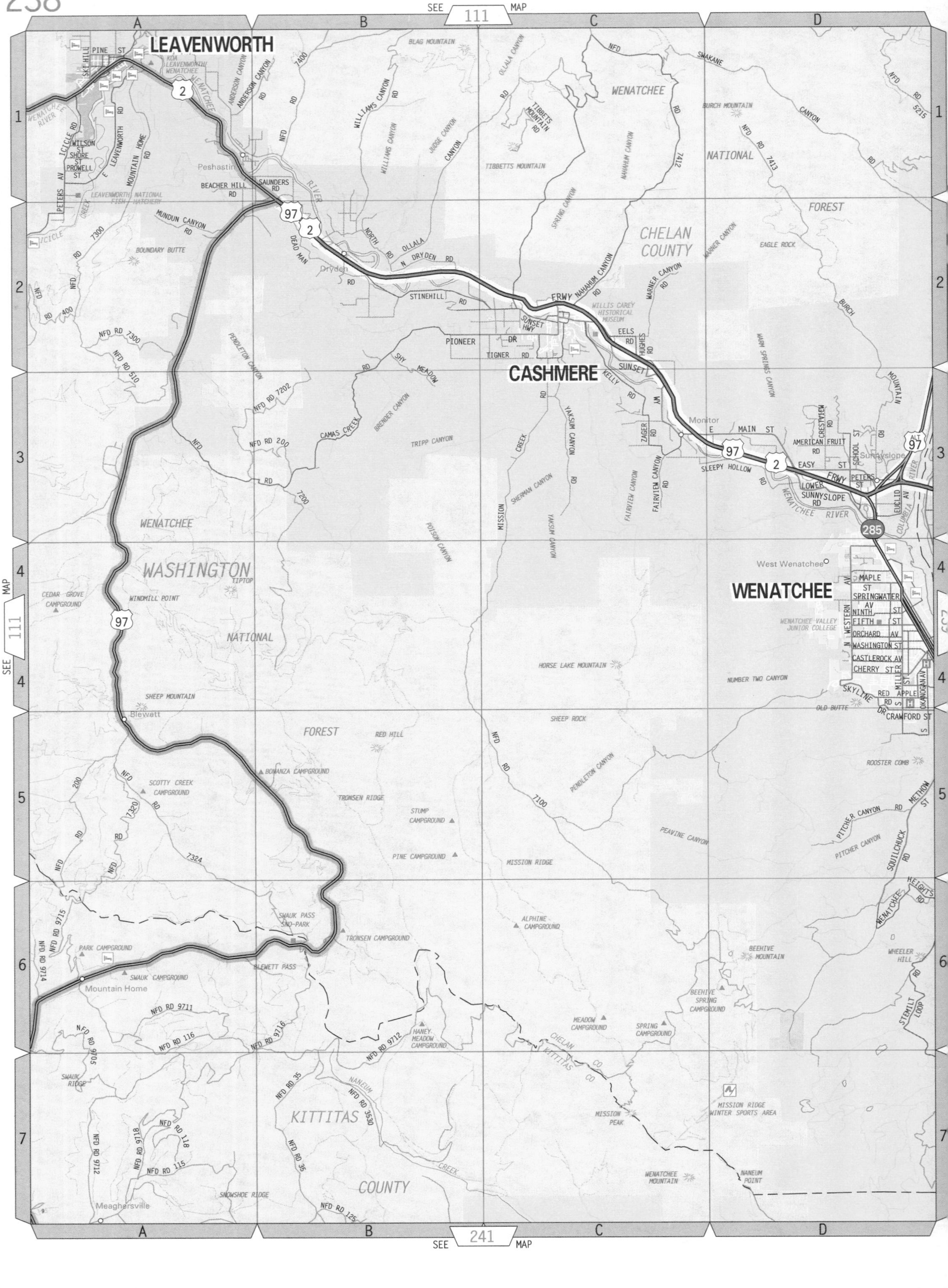
SEE 111 MAP
A
B
C
D
1
2
3
4
5
6
7
LEAVENWORTH
CASHMERE
WENATCHEE
WENATCHEE NATIONAL FOREST
CHELAN COUNTY
WENATCHEE WASHINGTON NATIONAL FOREST
KITTITAS COUNTY
Peshastin
Dryden
Monitor
Sunnyslope
West Wenatchee
Blewett
Mountain Home
Meaghersville
PINE ST
SKI HILL
WENATCHEE RIVER
ICICLE RD
WILSON ST
SHORE ST
PROWELL ST
PETERS AV
E LEAVENWORTH RD
MOUNTAIN HOME RD
KOA LEAVENWORTH/WENATCHEE
LEAVENWORTH NATIONAL FISH HATCHERY
ICICLE CREEK
ANDERSON CANYON
ANDERSON CANYON RD
BEACHER HILL RD
SAUNDERS RD
MUNDUN CANYON RD
NFD RD 7300
BOUNDARY BUTTE
NFD RD 400
NFD RD 7300
NFD RD 510
DEAD MAN RD
NORTH RD
OLLALA
N DRYDEN RD
STINEHILL RD
FRWY
PIONEER DR
TIGNER RD
SUNSET HWY
EELS RD
HUGHES RD
KELLY RD
ZAGER RD
AV
WILLIS CAREY HISTORICAL MUSEUM
PENDLETON CANYON
NFD RD 7202
SHY MEADOW
CAMAS CREEK
BRENDER CANYON
TRIPP CANYON
NFD RD 200
NFD RD
RD 7200
BLAG MOUNTAIN
WILLIAMS CANYON
JUDGE CANYON
NFD RD 7400
OLALLA CANYON
TIBBETS MOUNTAIN RD
TIBBETTS MOUNTAIN
SPRING CANYON
NAHAHUM CANYON
NFD RD 7412
NFD SNAKANE CANYON RD 5215
BURCH MOUNTAIN
NFD RD 7413
EAGLE ROCK
WARNER CANYON
WARNER CANYON RD
WARM SPRINGS CANYON
BURCH MOUNTAIN
MISSION CREEK RD
YAKSUM CANYON RD
SHERMAN CANYON
POISON CANYON
FAIRVIEW CANYON
FAIRVIEW CANYON RD
E MAIN ST
CRESTVIEW RD
AMERICAN FRUIT RD
SCHOOL ST
EASY ST
SLEEPY HOLLOW RD
PETERS ST
LOWER SUNNYSLOPE RD
WENATCHEE RIVER
COLUMBIA RIVER
EUCLID AV
ALT 97
97
2
285
MAPLE ST
SPRINGWATER AV
NINTH ST
FIFTH ST
ORCHARD AV
WASHINGTON ST
CASTLEROCK AV
CHERRY ST
N WESTERN AV
MILLER ST
S
SKYLINE DR
RED APPLE RD
OKANOGAN AV
CRAWFORD ST
WENATCHEE VALLEY JUNIOR COLLEGE
OLD BUTTE
HORSE LAKE MOUNTAIN
NUMBER TWO CANYON
CEDAR GROVE CAMPGROUND
WINDMILL POINT
TIPTOP
SHEEP MOUNTAIN
SHEEP ROCK
RED HILL
NFD RD 7100
PENDLETON CANYON
ROOSTER COMB
METHOW ST
PITCHER CANYON RD
PITCHER CANYON
SQUILCHUCK RD
PEAVINE CANYON
BONANZA CAMPGROUND
SCOTTY CREEK CAMPGROUND
NFD RD 200
NFD 7320 RD
TRONSEN RIDGE
STUMP CAMPGROUND
PINE CAMPGROUND
MISSION RIDGE
7324
NFD RD
SWAUK PASS SNO-PARK
TRONSEN CAMPGROUND
ALPHINE CAMPGROUND
WENATCHEE HEIGHTS RD
WHEELER HILL RD
NFD RD 9715
NFD RD 9714
PARK CAMPGROUND
SWAUK CAMPGROUND
BLEWETT PASS
BEEHIVE MOUNTAIN
BEEHIVE SPRING CAMPGROUND
STEMILT LOOP
NFD RD 9711
NFD RD 116
NFD RD 9716
NFD RD 9712
HANEY MEADOW CAMPGROUND
MEADOW CAMPGROUND
SPRING CAMPGROUND
CHELAN CO
KITTITAS CO
NFD RD 9705
SWAUK RIDGE
NFD RD 35
NANEUM
NFD RD 3530
MISSION RIDGE WINTER SPORTS AREA
MISSION PEAK
NFD RD 9718
NFD RD 118
NFD RD 9712
NFD RD 115
NFD RD 35
CREEK
WENATCHEE MOUNTAIN
NANEUM POINT
SNOWSHOE RIDGE
NFD RD 125
SEE 241 MAP
SEE 111 MAP
239

PNW

METRO

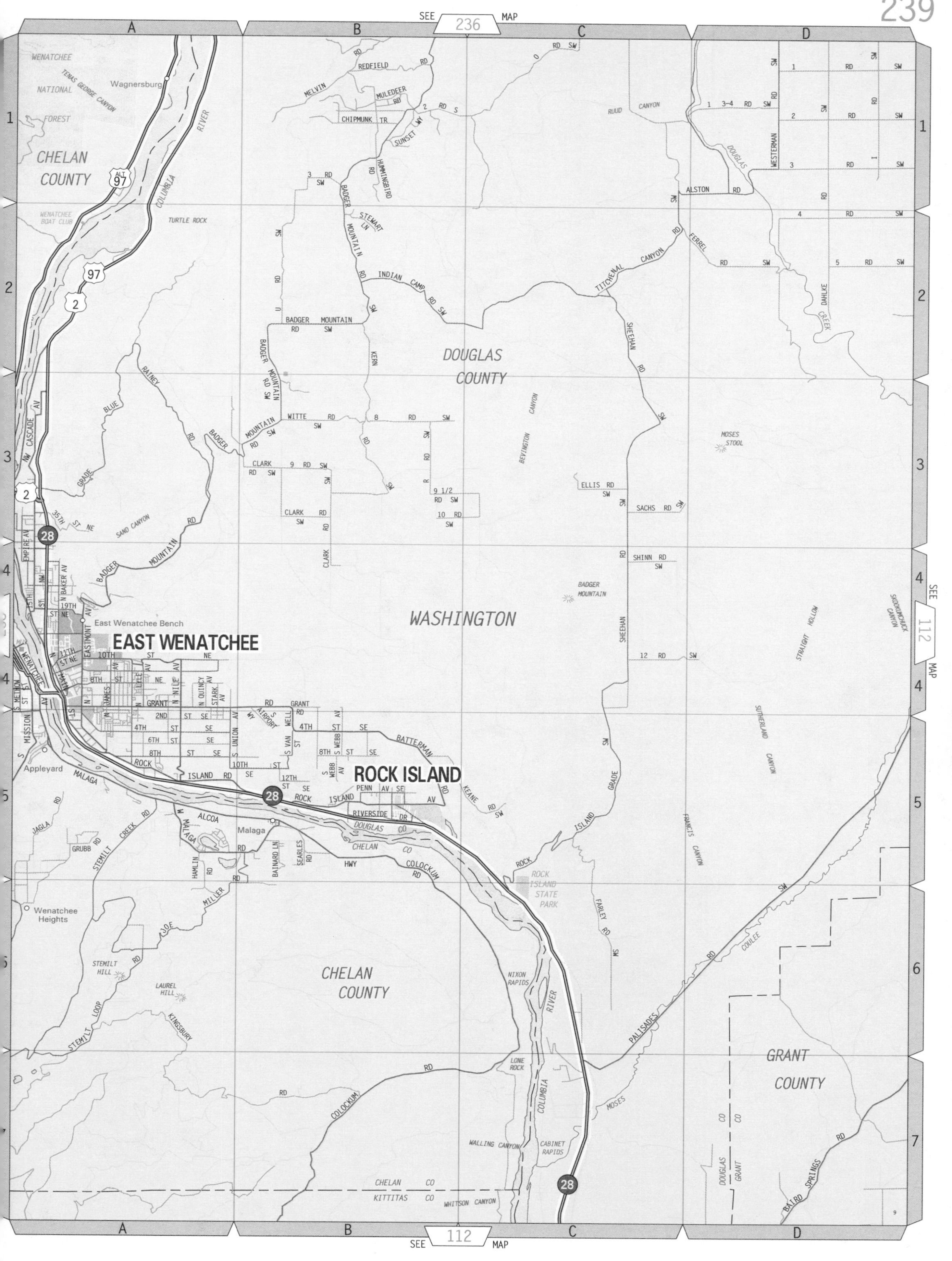

SEE 236 MAP
CHELAN COUNTY
DOUGLAS COUNTY
WASHINGTON
EAST WENATCHEE
ROCK ISLAND
CHELAN COUNTY
GRANT COUNTY
Wagnersburg
East Wenatchee Bench
Appleyard
Malaga
Wenatchee Heights
WENATCHEE NATIONAL FOREST
TEXAS GEORGE CANYON
WENATCHEE BOAT CLUB
TURTLE ROCK
COLUMBIA RIVER
BADGER MOUNTAIN
MOSES STOOL
ROCK ISLAND STATE PARK
NIXON RAPIDS
LONE ROCK
CABINET RAPIDS
WALLING CANYON
WHITSON CANYON
STEMILT HILL
LAUREL HILL
SEE 112 MAP
PNW
METRO

SEE 111 MAP

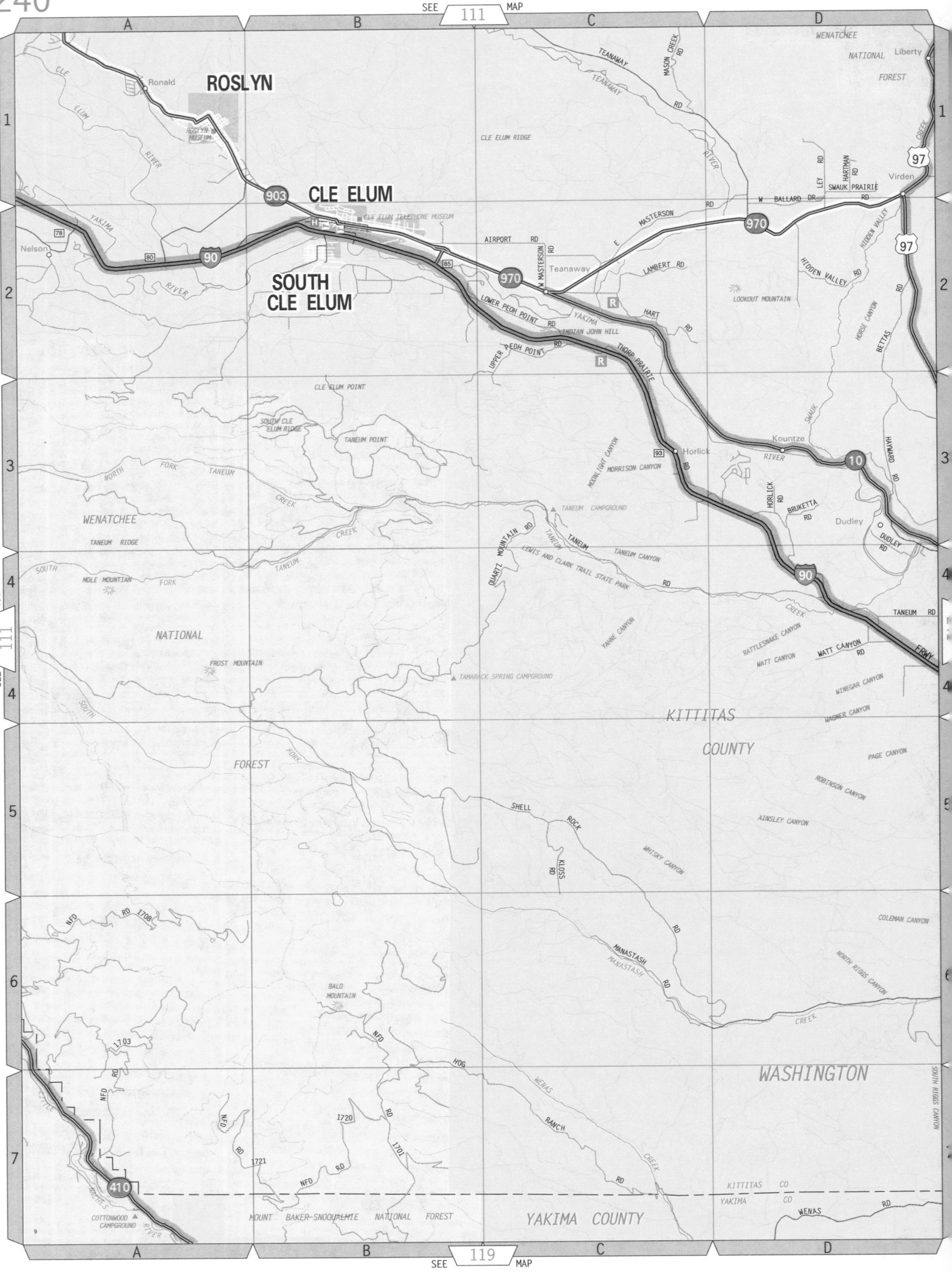

SEE 111 MAP

SEE 119 MAP

SEE 238 MAP

SEE 112 MAP

PNW

METRO

SEE 243 MAP

SEE 112 MAP

MOSES LAKE

GRANT COUNTY

WASHINGTON

THE POTHOLES RESERVOIR

POTHOLES STATE PARK

COLUMBIA NATIONAL WILDLIFE REFUGE

ADAMS COUNTY

Cascade Valley

Westlake

Mcdonald

SEE 112 MAP

SEE 120 MAP

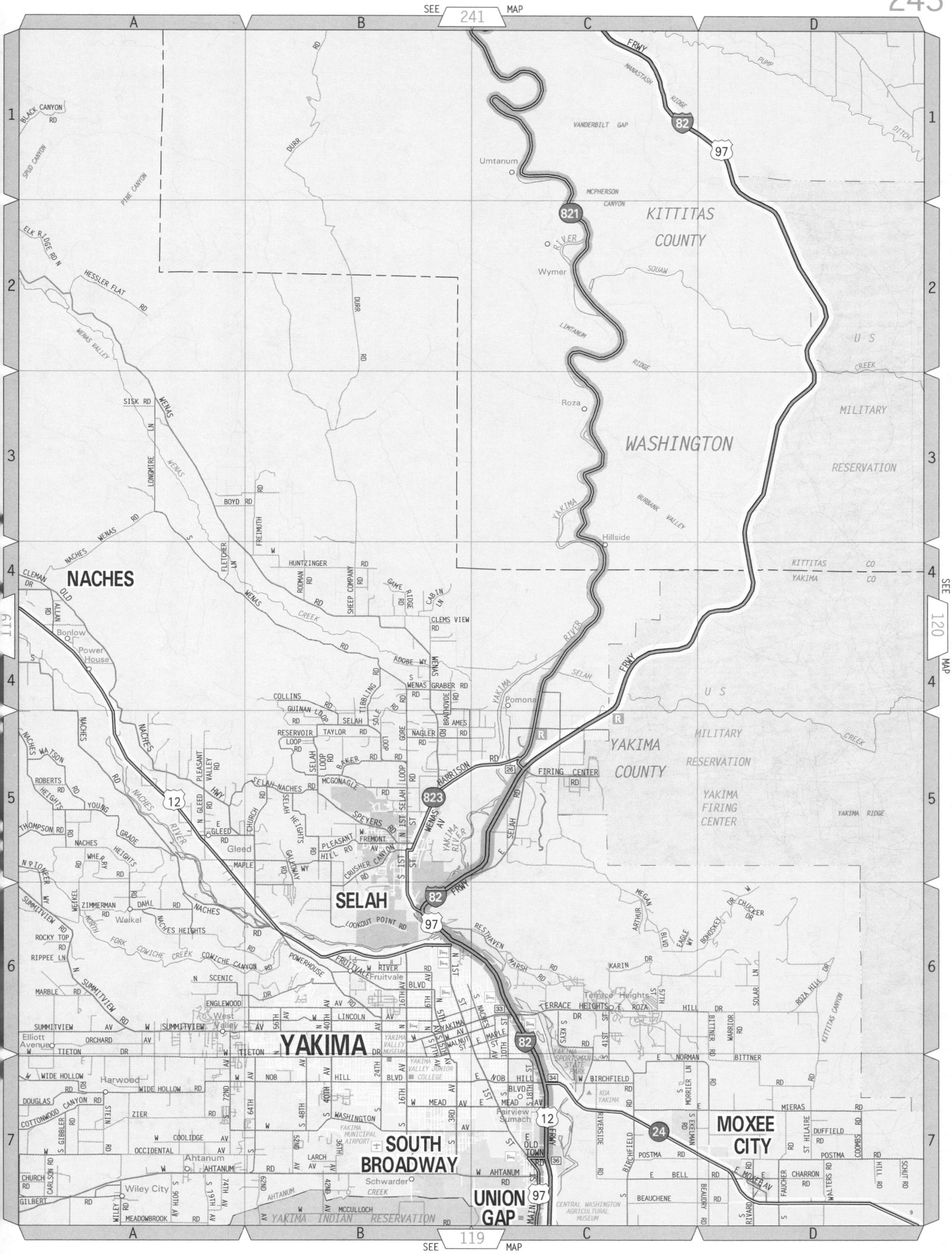
SEE 241 MAP
SEE 119 MAP
SEE 120 MAP
A
B
C
D
1
2
3
4
5
6
7
NACHES
SELAH
YAKIMA
SOUTH
BROADWAY
UNION
GAP
MOXEE
CITY
KITTITAS
COUNTY
WASHINGTON
YAKIMA
COUNTY
US
MILITARY
RESERVATION
YAKIMA
FIRING
CENTER
KITTITAS CO
YAKIMA CO
Umtanum
Wymer
Roza
Hillside
Pomona
Bonlow
Power House
Gleed
Weikel
Fruitvale
West Valley
Elliott Avenue
Harwood
Ahtanum
Wiley City
Schwarder
Fairview-Sumach
Terrace Heights
OLD TOWN
YAKIMA INDIAN RESERVATION
YAKIMA RIVER
NACHES RIVER
WENAS CREEK
COWICHE CREEK
AHTANUM CREEK
UMTANUM RIDGE
MANASTASH RIDGE
YAKIMA RIDGE
VANDERBILT GAP
MCPHERSON CANYON
BURBANK VALLEY
YAKIMA VALLEY MUSEUM
YAKIMA VALLEY JUNIOR COLLEGE
YAKIMA MUNICIPAL AIRPORT
YAKIMA SPORTSMAN STATE PARK
KOA YAKIMA
CENTRAL WASHINGTON AGRICULTURAL MUSEUM
82
97
12
24
821
823

SEE 107 MAP

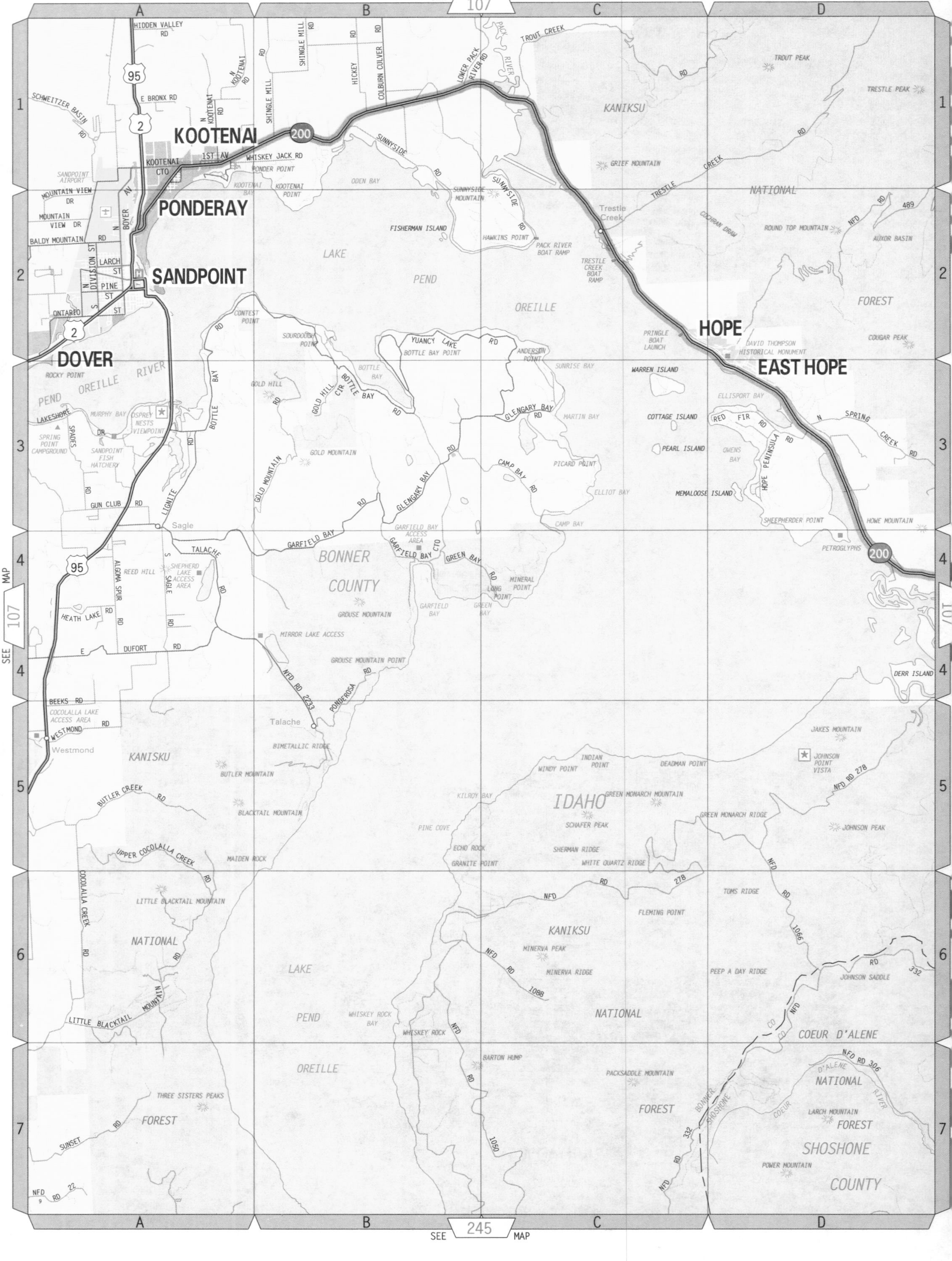

KOOTENAI
PONDERAY
SANDPOINT
DOVER
HOPE
EAST HOPE

Trestle Creek
Sagle
Talache
Westmond

LAKE PEND OREILLE
PEND OREILLE RIVER
BONNER COUNTY
KANIKSU NATIONAL FOREST
IDAHO
COEUR D'ALENE NATIONAL FOREST
SHOSHONE COUNTY

HIDDEN VALLEY RD
SCHWEITZER BASIN RD
E BRONX RD
KOOTENAI CTO
1ST AV
WHISKEY JACK RD
SANDPOINT AIRPORT
MOUNTAIN VIEW DR
BALDY MOUNTAIN RD
BOYER AV
DIVISION ST
LARCH ST
PINE ST
ONTARIO ST
ROCKY POINT
LAKESHORE DR
MURPHY BAY
OSPREY NESTS VIEWPOINT
SPRING POINT CAMPGROUND
SANDPOINT FISH HATCHERY
GUN CLUB RD
LIGNITE RD
BOTTLE BAY RD
TALACHE RD
SHEPHERD LAKE ACCESS AREA
REED HILL
ALGOMA SPUR RD
HEATH LAKE RD
E DUFORT RD
BEEKS RD
COCOLALLA LAKE ACCESS AREA
WESTMOND RD
BUTLER CREEK RD
UPPER COCOLALLA CREEK RD
COCOLALLA CREEK RD
LITTLE BLACKTAIL MOUNTAIN RD
SUNSET RD
NFD RD 22
THREE SISTERS PEAKS
SHINGLE MILL RD
HICKEY RD
COLBURN CULVER RD
LOWER PACK RIVER RD
PACK RIVER
TROUT CREEK RD
SUNNYSIDE RD
PONDER POINT
KOOTENAI BAY
KOOTENAI POINT
ODEN BAY
SUNNYSIDE MOUNTAIN
HAWKINS POINT
PACK RIVER BOAT RAMP
FISHERMAN ISLAND
CONTEST POINT
SOURDOUGH POINT
GOLD HILL
GOLD HILL CIR
GOLD MOUNTAIN RD
GOLD MOUNTAIN
GLENGARY BAY RD
GARFIELD BAY RD
GARFIELD BAY ACCESS AREA
GARFIELD BAY CTO
GREEN BAY RD
LONG POINT
MINERAL POINT
GROUSE MOUNTAIN
GROUSE MOUNTAIN POINT
MIRROR LAKE ACCESS
NFD RD 2233
PONDEROSA RD
BIMETALLIC RIDGE
BUTLER MOUNTAIN
BLACKTAIL MOUNTAIN
MAIDEN ROCK
YUANCY LAKE RD
BOTTLE BAY POINT
ANDERSON POINT
SUNRISE BAY
MARTIN BAY
CAMP BAY RD
PICARD POINT
ELLIOT BAY
CAMP BAY
TRESTLE CREEK RD
TRESTLE CREEK BOAT RAMP
GRIEF MOUNTAIN
PRINGLE BOAT LAUNCH
DAVID THOMPSON HISTORICAL MONUMENT
WARREN ISLAND
ELLISPORT BAY
COTTAGE ISLAND
PEARL ISLAND
RED FIR RD
OWENS BAY
HOPE PENINSULA RD
MEMALOOSE ISLAND
SHEEPHERDER POINT
PETROGLYPHS
TROUT PEAK
TRESTLE PEAK
COCHRAN DRAW
ROUND TOP MOUNTAIN
NFD RD 489
AUXOR BASIN
COUGAR PEAK
N SPRING CREEK RD
HOWE MOUNTAIN
DERR ISLAND
JAKES MOUNTAIN
JOHNSON POINT VISTA
NFD RD 278
JOHNSON PEAK
INDIAN POINT
WINDY POINT
DEADMAN POINT
GREEN MONARCH MOUNTAIN
GREEN MONARCH RIDGE
KILROY BAY
SCHAFER PEAK
SHERMAN RIDGE
WHITE QUARTZ RIDGE
PINE COVE
ECHO ROCK
GRANITE POINT
NFD RD 278
TOMS RIDGE
NFD RD 1066
FLEMING POINT
MINERVA PEAK
MINERVA RIDGE
NFD RD 1088
PEEP A DAY RIDGE
JOHNSON SADDLE
RD 332
WHISKEY ROCK BAY
WHISKEY ROCK
NFD RD 1050
BARTON HUMP
PACKSADDLE MOUNTAIN
NFD RD 306
COEUR D'ALENE RIVER
LARCH MOUNTAIN
POWER MOUNTAIN
NFD RD 332
BONNER CO
SHOSHONE CO

SEE 107 MAP

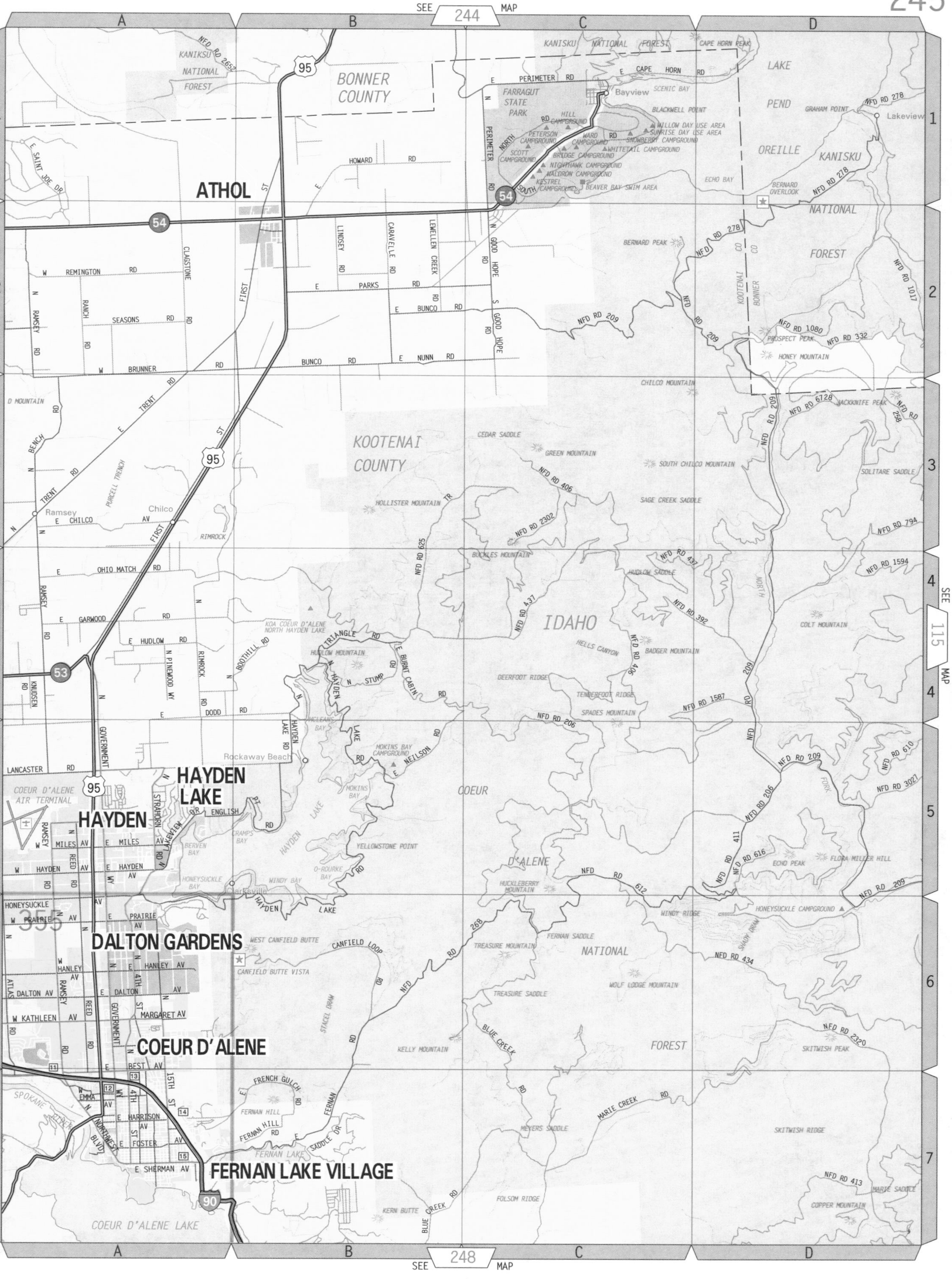
SEE MAP 244
A
B
C
D
1
2
3
4
5
6
7
SEE MAP 115
SEE MAP 248
247
355
KANIKSU NATIONAL FOREST
NFD RD 2652
BONNER COUNTY
KANISKU NATIONAL FOREST
CAPE HORN PEAK
E CAPE HORN RD
PERIMETER RD
FARRAGUT STATE PARK
Bayview
SCENIC BAY
BLACKWELL POINT
WILLOW DAY USE AREA
SUNRISE DAY USE AREA
SNOWBERRY CAMPGROUND
WHITETAIL CAMPGROUND
HILL CAMPGROUND
PETERSON CAMPGROUND
WARD CAMPGROUND
SCOTT CAMPGROUND
BRIDGE CAMPGROUND
NIGHTHAWK CAMPGROUND
WALDRON CAMPGROUND
KESTREL CAMPGROUND
BEAVER BAY SWIM AREA
ECHO BAY
LAKE PEND OREILLE
GRAHAM POINT
NFD RD 278
Lakeview
KANISKU NATIONAL FOREST
BERNARD OVERLOOK
BERNARD PEAK
ATHOL
HOWARD RD
E SAINT JOE DR
54
95
W REMINGTON RD
CLAGSTONE
LINDSEY RD
CARAVELLE RD
LEWELLEN CREEK
N GOOD HOPE RD
S GOOD HOPE RD
E PARKS RD
E BUNCO RD
N RAMSEY RD
RANCH RD
SEASONS RD
W BRUNNER RD
BUNCO RD
E NUNN RD
FIRST ST
NFD RD 209
KOOTENAI CO
BONNER CO
NFD RD 1080
PROSPECT PEAK
NFD RD 332
HONEY MOUNTAIN
NFD RD 1017
CHILCO MOUNTAIN
NFD RD 6728
JACKKNIFE PEAK
NFD RD 258
D MOUNTAIN
N BENCH RD
E TRENT RD
N TRENT RD
PURCELL TRENCH
KOOTENAI COUNTY
CEDAR SADDLE
GREEN MOUNTAIN
SOUTH CHILCO MOUNTAIN
SOLITARE SADDLE
NFD RD 406
SAGE CREEK SADDLE
Ramsey
Chilco
E CHILCO AV
RIMROCK
HOLLISTER MOUNTAIN TR
NFD RD 2302
NFD RD 625
NFD RD 794
BUCKLES MOUNTAIN
NFD RD 437
HUDLOW SADDLE
NFD RD 1594
E OHIO MATCH RD
E GARWOOD RD
E HUDLOW RD
N PINEWOOD WY
RIMROCK RD
BOOTHILL RD
KOA COEUR D'ALENE NORTH HAYDEN LAKE
TRIANGLE RD
IDAHO
NFD RD 392
COLT MOUNTAIN
HUDLOW MOUNTAIN
HELLS CANYON
BADGER MOUNTAIN
N STUMP
BURNT CABIN RD
DEERFOOT RIDGE
TENDERFOOT RIDGE
SPADES MOUNTAIN
NFD RD 1587
NORTH FORK
53
KNUDSEN RD
E DODD RD
NFD RD 206
GOVERNMENT
HAYDEN LAKE RD
MCLEANS BAY
Rockaway Beach
MOKINS BAY CAMPGROUND
E NEILSON RD
LAKE
NFD RD 610
NFD RD 209
NFD RD 3027
LANCASTER RD
COEUR D'ALENE AIR TERMINAL
HAYDEN LAKE
HAYDEN
STRAHORN
LAKEVIEW DR
ENGLISH PT RD
MOKINS BAY
COEUR D'ALENE NATIONAL FOREST
RAMSEY
MILES AV
E MILES AV
REED RD
BERVEN BAY
CRAMPS BAY
HAYDEN LAKE
YELLOWSTONE POINT
NFD RD 411
NFD RD 616
ECHO PEAK
FLORA MILLER HILL
W HAYDEN AV
E HAYDEN AV
HONEYSUCKLE BAY
Clarksville
WINDY BAY
O-ROURKE BAY
NFD RD 612
HUCKLEBERRY MOUNTAIN
WINDY RIDGE
HONEYSUCKLE CAMPGROUND
SHADY DRAW
HONEYSUCKLE AV
W PRAIRIE AV
E PRAIRIE AV
DALTON GARDENS
WEST CANFIELD BUTTE
CANFIELD LOOP RD
CANFIELD BUTTE VISTA
NFD RD 268
TREASURE MOUNTAIN
FERNAN SADDLE
NFD RD 434
W HANLEY AV
HANLEY AV
4TH ST
ATLAS
DALTON AV
E DALTON AV
WOLF LODGE MOUNTAIN
TREASURE SADDLE
W KATHLEEN AV
MARGARET AV
STACEL DRAW
BLUE CREEK RD
NFD RD 2320
COEUR D'ALENE
KELLY MOUNTAIN
SKITWISH PEAK
BEST AV
15TH ST
E FRENCH GULCH RD
FERNAN RD
SPOKANE RIVER
EMMA AV
NORTHWEST BLVD
HARRISON AV
FERNAN HILL
FERNAN HILL RD
E SADDLE DR
MEYERS SADDLE
MARIE CREEK RD
SKITWISH RIDGE
E FOSTER AV
FERNAN LAKE
E SHERMAN AV
FERNAN LAKE VILLAGE
11
12
13
14
15
90
NFD RD 413
MARIE SADDLE
COPPER MOUNTAIN
KERN BUTTE
FOLSOM RIDGE
COEUR D'ALENE LAKE

PNW

METRO

SEE 114 MAP

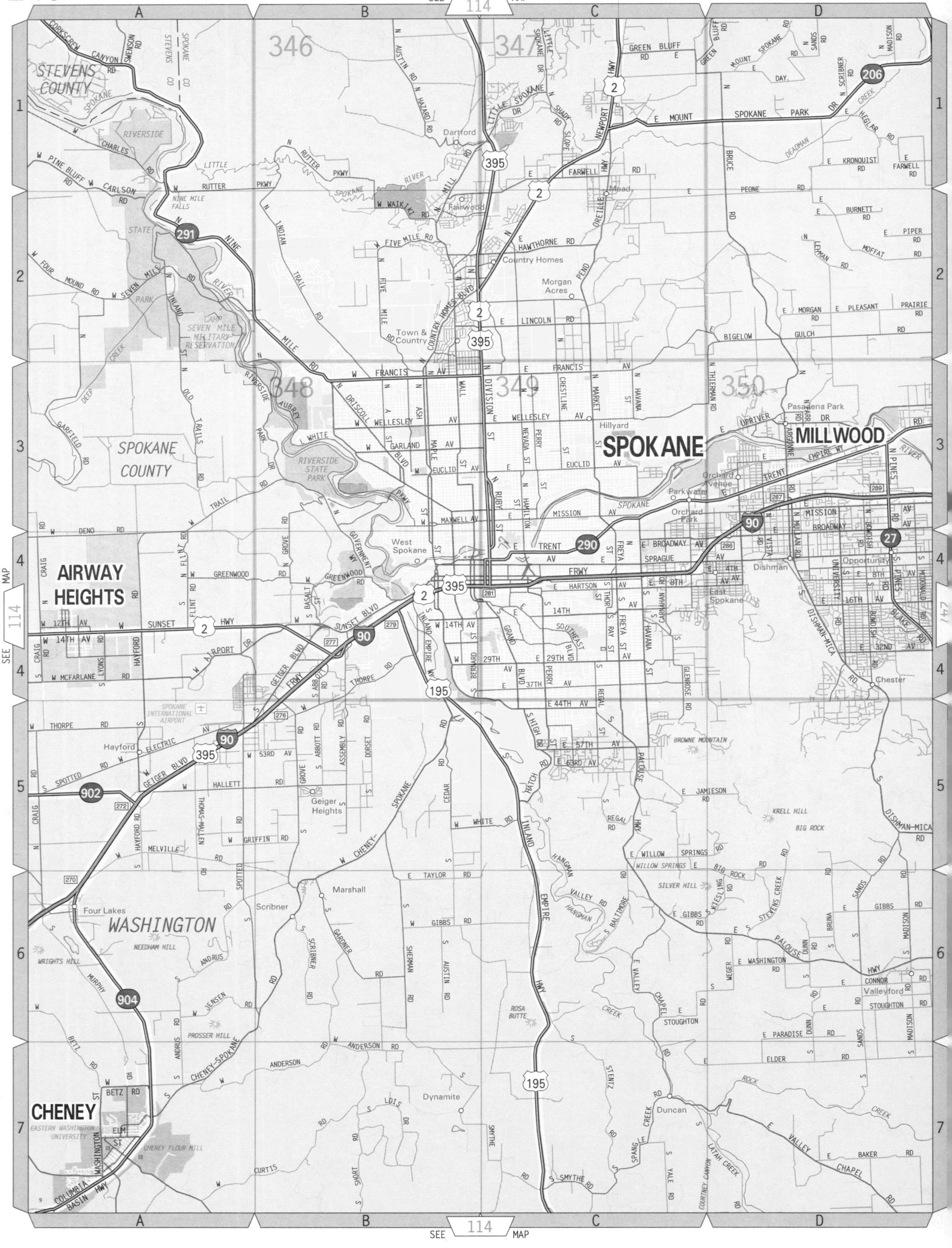

A B C D

346 347 348 349 350

STEVENS COUNTY

SPOKANE COUNTY

AIRWAY HEIGHTS

SPOKANE

MILLWOOD

CHENEY

WASHINGTON

Dartford
Fairwood
Mead
Country Homes
Morgan Acres
Town & Country
Hillyard
Pasadena Park
Orchard Avenue
Parkwater
Orchard Park
West Spokane
Dishman
East Spokane
Opportunity
Chester
Hayford
Geiger Heights
Marshall
Scribner
Four Lakes
Valleyford
Duncan
Dynamite

NINE MILE FALLS
RIVERSIDE STATE PARK
CAMP SEVEN MILE MILITARY RESERVATION
SPOKANE INTERNATIONAL AIRPORT
EASTERN WASHINGTON UNIVERSITY
CHENEY FLOUR MILL
BROWNE MOUNTAIN
KRELL HILL
BIG ROCK
SILVER HILL
ROSA BUTTE
NEEDHAM HILL
WRIGHTS HILL
PROSSER HILL

SEE 114 MAP

SEE 114 MAP

147

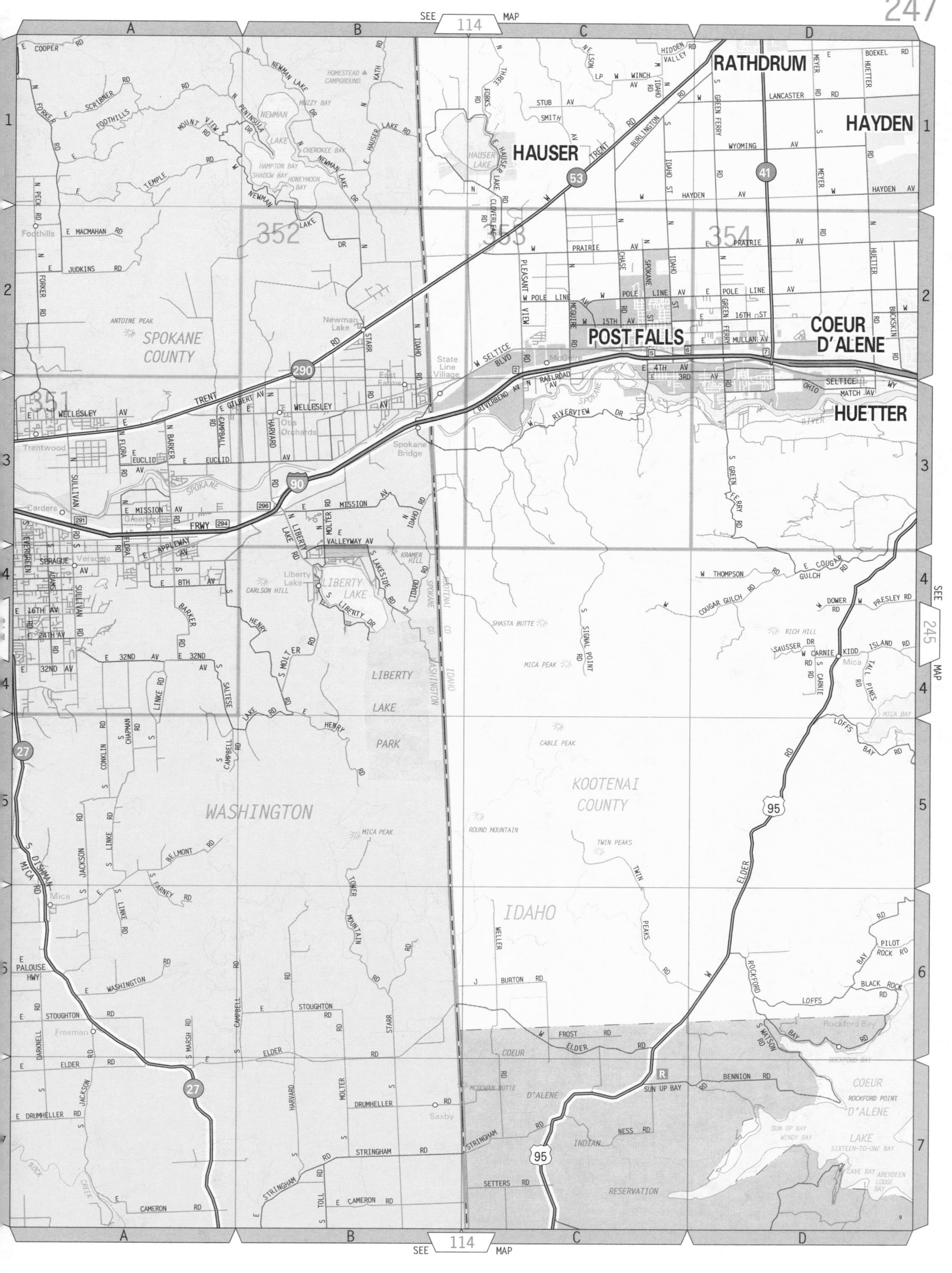
SEE 114 MAP
RATHDRUM
HAYDEN
HAUSER
POST FALLS
COEUR D'ALENE
HUETTER
SPOKANE COUNTY
KOOTENAI COUNTY
WASHINGTON
IDAHO
LIBERTY LAKE PARK
COEUR D'ALENE INDIAN RESERVATION
COEUR D'ALENE LAKE
Newman Lake
Liberty Lake
Hauser Lake
Trentwood
Otis Orchards
East Farms
State Line Village
Spokane Bridge
Greenacres
Veradale
Carders
Foothills
Freeman
Mica
Saxby
McGuire
Rockford Bay
MICA PEAK
CABLE PEAK
ROUND MOUNTAIN
TWIN PEAKS
SHASTA BUTTE
RICH HILL
ANTOINE PEAK
CARLSON HILL
KRAMER HILL
MCGOWAN BUTTE
351
352
353
354
SEE 245 MAP
PNW
METRO

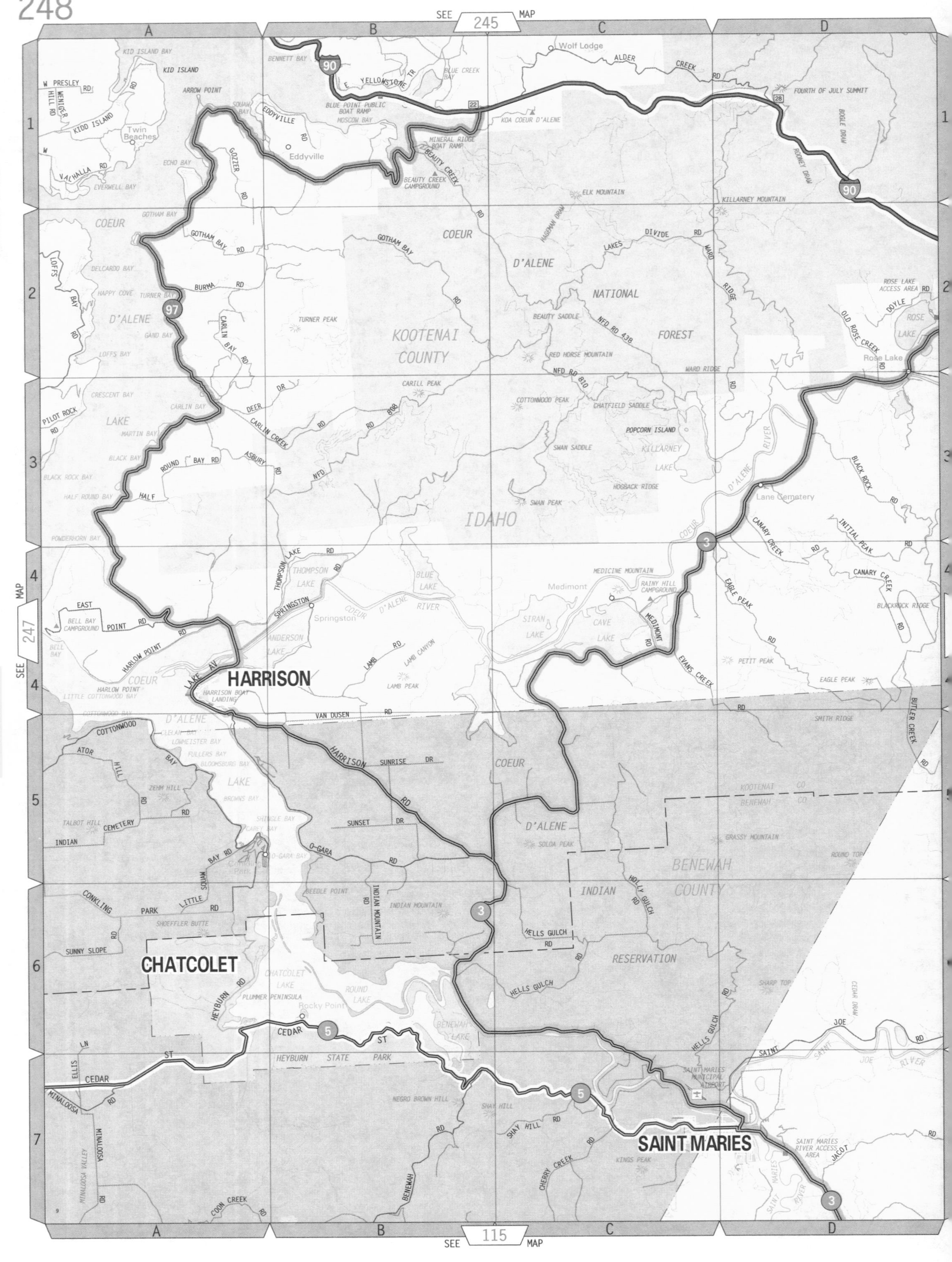

SEE 245 MAP
SEE 247 MAP
SEE 115 MAP
PNW
METRO
HARRISON
CHATCOLET
SAINT MARIES
KOOTENAI COUNTY
BENEWAH COUNTY
COEUR D'ALENE NATIONAL FOREST
IDAHO
COEUR D'ALENE LAKE
COEUR D'ALENE INDIAN RESERVATION
Wolf Lodge
Eddyville
Twin Beaches
Springston
Medimont
Rose Lake
Lane Cemetery
Rocky Point
KID ISLAND BAY
KID ISLAND
ARROW POINT
SQUAW BAY
BENNETT BAY
BLUE POINT PUBLIC BOAT RAMP
MOSCOW BAY
MINERAL RIDGE BOAT RAMP
BEAUTY CREEK CAMPGROUND
KOA COEUR D'ALENE
ALDER CREEK RD
FOURTH OF JULY SUMMIT
BOGLE DRAW
RODNEY DRAW
KILLARNEY MOUNTAIN
ELK MOUNTAIN
ECHO BAY
EVERWELL BAY
GOTHAM BAY
DELCARDO BAY
HAPPY COVE
TURNER BAY
GAND BAY
LOFFS BAY
CRESCENT BAY
CARLIN BAY
MARTIN BAY
BLACK BAY
BLACK ROCK BAY
HALF ROUND BAY
POWDERHORN BAY
BELL BAY
BELL BAY CAMPGROUND
HARLOW POINT
LITTLE COTTONWOOD BAY
COTTONWOOD BAY
HARRISON BOAT LANDING
CLEAR BAY
LOWMEISTER BAY
FULLERS BAY
BLOOMSBURG BAY
BROWNS BAY
SHINGLE BAY
CAREY BAY
O-GARA BAY
BEEDLE POINT
INDIAN MOUNTAIN
SHOEFFLER BUTTE
ZEHM HILL
TALBOT HILL
CHATCOLET LAKE
ROUND LAKE
BENEWAH LAKE
PLUMMER PENINSULA
HEYBURN STATE PARK
TURNER PEAK
CARILL PEAK
COTTONWOOD PEAK
RED HORSE MOUNTAIN
BEAUTY SADDLE
CHATFIELD SADDLE
POPCORN ISLAND
SWAN SADDLE
KILLARNEY LAKE
HOGBACK RIDGE
SWAN PEAK
THOMPSON LAKE
BLUE LAKE
ANDERSON LAKE
SIRAN LAKE
CAVE LAKE
MEDICINE MOUNTAIN
RAINY HILL CAMPGROUND
LAMB PEAK
LAMB CANYON
PETTIT PEAK
EAGLE PEAK
SMITH RIDGE
BLACKROCK RIDGE
ROSE LAKE ACCESS AREA
WARD RIDGE
SOLOA PEAK
GRASSY MOUNTAIN
ROUND TOP
SHARP TOP
CEDAR DRAW
NEGRO BROWN HILL
SHAY HILL
KINGS PEAK
SAINT MARIES MUNICIPAL AIRPORT
SAINT MARIES RIVER ACCESS AREA
COEUR D'ALENE RIVER
SAINT JOE RIVER
SAINT MARIES RIVER
HARRISON RD
VAN DUSEN RD
SUNRISE DR
SUNSET DR
O-GARA RD
HELLS GULCH RD
HOLLY GULCH RD
CEDAR ST
HEYBURN RD
MINALOOSA RD
MINALOOSA VALLEY RD
COON CREEK RD
CHERRY CREEK RD
SHAY HILL RD
BENEWAH RD
SAINT JOE RD
JACOT RD
ELLIS LN
CONKLING PARK RD
SUNNY SLOPE
LITTLE SQUAW BAY RD
INDIAN CEMETERY RD
ATOR HILL RD
LAKE AV
EAST POINT RD
HARLOW POINT RD
SPRINGSTON
THOMPSON LAKE RD
LAMB RD
MEDIMONT RD
EVANS CREEK RD
EAGLE PEAK RD
CANARY CREEK RD
INITIAL PEAK RD
BLACK ROCK RD
OLD ROSE CREEK RD
DOYLE RD
BUTLER CREEK RD
LAKES DIVIDE RD
WARD RIDGE RD
NFD RD 438
NFD RD 810
NFD RD 808
GOTHAM BAY RD
BURMA RD
CARLIN BAY RD
GOZZER RD
DEER CREEK DR
CARLIN CREEK RD
ASBURY RD
ROUND BAY RD
HALF ROUND BAY RD
PILOT ROCK RD
LOFFS BAY RD
E YELLOWSTONE TR
EDDYVILLE RD
BEAUTY CREEK RD
BLUE CREEK BAY
W PRESLEY RD
WENIG RD
KIDD ISLAND RD
VALHALLA RD
HAGEMAN DRAW
90
97
3
5
22
28
A B C D
1 2 3 4 5 6 7

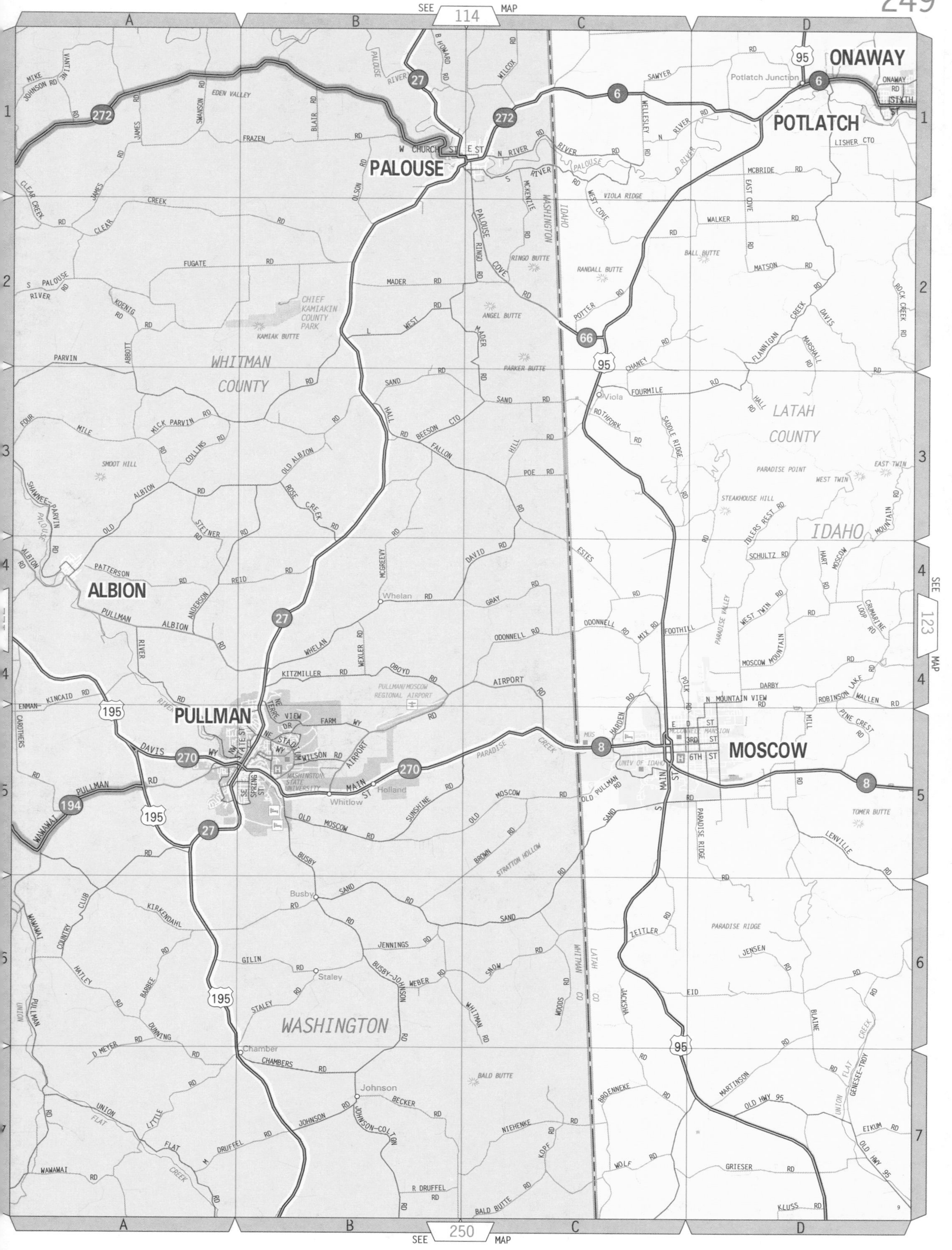

SEE 114 MAP
PALOUSE
POTLATCH
ONAWAY
Potlatch Junction
WHITMAN COUNTY
LATAH COUNTY
IDAHO
WASHINGTON
ALBION
PULLMAN
MOSCOW
Viola
Whelan
Whitlow
Holland
Busby
Staley
Chamber
Johnson
PULLMAN/MOSCOW REGIONAL AIRPORT
WASHINGTON STATE UNIVERSITY
UNIV OF IDAHO
CHIEF KAMIAKIN COUNTY PARK
KAMIAK BUTTE
SMOOT HILL
RINGO BUTTE
RANDALL BUTTE
ANGEL BUTTE
PARKER BUTTE
BALL BUTTE
PARADISE POINT
STEAKHOUSE HILL
WEST TWIN
EAST TWIN
TOMER BUTTE
PARADISE RIDGE
BALD BUTTE
SEE 123 MAP
SEE 250 MAP
PNW
METRO

SEE 249 MAP

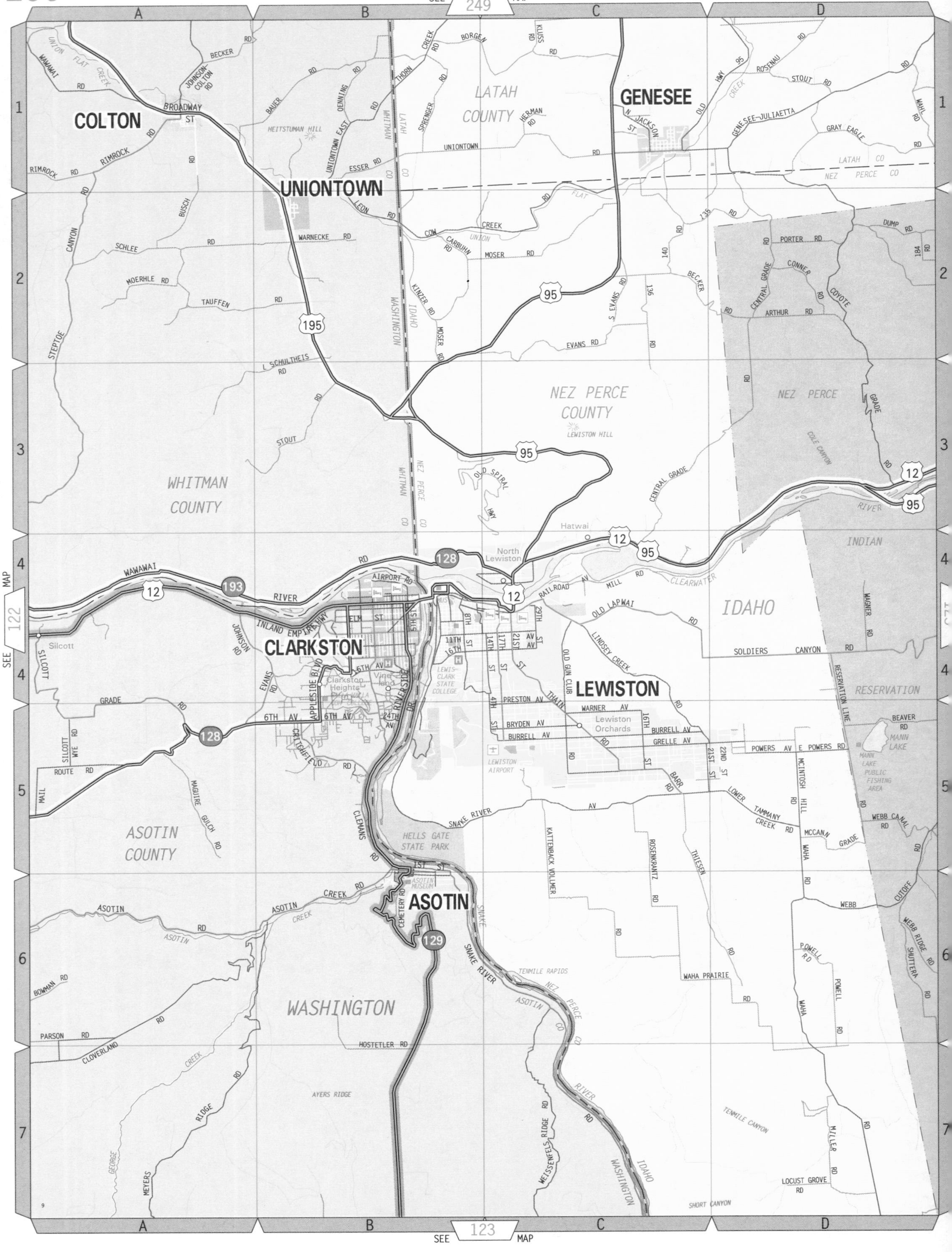

COLTON

UNIONTOWN

GENESEE

CLARKSTON

LEWISTON

ASOTIN

WHITMAN COUNTY

LATAH COUNTY

NEZ PERCE COUNTY

ASOTIN COUNTY

WASHINGTON

IDAHO

NEZ PERCE INDIAN RESERVATION

HELLS GATE STATE PARK

North Lewiston

Hatwai

Silcott

Clarkston Heights

Vineland

Lewiston Orchards

LEWIS-CLARK STATE COLLEGE

LEWISTON AIRPORT

LEWISTON HILL

HEITSTUMAN HILL

MANN LAKE PUBLIC FISHING AREA

SNAKE RIVER

CLEARWATER RIVER

TENMILE RAPIDS

SEE 122 MAP

SEE 123 MAP

SEE 131 MAP

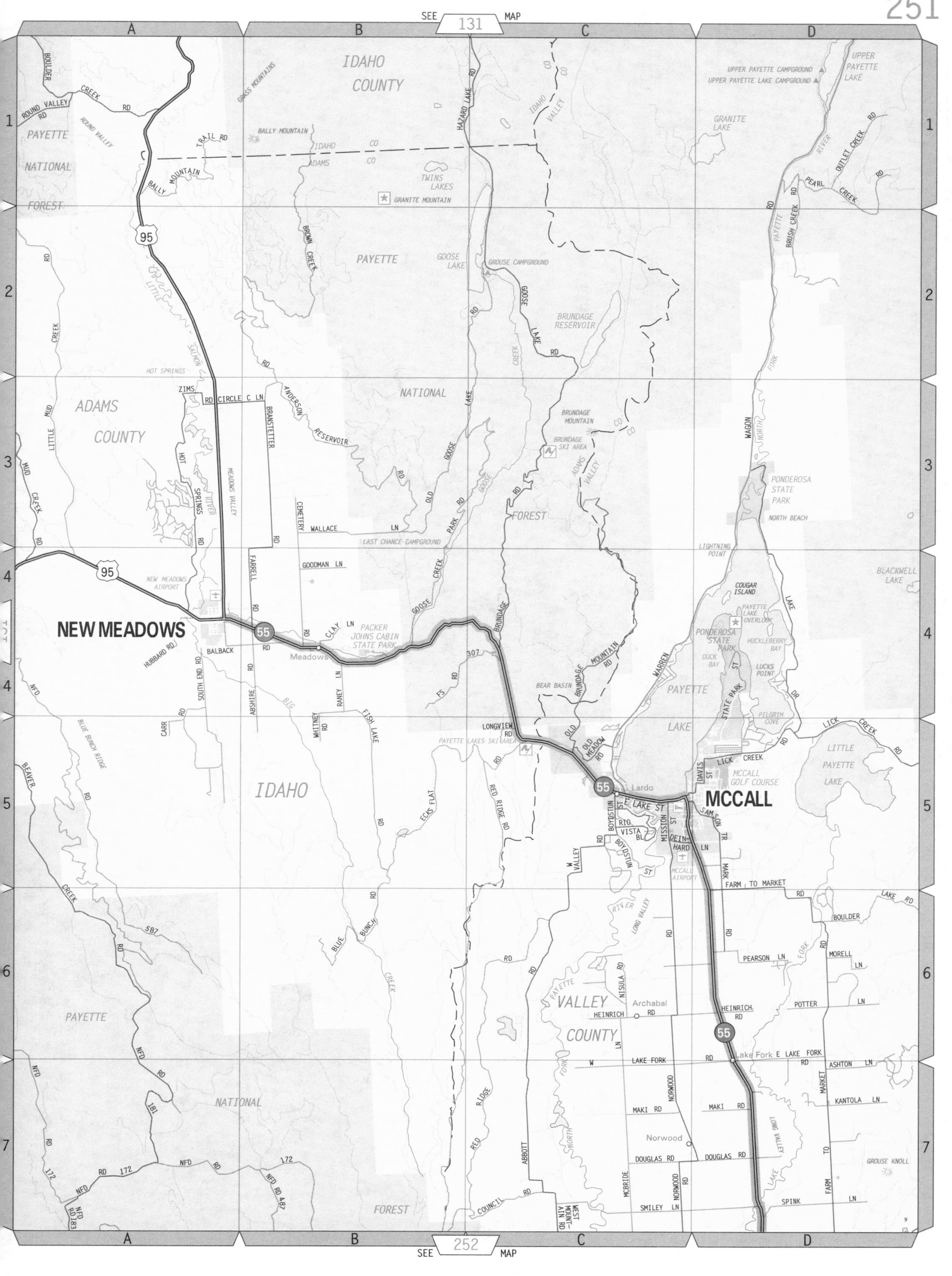

SEE 252 MAP

SEE MAP 251

SEE MAP 139

PNW

METRO

PAYETTE NATIONAL FOREST

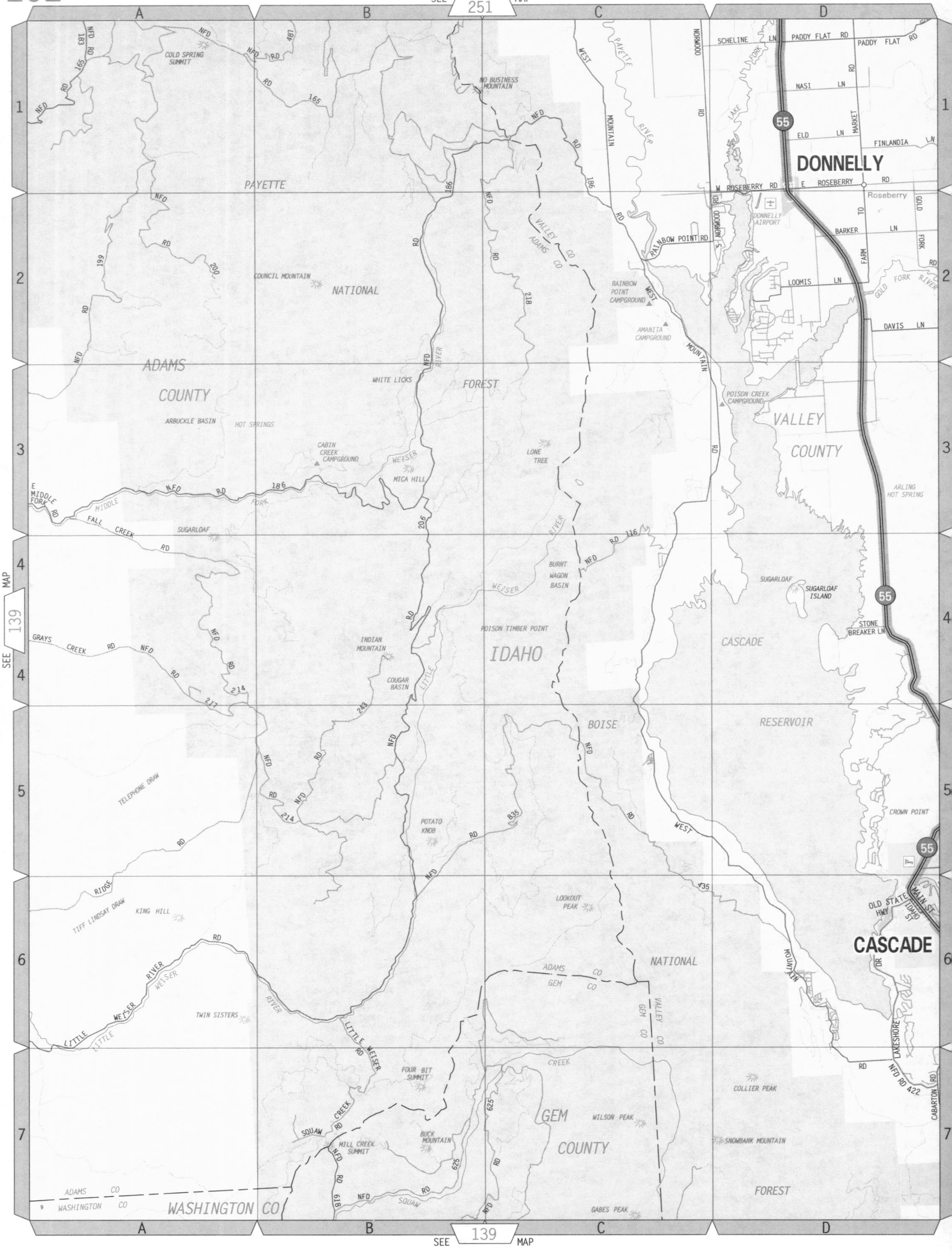

ADAMS COUNTY

VALLEY COUNTY

IDAHO

BOISE NATIONAL FOREST

GEM COUNTY

WASHINGTON CO

DONNELLY

CASCADE

CASCADE RESERVOIR

SEE MAP 139

SEE 139 MAP

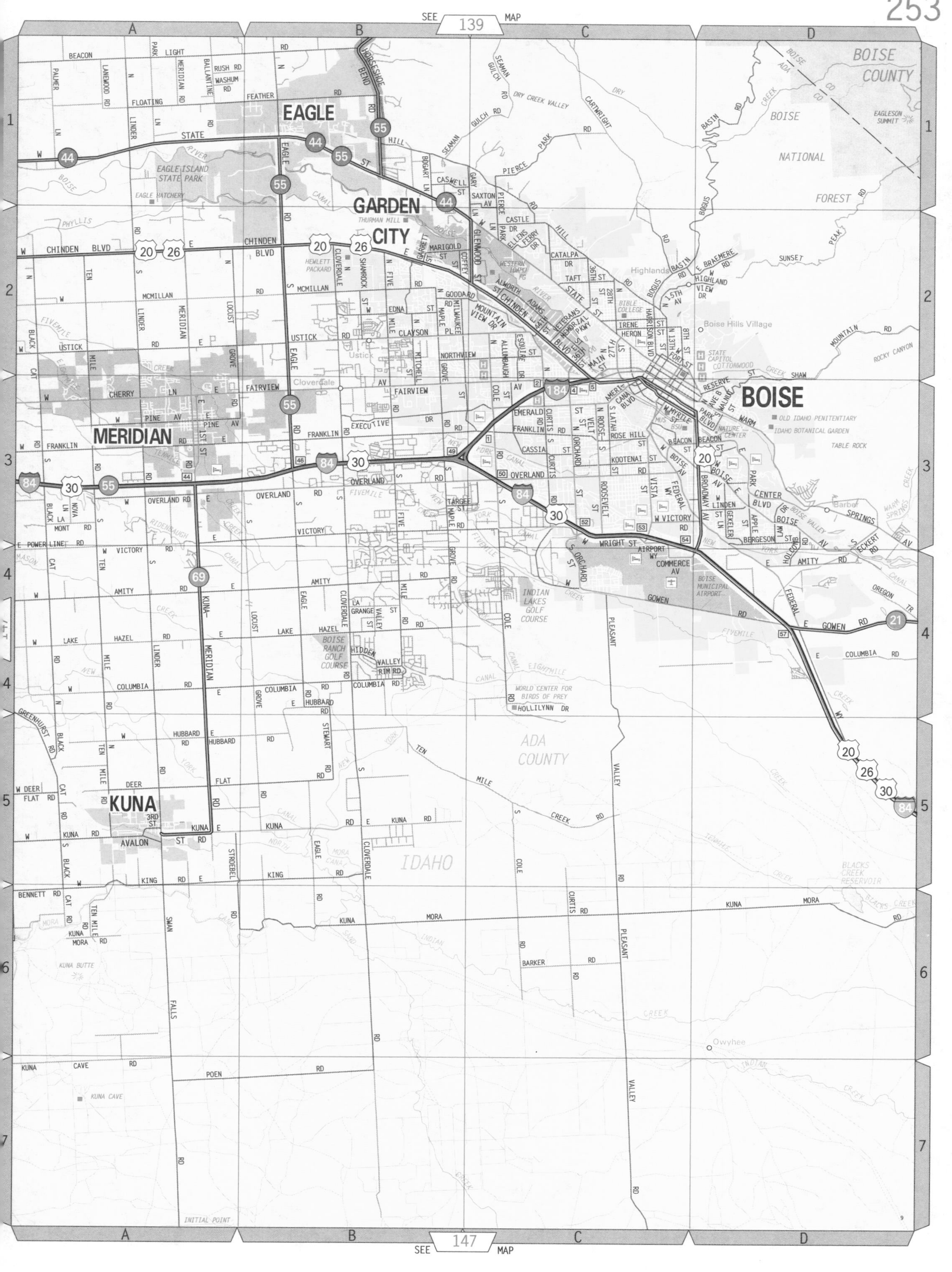

SEE 147 MAP

PNW

METRO

SEE 156 MAP

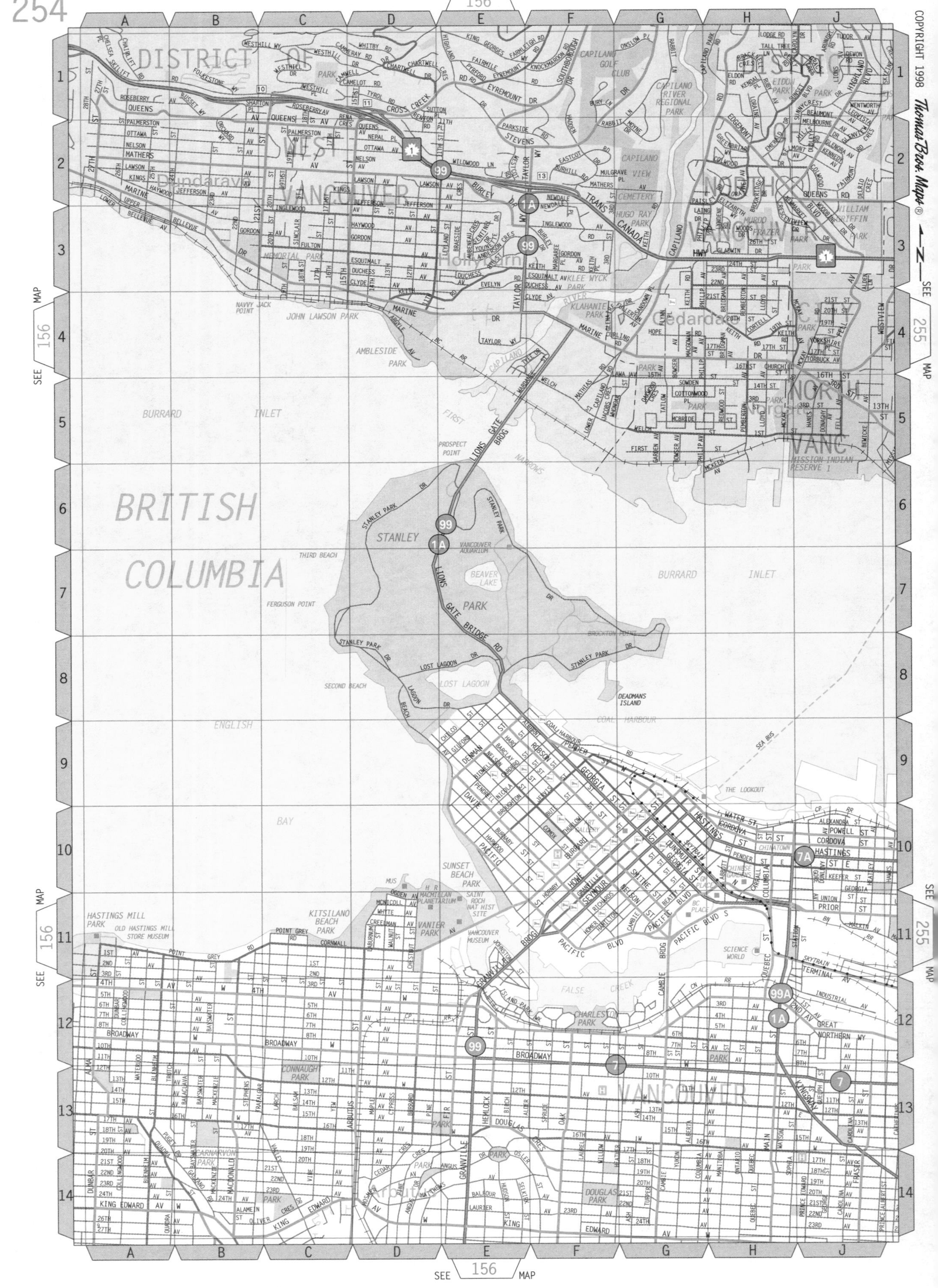

SEE 156 MAP
SEE 255 MAP
SEE 156 MAP

PNW

DETAIL

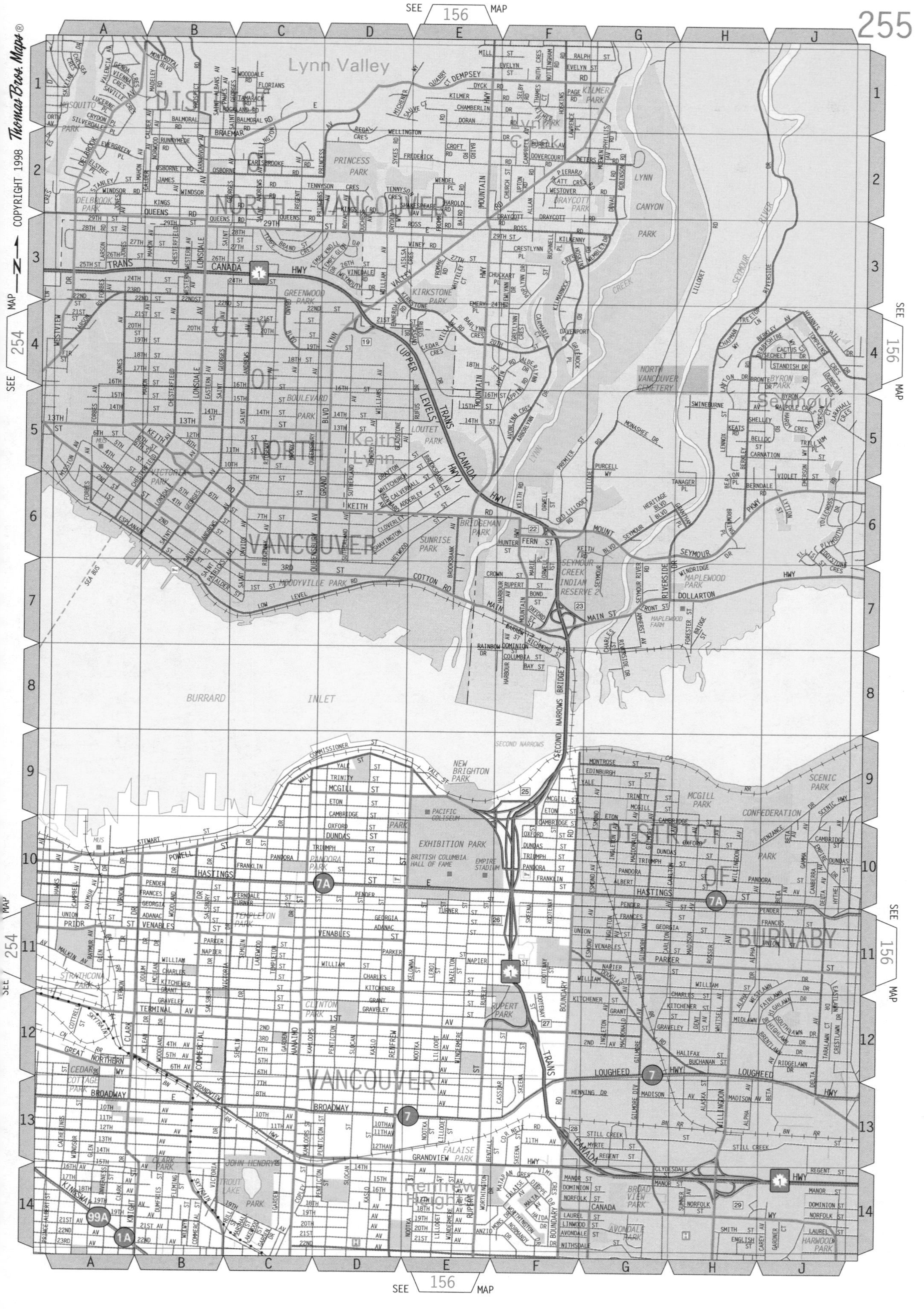
SEE 156 MAP
SEE 254 MAP
SEE 156 MAP
SEE 156 MAP
PNW
DETAIL
A
B
C
D
E
F
G
H
J
Lynn Valley
DISTRICT OF NORTH VANCOUVER
CITY OF NORTH VANCOUVER
Lynn Creek
PRINCESS PARK
DELBROOK PARK
DRAYCOTT PARK
LYNN CANYON PARK
GREENWOOD PARK
KIRKSTONE PARK
NORTH VANCOUVER CEMETERY
Seymour
BYRON PARK
BOULEVARD PARK
Keith Lynn
LOUTET PARK
VICTORIA PARK
BRIDGEMAN PARK
SUNRISE PARK
SEYMOUR CREEK INDIAN RESERVE 2
MOODYVILLE PARK
MAPLEWOOD PARK
MAPLEWOOD FARM
SEA BUS
BURRARD
INLET
SECOND NARROWS
SECOND NARROWS BRIDGE
NEW BRIGHTON PARK
PACIFIC COLISEUM
EXHIBITION PARK
BRITISH COLUMBIA HALL OF FAME
EMPIRE STADIUM
PANDORA PARK
TEMPLETON PARK
STRATHCONA PARK
CLINTON PARK
RUPERT PARK
CEDAR COTTAGE PARK
CLARK PARK
JOHN HENDRY PARK
TROUT LAKE
FALAISE PARK
Renfrew Heights
VANCOUVER
MCGILL PARK
SCENIC PARK
CONFEDERATION PARK
DISTRICT OF BURNABY
BROADVIEW PARK
AVONDALE PARK
HARWOOD PARK
TRANS CANADA HWY
UPPER LEVELS TRANS CANADA HWY
LOW LEVEL RD
COTTON RD
MAIN ST
DOLLARTON HWY
MOUNT SEYMOUR PKWY
LILLOOET RD
HASTINGS ST
LOUGHEED HWY
BROADWAY
GRANDVIEW HWY
KINGSWAY
GREAT NORTHERN WY
STILL CREEK
SKYTRAIN

SEE 159 MAP
SEE 165 MAP
SEE 257 MAP
SEE 159 MAP
DISTRICT OF SAANICH
TOWN OF VIEW ROYAL
TOWN OF ESQUIMALT
CITY OF VICTORIA
THOMAS FRANCIS PARK
COPLEY MEMORIAL PARK
BLENKINSOP LAKE
BLENKINSOP VALLEY GOLF COURSE
MOUNT DOUGLAS GOLF COURSE
HYACINTH PARK
CHRISTMAS HILL PARK
KNOCKAN HILL PARK
BRAEFOOT PARK
SWAN LAKE
SWAN LAKE NATURE SANCTUARY
PLAYFAIR PARK
CEDAR HILL GOLF COURSE
CHRISTIE POINT
PORTAGE LAKE
TILLICUM PARK
MAPLE POINT
DYKE POINT
THETIS COVE
KINSMEN GORGE PARK
GORGE VALE GOLF COURSE
AARON POINT
ESQUIMALT INDIAN RESERVE 1
PLUMPER BAY
SUMMIT PARK
TOPAZ PARK
CHAPMAN POINT
PILGRIM COVE
CONSTANCE COVE
LANG COVE
POINT ELLICE HOUSE
UPPER HARBOUR
HOPE POINT
LIMIT POINT
C F B ESQUIMALT
SAXE POINT PARK
SAXE POINT
ANNE HATHAWAYS COTTAGE
DEPARTMENT OF NATIONAL DEFENCE
WORK ISLAND
WORK POINT
VICTORIA HARBOUR
SHOAL POINT
RAYNOR POINT
INNER HARBOUR
SHIP PT
CANADIAN COAST GUARD
MCLOUGHLIN POINT
CAMEL POINT
OGDEN POINT
GILLINGHAM ISLAND
HARRISON ISLAND
MACDONALD PARK
BEACON HILL PARK
HOLLAND POINT
FINLAYSON POINT
CLOVER POINT
GOVERNMENT HOUSE GARDENS
CRAIGDARROCH CASTLE
ROYAL THEATRE
PARLIAMENT BLDGS
TRANS CANADA HWY
PATRICIA BAY HWY
BLANSHARD
QUADRA
DOUGLAS
GORGE
ESQUIMALT
CRAIGFLOWER
TILLICUM
BURNSIDE
HILLSIDE
MCKENZIE
CEDAR HILL CROSS
FORT
YATES
JOHNSON
PANDORA
BELLEVILLE
DALLAS
VICTORIA FERRY
PORT ANGELES VICTORIA FERRY
VICTORIA SEATTLE FERRY
BRITISH COLUMBIA
STRAIT OF JUAN DE FUCA
A B C D E F G H J
1 2 3 4 5 6 7 8 9 10 11 12 13 14

PNW

DETAIL

SEE 159 MAP

SEE 256 MAP
SEE 101 MAP
SEE 165 MAP

PNW

DETAIL

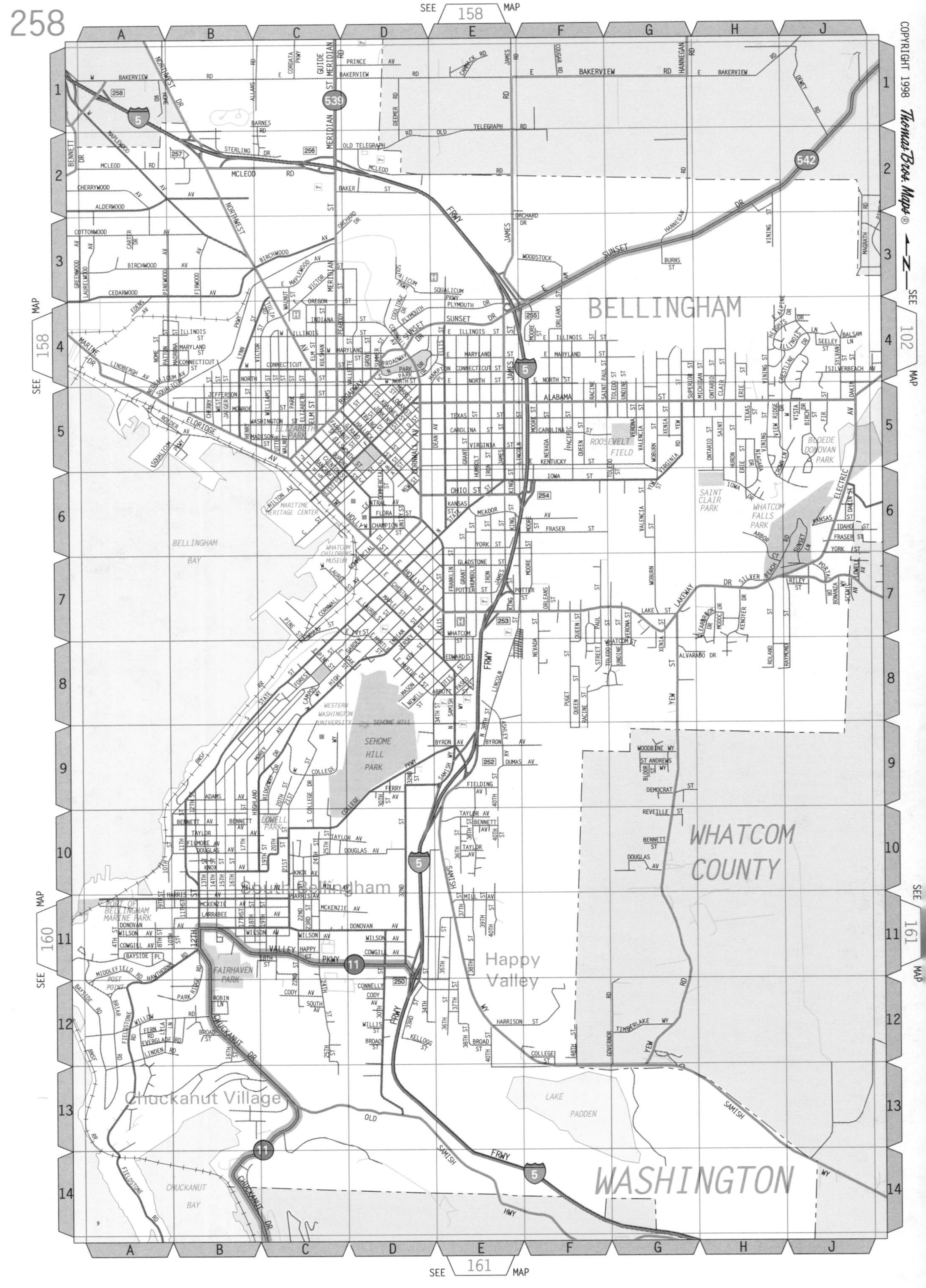
SEE 158 MAP
SEE 158 MAP
SEE 102 MAP
SEE 160 MAP
SEE 161 MAP
SEE 161 MAP
A
B
C
D
E
F
G
H
J
BELLINGHAM
WHATCOM COUNTY
WASHINGTON
South Bellingham
Happy Valley
Chuckanut Village
BELLINGHAM BAY
CHUCKANUT BAY
LAKE PADDEN
SEHOME HILL PARK
WESTERN WASHINGTON UNIVERSITY
FAIRHAVEN PARK
LOWELL PARK
ELIZABETH PARK
ROOSEVELT FIELD
SAINT CLAIR PARK
WHATCOM FALLS PARK
BLOEDE DONOVAN PARK
MARITIME HERITAGE CENTER
WHATCOM CHILDRENS MUSEUM
PORT OF BELLINGHAM MARINE PARK
POST POINT
BAKERVIEW RD
MCLEOD RD
OLD TELEGRAPH
TELEGRAPH RD
NORTHWEST DR
GUIDE MERIDIAN ST
E SUNSET DR
ELDRIDGE AV
SQUALICUM PKWY
ALABAMA ST
LAKEWAY DR
SILVER BEACH
E HOLLY ST
STATE ST
SAMISH WY
VALLEY PKWY
CHUCKANUT DR
OLD SAMISH
FRWY
HWY
YEW ST RD
COLLEGE WY
ELECTRIC AV

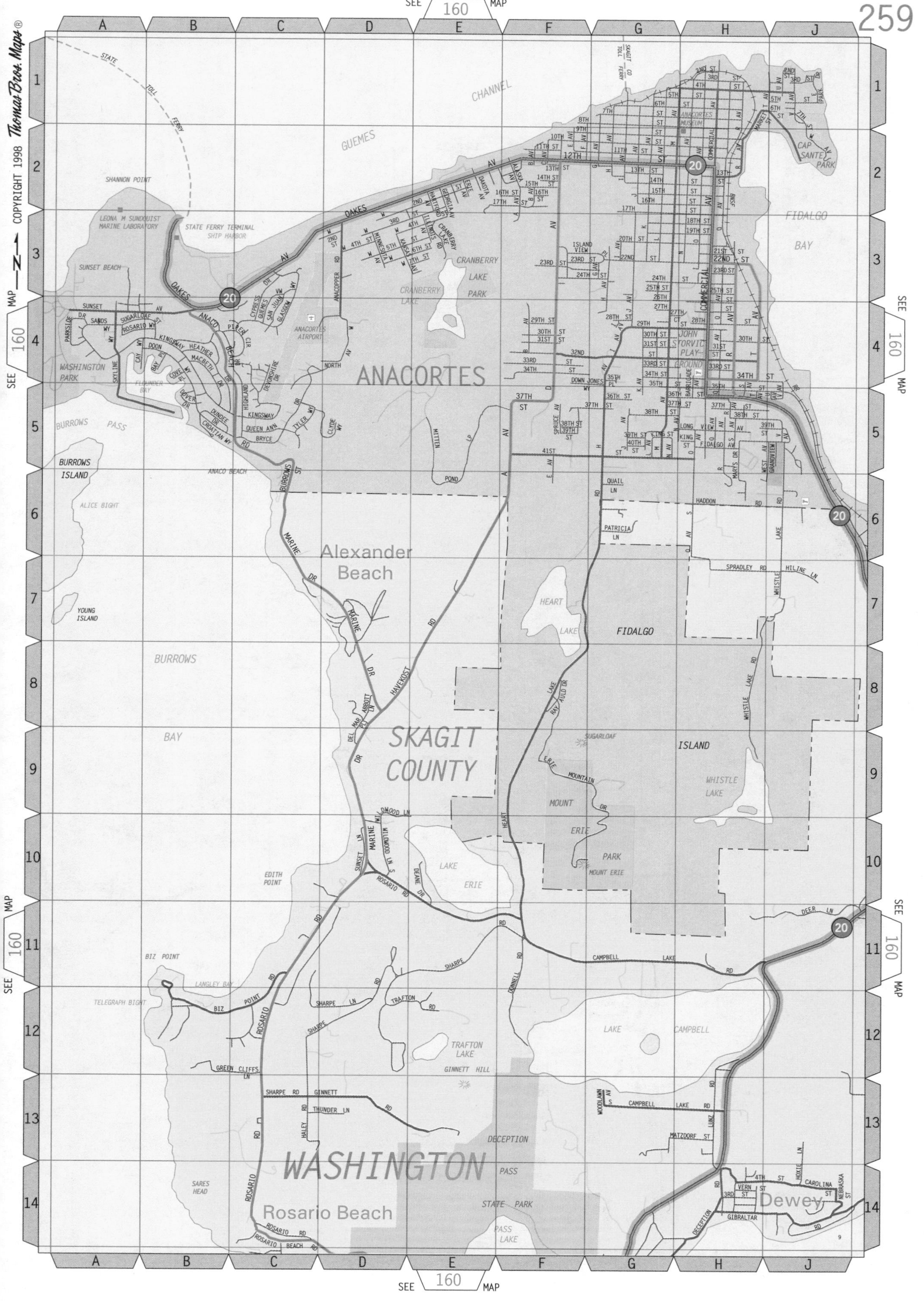
ANACORTES
Alexander Beach
SKAGIT COUNTY
WASHINGTON
Rosario Beach
Dewey
FIDALGO
ISLAND
BURROWS
BAY
GUEMES
CHANNEL
FIDALGO
BAY
BURROWS ISLAND
YOUNG ISLAND
HEART LAKE
LAKE ERIE
LAKE CAMPBELL
WHISTLE LAKE
CRANBERRY LAKE PARK
MOUNT ERIE PARK
DECEPTION PASS STATE PARK
TRAFTON LAKE
PASS LAKE
WASHINGTON PARK
SEE 160 MAP

PNW
DETAIL

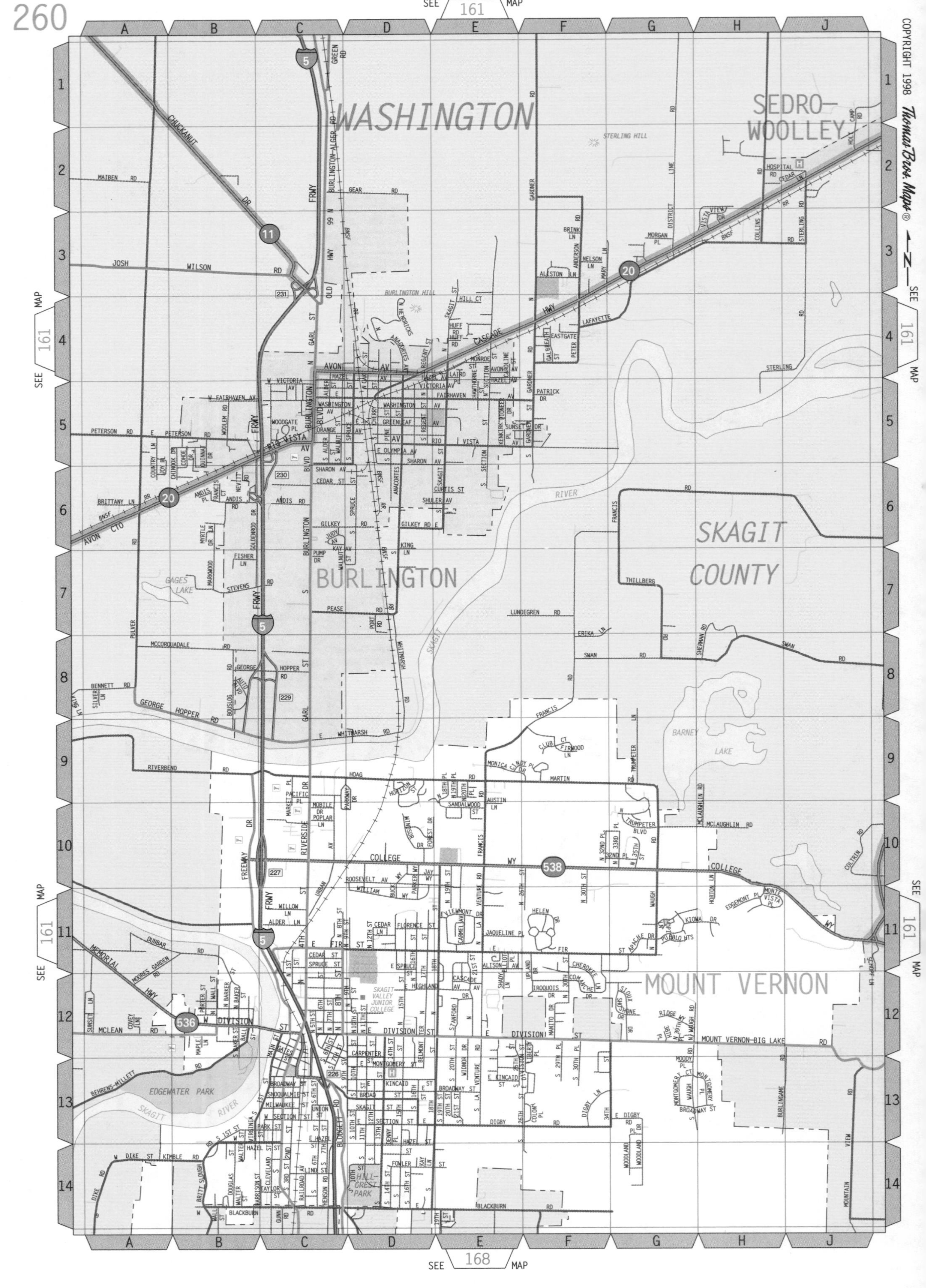

SEE 161 MAP
SEE 168 MAP

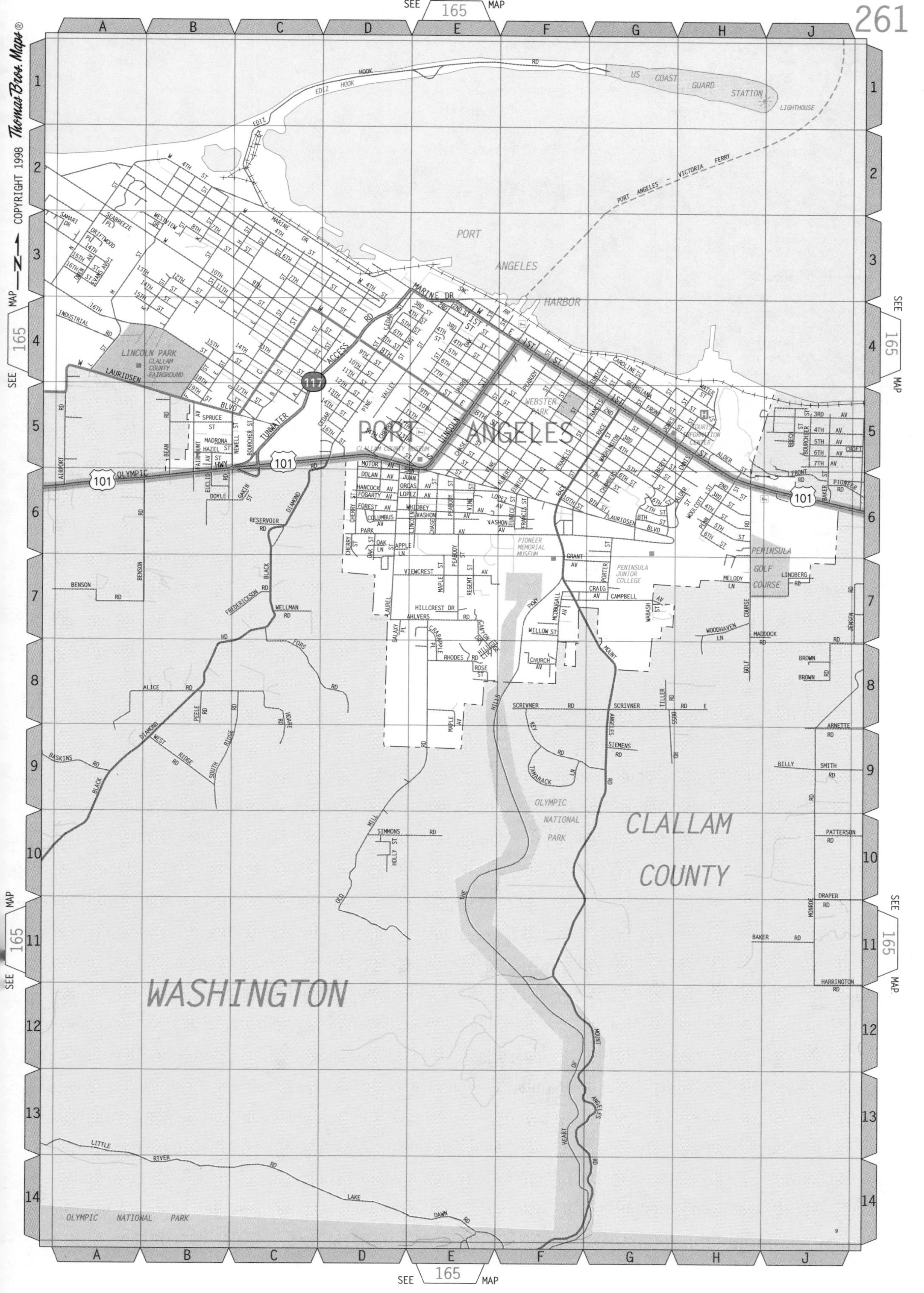

PORT ANGELES
PORT ANGELES HARBOR
US COAST GUARD STATION
LIGHTHOUSE
PORT ANGELES VICTORIA FERRY
LINCOLN PARK
CLALLAM COUNTY FAIRGROUND
WEBSTER PARK
CLALLAM COUNTY MUSEUM
PIONEER MEMORIAL MUSEUM
PENINSULA JUNIOR COLLEGE
PENINSULA GOLF COURSE
OLYMPIC NATIONAL PARK
CLALLAM COUNTY
WASHINGTON
SEE 165 MAP

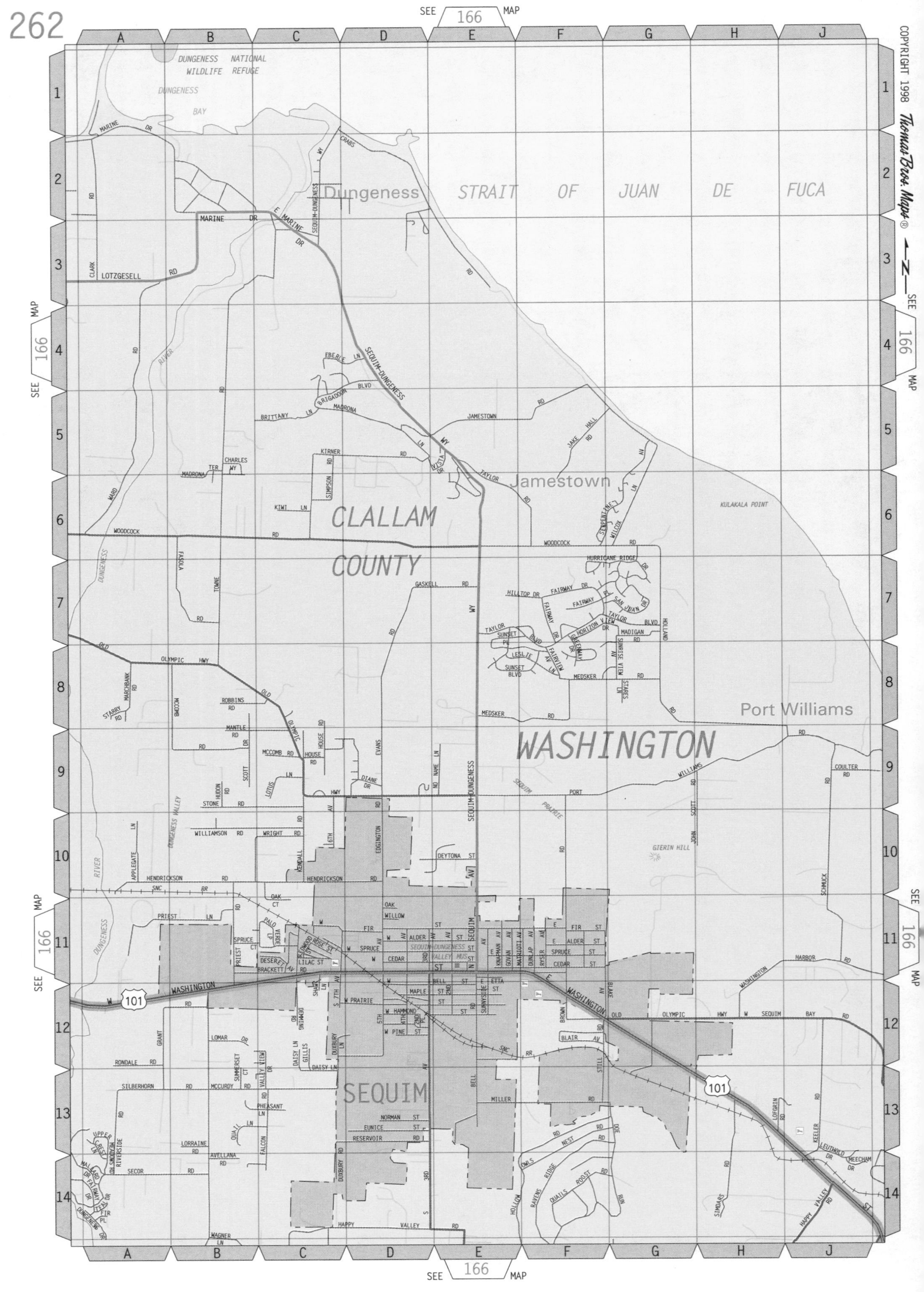
SEE 166 MAP
DUNGENESS NATIONAL WILDLIFE REFUGE
DUNGENESS BAY
Dungeness
STRAIT OF JUAN DE FUCA
Jamestown
KULAKALA POINT
CLALLAM COUNTY
WASHINGTON
Port Williams
SEQUIM
GIERIN HILL
MARINE DR
LOTZGESELL RD
SEQUIM-DUNGENESS WY
WOODCOCK RD
OLD OLYMPIC HWY
W WASHINGTON
101
DUNGENESS RIVER
SEQUIM PRAIRIE
PORT WILLIAMS RD
SEQUIM BAY RD
HAPPY VALLEY RD
A B C D E F G H J
1 2 3 4 5 6 7 8 9 10 11 12 13 14
COPYRIGHT 1998 Thomas Bros. Maps®

PNW

DETAIL

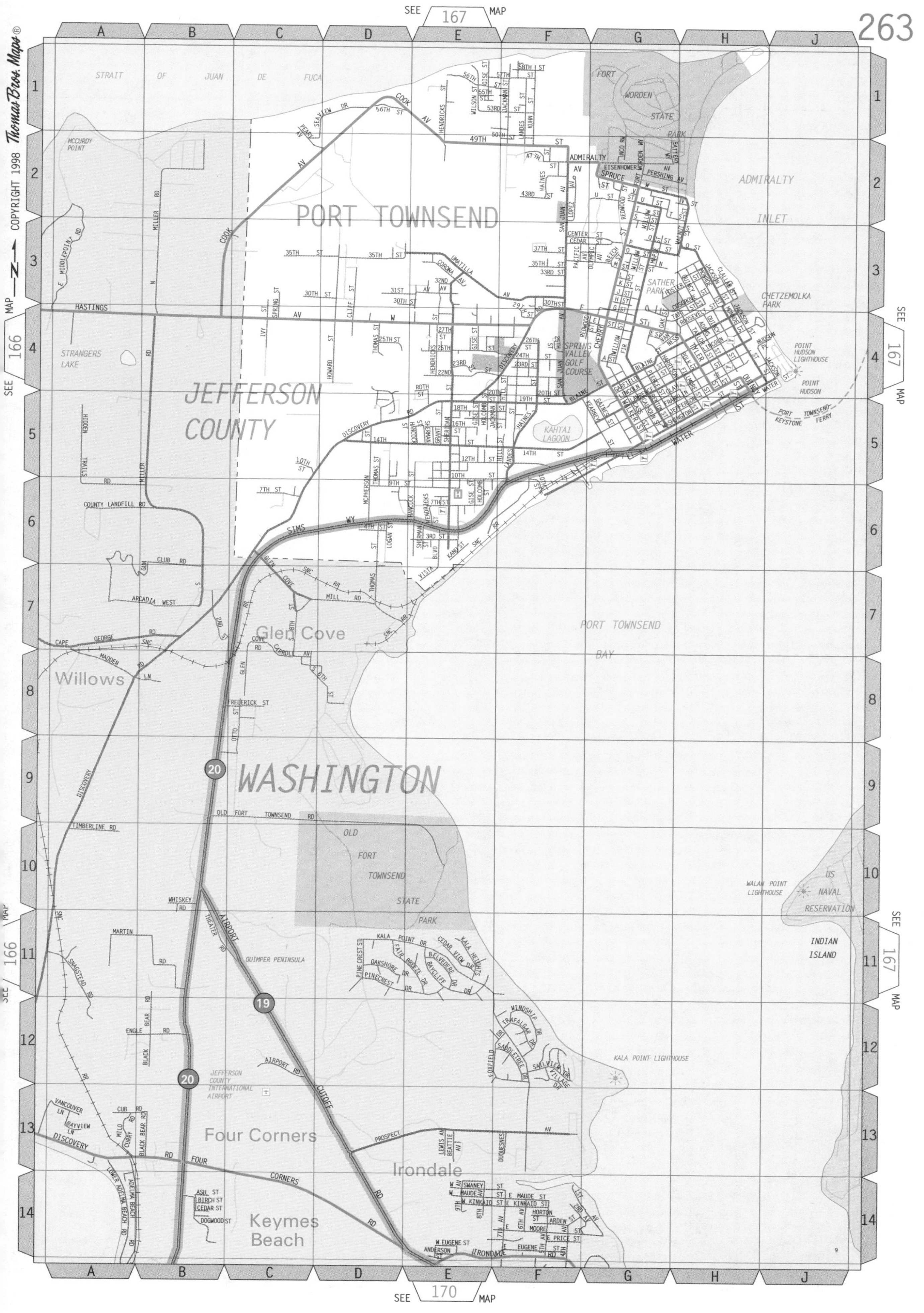
SEE 167 MAP
PORT TOWNSEND
JEFFERSON COUNTY
WASHINGTON
STRAIT OF JUAN DE FUCA
ADMIRALTY INLET
PORT TOWNSEND BAY
FORT WORDEN STATE PARK
OLD FORT TOWNSEND STATE PARK
SPRING VALLEY GOLF COURSE
KAHTAI LAGOON
SATHER PARK
CHETZEMOLKA PARK
POINT HUDSON LIGHTHOUSE
POINT HUDSON
PORT TOWNSEND-KEYSTONE FERRY
MCCURDY POINT
STRANGERS LAKE
Glen Cove
Willows
Four Corners
Irondale
Keymes Beach
JEFFERSON COUNTY INTERNATIONAL AIRPORT
KALA POINT LIGHTHOUSE
WALAN POINT LIGHTHOUSE
US NAVAL RESERVATION
INDIAN ISLAND
SEE 166 MAP
SEE 170 MAP

PNW

DETAIL

SEE 171 MAP
SEE 171 MAP
SEE 268 MAP
POSSESSION
SOUND
PORT GARDNER CHANNEL
PORT GARDNER
MARINA VILLAGE
NAVAL STATION EVERETT
PIER 3
PIER 1
W MARINE VIEW DR
EVERETT
FOREST PARK
HOWARTH PARK
MEMORIAL STADIUM
EVERGREEN CEM
PIGEON CREEK
MUKILTEO BLVD
BROADWAY
PACIFIC
HEWITT
CALIFORNIA
41ST ST SE
RUCKER
COLBY
GRAND AV
EVERGREEN WY
SHARON CREST
PDNW
DETAIL

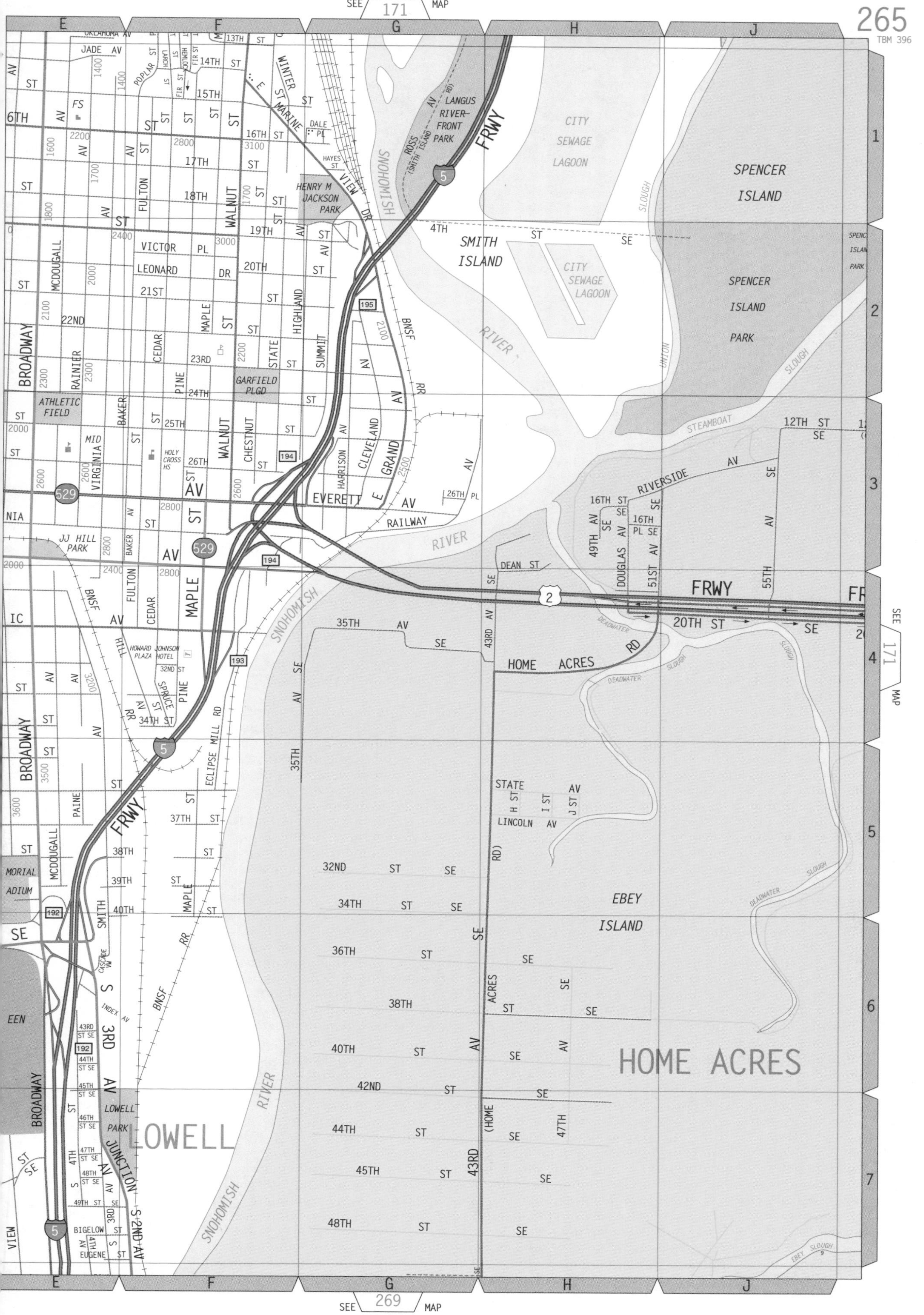
SEE 171 MAP
SEE 269 MAP
SEE 171 MAP
SPENCER ISLAND
SPENCER ISLAND PARK
CITY SEWAGE LAGOON
SMITH ISLAND
LANGUS RIVERFRONT PARK
HENRY M JACKSON PARK
GARFIELD PLGD
ATHLETIC FIELD
JJ HILL PARK
HOLY CROSS HS
HOWARD JOHNSON PLAZA HOTEL
SNOHOMISH RIVER
EBEY ISLAND
HOME ACRES
LOWELL
LOWELL PARK
FRWY
BROADWAY
EVERETT AV
HOME ACRES RD
20TH ST SE
RIVERSIDE AV
STEAMBOAT SLOUGH
UNION SLOUGH
EBEY SLOUGH
DEADWATER SLOUGH
PNW
DETAIL

SEE 171 MAP

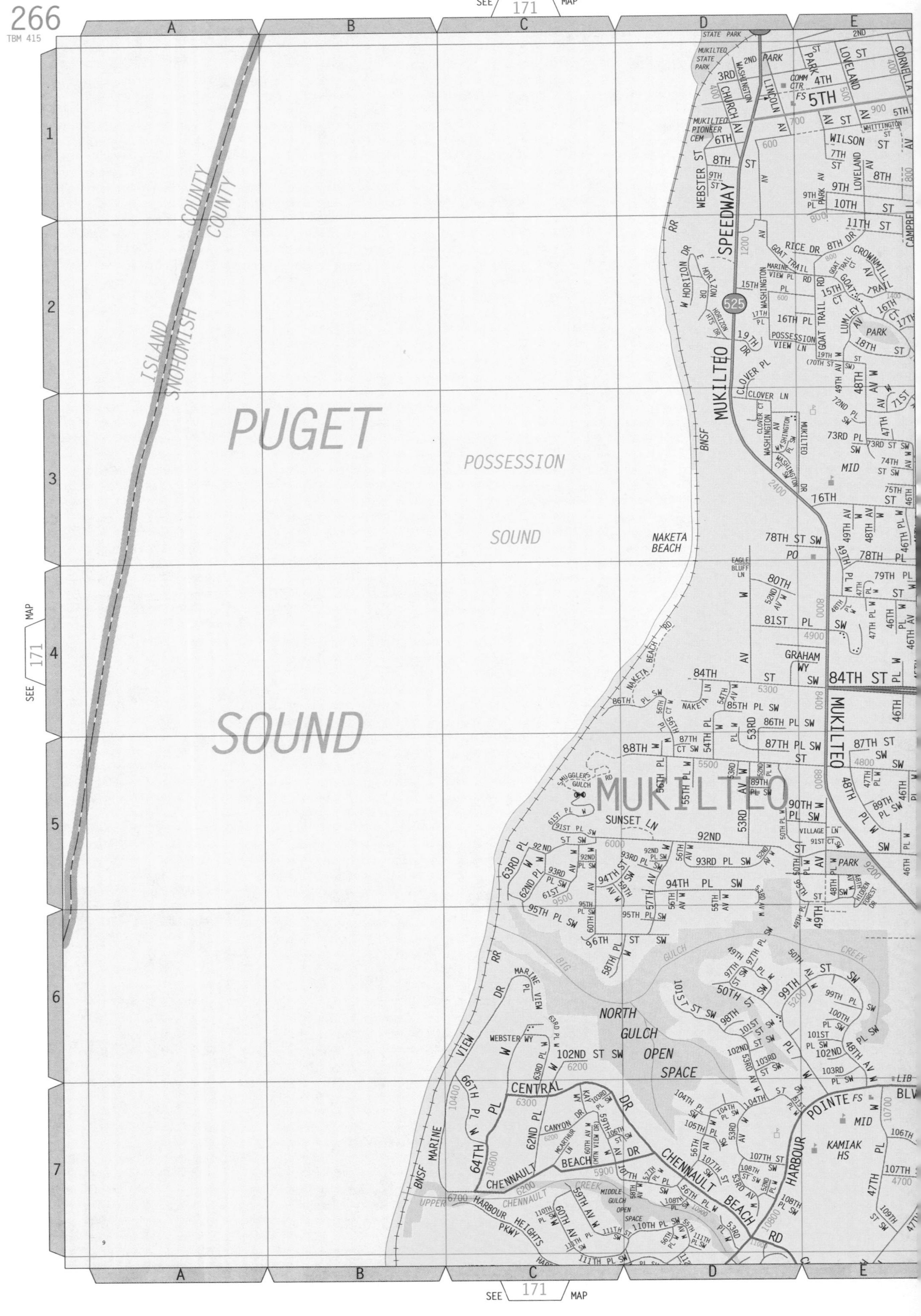

SEE 171 MAP

SEE 171 MAP

SEE 171 MAP

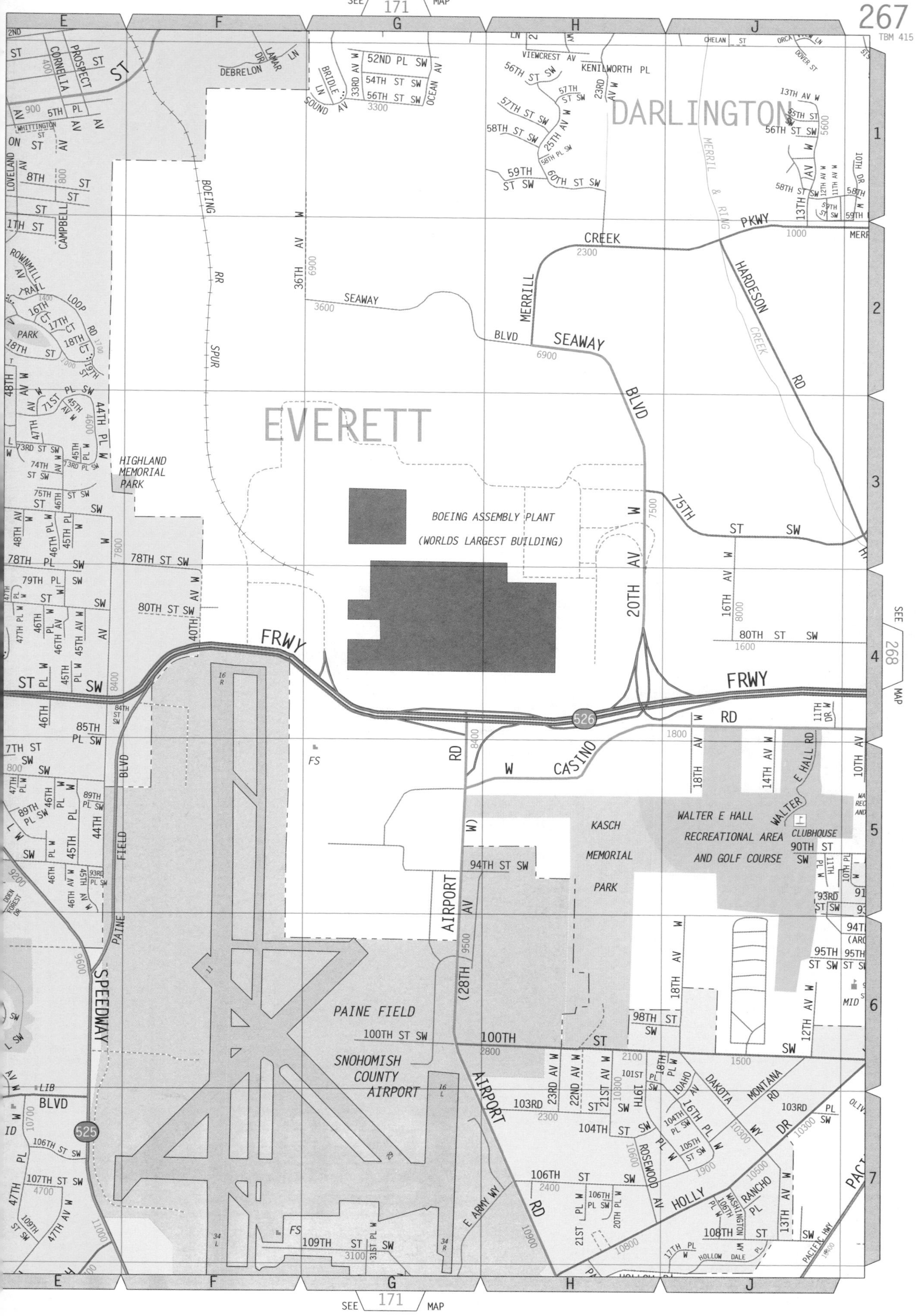

SEE 268 MAP

SEE 171 MAP

PNW

DETAIL

SEE 264 MAP

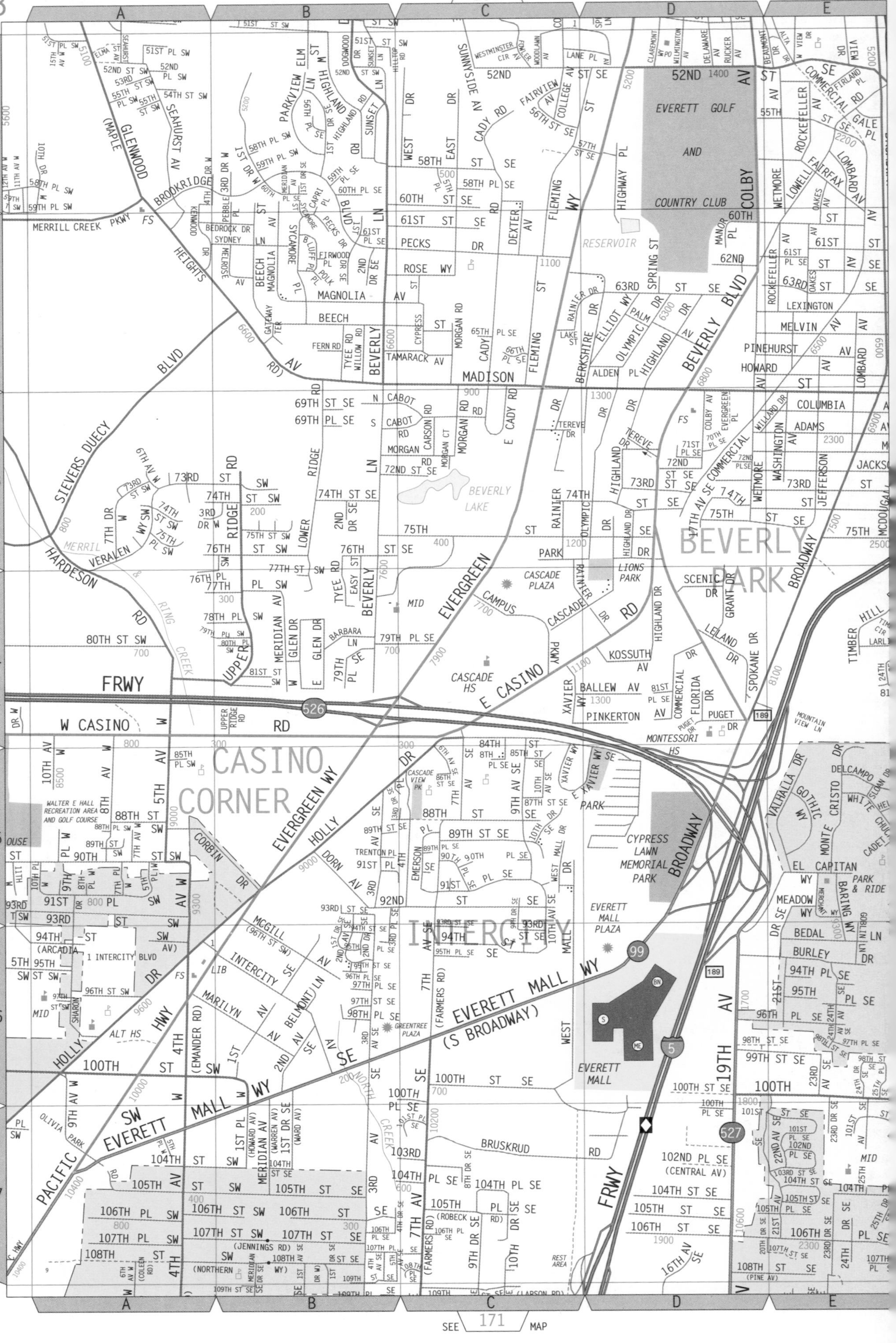

A B C D E

1 2 3 4 5 6 7

PNW

DETAIL

SEE 267 MAP

GLENWOOD (MAPLE
SEAHURST AV
BROOKRIDGE
MERRILL CREEK PKWY
HEIGHTS
KENWOOD DR
BEDROCK DR
SYDNEY LN
MELROSE AV
BEECH
MAGNOLIA AV
PARKVIEW ELM ST
HIGHLAND
SYCAMORE PL
CAPRI PL
PECKS DR
BLUFF PL
POLK
FIRWOOD
1ST HIGHLAND
SUNSET LN
WEST DR
EAST DR
58TH ST SE
60TH ST SE
61ST ST SE
PECKS DR
ROSE WY
CYPRESS ST
MORGAN RD
TAMARACK AV
FERN RD
WILLOW RD
TYEE RD
BEVERLY LN
SUNNYSIDE AV
CADY RD
FAIRVIEW AV
COLLEGE AV
56TH ST SE
57TH ST SE
DEXTER AV
FLEMING WY
FLEMING ST
HIGHWAY PL
RESERVOIR
SPRING ST
52ND ST SE
LANE PL
EVERETT GOLF AND COUNTRY CLUB
COLBY AV
60TH PL
MANOR PL
62ND
63RD ST SE
BEVERLY BLVD
BERKSHIRE DR
ELLIOT WY
PALM DR
OLYMPIC
HIGHLAND DR
RAINIER DR
LAKE ST
ALDEN PL
MADISON ST
SIEVERS DUECY BLVD
GATEWAY TER
RD) AV
COMMERCIAL
ROCKEFELLER AV
WETMORE AV
LOWELL
FAIRFAX
LOMBARD AV
OAKES AV
61ST ST
LEXINGTON
MELVIN AV
PINEHURST AV
HOWARD AV
COLUMBIA
ADAMS
WASHINGTON AV
JACKSON
JEFFERSON
73RD ST
74TH
75TH ST
MCDOUGALL
55TH
GALE PL
FIRLAND
69TH ST SE
69TH PL SE
N CABOT RD
S CABOT RD
CARSON RD
MORGAN CT
MORGAN RD
E CADY RD
72ND ST SE
TEREVE DR
BEVERLY LAKE
73RD ST SW
74TH ST SW
75TH ST SW
76TH ST SW
77TH PL SW
78TH PL SW
80TH ST SW
81ST ST SW
UPPER RIDGE RD
LOWER RIDGE
MERIDIAN AV
GLEN DR
E GLEN DR
BARBARA LN
79TH PL SE
79TH PL SE
EASY ST
7TH DR
VERALEN WY SW
HARDESON RD
MERRIL & RING CREEK
EVERGREEN
CASCADE PLAZA
CAMPUS PKWY
CASCADE
MID
CASCADE HS
E CASINO
LIONS PARK
KOSSUTH AV
XAVIER WY
BALLEW AV
PINKERTON
COMMERCIAL AV
FLORIDA DR
PUGET DR
MONTESSORI HS
BEVERLY PARK
SCENIC DR
GRANT DR
LELAND DR
SPOKANE DR
BROADWAY
TIMBER HILL
MOUNTAIN VIEW LN
FRWY
526
W CASINO RD
CASINO CORNER
10TH AV W
8TH AV W
5TH AV W
WALTER E HALL RECREATION AREA AND GOLF COURSE
88TH ST
90TH ST
91ST PL SW
93RD ST SW
94TH ST
95TH
96TH ST SW
1 INTERCITY BLVD
(ARCADIA AV)
DR
FS
LIB
MID
ALT HS
SHARON
HOLLY HWY
EVERGREEN WY
CORBIN DR
HOLLY DR
DORN AV
MCGILL (96TH ST SW)
INTERCITY AV SE
MARILYN AV
BELMONT LN
1ST AV
2ND AV SE
CASCADE VIEW PK
84TH ST
85TH ST SE
86TH ST SE
87TH ST SE
88TH ST SE
89TH ST SE
TRENTON PL
91ST PL
92ND ST SE
93RD ST SE
94TH ST
95TH PL SE
97TH PL SE
98TH PL SE
EMERSON
WEST MALL DR
INTERCITY
EVERETT MALL WY
(S BROADWAY)
GREENTREE PLAZA
XAVIER WY SE
E XAVIER WY
PARK
CYPRESS LAWN MEMORIAL PARK
EVERETT MALL PLAZA
99
189
EVERETT MALL
5
VALHALLA DR
GOTHIC WY
MONTE CRISTO
DELCAMPO
WHITE CHUCK
CADET
EL CAPITAN WY
PARK & RIDE
MEADOW WY
BARING WY
BEDAL LN
BURLEY DR
94TH PL SE
95TH PL SE
96TH PL SE
98TH ST SE
99TH ST SE
100TH
19TH AV
21ST
23RD AV
24TH
100TH ST
PACIFIC HWY
SW EVERETT MALL WY
OLIVIA PARK
9TH AV W
4TH (EMANDER RD)
1ST PL (HOWARD AV)
MERIDIAN AV (WARREN AV)
1ST DR SE (WARD AV)
NORTH CREEK
7TH AV
(FARMERS RD)
100TH PL SE
103RD
104TH PL SE
BRUSKRUD RD
100TH ST SE
102ND PL SE (CENTRAL AV)
527
104TH ST SE
105TH ST SE
106TH ST SE
108TH ST SE
(PINE AV)
16TH AV SE
REST AREA
FRWY
104TH ST SW
105TH ST SW
106TH PL SW
106TH ST SW
107TH PL SW
107TH ST SW
108TH ST SW
(JENNINGS RD)
(NORTHERN WY)
(COLEEN RD)
105TH (ROBECK RD)
9TH DR SE
10TH DR SE
109TH ST SE
(LARSON RD)

A B C D E

SEE 171 MAP

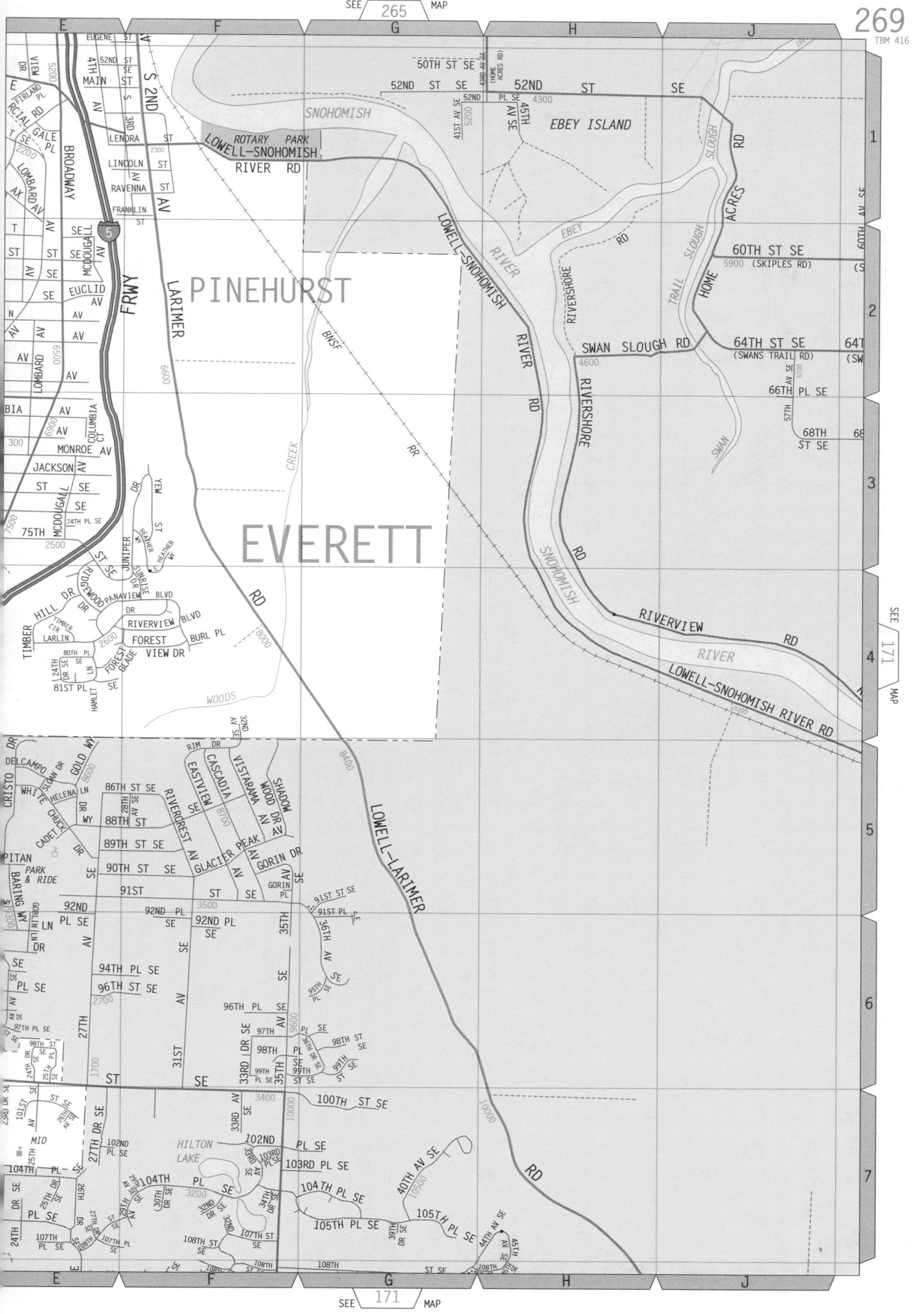
SEE 265 MAP
EVERETT
PINEHURST
EBEY ISLAND
SNOHOMISH RIVER
ROTARY PARK
LOWELL-SNOHOMISH RIVER RD
LOWELL-LARIMER RD
LARIMER RD
RIVERSHORE RD
RIVERVIEW RD
SWAN SLOUGH RD
HOME ACRES RD
EBEY RD
52ND ST SE
50TH ST SE
60TH ST SE (SKIPLES RD)
64TH ST SE (SWANS TRAIL RD)
66TH PL SE
68TH ST SE
BROADWAY
S 2ND AV
FRWY
HILTON LAKE
PARK & RIDE
WOODS CREEK
BNSF RR
SEE 171 MAP
PNW
DETAIL

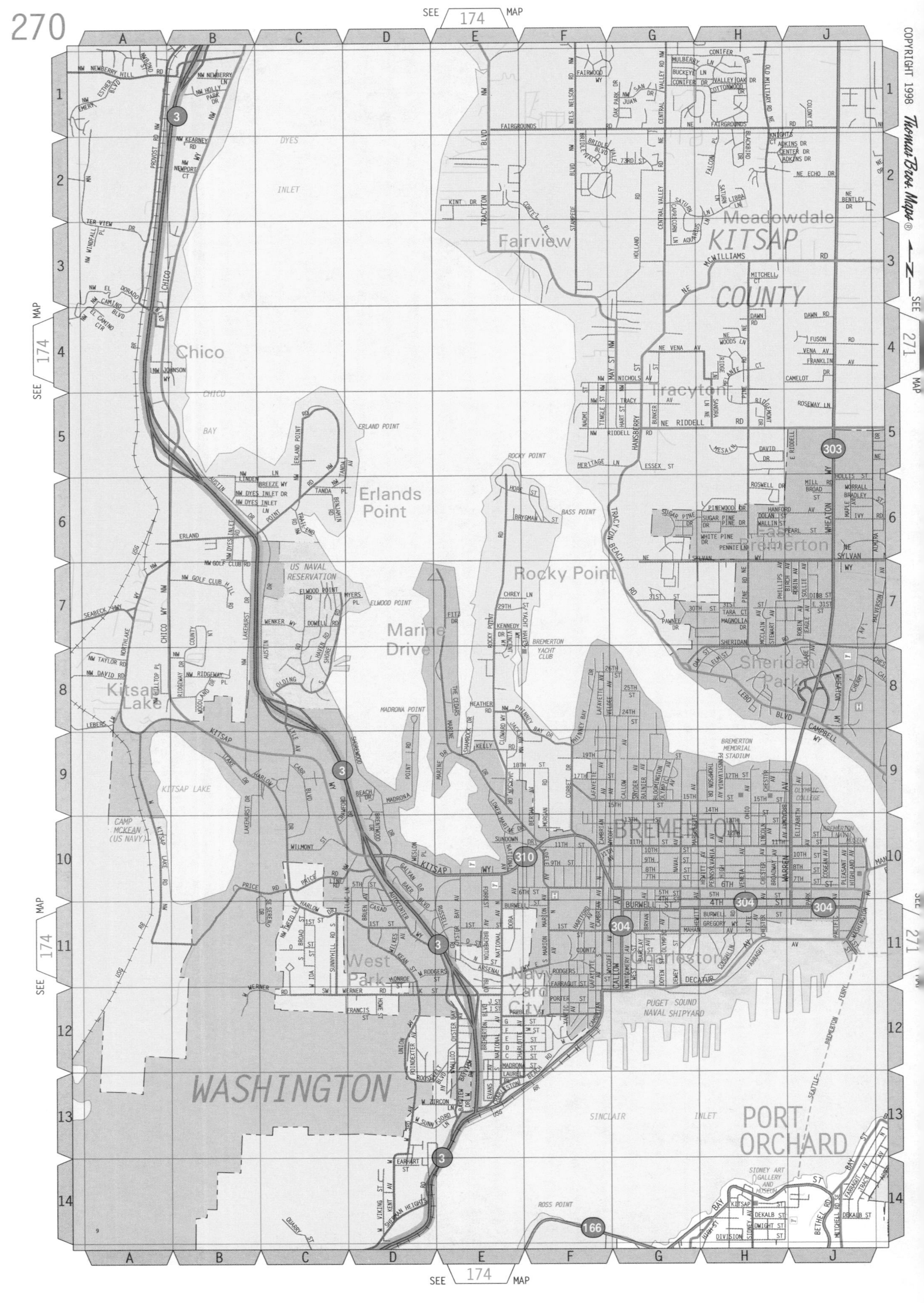

SEE 174 MAP
KITSAP
COUNTY
WASHINGTON
Chico
Fairview
Meadowdale
Tracyton
East Bremerton
Rocky Point
Erlands Point
Marine Drive
Sheridan Park
Kitsap Lake
BREMERTON
Charleston
West Park
Navy Yard City
PORT ORCHARD
DYES INLET
CHICO BAY
KITSAP LAKE
SINCLAIR INLET
PUGET SOUND NAVAL SHIPYARD
US NAVAL RESERVATION
CAMP MCKEAN (US NAVY)
BREMERTON MEMORIAL STADIUM
OLYMPIC COLLEGE
BREMERTON YACHT CLUB
SIDNEY ART GALLERY AND MUSEUM
ERLAND POINT
ROCKY POINT
BASS POINT
MADRONA POINT
ELWOOD POINT
ROSS POINT
SEATTLE - BREMERTON FERRY
PNW
DETAIL
COPYRIGHT 1998 Thomas Bros. Maps®

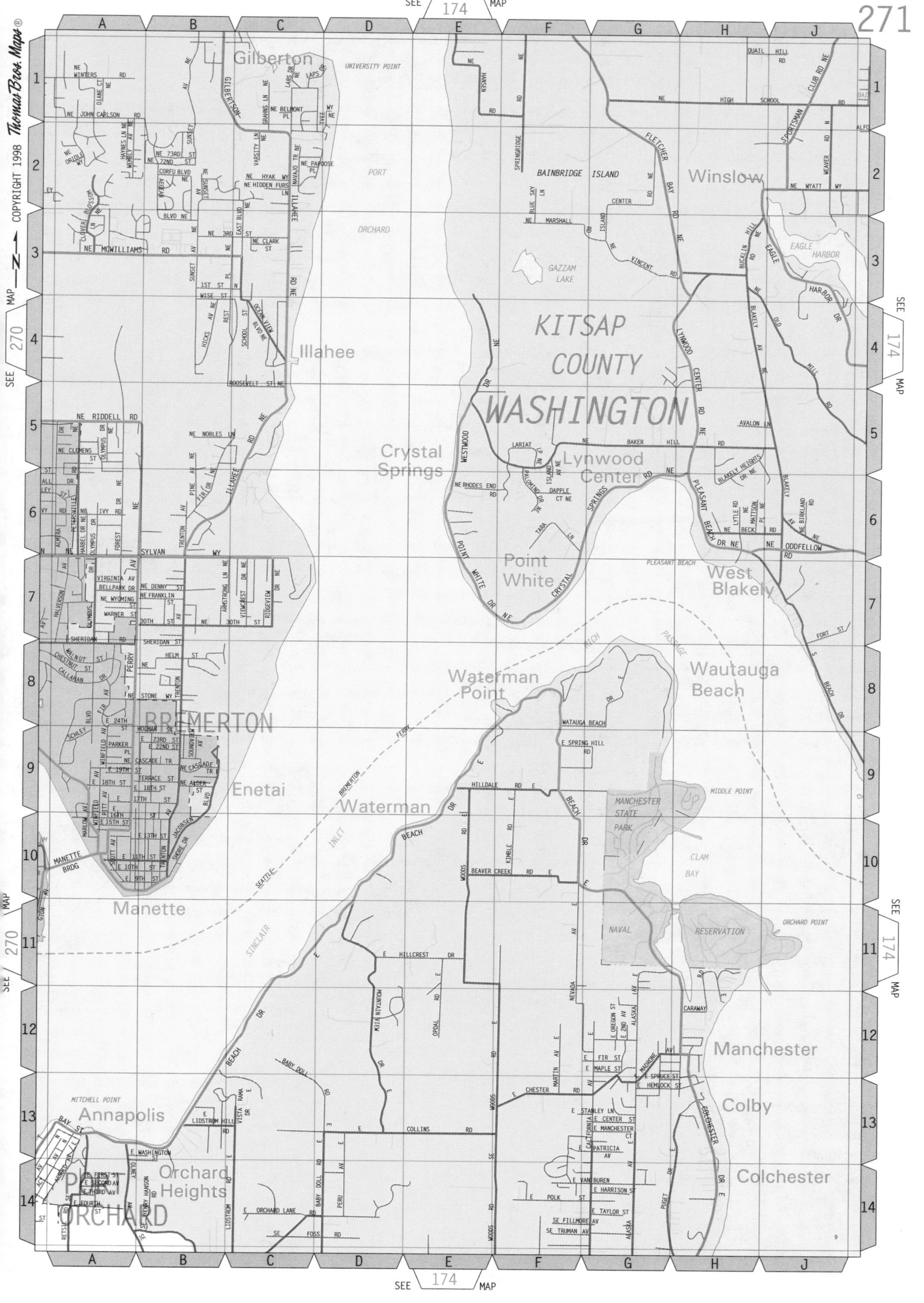
SEE 174 MAP
SEE 270 MAP
SEE 174 MAP
SEE 270 MAP
SEE 174 MAP
SEE 174 MAP
PNW
DETAIL
KITSAP
COUNTY
WASHINGTON
Gilberton
University Point
Port
Orchard
Illahee
Crystal Springs
Bainbridge Island
Winslow
Gazzam Lake
Eagle Harbor
Lynwood Center
Point White
Pleasant Beach
West Blakely
Rich Passage
Waterman Point
Wautauga Beach
Bremerton
Enetai
Waterman
Manette
Middle Point
Manchester State Park
Clam Bay
Naval Reservation
Orchard Point
Sinclair Inlet
Seattle Bremerton Ferry
Manchester
Colby
Colchester
Mitchell Point
Annapolis
Port Orchard
Orchard Heights
Manette Brdg
NE Winters Rd
NE John Carlson Rd
NE McWilliams Rd
NE Riddell Rd
Sylvan Wy
Illahee Rd NE
Gilberton Rd
Fletcher Bay Rd NE
NE High School Rd
Quail Hill Rd
Sportsman Club Rd NE
NE Wyatt Wy
Lynwood Center Rd NE
Bucklin Hill Rd
Eagle Harbor Dr
Blakely Av NE
Old Mill Rd
NE Baker Hill Rd
Pleasant Beach Dr NE
NE Oddfellow Rd
Fort St
S Beach Dr
Crystal Springs Rd NE
Point White Dr NE
Westwood Dr NE
Beach Dr E
Hilldale Rd E
Beaver Creek Rd E
E Hillcrest Dr
E Collins Rd
Woods Rd SE
Colchester Dr E
Puget Dr E
E Spring Hill Rd
Watauga Beach Dr
Mountain View Dr
Lidstrom Hill Rd
E Orchard Lane Rd
SE Foss Rd
Baby Doll Rd

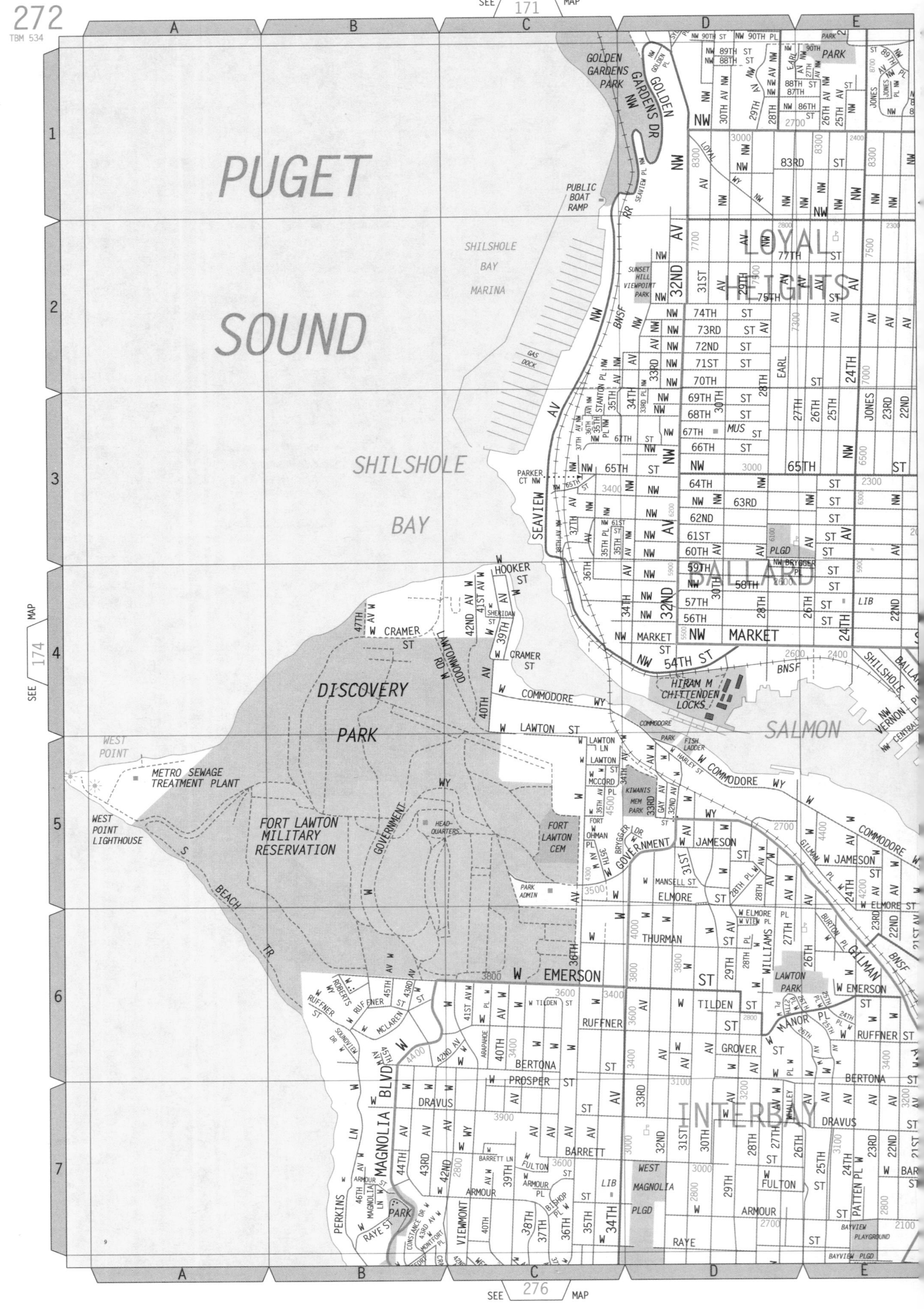
SEE 171 MAP
SEE 174 MAP
SEE 276 MAP
A
B
C
D
E
1
2
3
4
5
6
7
PUGET
SOUND
SHILSHOLE
BAY
SHILSHOLE
BAY
MARINA
GAS
DOCK
PUBLIC
BOAT
RAMP
GOLDEN
GARDENS
PARK
NW GOLDEN GARDENS DR
SEAVIEW AV NW
LOYAL
HEIGHTS
BALLARD
SUNSET
HILL
VIEWPOINT
PARK
PARKER
CT NW
NW MARKET ST
NW 54TH ST
HIRAM M
CHITTENDEN
LOCKS
FISH
LADDER
SALMON
W COMMODORE WY
W LAWTON ST
W CRAMER ST
W HOOKER ST
LAWTONWOOD RD W
DISCOVERY
PARK
WEST
POINT
METRO SEWAGE
TREATMENT PLANT
WEST
POINT
LIGHTHOUSE
S BEACH TR
FORT LAWTON
MILITARY
RESERVATION
GOVERNMENT WY
HEAD-
QUARTERS
FORT
LAWTON
CEM
PARK
ADMIN
KIWANIS
MEM
PARK
W EMERSON
W JAMESON
W ELMORE ST
THURMAN
W TILDEN ST
RUFFNER
BERTONA
PROSPER
DRAVUS
BARRETT
FULTON
ARMOUR
RAYE
MAGNOLIA BLVD W
PERKINS LN
LAWTON
PARK
INTERBAY
WEST
MAGNOLIA
PLGD
LIB
GILMAN
BNSF
BAYVIEW
PLAYGROUND
BAYVIEW PLGD
VIEWMONT
PLGD
MUS

SEE 171 MAP

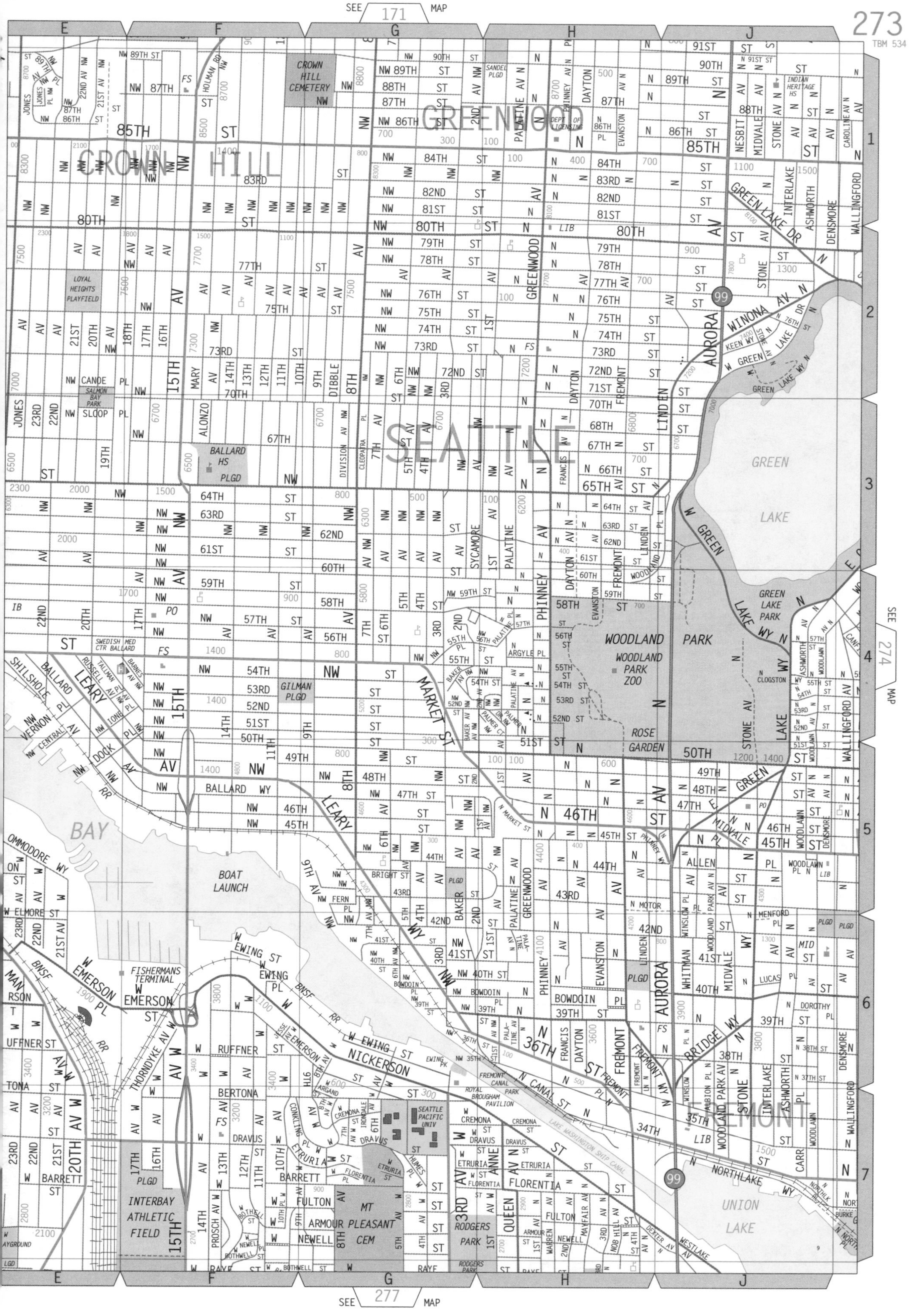

SEE 274 MAP
SEE 277 MAP
PNW
DETAIL

SEE 171 MAP

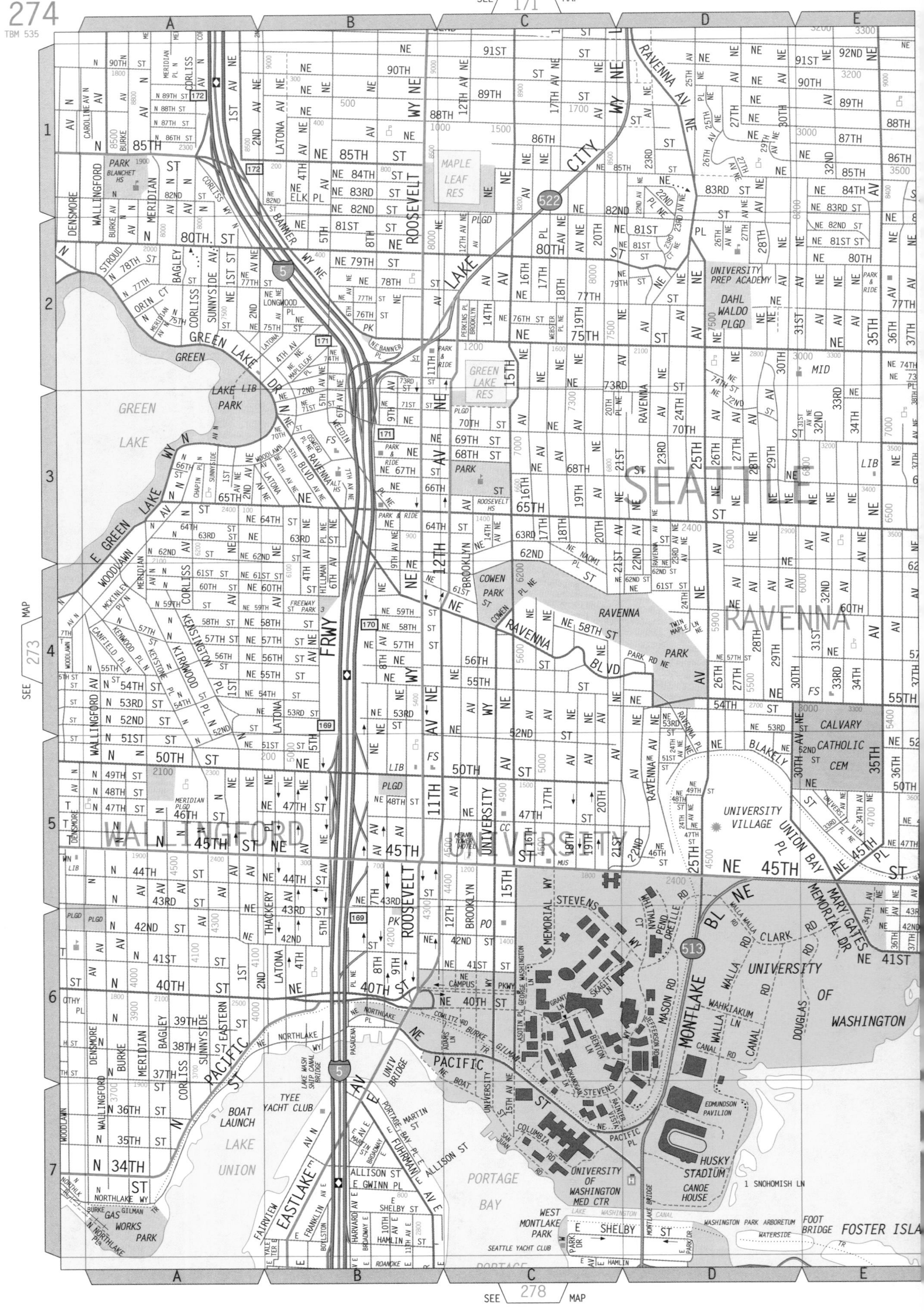

SEE 273 MAP

SEE 278 MAP

SEE 171 MAP

SEE 175 MAP
SEE 279 MAP
PNW
DETAIL

SEE 272 MAP

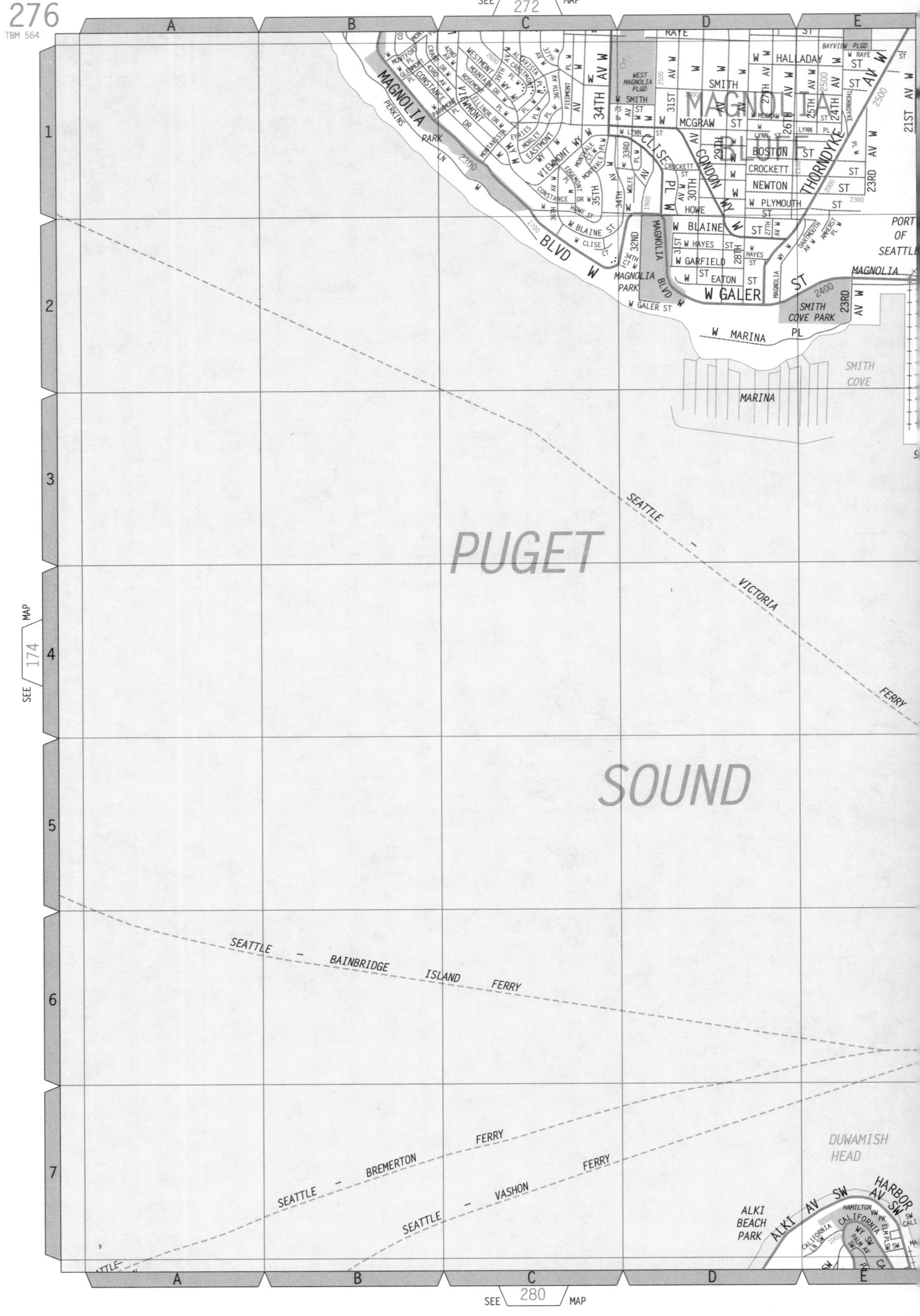

SEE 174 MAP

SEE 280 MAP

SEE 273 MAP

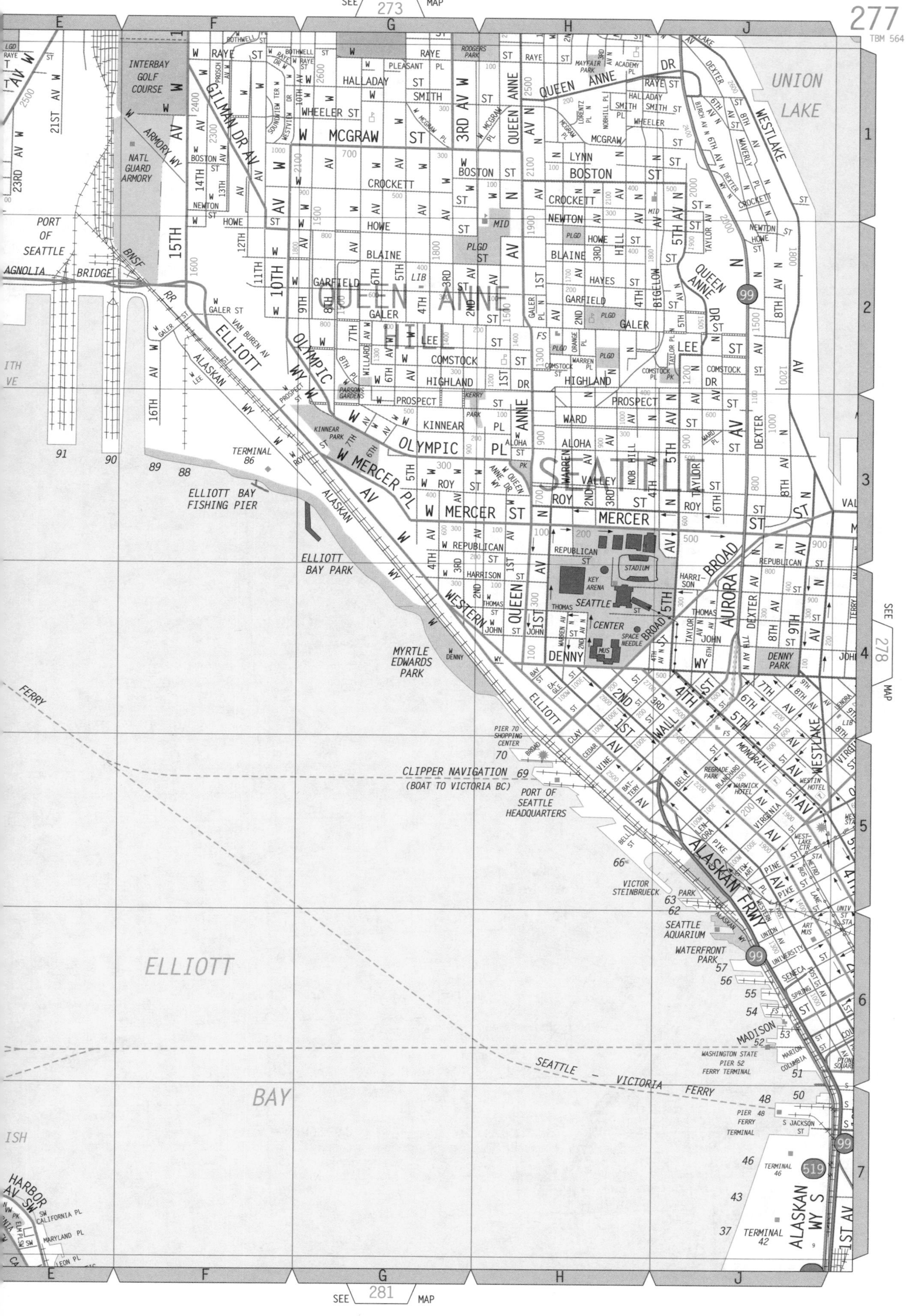

SEE 278 MAP

SEE 281 MAP

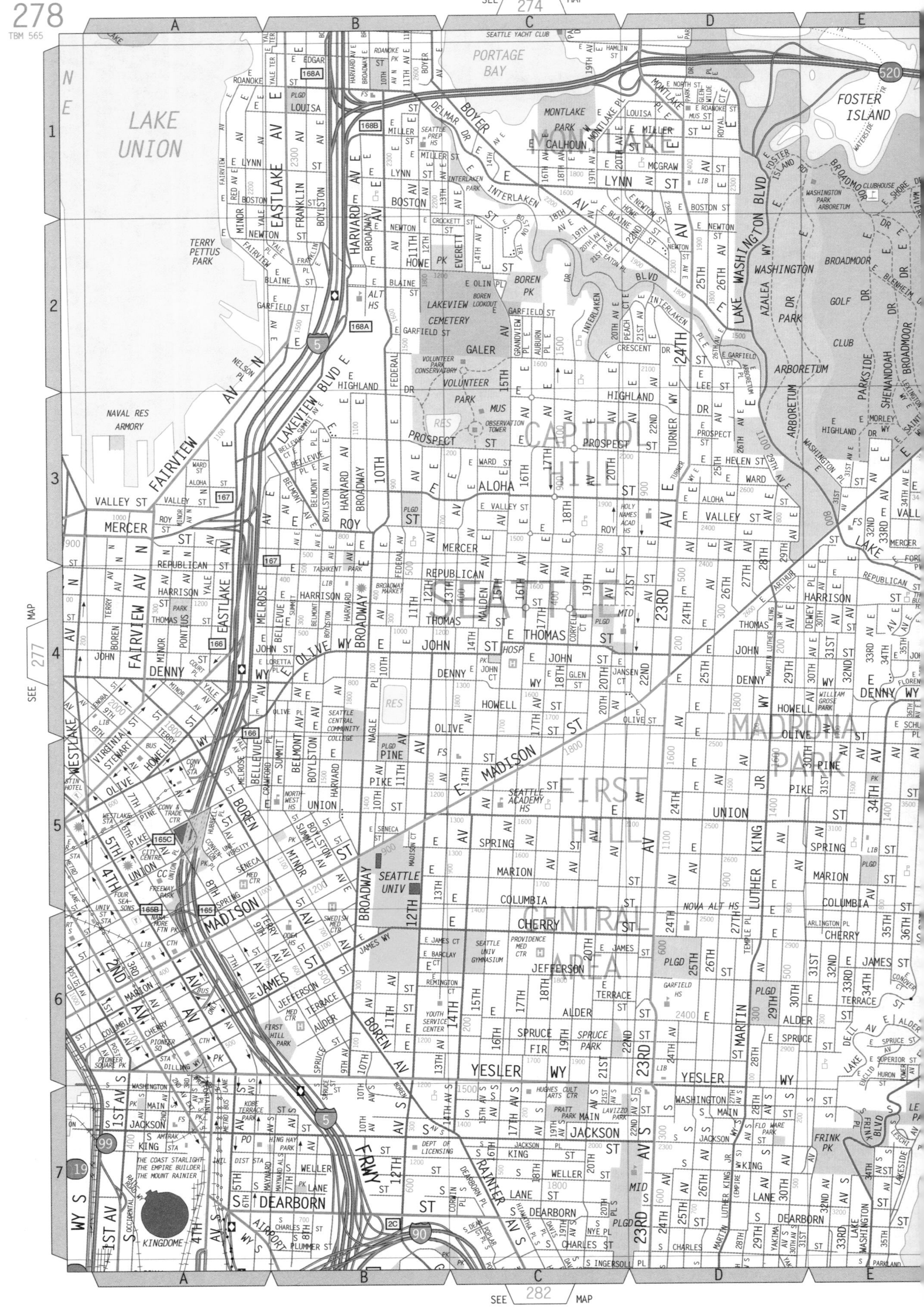
SEE 274 MAP
SEE 277 MAP
SEE 282 MAP
A
B
C
D
E
1
2
3
4
5
6
7
PNW
DETAIL
LAKE UNION
PORTAGE BAY
SEATTLE YACHT CLUB
FOSTER ISLAND
MONTLAKE
TERRY PETTUS PARK
LAKEVIEW CEMETERY
VOLUNTEER PARK
CAPITOL HILL
SEATTLE
FIRST HILL
CENTRAL AREA
MADRONA PARK
ARBORETUM
WASHINGTON PARK ARBORETUM
BROADMOOR GOLF CLUB
NAVAL RES ARMORY
SEATTLE UNIV
SEATTLE CENTRAL COMMUNITY COLLEGE
SEATTLE ACADEMY HS
KINGDOME
THE COAST STARLIGHT
THE EMPIRE BUILDER
THE MOUNT RAINIER
FRINK PK
FAIRVIEW AV N
EASTLAKE AV E
MERCER
VALLEY ST
DENNY
MADISON
BROADWAY
YESLER WY
JACKSON ST
DEARBORN
RAINIER AV S
MARTIN LUTHER KING JR WY S
LAKE WASHINGTON BLVD
23RD AV
UNION
JEFFERSON
PINE
PIKE
INTERLAKEN BLVD
BOREN AV
12TH AV
15TH AV E
24TH AV E
520
5
90
99

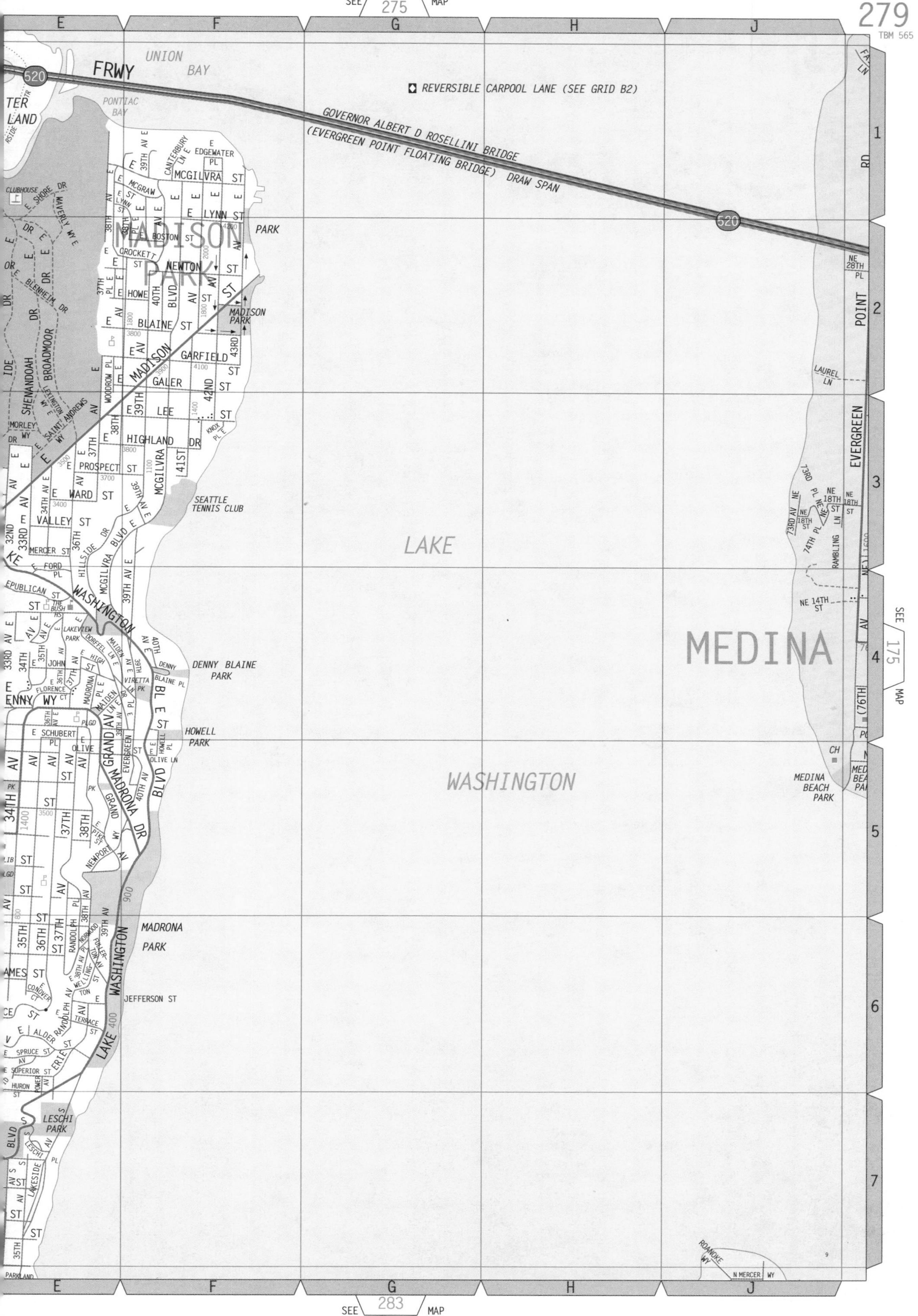
SEE 275 MAP
E
F
G
H
J
UNION BAY
FRWY
520
PONTIAC BAY
REVERSIBLE CARPOOL LANE (SEE GRID B2)
GOVERNOR ALBERT D ROSELLINI BRIDGE
(EVERGREEN POINT FLOATING BRIDGE) DRAW SPAN
MADISON PARK
PARK
MCGILVRA ST
E EDGEWATER PL
CANTERBURY LN E
MCGRAW
LYNN ST
BOSTON ST
CROCKETT
NEWTON ST
HOWE
BLAINE ST
GARFIELD ST
GALER ST
LEE ST
HIGHLAND DR
PROSPECT ST
WARD ST
VALLEY ST
MERCER ST
FORD PL
MADISON
40TH
BLVD
42ND
43RD
39TH
38TH
37TH
41ST
KNOX PL E
WOODROW PL
CLUBHOUSE
E SHORE DR
WAVERLY WY E
BLENHEIM DR
BROADMOOR DR
SHENANDOAH DR
LEXINGTON WY E
SAINT ANDREWS WY
MORLEY WY
SEATTLE TENNIS CLUB
HILLSIDE DR
MCGILVRA BLVD
REPUBLICAN ST
THE BUSH
LAKE WASHINGTON BLVD
LAKEVIEW PARK
DORFFEL
JOHN
HIGH
DENNY BLAINE PARK
DENNY BLAINE PL
VIRETTA PK
FLORENCE CT
DENNY WY
E SCHUBERT PL
OLIVE
GRAND AV
MADRONA DR
EVERGREEN PL
OLIVE LN
HOWELL PARK
NEWPORT WY
PIKE
34TH
35TH
36TH
RANDOLPH
NORWOOD
WELLINGTON AV
MADRONA PARK
JEFFERSON ST
JAMES ST
CONOVER CT
ALDER
TERRACE
SPRUCE ST
ERIE
SUPERIOR ST
HURON ST
POWER
LESCHI PARK
LESCHI PL
LAKESIDE
PARKLAND
900
400
LAKE
WASHINGTON
MEDINA
EVERGREEN POINT RD
NE 28TH PL
LAUREL LN
73RD PL NE
73RD AV NE
74TH PL NE
NE 18TH ST
RAMBLING LN
NE 14TH ST
76TH
CH
MEDINA BEACH PARK
ROANOKE WY
N MERCER WY
SEE 175 MAP
SEE 283 MAP
1
2
3
4
5
6
7
PNW
DETAIL

SEE 276 MAP

SEE 174 MAP
SEE 284 MAP

PNW

DETAIL

SEE 277 MAP

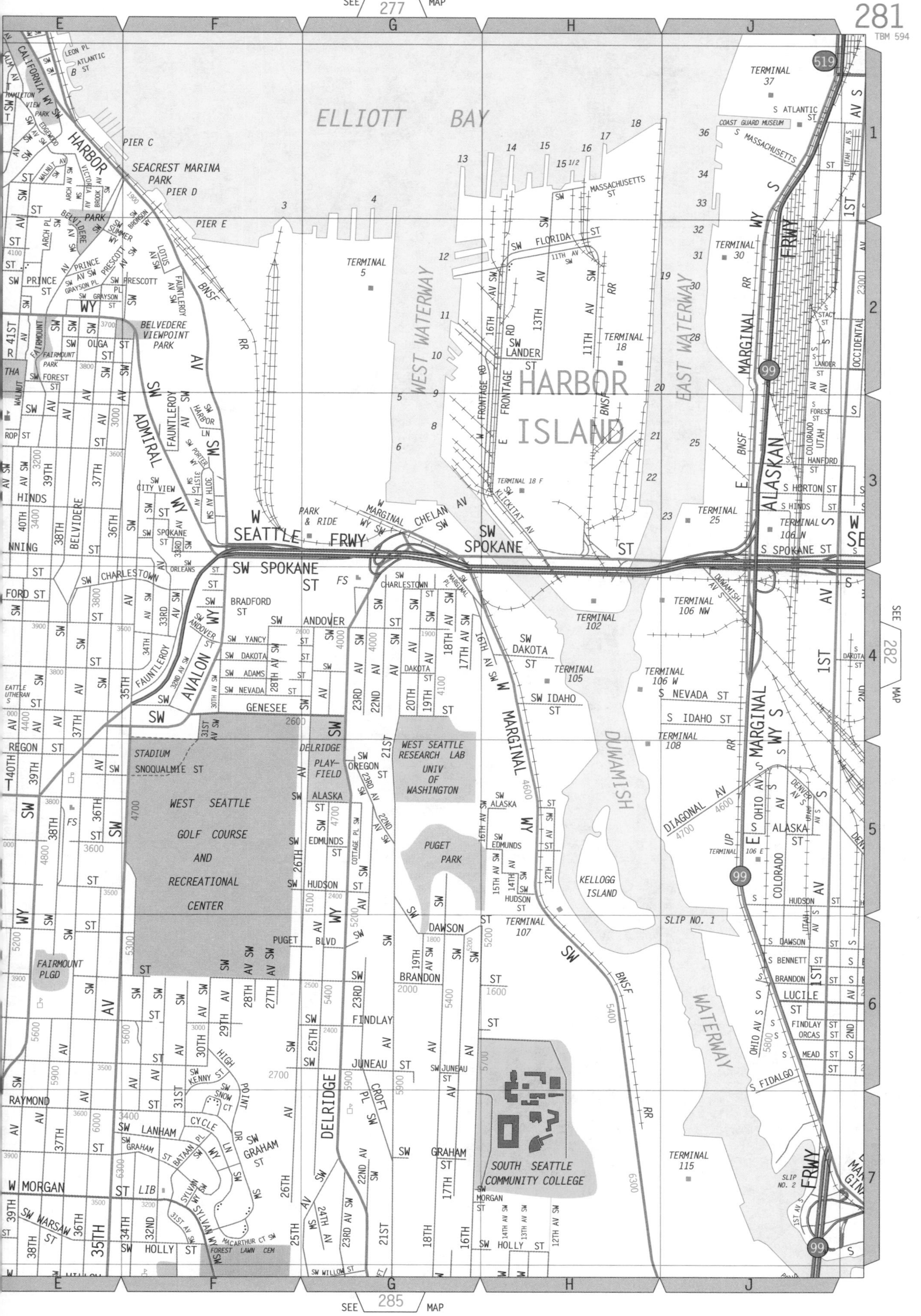

SEE 282 MAP
SEE 285 MAP

SEE 278 MAP

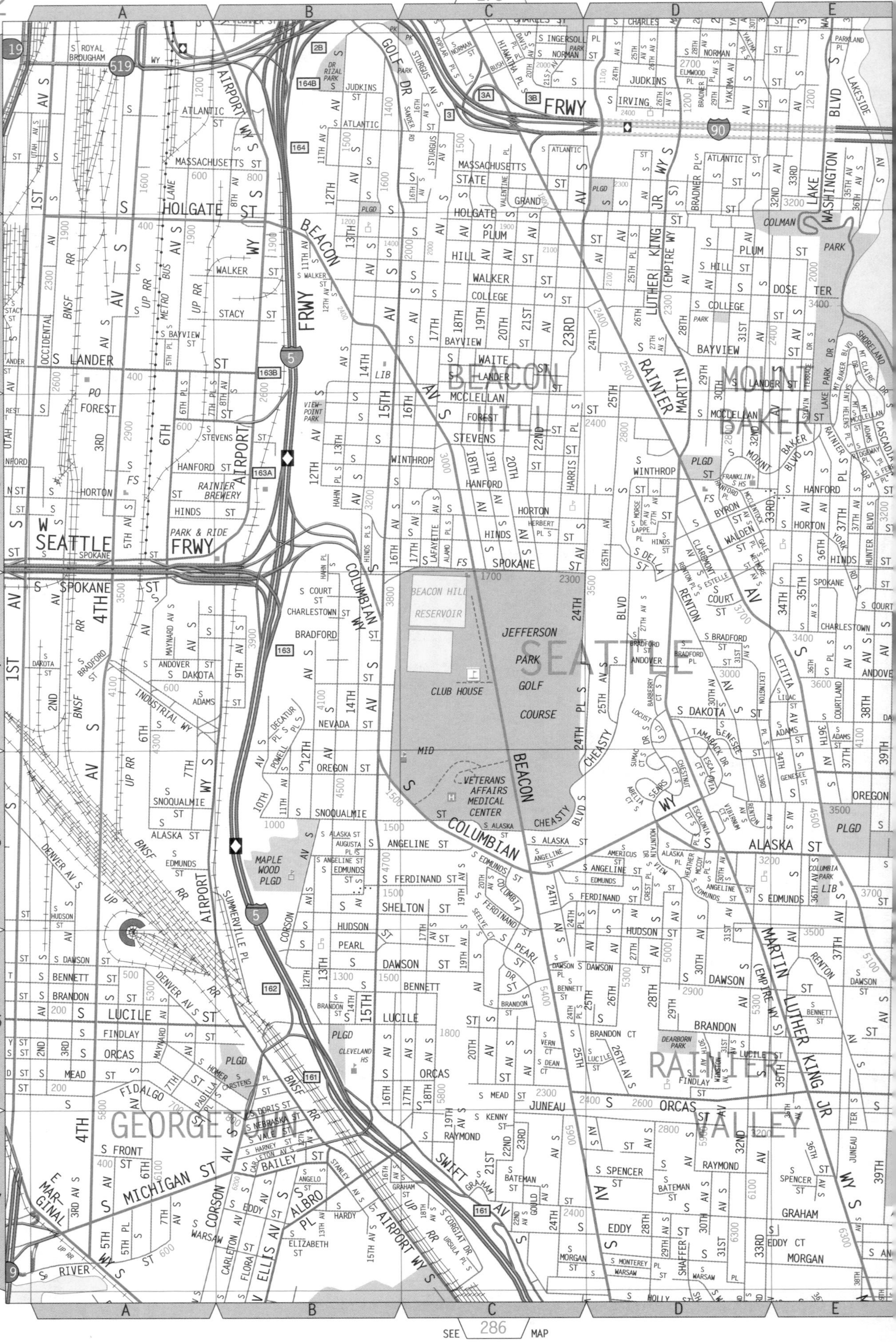

SEE 281 MAP

SEE 286 MAP

A B C D E

1 2 3 4 5 6 7

PNW

DETAIL

BEACON HILL
MOUNT BAKER
SEATTLE
GEORGETOWN
RAINIER VALLEY

JEFFERSON PARK GOLF COURSE
BEACON HILL RESERVOIR
CLUB HOUSE
VETERANS AFFAIRS MEDICAL CENTER
COLMAN PARK
DR RIZAL PARK
VIEWPOINT PARK
MAPLE WOOD PLGD
RAINIER BREWERY
PARK & RIDE
CLEVELAND HS
FRANKLIN SR HS
DEARBORN PARK
COLUMBIA PARK
LIB

S HOLGATE ST
S LANDER ST
S SPOKANE ST
S ATLANTIC ST
S MASSACHUSETTS ST
S ALASKA ST
S ORCAS ST
S MICHIGAN ST
E MARGINAL WY S
AIRPORT WY S
BEACON AV S
COLUMBIAN WY
RAINIER AV S
MARTIN LUTHER KING JR WY S
LAKE WASHINGTON BLVD
SWIFT AV S
CORSON AV S
ELLIS AV S
4TH AV S
1ST AV S
W SEATTLE FRWY
FRWY
GOLF DR S
RIVER ST

SEE 279 MAP

SEE 175 MAP

SEE 287 MAP

PNW

DETAIL

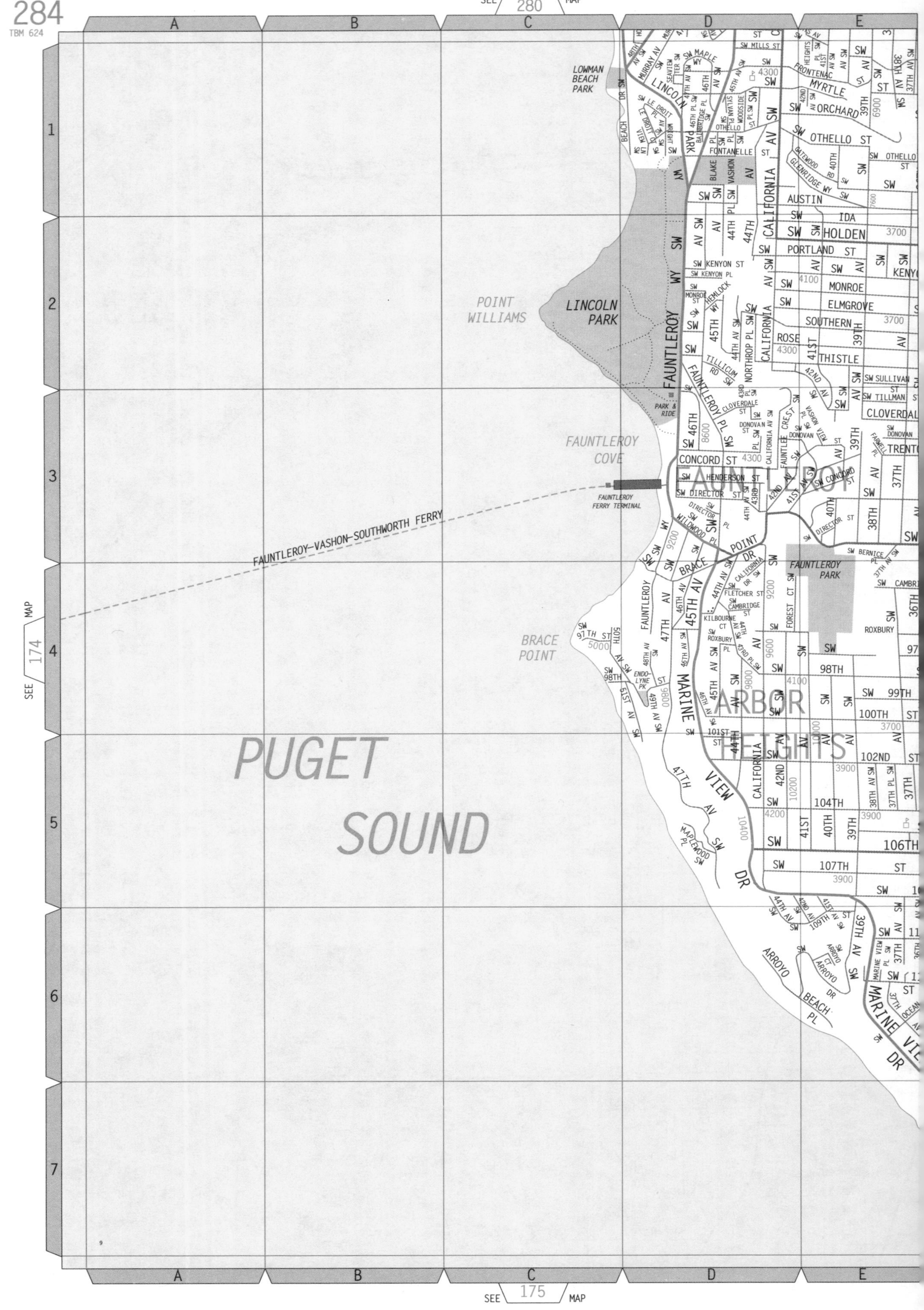
SEE 280 MAP
SEE 174 MAP
SEE 175 MAP
PUGET
SOUND
POINT WILLIAMS
LINCOLN PARK
LOWMAN BEACH PARK
FAUNTLEROY COVE
FAUNTLEROY FERRY TERMINAL
FAUNTLEROY-VASHON-SOUTHWORTH FERRY
BRACE POINT
FAUNTLEROY
FAUNTLEROY PARK
ARBOR HEIGHTS
PARK & RIDE
FAUNTLEROY WY SW
CALIFORNIA AV SW
MARINE VIEW DR SW
ARROYO BEACH PL
A
B
C
D
E
1
2
3
4
5
6
7

SEE 281 MAP

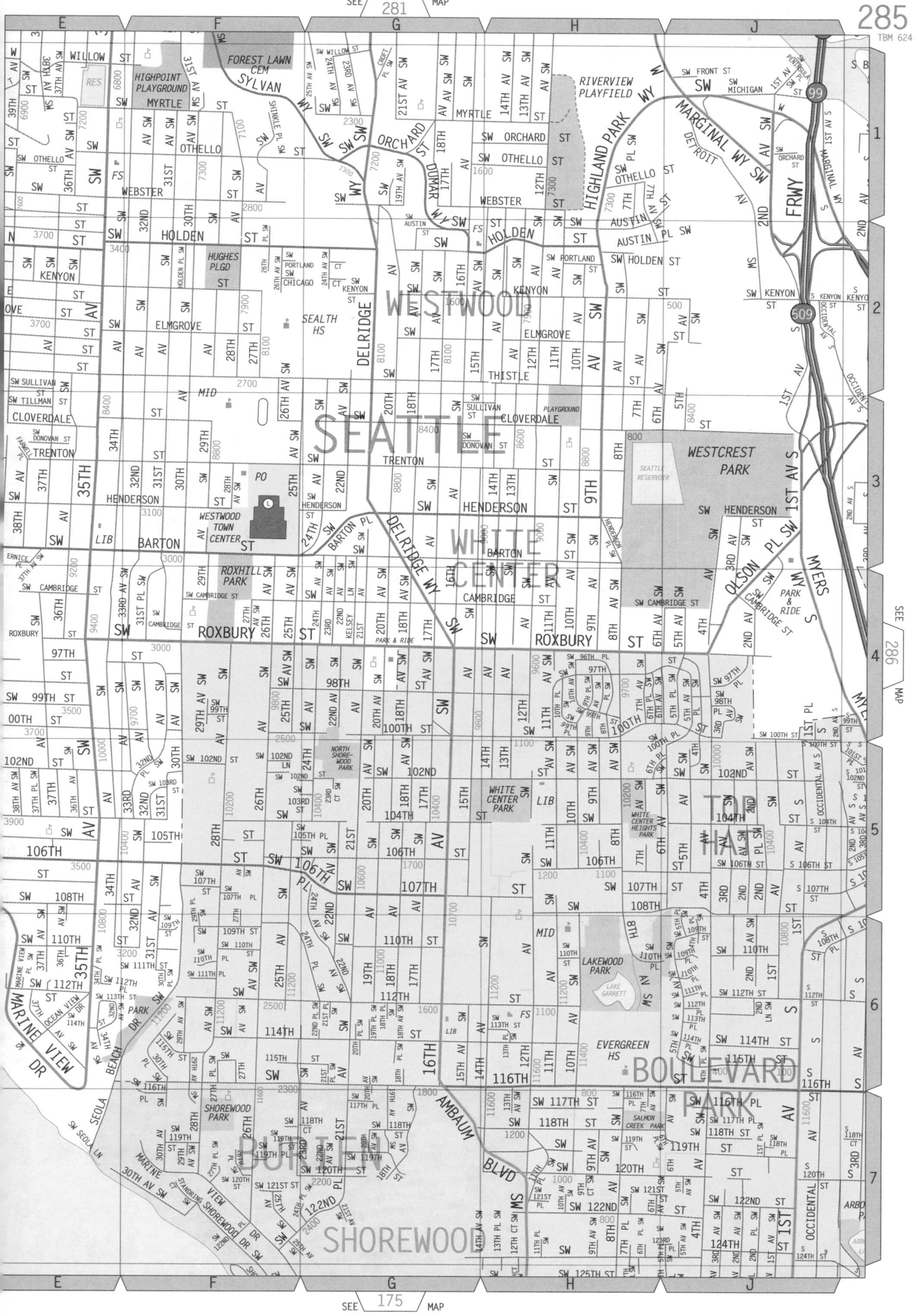

SEE 286 MAP

SEE 175 MAP

SEE 282 MAP

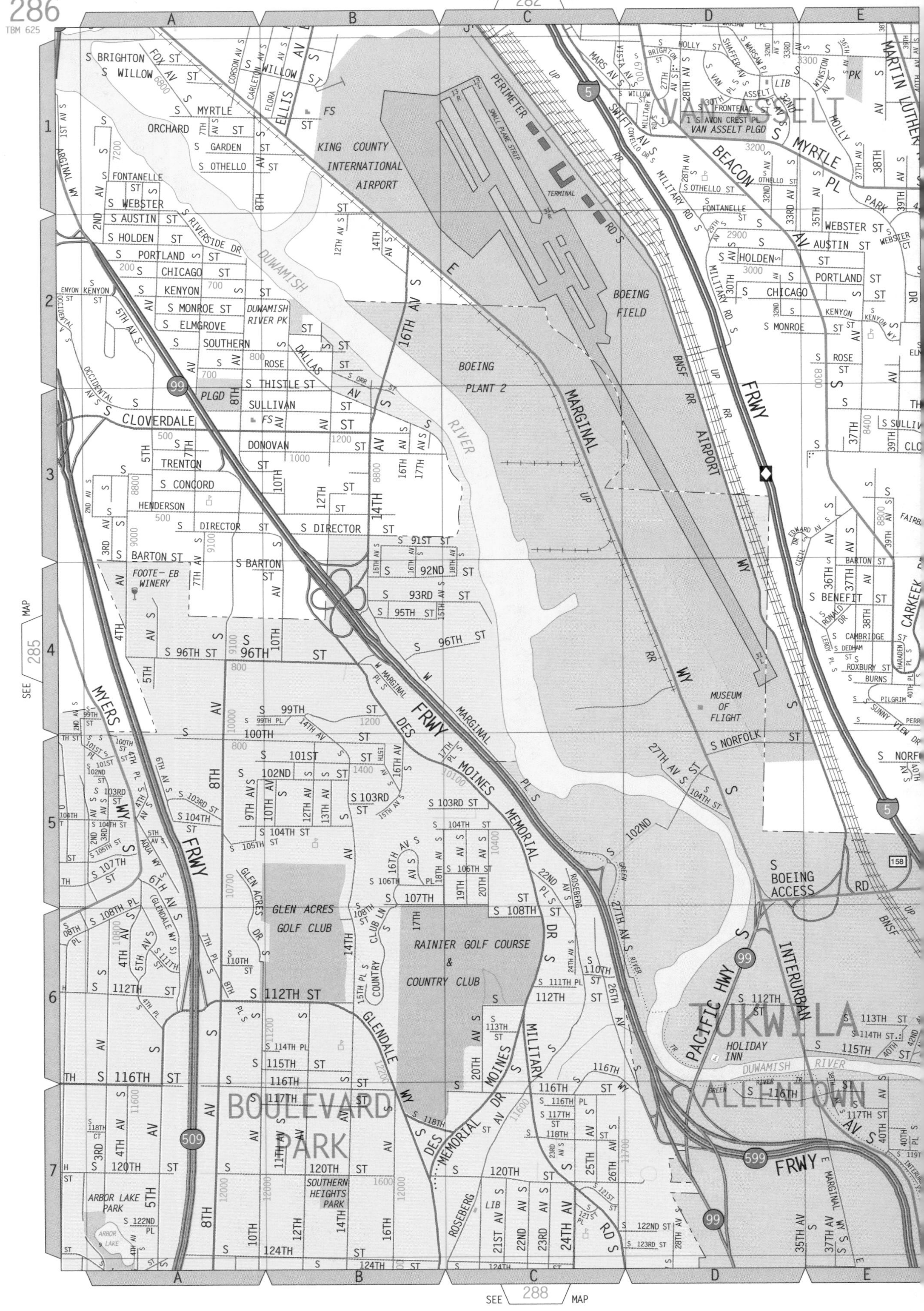

SEE 285 MAP

SEE 288 MAP

SEE 283 MAP

SEE 175 MAP
SEE 289 MAP

SEE 286 MAP

SEE 175 MAP

SEE 290 MAP

PNW

DETAIL

SEE 287 MAP

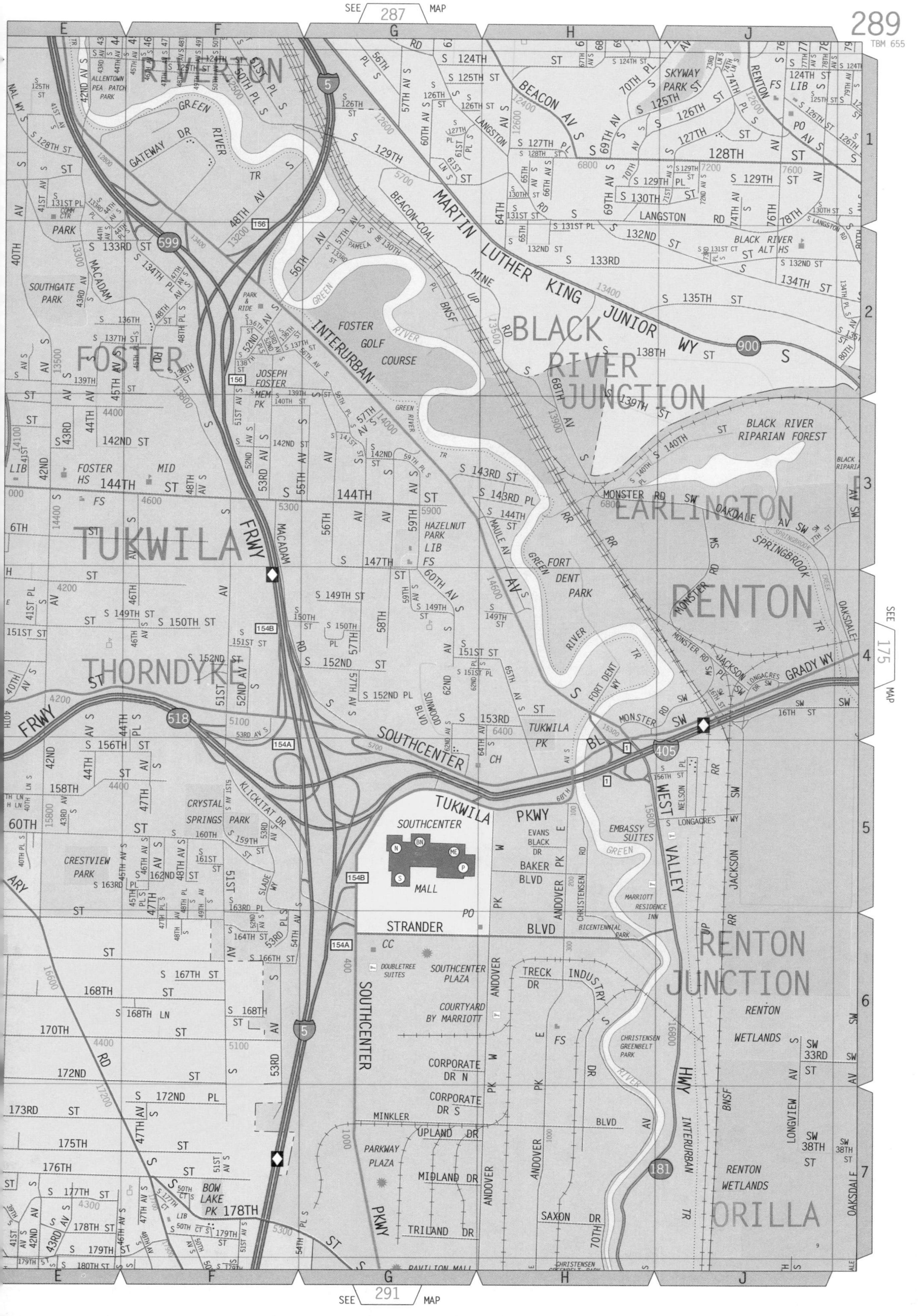

SEE 175 MAP

SEE 291 MAP

PNW
DETAIL

SEE 288 MAP

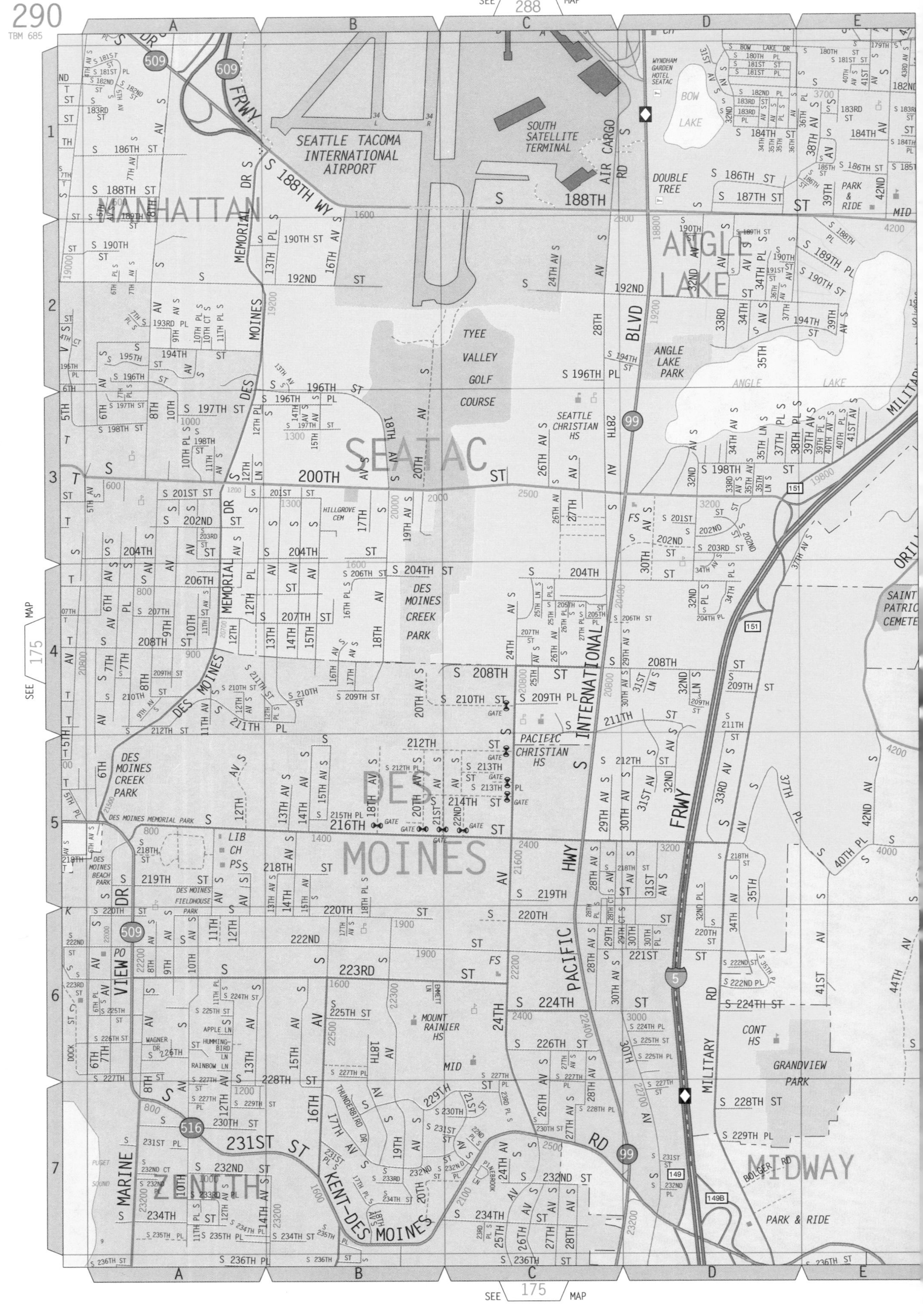

SEE 175 MAP

SEE 175 MAP

SEE 289 MAP
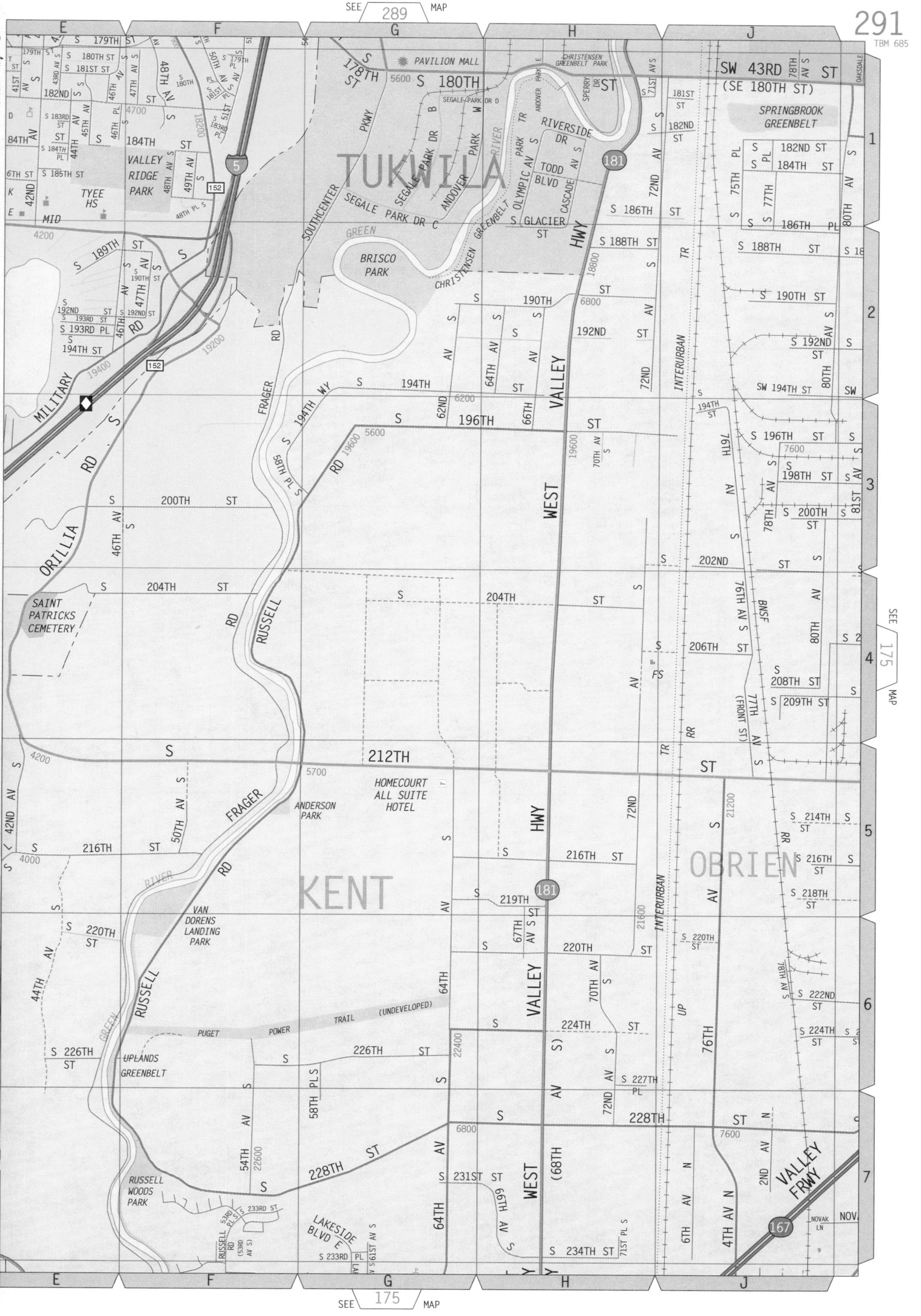

SEE 175 MAP
SEE 175 MAP

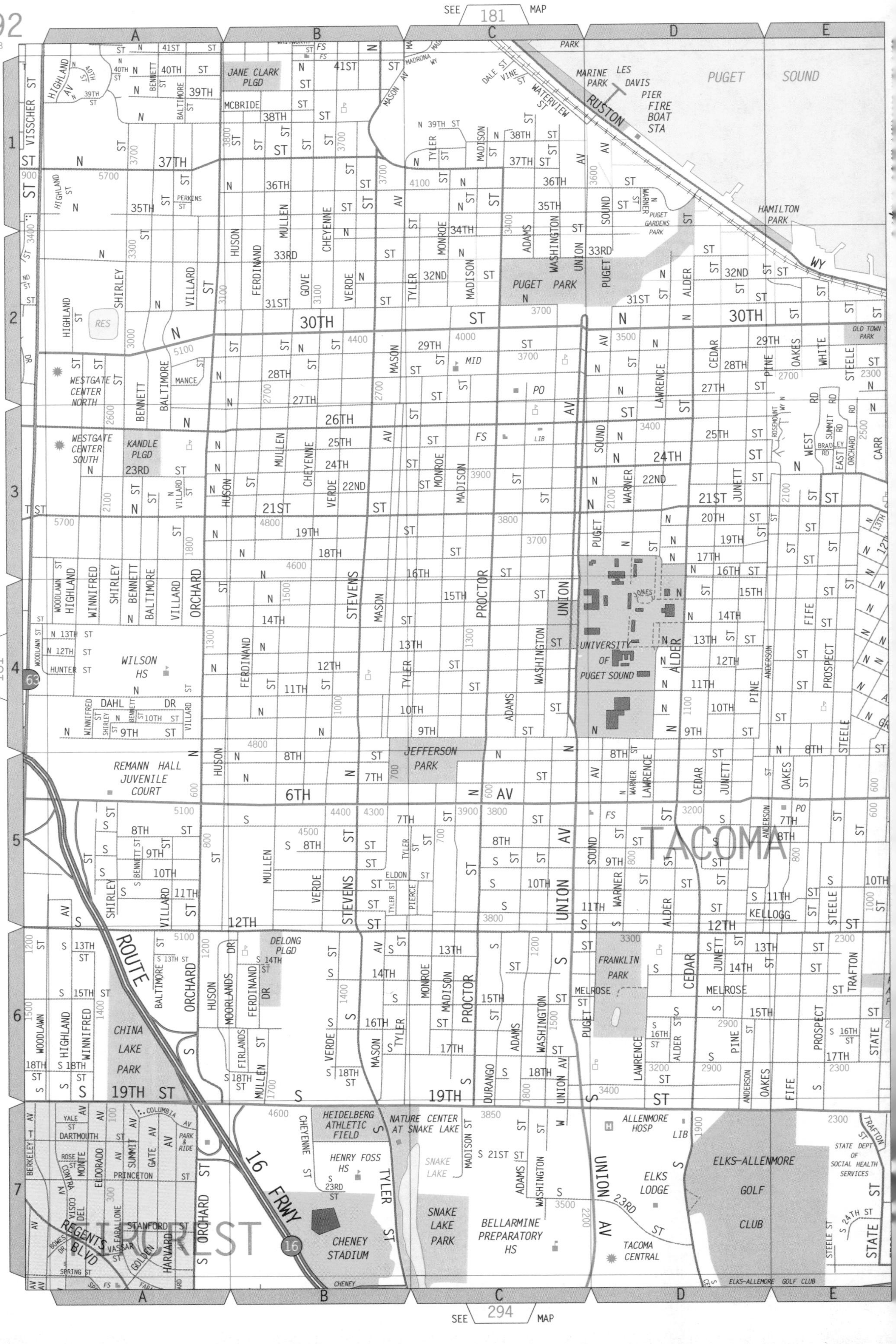

SEE 181 MAP

PNW

DETAIL

A B C D E

1 2 3 4 5 6 7

PUGET SOUND

MARINE PARK
LES DAVIS PIER
FIRE BOAT STA
RUSTON WY
HAMILTON PARK
PUGET GARDENS PARK
PUGET PARK
OLD TOWN PARK
JANE CLARK PLGD
KANDLE PLGD
WESTGATE CENTER NORTH
WESTGATE CENTER SOUTH
RES
MID
PO
LIB
FS
WILSON HS
UNIVERSITY OF PUGET SOUND
JONES
REMANN HALL JUVENILE COURT
JEFFERSON PARK
TACOMA
DELONG PLGD
CHINA LAKE PARK
FRANKLIN PARK
HEIDELBERG ATHLETIC FIELD
NATURE CENTER AT SNAKE LAKE
SNAKE LAKE
SNAKE LAKE PARK
HENRY FOSS HS
CHENEY STADIUM
BELLARMINE PREPARATORY HS
ALLENMORE HOSP
ELKS LODGE
TACOMA CENTRAL
ELKS-ALLENMORE GOLF CLUB
STATE DEPT OF SOCIAL HEALTH SERVICES
FIRCREST
PARK & RIDE
ROUTE 16 FRWY
N 30TH ST
N 26TH ST
N 21ST ST
6TH AV
S 12TH ST
S 19TH ST
UNION AV
STEVENS ST
PROCTOR ST
PEARL ST
REGENTS BLVD

SEE 294 MAP

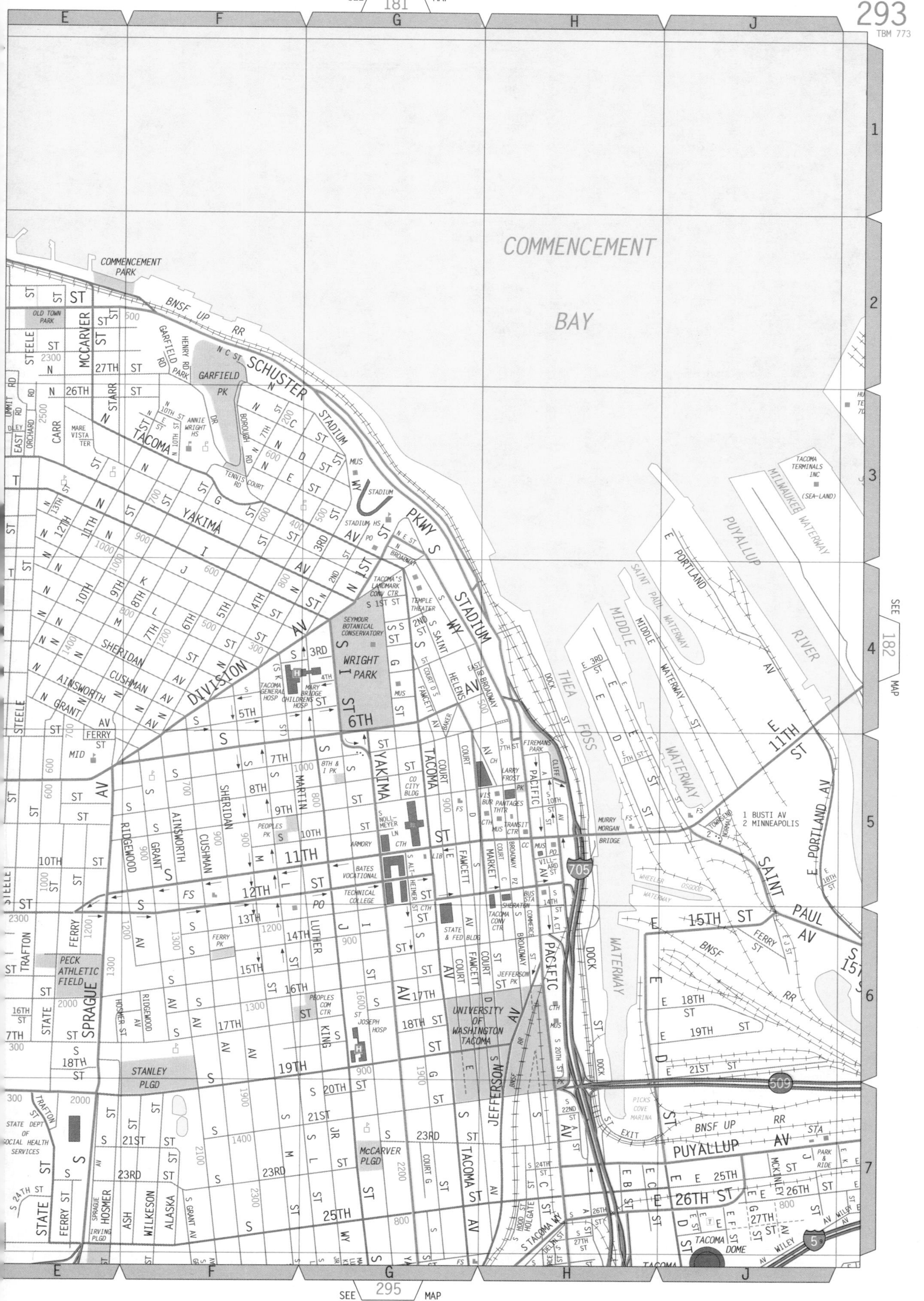
SEE 181 MAP
COMMENCEMENT BAY
COMMENCEMENT PARK
GARFIELD PK
WRIGHT PARK
PECK ATHLETIC FIELD
STANLEY PLGD
McCARVER PLGD
UNIVERSITY OF WASHINGTON TACOMA
TACOMA DOME
THEA FOSS WATERWAY
PUYALLUP RIVER
SEE 182 MAP
SEE 295 MAP
PNW
DETAIL

SEE 292 MAP

SEE 181 MAP

FIRCREST

UNIVERSITY PLACE

SOUTH TACOMA

LAKEWOOD

SEE 181 MAP

PNW

DETAIL

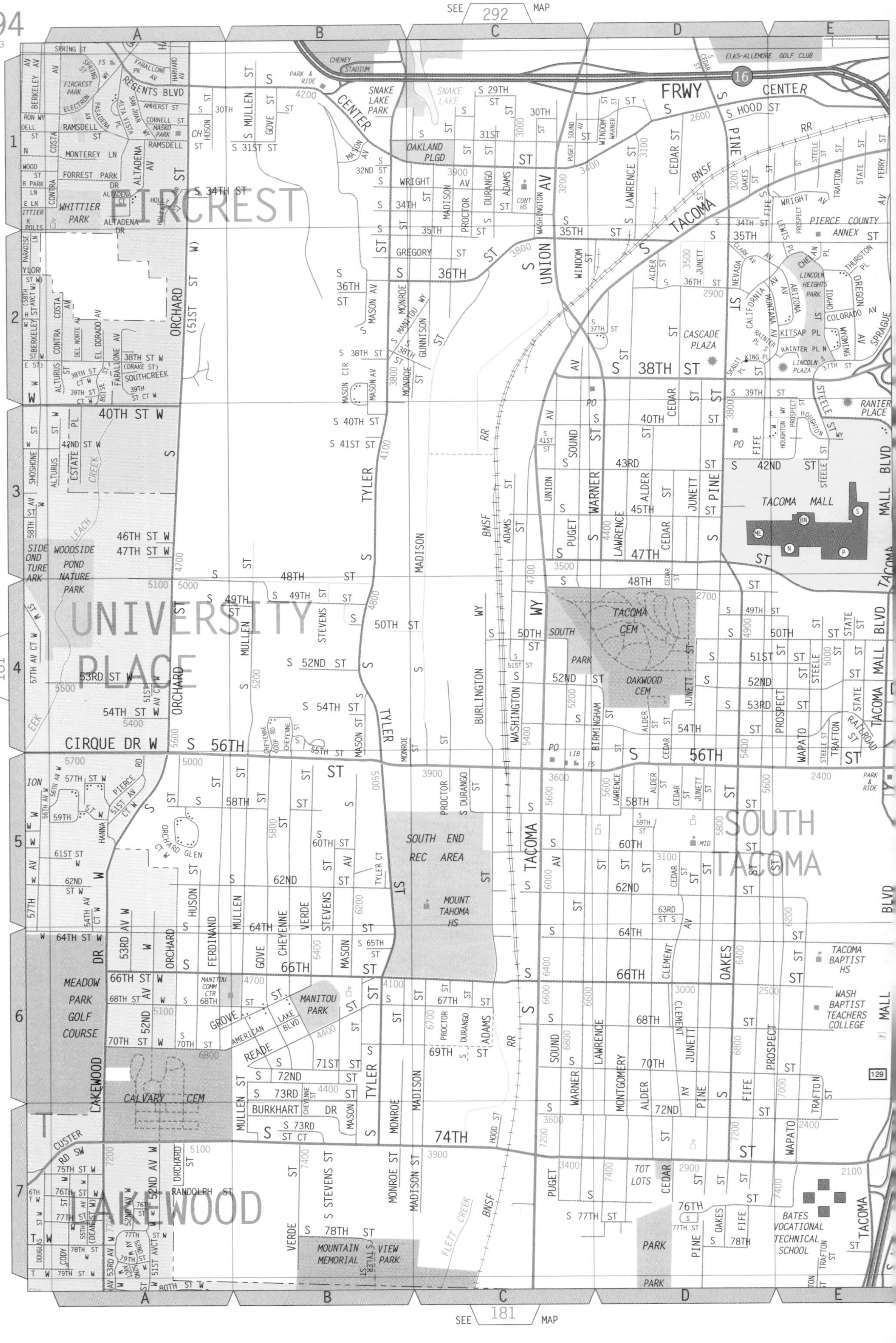

SEE 293 MAP

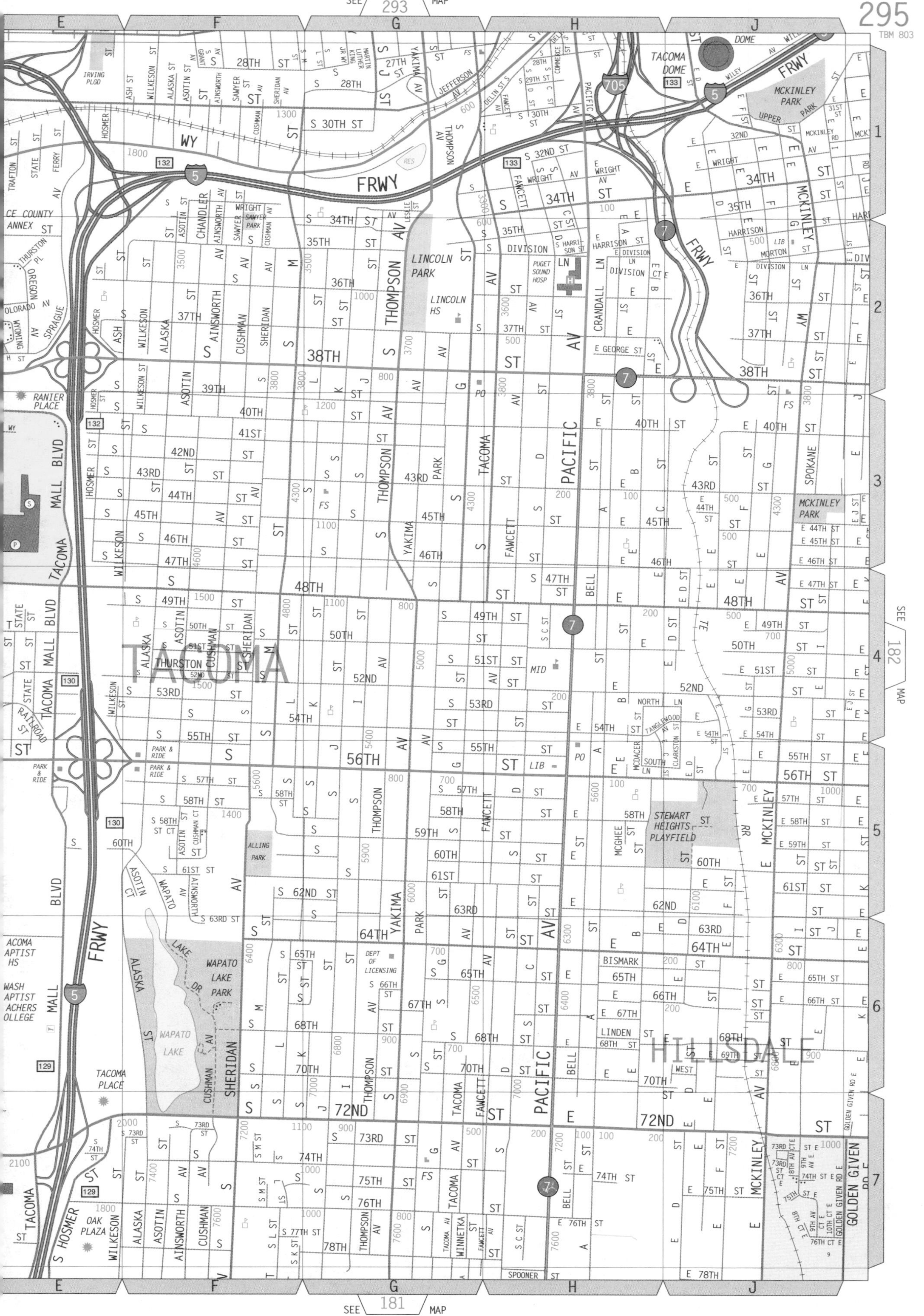

SEE 182 MAP
SEE 181 MAP

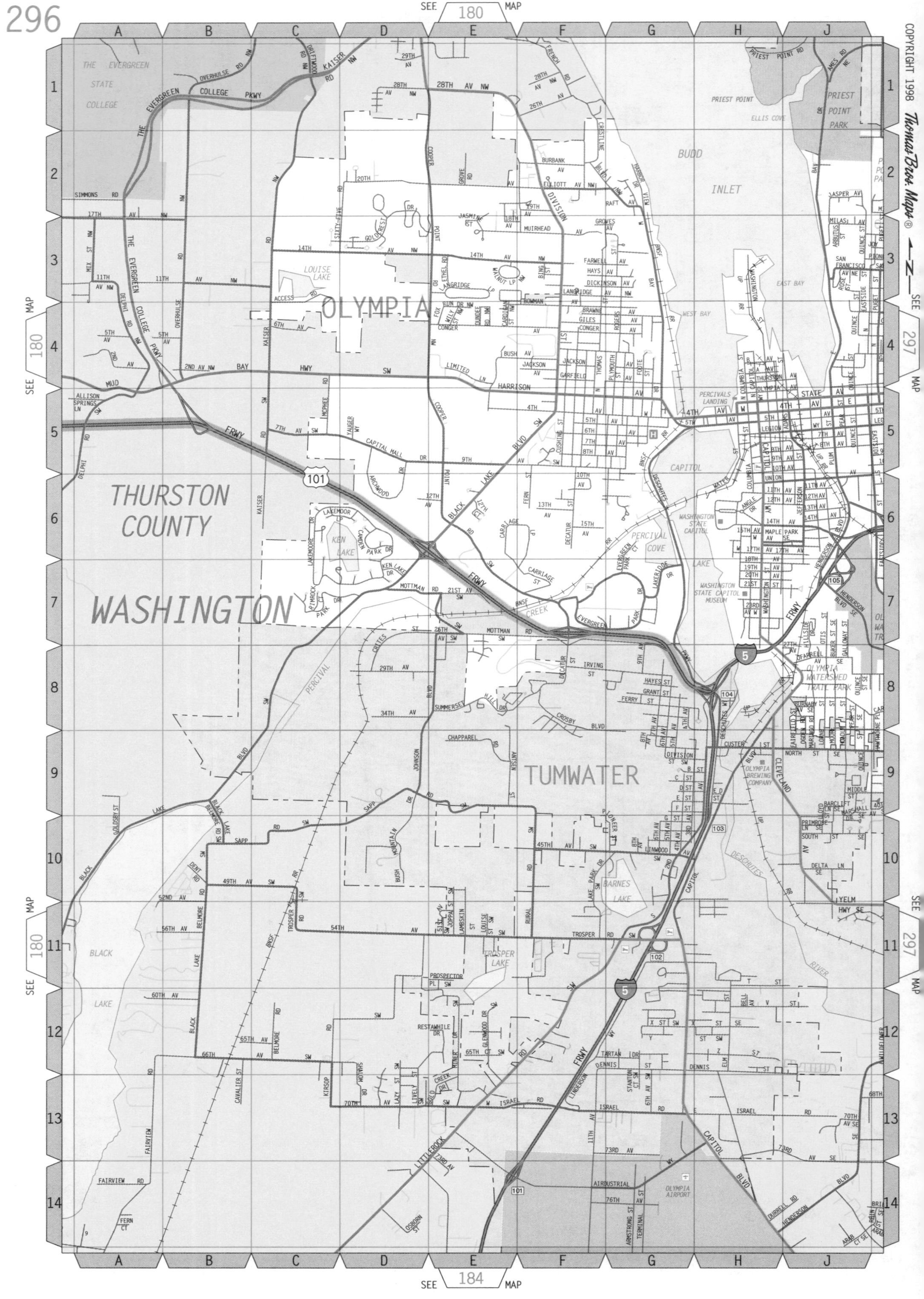
SEE 180 MAP
SEE 297 MAP
SEE 184 MAP
PNW
DETAIL
THE EVERGREEN STATE COLLEGE
OLYMPIA
THURSTON COUNTY
WASHINGTON
TUMWATER
BUDD INLET
PRIEST POINT PARK
LOUISE LAKE
KEN LAKE
PERCIVAL COVE
CAPITOL LAKE
WASHINGTON STATE CAPITOL
WASHINGTON STATE CAPITOL MUSEUM
OLYMPIA WATERSHED TRAIL PARK
OLYMPIA BREWING COMPANY
BARNES LAKE
TROSPER LAKE
BLACK LAKE
OLYMPIA AIRPORT
DESCHUTES RIVER
EVERGREEN PARK DR
BLACK LAKE BLVD
CAPITOL BLVD
HARRISON AV
STATE AV
MUD BAY HWY
COOPER POINT RD
KAISER RD
ISRAEL RD
TROSPER RD
YELM HWY SE
LITTLEROCK RD

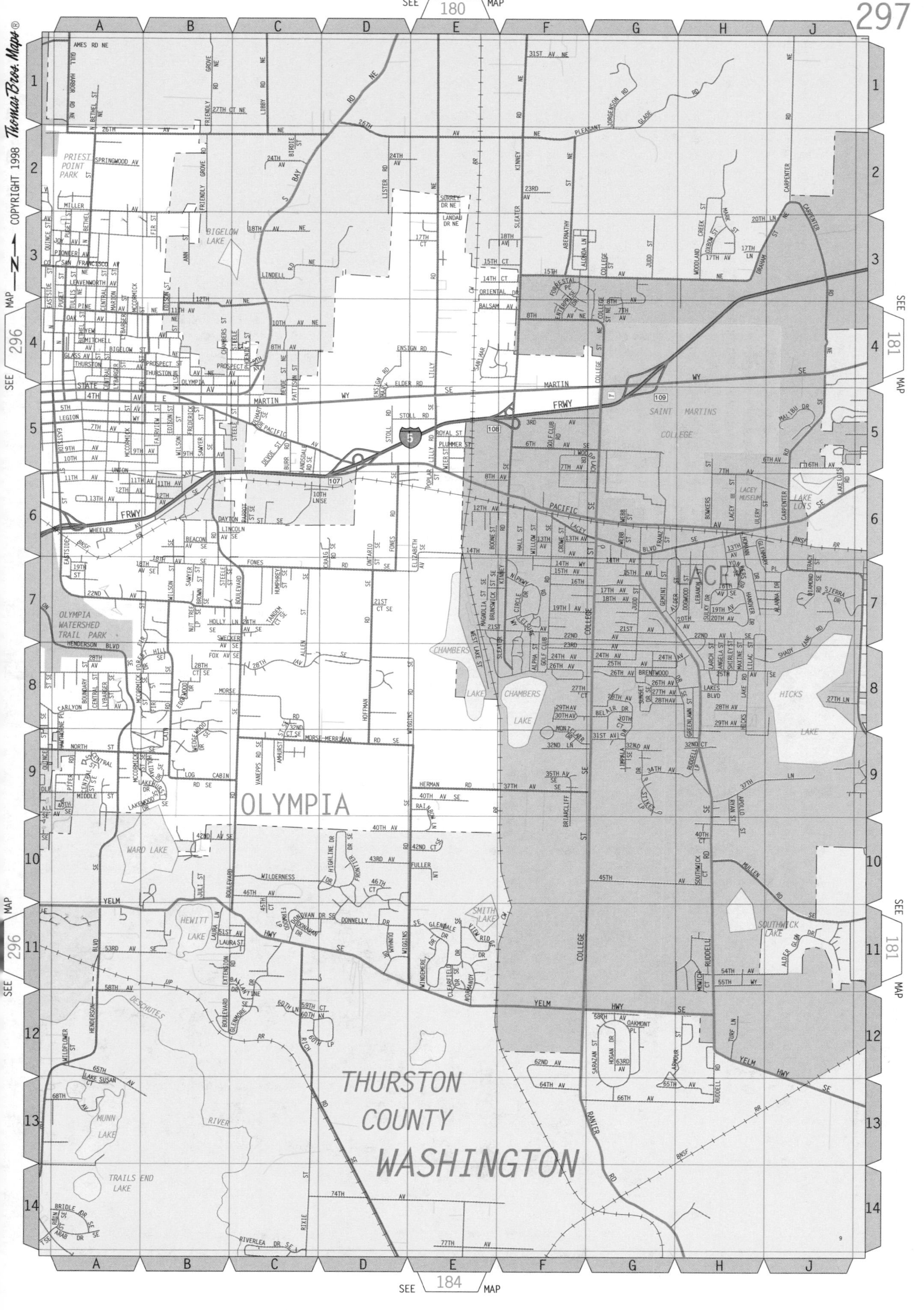
SEE 180 MAP
SEE 296 MAP
SEE 181 MAP
SEE 184 MAP
Thomas Bros. Maps®
COPYRIGHT 1998
PNW
DETAIL
A
B
C
D
E
F
G
H
J
1
2
3
4
5
6
7
8
9
10
11
12
13
14
OLYMPIA
LACEY
THURSTON
COUNTY
WASHINGTON
PRIEST POINT PARK
BIGELOW LAKE
OLYMPIA WATERSHED TRAIL PARK
WARD LAKE
HEWITT LAKE
SMITH LAKE
CHAMBERS LAKE
HICKS LAKE
SOUTHWICK LAKE
LAKE LOIS
MUNN LAKE
TRAILS END LAKE
SAINT MARTINS COLLEGE
LACEY MUSEUM
DESCHUTES
RIVER
MARTIN WY
PACIFIC AV
FRWY
YELM HWY
26TH AV NE
PLEASANT GLADE RD
S BAY RD
SLEATER KINNEY RD
COLLEGE ST
CARPENTER RD
HENDERSON BLVD
BOULEVARD RD
RIXIE RD
RUDDELL RD
RANIER RD
MULLEN RD
MORSE-MERRIMAN RD SE
LOG CABIN RD SE
HERMAN RD
WILDERNESS
77TH AV
74TH AV
BNSF

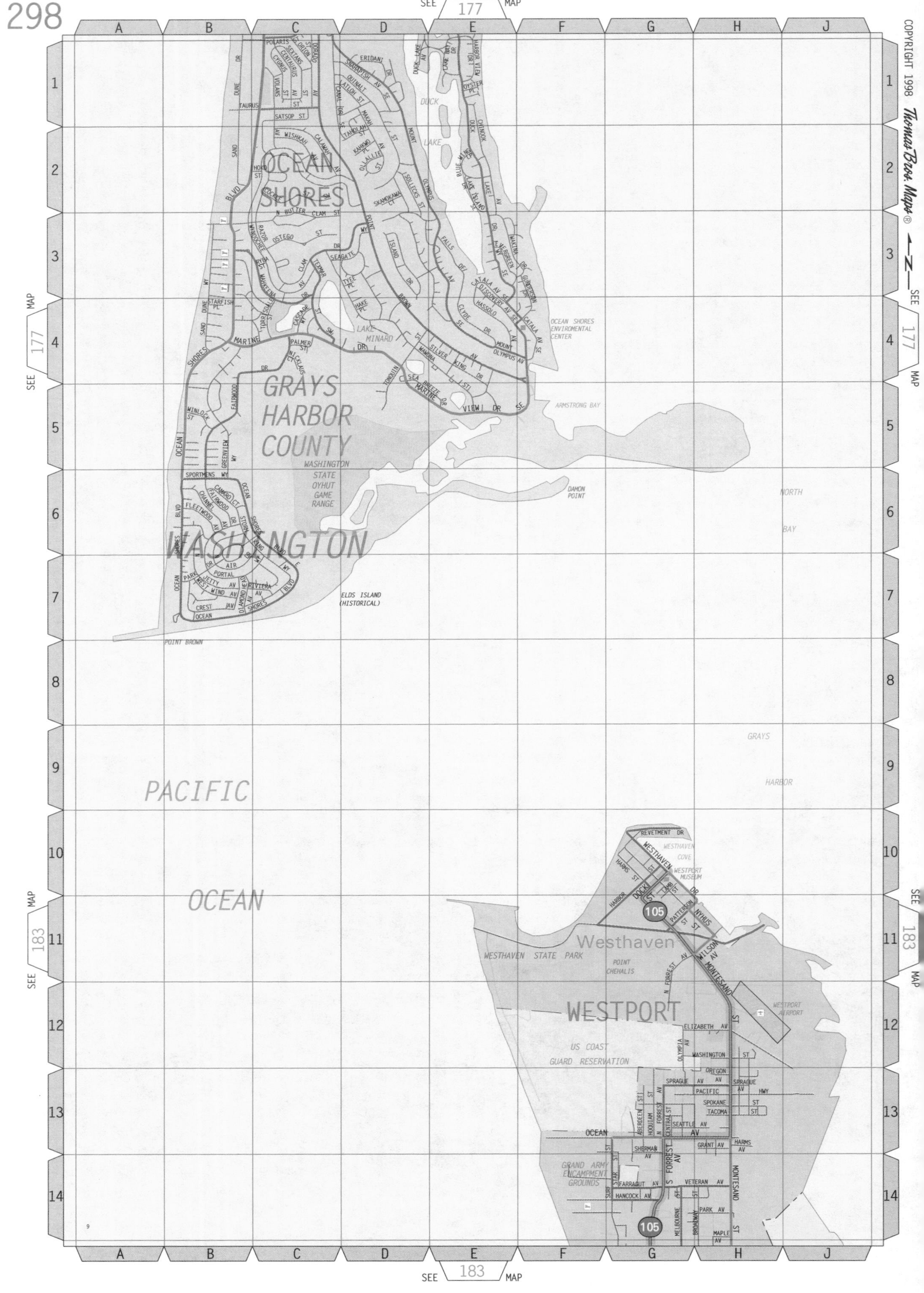
SEE 177 MAP
OCEAN SHORES
GRAYS HARBOR COUNTY
WASHINGTON
WASHINGTON STATE OYHUT GAME RANGE
DUCK LAKE
LAKE MINARD
OCEAN SHORES ENVIROMENTAL CENTER
ARMSTRONG BAY
DAMON POINT
NORTH BAY
ELDS ISLAND (HISTORICAL)
POINT BROWN
PACIFIC OCEAN
GRAYS HARBOR
WESTHAVEN COVE
WESTPORT MUSEUM
Westhaven
WESTHAVEN STATE PARK
POINT CHEHALIS
WESTPORT
WESTPORT AIRPORT
US COAST GUARD RESERVATION
GRAND ARMY ENCAMPMENT GROUNDS
105
SEE 183 MAP
PNW
DETAIL

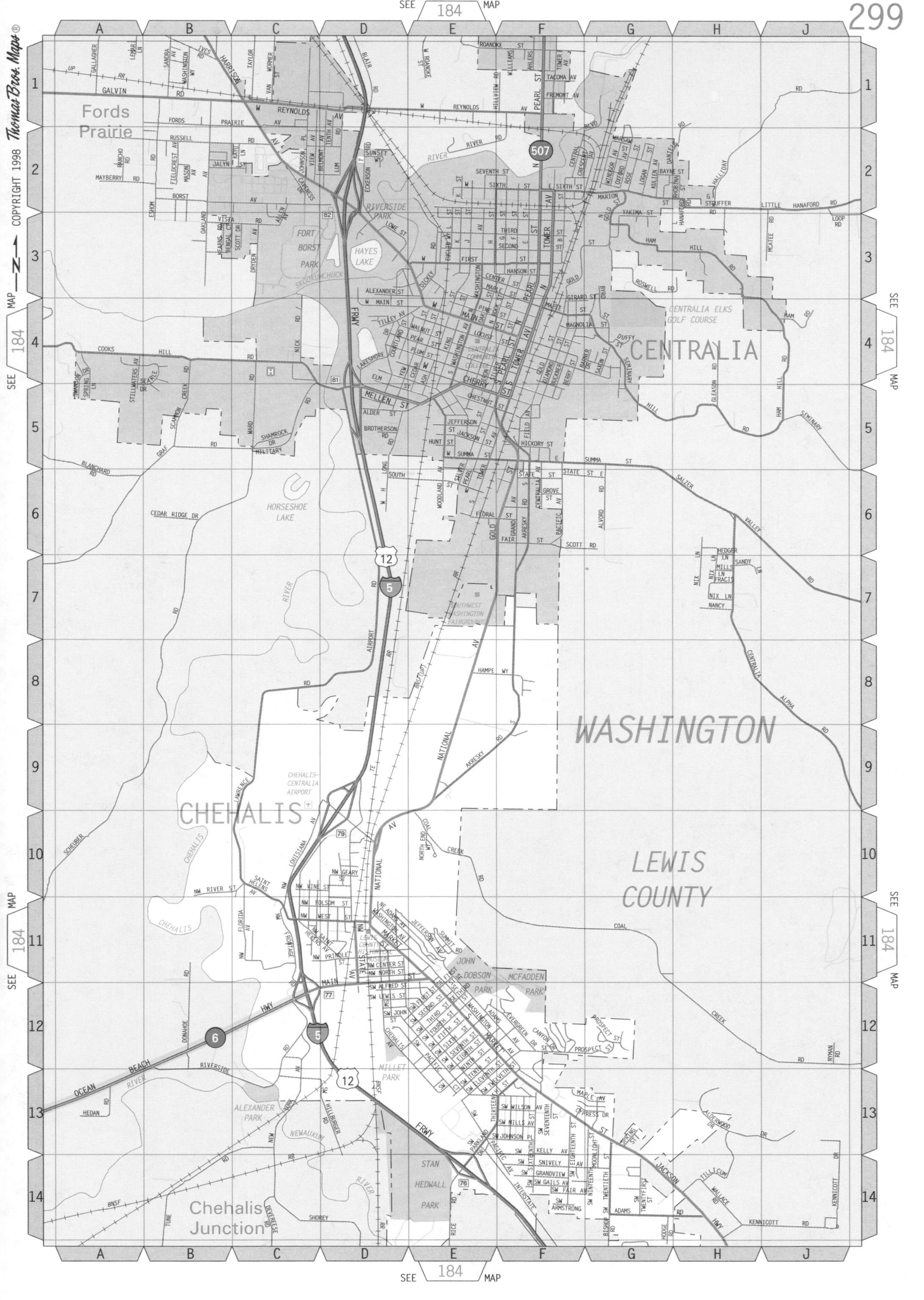
SEE 184 MAP
Fords Prairie
CENTRALIA
CENTRALIA ELKS GOLF COURSE
RIVERSIDE PARK
FORT BORST PARK
HAYES LAKE
HORSESHOE LAKE
SOUTHWEST WASHINGTON FAIRGROUNDS
WASHINGTON
CHEHALIS
CHEHALIS-CENTRALIA AIRPORT
LEWIS COUNTY
JOHN DOBSON PARK
MCFADDEN PARK
MILLET PARK
ALEXANDER PARK
STAN HEDWALL PARK
Chehalis Junction
PNW
DETAIL

COLUMBIA
RIVER
ASTORIA
Emerald Heights
CLATSOP COUNTY
OREGON
Jeffers Garden
Miles Crossing
YOUNGS BAY
MARITIME PARK
COLUMBIA RIVER MARITIME MUSEUM
UPPERTOWN FIREFIGHTERS MUSEUM
COLUMBIA FIELD
FORT ASTORIA
CLATSOP COMMUNITY COLLEGE
COXCOMB HILL
ASTORIA COLUMN
SHIVELY PARK
TAPIOLA PARK
CLATSOP STATE FOREST
FORESTRY HEADQUARTERS
4TH FAIRGROUNDS
DAGGETT POINT
FRY ISLAND
GRANT ISLAND
HAVEN ISLAND
YOUNGS BAY LIGHT
QUARANTINE ANCHORAGE
WARRENTON-ASTORIA HWY
NEHALEM HWY
WALLUSKI LOOP RD
LEWIS AND CLARK RD
YOUNGS RIVER LOOP RD
OREGON COAST HWY
COLUMBIA RIVER HWY

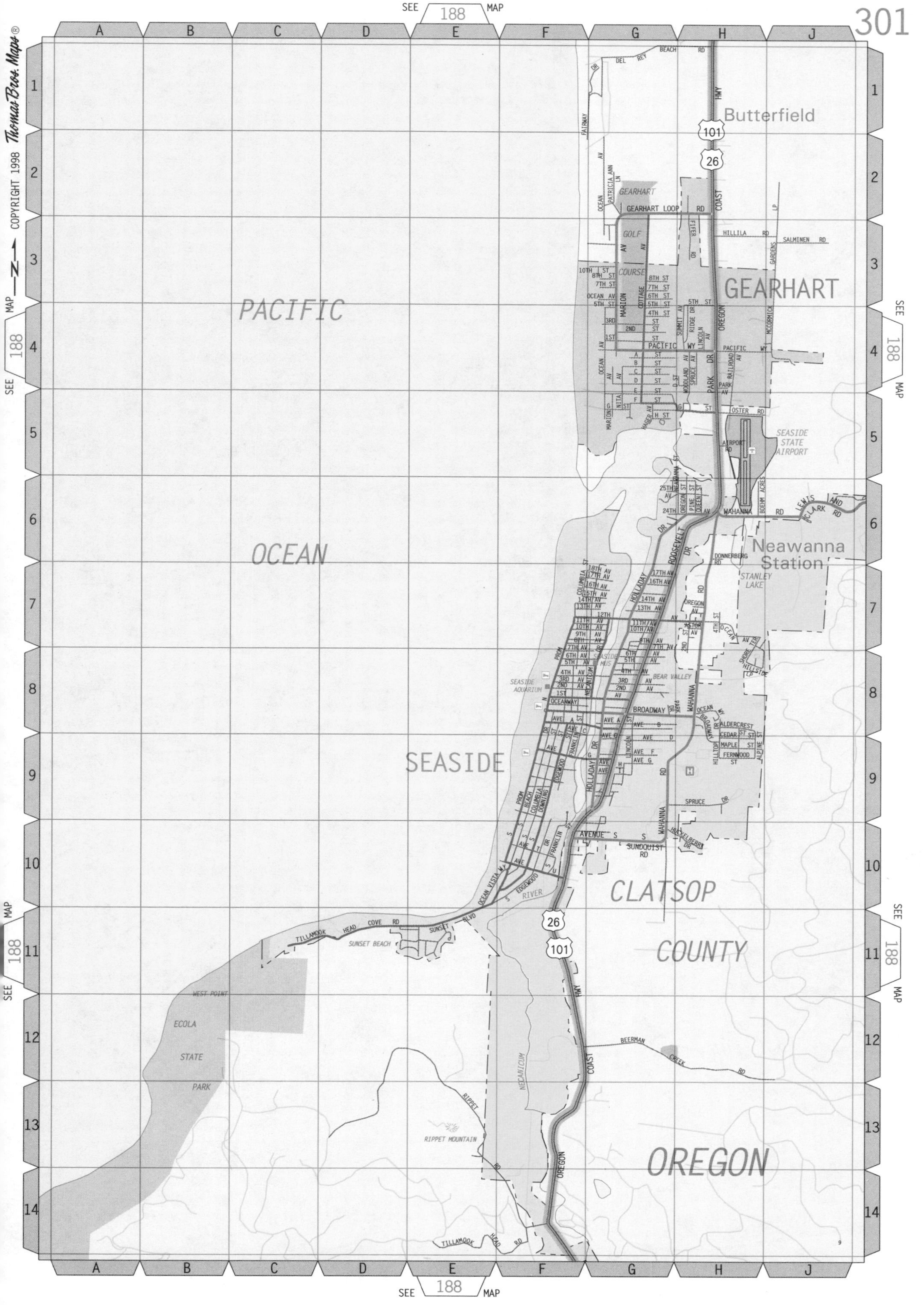
PACIFIC
OCEAN
Butterfield
GEARHART
Neawanna Station
SEASIDE
CLATSOP
COUNTY
OREGON
SEASIDE STATE AIRPORT
STANLEY LAKE
ECOLA STATE PARK
RIPPET MOUNTAIN
SUNSET BEACH
NECANICUM
SEE 188 MAP
Thomas Bros. Maps®
COPYRIGHT 1998
PNW
DETAIL

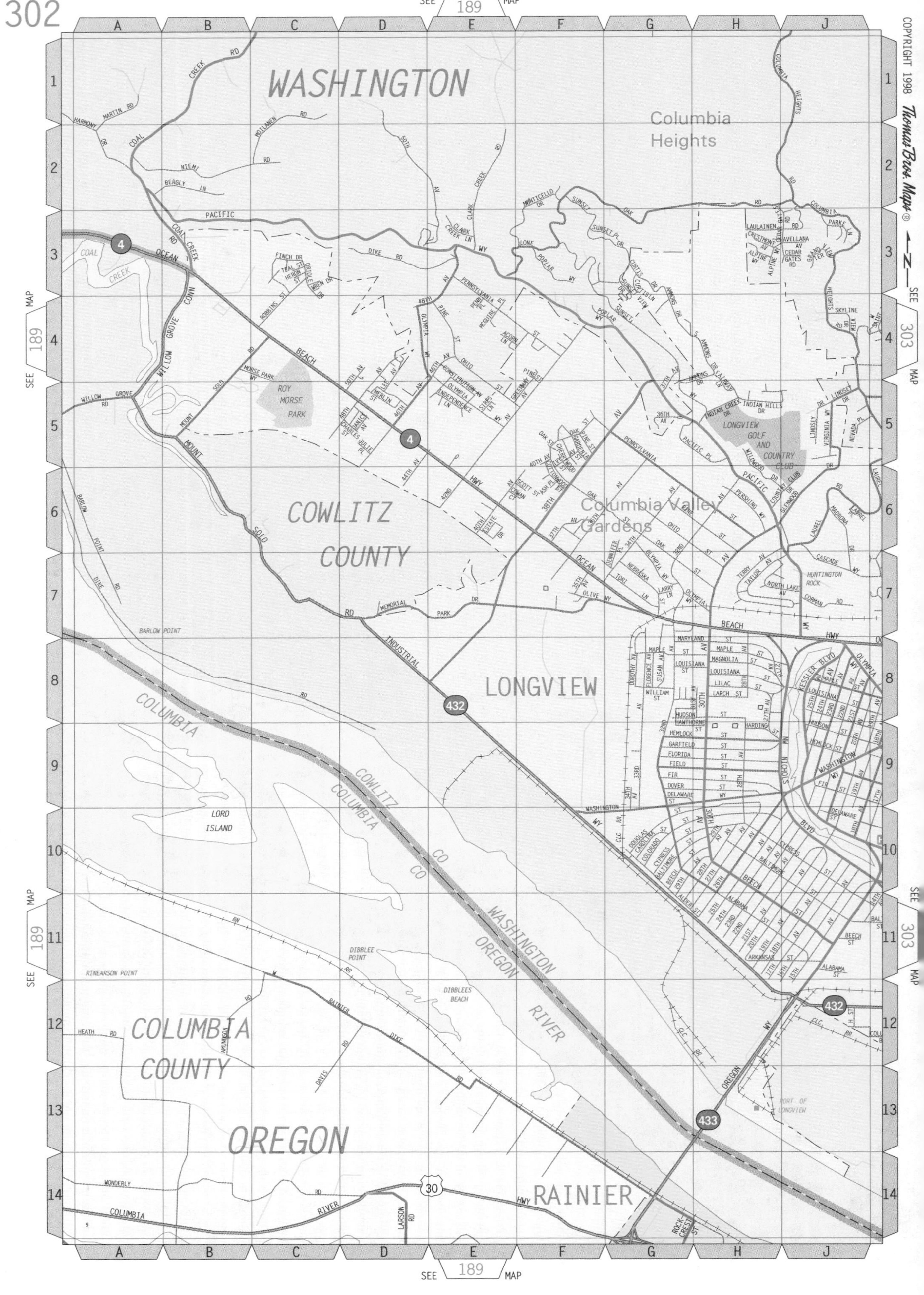

WASHINGTON
Columbia Heights
COWLITZ COUNTY
Columbia Valley Gardens
LONGVIEW
COLUMBIA COUNTY
OREGON
RAINIER
ROY MORSE PARK
LONGVIEW GOLF AND COUNTRY CLUB
LORD ISLAND
BARLOW POINT
DIBBLEE POINT
DIBBLEES BEACH
RINEARSON POINT
PORT OF LONGVIEW
COLUMBIA RIVER
WASHINGTON OREGON
OCEAN BEACH HWY
INDUSTRIAL WY
PACIFIC
COAL CREEK RD
WILLOW GROVE RD
MEMORIAL PARK DR
COLUMBIA RIVER HWY
SEE 189 MAP
SEE 303 MAP

PNW
DETAIL

SEE 189 MAP

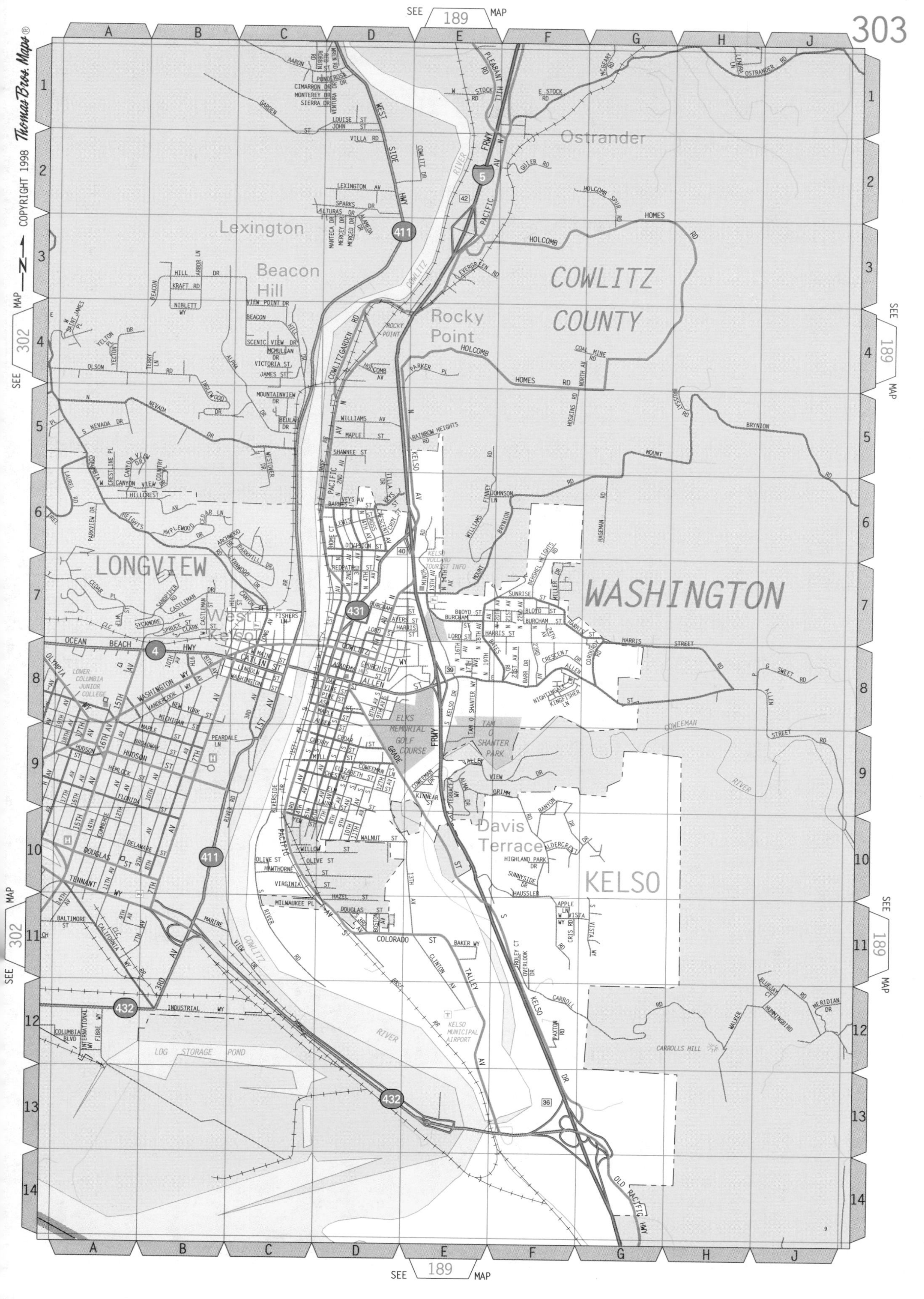

SEE 189 MAP

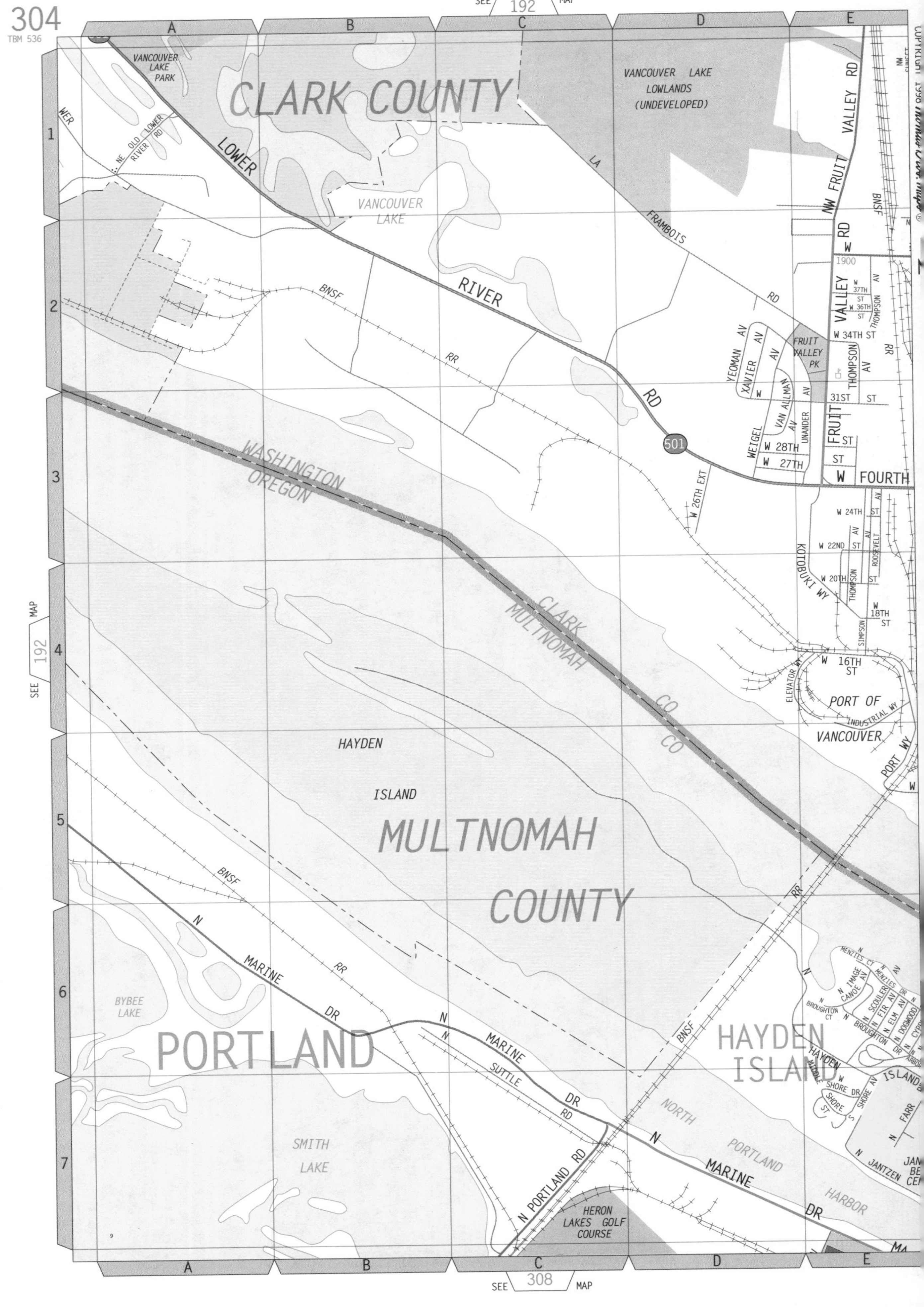
SEE 192 MAP
A
B
C
D
E
1
2
3
4
5
6
7
VANCOUVER LAKE PARK
CLARK COUNTY
VANCOUVER LAKE LOWLANDS (UNDEVELOPED)
NE OLD LOWER RIVER RD
LOWER RIVER RD
VANCOUVER LAKE
LA FRAMBOIS RD
NW FRUIT VALLEY RD
BNSF
BNSF RR
RR
501
W 26TH EXT
YEOMAN AV
XAVIER AV
VAN ALLMAN AV
UNANDER AV
WEIGEL AV
W 28TH
W 27TH
FRUIT VALLEY PK
THOMPSON AV
W 34TH ST
W 37TH ST
W 36TH ST
31ST ST
W FOURTH
FRUIT VALLEY RD
1900
WASHINGTON
OREGON
W 24TH ST
W 22ND ST
W 20TH ST
ROOSEVELT
KOTOBUKI WY
SIMPSON
W 18TH ST
W 16TH ST
ELEVATOR WY
PORT OF VANCOUVER
INDUSTRIAL WY
PORT WY
CLARK CO
MULTNOMAH CO
HAYDEN ISLAND
MULTNOMAH COUNTY
N MARINE DR
N SUTTLE RD
BYBEE LAKE
PORTLAND
SMITH LAKE
N PORTLAND RD
HERON LAKES GOLF COURSE
NORTH PORTLAND HARBOR
HAYDEN ISLAND
N MENZIES CT
N IMAGE AV
N CANOE AV
N BROUGHTON CT
N SCOULER AV
N FIR AV
N ELM AV
N BROUGHTON DR
N DOGWOOD
HAYDEN MIDDLE SHORE ST
W SHORE DR
SHORE AV
N JANTZEN
N FARR
SEE 192 MAP
SEE 308 MAP

PNW

DETAIL

SEE 192 MAP
SEE 306 MAP
SEE 309 MAP
PNW
DETAIL
E
F
G
H
J
1
2
3
4
5
6
7
VANCOUVER
MINNEHAHA
KIGGINS BOWL
LEVERICH PK
ARNOLD PARK
HIDDEN PK
SOUTHWEST WASH MED CTR (MEM CAMPUS)
CARTER PK
SCHOOL OF ARTS AND ACADEMICS HS
LEACH PARK
SAINT JAMES CEM
MILITARY CEM
ARNADA PK
JOHN BALL PK
CENTRAL PARK NORTH
REST AREA
VETERANS ADMINISTRATION HOSPITAL
WATERWORKS PARK
FIRE DEPT TRAINING CENTER
CLARK COMMUNITY COLLEGE
GENERAL GEORGE E MARSHALL PK
CLARK CO HIST MUS
CIVIC CENTER
SHERIFF
AMTRAK STATION
HUDSONS BAY HS
STATE SCHOOL FOR THE BLIND
QUARNBERG PK
VANCOUVER CITY CEMETERY
OFFICERS RW
FORT VANCOUVER NATIONAL HISTORIC SITE
PEARSON AIR MUSEUM
PEARSON AIRPORT
ESTHER SHORT PARK
OLD APPLE TREE PK
DOUBLETREE HOTEL AT THE QUAY
WATERFRONT PARK
COLUMBIA HOUSE
DOUBLETREE HOTEL COLUMBIA RIVER
DOUBLETREE HOTEL JANTZEN BEACH
JANTZEN BEACH CENTER
COLUMBIA RIVER
FOURTH PLAIN BLVD
MILL PLAIN BLVD
MCLOUGHLIN BLVD
EVERGREEN BLVD
FORT VANCOUVER WY
SAINT JOHNS BLVD
LEWIS AND CLARK HWY
COLUMBIA WY
FRWY
BNSF RR
HAYDEN ISLAND DR
WASHINGTON ST
MAIN ST
BROADWAY
COLUMBIA ST
GRAND BLVD

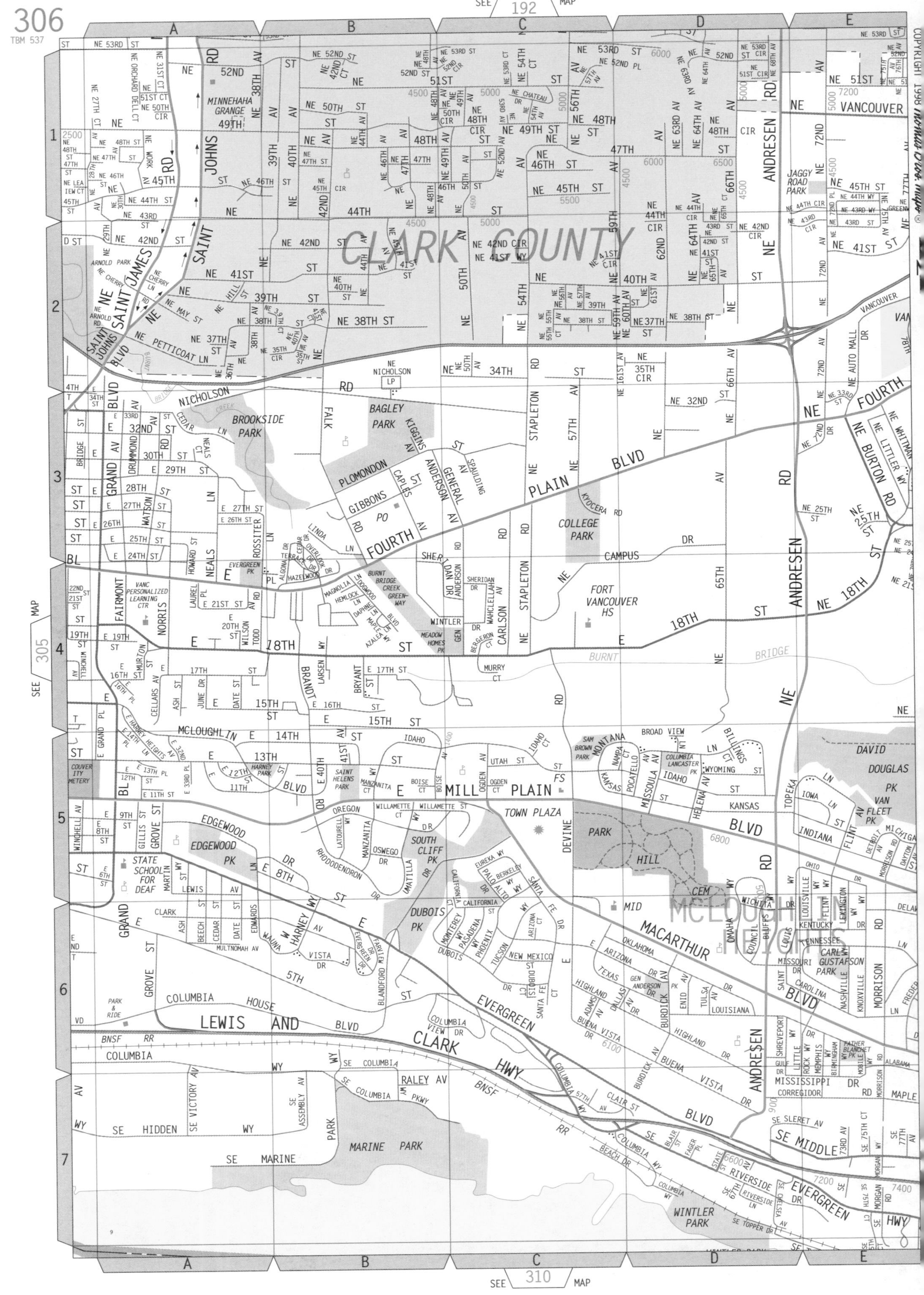
SEE 192 MAP
SEE 305 MAP
SEE 310 MAP
A
B
C
D
E
1
2
3
4
5
6
7
CLARK COUNTY
MINNEHAHA GRANGE
JAGGY ROAD PARK
ARNOLD PARK
BROOKSIDE PARK
BAGLEY PARK
COLLEGE PARK
FORT VANCOUVER HS
VANC PERSONALIZED LEARNING CTR
BURNT BRIDGE CREEK GREENWAY
MEADOW HOMES PK
SAM BROWN PARK
COLUMBIA LANCASTER PK
DAVID DOUGLAS PK
VAN FLEET PK
SAINT HELENS PARK
HARNEY PARK
EDGEWOOD PK
SOUTH CLIFF PK
DUBOIS PK
TOWN PLAZA
PARK HILL CEM
STATE SCHOOL FOR DEAF
MCLOUGHLIN HEIGHTS
CARL GUSTAFSON PARK
FATHER BLANCHET PK
PARK & RIDE
MARINE PARK
WINTLER PARK
SAINT JOHNS RD
SAINT JAMES RD
NE FOURTH PLAIN BLVD
E FOURTH PLAIN BLVD
NICHOLSON RD
E 18TH ST
NE 18TH ST
E MILL PLAIN BLVD
MCLOUGHLIN BLVD
E EVERGREEN BLVD
MACARTHUR BLVD
LEWIS AND CLARK HWY
COLUMBIA HOUSE BLVD
SE MIDDLE WY
SE EVERGREEN HWY
SE HIDDEN WY
SE MARINE PARK WY
ANDRESEN RD
NE ANDRESEN RD
STAPLETON RD
FALK RD
BRANDT RD
DEVINE RD
GRAND BLVD
BNSF RR
BURNT BRIDGE CREEK
NE VANCOUVER MALL DR
NE BURTON RD
SEE 192 MAP
SEE 310 MAP
COPYRIGHT 1998 Thomas Bros. Maps ®

SEE 192 MAP

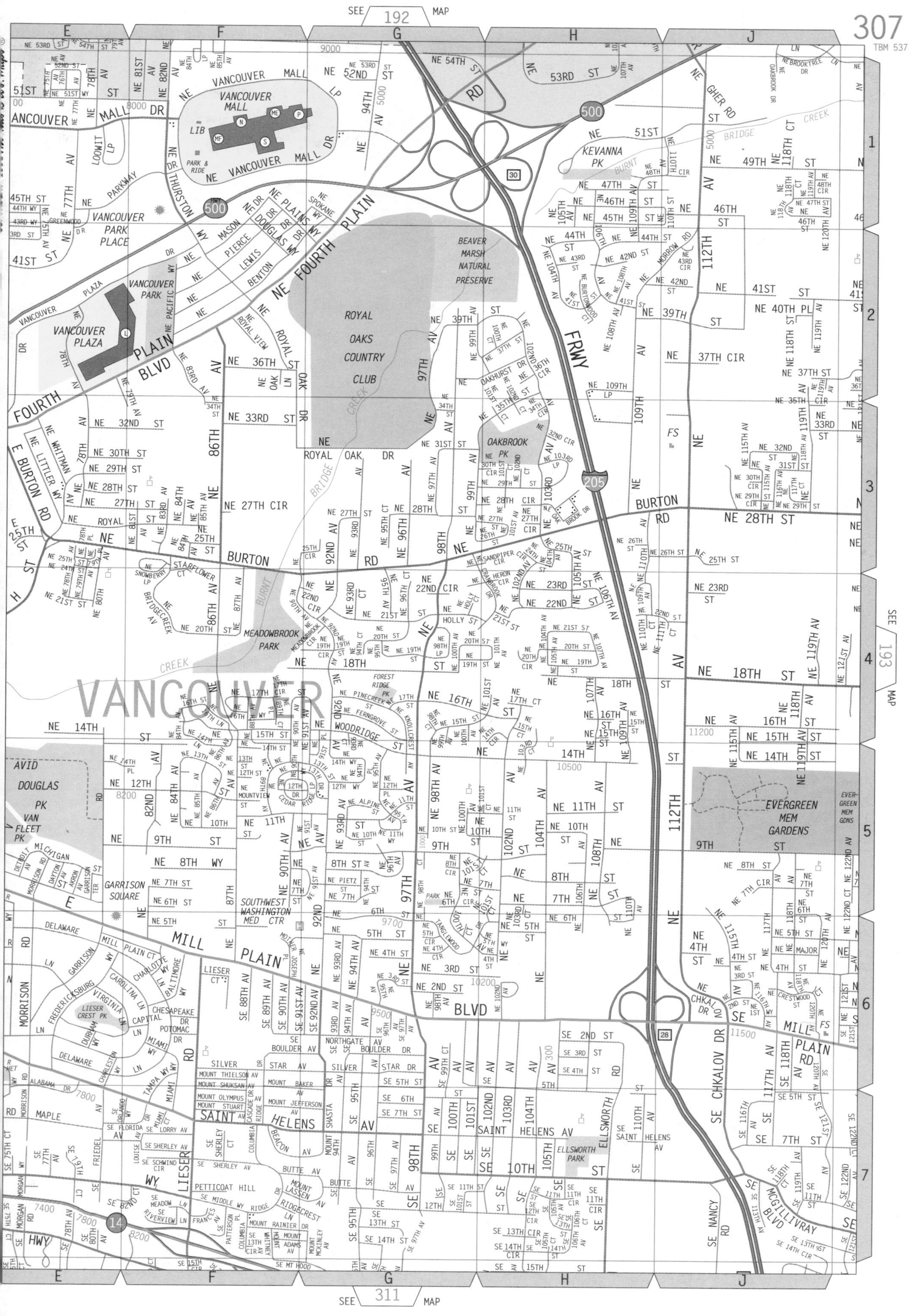

SEE 193 MAP
SEE 311 MAP

SEE 304 MAP

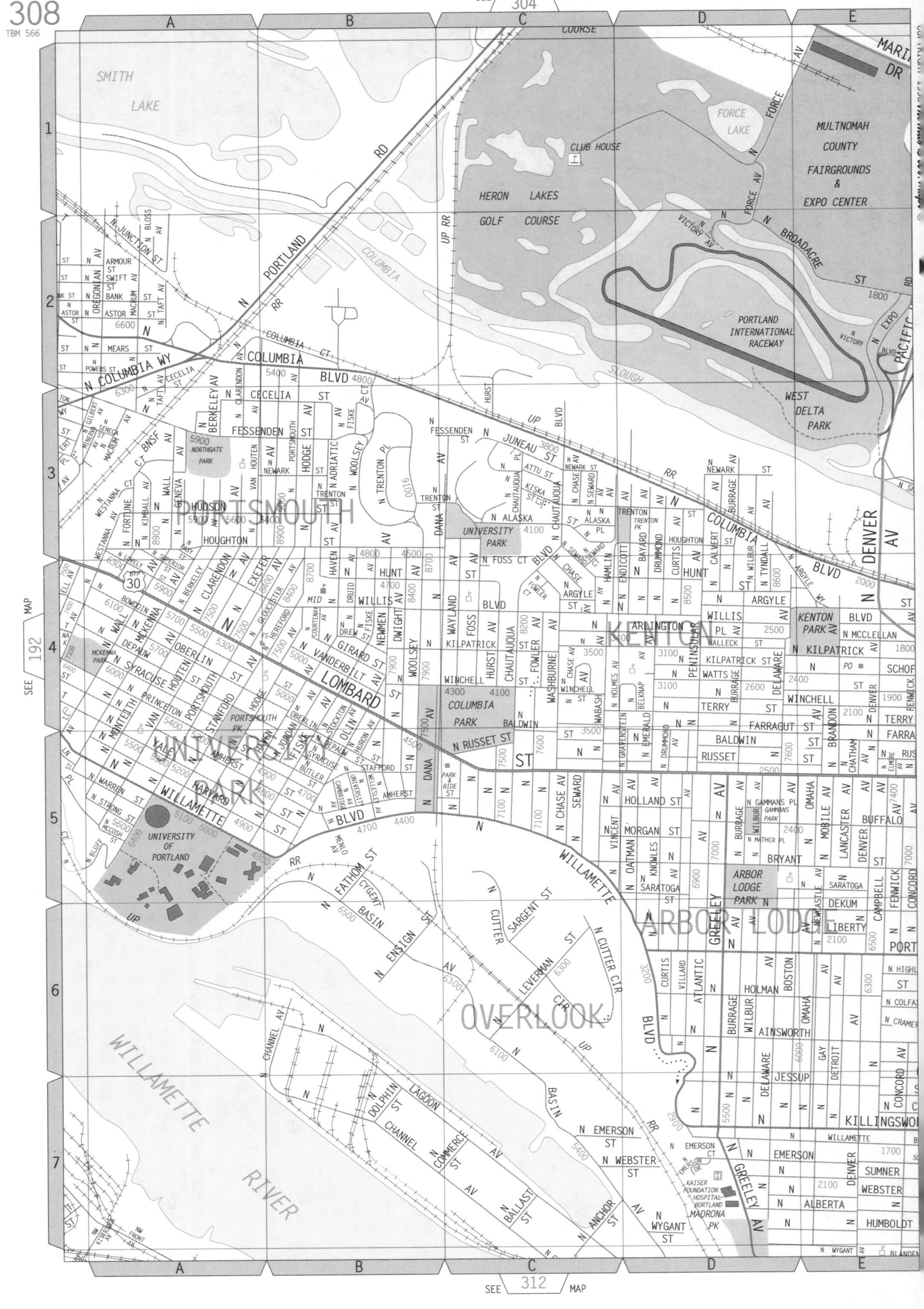

SEE 192 MAP

SEE 312 MAP

PNW

DETAIL

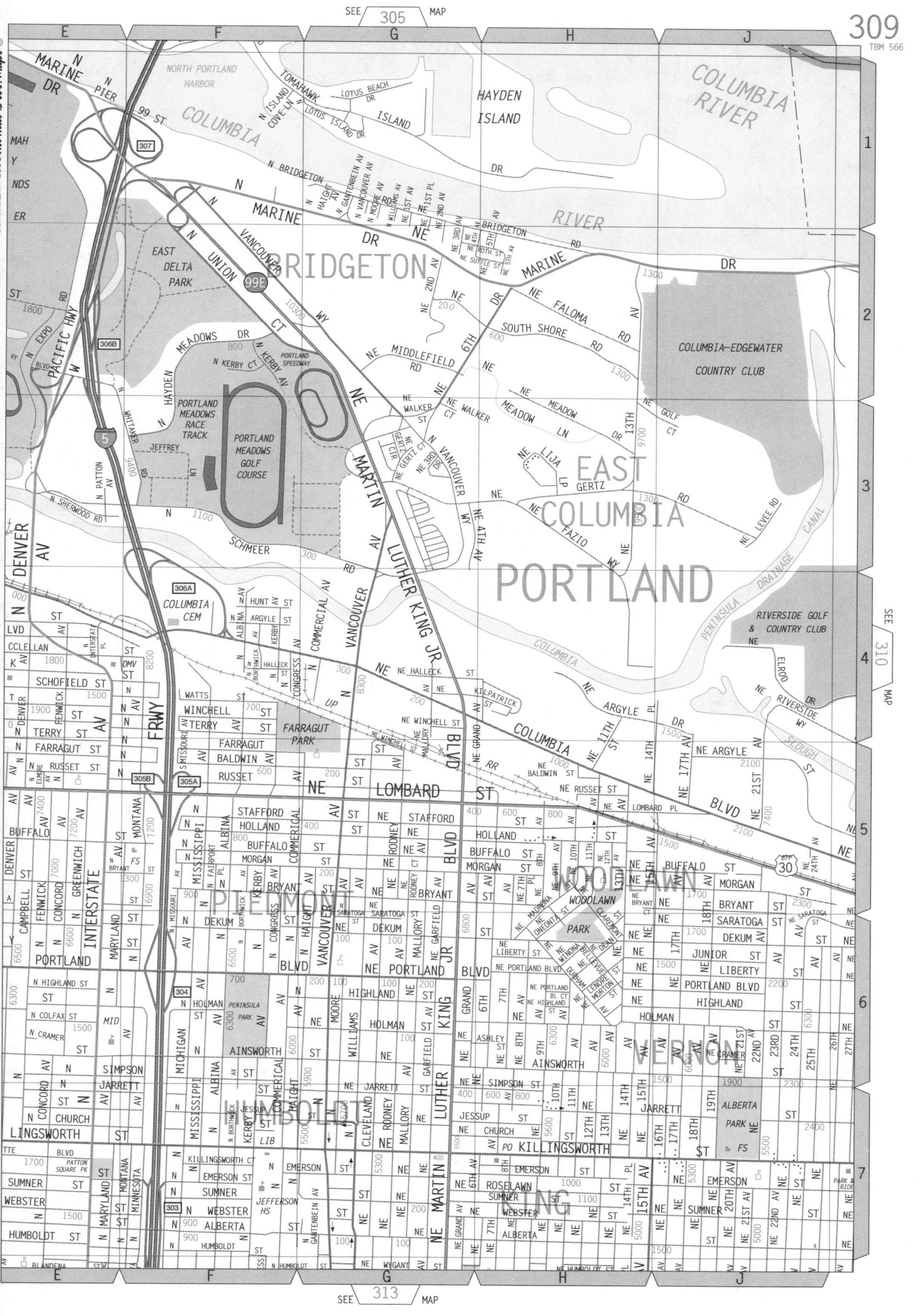
SEE 305 MAP
COLUMBIA RIVER
HAYDEN ISLAND
NORTH PORTLAND HARBOR
BRIDGETON
EAST DELTA PARK
PORTLAND MEADOWS RACE TRACK
PORTLAND MEADOWS GOLF COURSE
COLUMBIA-EDGEWATER COUNTRY CLUB
EAST COLUMBIA
PORTLAND
RIVERSIDE GOLF & COUNTRY CLUB
PENINSULA DRAINAGE CANAL
COLUMBIA SLOUGH
COLUMBIA CEM
FARRAGUT PARK
PIEDMONT
WOODLAWN
WOODLAWN PARK
VERNON
HUMBOLDT
KING
PENINSULA PARK
ALBERTA PARK
JEFFERSON HS
PATTON SQUARE PK
MARTIN LUTHER KING JR BLVD
INTERSTATE AV
FRWY
NE LOMBARD ST
COLUMBIA BLVD
PORTLAND BLVD
KILLINGSWORTH
SEE 310 MAP
SEE 313 MAP
PNW
DETAIL

SEE 306 MAP

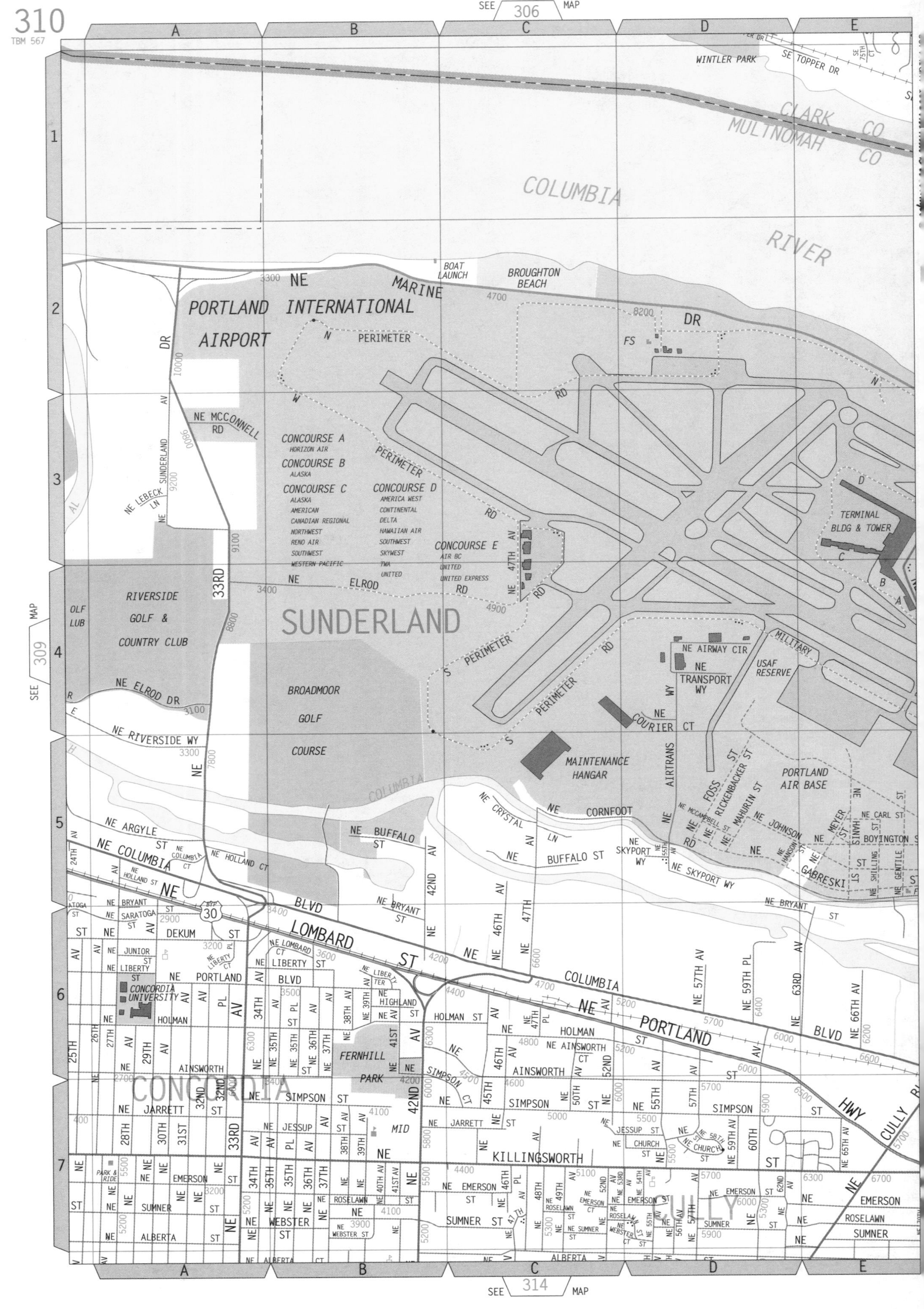

SEE 309 MAP
SEE 314 MAP

SEE 307 MAP

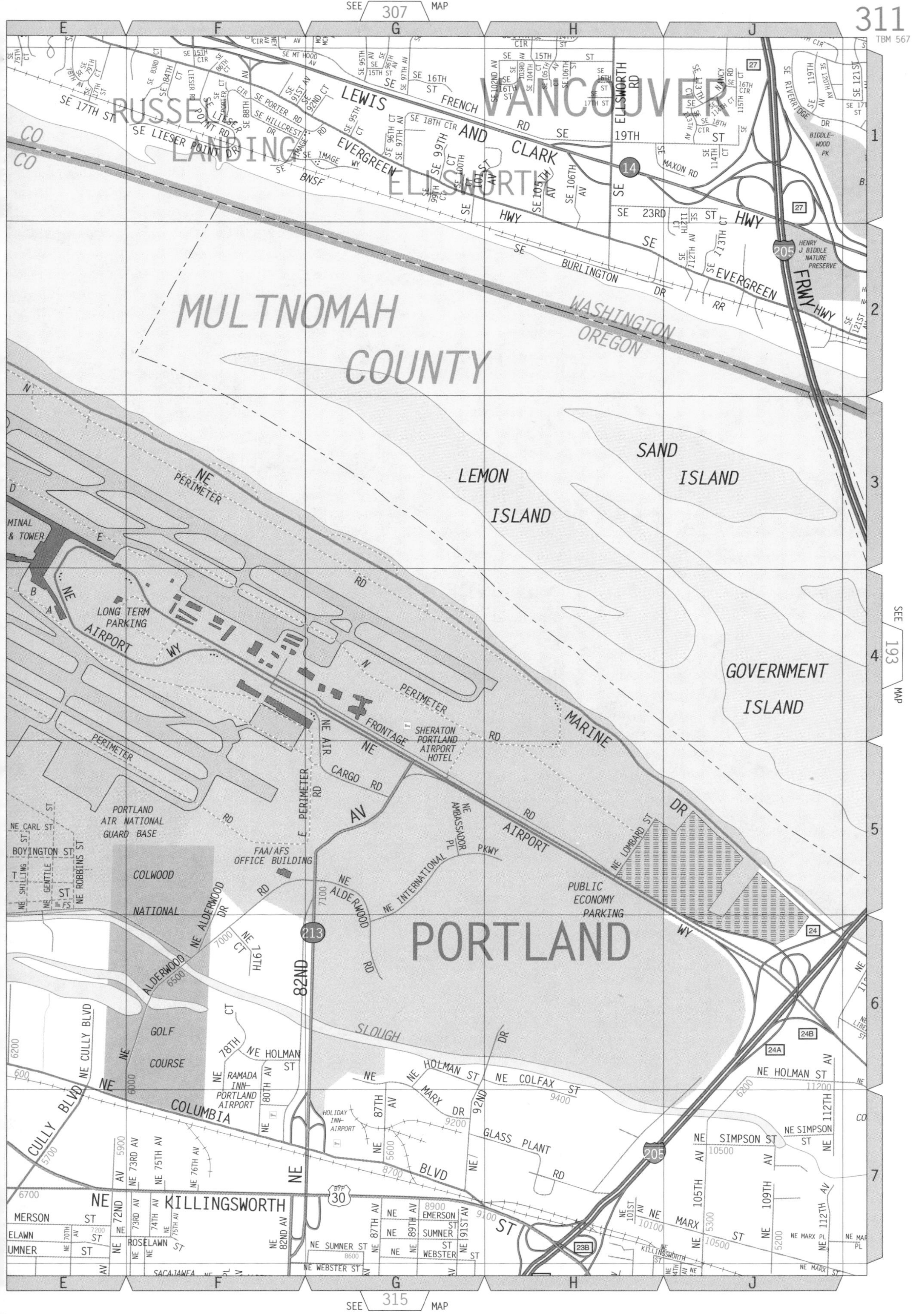

SEE 193 MAP

SEE 315 MAP

SEE 308 MAP

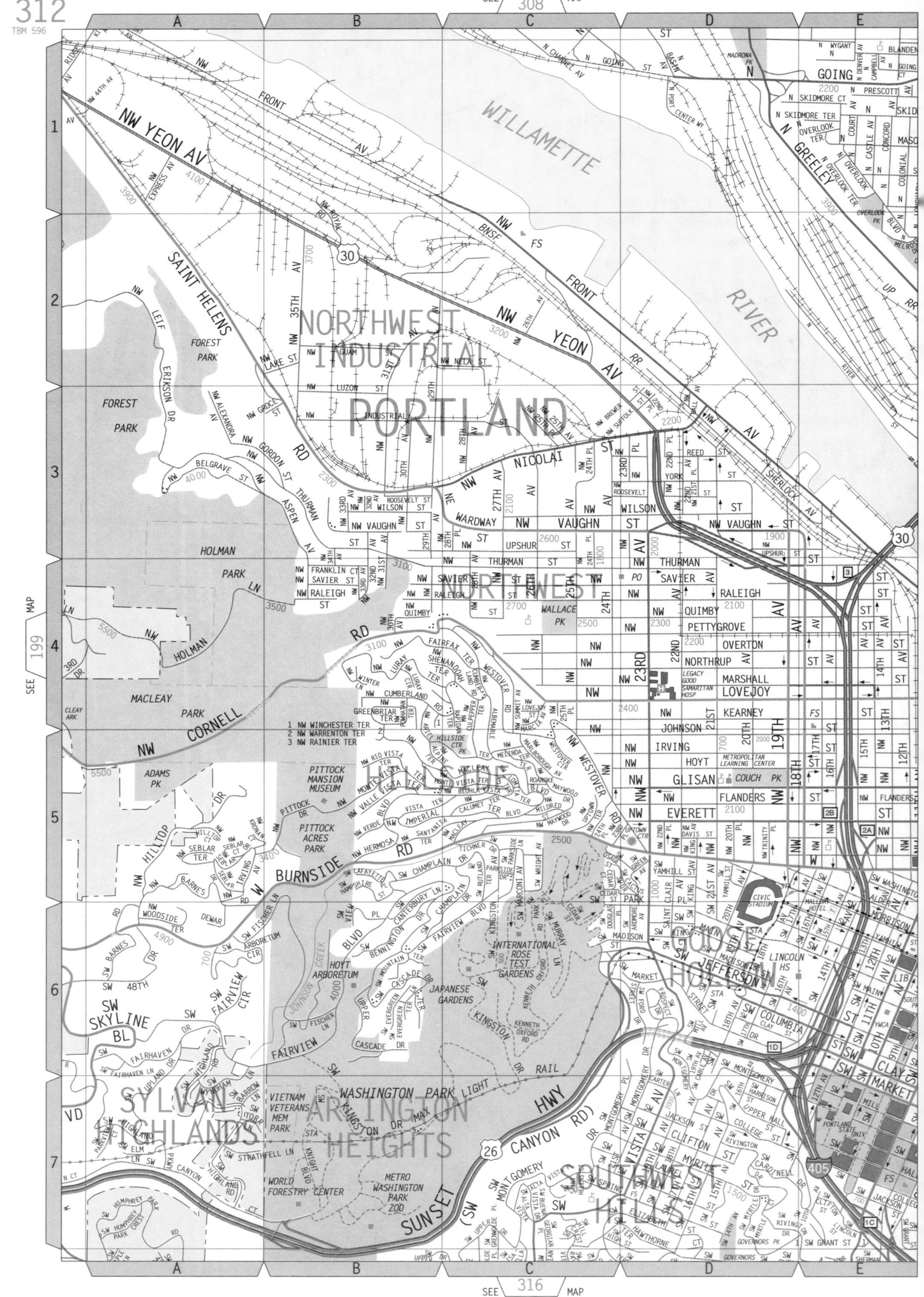

SEE 199 MAP

SEE 316 MAP

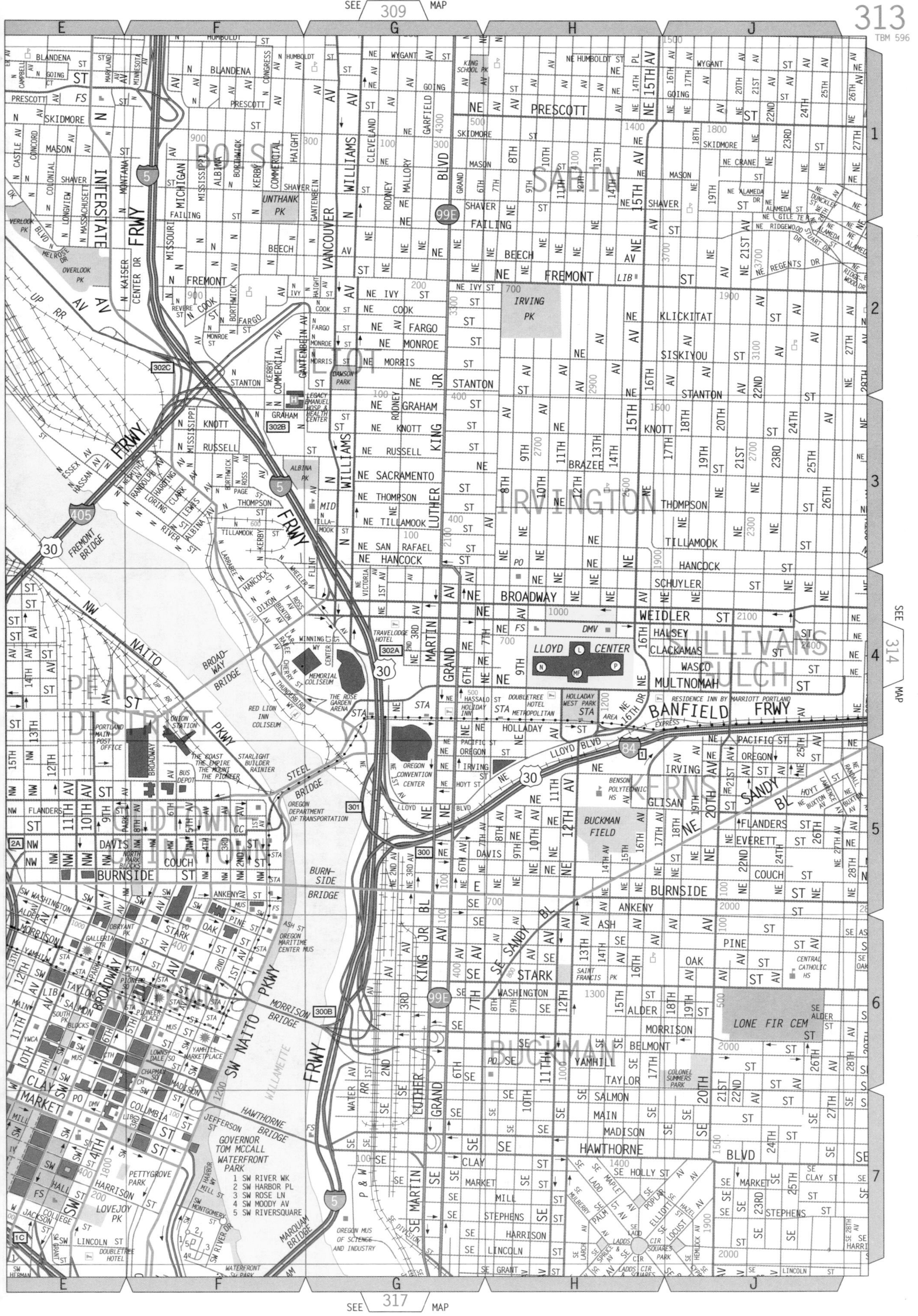
SEE 309 MAP
E
F
G
H
J
1
2
3
4
5
6
7
BOISE
SABIN
ELIOT
IRVINGTON
SULLIVANS GULCH
PEARL DISTRICT
OLD TOWN CHINATOWN
KERNS
BUCKMAN
LLOYD CENTER
LONE FIR CEM
IRVING PK
UNTHANK PK
BUCKMAN FIELD
BANFIELD FRWY
INTERSTATE AV
FRWY
BROADWAY
BURNSIDE
HAWTHORNE BLVD
FREMONT
MARTIN LUTHER KING JR BLVD
GRAND AV
WILLIAMS AV
VANCOUVER AV
FREMONT BRIDGE
BROADWAY BRIDGE
STEEL BRIDGE
BURNSIDE BRIDGE
MORRISON BRIDGE
HAWTHORNE BRIDGE
MARQUAM BRIDGE
SW NAITO PKWY
WILLAMETTE
GOVERNOR TOM MCCALL WATERFRONT PARK
1 SW RIVER WK
2 SW HARBOR PL
3 SW ROSE LN
4 SW MOODY AV
5 SW RIVERSQUARE
MEMORIAL COLISEUM
THE ROSE GARDEN ARENA
OREGON CONVENTION CENTER
OREGON MUS OF SCIENCE AND INDUSTRY
SEE 314 MAP
SEE 317 MAP

SEE 310 MAP 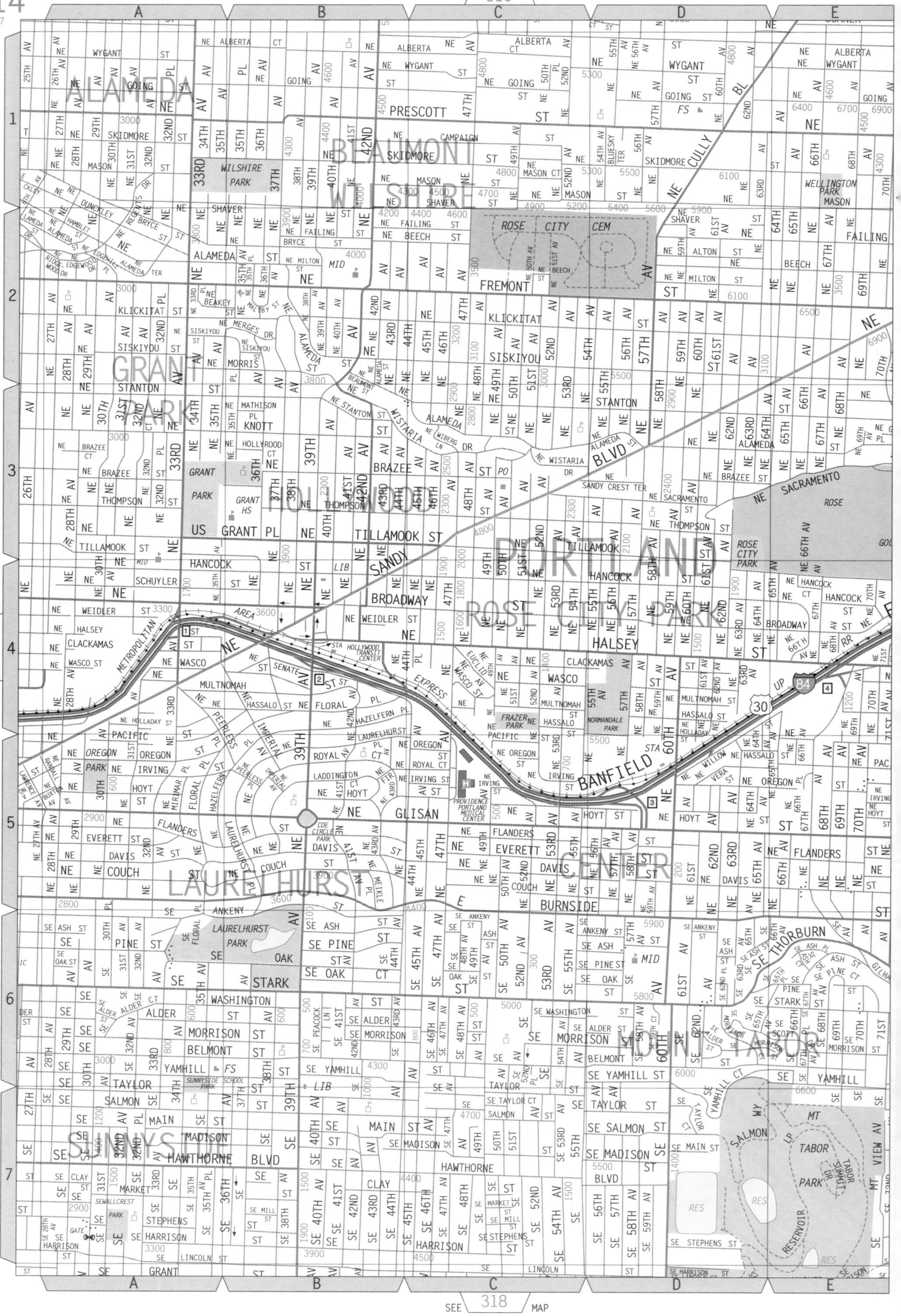
SEE 313 MAP
SEE 318 MAP

A B C D E

1 2 3 4 5 6 7

ALAMEDA
BEAUMONT WILSHIRE
GRANT PARK
HOLLYWOOD
PORTLAND
ROSE CITY PARK
LAURELHURST
CENTER
MOUNT TABOR
SUNNYSIDE

WILSHIRE PARK
ROSE CITY CEM
GRANT PARK
GRANT HS
ROSE CITY PARK
FRAZER PARK
NORMANDALE PARK
LAURELHURST PARK
SUNNYSIDE SCHOOL PARK
SEWALLCREST PARK
WELLINGTON PARK
COE CIRCLE PARK
MT TABOR PARK
PROVIDENCE PORTLAND MEDICAL CENTER
HOLLYWOOD TRANSIT CENTER

NE SANDY BLVD
NE ALAMEDA
NE FREMONT ST
NE BROADWAY
NE HALSEY ST
BANFIELD EXPRESSWAY
NE GLISAN ST
E BURNSIDE ST
SE STARK ST
SE HAWTHORNE BLVD
SE BELMONT ST
NE CULLY BL
METROPOLITAN AREA EXPRESS

SEE 311 MAP

E F G H J

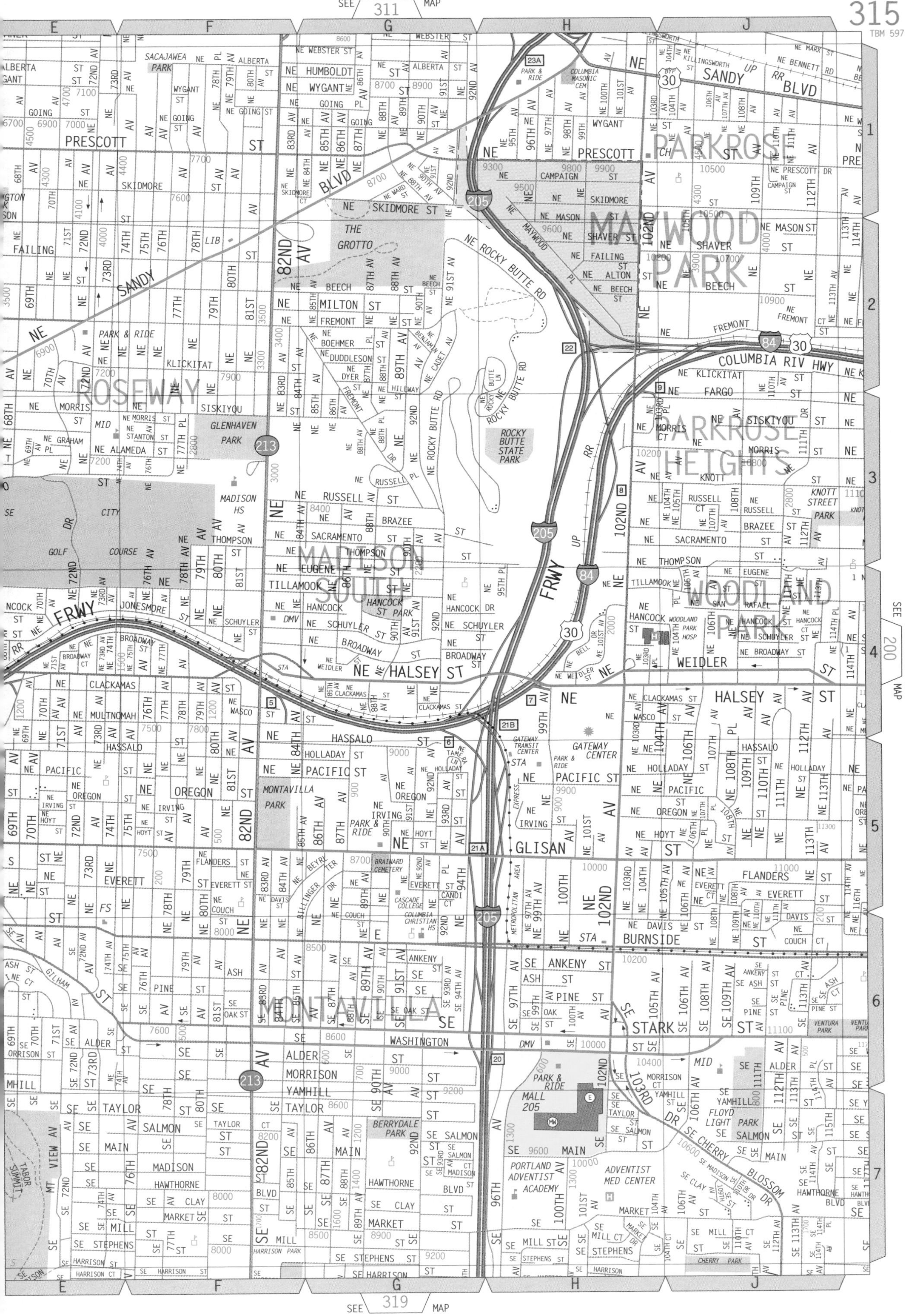

1 2 3 4 5 6 7

PNW

DETAIL

SEE 200 MAP

E F G H J

SEE 319 MAP

SEE 312 MAP

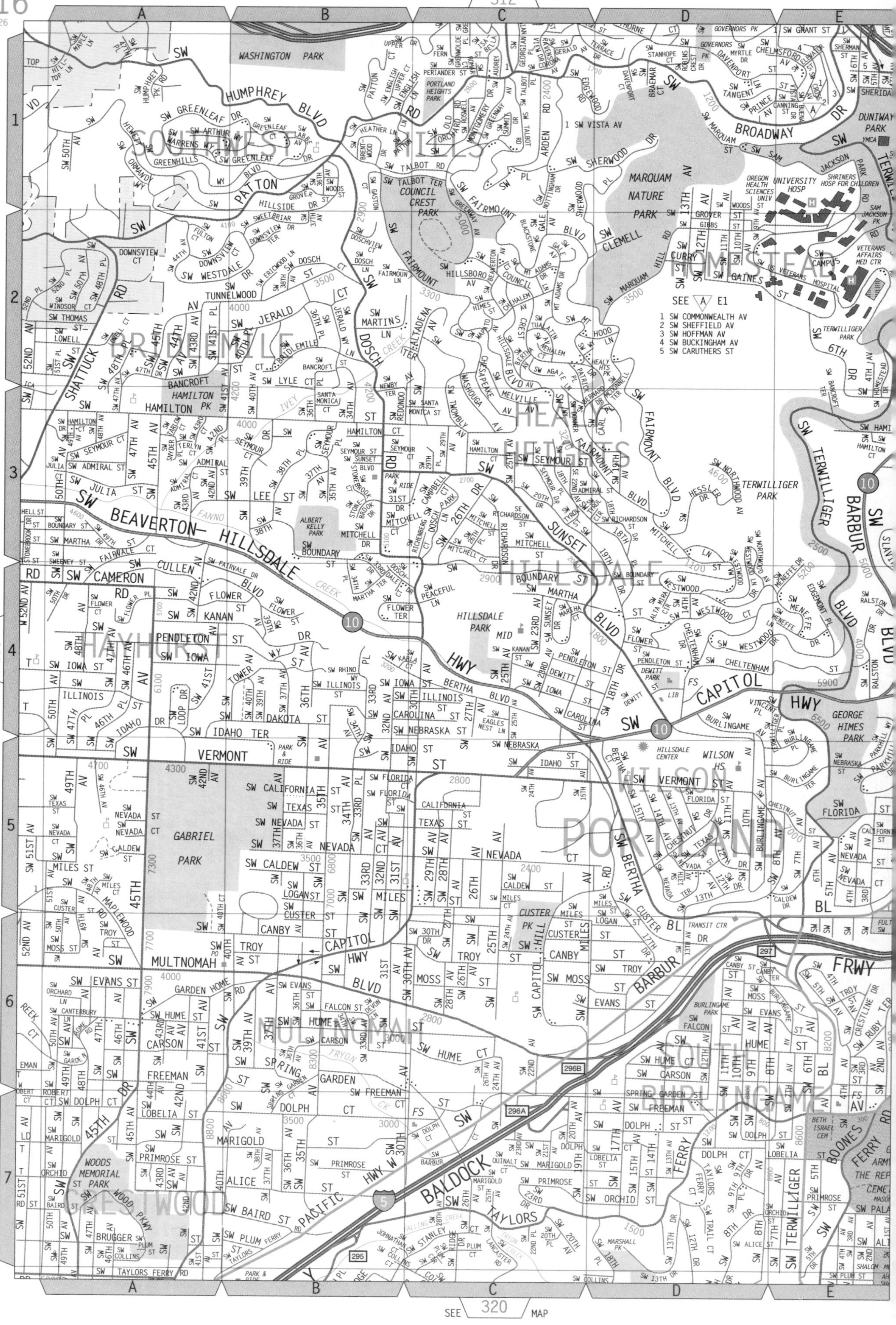

SEE 199 MAP

SOUTHWEST HILLS

WASHINGTON PARK

PORTLAND HEIGHTS PARK

COUNCIL CREST PARK

MARQUAM NATURE PARK

DUNIWAY PARK

HOMESTEAD

OREGON HEALTH SCIENCES UNIV

UNIVERSITY HOSP

SHRINERS HOSP FOR CHILDREN

VETERANS AFFAIRS MED CTR

BRIDLEMILE

HAMILTON PK

ALBERT KELLY PARK

HEALY HEIGHTS

TERWILLIGER PARK

HILLSDALE

HILLSDALE PARK

HAYHURST

WILSON HS

PORTLAND

GABRIEL PARK

CUSTER PK

GEORGE HIMES PARK

MULTNOMAH

SOUTH BURLINGAME

BURLINGAME PARK

BETH ISRAEL CEM

WOODS MEMORIAL PARK

CRESTWOOD

MARSHALL PK

SEE A E1
1 SW COMMONWEALTH AV
2 SW SHEFFIELD AV
3 SW HOFFMAN AV
4 SW BUCKINGHAM AV
5 SW CARUTHERS ST

SW BEAVERTON-HILLSDALE HWY

SW CAPITOL HWY

SW BARBUR BLVD

SW TERWILLIGER BLVD

SW BROADWAY DR

SW HUMPHREY BLVD

SW PATTON RD

SW VERMONT ST

SW MULTNOMAH BLVD

SW TAYLORS FERRY RD

BALDOCK FRWY

SEE 320 MAP

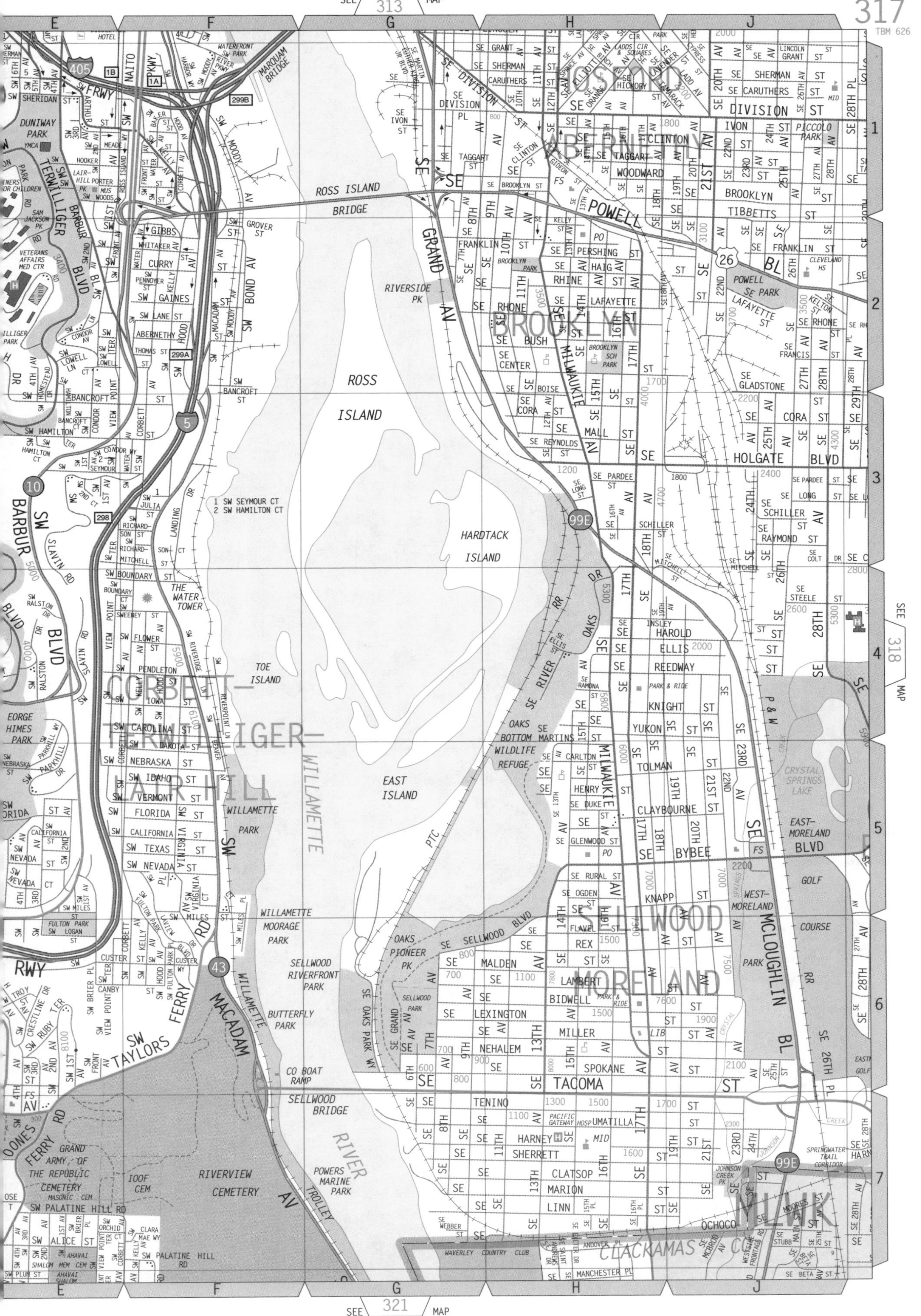
SEE 313 MAP
SEE 321 MAP
SEE 318 MAP
ROSS ISLAND BRIDGE
ROSS ISLAND
HARDTACK ISLAND
TOE ISLAND
EAST ISLAND
WILLAMETTE RIVER
SELLWOOD BRIDGE
BROOKLYN
SELLWOOD
MORELAND
CORBETT-TERWILLIGER-LAIR HILL
HOSFORD ABERNETHY
MLWK
CLACKAMAS CO
DUNIWAY PARK
VETERANS AFFAIRS MED CTR
EORGE HIMES PARK
RIVERSIDE PK
OAKS BOTTOM WILDLIFE REFUGE
OAKS PIONEER PK
WILLAMETTE PARK
WILLAMETTE MOORAGE PARK
SELLWOOD RIVERFRONT PARK
BUTTERFLY PARK
SELLWOOD PARK
POWERS MARINE PARK
CO BOAT RAMP
RIVERVIEW CEMETERY
IOOF CEM
GRAND ARMY OF THE REPUBLIC CEMETERY
MASONIC CEM
CRYSTAL SPRINGS LAKE
EAST-MORELAND GOLF COURSE
WEST-MORELAND PARK
POWELL SE PARK
CLEVELAND HS
BROOKLYN SCH PARK
THE WATER TOWER
WAVERLEY COUNTRY CLUB
PACIFIC GATEWAY HOSP
SPRINGWATER TRAIL CORRIDOR
JOHNSON CREEK PK
SE DIVISION ST
SE POWELL BL
SE HOLGATE BLVD
SE BYBEE BLVD
SE TACOMA ST
SE MILWAUKIE AV
SE MCLOUGHLIN BL
SE GRAND AV
SE SELLWOOD BLVD
SW MACADAM AV
SW BARBUR BLVD
SW TERWILLIGER BLVD
SW TAYLORS FERRY RD
SW PALATINE HILL RD
SE RIVER DR
SE OAKS PARK WY
405
5
10
26
43
99E
1 SW SEYMOUR CT
2 SW HAMILTON CT
E F G H J
1 2 3 4 5 6 7

SEE 314 MAP

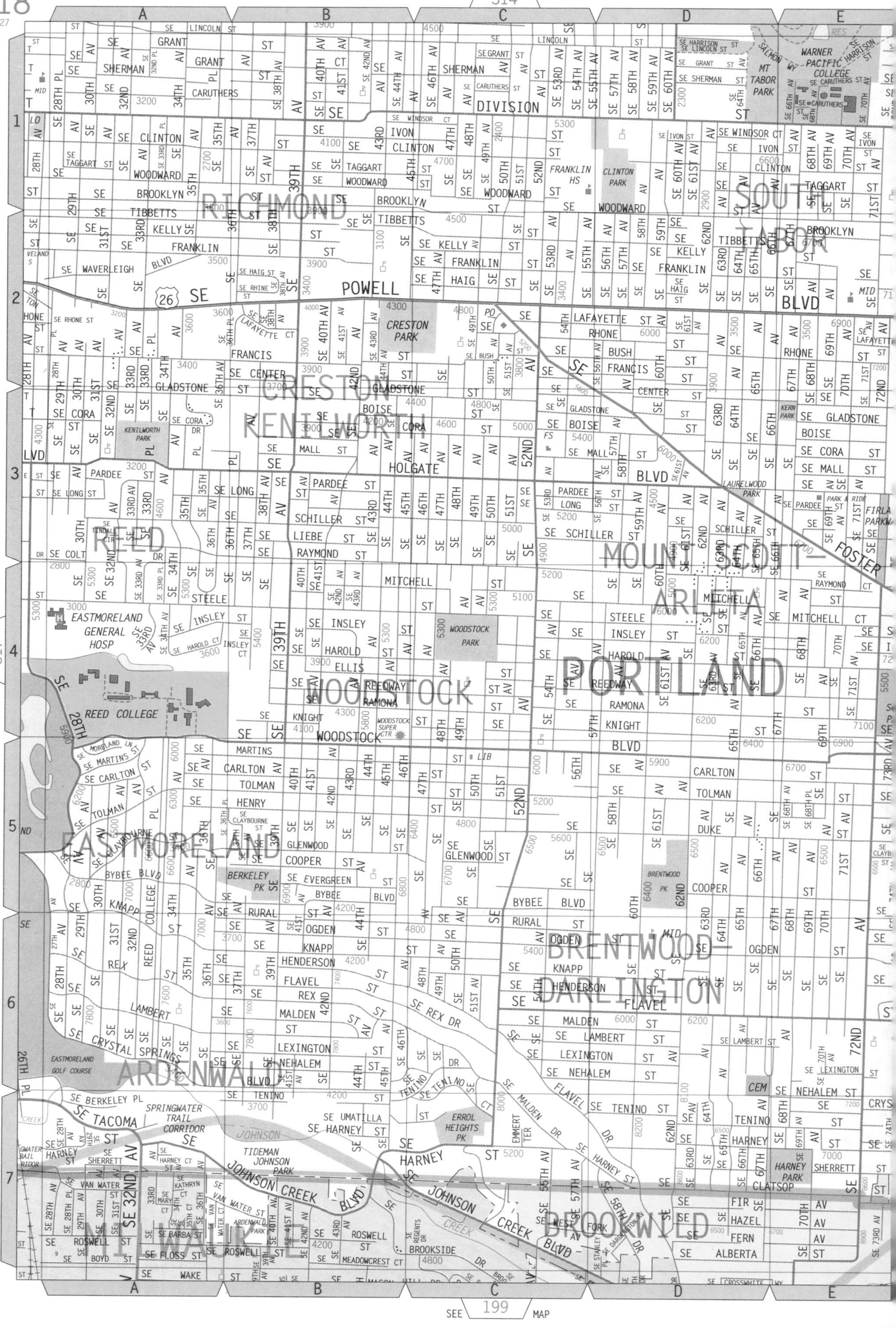

A B C D E

1 2 3 4 5 6 7

RICHMOND

SOUTH TABOR

CRESTON KENILWORTH

REED

MOUNT SCOTT-ARLETA

PORTLAND

WOODSTOCK

EASTMORELAND

BRENTWOOD-DARLINGTON

ARDENWALD

MILWAUKIE

BROOKWILD

SE DIVISION ST

SE POWELL BLVD

26

SE HOLGATE BLVD

SE WOODSTOCK BLVD

SE FOSTER

SE 39TH AV

SE 52ND AV

SE 28TH AV

SE 32ND AV

SE FLAVEL

SE TACOMA ST

SE JOHNSON CREEK BLVD

SE CRYSTAL SPRINGS BLVD

SE BYBEE BLVD

SE REX DR

WARNER PACIFIC COLLEGE

MT TABOR PARK

FRANKLIN HS

CLINTON PARK

CRESTON PARK

KENILWORTH PARK

KERN PARK

LAURELWOOD PARK

WOODSTOCK PARK

WOODSTOCK SUPER CTR

EASTMORELAND GENERAL HOSP

REED COLLEGE

BERKELEY PK

BRENTWOOD PK

EASTMORELAND GOLF COURSE

SPRINGWATER TRAIL CORRIDOR

TIDEMAN JOHNSON PARK

ERROL HEIGHTS PK

ARDENWALD PARK

HARNEY PARK

CEM

LIB

PO

FS

MID

RES

SEE 317 MAP

SEE 199 MAP

PNW

DETAIL

SEE 315 MAP

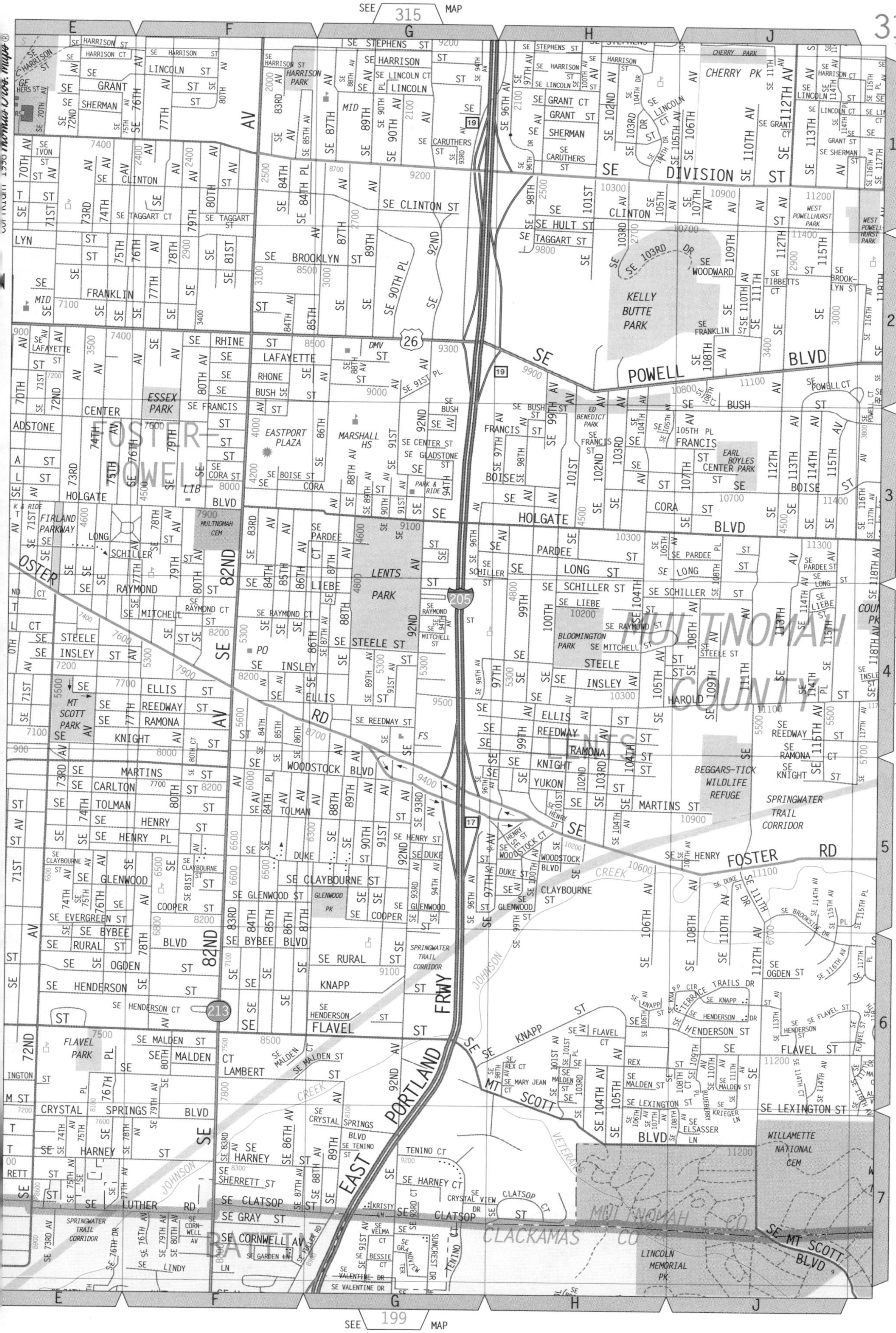

E F G H J

1 2 3 4 5 6 7

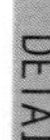

SEE 200 MAP

FOSTER-POWELL
MULTNOMAH COUNTY
LENTS

HARRISON PARK
CHERRY PK
WEST POWELLHURST PARK
KELLY BUTTE PARK
ESSEX PARK
EASTPORT PLAZA
MARSHALL HS
ED BENEDICT PARK
EARL BOYLES CENTER PARK
FIRLAND PARKWAY
MULTNOMAH CEM
LENTS PARK
BLOOMINGTON PARK
MT SCOTT PARK
BEGGARS-TICK WILDLIFE REFUGE
SPRINGWATER TRAIL CORRIDOR
GLENWOOD PK
FLAVEL PARK
WILLAMETTE NATIONAL CEM
LINCOLN MEMORIAL PK
DMV
LIB
PO
FS
PARK & RIDE

SE DIVISION ST
SE POWELL BLVD
SE HOLGATE BLVD
SE FOSTER RD
SE 82ND AV
EAST PORTLAND FRWY
SE WOODSTOCK BLVD
SE FLAVEL ST
SE MT SCOTT BLVD
SE LUTHER RD
SE JOHNSON CREEK BLVD
SE CLATSOP ST

MULTNOMAH CO
CLACKAMAS CO

SEE 199 MAP

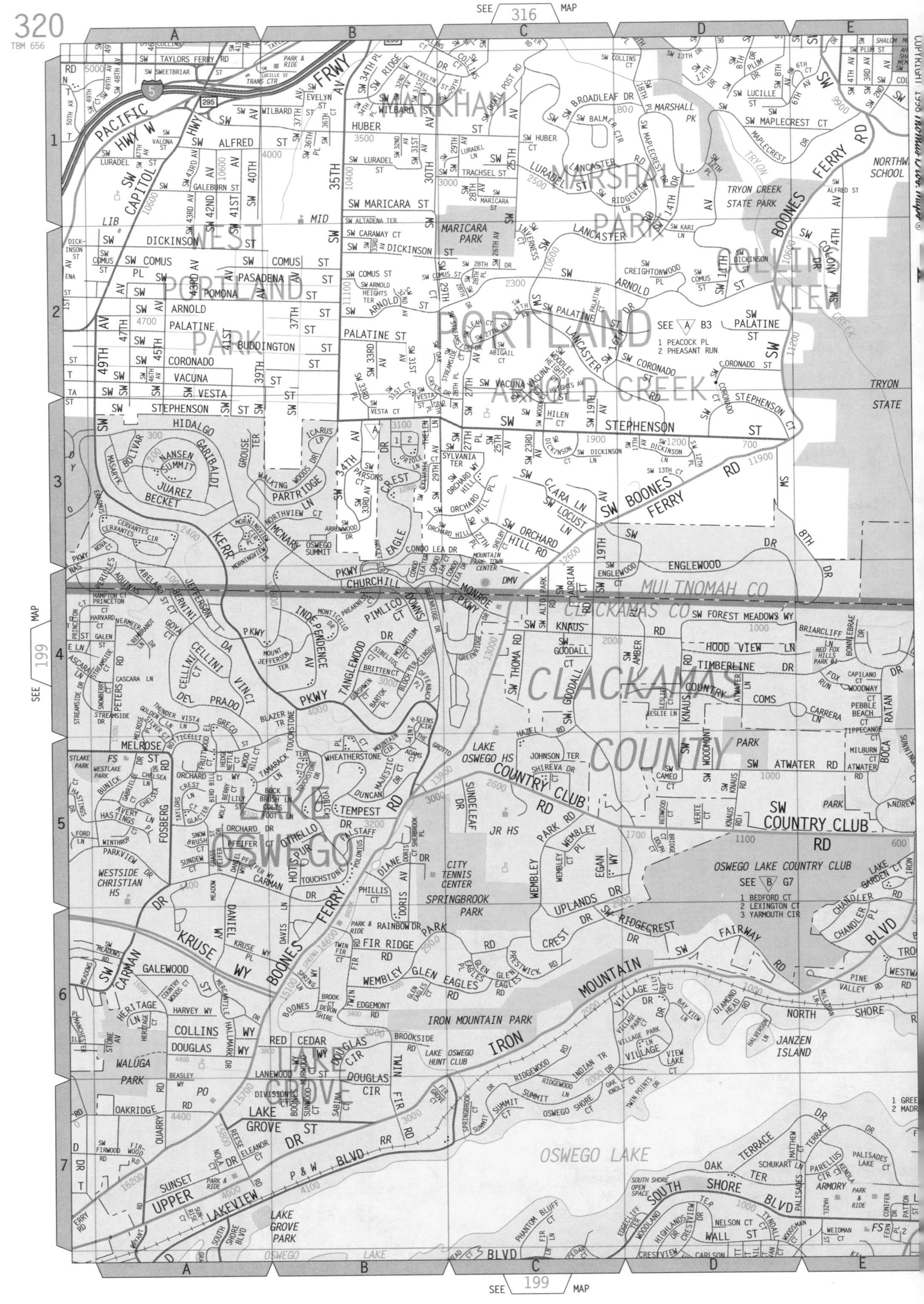
SEE 316 MAP
SEE 199 MAP
A
B
C
D
E
1
2
3
4
5
6
7
PNW
DETAIL
PACIFIC HWY W
CAPITOL HWY
FRWY
MARKHAM
MARSHALL PARK
WEST PORTLAND PARK
PORTLAND
ARNOLD CREEK
COLLINS VIEW
TRYON CREEK STATE PARK
TRYON STATE
NORTHWEST SCHOOL
MARICARA PARK
MARSHALL PK
SW BOONES FERRY RD
MULTNOMAH CO
CLACKAMAS CO
CLACKAMAS COUNTY
LAKE OSWEGO
LAKE GROVE
WESTLAKE PARK
WESTSIDE CHRISTIAN HS
LAKE OSWEGO HS
JR HS
CITY TENNIS CENTER
SPRINGBROOK PARK
OSWEGO LAKE COUNTRY CLUB
SEE B G7
1 BEDFORD CT
2 LEXINGTON CT
3 YARMOUTH CIR
SEE A B3
1 PEACOCK PL
2 PHEASANT RUN
IRON MOUNTAIN PARK
LAKE OSWEGO HUNT CLUB
JANZEN ISLAND
OSWEGO LAKE
WALUGA PARK
LAKE GROVE PARK
SOUTH SHORE OPEN SPACE
OSWEGO SUMMIT
MOUNTAIN PARK TOWN CENTER
DMV
KRUSE WY
COUNTRY CLUB RD
SW COUNTRY CLUB RD
IRON MOUNTAIN BLVD
NORTH SHORE RD
SOUTH SHORE BLVD
UPPER DR
LAKEVIEW BLVD
P & W RR
LAKE GROVE ST
KERR PKWY
INDEPENDENCE AV
SW STEPHENSON ST
SW ARNOLD ST
SW PALATINE ST
SW TAYLORS FERRY RD
SW MULTNOMAH BLVD
SW HUBER ST
SW DICKINSON ST
SW VACUNA ST
SW LANCASTER RD
SW 35TH AV
SW 49TH AV
SW ATWATER RD
SW KNAUS RD
SW MAPLECREST DR
ARMORY
PARK & RIDE
FS
PO
LIB
MID

SEE 317 MAP

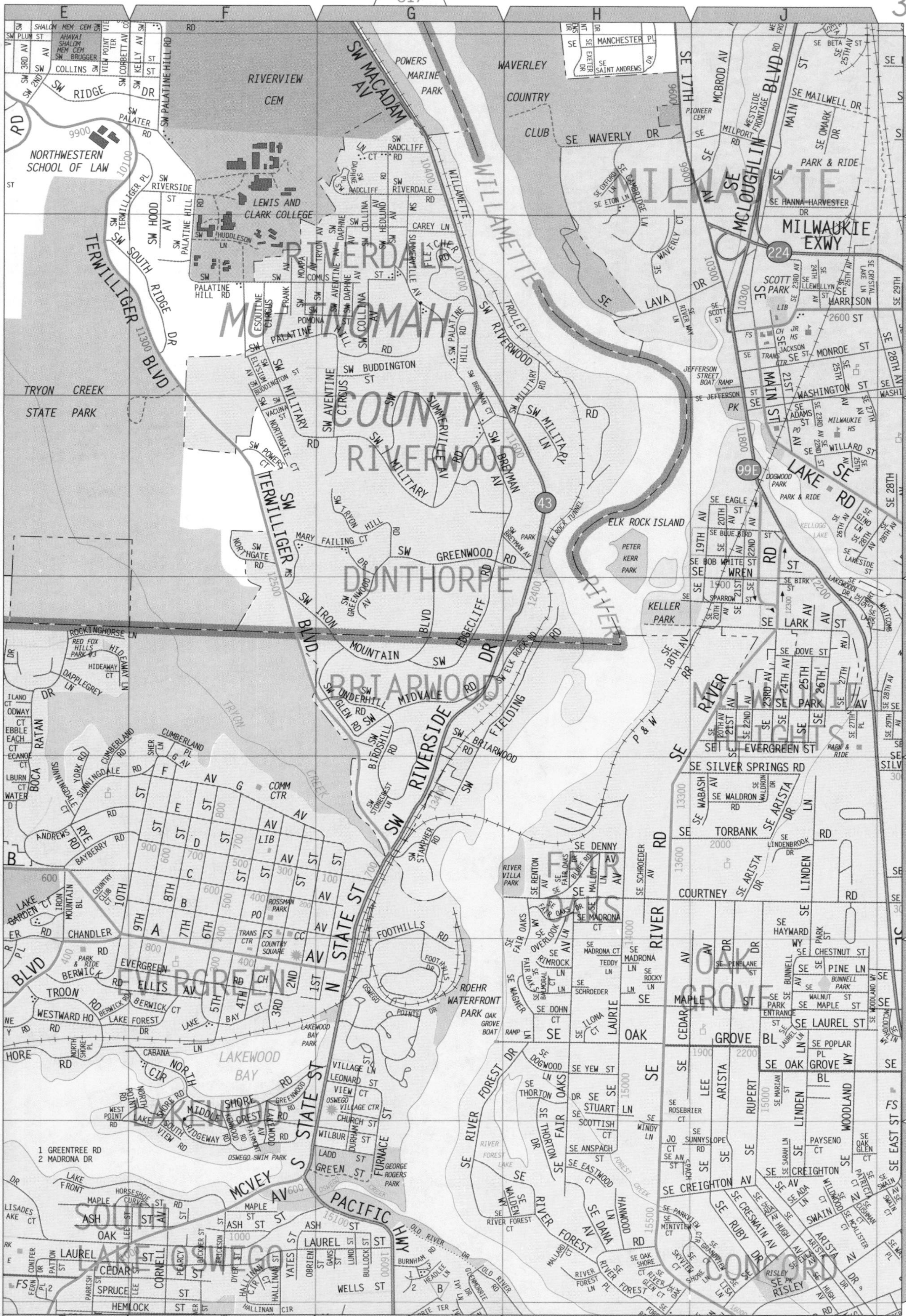

SEE 199 MAP

SEE 199 MAP

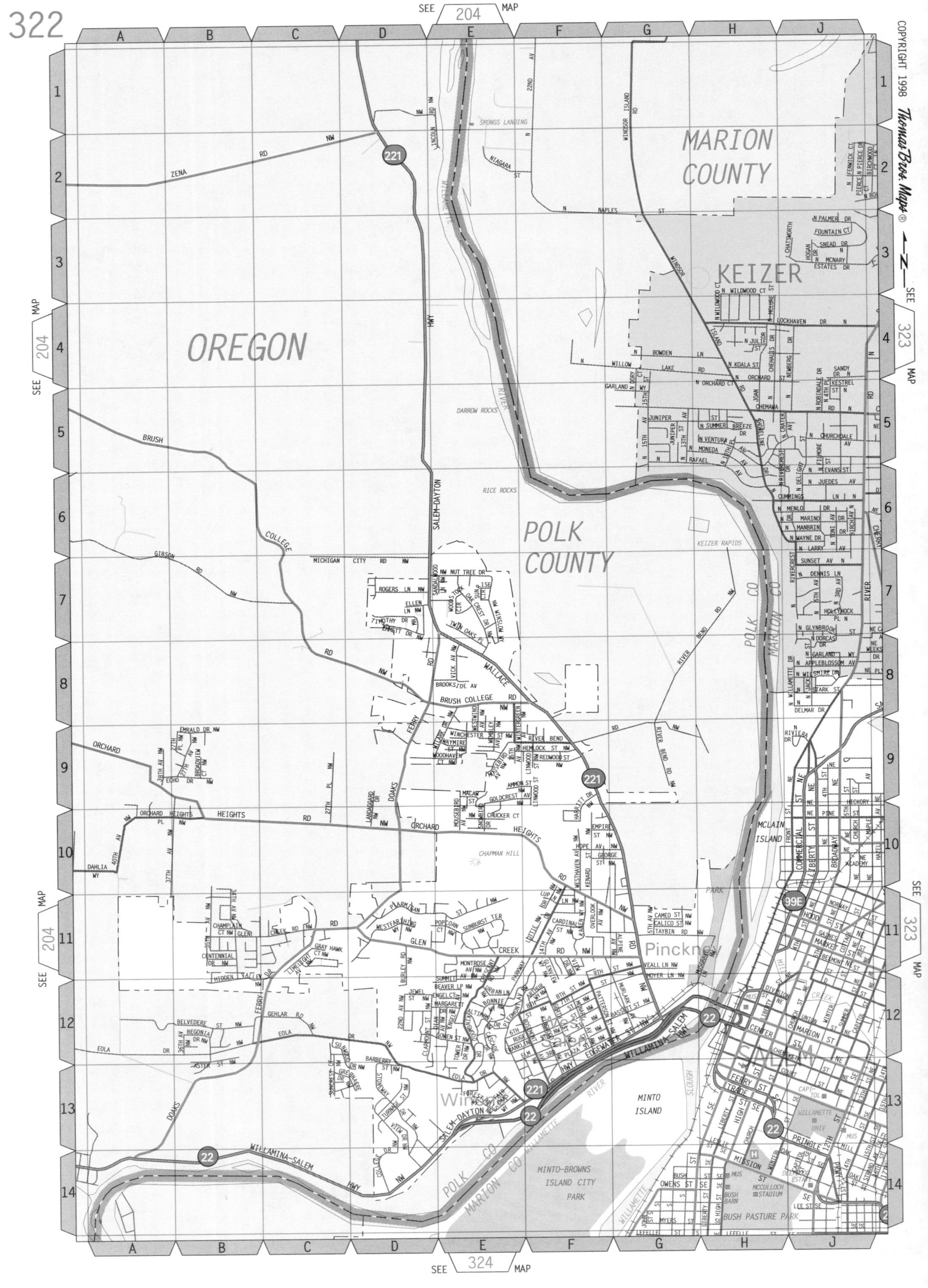
SEE 204 MAP
SEE 323 MAP
SEE 324 MAP
OREGON
MARION COUNTY
POLK COUNTY
KEIZER
SALEM
Pinckney
MINTO ISLAND
MINTO-BROWNS ISLAND CITY PARK
MCLAIN ISLAND
BUSH PASTURE PARK
WILLAMETTE RIVER
SALEM-DAYTON HWY
WILLAMINA-SALEM HWY
BRUSH COLLEGE RD NW
ORCHARD HEIGHTS RD NW
GLEN CREEK RD NW
ZENA RD NW
WALLACE RD
RIVER BEND RD NW
WINDSOR ISLAND RD
CHAPMAN HILL
KEIZER RAPIDS
DARROW ROCKS
RICE ROCKS
SPONGS LANDING
PNW
DETAIL

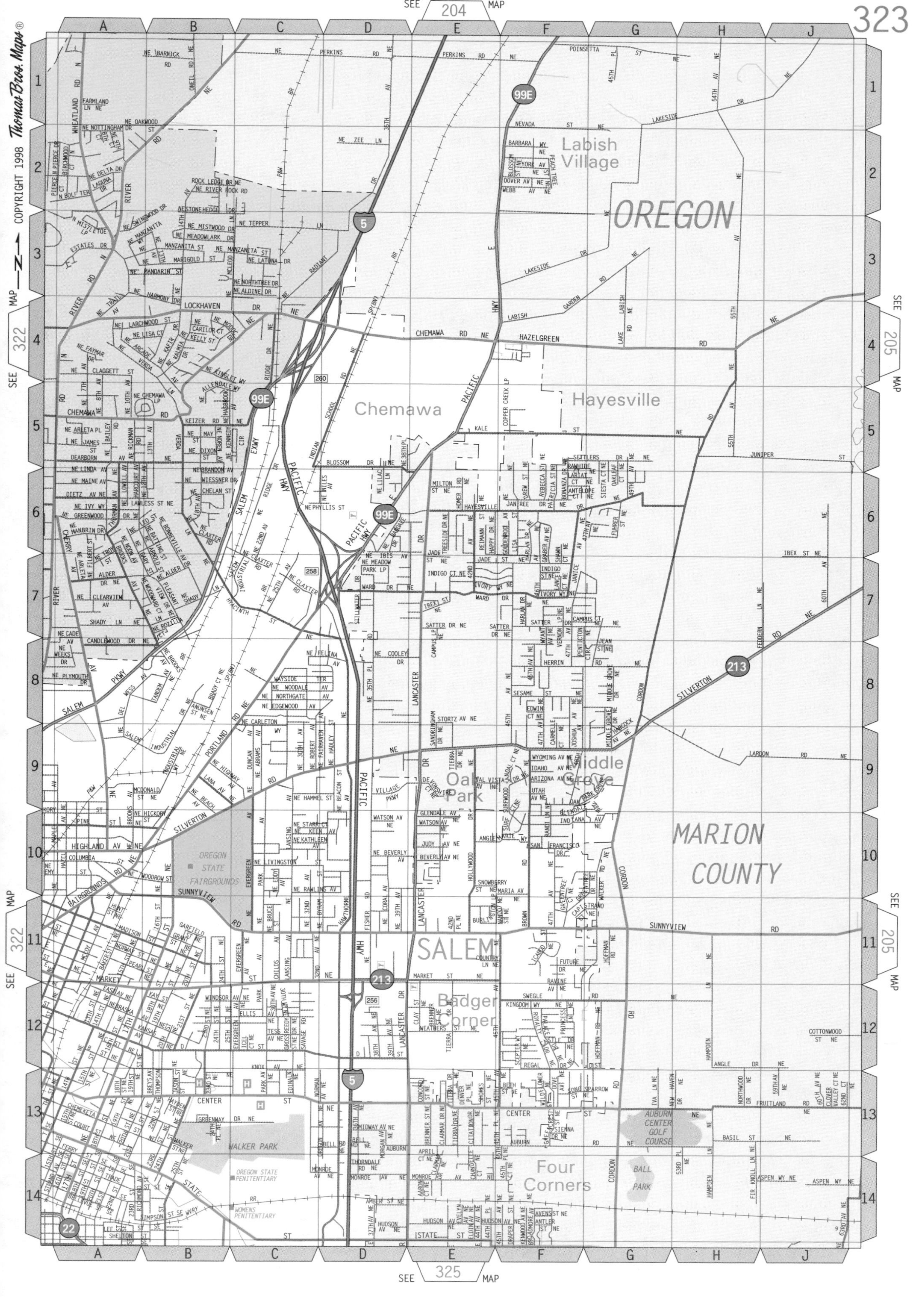

SEE 204 MAP
SEE 322 MAP
SEE 205 MAP
SEE 325 MAP
OREGON
MARION COUNTY
SALEM
Labish Village
Chemawa
Hayesville
Oak Park
Middle Grove
Badger Corner
Four Corners
OREGON STATE FAIRGROUNDS
WALKER PARK
OREGON STATE PENITENTIARY
WOMENS PENITENTIARY
AUBURN CENTER GOLF COURSE
BALL PARK
PNW
DETAIL

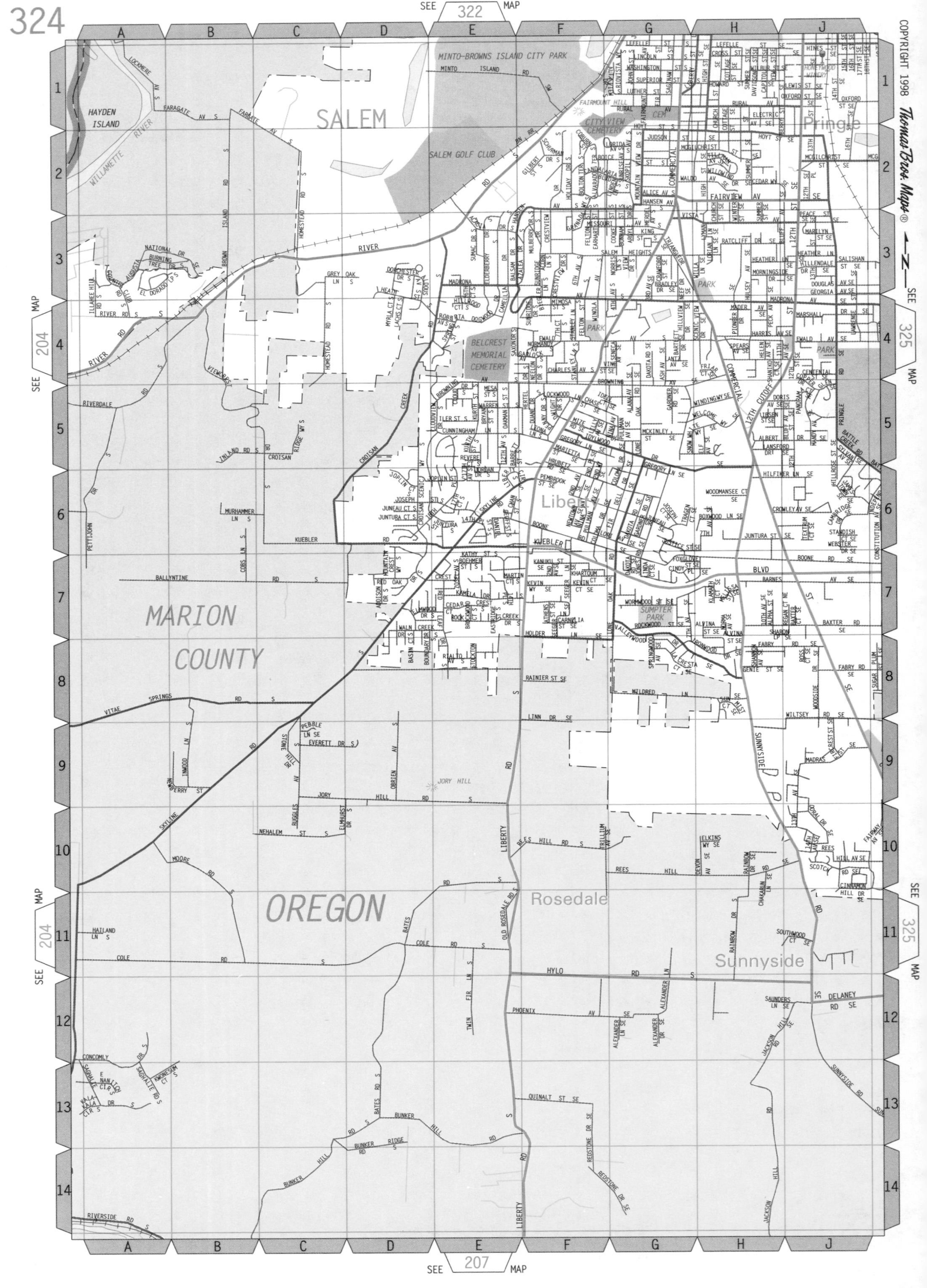

SEE 322 MAP
SEE 207 MAP
SEE MAP 204
SEE MAP 325
MINTO-BROWNS ISLAND CITY PARK
SALEM
HAYDEN ISLAND
WILLAMETTE RIVER
SALEM GOLF CLUB
CITY VIEW CEMETERY
FAIRMOUNT HILL
Pringle
BELCREST MEMORIAL CEMETERY
PARK
SUMPTER PARK
Liberty
MARION COUNTY
OREGON
JORY HILL
Rosedale
Sunnyside
RIVER RD
COMMERCIAL
12TH CUTOFF
KUEBLER BLVD
LIBERTY RD
SKYLINE RD
VITAE SPRINGS RD
CROISAN CREEK
BATES RD
COLE RD
HYLO RD
PHOENIX AV
SUNNYSIDE RD
JACKSON HILL RD
BUNKER HILL RD
DELANEY RD SE
RIVERSIDE RD
JORY HILL RD
REES HILL RD
WOODMANSEE CT
HILLROSE ST SE
BATTLE CREEK RD
BAXTER RD SE
FABRY RD SE
WILTSEY RD SE
MADRAS
SALISHAN
KATHY ST S
ROBERTA AV S
WOODSIDE DR
TEXTRUM
BROWN RD
HOMESTEAD RD S
ISLAND RD

PNW

DETAIL

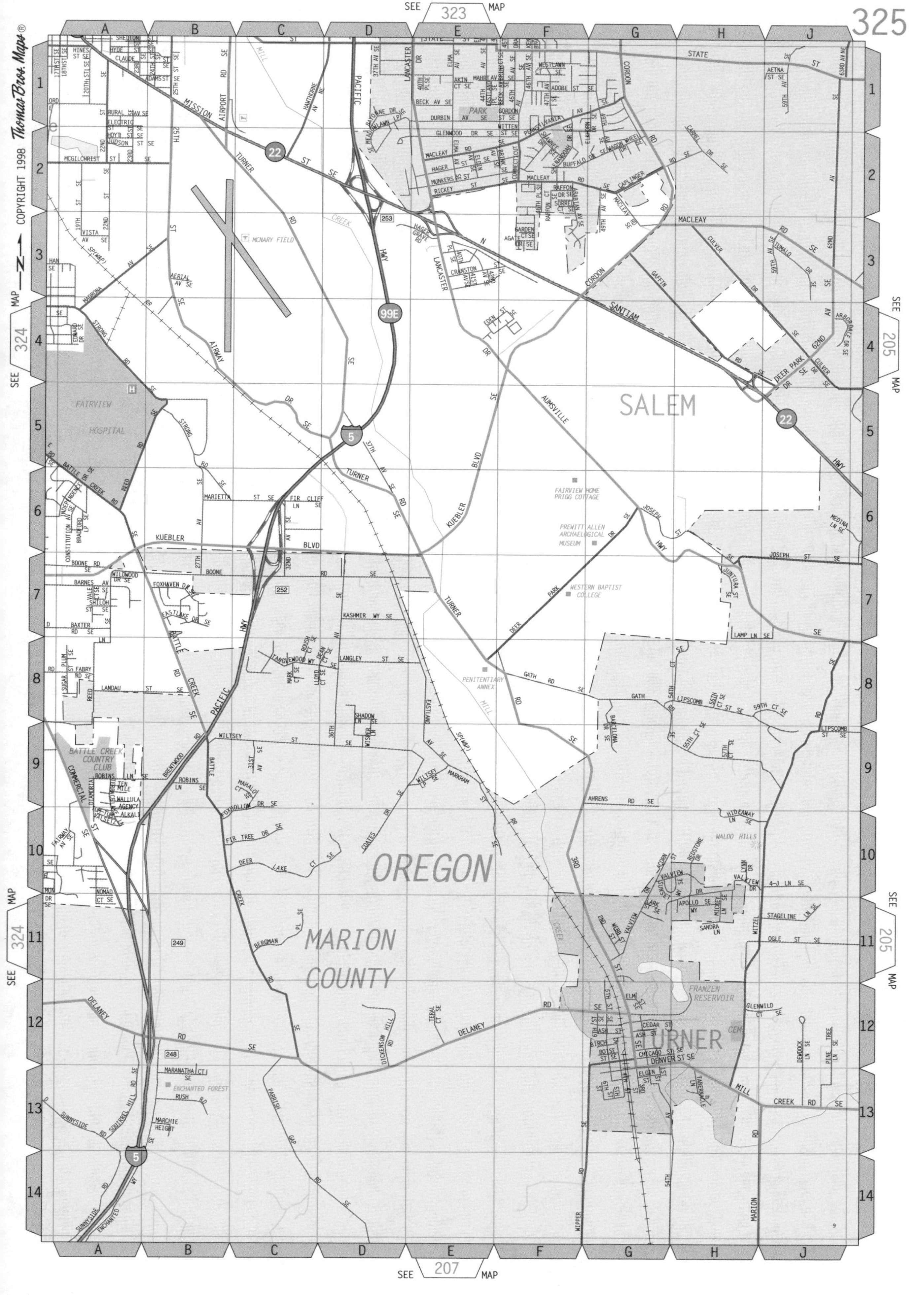
SALEM
OREGON
MARION
COUNTY
TURNER
FAIRVIEW HOSPITAL
BATTLE CREEK COUNTRY CLUB
MCNARY FIELD
FAIRVIEW HOME PRIGG COTTAGE
PREWITT ALLEN ARCHAEOLOGICAL MUSEUM
WESTERN BAPTIST COLLEGE
PENITENTIARY ANNEX
FRANZEN RESERVOIR
WALDO HILLS
ENCHANTED FOREST
SEE 323 MAP
SEE 324 MAP
SEE 205 MAP
SEE 207 MAP
PNW
DETAIL

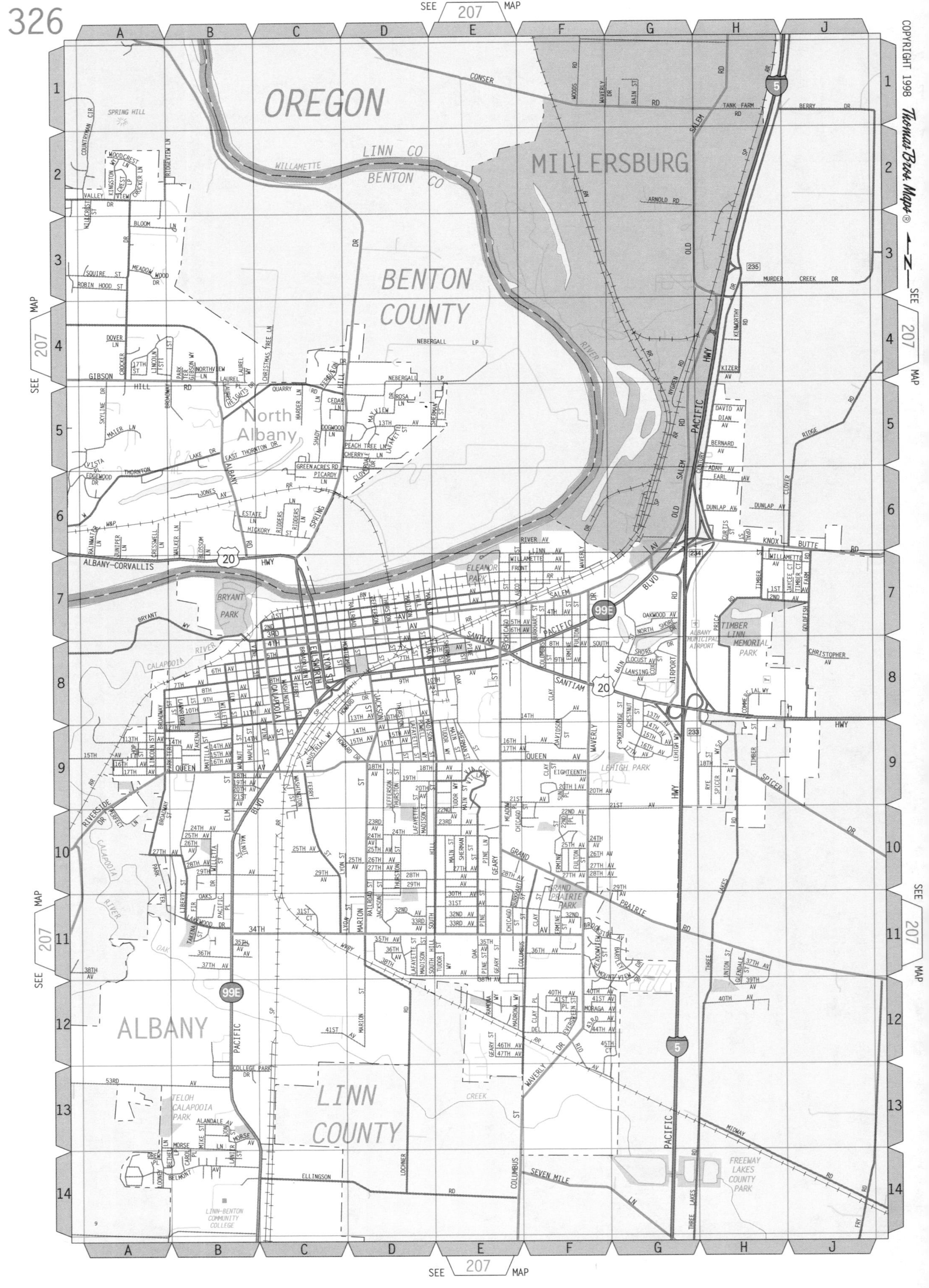
SEE 207 MAP
A
B
C
D
E
F
G
H
J
1
2
3
4
5
6
7
8
9
10
11
12
13
14
OREGON
LINN CO
BENTON CO
WILLAMETTE
MILLERSBURG
BENTON
COUNTY
North
Albany
ALBANY
LINN
COUNTY
SPRING HILL
CONSER
TANK FARM RD
BERRY DR
ARNOLD RD
MURDER CREEK DR
NEBERGALL LP
GIBSON HILL RD
ALBANY-CORVALLIS HWY
BRYANT PARK
ELEANOR PARK
CALAPOOIA RIVER
SANTIAM HWY
PACIFIC BLVD
PACIFIC HWY
OLD SALEM RD
KNOX BUTTE RD
TIMBER LINN MEMORIAL PARK
ALBANY MUNICIPAL AIRPORT
LEHIGH PARK
GRAND PRAIRIE PARK
GRAND PRAIRIE RD
QUEEN AV
34TH
WAVERLY
COLUMBUS ST
THREE LAKES RD
TELOH CALAPOOIA PARK
ELLINGSON RD
SEVEN MILE LN
FREEWAY LAKES COUNTY PARK
LINN-BENTON COMMUNITY COLLEGE
MIDWAY
SPICER DR
CREEK
9
SEE 207 MAP
PNW
DETAIL

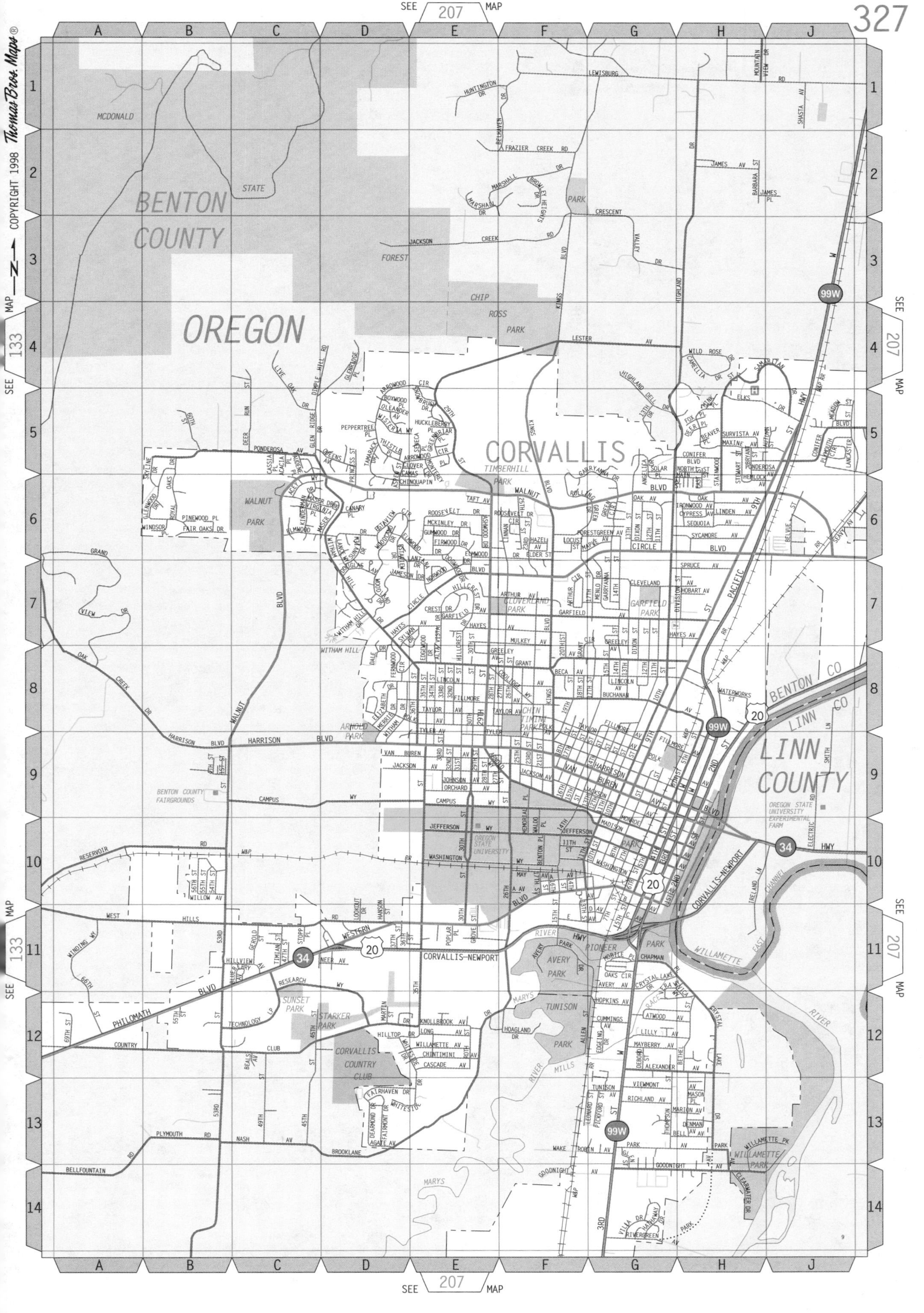
BENTON COUNTY
OREGON
CORVALLIS
LINN COUNTY
WALNUT PARK
CHIP ROSS PARK
TIMBERHILL PARK
CLOVERLAND PARK
GARFIELD PARK
CHINTIMINI PARK
ARNOLD PARK
OREGON STATE UNIVERSITY
AVERY PARK
PIONEER PARK
TUNISON PARK
SUNSET PARK
STARKER PARK
CORVALLIS COUNTRY CLUB
WILLAMETTE PARK
BENTON COUNTY FAIRGROUNDS
OREGON STATE UNIVERSITY EXPERIMENTAL FARM
WILLAMETTE RIVER
MARYS RIVER
SEE 207 MAP
SEE 133 MAP
PNW
DETAIL
Thomas Bros. Maps® COPYRIGHT 1998

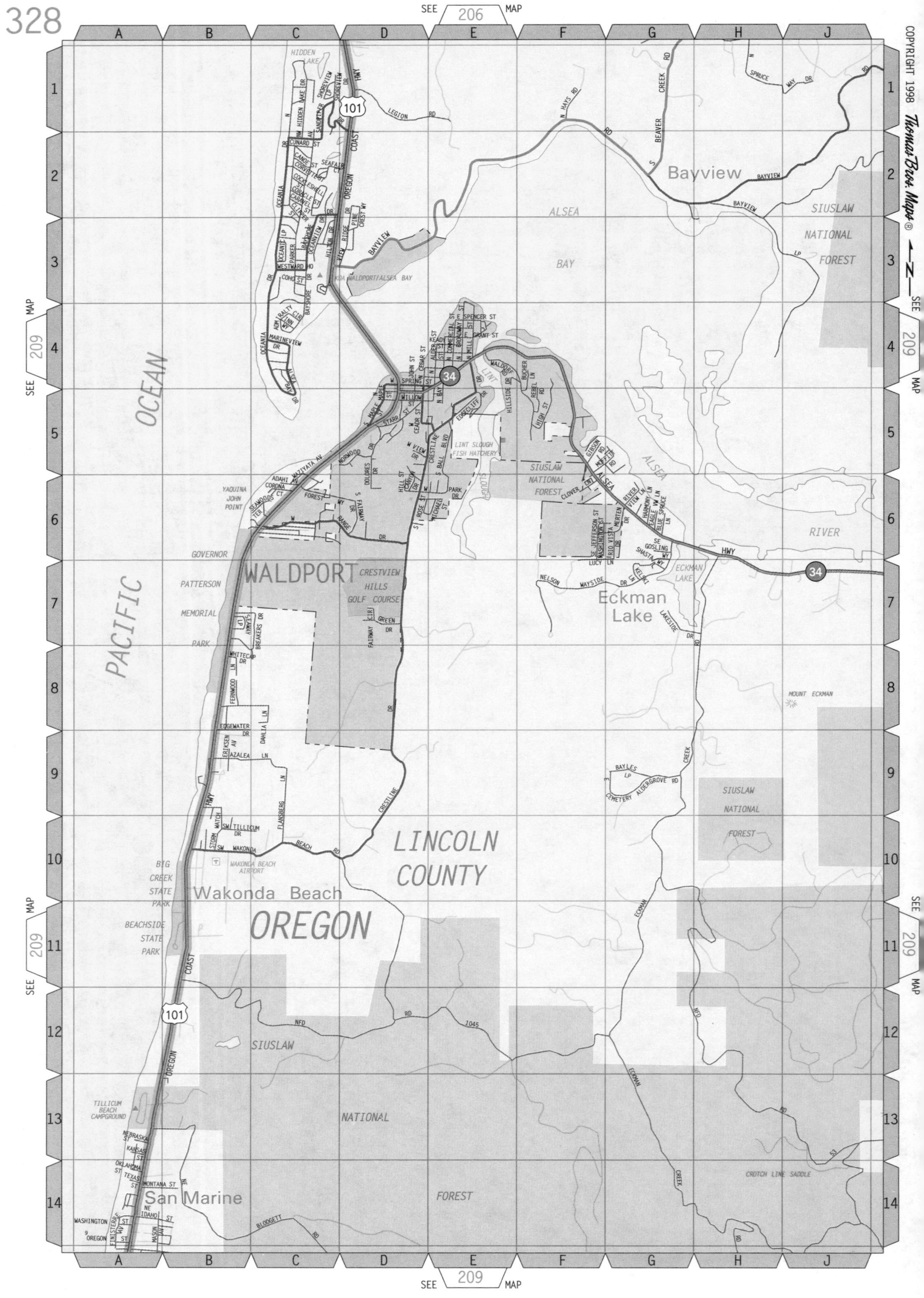
SEE 206 MAP
SEE 209 MAP
WALDPORT
Bayview
Eckman Lake
Wakonda Beach
San Marine
LINCOLN COUNTY
OREGON
PACIFIC OCEAN
ALSEA BAY
ALSEA RIVER
SIUSLAW NATIONAL FOREST
CRESTVIEW HILLS GOLF COURSE
GOVERNOR PATTERSON MEMORIAL PARK
BIG CREEK STATE PARK
BEACHSIDE STATE PARK
TILLICUM BEACH CAMPGROUND
LINT SLOUGH FISH HATCHERY
WAKONDA BEACH AIRPORT
YAQUINA JOHN POINT
MOUNT ECKMAN
CROTCH LINE SADDLE
HIDDEN LAKE
KOA WALDPORT/ALSEA BAY
OREGON COAST HWY
101
34

PNW
DETAIL

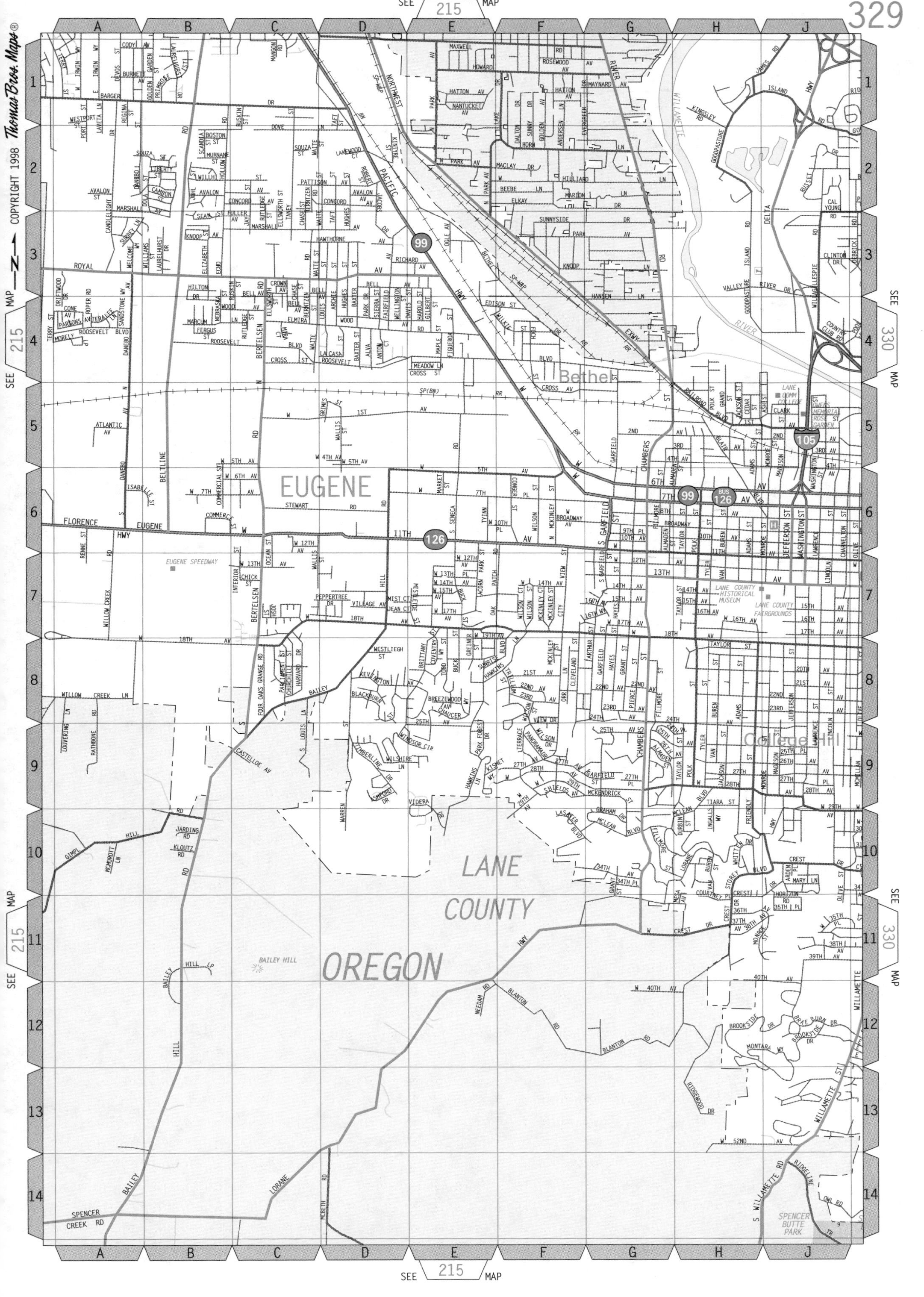

SEE 215 MAP
SEE 330 MAP
Thomas Bros. Maps ® COPYRIGHT 1998
PNW
DETAIL
A B C D E F G H J
1 2 3 4 5 6 7 8 9 10 11 12 13 14
EUGENE
Bethel
College Hill
LANE COUNTY
OREGON
EUGENE SPEEDWAY
BAILEY HILL
LANE COMM COLLEGE
OWENS MEMORIAL ROSE GARDEN
LANE COUNTY HISTORICAL MUSEUM
LANE COUNTY FAIRGROUNDS
SPENCER BUTTE PARK
WILLAMETTE RIVER
FLORENCE EUGENE HWY
NORTHWEST EXWY
PACIFIC HWY
BELTLINE

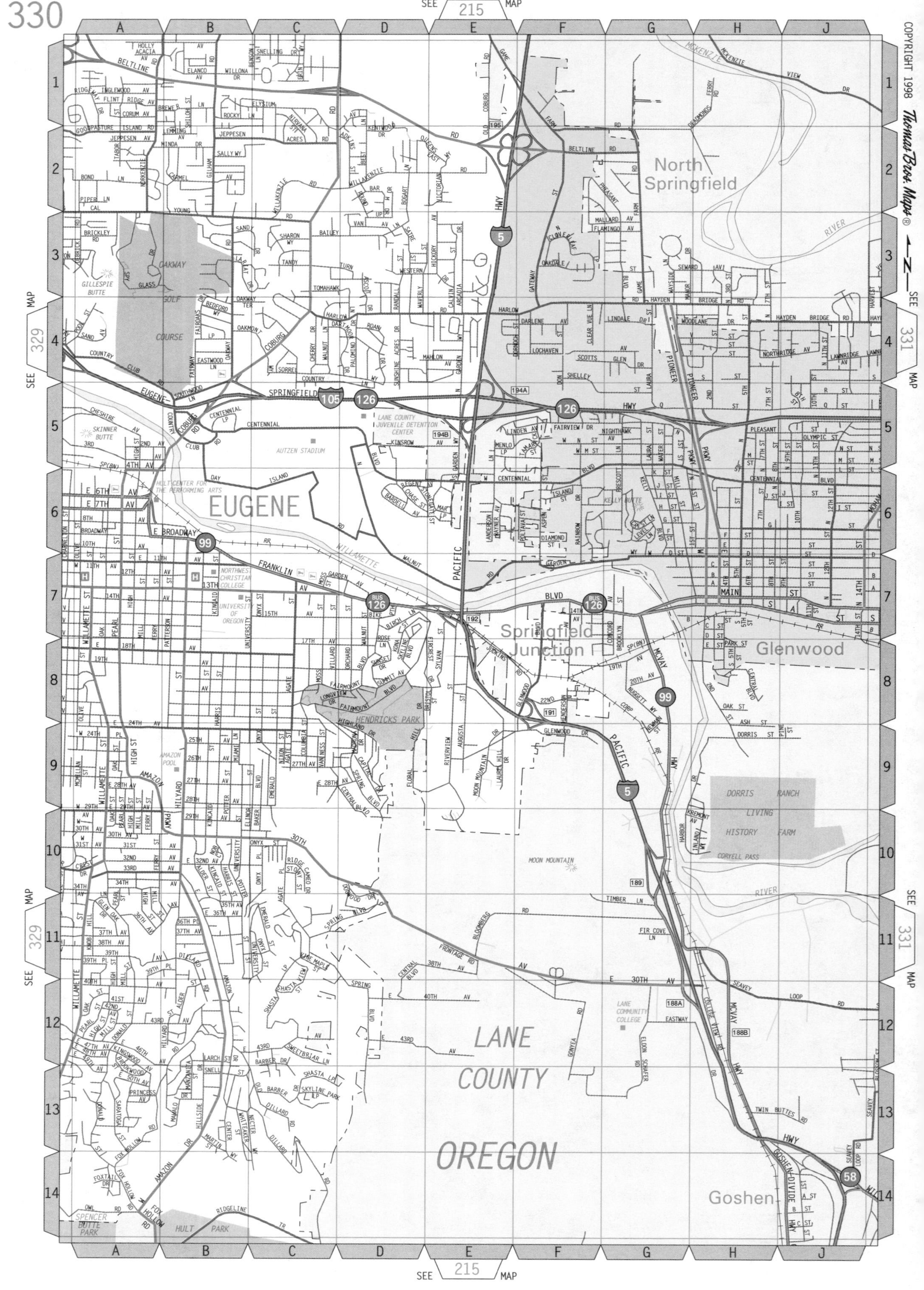
SEE 215 MAP
SEE 329 MAP
SEE 331 MAP
A B C D E F G H J
1 2 3 4 5 6 7 8 9 10 11 12 13 14
EUGENE
North Springfield
Springfield Junction
Glenwood
Goshen
LANE COUNTY
OREGON
OAKWAY GOLF COURSE
GILLESPIE BUTTE
SKINNER BUTTE
HULT CENTER FOR THE PERFORMING ARTS
AUTZEN STADIUM
LANE COUNTY JUVENILE DETENTION CENTER
NORTHWEST CHRISTIAN COLLEGE
UNIVERSITY OF OREGON
HENDRICKS PARK
AMAZON POOL
MOON MOUNTAIN
KELLY BUTTE
DORRIS RANCH LIVING HISTORY FARM
LANE COMMUNITY COLLEGE
SPENCER BUTTE PARK
HULT PARK
WILLAMETTE
MCKENZIE
RIVER
BELTLINE
SPRINGFIELD
PACIFIC HWY
FRANKLIN
BLVD
HARLOW
HAYDEN BRIDGE RD
CENTENNIAL
MAIN
MCVAY HWY
E 30TH AV
AMAZON
HILYARD
WILLAMETTE
PIONEER PKWY
GOSHEN-DIVIDE HWY
5
99
105
126
BUS 126
58
191
192
194A
194B
195
188A
188B
189

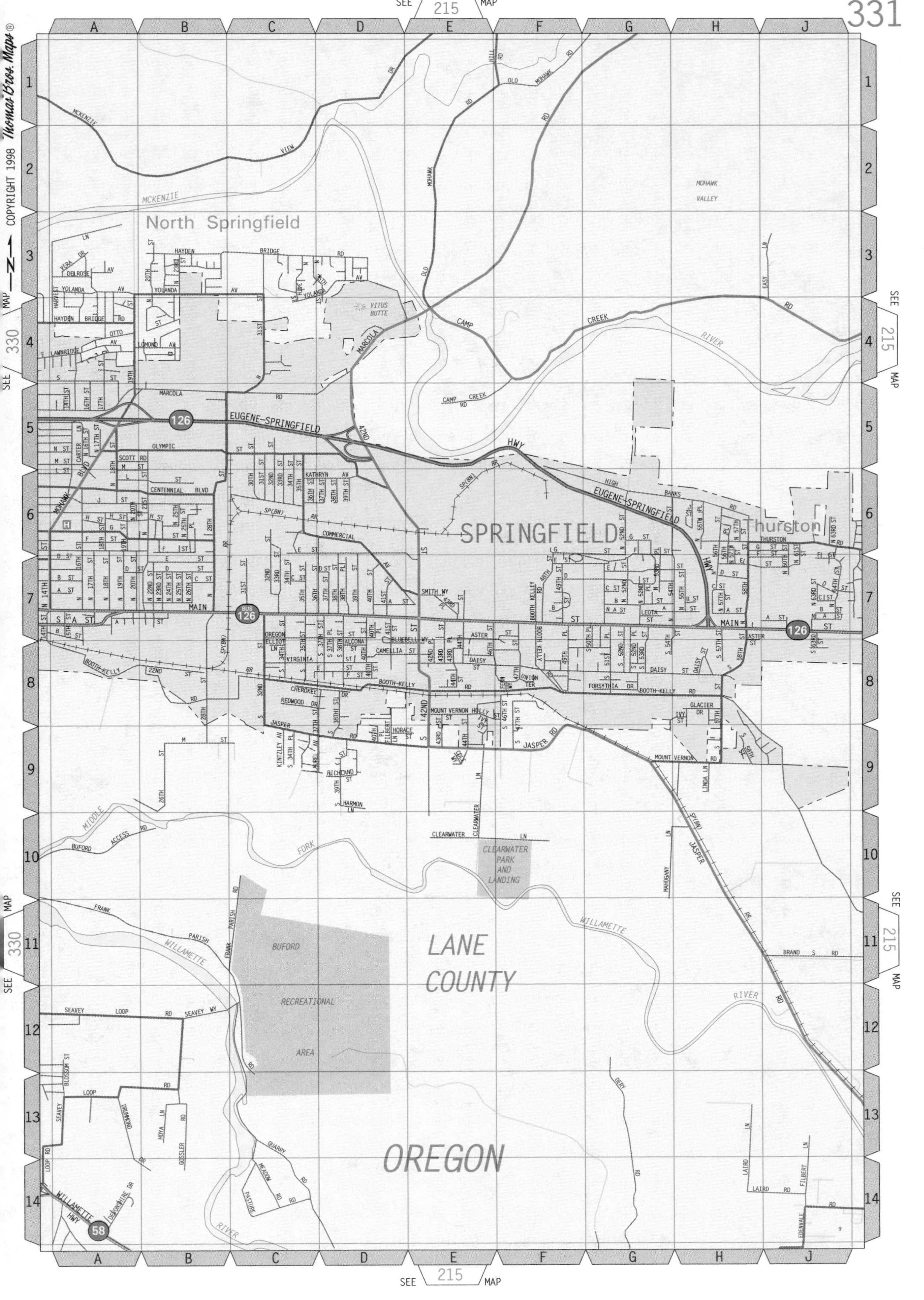
North Springfield
SPRINGFIELD
Thurston
LANE COUNTY
OREGON
BUFORD RECREATIONAL AREA
CLEARWATER PARK AND LANDING
MOHAWK VALLEY
VITUS BUTTE
EUGENE-SPRINGFIELD HWY
MAIN ST
CAMP CREEK RD
MARCOLA RD
JASPER RD
BOOTH-KELLY RD
MCKENZIE VIEW DR
MOHAWK BLVD
CENTENNIAL BLVD
WILLAMETTE HWY
SEE 215 MAP
SEE 330 MAP
PNW
DETAIL

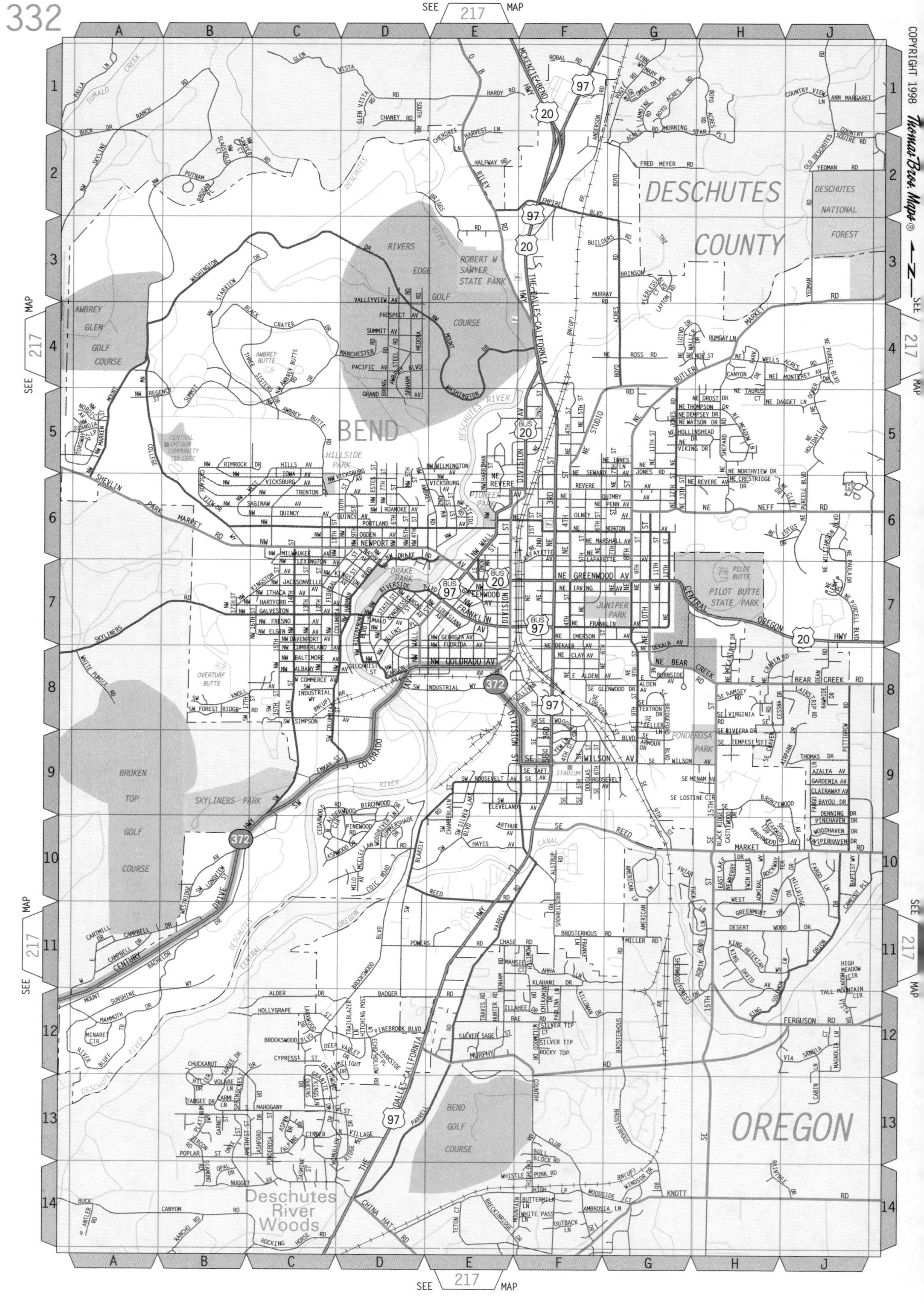

SEE 217 MAP
BEND
DESCHUTES COUNTY
OREGON
DESCHUTES NATIONAL FOREST
AWBREY GLEN GOLF COURSE
RIVERS EDGE GOLF COURSE
ROBERT W SAWYER STATE PARK
CENTRAL OREGON COMMUNITY COLLEGE
HILLSIDE PARK
PIONEER PARK
DRAKE PARK
JUNIPER PARK
PILOT BUTTE STATE PARK
PONDEROSA PARK
OVERTURF BUTTE
AWBREY BUTTE
PILOT BUTTE
BROKEN TOP GOLF COURSE
SKYLINERS PARK
BEND GOLF COURSE
Deschutes River Woods
DESCHUTES RIVER
TUMALO CREEK
MCKENZIE-BEND HWY
THE DALLES-CALIFORNIA HWY
CENTURY DRIVE
DIVISION ST
GREENWOOD AV
FRANKLIN AV
WALL ST
COLORADO AV
SHEVLIN PARK RD
MT WASHINGTON DR
NEFF RD
REED MARKET RD
CHINA HAT RD
KNOTT RD
FERGUSON RD
BEAR CREEK RD
EMPIRE BLVD
BUTLER MARKET RD
27TH ST
15TH ST
BROSTERHOUS RD
PARRELL RD
POWERS RD
BROOKSWOOD BLVD
97
20
BUS 97
BUS 20
372
A B C D E F G H J
1 2 3 4 5 6 7 8 9 10 11 12 13 14

SEE 218 MAP

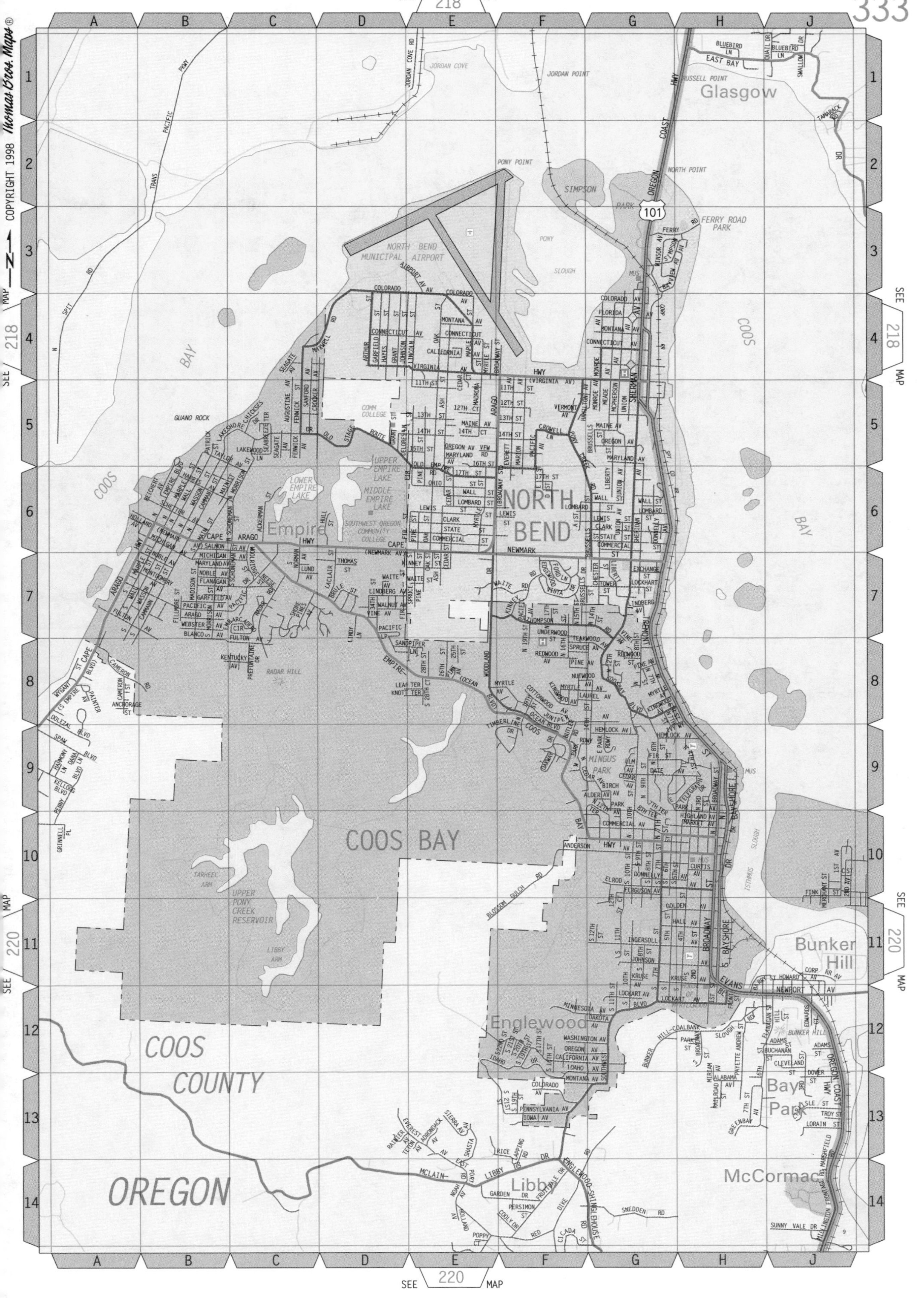

SEE 218 MAP
SEE 220 MAP
SEE 220 MAP
SEE 220 MAP

PNW

DETAIL

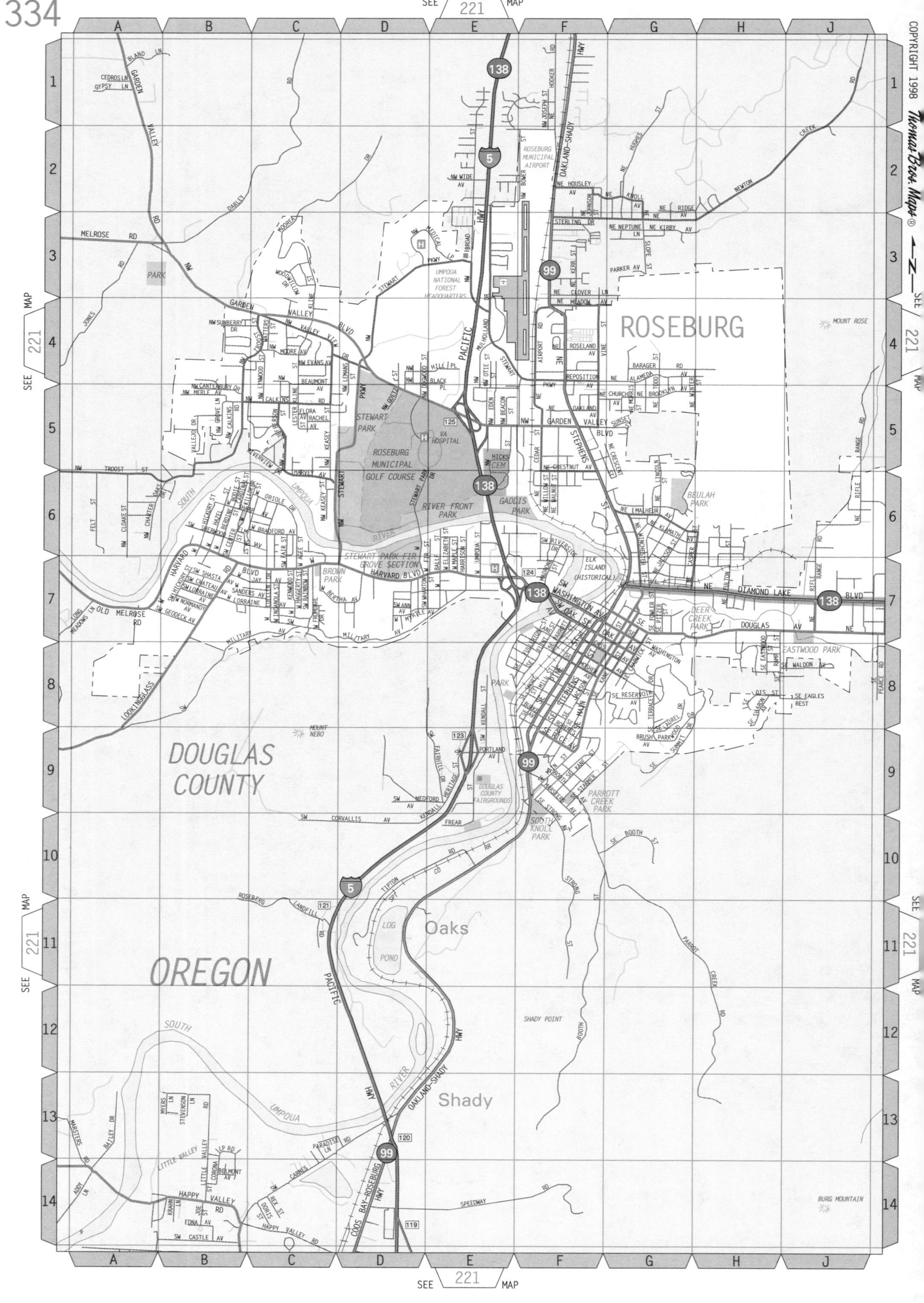

ROSEBURG
DOUGLAS COUNTY
OREGON
Oaks
Shady
ROSEBURG MUNICIPAL AIRPORT
UMPQUA NATIONAL FOREST HEADQUARTERS
STEWART PARK
ROSEBURG MUNICIPAL GOLF COURSE
RIVER FRONT PARK
VA HOSPITAL
HICKS CEM
GADDIS PARK
BEULAH PARK
ELK ISLAND (HISTORICAL)
STEWART PARK FIR GROVE SECTION
BROWN PARK
DEER CREEK PARK
EASTWOOD PARK
DOUGLAS COUNTY FAIRGROUNDS
SOUTH KNOLL PARK
PARROTT CREEK PARK
LOG POND
MOUNT NEBO
MOUNT ROSE
SHADY POINT
BURG MOUNTAIN
SOUTH UMPQUA RIVER
GARDEN VALLEY BLVD
DIAMOND LAKE BLVD
HARVARD BLVD
MELROSE RD
LOOKINGGLASS RD
PACIFIC HWY
OAKLAND-SHADY HWY
COOS BAY-ROSEBURG HWY
HAPPY VALLEY RD
SEE 221 MAP
COPYRIGHT 1998 Thomas Bros. Maps ®

SEE 221 MAP

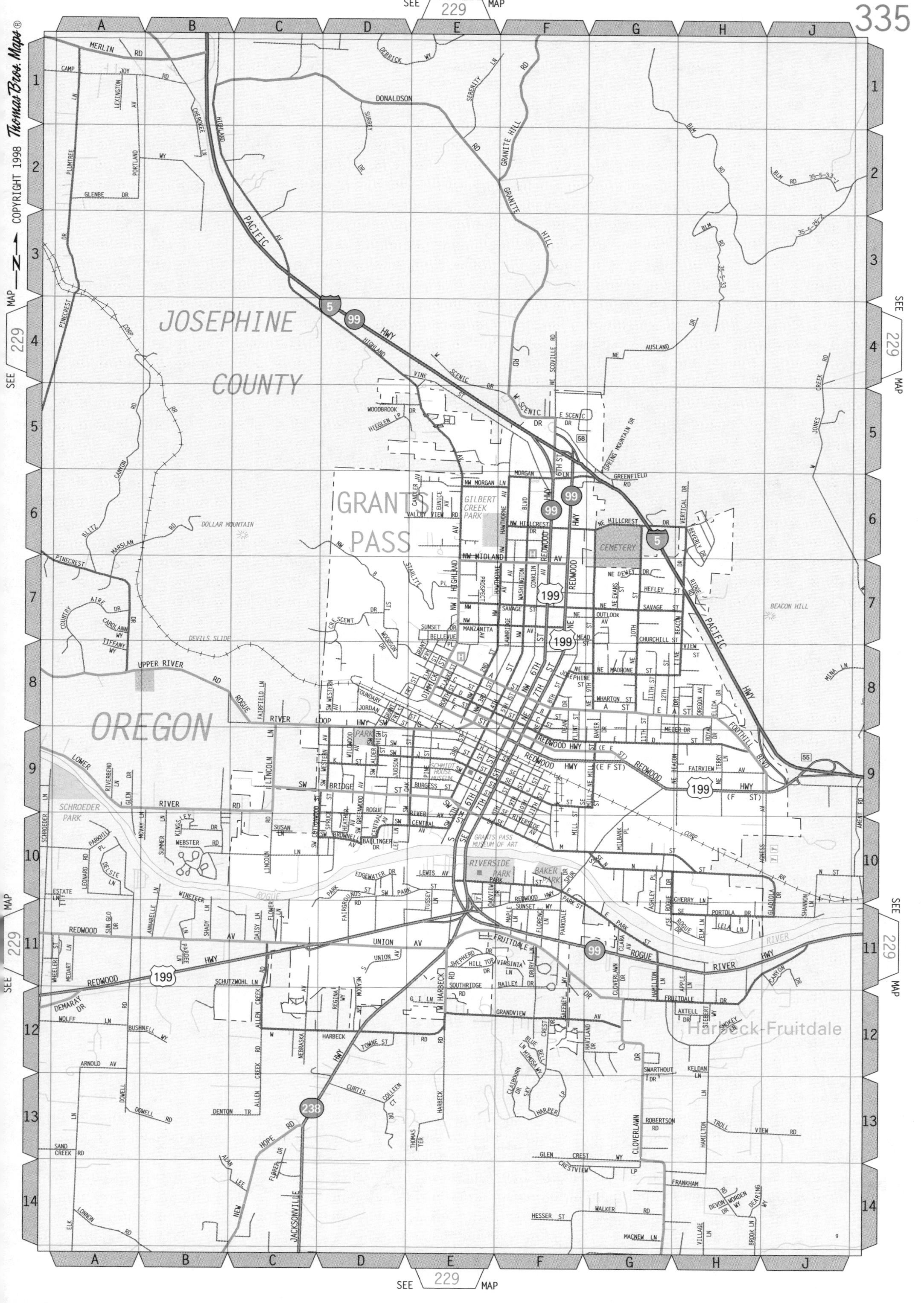

SEE 229 MAP
JOSEPHINE
COUNTY
OREGON
GRANTS PASS
Harbeck-Fruitdale
MERLIN RD
DONALDSON
PACIFIC HWY
REDWOOD HWY
ROGUE RIVER HWY
UNION AV
GILBERT CREEK PARK
CEMETERY
RIVERSIDE PARK
BAKER PARK
SCHROEDER PARK
SCHMIDT HOUSE MUSEUM
GRANTS PASS MUSEUM OF ART
DOLLAR MOUNTAIN
BEACON HILL
DEVILS SLIDE
PNW
DETAIL

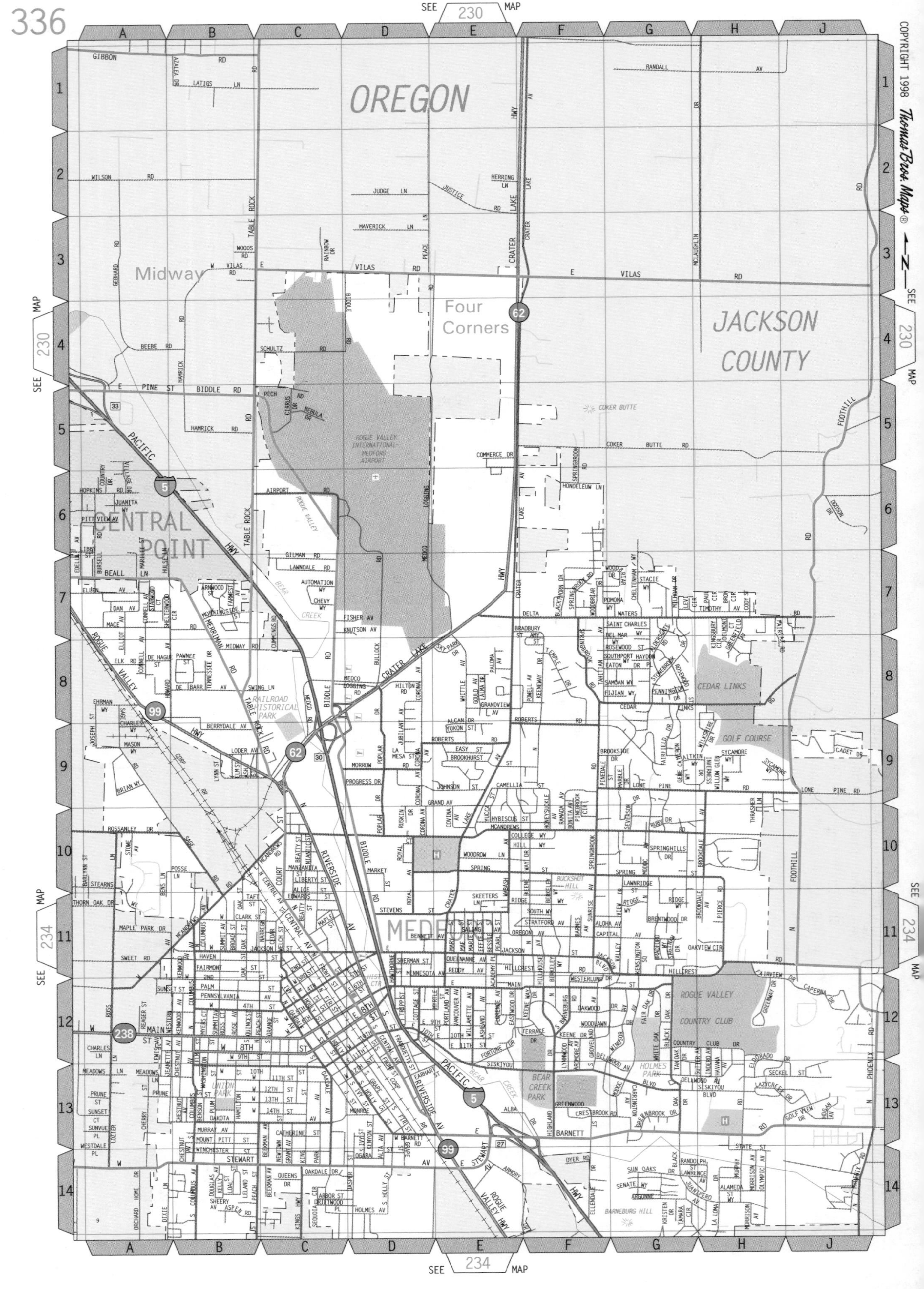
SEE 230 MAP
SEE 234 MAP
OREGON
JACKSON COUNTY
Midway
Four Corners
CENTRAL POINT
MEDFORD
ROGUE VALLEY INTERNATIONAL-MEDFORD AIRPORT
RAILROAD HISTORICAL PARK
CEDAR LINKS
GOLF COURSE
ROGUE VALLEY COUNTRY CLUB
BEAR CREEK PARK
HOLMES PARK
UNION PARK
BUCKSHOT HILL
COKER BUTTE
BARNEBURG HILL
GIBBON RD
LATIGS LN
WILSON RD
JUDGE LN
MAVERICK LN
HERRING LN
JUSTICE RD
RANDALL AV
E VILAS RD
BEEBE RD
E PINE ST
BIDDLE RD
HAMRICK RD
COKER BUTTE RD
COMMERCE DR
AIRPORT RD
TABLE ROCK RD
CRATER LAKE HWY
CRATER LAKE AV
PACIFIC HWY
ROGUE VALLEY HWY
DELTA WATERS RD
ROBERTS RD
LONE PINE RD
MCANDREWS RD
SPRING ST
JACKSON ST
MAIN ST
8TH ST
STEWART AV
BARNETT RD
SISKIYOU BLVD
RIVERSIDE AV
CENTRAL AV
FOOTHILL RD
PHOENIX RD
ROSSANLEY DR
MIDWAY RD
BERRYDALE AV
GARDEN AV
HIGHLAND DR
STATE ST
N
PNW
DETAIL

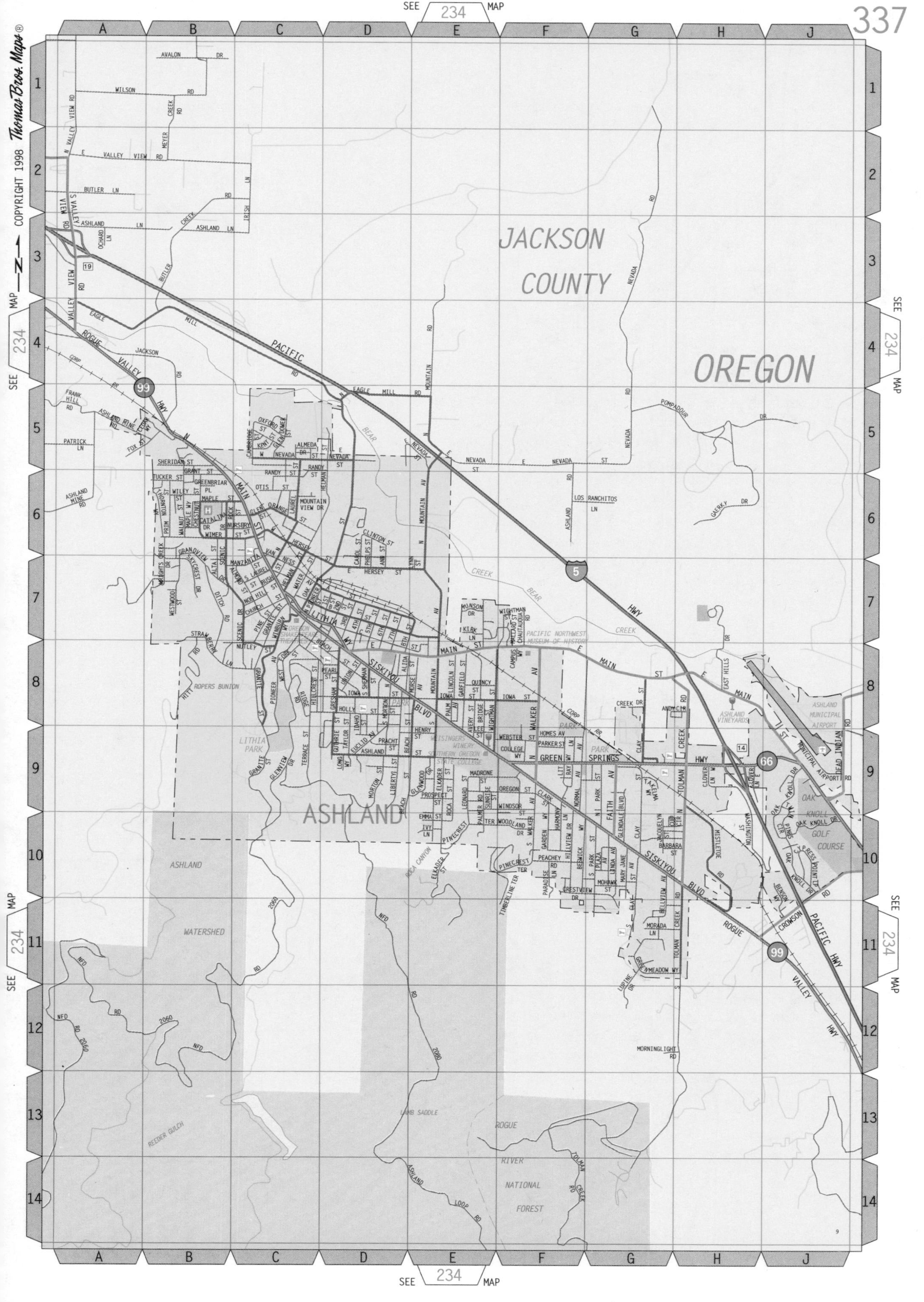

JACKSON COUNTY
OREGON
ASHLAND
ASHLAND WATERSHED
ROGUE RIVER NATIONAL FOREST
LITHIA PARK
ASHLAND MUNICIPAL AIRPORT
OAK KNOLL GOLF COURSE
ASHLAND VINEYARDS
PACIFIC NORTHWEST MUSEUM OF HISTORY
SOUTHERN OREGON STATE COLLEGE
WEISINGERS WINERY
OREGON SHAKESPEARE THEATERS
ROPERS BUNION
LAMB SADDLE
REEDER GULCH
PACIFIC HWY
ROGUE VALLEY HWY
SISKIYOU BLVD
GREEN SPRINGS HWY
E MAIN ST
N MAIN ST
LITHIA WY
TOLMAN CREEK RD
DEAD INDIAN RD
NEVADA ST
MOUNTAIN AV
WALKER AV
PACIFIC NORTHWEST MUSEUM OF HISTORY
SEE 234 MAP

PNW

DETAIL

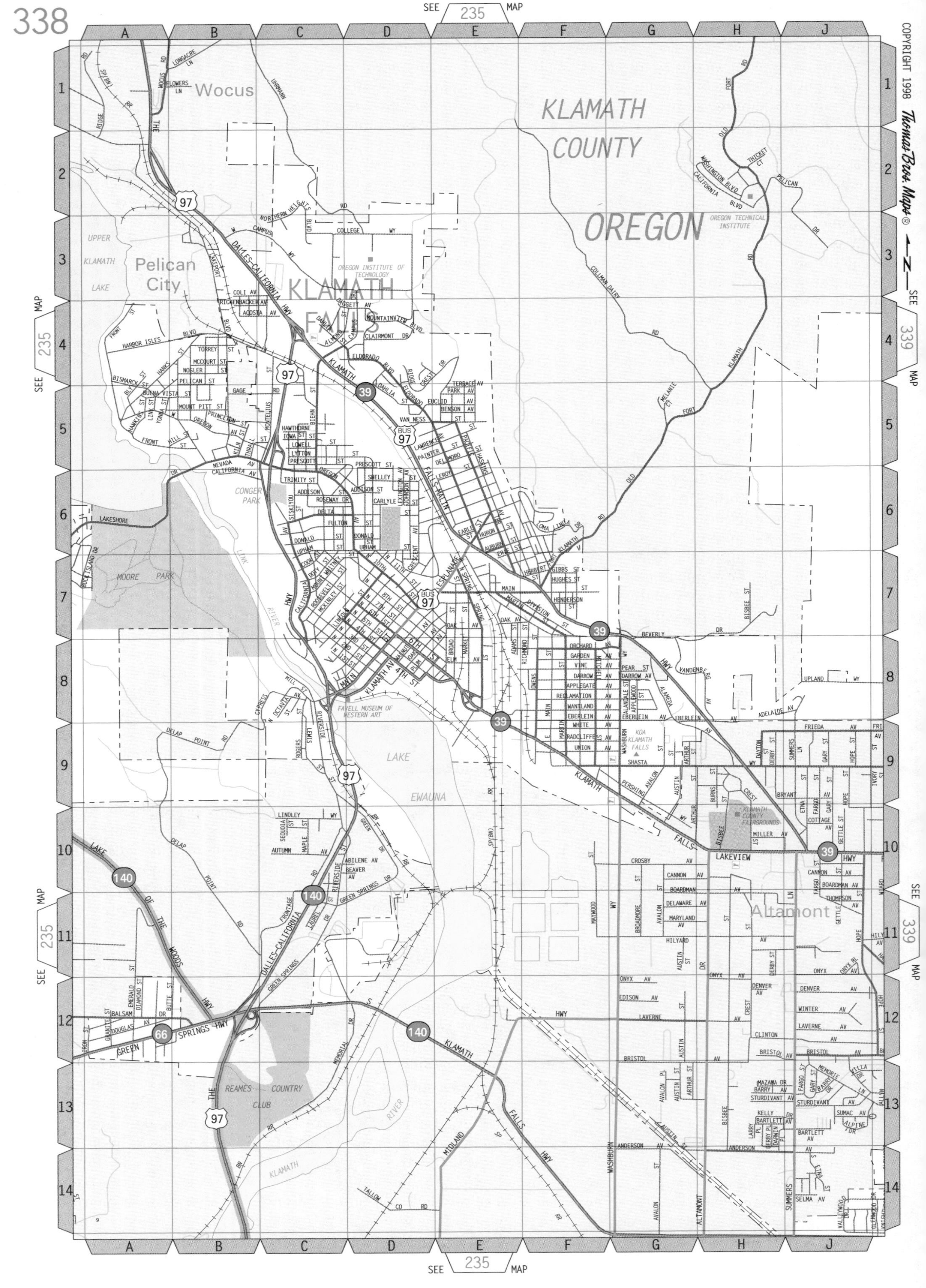
SEE 235 MAP
SEE 339 MAP
COPYRIGHT 1998 Thomas Bros. Maps ®
Wocus
KLAMATH COUNTY
OREGON
Pelican City
UPPER KLAMATH LAKE
KLAMATH FALLS
OREGON INSTITUTE OF TECHNOLOGY
OREGON TECHNICAL INSTITUTE
CONGER PARK
MOORE PARK
LINK RIVER
FAVELL MUSEUM OF WESTERN ART
LAKE EWAUNA
KOA KLAMATH FALLS
KLAMATH COUNTY FAIRGROUNDS
Altamont
REAMES COUNTRY CLUB
KLAMATH RIVER
DALLES-CALIFORNIA HWY
LAKE OF THE WOODS HWY
GREEN SPRINGS HWY
KLAMATH FALLS HWY
LAKEVIEW HWY
SOUTH SIXTH ST
MIDLAND RD
BEVERLY DR
LAKESHORE DR
DELAP RD
FORT KLAMATH RD
COLLMAN DAIRY RD
97
39
140
66

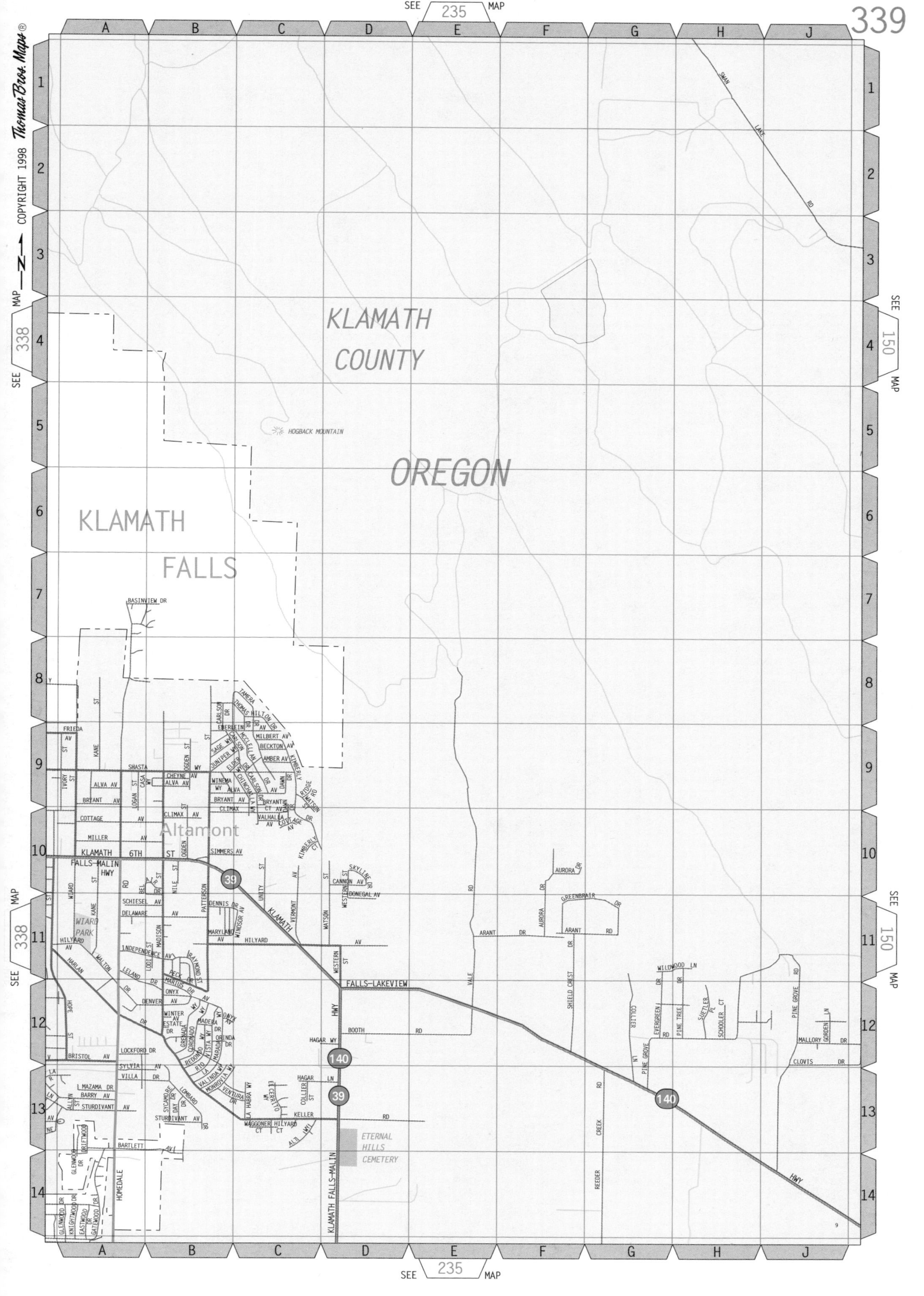
SEE 235 MAP
KLAMATH COUNTY
OREGON
KLAMATH FALLS
Altamont
HOGBACK MOUNTAIN
SEE 338 MAP
SEE 150 MAP
SWAN LAKE RD
FALLS-LAKEVIEW HWY
KLAMATH FALLS-MALIN HWY
ETERNAL HILLS CEMETERY
WIARD PARK
KLAMATH 6TH ST
ARANT DR
BOOTH RD
KELLER RD
REEDER RD
CREEK RD
SHIELD CREST DR
VALE RD
PINE GROVE RD
MALLORY DR
CLOVIS DR
WILDWOOD LN
HOMEDALE
BASINVIEW DR
PNW
DETAIL

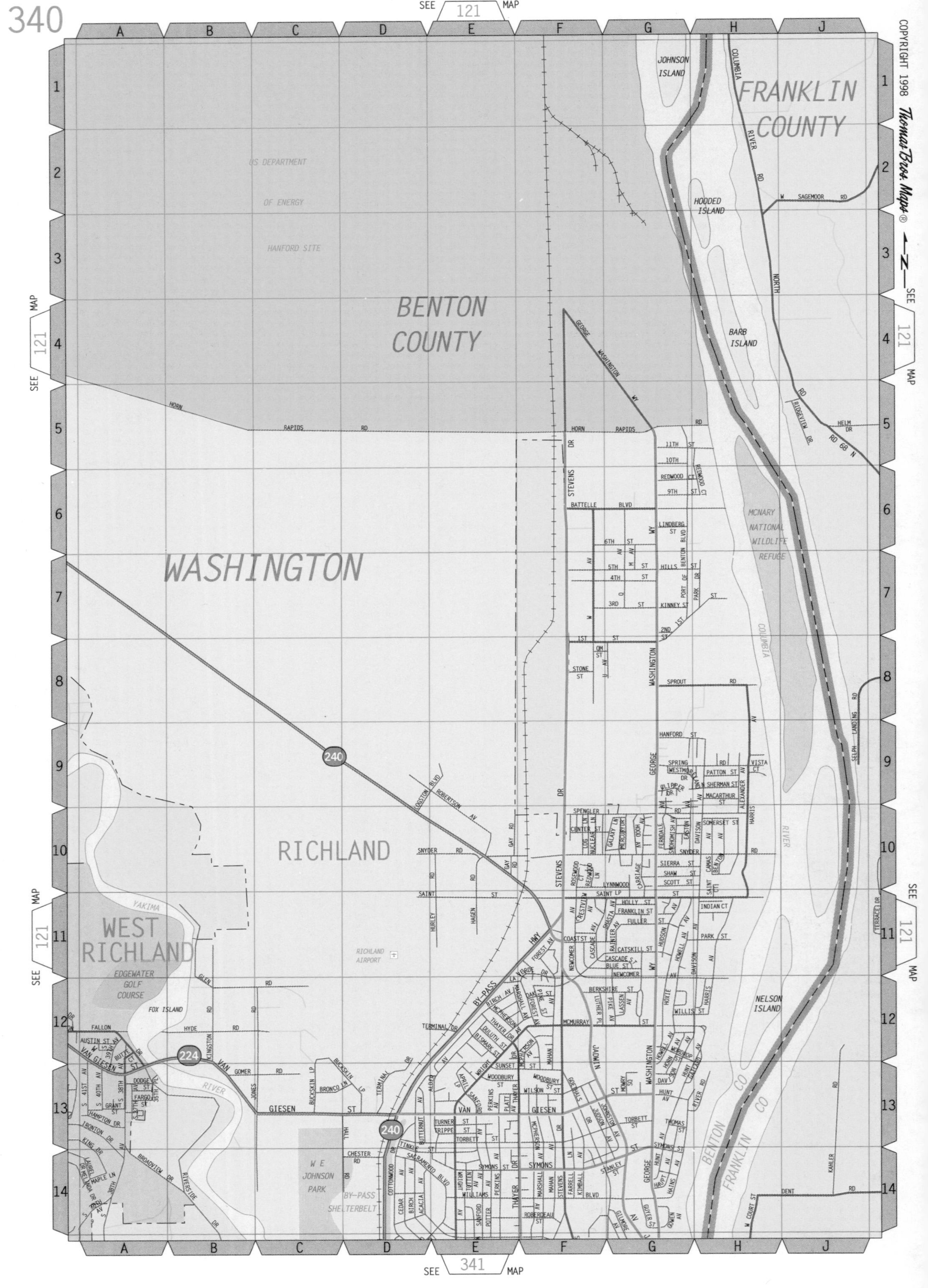

SEE 121 MAP
SEE 341 MAP

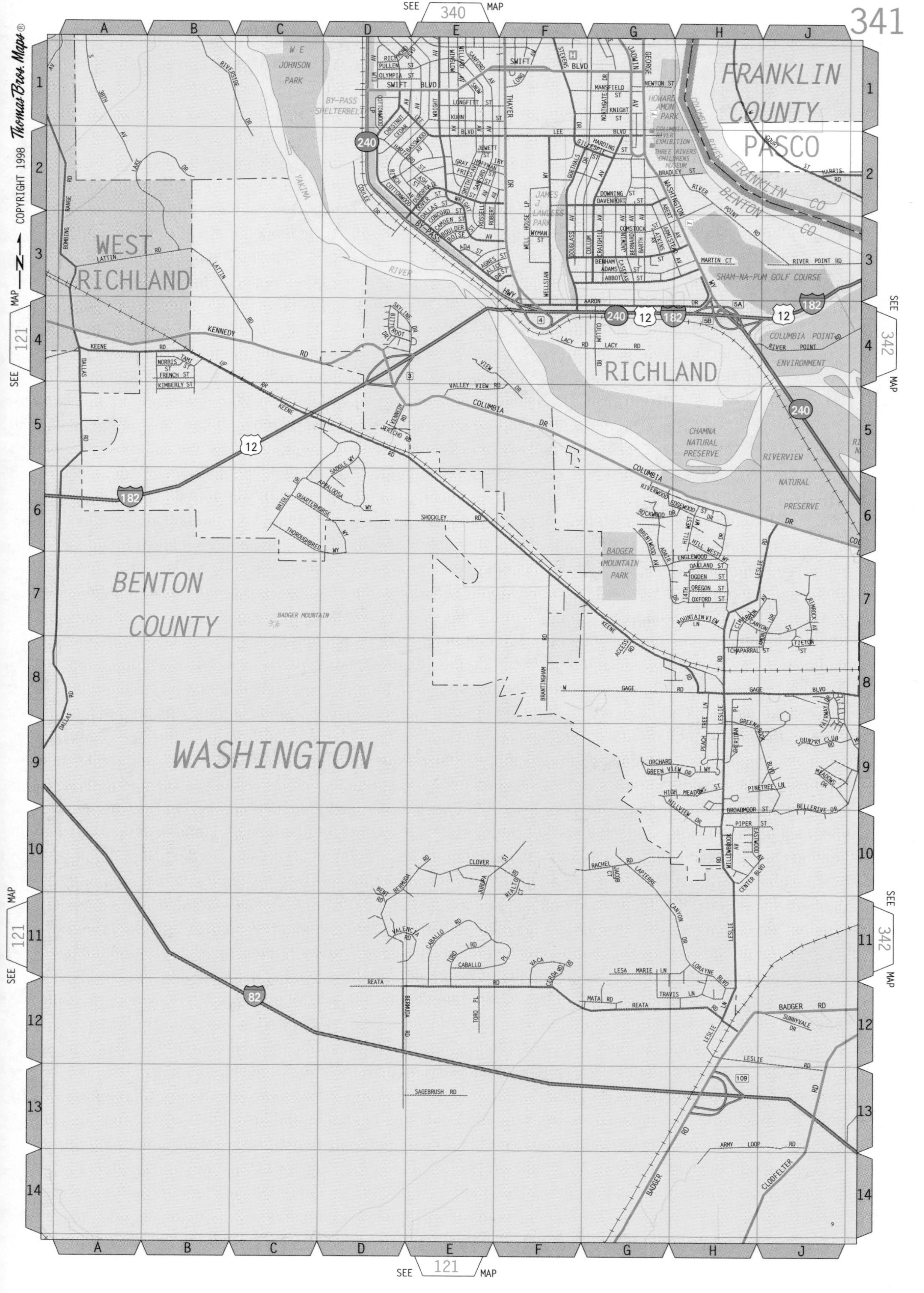
WEST RICHLAND
RICHLAND
FRANKLIN COUNTY
PASCO
BENTON COUNTY
WASHINGTON
W E JOHNSON PARK
BY-PASS SHELTERBELT
HOWARD AMON PARK
COLUMBIA RIVER EXHIBITION
THREE RIVERS CHILDRENS MUSEUM
JAMES J LAWLESS PARK
SHAM-NA-PUM GOLF COURSE
COLUMBIA POINT ENVIRONMENT
CHAMNA NATURAL PRESERVE
RIVERVIEW NATURAL PRESERVE
BADGER MOUNTAIN PARK
BADGER MOUNTAIN
KENNEDY RD
KEENE RD
COLUMBIA DR
GAGE BLVD
SHOCKLEY RD
REATA RD
BADGER RD
LESLIE RD
SAGEBRUSH RD
ARMY LOOP RD
CLODFELTER RD
DALLAS RD
BOMBING RANGE RD
SEE 340 MAP
SEE 342 MAP
SEE 121 MAP
PNW
DETAIL

SEE 121 MAP

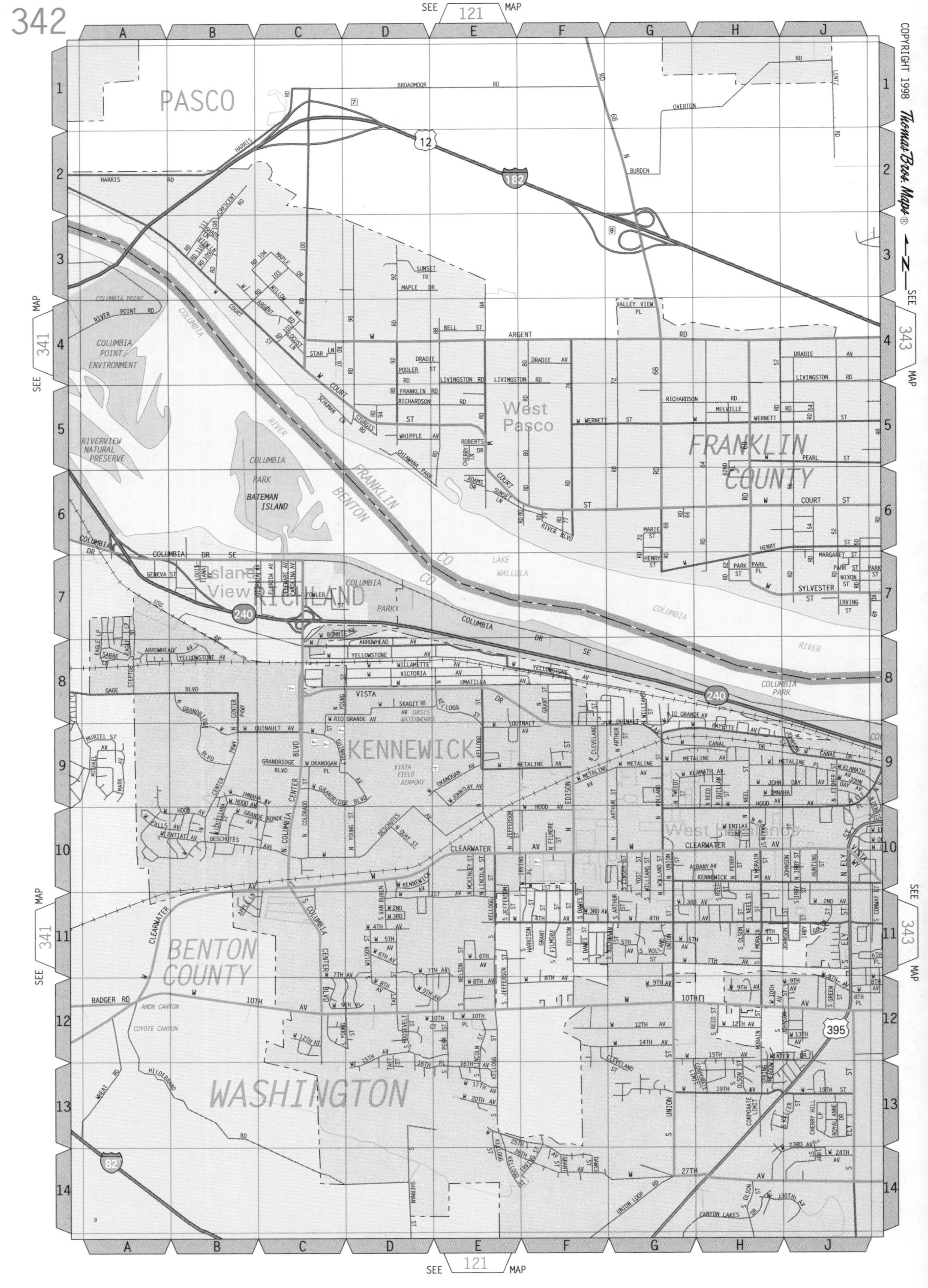

SEE 341 MAP
SEE 343 MAP
SEE 121 MAP

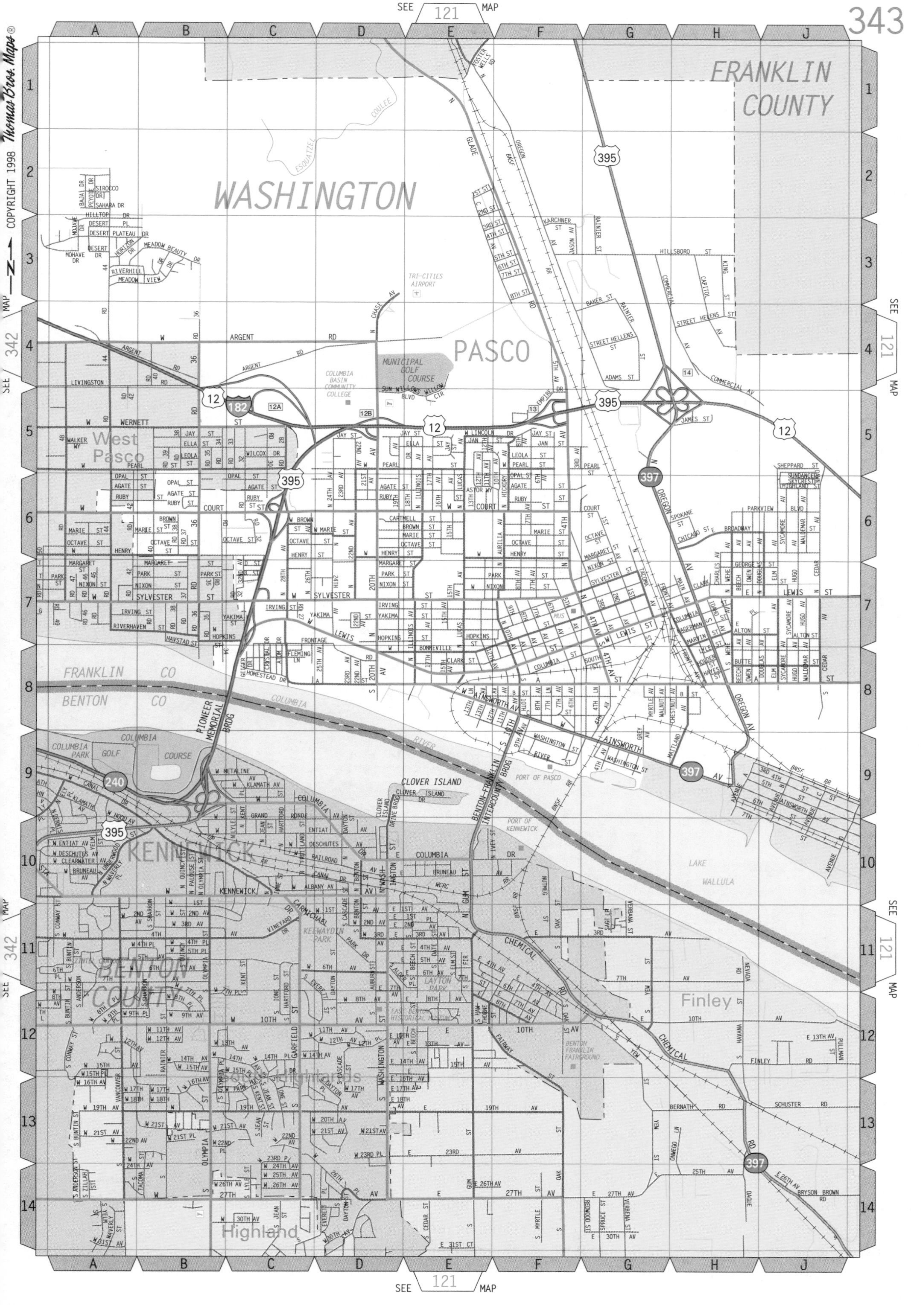
SEE 121 MAP
SEE 342 MAP
SEE 121 MAP
SEE 342 MAP
SEE 121 MAP
SEE 121 MAP
WASHINGTON
FRANKLIN COUNTY
PASCO
West Pasco
KENNEWICK
BENTON COUNTY
Finley
Highland
FRANKLIN CO
BENTON CO
COLUMBIA RIVER
LAKE WALLULA
CLOVER ISLAND
TRI-CITIES AIRPORT
MUNICIPAL GOLF COURSE
COLUMBIA BASIN COMMUNITY COLLEGE
COLUMBIA PARK GOLF COURSE
PIONEER MEMORIAL BRDG
BENTON-FRANKLIN INTERCOUNTY BRDG
PORT OF PASCO
PORT OF KENNEWICK
KEEWAYDIN PARK
LAYTON PARK
EAST BENTON HISTORICAL MUSEUM
BENTON FRANKLIN FAIRGROUND
ESQUATZEL COULEE
ARGENT RD
COURT ST
LEWIS ST
SYLVESTER ST
AINSWORTH AV
OREGON AV
COLUMBIA DR
CHEMICAL DR
CLEARWATER AV
KENNEWICK AV
10TH AV
19TH AV
27TH AV
HILLSBORO ST
COMMERCIAL AV
BERNATH RD
SCHUSTER RD
FINLEY RD
BRYSON BROWN RD
PNW
DETAIL

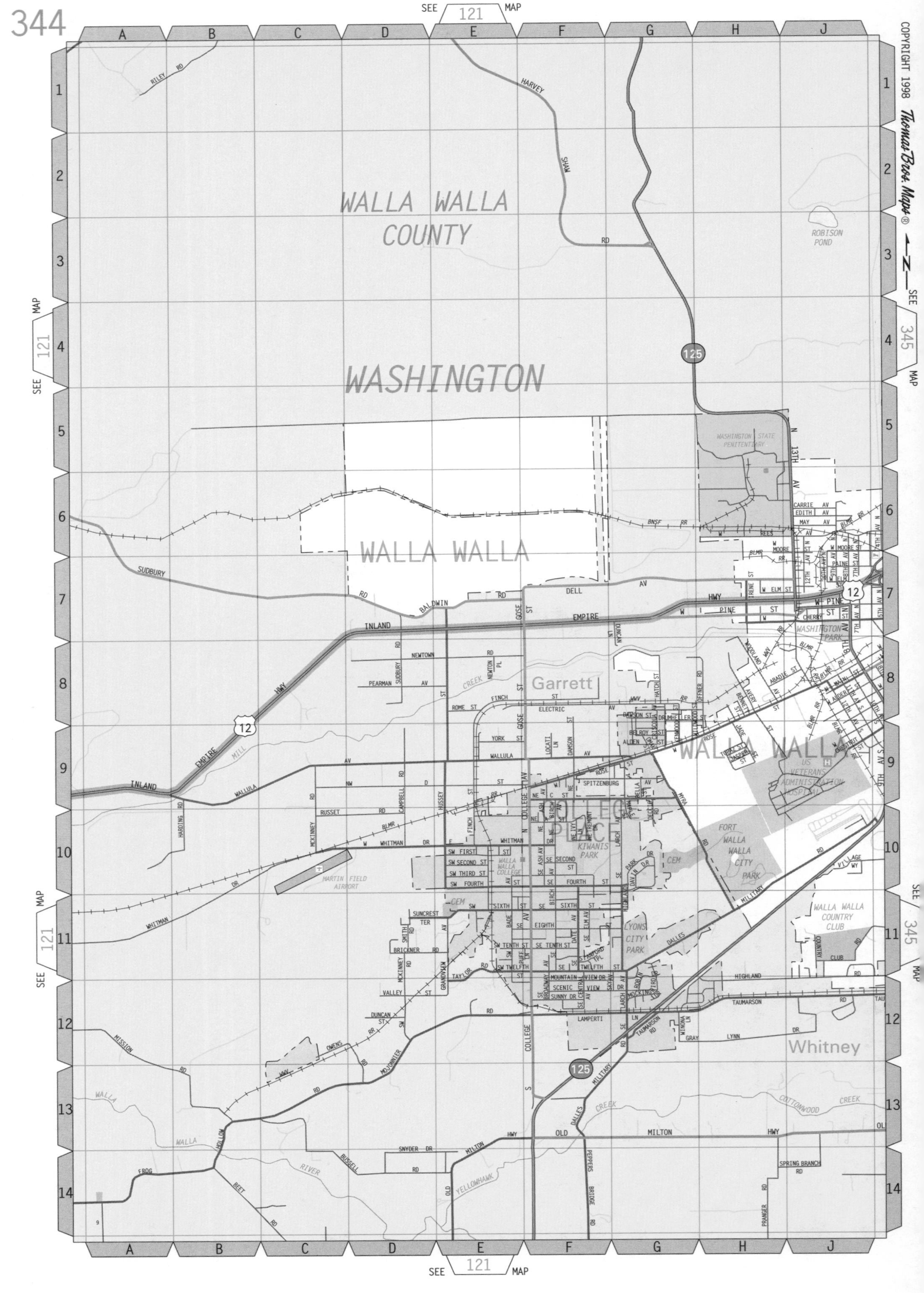

SEE 121 MAP
WALLA WALLA COUNTY
WASHINGTON
WALLA WALLA
Garrett
COLLEGE PLACE
Whitney
ROBISON POND
WASHINGTON STATE PENITENTIARY
WASHINGTON PARK
US VETERANS ADMINISTRATION HOSPITAL
FORT WALLA WALLA CITY PARK
KIWANIS PARK
WALLA WALLA COLLEGE
LYONS CITY PARK
WALLA WALLA COUNTRY CLUB
MARTIN FIELD AIRPORT
CEM
INLAND EMPIRE HWY
SUDBURY RD
DELL AV
BALDWIN RD
WALLULA AV
WHITMAN DR
MISSION RD
MOJONNIER RD
OLD MILTON HWY
HOLLOW
FROG
BEET RD
RUSSELL RD
SNYDER DR
YELLOWHAWK
PEPPERS BRIDGE RD
DALLES MILITARY RD
TAUMARSON RD
HIGHLAND
LYNN DR
GRAY
COTTONWOOD CREEK
SPRING BRANCH RD
PRANGER RD
RILEY RD
HARVEY SHAW RD
N 13TH AV
GOSE ST
COLLEGE AV
BNSF RR
BLMR RR
WALLA WALLA RIVER
MILL CREEK
SEE 345 MAP

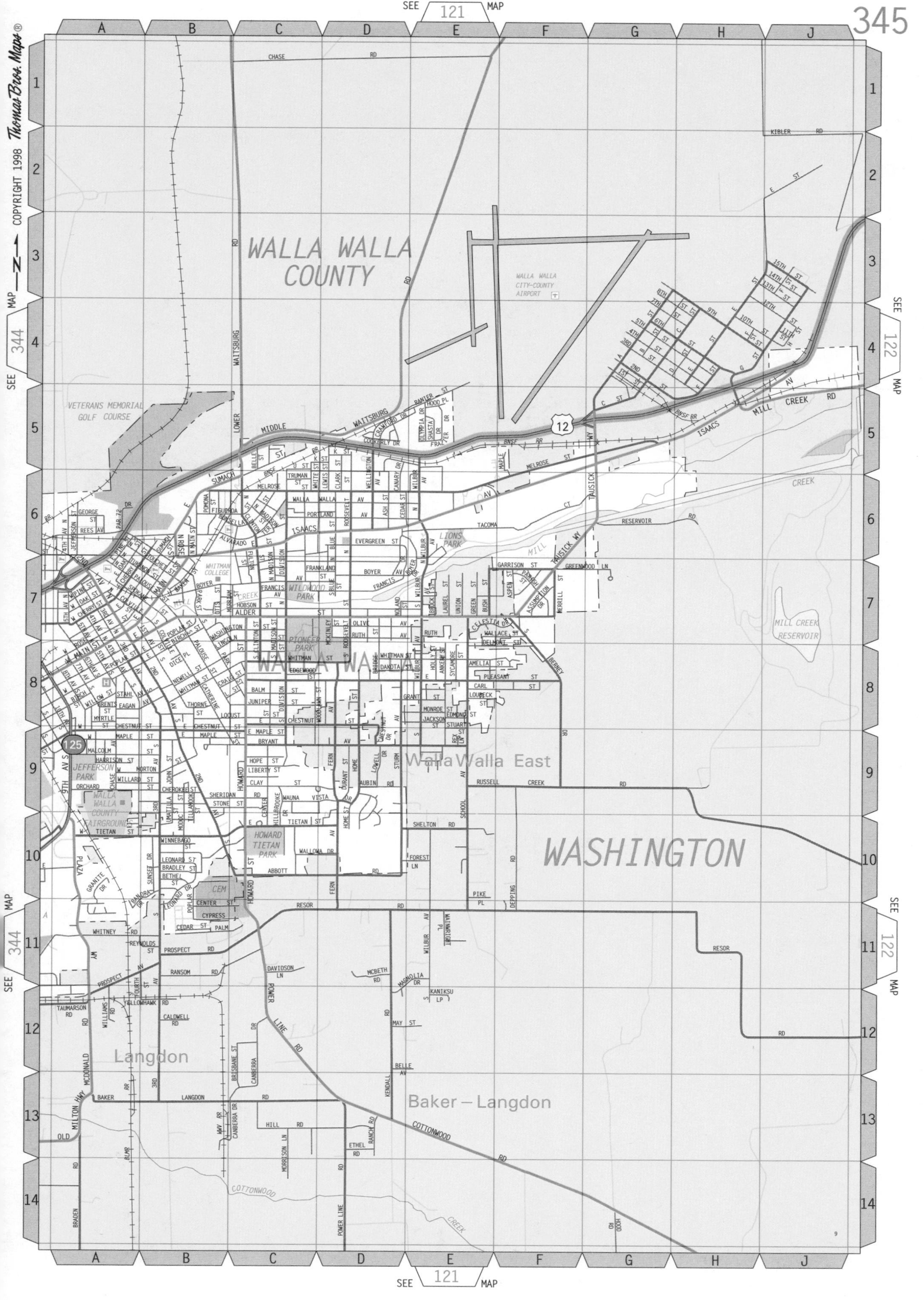
WALLA WALLA
COUNTY
WALLA WALLA CITY-COUNTY AIRPORT
VETERANS MEMORIAL GOLF COURSE
WHITMAN COLLEGE
WILDWOOD PARK
LIONS PARK
PIONEER PARK
JEFFERSON PARK
WALLA WALLA COUNTY FAIRGROUND
HOWARD TIETAN PARK
CEM
MILL CREEK RESERVOIR
Walla Walla East
WASHINGTON
Langdon
Baker – Langdon
SEE 121 MAP
SEE 122 MAP
SEE 344 MAP
DETAIL
PNW
Thomas Bros. Maps® COPYRIGHT 1998

SEE 114 MAP

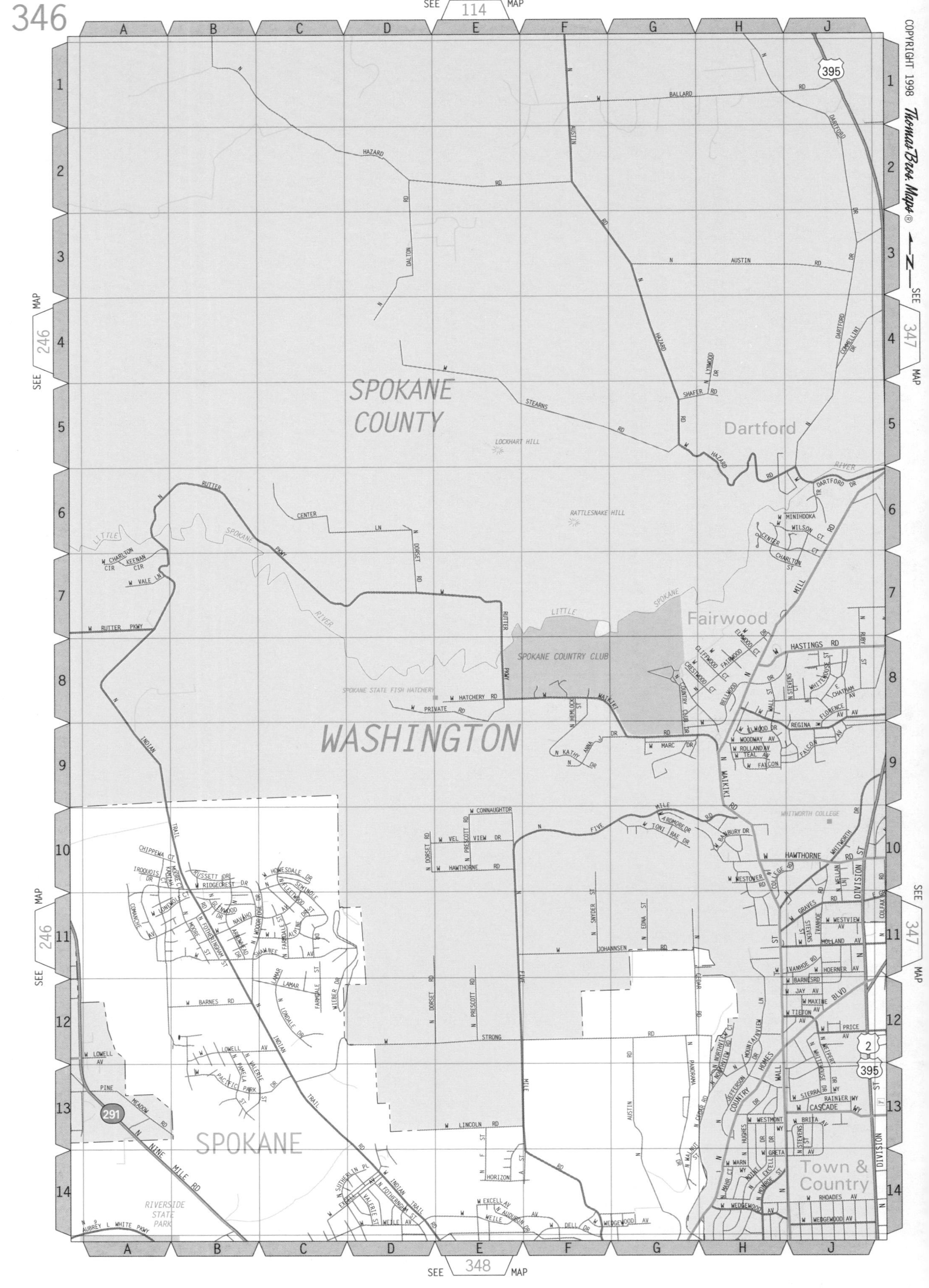

SEE 246 MAP
SEE 347 MAP
SEE 348 MAP

PNW

DETAIL

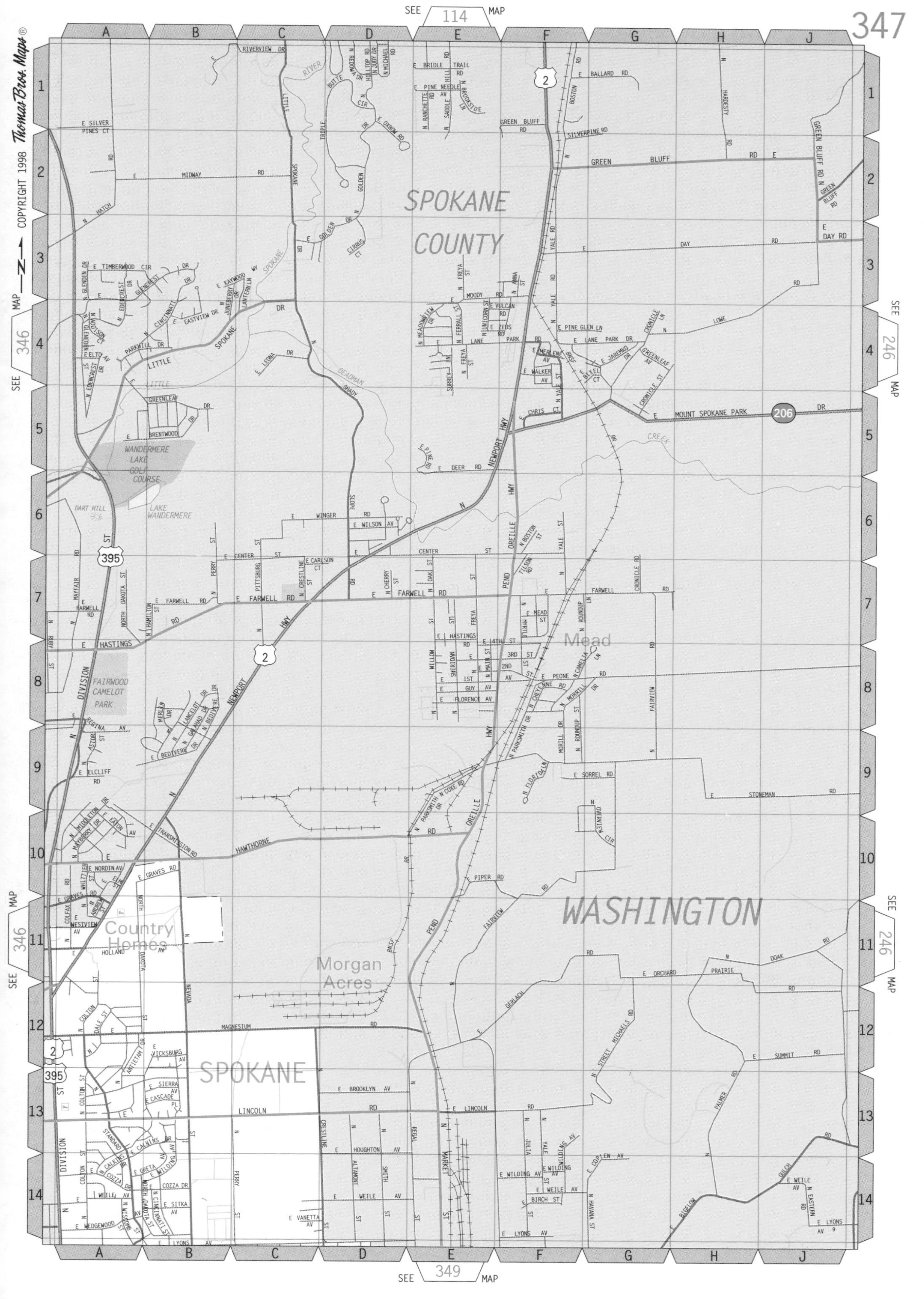

SEE 114 MAP
SEE 349 MAP
SEE 346 MAP
SEE 246 MAP
SPOKANE COUNTY
WASHINGTON
SPOKANE
Mead
Country Homes
Morgan Acres
WANDERMERE LAKE GOLF COURSE
LAKE WANDERMERE
DART HILL
FAIRWOOD CAMELOT PARK
LITTLE SPOKANE RIVER
DEADMAN CREEK
NEWPORT HWY
PEND OREILLE HWY
DIVISION ST
GREEN BLUFF RD
MOUNT SPOKANE PARK DR
E FARWELL RD
E HASTINGS RD
HAWTHORNE RD
MAGNESIUM RD
LINCOLN RD
E DAY RD
E MIDWAY RD
E CENTER ST
E PEONE RD
E STONEMAN RD
E ORCHARD PRAIRIE RD
E SUMMIT RD
E BIGELOW GULCH RD
Thomas Bros. Maps®
COPYRIGHT 1998
PNW
DETAIL

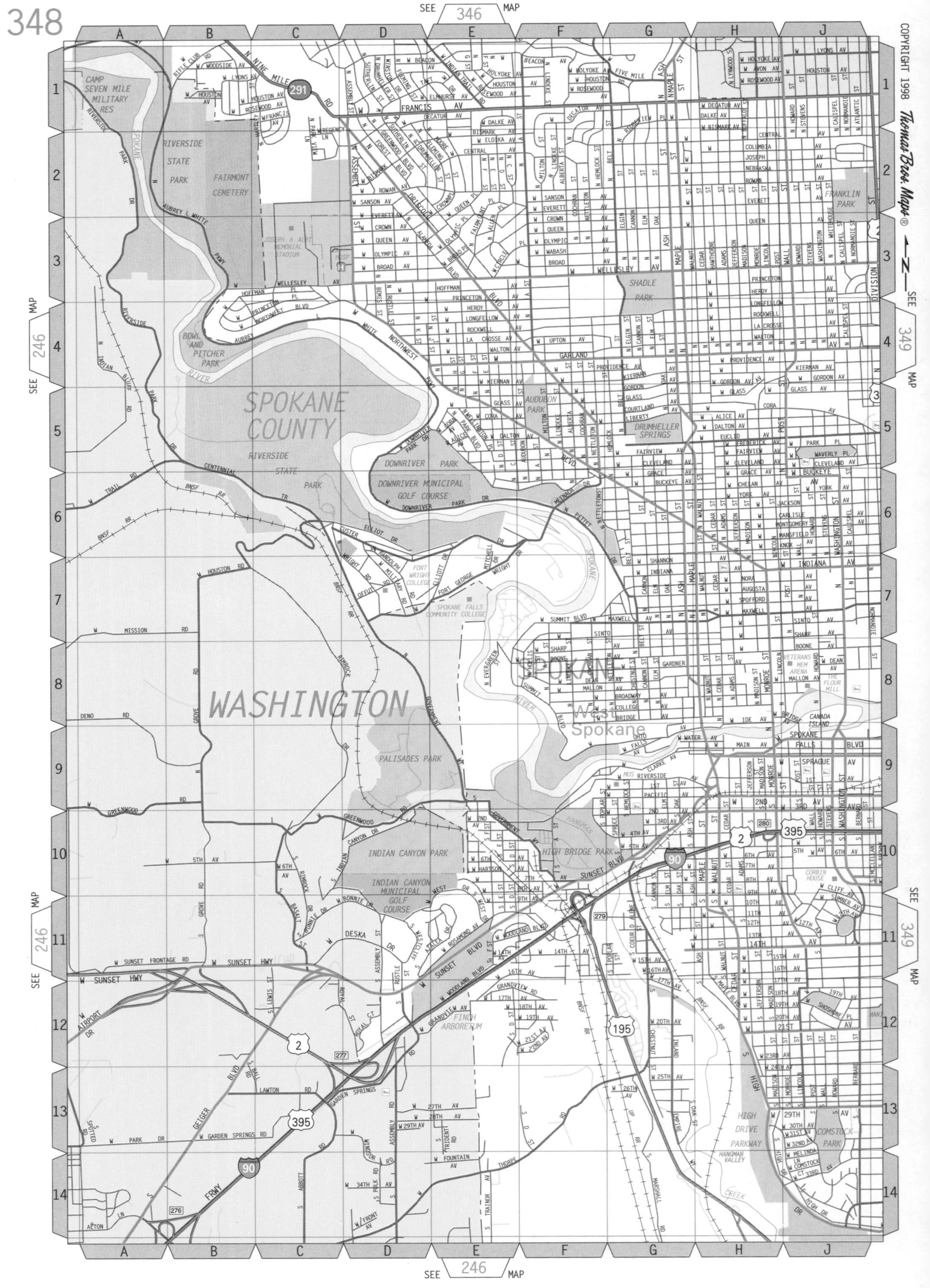
SEE 346 MAP
SPOKANE COUNTY
WASHINGTON
CAMP SEVEN MILE MILITARY RES
RIVERSIDE STATE PARK
FAIRMONT CEMETERY
JOSEPH A. ALBI MEMORIAL STADIUM
BOWL AND PITCHER PARK
DOWNRIVER PARK
DOWNRIVER MUNICIPAL GOLF COURSE
AUDUBON PARK
DRUMHELLER SPRINGS
SHADLE PARK
FRANKLIN PARK
FORT WRIGHT COLLEGE
SPOKANE FALLS COMMUNITY COLLEGE
SPOKANE
West Spokane
VETERANS MEM ARENA
THE FLOUR MILL
CANADA ISLAND
PALISADES PARK
INDIAN CANYON PARK
INDIAN CANYON MUNICIPAL GOLF COURSE
HIGH BRIDGE PARK
FINCH ARBORETUM
CORBIN HOUSE
HIGH DRIVE PARKWAY
HANGMAN VALLEY
COMSTOCK PARK
SEE 246 MAP
SEE 349 MAP
DIVISION
COPYRIGHT 1998 Thomas Bros. Maps ®

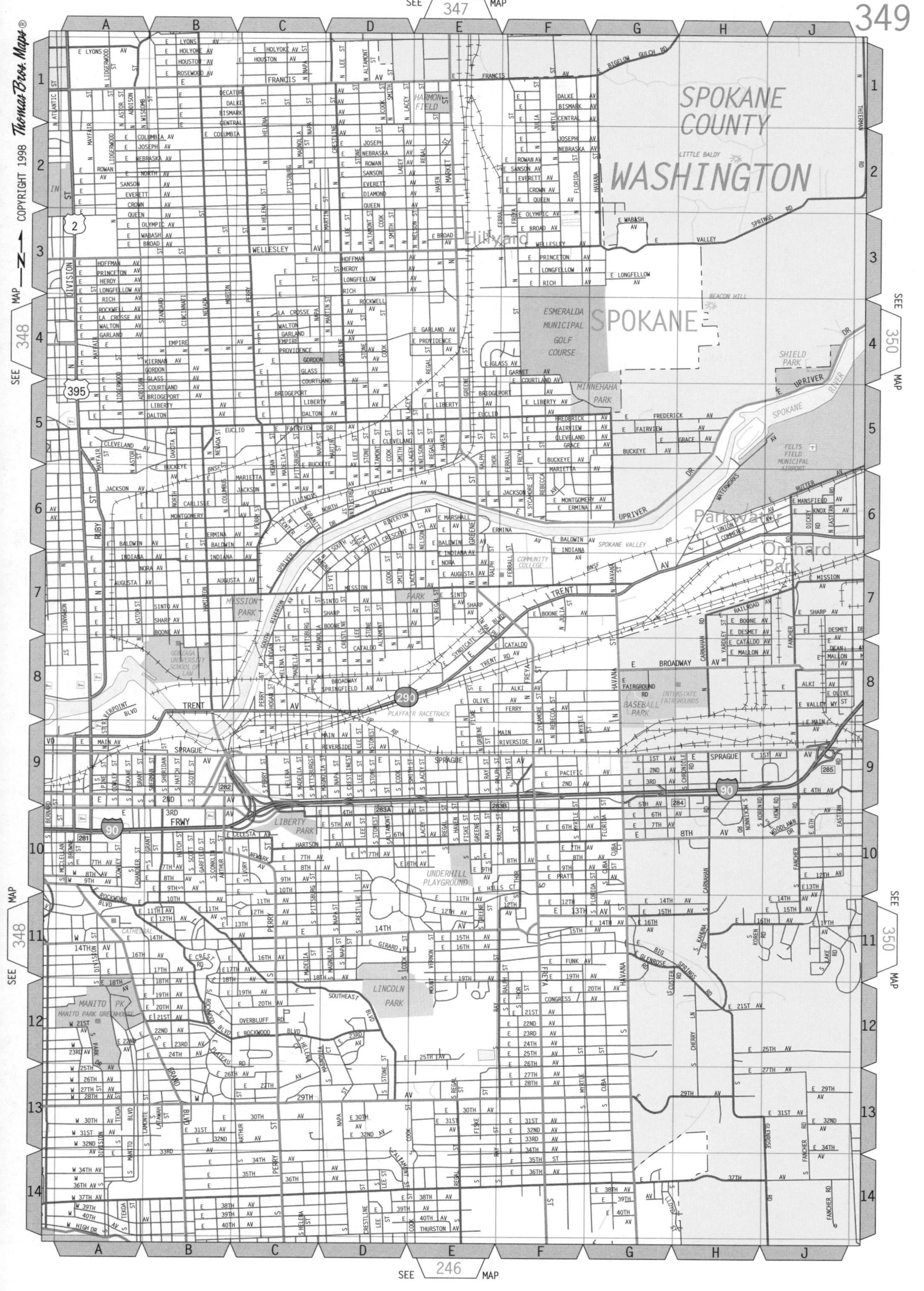

349
SEE 347 MAP
SEE 348 MAP
SEE 350 MAP
SEE 246 MAP
Thomas Bros. Maps ®
COPYRIGHT 1998
SPOKANE COUNTY
WASHINGTON
SPOKANE
Hillyard
Parkwater
Orchard Park
LITTLE BALDY
BEACON HILL
HARMON FIELD
ESMERALDA MUNICIPAL GOLF COURSE
MINNEHAHA PARK
SHIELD PARK
FELTS FIELD MUNICIPAL AIRPORT
SPOKANE RIVER
SPOKANE VALLEY
COMMUNITY COLLEGE
MISSION PARK
GONZAGA UNIVERSITY SCHOOL OF LAW
PLAYFAIR RACETRACK
FAIRGROUND
BASEBALL PARK
INTERSTATE FAIRGROUNDS
LIBERTY PARK
UNDERHILL PLAYGROUND
LINCOLN PARK
MANITO PK
MANITO PARK GREENHOUSE
CATHEDRAL
DIVISION
TRENT
SPRAGUE
WELLESLEY
FRANCIS
UPRIVER DR
BROADWAY
2ND
3RD
FRWY
14TH
29TH
37TH
GRAND BLVD
HAVANA
FREYA
PNW
DETAIL

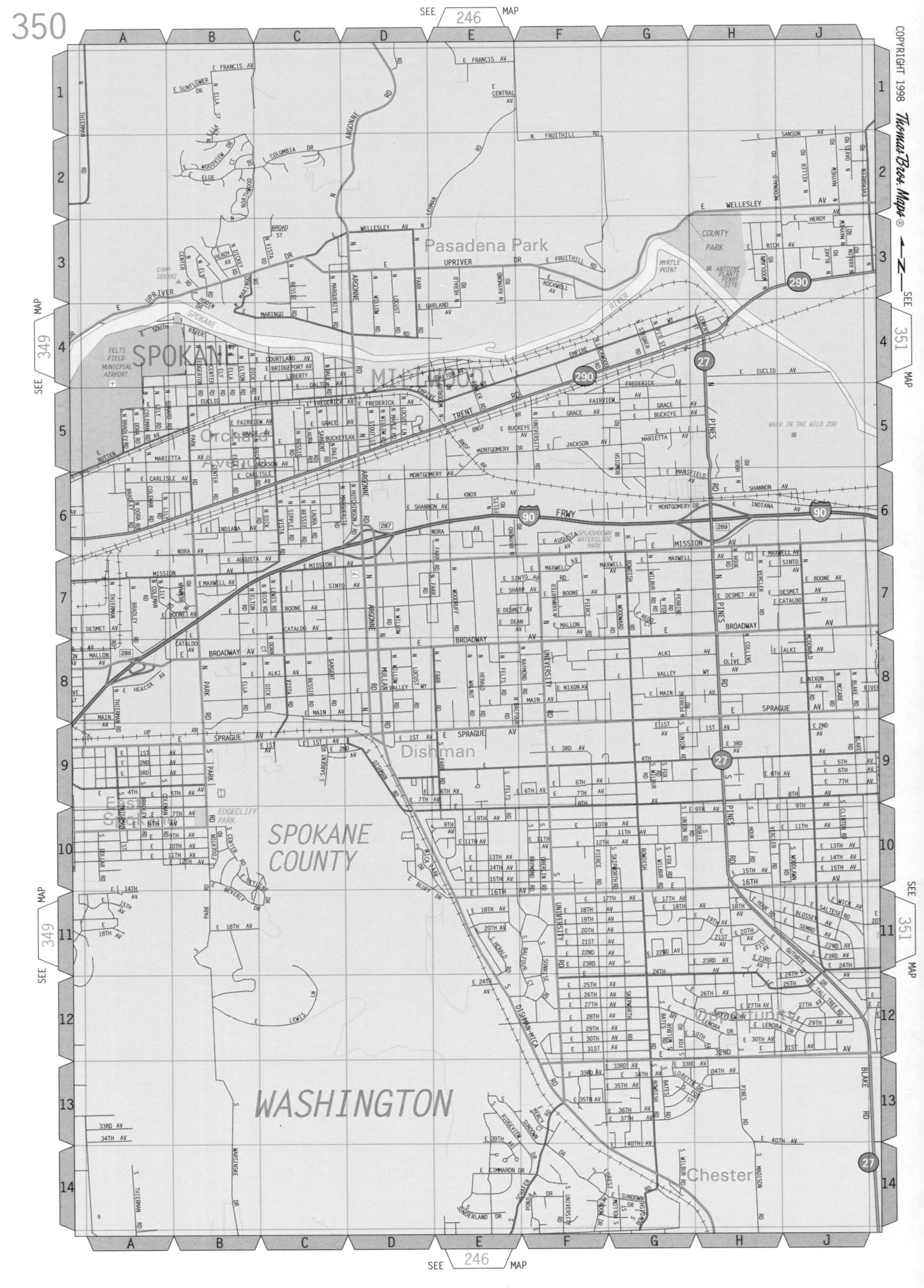

SEE 246 MAP
SEE 349 MAP
SEE 351 MAP
SPOKANE
MILLWOOD
Pasadena Park
Orchard Avenue
Dishman
East Spokane
SPOKANE COUNTY
WASHINGTON
Opportunity
Chester
FELTS FIELD MUNICIPAL AIRPORT
COUNTY PARK
ANTOINE PLANTE FERRY SITE
MYRTLE POINT
CAMP SEKANI
WALK IN THE WILD ZOO
SPLASHDOWN WATERSLIDE PARK
EDGECLIFF PARK
SPOKANE RIVER
E FRANCIS AV
E WELLESLEY AV
UPRIVER DR
N ARGONNE RD
E TRENT AV
FRWY
E MISSION AV
BROADWAY AV
E SPRAGUE AV
N UNIVERSITY RD
PINES RD
DISHMAN-MICA RD
S PARK RD
E 32ND AV
BLAKE RD

PNW

DETAIL

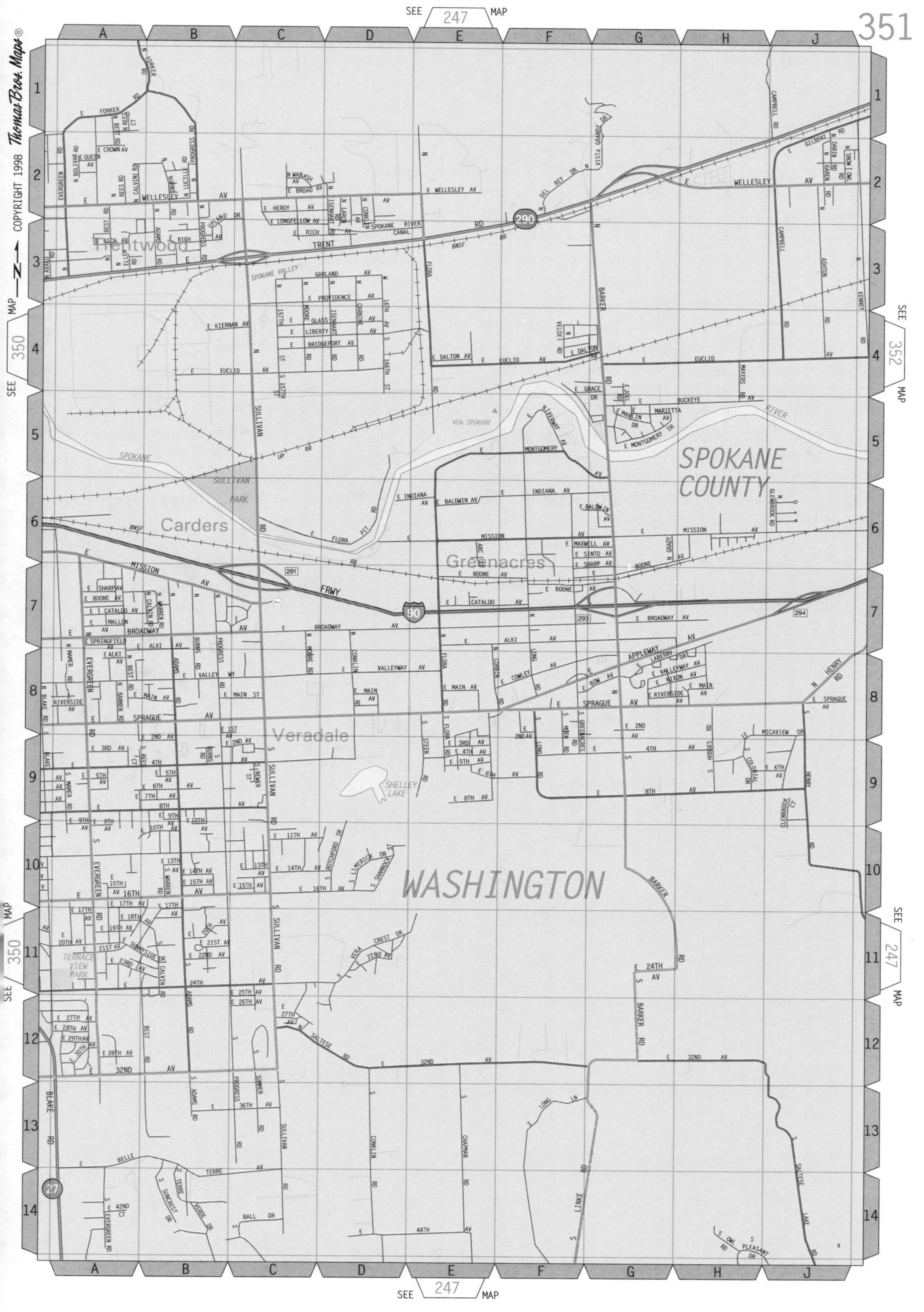

SEE 247 MAP
A
B
C
D
E
F
G
H
J
1
2
3
4
5
6
7
8
9
10
11
12
13
14
SEE 350 MAP
SEE 352 MAP
SEE 247 MAP
SEE 350 MAP
SEE 247 MAP
SPOKANE COUNTY
WASHINGTON
Trentwood
Carders
Greenacres
Veradale
SULLIVAN PARK
TERRACE VIEW PARK
SHELLEY LAKE
KOA SPOKANE
SPOKANE
RIVER
SPOKANE RIVER
WELLESLEY AV
TRENT RD
EUCLID AV
MISSION AV
BROADWAY AV
SPRAGUE AV
APPLEWAY AV
FRWY
SULLIVAN RD
BARKER RD
EVERGREEN RD
FLORA RD
ADAMS RD
PROGRESS RD
CONKLIN RD
CHAPMAN RD
LINKE RD
HENRY RD
CAMPBELL RD
SALTESE RD
SALTESE LAKE RD
BLAKE RD
32ND AV
24TH AV
16TH AV
8TH AV
44TH AV
BELLE TERRE AV
MONTGOMERY AV
INDIANA AV
VALLEYWAY AV
BNSF
UP RR
290
291
293
294
90
27

PNW

DETAIL

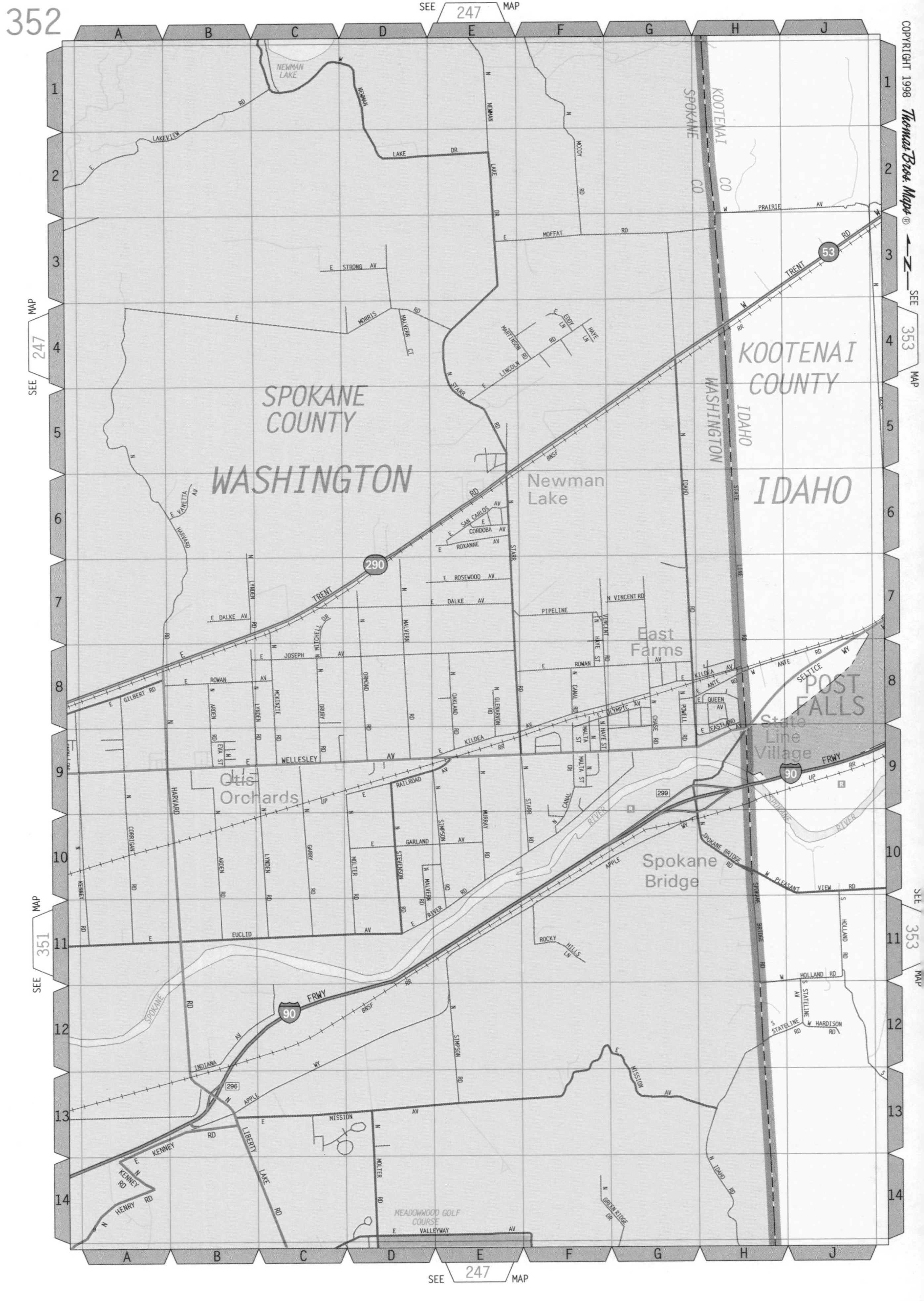
SEE 247 MAP
SPOKANE COUNTY
WASHINGTON
KOOTENAI COUNTY
IDAHO
Newman Lake
East Farms
Otis Orchards
State Line Village
POST FALLS
Spokane Bridge
NEWMAN LAKE
SPOKANE CO
KOOTENAI CO
WASHINGTON
IDAHO
MEADOWWOOD GOLF COURSE
SEE 353 MAP
SEE 351 MAP
SEE 247 MAP
COPYRIGHT 1998 Thomas Bros. Maps®

PNW
DETAIL

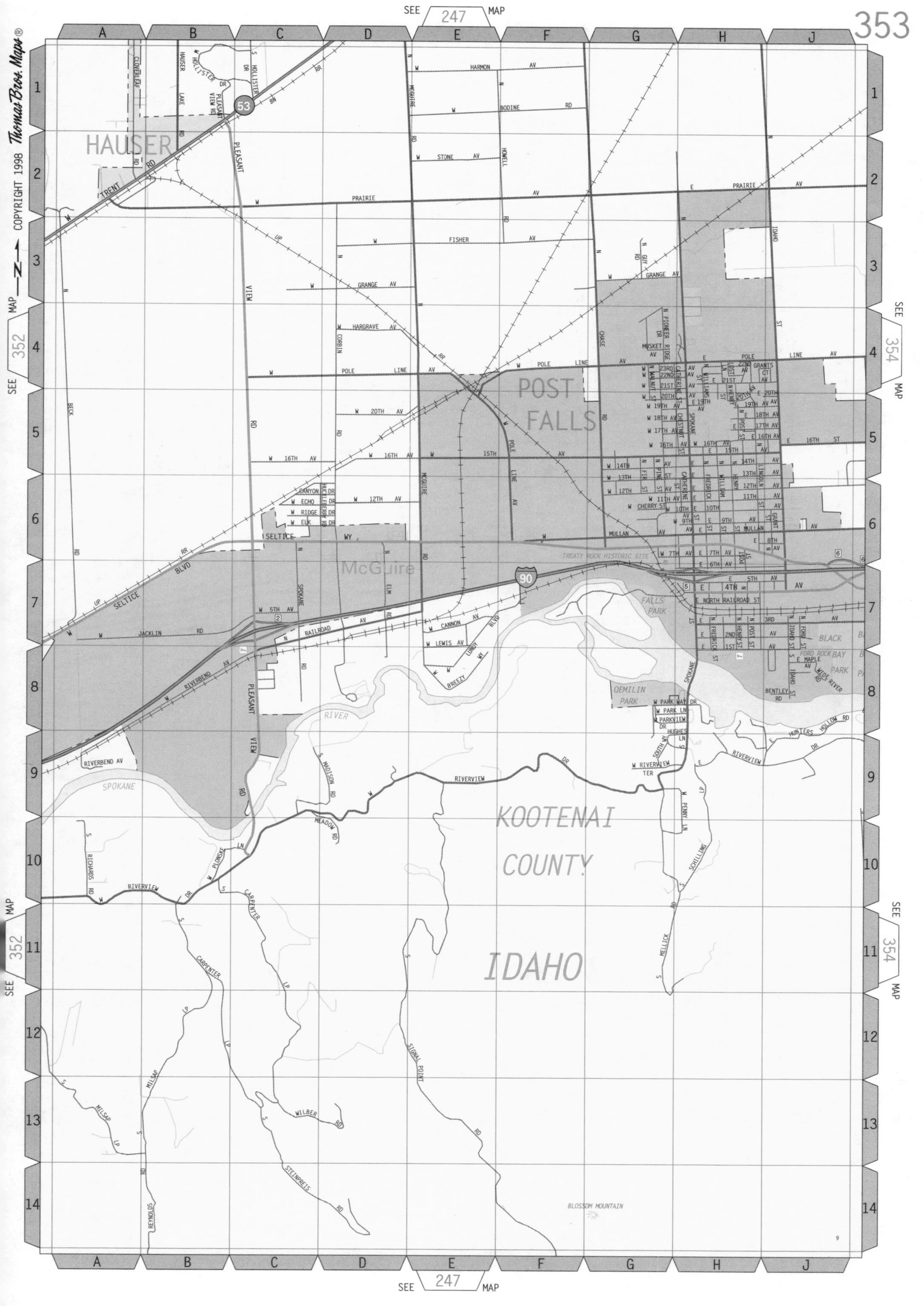

SEE 247 MAP
SEE 352 MAP
SEE 354 MAP
HAUSER
POST FALLS
McGuire
KOOTENAI COUNTY
IDAHO
FALLS PARK
QEMILIN PARK
BLACK BAY PARK
TREATY ROCK HISTORIC SITE
BLOSSOM MOUNTAIN
PRAIRIE AV
POLE LINE AV
SELTICE WY
SELTICE BLVD
RIVERVIEW DR
PLEASANT VIEW RD
SPOKANE RIVER

PNW

DETAIL

SEE 247 MAP
SEE 353 MAP
SEE 355 MAP
HAYDEN
COEUR D'ALENE
POST FALLS
HUETTER
KOOTENAI COUNTY
IDAHO
PRAIRIE AV
POLE LINE AV
MULLAN AV
SELTICE WY
SPOKANE RIVER
HIGHLAND DR
GREEN FERRY RD
POINT-RATHDRUM HWY
HUETTER RD
MEYER RD
RIVERVIEW DR
MEADOWBROOK RD
CLEMETSON RD
STACH RD
BUNN RD
COUGAR GULCH
PURCELL TRENCH
BLACK BAY PARK
HARBOR ISLAND
ROSS POINT

PNW

DETAIL

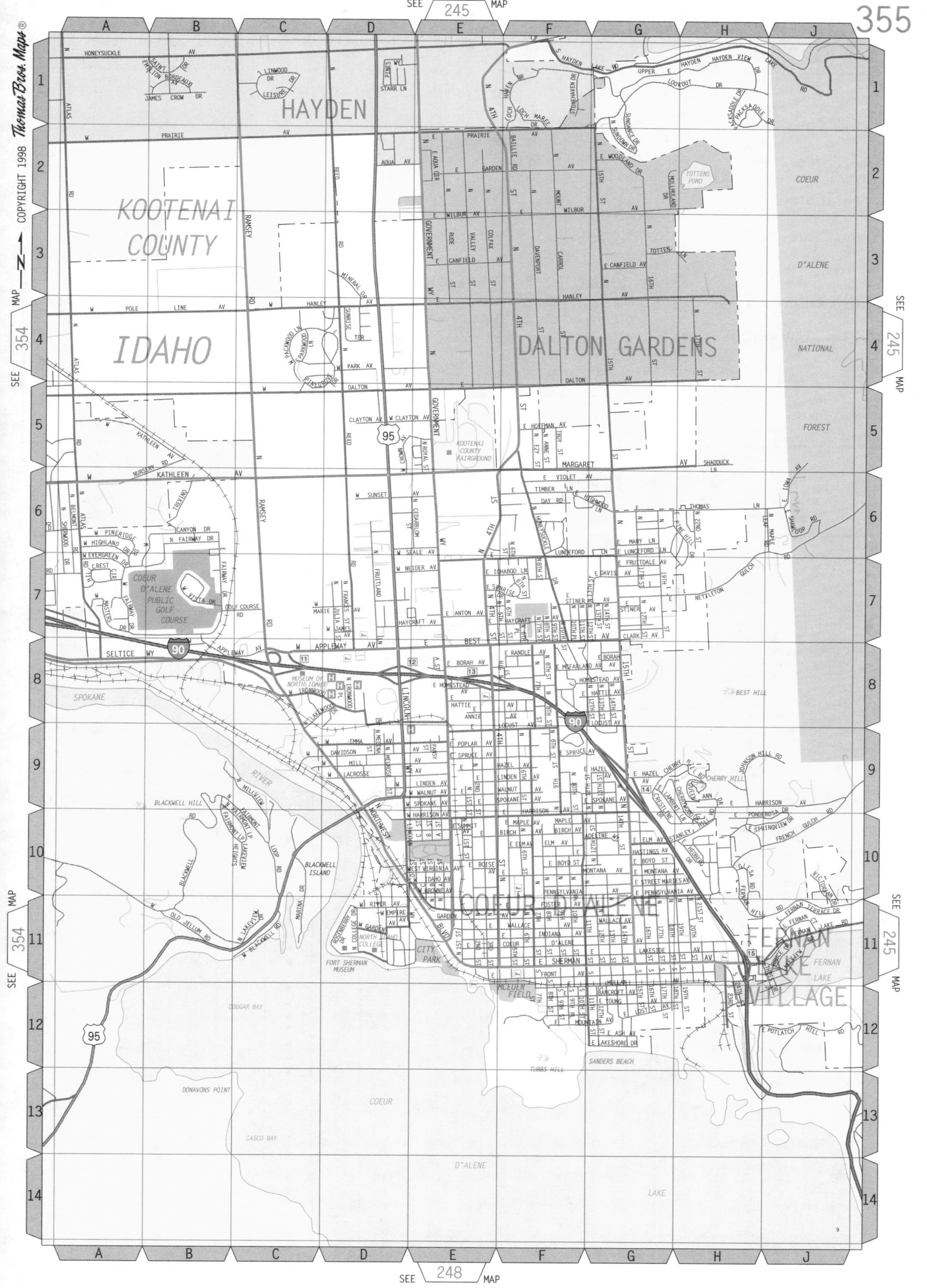

SEE 245 MAP
HAYDEN
KOOTENAI COUNTY
IDAHO
DALTON GARDENS
COEUR D'ALENE
FERNAN LAKE VILLAGE
COEUR D'ALENE NATIONAL FOREST
COEUR D'ALENE LAKE
SEE 354 MAP
SEE 248 MAP
PNW
DETAIL
Thomas Bros. Maps®
COPYRIGHT 1998

Pacific Northwest National & State Park Information

Camping & Lodging Information

British Columbia — Travel Canada
www.Travelcanada.ca/index-0.html

Washington State — Washington State Online Travel Information
www.tourism.wa.gov

Oregon State — Oregon Economic Developement Dept. Tourism Commission: (503) 986-0000
www.state.or.us/quality-.htm

Idaho State — Discover Idaho
www.visitid.org/

National & State Park Information

British Columbia — British Columbia Ministry of Environment Lands & Parks: (800) 689-9025
www.env.gov.bc.ca/bcparks/reserv/campers.htm

Washington State — Washington State Parks & Recreation Commission
www.parks.wa.gov

Oregon State — Oregon Online Highways
www.ohwy.com/or/oloprd.htm

Idaho State — Idaho State Parks
http://www.idoc.state.id.us/Lasso/InfoNet/questframe.html

Selected National & State Parks Including Recreation Areas, Forests, and National Monuments

Prov	Park	Page & Grid	Camping	Trailer / RV	Picnicking	Swimming	Fishing	Hiking	Boating	Beach
BC	**National Parks**									
	Pacific Rim National Park	100, A1	●	●	●	●	●	●	●	●
	Provincial Parks									
	Carmanah Pacific Provincial Park	92, B2	●		●			●		
	Cathedral Provincial Park	104, A1	●	●	●		●	●		
	Cultus Lake Provincial Park	102, C1	●	●	●	●	●	●	●	●
	Desolation Sound Provincial Marine Park	92, B1	●			●	●	●		
	Garibaldi Provincial Park	94, A1	●		●		●	●		
	Golden Ears Provincial Park	94, B2	●	●	●	●	●	●	●	●
	Manning Provincial Park	95, C3	●	●	●	●	●	●	●	●
	Skagit Valley Provincial Park	103, B1	●	●	●	●	●	●	●	●
	Strathcona Provincial Park	92, A2	●	●	●	●	●	●	●	●
State	**Park**									
WA	**National Parks**									
	Mount Rainier National Park	118, C1	●	●	●		●	●	●	
	North Cascades National Park	103, A1	●	●	●		●	●	●	
	Olympic National Park	109, B1	●	●	●		●	●	●	
	National / State Forests									
	Colville National Forest	105, C2	●	●	●	●	●	●	●	●
	Gifford Pinchot National Forest	118, C2	●	●	●	●	●	●	●	●
	Kaniksu National Forest	106, C2	●	●	●	●	●	●	●	●
	Mount Baker National Forest	103, A2	●	●	●	●	●	●	●	●
	Mount Baker-Snoqualmie National Forest	111, A2	●	●	●	●	●	●	●	●
	Okanogan National Forest	104, B2	●	●	●	●	●	●	●	●
	Olympic National Forest	109, B2	●	●	●	●	●	●	●	●
	Wenatchee National Forest	112, A1	●	●	●	●	●	●	●	●
	Parks / Recreation Areas / Monuments									
	Beacon Rock State Park	194, B6	●	●	●		●		●	●
	Birch Bay State Park	158, B5	●	●	●		●			●
	Bogachiel State Park	169, D3	●	●	●		●			●
	Brooks Memorial State Park	119, C3	●	●	●		●			
	Columbia River Gorge National Scenic Area	200, C1	●	●	●		●	●	●	
	Coulee Dam National Recreation Area	237, D3	●	●	●	●	●	●	●	●
	Fort Canby State Park	186, A6	●	●	●		●		●	●
	Fort Flagler State Park	167, B6	●	●	●		●		●	●
	Fort Worden State Park	167, A6	●	●	●		●		●	●
	Kanaskat-Palmer State Park	110, C3	●	●	●				●	●
	Lake Chelan National Recreation Area	103, C3	●	●	●		●	●	●	
	Larrabee State Park	160, D2	●	●	●		●		●	●
	Millersylvania State Park	184, C2	●	●	●	●	●			
	Mount Saint Helens National Volcanic Monument	190, B1						●		
	Mount Spokane State Park	114, C1	●		●					
	Ocean City State Park	177, B6	●	●	●		●			●
	Pacific Beach State Park	177, B2	●	●	●		●			●
	Potholes State Park	242, C6	●	●	●		●		●	●
	Ross Lake National Recreation Area	103, B1	●	●	●		●	●	●	
	Schafer State Park	179, A5	●	●	●		●			●
	Seaquest State Park	187, D7	●	●	●		●			
	Sequim Bay State Park	166, C7	●	●	●		●		●	●

Selected National & State Parks Including Recreation Areas, Forests, and National Monuments

State	Park	Page & Grid	Camping	Trailer / RV	Picnicking	Swimming	Fishing	Hiking	Boating	Beach
WA	**Parks/Recreation Areas/Monuments cont...**									
	Sun Lakes State Park	112, C2	●	●	●	●	●		●	
	Twanoh State Park	173, C7	●	●	●	●	●		●	●
	Wenberg State Park	168, B6	●	●	●		●		●	●
	Yakima Sportsman State Park	243, C7	●	●	●		●			●
OR	**National Parks**									
	Crater Lake National Park	227, C3	●	●	●			●		
	National/State Forests									
	Clatsop State Forest	191, D2	●	●	●	●	●	●	●	●
	Deschutes National Forest	143, A1	●	●	●	●	●	●	●	●
	Elliott State Forest	140, C1	●	●	●	●	●	●	●	●
	Fremont National Forest	151, C2	●	●	●	●	●	●	●	●
	Malheur National Forest	137, B1	●	●	●	●	●	●	●	●
	McDonald State Forest	207, A5	●	●	●	●	●	●	●	●
	Mount Hood National Forest	202, B2	●	●	●	●	●	●	●	●
	Ochoco National Forest	136, B2	●	●	●	●	●	●	●	●
	Rogue River National Forest	149, B3	●	●	●	●	●	●	●	●
	Santiam State Forest	134, A1	●	●	●	●	●	●	●	●
	Siskiyou National Forest	148, B2	●	●	●	●	●	●	●	●
	Siuslaw National Forest	132, C2	●	●	●	●	●	●	●	●
	Tillamook State Forest	125, A1	●	●	●	●	●	●	●	●
	Umatilla National Forest	129, B3	●	●	●	●	●	●	●	●
	Umpqua National Forest	142, A2	●	●	●	●	●	●	●	●
	Wallowa-Whitman National Forest	138, A1	●	●	●	●	●	●	●	●
	Willamette National Forest	134, B1	●	●	●	●	●	●	●	●
	Winema National Forest	142, C2	●	●	●	●	●	●	●	●
	Parks/Recreation Areas/Monuments									
	Beachside State Park	328, A11	●	●	●		●			
	Beverly Beach State Park	206, B2	●	●	●		●	●		
	Bullards Beach State Park	220, B5	●	●	●		●	●	●	
	Cape Blanco State Park	224, A4	●	●	●		●	●		●
	Cape Lookout State Park	197, A3	●	●	●		●	●		●
	Champoeg State Park	199, A6	●	●	●		●	●	●	
	Collier Memorial State Park	231, D2	●	●	●		●	●		
	Columbia River Gorge National Scenic Area	200, C1	●	●	●		●	●	●	
	Detroit Lake State Park	134, B1	●	●	●	●	●		●	●
	Emigrant Lake County Recreation Area	243, D4								
	Fort Stevens State Park	188, B1	●	●	●	●	●	●	●	●
	Harris Beach State Park	232, C6	●	●	●		●	●		●
	Hells Canyon National Recreation Area	131, B1	●	●	●	●	●	●	●	●
	Humbug Mountain State Park	224, B7	●	●	●		●	●		●
	Jessie M Honeyman Memorial State Park	214, B4	●	●	●	●	●	●	●	●
	John Day Fossil Beds National Monument	136, C1			●			●		
	Joseph Stewart State Park	149, C1	●	●	●	●	●	●	●	●
	Lake Owyhee State Park	147, A1	●	●	●		●		●	
	Memaloose State Park	196, A5	●	●						
	Milo McIver State Park	200, B6	●	●	●		●	●	●	
	Nehalem Bay State Park	191, B5	●	●	●		●		●	●
	Newberry National Volcanic Monument	143, B1						●		
	Oregon Cascades Recreation Area	142, B1	●	●	●	●	●	●	●	●
	Oregon Caves National Monument	149, D5			●			●		
	Oregon Dunes National Recreation Area	214, A5	●		●		●	●		●
	Silver Falls State Park	205, D7	●	●	●	●	●	●		●
	South Beach State Park	206, B5	●	●	●		●	●		
	Sunset Bay State Park	220, B1	●	●	●	●	●	●		●
	The Cove Palisades State Park	208, A6	●	●	●	●	●	●	●	●
	Umpqua Lighthouse State Park	218, B2	●	●	●		●	●	●	
	Valley of the Rogue State Park	229, D6	●	●	●		●	●	●	
	Viento State Park	195, B5	●	●	●					
	Wallowa Lake State Park	130, C2	●	●	●	●	●	●	●	●
	William M Tugman State Park	218, C3	●	●	●	●	●		●	●
ID	**National/State Forest**									
	Coeur d'Alene National Forest	115. B1	●	●	●	●	●	●	●	●
	Kaniksu National Forest	106, C2	●	●	●	●	●	●	●	●
	Nez Perce	131, C1	●	●	●	●	●	●	●	●
	Payette National Forest	131, B3	●	●	●	●	●	●	●	●
	Saint Joe National Forest	115, B3	●	●	●	●	●	●	●	●
	Parks/Recreation Areas/Monuments									
	Farragut State Park	245, C1	●	●	●	●	●	●	●	
	Heyburn State Park	248, A6	●	●	●	●	●	●	●	
CA	**National Parks**									
	Redwood National Park	148, B3	●	●	●		●	●	●	
	National/State Forests									
	Klamath National Forest	149, B3	●	●	●	●	●	●	●	●
	Modoc National Forest	151, B3	●	●	●	●	●	●	●	●
	Siskiyou National Forest	148, B2	●	●	●	●	●	●	●	●
	Six River National Forest	148, C3	●	●	●	●	●	●	●	●
	Parks/Recreation Areas/Monuments									
	Del Norte Coast Redwoods State Park	148, B3	●	●	●		●	●		●
	Lava Beds National Monument	151, A3	●		●			●		
	Smith River National Recreation Area	148, C3	●	●	●	●	●	●	●	●
NV	**National/State Forests**									
	Humboldt National Forest	154, C3	●	●	●		●	●	●	●
MT	**National/State Forests**									
	Kootenai National Forest	107, C1	●	●	●		●	●	●	●

LIST OF ABBREVIATIONS

PREFIXES AND SUFFIXES

AL . . . . ALLEY
ARC . . . . ARCADE
AV, AVE . . . . AVENUE
AVCT . . . . AVENUE COURT
AVDR . . . . AVENUE DRIVE
AVEX . . . . AVENUE EXTENSION
AVPL . . . . AVENUE PLACE
BLEX . . . . BOULEVARD EXTENSION
BL, BLVD . . . . BOULEVARD
BLCT . . . . BOULEVARD COURT
BRCH . . . . BRANCH
BRDG . . . . BRIDGE
BYPS . . . . BYPASS
BYWY . . . . BYWAY
CIDR . . . . CIRCLE DRIVE
CIR . . . . CIRCLE
CLTR . . . . CLUSTER
COM . . . . COMMON
COMS . . . . COMMONS
CORR . . . . CORRIDOR
CRES . . . . CRESCENT
CRSG . . . . CROSSING
CSWY . . . . CAUSEWAY
CT . . . . COURT
CTAV . . . . COURT AVENUE
CTO . . . . CUT OFF
CTR . . . . CENTER
CTST . . . . COURT STREET
CUR . . . . CURVE
CV . . . . COVE
DIAG . . . . DIAGONAL
DR . . . . DRIVE
DRAV . . . . DRIVE AVENUE
DRCT . . . . DRIVE COURT
DRLP . . . . DRIVE LOOP
DRWY . . . . DRIVEWAY
DVDR . . . . DIVISION DRIVE
EXAV . . . . EXTENSION AVENUE
EXBL . . . . EXTENSION BOULEVARD
EXRD . . . . EXTENSION ROAD
EXST . . . . EXTENSION STREET
EXT . . . . EXTENSION
EXWY . . . . EXPRESSWAY
FRWY . . . . FREEWAY
GDNS . . . . GARDENS
GN . . . . GLEN
GRN . . . . GREEN
GRV . . . . GROVE
HTS . . . . HEIGHTS
HWY . . . . HIGHWAY
ISL . . . . ISLE
JCT . . . . JUNCTION
LN . . . . LANE
LNDG . . . . LANDING
LNLP . . . . LANE LOOP
LP . . . . LOOP
MNR . . . . MANOR
MTWY . . . . MOTORWAY
NFD . . NATIONAL FOREST DEVELOPMENT
NK . . . . NOOK
OH . . . . OUTER HIGHWAY
OVL . . . . OVAL
OVLK . . . . OVERLOOK
OVPS . . . . OVERPASS
PK . . . . PARK
PKWY . . . . PARKWAY
PL . . . . PLACE
PLZ,PZ . . . . PLAZA
PASG . . . . PASSAGE
PT . . . . POINT
PTH . . . . PATH
PZWY . . . . PLAZA WAY
RD . . . . ROAD
RDAV . . . . ROAD AVENUE
RDEX . . . . ROAD EXTENSION
RDWY . . . . ROADWAY
RDGE . . . . RIDGE
RR . . . . RAILROAD
RT . . . . ROUTE
RW . . . . ROW
RY . . . . RAILWAY
SKWY . . . . SKYWAY
SQ . . . . SQUARE
ST . . . . STREET
STAV . . . . STREET AVENUE
STCT . . . . STREET COURT
STDR . . . . STREET DRIVE
STEX . . . . STREET EXTENSION
STLN . . . . STREET LANE
STLP . . . . STREET LOOP
STOV . . . . STREET OVERPASS
STPL . . . . STREET PLACE
STPM . . . . STREET PROMENADE
STXP . . . . STREET EXPRESSWAY
TER . . . . TERRACE
TFWY . . . . TRAFFICWAY
THWY . . . . THROUGHWAY
TKTR . . . . TRUCKTRAIL
TPKE . . . . TURNPIKE
TR . . . . TRAIL
TRC . . . . TRACE
TRCT . . . . TERRACE COURT
TTSP . . . . TRUCKTRAIL SPUR
TUN . . . . TUNNEL
UNPS . . . . UNDERPASS
VW . . . . VIEW
WK . . . . WALK
WY . . . . WAY
WYPL . . . . WAY PLACE

DIRECTIONS

E . . . . EAST
KPN . . . . KEY PENINSULA NORTH
KPS . . . . KEY PENINSULA SOUTH
N . . . . NORTH
NE . . . . NORTHEAST
NW . . . . NORTHWEST
S . . . . SOUTH
SE . . . . SOUTHEAST
SW . . . . SOUTHWEST
W . . . . WEST

DEPARTMENT STORES

BN . . . . THE BON MARCHE
E . . . . EMPORIUM
L . . . . LAMONTS
ME . . . . MERVYNS
MF . . . . MEIER & FRANK
MW . . . . MONTGOMERY WARD
N . . . . NORDSTROM
P . . . . J C PENNEY
S . . . . SEARS

BUILDINGS

CC . . . . CHAMBER OF COMMERCE
CH . . . . CITY HALL
COMM CTR . . . . COMMUNITY CENTER
CON CTR . . . . CONVENTION CENTER
CONT HS . CONTINUATION HIGH SCHOOL
CTH . . . . COURTHOUSE
DMV . . . . DEPT OF MOTOR VEHICLES
FAA . . . . FEDERAL AVIATION ADMIN
FS . . . . FIRE STATION
HOSP . . . . HOSPITAL
HS . . . . HIGH SCHOOL
INT . . . . INTERMEDIATE SCHOOL
JR HS . . . . JUNIOR HIGH SCHOOL
LIB . . . . LIBRARY
MID . . . . MIDDLE SCHOOL
MUS . . . . MUSEUM
PO . . . . POST OFFICE
PS . . . . POLICE STATION
SR CIT CTR . . . SENIOR CITIZENS CENTER
STA . . . . STATION
THTR . . . . THEATER
VIS BUR . . . . VISITORS BUREAU

OTHER ABBREVIATIONS

BCH . . . . BEACH
BLDG . . . . BUILDING
BLM . . BUREAU OF LAND MANAGEMENT
CEM . . . . CEMETERY
CK . . . . CREEK
CO . . . . COUNTY
CTR . . . . CENTER
COMM . . . . COMMUNITY
EST, ESTS . . . . ESTATE(S)
HIST . . . . HISTORIC
HTS . . . . HEIGHTS
LK . . . . LAKE
MDW . . . . MEADOW
MED . . . . MEDICAL
MEM . . . . MEMORIAL
MHP . . . . MOBILE HOME PARK
MT . . . . MOUNT
MTN . . . . MOUNTAIN
NATL . . . . NATIONAL
PKG . . . . PARKING
PLGD . . . . PLAYGROUND
RCH . . . . RANCH
REC . . . . RECREATION
RES . . . . RESERVOIR
RIV . . . . RIVER
RT # . . . . ROUTE NUMBER
SPG . . . . SPRING
VLG . . . . VILLAGE
VLY . . . . VALLEY
VW . . . . VIEW

STREET City State Page-Grid

A

A U.S.-95
COTTONWOOD ID 123-C3
GRANGEVILLE ID 123-C3
IDAHO CO ID 123-B3
A AV
ANACORTES WA 259-F5
LAKE OSWEGO OR 321-F5
A RD SW
DOUGLAS CO WA 112-B2
A ST
ASHLAND OR 337-D7
CASTLE ROCK WA 187-C7
GRANTS PASS OR 335-E8
PIERCE CO WA 181-D5
WALLA WALLA CO WA 345-G4
A ST Rt#-38
DOUGLAS CO OR 141-A1
ELKTON OR 141-A1
E A ST
FRANKLIN CO WA 121-A3
GRANTS PASS OR 335-G8
PASCO WA 121-A3
PASCO WA 343-H8
N A ST
ELLENSBURG WA 241-B5
SPOKANE WA 348-F2
S A ST
LANE CO OR 330-J7
SPOKANE WA 348-F10
SPRINGFIELD OR 330-J7
SPRINGFIELD OR 331-A7
W A ST
PASCO WA 343-D8
A ST E U.S.-20
VALE OR 139-A3
A ST SE
AUBURN WA 182-B1
EPHRATA WA 112-C3
GRANT CO WA 112-C3
KING CO WA 182-B1
A ST W
MALHEUR CO OR 138-C3
VALE OR 138-C3
A ST W U.S.-20
VALE OR 139-A3
A900 RD
GRAYS HARBOR CO WA 179-B6
A 1000 RD
GRAYS HARBOR CO WA 179-A5
A2000 RD
GRAYS HARBOR CO WA 179-A5
A3030 RD
GRAYS HARBOR CO WA 178-D4
A4000 RD
GRAYS HARBOR CO WA 179-D7
A5000 RD
GRAYS HARBOR CO WA 178-D4
A6000 RD
GRAYS HARBOR CO WA 178-D4
A7200 RD
GRAYS HARBOR CO WA 178-D3
AALVIK RD
SKAMANIA CO WA 194-C5
AARON DR
RICHLAND WA 341-F4
ABBEY RD
YAMHILL CO OR 198-B6
ABBOT ST
RICHLAND WA 341-G3
ABBOTSFORD-MISSION HWY Rt#-11
DISTRICT OF ABBOTSFORD BC 102-B1
DISTRICT OF MATSQUI BC 94-B3
DISTRICT OF MATSQUI BC 102-B1
ABBOTT RD
CLACKAMAS CO OR 126-C3
CLACKAMAS CO OR 201-A7
VALLEY CO ID 251-C7
WALLA WALLA WA 345-C10
WALLA WALLA CO WA 122-A3
WALLA WALLA CO WA 345-C10
WALLA WALLA EAST WA 345-D10
WHITMAN CO WA 249-A2
S ABBOTT RD
SPOKANE CO WA 246-B5
SPOKANE CO WA 348-C14
ABBOTT CREEK RD
JACKSON CO OR 226-C4
ABERDEEN GARDENS RD
GRAYS HARBOR CO WA 178-B6
ABERNATHY ST NE
LACEY WA 297-F3
THURSTON CO WA 297-F3
ABERNATHY TKTR
COWLITZ CO WA 187-A6
ABIQUA RD NE
MARION CO OR 205-D4
ABRAHAM DR
LINN CO OR 210-A1
ABSHIRE RD
ADAMS CO ID 251-B4
ACADEMY ST
KELSO WA 303-D8
LEBANON OR 133-C1
ACADIA RD
UNIV ENDOWMENT LANDS BC 156-A4
ACKLEY CAMP RD
HARNEY CO OR 153-A2
ACME RD
KLICKITAT CO WA 196-A3
ADA RD
DOUGLAS CO OR 214-B5
N ADAIR ST Rt#-8
CORNELIUS OR 198-C1
FOREST GROVE OR 198-C1
ADAMS AV U.S.-30
LA GRANDE OR 130-A2
ADAMS DR
MADRAS OR 208-C5
N ADAMS DR
JEFFERSON CO OR 208-C3
S ADAMS DR
JEFFERSON CO OR 208-C6
MADRAS OR 208-C6
ADAMS RD
CHEHALIS WA 299-G14
JACKSON CO OR 234-B3
ADAMS RD
LEWIS CO WA 299-G14
POLK CO OR 204-B6
N ADAMS RD
VERADALE WA 351-B8
S ADAMS RD
VERADALE WA 351-B11
ADAMS ST
GARDEN CITY ID 253-C2
HOQUIAM WA 178-A7
OLYMPIA WA 296-J5
N ADAMS ST
MCMINNVILLE OR 198-A7
N ADAMS ST Rt#-42
COQUILLE OR 220-D5
N ADAMS ST Rt#-99W
MCMINNVILLE OR 198-A7
NE ADAMS ST Rt#-14
CAMAS WA 193-B7
S ADAMS ST Rt#-99W
MCMINNVILLE OR 198-A7
ADAMS CREEK RD
DOUGLAS CO OR 219-B4
ADCOCK RD
YAMHILL CO OR 198-B4
E ADDISON DR
SPOKANE WA 349-A1
N ADDISON ST
SPOKANE WA 349-A1
ADDY-GIFFORD RD
STEVENS CO WA 106-A3
ADELE AV
BREMERTON WA 270-F10
ADKISSON MARKET RD
WASCO CO OR 127-B2
ADLER RD
FRANKLIN CO WA 121-A2
SW ADMIRAL WY
SEATTLE WA 280-D2
SEATTLE WA 281-F3
ADMIRALS RD
BRITISH COLUMBIA 256-B6
DISTRICT OF SAANICH BC 256-B5
TOWN OF ESQUILMALT BC 256-B6
TOWN OF VIEW ROYAL BC 256-B5
ADMIRALTY AV
PORT TOWNSEND WA 263-F2
ADMIRALTY DR
ISLAND CO WA 170-C2
ADOBE WY
YAKIMA CO WA 243-B4
ADRIAN BLVD Rt#-201
NYSSA OR 139-A3
ADRIAN BLVD W Rt#-201
NYSSA OR 139-A3
SW ADVANCE RD
CLACKAMAS CO OR 199-B5
WILSONVILLE OR 199-B5
ADVENT RD
PITT MEADOWS BC 157-B5
AENEAS VALLEY RD
OKANOGAN CO WA 105-A2
AGAN RD
LINN CO OR 207-D7
AGATE RD
JACKSON CO OR 230-D6
MASON CO WA 180-B3
AGATE ST
ASTORIA WA 300-A5
EUGENE OR 330-C8
AGATE POINT RD NE
KITSAP CO WA 170-C7
AGEE DR
JOSEPHINE CO OR 229-C3
AGENCY-HOT SPRINGS RD
JEFFERSON CO OR 208-A2
WARM SPRINGS OR 208-A2
AGER RD
SISKIYOU CO CA 150-A3
SISKIYOU CO CA 151-A3
AGER BESWICK RD
SISKIYOU CO CA 150-A3
NE AGNESS AV
GRANTS PASS OR 335-J9
AGNESS RD
CURRY CO OR 148-B1
CURRY CO OR 228-C4
AGNESS-ILLAHE RD
CURRY CO OR 148-B1
AGREN RD
COWLITZ CO WA 187-B5
AHSAHKA RD Rt#-7
OROFINO ID 123-C2
AHTANUM RD
SOUTH BROADWAY WA 243-A7
UNION GAP WA 243-A7
YAKIMA CO WA 119-C2
YAKIMA CO WA 243-A7
W AHTANUM RD
UNION GAP WA 243-C7
AINSLEE AV
DEPOE BAY OR 206-B1
E AINSWORTH AV Rt#-397
PASCO WA 343-G9
W AINSWORTH AV
PASCO WA 343-E8
W AINSWORTH AV Rt#-397
PASCO WA 343-G9
AINSWORTH AV S
PIERCE CO WA 181-D4
AIR CARGO RD N
SEATAC WA 288-C4
AIRDUSTRIAL WY
TUMWATER WA 296-F14
AIRLIE RD
POLK CO OR 133-B1
POLK CO OR 207-A2
AIRPLANE RESERVOIR RD
MALHEUR CO OR 154-C2
MALHEUR CO OR 155-A2
AIRPORT AV
BENTON CO OR 133-B1
BENTON CO OR 207-A7
AIRPORT DR
JOSEPHINE CO OR 233-A5
LEBANON OR 133-C1
LINN CO OR 133-C1
WHATCOM CO WA 158-D7
WHATCOM CO WA 258-A1
W AIRPORT DR
SPOKANE CO WA 246-A4
SPOKANE CO WA 348-A12
AIRPORT RD
ALBANY OR 326-G8
BENTON CO OR 133-B1
CANYON CO ID 147-C1
CENTRALIA WA 299-D8
CLACKAMAS CO OR 199-B6
CLALLAM CO WA 261-A4
CLARKSTON WA 250-B4
CURRY CO OR 224-A4
EUGENE OR 215-A1
EVERETT WA 267-G6
GRANT CO WA 237-B3
HARNEY CO OR 145-B1
KITTITAS CO WA 240-C2
KITTITAS CO WA 241-B5
LEWIS CO WA 299-D8
MALHEUR CO OR 138-C3
MEDFORD OR 336-C6
OKANOGAN WA 104-C3
OKANOGAN CO WA 104-C3
PORT ANGELES WA 261-A4
PULLMAN WA 249-C4
SISKIYOU CO CA 150-A3
SNOHOMISH WA 267-G6
SNOHOMISH CO WA 171-B4
WHITMAN CO WA 249-C4
NE AIRPORT RD
ROSEBURG OR 334-F4
SE AIRPORT RD
YAMHILL CO OR 204-C1
W AIRPORT RD
BAKER CO OR 130-B3
BAKER CO OR 138-B1
AIRPORT RD NE
MARION CO OR 199-B6
AIRPORT RD SE
SALEM OR 323-B14
SALEM OR 325-B1
AIRPORT WY
BOISE ID 253-C3
GRAYS HARBOR CO WA 178-A7
LAKESIDE OR 218-B4
SNOHOMISH CO WA 171-D3
TILLAMOOK CO OR 197-A7
WHATCOM CO WA 258-A1
NE AIRPORT WY
PORTLAND OR 311-E4
S AIRPORT WY
DOUGLAS CO WA 239-B4
SE AIRPORT WY
REDMOND OR 212-D6
AIRPORT WY S
KING WA 286-D3
SEATTLE WA 278-A7
SEATTLE WA 282-B1
SEATTLE WA 286-D3
TUKWILA WA 286-D3
AIRPORT CUTOFF RD Rt#-19
HADLOCK-IRONDALE WA 263-B11
JEFFERSON CO WA 263-B11
AIRSTRIP RD
COLUMBIA CO OR 189-A6
MALHEUR CO OR 146-B3
AIRWAY DR
CASCADE VALLEY WA 242-C2
GRANT CO WA 242-C2
KLAMATH CO OR 235-D5
MOSES LAKE WA 242-C2
AIRWAY DR SE
SALEM OR 325-B4
A J WARRIN RD
DESCHUTES CO OR 212-A5
AKINS DR
CROOK CO OR 213-D6
AKRESKY RD S
CENTRALIA WA 299-F6
CHEHALIS WA 299-E9
LEWIS CO WA 299-F6
ALABAMA ST
BELLINGHAM WA 258-F5
LONGVIEW WA 302-G10
ALAMEDA AV
ASTORIA WA 300-A5
ALAMEDA AV W
FIRCREST WA 181-C3
ALAMEDA ST
ASTORIA WA 300-A5
ALAMO LN
CANYON CO ID 147-B1
ALASKA AV E
MANCHESTER WA 271-G14
S ALASKA ST
SEATTLE WA 282-D5
SW ALASKA ST
SEATTLE WA 280-D5
SEATTLE WA 281-E5
ALASKA ST SE
MANCHESTER WA 271-G14
ALASKAN FRWY Rt#-99
SEATTLE WA 277-J5
SEATTLE WA 278-A6
SEATTLE WA 281-J3
SEATTLE WA 282-A1
ALASKAN WY S
SEATTLE WA 277-J7
SEATTLE WA 281-J1
ALASKAN WY S Rt#-519
SEATTLE WA 277-J7
SEATTLE WA 278-A7
ALBANY RD
ALBANY OR 326-B5
ALBANY RD U.S.-2
BONNER CO ID 107-A3
PRIEST RIVER ID 107-A3
ALBANY ST Rt#-82
ELGIN OR 130-A1
ALBANY ST SW
ROCHESTER WA 184-A3
THURSTON CO WA 184-A4
ALBANY-CORVALLIS HWY U.S.-20
ALBANY OR 207-B5
ALBANY OR 326-A6
BENTON CO OR 207-B5
BENTON CO OR 326-A6
BENTON CO OR 327-J8
CORVALLIS OR 207-B5
ALBANY-CORVALLIS HWY U.S.-20
CORVALLIS OR 327-J8
ALBANY-JCT CITY HWY U.S.-99E
ALBANY OR 207-C7
ALBANY OR 326-C14
HALSEY OR 210-A4
HARRISBURG OR 210-A5
JUNCTION CITY OR 210-A5
LANE CO OR 210-A5
LINN CO OR 207-C7
LINN CO OR 210-A4
TANGENT OR 207-C7
ALBANY-LYONS HWY Rt#-226
LINN CO OR 133-C1
LINN CO OR 134-A1
SCIO OR 133-C1
ALBATROSS ST
OCEAN SHORES WA 177-B6
ALBERT ST
NANAIMO BC 93-A3
SE ALBERTA ST
CLACKAMAS OR 318-E7
ALBERTSON RD
YAMHILL CO OR 198-C4
ALBION RD
ALBION WA 249-A4
WHITMAN CO WA 122-C1
WHITMAN CO WA 249-A4
S ALBRO PL
SEATTLE WA 282-B7
ALCAN RD
GRAND COULEE WA 237-C3
ALCORT RD
MALHEUR CO OR 154-B2
ALDER AV
SUMNER WA 182-B3
N ALDER AV
GRANITE FALLS WA 102-C3
ALDER DR NE
KEIZER OR 323-A7
ALDER ST
CATHLAMET WA 117-B3
LA GRANDE OR 130-A2
MOSES LAKE WA 242-C3
ALDER ST Rt#-507
CENTRALIA WA 299-E4
E ALDER ST
WALLA WALLA WA 345-C7
WALLA WALLA EAST WA 345-C7
N ALDER ST
TACOMA WA 292-D4
N ALDER ST U.S.-101
ABERDEEN WA 178-B7
S ALDER ST Rt#-21
ODESSA WA 113-B3
S ALDER ST U.S.-101
ABERDEEN WA 178-B7
SW ALDER ST
GRANTS PASS OR 335-D9
PORTLAND OR 313-F6
ALDER BRANCH RD
LANE CO OR 215-D1
ALDERBRIDGE WY
CITY OF RICHMOND BC 156-B6
ALDERBROOK RD
BAY CITY OR 197-B1
TILLAMOOK CO OR 197-B1
ALDER CREEK LN
CLACKAMAS CO OR 201-A4
ALDER CREEK RD
BAKER CO OR 138-B1
KOOTENAI CO ID 248-C1
WHEELER CO OR 128-B3
WHEELER CO OR 136-B1
ALDER CUTOFF RD
EATONVILLE WA 118-B1
PIERCE CO WA 118-B1
ALDERDALE RD
KLICKITAT CO WA 120-B3
KLICKITAT CO WA 128-B1
YAKIMA CO WA 120-B3
ALDERDALE WYE
YAKIMA CO WA 120-B3
ALDERGROVE RD
BIRCH BAY WA 158-B5
WHATCOM CO WA 158-C5
SE ALDERMAN RD
YAMHILL CO OR 204-C1
NE ALDERMEADOWS RD
MULTNOMAH CO OR 200-D1
ALDER SPRING RD
JACKSON CO OR 227-A5
ALDERWOOD AV
BELLINGHAM WA 158-D7
BELLINGHAM WA 258-A2
ALDRICH RD
WHATCOM CO WA 158-D5
ALECK BAY RD
SAN JUAN CO WA 160-A7
ALEXANDER AV
BENTON CO OR 327-G12
CORVALLIS OR 327-G12
ALEXANDER AV E
TACOMA WA 182-A2
ALEXANDER RD
SUNNYSIDE WA 120-B2
YAKIMA CO WA 120-B2
ALEXANDER RD Rt#-241
SUNNYSIDE WA 120-B2
YAKIMA CO WA 120-B2
ALFALFA RD
CROOK CO OR 135-B3
CROOK CO OR 213-A7
ALFALFA-GRANGER RD Rt#-223
SATUS WA 120-A2
YAKIMA CO WA 120-A2
ALFALFA MARKET RD
DESCHUTES CO OR 135-B3
DESCHUTES CO OR 217-D2
ALFRED JOHNSON RD
SKAGIT CO WA 168-B1
SKAGIT CO WA 260-C14
ALGER HILL LOGGING TR
SKAGIT CO WA 161-B3
ALGOMA RD
KLAMATH CO OR 235-B1
ALGOMA SPUR RD
BONNER CO ID 244-A4
ALICE AV S
SALEM OR 324-G2
ALKALI FLATS RD
MALHEUR CO OR 139-A3
ALKALI GULCH RD
MALHEUR CO OR 139-A2
ALKI AV SW
SEATTLE WA 276-D7
SEATTLE WA 280-D1
ALLAN RD
YAKIMA CO WA 243-A4
ALLARD CRES
TOWNSHIP OF LANGLEY BC 157-C6
SW ALLEN BLVD
BEAVERTON OR 199-B2
ALLEN RD
DESCHUTES CO OR 212-B7
LEWIS CO WA 187-D1
SUNNYSIDE WA 120-B2
YAKIMA CO WA 120-B2
ALLEN ST Rt#-4
KELSO WA 303-D8
E ALLEN ST
COWLITZ CO WA 303-F8
KELSO WA 303-F8
ALLEN CREEK RD
CROOK CO OR 213-D2
GRANTS PASS OR 335-C12
JOSEPHINE CO OR 335-C12
ALLEN WEST RD
SKAGIT CO WA 161-A5
ALLINGHAM CTO
JEFFERSON CO OR 211-C1
ALLISON RD
LEWIS CO WA 187-D3
ALLUMBAUGH ST
BOISE ID 253-C2
ALLWORTH RD
CLARK CO WA 193-A3
NE ALLWORTH RD
CLARK CO WA 193-B3
ALMA LN
JEFFERSON CO OR 208-B5
SW ALMA LN
JEFFERSON CO OR 208-A5
ALMA ST
UNIV ENDOWMENT LANDS BC 254-A13
VANCOUVER BC 254-A13
NW ALMETER WY
DESCHUTES CO OR 212-D4
N ALMIRA RD
LINCOLN CO WA 237-D7
ALMIRA RD S
LINCOLN CO WA 113-B2
LINCOLN CO WA 237-D7
ALM LANE RD
STEVENS CO WA 106-B3
ALMOTA RD
WHITMAN CO WA 122-C1
ALMOTA RD Rt#-194
WHITMAN CO WA 122-B1
ALMOTA ST Rt#-27
PALOUSE WA 249-B1
ALMOTA FERRY RD
GARFIELD CO WA 122-B1
E ALOHA ST
SEATTLE WA 278-C3
ALPINE DR SW
THURSTON CO WA 180-B7
ALPINE RD
BENTON CO OR 133-B2
SE ALPINE RD
KITSAP CO WA 174-C6
ALSEA HWY Rt#-34
BENTON CO OR 133-A1
LINCOLN CO OR 133-A2
LINCOLN CO OR 209-D2
LINCOLN CO OR 328-F6
WALDPORT OR 328-F6
ALSEA BAY DR
LINCOLN CO OR 328-C4
ALSEA-DEADWOOD HWY
BENTON CO OR 133-A2
ALSIP RD
POLK CO OR 204-A7
ALSTON RD W
DOUGLAS CO WA 239-C1
ALSTON-MAYGER RD
COLUMBIA CO OR 189-A3
ALTA LAKE RD
BRITISH COLUMBIA 93-C1
WHISTLER BC 93-C1
ALTAMONT DR
ALTAMONT OR 235-C5
ALTAMONT OR 338-H14
KLAMATH FALLS OR 338-H14
SW ALTA VISTA DR
KITSAP CO WA 174-A6
ALTA VISTA RD
EAGLE POINT OR 230-D6
JACKSON CO OR 230-D6
ALTHOUSE CREEK RD
JOSEPHINE CO OR 233-C5
ALTNOW-BEULAH RD
HARNEY CO OR 138-A3
ALTO RD
COLUMBIA CO WA 122-A2
E ALTON ST
PASCO WA 343-H7
ALTOONA PILLAR ROCK RD
WAHKIAKUM CO WA 117-A2
ALVADORE RD
LANE CO OR 133-B2
ALVADORE RD S
LANE CO OR 133-B3
NE ALVAS RD
CLARK CO WA 193-B3
ALVILLE LN
GILLIAM CO OR 128-A2
ALWORTH ST
GARDEN CITY ID 253-C2
W AMAZON DR
EUGENE OR 330-B10
AMAZON PKWY
EUGENE OR 330-A9
AMBAUM BLVD S
BURIEN WA 175-A5
AMBAUM BLVD S Rt#-509
BURIEN WA 175-A5
BURIEN WA 288-A7
KING WA 288-A7
KING CO WA 175-A5
AMBAUM BLVD SW
BURIEN WA 175-A5
BURIEN WA 285-G7
KING WA 285-G7
KING CO WA 175-A5
AMBERJACK AV
KITSAP CO WA 170-B6
S AMBLE RD
ISLAND CO WA 167-D7
AMBOY RD
CLARK CO WA 193-B1
AMERICAN DR
HALSEY OR 210-A2
LINN CO OR 210-A2
AMERICANA BLVD
BOISE ID 253-C3
AMERICAN FRUIT RD
SUNNYSLOPE WA 238-D3
AMERICAN MILL RD
GRAYS HARBOR CO WA 183-D3
AMES RD
YAKIMA CO WA 243-B5
AMES RD NE
OLYMPIA WA 296-J1
THURSTON CO WA 296-J1
THURSTON CO WA 297-A1
NE AMES LAKE RD
KING CO WA 176-A2
AMES LAKE CARNATION RD NE
KING CO WA 176-A1
AMICK RD
SKAGIT CO WA 168-C1
AMISIGGER RD
CLACKAMAS CO OR 200-B4
E AMITY RD
ADA CO ID 253-B4
BOISE ID 253-D4
SE AMITY RD
AMITY OR 204-C2
YAMHILL CO OR 204-C2
W AMITY RD
ADA CO ID 253-A4
AMITY DAYTON HWY
DAYTON OR 198-C7
YAMHILL CO OR 198-B7
AMITY DAYTON HWY Rt#-233
YAMHILL CO OR 198-B7
YAMHILL CO OR 204-C1
SE AMITY-DAYTON HWY Rt#-233
YAMHILL CO OR 204-C1
NE AMMETER RD
CLARK CO WA 193-C6
AMNEN RD
LINCOLN CO WA 113-C3
ANACO BEACH RD
ANACORTES WA 259-B4
ANACOPPER RD
ANACORTES WA 259-D4
N ANACORTES AV
BURLINGTON WA 260-D4
S ANACORTES ST
BURLINGTON WA 260-D6
SKAGIT CO WA 260-D6
SW ANCHOR AV
LINCOLN CITY OR 203-A5
ANDERSON AV
ALTAMONT OR 338-H14
COOS BAY OR 333-G10
ANDERSON RD
GRAYS HARBOR CO WA 184-A3
LEWIS CO WA 184-D6
MASON CO WA 179-B2
THURSTON CO WA 184-A3
WHITMAN CO WA 249-A4
NE ANDERSON RD
CLACKAMAS CO OR 199-B7
W ANDERSON RD
SPOKANE CO WA 246-B7
ANDERSON RD SE
MARION CO OR 205-B7
ANDERSON RD SE Rt#-214
MARION CO OR 205-B7
ANDERSON CANYON RD
CHELAN CO WA 238-A1
ANDERSON CREEK RD
JACKSON CO OR 234-B3
LINCOLN CO OR 203-B5
NW ANDERSON HILL RD
KITSAP CO WA 174-A1
ANDERSON HILL RD SW
KITSAP CO WA 174-B4
ANDERSON LAKE RD
JEFFERSON CO WA 170-A1
ANDERSON RESERVOIR RD
ADAMS CO ID 251-B3
ANDERSON VALLEY RD
HARNEY CO OR 145-C2
ANDRESEN RD
VANCOUVER WA 306-D7
NE ANDRESEN RD
CLARK WA 306-D1
CLARK CO WA 192-D5
VANCOUVER WA 306-D1
ANDREWS RD
DOUGLAS CO OR 219-A4
JACKSON CO OR 234-A2
S ANDRUS RD
SPOKANE CO WA 246-A6
ANGELINE RD
BONNEY LAKE WA 182-C4
PIERCE CO WA 182-C4
ANGUS DR
THURSTON CO WA 184-D2
ANKENY HILL RD
MARION CO OR 207-D1
ANKENY HILL RD SE
MARION CO OR 207-D2
ANKERTON RD
SHERMAN CO OR 127-C2
ANLIKER RD
COLUMBIA CO OR 189-B7
ANNACIS HWY Rt#-91
CITY OF RICHMOND BC 156-D6

STREET
City State Page-Grid

ANNACIS HWY Rt#-91
DISTRICT OF DELTA BC 156-D6
NEW WESTMINSTER BC 156-D6
ANNACIS HWY Rt#-91A
CITY OF RICHMOND BC 156-D6
ANNASIS HWY
DISTRICT OF DELTA BC 101-C1
ANNAWALT RD
MALHEUR CO OR 146-C3
ANNEX RD
MALHEUR CO OR 139-A2
ANNONEN RD
LEWIS CO WA 187-B5
ANSELL ST
MAPLE RIDGE BC 157-D5
ANTELOPE
CROOK CO OR 213-D6
ANTELOPE HWY Rt#-293
JEFFERSON CO OR 135-C1
WASCO CO OR 127-C3
WASCO CO OR 135-C1
ANTELOPE RD
JACKSON CO OR 230-C6
WHITE CITY OR 230-D6
E ANTELOPE RD
JACKSON CO OR 149-C1
JACKSON CO OR 234-D1
ANTELOPE CANAL RD
MALHEUR CO OR 147-A3
ANTELOPE FLAT RD
MALHEUR CO OR 146-B2
ANTELOPE SPRINGS RD
OWYHEE CO ID 147-C3
ANT FLAT RD
ENTERPRISE OR 130-C2
WALLOWA CO OR 130-C2
ANTHONY LAKES HWY
BAKER CO OR 130-A3
HAINES OR 130-A3
ANTHONY LAKES RD
BAKER CO OR 130-A3
ANTIOCH RD
JACKSON CO OR 230-C5
W ANTLER AV
DESCHUTES CO OR 212-D5
ANTLES RD
UNION CO OR 130-B2
ANTOINE CREEK RD
CHELAN CO WA 236-D1
ANTRIM RD
LEWIS CO WA 187-C2
A-P-A RD
WHATCOM CO WA 101-C1
APEL DR
PORT COQUITLAM BC 157-B4
APIARY RD
COLUMBIA CO OR 117-B3
COLUMBIA CO OR 189-B4
APPLE ST
BOISE ID 253-D3
APPLE ACRES RD
CHELAN CO WA 112-B1
CHELAN CO WA 236-D2
APPLEFORD RD
ASOTIN CO WA 123-A3
APPLEGATE AV
DOUGLAS CO OR 219-A4
JOSEPHINE CO OR 229-A6
APPLEGATE RD
JACKSON CO OR 149-B2
N APPLEGATE RD
JACKSON CO OR 149-B2
JOSEPHINE CO OR 149-B2
APPLEGATE ST
JACKSON CO OR 149-B2
JACKSONVILLE OR 149-B2
APPLESIDE BLVD Rt#-128
ASOTIN CO WA 250-B5
VINELAND WA 250-B5
APPLETON RD
KLICKITAT CO WA 196-B3
APPLE VALLEY RD
CANYON CO ID 139-A3
E APPLEWAY AV
GREEN ACRES WA 351-G8
SPOKANE CO WA 351-G8
W APPLEWAY AV
COEUR D'ALENE ID 355-C8
A P TUBBS RD
CARBONADO WA 182-D5
PIERCE CO WA 182-D5
ARAB LN SE
KITSAP CO WA 174-C6
ARAGO LN
COOS CO OR 220-D6
ARAGO-ARAGO JCT
COOS CO OR 220-D6
ARAGO CROSS RD
COOS CO OR 220-D6
ARBORETUM RD
BENTON CO OR 207-B4
ARBOR GROVE RD
MARION CO OR 199-A7
ARBOR GROVE RD NE
MARION CO OR 205-A1
ARBORLYNN DR
DIST OF N VANCOUVER BC 255-F4
ARBUTUS RD
DISTRICT OF SAANICH BC 257-D2
ARBUTUS ST
VANCOUVER BC 156-B5
VANCOUVER BC 254-D13
E ARCADIA AV
MASON CO WA 180-A3
SHELTON WA 180-A3
ARCADIA DR NE
LINCOLN CO OR 206-C4
ARCADIA RD
MASON CO WA 180-B3
ARCHERFISH RD
KITSAP CO WA 170-B7
ARCHIE MYERS RANCH RD
MALHEUR CO OR 154-B2
ARDMORE DR
LAKEWOOD WA 181-C4
W ARGENT RD
PASCO WA 342-E4
PASCO WA 343-C4
WEST PASCO WA 342-E4
WEST PASCO WA 343-C4

N ARGONNE RD
DISHMAN WA 350-D7
MILLWOOD WA 350-D3
SPOKANE CO WA 246-D2
SPOKANE CO WA 350-D2
ARGYLE DR
VANCOUVER BC 156-C5
ARGYLE DR S
SALEM OR 324-G3
ARGYLE ST
VANCOUVER BC 156-C5
ARID AV
DESCHUTES CO OR 212-C7
W ARLINGTON ST
GLADSTONE OR 199-D4
ARLINGTON HEIGHTS RD
SNOHOMISH CO WA 168-D4
ARMAR RD
MARYSVILLE WA 168-C7
ARMITAGE RD
SAN JUAN CO WA 160-A5
ARMSTRONG RD
TOWNSHIP OF LANGLEY BC 157-D7
ARMSTRONG ST
PACIFIC CO WA 117-A1
ARMSWORTHY ST
WASCO OR 127-C1
ARMSWORTHY ST Rt#-206
WASCO OR 127-C1
ARNDT RD
CLACKAMAS CO OR 199-B6
MARION CO OR 199-A6
ARNEY RD NE
MARION CO OR 205-B1
ARNIE RD
WHATCOM CO WA 158-B4
ARNOLD LN
JACKSON CO OR 234-A1
W ARNOLD RD
ISLAND CO WA 167-B4
ARNOLD WY
CORVALLIS OR 327-E9
ARNOLD MARKET LOOP RD
DESCHUTES CO OR 217-C3
AROCK RD
MALHEUR CO OR 146-C3
ARRAH WANNA BLVD
CLACKAMAS CO OR 201-C5
ARRITOLA PLACE RD
MALHEUR CO OR 146-C3
MALHEUR CO OR 147-A3
ARROW AV U.S.-12
NEZ PERCE CO ID 123-A2
W ARROWHEAD AV
BENTON CO WA 342-D8
KENNEWICK WA 342-D8
RICHLAND WA 342-D8
N ARROWHEAD RD
ISLAND CO WA 167-D4
ARSENAL WY E
BREMERTON WA 270-E11
NAVY YARD CITY WA 270-E11
ART DALZELL RD
MORROW CO OR 128-B2
ARTHUR BLVD
YAKIMA CO WA 243-C6
ARTHUR DR
DISTRICT OF DELTA BC 101-C1
ARTHUR RD
NEZ PERCE CO ID 250-D2
ARTHUR ST
NORTH BEND OR 333-D4
S ARTHUR ST
SPOKANE WA 349-B10
SW ARTHUR ST
PORTLAND OR 317-E1
ARTHUR LAING BRDG
CITY OF RICHMOND BC 156-B5
ARTONDALE DR NW
PIERCE CO WA 181-B1
ARVICK RD SE
KITSAP CO WA 174-C4
ARVID NELSON RD
CROOK CO OR 136-A2
ASBURY RD
KOOTENAI CO ID 248-A3
ASCHOFF RD
CLACKAMAS CO OR 201-B3
N ASH AV
WARDEN WA 121-A1
S ASH AV
WARDEN WA 121-A1
ASH RD
DISTRICT OF SAANICH BC 159-D5
ASH ST
BROWNSVILLE OR 210-C2
KELSO WA 303-D8
SODAVILLE OR 133-C2
N ASH ST
SPOKANE WA 346-G14
SPOKANE WA 348-G1
NE ASH ST
PULLMAN WA 249-B5
ASH ST N
OMAK WA 104-C2
ASH ST S
OMAK WA 104-C3
ASH WY
SNOHOMISH CO WA 171-B4
ASHBROOK LN
JOSEPHINE CO OR 229-A5
ASH CREEK
SISKIYOU CO CA 150-A3
ASH CREEK RD
DOUGLAS CO OR 225-C3
ASH LAKE RD
SKAMANIA CO WA 194-C5
ASHLAND ST
ASHLAND OR 337-D9
ASHLAND LOOP RD
JACKSON CO OR 234-C6
ASHTON LN
VALLEY CO ID 251-D7
SW ASHWOOD LN
JEFFERSON CO OR 208-B5
ASHWOOD RD
JEFFERSON CO OR 208-C5
ASHWORTH AV N
SHORELINE WA 171-A7

ASOTIN RD
ASOTIN CO WA 122-C2
ASOTIN CO WA 250-A6
ASOTIN CREEK RD
ASOTIN WA 250-B6
ASOTIN CO WA 250-B6
N ASPEN ST Rt#-231
LINCOLN CO WA 114-A2
REARDAN WA 114-A2
ASPEN WY
YAMHILL CO OR 198-D5
ASPEN LAKE RD
KLAMATH CO OR 235-A1
ASPENWALL RD
THURSTON CO WA 180-B6
S ASSEMBLY RD
SPOKANE CO WA 246-B5
SPOKANE CO WA 348-D13
N ASSEMBLY ST
SPOKANE WA 348-D2
ATHENA-HOLDMAN HWY
UMATILLA CO OR 129-B1
WASCO OR 129-B1
E ATHENA-HOLDMAN HWY
WASCO OR 129-C1
ATKINS AV
DISTRICT OF LANGFORD BC 159-B6
TOWN OF VIEW ROYAL BC 159-B6
ATKINS RD
COLUMBIA CO OR 189-A4
ATKINSON AV
DESCHUTES CO OR 212-C4
NW ATKINSON AV
DESCHUTES CO OR 212-C4
N ATLAS RD
COEUR D'ALENE ID 355-A4
HAYDEN ID 355-A1
KOOTENAI CO ID 355-A6
ATOR HILL RD
KOOTENAI CO ID 248-A5
ATWOOD RD
KLICKITAT CO WA 196-A5
AUBREY L WHITE PKWY
SPOKANE WA 348-B4
SPOKANE CO WA 348-B4
N AUBREY L WHITE PKWY
SPOKANE WA 246-A2
SPOKANE WA 346-A14
SPOKANE WA 348-B2
SPOKANE CO WA 348-B2
AUBURN AV
AUBURN WA 182-B2
BAKER CITY OR 138-B1
AUBURN AV U.S.-30
BAKER CITY OR 138-B1
AUBURN AV NE
AUBURN WA 182-C1
AUBURN ST
KLAMATH FALLS OR 338-E6
AUBURN WY N
AUBURN WA 175-C7
AUBURN WA 182-C1
KING CO WA 175-C7
AUBURN WY N Rt#-164
AUBURN WA 182-C1
AUBURN WY S Rt#-164
AUBURN WA 182-C1
AUBURN BLACK DIAMOND RD
AUBURN WA 182-D1
BLACK DIAMOND WA 110-C3
KING CO WA 110-C3
KING CO WA 182-D1
SE AUBURN BLACK DIAMOND RD
KING CO WA 182-C1
AUBURN-ECHO LAKE CTO Rt#-18
AUBURN WA 182-C1
KENT WA 175-D7
KING CO WA 175-D7
KING CO WA 176-A6
KING CO WA 182-C1
AUBURN ENUMCLAW RD Rt#-164
AUBURN WA 182-C2
KING CO WA 182-C2
S AUDUBON ST
SPOKANE WA 348-F10
AUFDERHEIDE SCENIC BYWY
LANE CO OR 134-A3
LANE CO OR 142-A1
WESTFIR OR 142-A1
W AUGUSTA AV
SPOKANE WA 348-H7
AUGUSTA AV NE
SUQUAMISH WA 170-C7
AULT FIELD RD
AULT FIELD WA 167-B2
ISLAND CO WA 167-B2
AUMSVILLE HWY SE
AUMSVILLE OR 133-C1
AUMSVILLE OR 205-B7
MARION CO OR 205-A7
MARION CO OR 325-F5
SALEM OR 325-F5
AUNE HALL RD
WHITMAN CO WA 122-A1
N AURILIA AV
PASCO WA 343-F6
AURORA AV N Rt#-99
EDMONDS WA 171-A7
SEATTLE WA 171-A7
SEATTLE WA 273-J2
SEATTLE WA 277-J4
SHORELINE WA 171-A7
AUSTIN AV
COQUITLAM BC 157-A5
DISTRICT OF COQUITLAM BC 156-D5
AUSTIN DR
BREMERTON WA 270-C8
AUSTIN RD
DISTRICT OF BURNABY BC 156-D5
DISTRICT OF COQUITLAM BC 156-D5
SKAGIT CO WA 161-C7
N AUSTIN RD
SPOKANE CO WA 346-F1
S AUSTIN RD
SPOKANE CO WA 246-B6
AUTOCENTER WY
BREMERTON WA 270-D10

AVALON ST Rt#-69
ADA CO ID 253-A5
KUNA ID 253-A5
SW AVALON WY
SEATTLE WA 281-F4
AVENUE A
SEASIDE WA 301-F8
AVENUE B
GRANDVIEW WA 120-B3
SEASIDE WA 301-G8
N AVENUE B
BOISE ID 253-D3
GRANDVIEW WA 120-B3
AVENUE D
SNOHOMISH WA 171-D3
SNOHOMISH CO WA 171-D3
AVENUE G
SEASIDE WA 301-G9
AVENUE S
SEASIDE WA 301-G10
CLATSOP CO WA 301-F10
AVENUE U
CLATSOP CO WA 301-F10
SEASIDE WA 301-F10
AVERY RD E
LEWIS CO WA 187-D2
AVERY RD W
LEWIS CO WA 187-C2
SW AVERY ST
TUALATIN OR 199-B4
AVON AV Rt#-20
BURLINGTON WA 260-C4
AVON CTO Rt#-20
SKAGIT CO WA 161-A6
SKAGIT CO WA 260-A6
AVON-ALLEN RD
SKAGIT CO WA 161-A6
AVONDALE RD NE
KING CO WA 171-D7
KING CO WA 175-D1
REDMOND WA 171-D7
REDMOND WA 175-D1
AVONDALE WY NE
REDMOND WA 175-D1
AWMILLER RD
LEWIS CO WA 187-B4
AXFORD RD
CLARK CO WA 193-A3
AXLING RD
WHATCOM CO WA 158-D3
AXTEL CREEK RD
LINCOLN CO OR 209-B4
E AXTON RD
WHATCOM CO WA 102-B1
WHATCOM CO WA 158-D6
W AXTON RD
FERNDALE WA 158-D6
WHATCOM CO WA 158-D6
AYER RD
WALLA WALLA CO WA 121-C2
AYRES RD
EUGENE OR 215-B1
AZALEA DR
JOSEPHINE CO OR 229-A5

B

B AV
DESCHUTES CO OR 212-D4
TERREBONNE OR 212-D4
W B AV Rt#-99
DRAIN OR 219-A3
B ST
ABERDEEN WA 178-B7
ASHLAND OR 337-D7
TILLAMOOK CO OR 191-B4
B ST Rt#-82
ISLAND CITY OR 130-A2
E B ST U.S.-30
RAINIER OR 189-C4
NE B ST
MADRAS OR 208-C5
S B ST
ISLAND CITY OR 130-A2
W B ST
RAINIER OR 189-B4
W B ST U.S.-30
RAINIER OR 189-C4
B ST E
PIERCE CO WA 181-D5
B 1/2-NE RD
GRANT CO WA 112-C3
B 5-NE
GRANT CO WA 112-C2
E BABB RD
SPOKANE CO WA 114-C3
BABCOCK RD
WALLA WALLA CO WA 121-C2
S BABCOCK RD
CLACKAMAS CO OR 205-D2
NE BABCOCK ST
KITSAP CO WA 170-C4
B A BENSON RD
SKAGIT CO WA 161-A5
BABY DOLL RD E
KITSAP CO WA 271-D14
BABY DOLL RD SE
KITSAP CO WA 271-D14
BABY ISLAND RD
ISLAND CO WA 167-D7
BACHELOR DR
LINCOLN CO WA 113-C1
BACHELOR FLAT RD
COLUMBIA CO OR 192-A2
BACONA RD
WASHINGTON CO OR 125-C1
BACON CAMP RD
HARNEY CO OR 144-B3
BACUS RD
SKAGIT CO WA 161-D5
BADGER RD
BENTON CO WA 120-C3
BENTON CO WA 121-A2
BENTON CO WA 341-J12
BENTON CO WA 342-A12
FRANKLIN CO WA 121-A2
GRAYS HARBOR CO WA 177-D2
E BADGER RD Rt#-546
WHATCOM CO WA 102-B1
WHATCOM CO WA 158-D3

E BADGER RD Rt#-547
WHATCOM CO WA 102-B1
W BADGER RD
WHATCOM CO WA 158-D3
BADGER CANYON RD
BENTON CO WA 120-C3
BADGER CREEK RD
CROOK CO OR 136-A2
WASCO CO OR 127-A3
WHEELER CO OR 136-B2
BADGER MOUNTAIN RD
DOUGLAS CO WA 239-A4
BADGER MOUNTAIN RD SW
DOUGLAS CO WA 239-B2
BADGER POCKET RD
KITTITAS WA 241-C6
KITTITAS CO WA 241-C6
BAGBY RD
CLACKAMAS CO OR 126-B3
BAGDAD RD
LINCOLN CO WA 113-B1
LINCOLN CO WA 237-D4
BAILER HILL RD
SAN JUAN CO WA 101-C2
BAILEY RD
DISTRICT OF CHILLIWACK BC 94-C3
S BAILEY RD
ISLAND CO WA 171-A3
S BAILEY ST
SEATTLE WA 282-B7
BAILEY HILL RD
EUGENE OR 329-C8
LANE CO OR 329-A14
BAINARD LN
CHELAN CO WA 239-B5
BAINBRIDGE ISLND-SEATTLE FERRY
KING CO WA 174-D2
KITSAP CO WA 174-D2
WINSLOW WA 174-D2
BAIRD RD NE
THURSTON CO WA 180-D4
BAIRD SPRINGS RD
GRANT CO WA 112-B3
GRANT CO WA 239-D7
BAKEOVEN RD
MAUPIN OR 127-B3
WASCO CO OR 127-B3
BAKEOVEN MARKET RD
WASCO CO OR 127-B3
N BAKER AV
EAST WENATCHEE BENCH WA 239-A4
BAKER RD
CLACKAMAS CO OR 199-A5
COOS CO OR 220-C5
JACKSON CO OR 234-B2
KLICKITAT CO WA 196-B3
MORROW CO OR 128-B1
SHERWOOD OR 199-A5
WASHINGTON CO OR 199-A5
YAKIMA CO WA 243-B5
E BAKER RD
SPOKANE CO WA 246-D7
SE BAKER RD
KITSAP CO WA 174-C4
BAKER RD SW
THURSTON CO WA 180-B6
N BAKER ST
MCMINNVILLE OR 198-A7
N BAKER ST Rt#-99W
MCMINNVILLE OR 198-A7
S BAKER ST Rt#-99W
MCMINNVILLE OR 198-A7
BAKER-COPPERFIELD HWY Rt#-86
BAKER CO OR 130-B3
BAKER CO OR 131-A3
BAKER CO OR 138-C1
BAKER CO OR 139-A1
RICHLAND OR 139-A1
BAKER CREEK RD
YAMHILL CO OR 125-B2
YAMHILL CO OR 198-A7
NW BAKER CREEK RD
YAMHILL CO OR 125-B2
SW BAKER CREEK RD
MCMINNVILLE OR 198-A7
YAMHILL CO OR 198-A7
BAKER HEIGHTS RD
SKAGIT CO WA 161-C7
NE BAKER HILL RD
KITSAP CO WA 271-G5
BAKER LAKE HWY
WHATCOM CO WA 102-C2
BAKER LAKE RD
SKAGIT CO WA 102-C2
BAKER LANGDON RD
WALLA WALLA CO WA 345-A13
S BAKERS FERRY RD
CLACKAMAS CO OR 200-A4
E BAKERVIEW RD
WHATCOM CO WA 258-F1
BALBACK RD
ADAMS CO ID 251-A4
BALCH RD
KLICKITAT CO WA 196-B5
BALDA RD
ISLAND CO WA 167-B3
BALD BUTTE RD
WHITMAN CO WA 249-C7
BALD HILLS RD SE
THURSTON CO WA 118-A1
BALDOCK FRWY I-5
PORTLAND OR 316-C7
PORTLAND OR 317-F2
PORTLAND OR 320-B1
BALD PEAK RD
WASHINGTON CO OR 198-C3
YAMHILL CO OR 198-C4
SE BALDWIN DR
JEFFERSON CO OR 208-C6
BALDWIN RD
CROOK CO OR 213-C5
HOOD RIVER CO OR 202-D4
WALLA WALLA WA 344-D7
WALLA WALLA WEST WA 344-D7
WASCO CO OR 127-A2
WASCO CO OR 202-D4
BALDY MOUNTAIN RD
BONNER CO ID 107-A3

BALDY MOUNTAIN RD
BONNER CO ID 244-A2
BALL RD
JACKSON CO OR 230-D4
BALL ST
MOUNT VERNON WA 260-B12
BALLANTINE RD
ADA CO ID 253-A1
W BALLARD DR
KITTITAS CO WA 240-D2
BALLARD RD
POLK CO OR 204-A7
BALLARD RD NW
DOUGLAS CO WA 236-D7
BALLINGER DR
GRANTS PASS OR 335-D10
NE BALLINGER WY Rt#-104
KING CO WA 171-B6
LAKE FOREST PARK WA 171-B6
BALL MOUNTAIN LITTLE SHASTA RD
SISKIYOU CO CA 150-A3
BALLOW RD
MASON CO WA 180-D2
BALLSTON RD
POLK CO OR 204-A3
SW BALLSTON RD
YAMHILL CO OR 125-B3
YAMHILL CO OR 204-A3
BALLY MOUNTAIN TRAIL RD
ADAMS CO ID 251-A1
BALM FORK RD
MORROW CO OR 128-C2
BALSAM DR
KLAMATH CO OR 235-A4
KLAMATH CO OR 338-A12
KLAMATH FALLS OR 338-A12
BALSAM DR S
SALEM OR 324-F3
S BALTIMORE RD
SPOKANE CO WA 246-C6
BANDIX RD SE
KITSAP CO WA 174-C6
BANDY RD
BONNER CO ID 107-A3
BANFIELD FRWY I-84
PORTLAND OR 313-H4
PORTLAND OR 314-C5
PORTLAND OR 315-J2
S BANGOR ST
SEATTLE WA 287-G6
N BANK RD
COOS CO OR 220-C4
S BANK RD
GRAYS HARBOR CO WA 117-B1
S BANK RD Rt#-107
GRAYS HARBOR CO WA 117-A1
SW BANK RD
KING CO WA 174-D5
NE BANNER PL
SEATTLE WA 274-B2
N BANNER RD
KITSAP CO WA 174-C4
BANNER RD SE
KITSAP CO WA 174-C5
BANNER WY NE
SEATTLE WA 274-B1
BANNISTER RD
UMATILLA CO OR 129-C1
WESTON OR 129-C1
BANTA RD
BAKER CO OR 130-B3
BAPTIST CHURCH DR
LINN CO OR 133-C1
BAR 14 RD
KITTITAS CO WA 241-C4
BARBARA DR
JOSEPHINE CO OR 229-A5
BARBARA WY
DESCHUTES CO OR 212-A7
BARBEE RD
WHITMAN CO WA 249-A6
BARBER RD NW
DOUGLAS CO WA 236-B5
SW BARBUR BLVD
PORTLAND OR 316-D6
PORTLAND OR 317-E1
SW BARBUR BLVD Rt#-10
PORTLAND OR 316-E3
PORTLAND OR 317-E2
BARCLAY DR
DESCHUTES CO OR 211-D5
BARD RD
UMATILLA CO OR 129-A1
BARGER DR
EUGENE OR 329-A1
BARKER LN
VALLEY CO ID 252-D2
BARKER RD
ADA CO ID 253-C6
COLUMBIA CO OR 189-B5
LANE CO OR 133-B3
N BARKER RD
GREEN ACRES WA 351-G3
SPOKANE CO WA 351-G3
S BARKER RD
GREEN ACRES WA 351-G8
SPOKANE CO WA 351-G10
BARKER CANYON RD
DOUGLAS CO WA 237-A4
BARKES RD
WHITE SWAN WA 119-C2
BARLOW RD
BARLOW OR 199-B7
CLACKAMAS CO OR 199-B7
CLACKAMAS CO OR 205-C1
HOOD RIVER CO OR 202-B7
S BARLOW RD
CLACKAMAS CO OR 205-C1
S BARLOW MONTE CRSTO RD
CLACKAMAS CO OR 205-C2
MARION CO OR 205-C2
BARLOW TRAIL RD
CLACKAMAS CO OR 201-B4
BARNARDS RD
CLACKAMAS CO OR 126-B3
CLACKAMAS CO OR 205-D1
S BARNARDS RD
CLACKAMAS CO OR 205-D1

PNW
INDEX

STREET City State Page-Grid

S BARNEBURG RD
MEDFORD OR 336-F12
BARNEKOFF RD
COOS CO OR 220-B7
BARNES AV U.S.-395
SENECA OR 137-B3
BARNES DR
COWLITZ CO WA 187-C6
LEWIS CO WA 187-C6
NE BARNES DR
JEFFERSON CO OR 208-C3
BARNES RD
KITTITAS CO WA 241-A6
NW BARNES RD
WASHINGTON CO OR 199-B1
SW BARNES RD
WASHINGTON CO OR 199-B1
BARNES RD NW
DOUGLAS CO WA 236-D7
BARNES ST
KELSO WA 303-D6
BARNES BUTTE RD
CROOK CO OR 213-D4
BARNET HWY Rt#-7A
COQUITLAM BC 157-A4
DISTRICT OF BURNABY BC 156-D4
PORT MOODY BC 157-A4
BARNETT RD
GILLIAM CO OR 128-A2
E BARNETT RD
MEDFORD OR 234-B1
MEDFORD OR 336-F13
W BARNETT RD
MEDFORD OR 336-D13
BARNHART RD
SATUS WA 120-A2
WHATCOM CO WA 158-D3
BARNSTON DR E
DISTRICT OF SURREY BC 157-B6
BARNSTON DR W
DISTRICT OF SURREY BC 157-B6
BARON RD NE
MARION CO OR 205-B3
BARR RD
CLALLAM CO WA 165-D7
DESCHUTES CO OR 212-B5
LEWISTON ID 250-C5
NEZ PERCE CO ID 250-C5
WHATCOM CO WA 158-C6
BARRELL SPRINGS RD
SKAGIT CO WA 161-B3
BARRETT RD
HOOD RIVER CO OR 195-C5
BARRY RD
DOUGLAS CO WA 237-C1
BARRY REX RD
DOUGLAS CO WA 237-C2
BARSTOW-PIERRE LAKE RD
STEVENS CO WA 105-C1
SE BARTEL RD
CLACKAMAS CO OR 200-B4
BARTLEMAY RD
CLACKAMAS CO OR 200-B4
BARTLETTE RD
PEND OREILLE CO WA 106-B3
SW BARTON PL
SEATTLE WA 285-G3
BARTON RD
DOUGLAS CO OR 225-C6
S BARTON RD
ADAMS CO WA 242-C7
SW BARTON ST
SEATTLE WA 284-D3
SEATTLE WA 285-F3
S BASALT ST
SPOKANE CO WA 348-C11
BASE LINE DR
HOOD RIVER CO OR 202-C2
BASE LINE RD
GILLIAM CO OR 128-A2
BASELINE RD
BAY CITY OR 197-B1
DOUGLAS CO WA 236-C7
GRANT CO WA 112-B3
SW BASELINE RD
HILLSBORO OR 199-A1
WASHINGTON CO OR 199-A1
W BASELINE RD
HILLSBORO OR 198-D1
HILLSBORO OR 199-A1
WASHINGTON CO OR 198-D1
WASHINGTON CO OR 199-A1
BASELINE RD E
GRANT CO WA 242-C4
E BASELINE ST Rt#-8
CORNELIUS OR 198-C1
SE BASELINE ST Rt#-8
HILLSBORO OR 198-D1
SW BASELINE ST Rt#-8
HILLSBORO OR 198-D1
W BASELINE ST Rt#-8
CORNELIUS OR 198-C1
BASELINE 1/2 RD SE
GRANT CO WA 242-D4
BASELINE RIDGE RD
WASHINGTON CO OR 198-A1
BASEY CANYON RD
MORROW CO OR 128-C2
W BASIN RD
DESCHUTES CO OR 135-B3
BASIN ST N Rt#-28
EPHRATA WA 112-C3
GRANT CO WA 112-C3
BASIN ST NW Rt#-28
EPHRATA WA 112-C3
GRANT CO WA 112-C3
BASIN ST S Rt#-28
EPHRATA WA 112-C3
GRANT CO WA 112-C3
BASKET BUTTE RD
DOUGLAS CO OR 223-A3
NE BASKET FLAT RD
CLARK CO WA 193-B2
BASL HILL RD
MARION CO OR 134-A1
BASSET RD
SKAGIT CO WA 161-C5
BATES RD
COOS CO OR 220-B6
DOUGLAS CO OR 225-C4

BATES RD
KELSO WA 303-E8
KLICKITAT CO WA 195-D4
BATTELLE BLVD
RICHLAND WA 340-F6
BATTERMAN RD
DOUGLAS CO WA 239-B5
BATTERY ST
SEATTLE WA 277-J4
BATTLE CREEK RD
JACKSON CO OR 230-A2
OWYHEE CO ID 155-C1
BATTLE CREEK RD SE
MARION CO OR 325-B9
SALEM OR 324-J5
SALEM OR 325-A5
BATTLE CREEK RANCH RD
MALHEUR CO OR 154-B2
BATTLE POINT RD NE
KITSAP CO WA 174-C1
BATUM RD
ADAMS CO WA 113-B3
LINCOLN CO WA 113-B3
BATY RD
CLACKAMAS CO OR 201-A4
BAUER RD
WHITMAN CO WA 250-B1
BAUMAN RD
ADAMS CO WA 113-C3
ADAMS CO WA 121-C1
RITZVILLE WA 113-C3
BAUMEISTER DR
ASOTIN WA 250-B5
BAY AV
HOQUIAM WA 178-A7
BAY AV Rt#-103
OCEAN PARK WA 186-A2
SE BAY BLVD
NEWPORT OR 206-B4
SW BAY BLVD
NEWPORT OR 206-B4
E BAY DR
OLYMPIA WA 296-J2
W BAY DR
OLYMPIA WA 296-G3
E BAY DR NW
PIERCE CO WA 181-C1
S BAY LP NE
THURSTON CO WA 180-D5
BAY PL
DESCHUTES CO OR 211-D5
BAY RD
BIRCH BAY WA 158-B4
LEWIS CO WA 187-C3
S BAY RD NE
OLYMPIA WA 297-C2
THURSTON CO WA 180-D5
THURSTON CO WA 297-C2
BAY ST
CITY OF VICTORIA BC 256-G7
CITY OF VICTORIA BC 257-A8
EAST PORT ORCHARD WA 271-A13
PORT ORCHARD WA 270-J14
PORT ORCHARD WA 271-A13
BAY ST Rt#-166
KITSAP CO WA 174-B4
PORT ORCHARD WA 174-B4
PORT ORCHARD WA 270-H14
BAY ST Rt#-167
TACOMA WA 182-A2
S BAY ST
WALDPORT OR 328-E5
SW BAY ST
NEWPORT OR 206-B4
BAYARD ST Rt#-206
CONDON OR 128-A2
E BAYARD ST Rt#-206
CONDON OR 128-A2
BAY CENTER RD
PACIFIC CO WA 183-C7
BAY CENTER DIKE RD
PACIFIC CO WA 183-C7
BAYLEY RD
YAMHILL CO OR 198-C5
BAYLISS RD
YAMHILL CO OR 198-B6
BAYNES RD
DISTRICT OF SAANICH BC 257-G5
BAYOCEAN RD NW
TILLAMOOK CO OR 197-B1
BAYOCEAN DIKE RD
TILLAMOOK CO OR 191-A7
TILLAMOOK CO OR 197-A1
BAYSHORE DR
LINCOLN CO OR 328-C3
N BAYSHORE DR
COOS BAY OR 333-H9
S BAYSHORE DR
COOS BAY OR 333-H11
BAYVIEW DR
WHATCOM CO WA 101-C1
BAYVIEW DR W
BREMERTON WA 270-E13
NAVY YARD CITY WA 270-E13
BAYVIEW RD
LINCOLN CO OR 328-H2
SKAGIT CO WA 161-A6
WALDPORT OR 328-D3
S BAYVIEW RD
ISLAND CO WA 170-D2
BAYVIEW RD KPN
PIERCE CO WA 174-A7
BAY VIEW EDISON RD
SKAGIT CO WA 160-D5
SKAGIT CO WA 161-A4
B D MINKLER RD
SKAGIT CO WA 161-C5
BEACH DR
CITY OF VICTORIA BC 257-B10
DISTRICT OF OAK BAY BC 257-E5
S BEACH DR
ISLAND CO WA 167-D7
KITSAP CO WA 271-J8
SEASIDE WA 301-F10
BEACH DR E
EAST PORT ORCHARD WA 271-B12
KITSAP CO WA 271-F9
MANCHESTER WA 271-F9
BEACH DR NE
KITSAP CO WA 170-B5

BEACH DR SW
SEATTLE WA 280-B3
SEATTLE WA 284-D1
BEACH RD
LANE CO OR 215-B6
W BEACH RD
AULT FIELD WA 167-B3
ISLAND CO WA 167-B3
BEACH ST
ASHLAND OR 337-E9
BEACHER HILL RD
CHELAN CO WA 238-A1
BEACH LOOP DR SW
BANDON OR 220-A6
BEACH LOOP RD
BANDON OR 220-A7
COOS CO OR 220-A7
BEACON AV E
MONTESANO WA 178-D7
BEACON AV S
KING WA 287-F4
KING WA 289-H1
SEATTLE WA 282-B2
SEATTLE WA 286-D1
SEATTLE WA 287-F4
TUKWILA WA 287-F4
E BEACON DR
LANE CO OR 210-A7
SANTA CLARA OR 210-A7
NE BEACON DR
GRANTS PASS OR 335-H7
W BEACON DR
LANE CO OR 210-A7
BEACON LN
DIST OF WEST VANCOUVER BC 156-A3
BEACON RD
GRAYS HARBOR CO WA 178-D7
WHITMAN CO WA 122-A1
BEACON ST
BOISE ID 253-C3
BEACON LIGHT RD
ADA CO ID 253-A1
BEAGLE RD
JACKSON CO OR 230-C4
E BEAKMAN ST Rt#-203
UNION OR 130-B2
BEALL LN
CENTRAL POINT OR 230-C7
CENTRAL POINT OR 336-A7
JACKSON CO OR 230-C7
JACKSON CO OR 336-A7
MEDFORD OR 230-C7
MEDFORD OR 336-A7
BEALL RD SW
KING CO WA 174-D6
BEALS CREEK RD
DOUGLAS CO OR 225-D3
BEAM RD
YAKIMA CO WA 120-A2
BEAR AV
CITY OF HARRISN HT SPGS BC 94-C3
BEAR DR
JEFFERSON CO OR 208-B7
SW BEAR DR
JEFFERSON CO OR 208-B6
BEAR BASIN RD
DEL NORTE CO CA 148-C3
BEAR CREEK RD
COOS CO OR 220-B6
CROOK CO OR 136-A1
DESCHUTES CO OR 217-D3
DOUGLAS CO OR 219-B1
DOUGLAS CO OR 223-B5
GRANT CO OR 137-B2
JOSEPHINE CO OR 233-C4
LANE CO OR 215-C5
LINCOLN CO OR 203-C4
LINCOLN CO OR 209-B2
SKAMANIA CO WA 194-D4
WALLOWA CO OR 130-B2
E BEAR CREEK RD
BEND OR 217-C3
BEND OR 332-J8
DESCHUTES CO OR 217-C3
DESCHUTES CO OR 332-J8
N BEAR CREEK RD
DOUGLAS CO OR 219-C1
NE BEAR CREEK RD
BEND OR 332-G8
W BEAR CREEK RD
KITSAP CO WA 173-C4
MASON CO WA 173-C4
BEAR CREEK RD NE
KING CO WA 171-D7
BEAR CREEK DEWATTO RD
KITSAP CO WA 173-C4
MASON CO WA 173-C4
BEAR CREEK-FIFE RD
CROOK CO OR 135-C3
CROOK CO OR 136-A3
CROOK CO OR 144-B1
BEAR CREST DR Rt#-99
JACKSON CO OR 234-B2
PHOENIX OR 234-B2
BEAR FLAT RD
KLAMATH CO OR 143-A2
LAKE CO OR 143-A2
BEAR MOUNTAIN RD
CHELAN CO WA 236-B3
LANE CO OR 215-C5
BEAR RIVER RD
PACIFIC CO WA 186-B6
BEAR SPURS LP
JEFFERSON CO OR 211-D1
BEAR SPURS RD
JEFFERSON CO OR 211-D1
BEAR WALLOW BUTTE RD
DESCHUTES CO OR 216-D1
BEATYS BUTTE RD
LAKE CO OR 152-C2
E BEAUCHENE RD
YAKIMA CO WA 243-C7
S BEAUDRY RD
YAKIMA CO WA 243-D7
BEAUTY CREEK RD
KOOTENAI CO ID 248-B1
BEAVER RD
DIST OF N VANCOUVER BC 255-B1
NEZ PERCE CO ID 250-D5

BEAVERBROOK DR
DISTRICT OF BURNABY BC 156-D4
NE BEAVER BROOK RD
CLARK CO WA 193-A1
BEAVER BUTTE RD
WASCO CO OR 127-A3
BEAVER CREEK RD
ADAMS CO ID 131-C3
ADAMS CO ID 251-A5
COOS CO OR 220-D3
CROOK CO OR 136-B3
LEWIS CO WA 187-A1
LINCOLN CO OR 206-B6
WAHKIAKUM CO WA 117-B3
E BEAVER CREEK RD
KITSAP CO WA 271-E10
MANCHESTER WA 271-F10
N BEAVER CREEK RD
LINCOLN CO OR 206-B6
S BEAVER CREEK RD
LINCOLN CO OR 206-B7
LINCOLN CO OR 328-G2
S BEAVERCREEK RD
CLACKAMAS CO OR 126-A3
CLACKAMAS CO OR 199-D5
CLACKAMAS CO OR 200-A6
OREGON CITY OR 199-D5
BEAVER FALLS RD
CLATSKANIE OR 117-B3
COLUMBIA CO OR 117-B3
COLUMBIA CO OR 189-A3
E BEAVER HILL RD
COOS CO OR 220-C4
W BEAVER HILL RD
COOS CO OR 220-B3
BEAVER LAKE RD
SKAGIT CO WA 161-C7
BEAVER MARSH RD
SKAGIT CO WA 168-A1
BEAVER SPRINGS RD
COLUMBIA CO OR 189-B5
SW BEAVRTN-HILLSDLE HWY Rt#-10
BEAVERTON OR 199-B2
PORTLAND OR 199-B2
PORTLAND OR 316-A3
WASHINGTON CO OR 199-B2
BEAVERTON-TIGARD FRWY Rt#-217
BEAVERTON OR 199-B2
WASHINGTON CO OR 199-B1
BEAVERTON-TIGARD HWY Rt#-217
BEAVERTON OR 199-B2
LAKE OSWEGO OR 199-B3
TIGARD OR 199-B3
BEAVERTON VALLEY RD
SAN JUAN CO WA 101-C2
BEAVER VALLEY RD Rt#-19
JEFFERSON CO WA 170-A1
BEBER RANCH RD
MALHEUR CO OR 154-B1
BECK RD
BENTON CO WA 121-A3
POLK CO OR 204-A4
STEVENS CO WA 106-A3
NE BECK RD
KITSAP CO WA 271-H6
BECKER RD
DOUGLAS CO OR 221-A3
NEZ PERCE CO ID 250-C2
WHITMAN CO WA 249-B7
WHITMAN CO WA 250-A1
BECKLEY RD
ADAMS CO WA 122-A1
BEDELL RD
COLUMBIA CO OR 189-B6
BED ROCK FLAT RD
WASHINGTON CO ID 139-B1
BEDWELL BAY RD
ANMORE BC 157-A3
BELCARRA BC 157-A3
CITY OF PORT MOODY BC 156-D3
MAPLE RIDGE BC 157-A3
VILLAGE OF BELCARRA BC 156-D3
BEEBE RD
COWLITZ CO WA 187-C6
BEECH ST
ARLINGTON OR 128-A1
LONGVIEW WA 302-H10
BEECH ST Rt#-64
LEWIS CO ID 123-C2
NEZPERCE ID 123-C2
E BEECH CREEK RD
GRANT CO OR 137-B1
SW BEEF BEND RD
WASHINGTON CO OR 199-A3
BEEKS RD
BONNER CO ID 244-A5
BEEKS CANYON RD
KLICKITAT CO WA 196-C1
BEE MILL RD
JEFFERSON CO WA 109-C1
BEERBOWER RD
MASON CO WA 179-A5
BEESON CTO
WHITMAN CO WA 249-B3
BEESON RD
CLACKAMAS CO OR 200-A7
BEET RD
CANYON CO ID 147-B1
BEEVILLE LOOP RD
MASON CO WA 179-B2
BEGBIE ST
CITY OF VICTORIA BC 256-J9
CITY OF VICTORIA BC 257-A9
BEHME RD
WHATCOM CO WA 158-C3
BEHRENS LN
UNION CO OR 130-A2
BEHRENS-MILLETT RD
MOUNT VERNON WA 260-A13
SKAGIT CO WA 260-A13
BEHRN RD
WASCO CO OR 196-A6
BEIRMAN RD
ADAMS CO WA 113-C3
BEITEY RD
STEVENS CO WA 106-B3

BELFAIR-TAHUYA RD
MASON CO WA 173-C5
BELKNAP SPRINGS HWY Rt#-126
LANE CO OR 134-B2
LINN CO OR 134-B2
SE BELL AV
CLACKAMAS OR 318-E7
BELL RD
WASHINGTON CO OR 199-A5
YAMHILL CO OR 198-D5
E BELL RD
YAKIMA CO WA 243-C7
SW BELL RD
CLACKAMAS CO OR 199-A5
BELL ST
DISTRICT OF MISSION BC 94-B3
BELL CANYON RD
KOOTENAI CO ID 248-B4
BELLE CENTER RD
SKAMANIA CO WA 193-D7
BELLE PASSI RD NE
MARION CO OR 205-B2
BELLEVILLE ST
CITY OF VICTORIA BC 256-G9
BELLEVUE HWY
AMITY OR 204-B2
YAMHILL CO OR 204-B2
SW BELLEVUE HWY
YAMHILL CO OR 204-A2
BELLEVUE WY NE
BELLEVUE WA 175-C2
BELLEVUE WY SE
BELLEVUE WA 175-C2
NE BELLEVUE REDMOND RD
BELLEVUE WA 175-C2
REDMOND WA 175-C2
BELLFOUNTAIN RD
BENTON CO OR 133-B2
BENTON CO OR 327-A14
BELLINGER LN
JACKSON CO OR 234-A1
BELLINGER SCALE RD
LINN CO OR 133-C1
BELL PLAIN DR
LINN CO OR 207-B7
BELL PLAIN RD
GARFIELD CO WA 122-B2
N BELLWOOD ST
UNION OR 130-B2
S BELLWOOD ST
UNION OR 130-B2
BELMONT AV E
SEATTLE WA 278-B3
BELMONT DR
HOOD RIVER CO OR 195-C5
SW BELMONT LN
JEFFERSON CO OR 208-B5
MADRAS OR 208-B5
BELMONT RD
HOOD RIVER OR 195-C5
HOOD RIVER CO OR 195-C5
E BELMONT RD
SPOKANE CO WA 247-A5
N BELMONT RD
COEUR D'ALENE ID 355-A6
SE BELMONT ST
PORTLAND OR 313-G6
BELMONT-FARMINGTON RD
FARMINGTON WA 115-A3
NW BELT RD
YAMHILL CO OR 198-A4
N BELT ST
SPOKANE WA 348-G2
BELTLINE RD
EUGENE OR 215-B1
EUGENE OR 329-B6
EUGENE OR 330-A1
LANE CO OR 215-B1
North Springfield OR 330-F2
Santa Clara OR 215-B1
SPRINGFIELD OR 330-F2
BELTS DR
LINN CO OR 210-B4
BELVEDERE RD
OKANOGAN CO WA 237-C1
BEN BUNCH RD
LANE CO OR 214-B1
S BEN BURR BLVD
SPOKANE WA 349-F11
N BENCH RD
KOOTENAI CO ID 245-A3
W BENCH RD
ADAMS CO WA 121-A1
BENCH MARK BUTTE RD
DESCHUTES CO OR 216-A7
BEND AV
WINSTON OR 221-B6
BEN DAY GULCH RD
GARFIELD CO WA 122-B2
BEND-DESCHUTES MRKT RD
BEND OR 217-C1
DESCHUTES CO OR 212-C7
DESCHUTES CO OR 217-C1
BENDER RD
KITTITAS CO WA 241-B5
LYNDEN WA 102-B1
WHATCOM CO WA 102-B1
BENDIRE RD
MALHEUR CO OR 138-A3
BEND ON RD N
OKANOGAN CO WA 104-C3
BENEKE RD
CLATSOP CO OR 117-B3
BENEWAH RD
BENEWAH CO ID 115-A3
BENEWAH CO ID 248-B7
S BEN GARNETT WY
SPOKANE WA 348-J10
BENGE WASHTUCNA RD
ADAMS CO WA 122-A1
BENGE-WASHTUCNA RD
ADAMS CO WA 121-C1
BENGE WINONA RD
ADAMS CO WA 122-A1
BENHAM ST
RICHLAND WA 341-G3
BENHAM FALLS RD
DESCHUTES CO OR 217-A5

BEN HOWARD RD
SNOHOMISH CO WA 110-C1
BENJAMIN RD
YAMHILL CO OR 198-D5
BEN MORE RD
DOUGLAS CO OR 219-B6
BENNETT DR
BELLINGHAM WA 158-D7
BELLINGHAM WA 258-A2
BENNETT RD
ADA CO ID 253-A6
CANYON CO ID 147-C1
COLUMBIA CO OR 192-A2
DESCHUTES CO OR 217-D3
PEND OREILLE CO WA 106-C3
WASCO CO OR 127-C3
BENNETT CREEK RD
LANE CO OR 215-B6
BENNION RD
KOOTENAI CO ID 247-D7
SE BENSON RD
LINCOLN CO OR 206-B4
NEWPORT OR 206-B4
BENSON RD S
RENTON WA 175-C5
BENSON RD SE Rt#-515
KING CO WA 175-C6
BENSON CREEK RD
COOS CO OR 218-D4
OKANOGAN CO WA 104-B3
BENTON ST
PORT TOWNSEND WA 263-G4
N BENTON ST
KENNEWICK WA 343-D10
S BENTON ST
KENNEWICK WA 343-D11
BENTON-FRANKLIN INTERCNTY BRDG
KENNEWICK WA 343-E10
PASCO WA 343-F9
BENTS RD
MARION CO OR 199-A6
BENVENUTO AV
DIST OF CENTRAL SAANICH BC 159-B4
BERCOT RD
AULT FIELD WA 170-D1
BERG RD
COLUMBIA CO OR 192-A2
DOUGLAS CO WA 112-C2
BERGE RD
SKAMANIA CO WA 195-A4
BERGER-FEELEY RD
HARNEY CO OR 136-C3
BERGESON ST
BOISE ID 253-D3
BERKLEY AV
DIST OF N VANCOUVER BC 255-H4
BERKLEY RD
DIST OF N VANCOUVER BC 255-H5
BERLIN RD
CRESWELL OR 133-C1
LEBANON OR 133-C1
LINN CO OR 133-C1
LOWELL OR 133-C1
BERMUDA RD
BENTON CO WA 341-D12
S BERNARD ST
SPOKANE WA 348-J13
BERNARDS ST
MARION CO OR 198-D7
S BERNEY DR
WALLA WALLA WA 345-F8
WALLA WALLA CO WA 345-F8
WALLA WALLA EAST WA 345-F8
BERNHARDT CREEK RD
LANE CO OR 214-C3
BERRY DR
LINN CO OR 326-J1
NE BERRY RD
CLARK CO WA 193-B3
BERRY CREEK RD
POLK CO OR 207-A2
NW BERRY CREEK RD
YAMHILL CO OR 198-A6
BERRY LAKES RD
KITSAP CO WA 174-B4
N BERTELSEN RD
EUGENE OR 329-C4
S BERTELSEN RD
EUGENE OR 329-C7
LANE CO OR 329-C7
SW BERTHA BLVD
PORTLAND OR 316-D5
BERTHUSEN RD
WHATCOM CO WA 158-D4
BESSEN RD
DESCHUTES CO OR 217-A6
BESSIE CREEK RD
JACKSON CO OR 226-C7
JACKSON CO OR 227-A7
E BEST AV
COEUR D'ALENE ID 355-E8
BEST RD
POLK CO OR 204-C5
SKAGIT CO WA 161-A7
SKAGIT CO WA 168-A1
BETA DR
LINN CO OR 207-C6
BETHANY RD
YAKIMA CO WA 120-B2
BETHANY-ALEXANDER Y
YAKIMA CO WA 120-B2
BETHEL RD
EAST PORT ORCHARD WA 174-B4
KITSAP CO WA 174-B4
POLK CO OR 204-B3
BETHEL RD Rt#-166
PORT ORCHARD WA 174-B4
PORT ORCHARD WA 270-J14
N BETHEL ST
OLYMPIA WA 297-A3
BETHEL-BURLEY RD SE
KITSAP CO WA 174-B5
BETHEL HEIGHTS RD
POLK CO OR 204-C3
BETTAS RD
KITTITAS CO WA 240-D2
W BETZ RD
CHENEY WA 246-A7
SPOKANE CO WA 246-A6

STREET City State Page-Grid

BEULAH RD
MALHEUR CO OR 138-A3
MALHEUR CO OR 146-A1
BEVERLY BLVD
EVERETT WA 268-D2
BEVERLY DR NE
THURSTON CO WA 181-A5
BEVERLY LN
EVERETT WA 268-B2
BEVERLY BURKE RD
GRANT CO WA 120-B1
BEVERLY PARK RD
MUKILTEO WA 171-B4
SNOHOMISH CO WA 171-B4
BEVERLY PARK EDMONDS RD
EVERETT WA 268-A6
SNOHOMISH WA 268-A6
BEVILLE RD
LEWIS CO WA 187-A1
BEWLEY CREEK RD
TILLAMOOK CO OR 197-C3
BEWLEYS ST
BAY CITY OR 197-B1
B HOWARD RD
WHITMAN CO WA 249-B1
BIA RD 10
OKANOGAN CO WA 105-A3
BIA RD 33
JEFFERSON CO OR 134-C1
JEFFERSON CO OR 135-A1
BIA RD 108
YAKIMA CO WA 119-A2
BIA RD 140
YAKIMA CO WA 119-B3
BIA RD 255
YAKIMA CO WA 119-A3
BIA RD 7047
GRAYS HARBOR CO WA 172-B5
BIA RD F-2
GRAYS HARBOR CO WA 177-C1
BIA RD F-4
GRAYS HARBOR CO WA 177-C1
BIA RD S-2
GRAYS HARBOR CO WA 177-B1
BIA RD S-26
GRAYS HARBOR CO WA 172-D7
GRAYS HARBOR CO WA 177-B1
BIBLE CREEK RD
TILLAMOOK CO OR 125-A2
SW BIBLE CREEK RD
TILLAMOOK CO OR 125-A2
YAMHILL CO OR 125-A2
BICKFORD AV
SNOHOMISH WA 171-D2
SNOHOMISH CO WA 171-D2
BIDDLE RD
JACKSON CO OR 336-B5
MEDFORD OR 336-C8
BIEHN ST
KLAMATH FALLS OR 338-C5
SE BIELMEIR RD
KITSAP CO WA 174-B5
BIENZ RD
YAMHILL CO OR 198-C6
BIG ALKALI RD
WHITMAN CO WA 122-A1
BIG BENCH RD
DOUGLAS CO WA 236-D4
BIG BEND RD
DOUGLAS CO OR 221-A3
BIG BUTTER CREEK RD
MORROW CO OR 128-C1
MORROW CO OR 129-A2
BIG CAMAS RD
DOUGLAS CO OR 222-C3
DOUGLAS CO OR 223-B4
BIG CREEK RD
BONNER CO ID 107-A3
COOS CO OR 218-D3
LANE CO OR 209-A6
SHOSHONE CO ID 115-C2
NE BIG CREEK RD
LINCOLN CO OR 206-B3
BIG ELK RD
JACKSON CO OR 150-A2
BIG ELK CREEK RD
LINCOLN CO OR 133-A1
LINCOLN CO OR 206-D4
BIGELOW ST NE
OLYMPIA WA 297-B4
E BIGELOW GULCH RD
SPOKANE CO WA 246-D2
SPOKANE CO WA 347-H14
SPOKANE CO WA 349-G1
BIG FALL CREEK RD
LANE CO OR 133-C3
LANE CO OR 134-A3
BIG FLAT RD
BAKER CO OR 138-A1
DEL NORTE CO CA 148-C3
WASHINGTON CO ID 139-C2
BIGHAM BROWN RD
JACKSON CO OR 230-D6
BIG HANAFORD RD
LEWIS CO WA 184-C5
BIG HUCKLEBERRY RD
SKAMANIA CO WA 195-A2
W BIG LAKE BLVD
SKAGIT CO WA 168-C1
BIG LICK LN
DOUGLAS CO OR 221-D7
E BIG MEADOWS RD
SPOKANE CO WA 114-C1
E BIG ROCK RD
SPOKANE CO WA 246-D5
BIG SANDY RD
CLACKAMAS CO OR 201-A4
BIG SPRING RD
DESCHUTES CO OR 216-D4
BIG SPRING BURN RD
DESCHUTES CO OR 216-D3
BIG SPRINGS RD
SISKIYOU CO CA 150-A3
E BIG SPRINGS RD
SPOKANE CO WA 349-G11
BIG SQUAWBACK RD
JEFFERSON CO OR 211-D1
BIG STICK RD
HARNEY CO OR 144-C2
HARNEY CO OR 145-A2

BIG VALLEY RD NE
KITSAP CO WA 170-B6
BIG WILLOW RD
PAYETTE CO ID 139-B3
BILGER CREEK RD
DOUGLAS CO OR 221-D7
BILLADEAU RD
DESCHUTES CO OR 217-D4
BILL CREEK RD
LEWIS CO WA 187-C4
BILL MOORE RD
KLICKITAT CO WA 196-B2
BILYEU CREEK RD
LINN CO OR 134-A1
BINGHAM AV E
PIERCE CO WA 182-A5
BINGHAM RD
UMATILLA CO OR 129-C1
BINGHAMPTON ST Rt#-507
RAINIER WA 118-A1
THURSTON CO WA 118-A1
BINNS HILL DR
HOOD RIVER CO OR 195-B6
BIRCH AV
LAPWAI ID 123-A2
WHITE SWAN WA 119-C2
NW BIRCH LN
JEFFERSON CO OR 208-B5
BIRCH PL
PACIFIC CO WA 186-A3
BIRCH RD
DIST OF NORTH SAANICH BC 159-B2
FRANKLIN CO WA 121-A2
BIRCH ST
BAKER CITY OR 138-B1
JUNCTION CITY OR 210-A6
PACIFIC CO WA 186-A4
N BIRCH ST Rt#-42S
COQUILLE OR 220-D5
BIRCH BAY DR
BIRCH BAY WA 158-B5
BIRCH BAY-LYNDEN RD
BIRCH BAY WA 158-B4
LYNDEN WA 158-D4
WHATCOM CO WA 158-C4
BIRCH CREEK RD
MALHEUR CO OR 146-C2
UMATILLA CO OR 121-C3
E BIRCH CREEK RD
PILOT ROCK OR 129-B2
UMATILLA CO OR 129-B2
S BIRCHFIELD RD
YAKIMA CO WA 243-C7
W BIRCHFIELD RD
YAKIMA WA 243-C7
YAKIMA CO WA 243-C7
BIRCH POINT RD
BIRCH BAY WA 158-A4
BIRCHWOOD AV
BELLINGHAM WA 258-C3
S BIRD RD
CLACKAMAS CO OR 126-A3
BIRDSEYE CREEK RD
JACKSON CO OR 229-D7
BISCAY ST NW
THURSTON CO WA 180-C5
BISCUIT BUTTE RD
MALHEUR CO OR 146-C2
BISHOP LN
LANE CO OR 210-A7
BISHOP RD
CLALLAM CO WA 164-D6
COLUMBIA CO OR 189-C5
GRAYS HARBOR CO WA 183-D3
WASHINGTON CO OR 192-A6
BISHOP CREEK RD
COLUMBIA CO OR 189-B7
NW BISHOP-SCOTT RD
YAMHILL CO OR 198-A4
BISSELL RD
STEVENS CO WA 105-C3
STEVENS CO WA 106-A3
BISSINGER RD
UMATILLA CO OR 129-B1
BITTERS RD
KOOTENAI CO ID 115-A2
BITTNER RD
YAKIMA CO WA 243-D6
E BITTNER RD
YAKIMA CO WA 243-D7
BIXBY RD
TILLAMOOK CO OR 197-C6
BIZ POINT RD
SKAGIT CO WA 259-B12
BLACK RD
LEWIS CO WA 187-A1
N BLACK RD
SPOKANE CO WA 347-F4
SE BLACK RD
KITSAP CO WA 174-C5
W BLACK RD
COUPEVILLE WA 167-B4
ISLAND CO WA 167-B4
BLACK BRIDGE RD
PAYETTE CO ID 139-B3
BLACKBURN RD
DISTRICT OF CHILLIWACK BC 102-C1
YAMHILL CO OR 198-B5
E BLACKBURN RD
MOUNT VERNON WA 260-E14
SKAGIT CO WA 260-E14
W BLACKBURN RD
MOUNT VERNON WA 260-B14
SKAGIT CO WA 260-B14
BLACK BUTTE LN
WHEELER CO OR 128-A3
BLACK BUTTE RD
JEFFERSON CO OR 211-C2
JEFFERSON CO OR 212-A2
E BLACK CANYON HWY Rt#-52
GEM CO ID 139-C3
W BLACK CANYON HWY
GEM CO ID 139-B3
BLACK CANYON RD
LANE CO OR 215-C1
YAKIMA CO WA 243-A1
N BLACK CAT RD
ADA CO ID 253-A2

S BLACK CAT RD
ADA CO ID 253-A5
BLACK CREEK RD
GRAYS HARBOR CO WA 178-D6
BLACK DIAMOND RD
CLALLAM CO WA 261-C7
BLACK DOG RD
LINN CO OR 207-C3
BLACKFORD RD
COLUMBIA CO OR 189-A3
BLACK LAKE BLVD SW
OLYMPIA WA 296-E6
THURSTON CO WA 296-A10
TUMWATER WA 296-E6
BLACK LK BELMORE RD SW
THURSTON CO WA 296-B9
BLACKLEDGE RD
SKAMANIA CO WA 194-C3
BLACK MOUNTAIN RD
BAKER CO OR 138-A1
BLACK OAK DR
MEDFORD OR 336-G12
BLACK ROCK LN
DESCHUTES CO OR 217-C1
BLACK ROCK RD
DOUGLAS CO OR 222-B7
KOOTENAI CO ID 247-D6
KOOTENAI CO ID 248-D3
BLACK SNAG RD
HARNEY CO OR 136-C3
BLACKTAIL DR
JEFFERSON CO OR 212-C3
BLACKWELL RD
JACKSON CO OR 230-B6
BLAHA RDEX
COLUMBIA CO OR 192-A2
BLAINE RD
LATAH CO ID 249-D6
PAYETTE CO ID 139-B3
TILLAMOOK CO OR 197-C6
WHATCOM CO WA 158-B3
BLAINE RD Rt#-548
BIRCH BAY WA 158-B4
BLAINE WA 158-B3
WHATCOM CO WA 158-B3
BLAINE ST
PORT TOWNSEND WA 263-G4
BLAINE ST U.S.-30
CALDWELL ID 147-B1
W BLAINE ST
SEATTLE WA 276-D2
BLAIR RD
WHITMAN CO WA 249-B1
NE BLAIR RD
CLARK CO WA 193-B6
S BLAIR RD
CLACKAMAS CO OR 205-D3
BLAIR KNOB LOOP RD
MARION CO OR 205-D4
BLAKE RD
GRAYS HARBOR CO WA 183-B3
LEWIS CO WA 187-D5
BLAKE RD Rt#-27
OPPORTUNITY WA 350-H10
OPPORTUNITY WA 351-A13
SPOKANE CO WA 351-A13
BLAKELEY LN
LEWIS CO WA 187-D4
BLAKELY AV NE
KITSAP CO WA 174-D2
KITSAP CO WA 271-H4
W BLAKELY AV NE
KITSAP CO WA 271-J6
SW BLAKELY RD
BEND OR 332-D10
BLALOCK CANYON RD
GILLIAM CO OR 128-A1
BLANCA ST
UNIV ENDOWMENT LANDS BC 156-A4
BLANCHARD RD
TILLAMOOK CO OR 197-C5
E BLANCHARD RD
SPOKANE CO WA 114-C1
BLANK RD
WHITMAN CO WA 114-C3
BLANSHARD ST
CITY OF VICTORIA BC 256-H9
DISTRICT OF SAANICH BC 256-F4
BLANSHARD ST Rt#-17
CITY OF VICTORIA BC 256-G6
DISTRICT OF SAANICH BC 256-G5
BLANTON RD
FRANKLIN CO WA 121-B2
BLANTON RD Rt#-260
FRANKLIN CO WA 121-B1
BLATCHFORD RD
LINN CO OR 207-D7
BLENHEIM ST
VANCOUVER BC 156-B5
VANCOUVER BC 254-A13
BLENKINSOP RD
DISTRICT OF SAANICH BC 159-C5
DISTRICT OF SAANICH BC 256-J1
BLIMP BLVD
TILLAMOOK CO OR 197-C3
NW BLISS RD
CLARK CO WA 192-C4
BLISS-COCHRANE RD KPN
PIERCE CO WA 174-A7
BLIZZARD RD
WHATCOM CO WA 160-B1
BLM ACCESS RD
MAUPIN OR 127-B3
BLM RD 2-3
DOUGLAS CO OR 214-D6
BLM RD 23-4-26
DOUGLAS CO OR 219-C5
BLM RD 23-4-28-0
DOUGLAS CO OR 219-C5
BLM RD 23-4-90
DOUGLAS CO OR 219-B5
BLM RD 23-5-191
DOUGLAS CO OR 219-A5
BLM RD 24-1
DOUGLAS CO OR 214-D6
BLM RD 24-3-31-2
DOUGLAS CO OR 219-D7
BLM RD 24-5-10
DOUGLAS CO OR 219-B6

BLM RD 25-4-13-0
DOUGLAS CO OR 221-D1
BLM RD 25-7-5-1
DOUGLAS CO OR 141-A1
BLM RD 28-4-29-0
DOUGLAS CO OR 221-D6
BLM RD 29-4-20
DOUGLAS CO OR 225-D1
BLM RD 29-7-25-1
DOUGLAS CO OR 225-A1
BLM RD 30-70-50
DOUGLAS CO OR 225-A1
BLM RD 31-4-35-0
DOUGLAS CO OR 225-D4
BLM RD 32-4-9
DOUGLAS CO OR 225-D5
BLM RD 32-9-3
COOS CO OR 140-C3
BLM RD 33-0
DOUGLAS CO OR 214-D6
BLM RD 33-5-18
JOSEPHINE CO OR 229-C1
BLM RD 33-5-26
JOSEPHINE CO OR 229-C1
BLM RD 33-5-27
JOSEPHINE CO OR 229-C1
BLM RD 33-5-35-1
JOSEPHINE CO OR 229-C1
BLM RD 33-7-22
JOSEPHINE CO OR 229-A1
BLM RD 34-4-5
JOSEPHINE CO OR 229-C1
BLM RD 34-5-1
JOSEPHINE CO OR 229-C1
BLM RD 34-5-32
JOSEPHINE CO OR 229-C3
BLM RD 34-5-9
JOSEPHINE CO OR 229-C2
BLM RD 34-6-12
JOSEPHINE CO OR 229-B3
BLM RD 34-6-13
JOSEPHINE CO OR 229-B2
BLM RD 34-8-1
JOSEPHINE CO OR 141-A3
BLM RD 36-0
DOUGLAS CO OR 214-C7
BLM RD 37-6-36
JOSEPHINE CO OR 233-D3
BLM RD 39-6-9
JOSEPHINE CO OR 233-D3
BLM RD 39-7-16
JOSEPHINE CO OR 233-C4
BLM RD 61064
LAKE CO OR 152-C2
BLODGETT RD
LINCOLN CO OR 209-A3
MOUNT VERNON WA 260-D14
SKAGIT CO WA 168-B1
BLOMBERG RD SW
THURSTON CO WA 184-C1
BLOODGOOD RD
KLICKITAT CO WA 127-C1
BLOOMFIELD RD
MASON CO WA 180-B5
BLOOMING-FERN HILL RD
WASHINGTON CO OR 198-C2
NE BLOSSOM DR
HAYESVILLE OR 323-D5
SALEM OR 323-D5
S BLOUNT RD
CLACKAMAS CO OR 199-C6
BLOWOUT RESERVOIR RD
MALHEUR CO OR 146-C2
MALHEUR CO OR 147-A2
BLUE BUNCH RD
ADAMS CO ID 251-B6
BLUE CREEK RD
KOOTENAI CO ID 245-C6
BLUE CREEK RD W
STEVENS CO WA 106-A3
BLUE GRADE
DOUGLAS CO WA 239-A3
BLUEGRASS LN
DESCHUTES CO OR 211-C5
BLUE LAKE RD
FAIRVIEW OR 200-B1
OKANOGAN CO WA 104-C1
BLUE MOUNTAIN RD
CLALLAM CO WA 165-D7
WHATCOM CO WA 161-D1
BLUE MOUNTAIN ST
COQUITLAM BC 157-A5
BLUE MOUNTAIN LOGGNG RD
WHATCOM CO WA 161-C1
BLUE OX LOGGING RD
SKAMANIA CO WA 195-B4
BLUESTEM RD
LINCOLN CO WA 114-A2
BLUFF RD
CLACKAMAS CO OR 200-C3
PAYETTE CO ID 139-B3
SANDY OR 200-C3
N BLUFF RD
CITY OF WHITE ROCK BC 158-A2
DISTRICT OF SURREY BC 158-A2
ISLAND CO WA 167-C6
SE BLUFF RD
CLACKAMAS CO OR 200-C3
MULTNOMAH CO OR 200-C3
BLUFF ST
WINTHROP WA 104-A2
S BLUHM RD
CLACKAMAS CO OR 200-A6
BLUMAUER RD SE
THURSTON CO WA 184-D3
BLUNDELL RD
CITY OF RICHMOND BC 156-B6
BLUNT RD KPS
PIERCE CO WA 181-A2
BLY MOUNTAIN CTO
KLAMATH CO OR 151-A2
BOARDMAN IRRIGON RD
MORROW CO OR 128-C1
BOARD SHANTY RD
JOSEPHINE CO OR 229-C7
BOAT RD
COOS CO OR 220-A7
BOB GALBREATH RD
LANGLEY WA 171-A2

BOB HALL RD
WHATCOM CO WA 158-D4
BODINE RD
COLUMBIA CO OR 189-A2
COWLITZ CO WA 189-D4
BODINE RD N
COWLITZ CO WA 189-D4
BOE RD
SNOHOMISH CO WA 168-A4
BOECKMAN RD
WILSONVILLE OR 199-B5
BOEHMER RD NE
MARION CO OR 205-C3
S BOEING ACCESS RD
TUKWILA WA 286-D5
TUKWILA WA 287-E5
E BOEKEL RD
KOOTENAI CO ID 247-D1
S BOGACHIEL RD
JEFFERSON CO WA 169-D3
BOGACHIEL WY
CLALLAM CO WA 169-C2
BOGART LN
ADA CO ID 253-B1
BOG CREEK RD
BOUNDARY CO ID 106-C1
BOUNDARY CO ID 107-A1
BOGUS BASIN RD
ADA CO ID 253-D2
BOISE ID 253-C2
BOGUS RANCH RD
MALHEUR CO OR 146-C3
BOHLKEN DR
LINN CO OR 133-C1
LINN CO OR 207-D5
BOH MOUNTAIN RD
JOSEPHINE CO OR 229-A7
SE BOHNA PARK RD
CLACKAMAS CO OR 200-B3
BOHOSKEY DR W
YAKIMA CO WA 243-D6
BOISE AV
BENTON CO OR 133-B2
E BOISE AV
ADA CO ID 253-D3
BOISE ID 253-D3
W BOISE AV
BOISE ID 253-C3
NW BOISE DR
JEFFERSON CO OR 208-B3
BOISE ST
KOOTENAI ID 244-A1
BOISTFORT RD
LEWIS CO WA 187-A2
BOLAN LAKE RD
DEL NORTE CO CA 233-C7
JOSEPHINE CO OR 233-C7
BOLEN RD
CLARK CO WA 192-C1
LA CENTER WA 192-C1
BOLESKINE RD
DISTRICT OF SAANICH BC 256-F5
BOLLAND RD
CLACKAMAS CO OR 199-C7
BOLLENBAUGH HILL RD
SNOHOMISH CO WA 110-C1
BOLTON RD
LANE CO OR 133-B3
VENETA OR 133-B3
BOMBING RANGE RD
MORROW CO OR 128-C2
WEST RICHLAND WA 341-A3
BONAPARTE RD
OKANOGAN CO WA 105-A1
BONAPARTE LAKE RD
OKANOGAN CO WA 105-A2
BOND DR
COWLITZ CO WA 187-C7
COWLITZ CO WA 189-C1
BOND RD
COWLITZ CO WA 189-C1
LINN CO OR 207-D4
BOND RD NE
POULSBO WA 170-B6
BOND RD NE Rt#-307
KITSAP CO WA 170-C6
POULSBO WA 170-C6
BOND ST
ASTORIA WA 300-B4
COWLITZ CO WA 187-C7
DISTRICT OF BURNABY BC 156-C5
NW BOND ST
BEND OR 332-E6
W BOND ST
ASTORIA WA 300-B4
BOND BUTTE DR
LINN CO OR 210-B4
BOND CREEK RD
SHOSHONE CO ID 115-B2
BOND MILL RD
SAN JUAN CO WA 160-A3
BONITA RD
MALHEUR CO OR 138-B3
W BONNEVILLE ST
PASCO WA 343-E8
BONNEY MEADOWS TR
WASCO CO OR 202-C7
BONSON RD
BRITISH COLUMBIA 157-C6
PITT MEADOWS BC 157-C5
BONY RD
YAMHILL CO OR 198-B4
BOOKER RD
ADAMS CO WA 121-A1
BOOMER HILL RD
DOUGLAS CO OR 225-B1
N BOON RD
ISLAND CO WA 167-B3
BOONE RD
LEWIS CO WA 187-D3
N BOONE ST Rt#-105
ABERDEEN WA 178-B7
S BOONE ST Rt#-105
ABERDEEN WA 117-A1
ABERDEEN WA 178-B7
GRAYS HARBOR CO WA 117-A1
BOONE CREEK RD
COOS CO OR 220-D3
BOONES FERRY RD
CLACKAMAS OR 320-B6

BOONES FERRY RD
CLACKAMAS CO OR 199-B6
LAKE OSWEGO OR 320-B6
MARION CO OR 199-B7
MARION CO OR 205-C1
PORTLAND OR 199-B6
WASHINGTON CO OR 199-B6
WILSONVILLE OR 199-B6
SW BOONES FERRY RD
CLACKAMAS OR 320-D3
DURHAM OR 199-B4
LAKE OSWEGO OR 320-D3
MULTNOMAH OR 320-D3
PORTLAND OR 316-E7
PORTLAND OR 317-E7
PORTLAND OR 320-D2
TUALATIN OR 199-B4
WASHINGTON CO OR 199-B4
BOONES FERRY RD NE
MARION CO OR 205-B1
WOODBURN OR 205-B1
BOOTH LN
UNION CO OR 130-A2
BOOTH RD
DOUGLAS CO OR 214-A6
SE BOOTH BEND RD
YAMHILL CO OR 204-C1
W BOOTH BEND RD
MCMINNVILLE OR 198-A7
BOOTH HILL RD
HOOD RIVER CO OR 202-D1
N BOOTHILL RD
KOOTENAI CO ID 245-B4
BOOTH-KELLY RD
SPRINGFIELD OR 331-D8
BORBA RD
TILLAMOOK CO OR 197-C5
BORDEAUX RD SW
THURSTON CO WA 184-A2
BOREN AV
SEATTLE WA 278-A5
BOREN AV S
SEATTLE WA 278-B6
BORGEN RD
LATAH CO ID 250-B1
WALLA WALLA CO WA 121-C3
SE BORGES RD
CLACKAMAS CO OR 200-B3
NE BORIN RD
CLARK CO WA 193-D6
SW BORLAND RD
CLACKAMAS CO OR 199-C4
TUALATIN OR 199-C4
WEST LINN OR 199-C4
SE BORNSTEDT RD
CLACKAMAS CO OR 200-C4
N BORSETH ST Rt#-9
SEDRO-WOOLLEY WA 161-C5
S BORTON RD
YAKIMA CO WA 243-A7
BOSSBURG RD
STEVENS CO WA 106-A1
BOSTON ST
SEATTLE WA 277-H1
BOSTON HARBOR RD NE
THURSTON CO WA 180-C5
BOSTON MILL DR
LINN CO OR 210-B1
BOSWELL RD
DOUGLAS CO OR 219-B3
NE BOTHELL WY Rt#-522
BOTHELL WA 171-B6
KING CO WA 171-B6
LAKE FOREST PARK WA 171-B6
BOTHELL WY NE Rt#-522
BOTHELL WA 171-C6
LAKE FOREST PARK WA 171-B6
BOTHELL WY NE Rt#-527
BOTHELL WA 171-C6
BOTHELL EVERETT HWY Rt#-527
BOTHELL WA 171-C4
EVERETT WA 171-C4
MILL CREEK WA 171-C4
SNOHOMISH CO WA 171-C4
BOTTLE BAY RD
BONNER CO ID 244-A3
BOULDER CREEK RD
ADAMS CO ID 131-C3
ADAMS CO ID 251-A1
TILLAMOOK CO OR 197-C6
BOULDER LAKE RD
VALLEY CO ID 251-D6
BOULDER RIDGE RD
WASCO CO OR 202-C7
BOULEVARD PL
MERCER ISLAND WA 283-J3
BOULEVARD RD SE
OLYMPIA WA 297-C7
THURSTON CO WA 297-C10
BOUNDARY HWY Rt#-251
NORTHPORT WA 106-B1
STEVENS CO WA 106-B1
BOUNDARY RD
BRITISH COLUMBIA 102-C1
DISTRICT OF BURNABY BC 156-C5
DISTRICT OF BURNABY BC 255-F12
DISTRICT OF CHILLIWACK BC 102-C1
JACKSON CO OR 150-A1
PEND OREILLE CO WA 106-B1
VANCOUVER BC 156-C5
VANCOUVER BC 255-F12
W BOUNDARY RD
KLAMATH CO OR 142-C3
LANE CO OR 134-A3
BOUNDARY RD S
DISTRICT OF BURNABY BC 156-C5
VANCOUVER BC 156-C5
BOUNDARY BAY RD
DISTRICT OF DELTA BC 101-C1
WHATCOM CO WA 101-C1
BOUNDARY CREEK RD
BOUNDARY CO ID 107-A1
BOURBON RD
SHERMAN CO OR 127-C2
BOW RD
SKAGIT CO WA 161-A5
BOWDEN RANCH RD
MALHEUR CO OR 154-B1

PNW

INDEX

STREET / City State / Page-Grid

N BOWDISH RD
OPPORTUNITY WA 350-G7
S BOWDISH RD
OPPORTUNITY WA 350-G10
SPOKANE CO WA 350-G14
BOWDOIN WY
EDMONDS WA 171-A5
BOWEN RD
NANAIMO BC 93-A3
BOWERS BLVD
SAN JUAN CO WA 160-A5
BOWERS DR
LINN CO OR 210-B5
BOWES RD
GRAYS HARBOR CO WA 177-D2
BOW HILL RD
SKAGIT CO WA 161-A4
BOWLES RD
FINLEY WA 121-A3
BOWMAN RD
ASOTIN CO WA 250-A6
REEDSPORT OR 218-C2
WHATCOM CO WA 161-C2
BOWMAN HILL RD
COLUMBIA CO WA 122-A2
BOWMONT RD
CANYON CO ID 147-C1
BOX CANYON-LE CLERC RD
PEND OREILLE CO WA 106-B1
BOYD RD
CHELAN WA 236-C2
CHELAN CO WA 236-C2
JACKSON CO OR 230-A5
YAKIMA CO WA 243-A3
BOYD ST
NEW WESTMINSTER BC 156-D6
BOYD ACRES RD
BEND OR 332-G4
BOYD LOOP RD
DUFUR OR 127-B2
WASCO CO OR 127-B2
BOYDSTUN ST
VALLEY CO ID 251-C5
N BOYER AV
SANDPOINT ID 244-A2
BOYER AV E
SEATTLE WA 274-B7
SEATTLE WA 278-B1
BOYER RD
DOUGLAS CO OR 225-B2
JOSEPHINE CO OR 229-B3
BOZARTH RD
CROOK CO OR 213-B6
BOZY CREEK RD
GRAYS HARBOR CO WA 179-D6
SW BRACE POINT DR
SEATTLE WA 284-D3
BRADEN RD
WALLA WALLA CO WA 345-A14
BRADLEY RD
SKAGIT CO WA 161-A5
S BRADLEY RD
CLACKAMAS CO OR 200-A4
BRADNER RD
DISTRICT OF MATSQUI BC 94-B3
DISTRICT OF MATSQUI BC 102-B1
BRADSHAW RD
SKAGIT CO WA 161-A7
SKAGIT CO WA 168-A1
E BRADSHAW RD
SPOKANE CO WA 114-C2
BRADY LOOP RD
GRAYS HARBOR CO WA 179-A7
BRAEMAR RD E
DIST OF N VANCOUVER BC 255-B2
E BRAEMERE RD
BOISE ID 253-D2
BRAGG RD
JACKSON CO OR 234-B2
BRAID ST
NEW WESTMINSTER BC 156-D5
NEW WESTMINSTER BC 157-A5
BRAINER RD
ISLAND CO WA 167-D7
BRAMHALL RD
COLUMBIA CO WA 122-A2
BRANCH RD
WHITE SWAN WA 119-C2
YAKIMA CO WA 119-C2
YAKIMA CO WA 120-A2
BRANDON RD
LINN CO OR 210-B3
BRANDSTROM RD
SNOHOMISH CO WA 168-B3
BRANDYWINE RD
DESCHUTES CO OR 212-A7
BRANSTETTER RD
ADAMS CO ID 251-B3
BRATHOVDE RD
YAKIMA CO WA 243-B5
BRATTAIN DR
LINN CO OR 210-A1
BRAYS RD NW
DOUGLAS CO WA 236-B5
BRECHIN RD
NANAIMO BC 93-A3
BREITENBUSH RD
DETROIT OR 134-B1
MARION CO OR 134-B1
S BREMER RD
CLACKAMAS CO OR 199-C6
BRENNER RD NW
THURSTON CO WA 180-B6
BRENNER CANYON RD
MORROW CO OR 128-B2
BRETZ MINE RD
MALHEUR CO OR 154-B2
BREWER RD
KLICKITAT CO WA 196-C2
BREWERY GRADE ST
THE DALLES OR 196-C7
BREWSTER RD
LEBANON OR 133-C1
LINN CO OR 133-C1
BREYMAN ORCHARDS RD
YAMHILL CO OR 198-C6
BRIAN RANCH RD
CLACKAMAS CO OR 200-D5
BRIAR RD
CROOK CO OR 213-B6
BRICE CREEK RD
LANE CO OR 141-C1
BRICKEL CREEK RD
KOOTENAI CO ID 115-A1
BRICK PILE RD
JACKSON CO OR 234-B5
BRICKYARD RD
TILLAMOOK CO OR 197-C3
NW BRIDGE AV U.S.-30
PORTLAND OR 192-B7
BRIDGE LN
JOSEPHINE CO OR 229-B1
BRIDGE RD
UMATILLA CO OR 129-A1
BRIDGE ST
FALLS CITY OR 125-B3
MIDVALE ID 139-B1
UKIAH OR 129-B3
UMATILLA CO OR 129-B3
WINTHROP WA 104-A2
BRIDGE ST U.S.-12
CLARKSTON WA 250-B4
LEWISTON ID 250-B4
BRIDGE ST U.S.-30
BAKER CITY OR 138-B1
E BRIDGE ST Rt#-47
VERNONIA OR 125-B1
N BRIDGE ST Rt#-27
PALOUSE WA 249-B1
S BRIDGE ST
SHERIDAN OR 125-B3
YAMHILL CO OR 125-B3
S BRIDGE ST Rt#-27
PALOUSE WA 249-C1
SW BRIDGE ST
GRANTS PASS OR 335-D9
PRAIRIE CITY OR 137-B2
BRIDGE ST N Rt#-173
BREWSTER WA 104-B3
BRIDGE ST S Rt#-173
BREWSTER WA 104-B3
BRIDGE ST SW Rt#-162
ORTING WA 182-C5
BRIDGE WY N
SEATTLE WA 273-J6
BRIDGE CREEK RD
FERRY CO WA 105-B3
INCHELIUM WA 105-B3
LAKE CO OR 143-B3
WHEELER CO OR 136-A1
BRIDGE CREEK RD SE
MARION CO OR 205-D6
BRIDGEFARMER RD
YAMHILL CO OR 198-B3
BRIDGEPORT HWY Rt#-174
GRAND COULEE WA 237-C3
BRIDGEPORT RD
BAKER CO OR 138-B1
CITY OF RICHMOND BC 156-B6
MALHEUR CO OR 138-B2
POLK CO OR 125-B3
SW BRIDGEPORT RD
TUALATIN OR 199-B4
BRIDGEPORT WY
LAKEWOOD WA 181-C4
TACOMA WA 181-C2
UNIVERSITY PLACE WA 181-C2
BRIDGEPORT WY SW
LAKEWOOD WA 181-D4
PIERCE CO WA 181-D4
BRIDGEPORT WY W
LAKEWOOD WA 181-C3
UNIVERSITY PLACE WA 181-C3
BRIDGEPORT HILL RD NE
DOUGLAS CO WA 112-C1
BRIDGEVIEW-TAKILMA RD
JOSEPHINE CO OR 233-B5
BRIDGEWATER RD
SKAGIT CO WA 161-C5
SW BRIEDWELL RD
YAMHILL CO OR 204-B2
BRIER RD
BRIER WA 171-B6
BRIGHTWOOD LOOP RD
CLACKAMAS CO OR 201-B4
BRIM CREEK RD
LEWIS CO WA 187-B4
BRIMSTONE RD
JOSEPHINE CO OR 229-A2
BRINES RD
COLUMBIA CO WA 122-A2
BRINK RD
DOUGLAS CO OR 222-D4
WHITMAN CO WA 122-B1
BRINN RD
COLUMBIA CO OR 192-A1
BRISTOL AV
ALTAMONT OR 338-J12
ALTAMONT OR 339-A12
BRISTOL RD
KLICKITAT CO WA 196-A4
BRITT SLOUGH RD
MOUNT VERNON WA 260-B14
SKAGIT CO WA 260-B14
BROAD ST
BUTTE FALLS OR 150-A1
MOUNT VERNON WA 260-D13
SEATTLE WA 277-H4
BROADACRES RD NE
MARION CO OR 205-B1
BROADMEAD RD
POLK CO OR 204-A3
SW BROADMEAD RD
YAMHILL CO OR 204-B3
BROADWAY
BELLINGHAM WA 258-C5
DISTRICT OF BURNABY BC 156-D4
EVERETT WA 171-C1
EVERETT WA 264-E3
EVERETT WA 265-E5
EVERETT WA 268-E4
EVERETT WA 269-E1
HOQUIAM WA 178-A7
SEASIDE WA 301-G8
SEATTLE WA 278-B4
VANCOUVER WA 305-G4
BROADWAY Rt#-99
EVERETT WA 268-D5
E BROADWAY Rt#-99
EUGENE OR 330-B6
E BROADWAY Rt#-142
GOLDENDALE WA 127-C1
KLICKITAT CO WA 127-C1
NE BROADWAY
PORTLAND OR 313-H4
PORTLAND OR 314-B4
NW BROADWAY
PORTLAND OR 313-F5
S BROADWAY Rt#-99
EVERETT WA 268-D5
SW BROADWAY
PORTLAND OR 312-E7
PORTLAND OR 313-E6
W BROADWAY
MILTON-FREEWATER OR 121-C3
W BROADWAY Rt#-142
GOLDENDALE WA 127-C1
KLICKITAT CO WA 127-C1
BROADWAY E
SEATTLE WA 278-B3
BROADWAY E Rt#-7
VANCOUVER BC 254-H13
VANCOUVER BC 255-A13
BROADWAY NE
SALEM OR 322-J10
BROADWAY W
VANCOUVER BC 254-A12
BROADWAY W Rt#-7
VANCOUVER BC 254-E12
BROADWAY AV
BOISE ID 253-D4
MALDEN WA 114-B3
SNOHOMISH CO WA 171-D5
BROADWAY AV Rt#-171
GRANT CO WA 242-C3
MOSES LAKE WA 242-C3
BROADWAY AV U.S.-20
ADA CO ID 253-D3
BOISE ID 253-D3
E BROADWAY AV
DISHMAN WA 350-B8
OPPORTUNITY WA 350-H7
OPPORTUNITY WA 351-A7
SPOKANE CO WA 349-G8
SPOKANE CO WA 350-B8
VERADALE WA 351-A7
N BROADWAY AV U.S.-20
BURNS OR 145-B1
S BROADWAY AV Rt#-24
ADAMS CO WA 121-A1
OTHELLO WA 121-A1
SW BROADWAY DR
PORTLAND OR 312-E7
PORTLAND OR 316-D1
BROADWAY ST
ALBANY OR 326-A9
LINN CO OR 326-A9
MALIN OR 151-A3
NORTH BEND OR 333-E6
PORT COQUITLAM BC 157-B5
BROADWAY ST U.S.-30
BAKER CITY OR 138-B1
BROADWAY ST U.S.-195
COLTON WA 250-A1
E BROADWAY ST
MILTON-FREEWATER OR 121-C3
PASCO WA 343-H6
UMATILLA CO OR 121-C3
E BROADWAY ST U.S.-2
REARDAN WA 114-A2
N BROADWAY ST U.S.-101
COOS BAY OR 333-H9
NE BROADWAY ST
PORTLAND OR 314-B4
S BROADWAY ST U.S.-101
COOS BAY OR 333-H11
W BROADWAY ST U.S.-2
REARDAN WA 114-A2
BROCKDALE RD
MASON CO WA 180-A1
SW BROCKMAN RD
BEAVERTON OR 199-B2
BROCKWAY RD
DOUGLAS CO OR 221-A6
S BROCKWAY RD
CLACKAMAS CO OR 200-A7
BROENNEKE RD
LATAH CO ID 249-C7
BRONDT RD
KITTITAS CO WA 241-B6
BRONSON WY N Rt#-900
RENTON WA 175-C5
E BRONX RD
BONNER CO ID 244-A1
BROOKDALE AV
MEDFORD OR 336-H10
BROOKDALE RD E
PIERCE CO WA 182-A5
BROOKLAKE RD NE
MARION CO OR 204-D3
MARION CO OR 205-A3
BROOKLANE DR
BENTON CO OR 327-D13
CORVALLIS OR 327-D13
BROOKLEIGH RD
DISTRICT OF SAANICH BC 159-C4
SW BROOKMAN RD
WASHINGTON CO OR 199-A5
NE BROOKS AV
KEIZER OR 323-A6
MARION CO OR 323-A6
SALEM OR 323-A6
BROOKS LN SE
THURSTON CO WA 184-D1
N BROOKS RD
PIERCE CO WA 182-C7
S BROOKS RD
MEDICAL LAKE WA 114-B2
SPOKANE CO WA 114-B2
SE BROOKS RD
CLACKAMAS CO OR 200-C3
W BROOKS RD
MEDICAL LAKE WA 114-B2
N BROOKS ST
MEDICAL LAKE WA 114-B2
BROOKSBANK AV
CITY OF N VANCOUVER BC 255-E7
DIST OF N VANCOUVER BC 255-E7
BROOKS HILL RD
ISLAND CO WA 171-A1
LANGLEY WA 171-A1
BROOKSIDE BLVD
JOSEPHINE CO OR 229-B4
BROOKS MEADOW RD
HOOD RIVER CO OR 202-D3
WASCO CO OR 202-D3
BROOKS-SCANLON LOG RD
DESCHUTES CO OR 211-C3
DESCHUTES CO OR 212-A7
DESCHUTES CO OR 217-A1
NE BROOKWOOD PKWY
HILLSBORO OR 198-D1
BROOTEN RD
TILLAMOOK CO OR 197-A7
BROSI ORCHARD RD
WINSTON OR 221-B6
BROSTERHOUS RD
BEND OR 332-F10
BROWER RD
MULTNOMAH CO OR 200-D2
MULTNOMAH CO OR 201-A1
BROWN RD
COLUMBIA CO OR 192-B3
DOUGLAS CO OR 225-A7
GLENDALE OR 225-A7
KITTITAS CO WA 241-B6
KLAMATH CO OR 231-B3
WHATCOM CO WA 158-B5
WHITMAN CO WA 249-C5
WILSONVILLE OR 199-B5
NE BROWN RD
CLARK CO WA 193-C6
SW BROWN RD
DESCHUTES CO OR 212-B7
BROWN RD E
LEWIS CO WA 187-B1
BROWN RD NE
HAYESVILLE OR 323-F11
SALEM OR 323-F11
BROWN RD SW
THURSTON CO WA 180-B7
BROWN RD W
LEWIS CO WA 187-A1
W BROWN ST
PASCO WA 343-C6
BROWN CREEK RD
ADAMS CO ID 251-B2
GILLIAM CO OR 128-B3
LONEROCK OR 128-B3
N BROWNE ST U.S.-2
SPOKANE WA 349-A9
S BROWNE ST U.S.-2
SPOKANE WA 349-A10
SW BROWNELL AV
GRANTS PASS OR 335-D10
BROWNLEE RD
COLUMBIA CO OR 189-C5
BROWNSBORO EAGLE POINT HWY
JACKSON CO OR 149-C1
JACKSON CO OR 230-D5
BROWNS CANYON RD NW
DOUGLAS CO WA 236-B5
BROWNS CREEK RD
WASCO CO OR 196-B7
BROWNS POINT BLVD NE
TACOMA WA 181-D1
TACOMA WA 182-A1
BROWNSTOWN RD
WHITE SWAN WA 119-C2
YAKIMA CO WA 119-C2
BROWNSVILLE RD
BROWNSVILLE OR 210-C1
LINN CO OR 210-C1
BROZIO RD
DOUGLAS CO OR 221-B2
BRUCE AV
NANAIMO BC 93-A3
BRUCE AV SW
BREWSTER WA 104-B3
N BRUCE RD
SPOKANE CO WA 246-D1
NW BRUGGER RD
WASHINGTON CO OR 192-A7
BRUKETTA RD
KITTITAS CO WA 240-D3
S BRUNA RD
SPOKANE CO WA 246-D6
BRUNDAGE RD
ADAMS CO ID 251-C4
BRUNETTE AV
COQUITLAM BC 157-A5
NEW WESTMINSTER BC 156-D5
NEW WESTMINSTER BC 157-A5
BRUNNER RD Rt#-500
CLARK CO WA 193-B6
W BRUNNER RD
KOOTENAI CO ID 245-A2
BRUSH COLLEGE RD NW
POLK CO OR 204-C4
POLK CO OR 322-A5
SALEM OR 322-E8
BRUSH CREEK DR NE
MARION CO OR 205-B5
BRUSH CREEK RD
LANE CO OR 133-C2
LINN CO OR 133-C2
VALLEY CO ID 251-D2
BRUSHY GULCH RD
JOSEPHINE CO OR 229-A1
BRUSSELLS ST
NORTH BEND OR 333-G7
BRYANT AV
WALLA WALLA WA 345-C9
WALLA WALLA EAST WA 345-C9
BRYANT RD
CLACKAMAS OR 320-A7
LAKE OSWEGO OR 199-C4
LAKE OSWEGO OR 320-A7
BRYANT WY
ALBANY OR 326-A7
LINN CO OR 207-C5
LINN CO OR 326-A7
BRYDEN AV
LEWISTON ID 250-C5
BRYNION ST
COWLITZ CO WA 303-E7
KELSO WA 303-E7
BRYSON SEARS RD
LANE CO OR 215-C7
BUCHANAN AV
CORVALLIS OR 327-G8
BUCHANAN LN
LA GRANDE OR 130-A2
UNION CO OR 130-A2
BUCKAROO PASS RD
HARNEY CO OR 153-A2
BUCKAROO SPRING RD
MALHEUR CO OR 138-B3
BUCK CANYON RD
JOSEPHINE CO OR 233-A5
BUCK CREEK RD
CROOK CO OR 144-B1
DOUGLAS CO OR 219-B2
LANE CO OR 209-C5
BUCKET POINT BLVD
JEFFERSON CO WA 166-D7
W BUCKEYE AV
SPOKANE WA 348-J6
BUCKEYE ST
WOODLAND WA 192-B1
BUCKEYE CREEK RD
DOUGLAS CO OR 226-B1
SW BUCKHAVEN RD
WASHINGTON CO OR 198-D4
YAMHILL CO OR 198-D4
BUCK HOLLOW RD
CROOK CO OR 136-B2
WHEELER CO OR 136-B2
BUCKHORN LN
GILLIAM CO OR 128-A3
BUCKHORN RD
DESCHUTES CO OR 212-B5
DOUGLAS CO OR 141-B2
DOUGLAS CO OR 221-C4
LEWIS CO WA 187-B2
WALLOWA CO OR 131-A1
BUCK LAKE RD
KLAMATH CO OR 235-A4
BUCKLEY LN
JEFFERSON CO OR 208-C3
BUCKLEY RD
LEWIS CO WA 187-D3
BUCKLEY TAPPS HWY
PIERCE CO WA 182-D3
NE BUCKLIN HILL RD Rt#-303
KITSAP CO WA 174-B1
NW BUCKLIN HILL RD
SILVERDALE WA 174-B1
NW BUCKLIN HILL RD Rt#-303
KITSAP CO WA 174-B1
SILVERDALE WA 174-B1
BUCKLIN HILL RD NE
KITSAP CO WA 271-H3
BUCKNER CREEK RD
CLACKAMAS CO OR 199-D7
CLACKAMAS CO OR 200-A7
BUCK POINT RD
WHEELER CO OR 136-B2
N BUCKSKIN RD
COEUR D'ALENE ID 354-J6
COEUR D'ALENE ID 355-A7
KOOTENAI CO ID 354-J6
KOOTENAI CO ID 355-A7
BUCODA HWY Rt#-507
LEWIS CO WA 184-C5
BUENA RD Rt#-22
YAKIMA CO WA 120-A2
BUENA WY Rt#-22
TOPPENISH WA 120-A2
BUENA VISTA
LANE CO OR 215-C4
BUENA VISTA RD
BENTON CO OR 207-B3
POLK CO OR 207-C2
BUENA VISTA RD S
MARION CO OR 207-C2
BUESING RD
KLAMATH CO OR 235-D7
SE BUFF ST
MADRAS OR 208-C5
BUFFALO DR
DESCHUTES CO OR 212-A4
BUFFALO LAKE RD S
OKANOGAN CO WA 105-A3
OKANOGAN CO WA 237-D1
BUFFALO LAKE ACCESS RD
OKANOGAN CO WA 237-D1
BUHMAN RD
SKAMANIA CO WA 193-D6
BULLARD RD
PACIFIC CO WA 117-A1
BULLARDS-PROSPER JUNCTION RD
COOS CO OR 220-B5
BULL CREEK RD
JOSEPHINE CO OR 229-A7
JOSEPHINE CO OR 233-D1
BULL CREEK WEST RD
STEVENS CO WA 106-A3
BULLDOG RD
DOUGLAS CO OR 222-B1
BULL FLAT RD
DESCHUTES CO OR 217-A1
BULLHEAD RD
KITSAP CO WA 170-B7
BULL LAKE RD Rt#-56
LINCOLN CO MT 107-C3
SANDERS CO MT 107-C3
SW BULL MOUNTAIN RD
TIGARD OR 199-A3
WASHINGTON CO OR 199-A3
BULL RUN RD
DOUGLAS CO OR 225-C6
SE BULL RUN RD
CLACKAMAS CO OR 200-D3
BULL RUN TO BAKER RD
GRANITE OR 137-C1
GRANT CO OR 137-C1
GRANT CO OR 138-A1
BULL SPRING RD
CROOK CO OR 136-B2
DESCHUTES CO OR 217-A2
WHEELER CO OR 136-B2
BULLY CREEK RD
MALHEUR CO OR 138-B3
BULSON RD
SKAGIT CO WA 168-B2
BUNCH RD
OKANOGAN CO WA 105-A1
BUNCO RD
KOOTENAI CO ID 245-B2
E BUNCO RD
KOOTENAI CO ID 245-B2
BUNKER CREEK RD
LEWIS CO WA 117-B1
LEWIS CO WA 184-A6
BUNKER HILL RD
COLUMBIA CO OR 192-A1
BUNKER KEYS RD
SKAMANIA CO WA 195-B4
BUNK FOSS RD
SNOHOMISH CO WA 171-D2
BUNTTON HOLLOW GULCH
SISKIYOU CO CA 150-A3
BURBEE HILL RD
CONCRETE WA 102-C2
SKAGIT CO WA 102-C2
BURCHAM ST
KELSO WA 303-E7
BURCH MOUNTAIN RD
CHELAN CO WA 238-D2
SUNNYSLOPE WA 238-D2
BURDETT WY
WALLA WALLA CO WA 121-B3
BURGDORF RD
KLAMATH CO OR 151-A2
BURGESS RD
DESCHUTES CO OR 143-A1
BURGUNDY RD
MASON CO WA 180-D3
BURK RD
WHATCOM CO WA 158-C3
BURKE RD Rt#-4
SHOSHONE CO ID 115-C2
WALLACE ID 115-C2
BURKE ST
DISTRICT OF BURNABY BC 156-C5
BURKE-CANYON CREEK RD Rt#-4
SHOSHONE CO ID 115-C2
SW BURKHALTER RD
WASHINGTON CO OR 198-D2
BURKLAND RD
SKAGIT CO WA 168-B1
BURLEY DR
DIST OF WEST VANCOUVER BC 254-E2
SE BURLEY OLALLA RD
KITSAP CO WA 174-B6
BURLINGTON BLVD Rt#-20
BURLINGTON WA 260-C5
S BURLINGTON BLVD
BURLINGTON WA 260-C5
S BURLINGTON BLVD Rt#-20
BURLINGTON WA 260-C7
BURLINGTON RD
KOOTENAI CO ID 247-C1
BURLINGTON-ALGER RD
BURLINGTON WA 260-C2
SKAGIT CO WA 161-B5
SKAGIT CO WA 260-C2
BURLINGTON NORTHERN RD
MODOC CO CA 151-A3
BURMA RD
DOUGLAS CO OR 225-D6
JEFFERSON CO OR 213-D1
KOOTENAI CO ID 248-A2
OKANOGAN CO WA 104-B3
BURMASTER RD
SKAGIT CO WA 161-C5
BURN RD
ARLINGTON WA 168-D5
SNOHOMISH CO WA 102-C3
SNOHOMISH CO WA 168-D5
BURNETT RD
LEWIS CO WA 187-B3
E BURNETT RD
SPOKANE CO WA 246-D2
BURNETT-FAIRFAX Rt#-165
BUCKLEY WA 182-D5
CARBONADO WA 182-D5
PIERCE CO WA 182-D5
WILKESON WA 182-D5
BURNHAM DR NW
PIERCE CO WA 174-B7
NE BURNSIDE RD
GRESHAM OR 200-B2
SE BURNSIDE RD
GRESHAM OR 200-A1
W BURNSIDE RD
PORTLAND OR 199-B1
PORTLAND OR 312-B5
WASHINGTON CO OR 199-B1
BURNSIDE RD E
CITY OF VICTORIA BC 256-F6
BURNSIDE RD W
DISTRICT OF SAANICH BC 256-A2
TOWN OF VIEW ROYAL BC 256-C3
E BURNSIDE ST
PORTLAND OR 313-H5
PORTLAND OR 314-C5
PORTLAND OR 315-H6
W BURNSIDE ST
PORTLAND OR 312-C5
PORTLAND OR 313-E5
E BURNT CABIN RD
KOOTENAI CO ID 245-B4
BURNT MOUNTAIN RD Rt#-113
CLALLAM CO WA 163-B6
BRNT MOUNTAIN ACCESS RD
COOS CO OR 140-C2
BURNT RIVER CANYON RD
BAKER CO OR 138-B1
BURNT WOODS-HARLAN RD
LINCOLN CO OR 133-A1
BURRARD ST
VANCOUVER BC 254-F10
BURRELL AV
LEWISTON ID 250-C5
BURRES RD
CLARK CO WA 192-D1
BURRI RD
LEWIS CO WA 187-A2
BURRIS ST
DISTRICT OF BURNABY BC 156-D5

STREET
City State Page-Grid

BURROUGHS RD
KITTITAS CO WA 241-C5
BURROWS RD
GRAYS HARBOR CO WA 177-C6
WALLA WALLA CO WA 121-C3
BURROWS ST
ANACORTES WA 259-C6
BURSELL RD
POLK CO OR 204-A7
BURTON LN
WASHINGTON CO ID 139-B1
NE BURTON RD
VANCOUVER WA 306-E3
VANCOUVER WA 307-F3
BURTON-FRASER RD
TILLAMOOK CO OR 197-B2
BURWELL PL Rt#-304
BREMERTON WA 270-G11
BURWELL ST Rt#-304
BREMERTON WA 270-G11
BUSBY RD
WHITMAN CO WA 249-B5
BUSBY-JOHNSON RD
WHITMAN CO WA 249-B6
BUSCH RD
WHITMAN CO WA 250-A2
BUSH ST
WALLA WALLA EAST WA 345-E7
BUSH CREEK RD
GRAYS HARBOR CO WA 179-C6
SKAMANIA CO WA 195-A4
BUSH GARDEN DR
LINN CO OR 210-B6
BUSHLACH RD
SKAMANIA CO WA 193-D7
BUSH POINT RD
AULT FIELD WA 170-C1
ISLAND CO WA 170-C1
BUSH RANCH TO COUNTY LINE RD
GRANT CO OR 136-C3
BUSHWELL RD
GRAYS HARBOR CO WA 179-B7
NE BUTLER AV
DESCHUTES CO OR 213-A4
BUTLER BLVD
MALHEUR CO OR 139-A3
BUTLER RD
COLUMBIA CO OR 189-C6
CROOK CO OR 213-A3
SE BUTLER RD
GRESHAM OR 200-A2
BUTLER BRIDGE RD SE
LINCOLN CO OR 206-C5
TOLEDO OR 206-C4
BUTLER CREEK RD
BONNER CO ID 244-A5
DOUGLAS CO OR 218-D1
KOOTENAI CO ID 248-D4
SKAGIT CO WA 161-B3
BUTLER GRADE RD
UMATILLA CO OR 121-B3
BUTLER MARKET RD
DESCHUTES CO OR 217-D2
NE BUTLER MARKET RD
BEND OR 217-C2
BEND OR 332-G4
DESCHUTES CO OR 217-C2
BUTTE AV
JEFFERSON CO OR 208-B6
BUTTE CT
WEST RICHLAND WA 340-A12
BUTTE RD
CANYON CO ID 147-C2
CLACKAMAS CO OR 200-A7
E BUTTE ST
PASCO WA 343-H8
BUTTE CREEK RD
CLACKAMAS CO OR 205-D4
WHEELER CO OR 128-A3
BUTTE FALLS RD
BUTTE FALLS OR 150-A1
JACKSON CO OR 149-C1
JACKSON CO OR 150-A1
JACKSON CO OR 230-D4
BUTTE FALLS-FISH LAKE RD
JACKSON CO OR 150-A1
BUTTE FALLS-PROSPECT RD
BUTTE FALLS OR 150-A1
JACKSON CO OR 150-A1
JACKSON CO OR 226-C7
BUTTER CREEK RD
MORROW CO OR 128-C1
MORROW CO OR 129-A2
UMATILLA CO OR 128-C1
UMATILLA CO OR 129-A2
BUTTER CREEK RD Rt#-207
HERMISTON OR 129-A1
UMATILLA CO OR 129-A1
BUTTERMILK CANYON RD
GILLIAM CO OR 128-B3
MORROW CO OR 128-B3
BUTTEVILLE RD
CLACKAMAS CO OR 199-B6
BUTTEVILLE RD NE
DONALD OR 199-A7
GERVAIS OR 205-B2
MARION CO OR 199-A7
MARION CO OR 205-B1
BUTTEVILLE RD NE Rt#-219
MARION CO OR 205-B1
BUTTON BRIDGE RD U.S.-30
HOOD RIVER CO OR 195-D5
BUYSERIE RD
MARION CO OR 198-D7
BUZZARD MINE RD
JACKSON CO OR 226-B5
SE BYBEE BLVD
PORTLAND OR 317-J5
PORTLAND OR 318-A5
BYBEE CREEK RD
JACKSON CO OR 226-D3
BYBEE CREEK BRANCH RD
JACKSON CO OR 227-A3
SE BYERS AV
PENDLETON OR 129-B1
NW BYHAM RD
LEWIS CO WA 187-B3
BY-PASS HWY
RICHLAND WA 340-F11
BY-PASS HWY Rt#-240
RICHLAND WA 340-E12
RICHLAND WA 341-E3
BYRAM RD
DESCHUTES CO OR 217-D3
BYRNES RD
WALLA WALLA CO WA 121-B3
B Z CORNER-GLENWOOD RD
KLICKITAT CO WA 119-A3
KLICKITAT CO WA 195-D2
KLICKITAT CO WA 196-A1

C

C AV
LA GRANDE OR 130-A2
C RD NW Rt#-172
DOUGLAS CO WA 112-B1
C ST
CULVER OR 208-B7
NESPELEM WA 105-A3
PORT ANGELES WA 261-C4
VANCOUVER WA 305-G4
WALLA WALLA CO WA 345-H4
C ST Rt#-214
SILVERTON OR 205-C4
E C ST
RAINIER OR 189-C4
NE C ST
COLLEGE PLACE WA 344-F9
WALLA WALLA CO WA 344-F9
C ST NW
EPHRATA WA 112-C3
C ST S
PIERCE CO WA 181-D4
C ST SE
QUINCY WA 112-B3
C ST SW
AUBURN WA 182-B2
EPHRATA WA 112-C3
QUINCY WA 112-B3
CABIN LN
YAKIMA CO WA 243-B4
CABIN LAKE RD
LAKE CO OR 143-B2
CACHE CREEK RD
FERRY CO WA 105-B3
NESPELEM WA 105-A3
OKANOGAN CO WA 105-A3
CADBORO BAY RD
DISTRICT OF OAK BAY BC 257-D6
DISTRICT OF SAANICH BC 257-E5
CADLE RD
POLK CO OR 204-B5
CADY RD
JACKSON CO OR 149-B2
CAGEY RD
WHATCOM CO WA 158-C7
S CAHILL RD
SPOKANE CO WA 114-C2
CAIN RD SE
OLYMPIA WA 297-B9
CAIN LAKE RD
SKAGIT CO WA 161-B3
WHATCOM CO WA 161-B3
CALAMITY PEAK RD
SKAMANIA CO WA 190-C7
SKAMANIA CO WA 194-A1
CALAPOOIA ST
ALBANY OR 326-C8
CALAPOOYA ST Rt#-99
DOUGLAS CO OR 221-C1
SUTHERLIN OR 221-C1
CALAWAH WY
CLALLAM CO WA 169-D1
CALDWELL BLVD U.S.-30
CANYON CO ID 147-B1
NAMPA ID 147-B1
CALEB PIKE RD
BRITISH COLUMBIA 159-B5
CALHOUN RD
SKAGIT CO WA 168-A1
CALIFORNIA AV
KLAMATH FALLS OR 338-C7
CALIFORNIA AV E
MANCHESTER WA 271-G13
CALIFORNIA AV SE
MANCHESTER WA 271-G14
CALIFORNIA AV SW
SEATTLE WA 276-E7
SEATTLE WA 280-E3
SEATTLE WA 284-D2
CALIFORNIA ST Rt#-238
JACKSONVILLE OR 149-B2
E CALIFORNIA ST
JACKSONVILLE OR 149-B2
E CALIFORNIA ST Rt#-238
JACKSONVILLE OR 149-B2
W CALIFORNIA ST Rt#-238
JACKSONVILLE OR 149-B2
CALIFORNIA WY
LONGVIEW WA 303-A11
CALIFORNIA WY SW
SEATTLE WA 276-E7
SEATTLE WA 280-E1
SEATTLE WA 281-E1
N CALIMUS RD
KLAMATH CO OR 151-A1
S CALISPELL AV
NEWPORT WA 106-C3
CALISTOGA AV
ORTING WA 182-C5
PIERCE CO WA 182-C5
CALISTOGA ST W
ORTING WA 182-C5
PIERCE CO WA 182-C5
CALKINS LN
YAMHILL CO OR 198-C4
NW CALKINS RD
ROSEBURG OR 334-C5
CALLAHAN RD
CLACKAMAS CO OR 126-A3
COLUMBIA CO OR 192-A4
S CALLAHAN RD
CLACKAMAS CO OR 126-A3
CALLIGAN AV
MAPLE RIDGE BC 157-C5
CALLOW AV N Rt#-304
BREMERTON WA 270-G10
CALLOW AV S Rt#-304
BREMERTON WA 270-G12
CALLOW RD
SNOHOMISH CO WA 171-D1
CALLOWAY RD
ADAMS CO WA 121-B1
CALONE RD
LANE CO OR 210-D7
CALVERT DR
DISTRICT OF DELTA BC 101-C1
DISTRICT OF DELTA BC 156-C7
CALVIN RD
LEWIS CO WA 187-C4
CAL YOUNG RD
EUGENE OR 329-J2
EUGENE OR 330-A2
CAMANO AV
ISLAND CO WA 171-A1
LANGLEY WA 171-A1
E CAMANO DR
ISLAND CO WA 167-D5
ISLAND CO WA 168-A7
N CAMANO DR
ISLAND CO WA 167-D3
W CAMANO DR
ISLAND CO WA 167-D4
ISLAND CO WA 168-A6
CAMANO ST
STANWOOD WA 168-A4
CAMANO HILL RD
ISLAND CO WA 167-D5
ISLAND CO WA 168-A4
W CAMANO HILL RD
ISLAND CO WA 167-D5
CAMANO RIDGE RD
ISLAND CO WA 167-D5
CAMAS RD
LEWIS CO ID 123-B3
CAMAS ST
UKIAH OR 129-B3
WINCHESTER ID 123-B2
CAMAS CREEK RD
CHELAN CO WA 238-B3
CAMAS PRAIRIE RD
MORROW CO OR 128-C3
WASCO CO OR 127-A3
CAMAS SWALE RD
CRESWELL OR 215-A5
LANE CO OR 215-A5
CAMBIE BRDG
VANCOUVER BC 254-G12
CAMBIE RD
CITY OF RICHMOND BC 156-B6
CAMBIE ST
VANCOUVER BC 156-B5
VANCOUVER BC 254-G14
CAMBRIAN AV N
BREMERTON WA 270-F11
CAMBRIAN AV S
BREMERTON WA 270-F11
CAMBRIAN AV S Rt#-304
BREMERTON WA 270-F12
E CAMERON RD
SPOKANE CO WA 247-A7
SW CAMERON RD
PORTLAND OR 316-A4
CAMERON ST
DISTRICT OF BURNABY BC 156-D5
DISTRICT OF COQUITLAM BC 156-D5
CAMERON WY
MOUNT VERNON WA 260-C11
CAMP RD
WHITMAN CO WA 122-A1
CAMP 2 RD
WHATCOM CO WA 161-B3
CAMP 10 RD
COLUMBIA CO OR 189-A7
CAMP 12
CHELAN CO WA 111-C1
CAMP ADAIR RD
BENTON CO OR 207-B3
CAMP BAY RD
BONNER CO ID 244-C3
CAMPBELL RD
JACKSON CO OR 234-B2
KLAMATH CO OR 151-B1
OTIS ORCHARDS WA 351-J3
SPOKANE CO WA 351-J3
YAKIMA CO WA 120-A2
E CAMPBELL RD
ISLAND CO WA 171-A2
S CAMPBELL RD
SPOKANE CO WA 247-A5
SW CAMPBELL RD
WASHINGTON CO OR 198-D3
CAMPBELL ST
BAKER CITY OR 138-B1
CAMPBELL ST Rt#-7
BAKER CITY OR 138-B1
CAMPBELL WY
BREMERTON WA 270-J9
CAMPBELL LAKE RD
SKAGIT CO WA 259-G11
S CAMPBELL LAKE RD
SKAGIT CO WA 259-G13
CAMP CREEK RD
BAKER CO OR 137-C1
CROOK CO OR 136-A3
DOUGLAS CO OR 140-C1
GRAYS HARBOR CO WA 178-D7
LANE CO OR 133-C3
LANE CO OR 215-D2
LANE CO OR 331-E4
E CAMP CREEK RD
BAKER CO OR 138-A2
CAMP DAVID JR RD
CLALLAM CO WA 164-A6
CAMP DISCOVERY RD
JEFFERSON CO WA 170-A5
CAMP HARMONY RD
JEFFERSON CO WA 170-A6
CAMP HAYDEN RD
CLALLAM CO WA 164-D5
CAMP KETTLE CREEK RD
MALHEUR CO OR 147-A1
CAMP MORRISON DR
LINN CO OR 134-A1
CAMP POLK RD
DESCHUTES CO OR 211-D4
DESCHUTES CO OR 212-A4
CAMP SHERMAN RD
DESCHUTES CO OR 211-C2
JEFFERSON CO OR 211-C2
CAMP TWELVE LP
LINCOLN CO OR 206-C3
CAMPUS DR
KLAMATH FALLS OR 338-D4
SW CAMPUS DR
FEDERAL WAY WA 182-A1
CAMPUS WY
BENTON CO OR 327-C9
CORVALLIS OR 327-E9
CAMUS RD
LEWIS CO WA 187-C4
CAMWELL DR
DIST OF WEST VANCOUVER BC 254-C1
CANAAN RD
COLUMBIA CO OR 189-B7
S CANAAN RD
COLUMBIA CO OR 189-B7
CANAAN RD S
COLUMBIA CO OR 189-B7
CANADA WY
DISTRICT OF BURNABY BC 156-D5
DISTRICT OF BURNABY BC 255-G14
CANADY RD
LEWIS CO WA 187-B5
CANAL BLVD
DESCHUTES CO OR 212-D6
N CANAL BLVD
DESCHUTES CO OR 212-D5
REDMOND OR 212-D5
S CANAL BLVD
DESCHUTES CO OR 212-D6
REDMOND OR 212-D6
W CANAL DR
KENNEWICK WA 342-J9
KENNEWICK WA 343-A9
CANAL RD
UMATILLA CO OR 129-A1
CANAL CREEK RD
LINCOLN CO OR 209-C2
CANAL W-20
GRANT CO WA 242-A1
CANARY RD
DUNES CITY OR 214-B4
CANARY RD S
LANE CO OR 214-B4
CANARY CREEK RD
KOOTENAI CO ID 248-D3
CANBY-MARQUAM HWY
CLACKAMAS CO OR 205-D1
SE CANBY-MARQUAM HWY
CANBY OR 199-C7
CLACKAMAS CO OR 199-C7
CANDIANI RD
MARION CO OR 198-C7
NE CANDLEWOOD DR
KEIZER OR 323-A8
MARION CO OR 323-A8
SALEM OR 323-A8
CANFIELD LOOP RD
KOOTENAI CO ID 245-B6
CANNA ST N
SOAP LAKE WA 112-C2
CANNA ST S
SOAP LAKE WA 112-C2
CANNIBAL MOUNTAIN RD
LINCOLN CO OR 209-C3
CANORA RD
DIST OF NORTH SAANICH BC 159-C2
TOWN OF SIDNEY BC 159-C2
CANTON CREEK RD
DOUGLAS CO OR 141-C1
S CANYON BLVD U.S.-395
JOHN DAY OR 137-B2
CANYON DR
DESCHUTES CO OR 212-C7
CANYON DR SE Rt#-516
KENT WA 175-C7
CANYON RD
GRAYS HARBOR CO WA 178-D4
KLICKITAT CO WA 196-B3
LANE CO OR 134-B3
PIERCE CO WA 182-A5
WHITMAN CO WA 122-A1
CANYON RD Rt#-181
ELLENSBURG WA 241-B6
KITTITAS CO WA 241-B6
NE CANYON RD
CLARK CO WA 193-B3
SW CANYON RD
JEFFERSON CO OR 208-B5
SW CANYON RD Rt#-8
BEAVERTON OR 199-B2
WASHINGTON CO OR 199-B2
SW CANYON RD U.S.-26
PORTLAND OR 312-C6
E CANYON ST Rt#-272
COLFAX WA 122-C1
WHITMAN CO WA 122-C1
CANYON WY
WASCO CO OR 196-B5
CANYON CITY EAST RD
CANYON CITY OR 137-B2
GRANT CO OR 137-B2
CANYON CREEK RD
CROOK CO OR 136-A2
DOUGLAS CO OR 225-C3
GRANT CO OR 137-B2
JEFFERSON CO OR 211-B1
CANYON CREEK TR
SKAMANIA CO WA 193-D1
SKAMANIA CO WA 194-A1
CANYON CREST DR
DESCHUTES CO OR 212-A4
CANYONVIEW RD
YAMHILL CO OR 198-B3
CANYONVILLE-RIDDLE RD
CANYONVILLE OR 225-C3
DOUGLAS CO OR 225-C3
CAPE ARAGO HWY
BARVIEW OR 220-C1
COOS BAY OR 333-B6
COOS CO OR 220-B2
COOS CO OR 333-A8
NORTH BEND OR 333-D6
CAPE BLANCO HWY
CURRY CO OR 224-A4
CAPE CREEK RD
LANE CO OR 209-A7
CAPE FERRELO RD
CURRY CO OR 232-C4
CAPE GEORGE RD
JEFFERSON CO WA 166-D6
JEFFERSON CO WA 263-A7
CAPE GEORGE RD W
JEFFERSON CO WA 166-D6
CAPE HORN RD
SKAMANIA CO WA 193-D7
E CAPE HORN RD
KOOTENAI CO ID 245-C1
CAPE KIWANDA DR
TILLAMOOK CO OR 197-A7
CAPE LOOKOUT RD
TILLAMOOK CO OR 197-A4
CAPE MEARES LOOP RD
TILLAMOOK CO OR 197-A2
CAPE SAINT MARY RD
SAN JUAN CO WA 160-A7
CAPE SEBASTIAN FRONTAGE RD
CURRY CO OR 228-A7
CAPILANO RD
DIST OF N VANCOUVER BC 254-G3
CAPITAL MALL DR
OLYMPIA WA 296-D5
CAPITOL BLVD
OLYMPIA WA 296-H7
THURSTON CO WA 296-H13
TUMWATER WA 296-G10
S CAPITOL BLVD
BOISE ID 253-C3
SW CAPITOL HWY
PORTLAND OR 316-B6
PORTLAND OR 320-A1
SW CAPITOL HWY Rt#-10
PORTLAND OR 316-D4
PORTLAND OR 317-E4
CAPITOL ST NE
SALEM OR 322-J12
SALEM OR 323-A10
CAPITOL WY
OLYMPIA WA 296-H5
N CAPITOL WY
OLYMPIA WA 296-H5
CAPITOL HILL RD
MASON CO WA 180-B3
CAPLES RD
COWLITZ CO WA 192-B1
NE CAPLES RD
CLARK CO WA 193-A4
CAPLINGER RD SE
MARION CO OR 325-G2
SALEM OR 325-G2
CARAVELLE RD
KOOTENAI CO ID 245-B2
CARBERRY RD
JACKSON CO OR 149-B2
JOSEPHINE CO OR 149-B2
CARBUHN RD
NEZ PERCE CO ID 250-B2
NW CARDEN AV
PENDLETON OR 129-B1
CARDWELL RD
DESCHUTES CO OR 217-D2
CAREY RD
DISTRICT OF SAANICH BC 256-D1
CAREY ST
MANZANITA OR 191-B4
TILLAMOOK CO OR 191-B4
CARIBOO RD
DISTRICT OF BURNABY BC 156-D5
NEW WESTMINSTER BC 156-D5
N CARIBOU RD
KITTITAS CO WA 241-D5
CARICO HILLS RD
ADAMS CO WA 114-A3
CARKEEK DR S
SEATTLE WA 287-E4
CARL RD NE
MARION CO OR 205-B1
CARLIN BAY RD
KOOTENAI CO ID 248-A2
CARLIN CREEK RD
KOOTENAI CO ID 248-A3
CARLISLE AV
LEWIS CO WA 118-A2
CARLISLE GRADE
GRAYS HARBOR CO WA 177-C3
CARLOCK RD NW
DOUGLAS CO WA 236-C7
NW CARLON AV
BEND OR 332-D8
CARLON RD
LAKE CO OR 143-C3
CARLSBORG RD
CLALLAM CO WA 166-A7
CARLSON RD
KITTITAS CO WA 241-C4
LINCOLN CO WA 113-C2
S CARLSON RD
YAKIMA CO WA 243-A7
W CARLSON RD
SPOKANE CO WA 246-A1
SW CARMAN DR
CLACKAMAS OR 320-A6
CLACKAMAS CO OR 199-B3
LAKE OSWEGO OR 199-B3
LAKE OSWEGO OR 320-A6
CARMARIA CT
DIST OF N VANCOUVER BC 255-F4
CARMEL RD
COLUMBIA CO OR 189-B5
CARMICHAEL DR
KENNEWICK WA 343-C10
N CARNAHAN RD
SPOKANE CO WA 349-H8
S CARNAHAN RD
SPOKANE CO WA 349-H10
CARNATION-DUVALL RD Rt#-203
DUVALL WA 110-C1
KING CO WA 110-C1
CARNATION-DUVALL RD NE Rt#-203
KING CO WA 110-C1
KING CO WA 176-A1
NE CARNATION FARM RD
KING CO WA 176-B1
SW CARNES RD
DOUGLAS CO OR 221-B6
DOUGLAS CO OR 334-B14
CARNEY LAKE RD SW
KITSAP CO WA 174-A6
S CARNIE RD
KOOTENAI CO ID 247-D4
W CARNIE RD
KOOTENAI CO ID 247-D4
CARNINE RD
COWLITZ CO WA 187-D7
CAROLINA ST
SKAGIT CO WA 259-J14
CAROLINA ST U.S.-20
LEBANON OR 133-C1
CAROLYN DR
DIST OF N VANCOUVER BC 254-J1
CAROTHERS RD
WHITMAN CO WA 249-A5
CARPENTER RD
KITTITAS CO WA 241-C4
CARPENTER RD NE
LACEY WA 297-J2
THURSTON CO WA 297-J2
CARPENTER RD SE
LACEY WA 297-J6
THURSTON CO WA 181-A7
THURSTON CO WA 297-J6
CARPENTER CREEK RD
WASHINGTON CO OR 198-A1
CARPENTER HILL RD
JACKSON CO OR 234-A2
CARPENTERVILLE FRONTAGE RD
CURRY CO OR 232-C2
CARPER ST SW
THURSTON CO WA 184-B4
CARR RD
ADAMS CO ID 251-A5
KING CO WA 175-C5
RENTON WA 175-C5
CARRALL ST
VANCOUVER BC 254-H10
CARRIE ST
JOSEPHINE CO OR 229-C2
CARROL RD
WASCO CO OR 196-A6
CARROLL AV
BONANZA OR 151-A2
KLAMATH CO OR 151-A2
CARROLL RD
LEWIS CO WA 187-C1
CARROLL WY
LEWIS CO WA 187-A1
CARSON GULER RD
SKAMANIA CO WA 194-D1
SKAMANIA CO WA 195-A1
CARTER RD SE
MARION CO OR 205-C7
CARTNEY DR
LINN CO OR 210-A3
CARTWRIGHT RD
ADA CO ID 139-C3
ADA CO ID 253-C1
NW CARTY RD
CLARK CO WA 192-C3
S CARUS RD
CLACKAMAS CO OR 199-D6
CLACKAMAS CO OR 200-A6
SW CARUTHERS ST
PORTLAND OR 317-E1
CASCADE AV
LANGLEY WA 171-A1
CASCADE AV U.S.-30
HOOD RIVER OR 195-C5
HOOD RIVER CO OR 195-C5
NW CASCADE AV
DOUGLAS CO WA 239-A3
EAST WENATCHEE BENCH WA 239-A3
CASCADE DR
JOSEPHINE CO OR 233-A5
CASCADE HWY
BURLINGTON WA 260-D4
MARION CO OR 205-B6
SILVERTON OR 205-B6
CASCADE HWY Rt#-9
SEDRO-WOOLLEY WA 161-C6
CASCADE HWY Rt#-20
BURLINGTON WA 260-E4
SEDRO-WOOLLEY WA 161-C6
SEDRO-WOOLLEY WA 260-E4
SKAGIT CO WA 260-E4
CASCADE HWY Rt#-213
CLACKAMAS CO OR 126-A3
CLACKAMAS CO OR 199-D7
CLACKAMAS CO OR 205-C4
MARION CO OR 205-C4
MOLALLA OR 126-A3
SE CASCADE HWY Rt#-213
CLACKAMAS CO OR 199-D3
CASCADE HWY S Rt#-213
CLACKAMAS CO OR 199-D4
CLACKAMAS CO OR 205-D2
MARION CO OR 205-D3
OREGON CITY OR 199-D4
CASCADE HWY SE
MARION CO OR 133-C1
STAYTON OR 133-C1
SUBLIMITY OR 133-C1
CASCADE RD
GEM CO ID 139-B3
SKAGIT CO WA 103-A2
CASCADE ST U.S.-20
DESCHUTES CO OR 211-D5
SISTERS OR 211-D5
CASCADE VW
EVERETT WA 265-E6
CASCADE WY
ELLENSBURG WA 241-B5
W CASCADE WY
TOWN AND COUNTRY WA 346-J13
TOWN AND COUNTRY WA 347-A13
CASCADE CREEK RD
LINCOLN CO OR 209-C3
CASCADE CREST TR
SKAMANIA CO WA 195-A1
CASCADE ESTATES DR
DESCHUTES CO OR 212-A6

STREET City State Page-Grid
CASCADE HEAD RD
TILLAMOOK CO OR 203-B3
CASCADE LAKES HWY
DESCHUTES CO OR 216-B3
DOUGLAS CO OR 223-C4
CASCADE LOCKS HWY U.S.-30
CASCADE LOCKS OR 194-D6
HOOD RIVER CO OR 194-D6
CASCADIAN WY
SNOHOMISH CO WA 171-C4
CASE RD
MARION CO OR 199-A7
CASE RD SW
THURSTON CO WA 184-C1
CASEY RD
COWLITZ CO WA 187-C6
WALLA WALLA CO WA 121-C2
CASEY CREEK RD
GARFIELD CO WA 122-B1
CASHMUR CT
DESCHUTES CO OR 212-C5
CASHUP NORTH RD
WHITMAN CO WA 114-C3
E CASINO RD
EVERETT WA 268-C4
W CASINO RD
EVERETT WA 267-H5
EVERETT WA 268-A4
CASON RD
TILLAMOOK CO OR 197-D5
SE CASON RD
CLACKAMAS CO OR 199-D4
GLADSTONE OR 199-D4
NE CASPER ST
ROSEBURG OR 334-H7
CASPERS ST Rt#-524
EDMONDS WA 171-A5
SE CASS AV
ROSEBURG OR 334-F8
CASSIA RD
PAYETTE CO ID 139-B3
CASSIA ST
BOISE ID 253-C3
CASTLE DR
BOISE ID 253-C2
CASTLE CREEK RD
JACKSON CO OR 226-D3
JACKSON CO OR 227-A3
OWYHEE CO ID 147-C3
CASTLEMAN RD
DISTRICT OF CHILLIWACK BC 94-C3
CASTLEROCK AV
WENATCHEE WA 238-D4
CASTLE ROCK RD
MALHEUR CO OR 138-A3
CASTLE ROCK TKTR
COWLITZ CO WA 187-A6
CASWELL ST
ADA CO ID 253-B1
CATALA AV SE
OCEAN SHORES WA 298-F4
CATALPA DR
BOISE ID 253-C2
CATCHING CREEK RD
COOS CO OR 140-B3
COOS CO OR 220-D7
E CATCHING SLOUGH RD
COOS CO OR 140-B2
COOS CO OR 220-D1
CATER RD
COLUMBIA CO OR 125-C1
COLUMBIA CO OR 192-A2
CATHERINE ST
CITY OF VICTORIA BC 256-F8
CATHERINE CREEK LN
UNION CO OR 130-B3
CATLIN ST Rt#-4
KELSO WA 303-C8
CATLOW VALLEY RD
HARNEY CO OR 153-B2
CATLOW VALLEY RD Rt#-205
HARNEY CO OR 153-B1
CATRON RD
WASCO CO OR 196-A6
CATTLE POINT RD
SAN JUAN CO WA 101-C2
CAVALEROS RD
SNOHOMISH CO WA 171-D2
CAVE BAY
KOOTENAI CO ID 247-D7
CAVE CREEK RD
SKAMANIA CO WA 195-B1
CAVENDISH RD
CLEARWATER CO ID 123-B2
CAVITT CREEK RD
DOUGLAS CO OR 141-B2
CAYS RD
CLALLAM CO WA 166-A6
CAYUSE RD
MISSION OR 129-C1
UMATILLA CO OR 129-C1
CC ST
WOODLAND WA 192-B1
CECIL RD
MORROW CO OR 128-B1
S CEDAR AV
FRANKLIN CO WA 343-J8
PASCO WA 343-J8
CEDAR DR
COLUMBIA CO OR 189-B4
COQUITLAM BC 157-B4
PORT COQUITLAM BC 157-B4
W CEDAR DR
WALDPORT OR 328-D5
CEDAR RD
SNOHOMISH CO WA 171-D1
N CEDAR RD
SPOKANE CO WA 114-B1
S CEDAR RD
SPOKANE WA 246-B5
CEDAR ST
BAKER CITY OR 138-B1
BAKER CO OR 138-B1
BINGEN WA 195-D5
DISTRICT OF MISSION BC 94-B3
KELSO WA 303-D9
SANDPOINT ID 244-A2
CEDAR ST Rt#-5
BENEWAH CO ID 115-A2
CEDAR ST Rt#-5
BENEWAH CO ID 248-A7
PLUMMER ID 115-A2
CEDAR ST Rt#-231
STEVENS CO WA 106-B3
CEDAR ST U.S.-95
SANDPOINT ID 244-A2
N CEDAR ST
COLFAX WA 122-C1
WALDPORT OR 328-D4
N CEDAR ST Rt#-99
DRAIN OR 219-A3
NE CEDAR ST
ROSEBURG OR 334-F5
S CEDAR ST
SPOKANE WA 348-H12
TACOMA WA 292-D6
TACOMA WA 294-D1
WALDPORT OR 328-D5
S CEDAR ST Rt#-99
DRAIN OR 219-A3
CEDAR WY
MAPLE RIDGE BC 157-C5
CEDAR WY S
MOUNTLAKE TERRACE WA 171-B6
CEDAR BURN RD
WASCO CO OR 126-C3
CEDAR CREEK RD
LANE CO OR 219-C2
LATAH CO ID 123-B1
CLARK CO WA 118-A3
CLARK CO WA 192-C1
CLARK CO WA 193-B1
CEDARDALE RD
MOUNT VERNON WA 168-B2
MOUNT VERNON WA 260-C14
SKAGIT CO WA 168-B2
CEDAR FALLS RD SE
KING CO WA 176-C6
CEDAR FLAT RD
JOSEPHINE CO OR 149-A2
CEDAR FLATS RD SW
THURSTON CO WA 180-B6
CEDAR GROVE RD
COLUMBIA CO OR 189-A4
KING CO WA 175-D6
KING CO WA 176-A5
CEDAR HILL RD
DISTRICT OF SAANICH BC 159-D5
DISTRICT OF SAANICH BC 256-J6
DISTRICT OF SAANICH BC 257-A1
CEDAR HILL CROSS RD
DISTRICT OF OAK BAY BC 257-B4
DISTRICT OF SAANICH BC 256-H2
DISTRICT OF SAANICH BC 257-B4
SW CEDAR HILLS BLVD
BEAVERTON OR 199-B2
WASHINGTON CO OR 199-B2
CEDAR LINKS RD
JACKSON CO OR 336-G8
MEDFORD OR 336-G8
N CEDAR PARK RD
LANE CO OR 215-C7
CEDAR RIVER PIPELINE RD
KING CO WA 176-A7
CEDAR SPRINGS RD
GILLIAM CO OR 128-A1
CEDAR SWAMP RD
SKAMANIA CO WA 194-B6
N CEDARVALE LOOP RD
SNOHOMISH CO WA 168-D3
CEDARWOOD AV
BELLINGHAM WA 258-A3
CEDARWOOD RD
MARION CO OR 199-B7
CEDONIA-ADDY Y RD
STEVENS CO WA 105-C3
STEVENS CO WA 106-A3
E CELESTA AV
SPOKANE WA 349-C10
CELILO-WASCO HWY
SHERMAN CO OR 127-C1
CELILO-WASCO HWY Rt#-206
SHERMAN CO OR 127-C1
N CEMENT ST
SPOKANE CO WA 350-H4
CEMETERY RD
ADAMS CO ID 251-B3
ARLINGTON WA 168-C5
ASOTIN CO WA 250-B6
BENTON CO WA 120-C3
CANYON CO ID 147-B1
KLICKITAT CO WA 119-A3
LANE CO OR 215-B7
SNOHOMISH CO WA 168-C5
WINLOCK WA 187-C3
CEMETERY RD Rt#-55
MARSING ID 147-B1
OWYHEE CO ID 147-B1
CEMETERY RD U.S.-95
OWYHEE CO ID 147-B1
S CEMETERY RD
CLACKAMAS CO OR 205-D4
SW CEMETERY RD
KING CO WA 174-D6
CEMETERY HILL RD
COLUMBIA CO WA 122-A2
CENTENNIAL BLVD
EUGENE OR 330-C5
LANE CO OR 330-C5
SPRINGFIELD OR 330-H6
SPRINGFIELD OR 331-B6
W CENTENNIAL BLVD
LANE CO OR 330-E6
SPRINGFIELD OR 330-E6
E CENTENNIAL ST
CALDWELL ID 147-B1
CENTENNIAL TR
SPOKANE CO WA 348-B5
CENTENNIAL WY U.S.-30
CALDWELL ID 147-B1
CENTER AV Rt#-25
NORTHPORT WA 106-A1
STEVENS CO WA 106-A1
E CENTER AV
PAYETTE ID 139-A3
CENTER DR
DUPONT WA 181-B5
N CENTER PKWY
KENNEWICK WA 342-B8
CENTER RD
JEFFERSON CO WA 109-C1
CENTER ST
SUBLIMITY OR 133-C1
N CENTER ST
SPOKANE WA 349-C6
S CENTER ST
TACOMA WA 294-B1
TACOMA WA 295-E1
CENTER ST E
EATONVILLE WA 118-B1
CENTER ST NE
FOUR CORNERS OR 323-F13
MARION CO OR 323-F13
SALEM OR 322-H12
SALEM OR 323-B13
CENTER ST NE Rt#-22
SALEM OR 322-H12
CENTER ST W
EATONVILLE WA 118-B1
CENTER RIDGE MARKET RD
WASCO CO OR 127-B2
CENTER SCHOOL RD
LINN CO OR 210-C3
CENTER ST BRDG Rt#-22
SALEM OR 322-H12
CENTER ST BRDG NE Rt#-22
SALEM OR 322-H12
CENTERVILLE HWY
KLICKITAT CO WA 196-D5
CENTRAL
DESCHUTES CO OR 212-A6
CENTRAL AV
COOS BAY OR 333-G10
GRANTS PASS OR 335-D10
E CENTRAL AV
DOUGLAS CO OR 221-C1
SUTHERLIN OR 221-C1
N CENTRAL AV
MEDFORD OR 336-C11
S CENTRAL AV
MEDFORD OR 336-D12
S CENTRAL AV U.S.-2
WATERVILLE WA 236-C7
SW CENTRAL AV
GRANTS PASS OR 335-E10
CENTRAL AV N
KENT WA 175-C6
CENTRAL AV N Rt#-516
KENT WA 175-C7
CENTRAL AV S
AUBURN WA 175-C7
GRANT CO WA 112-B3
KENT WA 175-C7
KING CO WA 175-C7
QUINCY WA 112-B3
CENTRAL AV S Rt#-281
GRANT CO WA 112-B3
QUINCY WA 112-B3
CENTRAL AV S Rt#-516
KENT WA 175-C7
CENTRAL AV W
OROVILLE WA 104-C1
CENTRAL BLVD U.S.-95
CAMBRIDGE ID 139-B1
WASHINGTON CO ID 139-B1
N CENTRAL BLVD Rt#-42
COQUILLE OR 220-D4
W CENTRAL BLVD Rt#-42
COQUILLE OR 220-D4
CENTRAL DR
MUKILTEO WA 266-C7
CENTRAL RD
LANE CO OR 133-B3
CENTRAL WY NE
KIRKLAND WA 175-C1
CENTRAL FERRY CANYON RD
DOUGLAS CO WA 112-B1
CENTRAL GRADE RD
NEZ PERCE CO ID 250-C3
CENTRALIA ALPHA RD
LEWIS CO WA 118-A1
LEWIS CO WA 184-C6
LEWIS CO WA 299-H8
CENTRAL OREGON HWY U.S.-20
BEND OR 217-C2
BEND OR 332-G7
BURNS OR 145-A1
DESCHUTES CO OR 135-B3
DESCHUTES CO OR 143-C1
DESCHUTES CO OR 144-A1
DESCHUTES CO OR 217-C2
DESCHUTES CO OR 332-G7
HARNEY CO OR 138-A3
HARNEY CO OR 144-B1
HARNEY CO OR 145-A1
HARNEY CO OR 146-A1
HINES OR 145-A1
LAKE CO OR 144-A1
MALHEUR CO OR 138-C3
MALHEUR CO OR 139-A3
MALHEUR CO OR 146-A1
NYSSA OR 139-A3
VALE OR 138-C3
VALE OR 139-A3
S CENTRAL POINT RD
CLACKAMAS CO OR 199-C6
CENTRAL RIDGE RD
LEWIS CO ID 123-C2
NEZ PERCE CO ID 123-C2
PECK ID 123-C2
CENTRAL SAANICH RD
DIST OF CENTRAL SAANICH BC 159-C4
CENTRAL VALE DR
HOOD RIVER CO OR 195-C7
CENTRAL VALLEY RD NE
KITSAP CO WA 174-B1
KITSAP CO WA 270-G3
TRACYTON WA 270-G3
CENTRAL VALLEY RD NW
KITSAP CO WA 270-G1
CENTURY DR
ALBANY OR 326-H6
LINN CO OR 326-H6
S CENTURY DR
DESCHUTES CO OR 143-A1
DESCHUTES CO OR 216-D7
DESCHUTES CO OR 217-A6
THREE RIVERS OR 216-D7
S CENTURY DR
THREE RIVERS OR 217-A7
CENTURY LN
WALLOWA CO OR 130-C2
CENTURY DRIVE HWY Rt#-372
BEND OR 332-A11
DESCHUTES CO OR 216-C4
DESCHUTES CO OR 217-B3
DESCHUTES CO OR 332-A11
CERES HILL RD
LEWIS CO WA 184-A7
LEWIS CO WA 187-A1
SE CHADWICK ST
ROSEBURG OR 334-G8
CHAIN LAKE RD
SNOHOMISH CO WA 110-C1
CHALET RD
DIST OF NORTH SAANICH BC 159-B1
CHALK BUTTE RD
MALHEUR CO OR 139-A3
CHALK HILLS RD NE
DOUGLAS CO WA 112-C1
SW CHAMBERLAIN ST
BEND OR 332-E9
CHAMBERS LN W
UNIVERSITY PLACE WA 181-C3
CHAMBERS RD
WHITMAN CO WA 249-B7
CHAMBERS ST
EUGENE OR 329-G6
LANE CO OR 329-G9
CHAMBERS CREEK RD
LAKEWOOD WA 181-C3
STEILACOOM WA 181-C3
UNIVERSITY PLACE WA 181-C3
CHAMBERS CREEK RD W
UNIVERSITY PLACE WA 181-C3
CHAMPOEG RD
MARION CO OR 198-D6
MARION CO OR 199-A7
CHANCE RD
TILLAMOOK CO OR 197-C3
CHANCELLOR BLVD
UNIV ENDOWMENT LANDS BC 156-A4
CHANDLER LN
BAKER CO OR 130-B3
CHANDLER RD
LAKE OSWEGO OR 321-E5
CHANEY RD
LATAH CO ID 249-C3
CHANNEL DR
SKAGIT CO WA 160-D7
CHANNEL VIEW DR
SKAGIT CO WA 160-C5
CHANUTE ST
MOSES LAKE NORTH WA 242-C2
CHAPEL DR
BENTON CO OR 133-B1
PHILOMATH OR 133-B1
CHAPMAN PL
CORVALLIS OR 327-G11
CHAPMAN RD
WASHINGTON CO OR 199-A5
S CHAPMAN RD
LATAH WA 114-C3
SPOKANE CO WA 114-C3
SPOKANE CO WA 247-A5
CHARLES RD
CLALLAM CO WA 165-A5
W CHARLES RD
SPOKANE CO WA 246-A1
CHARLES ST
PORT MOODY BC 157-A4
CHARLESTON BEACH RD W
NAVY YARD CITY WA 270-E13
CHARLOTTE AV W
NAVY YARD CITY WA 270-F12
CHARLTON RD
KITTITAS CO WA 241-C3
CHAROLAIS RD
WALLOWA CO OR 130-C1
E CHARRON RD
YAKIMA CO WA 243-D7
CHARTWELL DR
DIST OF WEST VANCOUVER BC 254-D1
N CHASE AV
PASCO WA 343-D4
N CHASE RD
KOOTENAI CO ID 353-G4
POST FALLS ID 353-G4
CHASE MOUNTAIN RD
KLAMATH CO OR 235-A6
CHATCOLET RD
KOOTENAI CO ID 115-A2
CHATHAM HILL DR
SUNNYSLOPE WA 238-D3
CHAUFTY RD
LEWIS CO WA 187-B4
CHEAM AV Rt#-9
DISTRICT OF KENT BC 94-C3
CHEESE FACTORY RD
KLAMATH CO OR 151-A2
CHEHALEM DR
NEWBERG OR 198-D5
YAMHILL CO OR 198-D5
CHEHALIS AV
GRAYS HARBOR CO WA 183-A2
N CHELAN AV
DOUGLAS CO WA 236-C7
WATERVILLE WA 236-C7
N CHELAN AV Rt#-285
WENATCHEE WA 238-D4
N CHELAN AV U.S.-2
WATERVILLE WA 236-C7
S CHELAN AV
WATERVILLE WA 236-C7
S CHELAN AV Rt#-285
WENATCHEE WA 238-D4
WENATCHEE WA 239-A4
S CHELAN ST
RITZVILLE WA 113-C3
CHELAN BUTTE RD
CHELAN CO WA 236-C3
CHELAN FALLS RD
CHELAN CO WA 236-D3
CHELAN FALLS RD Rt#-150
CHELAN CO WA 236-D3
CHELAN FALLS RD U.S.-97
CHELAN CO WA 236-D3
CHELAN-OKANOGAN HWY
SUNNYSLOPE WA 238-D3
CHELAN-STEHEKIN FERRY
CHELAN WA 236-B2
CHELAN CO WA 112-A1
CHELAN CO WA 236-B2
CHEMAWA RD N
KEIZER OR 322-H5
KEIZER OR 323-A5
CHEMAWA RD NE
KEIZER OR 323-A5
MARION CO OR 323-E4
SALEM OR 323-E4
CHEMEKETA ST NE
SALEM OR 322-H12
CHEMICAL RD Rt#-397
BENTON CO WA 343-G12
FINLEY WA 121-A3
FINLEY WA 343-G12
KENNEWICK WA 343-F11
CHENEY CREEK RD
JOSEPHINE CO OR 229-A7
CHENEY-PLAZA RD
SPOKANE CO WA 114-B2
S CHENEY-PLAZA RD
CHENEY WA 246-A7
SPOKANE CO WA 114-B2
SPOKANE CO WA 246-A7
W CHENEY-SPANGLE RD
CHENEY WA 246-A7
SPOKANE CO WA 114-B2
SPOKANE CO WA 246-A7
S CHENEY-SPOKANE RD
SPOKANE WA 246-A7
SPOKANE WA 348-H14
SPOKANE CO WA 246-A7
W CHENEY-SPOKANE RD
SPOKANE WA 246-B5
SPOKANE CO WA 246-B5
CHENNAULT BEACH DR
MUKILTEO WA 266-C7
CHENNAULT BEACH RD
MUKILTEO WA 266-D7
MUKILTEO WA 267-E7
CHENOWETH RD
WASCO CO OR 196-B7
CHENOWETH CREEK RD
THE DALLES OR 196-B7
WASCO CO OR 196-B7
CHEROKEE
CROOK CO OR 213-D7
CHEROKEE RD
GRANT CO WA 242-D2
CHEROKEE CREEK RD
MALHEUR CO OR 154-B2
NE CHERRY AV
KEIZER OR 322-J6
KEIZER OR 323-A6
SALEM OR 323-A6
CHERRY LN
CANYON CO ID 147-B1
JACKSON CO OR 234-B1
LINN CO OR 207-C5
MEDFORD OR 234-B1
E CHERRY LN
CANYON CO ID 147-C1
NE CHERRY LN
JEFFERSON CO OR 208-C5
W CHERRY LN
ADA CO ID 147-C1
ADA CO ID 253-A3
MERIDIAN ID 253-A3
CHERRY ST
PORT TOWNSEND WA 263-G4
WENATCHEE WA 238-D4
E CHERRY ST
SEATTLE WA 278-C6
WALLA WALLA WA 345-A7
W CHERRY ST
WALLA WALLA WA 344-J7
WALLA WALLA WA 345-A7
WALLA WALLA WEST WA 344-J7
W CHERRY ST Rt#-507
CENTRALIA WA 299-E4
SE CHERRY BLOSSOM DR
PORTLAND OR 315-J7
CHERRY CREEK RD
BENEWAH CO ID 248-C7
WHITMAN CO WA 114-B3
CHERRY HEIGHTS RD
WASCO CO OR 196-B7
CHERRY HILL RD
GRANGER WA 120-A2
CHERRY LANE RD
NEZ PERCE CO ID 123-B2
CHESNIMNUS LN
WALLOWA CO OR 131-A1
CHESTER AV
GRAYS HARBOR CO WA 183-B3
E CHESTER RD
KITSAP CO WA 271-F13
MANCHESTER WA 271-F13
CHESTERFIELD AV
CITY OF N VANCOUVER BC 255-B5
E CHESTNUT AV
GENESEE ID 250-C1
NE CHESTNUT AV
ROSEBURG OR 334-F5
W CHESTNUT AV
GENESEE ID 250-C1
LATAH CO ID 250-C1
CHESTNUT DR
DESCHUTES CO OR 211-D5
WALLA WALLA EAST WA 345-D9
CHESTNUT ST
ASHLAND OR 337-B6
ASOTIN CO WA 250-B4
CLARKSTON WA 250-B4
KELSO WA 303-C9
E CHESTNUT ST
WALLA WALLA WA 345-C8
WALLA WALLA EAST WA 345-C8
S CHESTNUT ST
SPOKANE WA 348-G12
W CHESTNUT ST
WALLA WALLA WA 344-J9
WALLA WALLA WA 345-A9
CHETCO AV U.S.-101
BROOKINGS OR 232-C6
CHEVY CHASE RD
JEFFERSON CO WA 166-D7
W CHEWACK RD
OKANOGAN CO WA 104-A2
CHEWILIKEN RD
OKANOGAN CO WA 105-A2
CHEWILIKEN VALLEY RD
OKANOGAN CO WA 104-C2
E CHEWUCH RD
OKANOGAN CO WA 104-A2
CHEYNE RD
KLAMATH CO OR 235-D7
CHIAWA LOOP RD
CHELAN CO WA 111-C1
CHICAGO ST SE
TURNER OR 325-G12
CHICKADEE DR
JEFFERSON CO OR 212-C2
CHICKAHOMINY RD
LANE CO OR 133-A3
CHICKEN DINNER RD
CANYON CO ID 147-B1
CHICO WY NW
BREMERTON WA 270-B7
KITSAP CO WA 270-B3
SILVERDALE WA 270-B3
TRACYTON WA 270-B7
CHIEF MARTIN RD
WHATCOM CO WA 158-C7
CHILBERG RD
LA CONNER WA 167-D1
SKAGIT CO WA 167-D1
SKAGIT CO WA 168-A1
E CHILCO AV
KOOTENAI CO ID 245-A3
SW CHILDS RD
CLACKAMAS CO OR 199-C4
CHILKO DR
COQUITLAM BC 157-A5
CHILLIWACK LAKE RD
BRITISH COLUMBIA 102-C1
BRITISH COLUMBIA 103-A1
DISTRICT OF CHILLIWACK BC 102-C1
CHILOQUIN HWY
CHILOQUIN OR 231-C3
KLAMATH CO OR 231-C3
S CHILOQUIN RD
CHILOQUIN OR 231-D4
KLAMATH CO OR 231-D4
CHILOQUIN CAMP RD
KLAMATH CO OR 142-C3
CHILOQUIN RIDGE RD
KLAMATH CO OR 231-D4
CHILVERS RD
LEWIS CO WA 184-A7
CHIMACUM CENTER RD
HADLOCK-IRONDALE WA 170-A2
JEFFERSON CO WA 170-A2
CHIMNEY CREEK RD
MALHEUR CO OR 138-A3
MALHEUR CO OR 146-A1
CHIN RD
KLAMATH CO OR 235-D7
CHINA CREEK RD
DOUGLAS CO WA 105-A3
CHINA GARDEN RD
KALAMA WA 189-D6
CHINA GRADE RD
SISKIYOU CO CA 149-A3
CHINA HAT RD
DESCHUTES CO OR 135-B3
DESCHUTES CO OR 143-B1
DESCHUTES CO OR 217-C4
DESCHUTES CO OR 332-D14
DESCHUTES RIVER WOODS OR 332-D14
CHINA MOUNTAIN RD
CURRY CO OR 224-B6
E CHINDEN BLVD U.S.-20
ADA CO ID 253-B2
BOISE ID 253-B2
EAGLE ID 253-B2
GARDEN CITY ID 253-C2
W CHINDEN BLVD U.S.-20
ADA CO ID 147-C1
ADA CO ID 253-A2
CHINOOK PASS HWY Rt#-410
KING CO WA 110-C3
PIERCE CO WA 110-C3
PIERCE CO WA 111-A3
CHINOOK VALLEY RD
PACIFIC CO WA 186-B6
CHIPMUNK
JEFFERSON CO OR 212-C2
CHIPMUNK TR
DOUGLAS CO WA 239-B1
CHIPPEWA
CROOK CO OR 213-D7
CHIWAWA LP
CHELAN CO WA 111-C1
CHIWAWA RIVER RD
CHELAN CO WA 103-C3
CHELAN CO WA 111-C1
NE CHKALOV DR
VANCOUVER WA 307-J6
SE CHKALOV DR
VANCOUVER WA 307-J7
E CHOCKTOOT ST
CHILOQUIN OR 231-D4
N CHOCKTOOT ST
CHILOQUIN OR 231-D4
W CHOCKTOOT ST
CHILOQUIN OR 231-D3
E CHRIS CT
SPOKANE CO WA 347-F5
CHRISELLA RD E
EDGEWOOD WA 182-B3
CHRISTENSEN RD
CLARK CO WA 192-D1
SW CHRISTENSEN RD
YAMHILL CO OR 204-A2
CHRISTIANSEN RD
LINCOLN CO OR 206-C4
CHRISTIANSON RD
SKAGIT CO WA 160-C7
CHRISTIE RD
BENTON CO WA 120-C3
BENTON CO WA 121-A3
BENTON CO WA 128-C1

STREET City State Page-Grid

CHRISTMAS VALLEY-WAGONTIRE RD
LAKE CO OR 143-B2
LAKE CO OR 144-A2
CHROME RIDGE RD
JOSEPHINE CO OR 148-C1
W CHRUCH RD
MOUNT ANGEL OR 205-C3
CHUCKANUT DR Rt#-11
BELLINGHAM WA 258-B12
SKAGIT CO WA 160-D2
SKAGIT CO WA 161-A3
SKAGIT CO WA 260-B1
WHATCOM CO WA 160-D2
WHATCOM CO WA 258-B14
CHUCKER DR
YAKIMA CO WA 243-D6
CHURCH AV Rt#-219
MARION CO OR 198-D7
SAINT PAUL OR 198-D7
CHURCH DR
LINN CO OR 207-B7
CHURCH RD
COLUMBIA CO OR 192-A2
WHATCOM CO WA 158-C6
YAKIMA CO WA 243-B5
SE CHURCH RD
CLACKAMAS CO OR 200-B3
W CHURCH RD
MARION CO OR 205-B3
MOUNT ANGEL OR 205-B3
YAKIMA CO WA 243-A7
CHURCH ST Rt#-165
WILKESON WA 182-D5
CHURCH ST Rt#-216
GRASS VALLEY OR 127-C2
W CHURCH ST
MONMOUTH OR 204-B7
W CHURCH ST Rt#-272
PALOUSE WA 249-B1
WHITMAN CO WA 249-B1
CHURCH ST NE
SALEM OR 322-J12
CHURCH ST SE
SALEM OR 322-H14
CHURCH HILL RD
WHITMAN CO WA 122-B1
CHURCHILL RD
DOUGLAS CO OR 219-A1
CHURCHILL RD SE
THURSTON CO WA 184-D3
CHURCH LAKE RD E
BONNEY LAKE WA 182-C4
PIERCE CO WA 182-C4
CHYNOWETH RD
CLACKAMAS CO OR 200-B5
CINDER BUTTE RD
DESCHUTES CO OR 211-D3
CINDER HILL RD
DESCHUTES CO OR 135-B3
DESCHUTES CO OR 143-B1
CINEBAR RD
LEWIS CO WA 118-A2
CINNAMON BUTTE RD
DOUGLAS CO OR 223-C4
CIRCLE BLVD
BENTON CO OR 207-B5
BENTON CO OR 327-G6
CORVALLIS OR 207-B5
CORVALLIS OR 327-G6
CIRCLE C LN
ADAMS CO ID 251-A3
CIRQUE DR W
TACOMA WA 294-A4
UNIVERSITY PLACE WA 181-C3
UNIVERSITY PLACE WA 294-A4
CISPUS RD Rt#-131
LEWIS CO WA 118-C2
CITADEL DR
PORT COQUITLAM BC 157-A5
NW CLACKAMAS DR
JEFFERSON CO OR 208-B4
CLACKAMAS HWY Rt#-212
CLACKAMAS CO OR 199-D4
CLACKAMAS CO OR 200-A3
CLACKAMAS HWY Rt#-224
CLACKAMAS CO OR 126-B3
CLACKAMAS CO OR 200-B4
ESTACADA OR 200-C7
CLACKAMAS-BORING RD Rt#-212
CLACKAMAS CO OR 200-B3
S CLACKAMAS RIVER DR
CLACKAMAS CO OR 199-D4
CLACKAMAS CO OR 200-A4
OREGON CITY OR 199-D4
CLACKAMAS RIVER RD
CLACKAMAS CO OR 126-B3
MARION CO OR 126-C3
CLAGSTONE RD
KOOTENAI CO ID 245-A2
CLAIR CUT-OFF RD Rt#-510
THURSTON CO WA 181-A7
S CLARK AV Rt#-20
REPUBLIC WA 105-B2
CLARK BLVD
MALHEUR CO OR 139-A3
CLARK DR
VANCOUVER BC 255-A12
NE CLARK DR
JEFFERSON CO OR 208-C3
CLARK LN
HARNEY CO OR 137-C3
CLARK RD
CLALLAM CO WA 163-B6
COLUMBIA CO OR 189-B6
KLICKITAT CO WA 196-D4
LEWIS CO WA 187-D2
CLARK RD SW
DOUGLAS CO WA 239-B3
CLARK ST
BAKER CITY OR 138-B1
SHERMAN CO OR 127-C1
WASCO OR 127-C1
CLARK ST U.S.-95
LEWIS CO ID 123-B2
WINCHESTER ID 123-B2
E CLARK ST
CONNELL WA 121-B1
W CLARK ST
CONNELL WA 121-B1
FRANKLIN CO WA 121-B1
CLARK CREEK RD
UNION CO OR 130-B1
CLARKE RD
COQUITLAM BC 157-A4
DISTRICT OF COQUITLAM BC 156-D4
KITTITAS CO WA 241-A4
PORT MOODY BC 157-A4
SW CLARK HILL RD
WASHINGTON CO OR 199-A3
CLARK LAKE RD
STEVENS CO WA 106-A3
CLARKS BRANCH RD
DOUGLAS CO OR 221-C7
CLARKS CANYON RD
MORROW CO OR 128-C2
CLARKS CREEK RD
BAKER CO OR 138-B1
CLAUSSEN RD
PIERCE CO WA 181-A4
CLAY LN
ADAMS CO ID 251-B4
CLAY ST
ASHLAND OR 337-G9
DISTRICT OF MISSION BC 94-B3
JACKSON CO OR 337-G9
SW CLAY ST
PORTLAND OR 312-D6
PORTLAND OR 312-E6
CLAYBURN RD
DISTRICT OF MATSQUI BC 102-B1
NW CLAY PIT RD
YAMHILL CO OR 198-A5
CLAYSON PL
ADA CO ID 253-B2
BOISE ID 253-B2
CLAYTON RD
LANE CO OR 215-B5
CLEARBROOK RD
DISTRICT OF MATSQUI BC 102-B1
CLEAR CREEK RD
CLACKAMAS CO OR 200-B6
HOOD RIVER CO OR 202-C2
WHITMAN CO WA 249-A1
CLEAR CREEK RD NW
BANGOR TRIDENT BASE WA 170-B7
KITSAP CO WA 170-B7
KITSAP CO WA 174-B1
SILVERDALE WA 174-B1
CLEAR LAKE RD
DOUGLAS CO OR 214-A7
DUNES CITY OR 214-B4
LANE CO OR 133-B3
LANE CO OR 215-A1
MODOC CO CA 151-A3
CLEAR LAKE RD NE
KEIZER OR 204-D4
CLEARVIEW DR
DOUGLAS CO OR 221-B3
W CLEARWATER AV
BENTON CO WA 342-A11
KENNEWICK WA 342-E10
NE CLEARWATER DR
CLARK CO WA 193-C3
CLEARWATER RD
DOUGLAS CO OR 222-D4
DOUGLAS CO OR 223-A4
JEFFERSON CO WA 108-C1
JEFFERSON CO WA 172-B1
CLEARWATER FALLS RD
DOUGLAS CO OR 223-B4
CLEMAN RD
KITTITAS CO WA 241-C7
CLEMANS RD
ASOTIN WA 250-B5
ASOTIN CO WA 250-B5
NE CLEMENS DR
JEFFERSON CO OR 208-C2
CLEMENTS RD
TILLAMOOK CO OR 197-C3
CLEMS VIEW RD
YAKIMA CO WA 243-B4
CLETO RD
MALHEUR CO OR 154-B2
CLEVELAND AV
TUMWATER WA 296-H9
CLEVELAND BLVD U.S.-30
CALDWELL ID 147-B1
CANYON CO ID 147-B1
CLEVELAND ST Rt#-202
REDMOND WA 175-D1
CLEVELAND ST Rt#-908
REDMOND WA 175-D1
E CLEVELAND ST
WOODBURN OR 205-B2
CLEVELAND HILL RD
DOUGLAS CO OR 221-A3
CLEVELAND RIDGE RD
JACKSON CO OR 230-C1
S CLIFF AV
TACOMA WA 293-H5
CLIFFRIDGE AV
DIST OF N VANCOUVER BC 156-B2
CLIFTON RD
CLATSOP CO WA 117-B3
SW CLIFTON RD
KITSAP CO WA 174-B4
CLIFTON RD SW
KITSAP CO WA 174-B4
PORT ORCHARD WA 174-B4
CLINE RD
COWLITZ CO WA 187-C7
CLINE FALLS HWY
DESCHUTES CO OR 212-B7
DESCHUTES CO OR 217-B1
CLINTON RD
LEWIS CO WA 184-A7
N CLINTON ST
WALLA WALLA WA 345-C6
S CLINTON ST
WALLA WALLA WA 345-C8
CLISE PL W
SEATTLE WA 276-D1
CLIVEDEN AV
DISTRICT OF DELTA BC 156-D6
CLODFELTER RD
BENTON CO WA 121-A3
BENTON CO WA 341-J14
CLODFELTER RD
BENTON CO WA 342-A12
CLOQUALLUM RD
MASON CO WA 179-D4
MASON CO WA 180-A4
CLOQUALLUM LOST LAKE RD
GRAYS HARBOR CO WA 179-B5
CLOSE RD NW
DOUGLAS CO WA 236-C7
WATERVILLE WA 236-C7
CLOVER BLOSSOM LN NE
KITSAP CO WA 271-A3
CLOVER CREEK RD
KLAMATH CO OR 150-B2
KLAMATH CO OR 235-A4
CLOVERDALE AV
DISTRICT OF SAANICH BC 256-G5
CLOVERDALE BYPS Rt#-15
DISTRICT OF SURREY BC 157-B7
CLOVERDALE RD
COWLITZ CO WA 189-D6
CRESWELL OR 215-C5
DESCHUTES CO OR 212-A5
LANE CO OR 215-C5
LINCOLN CO WA 114-A2
MARION CO OR 207-D1
N CLOVERDALE RD
ADA CO ID 253-B2
S CLOVERDALE RD
ADA CO ID 253-B5
COWLITZ CO WA 189-D6
S CLOVERDALE ST
SEATTLE WA 285-J3
SEATTLE WA 286-A3
CLOVER ISLAND DR
KENNEWICK WA 343-D9
CLOVER ISLAND DRIVE BRDG
KENNEWICK WA 343-D10
CLOVERLAND RD
ASOTIN CO WA 122-C2
ASOTIN CO WA 250-A7
CLOVERLAWN DR
JOSEPHINE CO OR 229-B7
JOSEPHINE CO OR 335-G13
N CLOVERLEAF RD
HAUSER ID 247-C1
KOOTENAI CO ID 247-C1
CLOVER RIDGE RD
ALBANY OR 326-J6
LINN CO OR 326-J6
CLOVER VALLEY RD
AULT FIELD WA 167-B2
ISLAND CO WA 167-B2
CLOW CORNER RD
POLK CO OR 204-A6
E CLUB CT
SPOKANE WA 246-C5
CLUGSTON CREEK-ONION CREEK RD
STEVENS CO WA 106-A2
COAL CREEK PKWY SE
BELLEVUE WA 175-C3
KING CO WA 175-C3
NEWCASTLE WA 175-C3
COAL CREEK RD
COWLITZ CO WA 189-A1
COWLITZ CO WA 302-B3
LONGVIEW WA 302-B3
WEST LONGVIEW WA 302-B3
COALMAN RD
CLACKAMAS CO OR 200-D4
CLACKAMAS CO OR 201-A4
COAL MINE RD
JACKSON CO OR 234-B2
COAL MINE HILL RD
MORROW CO OR 129-A3
COAST DR
DEPOE BAY OR 206-B1
SW COAST CREEK RD
YAMHILL CO OR 125-A3
COAST MERIDIAN RD
COQUITLAM BC 157-B4
PORT COQUITLAM BC 157-B4
COBBLE HILL RD
BRITISH COLUMBIA 159-A2
COBURG RD
COBURG OR 210-B7
EUGENE OR 215-B1
EUGENE OR 330-C4
LANE CO OR 210-B6
LANE CO OR 215-B1
LINN CO OR 210-A5
COBURG RD Rt#-99
EUGENE OR 330-A6
N COBURG RD
COBURG OR 210-B7
LANE CO OR 210-B7
LINN CO OR 210-B5
COBURG BOTTOM LOOP RD
LANE CO OR 210-B7
N COCHRAN ST
SPOKANE WA 348-F5
COCHRAN CREEK DR
LINN CO OR 210-C2
COCOLALLA CREEK RD
BONNER CO ID 244-A5
W COE AV
STANFIELD OR 129-A1
E COEUR D'ALENE AV Rt#-97
HARRISON ID 248-A4
KOOTENAI CO ID 248-A4
E COEUR D'ALENE AV U.S.-95
BENEWAH CO ID 115-A3
TENSED ID 115-A3
COFFEE LN NE
MARION CO OR 204-D1
COFFEEPOT RD
LINCOLN CO WA 113-C2
COFFEY RD
BAKER CO OR 130-B3
COFFEY ST
GARDEN CITY ID 253-B2
COFFIN BUTTE RD
BENTON CO OR 207-A3
COGLAN BUTTE RD
LAKE CO OR 144-A3
LAKE CO OR 151-C1
LAKE CO OR 152-A1
COLBURN CULVER RD
BONNER CO ID 107-B2
BONNER CO ID 244-B1
COLBY AV
EVERETT WA 264-D2
EVERETT WA 268-D2
COLCHESTER DR E
MANCHESTER WA 271-H13
COLCHESTER DR SE
MANCHESTER WA 174-C4
MANCHESTER WA 271-H13
COLD CAMP RD
WASCO CO OR 135-C1
COLD CREEK RD
BENTON CO WA 120-B2
COLD SPRING RD
JACKSON CO OR 226-B4
JACKSON CO OR 230-B1
COLD SPRINGS RD
DESCHUTES CO OR 211-C4
LANE CO OR 214-B1
LEWIS CO ID 123-B2
WASCO CO OR 202-D4
S COLD SPRINGS RD
UMATILLA CO OR 129-B1
COLE RD
DOUGLAS CO OR 221-B1
MASON CO WA 180-B3
SAN JUAN CO WA 160-A7
N COLE RD
BOISE ID 253-C3
S COLE RD
ADA CO ID 253-C5
BOISE ID 253-C4
COLE ST
HAINES OR 130-A3
COLE ST Rt#-164
ENUMCLAW WA 110-C3
COLEMAN RD
KLAMATH CO OR 235-D2
MALHEUR CO OR 138-C3
NE COLEMAN RD
JEFFERSON CO OR 208-C1
COLEMAN CREEK RD
JACKSON CO OR 234-B3
COLEMAN VALLEY RD
LAKE CO OR 152-B2
WASHOE CO NV 152-C3
COLE MOUNTAIN RD
CLATSOP CO OR 191-D2
S COLES RD
ISLAND CO WA 171-A1
COLESTIN RD
JACKSON CO OR 234-D6
COLINWOOD RD
TOWN OF SIDNEY BC 159-C2
COLLAWASH RIVER RD
CLACKAMAS CO OR 126-B3
COLLEGE AV Rt#-5
SAINT MARIES ID 248-D7
N COLLEGE AV
COLLEGE PLACE WA 344-F10
WALLA WALLA WEST WA 344-F9
S COLLEGE AV
COLLEGE PLACE WA 344-F12
WALLA WALLA CO WA 344-F12
COLLEGE PKWY
BELLINGHAM WA 258-D10
E COLLEGE RD
MARION CO OR 205-C3
MOUNT ANGEL OR 205-C3
COLLEGE ST Rt#-219
NEWBERG OR 198-D5
YAMHILL CO OR 198-D5
N COLLEGE ST Rt#-219
NEWBERG OR 198-D5
SW COLLEGE ST
MILTON-FREEWATER OR 121-C3
COLLEGE ST NE
LACEY WA 297-G4
COLLEGE ST SE
LACEY WA 297-G7
THURSTON CO WA 297-F11
COLLEGE WY Rt#-47
FOREST GROVE OR 198-B1
COLLEGE WY Rt#-538
MOUNT VERNON WA 260-D10
SKAGIT CO WA 161-C7
SKAGIT CO WA 260-H10
NW COLLEGE WY
BEND OR 332-A5
N COLLIER ST
COQUILLE OR 220-D5
E COLLINS DR
KLICKITAT CO WA 127-C1
COLLINS RD
DESCHUTES CO OR 212-B7
DESCHUTES CO OR 217-B1
LEWIS CO WA 187-D4
SEDRO-WOOLLEY WA 260-H3
SKAGIT CO WA 161-B5
SKAGIT CO WA 260-H3
UNION CO OR 130-B3
WHITMAN CO WA 249-A3
YAKIMA CO WA 243-B4
E COLLINS RD
KITSAP CO WA 271-E13
COLOCKUM RD
CHELAN CO WA 239-B5
KITTITAS CO WA 112-A3
KITTITAS CO WA 239-B7
KITTITAS CO WA 241-D3
COLONIAL DR
JOSEPHINE CO OR 229-B4
COLONIAL RD
DOUGLAS CO OR 221-A5
COLONY RD
SKAGIT CO WA 161-B4
COLONY MT RD
SKAGIT CO WA 161-A4
COLORADO AV
NORTH BEND OR 333-D3
PIERCE CO WA 181-C5
NW COLORADO AV Rt#-372
BEND OR 332-E8
SW COLORADO AV Rt#-372
BEND OR 332-D9
COLORADO RD
CLACKAMAS CO OR 200-C4
COLORADO ST
KELSO WA 303-D11
NE COLORADO ST
PULLMAN WA 249-B5
COLTON RD
BAKER CO OR 130-B3
N COLTON ST
SPOKANE WA 347-A13
COLUMBIA AV
BRIDGEPORT WA 112-C1
DOUGLAS CO WA 112-C1
COLUMBIA AV Rt#-155
COULEE DAM WA 237-C2
COLUMBIA AV Rt#-173
BRIDGEPORT WA 112-C1
E COLUMBIA AV
COLUMBIA CO OR 192-A4
COLUMBIA BLVD
SAINT HELENS OR 192-B1
N COLUMBIA BLVD
PORTLAND OR 192-B7
PORTLAND OR 308-D3
PORTLAND OR 309-E4
NE COLUMBIA BLVD
PORTLAND OR 309-H4
PORTLAND OR 310-A5
PORTLAND OR 311-F7
NE COLUMBIA BLVD U.S.-30
PORTLAND OR 315-H1
COLUMBIA DR
BENTON CO WA 341-E5
JEFFERSON CO OR 208-B7
RICHLAND WA 341-G6
RICHLAND WA 342-A6
E COLUMBIA DR
KENNEWICK WA 343-E10
NW COLUMBIA DR
JEFFERSON CO OR 208-B3
SW COLUMBIA DR
JEFFERSON CO OR 208-B6
W COLUMBIA DR
KENNEWICK WA 343-C9
COLUMBIA DR SE
RICHLAND WA 342-A6
COLUMBIA RD
ADA CO ID 253-B4
DESCHUTES CO OR 217-A2
E COLUMBIA RD
ADA CO ID 253-B4
BOISE ID 253-D4
W COLUMBIA RD
ADA CO ID 253-A4
COLUMBIA ST
CATHLAMET WA 117-B3
DOUGLAS CO WA 112-B2
MESA WA 121-A2
NEW WESTMINSTER BC 156-D6
POMEROY WA 122-B2
VANCOUVER BC 254-H11
COLUMBIA ST Rt#-150
CHELAN WA 236-D3
COLUMBIA ST Rt#-544
NOOKSACK WA 102-B1
NE COLUMBIA ST
KITSAP CO WA 170-C6
SUQUAMISH WA 170-C6
NW COLUMBIA ST
BEND OR 332-D7
SW COLUMBIA ST
BEND OR 332-C9
PORTLAND OR 312-D6
COLUMBIA WY
VANCOUVER WA 306-C6
WALLA WALLA CO WA 121-B3
N COLUMBIA WY
PORTLAND OR 308-A3
COLUMBIA BASIN HWY I-90
ADAMS CO WA 113-C3
COLUMBIA BASIN HWY Rt#-904
CHENEY WA 246-A7
SPOKANE CO WA 246-A7
N COLUMBIA CENTER BLVD
KENNEWICK WA 342-C10
RICHLAND WA 342-C7
S COLUMBIA CENTER BLVD
KENNEWICK WA 342-C11
COLUMBIA HEIGHTS RD
COWLITZ CO WA 189-B2
COWLITZ CO WA 302-H1
KELSO WA 303-A5
LONGVIEW WA 303-A5
LONGVIEW HEIGHTS WA 302-H1
LONGVIEW HEIGHTS WA 303-A5
S COLUMBIAN WY
SEATTLE WA 282-B3
COLUMBIA RIVER HWY I-84
ARLINGTON OR 128-A1
BOARDMAN OR 128-B1
CASCADE LOCKS OR 194-C6
FAIRVIEW OR 200-B1
GILLIAM CO OR 127-C1
GILLIAM CO OR 128-A1
GRESHAM OR 200-B1
HOOD RIVER OR 195-A5
HOOD RIVER CO OR 194-C6
HOOD RIVER CO OR 195-A5
HOOD RIVER CO OR 195-A5
MORROW CO OR 128-B1
MOSIER OR 196-D7
MULTNOMAH CO OR 194-B7
MULTNOMAH CO OR 200-C1
MULTNOMAH CO OR 201-A1
PORTLAND OR 200-B1
PORTLAND OR 315-J2
RUFUS OR 127-C1
SHERMAN CO OR 127-C1
THE DALLES OR 196-D7
TROUTDALE OR 200-B1
WASCO CO OR 127-B1
WASCO CO OR 195-A5
WASCO CO OR 196-D7
WOOD VILLAGE OR 200-B1
COLUMBIA RIVER HWY Rt#-730
UMATILLA CO OR 121-A3
WALLA WALLA CO WA 121-A3
COLUMBIA RIVER HWY U.S.-30
ASTORIA WA 188-D1
COLUMBIA RIVER HWY U.S.-30
ASTORIA WA 300-E5
CLATSKANIE OR 117-B3
CLATSOP CO WA 117-A3
CLATSOP CO WA 188-D1
COLUMBIA CITY OR 192-A3
COLUMBIA CO OR 117-B3
COLUMBIA CO OR 189-A4
COLUMBIA CO OR 192-A3
COLUMBIA CO OR 302-A14
RAINIER OR 189-A4
SAINT HELENS OR 192-A3
SCAPPOOSE OR 192-A3
COLUMBIA RIVER HWY U.S.-730
IRRIGON OR 128-C1
MORROW CO OR 128-C1
UMATILLA OR 129-A1
UMATILLA CO OR 128-C1
UMATILLA CO OR 129-A1
COLUMBIA RIVER RD
FRANKLIN CO WA 121-A2
FRANKLIN CO WA 340-H1
COLUMBIA SCHOOL RD
BURBANK WA 121-A3
COLUMBIA TIE RD
CLARK CO WA 118-A3
COLUMBIA VIEW DR
THE DALLES OR 196-D7
N COLUMBUS AV
GOLDENDALE WA 127-C1
MEDFORD OR 336-B12
S COLUMBUS AV
GOLDENDALE WA 127-C1
JACKSON CO OR 234-A2
KLICKITAT CO WA 127-C1
MEDFORD OR 336-B13
S COLUMBUS AV Rt#-238
MEDFORD OR 336-B12
COLUMBUS ST
ALBANY OR 326-F11
LINN CO OR 207-C6
LINN CO OR 326-E14
COLVER RD
JACKSON CO OR 234-B2
PHOENIX OR 234-B2
TALENT OR 234-B2
COLVILLE RD
TOWN OF ESQUILMALT BC 256-C7
COLVILLE-ALADDIN-NORTHPORT RD
NORTHPORT WA 106-A1
STEVENS CO WA 106-A1
COLVILLE-TIGER RD Rt#-20
STEVENS CO WA 106-A2
COLWOOD DR
DIST OF N VANCOUVER BC 254-H2
COMA RD
LEWIS CO WA 187-B4
COMMERCE AV
BOISE ID 253-C4
LONGVIEW WA 303-A8
S COMMERCE ST
TACOMA WA 293-H4
COMMERCIAL AV
ANACORTES WA 259-H2
COOS BAY OR 333-G10
SPRINGFIELD OR 331-D6
COMMERCIAL AV Rt#-20
ANACORTES WA 259-H4
COMMERCIAL DR
VANCOUVER BC 156-C5
VANCOUVER BC 255-B12
COMMERCIAL ST
ASTORIA WA 300-B5
HARNEY CO OR 137-C3
SPOKANE CO WA 114-C2
WAVERLY WA 114-C2
COMMERCIAL ST U.S.-30
ASTORIA WA 300-C5
E COMMERCIAL ST
WEISER ID 139-A2
W COMMERCIAL ST
ASTORIA WA 300-B5
WEISER ID 139-A2
COMMERCIAL ST NE
SALEM OR 322-J9
COMMERCIAL ST NE Rt#-99E
SALEM OR 322-J10
COMMERCIAL ST SE
SALEM OR 322-H13
SALEM OR 324-G2
SALEM OR 325-A9
COMO LAKE AV
COQUITLAM BC 157-A4
DISTRICT OF COQUITLAM BC 156-D4
COMOX RD
NANAIMO BC 93-A3
COMPTON LN
LANE CO OR 210-A6
COMPTON RD
BRITISH COLUMBIA 159-B5
SE COMPTON RD
CLACKAMAS CO OR 200-C3
COMSTOCK RD
SUTHERLIN OR 221-C1
SW COMSTOCK RD
SUTHERLIN OR 221-C1
CONCOMLY RD NE
MARION CO OR 205-A3
CONCONULLY RD
CONCONULLY WA 104-B2
OKANOGAN CO WA 104-B2
CONCRETE SAUK VALLEY RD
CONCRETE WA 102-C2
SKAGIT CO WA 102-C2
SKAGIT CO WA 103-A2
CONDON RD
CLARK CO WA 193-A1
CONDON WY W
SEATTLE WA 276-D1
CONGER RD U.S.-199
GRANTS PASS OR 335-E10
CONGER CREEK RD
OKANOGAN CO WA 104-B2
CONIFER BLVD
CORVALLIS OR 207-B5
CORVALLIS OR 327-J5

STREET
City State Page-Grid

CONIFER ST NE
MARION CO OR 205-A5
CONKLIN RD
DESCHUTES CO OR 217-A5
S CONKLIN RD
SPOKANE CO WA 247-A5
CONKLING PARK RD
KOOTENAI CO ID 115-A2
KOOTENAI CO ID 248-A6
CONNARN RD
DESCHUTES CO OR 212-B7
CONNECTICUT AV
NORTH BEND OR 333-G4
CONNECTICUT AV SE
FOUR CORNERS OR 325-F2
W CONNECTICUT ST
BELLINGHAM WA 258-C4
CONNECTING RD
MAPLE RIDGE BC 157-C5
PITT MEADOWS BC 157-C5
CONNELL HILL RD
GARFIELD CO WA 122-B2
CONNELLS PRAIRIE RD
PIERCE CO WA 182-C4
CONNELLY RD
SNOHOMISH CO WA 171-D4
CONNER RD
NEZ PERCE CO ID 250-D2
CONNER RD SE
THURSTON CO WA 184-C4
CONNETT RD
CLACKAMAS CO OR 200-D3
E CONNOR RD
SPOKANE CO WA 246-D6
CONRAD RD
LEWIS CO WA 187-C2
CONRADI RD
LEWIS CO WA 187-C2
CONSER DR
CORVALLIS OR 207-B5
CONSER RD
LINN CO OR 207-C3
LINN CO OR 326-E1
MILLERSBURG OR 326-E1
CONSTANCE AV
TOWN OF ESQUIMALT BC 256-C8
CONWAY RD
SKAGIT CO WA 168-B2
COOK AV
DESCHUTES CO OR 217-B1
JEFFERSON CO WA 263-B3
PORT TOWNSEND WA 263-D1
SW COOK AV
WASHINGTON CO OR 198-C1
NE COOK LN
JEFFERSON CO OR 208-C2
COOK RD
BAKER CO OR 130-C3
ISLAND CO WA 167-B4
LEWIS CO WA 187-A2
SATUS WA 120-A2
SEDRO-WOOLLEY WA 161-B5
SKAGIT CO WA 161-B5
COOK ST
CITY OF VICTORIA BC 256-J6
DISTRICT OF SAANICH BC 256-H5
COOK CREEK RD
TILLAMOOK CO OR 191-D4
COOKE RD
KLICKITAT CO WA 196-A4
COOKE CANYON RD
KITTITAS CO WA 241-D4
COOKS CREEK RD
LINCOLN CO OR 206-D3
COOKS HILL RD
CENTRALIA WA 299-A4
LEWIS CO WA 299-A4
COOK-UNDERWOOD RD
SKAMANIA CO WA 195-B4
SKAMANIA CO WA 195-C4
COOLEY RD
DESCHUTES CO OR 217-C1
COOLEY RD NE
MARION CO OR 205-B2
WOODBURN OR 205-B2
W COOLIDGE AV
YAKIMA CO WA 243-A7
COOMBS RD
YAKIMA CO WA 243-D7
COOMBS CANYON RD
UMATILLA CO OR 129-B1
COON CREEK RD
BENEWAH CO ID 248-A7
COON HOLLOW RD
MARION CO OR 133-C1
COOPER RD
LEWIS CO WA 187-D4
LINN CO OR 207-C3
E COOPER RD
SPOKANE CO WA 247-A1
COOPER CREEK RD
DOUGLAS CO OR 221-C1
COOPER HOLLOW RD
POLK CO OR 204-A7
COOPER MOUNTAIN RD
CHELAN CO WA 236-C2
COOPER POINT RD NW
OLYMPIA WA 296-E2
THURSTON CO WA 180-C5
THURSTON CO WA 296-E2
COOPER POINT RD SW
OLYMPIA WA 296-E5
THURSTON CO WA 296-E5
COOPER SPUR RD
HOOD RIVER CO OR 202-C2
COOS BAY-ROSEBURG HWY Rt#-42
COOS CO OR 140-C2
COOS CO OR 220-D4
COQUILLE OR 220-D4
DOUGLAS CO OR 140-C3
DOUGLAS CO OR 141-A2
DOUGLAS CO OR 221-A6
MYRTLE POINT OR 140-C2
WINSTON OR 221-B6
COOS BAY-ROSEBURG HWY Rt#-99
DOUGLAS CO OR 221-B6
DOUGLAS CO OR 334-D14
WINSTON OR 221-B6

COOS BAY-WAGON RD
DOUGLAS CO OR 141-A2
DOUGLAS CO OR 221-A5
COOS CITY-SUMNER RD
COOS CO OR 140-B2
COOS CO OR 220-D2
COOS RIVER HWY
COOS BAY OR 220-D1
COOS CO OR 140-B2
COOS CO OR 218-D7
COOS CO OR 220-D1
COOS RIVER RD
COOS CO OR 140-B2
S COOS RIVER RD
COOS CO OR 140-C2
COPALIS BEACH RD
GRAYS HARBOR CO WA 177-B4
COPALIS CROSSING RD
GRAYS HARBOR CO WA 177-C4
COPCO RD
KLAMATH CO OR 231-C5
SISKIYOU CO CA 150-A3
COPE RD
LEWIS CO WA 187-B4
COPELAND CREEK RD
DOUGLAS CO OR 222-C4
COPLEY RD
CROOK CO OR 213-B6
COPPEI AV U.S.-12
WAITSBURG WA 122-A2
COPPER QUEEN RD
JOSEPHINE CO OR 229-B2
COQUILLE-BANDON HWY Rt#-42S
BANDON OR 220-B6
COOS CO OR 220-C4
COQUILLE OR 220-D5
COQUILLE-FAIRVIEW RD
COOS CO OR 140-C2
COOS CO OR 220-D4
COQUILLE OR 220-D4
COQUILLE-FAT ELK RD
COOS CO OR 220-D5
W CORAL SEA AV
OAK HARBOR WA 167-C3
CORBET DR
BREMERTON WA 270-F9
KITSAP CO WA 270-F9
CORBETT AV
PORTLAND OR 317-F1
CO RD 722
UMATILLA CO OR 129-C1
CO RD 725
UMATILLA CO OR 129-C1
CO RD 802
UMATILLA CO OR 129-B1
CO RD 821
UMATILLA CO OR 129-B1
CO RD 900
MISSION OR 129-B1
UMATILLA CO OR 129-B1
CO RD 900 U.S.-30
PENDLETON OR 129-B1
UMATILLA CO OR 129-B1
CO RD 1046
UMATILLA CO OR 129-C2
CORDATA PKWY
BELLINGHAM WA 158-D7
CORDON RD
FOUR CORNERS OR 323-G10
FOUR CORNERS OR 325-G1
HAYESVILLE OR 323-G8
MARION CO OR 323-G8
MARION CO OR 325-G1
SALEM OR 323-G10
SALEM OR 325-G3
CORDOVA ST
VANCOUVER BC 254-H10
VANCOUVER BC 255-A10
CORDOVA BAY RD
DISTRICT OF SAANICH BC 159-C5
CORDUROY RD
KELSO WA 303-G8
COREY RD
JACKSON CO OR 230-D6
CORKSCREW CANYON RD
STEVENS CO WA 114-A1
CORKSCREW CANYON RD Rt#-291
STEVENS CO WA 114-B1
STEVENS CO WA 246-A1
NW CORNELIUS PASS RD
HILLSBORO OR 199-A1
MULTNOMAH CO OR 192-A6
WASHINGTON CO OR 192-A7
WASHINGTON CO OR 199-A1
CORNELIUS-SCHEFFLIN RD
WASHINGTON CO OR 198-C1
NE CORNELL RD
HILLSBORO OR 198-D1
HILLSBORO OR 199-A1
NW CORNELL RD
BEAVERTON OR 199-B1
HILLSBORO OR 199-B1
MULTNOMAH CO OR 199-B1
PORTLAND OR 199-B1
PORTLAND OR 312-A5
WASHINGTON CO OR 199-B1
CORNETT RD
CROOK CO OR 213-B5
CORNWALL AV
BELLINGHAM WA 258-D6
VANCOUVER BC 254-C11
CORONA AV
MEDFORD OR 336-D9
CORRAL CREEK RD
MALHEUR CO OR 154-C2
YAMHILL CO OR 198-D5
YAMHILL CO OR 199-A6
CORRIN AV SW Rt#-162
ORTING WA 182-C5
CORSON AV S
SEATTLE WA 282-B7
CORVALLIS RD
INDEPENDENCE OR 204-B7
POLK CO OR 204-B7
POLK CO OR 207-B2
CORVALLIS-LEBANON HWY Rt#-34
LEBANON OR 133-C1

CORVALLIS-LEBANON HWY Rt#-34
LINN CO OR 133-C1
LINN CO OR 207-B6
TANGENT OR 207-B6
CORVALLIS-NEWPORT HWY Rt#-34
CORVALLIS OR 327-H11
LINN CO OR 207-B6
LINN CO OR 327-H11
CORVALLIS-NEWPORT HWY U.S.-20
BENTON CO OR 133-A1
CORVALLIS OR 133-A1
CORVALLIS OR 327-E11
LINCOLN CO OR 133-A1
LINCOLN CO OR 206-D3
NEWPORT OR 206-B4
PHILOMATH OR 133-A1
TOLEDO OR 206-C4
COTTAGE AV
CASHMERE WA 238-C2
CLATSOP CO WA 301-G4
GEARHART WA 301-G4
COTTAGE ST
MEDFORD OR 336-D12
E COTTAGE GROVE CONN
COTTAGE GROVE OR 215-B7
COTTAGE GROVE-LORANE RD
COTTAGE GROVE OR 215-A6
LANE CO OR 215-A6
COTTAGE GRV-LORANE RD
LANE CO OR 133-B3
COTTAGE GROVE RESERVOIR RD
LANE CO OR 219-D2
COTTON RD
CITY OF N VANCOUVER BC 255-E7
DIST OF N VANCOUVER BC 255-E7
COTTONWOOD BAY
KOOTENAI CO ID 115-A2
KOOTENAI CO ID 248-A5
COTTONWOOD DR
BIRCH BAY WA 158-B4
MAPLE RIDGE BC 157-D6
RICHLAND WA 341-D2
COTTONWOOD RD
ADAMS CO ID 139-C1
STEVENS CO WA 114-A1
WALLA WALLA CO WA 121-C3
WALLA WALLA CO WA 122-A3
WALLA WALLA CO WA 345-E13
COTTONWOOD ST Rt#-19
ARLINGTON OR 128-A1
SW COTTONWOOD ST
GRANTS PASS OR 335-C10
COTTONWOOD BUTTE RD
IDAHO CO ID 123-B3
COTTONWOOD CANYON RD
YAKIMA CO WA 119-C2
YAKIMA CO WA 243-A7
COTTONWOOD CREEK RD
NEZ PERCE CO ID 123-B2
STEVENS CO WA 106-B3
COUCH RD
DESCHUTES CO OR 217-A2
COUCH MARKET RD
DESCHUTES CO OR 212-B7
COUGAR RD
CROOK CO OR 135-C1
JEFFERSON CO OR 212-C3
COUGAR WY
SKAMANIA CO WA 195-B1
COUGAR BEND RD
LANE CO OR 219-D4
COUGAR CREEK RD
ASOTIN CO WA 122-C3
E COUGAR GULCH RD
KOOTENAI CO ID 247-D4
KOOTENAI CO ID 354-H14
KOOTENAI CO ID 355-A13
W COUGAR GULCH RD
KOOTENAI CO ID 247-D4
COUGAR MOUNTAIN RD
LANE CO OR 219-D3
COUGAR SMITH RD
GRAYS HARBOR CO WA 178-D3
GRAYS HARBOR CO WA 179-A3
COUGHANOUR LN
UNION CO OR 130-A3
COULEE BLVD Rt#-155
ELECTRIC CITY WA 237-C3
GRANT CO WA 237-C3
COULSON RD
LEWIS CO WA 187-D2
COUNCIL RD
ADAMS CO ID 139-C1
VALLEY CO ID 251-C7
COUNCIL ST Rt#-47
FOREST GROVE OR 198-B1
COUNTRY LN
LANE CO OR 210-B7
COUNTRY RD
LINN CO OR 207-B7
COUNTRY CLUB DR
BENTON CO OR 327-A12
CORVALLIS OR 327-A12
COUNTRY CLUB RD
CLACKAMAS OR 320-C5
EUGENE OR 329-J4
EUGENE OR 330-A4
HOOD RIVER CO OR 195-C6
LAKE OSWEGO OR 320-C5
WHITMAN CO WA 249-A6
SW COUNTRY CLUB RD
CLACKAMAS OR 320-D5
CLACKAMAS OR 321-E5
LAKE OSWEGO OR 320-D5
LAKE OSWEGO OR 321-E5
COUNTRY CLUB RD NE
KITSAP CO WA 174-D2
N COUNTRY HOMES BLVD
COUNTRY HOMES WA 346-H13
SPOKANE WA 346-H13
SPOKANE WA 347-A12
TOWN AND COUNTRY WA 346-H13
COUNTRY QUARRY RD
SKAMANIA CO WA 194-B6
COUNTY RD Rt#-27
WHITMAN CO WA 114-C3

COUNTY LINE RD
BENTON CO WA 120-B3
CLATSOP CO OR 191-D2
DOUGLAS CO OR 214-A5
GEM CO ID 139-B3
WASCO CO OR 135-A1
COUNTY RD 12
CLARK CO WA 193-C2
COUNTY RD 139
MODOC CO CA 152-A3
COUNTY WELL RD
BENTON CO WA 120-C3
COUPLAND RD
CLACKAMAS CO OR 200-C6
ESTACADA OR 200-C6
NW COURT AV
PENDLETON OR 129-B1
NW COURT AV U.S.-30
PENDLETON OR 129-B1
SE COURT AV U.S.-30
PENDLETON OR 129-B1
SW COURT AV U.S.-30
PENDLETON OR 129-B1
SE COURT PL
PENDLETON OR 129-B1
SW COURT PL
PENDLETON OR 129-B1
SW COURT PL Rt#-37
PENDLETON OR 129-B1
COURT ST
DUFUR OR 127-B2
JACKSON CO OR 336-C9
MEDFORD OR 336-C10
COURT ST Rt#-74
HEPPNER OR 128-C2
E COURT ST
GOLDENDALE WA 127-C1
NE COURT ST
DUFUR OR 127-B2
W COURT ST
FRANKLIN CO WA 340-H14
FRANKLIN CO WA 341-J2
FRANKLIN CO WA 342-B4
GOLDENDALE WA 127-C1
PASCO WA 341-J2
PASCO WA 343-B6
WEST PASCO WA 342-B4
WEST PASCO WA 343-B6
COURT ST NE
SALEM OR 322-H13
COURTNEY RD
WASHINGTON CO OR 198-D5
YAMHILL CO OR 198-D5
COURTNEY CREEK DR
LINN CO OR 210-D3
COURTNEY CREEK RD
LINN CO OR 210-D3
COUSE CREEK RD
ASOTIN CO WA 123-A3
COUSINS RD
LEWIS CO WA 187-B1
COVE HWY Rt#-237
COVE OR 130-A2
UNION OR 130-A2
UNION CO OR 130-A2
E COVE HWY Rt#-237
UNION OR 130-B2
COVE RD
KITTITAS CO WA 241-A6
WASHINGTON CO ID 139-B2
SW COVE RD
KING CO WA 174-D5
COVE ORCHARD RD
YAMHILL CO OR 198-B4
COVERED BRIDGE RD
WAHKIAKUM CO WA 117-A2
COVILLE RD
POLK CO OR 204-A5
COVINGTON WY SE
KING CO WA 175-D7
COVINGTON-SAWYER RD
KING CO WA 182-D1
COW CAMP RD
DESCHUTES CO OR 211-C5
WASHINGTON CO ID 139-A1
COW CREEK RD
DOUGLAS CO OR 141-A3
DOUGLAS CO OR 225-A3
NEZ PERCE CO ID 250-B2
RIDDLE OR 225-A3
WASHINGTON CO ID 139-B1
W COW CREEK RD
MALHEUR CO OR 146-C2
COWEN PL NE
SEATTLE WA 274-C4
COW HOLLOW RD
MALHEUR CO OR 139-A3
N COWICHE RD
YAKIMA CO WA 119-C1
W COWICHE CANYON RD
YAKIMA CO WA 243-A6
COWICHE MILL RD
YAKIMA CO WA 119-C1
COWICHE-TIETON RD
TIETON WA 119-C1
YAKIMA CO WA 119-C1
COWLITZ AV
CASTLE ROCK WA 187-C7
COWLITZ CO WA 187-C7
E COWLITZ AV
CASTLE ROCK WA 187-C7
COWLITZ ST Rt#-505
LEWIS CO WA 187-D4
TOLEDO WA 187-D4
COWLITZ WY
KELSO WA 303-D8
COWLITZ GARDEN RD
COWLITZ CO WA 303-D4
COWLITZ LOOP RD
LEWIS CO WA 187-C4
COWLITZ RIDGE RD
LEWIS CO WA 187-C4
COX RD
DOUGLAS CO OR 219-B3
COX CREEK RD
DOUGLAS CO OR 219-C3
NW COYER AV
DESCHUTES CO OR 212-C4
COYLE RD
JEFFERSON CO WA 170-A4

NW COYNER AV
DESCHUTES CO OR 212-D4
TERREBONNE OR 212-D4
COYOTE
CROOK CO OR 213-D6
SW COYOTE
DESCHUTES CO OR 212-C6
COYOTE CREEK RD
JOSEPHINE CO OR 229-B1
COYOTE GRADE RD
NEZ PERCE CO ID 250-D2
CRAB CREEK RD
GRANT CO WA 120-C1
E CRAB CREEK RD
LINCOLN CO OR 209-D4
CRACKER CREEK RD
BAKER CO OR 138-A1
CRAIG LN
CROOK CO OR 213-D6
N CRAIG RD
SPOKANE CO WA 246-A4
S CRAIG RD
SPOKANE CO WA 246-A4
CRAIGFLOWER RD
BRITISH COLUMBIA 256-D6
TOWN OF ESQUIMALT BC 256-D6
TOWN OF VIEW ROYAL BC 256-D6
CRAIGFLOWER RD Rt#-1A
TOWN OF VIEW ROYAL BC 256-A5
CRAIG JUNCTION RD
LEWIS CO ID 123-B2
CRAMER RD
CLARK CO WA 192-D4
CRAMER RD KPN
PIERCE CO WA 174-A7
CRANBERRY RD
GRAYS HARBOR CO WA 183-B3
PACIFIC CO WA 186-A4
N CRANE RD
WASHINGTON CO ID 139-C2
CRANE-BUCHANAN RD
HARNEY CO OR 145-C1
CRANE CREEK RD
WASHINGTON CO ID 139-B1
CRANE CREEK RESRVOIR RD
WASHINGTON CO ID 139-B2
CRANE ORCHARD
DOUGLAS CO WA 112-B1
CRANE ORCHARD RD
DOUGLAS CO WA 104-B3
CRANES RD NW
DOUGLAS CO WA 104-B3
CRANE-VENATOR RD
HARNEY CO OR 145-C2
HARNEY CO OR 146-A1
MALHEUR CO OR 146-A1
CRANLEY DR
DISTRICT OF SURREY BC 158-A2
CRATER LP
JEFFERSON CO OR 212-C2
CRATER CREEK MTWY
JACKSON CO OR 227-A2
CRATER CREEK RD
KLAMATH CO OR 227-C5
CRATER LAKE AV
JACKSON CO OR 336-F3
MEDFORD OR 336-E11
CRATER LAKE HWY Rt#-62
EAGLE POINT OR 230-D4
JACKSON CO OR 149-C1
JACKSON CO OR 150-A1
JACKSON CO OR 226-C7
JACKSON CO OR 227-D7
JACKSON CO OR 230-D4
JACKSON CO OR 336-F3
KLAMATH CO OR 227-D7
KLAMATH CO OR 231-C2
MEDFORD OR 336-D8
SHADY COVE OR 230-D4
WHITE CITY OR 230-D6
CRATER LAKE RD
MALHEUR CO OR 146-C2
CRATER LAKE NORTH HWY
DOUGLAS CO OR 223-C7
DOUGLAS CO OR 227-C2
KLAMATH CO OR 227-C2
E CRAW RD
ISLAND CO WA 171-A1
NE CRAWFORD DR
KITSAP CO WA 170-C5
CRAWFORD LN
YAMHILL CO OR 198-C6
CRAWFORD RD
DESCHUTES CO OR 217-A6
LINCOLN CO OR 206-C1
NE CRAWFORD RD
CLARK CO WA 193-B3
CRAWFORD ST
APPLEYARD WA 238-D5
APPLEYARD WA 239-A5
WENATCHEE WA 238-D5
WENATCHEE WA 239-A5
E CRAWFORD ST
DEER PARK WA 114-B1
W CRAWFORD ST
DEER PARK WA 114-B1
CREAMER RD
WHATCOM CO WA 158-B6
CREASY RD
WHATCOM CO WA 158-C4
CREEK DR
LINN CO OR 210-A2
CREEK RD
HARNEY CO OR 137-B3
SISKIYOU CO CA 149-A3
E CREEK RD
TILLAMOOK CO OR 197-D5
CREEK BEND RD
LINN CO OR 210-A2
CREGO HILL RD
LEWIS CO WA 187-A1
CRESCENT AV
EUGENE OR 215-B1
KELSO WA 303-D6
CRESCENT RD
CITY OF VICTORIA BC 257-B11
DISTRICT OF OAK BAY BC 257-B11
DISTRICT OF SURREY BC 158-A1
CRESCENT RD NW
SALEM OR 322-E12

CRESCENT BEACH RD
CLALLAM CO WA 164-C5
CRESCENT BEACH RD KPN
PIERCE CO WA 181-A1
CRESCENT CUT-OFF RD
KLAMATH CO OR 142-C1
E CRESCENT HARBOR RD
ISLAND CO WA 167-C2
OAK HARBOR WA 167-C2
CRESCENT LAKE HWY
KLAMATH CO OR 142-B1
CRESCENT VALLEY DR NW
PIERCE CO WA 174-C7
CRESCENT VALLEY RD SE
KITSAP CO WA 174-C6
CREST DR
EUGENE OR 329-J10
EUGENE OR 330-A10
LANE CO OR 329-H11
W CREST DR
EUGENE OR 329-H11
LANE CO OR 329-H11
CRESTLINE BLVD NW
OLYMPIA WA 296-G2
CRESTLINE DR
LINCOLN CO OR 328-D9
WALDPORT OR 328-E5
S CRESTLINE DR
WALDPORT OR 328-E5
N CRESTLINE ST
SPOKANE WA 347-D13
SPOKANE WA 349-D2
SPOKANE CO WA 347-D13
CRESTVIEW DR
MASON CO WA 180-B3
CRESTVIEW LN
SKAGIT CO WA 161-A6
CRESTVIEW RD
CROOK CO OR 213-D5
SUNNYSLOPE WA 238-D3
CREVISTON DR NW
PIERCE CO WA 174-B7
CREVISTON RD KPS
PIERCE CO WA 181-A3
CRISP LN
LANE CO OR 215-B5
CRITCHFIELD RD
ASOTIN CO WA 250-B5
VINELAND WA 250-B5
CRITES RD
SHERMAN CO OR 127-C2
CRITESER RD
DOUGLAS CO OR 221-A5
S CRITSER RD
CLACKAMAS CO OR 199-D6
CROCKER DR
ALBANY OR 326-A4
CROCKER RD
Santa Clara OR 215-A1
CROFT AV U.S.-2
GOLD BAR WA 110-C1
SNOHOMISH CO WA 110-C1
CROFT LAKE RD
COOS CO OR 224-B1
CROISAN CREEK RD S
MARION CO OR 324-D5
SALEM OR 324-D5
CROMWELL DR NW
PIERCE CO WA 181-B2
CRONIN RD
CROOK CO OR 213-A6
CROOK DR
LINN CO OR 210-A3
CROOKED CREEK RD
LANE CO OR 210-D5
MALHEUR CO OR 146-B3
MALHEUR CO OR 154-B1
CROOKED CREEK RANGE RD
MALHEUR CO OR 154-A1
CROOKED FINGER RD
MARION CO OR 205-D4
CROOKED MILE RD
SNOHOMISH CO WA 102-C3
CROOKED RIVER HWY Rt#-27
CROOK CO OR 135-C3
CROOK CO OR 213-C6
DESCHUTES CO OR 135-C3
PRINEVILLE OR 213-C6
CROOKS RD
GRANT CO WA 237-B3
CROOKS CREEK RD
JOSEPHINE CO OR 233-C1
CROSBY RD
AULT FIELD WA 167-B2
BENTON CO WA 120-C3
ISLAND CO WA 167-B2
W CROSBY RD
ISLAND CO WA 167-B2
CROSBY RD NE
MARION CO OR 205-A1
CROSBY ST Rt#-27
TEKOA WA 114-C3
CROSS RD
KLAMATH CO OR 235-C6
CROSS CREEK RD
DIST OF WEST VANCOUVER BC 254-D1
CROSS ISLAND RD
ISLAND CO WA 167-D4
E CROSSROAD LN
LANE CO OR 210-A6
N CROSS STATE HWY Rt#-20
SEDRO-WOOLLEY WA 161-C5
SKAGIT CO WA 161-C5
CROSSWINDS
DESCHUTES CO OR 217-C1
CROW RD
JOSEPHINE CO OR 229-A4
LANE CO OR 133-B3
LANE CO OR 215-A2
CROW CREEK RD
WALLOWA CO OR 130-C2
WALLOWA CO OR 131-A1
CROWELL LN
NORTH BEND OR 333-F5
CROWFOOT RD
JACKSON CO OR 149-C1
CROWLEY RD
MALHEUR CO OR 138-B3
MALHEUR CO OR 146-B1
POLK CO OR 204-B5

STREET
City State Page-Grid

CROWLEY-RIVERSIDE RD
MALHEUR CO OR 146-A1
SE CROWN RD
CLARK CO WA 193-B7
CROWN ST
VANCOUVER BC 156-A5
CROWN POINT HWY
MULTNOMAH CO OR 194-A7
MULTNOMAH CO OR 200-D1
MULTNOMAH CO OR 201-A1
E CROWN POINT HWY
MULTNOMAH CO OR 200-D1
MULTNOMAH CO OR 201-A1
CROWN POINT RD Rt#-174
DOUGLAS CO WA 237-C2
CROWN PT RD
COOS CO OR 220-C2
CROWSNEST HWY Rt#-3
BRITISH COLUMBIA 103-C1
CROWSON RD
JACKSON CO OR 234-D4
JACKSON CO OR 337-J11
W CROW VALLEY RD
SAN JUAN CO WA 101-C2
CROW-VAUGHN RD
LANE CO OR 133-A3
CRUIKSHANK RD
YAMHILL CO OR 198-B7
CRUMARINE LOOP RD
LATAH CO ID 249-D4
CRUM CANYON RD
CHELAN CO WA 236-A6
CRUSH CRES
TOWNSHIP OF LANGLEY BC 157-C7
CRUSHER CANYON RD
YAKIMA CO WA 243-B5
CRYSTAL CREEK RD
CROOK CO OR 136-A2
CURRY CO OR 224-B4
CRYSTAL LAKE DR
BENTON CO OR 327-H12
CORVALLIS OR 327-H12
CRYSTAL LAKE RD
SNOHOMISH CO WA 171-D6
CRYSTAL MOUNTAIN HWY
PIERCE CO WA 119-A1
CRYSTAL SPRINGS RD
KLAMATH CO OR 150-C2
KLAMATH CO OR 235-D5
CRYSTAL SPRINGS RD NE
KITSAP CO WA 271-F7
C-SW DODSON RD
GRANT CO WA 120-C1
ROYAL CITY WA 120-C1
CUB CREEK RD
OKANOGAN CO WA 104-A2
CULBERTSON DR
HOOD RIVER CO OR 202-C2
CULDESAC CUTOFF RD
CULDESAC ID 123-B2
CULLABY LAKE RD
CLATSOP CO WA 188-B3
CULLEN RD
YAMHILL CO OR 198-D5
CULLUM AV
RICHLAND WA 341-G3
NE CULLY BLVD
PORTLAND OR 310-E7
PORTLAND OR 311-E6
PORTLAND OR 314-D1
S CULTUS BAY RD
ISLAND CO WA 171-A3
CULTUS LAKE RD
BRITISH COLUMBIA 102-C1
DISTRICT OF CHILLIWACK BC 102-C1
CULVER DR SE
MARION CO OR 325-H3
CULVER HWY Rt#-361
CULVER OR 208-B7
JEFFERSON CO OR 208-B6
JEFFERSON CO OR 212-D1
MADRAS OR 208-B6
METOLIUS OR 208-B6
SW CULVER HWY
JEFFERSON CO OR 212-D2
CULVER RD
LANE CO OR 210-A6
CUMBERLAND ST
NEW WESTMINSTER BC 156-D5
CUMBERLAND-KANASKAT RD
KING CO WA 110-C3
CUMMINGS LN N
KEIZER OR 322-J6
CUMMINS CREEK RD
LANE CO OR 209-A4
CUMMINS PEAK RD
LINCOLN CO OR 209-A4
CUNNINGHAM LN
YAMHILL CO OR 198-C4
CUNNINGHAM RD
ADAMS CO WA 121-C1
W CUNNINGHAM RD
ADAMS CO WA 121-B1
W CURLEW LAKE RD
FERRY CO WA 105-B2
CURLY CREEK RD
SKAMANIA CO WA 118-C3
CURRIN RD
CLACKAMAS CO OR 200-C5
CURRY RD
DOUGLAS CO OR 221-B3
CURTIN RD
DOUGLAS CO OR 219-B2
CURTIS RD
BELLINGHAM WA 158-D7
LINN CO OR 210-A6
WHITE SWAN WA 119-C2
N CURTIS RD
BOISE ID 253-C3
S CURTIS RD
ADA CO ID 253-C6
BOISE ID 253-C3
W CURTIS RD
SPOKANE CO WA 246-A7
CURTIS ST
DISTRICT OF BURNABY BC 156-D4
W CURTIS ST U.S.-101
ABERDEEN WA 178-B7
CURTIS HILL RD
LEWIS CO WA 184-A7
LEWIS CO WA 187-A1
W CUSTER DR
SPOKANE WA 348-D6
CUSTER RD SW
LAKEWOOD WA 181-C3
LAKEWOOD WA 294-A7
CUSTER RD W
LAKEWOOD WA 181-C3
CUSTER ST
TUMWATER WA 296-H9
CUSTER SCHOOL RD
WHATCOM CO WA 158-C4
CUTOFF RD
JEFFERSON CO OR 211-D2
JEFFERSON CO OR 212-A2
C W HUGHES RD
WHITMAN CO WA 114-C3
C WILLIAMS RD
BENTON CO WA 121-A3
CY BINGHAM RD
HARNEY CO OR 137-C3
CYMIOTTI RD
KLICKITAT CO WA 196-B3
CYPRESS BOWL RD
DIST OF WEST VANCOUVER BC 156-A2

D

D AV
ANACORTES WA 259-F5
D ST
BAKER CITY OR 138-B1
CULVER OR 208-B7
GRANTS PASS OR 335-E8
HUBBARD OR 205-B1
SALEM OR 322-J12
SALEM OR 323-B12
SPRINGFIELD OR 330-H7
WASHOUGAL WA 193-C7
D ST Rt#-14
CLARK CO WA 193-C7
WASHOUGAL WA 193-C7
D ST Rt#-218
SHANIKO OR 127-C3
D ST Rt#-507
TENINO WA 184-D3
D ST U.S.-12
LEWISTON ID 250-B4
E D ST
GRANTS PASS OR 335-G9
MOSCOW ID 249-C5
TACOMA WA 293-H6
TACOMA WA 295-J1
SW D ST Rt#-361
MADRAS OR 208-C5
W D ST
SPRINGFIELD OR 330-G7
DABOB RD
JEFFERSON CO WA 170-A3
DABOB POST OFFICE RD
JEFFERSON CO WA 170-A4
DAHL RD
YAKIMA CO WA 243-A6
DAHLGREN RD
COLUMBIA CO OR 192-A3
DAHLIA WY
POLK CO OR 204-C5
POLK CO OR 322-A10
DAHLKE RD SW
DOUGLAS CO WA 239-D2
DAILY LN
JOSEPHINE CO OR 229-A6
DAIRY-BONANZA HWY Rt#-70
BONANZA OR 151-A2
KLAMATH CO OR 151-A2
SW DAISY ST
KITSAP CO WA 174-A6
DAISY ST N Rt#-17
GRANT CO WA 112-C2
SOAP LAKE WA 112-C2
DAISY ST S Rt#-17
SOAP LAKE WA 112-C2
DAISY MINE RD
JACKSON CO OR 229-D2
JOSEPHINE CO OR 229-C2
STEVENS CO WA 105-C3
STEVENS CO WA 106-A3
DAKIN ST
BELLINGHAM WA 258-J5
DAKOTA AV
MEDFORD OR 336-B13
DALBY RD
MASON CO WA 173-B7
DALE DR
LINN CO OR 210-B5
DALE LN
CLACKAMAS CO OR 200-B4
DALE RD
BRITISH COLUMBIA 94-B3
DALE ST
WOODLAND WA 192-B1
WOODLAND WA 192-C1
DALLAS RD
BENTON CO WA 341-A4
CITY OF VICTORIA BC 256-F10
CITY OF VICTORIA BC 257-A11
RICHLAND WA 341-A5
WEST RICHLAND WA 341-A4
NE DALLAS ST Rt#-500
CAMAS WA 193-B7
DALLAS-RICKREALL HWY Rt#-223
DALLAS OR 204-A6
POLK CO OR 204-A6
DALLES MILITARY RD
COLLEGE PLACE WA 344-G11
WALLA WALLA WA 344-G11
WALLA WALLA WA 345-A10
WALLA WALLA CO WA 344-F13
DALLES MOUNTAIN RD
KLICKITAT CO WA 127-B1
KLICKITAT CO WA 196-D6
DALLESPORT RD
KLICKITAT CO WA 196-C6
E DALLMAN RD
ISLAND CO WA 168-A7
E DALTON AV
COEUR D'ALENE ID 355-F4
DALTON GARDENS ID 355-F4
KOOTENAI CO ID 355-F4
W DALTON AV
COEUR D'ALENE ID 354-H5
COEUR D'ALENE ID 355-D5
KOOTENAI CO ID 354-H5
DALY CREEK RD
BAKER CO OR 139-A1
DAMMAN RD
KITTITAS CO WA 241-B6
DAMON RD
ADAMS CO WA 113-B3
ADAMS CO WA 121-B1
DAMON RD Rt#-115
GRAYS HARBOR CO WA 177-B6
OCEAN SHORES WA 177-B6
DAMSON RD
SNOHOMISH CO WA 171-C5
DANBY DR SW
THURSTON CO WA 184-B3
DANE LN
LANE CO OR 210-A6
N DANEBO AV
EUGENE OR 329-A4
S DANEBO AV
EUGENE OR 329-A6
DANEKAS RD
ADAMS CO WA 113-C3
ADAMS CO WA 114-A3
LINCOLN CO WA 114-A3
RITZVILLE WA 113-C3
DANIELS RD
MASON CO WA 180-B2
DAN KELLY RD
CLALLAM CO WA 165-A6
DANNEN RD
LINN CO OR 210-B2
DANNER LP
MALHEUR CO OR 147-A3
DANNER RD
MALHEUR CO OR 146-C3
MALHEUR CO OR 147-A3
DARBY RD
LATAH CO ID 249-D4
DARK HOLLOW RD
JACKSON CO OR 234-A2
S DARKNELL RD
SPOKANE CO WA 247-A7
E DARLAND ST
GOLDENDALE WA 127-C1
DARLEY RD
MARION CO OR 133-C1
DARRELL AV
WINSTON OR 221-B6
DARRINGTN BNTTS STR RD Rt#-530
DARRINGTON WA 103-A3
SKAGIT CO WA 103-A3
SNOHOMISH CO WA 103-A3
DART CREEK RD
COLUMBIA CO OR 192-A1
DARTER RD
KITSAP CO WA 170-B6
W DARTFORD DR
FAIRWOOD WA 346-J6
FAIRWOOD WA 347-A6
SPOKANE CO WA 346-J6
DARTMOUTH ST U.S.-95
ADAMS CO ID 139-C1
COUNCIL ID 139-C1
SW DASH POINT RD Rt#-509
FEDERAL WAY WA 182-A1
PIERCE CO WA 182-A1
SE DATE AV
COLLEGE PLACE WA 344-F11
DAVENPORT ST
RICHLAND WA 341-G2
DAVID AV
COQUITLAM BC 157-B4
DAVID RD
WHITMAN CO WA 249-C4
DAVID HILL RD
WASHINGTON CO OR 198-B1
DAVIDSON AV
WOODLAND WA 192-B1
DAVIDSON RD
POLK CO OR 207-B1
DAVIE ST
VANCOUVER BC 254-E9
DAVIES RD
BRITISH COLUMBIA 159-B5
N DAVIES RD
SNOHOMISH CO WA 171-D1
S DAVIES RD
SNOHOMISH CO WA 171-D2
DAVIS DR
HOOD RIVER CO OR 195-C7
DAVIS LN
VALLEY CO ID 252-D2
DAVIS RD
ADAMS CO WA 113-B3
ASOTIN CO WA 123-A3
BENTON CO WA 120-C3
COWLITZ CO WA 189-D1
CROOK CO OR 213-D6
LATAH CO ID 249-D2
LINCOLN CO WA 113-C3
LINN CO OR 207-C7
SISKIYOU CO CA 150-C3
SW DAVIS RD
BEAVERTON OR 199-A2
DAVIS ST
MCCALL ID 251-D5
DAVIS WY Rt#-270
PULLMAN WA 249-A5
WHITMAN CO WA 249-A5
DAVIS CREEK RD
JOSEPHINE CO OR 233-B1
DAVIS CREEK RD NE
MARION CO OR 205-D4
DAVIS PEAK RD
COWLITZ CO WA 118-A3
DAVISSON RD
LANE CO OR 215-C6
S DAVIS SPUR RD
COWLITZ CO WA 189-D1
DAWES HILL RD
COQUITLAM BC 157-A5
DAWSON RD
BENTON CO OR 133-B2
DAY RD
IDAHO CO ID 123-C3
WASHINGTON CO OR 199-B5
E DAY RD
SPOKANE CO WA 246-D1
SPOKANE CO WA 347-J3
S DAY RD
ISLAND CO WA 167-C7
NE DAY RD E
KITSAP CO WA 174-C1
NE DAY RD W
KITSAP CO WA 174-C1
DAY HILL RD
CLACKAMAS CO OR 200-C6
DAY ISLAND RD
EUGENE OR 330-B6
DAY SCHOOL RD
KLAMATH CO OR 231-D5
DAYS CREEK RD
DOUGLAS CO OR 141-B3
DAYS CREEK CUTOFF RD
DOUGLAS CO OR 225-C1
E DAYTON AV
DAYTON WA 122-A2
W DAYTON AV
DAYTON WA 122-A2
DAYTON AV N
SHORELINE WA 171-A7
DAYTON RD
DESCHUTES CO OR 212-B7
DAYTON ST
ALTAMONT OR 338-H9
S DAYTON ST
KENNEWICK WA 343-D14
DAYTON-AIRPORT RD
MASON CO WA 179-D2
DAYTON-AIRPORT RD Rt#-102
MASON CO WA 179-D2
MASON CO WA 180-A2
DAYTON BYPASS RD Rt#-18
YAMHILL CO OR 198-B7
DEAD INDIAN RD
ASHLAND OR 337-J9
JACKSON CO OR 150-A2
JACKSON CO OR 234-D4
JACKSON CO OR 337-J9
KLAMATH CO OR 150-B2
DEAD MAN RD
CHELAN CO WA 238-B2
N DEADMAN RD
GARFIELD CO WA 122-B2
DEADMAN CREEK RD
DOUGLAS CO OR 141-C3
DEADMAN GULCH RD
MALHEUR CO OR 146-C1
DEAD POINT RD
HOOD RIVER CO OR 195-B7
DEADY CROSSING RD
DOUGLAS CO OR 221-C2
DEAL RD
ADAMS CO WA 113-B3
ADAMS CO WA 121-B1
DEAN MOUNTAIN RD
COOS CO OR 218-C6
DOUGLAS CO OR 218-D2
DEAN PARK RD
DIST OF NORTH SAANICH BC 159-C3
DEARBORN AV NE
KEIZER OR 322-J5
KEIZER OR 323-A5
S DEARBORN ST
SEATTLE WA 278-A7
DE ARMOND RD
POLK CO OR 207-A3
DEBAST RD
COLUMBIA CO OR 189-B4
DE BERRY RD
LANE CO OR 215-B5
DECATUR AV
BREMERTON WA 270-G11
DECEPTION RD
SKAGIT CO WA 160-C7
SKAGIT CO WA 259-H14
DECKER RD
BENTON CO OR 133-B2
DECKERVILLE RD
MASON CO WA 179-B2
DEEGAN RD W
MASON CO WA 180-A3
DEEP CREEK RD
LEWIS CO WA 184-A7
DEEP LAKE BOUNDARY RD
STEVENS CO WA 106-B1
DEEP RIVER VALLEY RD
WAHKIAKUM CO WA 117-A2
DEER DR
KOOTENAI CO ID 248-A3
DEER RD
WHEELER CO OR 136-B2
N DEER ST
PRINEVILLE OR 213-D5
DEER CREEK RD
JACKSON CO OR 226-D3
JACKSON CO OR 227-A3
JOSEPHINE CO OR 233-B2
KLAMATH CO OR 227-A3
STEVENS CO WA 106-A3
S DEER CREEK RD
DOUGLAS CO OR 221-D5
DEER CREEK-BOULDER CREEK RD
FERRY CO WA 105-B1
DEER FLAT RD
ADA CO ID 253-A5
CANYON CO ID 147-B1
W DEER FLAT RD
ADA CO ID 253-A5
DEERHORN RD
LANE CO OR 133-C3
DEER LAKE AV
DISTRICT OF BURNABY BC 156-D5
DEER LAKE PL
DISTRICT OF BURNABY BC 156-D5
DEER LAKE LOOP RD
STEVENS CO WA 106-B3
DEER PARK DR SE
MARION CO OR 325-J4
SALEM OR 325-J4
DEER PARK RD
CLALLAM CO WA 165-C7
DEER PARK-MILAN RD
DEER PARK WA 114-B1
SPOKANE CO WA 114-B1
E DEER PARK-MILAN RD
SPOKANE CO WA 114-B1
W DEER PARK-MILAN RD
SPOKANE CO WA 114-B1
DEER RIDGE RD
DESCHUTES CO OR 211-D4
DEER TRAIL LN
JACKSON CO OR 234-B3
DEER VALLEY RD
NEWPORT WA 106-C3
PEND OREILLE CO WA 106-C3
DE FRATES RD
COLUMBIA CO OR 189-C6
DEGGLER RD
LEWIS CO WA 118-A2
SW DEHAVEN ST
MILTON-FREEWATER OR 121-C3
DEHLER RD
CROOK CO OR 213-C3
DEHLINGER LN
KLAMATH CO OR 235-D6
DEINHARD LN
MCCALL ID 251-C5
VALLEY CO ID 251-D5
DEJONG RD
POLK CO OR 204-A3
SW DEJONG RD
YAMHILL CO OR 204-A3
DEKAY RD
GRAYS HARBOR CO WA 177-D5
DEKKER RD
YAKIMA CO WA 120-B2
DELAMETER RD
COWLITZ CO WA 187-B7
COWLITZ CO WA 189-B1
DELANEY RD
FRANKLIN CO WA 121-B2
DELANEY RD SE
MARION CO OR 324-J12
MARION CO OR 325-A12
MARION CO OR 325-A12
TURNER OR 325-E12
DELANO RD KPS
PIERCE CO WA 181-A2
DELBROOK AV
DIST OF N VANCOUVER BC 255-A2
DELENA-MAYGER RD
COLUMBIA CO OR 189-A4
DELEZENNE RD
GRAYS HARBOR CO WA 117-B1
DELFATTI LN
KLAMATH CO OR 235-C5
DELICIOUS ST
DESCHUTES CO OR 212-A7
DELINTMENT LAKE RD
HARNEY CO OR 136-C3
DELL AV
WALLA WALLA WA 344-F7
WALLA WALLA WEST WA 344-F7
DELL RD W
WASCO CO OR 196-B6
DELL ADAMS RD
MASON CO WA 179-C3
DELLMOOR LP
CLATSOP CO WA 188-B4
DELMAR DR E
SEATTLE WA 278-B1
DELMAR RD
COOS CO OR 220-D3
DELPHI RD NW
THURSTON CO WA 296-A3
DELPHI RD SW
THURSTON CO WA 180-B7
THURSTON CO WA 184-B1
THURSTON CO WA 296-A6
DELRIDGE WY SW
KING WA 285-G3
SEATTLE WA 281-G7
SEATTLE WA 285-G2
DEL RIO RD
DOUGLAS CO WA 113-A1
DEL RIO RD E
DOUGLAS CO WA 237-A2
DEL RIO COULEE CITY RD
DOUGLAS CO WA 113-A1
DELTA AV
DISTRICT OF BURNABY BC 255-J13
DELTA HWY
EUGENE OR 329-J3
DELTA ST
KLAMATH FALLS OR 338-C6
DELTA LINE RD
WHATCOM CO WA 158-C4
DELTAPORT WY
DISTRICT OF DELTA BC 101-C1
DELTA WATERS RD
JACKSON CO OR 336-F7
MEDFORD OR 336-F7
DEMARAY DR
JOSEPHINE CO OR 229-A7
JOSEPHINE CO OR 335-A12
DEMPSEY RD
CLALLAM CO WA 164-D6
DIST OF N VANCOUVER BC 255-E1
E DENISON-CHATTAROY RD
SPOKANE CO WA 114-C1
W DENISON-CHATTAROY RD
SPOKANE CO WA 114-B1
DENMAN ST
VANCOUVER BC 254-E9
DENMARK ST SW
THURSTON CO WA 184-B4
SW DENNEY RD
BEAVERTON OR 199-B2
DENNIS RD
BENTON CO WA 120-C3
DENNY WY
SEATTLE WA 277-H4
SEATTLE WA 278-A4
E DENNY WY
SEATTLE WA 278-A4
SEATTLE WA 279-E4
W DENNY WY
SEATTLE WA 277-H4
DENNY SCHOOL RD
LINN CO OR 133-C1
W DENO RD
SPOKANE CO WA 246-A4
DENT RD
FRANKLIN CO WA 340-J14
N DENVER AV
PORTLAND OR 308-E4
DENVER RD
IDAHO CO ID 123-C3
S DENVER ST
ASTORIA WA 300-B6
DENVER ST SE
TURNER OR 325-G12
DEPARTURE BAY RD
NANAIMO BC 93-A3
DERRICK CAVES RD
LAKE CO OR 143-B2
DESAVADO RD
SISKIYOU CO CA 150-A3
DESCHUTES AV U.S.-197
MAUPIN OR 127-B3
DESCHUTES DR
JEFFERSON CO OR 208-B5
NW DESCHUTES DR
JEFFERSON CO OR 208-B3
DESCHUTES PKWY
OLYMPIA WA 296-G6
TUMWATER WA 296-G6
NW DESCHUTES PL U.S.-20
BEND OR 332-E6
E DESCHUTES RD
DESCHUTES CO OR 142-C1
DESCHUTES ST
WASCO OR 127-C1
DESCHUTES WY
TUMWATER WA 296-H9
DESCHUTES-PLEASNT RIDGE MRKT RD
DESCHUTES CO OR 212-C7
DESCHUTES RIVER RD
MAUPIN OR 127-B3
WASCO CO OR 127-B3
DESERT RD
GEM CO ID 139-B3
W DESKA DR
SPOKANE CO WA 348-D11
DES MOINES MEM DR S Rt#-509
BURIEN WA 288-A7
BURIEN WA 290-A1
KING WA 288-A7
KING WA 290-A1
SEATAC WA 290-A1
DES MOINES MEMORIAL DR S
BURIEN WA 288-A4
DES MOINES WA 290-A3
KING WA 286-B4
KING WA 288-A4
SEATAC WA 288-A4
SEATAC WA 290-A3
NW DESPAIN AV
PENDLETON OR 129-B1
DESPAIN RD
UMATILLA CO OR 129-A1
DESPAIN GULCH RD
UMATILLA CO OR 129-B1
DETHMAN RIDGE DR
HOOD RIVER CO OR 195-C6
DETROIT BLVD
ALGONA WA 182-B2
KING CO WA 182-B2
DEVELOPMENT AV
BOISE ID 253-C3
DEVER-CONNER RD
LINN CO OR 207-C3
DEVILLE RD
SKAMANIA CO WA 194-A6
DEVILS CANYON RD
FRANKLIN CO WA 121-B2
DEVILS GAP RD
LINCOLN CO WA 114-A1
E DEVILS LAKE RD
LINCOLN CITY OR 203-B4
LINCOLN CO OR 203-B4
W DEVILS LAKE RD
LINCOLN CITY OR 203-A4
LINCOLN CO OR 203-A4
DEVILS MTN RD
SKAGIT CO WA 168-B1
DEVILS WELL RD
LINCOLN CO OR 206-D4
DEVINE RIDGE RD
HARNEY CO OR 137-B3
DE VRIES RD
ISLAND CO WA 167-C2
DEWATO RD W
KITSAP CO WA 173-C4
DEWATTO RD
KITSAP CO WA 173-D4
MASON CO WA 173-D4
MASON CO WA 174-A4
DEWATTO-HOLLY RD
MASON CO WA 173-C4
DEWDNEY TRUNK RD
DISTRICT OF MISSION BC 94-B3
MAPLE RIDGE BC 94-B3
MAPLE RIDGE BC 157-C5
PITT MEADOWS BC 157-B5
DEWEY AV Rt#-7
BAKER CITY OR 138-B1
DEWEY ST
BREMERTON WA 270-G11
DEWEY CREEK LP
LINCOLN CO OR 206-C2
DEW VALLEY RD
COOS CO OR 220-A7
S DHOOGHE RD
CLACKAMAS CO OR 126-A3
DIAGONAL ST Rt#-129
CLARKSTON WA 250-B4
DIAL LN
UNION CO OR 130-A2
DIAMOND LN
HARNEY CO OR 145-B3
DIAMOND HILL DR
LINN CO OR 210-A4
DIAMOND HILL RD
HARRISBURG OR 210-A5
LINN CO OR 210-A5

STREET / City State / Page-Grid

NE DIAMOND LAKE BLVD Rt#-138
ROSEBURG OR 221-C4
ROSEBURG OR 334-H7
E DIAMOND LAKE HWY Rt#-138
DOUGLAS CO OR 223-D7
KLAMATH CO OR 142-B2
KLAMATH CO OR 223-D7
W DIAMOND LAKE HWY Rt#-230
DOUGLAS CO OR 223-B7
DOUGLAS CO OR 226-D3
DOUGLAS CO OR 227-A1
JACKSON CO OR 226-D3
KLAMATH CO OR 142-C3
DIAMOND MATCH CAMP RD
CLEARWATER CO ID 123-C1
DIAMOND POINT RD
CLALLAM CO WA 166-C7
JEFFERSON CO WA 166-C7
DICK RD
GRANT CO WA 242-C2
WASHINGTON CO OR 192-A7
DICKENSHEET RD
BONNER CO ID 107-A2
DICKENSON RD
BRITISH COLUMBIA 93-A3
NANAIMO BC 93-A3
DICKEY RD
DESCHUTES CO OR 217-D2
DICKEY RD NW
KITSAP CO WA 174-A2
DICKEY PRAIRIE RD
CLACKAMAS CO OR 126-A3
DICK GEORGE RD
JOSEPHINE CO OR 233-B5
DIETZ AV NE
KEIZER OR 322-J6
KEIZER OR 323-A6
E DIGBY RD
MOUNT VERNON WA 260-E13
DIGGER RD
WASCO CO OR 196-A6
DIKE BYPS U.S.-12
LEWISTON ID 250-B4
DIKE RD
COLUMBIA CO OR 189-D7
COLUMBIA CO OR 192-A4
COWLITZ CO WA 189-D7
COWLITZ CO WA 192-B1
SKAGIT CO WA 168-B1
SKAGIT CO WA 260-A14
SNOHOMISH CO WA 168-D5
WHATCOM CO WA 161-C1
W DIKE ST
MOUNT VERNON WA 260-A14
SKAGIT CO WA 260-A14
DIKE ACCESS RD
COWLITZ CO WA 189-D7
WOODLAND WA 189-D7
DILLARD HWY Rt#-99
DOUGLAS CO OR 221-B6
DILLARD RD
LANE CO OR 215-B4
DILLEY RD
WASHINGTON CO OR 198-B1
DILLON FALLS RD
DESCHUTES CO OR 217-A4
NW DIMMICK ST
GRANTS PASS OR 335-E8
DIMRILL DALE RD
SKAMANIA CO WA 194-A6
DINGO
JEFFERSON CO OR 212-C3
DINSMORE BRDG
CITY OF RICHMOND BC 156-B6
DINWITTY LN
MALHEUR CO OR 147-A3
DISASTER PEAK RD
MALHEUR CO OR 154-B2
DISCOVERY AV SE
OCEAN SHORES WA 298-F4
DISCOVERY RD
JEFFERSON CO WA 166-D7
JEFFERSON CO WA 263-A9
PORT TOWNSEND WA 263-F4
S DISHMAN RD
DISHMAN WA 350-D9
SPOKANE CO WA 350-D9
E DISHMAN-MICA RD
SPOKANE CO WA 246-D5
SPOKANE CO WA 247-A5
S DISHMAN-MICA RD
DISHMAN WA 350-E12
OPPORTUNITY WA 350-E12
SPOKANE CO WA 246-D5
SPOKANE CO WA 350-E12
S DISHMAN-MICA RD Rt#-27
SPOKANE CO WA 247-A5
DISTRICT LINE RD
BENTON CO WA 120-C3
DITCH RD
DESCHUTES CO OR 212-D4
DITCH CREEK RD
JACKSON CO OR 229-D3
DIVERS RD
CLACKAMAS CO OR 200-C6
NE DIVIDE RD
JEFFERSON CO OR 135-C1
DIVISION AV
EPHRATA WA 112-C3
TACOMA WA 293-F4
S DIVISION AV Rt#-225
BENTON CITY WA 120-C3
DIVISION AV E
EPHRATA WA 112-C3
DIVISION AV NE
SUQUAMISH WA 170-C7
DIVISION AV W
EPHRATA WA 112-C3
E DIVISION LN
TACOMA WA 295-J2
N DIVISION RD
DOUGLAS CO WA 112-B2
GRANT CO WA 242-A3
S DIVISION RD
DOUGLAS CO WA 112-B2
GRANT CO WA 242-A4
DIVISION ST
BEND OR 332-E7
CASHMERE WA 238-C2
DOUGLAS CO OR 225-C1
GRANT CO WA 242-C3
KELSO WA 303-D6
MOSES LAKE WA 242-C3
MYRTLE CREEK OR 225-C1
OLYMPIA WA 296-F2
THURSTON CO WA 296-F2
DIVISION ST Rt#-20
TWISP WA 104-A3
DIVISION ST Rt#-204
ELGIN OR 130-A1
UNION CO OR 130-A1
DIVISION ST Rt#-372
BEND OR 332-F8
DIVISION ST U.S.-20
BEND OR 332-F6
E DIVISION ST
MOUNT VERNON WA 260-D12
N DIVISION ST
CASHMERE WA 238-C2
CHELAN CO WA 238-C2
RITZVILLE WA 113-C3
SANDPOINT ID 244-A2
WALLA WALLA WA 345-C7
N DIVISION ST Rt#-21
ODESSA WA 113-B3
N DIVISION ST Rt#-27
PALOUSE WA 249-B1
N DIVISION ST U.S.-2
SPOKANE WA 346-J12
SPOKANE WA 347-A14
SPOKANE WA 349-A4
TOWN AND COUNTRY WA 346-J12
TOWN AND COUNTRY WA 347-A14
TOWN AND COUNTRY WA 349-A4
N DIVISION ST U.S.-395
COUNTRY HOMES WA 346-J11
COUNTRY HOMES WA 347-A8
FAIRWOOD WA 347-A8
SPOKANE WA 346-J11
TOWN AND COUNTRY WA 346-J11
NE DIVISION ST
GRESHAM OR 200-B2
NW DIVISION ST
GRESHAM OR 200-A2
MYRTLE CREEK OR 225-C1
S DIVISION ST
ADAMS CO WA 113-C3
CASHMERE WA 238-C2
MOSES LAKE WA 242-C3
RITZVILLE WA 113-C3
SANDPOINT ID 244-A2
WALLA WALLA WA 345-C8
S DIVISION ST Rt#-225
BENTON CITY WA 120-C3
S DIVISION ST U.S.-2
SPOKANE WA 349-A9
SE DIVISION ST
GRESHAM OR 200-A2
PORTLAND OR 200-A2
PORTLAND OR 313-G7
PORTLAND OR 317-G1
PORTLAND OR 318-C1
PORTLAND OR 319-H1
W DIVISION ST Rt#-536
MOUNT VERNON WA 260-B12
DIVISION ST E
QUINCY WA 112-B3
DIVISION ST N
SOAP LAKE WA 112-C2
DIVISION ST NE
SALEM OR 322-H12
DIVISION ST S
GRANT CO WA 112-C2
KELLOGG ID 115-C2
SOAP LAKE WA 112-C2
DIVISION FENCE RD
KLICKITAT CO WA 196-C1
DIXIE CREEK RD
BAKER CO OR 138-C2
GRANT CO OR 137-B2
WASHINGTON CO ID 139-B1
DIXIE MOUNTAIN RD
WASHINGTON CO OR 125-C1
SE DIXON DR
JEFFERSON CO OR 208-C6
DIXON LP
DESCHUTES CO OR 217-D2
DIXON RD
CROOK CO OR 213-B5
DIXON MILL RD
WASHINGTON CO OR 198-C3
DIXONVILLE RD
DOUGLAS CO OR 221-D5
D MEYER RD
WHITMAN CO WA 249-A7
DOAK RD
KLAMATH CO OR 231-D5
DOAKS FERRY RD
POLK CO OR 322-D9
SALEM OR 322-D9
DOAN RD
COLUMBIA CO OR 189-B4
E DOBBIE POINT LN
SHERMAN CO OR 127-C3
DOBBIN RD
WALLOWA CO OR 130-C2
DOBER RD
WASHINGTON CO OR 198-C2
DOCK RD
KLICKITAT CO WA 196-D7
DOCK ST Rt#-105
WESTPORT WA 298-G11
DOCKTON RD SW
KING CO WA 174-D6
E DODD RD
KOOTENAI CO ID 245-A4
DODDS RD
DESCHUTES CO OR 135-B3
DODES CREEK RD
JACKSON CO OR 226-A7
DODGE RD
JACKSON CO OR 230-C4
DODGE PARK BLVD
MULTNOMAH CO OR 200-C2
SE DODGE PARK BLVD
MULTNOMAH CO OR 200-C2
DODGE VALLEY RD
SKAGIT CO WA 167-D1
DODSON RD
EPHRATA WA 112-C3
GRANT CO WA 112-C3
DOE CREEK RD
DOUGLAS CO OR 225-A3
DOERFLER RD SE
MARION CO OR 205-C6
DOERNER CTO
DOUGLAS CO OR 221-A4
DOERNER RD
DOUGLAS CO OR 221-A4
DOETSCH RD
COLUMBIA CO OR 189-C7
DOG RD
GRANT CO OR 137-B2
DOG LAKE RD
LAKE CO OR 151-C2
LAKE CO OR 152-A2
DOG RIDGE RD
NEWBERG OR 198-D6
YAMHILL CO OR 198-D6
DOGWOOD DR
EVERETT WA 264-B7
EVERETT WA 268-B1
DOGWOOD LN
JEFFERSON CO OR 208-B4
NE DOGWOOD LN
JEFFERSON CO OR 208-C4
E DOGWOOD RD
FRANKLIN CO WA 121-A2
W DOLARWAY RD
ELLENSBURG WA 241-B5
DOLE RD
DOUGLAS CO OR 221-B7
DOUGLAS CO OR 225-C1
MYRTLE CREEK OR 225-C1
NE DOLE VALLEY RD
CLARK CO WA 193-C3
DOLLARHIDE RD
WHEELER CO OR 136-B1
DOLLARTON HWY
DIST OF N VANCOUVER BC 156-D3
DIST OF N VANCOUVER BC 255-H7
DOMINIC RD NE
MARION CO OR 205-B3
DONAHUE RD
MULTNOMAH CO OR 200-D2
MULTNOMAH CO OR 201-A2
DONALD RD
MARION CO OR 199-A7
WAPATO WA 120-A2
YAKIMA CO WA 120-A2
DONALDSON RD
JOSEPHINE CO OR 335-D1
DONALD-WAPATO RD
YAKIMA CO WA 120-A2
DONELLY RD
HARNEY CO OR 136-C3
HARNEY CO OR 144-C1
HARNEY CO OR 145-A1
DONEY RD
DESCHUTES CO OR 212-D3
JEFFERSON CO OR 212-D3
DONKEY CREEK RD
GRAYS HARBOR CO WA 109-A2
GRAYS HARBOR CO WA 178-A1
NW DONNELLY LN
YAMHILL CO OR 198-A6
DONNELLY RD
SKAGIT CO WA 161-A7
DONOVAN AV
BELLINGHAM WA 258-D11
DONRUSS DR
DOUGLAS CO OR 221-A3
DOOLEY MOUNTAIN HWY Rt#-245
BAKER CO OR 138-A1
DOPP RD
YAMHILL CO OR 198-C4
DORAN RD
WHATCOM CO WA 161-C2
SE DORION AV U.S.-30
PENDLETON OR 129-B1
SW DORION AV U.S.-30
PENDLETON OR 129-B1
DORMAIER RD
SHERMAN CO OR 127-C1
DORNING RD
LEWIS CO WA 187-C2
DORRANCE MEADOW RD
DESCHUTES CO OR 143-A1
DORRIS BROWNELL RD
SISKIYOU CO CA 150-C3
S DORSET RD
SPOKANE CO WA 246-B5
DORSEY RD
KLICKITAT CO WA 196-A3
SW DOSCH RD
PORTLAND OR 316-B2
DOSEWALLIPS RD
JEFFERSON CO WA 109-C1
DOT RD
KLICKITAT CO WA 120-A3
KLICKITAT CO WA 128-A1
S DOUBLE BLUFF RD
ISLAND CO WA 170-D2
DOUBLE CREEK LN
SKAGIT CO WA 161-B4
DOUBLEDAY RD
JACKSON CO OR 150-A1
DOUBLE O RD
HARNEY CO OR 145-A2
DOUGHERTY DR
CASTLE ROCK WA 187-C7
COWLITZ CO WA 187-C7
DOUGHTY RD
BAY CITY OR 197-B1
TILLAMOOK CO OR 197-B1
DOUGLAS AV
BELLINGHAM WA 258-C10
GERVAIS OR 205-A2
MARION CO OR 205-A2
SNOHOMISH WA 265-H4
N DOUGLAS AV
PASCO WA 343-J7
NE DOUGLAS AV
DOUGLAS CO OR 221-C4
ROSEBURG OR 221-C4
NE DOUGLAS AV
ROSEBURG OR 334-J7
SE DOUGLAS AV
ROSEBURG OR 334-H7
N DOUGLAS BLVD Rt#-99
WINSTON OR 221-B6
W DOUGLAS BLVD Rt#-42
WINSTON OR 221-B6
DOUGLAS CRES
LANGLEY BC 158-C1
VANCOUVER BC 254-E13
DOUGLAS DR
PACIFIC CO WA 186-A2
DOUGLAS RD
DISTRICT OF BURNABY BC 156-D4
DISTRICT OF BURNABY BC 255-G11
VALLEY CO ID 251-C7
WHATCOM CO WA 158-B6
YAKIMA CO WA 243-A7
DOUGLAS ST
LONGVIEW WA 302-J10
LONGVIEW WA 303-A10
DOUGLAS ST Rt#-1
CITY OF VICTORIA BC 256-G6
DISTRICT OF SAANICH BC 256-G6
DOUGLAS FALLS RD
STEVENS CO WA 106-A2
SE DOVER LN
JEFFERSON CO OR 208-C6
SW DOVER LN
JEFFERSON CO OR 208-B6
S DOVER RD
SPOKANE CO WA 114-B2
DOVER ST
DISTRICT OF BURNABY BC 156-C5
MOSES LAKE NORTH WA 242-C2
DOW RD
KLICKITAT CO WA 196-D7
DOWD RD
COLUMBIA CO OR 192-A1
W DOWER RD
KOOTENAI CO ID 247-D4
SE DOWLING RD
CLACKAMAS CO OR 200-D5
DOWNES RD
DISTRICT OF MATSQUI BC 102-B1
DOWNEY RD
DIST OF NORTH SAANICH BC 159-B2
SKAGIT CO WA 160-D7
DOWNEY GULCH RD
CHELAN CO WA 236-B4
S DOWNING DR
SEASIDE WA 301-F10
E DOWNING RD Rt#-507
CENTRALIA WA 184-C5
LEWIS CO WA 184-C5
S DOWNING ST
SEASIDE WA 301-F9
DOWN RIVER RD Rt#-128
LEWISTON ID 250-B4
W DOWNRIVER PARK DR
SPOKANE WA 348-D6
DOWNS RD NE
MARION CO OR 205-B4
DOWTY RD
CLACKAMAS CO OR 200-B5
DOYLE RD
CLARK CO WA 192-C1
N DOYLE RD
KOOTENAI CO ID 248-D2
DRAGICH RD
COWLITZ CO WA 189-A1
DRAHAM ST NE
THURSTON CO WA 297-H3
DRAIN RD
DOUGLAS CO OR 219-A3
DRAIN 10 RD
MODOC CO CA 151-A3
DRAIN-YONCALLA HWY Rt#-99
DOUGLAS CO OR 219-A3
DRAIN OR 219-A3
YONCALLA OR 219-A3
DRAKE RD
CLACKAMAS CO OR 205-D3
NW DRAKE RD
BEND OR 332-D6
DRAKE RD NE
CLACKAMAS CO OR 205-C3
MARION CO OR 205-C3
DRAPER SPRINGS RD
KLICKITAT CO WA 119-A3
DRAPER VALLEY RD
JOSEPHINE CO OR 233-B1
W DRAVUS ST
SEATTLE WA 273-E7
DRAYTON ST
LYNDEN WA 102-B1
DRAYTON HARBOR RD
BIRCH BAY WA 158-A3
BLAINE WA 158-A3
WHATCOM CO WA 158-A3
DRAZIL RD
KLAMATH CO OR 151-A2
DRECHSEL RD
KOOTENAI CO ID 247-C7
DRESSER RD Rt#-500
CLARK CO WA 193-B6
DREWS RD
KLAMATH CO OR 151-A1
DREWSEY RD
HARNEY CO OR 137-C3
HARNEY CO OR 145-C1
DREWSEY MARKET RD
HARNEY CO OR 137-C3
DREWS PRAIRIE RD
LEWIS CO WA 187-C4
D REX RD
DOUGLAS CO WA 105-A3
DRIFT CREEK RD
LINCOLN CO OR 203-A5
LINCOLN CO OR 209-B1
DRIFT CREEK RD NE
MARION CO OR 205-C5
DRIFT CREEK RD SE
MARION CO OR 205-C7
DRIFTWOOD RD NW
THURSTON CO WA 180-B5
THURSTON CO WA 296-C1
N DRISCOLL BLVD
SPOKANE WA 348-D2
DRIVER RD
LINN CO OR 207-C7
DRIVER VALLEY RD
DOUGLAS CO OR 219-B7
DRUMHELLER RD
SPOKANE CO WA 247-B7
E DRUMHELLER RD
SPOKANE CO WA 247-A7
DRY COULEE RD
GRANT CO WA 112-C2
DRY CREEK CTO
MALHEUR CO OR 146-B1
DRY CREEK LN
UNION CO OR 130-A2
DRY CREEK RD
CROOK CO OR 213-D3
IDAHO CO ID 131-B1
JEFFERSON CO OR 208-B2
KITTITAS CO WA 241-B5
MALHEUR CO OR 146-C1
PAYETTE CO ID 139-B2
WARM SPRINGS OR 208-B2
WASCO CO OR 196-A6
WHITMAN CO WA 114-C3
DRY CREEK RD U.S.-97
KITTITAS CO WA 241-A4
SISKIYOU CO CA 150-B3
DRY CREEK CANYON RD
DOUGLAS CO OR 225-C3
DRY CREEK TRAIL RD
WARM SPRINGS OR 208-A2
DRYDEN RD
JOSEPHINE CO OR 233-C2
N DRYDEN RD
CHELAN CO WA 238-B2
DRYDEN OVERLOOK RD
JOSEPHINE CO OR 233-C2
DRY HOLLOW RD
JEFFERSON CO OR 208-A4
THE DALLES OR 196-C7
WASCO CO OR 196-C7
WHEELER CO OR 136-A1
DRY LAKE RD
CHELAN CO WA 236-B1
ISLAND CO WA 167-D5
MALHEUR CO OR 146-B2
DRYLAND RD
CLACKAMAS CO OR 199-C7
S DRYLAND RD
CLACKAMAS CO OR 205-D1
DRY SLOUGH RD
SKAGIT CO WA 168-A2
DRY VALLEY HWY
HARNEY CO OR 144-B2
DRY VALLEY RD
HARNEY CO OR 144-C2
N DUBOIS RD
COWLITZ CO WA 118-A3
DUBUQUE RD
SNOHOMISH CO WA 110-C1
DUCKABUSH RD
JEFFERSON CO WA 173-C1
DUCK CREEK RD
BAKER CO OR 131-A3
DUCK LAKE DR
OCEAN SHORES WA 177-B7
DUCK LAKE DR SE
OCEAN SHORES WA 298-E1
DUCK LAKE RD
LINCOLN CO WA 113-B2
DUDLEY RD
KITTITAS CO WA 240-D3
KOOTENAI CO ID 115-B2
YAMHILL CO OR 198-C5
E DUFFIELD RD
YAKIMA CO WA 243-D7
DUFORT RD
BONNER CO ID 107-A3
E DUFORT RD
BONNER CO ID 244-A4
DUFUR BYPASS RD
WASCO CO OR 127-B2
DUFUR GAP RD
WASCO CO OR 127-B2
DUFUR VALLEY RD
WASCO CO OR 127-B2
DUGOUT LAKE RD
DESCHUTES CO OR 211-B4
DUGUALLA BAY RD
ISLAND CO WA 167-C1
DUKE LN
MARION CO OR 198-D7
W DUKE RD
DOUGLAS CO WA 221-C1
DULEY CREEK RD
CURRY CO OR 232-C5
DUMAR WY SW
SEATTLE WA 285-G1
DUMP RD
NEZ PERCE CO ID 250-D2
DUNBAR RD
SKAGIT CO WA 161-A7
DUNBAR ST
UNIV ENDOWMENT LANDS BC 156-B5
VANCOUVER BC 156-B5
VANCOUVER BC 254-A14
DUNBAR DIV
VANCOUVER BC 254-A13
DUNCAN CREEK RD
SKAMANIA CO WA 194-B6
DUNDAS ST
VANCOUVER BC 255-D10
DUNDEE RD
WASHINGTON CO OR 198-A2
DUNIVAN RD
LEWIS CO WA 187-B4
DUNIWAY RD
YAMHILL CO OR 198-B6
DUNKARD RD
KLICKITAT CO WA 196-B1
DUNLAP RD SW
THURSTON CO WA 184-C4
DUNN RD
CLARK CO WA 192-D1
S DUNN RD
SPOKANE CO WA 246-D6
SE DUNN RD
CLACKAMAS CO OR 200-C3
DUNNING RD
WHITMAN CO WA 249-A6
DUNSMUIR ST
VANCOUVER BC 254-G10
DUPONT ST
BELLINGHAM WA 258-C5
DUPORTAIL ST
RICHLAND WA 341-E2
DURBIN CREEK RD
BAKER CO OR 138-C2
DURGIN RD SE
THURSTON CO WA 181-A6
SW DURHAM LN
YAMHILL CO OR 204-B1
SW DURHAM RD
TIGARD OR 199-B3
DURR RD
KITTITAS CO WA 241-B7
KITTITAS CO WA 243-B1
YAKIMA CO WA 243-B2
DURRWACHTER RD
CLALLAM CO WA 164-D5
DURY RD
ADAMS CO WA 113-C3
DUSTY LP
DESCHUTES CO OR 212-B6
DUTCH CANYON RD
COLUMBIA CO OR 192-A4
SCAPPOOSE OR 192-A4
DUTCH HENRY RD
DOUGLAS CO OR 141-A3
DUTCHY CREEK RD
JOSEPHINE CO OR 148-C1
DUTHIE AV
DISTRICT OF BURNABY BC 156-D4
SE DUTHIE HILL RD
KING CO WA 176-A3
DUTTON RD
UNION CO OR 130-B2
DUUS RD
CLACKAMAS CO OR 200-C5
DUVAL RD
DIST OF N VANCOUVER BC 255-G2
DUVALL-MONROE RD Rt#-203
KING CO WA 110-C1
SNOHOMISH CO WA 110-C1
DUVALL-MONROE RD NE Rt#-203
KING CO WA 110-C1
DWIGHT HALSEY RD
ASOTIN CO WA 123-A3
DYKE RD
CITY OF RICHMOND BC 156-B7
PITT MEADOWS BC 157-B5

E

E RD
COTTONWOOD ID 123-C3
IDAHO CO ID 123-C3
E RD SE
DOUGLAS CO WA 112-C2
E ST
COLUMBIA CITY OR 192-B1
CULVER OR 208-B7
ENDICOTT WA 122-B1
GRANTS PASS OR 335-E8
NESPELEM WA 105-A3
NORTH POWDER OR 130-B3
WALLA WALLA CO WA 345-H4
WASHOUGAL WA 193-C7
WHITMAN CO WA 122-B1
E ST Rt#-8
FOREST GROVE OR 198-B1
WASHINGTON CO OR 198-B1
E ST Rt#-14
WASHOUGAL WA 193-C7
E ST Rt#-207
LEXINGTON OR 128-C2
E ST Rt#-272
PALOUSE WA 249-C1
E ST U.S.-97
SHANIKO OR 127-C3
E E ST
GRANTS PASS OR 335-G9
N E ST
TACOMA WA 293-G3
N E ST Rt#-272
PALOUSE WA 249-C1
S E ST
ABERDEEN WA 178-B7
E ST NE
GRANT CO WA 112-C2
EADEN RD
CLACKAMAS CO OR 200-B4
EADON RD
LEWIS CO WA 187-D4
NE EADS ST
NEWPORT OR 206-B4
EAGAR RD
COLUMBIA CO WA 122-A2
EAGLE DR
DESCHUTES CO OR 212-C5
JACKSON CO OR 230-C4
EAGLE LN
JEFFERSON CO OR 208-C2
E EAGLE RD
BAKER CO OR 130-C3
N EAGLE RD
ADA CO ID 253-B1
EAGLE ID 253-B1
S EAGLE RD
ADA CO ID 253-B4
S EAGLE RD Rt#-55
ADA CO ID 253-B2
EAGLE ID 253-B2
MERIDIAN ID 253-B2
EAGLE WY
YAKIMA CO WA 243-C6
EAGLE CREEK DR
BAKER CO OR 130-C3
EAGLE CREEK LN
UNION CO OR 130-B3
EAGLE CREEK RD
CHELAN CO WA 111-C2
CLACKAMAS CO OR 200-C5
EAGLE CREEK RANCH RD
CLALLAM CO WA 163-C7

STREET / City State Page-Grid

EAGLE CREEK-SANDY HWY Rt#-211
CLACKAMAS CO OR 200-C4
SANDY OR 200-C4
EAGLE CREST RD
POLK CO OR 204-C5
EAGLE FERN RD
CLACKAMAS CO OR 200-C5
NE EAGLE HARBOR DR
KITSAP CO WA 174-D2
KITSAP CO WA 271-J3
EAGLE MILL RD
JACKSON CO OR 337-A4
N EAGLE MILL RD
JACKSON CO OR 337-D5
EAGLEMOUNT RD
JEFFERSON CO WA 170-A2
EAGLE PEAK RD
KOOTENAI CO ID 248-D4
SW EAGLE POINT RD
YAMHILL CO OR 204-A1
EAGLE RIDGE RD
KLAMATH CO OR 231-B7
EAGLE ROCK RD
DESCHUTES CO OR 211-D5
EAGLE VALLEY RD Rt#-99
DOUGLAS CO OR 219-A3
EARLES ST
VANCOUVER BC 156-C5
EARLWOOD RD
CLACKAMAS CO OR 199-A6
YAMHILL CO OR 199-A6
EAST BLVD NE
KITSAP CO WA 271-C3
EAST MALL
UNIV ENDOWMENT LANDS BC 156-A4
EAST RD
ANMORE BC 157-A3
KLICKITAT CO WA 120-A3
KLICKITAT CO WA 128-A1
EAST RD W
SISKIYOU CO CA 150-C3
SISKIYOU CO CA 151-A3
EAST AND WEST TKTR
COWLITZ CO WA 187-A7
EAST BAY DR
COOS BAY OR 220-D1
COOS CO OR 140-B2
COOS CO OR 218-B7
COOS CO OR 220-D1
COOS CO OR 333-H1
EAST BEACH RD
CLALLAM CO WA 164-C6
EAST BEAVER CREEK RD
TILLAMOOK CO OR 197-C5
EAST COVE RD
LATAH CO ID 249-D1
EASTERDAY RD
WASHINGTON CO OR 198-B1
EASTERN BOUNDARY RD
KITSAP CO WA 170-B6
EAST FORK RD
DOUGLAS CO OR 225-B1
EAST FORK EVANS CREEK RD
JACKSON CO OR 230-C1
EAST FORK GLENN CK RD
COOS CO OR 140-C1
EAST FORK PINE CREEK RD
SHOSHONE CO ID 115-C2
EAST GATE RD
PIERCE CO WA 181-C6
WASCO CO OR 126-C3
WASCO CO OR 127-A3
SE EASTGATE WY
BELLEVUE WA 175-C3
EASTLAKE AV E
SEATTLE WA 274-B7
SEATTLE WA 278-B2
EASTLAKE DR
DISTRICT OF BURNABY BC 156-D4
NW EASTMAN PKWY
GRESHAM OR 200-B2
N EASTMONT AV
DOUGLAS CO WA 239-A4
EAST WENATCHEE WA 239-A4
EAST WENATCHEE BENCH WA 239-A4
EASTON CANYON RD
WASCO CO OR 127-B2
EAST POINT RD
KOOTENAI CO ID 248-A4
EAST PORTLAND FRWY I-205
PORTLAND OR 319-G7
EAST RIVERSIDE RD
OKANOGAN CO WA 104-C2
EAST SAANICH RD
DIST OF NORTH SAANICH BC 159-C3
EAST SHORE RD
BONNER CO ID 107-A1
EAST SIDE RD
UMATILLA CO OR 121-C3
EASTSIDE RD
BONNER CO ID 107-A2
HOOD RIVER CO OR 195-D6
EASTSIDE ST
OLYMPIA WA 297-A5
N EASTSIDE ST
OLYMPIA WA 296-J5
OLYMPIA WA 297-A5
EASTSIDE ACCESS RD
OKANOGAN CO WA 104-C3
EASTSIDE CHEWACK RD
OKANOGAN CO WA 104-A2
WINTHROP WA 104-A2
EASTSIDE OROVILLE RD
OKANOGAN CO WA 104-C1
EASTSIDE OSOYOOS RD
OKANOGAN CO WA 104-C1
EASTSIDE-SUMNER RD
COOS CO OR 140-B2
COOS CO OR 220-D2
EAST SOOKE RD
BRITISH COLUMBIA 164-D1
BRITISH COLUMBIA 165-A1
DISTRICT OF METCHOSIN BC 165-A1
EAST TWISP-WINTHROP RD
OKANOGAN CO WA 104-A2
TWISP WA 104-A2
EAST VALLEY HWY
AUBURN WA 182-B2
KING CO WA 182-B2
EAST VALLEY HWY
PACIFIC WA 182-B2
PIERCE CO WA 182-B2
SUMNER WA 182-B2
EAST WEST RD
SISKIYOU CO CA 151-A3
EASY ST
BROOKINGS OR 232-C6
SUNNYSLOPE WA 238-D3
S EASY ST
ROCKAWAY BEACH OR 191-B6
EATON RD
CLARK CO WA 118-A3
CLARK CO WA 193-B1
EATONVILLE HWY
EATONVILLE WA 118-B1
PIERCE CO WA 118-B1
EATONVILLE CUT-OFF RD
PIERCE CO WA 118-B1
EBELL CREEK RD
BAKER CO OR 138-B1
S EBEY RD
ISLAND CO WA 167-B4
NE EBY AV
DESCHUTES CO OR 212-D3
TERREBONNE OR 212-D3
S EBY RD
CLACKAMAS CO OR 205-D1
ECHAVE RANCH RD
MALHEUR CO OR 154-B2
ECHO LAKE CTO SE Rt#-18
KING CO WA 176-A6
ECHO LAKE RD
SNOHOMISH CO WA 171-D5
ECKENSTAM-JOHNSON RD
PIERCE CO WA 181-A4
S ECKERT RD
ADA CO ID 253-D3
ECKLER MOUNTAIN RD
COLUMBIA CO WA 122-B2
ECKMAN CREEK RD
LINCOLN CO OR 209-B3
ECKS FLAT RD
ADAMS CO ID 251-B5
EDDYVILLE RD
KOOTENAI CO ID 248-B1
EDDYVILLE BLODGETT HWY
BENTON CO OR 133-A1
LINCOLN CO OR 133-A1
EDENBOWER MILLWOOD RD
DOUGLAS CO OR 221-B2
EDENS RD
SKAGIT CO WA 160-C5
EDENVALE RD
LANE CO OR 215-D3
LANE CO OR 331-J14
EDEN VALLEY RD
CLALLAM CO WA 164-D6
CLALLAM CO WA 165-A6
EDEN VALLEY RD Rt#-403
WAHKIAKUM CO WA 117-A2
EDER RD
OKANOGAN CO WA 104-C1
EDGEMONT BLVD
DIST OF N VANCOUVER BC 254-H2
EDGEWATER ST NW Rt#-221
SALEM OR 322-F13
EDGEWOOD DR
CLALLAM CO WA 165-A6
CLALLAM CO WA 261-A5
PORT ANGELES WA 165-A6
PORT ANGELES WA 261-A5
EDGEWOOD LN
KLAMATH CO OR 235-D1
EDISON AV SW
BANDON OR 220-B6
N EDISON ST
BENTON CO WA 342-F9
KENNEWICK WA 342-F9
S EDISON ST
BENTON CO WA 342-F11
EDISON ICE CAVE RD
DESCHUTES CO OR 216-C5
EDLER RD
KLAMATH CO OR 151-B2
SW EDMINSTON RD
CLACKAMAS CO OR 199-A6
EDMONDS AV NE
RENTON WA 175-C5
EDMONDS ST
DISTRICT OF BURNABY BC 156-D5
EDMONDS WY Rt#-104
EDMONDS WA 171-A6
SNOHOMISH CO WA 171-A6
WOODWAY WA 171-A6
EDMONDS-KINGSTON FERRY
EDMONDS WA 171-A5
KINGSTON WA 170-D5
KITSAP CO WA 170-D5
SNOHOMISH CO WA 171-A5
EDMUNDSON RD
DESCHUTES CO OR 212-A4
EDMUNSON DR SE
MARION CO OR 205-B6
W EDNA ST
BOISE ID 253-B2
EDSON CREEK RD
CURRY CO OR 228-A4
EDWARDS DR
WHATCOM CO WA 101-C1
EDWARDS RD E
PIERCE CO WA 182-C2
EDWARDS BUTTE RD
TILLAMOOK CO OR 197-D3
ED WILLIAMS RD
CROOK CO OR 213-B6
SW EDY RD
WASHINGTON CO OR 199-A4
EELS RD
CHELAN CO WA 238-C2
S EGAN AV
BURNS OR 145-B1
HARNEY CO OR 145-B1
EGAN SPRINGS RD
KLAMATH CO OR 142-C3
EGG AND I RD
JEFFERSON CO WA 170-A2
NE EGLON RD
KITSAP CO WA 170-D4
EGYPT CANYON RD
HARNEY CO OR 144-C1
EHLEN RD
MARION CO OR 199-A7
N EHORN LN
CHEWELAH WA 106-B3
EICHER RD
LINN CO OR 207-D5
EID RD
LATAH CO ID 249-D6
EIGHT DOLLAR MOUNTAIN RD
JOSEPHINE CO OR 233-A2
EILERS RD
CLACKAMAS CO OR 199-B6
SW EISCHEN LN
WASHINGTON CO OR 198-C2
S EKELMAN RD
YAKIMA CO WA 243-C7
EKROTH RD
TILLAMOOK CO OR 191-B7
ELBE DR
JEFFERSON CO OR 212-D2
NW ELBE DR
JEFFERSON CO OR 208-B4
SW ELBE DR
JEFFERSON CO OR 208-B7
ELD LN
VALLEY CO ID 252-D1
ELDER RD
WHATCOM CO WA 158-C6
E ELDER RD
SPOKANE CO WA 246-D7
SPOKANE CO WA 247-B6
W ELDER RD
KOOTENAI CO ID 247-C6
W ELDER RD U.S.-95
KOOTENAI CO ID 247-D5
ELDORADO AV
KLAMATH FALLS OR 338-D5
ELDORADO BLVD
KLAMATH FALLS OR 338-D4
NW EL DORADO BLVD
KITSAP CO WA 270-A3
ELDORADO RD
CLACKAMAS CO OR 199-D7
ELDRIDGE AV
BELLINGHAM WA 258-B5
ELECTRIC AV
BELLINGHAM WA 258-J6
W ELECTRIC AV
SPOKANE CO WA 246-A5
ELEPHANT MOUNTAIN RD
DOUGLAS CO OR 223-B3
ELFENDAHL PASS RD
MASON CO WA 173-C5
ELGAROSE LOOP RD
DOUGLAS CO OR 221-A3
ELGER BAY RD
ISLAND CO WA 167-D5
ELGIN AV U.S.-20
CANYON CO ID 147-B1
NOTUS ID 147-B1
ELGIN RD
CITY OF SURREY BC 158-A1
PAYETTE CO ID 139-B3
ELGIN-CLIFTON Rt#-302
PIERCE CO WA 174-A7
ELIJAH RD
STEVENS CO WA 114-A1
ELISHA RD
CLACKAMAS CO OR 199-C7
CLACKAMAS CO OR 205-D1
ELIZA DR
SAN JUAN CO WA 160-A6
ELIZABETH ST Rt#-27
TEKOA WA 114-C3
NE ELIZABETH ST
MILTON-FREEWATER OR 121-C3
SW ELIZABETH ST
NEWPORT OR 206-B4
NW ELK DR
JEFFERSON CO OR 208-B5
SW ELK DR
JEFFERSON CO OR 208-B5
ELK RD
JACKSON CO OR 226-C5
ELK BUTTE RD
CLEARWATER CO ID 123-C1
N ELK- CHATTAROY RD
SPOKANE CO WA 114-C1
ELK CITY RD
LINCOLN CO OR 206-D4
ELK CREEK RD
COLUMBIA CO OR 189-A4
JACKSON CO OR 226-B6
SISKIYOU CO CA 149-A3
ELK CREEK RIDGE RD
CLALLAM CO WA 169-D1
ELKHEAD RD
DOUGLAS CO OR 219-B4
ELKHORN CREEK RD
LINCOLN CO OR 206-B6
ELKHORN RIDGE RD
JACKSON CO OR 226-A5
ELKINS RD
CROOK CO OR 213-A4
POLK CO OR 207-A1
ELK LAKE RD
IDAHO CO ID 131-C2
ELK MOUNTAIN RD
COOS CO OR 218-D7
ELKOFF RD
TILLAMOOK CO OR 197-B3
ELK PRAIRIE RD
PACIFIC CO WA 117-B2
ELK RIDGE RD N
YAKIMA CO WA 243-A2
ELK RIVER RD
CLEARWATER CO ID 123-C1
CURRY CO OR 140-B3
CURRY CO OR 224-B6
CURRY CO OR 228-C1
ELK RIVER RD Rt#-3
LATAH CO ID 123-B1
ELKTON-SUTHERLIN HWY Rt#-138
DOUGLAS CO OR 141-A1
DOUGLAS CO OR 221-B1
ELKTON OR 141-A1
SUTHERLIN OR 221-C1
E ELKTON-SUTHERLIN HWY Rt#-99
SUTHERLIN OR 221-C1
W ELKTON-SUTHERLIN HWY Rt#-138
DOUGLAS CO OR 221-C1
SUTHERLIN OR 221-C1
ELK VIEW RD
DISTRICT OF CHILLIWACK BC 102-C1
ELLA RD
MORROW CO OR 128-B2
E ELLENDALE AV Rt#-223
DALLAS OR 204-A6
W ELLENDALE AV
DALLAS OR 204-A6
ELLENDALE RD
DALLAS OR 204-A6
POLK CO OR 125-B3
POLK CO OR 204-A6
W ELLENDALE RD
POLK CO OR 125-B3
ELLENS FERRY DR
BOISE ID 253-C2
ELLIGSEN RD
WASHINGTON CO OR 199-B5
WILSONVILLE OR 199-B5
ELLINGSON RD
ALBANY OR 326-C14
ALGONA WA 182-B2
AUBURN WA 182-B2
KING CO WA 182-B2
LINN CO OR 326-C14
PACIFIC WA 182-B2
ELLIOT RD
CLARK CO WA 193-B1
DESCHUTES CO OR 213-A4
MULTNOMAH CO OR 192-A6
ELLIOT ST
DISTRICT OF DELTA BC 101-C1
ELLIOTT AV
SEATTLE WA 277-H4
ELLIOTT AV NW
OLYMPIA WA 296-F2
ELLIOTT AV W
SEATTLE WA 277-F2
ELLIOTT LN
CROOK CO OR 213-C4
ELLIOTT RD
SNOHOMISH CO WA 171-D5
ELLIOTT PRAIRIE RD NE
MARION CO OR 205-C2
ELLIS AV S
SEATTLE WA 282-B7
SEATTLE WA 286-B1
ELLIS LN
BENEWAH CO ID 248-A7
ELLIS RD
BAKER CO OR 130-A3
UNION CO OR 130-A3
ELLIS RD SW
DOUGLAS CO WA 239-C3
ELLIS ST
BELLINGHAM WA 258-E4
SE ELLSWORTH RD
VANCOUVER WA 307-H7
VANCOUVER WA 311-H1
ELLSWORTH ST U.S.-20
ALBANY OR 326-C8
ELM AV
TILLAMOOK OR 197-B2
E ELM AV
COEUR D'ALENE ID 355-G10
HERMISTON OR 129-A1
UMATILLA CO OR 129-A1
S ELM AV
PASCO WA 343-J8
W ELM AV
HERMISTON OR 129-A1
ELM LN
CANYON CO ID 147-C1
NE ELM LN
JEFFERSON CO OR 208-C4
NW ELM LN
JEFFERSON CO OR 208-B4
ELM ST
ALBANY OR 326-B8
ASOTIN CO WA 250-B4
BELLINGHAM WA 258-C5
CANNON BEACH WA 188-B7
CHENEY WA 246-A7
CLARKSTON WA 250-B4
SISTERS OR 211-D5
SUMNER WA 182-B3
WHATCOM CO WA 101-C1
ELM ST U.S.-30
BAKER CITY OR 138-B1
E ELM ST
DOUGLAS CO WA 236-C7
WATERVILLE WA 236-C7
S ELM ST Rt#-22
TOPPENISH WA 120-A2
ELMA-GATE RD
GRAYS HARBOR CO WA 117-B1
ELMA-HICKLIN RD
GRAYS HARBOR CO WA 179-C6
ELMA-MCCLEARY RD
GRAYS HARBOR CO WA 179-C6
MCCLEARY WA 179-C6
ELMORE RD
PAYETTE CO ID 139-A3
ELMWAY Rt#-20
OKANOGAN WA 104-C3
OKANOGAN CO WA 104-C3
OMAK WA 104-C3
ELOCHOMAN MAINLINE Rt#-407
WAHKIAKUM CO WA 117-B3
EL RIO LN
LANE CO OR 210-A6
ELROD AV
COOS BAY OR 333-G10
ELSNER RD
CLACKAMAS CO OR 200-D3
SW ELSNER RD
WASHINGTON CO OR 199-A4
ELTOPIA WEST RD
FRANKLIN CO WA 121-A2
ELTOPIA WEST RD W
FRANKLIN CO WA 121-A2
SW ELWERT RD
WASHINGTON CO OR 199-A4
ELWHA RIVER RD
CLALLAM CO WA 165-A6
ELWOOD DR SW
LAKEWOOD WA 181-C4
N ELY PL
KENNEWICK WA 342-J9
KENNEWICK WA 343-A9
N ELY ST U.S.-395
KENNEWICK WA 342-J10
S ELY ST
KENNEWICK WA 342-J13
S ELY ST U.S.-395
BENTON CO WA 342-J11
KENNEWICK WA 342-J11
EMANDER RD
EVERETT WA 268-A5
SNOHOMISH WA 268-A5
EMENS AV Rt#-530
DARRINGTON WA 103-A3
EMERALD RD
GRANGER WA 120-B2
YAKIMA CO WA 120-B2
EMERALD ST
BOISE ID 253-C3
EMERSON AV Rt#-109
HOQUIAM WA 178-A7
NE EMERSON DR
JEFFERSON CO OR 208-D3
EMERSON LN
JEFFERSON CO OR 208-D4
W EMERSON PL
SEATTLE WA 272-E6
SEATTLE WA 273-E6
EMERSON RD
DOUGLAS CO OR 222-B7
W EMERSON ST
SEATTLE WA 272-C6
SEATTLE WA 273-F6
EMERSON LOOP RD
WASCO CO OR 127-B2
WASCO CO OR 196-D7
EMERY RD
CLALLAM CO WA 165-D7
SE EMIGRANT AV Rt#-37
PENDLETON OR 129-B1
SW EMIGRANT AV Rt#-37
PENDLETON OR 129-B1
EMIGRANT CREEK RD
HARNEY CO OR 136-C3
HARNEY CO OR 137-A3
EMIGRANTS RD
UMATILLA CO OR 129-B1
EMIGRANT SPRINGS RD
SHERMAN CO OR 127-C1
W EMMA AV
COEUR D'ALENE ID 355-D9
KOOTENAI CO ID 355-D9
EMMA ST Rt#-278
ROCKFORD WA 114-C2
EMMETT HWY Rt#-16
ADA CO ID 139-C3
ADA CO ID 147-C1
EMMETT RD
ADAMS CO ID 139-C1
CANYON CO ID 147-B1
NW EMPIRE AV
EAST WENATCHEE BENCH WA 239-A4
EMPIRE BLVD
BEND OR 332-F2
DESCHUTES CO OR 332-F2
S EMPIRE BLVD
CLATSOP CO WA 188-B2
COOS BAY OR 333-A8
COOS CO OR 220-C1
COOS CO OR 333-A8
WARRENTON WA 188-B2
E EMPIRE WY
MILLWOOD WA 350-D5
SPOKANE CO WA 350-F4
EMPIRE WY S
SEATTLE WA 278-D7
SEATTLE WA 282-D1
SEATTLE WA 283-E7
SEATTLE WA 287-E1
TUKWILA WA 287-E5
EMPIRE WY S Rt#-900
TUKWILA WA 287-E5
EMPIRE-COOS BAY HWY
COOS BAY OR 333-C6
SW EM WATTS RD
SCAPPOOSE OR 192-A4
ENCHANTED PKWY Rt#-161
FEDERAL WAY WA 182-B1
KING CO WA 182-B2
ENCHANTED PKWY S Rt#-161
EDGEWOOD WA 182-B2
KING CO WA 182-B2
MILTON WA 182-B2
S ENDICOTT RD
ENDICOTT WA 122-B1
WHITMAN CO WA 122-B1
ENDICOTT RD E
WHITMAN CO WA 122-B1
ENDICOTT RD SW
THURSTON CO WA 184-B2
ENDICOTT RD W
ENDICOTT WA 122-A1
WHITMAN CO WA 122-A1
ENDICOTT-SAINT JOHN RD
ENDICOTT WA 122-B1
WHITMAN CO WA 114-B3
WHITMAN CO WA 122-B1
ENDICOTT-ST JOHN RD
WHITMAN CO WA 114-B3
ENDICOTT-ST JOHN RD Rt#-23
SAINT JOHN WA 114-B3
WHITMAN CO WA 114-B3
ENDRESEN RD
HOQUIAM WA 178-A7
ENETAI BEACH RD
BREMERTON WA 271-B9
KITSAP CO WA 271-B9
ENGEL RD
LINCOLN CO WA 113-C2
LINN CO OR 207-D5
S ENGLE RD
ISLAND CO WA 167-B5
ENGLEWOOD AV
YAKIMA WA 243-A6
ENGLEWOOD-SHINGLEHOUSE RD
COOS CO OR 220-D2
COOS CO OR 333-F14
ENGLISH RD
SKAGIT CO WA 168-B2
ENGLISH BLUFF RD
DISTRICT OF DELTA BC 101-C1
ENGLISH GRADE RD
SNOHOMISH CO WA 168-B3
ENGLISH PT RD
KOOTENAI CO ID 245-A5
E ENID RD
LANE CO OR 215-A1
ENMAN-KINCAID RD
WHITMAN CO WA 249-A4
ENNIS CREEK RD
WHATCOM CO WA 161-C3
W ENOCH RD
SPOKANE CO WA 114-B1
ENTERPRISE AV
MALHEUR CO OR 139-A3
ENTERPRISE RD
COLUMBIA CO OR 189-A6
FERNDALE WA 158-C5
POLK CO OR 125-B3
POLK CO OR 204-A4
WHATCOM CO WA 158-C5
E ENTERPRISE RD
LANE CO OR 215-C5
N ENTERPRISE RD
WHATCOM CO WA 158-D4
ENTERPRISE-LEWISTON HWY Rt#-3
WALLOWA CO OR 122-C3
WALLOWA CO OR 130-C1
ENTIAT RIVER RD
CHELAN CO WA 112-A1
CHELAN CO WA 236-A6
ENTRANCE MOUNTAIN RD
SAN JUAN CO WA 160-A3
ENUMCLW BLK DMND RD SE Rt#-169
BLACK DIAMOND WA 110-C3
KING CO WA 110-C3
ENUMCLAW BUCKLEY RD Rt#-410
ENUMCLAW WA 110-C3
KING CO WA 110-C3
S ENUMCLAW BUCKLEY RD Rt#-410
BUCKLEY WA 110-C3
BUCKLEY WA 182-D4
ENUMCLW CHNOOK PASS RD Rt#-410
KING CO WA 110-C3
EOLA DR NW
POLK CO OR 322-C12
SALEM OR 322-E13
SE EOLA HILLS RD
YAMHILL CO OR 204-B2
ERICKSON RD
DESCHUTES CO OR 217-D2
KITTITAS CO WA 241-C5
ERICKSON RD KPS
PIERCE CO WA 181-A3
ERIE ST
CITY OF VICTORIA BC 256-F9
NW ERLAND POINT RD
TRACYTON WA 270-C5
ERLAND POINT RD NW
TRACYTON WA 270-C5
ERMINE DR
JEFFERSON CO OR 212-C3
ERSHING RD
SKAGIT CO WA 161-A5
ERSKINE RD SW
THURSTON CO WA 184-B2
ERSKINE WY SW
SEATTLE WA 280-D6
ESCOLAR RD
KITSAP CO WA 170-A7
ESPANOLA RD
MEDICAL LAKE WA 114-B2
SPOKANE CO WA 114-B2
S ESPANOLA RD
SPOKANE CO WA 114-B2
ESPLANADE AV
CITY OF HARRISN HT SPGS BC 94-C3
ESPLANADE ST
CITY OF N VANCOUVER BC 255-A6
KLAMATH FALLS OR 338-E7
ESPY DR
PACIFIC CO WA 186-A1
ESQUIMALT RD
CITY OF VICTORIA BC 256-E8
TOWN OF ESQUIMALT BC 256-C8
ESQUIRE DR
BOISE ID 253-C2
ESSER RD
WHITMAN CO WA 250-B1
NE ESTES AV
WHITE SALMON WA 195-D4
ESTES RD
LATAH CO ID 249-C4
EUCHRE CREEK RD
CURRY CO OR 228-B3
EUCLID AV
GRANDVIEW WA 120-B3
SUNNYSLOPE WA 238-D3
YAKIMA CO WA 120-B3
E EUCLID AV
OTIS ORCHARDS WA 352-B11
SPOKANE WA 349-B5
SPOKANE CO WA 349-E5
SPOKANE CO WA 350-B5
SPOKANE CO WA 351-E4
SPOKANE CO WA 352-B11
W EUCLID AV
SPOKANE WA 348-H5
SPOKANE WA 349-A5
EUCLID RD
GRANDVIEW WA 120-B3
MABTON WA 120-B3
YAKIMA CO WA 120-B3
E EUCLID RD
YAKIMA CO WA 120-B3

STREET City State Page-Grid

N EUCLID RD
GRANDVIEW WA 120-B3
S EUCLID RD
YAKIMA CO WA 120-B3
EUFAULA HEIGHTS RD
COWLITZ CO WA 189-A1
EUGENE ST
HOOD RIVER OR 195-D5
EUGENE-SPRINGFIELD HWY I-105
EUGENE OR 329-J4
EUGENE OR 330-A5
LANE CO OR 330-A5
SPRINGFIELD OR 330-A5
EUGENE-SPRINGFIELD HWY Rt#-126
EUGENE OR 330-E5
LANE CO OR 330-F5
LANE CO OR 331-C5
SPRINGFIELD OR 330-E5
SPRINGFIELD OR 331-C5
SW EUREKA LN
JEFFERSON CO OR 208-B6
EUREKA RD N
WALLA WALLA CO WA 121-C2
EVANS BLVD U.S.-101
COOS BAY OR 333-H11
EVANS RD
ASOTIN CO WA 250-B4
KLAMATH CO OR 151-A3
WHITE SWAN WA 119-C2
YAKIMA CO WA 119-C2
S EVANS RD
NEZ PERCE CO ID 250-C2
EVANS CREEK RD
JACKSON CO OR 229-D4
JACKSON CO OR 230-C1
KOOTENAI CO ID 248-C4
E EVANS CREEK RD
JACKSON CO OR 229-D5
JACKSON CO OR 230-C3
ROGUE RIVER OR 229-D5
W EVANS CREEK RD
JACKSON CO OR 229-D4
EVANS HILL CUTOFF RD
STEVENS CO WA 106-A2
EVANS-LEAP RD
WALLOWA CO OR 130-C2
EVANS VALLEY LP
MARION CO OR 205-C4
EVANS VALLEY RD NE
MARION CO OR 205-C4
EVERETT AV
EVERETT WA 265-G3
EVERETT AV Rt#-529
EVERETT WA 264-D3
EVERETT WA 265-E3
SE EVERETT RD Rt#-500
CLARK CO WA 193-B6
NE EVERETT ST
PORTLAND OR 313-F5
NE EVERETT ST Rt#-500
CAMAS WA 193-B7
CLARK CO WA 193-B7
NW EVERETT ST
PORTLAND OR 312-D5
PORTLAND OR 313-F5
SE EVERETT MALL WY Rt#-99
EVERETT WA 268-C6
SW EVERETT MALL WY Rt#-99
EVERETT WA 268-A7
SE EVERGREEN AV Rt#-126
REDMOND OR 212-D5
EVERGREEN AV NE
SALEM OR 323-C10
EVERGREEN BLVD Rt#-14
CLARK CO WA 193-C7
WASHOUGAL WA 193-C7
E EVERGREEN BLVD
VANCOUVER WA 305-H5
VANCOUVER WA 306-C6
W EVERGREEN BLVD
VANCOUVER WA 305-G5
EVERGREEN DR Rt#-9
DISTRICT OF KENT BC 94-C3
EVERGREEN HWY
VANCOUVER WA 306-D7
VANCOUVER WA 307-E7
VANCOUVER WA 311-G1
EVERGREEN HWY Rt#-14
CARSON WA 194-C6
CARSON WA 195-B5
NORTH BONNEVILLE WA 194-C6
SKAMANIA CO WA 193-D7
SKAMANIA CO WA 194-A7
SKAMANIA CO WA 195-B5
SKAMANIA CO WA 200-D1
STEVENSON WA 194-C6
EVERGREEN HWY Rt#-22
TOPPENISH WA 120-A2
YAKIMA CO WA 120-A2
EVERGREEN HWY U.S.-97
TOPPENISH WA 120-A2
YAKIMA CO WA 120-A2
SE EVERGREEN HWY
CLARK CO WA 193-A7
VANCOUVER WA 311-J2
EVERGREEN LN
SKAGIT CO WA 160-C5
NW EVERGREEN PKWY
HILLSBORO OR 199-A1
WASHINGTON CO OR 199-A1
EVERGREEN RD
TILLAMOOK CO OR 197-B6
N EVERGREEN RD
OPPORTUNITY WA 351-A8
TRENTWOOD WA 351-A2
VERADALE WA 351-A8
NW EVERGREEN RD
WASHINGTON CO OR 198-D1
S EVERGREEN RD
OPPORTUNITY WA 351-A10
VERADALE WA 351-A8
EVERGREEN WY
EVERETT WA 264-D7
EVERETT WA 268-C4
EVERGREEN PARK DR
OLYMPIA WA 296-F7
EVERGREEN PARK RD
PACIFIC CO WA 183-B3
EVERSON AV Rt#-544
EVERSON WA 102-B1
NOOKSACK WA 102-B1
EVERSON GOSHEN RD
WHATCOM CO WA 102-B1
EVERSON GOSHEN RD Rt#-544
EVERSON WA 102-B1
WHATCOM CO WA 102-B1
EVES RD
CLACKAMAS CO OR 126-A3
EWARTSVILLE RD
WHITMAN CO WA 122-C1
WHITMAN CO WA 249-A6
EWE CREEK RD
JOSEPHINE CO OR 229-A5
S EWING RD
ISLAND CO WA 171-A2
NE EXCHANGE DR
ROSEBURG OR 334-F4
EXECUTIVE DR
ADA CO ID 253-B3
EXTENSION RD
BRITISH COLUMBIA 93-A3
NANAIMO BC 93-A3
EXTROM RD
DISTRICT OF CHILLIWACK BC 102-C1
EYREMOUNT DR
DIST OF WEST VANCOUVER BC 254-E1
EYREMOUNT RD
DIST OF WEST VANCOUVER BC 156-B2
DIST OF WEST VANCOUVER BC 254-E1

F

F ST
BELLINGHAM WA 258-D5
CHENEY WA 246-A7
GEARHART WA 301-G5
GRANT CO WA 237-C3
GRANTS PASS OR 335-E8
PORT TOWNSEND WA 263-F4
WALLA WALLA CO WA 345-H5
F ST U.S.-95
WORLEY ID 115-A2
F ST U.S.-199
GRANTS PASS OR 335-H9
JOSEPHINE CO OR 335-H9
E F ST
TACOMA WA 293-J5
E F ST U.S.-199
GRANTS PASS OR 335-G9
N F ST
ELMA WA 179-B7
F ST N U.S.-395
LAKEVIEW OR 152-A2
F ST S U.S.-395
LAKE CO OR 152-A2
LAKEVIEW OR 152-A2
F ST SE Rt#-28
GRANT CO WA 112-B3
QUINCY WA 112-B3
F ST SW Rt#-28
GRANT CO WA 112-B3
QUINCY WA 112-B3
FACTORY RD
YAKIMA CO WA 120-B2
FADJUR LN
DESCHUTES CO OR 212-A4
FAGAN RD
SKAGIT CO WA 168-B3
FAGERUD RD SE
KITSAP CO WA 174-C6
FAIRBANKS RD
WHITMAN CO WA 114-C3
FAIRBANKS-SEABURY RD
WHITMAN CO WA 114-C3
FAIRFIELD RD
CITY OF VICTORIA BC 256-J10
CITY OF VICTORIA BC 257-A11
NE FAIRGROUNDS RD
KITSAP CO WA 270-H1
NW FAIRGROUNDS RD
KITSAP CO WA 270-E1
FAIRGROUNDS RD NE
SALEM OR 322-J11
SALEM OR 323-A11
E FAIRHAVEN AV
BURLINGTON WA 260-E5
SKAGIT CO WA 260-E5
FAIROAKS RD
DOUGLAS CO OR 219-B7
DOUGLAS CO OR 221-D1
FAIROAKS RD SE
THURSTON CO WA 181-A7
FAIRVIEW AV
ADA CO ID 253-B3
BOISE ID 253-B3
GARDEN CITY ID 253-B3
PAYETTE CO ID 139-A3
E FAIRVIEW AV
ADA CO ID 253-B3
MERIDIAN ID 253-B3
NW FAIRVIEW AV
GRESHAM OR 200-B1
SW FAIRVIEW AV Rt#-223
DALLAS OR 204-A6
FAIRVIEW AV N
SEATTLE WA 278-A3
FAIRVIEW AV SE
SALEM OR 324-H2
FAIRVIEW DR
HOOD RIVER CO OR 195-C5
YAMHILL CO OR 198-C6
FAIRVIEW LN
GILLIAM CO OR 128-B1
FAIRVIEW RD
COLUMBIA CO OR 189-C6
KITTITAS CO WA 241-C5
LINN CO OR 133-C2
TILLAMOOK CO OR 197-C2
SE FAIRVIEW RD
YAMHILL CO OR 204-C2
FAIRVIEW RD SW
THURSTON CO WA 184-B1
N FAIRVIEW ST
PRINEVILLE OR 213-D5
S FAIRVIEW ST
CROOK CO OR 213-D5
PRINEVILLE OR 213-D5
FAIRVIEW CANYON RD
CHELAN CO WA 238-C3
FAIRVIEW LAKE RD SW
KITSAP CO WA 174-A6
FAIRVIEW-MCKINLEY RD
COOS CO OR 140-C2
FAIRVIEW MOUNTAIN RD
LANE CO OR 209-A6
FAIRWAY AV
CLACKAMAS CO OR 201-C5
FAIRWAY DR
LINCOLN CO OR 203-A6
FAIRWAY ST
BENTON CO WA 343-F12
KENNEWICK WA 343-F12
SE FAIRWOOD BLVD
KING CO WA 175-C5
FAIRWOOD DR
OCEAN SHORES WA 298-B5
FAITH AV
ASHLAND OR 337-G10
FAKKEMA RD
ISLAND CO WA 167-C2
FALCON LN
JEFFERSON CO OR 208-B7
FALES RD
SNOHOMISH CO WA 171-D5
FALK RD
LINN CO OR 210-B3
FALL CITY-CRNTON RD NE Rt#-203
CARNATION WA 176-B2
KING CO WA 176-B2
FALL CITY-DUVALL RD
KING CO WA 176-B3
FALL CITY-SNQUALMIE RD Rt#-202
KING CO WA 176-B3
SNOQUALMIE WA 176-B3
FALL CREEK RD
ADAMS CO ID 252-A3
CLACKAMAS CO OR 200-C6
LINCOLN CO OR 133-A2
FALLERT RD
COWLITZ CO WA 189-D5
FALLON DR
WEST RICHLAND WA 340-A12
FALLON RD
WHITMAN CO WA 249-B3
FALLS CITY HWY
MONMOUTH OR 204-B7
POLK CO OR 204-B7
FALLS CITY RD
FALLS CITY OR 125-B3
POLK CO OR 125-B3
FALLS CREEK RD
GRAYS HARBOR CO WA 179-B6
N FANCHER RD
SPOKANE WA 349-J8
SPOKANE CO WA 349-J8
S FANCHER RD
SPOKANE CO WA 349-J10
FANDANGO PASS RD
MODOC CO CA 152-A3
F AND S GRADE RD
SEDRO-WOOLLEY WA 161-B5
SKAGIT CO WA 161-B5
FANTON RD
CLACKAMAS CO OR 200-D7
FARADAY RD
CLACKAMAS CO OR 200-C7
FARGO RD
MARION CO OR 199-A7
FARLEY RD SW
DOUGLAS CO WA 239-C6
FARM RD
CLACKAMAS CO OR 205-D3
FARM WY
WHITMAN CO WA 249-B5
FARMER RD
POLK CO OR 204-B5
FARMER RD SE
MARION CO OR 207-D2
FARMER CREEK RD
TILLAMOOK CO OR 197-B6
FARMERS RD
EVERETT WA 268-C6
FARMINGTON RD Rt#-10
WASHINGTON CO OR 198-D2
SW FARMINGTON RD Rt#-10
BEAVERTON OR 199-A2
WASHINGTON CO OR 198-D3
WASHINGTON CO OR 199-A2
FARMS RD
BRITISH COLUMBIA 94-B3
FARM STATION RD
KLAMATH CO OR 231-D5
FARM TO MARKET RD
SKAGIT CO WA 161-A6
VALLEY CO ID 251-D5
VALLEY CO ID 252-D2
WASHINGTON CO ID 139-B2
FARM TO MARKET LOOP RD
STEVENS CO WA 106-A3
FARMWAY RD
CANYON CO ID 147-B1
S FARNEY RD
SPOKANE CO WA 247-A5
FARR RD
CLARK CO WA 193-A1
N FARR RD
DISHMAN WA 350-E8
SPOKANE CO WA 350-D3
S FARR RD
DISHMAN WA 350-E9
FARRAGUT AV
BREMERTON WA 270-H11
WESTPORT WA 298-G14
FARRAGUT ST Rt#-304
BREMERTON WA 270-F12
FARRELL RD
ADAMS CO ID 251-B4
FARRINGTON RD
CLALLAM CO WA 164-C5
E FARWELL RD
FAIRWOOD WA 347-C7
SPOKANE CO WA 246-D1
E FARWELL RD
SPOKANE CO WA 347-C7
FARWEST DR
LAKEWOOD WA 181-C4
S FAUCHER RD
YAKIMA CO WA 243-D7
FAUNTLEROY WY SW
SEATTLE WA 280-E7
SEATTLE WA 281-F4
SEATTLE WA 284-D3
FAUST RD
KITTITAS CO WA 241-B5
FAUST RD U.S.-97
KITTITAS CO WA 241-B5
FAWCETT CREEK RD
TILLAMOOK CO OR 197-C3
FAWN CREEK RD
JACKSON CO OR 230-A3
FAYETTEVILLE DR
LINN CO OR 210-A1
SW FEATHER DR
JEFFERSON CO OR 208-B7
JEFFERSON CO OR 212-D1
FEDERAL AV
GRAND COULEE WA 237-C3
FEDERAL WY
ADA CO ID 253-D4
BOISE ID 253-C3
FEEDVILLE RD
UMATILLA CO OR 129-A1
FEIGLEY RD W
KITSAP CO WA 174-B4
FELL AV
CITY OF N VANCOUVER BC 254-J4
DIST OF N VANCOUVER BC 254-J4
FELLER RD
MARION CO OR 199-A7
FELLOWS RD
CLACKAMAS CO OR 200-B6
FELTHAM RD
DISTRICT OF SAANICH BC 257-B2
FENK RD
TILLAMOOK CO OR 197-B2
FENTON LN
KLICKITAT CO WA 127-C1
FENTON RD
PITT MEADOWS BC 157-C4
FENWICK ST
COOS BAY OR 333-C5
FENWICK RANCH RD
MALHEUR CO OR 155-A1
FERGIE RD
UMATILLA CO OR 121-B3
UMATILLA CO OR 129-B1
FERGUSON AV
MAPLE RIDGE BC 157-D5
FERGUSON RD
DESCHUTES CO OR 332-J12
KLICKITAT CO WA 120-A3
S FERGUSON RD
CLACKAMAS CO OR 200-A5
FERGUSON DIV
DISTRICT OF SURREY BC 157-A6
FERN AV
WALLA WALLA WA 345-D9
WALLA WALLA EAST WA 345-D9
FERN CRES
MAPLE RIDGE BC 157-D5
NE FERN LN
JEFFERSON CO OR 208-C3
FERN RD
BENTON CO OR 133-B1
FERN ST
DIST OF N VANCOUVER BC 255-F6
E FERNAN RD
KOOTENAI CO ID 245-B7
FERNAN HILL RD
KOOTENAI CO ID 245-B7
E FERNAN LAKE RD
COEUR D'ALENE ID 355-J11
FERNAN LAKE VILLAGE ID 355-J11
KOOTENAI CO ID 355-J11
FERNCLIFF AV NE
KITSAP CO WA 174-D2
FERNDALE AV
DISTRICT OF MISSION BC 94-B3
FERNDALE RD
DISTRICT OF SAANICH BC 159-D5
DISTRICT OF SAANICH BC 257-D1
WHATCOM CO WA 158-C6
FERN HILL RD
COLUMBIA CO OR 189-B5
RAINIER OR 189-B5
WASHINGTON CO OR 198-B2
FERN HILL RD W
RAINIER OR 189-B4
FERN RIDGE RD
CURRY CO OR 224-B3
MARION CO OR 134-A1
FERN RIDGE RD SE
MARION CO OR 133-C1
STAYTON OR 133-C1
FERNS CORNER RD
POLK CO OR 204-A7
FERNVALE RD
DOUGLAS CO OR 225-B6
FERN VALLEY RD
JACKSON CO OR 234-B2
PHOENIX OR 234-B2
FERNWOOD DR
JOSEPHINE CO OR 233-A5
FERNWOOD RD
NEWBERG OR 198-D6
YAMHILL CO OR 198-D6
FERRALL RD
COLUMBIA CO WA 122-A2
S FERRALL ST
SPOKANE WA 349-F11
FERREL RD SW
DOUGLAS CO WA 239-C2
FERRIER RD
LEWIS CO WA 187-C4
FERRY
BRITISH COLUMBIA 101-A1
BRITISH COLUMBIA 159-C1
DIST OF CENTRAL SAANICH BC 159-B3
TOWN OF SIDNEY BC 159-C2
FERRY RD
JOSEPHINE CO OR 229-A5
TILLAMOOK CO OR 197-A6
FERRY ST
ALBANY OR 326-C8
DAYTON OR 198-C7
WENATCHEE WA 238-D4
WENATCHEE WA 239-A4
YAMHILL CO OR 198-C7
FERRY ST SE Rt#-22
SALEM OR 322-H13
FERRY CANYON RD
GILLIAM CO OR 128-A2
FERTILE VALLEY RD
PEND OREILLE CO WA 106-C3
FIDDLE CREEK RD
LANE CO OR 214-B5
FIELD AV
CENTRALIA WA 299-F5
LEWIS CO WA 299-F5
FIELD RD
POLK CO OR 207-B1
SKAGIT CO WA 161-A5
FIELD ST
LONGVIEW WA 302-G9
FIELD CREEK RD
GRANT CO OR 137-A2
MALHEUR CO OR 154-C2
MALHEUR CO OR 155-A2
FIELDER CREEK RD
JACKSON CO OR 229-D5
FIELDING AV
BELLINGHAM WA 258-E9
FIELDS CREEK RESERVOIR RD
MALHEUR CO OR 155-A1
FIELDS-DENIO RD
HARNEY CO OR 145-C3
HARNEY CO OR 146-A3
HARNEY CO OR 153-C1
FIELDS GULCH RD
COLUMBIA CO WA 122-A2
FIELDSTONE RD
BELLINGHAM WA 160-D2
BELLINGHAM WA 258-A12
FIFE ST
TACOMA WA 292-E3
FIFTEENMILE BOULE RD
WASCO CO OR 127-B2
FIFTEENMILE FAIRBANKS MRKT RD
WASCO CO OR 127-B1
WASCO CO OR 196-D7
FIFTEENMILE RESERVOIR RD
MALHEUR CO OR 154-A2
FIFTH AV
DOUGLAS CO OR 225-B2
YAKIMA CO WA 120-A2
FIFTH AV Rt#-172
DOUGLAS CO WA 112-C1
MANSFIELD WA 112-C1
FIFTH ST
BURBANK WA 121-A3
TOWN OF SIDNEY BC 159-C2
WALLA WALLA CO WA 121-A3
WALLACE ID 115-C2
WENATCHEE WA 238-D4
WEST WENATCHEE WA 238-D4
FILBERT DR
SNOHOMISH CO WA 171-C5
FILBERT RD
CLACKAMAS CO OR 200-C5
SNOHOMISH CO WA 171-C5
FILBERT RD Rt#-524
SNOHOMISH CO WA 171-B5
FILLMORE DR NW
PIERCE CO WA 181-C1
FINCH PL
TOWN OF SIDNEY BC 159-C2
FINCH RD
JOSEPHINE CO OR 233-A3
WHITMAN CO WA 114-C3
FINCH RD NE
KITSAP CO WA 271-J2
FINLANDIA LN
VALLEY CO ID 252-D1
FINLAY RD NE
MARION CO OR 205-B5
FINLAYSON ST
CITY OF VICTORIA BC 256-H6
FINLAYSON ARM RD
BRITISH COLUMBIA 159-B5
FINLEY BUTTE RD
DESCHUTES CO OR 143-A1
FINN RD
CITY OF RICHMOND BC 156-B7
FINNEGAN RD
SHERMAN CO OR 127-C2
FINNEGAN WY
BELLINGHAM WA 258-B10
FINNERTY RD
DISTRICT OF SAANICH BC 257-D3
FINNEY ST
CULDESAC ID 123-B2
FINN HALL RD
CLALLAM CO WA 165-D6
NE FINN HILL RD
CLARK CO WA 193-B4
NW FINN HILL RD
KITSAP CO WA 170-B6
FINNIGAN HILL RD
WASHINGTON CO OR 198-C4
FINN SETTLEMENT RD
SNOHOMISH CO WA 168-C3
NW FIR LN
JEFFERSON CO OR 208-B4
FIR RD
COOS CO OR 220-B4
FIR ST
COULEE DAM WA 237-C2
LEAVENWORTH WA 238-A1
NORTHPORT WA 106-A1
OLYMPIA WA 297-B5
PORT TOWNSEND WA 263-G4
STEVENS CO WA 106-A1
VANCOUVER BC 254-E13
E FIR ST
MOUNT VERNON WA 260-C11
FIR ST SE
TOLEDO OR 206-C5
NW FIR CREST RD
YAMHILL CO OR 198-A6
FIRDALE RD
WASHINGTON CO OR 198-C3
FIRE RD
DESCHUTES CO OR 217-A6
FIRECLAY RD
LANE CO OR 219-D4
FIRE WARDEN RD
MASON CO WA 179-B3
FIREWOOD RD
CLACKAMAS CO OR 126-A3
FIR GROVE LN SE
MARION CO OR 133-C1
FIRING CENTER RD
YAKIMA CO WA 243-C5
FIR ISLAND RD
SKAGIT CO WA 168-A2
FIRLANE RD
COWLITZ CO WA 189-D1
FIR MOUNTAIN RD
HOOD RIVER CO OR 195-D6
HOOD RIVER CO OR 202-D1
FIRST AV
SISKIYOU CO CA 150-A3
ZILLAH WA 120-A2
FIRST ST
ATHOL ID 245-B2
ELK RIVER ID 123-C1
KOOTENAI CO ID 245-B2
WALLA WALLA CO WA 121-B3
FIRST ST Rt#-8
ELK RIVER ID 123-C1
FIRST ST Rt#-27
FAIRFIELD WA 114-C2
FIRST ST Rt#-904
CHENEY WA 246-A7
FIRST ST U.S.-101
COSMOPOLIS WA 178-B7
E FIRST ST Rt#-903
CLE ELUM WA 240-B2
E FIRST ST U.S.-101
COSMOPOLIS WA 117-A1
N FIRST ST Rt#-903
ROSLYN WA 240-A1
S FIRST ST Rt#-903
ROSLYN WA 240-A1
W FIRST ST
CENTRALIA WA 299-E3
WAPATO WA 120-A2
YAKIMA CO WA 120-A2
W FIRST ST Rt#-21
LIND WA 121-B1
W FIRST ST Rt#-903
CLE ELUM WA 240-B2
W FIRST ST Rt#-904
CHENEY WA 246-A7
SW FIRST CREEK CTO
JEFFERSON CO OR 211-B2
FIRST CREEK RD
CHELAN CO WA 236-A2
N FIRST CREEK RD
JEFFERSON CO OR 211-B1
FIR TREE DR SE
THURSTON CO WA 184-D1
N FIR VILLA RD
POLK CO OR 204-A6
SE FIR VILLA RD
DALLAS OR 204-A6
POLK CO OR 204-A6
FIRWOOD RD
CLACKAMAS CO OR 200-D5
S FISCHERS MILL RD
CLACKAMAS CO OR 200-A5
FISH RD
AULT FIELD WA 170-D1
S FISH RD
AULT FIELD WA 170-D1
FISHBACK RD
POLK CO OR 207-A1
FISH CREEK RD
DOUGLAS CO OR 222-D5
FISHER RD
DOUGLAS CO OR 221-B3
LEWIS CO ID 123-B2
LEWIS CO WA 187-C2
SNOHOMISH CO WA 171-B4
FISHER CREEK RD
VALLEY CO ID 251-C1
FISHER HILL RD
KLICKITAT CO WA 196-B4
FISHERMAN RD
MALHEUR CO OR 147-A1
FISH HATCHERY DR
LINN CO OR 133-C1
FISH HATCHERY RD
ENTERPRISE OR 130-C2
JOSEPHINE CO OR 229-A7
MASON CO WA 179-B3
WALLOWA CO OR 130-C2
FISHHAWK RD
COLUMBIA CO OR 117-B3
FISHHAWK FALLS HWY
CLATSOP CO WA 117-A3
CLATSOP CO OR 125-A1
FISH HOOK RD
WALLA WALLA CO WA 121-B2
FISH LAKE RD
ADAMS CO ID 251-B4
HARNEY CO OR 145-B3
OKANOGAN CO WA 104-C2
FISH LAKE CREEK RD
DOUGLAS CO OR 222-B7
FISHOOK ELGIN RD
FRANKLIN CO WA 121-B2
FISH POND RD
COWLITZ CO WA 189-C4
FISHTRAP RD
COOS CO OR 220-D5
FISHTRAP LANDING RD
COOS CO OR 220-D6
FIVE CORNERS RD
LAKE CO OR 152-A2
FIVE FORKS RD SW
THURSTON CO WA 180-A6
FIVE MILE RD
WALLA WALLA CO WA 122-A3
FIVEMILE RD
BAKER CO OR 138-C1
WASCO CO OR 127-B2
WASCO CO OR 202-D3

STREET / City State / Page-Grid

N FIVE MILE RD
BOISE ID 253-B2
COUNTRY HOMES WA 346-F10
SPOKANE WA 346-E11
SPOKANE CO WA 346-E11
S FIVE MILE RD
ADA CO ID 253-B3
W FIVE MILE RD
SPOKANE WA 346-F14
SPOKANE WA 348-G1
FIVE RIVERS RD
LINCOLN CO OR 209-D3
FIVESTICKS RD
DOUGLAS CO OR 226-B2
FJORD DR NE
KITSAP CO WA 170-B7
FLAEGER RD
CLARK CO WA 192-C1
FLAGLER RD Rt#-116
HADLOCK-IRONDALE WA 170-B1
JEFFERSON CO WA 167-B7
JEFFERSON CO WA 170-B1
FLAG POINT RD
WASCO CO OR 202-D5
FLAGSTAFF LN
SKAGIT CO WA 160-D7
FLAGSTAFF LAKE RD
LAKE CO OR 152-B1
FLANNIGAN CREEK RD
LATAH CO ID 249-D2
SE FLAVEL ST
PORTLAND OR 318-D6
PORTLAND OR 319-G6
FLEMING RD
CROOK CO OR 213-B5
WHITMAN CO WA 122-A1
FLETCHER LN
YAKIMA CO WA 243-A4
FLETCHER RD
COLUMBIA CO WA 122-A2
LEWIS CO ID 123-B2
YAMHILL CO OR 198-B7
FLETCHER BAY RD NE
KITSAP CO WA 174-C1
KITSAP CO WA 271-G2
FLETT RD
YAMHILL CO OR 198-B3
FLIER RD
KITSAP CO WA 170-B7
FLINT RD
OWYHEE CO ID 147-B3
N FLINT RD
SPOKANE CO WA 246-A4
S FLINT RD
SPOKANE CO WA 246-A4
FLOATING FEATHER RD
ADA CO ID 253-A1
EAGLE ID 253-A1
FLORA LN
WALLOWA CO OR 122-C3
N FLORA RD
GREEN ACRES WA 351-E3
SPOKANE CO WA 351-E3
TRENTWOOD WA 351-E3
FLORA ST
BELLINGHAM WA 258-D6
FLORAL AV
ASTORIA WA 300-A5
FLORAS CREEK RD
CURRY CO OR 224-B3
FLORAS LAKE RD
CURRY CO OR 224-A3
FLORAS LAKE LOOP RD
CURRY CO OR 224-B3
FLORENCE AV
ASTORIA WA 300-A5
FLORENCE ACRES RD
SNOHOMISH CO WA 110-C1
FLORENCE EUGENE HWY Rt#-126
EUGENE OR 215-A2
EUGENE OR 329-A6
LANE CO OR 215-A2
FLORENCE-EUGENE HWY Rt#-126
FLORENCE OR 214-C2
LANE CO OR 132-C3
LANE CO OR 133-A3
LANE CO OR 214-C2
VENETA OR 133-B3
FLORIDA ST
LONGVIEW WA 302-J9
LONGVIEW WA 303-A9
FLOURNOY VALLEY RD
DOUGLAS CO OR 141-A2
DOUGLAS CO OR 221-A4
FLOWERY TRAIL RD
STEVENS CO WA 106-B3
SW FLUKE DR
WASHINGTON CO OR 198-B2
FLUME GULCH RD
JOSEPHINE CO OR 229-A2
FLUME RANCH RD
DESCHUTES CO OR 212-D3
FLYNN ST
BELLINGHAM WA 258-J6
FOBERT RD
MARION CO OR 205-C1
FOBERT RD NE
MARION CO OR 205-C1
FOBES RD
SNOHOMISH CO WA 171-D3
FOLEY DR
HARNEY CO OR 145-A1
N FOLEY DR
BURNS OR 145-B1
HARNEY CO OR 145-B1
FOLEY RD
ADAMS CO WA 121-A1
FOLLY FARM CTO
MALHEUR CO OR 146-A3
FOLLY FARM RD
MALHEUR CO OR 146-A3
FOLSOM RD
CLACKAMAS CO OR 200-B5
FONES RD SE
OLYMPIA WA 297-D6
FOOT PTH
FERRY CO WA 105-B1
FOOT TR
POLK CO OR 204-A7
FOOTHILL BLVD
GRANTS PASS OR 335-H8
FOOTHILL DR
MALHEUR CO OR 139-A3
FOOTHILL RD
BAKER CO OR 130-A3
CANYON CO ID 147-B1
JACKSON CO OR 230-D7
JACKSON CO OR 336-J5
LATAH CO ID 249-C4
UNION CO OR 130-A2
N FOOTHILL RD
JACKSON CO OR 336-J10
MEDFORD OR 336-J9
FOOTHILLS BLVD
JACKSON CO OR 229-D6
ROGUE RIVER OR 229-D6
E FOOTHILLS RD
SPOKANE CO WA 247-A1
FOOTS CREEK RD
JACKSON CO OR 229-D7
JACKSON CO OR 230-A7
FORBES AV
CITY OF N VANCOUVER BC 255-A6
SW FORD LN
JEFFERSON CO OR 208-B7
FORD RD
DESCHUTES CO OR 217-D4
DISTRICT OF CHILLIWACK BC 94-C3
JACKSON CO OR 229-D3
MASON CO WA 179-B2
PITT MEADOWS BC 157-B5
NW FORD RD
YAMHILL CO OR 198-A3
FORDAIR RD NE
GRANT CO WA 113-A2
FORD DETOUR RD
PITT MEADOWS BC 157-B5
FORD LOOP RD
MASON CO WA 179-B4
FORD-WELLPINIT RD
STEVENS CO WA 114-A1
FORDYCE RD
YAKIMA CO WA 120-B2
FOREMAN RD
GRAYS HARBOR CO WA 179-C6
FOREST DR SE
BELLEVUE WA 175-C3
FOREST RD
WALLA WALLA CO WA 121-C3
S FOREST ST
SEATTLE WA 282-A3
FOREST CANYON RD E
PIERCE CO WA 182-C3
FOREST CREEK RD
JOSEPHINE CO OR 233-C3
FOREST LAKE RD
CASCADE LOCKS OR 194-D5
FOREST RIDGE RD NE
MARION CO OR 205-C5
FOREST ROUTE 42N 12
SISKIYOU CO CA 150-B3
FOREST ROUTE 5E 01
SISKIYOU CO CA 149-A3
FOREST ROUTE 5E 02
DEL NORTE CO CA 148-C3
SISKIYOU CO CA 148-C3
SISKIYOU CO CA 149-A3
FORGERY RD
ASOTIN CO WA 122-C3
S FORK RD
ASOTIN CO WA 122-C2
FORKED HORN RD
DESCHUTES CO OR 212-A5
E FORKER RD
SPOKANE CO WA 351-A1
TRENTWOOD WA 351-A1
N FORKER RD
SPOKANE CO WA 247-A1
SPOKANE CO WA 351-A1
TRENTWOOD WA 351-A1
N FORK JOHN DAY RD
GRANT CO OR 129-A3
UMATILLA CO OR 129-A3
S FORK PISTOL RIVER RD
CURRY CO OR 232-C2
N FORK RYEGRASS CK RD
MALHEUR CO OR 146-A3
MALHEUR CO OR 154-B1
FORKS AV N U.S.-101
FORKS WA 169-D1
FORKS AV S U.S.-101
FORKS WA 169-D1
S FORK SMITH RIVER RD
DOUGLAS CO OR 219-A1
W FORK SMITH RIVER RD
DOUGLAS CO OR 133-A3
N FORK TEANAWAY RD
KITTITAS CO WA 111-C3
N FORK TOUCHET RIVER RD
COLUMBIA CO WA 122-A2
FORLORN LAKES RD
SKAMANIA CO WA 195-A1
E FORREST AV
OPPORTUNITY WA 350-J11
N FORREST AV
WESTPORT WA 298-G13
S FORREST AV Rt#-105
WESTPORT WA 298-G14
FORSMAN RD SE
KITSAP CO WA 174-C6
S FORSYTHE RD
CLACKAMAS CO OR 199-D4
CLACKAMAS CO OR 200-A4
FORT RD
WHITE SWAN WA 119-C2
YAKIMA CO WA 120-A2
FORT RD Rt#-220
WHITE SWAN WA 119-C2
YAKIMA CO WA 119-C2
FORT ST
CITY OF VICTORIA BC 256-H9
CITY OF VICTORIA BC 257-C8
DISTRICT OF OAK BAY BC 257-C8
E FORT ST
BOISE ID 253-D3
W FORT ST
ADA CO ID 253-C2
W FORT ST
BOISE ID 253-C2
SEATTLE WA 272-D5
FORT CANBY RD
PACIFIC CO WA 186-A7
FORT CASEY RD
COUPEVILLE WA 167-B4
ISLAND CO WA 167-B4
S FORT CASEY RD
ISLAND CO WA 167-B5
FORT CLATSOP RD
CLATSOP CO WA 188-C3
FORT CLATSOP LOOP RD
CLATSOP CO WA 188-C2
W FORT GEORGE WRIGHT DR
SPOKANE WA 348-E7
SPOKANE CO WA 348-E7
FORT HILL RD
POLK CO OR 125-A3
SW FORT HILL RD
POLK CO OR 125-A3
YAMHILL CO OR 125-A3
FORT JONES RD Rt#-3
YREKA CA 149-C3
FORT KLAMATH RD
KLAMATH CO OR 338-F7
KLAMATH FALLS OR 338-F7
FORT MCKAY RD
DOUGLAS CO OR 221-B1
SUTHERLIN OR 221-B1
W FORT NUGENT RD
ISLAND CO WA 167-B3
FORT ROCK RD
LAKE CO OR 143-B2
FORT STEVENS HWY
CLATSOP CO WA 188-B2
WARRENTON WA 188-B2
FORT STEVENS HWY SPUR
WARRENTON WA 188-B2
FORT VANCOUVER WY
VANCOUVER WA 305-H4
FORTY FIVE RD
SNOHOMISH CO WA 168-C6
FOSBERG RD
LAKE OSWEGO OR 320-A5
FOSS RD
JACKSON CO OR 234-B3
TILLAMOOK CO OR 125-A1
TILLAMOOK CO OR 191-C4
FOSSIL ST Rt#-218
ANTELOPE OR 127-C3
FOSTER AV
COQUITLAM BC 157-A4
COTTONWOOD ID 123-C3
DISTRICT OF COQUITLAM BC 156-D4
E FOSTER AV
COEUR D'ALENE ID 355-F11
FOSTER LN
JEFFERSON CO OR 208-C7
FOSTER RD
SKAMANIA CO WA 194-C3
SE FOSTER RD
CLACKAMAS CO OR 200-A3
MULTNOMAH CO OR 200-A2
PORTLAND OR 200-A2
PORTLAND OR 318-E3
PORTLAND OR 319-J5
FOSTER CREEK AV Rt#-173
BRIDGEPORT WA 112-C1
FOSTER CREEK RD
DOUGLAS CO OR 226-D1
FOSTER SLOUGH RD
SNOHOMISH CO WA 171-D3
FOSTER WELLS RD
FRANKLIN CO WA 343-E1
PASCO WA 343-E1
FOUL BAY RD
CITY OF VICTORIA BC 257-B8
DISTRICT OF OAK BAY BC 257-C6
DISTRICT OF SAANICH BC 257-B7
FOULKES RD
ADAMS CO WA 121-B1
FOUR CORNERS RD
JACKSON CO OR 234-C7
JEFFERSON CO WA 263-B13
FOUR MILE RD
WASHINGTON CO ID 139-B2
WHITMAN CO WA 249-A3
FOURMILE RD
GILLIAM CO OR 128-A1
LATAH CO ID 249-C3
FOURMILE BUTTE RD
DESCHUTES CO OR 211-C4
FOURMILE CANAL
KLAMATH CO OR 231-B3
FOURMILE CANYON RD
GILLIAM CO OR 128-B1
W FOUR MOUND RD
SPOKANE CO WA 114-B1
FOURTH AV Rt#-231
STEVENS CO WA 106-B3
W FOURTH AV Rt#-6
PE ELL WA 117-B2
FOURTH AV W Rt#-20
OMAK WA 104-C3
FOURTH ST
MALDEN WA 114-B3
UNION GAP WA 243-C7
WALLA WALLA CO WA 121-B3
SE FOURTH ST
COLLEGE PLACE WA 344-F10
SW FOURTH ST
COLLEGE PLACE WA 344-E10
E FOURTH PLAIN BLVD
VANCOUVER WA 305-H3
VANCOUVER WA 306-B4
E FOURTH PLAIN BLVD Rt#-501
VANCOUVER WA 305-G3
NE FOURTH PLAIN BLVD
VANCOUVER WA 306-E3
VANCOUVER WA 307-G1
W FOURTH PLAIN BLVD Rt#-501
VANCOUVER WA 304-E3
VANCOUVER WA 305-E3
NE FOURTH PLAIN RD
CLARK WA 307-F2
CLARK CO WA 192-D5
VANCOUVER WA 307-F2
NE FOURTH PLAIN RD Rt#-500
CLARK CO WA 192-D5
CLARK CO WA 193-A5
VANCOUVER WA 192-D5
VANCOUVER WA 193-A5
NW FOUR WHEEL DR
KITSAP CO WA 173-D2
FOWLER RD
DISTRICT OF SAANICH BC 159-C4
FOWLER ST
PACIFIC CO WA 117-A1
RAYMOND WA 117-A1
FOX RD
KITTITAS CO WA 241-D5
FOX RD SE
MARION CO OR 205-C6
FOX BUTTE RD
DESCHUTES CO OR 135-B3
FOX HOLLOW RD
EUGENE OR 215-B3
EUGENE OR 330-A14
LANE CO OR 215-B3
LANE CO OR 330-A14
FOX ISLAND BRIDGE RD NW
PIERCE CO WA 181-B2
SW FOXRIDGE RD
YAMHILL CO OR 198-A7
FOX-ROUND BASIN RD
GRANT CO OR 137-A1
FOX SPIT RD
ISLAND CO WA 167-D7
FR 613
BENEWAH CO ID 115-B2
SE FRAGARIA RD
KITSAP CO WA 174-C5
E FRANCIS AV
SPOKANE WA 349-C1
W FRANCIS AV Rt#-291
SPOKANE WA 348-D1
SPOKANE WA 349-A1
TOWN AND COUNTRY WA 348-D1
TOWN AND COUNTRY WA 349-A1
FRANCIS RD
CITY OF RICHMOND BC 156-B6
MOUNT VERNON WA 260-E10
SKAGIT CO WA 161-C6
SKAGIT CO WA 260-G6
FRANK RD
DESCHUTES CO OR 212-C5
FRANK CRANE RD
TILLAMOOK CO OR 191-C6
SE FRANK FOREST RD
JEFFERSON CO OR 208-D7
FRANKLIN AV
ASTORIA WA 300-F4
FRANKLIN AV U.S.-26
DAYVILLE OR 136-C2
GRANT CO OR 136-C2
NE FRANKLIN AV
BEND OR 332-F7
NE FRANKLIN AV U.S.-97
BEND OR 332-F7
NW FRANKLIN AV U.S.-97
BEND OR 332-E7
FRANKLIN BLVD Rt#-99
EUGENE OR 330-C7
LANE CO OR 330-C7
FRANKLIN LN
JEFFERSON CO OR 208-B6
FRANKLIN RD
BOISE ID 253-C3
NAMPA ID 147-C1
FRANKLIN RD U.S.-20
CALDWELL ID 147-B1
CANYON CO ID 147-B1
E FRANKLIN RD
ADA CO ID 253-B3
W FRANKLIN RD
ADA CO ID 253-A3
FRANKS CREEK RD
DAYVILLE OR 136-C2
GRANT CO OR 136-C1
FRANK SMITH RD
COWLITZ CO WA 118-A2
FRANKTON RD
HOOD RIVER CO OR 195-C5
FRANK WATERS RD
SNOHOMISH CO WA 168-B5
FRANZ RD
SKAMANIA CO WA 194-A7
FRASER HWY Rt#-1A
DISTRICT OF MATSQUI BC 102-B1
DISTRICT OF SURREY BC 157-A6
LANGLEY BC 157-B7
LANGLEY BC 158-D1
TOWNSHIP OF LANGLEY BC 102-B1
TOWNSHIP OF LANGLEY BC 158-D1
FRASER ST
VANCOUVER BC 156-B5
VANCOUVER BC 254-J14
FRAZEE-FREDERICK BUTTE RD
LAKE CO OR 143-C2
LAKE CO OR 144-A1
FRAZEN RD
WHITMAN CO WA 249-B1
SE FRAZER AV Rt#-37
PENDLETON OR 129-B1
SW FRAZER AV Rt#-37
PENDLETON OR 129-B1
SW FRAZIER DR
JEFFERSON CO OR 208-A7
FRAZIER RD
COWLITZ CO WA 190-A7
FRD 1400
CLALLAM CO WA 162-D4
FREDERICK BUTTE RD
DESCHUTES CO OR 144-A1
FREDRICKSON INDUSTRIAL PARK RD
PIERCE CO WA 182-A5
FRED SCHNEBLY RD
KITTITAS CO WA 241-C5
FREEMAN RD
CENTRAL POINT OR 230-C7
CLACKAMAS CO OR 199-D7
COLUMBIA CO OR 192-A3
FREEMAN RD E
EDGEWOOD WA 182-B3
FREEMAN RD E
PIERCE CO WA 182-B3
FREEWATER HWY
MILTON-FREEWATER OR 121-C3
UMATILLA CO OR 121-C3
WALLA WALLA CO WA 121-C3
FREEWAY I-5
BELLINGHAM WA 158-D6
BELLINGHAM WA 161-B4
BELLINGHAM WA 258-E2
BLAINE WA 158-C4
BURLINGTON WA 260-C5
CASTLE ROCK WA 187-C5
CENTRALIA WA 299-D4
CHEHALIS WA 299-E13
CLACKAMAS CO OR 199-B3
CLARK CO WA 192-C3
COWLITZ CO WA 187-C5
COWLITZ CO WA 189-C1
COWLITZ CO WA 192-C3
COWLITZ CO WA 303-E2
DES MOINES WA 290-D5
DUPONT WA 181-A6
EVERETT WA 171-B4
EVERETT WA 265-H1
EVERETT WA 268-D7
EVERETT WA 269-F2
FEDERAL WAY WA 175-B7
FEDERAL WAY WA 182-B2
FERNDALE WA 158-D6
FIFE WA 182-B2
GRAND MOUND WA 184-B4
KALAMA WA 189-C1
KELSO WA 189-C1
KELSO WA 303-E2
KENT WA 175-B7
KENT WA 290-D5
KING WA 289-F3
KING CO WA 171-B7
KING CO WA 175-B7
KING CO WA 182-B2
LACEY WA 181-A6
LACEY WA 297-F5
LAKE OSWEGO OR 199-B3
LAKEWOOD WA 181-A6
LEWIS CO WA 184-B4
LEWIS CO WA 187-C3
LEWIS CO WA 299-D4
LYNNWOOD WA 171-B4
MARION CO OR 199-B5
MARYSVILLE WA 171-B4
MILTON WA 182-B2
MOUNT VERNON WA 260-C11
MOUNTLAKE TERRACE WA 171-B4
OLYMPIA WA 296-J7
OLYMPIA WA 297-F5
PIERCE CO WA 181-A6
PIERCE CO WA 182-B2
PORTLAND OR 199-B3
PORTLAND OR 305-H3
PORTLAND OR 309-F5
PORTLAND OR 313-F2
PORTLAND OR 317-F1
PORTLAND OR 320-A1
SEATAC WA 289-F3
SEATAC WA 290-D5
SEATAC WA 291-F1
SEATTLE WA 171-B7
SEATTLE WA 274-B4
SEATTLE WA 278-B7
SEATTLE WA 282-B2
SEATTLE WA 286-D2
SEATTLE WA 287-E5
SHORELINE WA 171-B7
SISKIYOU CO CA 149-C3
SISKIYOU CO CA 150-A3
SKAGIT CO WA 161-B4
SKAGIT CO WA 168-B3
SKAGIT CO WA 260-C2
SNOHOMISH CO WA 168-C4
SNOHOMISH CO WA 171-B4
TACOMA WA 181-A6
TACOMA WA 182-B2
TACOMA WA 293-J7
TACOMA WA 295-G1
THURSTON CO WA 181-A6
THURSTON CO WA 184-B4
THURSTON CO WA 296-F12
THURSTON CO WA 297-A6
TIGARD OR 199-B3
TUALATIN OR 199-B3
TUKWILA WA 287-E5
TUKWILA WA 289-F3
TUKWILA WA 291-F1
TUMWATER WA 184-B4
TUMWATER WA 296-F12
VANCOUVER WA 192-C3
VANCOUVER WA 305-H3
WASHINGTON CO OR 199-B5
WHATCOM CO WA 158-C4
WHATCOM CO WA 161-B4
WHATCOM CO WA 258-E2
WILSONVILLE OR 199-B5
WOODLAND WA 189-C1
WOODLAND WA 192-C3
YREKA CA 149-C3
FREEWAY I-82
BENTON CO WA 120-B2
BENTON CO WA 121-A3
BENTON CO WA 341-A9
BENTON CO WA 342-A13
FAIRVIEW-SUMACH WA 243-C7
GRANDVIEW WA 120-B2
GRANGER WA 120-A2
KITTITAS CO WA 241-B6
KITTITAS CO WA 243-C1
PROSSER WA 120-B2
SUNNYSIDE WA 120-B2
UNION GAP WA 120-A2
UNION GAP WA 243-C7
YAKIMA WA 243-C7
YAKIMA CO WA 120-A2
YAKIMA CO WA 243-C4
ZILLAH WA 120-A2
FREEWAY I-84
ADA CO ID 147-C1
ADA CO ID 253-B3
BOISE ID 253-B3
CALDWELL ID 147-B1
CANYON CO ID 139-B3
FREEWAY I-84
CANYON CO ID 147-B1
MERIDIAN ID 253-B3
NAMPA ID 147-B1
PAYETTE CO ID 139-A3
FREEWAY I-90
ADAMS CO WA 113-C3
ADAMS CO WA 114-B2
BELLEVUE WA 175-C3
CLE ELUM WA 240-D4
COEUR D'ALENE ID 354-H7
COEUR D'ALENE ID 355-A7
DISHMAN WA 350-F6
ELLENSBURG WA 241-C6
FERNAN LAKE VILLAGE ID 355-H11
GRANT CO WA 112-C3
GRANT CO WA 113-C3
GRANT CO WA 120-B1
GRANT CO WA 242-D3
GREEN ACRES WA 351-C7
ISSAQUAH WA 175-C3
ISSAQUAH WA 176-B4
KELLOGG ID 115-C2
KING CO WA 111-A2
KING CO WA 175-C3
KING CO WA 176-B4
KITTITAS CO WA 111-A2
KITTITAS CO WA 120-A1
KITTITAS CO WA 240-D4
KITTITAS CO WA 241-C6
KOOTENAI CO ID 115-B2
KOOTENAI CO ID 245-B7
KOOTENAI CO ID 248-B1
KOOTENAI CO ID 352-J9
KOOTENAI CO ID 353-F7
KOOTENAI CO ID 354-B7
KOOTENAI CO ID 355-A7
LINCOLN CO WA 114-B2
MERCER ISLAND WA 175-C3
MERCER ISLAND WA 283-H1
MOSES LAKE WA 242-D3
NORTH BEND WA 176-B4
OPPORTUNITY WA 350-F6
OSBURN ID 115-C2
PINEHURST ID 115-C2
POST FALLS ID 352-J9
POST FALLS ID 353-G6
POST FALLS ID 354-B7
SEATTLE WA 278-B7
SEATTLE WA 282-C1
SEATTLE WA 283-H1
SHOSHONE CO ID 115-C2
SNOQUALMIE WA 176-B4
SPOKANE WA 348-B14
SPOKANE WA 349-B10
SPOKANE CO WA 114-B2
SPOKANE CO WA 246-B5
SPOKANE CO WA 348-B14
SPOKANE CO WA 349-J8
SPOKANE CO WA 350-F6
SPOKANE CO WA 351-C7
SPOKANE CO WA 352-C12
SPRAGUE WA 114-B2
VERADALE WA 351-C7
WALLACE ID 115-C2
FREEWAY I-99
DISTRICT OF DELTA BC 101-C1
DISTRICT OF SURREY BC 101-C1
FREEWAY I-182
BENTON CO WA 121-A3
BENTON CO WA 341-E4
FRANKLIN CO WA 342-B2
PASCO WA 342-C1
PASCO WA 343-A4
RICHLAND WA 341-J3
RICHLAND WA 342-A3
WEST PASCO WA 342-A3
WEST PASCO WA 343-A4
FREEWAY I-184
ADA CO ID 253-B3
BOISE ID 253-C3
FREEWAY I-205
CLARK WA 307-H2
CLARK CO WA 192-D5
MAYWOOD PARK OR 315-H4
PORTLAND OR 193-A7
PORTLAND OR 311-J2
PORTLAND OR 315-H4
PORTLAND OR 319-G1
VANCOUVER WA 192-D5
VANCOUVER WA 307-H2
VANCOUVER WA 311-J2
FREEWAY I-405
BELLEVUE WA 175-C4
BOTHELL WA 171-C6
KING CO WA 171-C7
KING CO WA 175-C4
KIRKLAND WA 171-C7
KIRKLAND WA 175-C4
NEWCASTLE WA 175-C4
PORTLAND OR 312-E3
PORTLAND OR 313-E3
PORTLAND OR 317-E1
RENTON WA 175-C4
RENTON WA 289-J4
SNOHOMISH CO WA 171-C6
TUKWILA WA 289-J4
FREEWAY I-705
TACOMA WA 293-H4
TACOMA WA 295-J2
FREEWAY Rt#-3
BREMERTON WA 174-B4
BREMERTON WA 270-C6
KITSAP CO WA 170-B6
KITSAP CO WA 174-B1
KITSAP CO WA 270-B1
NAVY YARD CITY WA 270-E11
SILVERDALE WA 174-B1
SILVERDALE WA 270-B1
TRACYTON WA 270-A4
FREEWAY Rt#-7
TACOMA WA 295-H1
FREEWAY Rt#-8
ELMA WA 179-D6
GRAYS HARBOR CO WA 179-D6
MCCLEARY WA 179-D6
THURSTON CO WA 179-D6
THURSTON CO WA 180-B6
FREEWAY Rt#-16
BREMERTON WA 174-B7

STREET City State Page-Grid

FREEWAY Rt#-16
GIG HARBOR WA 181-C2
KITSAP CO WA 174-B7
PIERCE CO WA 174-B7
PIERCE CO WA 181-C2
PORT ORCHARD WA 174-B7
TACOMA WA 181-C2
TACOMA WA 294-D1
TACOMA WA 295-E1
FREEWAY Rt#-18
AUBURN WA 182-B1
FEDERAL WAY WA 182-B1
KING CO WA 182-B1
FREEWAY Rt#-26
GRANT CO WA 120-B1
FREEWAY Rt#-91
CITY OF RICHMOND BC 156-B6
FREEWAY Rt#-99
BRITISH COLUMBIA 158-B3
CITY OF RICHMOND BC 156-B6
DISTRICT OF DELTA BC 156-C7
DISTRICT OF SURREY BC 158-A1
KING WA 286-B4
SEATTLE WA 281-J7
SEATTLE WA 285-J1
SEATTLE WA 286-B4
TUKWILA WA 286-B4
WHATCOM CO WA 158-B3
FREEWAY Rt#-167
AUBURN WA 182-B3
PACIFIC WA 182-B3
PIERCE CO WA 182-B3
PUYALLUP WA 182-B3
SUMNER WA 182-B3
FREEWAY Rt#-240
KENNEWICK WA 342-D7
KENNEWICK WA 343-A9
RICHLAND WA 341-H4
RICHLAND WA 342-A6
FREEWAY Rt#-410
PIERCE CO WA 182-C3
SUMNER WA 182-C3
FREEWAY Rt#-509
BURIEN WA 175-A5
BURIEN WA 288-A2
BURIEN WA 290-A1
KING WA 286-A5
KING WA 288-A2
SEATAC WA 288-A6
SEATAC WA 290-A1
SEATTLE WA 285-J1
SEATTLE WA 286-A5
TACOMA WA 182-A2
TACOMA WA 293-J6
FREEWAY Rt#-512
LAKEWOOD WA 181-D4
PIERCE CO WA 181-D4
PIERCE CO WA 182-A4
PUYALLUP WA 182-A4
FREEWAY Rt#-516
KENT WA 290-D7
FREEWAY Rt#-518
BURIEN WA 175-A5
BURIEN WA 288-B4
SEATAC WA 288-B4
TUKWILA WA 288-D5
TUKWILA WA 289-F4
FREEWAY Rt#-520
BELLEVUE WA 175-D1
CLYDE HILL WA 175-D1
HUNTS POINT WA 175-D1
KING CO WA 175-D1
MEDINA WA 175-D1
MEDINA WA 279-E1
REDMOND WA 175-D1
SEATTLE WA 278-D1
SEATTLE WA 279-E1
YARROW POINT WA 175-D1
FREEWAY Rt#-522
BOTHELL WA 171-C6
KING CO WA 171-C6
SNOHOMISH CO WA 171-C6
WOODINVILLE WA 171-C6
FREEWAY Rt#-526
EVERETT WA 267-F4
EVERETT WA 268-A4
MUKILTEO WA 267-F4
SNOHOMISH WA 267-F4
FREEWAY Rt#-599
TUKWILA WA 286-D7
TUKWILA WA 287-E7
TUKWILA WA 289-E1
FREEWAY U.S.-2
CASHMERE WA 238-C2
CHELAN CO WA 238-C2
DOUGLAS CO WA 239-A3
EAST WENATCHEE BENCH WA 238-C2
EAST WENATCHEE BENCH WA 239-A3
EVERETT WA 265-J4
SNOHOMISH WA 265-J4
SNOHOMISH CO WA 171-D2
SUNNYSLOPE WA 238-C2
FREEWAY U.S.-12
CENTRAL PARK WA 178-C7
ELMA WA 179-A7
GRAYS HARBOR CO WA 178-B7
GRAYS HARBOR CO WA 179-A7
MONTESANO WA 178-D7
PASCO WA 343-H5
FREEWAY U.S.-97
EAST WENATCHEE BENCH WA 238-D3
SUNNYSLOPE WA 238-D3
FREEWAY U.S.-101
MASON CO WA 180-B5
OLYMPIA WA 296-E7
THURSTON CO WA 180-B5
THURSTON CO WA 296-B5
TUMWATER WA 296-E7
FREEWAY U.S.-395
BENTON CO WA 121-A3
HIGHLAND WA 121-A3
KENNEWICK WA 343-B9
LEWISTON OR 121-A3
PASCO WA 343-D5
UMATILLA CO OR 121-A3
WEST PASCO WA 343-C5
FREEWAY DR
MOUNT VERNON WA 260-B10
FREIMUTH RD
YAKIMA CO WA 243-B4
E FREMONT AV
SELAH WA 243-B5
W FREMONT AV
SELAH WA 243-B5
FREMONT AV N
SEATTLE WA 273-H5
SHORELINE WA 171-A6
FREMONT HWY Rt#-31
DESCHUTES CO OR 143-A1
KLAMATH CO OR 143-A1
LAKE CO OR 143-B2
LAKE CO OR 151-C1
LAKE CO OR 152-A1
PAISLEY OR 151-C1
FREMONT HWY U.S.-395
LAKE CO OR 152-A2
LAKEVIEW OR 152-A2
MODOC CO CA 152-A3
FREMONT PL N
SEATTLE WA 273-H6
NE FREMONT ST
PORTLAND OR 313-H2
PORTLAND OR 314-C2
PORTLAND OR 315-E2
FREMONT ST E
THE DALLES OR 196-D7
FREMONT WY N
SEATTLE WA 273-H6
E FRENCH RD
ISLAND CO WA 171-A2
FRENCHGLEN HWY Rt#-205
HARNEY CO OR 145-B1
FRENCHGLEN RD
LAKE CO OR 152-C1
LAKE CO OR 153-A1
E FRENCH GULCH RD
KOOTENAI CO ID 245-B7
FRENCH HILL RD
DEL NORTE CO CA 148-B3
FRENCHMAN CREEK RD
MALHEUR CO OR 154-C2
FRENCHMAN HILL RD
GRANT CO WA 112-B3
GRANT CO WA 120-B1
FRENCH MOUNTAIN RD
JOSEPHINE CO OR 233-C5
FRENCH PRAIRIE RD
MARION CO OR 198-D7
MARION CO OR 199-A6
FRENCH PRAIRIE RD Rt#-219
MARION CO OR 198-D7
FRENCH PRAIRIE RD NE
MARION CO OR 205-A2
FRESHWATER BAY RD
CLALLAM CO WA 164-D5
N FREYA ST
SPOKANE WA 349-F8
S FREYA ST
SPOKANE WA 246-C5
SPOKANE WA 349-F11
SPOKANE CO WA 246-C5
FREYRER PARK RD
CLACKAMAS CO OR 126-A3
FRIDAY CREEK RD
SKAGIT CO WA 161-B4
FRIEDA AV
ALTAMONT OR 338-J9
ALTAMONT OR 339-A9
FRIEND RD
WASCO CO OR 127-A2
FRIENDLY ST
EUGENE OR 329-H10
FRIENDS RD
CANYON CO ID 147-B1
FRIES RD
LEWIS CO WA 187-B3
FRITZ HOEFT RD
UMATILLA CO OR 129-B2
FRIZZELL RD
POLK CO OR 204-B4
SW FROBASE RD
WASHINGTON CO OR 199-B5
FROG CREEK RD
WASCO CO OR 202-B7
FROG HOLLOW RD
WALLA WALLA CO WA 121-C3
WALLA WALLA CO WA 344-A14
FROG LAKE BUTTE RD
WASCO CO OR 202-B7
FROGNER RD
LEWIS CO WA 187-B1
NW FRONT AV
PORTLAND OR 312-C2
S FRONT AV
PASCO WA 343-H8
SW FRONT AV
PORTLAND OR 317-F1
W FRONT AV Rt#-21
LINCOLN CO WA 113-B1
WILBUR WA 113-B1
FRONT ST
COOS BAY OR 333-H12
IDAHO CO ID 123-B3
JOSEPHINE CO OR 229-B1
LYNDEN WA 102-B1
LYNDEN WA 158-D4
MARION CO OR 205-B1
SHOSHONE CO ID 115-C2
WALLACE ID 115-C2
WOODBURN OR 205-B1
FRONT ST Rt#-23
SAINT JOHN WA 114-B3
FRONT ST Rt#-47
GASTON OR 198-B3
GASTON OR 198-B3
FRONT ST Rt#-99
YONCALLA OR 219-B4
FRONT ST Rt#-409
CATHLAMET WA 117-B3
CLATSOP CO WA 117-B3
FRONT ST Rt#-507
BUCODA WA 184-D4
THURSTON CO WA 184-D4
FRONT ST Rt#-547
SUMAS WA 102-B1
WHATCOM CO WA 102-B1
FRONT ST U.S.-20
BOISE ID 253-C2
FRONT ST U.S.-26
GRANT CO OR 137-B2
PRAIRIE CITY OR 137-B2
FRONT ST U.S.-30
HOOD RIVER OR 195-D5
E FRONT ST
ALBION WA 249-A4
E FRONT ST Rt#-39
MERRILL OR 150-C2
N FRONT ST Rt#-99
CENTRAL POINT OR 230-C7
S FRONT ST Rt#-99
CENTRAL POINT OR 230-C7
OAKLAND OR 219-A7
SE FRONT ST Rt#-202
ASTORIA WA 300-D7
CLATSOP CO WA 300-D7
W FRONT ST
ALBION WA 249-A4
W FRONT ST Rt#-39
MERRILL OR 150-C2
FRONT ST N
ISSAQUAH WA 176-A4
FRONT ST NE
SALEM OR 322-J10
FRONT ST NE Rt#-22
SALEM OR 322-H12
FRONT ST NE Rt#-99E
SALEM OR 322-H12
FRONT ST S
ISSAQUAH WA 176-A4
FRONT ST SE Rt#-22
SALEM OR 322-H13
NW FRONT WY
CHEHALIS WA 299-D11
FRONTAGE RD
CURRY CO OR 232-B1
GRANT CO WA 242-A3
MORROW CO OR 128-C1
N FRONTAGE RD
GRANT CO WA 112-C3
GRANT CO WA 242-A3
JOSEPHINE CO OR 225-B7
W FRONTAGE RD
BAKER CO OR 130-B3
FROST RD
KOOTENAI CO ID 247-C6
LEWIS CO WA 187-C3
E FROSTAD RD
ISLAND CO WA 167-C2
W FROSTAD RD
ISLAND CO WA 167-C2
FROSTY CREEK RD
OKANOGAN CO WA 105-A2
FROZEN CREEK RD
DOUGLAS CO OR 221-D7
FRUITDALE DR
GRANTS PASS OR 335-E11
JOSEPHINE CO OR 335-E11
FRUITDALE LN
ISLAND CITY OR 130-A2
UNION CO OR 130-A2
FRUITDALE RD
SEDRO-WOOLLEY WA 161-C6
SKAGIT CO WA 161-C5
FRUIT FARM RD
POLK CO OR 207-B1
FRUITLAND AV E
PIERCE CO WA 182-A4
PUYALLUP WA 182-A4
FRUITLAND RD NE
MARION CO OR 323-H13
FRUITVALE BLVD
FRUITVALE WA 243-B6
YAKIMA WA 243-B6
W FRUITVALE BLVD
YAKIMA WA 243-B6
FRUITVALE RD
ADAMS CO ID 131-C3
LINCOLN CO OR 206-B4
FRUIT VALLEY RD
VANCOUVER WA 304-E3
NW FRUIT VALLEY RD
VANCOUVER WA 192-C5
VANCOUVER WA 304-E1
FRY LN
HARNEY CO OR 145-B1
FRY RD
LINN CO OR 207-D6
LINN CO OR 326-J14
MARION CO OR 199-A7
FRYER RD
YAMHILL CO OR 198-B5
FRYREAR RD
DESCHUTES CO OR 212-A5
FS RD 307
ADAMS CO ID 251-B4
FUGATE RD
WHITMAN CO WA 249-A2
FUHRMAN AV E
SEATTLE WA 274-B7
FULLER RD
LEWIS CO WA 187-A1
FULLER CANYON RD
MORROW CO OR 128-C2
FULLERTON RD
COLUMBIA CO OR 192-A3
FULTON AV
DIST OF WEST VANCOUVER BC 254-C3
FULTON RD
UMATILLA CO OR 129-B1
FUNKE RD
LANE CO OR 210-B7
LANE CO OR 215-B1

G

G ST
CLATSOP CO WA 301-H5
GEARHART WA 301-H5
LEWISTON ID 250-C4
SPRINGFIELD OR 330-H6
SPRINGFIELD OR 331-A6
WALLA WALLA CO WA 345-H4
E G ST
TACOMA WA 293-J7
N G ST
ABERDEEN WA 178-B7
S G ST
ABERDEEN WA 178-B7
S G ST
TACOMA WA 295-G2
S G ST U.S.-101
ABERDEEN WA 178-B7
SW G ST
GRANTS PASS OR 335-E9
G ST N U.S.-395
LAKEVIEW OR 152-A2
G 100 RD
GRAYS HARBOR CO WA 179-A6
G 1100 RD
GRAYS HARBOR CO WA 179-A5
SW GAARDE ST
TIGARD OR 199-B3
GABLE RD
SAINT HELENS OR 192-A2
GAFFIN RD SE
MARION CO OR 325-G3
SALEM OR 325-G3
GAGE BLVD
KENNEWICK WA 342-A8
RICHLAND WA 341-H8
RICHLAND WA 342-A8
GAGE RD
POLK CO OR 133-A1
SW GAGE RD
CLACKAMAS CO OR 199-B5
W GAGE RD
RICHLAND WA 341-H8
GAGLARDI WY
DISTRICT OF BURNABY BC 156-D4
GAITHER ST Rt#-229
LINCOLN CO OR 206-C2
SILETZ OR 206-C2
GALE RD
KLAMATH CO OR 151-A2
GALENA DR
DESCHUTES CO OR 212-C3
W GALER ST
SEATTLE WA 276-D2
GALES CREEK RD Rt#-8
FOREST GROVE OR 198-B1
WASHINGTON CO OR 125-B1
WASHINGTON CO OR 198-B1
GALICE RD
JOSEPHINE CO OR 148-C1
JOSEPHINE CO OR 149-A1
GALLAGHER RD
MASON CO WA 179-D3
GALLAHER RD
DOUGLAS CO WA 112-B1
GALLOWAY DR
JEFFERSON CO OR 208-B6
GALLOWAY RD
TILLAMOOK CO OR 197-A5
YAKIMA CO WA 243-B5
GALLS CREEK RD
JACKSON CO OR 230-A6
NW GALVESTON AV
BEND OR 332-C7
GALVIN RD
FORDS PRAIRIE WA 184-B5
FORDS PRAIRIE WA 299-A1
LEWIS CO WA 184-B5
GAMBLE PL NE
KITSAP CO WA 170-C5
S GAMBLE BAY RD NE
KITSAP CO WA 170-C5
GAME FARM RD
EUGENE OR 330-E1
KITTITAS CO WA 241-C5
LANE CO OR 330-E1
North Springfield OR 330-G3
SPRINGFIELD OR 330-E1
N GAME FARM RD
LANE CO OR 215-B1
GAME RIDGE RD
YAKIMA CO WA 243-B4
GANON ST SE
MARION CO OR 325-J5
GAP RD
BROWNSVILLE OR 210-C4
LINN CO OR 210-C4
N GAP RD
BENTON CO WA 120-B3
S GAP RD
BENTON CO WA 120-B3
PROSSER WA 120-B3
GAP RANCH-WAGONTIRE RD
HARNEY CO OR 144-B2
GARBAGE DUMP RD
CLALLAM CO WA 169-C2
GARD RD
CLACKAMAS CO OR 200-A7
GARDEN AV
BENTON CO OR 207-B5
W GARDEN AV
COEUR D'ALENE ID 355-D11
GARDEN WY
LANE CO OR 330-F7
SPRINGFIELD OR 330-F7
GARDENA RD
WALLA WALLA CO WA 121-B3
GARDENA SCHOOL RD
WALLA WALLA CO WA 121-B3
GARDEN CITY RD
CITY OF RICHMOND BC 156-B6
GARDEN SPRINGS RD
SPOKANE WA 348-C13
SPOKANE CO WA 348-C13
NE GARDEN VALLEY BLVD
ROSEBURG OR 334-F5
NW GARDEN VALLEY BLVD
DOUGLAS CO OR 334-B4
ROSEBURG OR 334-F5
GARDEN VALLEY RD
COOS CO OR 220-D4
DOUGLAS CO OR 221-B3
DOUGLAS CO OR 334-A1
GARDNER RD
POLK CO OR 125-B3
SKAGIT CO WA 260-F5
N GARDNER RD
SKAGIT CO WA 260-F2
S GARDNER RD
SPOKANE CO WA 246-B6
S GARDNER ST
BURLINGTON WA 260-F5
SKAGIT CO WA 260-F5
GARDNER RIDGE RD
CURRY CO OR 232-D4
GARFIELD AV
CORVALLIS OR 327-F7
GARFIELD AV SE
KITSAP CO WA 174-C4
N GARFIELD RD
SPOKANE CO WA 246-A3
NE GARFIELD ST Rt#-500
CAMAS WA 193-B7
S GARFIELD ST
HIGHLAND WA 343-C12
KENNEWICK WA 343-C12
S GARFIELD ST Rt#-126
EUGENE OR 329-G6
GARFIELD BAY CTO
BONNER CO ID 244-B4
GARFIELD BAY RD
BONNER CO ID 244-B4
GARFIELD-FARMINGTON RD
FARMINGTON WA 115-A3
GARFIELD WA 114-C3
WHITMAN CO WA 114-C3
WHITMAN CO WA 115-A3
GARIBALDI AV U.S.-101
GARIBALDI OR 191-B7
TILLAMOOK CO OR 191-B7
N GARL ST
BURLINGTON WA 260-C4
SKAGIT CO WA 260-C4
S GARL ST
BURLINGTON WA 260-C9
W GARLAND AV
SPOKANE WA 348-F4
SPOKANE WA 349-A4
GARLOCK RD
COWLITZ CO WA 189-B1
GARNER RD
CLARK CO WA 193-B2
JOSEPHINE CO OR 233-B4
KLICKITAT CO WA 127-B1
YACOLT WA 193-B2
NE GARNER RD
CLARK CO WA 193-B1
GARRARD CREEK RD
GRAYS HARBOR CO WA 117-B1
OAKVILLE WA 117-B1
GARRETT ST
GARDEN CITY ID 253-B2
GARRISON RD Rt#-547
WHATCOM CO WA 102-B1
GARRISON ST
WALLA WALLA WA 345-F7
WALLA WALLA EAST WA 345-F7
GARRISON BUTTE RD
JEFFERSON CO OR 211-D3
GARRITY BLVD
CANYON CO ID 147-C1
GARRITY BLVD U.S.-30
CANYON CO ID 147-C1
NAMPA ID 147-C1
S GARRY RD
LIBERTY LAKE WA 247-B4
SPOKANE CO WA 247-B4
E GARWOOD RD
KOOTENAI CO ID 245-A4
GARY LN
BOISE ID 253-C1
GASSY CREEK RD
DOUGLAS CO OR 219-C7
SW GASTON RD
GASTON OR 198-B3
WASHINGTON CO OR 198-B3
GATE CREEK RD
WASCO CO OR 202-D7
GATE MIMA RD
THURSTON CO WA 184-A3
GATENSBURY RD
COQUITLAM BC 157-A5
PORT MOODY BC 157-A5
GATENSBURY ST
COQUITLAM BC 157-A4
GATEWAY DR
COOS CO OR 220-C4
GATEWAY RD
COOS CO OR 220-C5
GATEWAY ST
SPRINGFIELD OR 330-F3
NE GATEWAY GRADE
JEFFERSON CO OR 208-C2
GATFIELD
GEM CO ID 139-C3
GAZLEY RD
DOUGLAS CO OR 225-C3
GAZLEY BRIDGE RD
DOUGLAS CO OR 225-C3
GAZLEY NORTH RD
DOUGLAS CO OR 225-C2
GAZLEY PACIFIC HWY
DOUGLAS CO OR 225-C3
GEARHART LOOP RD
CLATSOP CO WA 301-G2
GEARHART WA 301-G2
GEARIN RD
MARION CO OR 198-D7
GEARY ST
ALBANY OR 326-E10
S GEIGER BLVD
SPOKANE CO WA 246-B5
SPOKANE CO WA 348-B13
W GEIGER BLVD
SPOKANE CO WA 246-A5
SPOKANE CO WA 348-C11
GEIGER RD
FOREST GROVE OR 198-C1
WASHINGTON CO OR 198-C1
GEISSLER RD
GRAYS HARBOR CO WA 178-C6
W GEISSLER RD
GRAYS HARBOR CO WA 178-C7
GEKELER LN
BOISE ID 253-D3
LA GRANDE OR 130-B2
UNION CO OR 130-B2
GELLOR RD
CLALLAM CO WA 165-D7
GEM AV
MALHEUR CO OR 139-A3
SW GEM LN
JEFFERSON CO OR 208-B7
GEM HEIGHTS DR E
PIERCE CO WA 182-B5
GENE BROWN RD
JOSEPHINE CO OR 233-A6
S GENESEE ST
SEATTLE WA 282-E5
SEATTLE WA 283-F5
SW GENESEE ST
SEATTLE WA 281-F4
GENESEE-JULIAETTA RD
LATAH CO ID 250-D1
GENESEE-TROY RD
LATAH CO ID 249-D7
GENSMAN RD
COLUMBIA CO OR 192-A1
GENZER RD
WASHINGTON CO OR 125-B1
GEO CYPRUS RD
DESCHUTES CO OR 212-A5
GEORGE RD
CLACKAMAS CO OR 200-C5
GEORGE CLARK RD
GRAYS HARBOR CO WA 183-C2
GEORGE HOPPER RD
BURLINGTON WA 260-A8
SKAGIT CO WA 260-A8
GEORGE KNOTT RD
WHITMAN CO WA 114-A3
GEORGE MASSEY TUN Rt#-99
CITY OF RICHMOND BC 156-B7
DISTRICT OF DELTA BC 156-C7
GEORGE SMITH RD
MULTNOMAH CO OR 200-D1
GEORGE TAYLOR RD
COWLITZ CO WA 187-D6
GEORGE WASHINGTON WY
BENTON CO WA 340-F4
RICHLAND WA 340-G9
RICHLAND WA 341-G1
GEORGIA ST
VANCOUVER BC 254-G10
GEORGIA ST Rt#-99
VANCOUVER BC 254-F9
GERBER RD
CLACKAMAS CO OR 200-B4
KLAMATH CO OR 151-A2
NE GERBER RD
CLARK CO WA 193-B1
GERBER-MCKEE RD
CLARK CO WA 193-B1
GERBER RANCH RD
KLAMATH CO OR 151-B2
GERIG DR
LINN CO OR 207-D5
GERKE RD
CROOK CO OR 213-C3
GERKING MARKET RD
DESCHUTES CO OR 212-B7
NW GERMANTOWN RD
MULTNOMAH CO OR 192-A7
WASHINGTON CO OR 192-A7
GERMANY CREEK RD
COWLITZ CO WA 117-B3
COWLITZ CO WA 189-A1
NW GERRISH VALLEY RD
YAMHILL CO OR 198-A3
GERTH ST NW
SALEM OR 322-F12
GERTLER RD
FRANKLIN CO WA 121-B2
GESHWILL LN NE
MARION CO OR 205-B2
NE GHER RD
CLARK WA 307-J1
VANCOUVER WA 307-J1
S GIBBLER RD
YAKIMA CO WA 243-A7
GIBBON RD
JACKSON CO OR 230-C7
JACKSON CO OR 336-A1
E GIBBS RD
SPOKANE CO WA 246-C6
W GIBBS RD
SPOKANE CO WA 246-B6
GIBBS LAKE RD
JEFFERSON CO WA 170-A2
GIBRALTAR DR
SKAGIT CO WA 259-J14
GIBRALTAR RD
SKAGIT CO WA 259-H14
GIBSON RD
COWLITZ CO WA 187-D7
SNOHOMISH CO WA 171-B4
WASHINGTON CO OR 198-C3
S GIBSON RD
CLACKAMAS CO OR 205-D2
SE GIBSON RD
CLARK CO WA 193-C7
GIBSON RD NW
DOUGLAS CO WA 236-D5
POLK CO OR 204-C5
GIBSON RD SW
THURSTON CO WA 184-C3
GIBSON ST
CHELAN WA 236-C3
GIBSON CREEK RD
CROOK CO OR 135-C3
GIBSON HILL RD
ALBANY OR 207-C4
ALBANY OR 326-A4
GIENGER RD
TILLAMOOK CO OR 197-C2
GIFFORD RD SW
THURSTON CO WA 184-B2
GIFFORD LENORE GRADE
NEZ PERCE CO ID 123-B2
GIFFORD REUBENS RD
NEZ PERCE CO ID 123-B2
GIFT AV
DESCHUTES CO OR 212-C7
GIFT RD
DESCHUTES CO OR 212-C7
KLAMATH CO OR 151-A2
GILBERT AV
GLENDALE OR 225-A7
GILBERT RD
CITY OF RICHMOND BC 156-B7
YAKIMA CO WA 243-A7
E GILBERT RD
OTIS ORCHARDS WA 351-J2

STREET
City State Page-Grid

E GILBERT RD
OTIS ORCHARDS WA 352-A8
GILBERT CREEK RD
YAMHILL CO OR 125-A2
SW GILBERT CREEK RD
YAMHILL CO OR 125-A2
GILBERT GRADE Rt#-7
CLEARWATER CO ID 123-C2
GILBERT RANCH RD
MALHEUR CO OR 146-B3
GILBERTSON-ILLAHEE RD NE
KITSAP CO WA 174-C1
KITSAP CO WA 271-B1
NW GILCHRIST ST
BEND OR 332-D8
GILES RD
WHATCOM CO WA 158-C4
GILHAM RD
EUGENE OR 330-B2
GILHOULEY RD
HOOD RIVER CO OR 195-C7
GILIN RD
WHITMAN CO WA 249-B6
GILKEY RD
LINN CO OR 133-C1
GILKEY RD E
SKAGIT CO WA 260-D6
NW GILKINSON RD
MULTNOMAH CO OR 192-A4
GILLESPIE RD
BRITISH COLUMBIA 159-A7
BRITISH COLUMBIA 164-D1
BRITISH COLUMBIA 165-A1
DISTRICT OF METCHOSIN BC 159-A7
GILLESPIE ST
RICHLAND WA 341-F2
GILLEY AV
DISTRICT OF BURNABY BC 156-D5
GILLIAND MCKAY CREEK RD
UMATILLA CO OR 129-B2
GILLIHAN RD
MULTNOMAH CO OR 192-B6
W GILLIS RD
ADAMS CO WA 120-C1
ADAMS CO WA 121-A1
GILMAN AV W
SEATTLE WA 272-E6
SEATTLE WA 273-E6
NW GILMAN BLVD
ISSAQUAH WA 175-D4
ISSAQUAH WA 176-A4
GILMAN DRAV W
SEATTLE WA 277-F1
GILMORE AV
DISTRICT OF BURNABY BC 255-G10
GILMORE DIV
DISTRICT OF BURNABY BC 255-G13
GILMOUR RD S
MARION CO OR 207-C2
GIMPL HILL RD
EUGENE OR 329-B10
LANE CO OR 215-A3
LANE CO OR 329-A10
GINKGO RD
JACKSON CO OR 226-D6
JACKSON CO OR 227-A5
GINKGO ELK RD
JACKSON CO OR 226-C5
GINNETT RD
SKAGIT CO WA 259-C13
GIRL SCOUT RD
SKAMANIA CO WA 195-A5
GIRT RD
COLUMBIA CO OR 189-B5
GISH RD
LEWIS CO WA 187-D2
N GLADE RD
FRANKLIN CO WA 121-A2
FRANKLIN CO WA 343-E2
PASCO WA 343-E2
GLADE CREEK RD
JACKSON CO OR 234-B7
GLADIOLA DR
JOSEPHINE CO OR 335-J11
GLADWIN RD
DISTRICT OF MATSQUI BC 102-B1
GLANFORD AV
DISTRICT OF SAANICH BC 159-C5
DISTRICT OF SAANICH BC 256-E2
GLASER DR
LINN CO OR 207-D7
GLASS LN
JACKSON CO OR 230-C5
GLASS RD
CLACKAMAS CO OR 199-B6
GLASSER HILL RD
STEVENS CO WA 106-B3
E GLEED RD
YAKIMA CO WA 243-A5
N GLEED RD
YAKIMA CO WA 243-A5
GLEN DR
COQUITLAM BC 157-A4
GLEN ST
ASHLAND OR 337-C6
GLEN AIKEN CREEK RD
COOS CO OR 220-D5
GLENAYRE DR
PORT MOODY BC 157-A4
GLENBROOK LP
DOUGLAS CO OR 225-B3
GLENBROOK RD
BENTON CO OR 133-A2
NW GLENCOE RD
HILLSBORO OR 198-D1
GLEN COVE MILL RD
JEFFERSON CO WA 263-C6
PORT TOWNSEND WA 263-C6
GLEN CREEK RD NW
POLK CO OR 322-D11
SALEM OR 322-D11
GLENDALE RD
WHATCOM CO WA 158-D4
E GLENDALE RD
ISLAND CO WA 171-A3
GLENDALE WY S
KING WA 286-B6
GLENDALE VALLEY RD
DOUGLAS CO OR 225-B7
GLENGARY BAY
BONNER CO ID 244-B3
GLENGARY RD
DOUGLAS CO OR 221-C6
GLENGARY BAY RD
BONNER CO ID 244-C3
GLENN ST S
VALE OR 139-A3
GLEN RIDGE DR
CORVALLIS OR 327-C5
E GLENROSE RD
SPOKANE WA 349-G11
SPOKANE CO WA 349-G11
S GLENROSE RD
SPOKANE CO WA 246-C5
SPOKANE CO WA 349-J13
GLENWAY AV
PAYETTE CO ID 139-A3
GLENWOOD AV
EVERETT WA 264-A7
EVERETT WA 268-A1
GLENWOOD BLVD
EUGENE OR 330-F8
GLENWOOD DR
LONGVIEW WA 302-J6
GLENWOOD RD SW
KITSAP CO WA 174-B5
GLENWOOD ST Rt#-44
ADA CO ID 253-C2
BOISE CITY ID 253-C2
GARDEN CITY ID 253-C2
GLENWOOD-GLNDDALE HWY
KLICKITAT CO WA 127-B1
KLICKITAT CO WA 196-D1
GLENWOOD-GOLDNDALE RD
KLICKITAT CO WA 119-A3
G-LINE RD
GRAYS HARBOR CO WA 179-A5
NE GLISAN ST
FAIRVIEW OR 200-B1
GRESHAM OR 200-A1
MULTNOMAH CO OR 200-A1
PORTLAND OR 200-A1
PORTLAND OR 313-J5
PORTLAND OR 314-B5
PORTLAND OR 315-H5
NW GLISAN ST
PORTLAND OR 312-D5
PORTLAND OR 313-F5
GLORY DR SE
THURSTON CO WA 181-A7
GLOVER RD
TOWNSHIP OF LANGLEY BC 157-C7
GLOVER RD Rt#-10
TOWNSHIP OF LANGLEY BC 157-C7
G L WILLIAMS RD
CLARK CO WA 118-A3
GNAT CREEK RD
CLATSOP CO WA 117-A3
GNOS RD
WASHINGTON CO OR 198-C2
GOAT RANCH RD
COLUMBIA CO OR 189-A5
N GOBLE CREEK RD
COWLITZ CO WA 189-D3
S GOBLE CREEK RD
COWLITZ CO WA 189-D3
GODBERTSON RD
WASCO CO OR 196-A7
GODDARD RD
BOISE ID 253-B2
SW GODDARD RD
WASHINGTON CO OR 198-C2
GODOWA SPRINGS RD
KLAMATH CO OR 151-A1
SE GODSEY RD
DALLAS OR 204-A6
GODS VALLEY RD
TILLAMOOK CO OR 191-C3
GOERIG ST
WOODLAND WA 118-A3
WOODLAND WA 192-B1
WOODLAND WA 192-C1
GOERIG ST Rt#-503
WOODLAND WA 118-A3
WOODLAND WA 192-C1
GOETHALS DR
RICHLAND WA 341-F2
N GOING ST
PORTLAND OR 312-E1
PORTLAND OR 313-0
GOLD ST
CENTRALIA WA 299-F6
LEWIS CO WA 299-F6
N GOLD ST
CENTRALIA WA 299-G3
GOLD CREEK RD
TILLAMOOK CO OR 197-D3
GOLD CREEK RD W
KITSAP CO WA 173-D3
GOLDEN RD
SISKIYOU CO CA 151-A3
GOLDENDALE BICKLETON RD
KLICKITAT CO WA 120-A3
KLICKITAT CO WA 127-C1
KLICKITAT CO WA 128-A1
YAKIMA CO WA 120-A3
GOLDENDALE-CENTERVILLE RD
KLICKITAT CO WA 127-C1
GOLDNDALE-GLNWOOD HWY
KLICKITAT CO WA 119-A3
GOLDENDALE GOODNOE HILLS RD
KLICKITAT CO WA 127-C1
KLICKITAT CO WA 128-A1
GOLDEN GARDENS DR NW
SEATTLE WA 272-D1
GOLDEN GIVEN RD E
PIERCE WA 295-J7
PIERCE CO WA 181-D4
GOLDEN MANTEL
JEFFERSON CO OR 212-C2
GOLDFISH FARM RD
ALBANY OR 326-J7
LINN CO OR 326-J7
GOLD FORK RD
VALLEY CO ID 252-D2
GOLD HILL CIR
BONNER CO ID 244-B3
GOLD HILL SPUR Rt#-99
GOLD HILL OR 230-B6
JACKSON CO OR 230-B6
N GOLDIE RD
ISLAND CO WA 167-C2
OAK HARBOR WA 167-C2
GOLD LAKE RD
OKANOGAN CO WA 105-A3
GOLD MOUNTAIN RD
BONNER CO ID 244-B3
GOLD RAY RD
JACKSON CO OR 230-B6
GOLDSTREAM AV Rt#-1A
CITY OF COLWOOD BC 159-B6
DISTRICT OF LANGFORD BC 159-B6
GOLF DR
SEATTLE WA 278-B7
SEATTLE WA 282-B1
GOLF CLUB RD
MARION CO OR 133-C1
STAYTON OR 133-C1
GOLF CLUB RD SE
LACEY WA 297-F6
MARION CO OR 133-C1
STAYTON OR 133-C1
GOLF COURSE RD
AULT FIELD WA 167-B2
ISLAND CO WA 167-B2
PACIFIC CO WA 117-A1
WALLOWA CO OR 130-C2
SW GOLF COURSE RD
WASHINGTON CO OR 198-C2
GOLL RD NW
DOUGLAS CO WA 236-D7
GOLTRA RD
LINN CO OR 207-D6
GOOD RD
BENTON CO WA 120-C3
ISLAND CO WA 168-A3
GOODFELLOW LAKES RD
CLACKAMAS CO OR 201-B4
N GOOD HOPE RD
KOOTENAI CO ID 245-C2
S GOOD HOPE RD
KOOTENAI CO ID 245-C2
GOODMAN LN
ADAMS CO ID 251-B4
GOODMAN MAIN LINE RD
CLALLAM CO WA 169-B2
GOODNIGHT AV
BENTON CO OR 327-G14
CORVALLIS OR 327-G14
GOODNOE STATION RD
KLICKITAT CO WA 127-C1
KLICKITAT CO WA 128-A1
GOODPASTURE ISLAND RD
EUGENE OR 329-H2
EUGENE OR 330-A2
GOODRICH DR NW
KITSAP CO WA 174-B7
PIERCE CO WA 174-B7
GOODRICH HWY
DOUGLAS CO OR 219-A6
GOODRICH RD
DESCHUTES CO OR 212-A5
WASHINGTON CO ID 139-B1
GOODRICH CREEK RD
ADAMS CO ID 139-B1
GOODSPEED RD
TILLAMOOK CO OR 197-B1
SE GOODWIN AV
PENDLETON OR 129-B1
SW GOODWIN AV
PENDLETON OR 129-B1
SW GOODWIN LN
PENDLETON OR 129-B1
GOODWIN RD
KITTITAS CO WA 241-A4
NE GOODWIN RD
CLARK CO WA 193-A6
GOOSEBERRY RD
IONE OR 128-B2
MORROW CO OR 128-B2
GOOSE CREEK RD Rt#-194
WHITMAN CO WA 122-C1
GOOSE CREEK PARK RD
ADAMS CO ID 251-B4
GOOSE LAKE RD
ADAMS CO ID 251-C2
GOPHER VALLEY RD
YAMHILL CO OR 125-B3
SW GOPHER VALLEY RD
YAMHILL CO OR 125-B3
YAMHILL CO OR 204-A2
GORDON RD
WASHINGTON CO OR 125-C1
GORDON CREEK RD
MULTNOMAH CO OR 200-C2
GORDON HEAD RD
DISTRICT OF SAANICH BC 257-C3
GORDON RIDGE RD
SHERMAN CO OR 127-C1
GORE DR
LINN CO OR 207-D6
GORE RD
COWLITZ CO WA 189-D6
YAKIMA CO WA 243-B5
GORGE RD
CHELAN CO WA 236-D3
GORGE RD E Rt#-1A
CITY OF VICTORIA BC 256-F6
GORGE RD W Rt#-1A
CITY OF VICTORIA BC 256-C5
DISTRICT OF SAANICH BC 256-C5
GOSE ST
WALLA WALLA WEST WA 344-F7
GOSHEN-DIVIDE HWY Rt#-99
COTTAGE GROVE OR 215-B6
CRESWELL OR 215-C4
LANE CO OR 215-C4
LANE CO OR 219-C1
LANE CO OR 330-J14
N GOSHEN-DIVIDE HWY Rt#-99
COTTAGE GROVE OR 215-B7
N GOSHEN-DIVIDE ST Rt#-99
COTTAGE GROVE OR 215-B7
S GOSHEN-DIVIDE ST Rt#-99
CRESWELL OR 215-C5
GOSNER RD
JEFFERSON CO OR 136-A1
NE GOSNER RD
JEFFERSON CO OR 135-C1
GOSSETT RD
CLALLAM CO WA 164-C5
E GOSS LAKE RD
ISLAND CO WA 170-D1
GOTHAM BAY RD
KOOTENAI CO ID 248-A2
GOULD RD
PACIFIC CO WA 183-B4
GOULD CITY-MAYVIEW RD
GARFIELD CO WA 122-B2
GOVERNMENT RD
GRANT CO WA 120-B1
LANE CO OR 141-C1
LANE CO OR 215-C7
MATTAWA WA 120-B1
GOVERNMENT ST
BRITISH COLUMBIA 101-A1
CITY OF VICTORIA BC 256-G8
DISTRICT OF BURNABY BC 156-D5
DUNCAN BC 101-A1
N GOVERNMENT WY
COEUR D'ALENE ID 355-E5
DALTON GARDENS ID 355-E5
HAYDEN ID 245-A5
HAYDEN ID 355-E5
KOOTENAI CO ID 245-A5
KOOTENAI CO ID 355-E5
SPOKANE WA 348-D8
SPOKANE CO WA 348-D8
S GOVERNMENT WY
SPOKANE WA 348-E10
SPOKANE CO WA 348-E9
W GOVERNMENT WY
SEATTLE WA 272-D5
GOWDYVILLE RD
LANE CO OR 215-A7
E GOWEN RD Rt#-21
ADA CO ID 253-D4
BOISE ID 253-D4
W GOWEN RD
ADA CO ID 253-C4
BOISE ID 253-C4
GOZZER RD
KOOTENAI CO ID 248-A1
GRABER RD
YAKIMA CO WA 243-B4
GRABHORN RD
WASHINGTON CO OR 199-A3
GRADE CRES
LANGLEY BC 158-C1
GRADE RD
LAKE STEVENS WA 171-D1
GRADE RD SE
MARION CO OR 205-D6
GRADE ST
COWLITZ CO WA 303-D9
KELSO WA 303-D9
GRADE ST SE
THURSTON CO WA 184-C4
GRADE CREEK RD
CHELAN CO WA 236-B1
S GRADY WY
RENTON WA 175-C5
S GRADY WY Rt#-515
RENTON WA 175-C5
SW GRADY WY
RENTON WA 175-C5
RENTON WA 289-J4
TUKWILA WA 289-J4
GRAHAM BLVD
MALHEUR CO OR 138-C3
SW GRAHAM RD
JEFFERSON CO OR 135-A1
GRAHAM CREEK RD
JACKSON CO OR 226-C6
SW GRAHAMS FERRY RD
CLACKAMAS CO OR 199-B5
GRAND AV
ASTORIA WA 300-E5
SEATTLE WA 279-E5
E GRAND AV
EVERETT WA 265-G3
N GRAND AV Rt#-27
PULLMAN WA 249-B5
NE GRAND AV Rt#-99E
PORTLAND OR 313-G4
S GRAND AV Rt#-27
PULLMAN WA 249-B5
SE GRAND AV Rt#-99E
PORTLAND OR 313-G7
PORTLAND OR 317-G2
W GRAND AV
ASTORIA WA 300-B5
GRAND AV NE
KITSAP CO WA 174-D2
GRAND BLVD
CITY OF N VANCOUVER BC 255-C3
VANCOUVER WA 305-J6
VANCOUVER WA 306-A3
S GRAND BLVD
SPOKANE WA 246-C5
SPOKANE WA 349-B13
GRAND COULEE AV Rt#-155
ELECTRIC CITY WA 237-C3
GRAND COULEE WA 237-C3
GRANT CO WA 237-C3
GRAND COULEE AV E Rt#-174
GRAND COULEE WA 237-C3
GRANT CO WA 237-C3
GRAND COULEE AV W Rt#-174
GRAND COULEE WA 237-C3
GRAND COULEE HWY
LINCOLN CO WA 237-D5
GRAND COULEE HWY Rt#-155
GRAND COULEE WA 237-C3
GRANDE RONDE RD
ASOTIN CO WA 122-C3
WALLOWA CO OR 122-C3
GRANDE RONDE RIVER RD
UNION CO OR 129-C2
SE GRAND ISLAND LP
YAMHILL CO OR 204-D2
SE GRAND ISLAND RD
YAMHILL CO OR 204-D2
GRAND PRAIRIE RD
ALBANY OR 326-E10
LINN CO OR 207-D5
LINN CO OR 326-F11
GRAND RONDE RD
POLK CO OR 125-A3
SW GRAND RONDE RD
YAMHILL CO OR 125-A3
GRANDSTROM RD
SKAGIT CO WA 168-C3
GRANDVIEW AV
GRANTS PASS OR 335-F12
JOSEPHINE CO OR 335-F12
GRANDVIEW DR
DISTRICT OF SAANICH BC 257-D1
GRANDVIEW DR W
UNIVERSITY PLACE WA 181-C3
GRANDVIEW HWY
VANCOUVER BC 255-B13
GRANDVIEW RD
BIRCH BAY WA 158-B5
SNOHOMISH CO WA 168-D4
WHATCOM CO WA 158-C5
GRANDVIEW RD Rt#-548
BIRCH BAY WA 158-B5
WHATCOM CO WA 158-B5
SW GRANDVIEW LOOP RD
JEFFERSON CO OR 212-A2
GRANDVIEW PAVEMENT RD
GRANDVIEW WA 120-B3
YAKIMA CO WA 120-B3
GRANGE RD NE
DOUGLAS CO WA 104-C3
GRANGE ST
DISTRICT OF BURNABY BC 156-C5
GRANGEMONT RD
CLEARWATER CO ID 123-C2
OROFINO ID 123-C2
GRANGER AV
BENTON CO OR 207-B5
GRANGER RD
WASHINGTON CO ID 139-C2
GRANGEVIEW RD
KLICKITAT CO WA 195-D4
GRANITE RD
GRANITE OR 137-C1
GRANT CO OR 137-C1
GRANITE CREEK RD
MALHEUR CO OR 146-A1
GRANITE FALLS HWY Rt#-92
GRANITE FALLS WA 102-C3
SNOHOMISH CO WA 102-C3
SNOHOMISH CO WA 110-C1
GRANITE HILL RD
BAKER CO OR 138-A1
JOSEPHINE CO OR 229-C4
JOSEPHINE CO OR 335-F2
SUMPTER OR 138-A1
GRANT AV
CORVALLIS OR 327-F8
MAPLE RIDGE BC 157-D6
GRANT RD
BRITISH COLUMBIA 164-C1
DOUGLAS CO WA 239-B4
EAST WENATCHEE WA 239-A4
EAST WENATCHEE BENCH WA 239-A4
GRANT ST
LEBANON OR 133-C1
LINN CO OR 133-C1
PORT MOODY BC 157-A4
N GRANT ST
CANBY OR 199-C6
GRANTHAM PL
DIST OF N VANCOUVER BC 255-G6
GRANTHAM RD
CLARK CO WA 193-A1
GRANT MCCONACHIE WY
CITY OF RICHMOND BC 156-B6
GRANVILLE AV
CITY OF RICHMOND BC 156-B6
GRANVILLE BRDG
VANCOUVER BC 254-E12
GRANVILLE BRDG Rt#-99
VANCOUVER BC 254-E12
GRANVILLE ST
VANCOUVER BC 156-B5
VANCOUVER BC 254-F11
GRANVILLE ST Rt#-99
VANCOUVER BC 156-B5
VANCOUVER BC 254-E14
GRAPE AV W
OMAK WA 104-C2
GRAPEVIEW LOOP RD
MASON CO WA 173-D7
MASON CO WA 180-C1
S GRASLE RD
CLACKAMAS CO OR 200-A5
GRASS CREEK RD
BOUNDARY CO ID 107-A1
GRASSHOPPER RD
WASCO CO OR 202-D7
GRASS MOUNTAIN LP
MALHEUR CO OR 146-C3
GRASSY KNOB RD
CURRY CO OR 224-B5
GRAUL RD
CLALLAM CO WA 164-D6
GRAVE CREEK RD
IDAHO CO ID 123-C3
JACKSON CO OR 229-D2
GRAVELLY BEACH RD NW
THURSTON CO WA 180-B5
GRAVELLY LAKE DR SW
LAKEWOOD WA 181-C4
GRAVES RD
CLACKAMAS CO OR 199-D7
CLARK CO WA 192-D1
E GRAVES RD
COUNTRY HOMES WA 346-J11
COUNTRY HOMES WA 347-A11
SPOKANE WA 347-A11
W GRAVES RD
COUNTRY HOMES WA 346-J11
GRAVETT RD
CROOK CO OR 213-D6
GRAY RD
LEWIS CO WA 187-D3
PEND OREILLE CO WA 106-C3
WHITMAN CO WA 249-C4
GRAYBACK RD
JOSEPHINE CO OR 149-A2
JOSEPHINE CO OR 233-D4
GRAY EAGLE RD
LATAH CO ID 250-D1
GRAYS CORNER RD
UNION CO OR 130-A2
GRAYS CREEK RD
ADAMS CO ID 139-C1
ADAMS CO ID 252-A4
GREASY SPOON RD
CLATSOP CO WA 117-B3
GREAT NORTHERN RD
MODOC CO CA 151-A3
GREAT NORTHERN WY
VANCOUVER BC 254-J12
VANCOUVER BC 255-A12
N GREELEY AV
PORTLAND OR 308-D6
PORTLAND OR 312-D1
PORTLAND OR 313-E2
GREEN AV
CHELAN CO WA 236-B2
SW GREEN DR
JEFFERSON CO OR 208-A7
JEFFERSON CO OR 212-C1
GREEN RD
CLARK CO WA 192-D1
COLUMBIA CO OR 189-C7
HOOD RIVER CO OR 195-B7
SKAGIT CO WA 161-B5
SKAGIT CO WA 260-C1
N GREEN RD
ISLAND CO WA 167-D2
GREEN ST
IONE OR 128-B2
SE GREEN ACRE RD
YAMHILL CO OR 204-D1
GREEN ACRES RD
COOS CO OR 220-D3
GREENACRES RD
OKANOGAN CO WA 104-C2
GREENAWAY RD
OKANOGAN CO WA 104-C3
GREENBACK RD
LINN CO OR 210-A1
GREENBACK MINE RD
JOSEPHINE CO OR 229-C2
GREEN BAY RD
BONNER CO ID 244-B4
GREENBERRY RD
BENTON CO OR 133-B2
GREEN BLUFF RD
SPOKANE CO WA 347-J2
GREEN BLUFF RD E
SPOKANE CO WA 347-G2
GREEN BLUFF RD N
SPOKANE CO WA 347-J1
GREEN CREEK RD
LANE CO OR 209-D7
GREENCREEK RD
IDAHO CO ID 123-C3
N GREENE ST
SPOKANE WA 349-E6
N GREEN FERRY RD
KOOTENAI CO ID 354-B2
POST FALLS ID 354-B2
S GREEN FERRY RD
KOOTENAI CO ID 247-D1
KOOTENAI CO ID 354-B11
POST FALLS ID 354-B7
GREEN FORK RD
SKAMANIA CO WA 193-D2
SKAMANIA CO WA 194-A2
GREEN HILL RD
EUGENE OR 215-A2
LANE CO OR 210-A7
LANE CO OR 215-A1
GREEN HOLLOW RD
WHITMAN CO WA 114-C3
WHITMAN CO WA 122-C1
GREENHORN RD
BAKER CO OR 137-C1
SISKIYOU CO CA 149-C3
GREENHOUSE LN
HARNEY CO OR 145-A1
GREENHURST RD
ADA CO ID 253-A5
CANYON CO ID 147-B1
GREEN ISLAND RD
LANE CO OR 210-B7
GREEN LAKE DR N
SEATTLE WA 273-J1
SEATTLE WA 274-A2
E GREEN LAKE WY N
SEATTLE WA 273-J5
SEATTLE WA 274-A3
W GREEN LAKE WY N
SEATTLE WA 273-J3
GREEN MOUNTAIN RD
CLATSOP CO WA 188-D4
COWLITZ CO WA 189-D6
WASHINGTON CO OR 125-B1
GREEN RIDGE RD
DESCHUTES CO OR 211-D3
DESCHUTES CO OR 212-A4
JEFFERSON CO OR 211-D2
GREEN RIVER RD
LANE CO OR 209-D5
GREEN SPRINGS HWY Rt#-66
ASHLAND OR 337-F9
JACKSON CO OR 150-A2
JACKSON CO OR 234-D4
JACKSON CO OR 337-F9
KLAMATH CO OR 150-A2
KLAMATH CO OR 235-A5
KLAMATH CO OR 338-A12
KLAMATH FALLS OR 338-A12
GREEN SPRINGS HWY Rt#-140
KLAMATH CO OR 338-B12
GREEN TIMBER RD
TILLAMOOK CO OR 197-C4
GREEN VALLEY RD
DOUGLAS CO OR 141-A1
DOUGLAS CO OR 219-A7

PNW

INDEX

STREET
City State Page-Grid
GREEN VALLEY RD
LINN CO OR 207-B7
LINN CO OR 210-A1
SE GREEN VALLEY RD
KING CO WA 182-C2
GREENVILLE RD
WALLA WALLA CO WA 121-C2
WASHINGTON CO OR 125-B1
NE GREENWOOD AV U.S.-20
BEND OR 332-F7
NW GREENWOOD AV U.S.-20
BEND OR 332-E7
SW GREENWOOD AV
GRANTS PASS OR 335-D10
GREENWOOD AV N
SEATTLE WA 171-A7
SEATTLE WA 273-H2
GREENWOOD RD
DIST OF WEST VANCOUVER BC 156-B2
GRAYS HARBOR CO WA 178-B4
POLK CO OR 204-B6
N GREENWOOD RD
POLK CO OR 204-B5
W GREENWOOD RD
SPOKANE WA 348-E9
SPOKANE CO WA 246-A4
SPOKANE CO WA 348-A10
GREGORY RD
COLUMBIA CO OR 189-B6
E GREGORY RD
JACKSON CO OR 230-C6
GREINER LN
GILLIAM CO OR 128-A3
GRELLE AV
LEWISTON ID 250-C5
GRESHAM ST
ASHLAND OR 337-D8
GREY BLVD
MALHEUR CO OR 139-A3
GREY RD
JACKSON CO OR 226-B5
YAKIMA CO WA 120-B3
GRIBBLE RD
CLACKAMAS CO OR 199-C7
GRIBBLING RD
DESCHUTES CO OR 217-D3
GRIESER RD
LATAH CO ID 249-D7
GRIFFIN AV Rt#-164
ENUMCLAW WA 110-C3
KING CO WA 110-C3
GRIFFIN LN
JACKSON CO OR 234-A3
W GRIFFIN RD
SPOKANE CO WA 246-A5
GRIFFIN CREEK RD
JACKSON CO OR 234-A2
W GRIFFIN CREEK RD
JACKSON CO OR 234-A2
E GRIFFIN CREEK RD NE
KING CO WA 176-B2
NE GRIM RD
MARION CO OR 199-B7
GRIMES RD
CROOK CO OR 213-C3
LEWIS CO WA 184-C6
GRINDSTONE RD
CROOK CO OR 136-B3
GRINNEL RD
CLARK CO WA 118-A3
GRINROD RD
KITTITAS CO WA 241-D5
GRIPP RD
SKAGIT CO WA 161-C5
GRIZZLY RD
CROOK CO OR 213-C1
JEFFERSON CO OR 213-C1
SE GRIZZLY RD
JEFFERSON CO OR 208-C5
GRIZZLY MOUNTAIN RD
JEFFERSON CO OR 213-C1
S GRONLUND RD
CLACKAMAS CO OR 200-A4
GROSHONG RD
LINN CO OR 207-C3
S GROSHONG RD
CLACKAMAS CO OR 126-A3
CLACKAMAS CO OR 205-D4
GROSS LN
DOUGLAS CO OR 221-B1
NW GROSS RD
KITSAP CO WA 174-A2
GROSS ST
WATERLOO OR 133-C1
GROSVENOR RD
DISTRICT OF SURREY BC 157-A6
GROUSE LN
CURRY CO OR 224-B3
GROUSE CREEK RD
STEVENS CO WA 106-B3
GROUSE FLAT RD
ASOTIN CO WA 122-C3
N GROVE RD
SPOKANE CO WA 348-B8
S GROVE RD
SPOKANE CO WA 246-B5
SPOKANE CO WA 348-B11
GROVE ST
MARYSVILLE WA 168-C7
SNOHOMISH CO WA 168-C7
E GROVE ST U.S.-95
CANYON CO ID 139-A3
PARMA ID 139-A3
S GROVE ST
SPOKANE WA 348-J11
W GROVE ST U.S.-95
PARMA ID 139-A3
GROWLERS GULCH RD
COWLITZ CO WA 187-B7
GRUBB RD
CHELAN CO WA 239-A5
GRUBSTAKE WY
DESCHUTES CO OR 212-C4
G STOUFFER RD
CENTRALIA WA 299-H2
LEWIS CO WA 299-H2
GUARD ST
FRIDAY HARBOR WA 101-C2
GUEMES ISLAND RD
SKAGIT CO WA 160-C4
GUERANT RD
UMATILLA CO OR 129-B1
GUIBERSON RD
LEWIS CO WA 187-B3
GUIDE MERIDIAN RD Rt#-539
BELLINGHAM WA 158-D6
BELLINGHAM WA 258-C1
LYNDEN WA 158-D6
WHATCOM CO WA 158-D6
GUILD RD
COWLITZ CO WA 189-D7
GUILDFORD WY
COQUITLAM BC 157-A4
GUINAN LOOP RD
YAKIMA CO WA 243-B5
GULCH PLACE RD
MALHEUR CO OR 147-A3
GULF RD
WHATCOM CO WA 158-B5
GULL HARBOR RD NE
OLYMPIA WA 297-A1
THURSTON CO WA 180-C5
THURSTON CO WA 297-A1
N GUM ST Rt#-397
KENNEWICK WA 343-E10
S GUM ST
BENTON CO WA 343-E14
KENNEWICK WA 343-E14
GUMBOOT RD
CLARK CO WA 193-D2
SKAMANIA CO WA 193-D1
NW GUMWOOD LN
JEFFERSON CO OR 208-B3
GUN CLUB RD
BONNER CO ID 244-A3
YAMHILL CO OR 198-B6
N GUN CLUB RD
INDEPENDENCE OR 204-B7
POLK CO OR 204-B7
GUNDERSEN RD
SKAGIT CO WA 161-C7
GUNDERSON RD
SKAGIT CO WA 161-C7
NE GUNDERSON RD
KITSAP CO WA 170-C6
SE GUNDERSON RD
CLACKAMAS CO OR 200-C4
GUNN RD
CLALLAM CO WA 165-D6
GUNNELL RD
JOSEPHINE CO OR 229-A5
LEWIS CO WA 187-B3
GUN STONE ST SW
THURSTON CO WA 184-C2
GUTHRIE RD
PIERCE CO WA 181-B4
GUTHRIE ST
ASHLAND OR 337-D9
GWINN RD
COLUMBIA CO WA 122-B2

H

H AV
ANACORTES WA 259-G5
E H AV U.S.-30
LA GRANDE OR 130-A2
H RD
POLK CO OR 204-C4
H RD NE
DOUGLAS CO WA 112-C2
H RD SE
DOUGLAS CO WA 112-C2
H ST
CENTRALIA WA 299-E3
CULVER OR 208-B7
JEFFERSON CO OR 208-B7
THE DALLES OR 196-C7
H ST U.S.-101
NEHALEM OR 191-B4
N H ST
ABERDEEN WA 178-B7
S H ST
ABERDEEN WA 178-B7
S H ST U.S.-101
ABERDEEN WA 178-B7
HAAS RD
WASHINGTON CO ID 139-A2
HAASE RD
ADAMS CO WA 121-C1
HABBERMAN RD
KITTITAS CO WA 241-A2
HABELT RD
CLACKAMAS CO OR 200-C7
HACKER RD
CROOK CO OR 213-A5
HACKETT RD
COWLITZ CO WA 189-A1
HACKLER RD
KLAMATH CO OR 231-B1
HADEN RD
OKANOGAN CO WA 105-A2
HAEFER LN
UNION CO OR 130-B2
HAENER RD
POLK CO OR 207-C1
HAFER RD
STEVENS CO WA 106-B3
HAGEN RD
GARFIELD CO WA 122-B2
HAGEY RD
YAMHILL CO OR 198-C6
HAGMAN LN
JEFFERSON CO OR 213-A2
HAHLEN AV W
CROOK CO OR 213-A7
HAIG HWY Rt#-9
DISTRICT OF KENT BC 94-C3
HAIGHT RD
LEWIS CO WA 187-C1
SW HAILEY AV
PENDLETON OR 129-B1
UMATILLA CO OR 129-B1
E HAINES RD
MULTNOMAH CO OR 200-D1
NE HAINES RD
MULTNOMAH CO OR 200-D1
S HAINES RD
CLACKAMAS CO OR 199-C6
HAINES ST
PORT TOWNSEND WA 263-F5
HAINES CEMETERY RD
BAKER CO OR 130-A3
HALE RD
PITT MEADOWS BC 157-C5
HALE RD W
LEWIS CO WA 187-B2
HALEY RD
POLK CO OR 207-B1
SE HALEY RD
CLACKAMAS CO OR 200-B3
HALFMILE RD
DOUGLAS CO OR 221-C2
HALF ROUND BAY RD
KOOTENAI CO ID 248-A3
HALFWAY SPUR
BAKER CO OR 131-A3
HALFWAY OR 131-A3
HALFWAY-CORNUCOPIA HWY
BAKER CO OR 131-A3
HALFWAY OR 131-A3
SW HALL BLVD
BEAVERTON OR 199-B2
TIGARD OR 199-B2
WASHINGTON CO OR 199-B2
HALL RD
LATAH CO ID 249-D3
SNOHOMISH CO WA 168-B3
WHITMAN CO WA 249-B3
HALL ST
STEVENS CO WA 106-A3
HALLADAY ST
SEATTLE WA 277-J1
HALL CREEK RD
COOS CO OR 220-C7
HALLECK ST
BELLINGHAM WA 258-D5
W HALLETT RD
SPOKANE CO WA 246-A5
W HALLETT RD Rt#-902
SPOKANE CO WA 246-A5
HALLIDAY RD
LEWIS CO WA 184-C5
HALLMAN RD NW
KITSAP CO WA 170-B7
HALLORAN RD
SKAGIT CO WA 160-D4
HALLS FERRY RD
POLK CO OR 204-B7
NE HALLS HILL RD
KITSAP CO WA 174-D2
HALLSTROM DR NW
PIERCE CO WA 174-C7
HALO TRAIL RD
DOUGLAS CO OR 219-B4
NE HALSEY ST
GRESHAM OR 200-A1
PORTLAND OR 200-A1
PORTLAND OR 314-D4
PORTLAND OR 315-G4
HALSEY-SWEET HOME HWY Rt#-228
BROWNSVILLE OR 210-B2
HALSEY OR 210-B2
LINN CO OR 133-C2
LINN CO OR 210-B2
SWEET HOME OR 133-C2
HALVERSTICK RD
WHATCOM CO WA 102-B1
HALVERSTICK RD Rt#-547
SUMAS WA 102-B1
WHATCOM CO WA 102-B1
HAM RD
COWLITZ CO WA 190-A6
WHATCOM CO WA 158-B5
HAMAKER RD
DOUGLAS CO OR 227-A1
HAMBY RD
DESCHUTES CO OR 217-C2
HAMER RD
LINCOLN CO OR 206-D2
HAM HILL RD
CENTRALIA WA 299-G3
LEWIS CO WA 299-J5
HAMILTON LN
JOSEPHINE CO OR 335-G12
HAMILTON RD
DEL NORTE CO CA 148-B3
WHITMAN CO WA 122-B1
N HAMILTON ST
SPOKANE WA 349-B7
HAMILTON CEMETERY RD
SKAGIT CO WA 102-C2
HAMLTON TO COURTRCK RD
GRANT CO OR 137-A1
HAMLET RD
CLATSOP CO OR 191-D1
HAMLIN RD
CHELAN CO WA 239-A5
HAMM RD
LANE CO OR 133-B3
LANE CO OR 215-A5
N HAMMA HAMMA RD
MASON CO WA 173-B2
HAMMELL RD
JACKSON CO OR 230-D4
HAMMER GRADE RD
WHITMAN CO WA 122-A1
HAMMOND RD
COLUMBIA CO OR 189-B5
MAPLE RIDGE BC 157-C5
PITT MEADOWS BC 157-B5
HAMMOND BAY RD
NANAIMO BC 93-A3
HAMPTON RD
ADAMS CO WA 121-C1
HANAFORD RD
CENTRALIA WA 299-H3
LEWIS CO WA 299-H3
HANCOCK AV
WESTPORT WA 298-G14
HANCOCK RD
GEM CO ID 139-C2
E HANCOCK ST Rt#-99W
NEWBERG OR 198-D5
W HANCOCK ST Rt#-99W
NEWBERG OR 198-D5
HANEY BYPS
MAPLE RIDGE BC 157-C5
HANFORD RD Rt#-24
YAKIMA CO WA 120-A2
S HANGMAN VALLEY RD
SPOKANE CO WA 246-C5
HANKS RD
BENTON CO WA 120-B3
HANKS BUTTE RD
PEND OREILLE CO WA 106-B2
HANKY RD
COLUMBIA CO OR 192-A1
E HANLEY AV
DALTON GARDENS ID 355-F4
W HANLEY AV
COEUR D'ALENE ID 355-C4
HANLEY RD
CENTRAL POINT OR 230-C7
JACKSON CO OR 230-C7
JACKSON CO OR 234-A1
HANNA AV
GEM CO ID 139-B3
HANNA RD
POLK CO OR 204-B7
HANNEGAN RD
WHATCOM CO WA 102-B1
WHATCOM CO WA 258-G1
HANSBERRY ST
KITSAP CO WA 270-G5
TRACYTON WA 270-G5
HANSEN AV S
SALEM OR 324-F3
HANSEN DR
GRANT CO WA 242-C3
MOSES LAKE WA 242-C3
NE HANSEN RD
KITSAP CO WA 271-E1
HANSON RD
KITTITAS CO WA 241-A6
LEWIS CO WA 187-D3
YAKIMA CO WA 241-A7
HANSON LOOP RD
BURBANK WA 121-A3
WALLA WALLA CO WA 121-A3
HANSON STATION RD
LINCOLN CO WA 237-C7
HANSVILLE RD NE
KITSAP CO WA 170-C4
HAPPY CAMP RD
JOSEPHINE CO OR 233-B6
HAPPY HOLLOW RD
SNOHOMISH CO WA 168-B5
HAPPY VALLEY RD
CLALLAM CO WA 166-B7
CLALLAM CO WA 262-J14
DISTRICT OF LANGFORD BC 159-A7
DISTRICT OF METCHOSIN BC 159-A7
DOUGLAS CO OR 221-A5
DOUGLAS CO OR 334-B14
HARNEY CO OR 145-C2
SNOHOMISH CO WA 168-B5
W HARBECK RD
GRANTS PASS OR 335-D12
JOSEPHINE CO OR 335-D12
HARBER RD
LINN CO OR 207-D5
NW HARBOR AV
LINCOLN CITY OR 203-A4
HARBOR AV SW
SEATTLE WA 276-E7
SEATTLE WA 277-E7
SEATTLE WA 281-E1
HARBOR RD Rt#-20
ISLAND CO WA 167-B4
E HARBOR RD
AULT FIELD WA 170-D1
ISLAND CO WA 167-D7
ISLAND CO WA 170-D1
HARBOR ST
WESTPORT WA 298-G11
E HARBOR ST
WARRENTON WA 188-B2
HARBORVIEW DR
GIG HARBOR WA 181-C1
HARBOR VIEW RD
BIRCH BAY WA 158-B4
HARBOUR POINTE BLVD
MUKILTEO WA 171-B4
MUKILTEO WA 266-D7
MUKILTEO WA 267-E7
E HARDCASTLE AV
MARION CO OR 205-B2
WOODBURN OR 205-B2
HARDEN RD
LATAH CO ID 249-C5
MOSCOW ID 249-C5
HARDESON RD
EVERETT WA 267-J2
EVERETT WA 268-A3
HARDIN RD NW
DOUGLAS CO WA 236-B6
HARDING RD
ABERDEEN WA 178-B7
CLACKAMAS CO OR 200-B5
HARDING RD Rt#-380
CROOK CO OR 213-D5
HARDING ST
RICHLAND WA 341-G2
HARDSCRABBLE RD
DOUGLAS CO OR 219-A2
HARDY RD
DISTRICT OF KENT BC 94-C3
HAREWOOD RD
NANAIMO BC 93-A3
HAREWOOD MINES RD
BRITISH COLUMBIA 93-A3
NANAIMO BC 93-A3
HARKINS RD
LEWIS CO WA 187-C3
HARKINS ST
BREMERTON WA 271-A10
HARKSELL RD
WHATCOM CO WA 158-C5
HARLAN DR
ALTAMONT OR 338-J11
ALTAMONT OR 339-A11
HARLAN RD
LINCOLN CO OR 133-A1
HARL BUTTE RD
WALLOWA CO OR 131-A2
HARLOW DR
BREMERTON WA 270-B9
HARLOW DR
KITSAP CO WA 270-B9
HARLOW DR NW
BREMERTON WA 270-C11
KITSAP CO WA 270-C11
HARLOW RD
EUGENE OR 330-C4
SPRINGFIELD OR 330-E4
HARLOW POINT RD
KOOTENAI CO ID 248-A4
HARMAN RD
DESCHUTES CO OR 144-A1
NW HARMON BLVD
BEND OR 332-D7
HARMON RD
LEWIS CO WA 187-C1
HARMON WY S Rt#-162
ORTING WA 182-C5
PIERCE CO WA 182-C5
HARMONY DR
COWLITZ CO WA 189-A2
COWLITZ CO WA 302-A2
HARMONY RD
LINN CO OR 210-A2
POLK CO OR 125-B3
YAMHILL CO OR 125-B3
HARMONY RD Rt#-122
LEWIS CO WA 118-A2
MOSSYROCK WA 118-A2
SE HARMONY RD
CLACKAMAS CO OR 199-D3
MILWAUKIE OR 199-D3
SW HARMONY RD
YAMHILL CO OR 125-B3
HARMS RD
CLACKAMAS CO OR 199-C7
HARMS ST
WESTPORT WA 298-G10
HARMS CREEK RD
LANE CO OR 215-D7
NE HARNEY DR
NEWPORT OR 206-B3
N HARNEY RD
HARNEY CO OR 145-B1
SE HARNEY ST
PORTLAND OR 318-B7
HARNISH RD
LINN CO OR 207-C3
HAROLD YOUNG RD
PACIFIC CO WA 183-D7
HARPER RD
DESCHUTES CO OR 212-C7
LANE CO OR 210-A6
HARPER BRIDGE RD
DESCHUTES CO OR 217-A6
THREE RIVERS OR 217-A6
HARPER-WESTFALL RD
MALHEUR CO OR 138-B3
HARPOLD RD
KLAMATH CO OR 151-A2
MODOC CO CA 151-A2
SISKIYOU CO CA 151-A2
HARPSTER GRADE RD Rt#-13
IDAHO CO ID 123-C3
S HARRAH RD
YAKIMA CO WA 119-C2
HARRIET
CITY OF VICTORIA BC 256-F5
DISTRICT OF SAANICH BC 256-F5
HARRIET RD
DISTRICT OF SAANICH BC 256-E6
HARRINGTON LP
DESCHUTES CO OR 212-A6
HARRIS AV
BELLINGHAM WA 258-A11
HARRIS DR
LINN CO OR 210-B4
HARRIS RD
CLACKAMAS CO OR 200-B4
DISTRICT OF MATSQUI BC 102-B1
FRANKLIN CO WA 341-J2
FRANKLIN CO WA 342-A2
PASCO WA 342-B2
PITT MEADOWS BC 157-B6
RICHLAND WA 340-H10
HARRIS ST
KELSO WA 303-F7
HARRISON AV
CENTRALIA WA 299-B1
FORDS PRAIRIE WA 184-B5
FORDS PRAIRIE WA 299-B1
OLYMPIA WA 296-E5
E HARRISON AV
COEUR D'ALENE ID 355-F10
W HARRISON AV
COEUR D'ALENE ID 355-E10
HARRISON BLVD
BENTON CO OR 327-B9
BOISE ID 253-C2
CORVALLIS OR 327-C9
HARRISON BLVD Rt#-34
CORVALLIS OR 327-G9
LINN CO OR 327-G9
HARRISON RD
COWLITZ CO WA 189-D4
LINN CO OR 210-C1
HARRISON RD Rt#-97
KOOTENAI CO ID 248-B5
HARRISON RD Rt#-823
YAKIMA CO WA 243-B5
SE HARRISON ST
MILWAUKIE OR 199-D3
MILWAUKIE OR 321-J2
HARRIS STREET RD
COWLITZ CO WA 303-G8
KELSO WA 303-G8
HARRY CASH RD
SISKIYOU CO CA 150-A3
HART RD
KITTITAS CO WA 240-C2
LATAH CO ID 249-D4
LEWIS CO WA 187-C3
WALLA WALLA CO WA 121-C3
SW HART RD
BEAVERTON OR 199-A2
HART RD SE
THURSTON CO WA 184-C1
HARTEL RD
UMATILLA CO OR 121-B3
UMATILLA CO OR 129-B1
HARTFORD ST
ELGIN OR 130-A1
HARTLEY RD
BRITISH COLUMBIA 94-B3
HARTMAN RD
KITTITAS CO WA 240-D1
S HARTMAN RD
CLACKAMAS CO OR 205-D3
HART MOUNTAIN RD
LAKE CO OR 152-B1
HARTS LAKE RD S
PIERCE CO WA 118-A1
E HARTSON AV
SPOKANE WA 349-C10
W HARTSON AV
SPOKANE WA 348-F10
HARTSTENE ISLAND NORTH RD
MASON CO WA 180-D2
HARTSTENE ISLAND SOUTH RD
MASON CO WA 180-D3
HARVARD AV E
SEATTLE WA 278-B2
SW HARVARD BLVD Rt#-138
ROSEBURG OR 334-F7
W HARVARD BLVD
ROSEBURG OR 334-B7
W HARVARD BLVD Rt#-138
ROSEBURG OR 334-E7
N HARVARD RD
OTIS ORCHARDS WA 352-B9
SPOKANE CO WA 352-B9
S HARVARD RD
SPOKANE CO WA 247-B7
HARVEST DR
LINN CO OR 207-B7
SW HARVEST LN
DESCHUTES CO OR 212-C6
HARVEY AV
ROSEBURG OR 334-C6
HARVEY RD
CLACKAMAS CO OR 200-D6
LANE CO OR 215-C4
WHATCOM CO WA 158-B3
HARVEY RD NE
AUBURN WA 182-C1
HARVEY RD SE
AUBURN WA 182-C1
HARVEY SHAW RD
WALLA WALLA CO WA 121-C3
WALLA WALLA CO WA 344-F1
HARVIE RD
DISTRICT OF SURREY BC 157-B7
HARWOOD ST
PRINEVILLE OR 213-D5
HARYU RD
COWLITZ CO WA 189-A2
HASIS DR
JOSEPHINE CO OR 229-B3
HASKINS RD
KLAMATH CO OR 151-A2
SISKIYOU CO CA 151-A3
W HASTIE LAKE RD
ISLAND CO WA 167-B3
HASTINGS AV W
JEFFERSON CO WA 166-D6
JEFFERSON CO WA 263-A4
PORT TOWNSEND WA 263-A4
E HASTINGS RD
FAIRWOOD WA 346-J8
FAIRWOOD WA 347-A8
SPOKANE CO WA 347-A8
W HASTINGS RD
FAIRWOOD WA 346-J8
HASTINGS ST
VANCOUVER BC 254-G10
HASTINGS ST Rt#-7A
DISTRICT OF BURNABY BC 156-D4
DISTRICT OF BURNABY BC 255-G10
VANCOUVER BC 255-F10
HASTINGS ST E Rt#-7A
VANCOUVER BC 254-J10
VANCOUVER BC 255-B10
HASTINGS HILL RD
GARFIELD CO WA 122-B1
S HATCH RD
SPOKANE WA 246-C5
SPOKANE CO WA 246-C5
HATCHET SLOUGH RD
COOS CO OR 220-C4
HATFIELD HWY Rt#-39
KLAMATH CO OR 151-A2
SISKIYOU CO CA 151-A3
HATLEY RD
WHITMAN CO WA 249-A6
S HATTAN RD
CLACKAMAS CO OR 200-A4
W HATTON RD
ADAMS CO WA 121-A1
HAUGEN RD
SKAGIT CO WA 168-B3
WASHINGTON CO OR 199-A5
YAMHILL CO OR 199-A5
SE HAUGLUM RD
CLACKAMAS CO OR 200-C3
HAUSER LAKE RD
HAUSER ID 353-B1
KOOTENAI CO ID 353-B1
E HAUSER LAKE RD
HAUSER ID 247-C1
SPOKANE CO WA 247-B1
N HAVANA ST
SPOKANE WA 349-G2
SPOKANE CO WA 349-G8
S HAVANA ST
SPOKANE WA 246-C5
SPOKANE WA 349-G12
SPOKANE CO WA 246-C5
SPOKANE CO WA 349-G12
HAVANA-HELIX HWY
HELIX OR 129-B1
UMATILLA CO OR 129-B1
HAVEKOST RD
ANACORTES WA 259-D8
SKAGIT CO WA 259-D8
HAVERLAND KOONTZ RD
FRANKLIN CO WA 121-B2
HAVLINA RD Rt#-260
FRANKLIN CO WA 121-B1

STREET City State Page-Grid

HAWKINS RD
LEWIS CO WA 187-C3
HAWKINS RD S
LEWIS CO WA 187-C3
HAWKS CLIFF RD NE
DOUGLAS CO WA 113-A1
DOUGLAS CO WA 237-A5
HAWKS PRAIRIE RD NE
THURSTON CO WA 180-D5
THURSTON CO WA 181-A5
HAWLEY CREEK RD
LANE CO OR 215-A6
HAWN CREEK RD
YAMHILL CO OR 198-B7
HAWORTH AV
NEWBERG OR 198-D5
HAWTHORNE AV
MEDFORD OR 336-D12
NW HAWTHORNE AV
GRANTS PASS OR 335-F6
HAWTHORNE AV NE
SALEM OR 323-D11
SALEM OR 325-C1
SE HAWTHORNE BLVD
PORTLAND OR 313-H7
PORTLAND OR 314-A7
HAWTHORNE RD
BELLINGHAM WA 258-A12
E HAWTHORNE RD
COUNTRY HOMES WA 346-J10
COUNTRY HOMES WA 347-A10
SPOKANE WA 347-B10
SPOKANE CO WA 347-C10
W HAWTHORNE RD
COUNTRY HOMES WA 346-J10
S HAWTHORNE ST
BENTON CO WA 343-E12
KENNEWICK WA 343-E12
HAXTON WY
WHATCOM CO WA 158-C7
WHATCOM CO WA 160-B1
NE HAY CREEK RD
JEFFERSON CO OR 135-B1
JEFFERSON CO OR 208-D4
SE HAY CREEK RD
JEFFERSON CO OR 135-B1
JEFFERSON CO OR 213-C1
E HAYDEN AV
HAYDEN ID 245-A5
W HAYDEN AV
HAYDEN ID 245-A5
HAYDEN ID 247-D1
KOOTENAI CO ID 247-C1
HAYDEN RD
CLACKAMAS CO OR 200-B6
LINN CO OR 133-C1
HAYDEN BRIDGE RD
North Springfield OR 330-G4
North Springfield OR 331-A4
SPRINGFIELD OR 330-G4
E HAYDEN LAKE RD
KOOTENAI CO ID 245-B5
N HAYDEN LAKE RD
KOOTENAI CO ID 245-B4
S HAYDEN LAKE RD
HAYDEN ID 355-F1
KOOTENAI CO ID 355-F1
HAYES LN
LANE CO OR 210-A6
S HAYES ST
MOSCOW ID 249-D5
W HAYES ST
WOODBURN OR 205-B2
HAYES HILL RD
JOSEPHINE CO OR 233-B1
HAYESVILLE DR NE
HAYESVILLE OR 323-E6
MARION CO OR 323-E6
SALEM OR 323-E6
S HAYFORD RD
AIRWAY HEIGHTS WA 246-A4
SPOKANE CO WA 246-A5
HAYHURST RD
DOUGLAS CO OR 219-A3
HAY-LA CROSSE RD
WHITMAN CO WA 122-A1
HAYNES WY
COOS CO OR 218-C6
HAYNIE RD
WHATCOM CO WA 158-C3
HAYSTACK DR
JEFFERSON CO OR 212-D1
HAYSTACK ROCK RD
MALHEUR CO OR 146-C1
HAYWARD RD
KITTITAS CO WA 240-D3
HAYWIRE RD
LEWIS CO WA 187-C1
N HAZARD RD
SPOKANE CO WA 346-G4
W HAZARD RD
SPOKANE CO WA 346-H5
HAZARD LAKE RD
IDAHO CO ID 131-C2
IDAHO CO ID 251-B1
HAZEL AV
BENTON CITY WA 120-C3
N HAZEL ST Rt#-9
ARLINGTON WA 168-D5
S HAZEL ST Rt#-9
ARLINGTON WA 168-D5
W HAZEL ST
MOUNT VERNON WA 260-B13
HAZEL CAMP RD
CURRY CO OR 232-D3
NE HAZEL DELL AV
CLARK WA 305-G1
CLARK CO WA 192-C5
VANCOUVER WA 305-G1
HAZEL DELL RD
COWLITZ CO WA 187-B7
COWLITZ CO WA 189-B1
HAZELGREEN RD NE
HAYESVILLE OR 323-F4
MARION CO OR 205-B4
MARION CO OR 323-F4
SALEM OR 323-F4
HAZELNUT RIDGE RD NE
MARION CO OR 205-D4

HAZEL POINT RD
JEFFERSON CO WA 170-A7
HAZEN RD
CLARK CO WA 193-A1
COLUMBIA CO OR 192-A2
H COOKE RD
KITTITAS CO WA 241-C5
HEADQUARTERS RD
COWLITZ CO WA 189-D1
HEADQUATERS RD
COWLITZ CO WA 189-C1
HEALY RD
CLARK CO WA 190-A7
HEART LAKE RD
ANACORTES WA 259-F10
SKAGIT CO WA 259-G6
HEART OF THE HILLS
CLALLAM CO WA 109-B1
HEART OF THE HILLS PKWY
CLALLAM CO WA 261-G14
HEATER RD
CLACKAMAS CO OR 199-A6
HEATHER OAK DR
LANE CO OR 210-A7
HEATH LAKE RD
BONNER CO ID 244-A4
HEBER RD
UNION CO OR 130-A3
HECETA BEACH RD
LANE CO OR 214-A2
HECKARD RD
PACIFIC CO WA 117-A1
E HEDGER AV Rt#-225
BENTON CITY WA 120-C3
HEGGENESS RD
LANGLEY WA 171-A2
E HEGLAR RD
SPOKANE CO WA 246-D1
HEIGHTS LN NE
THURSTON CO WA 180-D5
HEIMER RD
SNOHOMISH CO WA 168-D3
HEIMRICH ST
DUFUR OR 127-B2
WASCO CO OR 127-B2
HEINE RD
STEVENS CO WA 106-A3
HEINEMAN RD
ADAMS CO WA 113-C3
HEINRICH RD
VALLEY CO ID 251-C6
HEINZ BLVD
MALHEUR CO OR 139-A3
S HEINZ RD
CLACKAMAS CO OR 205-D1
HEINZ RD NE
MARION CO OR 205-D4
HEIPLE RD
CLACKAMAS CO OR 200-B5
HEISSEN RD
BATTLE GROUND WA 193-A3
CLARK CO WA 193-A3
HELIX-VANCYCLE RD
HELIX OR 129-B1
UMATILLA CO OR 121-B3
UMATILLA CO OR 129-B1
HELLER RD
AULT FIELD WA 167-B2
ISLAND CO WA 167-B2
OAK HARBOR WA 167-B2
HELLS CANYON RD
WASHINGTON CO OR 199-A5
HELLS GULCH RD
BENEWAH CO ID 248-C6
KOOTENAI CO ID 248-C6
HELM RD
JOSEPHINE CO OR 229-A6
HELMAN ST
ASHLAND OR 337-C7
HELMCKEN RD
DISTRICT OF SAANICH BC 256-C2
TOWN OF VIEW ROYAL BC 256-A4
NW HELMHOLTZ WY
DESCHUTES CO OR 212-D5
SW HELMHOLTZ WY
DESCHUTES CO OR 212-D5
HELMICK RD
POLK CO OR 207-B1
SKAGIT CO WA 161-C5
HELVETIA RD
WASHINGTON CO OR 125-C1
HEMENWAY RD
LEWIS CO WA 187-B4
NE HEMLOCK AV
DESCHUTES CO OR 212-D5
NW HEMLOCK AV
DESCHUTES CO OR 212-D5
HEMLOCK RD
SKAMANIA CO WA 194-C3
HEMLOCK ST
LONGVIEW WA 302-G9
VANCOUVER BC 254-E13
N HEMLOCK ST
CANNON BEACH WA 188-A7
S HEMLOCK ST
CANNON BEACH WA 188-A7
CANNON BEACH OR 191-A1
W HEMLOCK ST Rt#-34
WALDPORT OR 328-E4
HEMLOCK BUTTE RD
DOUGLAS CO OR 223-B6
HEMLOCK VALLEY RD
BRITISH COLUMBIA 94-C3
HEMMERING RD
LINCOLN CO WA 113-B2
W HEMMI RD
WHATCOM CO WA 158-D5
HENDERER RD
DOUGLAS CO OR 141-A1
HENDERSON BLVD
OLYMPIA WA 296-J7
HENDERSON BLVD SE
OLYMPIA WA 296-J7
OLYMPIA WA 297-A8
THURSTON CO WA 296-J7
THURSTON CO WA 297-A8
TUMWATER WA 297-A8
NE HENDERSON DR
JEFFERSON CO OR 208-C5

HENDERSON LN
OWYHEE CO ID 147-C2
HENDERSON RD
DISTRICT OF OAK BAY BC 257-C5
S HENDERSON ST
SEATTLE WA 287-F3
SW HENDERSON ST
SEATTLE WA 285-G3
HENDERSON CREEK RD
LANE CO OR 214-C3
HENDRICKS RD
YAMHILL CO OR 198-B5
HENDRICKSON RD
LEWIS CO WA 187-B5
HENKLE ST Rt#-6
PACIFIC CO WA 117-A1
RAYMOND WA 117-A1
HENKLE BUTTE DR
DESCHUTES CO OR 212-A4
HENLEY RD
KLAMATH CO OR 235-D5
HENLEY-HORNBROOK WY
SISKIYOU CO CA 150-A3
W HENNI RD
ISLAND CO WA 167-C1
HENRICHS RD
SHERMAN CO OR 127-C2
S HENRICI RD
CLACKAMAS CO OR 199-D5
CLACKAMAS CO OR 200-A5
HENRIOT RD
LEWIS CO WA 187-C3
HENRY RD
DOUGLAS CO OR 221-B2
LINCOLN CO OR 133-A1
WHATCOM CO WA 158-B5
E HENRY RD
SPOKANE CO WA 247-B5
N HENRY RD
GREEN ACRES WA 351-J8
SPOKANE CO WA 247-B4
SPOKANE CO WA 351-J8
SPOKANE CO WA 352-A14
S HENRY RD
GREEN ACRES WA 351-J9
SPOKANE CO WA 247-B4
SPOKANE CO WA 351-J9
W HENRY ST
PASCO WA 343-D6
WEST PASCO WA 342-H7
WEST PASCO WA 343-A6
HENRY CREEK RD
WHEELER CO OR 128-C3
HENRY FOSTER RD
GRAYS HARBOR CO WA 179-A7
HENSEL RD
GRAYS HARBOR CO WA 178-A3
HENSON RD
BENTON CO WA 120-C3
HEPPNER HWY Rt#-74
GILLIAM CO OR 128-B1
HEPPNER OR 128-C2
IONE OR 128-B1
LEXINGTON OR 128-C2
MORROW CO OR 128-B1
MORROW CO OR 129-A2
UMATILLA CO OR 129-A2
HEPPNER-SPRAY HWY Rt#-207
MORROW CO OR 128-C2
WHEELER CO OR 128-C2
WHEELER CO OR 136-C1
HERD RD
YAMHILL CO OR 198-D5
NE HEREFORD LN
JEFFERSON CO OR 208-D3
HEREFORD RD
CURRY CO OR 224-B4
HERFERD RD
LANE CO OR 210-C7
S HERGERT RD
WASHINGTON CO OR 198-C2
HERITAGE MOUNTAIN RD
PORT MOODY BC 157-A4
HERITAGE MOUNTAIN WY
PORT MOODY BC 157-A4
HERMAN RD
ADAMS CO WA 121-C1
LANE CO OR 210-B6
LATAH CO ID 250-C1
OLYMPIA WA 297-E9
HERMAN CREEK RD
HOOD RIVER CO OR 194-D5
HOOD RIVER CO OR 195-A5
W HERMISTON AV Rt#-207
HERMISTON OR 129-A1
HERMISTON HWY Rt#-207
HERMISTON OR 129-A1
UMATILLA CO OR 129-A1
HERMISTON-HINKLE RD
HERMISTON OR 129-A1
UMATILLA CO OR 129-A1
HERMISTON LOOP RD
HERMISTON OR 129-A1
UMATILLA CO OR 129-A1
HERON ST
BOISE ID 253-C2
E HERON ST U.S.-101
ABERDEEN WA 178-B7
W HERON ST U.S.-101
ABERDEEN WA 178-B7
HERRIN RD
SHERMAN CO OR 127-C1
HERRING LN
YAMHILL CO OR 198-C5
HERRING RD
WASHINGTON CO OR 198-A2
S HERRON RD KPN
PIERCE CO WA 181-A2
E HERSEY ST
ASHLAND OR 337-D7
W HERSEY ST
ASHLAND OR 337-C6
HERSHBERGER RD
DOUGLAS CO OR 226-C1
HESS RD
BENTON CO WA 120-C3
HESSELTINE RD
STEVENS CO WA 106-A3

HESSLER FLAT RD
YAKIMA CO WA 243-A2
HEWITT AV
EVERETT WA 264-D3
EVERETT WA 265-E3
HEWITT PARK HWY
BAKER CO OR 139-A1
HEYBURN RD
CHATCOLET ID 248-A6
KOOTENAI CO ID 248-A6
HEYDON RD
DOUGLAS CO OR 221-A3
HIACK RD
TILLAMOOK CO OR 203-D2
HIBBARD RD NE
MARION CO OR 205-B5
HICKEY RD
BONNER CO ID 244-B1
N HICKORY AV
PASCO WA 343-F6
NW HICKORY LN
JEFFERSON CO OR 208-B3
HICKOX RD
SKAGIT CO WA 168-B1
HIDDEN ACRES RD
LEWIS CO WA 187-C4
NE HIDDEN COVE LN
KITSAP CO WA 174-C1
NE HIDDEN COVE RD
KITSAP CO WA 174-C1
HIDDEN FALLS RD
CLARK CO WA 193-C7
HIDDEN SPRINGS RD
YAMHILL CO OR 198-C6
HIDDEN VALLEY RD
BONNER CO ID 244-A1
KITTITAS CO WA 240-D2
LINCOLN CO OR 206-B5
W HIDDEN VALLEY RD
KOOTENAI CO ID 247-C1
HIDDEN VALLEY RIM RD
ADA CO ID 253-B4
HIGGINS AIRPORT WY
SKAGIT CO WA 161-A7
HIGGINS LOOP RD NW
DOUGLAS CO WA 236-B5
E HIGH DR
SPOKANE WA 246-C5
S HIGH DR
SPOKANE WA 246-C5
SPOKANE WA 348-H13
SPOKANE CO WA 246-C5
W HIGH DR
SPOKANE WA 246-C5
SPOKANE WA 348-J14
SPOKANE WA 349-A14
HIGH ST
BAY CITY OR 191-B7
BELLINGHAM WA 258-C8
EUGENE OR 330-A9
PORT ORCHARD WA 174-B4
PORT ORCHARD WA 270-H14
PRIEST RIVER ID 107-A3
SW HIGH ST
GRANTS PASS OR 335-D9
HIGH ST NE
SALEM OR 322-H13
HIGH ST SE
SALEM OR 322-H14
SALEM OR 324-H1
HIGH BRIDGE RD
SNOHOMISH CO WA 110-C1
HIGHGRADE RD
MODOC CO CA 152-A3
HIGHLAND AV
ASOTIN CO WA 250-B4
CLARKSTON WA 250-B4
GRANTS PASS OR 335-D4
JOSEPHINE CO OR 335-B1
E HIGHLAND AV
HERMISTON OR 129-A1
NW HIGHLAND AV
GRANTS PASS OR 335-E7
SW HIGHLAND AV Rt#-126
DESCHUTES CO OR 212-D5
REDMOND OR 212-D5
W HIGHLAND AV
HERMISTON OR 129-A1
UMATILLA CO OR 129-A1
HIGHLAND AV NE
SALEM OR 322-J10
SALEM OR 323-A10
HIGHLAND BLVD
DIST OF N VANCOUVER BC 156-B2
DIST OF N VANCOUVER BC 254-J1
E HIGHLAND BLVD
SPOKANE WA 349-B12
HIGHLAND DR
BELLEVUE WA 175-C3
BELLINGHAM WA 258-C10
BENTON CO OR 327-H4
CORVALLIS OR 327-H4
ISLAND CO WA 168-A6
MEDFORD OR 336-F13
YAKIMA CO WA 120-A2
E HIGHLAND DR
ARLINGTON WA 168-D5
SW HIGHLAND LN
JEFFERSON CO OR 208-B7
HIGHLAND RD
BRITISH COLUMBIA 159-B6
COLUMBIA CO WA 122-B2
COLUMBIA CO OR 189-C6
MASON CO WA 179-D4
POLK CO OR 207-B1
TOWN OF VIEW ROYAL BC 159-B6
HIGHLAND RD NE
KITSAP CO WA 170-C5
HIGHLAND FLATS RD
BOUNDARY CO ID 107-B2
HIGHLAND PARK WY SW
SEATTLE WA 285-H1
HIGHLAND SCHOOL RD SE
DOUGLAS CO WA 112-C2
W HIGHLAND VIEW DR
BOISE ID 253-D2
S HIGHLINE DR
EAST WENATCHEE WA 239-A4
EAST WENATCHEE BENCH WA 239-A4

HIGHLINE RD
DESCHUTES CO OR 217-A2
HIGH PASS RD
JUNCTION CITY OR 210-A6
LANE CO OR 133-A2
LANE CO OR 210-A6
SE HIGH POINT WY
KING CO WA 176-A4
HIGH PRAIRIE RD
KLICKITAT CO WA 196-C4
LANE CO OR 134-A3
HIGH RIM RD
DOUGLAS CO WA 236-D4
HIGH SCHOOL DR
LINCOLN CITY OR 203-A5
NE HIGH SCHOOL RD
KITSAP CO WA 271-H1
WINSLOW WA 271-H1
HIGH VALLEY RD
UNION CO OR 130-B2
HIGHWAY ADRIAN RD
CANYON CO ID 139-A3
HILDERBRAND LN
SHERMAN CO OR 127-C1
HILL AV
MOSES LAKE WA 242-C3
E HILL AV
MOSES LAKE WA 242-C3
HILL RD
ADA CO ID 253-B1
BOISE ID 253-C2
CANYON CO ID 147-C2
KLAMATH CO OR 235-D5
LANE CO OR 215-C1
LANE CO OR 331-F1
MODOC CO CA 151-A3
OWYHEE CO ID 147-A1
SISKIYOU CO CA 150-C3
SISKIYOU CO CA 151-A3
WASHINGTON CO ID 139-A2
WHITMAN CO WA 249-C3
YAKIMA CO WA 243-D7
N HILL RD
YAMHILL CO OR 198-A6
NW HILL RD
YAMHILL CO OR 198-A7
W HILL RD
ISLAND CO WA 167-B5
HILL RD NE
THURSTON CO WA 181-A5
HILL RD S
MCMINNVILLE OR 198-A7
YAMHILL CO OR 198-A7
YAMHILL CO OR 204-B1
HILL ST
ALBANY OR 326-D7
KLICKITAT CO WA 196-C7
HILL ST Rt#-162
KAMIAH ID 123-C2
HILLAIRE RD
WHATCOM CO WA 158-C7
HILLARY GRADE
WASCO CO OR 202-D2
E HILLCREST DR
KITSAP CO WA 271-D11
NE HILLCREST DR
GRANTS PASS OR 335-G6
JOSEPHINE CO OR 335-G6
NW HILLCREST DR
GRANTS PASS OR 335-F6
HILLCREST RD
HOOD RIVER CO OR 195-C7
JACKSON CO OR 234-C1
JACKSON CO OR 336-G11
MEDFORD OR 234-C1
MEDFORD OR 336-G11
HILLCREST LOOP RD
CLATSOP CO WA 117-A3
HILLDALE RD E
KITSAP CO WA 271-E9
S HILLHURST RD
RIDGEFIELD WA 192-C3
HILL LOOP RD
STEVENS CO WA 106-A1
HILLOCKBURN RD
CLACKAMAS CO OR 200-C7
HILLS AV
LEWIS CO WA 187-D3
S HILLS DR
WENATCHEE WA 238-D4
WEST WENATCHEE WA 238-D4
HILLS RD
ADAMS CO WA 113-C3
HILLSBORO HWY Rt#-219
NEWBERG OR 198-D5
WASHINGTON CO OR 198-D4
YAMHILL CO OR 198-D5
SW HILLSBORO HWY Rt#-219
HILLSBORO OR 198-D2
WASHINGTON CO OR 198-D2
HILLSBORO-SILVRTON HWY Rt#-214
MARION CO OR 205-C3
MOUNT ANGEL OR 205-C3
SILVERTON OR 205-C3
WOODBURN OR 205-C3
HLLSBORO-SLVRTN HWY NE Rt#-219
MARION CO OR 205-A1
HILLSHAVEN AV
COLUMBIA CO OR 189-C7
HILLSIDE AV
CITY OF VICTORIA BC 256-H7
CITY OF VICTORIA BC 257-A6
HILLSIDE DR
PIERCE CO WA 181-C5
YAMHILL CO OR 198-C5
HILLSIDE RD
WASHINGTON CO OR 125-B1
HILLTOP
CROOK CO OR 213-D6
HILLTOP DR
LANE CO OR 215-D4
HILLVIEW RD
GEM CO ID 139-B3
LANE CO OR 215-C5
HILYARD AV
ALTAMONT OR 339-C11
HILYARD ST
EUGENE OR 330-B10

HINCH RD
COOS CO OR 220-C2
HINCK RD
LINN CO OR 207-C6
HINES ST SE
SALEM OR 324-J1
SALEM OR 325-A1
HINES LOGGING RD
HARNEY CO OR 137-A3
HARNEY CO OR 145-A1
HINKLE CREEK RD
DOUGLAS CO OR 219-D7
NE HINNESS RD
CLARK CO WA 193-B4
HINTON RD
WASCO CO OR 127-C3
HINTZVILLE RD NW
KITSAP CO WA 173-D3
HIPKINS RD SW
LAKEWOOD WA 181-C4
HIRTZEL RD
COLUMBIA CO OR 189-B4
E HISTORIC COLUMBIA RIVER HWY
MULTNOMAH CO OR 200-C1
TROUTDALE OR 200-C1
NW HITE CENTER RD
KITSAP CO WA 173-D2
H LAWRENCE RD
CLARK CO WA 193-A1
HOAG RD
MOUNT VERNON WA 260-D9
HOBART RD NE
MARION CO OR 205-C4
SILVERTON OR 205-C4
NW HOBBS RD
WASHINGTON CO OR 198-C1
HOBO PASS RD
SHOSHONE CO ID 115-C3
HOBSON RD
SKAGIT CO WA 161-B5
HOBSON RD SW
THURSTON CO WA 184-B4
HOBSONVILLE POINT DR
BAY CITY OR 191-B7
TILLAMOOK CO OR 191-B7
HODGEN RD
UMATILLA CO OR 121-C3
NW HODGEN RD
MILTON-FREEWATER OR 121-C3
HOEHN RD
SKAGIT CO WA 161-D6
HOERSTER LN
JACKSON CO OR 229-D4
HOFF RD
PIERCE CO WA 181-A2
HOFFMAN RD
CLACKAMAS CO OR 199-C5
INDEPENDENCE OR 204-B7
POLK CO OR 204-B7
WASHINGTON CO OR 125-B1
HOFFMAN RD NE
KITSAP CO WA 170-D4
HOFFMAN RD NW
THURSTON CO WA 180-B5
HOFFMAN RD SE
OLYMPIA WA 297-D8
HOFFMAN ST
WOODLAND WA 192-C1
SE HOFFMEISTER RD
CLACKAMAS CO OR 200-B3
SE HOGAN AV
GRESHAM OR 200-B2
NE HOGAN DR
GRESHAM OR 200-B2
HOGAN RD
DOUGLAS CO OR 219-A6
GRAYS HARBOR CO WA 177-C5
HOGBACK RD
LAKE CO OR 144-B3
LAKE CO OR 152-B1
HOG CREEK RD
WASHINGTON CO ID 139-B1
HOGEN RANCH RD
COLUMBIA CO OR 192-A3
HOGG HILL RD
MULTNOMAH CO OR 200-D3
HOG RANCH RD
KITTITAS CO WA 240-B6
HOGUM BAY RD NE
LACEY WA 181-A6
HOGUM CREEK RD
DOUGLAS CO OR 225-D6
HOH VILLAGE RD
JEFFERSON CO WA 169-C5
HOIER RD
WHATCOM CO WA 158-B3
HOKO OZETTE RD
CLALLAM CO WA 162-C4
CLALLAM CO WA 163-A3
HOLBROOK RD
COLUMBIA CO OR 189-C6
S HOLCOMB BLVD
CLACKAMAS CO OR 199-D4
CLACKAMAS CO OR 200-A4
HOLCOMB RD
ADA CO ID 253-D4
BOISE CITY ID 253-D4
HOLCOMB HOMES RD
COWLITZ CO WA 303-F3
HOLCOMB SPRING RD
KLAMATH CO OR 235-D2
HOLCUM RD
LEWIS CO WA 187-C1
HOLDEN RD SW
LAKEWOOD WA 181-C4
SW HOLDEN ST
SEATTLE WA 284-E2
SEATTLE WA 285-F2
HOLDER LN SE
MARION CO OR 324-F7
SALEM OR 324-F7
HOLDMAN RD
HELIX OR 129-B1
UMATILLA CO OR 129-B1
HOLDOM AV
DISTRICT OF BURNABY BC 156-D4
SE HOLGATE BLVD
PORTLAND OR 317-J3
PORTLAND OR 318-B3

STREET
City State Page-Grid

SE HOLGATE BLVD
PORTLAND OR 319-H3
S HOLGATE ST
SEATTLE WA 282-A2
HOLIDAY BLVD
SKAGIT CO WA 160-C5
HOLIDAY VALLEY DR NW
THURSTON CO WA 180-B5
N HOLLADAY DR
SEASIDE WA 301-G7
S HOLLADAY DR
SEASIDE WA 301-G9
E HOLLAND AV
SPOKANE WA 346-J11
SPOKANE WA 347-A11
W HOLLAND AV
COUNTRY HOMES WA 346-J11
HOLLAND LP
JOSEPHINE CO OR 233-B4
HOLLILYNN DR
ADA CO ID 253-C4
HOLLY DR
EVERETT WA 268-B5
SNOHOMISH WA 267-J7
SNOHOMISH WA 268-A6
SE HOLLY LN
JEFFERSON CO OR 208-C7
HOLLY RD
MALHEUR CO OR 139-A2
NW HOLLY RD
KITSAP CO WA 173-D2
KITSAP CO WA 174-A2
HOLLY ST
MAPLE RIDGE BC 157-C5
E HOLLY ST
BELLINGHAM WA 258-D7
N HOLLY ST
CLACKAMAS CO OR 199-C6
MEDFORD OR 336-C12
S HOLLY ST
MEDFORD OR 336-C12
W HOLLY ST
BELLINGHAM WA 258-D6
HOLLY GULCH RD
BENEWAH CO ID 248-C5
HOLLY HILL RD
WASHINGTON CO OR 198-C3
HOLLYWOOD CRES
CITY OF VICTORIA BC 257-A11
HOLLYWOOD DR NE
HAYESVILLE OR 323-E9
SALEM OR 323-E10
HOLM RD SW
THURSTON CO WA 184-A3
HOLMAN RD NW
SEATTLE WA 171-A7
SEATTLE WA 273-F1
HOLMES RD
DESCHUTES CO OR 212-B4
HOLMES POINT DR NE
KING CO WA 171-B7
HOLST RD
CLACKAMAS CO OR 200-B4
S HOLST RD
ISLAND CO WA 171-A2
HOLTON RD
JACKSON CO OR 234-B3
HOLYOKE PL S
SEATTLE WA 287-H5
HOLYOKE WY S
SEATTLE WA 287-H5
HOME ST
WALLA WALLA WA 345-D9
WALLA WALLA EAST WA 345-D9
HOME ACRES RD
SNOHOMISH WA 265-H4
SNOHOMISH WA 269-J2
HOME ACRES RANCH RD
KLICKITAT CO WA 196-D2
HOMEDALE RD
ALTAMONT OR 235-D5
ALTAMONT OR 339-A14
CANYON CO ID 147-B1
KLAMATH CO OR 235-D5
KLAMATH CO OR 339-A14
KLAMATH FALLS OR 339-A14
HOMER RD
ADA CO ID 139-C3
HOMESTEAD RD
MORROW CO OR 128-C1
SAN JUAN CO WA 160-A3
HOMESTEAD WY
DESCHUTES CO OR 212-C4
HOMESTEADER RD
CLACKAMAS CO OR 199-B5
WASHINGTON CO OR 199-B5
WHATCOM CO WA 161-C1
SE HOMESTEAD VALLEY RD
I-90
KING CO WA 111-A2
E HONEYMAN RD
COLUMBIA CO OR 192-B4
N HONEYMAN RD
COLUMBIA CO OR 192-A3
HONEYMOON BAY RD
AULT FIELD WA 170-C1
ISLAND CO WA 167-C7
HONEYSUCKLE AV
HAYDEN ID 355-A1
KOOTENAI CO ID 355-A1
N HONEYSUCKLE DR
COEUR D'ALENE ID 355-F6
W HOOD AV
KENNEWICK WA 342-H10
HOOD ST NE
SALEM OR 322-J11
HOOD CANAL DR NE
KITSAP CO WA 170-C3
HOOD RIVER HWY
HOOD RIVER CO OR 195-B7
HOOD RIVER CO OR 202-C1
HOOD RIVER RD
MOSIER OR 196-A5
WASCO CO OR 196-A5
HOOGDAL RD
SKAGIT CO WA 161-C5
SW HOOK AND EYE LN
YAMHILL CO OR 204-B2
HOOKER RD
CLALLAM CO WA 166-A7
HOOPER WOOLAM RD
CLARK CO WA 193-A1
HOOT N HOLLER LN
DOUGLAS CO OR 221-D5
HOOVER CREEK LN
WHEELER CO OR 128-A3
HOOVER HILL RD
DOUGLAS CO OR 221-A7
HOP CREEK RD
JACKSON CO OR 226-B5
HOPE ST
ALTAMONT OR 338-J11
ALTAMONT OR 339-A12
HOPE PENINSULA RD
BONNER CO ID 244-D3
HOPEWELL RD Rt#-9
WHATCOM CO WA 102-B1
HOPEWELL RD NW
POLK CO OR 204-C3
YAMHILL CO OR 204-C3
W HOPKINS ST
PASCO WA 343-B7
WEST PASCO WA 343-B7
HOPPER AV Rt#-71
CAMBRIDGE ID 139-B1
WASHINGTON CO ID 139-B1
E HOQUIAM RD
GRAYS HARBOR CO WA 178-B4
HOQUIAM WA 178-A6
HOQUIAM WISHKAH RD
GRAYS HARBOR CO WA 178-B4
HORLICK RD
KITTITAS CO WA 240-D3
HORN LN
EUGENE OR 329-F2
LANE CO OR 329-F2
HORN RD Rt#-225
BENTON CITY WA 120-C2
BENTON CO WA 120-C2
NW HORNECKER RD
WASHINGTON CO OR 198-C1
HORNER RD
DESCHUTES CO OR 212-D7
N HORNET CREEK RD
ADAMS CO ID 131-B3
ADAMS CO ID 139-B1
WASHINGTON CO ID 131-B3
HORNY HOLLOW TR
JEFFERSON CO OR 212-C2
HORRIGAN RD
BENTON CO WA 120-B3
HORSE CREEK RD
LINCOLN CO OR 206-C5
SISKIYOU CO CA 149-B3
WALLOWA CO OR 123-A3
HORSEFALL BEACH RD
COOS CO OR 218-A6
HORSEMAN LN
DESCHUTES CO OR 217-B1
HORSESHOE LN
LINN CO OR 207-B5
HORSESHOE BEND RD
ADA CO ID 253-B1
EAGLE ID 253-B1
KLICKITAT CO WA 196-D3
SHERMAN CO OR 127-C3
HORSESHOE BEND RD Rt#-55
ADA CO ID 139-C3
ADA CO ID 253-B1
BOISE CO ID 139-C3
EAGLE ID 253-B1
HORSESHOE BEND ID 139-C3
HORSESHOE LAKE RD
MARION CO OR 198-C7
HORTON RD
LANE CO OR 133-A2
HORTON GRADE RD
WHITMAN CO WA 122-B1
SE HORTSMAN RD
KITSAP CO WA 271-C14
PORT ORCHARD WA 271-A14
HOSKINS RD
DIST OF N VANCOUVER BC 255-F1
HOSKINS-SUMMIT RD
BENTON CO OR 133-A1
S HOSMER ST
PIERCE CO WA 181-D4
TACOMA WA 181-D4
TACOMA WA 295-E7
HOSPITAL WY
BREWSTER WA 104-B3
HOSTETLER RD
ASOTIN CO WA 250-B7
HOSTETLER ST W
THE DALLES OR 196-C7
WASCO CO OR 196-C7
NE HOSTMARK ST
POULSBO WA 170-B7
HOTCHKISS LN
HARNEY CO OR 145-A1
HOT SPRINGS AV
CARSON WA 194-D4
CARSON WA 195-A4
HOT SPRINGS RD
ADAMS CO ID 251-A3
MALHEUR CO OR 154-B2
HOT SPRINGS RD Rt#-9
CITY OF HARRISN HT SPGS BC 94-C3
DISTRICT OF KENT BC 94-C3
HOUSER WY S Rt#-900
RENTON WA 175-C5
NE HOUSLEY AV
DOUGLAS CO OR 334-F2
W HOUSTON AV
SPOKANE CO WA 348-B6
HOUSTON RD
ISLAND CO WA 167-C5
JACKSON CO OR 234-B2
LEWIS CO ID 123-B3
N HOUSTON RD
SPOKANE CO WA 348-B6
W HOUSTON RD
SPOKANE CO WA 348-B7
HOUSTON LAKE RD
CROOK CO OR 213-C5
HOUTCHEN ST
PACIFIC CO WA 186-B7
HOVANDER RD
FERNDALE WA 158-C6
WHATCOM CO WA 158-C6
HOVENDEN RD NE
MARION CO OR 205-B1
HOWARD AV
EUGENE OR 329-E1
LANE CO OR 329-E1
HOWARD LN
LANE CO OR 210-A5
HOWARD RD
KITTITAS CO WA 241-A4
MULTNOMAH CO OR 200-D2
E HOWARD RD
KOOTENAI CO ID 245-B1
HOWARD ST
WALLA WALLA WA 345-C9
WALLA WALLA CO WA 345-C9
WALLA WALLA EAST WA 345-C9
S HOWARD ST
WALLA WALLA WA 345-C11
WALLA WALLA CO WA 345-C11
HOWARD CREEK RD
CROOK CO OR 136-A2
HOWARD FLAT RD
CHELAN CO WA 236-D2
HOWARDS MILL RD
CLACKAMAS CO OR 199-D7
CLACKAMAS CO OR 200-A7
HOWE LN
LANE CO OR 215-B5
HOWE ST
VANCOUVER BC 254-G9
HOWE ST Rt#-99
VANCOUVER BC 254-F10
W HOWE ST
SEATTLE WA 276-D1
SEATTLE WA 277-F2
HOWELL ST
SEATTLE WA 278-A5
HOWELL GRADE RD
GARFIELD CO WA 122-C2
HOWELL PRAIRIE RD
MARION CO OR 205-B5
HOWLETT RD
CLACKAMAS CO OR 200-C4
E HOXIE RD
SPOKANE CO WA 115-A2
E HOXIE RD Rt#-278
ROCKFORD WA 114-C2
SPOKANE CO WA 114-C2
HOYT RD SW
FEDERAL WAY WA 182-A1
NW HOYT ST
PORTLAND OR 313-E5
HOYT ST S
SALEM OR 324-G2
HOYT ST SE
SALEM OR 324-H2
H STREET RD
BLAINE WA 158-C3
WHATCOM CO WA 158-C3
HUBBARD RD
ADAMS CO ID 251-A4
LEWIS CO WA 187-A2
E HUBBARD RD
ADA CO ID 253-B4
W HUBBARD RD
ADA CO ID 253-A5
N HUBBARD ST
COEUR D'ALENE ID 355-D11
HUBBARD CREEK RD
DOUGLAS CO OR 221-A1
HUBBARD GULCH RD
NEZ PERCE CO ID 123-B2
HUBER LN
JEFFERSON CO OR 208-B7
HUBER RD
PACIFIC CO WA 117-B2
HUCKELBERRY LN
COOS CO OR 220-B4
HUCKLEBERRY RD
JACKSON CO OR 226-D5
JACKSON CO OR 227-A4
HUDDLESTON RD
WHEELER CO OR 128-B3
E HUDLOW RD
KOOTENAI CO ID 245-A4
HUDSON RD
SKAMANIA CO WA 193-D7
SE HUDSON RD
CLACKAMAS CO OR 200-C3
HUDSON ST
CITY OF RICHMOND BC 156-B5
LONGVIEW WA 303-A9
VANCOUVER BC 156-B5
SW HUDSON ST
SEATTLE WA 280-C5
HUETTER RD
HAYDEN ID 247-D1
HAYDEN ID 354-H2
KOOTENAI CO ID 247-D1
KOOTENAI CO ID 354-H2
N HUETTER RD
KOOTENAI CO ID 354-H6
POST FALLS ID 354-H6
NE HUFF RD
CLARK CO WA 193-A1
HUGHES AV
BLAINE WA 158-B3
WHATCOM CO WA 158-B3
HUGHES RD
CHELAN CO WA 238-C2
NE HUGHES RD
CLARK CO WA 193-C6
HUGHEY LN
TILLAMOOK CO OR 197-C2
HUGO RD
JOSEPHINE CO OR 229-A4
HUHTALA RD
LINCOLN CO OR 206-C2
HULL RD
JACKSON CO OR 234-A2
HULL ST
PORT ORCHARD WA 174-B4
HULSE RD
CLALLAM CO WA 165-D6
HULTMAN RD
POLK CO OR 207-C1
HUMBOLDT ST
CITY OF VICTORIA BC 256-H9
HUME RD
WHITMAN CO WA 114-C3
HUMMINGBIRD RD
DOUGLAS CO WA 239-B1
HUMORIST RD
BURBANK WA 121-B3
WALLA WALLA CO WA 121-B3
HUMPBACK RD
BRITISH COLUMBIA 159-A6
DISTRICT OF LANGFORD BC 159-A6
HUMPERT LN NE
MARION CO OR 205-C4
SW HUMPHREY BLVD
MULTNOMAH OR 316-A1
PORTLAND OR 316-A1
S HUMPHREY RD
LANGLEY WA 171-A2
HUMPHREY HILL RD
SKAGIT CO WA 161-B4
E HUMPHREYS RD
COOS CO OR 220-B4
W HUMPHREYS RD
COOS CO OR 220-B4
E HUMPTULIPS RD
GRAYS HARBOR CO WA 178-B2
HUMPTULIPS VALLEY RD
GRAYS HARBOR CO WA 177-D3
HUMPTULIPS VALLEY DIKE RD
GRAYS HARBOR CO WA 177-C5
HUNGRY HILL RD
LANE CO OR 215-B5
HUNGRY JUNCTION RD
KITTITAS CO WA 241-B5
HUNNELL RD
DESCHUTES CO OR 217-C1
HUNT LN
JOSEPHINE CO OR 229-A6
HUNT RD
CLALLAM CO WA 165-A5
DESCHUTES CO OR 212-B4
HUNT ST NW
GIG HARBOR WA 181-B1
PIERCE CO WA 181-B1
HUNT CLUB RD
GRAYS HARBOR CO WA 183-B2
HUNTER RD
ISLAND CITY OR 130-A2
KITTITAS CO WA 241-A5
UNION CO OR 130-A2
SW HUNTER RD
KITSAP CO WA 174-B6
HUNTER RD SW
THURSTON CO WA 184-A3
HUNTER CREEK LP
CURRY CO OR 228-A6
HUNTER CREEK RD
CURRY CO OR 228-A6
HUNTER POINT RD NW
THURSTON CO WA 180-C4
HUNTINGDON RD
DISTRICT OF ABBOTSFORD BC 102-B1
DISTRICT OF MATSQUI BC 102-B1
HUNTINGTON AV
CASTLE ROCK WA 187-C7
CASTLE ROCK WA 189-C1
COWLITZ CO WA 187-C7
COWLITZ CO WA 189-C1
HUNTINGTON HWY U.S.-30
BAKER CO OR 138-C2
BAKER CO OR 139-A2
HUNTINGTON OR 138-C2
MALHEUR CO OR 139-A2
HUNTINGTON PL
LONGVIEW WA 302-J6
HUNTINGTON RD
MALHEUR CO OR 138-B2
W HUNTLEY ST
ABERDEEN WA 178-B7
COSMOPOLIS WA 178-B7
W HUNTZINGER RD
YAKIMA CO WA 243-B4
HURD RD
GRAYS HARBOR CO WA 179-B7
SE HURLBURT RD
MULTNOMAH CO OR 200-C2
HURLEY-WALDRIP RD
MASON CO WA 180-A5
HURRICANE CREEK RD
ENTERPRISE OR 130-C2
JOSEPH OR 130-C2
WALLOWA CO OR 130-C2
HURTLEY RANCH RD
DESCHUTES CO OR 212-A5
HUSKEY RD
HOOD RIVER CO OR 195-D7
WASCO CO OR 196-A6
HUSSEY ST
COLLEGE PLACE WA 344-E10
WALLA WALLA WA 344-E7
WALLA WALLA CO WA 344-E8
WALLA WALLA WEST WA 344-E10
HUTCHENS HILL RD
GARFIELD CO WA 122-B2
HUTCHINSON RD
BRITISH COLUMBIA 159-A1
COLUMBIA CO OR 189-B5
HUTSON DR
HOOD RIVER CO OR 202-C2
HWY Rt#-9
SNOHOMISH CO WA 171-D4
HYACINTH ST NE
SALEM OR 323-B7
HYANNIS DR
DIST OF N VANCOUVER BC 255-J4
HYATT RD SE
THURSTON CO WA 184-D2
HYATT PRAIRIE RD
JACKSON CO OR 150-A2
HYLINE RD
MALHEUR CO OR 139-A2
HYLO RD S
MARION CO OR 324-F12

I

I AV
ANACORTES WA 259-G4
I RD SW
DOUGLAS CO WA 239-D1
I ST
COLUMBIA CITY OR 192-B1
I ST
NEHALEM OR 191-B4
N I ST
LIND WA 121-B1
TACOMA WA 293-F3
S I ST
TACOMA WA 293-G4
SW I ST
GRANTS PASS OR 335-D9
ICE HARBOR DR
WALLA WALLA CO WA 121-B3
ICE HARBOR DR Rt#-124
WALLA WALLA CO WA 121-B3
ICICLE RD
CHELAN CO WA 238-A1
IDAHO AV U.S.-30
ONTARIO OR 139-A3
E IDAHO AV U.S.-95
HOMEDALE ID 147-A1
W IDAHO AV
ONTARIO OR 139-A3
W IDAHO AV Rt#-19
HOMEDALE ID 147-A1
W IDAHO BLVD
GEM CO ID 139-B3
N IDAHO RD
KOOTENAI CO ID 247-C1
OTIS ORCHARDS WA 352-G6
SPOKANE CO WA 352-G6
S IDAHO RD
SPOKANE CO WA 247-B4
IDAHO ST
CASCADE ID 252-D6
N IDAHO ST
KOOTENAI CO ID 353-J3
POST FALLS ID 353-J3
S IDAHO ST
KOOTENAI CO ID 247-C1
W IDAHO ST U.S.-95
WEISER ID 139-A2
IDAHO-OREGN-NEVADA HWY U.S.-95
HUMBOLDT CO NV 154-B3
JORDAN VALLEY OR 147-A2
MALHEUR CO OR 146-C3
MALHEUR CO OR 147-A2
MALHEUR CO OR 154-B1
OWYHEE CO ID 147-A2
IDAHO POWER RD
BAKER CO OR 131-A3
IDLERS REST RD
LATAH CO ID 249-D4
IDYLWOOD DR SE
SALEM OR 324-F5
IGO RD
GILLIAM CO OR 128-A2
IHRIG RD
WASHINGTON CO OR 198-B1
S ILER ST
MOXEE CITY WA 243-D7
ILLAHEE RD NE
KITSAP CO WA 174-C1
KITSAP CO WA 271-C6
ILLINOIS AV U.S.-95
COUNCIL ID 139-C1
N ILLINOIS AV
PASCO WA 343-E6
S ILLINOIS AV
PASCO WA 343-E8
ILLINOIS RIVER RD
JOSEPHINE CO OR 233-A1
ILLINOIS VALLEY PARK RD
CAVE JUNCTION OR 233-B4
JOSEPHINE CO OR 233-B4
ILMARI RD
COLUMBIA CO OR 189-A3
IMBLER LN
JEFFERSON CO OR 208-C7
IMBODEN RD
LEWIS CO WA 187-B5
IMHOFF RD
WHATCOM CO WA 158-C6
IMMIGRANT RD
LANE CO OR 215-D4
S IMMONEN RD
LINCOLN CO OR 203-A6
IMPERIAL ST
DISTRICT OF BURNABY BC 156-C5
INCHELIUM-KETTLE FALLS RD
FERRY CO WA 105-C2
INCHELIUM WA 105-C2
INDEPENDENCE HWY
BENTON CO OR 207-B4
INDEPENDENCE HWY Rt#-51
POLK CO OR 204-B6
INDEPENDENCE RD
YAKIMA CO WA 120-B2
INDEPENDENCE RD SW
LEWIS CO WA 117-B1
INDEX-GALENA RD
SNOHOMISH CO WA 111-A1
INDIAN RD
SHELTER BAY WA 167-D1
SKAGIT CO WA 160-D7
SKAGIT CO WA 167-D1
INDIAN ST
BELLINGHAM WA 258-D8
E INDIANA AV
SPOKANE WA 349-A7
S INDIANA AV
CANYON CO ID 147-B1
W INDIANA AV
SPOKANE WA 348-J7
SPOKANE WA 349-A7
INDIAN CAMP RD SW
DOUGLAS CO WA 239-B2
INDIAN CEMETERY RD
KOOTENAI CO ID 248-A5
INDIAN CHURCH RD
GRANGER WA 120-A2
SATUS WA 120-A2
YAKIMA CO WA 120-A2
INDIAN CREEK DR
DOUGLAS CO OR 219-A6
INDIAN CREEK RD
DESCHUTES CO OR 216-C7
GRANT CO OR 137-B2
HOOD RIVER CO OR 195-C5
JOSEPHINE CO OR 233-B1
INDIAN CREEK RD
LANE CO OR 209-D7
INDIAN CREEK-CANYON CREEK RD
HUMBOLDT CO NV 154-C3
INDIAN FORD RD
DESCHUTES CO OR 211-C4
INDIAN FORT CREEK RD
MALHEUR CO OR 146-C3
INDIAN GULCH RD
MALHEUR CO OR 138-B2
INDIAN HEAD RD
WASHINGTON CO ID 139-A2
INDIAN MOUNTAIN RD
KOOTENAI CO ID 248-B6
INDIANOLA RD NE
INDIANOLA A 170-C6
NE INDIAN SCHOOL RD
SALEM OR 323-C5
N INDIAN TRAIL RD
SPOKANE WA 346-C12
SPOKANE CO WA 346-A9
W INDIAN TRAIL RD
SPOKANE WA 346-D14
SPOKANE WA 348-E1
INDIAN VALLEY RD
ADAMS CO ID 139-C1
INDUSTRIAL RD
ABERDEEN WA 178-A7
DISTRICT OF SURREY BC 157-A5
HOQUIAM WA 178-A7
INDUSTRIAL WY Rt#-432
COWLITZ CO WA 302-D8
LONGVIEW WA 302-D8
LONGVIEW WA 303-A12
INGALLS LN
JOSEPHINE CO OR 229-A7
INGALLS RD
LEWIS CO WA 117-B1
WAHKIAKUM CO WA 117-B2
INGLE CREEK RD
GRANT CO OR 137-A2
INGLEWOOD AV
DIST OF WEST VANCOUVER BC 254-C3
INGLEWOOD HILL RD
KING CO WA 175-D2
INGRAM LN NW
YAMHILL CO OR 204-C2
INGRAM ISLAND RD
BENTON CO OR 133-B2
INITIAL PEAK RD
KOOTENAI CO ID 248-D3
INLAND ST U.S.-195
WHITMAN CO WA 114-C3
N INLAND ST
SPOKANE CO WA 246-A2
INLAND EMPIRE HWY
GRANDVIEW WA 120-B3
SUNNYSIDE WA 120-B2
YAKIMA CO WA 120-A2
INLAND EMPIRE HWY U.S.-12
ASOTIN CO WA 250-B4
WALLA WALLA CO WA 344-D7
WALLA WALLA WEST WA 344-D7
S INLAND EMPIRE HWY U.S.-195
SPOKANE WA 246-C5
SPOKANE CO WA 246-C5
N INLAND EMPIRE RD
GRANDVIEW WA 120-B3
S INLAND EMPIRE WY
SPOKANE WA 348-G12
NW INLET AV
LINCOLN CITY OR 203-A4
INLET DR Rt#-7A
DISTRICT OF BURNABY BC 156-D4
INNES RD
DESCHUTES CO OR 212-B7
INTERLAAKEN DR SW
LAKEWOOD WA 181-C4
INTERNATIONAL BLVD Rt#-99
DES MOINES WA 290-C5
SEATAC WA 288-D7
SEATAC WA 290-C5
TUKWILA WA 288-D7
INTER-PROVINCIAL HWY
DISTRICT OF ABBOTSFORD BC 94-B3
DISTRICT OF ABBOTSFORD BC 102-B1
DISTRICT OF MATSQUI BC 102-B1
N INTERSTATE AV
PORTLAND OR 308-E4
PORTLAND OR 309-E6
PORTLAND OR 313-E1
INTERURBAN AV S
TUKWILA WA 286-D6
TUKWILA WA 287-E7
TUKWILA WA 289-G2
INTERURBAN RD
DISTRICT OF SAANICH BC 159-C5
DISTRICT OF SAANICH BC 256-D1
INTERVALE RD
YAMHILL CO OR 198-B5
IOCO RD
PORT MOODY BC 157-A4
IOLANDA PL
WHATCOM CO WA 101-C1
IONE RD
FRANKLIN CO WA 121-A2
N IONE ST
KENNEWICK WA 343-C10
IONE-BOARDMAN RD
MORROW CO OR 128-B2
IONE-GOOSEBERRY RD
MORROW CO OR 128-B2
IOWA
CROOK CO OR 213-D6
S IOWA AV
EAST WENATCHEE BENCH WA 239-A5
PAYETTE ID 139-A3
PAYETTE CO ID 139-A3
IOWA AV N
PAYETTE ID 139-A3
PAYETTE CO ID 139-A3
IOWA ST
ASHLAND OR 337-D8
BELLINGHAM WA 258-F6
IOWA HEIGHTS RD
WHATCOM CO WA 161-B2

STREET / City State / Page-Grid

IOWA HILL RD
- WASHINGTON CO OR 198-C2

IRELAND RD
- WALLA WALLA CO WA 121-C3

NE IRELAND RD
- CLARK CO WA 193-C6

IRENE ST
- BOISE ID 253-C2
- WALLA WALLA WA 344-H7
- WALLA WALLA WEST WA 344-H7

SW IRIS LN
- CULVER OR 208-B7
- JEFFERSON CO OR 208-A7

IRISH RD
- TILLAMOOK CO OR 203-C1

IRISH BEND LP
- LINN CO OR 210-A3

IRONDALE RD
- HADLOCK-IRONDALE WA 170-A1
- HADLOCK-IRONDALE WA 263-E14

IRON MOUNTAIN BLVD
- LAKE OSWEGO OR 320-C6
- LAKE OSWEGO OR 321-E6

IRON MOUNTAIN RD
- MALHEUR CO OR 146-A3

IRONWOOD DR
- JACKSON CO OR 230-D4

W IRONWOOD DR
- COEUR D'ALENE ID 355-C8

IRVING AV
- ASTORIA WA 300-F5

W IRVING AV
- ASTORIA WA 300-B5

SW IRVING LN
- JEFFERSON CO OR 208-B7

IRVING RD
- EUGENE OR 215-A1
- LANE CO OR 215-A1
- Santa Clara OR 215-A1

IRVINGTON DR
- Santa Clara OR 215-A1

SE ISAAC AV
- PENDLETON OR 129-B1

SW ISAAC AV
- PENDLETON OR 129-B1

E ISAACS AV
- WALLA WALLA WA 345-C6
- WALLA WALLA CO WA 345-H5

ISLAND BLVD FI
- PIERCE CO WA 181-B2

ISLAND DR
- COLUMBIA CO OR 189-D7

N ISLAND DR
- MASON CO WA 180-C2

S ISLAND DR
- MASON CO WA 180-C2

ISLAND HWY Rt#-1
- BRITISH COLUMBIA 101-A1
- BRITISH COLUMBIA 159-A2
- DISTRICT OF LANGFORD BC 159-A2
- DISTRICT OF SAANICH BC 256-D4
- DUNCAN BC 101-A1
- TOWN OF VIEW ROYAL BC 159-A2
- TOWN OF VIEW ROYAL BC 256-D4

ISLAND HWY N Rt#-19
- BRITISH COLUMBIA 93-A3
- NANAIMO BC 93-A3

SE ISLAND CREST WY
- MERCER ISLAND WA 175-C4

ISLAND SHORE RD
- MASON CO WA 180-D3

ISOM RD
- LINN CO OR 210-A4

W ISRAEL RD
- TUMWATER WA 296-E13

ISSAQUAH FALL CITY RD
- KING CO WA 176-A3

ISSAQUAH HOBART RD
- ISSAQUAH WA 176-A5
- KING CO WA 176-A5

ISSAQUAH PINE LAKE RD
- KING CO WA 176-A3

IVANHOE AV
- MALHEUR CO OR 139-A3

IVAN MORSE RD
- CHELAN CO WA 236-B1

IVERSON RD
- DOUGLAS CO OR 221-A2
- ISLAND CO WA 168-A4
- YAKIMA CO WA 120-A2

NE IVERSON RD
- KITSAP CO WA 170-C6

IVORY PINE RD
- KLAMATH CO OR 151-B1

IVY AV
- GERVAIS OR 205-B2

IVY LN
- DESCHUTES CO OR 212-A6
- JEFFERSON CO OR 208-D3

NW IVY LN
- JEFFERSON CO OR 208-B3

IVY ST Rt#-99
- JUNCTION CITY OR 210-A5

N IVY ST
- CANBY OR 199-C6

S IVY ST
- CANBY OR 199-C6

IZEE-OFFICER RANCH RD
- GRANT CO OR 137-A3

IZEE RD TO BUSH RANCH RD
- GRANT CO OR 137-A3

J

J ST
- COSMOPOLIS WA 178-B7
- HUBBARD OR 205-B1
- MARION CO OR 205-B1
- VANCOUVER WA 305-G3

E J ST
- HUBBARD OR 205-C1

S J ST
- TACOMA WA 293-G6
- TACOMA WA 295-G1

SE J ST
- GRANTS PASS OR 335-F9
- MADRAS OR 208-C5

SW J ST
- GRANTS PASS OR 335-E9
- MADRAS OR 208-C5

J ST SE
- QUINCY WA 112-B3

J ST SW
- QUINCY WA 112-B3

JACKADEL LN
- JOSEPHINE CO OR 233-B5

JACK CREEK RD
- JEFFERSON CO OR 211-B1
- JOSEPHINE CO OR 229-C3

S JACK CREEK RD
- JEFFERSON CO OR 211-B1

SW JACK CREEK LOOP RD
- JEFFERSON CO OR 211-B1

JACK LAKE RD
- JEFFERSON CO OR 211-B1

JACKLIN RD
- DISTRICT OF LANGFORD BC 159-B6

JACKMAN RD
- WHATCOM CO WA 158-D3

JACK MOUNTAIN RD
- HARNEY CO OR 145-B3

JACK MOUNTAIN SPUR
- HARNEY CO OR 145-B2

JACKSHA RD
- LATAH CO ID 249-C6

JACKSON AV
- KITSAP CO WA 174-C4
- PIERCE CO WA 181-C5
- TACOMA WA 181-C5

S JACKSON AV
- TACOMA WA 181-C2

E JACKSON BLVD
- MEDFORD OR 336-F11

JACKSON DR
- BREMERTON WA 270-E9
- KITSAP CO WA 270-E9

JACKSON DR NW
- KITSAP CO WA 270-E9

JACKSON HWY
- CHEHALIS WA 299-G14
- LEWIS CO WA 184-C7
- LEWIS CO WA 187-D1
- LEWIS CO WA 299-G14

JACKSON HWY S
- LEWIS CO WA 187-C5

JACKSON RD
- BIRCH BAY WA 158-B5
- COWLITZ CO WA 189-A2
- WASHINGTON CO ID 139-A2

E JACKSON RD
- SPOKANE CO WA 247-A5

S JACKSON RD
- CLACKAMAS CO OR 205-D1
- SPOKANE CO WA 114-C2
- SPOKANE CO WA 247-A5

JACKSON ST
- ALBANY OR 326-D8
- PORT TOWNSEND WA 263-H3

E JACKSON ST
- MEDFORD OR 336-E11

N JACKSON ST
- GENESEE ID 250-C1

N JACKSON ST U.S.-95
- MOSCOW ID 249-C5

NE JACKSON ST
- ROSEBURG OR 334-G7

S JACKSON ST
- SEATTLE WA 277-J7
- SEATTLE WA 278-A7

S JACKSON ST U.S.-95
- MOSCOW ID 249-C5

SE JACKSON ST
- ROSEBURG OR 334-F8

W JACKSON ST
- MEDFORD OR 336-B11

JACKSON CANYON RD
- DOUGLAS CO WA 236-D4

JACKSON CREEK RD
- DOUGLAS CO OR 141-C3
- DOUGLAS CO OR 226-A2
- MALHEUR CO OR 154-B2

JACKSON HILL RD
- MARION CO OR 207-D1

JACKSON LAKE RD KPN
- PIERCE CO WA 181-A1

NE JACKSON SCHOOL RD
- HILLSBORO OR 198-D1

NW JACKSON SCHOOL RD
- WASHINGTON CO OR 125-C1

JACKSON TRAIL RD
- JEFFERSON CO OR 208-A5

JACKSONVILLE HWY Rt#-238
- GRANTS PASS OR 335-C14
- JACKSON CO OR 149-B2
- JACKSON CO OR 234-A1
- JACKSONVILLE OR 149-B2
- JACKSONVILLE OR 234-A1
- JOSEPHINE CO OR 149-A2
- JOSEPHINE CO OR 229-B7
- JOSEPHINE CO OR 335-C14

JACK VAUGHN RD
- GRANT CO OR 137-A1

JACOBSEN BLVD
- BREMERTON WA 271-B10
- KITSAP CO WA 271-B9

SW JACOBSEN RD
- SEATTLE WA 280-C5

JACOBSON RD
- LINCOLN CO OR 206-C4
- PACIFIC CO WA 183-B4

JACOMBS RD
- CITY OF RICHMOND BC 156-C6

JACOT RD
- BENEWAH CO ID 248-D7

JADWIN AV
- RICHLAND WA 340-F12
- RICHLAND WA 341-G1

JAEGER RD
- DESCHUTES CO OR 212-B4

JAGER LN
- LANE CO OR 210-A5

JAGLA RD
- CHELAN CO WA 239-A5

N JAMES AV
- EAST WENATCHEE BENCH WA 239-A4

JAMES RD
- BELLINGHAM WA 258-E3
- CLALLAM CO WA 169-A2
- EUGENE OR 329-H1
- WHATCOM CO WA 258-E3

JAMES RD
- WHITMAN CO WA 249-A1

JAMES RD SW
- THURSTON CO WA 184-A4

JAMES ST
- BELLINGHAM WA 258-E4
- SEATTLE WA 278-A6

E JAMES ST
- KENT WA 175-C7

E JAMES ST U.S.-195
- COLFAX WA 122-C1

N JAMES ST
- MARION CO OR 205-C4
- SILVERTON OR 205-C4

S JAMES ST
- SILVERTON OR 205-C4

W JAMES ST
- KENT WA 175-B7

E JAMES WY
- SEATTLE WA 278-B6

JAMES BROOKS RD
- COLUMBIA CO OR 192-A2

JAMES HOWE RD
- POLK CO OR 204-A5

JAMESON ST
- SEDRO-WOOLLEY WA 161-C6

JAMESON LAKE RD
- DOUGLAS CO WA 112-C2

JAMESON LAKE EAST ACCESS RD NE
- DOUGLAS CO WA 112-C2

JAMES SCHOOLHOUSE LN
- BAKER CO OR 138-B1

JAMESTOWN AV
- BENTON CO OR 133-B2

E JAMIESON RD
- SPOKANE CO WA 246-C5

JANETA AV
- MALHEUR CO OR 139-A3

JANICE AV NE
- HAYESVILLE OR 323-F7

JANICKI RD
- SKAGIT CO WA 161-C7

JANIS-OROVILLE WESTSIDE RD
- OKANOGAN CO WA 104-C1
- OROVILLE WA 104-C1

JANSHAW RD
- COLUMBIA CO OR 189-B7

JANSKY RD E
- PIERCE CO WA 182-C6

JANTZ RD
- ADAMS CO WA 121-B1

JAPANESE HOLLOW RD
- WASCO CO OR 127-B2

JAQUITH RD
- WASHINGTON CO OR 198-D4
- YAMHILL CO OR 198-D4

JARE ST SW
- GRAND MOUND WA 184-B4
- THURSTON CO WA 184-B4

JARED RD
- MASON CO WA 180-D3

JASPER RD
- JEFFERSON CO OR 208-C7
- JEFFERSON CO OR 213-A1
- LANE CO OR 215-D3
- LANE CO OR 331-F9
- SPRINGFIELD OR 331-C8

JASPER-LOWELL RD
- LANE CO OR 133-C3
- LANE CO OR 215-D3
- LOWELL OR 133-C3

JAYNES DR
- JOSEPHINE CO OR 229-B7

J BURTON RD
- KOOTENAI CO ID 247-C6

JEFFERS CREEK RD
- DOUGLAS CO OR 219-C7

JEFFERSON AV
- CORVALLIS OR 327-G10

JEFFERSON AV Rt#-361
- JEFFERSON CO OR 208-B6
- METOLIUS OR 208-B6

S JEFFERSON AV
- TACOMA WA 293-H7
- TACOMA WA 295-G1

JEFFERSON DR
- MALHEUR CO OR 139-A3

JEFFERSON HWY
- JEFFERSON OR 207-D2
- LINN CO OR 207-D2
- MARION CO OR 207-D2

JEFFERSON HWY U.S.-99E
- LINN CO OR 207-D3

JEFFERSON ST
- BINGEN WA 195-D5
- EUGENE OR 329-J7
- OLYMPIA WA 296-J6
- PORT TOWNSEND WA 263-G5

E JEFFERSON ST
- BOISE ID 253-D3
- STAYTON OR 133-C1

N JEFFERSON ST
- BENTON CO WA 342-E8

NW JEFFERSON ST
- ROSEBURG OR 334-C5

SE JEFFERSON ST Rt#-223
- DALLAS OR 204-A6

SW JEFFERSON ST
- PORTLAND OR 312-D6

JEFFERSON WY
- CORVALLIS OR 327-E10
- SNOHOMISH CO WA 171-B4

JEFFERSON-MARION RD
- JEFFERSON OR 207-D3
- MARION CO OR 133-C1
- MARION CO OR 207-D3

JEFFERSON-SCIO DR
- JEFFERSON OR 207-D3
- LINN CO OR 133-C1
- MARION CO OR 133-C1
- MARION CO OR 207-D3
- SCIO OR 133-C1

JEFFRIES RD
- LEWIS CO WA 184-A7

J E JOHNSON RD
- COWLITZ CO WA 189-D6

JELDNESS RD
- PACIFIC CO WA 186-B5

JEMTEGAARD RD
- SKAMANIA CO WA 193-D7

JENCK RD
- TILLAMOOK CO OR 197-B7

JENKINS CREEK RD
- WASHINGTON CO ID 139-A2

JENNY CREEK RD
- CLARK CO WA 192-C1

JENNINGS RD
- WHITMAN CO WA 249-B6

JENSEN RD
- LATAH CO ID 249-D6

W JENSEN RD
- SPOKANE CO WA 246-A6

JENTGES RD
- IDAHO CO ID 123-C3

JEPPESEN ACRES RD
- EUGENE OR 330-B2

JERICHO LN
- JEFFERSON CO OR 212-D1

JERNSTEDT RD
- YAMHILL CO OR 198-B6

JEROME PRAIRIE RD
- JOSEPHINE CO OR 229-A7

JERRYS FLAT RD
- CURRY CO OR 228-A5
- GOLD BEACH OR 228-A5

JERUSALEM HILL RD NW
- YAMHILL CO OR 204-C3

JERVIS ST
- VANCOUVER BC 254-F9

JESS RD
- WHATCOM CO WA 158-C4

JESSUP RD
- IDAHO CO ID 123-C3

NE JESSUP ST
- PORTLAND OR 309-G7

JETTY AV
- LINCOLN CITY OR 203-A4

JETTY RD
- CLATSOP CO WA 188-A1

N JETTY RD Rt#-115
- GRAYS HARBOR CO WA 177-B6

E JEWETT BLVD Rt#-141
- WHITE SALMON WA 195-D4

W JEWETT BLVD Rt#-141
- KLICKITAT CO WA 195-D4
- WHITE SALMON WA 195-D4

S JEWETT RD
- ISLAND CO WA 171-A3

JIM ST
- PACIFIC CO WA 186-A5

JIM CREEK SPUR
- JACKSON CO OR 226-B5

JIM DAVIS RD
- WHITMAN CO WA 114-B3

JIM TOWN LN
- LOSTINE OR 130-C1
- WALLOWA CO OR 130-C1

JINGLE POT RD
- BRITISH COLUMBIA 93-A3
- NANAIMO BC 93-A3

J LINE RD
- GRAYS HARBOR CO WA 117-B1

J MCCUTCHEON RD
- PIERCE CO WA 182-B5

J M DICKENSON RD SW
- KITSAP CO WA 174-A5

JOE JOHNS RD
- OCEAN PARK WA 186-A2
- PACIFIC CO WA 186-A2

JOELSON RD
- DOUGLAS CO OR 221-A2

JOE MILLER RD
- CHELAN CO WA 239-A6

JOE NEY-DAVIS SL RD
- COOS CO OR 220-C2

JOE SHERWOOD RD
- STEVENS CO WA 114-A1

JOE WRIGHT RD
- KLAMATH CO OR 235-C5

SE JOHANNESEN RD
- MULTNOMAH CO OR 200-D2

JOHN RD
- DIST OF NORTH SAANICH BC 159-C2
- LEWIS CO WA 187-D2

E JOHN ST
- SEATTLE WA 278-B4

JOHN DAY DR
- JACKSON CO OR 230-B5

JOHN DAY HWY Rt#-19
- ARLINGTON OR 128-A2
- CONDON OR 128-A2
- FOSSIL OR 128-A3
- GILLIAM CO OR 128-A2
- GRANT CO OR 136-B1
- SPRAY OR 136-B1
- WHEELER CO OR 128-A3
- WHEELER CO OR 136-B1

JOHN DAY HWY U.S.-26
- BAKER CO OR 137-C2
- BAKER CO OR 138-A2
- DAYVILLE OR 136-C1
- GRANT CO OR 136-C1
- GRANT CO OR 137-C2
- JOHN DAY OR 137-C2
- MALHEUR CO OR 138-B2
- MALHEUR CO OR 139-A3
- MOUNT VERNON OR 137-C2
- UNITY OR 138-A2
- VALE OR 139-A3

JOHN DAY HWY U.S.-395
- GRANT CO OR 137-A2
- JOHN DAY OR 137-A2
- MOUNT VERNON OR 137-A2

JOHN DAY-BURNS HWY U.S.-395
- CANYON CITY OR 137-B2
- GRANT CO OR 137-B2
- HARNEY CO OR 137-B3
- HARNEY CO OR 145-B1
- JOHN DAY OR 137-B2
- SENECA OR 137-B3

JOHN DAY RD TO COUNTY LINE RD
- GRANT CO OR 137-A3

JOHN HENLEY RD
- WHITMAN CO WA 122-A1

JOHN LONG RD NW
- DOUGLAS CO WA 236-C5

S JOHNS AV
- GEM CO ID 139-C3

JOHNS RD
- PIERCE CO WA 182-D5

JOHNS MILL RD
- WASCO CO OR 202-D2

JOHNSON AV
- MAPLE RIDGE BC 157-D5

JOHNSON BLVD
- TUMWATER WA 296-D9

JOHNSON RD
- ASOTIN CO WA 122-C2
- ASOTIN CO WA 250-A4
- BENTON CO WA 120-B3
- DESCHUTES CO OR 217-B1
- KLAMATH CO OR 151-A2
- KLICKITAT CO WA 196-A4
- LEWIS CO WA 187-C2
- MULTNOMAH CO OR 192-A6
- WHITMAN CO WA 249-B7

SE JOHNSON RD
- CLACKAMAS CO OR 199-D3

SW JOHNSON RD
- CLACKAMAS CO OR 199-C4

W JOHNSON RD
- SKAGIT CO WA 168-B1

JOHNSON ST
- BENTON CO OR 133-B2
- CITY OF VICTORIA BC 256-J9
- CITY OF VICTORIA BC 257-A9
- COQUITLAM BC 157-A4

N JOHNSON ST
- KENNEWICK WA 342-J9
- MCMINNVILLE OR 198-A7

NE JOHNSON ST
- DOUGLAS CO OR 334-F3

SW JOHNSON ST
- STANFIELD OR 129-A1
- UMATILLA CO OR 129-A1

JOHNSON-COLTON RD
- WHITMAN CO WA 249-B7
- WHITMAN CO WA 250-A1

SE JOHNSON CREEK BLVD
- CLACKAMAS OR 318-B7
- CLACKAMAS CO OR 199-D3
- MILWAUKIE OR 318-B7
- PORTLAND OR 318-B7
- PORTLAND OR 318-B7

JOHNSON GRADE RD
- MORROW CO OR 128-B2
- STEVENS CO WA 106-A1

JOHNSON MARKET RD
- DESCHUTES CO OR 135-B3

JOHNSON POINT RD NE
- THURSTON CO WA 180-D5

JOHNSON SCHOOL RD
- WASHINGTON CO OR 198-C2

JOHNS PRAIRIE RD
- MASON CO WA 180-B2

JOHNS RIVER RD
- GRAYS HARBOR CO WA 183-C2

JOHNSTON RD
- CITY OF WHITE ROCK BC 158-A2
- DISTRICT OF SURREY BC 158-A2

JOHNSTONE RD
- OWYHEE CO ID 147-A1

JOHN WAYNE TR
- ADAMS CO WA 114-A3
- ADAMS CO WA 121-C1

JOHN WIDMAN RD
- BAKER CO OR 138-C1

JOLLIFF RD
- STEVENS CO WA 106-B2

JONATHAN RD
- WASHINGTON CO ID 139-A2

JONATHAN ST
- TONASKET WA 104-C2

JONES AV
- CITY OF N VANCOUVER BC 255-A4

JONES RD
- COLUMBIA CO OR 189-C6
- JACKSON CO OR 230-C4
- KING CO WA 175-D5
- LEWIS CO WA 184-D6
- LEWIS CO WA 187-A3
- WHITMAN CO WA 114-B3

E JONES RD
- ISLAND CO WA 167-C1

N JONES RD
- ISLAND CO WA 167-C1

NE JONES RD
- BEND OR 332-G5

JONES RD NW
- DOUGLAS CO WA 236-C6

JONES RD SW
- THURSTON CO WA 184-C1

JONES ACRES RD
- LANE CO OR 210-D7

JORDAN RD
- DESCHUTES CO OR 212-A5
- GRANITE FALLS WA 102-C3
- LEWIS CO WA 187-C2
- SNOHOMISH CO WA 102-C3
- SNOHOMISH CO WA 168-D5

SW JORDAN RD
- JEFFERSON CO OR 135-A1
- JEFFERSON CO OR 208-A7

JORDAN ST SW
- ROCHESTER WA 184-A3
- THURSTON CO WA 184-A4

JORDAN CRATERS RD
- MALHEUR CO OR 147-A2

JORDAN CREEK RD
- WASCO CO OR 202-D5

JORDAN MEADOW RD
- HUMBOLDT CO NV 154-B3

JOSELYN SW
- THURSTON CO WA 184-B4

JOSEPH AV U.S.-95
- WINCHESTER ID 123-B2

JOSEPH ST SE
- MARION CO OR 205-A7
- MARION CO OR 325-J7

JOSEPH CREEK RD
- ASOTIN CO WA 123-A3

NE JOSEPHINE ST
- GRANTS PASS OR 335-F8

JOSPH-WALLOWA LAKE HWY Rt#-82
- WALLOWA CO OR 130-C2

JOSH WILSON RD
- SKAGIT CO WA 160-D6
- SKAGIT CO WA 161-A6
- SKAGIT CO WA 260-A3

JOVITA BLVD E
- EDGEWOOD WA 182-B2
- PACIFIC WA 182-B2
- PIERCE CO WA 182-B2

JOYCE ST
- VANCOUVER BC 156-C5

SW JP WEST RD
- COLUMBIA CO OR 192-A3

J SCHNEBLY RD
- KITTITAS CO WA 241-C4

JUANITA DR NE
- KING CO WA 171-C7
- KIRKLAND WA 171-C7

JUANITA-WOODINVILLE WY NE
- KING CO WA 171-C7

JUBB RD
- CLACKAMAS CO OR 200-B6

JUDD RD
- CLACKAMAS CO OR 200-B4

E JUDKINS RD
- SPOKANE CO WA 247-A2

E JUMPOFF RD
- STEVENS CO WA 106-B3

JUMP-OFF JOE RD
- JOSEPHINE CO OR 229-C3

JUMP-OFF JOE CREEK RD
- JOSEPHINE CO OR 229-B3

JUMPOFF RIDGE RD
- KITTITAS CO WA 241-D1

JUNCTION AV
- EVERETT WA 265-E7

JUNCTION RD
- DOUGLAS CO OR 225-B6

JUNGQUIST RD
- SKAGIT CO WA 161-A7

NE JUNIPER LN
- JEFFERSON CO OR 208-C2

NW JUNIPER LN
- JEFFERSON CO OR 208-B2

JUNIPER RD
- MORROW CO OR 128-C1

JUNIPER BEACH RD
- ISLAND CO WA 168-A4

JUNIPER CANYON RD
- CROOK CO OR 135-C3
- CROOK CO OR 213-D5

N JUNIPER CANYON RD
- UMATILLA CO OR 121-B3

S JUNIPER CANYON RD
- UMATILLA CO OR 129-B1

JUNIPER MOUNTAIN RD
- OWYHEE CO ID 155-A1

JUNTURA CUTOFF RD
- HARNEY CO OR 138-A3

JUNTURA-RIVERSIDE RD
- MALHEUR CO OR 146-A1

JUSTICE RANCH WEST RD
- GRANT CO OR 137-A1

K

K AV
- LA GRANDE OR 130-A2

K ST
- BREMERTON WA 270-D12
- NAVY YARD CITY WA 270-D12

SW K ST
- GRANTS PASS OR 335-D9

K 4-10-NE
- GRANT CO WA 242-C1

KACHESS LAKE RD
- KITTITAS CO WA 111-A3

NW KACHINA AV
- DESCHUTES CO OR 212-C5

KACKMAN RD
- WHITMAN CO WA 114-B3
- WHITMAN CO WA 122-B1

KAGY ST SE
- THURSTON CO WA 181-A7

KAHLER BASIN RD
- WHEELER CO OR 128-B3
- WHEELER CO OR 136-B1

KAHOUT RD
- LEWIS CO WA 187-A2

KAHUT LN NE
- MARION CO OR 205-B2

NW KAISER RD
- MULTNOMAH CO OR 192-A7
- WASHINGTON CO OR 192-A7

KAISER RD NW
- OLYMPIA WA 296-C1
- THURSTON CO WA 180-C5
- THURSTON CO WA 296-C1

KAISER RD SW
- THURSTON CO WA 296-C6

KAKELA RD
- LEWIS CO WA 187-C3

KALAMA RIVER RD
- COWLITZ CO WA 118-A3
- COWLITZ CO WA 189-D5

KALE ST Rt#-544
- EVERSON WA 102-B1

KALE ST NE
- HAYESVILLE OR 323-E5
- SALEM OR 323-E5

KALMBACH RD
- COWLITZ CO WA 187-C7
- COWLITZ CO WA 189-C1

KAMB RD
- SKAGIT CO WA 168-A1

KAME TER
- CLACKAMAS CO OR 199-B5

NE KAMIAKEN ST
- PULLMAN WA 249-B5

NE KAMIAKEN ST Rt#-270
- PULLMAN WA 249-B5

KAMILCHE POINT RD
- MASON CO WA 180-B4

KAMMEYER RD
- COLUMBIA CO OR 192-A4

KAMPH RD
- LINN CO OR 207-D4

S KAMRATH RD
- CLACKAMAS CO OR 200-A6

PNW

INDEX

STREET City State Page-Grid

KANAKA CREEK RD
MAPLE RIDGE BC 157-D6
SKAMANIA CO WA 194-D5
KANASKAT KANGLEY RD SE
KING CO WA 110-C3
KING CO WA 176-B7
SE KANE RD
GRESHAM OR 200-B2
SE KANE ST
ROSEBURG OR 334-G8
KANE CREEK RD
JACKSON CO OR 230-B7
KANGAROO RD
DISTRICT OF METCHOSIN BC 159-A7
KANGAS RD
LEWIS CO WA 187-D4
KANNIWAI CREEK RD
GRANT CO WA 113-A2
KANSAS CITY RD
WASHINGTON CO OR 125-B1
KANTOLA LN
VALLEY CO ID 251-D7
KAPKA BUTTE RD
DESCHUTES CO OR 216-D5
KAPOWSIN HWY
PIERCE CO WA 118-B1
KAPPLER RD
COLUMBIA CO OR 192-A2
KARCHER RD Rt#-55
CANYON CO ID 147-B1
NAMPA ID 147-B1
KARIN DR
TERRACE HEIGHTS WA 243-C6
YAKIMA CO WA 243-C6
KARNOWSKY CREEK RD
LANE CO OR 214-C2
KARTH RD
COLUMBIA CO OR 189-A7
N KATH RD
SPOKANE CO WA 247-B1
W KATHLEEN AV
COEUR D'ALENE ID 355-B6
KOOTENAI CO ID 355-B6
KATON RD
GRAYS HARBOR CO WA 178-D7
KATTENBACK VOLLMER RD
NEZ PERCE CO ID 250-C5
KAUFFMAN RD
CLACKAMAS CO OR 205-D2
KAUFMAN RD NE
MARION CO OR 205-B5
KAYAK POINT RD
SNOHOMISH CO WA 168-B6
KEAN ST
BREMERTON WA 270-D11
KEANE RD SW
DOUGLAS CO WA 239-C5
KEASEY RD
COLUMBIA CO OR 125-B1
NW KEASEY ST
ROSEBURG OR 334-C5
KEASLING RD
LEWIS CO WA 187-D2
KEATING RD NW
THURSTON CO WA 180-B5
KEATING CROSS RD
DIST OF CENTRAL SAANICH BC 159-C4
KEATING CUTOFF RD
BAKER CO OR 130-B3
BAKER CO OR 138-B1
KEATING GRANGE HALL RD
BAKER CO OR 130-C3
KEEFER RD
DESCHUTES CO OR 142-C1
KEENE RD
BENTON CO WA 341-C5
RICHLAND WA 341-C5
KEENE RD NE
MARION CO OR 205-A2
SW KEENEY LN
JEFFERSON CO OR 212-C2
KEENEY FORKS RD
GRANT CO OR 137-B1
LONG CREEK OR 137-B1
E KEEVEY RD
SPOKANE CO WA 114-C2
KEIL RD NE
MARION CO OR 199-B7
KEITH RD
CITY OF N VANCOUVER BC 255-B5
DIST OF N VANCOUVER BC 254-G4
DIST OF N VANCOUVER BC 255-D6
DIST OF WEST VANCOUVER BC 254-D4
KEITHLY CREEK RD
WASHINGTON CO ID 139-B1
KEITH WILSON RD
DISTRICT OF CHILLIWACK BC 102-C1
NE KEIZER RD
KEIZER OR 323-B5
KELLEHER RD
SKAGIT CO WA 161-B5
KELLER RD
ALTAMONT OR 339-C13
KELLOGG RD
DEL NORTE CO CA 148-B3
N KELLOGG ST
KENNEWICK WA 342-E9
S KELLOGG ST
KENNEWICK WA 342-E11
KELLOGG LAKE RD
SNOHOMISH CO WA 110-C1
SW KELLY AV
PORTLAND OR 317-F1
KELLY RD
CHELAN CO WA 238-C3
CITY OF COLWOOD BC 159-B6
DISTRICT OF LANGFORD BC 159-B6
GRAYS HARBOR CO WA 179-A1
LINN CO OR 133-C1
NE KELLY RD
CLARK CO WA 193-A2
KELLY CREEK RD
LANE CO OR 215-A7
KELLY CUTOFF RD
WASCO CO OR 127-B1
KELLY HALL RD
MASON CO WA 179-B1
KELSAY MOUNTAIN RD
DOUGLAS CO OR 223-C2
KELSAY POINT RD
DOUGLAS CO OR 223-C3
N KELSO AV
COWLITZ CO WA 303-E5
KELSO WA 303-E5
S KELSO DR
KELSO WA 303-F12
SE KELSO RD
CLACKAMAS CO OR 200-C3
KEMP RD
CLACKAMAS CO OR 200-C6
KEMP LAKE RD
BRITISH COLUMBIA 101-A2
BRITISH COLUMBIA 164-C1
KENDALL RD
WALLA WALLA CO WA 345-D13
WALLA WALLA EAST WA 345-D13
KENDALL RD Rt#-547
WHATCOM CO WA 102-B1
KENNEDY LN
LANE CO OR 219-C1
KENNEDY RD
BENTON CO WA 120-C3
BENTON CO WA 121-A3
BENTON CO WA 341-B4
RICHLAND WA 341-B4
WEST RICHLAND WA 121-A3
WEST RICHLAND WA 341-B4
KENNEDY RD Rt#-224
BENTON CO WA 120-C3
KENNEL RD
LINN CO OR 207-D5
W KENNEWICK AV
KENNEWICK WA 342-H10
KENNEWICK WA 343-B10
E KENNEY RD
SPOKANE CO WA 352-A13
N KENNEY RD
SPOKANE CO WA 352-A14
KENO WORDEN RD
KLAMATH CO OR 235-A6
KENSINGTON AV
ASTORIA WA 300-C5
DISTRICT OF BURNABY BC 156-D4
W KENSINGTON AV
ASTORIA WA 300-B5
KENT AV W
KITSAP CO WA 270-D14
NAVY YARD CITY WA 270-D14
SW KENT LN
JEFFERSON CO OR 212-C1
KENT RD
DESCHUTES CO OR 212-A5
KENT BLACK DIAMOND RD
KING CO WA 175-C7
KING CO WA 182-D1
KENT CREEK RD
DOUGLAS CO OR 221-A7
KENT-DES MOINES RD Rt#-516
DES MOINES WA 290-B7
KENT WA 175-B7
KENT WA 290-B7
KENT-DES MOINES RD S Rt#-516
KENT WA 175-B7
KENT WA 290-E7
KING WA 290-E7
KING CO WA 175-B7
KENT-GRASS VALLEY RD
SHERMAN CO OR 127-C2
KENT KANGLEY RD
KENT WA 176-A7
KING CO WA 176-A7
KENT KANGLEY RD Rt#-516
KENT WA 175-C7
KING CO WA 175-C7
KING CO WA 176-A7
KENTUCK WY
COOS CO OR 218-C7
N KENTUCKY AV
EAST WENATCHEE BENCH WA 239-A4
KENWORTHY RD
LINN CO OR 326-H4
KERBY CREEK RD
JACKSON CO OR 227-A7
KERBY MAINLINE RD
JOSEPHINE CO OR 233-B3
KERN RD SW
DOUGLAS CO WA 239-B2
KERN SWAMP RD
KLAMATH CO OR 235-B6
KERR PKWY
LAKE OSWEGO OR 320-A3
LAKE OSWEGO OR 320-A3
PORTLAND OR 320-A3
KERR ST
VANCOUVER BC 156-C5
KERRON AV
LEWIS CO WA 187-C2
NAPAVINE WA 187-C2
WINLOCK WA 187-C2
KERRON AV Rt#-505
WINLOCK WA 187-C3
W KERRON AV
NAPAVINE WA 187-C1
KERRY RD
COLUMBIA CO OR 117-B3
KERSEY WY
AUBURN WA 182-C2
KERSHAW RD
JACKSON CO OR 230-D6
KESSLER BLVD
LONGVIEW WA 302-J8
LONGVIEW WA 303-A10
W KETTLE RIVER RD
FERRY CO WA 105-B1
KEY RD
UMATILLA CO OR 129-C1
WESTON OR 129-C1
KEYES RD
GRAYS HARBOR CO WA 179-A7
KEY PENINSULA HWY
PIERCE CO WA 174-B7
PIERCE CO WA 181-A2
KEY PENINSULA HWY Rt#-302
PIERCE CO WA 174-A7
S KEYS RD
YAKIMA CO WA 243-C6
KEYSTONE AV
DISTRICT OF MISSION BC 94-B3
W KEYSTONE AV
ISLAND CO WA 167-C5
KEYSTONE RD
OKANOGAN CO WA 104-C2
S KEYSTONE RD
ISLAND CO WA 167-C5
KEYSTONE RANCH RD
CROOK CO OR 135-C2
KIACUT RD
YAMHILL CO OR 198-A3
KICKERVILLE RD
BIRCH BAY WA 158-B4
WHATCOM CO WA 158-B4
KIDD ISLAND RD
KOOTENAI CO ID 247-D4
KOOTENAI CO ID 248-A1
S KIESLING RD
SPOKANE CO WA 246-D6
KIGER RD
MALHEUR CO OR 146-B3
KIGER ISLAND DR
BENTON CO OR 207-A7
KILCHIS FOREST RD
TILLAMOOK CO OR 197-C1
KILCHIS RIVER RD
TILLAMOOK CO OR 191-C7
TILLAMOOK CO OR 197-C1
KILLDEER RD
CLACKAMAS CO OR 200-A6
KILLEBREW DR
PAYETTE CO ID 139-A3
N KILLINGSWORTH ST
PORTLAND OR 308-E7
PORTLAND OR 309-E7
NE KILLINGSWORTH ST
PORTLAND OR 309-H7
PORTLAND OR 310-C7
PORTLAND OR 311-E7
NE KILLINGSWORTH ST U.S.-30
PORTLAND OR 311-F7
KILLMORE RD
KITTITAS CO WA 241-A5
KILMER RD
CLALLAM CO WA 169-B2
KIMBALL RD
LANE CO OR 215-D5
KIMBERLY-LONG CREEK HWY
GRANT CO OR 136-C1
GRANT CO OR 137-A1
LONG CREEK OR 137-A1
MONUMENT OR 136-C1
KIMBLE RD
MOUNT VERNON WA 260-A14
SKAGIT CO WA 260-A14
KINCAID RD
JOSEPHINE CO OR 149-A2
YAMHILL CO OR 198-D5
KINCAID ST Rt#-536
MOUNT VERNON WA 260-C13
KINDER DR
GRANT CO WA 242-C2
KING LN
JEFFERSON CO OR 212-D1
SW KING LN
JEFFERSON CO OR 212-C1
JEFFERSON CO OR 213-A1
KING RD
CROOK CO OR 213-C4
DISTRICT OF MATSQUI BC 102-B1
DISTRICT OF SURREY BC 157-A5
LEWIS CO WA 187-B3
E KING RD
ADA CO ID 253-B5
SE KING RD
CLACKAMAS CO OR 199-D3
CLACKAMAS CO OR 200-A3
HAPPY VALLEY OR 200-A3
KITSAP CO WA 174-C4
MILWAUKIE OR 199-D3
W KING RD
ADA CO ID 253-A5
KING ST
COTTONWOOD ID 123-C3
IDAHO CO ID 123-C3
YACHATS OR 209-A3
N KING ST
GOLDENDALE WA 127-C1
NE KING WY
DESCHUTES CO OR 212-D5
KING EDWARD AV E
VANCOUVER BC 156-B5
KING EDWARD AV W
VANCOUVER BC 156-B5
VANCOUVER BC 254-A14
KINGFISHER DR
BRITISH COLUMBIA 104-C1
OSOYOOS BC 104-C1
KING GEORGE HWY Rt#-99A
DISTRICT OF SURREY BC 156-D5
DISTRICT OF SURREY BC 157-A7
DISTRICT OF SURREY BC 158-A1
KING GEORGE TR
DISTRICT OF OAK BAY BC 257-C11
KING GRADE RD
COLUMBIA CO WA 122-B2
KING HEZEKIAH WY
DESCHUTES CO OR 332-H11
KING MOUNTAIN RD
JOSEPHINE CO OR 229-C2
KINGS BLVD
BENTON CO OR 327-F4
CORVALLIS OR 327-F5
KINGS HWY
JACKSON CO OR 234-A2
JACKSON CO OR 336-C14
MEDFORD OR 336-C14
KINGSBURY RD
CHELAN CO WA 239-A6
KINGS CORNER RD
UMATILLA CO OR 129-B1
KINGS GRADE
YAMHILL CO OR 198-C4
KINGSLEY RD
HOOD RIVER CO OR 195-B6
HOOD RIVER CO OR 195-B6
PACIFIC CO WA 183-D7
KINGSLEY-FRIEND MARKET RD
WASCO CO OR 127-B2
KING SOLOMON LN
DESCHUTES CO OR 332-H12
KINGS RIVER RD
HUMBOLDT CO NV 154-A3
KINGS RIVER RD Rt#-293
HUMBOLDT CO NV 154-A3
S KINGSTON RD NE
INDIANOLA WA 170-D6
KITSAP CO WA 170-D6
W KINGSTON RD NE
KITSAP CO WA 170-C5
KINGSTON ST
CITY OF VICTORIA BC 256-F9
KINGSTON-JORDAN DR
LINN CO OR 133-C1
KINGSTON-JORDAN RD
LINN CO OR 134-A1
KINGS VALLEY HWY Rt#-223
BENTON CO OR 133-A1
DALLAS OR 204-A5
POLK CO OR 125-B3
POLK CO OR 133-B1
POLK CO OR 204-A5
KINGS VALLEY RD
DEL NORTE CO CA 148-B3
KINGSWAY
VANCOUVER BC 254-H13
KINGSWAY Rt#-1A
VANCOUVER BC 156-C5
VANCOUVER BC 254-J13
VANCOUVER BC 255-A14
KINGSWAY Rt#-99A
DISTRICT OF BURNABY BC 156-C5
NEW WESTMINSTER BC 156-C5
KINGSWAY AV
PORT COQUITLAM BC 157-B4
KING TULL RD
BENTON CO WA 120-C3
E KING TULL RD
BENTON CO WA 120-B3
W KING TUT RD
WHATCOM CO WA 158-D5
KINGWOOD AV
MILL CITY OR 134-A1
KINGWOOD DR NW
SALEM OR 322-E12
KINNEY RD
YAMHILL CO OR 198-C5
KINNS LN NE
MARION CO OR 205-A1
KINZEL CREEK RD
CLACKAMAS CO OR 201-D7
CLACKAMAS CO OR 202-A7
KINZER RD
NEZ PERCE CO ID 250-B2
KINZUA LN
WHEELER CO OR 128-A3
KINZUA RD
MORROW CO OR 128-C3
WHEELER CO OR 128-B3
KINZY RD
CLACKAMAS CO OR 200-C7
KIPLING RD
OKANOGAN CO WA 105-A1
KIRBY MAYVIEW RD
GARFIELD CO WA 122-C2
KIRK AV
BROWNSVILLE OR 210-C2
LINN CO OR 210-C2
KIRK DR
LINN CO OR 210-D2
KIRK RD
BENTON CO WA 121-A3
KIRKENDAHL RD
WHITMAN CO WA 249-A6
KIRKHAM RD
JOSEPHINE CO OR 233-B5
KIRKLAND RD
LEWIS CO WA 187-C1
KIRKSTONE RD
DIST OF N VANCOUVER BC 255-D3
KIRKWOOD RD NW
YAMHILL CO OR 204-C3
KIRSOP RD SW
THURSTON CO WA 296-C13
KIRTLAND RD
JACKSON CO OR 230-C6
KISSLER RD
CROOK CO OR 213-B6
KITER CREEK RD
JACKSON CO OR 226-B6
KITER CREEK SPUR
JACKSON CO OR 226-C6
KITSAP CT NW
SILVERDALE WA 174-B1
KITSAP WY
BREMERTON WA 270-B9
KITSAP WY Rt#-310
BREMERTON WA 270-D10
W KITSAP LAKE RD NW
BREMERTON WA 270-A9
ERLANDS PT-KITSAP LAKE WA 270-A10
KITSILANO DIV
VANCOUVER BC 254-B12
KITSON SPRINGS RD
LANE CO OR 142-A1
KITTITAS HWY
ELLENSBURG WA 241-B6
KITTITAS WA 241-C6
KITTITAS CO WA 241-B6
KITTSON PKWY
DISTRICT OF DELTA BC 156-D7
DISTRICT OF SURREY BC 156-D7
KITZMILLER RD
CLACKAMAS CO OR 200-C5
WHITMAN CO WA 249-B4
KIWANIS WY
CITY OF VICTORIA BC 256-J6
KIWA SPRING RD
DESCHUTES CO OR 217-A5
KIZER AV
LINN CO OR 326-H4
SE KLAHANIE BLVD
KING CO WA 176-A3
KLAHOWYA LN
DOUGLAS CO OR 221-B3
NW KLAHOWYA TR
KITSAP CO WA 174-A2
KLAK BUTTE RD
DESCHUTES CO OR 216-C6
KLAMATH AV Rt#-39
KLAMATH FALLS OR 338-D8
S KLAMATH FALLS HWY Rt#-140
ALTAMONT OR 235-D5
KLAMATH CO OR 235-C5
KLAMATH CO OR 338-D12
KLAMATH FALLS OR 235-C5
KLAMATH FALLS OR 338-C12
KLAMATH FALLS-LKVW HWY Rt#-39
ALTAMONT OR 338-F9
ALTAMONT OR 339-C11
KLAMATH CO OR 150-C2
KLAMATH CO OR 151-A1
KLAMATH CO OR 339-E12
KLAMATH FALLS OR 338-F9
LAKE CO OR 151-C2
LAKE CO OR 152-A2
KLAMATH FALLS-MALIN HWY
KLAMATH CO OR 151-A3
KLAMATH FALLS OR 338-C4
MALIN OR 151-A3
KLAMATH FALLS-MALIN HWY Rt#-39
ALTAMONT OR 338-C4
ALTAMONT OR 339-A10
KLAMATH CO OR 150-C2
KLAMATH CO OR 151-A2
KLAMATH CO OR 235-D5
KLAMATH CO OR 338-C4
KLAMATH FALLS OR 338-C4
MERRILL OR 150-C2
KLAMATH FALLS-MALN HWY Rt#-140
ALTAMONT OR 339-D14
KLAMATH CO OR 235-D5
KLAMATH CO OR 339-D14
KLAMATHON RD
SISKIYOU CO CA 150-A3
KLASKANINE AV
ASTORIA WA 300-C6
KLEIN RD
ADAMS CO WA 113-C3
KLEINSMITH RD
CLACKAMAS CO OR 200-D5
KLEMGARD RD
WHITMAN CO WA 249-A6
KLICKITAT APPLETON RD
KLICKITAT CO WA 196-C3
KLICKITAT TRAIL RD
LANE CO OR 209-B5
KLONDIKE RD
FERRY CO WA 105-B2
SHERMAN CO OR 127-C1
N KLONDIKE RD
SHERMAN CO OR 127-C1
KLOOCHMAN CREEK RD
CROOK CO OR 136-A3
KLUPENGER RD
MARION CO OR 199-B6
KLUSS RD
LATAH CO ID 249-D7
LATAH CO ID 250-C1
KNAPPA RD
CLATSOP CO WA 117-A3
KNAPPTON FERRY RD Rt#-401
PACIFIC CO WA 186-C7
NW KNICKERBOCKER AV
DESCHUTES CO OR 212-D4
KNIERIEM RD
MULTNOMAH CO OR 200-C1
KNIGHT RD
KLICKITAT CO WA 127-C1
KLICKITAT CO WA 196-C4
LANE CO OR 133-A3
KNIGHT ST
CITY OF RICHMOND BC 156-C5
VANCOUVER BC 156-C5
VANCOUVER BC 255-B14
KNIGHTS BRIDGE RD
CANBY OR 199-C6
CLACKAMAS CO OR 199-C6
NW KNIGHTS BRIDGE RD
CANBY OR 199-C6
KNOB HILL RD
WASCO CO OR 196-C7
KNOB HILL-TROUT CREEK RD
FERRY CO WA 105-B2
KNOBLE RD E
PIERCE CO WA 182-A6
NE KNOLL AV
DOUGLAS CO OR 334-G2
KNOTGRASS RIDGE RD
ASOTIN CO WA 122-C2
KNOTT RD
DESCHUTES CO OR 217-B4
DESCHUTES CO OR 332-G14
KNOTT CREEK RD
HUMBOLDT CO NV 153-B3
KNOWLES RD
JACKSON CO OR 234-A2
KNOWLES RD SE
THURSTON CO WA 184-D3
KNOX AV
BELLINGHAM WA 258-B10
KNOX RD
CLACKAMAS CO OR 200-B4
KNOX BUTTE RD
ALBANY OR 207-D4
ALBANY OR 326-H6
LINN CO OR 133-C1
LINN CO OR 207-D4
LINN CO OR 326-H6
KNUDSEN RD
KOOTENAI CO ID 245-A4
KOCH RD
ADAMS CO WA 113-B3
KOENIG RD
WHITMAN CO WA 249-A2
KOHFIELD RD
DESCHUTES CO OR 212-A7
KOLLOCK-KNAPP RD
SKAMANIA CO WA 195-C4
KONKOLVILLE RD
CLEARWATER CO ID 123-C2
OROFINO ID 123-C2
KOOL RD
COWLITZ CO WA 189-D4
KOONTZ RD
LEWIS CO WA 187-C2
KOOSBAY BLVD
COOS BAY OR 333-G8
NORTH BEND OR 333-G8
KOOTENAI CTO
PONDERAY ID 244-A1
N KOOTENAI RD
BONNER CO ID 244-A1
KOOTENAI ST
BOISE ID 253-C3
BONNERS FERRY ID 107-B2
KOPACHUCK DR NW
PIERCE CO WA 181-B1
KOPF RD
WHITMAN CO WA 249-C7
KOSYDAR RD
LINCOLN CO OR 206-C1
KOWITZ RD
LINN CO OR 133-C1
KRAIMIEN RD
YAMHILL CO OR 199-A6
KRAUSS RD
JOSEPHINE CO OR 233-A5
KRAXBERGER RD
CLACKAMAS CO OR 199-C7
KRIEGER RD
DESCHUTES CO OR 212-C7
KROENIG RD
POLK CO OR 204-A3
SE KROHN RD
CLARK CO WA 193-C6
KROLL RD
COWLITZ CO WA 187-C6
E KRONQUIST RD
SPOKANE CO WA 246-D1
S KROPF RD
CLACKAMAS CO OR 205-D3
SW KRUGER RD
WASHINGTON CO OR 199-A4
SW KRUSE RD
CLACKAMAS CO OR 199-B5
KRUSE WY
CLACKAMAS OR 320-A6
CLACKAMAS CO OR 199-B3
LAKE OSWEGO OR 199-B3
LAKE OSWEGO OR 320-A6
KUEBLER BLVD SE
MARION CO OR 325-B6
SALEM OR 324-F6
SALEM OR 325-B6
KUEBLER RD
MARION CO OR 324-C6
SALEM OR 324-C6
KUEFFLER RD
SKAMANIA CO WA 194-B6
KUHNIS RD
COWLITZ CO WA 192-B1
KULM RD
GRANT CO WA 242-C7
KUNA RD Rt#-69
ADA CO ID 253-A5
E KUNA RD
ADA CO ID 253-B5
W KUNA RD
ADA CO ID 147-C1
ADA CO ID 253-A5
KUNA CAVE RD
ADA CO ID 253-A7
KUNA-MERIDIAN RD Rt#-69
ADA CO ID 253-A3
MERIDIAN ID 253-A3
KUNA MORA RD
ADA CO ID 253-A6
KUNZE RD
MORROW CO OR 128-B1
KUNZE RD SW
BOARDMAN OR 128-C1
MORROW CO OR 128-C1
KURTZ RD
POLK CO OR 204-A4
NW KUYKENDALL RD
YAMHILL CO OR 198-A5
KWINA RD
WHATCOM CO WA 158-C7
KWNEESUM RD
SKAMANIA CO WA 193-D5

L

L RD NE
DOUGLAS CO WA 112-C1
L RD NW
DOUGLAS CO WA 236-D5
L RD SE
DOUGLAS CO WA 112-C2
L ST U.S.-101
CRESCENT CITY CA 148-B3
E L ST
TACOMA WA 182-A3
N L ST
TOPPENISH WA 120-A2
YAKIMA CO WA 120-A2
S L ST
TOPPENISH WA 120-A2
YAKIMA CO WA 120-A2
L 1/2-SW RD
GRANT CO WA 112-B3
LABARRE RD
SKAMANIA CO WA 193-D6
LABIEUX RD
NANAIMO BC 93-A3
LABISH CENTER RD NE
MARION CO OR 205-A4
LABISKE RD
CLATSOP CO WA 188-D3
LABOR CAMP
CANYON CO ID 147-B1
NW LA CENTER RD
CLARK CO WA 192-C2
LA CENTER WA 192-C2
LACEY BLVD SE
LACEY WA 297-F6
LACKEY RD
PIERCE CO WA 181-A1

STREET / City State / Page-Grid

LACOMB DR
LINN CO OR 133-C1
LA CROSSE AIRPORT RD
LA CROSSE WA 122-A1
WHITMAN CO WA 122-A1
LADD CREEK RD
UNION CO OR 130-A3
SW LADD HILL RD
CLACKAMAS CO OR 199-A6
SHERWOOD OR 199-A6
WASHINGTON CO OR 199-A6
LADNER TRUNK RD
DISTRICT OF DELTA BC 101-C1
LADNER TRUNK RD Rt#-10
DISTRICT OF DELTA BC 156-D7
LAEL-FLAT CREEK RD
STEVENS CO WA 106-A1
LAFAYETTE AV
MCMINNVILLE OR 198-A7
YAMHILL CO OR 198-A7
LAFAYETTE HWY
LAFAYETTE OR 198-B7
YAMHILL CO OR 198-B7
YAMHILL CO OR 204-C1
SE LAFAYETTE HWY
YAMHILL CO OR 204-C1
LAFAYETTE RD
SKAGIT CO WA 260-F4
LAFAYETTE ST
STEILACOOM WA 181-C4
SW LAFOLLETT RD
WASHINGTON CO OR 198-C2
LAGOON DR
MALHEUR CO OR 139-A3
VALE OR 139-A3
LAGOON RD
ISLAND CO WA 167-C7
LA GRANDE-BAKER HWY Rt#-30
NORTH POWDER OR 130-B3
UNION CO OR 130-B3
LA GRANDE-BAKER HWY Rt#-203
UNION OR 130-A2
UNION CO OR 130-A2
LA GRANDE-BAKER HWY Rt#-237
NORTH POWDER OR 130-B3
UNION OR 130-B3
UNION CO OR 130-B3
LA GRANDE-BAKER HWY U.S.-30
BAKER CITY OR 138-B1
BAKER CO OR 130-A3
BAKER CO OR 138-B1
HAINES OR 130-B3
LA GRANDE OR 130-A3
UNION CO OR 130-A3
LA GRANGE ST
ADA CO ID 253-B4
LAIRD RD
CLALLAM CO WA 165-A6
LAITY ST
MAPLE RIDGE BC 157-C5
LAKE AV
CANYON CO ID 147-B1
LAKE AV Rt#-97
HARRISON ID 248-A4
LAKE DR
DESCHUTES CO OR 212-A4
EUGENE OR 329-F1
LANE CO OR 329-F1
VALLEY CO ID 251-D4
WARRENTON WA 188-B1
LAKE RD
ASOTIN CO WA 122-C3
KLICKITAT CO WA 119-A3
N LAKE RD
WALLA WALLA CO WA 121-B3
S LAKE RD
BURBANK WA 121-B3
WALLA WALLA CO WA 121-B3
SE LAKE RD
CLACKAMAS CO OR 199-D3
MILWAUKIE OR 199-D3
MILWAUKIE OR 321-J3
E LAKE ST Rt#-55
MCCALL ID 251-C5
LAKE ST S
KIRKLAND WA 175-C1
LAKE CAVANAUGH RD
SKAGIT CO WA 168-C2
LAKE CITY WY NE
SEATTLE WA 171-B7
SEATTLE WA 274-C2
LAKE CITY WY NE Rt#-522
SEATTLE WA 171-B7
SEATTLE WA 274-C2
LAKE CREEK DR
LINN CO OR 207-C6
LINN CO OR 210-A3
TANGENT OR 207-C6
LAKE CREEK RD
DOUGLAS CO OR 223-C5
JACKSON CO OR 234-D1
LEWIS CO WA 187-A1
LAKE CUSHMAN RD Rt#-119
MASON CO WA 109-B2
MASON CO WA 173-A6
LAKE EARL DR Rt#-D3
DEL NORTE CO CA 148-B3
SW LAKE FLORA RD
KITSAP CO WA 174-A5
E LAKE FORK RD
VALLEY CO ID 251-D6
W LAKE FORK RD
VALLEY CO ID 251-C7
E LAKE GOODWIN RD Rt#-531
SNOHOMISH CO WA 168-B5
W LAKE GOODWIN RD
SNOHOMISH CO WA 168-B5
LAKE GROVE ST
LAKE OSWEGO OR 320-A7
E LAKE HAZEL RD
ADA CO ID 253-B4
W LAKE HAZEL RD
ADA CO ID 253-A4
SW LAKE HELENA RD
KITSAP CO WA 174-A5
LAKE HILLS BLVD
BELLEVUE WA 175-C2
LAKE HILLS CONNECTOR
BELLEVUE WA 175-C2
SE LAKE HOLM RD
KING CO WA 182-C1
LAKE JOSEPHINE AV
PIERCE CO WA 181-B4
LAKE LOUISE RD
SUDDEN VALLEY WA 161-A1
WHATCOM CO WA 161-A1
LAKE LOWELL AV
CANYON CO ID 147-B1
LAKEMONT BLVD SE
BELLEVUE WA 175-D3
LAKE OF THE WOODS HWY Rt#-96
SISKIYOU CO CA 149-A3
LAKE OF THE WOODS HWY Rt#-99
CENTRAL POINT OR 230-C7
JACKSON CO OR 230-C7
LAKE OF THE WOODS HWY Rt#-140
JACKSON CO OR 149-C1
JACKSON CO OR 150-A1
JACKSON CO OR 230-D6
KLAMATH CO OR 150-B1
KLAMATH CO OR 231-A6
KLAMATH CO OR 235-A1
KLAMATH CO OR 338-A10
KLAMATH FALLS OR 235-A1
KLAMATH FALLS OR 338-B12
WHITE CITY OR 230-D6
LAKE OF THE WOODS HWY Rt#-263
SISKIYOU CO CA 149-C3
YREKA CA 149-C3
N LAKE OF THE WOODS HWY Rt#-3
SISKIYOU CO CA 149-C3
W LAKE OF THE WOODS HWY Rt#-3
SISKIYOU CO CA 149-C3
YREKA CA 149-C3
LAKE PLEASANT RD
CLALLAM CO WA 163-A6
E LAKE PLEASANT RD
CLALLAM CO WA 163-A6
LAKERIDGE DR
OLYMPIA WA 296-G7
LAKE SAMISH DR
WHATCOM CO WA 161-A2
LAKE SAMISH RD
SKAGIT CO WA 161-A3
WHATCOM CO WA 161-A3
E LK SAMMAMISH PKWY NE
KING CO WA 175-D2
REDMOND WA 175-D2
W LK SAMMAMISH PKWY NE
BELLEVUE WA 175-D1
KING CO WA 175-D1
REDMOND WA 175-D1
E LK SAMMAMISH PKWY SE
ISSAQUAH WA 176-A4
KING CO WA 175-D3
KING CO WA 176-A3
W LK SAMMAMISH PKWY SE
BELLEVUE WA 175-D2
KING CO WA 175-D2
LAKES DIVIDE RD
KOOTENAI CO ID 248-C2
LAKE SHORE DR
CANYON CO ID 147-B1
LAKESHORE DR
BONNER CO ID 107-A3
BONNER CO ID 244-A3
CASCADE ID 252-D7
CLARK CO WA 192-C1
COOS BAY OR 333-B5
COWLITZ CO WA 192-C1
JOSEPHINE CO OR 233-B2
KLAMATH CO OR 235-B3
KLAMATH CO OR 338-A6
KLAMATH FALLS OR 338-A6
VALLEY CO ID 252-D7
WOODLAND WA 192-C1
WOODLAND WA 192-C1
E LAKESHORE DR
LAKE STEVENS WA 171-D1
N LAKESHORE DR
LAKE STEVENS WA 171-D1
S LAKESHORE RD
CHELAN CO WA 236-B3
LAKESIDE RD
KLICKITAT CO WA 119-A3
S LAKESIDE RD
LIBERTY LAKE WA 247-B4
LIBERTY LAKE WA 352-F14
SPOKANE CO WA 247-B4
SPOKANE CO WA 352-F14
E LAKE STEVENS RD
LAKE STEVENS WA 171-D2
SNOHOMISH CO WA 171-D2
S LAKE STEVENS RD
SNOHOMISH CO WA 171-D2
LAKE TERRELL RD
WHATCOM CO WA 158-B6
LAKEVIEW BLVD
LAKE OSWEGO OR 320-A7
LAKEVIEW BLVD E
SEATTLE WA 278-B3
N LAKEVIEW DR
HAYDEN LAKE ID 245-A5
LAKEVIEW-BURNS HWY U.S.-395
HARNEY CO OR 144-C2
LAKE CO OR 144-B3
LAKE CO OR 152-A1
LAKE VISTA DR
GRANT CO WA 242-B1
LAKE WASHINGTON BLVD
SEATTLE WA 279-E6
LAKE WASHINGTON BLVD E
SEATTLE WA 278-D2
SEATTLE WA 279-E4
LAKE WASHINGTON BLVD N
RENTON WA 175-C4
LAKE WASHINGTON BLVD NE
BELLEVUE WA 175-C2
LAKE WASHINGTON BLVD NE
KIRKLAND WA 175-C1
LAKE WASHINGTON BLVD S
SEATTLE WA 278-E7
SEATTLE WA 282-E1
SEATTLE WA 283-E3
LAKE WASHINGTON BLVD SE
BELLEVUE WA 175-C3
NEWCASTLE WA 175-C3
RENTON WA 175-C4
LAKEWAY DR
BELLINGHAM WA 258-G7
WHATCOM CO WA 161-A1
WHATCOM CO WA 258-G7
LAKE WHATCOM BLVD
SUDDEN VALLEY WA 161-A1
WHATCOM CO WA 161-A1
LAKEWOOD DR
ALBANY OR 326-B11
LAKEWOOD DR W
LAKEWOOD WA 294-A7
PIERCE CO WA 294-A7
TACOMA WA 294-A7
UNIVERSITY PLACE WA 294-A7
LAKEWOOD RD
SNOHOMISH CO WA 168-B5
LAKEWOOD RD Rt#-531
SNOHOMISH CO WA 168-B5
LAMAR RD
WALLA WALLA CO WA 121-C2
LAMB RD
KOOTENAI CO ID 248-B4
UMATILLA CO OR 128-C1
UMATILLA CO OR 129-A1
LAMBERSON RD
GILLIAM CO OR 128-A2
SW LAMBERT LN
WASHINGTON CO OR 198-C3
LAMBERT RD
KITTITAS CO WA 240-C2
W LAMBERT RD
DESCHUTES CO OR 212-B3
LAMBERTIANA RD
DESCHUTES CO OR 217-A7
LAMERS RD
POLK CO OR 207-B1
LAMOINE RD NW
DOUGLAS CO WA 112-B1
DOUGLAS CO WA 236-C5
LA MONT RD
ADA CO ID 253-A3
LAMONT RD
WHITMAN CO WA 114-A3
LAMONTA RD
CROOK CO OR 213-C3
LAMPA VALLEY RD
COOS CO OR 220-C6
LAMPERTI LN
COLLEGE PLACE WA 344-F12
WALLA WALLA CO WA 344-F12
LAMPMAN RD
WHATCOM CO WA 158-C6
LAMPSON ST
TOWN OF ESQUIMALT BC 256-C9
LANA AV NE
SALEM OR 323-B9
LANCASTER DR
FOUR CORNERS OR 323-E12
FOUR CORNERS OR 325-E1
HAYESVILLE OR 323-E8
SALEM OR 323-E12
SALEM OR 325-E3
LANCASTER DR Rt#-213
HAYESVILLE OR 323-E11
SALEM OR 323-E11
LANCASTER RD
AULT FIELD WA 170-D2
CLARK CO WA 192-B1
KOOTENAI CO ID 245-A5
SAINT JOHN WA 114-B3
WHITMAN CO WA 114-B3
WHITMAN CO WA 122-B1
W LANCASTER RD
HAYDEN ID 247-D1
KOOTENAI CO ID 247-D1
SW LANCEFIELD RD
YAMHILL CO OR 204-B2
S LANDER ST
SEATTLE WA 282-A2
NE LANDERHOLM RD
CLARK CO WA 192-D2
LANDES ST
PORT TOWNSEND WA 263-F5
LANDING RD
COOS CO OR 220-D6
SKAGIT CO WA 168-A1
LANDRITH RD
COOS CO OR 140-C2
LANDSBERG RD SE
KING CO WA 176-A7
LANDSBURG RD SE
KING CO WA 176-A7
LANDS END RD
DIST OF NORTH SAANICH BC 159-B1
LANE AV
ROSEBURG OR 334-F7
LANEDA AV
MANZANITA OR 191-A4
E LANE PARK RD
SPOKANE CO WA 347-E4
LANES TURN RD
LANE CO OR 210-A6
LANEWOOD RD
ADA CO ID 253-A1
LANEY RD
LINCOLN CO WA 113-C3
LANGE RD
SKAGIT CO WA 161-C7
LANGE GATEWAY RD
TILLAMOOK CO OR 191-B4
E LANGELL VALLEY RD
BONANZA OR 151-A2
KLAMATH CO OR 151-A2
W LANGELL VALLEY RD
KLAMATH CO OR 151-A2
LANGENSAND RD
CLACKAMAS CO OR 200-D4
SANDY OR 200-D4
LANGFORD RD
FRANKLIN CO WA 121-A2
LANGLEY BYPS
LANGLEY BC 158-C1
LANGLEY BYPS Rt#-10
DISTRICT OF SURREY BC 157-C7
DISTRICT OF SURREY BC 158-B1
LANGLEY BC 157-C7
LANGLEY RD
ISLAND CO WA 171-A1
LANGLEY WA 171-A1
LANGLOIS MOUNTAIN RD
CURRY CO OR 224-B2
LANGWORTHY RD SW
THURSTON CO WA 184-A4
LANSDOWNE RD
DISTRICT OF OAK BAY BC 257-C6
DISTRICT OF SAANICH BC 257-B6
LANSKY DR
MASON CO WA 180-D3
LANTZ LN
UNION CO OR 130-B2
LA PUSH RD
CLALLAM CO WA 169-A2
LA PUSH RD Rt#-110
CLALLAM CO WA 169-C1
FORKS WA 169-C1
SE LARCH AV
COLLEGE PLACE WA 344-G12
WALLA WALLA CO WA 344-G12
W LARCH AV
YAKIMA CO WA 243-B7
LARCH DR
DESCHUTES CO OR 212-C5
LARCH ST
LONGVIEW WA 303-A9
SANDPOINT ID 244-A2
VANCOUVER BC 156-B5
LARCH WY SW
SNOHOMISH CO WA 171-B5
LARCH MOUNTAIN RD
HOOD RIVER CO OR 195-B6
MULTNOMAH CO OR 200-D1
MULTNOMAH CO OR 201-A1
LARGENT RD
FRANKLIN CO WA 121-B2
LARIMER RD
EVERETT WA 269-G5
SNOHOMISH WA 269-G5
LARKIN RD
PACIFIC CO WA 183-B4
S LARKIN RD
CLACKAMAS CO OR 200-A7
SW LARKINS MILL RD
WASHINGTON CO OR 198-C3
LARMON RD
LEWIS CO WA 187-D2
LARSON LN NW
KITSAP CO WA 173-D2
LARSON RD
CITY OF N VANCOUVER BC 254-J4
CITY OF N VANCOUVER BC 255-A4
COLUMBIA CO OR 189-B4
COLUMBIA CO OR 302-D14
DOUGLAS CO OR 221-A5
KITSAP CO WA 174-A2
SNOHOMISH CO WA 168-B4
LARSON ST
EATONVILLE WA 118-B1
LARSON WY
COOS CO OR 218-C6
LARSON BCH SHRE ACCESS RD
STEVENS CO WA 106-B3
LARSON CREEK RD
JACKSON CO OR 226-C6
LARSON LAKE RD
JEFFERSON CO WA 170-A3
SW LA SALLE LN
JEFFERSON CO OR 212-C1
LA SALLE RD
WASHINGTON CO OR 198-B3
LA SALLE ST
HARRISBURG OR 210-A5
LASSEN LN
LANE CO OR 210-A7
LAST CHANCE CREEK RD
JACKSON CO OR 225-D7
S LATAH ST
BOISE ID 253-C3
S LATAH CREEK RD
SPOKANE CO WA 246-D7
SW LATHAM RD
YAMHILL CO OR 204-A2
LATIMER RD
TILLAMOOK CO OR 197-C2
LATORIA RD
CITY OF COLWOOD BC 159-B7
DISTRICT OF LANGFORD BC 159-B7
LAUER CROSSING RD U.S.-95
IDAHO CO ID 123-B3
LAUFERS RD
LEWIS CO ID 123-B2
LAUGHLIN RD
PRINEVILLE OR 213-D5
YAMHILL CO OR 198-B5
LAURANCE LAKE DR
HOOD RIVER CO OR 202-B3
LAUREL AV
BUTTE FALLS OR 150-A1
JOSEPHINE CO OR 229-A6
LAUREL LN
JEFFERSON CO OR 213-A1
LAUREL PL
NAVY YARD CITY WA 270-E13
LAUREL RD
CAVE JUNCTION OR 233-B4
JOSEPHINE CO OR 233-B4
LONGVIEW WA 302-J6
LONGVIEW WA 303-A6
SW LAUREL RD
WASHINGTON CO OR 198-D3
W LAUREL RD
WHATCOM CO WA 158-D6
N LAUREL ST
ASHLAND OR 337-C6
LAUREL HILLS RD
DOUGLAS CO OR 219-A2
LAURELVIEW RD
WASHINGTON CO OR 198-C3
LAURELWOOD RD
WASHINGTON CO OR 198-C3
W LAURIDSEN BLVD
CLALLAM CO WA 261-A4
PORT ANGELES WA 261-A4
SW LAVA AV
DESCHUTES CO OR 212-C5
LAVA BEDS RD
HARNEY CO OR 145-B3
LAVA BEDS NATIONAL MONUMENT RD
MODOC CO CA 151-A3
LAVA CAST FOREST RD
DESCHUTES CO OR 217-B6
LAVA LAKE RD
DESCHUTES CO OR 142-C1
DESCHUTES CO OR 216-A5
LAVA-ODELL RD
KLAMATH CO OR 142-B1
N LA VENTURE RD
MOUNT VERNON WA 260-E11
LAVERNE AV
ALTAMONT OR 338-G12
LAVERNE PARK NORTH RD
COOS CO OR 140-C2
LAW DR
BOISE ID 253-D3
LAWEN LN
HARNEY CO OR 145-B2
LAWEN-HARNEY RD
HARNEY CO OR 145-B1
LAWRENCE RD
CHEHALIS WA 299-C9
COLUMBIA CO OR 189-C7
LANE CO OR 133-B2
LEWIS CO WA 299-C9
LAWRENCE RD Rt#-9
WHATCOM CO WA 102-B1
LAWRENCE ST
PORT TOWNSEND WA 263-G5
LAWTON RD
SPOKANE CO WA 348-C13
LAWYERS CANYON RD Rt#-162
LEWIS CO ID 123-C3
NEZPERCE ID 123-C3
LAYALL RD
KLICKITAT CO WA 196-B2
LAYNG RD
LANE CO OR 215-C7
LAZY ALLEN OAKS RD
KLICKITAT CO WA 196-A4
L COOKE RD
KITTITAS CO WA 241-D5
NE LEADBETTER RD
CLARK CO WA 193-B6
LEAFWOOD DR
JACKSON CO OR 230-D4
LEA HILL RD SE
KING CO WA 182-C1
LEAHY RD N
DOUGLAS CO WA 112-C1
LEAHY RD S Rt#-17
DOUGLAS CO WA 112-C1
LEAHY-MANSFIELD-MAYFIELD RD NE
DOUGLAS CO WA 112-C1
LEANDER DR
YAMHILL CO OR 198-D5
LEAP LN
WALLOWA CO OR 130-C1
LEARY AV NW
SEATTLE WA 273-E4
LEARY RD NE
MARION CO OR 205-A1
LEARY WY NW
SEATTLE WA 273-G5
E LEAVENWORTH RD
CHELAN CO WA 238-A1
LEBANON ST
ARLINGTON WA 168-D5
SNOHOMISH CO WA 168-D5
SW LEBEAU RD
WASHINGTON CO OR 199-A4
LEBO BLVD
BREMERTON WA 270-H8
LE BRUN RD NE
MARION CO OR 205-A2
LE CLERC CREEK RD
PEND OREILLE CO WA 106-C3
LEDGERWOOD SPUR RD
GARFIELD CO WA 122-C2
LEE BLVD
RICHLAND WA 341-E1
LEE RD
WASHINGTON CO OR 198-A2
LEE ST
SEATTLE WA 277-J2
LEE MCKINLEY RD
COOS CO OR 140-B2
LEES CREEK RD
DOUGLAS CO OR 219-B3
LEFEUVRE RD
DISTRICT OF MATSQUI BC 102-B1
LEFEVRE ST Rt#-902
MEDICAL LAKE WA 114-B2
LEFFEL RD
UNION CO OR 130-A2
LEFT FORK FOOTS CREEK RD
JACKSON CO OR 230-A7
LEFT FORK SARDINE CREEK RD
JACKSON CO OR 230-A5
LEGALL RD
KLICKITAT CO WA 196-B2
LEGION WY
OLYMPIA WA 296-H5
OLYMPIA WA 297-A5
LEGOE BAY RD
WHATCOM CO WA 160-B1
N LEHMAN RD
SPOKANE CO WA 246-D2
LEISLE RD
ADAMS CO WA 113-B3
LEITNER ST SW
THURSTON CO WA 184-B3
LELAND RD
JOSEPHINE CO OR 229-A1
S LELAND RD
CLACKAMAS CO OR 199-D6
LE-LOU-WA PL
PIERCE CO WA 181-D1
S LE MAIRE ST
MOXEE CITY WA 243-D7
LEMLEY RD
BENTON CO WA 120-B3
LEMMON RD NE
THURSTON CO WA 180-D5
LEMOLO RD
DOUGLAS CO OR 223-B3
E LEMOLO LAKE RD
DOUGLAS CO OR 223-C3
LEMOLO SHORE DR NE
KITSAP CO WA 170-B7
SUQUAMISH WA 170-B7
LEMON RD
CLALLAM CO WA 165-D6
LEMONDS RD
JEFFERSON CO WA 170-A6
LENORA ST
EVERETT WA 269-F1
LENTZ RD
COLUMBIA CO OR 189-B5
LEWIS CO WA 187-B2
LENTZ RD N
LEWIS CO WA 187-B2
LENVILLE RD
LATAH CO ID 123-A1
LATAH CO ID 249-D5
LEON RD
WHITMAN CO WA 250-B2
LEONARD RD
JOSEPHINE CO OR 229-A6
LEWIS CO WA 118-A2
LESLIE AV
LA CROSSE WA 122-A1
WHITMAN CO WA 122-A1
LESLIE LN
BENTON CO WA 341-H12
LESLIE RD
BENTON CO WA 341-H11
RICHLAND WA 341-H7
YAMHILL CO OR 199-A6
LESLIE GULCH RD
MALHEUR CO OR 146-C2
MALHEUR CO OR 147-A2
NE LESSARD RD
CLARK CO WA 193-C5
LESSIG SOUTH FORK RD
STEVENS CO WA 106-A3
LESTER AV
BENTON CO OR 327-F4
CORVALLIS OR 327-F4
LESTER CAMP RD
WHITMAN CO WA 122-B1
LEVEE
KLAMATH CO OR 231-C3
LEVEE ST U.S.-101
HOQUIAM WA 178-A7
LEWELLEN RD
CLACKAMAS CO OR 200-B7
LEWELLEN CREEK RD
KOOTENAI CO ID 245-B2
LEWIS AV
CLATSOP CO WA 188-B3
LEWIS DR
PIERCE CO WA 181-B5
LEWIS LN
CANYON CO ID 147-C1
W LEWIS LN
CANYON CO ID 147-B1
LEWIS RD
CLALLAM CO WA 165-D6
GARFIELD CO WA 122-B2
WALLOWA CO OR 131-A1
LEWIS RD W
KITSAP CO WA 173-D3
LEWIS ST Rt#-214
SILVERTON OR 205-C4
E LEWIS ST
FRANKLIN CO WA 121-A3
FRANKLIN CO WA 343-J7
PASCO WA 121-A3
PASCO WA 343-J7
N LEWIS ST Rt#-203
MONROE WA 110-C1
S LEWIS ST Rt#-203
MONROE WA 110-C1
SNOHOMISH CO WA 110-C1
W LEWIS ST
PASCO WA 343-D7
LEWIS AND CLARK HWY Rt#-14
BINGEN WA 195-C5
CAMAS WA 193-A7
CLARK CO WA 193-A7
CLARK CO WA 200-C1
KLICKITAT CO WA 127-B1
KLICKITAT CO WA 195-C5
KLICKITAT CO WA 196-C6
SKAMANIA CO WA 195-C5
VANCOUVER WA 305-G6
VANCOUVER WA 306-A6
VANCOUVER WA 307-E7
VANCOUVER WA 311-G1
WASHOUGAL WA 193-C7
WHITE SALMON WA 195-C5
LEWIS AND CLARK RD
CLATSOP CO WA 188-C5
CLATSOP CO WA 300-A11
CLATSOP CO WA 301-J6
SEASIDE WA 188-C5
SEASIDE WA 301-J6
LEWIS GULCH RD
COLUMBIA CO WA 122-B2
LEWIS RIVER DR Rt#-503
COWLITZ CO WA 118-A3
COWLITZ CO WA 190-A6
WOODLAND WA 118-A3
LEWIS RIVER RD Rt#-503
COWLITZ CO WA 190-A6
LEWIS ROGERS LN
YAMHILL CO OR 198-C5
LEWISTON RD
WALLA WALLA CO WA 122-A3
NE LEWISVILLE HWY
CLARK CO WA 193-A1
LEXINGTON AV
ASTORIA WA 300-C5

PNW

INDEX

STREET City State Page-Grid

W LEXINGTON AV
ASTORIA WA 300-B6
LEXINGTON-ECHO HWY
UMATILLA CO OR 129-A1
LEXINGTON-ECHO HWY Rt#-207
LEXINGTON OR 128-C2
MORROW CO OR 128-C2
UMATILLA CO OR 128-C2
SW LEXINGTON-ECHO HWY Rt#-207
UMATILLA CO OR 128-C1
UMATILLA CO OR 129-A1
LEY RD
KITTITAS CO WA 240-D1
L GILBERT RD
KITTITAS CO WA 241-D5
W LIBBEY RD
ISLAND CO WA 167-A4
LIBBY RD NE
THURSTON CO WA 180-D4
THURSTON CO WA 297-C1
LIBBY CREEK RD
OKANOGAN CO WA 104-A3
S LIBERTY DR
LIBERTY LAKE WA 247-B4
SPOKANE CO WA 247-B4
LIBERTY RD
KITTITAS CO WA 241-A1
POLK CO OR 204-A6
SHERMAN CO OR 127-C2
LIBERTY RD S
MARION CO OR 207-D1
MARION CO OR 324-E10
MARION CO OR 324-F14
SALEM OR 324-G2
LIBERTY ST
ALBANY OR 326-B11
LIBERTY ST NE
SALEM OR 322-H12
LIBERTY ST NE Rt#-99E
SALEM OR 322-J10
LIBERTY ST SE
SALEM OR 322-H13
SALEM OR 324-G1
N LIBERTY LAKE RD
LIBERTY LAKE WA 247-B4
LIBERTY LAKE WA 352-B13
SPOKANE CO WA 247-B4
SPOKANE CO WA 352-B13
S LIBERTY LAKE RD
LIBERTY LAKE WA 247-B4
LIBERTY PARK PL
SPOKANE WA 349-C9
LICK CREEK RD
MCCALL ID 251-D5
VALLEY CO ID 251-D5
LICKFORK RD
ASOTIN CO WA 122-C2
LICKMAN RD
DISTRICT OF CHILLIWACK BC 94-C3
DISTRICT OF CHILLIWACK BC 102-C1
SE LIDER RD
KITSAP CO WA 174-B5
LIDSTROM RD
CROOK CO OR 213-D4
LIDSTROM RD E
KITSAP CO WA 271-C14
E LIDSTROM HILL RD
KITSAP CO WA 271-B13
LIESER RD
VANCOUVER WA 307-F7
LIGHTNING CREEK RD Rt#-200
CLARK FORK ID 107-C3
LIGNITE RD
BONNER CO ID 244-A3
LILAC HILL RD
YAMHILL CO OR 198-A4
LILLENAS RD
CLATSOP CO WA 188-D3
LILLIAN ST
DOUGLAS CO OR 225-C1
MYRTLE CREEK OR 225-C1
LILLOOET AV
CITY OF HARRISN HT SPGS BC 94-C3
LILLOOET RD
DIST OF N VANCOUVER BC 156-C2
DIST OF N VANCOUVER BC 255-G6
LILLY RD NE
OLYMPIA WA 297-E4
THURSTON CO WA 297-E4
LILLY RD SE
OLYMPIA WA 297-E5
LILLY WHEATON RD
PACIFIC CO WA 117-A1
LIMBERT RD
DISTRICT OF KENT BC 94-C3
LIME KILN RD
WALLOWA CO OR 130-C2
LIMESTONE AV
DESCHUTES CO OR 212-C7
LINCOLN AV
COQUITLAM BC 157-A4
KENT WA 175-B7
PORT COQUITLAM BC 157-A4
SNOHOMISH WA 171-D3
SNOHOMISH CO WA 171-D3
TACOMA WA 182-A2
YAMHILL CO OR 198-B4
E LINCOLN AV
SUNNYSIDE WA 120-B2
W LINCOLN AV
CHEWELAH WA 106-B3
YAKIMA WA 243-B6
LINCOLN AV SE
EAST PORT ORCHARD WA 174-B4
NE LINCOLN DR
POULSBO WA 170-C6
W LINCOLN DR
PASCO WA 343-E5
LINCOLN LN
GRANTS PASS OR 335-C9
JOSEPHINE CO OR 335-C9
LINCOLN PKWY SW
SEATTLE WA 284-D1
LINCOLN RD
JOSEPHINE CO OR 335-C9
LINCOLN CO WA 113-C1

E LINCOLN RD
PIERCE CO WA 181-C5
SPOKANE WA 347-C13
SPOKANE CO WA 347-C13
TOWN AND COUNTRY WA 347-C13
LINCOLN RD NE
MARION CO OR 205-B2
LINCOLN ST
ASTORIA WA 300-B5
KLAMATH FALLS OR 338-C7
PIERCE CO WA 181-C5
LINCOLN ST U.S.-101
HOQUIAM WA 178-A7
S LINCOLN ST
SPOKANE WA 348-J13
S LINCOLN ST U.S.-101
PORT ANGELES WA 261-E5
LINCOLN WY U.S.-95
COEUR D'ALENE ID 355-D8
N LINCOLN WY
COEUR D'ALENE ID 355-D10
KOOTENAI CO ID 355-D10
LINCOLN CREEK RD
LEWIS CO WA 117-B1
LEWIS CO WA 184-B5
LINCOLN MOUNTAIN RD
UMATILLA CO OR 129-C1
LINCOLN PARK WY
SEATTLE WA 284-D1
LINCOLN-ZENA RD
POLK CO OR 204-C4
LINCTON MOUNTAIN RD
UMATILLA CO OR 130-A1
LIND AV SW
RENTON WA 175-C5
LIND RD
FRANKLIN CO WA 121-B1
LINDBECK RD
LEWIS CO WA 187-C2
LINDBERG RD
COLUMBIA CO OR 189-A4
LINDEN AV N
SEATTLE WA 273-J3
LINDEN LN
POLK CO OR 207-B1
LINDEN ST
MILTON-FREEWATER OR 121-C3
W LINDEN ST
BOISE ID 253-D3
W LINDEN WY Rt#-74
HEPPNER OR 128-C2
N LINDER RD
ADA CO ID 253-A1
S LINDER RD
ADA CO ID 253-A4
MERIDIAN ID 253-A2
LINDGREN RD
PACIFIC CO WA 183-B4
LIND-HATTON RD
ADAMS CO WA 121-B1
LINDHOLM RD
DISTRICT OF METCHOSIN BC 159-A7
LIND-KAHLOTUS RD Rt#-21
ADAMS CO WA 121-C1
FRANKLIN CO WA 121-C1
KAHLOTUS WA 121-C1
LINDSAY DR
LINN CO OR 207-B7
LINDSEY DR
LONGVIEW HEIGHTS WA 302-J5
LINDSEY RD
KOOTENAI CO ID 245-B2
LINDSEY CREEK RD
NEZ PERCE CO ID 250-C4
LIND-WARDEN RD
ADAMS CO WA 121-B1
LINGENFELTER RD
PACIFIC CO WA 186-B7
LINGER LONGER RD
JEFFERSON CO WA 109-C1
LINGO LN
LANE CO OR 210-A5
LINK LN
LANE CO OR 210-A5
S LINKE RD
SPOKANE CO WA 247-A5
SPOKANE CO WA 351-F14
W LINN RD
JACKSON CO OR 230-D5
LINN WY
BROWNSVILLE OR 210-C2
LINNEY CREEK RD
CLACKAMAS CO OR 201-D7
LINN WEST DR
LINN CO OR 210-B2
LINTON ST
COQUITLAM BC 157-A5
LINVILLE GULCH RD
GARFIELD CO WA 122-B2
LINVILLE RIDGE RD
GARFIELD CO WA 122-B2
SE LINWOOD AV
CLACKAMAS CO OR 199-D3
MILWAUKIE OR 199-D3
LINWOOD AV SW
TUMWATER WA 296-G10
SE LION LAKE RD
REDMOND OR 212-D5
LIONS GATE BRDG Rt#-99
DIST OF WEST VANCOUVER BC 254-E6
VANCOUVER BC 254-E6
LIONS GATE BRIDGE RD Rt#-99
DIST OF WEST VANCOUVER BC 254-D7
VANCOUVER BC 254-D7
LIPPMAN RD
HOOD RIVER CO OR 195-C6
LISHER CTO
LATAH CO ID 249-D1
LITHIA WY
ASHLAND OR 337-C7
LITHIA WY Rt#-99
ASHLAND OR 337-C7
LITTLE RD
WHITMAN CO WA 249-A7
LITTLE ALKALI RD
WHITMAN CO WA 122-B1
LITTLE APPLEGATE RD
JACKSON CO OR 234-A5

LITTLE BEAR CREEK RD
CROOK CO OR 135-C3
LITTLE BLACKTAIL MOUNTAIN RD
BONNER CO ID 244-A6
LITTLE BOSTON RD NE
KITSAP CO WA 170-C4
LITTLE BURMA RD
DOUGLAS CO OR 214-D6
LITTLE BUTTER CREEK RD
MORROW CO OR 128-C2
MORROW CO OR 129-A2
LITTLE EGYPT RD
MASON CO WA 179-D3
LITTLE FALL CREEK RD
LANE CO OR 134-A3
LITTLE FALLS RD
LINCOLN CO WA 114-A1
LITTLE FALLS CHAMOKANA RD
STEVENS CO WA 114-A1
LITTLE FALLS LONGLAKE RD
STEVENS CO WA 114-A1
LITTLE GOOSE DAM RD
COLUMBIA CO WA 122-A2
LITTLE GREYBACK RD
JOSEPHINE CO OR 233-C4
LITTLE HANAFORD RD
LEWIS CO WA 184-D6
LEWIS CO WA 299-J2
LITTLE JUNIPER RD
HARNEY CO OR 144-B3
LITTLE KALAMA RIVER RD
COWLITZ CO WA 118-A3
LITTLE MCKAY RD
CROOK CO OR 135-C2
LITTLE MOUNTAIN RD
KLICKITAT CO WA 119-A3
SKAGIT CO WA 168-B1
SKAGIT CO WA 260-F14
LITTLE MUD CREEK RD
ADAMS CO ID 251-A3
LITTLE NESTUCCA HWY
TILLAMOOK CO OR 203-D2
LITTLE NESTUCCA RIVER RD
TILLAMOOK CO OR 203-C1
LITTLE RIVER RD
CLALLAM CO WA 165-A7
DOUGLAS CO OR 141-B2
DOUGLAS CO OR 222-A5
LITTLEROCK RD SW
ROCHESTER WA 184-A3
THURSTON CO WA 184-B1
THURSTON CO WA 296-D14
TUMWATER WA 296-D14
LITTLE SHEEP CREEK HWY
JOSEPH OR 130-C2
WALLOWA CO OR 130-C2
WALLOWA CO OR 131-A2
LITTLE SHEEP CREEK RD Rt#-25
STEVENS CO WA 106-A1
LITTLE SPOKANE DR
SPOKANE CO WA 347-C1
SW LITTLE SQUAWBACK RD
JEFFERSON CO OR 211-D2
LITTLE SQUAW BAY RD
KOOTENAI CO ID 248-A6
LITTLE VALLEY LN
LINN CO OR 210-D4
LITTLE WEISER RD
ADAMS CO ID 252-B6
LITTLE WEISER RD U.S.-95
ADAMS CO ID 139-B1
LITTLE WEISER RIVER RD
ADAMS CO ID 252-A6
LITTLE WILLOW RD
PAYETTE CO ID 139-B3
LIVERMORE RD
POLK CO OR 204-B4
LIVESAY RD
DESCHUTES CO OR 211-D7
LIVINGSTON RD
CLARK CO WA 193-C5
LIZARD CREEK RD
DESCHUTES CO OR 144-A1
L JOHNSON RD
CLARK CO WA 192-D1
LLEWELLYN RD
BENTON CO OR 133-B2
NE LLOYD BLVD
PORTLAND OR 313-H4
LLOYD DR
JOSEPHINE CO OR 229-B4
LLOYD WY
DESCHUTES CO OR 216-D7
DESCHUTES CO OR 217-A6
THREE RIVERS OR 217-A6
LOBSTER CREEK RD
CURRY CO OR 228-B3
LINCOLN CO OR 209-D3
LOBSTER VALLEY RD
BENTON CO OR 133-A2
BENTON CO OR 209-D3
LOCARNO CRES
UNIV ENDOWMENT LANDS BC 156-A4
LOCHNER RD
ALBANY OR 326-D14
LINN CO OR 326-D14
LOCHSIDE DR
DIST OF NORTH SAANICH BC 159-C3
TOWN OF SIDNEY BC 159-C3
LOCKART AV
COOS BAY OR 333-G12
LOCKER RD SE
KITSAP CO WA 174-C4
LOCKETT RD
MALHEUR CO OR 139-A2
LOCKHAVEN DR N
KEIZER OR 322-J4
KEIZER OR 323-A4
LOCKHAVEN DR NE
KEIZER OR 323-B4
LOCKITT BUTTE RD
DESCHUTES CO OR 217-C5
LOCKS RD
YAMHILL CO OR 198-B7
LOCKWOOD RD
SNOHOMISH CO WA 171-B6

NE LOCKWOOD CREEK RD
CLARK CO WA 192-D2
LOCUST AV
BROWNSVILLE OR 210-C2
E LOCUST AV
COEUR D'ALENE ID 355-E9
LOCUST LN
CANYON CO ID 147-C1
LOCUST ST
ALMIRA WA 237-D7
DESCHUTES CO OR 211-D5
OAKLAND OR 219-A7
SISTERS OR 211-D5
LOCUST ST Rt#-19
ARLINGTON OR 128-A1
N LOCUST ST Rt#-19
ARLINGTON OR 128-A1
GILLIAM CO OR 128-A1
S LOCUST ST Rt#-19
ARLINGTON OR 128-A1
LOCUST WY
SNOHOMISH CO WA 171-B6
LOCUST GROVE RD
BENTON CO WA 121-A3
NEZ PERCE CO ID 250-D7
N LOCUST GROVE RD
ADA CO ID 253-A2
S LOCUST GROVE RD
ADA CO ID 253-B4
LODGEPOLE RD
JACKSON CO OR 150-A1
LOERLAND LN
ISLAND CO WA 167-B3
LOFFS BAY RD
KOOTENAI CO ID 247-D6
KOOTENAI CO ID 248-A2
LOFTON CREEK RD
CROOK CO OR 213-D2
LOGAN RD
CLATSOP CO WA 188-C3
NE LOGAN RD
LINCOLN CO OR 203-A4
NW LOGAN RD
LINCOLN CO OR 203-A4
SW LOGANBERRY LN
SHERIDAN OR 125-B3
YAMHILL CO OR 125-B3
YAMHILL CO OR 204-A2
LOGAN HILL RD
LEWIS CO WA 184-D7
LOGAN VALLEY RD
GRANT CO OR 137-B3
SENECA OR 137-B3
LOG CABIN RD SE
OLYMPIA WA 297-B9
LOG CORRAL RD
KLICKITAT CO WA 196-B1
LOGEN RD
SNOHOMISH CO WA 168-A3
LOGGING RD
CLACKAMAS CO OR 205-D1
LOGGING 1600 RD
COWLITZ CO WA 118-A3
COWLITZ CO WA 189-D1
LOGIE TRAIL RD
MULTNOMAH CO OR 192-A6
LOGSDEN RD
LINCOLN CO OR 133-A1
LINCOLN CO OR 206-D2
SILETZ OR 206-D2
S LOIS DR
SPOKANE CO WA 246-B7
W LOLAH BUTTE RD
DESCHUTES CO OR 216-B7
LOLO BUTTE RD
DESCHUTES CO OR 216-C6
LOLO PASS RD
BENEWAH CO ID 115-A3
CLACKAMAS CO OR 201-D4
HOOD RIVER CO OR 202-A3
LOMBARD DR NW
PIERCE CO WA 181-B1
N LOMBARD ST
PORTLAND OR 192-B6
N LOMBARD ST U.S.-30
PORTLAND OR 192-B7
PORTLAND OR 308-B4
PORTLAND OR 309-E5
NE LOMBARD ST U.S.-30
PORTLAND OR 309-G5
PORTLAND OR 310-B6
LOMBARDY LN
KLAMATH CO OR 235-C5
LONDON DR
HOOD RIVER CO OR 202-C2
LONDON RD
LANE CO OR 219-D1
LONDON HILL RD
DOUGLAS CO OR 219-C4
NE LONE ELDER RD
CLACKAMAS CO OR 199-C7
LONE FIR RD
BAKER CO OR 131-A3
S LONE LAKE RD
ISLAND CO WA 167-D7
ISLAND CO WA 170-D1
LONE MOUNTAIN RD
JOSEPHINE CO OR 233-A6
LONE OAK RD
LONGVIEW WA 302-F3
LONGVIEW HEIGHTS WA 302-F3
WEST LONGVIEW WA 302-F3
LONE OAK RD SE
SALEM OR 324-G7
LONE PINE DR
LANE CO OR 210-A7
LONE PINE RD
CROOK CO OR 213-A4
JACKSON CO OR 336-G9
JEFFERSON CO OR 213-A3
MEDFORD OR 336-G9
LONE PINE-DORA RD
COOS CO OR 140-C2
LONE PINE SCHOOL RD
CROOK CO OR 213-A3
LONE ROCK RD
MORO OR 127-C2
SHERMAN CO OR 127-C2
LONEROCK RD
GILLIAM CO OR 128-B3

LONEROCK RD
WHEELER CO OR 128-B3
LONE STAR RD NW
POLK CO OR 204-C3
LONE YEW RD
LEWIS CO WA 187-D5
LONG AV
KELSO WA 303-C8
LONG RD
KLICKITAT CO WA 196-D2
WASHINGTON CO OR 198-C1
S LONG RD
GREEN ACRES WA 351-F9
LONG CREEK RD
GRANT CO OR 129-A3
GRANT CO OR 137-A1
LONG HOLLOW RD
WHITMAN CO WA 122-A1
LONG HOLLOW MARKET RD
WASCO CO OR 127-B2
LONG JOHN MORASCH RD
WHITMAN CO WA 122-B1
LONG LAKE RD
KLAMATH CO OR 235-A3
LINCOLN CO WA 114-A1
W LONG LAKE RD
SPOKANE CO WA 114-B1
LONG LAKE RD SE
KITSAP CO WA 174-C4
LONGMIRE LN
YAKIMA CO WA 243-A3
LONG PRAIRIE RD
STEVENS CO WA 106-B3
TILLAMOOK CO OR 197-C3
LONG RIDGE RD
DOUGLAS CO OR 141-A2
LONG VALLEY RD
DOUGLAS CO OR 219-C7
LONGVIEW RD
ADAMS CO ID 251-C5
LONGWOOD DR
REEDSPORT OR 218-C2
LONSDALE AV
CITY OF N VANCOUVER BC 255-B3
DIST OF N VANCOUVER BC 255-B3
LONSETH RD
WHATCOM CO WA 158-B5
LOOK RD
KITTITAS CO WA 241-B5
LOOKINGGLASS RD
DOUGLAS CO OR 221-A5
DOUGLAS CO OR 334-A8
ROSEBURG OR 334-A8
WINSTON OR 221-A5
NW LOOKINGGLASS RD
WINSTON OR 221-B6
LOOKNGGLASS-BRCKWY RD
DOUGLAS CO OR 221-A5
LOOKOUT RD
KLAMATH CO OR 151-A1
N LOOKOUT RD
DESCHUTES CO OR 216-B7
LOOKOUT MOUNTAIN RD
DESCHUTES CO OR 216-B7
MARION CO OR 134-A1
UNION CO OR 130-B1
LOOKOUT POINT RD
SELAH WA 243-B6
LOOMIS LN
VALLEY CO ID 252-D2
LOOMIS-OROVILLE RD
OKANOGAN CO WA 104-C1
LOOMIS TRAIL RD
WHATCOM CO WA 158-C4
LOON LAKE RD
DOUGLAS CO OR 140-C1
LOON LAKE-MCVAY PIT RD
STEVENS CO WA 106-B3
LOON LAKE SOUTHSIDE RD
STEVENS CO WA 106-B3
STEVENS CO WA 114-B1
LOOP RD
JACKSON CO OR 226-C5
SKAMANIA CO WA 194-D4
STEVENS CO WA 114-A1
N LOOP RD
UMATILLA CO OR 129-A1
SE LOOP RD
YAMHILL CO OR 198-B7
LOOSLEY RD
KLAMATH CO OR 231-C2
LOPER AV
PRINEVILLE OR 213-D4
LORAINE AV
DIST OF N VANCOUVER BC 254-H2
LORANE HWY
EUGENE OR 329-C14
LANE CO OR 133-B3
LANE CO OR 215-A4
LANE CO OR 329-C14
LORD ST
KELSO WA 303-D7
LORDS LAKE LOOP RD
JEFFERSON CO WA 109-C1
LORIMER RD
BRITISH COLUMBIA 159-B5
LOST HWY W
KITSAP CO WA 173-D4
LOST CREEK RD
COLUMBIA CO OR 189-A4
DOUGLAS CO OR 223-B4
LANE CO OR 133-C3
SKAMANIA CO WA 195-B3
LOSTINE RIVER RD
WALLOWA CO OR 130-C2
LOST LAKE RD
HOOD RIVER CO OR 195-B7
HOOD RIVER CO OR 202-A1
MASON CO WA 179-D4
MASON CO WA 180-A3
SHELTON WA 180-A3
LOST MOUNTAIN RD
CLALLAM CO WA 109-C1
LOST PRAIRIE RD
WALLOWA CO OR 122-C3
LOST RIVER RD
OKANOGAN CO WA 104-A2
LOST VALLEY RD
WHEELER CO OR 128-B3

LOTZGESELL DR
CLALLAM CO WA 262-B3
LOTZGESELL RD
CLALLAM CO WA 166-A5
CLALLAM CO WA 262-A3
NE LOUCKS RD
JEFFERSON CO OR 208-C5
LOUDEN RD
MULTNOMAH CO OR 200-D2
LOUGHEED HWY Rt#-7
BRITISH COLUMBIA 94-B3
COQUITLAM BC 157-A5
DISTRICT OF BURNABY BC 156-D4
DISTRICT OF BURNABY BC 255-G12
DISTRICT OF COQUITLAM BC 156-D4
DISTRICT OF KENT BC 94-B3
DISTRICT OF MISSION BC 94-B3
MAPLE RIDGE BC 94-B3
MAPLE RIDGE BC 157-D6
PITT MEADOWS BC 157-B4
PORT COQUITLAM BC 157-B4
LOUIE FAVE RD
WASHINGTON CO ID 139-B1
LOUISIANA ST
LONGVIEW WA 303-A8
NW LOVEJOY ST
PORTLAND OR 312-D4
PORTLAND OR 313-F4
LOVE LAKE RD
LANE CO OR 210-A5
LOVELL VALLEY RD
BENEWAH CO ID 115-A3
LOVE RESERVOIR RD
BAKER CO OR 138-C1
LOVES ST
WOODLAND WA 192-B1
NE LOVGREN RD W
KITSAP CO WA 174-C1
LOWDEN GARDENA RD
WALLA WALLA CO WA 121-C3
LOW DIVIDE RD
DEL NORTE CO CA 148-B3
W LOWELL AV
SPOKANE CO WA 246-A2
SPOKANE CO WA 346-A12
LOWELL-LARIMER RD
SNOHOMISH WA 269-H7
SNOHOMISH CO WA 171-C4
E LOWELL-LARIMER RD Rt#-96
SNOHOMISH CO WA 171-D4
LOWELL-SNOHOMISH RIVER RD
EVERETT WA 269-F1
SNOHOMISH WA 269-G1
SNOHOMISH CO WA 171-D3
LOWER ANTELOPE RD Rt#-293
ANTELOPE OR 127-C3
WASCO CO OR 127-C3
LOWER BENCH RD
GEM CO ID 139-B3
SW LOWER BEND RD
JEFFERSON CO OR 208-A5
LOWER BOONES FERRY RD
PORTLAND OR 199-B4
TUALATIN OR 199-B4
SW LOWR BOONES FERRY RD
DURHAM OR 199-B4
TUALATIN OR 199-B4
LOWER BRIDGE RD
DESCHUTES CO OR 212-B3
SW LOWER BRIDGE RD
JEFFERSON CO OR 212-B3
LOWER BURNETT RD E
PIERCE CO WA 182-D5
LOWER COVE RD
UNION CO OR 130-B2
LOWER COW CREEK RD
MALHEUR CO OR 146-C2
MALHEUR CO OR 147-A3
LOWER CRAB CREEK RD
GRANT CO WA 120-B1
LOWER DEADMAN RD
GARFIELD CO WA 122-B1
LOWER DEADWOOD CK RD
LANE CO OR 133-A2
LOWER DIAMOND RD
WALLOWA CO OR 130-B1
LOWER DRY CREEK RD
WALLA WALLA CO WA 121-C3
LOWER EIGHTMILE RD
WASCO CO OR 127-B2
WASCO CO OR 196-D7
LOWER ELWHA RD
CLALLAM CO WA 165-A5
LOWER FORDS CREEK RD
CLEARWATER CO ID 123-C2
LOWER FOURMILE RD
COOS CO OR 224-B1
LOWER FOX HOLLOW RD
LANE CO OR 215-A4
LOWER GRAVE CREEK RD
JOSEPHINE CO OR 149-A1
JOSEPHINE CO OR 229-A2
LOWER GREEN CANYON RD
KITTITAS CO WA 241-A4
LOWER HIGHLAND RD
CLACKAMAS CO OR 200-A6
LOWER HOGEYE RD
COLUMBIA CO WA 122-A2
LOWER HOH RD
JEFFERSON CO WA 169-C5
SE LOWER ISLAND RD
YAMHILL CO OR 204-D1
LOWER JOE CREEK RD
CHELAN CO WA 236-B1
LOWER KEITH RD
CITY OF N VANCOUVER BC 255-B5
LOWER KLAMATH LAKE RD
KLAMATH CO OR 150-C3
KLAMATH CO OR 235-C6
LOWER LITTLE SHASTA RD
SISKIYOU CO CA 150-A3
LOWER MONITOR RD
SUNNYSLOPE WA 238-D3
LOWER MONUMENTAL RD
WALLA WALLA CO WA 121-C2
LOWER NEHALEM RD
CLATSOP CO OR 125-A1

PNW

INDEX

STREET / City State / Page-Grid

LOWER NORWAY RD
COOS CO OR 220-D6
LOWER PACK RIVER RD
BONNER CO ID 244-B1
LOWER PEOH POINT RD
KITTITAS CO WA 240-C2
LOWER PLEASANT RIDGE RD
CANYON CO ID 147-B1
LOWER RIVER RD
JOSEPHINE CO OR 229-B6
JOSEPHINE CO OR 335-A9
LOWER RIVER RD Rt#-501
CLARK WA 304-A1
CLARK CO WA 192-B5
CLARK CO WA 192-B5
VANCOUVER WA 192-B5
VANCOUVER WA 192-B5
VANCOUVER WA 304-A1
NW LOWER RIVER RD
CLARK CO WA 192-B4
NW LOWER RIVER RD Rt#-501
CLARK CO WA 192-B5
VANCOUVER WA 192-B5
LOWER SMITH RIVER RD
DOUGLAS CO OR 214-B7
DOUGLAS CO OR 218-D1
LOWER SUMAS MOUNTAIN RD
DISTRICT OF ABBOTSFORD BC 102-B1
LOWER SUNNYSLOPE RD
SUNNYSLOPE WA 238-D3
LOWER TAMMANY CREEK RD
NEZ PERCE CO ID 250-D5
LOWER WAITSBURG RD
WALLA WALLA WA 345-C5
WALLA WALLA CO WA 121-C3
WALLA WALLA CO WA 345-C5
LOWER WAITSBURG RD Rt#-124
WALLA WALLA CO WA 122-A2
LOWER WHETSTONE RD
COLUMBIA CO WA 122-A2
LOWER WOLF CREEK RD
JOSEPHINE CO OR 229-A1
LOW LEVEL RD
CITY OF N VANCOUVER BC 255-C7
LOYAL AV NW
SEATTLE WA 272-D1
LOZIER LN
JACKSON CO OR 336-A13
L SCHULTHEIS RD
WHITMAN CO WA 250-B3
SW LUANA BEACH RD
KING CO WA 175-A6
N LUCAS AV
PASCO WA 343-E6
S LUCAS AV
PASCO WA 343-E8
NE LUCIA FALLS RD
CLARK CO WA 193-B2
S LUCILE ST
SEATTLE WA 281-J6
SEATTLE WA 282-A6
LUCKENBILL RD
WALLA WALLA CO WA 121-B3
LUCKIAMUTE RD
BENTON CO OR 133-A1
LUCKY SEVEN COW CAMP RD
MALHEUR CO OR 154-C2
LUCKY STRIKE RD
JOSEPHINE CO OR 233-B7
LUCY REEDER RD
MULTNOMAH CO OR 192-A5
LUDEMAN RD NW
DOUGLAS CO WA 236-D5
LUDLOW BAY RD
JEFFERSON CO WA 170-B3
LUDLOW PARADISE RD
JEFFERSON CO WA 170-B3
E LUDLOW RIDGE RD
JEFFERSON CO WA 170-B3
LUFT RD
WHITMAN CO WA 122-B1
SW LUKAS RD
WASHINGTON CO OR 198-D3
LUMMI SHORE DR
WHATCOM CO WA 158-C7
LUMMI SHORE RD
WHATCOM CO WA 158-C7
WHATCOM CO WA 160-C1
LUMMI VIEW DR
WHATCOM CO WA 160-C1
E LUNCEFORD LN
COEUR D'ALENE ID 355-F7
KOOTENAI CO ID 355-F7
SE LUND AV
EAST PORT ORCHARD WA 174-B4
LUNDEEN RD SW
THURSTON CO WA 184-A4
LUNDGREN MILL RD
DESCHUTES CO OR 211-D4
LUNDY RD
DESCHUTES CO OR 211-D4
NW LUOTO RD Rt#-308
KITSAP CO WA 170-B7
LUSK CREEK RD
SKAMANIA CO WA 195-B1
LUSTED RD
CLACKAMAS CO OR 200-C3
SE LUSTED RD
GRESHAM OR 200-B2
MULTNOMAH CO OR 200-B2
LUTZ LN
WASCO CO OR 196-B7
L WEST RD
WHITMAN CO WA 249-B2
LYLE AV
BREMERTON WA 270-C8
N LYLE AV
EAST WENATCHEE BENCH WA 239-A4
LYLE GOLDENDALE RD
KLICKITAT CO WA 127-B1
LYLE SNOWDEN RD
KLICKITAT CO WA 196-B3
LYMAN HAMILTON RD
SKAGIT CO WA 161-D5
LYMAN LAKE-MOSES MOUNTAIN RD
OKANOGAN CO WA 105-A3
LYNCH RD
MASON CO WA 180-B4
LYNN BLVD
CROOK CO OR 213-D5
PRINEVILLE OR 213-D5
LYNN ST
BELLINGHAM WA 258-B4
E LYNN ST
SEATTLE WA 278-C1
W LYNN ST
SEATTLE WA 276-C1
LYNN VALLEY RD
CITY OF N VANCOUVER BC 255-D4
DIST OF N VANCOUVER BC 255-D4
LYNWOOD RD
CANYON CO ID 147-B1
LYNWOOD CENTER RD NE
KITSAP CO WA 271-G4
LYNX HOLLOW RD
LANE CO OR 215-B6
LYON ST U.S.-20
ALBANY OR 326-C8
E LYONS AV
SPOKANE WA 349-A1
TOWN AND COUNTRY WA 349-A1
W LYONS AV
TOWN AND COUNTRY WA 348-J1
TOWN AND COUNTRY WA 349-A1
LYONS DR S
PIERCE CO WA 181-C7
LYONS RD
CLARK CO WA 118-A3
CLARK CO WA 192-C1
KITTITAS CO WA 241-C5
SISKIYOU CO CA 151-A3
S LYONS RD
AIRWAY HEIGHTS WA 246-A4
CLACKAMAS CO OR 200-A6
LYONS FERRY RD
WALLA WALLA CO WA 121-C2
LYONS-MILL CITY DR
LINN CO OR 134-A1
W LYRE RIVER RD
CLALLAM CO WA 164-B5
LYTLE BLVD
MALHEUR CO OR 139-A3

M

M AV
ANACORTES WA 259-G2
S M ST
TACOMA WA 295-F2
SE M ST
GRANTS PASS OR 335-F10
SW M ST
GRANTS PASS OR 335-E9
MABEE MINES RD
SKAMANIA CO WA 194-A6
MABLES CT
LEWIS CO WA 187-D2
MABTON-BICKLETON RD
MABTON WA 120-B3
YAKIMA CO WA 120-A3
MABTON-SUNNYSIDE RD
SUNNYSIDE WA 120-B2
YAKIMA CO WA 120-B2
MABTON-SUNNYSIDE RD Rt#-241
SATUS WA 120-B3
SUNNYSIDE WA 120-B3
YAKIMA CO WA 120-B3
SW MACADAM AV
PORTLAND OR 317-F6
SW MACADAM AV Rt#-43
MULTNOMAH OR 321-G1
PORTLAND OR 317-F6
PORTLAND OR 321-G1
MACARTHUR BLVD
VANCOUVER WA 306-D6
VANCOUVER WA 307-E6
MACDONALD ST
VANCOUVER BC 156-B5
VANCOUVER BC 254-B14
MACHIAS CTO
SNOHOMISH CO WA 171-D2
N MACHIAS RD
LAKE STEVENS WA 110-C1
SNOHOMISH CO WA 110-C1
S MACHIAS RD
SNOHOMISH WA 171-D2
SNOHOMISH CO WA 110-C1
SNOHOMISH CO WA 171-D2
MACHIAS CUTOFF
SNOHOMISH CO WA 110-C1
SNOHOMISH CO WA 171-D2
MAC HOKE RD
UMATILLA CO OR 129-A1
MACK RD
ADAMS CO WA 122-A1
MACKENZIE ST
VANCOUVER BC 156-B5
VANCOUVER BC 254-B14
MACKSBURG RD
CLACKAMAS CO OR 199-C7
MACLEAY RD SE
FOUR CORNERS OR 325-E2
MARION CO OR 205-A6
MARION CO OR 325-H3
SALEM OR 325-F2
MACLURE RD
DISTRICT OF MATSQUI BC 102-B1
E MACMAHAN RD
SPOKANE CO WA 247-A2
S MADELIA ST
SPOKANE WA 349-C9
MADER RD
WHITMAN CO WA 122-B1
WHITMAN CO WA 249-B2
MADISON AV
CORVALLIS OR 327-G10
N MADISON AV NE
KITSAP CO WA 174-D1
MADISON AV S
KITSAP CO WA 174-D2
N MADISON RD
SPOKANE CO WA 246-D1
NE MADISON RD
KITSAP CO WA 174-B1
S MADISON RD
SPOKANE CO WA 246-D6
MADISON ST
ALTAMONT OR 339-B11
EVERETT WA 268-C2
EVERETT WA 269-E3
LAFAYETTE OR 198-B7
SEATTLE WA 277-J6
SEATTLE WA 278-A6
E MADISON ST
CALDWELL ID 147-B1
SEATTLE WA 278-C5
SEATTLE WA 279-F2
N MADISON ST Rt#-82
WALLOWA OR 130-B1
SE MADISON ST
PORTLAND OR 313-H7
SW MADISON ST
PORTLAND OR 313-E6
MADISON ST NE
SALEM OR 322-J10
SALEM OR 323-A11
MADRAS-PRINEVILLE HWY U.S.-26
CROOK CO OR 213-C3
JEFFERSON CO OR 213-C3
PRINEVILLE OR 213-C3
SE MADRAS-PRINEVILLE HWY
JEFFERSON CO OR 213-B2
SE MADRAS-PRNEVLLE HWY U.S.-26
JEFFERSON CO OR 208-C7
JEFFERSON CO OR 213-B2
SW MADRAS-PRNEVLLE HWY U.S.-26
JEFFERSON CO OR 208-C6
MADRONA AV S
SALEM OR 324-E3
MADRONA AV SE
SALEM OR 324-H4
SALEM OR 325-A4
NE MADRONA BLVD
KITSAP CO WA 170-C3
MADRONA DR
DIST OF NORTH SAANICH BC 159-B2
SEATTLE WA 279-E5
MADRONA RD SW
KITSAP CO WA 174-B6
MADRONA WY
ISLAND CO WA 167-B4
E MADRONE AV
MANCHESTER WA 271-G12
NE MADRONE ST
GRANTS PASS OR 335-G8
MAE VALLEY RD
GRANT CO WA 242-A3
NE MAFFET RD
MULTNOMAH CO OR 200-D1
E MAGNESIUM RD
SPOKANE WA 346-J12
SPOKANE WA 347-B12
SPOKANE CO WA 347-B12
TOWN AND COUNTRY WA 346-J12
MAGNOLIA BLVD W
SEATTLE WA 272-B7
SEATTLE WA 276-B1
MAGNOLIA BRDG
SEATTLE WA 276-E2
SEATTLE WA 277-E2
MAGNOLIA WY W
SEATTLE WA 276-E2
MAGPIE GRADE
NEZ PERCE CO ID 123-B2
MAGUIRE GULCH RD
ASOTIN CO WA 250-A5
MAHNCKE RD KPS
PIERCE CO WA 181-A3
MAHOGANY RD
MALHEUR CO OR 146-C2
MAHOGANY GAP RD
MALHEUR CO OR 147-A2
MAHONY RD NE
MARION CO OR 205-A2
MAIDEN LN
WENATCHEE WA 238-D4
WEST WENATCHEE WA 238-D4
MAIL ROUTE RD
ASOTIN CO WA 250-A5
MAIN AV
LA CROSSE WA 122-A1
PINEHURST ID 115-C2
SHOSHONE CO ID 115-C2
WHITMAN CO WA 122-A1
MAIN AV Rt#-5
SAINT MARIES ID 248-C7
MAIN AV Rt#-508
MORTON WA 118-B2
MAIN AV U.S.-101
TILLAMOOK OR 197-B2
TILLAMOOK CO OR 197-B2
E MAIN AV
BREWSTER WA 104-B3
CHEWELAH WA 106-B3
PIERCE CO WA 182-B3
PUYALLUP WA 182-B3
SUMNER WA 182-B3
E MAIN AV U.S.-2
LINCOLN CO WA 113-B1
WILBUR WA 113-B1
N MAIN AV
GRESHAM OR 200-B2
KLICKITAT CO WA 195-D4
WARRENTON WA 188-B2
WHITE SALMON WA 195-D4
S MAIN AV
MORROW CO OR 128-C1
WARRENTON WA 188-B2
W MAIN AV
BREWSTER WA 104-B3
OKANOGAN CO WA 104-B3
W MAIN AV U.S.-2
WILBUR WA 113-B1
MAIN AV E
SOAP LAKE WA 112-C2
MAIN AV E U.S.-730
IRRIGON OR 128-C1
S MAIN AV E
IRRIGON OR 128-C1
MAIN AV S
RENTON WA 175-C5
MAIN AV S Rt#-515
RENTON WA 175-C5
MAIN AV S Rt#-900
RENTON WA 175-C5
MAIN AV W
GRANT CO WA 112-C2
SOAP LAKE WA 112-C2
S MAIN AV W
IRRIGON OR 128-C1
MORROW CO OR 128-C1
MAIN RD
BREWSTER WA 104-B3
LEBANON OR 133-C1
OKANOGAN CO WA 104-B3
W MAIN RD
COTTAGE GROVE OR 215-B7
LANE CO OR 215-B7
MAIN ST
ALBANY OR 326-D7
AULT FIELD WA 170-D1
AUMSVILLE OR 133-C1
BAKER CITY OR 138-B1
BELLEVUE WA 175-C2
BOISE ID 253-C2
BONNERS FERRY ID 107-B2
BOTHELL WA 171-C6
BROWNSVILLE OR 210-C2
CANYON CITY OR 137-B2
CHEHALIS WA 299-D12
CHELAN CO WA 238-C3
CONCONULLY WA 104-B2
COTTONWOOD ID 123-B2
CRAIGMONT ID 123-B2
CULDESAC ID 123-B2
DIST OF N VANCOUVER BC 255-E7
DOUGLAS CO OR 225-B3
DUFUR OR 127-B2
ECHO OR 129-A1
EDMONDS WA 171-A5
ELLENSBURG WA 241-B6
FERNDALE WA 158-C6
FOREST GROVE OR 198-B1
GRANGER WA 120-A2
HALFWAY OR 131-A3
IONE OR 128-B2
KITTITAS WA 241-C6
KLAMATH FALLS OR 338-E7
KLICKITAT CO WA 119-A3
LANE CO OR 330-H7
LAPWAI ID 123-B2
LEWISTON ID 250-B4
LINN CO OR 133-C1
LYNDEN WA 102-B1
MABTON WA 120-B3
MALIN OR 151-A3
MARION CO OR 198-D7
MILTON-FREEWATER OR 121-C3
MOUNT VERNON WA 260-C13
NEZ PERCE CO ID 123-B2
PACIFIC CO WA 117-A1
PECK ID 123-B2
POLK CO OR 207-C2
RIDDLE OR 225-B2
RUFUS OR 127-C1
SAINT PAUL OR 198-D7
SCIO OR 133-C1
SODAVILLE OR 133-C2
SOUTH LEBANON OR 133-C1
SPRINGFIELD OR 330-H7
SPRINGFIELD OR 331-B7
STEVENS CO WA 106-A3
SUMNER WA 182-B3
TROY ID 123-B2
UNION GAP WA 243-C7
VANCOUVER BC 156-B5
VANCOUVER BC 254-H14
VANCOUVER WA 305-G3
WAITSBURG WA 122-A2
WARDNER ID 115-C2
WINTHROP WA 104-A2
YAKIMA CO WA 120-A2
YAMHILL OR 198-D7
YAMHILL CO OR 198-D7
MAIN ST Rt#-3
BRITISH COLUMBIA 104-C1
JULIAETTA ID 123-B1
KENDRICK ID 123-B1
OSOYOOS BC 104-C1
MAIN ST Rt#-5
SAINT MARIES ID 248-D7
MAIN ST Rt#-6
PE ELL WA 117-B2
MAIN ST Rt#-7
BAKER CITY OR 138-B1
MAIN ST Rt#-8
TROY ID 123-A1
MAIN ST Rt#-9
SKAGIT CO WA 168-C2
MAIN ST Rt#-19
CANYON CO ID 147-B1
GREENLEAF ID 147-B1
MAIN ST Rt#-31
PAISLEY OR 151-C1
MAIN ST Rt#-39
KLAMATH FALLS OR 338-D8
MAIN ST Rt#-44
CANYON CO ID 147-B1
MAIN ST Rt#-55
MARSING ID 147-B1
OWYHEE CO ID 147-B1
MAIN ST Rt#-62
CRAIGMONT ID 123-B2
MAIN ST Rt#-74
HEPPNER OR 128-C2
LEXINGTON OR 128-C2
MAIN ST Rt#-86
RICHLAND OR 139-A1
MAIN ST Rt#-99
CANYONVILLE OR 225-C3
DOUGLAS CO OR 225-C3
PHOENIX OR 234-B2
MAIN ST Rt#-124
WAITSBURG WA 122-A2
MAIN ST Rt#-126
SPRINGFIELD OR 215-D2
SPRINGFIELD OR 331-H7
MAIN ST Rt#-203
DUVALL WA 110-C1
KING CO WA 110-C1
MAIN ST Rt#-206
HEPPNER OR 128-C2
MAIN ST Rt#-212
OREGON CITY OR 199-D4
MAIN ST Rt#-214
MOUNT ANGEL OR 205-C3
MAIN ST Rt#-219
SAINT PAUL OR 198-D7
MAIN ST Rt#-226
LINN CO OR 133-C1
LYONS OR 134-A1
SCIO OR 133-C1
MAIN ST Rt#-231
LINCOLN CO WA 114-A2
MAIN ST Rt#-237
COVE OR 130-B2
UNION CO OR 130-B2
MAIN ST Rt#-240
YAMHILL OR 198-B5
YAMHILL CO OR 198-B5
MAIN ST Rt#-260
WASHTUCNA WA 121-C1
MAIN ST Rt#-261
WASHTUCNA WA 121-C1
MAIN ST Rt#-409
CATHLAMET WA 117-B3
MAIN ST Rt#-524
EDMONDS WA 171-A5
MAIN ST Rt#-544
NOOKSACK WA 102-B1
MAIN ST U.S.-12
DAYTON WA 122-A2
LEWISTON ID 250-C4
MAIN ST U.S.-20
BENTON CO OR 133-B1
LEBANON OR 133-C1
LINN CO OR 133-C1
MALHEUR CO OR 139-A3
NYSSA OR 139-A3
PHILOMATH OR 133-B1
SWEET HOME OR 133-C2
MAIN ST U.S.-30
BAKER CITY OR 138-B1
MAIN ST U.S.-95
BONNERS FERRY ID 107-B2
FERDINAND ID 123-B3
HOMEDALE ID 147-A1
IDAHO CO ID 123-B3
MAIN ST U.S.-97
MORO OR 127-C2
OKANOGAN CO WA 104-C1
OROVILLE WA 104-C1
UNION GAP WA 120-A2
UNION GAP WA 243-C7
YAKIMA CO WA 120-A2
E MAIN ST
ALMIRA WA 237-D7
ASHLAND OR 337-E8
AUBURN WA 182-C1
BATTLE GROUND WA 193-A3
CANYON CITY OR 137-B2
CHELAN CO WA 238-D3
COTTAGE GROVE OR 215-B7
ELMA WA 179-B7
FERNDALE WA 158-D6
GRANDVIEW WA 120-B3
HERMISTON OR 129-A1
HILLSBORO OR 198-D1
JACKSON CO OR 337-G8
LEWISTON ID 250-C4
LINCOLN CO WA 237-D7
LONG CREEK OR 137-A1
LYNDEN WA 102-B1
LYNDEN WA 158-D4
MANCHESTER WA 271-H12
MEDFORD OR 336-E12
MONMOUTH OR 204-B7
MONROE WA 110-C1
PULLMAN WA 249-B5
ROGUE RIVER OR 229-D6
SUNNYSLOPE WA 238-D3
WALLA WALLA WA 345-B7
YAKIMA CO WA 120-B3
E MAIN ST Rt#-13
GRANGEVILLE ID 123-C3
IDAHO CO ID 123-C3
E MAIN ST Rt#-18
SHERIDAN OR 125-B3
WILLAMINA OR 125-A3
E MAIN ST Rt#-23
HARRINGTON WA 113-C2
E MAIN ST Rt#-27
GARFIELD WA 114-C3
E MAIN ST Rt#-51
MONMOUTH OR 204-B7
E MAIN ST Rt#-211
MOLALLA OR 126-A3
E MAIN ST Rt#-238
MEDFORD OR 336-D12
E MAIN ST Rt#-270
PULLMAN WA 249-B5
E MAIN ST Rt#-272
PALOUSE WA 249-C1
E MAIN ST U.S.-12
COLUMBIA CO WA 122-A2
DAYTON WA 122-A2
LEWISTON ID 250-C4
E MAIN ST U.S.-26
GRANT CO OR 137-B2
JOHN DAY OR 137-B2
E MAIN ST U.S.-95
WEISER ID 139-A2
E MAIN ST U.S.-395
MOUNT VERNON OR 137-A2
N MAIN ST
BOARDMAN OR 128-C1
EAST WENATCHEE WA 239-A4
EAST WENATCHEE BENCH WA 239-A4
ELLENSBURG WA 241-B5
FALLS CITY OR 125-B3
MABTON WA 120-B3
MILTON-FREEWATER OR 121-C3
MOSCOW ID 249-C5
PENDLETON OR 129-B1
PRINEVILLE OR 213-D4
SPANGLE WA 114-C2
TOLEDO OR 206-C4
N MAIN ST Rt#-3
YREKA CA 149-C3
N MAIN ST Rt#-47
BANKS OR 125-B1
N MAIN ST Rt#-51
INDEPENDENCE OR 204-B7
POLK CO OR 204-B7
N MAIN ST Rt#-82
JOSEPH OR 130-C2
WALLOWA CO OR 130-C2
N MAIN ST Rt#-99
ASHLAND OR 337-C6
CANYONVILLE OR 225-C3
JACKSON CO OR 337-C6
PHOENIX OR 234-B2
N MAIN ST Rt#-203
UNION OR 130-B2
N MAIN ST Rt#-214
MOUNT ANGEL OR 205-C3
N MAIN ST Rt#-231
SPRINGDALE WA 106-B3
N MAIN ST Rt#-240
NEWBERG OR 198-D5
N MAIN ST Rt#-263
YREKA CA 149-C3
N MAIN ST U.S.-95
LATAH CO ID 249-C4
MOSCOW ID 249-C5
N MAIN ST U.S.-195
COLFAX WA 122-C1
N MAIN ST U.S.-395
COLVILLE WA 106-A2
NW MAIN ST
SHERWOOD OR 199-A4
S MAIN ST
BOARDMAN OR 128-C1
DALLAS OR 204-A6
FALLS CITY OR 125-B3
INDEPENDENCE OR 204-A6
JEFFERSON OR 207-D3
KLAMATH CO OR 150-C3
MARION CO OR 205-C3
MARION CO OR 207-D3
MERRILL OR 150-C2
MILTON-FREEWATER OR 121-C3
MOUNT ANGEL OR 205-C3
PENDLETON OR 129-B1
SPANGLE WA 114-C2
SPOKANE CO WA 114-C2
TOLEDO OR 206-C4
S MAIN ST Rt#-3
YREKA CA 149-C3
S MAIN ST Rt#-11
MILTON-FREEWATER OR 121-C3
S MAIN ST Rt#-18
WILLAMINA OR 125-A3
S MAIN ST Rt#-19
CONDON OR 128-A2
S MAIN ST Rt#-47
BANKS OR 125-B1
WASHINGTON CO OR 125-B1
S MAIN ST Rt#-51
INDEPENDENCE OR 204-B7
S MAIN ST Rt#-82
JOSEPH OR 130-C2
S MAIN ST Rt#-99
CANYONVILLE OR 225-C3
WINSTON OR 221-B6
S MAIN ST Rt#-223
DALLAS OR 204-A6
S MAIN ST Rt#-237
UNION OR 130-B2
S MAIN ST U.S.-95
BONNERS FERRY ID 107-B2
MOSCOW ID 249-C5
S MAIN ST U.S.-195
COLFAX WA 122-C1
S MAIN ST U.S.-395
COLVILLE WA 106-A2
SE MAIN ST
MILWAUKIE OR 321-J2
ROSEBURG OR 334-F8
SW MAIN ST
PORTLAND OR 313-E6
W MAIN ST
ALMIRA WA 237-D7
AUBURN WA 182-C1
BATTLE GROUND WA 193-A3
CARLTON OR 198-B6
CENTRALIA WA 299-E4
COTTAGE GROVE OR 215-B7
ELMA WA 179-B7
GRANDVIEW WA 120-B3
LANE CO OR 215-B7
LONG CREEK OR 137-A1
LYNDEN WA 158-D4
MARION CO OR 205-C4
MONMOUTH OR 204-B7
MONROE WA 110-C1
PULLMAN WA 249-A5
ROGUE RIVER OR 229-D6
SANDPOINT ID 244-A2
SILVERTON OR 205-C4
WALLA WALLA WA 344-J8
WALLA WALLA WA 345-A8
WHATCOM CO WA 158-D4
WHITMAN CO WA 249-A5
WILLAMINA OR 125-A3
YAMHILL OR 198-A5
YAMHILL CO OR 198-A5
W MAIN ST Rt#-13
GRANGEVILLE ID 123-C3
IDAHO CO ID 123-C3
W MAIN ST Rt#-18
SHERIDAN OR 125-B3
W MAIN ST Rt#-27
GARFIELD WA 114-C3
W MAIN ST Rt#-44
CANYON CO ID 147-B1
MIDDLETON ID 147-B1
W MAIN ST Rt#-47
CARLTON OR 198-B6
W MAIN ST Rt#-99
CANYONVILLE OR 225-C3
W MAIN ST Rt#-211
CLACKAMAS CO OR 126-A3
MOLALLA OR 126-A3
W MAIN ST Rt#-213
SILVERTON OR 205-C4
W MAIN ST Rt#-238
JACKSON CO OR 234-A1
JACKSON CO OR 336-A12

STREET City State Page-Grid

W MAIN ST Rt#-238
MEDFORD OR 336-C12
W MAIN ST Rt#-502
BATTLE GROUND WA 192-D3
BATTLE GROUND WA 193-A3
CLARK CO WA 192-D3
W MAIN ST U.S.-12
DAYTON WA 122-A2
W MAIN ST U.S.-26
MOUNT VERNON OR 137-A2
W MAIN ST U.S.-95
WEISER ID 139-A2
W MAIN ST U.S.-395
GRANT CO OR 137-B2
JOHN DAY OR 137-B2
MAIN ST N
COUPEVILLE WA 167-B4
MAIN ST S
MONTESANO WA 178-D7
MAIN ST S Rt#-20
OMAK WA 104-C3
MAIN EAST WEST RD
MODOC CO CA 151-A3
MAIN LINE RD
CLALLAM CO WA 162-C2
MAINLINE RD
MASON CO WA 180-A4
S MAITLAND AV
PASCO WA 343-H9
MAJOR CREEK RD
KLICKITAT CO WA 196-A4
MAKI RD
VALLEY CO ID 251-C7
MAKINSTER RD
TILLAMOOK CO OR 197-B1
W MALAGA RD
CHELAN CO WA 239-A5
MALAGA ALCOA HWY
APPLEYARD WA 239-A5
CHELAN CO WA 239-A5
MALAVIEW AV
TOWN OF SIDNEY BC 159-C2
MALAVIEW ST
TOWN OF SIDNEY BC 159-C2
MALCOM MCCLARTY
PIERCE CO WA 182-A4
MALDEN RD
MALDEN WA 114-C3
WHITMAN CO WA 114-C3
NE MALHEUR AV
ROSEBURG OR 334-G6
MALHEUR CAVE RD
HARNEY CO OR 146-A2
MALHEUR LINE RD
BAKER CO OR 138-C2
MALHEUR RESERVOIR RD
BAKER CO OR 138-B2
MALHEUR CO OR 138-B2
MALIN LP
KLAMATH CO OR 151-A2
N MALIN RD
KLAMATH CO OR 151-A2
MALLIS LANDING RD
PACIFIC CO WA 117-A1
MALONEY MOUNTAIN RD
COLUMBIA CO WA 122-B2
MALPASS RD
LINN CO OR 210-A4
MALTBY RD
BOTHELL WA 171-C5
SNOHOMISH CO WA 171-C5
MALTBY RD Rt#-524
SNOHOMISH CO WA 171-C5
MANASTASH RD
KITTITAS CO WA 240-C6
KITTITAS CO WA 241-A6
MANDY RD
LEWIS CO WA 187-C5
MANETTE BRDG
BREMERTON WA 270-J10
BREMERTON WA 271-A10
MANILA CREEK RD
FERRY CO WA 113-B1
MANION RD
CLATSOP CO WA 188-B4
NE MANITOU BEACH DR
KITSAP CO WA 174-D1
MANLEY RD
WHATCOM CO WA 161-B2
MANLEY RD NW
KITSAP CO WA 174-A1
MANN RD
KLAMATH CO OR 235-C6
LANE CO OR 209-D6
SKAGIT CO WA 168-A2
SNOHOMISH CO WA 110-C1
UMATILLA CO OR 129-C1
MANN CREEK RD
WASHINGTON CO ID 139-B2
MANNERS RD
LEWIS CO WA 117-B1
LEWIS CO WA 184-A4
THURSTON CO WA 184-A4
MANNERS RD SW
LEWIS CO WA 117-B1
MANNING DR
LINN CO OR 210-C1
MANNING BASIN RD
BAKER CO OR 138-C1
MANNTHEY RD
MULTNOMAH CO OR 200-D2
W MANOR PL
SEATTLE WA 272-D6
MANOR WY
SNOHOMISH CO WA 171-B4
MANSFIELD RD NE
DOUGLAS CO WA 112-C1
MANSFIELD BARKER RD
KLICKITAT CO WA 196-A5
MANSON BLVD
CHELAN CO WA 236-B2
MANSON RD
DISTRICT OF MISSION BC 94-B3
NW MANZANITA AV
GRANTS PASS OR 335-E7
MANZANITA RD NE
KITSAP CO WA 174-C1
MANZER ST
DISTRICT OF MISSION BC 94-B3

MAPLE AV
LA CONNER WA 167-D1
SNOHOMISH WA 171-D3
NE MAPLE AV
DESCHUTES CO OR 212-D5
REDMOND OR 212-D5
NW MAPLE AV
DESCHUTES CO OR 212-D5
MAPLE AV E
EAST PORT ORCHARD WA 271-A14
PORT ORCHARD WA 271-A14
MAPLE CRES
MAPLE RIDGE BC 157-C5
MAPLE DR
GRANT CO WA 242-C2
LANE CO OR 210-A7
MAPLE RD
SNOHOMISH CO WA 171-B5
MAPLE ST
ASHLAND OR 337-B6
BELLINGHAM WA 258-D7
LONGVIEW WA 302-J8
LONGVIEW WA 303-A9
NORTH BEND OR 333-E4
SODAVILLE OR 133-C2
WENATCHEE WA 238-D4
WEST WENATCHEE WA 238-D4
MAPLE ST Rt#-47
YAMHILL OR 198-B5
MAPLE ST Rt#-173
BRIDGEPORT WA 112-C1
DOUGLAS CO WA 112-C1
MAPLE ST Rt#-529
EVERETT WA 265-F4
E MAPLE ST
CENTRALIA WA 299-F4
YAKIMA WA 243-C6
N MAPLE ST
SPOKANE WA 348-G1
WALDPORT OR 328-D5
NE MAPLE ST
PULLMAN WA 249-B5
S MAPLE ST
SPOKANE WA 348-H10
WALDPORT OR 328-D5
MAPLE WY
YAKIMA CO WA 243-A5
MAPLE DELL RD
JACKSON CO OR 234-A7
MAPLE GROVE RD
CLACKAMAS CO OR 205-D4
POLK CO OR 133-B1
N MAPLE GROVE RD
BOISE ID 253-B2
S MAPLE GROVE RD
ADA CO ID 253-B3
CLACKAMAS CO OR 126-A3
MAPLE GULCH RD
JACKSON CO OR 230-B3
MAPLE HEIGHTS RD
EVERETT WA 268-A1
S MAPLELANE RD
CLACKAMAS CO OR 199-D5
MAPLE PARK AV SE
OLYMPIA WA 296-H6
E MAPLETON RD
LANE CO OR 214-D2
MAPLTN-JUNCTION CTY HWY Rt#-36
LANE CO OR 132-C3
LANE CO OR 133-B2
LANE CO OR 210-A6
LANE CO OR 214-D1
MAPLE VALLEY RD Rt#-169
KING CO WA 175-C5
RENTON WA 175-C5
MAPLE VALLEY RD SW
THURSTON CO WA 180-B6
MPLE VLY-BLCK DMND RD Rt#-169
BLACK DIAMOND WA 110-C3
KING CO WA 110-C3
KING CO WA 175-D7
KING CO WA 176-A7
MAPLEWILD AV SW
BURIEN WA 175-A5
W MAPLEWOOD AV
BELLINGHAM WA 158-D7
BELLINGHAM WA 258-A2
WHATCOM CO WA 158-D7
WHATCOM CO WA 258-A2
MAPLEWOOD RD
DISTRICT OF SAANICH BC 256-J5
MAP ROCK RD
CANYON CO ID 147-B1
MARBLE RD
SKAMANIA CO WA 200-D1
W MARBLE RD
YAKIMA CO WA 243-A6
MARBLE CREEK RD
SHOSHONE CO ID 115-C3
MARBLE FRONT RD
CALDWELL ID 147-B1
MARBLE MOUNTAIN RD
JOSEPHINE CO OR 229-A7
MARBLE VALLEY SOUTH BASIN RD
STEVENS CO WA 106-A2
MARCELLUS RD
ADAMS CO WA 113-C3
ADAMS CO WA 121-C1
RITZVILLE WA 113-C3
MARCH POINT RD
SKAGIT CO WA 160-C6
E MARCH POINT RD
SKAGIT CO WA 160-D6
S MARCH POINT RD
SKAGIT CO WA 160-D6
W MARCH POINT RD
SKAGIT CO WA 160-C6
MARCOLA RD
LANE CO OR 133-C2
LANE CO OR 210-D7
LANE CO OR 215-D1
LANE CO OR 331-E4
SPRINGFIELD OR 331-D4
MARCY LP
JOSEPHINE CO OR 229-A6
MARGARET AV
COEUR D'ALENE ID 355-F5

MARGIN ST
ENDICOTT WA 122-B1
E MARGINAL WY S
SEATTLE WA 281-J2
SEATTLE WA 282-A7
SEATTLE WA 286-C3
TUKWILA WA 286-C3
E MARGINAL WY S Rt#-99
SEATTLE WA 281-J5
W MARGINAL WY S
SEATTLE WA 285-J1
W MARGINAL WY SW
SEATTLE WA 281-H4
SEATTLE WA 285-J1
S MARGUERITE RD
DISHMAN WA 350-D9
W MARIE ST
PASCO WA 343-D6
MARIE CREEK RD
KOOTENAI CO ID 245-C7
MARIGOLD ST
GARDEN CITY ID 253-B2
MARIHUGH RD
SKAGIT CO WA 161-A6
MARINA DR
WHATCOM CO WA 101-C1
W MARINA DR
MOSES LAKE WA 242-C3
MARINE DR
ANACORTES WA 259-C6
BELLINGHAM WA 158-D7
BELLINGHAM WA 258-A4
BREMERTON WA 270-E8
CITY OF N VANCOUVER BC 254-F4
CITY OF WHITE ROCK BC 158-A2
CLALLAM CO WA 262-B2
DIST OF N VANCOUVER BC 254-F4
DIST OF WEST VANCOUVER BC 156-A2
DIST OF WEST VANCOUVER BC 254-A2
DISTRICT OF BURNABY BC 156-C5
DISTRICT OF SURREY BC 158-A2
NEW WESTMINSTER BC 156-C5
SKAGIT CO WA 259-C6
SNOHOMISH CO WA 168-B4
SNOHOMISH CO WA 171-C1
STANWOOD WA 168-B4
WHATCOM CO WA 101-C1
WHATCOM CO WA 158-C7
MARINE DR Rt#-99
DIST OF WEST VANCOUVER BC 254-E4
MARINE DR Rt#-117
PORT ANGELES WA 261-E3
MARINE DR U.S.-30
ASTORIA WA 300-C5
E MARINE DR
CLALLAM CO WA 262-C3
N MARINE DR
PORTLAND OR 192-B6
PORTLAND OR 304-A6
PORTLAND OR 308-E1
PORTLAND OR 309-F1
NE MARINE DR
GRESHAM OR 200-A1
PORTLAND OR 200-A1
PORTLAND OR 309-H2
PORTLAND OR 310-B2
PORTLAND OR 311-H4
NW MARINE DR
UNIV ENDOWMENT LANDS BC 156-A4
SE MARINE DR
VANCOUVER BC 156-C5
SW MARINE DR
UNIV ENDOWMENT LANDS BC 156-A5
VANCOUVER BC 156-B5
W MARINE DR Rt#-202
ASTORIA WA 300-A6
W MARINE DR U.S.-30
ASTORIA WA 300-B4
W MARINE DR U.S.-101
ASTORIA WA 300-A5
MARINE DR NE
SNOHOMISH CO WA 168-C7
SNOHOMISH CO WA 171-C1
MARINE WY
DISTRICT OF BURNABY BC 156-C5
NEW WESTMINSTER BC 156-C5
VANCOUVER BC 156-C5
MARINER WY
COQUITLAM BC 157-A5
MARINE VIEW DR
DES MOINES WA 175-B7
DES MOINES WA 290-A7
KING CO WA 175-B7
OCEAN SHORES WA 298-B4
SEATTLE WA 284-D4
SEATTLE WA 285-E6
MARINE VIEW DR Rt#-509
DES MOINES WA 290-A7
PIERCE CO WA 181-D1
PIERCE CO WA 182-A1
TACOMA WA 181-D1
TACOMA WA 182-A1
MARINEVIEW DR
LINCOLN CO OR 328-C4
E MARINE VIEW DR
EVERETT WA 171-C1
EVERETT WA 265-F1
E MARINE VIEW DR Rt#-529
EVERETT WA 171-C1
W MARINE VIEW DR
EVERETT WA 264-D4
W MARINE VIEW DR Rt#-529
EVERETT WA 171-C1
EVERETT WA 264-D3
MARINE VIEW DR S
KING CO WA 175-B7
MARINE VIEW DR SE
OCEAN SHORES WA 298-D5
N MARINGO DR
SPOKANE CO WA 350-B3
E MARINGO RD
SPOKANE CO WA 350-C4
MARION AV
CLATSOP CO WA 301-G4
GEARHART WA 301-G4
S MARION AV
BREMERTON WA 270-F11
MARION AV N
BREMERTON WA 270-F10

MARION RD
DISTRICT OF ABBOTSFORD BC 102-B1
MARION CO OR 133-C1
MARION CO OR 325-H14
MARION ST
ALBANY OR 326-D11
CENTRALIA WA 299-G2
SALEM OR 322-J12
SALEM OR 323-A13
SEATTLE WA 277-J6
SEATTLE WA 278-A6
MARION ST Rt#-22
SALEM OR 322-H12
MARION DRAIN RD
YAKIMA CO WA 120-A2
MARION ST BRDG Rt#-22
SALEM OR 322-H12
MARK RD
CLACKAMAS CO OR 199-C7
VALLEY CO ID 251-D5
N MARKET EXT
SPOKANE WA 349-E5
MARKET LN
UNION CO OR 130-A2
MARKET RD
SHERMAN CO OR 127-C3
E MARKET RD
OWYHEE CO ID 147-B1
MARKET ST
ANACORTES WA 259-H1
BONANZA OR 151-A2
CHEHALIS WA 299-D11
KIRKLAND WA 175-C1
KLAMATH CO OR 151-A2
KLICKITAT CO WA 120-A3
MALIN OR 151-A3
MARKET ST Rt#-27
LATAH WA 114-C3
E MARKET ST
ABERDEEN WA 178-B7
N MARKET ST
SEATTLE WA 273-H5
SPOKANE WA 349-E2
SPOKANE CO WA 347-E13
SPOKANE CO WA 349-E2
NE MARKET ST
JEFFERSON CO OR 208-C2
NW MARKET ST
SEATTLE WA 272-D4
SEATTLE WA 273-G4
S MARKET ST
TACOMA WA 293-H5
SW MARKET ST
PORTLAND OR 312-E7
PORTLAND OR 313-0
MARKET ST NE
SALEM OR 322-J11
SALEM OR 323-E11
MARKET ST NE Rt#-213
SALEM OR 323-D11
MARKSMAN ST SW
THURSTON CO WA 184-B2
MARKWORTH RD
WHATCOM CO WA 158-D3
MARLATT RD S
MARION CO OR 207-C2
MARMONT ST
COQUITLAM BC 157-A5
MARMOT RD
CLACKAMAS CO OR 201-A4
E MARQUAM ST
MARION CO OR 205-C3
MOUNT ANGEL OR 205-C3
W MARQUAM ST
MARION CO OR 205-B3
MOUNT ANGEL OR 205-B3
E MARROWSTONE RD
JEFFERSON CO WA 170-B1
MARSH CTO
WASCO CO OR 196-B5
MARSH RD
DESCHUTES CO OR 212-B7
YAKIMA CO WA 243-C6
S MARSH RD
SPOKANE CO WA 114-C2
SPOKANE CO WA 247-A6
SE MARSH RD
CLACKAMAS CO OR 200-D3
MARSHALL AV
MAPLE RIDGE BC 157-D5
SW MARSHALL AV
PENDLETON OR 129-B1
MARSHALL RD
CHENEY WA 246-A7
DISTRICT OF ABBOTSFORD BC 102-B1
DISTRICT OF MATSQUI BC 102-B1
LATAH CO ID 249-D2
SPOKANE CO WA 246-A7
NW MARSHALL ST
PORTLAND OR 312-D4
MARSING RD
CANYON CO ID 147-B1
MARSING-MURPHY RD Rt#-78
MARSING ID 147-B1
OWYHEE CO ID 147-B1
MARTHA BOARDMAN RD
STEVENS CO WA 114-A1
MARTHALER RD NE
MARION CO OR 204-D2
MARION CO OR 205-A2
MARTIN RD
CLARK CO WA 192-D1
FOREST GROVE OR 198-C1
JOSEPHINE CO OR 233-B4
MOUNT VERNON WA 260-F9
SHERMAN CO OR 127-C2
SKAGIT CO WA 260-F9
WASHINGTON CO OR 198-C1
W MARTIN RD
SPOKANE CO WA 114-B3
MARTIN ST
KLAMATH FALLS OR 338-E7
W MARTIN ST
ELMA WA 179-B7
MARTIN WY SE
LACEY WA 181-A6
LACEY WA 297-F5
OLYMPIA WA 297-C5
THURSTON CO WA 181-A6
THURSTON CO WA 297-F5

MARTIN CREEK RD
LANE CO OR 219-C1
NE MLK JR BLVD Rt#-99E
PORTLAND OR 309-G3
PORTLAND OR 313-G4
SE MLK JR BLVD Rt#-99E
PORTLAND OR 313-G7
PORTLAND OR 317-G1
MARTIN LUTHER KING JR WY
SEATTLE WA 278-D6
MARTIN LUTHER KING JR WY E
SEATTLE WA 278-D4
MARTIN LUTHER KING JR WY S
SEATTLE WA 278-D7
SEATTLE WA 282-D6
SEATTLE WA 283-E7
SEATTLE WA 287-E4
TUKWILA WA 287-E4
MLK JR WY S Rt#-900
KING WA 287-E6
KING WA 289-G1
KING CO WA 175-C5
SEATTLE WA 287-E6
TUKWILA WA 287-E6
TUKWILA WA 289-G1
MARTIN RANCH RD
CURRY CO OR 232-C4
MARTINSON RD
LATAH CO ID 249-D7
MARTLETT DR
BRITISH COLUMBIA 159-B5
MARVIN RD NE
LACEY WA 181-A5
THURSTON CO WA 181-A5
MARVIN RD NE Rt#-510
LACEY WA 181-A6
MARVIN RD SE
THURSTON CO WA 181-A7
MARVIN RD SE Rt#-510
LACEY WA 181-A6
THURSTON CO WA 181-A6
E MARVIN ST
PASCO WA 343-H7
MARX ST U.S.-95
IDAHO CO ID 131-C2
RIGGINS ID 131-C2
MARY GATES MEMORIAL DR
SEATTLE WA 274-E5
MARY HILL BYPS
PORT COQUITLAM BC 157-B5
MARY HILL RD
PORT COQUITLAM BC 157-A5
MARYLAND AV Rt#-42
MYRTLE POINT OR 140-B2
MARY M KNIGHT RD
MASON CO WA 179-A3
MARYS PEAK RD
BENTON CO OR 133-A1
MARYS RIVER RD
BENTON CO OR 133-A1
MASCHER RD NE
MARION CO OR 205-B5
MASCHKE RD
LEWIS CO WA 187-B5
MASHELL AV Rt#-161
EATONVILLE WA 118-B1
PIERCE CO WA 118-B1
W MASON AV
BUCKLEY WA 110-C3
BUCKLEY WA 182-D4
MASON DR
CROOK CO OR 213-D5
PRINEVILLE OR 213-D5
MASON RD
WASCO CO OR 127-B2
MASON ANDERSON RD
TILLAMOOK CO OR 191-B3
MASON BENSON RD
MASON CO WA 173-C7
MASON CO WA 180-C1
MASON CREEK RD
KITTITAS CO WA 240-C1
NE MASON CREEK RD
CLARK CO WA 192-D2
MASON LAKE DR W
MASON CO WA 173-C7
MASON CO WA 180-C1
MASON LAKE RD W
MASON CO WA 180-B1
SW MASONVILLE RD
YAMHILL CO OR 204-A1
E MASTERSON RD
KITTITAS CO WA 240-C2
W MASTERSON RD
KITTITAS CO WA 240-C2
MATEJECK RD
TILLAMOOK CO OR 197-B2
MATHENY RD N
MARION CO OR 204-D3
MATHENY RD NE
MARION CO OR 204-D3
MATHENY CREEK RD
COOS CO OR 220-D7
MATHER MEMORIAL PKWY Rt#-410
PIERCE CO WA 119-A1
MATHERS AV
DIST OF WEST VANCOUVER BC 254-A2
MATHIAS RD
CLACKAMAS CO OR 126-A3
MOLALLA OR 126-A3
MATHIAS RD E
PIERCE CO WA 182-A6
MATLOCK-BRADY RD
MASON CO WA 179-A4
MATNEY RD
KLAMATH CO OR 235-D6
MATNEY WY
KLAMATH CO OR 235-D6
MATSEN RD
KLICKITAT CO WA 120-A3
MATSON RD
LATAH CO ID 249-D2
MATTESON RD
YAMHILL CO OR 198-B3
MATTHIEU LN
MARION CO OR 199-A7

MATTOON RD
CLACKAMAS CO OR 200-B5
MATTSON RD
LEWIS CO WA 184-B5
MAUI AV
OAK HARBOR WA 167-C3
MAUPIN RD
DOUGLAS CO OR 141-A1
SKAGIT CO WA 168-A2
MAXFIELD CREEK RD
BENTON CO OR 133-B1
POLK CO OR 133-B1
POLK CO OR 207-A2
W MAXWELL AV
SPOKANE WA 348-G7
MAXWELL CRES
TOWNSHIP OF LANGLEY BC 157-C7
MAXWELL RD
COOS BAY OR 333-C4
EUGENE OR 329-E1
LANE CO OR 329-E1
NORTH BEND OR 333-C4
S MAXWELTON RD
ISLAND CO WA 171-A2
MAY AV
HOOD RIVER OR 195-D5
W MAY AV Rt#-21
ODESSA WA 113-B3
MAY DR
HOOD RIVER OR 195-C5
HOOD RIVER CO OR 195-C5
MAY RD
POLK CO OR 204-A5
S MAY RD
ADAMS CO WA 242-C7
E MAY ST Rt#-74
HEPPNER OR 128-C2
MAY ST NW
TRACYTON WA 270-G4
MAYFIELD RD NE
DOUGLAS CO WA 112-C1
MAYGER RD
COLUMBIA CO OR 117-B3
MAYS CREEK RD
JACKSON CO OR 230-A2
MAYTOWN RD SW
THURSTON CO WA 184-B2
MAYTOWN RD SW Rt#-121
THURSTON CO WA 184-C2
SE MAY VALLEY RD
KING CO WA 175-D5
KING CO WA 176-A5
MAZAMA RD
OKANOGAN CO WA 104-A2
MCADAMS CREEK RD
SISKIYOU CO CA 149-C3
S MCALISTER RD
ISLAND CITY OR 130-A2
UNION CO OR 130-A2
E MCANDREWS RD
JACKSON CO OR 336-C10
MEDFORD OR 336-E10
W MCANDREWS RD
JACKSON CO OR 336-B11
MEDFORD OR 336-B11
MCARDLE RD
DESCHUTES CO OR 217-D3
MCBEE RD
BENTON CO WA 120-C3
MCBETH RD
LANE CO OR 215-A3
LANE CO OR 329-D14
MCBRIDE BLVD
NEW WESTMINSTER BC 156-D5
MCBRIDE BLVD Rt#-99A
NEW WESTMINSTER BC 156-D5
MCBRIDE DR
DISTRICT OF SURREY BC 157-A5
MCBRIDE LN
VALLEY CO ID 251-C7
MCBRIDE RD
LATAH CO ID 249-D1
MALHEUR CO OR 147-A2
NW MCBRIDE CEM RD
YAMHILL CO OR 198-A5
MCBRYDE AV E
MONTESANO WA 178-D7
MCCABE RD
CLACKAMAS CO OR 200-D5
CROOK CO OR 213-C3
MCCAFFERY RD
CROOK CO OR 213-A6
MCCALEB RD
POLK CO OR 204-A7
MCCALL BLVD
NAVY YARD CITY WA 270-F13
MCCALLAN RD
CITY OF RICHMOND BC 156-B6
MCCALLUM RD
BRITISH COLUMBIA 102-B1
DISTRICT OF ABBOTSFORD BC 102-B1
DISTRICT OF KENT BC 94-C3
DISTRICT OF MATSQUI BC 102-B1
MCCANLIES RD
HARNEY CO OR 144-C1
MCCANN RD
LEWIS CO OR 123-B3
POLK CO OR 204-A3
MCCANN GRADE
NEZ PERCE CO ID 250-D5
MCCANSE RD
UNION CO OR 130-A3
MCCARVER ST
TACOMA WA 293-E2
MCCLAINE ST Rt#-213
MARION CO OR 205-C4
SILVERTON OR 205-C4
MCCLAIN TUTHILL RD
KLICKITAT CO WA 196-B5
S MCCLELLAN ST
SPOKANE WA 349-A10
MCCLENNY RD
FRANKLIN CO WA 121-B2
MCCLOSKEY CREEK RD
SKAMANIA CO WA 194-A6
MCCLURE RD
LEWIS CO WA 187-C4
MCCOIN RD
CROOK CO OR 213-B2

STREET
City State Page-Grid

MCCONIHE RD
GRANT CO WA 242-B2
SW MCCONNELL RD
CLACKAMAS CO OR 199-A5
MCCORKLE RD SE
THURSTON CO WA 184-D2
MCCORMICK LP
TILLAMOOK CO OR 197-C2
MCCORMICK HILL RD
WASHINGTON CO OR 198-D4
YAMHILL CO OR 198-D4
MCCOY RD
COLUMBIA CO OR 189-C6
POLK CO OR 204-B4
MCCRORY RD
COWLITZ CO WA 187-B5
MCCROSKEY RD
WHITMAN CO WA 114-C3
W MCCULLOCH RD
YAKIMA CO WA 243-B7
MCCULLOUGH CREEK RD
DOUGLAS CO OR 225-A6
MCCUNE RD
LEWIS CO WA 187-D2
MCDANIEL RD
CROOK CO OR 213-B5
MCDERMITT RD
MALHEUR CO OR 154-B2
MCDERMOTT RD
COLUMBIA CO OR 189-C7
S MCDERMOTT RD
ADA CO ID 147-C1
CANYON CO ID 147-C1
MCDONALD DR
CROOK CO OR 213-B6
MCDONALD RD
COLUMBIA CO OR 125-B1
SKAMANIA CO WA 193-D7
TILLAMOOK CO OR 191-B3
TILLAMOOK CO OR 191-B3
WALLA WALLA CO WA 121-C3
WALLA WALLA CO WA 345-A13
N MCDONALD RD
OPPORTUNITY WA 350-J7
S MCDONALD RD
OPPORTUNITY WA 350-J8
MCDONALD RDG
SKAMANIA CO WA 119-A3
SW MCDONALD ST
TIGARD OR 199-B3
MCDOUGALL RD
YAMHILL CO OR 198-C7
MCDOWELL CREEK DR
LINN CO OR 133-C2
LINN CO OR 134-A2
MCDUFF RD SE
THURSTON CO WA 184-D3
MCELLIGOTT RD
MORROW CO OR 128-B2
MCELROY RD
SNOHOMISH CO WA 168-D6
MCEWAN RD KPN
PIERCE CO WA 181-A2
MCEWAN PRAIRIE RD
MASON CO WA 180-A2
MCEWEN RD
MALHEUR CO OR 146-A1
NE MCFARLAND LN
JEFFERSON CO OR 208-C2
MCFARLAND RD
TANGENT OR 207-C6
W MCFARLANE RD
AIRWAY HEIGHTS WA 246-A4
SPOKANE CO WA 114-B2
SPOKANE CO WA 246-A4
SW MCFEE PL
WASHINGTON CO OR 198-C4
MCFEELY RD
WALLA WALLA CO WA 121-C2
MCGARIGLE RD
SEDRO-WOOLLEY WA 161-C5
SKAGIT CO WA 161-C5
MCGILCHRIST ST SE
SALEM OR 324-J2
SALEM OR 325-A2
MCGILL ST
VANCOUVER BC 255-D9
SE MCGILLIVRAY BLVD
CLARK CO WA 193-A7
VANCOUVER WA 307-J7
MCGINNIS LAKE RD
OKANOGAN CO WA 237-D1
MCGLAUGHLIN RD
LEWIS CO WA 187-C4
MCGONAGLE RD
YAKIMA CO WA 243-B5
MCGOWAN CREEK RD
LANE CO OR 210-C7
MCGOWEN RD
KLICKITAT CO WA 196-B4
MCGRADY RD
WHITMAN CO WA 114-C3
MCGRATH RD
DESCHUTES CO OR 217-D1
W MCGRAW ST
SEATTLE WA 276-C1
SEATTLE WA 277-G1
MCGREEVY RD
WHITMAN CO WA 249-B4
MCGREGOR RD
WHITMAN CO WA 122-A1
MCGUIRE RD
DISTRICT OF CHILLIWACK BC 94-C3
N MCGUIRE RD
KOOTENAI CO ID 353-D1
POST FALLS ID 353-E5
MCINTOSH RD
DOUGLAS CO WA 237-A2
HOOD RIVER CO OR 202-C2
WHITMAN CO WA 122-A1
MCINTOSH HILL RD
NEZ PERCE CO ID 250-D5
MCINTYRE SPRING RD
MALHEUR CO OR 147-A1
MCKAY AV
CITY OF N VANCOUVER BC 254-J4
DIST OF N VANCOUVER BC 254-J4
MCKAY DR
UMATILLA CO OR 129-B1
MCKAY RD
CROOK CO OR 213-D3
MARION CO OR 199-A7
PRINEVILLE OR 213-D4
WALLA WALLA CO WA 121-B3
MCKAY CREEK RD
CROOK CO OR 135-C2
CROOK CO OR 213-D2
MCKECHNIE RD
PITT MEADOWS BC 157-C5
MCKEE RD
COWLITZ CO WA 189-B1
SW MCKEE RD
YAMHILL CO OR 204-B2
MCKEE SCHOOL RD NE
MARION CO OR 205-B2
MCKENNA TANWAX Rt#-702
PIERCE CO WA 118-A1
MCKENNA-YELM HWY Rt#-507
PIERCE CO WA 118-A1
THURSTON CO WA 118-A1
MCKENZIE AV
DISTRICT OF SAANICH BC 256-G3
DISTRICT OF SAANICH BC 257-A3
MCKENZIE HWY Rt#-126
DESCHUTES CO OR 211-D5
DESCHUTES CO OR 212-A5
LANE CO OR 133-C3
LANE CO OR 134-B2
LANE CO OR 215-D2
LINN CO OR 134-B2
SPRINGFIELD OR 215-D2
MCKENZIE HWY Rt#-242
DESCHUTES CO OR 211-C4
LANE CO OR 134-C2
LANE CO OR 211-A6
LINN CO OR 211-A6
SISTERS OR 211-C4
MCKENZIE LN
SUMMERVILLE OR 130-A2
UNION CO OR 130-A2
MCKENZIE RD
CURRY CO OR 224-A5
WHITMAN CO WA 249-C1
MCKENZIE RD SW
THURSTON CO WA 180-B6
MCKENZIE-BEND HWY U.S.-20
BEND OR 332-F1
DESCHUTES CO OR 211-D5
DESCHUTES CO OR 212-A6
DESCHUTES CO OR 217-B1
DESCHUTES CO OR 332-F1
MCKENZIE CANYON RD
DESCHUTES CO OR 212-B4
MCKENZIE VIEW DR
LANE CO OR 215-C1
LANE CO OR 330-H1
LANE CO OR 331-A1
MCKERN-SCOTT RD
STEVENS CO WA 106-A3
MCKIBBIN RD
WASHINGTON CO OR 198-C1
MCKILLOP RD NE
MARION CO OR 205-D4
MCKIMMENS RD
TILLAMOOK CO OR 191-B4
MCKINLEY AV
PIERCE CO WA 181-D4
TACOMA WA 181-D4
E MCKINLEY AV
PIERCE WA 295-J7
TACOMA WA 295-J5
MCKINLEY AV W
KELLOGG ID 115-C2
SHOSHONE CO ID 115-C2
W MCKINLEY RD
SMELTERVILLE ID 115-C2
MCKINLEY ST
COLTON WA 250-A1
E MCKINLEY WY
TACOMA WA 295-J1
MCKINLEY SPRINGS RD
BENTON CO WA 120-B3
MCKINNEY RD
ADAMS CO WA 121-A1
MCKINNON CRES
TOWNSHIP OF LANGLEY BC 157-C6
MCKNIGHT RD
GRAYS HARBOR CO WA 179-C6
MCLAGEN RD
LINN CO OR 207-C7
MCLAIN-LIBBY DR
BARVIEW OR 220-C1
COOS CO OR 220-C1
COOS CO OR 333-A12
MCLAUGHLIN DR
JACKSON CO OR 336-H3
MCLEAN AV
PORT COQUITLAM BC 157-B5
MCLEAN RD
MOUNT VERNON WA 260-A12
SKAGIT CO WA 160-D7
SKAGIT CO WA 161-A7
SKAGIT CO WA 260-A12
UMATILLA CO OR 129-C1
MCLEOD RD
BELLINGHAM WA 258-B2
E MCLOUGHLIN BLVD
VANCOUVER WA 305-H4
VANCOUVER WA 306-A4
SE MCLOUGHLIN BLVD Rt#-99E
CLACKAMAS OR 321-J2
CLACKAMAS CO OR 199-D3
GLADSTONE OR 199-D3
MILWAUKIE OR 317-J5
MILWAUKIE OR 321-J2
OREGON CITY OR 199-D3
PORTLAND OR 317-J5
W MCLOUGHLIN BLVD
VANCOUVER WA 305-G4
MCLOUGHLIN BLVD E Rt#-99E
CLACKAMAS CO OR 199-D5
OREGON CITY OR 199-D5
E MCLOUGHLIN ST
VANCOUVER WA 305-G4
MCMANAMY RD
KITTITAS CO WA 241-A4
MCMANOMON RD
ADAMS CO WA 121-A1
ADAMS CO WA 242-C7
MCMILLAN RD
ADA CO ID 253-B2
W MCMILLAN RD
ADA CO ID 253-A2
W MCMINNVILLE BYPS Rt#-18
MCMINNVILLE OR 204-B1
YAMHILL CO OR 204-B1
MCMULLEN LN
LANE CO OR 210-A5
MCMULLIN CREEK RD
JOSEPHINE CO OR 233-C2
E MCMULLIN CREEK RD
JOSEPHINE CO OR 233-C3
MCMURRAY RD
TACOMA WA 182-A2
MCMURRAY ST
RICHLAND WA 340-F12
MCNABB CREEK RD
DOUGLAS CO OR 221-A7
MCNAIR DR
DIST OF N VANCOUVER BC 156-C2
NW MCNAMEE RD
MULTNOMAH CO OR 192-A6
MCNARY HWY I-82
UMATILLA OR 129-A1
UMATILLA CO OR 129-A1
MCNARY HWY U.S.-395
UMATILLA OR 129-A1
UMATILLA CO OR 129-A1
SW MCNAY RD
WASHINGTON CO OR 198-D3
MCNEALY WY
COOS CO OR 220-D6
MCNEIL RD
KITTITAS CO WA 241-A6
PITT MEADOWS BC 157-B4
MCNEIL CANYON RD NW
DOUGLAS CO WA 112-B1
DOUGLAS CO WA 236-D3
MCNEILLY RD
WHITMAN CO WA 122-B1
MCNULTY RD
LEWIS CO WA 187-D4
MCNUTT RD
GRAYS HARBOR CO WA 178-A2
MCPHILLIPS RD
TILLAMOOK CO OR 197-A7
MCQUISTON RD
KLAMATH CO OR 231-B2
MCRAE RD NE
SNOHOMISH CO WA 168-C6
MCREAVY RD
MASON CO WA 173-A7
MASON CO WA 180-A1
MCSWEEN RD
DISTRICT OF CHILLIWACK BC 94-C3
MCTAVISH RD
DIST OF NORTH SAANICH BC 159-B3
MCVAY HWY Rt#-99
LANE CO OR 330-G8
MCVEY AV
LAKE OSWEGO OR 321-F7
NE MCWILLIAMS RD
KITSAP CO WA 270-H3
KITSAP CO WA 271-A3
TRACYTON WA 270-H3
M DRUFFEL RD
WHITMAN CO WA 249-A7
E MEAD AV
FAIRVIEW-SUMACH WA 243-C7
YAKIMA WA 243-C7
W MEAD AV
SOUTH BROADWAY WA 243-B7
YAKIMA WA 243-B7
MEAD RD
COLUMBIA CO WA 122-A2
NE MEADOW AV
DOUGLAS CO OR 334-F4
ROSEBURG OR 334-F4
MEADOW LN
COOS CO OR 218-B6
MEADOW RD
LINN CO OR 207-B5
SNOHOMISH CO WA 171-C4
W MEADOWBROOK RD
YAKIMA CO WA 243-A7
MEADOW CREEK RD
BOUNDARY CO ID 107-B1
GARFIELD CO WA 122-B2
PEND OREILLE CO WA 106-B2
SKAMANIA CO WA 118-C3
SKAMANIA CO WA 194-C1
STEVENS CO WA 106-B1
MEADOW CREEK RD U.S.-95
IDAHO CO ID 123-B3
NW MEADOW LAKE RD
YAMHILL CO OR 125-B2
YAMHILL CO OR 198-A6
MEADOWLARK DR
JEFFERSON CO OR 212-C2
MEADOWS RD
JACKSON CO OR 230-C3
MEDA LOOP RD
TILLAMOOK CO OR 203-B1
MEDCO RD
JACKSON CO OR 336-C9
MEDFORD OR 336-C9
MEDICAL LAKE RD Rt#-902
MEDICAL LAKE WA 114-B2
SPOKANE CO WA 114-B2
S MEDICAL LK TYLER RD Rt#-902
MEDICAL LAKE WA 114-B2
MEDICAL SPRINGS HWY Rt#-203
BAKER CO OR 130-B3
UNION OR 130-B2
UNION CO OR 130-B2
E MEDICAL SPRINGS HWY Rt#-203
UNION OR 130-B2
MEDIMONT RD
KOOTENAI CO ID 248-C4
MEDLEYS ELKHEAD RD
DOUGLAS CO OR 219-B5
MEDOHILL RD
COOS CO OR 220-B4
MEEKER DR
COWLITZ CO WA 189-C4
N MEEKER DR
COWLITZ CO WA 189-C5
MEEKER RD
CROOK CO OR 213-B6
W MEEKER ST
KENT WA 175-B7
MEENACH DR
SPOKANE WA 348-F6
MEGAN BLVD
YAKIMA CO WA 243-C6
MEHL CREEK RD
DOUGLAS CO OR 141-A1
MEIER RD
LEWIS CO WA 187-D2
WASHINGTON CO OR 192-A6
MEISS LAKE
SISKIYOU CO CA 150-B3
MEISS LAKE SAMS NECK RD
SISKIYOU CO CA 150-B3
MEISSNER RD
COLUMBIA CO OR 189-A6
MELBA RD
CANYON CO ID 147-B1
MELBOURNE ST
WESTPORT WA 183-B2
WESTPORT WA 298-G14
MELLEN ST
CENTRALIA WA 299-D5
MELLEN ST Rt#-507
CENTRALIA WA 299-D5
MELMONT RD
CANYON CO ID 147-B1
MELODY LN
LANE CO OR 215-B5
MELOTT RD
YAMHILL CO OR 198-C4
MELQUA RD
DOUGLAS CO OR 221-A2
MELROSE RD
DOUGLAS CO OR 221-A4
DOUGLAS CO OR 334-A3
MELROSE ST
LAKE OSWEGO OR 320-A5
WALLA WALLA WA 345-C6
WALLA WALLA CO WA 345-F5
W MELVILLE RD
SPOKANE CO WA 246-A5
MELVILLE ST
VANCOUVER BC 254-F9
MELVILLE ST SE
THURSTON CO WA 184-C3
MELVIN RD
DOUGLAS CO WA 239-B1
MEMORIAL HWY Rt#-20
SKAGIT CO WA 160-D6
SKAGIT CO WA 161-A7
MEMORIAL HWY Rt#-536
MOUNT VERNON WA 260-A11
SKAGIT CO WA 161-A7
SKAGIT CO WA 260-A11
MEMORIAL PARK DR
COWLITZ CO WA 302-D7
LONGVIEW WA 302-D7
MENLO SOUTH FORK RD
PACIFIC CO WA 117-A1
MENZEL LAKE RD
SNOHOMISH CO WA 102-C3
MENZIE RD SE
KITSAP CO WA 174-C4
W MERCER PL
SEATTLE WA 277-G3
MERCER ST
SEATTLE WA 277-H3
SEATTLE WA 278-A3
W MERCER ST
SEATTLE WA 277-G3
E MERCER WY
MERCER ISLAND WA 175-C4
W MERCER WY
MERCER ISLAND WA 175-C3
MERCER ISLAND WA 283-J3
MERCER ISLAND WA 287-J2
MERCER LAKE RD
LANE CO OR 214-B2
MERCHANTS RD
CLALLAM CO WA 169-D1
N MERIDIAN
PUYALLUP WA 182-B3
N MERIDIAN Rt#-161
PUYALLUP WA 182-B3
N MERIDIAN Rt#-167
PUYALLUP WA 182-B3
S MERIDIAN
PUYALLUP WA 182-B4
S MERIDIAN Rt#-161
PUYALLUP WA 182-B4
MERIDIAN E Rt#-161
EDGEWOOD WA 182-B3
MILTON WA 182-B3
PIERCE CO WA 182-B6
PUYALLUP WA 182-B3
MERIDIAN AV E Rt#-161
EATONVILLE WA 118-B1
PIERCE CO WA 118-B1
PIERCE CO WA 182-B7
MERIDIAN AV N
SEATTLE WA 171-B7
SHORELINE WA 171-B7
MERIDIAN AV S
BOTHELL WA 171-C6
MERIDIAN RD
ADA CO ID 253-A1
ANMORE BC 157-A4
COQUITLAM BC 157-A4
LINN CO OR 133-C1
MARION CO OR 205-C4
MERIDIAN ID 253-A2
MOSES LAKE WA 242-C3
PORT MOODY BC 157-A4
SILVERTON OR 205-C4
NE MERIDIAN RD
CLACKAMAS CO OR 199-B7
S MERIDIAN RD
CLACKAMAS CO OR 205-C2
MERIDIAN RD NE
LACEY WA 181-A6
MERIDIAN RD NE
MARION CO OR 205-C3
MERIDIAN RD SE
THURSTON CO WA 181-A7
MERIDIAN ST
BELLINGHAM WA 258-C3
MERIDIAN ST Rt#-539
BELLINGHAM WA 258-C2
E MERLENE AV
SPOKANE CO WA 347-F4
MERLIN RD
JOSEPHINE CO OR 229-A4
JOSEPHINE CO OR 335-A1
MERLIN-GALICE RD
JOSEPHINE CO OR 149-A1
JOSEPHINE CO OR 229-A4
MERRILL RD
DESCHUTES CO OR 136-A3
S MERRILL RD
KLAMATH CO OR 150-C3
SISKIYOU CO CA 150-C3
MERRILL ST
WALLA WALLA WA 345-F7
MERRILL CREEK PKWY
EVERETT WA 267-H2
EVERETT WA 268-A2
MERRILL CREEK RD
COLUMBIA CO OR 189-C7
MERRIMAN RD
CENTRAL POINT OR 336-B7
JACKSON CO OR 336-B7
MEDFORD OR 336-B7
MERRITT LN
UNION CO OR 130-B1
MERRY CREEK RD
SHOSHONE CO ID 115-C3
MESA KAHLOTUS RD
FRANKLIN CO WA 121-B2
MESERVE RD
COLUMBIA CO WA 189-B4
NE MESFORD RD
POULSBO WA 170-C7
MESKILL RD
LEWIS CO WA 184-A7
MESSNER RD
COLUMBIA CO WA 122-A2
W METALINE AV
KENNEWICK WA 342-F9
METCHOSIN RD
CITY OF COLWOOD BC 159-B6
DISTRICT OF METCHOSIN BC 159-B7
DISTRICT OF METCHOSIN BC 165-B1
METGE AV
BENTON CO OR 207-B4
METHODIST DR
HOOD RIVER CO OR 195-C5
METHOW ST
CHELAN CO WA 238-D5
CHELAN CO WA 239-A5
S METHOW ST
WENATCHEE WA 239-A4
E METHOW VALLEY HWY Rt#-20
OKANOGAN CO WA 104-B3
TWISP WA 104-A3
METOLIUS BENCH RD
JEFFERSON CO OR 208-A5
METOLIUS RIVER RD
JEFFERSON CO OR 211-C1
METTMAN CREEK RD
COOS CO OR 218-C7
METZ HILL RD
DOUGLAS CO OR 219-A7
N MEYER RD
KOOTENAI CO ID 354-F2
S MEYER RD
KOOTENAI CO ID 247-D1
MEYERS ST
KETTLE FALLS WA 106-A2
MEYERS RIDGE RD
ASOTIN CO WA 122-C3
ASOTIN CO WA 250-A7
MIAMI RIVER RD
TILLAMOOK CO OR 191-B6
TILLAMOOK CO OR 191-C5
MICHELBOOK LN
MCMINNVILLE OR 198-A7
MICHIGAN AV
OROFINO ID 123-C2
E MICHIGAN AV
CLEARWATER CO ID 123-C2
OROFINO ID 123-C2
MICHIGAN ST U.S.-95
COUNCIL ID 139-C1
S MICHIGAN ST
SEATTLE WA 282-A7
MICHIGAN HILL RD SW
THURSTON CO WA 184-A4
MICK PARVIN RD
WHITMAN CO WA 249-A3
MIDDLE RD
KLICKITAT CO WA 128-A1
SE MIDDLE WY
VANCOUVER WA 306-D7
VANCOUVER WA 307-E7
MIDDLE CREEK RD
DOUGLAS CO OR 225-A5
MIDDLE CREEK ACCESS RD
COOS CO OR 140-C2
MIDDLE FORK RD
LEWIS CO WA 118-A2
LEWIS CO WA 187-D1
MIDDLEFORK RD
CLACKAMAS CO OR 126-A3
E MIDDLE FORK RD
ADAMS CO ID 139-C1
ADAMS CO ID 252-A3
MIDDLE FORK FOOTS CREEK RD
JACKSON CO OR 230-A7
MIDDLE FORK MILL CREEK RD
STEVENS CO WA 106-B2
MIDDLE RIDGE DR
LINN CO OR 210-D1
MIDDLE SATSOP RD
GRAYS HARBOR CO WA 179-A3
MIDDLETON RD
CANYON CO ID 147-B1
MIDDLE WAITSBURG RD
WALLA WALLA WA 345-C5
WALLA WALLA CO WA 121-C3
WALLA WALLA CO WA 122-A3
WALLA WALLA CO WA 345-C5
NW MIDLAND AV
GRANTS PASS OR 335-E7
MIDLAND BLVD
CANYON CO ID 147-B1
MIDLAND HWY
KLAMATH CO OR 235-C5
KLAMATH CO OR 338-E14
KLAMATH FALLS OR 235-C5
KLAMATH FALLS OR 338-E14
N MIDVALE PL
SEATTLE WA 273-J5
MIDVALE RD
SUNNYSIDE WA 120-B3
YAKIMA CO WA 120-B3
MIDWAY AV
JOSEPHINE CO OR 229-A6
MIDWAY BLVD
OAK HARBOR WA 167-C3
MIDWAY RD
CANYON CO ID 147-B1
LINN CO OR 207-D5
LINN CO OR 326-H13
WASHINGTON CO OR 198-D3
MIDWAY BEACH RD
PACIFIC CO WA 183-B4
E MIERAS RD
YAKIMA CO WA 243-D7
MIKE JOHNSON RD
WHITMAN CO WA 249-A1
MIKKALO RD
GILLIAM CO OR 128-A2
MILAN-ELK RD
SPOKANE CO WA 114-C1
S MILDRED ST
TACOMA WA 181-C2
E MILES AV
HAYDEN ID 245-A5
W MILES AV
HAYDEN ID 245-A5
MILES RD
STEVENS CO WA 106-A3
MILES BRIDGE RD
BAKER CO OR 130-B3
MILES CRESTON RD
LINCOLN CO WA 113-C1
MILEY RD
WILSONVILLE OR 199-B6
MILITARY RD
COWLITZ CO WA 187-B7
FEDERAL WAY WA 175-B7
LAKEWOOD WA 181-C4
N MILITARY RD
LEWIS CO WA 187-C3
S MILITARY RD
LEWIS CO WA 187-C4
MILITARY RD E
PIERCE CO WA 182-A5
MILITARY RD S
FEDERAL WAY WA 175-B7
FEDERAL WAY WA 182-B1
KENT WA 175-B7
KENT WA 290-D7
KING WA 286-C6
KING WA 288-D1
KING WA 290-D7
KING CO WA 175-B7
KING CO WA 182-B1
PIERCE CO WA 181-D5
SEATAC WA 288-E5
SEATAC WA 289-E6
SEATAC WA 290-D7
SEATAC WA 291-E3
TUKWILA WA 288-D1
MILITARY CROSSING RD
KLAMATH CO OR 142-C3
MILL AV S Rt#-900
RENTON WA 175-C5
MILL DR
KLICKITAT CO WA 196-D2
MILL RD
ASOTIN CO WA 122-C3
LATAH CO ID 249-D5
LEWIS CO WA 187-C2
NEZ PERCE CO ID 250-C4
WASHINGTON CO ID 139-B1
N MILL RD
FAIRWOOD WA 346-J7
FAIRWOOD WA 347-A6
SPOKANE CO WA 347-A6
MILL ST
CHENEY WA 246-A7
CLEARWATER CO ID 123-C1
ELK RIVER ID 123-C1
KELSO WA 303-C9
MAPLE RIDGE BC 157-D5
SPOKANE CO WA 246-A7
NE MILL ST
GRANTS PASS OR 335-G9
SE MILL ST
DALLAS OR 204-A6
GRANTS PASS OR 335-G9
SW MILL ST
SHERIDAN OR 125-B3
YAMHILL CO OR 125-B3
MILLARD RD
COLUMBIA CO OR 192-A2
MILL BAY RD
BRITISH COLUMBIA 159-B2
MILL CREEK BLVD
MILL CREEK WA 171-C4
MILL CREEK DR
JACKSON CO OR 226-C7
MILL CREEK RD
ADAMS CO ID 139-C1
AUMSVILLE OR 133-C1
COWLITZ CO WA 117-B3
CROOK CO OR 135-C2
JACKSON CO OR 234-C7
LINCOLN CO OR 206-C5
MARION CO OR 133-C1
MARION CO OR 325-H13
PACIFIC CO WA 117-A1
POLK CO OR 125-B3
TURNER OR 325-H13
UNION CO OR 130-B2

STREET / City State / Page-Grid

MILL CREEK RD
WALLA WALLA WA 122-A3
WALLA WALLA WA 345-H5
WALLA WALLA CO WA 122-A3
WALLA WALLA CO WA 345-H5
WASCO CO OR 127-A2
WASCO CO OR 196-C7
MILL CREEK RD SE
TURNER OR 325-H12
MILL CREEK LOOKOUT RD
WASCO CO OR 202-D2
MILL CREEK RIDGE RD
JACKSON CO OR 226-C5
SE MILLER AV
DALLAS OR 204-A6
POLK CO OR 204-A6
MILLER RD
CLACKAMAS CO OR 205-C1
CLALLAM CO WA 164-C6
KITTITAS CO WA 241-A5
MARION CO OR 199-A7
NEZ PERCE CO ID 250-D7
SNOHOMISH CO WA 168-B4
S MILLER RD
JEFFERSON CO WA 263-B6
MILLER RD NE
KITSAP CO WA 174-C1
MARION CO OR 205-B3
MILLER RD NW
KITSAP CO WA 174-C1
E MILLER ST
SEATTLE WA 278-B1
N MILLER ST
WENATCHEE WA 238-D4
N MILLER ST Rt#-285
WENATCHEE WA 238-D4
S MILLER ST
WENATCHEE WA 238-D4
MILLER BAY RD NE
KITSAP CO WA 170-C6
SUQUAMISH WA 170-C6
MILLER CANYON RD
HARNEY CO OR 144-C1
MILLER CEMETERY RD
LINN CO OR 133-C1
MILLER ISLAND RD
KLAMATH CO OR 235-B5
MILLERS CEMETERY RD
LINN CO OR 207-C3
MILLERS CREEK RD
POLK CO OR 207-A2
MILLICAN RD
CROOK CO OR 135-B3
CROOK CO OR 213-C7
LAKE CO OR 143-C1
W MILLIRON RD
LANE CO OR 210-A7
E MILLMAN RD
ISLAND CO WA 170-D1
E MILL PLAIN BLVD
VANCOUVER WA 305-H5
VANCOUVER WA 306-B5
VANCOUVER WA 307-F6
W MILL PLAIN BLVD
VANCOUVER WA 305-G4
SE MILL PLAIN RD
CLARK CO WA 193-A6
VANCOUVER WA 307-J6
MILL RIDGE RD
WASCO CO OR 202-D2
MILLS RD
DIST OF NORTH SAANICH BC 159-C2
TOWN OF SIDNEY BC 159-C2
MILLS CANYON RD
CHELAN CO WA 236-A7
MILLSTREAM RD
DISTRICT OF LANGFORD BC 159-B5
MILLSTREAM LAKE RD
BRITISH COLUMBIA 159-B5
MILLTOWN RD
SKAGIT CO WA 168-B2
MILTON WY
MILTON WA 182-B2
MILTON CEMETERY RD
MILTON-FREEWATER OR 121-C3
UMATILLA CO OR 121-C3
MILWAUKEE DR
COEUR D'ALENE ID 355-E10
N MILWAUKEE ST
BOISE ID 253-B2
MILWAUKEE WY
TACOMA WA 182-A2
SE MILWAUKIE AV
PORTLAND OR 317-H2
MILWAUKIE EXWY Rt#-224
CLACKAMAS CO OR 199-D3
MILWAUKIE OR 199-D3
MILWAUKIE OR 321-J2
MIMA ACRES RD SE
THURSTON CO WA 184-D3
MINALOOSA RD
BENEWAH CO ID 248-A7
MINARD RD W
KITSAP CO WA 174-A4
MINA SMITH RD
CLALLAM CO WA 169-B1
MINERAL RD
WASHINGTON CO ID 139-A1
MINERAL SPRINGS RD
SKAMANIA CO WA 194-C1
YAMHILL CO OR 198-B6
MINK RD
CANYON CO ID 147-B1
MINK RD NE
KING CO WA 171-D7
MINKLER RD
LEWIS CO WA 187-C3
NE MINNEHAHA ST
CLARK CO WA 192-D5
MINNESOTA AV
RAINIER WA 118-A1
MINOR RD
KELSO WA 303-E7
MINSON RD
CROOK CO OR 213-B6
SW MINTERBROOK RD
KITSAP CO WA 174-B6
MIRROR LN
DOUGLAS CO OR 221-A5

MISERY POINT LOOP RD NW
KITSAP CO WA 173-D1
MISSILE SITE RD
LINCOLN CO WA 114-A1
E MISSION AV
DISHMAN WA 350-C7
GREEN ACRES WA 351-A7
LIBERTY LAKE WA 352-C13
OPPORTUNITY WA 350-G6
OPPORTUNITY WA 351-A7
SPOKANE WA 349-D7
SPOKANE CO WA 349-J7
SPOKANE CO WA 350-A7
SPOKANE CO WA 351-A7
SPOKANE CO WA 352-G12
VERADALE WA 351-A7
W MISSION AV
SPOKANE WA 348-J7
SPOKANE WA 349-A7
MISSION RD
MARION CO OR 198-D7
SAINT PAUL OR 198-D7
MISSION ST
MCCALL ID 251-C5
N MISSION ST Rt#-285
WENATCHEE WA 238-D4
S MISSION ST
APPLEYARD WA 239-A5
WENATCHEE WA 239-A5
S MISSION ST Rt#-285
WENATCHEE WA 238-D4
WENATCHEE WA 239-A4
MISSION ST SE
SALEM OR 322-H14
MISSION ST SE Rt#-22
SALEM OR 322-J14
SALEM OR 323-A14
SALEM OR 325-B1
MISSION CREEK RD
CHELAN CO WA 238-C3
MISSOULA AV U.S.-2
LINCOLN CO MT 107-C2
TROY MT 107-C2
E MISSOULA AV U.S.-2
TROY MT 107-C2
MISSOURI AV
CANYON CO ID 147-B1
MIST DR Rt#-47
COLUMBIA CO OR 125-B1
VERNONIA OR 125-B1
MIST-CLATSKANIE HWY Rt#-47
CLATSKANIE OR 117-B3
COLUMBIA CO OR 117-B3
MISTLETOE RD
ASHLAND OR 337-H10
DALLAS OR 204-A7
MONMOUTH OR 204-A7
POLK CO OR 204-A7
MISTY CREEK RD
JACKSON CO OR 230-B1
MITCHELL RD SE
EAST PORT ORCHARD WA 174-B4
PORT ORCHARD WA 174-B4
PORT ORCHARD WA 270-J14
MITCHELL ST
KLAMATH FALLS OR 338-F8
N MITCHELL ST
ADA CO ID 253-B2
MITCHELL BUTTE RD
MALHEUR CO OR 139-A3
MALHEUR CO OR 146-C1
MIX RD
LATAH CO ID 249-C4
MIX ST NW
THURSTON CO WA 296-A3
MOCK RD
DESCHUTES CO OR 217-B1
MOCLIPS HWY
GRAYS HARBOR CO WA 108-C2
GRAYS HARBOR CO WA 109-A2
MOCTILEME RD Rt#-60
BENEWAH CO ID 115-A3
MODOC RD
JACKSON CO OR 230-C6
MODOC POINT RD
KLAMATH CO OR 231-C3
MODROW RD
COWLITZ CO WA 189-D5
MOE RD NE
DOUGLAS CO WA 104-C3
MOELLERING RD
LINCOLN CO WA 113-C2
MOERHLE RD
WHITMAN CO WA 250-A2
E MOFFAT RD
SPOKANE CO WA 246-D2
MOFFATT RD
CROOK CO OR 213-C6
SE MOFFET RD
CLARK CO WA 193-D7
MOHAWK BLVD
SPRINGFIELD OR 330-J6
SPRINGFIELD OR 331-A6
MOHAWK HILL RD
LANE CO OR 210-D7
MOHLER RD
LINCOLN CO WA 113-C2
LINCOLN CO WA 114-A2
MOHLER CHEESE FACTRY RD
TILLAMOOK CO OR 191-B4
MOHORIC RD
LEWIS CO WA 187-B1
MOJONNIER RD
WALLA WALLA CO WA 344-D13
MOLALLA AV
CLACKAMAS CO OR 126-A3
CLACKAMAS CO OR 199-D5
MOLALLA OR 126-A3
OREGON CITY OR 199-D5
MOLITOR HILL RD
LANE CO OR 215-C7
MOLSON RD
OKANOGAN CO WA 105-A1
N MOLTER RD
LIBERTY LAKE WA 352-D14
S MOLTER RD
LIBERTY LAKE WA 247-B4
SPOKANE CO WA 247-B4

MONAHAN RD
COWLITZ CO WA 187-B7
MONCTON ST
CITY OF RICHMOND BC 156-B7
MONITOR-MCKEE RD NE
MARION CO OR 205-B2
MONKLAND RD
SHERMAN CO OR 127-C2
N MONMOUTH AV
MONMOUTH OR 204-B7
MONMOUTH CTO
DALLAS OR 204-A6
POLK CO OR 204-A6
MONMOUTH HWY
POLK CO OR 125-B3
POLK CO OR 133-B1
POLK CO OR 204-A7
POLK CO OR 207-A1
MONMOUTH ST Rt#-51
INDEPENDENCE OR 204-B7
MONMOUTH-INDPNDNCE HWY Rt#-51
INDEPENDENCE OR 204-B7
MONMOUTH OR 204-B7
POLK CO OR 204-B7
MONNIER RD NE
MARION CO OR 205-C1
MONROE AV
CORVALLIS OR 327-G10
LA GRANDE OR 130-A2
NORTH BEND OR 333-G4
SW MONROE LN
JEFFERSON CO OR 212-C1
MONROE RD
LEWIS CO WA 187-C2
N MONROE RD
SPOKANE CO WA 114-B1
W MONROE RD
DEER PARK WA 114-B1
SPOKANE CO WA 114-B1
MONROE ST
PORT TOWNSEND WA 263-H3
E MONROE ST Rt#-78
BURNS OR 145-B1
HARNEY CO OR 145-B1
N MONROE ST
SPOKANE WA 348-H8
TOWN AND COUNTRY WA 346-H14
TOWN AND COUNTRY WA 348-H8
S MONROE ST
SPOKANE WA 348-H9
W MONROE ST U.S.-20
BURNS OR 145-B1
MONROE CREEK RD
WASHINGTON CO ID 139-A2
N MONROE LANDING RD
ISLAND CO WA 167-B4
MONSE SOUTH RD
OKANOGAN CO WA 104-C3
MONSOR RD
LINCOLN CO WA 113-B2
MONSOR RD Rt#-21
LINCOLN CO WA 113-B2
MONTAGUE RD
MONTAGUE CA 150-A3
SISKIYOU CO CA 150-A3
MONTAGUE RD Rt#-3
YREKA CA 149-C3
MONTAGUE GRENADA RD
MONTAGUE CA 150-A3
SISKIYOU CO CA 150-A3
MONTAGUE-YREKA RD Rt#-3
MONTAGUE CA 150-A3
SISKIYOU CO CA 149-C3
SISKIYOU CO CA 150-A3
YREKA CA 149-C3
MONTE CRISTO RD
SNOHOMISH CO WA 111-A1
S MONTE CRISTO RD
CLACKAMAS CO OR 205-D3
SW MONTEE DR
PENDLETON OR 129-B1
UMATILLA CO OR 129-B1
MONTERAY AV
DIST OF N VANCOUVER BC 255-B1
MONTESANO ST
GRAYS HARBOR CO WA 183-B2
WESTPORT WA 183-B2
WESTPORT WA 298-H14
MONTESANO ST Rt#-105
WESTPORT WA 298-H11
MONTESANO-ABERDEEN RD
GRAYS HARBOR CO WA 178-D7
E MONTGOMERY AV
GREEN ACRES WA 351-F5
MONTGOMERY RD
DESCHUTES CO OR 136-A3
DESCHUTES CO OR 144-A1
JEFFERSON CO OR 135-A1
MONTGOMERY RIDGE RD
ASOTIN CO WA 123-A3
MONTI DR
LINCOLN CO OR 203-B3
MONTICELLO DR
ISLAND CO WA 167-D5
MONTLAKE BLVD NE Rt#-513
SEATTLE WA 274-D6
SEATTLE WA 278-D1
MONTLAKE PL E
SEATTLE WA 278-D1
MONTMORENCE DR
LANE CO OR 210-A7
MONTOUR RD
GEM CO ID 139-C3
MONTREAL ST
CITY OF VICTORIA BC 256-F9
MONTROSE ST
DISTRICT OF BURNABY BC 255-G9
MONTROYAL BLVD
DIST OF N VANCOUVER BC 156-B2
DIST OF N VANCOUVER BC 255-A1
MONUMENT DR
JOSEPHINE CO OR 229-B3
JOSEPHINE CO OR 335-B1
MONUMENT RD
GRANT CO WA 112-B3
GRANT CO OR 136-C1
MONUMENT RD SW
KING CO WA 174-D6

MONUMENT TO COUNTY LINE
GRANT CO OR 128-C3
GRANT CO OR 136-C1
MONUMNT TO COURTRCK RD
GRANT CO OR 136-C1
GRANT CO OR 137-A1
MOODY RD
GRAYS HARBOR CO WA 177-D2
MOODY ST
PORT MOODY BC 157-A4
MOON RD SW
THURSTON CO WA 184-A3
MOON CREEK RD
TILLAMOOK CO OR 197-D5
MOONEY MOUNTAIN RD
JOSEPHINE CO OR 233-C1
MOON HILL RD
LEWIS CO WA 187-A1
MOONSHINE PARK RD
LINCOLN CO OR 206-D1
MOON VALLEY RD
KING CO WA 176-D4
MOORE LN
SHERMAN CO OR 127-C2
MOORE RD
GRAYS HARBOR CO WA 179-A7
SKAGIT CO WA 168-A1
NE MOORE RD
CLARK CO WA 192-D2
MOORE ST Rt#-9
SEDRO-WOOLLEY WA 161-C5
MOOREA DR
DOUGLAS CO OR 221-B3
MOOREHOUSE RD
UMATILLA CO OR 129-A1
MOORES HOLLOW RD
MALHEUR CO OR 139-A2
NW MOORES VALLEY RD
YAMHILL OR 198-A5
YAMHILL CO OR 198-A5
MORA RD
CLALLAM CO WA 169-A2
MORA RD Rt#-110
CLALLAM CO WA 169-B2
N MORAIN ST
KENNEWICK WA 342-H10
S MORAIN ST
BENTON CO WA 342-H11
KENNEWICK WA 342-H11
MORAY BRDG
CITY OF RICHMOND BC 156-B6
MORCOM RD
MALHEUR CO OR 146-C2
MOREHEAD RD
DEL NORTE CO CA 148-B3
MORELAND AV
MALDEN WA 114-B3
MORELL LN
VALLEY CO ID 251-D6
MORFORD RD
SKAGIT CO WA 161-C6
MORGAN AV
MALHEUR CO OR 139-A3
MORGAN DR
BIRCH BAY WA 158-B4
LINN CO OR 210-C1
MORGAN LN
LANE CO OR 210-A6
NE MORGAN LN
GRANTS PASS OR 335-F6
NW MORGAN LN
GRANTS PASS OR 335-E6
MORGAN RD
CLACKAMAS CO OR 200-C7
MORROW CO OR 128-B2
MULTNOMAH CO OR 192-A5
E MORGAN RD
SPOKANE CO WA 246-D2
MORGAN ST U.S.-2
DAVENPORT WA 114-A2
LINCOLN CO WA 114-A2
SW MORGAN ST
SEATTLE WA 280-E7
SEATTLE WA 281-E7
MORGAN LAKE RD
ADAMS CO WA 242-D7
MORGANSON RD
WASCO CO OR 196-A6
MORIARTY RD
CLALLAM CO WA 169-B2
MORMON BASIN RD
MALHEUR CO OR 138-B2
MORMON BASIN CUTOFF RD
MALHEUR CO OR 138-B2
MORNING STAR RD
LINN CO OR 207-D3
N MORNING-STAR RD
LANE CO OR 215-D4
MORRELLI DR
YAMHILL CO OR 198-B5
MORRILL RD
DESCHUTES CO OR 212-D5
MORRIS RD
ISLAND CO WA 167-C4
KLICKITAT CO WA 196-D4
POLK CO OR 204-A5
MORRIS ST
LA CONNER WA 167-D1
MORRISON RD
COOS CO OR 220-B6
SE MORRISON ST
PORTLAND OR 313-G6
MORRIS VALLEY RD
BRITISH COLUMBIA 94-C3
MORROW RD
MEDFORD OR 336-D9
POLK CO OR 204-B6
MORSE RD N
COLUMBIA CO OR 192-A2
MORSE RD S
COLUMBIA CO OR 192-A2
MORSE ST
COWLITZ CO WA 187-B5
MORSE-MERRIMAN RD SE
OLYMPIA WA 297-C9
MORTON RD
LEWIS CO WA 187-C3
MORTON RD Rt#-7
LEWIS CO WA 118-B2
MORTON WA 118-B2

MORTON ST Rt#-34
LEBANON OR 133-C1
N MORTON ST
COLFAX WA 122-C1
MORTON-BEAR CANYON RD Rt#-508
LEWIS CO WA 118-B2
MORTON WA 118-B2
MOSBY CREEK RD
COTTAGE GROVE OR 215-B7
LANE CO OR 141-C1
LANE CO OR 215-B7
MOSCOW RD Rt#-27
PALOUSE WA 249-B1
MOSCOW MOUNTAIN RD
LATAH CO ID 249-D4
MOSCROP ST
DISTRICT OF BURNABY BC 156-C5
MOSE RD
SNOHOMISH CO WA 168-D4
MOSELEY RD
DEL NORTE CO CA 148-B3
MOSER RD
NEZ PERCE CO ID 250-B2
MOSES RD
OKANOGAN CO WA 105-B3
MOSES COULEE RD SE
DOUGLAS CO WA 112-C2
MOSES CREEK LN
UNION CO OR 130-A1
SE MOSHER AV
ROSEBURG OR 334-F8
MOSIER RD
CLACKAMAS CO OR 200-A6
COLUMBIA CO OR 189-A4
SKAGIT CO WA 161-C5
MOSIER CREEK RD
WASCO CO OR 196-A6
MOSIER-THE DALLES HWY U.S.-30
MOSIER OR 196-A5
THE DALLES OR 196-A5
WASCO CO OR 196-A5
MOSQUITO CREEK RD
COWLITZ CO WA 187-A7
MOSQUITO LAKE RD
WHATCOM CO WA 102-B1
WHATCOM CO WA 161-D1
MOSS ST
CITY OF VICTORIA BC 256-J11
MOSS CREEK RD
TILLAMOOK CO OR 191-B7
MOSS HILL RD
CLACKAMAS CO OR 200-C6
MOSSYROCK RD W
LEWIS CO WA 118-A2
MOTTMAN RD SW
OLYMPIA WA 296-D7
TUMWATER WA 296-D7
MOUNT ADAMS RD
KLICKITAT CO WA 119-A3
MOUNT ADAMS ST
HARRAH WA 119-C2
YAKIMA CO WA 119-C2
MOUNT ADAMS RECREATION AREA RD
KLICKITAT CO WA 119-A3
YAKIMA CO WA 119-A3
N MOUNTAIN AV
ASHLAND OR 337-E6
JACKSON CO OR 337-E6
S MOUNTAIN AV
ASHLAND OR 337-E8
MOUNTAIN BLVD U.S.-395
MOUNT VERNON OR 137-A2
MOUNTAIN HWY
DIST OF N VANCOUVER BC 255-E2
MOUNTAIN HWY E Rt#-7
PIERCE CO WA 118-B1
PIERCE CO WA 181-D6
PIERCE CO WA 182-A6
MOUNTAIN HWY E Rt#-706
PIERCE CO WA 118-B1
PIERCE CO WA 185-A5
MOUNTAIN RD
ASOTIN CO WA 122-C3
GARFIELD CO WA 122-B2
KLAMATH CO OR 231-C1
SW MOUNTAIN RD
CLACKAMAS CO OR 199-C5
MOUNTAIN HOME DR
LINN CO OR 210-D2
MOUNTAIN HOME RD
CHELAN CO WA 238-A1
WASHINGTON CO OR 198-D4
YAMHILL CO OR 198-D5
MOUNTAIN LOOP HWY
GRANITE FALLS WA 102-C3
SNOHOMISH CO WA 102-C3
SNOHOMISH CO WA 103-A3
SNOHOMISH CO WA 111-A1
MOUNTAIN MEADOWS RD
PIERCE CO WA 185-A2
MOUNTAIN MEADOWS RD Rt#-165
PIERCE CO WA 118-C1
PIERCE CO WA 185-A2
MOUNTAIN TOP RD
YAMHILL CO OR 198-D4
MOUNTAIN VIEW AV
ISLAND CO WA 167-D6
ISLAND CO WA 168-A6
E MOUNTAIN VIEW AV
ELLENSBURG WA 241-B6
KITTITAS CO WA 241-B6
W MOUNTAIN VIEW AV
ELLENSBURG WA 241-B6
MOUNTAIN VIEW DR
BENTON CO OR 207-A4
BENTON CO OR 327-H1
BOISE ID 253-C2
BONNER CO ID 244-A2
COLUMBIA CO OR 192-A3
GARDEN CITY ID 253-C2
MOUNTAINVIEW DR
NEWBERG OR 198-D5
YAMHILL CO OR 198-D5
SW MOUNTAIN VIEW DR
JEFFERSON CO OR 208-A6

MOUNTAIN VIEW DR E
KITSAP CO WA 271-D12
MOUNTAIN VIEW DR S
SALEM OR 324-G2
MOUNTAIN VIEW RD
CLACKAMAS CO OR 201-C5
COWLITZ CO WA 189-D5
DESCHUTES CO OR 212-A4
FERNDALE WA 158-B6
SKAGIT CO WA 260-J14
WHATCOM CO WA 158-B6
N MOUNTAIN VIEW RD
LATAH CO ID 249-D4
MOUNT ANGEL HWY NE
MARION CO OR 205-B4
MOUNT ANGELES RD
CLALLAM CO WA 261-G8
PORT ANGELES WA 261-G8
MOUNT ANGEL-GERVAIS RD NE
MARION CO OR 205-B3
MOUNT ANGEL-SCOTTS MILLS RD NE
MARION CO OR 205-C3
MARION CO OR 205-D4
MOUNT ASHLAND SKI RD
JACKSON CO OR 234-D6
MOUNT BAKER Rt#-542
WHATCOM CO WA 103-A1
MOUNT BAKER HWY Rt#-542
WHATCOM CO WA 102-B1
MOUNT BRYNION RD
COWLITZ CO WA 303-H5
N MOUNT CARROL ST
DALTON GARDENS ID 355-F2
MOUNT GLEN RD
UNION CO OR 130-A2
MOUNT HOOD AV Rt#-214
MARION CO OR 205-B1
WOODBURN OR 205-B1
MOUNT HOOD HWY Rt#-35
CLACKAMAS CO OR 202-C5
HOOD RIVER CO OR 195-C7
HOOD RIVER CO OR 202-C1
HOOD RIVER CO OR 202-C5
MOUNT HOOD HWY U.S.-26
CLACKAMAS CO OR 200-C3
CLACKAMAS CO OR 201-B4
CLACKAMAS CO OR 202-A6
GRESHAM OR 200-C3
MULTNOMAH CO OR 200-C3
SANDY OR 200-C3
SE MOUNT HOOD HWY U.S.-26
GRESHAM OR 200-A2
MULTNOMAH CO OR 200-A2
PORTLAND OR 200-A2
S MOUNT HOPE RD
CLACKAMAS CO OR 205-D2
MOUNT HOREB RD SE
MARION CO OR 134-A1
MOUNT JUPITER RD
JEFFERSON CO WA 173-C1
MOUNT LEHMAN RD
DISTRICT OF MATSQUI BC 102-B1
MOUNT MATHESON RD
BRITISH COLUMBIA 165-A1
DISTRICT OF METCHOSIN BC 165-A1
MOUNT NEWTON CROSS RD
DIST OF CENTRAL SAANICH BC 159-B3
MOUNT NORWAY DR
CLARK CO WA 193-C6
MOUNT OLYMPUS AV
OCEAN SHORES WA 298-E4
MOUNT OLYMPUS AV SE
OCEAN SHORES WA 298-D2
MOUNT PLEASANT RD
COWLITZ CO WA 189-D4
SKAMANIA CO WA 193-D7
MOUNT REUBEN RD
DOUGLAS CO OR 225-A7
NW MOUNT RICHMOND RD
YAMHILL CO OR 198-A4
SE MOUNT SCOTT BLVD
CLACKAMAS OR 319-J7
CLACKAMAS CO OR 200-A3
HAPPY VALLEY OR 200-A3
MULTNOMAH OR 319-H6
PORTLAND OR 200-A3
PORTLAND OR 319-H6
PORTLAND OR 319-J7
MOUNT SEYMOUR PKWY
DIST OF N VANCOUVER BC 156-D3
DIST OF N VANCOUVER BC 255-H6
MOUNT SEYMOUR RD
DIST OF N VANCOUVER BC 156-D3
MOUNT SHASTA DR
VANCOUVER WA 307-G7
MOUNT SOLO RD
COWLITZ CO WA 302-B5
WEST LONGVIEW WA 302-B5
MOUNT SOLO RD Rt#-432
COWLITZ CO WA 302-C6
MOUNT SPOKANE RD
SPOKANE CO WA 246-D1
E MOUNT SPOKANE PK DR Rt#-206
SPOKANE CO WA 114-C1
SPOKANE CO WA 246-D1
SPOKANE CO WA 247-A1
SPOKANE CO WA 347-H5
N MOUNT SPOKANE PK DR Rt#-206
SPOKANE CO WA 114-C1
MOUNT STELLA RD
JACKSON CO OR 226-D3
MOUNT TOM DR
LINN CO OR 210-B6
MOUNT TOM RD
LANE CO OR 210-C7
MOUNT VERNON RD
LANE CO OR 331-H9
SPRINGFIELD OR 331-H9
MOUNT VERNON RD S
SKAGIT CO WA 168-B1
MOUNT VRNON-BIG LAKE RD
MOUNT VERNON WA 260-H12
SKAGIT CO WA 161-C7
SKAGIT CO WA 260-H12

STREET / City State Page-Grid

MOUNT VIEW RD
SPOKANE CO WA 247-A1
NW MOUNT WASHINGTON DR
BEND OR 332-B3
MOWICH RD
DOUGLAS CO OR 223-A4
MOWICH SECTION Rt#-165
CARBONADO WA 182-D6
PIERCE CO WA 110-C3
PIERCE CO WA 118-C1
PIERCE CO WA 182-D6
MOWREY RD
CHELAN CO WA 236-B3
MOX-CHEHALIS RD
GRAYS HARBOR CO WA 117-B1
GRAYS HARBOR CO WA 179-C7
E MOXEE AV
MOXEE CITY WA 243-D7
YAKIMA CO WA 243-D7
MOYIE RIVER RD
BOUNDARY CO ID 107-B1
MUD BAY HWY SW
THURSTON CO WA 180-B6
THURSTON CO WA 296-A5
MUD BAY RD
SAN JUAN CO WA 160-A7
MUD CREEK RD
ADAMS CO ID 251-A3
MUDDY RD
WASCO CO OR 135-C1
MUDDY CREEK RD
BAKER CO OR 130-A3
SW MUDDY VALLEY RD
YAMHILL CO OR 204-A2
MUD FLAT RD
MALHEUR CO OR 146-C2
OWYHEE CO ID 147-C3
OWYHEE CO ID 155-B1
WHITMAN CO WA 122-B1
MUD LAKE RD
DESCHUTES CO OR 216-A4
SKAGIT CO WA 161-C6
MUD SPRING RD
MALHEUR CO OR 154-A2
MUD SPRINGS RD NE
DOUGLAS CO WA 112-C1
MUD SPRINGS RD NW
DOUGLAS CO WA 112-B1
MUEKE RD
CLACKAMAS CO OR 199-B6
MUELLER RD
UMATILLA CO OR 121-C3
MUFFORD AV
LANGLEY BC 157-C7
TOWNSHIP OF LANGLEY BC 157-C7
MUIR CREEK RD
DOUGLAS CO OR 223-A7
DOUGLAS CO OR 227-A1
MUKILTEO BLVD
EVERETT WA 171-B2
EVERETT WA 264-A7
MUKILTEO WA 171-B2
MUKILTEO BLVD SE
EVERETT WA 264-C6
MUKILTEO BLVD SW
EVERETT WA 264-B7
MUKILTEO-CLINTON FERRY
ISLAND CO WA 171-B2
LANGLEY WA 171-A2
MUKILTEO WA 171-B2
SNOHOMISH CO WA 171-B2
MUKILTEO SPEEDWAY Rt#-525
MUKILTEO WA 171-B4
MUKILTEO WA 266-D3
MUKILTEO WA 267-E6
SNOHOMISH WA 267-E6
SNOHOMISH CO WA 171-B4
MULEDEER RD
DOUGLAS CO WA 239-B1
MULE SPRING RD
HARNEY CO OR 144-C3
MULFORD RD
LEWIS CO WA 187-C4
NW MULHOLLAND DR
ROSEBURG OR 334-E4
MULINO RD
CLACKAMAS CO OR 199-C7
S MULINO RD
CLACKAMAS CO OR 199-C6
MULKEY RD
WHITMAN CO WA 114-B3
E MULLAN AV
KOOTENAI CO ID 353-H6
KOOTENAI CO ID 354-B6
OSBURN ID 115-C2
POST FALLS ID 353-H6
POST FALLS ID 354-B6
W MULLAN AV
KOOTENAI CO ID 354-H6
POST FALLS ID 353-G6
MULLAN RD
ADAMS CO WA 122-A1
N MULLAN RD
DISHMAN WA 350-D8
SPOKANE CO WA 350-D8
MULLEN RD SE
LACEY WA 297-H10
THURSTON CO WA 181-A7
THURSTON CO WA 297-J11
SE MULLENIX RD
KITSAP CO WA 174-C5
MULLER DR
LINN CO OR 207-D5
S MULLINIX RD
SPOKANE CO WA 114-B2
SW MULTNOMAH BLVD
PORTLAND OR 199-B2
PORTLAND OR 199-B2
PORTLAND OR 316-A6
MULTNOMAH DR
HOOD RIVER CO OR 195-C5
NE MULTNOMAH ST
PORTLAND OR 313-H4
PORTLAND OR 314-A4
MULTNOMAH BASIN RD
MULTNOMAH CO OR 201-A1
MUNCH RD
CLARK CO WA 193-A1
MUNDUN CANYON RD
CHELAN CO WA 238-A2
MUNDY ST
COQUITLAM BC 157-A5
MUNDY LOSS RD
PIERCE CO WA 182-D4
MUNN RD
BRITISH COLUMBIA 159-B5
DISTRICT OF SAANICH BC 256-A1
MUNSEL LAKE RD
FLORENCE OR 214-B2
LANE CO OR 214-B2
MUNSON DR SW
THURSTON CO WA 180-B6
MUNSON CREEK RD
TILLAMOOK CO OR 197-C4
MURCHIE RD
TOWNSHIP OF LANGLEY BC 158-B2
MURDER CREEK DR
LINN CO OR 326-H3
MURPHY DR NW
PIERCE CO WA 181-C1
MURPHY RD
BEND OR 332-E12
DESCHUTES CO OR 332-E12
DOUGLAS CO OR 225-C7
FRANKLIN CO WA 121-B2
LINCOLN CO OR 203-D4
S MURPHY RD
SPOKANE CO WA 246-A6
MURPHY CREEK RD
JOSEPHINE CO OR 149-A2
MURPHY-GRANDVIEW RD Rt#-78
OWYHEE CO ID 147-C2
MURPHY GULCH RD
JACKSON CO OR 230-A4
NW MURRAY BLVD
WASHINGTON CO OR 199-B1
SW MURRAY BLVD
BEAVERTON OR 199-A2
WASHINGTON CO OR 199-A2
MURRAY RD SW
LAKEWOOD WA 181-C5
PIERCE CO WA 181-C5
MURRAY ST
PORT MOODY BC 157-A4
MUSTANG RESERVOIR RD
MALHEUR CO OR 146-C3
MALHEUR CO OR 154-C1
MUTCH CREEK RD
BENEWAH CO ID 248-C7
S MUTINY BAY RD
AULT FIELD WA 170-C1
MYERS RD
POLK CO OR 204-A5
TOPPENISH WA 120-A2
YAKIMA CO WA 120-A2
MYERS RD E
BONNEY LAKE WA 182-C4
MYERS WY S
KING WA 285-J3
KING WA 286-A4
SEATTLE WA 285-J3
SEATTLE WA 286-A4
MYERS CREEK RD
CURRY CO OR 232-B1
MYRA RD
COLLEGE PLACE WA 344-G9
WALLA WALLA WA 344-G9
WALLA WALLA CO WA 344-G9
MYRNA LN
JOSEPHINE CO OR 233-A4
S MYRTLE PL
SEATTLE WA 286-D1
E MYRTLE ST U.S.-20
BOISE ID 253-C3
S MYRTLE ST
SEATTLE WA 286-D1
W MYRTLE ST U.S.-20
BOISE ID 253-C3
MYRTLE CREEK RD
COOS CO OR 140-C3
N MYRTLE CREEK RD
DOUGLAS CO OR 141-B2
DOUGLAS CO OR 221-D7
DOUGLAS CO OR 225-D1
S MYRTLE CREEK RD
DOUGLAS CO OR 225-D1
MYRTLE PARK RD
HARNEY CO OR 137-A3
MYRTLE POINT-COOPER BRIDGE RD
COOS CO OR 140-B2
MYRTLE POINT OR 140-B2
MYRTLE POINT-LAMPA RD
COOS CO OR 140-B2
COOS CO OR 220-C6
MYRTLE POINT OR 140-B2
MYRTLE POINT-SITKUM RD
COOS CO OR 140-C2

N

N ST
GRANTS PASS OR 335-G10
JOSEPHINE CO OR 335-H10
SE N ST
GRANTS PASS OR 335-G10
NACHES AV
TIETON WA 119-C1
E NACHES AV Rt#-823
SELAH WA 243-B5
S NACHES AV
YAKIMA WA 243-C6
S NACHES RD
NACHES WA 119-C1
YAKIMA CO WA 119-C1
YAKIMA CO WA 243-A5
S NACHES WY
YAKIMA CO WA 119-C1
W NACHES WY
YAKIMA CO WA 119-C1
NACHES HEIGHTS RD
YAKIMA CO WA 243-A5
NACHES-TIETON RD
TIETON WA 119-C1
YAKIMA CO WA 119-C1
NACHES WENAS RD
YAKIMA CO WA 243-A4
NAGLER RD
YAKIMA CO WA 243-B5
NAHAHUM CANYON RD
CHELAN CO WA 238-C2
NAITO PKWY
PORTLAND OR 312-E3
PORTLAND OR 313-F5
NW NAITO PKWY
PORTLAND OR 312-E4
PORTLAND OR 313-F4
SW NAITO PKWY
PORTLAND OR 313-F6
PORTLAND OR 317-F1
NAMPA BLVD Rt#-55
NAMPA ID 147-B1
NANAIMO ST
VANCOUVER BC 156-C5
VANCOUVER BC 255-C12
NANAIMO-HRSSHOE FERRY
BRITISH COLUMBIA 93-A3
NANAIMO LAKES RD
NANAIMO BC 93-A3
NANAIMO-TSAWASN FERRY
BRITISH COLUMBIA 93-A3
BRITISH COLUMBIA 101-B1
NANAIMO BC 93-A3
NANCY GREENE WY
DIST OF N VANCOUVER BC 156-B2
NANEUM RD
KITTITAS CO WA 241-C4
NANEUM RIDGE RD
KITTITAS CO WA 241-D1
NAPOLEON-BARSTOW RD
STEVENS CO WA 106-A1
NAPTON RD
MALHEUR CO OR 147-A1
NARROWS DR
TACOMA WA 181-C2
NARROWS-PRINCETON RD
HARNEY CO OR 145-B2
NASH AV
BENTON CO OR 327-C13
NASH LN
CANYON CO ID 147-B1
NASHUA LN
DESCHUTES CO OR 212-A4
NW NASHVILLE AV
BEND OR 332-D6
NASI LN
VALLEY CO ID 252-D1
NASTY FLAT RD
HARNEY CO OR 144-B3
SW NATERLIN DR
NEWPORT OR 206-B4
NATIONAL AV
CHEHALIS WA 299-E9
LEWIS CO WA 299-E9
S NATIONAL AV
NAVY YARD CITY WA 270-E12
NATIONAL AV N
BREMERTON WA 270-E11
NAVY YARD CITY WA 270-E11
NATIONAL PARK HWY
LEWIS CO WA 185-B5
PIERCE CO WA 185-B5
NATIONAL PARK HWY Rt#-62
KLAMATH CO OR 227-B4
NATIONAL PARK HWY U.S.-12
LEWIS CO WA 118-B2
MORTON WA 118-B2
NAVAL AV
BREMERTON WA 270-G10
NAVARRE ST
CHELAN WA 236-D3
NAVARRE COULEE RD Rt#-971
CHELAN CO WA 236-B3
NEACOXIE DR
GEARHART WA 301-G5
NEAH BAY RD
CLALLAM CO WA 100-B2
NEAH BAY RD Rt#-112
CLALLAM CO WA 100-B2
NEAL LN
DOUGLAS CO OR 225-C1
NEAL CREEK RD
HOOD RIVER CO OR 195-C7
NEALEY RD
OKANOGAN CO WA 105-A1
NEATHAMMER GULCH RD
JACKSON CO OR 230-A3
NEAVES RD
PITT MEADOWS BC 157-C5
NEBRASKA ST
SKAGIT CO WA 259-J14
NECANICUM DR
SEASIDE WA 301-G8
NECANICUM HWY Rt#-53
CLATSOP CO WA 188-D7
CLATSOP CO OR 191-C3
TILLAMOOK CO OR 191-C3
TILLAMOOK CO OR 191-C3
NECK RD
YAMHILL CO OR 198-C7
NEEDLE CREEK RD
JACKSON CO OR 226-C5
NEEDLE RIDGE RD
JACKSON CO OR 226-B5
NEEDLE ROCK RD
JACKSON CO OR 226-B5
S NEEDY RD
CLACKAMAS CO OR 205-D1
NEER CITY RD
COLUMBIA CO OR 189-C4
NEER CITY CEMETERY RD
COLUMBIA CO OR 189-C5
NEERGAARD RD
ADAMS CO WA 113-B3
NEFF RD
BEND OR 217-C2
DESCHUTES CO OR 217-C2
JEFFERSON CO OR 208-C3
NE NEFF RD
BEND OR 217-C2
BEND OR 332-H6
NEGUS WY
DESCHUTES CO OR 212-D5
NEHALEM DR
CLATSOP CO OR 191-D1
NEHALEM HWY Rt#-47
COLUMBIA CO OR 117-B3
COLUMBIA CO OR 125-B1
WASHINGTON CO OR 125-B1
NEHALEM HWY Rt#-202
CLATSOP CO WA 117-B3
CLATSOP CO WA 188-C3
CLATSOP CO WA 300-F8
COLUMBIA CO OR 117-B3
NEHALEM RD
TILLAMOOK CO OR 191-A4
NEHALEM ST
CLATSKANIE OR 117-B3
NEHALEM QUARRY RD
TILLAMOOK CO OR 191-B3
NEILL RD
WASHINGTON CO OR 198-D5
NEILSEN RD
WHATCOM CO WA 158-C6
E NEILSON RD
KOOTENAI CO ID 245-B5
NELLITA RD NW
KITSAP CO WA 173-C2
NELS NELSON RD NW
DOUGLAS CO WA 236-B6
KITSAP CO WA 174-B1
KITSAP CO WA 270-F1
SILVERDALE WA 174-B1
NELSON AV
DISTRICT OF BURNABY BC 156-C5
NELSON LP
KOOTENAI CO ID 247-C1
NELSON RD
DESCHUTES CO OR 217-D2
DOUGLAS CO OR 219-B1
LEWIS CO WA 187-B2
WALLA WALLA CO WA 121-B3
WASHINGTON CO OR 198-A1
E NELSON RD
GRANT CO WA 242-D3
SE NELSON RD
KITSAP CO WA 174-C6
NELSON ST
TOWN OF ESQUILMALT BC 256-B8
VANCOUVER BC 254-E9
NELSON SIDING RD
KITTITAS CO WA 111-B3
NESIKA RD
CURRY CO OR 228-A4
NESS RD
KOOTENAI CO ID 247-C7
NESS RD Rt#-116
HADLOCK-IRONDALE WA 170-A1
JEFFERSON CO WA 170-A1
NESS CORNER RD Rt#-116
HADLOCK-IRONDALE WA 170-A1
NESTUCCA RIVER RD
TILLAMOOK CO OR 125-B2
YAMHILL CO OR 125-B2
NW NESTUCCA RIVER RD
YAMHILL CO OR 125-B2
NETARTS HWY
TILLAMOOK OR 197-B2
TILLAMOOK CO OR 197-A2
NETARTS BAY DR
TILLAMOOK CO OR 197-A2
N NETTLETON ST
SPOKANE WA 348-F5
NEUGERBAUER RD
WASHINGTON CO OR 198-D4
NEVADA AV
KLAMATH FALLS OR 338-B5
W NEVADA AV Rt#-903
ROSLYN WA 240-A1
N NEVADA DR
COWLITZ CO WA 303-B5
LONGVIEW HEIGHTS WA 302-J5
LONGVIEW HEIGHTS WA 303-B5
E NEVADA ST
ASHLAND OR 337-D5
N NEVADA ST
SPOKANE WA 347-B12
SPOKANE WA 349-B4
SPOKANE CO WA 347-B12
W NEVADA ST
ASHLAND OR 337-C5
NEVADA STATE ROUTE Rt#-140
HARNEY CO OR 153-A3
HUMBOLDT CO NV 153-C3
NEVADA STATE ROUTE Rt#-292
HUMBOLDT CO NV 153-C3
NEVIL RD
LEWIS CO WA 187-C3
NEVILLE LN
JACKSON CO OR 234-A2
NEVIN RD
DISTRICT OF CHILLIWACK BC 94-C3
E NEWARK AV
SPOKANE WA 349-C10
NEWBERG HWY Rt#-214
WOODBURN OR 205-B1
NEWBERG HWY Rt#-219
MARION CO OR 205-B1
WOODBURN OR 205-B1
NEWBERG RD
TILLAMOOK CO OR 197-B5
NW NEWBERRY RD
MULTNOMAH CO OR 192-B7
PORTLAND OR 192-B7
NEWBERRY CRATER RD
DESCHUTES CO OR 143-A1
NW NEWBERRY HILL RD
KITSAP CO WA 174-A2
SILVERDALE WA 270-A1
NEW BRIDGE RD
BAKER CO OR 139-A1
NE NEW BROOKLYN RD
KITSAP CO WA 174-C1
NEWBURY RD
GRAYS HARBOR CO WA 178-A2
NEWCASTLE COAL CREEK RD
KING CO WA 175-C4
NEWCASTLE WA 175-C4
NEWCOMB RD
DESCHUTES CO OR 212-C6
NEW CREEK RD
MALHEUR CO OR 146-B1
S NEW ERA RD
CLACKAMAS CO OR 199-C6
NEW HOPE RD
JOSEPHINE CO OR 149-A2
JOSEPHINE CO OR 229-B7
JOSEPHINE CO OR 335-C14
NEW JONES RD
JACKSON CO OR 230-C4
S NEW KIRCHNER RD
CLACKAMAS CO OR 199-D7
NEW LAKE RD
COOS CO OR 224-B2
NEWLAND RD
CLACKAMAS CO OR 199-C5
JACKSON CO OR 230-C6
E NEWMAN RD
ISLAND CO WA 170-D1
S NEWMAN RD
CLACKAMAS CO OR 205-C2
NEWMAN CREEK RD
GRAYS HARBOR CO WA 179-B7
N NEWMAN LAKE DR
SPOKANE CO WA 247-B1
SPOKANE CO WA 352-E1
W NEWMAN LAKE DR
SPOKANE CO WA 247-B1
SPOKANE CO WA 352-D1
NEWMARK AV
COOS BAY OR 333-B6
NORTH BEND OR 333-D6
NEWMARK ST
NORTH BEND OR 333-F7
NEW OMAK LAKE RD
OKANOGAN CO WA 104-C3
NEW PINE RD
MODOC CO CA 152-A3
NEWPORT AV
BUNKER HILL OR 220-D1
BUNKER HILL OR 333-J12
COOS CO OR 220-D1
DISTRICT OF OAK BAY BC 257-C9
NEWPORT AV U.S.-101
BUNKER HILL OR 333-J12
COOS BAY OR 333-J12
NW NEWPORT AV
BEND OR 332-D6
N NEWPORT HWY U.S.-2
FAIRWOOD WA 347-C8
SPOKANE CO WA 347-E5
SE NEWPORT WY
BELLEVUE WA 175-D3
ISSAQUAH WA 175-D3
ISSAQUAH WA 176-A4
KING CO WA 175-D3
NEWSKAH RD
GRAYS HARBOR CO WA 183-D1
NEWSOME CREEK RD
CROOK CO OR 136-A3
NEWTON RD
STEVENS CO WA 106-B3
NEWTON ST
CITY OF VICTORIA BC 257-A7
DISTRICT OF SAANICH BC 257-A7
NE NEWTON CREEK RD
DOUGLAS CO OR 334-H2
ROSEBURG OR 334-H2
NEWTON HILL RD
LINCOLN CO OR 206-B3
NEZ PERCE AV
WINCHESTER ID 123-B2
W NEZ PERCE RD
COEUR D'ALENE ID 354-J6
COEUR D'ALENE ID 355-A6
NEZPERCE-CRAIGMONT RD
LEWIS CO ID 123-B2
NFD RD 2
ADAMS CO ID 131-B3
NFD RD 9
SHOSHONE CO ID 115-C1
WASHINGTON CO ID 139-A1
NFD RD 10
CLACKAMAS CO OR 201-A3
GRANT CO OR 129-B3
GRANT CO OR 137-B1
MULTNOMAH CO OR 201-B2
NFD RD 11
JOSEPHINE CO OR 233-A5
NFD RD 12
CLACKAMAS CO OR 201-A3
JEFFERSON CO OR 134-C1
JEFFERSON CO OR 211-B2
LEWIS CO WA 185-A6
MULTNOMAH CO OR 201-B2
TILLAMOOK CO OR 203-C3
NFD RD 13
BAKER CO OR 137-C2
GRANT CO OR 137-C2
HOOD RIVER CO OR 201-D2
HOOD RIVER CO OR 202-A1
NFD RD 14
CLACKAMAS CO OR 201-A3
GRANT CO OR 137-C3
LEWIS CO WA 185-A7
TILLAMOOK CO OR 197-C6
YAMHILL CO OR 197-D7
NFD RD 15
GRANT CO OR 137-B3
JOSEPHINE CO OR 233-B7
TILLAMOOK CO OR 203-C2
NFD RD 16
BAKER CO OR 138-A2
GRANT CO OR 137-C2
GRANT CO OR 138-A2
HOOD RIVER CO OR 202-A2
JOSEPHINE CO OR 233-A1
NFD RD 17
HOOD RIVER CO OR 202-C3
JOSEPHINE CO OR 233-C7
LINCOLN CO OR 203-C4
NFD RD 18
LAKE CO OR 143-B1
NFD RD 19
LINCOLN CO OR 203-B6
NFD RD 20
CURRY CO OR 224-B7
MULTNOMAH CO OR 201-A1
NFD RD 21
GRANT CO OR 137-A2
LANE CO OR 142-A1
MORROW CO OR 128-C3
UMATILLA CO OR 129-C3
UNION CO OR 129-C2
NFD RD 22
BONNER CO ID 244-A7
GRAYS HARBOR CO WA 109-A2
KLAMATH CO OR 143-A1
LAKE CO OR 143-A1
LANE CO OR 142-A1
NFD RD 23
CURRY CO OR 148-C1
DOUGLAS CO OR 214-C6
LANE CO OR 142-B1
LEWIS CO WA 118-C2
MASON CO WA 109-B2
SKAMANIA CO WA 119-A3
NFD RD 24
GRANT CO OR 136-C2
GRANT CO OR 137-A2
LAKE CO OR 143-A1
LANE CO OR 142-B1
MASON CO WA 109-B2
MASON CO WA 173-A4
NFD RD 25
LANE CO OR 209-C6
LEWIS CO WA 118-C2
MASON CO WA 173-A2
SKAMANIA CO WA 118-C2
SKAMANIA CO WA 190-D3
WASHINGTON CO ID 139-A1
WHEELER CO OR 128-B3
NFD RD 28
GRANT CO OR 137-B3
NFD RD 29
CLALLAM CO WA 163-C7
NFD RD 30
CLALLAM CO WA 163-C6
CLALLAM CO WA 164-A6
COWLITZ CO WA 190-A3
DESCHUTES CO OR 217-C5
NFD RD 31
GRANT CO OR 137-A3
UMATILLA CO OR 130-A1
WASHINGTON CO ID 139-B1
NFD RD 32
LANE CO OR 209-D6
OKANOGAN CO WA 105-A1
UMATILLA CO OR 130-A1
NFD RD 33
CURRY CO OR 140-B3
CURRY CO OR 148-B1
KLAMATH CO OR 231-B1
NFD RD 34
DOUGLAS CO OR 222-D2
DOUGLAS CO OR 223-A2
NFD RD 35
DOUGLAS CO OR 222-D4
KITTITAS CO WA 238-B7
NFD RD 36
GRANT CO OR 137-B1
NFD RD 37
GRANT CO OR 137-A3
NFD RD 38
LANE CO OR 142-A1
OKANOGAN CO WA 104-B2
NFD RD 40
GARFIELD CO WA 122-B2
NFD RD 41
JOSEPHINE CO OR 233-D7
NFD RD 42
JOSEPHINE CO OR 233-C5
SKAMANIA CO WA 194-A2
NFD RD 43
KLAMATH CO OR 142-C3
SKAMANIA CO WA 194-B3
NFD RD 44
HOOD RIVER CO OR 202-C4
LEWIS CO WA 185-D6
OKANOGAN CO WA 104-A3
NFD RD 46
KLAMATH CO OR 151-A1
LEWIS CO WA 185-D7
MARION CO OR 134-C1
NFD RD 48
HOOD RIVER CO OR 202-B6
HOOD RIVER CO OR 202-B6
LANE CO OR 214-D4
WASCO CO OR 127-A3
WASCO CO OR 202-B6
WASCO CO OR 202-C7
NFD RD 48N
KLAMATH CO OR 151-B3
LAKE CO OR 151-B3
MODOC CO CA 151-B3
NFD RD 49
KLAMATH CO OR 143-A3
NFD RD 50
KING CO WA 176-D7
LINCOLN CO OR 206-C7
SHOSHONE CO ID 115-B2
NFD RD 51
GRANT CO OR 129-C3
UNION CO OR 129-C3
NFD RD 52
GRANT CO OR 129-C3
JEFFERSON CO OR 211-C2
LANE CO OR 209-A7
LINCOLN CO OR 206-D7
UMATILLA CO OR 129-B3
NFD RD 53
MORROW CO OR 129-A3
SKAMANIA CO WA 193-D2
UMATILLA CO OR 129-A3
NFD RD 54
LANE CO OR 209-C4
SKAMANIA CO WA 190-B7
SKAMANIA CO WA 193-D1
SKAMANIA CO WA 194-A1
NFD RD 55
WASHINGTON CO ID 131-B3
NFD RD 58
CROOK CO OR 136-C2
GRANT CO OR 136-C2
LANE CO OR 209-C5
SKAMANIA CO WA 194-A1
NFD RD 59
DOUGLAS CO OR 214-B6
NFD RD 60
DOUGLAS CO OR 223-D2
KLAMATH CO OR 142-B1

STREET City State Page-Grid

NFD RD 62
UNION CO OR 130-B1
NFD RD 63
UNION CO OR 130-A1
NFD RD 64
SKAMANIA CO WA 190-D6
UNION CO OR 130-A1
NFD RD 65
CHELAN CO WA 111-B1
SKAMANIA CO WA 194-D1
NFD RD 67
JOSEPHINE CO OR 233-A1
NFD RD 68
SKAMANIA CO WA 195-A3
NFD RD 70
CURRY CO OR 232-C1
NFD RD 73
GRANITE OR 137-C1
GRANT CO OR 129-C3
GRANT CO OR 130-A3
GRANT CO OR 137-C1
UNION CO OR 130-A3
NFD RD 75
DOUGLAS CO OR 222-D4
NFD RD 77
BAKER CO OR 130-C3
NFD RD 80
GRAYS HARBOR CO WA 109-A2
JOSEPHINE CO OR 233-D6
NFD RD 81
COWLITZ CO WA 190-A3
SKAMANIA CO WA 190-B3
NFD RD 83
HUMBOLDT CO NV 154-C3
HUMBOLDT CO NV 155-A3
SKAMANIA CO WA 190-D2
NFD RD 84
HUMBOLDT CO NV 154-C3
LEWIS CO WA 185-A6
LINCOLN CO OR 203-C7
NFD RD 85
JOSEPHINE CO OR 233-C7
TILLAMOOK CO OR 125-A2
TILLAMOOK CO OR 197-D6
NFD RD 87
HUMBOLDT CO NV 154-C3
NFD RD 89
ADAMS CO ID 131-C3
NFD RD 90
SKAMANIA CO WA 118-C3
SKAMANIA CO WA 190-D5
NFD RD 92 Rt#-508
LINCOLN CO MT 107-C1
NFD RD 94
SKAMANIA CO WA 190-D1
NFD RD 96
HUMBOLDT CO NV 154-C3
HUMBOLDT CO NV 155-A3
NFD RD 98
JOSEPHINE CO OR 233-D7
NFD RD 99
SKAMANIA CO WA 190-C1
NFD RD 100
DESCHUTES CO OR 211-D6
OKANOGAN CO WA 105-B2
DOUGLAS CO OR 222-B1
NFD RD 105
ADAMS CO ID 131-B3
NFD RD 110
CURRY CO OR 228-D1
KLAMATH CO OR 231-A2
NFD RD 111
KITTITAS CO WA 241-B1
NFD RD 112
CHELAN CO WA 111-C2
KITTITAS CO WA 241-A2
TILLAMOOK CO OR 125-A2
NFD RD 113
KITTITAS CO WA 241-B1
NFD RD 114
KITTITAS CO WA 241-A1
NFD RD 115
KITTITAS CO WA 238-A7
KITTITAS CO WA 241-B2
NFD RD 116
KITTITAS CO WA 238-A7
KITTITAS CO WA 241-B2
VALLEY CO ID 252-C4
NFD RD 118
KITTITAS CO WA 238-A7
NFD RD 128
ADAMS CO ID 131-B3
NFD RD 129
LINCOLN CO OR 203-B4
NFD RD 130
CURRY CO OR 232-D2
JEFFERSON CO OR 211-C2
NFD RD 134
LEWIS CO WA 185-A7
NFD RD 150
CURRY CO OR 228-B1
GRANT CO OR 129-A3
LANE CO OR 211-A6
NFD RD 151
SHOSHONE CO ID 115-C1
NFD RD 160
DESCHUTES CO OR 211-C4
DESCHUTES CO OR 216-D6
NFD RD 165
ADAMS CO ID 139-C1
ADAMS CO ID 252-A1
NFD RD 172
ADAMS CO ID 251-A7
NFD RD 181
ADAMS CO ID 251-A7
NFD RD 183
ADAMS CO ID 251-A7
ADAMS CO ID 252-A1
NFD RD 186
ADAMS CO ID 252-B2
VALLEY CO ID 252-C1
NFD RD 199
ADAMS CO ID 252-A2
NFD RD 200
ADAMS CO ID 252-A2
CHELAN CO WA 238-A5
DESCHUTES CO OR 217-A5
DOUGLAS CO OR 222-B2
JEFFERSON CO OR 211-B1
OKANOGAN CO WA 105-B2

NFD RD 201
CLACKAMAS CO OR 201-A3
NFD RD 203
SKAMANIA CO WA 190-D7
NFD RD 206
ADAMS CO ID 252-B4
KOOTENAI CO ID 245-C4
NFD RD 207
SKAMANIA CO WA 190-D6
NFD RD 208
SHOSHONE CO ID 115-C1
NFD RD 209
KOOTENAI CO ID 245-C2
NFD RD 213
KITTITAS CO WA 241-A1
NFD RD 214
ADAMS CO ID 252-A4
NFD RD 217
ADAMS CO ID 252-A4
NFD RD 218
ADAMS CO ID 252-C2
NFD RD 230
CURRY CO OR 232-D1
DESCHUTES CO OR 217-D5
KLAMATH CO OR 231-A2
CURRY CO OR 232-D1
DESCHUTES CO OR 217-D5
KLAMATH CO OR 231-A2
NFD RD 231
BOUNDARY CO ID 107-A2
NFD RD 243
ADAMS CO ID 252-B5
NFD RD 250
DESCHUTES CO OR 217-D7
NFD RD 255
CLACKAMAS CO OR 201-A6
NFD RD 258
KOOTENAI CO ID 245-D3
NFD RD 268
KOOTENAI CO ID 245-B6
NFD RD 270
SKAMANIA CO WA 190-D2
NFD RD 278
BONNER CO ID 244-D5
BONNER CO ID 245-D1
KOOTENAI CO ID 245-D2
NFD RD 280
JEFFERSON CO OR 211-B1
NFD RD 281
DOUGLAS CO OR 223-A7
NFD RD 288
KLAMATH CO OR 143-B3
KLAMATH CO OR 151-B1
KLAMATH CO OR 151-B1
LAKE CO OR 143-B3
NFD RD 291
BOUNDARY CO ID 107-B2
NFD RD 294
BOUNDARY CO ID 107-B2
NFD RD 300
DESCHUTES CO OR 217-A3
NFD RD 301
SHOSHONE CO ID 115-C3
NFD RD 302
BONNER CO ID 106-C2
NFD RD 306
SHOSHONE CO ID 244-D7
NFD RD 317
SKAMANIA CO WA 190-D7
NFD RD 320
SKAMANIA CO WA 190-C7
NFD RD 331
KLAMATH CO OR 151-B1
NFD RD 332
BONNER CO ID 244-C7
BONNER CO ID 245-D2
SHOSHONE CO ID 244-D6
NFD RD 348
KLAMATH CO OR 151-B1
LAKE CO OR 151-C1
NFD RD 350
KLAMATH CO OR 231-A4
NFD RD 360
KLAMATH CO OR 231-A4
NFD RD 370
DESCHUTES CO OR 216-C1
NFD RD 375
KLAMATH CO OR 151-B2
NFD RD 380
SKAMANIA CO WA 190-D2
NFD RD 381
KLAMATH CO OR 151-B2
NFD RD 382
CLACKAMAS CO OR 201-D4
NFD RD 392
KOOTENAI CO ID 245-C4
NFD RD 400
CHELAN CO WA 238-A2
DESCHUTES CO OR 211-C5
DESCHUTES CO OR 216-D5
JEFFERSON CO OR 211-B1
SHOSHONE CO ID 115-C1
NFD RD 406
KOOTENAI CO ID 245-C3
NFD RD 410
CLACKAMAS CO OR 201-A3
NFD RD 411
KOOTENAI CO ID 245-D5
NFD RD 413
KOOTENAI CO ID 245-D7
SKAMANIA CO WA 194-B2
NFD RD 422
VALLEY CO ID 252-D7
NFD RD 434
KOOTENAI CO ID 245-D6
NFD RD 435
VALLEY CO ID 252-C5
NFD RD 437
KOOTENAI CO ID 245-C4
NFD RD 438
KOOTENAI CO ID 248-C2
NFD RD 450
DESCHUTES CO OR 216-A3
NFD RD 454
ADAMS CO ID 131-A3
NFD RD 456
SHOSHONE CO ID 115-C2
NFD RD 471
HUMBOLDT CO NV 154-C3

NFD RD 472
JOSEPHINE CO OR 233-D6
NFD RD 480
LANE CO OR 142-A1
NFD RD 487
ADAMS CO ID 251-B7
ADAMS CO ID 252-B1
NFD RD 489
BONNER CO ID 244-D2
NFD RD 500
DOUGLAS CO OR 222-B2
NFD RD 503
SHOSHONE CO ID 115-C1
NFD RD 508 Rt#-508
LINCOLN CO MT 107-C2
NFD RD 510
CHELAN CO WA 238-A2
NFD RD 527
SKAMANIA CO WA 194-A1
NFD RD 529
HUMBOLDT CO NV 154-C3
NFD RD 531
HUMBOLDT CO NV 154-C3
NFD RD 587
ADAMS CO ID 251-A5
NFD RD 600
DESCHUTES CO OR 211-C7
DESCHUTES CO OR 217-C4
JEFFERSON CO OR 211-B2
NFD RD 610
KOOTENAI CO ID 245-D5
NFD RD 612
KOOTENAI CO ID 245-C5
NFD RD 616
KOOTENAI CO ID 245-D5
NFD RD 618
GEM CO ID 139-C2
GEM CO ID 252-B7
NFD RD 625
GEM CO ID 252-B7
KOOTENAI CO ID 245-B4
NFD RD 700
DOUGLAS CO OR 223-C2
LINN CO OR 134-A2
SKAMANIA CO WA 190-D3
NFD RD 719
LANE CO OR 214-C1
NFD RD 760
DOUGLAS CO OR 223-C7
NFD RD 794
KOOTENAI CO ID 245-D3
NFD RD 800
DESCHUTES CO OR 211-B3
NFD RD 808
KOOTENAI CO ID 248-B3
NFD RD 810
KOOTENAI CO ID 248-C3
SKAMANIA CO WA 190-D3
NFD RD 831
LANE CO OR 214-D3
NFD RD 835
ADAMS CO ID 252-B5
NFD RD 855
KLAMATH CO OR 142-C1
NFD RD 950
DOUGLAS CO OR 222-C6
DOUGLAS CO OR 226-B3
NFD RD 953
LANE CO OR 214-B4
NFD RD 958
LANE CO OR 214-C4
NFD RD 980
KLAMATH CO OR 231-A4
NFD RD 1000
LINCOLN CO OR 206-D7
NFD RD 1008
MULTNOMAH CO OR 201-A2
NFD RD 1010
MULTNOMAH CO OR 201-A2
NFD RD 1012
DESCHUTES CO OR 211-C4
NFD RD 1013
BOUNDARY CO ID 106-C1
NFD RD 1014
LINCOLN CO OR 206-D7
NFD RD 1017
BONNER CO ID 245-D2
NFD RD 1018
DESCHUTES CO OR 211-B6
NFD RD 1024
DESCHUTES CO OR 211-B6
NFD RD 1026
DESCHUTES CO OR 211-B6
NFD RD 1027
CLACKAMAS CO OR 201-C3
NFD RD 1028
DESCHUTES CO OR 211-B4
NFD RD 1030
LINCOLN CO OR 206-D7
NFD RD 1031
TILLAMOOK CO OR 203-B1
NFD RD 1050
BONNER CO ID 244-B7
NFD RD 1066
BONNER CO ID 244-D6
NFD RD 1078
BONNER CO ID 245-D2
NFD RD 1080
BONNER CO ID 245-D2
NFD RD 1088
BONNER CO ID 244-C6
NFD RD 1101
CURRY CO OR 232-D7
NFD RD 1110
JEFFERSON CO OR 211-C2
NFD RD 1176
JEFFERSON CO OR 208-C5
NFD RD 1179
JEFFERSON CO OR 212-A2
NFD RD 1207
YAKIMA CO WA 119-A2
NFD RD 1210
CLACKAMAS CO OR 201-B3
NFD RD 1217
CLACKAMAS CO OR 201-C2
MULTNOMAH CO OR 201-C2
NFD RD 1228
CLACKAMAS CO OR 201-C4
NFD RD 1268
TILLAMOOK CO OR 203-B2

NFD RD 1270
LEWIS CO WA 185-D7
NFD RD 1280
TILLAMOOK CO OR 203-C2
NFD RD 1310
HOOD RIVER CO OR 202-A1
NFD RD 1340
HOOD RIVER CO OR 202-A2
NFD RD 1341
BONNER CO ID 107-A1
NFD RD 1376
CURRY CO OR 148-B2
NFD RD 1393
JEFFERSON CO OR 212-B3
NFD RD 1394
JEFFERSON CO OR 213-A2
NFD RD 1395
JEFFERSON CO OR 213-A2
NFD RD 1399
JEFFERSON CO OR 212-B1
NFD RD 1414
CLACKAMAS CO OR 201-B3
NFD RD 1425
JEFFERSON CO OR 211-C1
NFD RD 1432
TILLAMOOK CO OR 197-C7
NFD RD 1441
CHELAN CO WA 103-C3
NFD RD 1491
TILLAMOOK CO OR 197-C7
NFD RD 1509
MULTNOMAH CO OR 201-A2
NFD RD 1510
DESCHUTES CO OR 211-C5
NFD RD 1514
DESCHUTES CO OR 211-C6
NFD RD 1516
DESCHUTES CO OR 211-C7
NFD RD 1520
DESCHUTES CO OR 211-C5
NFD RD 1522
DESCHUTES CO OR 211-C6
NFD RD 1526
DESCHUTES CO OR 211-C7
NFD RD 1587
KOOTENAI CO ID 245-C4
NFD RD 1590
TILLAMOOK CO OR 197-B7
NFD RD 1594
KOOTENAI CO ID 245-D4
NFD RD 1608
DESCHUTES CO OR 211-D6
NFD RD 1610
DESCHUTES CO OR 211-D7
HOOD RIVER CO OR 202-B2
NFD RD 1611
HOOD RIVER CO OR 202-B2
NFD RD 1614
IDAHO CO ID 131-C2
NFD RD 1620
DESCHUTES CO OR 211-C7
NFD RD 1628
DESCHUTES CO OR 211-C7
DESCHUTES CO OR 216-C1
NFD RD 1631
HOOD RIVER CO OR 202-B3
NFD RD 1633
TILLAMOOK CO OR 203-C2
NFD RD 1640
HOOD RIVER CO OR 202-A2
NFD RD 1650
HOOD RIVER CO OR 202-A3
TILLAMOOK CO OR 203-C2
NFD RD 1660
HOOD RIVER CO OR 202-A3
NFD RD 1670
HOOD RIVER CO OR 202-A3
NFD RD 1686
TILLAMOOK CO OR 203-D2
NFD RD 1700
MASON CO WA 179-B2
NFD RD 1701
LINCOLN CO OR 203-C5
YAKIMA CO WA 240-B7
NFD RD 1703
KITTITAS CO WA 240-A7
NFD RD 1708
KITTITAS CO WA 240-A6
NFD RD 1710
HOOD RIVER CO OR 202-D1
NFD RD 1711
HOOD RIVER CO OR 202-D1
NFD RD 1720
HOOD RIVER CO OR 202-D3
KITTITAS CO WA 240-B7
NFD RD 1721
KITTITAS CO WA 240-A7
NFD RD 1726
LINCOLN CO OR 203-B4
NFD RD 1770
LINCOLN CO OR 203-C6
NFD RD 1783
LINCOLN CO OR 203-B5
NFD RD 1800
YAKIMA CO WA 119-B1
NFD RD 1810
DESCHUTES CO OR 217-C7
HOOD RIVER CO OR 202-A3
NFD RD 1814
DESCHUTES CO OR 217-C5
NFD RD 1815
DESCHUTES CO OR 217-C4
NFD RD 1818
DESCHUTES CO OR 217-D7
NFD RD 1819
DESCHUTES CO OR 217-D5
NFD RD 1820
DESCHUTES CO OR 217-D6
NFD RD 1825
CLACKAMAS CO OR 201-D4
DESCHUTES CO OR 217-D7
NFD RD 1828
CLACKAMAS CO OR 201-D4
NFD RD 1846
CURRY CO OR 232-D2
NFD RD 1888
LINCOLN CO OR 203-C3
ROSE LODGE OR 203-C3
NFD RD 1928
LINCOLN CO OR 203-B6

NFD RD 1929
LINCOLN CO OR 203-B6
NFD RD 1956
LINCOLN CO OR 203-B6
NFD RD 1980
LINCOLN CO OR 203-C6
NFD RD 2022
LINN CO OR 134-A2
NFD RD 2025
JACKSON CO OR 234-A7
NFD RD 2026
LINN CO OR 134-A2
NFD RD 2040
JACKSON CO OR 234-B5
NFD RD 2050
JEFFERSON CO OR 212-A3
NFD RD 2060
DESCHUTES CO OR 211-B4
JACKSON CO OR 234-C5
NFD RD 2061
DESCHUTES CO OR 211-B3
NFD RD 2066
JEFFERSON CO OR 211-B2
NFD RD 2068
JEFFERSON CO OR 211-B3
NFD RD 2076
JEFFERSON CO OR 211-A3
NFD RD 2134
DOUGLAS CO OR 223-A1
LANE CO OR 142-A1
NFD RD 2153
DOUGLAS CO OR 223-C1
GRAYS HARBOR CO WA 179-A1
NFD RD 2160
LANE CO OR 209-D6
NFD RD 2199
MASON CO WA 179-C1
NFD RD 2207
MARION CO OR 134-A1
NFD RD 2210
YAMHILL CO OR 197-D7
NFD RD 2233
BONNER CO ID 244-B4
NFD RD 2234
YAMHILL CO OR 203-D2
NFD RD 2255
MASON CO WA 179-B1
NFD RD 2260
GRAYS HARBOR CO WA 109-B2
NFD RD 2282
YAMHILL CO OR 203-D1
NFD RD 2283
YAMHILL CO OR 197-D7
NFD RD 2302
GRAYS HARBOR CO WA 109-A2
KOOTENAI CO ID 245-C3
NFD RD 2308
CURRY CO OR 148-C1
NFD RD 2312
GRAYS HARBOR CO WA 109-B2
NFD RD 2320
KOOTENAI CO ID 245-D6
NFD RD 2341
MASON CO WA 179-B1
NFD RD 2399
MASON CO WA 179-B1
NFD RD 2401
MASON CO WA 173-A3
NFD RD 2403
JEFFERSON CO WA 173-B2
NFD RD 2420
MASON CO WA 173-A3
NFD RD 2421
MASON CO WA 173-A2
NFD RD 2464
MASON CO WA 173-A4
NFD RD 2469
MASON CO WA 173-A3
NFD RD 2470
MASON CO WA 173-A3
NFD RD 2472
MASON CO WA 173-B2
NFD RD 2480
LANE CO OR 214-D4
MASON CO WA 173-B3
NFD RD 2510
JEFFERSON CO WA 109-C1
JEFFERSON CO WA 173-B1
NFD RD 2512
BONNER CO ID 107-A2
NFD RD 2515
JEFFERSON CO WA 173-C1
NFD RD 2516
KLAMATH CO OR 143-A2
LAKE CO OR 143-A2
NFD RD 2524
JEFFERSON CO WA 173-B2
NFD RD 2530
JEFFERSON CO WA 173-B1
NFD RD 2540
JEFFERSON CO WA 173-B1
NFD RD 2546
JEFFERSON CO WA 173-B1
NFD RD 2550
BONNER CO ID 107-A3
NFD RD 2560
SKAMANIA CO WA 190-D1
NFD RD 2586
SKAMANIA CO WA 190-D3
NFD RD 2588
SKAMANIA CO WA 190-D3
NFD RD 2605
BOUNDARY CO ID 107-A2
NFD RD 2610
LANE CO OR 214-C2
NFD RD 2612
CLACKAMAS CO OR 201-C6
NFD RD 2618
CLACKAMAS CO OR 201-C6
NFD RD 2652
BONNER CO ID 245-A1
NFD RD 2654
LINN CO OR 134-B2
NFD RD 2720
WASCO CO OR 202-D5
NFD RD 2820
HOOD RIVER CO OR 195-A6
NFD RD 2823
LAKE CO OR 143-B3
LAKE CO OR 151-C1

NFD RD 2840
HOOD RIVER CO OR 202-B3
NFD RD 2902
CLALLAM CO WA 163-B7
CLALLAM CO WA 169-D1
NFD RD 2903
CLALLAM CO WA 163-B7
NFD RD 2918
CLALLAM CO WA 109-A1
NFD RD 2922
CLALLAM CO WA 163-C7
NFD RD 2923
CLALLAM CO WA 163-C7
NFD RD 2924
CLALLAM CO WA 169-D1
NFD RD 2929
CLALLAM CO WA 163-D7
NFD RD 2933
CLALLAM CO WA 163-A7
NFD RD 2937
CLALLAM CO WA 163-B7
NFD RD 2938
CLALLAM CO WA 163-B7
NFD RD 2946
CLALLAM CO WA 164-A7
NFD RD 2978
CLALLAM CO WA 163-D7
NFD RD 3006
CLALLAM CO WA 163-B5
NFD RD 3007
CLALLAM CO WA 163-B6
NFD RD 3010
OKANOGAN CO WA 105-A2
NFD RD 3027
KOOTENAI CO ID 245-D5
NFD RD 3028
CLALLAM CO WA 163-D5
NFD RD 3029
CLALLAM CO WA 163-D5
NFD RD 3030
CLALLAM CO WA 165-A7
NFD RD 3031
CLALLAM CO WA 163-C5
NFD RD 3040
CLALLAM CO WA 163-C6
CLALLAM CO WA 164-A6
NFD RD 3041
CLALLAM CO WA 163-C6
NFD RD 3062
SKAMANIA CO WA 194-C1
NFD RD 3067
CLALLAM CO WA 163-D6
NFD RD 3068
CLALLAM CO WA 164-A6
NFD RD 3069
CLALLAM CO WA 163-D6
NFD RD 3080
SKAMANIA CO WA 194-C2
NFD RD 3105
SKAMANIA CO WA 190-D6
NFD RD 3116
CLALLAM CO WA 163-B5
NFD RD 3117
CLALLAM CO WA 163-B5
NFD RD 3120
LINCOLN CO OR 206-D6
NFD RD 3142
LAKE CO OR 143-B3
NFD RD 3230
DOUGLAS CO OR 141-C3
NFD RD 3310
CURRY CO OR 228-D1
NFD RD 3312
KLAMATH CO OR 151-B1
NFD RD 3313
CURRY CO OR 228-C5
NFD RD 3334
KLAMATH CO OR 231-A1
NFD RD 3340
CURRY CO OR 228-D3
NFD RD 3348
COOS CO OR 140-C3
NFD RD 3384
KLAMATH CO OR 231-A1
NFD RD 3402
CURRY CO OR 228-B1
NFD RD 3413
KLAMATH CO OR 231-A2
NFD RD 3414
KLAMATH CO OR 231-A2
NFD RD 3419
KLAMATH CO OR 231-A4
NFD RD 3449
KLAMATH CO OR 231-A2
NFD RD 3450
KLAMATH CO OR 231-A3
NFD RD 3454
KLAMATH CO OR 231-A6
NFD RD 3455
KLAMATH CO OR 231-A5
NFD RD 3484
KLAMATH CO OR 231-A3
NFD RD 3506
KITTITAS CO WA 241-A2
NFD RD 3507
KITTITAS CO WA 241-A1
NFD RD 3512
HOOD RIVER CO OR 202-B3
NFD RD 3517
KITTITAS CO WA 241-B2
NFD RD 3521
KITTITAS CO WA 241-B1
NFD RD 3530
KITTITAS CO WA 238-B7
NFD RD 3533
CURRY CO OR 228-C4
NFD RD 3540
HOOD RIVER CO OR 202-C6
NFD RD 3550
HOOD RIVER CO OR 202-C6
NFD RD 3610
KLAMATH CO OR 231-A7
NFD RD 3640
GRANT CO OR 137-B1
NFD RD 3660
GRANT CO OR 137-B1
NFD RD 3670
GRANT CO OR 137-B1
NFD RD 3680
CURRY CO OR 228-B6

STREET City State Page-Grid

NFD RD 3817
DOUGLAS CO OR 222-B1
NFD RD 4000
DESCHUTES CO OR 217-A6
NFD RD 4017
LAKE CO OR 151-C3
NFD RD 4050
JACKSON CO OR 234-C7
NFD RD 4104
SKAMANIA CO WA 193-D3
NFD RD 4105
JOSEPHINE CO OR 233-A1
NFD RD 4109
SKAMANIA CO WA 193-D3
NFD RD 4130
DESCHUTES CO OR 217-A4
NFD RD 4180
DESCHUTES CO OR 216-D5
NFD RD 4201
JOSEPHINE CO OR 233-A2
NFD RD 4211
SKAMANIA CO WA 193-D2
NFD RD 4220
DESCHUTES CO OR 216-D6
NFD RD 4235
CROOK CO OR 136-A2
NFD RD 4240
WALLOWA CO OR 131-B2
NFD RD 4260
WALLOWA CO OR 131-A1
NFD RD 4273
DESCHUTES CO OR 142-C1
NFD RD 4305
UNION CO OR 129-C3
NFD RD 4306
SKAMANIA CO WA 194-B2
NFD RD 4410
HOOD RIVER CO OR 202-C4
NFD RD 4420
HOOD RIVER CO OR 202-D5
NFD RD 4430
WASCO CO OR 202-D3
NFD RD 4450
WASCO CO OR 202-D4
NFD RD 4510
LEWIS CO WA 185-D6
NFD RD 4601
DESCHUTES CO OR 216-D3
NFD RD 4609
JOSEPHINE CO OR 233-D4
NFD RD 4610
DESCHUTES CO OR 217-A3
NFD RD 4612
DESCHUTES CO OR 216-D3
JOSEPHINE CO OR 233-D6
LEWIS CO WA 185-D7
NFD RD 4613
CLACKAMAS CO OR 201-A7
DESCHUTES CO OR 216-D4
JOSEPHINE CO OR 233-D5
NFD RD 4614
CLACKAMAS CO OR 200-D7
NFD RD 4615
CLACKAMAS CO OR 201-A7
DESCHUTES CO OR 216-D3
NFD RD 4630
DESCHUTES CO OR 216-A7
NFD RD 4635
DESCHUTES CO OR 216-A7
NFD RD 4650
DESCHUTES CO OR 142-C1
NFD RD 4703
JOSEPHINE CO OR 233-C7
NFD RD 4720
LEWIS CO WA 185-B7
NFD RD 4803
JOSEPHINE CO OR 233-A7
NFD RD 4808
JOSEPHINE CO OR 233-B7
NFD RD 4811
DOUGLAS CO OR 214-D5
HOOD RIVER CO OR 202-C6
WASCO CO OR 202-C6
NFD RD 4814
WASCO CO OR 202-D7
NFD RD 4820
DOUGLAS CO OR 214-D5
WASCO CO OR 202-D7
NFD RD 4830
LANE CO OR 214-C4
NFD RD 4860
HOOD RIVER CO OR 202-C6
NFD RD 4870
WASCO CO OR 202-C7
NFD RD 4880
HOOD RIVER CO OR 202-C6
WASCO CO OR 202-C7
NFD RD 5087
LINCOLN CO OR 206-C7
NFD RD 5125
UNION CO OR 129-C3
UNION CO OR 130-A3
NFD RD 5130
OKANOGAN CO WA 104-A2
NFD RD 5185
BAKER CO OR 130-A3
GRANT CO OR 130-A3
UNION CO OR 130-A3
NFD RD 5210
LEWIS CO WA 185-A6
NFD RD 5260
LEWIS CO WA 185-B7
NFD RD 5270
LEWIS CO WA 185-C6
NFD RD 5400
CURRY CO OR 224-B7
OKANOGAN CO WA 103-C2
NFD RD 5701
SKAMANIA CO WA 190-B7
NFD RD 5842
LANE CO OR 209-A7
LANE CO OR 214-B1
NFD RD 5850
LANE CO OR 142-A1
NFD RD 5875
LANE CO OR 142-A1
NFD RD 6020
KLAMATH CO OR 142-C2
NFD RD 6052
SKAMANIA CO WA 194-D1
NFD RD 6210
KLAMATH CO OR 231-C2
NFD RD 6214
KLAMATH CO OR 231-C1
NFD RD 6231
UNION CO OR 130-B1
NFD RD 6401
SKAMANIA CO WA 190-D7
NFD RD 6403
SKAMANIA CO WA 190-D6
NFD RD 6406
SKAMANIA CO WA 190-D7
NFD RD 6420
KING CO WA 111-A1
NFD RD 6500
CHELAN CO WA 111-B1
NFD RD 6517
SKAMANIA CO WA 194-D3
NFD RD 6728
KOOTENAI CO ID 245-D3
NFD RD 6750
CHELAN CO WA 111-C1
NFD RD 7184 Rt#-410
PIERCE CO WA 111-A3
NFD RD 7200
CHELAN CO WA 238-B3
NFD RD 7202
CHELAN CO WA 238-B3
NFD RD 7300
CHELAN CO WA 238-A2
NFD RD 7320
CHELAN CO WA 238-A5
NFD RD 7324
CHELAN CO WA 238-A5
NFD RD 7400
CHELAN CO WA 238-B1
NFD RD 7412
CHELAN CO WA 238-C1
NFD RD 7600
CHELAN CO WA 111-B2
NFD RD 7601
CHELAN CO WA 111-C2
NFD RD 7755
BAKER CO OR 130-C3
NFD RD 8123
COWLITZ CO WA 190-B3
NFD RD 8170
TILLAMOOK CO OR 197-C5
NFD RD 8171
TILLAMOOK CO OR 197-C4
NFD RD 8172
TILLAMOOK CO OR 197-C5
NFD RD 8208
TILLAMOOK CO OR 197-A5
NFD RD 8303
SKAMANIA CO WA 190-B4
NFD RD 8320
SKAMANIA CO WA 190-D3
NFD RD 8376
TILLAMOOK CO OR 197-D6
NFD RD 8410
LEWIS CO WA 185-A6
NFD RD 8415
LEWIS CO WA 185-A6
NFD RD 8420
LEWIS CO WA 185-A6
NFD RD 8425
LEWIS CO WA 185-A6
NFD RD 8430
LEWIS CO WA 185-A6
NFD RD 8440
LEWIS CO WA 185-A7
NFD RD 8594
LEWIS CO WA 185-A7
NFD RD 9015
TILLAMOOK CO OR 197-D6
NFD RD 9403
SKAMANIA CO WA 190-C4
NFD RD 9701
SKAMANIA CO WA 190-D1
NFD RD 9705
DESCHUTES CO OR 217-C5
NFD RD 9711
KITTITAS CO WA 238-A6
NFD RD 9712
KITTITAS CO WA 238-A6
NFD RD 9713
KITTITAS CO WA 238-A7
NFD RD 9714
KLAMATH CO OR 231-D5
NF RD 9715
KITTITAS CO WA 238-A6
NFD RD 9716
KITTITAS CO WA 238-A6
KLAMATH CO OR 231-D5
NFD RD 9717
KITTITAS CO WA 238-A6
NFD RD 9718
KLAMATH CO OR 231-D5
NFD RD 9720
KITTITAS CO WA 238-A7
NFD RD 9723
DESCHUTES CO OR 217-A6
NFD RD 9724
DESCHUTES CO OR 217-B6
NFD RD 9726
DESCHUTES CO OR 217-B7
NFD RD 9730
KITTITAS CO WA 241-A1
NFD RD 9734
KLAMATH CO OR 231-D2
NFD RD 9938
KLAMATH CO OR 231-D1
NFD RD 91013
JOSEPHINE CO OR 233-A7
NFH 50
SKAMANIA CO WA 190-C4
NF HWY 50
BENEWAH CO ID 115-B2
NHS 11 Rt#-60
SHOSHONE CO ID 115-C3
W NIAGARA AV
BENEWAH CO ID 115-A3
NICE RD
ASTORIA WA 300-D6
NICEWOOD DR
UNION CO OR 130-A3
NICEWOOD LN
LINN CO OR 210-A2
LINN CO OR 210-A3
NW NICHOLS AV
TRACYTON WA 270-G4
NW NICHOLS BLVD
LONGVIEW WA 302-J9
LONGVIEW WA 303-A10
NICHOLS LN
FOREST GROVE OR 198-B1
LANE CO OR 219-D1
WASHINGTON CO OR 198-B1
SE NICHOLS RD
YAMHILL CO OR 204-D1
NICHOLSON RD
KLAMATH CO OR 231-B1
LEWIS CO WA 187-D3
NICKEL MINE RD
DOUGLAS CO OR 225-B3
NICKERSON ST
SEATTLE WA 273-H7
W NICKERSON ST
SEATTLE WA 273-G6
NICK THOMAS RD
COLUMBIA CO OR 189-C5
NICK YOUNG RD
EAGLE POINT OR 230-D5
JACKSON CO OR 230-D5
NICOLAI RD
COLUMBIA CO OR 189-C6
NW NICOLAI ST
PORTLAND OR 312-C3
NICOLAI CUTOFF RD
COLUMBIA CO OR 189-C6
NIEHENKE RD
WHITMAN CO WA 249-C7
NIELSON RD
TILLAMOOK CO OR 197-C2
NIKULA RD
LEWIS CO WA 187-C3
N NILE AV
DOUGLAS CO WA 239-A4
S NILE AV
DOUGLAS CO WA 239-A4
NILLES RD
DOUGLAS CO WA 112-C1
NINE CANYON RD
BENTON CO WA 121-A3
NINEMILE RD
HUMBOLDT CO NV 154-A3
N NINE MILE RD Rt#-291
SPOKANE WA 246-A2
SPOKANE WA 346-A13
SPOKANE WA 348-C1
SPOKANE CO WA 246-A2
SPOKANE CO WA 346-A13
NINTH ST
WENATCHEE WA 238-D4
NISQUALLY RD SW
PIERCE CO WA 181-B6
NISULA RD
VALLEY CO ID 251-C6
NIXON DR
LINN CO OR 210-A3
W NIXON ST
PASCO WA 343-E7
NO 1 RD
CITY OF RICHMOND BC 156-A7
DISTRICT OF ABBOTSFORD BC 94-B3
NO 2 RD
CITY OF RICHMOND BC 156-B7
NO 3 RD
CITY OF RICHMOND BC 156-B7
DISTRICT OF ABBOTSFORD BC 102-B1
NO 4 RD
CITY OF RICHMOND BC 156-B7
NO 5 RD
CITY OF RICHMOND BC 156-B6
NO 6 RD
CITY OF RICHMOND BC 156-C6
NO 7 RD
CITY OF RICHMOND BC 156-C6
E NOB HILL BLVD
FAIRVIEW-SUMACH WA 243-C7
YAKIMA WA 243-C7
W NOB HILL BLVD
YAKIMA WA 243-B7
NOBLE RD
GRAND COULEE WA 237-C3
NOBLE CREEK RD
COOS CO OR 218-D4
NOLL RD NE
KITSAP CO WA 170-C7
NONPAREIL RD
DOUGLAS CO OR 219-C7
NOOKSACK AV Rt#-9
NOOKSACK WA 102-B1
NOOKSACK RD Rt#-9
NOOKSACK WA 102-B1
WHATCOM CO WA 102-B1
NORATEN RD
LANE CO OR 210-A5
NORDEL WY
DISTRICT OF DELTA BC 156-D6
NORKENZIE RD
EUGENE OR 330-A2
NORMAN RD
SNOHOMISH CO WA 168-B4
E NORMAN RD
YAKIMA CO WA 243-C7
S NORMANDY RD
KING WA 288-A7
NORPOINT WY NE
TACOMA WA 182-A2
NORRIS AV Rt#-55
NEW MEADOWS ID 251-A4
NORRIS AV U.S.-95
ADAMS CO ID 251-A4
NEW MEADOWS ID 251-A4
NORRIS LN
JEFFERSON CO OR 212-D2
NORTH AV
JEFFERSON OR 207-D3
NORTH RD
CHELAN CO WA 238-A1
DISTRICT OF COQUITLAM BC 156-D5
FRANKLIN CO WA 340-H3
KOOTENAI CO ID 245-C1
NEW WESTMINSTER BC 156-D5
SNOHOMISH CO WA 171-C5
NORTH RD NW
DOUGLAS CO WA 236-C6
NORTH SPUR
JACKSON CO OR 227-A5
NORTH ST Rt#-26
WASHTUCNA WA 121-C1
E NORTH ST
ENTERPRISE OR 130-C2
W NORTH ST Rt#-82
ENTERPRISE OR 130-C2
NORTH ST SE
OLYMPIA WA 296-J9
OLYMPIA WA 297-A9
TUMWATER WA 296-J9
TUMWATER WA 297-A9
NORTH WY
COOS CO OR 218-B5
NORTH BANK RD
DOUGLAS CO OR 141-B2
DOUGLAS CO OR 221-C2
LINCOLN CO OR 203-B4
ROSE LODGE OR 203-B4
NORTH BANK RD U.S.-197
DEL NORTE CO CA 148-B3
NORTH BANK CHETCO RIVER RD
CURRY CO OR 232-D5
NORTH BANK PISTOL RIVER RD
CURRY CO OR 232-C1
NORTH BANK ROGUE RIVER RD
CURRY CO OR 228-B4
NORTH BAY DR
COOS CO OR 218-B6
NORTH BEND BLVD N Rt#-202
NORTH BEND WA 176-C4
NORTH BEND BLVD S Rt#-202
NORTH BEND WA 176-C5
SE NORTH BEND WY
KING CO WA 176-C4
NORTH BEND WA 176-C4
SNOQUALMIE WA 176-C4
NORTH CASCADES HWY Rt#-20
CHELAN CO WA 103-C2
OKANOGAN CO WA 103-C2
SKAGIT CO WA 103-A2
WHATCOM CO WA 103-A2
N NORTHCLIFF RD
SHELTON WA 180-A2
NORTHCRAFT RD SE
THURSTON CO WA 184-D3
NORTHCREST DR Rt#-D3
CRESCENT CITY CA 148-B3
DEL NORTE CO CA 148-B3
NORTH DAIRY RD
CITY OF VICTORIA BC 257-A6
DISTRICT OF SAANICH BC 257-A6
NORTH END OMAK LAKE RD
OKANOGAN CO WA 104-C3
NORTHERN DR
LINN CO OR 210-C2
NORTHERNWOOD DR
LINN CO OR 210-C4
NORTH FORK RD
CLACKAMAS CO OR 200-D7
DOUGLAS CO OR 214-C6
LANE CO OR 134-A3
LANE CO OR 142-A1
LEWIS CO WA 184-D7
LEWIS CO WA 187-D1
MARION CO OR 134-A1
NEHALEM OR 191-B4
SKAMANIA CO WA 193-D6
TILLAMOOK CO OR 191-B4
TILLAMOOK CO OR 191-B4
TILLAMOOK CO OR 197-D2
WESTFIR OR 142-A1
NORTH FORK AHTANUM RD
YAKIMA CO WA 119-B2
NORTH FORK BURNT RIVER RD
BAKER CO OR 138-A1
NORTH FORK COUNTY RD
KING CO WA 176-D3
NORTH FORK SIUSLAW RD
FLORENCE OR 214-B3
LANE CO OR 214-B3
NORTH FORK YACHATS RD
LINCOLN CO OR 209-B3
NORTH FOURMILE RD
COOS CO OR 224-C1
NORTH GATE RD
PIERCE CO WA 181-C4
N NORTHGATE WY
SEATTLE WA 171-B7
NE NORTHGATE WY
SEATTLE WA 171-B7
NORTH HEAD RD
ILWACO WA 186-A6
PACIFIC CO WA 186-A6
NORTH HEAD LIGHTHSE RD
PACIFIC CO WA 186-A6
NORTH LAKE RD
COOS CO OR 218-C4
NORTHLAKE WY NW
BREMERTON WA 270-A8
TRACYTON WA 270-A8
NORTH MISSION RD W
KITSAP CO WA 173-D3
NORTH MOUNTAIN RD
CLACKAMAS CO OR 201-C4
NORTH PINE CREEK RD
BAKER CO OR 131-A3
NORTHPORT-FLAT CREEK RD
STEVENS CO WA 106-A1
NORTH POWDER-LADD CANYON RD
NORTH POWDER OR 130-B3
UNION CO OR 130-A3
NORTH POWDER RIVER LN
UNION CO OR 130-A3
NORTH POWDER RIVER RD
NORTH POWDER OR 130-A3
UNION CO OR 130-A3
NORTH PRAIRIE RD
LEWIS CO WA 187-D2
NORTH RAILWAY AV Rt#-7
DISTRICT OF MISSION BC 94-B3
NORTH RIVER DR
LINN CO OR 134-A2
NORTH RIVER RD
GRAYS HARBOR CO WA 117-A1
IDAHO CO ID 123-C3
NORTH RIVER VALLEY RD
PACIFIC CO WA 117-B1
NORTHRUP RD
GRANT CO WA 237-B4
NORTH SHORE DR
BELLINGHAM WA 102-B1
BELLINGHAM WA 161-A1
BELLINGHAM WA 258-J5
LOWELL OR 133-C3
WHATCOM CO WA 102-B1
WHATCOM CO WA 161-A1
NORTHSHORE PKWY
PIERCE CO WA 182-A1
TACOMA WA 182-A1
NORTH SHORE RD
MASON CO WA 173-A6
NORTH SHORE RD Rt#-300
MASON CO WA 173-D6
NORTHSHORE RD Rt#-150
CHELAN CO WA 236-C2
NORTH SIDE DR
LINN CO OR 133-C2
NORTH SIDE RD
DOUGLAS CO OR 221-D1
SHOSHONE CO ID 115-C3
NORTHSIDE RD
CANYON CO ID 147-B1
NORTH STAR RD
WHATCOM CO WA 158-C5
NORTH UMPQUA HWY Rt#-138
DOUGLAS CO OR 141-C2
DOUGLAS CO OR 221-D4
DOUGLAS CO OR 222-B3
DOUGLAS CO OR 223-A4
ROSEBURG OR 221-D4
NORTHUP WY
BELLEVUE WA 175-D2
NORTH VALLEY RD
YAMHILL CO OR 198-C5
NORTHVIEW ST
BOISE ID 253-B2
NORTHWEST AV
BELLINGHAM WA 258-B2
N NORTHWEST BLVD
COEUR D'ALENE ID 355-D10
KOOTENAI CO ID 355-C9
W NORTHWEST BLVD
SPOKANE WA 348-D4
NORTHWEST DR
BELLINGHAM WA 158-D6
BELLINGHAM WA 258-A1
WHATCOM CO WA 158-D6
WHATCOM CO WA 258-A1
NORTHWEST EXWY
EUGENE OR 215-A1
EUGENE OR 329-D1
LANE CO OR 215-A1
LANE CO OR 329-D1
Santa Clara OR 215-A1
NORTHWEST WY
DESCHUTES CO OR 212-D4
TERREBONNE OR 212-D4
NORTHWESTERN LAKE RD
KLICKITAT CO WA 195-C3
NE NORTH WOODINVILLE WY
WOODINVILLE WA 171-C6
NE NORTON AV
BEND OR 332-G6
NORWAY-LEE-FAIRVIEW RD
COOS CO OR 140-B2
NORWELL DR
NANAIMO BC 93-A3
NORWOOD RD
VALLEY CO ID 251-C7
VALLEY CO ID 252-C1
S NORWOOD RD
VALLEY CO ID 252-D2
NOTUS RD
CANYON CO ID 147-B1
NOUQUE RANCH RD
MALHEUR CO OR 154-C2
NOVA LN
ADA CO ID 253-A3
NOVELTY HILL RD
KING CO WA 110-C1
KING CO WA 175-D1
KING CO WA 176-A1
REDMOND WA 175-D1
NOWLENS BRIDGE RD
CLACKAMAS CO OR 205-D3
SCOTTS MILLS OR 205-D3
NUGENT RD
WHATCOM CO WA 160-B1
N NUGENT RD
WHATCOM CO WA 160-B1
S NUGENT RD
WHATCOM CO WA 160-B1
NULLE RD
SKAGIT CO WA 161-A3
WHATCOM CO WA 161-B3
NUMBER 4 RD
KLICKITAT CO WA 127-C1
NUMBER 81 RD
KITTITAS CO WA 241-C5
NUMBER TWO CANYON RD
WENATCHEE WA 238-D4
E NUNN RD
KOOTENAI CO ID 245-B2
NURSERY AV
AMITY OR 204-B2
SW NURSERY RD
WASHINGTON CO OR 198-C2
NUSOM RD NE
MARION CO OR 205-B4
NUTLEY ST
ASHLAND OR 337-C8
NUTMEG ST SW
GRAND MOUND WA 184-B4
NYANZA RD SW
LAKEWOOD WA 181-C4
SW NYBERG ST
TUALATIN OR 199-B4
SE NYE AV
PENDLETON OR 129-B1
SW NYE AV
PENDLETON OR 129-B1
NW NYE ST
NEWPORT OR 206-B4
NYHUS ST
WESTPORT WA 298-H11

O

O RD NW
DOUGLAS CO WA 236-C7
O RD SW
DOUGLAS CO WA 239-C1
OAK AV
LAKE CO OR 152-A2
SE OAK AV
ROSEBURG OR 334-F7
SE OAK AV Rt#-138
ROSEBURG OR 334-F7
SW OAK AV Rt#-138
ROSEBURG OR 334-F7
OAK RD
DESCHUTES CO OR 212-C5
OAK RD NW
YAMHILL CO OR 204-C2
OAK ST
ALBANY OR 326-E11
ASHLAND OR 337-C7
JACKSON CO OR 337-C7
LEBANON OR 133-C1
LINN CO OR 133-C1
MILTON WA 182-B2
OKANOGAN WA 104-C3
OKANOGAN CO WA 104-C3
VANCOUVER BC 156-B5
VANCOUVER BC 254-F13
WASHINGTON CO OR 198-A2
OAK ST Rt#-99
CITY OF RICHMOND BC 156-B5
VANCOUVER BC 156-B5
OAK ST Rt#-141
BINGEN WA 195-D5
OAK ST Rt#-162
NEZPERCE ID 123-C2
OAK ST Rt#-213
MARION CO OR 205-C4
SILVERTON OR 205-C4
OAK ST U.S.-30
HOOD RIVER OR 195-C5
S OAK ST
BENTON CO WA 121-A3
BENTON CO WA 343-F14
FINLEY WA 121-A3
FINLEY WA 343-F14
HIGHLAND WA 121-A3
SE OAK ST Rt#-8
HILLSBORO OR 198-D1
SW OAK ST
GRANTS PASS OR 335-E9
SW OAK ST Rt#-8
HILLSBORO OR 198-D1
OAK BAY AV
CITY OF VICTORIA BC 257-B9
DISTRICT OF OAK BAY BC 257-B9
OAK BAY RD
JEFFERSON CO WA 170-B1
OAK BAY RD Rt#-116
HADLOCK-IRONDALE WA 170-A1
JEFFERSON CO WA 170-A1
OAK CREEK DR
BENTON CO OR 327-A8
OAK CREST RD
LANE CO OR 210-C7
N OAKDALE AV
MEDFORD OR 336-C12
S OAKDALE AV
MEDFORD OR 336-C13
SW OAKDALE AV
DALLAS OR 204-A6
OAKDALE RD
POLK CO OR 125-B3
POLK CO OR 204-A6
OAKES AV Rt#-20
ANACORTES WA 259-B3
S OAKES ST
TACOMA WA 294-D6
OAK FLAT RD
CURRY CO OR 148-B1
KLICKITAT CO WA 127-C1
SE OAK GROVE BLVD
CLACKAMAS OR 321-H6
OAK GROVE DR
BENTON CO OR 207-B4
OAK GROVE RD
CLACKAMAS CO OR 199-D7
POLK CO OR 204-B3
OAK GROVE FORK RD
CLACKAMAS CO OR 126-B3
N OAK HARBOR RD
ISLAND CO WA 167-B2
OAK HILL RD
POLK CO OR 207-B2
YAMHILL CO OR 198-A4
OAKHURST RD
ELMA WA 179-B7
OAK ISLAND RD
MULTNOMAH CO OR 192-A5
OAK KNOLL RD NW
POLK CO OR 204-C4
OAKLAND ST
DISTRICT OF BURNABY BC 156-D5
OAKLAND-SHADY HWY Rt#-99
DOUGLAS CO OR 219-A7
DOUGLAS CO OR 221-C1
DOUGLAS CO OR 334-F2
OAKLAND OR 219-A7
ROSEBURG OR 334-F2
SUTHERLIN OR 221-C1
OAKLEA DR
LANE CO OR 210-A5
OAKMEADE LN
YAMHILL CO OR 198-D6
OAK PLAIN DR
LINN CO OR 210-A2
OAKRIDGE DR SW
KITSAP CO WA 174-A6
OAK RIDGE RD
KLICKITAT CO WA 195-D2
NW OAK RIDGE RD
YAMHILL CO OR 198-A5

STREET
City State Page-Grid

OAK SPRINGS FARM RD
YAMHILL CO OR 198-B6
OAKVIEW DR
LINN CO OR 210-C2
OAK VILLA RD
POLK CO OR 204-A6
OAKVILLE RD
GRAYS HARBOR CO WA 117-B1
LINN CO OR 207-B6
LINN CO OR 326-A10
OAKVILLE CEMETERY RD
GRAYS HARBOR CO WA 117-B1
OAKWAY RD
EUGENE OR 330-B4
OAKWOOD DR
DOUGLAS CO OR 219-A6
OASIS RD
CANYON CO ID 139-B3
GEM CO ID 139-B3
PAYETTE CO ID 139-B3
OATFIELD RD
CLACKAMAS CO OR 199-D4
CLARK CO WA 193-A1
GLADSTONE OR 199-D4
SE OATFIELD RD
CLACKAMAS CO OR 199-D3
MILWAUKIE OR 199-D3
OBERLIN RD
SISKIYOU CO CA 149-C3
YREKA CA 149-C3
OBOYD RD
WHITMAN CO WA 249-B4
OBRIAN RD
BENTON CO WA 120-C3
OBRIEN RD
CLALLAM CO WA 165-D7
JOSEPHINE CO OR 233-A6
O B RILEY RD
BEND OR 332-E1
DESCHUTES CO OR 217-B1
DESCHUTES CO OR 332-E1
SW OBSIDIAN AV
DESCHUTES CO OR 212-C5
OBSTRUCTION PASS RD
SAN JUAN CO WA 160-A3
W OCCIDENTAL AV
YAKIMA CO WA 243-A7
OCEAN AV
MANZANITA OR 191-B4
WESTPORT WA 298-G13
OCEAN AV Rt#-105
WESTPORT WA 298-F13
OCEAN AV U.S.-101
RAYMOND WA 117-A1
OCEAN BLVD
CITY OF COLWOOD BC 159-B6
COOS BAY OR 333-E8
OCEAN BLVD SW
BANDON OR 220-A6
OCEAN DR
CLATSOP CO WA 188-B4
OCEAN RD
MANZANITA OR 191-B4
TILLAMOOK CO OR 191-B4
OCEAN BEACH HWY Rt#-4
CATHLAMET WA 117-B3
COWLITZ CO WA 117-B3
COWLITZ CO WA 189-A2
COWLITZ CO WA 302-A3
LONGVIEW WA 302-F7
LONGVIEW WA 303-A8
WAHKIAKUM CO WA 117-B3
WEST LONGVIEW WA 302-A3
OCEAN BEACH HWY Rt#-6
CHEHALIS WA 299-A13
LEWIS CO WA 117-B1
LEWIS CO WA 184-B7
LEWIS CO WA 187-A1
LEWIS CO WA 299-A13
PE ELL WA 117-B2
OCEAN BEACH HWY Rt#-103
LONG BEACH WA 186-A5
PACIFIC CO WA 186-A5
OCEAN BEACH RD
GRAYS HARBOR CO WA 177-B2
GRAYS HARBOR CO WA 178-A6
OCEANIA DR
LINCOLN CO OR 328-C4
OCEANIA DR N
LINCOLN CO OR 328-C2
OCEAN LAKE WY
OCEAN SHORES WA 177-B7
OCEAN SHORES BLVD
OCEAN SHORES WA 177-B6
OCEAN SHORES WA 298-B5
OCEAN SHORES BLVD E
OCEAN SHORES WA 298-B6
OCEAN SHORES BLVD SW
OCEAN SHORES WA 177-B7
OCEAN VIEW BLVD NE
KITSAP CO WA 271-C4
OCEAN VIEW DR
CURRY CO OR 232-D6
HARBOR OR 232-D6
NEWPORT OR 206-B4
YACHATS OR 209-A3
OCEAN VIEW DR Rt#-D5
DEL NORTE CO CA 232-D7
OCEANVIEW CEMETERY RD
CLATSOP CO WA 188-B2
WARRENTON WA 188-B2
OCHOCO HWY Rt#-126
CROOK CO OR 213-A5
DESCHUTES CO OR 212-D5
DESCHUTES CO OR 213-A5
PRINEVILLE OR 213-B6
REDMOND OR 212-D5
REDMOND OR 213-A5
OCHOCO HWY U.S.-26
CROOK CO OR 135-C2
CROOK CO OR 136-A2
CROOK CO OR 213-D5
GRANT CO OR 136-B1
MITCHELL OR 136-B1
PRINEVILLE OR 213-D5
WHEELER CO OR 136-B1
OCHOCO CREEK RD
CROOK CO OR 135-C2
CROOK CO OR 136-A2
OCONNER RD SE
THURSTON CO WA 184-C4
OCONNOR RD
KLAMATH CO OR 235-C6
NE ODDFELLOW RD
KITSAP CO WA 271-J6
ODELL HWY
HOOD RIVER CO OR 195-C6
ODELL RD
DESCHUTES CO OR 142-C1
ODELL ST
WHATCOM CO WA 158-B3
NW ODEM AV
DESCHUTES CO OR 212-D4
TERREBONNE OR 212-D4
ODONNELL RD
LATAH CO ID 249-C4
WHITMAN CO WA 249-C4
OENNING RD
WHITMAN CO WA 250-B1
OFFUTT LAKE RD SE
THURSTON CO WA 184-D2
O-GARA RD
KOOTENAI CO ID 248-B5
OGDEN RD
COWLITZ CO WA 187-B7
OGLE RD NE
KITSAP CO WA 174-C1
OHARA RD
UMATILLA CO OR 129-C1
WESTON OR 129-C1
OHIO ST
BELLINGHAM WA 258-E6
OHIO MATCH AV
KOOTENAI CO ID 354-E8
POST FALLS ID 354-E8
E OHIO MATCH AV
KOOTENAI CO ID 354-D7
POST FALLS ID 354-D7
E OHIO MATCH RD
KOOTENAI CO ID 245-A4
OHOP VALLEY RD E
PIERCE CO WA 118-B1
S OKANOGAN AV
WENATCHEE WA 238-D5
OKLAHOMA RD
SKAMANIA CO WA 195-B2
OKLAHOMA GULCH RD
CHELAN CO WA 236-A4
OKOMA DR Rt#-20
OKANOGAN CO WA 104-C3
OMAK WA 104-C3
OLA HWY
GEM CO ID 139-C3
OLALLA RD
DOUGLAS CO OR 141-A2
DOUGLAS CO OR 221-A7
LINCOLN CO OR 206-C4
SE OLALLA VALLEY RD
KITSAP CO WA 174-C6
OLALLA VALLEY RD SE
KITSAP CO WA 174-C5
OLANDER RD
LEWIS CO ID 123-B3
OLD HWY
DOUGLAS CO OR 221-B1
KLICKITAT CO WA 196-A5
OLD HWY Rt#-99
DOUGLAS CO OR 221-B7
WINSTON OR 221-B7
OLD 26 RD
ADAMS CO WA 122-A1
OLD 410 HWY
ELMA WA 179-A7
GRAYS HARBOR CO WA 178-D7
GRAYS HARBOR CO WA 179-C6
OLD ALBION RD
WHITMAN CO WA 249-A3
OLD ALTURAS HWY
KLAMATH CO OR 151-A3
MODOC CO CA 151-A3
OLD APPLETON GRADE RD
KLICKITAT CO WA 196-C3
SW OLD BARNEY WHITE LN
KITSAP CO WA 174-A4
OLD BEAVER HILL RD
COOS CO OR 220-C3
OLD BELFAIR HWY
MASON CO WA 173-D5
OLD BELFAIR HWY Rt#-300
MASON CO WA 173-D5
NE OLD BELFAIR HWY
MASON CO WA 174-A4
W OLD BELFAIR VALLEY RD
BREMERTON WA 174-A4
KITSAP CO WA 174-A4
SE OLD BETHEL RD
YAMHILL CO OR 204-B3
OLD BRIDGE DR
LINN CO OR 133-C1
OLD BRUNDAGE MTN RD
MCCALL ID 251-C5
OLD BUZZARD MINE RD
JACKSON CO OR 226-B4
OLD CONDOR RD N
TILLAMOOK CO OR 197-B6
OLD CORNELIUS PASS RD
WASHINGTON CO OR 192-A7
OLD COULEE RD
GRANT CO WA 237-C4
LINCOLN CO WA 237-C4
OLD CRATER LAKE HWY
EAGLE POINT OR 230-D5
JACKSON CO OR 230-D5
OLD DALLES DR
HOOD RIVER CO OR 195-D5
OLD DALLES RD
HOOD RIVER CO OR 195-D6
OLD DAY CREEK RD
SKAGIT CO WA 161-C6
OLD DIAMOND LAKE RD
DOUGLAS CO OR 227-A2
JACKSON CO OR 226-D3
OLD DUFUR RD
THE DALLES OR 196-D7
WASCO CO OR 196-D7
OLD EASTSIDE RD
BONNER CO ID 107-A3
OLD EMGRNT HIL SCENC FRNTG RD
UNION CO OR 129-C2
OLD EMPIRE RD
NORTH BEND OR 333-E6
OLD EXPERIMENT RD
HARNEY CO OR 145-B1
OLD FAIRHAVEN PKWY Rt#-11
BELLINGHAM WA 258-B11
OLDFIELD RD
DIST OF CENTRAL SAANICH BC 159-C5
DISTRICT OF SAANICH BC 159-C5
OLD FORT RD
KLAMATH CO OR 235-C1
KLAMATH CO OR 338-H2
POLK CO OR 207-B1
OLD FORT HARNEY RD
HARNEY CO OR 137-B3
HARNEY CO OR 145-B1
OLD FORT KLAMATH RD
KLAMATH CO OR 338-G6
OLD FRONTIER RD NW
KITSAP CO WA 174-B1
OLD GASQUET TOLL RD
DEL NORTE CO CA 148-C3
OLD GOOSE LAKE RD
ADAMS CO ID 251-B3
OLD GRAND COULEE WILBUR HWY
GRANT CO WA 237-C3
OLD GUN CLUB RD
LEWISTON ID 250-C4
NEZ PERCE CO ID 250-C4
OLDHAM CREEK RD
DOUGLAS CO OR 219-C7
OLD HARTFORD RD
LAKE STEVENS WA 110-C1
SNOHOMISH CO WA 110-C1
OLD HIGHWAY RD
WASHINGTON CO ID 139-B1
OLD HIGHWAY 22 CUTOFF RD
STEVENS CO WA 113-C1
OLD HIGHWAY 47
WASHINGTON CO OR 198-B2
OLD HIGHWAY 99
SISKIYOU CO CA 149-C3
SISKIYOU CO CA 150-A3
OLD HOG JOHN RD
HUMBOLDT CO NV 154-A3
OLD HWY RD
MIDVALE ID 139-B1
WASHINGTON CO ID 139-B1
OLD HWY 30 E
BAKER CITY OR 138-B1
BAKER CO OR 138-B1
SW OLD HWY 47 Rt#-47
FOREST GROVE OR 198-B1
WASHINGTON CO OR 198-B1
OLD HWY 95
LATAH CO ID 249-D7
OLD HWY 97
BREWSTER WA 104-C3
JEFFERSON CO OR 208-D3
OKANOGAN CO WA 104-C3
OLD HWY 99 N
BURLINGTON WA 260-C4
SKAGIT CO WA 161-B3
SKAGIT CO WA 260-C4
WHATCOM CO WA 161-B3
OLD HWY 99N
SKAGIT CO WA 168-B2
SNOHOMISH CO WA 168-B3
OLD HWY 99 SE
THURSTON CO WA 296-H14
OLD HWY 99 SW
GRAND MOUND WA 184-B4
THURSTON CO WA 184-B4
OLD HWY 101
CANNON BEACH WA 188-B7
CLATSOP CO WA 188-B7
OLD HWY 160
KITSAP CO WA 174-D4
OLD HWY 195
WHITMAN CO WA 114-C3
OLD HWY-NW CHEWELAH RD
CHEWELAH WA 106-B3
OLD HWY EAST SPRINGDALE RD
STEVENS CO WA 106-B3
OLD HWY NORTHPORT RD
STEVENS CO WA 106-A1
OLD IDAHO-OREGON-NEVADA HWY
MALHEUR CO OR 146-B3
MALHEUR CO OR 154-B1
OLD IMNAHA RD
WALLOWA CO OR 131-A2
OLDING RD
BREMERTON WA 270-C8
OLD INLAND EMPIRE HWY
BENTON CITY WA 120-C3
BENTON CO WA 120-C3
OLD ISLAND HWY
CITY OF COLWOOD BC 159-B6
OLD ISLAND HWY Rt#-1A
CITY OF COLWOOD BC 159-B6
DISTRICT OF SAANICH BC 256-B5
TOWN OF ESQUIMALT BC 256-B5
TOWN OF VIEW ROYAL BC 159-B6
TOWN OF VIEW ROYAL BC 256-A4
OLD KETTLE RD
STEVENS CO WA 106-A2
W OLD KETTLE RD
KETTLE FALLS WA 106-A2
STEVENS CO WA 106-A2
OLD LAKE RD
LAKE CO OR 143-C2
OLD LAPWAI RD
LEWISTON ID 250-C4
NEZ PERCE CO ID 250-C4
OLD LINDBERG HWY
COLUMBIA CO OR 189-C5
OLD LORANE RD
LANE CO OR 133-B3
OLD MARINE DR
BELLINGHAM WA 158-D7
OLD MCMINNVILLE HWY
YAMHILL CO OR 198-B6
OLD MEADOW RD
MCCALL ID 251-C5
OLD MEHAMA RD SE
MARION CO OR 133-C1
STAYTON OR 133-C1
OLD MELROSE RD
DOUGLAS CO OR 221-B4
DOUGLAS CO OR 334-A7
ROSEBURG OR 334-A7
OLD MIDLAND RD
KLAMATH CO OR 235-C5
OLD MILITARY RD NE
KITSAP CO WA 174-B1
KITSAP CO WA 270-H1
OLD MILITARY RD SE
THURSTON CO WA 184-D3
NE OLD MILL RD
KITSAP CO WA 271-J4
OLD MILL RD SW
KING CO WA 174-D7
OLD MILL SCHOOLIE RD
WASCO CO OR 127-A3
OLD MILTON HWY
WALLA WALLA CO WA 344-F13
WALLA WALLA CO WA 345-A13
OLD MOHAWK RD
LANE CO OR 215-D1
LANE CO OR 331-E3
OLD MONITOR RD
CASHMERE WA 238-C2
CHELAN CO WA 238-C2
OLD MOSCOW RD
WHITMAN CO WA 249-B5
OLD MOSES LAKE HWY
GRANT CO WA 242-B1
OLD NACHES HWY
NACHES WA 119-C1
YAKIMA CO WA 119-C1
YAKIMA CO WA 243-A4
OLD NORTHERN STATE HOSPITAL RD
SKAGIT CO WA 161-C4
OLD NORTHPORT HWY
STEVENS CO WA 106-A1
OLD OCHOCO HWY
CROOK CO OR 136-A2
OLD OLYMPIC HWY
CLALLAM CO WA 165-D6
CLALLAM CO WA 166-A6
CLALLAM CO WA 262-C8
MASON CO WA 180-A4
OLD OLYMPIC HWY Rt#-3
MASON CO WA 180-A3
SHELTON WA 180-A3
OLD OLYMPIC HWY SW
THURSTON CO WA 180-B6
OLD OREGON TRAIL HWY I-84
BAKER CITY OR 138-B1
BAKER CO OR 130-A3
BAKER CO OR 138-B1
LA GRANDE OR 130-A2
MALHEUR CO OR 138-B1
MALHEUR CO OR 139-A2
MORROW CO OR 128-C1
NORTH POWDER OR 130-A3
ONTARIO OR 139-A2
PAYETTE CO ID 139-A2
PENDLETON OR 129-A1
UMATILLA CO OR 128-C1
UMATILLA CO OR 129-A1
UNION CO OR 129-C2
UNION CO OR 130-A2
OLD OWEN RD
MONROE WA 110-C1
SNOHOMISH CO WA 110-C1
OLD PACIFIC HWY
COWLITZ CO WA 118-A3
COWLITZ CO WA 187-C6
COWLITZ CO WA 189-D3
COWLITZ CO WA 303-G14
DOUGLAS CO OR 225-C6
KELSO WA 303-G14
LA CENTER WA 192-C1
SNOHOMISH CO WA 168-A4
WOODLAND WA 118-A3
WOODLAND WA 189-D3
OLD PACIFIC HWY Rt#-99
DOUGLAS CO OR 225-C2
MYRTLE CREEK OR 225-C2
TRI-CITY OR 225-C2
OLD PACIFIC HWY Rt#-432
KELSO WA 303-F13
OLD PACIFIC HWY N
CASTLE ROCK WA 187-C7
COWLITZ CO WA 187-C6
OLD PACIFIC HWY S
COWLITZ CO WA 189-D6
OLD PACIFIC HWY SE
THURSTON CO WA 181-A6
OLD PARRETT MOUNTAIN RD
YAMHILL CO OR 199-A5
OLD PENDLETON RIVER RD
ECHO OR 129-A1
UMATILLA CO OR 129-A1
OLD PENGRA RD
LANE CO OR 133-C3
LOWELL OR 133-C3
OLD PORTLAND RD
COLUMBIA CO OR 192-A2
OLD PULLMAN RD
MOSCOW ID 249-C5
OLD RAINIER RD
COLUMBIA CO OR 189-A4
NE OLD REDMOND RD
KING CO WA 175-C1
REDMOND WA 175-C1
OLD REDWOOD HWY
JOSEPHINE CO OR 229-A7
OLD RIVER RD
BENTON CO OR 133-B2
BENTON CO OR 210-A4
LINCOLN CO OR 206-C2
OLD ROSE CREEK RD
KOOTENAI CO ID 248-D2
OLD RR GRADE
YAMHILL CO OR 198-A4
NW OLD RR GRADE
YAMHILL CO OR 198-A5
OLD SALEM RD
MILLERSBURG OR 207-D3
MILLERSBURG OR 326-H3
OLD SAMISH HWY
BELLINGHAM WA 258-D13
WHATCOM CO WA 161-A2
WHATCOM CO WA 258-D13
OLD SAMS VALLEY RD
JACKSON CO OR 230-B5
OLD SAND CREEK RD
DOUGLAS CO OR 219-B2
GRAYS HARBOR CO WA 179-C6
OLD SANDERS RD
BENEWAH CO ID 115-A3
OLD SANTIAM WAGON RD
DESCHUTES CO OR 211-A3
OLD SCENIC HWY 101
LINCOLN CO OR 203-B3
ROSE LODGE OR 203-B3
SW OLD SCHOLLS FERRY RD Rt#-21
BEAVERTON OR 199-B3
WASHINGTON CO OR 199-A3
OLD SEEKSEEQUA RD
JEFFERSON CO OR 208-A4
OLDS FERRY RD
WASHINGTON CO ID 139-A2
OLDS FERRY-ONTARIO HWY Rt#-201
MALHEUR CO OR 139-A2
ONTARIO OR 139-A2
OLDS FERRY-ONTARIO HWY U.S.-30
MALHEUR CO OR 139-A3
ONTARIO OR 139-A3
SW OLD SHERIDAN RD
MCMINNVILLE OR 198-A7
YAMHILL CO OR 198-A7
YAMHILL CO OR 204-B1
OLD SHERMAN HWY
SHERMAN CO OR 127-C1
OLD SILETZ-TOLEDO RD
LINCOLN CO OR 206-C3
OLD SISKIYOU HWY
JACKSON CO OR 150-A2
JACKSON CO OR 234-D5
OLD SNOHOMISH MNRO HWY
SNOHOMISH CO WA 110-C1
OLD SNOHOMISH MONROE HWY SE
MONROE WA 110-C1
SNOHOMISH CO WA 110-C1
OLD SNOHOMISH MONROE RD
SNOHOMISH CO WA 171-D4
NW OLD SOLDIERS RD
YAMHILL CO OR 198-A5
OLD SOLDIERS GRADE
LAPWAI ID 123-A2
NEZ PERCE CO ID 123-A2
NEZ PERCE CO ID 250-D4
OLD SOUTH RD
CLEARWATER CO ID 123-B2
OLD SPIRAL HWY
NEZ PERCE CO ID 250-B3
OLD SPIRAL HWY Rt#-128
LEWISTON ID 250-B4
OLD SPREADBOROUGH RD
COWLITZ CO WA 189-D5
OLD SR 195
SPOKANE CO WA 114-C2
OLD STAGE RD
CAVE JUNCTION OR 233-B4
JACKSON CO OR 149-B2
JACKSON CO OR 230-B6
JACKSON CO OR 234-A1
JOSEPHINE CO OR 233-B4
OLD STAGE RD Rt#-99
JACKSON CO OR 230-B6
OLD STAGE ROUTE
COOS BAY OR 333-D5
COOS CO OR 333-D5
NORTH BEND OR 333-D5
OLD STATE HWY
CASCADE ID 252-D6
SISKIYOU CO CA 150-B3
WHITMAN CO WA 114-C3
OLD STITES STAGE RD
IDAHO CO ID 123-C3
SW OLDSVILLE RD
YAMHILL CO OR 204-A2
OLD THORNTON HWY
WHITMAN CO WA 114-C3
E OLD TOWN RD U.S.-97
UNION GAP WA 243-C7
OLD TRAIL CREEK RD
JACKSON CO OR 230-D2
N OLD TRAILS RD
SPOKANE CO WA 246-A3
OLD TYGH MARKET RD
WASCO CO OR 127-B2
OLD US HWY 2
BOUNDARY CO ID 107-B1
MOYIE SPRINGS ID 107-B1
OLD US HWY 30
CLATSOP CO WA 117-A3
OLD WAPINITIA RD
WASCO CO OR 127-A3
OLD WILLAMETTE HWY
LANE CO OR 142-A1
OLD WILLAPA
PACIFIC CO WA 117-A1
OLD WOODS RD
TILLAMOOK CO OR 197-A7
OLD WYNOOCHEE RD
GRAYS HARBOR CO WA 178-C5
OLD YALE RD
DISTRICT OF ABBOTSFORD BC 102-B1
DISTRICT OF MATSQUI BC 102-B1
DISTRICT OF SURREY BC 157-A6
TOWNSHIP OF LANGLEY BC 158-C1
SW OLESON RD
PORTLAND OR 199-B2
WASHINGTON CO OR 199-B2
OLEX-MCNAB RD
MORROW CO OR 128-B2
OLGA TO PT LAWRENCE RD
SAN JUAN CO WA 160-A3
E OLIPHANT RD
GARFIELD CO WA 122-B2
E OLIPHANT RD Rt#-126
COLUMBIA CO WA 122-B2
GARFIELD CO WA 122-B2
OLIVE ST
LINCOLN CO OR 206-B4
NEWPORT OR 206-B4
OLIVE ST U.S.-20
NEWPORT OR 206-B4
E OLIVE ST U.S.-20
NEWPORT OR 206-B4
W OLIVE ST
NEWPORT OR 206-A4
OLIVE WY
LONGVIEW WA 302-F7
SEATTLE WA 277-J5
SEATTLE WA 278-A5
E OLIVE WY
SEATTLE WA 278-B4
OLIVE BARBER RD
COOS CO OR 220-D2
OLIVER RD
COQUITLAM BC 157-B4
OLLALA CANYON RD
CHELAN CO WA 238-B2
OLMSTEAD RD
MARION CO OR 199-A7
OLMSTEAD RD NW
DOUGLAS CO WA 236-D4
OLNEY AV Rt#-202
ASTORIA WA 300-C7
NE OLNEY AV
BEND OR 332-F6
NW OLNEY AV
BEND OR 332-E6
OLNEY AV SE
KITSAP CO WA 271-A14
PORT ORCHARD WA 271-A14
OLNEY CUTOFF RD
CLATSOP CO WA 188-D3
OLSEN RD
CLALLAM CO WA 166-A7
TILLAMOOK CO OR 197-C2
SE OLSEN ST Rt#-270
PULLMAN WA 249-B5
OLSON DR KPN
PIERCE CO WA 174-A7
OLSON PL SW
SEATTLE WA 285-J4
OLSON RD
COLUMBIA CO OR 189-C7
COWLITZ CO WA 189-D4
DESCHUTES CO OR 212-B7
WHATCOM CO WA 158-C6
WHITMAN CO WA 249-B2
YAMHILL CO OR 198-B3
S OLYMPIA ST
BENTON CO WA 121-A3
BENTON CO WA 343-B14
KENNEWICK WA 343-B11
OLYMPIA WY
LONGVIEW WA 302-D4
LONGVIEW WA 303-A8
WEST LONGVIEW WA 302-D4
SE OLYMPIAD DR
KITSAP CO WA 174-D4
OLYMPIA TENINO HWY N
TENINO WA 184-D3
OLYMPIA TENINO HWY SE
THURSTON CO WA 184-D3
OLYMPIA-YELM HWY Rt#-510
THURSTON CO WA 118-A1
THURSTON CO WA 181-B7
YELM WA 118-A1
N OLYMPIC AV
ARLINGTON WA 168-D5
S OLYMPIC AV
ARLINGTON WA 168-D5
OLYMPIC BLVD
EVERETT WA 264-A6
OLYMPIC DR NW
GIG HARBOR WA 181-C1
PIERCE CO WA 181-C1
OLYMPIC DR SE
KITSAP CO WA 174-B6
OLYMPIC HWY U.S.-101
CLALLAM CO WA 164-A6
CLALLAM CO WA 165-B6
CLALLAM CO WA 166-C7
CLALLAM CO WA 261-A6
JEFFERSON CO WA 109-C1
JEFFERSON CO WA 166-C7
PORT ANGELES WA 261-A6
W OLYMPIC PL
SEATTLE WA 277-G3
OLYMPIC ST
SPRINGFIELD OR 331-B5
OLYMPIC WK NE
SHORELINE WA 171-B6
OLYMPIC WY SE Rt#-305
WINSLOW WA 174-D2
OLYMPIC WY W
SEATTLE WA 277-F2
OLYMPIC HOT SPRINGS RD
CLALLAM CO WA 109-A1
CLALLAM CO WA 165-A7
OLYMPIC VIEW DR
EDMONDS WA 171-A5
LYNNWOOD WA 171-A5
SNOHOMISH CO WA 171-A5
OLYMPIC VIEW RD NW
KITSAP CO WA 174-A1
OLYMPIC VIEW WY
OCEAN SHORES WA 177-B6
OLYMPIC VIEW LOOP RD NW
KITSAP CO WA 170-A7
OLYMPUS BLVD
JEFFERSON CO WA 170-B2
OLYMPUS DR
BREMERTON WA 271-A7
KITSAP CO WA 271-A7
OMAK AV E Rt#-155
OKANOGAN CO WA 104-C3
OMAK WA 104-C3
OMAK LAKE RD
OKANOGAN CO WA 104-C3
OMAK LAKE COLUMBIA RIVER RD
OKANOGAN CO WA 105-A3
ONA RD
LINCOLN CO OR 206-B7

STREET / City State / Page-Grid

ONAWAY RD
LATAH CO ID 249-D1
ONEAL RD
KLICKITAT CO WA 196-B2
ONEIL HWY
CROOK CO OR 213-B4
DESCHUTES CO OR 212-D4
DESCHUTES CO OR 213-A4
ONEILL RD
GRAYS HARBOR CO WA 179-A7
ONION MOUNTAIN RD
JOSEPHINE CO OR 148-C1
ONTARIO ST
SANDPOINT ID 244-A2
VANCOUVER BC 156-B5
OPAL LN
JEFFERSON CO OR 212-D2
OPHIR RD
CURRY CO OR 228-A3
NW OPPENLANDER LN
WASHINGTON CO OR 198-B1
ORAL HULL RD
CLACKAMAS CO OR 200-D4
ORANGE ST
ASHLAND OR 337-C6
S ORCAS ST
SEATTLE WA 282-C6
SEATTLE WA 283-E6
ORCAS TO OLGA RD
SAN JUAN CO WA 101-C2
SAN JUAN CO WA 160-A2
ORCHARD AV
CANYON CO ID 147-B1
KLAMATH CO OR 338-F8
KLAMATH FALLS OR 338-F8
WENATCHEE WA 238-D4
YAKIMA CO WA 243-A6
N ORCHARD AV
DALLAS OR 204-A6
POLK CO OR 204-A6
ORCHARD AV SE
KITSAP CO WA 174-C6
ORCHARD DR
GRANT CO WA 242-C2
ORCHARD LN
DOUGLAS CO OR 221-A4
N ORCHARD ST
BOISE ID 253-C3
TACOMA WA 292-A4
S ORCHARD ST
BOISE ID 253-C4
FIRCREST WA 292-A7
FIRCREST WA 294-A2
TACOMA WA 292-A6
TACOMA WA 294-A4
UNIVERSITY PLACE WA 294-A2
SW ORCHARD ST
SEATTLE WA 285-G1
ORCHARD GRADE
OKANOGAN CO WA 104-C3
ORCHARD HEIGHTS PL NW
POLK CO OR 322-A10
ORCHARD HEIGHTS RD NW
POLK CO OR 204-C5
POLK CO OR 322-A9
SALEM OR 322-E10
ORCHARD KNOB RD
POLK CO OR 204-A5
OREANA RD
OWYHEE CO ID 147-C2
OREGON AV
KLAMATH FALLS OR 338-C6
E OREGON AV
CRESWELL OR 215-C5
N OREGON AV Rt#-397
PASCO WA 343-G6
S OREGON AV Rt#-397
FRANKLIN CO WA 343-H8
PASCO WA 343-H8
W OREGON AV
CRESWELL OR 215-C5
OREGON RD
SISKIYOU CO CA 150-A3
OREGON ST
ASTORIA WA 300-A5
BENTON CO WA 120-C2
FRANKLIN CO WA 343-E1
PRINEVILLE OR 213-D5
OREGON ST Rt#-231
LINCOLN CO WA 114-A2
OREGON ST U.S.-30
MALHEUR CO OR 139-A3
ONTARIO OR 139-A3
OREGON ST U.S.-101
PORT ORFORD OR 224-A6
N OREGON ST
JACKSON CO OR 149-B2
JACKSONVILLE OR 149-B2
N OREGON ST U.S.-30
ONTARIO OR 139-A3
NE OREGON ST
PORTLAND OR 313-G5
SHERWOOD OR 199-A4
S OREGON ST
ONTARIO OR 139-A3
OREGON WY
LONGVIEW WA 302-H13
LONGVIEW WA 303-A10
OREGON WY Rt#-433
COLUMBIA CO OR 189-B4
COWLITZ CO WA 302-H13
LONGVIEW WA 302-J12
RAINIER OR 189-B4
RAINIER OR 302-H13
OREGON CANYON RD
MALHEUR CO OR 154-B2
OREGON CAVES HWY Rt#-46
CAVE JUNCTION OR 233-B4
JOSEPHINE CO OR 233-B4
OREGON CENTRAL HWY U.S.-20
CANYON CO ID 139-A3
OREGON COAST HWY
CLATSOP CO WA 188-B6
OREGON COAST HWY U.S.-101
ASTORIA WA 188-C1
ASTORIA WA 300-A1
BANDON OR 220-C4
BAY CITY OR 191-B5
BAY CITY OR 197-B1
BROOKINGS OR 232-C5
BUNKER HILL OR 333-J12
CANNON BEACH WA 188-B7
CANNON BEACH OR 191-A2
CLATSOP CO WA 188-C1
CLATSOP CO OR 191-A2
CLATSOP CO WA 300-A1
CLATSOP CO WA 301-F14
COOS CO OR 218-B5
COOS CO OR 220-C4
COOS CO OR 224-B4
COOS CO OR 333-G2
CURRY CO OR 224-B4
CURRY CO OR 228-A1
CURRY CO OR 232-B2
DEPOE BAY OR 203-A7
DEPOE BAY OR 206-B3
DOUGLAS CO OR 214-A7
DOUGLAS CO OR 218-B2
DUNES CITY OR 214-B4
FLORENCE OR 214-B4
GARIBALDI OR 191-B5
GEARHART WA 301-H4
GOLD BEACH OR 228-A6
HARBOR OR 232-D6
LAKESIDE OR 218-B2
LANE CO OR 132-B2
LANE CO OR 209-A6
LANE CO OR 214-B4
LINCOLN BEACH OR 203-A7
LINCOLN CITY OR 203-B3
LINCOLN CO OR 203-B3
LINCOLN CO OR 206-B3
LINCOLN CO OR 209-A3
LINCOLN CO OR 328-D2
MANZANITA OR 191-B5
NEWPORT OR 206-B3
NORTH BEND OR 333-G2
PORT ORFORD OR 224-B6
REEDSPORT OR 218-B2
ROCKAWAY BEACH OR 191-B5
SEASIDE WA 188-B7
SEASIDE WA 301-H4
TILLAMOOK CO OR 191-B5
TILLAMOOK CO OR 197-B7
TILLAMOOK CO OR 197-C4
TILLAMOOK CO OR 203-B3
WALDPORT OR 328-D2
WARRENTON WA 188-B2
WHEELER OR 191-B5
YACHATS OR 209-A3
OREGON LAKE RESERVR RD
MALHEUR CO OR 155-A1
OREGON SKYLINE RD
CLACKAMAS CO OR 126-C3
WASCO CO OR 126-C3
OREGON TRAIL RD
UNION CO OR 130-A3
OREGON-WASHINGTON HWY Rt#-11
MILTON-FREEWATER OR 121-C3
PENDLETON OR 129-B1
UMATILLA CO OR 121-C3
UMATILLA CO OR 129-B1
WALLA WALLA CO WA 121-C3
WASCO OR 129-B1
SE ORIENT DR
CLACKAMAS CO OR 200-C3
GRESHAM OR 200-B2
MULTNOMAH CO OR 200-B2
ORILLIA RD S
KENT WA 290-E4
KING WA 290-E4
KING WA 291-E4
SEATAC WA 290-E4
SEATAC WA 291-E4
ORINDALE RD
KLAMATH CO OR 235-B4
ORION DR
DESCHUTES CO OR 332-J11
ORNDUFF RD
YAMHILL CO OR 198-C4
ORO BAY RD
PIERCE CO WA 181-A4
ORONDO AV
WENATCHEE WA 238-D4
WENATCHEE WA 239-A4
E ORONDO AV
WENATCHEE WA 239-A4
S ORONDO AV
WENATCHEE WA 238-D4
OROVILLE-TORODA CK RD
OKANOGAN CO WA 104-C1
OKANOGAN CO WA 105-A1
OROVILLE WA 104-C1
ORR RD
COLUMBIA CO OR 189-C6
ORRS CORNER RD
POLK CO OR 204-A6
ORTING-KAPOWSIN HWY
PIERCE CO WA 118-B1
PIERCE CO WA 182-B7
ORVILLE RD E
EATONVILLE WA 118-B1
PIERCE CO WA 118-B1
PIERCE CO WA 182-C7
ORVILLE RD S
MARION CO OR 204-C7
OSBORN RD
MODOC CO CA 151-A3
SISKIYOU CO CA 151-A3
OSBORNE RD
DIST OF N VANCOUVER BC 255-B2
OSBURN CUTOFF RD
WASCO CO OR 196-A6
S OSTER RD
CLACKAMAS CO OR 205-D3
OSTRANDER RD
COWLITZ CO WA 303-H1
OSULLIVAN DAM RD Rt#-262
GRANT CO WA 121-A1
GRANT CO WA 242-B6
S OTHELLO ST
SEATTLE WA 286-E1
SEATTLE WA 287-E1
OTIS VALLEY RD
HARNEY CO OR 137-C3
HARNEY CO OR 138-A3
OTSO POINT RD
PIERCE CO WA 181-A4
OTTER POINT RD
BRITISH COLUMBIA 101-A2
OTTER SLOUGH RD
DOUGLAS CO OR 218-D1
OTTMAR RD
CASCADE VALLEY WA 242-C3
OUTLET CREEK RD
VALLEY CO ID 251-D1
OUTLOOK RD
SUNNYSIDE WA 120-B2
YAKIMA CO WA 120-B2
N OUTLOOK RD
YAKIMA CO WA 120-B2
OUTLOOK RD W
YAKIMA CO WA 120-B2
OVENELL RD
SKAGIT CO WA 161-A6
OVERHULSE RD NW
THURSTON CO WA 296-B1
OVERLAND RD
ADA CO ID 253-B3
BOISE ID 253-C3
COOS CO OR 220-D3
E OVERLAND RD
ADA CO ID 253-B3
MERIDIAN ID 253-B3
W OVERLAND RD
ADA CO ID 147-C1
ADA CO ID 253-A3
OVERLOOK RD
LINCOLN CO OR 209-A4
SE OVERRA RD
KITSAP CO WA 174-C4
OVERSTREET RD
MALHEUR CO OR 139-A3
OWENS RD
BENTON CO WA 121-A3
COLUMBIA CO WA 122-B2
HIGHLAND WA 121-A3
OWENS ST
KLAMATH FALLS OR 338-F8
OWENS ST S
SALEM OR 322-G14
OWHI LAKE RD
OKANOGAN CO WA 105-B3
OWHI LOOP RD
FERRY CO WA 105-B3
OWL CAMP RD
TILLAMOOK CO OR 125-B1
OWSLEY CANYON RD
UNION CO OR 130-A2
OWSLEY GRADE RD Rt#-126
GARFIELD CO WA 122-B2
OWYHEE AV
MALHEUR CO OR 139-A3
OWYHEE BLVD Rt#-19
OWYHEE CO ID 147-A1
OWYHEE LAKE RD
MALHEUR CO OR 139-A3
MALHEUR CO OR 147-A1
OWYHEE TUNNEL RD
MALHEUR CO OR 147-A1
OXENFORD RD
CLALLAM CO WA 165-A6
OXFORD ST
COQUITLAM BC 157-B4
PORT COQUITLAM BC 157-B4
OYSTER BAY AV
BREMERTON WA 270-E12
NAVY YARD CITY WA 270-E12
OYSTER BAY RD NW
THURSTON CO WA 180-B5
OYSTERVILLE RD
PACIFIC CO WA 186-A1
OZETTE MAINLINE RD
CLALLAM CO WA 162-B5

P

P RD NW
DOUGLAS CO WA 236-C7
P ST
PORT TOWNSEND WA 263-G3
PACIFIC AV
EVERETT WA 264-D4
EVERETT WA 265-E4
GLENDALE OR 225-A7
NORTH BEND OR 333-F5
OLYMPIA WA 297-C5
PIERCE CO WA 182-B3
SUMNER WA 182-B3
TACOMA WA 293-H5
TACOMA WA 295-H1
THURSTON CO WA 297-C5
TILLAMOOK CO OR 197-A7
PACIFIC AV Rt#-7
PIERCE CO WA 181-D4
TACOMA WA 181-D4
TACOMA WA 295-H3
PACIFIC AV Rt#-8
CORNELIUS OR 198-C1
FOREST GROVE OR 198-C1
PACIFIC AV Rt#-11
TACOMA WA 293-H6
TACOMA WA 295-H1
PACIFIC AV Rt#-529
EVERETT WA 265-F4
PACIFIC AV U.S.-101
TILLAMOOK OR 197-B2
TILLAMOOK CO OR 197-B2
N PACIFIC AV Rt#-99W
MONMOUTH OR 204-B7
POLK CO OR 204-B7
S PACIFIC AV Rt#-99W
MONMOUTH OR 204-B7
PACIFIC AV N
COWLITZ CO WA 189-C2
COWLITZ CO WA 303-E3
KELSO WA 303-D6
PACIFIC AV N Rt#-431
KELSO WA 303-D7
PACIFIC AV S
ALGONA WA 182-B2
AUBURN WA 182-B2
COWLITZ CO WA 303-C10
KELSO WA 303-C10
PACIFIC AV S Rt#-7
PIERCE CO WA 181-D5
PACIFIC AV SE
LACEY WA 297-F6
OLYMPIA WA 297-F6
THURSTON CO WA 181-A6
THURSTON CO WA 297-F6
PACIFIC AV SE Rt#-510
THURSTON CO WA 181-A6
PACIFIC BLVD
VANCOUVER BC 254-F11
PACIFIC BLVD U.S.-99E
ALBANY OR 326-F8
LINN CO OR 326-F8
MILLERSBURG OR 326-F8
PACIFIC BLVD N
VANCOUVER BC 254-G11
PACIFIC BLVD S
VANCOUVER BC 254-G11
PACIFIC HWY
EVERETT WA 268-B5
GEARHART WA 301-G4
SNOHOMISH CO WA 171-B4
WARRENTON WA 188-B1
CLARK CO WA 192-C1
PACIFIC HWY I-5
ALBANY OR 326-H5
ASHLAND OR 337-C4
CANYONVILLE OR 225-C1
CENTRAL POINT OR 230-B6
CENTRAL POINT OR 336-A5
CLACKAMAS CO OR 199-B6
COBURG OR 210-B6
COBURG OR 215-C5
COTTAGE GROVE OR 215-B7
CRESWELL OR 215-C5
DOUGLAS CO OR 219-C1
DOUGLAS CO OR 221-C2
DOUGLAS CO OR 225-C1
DOUGLAS CO OR 334-C11
EUGENE OR 330-E7
FOUR CORNERS OR 323-D9
FOUR CORNERS OR 325-D1
GRANTS PASS OR 335-H7
HAYESVILLE OR 323-D9
JACKSON CO OR 149-C3
JACKSON CO OR 150-A2
JACKSON CO OR 229-B4
JACKSON CO OR 230-B6
JACKSON CO OR 234-B2
JACKSON CO OR 336-A5
JACKSON CO OR 337-C4
JOSEPHINE CO OR 225-C5
JOSEPHINE CO OR 229-B1
JOSEPHINE CO OR 335-C3
KEIZER OR 323-C5
LANE CO OR 210-B6
LANE CO OR 215-C5
LANE CO OR 219-C1
LANE CO OR 330-G9
LINN CO OR 207-C7
LINN CO OR 210-B6
LINN CO OR 326-G14
MARION CO OR 199-B6
MARION CO OR 205-A2
MARION CO OR 207-D2
MARION CO OR 323-C5
MARION CO OR 325-B8
MARYSVILLE WA 168-C7
MARYSVILLE WA 171-C1
MEDFORD OR 234-B2
MEDFORD OR 336-E13
MILLERSBURG OR 326-H5
PHOENIX OR 234-B2
ROGUE RIVER OR 229-B4
ROSEBURG OR 334-C11
SALEM OR 323-C5
SALEM OR 325-D1
SISKIYOU CO CA 149-C3
SNOHOMISH CO WA 168-C7
SNOHOMISH CO WA 171-C1
SPRINGFIELD OR 330-E7
SUTHERLIN OR 221-C2
TRI-CITY OR 225-C1
VANCOUVER WA 305-G1
WOODBURN OR 205-A2
PACIFIC HWY Rt#-15
DISTRICT OF SURREY BC 158-B1
PACIFIC HWY Rt#-43
LAKE OSWEGO OR 199-C4
LAKE OSWEGO OR 321-G7
WEST LINN OR 199-C4
PACIFIC HWY Rt#-99
EDMONDS WA 171-B5
EVERETT WA 171-B5
EVERETT WA 267-J7
EVERETT WA 268-A7
FEDERAL WAY WA 182-A2
LYNNWOOD WA 171-B5
SNOHOMISH CO WA 171-B5
PACIFIC HWY Rt#-99E
MARION CO OR 205-B2
WOODBURN OR 205-B1
PACIFIC HWY Rt#-103
OCEAN PARK WA 186-A2
PACIFIC CO WA 186-A3
PACIFIC HWY Rt#-529
EVERETT WA 171-C1
MARYSVILLE WA 171-C1
SNOHOMISH CO WA 171-C1
PACIFIC HWY E Rt#-99
FEDERAL WAY WA 182-A2
FIFE WA 182-A2
MILTON WA 182-A2
PIERCE CO WA 182-A2
PACIFIC HWY E Rt#-99E
AURORA OR 199-B7
BARLOW OR 199-C6
CANBY OR 199-C6
CLACKAMAS CO OR 199-D4
GERVAIS OR 205-B1
GLADSTONE OR 199-D4
HAYESVILLE OR 323-E5
HUBBARD OR 205-B1
MARION CO OR 199-B7
MARION CO OR 205-A3
MARION CO OR 323-E5
OREGON CITY OR 199-D4
SALEM OR 323-E5
WOODBURN OR 205-B1
PACIFIC HWY N Rt#-431
KELSO WA 303-E6
PACIFIC HWY S Rt#-99
DES MOINES WA 175-B7
DES MOINES WA 290-C6
FEDERAL WAY WA 175-B7
FEDERAL WAY WA 182-B1
KENT WA 175-B7
KENT WA 290-C6
KING WA 286-D6
KING CO WA 175-B7
SEATAC WA 288-D1
TUKWILA WA 286-D6
TUKWILA WA 288-D1
PACIFIC HWY S Rt#-103
LONG BEACH WA 186-A5
PACIFIC HWY SE
TENINO WA 184-D2
THURSTON CO WA 184-C1
PACIFIC HWY SE Rt#-510
THURSTON CO WA 181-A6
PACIFIC HWY SW
GRAND MOUND WA 184-B4
LAKEWOOD WA 181-C4
THURSTON CO WA 184-B4
PACIFIC HWY W
PORTLAND OR 308-E3
PORTLAND OR 309-E2
PORTLAND OR 316-B7
PORTLAND OR 320-A1
PACIFIC HWY W Rt#-99
EUGENE OR 215-A1
EUGENE OR 329-D2
JUNCTION CITY OR 210-A7
LANE CO OR 210-A7
LANE CO OR 215-A1
PACIFIC HWY W Rt#-99W
ADAIR VILLAGE OR 207-B3
BENTON CO OR 133-B2
BENTON CO OR 207-A7
BENTON CO OR 327-H7
CORVALLIS OR 207-A7
CORVALLIS OR 327-H7
JUNCTION CITY OR 210-A5
KING CITY OR 199-B3
LANE CO OR 133-B2
LANE CO OR 210-A5
MONMOUTH OR 204-B6
MONROE OR 133-B2
NEWBERG OR 198-D5
POLK CO OR 204-B6
POLK CO OR 207-B3
PORTLAND OR 199-B3
SHERWOOD OR 199-A4
TIGARD OR 199-B3
TUALATIN OR 199-B3
WASHINGTON CO OR 199-B3
YAMHILL CO OR 198-C6
YAMHILL CO OR 199-A4
YAMHILL CO OR 204-B6
PACIFIC HWY W Rt#-103
LONG BEACH WA 186-A5
NE PACIFIC PL
SEATTLE WA 274-C7
PACIFIC ST
VANCOUVER BC 254-E10
WOODLAND WA 189-D7
WOODLAND WA 192-B1
WOODLAND WA 192-C1
N PACIFIC ST
SEATTLE WA 274-A7
NE PACIFIC ST
SEATTLE WA 274-B6
PACIFIC TER
KLAMATH FALLS OR 338-E5
PACIFIC VW
CURRY CO OR 224-B3
PACIFIC WY
COWLITZ CO WA 302-B3
LONGVIEW WA 302-H6
LONGVIEW HEIGHTS WA 302-B3
WEST LONGVIEW WA 302-B3
PACIFIC CREST TR
BRITISH COLUMBIA 103-C1
CASCADE LOCKS OR 194-D6
CHELAN CO WA 111-B1
CLACKAMAS CO OR 126-C3
CLACKAMAS CO OR 202-A5
DESCHUTES CO OR 134-C3
DESCHUTES CO OR 216-A4
DOUGLAS CO OR 223-D6
HOOD RIVER CO OR 194-D6
HOOD RIVER CO OR 201-D2
HOOD RIVER CO OR 202-A5
JACKSON CO OR 150-A2
JEFFERSON CO OR 211-A2
KING CO WA 111-A3
KLAMATH CO OR 142-B1
KLAMATH CO OR 150-A2
KLAMATH CO OR 223-D6
KLAMATH CO OR 227-B7
LANE CO OR 134-C3
LANE CO OR 142-B1
LANE CO OR 211-A6
LANE CO OR 216-A4
LEWIS CO WA 119-A2
LINN CO OR 211-A2
MARION CO OR 126-C3
OKANOGAN CO WA 103-C1
PIERCE CO WA 119-A1
SKAMANIA CO WA 118-C3
SKAMANIA CO WA 194-B4
SKAMANIA CO WA 195-A3
SNOHOMISH CO WA 103-B3
SNOHOMISH CO WA 111-B1
WASCO CO OR 126-C3
YAKIMA CO WA 119-A1
PACK RIVER RD
BONNER CO ID 107-B2
PADDY FLAT RD
VALLEY CO ID 252-D1
PAGE RD
DISTRICT OF MATSQUI BC 94-B3
DOUGLAS CO OR 221-C3
PAGE CREEK RD
JOSEPHINE CO OR 233-B7
PAGE PLACE RD
MALHEUR CO OR 146-C2
PAGH RD
CLACKAMAS CO OR 200-D5
PAHA PACKARD RD
ADAMS CO WA 113-C3
PAINE AV
EVERETT WA 265-E4
PAINE RD
COWLITZ CO WA 187-D7
PAINE FIELD BLVD
MUKILTEO WA 267-E6
SNOHOMISH WA 267-E6
PAINTER LP NE
MARION CO OR 205-C1
E PAINTER RD
SPOKANE CO WA 114-C2
PAISLEY RD
DIST OF N VANCOUVER BC 254-G3
PAIUTE
CROOK CO OR 213-D7
PALA RD
DEL NORTE CO CA 148-B3
PALERMO DR SW
THURSTON CO WA 184-B1
PALESTINE AV
BENTON CO OR 207-B3
PALISADES RD SW
DOUGLAS CO WA 112-B2
DOUGLAS CO WA 239-C6
S PALIX RD
PACIFIC CO WA 186-B1
PALM CREEK RD
COLUMBIA CO OR 189-A4
PALMER AV
OKANOGAN CO WA 104-C1
PALMER LN
ADA CO ID 253-A1
PALMER RD
CLACKAMAS CO OR 200-B5
CLATSOP CO WA 188-D3
LEWIS CO WA 187-D2
S PALMER RD
CLACKAMAS CO OR 205-D2
SE PALMER CREEK RD
YAMHILL CO OR 204-C1
PALMER JUNCTION RD
ELGIN OR 130-A1
UNION CO OR 130-A1
PALMER MILL RD
MULTNOMAH CO OR 201-A1
PALO ALTO RD
CLALLAM CO WA 109-C1
PALOUSE HWY
SPOKANE CO WA 114-C2
WAVERLY WA 114-C2
E PALOUSE HWY
SPOKANE CO WA 246-D6
SPOKANE CO WA 247-A6
S PALOUSE HWY
SPOKANE CO WA 246-C5
N PALOUSE RD
COLFAX WA 122-C1
WHITMAN CO WA 122-C1
PALOUSE ST
ENDICOTT WA 122-B1
PALOUSE COVE RD
PALOUSE WA 249-C2
WHITMAN CO WA 249-C2
PALOUSE COVE RD Rt#-66
LATAH CO ID 249-C2
S PALOUSE RIVER RD
WHITMAN CO WA 249-A2
PANAKANIC RD
KLICKITAT CO WA 196-B1
PANDA RD
SKAMANIA CO WA 193-D6
PANDORA AV
CITY OF VICTORIA BC 256-J9
CITY OF VICTORIA BC 257-A9
PANDORA RD
ROSALIA WA 114-C3
WHITMAN CO WA 114-C3
PANORAMA DR
COQUITLAM BC 157-A4
PANORAMA RD
LANE CO OR 215-D3
PANTHER CREEK RD
SKAMANIA CO WA 194-D3
PANTHER LAKE RD W
KITSAP CO WA 173-D4
PARADISE DR
WALLA WALLA CO WA 121-B3
SW PARADISE LN
KITSAP CO WA 174-A6
PARADISE LP
WALLA WALLA CO WA 121-B3
PARADISE RD
WHATCOM CO WA 158-D6
E PARADISE RD
SPOKANE CO WA 246-D6
PARADISE WY
COOS CO OR 220-D6
PARADISE CREEK RD
DOUGLAS CO OR 141-A1
PARADISE HILL RD
OKANOGAN CO WA 104-B3
PARADISE LAKE RD
SNOHOMISH CO WA 171-D5
PARADISE LAKE RD Rt#-524
SNOHOMISH CO WA 171-D5
PARADISE RIDGE RD
LATAH CO ID 249-D5
PARADISE SPRING RD
KLICKITAT CO WA 196-C2
PARALLEL AV
KLICKITAT CO WA 196-D6
PARCELL RD NE
KITSAP CO WA 170-D5
PARENT AV SW
KITSAP CO WA 174-A5
PARISH LN
CROOK CO OR 213-B6
PARK AV
BENTON CO OR 327-H13
MALHEUR CO OR 139-A3
PACIFIC CO WA 117-A1
RAYMOND WA 117-A1
SNOHOMISH WA 171-D3
WINTHROP WA 104-A2
WOODBURN OR 205-B2
PARK AV Rt#-3
BOVILL ID 123-B1
LATAH CO ID 123-B1

STREET / City State / Page-Grid

PARK AV Rt#-105
RAYMOND WA 117-A1
N PARK AV
EUGENE OR 329-E1
LANE CO OR 329-E2
PARK AV N
RENTON WA 175-C5
PARK BLVD
BOISE ID 253-D3
ONTARIO OR 139-A3
SW PARK BLVD
ONTARIO OR 139-A3
PARK DR U.S.-101
GEARHART WA 301-H5
N PARK DR
RENTON WA 175-C4
NE PARK DR Rt#-900
RENTON WA 175-C4
W PARK DR
SPOKANE CO WA 348-A13
PARK LN
ADA CO ID 253-A1
JEFFERSON CO OR 212-D2
MAPLE RIDGE BC 157-C5
NE PARK LN
LINCOLN CO OR 203-B4
PARK RD
BANDON OR 220-B5
DISTRICT OF DELTA BC 156-D6
LEWIS CO WA 187-D3
WHATCOM CO WA 161-C2
PARK RD Rt#-150
CHELAN WA 236-C3
N PARK RD
DISHMAN WA 350-B8
SPOKANE CO WA 350-B5
S PARK RD
SPOKANE CO WA 350-B9
PARK ST
GRANTS PASS OR 335-E10
POLK CO OR 207-C2
TEKOA WA 114-C3
WOODLAND WA 192-B1
WOODLAND WA 192-C1
PARK ST U.S.-20
LEBANON OR 133-C1
E PARK ST
GRANTS PASS OR 335-F10
JOSEPHINE CO OR 335-G11
WEISER ID 139-A2
N PARK ST U.S.-101
ABERDEEN WA 178-B7
N PARK ST U.S.-395
CHEWELAH WA 106-B3
STEVENS CO WA 106-B3
S PARK ST U.S.-101
ABERDEEN WA 178-B7
S PARK ST U.S.-395
CHEWELAH WA 106-B3
STEVENS CO WA 106-B3
W PARK ST Rt#-27
TEKOA WA 114-C3
PARKATO RD
YAKIMA CO WA 120-A2
E PARK CENTER BLVD
ADA CO ID 253-D3
BOISE ID 253-D3
PARK CITY LOOP RD
OKANOGAN CO WA 105-A3
PARKE CREEK RD
KITTITAS CO WA 241-D5
PARKER RD
LEWIS CO WA 187-A1
LINN CO OR 207-D7
POLK CO OR 207-B1
NE PARKER RD
ISLAND CO WA 167-B4
SW PARKER RD
WEST LINN OR 199-C4
PARKER ST
DISTRICT OF BURNABY BC 156-D4
DISTRICT OF BURNABY BC 255-G11
PARKER BRIDGE RD
YAKIMA CO WA 120-A2
PARKERBURG-PROSPER JUNCTION RD
COOS CO OR 220-B5
PARKER MEADOWS RD
JACKSON CO OR 226-D7
PARKER RESERVOIR RD
MALHEUR CO OR 155-A1
PARKEY DR
DESCHUTES CO OR 212-C3
PARK HILL LN
DOUGLAS CO OR 221-C1
SUTHERLIN OR 221-C1
SW PARKLAND DR
CHEHALIS WA 299-E13
PARK ORCHARD DR
GRANT CO WA 242-C2
PARK RIDGE LN
SKAGIT CO WA 161-B4
PARKS RD
DOUGLAS CO WA 237-B1
E PARKS RD
KOOTENAI CO ID 245-B2
PARKWAY DR NW
SALEM OR 322-E12
PARKWAY RD
LANE CO OR 215-D4
PARPALA RD
PACIFIC CO WA 186-C4
PARR RD NE
MARION CO OR 205-B2
PARRELL RD
BEND OR 332-E11
DESCHUTES CO OR 332-D13
DESCHUTES RIVER WOODS OR 332-D13
SW PARRETT MOUNTAIN RD
WASHINGTON CO OR 199-A5
YAMHILL CO OR 199-A5
PARRISH RD
YAMHILL CO OR 198-D6
PARRISH CREEK RD
SPRAY OR 136-B1
WHEELER CO OR 136-B1
PARRISH GAP RD
MARION CO OR 133-C1
MARION CO OR 207-D2

SE PARROTT ST
ROSEBURG OR 334-F7
PARSON RD
ASOTIN CO WA 122-C3
ASOTIN CO WA 250-A6
PARSON CREEK RD
SKAGIT CO WA 161-B4
PARSONS CREEK RD
LANE CO OR 210-D6
PARTON RD
DESCHUTES CO OR 211-D7
PARVIN RD
WHITMAN CO WA 122-C1
WHITMAN CO WA 249-A2
PASCOE AV
LEWIS CO WA 187-D2
PASCO-KAHLOTUS RD
FRANKLIN CO WA 121-B2
KAHLOTUS WA 121-B2
PASCO WA 121-B2
PASSMORE RD
KITTITAS CO WA 241-A4
PATAHA CREEK RD
GARFIELD CO WA 122-B2
PATAHA CREEK RD Rt#-128
GARFIELD CO WA 122-B2
PATEROS FERRY RD
DOUGLAS CO WA 112-B1
PATERSON RD
PROSSER WA 120-C3
PATIT RD
COLUMBIA CO WA 122-A2
PAT MARX RD
KLICKITAT CO WA 196-D4
PATMORE RD
ISLAND CO WA 167-B5
PATRICIA BAY HWY Rt#-17
DIST OF CENTRAL SAANICH BC 159-C2
DIST OF NORTH SAANICH BC 159-C2
DISTRICT OF SAANICH BC 159-C2
DISTRICT OF SAANICH BC 256-F2
TOWN OF SIDNEY BC 159-C2
PATRICK AV
KITTITAS WA 241-C6
PATRICK CREEK RD
DEL NORTE CO CA 148-C3
PATSY DR SE
THURSTON CO WA 184-D2
PATTEE RD
LEWIS CO WA 184-D7
PATTERSON AV
DISTRICT OF BURNABY BC 156-C5
PATTERSON RD
PIERCE CO WA 182-C6
WHITMAN CO WA 249-A4
PATTERSON ST
ALTAMONT OR 339-B11
WESTPORT WA 298-G11
PATTERSON ST NW
SALEM OR 322-F12
PATTERSON FERRY RD
MORROW CO OR 128-C1
PATTERSON LAKE RD
OKANOGAN CO WA 104-A2
PATTON BLVD
GRANT CO WA 242-C2
MOSES LAKE NORTH WA 242-C2
SW PATTON RD
MULTNOMAH OR 316-B1
PORTLAND OR 316-B1
PATTON VALLEY RD
WASHINGTON CO OR 198-A2
PATTULLO BRDG Rt#-99A
DISTRICT OF SURREY BC 156-D5
PATTY RD
ASOTIN CO WA 122-C3
PAULINA HWY
CROOK CO OR 136-B3
PAULINA HWY Rt#-380
CROOK CO OR 135-C2
CROOK CO OR 136-A3
CROOK CO OR 213-D5
PRINEVILLE OR 213-D5
PAULINA-EAST LAKE RD
DESCHUTES CO OR 143-A1
PAULINA SUPLEE RD
CROOK CO OR 136-B3
PAULSON RD
HOQUIAM WA 178-A7
PAVEL RD
CLALLAM CO WA 163-A6
PAWNEE
CROOK CO OR 213-D7
W PAYETTE AV
BENTON CO WA 342-H9
KENNEWICK WA 342-H9
PAYETTE RIVER SCENIC RT Rt#-55
BOISE CO ID 139-C3
PAYNE RD
BENTON CO OR 207-A7
JACKSON CO OR 234-C2
PEACE PORTAL DR
WHATCOM CO WA 158-B3
S PEACH ST
JACKSON CO OR 336-B14
MEDFORD OR 336-B14
W PEACH ST
YAKIMA WA 243-B7
PEACHEY ST Rt#-285
WENATCHEE WA 239-A4
PEACOCK WK
CROOK CO OR 213-C4
PEACOCK HILL AV NW
KITSAP CO WA 174-C6
PIERCE CO WA 174-C7
PEARCE RD
KLICKITAT CO WA 196-A3
PEARDALE LN Rt#-411
LONGVIEW WA 303-C9
PEARDONVILLE RD
DISTRICT OF MATSQUI BC 102-B1
PEARL RD
CANYON CO ID 139-A3
PAYETTE CO ID 139-B3
PEARL ST
COBURG OR 210-B7
EUGENE OR 330-A7
LANE CO OR 210-B7

PEARL ST Rt#-163
RUSTON WA 181-C2
TACOMA WA 181-C2
N PEARL ST Rt#-507
CENTRALIA WA 184-C5
CENTRALIA WA 299-F1
LEWIS CO WA 184-C5
S PEARL ST
TACOMA WA 181-C2
S PEARL ST Rt#-507
CENTRALIA WA 299-F4
W PEARL ST
PASCO WA 343-D5
WEST PASCO WA 342-J5
WEST PASCO WA 343-A5
PEARL CREEK RD
VALLEY CO ID 251-D1
PEARL HILL RD
DOUGLAS CO WA 112-C1
PEARSON LN
VALLEY CO ID 251-D6
PEARSON CREEK RD
UMATILLA CO OR 129-B2
PEART RD
CLARK CO WA 192-D1
NE PEART RD
CLARK CO WA 193-A1
PEASE RD
BURLINGTON WA 260-C7
SKAGIT CO WA 260-C7
PEASLEE AV
ASOTIN CO WA 250-B5
VINELAND WA 250-B5
S PEASLEY CANYON RD
AUBURN WA 182-B1
KING CO WA 182-B1
SW PEAVINE RD
YAMHILL CO OR 198-A7
YAMHILL CO OR 204-B1
PEAVINE VALLEY RD
JOSEPHINE CO OR 148-C1
PEBBLE CREEK RD
COLUMBIA CO OR 125-B1
PECK DR
ALTAMONT OR 339-B11
N PECK RD
SPOKANE CO WA 247-A1
SW PECK RD
JEFFERSON CO OR 208-A7
PECKENPAUGH RD
LINN CO OR 210-A1
PECKHAM RD
CANYON CO ID 147-A1
PECK RIDGE RD
LEWIS CO ID 123-B2
E PE ELL AV
PE ELL WA 117-B2
PE ELL-MCDONALD RD
LEWIS CO WA 117-B2
LEWIS CO WA 187-A2
PE ELL WA 117-B2
PEER-HOPE RD
BAKER CO OR 131-A3
S PEKIN RD
COWLITZ CO WA 192-C1
PELHAM HILL RD
COLUMBIA CO OR 189-B5
PEMBERTON AV
DIST OF N VANCOUVER BC 254-H5
PENAWAWA RD
WHITMAN CO WA 122-B1
PENDALL RD
DOUGLAS CO WA 237-C1
PENDER ST E
VANCOUVER BC 254-H10
VANCOUVER BC 255-A10
PENDER ST W
VANCOUVER BC 254-F9
PENDLETON AV
PIERCE CO WA 181-C5
PENDLETON CTO
ECHO OR 129-A1
UMATILLA CO OR 129-A1
PENDLETON HWY U.S.-30
UMATILLA CO OR 129-B1
NW PENDLETON HWY U.S.-30
PENDLETON OR 129-B1
UMATILLA CO OR 129-B1
PENDLETON RD
PIERCE CO WA 181-B5
PENDLETON ST SW
ROCHESTER WA 184-A3
PENDLETON-CLD SPGS HWY Rt#-37
PENDLETON OR 129-B1
UMATILLA CO OR 129-A1
PENDLETON-JHN DAY HWY U.S.-395
GRANT CO OR 129-B3
GRANT CO OR 137-A1
LONG CREEK OR 137-A1
MOUNT VERNON OR 137-A1
PENDLETON OR 129-B2
PILOT ROCK OR 129-B2
UMATILLA CO OR 129-B2
PENDLETON RIVER RD
PENDLETON OR 129-B1
UMATILLA CO OR 129-B1
PEND OREILLE HWY
SPOKANE CO WA 347-F7
PENGRA-HUNTINGTON RD
DESCHUTES CO OR 143-A1
DESCHUTES CO OR 217-A7
THREE RIVERS OR 143-A1
THREE RIVERS OR 217-A7
PENINSULA DR
JEFFERSON CO OR 212-C2
N PENINSULA DR
SPOKANE CO WA 247-A1
W PENINSULA DR
MOSES LAKE WA 242-C4
PENINSULA RD
BONNER CO ID 107-A3
SW PENINSULA RD
JEFFERSON CO OR 212-C1
S PENMAN RD
CLACKAMAS CO OR 199-D6
PENN AV SE
DOUGLAS CO WA 239-B5

PENN RD
SKAGIT CO WA 161-A7
PENN COVE RD
ISLAND CO WA 167-B4
PENNING RD
LEWIS CO WA 187-A1
PENNSYLVANIA AV U.S.-95
PAYETTE CO ID 139-A3
E PENNSYLVANIA AV
COEUR D'ALENE ID 355-G10
S PENNSYLVANIA AV U.S.-95
FRUITLAND ID 139-A3
PAYETTE CO ID 139-A3
PENNSYLVANIA AV SE
FOUR CORNERS OR 325-F2
PENNSYLVANIA ST
LONGVIEW WA 302-G5
PENNY CREEK RD
JEFFERSON CO WA 109-C1
E PEONE RD
SPOKANE CO WA 246-D2
PEORIA RD
HARRISBURG OR 210-A2
LINN CO OR 207-B6
LINN CO OR 210-A2
PEPIOT RD
FRANKLIN CO WA 121-B2
MESA WA 121-B2
PEPPERMINT RD
CROOK CO OR 213-D4
PEPPERS BRIDGE RD
WALLA WALLA CO WA 344-F14
PERCH RD
JEFFERSON CO OR 212-C2
PERDITA ST
OCEAN SHORES WA 298-F4
PERIMETER RD
PIERCE CO WA 181-D5
E PERIMETER RD
KOOTENAI CO ID 245-C1
N PERIMETER RD
KOOTENAI CO ID 245-C1
PERKINS RD
CLATSOP CO WA 188-B3
PERKINS ST NE
MARION CO OR 205-A4
PERRY AV U.S.-101
HOQUIAM WA 178-A7
PERRY AV NE
BREMERTON WA 271-A8
KITSAP CO WA 271-A8
PERRY RD
JACKSON CO OR 230-C5
LANE CO OR 215-A4
N PERRY RD
SPOKANE CO WA 114-C1
PERRY ST
WINTHROP WA 104-A2
N PERRY ST
SPOKANE WA 349-C4
S PERRY ST
SPOKANE WA 246-C5
SPOKANE WA 349-C9
SPOKANE CO WA 246-C5
PERRY CREEK RD
COLUMBIA CO OR 192-A1
PERRYDALE RD
DALLAS OR 204-A5
POLK CO OR 204-A4
W PERRYDALE RD
POLK CO OR 204-A3
N PERRY NB CONNECTION ST
SPOKANE WA 349-C6
E PERSHALL RD
OWYHEE CO ID 147-B1
NW PERSHALL WY
DESCHUTES CO OR 212-D4
TERREBONNE OR 212-D4
PERSONS RD
SKAGIT CO WA 160-D6
PETER ANDERSON RD
SKAGIT CO WA 260-F4
PETER BURNS RD
SKAGIT CO WA 168-C1
PETER DAM RD
OKANOGAN CO WA 113-B1
OKANOGAN CO WA 237-D1
PETER HAGEN RD NW
KITSAP CO WA 173-D3
PETER JOHNSON RD
CLARK CO WA 192-D1
CLATSOP CO WA 188-C3
PETERS AV
CHELAN CO WA 238-A2
PETERS RD
CLALLAM CO WA 165-A6
CROOK CO OR 213-D4
DIST OF N VANCOUVER BC 255-F2
PETERS ST
SUNNYSLOPE WA 238-D3
PETERSON RD
DESCHUTES CO OR 212-C7
JEFFERSON CO WA 109-C1
KLICKITAT CO WA 120-B3
KLICKITAT CO WA 128-B1
SKAGIT CO WA 161-A6
SKAGIT CO WA 260-A5
E PETERSON RD
BURLINGTON WA 260-A5
SKAGIT CO WA 260-A5
PETERSON BURN RD
DESCHUTES CO OR 211-D6
PETERSON CREEK RD
CROOK CO OR 136-A2
PETERSON RIDGE RD
DESCHUTES CO OR 211-D6
PETERS PASTURE RD
JEFFERSON CO OR 135-A1
PETERSVILLE RD NE
BREMERTON WA 271-A6
KITSAP CO WA 271-A6
PETES MOUNTAIN RD
CLACKAMAS CO OR 199-C5
PETROVITSKY RD
KING CO WA 175-D6
N PETTET DR
SPOKANE WA 348-F6
PETTIBONE DR
BENTON CO OR 207-B4

PETTIGREW RD
BEND OR 332-J9
DESCHUTES CO OR 332-J9
PETTYJOHN RD
WALLA WALLA CO WA 121-C3
PETZOLD RD
LANE CO OR 133-B3
PFEIFER RD
LINCOLN CO WA 113-A2
PH 15
FRANKLIN CO WA 121-B2
PHARR RD
OKANOGAN CO WA 104-C2
PHEASANT LN
LANE CO OR 215-D4
PHELPS RD
CLACKAMAS CO OR 200-D3
PHELPS RD NE
KITSAP CO WA 174-C1
N PHILADELPHIA AV U.S.-30
PORTLAND OR 192-B7
PHILLIPS RD
WASHINGTON CO OR 192-A7
YAMHILL CO OR 198-B3
W PHILLIPS RD
ADAMS CO WA 242-C7
PHILLIPS RD SE
KITSAP CO WA 174-C5
PHILOMATH BLVD U.S.-20
BENTON CO OR 133-B1
BENTON CO OR 327-A12
CORVALLIS OR 133-B1
CORVALLIS OR 327-A12
PHILOMATH RD
BENTON CO OR 133-B1
PHINNEY AV N
SEATTLE WA 273-H4
N PHINNEY WY
SEATTLE WA 273-H5
NW PHINNEY BAY DR
BREMERTON WA 270-E8
KITSAP CO WA 270-E8
PH NO 10
CASTLE ROCK WA 187-C7
COWLITZ CO WA 187-C7
N PHOENIX RD
JACKSON CO OR 234-B2
JACKSON CO OR 336-J14
MEDFORD OR 234-B1
MEDFORD OR 336-J14
PHYS POINT RD
UNION CO OR 130-B2
PICARD RD
SISKIYOU CO CA 150-B3
PICKERING RD
MASON CO WA 180-C2
PICKETT RD
KLAMATH CO OR 151-A2
PICNIC POINT RD
SNOHOMISH CO WA 171-B4
PICTURE LN
LAKE CO OR 143-B2
PIEDMONT RD
CLALLAM CO WA 164-C6
PIEDMONT RD Rt#-112
CLALLAM CO WA 164-C5
CLALLAM CO WA 165-A6
PIERCE RD
MEDFORD OR 336-H11
UNION CO OR 130-A2
PIERCE RD NW
DOUGLAS CO WA 236-D5
PIERCE PARK LN
BOISE ID 253-C1
PIERCE PARK RD
ADA CO ID 253-C1
PIERSON RD
WHITMAN CO WA 114-B3
PIKE RD
YAMHILL OR 198-A4
YAMHILL CO OR 198-B4
NW PIKE RD
YAMHILL OR 198-A4
YAMHILL CO OR 198-A4
SW PIKE RD
JEFFERSON CO OR 212-C1
S PILCHUCK DR
ISLAND CO WA 168-A6
PILLER PL
JOSEPHINE CO OR 233-A4
PILOT ROCK RD
KOOTENAI CO ID 247-D6
KOOTENAI CO ID 248-A3
N PINE
LA GRANDE OR 130-A2
PINE AV
SNOHOMISH WA 171-D3
E PINE AV
MERIDIAN ID 253-A3
W PINE AV
MERIDIAN ID 253-A3
PINE AV NE
OLYMPIA WA 297-A4
THURSTON CO WA 297-A4
PINE LN
COOS CO OR 220-B4
SE PINE RD
KITSAP CO WA 174-B6
SW PINE RD
KITSAP CO WA 174-B6
PINE RD NE
BREMERTON WA 270-H7
KITSAP CO WA 270-H5
TRACYTON WA 270-H5
PINE ST
CHELAN CO WA 238-A1
LEAVENWORTH WA 238-A1
MARION CO OR 205-C4
NORTHPORT WA 106-A1
ROGUE RIVER OR 229-D6
SANDPOINT ID 244-A2
SILVERTON OR 205-C4
PINE ST U.S.-2
SANDPOINT ID 244-A2
PINE ST U.S.-12
OAKVILLE WA 117-B1
PINE ST U.S.-95
SANDPOINT ID 244-A2

E PINE ST
CENTRAL POINT OR 230-C7
JACKSON CO OR 230-C7
JACKSON CO OR 336-A5
E PINE ST Rt#-3
MASON CO WA 180-A3
SHELTON WA 180-A3
N PINE ST
CANBY OR 199-C6
NE PINE ST
SALEM OR 322-J10
SALEM OR 323-A10
S PINE ST
TACOMA WA 294-D1
SE PINE ST Rt#-99
ROSEBURG OR 334-F8
SE PINE ST Rt#-138
ROSEBURG OR 334-G7
W PINE ST
CENTRAL POINT OR 230-C7
WALLA WALLA WA 344-H7
WALLA WALLA WEST WA 344-H7
W PINE ST Rt#-125
WALLA WALLA WA 344-J7
PINE ST NE
MARION CO OR 205-B4
SALEM OR 322-J10
SILVERTON OR 205-B4
W PINE BLUFF RD
SPOKANE CO WA 114-B1
SPOKANE CO WA 246-A1
N PINE BLUFF WYE RD
SPOKANE CO WA 114-B1
PINE CITY RD
MALDEN WA 114-B3
WHITMAN CO WA 114-B3
PINECONE DR
JOSEPHINE CO OR 233-B5
PINE CREEK HWY
BAKER CO OR 131-A3
HALFWAY OR 131-A3
PINE CREEK RD
GRANT CO OR 137-B2
HARNEY CO OR 137-C3
HARNEY CO OR 145-C1
OKANOGAN CO WA 104-C2
SHOSHONE CO ID 115-C2
UMATILLA CO OR 129-C1
WALLOWA CO OR 131-A1
E PINE CREEK RD
BAKER CO OR 131-A3
N PINE CREEK RD
OKANOGAN CO WA 104-C2
PINECREST DR
JOSEPHINE CO OR 229-B5
JOSEPHINE CO OR 335-A7
LA GRANDE OR 130-A2
PINE CREST RD
LATAH CO ID 249-D5
PINE GROVE RD
LANE CO OR 133-B3
PINEHURST RD
DESCHUTES CO OR 217-B1
PINE MOUNT DR
HOOD RIVER CO OR 195-C7
HOOD RIVER CO OR 202-C1
N PINES RD Rt#-27
OPPORTUNITY WA 350-H7
SPOKANE CO WA 350-H5
S PINES RD Rt#-27
OPPORTUNITY WA 350-H10
S PINE SPRING RD
SPOKANE CO WA 114-B2
S PINE SPRINGS RD
SPOKANE CO WA 114-B2
PINE TOWN RD
BAKER CO OR 131-A3
PINE TREE RD
LEWIS CO WA 187-D3
PINETREE WY
COQUITLAM BC 157-A4
N PINEWOOD WY
KOOTENAI CO ID 245-A4
PING GULCH RD
GARFIELD CO WA 122-B1
PINKNEY RD
COLUMBIA CO OR 189-B7
PINTO RIDGE RD
GRANT CO WA 113-A2
PIOCH LN
LANE CO OR 210-D7
PIONEER AV
CASHMERE WA 238-C2
E PIONEER AV
PUYALLUP WA 182-B3
W PIONEER AV
PUYALLUP WA 182-B3
PIONEER AV E
GRAYS HARBOR CO WA 178-D7
MONTESANO WA 178-D7
PIONEER AV W
GRAYS HARBOR CO WA 178-D7
MONTESANO WA 178-D7
PIONEER BLVD U.S.-26
SANDY OR 200-C4
PIONEER DR
CASHMERE WA 238-B2
CHELAN CO WA 238-B2
PIONEER HWY
SKAGIT CO WA 168-B2
SNOHOMISH CO WA 168-B4
STANWOOD WA 168-B4
PIONEER HWY E
SNOHOMISH CO WA 168-C5
PIONEER LP
DESCHUTES CO OR 217-C1
PIONEER PKWY
SKAGIT CO WA 160-D7
SWINOMISH VILLAGE WA 167-D1
PIONEER PKWY E
North Springfield OR 330-G4
SPRINGFIELD OR 330-G4
PIONEER PKWY W
North Springfield OR 330-G4
SPRINGFIELD OR 330-G4
PIONEER RD
JACKSON CO OR 234-A2
LONG BEACH WA 186-A5
OWYHEE CO ID 147-A1
PACIFIC CO WA 186-A5

STREET City State Page-Grid

PIONEER RD NW
KITSAP CO WA 174-A1
PIONEER ST
LANE CO OR 133-C3
LOWELL OR 133-C3
PIONEER ST Rt#-501
CLARK CO WA 192-C2
KNAPP WA 192-B2
RIDGEFIELD WA 192-C2
PIONEER WY
CHELAN CO WA 238-C3
GIG HARBOR WA 181-C1
MOSES LAKE WA 242-C3
PIONEER WY Rt#-162
ORTING WA 182-B5
PIERCE CO WA 182-B5
SOUTH PRAIRIE WA 182-B5
SUMNER WA 182-B5
E PIONEER WY
OAK HARBOR WA 167-C3
PIERCE CO WA 182-A3
PUYALLUP WA 182-A3
TACOMA WA 182-A3
E PIONEER WY Rt#-162
SOUTH PRAIRIE WA 182-D4
N PIONEER WY
YAKIMA CO WA 243-A5
S PIONEER WY
SHELTON WA 180-A3
S PIONEER WY Rt#-162
PIERCE CO WA 182-C6
W PIONEER WY Rt#-20
OAK HARBOR WA 167-B3
W PIONEER WY Rt#-162
PIERCE CO WA 182-D5
SOUTH PRAIRIE WA 182-D5
PIONEER WY E
PIERCE CO WA 182-B4
PUYALLUP WA 182-B4
PIONEER WY NW
KITSAP CO WA 170-B6
NW PIONEER HILL RD
KITSAP CO WA 170-B6
PIONEER MEMORIAL BRDG U.S.-395
KENNEWICK WA 343-B9
PASCO WA 343-B9
PIONEER PARKWAY RD
LA CONNER WA 167-D1
SHELTER BAY WA 167-D1
SKAGIT CO WA 167-D1
SWINOMISH VILLAGE WA 167-D1
PIPELINE RD
COQUITLAM BC 157-B4
DOUGLAS CO OR 221-B2
WHATCOM CO WA 158-B3
SE PIPE LINE RD
MULTNOMAH CO OR 200-C2
PIPER RD
WHATCOM CO WA 158-D5
E PIPER RD
SPOKANE CO WA 246-D2
PIPER CANYON RD
WALLA WALLA CO WA 121-C2
PISCALE LOOKOUT RD
CROOK CO OR 136-A2
PISTOL BUTTE RD
DESCHUTES CO OR 216-D7
PISTOL RIVER LP
CURRY CO OR 232-B1
PITCHER CANYON RD
CHELAN CO WA 238-D5
PITNEY LN
LANE CO OR 210-A6
PITSUA BUTTE RD
DESCHUTES CO OR 216-D5
PITT AV
BREMERTON WA 271-A10
PITT RIVER RD
COQUITLAM BC 157-A5
PORT COQUITLAM BC 157-A5
PITTSBURG RD
COLUMBIA CO OR 192-A1
PLACE RD
CLALLAM CO WA 165-A5
LANE CO OR 133-C3
PLACER RD
JOSEPHINE CO OR 229-B2
PLAINVIEW DR
LINN CO OR 210-C1
PLANETZ RD NW
DOUGLAS CO WA 236-C7
PLANK RD
SATUS WA 120-A3
YAKIMA CO WA 120-A3
PLATEAU BLVD
COQUITLAM BC 157-B4
PLAT I RD
DOUGLAS CO OR 221-D1
PLAT K RD
DOUGLAS CO OR 221-D1
PLAT M RD
DOUGLAS CO OR 221-C1
PLATT RD
KLICKITAT CO WA 196-A4
PLAZA WY
WALLA WALLA WA 345-A10
WALLA WALLA CO WA 345-A11
E PLEASANT ST
WALLA WALLA WA 345-E8
WALLA WALLA CO WA 345-E8
WALLA WALLA EAST WA 345-E8
PLEASANT BEACH DR NE
KITSAP CO WA 271-H6
PLEASANT CREEK RD
JACKSON CO OR 229-D2
PLEASANT HILL RD
COWLITZ CO WA 189-C2
COWLITZ CO WA 303-E1
GRANT CO OR 137-A2
POLK CO OR 204-A3
YAKIMA CO WA 243-B5
E PLEASANT PRAIRIE RD
SPOKANE CO WA 246-D2
PLEASANT RIDGE RD
WASCO CO OR 127-B2
PLEASANT VALLEY RD
ADA CO ID 253-C6
COOS CO OR 220-D7
DOUGLAS CO OR 219-B5
PLEASANT VALLEY RD
JOSEPHINE CO OR 229-A4
LEWIS CO WA 187-B1
LINN CO OR 133-C2
OWYHEE CO ID 155-C2
YAKIMA CO WA 243-A5
SW PLEASANT VALLEY RD
WASHINGTON CO OR 199-A3
PLEASANT VIEW RD
KOOTENAI CO ID 353-B1
POST FALLS ID 353-C8
E PLEASANT VIEW RD
SPOKANE CO WA 352-H10
W PLEASANT VIEW RD
KOOTENAI CO ID 352-H10
PLOMONDON RD
LEWIS CO WA 187-D4
PLUG MILL RD
MASON CO WA 179-B5
PLUM ST
OLYMPIA WA 296-J5
PLUMLEE RD
WASHINGTON CO OR 198-B1
PLUMTREE LN
JOSEPHINE CO OR 335-A2
PLUSH CUTOFF RD
LAKE CO OR 152-B2
PLYMOUTH AV U.S.-30
NEW PLYMOUTH ID 139-B3
PLYMOUTH RD
BENTON CO WA 121-A3
BENTON CO OR 327-B13
PLYMPTON CREEK Rt#-409
CLATSOP CO WA 117-B3
POCAHONTAS RD
BAKER CITY OR 138-A1
BAKER CO OR 130-A3
BAKER CO OR 138-A1
POE RD
WHITMAN CO WA 249-C3
POEN RD
ADA CO ID 253-A7
POETSCH RD
LEWIS CO WA 187-D4
N POE VALLEY RD
KLAMATH CO OR 151-A2
S POE VALLEY RD
KLAMATH CO OR 150-C2
KLAMATH CO OR 151-A2
POGGENSEE RD Rt#-20
ISLAND CO WA 167-C5
W POINT RD
DOUGLAS CO OR 223-A4
POINT BROWN AV
OCEAN SHORES WA 177-B6
OCEAN SHORES WA 298-D3
POINT DEFIANCE TAHLEQUAH FERRY
KING CO WA 181-D1
PIERCE CO WA 181-D1
TACOMA WA 181-D1
POINT FOSDICK DR NW
PIERCE CO WA 181-C1
POINT GREY RD
VANCOUVER BC 254-A11
POINT ROBERTS RD
DISTRICT OF DELTA BC 101-C1
SW POINT ROBINSON RD
KING CO WA 175-A6
S POINT THORNDYKE RD
JEFFERSON CO WA 170-A5
POINT WHITE DR NE
KITSAP CO WA 271-E6
POINT WHITEHORN RD
BIRCH BAY WA 158-B5
POINT WILSON RD
MASON CO WA 180-D3
POISON CREEK CTO
OWYHEE CO ID 147-C3
POKORNY RD
MARION CO OR 199-A7
E POLE RD Rt#-544
EVERSON WA 102-B1
WHATCOM CO WA 102-B1
WHATCOM CO WA 158-D5
W POLE RD
WHATCOM CO WA 158-D5
POLE CREEK RD
DESCHUTES CO OR 211-C6
MALHEUR CO OR 138-B3
MALHEUR CO OR 154-B2
MALHEUR CO OR 155-A1
POLEHN RD SW
THURSTON CO WA 184-B3
E POLE LINE AV
KOOTENAI CO ID 353-H4
KOOTENAI CO ID 354-A4
POST FALLS ID 353-H4
W POLE LINE AV
COEUR D'ALENE ID 355-A4
KOOTENAI CO ID 353-D4
KOOTENAI CO ID 354-H4
KOOTENAI CO ID 355-A4
POST FALLS ID 353-F5
POLE LINE RD
BAKER CO OR 130-A3
MORROW CO OR 128-C1
POLK RD
LATAH CO ID 249-C4
POLK ST
EUGENE OR 329-H6
INDEPENDENCE OR 204-B7
POLLMAN RD
LEWIS CO WA 184-D7
POLNELL RD
ISLAND CO WA 167-D3
POLSON RD
SKAGIT CO WA 168-A1
POMEROY RD
JACKSON CO OR 230-C2
PONDEROSA AV
CORVALLIS OR 327-C5
E PONDEROSA BLVD
POST FALLS ID 354-B8
PONDEROSA DR
DOUGLAS CO OR 221-A3
PONDEROSA RD
BONNER CO ID 244-B5
PONY BUTTE RD
JEFFERSON CO OR 135-B1
PONY CREEK RD
NORTH BEND OR 333-F5
POODLE CREEK RD
LANE CO OR 133-A3
POPLAR AV
DISTRICT OF SAANICH BC 257-B4
POPLAR DR
DESCHUTES CO OR 212-C5
MEDFORD OR 336-D9
POPLAR LN
POLK CO OR 204-B6
POPLAR ST
POWERS OR 140-B3
E POPLAR ST U.S.-2
DOUGLAS CO WA 236-C7
WATERVILLE WA 236-C7
NW POPLAR ST
MILTON-FREEWATER OR 121-C3
W POPLAR ST
WALLA WALLA WA 345-A8
POPULAR ST Rt#-27
TEKOA WA 114-C3
POPULAR ST Rt#-274
TEKOA WA 114-C3
PORCUPINE BAY RD
LINCOLN CO WA 114-A1
PORCUPINE RIDGE RD
MORROW CO OR 129-A3
PORTAL WY
FERNDALE WA 158-C5
WHATCOM CO WA 158-C4
PORTER RD
CLACKAMAS CO OR 200-C6
NEZ PERCE CO ID 250-D2
WASHINGTON CO OR 198-C1
PORTER RD NW
DOUGLAS CO WA 236-B6
PORTER ST Rt#-169
ENUMCLAW WA 110-C3
KING CO WA 110-C3
PORTER WY
MILTON WA 182-A2
PORTER CREEK RD
DOUGLAS CO OR 221-A6
GRAYS HARBOR CO WA 117-B1
GRAYS HARBOR CO WA 179-C7
PORT GAMBLE RD NE
KITSAP CO WA 170-C5
PORT INDUSTRIAL RD
ABERDEEN WA 178-B7
PORTLAND AV
FAIRFIELD WA 114-C2
SPOKANE CO WA 114-C2
TACOMA WA 293-J5
E PORTLAND AV
TACOMA WA 182-A3
TACOMA WA 293-J5
NW PORTLAND AV
BEND OR 332-D6
PORTLAND AV E
PIERCE CO WA 182-A4
TACOMA WA 182-A4
N PORTLAND BLVD
PORTLAND OR 308-D6
PORTLAND OR 309-G6
NE PORTLAND BLVD
PORTLAND OR 309-G6
PORTLAND DR
HOOD RIVER CO OR 195-C6
E PORTLAND FRWY I-205
CLACKAMAS OR 319-G7
CLACKAMAS CO OR 199-D4
GLADSTONE OR 199-D4
OREGON CITY OR 199-D4
PORTLAND OR 319-G7
WASHINGTON CO OR 199-D4
WEST LINN OR 199-D4
NE PORTLAND HWY U.S.-30
PORTLAND OR 310-D6
PORTLAND OR 311-E7
N PORTLAND RD
PORTLAND OR 304-C7
PORTLAND OR 308-B2
PORTLAND RD NE
SALEM OR 323-B9
N PORTLAND ST
WILBUR WA 113-B1
PORTLAND HUBBARD HWY
CLACKAMAS CO OR 199-B6
W PORT MADISON RD
KITSAP CO WA 170-C7
PORT OF TACOMA RD
FIFE WA 182-A2
TACOMA WA 182-A2
SE PORTOLA DR
GRANTS PASS OR 335-H11
JOSEPHINE CO OR 335-H11
PORT ORFORD HWY
CURRY CO OR 224-A6
PORT ORFORD OR 224-A6
PORT TOWNSEND-KEYSTONE FERRY
ISLAND CO WA 167-B6
POSSESSION RD
ISLAND CO WA 171-A3
N POST ST
SPOKANE WA 348-J5
POST CANYON DR
HOOD RIVER CO OR 195-C5
POSTGREN RD
KLICKITAT CO WA 195-D2
POSTMA RD
YAKIMA CO WA 243-D7
E POSTMA RD
YAKIMA CO WA 243-C7
POTATO HILL RD
GRANT CO WA 242-C4
POTOMAC RANCH RD
MALHEUR CO OR 154-C1
POTTER LN
VALLEY CO ID 251-D6
POTTER RD
LATAH CO ID 249-C2
LINN CO OR 210-A2
POTTERY AV
PORT ORCHARD WA 174-B4
POTTS RD
WHITMAN CO WA 114-A3
POVERTY BEND RD
YAMHILL CO OR 198-A6
POWDER CREEK RD
TILLAMOOK CO OR 197-D6
E POWELL BLVD U.S.-26
GRESHAM OR 200-B2
SE POWELL BLVD U.S.-26
GRESHAM OR 200-A2
PORTLAND OR 200-A2
PORTLAND OR 317-H1
PORTLAND OR 318-B2
PORTLAND OR 319-H2
W POWELL BLVD U.S.-26
GRESHAM OR 200-A2
POWELL RD
COWLITZ CO WA 187-C7
GRAYS HARBOR CO WA 177-C5
NEZ PERCE CO ID 250-D6
NE POWELL RD
CLARK CO WA 193-B4
POWELL ST
VANCOUVER BC 254-J10
VANCOUVER BC 255-B10
POWELL BUTTE HWY
CROOK CO OR 213-A7
DESCHUTES CO OR 135-B3
DESCHUTES CO OR 213-A7
DESCHUTES CO OR 217-D1
POWELL BUTTE CEM RD
CROOK CO OR 213-B6
SE POWELL VALLEY RD
GRESHAM OR 200-B2
POWER RD
MALHEUR CO OR 139-A2
POWER CREEK RD
GRAYS HARBOR CO WA 179-C6
POWERHOUSE RD
FRUITVALE WA 243-B6
KLICKITAT CO WA 195-C4
YAKIMA WA 243-B6
YAKIMA CO WA 243-B6
SW POWER HOUSE HILL RD
YAMHILL CO OR 125-B2
POWER LINE RD
UMATILLA CO OR 121-C3
WALLA WALLA CO WA 345-C11
POWERLINE RD
IDAHO CO ID 123-C3
LANE CO OR 210-B6
LEWIS CO ID 123-B2
LINN CO OR 210-B3
E POWER LINE RD
ADA CO ID 253-A4
CANYON CO ID 147-C1
POWERLINE RD SW
THURSTON CO WA 180-A7
POWER LINE EASEMENT RD
JOSEPHINE CO OR 233-B5
POWERS AV
NEZ PERCE CO ID 250-D5
POWERS HWY
COOS CO OR 140-B3
POWERS RD
COLUMBIA CO WA 122-A2
E POWERS RD
NEZ PERCE CO ID 250-D5
POWERS CREEK LP NE
MARION CO OR 205-D5
POWERS SOUTH RD
COOS CO OR 140-B3
CURRY CO OR 140-B3
POWERS OR 140-B3
POW WAH KEE RD
GARFIELD CO WA 122-C2
PRAIRIE AV
PORT COQUITLAM BC 157-B4
PRAIRIE AV U.S.-95
CRAIGMONT ID 123-B2
E PRAIRIE AV
DALTON GARDENS ID 355-E2
KOOTENAI CO ID 353-H2
KOOTENAI CO ID 354-B2
KOOTENAI CO ID 355-E2
W PRAIRIE AV
COEUR D'ALENE ID 354-J3
COEUR D'ALENE ID 355-B2
DALTON GARDENS ID 355-B2
HAYDEN ID 354-G2
HAYDEN ID 355-B2
KOOTENAI CO ID 353-D2
KOOTENAI CO ID 354-J3
KOOTENAI CO ID 355-B2
PRAIRIE RD
JUNCTION CITY OR 210-A6
LANE CO OR 210-A6
LANE CO OR 215-A1
SKAGIT CO WA 161-B4
S PRAIRIE RD
LEWIS CO WA 187-D2
SKAMANIA CO WA 195-A1
PRAIRIE CENTRAL RD
DISTRICT OF CHILLIWACK BC 94-C3
PRAIRIE CITY S SIDE OF RIV RD
GRANT CO OR 137-C2
PRAIRIE CITY OR 137-C2
PRAIRIE CREEK RD
DOUGLAS CO OR 226-D2
S PRAIRIE CREEK RD
PIERCE CO WA 182-C5
PRAIRIE FARM CTO
JEFFERSON CO OR 135-A1
JEFFERSON CO OR 211-D1
PRAIRIE PKWY LN SW
THURSTON CO WA 184-B2
PRAIRIE RIDGE DR E
PIERCE CO WA 182-C5
PRAIRIE ROAD CONN
LANE CO OR 210-A6
PRAIRIE ROAD CONN Rt#-36
LANE CO OR 210-A6
S PRAIRIE VIEW RD
SPOKANE CO WA 114-C2
PRATER RD
DESCHUTES CO OR 216-C6
PRATHER RD
POLK CO OR 207-B2
PRATHER RD SW
THURSTON CO WA 184-A4
PRATT RD
WALLOWA CO OR 130-C2
PREACHER CREEK RD
LANE CO OR 133-A2
PREBLE ST
BREMERTON WA 270-E12
NAVY YARD CITY WA 270-E12
NE PRESCOTT ST
MAYWOOD PARK OR 315-H1
PORTLAND OR 313-H1
PORTLAND OR 314-B1
PORTLAND OR 315-E1
W PRESLEY RD
KOOTENAI CO ID 247-D4
KOOTENAI CO ID 248-A1
PRESTON AV
LEWISTON ID 250-C5
PRESTON AV U.S.-12
WAITSBURG WA 122-A2
PRESTON-FALL CITY RD SE
KING CO WA 176-B4
W PREWETT RD
SPOKANE CO WA 114-B1
W PRICE AV
TOWN AND COUNTRY WA 346-J12
PRICE RD
ALBANY OR 326-H7
BREMERTON WA 270-B10
KITSAP CO WA 270-C10
YAKIMA CO WA 120-B2
N PRICE RD
YAKIMA CO WA 120-B2
PRICE RD NW
BREMERTON WA 270-D10
KITSAP CO WA 270-C10
PRICEBORO DR
LINN CO OR 210-A5
PRICE-TWELVEMILE RD
CROOK CO OR 136-B3
PRIEST RAPIDS RD
BENTON CO WA 120-B2
YAKIMA CO WA 120-B2
PRINCESS AV
DIST OF N VANCOUVER BC 255-D2
PRINCETON AV NE
SEATTLE WA 275-F4
NE PRINCETON WY
SEATTLE WA 275-F3
PRINGLE PKWY SE Rt#-22
SALEM OR 322-J13
PRINGLE RD
WASHINGTON CO ID 139-A2
PRINGLE RD SE
SALEM OR 324-J5
PRINGLE FALLS LP
DESCHUTES CO OR 142-C1
DESCHUTES CO OR 143-A1
PRINGLE FLAT RD
CROOK CO OR 136-A3
PRIOR ST
VANCOUVER BC 254-J11
VANCOUVER BC 255-A11
PRIVATE RD
CLARK CO WA 190-A7
PROCTOR BLVD U.S.-26
SANDY OR 200-C4
N PROCTOR ST
TACOMA WA 292-C4
S PROCTOR ST
TACOMA WA 292-C6
PROFFITT RD
LEWIS CO WA 184-D6
N PROGRESS RD
SPOKANE CO WA 351-B2
TRENTWOOD WA 351-B2
W PROGRESS RD
UMATILLA CO OR 129-A1
PROGRESSIVE RD
WHITE SWAN WA 119-C2
N PROM
SEASIDE WA 301-F8
S PROM
SEASIDE WA 301-F9
PROMISE RD
WALLOWA CO OR 130-B1
PROMONTORY RD
DISTRICT OF CHILLIWACK BC 102-C1
PROSPECT AV
HADLOCK-IRONDALE WA 263-D13
WALLA WALLA CO WA 345-A12
PROSPECT DR
BENTON CITY WA 120-C3
PROSPECT RD
DIST OF N VANCOUVER BC 255-B1
WALLA WALLA CO WA 345-B11
WALLA WALLA EAST WA 345-B11
PROSPECT ST
BELLINGHAM WA 258-D6
PROSPECT LAKE RD
DISTRICT OF SAANICH BC 159-B5
DISTRICT OF SAANICH BC 256-A1
PROTEST RD
BOISE ID 253-C3
PROVIDENCE RD
ADAMS CO WA 121-C1
PROVIDENCE RD Rt#-261
ADAMS CO WA 121-C1
PROVOST RD NW
KITSAP CO WA 270-A2
SILVERDALE WA 270-A2
PROWELL ST
CHELAN CO WA 238-A1
PRUNEDALE RD
UMATILLA CO OR 121-C3
PRUNER RD
DOUGLAS CO OR 225-B2
RIDDLE OR 225-B2
P S OGDEN RD
DESCHUTES CO OR 212-D3
SW PUCKER HUDDLE RD Rt#-141
KLICKITAT CO WA 195-D4
PUCKETT RD
CROOK CO OR 213-C3
PUDDING RIVER RD NE
MARION CO OR 205-C1
NW PUDDY GULCH RD
YAMHILL CO OR 198-A5
PUGET DR
VANCOUVER BC 254-B14
PUGET DR Rt#-524
EDMONDS WA 171-A5
PUGET DR E
MANCHESTER WA 271-G14
PUGET DR SE
MANCHESTER WA 271-G14
RENTON WA 175-C5
PUGET RD NE
THURSTON CO WA 180-D5
N PUGET ST
OLYMPIA WA 297-A4
PUGET BEACH RD NE
THURSTON CO WA 181-A4
PUGH RD NE
KITSAP CO WA 170-C6
PUITT RD
CROOK CO OR 136-B2
PULLEN LN
JOSEPHINE CO OR 233-B5
PULLMAN ALBION RD
ALBION WA 249-A4
WHITMAN CO WA 249-A4
PULVER RD
SKAGIT CO WA 260-A8
SW PUMA DR
WASHINGTON CO OR 198-B2
PUMP RD
CANYON CO ID 147-B1
PUMPKIN RIDGE RD
WASHINGTON CO OR 125-C1
PUNCH BOWL RD
HOOD RIVER CO OR 195-B7
PUNKIN CENTER RD
UMATILLA CO OR 129-A1
PURDIN RD
WASHINGTON CO OR 198-B1
PURDY DR Rt#-302
KITSAP CO WA 174-B6
PIERCE CO WA 174-B6
PURDY CUTOFF RD
MASON CO WA 180-A1
PURTTEMAN GULCH RD
CHELAN CO WA 236-C2
PUYALLUP AV
TACOMA WA 182-A2
TACOMA WA 293-J7
PUYALLUP AV Rt#-99
TACOMA WA 293-J7
S PUYALLUP AV Rt#-99
TACOMA WA 293-H7
PUYALLUP ST
STEILACOOM WA 181-C4
N PUYALLUP MOTOR NATURE TR
PIERCE CO WA 185-A3
PYLE RD
KLICKITAT CO WA 196-B3

Q

Q RD NW
DOUGLAS CO WA 236-C7
Q ST
PORT TOWNSEND WA 263-H3
NE QUAALE RD
JEFFERSON CO OR 208-D3
QUADRA ST
CITY OF VICTORIA BC 256-H6
DISTRICT OF SAANICH BC 159-C5
DISTRICT OF SAANICH BC 256-F1
VANCOUVER BC 254-A13
S QUADRANT ST
ROCKAWAY BEACH OR 191-B6
QUARRY RD
ALBANY OR 326-C4
COQUITLAM BC 157-B3
YAMHILL CO OR 198-D5
QUARTZ CREEK RD
DOUGLAS CO OR 222-B7
JOSEPHINE CO OR 229-A3
QUARTZ MOUNTAIN RD
DOUGLAS CO OR 222-A5
KITTITAS CO WA 240-C4
QUARTZVILLE DR
LINN CO OR 134-A1
QUEBEC ST
CITY OF VICTORIA BC 256-F9
VANCOUVER BC 254-H12
QUEEN AV
ALBANY OR 326-B9
LINN CO OR 326-B9
S QUEEN ANN BLVD
YAKIMA WA 243-B7
QUEEN ANNE AV N
SEATTLE WA 273-H7
SEATTLE WA 277-H1
QUEEN ANNE DR
SEATTLE WA 277-H1
W QUEEN ANNE DR WY
SEATTLE WA 277-H3
QUEEN MARY BLVD
DISTRICT OF SURREY BC 157-A6
QUEENS AV
DIST OF WEST VANCOUVER BC 254-A1
QUEENS RD
DIST OF N VANCOUVER BC 254-J2
DIST OF N VANCOUVER BC 255-A3
QUEENSBOROUGH BRDG Rt#-91A
CITY OF RICHMOND BC 156-D6
NEW WESTMINSTER BC 156-D6
QUEENS BRANCH RD
JACKSON CO OR 229-D4
QUEENSBURY AV
CITY OF N VANCOUVER BC 255-C7
QUEETS RIVER RD
JEFFERSON CO WA 172-D2
QUESNEL DR
VANCOUVER BC 254-B14
QUICK RD
COWLITZ CO WA 187-C7
E QUILCENE RD
JEFFERSON CO WA 109-C1
QUILLAYUTE RD
CLALLAM CO WA 169-B2
QUINABY RD NE
MARION CO OR 204-D4
MARION CO OR 205-A4
W QUINAULT AV
KENNEWICK WA 342-C9
QUINCE AV
DESCHUTES CO OR 212-C5

STREET City State Page-Grid

N QUINCY AV
DOUGLAS CO WA 239-A4
QUINCY ST
PORT TOWNSEND WA 263-H4
QUINCY-MAYGER RD
COLUMBIA CO OR 117-B3
COLUMBIA CO OR 189-A2
QUINES CREEK RD
DOUGLAS CO OR 225-C6
QUINN RD
GILLIAM CO OR 128-A3

R

R AV
ANACORTES WA 259-H2
R RD NE Rt#-17
DOUGLAS CO WA 112-C1
R RD SW
DOUGLAS CO WA 239-B3
S R ST
COTTAGE GROVE OR 215-B7
R ST SE
AUBURN WA 182-C2
KING CO WA 182-C2
NW RABAUL DR
KITSAP CO WA 170-B7
RABBIT CAMP RD
LINN CO OR 134-B2
RABY LN
PAYETTE CO ID 139-A3
RACCOON DR
DOUGLAS CO OR 219-A5
RACE RD
EPHRATA WA 112-C3
GRANT CO WA 112-C3
S RACE RD
ISLAND CO WA 167-C5
RACE ST
PORT ANGELES WA 261-G5
RADAR RD
HARNEY CO OR 145-A1
RADAR HILL RD
ADAMS CO WA 121-A1
FRANKLIN CO WA 121-A1
RADER RD
KITTITAS CO WA 241-C4
RAFT AV
OLYMPIA WA 296-G2
RAGER RD
CROOK CO OR 136-B2
RAGLAND RD
COWLITZ CO WA 189-B1
RAIL HOLLOW RD
HOOD RIVER CO OR 202-D4
WASCO CO OR 127-B2
WASCO CO OR 202-D4
RAILROAD AV
COLUMBIA CO OR 192-B2
JOSEPHINE CO OR 225-B7
JOSEPHINE CO OR 229-B1
KITTITAS WA 241-C6
LEWISTON ID 250-C4
MALHEUR CO OR 139-A3
MOUNT ANGEL OR 205-C3
POWERS OR 140-B3
SAINT HELENS OR 192-B2
RAILROAD AV Rt#-200
KOOTENAI ID 244-A1
E RAILROAD AV
OTIS ORCHARDS WA 352-D9
SPOKANE CO WA 349-H7
N RAILROAD AV
COOS CO OR 140-B3
KOOTENAI CO ID 353-C7
POST FALLS ID 353-C7
POWERS OR 140-B3
NE RAILROAD AV
CLARK CO WA 193-B2
W RAILROAD AV
MASON CO WA 180-A3
SHELTON WA 180-A3
RAILROAD AV SE Rt#-202
KING CO WA 176-C4
NORTH BEND WA 176-C4
SNOQUALMIE WA 176-C4
RAILROAD BLVD
EUGENE OR 329-H5
RAILROAD ST Rt#-27
ROCKFORD WA 114-C2
SPOKANE CO WA 114-C2
RAILROAD ST U.S.-95
MIDVALE ID 139-B1
SW RAILROAD ST
SHERIDAN OR 125-B3
SHERWOOD OR 199-A4
RAILWAY AV
CITY OF RICHMOND BC 156-B7
RAINBOW DR
JEFFERSON CO OR 212-C2
NW RAINBOW DR
DESCHUTES CO OR 212-C3
RAINBOW RD
WHATCOM CO WA 158-B5
RAINBOW POINT RD
VALLEY CO ID 252-C2
RAINBOW ROCK RD
CURRY CO OR 232-C5
RAINEY RD
DOUGLAS CO WA 239-A2
RAINIER AV N
KING CO WA 175-C4
RENTON WA 175-C4
RAINIER AV S
KING WA 287-F4
KING CO WA 175-C4
RENTON WA 175-C4
SEATTLE WA 278-C7
SEATTLE WA 282-D2
SEATTLE WA 283-E6
SEATTLE WA 287-F1
RAINIER AV S Rt#-167
RENTON WA 175-C5
RAINIER DR
PIERCE CO WA 181-C5
RAINIER RD SE
RAINIER WA 118-A1
THURSTON CO WA 118-A1
RAINIER ST
STEILACOOM WA 181-C4
RAINIER DIKE RD
RAINIER OR 302-G14
W RAINIER DIKE RD
COLUMBIA CO OR 302-C12
RAINIER OR 302-C12
RAINIER-YELM HWY Rt#-507
THURSTON CO WA 118-A1
YELM WA 118-A1
RAISOR RD
LANE CO OR 219-D3
RALSTON-BENGE RD
ADAMS CO WA 121-C1
ADAMS CO WA 122-A1
RAMBLER DR NE
MARION CO OR 205-B4
N RAMBO RD
SPOKANE CO WA 114-B2
RAMMS RD
JEFFERSON CO OR 213-A1
S RAMSBY RD
CLACKAMAS CO OR 126-A3
RAMSEY LN
KLICKITAT CO WA 195-D5
RAMSEY RD
COEUR D'ALENE ID 355-C3
HAYDEN ID 245-A5
HAYDEN ID 355-C3
JACKSON CO OR 230-B4
KOOTENAI CO ID 245-A5
KOOTENAI CO ID 355-C3
N RAMSEY RD
COEUR D'ALENE ID 355-C6
KOOTENAI CO ID 245-A2
S RAMSEY ST Rt#-27
TEKOA WA 114-C3
RAMSEY-CANYON RD
JACKSON CO OR 230-B3
RANCH RD
DESCHUTES CO OR 144-B1
DOUGLAS CO OR 218-C1
KOOTENAI CO ID 245-A2
RANCHERO RD
DOUGLAS CO OR 225-C6
RAND RD
HOOD RIVER OR 195-C5
RANDAL RD
COOS CO OR 220-B6
RANDALL RD SW
THURSTON CO WA 180-B6
RANDOLPH RD
GRANT CO WA 242-C2
RANEY LN
ADAMS CO ID 251-B4
W RANGE DR
LINCOLN CO OR 328-C6
WALDPORT OR 328-C6
RANGER RD
CLALLAM CO WA 165-A5
RANIER RD
LACEY WA 297-F13
THURSTON CO WA 297-F13
RANIER RD SE
THURSTON CO WA 184-D1
RANKIN RD
WHATCOM CO WA 158-C6
RANKIN HILL RD
VINELAND WA 250-B5
RAT CREEK RD
LANE CO OR 215-D7
RATHERT RD
KLICKITAT CO WA 196-C1
RATTLESNAKE RD
HARNEY CO OR 145-B1
KLICKITAT CO WA 195-D3
KLICKITAT CO WA 196-A1
RATTLESNAKE CREEK RD
MALHEUR CO OR 154-B1
RAUBUCK RD
LEWIS CO WA 187-B2
RAVENA DR N
MARION CO OR 204-D3
RAVENNA AV NE
SEATTLE WA 274-D1
NE RAVENNA BLVD
SEATTLE WA 274-B3
RAWLINS RD
SKAGIT CO WA 168-A1
RAWLISON CRES
TOWNSHIP OF LANGLEY BC 157-D7
NE RAWSON RD
CLARK CO WA 193-B4
RAY RD
LEWIS CO WA 187-D4
S RAY ST
SPOKANE WA 349-F12
RAY BELL RD
MARION CO OR 198-D6
RAYE ST
SEATTLE WA 277-H1
RAYMOND CREEK RD
COLUMBIA CO OR 192-A4
RAY NASH DR NW
PIERCE CO WA 181-B1
RAZOR CLAM DR
OCEAN SHORES WA 298-C3
R DRUFFEL RD
WHITMAN CO WA 249-B7
REASON CT
DESCHUTES CO OR 212-C5
REATA RD
BENTON CO WA 341-D12
REAVIS LN
WALLOWA CO OR 130-C2
SE REBMAN RD
CLACKAMAS CO OR 200-B4
RECORD ST
BAKER CO OR 131-A3
HALFWAY OR 131-A3
RECREATIONAL CORR
GRANT CO WA 121-A1
RED APPLE RD
WENATCHEE WA 238-D4
REDBERG RD
TILLAMOOK CO OR 203-B1
RED BLANKET RD
JACKSON CO OR 226-C7
S RED BLANKET RD
JACKSON CO OR 226-D7
RED BLANKET MOUNTAIN RD
JACKSON CO OR 226-D6
JACKSON CO OR 227-A6
RED BRIDGE RD
LINN CO OR 207-D6
RED CLOUD LN
CROOK CO OR 213-B6
RED CLOUD RD
CROOK CO OR 213-B6
REDDING RD
MORROW CO OR 128-B2
REDFIELD RD
DOUGLAS CO WA 239-B1
RED FIR RD
BONNER CO ID 244-D3
KLAMATH CO OR 151-B1
RED HILL RD
DOUGLAS CO OR 219-B5
HOOD RIVER CO OR 202-B2
WALLOWA CO OR 131-A1
RED HILLS RD
YAMHILL CO OR 198-C6
RED HOUSE RD
LAKE CO OR 152-A1
S REDLAND RD
CLACKAMAS CO OR 199-D4
CLACKAMAS CO OR 200-A5
OREGON CITY OR 199-D4
RED MARBLE RD
STEVENS CO WA 106-A3
NE REDMOND DR Rt#-908
REDMOND WA 175-C1
REDMOND RD
MCMINNVILLE OR 198-A7
YAMHILL CO OR 198-A7
NE REDMOND WY Rt#-202
REDMOND WA 175-D1
NE REDMOND WY Rt#-908
REDMOND WA 175-C1
REDMOND-BEND HWY
DESCHUTES CO OR 212-C7
DESCHUTES CO OR 217-C1
REDMOND FALL CITY RD Rt#-202
KING CO WA 175-D1
KING CO WA 176-A1
REDMOND WA 175-D1
SE REDMND FALL CITY RD Rt#-202
KING CO WA 176-A3
REDMND FALL CITY RD NE Rt#-202
KING CO WA 176-A2
REDMOND GRADE RD
WALLOWA CO OR 122-C3
REDMOND-POWELL BUTE RD
DESCHUTES CO OR 212-D5
REDONDO WY S
FEDERAL WAY WA 175-B7
KING CO WA 175-B7
RED RIDGE RD
ADAMS CO ID 251-C5
VALLEY CO ID 251-C7
N RED RIVER RD
WHATCOM CO WA 158-C6
RED ROCK RD
SISKIYOU CO CA 150-B3
REDWOOD AV
GRANTS PASS OR 335-A11
JOSEPHINE CO OR 229-B6
JOSEPHINE CO OR 335-A11
REDWOOD HWY
GRANTS PASS OR 335-F9
REDWOOD HWY U.S.-101
CRESCENT CITY CA 148-B3
DEL NORTE CO CA 148-B3
DEL NORTE CO CA 232-D7
REDWOOD HWY U.S.-199
CAVE JUNCTION OR 233-B3
DEL NORTE CO CA 148-B3
DEL NORTE CO CA 233-A6
GRANTS PASS OR 335-F7
JOSEPHINE CO OR 149-A1
JOSEPHINE CO OR 229-A7
JOSEPHINE CO OR 233-B3
JOSEPHINE CO OR 335-A12
NE REDWOOD HWY U.S.-199
GRANTS PASS OR 335-F7
REECER CREEK RD
KITTITAS CO WA 241-B2
REED RD
BEND OR 332-E10
HOOD RIVER CO OR 195-C6
LEWIS CO WA 187-C4
N REED RD
COEUR D'ALENE ID 355-D5
HAYDEN ID 245-A5
HAYDEN ID 355-D2
KOOTENAI CO ID 355-D2
REED RD SE
SALEM OR 325-A6
REEDER RD
KLAMATH CO OR 235-D5
MULTNOMAH CO OR 192-B5
REEDER RD SW
THURSTON CO WA 184-C2
SE REED MARKET RD
BEND OR 332-G10
DESCHUTES CO OR 217-C3
DESCHUTES CO OR 332-G10
REESE RD
LAKE OSWEGO OR 320-A7
REESE CREEK RD
JACKSON CO OR 230-D5
REESE HILL RD Rt#-547
WHATCOM CO WA 102-B1
REEVES RD KPS
PIERCE CO WA 181-A3
REEVES CREEK RD
JOSEPHINE CO OR 233-B3
S REGAL RD
SPOKANE CO WA 246-C5
S REGAL ST
SPOKANE WA 349-E14
REGENTS BLVD
FIRCREST WA 181-C2
FIRCREST WA 292-A7
FIRCREST WA 294-A1
E REGINA AV
FAIRWOOD WA 346-J8
FAIRWOOD WA 347-A8
W REGINA AV
FAIRWOOD WA 346-J9
SE REGNER RD
CLACKAMAS CO OR 200-B3
GRESHAM OR 200-B2
MULTNOMAH CO OR 200-B2
REHKLAU RD SE
THURSTON CO WA 181-A7
REHN RD
ADAMS CO WA 113-C3
REICHENBACK RD
PITT MEADOWS BC 157-B5
REID DR NW
GIG HARBOR WA 181-C1
PIERCE CO WA 181-C1
REID RD
CLARK CO WA 193-A1
WHITMAN CO WA 249-A4
REIMANN ST NE
HAYESVILLE OR 323-E6
SE REINIG RD
KING CO WA 176-C4
REITER RD
SNOHOMISH CO WA 111-A1
REITH RD
KENT WA 175-B7
REKDAL RD
ISLAND CO WA 168-A4
W REMINGTON RD
KOOTENAI CO ID 245-A2
REMY LN
LEWIS CO WA 187-D1
RENFREW ST
VANCOUVER BC 255-D12
RENFRO CREEK RD
BENEWAH CO ID 115-B3
RENNE RD
YAMHILL CO OR 198-D6
RENTON AV S
KING WA 287-G5
KING WA 289-J1
SEATTLE WA 287-F3
SE RENTON ISSAQUAH RD Rt#-900
KING CO WA 175-D4
RENTON WA 175-C4
RENTON ISSAQUAH RD SE Rt#-900
ISSAQUAH WA 175-D4
KING CO WA 175-D4
RENTON MAPLE VALLEY RD Rt#-169
KING CO WA 175-D5
KING CO WA 176-A6
REPOSITION AV
ROSEBURG OR 334-F4
RESEARCH WY
CORVALLIS OR 327-C11
RESERVATION RD
SKAGIT CO WA 160-D7
WASCO CO OR 127-A3
RESERVATION RD Rt#-241
SATUS WA 120-B3
N RESERVATION RD
ISLAND CO WA 167-C2
OAK HARBOR WA 167-C2
W RESERVATION RD Rt#-241
SATUS WA 120-B3
RESERVATION RD SE
THURSTON CO WA 181-A6
RESERVATION LINE RD
IDAHO CO ID 123-C3
NEZ PERCE CO ID 250-D4
RESERVE ST
BOISE ID 253-D3
RESERVOIR RD
BENTON CO OR 327-A10
CORVALLIS OR 327-A10
CROOK CO OR 135-B3
MALHEUR CO OR 138-C3
MALHEUR CO OR 146-A1
RESERVOIR LOOP RD
YAKIMA CO WA 243-B5
RESOR RD
WALLA WALLA CO WA 345-H11
WALLA WALLA EAST WA 345-C11
RESORT DR
TILLAMOOK CO OR 197-A7
RESTHAVEN DR
TOWN OF SIDNEY BC 159-C2
E RESTHAVEN RD
YAKIMA CO WA 243-C6
RESTON RD
DOUGLAS CO OR 141-A2
RETREAT KANASKAT RD
KING CO WA 110-C3
RETSIL RD SE
EAST PORT ORCHARD WA 271-A14
PORT ORCHARD WA 271-A14
REUBEN RD
DOUGLAS CO OR 225-A7
N REUBEN RD
DOUGLAS CO OR 225-A6
REUBENS RD
LEWIS CO ID 123-B2
REUBENS GRADE
NEZ PERCE CO ID 123-B2
SE REVENUE RD
CLACKAMAS CO OR 200-C3
NE REVERE AV U.S.-20
BEND OR 332-E6
REVETMENT DR
WESTPORT WA 298-G10
REX RD
DOUGLAS CO WA 237-B1
REYNOLD RD
CLALLAM CO WA 164-B5
W REYNOLDS AV
CENTRALIA WA 299-C1
LEWIS CO WA 299-E1
REYNOLDS RD
FRANKLIN CO WA 121-B2
REYNOLDS CREEK RD
DOUGLAS CO OR 222-B1
REYNOLDS CREEK STAGE RD
OWYHEE CO ID 147-B2
REYNOLDS RIDGE RD
DOUGLAS CO OR 222-B3
RHEA RD
GILLIAM CO OR 128-A1
RHEA CREEK RD
MORROW CO OR 128-B2
RHINEHART RD
UNION CO OR 130-A2
RHODES RD
LEWIS CO WA 187-C3
RHODESIA BEACH RD
PACIFIC CO WA 183-C7
RHODESIDE RD
DESCHUTES CO OR 213-A4
RHODES LAKE RD E
PIERCE CO WA 182-C4
RHODODENDRON DR
FLORENCE OR 214-A2
LANE CO OR 214-A2
RHODODENDRON LN NW
KITSAP CO WA 170-B6
RHODODENDRON RD
DOUGLAS CO OR 222-C5
RHODY DR Rt#-19
HADLOCK-IRONDALE WA 170-A1
HADLOCK-IRONDALE WA 263-E14
JEFFERSON CO WA 170-A1
JEFFERSON CO WA 263-E14
RIBBON RIDGE RD
YAMHILL CO OR 198-C4
SE RICE AV
ROSEBURG OR 334-F9
RICE RD
BAKER CO OR 138-A1
RICE ST
MYRTLE CREEK OR 225-C1
RICE CREEK RD
DOUGLAS CO OR 221-B7
DOUGLAS CO OR 225-A1
RICE KANDLE
PIERCE CO WA 181-D7
RICE-ORIN RD
STEVENS CO WA 105-C2
STEVENS CO WA 106-A2
RICE VALLEY RD
DOUGLAS CO OR 219-A5
RICH RD SE
THURSTON CO WA 184-D1
THURSTON CO WA 297-C12
RICHARDS RD
KITTITAS CO WA 241-A6
RICHARDSON RD
DOUGLAS CO OR 221-C7
LINCOLN CO WA 113-C2
PITT MEADOWS BC 157-C4
SISKIYOU CO CA 150-B3
RICHARDSON RD NE
MARION CO OR 205-D5
RICHARDSONS GAP RD
LINN CO OR 133-C1
RICHART RD
FRANKLIN CO WA 121-A2
RICHES RD SE
MARION CO OR 205-C6
RICHMOND AV
CITY OF VICTORIA BC 257-B8
DISTRICT OF SAANICH BC 257-B8
RICHMOND FRWY Rt#-91
CITY OF RICHMOND BC 156-C6
RICHMOND RD
DISTRICT OF SAANICH BC 257-B4
GILLIAM CO OR 128-A2
N RICHMOND BEACH RD
SHORELINE WA 171-A6
NW RICHMOND BEACH RD
SHORELINE WA 171-A6
RICHMOND SIXSHOOTER RD
WHEELER CO OR 136-B1
RICKARD RD
BENTON CO OR 210-A4
DESCHUTES CO OR 217-C3
RICKEY ST SE
FOUR CORNERS OR 325-E2
SALEM OR 325-E2
RICKREALL RD
POLK CO OR 204-B6
RIDDELL RD
POLK CO OR 204-B7
NE RIDDELL RD
BREMERTON WA 270-G5
KITSAP CO WA 270-G5
KITSAP CO WA 271-A5
TRACYTON WA 270-G5
NW RIDDELL RD
KITSAP CO WA 270-G5
RIDDLE BYPS
DOUGLAS CO OR 225-B2
RIDDLE OR 225-B2
TRI-CITY OR 225-B2
RIDGE DR
ASTORIA WA 300-C6
HOOD RIVER CO OR 195-C6
LINN CO OR 207-C7
OROVILLE WA 104-C1
NE RIDGE DR
KEIZER OR 323-C4
RIDGE RD
ADAMS CO ID 252-A6
CLACKAMAS CO OR 200-B5
COOS CO OR 218-B6
GILLIAM CO OR 128-B2
HARNEY CO OR 137-B3
MORROW CO OR 128-B2
WARRENTON WA 188-B2
YAMHILL CO OR 198-B4
RIDGE TR
SKAMANIA CO WA 194-B1
SE RIDGECREST RD
CLACKAMAS CO OR 200-A3
HAPPY VALLEY OR 200-A3
RIDGELINE TR
EUGENE OR 330-B14
LANE CO OR 215-B3
LANE CO OR 329-J14
RIDGETOP BLVD
SILVERDALE WA 174-B1
RIDGEVIEW DR NE
KITSAP CO WA 271-C7
RIDGEWAY DR
REEDSPORT OR 218-C1
RIDGEWAY DR SE
MARION CO OR 207-D1
SW RIEDWEG RD
WASHINGTON CO OR 198-C2
RIETH RD
UMATILLA CO OR 129-A1
RIFE RD
CLALLAM CO WA 165-A6
RIFLE RANGE RD
BENTON CO OR 207-B3
NE RIFLE RANGE RD
ROSEBURG OR 334-J7
RIGDON RD
LANE CO OR 142-A1
SW RIGERT RD
WASHINGTON CO OR 199-A2
RIGGS RD
CROOK CO OR 213-B6
WALLA WALLA CO WA 121-B3
RIGHT FORK RD
DOUGLAS CO OR 221-D6
RIGHT FORK FOOTS CK RD
JACKSON CO OR 229-D7
RIGHT FORK SARDINE CREEK RD
JACKSON CO OR 230-B4
RIM DR
KLAMATH CO OR 227-C2
RIM RD
CANYON CO ID 147-B1
JEFFERSON CO OR 212-C2
RIMROCK RD
COLTON WA 250-A1
WHITMAN CO WA 250-A1
N RIMROCK RD
KOOTENAI CO ID 245-A4
NW RIMROCK RD
JEFFERSON CO OR 208-B3
RIMROCK ACRES RD
CROOK CO OR 213-C4
RIM VIEW RD
KLICKITAT CO WA 196-A5
RINEHART RD
MALHEUR CO OR 146-C2
RINEHART RANCH RD
MALHEUR CO OR 146-B2
RINGO RD
CLACKAMAS CO OR 199-D7
WHITMAN CO WA 249-C2
RINGOLD RD
FRANKLIN CO WA 121-A2
RINK CREEK RD
COOS CO OR 220-D5
RIO NES LN
DOUGLAS CO OR 221-C3
RIORDAN HILL DR
HOOD RIVER CO OR 195-B6
RIO VISTA AV
BURLINGTON WA 260-E5
SKAGIT CO WA 260-E5
RIO VISTA AV Rt#-20
BURLINGTON WA 260-C5
RIO VISTA BLVD
VALLEY CO ID 251-C5
RIPON AV
LEWISTON ID 250-C5
RIPPEE LN
YAKIMA CO WA 243-A6
RIPPINGTON RD
PITT MEADOWS BC 157-B5
RISLEY CREEK RD
LINCOLN CO OR 209-C1
NE RISTO RD
CLARK CO WA 193-A3
RITCHEY RD
WASHINGTON CO OR 198-B1
RITTER RD
WHATCOM CO WA 158-D5
RITTER SPRINGS RD
GRANT CO OR 129-A3
S RIVARD RD
YAKIMA CO WA 243-D7
RIVER AV
EUGENE OR 215-B1
TILLAMOOK CO OR 197-A7
RIVER DR
LANE CO OR 215-C5
RIVER DR Rt#-155
COULEE DAM WA 237-C2
OKANOGAN CO WA 237-C2
N RIVER DR
LINN CO OR 133-C2
RIVER RD
CITY OF RICHMOND BC 156-B6
DISTRICT OF DELTA BC 156-C7
DISTRICT OF SURREY BC 156-D6
EUGENE OR 215-A1
EUGENE OR 329-G1
JACKSON CO OR 150-A1
JACKSON CO OR 226-C6
JACKSON CO OR 230-B3
JUNCTION CITY OR 210-A6
KOOTENAI CO ID 115-B2
LAKE CO OR 151-C1
LANE CO OR 210-A6
LANE CO OR 215-A1
LANE CO OR 329-G1
LINN CO OR 134-B2
MARION CO OR 205-A1
SANTA CLARA OR 210-A7
Santa Clara OR 215-A1
SKAGIT CO WA 161-C6
TOWNSHIP OF LANGLEY BC 157-D6
UMATILLA OR 129-A1
UMATILLA CO OR 129-A1
WASCO CO OR 196-C6
WHITMAN CO WA 249-A4
RIVER RD Rt#-155
ELMER CITY WA 237-C1
OKANOGAN CO WA 237-C1
RIVER RD Rt#-167
PIERCE CO WA 182-A3
PUYALLUP WA 182-A3
TACOMA WA 182-A3
E RIVER RD
PUYALLUP WA 182-B3
N RIVER RD
JACKSON CO OR 229-D6
JACKSON CO OR 230-A6
LATAH CO ID 249-C1
ROGUE RIVER OR 229-D6
WHITMAN CO WA 249-C1
S RIVER RD
COTTAGE GROVE OR 215-B7

STREET
City State Page-Grid

S RIVER RD
WHITMAN CO WA 249-C1
SE RIVER RD
CLACKAMAS OR 321-J4
CLACKAMAS CO OR 199-C4
GLADSTONE OR 199-D4
HILLSBORO OR 198-D2
MILWAUKIE OR 321-J4
WASHINGTON CO OR 198-D2
SW RIVER RD
HILLSBORO OR 198-D3
WASHINGTON CO OR 198-D3
W RIVER RD
YAKIMA WA 243-B6
RIVER RD N
KEIZER OR 322-J5
KEIZER OR 323-A4
SALEM OR 322-J8
RIVER RD NE
KEIZER OR 323-A2
MARION CO OR 204-D1
MARION CO OR 205-A1
MARION CO OR 323-A2
RIVER RD S
MARION CO OR 204-B7
MARION CO OR 324-D3
SALEM OR 322-G14
SALEM OR 324-D3
S RIVER RD S
INDEPENDENCE OR 204-B7
RIVER RD W
DISTRICT OF DELTA BC 101-C1
RIVER ST
CAVE JUNCTION OR 233-B4
JOSEPHINE CO OR 233-B4
LEBANON OR 133-C1
N RIVER ST
NEWBERG OR 198-D5
N RIVER ST Rt#-82
ENTERPRISE OR 130-C2
S RIVER ST Rt#-82
ENTERPRISE OR 130-C2
W RIVER ST
CAVE JUNCTION OR 233-A4
RIVER BEND RD
SALEM OR 322-F9
RIVERBEND RD
MOUNT VERNON WA 260-A9
SKAGIT CO WA 161-A7
SKAGIT CO WA 260-A9
SW RIVER BEND RD
YAMHILL CO OR 204-B1
RIVER BOTTOM RD
KITTITAS CO WA 241-B6
RIVERCREST DR N
KEIZER OR 322-J6
NW RIVERFRONT BLVD
BEND OR 332-D8
RIVERFRONT RD
COLUMBIA CO OR 117-B3
RIVERGREEN AV
BENTON CO OR 327-G14
CORVALLIS OR 327-G14
RIVERHAVEN ST
WEST PASCO WA 343-A7
RIVERIA RD
COLUMBIA CO WA 122-A2
RIVERSHORE RD
SNOHOMISH WA 269-H2
RIVERSIDE AV Rt#-7
OROFINO ID 123-C2
RIVERSIDE AV Rt#-20
OKANOGAN CO WA 104-A2
WINTHROP WA 104-A2
RIVERSIDE AV U.S.-101
HOQUIAM WA 178-A7
N RIVERSIDE AV Rt#-99
MEDFORD OR 336-C10
S RIVERSIDE AV Rt#-99
MEDFORD OR 336-D13
W RIVERSIDE AV
SPOKANE WA 348-H9
NW RIVERSIDE BLVD
BEND OR 332-D7
RIVERSIDE DR
BANDON OR 220-B5
COOS CO OR 220-B5
DIST OF N VANCOUVER BC 255-J3
DOUGLAS CO OR 225-C1
DOUGLAS CO WA 239-B5
LINN CO OR 207-C5
LINN CO OR 326-A10
MARION CO OR 198-D6
MCMINNVILLE OR 198-B7
MOUNT VERNON WA 260-C10
MYRTLE CREEK OR 225-C1
PIERCE CO WA 182-C3
YAMHILL CO OR 198-B7
RIVERSIDE DR Rt#-20
OKANOGAN CO WA 104-C2
OMAK WA 104-C2
RIVERSIDE DR Rt#-129
ASOTIN CO WA 250-B5
VINELAND WA 250-B5
RIVERSIDE DR U.S.-101
NEHALEM OR 191-B4
SE RIVERSIDE DR
VANCOUVER WA 306-C7
SW RIVERSIDE DR Rt#-43
CLACKAMAS OR 321-G5
LAKE OSWEGO OR 321-G5
MULTNOMAH OR 321-G5
RIVERSIDE DR NE
BANDON OR 220-B6
S RIVERSIDE RD
YAKIMA CO WA 243-C7
RIVERSIDE RD S
MARION CO OR 207-C1
MARION CO OR 324-A14
RIVERSIDE ST
BONNERS FERRY ID 107-B2
BOUNDARY CO ID 107-B2
RIVERSIDE CUTOFF RD
OKANOGAN CO WA 104-C2
RIVERSIDE WA 104-C2
RIVERSIDE PARK DR
SPOKANE CO WA 348-A1
RIVERVIEW BLVD
CLARKSTON WA 250-B4
RIVERVIEW DR
DESCHUTES CO OR 143-A1
LANE CO OR 210-A7
ROSEBURG OR 334-C5
W RIVERVIEW DR
KOOTENAI CO ID 353-E9
RIVERVIEW RD
JEFFERSON CO OR 208-A6
SNOHOMISH WA 171-D3
SNOHOMISH WA 269-H4
SNOHOMISH CO WA 171-D3
RIVERWOOD RD
YAMHILL CO OR 198-C7
RIXIE DR SE
THURSTON CO WA 184-D1
RIXON RD
PACIFIC CO WA 183-D7
ROAD 1-NE
GRANT CO WA 242-D3
ROAD 1-NW
GRANT CO WA 112-B3
ROAD 1-SW
GRANT CO WA 112-B3
GRANT CO WA 242-A4
ROAD 2-NE
GRANT CO WA 242-A3
ROAD 2-NW
GRANT CO WA 112-B3
GRANT CO WA 242-A3
ROAD 3-NE
GRANT CO WA 113-A2
GRANT CO WA 242-A3
MOSES LAKE WA 242-D3
ROAD 3-NW
GRANT CO WA 242-A3
ROAD 3-SE
GRANT CO WA 113-A3
GRANT CO WA 242-D4
ROAD 3-SW
GRANT CO WA 112-B3
ROAD 4-NE
GRANT CO WA 242-B2
ROAD 4-NW
GRANT CO WA 112-C3
GRANT CO WA 242-A2
ROAD 4-SE
GRANT CO WA 242-D5
ROAD 4-SW
GRANT CO WA 112-C3
ROAD 4-10-NE
GRANT CO WA 113-A2
ROAD 5-NE
GRANT CO WA 242-A2
ROAD 5-NW
GRANT CO WA 112-C3
GRANT CO WA 242-A2
ROAD 5-SE
GRANT CO WA 242-C5
ROAD 5-SW
GRANT CO WA 112-B3
ROAD 6-NE
GRANT CO WA 242-D2
ROAD 6-NW
GRANT CO WA 112-B3
ROAD 6-SW
GRANT CO WA 112-B3
ROAD 7-NE
GRANT CO WA 113-A3
GRANT CO WA 242-D2
ROAD 7-NW
GRANT CO WA 112-C3
GRANT CO WA 242-A2
ROAD 7-SW
GRANT CO WA 120-B1
GRANT CO WA 242-A6
W ROAD 7-10-NE
GRANT CO WA 113-A2
ROAD 8-NE
GRANT CO WA 242-D1
ROAD 8-NW
GRANT CO WA 242-A1
ROAD 8-SE Rt#-170
GRANT CO WA 121-A1
WARDEN WA 121-A1
ROAD 9-NE
GRANT CO WA 113-A3
GRANT CO WA 242-D1
ROAD 9-NW
GRANT CO WA 112-C3
GRANT CO WA 242-A1
ROAD 10-NE
GRANT CO WA 242-C1
ROAD 10-NW Rt#-28
GRANT CO WA 112-B3
ROAD 10-NW Rt#-281
GRANT CO WA 112-B3
ROAD 11-NW Rt#-28
GRANT CO WA 112-C3
ROAD 11-SW
GRANT CO WA 120-B1
GRANT CO WA 242-A7
ROAD 12-NE
GRANT CO WA 113-A3
ROAD 12-NW
GRANT CO WA 112-B3
ROAD 12 SE
ADAMS CO WA 242-C7
GRANT CO WA 242-C7
ROAD 12-SE
GRANT CO WA 242-B7
ROAD 13-SE
GRANT CO WA 242-B7
ROAD 13-SW
GRANT CO WA 242-A7
ROAD 13-SW Rt#-26
GRANT CO WA 120-B1
ROAD 15-NE
GRANT CO WA 113-A3
ROAD 15-1-31
LANE CO OR 210-D5
LINN CO OR 210-D5
ROAD 15-2-25
LANE CO OR 210-D5
ROAD 15-2-25-1
LANE CO OR 210-D6
ROAD 15-2-26-1
LINN CO OR 210-D5
ROAD 16-NE
GRANT CO WA 113-A3
ROAD 16-2-10
LANE CO OR 210-D6
ROAD 16-2-10-2
LANE CO OR 210-D6
ROAD 16-2-17-1
LANE CO OR 210-C7
ROAD 16-2-18
LANE CO OR 210-D7
ROAD 16-2-18-1
LANE CO OR 210-C6
ROAD 16-2-27
LANE CO OR 210-C7
ROAD 16-2-28
LANE CO OR 210-D7
ROAD 16-2-29
LANE CO OR 210-C7
ROAD 16-2-7-1
LANE CO OR 210-C6
ROAD 16-3-13-2
LANE CO OR 210-C7
ROAD 19-NE
GRANT CO WA 112-C2
ROAD 19-NW
GRANT CO WA 112-C2
ROAD 20-NE
GRANT CO WA 112-C2
GRANT CO WA 113-A2
ROAD 20-NW
GRANT CO WA 112-C2
ROAD 21 1/2-NE
GRANT CO WA 113-A2
ROAD 22-NE
GRANT CO WA 113-A2
ROAD 23-NE
GRANT CO WA 112-C2
GRANT CO WA 113-A2
ROAD 23 SW
GRANT CO WA 120-B1
ROAD 24-NW
GRANT CO WA 112-B2
ROAD 24-SW
GRANT CO WA 120-B1
MATTAWA WA 120-B1
ROAD 25-NE
GRANT CO WA 112-C2
ROAD 27-SW
GRANT CO WA 120-B1
ROAD 28
WEST PASCO WA 343-C5
ROAD 29-NE
GRANT CO WA 112-C2
ROAD 31-NE
GRANT CO WA 113-A2
ROAD 36
PASCO WA 343-B6
WEST PASCO WA 343-B4
ROAD 36-NE
GRANT CO WA 113-A2
ROAD 42-NE
GRANT CO WA 113-A2
ROAD 43-NE
GRANT CO WA 237-B7
ROAD 44
PASCO WA 343-A6
WEST PASCO WA 343-A4
ROAD 44-NE
GRANT CO WA 237-A7
ROAD 45-NE
GRANT CO WA 237-B7
ROAD 46-NE
GRANT CO WA 237-B6
ROAD 47-NE
GRANT CO WA 237-B6
ROAD 48
WEST PASCO WA 343-A5
ROAD 48-NE
GRANT CO WA 237-B6
ROAD 49-NE
GRANT CO WA 237-B6
ROAD 50-NE
GRANT CO WA 237-C5
ROAD 51-NE
GRANT CO WA 237-C5
ROAD 52-NE
GRANT CO WA 237-C5
ROAD 60
WEST PASCO WA 342-H5
ROAD 68
PASCO WA 342-G6
WEST PASCO WA 342-G6
ROAD 68 N
FRANKLIN CO WA 121-A2
FRANKLIN CO WA 340-J5
PASCO WA 121-A2
PASCO WA 342-G1
ROAD 76
PASCO WA 342-F5
WEST PASCO WA 342-F5
ROAD 84
WEST PASCO WA 342-E4
ROAD 92
WEST PASCO WA 342-D4
ROAD 100
PASCO WA 342-C3
WEST PASCO WA 342-C3
ROAD 170
FRANKLIN CO WA 121-A2
ROAD 4370
LINCOLN CO WA 113-B1
WILBUR WA 113-B1
ROAD 5215
CHELAN CO WA 238-D1
ROAD 5300
CHELAN CO WA 236-A4
ROAD 5900
CHELAN CO WA 112-A1
ROAD 7009
GRAYS HARBOR CO WA 177-D1
ROAD 7100
CHELAN CO WA 238-C5
ROAD 7413
CHELAN CO WA 238-D1
ROAD 8002
GRAYS HARBOR CO WA 178-A1
ROAD 8020
CHELAN CO WA 236-C1
ROAD 8410
CHELAN CO WA 236-A1
ROAD 8500
CHELAN CO WA 236-A3
ROAD 8550
CHELAN CO WA 236-B4
ROAD A-NE
GRANT CO WA 112-C2
GRANT CO WA 242-A2
ROAD A-NW
GRANT CO WA 242-A1
ROAD A-SE
GRANT CO WA 120-C1
GRANT CO WA 242-A4
ROAD A-SE Rt#-262
GRANT CO WA 120-C1
GRANT CO WA 242-A7
ROAD A-LINE
GRAYS HARBOR CO WA 117-B1
GRAYS HARBOR CO WA 178-D4
GRAYS HARBOR CO WA 179-A4
ROAD B-NE
GRANT CO WA 112-C2
GRANT CO WA 242-A1
ROAD B-NW
GRANT CO WA 112-C2
GRANT CO WA 242-A2
ROAD B-SE
GRANT CO WA 120-C1
GRANT CO WA 242-B7
ROAD B-210
WASCO CO OR 135-A1
ROAD B-1000
GRAYS HARBOR CO WA 179-D7
ROAD B-LINE
GRAYS HARBOR CO WA 179-A4
ROAD C-NW
EPHRATA WA 112-C3
GRANT CO WA 112-C3
ROAD C-SE
GRANT CO WA 242-B4
ROAD C-LINE RD
GRAYS HARBOR CO WA 179-D7
ROAD CS30
MASON CO WA 179-B4
ROAD D-NE
GRANT CO WA 112-C2
GRANT CO WA 242-B3
ROAD D-SE
GRANT CO WA 120-C1
ROAD D-LINE
GRAYS HARBOR CO WA 178-D4
ROAD E-NE
GRANT CO WA 242-B3
ROAD E-NW
GRANT CO WA 112-C3
ROAD E-SW
GRANT CO WA 120-C1
ROAD F-NE
GRANT CO WA 112-C2
GRANT CO WA 242-B2
ROAD H SE
GRANT CO WA 242-C7
ROAD I-NE
GRANT CO WA 242-C2
ROAD J-NE
GRANT CO WA 113-A2
ROAD K-NE
GRANT CO WA 113-A3
GRANT CO WA 242-D2
ROAD K-NW
GRANT CO WA 112-C3
ROAD K-SE
GRANT CO WA 242-D4
MOSES LAKE WA 242-D4
ROAD K-SW
GRANT CO WA 112-C3
ROAD L-NE
GRANT CO WA 113-A2
GRANT CO WA 242-D1
ROAD L-SE
GRANT CO WA 242-D5
ROAD L-SW
GRANT CO WA 120-B1
ROAD L-5-SW
GRANT CO WA 112-B3
GRANT CO WA 120-B1
ROAD L 7-NE
GRANT CO WA 237-A7
ROAD M-NW
GRANT CO WA 112-B3
ROAD M-SE
GRANT CO WA 242-D5
ROAD M-SW
GRANT CO WA 112-B3
GRANT CO WA 120-B1
ROAD M-110
JEFFERSON CO OR 208-A6
ROAD N-NE
GRANT CO WA 237-A7
GRANT CO WA 242-D1
ROAD N-SE
GRANT CO WA 242-D4
ROAD O-NE
GRANT CO WA 237-A6
GRANT CO WA 242-D1
ROAD O-SE
GRANT CO WA 242-D4
ROAD O-SW
GRANT CO WA 120-B1
ROAD P-NE
GRANT CO WA 113-A3
GRANT CO WA 237-B6
ROAD P-NW
GRANT CO WA 112-B3
ROAD P-110
JEFFERSON CO OR 208-A4
ROAD Q-NE
GRANT CO WA 113-A3
GRANT CO WA 237-B6
ROAD Q-SE
GRANT CO WA 113-A3
ROAD Q-SW
GEORGE WA 112-B3
GRANT CO WA 112-B3
GRANT CO WA 120-B1
ROAD R-NE
GRANT CO WA 113-A2
GRANT CO WA 237-B6
HARTLINE WA 113-A2
ROAD R-NW
GRANT CO WA 112-B3
ROAD R-SW
GRANT CO WA 112-B3
GRANT CO WA 120-B1
ROAD S-NE
GRANT CO WA 113-A3
GRANT CO WA 237-B6
ROAD S-NW
GRANT CO WA 112-B3
ROAD S-322
WASCO CO OR 127-B3
ROAD T-NE
GRANT CO WA 237-B6
ROAD T-2 NE
GRANT CO WA 237-B5
ROAD U-NE
GRANT CO WA 113-A3
GRANT CO WA 237-C5
ROAD U-NW
GRANT CO WA 112-B3
ROAD U-SE
GRANT CO WA 113-A3
GRANT CO WA 121-A1
WARDEN WA 121-A1
ROAD U-SW
GRANT CO WA 112-B3
GRANT CO WA 120-B1
ROAD V-NE
GRANT CO WA 237-C5
ROAD W-NE
GRANT CO WA 113-A2
GRANT CO WA 237-C4
KRUPP WA 113-A2
LINCOLN CO WA 113-A2
ROAD W-SE
GRANT CO WA 121-A1
ROANOKE DR NE
MARION CO OR 205-A3
E ROANOKE ST
SEATTLE WA 278-B1
ROARING CREEK RD
WASHINGTON CO OR 198-A3
ROBBINS RD
KITTITAS CO WA 241-B4
ROBERTA AV
LAKE CO OR 152-A2
ROBERT BUSH DR U.S.-101
PACIFIC CO WA 183-D6
SOUTH BEND WA 117-A1
SOUTH BEND WA 183-D6
ROBERT CREEK RD
COOS CO OR 218-D4
ROBERT GRAY DR
PACIFIC CO WA 186-A6
SE ROBERTS AV
GRESHAM OR 200-B2
ROBERTS DR
BLACK DIAMOND WA 110-C3
ROBERTS RD
CROOK CO OR 135-C3
CROOK CO OR 136-A3
GRAYS HARBOR CO WA 183-B2
LEWIS CO WA 187-D1
LINN CO OR 210-B1
MEDFORD OR 336-E9
YAKIMA CO WA 243-A5
ROBERTS RD KPN
PIERCE CO WA 181-A1
ROBERTS BANK SUPERPORT CSWY
DISTRICT OF DELTA BC 101-C1
ROBERTS BUTTE RD
WALLOWA CO OR 130-C1
ROBERTS CREEK RD
DOUGLAS CO OR 221-B6
ROBERTS MOUNTAIN RD
DOUGLAS CO OR 221-B6
ROBERTSON CRES
TOWNSHIP OF LANGLEY BC 158-D1
ROBERTSON ST
CITY OF VICTORIA BC 257-A11
ROBERTSON BRIDGE RD
JOSEPHINE CO OR 229-A4
ROBIN DR
JEFFERSON CO OR 212-C2
ROBINETTE RD
COLUMBIA CO OR 192-A1
ROBINSON RD
JOSEPHINE CO OR 233-C4
ROBINSON ST
COQUITLAM BC 157-A5
ROBINSON CANYON RD
KITTITAS CO WA 241-A5
ROBINSON LAKE RD
LATAH CO ID 249-D4
ROBINSON PARK RD
LATAH CO ID 249-D4
ROBISON RD
BENTON CO OR 207-A3
POLK CO OR 207-A3
ROBSON DR
COQUITLAM BC 157-B4
ROBSON ST
VANCOUVER BC 254-F9
ROCHAT RD
KOOTENAI CO ID 115-B2
ROCHAT DIVIDE RD
BENEWAH CO ID 115-B2
ROCHE HARBOR RD
FRIDAY HARBOR WA 101-C2
SAN JUAN CO WA 101-C2
ROCK RD Rt#-547
WHATCOM CO WA 102-B1
ROCK RD NW
DOUGLAS CO WA 236-C6
ROCKAWAY BEACH RD
KITSAP CO WA 174-D2
ROCK CANDY MOUNTAIN RD SW
THURSTON CO WA 180-A7
ROCK CANYON RD
MALHEUR CO OR 146-C1
ROCK CREEK RD
COLUMBIA CO OR 125-B1
COOS CO OR 140-C3
DOUGLAS CO OR 141-C2
DOUGLAS CO OR 219-B2
HARNEY CO OR 145-A3
HARNEY CO OR 153-A1
JACKSON CO OR 227-A3
JACKSON CO OR 230-B1
KLICKITAT CO WA 128-A1
ROCK CREEK RD
LINCOLN CO OR 133-A1
MALHEUR CO OR 146-C3
WASHINGTON CO ID 139-A2
NW ROCK CREEK RD
MULTNOMAH CO OR 192-A6
S ROCK CREEK RD
BAKER CO OR 130-A3
ROCK CREEK DAM RD
WASCO CO OR 127-A3
ROCKCREST ST
COLUMBIA CO OR 189-B4
RAINIER OR 189-B4
RAINIER OR 302-H14
ROCK CUT RD
STEVENS CO WA 105-C1
ROCKFORD BAY RD
KOOTENAI CO ID 247-D6
ROCK HILL DR
LANE CO OR 215-B4
LINN CO OR 133-C1
LINN CO OR 210-C1
SOUTH LEBANON OR 133-C1
ROCK ISLAND AV
DOUGLAS CO WA 239-B5
ROCK ISLAND WA 239-B5
ROCK ISLAND RD
DOUGLAS CO WA 239-A5
EAST WENATCHEE BENCH WA 239-A5
ROCK ISLAND GRADE SW
DOUGLAS CO WA 239-C5
ROCK LAKE RD
WHITMAN CO WA 114-B3
S ROCK LAKE RD
SPOKANE CO WA 114-B3
ROCKLAND AV
CITY OF VICTORIA BC 256-J9
CITY OF VICTORIA BC 257-A10
W ROCKLAND RD
DIST OF N VANCOUVER BC 255-B1
ROCKLYN RD
LINCOLN CO WA 113-C2
ROCKPORT CASCADE RD
SKAGIT CO WA 103-A2
ROCK SPRINGS RD
JEFFERSON CO OR 211-D3
WHITMAN CO WA 122-A1
ROCKWELL DR
CITY OF HARRISN HT SPGS BC 94-C3
DISTRICT OF KENT BC 94-C3
E ROCKWOOD BLVD
SPOKANE WA 349-A11
S ROCKWOOD BLVD
SPOKANE WA 349-B12
ROCKY RD
DOUGLAS CO WA 236-D4
ROCKY BAY PT Rt#-302
MASON CO WA 173-D7
MASON CO WA 174-A7
PIERCE CO WA 174-A7
ROCKY BUTTE RD
WASCO CO OR 202-D7
ROCKY CANYON RD
IDAHO CO ID 123-B3
IDAHO CO ID 131-C1
ROCKY CREEK RD KPN
PIERCE CO WA 174-A6
ROCKYDALE RD
JOSEPHINE CO OR 233-B6
ROCKY FORD RD
LINCOLN CO WA 113-C2
YAKIMA CO WA 120-A2
NW ROCKYFORD RD
YAMHILL CO OR 198-A4
ROCKY POINT RD
DISTRICT OF METCHOSIN BC 159-A7
DISTRICT OF METCHOSIN BC 165-A1
KITSAP CO WA 270-E8
MULTNOMAH CO OR 192-A5
ROCKY TOP RD
YAKIMA CO WA 243-A6
RODGERS RD
LANE CO OR 215-C5
RODMAN RD
YAKIMA CO WA 243-B4
ROE RD
LEWIS CO WA 187-B4
ROE RD E
LEWIS CO WA 187-B3
ROE ST
STEILACOOM WA 181-C4
ROGERS RD
COWLITZ CO WA 189-D5
DOUGLAS CO OR 221-C2
LEWIS CO WA 187-C5
POLK CO OR 204-B7
ROGERS AND HOBSON RD
CHELAN CO WA 236-C2
ROGERSON RD
LEWIS CO WA 184-D7
SE ROGUE DR
GRANTS PASS OR 335-G11
ROGUE RIVER DR
JACKSON CO OR 230-D4
SHADY COVE OR 230-D4
ROGUE RIVER HWY Rt#-99
GRANTS PASS OR 335-F11
JACKSON CO OR 229-C6
JACKSON CO OR 230-A6
JOSEPHINE CO OR 229-C6
JOSEPHINE CO OR 335-J11
ROGUE RIVER OR 229-C6
ROGUE RIVER HWY U.S.-199
GRANTS PASS OR 335-G11
ROGUE RIVER LOOP HWY
JOSEPHINE CO OR 149-A1
JOSEPHINE CO OR 229-A5
JOSEPHINE CO OR 335-C8
SW ROGUE RIVER LOOP HWY
GRANTS PASS OR 335-D8
ROGUE VALLEY HWY Rt#-99
ASHLAND OR 337-A4
CENTRAL POINT OR 230-C7
JACKSON CO OR 230-C7
JACKSON CO OR 234-B2
JACKSON CO OR 336-A7
JACKSON CO OR 337-A4
MEDFORD OR 230-C7
MEDFORD OR 234-B2
MEDFORD OR 336-A7

PNW
INDEX

STREET City State Page-Grid

ROGUE VALLEY HWY Rt#-99
PHOENIX OR 234-B2
TALENT OR 234-B2
ROITZ RD
STEVENS CO WA 106-B3
ROLLING HILLS RD
POLK CO OR 207-B2
ROLOFF RD
ADAMS CO WA 113-C3
ROME RD
MALHEUR CO OR 146-C3
ROMIE HOWARD RD
DOUGLAS CO OR 219-C5
ROMINE CREEK RD
JACKSON CO OR 230-C1
ROMMERMAN RD
LEWIS CO WA 187-C1
SW ROOD BRIDGE RD
WASHINGTON CO OR 198-D2
ROOSEVELT AV Rt#-410
ENUMCLAW WA 110-C3
SW ROOSEVELT AV
BEND OR 332-E9
W ROOSEVELT AV
CANYON CO ID 147-B1
ROOSEVELT AV E Rt#-410
ENUMCLAW WA 110-C3
KING CO WA 110-C3
ROOSEVELT DR U.S.-101
SEASIDE WA 301-H7
ROOSEVELT ST
ABERDEEN WA 178-B7
N ROOSEVELT ST
BOISE ID 253-C3
WALLA WALLA WA 345-D6
S ROOSEVELT ST
BOISE ID 253-C3
WALLA WALLA WA 345-D8
ROOSEVELT WY
WHATCOM CO WA 101-C1
ROOSEVELT WY NE
SEATTLE WA 171-B7
SEATTLE WA 274-B2
ROOSEVELT GRADE RD
KLICKITAT CO WA 128-A1
ROPPERT RD
LEWIS CO WA 187-C3
ROSA RD
COOS CO OR 220-B7
ROSARIO RD
SKAGIT CO WA 160-C7
SKAGIT CO WA 259-D10
ROSARIO BEACH RD
SKAGIT CO WA 259-C14
ROSE AV Rt#-47
COLUMBIA CO OR 125-B1
VERNONIA OR 125-B1
ROSE RD
LANE CO OR 210-D6
SISKIYOU CO CA 151-A3
SNOHOMISH CO WA 168-C4
ROSE ST
PHOENIX OR 234-B2
N ROSE ST
WALLA WALLA WA 345-B6
W ROSE ST
COLLEGE PLACE WA 344-F9
WALLA WALLA WA 344-H9
ROSEBERG ST SW
THURSTON CO WA 184-A4
E ROSEBERRY RD
DONNELLY ID 252-D1
VALLEY CO ID 252-D1
W ROSEBERRY RD
VALLEY CO ID 252-D2
ROSEBROOK RD
LEWIS CO WA 187-D1
ROSE CREEK RD
MALHEUR CO OR 138-A2
WHITMAN CO WA 249-B3
ROSEDALE RD
CATHLAMET WA 117-B3
WAHKIAKUM CO WA 117-B3
SW ROSEDALE RD
WASHINGTON CO OR 198-D2
WASHINGTON CO OR 199-A2
ROSEDALE ST NW
GIG HARBOR WA 181-B1
PIERCE CO WA 181-B1
ROSE HILL ST
BOISE ID 253-C3
ROSEMONT AV NW
SALEM OR 322-F12
SW ROSEMONT RD
CLACKAMAS CO OR 199-C4
ROSENAU RD
LATAH CO ID 250-D1
ROSENKRANTZ RD
NEZ PERCE CO ID 250-C5
ROSENOFF RD
ADAMS CO WA 113-B3
RITZVILLE WA 113-B3
ROSENOFF RD Rt#-21
ADAMS CO WA 113-B3
ROSE VALLEY RD
COWLITZ CO WA 118-A3
COWLITZ CO WA 189-C4
ROSS LN
JACKSON CO OR 234-A1
JACKSON CO OR 336-A12
LANE CO OR 215-C7
MEDFORD OR 336-A12
ROSS LN Rt#-238
JACKSON CO OR 336-A12
ROSS RD
DIST OF N VANCOUVER BC 255-F3
DISTRICT OF MATSQUI BC 102-B1
ROSSANLEY DR
JACKSON CO OR 234-A1
JACKSON CO OR 336-A10
MEDFORD OR 336-A10
ROSS INLET RD
COOS CO OR 220-D2
S ROSS POINT RD
KOOTENAI CO ID 354-D7
POST FALLS ID 354-D7
ROSS POINT-RATHDRUM HWY Rt#-41
KOOTENAI CO ID 247-D1
KOOTENAI CO ID 354-D2
ROSS POINT-RATHDRUM HWY Rt#-41
POST FALLS ID 354-D2
ROSWELL RD
MALHEUR CO OR 147-A1
ROTH RD
LEWIS CO WA 187-C3
ROTHFORK RD
LATAH CO ID 249-C3
ROTHROCK RD
BENTON CO WA 120-C2
NE ROTSCHY RD
CLARK CO WA 193-B1
ROUGH & RUGGED RD
JACKSON CO OR 230-B7
SW ROUND BUTTE DR
JEFFERSON CO OR 208-A6
ROUND BUTTE LOOP RD
KLAMATH CO OR 142-C3
ROUND LAKE RD
JEFFERSON CO OR 211-B1
KLAMATH CO OR 235-A2
ROUNDS AV
JOSEPHINE CO OR 229-A6
ROUND TOP RD
JACKSON CO OR 230-B1
ROUNDTREE RD
LEWIS CO WA 187-A2
ROUND VALLEY RD
ADAMS CO ID 131-C3
ADAMS CO ID 251-A1
ROUPE RD
ASOTIN CO WA 122-C2
ROUSE RD KPS
PIERCE CO WA 181-A3
ROUTE 16 FRWY Rt#-16
TACOMA WA 292-A6
TACOMA WA 294-B1
TACOMA WA 295-E1
NE ROVA RD
KITSAP CO WA 170-C6
ROWDY CREEK RD
DEL NORTE CO CA 148-B3
ROWE CREEK RD
WHEELER CO OR 128-A3
WHEELER CO OR 136-A1
ROWLAND RD
LINN CO OR 210-B4
YAMHILL CO OR 198-B5
ROW RIVER RD
COTTAGE GROVE OR 215-C7
LANE CO OR 141-C1
LANE CO OR 215-C7
ROW RIVER CUTOFF RD
COTTAGE GROVE OR 215-B7
SW ROXBURY ST
KING WA 285-F4
SEATTLE WA 285-F4
ROXY ANN RD
JACKSON CO OR 234-C1
ROY RD
WASHINGTON CO OR 125-C1
WHATCOM CO WA 161-A2
ROY ST
SEATTLE WA 277-H3
E ROY ST
SEATTLE WA 278-B3
ROYAL AV
EUGENE OR 215-A2
EUGENE OR 329-A3
LANE CO OR 215-A2
MEDFORD OR 336-D11
NEW WESTMINSTER BC 156-D5
ROYAL AV N
EAGLE POINT OR 230-D5
JACKSON CO OR 230-D5
ROYAL AV S
EAGLE POINT OR 230-D5
S ROYAL BROUGHAM WY
SEATTLE WA 282-A1
S ROYAL BROUGHAM WY Rt#-519
SEATTLE WA 281-J1
SEATTLE WA 282-A1
ROYAL OAK AV
DISTRICT OF BURNABY BC 156-C5
ROYAL OAK DR
DISTRICT OF SAANICH BC 159-C5
SE ROYER RD
CLACKAMAS CO OR 200-B3
ROY JONES RD
SISKIYOU CO CA 150-A3
ROY PAYNE RD
LANE CO OR 219-D1
ROZA HILL DR
YAKIMA CO WA 243-D6
E ROZA HILL DR
TERRACE HEIGHTS WA 243-C6
YAKIMA CO WA 243-C6
N RUBY ST U.S.-2
SPOKANE WA 349-A6
RUCKEL RD
UNION CO OR 130-A1
RUCKER AV
EVERETT WA 264-D3
RUCKMAN AV Rt#-82
IMBLER OR 130-A2
RUDDELL RD SE
LACEY WA 297-H11
THURSTON CO WA 297-H11
NW RUDE RD
KITSAP CO WA 170-B6
SE RUDE RD
CLACKAMAS CO OR 200-C5
RUDI RD
DESCHUTES CO OR 212-B7
RUE CREEK RD
PACIFIC CO WA 117-A1
RUEPPELL ST
TILLAMOOK CO OR 197-A7
RUMBLE ST
DISTRICT OF BURNABY BC 156-C5
SE RUPERT DR
CLACKAMAS OR 321-J6
RUPERT RD
COLUMBIA CO OR 189-A7
RUPERT ST
VANCOUVER BC 156-C5
VANCOUVER BC 255-E14
RUPP RD
LEWIS CO WA 187-C5
RUPPERT RD
BENTON CO WA 120-C2
RURAL AV
BELLINGHAM WA 158-C7
RURAL AV SE
SALEM OR 324-H1
RURAL RD SW
THURSTON CO WA 296-F11
TUMWATER WA 296-F11
RURAL S ST
HARNEY CO OR 145-B2
RUSH AV
KLAMATH CO OR 151-A3
MALIN OR 151-A3
RUSH RD
ADA CO ID 253-A1
LEWIS CO WA 187-C1
RUSH CREEK RD
WASHINGTON CO ID 139-B1
RUSS BAKER WY
CITY OF RICHMOND BC 156-B6
RUSSEL RD
JOSEPHINE CO OR 229-B3
RUSSELL LN
JOSEPH OR 130-C2
WALLOWA CO OR 130-C2
RUSSELL RD
KENT WA 291-F4
LEWIS CO WA 187-B3
MALHEUR CO OR 138-C3
RUSSELL ST
WENATCHEE WA 238-D4
RUSSELL CREEK RD
WALLA WALLA CO WA 345-E9
WALLA WALLA EAST WA 345-E9
RUSSELL RIDGE RD
LEWIS CO ID 123-C2
RUSSELL RIDGE RD Rt#-7
CLEARWATER CO ID 123-C2
RUSTEMEYER RD
GRAYS HARBOR CO WA 183-C1
RUSTIC LN
LANE CO OR 214-B1
S RUSTLE ST
SPOKANE WA 348-D12
RUSTON WY
TACOMA WA 181-D1
TACOMA WA 292-D1
TACOMA WA 293-E2
RUTLEDGE LN
SHERMAN CO OR 127-C2
RUTLEDGE RD
SHERMAN CO OR 127-C2
E RUTTER AV
SPOKANE WA 349-J6
SPOKANE WA 350-A5
SPOKANE CO WA 349-J6
SPOKANE CO WA 350-A5
N RUTTER PKWY
SPOKANE CO WA 346-B6
W RUTTER PKWY
FAIRWOOD WA 346-A7
SPOKANE CO WA 246-A2
SPOKANE CO WA 346-A7
RYALS AV
BENTON CO OR 207-B4
RYAN RD
DESCHUTES CO OR 213-A4
RYAN-ALLEN RD
SKAMANIA CO WA 194-C5
RYAN-TAVELLI RD
SKAMANIA CO WA 194-A7
RYE GRASS LN
HARNEY CO OR 145-B1
RYEGRASS RD
CROOK CO OR 213-B3
RYE VALLEY-MORMON BASIN RD
BAKER CO OR 138-C2

S

SAANICH RD
DISTRICT OF SAANICH BC 256-G5
SAARI RD
LEWIS CO WA 187-C4
SACHS RD SW
DOUGLAS CO WA 239-C3
SADDLE DR
KOOTENAI CO ID 245-B7
SADDLE BUTTE RD
HARNEY CO OR 145-C2
SADDLE MOUNTAIN RD
CLATSOP CO WA 188-D4
SADDLE RIDGE RD
LATAH CO ID 249-C3
SAGE RD
GRANT CO WA 242-C3
JACKSON CO OR 336-B10
MALHEUR CO OR 139-A3
MEDFORD OR 336-B10
OWYHEE CO ID 147-A1
SAGEBRUSH FLAT RD
EPHRATA WA 112-C2
GRANT CO WA 112-C2
SAGEHILL RD
FRANKLIN CO WA 121-A1
W SAGEMOOR RD
FRANKLIN CO WA 121-A2
FRANKLIN CO WA 340-J2
SAGINAW EAST RD
LANE CO OR 215-B6
SAGINAW WEST RD
LANE CO OR 215-B6
S SAGLE RD
BONNER CO ID 244-A4
SAHALEE WY NE
KING CO WA 175-D1
KING CO WA 176-A2
SAINT ST
RICHLAND WA 340-F11
SAINT ANDREWS AV
CITY OF N VANCOUVER BC 255-C5
SAINT ANDREWS RD E
DOUGLAS CO WA 112-C2
SAINT ANDREWS RD S
DOUGLAS CO WA 112-C2
SAINT ANDREWS RD W
DOUGLAS CO WA 112-C2
SAINT CHARLES ST
CITY OF VICTORIA BC 257-A9
SAINT CLAIR RD
DESCHUTES CO OR 135-B3
DESCHUTES CO OR 217-D3
SAINT GEORGES AV
CITY OF N VANCOUVER BC 255-B5
SAINT HELENS AV
CHEHALIS WA 299-C10
SAINT HELENS AV
VANCOUVER WA 307-F7
S SAINT HELENS AV
TACOMA WA 293-G4
SAINT HELENS RD
PORTLAND OR 199-B1
PORTLAND OR 312-A2
NW SAINT HELENS RD
PORTLAND OR 199-B1
NW SAINT HELENS RD U.S.-30
MULTNOMAH CO OR 192-A5
PORTLAND OR 192-A5
PORTLAND OR 199-B1
SAINT HELENS ST
SAINT HELENS OR 192-B1
NE SAINT JAMES RD
VANCOUVER WA 192-D5
VANCOUVER WA 306-A2
E SAINT JOE DR
KOOTENAI CO ID 245-A1
SAINT JOE RD
BENEWAH CO ID 248-D7
SAINT JOHN RD
WHITMAN CO WA 114-C3
SAINT JOHNS BLVD
CLARK WA 306-A2
VANCOUVER WA 305-H3
VANCOUVER WA 306-A2
NE SAINT JOHNS RD
CLARK WA 306-A2
CLARK CO WA 192-D5
VANCOUVER WA 192-D5
VANCOUVER WA 306-A2
SAINT JOHNS ST Rt#-7A
DISTRICT OF BURNABY BC 156-D4
PORT MOODY BC 156-D4
PORT MOODY BC 157-A4
SAINT LAWRENCE ST
CITY OF VICTORIA BC 256-F9
SAINT LOUIS RD NE
MARION CO OR 205-A2
SAINT PAUL AV
TACOMA WA 182-A2
TACOMA WA 293-J5
SAINT PAUL HWY
MARION CO OR 198-D7
MARION CO OR 199-A7
MARION CO OR 205-B1
SAINT PAUL HWY Rt#-219
MARION CO OR 198-D7
NEWBERG OR 198-D7
SAINT PAUL OR 198-D7
YAMHILL CO OR 198-D7
SAINT PAUL HWY NE
MARION CO OR 205-B1
SALAL LN
COOS CO OR 220-C2
SALEM AV
ALBANY OR 326-F7
LINN CO OR 326-F7
MILLERSBURG OR 326-F7
SALEM EXWY Rt#-99E
KEIZER OR 323-B6
SALEM OR 323-B6
SALEM HWY Rt#-22
SALEM OR 322-J14
SALEM PKWY Rt#-99E
KEIZER OR 323-A8
MARION CO OR 323-A8
SALEM OR 322-J8
SALEM OR 323-A8
SALEM-DAYTON HWY Rt#-221
POLK CO OR 204-D2
POLK CO OR 322-E6
YAMHILL CO OR 204-D2
SALEM-DAYTON HWY NW Rt#-221
SALEM OR 322-E13
SALMI RD
LEWIS CO WA 187-B2
SW SALMON AV
REDMOND OR 212-D6
SALMON DR U.S.-95
IDAHO CO ID 131-C2
SE SALMONBERRY RD
EAST PORT ORCHARD WA 174-B4
SALMON BUTTE RD
CLACKAMAS CO OR 201-C7
NE SALMON CREEK AV
CLARK CO WA 192-D4
SALMON CREEK RD
LANE CO OR 142-A1
OKANOGAN CO WA 104-C3
WAHKIAKUM CO WA 117-A2
WAHKIAKUM CO WA 186-D5
SALMON FALLS RD
SKAMANIA CO WA 193-D7
SALMON HARBOR DR
DOUGLAS CO OR 218-B2
SALMON LA SAC RD
KITTITAS CO WA 111-B3
SALMON LA SAC RD Rt#-903
KITTITAS CO WA 111-B3
KITTITAS CO WA 240-A1
SALMON RIVER HWY Rt#-18
LINCOLN CO OR 203-B4
LINCOLN CO OR 203-D3
MCMINNVILLE OR 198-A7
MCMINNVILLE OR 204-A2
POLK CO OR 125-A3
ROSE LODGE OR 203-D3
SHERIDAN OR 125-B3
TILLAMOOK CO OR 125-A3
TILLAMOOK CO OR 203-D3
YAMHILL CO OR 125-B3
YAMHILL CO OR 198-A7
YAMHILL CO OR 204-A2
SALMON RIVER RD
CLACKAMAS CO OR 201-C5
W SALNAVE RD
SPOKANE CO WA 114-B2
SPOKANE CO WA 246-A7
W SALNAVE RD Rt#-902
MEDICAL LAKE WA 114-B2
SPOKANE CO WA 114-B2
W SALNAVE MEDICAL LAKE RD
CHENEY WA 246-A7
SPOKANE CO WA 246-A7
SALT CREEK RD
CROOK CO OR 135-C3
JACKSON CO OR 230-B2
N SALTESE RD
SPOKANE CO WA 351-C12
VERADALE WA 351-C12
S SALTESE LAKE RD
SPOKANE CO WA 351-J13
SALTY DR NW
THURSTON CO WA 180-C4
NW SALTZMAN RD
WASHINGTON CO OR 199-B1
SALZER VALLEY RD
LEWIS CO WA 184-C6
LEWIS CO WA 299-H6
NE SALZMAN RD
MULTNOMAH CO OR 200-D1
SAMARITAN DR
CORVALLIS OR 327-H4
SAM BELL RD
SKAGIT CO WA 161-A5
SAMISH WY
BELLINGHAM WA 258-E9
WHATCOM CO WA 161-A2
WHATCOM CO WA 258-H13
N SAMISH WY
BELLINGHAM WA 258-E8
SAMISH ISLAND RD
SKAGIT CO WA 160-D4
SAMISH POINT RD
SKAGIT CO WA 160-D4
NW SAMMAMISH RD
ISSAQUAH WA 175-D3
KING CO WA 175-D3
SAMS CREEK RD
LINCOLN CO OR 206-D3
SAMSON TR
MCCALL ID 251-D5
SAMS VALLEY AV Rt#-234
GOLD HILL OR 230-B6
JACKSON CO OR 230-B6
SAMS VALLEY HWY Rt#-99
GOLD HILL OR 230-A6
JACKSON CO OR 230-A6
SAMS VALLEY HWY Rt#-234
JACKSON CO OR 230-B6
SAMUELS RD
CLACKAMAS CO OR 200-B5
SANBORN RD
KLICKITAT CO WA 195-D3
SAND RD
LATAH CO ID 249-C5
WHITMAN CO WA 249-B3
SAND CANYON RD
CHEWELAH WA 106-B3
STEVENS CO WA 106-B3
SAND CREEK RD
DOUGLAS CO OR 219-B1
KLAMATH CO OR 142-C3
STEVENS CO WA 105-C1
SAND DUNES RD
GRANT CO WA 242-C4
SANDERS RD
BENEWAH CO ID 115-A3
SANDERS ST
CHELAN WA 236-D3
SAND FLATS-ICE CAVE RD
DESCHUTES CO OR 143-A1
SAND HILL RD
MASON CO WA 173-D4
SAND HILL RD U.S.-2
BOUNDARY CO ID 107-B1
SAND HOLLOW RD
MALHEUR CO OR 138-C3
PAYETTE CO ID 139-B3
UMATILLA CO OR 129-C1
WASCO OR 129-C1
SAND LAKE RD
TILLAMOOK CO OR 197-B4
SAND LAKE SUMMIT RD
TILLAMOOK CO OR 197-B4
SANDLIN RD
WASCO CO OR 196-B7
SANDNER DR
LINN CO OR 133-C1
SAND PASS RD
HUMBOLDT CO NV 154-A3
SANDPIPER DR
LINCOLN CO OR 328-C2
SAND PIT RD
WALLA WALLA CO WA 121-B3
SAND POINT WY NE
SEATTLE WA 171-B7
SAND POINT WY NE Rt#-513
SEATTLE WA 171-B7
SEATTLE WA 275-G1
SANDRA LN NE
KITSAP CO WA 270-H5
TRACYTON WA 270-H5
SAND RIDGE RD
KLICKITAT CO WA 120-B3
KLICKITAT CO WA 128-B1
LINN CO OR 133-C1
LINN CO OR 207-D7
LINN CO OR 210-C1
SANDRIDGE RD
ILWACO WA 186-A5
OCEAN PARK WA 186-A5
PACIFIC CO WA 186-A5
N SANDS RD
SPOKANE CO WA 246-D1
S SANDS RD
SPOKANE CO WA 246-D6
SAND SPRINGS RD
DESCHUTES CO OR 135-B3
DESCHUTES CO OR 143-B1
SANDSTROM RD
WASHINGTON CO OR 198-B2
NE SANDY BLVD
PORTLAND OR 200-A1
PORTLAND OR 313-J5
PORTLAND OR 314-B4
PORTLAND OR 315-F2
NE SANDY BLVD U.S.-30
FAIRVIEW OR 200-A1
GRESHAM OR 200-A1
PORTLAND OR 200-A1
PORTLAND OR 315-J1
SE SANDY BLVD
PORTLAND OR 313-H6
SANDY BEACH LN NE
KITSAP CO WA 170-D5
SANDY BEND RD
COWLITZ CO WA 189-C1
SANDY CREEK RD
COOS CO OR 140-C3
SANDY POINT RD NE
THURSTON CO WA 181-A5
SANDY SHORE LAKE RD
JEFFERSON CO WA 170-A3
SANFORD CANYON RD
MORROW CO OR 128-C2
SAN FRANCISCO AV NE
OLYMPIA WA 296-J3
OLYMPIA WA 297-A3
SANGSTER RD
ASOTIN CO WA 122-C3
SAN JUAN AV
PORT TOWNSEND WA 263-F3
SAN SALVADOR RD
MEDICAL LAKE WA 114-B2
SANTIAM HWY Rt#-20
LEBANON OR 133-C1
LINN CO OR 133-C1
SOUTH LEBANON OR 133-C1
SANTIAM HWY U.S.-20
ALBANY OR 326-F8
DESCHUTES CO OR 211-C3
JEFFERSON CO OR 211-A2
LINN CO OR 133-C1
LINN CO OR 134-A2
LINN CO OR 207-D5
LINN CO OR 211-A2
LINN CO OR 326-F8
SISTERS OR 211-C3
SWEET HOME OR 133-C2
SWEET HOME OR 134-A2
N SANTIAM HWY Rt#-22
AUMSVILLE OR 205-A7
DETROIT OR 134-A1
FOUR CORNERS OR 325-G4
GATES OR 134-A1
IDANHA OR 134-A1
LINN CO OR 134-C1
MARION CO OR 133-C1
MARION CO OR 134-A1
MARION CO OR 205-A7
MARION CO OR 325-G4
MILL CITY OR 134-A1
SALEM OR 325-G4
STAYTON OR 133-C1
SUBLIMITY OR 133-C1
SANTIAM RD
ALBANY OR 326-E7
E SANTIAM ST
MARION CO OR 133-C1
STAYTON OR 133-C1
SAPP RD
SEDRO-WOOLLEY WA 161-C5
SAPP RD SW
THURSTON CO WA 296-B10
TUMWATER WA 296-D9
SARATOGA DR NE
MARION CO OR 205-B3
SARATOGA RD
ISLAND CO WA 167-D7
ISLAND CO WA 168-A7
ISLAND CO WA 171-A1
LANGLEY WA 171-A1
SARDINE CREEK RD
BAKER CO OR 138-C1
JACKSON CO OR 230-A5
SAREAULT RD
LEWIS CO WA 187-D3
SARGENT RD
LEWIS CO WA 187-C3
SARGENT RD SW
THURSTON CO WA 184-B3
SARINA RD
DEL NORTE CO CA 148-B3
E SATSOP RD
GRAYS HARBOR CO WA 179-A6
W SATSOP RD
GRAYS HARBOR CO WA 179-A5
SATSOP- CLOQUALLUM RD
MASON CO WA 179-B5
SATTERLEE RD
SKAGIT CO WA 160-C7
SATTLER DR
COLUMBIA CO OR 192-A4
N SATUS RD
SATUS WA 120-A2
W SATUS RD
SATUS WA 120-A3
SAUERKRAUT RD
POLK CO OR 207-A2
SAUK VALLEY RD Rt#-530
SKAGIT CO WA 103-A2
SAULSER RD
COLUMBIA CO OR 192-A2
SAUNDERS RD
CHELAN CO WA 238-B1
SAUNDERS ST
DOUGLAS CO WA 239-B5
ROCK ISLAND WA 239-B5
SAUNDERS CREEK RD
CURRY CO OR 228-B5
SAUSSER DR
KOOTENAI CO ID 247-D4
SAUVIE ISLAND RD
MULTNOMAH CO OR 192-A5
SAVAGE RD
TILLAMOOK CO OR 203-A3
NE SAVAGE ST
GRANTS PASS OR 335-G7
NW SAVAGE ST
GRANTS PASS OR 335-F7

STREET / City State Page-Grid

SAVAGE CREEK RD
JACKSON CO OR 229-D7
NE SAWDUST HILL RD
KITSAP CO WA 170-C6
SAWMILL CREEK RD
HARNEY CO OR 144-C1
SAWMILL CUTOFF RD
BAKER CO OR 131-A3
SAWTELL RD
CLACKAMAS CO OR 126-A3
S SAWTELL RD
CLACKAMAS CO OR 126-A3
SAWYER RD
JACKSON CO OR 230-D2
LATAH CO ID 249-C1
SAWYER CREEK RD
DOUGLAS CO OR 141-A1
SAXON RD
WHATCOM CO WA 161-C2
SAXTON AV
BOISE ID 253-C1
SAYWARD RD
DISTRICT OF SAANICH BC 159-C4
SCAPPOOSE-VERNONIA RD
COLUMBIA CO OR 125-B1
COLUMBIA CO OR 192-A3
SCAPPOOSE OR 192-A3
SCARIFICATION RD
MASON CO WA 173-D4
SCENIC AV
JACKSON CO OR 230-B7
SCENIC DR
ALBANY OR 207-C4
ASHLAND OR 337-B7
AULT FIELD WA 170-D1
BENTON CO OR 207-C4
DESCHUTES CO OR 217-C1
Santa Clara OR 215-B1
N SCENIC DR
YAKIMA CO WA 243-A6
W SCENIC DR
GRANTS PASS OR 335-F5
JOSEPHINE CO OR 335-F5
THE DALLES OR 196-C7
SCENIC WY Rt#-128
ASOTIN CO WA 250-B4
VINELAND WA 250-B4
N SCENIC HEIGHTS RD
ISLAND CO WA 167-B3
SCHAD RD
DOUGLAS CO OR 141-A1
SCHAEFFER RD
UMATILLA CO OR 129-B1
SW SCHAEFFER RD
CLACKAMAS CO OR 199-C5
S SCHAFER RD
OPPORTUNITY WA 350-F14
SPOKANE CO WA 350-F14
SCHAFER PARK RD
MASON CO WA 179-A5
SCHAFFER RD
COLUMBIA CO OR 189-A7
SCHAFFRAN RD
COWLITZ CO WA 187-C7
SCHARPENBERG HILL RD
LA CROSSE WA 122-A1
WHITMAN CO WA 122-A1
SCHELINE LN
VALLEY CO ID 252-D1
SCHERZINGER RD
TILLAMOOK CO OR 203-B1
SCHIEFFELIN GULCH RD
JACKSON CO OR 229-D7
SCHILLING RD
KLICKITAT CO WA 196-D4
SCHLEE RD
WHITMAN CO WA 250-A2
SCHMEIRER RD
LINCOLN CO WA 113-B2
SCHMELTZER RD
WASHINGTON CO OR 198-D4
SCHMIDLEKOFER RD
CHEWELAH WA 106-B3
STEVENS CO WA 106-B3
SCHMITT RD
CLALLAM CO WA 164-C5
S SCHNEIDER RD
CLACKAMAS CO OR 205-D2
SCHNIEDER WY
CROOK CO OR 213-D2
SCHOCKLEY RD
CLACKAMAS CO OR 200-B7
SCHOESSLER RD
ADAMS CO WA 113-B3
SCHOLFIELD RD
DOUGLAS CO OR 218-D2
SCHOLFIELD RIDGE RD
DOUGLAS CO OR 218-D2
SCHOLLS FERRY Rt#-210
BEAVERTON OR 199-B2
TIGARD OR 199-B2
SW SCHOLLS FERRY RD
BEAVERTON OR 199-A3
TIGARD OR 199-A3
WASHINGTON CO OR 199-A3
SW SCHOLLS FERRY RD Rt#-210
BEAVERTON OR 199-B2
TIGARD OR 199-B2
WASHINGTON CO OR 198-D3
WASHINGTON CO OR 199-A3
SW SCHOLLS-SHERWOOD RD
WASHINGTON CO OR 199-A4
SCHOOL AV
WALLA WALLA WA 345-E7
WALLA WALLA CO WA 345-E8
WALLA WALLA EAST WA 345-E10
SCHOOL DR
KLICKITAT CO WA 196-D3
SCHOOL ST
SUNNYSLOPE WA 238-D3
SCHOOL FLAT LN
WALLOWA CO OR 130-C2
SCHOOLHOUSE LN
LEWIS CO WA 187-D3
SCHOOLHOUSE ST
COQUITLAM BC 157-A5
SCHOOLHOUSE LOOP RD
NESPELEM WA 105-A3
OKANOGAN CO WA 105-A3
SCHOOLIE MT WILSON RD
WASCO CO OR 126-C3
SCHOOL LAND RD SW
THURSTON CO WA 184-A3
SCHOOLMARM SPUR
JACKSON CO OR 226-C7
S SCHOONER CREEK RD
LINCOLN CITY OR 203-B5
LINCOLN CO OR 203-B5
SCHOONOVER RD
LINCOLN CO WA 113-B3
SCHOONOVER RD Rt#-407
WAHKIAKUM CO WA 117-B2
SCHRAEDER RD
DESCHUTES CO OR 144-B1
SCHRAG RD
ADAMS CO WA 113-B3
SCHRAM RD
CLACKAMAS CO OR 200-B7
SCHULER RD
MARION CO OR 199-A6
SCHULTZ RD
LATAH CO ID 249-D4
MARION CO OR 199-A6
SCHUSTER PKWY
TACOMA WA 293-F2
SCHUT RD
YAKIMA CO WA 243-D7
SCHWARTZ RD
JEFFERSON CO WA 167-B7
SCHWEITZER CTO
PONDERAY ID 244-A1
SANDPOINT ID 244-A1
SCHWEITZER BASIN RD
BONNER CO ID 244-A1
SCISM RD NE
MARION CO OR 205-B4
SCOGGINS VALLEY RD
WASHINGTON CO OR 198-B2
S SCONCE RD
CLACKAMAS CO OR 205-C1
SCOTIA RD
PEND OREILLE CO WA 106-C3
E SCOTT AV
WOODLAND WA 118-A3
SCOTT RD
DISTRICT OF DELTA BC 156-D7
DISTRICT OF SURREY BC 156-D6
DISTRICT OF SURREY BC 157-A5
SKAMANIA CO WA 194-B6
WHATCOM CO WA 158-C7
WHITMAN CO WA 122-A1
SCOTT RD NW
THURSTON CO WA 180-B5
SCOTT ST
CITY OF VICTORIA BC 257-A6
SCOTT CAMP RD
CROOK CO OR 136-B2
SCOTT CANYON RD
RUFUS OR 127-C1
SHERMAN CO OR 127-C1
SCOTT CREEK RD
LINCOLN CO OR 209-D2
SCOTT HILL RD
WASHINGTON CO OR 198-A2
SCOTT RIVER RD
SISKIYOU CO CA 149-B3
SCOTTS VALLEY RD
DOUGLAS CO OR 219-C5
SCOUT LAKE RD
JEFFERSON CO OR 211-B2
NE SCOVILLE RD
GRANTS PASS OR 335-F4
SCRAVEL HILL RD
LINN CO OR 207-D3
E SCRIBNER RD
SPOKANE CO WA 247-A1
N SCRIBNER RD
SPOKANE CO WA 246-D1
S SCRIBNER RD
SPOKANE CO WA 246-B6
SEA ACRES RD
SAN JUAN CO WA 160-B2
SEABECK HWY
KITSAP CO WA 270-A7
TRACYTON WA 270-A7
SEABECK HWY NW
KITSAP CO WA 174-A1
NW SEABECK-HOLLY RD
KITSAP CO WA 173-D2
SEABECK HOLLY RD NW
KITSAP CO WA 173-C3
SEA BIRD DR
BANDON OR 220-A6
COOS CO OR 220-A6
SEACREST DR
WHATCOM CO WA 160-B1
SEAGULL DR
CLALLAM CO WA 164-D5
SEAHURST ACCESS RD
PACIFIC CO WA 183-B4
SEA ISLAND WY
CITY OF RICHMOND BC 156-B6
SEALION RD
KITSAP CO WA 170-A7
SEAMAN GULCH RD
ADA CO ID 253-B1
SEAMOUNT DR
JEFFERSON CO WA 173-C1
SEARLES RD
CHELAN CO WA 239-B5
SEARS RD
LANE CO OR 215-B7
LEWIS CO WA 187-B2
NANAIMO BC 93-A3
SEASONS RD
KOOTENAI CO ID 245-A2
N SEASONS RD
KOOTENAI CO ID 115-A1
SEA TO SKY HWY Rt#-1
DIST OF WEST VANCOUVER BC 156-A2
E SEATTLE AV
MOXEE CITY WA 243-D7
W SEATTLE AV
MOXEE CITY WA 243-D7
W SEATTLE FRWY
SEATTLE WA 281-F3
SEATTLE WA 282-A3
SEATTLE HILL RD
SNOHOMISH CO WA 171-C4
SEATTLE HILL RD Rt#-96
SNOHOMISH CO WA 171-D4
SEATTLE-VASHON FERRY
KING CO WA 174-D4
SEATTLE-VICTORIA FERRY
ISLAND CO WA 167-B6
ISLAND CO WA 170-C2
JEFFERSON CO WA 167-A5
KING CO WA 174-D1
KITSAP CO WA 170-C2
SEAVEY LOOP RD
LANE CO OR 330-G12
LANE CO OR 331-A12
SEAVIEW AV NW
SEATTLE WA 272-C3
SEAVIEW PL NW
SEATTLE WA 272-D1
SEAVIEW RD
DISTRICT OF SAANICH BC 257-F4
SEAWAY BLVD
EVERETT WA 267-H2
SEAWOLF RD
KITSAP CO WA 170-B6
SECHELT DR
DIST OF N VANCOUVER BC 255-H4
SECOND AV
YAKIMA CO WA 120-A2
ZILLAH WA 120-A2
SECOND AV Rt#-3
DEARY ID 123-B1
LATAH CO ID 123-B1
SECOND AV Rt#-8
DEARY ID 123-B1
LATAH CO ID 123-B1
S SECOND AV Rt#-31
IONE WA 106-B1
SECOND AV N Rt#-20
OKANOGAN WA 104-C3
SECOND AV NW Rt#-20
OKANOGAN WA 104-C3
SECOND AV SW Rt#-20
OKANOGAN WA 104-C3
W SECOND RD
CHENEY WA 246-A7
SECOND ST
FRIDAY HARBOR WA 101-C2
LANGLEY WA 171-A1
SECOND ST Rt#-124
PRESCOTT WA 121-C2
WALLA WALLA CO WA 121-C2
E SECOND ST
ABERDEEN WA 178-B7
E SECOND ST Rt#-21
LIND WA 121-B1
N SECOND ST Rt#-231
SPRINGDALE WA 106-B3
S SECOND ST
BURBANK WA 121-A3
WALLA WALLA CO WA 121-A3
S SECOND ST Rt#-231
SPRINGDALE WA 106-B3
W SECOND ST
ABERDEEN WA 178-B7
W SECOND ST Rt#-903
CLE ELUM WA 240-B2
SECOND ST W Rt#-903
CLE ELUM WA 240-B2
SECOND NARROWS BRDG Rt#-1
DIST OF N VANCOUVER BC 255-F9
VANCOUVER BC 255-F9
NW SEDGEWICK AV
DESCHUTES CO OR 212-D4
SE SEDGWICK RD Rt#-160
KITSAP CO WA 174-C4
PORT ORCHARD WA 174-C4
SEEFELD DR
LINN CO OR 210-B3
SEEKSEEQUA CREEK RD
JEFFERSON CO OR 208-A4
SEELANDER RD
COOS CO OR 140-B2
SEEMANN ST Rt#-530
DARRINGTON WA 103-A3
SW SEGHERS RD
WASHINGTON CO OR 198-B2
SEHMEL DR NW
PIERCE CO WA 174-B7
SW SEIFFERT RD
WASHINGTON CO OR 198-D4
SELAH RD Rt#-823
YAKIMA CO WA 243-B6
E SELAH RD
YAKIMA CO WA 243-C5
SELAH HEIGHTS RD
YAKIMA CO WA 243-B5
SELAH LOOP RD
SELAH WA 243-B5
YAKIMA CO WA 243-B5
SELAH-NACHES RD
YAKIMA CO WA 243-B5
SELAH SPRINGS DR NE
MARION CO OR 205-B5
SELDON RD
DISTRICT OF MATSQUI BC 102-B1
SELLARDS RD
BENTON CO WA 120-B3
E SELLE RD
BONNER CO ID 107-B2
SELPH LANDING RD
FRANKLIN CO WA 121-A2
FRANKLIN CO WA 340-J9
SELTICE BLVD
KOOTENAI CO ID 353-A7
POST FALLS ID 353-A7
SELTICE WY
COEUR D'ALENE ID 355-A8
HAUSER ID 352-J8
KOOTENAI CO ID 352-J8
KOOTENAI CO ID 353-C6
KOOTENAI CO ID 354-H7
KOOTENAI CO ID 355-A8
POST FALLS ID 352-J8
POST FALLS ID 353-C6
POST FALLS ID 354-A7
SEMIAHMOO DR
BIRCH BAY WA 158-A4
BLAINE WA 158-A4
WHATCOM CO WA 158-A4
SEMINARY HILL RD
CENTRALIA WA 299-G4
LEWIS CO WA 299-G4
N SEQUIM AV
NEAH BAY WA 262-E12
S SEQUIM RD
CLALLAM CO WA 262-E10
NEAH BAY WA 262-E10
E SEQUIM BAY RD
CLALLAM CO WA 166-C7
W SEQUIM BAY RD
CLALLAM CO WA 262-G12
NEAH BAY WA 262-F12
SEQUIM-DUNGENESS WY
CLALLAM CO WA 262-D4
SERVICE CK-MITCHLL HWY Rt#-207
MITCHELL OR 136-A1
WHEELER CO OR 136-A1
NE SERWOLD RD
POULSBO WA 170-C7
SESAME ST NW
KITSAP CO WA 174-A2
SETHER AV
DOUGLAS CO OR 225-B7
GLENDALE OR 225-A7
SETTERS RD
KOOTENAI CO ID 247-C7
SETTLEMIER AV
MARION CO OR 205-B2
WOODBURN OR 205-B1
SEVEN DEVILS RD
COOS CO OR 220-B2
N SEVEN MILE EXT
SPOKANE CO WA 246-A2
SEVEN MILE LN
BROWNSVILLE OR 210-C2
LINN CO OR 207-C6
LINN CO OR 210-C1
LINN CO OR 326-F14
SEVEN MILE RD
COOS CO OR 220-B5
SEVEN MILE RD Rt#-62
IDAHO CO ID 123-C3
SEVEN MILE RD Rt#-162
KAMIAH ID 123-C2
LEWIS CO ID 123-C2
SEVENMILE RD
KLAMATH CO OR 231-B2
W SEVEN MILE RD
SPOKANE CO WA 246-A2
SEVENMILE HILL RD
WASCO CO OR 196-B6
SEVENMILE RANCH RD
KLAMATH CO OR 231-B2
SEVENTH ST U.S.-101
HOQUIAM WA 178-A7
E SEVENTH ST
ROSALIA WA 114-C3
N SEVENTH ST Rt#-903
ROSLYN WA 240-A1
SEWARD DR
LINN CO OR 207-B7
SEWARD PARK AV S
SEATTLE WA 283-G7
SEATTLE WA 287-G1
SEYMOUR BLVD
DIST OF N VANCOUVER BC 255-G6
SEYMOUR ST Rt#-99
VANCOUVER BC 254-F11
SHAD RD
JEFFERSON CO OR 212-C2
SHADY LN
KLICKITAT CO WA 196-B4
SHADY PINE RD
KLAMATH CO OR 235-C1
N SHADY SLOPE RD
SPOKANE CO WA 347-D5
SHAFF RD
MARION CO OR 133-C1
SHAFF RD SE
MARION CO OR 133-C1
STAYTON OR 133-C1
W SHAFFER AV Rt#-231
SPRINGDALE WA 106-B3
SHAMROCK ST
ADA CO ID 253-B2
BOISE ID 253-B2
SHANIKO-FOSSIL HWY Rt#-218
ANTELOPE OR 127-C3
FOSSIL OR 128-A3
SHANIKO OR 127-C3
WASCO CO OR 127-C3
WASCO CO OR 128-A3
WHEELER CO OR 128-A3
SHARON AV
BURLINGTON WA 260-C5
SHARON CREEK RESERVOIR RD
MALHEUR CO OR 155-A2
SHARPE RD
PITT MEADOWS BC 157-C5
SKAGIT CO WA 259-C13
SHARPS CREEK RD
LANE CO OR 141-C1
LANE CO OR 142-A1
S SHASTA AV
EAGLE POINT OR 230-D5
SHASTA WY
ALTAMONT OR 338-G9
ALTAMONT OR 339-A9
KLAMATH CO OR 338-G9
KLAMATH FALLS OR 338-G9
SHATTUCK RD
DESCHUTES CO OR 211-D6
SW SHATTUCK RD
MULTNOMAH OR 316-A3
PORTLAND OR 199-B2
PORTLAND OR 316-A3
SHAUGHNESSY ST
COQUITLAM BC 157-B4
PORT COQUITLAM BC 157-B4
SHAW HWY SE
AUMSVILLE OR 205-B7
MARION CO OR 205-B7
SHAW RD
PIERCE CO WA 182-B4
PUYALLUP WA 182-B4
SHAW RD E
PIERCE CO WA 182-B4
SHAW-HOLMES RD
UMATILLA CO OR 129-B2
SHAW MOUNTAIN RD
ADA CO ID 253-D2
SHAWNEE
CROOK CO OR 213-D7
SHAWNEE-PARVIN RD
WHITMAN CO WA 249-A3
SHAWNIGAN LAKE RD
BRITISH COLUMBIA 159-A3
SHAY LN
DESCHUTES CO OR 143-A1
SHAY HILL RD
BENEWAH CO ID 248-C7
SHEARERS BRIDGE HWY Rt#-216
WASCO CO OR 127-A3
SHEDD CEMETERY RD
LINN CO OR 210-B1
SHEEHAN RD SW
DOUGLAS CO WA 239-C2
NW SHEELAR LN
WASHINGTON CO OR 198-B1
SHEEP CANYON RD
GRANT CO WA 112-C2
SHEEP COMPANY RD
YAKIMA CO WA 243-B4
SHEEP CREEK RD
STEVENS CO WA 106-A1
WASHINGTON CO ID 139-C2
SHEEPY CREEK RD
SISKIYOU CO CA 150-C3
SHEFFIELD RD
FRANKLIN CO WA 121-A2
MESA WA 121-A2
SHEFFLER RD
WALLA WALLA CO WA 121-B2
SHELBOURNE ST
CITY OF VICTORIA BC 257-A7
DISTRICT OF SAANICH BC 159-D5
DISTRICT OF SAANICH BC 257-A1
SHELBURN DR
LINN CO OR 133-C1
SHELBY RD
SNOHOMISH CO WA 171-B4
SHELDON RD SE
THURSTON CO WA 184-D1
SHELDON ST
FALLS CITY OR 125-B3
POLK CO OR 125-B3
SHELGRIN RD
GRAYS HARBOR CO WA 177-C4
SHELL RD
CITY OF RICHMOND BC 156-B6
SHELLER RD
YAKIMA CO WA 120-B2
SHELLEY RD
COOS CO OR 220-D5
SHELLRIDGE RD NW
THURSTON CO WA 180-B5
SHELL ROCK RD
CLACKAMAS CO OR 126-C3
KITTITAS CO WA 240-C6
SHELTER BAY DR
SHELTER BAY WA 167-D1
SHELTON RD
WALLA WALLA WA 345-E10
WALLA WALLA EAST WA 345-E10
NW SHELTON RD
YAMHILL CO OR 198-A6
SHELTON-MATLOCK RD
MASON CO WA 179-C2
MASON CO WA 180-A3
SHELTON VALLEY RD
MASON CO WA 180-A3
SHEPARD RD
COLUMBIA CO OR 189-A3
SHERARS BRIDGE HWY Rt#-216
GRASS VALLEY OR 127-B2
SHERMAN CO OR 127-B2
SHERIDAN AV U.S.-101
NORTH BEND OR 333-G4
S SHERIDAN AV
TACOMA WA 295-F7
SHERIDAN RD
BREMERTON WA 270-H8
BREMERTON WA 271-A8
KITSAP CO WA 271-A8
SHERIDAN ST
PORT TOWNSEND WA 263-E5
SE SHERIDAN ST
SHERIDAN OR 125-B3
SHER KHAN RD
LANE CO OR 215-B4
NW SHERLOCK AV
PORTLAND OR 312-B1
E SHERLOCK ST Rt#-23
HARRINGTON WA 113-C2
SHERMAN AV
NORTH BEND OR 333-G5
SHERMAN AV U.S.-101
NORTH BEND OR 333-G5
E SHERMAN AV
COEUR D'ALENE ID 355-F11
KOOTENAI CO ID 355-F11
SHERMAN HWY U.S.-97
GRASS VALLEY OR 127-C2
MORO OR 127-C2
SHANIKO OR 127-C2
SHERMAN CO OR 127-C1
WASCO CO OR 127-B3
SHERMAN RD
ISLAND CO WA 167-B4
S SHERMAN RD
SPOKANE CO WA 246-B6
SHERMAN RD SE
MARION CO OR 205-B7
S SHERMAN ST
ASHLAND OR 337-D8
SPOKANE WA 349-B9
SHERMAN HEIGHTS RD
KITSAP CO WA 270-D14
NAVY YARD CITY WA 270-D14
S SHERWOOD BLVD
SHERWOOD OR 199-A4
SHERWOOD DR
JEFFERSON CO OR 212-D2
SHERWOOD RD
CROOK CO OR 136-A3
NW SHEVLIN PARK MARKET RD
BEND OR 217-B2
BEND OR 332-A6
DESCHUTES CO OR 217-B2
DESCHUTES CO OR 332-A6
SHIBLEY RD
CLACKAMAS CO OR 200-B7
SHIFFMAN RD
TILLAMOOK CO OR 191-C4
SHILOH RD
JACKSON CO OR 230-C4
SHINCKE RD NE
THURSTON CO WA 180-D5
SHINGLEBOLT RD
TILLAMOOK CO OR 203-B3
E SHINGLE MILL RD
BONNER CO ID 244-B1
W SHINGLE MILL RD
BONNER CO ID 244-B1
SHINN RD SW
DOUGLAS CO WA 239-C4
SHIPLEY RD
CLACKAMAS CO OR 200-D4
SHIRTTAIL CREEK RD
BAKER CO OR 138-C2
SHIVELY CREEK RD
DOUGLAS CO OR 225-D2
SHOALWATER BAY
PACIFIC CO WA 186-B6
SHOEPEG RD
WASHINGTON CO ID 139-B1
SHOESTRING RD
DOUGLAS CO OR 225-B3
LANE CO OR 219-C3
SHOLLMEYER RD
TILLAMOOK CO OR 191-B4
SHORE DR
BREMERTON WA 271-B10
S SHORE DR
SKAGIT CO WA 160-C5
W SHORE DR
SKAGIT CO WA 160-C4
WHATCOM CO WA 160-B1
SHORE RD
CLALLAM CO WA 165-D6
S SHORE RD
BREMERTON WA 270-C8
LINCOLN CO OR 206-C5
SKAGIT CO WA 160-C5
SHORE ST
CHELAN CO WA 238-A1
SHORELINE DR N
KEIZER OR 322-H5
SHORELINE LN
BOISE ID 253-C2
SHORE PINE RD
CURRY CO OR 232-C4
SHOREVIEW DR
LINCOLN CO OR 328-C1
SHOREWOOD
SAN JUAN CO WA 160-A3
SHORT RD
KLAMATH CO OR 235-D5
N SHORT RD
SPOKANE CO WA 114-B1
S SHORT RD
SPOKANE CO WA 246-B7
SHORT ST
ASTORIA WA 300-B5
SHORT HORN GULCH RD
JOSEPHINE CO OR 229-B2
SHORT ROAD BEECH CREEK
GRANT CO OR 137-A1
SHORT ROAD IN FOX
GRANT CO OR 137-A1
SHORT SAND CROSS OVR RD
TILLAMOOK CO OR 191-B3
SHORT SCHOOL RD
SNOHOMISH CO WA 171-D4
NE SHORTY CAMPBELL RD
KINGSTON WA 170-D5
KITSAP CO WA 170-D5
SHOSHONI LN
LANE CO OR 215-D5
SHROPSHIRE RD
WHITMAN CO WA 122-A1
SHUFFIELD RD
LAKE CO OR 143-C3
SHUKSAN DR
ISLAND CO WA 168-A6
SHUMAKER RD
ASOTIN CO WA 123-A3
SHUMWAY RD
CROOK CO OR 213-A7
MALHEUR CO OR 146-A1
SHUMWAY CUTOFF RD
MALHEUR CO OR 146-B1
SHUMWAY RANCH RD
MALHEUR CO OR 146-B1
NE SHUTE RD
HILLSBORO OR 198-D1
SHUTTERA RD
NEZ PERCE CO ID 250-D6
SHUTTERS LANDING RD
COOS CO OR 218-C4
SHY MEADOW
CHELAN CO WA 238-B2
SIAH BUTTE RD
DESCHUTES CO OR 216-C6
SIDAWAY RD
CITY OF RICHMOND BC 156-C7
S SIDE RD
DOUGLAS CO OR 219-A3
W SIDE RD
BOUNDARY CO ID 107-B1
SIDE HILL RD
DESCHUTES CO OR 211-B3
SIDNEY AV
PORT ORCHARD WA 174-B4
PORT ORCHARD WA 270-H14
SIDNEY DR S
MARION CO OR 207-C1
SIDNEY RD SW
KITSAP CO WA 174-B5
PIERCE CO WA 174-B6
PORT ORCHARD WA 174-B4

STREET / City State / Page-Grid

SIDNEY-ANACORTES FERRY
- BRITISH COLUMBIA 101-C2
- BRITISH COLUMBIA 159-C2
- SAN JUAN CO WA 101-C2
- TOWN OF SIDNEY BC 159-C2

SIEVERS DUECY BLVD
- EVERETT WA 268-A3

SIGHTLY RD
- COWLITZ CO WA 118-A2

SIGNAL PEAK RD
- WHITE SWAN WA 119-C2

SIGNAL PEAK RD Rt#-220
- WHITE SWAN WA 119-C2

SILCOTT GRADE RD
- ASOTIN CO WA 250-A4

SILCOTT WYE RD
- ASOTIN CO WA 250-A5

SILETZ HWY Rt#-229
- LINCOLN CO OR 203-A6
- LINCOLN CO OR 206-C1
- SILETZ OR 206-C1
- TOLEDO OR 206-C4

SILL RD
- SNOHOMISH CO WA 168-C5

SILLS RD
- ISLAND CO WA 170-D2

S SILLS RD
- ISLAND CO WA 171-A2

SILTCOOS STATION RD
- LANE CO OR 214-B5

SILVA RD
- SISKIYOU CO CA 150-A3

SILVER ST
- PORT TOWNSEND WA 263-E3

SILVER CITY RD
- OWYHEE CO ID 147-B2

SILVER CREEK RD
- FERRY CO WA 105-B3
- HARNEY CO OR 144-C1
- JOSEPHINE CO OR 148-C1

SILVERCREEK RD Rt#-122
- LEWIS CO WA 118-A2

SILVER CROWN AV
- NORTHPORT WA 106-A1

SILVERDALE WY NW
- KITSAP CO WA 170-B7
- KITSAP CO WA 174-B1
- SILVERDALE WA 174-B1
- SILVERDALE WA 270-B1

SILVER FALLS HWY Rt#-214
- MARION CO OR 205-A7

SILVER FALLS HWY NE Rt#-214
- MARION CO OR 205-C5
- MARION CO OR 205-C5
- SILVERTON OR 205-C5

SILVER FALLS HWY NW Rt#-214
- MARION CO OR 205-B7

SILVER FALLS HWY SE Rt#-214
- MARION CO OR 205-B7
- MARION CO OR 205-D6

SILVER LAKE RD
- KLAMATH CO OR 142-C3
- KLAMATH CO OR 143-A3
- WHATCOM CO WA 102-C1

E SILVER LAKE RD
- ISLAND CO WA 167-C2

S SILVER LAKE RD
- COWLITZ CO WA 187-C7
- COWLITZ CO WA 189-D1

SILVERNAIL RD
- SKAGIT CO WA 168-B3

SILVER RIDGE RD SE
- MARION CO OR 205-D7

SILVERTON AV Rt#-214
- MARION CO OR 205-B2
- WOODBURN OR 205-B2

SILVERTON HWY Rt#-214
- WOODBURN OR 205-B2

NE SILVERTON HWY Rt#-213
- MARION CO OR 205-B4

SILVERTON RD NE
- HAYESVILLE OR 323-H8
- SALEM OR 323-B10

SILVERTON RD NE Rt#-213
- HAYESVILLE OR 323-G9
- MARION CO OR 205-A5
- MARION CO OR 323-J7

SILVER VALLEY RD
- SHOSHONE CO ID 115-B2

SILVIES-HOPPER RANCH RD
- GRANT CO OR 137-B3

SILVIS RD
- DESCHUTES CO OR 217-D2

SIMCOE MOUNTAIN RD
- KLICKITAT CO WA 127-B1

SIMILKAMEEN RD
- OKANOGAN CO WA 104-C1

SIMMONS RD
- KLICKITAT CO WA 195-D4
- YAKIMA CO WA 119-C1

SIMMONS RD NW
- THURSTON CO WA 180-B6

SIMMONS CREEK RD
- TILLAMOOK CO OR 197-C4

SIMMONS RIDGE RD
- TILLAMOOK CO OR 197-D4

SIMNASHO RD
- WASCO CO OR 127-A3

SIMNASHO HOT SPRINGS RD
- WASCO CO OR 127-A3
- WASCO CO OR 208-B1

SIMONDS RD NE
- KING CO WA 171-C6

SIMPLOT BLVD Rt#-19
- CALDWELL ID 147-B1
- CANYON CO ID 147-B1
- WILDER ID 147-B1

SIMPSON AV
- MCCLEARY WA 179-D6

SIMPSON AV U.S.-101
- ABERDEEN WA 178-B7
- HOQUIAM WA 178-A7

SIMPSON RD
- DISTRICT OF MATSQUI BC 102-B1
- POLK CO OR 207-A2
- UMATILLA CO OR 129-B1

SIMPSON RD NW
- THURSTON CO WA 180-B5

SIMPSON CANYON RD
- KLAMATH CO OR 235-C1

SIMS WY Rt#-20
- PORT TOWNSEND WA 263-C6

SINCLAIR RD
- BAKER CO OR 138-C1
- DISTRICT OF CHILLIWACK BC 102-C1
- DISTRICT OF SAANICH BC 257-D3

SINE RD
- GRAYS HARBOR CO WA 179-D6

SINE RD Rt#-108
- GRAYS HARBOR CO WA 179-D6
- MCCLEARY WA 179-D6

SINGLE CREEK RD
- DOUGLAS CO OR 222-B2

SINGLE TREE TR
- HUMBOLDT CO NV 154-C3

SINK RD
- LAKE CO OR 143-C2

SINLAHEKIN RD
- OKANOGAN CO WA 104-C2

SISEMORE RD
- DESCHUTES CO OR 212-A7

SISK RD
- YAKIMA CO WA 243-A3

SISKIYOU BLVD
- MEDFORD OR 336-E13

SISKIYOU BLVD Rt#-99
- ASHLAND OR 337-D8
- JACKSON CO OR 337-H10

SISKIYOU HWY
- JACKSON CO OR 150-A2

SISKIYOU SUMMIT RD
- JACKSON CO OR 234-D5

S SISTER RD
- DOUGLAS CO OR 133-A3
- LANE CO OR 133-A3

SISTERS AV
- DESCHUTES CO OR 212-D5
- REDMOND OR 212-D5

SITKUM-COUNTY LINE RD
- COOS CO OR 140-C2
- COOS CO OR 141-A2

SI TOWN RD
- COWLITZ CO WA 187-C7

SITZ RIDGE RD
- LINCOLN CO OR 209-C3

SIUSLAW RIVER RD
- LANE CO OR 133-A3

SIXES RIVER RD
- CURRY CO OR 224-B5

SIX PRONG RD
- KLICKITAT CO WA 128-A1

SIXTH ST Rt#-6
- POTLATCH ID 249-D1

SIXTH ST Rt#-20
- OKANOGAN CO WA 104-C2
- TONASKET WA 104-C2

SIXTH ST Rt#-507
- TENINO WA 184-D3

SIXTH ST U.S.-101
- RAYMOND WA 117-A1

E SIXTH ST
- CENTRALIA WA 299-F2
- LANGLEY WA 171-A1

E SIXTH ST Rt#-507
- CENTRALIA WA 299-F2

SE SIXTH ST
- COLLEGE PLACE WA 344-F11
- WALLA WALLA CO WA 344-F11

SW SIXTH ST
- COLLEGE PLACE WA 344-E11
- WALLA WALLA CO WA 344-E11

W SIXTH ST
- CENTRALIA WA 299-F2

SKAAR RD
- SKAMANIA CO WA 194-D4

S SKAGIT HWY
- SKAGIT CO WA 102-C2
- SKAGIT CO WA 161-C6

N SKAGIT ST
- BURLINGTON WA 260-E4

S SKAGIT ST
- BURLINGTON WA 260-E6
- SKAGIT CO WA 260-E6

SKAGIT CITY RD
- SKAGIT CO WA 168-A1

SKAMANIA MINES RD
- SKAMANIA CO WA 193-D5

SKATE CREEK RD N
- LEWIS CO WA 118-C1

SKATE CREEK RD S
- LEWIS CO WA 185-B6

SKEANS RD
- COLUMBIA CO OR 189-B5

SKELLEY RD
- DOUGLAS CO OR 219-A4

SKELLEY RD S
- DOUGLAS CO OR 219-A4

SKELTON RD SE
- MARION CO OR 207-D2

SKI HILL RD
- CHELAN CO WA 238-A1
- LEAVENWORTH WA 238-A1

SKINNER RD
- CLACKAMAS CO OR 200-C7

SKINNER ST
- CITY OF VICTORIA BC 256-E7

SKIPLEY RD
- SNOHOMISH CO WA 171-D3

SKI RUN RD
- WALLOWA CO OR 130-C2

SKOKOMISH VALLEY RD
- MASON CO WA 179-D1

SKOOKUM CANYON RD
- KLICKITAT CO WA 196-C1

SKOOKUMCHUCK RD SE
- THURSTON CO WA 184-D4

SKULL CREEK RD
- MALHEUR CO OR 146-C3
- MALHEUR CO OR 155-A1

SKYE RD
- SKAMANIA CO WA 193-D6

W SKYLINE AV
- ASTORIA WA 300-B5

NW SKYLINE BLVD
- MULTNOMAH CO OR 192-A5
- PORTLAND OR 192-B7

SW SKYLINE BLVD
- MULTNOMAH OR 312-A6
- MULTNOMAH CO OR 199-B1
- PORTLAND OR 199-B1
- PORTLAND OR 312-A6

SKYLINE DR
- COLUMBIA CO WA 122-B3
- WENATCHEE WA 238-D4
- WEST WENATCHEE WA 238-D4

NW SKYLINE DR
- TOLEDO OR 206-C4

SKYLINE RD
- BAKER CO OR 138-A1
- CANYON CO ID 147-B1
- WASCO CO OR 196-C7

SKYLINE RD S
- MARION CO OR 207-C1
- MARION CO OR 324-A10
- SALEM OR 324-E6

SKYLINE WY
- ANACORTES WA 259-A5

SKYLINERS RD
- BEND OR 332-A7
- DESCHUTES CO OR 217-A3
- DESCHUTES CO OR 332-A7

SLAB CREEK RD
- TILLAMOOK CO OR 203-B2

SLACK CANYON RD SW
- DOUGLAS CO WA 112-B2

SLATE CREEK RD
- IDAHO CO ID 131-C1

SLATER RD
- WHATCOM CO WA 158-B6

SLATER RD Rt#-540
- BELLINGHAM WA 158-C6
- FERNDALE WA 158-C6
- WHATCOM CO WA 158-C6

SLAVENS WY
- COLUMBIA CO OR 192-A3

SLEATER KINNEY RD NE
- LACEY WA 297-F3
- OLYMPIA WA 297-F3
- THURSTON CO WA 297-F3

SLEATER KINNEY RD SE
- LACEY WA 297-F8
- OLYMPIA WA 297-F8

SLEEPER RD
- ISLAND CO WA 167-C2

SLEEPY HOLLOW LP
- JOSEPHINE CO OR 229-A7

SLEEPY HOLLOW RD
- CHELAN CO WA 238-C3
- KLICKITAT CO WA 196-A3

SLEEPY HOLLOW RD NE
- MARION CO OR 205-B1

N SLICK ROCK CREEK RD
- LINCOLN CO OR 203-C4

SLIDE CREEK RD
- COWLITZ CO WA 117-B3

SLIVA LN
- MASON CO WA 180-D3

E SLOPE RD
- LINCOLN CO OR 206-C4
- TOLEDO OR 206-C4

E SLOPE RD SE
- TOLEDO OR 206-C4

NE SLOPE ST
- DOUGLAS CO OR 334-G3

SLUSSER RD NW
- DOUGLAS CO WA 112-B2
- DOUGLAS CO WA 236-C6

SMILEY LN
- VALLEY CO ID 251-C7

SMITH AV
- DISTRICT OF BURNABY BC 156-C5
- DISTRICT OF BURNABY BC 255-G14
- KOOTENAI CO ID 247-C1

SMITH LN
- JEFFERSON CO OR 212-D1

SMITH RD
- CLACKAMAS CO OR 199-A5
- COLUMBIA CO OR 192-A1
- KLICKITAT CO WA 120-B3
- POLK CO OR 207-A1
- WALLA WALLA CO WA 121-C3
- WALLA WALLA CO WA 122-A3
- WHITE SWAN WA 119-C2
- YAMHILL CO OR 199-A5

E SMITH RD
- WHATCOM CO WA 102-B1
- WHATCOM CO WA 158-D6

W SMITH RD
- FERNDALE WA 158-D6
- WHATCOM CO WA 158-D6

SMITH ST
- HARRISBURG OR 210-A5

E SMITH ST Rt#-516
- KENT WA 175-C7

W SMITH ST
- KENT WA 175-B7

SMITH ANDERSON RD
- PACIFIC CO WA 183-B5

SMITH CANYON RD
- FRANKLIN CO WA 121-B2

SMITH COLUMBIA CITY RD
- COLUMBIA CO OR 192-A1

SMITH CREEK RD
- PACIFIC CO WA 117-A1

SMITHE ST
- VANCOUVER BC 254-G10

SMITHFIELD RD
- POLK CO OR 204-A5

SMITH HOLLOW RD
- COLUMBIA CO WA 122-A2

SMITH LAKE RD
- MASON CO WA 237-B2

NE SMITH POINT RD
- MULTNOMAH CO OR 194-B7
- MULTNOMAH CO OR 201-B1

SMITH RIVER RD
- DOUGLAS CO OR 132-C3
- DOUGLAS CO OR 133-A3
- DOUGLAS CO OR 141-A1
- DOUGLAS CO OR 214-D7

SMITH ROCK WY
- DESCHUTES CO OR 212-D4
- DESCHUTES CO OR 213-A4

SMITHSON RD
- KITTITAS CO WA 241-A3

SMITH SPRINGS RD
- PRESCOTT WA 121-C2
- WALLA WALLA CO WA 121-C2

SMOCK RD
- WASCO CO OR 127-A3

SMOKEHOUSE RD
- WHATCOM CO WA 160-C1

SMOKEY POINT BLVD
- MARYSVILLE WA 168-C5
- SNOHOMISH CO WA 168-C5

SMOKEY VALLEY RD
- LEWIS CO WA 187-C5

SMOKY BUTTE DR
- DESCHUTES CO OR 212-B7

SMOOTHING IRON RD
- ASOTIN CO WA 122-C3

SMUGGLERS COVE RD
- ISLAND CO WA 167-C7
- ISLAND CO WA 170-C1

S SMUGGLERS COVE RD
- ISLAND CO WA 167-C7

S SMYTHE RD
- SPOKANE CO WA 246-C7

SNAG CREEK TR
- SKAMANIA CO WA 194-C4

SNAKE CREEK RD
- JACKSON CO OR 230-A3

SNAKE RIVER AV
- LEWISTON ID 250-B5

SNAKE RIVER RD
- ASOTIN CO WA 123-A3
- ASOTIN CO WA 250-B6
- BAKER CO OR 138-C2
- BAKER CO OR 139-A1
- HUNTINGTON OR 138-C2

N SNAKE RIVER RD
- BAKER CO OR 139-A1
- RICHLAND OR 139-A1

SNEE-OOSH RD
- SHELTER BAY WA 167-D1
- SKAGIT CO WA 160-D7
- SKAGIT CO WA 167-D1
- SNEE OOSH WA 167-D1
- SWINOMISH VILLAGE WA 167-D1

SNEIDER-BARKS RD
- SKAMANIA CO WA 194-A7

SNIPES RD
- BENTON CO WA 120-B2

SNIVELY GULCH RD
- MALHEUR CO OR 147-A1

SNODGRASS RD
- KITTITAS CO WA 241-C5

SNOHOMISH AV
- SNOHOMISH CO WA 171-D5

W SNOQUALMIE VALLEY RD
- KING CO WA 110-C1

W SNOQUALMIE VALLEY RD NE
- KING CO WA 110-C1
- KING CO WA 176-A1

SNOW RD
- WHITMAN CO WA 249-C6

SNOWBIRD RD
- DOUGLAS CO OR 222-B5

SNOW CREEK RD
- DESCHUTES CO OR 212-A7
- DESCHUTES CO OR 216-D1
- DESCHUTES CO OR 217-A1
- DOUGLAS CO OR 141-B3

SNOWDEN RD
- KLICKITAT CO WA 196-A3

SNOWDEN HOVEY GULCH RD
- SISKIYOU CO CA 150-A3

SNOWDEN WHITE SALMN RD
- KLICKITAT CO WA 195-D4

SNUFFIN RD
- CLACKAMAS CO OR 200-C6

SOAP CREEK RD
- BENTON CO OR 207-A4

SOAP HILL RD
- UMATILLA CO OR 129-B3

SODA PEAK TR
- SKAMANIA CO WA 194-B1

SODA SPRINGS RD
- KLICKITAT CO WA 196-D1

SODAVILLE RD
- LINN CO OR 133-C1
- SODAVILLE OR 133-C1

SODAVILLE-WATERLOO DR
- LINN CO OR 133-C1
- SODAVILLE OR 133-C2

SOLAR LN
- YAKIMA CO WA 243-D6

SOLDIER CREEK RD
- JOSEPHINE CO OR 229-B4
- MALHEUR CO OR 147-A3

SOLDIERS CANYON RD
- NEZ PERCE CO ID 250-D4

SOLDIERS MEADOW RD
- NEZ PERCE CO ID 123-A3

SOLE RD
- YAKIMA CO WA 243-B5

SOLEDUCK VALLEY RD
- CLALLAM CO WA 163-B7

SOLKI RD
- CENTRAL PARK WA 178-C7

SOMMER CAMP RD
- OWYHEE CO ID 147-B1

SOMMERS RD
- WHITMAN CO WA 122-B1

SOMMERVILLE RD
- LEWIS CO WA 187-C1

SOOKE RD
- CITY OF COLWOOD BC 159-A7
- DISTRICT OF LANGFORD BC 159-A7

SOOKE RD Rt#-14
- BRITISH COLUMBIA 101-A2
- BRITISH COLUMBIA 159-A7
- DISTRICT OF LANGFORD BC 159-A7
- DISTRICT OF METCHOSIN BC 159-A7

SOPER HILL RD
- SNOHOMISH CO WA 171-D1

SOUNDVIEW DR
- GIG HARBOR WA 181-C1
- PIERCE CO WA 181-C1

W SOUTH AV
- CHEWELAH WA 106-B3
- STEVENS CO WA 106-B3

SOUTH DR
- PIERCE CO WA 181-A4

SOUTH RD
- KOOTENAI CO ID 245-C1
- WASHINGTON CO OR 198-A3
- YAMHILL CO OR 198-B3

SOUTH ST Rt#-293
- ANTELOPE OR 127-C3

SOUTH BANK RD
- DOUGLAS CO OR 221-D3
- GRAYS HARBOR CO WA 178-D7
- GRAYS HARBOR CO WA 179-B7

SOUTH BANK RD Rt#-107
- GRAYS HARBOR CO WA 178-D7

W SOUTH BANK RD
- SPOKANE CO WA 114-B1

SOUTH BANK CHETCO RIVER RD
- CURRY CO OR 232-D6

SOUTH BANK MAPLETON WEST RD
- LANE CO OR 214-D2

SOUTH BAY DR
- WHATCOM CO WA 161-B2

SOUTHBAY RD
- LINCOLN CO OR 206-C5

SOUTH BEND PALIX RD
- PACIFIC CO WA 183-D7

SOUTHBOROUGH DR
- DIST OF WEST VANCOUVER BC 156-B2
- DIST OF WEST VANCOUVER BC 254-F1

SOUTHCENTER BLVD
- TUKWILA WA 289-G4

SOUTHCENTER PKWY
- TUKWILA WA 289-G6
- TUKWILA WA 291-G1

SOUTH CRANE CREEK RD
- WASHINGTON CO ID 139-B2

SOUTHEAST AV U.S.-30
- NEW PLYMOUTH ID 139-B3
- PAYETTE CO ID 139-B3

SOUTHEAST BLVD
- EPHRATA WA 112-C3

E SOUTHEAST BLVD
- SPOKANE WA 349-D12

S SOUTHEAST BLVD
- SPOKANE WA 349-B11

SOUTH END RD
- ADAMS CO ID 251-A4
- CLACKAMAS CO OR 199-C5

SOUTHERN RD
- DESCHUTES CO OR 217-A1

SOUTH FORK RD
- BENTON CO OR 133-A2
- DEL NORTE CO CA 148-B3
- GRANT CO OR 136-C2
- LANE CO OR 134-B3
- TILLAMOOK CO OR 125-A2

SOUTH FORK AHTANUM RD
- YAKIMA CO WA 119-B2

SOUTH FORK BURNT RIVER RD
- BAKER CO OR 138-A2

SOUTH FORK JOHN DAY RD
- GRANT CO OR 136-C2

SOUTH FORK LITTLE BUTTE RD
- JACKSON CO OR 150-A1

SOUTH FORK MILL CREEK RD
- STEVENS CO WA 106-B2

SOUTH FRASER WY
- DISTRICT OF ABBOTSFORD BC 102-B1
- DISTRICT OF MATSQUI BC 102-B1

SOUTHGATE PL
- PENDLETON OR 129-B1
- UMATILLA CO OR 129-B1

SW SOUTHGATE PL
- UMATILLA CO OR 129-B1

SOUTHGATE ST
- CITY OF VICTORIA BC 256-G10

SOUTH HILL ST
- ALBANY OR 326-E11

SOUTH JUNCTION RD
- WASCO CO OR 208-C1

SOUTH PASS RD
- WHATCOM CO WA 102-B1

SOUTH POST RD
- CLATSOP CO WA 188-B3

SOUTH PRAIRIE RD
- TILLAMOOK CO OR 197-C3

SOUTH PRAIRIE RD E
- BONNEY LAKE WA 182-C4

SOUTH PRAIRIE CARBON RIVER RD
- PIERCE CO WA 182-C5

SOUTH ROCK CREEK RD
- BAKER CO OR 130-A3

SOUTH SHORE BLVD
- LAKE OSWEGO OR 199-C4
- LAKE OSWEGO OR 320-A7
- LAKE OSWEGO OR 321-E7

SOUTH SHORE RD
- CLALLAM CO WA 164-C6
- GRAYS HARBOR CO WA 109-A2
- JEFFERSON CO WA 109-A2

SOUTHSIDE BLVD
- CANYON CO ID 147-C1

SOUTH SIDE RD
- DOUGLAS CO OR 218-D1
- DOUGLAS CO OR 221-C1
- JOSEPHINE CO OR 149-A2
- JOSEPHINE CO OR 229-B7

SOUTH SLOPE RD
- GEM CO ID 139-B3

SOUTH SLOUGH RD
- LANE CO OR 214-B4

SOUTH SUMAS RD
- DISTRICT OF CHILLIWACK BC 94-C3

SOUTH TOUTLE RD
- COWLITZ CO WA 118-A2

SOUTH UNION RD
- GRAYS HARBOR CO WA 179-C7

SOUTH VALLEY RD
- WASCO CO OR 127-A2

SOUTHWEST AV
- NEW PLYMOUTH ID 139-B3

SOUTHWEST BLVD
- COOS BAY OR 333-G13
- COOS CO OR 333-G13

SOUTHWOOD LN
- EUGENE OR 330-B5

SOVERN LN
- LANE CO OR 210-A6

SPADES RD
- BONNER CO ID 244-A3

SPANAWAY LOOP RD S
- PIERCE CO WA 181-D5

SPANAWAY-MCKENNA HWY Rt#-507
- PIERCE CO WA 118-A1
- PIERCE CO WA 181-C7
- ROY WA 181-C7

W SPANGLE RD
- CHENEY WA 246-A7
- SPOKANE CO WA 246-A7

S SPANGLE CREEK RD
- SPOKANE CO WA 246-C7

S SPANGLER RD
- CLACKAMAS CO OR 199-D6

E SPANGLE WAVERLY RD
- SPOKANE CO WA 114-C2

SPARROW DR
- JEFFERSON CO OR 212-C2

SE SPARROW ST
- MILWAUKIE OR 321-J4

SPARROW PARK RD
- DOUGLAS CO OR 214-A7

SPARTA RD
- BAKER CO OR 130-C3
- BAKER CO OR 138-C1
- BAKER CO OR 139-A1

SPEAKER RD
- JOSEPHINE CO OR 225-C7

SPEARE CANYON RD
- UMATILLA CO OR 129-A1

SPENCER RD
- LEWIS CO WA 187-D3

SPENCER CREEK RD
- COWLITZ CO WA 189-D5
- DOUGLAS CO OR 214-D6
- LANE CO OR 133-B3
- LANE CO OR 215-A3
- LANE CO OR 329-A14

SPENCER LAKE RD
- MASON CO WA 180-B2

SPENCER WELLS RD
- DESCHUTES CO OR 135-B3

SPEOS RD
- PAYETTE CO ID 139-A3

SPERLING AV
- DISTRICT OF BURNABY BC 156-D4

SPERRY RD
- SAN JUAN CO WA 160-A6

SPEYERS RD
- SELAH WA 243-B5
- YAKIMA CO WA 243-B5

SPICER DR
- ALBANY OR 326-H9
- LINN CO OR 133-C1
- LINN CO OR 207-D5
- LINN CO OR 326-H9

SPINK LN
- VALLEY CO ID 251-D7

SPIRIT LAKE HWY Rt#-504
- CASTLE ROCK WA 187-C7
- COWLITZ CO WA 118-A2
- COWLITZ CO WA 187-C7

SPIRIT LAKE RD
- BONNER CO ID 107-A3
- KOOTENAI CO ID 115-A1

SPOFFORD RD
- UMATILLA CO OR 121-C3

N SPOKANE ST
- KOOTENAI CO ID 353-H5
- POST FALLS ID 353-H5

S SPOKANE ST
- KOOTENAI CO ID 353-H8
- POST FALLS ID 353-H8
- SEATTLE WA 281-J3
- SEATTLE WA 282-A3

SW SPOKANE ST
- SEATTLE WA 281-G3

SPOKANE WY
- GRAND COULEE WA 237-C3
- GRANT CO WA 237-C3

N SPOKANE BRIDGE RD
- SPOKANE CO WA 352-H10

W SPOKANE FALLS BLVD
- SPOKANE WA 348-J9
- SPOKANE WA 349-A9

W SPOKANE FALLS BLVD U.S.-2
- SPOKANE WA 349-A9

SPOONER RD
- LEWIS CO WA 184-A7

SPORTMENS WY
- OCEAN SHORES WA 298-B6

SPORTSMAN CLUB RD NE
- KITSAP CO WA 174-D1
- KITSAP CO WA 271-J2

S SPOTTED RD
- SPOKANE CO WA 348-A13

SPOUT CREEK RD
- LINCOLN CO OR 133-A1

SPRAGUE AV
- WESTPORT WA 298-G13

E SPRAGUE AV
- DISHMAN WA 350-E9
- GREEN ACRES WA 351-F8
- OPPORTUNITY WA 350-H8
- OPPORTUNITY WA 351-A8
- SPOKANE WA 349-B9
- SPOKANE CO WA 349-H9
- SPOKANE CO WA 350-B9
- SPOKANE CO WA 351-A8
- VERADALE WA 351-A8

S SPRAGUE AV
- TACOMA WA 293-E6

W SPRAGUE AV
- SPOKANE WA 348-J9
- SPOKANE WA 349-A9

S SPRAGUE RD
- CLACKAMAS CO OR 200-A5

SPRAGUE ST
- WILSON CREEK WA 113-A2

E SPRAGUE AVE ACCESS 1
- SPOKANE WA 349-C9

E SPRAGUE AVE ACCESS 3
- SPOKANE WA 349-B9

SPRAGUE RIVER RD
- KLAMATH CO OR 150-C1

STREET
City State Page-Grid

SPRAGUE RIVER RD
KLAMATH CO OR 151-A1
KLAMATH CO OR 231-D3
SPRAUER RD NW
DOUGLAS CO WA 112-B1
SPRENGER RD
LATAH CO ID 250-B1
SPRING ST
IONE OR 128-B2
KLAMATH FALLS OR 338-E7
KLICKITAT CO WA 195-D4
MAUPIN OR 127-B3
MEDFORD OR 336-E10
WHITE SALMON WA 195-D4
N SPRING ST
KLAMATH FALLS OR 338-E7
SE SPRING ST
PULLMAN WA 249-B5
W SPRING ST
WALDPORT OR 328-D4
SPRING BROOK RD
DOUGLAS CO OR 225-C1
SPRINGBROOK RD
MEDFORD OR 336-F7
YAMHILL CO OR 198-D5
SPRINGBROOK ST
NEWBERG OR 198-D6
YAMHILL CO OR 198-D6
SPRING COULEE RD
OKANOGAN CO WA 104-C3
SPRING CREEK RD
UNION CO OR 129-C2
SPRING CREEK RD Rt#-231
LINCOLN CO WA 114-A1
N SPRING CREEK RD
BONNER CO ID 244-D3
SPRINGDALE-HUNTERS RD
SPRINGDALE WA 106-A3
STEVENS CO WA 105-C3
STEVENS CO WA 106-A3
STEVENS CO WA 114-A1
SPRINGER RD
JEFFERSON CO OR 213-A1
SPRING HILL DR
ALBANY OR 326-C6
BENTON CO OR 207-B3
BENTON CO OR 326-C6
SPRING HILL RD
WASHINGTON CO OR 198-B3
SPRING HOLLOW RD
UMATILLA CO OR 129-C1
SPRING LAKE RD
KLAMATH CO OR 235-C5
SPRINGRIDGE RD NE
KITSAP CO WA 271-F2
SPRING RIVER RD
DESCHUTES CO OR 217-A5
SPRINGS RD
JEFFERSON CO OR 211-D2
SPRINGSTON RD
KOOTENAI CO ID 248-B4
SPRING VALLEY RD
WHITMAN CO WA 114-C3
E SPRING VALLEY RD
SPOKANE CO WA 114-C3
SPRING VALLEY RD NW
POLK CO OR 204-C4
NW SPRINGVILLE RD
WASHINGTON CO OR 192-A7
SPRINGWATER AV
WENATCHEE WA 238-D4
WEST WENATCHEE WA 238-D4
SPRINGWATER RD
CLACKAMAS CO OR 200-B6
S SPRINGWATER RD
CLACKAMAS CO OR 200-A4
SPROTT ST
DISTRICT OF BURNABY BC 156-D5
SPROUT RD
RICHLAND WA 340-G8
NW SPRUCE
DESCHUTES CO OR 212-D5
NW SPRUCE AV
DESCHUTES CO OR 212-C5
SW SPRUCE RD
KITSAP CO WA 174-B6
SPRUCE ST
CANNON BEACH WA 188-B7
MYRTLE POINT OR 140-B2
PACIFIC CO WA 186-A5
PORT TOWNSEND WA 263-G2
N SPRUCE ST
BURLINGTON WA 260-D4
LA GRANDE OR 130-A2
S SPRUCE ST
BURLINGTON WA 260-D5
SE SPRUCE ST
ROSEBURG OR 334-F7
SPRUCE ST E U.S.-101
ILWACO WA 186-A6
SPRUCE ST W
ILWACO WA 186-A6
SPRUCE TRAIL RD
CLALLAM CO WA 164-B6
SPURAWAY DR
COQUITLAM BC 157-A4
SQUAW RD
WHITMAN CO WA 114-B3
SQUAWBACK RIDGE RD
JEFFERSON CO OR 135-A1
JEFFERSON CO OR 211-D1
SQUAW BUTTE RD
HARNEY CO OR 144-C1
SQUAW CREEK DR
DESCHUTES CO OR 212-A4
SQUAW CREEK RD
ADAMS CO ID 252-B7
DOUGLAS CO OR 221-A7
TILLAMOOK CO OR 203-C2
S SQUAW CREEK RD
SPOKANE CO WA 114-B3
SW SQUAW CREEK RD
JEFFERSON CO OR 212-A2
SQUAW FLAT RD
KLAMATH CO OR 151-A2
SW SQUAW FLAT RD
JEFFERSON CO OR 212-B1
SW SQUAW GULCH RD
JEFFERSON CO OR 212-A2

SQUAW MOUNTAIN RD
CLACKAMAS CO OR 200-C6
CLACKAMAS CO OR 201-A7
SE SQUAW MOUNTAIN RD
CLACKAMAS CO OR 200-D7
SQUAW VALLEY RD
CURRY CO OR 228-B3
SQUEEDUNK RD
TILLAMOOK CO OR 197-B1
SQUILCHUCK RD
CHELAN CO WA 238-D5
STACKPOLE RD
PACIFIC CO WA 186-A1
NE STADIUM WY
PULLMAN WA 249-B5
NW STADIUM WY
PULLMAN WA 249-B5
S STADIUM WY
TACOMA WA 293-G4
SE STADIUM WY
PULLMAN WA 249-B5
STADSVOLD RD
WHATCOM CO WA 158-B3
NE STAFFER RD
CLARK CO WA 193-C6
STAFFORD AV Rt#-903
CLE ELUM WA 240-B2
STAFFORD RD
CLACKAMAS CO OR 199-B5
SW STAFFORD RD
CLACKAMAS CO OR 199-C4
LAKE OSWEGO OR 199-C4
LAKE OSWEGO OR 321-E7
STAGE RD
COOS CO OR 218-B5
S STAGE RD
JACKSON CO OR 234-A2
STAGE RD S
JACKSON CO OR 234-A2
JACKSONVILLE OR 149-B2
JACKSONVILLE OR 234-A2
STAGECOACH RD
LANE CO OR 133-A3
STAG HOLLOW RD
YAMHILL CO OR 198-B5
STAHANCYK LN
CROOK CO OR 213-C4
STAINWOOD ST
BENTON CO OR 327-H6
CORVALLIS OR 327-H6
STALEY RD
WHITMAN CO WA 249-B6
W STALEY RD
SPOKANE CO WA 114-B1
STAMPEDE BLVD NW
KITSAP CO WA 270-F3
STAMPER RD
ELMA WA 179-B7
GRAYS HARBOR CO WA 179-B7
N STANDARD ST
SPOKANE WA 347-A13
STANDLEY LN
UNION CO OR 130-A2
STANFIELD MEADOWS RD
UMATILLA CO OR 129-A1
STANKEY RD
COWLITZ CO WA 187-D7
STANLEY AV S
SEATTLE WA 282-B7
E STANLEY ST Rt#-92
GRANITE FALLS WA 102-C3
W STANLEY ST Rt#-92
GRANITE FALLS WA 102-C3
STANTON BLVD
MALHEUR CO OR 139-A3
STANTON PARK RD Rt#-99
DOUGLAS CO OR 225-C3
STANWOOD-BRYANT RD
SNOHOMISH CO WA 168-C4
STAPLETON RD
POLK CO OR 207-B1
STAR BLVD Rt#-44
CANYON CO ID 147-B1
MIDDLETON ID 147-B1
STARBIRD RD
SKAGIT CO WA 168-B2
N STARK AV
DOUGLAS CO WA 239-A4
SE STARK ST
GRESHAM OR 200-B1
MULTNOMAH CO OR 200-B1
PORTLAND OR 200-A1
PORTLAND OR 313-H6
PORTLAND OR 314-B6
PORTLAND OR 315-H6
TROUTDALE OR 200-B1
SW STARK ST
PORTLAND OR 313-E5
STAR LAKE RD
MASON CO WA 179-C4
STARLING ST
STEILACOOM WA 181-C4
STARR RD
POLK CO OR 204-A4
N STARR RD
OTIS ORCHARDS WA 352-E6
SPOKANE CO WA 352-E4
S STARR RD
SPOKANE CO WA 247-B6
STARR ST
MARION CO OR 133-C1
SUBLIMITY OR 133-C1
STAR RANCH RD
MALHEUR CO OR 146-A2
STARR CREEK RD
LINCOLN CO OR 209-A3
SE STARR QUARRY RD
YAMHILL CO OR 204-C1
STARVEOUT CREEK RD
DOUGLAS CO OR 225-D6
STATE AV
COLUMBIA CO OR 125-B1
MARYSVILLE WA 168-C7
MARYSVILLE WA 171-C1
OLYMPIA WA 296-J5
OLYMPIA WA 297-A5
VERNONIA OR 125-B1
STATE AV Rt#-529
MARYSVILLE WA 171-C1

STATE AV U.S.-30
HOOD RIVER OR 195-D5
HOOD RIVER CO OR 195-D5
N STATE AV Rt#-41
OLDTOWN ID 106-C3
NW STATE AV
CHEHALIS WA 299-D11
S STATE AV Rt#-41
NEWPORT WA 106-C3
OLDTOWN ID 106-C3
STATE RD
THE DALLES OR 196-D7
WASCO CO OR 127-B2
WASCO CO OR 196-A5
STATE ST
FOUR CORNERS OR 323-E14
FOUR CORNERS OR 325-H1
MARION CO OR 205-A6
MARION CO OR 325-H1
OAKVILLE WA 117-B1
SALEM OR 322-H13
SALEM OR 323-B14
SALEM OR 325-H1
SEDRO-WOOLLEY WA 161-C6
SKAGIT CO WA 161-C6
VANCOUVER WA 306-D7
STATE ST Rt#-82
LOSTINE OR 130-C2
STATE ST U.S.-95
WEISER ID 139-A2
STATE ST U.S.-101
NORTH BEND OR 333-G6
E STATE ST
SEDRO-WOOLLEY WA 161-C6
N STATE ST
BELLINGHAM WA 258-E6
N STATE ST Rt#-43
CLACKAMAS OR 321-G6
LAKE OSWEGO OR 321-G6
NE STATE ST Rt#-99
DOUGLAS CO OR 221-C1
SUTHERLIN OR 221-C1
NW STATE ST
PULLMAN WA 249-B5
S STATE ST
BELLINGHAM WA 258-C8
TACOMA WA 293-E7
S STATE ST Rt#-43
LAKE OSWEGO OR 321-F7
W STATE ST
ADA CO ID 253-C2
BOISE ID 253-C2
GARDEN CITY ID 253-C2
SEDRO-WOOLLEY WA 161-C6
W STATE ST Rt#-44
ADA CO ID 147-C1
ADA CO ID 253-A1
BOISE ID 253-A1
EAGLE ID 253-A1
STATE FARM RD
POLK CO OR 204-C6
STATE FOREST RD
CLALLAM CO WA 165-A6
STATE LINE RD
CANYON CO ID 147-A1
MALHEUR CO OR 147-A1
MODOC CO CA 151-A3
OWYHEE CO ID 155-C2
STATE LINE RD Rt#-161
SISKIYOU CO CA 150-C3
SISKIYOU CO CA 151-A3
STATE PARK ST
MCCALL ID 251-D5
VALLEY CO ID 251-D5
STATE TOLL FERRY
SAN JUAN CO WA 160-B5
SKAGIT CO WA 160-B5
STAUCH RD
KLICKITAT CO WA 196-A2
STAUFFER RD NE
MARION CO OR 205-C1
STAVE LAKE RD
BRITISH COLUMBIA 94-B3
STAVE LAKE ST
DISTRICT OF MISSION BC 94-B3
NW STAVIS BAY RD
KITSAP CO WA 173-D2
STAYMAN RD
CHELAN CO WA 236-B4
STAYTE RD
CITY OF WHITE ROCK BC 158-B2
DISTRICT OF SURREY BC 158-B2
W STAYTON
MARION CO OR 133-C1
STAYTON RD
MARION CO OR 133-C1
STAYTON OR 133-C1
W STAYTON RD
AUMSVILLE OR 133-C1
MARION CO OR 133-C1
STAYTON RD SE
MARION CO OR 133-C1
STAYTON-SCIO RD
LINN CO OR 133-C1
MARION CO OR 133-C1
STAYTON OR 133-C1
STEAMBOAT CREEK RD
DOUGLAS CO OR 142-A1
DOUGLAS CO OR 222-A2
STEAMBOAT ISLAND RD NW
THURSTON CO WA 180-B5
STEARNS LN
DOUGLAS CO OR 219-A7
DOUGLAS CO OR 221-C1
STEARNS RD
CROOK CO OR 135-B3
STECKLEY RD
LINN CO OR 207-D7
STEDMAN RD SE
THURSTON CO WA 184-D1
STEELE RD
WASCO CO OR 127-B2
WASCO CO OR 196-C7
S STEELE ST
TACOMA WA 294-E2
STEELE ST S
LAKEWOOD WA 181-D4
PIERCE CO WA 181-D4
TACOMA WA 181-D4

STEELE SWAMP RD
MODOC CO CA 151-B3
STEELHEAD RD
JEFFERSON CO OR 212-C2
SW STEELHEAD FALLS DR
DESCHUTES CO OR 212-C3
JEFFERSON CO OR 212-C3
STEELMAN RD
COLUMBIA CO OR 192-A4
STEENS HWY Rt#-78
HARNEY CO OR 145-B1
HARNEY CO OR 146-A2
MALHEUR CO OR 146-B3
STEENS MOUNTAIN LOOP RD
HARNEY CO OR 153-B1
STEFFENSEN RD
PIERCE CO WA 181-A4
STEFFY LN
CROOK CO OR 213-C6
STEGEMAN RD
KLICKITAT CO WA 120-A3
STEHEKIN VALLEY RD
CHELAN CO WA 103-B2
STEILACOOM BLVD
LAKEWOOD WA 181-C4
STEILACOOM WA 181-C4
STEILACOOM BLVD SW
LAKEWOOD WA 181-C4
STEILACOOM WA 181-C4
STEILACOOM RD SE
THURSTON CO WA 181-A6
STEILACOOM-ANDERSON ISL FERRY
PIERCE CO WA 181-B4
STEILACOOM WA 181-B4
STEILACOOM-DUPONT RD SW
DUPONT WA 181-B5
PIERCE CO WA 181-B5
STEILACOOM-KETRON ISLAND FERRY
PIERCE CO WA 181-B4
STEILACOOM WA 181-B4
STEIN RD
WHATCOM CO WA 158-C4
S STEIN RD
YAKIMA CO WA 243-A7
STEINER RD
TILLAMOOK CO OR 197-C3
WHITMAN CO WA 249-A3
S STEINER RD
CLACKAMAS CO OR 200-A6
STEIWER RD SE
MARION CO OR 207-D2
STELLA RD
COWLITZ CO WA 189-A2
STELLYS CROSS RD
DIST OF CENTRAL SAANICH BC 159-B4
STEMILT CREEK RD
CHELAN CO WA 239-A5
STEMILT LOOP RD
CHELAN CO WA 238-D6
CHELAN CO WA 239-A6
STENKAMP RD
DESCHUTES CO OR 217-D2
S STENTZ RD
SPOKANE CO WA 246-C7
STEPHEN RD
GRAYS HARBOR CO WA 179-A6
NE STEPHENS ST Rt#-99
ROSEBURG OR 334-F5
SE STEPHENS ST Rt#-99
ROSEBURG OR 334-G7
SE STEPHENS ST Rt#-138
ROSEBURG OR 334-F8
SW STEPHENSON ST
LAKE OSWEGO OR 320-C3
PORTLAND OR 320-C3
STEPIEN RD
WASHINGTON CO OR 198-A1
STEPTOE AV Rt#-27
OAKESDALE WA 114-C3
STEPTOE ST
COLTON WA 250-A1
STEPTOE CANYON RD
WHITMAN CO WA 122-C2
WHITMAN CO WA 250-A2
STERLING RD
SEDRO-WOOLLEY WA 260-J3
SKAGIT CO WA 260-J3
STERLING CREEK RD
JACKSON CO OR 149-B2
JACKSON CO OR 234-A4
STEUBEN ST Rt#-14
BINGEN WA 195-D5
STEVENS DR
BENTON CO WA 340-F6
DIST OF WEST VANCOUVER BC 156-B2
DIST OF WEST VANCOUVER BC 254-E2
RICHLAND WA 340-F10
RICHLAND WA 341-F1
STEVENS RD
DESCHUTES CO OR 217-C3
STEVENS RD SE
KITSAP CO WA 174-B6
STEVENS ST
CHEWELAH WA 106-B3
MEDFORD OR 336-D11
STEVENS CO WA 106-B3
STEVENS ST Rt#-285
WENATCHEE WA 239-A4
N STEVENS ST
TACOMA WA 292-B4
S STEVENS ST
SPOKANE WA 348-J10
TACOMA WA 292-B6
STEVENS CANYON RD
DESCHUTES CO OR 211-D4
DESCHUTES CO OR 212-A3
LEWIS CO WA 185-C5
S STEVENS CREEK RD
SPOKANE CO WA 246-D6
STEVENSON RD
POLK CO OR 204-B4
SKAGIT CO WA 160-C6
N STEVENSON RD
OTIS ORCHARDS WA 352-D10
STEVENSON RIDGE TR
CARSON WA 194-D4
SKAMANIA CO WA 194-D4

STEVENS PASS HWY
SNOHOMISH CO WA 171-D2
STEVENS PASS HWY U.S.-2
GOLD BAR WA 110-C1
KING CO WA 111-B1
MONROE WA 110-C1
SNOHOMISH WA 171-D3
SNOHOMISH CO WA 110-C1
SNOHOMISH CO WA 111-A1
SNOHOMISH CO WA 171-D3
SULTAN WA 110-C1
NE STEVENS PASS HWY Rt#-2
KING CO WA 111-A1
SKYKOMISH WA 111-A1
NE STEVENS PASS HWY U.S.-2
KING CO WA 111-A1
SNOHOMISH CO WA 111-A1
STEVESTON HWY
CITY OF RICHMOND BC 156-B7
STEWARD RD SE
PACIFIC WA 182-B2
STEWARD RD SW
PACIFIC WA 182-B2
STEWARDSON WY
NEW WESTMINSTER BC 156-D5
STEWART AV
PIERCE CO WA 182-A3
PUYALLUP WA 182-A3
E STEWART AV
MEDFORD OR 336-E14
W STEWART AV
JACKSON CO OR 234-A1
JACKSON CO OR 336-B14
MEDFORD OR 336-B14
PUYALLUP WA 182-B3
STEWART LN
DOUGLAS CO WA 239-B2
STEWART PKWY
ROSEBURG OR 334-E4
NE STEWART PKWY
ROSEBURG OR 334-F4
NW STEWART PKWY
ROSEBURG OR 334-D3
STEWART RD
ADA CO ID 253-B5
COOS CO OR 224-B1
JOSEPHINE CO OR 229-A6
STEWART ST
SEATTLE WA 277-J5
SEATTLE WA 278-A5
STEWART CREEK RD
COLUMBIA CO OR 189-A3
S STILLAGUAMISH AV
ARLINGTON WA 168-D5
STILL CREEK RD
CLACKAMAS CO OR 201-D6
CLACKAMAS CO OR 202-A6
STILLMAN RD
CROOK CO OR 213-B6
STILLWATER TKTR
COWLITZ CO WA 187-B6
STIMSON RD
SNOHOMISH CO WA 168-C6
STINEHILL RD
CHELAN CO WA 238-B2
STINSON AV
GIG HARBOR WA 181-C1
STIRLING DR
DESCHUTES CO OR 217-D4
STITZEL RD
MALHEUR CO OR 146-C3
STOCK DRIVE RD
LAKE CO OR 152-A2
SE STOCKHOFF RD
YAMHILL CO OR 204-C1
STOCKYARD RD
KLICKITAT CO WA 127-C1
STOLTE CANYON RD
NEZ PERCE CO ID 123-B2
STOLTZ HILL RD
LEBANON OR 133-C1
LINN CO OR 133-C1
SOUTH LEBANON OR 133-C1
STONE DR NW
PIERCE CO WA 181-C2
STONE RD
COLUMBIA CO OR 192-A2
TILLAMOOK CO OR 197-D3
YAMHILL CO OR 198-C5
STONE WY N
SEATTLE WA 273-J7
STONE BREAKER LN
VALLEY CO ID 252-D4
STONE CABIN RD
WHEELER CO OR 128-A3
STONECIPHER RD
WALLA WALLA CO WA 122-A3
STONECREST RD
GRANT CO WA 242-B1
STOREY BLVD
EUGENE OR 329-H10
N STORIE ST
WALLOWA OR 130-C1
STORMER RD
CLACKAMAS CO OR 200-B6
STOTTLEMEYER RD NE
KITSAP CO WA 170-C6
STOTTS RD SW
DOUGLAS CO WA 112-B2
E STOUGHTON RD
SPOKANE CO WA 246-C6
SPOKANE CO WA 247-A6
STOUT RD
LATAH CO ID 250-D1
WHITMAN CO WA 250-B3
E STOVER RD
YAKIMA CO WA 120-B3
STRAHL RD
DOUGLAS CO WA 105-A3
DOUGLAS CO WA 237-A1
STRAHL CANYON RD
DOUGLAS CO WA 105-A3
N STRAHORN RD
HAYDEN ID 245-A5
HAYDEN ID 355-F1
HAYDEN LAKE ID 245-A5
KOOTENAI CO ID 245-A5
KOOTENAI CO ID 355-F1

STRAND RD
WHATCOM CO WA 161-C1
STRANDER BLVD
TUKWILA WA 289-G6
STRATFORD DR NE
MARION CO OR 205-A3
STRATFORD RD
GRANT CO WA 113-A2
GRANT CO WA 242-C1
MOSES LAKE WA 242-C1
STRATTON RD
CLALLAM CO WA 165-A5
STRAWBERRY RD
GRANT CO OR 137-B2
N STRAWBERRY POINT RD
ISLAND CO WA 167-D3
STRAWN LN SE
THURSTON CO WA 184-D3
STREET HILAIRE RD
YAKIMA CO WA 243-D7
STRICKLAND CANYON RD
DOUGLAS CO OR 221-A6
STRIEBEL RD
JEFFERSON CO OR 211-C1
STRIKER LN
IMBLER OR 130-A2
STRINGER GAP RD
JOSEPHINE CO OR 229-B7
STRINGHAM RD
KOOTENAI CO ID 247-C7
LEWIS CO WA 187-D2
E STRINGHAM RD
ROCKFORD WA 114-C2
SPOKANE CO WA 247-B7
STRING TOWN RD
YAMHILL CO OR 198-C7
STRINGTOWN RD
PACIFIC CO WA 186-A6
WASHINGTON CO OR 198-B1
STRODA DR
LINN CO OR 210-A5
STROEBEL RD
ADA CO ID 253-A5
STROME LN
LANE CO OR 210-A6
STRONG RD SE
SALEM OR 325-A4
STRUCK RD
KLICKITAT CO WA 196-C5
STRYKER AV
PIERCE CO WA 181-B5
STRYKER RD
INDEPENDENCE OR 204-B7
STUB AV
KOOTENAI CO ID 247-C1
NE STUDIO RD
BEND OR 332-F5
N STUMP RD
KOOTENAI CO ID 245-B4
STURDAVENT RD
LINCOLN CO OR 206-C4
TOLEDO OR 206-C4
STURGEON RD
DESCHUTES CO OR 212-C7
STURGEON ST
KITSAP CO WA 170-A7
STURM AV
WALLA WALLA WA 345-D9
WALLA WALLA EAST WA 345-D9
S STUWE RD
CLACKAMAS CO OR 205-D1
SUBLIMITY RD
MARION CO OR 133-C1
SUBLIMITY OR 133-C1
SUBSTATION DR
LINN CO OR 210-A4
SUCCOR CREEK HWY Rt#-201
ADRIAN OR 147-A1
MALHEUR CO OR 139-A3
MALHEUR CO OR 147-A1
NYSSA OR 139-A3
SUCCOR CREEK RD
MALHEUR CO OR 147-A1
SUCIA DR
WHATCOM CO WA 158-B6
SUCKER CREEK RD
JOSEPHINE CO OR 233-D5
SUDBURY RD
WALLA WALLA WA 344-A7
WALLA WALLA CO WA 121-C3
WALLA WALLA CO WA 344-A7
SUGAR PINE RD
JACKSON CO OR 226-A6
SUGARPINE BUTTE RD
DESCHUTES CO OR 217-B7
SUICIDE GULCH RD
DESCHUTES CO OR 211-B4
SULLIVAN LN
YAMHILL CO OR 198-C5
SULLIVAN RD
SKAGIT CO WA 161-A5
N SULLIVAN RD
SPOKANE CO WA 351-C5
TRENTWOOD WA 351-C5
VERADALE WA 351-C5
S SULLIVAN RD
VERADALE WA 351-C11
SULLIVAN CREEK RD
PEND OREILLE CO WA 106-C1
SULLIVAN LAKE RD
PEND OREILLE CO WA 106-B2
SULPHUR SPRINGS RD
BENTON CO OR 207-A4
SULTAN BASIN RD
SNOHOMISH CO WA 110-C1
SULTAN WA 110-C1
E SUMACH ST
WALLA WALLA WA 345-B6
SUMAS RD Rt#-547
WHATCOM CO WA 102-B1
SUMAS WY
BRITISH COLUMBIA 102-B1
DISTRICT OF ABBOTSFORD BC 102-B1
DISTRICT OF MATSQUI BC 102-B1
SUMAS CENTRAL RD
DISTRICT OF CHILLIWACK BC 94-C3
E SUMMA ST
CENTRALIA WA 299-G5
LEWIS CO WA 299-G5

STREET City State Page-Grid

W SUMMA ST
CENTRALIA WA 299-E5
SUMMER ST
BELLINGHAM WA 258-D4
SUMMER ST NE
SALEM OR 322-J12
SALEM OR 323-A11
SUMMER CREEK RD
LANE CO OR 215-D4
SUMMERHURST WK SW
KING CO WA 174-D7
SUMMERLAND RD
WHATCOM CO WA 161-A2
SUMMERS LN
ALTAMONT OR 235-C5
ALTAMONT OR 338-J14
KLAMATH FALLS OR 235-C5
KLAMATH FALLS OR 338-J14
SUMMERVILLE RD
IMBLER OR 130-A2
SUMMERVILLE OR 130-A2
UNION CO OR 130-A2
SUMMIT AV
WASHINGTON CO OR 198-A2
SUMMIT DR
HOOD RIVER CO OR 195-C6
SUMMIT HWY
BENTON CO OR 133-A1
SUMMIT LP
MARION CO OR 207-D2
SUMMIT RD
JACKSON CO OR 149-B2
JACKSON CO OR 234-A6
JEFFERSON CO OR 211-D2
WHEELER CO OR 136-A2
SUMMIT RD Rt#-108
GRAYS HARBOR CO WA 179-D6
MCCLEARY WA 179-D6
SUMMIT LAKE RD NW
THURSTON CO WA 180-A6
SUMMIT LAKE SHORE RD NW
THURSTON CO WA 180-A6
SE SUMMIT LANDSBURG RD
KING CO WA 176-A7
E SUMMIT MEADOW RD
CLACKAMAS CO OR 202-A6
SUMMIT ROCK RD
DOUGLAS CO OR 223-C6
SUMMIT VALLEY RD
STEVENS CO WA 106-A3
W SUMMITVIEW AV
WEST VALLEY WA 243-A6
YAKIMA WA 243-A6
YAKIMA CO WA 243-A6
SUMMITVIEW RD
YAKIMA CO WA 119-C1
YAKIMA CO WA 243-A6
N SUMMITVIEW RD
YAKIMA CO WA 243-A6
SUMNER AV U.S.-101
HOQUIAM WA 178-A7
SUMNER ST Rt#-507
BUCODA WA 184-D4
TENINO WA 184-D4
THURSTON CO WA 184-D4
SUMNER ST U.S.-101
ABERDEEN WA 178-B7
HOQUIAM WA 178-A7
SUMNER-BUCKLEY HWY Rt#-410
PIERCE CO WA 182-B3
SUMNER WA 182-B3
SUMNER BUCKLEY HWY E
BONNEY LAKE WA 182-C4
BUCKLEY WA 182-C4
PIERCE CO WA 182-C4
SUMNER-FAIRVIEW RD
COOS CO OR 140-B2
SUMNER-HEIGHTS DR E
SUMNER WA 182-B3
SUMNER TAPPS HWY
PIERCE CO WA 182-C3
SUMPTER HWY
BAKER CO OR 138-A1
SUMPTER OR 138-A1
SE SUN DR
JEFFERSON CO OR 208-C5
MADRAS OR 208-C5
SUNCREST TER
COLLEGE PLACE WA 344-D11
WALLA WALLA CO WA 344-D11
NW SUNDE RD
KITSAP CO WA 174-B1
SUNDERMAN RD
LANE CO OR 210-D7
SUNDOWN RD
CURRY CO OR 232-C4
DESCHUTES CO OR 211-D3
S SUNDQUIST RD
SEASIDE WA 301-G10
SUNFLOWER RD
MORROW CO OR 128-C3
SUNFLOWER FLAT RD
MORROW CO OR 128-C3
SUN MOUNTAIN RD
KLAMATH CO OR 142-B3
SUNNY COVE DR SE
KITSAP CO WA 174-C6
SUNNYCREST RD
YAMHILL CO OR 198-C5
SUNNY DELL RD
BAKER CO OR 131-A3
SUNNYGLEN WY
JOSEPHINE CO OR 229-B2
SUNNYHILL RD S
BREMERTON WA 270-C11
KITSAP CO WA 270-C11
SUNNY RIDGE RD
YAMHILL CO OR 204-A2
SUNNYSIDE AV
GRANGER WA 120-A2
SUNNYSIDE BLVD
MARYSVILLE WA 171-D1
SNOHOMISH CO WA 171-D1
SUNNYSIDE BLVD NE
MARYSVILLE WA 171-D1
SUNNYSIDE BLVD SE
SNOHOMISH CO WA 171-D1
SUNNYSIDE RD
ANMORE BC 157-A3

STREET City State Page-Grid

SUNNYSIDE RD
BONNER CO ID 244-B1
LINN CO OR 134-A2
POLK CO OR 204-A4
SE SUNNYSIDE RD
CLACKAMAS CO OR 199-D3
CLACKAMAS CO OR 200-A3
SUNNYSIDE RD SE
MARION CO OR 324-H9
SALEM OR 324-H9
SUNNYSIDE-UMAPINE HWY
UMATILLA CO OR 121-C3
SUNNY SLOPE LN
BAKER CO OR 130-B3
SUNNYSLOPE LN
BAKER CO OR 138-B1
SUNNY SLOPE RD
KOOTENAI CO ID 248-A6
SUNNY SLOPE RD Rt#-55
CANYON CO ID 147-B1
SUNNYSLOPE RD SW
KITSAP CO WA 174-A5
SUNNY VALLEY LP
JOSEPHINE CO OR 229-B2
SUNNYVIEW RD
FOUR CORNERS OR 323-G11
MARION CO OR 205-B5
MARION CO OR 323-G11
SALEM OR 323-B11
SUN RAY
CURRY CO OR 232-C4
SUNRISE AV
MEDFORD OR 336-F11
N SUNRISE BLVD
ISLAND CO WA 167-D4
SUNRISE DR
KOOTENAI CO ID 248-B5
SUNRISE DR NE
KITSAP CO WA 170-D7
KITSAP CO WA 174-D1
SUNRISE LN
DOUGLAS CO OR 221-A5
SUNRISE PKWY E
PIERCE CO WA 182-B5
SUNRISE RD
WALLOWA CO OR 130-C2
WHATCOM CO WA 158-C3
WHATCOM CO WA 160-B2
SUNRISE ST
KELSO WA 303-F7
SUNRISE BEACH RD NW
THURSTON CO WA 180-B5
SUNRISE PARK RD
PIERCE CO WA 119-A1
PIERCE CO WA 185-D2
SUNSET AV
ANACORTES WA 259-A4
SUNSET AV N
KEIZER OR 322-J7
SUNSET BLVD
CANNON BEACH WA 188-B7
DIST OF N VANCOUVER BC 254-J1
SEASIDE WA 301-E11
E SUNSET BLVD
CANNON BEACH WA 188-B7
NE SUNSET BLVD Rt#-900
RENTON WA 175-C4
S SUNSET BLVD
SPOKANE WA 348-G10
SW SUNSET BLVD
PORTLAND OR 316-C3
SHERWOOD OR 199-A5
SW SUNSET BLVD Rt#-900
KING CO WA 175-C5
RENTON WA 175-C5
W SUNSET BLVD
SPOKANE WA 348-F10
SPOKANE CO WA 348-E12
SUNSET BLVD NE
RENTON WA 175-C4
SUNSET BLVD NE Rt#-900
RENTON WA 175-C5
SUNSET DR
BELLINGHAM WA 258-D4
ISLAND CO WA 167-D4
KOOTENAI CO ID 248-B5
LA GRANDE OR 130-A2
WALLA WALLA CO WA 121-B3
SUNSET DR Rt#-47
FOREST GROVE OR 198-B1
WASHINGTON CO OR 198-B1
E SUNSET DR Rt#-542
BELLINGHAM WA 258-G3
WHATCOM CO WA 102-B1
WHATCOM CO WA 258-G3
SUNSET DR W
UNIVERSITY PLACE WA 181-C3
SUNSET FRWY U.S.-2
DOUGLAS CO WA 238-D3
EAST WENATCHEE BENCH WA 238-D3
SUNNYSLOPE WA 238-D3
SUNSET HWY
CHELAN CO WA 238-C2
SUNSET HWY Rt#-970
KITTITAS CO WA 240-B2
SUNSET HWY U.S.-26
BEAVERTON OR 199-A1
CLATSOP CO WA 117-A3
CLATSOP CO OR 125-A1
CLATSOP CO WA 188-C7
COLUMBIA CO OR 125-A1
HILLSBORO OR 125-C1
HILLSBORO OR 192-A7
HILLSBORO OR 199-A1
MULTNOMAH CO OR 312-B7
MULTNOMAH CO OR 199-A1
NORTH PLAINS OR 125-C1
PORTLAND OR 199-A1
PORTLAND OR 312-B7
PORTLAND OR 316-B1
TILLAMOOK CO OR 125-A1
WASHINGTON CO OR 125-C1
WASHINGTON CO OR 192-A7
WASHINGTON CO OR 199-A1
W SUNSET HWY
SPOKANE WA 348-B11
SPOKANE CO WA 348-B11
W SUNSET HWY U.S.-2
AIRWAY HEIGHTS WA 246-A4
SPOKANE CO WA 246-A4

STREET City State Page-Grid

W SUNSET HWY U.S.-2
SPOKANE CO WA 348-A11
SUNSET LN
CROOK CO OR 213-C4
SUNSET RD
BONNER CO ID 244-A7
SKAGIT CO WA 161-A5
WHITMAN CO WA 114-B3
SE SUNSET VW
CLARK CO WA 193-C7
SUNSET WY
CHELAN CO WA 238-C2
DOUGLAS CO WA 239-B1
E SUNSET WY
ISSAQUAH WA 176-A4
W SUNSET WY
ISSAQUAH WA 176-A4
SUNSET BEACH RD
CLATSOP CO WA 188-B3
SUNSET HEMLOCK RD
SKAMANIA CO WA 193-D3
SKAMANIA CO WA 194-A3
SUNSET PEAK RD
ADA CO ID 253-D2
SUNSHINE RD
DOUGLAS CO OR 221-D4
WHITMAN CO WA 249-B5
SUNSHINE CREEK RD
JACKSON CO OR 226-C4
SE SUNSHINE VALLEY RD
CLACKAMAS CO OR 200-B3
SUN UP BAY RD
KOOTENAI CO ID 247-C7
SUPERIOR AV
CONCRETE WA 102-C2
SUPERIOR ST
CITY OF VICTORIA BC 256-F10
SUPERIOR ST U.S.-95
CAMBRIDGE ID 139-B1
SANDPOINT ID 244-A2
S SUPERIOR ST U.S.-95
CAMBRIDGE ID 139-B1
SUQUAMISH WY NE
SUQUAMISH WA 170-C7
SURBER DR NE
SEATTLE WA 275-E6
SURF ST
WESTPORT WA 298-G14
SURFACE RD
ISLAND CO WA 171-A2
LANGLEY WA 171-A2
SURF PINES RD
CLATSOP CO WA 188-B4
SURPRISE VALLEY RD
MODOC CO CA 152-B3
SUSAN RD
KITTITAS CO WA 241-A6
SUSBAUER RD
WASHINGTON CO OR 198-C1
SUSSEX ST Rt#-507
TENINO WA 184-D3
THURSTON CO WA 184-D3
SUTHERLIN-NONPAREIL RD
DOUGLAS CO OR 141-B2
DOUGLAS CO OR 221-D1
SUTHERLIN-UMPQUA RD
DOUGLAS CO OR 221-B1
SUTTER RD
CLALLAM CO WA 165-D6
SUTTLE RD
CLACKAMAS CO OR 200-B4
LANE CO OR 133-A3
SUTTLE LAKE LP
JEFFERSON CO OR 211-B2
SUTTLE-SHERMAN RD
JEFFERSON CO OR 211-B2
SUTTON RD
ADAMS CO WA 121-C1
SUTTON BEACH RD
LANE CO OR 214-B1
SUTTON CREEK RD
TILLAMOOK CO OR 197-B3
SUTTON LAKE RD
LANE CO OR 214-B1
SUVER RD
POLK CO OR 207-B2
SWAKANE CANYON RD
CHELAN CO WA 238-C1
SWALLEY RD
DESCHUTES CO OR 212-C7
SWALLOW DR
JEFFERSON CO OR 212-C2
SWAMP CREEK RD
MALHEUR CO OR 146-A1
SWAMP CREEK TO COUNTY LINE RD
GRANT CO OR 136-C3
SWAMP WELLS RD
DESCHUTES CO OR 217-C6
E SWAN AV
SILETZ OR 206-C2
SWAN RD
SKAGIT CO WA 260-H8
SWAN FALLS RD
ADA CO ID 147-C2
ADA CO ID 253-A6
SWAN HILL RD
DOUGLAS CO OR 221-A6
SWANK DR
LINN CO OR 207-D6
SWAN LAKE RD
FERRY CO WA 105-B2
KLAMATH CO OR 235-C1
SWAN SLOUGH RD
SNOHOMISH WA 269-H2
SWANSON RD
WHITMAN CO WA 249-A1
SWANSON GULCH RD
CHELAN CO WA 236-C1
SWANSONVILLE RD
JEFFERSON CO WA 170-B2
SWANS TRAIL RD
SNOHOMISH WA 269-J2
W SWANTOWN RD
ISLAND CO WA 167-B2
OAK HARBOR WA 167-B2
SWARTZ BAY-TSAWWASSEN FERRY
BRITISH COLUMBIA 101-B1
BRITISH COLUMBIA 159-C1

STREET City State Page-Grid

SWARTZ BAY-TSAWWASSEN FERRY
DIST OF NORTH SAANICH BC 159-C1
SWARTZ CANYON RD
CROOK CO OR 213-C7
SWAUK PRAIRIE RD
KITTITAS CO WA 240-D1
SWAWILLA BASIN RD
FERRY CO WA 113-B1
SWEDE BASIN RD
JOSEPHINE CO OR 148-C1
JOSEPHINE CO OR 233-B1
E SWEDE HILL RD
ISLAND CO WA 171-A3
SWEDE RIDGE RD
DESCHUTES CO OR 216-D3
DESCHUTES CO OR 217-A3
SWEDETOWN RD
COLUMBIA CO OR 117-B3
COLUMBIA CO OR 189-A5
SWEENEY RD SE
KING CO WA 175-D6
SWEENEY GULCH RD
GARFIELD CO WA 122-B2
SWEET RD
WHATCOM CO WA 158-B3
SWEET CREEK RD
LANE CO OR 214-D4
SWEGLE RD NE
FOUR CORNERS OR 323-F12
SALEM OR 323-F12
SWENSON RD
STEVENS CO WA 114-B1
STEVENS CO WA 246-A1
SWENSON-WILLIAMS VALLEY RD
STEVENS CO WA 114-B1
SWIFT AV S
SEATTLE WA 282-C7
SEATTLE WA 286-C1
SWIFT BLVD
RICHLAND WA 341-D1
SWINDLER RD
LEWIS CO WA 187-C4
SYDNAM RD
COOS CO OR 224-B1
SYKES RD
SAINT HELENS OR 192-A2
NE SYLVAN WY
BREMERTON WA 270-J7
BREMERTON WA 271-A7
KITSAP CO WA 270-G7
KITSAP CO WA 271-A7
SYLVAN WY SW
SEATTLE WA 281-F7
SEATTLE WA 285-F1
SYLVESTER RD
BRITISH COLUMBIA 94-B3
W SYLVESTER ST
PASCO WA 343-C7
WEST PASCO WA 342-J7
WEST PASCO WA 343-A7
SYLVIA LAKE RD
MONTESANO WA 178-D7
SYMONS ST
RICHLAND WA 340-F14

T

T AV
ANACORTES WA 259-H4
T RD NW
DOUGLAS CO WA 236-B5
T 1-2-SW ST
GRANT CO WA 120-B1
TABLE ROCK RD
JACKSON CO OR 230-C6
JACKSON CO OR 336-C3
MEDFORD OR 336-B8
TABLE ROCK TRAIL RD
JACKSON CO OR 230-C5
N TACOMA AV
PASCO WA 343-G7
TACOMA WA 293-F3
S TACOMA AV
TACOMA WA 293-G5
TACOMA WA 295-H3
SE TACOMA ST
PORTLAND OR 317-H6
PORTLAND OR 318-A7
S TACOMA WY
LAKEWOOD WA 181-D4
TACOMA WA 181-D4
TACOMA WA 293-H7
TACOMA WA 294-D2
TACOMA WA 295-H1
TACOMA MALL
TACOMA WA 295-E5
TACOMA MALL BLVD
TACOMA WA 295-E7
S TACOMA MALL BLVD
TACOMA WA 294-E3
TACOMA WA 295-E4
TAFT ST
BOISE ID 253-C2
TAFT ST Rt#-8
ELK RIVER ID 123-C1
TAHUYA BLACKSMITH RD
MASON CO WA 173-B5
TAHUYA LAKE RD NW
KITSAP CO WA 173-D2
TAHUYA RIVER DR
MASON CO WA 173-C6
TAHUYA RIVER RD
MASON CO WA 173-B6
TALACHE RD
BONNER CO ID 244-A4
TALAPUS RIDGE RD
MULTNOMAH CO OR 194-C7
MULTNOMAH CO OR 201-C1
TALA SHORE DR
JEFFERSON CO WA 170-B3
TALBOT RD
MARION CO OR 207-D2
TALBOT RD S
KING CO WA 175-C6
MARION CO OR 207-D2
RENTON WA 175-C6
TALBOT RD SE
MARION CO OR 207-C2

STREET City State Page-Grid

TALBOTT LN
LANE CO OR 210-A5
TALLEY AV
KELSO WA 303-E11
TALLEY WY
KELSO WA 303-E11
TALLMAN RD
LINN CO OR 207-D6
TALL PINES RD
KOOTENAI CO ID 247-D4
TALMAGE RD
POLK CO OR 204-B7
TALMAKS RD
LEWIS CO ID 123-B2
TAMARACK LN
MAPLE RIDGE BC 157-D6
TAMPICO RD
BENTON CO OR 207-A3
TANDY LN
LINN CO OR 210-A4
TANEUM RD
KITTITAS CO WA 240-D4
TANGELWOOD LN
DOUGLAS CO OR 221-A4
TANGEN RD
YAMHILL CO OR 198-C5
TANGENT DR
LINN CO OR 207-B6
TANGENT OR 207-C6
TANGENT LP
LINN CO OR 207-C7
TANGENT ST Rt#-34
LEBANON OR 133-C1
TANKE RD
LINCOLN CO WA 113-C2
TANNER RD
DIST OF CENTRAL SAANICH BC 159-C4
TANNER CREEK RD
MULTNOMAH CO OR 194-C7
WASHINGTON CO OR 198-A1
S TAPPS DR E
PIERCE CO WA 182-C3
W TAPPS DR E
PIERCE CO WA 182-C3
W TAPPS HWY
BONNEY LAKE WA 182-C3
TARBOO LAKE RD
JEFFERSON CO WA 109-C1
TARGEE ST
ADA CO ID 253-B3
TARLATT RD
PACIFIC CO WA 186-A5
TARTAR GULCH RD
JOSEPHINE CO OR 233-C5
TATLOW RD
DIST OF NORTH SAANICH BC 159-B1
TATTERSALL DR
DISTRICT OF SAANICH BC 256-G5
TAUFFEN RD
WHITMAN CO WA 250-A2
TAUMARSON RD
COLLEGE PLACE WA 344-G12
WALLA WALLA CO WA 344-H12
WALLA WALLA CO WA 345-A12
TAURUS ST
OCEAN SHORES WA 298-B1
TAUSCHER RD
LEWIS CO WA 187-D1
TAUSICK WY
WALLA WALLA WA 345-G6
WALLA WALLA CO WA 345-G6
TAYLOR AV
ASTORIA WA 300-A5
BELLINGHAM WA 258-C10
TAYLOR AV N
SEATTLE WA 277-J2
TAYLOR RD
JACKSON CO OR 230-C7
LEWIS CO WA 187-D1
WALLA WALLA CO WA 344-E12
YAKIMA CO WA 243-B5
E TAYLOR RD
SPOKANE CO WA 246-B6
N TAYLOR RD
ISLAND CO WA 167-C2
TAYLOR ST E
EDGEWOOD WA 182-B2
MILTON WA 182-B2
TAYLOR WY
DIST OF WEST VANCOUVER BC 254-F2
FIFE WA 182-A2
PIERCE CO WA 182-A2
TACOMA WA 182-A2
TAYLOR WY Rt#-99
DIST OF WEST VANCOUVER BC 254-E4
TAYLOR FLATS RD
FRANKLIN CO WA 121-A2
TAYLOR RANCH RD
JEFFERSON CO WA 109-C1
TAYLOR VALLEY RD
CLARK CO WA 192-D1
SW TAYLORS FERRY RD
PORTLAND OR 316-B7
PORTLAND OR 317-E6
PORTLAND OR 320-A1
T CARRY RD
CLARK CO WA 193-A1
TEAGUE RD
LEWIS CO WA 184-A5
TEAL RD
DESCHUTES CO OR 217-D3
TEAL LAKE RD
JEFFERSON CO WA 170-B4
TEANAWAY RD
KITTITAS CO WA 240-C1
TEANAWAY WILSN STOCK TR
KITTITAS CO WA 241-B1
TEATERS RD
CROOK CO OR 136-A3
TECHNOLOGY LP
CORVALLIS OR 327-B12
TECHNOR ROBISON RD
SISKIYOU CO CA 150-B3
TEITZEL RD
LEWIS CO WA 184-C5
TEKOA-FARMINGTON RD
TEKOA WA 114-C3
WHITMAN CO WA 114-C3
WHITMAN CO WA 115-A3

STREET City State Page-Grid

TEKOA OAKSDALE RD Rt#-27
OAKESDALE WA 114-C3
WHITMAN CO WA 114-C3
TELEGRAPH RD
BRITISH COLUMBIA 159-A1
LEWIS CO WA 187-C4
TELEGRAPH TR
TOWNSHIP OF LANGLEY BC 157-C7
TELEPHONE RD
DESCHUTES CO OR 216-D5
TELEPHONE POLE RD
UMATILLA CO OR 121-C3
SE TELFORD RD
CLACKAMAS CO OR 200-B3
MULTNOMAH CO OR 200-B2
TELOCASET LN
UNION CO OR 130-B3
E TEMPLE RD
SPOKANE CO WA 247-A1
TEMPLETON RD
COOS CO OR 218-C4
TEN BAR RD
DESCHUTES CO OR 217-D3
TEN EYCK RD
CLACKAMAS CO OR 200-D3
SANDY OR 200-D3
NW TENINO RD
JEFFERSON CO OR 135-A1
WARM SPRINGS OR 208-A3
TEN MILE RD
ADA CO ID 253-A2
TENMILE RD
MALHEUR CO OR 154-B2
N TEN MILE RD
ADA CO ID 253-A5
S TEN MILE RD
ADA CO ID 253-A4
TEN MILE CREEK RD
ADA CO ID 253-B5
TENMILE CREEK RD
LANE CO OR 209-A5
TENNANT WY
LONGVIEW WA 303-A10
TENNANT WY Rt#-432
COWLITZ CO WA 303-C12
LONGVIEW WA 303-B11
TENNESSEE RD
LEWIS CO WA 187-C3
LINN CO OR 133-C1
TENT CREEK RD
MALHEUR CO OR 155-A2
TENTH ST
KETTLE FALLS WA 106-A2
NESPELEM WA 105-A3
TERMINAL AV
VANCOUVER BC 254-J11
VANCOUVER BC 255-B12
SW TERRA DR
JEFFERSON CO OR 212-C1
TERRACE HEIGHTS DR
TERRACE HEIGHTS WA 243-C6
YAKIMA WA 243-C6
YAKIMA CO WA 243-C6
TERRA FERN DR
CLACKAMAS CO OR 201-A4
TERREBONNE-LWR BRDG WY
DESCHUTES CO OR 212-C3
TERREBONNE OR 212-C3
NE TERRE VIEW DR
PULLMAN WA 249-B4
TERRI DR
JACKSON CO OR 234-C2
TERRITORIAL HWY
BENTON CO OR 133-B2
DOUGLAS CO OR 133-B3
LANE CO OR 133-B2
VENETA OR 133-B3
TERRITORIAL RD
COLUMBIA CO OR 122-A2
DOUGLAS CO OR 219-B1
NE TERRITORIAL RD
CANBY OR 199-C6
CLACKAMAS CO OR 199-C6
TERRITORIAL ST
HARRISBURG OR 210-A5
LINN CO OR 210-A5
TERRY RD
COUPEVILLE WA 167-B4
ISLAND CO WA 167-B4
SW TERWILLIGER BLVD
CLACKAMAS OR 321-F3
LAKE OSWEGO OR 321-F3
MULTNOMAH OR 321-E2
PORTLAND OR 316-E3
PORTLAND OR 317-E1
PORTLAND OR 320-E1
PORTLAND OR 321-E2
TETHEROW RD
DESCHUTES CO OR 212-C5
N TEXAS RD
SKAGIT CO WA 160-C6
TEXAS LAKE RD
WHITMAN CO WA 114-A3
TEXMAR ST SW
OCEAN SHORES WA 298-C3
THAIN RD
LEWISTON ID 250-C4
THATCHER RD
FOREST GROVE OR 198-B1
WASHINGTON CO OR 125-B1
WASHINGTON CO OR 198-B1
THATCHER PASS RD
SAN JUAN CO WA 160-A5
THAYER DR
RICHLAND WA 340-F13
RICHLAND WA 341-F1
THAYER RD
LEWIS CO WA 187-D3
S THAYER RD
CLACKAMAS CO OR 199-D5
NW THEATER AV
DESCHUTES CO OR 212-C4
THE DALLES-CALIF HWY U.S.-97
BEND OR 332-D14
BEND OR 332-F3
CHILOQUIN OR 231-D3
DESCHUTES CO OR 143-A1
DESCHUTES CO OR 212-C7
DESCHUTES CO OR 217-C1

STREET City State Page-Grid

THE DALLES-CALIF HWY U.S.-97
DESCHUTES CO OR 332-D14
DESCHUTES CO OR 332-G3
DESCHUTES RIVER WOODS OR 217-C1
DESCHUTES RIVER WOODS OR 332-D14
DUFUR OR 127-B2
JEFFERSON CO OR 135-B1
JEFFERSON CO OR 208-C4
JEFFERSON CO OR 208-C6
JEFFERSON CO OR 212-D3
KLAMATH CO OR 142-C3
KLAMATH CO OR 143-A1
KLAMATH CO OR 150-C1
KLAMATH CO OR 231-D3
KLAMATH CO OR 235-C1
KLAMATH CO OR 338-A1
KLAMATH FALLS OR 338-A1
MADRAS OR 208-C4
MADRAS OR 208-C5
MAUPIN OR 127-B3
REDMOND OR 212-D3
TERREBONNE OR 212-D3
THE DALLES OR 196-D7
WASCO CO OR 127-B2
WASCO CO OR 127-B3
WASCO CO OR 135-B1
WASCO CO OR 196-D7
THE EVERGREEN COLLEGE PKWY
THURSTON CO WA 296-A2
THERMAL DR
COQUITLAM BC 157-A4
THIEF CREEK RD
DOUGLAS CO OR 219-B3
THIELSON ST
ECHO OR 129-A1
UMATILLA CO OR 129-A1
N THIERMAN RD
SPOKANE CO WA 350-A1
S THIERMAN ST
SPOKANE CO WA 350-A9
THIESEN RD
NEZ PERCE CO ID 250-C5
SE THIESSEN RD
CLACKAMAS CO OR 199-D3
THILLBERG RD
SKAGIT CO WA 260-G7
THIRD
DESCHUTES CO OR 212-A6
THIRD AV
FERNDALE WA 158-C6
E THIRD AV
EAST PORT ORCHARD WA 271-A14
THIRD AV NW
OKANOGAN WA 104-C3
THIRD AV SW
OKANOGAN WA 104-C3
THIRD ST
FARMINGTON WA 115-A3
LINCOLN CO WA 114-A2
WHITMAN CO WA 115-A3
THIRD ST Rt#-507
TENINO WA 184-D3
THIRD FORK RD
GEM CO ID 139-C2
SW THIRTEENTH ST
CHEHALIS WA 299-F13
THOMAS
CROOK CO OR 213-D6
THOMAS RD
CLACKAMAS CO OR 126-A3
CLACKAMAS CO OR 200-D3
KING CO WA 182-D1
KITTITAS CO WA 241-C4
SKAGIT CO WA 161-A5
STEVENS CO WA 105-C3
STEVENS CO WA 106-A3
THOMAS RD KPN
PIERCE CO WA 174-A7
E THOMAS ST
SEATTLE WA 278-C4
THOMAS CREEK DR
LINN CO OR 134-A1
THOMAS CREEK RD
LAKE CO OR 152-A2
S THOMAS-MALLEN RD
SPOKANE CO WA 246-A5
THOMLE RD
SNOHOMISH CO WA 168-A4
THOMPSON AV
DOUGLAS CO OR 221-B6
WINSTON OR 221-B6
S THOMPSON AV
TACOMA WA 295-G1
THOMPSON LN
YAMHILL CO OR 198-C7
THOMPSON RD
CLALLAM CO WA 166-C7
COOS BAY OR 333-F7
YAKIMA CO WA 243-A5
E THOMPSON RD
OWYHEE CO ID 147-B1
W THOMPSON RD
KOOTENAI CO ID 247-D4
THOMPSON ST
SUMNER WA 182-B3
THOMPSON CREEK RD
JACKSON CO OR 149-B2
JOSEPHINE CO OR 149-B2
JOSEPHINE CO OR 233-C2
LANE CO OR 209-C7
LANE CO OR 214-D1
THOMPSON LAKE RD
KOOTENAI CO ID 248-B4
THOMPSON MILL RD
MULTNOMAH CO OR 200-D1
THOMSEN RD
HOOD RIVER CO OR 195-D7
S THOR ST
SPOKANE WA 349-F10
SE THORBURN ST
PORTLAND OR 314-E6
PORTLAND OR 315-E6
NE THORMAN AV
KEIZER OR 323-A6
THORN CREEK RD
WHITMAN CO WA 114-B3
THORNDYKE AV W
SEATTLE WA 273-E7

THORNDYKE AV W
SEATTLE WA 276-E1
SEATTLE WA 277-E1
N THORNE LN SW
LAKEWOOD WA 181-C5
THORN HOLLOW RD
COLUMBIA CO WA 122-A2
THORN PRAIRIE RD
DOUGLAS CO OR 223-A3
THORN SPRING RD
JEFFERSON CO OR 211-D1
THORNTON RD
WHATCOM CO WA 158-C5
THORNTON CREEK RD
LINCOLN CO OR 206-D4
W THORNTON LAKE DR
ALBANY OR 326-A6
THORP HWY
KITTITAS CO WA 241-A4
S THORPE RD
SPOKANE WA 348-G12
W THORPE RD
SPOKANE WA 348-E14
SPOKANE CO WA 114-B2
SPOKANE CO WA 246-A5
SPOKANE CO WA 348-E14
THORP PRAIRIE RD
KITTITAS CO WA 240-C2
THOUSAND SPRINGS RD
JACKSON CO OR 227-A4
THRALL RD
KITTITAS CO WA 241-C7
THRALL RD Rt#-821
KITTITAS CO WA 241-B7
THREE CREEKS LAKE RD
DESCHUTES CO OR 211-D5
DESCHUTES CO OR 216-C1
SISTERS OR 211-D5
THREE DEVILS GRADE RD SW
DOUGLAS CO WA 112-B2
THREE FORKS RD
MALHEUR CO OR 146-C3
MALHEUR CO OR 147-A3
MALHEUR CO OR 155-A1
N THREE FORKS RD
KOOTENAI CO ID 247-C1
THREE FRKS RESERVOIR RD
MALHEUR CO OR 146-A3
THREE LAKES RD
ALBANY OR 326-H11
LINN CO OR 326-H11
SNOHOMISH CO WA 110-C1
SNOHOMISH CO WA 171-D3
THREE MILE LN
MCMINNVILLE OR 198-A7
YAMHILL CO OR 198-A7
THREEMILE RD
WASCO CO OR 127-A2
WASCO CO OR 196-C7
THREE PINES RD
JOSEPHINE CO OR 229-B3
THREE RIVERS HWY Rt#-22
POLK CO OR 125-A3
TILLAMOOK CO OR 197-B6
TILLAMOOK CO OR 203-D1
YAMHILL CO OR 125-A3
YAMHILL CO OR 203-D1
THREE ROCKS RD
LINCOLN CO OR 203-B3
THREE TRAPPER RD
DESCHUTES CO OR 216-C7
THRESHER AV
BANGOR TRIDENT BASE WA 170-B7
THUMPER RD
DESCHUTES CO OR 211-C5
NW THURMAN ST
PORTLAND OR 312-E4
THURNER RD
WASHINGTON CO OR 198-C3
THURSTON RD
LANE CO OR 215-D2
SPRINGFIELD OR 215-D2
SPRINGFIELD OR 331-J6
NE THURSTON WY
VANCOUVER WA 307-F1
TIBBETS MOUNTAIN RD
CHELAN CO WA 238-C1
TIBBLING RD
YAKIMA CO WA 243-B5
TICKLE CREEK RD
CLACKAMAS CO OR 200-B3
TIDE AV
TILLAMOOK CO OR 191-A3
TIDE CREEK RD
COLUMBIA CO OR 189-C6
TIDELAND RD
TILLAMOOK CO OR 191-B4
TIDEWATER RD
LINCOLN CO OR 209-D2
TIEDMAN RD KPS
PIERCE CO WA 180-D2
E TIETAN ST
WALLA WALLA WA 345-C10
W TIETAN ST
WALLA WALLA WA 345-A10
WALLA WALLA CO WA 345-A10
W TIETON AV
COUNTRY HOMES WA 346-J12
TIETON DR
YAKIMA CO WA 243-A7
W TIETON DR
YAKIMA WA 243-A7
TIETON RESERVOIR RD
YAKIMA CO WA 119-B2
SE TIGER MOUNTAIN RD
KING CO WA 176-A5
TIGNER RD
CHELAN CO WA 238-C2
W TILDEN ST
SEATTLE WA 272-D6
TILE FLAT RD
WASHINGTON CO OR 198-D3
WASHINGTON CO OR 199-A3
TILLAMOOK
CROOK CO OR 213-D7
TILLAMOOK AV
BAY CITY OR 197-B1
NE TILLAMOOK ST
PORTLAND OR 314-B3

TILLAMOOK HEAD COVE RD
CLATSOP CO WA 301-C11
SEASIDE WA 301-C11
TILLAMOOK RIVER RD
TILLAMOOK OR 197-B3
TILLAMOOK CO OR 197-B3
TILLAMOOK CO OR 197-B3
TILLER-SOUTH UMPQUA CAMP RD
DOUGLAS CO OR 141-C3
DOUGLAS CO OR 222-A7
DOUGLAS CO OR 226-A1
TILLER-TRAIL HWY Rt#-227
CANYONVILLE OR 225-C3
DOUGLAS CO OR 141-B3
DOUGLAS CO OR 225-C3
JACKSON CO OR 141-C3
JACKSON CO OR 230-D1
TILLEY RD SW
THURSTON CO WA 184-C3
TILLEY RD SW Rt#-121
THURSTON CO WA 184-C2
TILLICUM RD
DISTRICT OF SAANICH BC 256-D5
TOWN OF ESQUILMALT BC 256-D7
SE TILLSTROM RD
CLACKAMAS CO OR 200-B3
TIMBER RD
COLUMBIA CO OR 125-B1
LINN CO OR 210-D3
WASHINGTON CO OR 125-B1
TIMBER ST
ALBANY OR 326-H7
TIMBER TR NE
MARION CO OR 205-D5
TIMBER WY
COOS CO OR 220-D3
TIMBER CREEK RD
JACKSON CO OR 226-A6
TIMBERLINE HWY
CLACKAMAS CO OR 202-A6
TIMBERLINE EAST LEG
CLACKAMAS CO OR 202-A6
TIMBERLINE WEST LEG
CLACKAMAS CO OR 202-A6
NE TIMMEN RD
CLARK CO WA 192-C2
NW TIMMEN RD
CLARK CO WA 192-C2
TIMOTHY LAKE RD
CLACKAMAS CO OR 126-C3
TINGLE RD
LEWIS CO WA 187-C2
TINGLEY LN
KLAMATH CO OR 235-C5
TIPTON RD
KITTITAS CO WA 241-B4
TITCHENAL CANYON RD SW
DOUGLAS CO WA 239-C2
TOAD RD
JACKSON CO OR 229-D3
TOANDOS RD
JEFFERSON CO WA 170-A5
TODEY RD
LEWIS CO WA 187-D5
TOE JAM HILL RD NE
KITSAP CO WA 174-D3
TOFTDAHL RD N
LANE CO OR 210-A5
NE TOHOMISH ST
WHITE SALMON WA 195-D4
TOKELAND RD
PACIFIC CO WA 183-C5
TOKIO RD
ADAMS CO WA 113-B3
HARRINGTON WA 113-C3
LINCOLN CO WA 113-C3
TOLEDO SALMON CREEK RD
LEWIS CO WA 187-D5
TOLEDO SALMON HANKIN RD
LEWIS CO WA 187-D4
TOLEDO VADER RD
LEWIS CO WA 187-C4
TOLEDO WA 187-C4
TOLER RD NW
DOUGLAS CO WA 236-D7
TOLIVER RD
CLACKAMAS CO OR 205-D1
S TOLL RD
SPOKANE CO WA 247-B7
TOLL STATION RD
DESCHUTES CO OR 211-B3
JEFFERSON CO OR 211-B2
TOLMAN RD
LANE CO OR 215-A4
SE TOLMAN ST
PORTLAND OR 318-A5
TOLMAN CREEK RD
JACKSON CO OR 234-D5
N TOLMAN CREEK RD
ASHLAND OR 337-H9
JACKSON CO OR 337-H9
S TOLMAN CREEK RD
ASHLAND OR 337-H11
TOLMIE RD
DISTRICT OF ABBOTSFORD BC 102-B1
TOLO RD
JACKSON CO OR 230-B7
TOLT AV Rt#-203
CARNATION WA 176-B2
KING CO WA 176-B2
NE TOLT HILL RD
KING CO WA 176-A2
TOMLINSON RD
TILLAMOOK CO OR 197-B2
TOM SMITH RD
COOS CO OR 220-B5
TONASKET-HAVILLAH RD
OKANOGAN CO WA 104-C2
OKANOGAN CO WA 105-A1
TONASKET WA 104-C2
TONE RD
TILLAMOOK CO OR 197-B2
TONGUE LN
WASHINGTON CO OR 198-C2
TONO RD SE
THURSTON CO WA 184-D4
SW TONQUIN RD
WASHINGTON CO OR 199-B5

TONY CREEK RD
HOOD RIVER CO OR 202-B1
TOONERVILLE DR
MASON CO WA 173-D4
SW TOOZE RD
CLACKAMAS CO OR 199-A5
TOPE RD
WALLOWA CO OR 130-C1
E TOPPENISH AV
TOPPENISH WA 120-A2
S TOPPENISH AV
TOPPENISH WA 120-A2
TOPPENISH-ZILLAH RD
YAKIMA CO WA 120-A2
ZILLAH WA 120-A2
TOQUA RD
KLAMATH CO OR 231-C5
TORNQUIST RD
GRAYS HARBOR CO WA 179-D5
TORODA BRIDGE CUSTMS RD
FERRY CO WA 105-B1
TORODA CREEK RD
FERRY CO WA 105-B1
OKANOGAN CO WA 105-A2
TORPEDO RD
ISLAND CO WA 167-C2
OAK HARBOR WA 167-C2
TORVEND RD NE
MARION CO OR 205-B4
TOTTEN RD NE
SUQUAMISH WA 170-C7
TOUCHET RD
WALLA WALLA CO WA 121-B3
S TOUCHET RD
COLUMBIA CO WA 122-A3
TOUCHET-GARDENA RD
WALLA WALLA CO WA 121-B3
TOUVELLE RD
JACKSON CO OR 230-C5
N TOWER AV Rt#-507
CENTRALIA WA 299-F3
S TOWER AV
CENTRALIA WA 299-F5
S TOWER AV Rt#-507
CENTRALIA WA 299-F4
TOWER RD
COWLITZ CO WA 118-A2
COWLITZ CO WA 187-C6
MORROW CO OR 128-B1
WHATCOM CO WA 161-A1
TOWER MOUNTAIN RD
SPOKANE CO WA 247-B5
SW TOWLE AV
GRESHAM OR 200-B2
TOWN RD
BRITISH COLUMBIA 102-B1
DISTRICT OF ABBOTSFORD BC 102-B1
TOWNSEND-SACKMAN RD
STEVENS CO WA 106-A2
TOWNSHIP RD
KLAMATH CO OR 235-B7
TOWNSHIP RD Rt#-9
SEDRO-WOOLLEY WA 161-C5
SKAGIT CO WA 161-C5
SE TOWNSHIP RD
CLACKAMAS CO OR 199-C6
TOWNSHIP LINE RD
CLALLAM CO WA 165-D7
N TRACK RD
WAPATO WA 120-A2
YAKIMA CO WA 120-A2
TRACY RD
CLACKAMAS CO OR 200-C6
TRACYTON BLVD NW
KITSAP CO WA 270-E3
SILVERDALE WA 174-B1
SILVERDALE WA 270-E3
TRACYTON WA 270-E3
TRACYTON BEACH RD NW
BREMERTON WA 270-G6
KITSAP CO WA 270-G6
TRACYTON WA 270-G6
TRADE ST Rt#-99W
AMITY OR 204-B2
S TRADE ST Rt#-99W
AMITY OR 204-B2
TRADE ST SE Rt#-22
SALEM OR 322-H13
S TRAFTON ST
TACOMA WA 293-E7
W TRAIL RD
SPOKANE CO WA 246-A3
SPOKANE CO WA 348-A6
TRAIL BUTTE RD
COOS CO OR 218-D6
TRAIL CREEK RD
JACKSON CO OR 230-D1
LANE CO OR 209-C7
TRAIL FORK RD
GILLIAM CO OR 128-A3
TRAILS RD
MASON CO WA 173-C7
TRAM RD
IDAHO CO ID 123-C3
TRAMWAY RD
GARFIELD CO WA 122-C1
TRANS CANADA HWY Rt#-1
BRITISH COLUMBIA 93-C1
BRITISH COLUMBIA 94-C3
BRITISH COLUMBIA 95-A1
BRITISH COLUMBIA 101-A1
BRITISH COLUMBIA 102-B1
BRITISH COLUMBIA 156-A2
BRITISH COLUMBIA 159-A1
CITY OF N VANCOUVER BC 255-A3
CITY OF VICTORIA BC 256-G11
COQUITLAM BC 157-B6
DIST OF N VANCOUVER BC 254-F2
DIST OF N VANCOUVER BC 255-A3
DIST OF WEST VANCOUVER BC 156-A2
DIST OF WEST VANCOUVER BC 254-F2
DISTRICT OF ABBOTSFORD BC 94-C3
DISTRICT OF ABBOTSFORD BC 102-B1
DISTRICT OF BURNABY BC 156-D4
DISTRICT OF BURNABY BC 255-F12
DISTRICT OF CHILLIWACK BC 94-C3
DISTRICT OF COQUITLAM BC 156-D4
DISTRICT OF LANGFORD BC 159-A6
DISTRICT OF MATSQUI BC 102-B1
DISTRICT OF SAANICH BC 256-G5

TRANS CANADA HWY Rt#-1
DISTRICT OF SURREY BC 157-B6
DUNCAN BC 101-A1
HOPE BC 95-A3
NANAIMO BC 93-A3
SQUAMISH BC 93-C1
TOWN OF VIEW ROYAL BC 159-A6
TOWN OF VIEW ROYAL BC 256-B3
TOWNSHIP OF LANGLEY BC 102-B1
TOWNSHIP OF LANGLEY BC 157-B6
TOWNSHIP OF LANGLEY BC 158-D1
VANCOUVER BC 255-F12
WHISTLER BC 93-C1
TRANSFORMER RD
KLAMATH CO OR 151-A2
TRANS PACIFIC PKWY
COOS CO OR 218-A6
TRAP CREEK RD
LINCOLN CO OR 206-D4
TRAP MOUNTAIN RD
DOUGLAS CO OR 223-A4
TRASK RIVER RD
TILLAMOOK CO OR 125-A2
TILLAMOOK CO OR 197-D2
TRAVIS RD
BENTON CO WA 120-C3
TREADWELL RD
LANE CO OR 215-C5
TREE FARM RD
LANE CO OR 215-D1
TREMONT ST
COOS BAY OR 333-H9
TREMONT ST U.S.-101
COOS BAY OR 333-G7
NORTH BEND OR 333-G7
TREMONT ST W
PORT ORCHARD WA 174-B4
E TRENT AV Rt#-290
MILLWOOD WA 350-C5
SPOKANE WA 349-F7
SPOKANE CO WA 349-F7
SPOKANE CO WA 350-C6
TRENT RD Rt#-53
KOOTENAI CO ID 247-C1
E TRENT RD
KOOTENAI CO ID 245-A3
E TRENT RD Rt#-290
MILLWOOD WA 350-E5
OTIS ORCHARDS WA 351-C3
OTIS ORCHARDS WA 352-C7
SPOKANE CO WA 350-E5
SPOKANE CO WA 351-C3
SPOKANE CO WA 352-C7
TRENTWOOD WA 350-E5
TRENTWOOD WA 351-C3
N TRENT RD
KOOTENAI CO ID 115-A1
KOOTENAI CO ID 245-A3
W TRENT RD Rt#-53
KOOTENAI CO ID 247-C1
KOOTENAI CO ID 352-J3
KOOTENAI CO ID 353-A2
TRENTON AV
BREMERTON WA 271-B10
KITSAP CO WA 271-B8
TRESHAM LN
JACKSON CO OR 230-C5
TRESTLE RD
KLAMATH CO OR 235-C1
TRESTLE CREEK RD
BONNER CO ID 244-C2
TREVITT ST
THE DALLES OR 196-C7
TRIANGLE RD
KOOTENAI CO ID 245-B4
OWYHEE CO ID 147-B3
TRIANGLE HILL RD
DESCHUTES CO OR 217-A2
TRIGGER AV
BANGOR TRIDENT BASE WA 170-A7
KITSAP CO WA 170-A7
TRILLIUM LAKE RD
CLACKAMAS CO OR 202-A7
TRIPLE OAK DR
LANE CO OR 210-C7
TRIPOD CAMP RD
JACKSON CO OR 226-B4
NW TROOST ST
DOUGLAS CO OR 334-A6
ROSEBURG OR 334-C4
TROSPER RD SW
THURSTON CO WA 296-C11
TUMWATER WA 296-F11
TROUT LN
DESCHUTES CO OR 212-A6
TROUT CREEK RD
BONNER CO ID 244-C1
CROOK CO OR 135-C1
HOOD RIVER CO OR 202-B1
MALHEUR CO OR 154-A2
MULTNOMAH CO OR 200-D2
NE TROUT CREEK RD
JEFFERSON CO OR 135-C1
SE TROUT CREEK RD
JEFFERSON CO OR 135-C1
TROUT CREEK BUTTE RD
DESCHUTES CO OR 211-B6
SE TROUTDALE RD
TROUTDALE OR 200-B1
TROUT LAKE HWY
KLICKITAT CO WA 119-A3
TROUT LK GREENWOOD RD
KLICKITAT CO WA 119-A3
TROUT LODGE RD
GRANT CO WA 112-C3
TROXELL RD
ISLAND CO WA 167-C1
TROY RD
WALLOWA CO OR 122-C3
WALLOWA CO OR 130-C1
TRUAX RD
SPOKANE CO WA 114-C2
TRUBEL RD
CLACKAMAS CO OR 200-C4
NW TRUE ST
PULLMAN WA 249-B5
TRUITT RD
DOUGLAS CO OR 219-A7
TRUNK RD
DUNCAN BC 101-A1

TRUNK RD
YAMHILL CO OR 198-C6
TSAWWASSEN FERRY CSWY
DISTRICT OF DELTA BC 101-C1
SW TUALATIN RD
TUALATIN OR 199-B4
SW TUALATIN-SHERWOOD RD
SHERWOOD OR 199-B4
TUALATIN OR 199-B4
WASHINGTON CO OR 199-B4
TUALATIN VALLEY HWY Rt#-8
CORNELIUS OR 198-D1
HILLSBORO OR 198-D1
HILLSBORO OR 199-A2
WASHINGTON CO OR 198-D1
WASHINGTON CO OR 199-A2
TUALATIN VALLEY HWY Rt#-47
CARLTON OR 198-B6
FOREST GROVE OR 198-B4
GASTON OR 198-B4
WASHINGTON CO OR 198-B4
YAMHILL OR 198-B4
YAMHILL CO OR 198-B4
SW TUALATIN VALLEY HWY Rt#-8
BEAVERTON OR 199-A2
WASHINGTON CO OR 199-A2
TUB SPRINGS RD
MALHEUR CO OR 146-B3
WASCO CO OR 135-C1
TUCANNON RD
COLUMBIA CO WA 122-A2
TUCKER AV
FRIDAY HARBOR WA 101-C2
TUCKER RD
HOOD RIVER CO OR 195-C5
LEWIS CO WA 118-A2
LEWIS CO WA 187-D3
POLK CO OR 204-A3
TUCKER CREEK CTO
CLATSOP CO WA 188-C3
TUCKNESS RD
MALHEUR CO OR 146-C3
SE TUCKRIDGE RD
CLACKAMAS CO OR 200-D3
TUDOR AV
DISTRICT OF SAANICH BC 257-F5
TUFFRE RD
GRAYS HARBOR CO WA 178-A2
TUKWILA PKWY
TUKWILA WA 289-G5
TULE LAKE RD S
PIERCE CO WA 181-D4
TULIN RD NE
KITSAP CO WA 170-D6
TULL RD
COLUMBIA CO WA 122-A2
NW TUMALO AV
BEND OR 332-D7
TUMALO CREEK RD
DESCHUTES CO OR 217-B1
TUMALO-DESCHUTES HWY
DESCHUTES CO OR 212-C7
DESCHUTES CO OR 217-C1
TUMALO FALLS RD
DESCHUTES CO OR 216-D3
TUMALO LOOP RD
DESCHUTES CO OR 216-D2
DESCHUTES CO OR 217-A3
TUMALO RESERVOIR RD
DESCHUTES CO OR 217-B1
TUM-A-LUM RD
UMATILLA CO OR 121-C3
TUM TUM RD
BENTON CO OR 133-A1
TUMWIT RD
MULTNOMAH CO OR 194-B7
TUNK CREEK RD
OKANOGAN CO WA 104-C2
OKANOGAN CO WA 105-A2
TUNNEL RD
DOUGLAS CO OR 225-B7
KLICKITAT CO WA 195-D4
TUNNEL CREEK RD
JOSEPHINE CO OR 229-A3
TUNNEL HILL RD
LAKE CO OR 152-A2
TUNNEL LOOP RD
JOSEPHINE CO OR 229-A3
TUNWATER ACCESS RD Rt#-117
CLALLAM CO WA 261-C5
PORT ANGELES WA 261-C5
TUPPER RD
MORROW CO OR 128-C3
NW TUPPER RD
YAMHILL CO OR 198-A4
TURK DR
SNOHOMISH CO WA 168-B7
TURKEY CRICK LN
DOUGLAS CO OR 221-B2
TURKEY RANCH RD
WALLA WALLA CO WA 121-C3
TURKEY RUN RD
LANE CO OR 215-B6
TURKINGTON RD
WHATCOM CO WA 161-C1
TURNER RD
COLUMBIA CO WA 122-B2
TURNER RD SE
MARION CO OR 325-E7
SALEM OR 325-B2
TURNER CREEK RD
JEFFERSON CO OR 213-D1
NW TURNER CREEK RD
YAMHILL CO OR 198-A3
TURNER RANCH RD
MALHEUR CO OR 154-A2
TURNERS CUTOFF RD
OKANOGAN CO WA 105-A1
TURNIDGE RD
LINN CO OR 207-C2
TUTTLE LN
WHATCOM CO WA 160-B1
SW TUTUILLA CREEK RD
PENDLETON OR 129-B1
UMATILLA CO OR 129-B1

STREET INDEX

STREET / City State / Page-Grid

TVEIT RD
SNOHOMISH CO WA 168-D5
TWEED RD
DESCHUTES CO OR 212-B7
TWELFTH ST Rt#-28
DAVENPORT WA 114-A2
SE TWELFTH ST
COLLEGE PLACE WA 344-F11
SW TWELFTH ST
COLLEGE PLACE WA 344-E11
WALLA WALLA CO WA 344-E11
TWELVE MILE RD
STEVENS CO WA 106-A2
SW TWENTIETH ST
CHEHALIS WA 299-G14
TWENTYMILE RD
LAKE CO OR 152-B3
MODOC CO CA 152-B3
N TWICKENHAM RD
WHEELER CO OR 136-A1
S TWICKENHAM RD
WHEELER CO OR 136-A1
TWIN BRIDGE RD
FERRY CO WA 106-A2
TWIN BRIDGES RD
CLACKAMAS CO OR 201-D6
TWIN BUTTES W DR
LINN CO OR 210-B3
TWIN HOUSE RD
IDAHO CO ID 123-B3
TWIN LAKES RD
FERRY CO WA 105-C3
N TWIN LAKES RD
DESCHUTES CO OR 142-C1
TWIN OAK RD
KLICKITAT CO WA 196-D6
TWIN PEAKS RD
KOOTENAI CO ID 247-C5
NE TWIN SPITS RD
KITSAP CO WA 170-C3
TWIN SPRINGS RD
MALHEUR CO OR 146-C1
TWISP-CARLTON RD
OKANOGAN CO WA 104-B3
TWISP RIVER RD
OKANOGAN CO WA 104-A3
TWISP-WINTHROP EAST RD
WINTHROP WA 104-A2
TWOMILE RD
COOS CO OR 220-B7
T W WALTERS RD Rt#-26
COLFAX WA 122-C1
TYADMAN RD
KLICKITAT CO WA 196-C7
TYEE DR
WHATCOM CO WA 101-C1
TYEE RD
DOUGLAS CO OR 141-A1
DOUGLAS CO OR 221-A1
TYGH BURN RD
WASCO CO OR 202-D5
TYGH RIDGE MARKET RD
WASCO CO OR 127-B2
TYKESON RD
YAMHILL CO OR 198-C4
TYLER RD
DESCHUTES CO OR 217-B1
TYLER ST
PORT TOWNSEND WA 263-H4
S TYLER ST
TACOMA WA 292-B7
TACOMA WA 294-B3
TYNDALL AV
DISTRICT OF SAANICH BC 257-C2
TYNDALL RD
GRANT CO WA 242-C1
TYNE ST
VANCOUVER BC 156-C5
TYNER ST
PORT COQUITLAM BC 157-B5
TYRELL RD
BENTON CO WA 120-C3
TYRELL RD SE
THURSTON CO WA 184-D4
TY VALLEY RD
LINN CO OR 210-D1
TZOUHALEM RD
BRITISH COLUMBIA 101-A1
DUNCAN BC 101-A1

U

U RD NE
DOUGLAS CO WA 113-A1
U RD SW
DOUGLAS CO WA 239-B2
U ST
PORT TOWNSEND WA 263-G2
U 1-2 RD NW
DOUGLAS CO WA 236-B7
UDELL RD
SNOHOMISH CO WA 168-D3
UDELL HANSEN RD
PACIFIC CO WA 183-B4
SE UGLOW AV
DALLAS OR 204-A6
POLK CO OR 204-A6
UKIAH-ALBEE RD
UKIAH OR 129-B3
UMATILLA CO OR 129-B3
UKIAH-HILGARD HWY Rt#-244
UKIAH OR 129-B3
UMATILLA CO OR 129-B3
UNION CO OR 129-C3
UNION CO OR 130-A2
ULRICH RD
JACKSON CO OR 226-B7
ULRICK RD
WHATCOM CO WA 158-C6
UMAPINE RD
UMATILLA CO OR 121-C3
UMAPINE-BEAUCHAMP RD
UMATILLA CO OR 121-C3
UMATILLA
CROOK CO OR 213-D7
UMATILLA AV
PORT TOWNSEND WA 263-E3
UMATILLA MISSION HWY
MISSION OR 129-B1
UMATILLA CO OR 129-B1
UMATILLA RIVER RD
HERMISTON OR 129-A1
UMATILLA CO OR 129-A1
UMATILLA-STANFLD HWY U.S.-395
HERMISTON OR 129-A1
STANFIELD OR 129-A1
UMATILLA OR 129-A1
UMATILLA CO OR 129-A1
UMIKER RD
COWLITZ CO WA 118-A2
UMPQUA AV Rt#-38
REEDSPORT OR 218-C1
UMPQUA HWY Rt#-38
DOUGLAS CO OR 140-C1
DOUGLAS CO OR 141-A1
DOUGLAS CO OR 218-D2
DOUGLAS CO OR 219-A2
DRAIN OR 219-A2
ELKTON OR 141-A1
REEDSPORT OR 218-D2
UMPQUA HWY Rt#-99
DOUGLAS CO OR 219-A2
DRAIN OR 219-A2
N UMPQUA RD
DOUGLAS CO OR 222-D3
DOUGLAS CO OR 223-B2
UMPQUA ST NE
MARION CO OR 205-A3
UMPTANUM RD
KITTITAS CO WA 241-B7
UNDERHILL AV
DISTRICT OF BURNABY BC 156-D4
UNDERPASS RD
DOUGLAS CO OR 219-A7
DOUGLAS CO OR 221-C1
UNDERWOOD RD
CLARK CO WA 192-D1
N UNDERWOOD ST
KENNEWICK WA 343-A10
UNDIE RD
CLALLAM CO WA 169-D3
UNGER RD
CLACKAMAS CO OR 126-A3
CLACKAMAS CO OR 200-A7
S UNGER RD
CLACKAMAS CO OR 126-A3
SW UNGER RD
WASHINGTON CO OR 198-C2
UNICK RD
WHATCOM CO WA 158-B6
UNION AV
BREMERTON WA 270-D12
GRANTS PASS OR 335-D11
NAVY YARD CITY WA 270-D12
OLYMPIA WA 296-H6
OLYMPIA WA 297-A6
PIERCE CO WA 181-C4
STEILACOOM WA 181-C4
N UNION AV
TACOMA WA 292-C4
S UNION AV
DOUGLAS CO WA 239-B5
TACOMA WA 292-C5
TACOMA WA 294-C2
W UNION AV
PALOUSE WA 249-B1
UNION AV NE
RENTON WA 175-C4
N UNION CT
PORTLAND OR 309-F2
NE UNION RD
CLARK CO WA 192-C4
E UNION ST
SEATTLE WA 278-D5
N UNION ST
KENNEWICK WA 342-G10
S UNION ST
BENTON CO WA 342-G11
KENNEWICK WA 342-G11
SE UNION ST Rt#-500
CAMAS WA 193-B7
UNION ST NE
SALEM OR 322-J12
UNION BAY PL
SEATTLE WA 274-D5
UNION CREEK RD
JACKSON CO OR 226-D4
JACKSON CO OR 227-A4
UNION FLAT RD
WHITMAN CO WA 122-C1
WHITMAN CO WA 249-A7
UNION FLAT CREEK RD
WHITMAN CO WA 122-B1
UNION HALL RD
CLACKAMAS CO OR 199-D7
NE UNION HILL RD
KING CO WA 175-D1
KING CO WA 176-A1
UNION MILLS RD
CLACKAMAS CO OR 126-A3
S UNION MILLS RD
CLACKAMAS CO OR 126-A3
UNION MILLS RD SE
THURSTON CO WA 181-A6
UNION SCHOOL RD NE
MARION CO OR 205-C2
UNIONTOWN RD
LATAH CO ID 250-B1
UNIONTOWN EAST RD
WHITMAN CO WA 250-B1
SE UNIONVALE RD
YAMHILL CO OR 204-D2
UNION VALLEY LOOP RD
CHELAN CO WA 236-C2
UNITED BLVD
COQUITLAM BC 157-A5
UNIVERSITY AV Rt#-47
FOREST GROVE OR 198-B1
UNIVERSITY BLVD
UNIV ENDOWMENT LANDS BC 156-A4
UNIVERSITY DR
DISTRICT OF BURNABY BC 156-D4
N UNIVERSITY RD
OPPORTUNITY WA 350-F8
S UNIVERSITY RD
DISHMAN WA 350-F11
OPPORTUNITY WA 350-F11
UNIVERSITY WY
SEATTLE WA 274-C5
UPAS AV
DESCHUTES CO OR 212-D5
DESCHUTES CO OR 213-A5
UPDIKE BEAR CREEK RD
LINCOLN CO OR 206-D5
UPHAM ST
KLAMATH FALLS OR 338-D6
UPPER AV
GEM CO ID 139-B3
UPPER DR
CLACKAMAS OR 320-A7
CLACKAMAS CO OR 199-B3
LAKE OSWEGO OR 320-A7
PORTLAND OR 199-B4
SW UPPER BOONS FERRY DR
TIGARD OR 199-B3
SW UPPER BOONS FERRY RD
DURHAM OR 199-B4
TIGARD OR 199-B4
TUALATIN OR 199-B4
UPPER CALAPOOIA DR
LINN CO OR 133-C2
LINN CO OR 134-A2
UPPER CLEVELAND RAPIDS RD
DOUGLAS CO OR 221-B3
UPPER COCOLALLA CK RD
BONNER CO ID 244-A5
UPPER COW CREEK RD
DOUGLAS CO OR 225-D6
UPPER CROSSING RD
JEFFERSON CO OR 135-A1
UPPER DEADWOOD CK RD
LINCOLN CO OR 209-D4
UPPER DESCHUTES RD
DESCHUTES CO OR 216-C7
UPPER DIAMOND RD
WALLOWA CO OR 130-B1
UPPER DRY CREEK RD
WALLA WALLA CO WA 122-A3
WARM SPRINGS OR 208-A2
UPPER EIGHTMILE RD
WASCO CO OR 127-A2
UPPER FERRY LN
UNION CO OR 130-A2
UPPER FORDS CREEK RD
CLEARWATER CO ID 123-C2
UPPER GREEN CANYON RD
KITTITAS CO WA 241-A2
UPPER HAYDEN LAKE RD
KOOTENAI CO ID 355-G1
UPPER HIGHLAND RD
CLACKAMAS CO OR 200-A7
UPPER HOH RD
JEFFERSON CO WA 108-C1
JEFFERSON CO WA 109-A1
UPPER HORSE CAMP RESERVOIR RD
MALHEUR CO OR 154-C1
MALHEUR CO OR 155-A1
UPPER IMNAHA RD
WALLOWA CO OR 131-A2
UPPER INJUN CREEK RD
JACKSON CO OR 226-D5
UPPER JOE CREEK RD
CHELAN CO WA 236-B1
UPPER KEITH RD
CITY OF N VANCOUVER BC 255-B5
UPPER LEVELS HWY Rt#-1
CITY OF N VANCOUVER BC 255-D4
DIST OF N VANCOUVER BC 254-H3
DIST OF N VANCOUVER BC 255-D4
DIST OF WEST VANCOUVER BC 156-A2
DIST OF WEST VANCOUVER BC 254-A1
UPPER LOOP RD
COOS CO OR 220-D3
UPPER MAPLE CREEK RD
LANE CO OR 214-B4
UPPER MIDDLE FORK RD
GRANT CO OR 137-B1
UPPER MOUNTAIN RD
WALLOWA CO OR 131-A3
UPPER NESTUCCA RD
TILLAMOOK CO OR 197-D6
UPPER NORTH FORK RD
LANE CO OR 209-C7
LANE CO OR 214-C1
UPPER OLALLA RD
DOUGLAS CO OR 141-A3
UPPER PEOH POINT RD
KITTITAS CO WA 240-C2
UPPER REYNOLDS CREEK RD
OWYHEE CO ID 147-B2
UPPER RHEA CREEK RD
MORROW CO OR 128-C2
UPPER RIDGE RD
DOUGLAS CO OR 219-A5
EVERETT WA 268-B4
UPPER RIVER RD
JACKSON CO OR 230-B6
JOSEPHINE CO OR 229-B6
JOSEPHINE CO OR 335-A8
UPPER ROCK CREEK RD
GILLIAM CO OR 128-A2
UPPER SAMISH RD
SKAGIT CO WA 161-C4
UPPER SMITH RIVER RD
DOUGLAS CO OR 133-A3
DOUGLAS CO OR 219-A1
UPPER SUMAS MOUNTAIN RD
DISTRICT OF ABBOTSFORD BC 102-B1
S UPPER TERRACE RD
SPOKANE WA 349-B11
UPPER WHETSTONE RD
COLUMBIA CO WA 122-A2
E UPRIVER DR
SPOKANE WA 349-C7
SPOKANE WA 350-A4
SPOKANE CO WA 349-G6
SPOKANE CO WA 350-E3
TRENTWOOD WA 350-E3
UPTON RD
CENTRAL POINT OR 230-C7
JACKSON CO OR 230-C7
URAN RD
SKAMANIA CO WA 193-D7
URQUHART RD
ADAMS CO WA 113-B3
NE U S GRANT PL
PORTLAND OR 314-A3
US RESERVATION RD
BENTON CO WA 120-C2
US RESERVATION RD Rt#-225
BENTON CO WA 120-C2
USTICK RD
CANYON CO ID 147-B1
E USTICK RD
ADA CO ID 253-B2
BOISE ID 253-B2
W USTICK RD
ADA CO ID 253-A2
CANYON CO ID 147-C1
UTSALADY RD
ISLAND CO WA 168-A3

V

V PL
PACIFIC CO WA 186-A1
V RD
WHATCOM CO WA 102-B1
V ST
PACIFIC CO WA 186-A3
VACHTER RD NE
MARION CO OR 205-A1
VAIL LOOP RD SE
THURSTON CO WA 118-A1
VALBY RD
MORROW CO OR 128-B2
VALDE RD
SNOHOMISH CO WA 168-B4
VALE GARDEN RD
CLACKAMAS CO OR 199-C7
VALENTINE RD
SKAGIT CO WA 168-A1
VALENTINE RIDGE RD
GARFIELD CO WA 122-C2
VALE WEST HWY
MALHEUR CO OR 138-C3
VALE-WEST HWY U.S.-20
VALE OR 139-A3
W VALHALLA RD
KOOTENAI CO ID 248-A1
VALLEY AV
SUMNER WA 182-B3
VALLEY AV Rt#-162
PIERCE CO WA 182-B3
SUMNER WA 182-B3
VALLEY AV E
EDGEWOOD WA 182-B3
FIFE WA 182-B3
PIERCE CO WA 182-B3
PUYALLUP WA 182-B3
SUMNER WA 182-B3
VALLEY FRWY Rt#-167
ALGONA WA 182-B2
AUBURN WA 175-B7
AUBURN WA 182-B2
KENT WA 175-B7
KENT WA 291-J7
KING CO WA 175-B7
PACIFIC WA 182-B2
PACIFIC WA 182-B2
RENTON WA 175-B7
VALLEY HWY Rt#-9
WHATCOM CO WA 102-B1
WHATCOM CO WA 161-C2
E VALLEY HWY
KENT WA 175-C6
W VALLEY HWY Rt#-18
SHERIDAN OR 125-B3
WILLAMINA OR 125-B3
YAMHILL CO OR 125-B3
VALLEY PKWY Rt#-11
BELLINGHAM WA 258-C11
VALLEY RD
CASCADE VALLEY WA 242-C3
DOUGLAS CO OR 221-A4
GRANT CO WA 242-C3
HUMBOLDT CO NV 154-A3
LANE CO OR 215-D4
MOSES LAKE WA 242-C3
VALLEY RD Rt#-D2
DEL NORTE CO CA 148-B3
E VALLEY RD
KENT WA 175-C5
RENTON WA 175-C5
NE VALLEY RD
KITSAP CO WA 174-D1
W VALLEY RD
VALLEY CO ID 251-C5
VALLEY ST
ADA CO ID 253-B4
SEATTLE WA 277-J3
SEATTLE WA 278-A3
E VALLEY CHAPEL RD
SPOKANE CO WA 114-C2
SPOKANE CO WA 246-C6
VALLEY CREEK RD NW
POLK CO OR 204-C4
VALLEY GROVE RD
WALLA WALLA CO WA 121-C3
E VALLEY SPRINGS RD
SPOKANE WA 349-H3
SPOKANE CO WA 349-H3
SPOKANE CO WA 350-A2
VALLEY VIEW DR
ALBANY OR 326-A2
MEDFORD OR 336-G11
NW VALLEY VIEW DR
ROSEBURG OR 334-C4
VALLEY VIEW RD
CROOK CO OR 213-B6
DOUGLAS CO OR 221-D1
JACKSON CO OR 234-C2
JACKSON CO OR 337-A4
WHATCOM CO WA 158-C3
S VALLEY VIEW RD
JACKSON CO OR 337-A2
W VALLEY VIEW RD
JACKSON CO OR 234-C3
JACKSON CO OR 337-A2
TALENT OR 234-C3
VALLEY VISTA RD
WASHINGTON CO OR 192-A7
E VALLEYWAY AV
LIBERTY LAKE WA 352-D14
SPOKANE CO WA 352-D14
VALLEY-WESTSIDE RD
STEVENS CO WA 106-A2
VALLEYWOOD DR SE
SALEM OR 324-G7
VAN BELLE RD
YAKIMA CO WA 120-B2
VAN BELLE RD Rt#-223
GRANGER WA 120-A2
YAKIMA CO WA 120-A2
VAN BUREN AV
CORVALLIS OR 327-F9
VAN BUREN AV Rt#-34
CORVALLIS OR 327-F9
LINN CO OR 327-F9
N VANCOUVER AV
PORTLAND OR 309-G4
PORTLAND OR 313-G2
S VANCOUVER ST
BENTON CO WA 343-A13
KENNEWICK WA 343-A13
N VANCOUVER WY
PORTLAND OR 309-F2
NE VANCOUVER MALL DR
VANCOUVER WA 306-E1
VANCOUVER WA 307-F1
VAN CUREN RD
CLACKAMAS CO OR 200-C5
W VAN DAM RD
ISLAND CO WA 167-B3
SW VANDERMOST RD
WASHINGTON CO OR 199-A3
VANDERSCHUERE RD
WASHINGTON CO OR 198-D4
VAN DEUSEN RD
GEM CO ID 139-C3
VANDEVERT RD
DESCHUTES CO OR 217-A7
VAN-DREWSEY RD
HARNEY CO OR 137-C3
VAN DUSEN RD
KOOTENAI CO ID 248-B5
VAN DUYN RD
LANE CO OR 210-B7
N VAN DUYN RD
OKANOGAN WA 104-C3
OKANOGAN CO WA 104-C3
VAN DUYN ST
COBURG OR 210-B7
VAN DYKE RD SW
THURSTON CO WA 184-A4
VAN GIESEN ST
RICHLAND WA 340-E13
VAN GIESEN ST Rt#-224
RICHLAND WA 340-B13
WEST RICHLAND WA 120-C2
W VAN GIESEN ST Rt#-224
BENTON CO WA 340-A12
RICHLAND WA 340-A12
WEST RICHLAND WA 121-A2
WEST RICHLAND WA 340-A12
VAN GILDER RD
SHERMAN CO OR 127-C1
VAN LAKE RD
DESCHUTES CO OR 144-A1
VAN NESS RD
COWLITZ CO WA 187-B7
VAN NESS ST
KLAMATH FALLS OR 338-D5
VANTAGE HWY
KITTITAS CO WA 120-A1
KITTITAS CO WA 241-C5
VANTINE RD
WHITMAN CO WA 249-A1
VANTINE RD SE
THURSTON CO WA 184-D3
VAN TROJAN RD
JEFFERSON CO WA 170-A1
VAN WELL RD
POLK CO OR 204-A4
S VAN WELL ST
DOUGLAS CO WA 239-B5
VARCO RD
DESCHUTES CO OR 212-A6
VASHON HWY SW
KING CO WA 174-D7
KING CO WA 181-D1
VASSAULT ST
TACOMA WA 181-C1
VAUGHN RD
MARION CO OR 207-D2
TILLAMOOK CO OR 197-B1
S VAUGHN RD KPN
PIERCE CO WA 174-A7
NW VAUGHN ST
PORTLAND OR 312-C3
VAY EDGEMERE RD
BONNER CO ID 107-A3
VEAZIE-CUMBERLAND RD
KING CO WA 110-C3
VEDDER RD
DISTRICT OF CHILLIWACK BC 94-C3
DISTRICT OF CHILLIWACK BC 102-C1
VEDDER RD Rt#-1A
DISTRICT OF CHILLIWACK BC 94-C3
VEDDER MOUNTAIN RD
BRITISH COLUMBIA 102-C1
DISTRICT OF CHILLIWACK BC 102-C1
NE VENA AV
TRACYTON WA 270-G4
NW VENA AV
TRACYTON WA 270-G4
VENABLES ST
VANCOUVER BC 255-B11
VENTURA CRES
DIST OF N VANCOUVER BC 255-B1
VERDA LN NE
KEIZER OR 323-B5
SALEM OR 323-B5
N VERDE DR
MALHEUR CO OR 139-A3
ONTARIO OR 139-A3
NW VERDE DR
ONTARIO OR 139-A3
SW VERDE DR
ONTARIO OR 139-A3
VERGEN RD
CLACKAMAS CO OR 199-B6
SW VERMONT ST
PORTLAND OR 316-A5
VERNON AV
DISTRICT OF SAANICH BC 256-F4
VERNON RD
LAKE STEVENS WA 171-D1
SNOHOMISH CO WA 171-D1
SE VERNON RD
CLARK CO WA 193-C6
VERNONIA RD
SAINT HELENS OR 192-B2
WASHINGTON CO OR 125-B1
VETERAN AV
WESTPORT WA 298-G14
VETERANS DR SW
LAKEWOOD WA 181-C5
PIERCE CO WA 181-C5
VETERANS MEMORIAL PKWY
GARDEN CITY ID 253-C2
VEYS DR
KELSO WA 303-D6
VEYS ST
COWLITZ CO WA 303-D6
VIA CASA VILLA
ALBANY OR 326-E9
VIA KACHESS RD
KITTITAS CO WA 111-B3
VICKERY AV E
PIERCE CO WA 182-A4
VICTOR RD
WASCO CO OR 127-A3
VICTOR CUT-OFF RD Rt#-302
MASON CO WA 173-D6
VICTORIA DR
COQUITLAM BC 157-B4
VANCOUVER BC 156-C5
VICTORIA DR S
VANCOUVER BC 255-C11
VICTORIA-SEATTLE FERRY
BRITISH COLUMBIA 165-C1
VICTOR POINT RD NE
MARION CO OR 205-C5
VICTOR POINT RD SE
MARION CO OR 205-C6
VICTORY DR SW
KITSAP CO WA 174-A4
VICTORY RD
LANE CO OR 210-A7
E VICTORY RD
ADA CO ID 253-B3
W VICTORY RD
ADA CO ID 253-A3
BOISE ID 253-C3
SE VIEWPARK RD
KITSAP CO WA 174-C5
VIEWPOINT DR
CULVER OR 208-B7
VIEW POINT RD
CLEARWATER CO ID 123-C2
VIKING WY NW
KITSAP CO WA 170-B7
POULSBO WA 170-B7
E VILAS RD
JACKSON CO OR 230-D7
JACKSON CO OR 336-D3
MEDFORD OR 336-D3
N VILLA RD
NEWBERG OR 198-D5
VILLAGE RD
SNOHOMISH CO WA 168-B3
VILLAGE PARK DR SE
BELLEVUE WA 175-D3
VINE RD
BRIER WA 171-B5
NE VINE ST
ROSEBURG OR 334-G4
VINEYARD DR
KENNEWICK WA 343-C11
VINGIE CREEK RD
LINCOLN CO OR 209-A3
VIOLA WELCHES RD
CLACKAMAS CO OR 200-B6
VIOLET AV Rt#-21
KAHLOTUS WA 121-C1
VIRGINIA AV
NORTH BEND OR 333-E4
VIRGINIA RD
BELLINGHAM WA 258-G6
VIRGINIA ST
MOUNT VERNON WA 260-B13
SEATTLE WA 277-J5
SEATTLE WA 278-A5
VIRGINIA ST Rt#-55
NEW MEADOWS ID 251-A4
VIRGINIA ST U.S.-95
ADAMS CO ID 251-A4
NEW MEADOWS ID 251-A4
VIRGINIA WY
LONGVIEW WA 302-J5
LONGVIEW HEIGHTS WA 302-J5
VIRGINIA VALLEY RD
HARNEY CO OR 145-C2
VIRGIN VALLEY RANCH RD
HUMBOLDT CO NV 153-B3
VISTA AV
BOISE ID 253-C3
SW VISTA AV
PORTLAND OR 312-D7
PORTLAND OR 316-C1
VISTA AV SE
SALEM OR 324-G3
VISTA DR
ASTORIA WA 300-B7
FERNDALE WA 158-C5
KENNEWICK WA 342-D8
WHATCOM CO WA 158-C5
N VISTA RD
DISHMAN WA 350-C8
SPOKANE CO WA 350-C6
VISTA WY
KENNEWICK WA 342-J10
KENNEWICK WA 343-A10
VISTA RAMA DR E
KITSAP CO WA 271-C13
VITAE SPRINGS RD S
MARION CO OR 204-C7
MARION CO OR 324-A8
N VOLLAND ST
KENNEWICK WA 342-G10

STREET / City State / Page-Grid

VOORHIES RD
JACKSON CO OR 234-B2
VULCAN WY
CITY OF RICHMOND BC 156-B6
VYE RD
DISTRICT OF ABBOTSFORD BC 102-B1

W

W AV
RICHLAND WA 340-F6
W ST
CLARK CO WA 193-C7
PORT TOWNSEND WA 263-G2
WAAGA WY Rt#-303
KITSAP CO WA 174-B1
SILVERDALE WA 174-B1
WABASH AV
MEDFORD OR 336-E11
WABASH DR NE
MARION CO OR 205-A3
WABASH RD
DOUGLAS CO OR 222-B1
WACONDA RD NE
MARION CO OR 205-A3
WADDELL CREEK RD SW
THURSTON CO WA 184-B1
WADE RD
LINCOLN CO OR 206-C2
SNOHOMISH CO WA 168-D6
WADSWORTH DR
BOISE ID 253-C3
WADSWORTH RD
CLATSOP CO WA 188-C4
WAGGENER RD
LINN CO OR 210-B4
WAGHORN RD NW
KITSAP CO WA 170-B6
WAGNER RD
CANYON CO ID 147-B1
NEZ PERCE CO ID 250-D4
SNOHOMISH CO WA 110-C1
WALLA WALLA CO WA 121-B3
WHITMAN CO WA 114-A3
WAGNER ST
TWISP WA 104-A3
WAGNER BUTTE TRAIL RD
JACKSON CO OR 234-B5
WAGNER CREEK RD
JACKSON CO OR 234-B3
WAGNER GAP RD
JACKSON CO OR 234-B5
WAGON RD NE
MARION CO OR 205-C3
WAHA RD
NEZ PERCE CO ID 250-D5
WAHANNA RD
CLATSOP CO WA 301-H6
SEASIDE WA 301-H6
WAHA PRAIRIE RD
NEZ PERCE CO ID 250-C6
WAHKEENA DR
OCEAN SHORES WA 298-C3
WAHKIACUS HEIGHTS RD
KLICKITAT CO WA 196-C1
WAHKIACUS HIGH PRAIRIE RD
KLICKITAT CO WA 196-D3
WAHKIAKUM ST
CROOK CO OR 213-B6
WAHL RD
ADAMS CO WA 113-B3
ADAMS CO WA 121-B1
LATAH CO ID 250-D1
S WAHL RD
ISLAND CO WA 170-D2
WAHL LAKE RD
JEFFERSON CO WA 170-A4
WAHLUKE SLOPE RD
GRANT CO WA 120-C1
WAHTONKA RD W
WASCO CO OR 196-B7
WAHTUM LAKE TR
HOOD RIVER CO OR 195-A7
HOOD RIVER CO OR 201-D2
N WAIKIKI RD
COUNTRY HOMES WA 346-H9
FAIRWOOD WA 346-H9
W WAIKIKI RD
FAIRWOOD WA 346-F8
SPOKANE CO WA 346-F8
WAIN RD Rt#-17A
DIST OF NORTH SAANICH BC 159-B2
WAKEFIELD RD
GRAYS HARBOR CO WA 179-B7
S WAKEFIELD RD
ELMA WA 179-B7
GRAYS HARBOR CO WA 179-B7
WAKEFIELD CAMERON LAKE RD
OKANOGAN CO WA 104-C3
WAKLY LN
THURSTON CO WA 184-B3
WAKONDA BEACH RD
LINCOLN CO OR 328-B10
SW WAKONDA BEACH RD
LINCOLN CO OR 328-B10
WALBERG RD
SKAGIT CO WA 161-D6
WALDO RD
JOSEPHINE CO OR 233-A6
WALDO HILLS DR SE
MARION CO OR 205-B6
WALDRICK RD SE
THURSTON CO WA 184-D2
N WALKER AV
ASHLAND OR 337-F9
WALKER RD
COLUMBIA CO OR 189-B5
DESCHUTES CO OR 217-D2
GRAYS HARBOR CO WA 177-D3
LEWIS CO WA 187-C5
UMATILLA CO OR 129-A1
WALLA WALLA CO WA 122-A3
E WALKER RD
LATAH CO ID 249-D2
NW WALKER RD
BEAVERTON OR 199-A1
SW WALKER RD
WASHINGTON CO OR 199-B1
WALKER ST
PORT TOWNSEND WA 263-G5
WALKER VALLEY RD
SKAGIT CO WA 168-C1
WALKING WOODS DR
PORTLAND OR 320-B1
WALL ST
SEATTLE WA 277-J5
VANCOUVER BC 255-C9
N WALL ST
COUNTRY HOMES WA 346-J13
SPOKANE WA 348-J3
TOWN AND COUNTRY WA 346-J13
TOWN AND COUNTRY WA 348-J3
NW WALL ST
BEND OR 332-D8
NW WALL ST U.S.-20
BEND OR 332-E6
S WALL ST
MOUNT VERNON WA 260-B12
WALLACE DR
DIST OF CENTRAL SAANICH BC 159-C3
DISTRICT OF SAANICH BC 159-C3
WALLACE LN
ADAMS CO ID 251-B3
WALLACE RD
MCMINNVILLE OR 198-A7
WALLACE RD Rt#-221
DAYTON OR 198-C7
YAMHILL CO OR 198-C7
YAMHILL CO OR 204-D1
WALLACE RD NW Rt#-221
POLK CO OR 322-E8
SALEM OR 322-E8
WALLACE CREEK RD
LANE CO OR 215-D3
WALLA WALLA RIVER RD
UMATILLA CO OR 129-C1
WALLEN RD
LATAH CO ID 249-D4
WALLENS RD
CLACKAMAS CO OR 200-B7
WALLER RD
PIERCE CO WA 182-A4
WALLER RD S
PIERCE CO WA 182-A5
WALLINGFORD AV N
SEATTLE WA 274-A1
WALLOWA AV
JOSEPH OR 130-C2
WALLOWA LAKE HWY Rt#-82
ELGIN OR 130-B1
ENTERPRISE OR 130-C2
IMBLER OR 130-A2
ISLAND CITY OR 130-A2
LA GRANDE OR 130-A2
LOSTINE OR 130-C2
UNION CO OR 130-B1
WALLOWA OR 130-B1
WALLOWA CO OR 130-B1
WALLOWA MOUNTAIN LP
BAKER CO OR 131-A3
WALLOWA CO OR 131-A3
WALLOWA MOUNTAIN RD
WALLOWA CO OR 131-A2
WALLULA AV
COLLEGE PLACE WA 344-E9
WALLA WALLA CO WA 344-B9
WALLA WALLA WEST WA 344-E9
WALLUPA RD
WALLOWA CO OR 122-C3
WALLOWA CO OR 130-B1
WALLUSKI LOOP RD
CLATSOP CO WA 300-H10
WALNUT AV
BROWNSVILLE OR 210-C2
DESCHUTES CO OR 213-A4
W WALNUT AV
COEUR D'ALENE ID 355-E9
WALNUT BLVD
BENTON CO OR 327-C8
CORVALLIS OR 327-F6
WALNUT DR
LINN CO OR 207-B5
S WALNUT PL
SPOKANE WA 348-H11
N WALNUT RD
EUGENE OR 330-D7
LANE CO OR 330-D7
SPRINGFIELD OR 330-D7
WALNUT ST
EVERETT WA 265-F2
PORT TOWNSEND WA 263-H3
WALLA WALLA CO WA 121-B3
WALNUT ST U.S.-2
NEWPORT WA 106-C3
OLDTOWN ID 106-C3
E WALNUT ST
YAKIMA WA 243-C6
E WALNUT ST Rt#-19
CONDON OR 128-A2
E WALNUT ST Rt#-505
WINLOCK WA 187-C3
N WALNUT ST
SPOKANE WA 348-H8
S WALNUT ST
BOISE ID 253-D3
SPOKANE WA 348-H10
SW WALNUT ST
TIGARD OR 199-B3
WASHINGTON CO OR 199-B3
W WALNUT ST
YAKIMA WA 243-B6
W WALNUT ST Rt#-206
CONDON OR 128-A2
GILLIAM CO OR 128-A2
WALTERS RD
YAKIMA CO WA 243-D7
WALTERS RD S
TACOMA WA 181-C2
WALTON RD
DESCHUTES CO OR 217-B1
WALTRINE RD
WHATCOM CO WA 158-B6
WAMIC MARKET RD
WASCO CO OR 127-A2
WAMIC MILL RD
WASCO CO OR 202-D7
WAMPUM LN
POLK CO OR 204-A5
WAMSTAD RD
CANYON CO ID 139-A3
W WANAMAKER RD
ISLAND CO WA 167-B5
WANETA RD
SUNNYSIDE WA 120-B3
YAKIMA CO WA 120-B3
WANETA RD Rt#-241
SUNNYSIDE WA 120-B2
YAKIMA CO WA 120-B2
WANNACUT LAKE RD
OKANOGAN CO WA 104-C1
WANOGA LOOKOUT RD
DESCHUTES CO OR 216-D5
S WAPATO RD
YAKIMA CO WA 120-A2
W WAPATO RD
YAKIMA CO WA 119-C2
YAKIMA CO WA 120-A2
WAPATO WY Rt#-150
CHELAN CO WA 236-B2
WAPATO LAKE RD
CHELAN CO WA 236-B2
WAPATO SCHOOL RD
YAMHILL CO OR 198-B4
WAPENISH RD
TOPPENISH WA 120-A2
WAPATO WA 120-A2
YAKIMA CO WA 120-A2
WAPENISH RD Rt#-22
SATUS WA 120-A2
YAKIMA CO WA 120-A2
WAPINITIA HWY Rt#-216
WASCO CO OR 127-A3
WAPINITIA RD
WASCO CO OR 127-A3
WAPINITIA MARKET RD
WASCO CO OR 127-A3
WAPITI LN
DOUGLAS CO OR 221-A1
NE WARD DR
HAYESVILLE OR 323-D7
SALEM OR 323-D7
NE WARD DR NE
HAYESVILLE OR 323-D7
WARD RD
DESCHUTES CO OR 217-C3
WASCO CO OR 127-B2
NE WARD RD
CLARK CO WA 193-A5
WARD CREEK RD
COOS CO OR 220-C7
PACIFIC CO WA 117-A1
WARD GAP RD
BENTON CO WA 120-B3
WARD RIDGE RD
KOOTENAI CO ID 248-C2
WARDS BUTTE RD
DOUGLAS CO OR 219-C1
WARDS CREEK RD
JACKSON CO OR 230-A6
NE WARDWAY ST
PORTLAND OR 312-C3
WARMINGTON RD
YAMHILL CO OR 198-B7
WARM LAKE RD
CASCADE ID 252-D5
VALLEY CO ID 252-D5
WARM SPRING RD
WASCO CO OR 208-B1
WARM SPRINGS AV
ADA CO ID 253-D3
BOISE ID 253-D3
WARM SPRINGS HWY U.S.-26
CLACKAMAS CO OR 202-A6
JEFFERSON CO OR 135-A1
JEFFERSON CO OR 208-B3
MADRAS OR 208-B3
WARM SPRINGS OR 135-A1
WARM SPRINGS OR 208-A2
WASCO CO OR 126-C3
WASCO CO OR 127-A3
WASCO CO OR 135-A1
WASCO CO OR 202-A6
WARM SPRINGS RD
HARNEY CO OR 145-C1
HARNEY CO OR 146-A1
JEFFERSON CO OR 211-C1
WARNECKE RD
WHITMAN CO WA 250-B2
WARNER AV
KING CO WA 110-C3
NEZ PERCE CO ID 250-C5
WARNER DR SE
MARION CO OR 205-B6
WARNER HWY Rt#-140
HARNEY CO OR 153-A3
LAKE CO OR 152-A2
LAKE CO OR 153-A3
S WARNER ST
TACOMA WA 294-D3
WARNER CANYON RD
CHELAN CO WA 238-C2
WARNOCK RD
WALLOWA CO OR 130-C1
WARREN AV Rt#-303
BREMERTON WA 270-J10
N WARREN AV
NEWPORT WA 106-C3
S WARREN AV
NEWPORT WA 106-C3
WARREN DR NW
PIERCE CO WA 181-B1
WARREN RD
COLUMBIA CO OR 189-A3
YAMHILL CO OR 198-C6
WARRENS SPUR
CANYON CO ID 147-C2
NW WARRENTON DR
WARRENTON WA 188-B1
WARRENTON-ASTORIA HWY
ASTORIA WA 300-C9
CLATSOP CO WA 300-C9
WARRENTON-ASTORIA HWY U.S.-101
CLATSOP CO WA 188-C2
CLATSOP CO WA 300-A10
WARRENTON WA 188-B2
WARRENTON DUMP SCHL RD
WARRENTON WA 188-B2
WARREN WAGON RD
MCCALL ID 251-C4
VALLEY CO ID 251-C4
WARRINER RD
CLACKAMAS CO OR 200-D3
S WARRIOR RD
YAKIMA CO WA 243-D6
WARTHEN RD
LANE CO OR 133-A3
WASANKARI RD
CLALLAM CO WA 164-D6
WASCO-HEPPNER HWY
SHERMAN CO OR 127-C1
WASCO OR 127-C1
WASCO-HEPPNER HWY Rt#-206
CONDON OR 128-A2
GILLIAM CO OR 128-A2
HEPPNER OR 128-C2
MORROW CO OR 128-C2
SHERMAN CO OR 127-C1
SHERMAN CO OR 128-A2
WASCO OR 127-C1
WASCO RUFUS RD
SHERMAN CO OR 127-C1
WASCO OR 127-C1
WASHBOARD RD
GARFIELD CO WA 122-B1
WASHBURN ST
BROWNSVILLE OR 210-C2
WASHBURN WY
ALTAMONT OR 235-C5
ALTAMONT OR 338-G14
KLAMATH CO OR 235-C5
KLAMATH CO OR 338-G9
KLAMATH FALLS OR 338-G9
WASHINGTON AV
BREMERTON WA 270-J10
CHELAN CO WA 236-D4
KENT WA 175-B7
LA GRANDE OR 130-A2
WASHINGTON AV Rt#-161
EATONVILLE WA 118-B1
PIERCE CO WA 118-B1
WASHINGTON AV Rt#-169
ENUMCLAW WA 110-C3
WASHINGTON AV Rt#-181
KENT WA 175-B7
WASHINGTON AV Rt#-304
BREMERTON WA 270-J11
N WASHINGTON AV
CENTRALIA WA 299-E4
N WASHINGTON AV Rt#-52
GEM CO ID 139-C3
N WASHINGTON AV U.S.-2
NEWPORT WA 106-C3
S WASHINGTON AV
CENTRALIA WA 299-E4
S WASHINGTON AV Rt#-52
EMMETT ID 139-C3
GEM CO ID 139-C3
S WASHINGTON AV U.S.-2
NEWPORT WA 106-C3
SE WASHINGTON AV
ROSEBURG OR 334-G8
SW WASHINGTON AV Rt#-138
ROSEBURG OR 334-F7
W WASHINGTON AV
YAKIMA WA 243-B7
WASHINGTON AV N Rt#-162
ORTING WA 182-C5
WASHINGTON AV S
LONG BEACH WA 186-A5
WASHINGTON AV S Rt#-162
ORTING WA 182-C5
WASHINGTON BLVD
LAKEWOOD WA 181-C4
NW WASHINGTON BLVD
GRANTS PASS OR 335-F7
E WASHINGTON RD
SPOKANE CO WA 246-D6
SPOKANE CO WA 247-A6
WASHINGTON ST
ASTORIA WA 300-B4
CHELAN CO WA 236-B1
CHENEY WA 246-A7
EUGENE OR 329-J7
FERNDALE WA 158-C6
LEWIS CO WA 187-C1
MABTON WA 120-B3
MORROW CO OR 128-C1
NAPAVINE WA 187-C1
OREGON CITY OR 199-D4
PORT TOWNSEND WA 263-G5
SEDRO-WOOLLEY WA 161-C5
SKAGIT CO WA 259-H14
SODAVILLE OR 133-C2
SPOKANE CO WA 246-A7
VANCOUVER WA 305-F5
WENATCHEE WA 238-D4
WOODLAND WA 192-C1
WASHINGTON ST Rt#-26
ADAMS CO WA 121-A1
OTHELLO WA 121-A1
WASHINGTON ST Rt#-129
ASOTIN WA 250-B5
WASHINGTON ST Rt#-218
FOSSIL OR 128-A3
E WASHINGTON ST
STAYTON OR 133-C1
E WASHINGTON ST U.S.-101
CLALLAM CO WA 166-B7
NEAH BAY WA 262-E11
N WASHINGTON ST
KENNEWICK WA 343-D10
SPOKANE WA 348-J7
N WASHINGTON ST Rt#-19
CONDON OR 128-A2
S WASHINGTON ST
KENNEWICK WA 343-D13
SPOKANE WA 348-J10
S WASHINGTON ST Rt#-19
CONDON OR 128-A2
S WASHINGTON ST U.S.-95
MOSCOW ID 249-C5
SE WASHINGTON ST
PORTLAND OR 315-G6
SE WASHINGTON ST Rt#-223
DALLAS OR 204-A6
SW WASHINGTON ST
PORTLAND OR 313-F6
SW WASHINGTON ST Rt#-223
DALLAS OR 204-A6
W WASHINGTON ST
STAYTON OR 133-C1
W WASHINGTON ST U.S.-101
CLALLAM CO WA 165-D6
CLALLAM CO WA 166-A6
NEAH BAY WA 262-D11
WASHINGTON ST E
HUNTINGTON OR 138-C2
WASHINGTON ST E U.S.-20
VALE OR 139-A3
WASHINGTON ST E U.S.-30
HUNTINGTON OR 138-C2
WASHINGTON ST W U.S.-20
VALE OR 139-A3
WASHINGTON ST W U.S.-30
HUNTINGTON OR 138-C2
WASHINGTON WY
COLUMBIA CO OR 189-B4
GEORGE WA 112-B3
GRANT CO WA 112-B3
LONGVIEW WA 302-J9
LONGVIEW WA 303-A8
RAINIER OR 189-B4
WASHOUGAL RIVER RD
CLARK CO WA 193-C7
SKAMANIA CO WA 193-D7
SKAMANIA CO WA 194-A6
WASHOUGAL WA 193-C7
WASHUM RD
ADA CO ID 253-A1
WASSER RD
COLUMBIA CO OR 189-C6
WATER ST
PORT MOODY BC 157-A4
PORT TOWNSEND WA 263-H4
VANCOUVER BC 254-H10
WATER ST Rt#-20
PORT TOWNSEND WA 263-G5
WATER ST Rt#-27
TEKOA WA 114-C3
WHITMAN CO WA 114-C3
WATER ST Rt#-82
LOSTINE OR 130-C2
N WATER ST
OLYMPIA WA 296-H5
SILVERTON OR 205-C4
WESTON OR 129-C1
N WATER ST Rt#-214
SILVERTON OR 205-C4
S WATER ST
WESTON OR 129-C1
S WATER ST Rt#-214
SILVERTON OR 205-C4
WATERFRONT ST
YAMHILL CO OR 198-D6
WATER GAP RD
JOSEPHINE CO OR 149-B2
WATER GULCH RD
BAKER CO OR 138-A1
WATERLOO RD
LINN CO OR 133-C1
WATERLOO OR 133-C1
WATERMAN RD
WHITMAN CO WA 114-C3
WATERS AV S
SEATTLE WA 287-H5
WATERS RD
COWLITZ CO WA 189-C1
WATER TANK RD
SKAGIT CO WA 161-A6
WATER WHEEL RD
GEM CO ID 139-C3
WATERWORKS RD
CLACKAMAS CO OR 200-D3
SNOHOMISH CO WA 168-B7
SW WATSON AV
BEAVERTON OR 199-B2
WATSON RD
JEFFERSON CO WA 170-B3
KITTITAS CO WA 241-C5
WALLA WALLA CO WA 121-B3
YAKIMA CO WA 243-A5
S WATSON RD
KOOTENAI CO ID 247-D6
WATSON ST U.S.-2
CRESTON WA 113-C1
WATT CANYON RD
KITTITAS CO WA 240-D4
WAUGH RD
DESCHUTES CO OR 217-D2
LINCOLN CO OR 206-C2
N WAUGH RD
MOUNT VERNON WA 260-G11
WAUKON RD
LINCOLN CO WA 114-A2
WAUNA VISTA DR
WALLA WALLA WA 345-C9
WAUNCHER GULCH RD
LATAH CO ID 123-B1
NEZ PERCE CO ID 123-B1
SW WAVA LN
KITSAP CO WA 174-A6
WAVERLY DR
ALBANY OR 326-F9
E WAVERLY RD
SPOKANE CO WA 114-C2
WAVERLY WA 114-C2
WAWAWAI RD
WHITMAN CO WA 249-A7
WHITMAN CO WA 250-A1
WAWAWAI GRADE RD
WHITMAN CO WA 122-C1
WAWAWAI-PULLMAN RD
PULLMAN WA 249-A5
WHITMAN CO WA 249-A5
WAWAWAI-PULLMAN RD Rt#-194
WHITMAN CO WA 249-A5
WAWAWAI RIVER RD
WHITMAN CO WA 122-C2
WHITMAN CO WA 250-B4
WAWAWAI RIVER RD Rt#-193
WHITMAN CO WA 122-C2
WHITMAN CO WA 250-A4
SE WAX RD
KING CO WA 175-D7
WAX ORCHARD RD SW
KING CO WA 174-D7
WAYNE DR N
KEIZER OR 322-J6
WAYNITA WY NE
BOTHELL WA 171-C6
WAYPARK DR NE
MARION CO OR 205-B3
WEATHERFORD RD
LINN CO OR 210-B5
WEAVER RD
DOUGLAS CO OR 225-C2
KITTITAS CO WA 241-A5
WEAVER RD N
KITSAP CO WA 271-J2
S WEBB AV
DOUGLAS CO WA 239-B5
WEBB CANAL RD
NEZ PERCE CO ID 250-D5
WEBB CUTOFF RD
NEZ PERCE CO ID 250-D6
WEBB DISTRICT RD
COLUMBIA CO OR 117-B3
WEBBER CANYON RD
BENTON CO WA 120-C3
WEBBER CANYON RD Rt#-224
BENTON CO WA 120-C3
WEBBER CANYON RD Rt#-225
BENTON CO WA 120-C3
WEBB HILL RD
MASON CO WA 180-A1
WEBB RIDGE RD
NEZ PERCE CO ID 250-D6
WEBER RD
ADAMS CO WA 113-C3
CLACKAMAS CO OR 201-A5
LINCOLN CO WA 113-C3
LINN CO OR 210-C3
WHITMAN CO WA 249-B6
S WEBER COULEE RD
ADAMS CO WA 113-B3
WEBERG RD
CROOK CO OR 136-C3
WEBFOOT RD
DAYTON OR 198-C7
YAMHILL CO OR 198-C7
SE WEBFOOT RD
YAMHILL CO OR 204-C2
WEBSTER AV
CHELAN WA 236-D3
W WEBSTER AV
CHEWELAH WA 106-B3
WEBSTER RD
GLADSTONE OR 199-D4
PIERCE CO WA 118-B1
SE WEBSTER RD
CLACKAMAS CO OR 199-D3
GLADSTONE OR 199-D3
WEBSTER RD E
PIERCE CO WA 182-A7
WEBSTER ST
MAPLE RIDGE BC 157-D5
WEBSTER FLAT RD
JEFFERSON CO OR 208-B1
W WEDGEWOOD AV
TOWN AND COUNTRY WA 346-H14
TOWN AND COUNTRY WA 347-A14
WEED RD
KLAMATH CO OR 231-C2
S WEGER RD
SPOKANE CO WA 246-D6
N WEHE AV
PASCO WA 343-H7
S WEHE AV
PASCO WA 343-H8
WEHRLI CANYON RD
GILLIAM CO OR 128-A3
WEIDKAMP RD
WHATCOM CO WA 158-D3
NE WEIDLER ST
PORTLAND OR 313-H4
PORTLAND OR 315-J4
WEIGAND RD
CROOK CO OR 213-B6
WEIKEL RD
YAKIMA CO WA 243-A6
N WEIPERT DR
COUNTRY HOMES WA 346-J12
TOWN AND COUNTRY WA 346-J12
SW WEIR RD
BEAVERTON OR 199-A3
WEISER SPUR U.S.-95
MALHEUR CO OR 139-A2
WEISER RIVER RD
WASHINGTON CO ID 139-A2
WEISER ID 139-A2
WEISS RD
LANE CO OR 215-A5
WEISSENFELS RIDGE RD
ASOTIN CO WA 123-A3
ASOTIN CO WA 250-C7
WEITZ LN
CLACKAMAS CO OR 200-B5
WEITZ RD
CANYON CO ID 147-B1
WELCH ST
DIST OF N VANCOUVER BC 254-G5
WELCHER RD
ISLAND CO WA 167-C5
WELCHES RD
CLACKAMAS CO OR 201-C5
WELLER RD
KOOTENAI CO ID 247-C6
E WELLESLEY AV
OTIS ORCHARDS WA 351-H2
OTIS ORCHARDS WA 352-C9
SPOKANE WA 349-C3
SPOKANE CO WA 350-D3
SPOKANE CO WA 351-H2
TRENTWOOD WA 350-H2
TRENTWOOD WA 351-A2
W WELLESLEY AV
SPOKANE WA 348-F3
SPOKANE WA 349-A3
WELLESLEY RD
LATAH CO ID 249-C1
WELLINGTON AV
WALLA WALLA WA 345-D6
E WELLINGTON RD
NANAIMO BC 93-A3

STREET City State Page-Grid

WELLPINIT-LITTLE FALLS RD
STEVENS CO WA 114-A1
WELLPINIT-MCCOY LAKE RD
STEVENS CO WA 113-C1
STEVENS CO WA 114-A1
WELLS RD
DOUGLAS CO OR 141-A1
S WELLS RD
SPOKANE CO WA 114-B2
WELLSANDT RD
ADAMS CO WA 113-C3
ADAMS CO WA 114-A3
RITZVILLE WA 113-C3
WELLS BENCH RD
CLEARWATER CO ID 123-C2
WELLSIAN WY
RICHLAND WA 341-F3
WELLS LANDING RD
POLK CO OR 207-C2
WELLS LINE
DISTRICT OF ABBOTSFORD BC 102-B1
WELLS STATION RD
UMATILLA CO OR 129-A1
WEMBLEY DR
DIST OF N VANCOUVER BC 255-G3
WENAS AV Rt#-823
SELAH WA 243-B5
YAKIMA CO WA 243-B5
WENAS RD
YAKIMA CO WA 119-C1
YAKIMA CO WA 240-D7
YAKIMA CO WA 241-A7
YAKIMA CO WA 243-A3
S WENAS RD
YAKIMA CO WA 243-B4
WENATCHEE AV
WENATCHEE WA 238-D4
WENATCHEE WA 239-A4
WENATCHEE AV Rt#-285
WENATCHEE WA 239-A4
N WENATCHEE AV Rt#-285
WENATCHEE WA 238-D4
WEST WENATCHEE WA 238-D4
S WENATCHEE AV
APPLEYARD WA 239-A5
WENATCHEE WA 239-A4
S WENATCHEE AV Rt#-285
WENATCHEE WA 239-A4
WENATCHEE HEIGHTS RD
CHELAN CO WA 238-D6
WENIGER HILL RD
KOOTENAI CO ID 248-A1
WENTWORTH RD
CLALLAM CO WA 169-B1
WENTWORTH ST
NANAIMO BC 93-A3
WENZEL SLOUGH RD
GRAYS HARBOR CO WA 179-A7
SW WERNER RD
BREMERTON WA 270-C12
KITSAP CO WA 270-C12
W WERNETT ST
PASCO WA 343-A5
WEST PASCO WA 342-F5
WEST PASCO WA 343-A5
WESGATE PL
PENDLETON OR 129-B1
UMATILLA CO OR 129-B1
WESLEY RD
WHITE SWAN WA 119-C2
WEST BLVD
VANCOUVER BC 156-B5
S WEST BLVD U.S.-101
ABERDEEN WA 178-B7
COSMOPOLIS WA 178-B7
WEST LN
COLUMBIA CO OR 192-A3
WEST MALL
UNIV ENDOWMENT LANDS BC 156-A4
WEST RD
PIERCE CO WA 181-D4
WEST SPUR
JACKSON CO OR 226-C4
WEST ST
DESCHUTES CO OR 212-A6
LINCOLN CO WA 114-A2
SAINT HELENS OR 192-B1
NW WEST ST
CHEHALIS WA 299-C11
S WEST ST Rt#-21
WILBUR WA 113-B1
WEST BOUNDARY DR
LANE CO OR 133-C3
WESTBROOK MALL
UNIV ENDOWMENT LANDS BC 156-A4
WESTBROOK RD SW
KITSAP CO WA 174-B6
WEST COAST RD Rt#-14
BRITISH COLUMBIA 101-A2
BRITISH COLUMBIA 164-C1
WEST COVE RD
LATAH CO ID 249-C1
NE WESTERHOLM RD
CLARK CO WA 193-B4
WESTERMAN RD SW
DOUGLAS CO WA 239-D1
WESTERN AV
SEATTLE WA 277-G4
N WESTERN AV
WENATCHEE WA 238-D4
WEST WENATCHEE WA 238-D4
S WESTERN AV
WENATCHEE WA 238-D4
WEST WENATCHEE WA 238-D4
SW WESTERN AV
GRANTS PASS OR 335-D9
WESTERN BLVD
BENTON CO OR 327-D11
CORVALLIS OR 327-D11
WESTERN ST
ALTAMONT OR 339-D11
WESTERN ROUTE RD
MORROW CO OR 128-C3
SW WESTFALL RD
CLACKAMAS CO OR 199-A5
WESTFIR RD
LANE CO OR 142-A1
WESTFIR OR 142-A1

WEST FORK RD
OKANOGAN CO WA 104-B2
WEST FORK EVANS CK RD
JACKSON CO OR 230-A1
WEST FORK INDIAN CREEK RD
LANE CO OR 209-C7
WEST FORK-MILLICOMA RD
COOS CO OR 218-D6
WESTGATE AV U.S.-30
PENDLETON OR 129-B1
WESTHAVEN DR
WESTPORT WA 298-G10
WEST HILLS RD
BENTON CO OR 133-B1
BENTON CO OR 327-A11
CORVALLIS OR 327-A11
WESTLAKE AV
SEATTLE WA 273-J7
SEATTLE WA 277-J1
WESTLAKE AV N
SEATTLE WA 277-J5
WESTLAKE RD
LEWIS CO ID 123-B2
WESTLAND RD
UMATILLA CO OR 129-A1
WESTMINSTER HWY
CITY OF RICHMOND BC 156-A6
WESTMINSTER HWY S
CITY OF RICHMOND BC 156-C6
WESTMINSTER WY N
SHORELINE WA 171-A7
WESTMOND RD
BONNER CO ID 244-A5
WEST MOUNTAIN RD
VALLEY CO ID 251-C7
VALLEY CO ID 252-C1
SW WEST OAK RD
KITSAP CO WA 174-B6
WESTON-ELGIN HWY Rt#-204
UMATILLA CO OR 129-C1
UMATILLA CO OR 130-A1
UNION CO OR 130-A1
WESTPORT RD Rt#-105
GRAYS HARBOR CO WA 117-A1
WESTPORT DOCK RD Rt#-409
CLATSOP CO OR 117-B3
WEST SAANICH RD
DIST OF NORTH SAANICH BC 159-B2
WEST SAANICH RD Rt#-17A
DIST OF CENTRAL SAANICH BC 159-B3
DIST OF NORTH SAANICH BC 159-B3
DISTRICT OF SAANICH BC 159-C5
WEST SHORE DR
WASHINGTON CO OR 198-A2
WESTSHORE DR
GRANT CO WA 242-C2
MOSES LAKE WA 242-C3
WEST SIDE HWY Rt#-411
COWLITZ CO WA 187-C6
COWLITZ CO WA 189-C1
COWLITZ CO WA 303-D1
KELSO WA 303-C7
LEWIS CO WA 187-C6
LONGVIEW WA 303-C6
LONGVIEW HEIGHTS WA 303-C5
VADER WA 187-C6
WESTSIDE HWY SW
KING CO WA 174-D6
WEST SIDE RD
COOS CO OR 140-B3
COOS CO OR 220-D7
JOSEPHINE CO OR 233-A4
KLAMATH CO OR 231-B2
LAKE CO OR 151-C3
LAKE CO OR 152-A2
MODOC CO CA 151-C3
MODOC CO CA 152-A3
MYRTLE POINT OR 140-B3
WESTSIDE RD
MCMINNVILLE OR 198-A6
MODOC CO CA 151-C3
PIERCE CO WA 185-A5
YAMHILL CO OR 198-A5
NW WEST SIDE RD
YAMHILL CO OR 198-A7
WEST TWIN RD
LATAH CO ID 249-D4
NW WEST UNION RD
WASHINGTON CO OR 125-C1
WASHINGTON CO OR 192-A7
WASHINGTON CO OR 199-A1
WEST VALLEY HWY
ALGONA WA 182-B1
AUBURN WA 175-B7
AUBURN WA 182-B1
EDGEWOOD WA 182-B1
KENT WA 175-B7
KING CO WA 175-B7
PACIFIC WA 182-B1
PIERCE CO WA 182-B1
SUMNER WA 182-B3
WEST VALLEY HWY Rt#-181
KENT WA 175-B7
KENT WA 291-H3
TUKWILA WA 289-J5
TUKWILA WA 291-H3
WEST VALLEY HWY S
KING CO WA 182-B2
PACIFIC WA 182-B2
WEST VALLEY RD
JEFFERSON CO WA 170-A2
WESTVIEW DR
CITY OF N VANCOUVER BC 254-J4
CITY OF N VANCOUVER BC 255-A4
DIST OF N VANCOUVER BC 255-A4
DISTRICT OF DELTA BC 156-D7
DOUGLAS CO OR 221-B2
WESTWARD HO
LINCOLN CO OR 328-C3
WESTWOOD DR NE
KITSAP CO WA 271-E5
WESTWOOD ST
PORT COQUITLAM BC 157-A4
WETHERBEE RD
JOSEPHINE CO OR 229-A7
WEXLER RD
WHITMAN CO WA 249-B4
WEYERHAUSER RD
LANE CO OR 219-D1

WHALEN RD
COWLITZ CO WA 192-B1
WHARF ST
CITY OF VICTORIA BC 256-G9
WHATCOM RD
DISTRICT OF ABBOTSFORD BC 102-B1
SE WHEATLAND RD
YAMHILL CO OR 204-D2
WHEATLAND RD N
KEIZER OR 204-D3
KEIZER OR 323-A2
MARION CO OR 204-D3
WHEATON WY
BREMERTON WA 270-J8
BREMERTON WA 271-A9
WHEATON WY Rt#-303
BREMERTON WA 270-J6
KITSAP CO WA 270-J6
WHEELER RD
CLALLAM CO WA 163-A7
GRANT CO WA 242-D3
JACKSON CO OR 230-C5
LANE CO OR 215-D4
MOSES LAKE WA 242-D3
E WHEELER RD
MOSES LAKE WA 242-C3
S WHEELER RD
SPOKANE CO WA 114-C3
WHELAN RD
WHITMAN CO WA 249-B4
WHERRY RD
YAKIMA CO WA 243-A5
WHETSTONE RD
COLUMBIA CO WA 122-A2
WHIFFIN SPIT RD
BRITISH COLUMBIA 164-C1
WHISKEY CREEK DR
HOOD RIVER CO OR 195-D5
WHISKEY CREEK RD
COLUMBIA CO WA 122-A3
JACKSON CO OR 226-D3
MALHEUR CO OR 146-A1
TILLAMOOK CO OR 197-A3
WALLOWA OR 130-C1
WALLOWA CO OR 130-C1
E WHISKEY CREEK RD
WALLOWA OR 130-C1
S WHISKEY HILL RD
CLACKAMAS CO OR 205-C1
WHISKEY HILL RD NE
HUBBARD OR 205-C1
MARION CO OR 205-C1
WHISKEY JACK RD
BONNER CO ID 244-A1
JEFFERSON CO OR 211-B1
WHISKEY RUN RD
COOS CO OR 220-B4
WHISKEY SPRING CREEK RD
CROOK CO OR 135-C2
WHISKEY SPRINGS RD
JEFFERSON CO OR 211-D2
WHISTLE CREEK RD
HARNEY CO OR 136-C3
WHISTLERS LN
DOUGLAS CO OR 221-D3
WHISTLERS BEND PARK RD
DOUGLAS CO OR 221-D3
WHITAKER RD
POLK CO OR 204-A6
WHITCOMB AV U.S.-97
OKANOGAN CO WA 104-C2
TONASKET WA 104-C2
WHITE RD
WALLA WALLA CO WA 121-B3
W WHITE RD
SPOKANE CO WA 246-B5
E WHITEAKER AV
COTTAGE GROVE OR 215-B7
WHITE CREEK RD
JOSEPHINE CO OR 233-C3
E WHITE CREEK RD
JOSEPHINE CO OR 233-D3
WHITEHALL RD SE
DOUGLAS CO WA 112-C2
WHITEHORSE CTO
MALHEUR CO OR 154-B1
WHITEHORSE RD
MALHEUR CO OR 154-A1
WHITEHORSE CREEK RD
DOUGLAS CO OR 225-D6
WHITEHORSE RANCH RD
HARNEY CO OR 153-C2
HARNEY CO OR 154-A2
WHITELINE RD
KLAMATH CO OR 235-D1
WHITEMAN RD KPS
PIERCE CO WA 181-A3
WHITE OAK RD
LINN CO OR 207-B6
WHITE PINE DR Rt#-6
BENEWAH CO ID 115-B3
LATAH CO ID 115-B3
WHITE RIVER RD
CHELAN CO WA 111-B1
WASCO CO OR 127-A3
WHITE ROCK LOOP RD
DESCHUTES CO OR 212-B7
WHITE SCHOOL HOUSE RD
JOSEPHINE CO OR 233-B4
WHITES CREEK RD
LANE CO OR 219-D1
SE WHITESON RD
YAMHILL CO OR 204-B1
N WHITE SWAN RD
WHITE SWAN WA 119-C2
W WHITE SWAN RD Rt#-220
WHITE SWAN WA 119-C2
WHITHAM RD NE
THURSTON CO WA 180-D4
WHITING WY
DISTRICT OF COQUITLAM BC 156-D5
WHITLEY DR U.S.-95
FRUITLAND ID 139-A3
N WHITLEY DR U.S.-95
FRUITLAND ID 139-A3
PAYETTE CO ID 139-A3
E WHITMAN DR
COLLEGE PLACE WA 344-F10
W WHITMAN DR
COLLEGE PLACE WA 344-E10

W WHITMAN DR
WALLA WALLA CO WA 344-D10
WHITMAN RD
WHITMAN CO WA 249-C6
E WHITMAN RD
SPOKANE CO WA 114-C3
WHITMAN ST
WALLA WALLA WA 345-C8
S WHITMAN ST
MONMOUTH OR 204-B7
ROSALIA WA 114-C3
WHITMAN CO WA 114-C3
W WHITMAN ST
ROSALIA WA 114-C3
WHITMORE DR NW
PIERCE CO WA 181-B1
WHITMORE RD
WASHINGTON CO OR 198-C3
WHITNEY HWY Rt#-7
BAKER CITY OR 138-B1
BAKER CO OR 137-C1
BAKER CO OR 138-A1
GRANT CO OR 137-C1
WHITNEY RD
ADAMS CO ID 251-B5
COLUMBIA CO OR 189-B6
COOS CO OR 140-B3
WHITNEY-LA CONNER RD
SKAGIT CO WA 160-D7
SKAGIT CO WA 167-D1
WHITTAKER RD NW
THURSTON CO WA 180-B6
WHITTEMORE RD
DESCHUTES CO OR 212-C6
N WHITWORTH DR
COUNTRY HOMES WA 346-J10
FAIRWOOD WA 346-J9
FAIRWOOD WA 347-A9
WHOOPEMUP RD
COLUMBIA CO WA 122-A2
WIARD ST
ALTAMONT OR 339-A9
WICKERSHAM TRUCK TR
WHATCOM CO WA 161-C2
SW WICKIUP AV
DESCHUTES CO OR 212-D6
WICKIUP RD
DESCHUTES CO OR 142-C1
W WIDE HOLLOW RD
YAKIMA CO WA 243-A7
WIDME RD NE
SUQUAMISH WA 170-C7
WIDOW CREEK RD
LINCOLN CO OR 203-C3
ROSE LODGE OR 203-C3
SE WIESE RD
CLACKAMAS CO OR 200-B3
WIGGINS RD SE
OLYMPIA WA 297-E11
THURSTON CO WA 297-E11
WIGHTMAN ST
ASHLAND OR 337-E9
WIGRICH RD
POLK CO OR 207-C1
WIKSTROM RD
COLUMBIA CO OR 192-A3
WILBUR AV
WALLA WALLA WA 345-E5
N WILBUR AV
WALLA WALLA WA 345-E6
S WILBUR AV
WALLA WALLA WA 345-E7
WALLA WALLA EAST WA 345-E7
WILBUR RD
DOUGLAS CO OR 221-B2
WILBUR-GARDEN VALLEY RD
DOUGLAS CO OR 221-B3
WILBUR GULCH RD Rt#-194
WHITMAN CO WA 122-C1
WHITMAN CO WA 249-A5
WILBUR-UMPQUA RD
DOUGLAS CO OR 221-B1
WILCO RD
MARION CO OR 133-C1
STAYTON OR 133-C1
NE WILCOX AV
DESCHUTES CO OR 212-D4
WILCOX RD
DOUGLAS CO OR 221-B1
WHITMAN CO WA 122-B1
WHITMAN CO WA 249-C1
WILDCAT RD
MALHEUR CO OR 146-A3
S WILDCAT RD
CLACKAMAS CO OR 126-A3
CLACKAMAS CO OR 205-D3
NW WILDCAT LAKE RD
KITSAP CO WA 174-A2
WILDCAT MOUNTAIN DR
CLACKAMAS CO OR 200-C5
CLACKAMAS CO OR 201-A5
WILDERNESS LN
KITTITAS CO WA 111-B3
WILD FERN DR
DOUGLAS CO OR 221-C3
WILDHORSE RD
UMATILLA CO OR 129-C1
WILDWOOD DR
COOS CO OR 218-B5
SW WILDWOOD PL
SEATTLE WA 284-D3
WILDWOOD RD
LEWIS CO WA 187-A3
SW WILDWOOD RD
KITSAP CO WA 174-B5
WILES RD
BENTON CO OR 207-B3
WILEY RD
CROOK CO OR 213-C5
W WILEY RD
YAKIMA CO WA 243-A7
WILEY CREEK DR
LINN CO OR 134-A2
WILHOIT RD
CLACKAMAS CO OR 126-A3
MOLALLA OR 126-A3
S WILKENSON RD
ISLAND CO WA 171-A1
WILKES DR
Santa Clara OR 215-A1

WILKINS RD
LANE CO OR 210-B7
WILKINSON RD
CLACKAMAS CO OR 200-D3
DISTRICT OF SAANICH BC 159-C5
DISTRICT OF SAANICH BC 256-D1
MALHEUR CO OR 154-C2
MULTNOMAH CO OR 200-D3
WILLAGILLESPIE RD
EUGENE OR 329-J4
WILLAMETTE AV
MEDFORD OR 336-E12
N WILLAMETTE BLVD
PORTLAND OR 192-B7
PORTLAND OR 308-A5
WILLAMETTE DR
LANE CO OR 210-A6
WILLAMETTE HWY Rt#-58
KLAMATH CO OR 142-C2
LANE CO OR 133-C3
LANE CO OR 134-A3
LANE CO OR 142-B1
LANE CO OR 215-C3
LANE CO OR 330-J14
LANE CO OR 331-A14
OAKRIDGE OR 142-B1
S WILLAMETTE RD
LANE CO OR 215-B3
LANE CO OR 329-J14
WILLAMETTE ST
COBURG OR 210-B7
EUGENE OR 329-J13
EUGENE OR 330-A8
LANE CO OR 210-B7
LANE CO OR 329-H14
WILLAMETTE FALLS DR
WEST LINN OR 199-C5
WILLAMETTE FERRY ST
MARION CO OR 207-C2
POLK CO OR 207-C2
WILLAMETTE-MERIDIAN RD
KITSAP CO WA 174-A1
SW WILLAMINA CREEK RD
WILLAMINA OR 125-A3
YAMHILL CO OR 125-A3
WILLAMINA-SALEM HWY Rt#-22
POLK CO OR 125-B3
POLK CO OR 204-A4
POLK CO OR 322-G13
SALEM OR 322-G13
WILLAMINA-SALEM HWY NW Rt#-22
POLK CO OR 204-B6
POLK CO OR 322-B14
SALEM OR 322-B14
WILLAMINA-SHERIDAN HWY Rt#-18
POLK CO OR 125-A3
WILLAMINA OR 125-A3
WILLANCH WY
COOS CO OR 218-C7
WILLAPA RD
PACIFIC CO WA 117-A1
WILLAPA-MONOHAN LANDING RD
PACIFIC CO WA 117-A1
RAYMOND WA 117-A1
WILLARD RD
DESCHUTES CO OR 135-B3
SKAMANIA CO WA 195-B4
WILLEYS LAKE RD
WHATCOM CO WA 158-C4
WILLIAM H BUNDY BLVD U.S.-95
LAPWAI ID 123-A2
NEZ PERCE CO ID 123-A2
WILLIAM HEAD RD
DISTRICT OF METCHOSIN BC 165-A1
WILLIAMS AV
DEPOE BAY OR 203-A7
N WILLIAMS AV
PORTLAND OR 309-G7
PORTLAND OR 313-G1
WILLIAMS RD
ADAMS CO WA 121-B1
BENTON CO WA 120-B3
CITY OF RICHMOND BC 156-B7
COWLITZ CO WA 190-A6
CROOK CO OR 213-C4
WILLIAMS CANYON RD
CHELAN CO WA 238-B1
NW WILLIAMS CANYON RD
YAMHILL CO OR 198-A3
WILLIAMS CREEK RD
GRAYS HARBOR CO WA 117-B1
LANE CO OR 219-D2
WILLIAMS LAKE RD
LINCOLN CO WA 114-A3
STEVENS CO WA 106-A1
W WILLIAMS LAKE RD
SPOKANE CO WA 114-B2
WILLIAMSON RD
YAMHILL CO OR 198-C5
WILLIAMSON MOUNTAIN RD
DESCHUTES CO OR 216-A6
WILLIAMSON RIVER RD
KLAMATH CO OR 143-A3
KLAMATH CO OR 151-A1
WILLIAMSPORT RD
ASTORIA WA 300-D6
WILLIAMS RIVER RD
KLAMATH CO OR 150-C1
WILLIAMS VALLEY RD
STEVENS CO WA 114-B1
WILLIMINA CREEK RD
YAMHILL CO OR 125-A3
WILLINGDON AV
DISTRICT OF BURNABY BC 156-C5
DISTRICT OF BURNABY BC 255-H13
E WILLIS RD
CANYON CO ID 147-B1
NW WILLIS RD
YAMHILL CO OR 198-A6
W WILLIS ST Rt#-516
KENT WA 175-C7
WILLIS CANYON RD
KLICKITAT CO WA 196-C1
WILLIS CREEK RD
DOUGLAS CO OR 221-B7

WILLIS CREEK RD
DOUGLAS CO OR 225-B1
WILLIS POINT RD
DISTRICT OF SAANICH BC 159-B4
WILLOW AV Rt#-39
KLAMATH FALLS OR 338-D8
WILLOW RD SE
KITSAP CO WA 174-B6
N WILLOW ST
LA GRANDE OR 130-A2
WILLOW CREEK RD
COLUMBIA CO WA 122-A2
JEFFERSON CO OR 208-B4
MALHEUR CO OR 138-B2
MORROW CO OR 128-C2
MORROW CO OR 129-A2
WILLOW GROVE RD
COWLITZ CO WA 189-A2
COWLITZ CO WA 302-A5
WEST LONGVIEW WA 302-A5
WILLOW GROVE RD Rt#-432
COWLITZ CO WA 302-A5
WEST LONGVIEW WA 302-A5
WILLOW GROVE CONN Rt#-432
COWLITZ CO WA 302-A4
LONGVIEW WA 302-A4
WEST LONGVIEW WA 302-A4
WILLOWLAKE RD
GRANT CO WA 112-C2
WILLOWS RD
ILWACO WA 186-A6
PACIFIC CO WA 186-A6
REDMOND WA 171-C7
E WILLOW SPRINGS RD
SPOKANE CO WA 246-C5
WILLOW VALLEY RD
KLAMATH CO OR 151-B2
MODOC CO CA 151-B2
WILLS RD
LANE CO OR 215-D5
WILSON AV
WESTPORT WA 298-H11
SE WILSON AV
BEND OR 332-G9
SE WILSON AV Rt#-372
BEND OR 332-F9
WILSON AV S
SEATTLE WA 283-F6
WILSON HWY
YAKIMA CO WA 120-B2
WILSON LN
SKAGIT CO WA 161-A6
WILSON RD
BOARDMAN OR 128-C1
CLACKAMAS CO OR 126-C3
DOUGLAS CO OR 219-B4
GRANDVIEW WA 120-B3
LEWIS CO ID 123-C2
LEWIS CO WA 187-C2
MORROW CO OR 128-C1
WASCO CO OR 127-C3
WASCO CO OR 196-A6
WHITMAN CO WA 249-B5
YAKIMA CO WA 120-B3
YONCALLA OR 219-B4
S WILSON RD
CLACKAMAS CO OR 200-A6
WILSON RD NW
THURSTON CO WA 180-A6
WILSON ST
ASOTIN WA 250-B5
CHELAN CO WA 238-A1
DISTRICT OF MISSION BC 94-B3
MAPLE RIDGE BC 94-B3
THURSTON CO WA 297-B5
N WILSON ST
POST FALLS ID 353-F6
WILSON CREEK RD
KITTITAS CO WA 241-B2
LINCOLN CO OR 209-C4
WILSON RIVER HWY Rt#-6
BANKS OR 125-B1
TILLAMOOK OR 197-C2
TILLAMOOK CO OR 125-B1
TILLAMOOK CO OR 197-C2
WASHINGTON CO OR 125-B1
WILSON RIVER LP
TILLAMOOK CO OR 197-C2
WILSONVILLE RD
CLACKAMAS CO OR 199-B6
NEWBERG OR 198-D6
WILSONVILLE OR 199-B6
YAMHILL CO OR 198-D6
YAMHILL CO OR 199-A6
WILSONVILLE HUBBARD HWY
MARION CO OR 199-B7
WILT RD
DESCHUTES CO OR 211-D4
DESCHUTES CO OR 212-A4
WIMER RD
JOSEPHINE CO OR 148-C2
WIMER ST
ASHLAND OR 337-B6
NW WIMP WY
DESCHUTES CO OR 212-D3
WINBERRY CREEK RD
LANE CO OR 133-C3
LANE CO OR 134-A3
WINBURN WY
ASHLAND OR 337-C7
W WINCH AV
KOOTENAI CO ID 247-C1
WINCHELL ST
DEPOE BAY OR 206-B1
WINCHESTER AV
REEDSPORT OR 218-D1
WINCHESTER AV U.S.-101
REEDSPORT OR 218-C1
WINCHESTER RD
DOUGLAS CO OR 221-B3
LEWIS CO ID 123-B2
NE WINCHESTER ST
ROSEBURG OR 334-G6
WINCHUCK RIVER RD
CURRY CO OR 232-D7
WINDHURST RD
COOS CO OR 220-B6
WINDIGO PASS RD
DOUGLAS CO OR 223-D3

STREET City State Page-Grid

WINDIGO PASS RD
KLAMATH CO OR 142-B2
WIND MOUNTAIN RD
SKAMANIA CO WA 195-A5
WIND RIDGE RD
YAMHILL CO OR 198-C4
WIND RIVER RD
CARSON WA 194-D3
SKAMANIA CO WA 194-D3
WINDSOR RD
DISTRICT OF OAK BAY BC 257-D9
PITT MEADOWS BC 157-B5
WINDSOR ISLAND RD
KEIZER OR 322-G3
MARION CO OR 204-D4
MARION CO OR 322-G2
WINDY CITY RD
CLACKAMAS CO OR 200-A7
WINDY RIDGE DR
COWLITZ CO WA 189-B1
WINESAP AV
CHELAN CO WA 236-C2
WINGVILLE RD
BAKER CO OR 130-A3
BAKER CO OR 138-A1
WINLOCK LN
WHEELER CO OR 128-B3
WINLOCK-TOLEDO RD Rt#-505
LEWIS CO WA 187-C3
WINLOCK-VADER RD
LEWIS CO WA 187-B4
WINLOCK WA 187-B4
WINONA AV N
SEATTLE WA 273-J2
WINONA RD
JOSEPHINE CO OR 229-C3
WINONA SOUTH RD
WHITMAN CO WA 122-A1
WINSLOW RD
WASCO CO OR 127-B2
WINSTON RD
DOUGLAS CO OR 221-B6
WINSTON OR 221-B6
WINSTON ST
DISTRICT OF BURNABY BC 156-D4
WINTEL RD S
MARION CO OR 207-C2
WINTER ST SE
SALEM OR 322-H14
WINTERCREEK RD
MARION CO OR 207-D2
WINTERGREEN AV NW
SALEM OR 322-E9
W WINTERGREEN LN
KITSAP CO WA 173-D3
WINTERS RD
WASHINGTON CO OR 198-C2
NE WINTERS RD
CLARK CO WA 193-C5
SW WINTERS RD
WASHINGTON CO OR 198-C2
WINTERS HILL RD
YAMHILL CO OR 198-C6
WIPPER RD SE
MARION CO OR 325-F14
TURNER OR 325-F14
WIRTA RD
LEWIS CO WA 187-B2
WIRTH RD
LINN CO OR 207-C7
WISCONSIN ST
PRIEST RIVER ID 107-A3
WISCONSIN TKTR
COWLITZ CO WA 117-B2
COWLITZ CO WA 187-A7
WISEACRE LN NE
MARION CO OR 205-B1
W WISER LAKE RD
WHATCOM CO WA 158-D5
WISHKAH RD
ABERDEEN WA 178-B6
GRAYS HARBOR CO WA 178-C3
W WISHKAH RD
GRAYS HARBOR CO WA 178-B4
WISHKAH ST
ABERDEEN WA 178-B7
WISHKAH ST U.S.-12
ABERDEEN WA 178-B7
GRAYS HARBOR CO WA 178-B7
WISHKAH ST U.S.-101
ABERDEEN WA 178-B7
E WISHKAH ST U.S.-101
ABERDEEN WA 178-B7
W WISHKAH ST U.S.-101
ABERDEEN WA 178-B7
NE WISTARIA DR
PORTLAND OR 314-B2
WITCHER GATEWAY RD
LANE CO OR 215-C6
WITHAM HILL DR
CORVALLIS OR 327-D6
WITHROW RD NW
DOUGLAS CO WA 112-B2
WITHYCOMBE RD
WASHINGTON CO OR 198-B2
WITT DR
LINN CO OR 207-C7
WITTE RD SE
KING CO WA 175-D7
WITTE RD SW
DOUGLAS CO WA 239-B3
WITTIG RD NE
DOUGLAS CO WA 112-C1
WITZEL RD SE
MARION CO OR 325-H11
TURNER OR 325-H11
NE W KINGSON RD
KITSAP CO WA 170-D5
WNUK RD
KLICKITAT CO WA 195-D4
WOCUS RD
KLAMATH CO OR 235-C2
KLAMATH CO OR 338-A1
WOHL RD
COWLITZ CO WA 189-A2
WOLCOTT AV S
SEATTLE WA 287-G3
WOLCOTT RD
LINN CO OR 207-B6

WOLF RD
LATAH CO ID 249-C7
WOLF CREEK LN
UNION CO OR 130-A3
WOLF CREEK RD
LANE CO OR 133-A3
WOLFE RD
DISTRICT OF CHILLIWACK BC 94-C3
WOLF HOLLOW LN
GILLIAM CO OR 128-B2
WOLFORD CANYON RD
JEFFERSON CO OR 208-A2
WOLLOCHET DR NW
GIG HARBOR WA 181-B1
PIERCE CO WA 181-B1
N WOLVERTON CT
SPOKANE WA 349-B5
WONDERLY RD
COLUMBIA CO OR 302-D14
S WOOD DR
CROOK CO OR 213-D7
WOOD RD
SKAGIT CO WA 161-A4
WOODARD RD
LEWIS CO WA 187-C1
WOODARD BAY RD NE
THURSTON CO WA 180-D5
WOODBROOK RD
LAKEWOOD WA 181-C4
WOODBROOK RD SW
LAKEWOOD WA 181-C5
PIERCE CO WA 181-C5
WOODBROOK COUNTY PK RD
COWLITZ CO WA 303-J1
WOODBURN-ESTACADA HWY Rt#-211
CLACKAMAS CO OR 126-A3
CLACKAMAS CO OR 200-C6
CLACKAMAS CO OR 205-D2
ESTACADA OR 200-C6
MARION CO OR 205-B1
MOLALLA OR 126-A3
WOODBURN OR 205-B1
S WOODBURN-ESTCDA HWY Rt#-211
CLACKAMAS CO OR 126-A3
WOODBURN HUBBARD HWY
HUBBARD OR 205-B1
MARION CO OR 205-B1
WOODBURN-MONITOR RD NE
MARION CO OR 205-C2
WOODCOCK RD
CLALLAM CO WA 262-A6
WOODELL LN
UNION CO OR 130-A2
WOODGATE RD
PACIFIC CO WA 186-A5
WOODIN AV
CHELAN WA 236-C3
CHELAN CO WA 236-C3
WOODIN AV Rt#-150
CHELAN WA 236-D3
SE WOODING RD
CLARK CO WA 193-C7
WOODINVILLE DR Rt#-522
BOTHELL WA 171-C6
NE WOODINVILLE-DUVALL RD
DUVALL WA 110-C1
KING CO WA 110-C1
KING CO WA 171-D6
WOODINVILLE WA 171-D6
WOODINVILLE REDMOND RD Rt#-202
KING CO WA 171-D7
REDMOND WA 171-D7
WOODINVILLE WA 171-D7
WOODINVILLE RDMD RD NE Rt#-202
REDMOND WA 171-D7
REDMOND WA 175-D1
WOODINVILLE SNOHOMSH RD
KING CO WA 171-C6
SNOHOMISH CO WA 171-D6
WOODINVILLE WA 171-C6
WOODINVILLE SNOMISH RD Rt#-202
BOTHELL WA 171-C6
WOODINVILLE WA 171-C6
WOODLAND AV
CENTRALIA WA 299-E5
WOODLAND AV E
PIERCE CO WA 182-A4
WOODLAND DR
COOS BAY OR 333-E8
NORTH BEND OR 333-E8
WOODLAND LP
YAMHILL CO OR 198-B4
WOODLAND RD
IDAHO CO ID 123-C2
WOODLAND GRADE RD
IDAHO CO ID 123-C2
WOODLAND PARK RD
JOSEPHINE CO OR 229-A7
WOODLAWN AV
SKAGIT CO WA 259-G13
WOODLYN RD
WHATCOM CO WA 158-D5
WOODMONT DR S
KING CO WA 175-B7
WOODRIDGE PL
BRITISH COLUMBIA 159-B5
WOOD RIVER CANAL
KLAMATH CO OR 231-C3
WOODRUFF RD
DOUGLAS CO OR 221-A3
WOODRUFF CREEK RD
JACKSON CO OR 226-C4
WOODS RD
WHITMAN CO WA 249-C6
E WOODS RD
KITSAP CO WA 271-E9
WOODS RD E
KITSAP CO WA 271-E10
WOODS RD NE
DOUGLAS CO WA 112-C2
WOODS RD SE
KITSAP CO WA 271-F14
WOODS CREEK RD
DOUGLAS CO OR 225-B6

WOODS CREEK RD Rt#-131
LEWIS CO WA 118-C2
WOODSIDE DR
COWLITZ CO WA 189-B1
WOODS LAKE RD
SNOHOMISH CO WA 110-C1
SE WOODSTOCK BLVD
PORTLAND OR 318-B5
PORTLAND OR 319-E5
WOODWARD RD
AULT FIELD WA 170-D1
SW WOODWARD RD
JEFFERSON CO OR 212-C1
WOODWARD CREEK RD
SKAMANIA CO WA 194-B6
WOODWORTH DR
HOOD RIVER CO OR 202-C1
WOODY RD
CLARK CO WA 192-D1
E WOOLARD RD
SPOKANE CO WA 114-C1
WOOLRIDGE RD
PITT MEADOWS BC 157-B5
WORDEN HILL RD
YAMHILL CO OR 198-C5
WORKMAN CREEK RD
GRAYS HARBOR CO WA 179-B7
WORLINE RD
SKAGIT CO WA 161-A5
NE WORTHINGTON RD
CLARK CO WA 193-B1
WREN ST
DISTRICT OF MISSION BC 94-B3
WRENTHAM MARKET RD
WASCO CO OR 127-B2
WRIGHT AV
RICHLAND WA 340-E13
RICHLAND WA 341-E1
WRIGHT RD
SISKIYOU CO CA 151-A3
S WRIGHT RD
CLACKAMAS CO OR 126-A3
WRIGHT RD SE
THURSTON CO WA 184-C3
W WRIGHT ST
BOISE ID 253-C3
WRIGHT-BLISS RD KPN
PIERCE CO WA 174-A7
WRIGHT CREEK RD
LINCOLN CO OR 206-B6
WTC 8000 RD
DOUGLAS CO OR 140-C2
WULFF LN
DOUGLAS CO OR 221-A4
WYATT DR
LINN CO OR 210-A6
NE WYATT WY
KITSAP CO WA 271-J2
WINSLOW WA 271-J2
WYATT WY NW
KITSAP CO WA 271-J2
WINSLOW WA 271-J2
WYEAST RD
HOOD RIVER CO OR 195-C7
WYNOOCHEE VALLEY RD
ABERDEEN WA 178-C5
GRAYS HARBOR CO WA 109-A2
GRAYS HARBOR CO WA 178-C5
MONTESANO WA 178-D6
WYNOOCHEE WISHKAH RD
GRAYS HARBOR CO WA 178-B5
S WYNOOSKI RD
NEWBERG OR 198-D6
YAMHILL CO OR 198-D6
WYOMING AV
HAYDEN ID 245-A5
KOOTENAI CO ID 245-A5
KOOTENAI CO ID 247-D1
WYOMING ST Rt#-3
DEARY ID 123-B1
LATAH CO ID 123-B1
WYSE RD
WASCO CO OR 196-A7

X

X RD NE
GRANT CO WA 237-C6
LINCOLN CO WA 237-C5
XL RANCH RD
LAKE CO OR 144-A3

Y

Y AV
LA GRANDE OR 130-A2
Y PL
PACIFIC CO WA 186-A4
Y RD
WHATCOM CO WA 102-B1
WHATCOM CO WA 161-B1
Y RD NE
DOUGLAS CO WA 237-A2
Y 1/2 RD NE
DOUGLAS CO WA 237-A2
YACHATS OCEAN RD
YACHATS OR 209-A4
YACHATS RIVER RD
LINCOLN CO OR 209-A3
YACHATS OR 209-A3
YAKIMA
CROOK CO OR 213-D7
YAKIMA AV
TACOMA WA 293-G5
TACOMA WA 295-G1
E YAKIMA AV
YAKIMA WA 243-C6
N YAKIMA AV
TACOMA WA 292-E3
TACOMA WA 293-F3
S YAKIMA AV
TACOMA WA 293-G4
TACOMA WA 295-G6
W YAKIMA AV
YAKIMA WA 243-B6
YAKIMA VALLEY HWY
GRANGER WA 120-A2
SUNNYSIDE WA 120-A2
YAKIMA CO WA 120-A2

YAKSUM CANYON RD
CHELAN CO WA 238-C3
S YALE RD
SPOKANE CO WA 246-C7
YALE RD E Rt#-1A
BRITISH COLUMBIA 94-C3
DISTRICT OF CHILLIWACK BC 94-C3
YALE RD W Rt#-1A
DISTRICT OF CHILLIWACK BC 94-C3
N YALE ST
SPOKANE CO WA 347-F5
YALE CREEK RD
JACKSON CO OR 234-A5
YAMHILL RD
YAMHILL CO OR 198-B5
N YAMHILL ST Rt#-47
CARLTON OR 198-B5
YAMHILL NEWBERG HWY Rt#-240
NEWBERG OR 198-B5
YAMHILL CO OR 198-B5
YAMPO RD
POLK CO OR 204-B3
YAMHILL CO OR 204-C3
YANK GULCH RD
JACKSON CO OR 234-B4
YAQUINA BAY RD
LINCOLN CO OR 206-B4
NEWPORT OR 206-B4
TOLEDO OR 206-B4
NE YAQUINA HEIGHTS DR
LINCOLN CO OR 206-B4
YARRINGTON RD
UNION CO OR 130-B1
YARROW CENTRAL RD
DISTRICT OF CHILLIWACK BC 102-C1
YATES RD
CROOK CO OR 213-B6
LEWIS CO WA 184-D7
MASON CO WA 180-D2
YATES ST
CITY OF VICTORIA BC 256-H9
YEAGENS LANDING RD
MARION CO OR 198-D6
YELLOW FIR RD
TILLAMOOK CO OR 197-B4
YELLOW JACKET RD
UMATILLA CO OR 129-B2
YELLOWSTONE AV
OSBURN ID 115-C2
W YELLOWSTONE AV
BENTON CO WA 342-F8
E YELLOWSTONE TR
KOOTENAI CO ID 248-B1
YELM AV Rt#-507
THURSTON CO WA 118-A1
YELM WA 118-A1
YELM AV Rt#-510
YELM WA 118-A1
YELM HWY SE
LACEY WA 297-F12
THURSTON CO WA 181-A7
THURSTON CO WA 296-J11
THURSTON CO WA 297-A11
TUMWATER WA 296-J11
NW YEON AV U.S.-30
PORTLAND OR 199-B1
PORTLAND OR 312-A1
YESLER WY
SEATTLE WA 277-J6
SEATTLE WA 278-C6
YEW AV
OLYMPIA WA 297-B4
SW YEW AV
DESCHUTES CO OR 212-C6
YEW RD
BELLINGHAM WA 258-G12
WHATCOM CO WA 258-G12
YEW ST
BELLINGHAM WA 258-G5
KELSO WA 303-C10
S YEW ST
FINLEY WA 343-G12
YEW WY
SNOHOMISH CO WA 171-D5
YEW WY Rt#-524
SNOHOMISH CO WA 171-D5
YOAKUM GRADE RD
UMATILLA CO OR 129-B1
YOKEKO DR
SKAGIT CO WA 160-C7
YOKUM RD
DOUGLAS CO OR 225-C3
RIDDLE OR 225-C3
YOLANDA AV
North Springfield OR 331-B3
SPRINGFIELD OR 331-B3
YOMAN RD
PIERCE CO WA 181-A4
YONCALLA-ELKHEAD RD
DOUGLAS CO OR 219-B4
YORK RD
SISKIYOU CO CA 150-A3
SNOHOMISH CO WA 171-C5
UMATILLA CO OR 129-C1
WALLA WALLA CO WA 121-C3
YORK ST
BELLINGHAM WA 258-D6
YORK HILL DR
HOOD RIVER CO OR 195-C6
YOST RD
WHITE SWAN WA 119-C2
YAKIMA CO WA 119-C2
YAKIMA CO WA 120-A2
YOUMANS RD
GRAYS HARBOR CO WA 178-A3
YOUNG RD
COWLITZ CO WA 189-D3
DISTRICT OF CHILLIWACK BC 94-C3
YOUNG RD NW
THURSTON CO WA 180-C5
YOUNG ST
ABERDEEN WA 178-B7
WOODBURN OR 205-B2
E YOUNG ST
ELMA WA 179-B7
YOUNG GRADE
YAKIMA CO WA 243-A5
YOUNGS RIVER LOOP RD
CLATSOP CO WA 188-C3

YOUNGS RIVER LOOP RD
CLATSOP CO WA 300-C10
YREKA CREEK
SISKIYOU CO CA 150-A3
YREKA WALKER RD
SISKIYOU CO CA 149-C3
YTURRI BLVD
MALHEUR CO OR 147-A3
YUANCY LAKE RD
BONNER CO ID 244-B2
YUCCA AV
DESCHUTES CO OR 212-C4
NE YUCCA AV
DESCHUTES CO OR 212-D4
DESCHUTES CO OR 213-A4
YUMA ST
EDGEWOOD WA 182-B2
MILTON WA 182-B2
YUNGEN RD
WASHINGTON CO OR 192-A6

Z

ZAGER RD
CHELAN CO WA 238-C3
ZANDECKI RD
LEWIS CO WA 187-D2
ZANGLE RD NE
THURSTON CO WA 180-D5
ZARA DR
COOS CO OR 218-B5
ZAZA RD
NEZ PERCE CO ID 123-A3
ZEEK RD
CLARK CO WA 193-C6
ZEITLER RD
LATAH CO ID 249-C6
ZELATCHED POINT RD
JEFFERSON CO WA 170-A7
ZELL RD
WHATCOM CO WA 158-C4
ZEMKE RD
JACKSON CO OR 234-B3
ZENA RD
POLK CO OR 204-B4
ZENA RD NW
POLK CO OR 204-C4
POLK CO OR 322-B2
SW ZENITH
DESCHUTES CO OR 212-C6
ZENKER RD SW
THURSTON CO WA 184-C4
ZIAK-GNAT CREEK RD
CLATSOP CO WA 117-A3
W ZIER RD
WEST VALLEY WA 243-A7
YAKIMA CO WA 243-A7
ZIGZAG MOUNTAIN RD
CLACKAMAS CO OR 201-D5
E ZILLAH DR
YAKIMA CO WA 120-A2
ZILLIG RD
COWLITZ CO WA 118-A3
ZIMMER RD
STEVENS CO WA 106-A3
ZIMMERMAN RD
COLUMBIA CO OR 189-B5
YAKIMA CO WA 243-A6
S ZIMMERMAN RD
CLACKAMAS CO OR 205-C1
ZIMMERMAN RANCH RD
MALHEUR CO OR 154-A2
ZIMRI DR
NEWBERG OR 198-D5
YAMHILL CO OR 198-D5
ZIMS RD
ADAMS CO ID 251-A3
SE ZITZELSBERGER RD
CLARK CO WA 193-D7
ZUMWALT RD
POLK CO OR 207-A1
WALLOWA CO OR 131-A2
N ZYLSTRA RD
ISLAND CO WA 167-B3

#

1ST AV
ALBANY OR 326-C7
BONNER CO ID 244-A1
DISTRICT OF BURNABY BC 255-D12
DISTRICT OF DELTA BC 101-C1
KOOTENAI ID 244-A1
POWERS OR 140-B3
RIDDLE OR 225-B3
SEASIDE WA 301-F8
SEATTLE WA 277-H4
SEATTLE WA 278-A6
SHOSHONE CO ID 115-C2
SMELTERVILLE ID 115-C2
VANCOUVER BC 255-D12
1ST AV Rt#-3
BOVILL ID 123-B1
1ST AV Rt#-7
DISTRICT OF MISSION BC 94-B3
1ST AV Rt#-226
SCIO OR 133-C1
1ST AV Rt#-241
MABTON WA 120-B3
SATUS WA 120-B3
1ST AV Rt#-361
CULVER OR 208-B7
1ST AV Rt#-411
KELSO WA 303-C9
LONGVIEW WA 303-C9
E 1ST AV
JUNCTION CITY OR 210-A6
JUNCTION CITY OR 210-A6
LANE CO OR 210-A6
LANE CO OR 210-A6
RITZVILLE WA 113-C3
RITZVILLE WA 113-C3
E 1ST AV Rt#-28
ODESSA WA 113-B3
N 1ST AV
CHILOQUIN OR 231-D3
KLAMATH CO OR 231-D3
STAYTON OR 133-C1
N 1ST AV Rt#-99
DRAIN OR 219-A3

N 1ST AV U.S.-95
SANDPOINT ID 244-A2
NW 1ST AV
CANBY OR 199-C6
MILTON FREEWATER OR 121-C3
PAYETTE CO ID 139-B3
S 1ST AV
STAYTON OR 133-C1
S 1ST AV U.S.-95
SANDPOINT ID 244-A2
SE 1ST AV
CLACKAMAS CO OR 199-C6
SE 1ST AV Rt#-99E
CANBY OR 199-C6
SW 1ST AV
NEW PLYMOUTH ID 139-B3
PAYETTE CO ID 139-B3
PORTLAND OR 317-F1
SW 1ST AV Rt#-99E
CANBY OR 199-C6
W 1ST AV
ADAMS CO WA 113-C3
EUGENE OR 329-H5
JUNCTION CITY OR 210-A6
LANE CO OR 210-A6
RITZVILLE WA 113-C3
TOPPENISH WA 120-A2
YAKIMA CO WA 120-A2
W 1ST AV Rt#-21
ODESSA WA 113-B3
W 1ST AV Rt#-28
ODESSA WA 113-B3
1ST AV N
KELSO WA 303-D7
SEATTLE WA 277-H4
1ST AV N U.S.-101
ILWACO WA 186-A6
PACIFIC CO WA 186-A6
1ST AV NE
SEATTLE WA 171-B7
SEATTLE WA 274-A1
SHORELINE WA 171-B6
1ST AV NW
EPHRATA WA 112-C3
GRANT CO WA 112-C3
1ST AV NW Rt#-411
KELSO WA 303-C7
1ST AV S
ALGONA WA 182-B2
BURIEN WA 175-A5
FEDERAL WAY WA 182-A1
KELSO WA 303-D8
KING WA 285-J6
KING CO WA 175-A5
NORMANDY PARK WA 175-A5
SEATTLE WA 278-A7
SEATTLE WA 281-J4
SEATTLE WA 282-A1
SEATTLE WA 285-J3
1ST AV S Rt#-509
DES MOINES WA 175-A6
KING CO WA 175-A6
NORMANDY PARK WA 175-A6
1ST AV SW
QUINCY WA 112-B3
1ST PL
HERMISTON OR 129-A1
1ST PL W
EVERETT WA 268-B6
1ST RD
POWERS OR 140-B3
1 RD NE
DOUGLAS CO WA 112-C2
1 RD SE U.S.-2
DOUGLAS CO WA 112-C2
1 RD SW
DOUGLAS CO WA 239-D1
1ST ST
ASOTIN WA 250-B5
BANDON OR 220-B6
BENTON CO WA 340-F8
BREMERTON WA 270-D11
CANYONVILLE OR 225-C3
CITY OF N VANCOUVER BC 254-H5
CLARKSTON WA 250-B5
DESCHUTES CO OR 212-A6
DIST OF N VANCOUVER BC 254-H5
HERMISTON OR 129-A1
LINN CO OR 133-C1
LYNDEN WA 102-B1
MORO OR 127-C2
NEWPORT WA 106-C3
OAKLAND OR 219-A7
RICHLAND OR 139-A1
RICHLAND WA 340-F8
RUFUS OR 127-C1
WATERLOO OR 133-C1
WHATCOM CO WA 102-B1
WILSON CREEK WA 113-A2
YONCALLA OR 219-A4
1ST ST Rt#-4
SHOSHONE CO ID 115-C2
1ST ST Rt#-6
TILLAMOOK OR 197-B2
1ST ST Rt#-27
OAKESDALE WA 114-C3
1ST ST Rt#-82
ISLAND CITY OR 130-A2
1ST ST Rt#-129
ASOTIN WA 250-B5
1ST ST Rt#-214
SILVERTON OR 205-C4
1ST ST Rt#-237
ISLAND CITY OR 130-A2
UNION CO OR 130-A2
1ST ST Rt#-304
BREMERTON WA 270-J11
1ST ST U.S.-12
LEWISTON ID 250-B4
E 1ST ST
COLFAX WA 122-C1
COQUILLE OR 220-D5
MCMINNVILLE OR 198-A7
MERIDIAN ID 253-A3
WEISER ID 139-A2
E 1ST ST Rt#-82
WALLOWA OR 130-C1
E 1ST ST Rt#-117
PORT ANGELES WA 261-F4

STREET / City State / Page-Grid

E 1ST ST Rt#-170
GRANT CO WA 121-A1
WARDEN WA 121-A1
E 1ST ST Rt#-219
NEWBERG OR 198-D5
YAMHILL CO OR 198-D5
E 1ST ST U.S.-101
PORT ANGELES WA 261-F4
N 1ST ST
AUMSVILLE OR 133-C1
AUMSVILLE OR 205-B7
MARION CO OR 205-B7
MOUNT VERNON WA 260-C12
SELAH WA 243-B5
TACOMA WA 293-G4
YAKIMA WA 243-B6
YAKIMA CO WA 243-B5
N 1ST ST Rt#-21
ODESSA WA 113-B3
N 1ST ST Rt#-99
OAKLAND OR 219-A7
N 1ST ST Rt#-99W
NEWBERG OR 198-D5
N 1ST ST Rt#-214
SILVERTON OR 205-C4
N 1ST ST U.S.-395
HERMISTON OR 129-A1
NE 1ST ST
BELLEVUE WA 175-C2
DESCHUTES CO OR 212-D4
MEDINA WA 175-C2
NW 1ST ST Rt#-3
ENTERPRISE OR 130-C2
WALLOWA CO OR 130-C2
S 1ST ST
FAIRVIEW SUMACH WA 243-C7
MOUNT VERNON WA 260-C13
SHELTON WA 180-A3
SUNNYSIDE WA 120-B2
UNION GAP WA 243-C7
YAKIMA WA 243-C7
YAKIMA CO WA 243-C7
S 1ST ST Rt#-823
SELAH WA 243-B5
YAKIMA CO WA 243-B5
SE 1ST ST
CLARK CO WA 193-A6
PENDLETON OR 129-B1
SW 1ST ST
MADRAS OR 208-C5
ONTARIO OR 139-A3
PENDLETON OR 129-B1
W 1ST ST
MEDFORD OR 336-C11
NEWPORT WA 106-C3
PEND OREILLE CO WA 106-C3
WALLOWA OR 130-B1
WALLOWA CO OR 130-B1
W 1ST ST Rt#-82
WALLOWA OR 130-B1
W 1ST ST Rt#-117
PORT ANGELES WA 261-E4
W 1ST ST Rt#-170
WARDEN WA 121-A1
W 1ST ST Rt#-219
NEWBERG OR 198-D5
1ST ST N
MONTESANO WA 178-D7
1ST ST S
POULSBO WA 170-B6
1ST ST SW
BANDON OR 220-A6
1ST WY S
FEDERAL WAY WA 182-A1
1 1 2 RD NW
DOUGLAS CO WA 236-A7
1/2 NE RD
GRANT CO WA 112-C2
SOAP LAKE WA 112-C2
1-2-SE RD
GRANT CO WA 121-A1
1 3 4 RD SW
DOUGLAS CO WA 239-D1
2ND AV
ALBANY OR 326-C7
ASTORIA WA 300-C5
DESCHUTES CO OR 212-A6
SEATTLE WA 277-H4
SEATTLE WA 278-A6
TOWNSHIP OF LANGLEY BC 158-C3
VANCOUVER BC 254-H12
2ND AV Rt#-7
MORTON WA 118-B2
2ND AV Rt#-99
GOLD HILL OR 230-A6
2ND AV Rt#-903
KITTITAS CO WA 240-A1
E 2ND AV
SPOKANE WA 349-B9
NW 2ND AV
MYRTLE CREEK OR 225-C1
PAYETTE CO ID 139-B3
PORTLAND OR 313-F5
S 2ND AV
CHILOQUIN OR 231-D4
EVERETT WA 265-F7
EVERETT WA 269-F1
ROCKAWAY BEACH OR 191-B6
TUMWATER WA 296-G10
W 2ND AV
SPOKANE WA 348-H9
SPOKANE WA 349-A9
2ND AV N
WALLA WALLA WA 345-A7
2ND AV S
WALLA WALLA WA 345-B8
WALLA WALLA CO WA 345-B9
2ND AV S Rt#-52
PAYETTE ID 139-A3
2ND AV SE
SOAP LAKE WA 112-C2
2ND AV SW
SEATTLE WA 285-J2
SOAP LAKE WA 112-C2
2ND AVEX S
SEATTLE WA 278-A6
NW 2ND DR
LINCOLN CITY OR 203-A4
2 RD NW
DOUGLAS CO WA 236-B7

2 RD NW
WATERVILLE WA 236-B7
2 RD S
DOUGLAS CO WA 239-B1
2 RD SE
DOUGLAS CO WA 112-C2
2 RD SW
DOUGLAS CO WA 239-D1
2ND ST
ASOTIN WA 250-B5
ASOTIN CO WA 250-B4
CLARKSTON WA 250-B4
CORVALLIS OR 327-G10
ILWACO WA 186-A6
JEFFERSON OR 207-D3
LA GRANDE OR 130-A2
LEBANON OR 133-C1
MARION CO OR 199-A6
MARION CO OR 207-D3
NACHES WA 119-C1
NEW WESTMINSTER BC 156-D5
PACIFIC CO WA 186-A6
SHERMAN CO OR 127-C3
SNOHOMISH WA 171-D3
WALLA WALLA CO WA 345-G4
WHITE SWAN WA 119-C2
YAKIMA CO WA 119-C1
2ND ST Rt#-30
NORTH POWDER OR 130-B3
2ND ST Rt#-34
LEBANON OR 133-C1
2ND ST Rt#-42S
COQUILLE OR 220-D5
2ND ST Rt#-237
NORTH POWDER OR 130-B3
2ND ST U.S.-20
BENTON CO OR 327-H9
CORVALLIS OR 327-H9
2ND ST U.S.-99E
HALSEY OR 210-B2
E 2ND ST
COQUILLE OR 220-D5
WARDEN WA 121-A1
N 2ND ST
CENTRAL POINT OR 230-C7
LA GRANDE OR 130-A2
REEDSPORT OR 218-D1
SILVERTON OR 205-C4
NE 2ND ST
BEND OR 332-F6
NW 2ND ST
GRANTS PASS OR 335-E8
S 2ND ST
MOUNT VERNON WA 260-C14
SKAGIT CO WA 260-C14
S 2ND ST Rt#-900
RENTON WA 175-C5
W 2ND ST
MCMINNVILLE OR 198-A7
THE DALLES OR 196-C7
WARDEN WA 121-A1
WASCO CO OR 196-C7
W 2ND ST Rt#-124
WAITSBURG WA 122-A2
WALLA WALLA CO WA 122-A2
2ND ST E
PIERCE CO WA 182-C2
2ND ST NE
PUYALLUP WA 182-B3
2ND ST S
CANYON CO ID 147-C1
NAMPA ID 147-C1
2ND ST S U.S.-30
NAMPA ID 147-B1
2ND ST SE
DOUGLAS CO WA 239-A5
2ND ST SE U.S.-101
BANDON OR 220-B6
N 2ND ST W
CHEWELAH WA 106-B3
S 2ND ST W
CHEWELAH WA 106-B3
STEVENS CO WA 106-B3
2 1/2 RD NW U.S.-2
DOUGLAS CO WA 236-C7
WATERVILLE WA 236-C7
2 1/4 RD NW
DOUGLAS CO WA 236-B7
2ND DIVISION DR
PIERCE CO WA 181-C6
2ND DIVISION RANGE RD
PIERCE CO WA 181-B6
3RD AV
ALBANY OR 326-C7
BREWSTER WA 104-B3
KELSO WA 303-C8
LONGVIEW WA 303-C8
MOSIER OR 196-A5
TOWNSHIP OF LANGLEY BC 158-C2
WASCO CO OR 196-A5
3RD AV Rt#-169
BLACK DIAMOND WA 110-C3
3RD AV Rt#-411
LONGVIEW WA 303-C9
3RD AV Rt#-432
LONGVIEW WA 303-B12
E 3RD AV
FINLEY WA 343-G11
KENNEWICK WA 343-E11
POST FALLS ID 353-J7
POST FALLS ID 354-A7
SPOKANE WA 349-B10
E 3RD AV Rt#-20
COLVILLE WA 106-A2
STEVENS CO WA 106-A2
N 3RD AV
ROCKAWAY BEACH OR 191-B6
STAYTON OR 133-C1
NE 3RD AV
GOLDENDALE WA 127-C1
KLICKITAT CO WA 127-C1
NE 3RD AV Rt#-14
CAMAS WA 193-B7
CLARK CO WA 193-B7
WASHOUGAL WA 193-B7
NE 3RD AV Rt#-500
CAMAS WA 193-B7
NW 3RD AV
KELSO WA 303-C8

S 3RD AV
CLALLAM CO WA 262-D14
EVERETT WA 265-E6
NEAH BAY WA 262-D14
SOUTH BROADWAY WA 243-B7
UNION GAP WA 243-B7
YAKIMA WA 243-B7
S 3RD AV NE
POULSBO WA 170-B7
SW 3RD AV
KELSO WA 303-C8
PAYETTE CO ID 139-A3
W 3RD AV
KENNEWICK WA 343-D11
SPOKANE WA 348-J10
SPOKANE WA 349-A10
3RD AV FI
PIERCE CO WA 181-B2
3RD AV N
KELSO WA 303-D7
PAYETTE ID 139-A3
3RD AV N Rt#-524
EDMONDS WA 171-A5
3RD AV NE
SNOHOMISH CO WA 168-C5
3RD AV NW
SHORELINE WA 171-A6
3RD AV S
EDMONDS WA 171-A5
KELSO WA 303-C10
WALLA WALLA WA 345-B9
WALLA WALLA CO WA 345-B13
3RD AV SE
PACIFIC WA 182-B2
QUINCY WA 112-B3
3RD AV SW
EPHRATA WA 112-C3
3RD AV W
BREMERTON WA 270-D13
NAVY YARD CITY WA 270-D13
SEATTLE WA 273-G7
SEATTLE WA 277-G1
SE 3RD DR
PENDLETON OR 129-B1
3RD PL
THE DALLES OR 196-C7
3 RD NE
DOUGLAS CO WA 112-C2
3 RD NW
DOUGLAS CO WA 236-B7
3 RD SW
DOUGLAS CO WA 239-B1
3RD ST
ASOTIN CO WA 250-B4
ASTORIA WA 300-C6
CANNON BEACH WA 188-B7
CITY OF N VANCOUVER BC 254-J5
CITY OF N VANCOUVER BC 255-A5
CLARKSTON WA 250-B4
HAINES OR 130-A3
HUBBARD OR 205-B1
KUNA ID 253-A5
LEAVENWORTH WA 238-A1
MANZANITA OR 191-B4
MARYSVILLE WA 171-C1
NACHES WA 119-C1
NEWPORT WA 106-C3
OAKESDALE WA 114-C3
SEDRO WOOLLEY WA 161-C6
THE DALLES OR 196-C7
TILLAMOOK OR 197-C2
TILLAMOOK OR 197-C2
TILLAMOOK CO OR 197-C2
WHEELER OR 191-B4
WHITMAN CO WA 114-C3
YAKIMA CO WA 119-C1
3RD ST Rt#-6
TILLAMOOK OR 197-B2
TILLAMOOK OR 197-C2
3RD ST Rt#-42
COQUILLE OR 220-D5
3RD ST Rt#-99W
LAFAYETTE OR 198-B7
YAMHILL CO OR 198-B7
3RD ST Rt#-108
MCCLEARY WA 179-D6
3RD ST Rt#-112
CLALLAM CO WA 100-B2
3RD ST Rt#-221
DAYTON OR 198-C7
YAMHILL CO OR 198-C7
3RD ST U.S.-99E
HARRISBURG OR 210-A5
E 3RD ST
MCMINNVILLE OR 198-A7
MOSCOW ID 249-C5
E 3RD ST Rt#-8
MOSCOW ID 249-C5
N 3RD ST
ALMIRA WA 237-D7
CENTRAL POINT OR 230-C7
DAYTON WA 122-A2
DUFUR OR 127-B2
JACKSON CO OR 230-C7
OSBURN ID 115-C2
WASCO CO OR 127-B2
NE 3RD ST U.S.-20
BEND OR 332-F4
NE 3RD ST U.S.-97
BEND OR 332-F6
NE 3RD ST Rt#-500
CLARK CO WA 193-B6
NE 3RD ST
MALHEUR CO OR 139-A3
ONTARIO OR 139-A3
RENTON WA 175-C5
NW 3RD ST
GRANTS PASS OR 335-E8
S 3RD ST
ELMA WA 179-B7
S 3RD ST Rt#-23
HARRINGTON WA 113-C2
S 3RD ST Rt#-536
MOUNT VERNON WA 260-C12
S 3RD ST Rt#-900
RENTON WA 175-C5
S 3RD ST U.S.-95
FRUITLAND ID 139-A3
SE 3RD ST
LINCOLN CITY OR 203-A5

SE 3RD ST
ONTARIO OR 139-A3
PENDLETON OR 129-B1
SE 3RD ST Rt#-14
CAMAS WA 193-B7
WASHOUGAL WA 193-B7
SE 3RD ST U.S.-97
BEND OR 332-F9
W 3RD ST Rt#-8
MOSCOW ID 249-C5
W 3RD ST Rt#-126
CROOK CO OR 213-D5
PRINEVILLE OR 213-D5
3RD ST N
MONTESANO WA 178-D7
3RD ST S
NAMPA ID 147-B1
3RD ST S U.S.-30
NAMPA ID 147-B1
3RD ST SE
MARION CO OR 325-F10
PUYALLUP WA 182-B3
TURNER OR 325-F10
TURNER OR 325-G13
3RD ST W Rt#-99W
CORVALLIS OR 207-A7
CORVALLIS OR 327-G14
3RD ST W U.S.-20
CORVALLIS OR 327-G10
3 AV
DISTRICT OF DELTA BC 101-C1
4TH AV
ALBANY OR 326-C8
GOLD HILL OR 230-A6
KITTITAS WA 241-C6
SCIO OR 133-C1
SEATTLE WA 277-J4
SEATTLE WA 278-A5
TOWNSHIP OF LANGLEY BC 158-C2
UNIV ENDOWMENT LANDS BC 156-A4
4TH AV Rt#-234
GOLD HILL OR 230-B6
E 4TH AV
DISHMAN WA 350-G9
EUGENE OR 330-A5
OPPORTUNITY WA 350-G9
OPPORTUNITY WA 351-B9
POST FALLS ID 353-H7
POST FALLS ID 354-A7
SPOKANE WA 349-D10
SPOKANE CO WA 349-J9
SPOKANE CO WA 350-A9
VERADALE WA 351-B9
N 4TH AV
KENT WA 291-J7
PASCO WA 343-F6
NW 4TH AV
ONTARIO OR 139-B3
PAYETTE CO ID 139-B3
S 4TH AV
PASCO WA 343-G7
YAKIMA WA 243-B7
SW 4TH AV
PORTLAND OR 313-E7
PORTLAND OR 317-E1
SW 4TH AV Rt#-201
ONTARIO OR 139-A3
W 4TH AV
BENTON CO WA 342-F11
KENNEWICK WA 342-G11
KENNEWICK WA 343-B11
4TH AV E
OLYMPIA WA 296-J5
OLYMPIA WA 297-A5
4TH AV N
KELSO WA 303-D7
KENT WA 175-B7
KENT WA 291-J7
4TH AV NW
SNOHOMISH CO WA 168-C4
4TH AV S
SEATTLE WA 278-A7
SEATTLE WA 282-A4
4TH AV W
BOTHELL WA 171-C6
EVERETT WA 268-A6
OLYMPIA WA 296-G5
SNOHOMISH WA 268-A6
SNOHOMISH CO WA 171-C4
UNIV ENDOWMENT LANDS BC 156-A4
VANCOUVER BC 156-A4
VANCOUVER BC 254-A12
4TH ST
ANACORTES WA 259-H1
GERVAIS OR 205-B2
GRANTS PASS OR 335-E8
HAINES OR 130-A3
LA GRANDE OR 130-A2
LEWISTON ID 250-C4
NANAIMO BC 93-A3
NORTHPORT WA 106-A1
PHOENIX OR 234-B2
SKAGIT CO WA 259-H14
SNOHOMISH CO WA 171-C1
4TH ST Rt#-528
SNOHOMISH CO WA 171-C1
4TH ST
SUMMERVILLE OT 130-A2
4TH ST Rt#-5
SAINT MARIES ID 248-D7
4TH ST Rt#-27
GARFIELD WA 114-C3
4TH ST Rt#-39
KLAMATH FALLS OR 338-D8
4TH ST Rt#-234
GOLD HILL OR 230-B6
4TH ST Rt#-304
BREMERTON WA 270-H11
4TH ST Rt#-528
MARYSVILLE WA 171-C1
4TH ST U.S.-97
GRASS VALLEY OR 127-C2
SHANIKO OR 127-C3
WASCO CO OR 127-C3
E 4TH ST
MEDFORD OR 336-D11
THE DALLES OR 196-C7
N 4TH ST
ALMIRA WA 237-D7
COEUR D'ALENE ID 355-E6

N 4TH ST
DALTON GARDENS ID 355-F4
HAYDEN ID 355-E1
KLAMATH FALLS OR 338-D7
KOOTENAI CO ID 355-E1
MOUNT VERNON WA 260-C11
NE 4TH ST
BEND OR 332-F6
ENTERPRISE OR 130-C2
KING CO WA 175-C5
RENTON WA 175-C5
NW 4TH ST U.S.-26
MADRAS OR 208-C5
S 4TH ST
COLUMBIA CO WA 122-A2
DAYTON WA 122-A2
SW 4TH ST
MALHEUR CO OR 139-A3
ONTARIO OR 139-A3
PENDLETON OR 129-B1
SW 4TH ST U.S.-26
MADRAS OR 208-C5
W 4TH ST
MEDFORD OR 336-B12
THE DALLES OR 196-C7
4TH ST N Rt#-140
LAKE CO OR 152-A2
LAKEVIEW OR 152-A2
4TH ST NE
SNOHOMISH CO WA 171-D2
4TH ST NW
BREWSTER WA 104-B3
OKANOGAN CO WA 104-B3
4TH ST SE
DOUGLAS CO WA 239-B5
EAST WENATCHEE BENCH WA 239-A5
4TH ST SW
BANDON OR 220-A6
BREWSTER WA 104-B3
OKANOGAN CO WA 104-B3
4TH ST W Rt#-99W
CORVALLIS OR 327-H9
4TH ST W U.S.-20
CORVALLIS OR 327-H9
4 1/2 RD NW
DOUGLAS CO WA 112-B2
4TH DIVISION DR
PIERCE CO WA 181-C6
4TH ST GRADE
THE DALLES OR 196-C7
4 RD SW
DOUGLAS CO WA 239-D2
5TH AV
ALBANY OR 326-C8
BENTON CO OR 133-B2
MONROE OR 133-B2
OLYMPIA WA 296-G5
RIDDLE OR 225-B3
SEATTLE WA 277-J4
SEATTLE WA 278-A5
5TH AV Rt#-41
SPIRIT LAKE ID 115-A1
5TH AV Rt#-99W
MONROE OR 133-B2
5TH AV U.S.-95
SANDPOINT ID 244-A2
N 5TH AV
YAKIMA WA 243-B6
N 5TH AV U.S.-95
SANDPOINT ID 244-A2
S 5TH AV
YAKIMA WA 243-B6
SE 5TH AV
MALHEUR CO OR 139-A3
ONTARIO OR 139-A3
SW 5TH AV
ONTARIO OR 139-A3
PORTLAND OR 312-E7
PORTLAND OR 316-E1
PORTLAND OR 317-E1
W 5TH AV
EUGENE OR 329-E6
W 5TH AV U.S.-395
COLVILLE WA 106-A2
5TH AV N
KELSO WA 303-D7
SEATTLE WA 277-J2
5TH AV NE
SEATTLE WA 171-B7
SHORELINE WA 171-B6
5TH AV NW
KELSO WA 303-C8
5TH AV S
EDMONDS WA 171-A5
KELSO WA 303-C10
KING WA 286-A6
SEATTLE WA 278-A7
5TH AV W
EVERETT WA 268-A5
5 RD NE
DOUGLAS CO WA 112-C2
5 RD NW
DOUGLAS CO WA 236-C6
5 RD SW
DOUGLAS CO WA 112-B2
DOUGLAS CO WA 239-D2
5TH ST
ASTORIA WA 300-C6
BAY CITY OR 197-B1
CLARKSTON WA 250-B4
CORVALLIS OR 327-H9
EVERETT WA 171-B2
HOQUIAM WA 178-A7
LEWISTON ID 250-B4
MUKILTEO WA 171-B2
MUKILTEO WA 266-E1
MUKILTEO WA 267-F1
OAKLAND OR 219-A7
YAKIMA CO WA 120-B3
5TH ST Rt#-39
KLAMATH FALLS OR 338-E8
5TH ST Rt#-129
ASOTIN CO WA 250-B4
CLARKSTON WA 250-B4
5TH ST Rt#-162
KAMIAH ID 123-C2
5TH ST Rt#-226
LINN CO OR 134-A1
LYONS OR 134-A1
MARION CO OR 134-A1

5TH ST U.S.-12
LEWISTON ID 250-B4
5TH ST U.S.-26
MADRAS OR 208-C5
5TH ST U.S.-95
CANYON CO ID 147-A1
WILDER ID 147-A1
N 5TH ST
DUFUR OR 127-B2
North Springfield OR 330-H5
SPRINGFIELD OR 330-H5
N 5TH ST Rt#-238
JACKSONVILLE OR 149-B2
N 5TH ST Rt#-505
LEWIS CO WA 187-D4
TOLEDO WA 187-D4
NE 5TH ST
CLATSKANIE OR 117-B3
DESCHUTES CO OR 212-D4
NW 5TH ST
CLATSKANIE OR 117-B3
COLUMBIA CO OR 117-B3
NW 5TH ST U.S.-97
REDMOND OR 212-D5
S 5TH ST
POMEROY WA 122-B2
SPRINGFIELD OR 330-H7
S 5TH ST Rt#-39
KLAMATH FALLS OR 338-D8
SE 5TH ST
PRINEVILLE OR 213-D5
SW 5TH ST
GRANTS PASS OR 335-E10
SW 5TH ST Rt#-99
CANYONVILLE OR 225-C3
SW 5TH ST U.S.-97
REDMOND OR 212-D5
W 5TH ST
GRANDVIEW WA 120-B3
WALLOWA OR 130-C1
YAKIMA CO WA 120-B3
5TH ST NE
EAST WENATCHEE BENCH WA 239-A4
SALEM OR 322-J11
6TH AV
NEW WESTMINSTER BC 156-D5
SEATTLE WA 278-A6
TACOMA WA 181-C2
TACOMA WA 292-B5
TACOMA WA 293-E5
TOWNSHIP OF LANGLEY BC 158-C2
VANCOUVER BC 254-G12
VINELAND WA 250-B5
6TH AV Rt#-128
ASOTIN CO WA 250-B5
VINELAND WA 250-B5
E 6TH AV
JUNCTION CITY OR 210-A6
E 6TH AV Rt#-21
ODESSA WA 113-B3
E 6TH AV Rt#-99
EUGENE OR 330-A6
N 6TH AV
RIDDLE OR 225-B3
YAKIMA WA 243-B6
NE 6TH AV
SUTHERLIN OR 221-C1
NW 6TH AV
SUTHERLIN OR 221-C1
NW 6TH AV Rt#-14
CAMAS WA 193-B7
S 6TH AV
TACOMA WA 293-G4
SE 6TH AV Rt#-500
CAMAS WA 193-B7
SW 6TH AV
PORTLAND OR 316-E1
W 6TH AV
JUNCTION CITY OR 210-A6
KENNEWICK WA 343-D11
LANE CO OR 210-A6
W 6TH AV Rt#-99
EUGENE OR 329-G6
EUGENE OR 330-A6
6TH AV NW
SHORELINE WA 171-A6
6TH AV S
SEATTLE WA 282-A3
6TH AV SE
GRANT CO WA 112-C2
LACEY WA 297-F5
SOAP LAKE WA 112-C2
6TH AV SW
GRANT CO WA 112-C2
SOAP LAKE WA 112-C2
NE 6TH DR
PORTLAND OR 309-G2
6 RD SE
DOUGLAS CO WA 112-C2
6TH ST
ANACORTES WA 259-J1
ASTORIA WA 300-C5
BREMERTON WA 270-H10
COLUMBIA CITY OR 192-B1
COWLITZ CO WA 192-B1
DESCHUTES CO OR 143-A1
HARRISBURG OR 210-A5
HOOD RIVER OR 195-D5
LANE CO OR 219-D1
NEW WESTMINSTER BC 156-D5
THE DALLES OR 196-C7
WALLA WALLA CO WA 345-G4
WOODLAND WA 192-B1
6TH ST Rt#-39
KLAMATH FALLS OR 338-D8
6TH ST Rt#-129
CLARKSTON WA 250-B4
6TH ST Rt#-226
LINN CO OR 134-A1
LYONS OR 134-A1
6TH ST Rt#-310
BREMERTON WA 270-G10
6TH ST U.S.-2
NEWPORT WA 106-C3
6TH ST U.S.-730
UMATILLA OR 129-A1
UMATILLA CO OR 129-A1
E 6TH ST
COLFAX WA 122-C1
MOSCOW ID 249-D5

PNW

INDEX

STREET / City State / Page-Grid

N 6TH ST
GRANTS PASS OR 335-F6
KLAMATH FALLS OR 338-D7
SAINT HELENS OR 192-B1
N 6TH ST Rt#-52
PAYETTE ID 139-A3
N 6TH ST U.S.-199
GRANTS PASS OR 335-F8
NW 6TH ST U.S.-97
REDMOND OR 212-D5
NW 6TH ST U.S.-199
GRANTS PASS OR 335-F8
S 6TH ST
COTTAGE GROVE OR 215-B7
LANE CO OR 215-B7
SUNNYSIDE WA 120-B2
S 6TH ST Rt#-39
KLAMATH FALLS OR 338-E8
S 6TH ST U.S.-199
GRANTS PASS OR 335-E9
SE 6TH ST
CLARK CO WA 193-C6
SW 6TH ST U.S.-97
REDMOND OR 212-D5
W 6TH ST
MOSCOW ID 249-C5
W 6TH ST Rt#-20
REPUBLIC WA 105-B2
6TH ST N
NAMPA ID 147-B1
6TH ST SE
DOUGLAS CO WA 239-A5
EAST WENATCHEE BENCH WA 239-A5
7TH AV
ALBANY OR 326-B8
CITY OF RICHMOND BC 156-A7
DISTRICT OF MISSION BC 94-B3
KELSO WA 303-B9
LONGVIEW WA 303-B9
E 7TH AV
SPOKANE WA 349-C10
E 7TH AV Rt#-99
EUGENE OR 330-A6
N 7TH AV
YAKIMA WA 243-B6
S 7TH AV
YAKIMA WA 243-B6
SE 7TH AV
PORTLAND OR 313-G6
W 7TH AV
SPOKANE WA 348-F10
W 7TH AV Rt#-99
EUGENE OR 329-G6
EUGENE OR 330-A6
7TH AV N
KELSO WA 303-D8
PAYETTE ID 139-A3
PAYETTE CO ID 139-A3
SEATTLE WA 277-J4
7TH AV S
DES MOINES WA 290-A5
KELSO WA 303-D10
7TH AV SE
EVERETT WA 268-C7
7TH AV SW
KELSO WA 303-C8
OLYMPIA WA 296-C5
THURSTON CO WA 296-C5
7 RD NE
DOUGLAS CO WA 112-C1
7 RD NW
DOUGLAS CO WA 236-C5
7TH ST
ASTORIA WA 300-C7
GOLD HILL OR 230-B6
HARRISBURG OR 210-A5
NEHALEM OR 191-B4
OREGON CITY OR 199-D5
PROSSER WA 120-B3
WEST LINN OR 199-D5
7TH ST Rt#-506
VADER WA 187-B5
7TH ST U.S.-95
WEISER ID 139-A2
7TH ST U.S.-101
NEHALEM OR 191-B4
E 7TH ST
PRINEVILLE OR 213-D5
E 7TH ST Rt#-19
FOSSIL OR 128-A3
E 7TH ST U.S.-95
WEISER ID 139-A2
N 7TH ST
BREWSTER WA 104-B3
COEUR D'ALENE ID 355-F8
COOS BAY OR 333-G10
N 7TH ST Rt#-52
PAYETTE ID 139-A3
NE 7TH ST U.S.-199
GRANTS PASS OR 335-F8
S 7TH ST
COOS BAY OR 333-G10
TACOMA WA 293-H5
S 7TH ST Rt#-52
PAYETTE ID 139-A3
S 7TH ST U.S.-95
PAYETTE ID 139-A3
SE 7TH ST U.S.-199
GRANTS PASS OR 335-E9
SE 7TH ST
WARRENTON WA 188-B2
7TH ST SW
BANDON OR 220-A6
7TH ST W
RAINIER OR 189-B4
7 1/2 RD NW
DOUGLAS CO WA 236-A5
7 3/4 RD NW
DOUGLAS CO WA 236-A5
8TH AV
CITY OF WHITE ROCK BC 158-B2
DISTRICT OF SURREY BC 158-B2
LONGVIEW WA 303-B10
NEW WESTMINSTER BC 156-D5
TOWNSHIP OF LANGLEY BC 158-C2
8TH AV Rt#-162
NEZPERCE ID 123-C2
E 8TH AV
DISHMAN WA 350-F10
GREEN ACRES WA 351-G9

E 8TH AV
KENNEWICK WA 343-F12
OPPORTUNITY WA 350-F10
OPPORTUNITY WA 351-B9
SPOKANE WA 349-G10
SPOKANE CO WA 349-H10
SPOKANE CO WA 350-A10
SPOKANE CO WA 351-G9
VERADALE WA 351-B9
N 8TH AV Rt#-82
ELGIN OR 130-A1
NE 8TH AV
MILTON FREEWATER OR 121-C3
NW 8TH AV
MILTON FREEWATER OR 121-C3
ONTARIO OR 139-A3
S 8TH AV Rt#-82
ELGIN OR 130-A1
UNION CO OR 130-A1
SW 8TH AV
MILTON FREEWATER OR 121-C3
W 8TH AV
SPOKANE WA 348-J10
SPOKANE WA 349-A10
8TH AV E
PIERCE CO WA 118-A1
PIERCE CO WA 181-D7
8TH AV N Rt#-125
WALLA WALLA WA 344-J8
8TH AV NE
LACEY WA 297-F4
8TH AV NW
SEATTLE WA 273-G2
SHORELINE WA 171-A6
8TH AV S
BURIEN WA 288-A2
KING WA 286-A5
KING WA 288-A2
PIERCE CO WA 118-A1
PIERCE CO WA 181-D7
SEATAC WA 288-A4
8 RD NW
DOUGLAS CO WA 236-B5
8 RD SE
DOUGLAS CO WA 112-C2
8 RD SW
DOUGLAS CO WA 239-B3
8TH ST
ASHLAND OR 337-D8
ASTORIA WA 300-C5
LEWISTON ID 250-B4
NEW WESTMINSTER BC 156-D5
PIERCE CO WA 181-B5
8TH ST Rt#-42
MYRTLE POINT OR 140-B2
8TH ST U.S.-30
ASTORIA WA 300-C5
E 8TH ST
MEDFORD OR 336-D12
PORT ANGELES WA 261-E5
E 8TH ST Rt#-82
JOSEPH OR 130-C2
WALLOWA CO OR 130-C2
E 8TH ST Rt#-238
MEDFORD OR 336-D12
N 8TH ST
BOISE ID 253-C2
MOUNT VERNON WA 260-C12
PAYETTE ID 139-A3
NE 8TH ST
BELLEVUE WA 175-C2
BEND OR 332-G6
GRANTS PASS OR 335-F8
KING CO WA 176-A2
S 8TH ST
AUMSVILLE OR 133-C1
BOISE ID 253-C3
JEFFERSON CO WA 263-C7
PAYETTE ID 139-A3
SE 8TH ST
PENDLETON OR 129-B1
W 8TH ST
PORT ANGELES WA 261-D4
W 8TH ST Rt#-238
MEDFORD OR 336-B12
8TH ST E
EDGEWOOD WA 182-B2
PACIFIC WA 182-B2
PIERCE CO WA 182-B2
8TH ST NE
EAST WENATCHEE BENCH WA 239-A4
8TH ST NW
SALEM OR 322-F12
8TH ST SE
DOUGLAS CO WA 239-B5
EAST WENATCHEE BENCH WA 239-A5
SNOHOMISH CO WA 171-D2
8TH ST SW
BANDON OR 220-A6
8-10-NE RD
GRANT CO WA 242-B1
8 1/2 RD NW
DOUGLAS CO WA 236-C5
9TH AV
ALBANY OR 326-D8
LONGVIEW WA 303-B8
SEATTLE WA 277-J4
SEATTLE WA 278-B6
SE 9TH AV
MILTON FREEWATER OR 121-C3
W 9TH AV
SPOKANE WA 348-J10
SPOKANE WA 349-A10
9TH AV FI
PIERCE CO WA 181-B2
9TH AV N
SEATTLE WA 277-J4
9TH AV N Rt#-524
EDMONDS WA 171-A5
9TH AV S
EDMONDS WA 171-A5
9TH AV S Rt#-125
WALLA WALLA WA 344-J8
WALLA WALLA WA 345-A9
9TH AV SW
OLYMPIA WA 296-E5
SEATTLE WA 285-H3
9 RD NW
DOUGLAS CO WA 236-D5

9 RD SW
DOUGLAS CO WA 239-B3
9TH ST
CORVALLIS OR 327-H6
FLORENCE OR 214-B3
HARRISBURG OR 210-A5
HOOD RIVER OR 195-D5
JEFFERSON CO OR 208-B6
ONTARIO OR 139-A3
PORT ORFORD OR 224-A6
WALLA WALLA CO WA 345-H4
9TH ST Rt#-57
BONNER CO ID 107-A3
PRIEST RIVER ID 107-A3
9TH ST Rt#-225
BENTON CITY WA 120-C3
BENTON CO WA 120-C3
E 9TH ST
THE DALLES OR 196-C7
N 9TH ST
BOISE ID 253-C2
COEUR D'ALENE ID 355-F9
TACOMA WA 181-C2
NE 9TH ST
BEND OR 332-G8
CLARK CO WA 193-C6
DESCHUTES CO OR 212-D5
GRANTS PASS OR 335-G8
JOSEPHINE CO OR 335-G8
TERREBONNE OR 212-D3
S 9TH ST
BOISE ID 253-C3
SE 9TH ST
BEND OR 332-G8
9TH ST E
PIERCE CO WA 182-C2
9TH ST NE
EAST WENATCHEE BENCH WA 239-A4
9TH ST NW
SALEM OR 322-F12
9TH ST S
LAKE CO OR 152-A2
LAKEVIEW OR 152-A2
9TH ST SW
PUYALLUP WA 182-B4
9 1 2 RD SW
DOUGLAS CO WA 239-B3
10TH AV
DISTRICT OF BURNABY BC 156-D5
NEW WESTMINSTER BC 156-D5
TOWNSHIP OF LANGLEY BC 158-D2
VANCOUVER BC 156-A4
VANCOUVER BC 254-A12
10TH AV Rt#-99A
DISTRICT OF BURNABY BC 156-D5
NEW WESTMINSTER BC 156-D5
E 10TH AV
BENTON CO WA 343-F12
KENNEWICK WA 343-F12
SPOKANE WA 349-B11
N 10TH AV
ELGIN OR 130-A1
PASCO WA 343-F7
STAYTON OR 133-C1
NE 10TH AV
CLARK CO WA 192-C3
PAYETTE ID 139-A3
PAYETTE CO ID 139-A3
NW 10TH AV
PORTLAND OR 313-E5
NE 10TH AV Rt#-502
CLARK CO WA 192-C3
S 10TH AV
CANYON CO ID 147-B1
CORNELIUS OR 198-C1
PASCO WA 343-F8
S 10TH AV Rt#-397
PASCO WA 343-F9
SE 10TH AV
HILLSBORO OR 198-D1
SE 10TH AV Rt#-8
HILLSBORO OR 198-D1
SW 10TH AV
BATTLE GROUND WA 193-A3
CLARK CO WA 193-A3
PORTLAND OR 312-E6
PORTLAND OR 313-0
W 10TH AV
BENTON CO WA 342-B12
KENNEWICK WA 342-B12
KENNEWICK WA 343-C12
10TH AV E
SEATTLE WA 278-B3
10TH AV NE
SHORELINE WA 171-B7
10TH AV SW
FEDERAL WAY WA 182-A1
QUINCY WA 112-B3
10TH AV W
SEATTLE WA 277-F2
10 RD NW
DOUGLAS CO WA 236-D5
10 RD SW
DOUGLAS CO WA 239-B3
10TH ST
CORVALLIS OR 327-G8
EVERETT WA 171-C1
NANAIMO BC 93-A3
SNOHOMISH WA 171-D3
10TH ST Rt#-173
BRIDGEPORT WA 112-C1
10TH ST U.S.-30
BAKER CITY OR 138-B1
E 10TH ST
MEDFORD OR 336-D12
THE DALLES OR 196-C7
N 10TH ST
CENTRAL POINT OR 230-C7
KLAMATH FALLS OR 338-D7
NE 10TH ST
BEND OR 332-G7
GRANTS PASS OR 335-G7
JOSEPHINE CO OR 335-G7
NW 10TH ST
DESCHUTES CO OR 212-D3
PENDLETON OR 129-B1
TERREBONNE OR 212-D4
NW 10TH ST U.S.-97
TERREBONNE OR 212-D3

S 10TH ST
COTTAGE GROVE OR 215-B7
FAIRVIEW SUMACH WA 243-C7
YAKIMA WA 243-C7
SE 10TH ST
PENDLETON OR 129-B1
VANCOUVER WA 307-H7
SE 10TH ST Rt#-37
PENDLETON OR 129-B1
SW 10TH ST
PENDLETON OR 129-B1
W 10TH ST
MEDFORD OR 336-D12
PRINEVILLE OR 213-D5
THE DALLES OR 196-C7
WASCO CO OR 196-C7
10TH ST NE
DOUGLAS CO WA 239-A4
EAST WENATCHEE WA 239-A4
EAST WENATCHEE BENCH WA 239-A4
10TH ST SE
DOUGLAS CO WA 239-A5
10 5 SE RD
GRANT CO WA 242-C7
11TH AV
BREMERTON WA 270-F10
LEWISTON ID 250-B4
NAMPA ID 147-B1
11TH AV Rt#-11
DISTRICT OF MISSION BC 94-B3
11TH AV U.S.-30
NAMPA ID 147-B1
E 11TH AV
EUGENE OR 330-A7
NE 11TH AV
PORTLAND OR 313-H4
NW 11TH AV
CLARK CO WA 192-C2
PORTLAND OR 313-E5
SE 11TH AV
PORTLAND OR 313-H6
PORTLAND OR 317-H1
SW 11TH AV
PORTLAND OR 312-E6
PORTLAND OR 313-E5
W 11TH AV
EUGENE OR 329-H7
EUGENE OR 330-A7
W 11TH AV Rt#-126
EUGENE OR 329-D6
11TH AV FI
PIERCE CO WA 181-B3
11TH AV N U.S.-30
NAMPA ID 147-C1
11TH AV NE
SEATTLE WA 274-B5
SNOHOMISH CO WA 168-C6
THURSTON CO WA 297-B4
11TH AV NW
OLYMPIA WA 296-A3
THURSTON CO WA 296-A3
11TH ST
BELLINGHAM WA 258-B10
BREMERTON WA 270-G10
CORVALLIS OR 327-F10
DIST OF WEST VANCOUVER BC 254-D4
WALLA WALLA CO WA 345-J4
E 11TH ST
BREMERTON WA 271-A10
TACOMA WA 182-A2
TACOMA WA 293-J4
E 11TH ST Rt#-11
TACOMA WA 293-J5
N 11TH ST
AUMSVILLE OR 133-C1
COEUR D'ALENE ID 355-G11
NE 11TH ST
DESCHUTES CO OR 212-D4
S 11TH ST
COEUR D'ALENE ID 355-G12
TACOMA WA 293-F5
S 11TH ST Rt#-11
TACOMA WA 293-H5
SW 11TH ST Rt#-207
HERMISTON OR 129-A1
UMATILLA CO OR 129-A1
W 11TH ST
KETTLE FALLS WA 106-A2
STEVENS CO WA 106-A2
WARDEN WA 121-A1
11TH ST NE
EAST WENATCHEE WA 239-A4
12TH AV
ALBANY OR 326-A9
CLATSOP CO WA 301-G7
DISTRICT OF DELTA BC 101-C1
SEASIDE WA 301-G7
SEATTLE WA 278-B6
TOWNSHIP OF LANGLEY BC 158-D2
VANCOUVER BC 254-J13
VANCOUVER BC 255-A13
E 12TH AV
SPOKANE WA 349-F11
NE 12TH AV
PORTLAND OR 313-H5
SE 12TH AV
PORTLAND OR 313-H6
PORTLAND OR 317-H1
SW 12TH AV
PORTLAND OR 312-E6
W 12TH AV
AIRWAY HEIGHTS WA 246-A4
12TH AV E
SEATTLE WA 278-B4
VANCOUVER BC 254-H13
12TH AV NE
SEATTLE WA 274-C4
THURSTON CO WA 297-B4
12TH AV S
SEATAC WA 288-B6
SEATTLE WA 278-B7
WALLA WALLA WA 344-J8
12TH AV S Rt#-45
NAMPA ID 147-B1
12TH AV W
VANCOUVER BC 254-C13
12 RD NE
DOUGLAS CO WA 112-C2
12 RD NE U.S.-2
DOUGLAS CO WA 112-C2

12 RD SW
DOUGLAS CO WA 239-C4
12TH ST
BELLINGHAM WA 258-B10
HOOD RIVER OR 195-D5
LEBANON OR 133-C1
LINN CO OR 133-C1
NEW WESTMINSTER BC 156-D5
TILLAMOOK OR 197-C2
TILLAMOOK CO OR 197-C2
12TH ST Rt#-11
BELLINGHAM WA 258-B11
12TH ST Rt#-20
ANACORTES WA 259-F2
E 12TH ST
MEDFORD OR 336-D12
N 12TH ST
SPRINGFIELD OR 330-J7
NE 12TH ST
BELLEVUE WA 175-C2
BEND OR 332-G6
CLYDE HILL WA 175-C2
MEDINA WA 175-C2
NEWPORT OR 206-B4
RENTON WA 175-C4
NW 12TH ST
LINCOLN CITY OR 203-A4
NEWPORT OR 206-A4
S 12TH ST
TACOMA WA 292-A6
TACOMA WA 293-F5
SE 12TH ST
PENDLETON OR 129-B1
12TH ST E
PIERCE CO WA 182-C2
12TH ST N U.S.-26
MALHEUR CO OR 139-A3
VALE OR 139-A3
12TH ST NE
SALEM OR 322-J12
12TH ST SE
DOUGLAS CO WA 239-B5
SALEM OR 322-J14
SALEM OR 324-J3
12TH ST SE Rt#-22
SALEM OR 322-J14
12TH AVENUE RD Rt#-45
CANYON CO ID 147-B1
NAMPA ID 147-B1
OWYHEE CO ID 147-B1
12TH CUTOFF ST SE
SALEM OR 324-H5
13TH AV
TOWNSHIP OF LANGLEY BC 158-D2
E 13TH AV
EUGENE OR 330-B7
SPOKANE WA 349-F11
NE 13TH AV
PORTLAND OR 313-H4
SE 13TH AV
PORTLAND OR 317-H6
SW 13TH AV
PORTLAND OR 312-E6
W 13TH AV
EUGENE OR 329-G7
EUGENE OR 330-A7
13TH AV N Rt#-125
WALLA WALLA WA 344-J5
13TH AV S
SEATTLE WA 282-B7
13TH AV W
SNOHOMISH CO WA 171-B4
13 RD NE
DOUGLAS CO WA 113-A1
13TH ST
ANACORTES WA 259-H2
ASOTIN CO WA 250-B4
CITY OF N VANCOUVER BC 254-J5
CITY OF N VANCOUVER BC 255-B5
CLARKSTON WA 250-B4
DESCHUTES CO OR 212-D3
HOOD RIVER OR 195-D5
SNOHOMISH WA 171-D3
VINELAND WA 250-B5
E 13TH ST
WASCO CO OR 196-D7
N 13TH ST
BOISE ID 253-C2
NE 13TH ST
DESCHUTES CO OR 212-D5
S 13TH ST
MOUNT VERNON WA 260-D13
SKAGIT CO WA 260-D13
TACOMA WA 293-H5
SW 13TH ST
PENDLETON OR 129-B1
W 13TH ST
THE DALLES OR 196-C7
WASCO CO OR 196-C7
13TH ST NE
SALEM OR 322-J13
SALEM OR 323-A13
14TH AV
OLYMPIA WA 296-H6
SEATTLE WA 278-C6
TOWNSHIP OF LANGLEY BC 158-D2
E 14TH AV
ELLENSBURG WA 241-B5
SPOKANE WA 349-D11
NE 14TH AV Rt#-500
CAMAS WA 193-B7
NW 14TH AV
PORTLAND OR 312-E4
W 14TH AV
SPOKANE WA 348-H11
SPOKANE WA 349-A11
W 14TH AV U.S.-2
AIRWAY HEIGHTS WA 246-A4
SPOKANE CO WA 246-A4
14TH AV NW
OLYMPIA WA 296-C3
PIERCE CO WA 174-C7
PIERCE CO WA 181-C1
THURSTON CO WA 296-C3
14TH AV S
KING WA 286-B3
SEATTLE WA 278-C7
SEATTLE WA 286-B3
14 RD NE
DOUGLAS CO WA 112-C1

14 RD NE Rt#-172
DOUGLAS CO WA 112-C1
14 RD NW Rt#-172
DOUGLAS CO WA 112-B1
14TH ST
LEWISTON ID 250-C4
PORT TOWNSEND WA 263-D5
REEDSPORT OR 218-C1
E 14TH ST
BREMERTON WA 271-A10
N 14TH ST
SPRINGFIELD OR 330-J7
NE 14TH ST
CLARK CO WA 193-B6
NW 14TH ST
BEND OR 332-C7
PENDLETON OR 129-B1
SE 14TH ST
CLARK CO WA 193-C7
SW 14TH ST
BEND OR 332-C8
DESCHUTES CO OR 332-C8
14TH ST NE
SALEM OR 322-J13
SALEM OR 323-A13
14TH ST SE
SALEM OR 322-J14
SALEM OR 324-J1
15TH AV
LONGVIEW WA 303-A8
E 15TH AV
POST FALLS ID 353-H5
SPOKANE WA 349-G11
SPOKANE CO WA 349-G11
N 15TH AV
BOISE ID 253-C2
NE 15TH AV
PORTLAND OR 309-H7
PORTLAND OR 313-H1
W 15TH AV
ELLENSBURG WA 241-B5
KITTITAS CO WA 241-B5
POST FALLS ID 353-E5
15TH AV E
SEATTLE WA 278-C4
15TH AV NE
KING CO WA 171-B7
LACEY WA 297-F3
SEATTLE WA 171-B7
SEATTLE WA 274-C3
SHORELINE WA 171-B7
SNOHOMISH CO WA 168-C4
THURSTON CO WA 297-F3
15TH AV NW
SEATTLE WA 273-F2
SHORELINE WA 171-A6
15TH AV S
SEATTLE WA 282-B3
15TH AV SW
EPHRATA WA 112-C3
15TH AV W
SEATTLE WA 273-F7
SEATTLE WA 277-F2
15 RD NE
DOUGLAS CO WA 112-C1
15TH ST
BREMERTON WA 270-G9
DIST OF WEST VANCOUVER BC 254-D3
OROVILLE WA 104-C1
WALLA WALLA CO WA 345-J3
WASHOUGAL WA 193-C7
15TH ST Rt#-128
ASOTIN CO WA 250-B4
CLARKSTON WA 250-B4
E 15TH ST
TACOMA WA 293-J6
VANCOUVER WA 305-G4
N 15TH ST
COEUR D'ALENE ID 355-G8
DALTON GARDENS ID 355-G2
KOOTENAI CO ID 355-G2
S 15TH ST Rt#-128
POMEROY WA 122-B2
SE 15TH ST
BEND OR 332-H10
CLARK CO WA 193-B7
DESCHUTES CO OR 332-H12
SW 15TH ST
PENDLETON OR 129-B1
15TH ST NE
AUBURN WA 182-C1
15TH ST NW
AUBURN WA 182-B1
EAST WENATCHEE BENCH WA 239-A4
15TH ST NW U.S.-2
EAST WENATCHEE BENCH WA 239-A4
15TH ST SW
AUBURN WA 182-B1
16TH AV
ASOTIN CO WA 250-B4
CITY OF WHITE ROCK BC 158-A2
DISTRICT OF SURREY BC 158-A2
LEWISTON ID 250-B4
LONGVIEW WA 303-A9
TOWNSHIP OF LANGLEY BC 102-B1
TOWNSHIP OF LANGLEY BC 158-C2
E 16TH AV
DISHMAN WA 350-E11
OPPORTUNITY WA 350-E11
OPPORTUNITY WA 351-A10
SPOKANE CO WA 349-H11
VERADALE WA 351-A10
N 16TH AV
FRUITVALE WA 243-B6
YAKIMA WA 243-B6
NE 16TH AV
PORTLAND OR 313-H4
S 16TH AV
SOUTH BROADWAY WA 243-B7
YAKIMA WA 243-B7
16TH AV NW
SNOHOMISH CO WA 168-C6
16TH AV S
DES MOINES WA 290-B7
KING WA 286-B2
KING CO WA 175-B7
SEATTLE WA 286-B3
TUKWILA WA 286-B2
16TH AV SW
KING WA 285-G6

STREET / City State / Page-Grid

16TH AV SW
SEATTLE WA 285-G6
16TH AV W
UNIV ENDOWMENT LANDS BC 156-A4
VANCOUVER BC 254-A13
NE 16TH DR
PORTLAND OR 313-H4
16 RD NE
DOUGLAS CO WA 112-C1
16TH ST
ASTORIA WA 300-D6
EVERETT WA 264-E1
EVERETT WA 265-E1
HOQUIAM WA 178-A7
LEWISTON ID 250-C5
NORTH BEND OR 333-E5
E 16TH ST
KOOTENAI CO ID 353-J5
KOOTENAI CO ID 354-B5
POST FALLS ID 353-J5
POST FALLS ID 354-B5
N 16TH ST U.S.-95
PAYETTE ID 139-A3
NE 16TH ST
FRUITLAND ID 139-A3
PAYETTE CO ID 139-A3
NE 16TH ST Rt#-30
FRUITLAND ID 139-A3
PAYETTE CO ID 139-A3
S 16TH ST
MOUNT VERNON WA 260-D13
SUNNYSIDE WA 120-B2
S 16TH ST U.S.-95
PAYETTE ID 139-A3
SE 16TH ST
BELLEVUE WA 175-D3
SW 16TH ST
RENTON WA 175-C5
16TH ST E
PIERCE CO WA 182-C2
16TH ST W
CITY OF N VANCOUVER BC 254-J5
17TH AV
LONGVIEW WA 303-A9
SE 17TH AV
CLACKAMAS OR 321-H1
MILWAUKIE OR 317-H7
MILWAUKIE OR 321-H1
PORTLAND OR 317-H2
PORTLAND OR 317-H7
PORTLAND OR 321-H1
17TH AV NW
THURSTON CO WA 296-A3
17TH AV NW Rt#-900
ISSAQUAH WA 175-D3
17TH ST
ASOTIN CO WA 250-C4
BAKER CITY OR 138-B1
LEWISTON ID 250-C4
NORTH BEND OR 333-E6
WASHOUGAL WA 193-C7
17TH ST Rt#-173
BRIDGEPORT WA 112-C1
NE 17TH ST
DESCHUTES CO OR 212-D4
SE 17TH ST
PENDLETON OR 129-B1
SW 17TH ST Rt#-37
PENDLETON OR 129-B1
17TH ST NE
SALEM OR 323-A12
17TH ST SE
SALEM OR 323-A14
18TH AV
LONGVIEW WA 302-J9
LONGVIEW WA 303-A9
TOWNSHIP OF LANGLEY BC 158-C2
E 18TH AV
EUGENE OR 330-A8
SPOKANE WA 349-B12
NW 18TH AV
PORTLAND OR 312-E5
SW 18TH AV
MALHEUR CO OR 139-A3
W 18TH AV
EUGENE OR 329-D7
EUGENE OR 330-A8
JUNCTION CITY OR 210-A5
LANE CO OR 210-A5
18TH AV N
KELSO WA 303-E8
18TH ST
LEWISTON ID 250-C4
18TH ST U.S.-12
LEWISTON ID 250-C4
E 18TH ST
THE DALLES OR 196-C7
VANCOUVER WA 305-G4
VANCOUVER WA 306-A4
WASCO CO OR 196-C7
N 18TH ST
MOUNT VERNON WA 260-E11
SPRINGFIELD OR 331-A6
NE 18TH ST
CLARK CO WA 193-A6
VANCOUVER WA 306-E4
VANCOUVER WA 307-J4
S 18TH ST
FAIRVIEW SUMACH WA 243-C7
MOUNT VERNON WA 260-E13
POMEROY WA 122-B2
SKAGIT CO WA 260-E13
S 18TH ST Rt#-52
PAYETTE ID 139-A3
W 18TH ST
VANCOUVER WA 305-G4
19TH AV
ALBANY OR 326-D9
TOWNSHIP OF LANGLEY BC 158-D2
19TH AV Rt#-8
FOREST GROVE OR 198-B1
19TH AV Rt#-527
EVERETT WA 171-C4
EVERETT WA 268-D6
E 19TH AV
BENTON CO WA 343-E13
KENNEWICK WA 343-E13
NW 19TH AV
PORTLAND OR 312-D5
W 19TH AV
BENTON CO WA 343-C13
KENNEWICK WA 342-H13
KENNEWICK WA 343-C13
19TH AV NE
SNOHOMISH CO WA 168-C4
19TH AV SE
BOTHELL WA 171-C6
19TH ST
BELLINGHAM WA 258-C10
BENTON CO OR 133-B1
CITY OF N VANCOUVER BC 254-H4
CITY OF N VANCOUVER BC 255-C4
DIST OF N VANCOUVER BC 254-H4
DISTRICT OF BURNABY BC 156-D5
EVERETT WA 264-E1
EVERETT WA 265-E2
North Springfield OR 331-A5
PHILOMATH OR 133-B1
PORT TOWNSEND WA 263-F5
SPRINGFIELD OR 331-A5
E 19TH ST
MCMINNVILLE OR 198-A7
THE DALLES OR 196-C7
NE 19TH ST
CLARK CO WA 193-B6
NW 19TH ST
DESCHUTES CO OR 212-D4
REDMOND OR 212-D5
TERREBONNE OR 212-D4
S 19TH ST
FIRCREST WA 181-C2
FIRCREST WA 292-A6
PIERCE CO WA 181-C2
TACOMA WA 181-C2
TACOMA WA 292-A6
TACOMA WA 293-F6
UNIVERSITY PLACE WA 181-C2
SW 19TH ST
DESCHUTES CO OR 212-D5
REDMOND OR 212-D5
W 19TH ST
KENNEWICK WA 342-J13
MCMINNVILLE OR 198-A7
19TH ST NE
EAST WENATCHEE BENCH WA 239-A4
19TH ST NW
EAST WENATCHEE BENCH WA 239-A4
19 20 ST DIV
DISTRICT OF BURNABY BC 156-D5
20TH AV
DISTRICT OF SURREY BC 158-A2
TOWNSHIP OF LANGLEY BC 158-D2
N 20TH AV
PASCO WA 343-D7
NE 20TH AV
CLARK CO WA 192-C4
PORTLAND OR 313-J5
NW 20TH AV
MALHEUR CO OR 139-A3
S 20TH AV
PASCO WA 343-D8
SE 20TH AV
PORTLAND OR 313-J7
PORTLAND OR 317-J1
SW 20TH AV
BATTLE GROUND WA 192-D3
CLARK CO WA 192-D3
20TH AV W
EVERETT WA 267-H4
SEATTLE WA 273-E7
20 RD NE
DOUGLAS CO WA 112-C1
DOUGLAS CO WA 113-A1
20TH ST
BELLINGHAM WA 258-C10
DIST OF N VANCOUVER BC 255-E4
LA GRANDE OR 130-A2
NEW WESTMINSTER BC 156-D5
NE 20TH ST
BELLEVUE WA 175-D2
SE 20TH ST
CLARK CO WA 193-C7
KING CO WA 175-D3
SW 20TH ST
PENDLETON OR 129-B1
20TH ST E
FIFE WA 182-A2
20TH ST KPN
PIERCE CO WA 181-A2
20TH ST NE
LAKE STEVENS WA 171-D1
20TH ST SE
SNOHOMISH WA 265-J4
SNOHOMISH CO WA 171-D2
21ST AV
LONGVIEW WA 302-J9
LONGVIEW WA 303-A8
TOWNSHIP OF LANGLEY BC 158-D2
E 21ST AV
SPOKANE WA 349-B12
NE 21ST AV
PORTLAND OR 313-J4
NW 21ST AV
CLARK CO WA 192-C5
SE 21ST AV
PORTLAND OR 317-J1
W 21ST AV
SPOKANE WA 348-H12
21ST AV SW
FEDERAL WAY WA 182-A1
21ST ST
BELLINGHAM WA 258-C10
DIST OF WEST VANCOUVER BC 254-C3
LEWISTON ID 250-C4
N 21ST ST
TACOMA WA 292-B3
TACOMA WA 293-E3
NW 21ST ST
LINCOLN CITY OR 203-A4
21ST ST NE
SALEM OR 323-B12
21ST ST SE
AUBURN WA 182-C2
22ND AV
MOSES LAKE NORTH WA 242-C2
OLYMPIA WA 297-A7
VANCOUVER BC 255-C14
N 22ND AV
PASCO WA 343-D6
NE 22ND AV
CLARK CO WA 192-C3
SE 22ND AV
MILWAUKIE OR 321-J3
22ND AV E
PIERCE CO WA 182-A6
22ND ST
ANACORTES WA 259-H3
DIST OF N VANCOUVER BC 254-H3
EVERETT WA 264-D2
HOOD RIVER OR 195-C5
HOOD RIVER CO OR 195-C5
HOQUIAM WA 178-A7
LEWISTON ID 250-D5
NEZ PERCE CO ID 250-D5
NE 22ND ST
LINCOLN CITY OR 203-A4
S 22ND ST
REEDSPORT OR 218-C1
22ND ST SE
SALEM OR 325-A2
23RD AV
LONGVIEW WA 302-J8
SEATTLE WA 278-D6
NW 23RD AV
PORTLAND OR 312-D4
23RD AV E
SEATTLE WA 278-D4
23RD AV NE
SNOHOMISH CO WA 168-C5
23RD AV S
SEATTLE WA 278-D7
SEATTLE WA 282-D1
23RD AV SE
PUYALLUP WA 182-B4
23RD ST
CITY OF N VANCOUVER BC 255-A3
S 23RD ST
COEUR D'ALENE ID 355-H12
KOOTENAI CO ID 355-H12
SE 23RD ST
CLARK CO WA 193-B7
SW 23RD ST
DESCHUTES CO OR 212-D5
23RD ST NE
SALEM OR 323-B13
24TH AV
ALBANY OR 326-B10
ASOTIN CO WA 250-B5
DISTRICT OF SURREY BC 158-A2
FOREST GROVE OR 198-C1
LONGVIEW WA 302-J8
SEASIDE WA 301-G6
TOWNSHIP OF LANGLEY BC 158-C2
E 24TH AV
EUGENE OR 330-A9
OPPORTUNITY WA 350-G12
OPPORTUNITY WA 351-B11
SPOKANE CO WA 351-G11
VERADALE WA 351-B11
N 24TH AV
PASCO WA 343-D6
NE 24TH AV
PORTLAND OR 313-J4
S 24TH AV
YAKIMA WA 243-B7
24TH AV E
SEATTLE WA 278-D2
24TH AV NE
SEATTLE WA 274-D2
SHORELINE WA 171-B6
24TH AV NW
SEATTLE WA 272-E2
24TH AV S
DES MOINES WA 290-C4
KING WA 286-C7
KING WA 288-C3
NAMPA ID 147-C1
SEATAC WA 288-C3
SEATAC WA 290-C4
24TH PL S
DES MOINES WA 290-C6
24 RD NW
DOUGLAS CO WA 112-B2
GRANT CO WA 112-B2
N 24TH ST
TACOMA WA 292-D3
NE 24TH ST
CLYDE HILL WA 175-C2
REDMOND WA 175-D2
SE 24TH ST
BELLEVUE WA 175-D3
24TH ST E
EDGEWOOD WA 182-B3
24TH ST NE
SALEM OR 323-B14
E 25TH AV
OPPORTUNITY WA 350-J12
25TH AV NE
KING CO WA 171-B7
SEATTLE WA 274-D3
SHORELINE WA 171-B7
25TH AV SW
TUMWATER WA 296-E7
25TH ST
DESCHUTES CO OR 213-A4
E 25TH ST
TACOMA WA 293-J7
S 25TH ST
TACOMA WA 293-G7
25TH ST SE
SALEM OR 323-B14
SALEM OR 325-B1
26TH AV
LONGVIEW WA 302-H10
TOWNSHIP OF LANGLEY BC 158-C2
N 26TH AV
PASCO WA 343-C7
26TH AV NE
OLYMPIA WA 297-A2
THURSTON CO WA 297-D1
W 26TH PL
KENNEWICK WA 343-D14
26TH ST
CORVALLIS OR 327-F10
E 26TH ST
TACOMA WA 293-J7
N 26TH ST
TACOMA WA 181-C2
TACOMA WA 292-B3
S 26TH ST
TACOMA WA 293-H7
27TH AV
ALBANY OR 326-A10
LINN CO OR 326-A10
E 27TH AV
BENTON CO WA 343-F14
HIGHLAND WA 343-F14
KENNEWICK WA 343-F14
W 27TH AV
BENTON CO WA 343-B14
HIGHLAND WA 343-B14
KENNEWICK WA 342-G14
KENNEWICK WA 343-B14
27TH AV NE
SNOHOMISH CO WA 168-C4
27TH ST
DIST OF WEST VANCOUVER BC 254-A2
N 27TH ST
BOISE ID 253-C2
NE 27TH ST
BEND OR 217-C2
DESCHUTES CO OR 217-C2
NW 27TH ST
DESCHUTES CO OR 212-D3
S 27TH ST
BOISE ID 253-C2
SE 27TH ST
BEND OR 217-C3
CLARK CO WA 193-C7
DESCHUTES CO OR 217-C3
SW 27TH ST
DESCHUTES CO OR 212-D6
REDMOND OR 212-D6
27TH ST W
UNIVERSITY PLACE WA 181-C2
27B AV
DISTRICT OF DELTA BC 101-C1
28 AV
DISTRICT OF DELTA BC 101-C1
28TH AV
TOWNSHIP OF LANGLEY BC 158-C2
N 28TH AV
PASCO WA 343-C7
SE 28TH AV
PORTLAND OR 317-J4
PORTLAND OR 318-A4
W 28TH AV
EUGENE OR 329-H9
28TH AV NW
SEATTLE WA 272-D1
SNOHOMISH CO WA 168-B4
THURSTON CO WA 296-E1
28TH AV S
KING CO WA 182-B2
28TH AV W
EVERETT WA 267-G4
SEATTLE WA 272-D6
SNOHOMISH WA 267-G5
NE 28TH CT
DESCHUTES CO OR 213-A4
N 28TH ST
BOISE ID 253-C2
SPRINGFIELD OR 331-B6
NE 28TH ST
CLARK CO WA 193-A6
VANCOUVER WA 307-J3
29TH AV
TOWNSHIP OF LANGLEY BC 158-C2
VANCOUVER BC 156-B5
E 29TH AV
EUGENE OR 330-A10
SPOKANE WA 349-H13
SPOKANE CO WA 349-H13
NE 29TH AV
CLARK CO WA 192-D3
W 29TH AV
EUGENE OR 329-J10
EUGENE OR 330-A10
SPOKANE WA 348-J13
SPOKANE WA 349-C13
29TH AV W
SEATTLE WA 272-D6
SEATTLE WA 276-D2
29TH ST
ANACORTES WA 259-G4
CORVALLIS OR 327-E5
LEWISTON ID 250-C4
MANZANITA OR 191-B4
NE 29TH ST
DESCHUTES CO OR 213-A4
29TH ST E
DIST OF N VANCOUVER BC 255-C3
29TH ST NE
FEDERAL WAY WA 182-A2
TACOMA WA 182-A2
29TH ST SE
AUBURN WA 182-C2
30TH AV
LINN CO OR 207-B5
LONGVIEW WA 302-H8
TOWNSHIP OF LANGLEY BC 158-D2
E 30TH AV
EUGENE OR 330-B10
LANE CO OR 330-H12
30TH AV NE
SEATTLE WA 274-E5
30TH PL W
SNOHOMISH CO WA 171-B5
30TH ST
BELLINGHAM WA 258-D12
CORVALLIS OR 327-E10
E 30TH ST
KITSAP CO WA 271-A7
N 30TH ST
RENTON WA 175-C4
TACOMA WA 181-C2
TACOMA WA 292-B2
TACOMA WA 293-E2
NE 30TH ST
KITSAP CO WA 271-B7
SE 30TH ST
CLARK CO WA 193-C7
SW 30TH ST
PENDLETON OR 129-B1
NW 31ST AV
CLARK CO WA 192-C2
31ST AV NE
LACEY WA 181-A6
31ST AV SW Rt#-161
PUYALLUP WA 182-B4
N 31ST ST
North Springfield OR 331-C4
SPRINGFIELD OR 331-C4
NW 31ST ST
DESCHUTES CO OR 212-D4
31ST ST NE
TACOMA WA 182-A2
32ND AV
DISTRICT OF SURREY BC 158-B1
LONGVIEW WA 302-G9
TOWNSHIP OF LANGLEY BC 158-C1
E 32ND AV
DISHMAN WA 350-H12
OPPORTUNITY WA 350-H12
OPPORTUNITY WA 351-A12
SPOKANE CO WA 350-H12
SPOKANE CO WA 351-E12
VERADALE WA 351-A12
NE 32ND AV
PORTLAND OR 314-A2
SE 32ND AV
HILLSBORO OR 198-D1
MILWAUKIE OR 199-D3
MILWAUKIE OR 318-A7
PORTLAND OR 318-A7
32ND AV NW
SEATTLE WA 272-D2
32ND AV S
KING CO WA 182-B2
32ND AV W
SEATTLE WA 272-D5
32ND ST
ANACORTES WA 259-F4
BELLINGHAM WA 258-D11
WASHOUGAL WA 193-C7
S 32ND ST
LANE CO OR 331-C8
SPRINGFIELD OR 331-C8
SE 32ND ST
KING CO WA 176-A3
32ND ST E
EDGEWOOD WA 182-B3
32ND ST KPN
PIERCE CO WA 181-A1
32ND ST NW
PIERCE CO WA 181-B1
32ND ST SE
SNOHOMISH CO WA 171-D2
32ND DIVISION DR
PIERCE CO WA 181-B5
33RD AV
VANCOUVER BC 156-B5
E 33RD AV
EUGENE OR 330-B10
NE 33RD AV
PORTLAND OR 310-A7
PORTLAND OR 314-A1
NE 33RD DR
PORTLAND OR 310-A4
33RD ST
ASTORIA WA 300-F5
E 33RD ST
VANCOUVER WA 305-H3
VANCOUVER WA 306-A3
33RD ST NE
TACOMA WA 182-A2
33A AV
DISTRICT OF DELTA BC 101-C1
34TH AV
ALBANY OR 326-B11
SEATTLE WA 278-E5
SEATTLE WA 279-E4
TOWNSHIP OF LANGLEY BC 158-D1
34TH AV E
PIERCE CO WA 182-A4
34TH AV W
SEATTLE WA 272-C7
SEATTLE WA 276-C1
34TH ST
ANACORTES WA 259-H4
CLARK CO WA 193-C7
MOUNT VERNON WA 260-G13
E 34TH ST
TACOMA WA 295-J1
N 34TH ST
SEATTLE WA 273-H7
SEATTLE WA 274-A7
S 34TH ST
TACOMA WA 295-H1
SW 35TH AV
PORTLAND OR 316-B7
PORTLAND OR 320-B1
35TH AV NE
LAKE FOREST PARK WA 171-B6
SEATTLE WA 274-E2
35TH AV SE
BOTHELL WA 171-C6
SNOHOMISH WA 269-F7
SNOHOMISH CO WA 171-C4
35TH AV SW
SEATTLE WA 281-E7
SEATTLE WA 285-E3
35TH AV W
SNOHOMISH CO WA 171-B4
SW 35TH DR
CLACKAMAS CO OR 199-C5
35TH ST
ASTORIA WA 300-F5
BENTON CO OR 327-E12
CORVALLIS OR 327-E12
FLORENCE OR 214-B2
SPRINGFIELD OR 331-C6
NW 35TH ST
DESCHUTES CO OR 212-D5
S 35TH ST
TACOMA WA 294-C2
SW 35TH ST
DESCHUTES CO OR 212-D6
REDMOND OR 212-D6
35TH ST NE
DOUGLAS CO WA 239-A3
35TH ST W
UNIVERSITY PLACE WA 181-C3
36 AV
DISTRICT OF DELTA BC 101-C1
36TH AV
TOWNSHIP OF LANGLEY BC 158-C1
NW 36TH AV
CLARK CO WA 192-C4
S 36TH AV
YAKIMA CO WA 243-B7
36TH AV NE
THURSTON CO WA 180-D5
36TH AV NW
SNOHOMISH CO WA 168-B4
THURSTON CO WA 180-C5
36TH AV S
KENT WA 175-B7
KING CO WA 175-B7
36TH AV W
LYNNWOOD WA 171-B5
SNOHOMISH CO WA 171-B5
NE 36TH DR
LINCOLN CITY OR 203-A4
36TH ST
CORVALLIS OR 327-E8
E 36TH ST
GARDEN CITY ID 253-C2
N 36TH ST
BOISE ID 253-C2
SEATTLE WA 273-H6
NW 36TH ST
SEATTLE WA 273-G6
S 36TH ST
TACOMA WA 294-C2
W 36TH ST
BOISE ID 253-C2
GARDEN CITY ID 253-C2
37TH AV
TOWNSHIP OF LANGLEY BC 158-C1
E 37TH AV
SPOKANE WA 349-H14
SPOKANE CO WA 349-H14
W 37TH AV
SPOKANE WA 348-J14
SPOKANE WA 349-A14
37TH AV SE
LACEY WA 297-F9
37TH AV W
LYNNWOOD WA 171-B5
37TH ST
ANACORTES WA 259-F5
N 37TH ST
TACOMA WA 292-A1
NE 37TH ST
DESCHUTES CO OR 213-A4
SW 37TH ST
PENDLETON OR 129-B1
UMATILLA CO OR 129-B1
37TH ST NW
AUBURN WA 182-B1
38TH AV
LONGVIEW WA 302-F6
TOWNSHIP OF LANGLEY BC 158-C1
WEST LONGVIEW WA 302-F6
S 38TH AV
WEST RICHLAND WA 340-A13
38TH AV E
PIERCE CO WA 182-A5
38TH AV NW
PIERCE CO WA 181-C1
NE 38TH PL
KIRKLAND WA 175-C1
38TH ST
EVERETT WA 265-E5
E 38TH ST
TACOMA WA 182-A3
TACOMA WA 295-J2
E 38TH ST Rt#-7
TACOMA WA 295-J2
NE 38TH ST
CLARK CO WA 193-B6
S 38TH ST
TACOMA WA 294-D2
TACOMA WA 295-G2
39TH AV
SKAMANIA CO WA 193-D6
NE 39TH AV
PORTLAND OR 314-B3
SE 39TH AV
PORTLAND OR 314-B7
PORTLAND OR 318-B1
39TH AV S
SEATTLE WA 287-E4
39TH AV SE
PUYALLUP WA 182-B4
SNOHOMISH CO WA 171-C6
39TH AV SW
PUYALLUP WA 182-B4
39TH ST
CLARK CO WA 193-C7
E 39TH ST
VANCOUVER WA 305-G2
N 39TH ST
SEATTLE WA 273-H6
NE 39TH ST
CLARK CO WA 193-D6
NW 39TH ST
SEATTLE WA 273-H6
W 39TH ST
VANCOUVER WA 304-E2
VANCOUVER WA 305-F2
40TH AV
DISTRICT OF SURREY BC 158-B1
TOWNSHIP OF LANGLEY BC 158-C1
N 40TH AV
YAKIMA WA 243-B6
S 40TH AV
YAKIMA WA 243-B7
40TH AV NW
POLK CO OR 322-A10
SNOHOMISH CO WA 168-B3
40TH AV S
PIERCE CO WA 118-A1
PIERCE CO WA 181-D7
NE 40TH CIR
CLARK CO WA 193-C6
N 40TH ST
SEATTLE WA 273-J6
SEATTLE WA 274-A6
NE 40TH ST
REDMOND WA 175-D2
SEATTLE WA 274-B6
NW 40TH ST
LINCOLN CITY OR 203-A4
SE 40TH ST
MERCER ISLAND WA 175-C3

STREET / City State Page-Grid

SE 40TH ST
MERCER ISLAND WA 283-J3
40TH ST E
PIERCE CO WA 182-C3
40TH ST NW
PIERCE CO WA 181-B1
40TH ST W
FIRCREST WA 294-A3
UNIVERSITY PLACE WA 181-C3
UNIVERSITY PLACE WA 294-A3
41ST AV
UNIV ENDOWMENT LANDS BC 156-B5
VANCOUVER BC 156-B5
NW 41ST AV
CLARK CO WA 192-C4
41ST AV NE
THURSTON CO WA 180-D5
41 PL
PACIFIC CO WA 186-A6
41ST ST
ANACORTES WA 259-F5
NE 41ST ST
SEATTLE WA 274-E6
SEATTLE WA 275-E6
S 41ST ST
TERRACE HEIGHTS WA 243-C6
41ST ST SE
AUBURN WA 182-B2
EVERETT WA 264-D6
EVERETT WA 265-E5
41B ST
DISTRICT OF DELTA BC 101-C1
41ST DIVISION DR
PIERCE CO WA 181-C5
41ST ST
CLARK CO WA 192-D1
NE 42ND AV
PORTLAND OR 310-B7
PORTLAND OR 314-B1
S 42ND AV
YAKIMA CO WA 243-B7
42ND AV E
PIERCE CO WA 182-A5
42ND AV NE
HAYESVILLE OR 323-E7
SEATTLE WA 275-F6
42ND AV NW
THURSTON CO WA 180-B5
42ND ST
SPRINGFIELD OR 331-D5
S 42ND ST
LANE CO OR 331-E8
SPRINGFIELD OR 331-E8
E 43RD AV
SPOKANE WA 246-C5
43RD AV NE
SEATTLE WA 275-F6
43RD AV NW
THURSTON CO WA 180-C5
43RD AV SE
PIERCE CO WA 182-B4
PUYALLUP WA 182-B4
SNOHOMISH WA 265-G7
SNOHOMISH WA 269-H1
NW 43RD ST
DESCHUTES CO OR 212-D3
S 43RD ST
RENTON WA 175-C6
SW 43RD ST
KENT WA 175-C6
KENT WA 291-J1
RENTON WA 175-C6
RENTON WA 291-J1
TUKWILA WA 291-J1
SE 43RD WY
KING CO WA 175-D3
KING CO WA 176-A3
44TH AV
TOWNSHIP OF LANGLEY BC 158-C1
E 44TH AV
SPOKANE WA 246-C5
44TH AV E
PIERCE CO WA 182-A3
44TH AV NW
SNOHOMISH CO WA 168-B3
44TH AV W
LYNNWOOD WA 171-B5
MOUNTLAKE TERRACE WA 171-B5
SNOHOMISH CO WA 171-B4
E 44TH ST
GARDEN CITY ID 253-C2
NE 44TH ST
RENTON WA 175-C4
NE 44TH ST Rt#-500
CLARK CO WA 193-B6
44TH ST NE
MARYSVILLE WA 171-D1
SNOHOMISH CO WA 171-D1
45TH AV
VANCOUVER BC 156-C5
E 45TH AV
HIGHLAND WA 121-A3
SW 45TH AV
PORTLAND OR 316-A5
W 45TH AV
BENTON CO WA 121-A3
HIGHLAND WA 121-A3
45TH AV NE
FOUR CORNERS OR 323-F13
SALEM OR 323-F12
45TH AV SE
SNOHOMISH CO WA 171-C6
45TH AV SW
SEATTLE WA 284-D4
THURSTON CO WA 296-F10
TUMWATER WA 296-F10
SW 45TH DR
PORTLAND OR 316-A7
NE 45TH PL
SEATTLE WA 274-E5
N 45TH ST
SEATTLE WA 273-J5
SEATTLE WA 274-A5
NE 45TH ST
DESCHUTES CO OR 213-A4
SEATTLE WA 274-B5
SEATTLE WA 275-E5
NE 45TH ST Rt#-513
SEATTLE WA 274-D5
SEATTLE WA 275-E5

46TH AV
LONGVIEW WA 302-D5
WEST LONGVIEW WA 302-D5
46TH AV E
PIERCE CO WA 182-A6
46TH AV NE
THURSTON CO WA 180-D5
THURSTON CO WA 181-A5
46TH AV NW
THURSTON CO WA 180-C5
N 46TH ST
SEATTLE WA 273-H5
TACOMA WA 181-D1
47TH AV
TOWNSHIP OF LANGLEY BC 158-D1
47TH AV NE
MARYSVILLE WA 168-C7
47TH AV SW
FEDERAL WAY WA 182-A1
S 47TH ST
TACOMA WA 294-D3
TACOMA WA 295-E4
47A AV
DISTRICT OF DELTA BC 101-C1
48TH AV
LANGLEY BC 158-C1
TOWNSHIP OF LANGLEY BC 158-C1
WEST LONGVIEW WA 302-D4
S 48TH AV
YAKIMA WA 243-B7
YAKIMA CO WA 243-B7
SW 48TH AV
PORTLAND OR 316-A7
PORTLAND OR 320-A1
48TH AV NW
SNOHOMISH CO WA 168-B5
48TH AV S
PIERCE CO WA 181-D7
48TH AV SW
SEATTLE WA 280-D7
SEATTLE WA 284-D1
48TH AV W
MOUNTLAKE TERRACE WA 171-B6
48 ST
DISTRICT OF DELTA BC 101-C1
E 48TH ST
TACOMA WA 295-J4
NE 48TH ST
CLARK CO WA 193-D6
S 48TH ST
TACOMA WA 295-F4
48TH ST E
EDGEWOOD WA 182-B3
PIERCE CO WA 182-A3
SW 49TH AV
LAKE OSWEGO OR 320-A2
PORTLAND OR 320-A2
49TH AV E
VANCOUVER BC 156-B5
49TH AV NE
TACOMA WA 182-A1
49TH AV SW
SEATTLE WA 280-D5
THURSTON CO WA 296-B10
49TH AV W
VANCOUVER BC 156-B5
49TH ST
CLARK CO WA 193-C7
PORT TOWNSEND WA 263-E2
50TH AV
TOWNSHIP OF LANGLEY BC 158-D1
NE 50TH AV
CLARK CO WA 192-D3
50TH AV E
PIERCE CO WA 182-A5
50TH AV NE
MARION CO OR 205-A3
50TH AV NW
PIERCE CO WA 181-C2
SNOHOMISH CO WA 168-B5
50TH AV S
SEATTLE WA 283-F6
N 50TH ST
SEATTLE WA 273-J5
SEATTLE WA 274-A5
NE 50TH ST
LINCOLN CO OR 203-B4
SEATTLE WA 274-C5
NW 50TH ST
SEATTLE WA 273-G5
NW 51ST AV
CLARK CO WA 192-C2
51ST AV NE
MARYSVILLE WA 168-C7
SNOHOMISH CO WA 168-C7
51ST AV S
KING CO WA 182-B1
51ST AV SE
SNOHOMISH WA 265-H4
SNOHOMISH CO WA 171-C5
N 51ST ST
RUSTON WA 181-D1
NE 51ST ST
REDMOND WA 175-D1
SE 51ST ST
LINCOLN CITY OR 203-A5
SW 51ST ST
DESCHUTES CO OR 212-C6
51ST ST W
FIRCREST WA 292-A7
FIRCREST WA 294-A2
TACOMA WA 292-A7
TACOMA WA 294-A2
UNIVERSITY PLACE WA 294-A2
52ND AV
TOWNSHIP OF LANGLEY BC 158-C1
S 52ND AV
YAKIMA CO WA 243-B7
SE 52ND AV
PORTLAND OR 318-C3
52ND AV NW
SNOHOMISH CO WA 168-B5
52ND AV W
LYNNWOOD WA 171-B5
SNOHOMISH CO WA 171-B4
52ND ST SE
EVERETT WA 268-D1
EVERETT WA 269-H1
SNOHOMISH WA 269-H1

W 53RD AV
SPOKANE CO WA 246-B5
53RD AV NE
TACOMA WA 182-A2
53RD AV NW
POLK CO OR 204-C6
53RD ST
BENTON CO OR 207-A7
BENTON CO OR 327-B11
CORVALLIS OR 327-B11
NE 53RD ST
CLARK CO WA 193-B6
53RD ST KPN
PIERCE CO WA 181-A1
54TH AV
TOWNSHIP OF LANGLEY BC 158-D1
VANCOUVER BC 156-C5
54TH AV E
FIFE WA 182-A2
PIERCE CO WA 182-A5
54TH AV E Rt#-99
FIFE WA 182-A2
54TH AV NW
PIERCE CO WA 174-C7
THURSTON CO WA 180-B5
54TH AV SW
THURSTON CO WA 296-C11
TUMWATER WA 296-C11
NE 54TH ST Rt#-500
CLARK CO WA 193-B6
NW 54TH ST
SEATTLE WA 272-D4
55TH AV NE
HAYESVILLE OR 323-H5
MARION CO OR 323-H5
SEATTLE WA 275-G3
SNOHOMISH CO WA 168-D4
55TH AV NW
POLK CO OR 204-C6
55TH AV S
KING CO WA 175-B7
SW 55TH PL
DESCHUTES CO OR 212-C5
55 ST
PACIFIC CO WA 186-A5
NE 55TH ST
SEATTLE WA 274-E4
SEATTLE WA 275-F4
SW 55TH ST
DESCHUTES CO OR 212-C5
56TH AV
DISTRICT OF SURREY BC 158-C1
LANGLEY BC 158-C1
TOWNSHIP OF LANGLEY BC 102-B1
TOWNSHIP OF LANGLEY BC 158-D1
56TH AV Rt#-10
DISTRICT OF SURREY BC 157-A7
DISTRICT OF SURREY BC 158-B1
N 56TH AV
YAKIMA WA 243-B6
56TH AV NW
SNOHOMISH CO WA 168-B4
56TH AV W
MOUNTLAKE TERRACE WA 171-B6
56 ST
DISTRICT OF DELTA BC 101-C1
E 56TH ST
TACOMA WA 295-J5
S 56TH ST
TACOMA WA 294-D5
TACOMA WA 295-G5
SE 56TH ST
KING CO WA 176-A3
56TH ST NW
PIERCE CO WA 181-C1
56TH ST SE
SNOHOMISH CO WA 171-D3
57TH AV
VANCOUVER BC 156-B5
E 57TH AV
SPOKANE WA 246-C5
SPOKANE CO WA 246-C5
NE 57TH AV
PORTLAND OR 314-D2
57TH AV SE
SNOHOMISH CO WA 171-C6
N 57TH ST
TERRACE HEIGHTS WA 243-C6
S 57TH ST
LANE CO OR 331-H8
SPRINGFIELD OR 331-H8
57TH ST KPN
PIERCE CO WA 181-A1
57TH ST NE
TACOMA WA 182-A1
57TH WY NW
THURSTON CO WA 180-C5
58TH AV Rt#-10
DISTRICT OF DELTA BC 156-D7
DISTRICT OF SURREY BC 156-D7
DISTRICT OF SURREY BC 157-A7
58TH AV E
PIERCE CO WA 182-A5
58TH AV SE
THURSTON CO WA 181-A7
N 58TH ST
SPRINGFIELD OR 331-H7
NE 58TH ST
CLARK CO WA 192-D5
NE 58TH ST Rt#-500
CLARK CO WA 193-B5
S 58TH ST
SPRINGFIELD OR 331-H8
SW 58TH ST
DESCHUTES CO OR 212-C6
59TH AV NE
ARLINGTON WA 168-D5
MARION CO OR 205-A3
SNOHOMISH CO WA 168-D4
59TH AV SW
SEATTLE WA 280-C3
NW 59TH ST
DESCHUTES CO OR 212-C5
60TH AV
DISTRICT OF SURREY BC 157-B7
TOWNSHIP OF LANGLEY BC 157-D7
NE 60TH AV
PORTLAND OR 314-D5
SE 60TH AV
PORTLAND OR 314-D6

SE 60TH AV
PORTLAND OR 318-D1
60TH AV E
PIERCE CO WA 182-A7
60TH AV W
LYNNWOOD WA 171-B5
60 ST
DISTRICT OF DELTA BC 101-C1
60TH ST Rt#-17
DISTRICT OF DELTA BC 156-C7
NE 60TH ST
SEATTLE WA 274-B4
NW 60TH ST
DESCHUTES CO OR 212-C4
SE 60TH ST
BELLEVUE WA 175-C3
60TH ST NE
SNOHOMISH CO WA 171-D1
60TH ST SE
SNOHOMISH WA 269-J2
SNOHOMISH CO WA 171-D3
61ST AV
TOWNSHIP OF LANGLEY BC 157-C7
NW 61ST AV
CLARK CO WA 192-C3
61ST AV NE
THURSTON CO WA 180-D5
THURSTON CO WA 181-A5
61ST AV NW
THURSTON CO WA 180-C5
61ST ST NE
MARYSVILLE WA 171-C1
62ND AV
TOWNSHIP OF LANGLEY BC 157-D7
S 62ND AV
YAKIMA CO WA 243-B7
62ND AV E
PIERCE CO WA 182-A4
62ND AV NE
MARION CO OR 205-A4
62ND AV NW
PIERCE CO WA 181-B2
62ND AV SE
MARION CO OR 325-J3
THURSTON CO WA 181-A7
62ND AV SW
THURSTON CO WA 180-B7
62A CRES
TOWNSHIP OF LANGLEY BC 157-D7
62B ST
DISTRICT OF DELTA BC 156-C7
E 63RD AV
SPOKANE CO WA 246-C5
63RD AV NE
MARION CO OR 205-A6
MARION CO OR 323-J14
MARION CO OR 325-J1
MARYSVILLE WA 171-D1
THURSTON CO WA 180-D5
63RD AV SW
SEATTLE WA 280-B3
NE 63RD ST
CLARK CO WA 192-D5
SE 63RD ST
BELLEVUE WA 175-C3
64TH AV
DISTRICT OF DELTA BC 156-D7
DISTRICT OF SURREY BC 156-D7
DISTRICT OF SURREY BC 157-A7
TOWNSHIP OF LANGLEY BC 157-C7
S 64TH AV
WEST VALLEY WA 243-B7
64TH AV NW
SNOHOMISH CO WA 168-B4
THURSTON CO WA 180-C5
64TH AV S
KENT WA 175-B7
KENT WA 291-G7
64TH PL W
MUKILTEO WA 266-C7
E 64TH ST
TACOMA WA 182-A3
TACOMA WA 295-J6
S 64TH ST
TACOMA WA 295-G6
64TH ST E
PIERCE CO WA 182-C3
SUMNER WA 182-C3
64TH ST KPN
PIERCE CO WA 181-A1
64TH ST KPS
PIERCE CO WA 181-A3
64TH ST NE Rt#-528
MARYSVILLE WA 168-D7
MARYSVILLE WA 171-C1
SNOHOMISH CO WA 168-D7
SNOHOMISH CO WA 171-D1
64TH ST SE
SNOHOMISH WA 269-J2
SNOHOMISH CO WA 171-D3
64TH ST W
UNIVERSITY PLACE WA 181-C3
65TH AV
TOWNSHIP OF LANGLEY BC 157-D7
SW 65TH AV
CLACKAMAS CO OR 199-B4
TUALATIN OR 199-B4
WASHINGTON CO OR 199-B4
65TH AV NE
MARION CO OR 205-A4
N 65TH ST
SEATTLE WA 273-H3
SEATTLE WA 274-A3
NE 65TH ST
SEATTLE WA 274-C3
SEATTLE WA 275-F3
NW 65TH ST
SEATTLE WA 272-D3
SEATTLE WA 273-E3
66TH AV
TOWNSHIP OF LANGLEY BC 157-C7
66TH AV E
PIERCE CO WA 182-A3
66TH AV NE
MARION CO OR 205-A4
66TH AV NW
SNOHOMISH CO WA 168-B6
THURSTON CO WA 180-C4
66TH AV SW
THURSTON CO WA 296-B12

66TH AV W
MOUNTLAKE TERRACE WA 171-B5
NW 66TH ST
DESCHUTES CO OR 212-C4
S 66TH ST
TACOMA WA 294-B6
66TH ST W
PIERCE WA 294-A6
67TH AV NE
ARLINGTON WA 168-D7
MARYSVILLE WA 168-D7
MARYSVILLE WA 171-D1
SNOHOMISH CO WA 168-D7
67TH AV SE
SNOHOMISH CO WA 171-D5
67TH AV W
UNIVERSITY PLACE WA 181-C3
67TH PL
PACIFIC CO WA 186-A5
68TH AV
TOWNSHIP OF LANGLEY BC 157-C7
68TH AV NW
SNOHOMISH CO WA 168-B3
68TH AV S
SEATTLE WA 287-H5
TUKWILA WA 289-H5
68TH AV S Rt#-181
KENT WA 291-H5
68TH AV SW
LAKEWOOD WA 181-C4
68TH AV W
LYNNWOOD WA 171-B5
NE 68TH ST
CLARK CO WA 192-C5
CLARK CO WA 193-A5
69TH AV NW
THURSTON CO WA 180-B4
69TH AV SE
SNOHOMISH CO WA 171-D3
SE 69TH WY
BELLEVUE WA 175-C4
NEWCASTLE WA 175-C4
70TH AV
VANCOUVER BC 156-B5
70TH AV Rt#-99
VANCOUVER BC 156-B5
70TH AV E
FIFE WA 182-A3
MILTON WA 182-A2
PIERCE CO WA 182-A5
70TH AV NW
PIERCE CO WA 174-B7
PIERCE CO WA 181-B1
SNOHOMISH CO WA 168-B6
70TH AV S
TUKWILA WA 289-H6
70TH AV SE
MARION CO OR 133-C1
70TH AV SW
THURSTON CO WA 296-D13
TUMWATER WA 296-D13
NE 70TH ST
KIRKLAND WA 175-C1
SEATTLE WA 274-E3
SEATTLE WA 275-F3
70TH ST KPS
PIERCE CO WA 181-A3
70TH ST NE
OAK HARBOR WA 167-C3
NW 71ST AV
CLARK CO WA 192-C2
71ST AV NE
SNOHOMISH CO WA 171-D1
71ST AV SE
MARION CO OR 205-A7
71ST ST KPN
PIERCE CO WA 181-A1
72ND AV
DISTRICT OF DELTA BC 156-D7
DISTRICT OF SURREY BC 156-D7
DISTRICT OF SURREY BC 157-A7
TOWNSHIP OF LANGLEY BC 157-C7
NE 72ND AV
CLARK CO WA 192-D3
S 72ND AV
WEST VALLEY WA 243-A7
SE 72ND AV
CLACKAMAS OR 318-E6
PORTLAND OR 318-E6
PORTLAND OR 319-E4
SW 72ND AV
TIGARD OR 199-B3
72ND AV NE
MARION CO OR 205-A3
72ND AV NW
STANWOOD WA 168-B4
72 ST
DISTRICT OF DELTA BC 101-C1
E 72ND ST
PIERCE WA 295-H7
PIERCE CO WA 182-A3
TACOMA WA 182-A3
TACOMA WA 295-H7
S 72ND ST
TACOMA WA 295-G7
SE 72ND ST
MERCER ISLAND WA 287-J1
72ND ST E
PIERCE CO WA 182-A3
72ND ST KPS
PIERCE CO WA 181-A3
72ND ST SE
SNOHOMISH CO WA 171-D3
73RD AV NE
KING CO WA 171-C6
73RD AV SE
SNOHOMISH CO WA 171-D5
73RD WY NE
THURSTON CO WA 180-C4
73A AV
TOWNSHIP OF LANGLEY BC 157-C7
S 74TH AV
YAKIMA CO WA 243-A7
NW 74TH ST
DESCHUTES CO OR 212-C4
S 74TH ST
LAKEWOOD WA 294-C7
TACOMA WA 294-C7
TACOMA WA 295-E7

74B AV
TOWNSHIP OF LANGLEY BC 157-C7
75TH AV SE
SNOHOMISH CO WA 171-D6
75TH AV W
UNIVERSITY PLACE WA 181-C3
NE 75TH ST
SEATTLE WA 274-C2
SEATTLE WA 275-E2
75TH ST SW
EVERETT WA 267-J3
EVERETT WA 268-A3
76TH AV NW
SNOHOMISH CO WA 168-B3
76TH AV S
KENT WA 291-J6
76TH AV W
EDMONDS WA 171-B5
LYNNWOOD WA 171-B5
NE 76TH ST
CLARK CO WA 192-D5
CLARK CO WA 193-A5
76TH ST KPS
PIERCE CO WA 181-A3
77TH AV NE
SNOHOMISH CO WA 168-D6
THURSTON CO WA 180-D4
NE 77TH ST Rt#-202
REDMOND WA 175-D1
77A AV
TOWNSHIP OF LANGLEY BC 157-C7
78TH AV
TOWNSHIP OF LANGLEY BC 157-C7
78TH AV E
PIERCE CO WA 182-A6
78TH AV NE
THURSTON CO WA 180-D4
78TH AV NW
THURSTON CO WA 180-B4
78TH ST
DESCHUTES CO OR 212-C7
NE 78TH ST
CLARK CO WA 192-C5
NW 78TH ST
CLARK CO WA 192-C5
78TH ST KPN
PIERCE CO WA 181-A1
S 79TH AV
YAKIMA CO WA 243-A7
79TH AV NW
THURSTON CO WA 180-C4
79TH AV SE
SNOHOMISH CO WA 171-D2
80TH AV
DISTRICT OF DELTA BC 156-D7
DISTRICT OF SURREY BC 156-D7
DISTRICT OF SURREY BC 157-A7
TOWNSHIP OF LANGLEY BC 157-C7
80TH AV NE
KING CO WA 171-C6
80TH AV NW
SNOHOMISH CO WA 168-B4
80TH PL S
KENT WA 175-C6
N 80TH ST
SEATTLE WA 273-H2
SEATTLE WA 274-A2
NE 80TH ST
KIRKLAND WA 175-C1
SEATTLE WA 274-C2
NW 80TH ST
SEATTLE WA 272-D2
SEATTLE WA 273-E2
80TH ST E
PIERCE CO WA 182-A4
80TH ST NE
MARYSVILLE WA 168-C7
81ST AV NE
THURSTON CO WA 180-D4
81ST AV NW
THURSTON CO WA 180-C4
81ST AV SW
THURSTON CO WA 184-C1
82ND AV
TOWNSHIP OF LANGLEY BC 157-C7
NE 82ND AV
CLARK CO WA 192-D2
PORTLAND OR 311-G6
NE 82ND AV Rt#-213
PORTLAND OR 311-F7
PORTLAND OR 315-F2
SE 82ND AV Rt#-213
CLACKAMAS OR 319-F6
CLACKAMAS CO OR 199-D3
MULTNOMAH OR 319-F6
PORTLAND OR 315-F7
PORTLAND OR 319-F4
82ND AV NE
MARION CO OR 205-B4
SE 82ND DR
CLACKAMAS CO OR 199-D3
SE 82ND ST
KING CO WA 176-B4
83RD AV
TOWNSHIP OF LANGLEY BC 157-C7
83RD AV NE
SNOHOMISH CO WA 171-D1
83RD AV SE
SNOHOMISH CO WA 171-D3
83RD AV SW
THURSTON CO WA 184-C1
TUMWATER WA 184-C1
NE 83RD ST
CLARK CO WA 193-A5
NW 83RD ST
DESCHUTES CO OR 212-C4
84TH AV
DISTRICT OF DELTA BC 156-D6
DISTRICT OF SURREY BC 157-A6
TOWNSHIP OF LANGLEY BC 157-C7
84TH AV NE
CLYDE HILL WA 175-C2
HUNTS POINT WA 175-C2
KING CO WA 171-C7
MEDINA WA 175-C2
84TH AV NW
SNOHOMISH CO WA 168-B4
84TH AV S
KENT WA 175-C6

STREET City State Page-Grid

84TH AV W
SNOHOMISH CO WA 171-A6
E 84TH ST
TACOMA WA 181-D4
S 84TH ST
PIERCE CO WA 181-D4
TACOMA WA 181-D4
84TH ST E
PIERCE CO WA 182-A4
84TH ST NE
SNOHOMISH CO WA 102-C3
SNOHOMISH CO WA 168-C7
84TH ST S
LAKEWOOD WA 181-D4
84TH ST SW Rt#-526
MUKILTEO WA 266-E4
MUKILTEO WA 267-0
85TH AV NW
THURSTON CO WA 180-C4
85TH ST
DESCHUTES CO OR 212-C7
N 85TH ST
SEATTLE WA 273-J1
SEATTLE WA 274-A1
NE 85TH ST
CLARK CO WA 193-C5
KIRKLAND WA 175-D1
REDMOND WA 175-D1
SEATTLE WA 274-B1
NE 85TH ST Rt#-908
KIRKLAND WA 175-C1
NW 85TH ST
SEATTLE WA 272-D1
SEATTLE WA 273-E1
85TH ST E
PIERCE CO WA 181-D4
PIERCE CO WA 182-A4
86TH AV
TOWNSHIP OF LANGLEY BC 157-C6
NE 86TH AV
VANCOUVER WA 307-F3
86TH AV E
PIERCE CO WA 182-A6
86TH AV NE
MARION CO OR 205-B3
86TH AV NW
PIERCE CO WA 174-B7
86TH ST NW
SNOHOMISH CO WA 168-B7
86A AV
TOWNSHIP OF LANGLEY BC 157-C6
87TH AV SE
SNOHOMISH CO WA 171-D2
NE 87TH ST
CLARK CO WA 192-D5
88TH AV
DISTRICT OF DELTA BC 156-D6
DISTRICT OF SURREY BC 156-D6
DISTRICT OF SURREY BC 157-A6
TOWNSHIP OF LANGLEY BC 157-C6
SE 88TH AV
VANCOUVER WA 311-F1
88TH AV SW
THURSTON CO WA 184-C1
TUMWATER WA 184-C1
88TH AV W
EDMONDS WA 171-A5
NE 88TH ST
CLARK CO WA 192-D5
SE 88TH ST
KING CO WA 176-D4
88TH ST NE
SNOHOMISH CO WA 168-C7
88TH ST SE
SNOHOMISH CO WA 171-D3
88TH ST SW
LAKEWOOD WA 181-C4
89TH AV SE
THURSTON CO WA 184-D1
89TH ST
BRITISH COLUMBIA 104-C1
90TH AV
DISTRICT OF DELTA BC 156-D6
S 90TH AV
YAKIMA CO WA 243-A7
90TH AV E
PIERCE CO WA 182-B6
90TH AV NE
KING CO WA 171-C7
90TH AV NW
THURSTON CO WA 180-C4
90TH ST SW
EVERETT WA 268-A5
91ST AV NE
SNOHOMISH CO WA 168-D6
NW 91ST ST
DESCHUTES CO OR 212-C4
91A AV
TOWNSHIP OF LANGLEY BC 157-C6
92ND AV
DISTRICT OF DELTA BC 156-D6
DISTRICT OF SURREY BC 157-A6
NE 92ND AV
CLARK CO WA 192-D3
SE 92ND AV
VANCOUVER WA 307-G6
92ND AV NE
CLYDE HILL WA 175-C2
SNOHOMISH CO WA 171-D1
YARROW POINT WA 175-C2
92ND AV NW
PIERCE CO WA 181-B1
92ND ST KPN
PIERCE CO WA 174-A7
92ND ST NW
SNOHOMISH CO WA 168-C7
92ND ST SE
SNOHOMISH WA 171-D3
SNOHOMISH CO WA 171-D3
92A AV
TOWNSHIP OF LANGLEY BC 157-C6
93RD AV SE
THURSTON CO WA 184-C1
93RD AV SW
THURSTON CO WA 184-C1
93RD AV SW Rt#-121
THURSTON CO WA 184-C1
93RD ST
DESCHUTES CO OR 212-C7

93RD ST SW
LAKEWOOD WA 181-C4
NE 94TH AV
CLARK CO WA 192-D5
94TH AV E
PIERCE CO WA 182-B5
94TH AV NW
PIERCE CO WA 174-B6
94TH AV S
KENT WA 175-C7
94TH ST
DESCHUTES CO OR 212-C7
95TH AV NE
MARION CO OR 205-B6
NE 95TH ST
SEATTLE WA 171-B7
96TH AV
DISTRICT OF DELTA BC 156-D6
DISTRICT OF SURREY BC 156-D6
DISTRICT OF SURREY BC 157-A6
MAPLE RIDGE BC 157-D6
TOWNSHIP OF LANGLEY BC 157-C6
S 96TH ST
KING WA 286-A4
PIERCE CO WA 181-D4
TACOMA WA 181-D4
96TH ST E
PIERCE CO WA 182-A4
96TH ST NW
GIG HARBOR WA 174-C7
NE 97TH AV
VANCOUVER WA 307-G5
98TH AV
MAPLE RIDGE BC 157-D6
TOWNSHIP OF LANGLEY BC 157-C6
NE 98TH AV
VANCOUVER WA 307-G3
SE 98TH AV
VANCOUVER WA 307-G7
98TH AV NE
BOTHELL WA 171-C7
KIRKLAND WA 171-C7
KIRKLAND WA 175-C1
99TH AV NE
SNOHOMISH CO WA 168-D7
SNOHOMISH CO WA 171-D1
99TH AV SE
SNOHOMISH CO WA 171-D2
99TH AV SW
KING CO WA 174-D7
NE 99TH ST
CLARK CO WA 192-C5
CLARK CO WA 193-A5
NW 99TH ST
CLARK CO WA 192-C5
99TH ST E
PIERCE CO WA 181-D4
100TH AV
DISTRICT OF SURREY BC 157-A6
MAPLE RIDGE BC 157-D6
TOWNSHIP OF LANGLEY BC 157-C6
100TH AV NE
BELLEVUE WA 175-C2
BOTHELL WA 171-C7
KING CO WA 171-C7
KIRKLAND WA 171-C7
100TH AV SE
THURSTON CO WA 184-C1
100TH AV W
EDMONDS WA 171-A6
SW 100TH ST U.S.-101
NEWPORT OR 206-A5
100TH ST NE
SNOHOMISH CO WA 168-C7
100TH ST SE
EVERETT WA 268-D6
EVERETT WA 269-G7
SNOHOMISH WA 268-D6
SNOHOMISH WA 269-G7
100TH ST SW
EVERETT WA 267-H6
EVERETT WA 268-A6
LAKEWOOD WA 181-D4
SNOHOMISH WA 267-G6
SNOHOMISH WA 268-A6
100TH WY
LINCOLN CO OR 206-B3
101ST AV
TOWNSHIP OF LANGLEY BC 157-C6
101ST AV SW
THURSTON CO WA 184-B1
NW 101 LN
DESCHUTES CO OR 212-C5
101 PL
PACIFIC CO WA 186-A5
102ND AV
DISTRICT OF SURREY BC 157-B6
MAPLE RIDGE BC 157-D6
TOWNSHIP OF LANGLEY BC 157-C6
NE 102ND AV
CLARK CO WA 192-D1
MAYWOOD PARK OR 315-H2
PORTLAND OR 315-H2
SE 102ND AV
PORTLAND OR 315-H6
102ND AV NW
STANWOOD WA 168-A4
102B AV
TOWNSHIP OF LANGLEY BC 157-C6
103RD AV
MAPLE RIDGE BC 157-D6
103RD AV SE
SNOHOMISH CO WA 171-D2
THURSTON CO WA 184-D1
103RD AV SW
THURSTON CO WA 184-B1
SE 103RD DR
PORTLAND OR 315-H6
104 AV
DISTRICT OF SURREY BC 156-D6
104TH AV
DISTRICT OF SURREY BC 157-A6
104TH AV SE Rt#-515
KENT WA 175-C7
KING CO WA 175-C7
104TH AV SW
THURSTON CO WA 184-C1
104 ST
DISTRICT OF DELTA BC 156-D7

NE 104TH ST
REDMOND WA 175-D1
104TH ST E
PIERCE CO WA 182-A4
104TH ST SW
LAKEWOOD WA 181-C4
N 105TH ST
SEATTLE WA 171-A7
NE 105TH ST
CLARK CO WA 193-B5
SW 106TH PL
KING WA 285-F5
SW 106TH ST
KING WA 285-F5
SEATTLE WA 284-E5
SEATTLE WA 285-E5
NE 107TH AV
CLARK CO WA 192-D5
107TH AV SW
THURSTON CO WA 184-C1
SW 107TH ST
KING WA 285-G5
108TH AV
DISTRICT OF SURREY BC 157-A6
MAPLE RIDGE BC 157-D6
108TH AV SE
KENT WA 175-C7
KING CO WA 175-C5
108TH AV SE Rt#-515
KING CO WA 175-C6
SW 108TH ST
SEATTLE WA 284-E5
108TH ST NE
SNOHOMISH CO WA 168-D7
108TH ST SW
LAKEWOOD WA 181-D4
109TH AV SE
SNOHOMISH CO WA 171-D5
NE 109TH ST
CLARK CO WA 192-D5
CLARK CO WA 193-B5
110TH AV
CLACKAMAS CO OR 199-B5
MAPLE RIDGE BC 157-D6
WILSONVILLE OR 199-B5
110TH AV E
PIERCE CO WA 182-B5
110TH AV SW
THURSTON CO WA 184-B1
111TH AV SW
KING CO WA 174-D6
112TH AV
DISTRICT OF SURREY BC 157-A5
MAPLE RIDGE BC 157-D6
NE 112TH AV
BATTLE GROUND WA 192-D3
CLARK CO WA 192-D2
VANCOUVER WA 307-J2
SE 112TH AV
MULTNOMAH OR 319-J1
PORTLAND OR 315-J7
PORTLAND OR 319-J1
112TH AV NE
BELLEVUE WA 175-C2
112TH AV SE
BELLEVUE WA 175-C3
KING CO WA 182-C1
112 ST
DISTRICT OF DELTA BC 156-D7
S 112TH ST
KING WA 286-A6
112TH ST E
PIERCE CO WA 181-D4
PIERCE CO WA 182-A4
112TH ST S
PIERCE CO WA 181-D4
112TH ST SE
EVERETT WA 171-C4
112TH ST SW
EVERETT WA 171-B4
LAKEWOOD WA 181-C4
SNOHOMISH CO WA 171-B4
113TH AV NE
LAKE STEVENS WA 171-D1
SNOHOMISH CO WA 171-D1
113TH AV SW
THURSTON CO WA 184-B1
113TH PL SE Rt#-527
EVERETT WA 171-C4
113 ST
PACIFIC CO WA 186-A5
114TH AV NE
MARION CO OR 205-B3
114TH ST NE
SNOHOMISH CO WA 168-C7
115TH AV NE
SNOHOMISH CO WA 168-D7
NE 115TH ST
SEATTLE WA 171-B7
116TH AV
DISTRICT OF SURREY BC 157-A5
MAPLE RIDGE BC 157-D5
116TH AV SE
KING CO WA 175-C6
NEWCASTLE WA 175-C4
116 ST
DISTRICT OF DELTA BC 156-D7
NE 116TH ST
KING CO WA 171-D7
KIRKLAND WA 171-C7
REDMOND WA 171-D7
S 116TH ST
KING WA 285-J6
KING WA 286-A6
SW 116TH ST
BURIEN WA 285-H6
KING WA 285-H6
116TH ST NE
SNOHOMISH CO WA 102-C3
SNOHOMISH CO WA 168-C7
116TH ST S
PIERCE CO WA 181-D4
116TH ST SE
SNOHOMISH CO WA 171-C4
117TH AV
MAPLE RIDGE BC 157-D5
NE 117TH AV
CLARK CO WA 192-D5
117TH AV NE
MARION CO OR 205-B6

118TH AV
MAPLE RIDGE BC 157-D5
118TH AV NW
KITSAP CO WA 174-B7
PIERCE CO WA 174-B7
118TH AV SE
BELLEVUE WA 175-C3
NE 118TH ST
CLARK CO WA 193-B5
S 118TH ST
KING WA 286-B7
118TH ST KPN
PIERCE CO WA 174-A7
118TH ST NE
SNOHOMISH CO WA 168-C7
109TH AV
CLARK CO WA 192-D1
119TH AV
PITT MEADOWS BC 157-B5
119TH AV SE
BELLEVUE WA 175-C3
NE 119TH ST
CLARK CO WA 192-D5
CLARK CO WA 193-A5
NW 119TH ST
CLARK CO WA 192-C5
120TH AV NE
KIRKLAND WA 171-C7
NE 120TH PL
KIRKLAND WA 171-C7
120 ST
DISTRICT OF DELTA BC 156-D7
DISTRICT OF SURREY BC 156-D7
120TH ST E
PIERCE CO WA 182-C4
SW 121ST AV
WASHINGTON CO OR 199-B3
121ST ST E
PIERCE CO WA 182-A4
122ND AV
MAPLE RIDGE BC 157-C5
NE 122ND AV
BATTLE GROUND WA 193-A3
CLARK CO WA 193-A3
PORTLAND OR 200-A1
SE 122ND AV
CLACKAMAS CO OR 200-A3
PORTLAND OR 200-A2
122ND AV E
EDGEWOOD WA 182-B3
PIERCE CO WA 182-B5
NE 122ND BLVD
PORTLAND OR 193-A7
PORTLAND OR 200-A1
NE 122ND ST
CLARK CO WA 193-B5
122ND ST E
PIERCE CO WA 182-B4
123RD AV NE
SNOHOMISH CO WA 168-D5
123RD AV SE
SNOHOMISH CO WA 171-D2
124TH AV
MAPLE RIDGE BC 157-C5
124TH AV NE
KING CO WA 171-C7
KIRKLAND WA 175-C1
LAKE STEVENS WA 110-C1
LAKE STEVENS WA 171-C7
WOODINVILLE WA 171-C7
124TH AV SE
KING CO WA 175-C6
NE 124TH ST
KING CO WA 171-C7
KIRKLAND WA 171-C7
REDMOND WA 171-C7
NE 124TH WY
KING CO WA 171-D7
125TH AV
MAPLE RIDGE BC 157-D5
NE 125TH ST
SEATTLE WA 171-B7
126TH AV E
PIERCE CO WA 182-B6
126TH AV KPN
PIERCE CO WA 174-B7
126TH ST NW
SNOHOMISH CO WA 168-B6
127TH AV
MAPLE RIDGE BC 157-D5
127TH AV SE
SNOHOMISH CO WA 171-D4
NW 127TH ST
CLARK CO WA 192-C4
128TH AV
MAPLE RIDGE BC 157-C5
128TH AV SE
BELLEVUE WA 175-C3
KING CO WA 175-C3
128TH ST
DISTRICT OF SURREY BC 157-A7
DISTRICT OF SURREY BC 158-A2
NE 128TH ST
KING CO WA 171-D7
S 128TH ST
BURIEN WA 288-A1
KING WA 288-A1
KING WA 289-J1
SEATAC WA 288-A1
SE 128TH ST
KING CO WA 175-D5
128TH ST E
PIERCE CO WA 182-A4
128TH ST KPN
PIERCE CO WA 174-A7
128TH ST NE
SNOHOMISH CO WA 168-C6
128TH ST SE
SNOHOMISH CO WA 171-C4
128TH ST SE Rt#-96
SNOHOMISH CO WA 171-C4
128TH ST SW
SNOHOMISH CO WA 171-C4
SE 128TH WY
KING CO WA 175-D5
129TH AV
MAPLE RIDGE BC 157-C5
PITT MEADOWS BC 157-B5
SE 129TH AV
HAPPY VALLEY OR 200-A3

129TH PL SE
BELLEVUE WA 175-C3
NE 130TH AV
CLARK CO WA 193-A5
130TH AV NE
BELLEVUE WA 175-C2
BOTHELL WA 171-C6
KING CO WA 171-C6
WOODINVILLE WA 171-C6
N 130TH ST
SEATTLE WA 171-A7
NE 130TH ST
KING CO WA 171-D7
NE 131ST AV
CLARK CO WA 193-A5
131ST AV NE Rt#-92
SNOHOMISH CO WA 110-C1
131ST AV SE
THURSTON CO WA 184-C2
131ST ST E
PIERCE CO WA 181-D4
131ST ST NW
SNOHOMISH CO WA 168-C6
132ND AV
MAPLE RIDGE BC 157-C5
PITT MEADOWS BC 157-C5
NE 132ND AV
CLARK CO WA 193-A2
132ND AV E
PIERCE CO WA 182-B7
132ND AV NE
BOTHELL WA 171-C6
KING CO WA 171-C7
KING CO WA 175-C1
KIRKLAND WA 175-C1
WOODINVILLE WA 171-C6
132ND AV SE
KENT WA 175-C7
KING CO WA 175-C7
KING CO WA 182-C1
132ND ST
DISTRICT OF SURREY BC 157-A7
NE 132ND ST
KING CO WA 171-C7
KIRKLAND WA 171-C7
132ND ST NE
SNOHOMISH CO WA 168-D6
132ND ST SE
SNOHOMISH CO WA 171-C4
132ND ST SE Rt#-96
MILL CREEK WA 171-C4
SNOHOMISH CO WA 171-C4
133RD AV SW
THURSTON CO WA 184-B2
NE 133RD ST
KING CO WA 171-D7
134TH AV E
PIERCE CO WA 182-B5
134TH AV NE
BELLEVUE WA 175-C2
NE 134TH ST
CLARK CO WA 192-C4
135 RD
NEZ PERCE CO ID 250-C2
SE 136TH AV
PORTLAND OR 200-A2
136 RD
NEZ PERCE CO ID 250-C2
S 136TH ST
BURIEN WA 288-A2
SEATAC WA 288-B2
136TH ST E
PIERCE CO WA 182-B5
136TH ST NE
MARYSVILLE WA 168-C6
SNOHOMISH CO WA 168-C6
NE 137TH AV
CLARK CO WA 193-A5
138TH AV SE
KING CO WA 175-C5
RENTON WA 175-C5
138TH ST S
PIERCE CO WA 181-D5
NE 139TH ST
CLARK CO WA 192-D4
CLARK CO WA 193-A4
NW 139TH ST
CLARK CO WA 192-C4
140TH AV NE
BELLEVUE WA 175-C2
WOODINVILLE WA 171-C6
140TH AV SE
BELLEVUE WA 175-C2
KING CO WA 175-C6
140TH AV SW
THURSTON CO WA 184-B2
140TH PL NE
KING CO WA 171-C6
140 RD
NEZ PERCE CO ID 250-C2
140TH ST
CITY OF WHITE ROCK BC 158-A2
DISTRICT OF SURREY BC 157-A6
DISTRICT OF SURREY BC 158-A2
140TH ST NE
SNOHOMISH CO WA 168-C6
140TH ST NW
SNOHOMISH CO WA 168-B6
140TH WY SE
KING CO WA 175-C5
NE 142ND AV
CLARK CO WA 193-A4
SE 142ND AV
CLACKAMAS CO OR 200-A3
NW 143RD AV
WASHINGTON CO OR 199-A1
143RD AV SE
THURSTON CO WA 184-C2
143RD AV SW
THURSTON CO WA 184-C2
144TH AV SE
KENT WA 175-C7
144TH ST
DISTRICT OF SURREY BC 158-A1
NE 144TH ST
CLARK CO WA 192-D4
CLARK CO WA 193-A4
S 144TH ST
SEATAC WA 288-D3
TUKWILA WA 288-D3

S 144TH ST
TUKWILA WA 289-E3
144TH ST E
PIERCE CO WA 182-A5
144TH ST KPN
PIERCE CO WA 174-A6
144TH ST NW
PIERCE CO WA 174-C6
SE 145TH AV
CLACKAMAS CO OR 200-A3
145TH PL SE
BELLEVUE WA 175-C2
N 145TH ST
SEATTLE WA 171-A7
SHORELINE WA 171-A7
N 145TH ST Rt#-523
SEATTLE WA 171-A7
SHORELINE WA 171-A7
NE 145TH ST
KING CO WA 171-C7
LAKE FOREST PARK WA 171-B7
SEATTLE WA 171-B7
SHORELINE WA 171-B7
NE 145TH ST Rt#-202
KING CO WA 171-D7
WOODINVILLE WA 171-C7
146TH AV E
PIERCE CO WA 182-B6
NE 147TH AV
CLARK CO WA 193-A2
NE 148TH AV
PORTLAND OR 200-A1
SE 148TH AV
PORTLAND OR 200-A2
148TH AV NE
BELLEVUE WA 175-C2
REDMOND WA 175-C2
148TH AV SE
BELLEVUE WA 175-C3
KING CO WA 175-C7
KING CO WA 182-C1
148TH ST
DISTRICT OF SURREY BC 157-A6
SW 148TH ST
BURIEN WA 175-A5
148TH ST SW
SNOHOMISH CO WA 171-B4
NW 149TH ST
CLARK CO WA 192-C4
150TH AV
PITT MEADOWS BC 157-C4
SW 150TH AV
WASHINGTON CO OR 199-A3
150TH AV E
PIERCE CO WA 182-B7
150TH AV SE
BELLEVUE WA 175-D3
KING CO WA 175-D3
150TH ST SW
LAKEWOOD WA 181-C5
PIERCE CO WA 181-C5
150 NW ST
OAK HARBOR WA 167-B2
NE 152ND AV
CLARK CO WA 193-A2
152ND AV SE
KENT WA 175-C7
KING CO WA 175-C7
152ND AV SW
THURSTON CO WA 184-B3
152ND ST
DISTRICT OF SURREY BC 157-A6
DISTRICT OF SURREY BC 158-A1
SW 152ND ST
BURIEN WA 175-A5
152ND ST E
PIERCE CO WA 182-A5
152ND ST NE
SNOHOMISH CO WA 168-C6
154TH AV E
PIERCE CO WA 182-B7
154TH AV SE
KING CO WA 182-C1
154TH PL SE
KING CO WA 175-D5
154TH ST
DISTRICT OF SURREY BC 157-A6
S 154TH ST
SEATAC WA 288-B4
TUKWILA WA 288-D4
TUKWILA WA 289-E4
N 155TH ST
SHORELINE WA 171-B7
155TH ST SW
LAKEWOOD WA 181-C5
PIERCE CO WA 181-C5
156TH AV NE
BELLEVUE WA 175-D2
REDMOND WA 175-D2
WOODINVILLE WA 171-D6
156TH AV SE
BELLEVUE WA 175-D3
KING CO WA 175-D5
156TH ST
DISTRICT OF SURREY BC 157-A6
NE 156TH ST
CLARK CO WA 192-D4
S 156TH ST
BURIEN WA 175-A5
BURIEN WA 288-A4
SE 156TH ST
KING CO WA 176-A5
SW 156TH ST
BURIEN WA 175-A5
156TH ST NE
SNOHOMISH CO WA 168-C6
156TH ST NW
SNOHOMISH CO WA 168-A6
156TH ST SE
SNOHOMISH CO WA 171-D4
S 156TH WY
SEATAC WA 288-B4
157TH ST
DISTRICT OF SURREY BC 158-A2
NW 158TH AV
BEAVERTON OR 199-A1
SW 158TH AV
BEAVERTON OR 199-A1
WASHINGTON CO OR 199-A1

STREET
City State Page-Grid

158TH AV E
PIERCE CO WA 182-B7
158TH AV KPS
PIERCE CO WA 181-A3
159TH AV NE
SNOHOMISH CO WA 102-C3
NE 159TH ST
CLARK CO WA 192-D4
CLARK CO WA 193-A4
159TH ST E
PIERCE CO WA 181-D5
160TH AV E
SUMNER WA 182-C3
160TH PL SE
KING CO WA 182-D2
160TH ST
DISTRICT OF SURREY BC 157-B6
NE 160TH ST
KING CO WA 171-D7
S 160TH ST
BURIEN WA 288-A5
SEATAC WA 288-A5
TUKWILA WA 288-A5
160TH ST E
PIERCE CO WA 181-D5
PIERCE CO WA 182-A5
NE 162ND AV
CLARK CO WA 193-A5
GRESHAM OR 200-A1
PORTLAND OR 200-A1
SE 162ND AV
MULTNOMAH CO OR 200-A2
PORTLAND OR 200-A2
162ND AV KPS
PIERCE CO WA 181-A3
162ND ST E
PIERCE CO WA 182-D5
162ND ST SE
MONROE WA 110-C1
163RD AV NE
SNOHOMISH CO WA 102-C3
163RD AV SW
THURSTON CO WA 184-B3
SE 164TH AV
CLARK CO WA 193-A6
164TH AV NE
BELLEVUE WA 175-D2
164TH AV SE
BELLEVUE WA 175-D2
KING CO WA 175-D7
164TH AV NE Rt#-202
REDMOND WA 175-D1
NE 164TH ST
CLARK CO WA 193-A4
NW 164TH ST
CLARK CO WA 192-C4
164TH ST NE
SNOHOMISH CO WA 168-D6
164TH ST SE
MILL CREEK WA 171-C4
MONROE WA 110-C1
SNOHOMISH CO WA 110-C1
SNOHOMISH CO WA 171-C4
164TH WY SE
KING CO WA 175-D3
NE 165TH ST
KING CO WA 171-D7
166TH AV E
PIERCE CO WA 182-C3
166TH AV NE
REDMOND WA 175-D1
NE 167TH AV
CLARK CO WA 193-A4
168TH AV NE
KING CO WA 171-D7
168TH ST
DISTRICT OF SURREY BC 157-B6
DISTRICT OF SURREY BC 158-B2
168TH ST SW
LYNNWOOD WA 171-B5
169TH AV SW
THURSTON CO WA 184-B3
NE 169TH ST
CLARK CO WA 193-B4
NW 169TH ST
CLARK CO WA 192-C4
169TH ST SE
SNOHOMISH CO WA 171-C5
SW 170TH AV
WASHINGTON CO OR 199-A2
S 170TH ST
SEATAC WA 288-C6
170TH ST E
PIERCE CO WA 182-A5
171ST AV SE
SNOHOMISH CO WA 110-C1
THURSTON CO WA 184-C3
171ST PL NE
KING CO WA 171-D7
NE 172ND AV
CLARK CO WA 193-A5
SE 172ND AV
CLACKAMAS CO OR 200-A3
SW 172ND ST
BURIEN WA 175-A5
172ND ST NE Rt#-531
ARLINGTON WA 168-C6
SNOHOMISH CO WA 168-C6
173RD AV SW
ROCHESTER WA 184-A3
THURSTON CO WA 184-A3
174TH AV KPS
PIERCE CO WA 181-A3
NE 174TH ST
CLARK CO WA 193-A4
S 174TH ST Rt#-509
BURIEN WA 175-A5
KING CO WA 175-A5
174TH ST S
PIERCE CO WA 181-D5
SW 175TH AV
WASHINGTON CO OR 199-A3
175TH AV SW
THURSTON CO WA 184-A3
NE 175TH ST
KING CO WA 171-D6
SHORELINE WA 171-B6
WOODINVILLE WA 171-B6
NE 176TH AV
CLARK CO WA 193-A3

176TH AV SW
THURSTON CO WA 184-A3
176TH ST
DISTRICT OF SURREY BC 157-B6
176TH ST Rt#-15
BRITISH COLUMBIA 158-B2
DISTRICT OF SURREY BC 157-B7
DISTRICT OF SURREY BC 158-B2
WHATCOM CO WA 158-B2
S 176TH ST
BURIEN WA 288-A7
SEATAC WA 288-A7
SEATAC WA 289-F7
SE 176TH ST
KING CO WA 175-C5
176TH ST E
PIERCE CO WA 181-D5
PIERCE CO WA 182-A5
176TH ST S
PIERCE CO WA 181-D5
176TH ST SW
LYNNWOOD WA 171-B5
177TH ST
PACIFIC CO WA 186-A4
177TH ST E
PIERCE CO WA 182-C5
S 178TH ST
SEATAC WA 289-F7
TUKWILA WA 289-F7
TUKWILA WA 291-G1
NE 179TH ST
CLARK CO WA 192-D4
NW 179TH ST
CLARK CO WA 192-C4
SE 179TH ST
KING CO WA 175-C5
RENTON WA 175-C5
180TH AV SE
KING CO WA 175-D7
KING CO WA 182-D3
S 180TH ST
TUKWILA WA 291-G1
SE 180TH ST
KENT WA 291-J1
RENTON WA 291-J1
TUKWILA WA 291-H1
180TH ST E
PIERCE CO WA 182-A5
180TH ST SE
SNOHOMISH CO WA 171-C5
180TH WY SW
THURSTON CO WA 184-B3
NE 181ST AV
GRESHAM OR 200-A1
NE 182ND AV
CLARK CO WA 193-A3
SE 182ND AV
GRESHAM OR 200-A2
182ND AV E
PIERCE CO WA 182-C2
182ND ST
DISTRICT OF SURREY BC 157-B6
183RD AV SW
ROCHESTER WA 184-B3
THURSTON CO WA 184-A3
183RD AV SW U.S.-12
ROCHESTER WA 184-A3
THURSTON CO WA 184-A3
184TH AV SE
KING CO WA 175-D6
184 RD
NEZ PERCE CO ID 250-D2
184TH ST
DISTRICT OF SURREY BC 157-B7
DISTRICT OF SURREY BC 158-B1
NW 184TH ST
CLARK CO WA 192-C4
184TH ST E
PIERCE CO WA 182-A5
NW 185TH AV
HILLSBORO OR 199-A1
WASHINGTON CO OR 192-A7
SW 185TH AV
WASHINGTON CO OR 199-A2
N 185TH ST
SHORELINE WA 171-B6
186TH AV E
PIERCE CO WA 182-C5
186TH AV KPN
PIERCE CO WA 174-A7
PIERCE CO WA 181-A2
186TH ST NE
SNOHOMISH CO WA 168-D5
187TH AV SE
KING CO WA 175-D7
187TH AV SW
THURSTON CO WA 184-B4
188TH AV SW
THURSTON CO WA 184-A4
188TH ST
PITT MEADOWS BC 157-B5
S 188TH ST
SEATAC WA 290-C1
SEATAC WA 291-E2
188TH ST NE
ARLINGTON WA 168-C5
SNOHOMISH CO WA 168-C5
188TH ST NW
SNOHOMISH CO WA 168-B5
188TH ST SW
LYNNWOOD WA 171-B5
S 188TH WY
SEATAC WA 290-B1
NE 189TH ST
CLARK CO WA 193-A4
NW 189TH ST
CLARK CO WA 192-C4
190TH AV E
PIERCE CO WA 182-C4
190TH AV KPS
PIERCE CO WA 181-A2
SE 190TH DR
MULTNOMAH CO OR 200-A2
191ST AV SW
THURSTON CO WA 184-B4
NE 192ND AV
CLARK CO WA 193-A5
SW 192ND AV
WASHINGTON CO OR 199-A4

192ND PL SE
KING CO WA 182-D3
192ND ST
DISTRICT OF SURREY BC 157-B6
DISTRICT OF SURREY BC 158-B1
SE 192ND ST
KING CO WA 175-C6
192ND ST E
PIERCE CO WA 182-A6
194TH PL SW
LYNNWOOD WA 171-B5
NW 194TH ST
CLARK CO WA 192-C3
195TH AV SW
THURSTON CO WA 184-B4
NW 195TH ST
SHORELINE WA 171-A6
196TH AV SE
KING CO WA 175-D6
KING CO WA 182-D3
196TH AV SW
GRAND MOUND WA 184-B4
196TH ST
DISTRICT OF SURREY BC 158-C2
S 196TH ST
KENT WA 291-G3
SE 196TH ST
KING CO WA 176-A6
196TH ST NW
SNOHOMISH CO WA 168-B5
196TH ST SE
SNOHOMISH CO WA 171-C5
196TH ST SW Rt#-524
EDMONDS WA 171-B5
LYNNWOOD WA 171-B5
SNOHOMISH CO WA 171-B5
196C ST
PITT MEADOWS BC 157-C4
197TH ST
TOWNSHIP OF LANGLEY BC 157-C7
SW 198TH AV
WASHINGTON CO OR 199-A2
198TH AV E
PIERCE CO WA 182-C5
198 PL
PACIFIC CO WA 186-A3
198TH ST
TOWNSHIP OF LANGLEY BC 157-C6
TOWNSHIP OF LANGLEY BC 158-C2
NE 199TH AV
CLARK CO WA 193-A6
NE 199TH ST
CLARK CO WA 192-D3
CLARK CO WA 193-A3
NW 199TH ST
CLARK CO WA 192-C3
S 199TH ST
DES MOINES WA 175-A6
DES MOINES WA 290-A3
199A ST
TOWNSHIP OF LANGLEY BC 157-C6
200TH AV SE
KING CO WA 182-D2
200TH ST
LANGLEY BC 157-C7
LANGLEY BC 158-C1
TOWNSHIP OF LANGLEY BC 157-C7
TOWNSHIP OF LANGLEY BC 158-C1
N 200TH ST
SHORELINE WA 171-A6
S 200TH ST
DES MOINES WA 290-B3
SEATAC WA 290-B3
SE 200TH ST
KING CO WA 176-A6
200TH ST E
PIERCE CO WA 182-A6
200TH ST NE
SNOHOMISH CO WA 168-C5
NE 202ND AV
CLARK CO WA 193-A4
202ND ST
TOWNSHIP OF LANGLEY BC 158-C2
202A ST
TOWNSHIP OF LANGLEY BC 157-C7
202B ST
TOWNSHIP OF LANGLEY BC 157-C7
203RD ST
MAPLE RIDGE BC 157-C5
PITT MEADOWS BC 157-C5
204TH PL NE
KING CO WA 175-D1
204TH ST
TOWNSHIP OF LANGLEY BC 157-C7
TOWNSHIP OF LANGLEY BC 158-C1
NE 204TH ST
CLARK CO WA 193-B3
SW 204TH ST
KING CO WA 174-D6
204TH ST NE
ARLINGTON WA 168-D5
SNOHOMISH CO WA 168-C5
SE 204TH WY
KING CO WA 175-C6
205TH AV KPS
PIERCE CO WA 180-D2
205TH ST
TOWNSHIP OF LANGLEY BC 157-C6
206TH AV NE
KING CO WA 171-D7
206TH ST
TOWNSHIP OF LANGLEY BC 158-C2
207TH ST
MAPLE RIDGE BC 157-C5
208TH AV NE
KING CO WA 175-D1
208TH AV SE
KING CO WA 175-D7
208 PL
PACIFIC CO WA 186-A3
208TH ST
LANGLEY BC 158-C2
TOWNSHIP OF LANGLEY BC 157-C7
TOWNSHIP OF LANGLEY BC 158-C2
S 208TH ST
SEATAC WA 290-C4
SE 208TH ST
KENT WA 175-C6
KING CO WA 175-C6

208TH ST E
PIERCE CO WA 181-D6
PIERCE CO WA 182-A6
208TH ST SE
BOTHELL WA 171-C5
SNOHOMISH CO WA 171-C5
208TH ST SW
LYNNWOOD WA 171-B5
SW 209TH AV
WASHINGTON CO OR 199-A2
209TH ST
MAPLE RIDGE BC 157-C5
NE 209TH ST
CLARK CO WA 193-B3
NW 209TH ST
CLARK CO WA 192-C3
209TH ST NE
ARLINGTON WA 168-D5
210TH AV SW
THURSTON CO WA 184-B4
210TH ST
MAPLE RIDGE BC 157-C5
TOWNSHIP OF LANGLEY BC 157-C7
TOWNSHIP OF LANGLEY BC 158-C2
211TH PL NE
ARLINGTON WA 168-D5
SNOHOMISH CO WA 168-D5
NE 212TH AV
CLARK CO WA 193-B2
212TH AV SE
KING CO WA 175-D3
KING CO WA 182-D2
212TH ST
TOWNSHIP OF LANGLEY BC 158-C2
S 212TH ST
KENT WA 175-C6
KENT WA 290-E4
KENT WA 291-G5
212TH ST NW
SNOHOMISH CO WA 168-C5
212TH ST SW
EDMONDS WA 171-B5
LYNNWOOD WA 171-B5
MOUNTLAKE TERRACE WA 171-B5
S 212TH WY
KENT WA 175-C6
KING CO WA 175-C6
NE 213TH AV
CLARK CO WA 193-B1
213TH AV SW
THURSTON CO WA 184-B4
213TH ST E
PIERCE CO WA 182-B6
214TH AV E
BONNEY LAKE WA 182-C4
PIERCE CO WA 182-C4
215 RD
CLEARWATER CO ID 123-B1
NEZ PERCE CO ID 123-B1
216TH AV NE
KING CO WA 175-D2
216TH AV SE
KING CO WA 175-D7
216TH AV SW
THURSTON CO WA 184-B4
S 216TH PL Rt#-509
DES MOINES WA 175-A6
NORMANDY PARK WA 175-A6
216TH ST
LANGLEY BC 158-C1
MAPLE RIDGE BC 157-C5
TOWNSHIP OF LANGLEY BC 157-C6
TOWNSHIP OF LANGLEY BC 158-C1
S 216TH ST
DES MOINES WA 290-B5
SEATAC WA 290-B5
S 216TH ST Rt#-509
DES MOINES WA 175-A6
DES MOINES WA 290-A5
NORMANDY PARK WA 175-A6
NORMANDY PARK WA 290-A5
SE 216TH ST
KING CO WA 176-A6
216TH ST E
PIERCE CO WA 182-B6
NE 217TH AV
CLARK CO WA 193-B5
218TH AV E
PIERCE CO WA 182-C3
218TH AV SE
KING CO WA 182-D2
219TH AV SW
THURSTON CO WA 184-B4
NE 219TH ST
BATTLE GROUND WA 193-A3
CLARK CO WA 193-A3
NE 219TH ST Rt#-502
CLARK CO WA 192-D3
NE 220TH AV
CLARK CO WA 193-B2
SW 220TH ST
KING CO WA 174-D6
220TH ST NW
SNOHOMISH CO WA 168-B5
220TH ST SW
EDMONDS WA 171-A5
NE 221ST AV
CLARK CO WA 193-B4
NE 222ND AV
CLARK CO WA 193-B5
SE 222ND AV
CLACKAMAS CO OR 200-B3
222ND ST
TOWNSHIP OF LANGLEY BC 157-C6
S 223RD ST
DES MOINES WA 290-B6
224TH AV SE
KING CO WA 182-D1
224TH ST
MAPLE RIDGE BC 157-C5
TOWNSHIP OF LANGLEY BC 158-C2
S 224TH ST
DES MOINES WA 290-C6
KENT WA 291-G6
SE 224TH ST
KING CO WA 175-D6
KING CO WA 176-A6
224TH ST E
PIERCE CO WA 182-A6

224TH ST SE
SNOHOMISH CO WA 171-D6
NE 225TH ST
CLARK CO WA 193-B3
226TH ST
TOWNSHIP OF LANGLEY BC 157-C7
NE 227TH AV
CLARK CO WA 193-B3
227 PL
PACIFIC CO WA 186-A3
227TH ST
TOWNSHIP OF LANGLEY BC 158-C2
228TH AV NE
KING CO WA 176-A2
228TH AV SE
KING CO WA 176-A3
KING CO WA 182-D1
228TH ST
TOWNSHIP OF LANGLEY BC 157-C7
TOWNSHIP OF LANGLEY BC 158-C1
S 228TH ST
KENT WA 291-G7
228TH ST NE
SNOHOMISH CO WA 168-D4
228TH ST SE
SNOHOMISH CO WA 171-B6
228TH ST SW
BRIER WA 171-B6
MOUNTLAKE TERRACE WA 171-B6
NW 229TH AV
HILLSBORO OR 199-A1
NE 229TH ST
CLARK CO WA 193-B3
230TH ST
TOWNSHIP OF LANGLEY BC 157-C7
NW 231ST AV
HILLSBORO OR 199-A1
WASHINGTON CO OR 199-A1
NE 232ND AV
CLARK CO WA 193-B4
NE 232ND AV Rt#-500
CLARK CO WA 193-B5
SE 232ND DR
CLACKAMAS CO OR 200-B4
232ND ST
MAPLE RIDGE BC 157-D5
TOWNSHIP OF LANGLEY BC 157-D7
TOWNSHIP OF LANGLEY BC 158-D1
232ND ST Rt#-10
TOWNSHIP OF LANGLEY BC 157-D7
SE 232ND ST
KING CO WA 175-D7
232ND ST E
PIERCE CO WA 182-A6
234TH AV E
PIERCE CO WA 182-D4
NE 234TH ST
CLARK CO WA 193-A3
234TH ST E
PIERCE CO WA 182-B6
235TH ST
MAPLE RIDGE BC 157-D5
236TH AV NE
KING CO WA 176-A2
236TH AV SE
KING CO WA 110-C3
236TH ST
MAPLE RIDGE BC 157-D6
TOWNSHIP OF LANGLEY BC 158-D1
236TH ST NE
SNOHOMISH CO WA 168-C4
236TH ST SW
MOUNTLAKE TERRACE WA 171-B6
NE 237TH AV Rt#-500
CLARK CO WA 193-B6
237TH ST
MAPLE RIDGE BC 157-D5
NE 237TH ST
CLARK CO WA 193-B3
NE 238TH AV Rt#-500
CLARK CO WA 193-B6
238TH AV E
PIERCE CO WA 182-D5
238TH AV NE
KING CO WA 176-A1
238TH ST
TOWNSHIP OF LANGLEY BC 157-D7
238TH ST E
PIERCE CO WA 182-B6
239TH ST
MAPLE RIDGE BC 157-D5
TOWNSHIP OF LANGLEY BC 158-D1
NE 239TH ST
CLARK CO WA 192-D3
240TH ST
KING CO WA 175-A6
MAPLE RIDGE BC 157-D5
TOWNSHIP OF LANGLEY BC 157-D7
TOWNSHIP OF LANGLEY BC 158-D2
S 240TH ST
DES MOINES WA 175-B7
SE 240TH ST
KENT WA 175-C7
KING CO WA 175-C7
240TH ST E
PIERCE CO WA 182-B6
240TH ST SE
BOTHELL WA 171-C6
SNOHOMISH CO WA 171-C6
NE 242ND AV
CLARK CO WA 193-B3
NE 242ND AV Rt#-500
CLARK CO WA 193-B6
SE 242ND AV
CLACKAMAS CO OR 200-B3
MULTNOMAH CO OR 200-B2
NE 242ND DR
TROUTDALE OR 200-B1
WOOD VILLAGE OR 200-B1
242ND ST
TOWNSHIP OF LANGLEY BC 158-D2
242ND ST NE
SNOHOMISH CO WA 102-C3
243RD ST
MAPLE RIDGE BC 157-D5
244TH AV NE
KING CO WA 176-A2
244TH AV SE
KING CO WA 176-A6

244TH ST
MAPLE RIDGE BC 157-D5
TOWNSHIP OF LANGLEY BC 158-D1
NE 244TH ST
CLARK CO WA 193-A3
SE 244TH ST
KING CO WA 175-C7
244TH ST SW
KING CO WA 171-B6
MOUNTLAKE TERRACE WA 171-B6
244TH ST SW Rt#-104
EDMONDS WA 171-B6
KING CO WA 171-B6
MOUNTLAKE TERRACE WA 171-B6
SHORELINE WA 171-B6
245 ST
OCEAN PARK WA 186-A3
PACIFIC CO WA 186-A3
246TH ST
MAPLE RIDGE BC 157-D5
248TH ST
MAPLE RIDGE BC 157-D5
TOWNSHIP OF LANGLEY BC 157-D5
TOWNSHIP OF LANGLEY BC 158-D2
SE 248TH ST
KENT WA 175-C7
250TH AV E
PIERCE CO WA 182-D4
250TH ST
TOWNSHIP OF LANGLEY BC 158-D2
252ND ST
MAPLE RIDGE BC 157-D5
TOWNSHIP OF LANGLEY BC 157-D7
TOWNSHIP OF LANGLEY BC 158-D2
252ND ST E
PIERCE CO WA 182-B7
252ND ST NE
SNOHOMISH CO WA 168-C4
254TH AV E
PIERCE CO WA 182-D4
254TH ST
TOWNSHIP OF LANGLEY BC 158-D1
NW 254TH ST
CLARK CO WA 192-C3
256TH ST
MAPLE RIDGE BC 157-D6
TOWNSHIP OF LANGLEY BC 157-D7
TOWNSHIP OF LANGLEY BC 158-D2
SE 256TH ST
KENT WA 175-C7
KING CO WA 175-C7
SE 256TH ST Rt#-516
KENT WA 175-C7
SW 257TH AV
TROUTDALE OR 200-B1
258TH AV E
PIERCE CO WA 182-D4
258TH ST
TOWNSHIP OF LANGLEY BC 157-D7
NE 259TH ST
CLARK CO WA 192-D3
CLARK CO WA 193-A3
260TH ST
MAPLE RIDGE BC 157-D5
S 260TH ST
KING CO WA 175-B7
260TH ST E
PIERCE CO WA 182-A7
261ST ST
MAPLE RIDGE BC 157-D5
NE 262ND AV
CLARK CO WA 193-B5
262ND ST
MAPLE RIDGE BC 157-D6
264TH AV SE Rt#-169
KING CO WA 110-C3
264TH ST
MAPLE RIDGE BC 157-D6
TOWNSHIP OF LANGLEY BC 157-D7
TOWNSHIP OF LANGLEY BC 158-D1
264TH ST Rt#-13
TOWNSHIP OF LANGLEY BC 158-D2
264TH ST E
PIERCE CO WA 182-B7
S 265TH PL
KING CO WA 175-B7
NE 267TH AV Rt#-500
CLARK CO WA 193-B6
268TH ST NW
SNOHOMISH CO WA 168-B4
STANWOOD WA 168-B4
268TH ST NW Rt#-532
ISLAND CO WA 167-D4
ISLAND CO WA 168-A4
SNOHOMISH CO WA 168-A4
STANWOOD WA 168-A4
NE 269TH ST
CLARK CO WA 192-D2
NW 269TH ST Rt#-501
CLARK CO WA 192-C2
RIDGEFIELD WA 192-C2
271ST ST NW
STANWOOD WA 168-A4
SE 272ND AV
CLACKAMAS CO OR 200-B3
272ND AV E
PIERCE CO WA 182-D5
272ND ST
MAPLE RIDGE BC 94-B3
TOWNSHIP OF LANGLEY BC 94-B3
TOWNSHIP OF LANGLEY BC 102-B1
TOWNSHIP OF LANGLEY BC 158-D1
S 272ND ST
FEDERAL WAY WA 175-B7
KENT WA 175-B7
KING CO WA 175-B7
272ND ST E
PIERCE CO WA 182-B7
S 272ND WY
KING CO WA 175-B7
274TH ST E
PIERCE CO WA 182-A7
276TH AV SE
KING CO WA 176-A7
276TH ST NW
SNOHOMISH CO WA 168-B4
NE 277TH AV
CLARK CO WA 193-B6
S 277TH ST
AUBURN WA 175-B7

PNW

INDEX

STREET / City State / Page-Grid

S 277TH ST
- KENT WA 175-B7
- KING CO WA 175-B7

278TH ST E
- PIERCE CO WA 182-B7

NE 279TH ST
- CLARK CO WA 192-D2
- CLARK CO WA 193-A2

NW 279TH ST
- CLARK CO WA 192-C2

280TH ST NW
- SNOHOMISH CO WA 168-B4

280TH ST S
- PIERCE CO WA 181-C7

SE 282ND AV
- CLACKAMAS CO OR 200-B3
- GRESHAM OR 200-B2

282ND ST NE
- SNOHOMISH CO WA 168-C4

SE 283RD AV
- CLARK CO WA 193-B7

284TH ST NE
- SNOHOMISH CO WA 168-C4

284TH ST NW
- SNOHOMISH CO WA 168-B3

NE 288TH ST
- KITSAP CO WA 170-C5

S 288TH ST
- KING CO WA 175-B7

288TH ST E
- PIERCE CO WA 181-D7
- PIERCE CO WA 182-A7

288TH ST NE
- SNOHOMISH CO WA 168-C3

288TH ST NW
- SNOHOMISH CO WA 168-B3

288TH ST S
- PIERCE CO WA 181-C7

NW 289TH ST
- CLARK CO WA 192-C2

NE 292ND AV
- CLARK CO WA 193-B6

292ND ST E
- PIERCE CO WA 182-A7

S 296TH ST
- KING CO WA 182-B1

296TH ST E
- PIERCE CO WA 182-A7

296TH ST S
- PIERCE CO WA 181-D7

299TH AV SE
- SNOHOMISH CO WA 110-C1

NE 299TH ST
- CLARK CO WA 192-D2
- CLARK CO WA 193-A2

NW 299TH ST
- CLARK CO WA 192-C2

300TH ST NE
- SNOHOMISH CO WA 168-C3

300TH ST NW
- SNOHOMISH CO WA 168-B3

SE 302ND AV
- MULTNOMAH CO OR 200-C2

S 304TH ST
- FEDERAL WAY WA 182-B1

SE 304TH ST
- KENT WA 182-C1
- KING CO WA 182-C1

304TH ST E
- PIERCE CO WA 118-A1

NE 312TH AV
- CLARK CO WA 193-C6

SE 312TH AV
- CLACKAMAS CO OR 200-C3

S 312TH ST
- FEDERAL WAY WA 182-A1

SE 312TH ST
- KING CO WA 110-C3

SW 312TH ST
- FEDERAL WAY WA 182-A1

NE 314TH ST
- CLARK CO WA 192-D2

316TH ST NW
- SNOHOMISH CO WA 168-C3

S 320TH ST
- FEDERAL WAY WA 182-B1
- KING CO WA 182-B1

SE 320TH ST
- KING CO WA 182-C1

SW 320TH ST
- FEDERAL WAY WA 182-A1

320TH ST E
- PIERCE CO WA 118-B1

SE 322ND AV
- CLACKAMAS CO OR 200-C4

324TH AV SE
- KING CO WA 176-B3

324TH ST NW
- SNOHOMISH CO WA 168-B3

SW 325TH AV
- WASHINGTON CO OR 198-C1

SE 327TH AV
- MULTNOMAH CO OR 200-C2

SE 329TH AV
- CLACKAMAS CO OR 200-C4

SW 331ST AV
- WASHINGTON CO OR 198-C1

332ND ST NW
- SKAGIT CO WA 168-B3

NW 334TH AV
- WASHINGTON CO OR 198-C1

S 336TH ST
- FEDERAL WAY WA 182-A1

SW 336TH ST
- FEDERAL WAY WA 182-A1

336TH ST S
- PIERCE CO WA 118-B1

SW 345TH AV
- WASHINGTON CO OR 198-C1

S 348TH ST
- FEDERAL WAY WA 182-A1

352ND AV
- CLACKAMAS CO OR 200-C3

S 352ND ST
- KING CO WA 182-B2

352ND ST E
- PIERCE CO WA 118-B1

S 356TH ST
- FEDERAL WAY WA 182-A2

SW 356TH ST
- FEDERAL WAY WA 182-A2

NE 360TH ST
- KITSAP CO WA 170-D4

S 360TH ST
- KING CO WA 182-B2

362ND AV
- CLACKAMAS CO OR 200-C3

SE 362ND AV
- CLACKAMAS CO OR 200-C3

362ND DR
- CLACKAMAS CO OR 200-C4

SE 368TH ST
- KING CO WA 182-D2

379TH ST
- CLARK CO WA 192-D1
- CLARK CO WA 193-A1

SE 384TH ST
- KING CO WA 182-D2

389TH ST
- CLARK CO WA 192-C1

SE 400TH ST
- KING CO WA 182-D2

SE 408TH ST
- KING CO WA 182-D3

408TH ST E
- PIERCE CO WA 118-B1

412TH AV
- CLARK CO WA 193-D6
- SKAMANIA CO WA 193-D6

SE 416TH ST
- KING CO WA 182-D3

422ND AV
- CLACKAMAS CO OR 200-D4
- SANDY OR 200-D4

SE 424TH ST
- KING CO WA 110-C3
- KING CO WA 182-D3

428TH AV SE
- KING CO WA 176-C4

SE 432ND ST
- KING CO WA 110-C3

436TH AV SE
- KING CO WA 176-C5

SE 436TH ST Rt#-164
- KING CO WA 110-C3
- KING CO WA 182-D3

SE 436TH WY Rt#-164
- ENUMCLAW WA 110-C3
- KING CO WA 110-C3

442ND AV
- CLACKAMAS CO OR 200-D5

SE 448TH ST
- KING CO WA 182-D3

SE 456TH WY
- KING CO WA 182-D4

2900 RD
- MASON CO WA 180-A4

7000 RD
- CLALLAM CO WA 162-D3

I-5 BALDOCK FRWY
- PORTLAND OR 316-C7
- PORTLAND OR 317-F2
- PORTLAND OR 320-B1

I-5 FRWY
- BELLINGHAM WA 158-D6
- BELLINGHAM WA 161-B4
- BELLINGHAM WA 258-E2
- BLAINE WA 158-C4
- BURLINGTON WA 260-C5
- CASTLE ROCK WA 187-C5
- CENTRALIA WA 299-D4
- CHEHALIS WA 299-E13
- CLACKAMAS CO OR 199-B3
- CLARK CO WA 192-C3
- COWLITZ CO WA 187-C5
- COWLITZ CO WA 189-C1
- COWLITZ CO WA 192-C3
- COWLITZ CO WA 303-E2
- DES MOINES WA 290-D5
- DUPONT WA 181-A6
- EVERETT WA 171-B4
- EVERETT WA 265-H1
- EVERETT WA 268-D7
- EVERETT WA 269-F2
- FEDERAL WAY WA 175-B7
- FEDERAL WAY WA 182-B2
- FERNDALE WA 158-D6
- FIFE WA 182-B2
- GRAND MOUND WA 184-B4
- KALAMA WA 189-C1
- KELSO WA 189-C1
- KELSO WA 303-E2
- KENT WA 175-B7
- KENT WA 290-D5
- KING WA 289-F3
- KING CO WA 171-B7
- KING CO WA 175-B7
- KING CO WA 182-B2
- LACEY WA 181-A6
- LACEY WA 297-F5
- LAKE OSWEGO OR 199-B3
- LAKEWOOD WA 181-A6
- LEWIS CO WA 184-B4
- LEWIS CO WA 187-C3
- LEWIS CO WA 299-D4
- LYNNWOOD WA 171-B4
- MARION CO OR 199-B5
- MARYSVILLE WA 171-B4
- MILTON WA 182-B2
- MOUNT VERNON WA 260-C11
- MOUNTLAKE TERRACE WA 171-B4
- OLYMPIA WA 296-J7
- OLYMPIA WA 297-F5
- PIERCE CO WA 181-A6
- PIERCE CO WA 182-B2
- PORTLAND OR 199-B3
- PORTLAND OR 305-H3
- PORTLAND OR 309-F5
- PORTLAND OR 313-F2
- PORTLAND OR 317-F1
- PORTLAND OR 320-A1
- SEATAC WA 289-F3
- SEATAC WA 290-D5
- SEATAC WA 291-F1
- SEATTLE WA 171-B7
- SEATTLE WA 274-B4
- SEATTLE WA 278-B7
- SEATTLE WA 282-B2
- SEATTLE WA 286-D2

I-5 FRWY
- SEATTLE WA 287-E5
- SHORELINE WA 171-B7
- SISKIYOU CO CA 149-C3
- SISKIYOU CO CA 150-A3
- SKAGIT CO WA 161-B4
- SKAGIT CO WA 168-B3
- SKAGIT CO WA 260-C2
- SNOHOMISH CO WA 168-C4
- SNOHOMISH CO WA 171-B4
- TACOMA WA 181-A6
- TACOMA WA 182-B2
- TACOMA WA 293-J7
- TACOMA WA 295-G1
- THURSTON CO WA 181-A6
- THURSTON CO WA 184-B4
- THURSTON CO WA 296-F12
- THURSTON CO WA 297-A6
- TIGARD OR 199-B3
- TUALATIN OR 199-B3
- TUKWILA WA 287-E5
- TUKWILA WA 289-F3
- TUKWILA WA 291-F1
- TUMWATER WA 184-B4
- TUMWATER WA 296-F12
- VANCOUVER WA 192-C3
- VANCOUVER WA 305-H3
- WASHINGTON CO OR 199-B5
- WHATCOM CO WA 158-C4
- WHATCOM CO WA 161-B4
- WHATCOM CO WA 258-E2
- WILSONVILLE OR 199-B5
- WOODLAND WA 189-C1
- WOODLAND WA 192-C3
- YREKA CA 149-C3

I-5 PACIFIC HWY
- ALBANY OR 326-H5
- ASHLAND OR 337-C4
- CANYONVILLE OR 225-C1
- CENTRAL POINT OR 230-B6
- CENTRAL POINT OR 336-A5
- CLACKAMAS CO OR 199-B6
- COBURG OR 210-B6
- COBURG OR 215-C5
- COTTAGE GROVE OR 215-B7
- CRESWELL OR 215-C5
- DOUGLAS CO OR 219-C1
- DOUGLAS CO OR 221-C2
- DOUGLAS CO OR 225-C1
- DOUGLAS CO OR 334-C11
- EUGENE OR 330-E7
- FOUR CORNERS OR 323-D9
- FOUR CORNERS OR 325-D1
- GRANTS PASS OR 335-H7
- HAYESVILLE OR 323-D9
- JACKSON CO OR 149-C3
- JACKSON CO OR 150-A2
- JACKSON CO OR 229-B4
- JACKSON CO OR 230-B6
- JACKSON CO OR 234-B2
- JACKSON CO OR 336-A5
- JACKSON CO OR 337-C4
- JOSEPHINE CO OR 225-C5
- JOSEPHINE CO OR 229-B1
- JOSEPHINE CO OR 335-C3
- KEIZER OR 323-C5
- LANE CO OR 210-B6
- LANE CO OR 215-C5
- LANE CO OR 219-C1
- LANE CO OR 330-G9
- LINN CO OR 207-C7
- LINN CO OR 210-B6
- LINN CO OR 326-G14
- MARION CO OR 199-B6
- MARION CO OR 205-A2
- MARION CO OR 207-D2
- MARION CO OR 323-C1
- MARION CO OR 325-B8
- MARYSVILLE WA 168-C7
- MARYSVILLE WA 171-C1
- MEDFORD OR 234-B2
- MEDFORD OR 336-E13
- MILLERSBURG OR 326-H5
- PHOENIX OR 234-B2
- ROGUE RIVER OR 229-B4
- ROSEBURG OR 334-C11
- SALEM OR 323-C5
- SALEM OR 325-D1
- SISKIYOU CO CA 149-C3
- SNOHOMISH CO WA 168-C7
- SNOHOMISH CO WA 171-C1
- SPRINGFIELD OR 330-E7
- SUTHERLIN OR 221-C2
- TRI-CITY OR 225-C1
- VANCOUVER WA 305-G1
- WOODBURN OR 205-A2

I-18 HIGHWAY
- BRITISH COLUMBIA 101-A1

I-82 FRWY
- BENTON CO WA 120-B2
- BENTON CO WA 121-A3
- BENTON CO WA 341-B9
- BENTON CO WA 342-A13
- FAIRVIEW-SUMACH WA 243-C7
- GRANDVIEW WA 120-B2
- GRANGER WA 120-A2
- KITTITAS CO WA 241-B6
- KITTITAS CO WA 243-C1
- PROSSER WA 120-B2
- SUNNYSIDE WA 120-B2
- UNION GAP WA 120-A2
- UNION GAP WA 243-C7
- YAKIMA WA 243-C7
- YAKIMA CO WA 243-C4
- ZILLAH WA 120-A2

I-82 MCNARY HWY
- UMATILLA OR 129-A1
- UMATILLA CO OR 129-A1

I-84 BANFIELD FRWY
- PORTLAND OR 313-H4
- PORTLAND OR 314-C5
- PORTLAND OR 315-J2

I-84 COLUMBIA RIVER HWY
- ARLINGTON OR 128-A1
- BOARDMAN OR 128-B1
- CASCADE LOCKS OR 194-C6
- FAIRVIEW OR 200-B1
- GILLIAM CO OR 127-C1
- GILLIAM CO OR 128-A1
- GRESHAM OR 200-B1

I-84 COLUMBIA RIVER HWY
- HOOD RIVER OR 195-A5
- HOOD RIVER CO OR 194-C6
- HOOD RIVER CO OR 195-A5
- MORROW CO OR 128-B1
- MOSIER OR 196-D7
- MULTNOMAH CO OR 194-B7
- MULTNOMAH CO OR 200-C1
- MULTNOMAH CO OR 201-A1
- PORTLAND OR 200-B1
- PORTLAND OR 315-J2
- RUFUS OR 127-C1
- SHERMAN CO OR 127-C1
- THE DALLES OR 196-D7
- TROUTDALE OR 200-B1
- WASCO CO OR 127-B1
- WASCO CO OR 195-A5
- WASCO CO OR 196-D7
- WOOD VILLAGE OR 200-B1

I-84 FRWY
- ADA CO ID 147-C1
- ADA CO ID 253-B3
- BOISE ID 253-B3
- CALDWELL ID 147-B1
- CANYON CO ID 139-B3
- CANYON CO ID 147-B1
- MERIDIAN ID 253-B3
- NAMPA ID 147-B1
- PAYETTE CO ID 139-A3

I-84 OLD OREGON TRAIL HWY
- BAKER CITY OR 138-B1
- BAKER CO OR 130-A3
- BAKER CO OR 138-B1
- LA GRANDE OR 130-A2
- MALHEUR CO OR 138-B1
- MALHEUR CO OR 139-A2
- MORROW CO OR 128-C1
- NORTH POWDER OR 130-A3
- ONTARIO OR 139-A2
- PAYETTE CO ID 139-A2
- PENDLETON OR 129-A1
- UMATILLA CO OR 128-C1
- UMATILLA CO OR 129-A1
- UNION CO OR 129-C2
- UNION CO OR 130-A2

I-90 COLUMBIA BASIN HWY
- ADAMS CO WA 113-C3

I-90 FRWY
- ADAMS CO WA 113-C3
- ADAMS CO WA 114-B2
- BELLEVUE WA 175-C3
- CLE ELUM WA 240-D4
- COEUR D'ALENE ID 354-H7
- COEUR D'ALENE ID 355-A7
- DISHMAN WA 350-F6
- ELLENSBURG WA 241-C6
- FERNAN LAKE VILLAGE ID 355-H11
- GRANT CO WA 112-C3
- GRANT CO WA 113-C3
- GRANT CO WA 120-B1
- GRANT CO WA 242-D3
- GREEN ACRES WA 351-C7
- ISSAQUAH WA 175-C3
- ISSAQUAH WA 176-B4
- KELLOGG ID 115-C2
- KING CO WA 111-A2
- KING CO WA 175-C3
- KING CO WA 176-B4
- KITTITAS CO WA 111-A2
- KITTITAS CO WA 120-A1
- KITTITAS CO WA 240-D4
- KITTITAS CO WA 241-C6
- KOOTENAI CO ID 115-B2
- KOOTENAI CO ID 245-B7
- KOOTENAI CO ID 248-B1
- KOOTENAI CO ID 352-J9
- KOOTENAI CO ID 353-F7
- KOOTENAI CO ID 354-B7
- KOOTENAI CO ID 355-A7
- LINCOLN CO WA 114-B2
- MERCER ISLAND WA 175-C3
- MERCER ISLAND WA 283-H1
- MOSES LAKE WA 242-D3
- NORTH BEND WA 176-B4
- OPPORTUNITY WA 350-F6
- OSBURN ID 115-C2
- PINEHURST ID 115-C2
- POST FALLS ID 352-J9
- POST FALLS ID 353-G6
- POST FALLS ID 354-B7
- SEATTLE WA 278-B7
- SEATTLE WA 282-C1
- SEATTLE WA 283-H1
- SHOSHONE CO ID 115-C2
- SNOQUALMIE WA 176-B4
- SPOKANE WA 348-B14
- SPOKANE WA 349-B10
- SPOKANE CO WA 114-B2
- SPOKANE CO WA 246-B5
- SPOKANE CO WA 348-B14
- SPOKANE CO WA 349-J8
- SPOKANE CO WA 350-F6
- SPOKANE CO WA 351-C7
- SPOKANE CO WA 352-C12
- SPRAGUE WA 114-B2
- VERADALE WA 351-C7
- WALLACE ID 115-C2

I-90 SE HOMESTEAD VALLEY RD
- KING CO WA 111-A2

I-99 FRWY
- DISTRICT OF DELTA BC 101-C1
- DISTRICT OF SURREY BC 101-C1

I-105 EUGENE-SPRINGFIELD HWY
- EUGENE OR 329-J4
- EUGENE OR 330-A5
- LANE CO OR 330-A5
- SPRINGFIELD OR 330-A5

I-182 FRWY
- BENTON CO WA 121-A3
- BENTON CO WA 341-E4
- FRANKLIN CO WA 342-B2
- PASCO WA 342-C1
- PASCO WA 343-A4
- RICHLAND WA 341-J3
- RICHLAND WA 342-A3
- WEST PASCO WA 342-A3
- WEST PASCO WA 343-A4

I-184 FRWY
- ADA CO ID 253-B3
- BOISE ID 253-C3

I-205 FRWY
- CLARK WA 307-H2
- CLARK CO WA 192-D5
- MAYWOOD PARK OR 315-H4
- PORTLAND OR 193-A7
- PORTLAND OR 311-J2
- PORTLAND OR 315-H4
- PORTLAND OR 319-G1
- VANCOUVER WA 192-D5
- VANCOUVER WA 307-H2
- VANCOUVER WA 311-J2

I-205 E PORTLAND FRWY
- CLACKAMAS OR 319-G7
- CLACKAMAS CO OR 199-D4
- GLADSTONE OR 199-D4
- OREGON CITY OR 199-D4
- PORTLAND OR 319-G7
- WASHINGTON CO OR 199-D4
- WEST LINN OR 199-D4

I-405 FRWY
- BELLEVUE WA 175-C4
- BOTHELL WA 171-C6
- KING CO WA 171-C7
- KING CO WA 175-C4
- KIRKLAND WA 171-C7
- KIRKLAND WA 175-C4
- NEWCASTLE WA 175-C4
- PORTLAND OR 312-E3
- PORTLAND OR 313-E3
- PORTLAND OR 317-E1
- RENTON WA 175-C4
- RENTON WA 289-J4
- SNOHOMISH CO WA 171-C6
- TUKWILA WA 289-J4

I-705 FRWY
- TACOMA WA 293-H4
- TACOMA WA 295-J2

Rt#-D2 VALLEY RD
- DEL NORTE CO CA 148-B3

Rt#-D3 LAKE EARL DR
- DEL NORTE CO CA 148-B3

Rt#-D3 NORTHCREST DR
- CRESCENT CITY CA 148-B3
- DEL NORTE CO CA 148-B3

Rt#-D5 OCEAN VIEW DR
- DEL NORTE CO CA 232-D7

Rt#-1 DOUGLAS ST
- CITY OF VICTORIA BC 256-G6
- DISTRICT OF SAANICH BC 256-G6

Rt#-1 HIGHWAY
- BOUNDARY CO ID 107-B1

Rt#-1 ISLAND HWY
- BRITISH COLUMBIA 101-A1
- BRITISH COLUMBIA 159-A2
- DISTRICT OF LANGFORD BC 159-A2
- DISTRICT OF SAANICH BC 256-D4
- DUNCAN BC 101-A1
- TOWN OF VIEW ROYAL BC 159-A2
- TOWN OF VIEW ROYAL BC 256-D4

Rt#-1 SEA TO SKY HWY
- DIST OF WEST VANCOUVER BC 156-A2

Rt#-1 SECOND NARROWS BRDG
- DIST OF VANCOUVER BC 255-F9
- VANCOUVER BC 255-F9

Rt#-1 TRANS CANADA HWY
- BRITISH COLUMBIA 93-C1
- BRITISH COLUMBIA 94-C3
- BRITISH COLUMBIA 95-A1
- BRITISH COLUMBIA 101-A1
- BRITISH COLUMBIA 102-B1
- BRITISH COLUMBIA 156-A2
- BRITISH COLUMBIA 159-A1
- CITY OF VANCOUVER BC 255-A3
- CITY OF VICTORIA BC 256-G11
- COQUITLAM BC 157-B6
- DIST OF VANCOUVER BC 254-F2
- DIST OF VANCOUVER BC 255-A3
- DIST OF WEST VANCOUVER BC 156-A2
- DIST OF WEST VANCOUVER BC 254-F2
- DISTRICT OF ABBOTSFORD BC 94-C3
- DISTRICT OF ABBOTSFORD BC 102-B1
- DISTRICT OF BURNABY BC 156-D4
- DISTRICT OF BURNABY BC 255-F12
- DISTRICT OF CHILLIWACK BC 94-C3
- DISTRICT OF COQUITLAM BC 156-D4
- DISTRICT OF LANGFORD BC 159-A6
- DISTRICT OF MATSQUI BC 102-B1
- DISTRICT OF SAANICH BC 256-G5
- DISTRICT OF SURREY BC 157-B6
- DUNCAN BC 101-A1
- HOPE BC 95-A3
- NANAIMO BC 93-A3
- SQUAMISH BC 93-C1
- TOWN OF VIEW ROYAL BC 159-A6
- TOWN OF VIEW ROYAL BC 256-B3
- TOWNSHIP OF LANGLEY BC 102-B1
- TOWNSHIP OF LANGLEY BC 157-B6
- TOWNSHIP OF LANGLEY BC 158-D1
- VANCOUVER BC 255-F12
- WHISTLER BC 93-C1

Rt#-1 UPPER LEVELS HWY
- CITY OF VANCOUVER BC 255-D4
- DIST OF VANCOUVER BC 254-H3
- DIST OF VANCOUVER BC 255-D4
- DIST OF WEST VANCOUVER BC 156-A2
- DIST OF WEST VANCOUVER BC 254-A1

Rt#-1A CRAIGFLOWER RD
- TOWN OF VIEW ROYAL BC 256-A5

Rt#-1A FRASER HWY
- DISTRICT OF MATSQUI BC 102-B1
- DISTRICT OF SURREY BC 157-A6
- LANGLEY BC 157-B7
- LANGLEY BC 158-D1
- TOWNSHIP OF LANGLEY BC 102-B1
- TOWNSHIP OF LANGLEY BC 158-D1

Rt#-1A GOLDSTREAM AV
- CITY OF COLWOOD BC 159-B6
- DISTRICT OF LANGFORD BC 159-B6

Rt#-1A GORGE RD E
- CITY OF VICTORIA BC 256-F6

Rt#-1A GORGE RD W
- CITY OF VICTORIA BC 256-C5
- DISTRICT OF SAANICH BC 256-C5

Rt#-1A HIGHWAY
- CITY OF VICTORIA BC 256-F6
- DISTRICT OF SAANICH BC 256-B5

Rt#-1A HIGHWAY
- LANGLEY BC 158-C1

Rt#-1A KINGSWAY
- VANCOUVER BC 156-C5
- VANCOUVER BC 254-J13
- VANCOUVER BC 255-A14

Rt#-1A OLD ISLAND HWY
- CITY OF COLWOOD BC 159-B6
- DISTRICT OF SAANICH BC 256-B5
- TOWN OF ESQUIMALT BC 256-B5
- TOWN OF VIEW ROYAL BC 159-B6
- TOWN OF VIEW ROYAL BC 256-A4

Rt#-1A VEDDER RD
- DISTRICT OF CHILLIWACK BC 94-C3

Rt#-1A YALE RD E
- BRITISH COLUMBIA 94-C3
- DISTRICT OF CHILLIWACK BC 94-C3

Rt#-1A YALE RD W
- DISTRICT OF CHILLIWACK BC 94-C3

Rt#-2 HIGHWAY
- CHELAN CO WA 111-C1

Rt#-2 NE STEVENS PASS HWY
- KING CO WA 111-A1
- SKYKOMISH WA 111-A1

Rt#-3 1ST AV
- BOVILL ID 123-B1

Rt#-3 NW 1ST ST
- ENTERPRISE OR 130-C2
- WALLOWA CO OR 130-C2

Rt#-3 CROWSNEST HWY
- BRITISH COLUMBIA 103-C1

Rt#-3 ELK RIVER RD
- LATAH CO ID 123-B1

Rt#-3 ENTERPRISE-LEWISTON HWY
- WALLOWA CO OR 122-C3
- WALLOWA CO OR 130-C1

Rt#-3 FORT JONES RD
- YREKA CA 149-C3

Rt#-3 FRWY
- BREMERTON WA 174-B4
- BREMERTON WA 270-C6
- KITSAP CO WA 170-B6
- KITSAP CO WA 174-B1
- KITSAP CO WA 270-B1
- NAVY YARD CITY WA 270-E11
- SILVERDALE WA 174-B1
- SILVERDALE WA 270-B1
- TRACYTON WA 270-A4

Rt#-3 HIGHWAY
- BENEWAH CO ID 115-B3
- BENEWAH CO ID 248-B6
- BREMERTON WA 174-B4
- BRITISH COLUMBIA 95-C3
- BRITISH COLUMBIA 104-B1
- BRITISH COLUMBIA 105-C1
- BRITISH COLUMBIA 106-C1
- GRAND FORKS BC 105-C1
- GREENWOOD BC 105-B1
- HOPE BC 95-A3
- JULIAETTA ID 123-B2
- KENDRICK ID 123-B1
- KITSAP CO WA 170-C4
- KITSAP CO WA 174-B4
- KOOTENAI CO ID 115-B2
- KOOTENAI CO ID 248-D2
- LATAH CO ID 115-B3
- LATAH CO ID 123-B1
- MASON CO WA 173-D5
- MASON CO WA 174-A5
- MASON CO WA 180-D1
- NEZ PERCE CO ID 123-A2
- PRINCETON BC 95-C3
- SAINT MARIES ID 248-D7
- SHOSHONE CO ID 115-B3

Rt#-3 N LAKE OF THE WOODS HWY
- SISKIYOU CO CA 149-C3

Rt#-3 W LAKE OF THE WOODS HWY
- SISKIYOU CO CA 149-C3
- YREKA CA 149-C3

Rt#-3 MAIN ST
- BRITISH COLUMBIA 104-C1
- JULIAETTA ID 123-B1
- KENDRICK ID 123-B1
- OSOYOOS BC 104-C1

Rt#-3 N MAIN ST
- YREKA CA 149-C3

Rt#-3 S MAIN ST
- YREKA CA 149-C3

Rt#-3 MONTAGUE RD
- YREKA CA 149-C3

Rt#-3 MONTAGUE-YREKA RD
- MONTAGUE CA 150-A3
- SISKIYOU CO CA 149-C3
- SISKIYOU CO CA 150-A3
- YREKA CA 149-C3

Rt#-3 OLD OLYMPIC HWY
- MASON CO WA 180-A3
- SHELTON WA 180-A3

Rt#-3 PARK AV
- BOVILL ID 123-B1
- LATAH CO ID 123-B1

Rt#-3 E PINE ST
- MASON CO WA 180-A3
- SHELTON WA 180-A3

Rt#-3 SECOND AV
- DEARY ID 123-B1
- LATAH CO ID 123-B1

Rt#-3 WYOMING ST
- DEARY ID 123-B1
- LATAH CO ID 123-B1

Rt#-3B HIGHWAY
- BRITISH COLUMBIA 106-A1
- MONTROSE BC 106-B1
- ROSSLAND BC 106-A1

Rt#-4 1ST ST
- SHOSHONE CO ID 115-C2

Rt#-4 ALLEN ST
- KELSO WA 303-D8

Rt#-4 BURKE-CANYON CREEK RD
- SHOSHONE CO ID 115-C2

Rt#-4 BURKE RD
- SHOSHONE CO ID 115-C2
- WALLACE ID 115-C2

Rt#-4 CATLIN ST
- KELSO WA 303-C8

STREET
City State Page-Grid

Rt#-4 HIGHWAY
BRITISH COLUMBIA 92-A3
CATHLAMET WA 117-B3
PACIFIC CO WA 186-C4
PORT ALBERNI BC 92-B3
SHOSHONE CO ID 115-C2
WAHKIAKUM CO WA 117-A2
WAHKIAKUM CO WA 186-D5
WALLACE ID 115-C2
Rt#-4 OCEAN BEACH HWY
CATHLAMET WA 117-B3
COWLITZ CO WA 117-B3
COWLITZ CO WA 189-A2
COWLITZ CO WA 302-A3
LONGVIEW WA 302-F7
LONGVIEW WA 303-A8
WAHKIAKUM CO WA 117-B3
WEST LONGVIEW WA 302-A3
Rt#-5 4TH ST
SAINT MARIES ID 248-D7
Rt#-5 CEDAR ST
BENEWAH CO ID 115-A2
BENEWAH CO ID 248-A7
PLUMMER ID 115-A2
Rt#-5 COLLEGE AV
SAINT MARIES ID 248-D7
Rt#-5 HIGHWAY
BENEWAH CO ID 248-A7
BRITISH COLUMBIA 95-C1
CHATCOLET ID 248-B6
HOPE BC 95-A3
SAINT MARIES ID 248-C7
Rt#-5 MAIN AV
SAINT MARIES ID 248-C7
Rt#-5 MAIN ST
SAINT MARIES ID 248-D7
Rt#-5A HIGHWAY
BRITISH COLUMBIA 95-C1
PRINCETON BC 95-C3
Rt#-6 1ST ST
TILLAMOOK OR 197-B2
TILLAMOOK OR 197-C2
Rt#-6 3RD ST
TILLAMOOK OR 197-B2
TILLAMOOK OR 197-C2
Rt#-6 W FOURTH AV
PE ELL WA 117-B2
Rt#-6 HENKLE ST
PACIFIC CO WA 117-A1
RAYMOND WA 117-A1
Rt#-6 HIGHWAY
BRITISH COLUMBIA 106-C1
LATAH CO ID 123-B1
LATAH CO ID 249-D1
LEWIS CO WA 117-B2
PACIFIC CO WA 117-A1
PE ELL WA 117-B2
POTLATCH ID 249-D1
Rt#-6 MAIN ST
PE ELL WA 117-B2
Rt#-6 OCEAN BEACH HWY
CHEHALIS WA 299-A13
LEWIS CO WA 117-B1
LEWIS CO WA 184-B7
LEWIS CO WA 187-A1
LEWIS CO WA 299-A13
PE ELL WA 117-B2
Rt#-6 SIXTH ST
POTLATCH ID 249-D1
Rt#-6 WHITE PINE DR
BENEWAH CO ID 115-B3
LATAH CO ID 115-B3
Rt#-6 WILSON RIVER HWY
BANKS OR 125-B1
TILLAMOOK OR 197-C2
TILLAMOOK CO OR 125-B1
TILLAMOOK CO OR 197-C2
WASHINGTON CO OR 125-B1
Rt#-7 1ST AV
DISTRICT OF MISSION BC 94-B3
Rt#-7 2ND AV
MORTON WA 118-B2
Rt#-7 E 38TH ST
TACOMA WA 295-J2
Rt#-7 AHSAHKA RD
OROFINO ID 123-C2
Rt#-7 BROADWAY E
VANCOUVER BC 254-H13
VANCOUVER BC 255-A13
Rt#-7 BROADWAY W
VANCOUVER BC 254-E12
Rt#-7 CAMPBELL ST
BAKER CITY OR 138-B1
Rt#-7 DEWEY AV
BAKER CITY OR 138-B1
Rt#-7 FRWY
TACOMA WA 295-H1
Rt#-7 GILBERT GRADE
CLEARWATER CO ID 123-C2
Rt#-7 HIGHWAY
BRITISH COLUMBIA 95-A3
CLEARWATER CO ID 123-C2
LEWIS CO WA 118-B1
OROFINO ID 123-C2
PIERCE CO WA 118-B1
Rt#-7 LOUGHEED HWY
BRITISH COLUMBIA 94-B3
COQUITLAM BC 157-A5
DISTRICT OF BURNABY BC 156-D4
DISTRICT OF BURNABY BC 255-G12
DISTRICT OF COQUITLAM BC 156-D4
DISTRICT OF KENT BC 94-B3
DISTRICT OF MISSION BC 94-B3
MAPLE RIDGE BC 94-B3
MAPLE RIDGE BC 157-D6
PITT MEADOWS BC 157-B4
PORT COQUITLAM BC 157-B4
Rt#-7 MAIN ST
BAKER CITY OR 138-B1
Rt#-7 MORTON RD
LEWIS CO WA 118-B2
MORTON WA 118-B2
Rt#-7 MOUNTAIN HWY E
PIERCE CO WA 118-B1
PIERCE CO WA 181-D6
PIERCE CO WA 182-A6
Rt#-7 NORTH RAILWAY AV
DISTRICT OF MISSION BC 94-B3
Rt#-7 PACIFIC AV
PIERCE CO WA 181-D4
Rt#-7 PACIFIC AV
TACOMA WA 181-D4
TACOMA WA 295-H3
Rt#-7 PACIFIC AV S
PIERCE CO WA 181-D5
Rt#-7 RIVERSIDE AV
OROFINO ID 123-C2
Rt#-7 RUSSELL RIDGE RD
CLEARWATER CO ID 123-C2
Rt#-7 WHITNEY HWY
BAKER CITY OR 138-B1
BAKER CO OR 137-C1
BAKER CO OR 138-A1
GRANT CO OR 137-C1
Rt#-7A BARNET HWY
COQUITLAM BC 157-A4
DISTRICT OF BURNABY BC 156-D4
PORT MOODY BC 157-A4
Rt#-7A HASTINGS ST
DISTRICT OF BURNABY BC 156-D4
DISTRICT OF BURNABY BC 255-G10
VANCOUVER BC 255-F10
Rt#-7A HASTINGS ST E
VANCOUVER BC 254-J10
VANCOUVER BC 255-B10
Rt#-7A HIGHWAY
DISTRICT OF BURNABY BC 156-D4
Rt#-7A INLET DR
DISTRICT OF BURNABY BC 156-D4
Rt#-7A SAINT JOHNS ST
DISTRICT OF BURNABY BC 156-D4
PORT MOODY BC 156-D4
PORT MOODY BC 157-A4
Rt#-8 E 3RD ST
MOSCOW ID 249-C5
Rt#-8 W 3RD ST
MOSCOW ID 249-C5
Rt#-8 SE 10TH AV
HILLSBORO OR 198-D1
Rt#-8 19TH AV
FOREST GROVE OR 198-B1
Rt#-8 N ADAIR ST
CORNELIUS OR 198-C1
FOREST GROVE OR 198-C1
Rt#-8 E BASELINE ST
CORNELIUS OR 198-C1
Rt#-8 W BASELINE ST
CORNELIUS OR 198-C1
Rt#-8 SE BASELINE ST
HILLSBORO OR 198-D1
Rt#-8 SW BASELINE ST
HILLSBORO OR 198-D1
Rt#-8 SW CANYON RD
BEAVERTON OR 199-B2
WASHINGTON CO OR 199-B2
Rt#-8 E ST
FOREST GROVE OR 198-B1
WASHINGTON CO OR 198-B1
Rt#-8 FIRST ST
ELK RIVER ID 123-C1
Rt#-8 FRWY
ELMA WA 179-D6
GRAYS HARBOR CO WA 179-D6
MCCLEARY WA 179-D6
THURSTON CO WA 179-D6
THURSTON CO WA 180-B6
Rt#-8 GALES CREEK RD
FOREST GROVE OR 198-B1
WASHINGTON CO OR 125-B1
WASHINGTON CO OR 198-B1
Rt#-8 HIGHWAY
BOVILL ID 123-B1
BRITISH COLUMBIA 95-C1
CLEARWATER CO ID 123-B1
ELK RIVER ID 123-C1
LATAH CO ID 123-B1
LATAH CO ID 249-D5
MOSCOW ID 249-C5
TROY ID 123-A1
Rt#-8 MAIN ST
TROY ID 123-A1
Rt#-8 SE OAK ST
HILLSBORO OR 198-D1
Rt#-8 SW OAK ST
HILLSBORO OR 198-D1
Rt#-8 PACIFIC AV
CORNELIUS OR 198-C1
FOREST GROVE OR 198-C1
Rt#-8 SECOND AV
DEARY ID 123-B1
LATAH CO ID 123-B1
Rt#-8 TAFT ST
ELK RIVER ID 123-C1
Rt#-8 TUALATIN VALLEY HWY
CORNELIUS OR 198-D1
HILLSBORO OR 198-D1
HILLSBORO OR 199-A2
WASHINGTON CO OR 198-D1
WASHINGTON CO OR 199-A2
Rt#-8 SW TUALATIN VALLEY HWY
BEAVERTON OR 199-A2
WASHINGTON CO OR 199-A2
Rt#-9 N BORSETH ST
SEDRO-WOOLLEY WA 161-C5
Rt#-9 CASCADE HWY
SEDRO-WOOLLEY WA 161-C6
Rt#-9 CHEAM AV
DISTRICT OF KENT BC 94-C3
Rt#-9 EVERGREEN DR
DISTRICT OF KENT BC 94-C3
Rt#-9 HAIG HWY
DISTRICT OF KENT BC 94-C3
Rt#-9 N HAZEL ST
ARLINGTON WA 168-D5
Rt#-9 S HAZEL ST
ARLINGTON WA 168-D5
Rt#-9 HIGHWAY
ARLINGTON WA 168-D5
BRITISH COLUMBIA 94-C3
DISTRICT OF KENT BC 94-C3
LATAH CO ID 123-A1
SEDRO-WOOLLEY WA 161-C6
SKAGIT CO WA 161-C3
SKAGIT CO WA 168-C1
SKAGIT CO WA 260-J11
SNOHOMISH WA 171-D3
SNOHOMISH CO WA 168-C3
SNOHOMISH CO WA 171-D1
Rt#-9 HOPEWELL RD
WHATCOM CO WA 102-B1
Rt#-9 HOT SPRINGS RD
CITY OF HARRISN HT SPGS BC 94-C3
DISTRICT OF KENT BC 94-C3
Rt#-9 LAWRENCE RD
WHATCOM CO WA 102-B1
Rt#-9 MAIN ST
SKAGIT CO WA 168-C2
Rt#-9 MOORE ST
SEDRO-WOOLLEY WA 161-C5
Rt#-9 NOOKSACK AV
NOOKSACK WA 102-B1
Rt#-9 NOOKSACK RD
NOOKSACK WA 102-B1
WHATCOM CO WA 102-B1
Rt#-9 TOWNSHIP RD
SEDRO-WOOLLEY WA 161-C5
SKAGIT CO WA 161-C5
Rt#-9 VALLEY HWY
WHATCOM CO WA 102-B1
WHATCOM CO WA 161-C2
Rt#-10 56TH AV
DISTRICT OF SURREY BC 157-A7
DISTRICT OF SURREY BC 158-B1
Rt#-10 58TH AV
DISTRICT OF DELTA BC 156-D7
DISTRICT OF SURREY BC 156-D7
DISTRICT OF SURREY BC 157-A7
Rt#-10 232ND ST
TOWNSHIP OF LANGLEY BC 157-D7
Rt#-10 SW BARBUR BLVD
PORTLAND OR 316-E3
PORTLAND OR 317-E2
Rt#-10 SW BEAVERTN-HLLSDL HWY
BEAVERTON OR 199-B2
PORTLAND OR 199-B2
PORTLAND OR 316-A3
WASHINGTON CO OR 199-B2
Rt#-10 SW CAPITOL HWY
PORTLAND OR 316-D4
PORTLAND OR 317-E4
Rt#-10 FARMINGTON RD
WASHINGTON CO OR 198-D2
Rt#-10 SW FARMINGTON RD
BEAVERTON OR 199-A2
WASHINGTON CO OR 198-D3
WASHINGTON CO OR 199-A2
Rt#-10 GLOVER RD
LANGLEY BC 157-C7
TOWNSHIP OF LANGLEY BC 157-C7
Rt#-10 HIGHWAY
KITTITAS CO WA 240-C2
KITTITAS CO WA 241-A3
TOWNSHIP OF LANGLEY BC 157-D7
Rt#-10 LADNER TRUNK RD
DISTRICT OF DELTA BC 156-D7
Rt#-10 LANGLEY BYPS
DISTRICT OF SURREY BC 157-C7
DISTRICT OF SURREY BC 158-B1
LANGLEY BC 157-C7
Rt#-10 RAWLISON CRES
TOWNSHIP OF LANGLEY BC 157-C7
Rt#-11 11TH AV
DISTRICT OF MISSION BC 94-B3
Rt#-11 E 11TH ST
TACOMA WA 293-J5
Rt#-11 S 11TH ST
TACOMA WA 293-H5
Rt#-11 12TH ST
BELLINGHAM WA 258-B11
Rt#-11 ABBOTSFORD-MISSION HWY
DISTRICT OF MATSQUI BC 94-B3
DISTRICT OF MATSQUI BC 102-B1
Rt#-11 CHUCKANUT DR
BELLINGHAM WA 258-B12
SKAGIT CO WA 160-D2
SKAGIT CO WA 161-A3
SKAGIT CO WA 260-B1
WHATCOM CO WA 160-D2
WHATCOM CO WA 258-B14
Rt#-11 HIGHWAY
CLEARWATER CO ID 123-C2
SKAGIT CO WA 161-A5
SKAGIT CO WA 260-A1
Rt#-11 S MAIN ST
MILTON-FREEWATER OR 121-C3
Rt#-11 OLD FAIRHAVEN PKWY
BELLINGHAM WA 258-B11
Rt#-11 OREGON-WASHINGTON HWY
MILTON-FREEWATER OR 121-C3
PENDLETON OR 129-B1
UMATILLA CO OR 121-C3
UMATILLA CO OR 129-B1
WALLA WALLA CO WA 121-C3
WASCO OR 129-B1
Rt#-11 PACIFIC AV
TACOMA WA 293-H6
TACOMA WA 295-H1
Rt#-11 VALLEY PKWY
BELLINGHAM WA 258-C11
Rt#-12 HIGHWAY
CLEARWATER CO ID 123-C2
Rt#-13 264TH ST
TOWNSHIP OF LANGLEY BC 158-D2
Rt#-13 HARPSTER GRADE RD
IDAHO CO ID 123-C3
Rt#-13 HIGHWAY
BRITISH COLUMBIA 158-D3
TOWNSHIP OF LANGLEY BC 158-D2
Rt#-13 E MAIN ST
GRANGEVILLE ID 123-C3
IDAHO CO ID 123-C3
Rt#-13 W MAIN ST
GRANGEVILLE ID 123-C3
IDAHO CO ID 123-C3
Rt#-14 NE 3RD AV
CAMAS WA 193-B7
CLARK CO WA 193-B7
WASHOUGAL WA 193-B7
Rt#-14 SE 3RD ST
CAMAS WA 193-B7
WASHOUGAL WA 193-B7
Rt#-14 NW 6TH AV
CAMAS WA 193-B7
Rt#-14 NE ADAMS ST
CAMAS WA 193-B7
Rt#-14 D ST
CLARK CO WA 193-C7
WASHOUGAL WA 193-C7
Rt#-14 EVERGREEN BLVD
CLARK CO WA 193-C7
WASHOUGAL WA 193-C7
Rt#-14 EVERGREEN HWY
CARSON WA 194-C6
CARSON WA 195-B5
NORTH BONNEVILLE WA 194-C6
SKAMANIA CO WA 193-D7
SKAMANIA CO WA 194-A7
SKAMANIA CO WA 195-B5
SKAMANIA CO WA 200-D1
STEVENSON WA 194-C6
Rt#-14 HIGHWAY
BENTON CO WA 120-C3
BENTON CO WA 121-A3
BENTON CO WA 128-C1
BRITISH COLUMBIA 100-C2
IDAHO CO ID 123-C3
KLICKITAT CO WA 128-B1
Rt#-14 LEWIS AND CLARK HWY
BINGEN WA 195-C5
CAMAS WA 193-A7
CLARK CO WA 193-A7
CLARK CO WA 200-C1
KLICKITAT CO WA 127-B1
KLICKITAT CO WA 195-C5
KLICKITAT CO WA 196-C6
SKAMANIA CO WA 195-C5
VANCOUVER WA 305-G6
VANCOUVER WA 306-A6
VANCOUVER WA 307-E7
VANCOUVER WA 311-G1
WASHOUGAL WA 193-C7
WHITE SALMON WA 195-C5
Rt#-14 SOOKE RD
BRITISH COLUMBIA 101-A2
BRITISH COLUMBIA 159-A7
DISTRICT OF LANGFORD BC 159-A7
DISTRICT OF METCHOSIN BC 159-A7
Rt#-14 STEUBEN ST
BINGEN WA 195-D5
Rt#-14 WEST COAST RD
BRITISH COLUMBIA 101-A2
BRITISH COLUMBIA 164-C1
Rt#-15 176TH ST
BRITISH COLUMBIA 158-B2
DISTRICT OF SURREY BC 157-B7
DISTRICT OF SURREY BC 158-B2
WHATCOM CO WA 158-B2
Rt#-15 CLOVERDALE BYPS
DISTRICT OF SURREY BC 157-B7
Rt#-15 PACIFIC HWY
DISTRICT OF SURREY BC 158-B1
Rt#-16 EMMETT HWY
ADA CO ID 139-C3
ADA CO ID 147-C1
Rt#-16 FRWY
BREMERTON WA 174-B7
GIG HARBOR WA 181-C2
KITSAP CO WA 174-B7
PIERCE CO WA 174-B7
PIERCE CO WA 181-C2
PORT ORCHARD WA 174-B7
TACOMA WA 181-C2
TACOMA WA 294-D1
TACOMA WA 295-E1
Rt#-16 HIGHWAY
ADA CO ID 139-C3
GEM CO ID 139-C3
Rt#-16 ROUTE 16 FRWY
TACOMA WA 292-A6
TACOMA WA 294-B1
TACOMA WA 295-E1
Rt#-17 60TH ST
DISTRICT OF DELTA BC 156-C7
Rt#-17 BLANSHARD ST
CITY OF VICTORIA BC 256-G6
DISTRICT OF SAANICH BC 256-G5
Rt#-17 DAISY ST N
GRANT CO WA 112-C2
SOAP LAKE WA 112-C2
Rt#-17 DAISY ST S
SOAP LAKE WA 112-C2
Rt#-17 HIGHWAY
ADAMS CO WA 121-A1
BRIDGEPORT WA 112-C1
CASCADE VALLEY WA 242-C2
DOUGLAS CO WA 112-C1
DOUGLAS CO WA 113-A2
FRANKLIN CO WA 121-A1
GRANT CO WA 112-C2
GRANT CO WA 113-A2
GRANT CO WA 121-A1
GRANT CO WA 242-B1
MESA WA 121-A2
MOSES LAKE WA 242-C2
MOSES LAKE NORTH WA 242-C2
OKANOGAN CO WA 104-C3
OKANOGAN CO WA 112-C1
SOAP LAKE WA 112-C2
Rt#-17 LEAHY RD S
DOUGLAS CO WA 112-C1
Rt#-17 PATRICIA BAY HWY
DIST OF CENTRAL SAANICH BC 159-C2
DIST OF NORTH SAANICH BC 159-C2
DISTRICT OF SAANICH BC 159-C2
DISTRICT OF SAANICH BC 256-F2
TOWN OF SIDNEY BC 159-C2
Rt#-17 R RD NE
DOUGLAS CO WA 112-C1
Rt#-17A HIGHWAY
DISTRICT OF SAANICH BC 159-C5
Rt#-17A WAIN RD
DIST OF NORTH SAANICH BC 159-B2
Rt#-17A WEST SAANICH RD
DIST OF CENTRAL SAANICH BC 159-B3
DIST OF NORTH SAANICH BC 159-B3
DISTRICT OF SAANICH BC 159-C5
Rt#-18 AUBURN-ECHO LAKE CTO
AUBURN WA 182-C1
KENT WA 175-D7
KING CO WA 175-D7
KING CO WA 176-A6
Rt#-18 AUBURN-ECHO LAKE CTO
KING CO WA 182-C1
Rt#-18 DAYTON BYPASS RD
YAMHILL CO OR 198-B7
Rt#-18 ECHO LAKE CTO SE
KING CO WA 176-A6
Rt#-18 FRWY
AUBURN WA 182-B1
FEDERAL WAY WA 182-B1
KING CO WA 182-B1
Rt#-18 HIGHWAY
BRITISH COLUMBIA 100-C1
Rt#-18 S HIGHWAY 99W
YAMHILL CO OR 204-B1
Rt#-18 E MAIN ST
SHERIDAN OR 125-B3
WILLAMINA OR 125-A3
Rt#-18 S MAIN ST
WILLAMINA OR 125-A3
Rt#-18 W MAIN ST
SHERIDAN OR 125-B3
Rt#-18 W MCMINNVILLE BYPS
MCMINNVILLE OR 204-B1
YAMHILL CO OR 204-B1
Rt#-18 SALMON RIVER HWY
LINCOLN CO OR 203-B4
LINCOLN CO OR 203-D3
MCMINNVILLE OR 198-A7
MCMINNVILLE OR 204-A2
POLK CO OR 125-A3
ROSE LODGE OR 203-D3
SHERIDAN OR 125-B3
TILLAMOOK CO OR 125-A3
TILLAMOOK CO OR 203-D3
YAMHILL CO OR 125-B3
YAMHILL CO OR 198-A7
YAMHILL CO OR 204-A2
Rt#-18 W VALLEY HWY
SHERIDAN OR 125-B3
WILLAMINA OR 125-B3
YAMHILL CO OR 125-B3
Rt#-18 WILLAMINA-SHERIDAN HWY
POLK CO OR 125-A3
WILLAMINA OR 125-A3
Rt#-19 E 7TH ST
FOSSIL OR 128-A3
Rt#-19 AIRPORT CUTOFF RD
HADLOCK-IRONDALE WA 263-B11
JEFFERSON CO WA 263-B11
Rt#-19 BEAVER VALLEY RD
JEFFERSON CO WA 170-A1
Rt#-19 COTTONWOOD ST
ARLINGTON OR 128-A1
Rt#-19 HIGHWAY
BRITISH COLUMBIA 92-A1
CAMPBELL RIVER BC 92-A1
COURTENAY BC 92-A2
PARKSVILLE BC 92-C3
Rt#-19 W IDAHO AV
HOMEDALE ID 147-A1
Rt#-19 ISLAND HWY N
BRITISH COLUMBIA 93-A3
NANAIMO BC 93-A3
Rt#-19 JOHN DAY HWY
ARLINGTON OR 128-A2
CONDON OR 128-A2
FOSSIL OR 128-A3
GILLIAM CO OR 128-A2
GRANT CO OR 136-B1
SPRAY OR 136-B1
WHEELER CO OR 128-A3
WHEELER CO OR 136-B1
Rt#-19 LOCUST ST
ARLINGTON OR 128-A1
Rt#-19 N LOCUST ST
ARLINGTON OR 128-A1
GILLIAM CO OR 128-A1
Rt#-19 S LOCUST ST
ARLINGTON OR 128-A1
Rt#-19 MAIN ST
CANYON CO ID 147-B1
GREENLEAF ID 147-B1
Rt#-19 S MAIN ST
CONDON OR 128-A2
Rt#-19 OWYHEE BLVD
OWYHEE CO ID 147-A1
Rt#-19 RHODY DR
HADLOCK-IRONDALE WA 170-A1
HADLOCK-IRONDALE WA 263-E14
JEFFERSON CO WA 170-A1
JEFFERSON CO WA 263-E14
Rt#-19 SIMPLOT BLVD
CALDWELL ID 147-B1
CANYON CO ID 147-B1
WILDER ID 147-B1
Rt#-19 E WALNUT ST
CONDON OR 128-A2
Rt#-19 N WASHINGTON ST
CONDON OR 128-A2
Rt#-19 S WASHINGTON ST
CONDON OR 128-A2
Rt#-20 12TH ST
ANACORTES WA 259-F2
Rt#-20 E 3RD AV
COLVILLE WA 106-A2
STEVENS CO WA 106-A2
Rt#-20 W 6TH ST
REPUBLIC WA 105-B2
Rt#-20 AVON AV
BURLINGTON WA 260-C4
Rt#-20 AVON CTO
SKAGIT CO WA 161-A6
SKAGIT CO WA 260-A6
Rt#-20 BURLINGTON BLVD
BURLINGTON WA 260-C5
Rt#-20 S BURLINGTON BLVD
BURLINGTON WA 260-C7
Rt#-20 CASCADE HWY
BURLINGTON WA 260-E4
SEDRO-WOOLLEY WA 161-C6
SEDRO-WOOLLEY WA 260-E4
SKAGIT CO WA 260-E4
Rt#-20 S CLARK AV
REPUBLIC WA 105-B2
Rt#-20 COLVILLE-TIGER RD
STEVENS CO WA 106-A2
Rt#-20 COMMERCIAL AV
ANACORTES WA 259-H4
Rt#-20 N CROSS STATE HWY
SEDRO-WOOLLEY WA 161-C5
SKAGIT CO WA 161-C5
Rt#-20 DIVISION ST
TWISP WA 104-A3
Rt#-20 ELMWAY
OKANOGAN WA 104-C3
OKANOGAN CO WA 104-C3
OMAK WA 104-C3
Rt#-20 FOURTH AV W
OMAK WA 104-C3
Rt#-20 HARBOR RD
ISLAND CO WA 167-B4
Rt#-20 HIGHWAY
ANACORTES WA 259-H5
AULT FIELD WA 167-C2
BURLINGTON WA 260-C5
CONCRETE WA 102-C2
COUPEVILLE WA 167-B4
CUSICK WA 106-C3
FERRY CO WA 105-B2
FERRY CO WA 106-A2
HAMILTON WA 102-C2
ISLAND CO WA 160-C7
ISLAND CO WA 167-C1
JEFFERSON CO WA 109-C1
JEFFERSON CO WA 170-A1
JEFFERSON CO WA 263-C6
LYMAN WA 102-C2
NEWPORT WA 106-C3
OAK HARBOR WA 167-C2
OKANOGAN WA 104-C3
OKANOGAN CO WA 104-C2
OKANOGAN CO WA 105-A2
PEND OREILLE CO WA 106-B2
PORT TOWNSEND WA 263-C6
REPUBLIC WA 105-B2
SKAGIT CO WA 102-C2
SKAGIT CO WA 160-C6
SKAGIT CO WA 161-D5
SKAGIT CO WA 259-J6
SKAGIT CO WA 260-B6
WINTHROP WA 104-A2
Rt#-20 MAIN ST S
OMAK WA 104-C3
Rt#-20 MEMORIAL HWY
SKAGIT CO WA 160-D6
SKAGIT CO WA 161-A7
Rt#-20 E METHOW VALLEY HWY
OKANOGAN CO WA 104-B3
TWISP WA 104-A3
Rt#-20 NORTH CASCADES HWY
CHELAN CO WA 103-C2
OKANOGAN CO WA 103-C2
OKANOGAN CO WA 103-A2
WHATCOM CO WA 103-A2
Rt#-20 OAKES AV
ANACORTES WA 259-B3
Rt#-20 OKOMA DR
OKANOGAN CO WA 104-C3
OMAK WA 104-C3
Rt#-20 W PIONEER WY
OAK HARBOR WA 167-B3
Rt#-20 POGGENSEE RD
ISLAND CO WA 167-C5
Rt#-20 RIO VISTA AV
BURLINGTON WA 260-C5
Rt#-20 RIVERSIDE AV
OKANOGAN CO WA 104-A2
WINTHROP WA 104-A2
Rt#-20 RIVERSIDE DR
OKANOGAN CO WA 104-C2
OMAK WA 104-C2
Rt#-20 SANTIAM HWY
LEBANON OR 133-C1
LINN CO OR 133-C1
SOUTH LEBANON OR 133-C1
Rt#-20 SECOND AV N
OKANOGAN WA 104-C3
Rt#-20 SECOND AV NW
OKANOGAN WA 104-C3
Rt#-20 SECOND AV SW
OKANOGAN WA 104-C3
Rt#-20 SIMS WY
PORT TOWNSEND WA 263-C6
Rt#-20 SIXTH ST
OKANOGAN CO WA 104-C2
TONASKET WA 104-C2
Rt#-20 WATER ST
PORT TOWNSEND WA 263-G5
Rt#-21 W 1ST AV
ODESSA WA 113-B3
Rt#-21 N 1ST ST
ODESSA WA 113-B3
Rt#-21 E 6TH AV
ODESSA WA 113-B3
Rt#-21 S ALDER ST
ODESSA WA 113-B3
Rt#-21 N DIVISION ST
ODESSA WA 113-B3
Rt#-21 W FIRST ST
LIND WA 121-B1
Rt#-21 W FRONT AV
LINCOLN CO WA 113-B1
WILBUR WA 113-B1
Rt#-21 E GOWEN RD
ADA CO ID 253-D4
BOISE ID 253-D4
Rt#-21 HIGHWAY
ADAMS CO WA 113-B3
ADAMS CO WA 121-B1
BOUNDARY CO ID 107-B1
BRITISH COLUMBIA 105-C1
BRITISH COLUMBIA 107-B1
FERRY CO WA 105-C1
FERRY CO WA 113-B1
GRAND FORKS BC 105-C1
LINCOLN CO WA 113-B1
LIND WA 121-B1
ODESSA WA 113-B3
REPUBLIC WA 105-B2
Rt#-21 LIND-KAHLOTUS RD
ADAMS CO WA 121-C1
FRANKLIN CO WA 121-C1
KAHLOTUS WA 121-C1

STREET
City State Page-Grid

Rt#-21 W MAY AV
ODESSA WA 113-B3
Rt#-21 MONSOR RD
LINCOLN CO WA 113-B2
Rt#-21 ROSENOFF RD
ADAMS CO WA 113-B3
Rt#-21 E SECOND ST
LIND WA 121-B1
Rt#-21 VIOLET AV
KAHLOTUS WA 121-C1
Rt#-21 S WEST ST
WILBUR WA 113-B1
Rt#-22 12TH ST SE
SALEM OR 322-J14
Rt#-22 BUENA RD
YAKIMA CO WA 120-A2
Rt#-22 BUENA WY
TOPPENISH WA 120-A2
Rt#-22 CENTER ST NE
SALEM OR 322-H12
Rt#-22 CENTER ST BRDG
SALEM OR 322-H12
SALEM OR 322-H12
Rt#-22 S ELM ST
TOPPENISH WR 120-A2
Rt#-22 EVERGREEN HWY
TOPPENISH WA 120-A2
YAKIMA CO WA 120-A2
Rt#-22 FERRY ST SE
SALEM OR 322-H13
Rt#-22 FRONT ST NE
SALEM OR 322-H12
Rt#-22 FRONT ST SE
SALEM OR 322-H13
Rt#-22 HIGHWAY
BENTON CO WA 120-B3
BRITISH COLUMBIA 106-A1
MABTON WA 120-B3
PROSSER WA 120-C3
SATUS WA 120-A2
TOPPENISH WA 120-A2
YAKIMA CO WA 120-A2
Rt#-22 MARION ST
SALEM OR 322-H12
Rt#-22 MARION ST BRDG
SALEM OR 322-H12
Rt#-22 MISSION ST SE
SALEM OR 322-J14
SALEM OR 323-A14
SALEM OR 325-B1
Rt#-22 PRINGLE PKWY
SALEM OR 322-J13
Rt#-22 SALEM HWY
SALEM OR 322-J14
Rt#-22 N SANTIAM HWY
AUMSVILLE OR 205-A7
DETROIT OR 134-A1
FOUR CORNERS OR 325-G4
GATES OR 134-A1
IDANHA OR 134-A1
LINN CO OR 134-C1
MARION CO OR 133-C1
MARION CO OR 134-A1
MARION CO OR 205-A7
MARION CO OR 325-G4
MILL CITY OR 134-A1
SALEM OR 325-G4
STAYTON OR 133-C1
SUBLIMITY OR 133-C1
Rt#-22 THREE RIVERS HWY
POLK CO OR 125-A3
TILLAMOOK CO OR 197-B6
TILLAMOOK CO OR 197-B6
TILLAMOOK CO OR 203-D1
YAMHILL CO OR 125-A3
YAMHILL CO OR 203-D1
Rt#-22 TRADE ST SE
SALEM OR 322-H13
Rt#-22 WAPENISH RD
SATUS WA 120-A2
YAKIMA CO WA 120-A1
Rt#-22 WILLAMINA-SALEM HWY
POLK CO OR 125-B3
POLK CO OR 204-A4
POLK CO OR 322-G13
SALEM OR 322-G13
Rt#-22 WILLAMINA-SALEM HWY NW
POLK CO OR 204-B6
POLK CO OR 322-B14
SALEM OR 322-B14
Rt#-22A HIGHWAY
BRITISH COLUMBIA 106-B1
Rt#-23 S 3RD ST
HARRINGTON WA 113-C2
Rt#-23 ENDICOTT-ST JOHN RD
SAINT JOHN WA 114-B3
WHITMAN CO WA 114-B3
Rt#-23 FRONT ST
SAINT JOHN WA 114-B3
Rt#-23 HIGHWAY
HARRINGTON WA 113-C2
LINCOLN CO WA 113-C2
LINCOLN CO WA 114-A2
SAINT JOHN WA 114-B3
SPRAGUE WA 114-A3
WHITMAN CO WA 114-A3
Rt#-23 E MAIN ST
HARRINGTON WA 113-C2
Rt#-23 E SHERLOCK ST
HARRINGTON WA 113-C2
Rt#-24 S BROADWAY AV
ADAMS CO WA 121-A1
OTHELLO WA 121-A1
Rt#-24 HANFORD RD
YAKIMA CO WA 120-A2
Rt#-24 HIGHWAY
ADAMS CO WA 120-C1
ADAMS CO WA 121-A1
BENTON CO WA 120-C1
GRANT CO WA 120-C1
MOXEE CITY WA 243-D7
YAKIMA WA 243-C7
YAKIMA CO WA 120-A2
YAKIMA CO WA 243-C7
Rt#-25 CENTER AV
NORTHPORT WA 106-A1
STEVENS CO WA 106-A1
Rt#-25 HIGHWAY
DAVENPORT WA 114-A2
LINCOLN CO WA 113-C1
LINCOLN CO WA 114-A1
MARCUS WA 106-A2
NORTHPORT WA 106-A1
STEVENS CO WA 105-C2
STEVENS CO WA 106-A1
STEVENS CO WA 113-C1
Rt#-25 LITTLE SHEEP CREEK RD
STEVENS CO WA 106-A1
Rt#-26 FRWY
GRANT CO WA 120-B1
Rt#-26 HIGHWAY
ADAMS CO WA 120-C1
ADAMS CO WA 121-A1
ADAMS CO WA 122-A1
COLFAX WA 122-C1
GRANT CO WA 120-B1
OTHELLO WA 121-A1
ROYAL CITY WA 120-C1
WASHTUCNA WA 121-C1
WHITMAN CO WA 122-C1
Rt#-26 NORTH ST
WASHTUCNA WA 121-C1
Rt#-26 ROAD 13-SW
GRANT CO WA 120-B1
Rt#-26 T WALTERS RD
COLFAX WA 122-C1
Rt#-26 WASHINGTON ST
ADAMS CO WA 121-A1
OTHELLO WA 121-A1
Rt#-27 1ST ST
OAKESDALE WA 114-C3
Rt#-27 4TH ST
GARFIELD WA 114-C3
Rt#-27 ALMOTA ST
PALOUSE WA 249-B1
Rt#-27 BLAKE RD
OPPORTUNITY WA 350-H10
OPPORTUNITY WA 351-A13
SPOKANE CO WA 351-A13
Rt#-27 N BRIDGE ST
PALOUSE WA 249-B1
Rt#-27 S BRIDGE ST
PALOUSE WA 249-C1
Rt#-27 COUNTY RD
WHITMAN CO WA 114-C3
Rt#-27 CROOKED RIVER HWY
CROOK CO OR 135-C3
CROOK CO OR 213-C6
DESCHUTES CO OR 135-C3
PRINEVILLE OR 213-C6
Rt#-27 CROSBY ST
TEKOA WA 114-C3
Rt#-27 S DISHMAN-MICA RD
SPOKANE CO WA 247-A5
Rt#-27 N DIVISION ST
PALOUSE WA 249-B1
Rt#-27 ELIZABETH ST
TEKOA WA 114-C3
Rt#-27 FIRST ST
FAIRFIELD WA 114-C2
Rt#-27 N GRAND AV
PULLMAN WA 249-B5
Rt#-27 S GRAND AV
PULLMAN WA 249-B5
Rt#-27 HIGHWAY
FAIRFIELD WA 114-C2
GARFIELD WA 114-C3
LATAH WA 114-C3
OAKESDALE WA 114-C3
PALOUSE WA 249-B1
PULLMAN WA 249-B4
SPOKANE CO WA 114-C2
SPOKANE CO WA 247-A5
SPOKANE CO WA 351-A14
TEKOA WA 114-C3
WHITMAN CO WA 114-C3
WHITMAN CO WA 249-B1
Rt#-27 E MAIN ST
GARFIELD WA 114-C3
Rt#-27 W MAIN ST
GARFIELD WA 114-C3
Rt#-27 MARKET ST
LATAH WA 114-C3
Rt#-27 MOSCOW RD
PALOUSE WA 249-B1
Rt#-27 W PARK ST
TEKOA WA 114-C3
Rt#-27 N PINES RD
OPPORTUNITY WA 350-H7
SPOKANE CO WA 350-H5
Rt#-27 S PINES RD
OPPORTUNITY WA 350-H10
Rt#-27 POPULAR ST
TEKOA WA 114-C3
Rt#-27 RAILROAD ST
ROCKFORD WA 114-C2
SPOKANE CO WA 114-C2
Rt#-27 S RAMSEY ST
TEKOA WA 114-C3
Rt#-27 STEPTOE AV
OAKESDALE WA 114-C3
Rt#-27 TEKOA OAKSDALE RD
OAKESDALE WA 114-C3
WHITMAN CO WA 114-C3
Rt#-27 WATER ST
TEKOA WA 114-C3
WHITMAN CO WA 114-C3
Rt#-28 E 1ST AV
ODESSA WA 113-B3
Rt#-28 W 1ST AV
ODESSA WA 113-B3
Rt#-28 BASIN ST N
EPHRATA WA 112-C3
GRANT CO WA 112-C3
Rt#-28 BASIN ST NW
EPHRATA WA 112-C3
GRANT CO WA 112-C3
Rt#-28 BASIN ST S
EPHRATA WA 112-C3
GRANT CO WA 112-C3
Rt#-28 F ST SE
GRANT CO WA 112-B3
QUINCY WA 112-B3
Rt#-28 F ST SW
GRANT CO WA 112-B3
QUINCY WA 112-B3
Rt#-28 HIGHWAY
DAVENPORT WA 114-A2
DOUGLAS CO WA 112-B3
DOUGLAS CO WA 239-A5
EAST WENATCHEE WA 239-A4
EAST WENATCHEE BENCH WA 239-A3
GRANT CO WA 112-C2
GRANT CO WA 113-A2
HARRINGTON WA 113-C2
LINCOLN CO WA 113-C2
LINCOLN CO WA 114-A2
ODESSA WA 113-B3
ROCK ISLAND WA 239-B5
SOAP LAKE WA 112-C2
Rt#-28 ROAD 10-NW
GRANT CO WA 112-B3
Rt#-28 ROAD 11-NW
GRANT CO WA 112-C3
Rt#-28 TWELFTH ST
DAVENPORT WA 114-A2
Rt#-30 2ND ST
NORTH POWDER OR 130-B3
Rt#-30 NE 16TH ST
FRUITLAND ID 139-A3
PAYETTE CO ID 139-A3
Rt#-30 LA GRANDE-BAKER HWY
NORTH POWDER OR 130-B3
UNION CO OR 130-B3
Rt#-31 FREMONT HWY
DESCHUTES CO OR 143-A1
KLAMATH CO OR 143-A1
LAKE CO OR 143-B2
LAKE CO OR 151-C1
LAKE CO OR 152-A1
PAISLEY OR 151-C1
Rt#-31 HIGHWAY
IONE WA 106-B1
METALINE WA 106-B1
METALINE FALLS WA 106-B1
PEND OREILLE CO WA 106-C1
Rt#-31 MAIN ST
PAISLEY OR 151-C1
Rt#-31 S SECOND AV
IONE WA 106-B1
Rt#-33 HIGHWAY
BRITISH COLUMBIA 105-A1
Rt#-34 2ND ST
LEBANON OR 133-C1
Rt#-34 ALSEA HWY
BENTON CO OR 133-A1
LINCOLN CO OR 133-A2
LINCOLN CO OR 209-D2
LINCOLN CO OR 328-F6
WALDPORT OR 328-F6
Rt#-34 CORVALLIS-LEBANON HWY
LEBANON OR 133-C1
LINN CO OR 133-C1
LINN CO OR 207-B6
TANGENT OR 207-B6
Rt#-34 CORVALLIS-NEWPORT HWY
CORVALLIS OR 327-H11
LINN CO OR 207-B6
LINN CO OR 327-H11
Rt#-34 HARRISON BLVD
CORVALLIS OR 327-G9
LINN CO OR 327-G9
Rt#-34 W HEMLOCK ST
WALDPORT OR 328-E4
Rt#-34 MORTON ST
LEBANON OR 133-C1
Rt#-34 TANGENT ST
LEBANON OR 133-C1
Rt#-34 VAN BUREN AV
CORVALLIS OR 327-F9
LINN CO OR 327-F9
Rt#-35 MOUNT HOOD HWY
CLACKAMAS CO OR 202-C5
HOOD RIVER CO OR 195-C7
HOOD RIVER CO OR 202-C1
HOOD RIVER CO OR 202-C5
Rt#-36 MAPLETON-JCT CITY HWY
LANE CO OR 132-C3
LANE CO OR 133-B2
LANE CO OR 210-A6
LANE CO OR 214-D1
Rt#-36 PRAIRIE ROAD CONN
LANE CO OR 210-A6
Rt#-37 SE 10TH ST
PENDLETON OR 129-B1
Rt#-37 SW 17TH ST
PENDLETON OR 129-B1
Rt#-37 SW COURT PL
PENDLETON OR 129-B1
Rt#-37 SW EMIGRANT AV
PENDLETON OR 129-B1
Rt#-37 SE EMIGRANT AV
PENDLETON OR 129-B1
Rt#-37 SW FRAZER AV
PENDLETON OR 129-B1
Rt#-37 SE FRAZER AV
PENDLETON OR 129-B1
Rt#-37 PENDLETON-COLD SPG HWY
PENDLETON OR 129-B1
UMATILLA CO OR 129-A1
Rt#-38 A ST
DOUGLAS CO OR 141-A1
ELKTON OR 141-A1
Rt#-38 UMPQUA AV
REEDSPORT OR 218-C1
Rt#-38 UMPQUA HWY
DOUGLAS CO OR 140-C1
DOUGLAS CO OR 141-A1
DOUGLAS CO OR 218-D2
DOUGLAS CO OR 219-A2
DRAIN OR 219-A2
ELKTON OR 141-A1
REEDSPORT OR 218-D2
Rt#-39 4TH ST
KLAMATH FALLS OR 338-D8
Rt#-39 5TH ST
KLAMATH FALLS OR 338-E8
Rt#-39 S 5TH ST
KLAMATH FALLS OR 338-D8
Rt#-39 6TH ST
KLAMATH FALLS OR 338-D8
Rt#-39 S 6TH ST
KLAMATH FALLS OR 338-E8
Rt#-39 E FRONT ST
MERRILL OR 150-C2
Rt#-39 W FRONT ST
MERRILL OR 150-C2
Rt#-39 HATFIELD HWY
KLAMATH CO OR 151-A2
SISKIYOU CO CA 151-A3
Rt#-39 KLAMATH AV
KLAMATH FALLS OR 338-D8
Rt#-39 KLAMATH FALLS-LKVW HWY
ALTAMONT OR 338-F9
ALTAMONT OR 339-C11
KLAMATH FALLS OR 338-F9
Rt#-39 KLAMATH FALS-MALIN HWY
ALTAMONT OR 338-C4
ALTAMONT OR 339-A10
KLAMATH CO OR 150-C2
KLAMATH CO OR 151-A2
KLAMATH CO OR 235-D5
KLAMATH CO OR 338-C4
KLAMATH FALLS OR 338-C4
MERRILL OR 150-C2
Rt#-39 MAIN ST
KLAMATH FALLS OR 338-D8
Rt#-39 WILLOW AV
KLAMATH FALLS OR 338-D8
Rt#-41 5TH AV
SPIRIT LAKE ID 115-A1
Rt#-41 HIGHWAY
BONNER CO ID 106-C3
BONNER CO ID 107-A3
BONNER CO ID 115-A1
KOOTENAI CO ID 115-A1
KOOTENAI CO ID 247-D1
NEWPORT WA 106-C3
OLDTOWN ID 106-C3
RATHDRUM ID 115-A1
RATHDRUM ID 247-D1
SPIRIT LAKE ID 115-A1
Rt#-41 ROSS PT-RATHDRUM HWY
KOOTENAI CO ID 247-D1
KOOTENAI CO ID 354-D2
POST FALLS ID 354-D2
Rt#-41 N STATE AV
OLDTOWN ID 106-C3
Rt#-41 S STATE AV
OLDTOWN ID 106-C3
NEWPORT WA 106-C3
Rt#-42 3RD ST
COQUILLE OR 220-D5
Rt#-42 8TH ST
MYRTLE POINT OR 140-B2
Rt#-42 N ADAMS ST
COQUILLE OR 220-D5
Rt#-42 N CENTRAL BLVD
COQUILLE OR 220-D4
Rt#-42 W CENTRAL BLVD
COQUILLE OR 220-D4
Rt#-42 COOS BAY-ROSEBURG HWY
COOS CO OR 140-C2
COOS CO OR 220-D4
COQUILLE OR 220-D4
DOUGLAS CO OR 140-C3
DOUGLAS CO OR 141-A2
DOUGLAS CO OR 221-A6
MYRTLE POINT OR 140-C2
WINSTON OR 221-B6
Rt#-42 W DOUGLAS BLVD
WINSTON OR 221-B6
Rt#-42 HIGHWAY
COOS CO OR 220-D2
DOUGLAS CO OR 140-C3
Rt#-42 MARYLAND AV
MYRTLE POINT OR 140-B2
Rt#-42S 2ND ST
COQUILLE OR 220-D5
Rt#-42S N BIRCH ST
COQUILLE OR 220-D5
Rt#-42S COQUILLE-BANDON HWY
BANDON OR 220-B6
COOS CO OR 220-C4
COQUILLE OR 220-D5
Rt#-43 SW MACADAM AV
MULTNOMAH OR 321-G1
PORTLAND OR 317-F6
PORTLAND OR 321-G1
Rt#-43 PACIFIC HWY
LAKE OSWEGO OR 199-C4
LAKE OSWEGO OR 321-G7
WEST LINN OR 199-C4
Rt#-43 SW RIVERSIDE DR
CLACKAMAS OR 321-G5
LAKE OSWEGO OR 321-G5
MULTNOMAH OR 321-G5
Rt#-43 N STATE ST
CLACKAMAS OR 321-G6
LAKE OSWEGO OR 321-G6
Rt#-43 S STATE ST
LAKE OSWEGO OR 321-F7
Rt#-44 GLENWOOD ST
ADA CO ID 253-C2
BOISE CITY ID 253-C2
GARDEN CITY ID 253-C2
Rt#-44 HIGHWAY
CANYON CO ID 147-B1
Rt#-44 MAIN ST
CANYON CO ID 147-B1
Rt#-44 W MAIN ST
CANYON CO ID 147-B1
MIDDLETON ID 147-B1
Rt#-44 STAR BLVD
CANYON CO ID 147-B1
MIDDLETON ID 147-B1
Rt#-44 W STATE ST
ADA CO ID 147-C1
ADA CO ID 253-A1
BOISE ID 253-A1
EAGLE ID 253-A1
Rt#-45 12TH AV S
NAMPA ID 147-B1
Rt#-45 12TH AVENUE RD
CANYON CO ID 147-B1
NAMPA ID 147-B1
Rt#-45 12TH AVENUE RD
OWYHEE CO ID 147-B1
Rt#-46 OREGON CAVES HWY
CAVE JUNCTION OR 233-B4
JOSEPHINE CO OR 233-B4
Rt#-47 E BRIDGE ST
VERNONIA OR 125-B1
Rt#-47 COLLEGE WY
FOREST GROVE OR 198-B1
Rt#-47 COUNCIL ST
FOREST GROVE OR 198-B1
Rt#-47 FRONT ST
GASTON OR 198-B3
GASTON OR 198-B3
Rt#-47 HIGHWAY 47 NW
FOREST GROVE OR 198-B1
WASHINGTON CO OR 125-B1
WASHINGTON CO OR 198-B1
Rt#-47 NW HIGHWAY 47
WASHINGTON CO OR 125-B1
Rt#-47 SW HIGHWAY 47
FOREST GROVE OR 198-C1
Rt#-47 N MAIN ST
BANKS OR 125-B1
Rt#-47 S MAIN ST
BANKS OR 125-B1
WASHINGTON CO OR 125-B1
Rt#-47 W MAIN ST
CARLTON OR 198-B6
Rt#-47 MAPLE ST
YAMHILL OR 198-B5
Rt#-47 MIST DR
COLUMBIA CO OR 125-B1
VERNONIA OR 125-B1
Rt#-47 MIST-CLATSKANIE HWY
CLATSKANIE OR 117-B3
COLUMBIA CO OR 117-B3
Rt#-47 NEHALEM HWY
COLUMBIA CO OR 117-B3
COLUMBIA CO OR 125-B1
WASHINGTON CO OR 125-B1
Rt#-47 SW OLD HWY 47
FOREST GROVE OR 198-B1
WASHINGTON CO OR 198-B1
Rt#-47 ROSE AV
COLUMBIA CO OR 125-B1
VERNONIA OR 125-B1
Rt#-47 SUNSET DR
FOREST GROVE OR 198-B1
WASHINGTON CO OR 198-B1
Rt#-47 TUALATIN VALLEY HWY
CARLTON OR 198-B6
FOREST GROVE OR 198-B4
GASTON OR 198-B4
WASHINGTON CO OR 198-B4
YAMHILL OR 198-B4
YAMHILL CO OR 198-B4
Rt#-47 UNIVERSITY AV
FOREST GROVE OR 198-B1
Rt#-47 N YAMHILL ST
CARLTON OR 198-B5
Rt#-51 INDEPENDENCE HWY
POLK CO OR 204-B6
Rt#-51 E MAIN ST
MONMOUTH OR 204-B7
Rt#-51 N MAIN ST
INDEPENDENCE OR 204-B7
POLK CO OR 204-B7
Rt#-51 S MAIN ST
INDEPENDENCE OR 204-B7
Rt#-51 MONMOUTH ST
INDEPENDENCE OR 204-B7
Rt#-51 MONMOUTH-INDPNDNC HWY
INDEPENDENCE OR 204-B7
MONMOUTH OR 204-B7
POLK CO OR 204-B7
Rt#-52 S 18TH ST
PAYETTE ID 139-A3
Rt#-52 2ND AV S
PAYETTE ID 139-A3
Rt#-52 N 6TH ST
PAYETTE ID 139-A3
Rt#-52 N 7TH ST
PAYETTE ID 139-A3
Rt#-52 S 7TH ST
PAYETTE ID 139-A3
Rt#-52 E BLACK CANYON HWY
GEM CO ID 139-C3
Rt#-52 HIGHWAY
BOISE CO ID 139-C3
GEM CO ID 139-C3
HORSESHOE BEND ID 139-C3
MALHEUR CO OR 139-A2
PAYETTE ID 139-A3
PAYETTE CO ID 139-A3
Rt#-52 N WASHINGTON AV
GEM CO ID 139-C3
Rt#-52 S WASHINGTON AV
EMMETT ID 139-C3
GEM CO ID 139-C3
Rt#-53 HIGHWAY
KOOTENAI CO ID 115-A1
KOOTENAI CO ID 245-A4
KOOTENAI CO ID 247-D1
RATHDRUM ID 115-A1
Rt#-53 NECANICUM HWY
CLATSOP CO OR 191-C3
CLATSOP CO WA 188-D7
TILLAMOOK CO OR 191-C3
TILLAMOOK CO OR 191-C3
Rt#-53 TRENT RD
KOOTENAI CO ID 247-C1
Rt#-53 W TRENT RD
KOOTENAI CO ID 247-C1
KOOTENAI CO ID 352-J3
KOOTENAI CO ID 353-A2
Rt#-54 HIGHWAY
ATHOL ID 245-B2
KOOTENAI CO ID 115-A1
KOOTENAI CO ID 245-C1
Rt#-55 CEMETERY RD
MARSING ID 147-B1
OWYHEE CO ID 147-B1
Rt#-55 S EAGLE RD
ADA CO ID 253-B2
EAGLE ID 253-B2
Rt#-55 S EAGLE RD
MERIDIAN ID 253-B2
Rt#-55 HIGHWAY
ADAMS CO ID 251-A4
CASCADE ID 252-D5
DONNELLY ID 252-D1
MCCALL ID 251-C5
NEW MEADOWS ID 251-A4
VALLEY CO ID 251-C5
VALLEY CO ID 252-D1
Rt#-55 HORSESHOE BEND RD
ADA CO ID 139-C3
ADA CO ID 253-B1
BOISE CO ID 139-C3
EAGLE ID 253-B1
HORSESHOE BEND ID 139-C3
Rt#-55 KARCHER RD
CANYON CO ID 147-B1
NAMPA ID 147-B1
Rt#-55 E LAKE ST
MCCALL ID 251-C5
Rt#-55 MAIN ST
MARSING ID 147-B1
OWYHEE CO ID 147-B1
Rt#-55 NAMPA BLVD
NAMPA ID 147-B1
Rt#-55 NORRIS AV
NEW MEADOWS ID 251-A4
Rt#-55 PAYETTE RIV SCENIC RT
BOISE CO ID 139-C3
Rt#-55 SUNNY SLOPE RD
CANYON CO ID 147-B1
Rt#-55 VIRGINIA ST
NEW MEADOWS ID 251-A4
Rt#-56 BULL LAKE RD
LINCOLN CO MA 107-C3
SANDERS CO MA 107-C3
Rt#-56 HIGHWAY
SANDERS CO MA 107-C3
Rt#-57 9TH ST
BONNER CO ID 107-A3
PRIEST RIVER ID 107-A3
Rt#-57 HIGHWAY
BONNER CO ID 106-C2
BONNER CO ID 107-A2
Rt#-58 HIGHWAY
KOOTENAI CO ID 115-A2
Rt#-58 WILLAMETTE HWY
KLAMATH CO OR 142-C2
LANE CO OR 133-C3
LANE CO OR 134-A3
LANE CO OR 142-B1
LANE CO OR 215-C3
LANE CO OR 330-J14
LANE CO OR 331-A14
OAKRIDGE OR 142-B1
Rt#-60 MOCTILEME RD
BENEWAH CO ID 115-A3
Rt#-60 NHS 11
BENEWAH CO ID 115-A3
Rt#-62 CRATER LAKE HWY
EAGLE POINT OR 230-D4
JACKSON CO OR 149-C1
JACKSON CO OR 150-A1
JACKSON CO OR 226-C7
JACKSON CO OR 227-D7
JACKSON CO OR 230-D4
JACKSON CO OR 336-F3
KLAMATH CO OR 227-D7
KLAMATH CO OR 231-C2
MEDFORD OR 336-D8
SHADY COVE OR 230-D4
WHITE CITY OR 230-D6
Rt#-62 HIGHWAY
CRAIGMONT ID 123-B2
IDAHO CO ID 123-C3
LEWIS CO ID 123-C2
NEZPERCE ID 123-C2
Rt#-62 MAIN ST
CRAIGMONT ID 123-B2
Rt#-62 NATIONAL PARK HWY
KLAMATH CO OR 227-B4
Rt#-62 SEVEN MILE RD
IDAHO CO ID 123-C3
Rt#-64 BEECH ST
LEWIS CO ID 123-C2
NEZPERCE ID 123-C2
Rt#-64 HIGHWAY
KAMIAH ID 123-C2
LEWIS CO ID 123-C2
NEZPERCE ID 123-C2
Rt#-66 GREEN SPRINGS HWY
ASHLAND OR 337-F9
JACKSON CO OR 150-A2
JACKSON CO OR 234-D4
JACKSON CO OR 337-F9
KLAMATH CO OR 150-A2
KLAMATH CO OR 235-A5
KLAMATH CO OR 338-A12
KLAMATH FALLS OR 338-A12
Rt#-66 PALOUSE COVE RD
LATAH CO ID 249-C2
Rt#-69 AVALON ST
ADA CO ID 253-A5
KUNA ID 253-A5
Rt#-69 KUNA RD
ADA CO ID 253-A5
Rt#-69 KUNA-MERIDIAN RD
ADA CO ID 253-A3
MERIDIAN ID 253-A3
Rt#-70 DAIRY-BONANZA HWY
BONANZA OR 151-A2
KLAMATH CO OR 151-A2
Rt#-71 HIGHWAY
ADAMS CO ID 131-A3
CAMBRIDGE ID 139-B1
WASHINGTON CO ID 131-A3
WASHINGTON CO ID 139-A1
Rt#-71 HOPPER AV
CAMBRIDGE ID 139-B1
WASHINGTON CO ID 139-B1
Rt#-72 HIGHWAY
PAYETTE CO ID 139-B3
Rt#-74 COURT ST
HEPPNER OR 128-C2
Rt#-74 HEPPNER HWY
GILLIAM CO OR 128-B1
HEPPNER OR 128-C2
IONE OR 128-B1

STREET
City State Page-Grid

Rt#-74 HEPPNER HWY
LEXINGTON OR 128-C2
MORROW CO OR 128-B1
MORROW CO OR 129-A2
UMATILLA CO OR 129-A2
Rt#-74 W LINDEN WY
HEPPNER OR 128-C2
Rt#-74 MAIN ST
HEPPNER OR 128-C2
LEXINGTON OR 128-C2
Rt#-74 E MAY ST
HEPPNER OR 128-C2
Rt#-78 MARSING-MURPHY RD
MARSING ID 147-B1
OWYHEE CO ID 147-B1
Rt#-78 E MONROE ST
BURNS OR 145-B1
HARNEY CO OR 145-B1
Rt#-78 MURPHY-GRANDVIEW RD
OWYHEE CO ID 147-C2
Rt#-78 STEENS HWY
HARNEY CO OR 145-B1
HARNEY CO OR 146-A2
MALHEUR CO OR 146-B3
Rt#-82 1ST ST
ISLAND CITY OR 130-A2
Rt#-82 E 1ST ST
WALLOWA OR 130-C1
Rt#-82 W 1ST ST
WALLOWA OR 130-B1
Rt#-82 N 8TH AV
ELGIN OR 130-A1
Rt#-82 S 8TH AV
ELGIN OR 130-A1
UNION CO OR 130-A1
Rt#-82 E 8TH ST
JOSEPH OR 130-C2
WALLOWA CO OR 130-C2
Rt#-82 ALBANY ST
ELGIN OR 130-A1
Rt#-82 B ST
ISLAND CITY OR 130-A2
Rt#-82 JOSEPH-WALLOWA LK HWY
WALLOWA CO OR 130-C2
Rt#-82 N MADISON ST
WALLOWA OR 130-B1
Rt#-82 N MAIN ST
JOSEPH OR 130-C2
WALLOWA CO OR 130-C2
Rt#-82 S MAIN ST
JOSEPH OR 130-C2
Rt#-82 W NORTH ST
ENTERPRISE OR 130-C2
Rt#-82 N RIVER ST
ENTERPRISE OR 130-C2
Rt#-82 S RIVER ST
ENTERPRISE OR 130-C2
Rt#-82 RUCKMAN AV
IMBLER OR 130-A2
Rt#-82 STATE ST
LOSTINE OR 130-C2
Rt#-82 WALLOWA LAKE HWY
ELGIN OR 130-B1
ENTERPRISE OR 130-C2
IMBLER OR 130-A2
ISLAND CITY OR 130-A2
LA GRANDE OR 130-A2
LOSTINE OR 130-C2
UNION CO OR 130-B1
WALLOWA OR 130-B1
WALLOWA CO OR 130-B1
Rt#-82 WATER ST
LOSTINE OR 130-C2
Rt#-86 BAKER-COPPERFIELD HWY
BAKER CO OR 130-B3
BAKER CO OR 131-A3
BAKER CO OR 138-C1
BAKER CO OR 139-A1
RICHLAND OR 139-A1
Rt#-86 MAIN ST
RICHLAND OR 139-A1
Rt#-91 ANNACIS HWY
CITY OF RICHMOND BC 156-D6
DISTRICT OF DELTA BC 156-D6
NEW WESTMINSTER BC 156-D6
Rt#-91 FRWY
CITY OF RICHMOND BC 156-B6
Rt#-91 RICHMOND FRWY
CITY OF RICHMOND BC 156-C6
Rt#-91A ANNACIS HWY
CITY OF RICHMOND BC 156-D6
Rt#-91A HIGHWAY
NEW WESTMINSTER BC 156-D6
Rt#-91A QUEENSBOROUGH BRDG
CITY OF RICHMOND BC 156-D6
NEW WESTMINSTER BC 156-D6
Rt#-92 131ST AV NE
SNOHOMISH CO WA 110-C1
Rt#-92 GRANITE FALLS HWY
GRANITE FALLS WA 102-C3
SNOHOMISH CO WA 102-C3
SNOHOMISH CO WA 110-C1
Rt#-92 HIGHWAY
LAKE STEVENS WA 171-D1
SNOHOMISH CO WA 110-C1
SNOHOMISH CO WA 171-D1
Rt#-92 E STANLEY ST
GRANITE FALLS WA 102-C3
Rt#-92 W STANLEY ST
GRANITE FALLS WA 102-C3
Rt#-95 HIGHWAY
BRITISH COLUMBIA 107-B1
Rt#-96 128TH ST SE
SNOHOMISH CO WA 171-C4
Rt#-96 132ND ST SE
MILL CREEK WA 171-C4
SNOHOMISH CO WA 171-C4
Rt#-96 HIGHWAY
SISKIYOU CO CA 150-A3
Rt#-96 LAKE OF THE WOODS HWY
SISKIYOU CO CA 149-A3
Rt#-96 E LOWELL-LARIMER RD
SNOHOMISH CO WA 171-D4
Rt#-96 SEATTLE HILL RD
SNOHOMISH CO WA 171-D4
Rt#-97 E COEUR D'ALENE AV
HARRISON ID 248-A4
KOOTENAI CO ID 248-A4
Rt#-97 HARRISON RD
KOOTENAI CO ID 248-B5
Rt#-97 HIGHWAY
BRITISH COLUMBIA 104-C1
HARRISON ID 248-A4
KOOTENAI CO ID 248-A1
OSOYOOS BC 104-C1
Rt#-97 LAKE AV
HARRISON ID 248-A4
Rt#-97C HIGHWAY
BRITISH COLUMBIA 95-C1
Rt#-99 N 1ST AV
DRAIN OR 219-A3
Rt#-99 N 1ST ST
OAKLAND OR 219-A7
Rt#-99 2ND AV
GOLD HILL OR 230-A6
Rt#-99 SW 5TH ST
CANYONVILLE OR 225-C3
Rt#-99 E 6TH AV
EUGENE OR 330-A6
Rt#-99 W 6TH AV
EUGENE OR 329-G6
EUGENE OR 330-A6
Rt#-99 E 7TH AV
EUGENE OR 330-A6
Rt#-99 W 7TH AV
EUGENE OR 329-G6
EUGENE OR 330-A6
Rt#-99 54TH AV E
FIFE WA 182-A2
Rt#-99 70TH AV
VANCOUVER BC 156-B5
Rt#-99 ALASKAN FRWY
SEATTLE WA 277-J5
SEATTLE WA 278-A6
SEATTLE WA 281-J3
SEATTLE WA 282-A1
Rt#-99 AURORA AV N
EDMONDS WA 171-A7
SEATTLE WA 171-A7
SEATTLE WA 273-J2
SEATTLE WA 277-J4
SHORELINE WA 171-A7
Rt#-99 W B AV
DRAIN OR 219-A3
Rt#-99 BEAR CREST DR
JACKSON CO OR 234-B2
PHOENIX OR 234-B2
Rt#-99 BROADWAY
EVERETT WA 268-D5
Rt#-99 E BROADWAY
EUGENE OR 330-B6
Rt#-99 S BROADWAY
EVERETT WA 268-D5
Rt#-99 CALAPOOYA ST
DOUGLAS CO OR 221-C1
SUTHERLIN OR 221-C1
Rt#-99 N CEDAR ST
DRAIN OR 219-A3
Rt#-99 S CEDAR ST
DRAIN OR 219-A3
Rt#-99 COBURG RD
EUGENE OR 330-A6
Rt#-99 COOS BAY-ROSEBURG HWY
DOUGLAS CO OR 221-B6
DOUGLAS CO OR 334-D14
WINSTON OR 221-B6
Rt#-99 DILLARD HWY
DOUGLAS CO OR 221-B6
Rt#-99 N DOUGLAS BLVD
WINSTON OR 221-B6
Rt#-99 DRAIN-YONCALLA HWY
DOUGLAS CO OR 219-A3
DRAIN OR 219-A3
YONCALLA OR 219-A3
Rt#-99 EAGLE VALLEY RD
DOUGLAS CO OR 219-A3
Rt#-99 E ELKTON-SUTHERLIN HWY
SUTHERLIN OR 221-C1
Rt#-99 SE EVERETT MALL WY
EVERETT WA 268-C6
Rt#-99 SW EVERETT MALL WY
EVERETT WA 268-A7
Rt#-99 FRANKLIN BLVD
EUGENE OR 330-C7
LANE CO OR 330-C7
Rt#-99 FRONT ST
YONCALLA OR 219-B4
Rt#-99 N FRONT ST
CENTRAL POINT OR 230-C7
Rt#-99 S FRONT ST
CENTRAL POINT OR 230-C7
OAKLAND OR 219-A7
Rt#-99 FRWY
BRITISH COLUMBIA 158-B3
CITY OF RICHMOND BC 156-B6
DISTRICT OF DELTA BC 156-C7
DISTRICT OF SURREY BC 158-A1
KING WA 286-B4
SEATTLE WA 281-J7
SEATTLE WA 285-J1
SEATTLE WA 286-B4
TUKWILA WA 286-B4
WHATCOM CO WA 158-B3
Rt#-99 GEORGE MASSEY TUN
CITY OF RICHMOND BC 156-B7
DISTRICT OF DELTA BC 156-C7
Rt#-99 GEORGIA ST
VANCOUVER BC 254-F9
Rt#-99 GOLD HILL SPUR
GOLD HILL OR 230-B6
JACKSON CO OR 230-B6
Rt#-99 GOSHEN-DIVIDE HWY
COTTAGE GROVE OR 215-B6
CRESWELL OR 215-C4
LANE CO OR 215-C4
LANE CO OR 219-C1
LANE CO OR 330-J14
Rt#-99 N GOSHEN-DIVIDE HWY
COTTAGE GROVE OR 215-B7
Rt#-99 N GOSHEN-DIVIDE ST
COTTAGE GROVE OR 215-B7
Rt#-99 S GOSHEN-DIVIDE ST
CRESWELL OR 215-C5
Rt#-99 GRANVILLE BRDG
VANCOUVER BC 254-E12
Rt#-99 GRANVILLE ST
VANCOUVER BC 156-B5
VANCOUVER BC 254-E14
Rt#-99 HIGHWAY
CITY OF RICHMOND BC 156-B5
KENDRICK ID 123-B1
LATAH CO ID 123-A1
SEATTLE WA 286-A2
TROY ID 123-A1
Rt#-99 HOWE ST
VANCOUVER BC 254-F10
Rt#-99 INTERNATIONAL BLVD
DES MOINES WA 290-C5
SEATAC WA 288-D7
SEATAC WA 290-C5
TUKWILA WA 288-D7
Rt#-99 IVY ST
JUNCTION CITY OR 210-A5
Rt#-99 LAKE OF THE WOODS HWY
CENTRAL POINT OR 230-C7
JACKSON CO OR 230-C7
Rt#-99 LIONS GATE BRDG
DIST OF WEST VANCOUVER BC 254-E6
VANCOUVER BC 254-E6
Rt#-99 LIONS GATE BRIDGE RD
DIST OF WEST VANCOUVER BC 254-D7
VANCOUVER BC 254-D7
Rt#-99 LITHIA WY
ASHLAND OR 337-C7
Rt#-99 MAIN ST
CANYONVILLE OR 225-C3
DOUGLAS CO OR 225-C3
PHOENIX OR 234-B2
Rt#-99 N MAIN ST
ASHLAND OR 337-C6
CANYONVILLE OR 225-C3
JACKSON CO OR 337-C6
PHOENIX OR 234-B2
Rt#-99 S MAIN ST
CANYONVILLE OR 225-C3
WINSTON OR 221-B6
Rt#-99 W MAIN ST
CANYONVILLE OR 225-C3
Rt#-99 E MARGINAL WY S
SEATTLE WA 281-J5
Rt#-99 MARINE DR
DIST OF WEST VANCOUVER BC 254-E4
Rt#-99 MCVAY HWY
LANE CO OR 330-G8
Rt#-99 OAK ST
CITY OF RICHMOND BC 156-B5
VANCOUVER BC 156-B5
Rt#-99 OAKLAND-SHADY HWY
DOUGLAS CO OR 219-A7
DOUGLAS CO OR 221-C1
DOUGLAS CO OR 334-F2
OAKLAND OR 219-A7
ROSEBURG OR 334-F2
SUTHERLIN OR 221-C1
Rt#-99 OLD HWY
DOUGLAS CO OR 221-B7
WINSTON OR 221-B7
Rt#-99 OLD PACIFIC HWY
DOUGLAS CO OR 225-C2
MYRTLE CREEK OR 225-C2
TRI-CITY OR 225-C2
Rt#-99 OLD STAGE RD
JACKSON CO OR 230-B6
Rt#-99 PACIFIC HWY
EDMONDS WA 171-B5
EVERETT WA 171-B5
EVERETT WA 267-J7
EVERETT WA 268-A7
FEDERAL WAY WA 182-A2
LYNNWOOD WA 171-B5
SNOHOMISH CO WA 171-B5
Rt#-99 PACIFIC HWY E
FEDERAL WAY WA 182-A2
FIFE WA 182-A2
MILTON WA 182-A2
PIERCE CO WA 182-A2
Rt#-99 PACIFIC HWY S
DES MOINES WA 175-B7
DES MOINES WA 290-C6
FEDERAL WAY WA 175-B7
FEDERAL WAY WA 182-B1
KENT WA 175-B7
KENT WA 290-C6
KING WA 286-D6
KING CO WA 175-B7
SEATAC WA 288-D1
TUKWILA WA 286-D6
TUKWILA WA 288-D1
Rt#-99 PACIFIC HWY W
EUGENE OR 215-A1
EUGENE OR 329-D2
JUNCTION CITY OR 210-A7
LANE CO OR 210-A7
LANE CO OR 215-A1
Rt#-99 SE PINE ST
ROSEBURG OR 334-F8
Rt#-99 PUYALLUP AV
TACOMA WA 293-J7
Rt#-99 S PUYALLUP AV
TACOMA WA 293-H7
Rt#-99 N RIVERSIDE AV
MEDFORD OR 336-C10
Rt#-99 S RIVERSIDE AV
MEDFORD OR 336-D13
Rt#-99 ROGUE RIVER HWY
GRANTS PASS OR 335-F11
JACKSON CO OR 229-C6
JACKSON CO OR 230-A6
JOSEPHINE CO OR 229-C6
JOSEPHINE CO OR 335-J11
ROGUE RIVER OR 229-C6
Rt#-99 ROGUE VALLEY HWY
ASHLAND OR 337-A4
CENTRAL POINT OR 230-C7
JACKSON CO OR 230-C7
JACKSON CO OR 234-B2
JACKSON CO OR 336-A7
JACKSON CO OR 337-A4
MEDFORD OR 230-C7
MEDFORD OR 234-B2
MEDFORD OR 336-A7
PHOENIX OR 234-B2
TALENT OR 234-B2
Rt#-99 SAMS VALLEY HWY
GOLD HILL OR 230-A6
JACKSON CO OR 230-A6
Rt#-99 SEYMOUR ST
VANCOUVER BC 254-F11
Rt#-99 SISKIYOU BLVD
ASHLAND OR 337-D8
JACKSON CO OR 337-H10
Rt#-99 STANTON PARK RD
DOUGLAS CO OR 225-C3
Rt#-99 NE STATE ST
DOUGLAS CO OR 221-C1
SUTHERLIN OR 221-C1
Rt#-99 NE STEPHENS ST
ROSEBURG OR 334-F5
Rt#-99 SE STEPHENS ST
ROSEBURG OR 334-G7
Rt#-99 TAYLOR WY
DIST OF WEST VANCOUVER BC 254-E4
Rt#-99 UMPQUA HWY
DOUGLAS CO OR 219-A2
DRAIN OR 219-A2
Rt#-99A 10TH AV
DISTRICT OF BURNABY BC 156-D5
NEW WESTMINSTER BC 156-D5
Rt#-99A HIGHWAY
DISTRICT OF SURREY BC 156-D5
NEW WESTMINSTER BC 156-D5
Rt#-99A KING GEORGE HWY
DISTRICT OF SURREY BC 156-D5
DISTRICT OF SURREY BC 157-A7
DISTRICT OF SURREY BC 158-A1
Rt#-99A KINGSWAY
DISTRICT OF BURNABY BC 156-C5
NEW WESTMINSTER BC 156-C5
Rt#-99A MCBRIDE BLVD
NEW WESTMINSTER BC 156-D5
Rt#-99A PATTULLO BRDG
DISTRICT OF SURREY BC 156-D5
Rt#-99E SE 1ST AV
CANBY OR 199-C6
Rt#-99E SW 1ST AV
CANBY OR 199-C6
Rt#-99E COMMERCIAL ST NE
SALEM OR 322-J10
Rt#-99E FRONT ST NE
SALEM OR 322-H12
Rt#-99E NE GRAND AV
PORTLAND OR 313-G4
Rt#-99E SE GRAND AV
PORTLAND OR 313-G7
PORTLAND OR 317-G2
Rt#-99E HIGHWAY
MILWAUKIE OR 321-J2
SALEM OR 322-H12
Rt#-99E LIBERTY ST NE
SALEM OR 322-J10
Rt#-99E NE MARTIN L KING BLVD
PORTLAND OR 309-G3
PORTLAND OR 313-G4
Rt#-99E SE MARTIN L KING BLVD
PORTLAND OR 313-G7
PORTLAND OR 317-G1
Rt#-99E MCLOUGHLIN BLVD
CLACKAMAS CO OR 199-D5
OREGON CITY OR 199-D5
Rt#-99E SE MCLOUGHLIN BLVD
CLACKAMAS OR 321-J2
CLACKAMAS CO OR 199-D3
GLADSTONE OR 199-D3
MILWAUKIE OR 317-J5
MILWAUKIE OR 321-J2
OREGON CITY OR 199-D3
PORTLAND OR 317-J5
Rt#-99E PACIFIC HWY
MARION CO OR 205-B2
WOODBURN OR 205-B1
Rt#-99E PACIFIC HWY E
AURORA OR 199-B7
BARLOW OR 199-C6
CANBY OR 199-C6
CLACKAMAS CO OR 199-D4
GERVAIS OR 205-B1
GLADSTONE OR 199-D4
HAYESVILLE OR 323-E5
HUBBARD OR 205-B1
MARION CO OR 199-B7
MARION CO OR 205-A3
MARION CO OR 323-E5
OREGON CITY OR 199-D4
SALEM OR 323-E5
WOODBURN OR 205-B1
Rt#-99E SALEM EXWY
KEIZER OR 323-B6
SALEM OR 323-B6
Rt#-99E SALEM PKWY
KEIZER OR 323-A8
MARION CO OR 323-A8
SALEM OR 322-J8
SALEM OR 323-A8
Rt#-99W N 1ST ST
NEWBERG OR 198-D5
Rt#-99W 3RD ST
LAFAYETTE OR 198-B7
YAMHILL CO OR 198-B7
Rt#-99W 3RD ST W
CORVALLIS OR 207-A7
CORVALLIS OR 327-G14
Rt#-99W 4TH ST W
CORVALLIS OR 327-H9
Rt#-99W 5TH AV
MONROE OR 133-B2
Rt#-99W N ADAMS ST
MCMINNVILLE OR 198-A7
Rt#-99W S ADAMS ST
MCMINNVILLE OR 198-A7
Rt#-99W N BAKER ST
MCMINNVILLE OR 198-A7
Rt#-99W S BAKER ST
MCMINNVILLE OR 198-A7
Rt#-99W E HANCOCK ST
NEWBERG OR 198-D5
Rt#-99W W HANCOCK ST
NEWBERG OR 198-D5
Rt#-99W HIGHWAY
AMITY OR 204-B2
YAMHILL CO OR 204-B1
Rt#-99W HIGHWAY 99W
DUNDEE OR 198-C6
MCMINNVILLE OR 198-B7
YAMHILL CO OR 198-C6
Rt#-99W N HIGHWAY 99W
MCMINNVILLE OR 198-B7
Rt#-99W S HIGHWAY 99W
MCMINNVILLE OR 198-A7
MCMINNVILLE OR 204-B1
YAMHILL CO OR 198-A7
YAMHILL CO OR 204-B1
Rt#-99W N PACIFIC AV
MONMOUTH OR 204-B7
POLK CO OR 204-B7
Rt#-99W S PACIFIC AV
MONMOUTH OR 204-B7
Rt#-99W PACIFIC HWY W
ADAIR VILLAGE OR 207-B3
BENTON CO OR 133-B2
BENTON CO OR 207-A7
BENTON CO OR 327-H7
CORVALLIS OR 207-A7
CORVALLIS OR 327-H7
JUNCTION CITY OR 210-A5
KING CITY OR 199-B3
LANE CO OR 133-B2
LANE CO OR 210-A5
MONMOUTH OR 204-B6
MONROE OR 133-B2
NEWBERG OR 198-D5
POLK CO OR 204-B6
POLK CO OR 207-B3
PORTLAND OR 199-B3
SHERWOOD OR 199-A4
TIGARD OR 199-B3
TUALATIN OR 199-B3
WASHINGTON CO OR 199-B3
YAMHILL CO OR 198-C6
YAMHILL CO OR 199-A4
YAMHILL CO OR 204-B6
Rt#-99W TRADE ST
AMITY OR 204-B2
Rt#-99W S TRADE ST
AMITY OR 204-B2
Rt#-101 HIGHWAY
BRITISH COLUMBIA 92-B1
BRITISH COLUMBIA 93-A1
GIBSON BC 93-B3
PACIFIC CO WA 186-C4
POWELL RIVER BC 92-C1
SECHEIT BC 93-A2
Rt#-102 DAYTON-AIRPORT RD
MASON CO WA 179-D2
MASON CO WA 180-A2
Rt#-103 BAY AV
OCEAN PARK WA 186-A2
Rt#-103 OCEAN BEACH HWY
LONG BEACH WA 186-A5
PACIFIC CO WA 186-A5
Rt#-103 PACIFIC HWY
OCEAN PARK WA 186-A2
PACIFIC CO WA 186-A3
Rt#-103 PACIFIC HWY S
LONG BEACH WA 186-A5
Rt#-103 PACIFIC HWY W
LONG BEACH WA 186-A5
Rt#-104 244TH ST SW
EDMONDS WA 171-B6
KING CO WA 171-B6
MOUNTLAKE TERRACE WA 171-B6
SHORELINE WA 171-B6
SHORELINE WA 171-B6
Rt#-104 NE BALLINGER WY
KING CO WA 171-B6
LAKE FOREST PARK WA 171-B6
Rt#-104 EDMONDS WY
EDMONDS WA 171-A6
SNOHOMISH CO WA 171-A6
WOODWAY WA 171-A6
Rt#-104 HIGHWAY
JEFFERSON CO WA 109-C1
JEFFERSON CO WA 170-A3
KINGSTON WA 170-D5
KITSAP CO WA 170-C4
Rt#-105 N BOONE ST
ABERDEEN WA 178-B7
Rt#-105 S BOONE ST
ABERDEEN WA 117-A1
ABERDEEN WA 178-B7
GRAYS HARBOR CO WA 117-A1
Rt#-105 DOCK ST
WESTPORT WA 298-G11
Rt#-105 S FORREST AV
WESTPORT WA 298-G14
Rt#-105 HIGHWAY
ABERDEEN WA 117-A1
GRAYS HARBOR CO WA 117-A1
GRAYS HARBOR CO WA 183-D1
PACIFIC CO WA 117-A1
PACIFIC CO WA 183-B3
RAYMOND WA 117-A1
WESTPORT WA 183-B2
WESTPORT WA 298-G11
Rt#-105 MONTESANO ST
WESTPORT WA 298-H11
Rt#-105 OCEAN AV
WESTPORT WA 298-F13
Rt#-105 PARK AV
RAYMOND WA 117-A1
Rt#-105 WESTPORT RD
GRAYS HARBOR CO WA 117-A1
Rt#-106 HIGHWAY
MASON CO WA 173-D5
MASON CO WA 180-A1
Rt#-107 S BANK RD
GRAYS HARBOR CO WA 117-A1
Rt#-107 HIGHWAY
GRAYS HARBOR CO WA 178-D7
MONTESANO WA 178-D7
Rt#-107 SOUTH BANK RD
GRAYS HARBOR CO WA 178-D7
Rt#-108 3RD ST
MCCLEARY WA 179-D6
Rt#-108 HIGHWAY
GRAYS HARBOR CO WA 179-D5
MASON CO WA 179-D5
MASON CO WA 180-A4
Rt#-108 SINE RD
GRAYS HARBOR CO WA 179-D6
MCCLEARY WA 179-D6
Rt#-108 SUMMIT RD
GRAYS HARBOR CO WA 179-D6
MCCLEARY WA 179-D6
Rt#-109 EMERSON AV
HOQUIAM WA 178-A7
Rt#-109 HIGHWAY
GRAYS HARBOR CO WA 172-B7
GRAYS HARBOR CO WA 177-B1
GRAYS HARBOR CO WA 178-A7
HOQUIAM WA 178-A7
TAHOLAH WA 172-B6
Rt#-110 LA PUSH RD
CLALLAM CO WA 169-C1
FORKS WA 169-C1
Rt#-110 MORA RD
CLALLAM CO WA 169-B2
Rt#-112 3RD ST
CLALLAM CO WA 100-B2
Rt#-112 HIGHWAY
CLALLAM CO WA 100-B2
CLALLAM CO WA 162-C1
CLALLAM CO WA 163-A2
CLALLAM CO WA 164-A4
CLALLAM CO WA 165-A6
Rt#-112 NEAH BAY RD
CLALLAM CO WA 100-B2
Rt#-112 PIEDMONT RD
CLALLAM CO WA 164-C5
CLALLAM CO WA 165-A6
Rt#-113 BURNT MOUNTAIN RD
CLALLAM CO WA 163-B6
Rt#-115 DAMON RD
GRAYS HARBOR CO WA 177-B6
OCEAN SHORES WA 177-B6
Rt#-115 N JETTY RD
GRAYS HARBOR CO WA 177-B6
Rt#-116 FLAGLER RD
HADLOCK-IRONDALE WA 170-B1
JEFFERSON CO WA 167-B7
JEFFERSON CO WA 170-B1
Rt#-116 NESS RD
HADLOCK-IRONDALE WA 170-A1
JEFFERSON CO WA 170-A1
Rt#-116 NESS CORNER RD
HADLOCK-IRONDALE WA 170-A1
Rt#-116 OAK BAY RD
HADLOCK-IRONDALE WA 170-A1
JEFFERSON CO WA 170-A1
Rt#-117 E 1ST ST
PORT ANGELES WA 261-F4
Rt#-117 W 1ST ST
PORT ANGELES WA 261-E4
Rt#-117 MARINE DR
PORT ANGELES WA 261-E3
Rt#-117 TUNWATER ACCESS RD
CLALLAM CO WA 261-C5
PORT ANGELES WA 261-C5
Rt#-119 HIGHWAY
MASON CO WA 109-B2
MASON CO WA 173-A6
Rt#-119 LAKE CUSHMAN RD
MASON CO WA 109-B2
MASON CO WA 173-A6
Rt#-121 93RD AV SW
THURSTON CO WA 184-C1
Rt#-121 MAYTOWN RD SW
THURSTON CO WA 184-C2
Rt#-121 TILLEY RD SW
THURSTON CO WA 184-C2
Rt#-122 HARMONY RD
LEWIS CO WA 118-A2
MOSSYROCK WA 118-A2
Rt#-122 SILVERCREEK RD
LEWIS CO WA 118-A2
Rt#-123 HIGHWAY
LEWIS CO WA 185-D5
PIERCE CO WA 119-A1
PIERCE CO WA 185-D4
Rt#-124 W 2ND ST
WAITSBURG WA 122-A2
WALLA WALLA CO WA 122-A2
Rt#-124 HIGHWAY
PRESCOTT WA 121-C2
WALLA WALLA CO WA 121-C2
WALLA WALLA CO WA 122-A2
Rt#-124 ICE HARBOR DR
WALLA WALLA CO WA 121-B3
Rt#-124 LOWER WAITSBURG RD
WALLA WALLA CO WA 122-A2
Rt#-124 MAIN ST
WAITSBURG WA 122-A2
Rt#-124 SECOND ST
PRESCOTT WA 121-C2
WALLA WALLA CO WA 121-C2
Rt#-125 8TH AV N
WALLA WALLA WA 344-J8
Rt#-125 9TH AV S
WALLA WALLA WA 344-J8
WALLA WALLA WA 345-A9
Rt#-125 13TH AV N
WALLA WALLA WA 344-J5
Rt#-125 HIGHWAY
COLLEGE PLACE WA 344-G12
WALLA WALLA WA 344-H5
WALLA WALLA WA 345-A10
WALLA WALLA CO WA 121-C2
WALLA WALLA CO WA 344-G1
Rt#-125 W PINE ST
WALLA WALLA WA 344-J7
Rt#-126 W 3RD ST
CROOK CO OR 213-D5
PRINEVILLE OR 213-D5

STREET
City State Page-Grid

Rt#-126 W 11TH AV
EUGENE OR 329-D6
Rt#-126 BELKNAP SPRINGS HWY
LANE CO OR 134-B2
LINN CO OR 134-B2
Rt#-126 EUGENE-SPRINGFIELD HW
EUGENE OR 330-E5
LANE CO OR 330-F5
LANE CO OR 331-C5
SPRINGFIELD OR 330-E5
SPRINGFIELD OR 331-C5
Rt#-126 SE EVERGREEN AV
REDMOND OR 212-D5
Rt#-126 FLORENCE EUGENE HWY
EUGENE OR 215-A2
EUGENE OR 329-A6
LANE CO OR 133-A3
LANE CO OR 215-A2
VENETA OR 133-B3
Rt#-126 FLORENCE-EUGENE HWY
FLORENCE OR 214-C2
LANE CO OR 132-C3
LANE CO OR 214-C2
Rt#-126 S GARFIELD ST
EUGENE OR 329-G6
Rt#-126 SW HIGHLAND AV
DESCHUTES CO OR 212-D5
REDMOND OR 212-D5
Rt#-126 HIGHWAY
COLUMBIA CO WA 122-B2
Rt#-126 MAIN ST
SPRINGFIELD OR 215-D2
SPRINGFIELD OR 331-H7
Rt#-126 MCKENZIE HWY
DESCHUTES CO OR 211-D5
DESCHUTES CO OR 212-A5
LANE CO OR 133-C3
LANE CO OR 134-B2
LANE CO OR 215-D2
LINN CO OR 134-B2
SPRINGFIELD OR 215-D2
Rt#-126 OCHOCO HWY
CROOK CO OR 213-A5
DESCHUTES CO OR 212-D5
DESCHUTES CO OR 213-A5
PRINEVILLE OR 213-B6
REDMOND OR 212-D5
REDMOND OR 213-A5
Rt#-126 E OLIPHANT RD
COLUMBIA CO WA 122-B2
GARFIELD CO WA 122-B2
Rt#-126 OWSLEY GRADE RD
GARFIELD CO WA 122-B2
Rt#-127 HIGHWAY
GARFIELD CO WA 122-B1
WHITMAN CO WA 122-B1
Rt#-128 6TH AV
ASOTIN CO WA 250-B5
VINELAND WA 250-B5
Rt#-128 15TH ST
ASOTIN CO WA 250-B4
CLARKSTON WA 250-B4
Rt#-128 S 15TH ST
POMEROY WA 122-B2
Rt#-128 APPLESIDE BLVD
ASOTIN CO WA 250-B5
VINELAND WA 250-B5
Rt#-128 DOWN RIVER RD
LEWISTON ID 250-B4
Rt#-128 HIGHWAY
ASOTIN CO WA 122-C2
ASOTIN CO WA 250-A5
GARFIELD CO WA 122-B2
LEWISTON ID 250-B4
POMEROY WA 122-B2
Rt#-128 OLD SPIRAL HWY
LEWISTON ID 250-B4
Rt#-128 PATAHA CREEK RD
GARFIELD CO WA 122-B2
Rt#-128 SCENIC WY
ASOTIN CO WA 250-B4
VINELAND WA 250-B4
Rt#-129 1ST ST
ASOTIN WA 250-B5
Rt#-129 5TH ST
ASOTIN CO WA 250-B4
CLARKSTON WA 250-B4
Rt#-129 6TH ST
CLARKSTON WA 250-B4
Rt#-129 DIAGONAL ST
CLARKSTON WA 250-B4
Rt#-129 HIGHWAY
ASOTIN WA 250-B5
ASOTIN CO WA 122-C3
ASOTIN CO WA 123-A3
ASOTIN CO WA 250-B5
CLARKSTON WA 250-B4
VINELAND WA 250-B5
Rt#-129 RIVERSIDE DR
ASOTIN CO WA 250-B5
VINELAND WA 250-B5
Rt#-129 WASHINGTON ST
ASOTIN WA 250-B5
Rt#-131 CISPUS RD
LEWIS CO WA 118-C2
Rt#-131 WOODS CREEK RD
LEWIS CO WA 118-C2
Rt#-138 NE DIAMOND LAKE BLVD
ROSEBURG OR 221-C4
ROSEBURG OR 334-H7
Rt#-138 E DIAMOND LAKE HWY
DOUGLAS CO OR 223-D7
KLAMATH CO OR 142-B2
KLAMATH CO OR 223-D7
Rt#-138 ELKTON-SUTHERLIN HWY
DOUGLAS CO OR 141-A1
DOUGLAS CO OR 221-B1
ELKTON OR 141-A1
SUTHERLIN OR 221-C1
Rt#-138 W ELKTON-SUTHERLN HWY
DOUGLAS CO OR 221-C1
SUTHERLIN OR 221-C1
Rt#-138 W HARVARD BLVD
ROSEBURG OR 334-E7
Rt#-138 SW HARVARD BLVD
ROSEBURG OR 334-F7
Rt#-138 NORTH UMPQUA HWY
DOUGLAS CO OR 141-C2
DOUGLAS CO OR 221-D4
DOUGLAS CO OR 222-B3
DOUGLAS CO OR 223-A4
ROSEBURG OR 221-D4
Rt#-138 SE OAK AV
ROSEBURG OR 334-F7
Rt#-138 SW OAK AV
ROSEBURG OR 334-F7
Rt#-138 SE PINE ST
ROSEBURG OR 334-G7
Rt#-138 SE STEPHENS ST
ROSEBURG OR 334-F8
Rt#-138 SW WASHINGTON AV
ROSEBURG OR 334-F7
Rt#-139 HIGHWAY
MODOC CO CA 151-A3
SISKIYOU CO CA 151-A3
Rt#-140 4TH ST N
LAKE CO OR 152-A2
LAKEVIEW OR 152-A2
Rt#-140 GREEN SPRINGS HWY
KLAMATH CO OR 338-B12
Rt#-140 S KLAMATH FALLS HWY
ALTAMONT OR 235-D5
KLAMATH CO OR 235-C5
KLAMATH CO OR 338-D12
KLAMATH FALLS OR 235-C5
KLAMATH FALLS OR 338-C12
Rt#-140 KLAMATH FALS-LKVW HWY
ALTAMONT OR 339-C11
KLAMATH CO OR 150-C2
KLAMATH CO OR 151-A1
KLAMATH CO OR 339-E12
LAKE CO OR 151-C2
LAKE CO OR 152-A2
Rt#-140 KLAMATH FALS-MALN HWY
ALTAMONT OR 339-D14
KLAMATH CO OR 235-D5
KLAMATH CO OR 339-D14
Rt#-140 LAKE OF THE WOODS HWY
JACKSON CO OR 149-C1
JACKSON CO OR 150-A1
JACKSON CO OR 230-D6
KLAMATH CO OR 150-B1
KLAMATH CO OR 231-A6
KLAMATH CO OR 235-A1
KLAMATH CO OR 338-A10
KLAMATH FALLS OR 235-A1
KLAMATH FALLS OR 338-B12
WHITE CITY OR 230-D6
Rt#-140 NEVADA STATE ROUTE
HARNEY CO OR 153-A3
HUMBOLDT CO NV 153-C3
Rt#-140 WARNER HWY
HARNEY CO OR 153-A3
LAKE CO OR 152-A2
LAKE CO OR 153-A3
Rt#-141 HIGHWAY
BINGEN WA 195-D5
KLICKITAT CO WA 119-A3
KLICKITAT CO WA 195-D1
WHITE SALMON WA 195-D4
Rt#-141 E JEWETT BLVD
WHITE SALMON WA 195-D4
Rt#-141 W JEWETT BLVD
KLICKITAT CO WA 195-D4
WHITE SALMON WA 195-D4
Rt#-141 OAK ST
BINGEN WA 195-D5
Rt#-141 SW PUCKER HUDDLE RD
KLICKITAT CO WA 195-D4
Rt#-142 E BROADWAY
GOLDENDALE WA 127-C1
KLICKITAT CO WA 127-C1
Rt#-142 W BROADWAY
GOLDENDALE WA 127-C1
KLICKITAT CO WA 127-C1
Rt#-142 HIGHWAY
KLICKITAT CO WA 127-B1
KLICKITAT CO WA 196-D2
Rt#-150 CHELAN FALLS RD
CHELAN CO WA 236-D3
Rt#-150 COLUMBIA ST
CHELAN WA 236-D3
Rt#-150 HIGHWAY
CHELAN WA 236-C3
CHELAN CO WA 236-C3
Rt#-150 NORTHSHORE RD
CHELAN CO WA 236-C2
Rt#-150 PARK RD
CHELAN WA 236-C3
Rt#-150 WAPATO WY
CHELAN CO WA 236-B2
Rt#-150 WOODIN AV
CHELAN WA 236-D3
Rt#-153 HIGHWAY
OKANOGAN CO WA 104-B3
OKANOGAN CO WA 112-B1
Rt#-155 COLUMBIA AV
COULEE DAM WA 237-C2
Rt#-155 COULEE BLVD
ELECTRIC CITY WA 237-C3
GRANT CO WA 237-C3
Rt#-155 GRAND COULEE AV
ELECTRIC CITY WA 237-C3
GRAND COULEE WA 237-C3
GRANT CO WA 237-C3
Rt#-155 GRAND COULEE HWY
GRAND COULEE WA 237-C3
Rt#-155 HIGHWAY
COULEE DAM WA 237-C2
COULEE DAM WA 237-C2
GRAND COULEE WA 237-C3
GRANT CO WA 113-A1
GRANT CO WA 237-C2
NESPELEM WA 105-A3
OKANOGAN CO WA 104-C3
Rt#-155 HIGHWAY
OKANOGAN CO WA 105-A3
OMAK WA 104-C3
Rt#-155 OMAK AV E
OKANOGAN CO WA 104-C3
OMAK WA 104-C3
Rt#-155 RIVER DR
COULEE DAM WA 237-C2
OKANOGAN CO WA 237-C2
Rt#-155 RIVER RD
ELMER CITY WA 237-C1
OKANOGAN CO WA 237-C1
Rt#-160 HIGHWAY
KITSAP CO WA 174-D4
Rt#-160 SE SEDGWICK RD
KITSAP CO WA 174-C4
PORT ORCHARD WA 174-C4
Rt#-161 31ST AV SW
PUYALLUP WA 182-B4
Rt#-161 ENCHANTED PKWY
FEDERAL WAY WA 182-B1
KING CO WA 182-B2
EDGEWOOD WA 182-B2
KING CO WA 182-B2
MILTON WA 182-B2
Rt#-161 HIGHWAY
SISKIYOU CO CA 150-C3
Rt#-161 MASHELL AV
EATONVILLE WA 118-B1
PIERCE CO WA 118-B1
Rt#-161 MERIDIAN E
EDGEWOOD WA 182-B3
MILTON WA 182-B3
PIERCE CO WA 182-B6
PUYALLUP WA 182-B3
Rt#-161 N MERIDIAN
PUYALLUP WA 182-B3
Rt#-161 S MERIDIAN
PUYALLUP WA 182-B4
Rt#-161 MERIDIAN AV E
EATONVILLE WA 118-B1
PIERCE CO WA 118-B1
PIERCE CO WA 182-B7
Rt#-161 STATE LINE RD
SISKIYOU CO CA 150-C3
SISKIYOU CO CA 151-A3
Rt#-161 WASHINGTON AV
EATONVILLE WA 118-B1
PIERCE CO WA 118-B1
Rt#-162 5TH ST
KAMIAH ID 123-C2
Rt#-162 8TH AV
NEZPERCE ID 123-C2
Rt#-162 BRIDGE ST SW
ORTING WA 182-C5
Rt#-162 CORRIN AV SW
ORTING WA 182-C5
Rt#-162 HARMON WY S
ORTING WA 182-C5
PIERCE CO WA 182-C5
Rt#-162 HILL ST
KAMIAH ID 123-C2
Rt#-162 LAWYERS CANYON RD
LEWIS CO ID 123-C3
NEZPERCE ID 123-C3
Rt#-162 OAK ST
NEZPERCE ID 123-C2
Rt#-162 PIONEER WY
ORTING WA 182-B5
PIERCE CO WA 182-B5
SOUTH PRAIRIE WA 182-B5
SUMNER WA 182-B5
Rt#-162 E PIONEER WY
SOUTH PRAIRIE WA 182-D4
Rt#-162 S PIONEER WY
PIERCE CO WA 182-C6
Rt#-162 W PIONEER WY
PIERCE CO WA 182-D5
SOUTH PRAIRIE WA 182-D5
Rt#-162 SEVEN MILE RD
KAMIAH ID 123-C2
LEWIS CO ID 123-C2
Rt#-162 VALLEY AV
PIERCE CO WA 182-B3
SUMNER WA 182-B3
Rt#-162 WASHINGTON AV N
ORTING WA 182-C5
Rt#-162 WASHINGTON AV S
ORTING WA 182-C5
Rt#-163 PEARL ST
RUSTON WA 181-C2
TACOMA WA 181-C2
Rt#-164 SE 436TH ST
KING CO WA 110-C3
KING CO WA 182-D3
Rt#-164 SE 436TH WY
ENUMCLAW WA 110-C3
KING CO WA 110-C3
Rt#-164 AUBURN WY N
AUBURN WA 182-C1
Rt#-164 AUBURN WY S
AUBURN WA 182-C1
Rt#-164 AUBURN ENUMCLAW RD
AUBURN WA 182-C2
KING CO WA 182-C2
Rt#-164 COLE ST
ENUMCLAW WA 110-C3
Rt#-164 GRIFFIN AV
ENUMCLAW WA 110-C3
KING CO WA 110-C3
Rt#-165 BURNETT-FAIRFAX
BUCKLEY WA 182-D5
CARBONADO WA 182-D5
PIERCE CO WA 182-D5
WILKESON WA 182-D5
Rt#-165 CHURCH ST
WILKESON WA 182-D5
Rt#-165 MOUNTAIN MEADOWS RD
PIERCE CO WA 118-C1
PIERCE CO WA 185-A2
Rt#-165 MOWICH SECTION
CARBONADO WA 182-D6
PIERCE CO WA 110-C3
PIERCE CO WA 118-C1
PIERCE CO WA 182-D6
Rt#-166 BAY ST
KITSAP CO WA 174-B4
Rt#-166 BAY ST
PORT ORCHARD WA 174-B4
PORT ORCHARD WA 270-H14
Rt#-166 BETHEL RD
PORT ORCHARD WA 174-B4
PORT ORCHARD WA 270-J14
Rt#-166 HIGHWAY
EAST PORT ORCHARD WA 174-C4
KITSAP CO WA 174-B4
KITSAP CO WA 270-F14
PORT ORCHARD WA 174-B4
Rt#-167 BAY ST
TACOMA WA 182-A2
Rt#-167 FRWY
AUBURN WA 182-B3
PACIFIC WA 182-B3
PIERCE CO WA 182-B3
PUYALLUP WA 182-B3
SUMNER WA 182-B3
Rt#-167 N MERIDIAN
PUYALLUP WA 182-B3
Rt#-167 RAINIER AV S
RENTON WA 175-C5
Rt#-167 RIVER RD
PIERCE CO WA 182-A3
PUYALLUP WA 182-A3
TACOMA WA 182-A3
Rt#-167 VALLEY FRWY
ALGONA WA 182-B2
AUBURN WA 175-B7
AUBURN WA 182-B2
KENT WA 175-B7
KENT WA 291-J7
KING CO WA 175-B7
PACIFIC WA 182-B2
PACIFIC WA 182-B2
RENTON WA 175-B7
Rt#-169 3RD AV
BLACK DIAMOND WA 110-C3
Rt#-169 264TH AV SE
KING CO WA 110-C3
Rt#-169 ENUMCLAW BLK DMND RD
BLACK DIAMOND WA 110-C3
KING CO WA 110-C3
Rt#-169 MAPLE VALLEY RD
KING CO WA 175-C5
RENTON WA 175-C5
Rt#-169 MAPLE VLY-BLK DMND RD
BLACK DIAMOND WA 110-C3
KING CO WA 110-C3
KING CO WA 175-D7
KING CO WA 176-A7
Rt#-169 PORTER ST
ENUMCLAW WA 110-C3
KING CO WA 110-C3
Rt#-169 RENTON MAPLE VLY RD
KING CO WA 175-D5
KING CO WA 176-A6
Rt#-169 WASHINGTON AV
ENUMCLAW WA 110-C3
Rt#-170 E 1ST ST
GRANT CO WA 121-A1
WARDEN WA 121-A1
Rt#-170 W 1ST ST
WARDEN WA 121-A1
Rt#-170 ROAD 8-SE
GRANT CO WA 121-A1
WARDEN WA 121-A1
Rt#-171 BROADWAY AV
GRANT CO WA 242-C3
MOSES LAKE WA 242-C3
Rt#-172 14 RD NE
DOUGLAS CO WA 112-C1
Rt#-172 14 RD NW
DOUGLAS CO WA 112-B1
Rt#-172 C RD NW
DOUGLAS CO WA 112-B1
Rt#-172 FIFTH AV
DOUGLAS CO WA 112-C1
MANSFIELD WA 112-C1
Rt#-173 10TH ST
BRIDGEPORT WA 112-C1
Rt#-173 17TH ST
BRIDGEPORT WA 112-C1
Rt#-173 BRIDGE ST N
BREWSTER WA 104-B3
Rt#-173 BRIDGE ST S
BREWSTER WA 104-B3
Rt#-173 COLUMBIA AV
BRIDGEPORT WA 112-C1
Rt#-173 FOSTER CREEK AV
BRIDGEPORT WA 112-C1
Rt#-173 HIGHWAY
BREWSTER WA 104-B3
BRIDGEPORT WA 112-C1
DOUGLAS CO WA 104-B3
DOUGLAS CO WA 112-C1
OKANOGAN CO WA 104-B3
Rt#-173 MAPLE ST
BRIDGEPORT WA 112-C1
DOUGLAS CO WA 112-C1
Rt#-174 BRIDGEPORT HWY
GRAND COULEE WA 237-C3
Rt#-174 CROWN POINT RD
DOUGLAS CO WA 237-C2
Rt#-174 GRAND COULEE AV E
GRAND COULEE WA 237-C3
GRANT CO WA 237-C3
Rt#-174 GRAND COULEE AV W
GRAND COULEE WA 237-C3
Rt#-174 HIGHWAY
DOUGLAS CO WA 112-C1
DOUGLAS CO WA 113-A1
DOUGLAS CO WA 237-C2
GRAND COULEE WA 237-C3
GRANT CO WA 237-C2
LINCOLN CO WA 113-B1
LINCOLN CO WA 237-C3
Rt#-181 68TH AV S
KENT WA 291-H5
Rt#-181 CANYON RD
ELLENSBURG WA 241-B6
KITTITAS CO WA 241-B6
Rt#-181 HIGHWAY
ELLENSBURG WA 241-B6
Rt#-181 WASHINGTON AV
KENT WA 175-B7
Rt#-181 WEST VALLEY HWY
KENT WA 175-B7
KENT WA 291-H3
TUKWILA WA 289-J5
TUKWILA WA 291-H3
Rt#-193 WAWAWAI RIVER RD
WHITMAN CO WA 122-C2
WHITMAN CO WA 250-A4
Rt#-194 ALMOTA RD
WHITMAN CO WA 122-B1
Rt#-194 GOOSE CREEK RD
WHITMAN CO WA 122-C1
Rt#-194 WAWAWAI-PULLMAN RD
WHITMAN CO WA 249-A5
Rt#-194 WILBUR GULCH RD
WHITMAN CO WA 122-C1
WHITMAN CO WA 249-A5
Rt#-200 HIGHWAY
BONNER CO ID 107-C3
BONNER CO ID 244-B1
CLARK FORK ID 107-C3
EAST HOPE ID 244-D2
HOPE ID 244-C2
KOOTENAI ID 244-A1
PONDERAY ID 244-A1
SANDERS CO MT 107-C3
Rt#-200 LIGHTNING CREEK RD
CLARK FORK ID 107-C3
Rt#-200 RAILROAD AV
KOOTENAI ID 244-A1
Rt#-201 SW 4TH AV
ONTARIO OR 139-A3
Rt#-201 ADRIAN BLVD
NYSSA OR 139-A3
NYSSA OR 139-A3
Rt#-201 OLDS FRRY-ONTARIO HWY
MALHEUR CO OR 139-A2
ONTARIO OR 139-A2
Rt#-201 SUCCOR CREEK HWY
ADRIAN OR 147-A1
MALHEUR CO OR 139-A3
MALHEUR CO OR 147-A1
NYSSA OR 139-A3
Rt#-202 NE 77TH ST
REDMOND WA 175-D1
Rt#-202 NE 145TH ST
KING CO WA 171-D7
WOODINVILLE WA 171-C7
Rt#-202 164TH AV NE
REDMOND WA 175-D1
Rt#-202 CLEVELAND ST
REDMOND WA 175-D1
Rt#-202 FLL CTY-CARNATN RD
KING CO WA 176-B3
KING CO WA 176-B3
Rt#-202 FALL CTY-SNQUALMIE RD
KING CO WA 176-B3
SNOQUALMIE WA 176-B3
Rt#-202 SE FRONT ST
ASTORIA WA 300-D7
CLATSOP CO WA 300-D7
Rt#-202 W MARINE DR
ASTORIA WA 300-A6
Rt#-202 NEHALEM HWY
CLATSOP CO WA 117-B3
CLATSOP CO WA 188-C3
CLATSOP CO WA 300-F8
COLUMBIA CO OR 117-B3
Rt#-202 NORTH BEND BLVD
NORTH BEND WA 176-C4
NORTH BEND WA 176-C5
Rt#-202 OLNEY AV
ASTORIA WA 300-C7
Rt#-202 RAILROAD AV SE
KING CO WA 176-C4
NORTH BEND WA 176-C4
SNOQUALMIE WA 176-C4
Rt#-202 REDMOND FALL CITY RD
KING CO WA 175-D1
KING CO WA 176-A1
REDMOND WA 175-D1
Rt#-202 SE REDMND FLL CTY RD
KING CO WA 176-A3
Rt#-202 NE REDMOND WY
REDMOND WA 175-D1
Rt#-202 WOODINVLLE REDMND RD
KING CO WA 171-D7
REDMOND WA 171-D7
REDMOND WA 171-D7
REDMOND WA 175-D1
WOODINVILLE WA 171-D7
Rt#-202 WOODNVLLE SNHOMSH RD
BOTHELL WA 171-C6
WOODINVILLE WA 171-C6
Rt#-203 E BEAKMAN ST
UNION OR 130-B2
Rt#-203 CARNATION-DUVALL RD
DUVALL WA 110-C1
KING CO WA 110-C1
KING CO WA 110-C1
KING CO WA 176-A1
Rt#-203 DUVALL-MONROE RD
KING CO WA 110-C1
SNOHOMISH CO WA 110-C1
Rt#-203 DUVALL-MONROE RD NE
KING CO WA 110-C1
Rt#-203 FLL CTY-CRNTN RD
CARNATION WA 176-B2
KING CO WA 176-B2
Rt#-203 LA GRANDE-BAKER HWY
UNION OR 130-A2
UNION CO OR 130-A2
Rt#-203 N LEWIS ST
MONROE WA 110-C1
Rt#-203 S LEWIS ST
MONROE WA 110-C1
Rt#-203 S LEWIS ST
SNOHOMISH CO WA 110-C1
Rt#-203 MAIN ST
DUVALL WA 110-C1
KING CO WA 110-C1
Rt#-203 N MAIN ST
UNION OR 130-B2
Rt#-203 MEDICAL SPRINGS HWY
BAKER CO OR 130-B3
UNION OR 130-B2
UNION CO OR 130-B2
Rt#-203 E MEDICAL SPRINGS HWY
UNION OR 130-B2
Rt#-203 TOLT AV
CARNATION WA 176-B2
KING CO WA 176-B2
Rt#-204 DIVISION ST
ELGIN OR 130-A1
UNION CO OR 130-A1
Rt#-204 HIGHWAY
SNOHOMISH CO WA 171-D2
Rt#-204 WESTON-ELGIN HWY
UMATILLA CO OR 129-C1
UMATILLA CO OR 130-A1
UNION CO OR 130-A1
Rt#-205 CATLOW VALLEY RD
HARNEY CO OR 153-B1
Rt#-205 FRENCHGLEN HWY
HARNEY CO OR 145-B1
Rt#-206 ARMSWORTHY ST
WASCO OR 127-C1
Rt#-206 BAYARD ST
CONDON OR 128-A2
Rt#-206 E BAYARD ST
CONDON OR 128-A2
Rt#-206 CELILO-WASCO HWY
SHERMAN CO OR 127-C1
Rt#-206 HIGHWAY
SPOKANE CO WA 114-C1
Rt#-206 MAIN ST
HEPPNER OR 128-C2
Rt#-206 E MOUNT SPOKANE PK DR
SPOKANE CO WA 114-C1
SPOKANE CO WA 246-D1
SPOKANE CO WA 247-A1
SPOKANE CO WA 347-H5
Rt#-206 N MOUNT SPOKANE PK DR
SPOKANE CO WA 114-C1
Rt#-206 W WALNUT ST
CONDON OR 128-A2
GILLIAM CO OR 128-A2
Rt#-206 WASCO-HEPPNER HWY
CONDON OR 128-A2
GILLIAM CO OR 128-A2
GILLIAM CO OR 128-A2
HEPPNER OR 128-C2
MORROW CO OR 128-C2
SHERMAN CO OR 127-C1
SHERMAN CO OR 128-A2
WASCO OR 127-C1
Rt#-207 SW 11TH ST
HERMISTON OR 129-A1
UMATILLA CO OR 129-A1
Rt#-207 BUTTER CREEK RD
HERMISTON OR 129-A1
UMATILLA CO OR 129-A1
Rt#-207 E ST
LEXINGTON OR 128-C2
Rt#-207 HEPPNER-SPRAY HWY
MORROW CO OR 128-C2
WHEELER CO OR 128-C2
WHEELER CO OR 136-C1
Rt#-207 W HERMISTON AV
HERMISTON OR 129-A1
Rt#-207 HERMISTON HWY
HERMISTON OR 129-A1
UMATILLA CO OR 129-A1
Rt#-207 HIGHWAY
CHELAN CO WA 111-C1
Rt#-207 LEXINGTON-ECHO HWY
LEXINGTON OR 128-C2
MORROW CO OR 128-C2
UMATILLA CO OR 128-C2
Rt#-207 SW LEXINGTON-ECHO HWY
UMATILLA CO OR 128-C1
UMATILLA CO OR 129-A1
Rt#-207 SERVCE CRK-MTCHLL HWY
MITCHELL OR 136-A1
WHEELER CO OR 136-A1
Rt#-210 SW OLD SCHOLLS FERRY
BEAVERTON OR 199-B3
WASHINGTON CO OR 199-A3
Rt#-210 SCHOLLS FERRY
BEAVERTON OR 199-B2
TIGARD OR 199-B2
Rt#-210 SW SCHOLLS FERRY RD
BEAVERTON OR 199-B2
TIGARD OR 199-B2
WASHINGTON CO OR 198-D3
WASHINGTON CO OR 199-A3
Rt#-211 EAGLE CREEK-SANDY HWY
CLACKAMAS CO OR 200-C4
SANDY OR 200-C4
Rt#-211 HIGHWAY
PEND OREILLE CO WA 106-C3
Rt#-211 E MAIN ST
MOLALLA OR 126-A3
Rt#-211 W MAIN ST
CLACKAMAS CO OR 126-A3
MOLALLA OR 126-A3
Rt#-211 WOODBURN-ESTACADA HWY
CLACKAMAS CO OR 126-A3
CLACKAMAS CO OR 200-C6
CLACKAMAS CO OR 205-D2
ESTACADA OR 200-C6
MARION CO OR 205-B1
MOLALLA OR 126-A3

PNW

INDEX

STREET City State Page-Grid

Rt#-211 WOODBURN-ESTACADA HWY
WOODBURN OR 205-B1
Rt#-211 S WOODBRN-ESTCADA HWY
CLACKAMAS CO OR 126-A3
Rt#-212 CLACKAMAS HWY
CLACKAMAS CO OR 199-D4
CLACKAMAS CO OR 200-A3
Rt#-212 CLACKAMAS-BORING RD
CLACKAMAS CO OR 200-B3
Rt#-212 MAIN ST
OREGON CITY OR 199-D4
Rt#-213 NE 82ND AV
PORTLAND OR 311-F7
PORTLAND OR 315-F2
Rt#-213 SE 82ND AV
CLACKAMAS OR 319-F6
CLACKAMAS CO OR 199-D3
MULTNOMAH OR 319-F6
PORTLAND OR 315-F7
PORTLAND OR 319-F4
Rt#-213 CASCADE HWY
CLACKAMAS CO OR 126-A3
CLACKAMAS CO OR 199-D7
CLACKAMAS CO OR 205-C4
MARION CO OR 205-C4
MOLALLA OR 126-A3
Rt#-213 SE CASCADE HWY
CLACKAMAS CO OR 199-D3
Rt#-213 CASCADE HWY S
CLACKAMAS CO OR 199-D4
CLACKAMAS CO OR 205-D2
MARION CO OR 205-D3
OREGON CITY OR 199-D4
Rt#-213 LANCASTER DR
HAYESVILLE OR 323-E11
SALEM OR 323-E11
Rt#-213 W MAIN ST
SILVERTON OR 205-C4
Rt#-213 MARKET ST NE
SALEM OR 323-D11
Rt#-213 MCCLAINE ST
MARION CO OR 205-C4
SILVERTON OR 205-C4
Rt#-213 OAK ST
MARION CO OR 205-C4
SILVERTON OR 205-C4
Rt#-213 NE SILVERTON HWY
MARION CO OR 205-B4
Rt#-213 SILVERTON RD NE
HAYESVILLE OR 323-G9
MARION CO OR 205-A5
MARION CO OR 323-J7
Rt#-214 1ST ST
SILVERTON OR 205-C4
Rt#-214 N 1ST ST
SILVERTON OR 205-C4
Rt#-214 ANDERSON RD SE
MARION CO OR 205-B7
Rt#-214 C ST
SILVERTON OR 205-C4
Rt#-214 HILLSBORO-SILVRTN HWY
MARION CO OR 205-C3
MOUNT ANGEL OR 205-C3
SILVERTON OR 205-C3
WOODBURN OR 205-C3
Rt#-214 LEWIS ST
SILVERTON OR 205-C4
Rt#-214 MAIN ST
MOUNT ANGEL OR 205-C3
Rt#-214 N MAIN ST
MOUNT ANGEL OR 205-C3
Rt#-214 MOUNT HOOD AV
MARION CO OR 205-B1
WOODBURN OR 205-B1
Rt#-214 NEWBERG HWY
WOODBURN OR 205-B1
Rt#-214 SILVER FALLS HWY
MARION CO OR 205-A7
Rt#-214 SILVER FALLS HWY NE
MARION CO OR 205-C5
MARION CO OR 205-C5
SILVERTON OR 205-C5
Rt#-214 SILVER FALLS HWY NW
MARION CO OR 205-B7
Rt#-214 SILVER FALLS HWY SE
MARION CO OR 205-B7
MARION CO OR 205-D6
Rt#-214 SILVERTON AV
MARION CO OR 205-B2
WOODBURN OR 205-B2
Rt#-214 SILVERTON HWY
WOODBURN OR 205-B2
Rt#-214 N WATER ST
SILVERTON OR 205-C4
Rt#-214 S WATER ST
SILVERTON OR 205-C4
Rt#-216 CHURCH ST
GRASS VALLEY OR 127-C2
Rt#-216 SHEARERS BRIDGE HWY
WASCO CO OR 127-A3
Rt#-216 SHERARS BRIDGE HWY
GRASS VALLEY OR 127-B2
SHERMAN CO OR 127-B2
Rt#-216 WAPINITIA HWY
WASCO CO OR 127-A3
Rt#-217 BEAVERTON-TIGARD FRWY
BEAVERTON OR 199-B2
WASHINGTON CO OR 199-B1
Rt#-217 BEAVERTON-TIGARD HWY
BEAVERTON OR 199-B2
LAKE OSWEGO OR 199-B3
LAKE OSWEGO OR 199-B3
TIGARD OR 199-B3
Rt#-218 D ST
SHANIKO OR 127-C3
Rt#-218 FOSSIL ST
ANTELOPE OR 127-C3

Rt#-218 SHANIKO-FOSSIL HWY
ANTELOPE OR 127-C3
FOSSIL OR 128-A3
SHANIKO OR 127-C3
WASCO CO OR 127-C3
WASCO CO OR 128-A3
WHEELER CO OR 128-A3
Rt#-218 WASHINGTON ST
FOSSIL OR 128-A3
Rt#-219 E 1ST ST
NEWBERG OR 198-D5
YAMHILL CO OR 198-D5
Rt#-219 W 1ST ST
NEWBERG OR 198-D5
Rt#-219 BUTTEVILLE RD NE
MARION CO OR 205-B1
Rt#-219 CHURCH AV
MARION CO OR 198-D7
SAINT PAUL OR 198-D7
Rt#-219 COLLEGE ST
NEWBERG OR 198-D5
YAMHILL CO OR 198-D5
Rt#-219 N COLLEGE ST
NEWBERG OR 198-D5
Rt#-219 FRENCH PRAIRIE RD
MARION CO OR 198-D7
Rt#-219 HILLSBORO HWY
NEWBERG OR 198-D5
WASHINGTON CO OR 198-D4
YAMHILL CO OR 198-D5
Rt#-219 SW HILLSBORO HWY
HILLSBORO OR 198-D2
WASHINGTON CO OR 198-D2
Rt#-219 HLLSBRO-SLVRTN HWY
MARION CO OR 205-A1
MARION CO OR 205-B1
Rt#-219 MAIN ST
SAINT PAUL OR 198-D7
Rt#-219 NEWBERG HWY
MARION CO OR 205-B1
WOODBURN OR 205-B1
Rt#-219 SAINT PAUL HWY
MARION CO OR 198-D7
MARION CO OR 198-D7
NEWBERG OR 198-D7
SAINT PAUL OR 198-D7
YAMHILL CO OR 198-D7
Rt#-220 FORT RD
WHITE SWAN WA 119-C2
YAKIMA CO WA 119-C2
Rt#-220 SIGNAL PEAK RD
WHITE SWAN WA 119-C2
Rt#-220 W WHITE SWAN RD
WHITE SWAN WA 119-C2
Rt#-221 3RD ST
DAYTON OR 198-C7
YAMHILL CO OR 198-C7
Rt#-221 EDGEWATER ST NW
SALEM OR 322-F13
Rt#-221 HIGHWAY
BENTON CO WA 120-C3
DAYTON OR 198-C7
PROSSER WA 120-C3
YAMHILL CO OR 198-C7
Rt#-221 SALEM-DAYTON HWY
POLK CO OR 204-D2
POLK CO OR 322-E6
YAMHILL CO OR 204-D2
Rt#-221 SALEM-DAYTON HWY NW
SALEM OR 322-E13
Rt#-221 WALLACE RD
DAYTON OR 198-C7
YAMHILL CO OR 198-C7
YAMHILL CO OR 204-D1
Rt#-221 WALLACE RD NW
POLK CO OR 322-E8
SALEM OR 322-E8
Rt#-223 ALFALFA-GRANGER RD
SATUS WA 120-A2
YAKIMA CO WA 120-A2
Rt#-223 DALLAS-RICKREALL HWY
DALLAS OR 204-A6
POLK CO OR 204-A6
Rt#-223 E ELLENDALE AV
DALLAS OR 204-A6
Rt#-223 SW FAIRVIEW AV
DALLAS OR 204-A6
Rt#-223 HIGHWAY
GRANGER WA 120-A2
SATUS WA 120-A2
YAKIMA CO WA 120-A2
Rt#-223 SE JEFFERSON ST
DALLAS OR 204-A6
Rt#-223 KINGS VALLEY HWY
BENTON CO OR 133-A1
DALLAS OR 204-A5
POLK CO OR 125-B3
POLK CO OR 133-B1
POLK CO OR 204-A5
Rt#-223 S MAIN ST
DALLAS OR 204-A6
Rt#-223 VAN BELLE RD
GRANGER WA 120-A2
YAKIMA CO WA 120-A2
Rt#-223 SE WASHINGTON ST
DALLAS OR 204-A6
Rt#-223 SW WASHINGTON ST
DALLAS OR 204-A6
Rt#-224 CLACKAMAS HWY
CLACKAMAS CO OR 126-B3
CLACKAMAS CO OR 200-B4
ESTACADA OR 200-C7
Rt#-224 HIGHWAY
BENTON CO WA 120-C2
WEST RICHLAND WA 120-C2
Rt#-224 KENNEDY RD
BENTON CO WA 120-C3
Rt#-224 MILWAUKIE EXWY
CLACKAMAS CO OR 199-D3
MILWAUKIE OR 199-D3
MILWAUKIE OR 321-J2
Rt#-224 VAN GIESEN ST
RICHLAND WA 340-B13
WEST RICHLAND WA 120-C2

Rt#-224 W VAN GIESEN ST
BENTON CO WA 340-A12
RICHLAND WA 340-A12
WEST RICHLAND WA 121-A2
WEST RICHLAND WA 340-A12
Rt#-224 WEBBER CANYON RD
BENTON CO WA 120-C3
Rt#-225 9TH ST
BENTON CITY WA 120-C3
BENTON CO WA 120-C3
Rt#-225 S DIVISION AV
BENTON CITY WA 120-C3
Rt#-225 S DIVISION ST
BENTON CITY WA 120-C3
Rt#-225 E HEDGER AV
BENTON CITY WA 120-C3
Rt#-225 HORN RD
BENTON CITY WA 120-C2
BENTON CO WA 120-C2
Rt#-225 US RESERVATION RD
BENTON CO WA 120-C2
Rt#-225 WEBBER CANYON RD
BENTON CO WA 120-C3
Rt#-226 1ST AV
SCIO OR 133-C1
Rt#-226 5TH ST
LINN CO OR 134-A1
LYONS OR 134-A1
MARION CO OR 134-A1
Rt#-226 6TH ST
LINN CO OR 134-A1
LYONS OR 134-A1
Rt#-226 ALBANY-LYONS HWY
LINN CO OR 133-C1
LINN CO OR 134-A1
SCIO OR 133-C1
Rt#-226 MAIN ST
LINN CO OR 133-C1
LYONS OR 134-A1
SCIO OR 133-C1
Rt#-227 TILLER-TRAIL HWY
CANYONVILLE OR 225-C3
DOUGLAS CO OR 141-B3
DOUGLAS CO OR 225-C3
JACKSON CO OR 141-C3
JACKSON CO OR 230-D1
Rt#-228 HALSEY-SWEET HOME HWY
BROWNSVILLE OR 210-B2
HALSEY OR 210-B2
LINN CO OR 133-C2
LINN CO OR 210-B2
SWEET HOME OR 133-C2
Rt#-229 GAITHER ST
LINCOLN CO OR 206-C2
SILETZ OR 206-C2
Rt#-229 SILETZ HWY
LINCOLN CO OR 203-A6
LINCOLN CO OR 206-C1
SILETZ OR 206-C1
TOLEDO OR 206-C4
Rt#-230 W DIAMOND LAKE HWY
DOUGLAS CO OR 223-B7
DOUGLAS CO OR 226-D3
DOUGLAS CO OR 227-A1
JACKSON CO OR 226-D3
KLAMATH CO OR 142-C3
Rt#-231 N ASPEN ST
LINCOLN CO WA 114-A2
REARDAN WA 114-A2
Rt#-231 CEDAR ST
STEVENS CO WA 106-B3
Rt#-231 FOURTH AV
STEVENS CO WA 106-B3
Rt#-231 HIGHWAY
LINCOLN CO WA 114-A1
SPRINGDALE WA 106-B3
STEVENS CO WA 106-B3
STEVENS CO WA 114-B1
Rt#-231 MAIN ST
LINCOLN CO WA 114-A2
Rt#-231 N MAIN ST
SPRINGDALE WA 106-B3
Rt#-231 OREGON ST
LINCOLN CO WA 114-A2
Rt#-231 N SECOND ST
SPRINGDALE WA 106-B3
Rt#-231 S SECOND ST
SPRINGDALE WA 106-B3
Rt#-231 W SHAFFER AV
SPRINGDALE WA 106-B3
Rt#-231 SPRING CREEK RD
LINCOLN CO WA 114-A1
Rt#-232 HIGHWAY
STEVENS CO WA 106-B3
Rt#-233 AMITY DAYTON HWY
YAMHILL CO OR 198-B7
YAMHILL CO OR 204-C1
Rt#-233 SE AMITY-DAYTON HWY
YAMHILL CO OR 204-C1
Rt#-234 4TH AV
GOLD HILL OR 230-B6
Rt#-234 4TH ST
GOLD HILL OR 230-B6
Rt#-234 SAMS VALLEY AV
GOLD HILL OR 230-B6
JACKSON CO OR 230-B6
Rt#-234 SAMS VALLEY HWY
JACKSON CO OR 230-B6
Rt#-237 1ST ST
ISLAND CITY OR 130-A2
UNION CO OR 130-A2
Rt#-237 2ND ST
NORTH POWDER OR 130-B3
Rt#-237 COVE HWY
COVE OR 130-A2
UNION OR 130-A2
UNION CO OR 130-A2
Rt#-237 E COVE HWY
UNION OR 130-B2
Rt#-237 LA GRANDE-BAKER HWY
NORTH POWDER OR 130-B3
UNION OR 130-B3
UNION CO OR 130-B3
Rt#-237 MAIN ST
COVE OR 130-B2

Rt#-237 MAIN ST
UNION CO OR 130-B2
Rt#-237 S MAIN ST
UNION OR 130-B2
Rt#-238 N 5TH ST
JACKSONVILLE OR 149-B2
Rt#-238 E 8TH ST
MEDFORD OR 336-D12
Rt#-238 W 8TH ST
MEDFORD OR 336-B12
Rt#-238 CALIFORNIA ST
JACKSONVILLE OR 149-B2
Rt#-238 E CALIFORNIA ST
JACKSONVILLE OR 149-B2
Rt#-238 W CALIFORNIA ST
JACKSONVILLE OR 149-B2
Rt#-238 S COLUMBUS AV
MEDFORD OR 336-B12
Rt#-238 JACKSONVILLE HWY
GRANTS PASS OR 335-C14
JACKSON CO OR 149-B2
JACKSON CO OR 234-A1
JACKSONVILLE OR 149-B2
JACKSONVILLE OR 234-A1
JOSEPHINE CO OR 149-A2
JOSEPHINE CO OR 229-B7
JOSEPHINE CO OR 335-C14
Rt#-238 E MAIN ST
MEDFORD OR 336-D12
Rt#-238 W MAIN ST
JACKSON CO OR 234-A1
JACKSON CO OR 336-A12
MEDFORD OR 336-C12
Rt#-238 ROSS LN
JACKSON CO OR 336-A12
Rt#-240 BY-PASS HWY
RICHLAND WA 340-E12
RICHLAND WA 341-E3
Rt#-240 FRWY
KENNEWICK WA 342-D7
KENNEWICK WA 343-A9
RICHLAND WA 341-H4
RICHLAND WA 342-A6
Rt#-240 HIGHWAY
BENTON CO WA 120-C2
RICHLAND WA 120-C2
RICHLAND WA 121-A2
RICHLAND WA 340-A7
Rt#-240 MAIN ST
YAMHILL OR 198-B5
YAMHILL CO OR 198-B5
Rt#-240 N MAIN ST
NEWBERG OR 198-D5
Rt#-240 YAMHILL NEWBERG HWY
NEWBERG OR 198-B5
YAMHILL CO OR 198-B5
Rt#-241 1ST AV
MABTON WA 120-B3
SATUS WA 120-B3
Rt#-241 ALEXANDER RD
SUNNYSIDE WA 120-B2
YAKIMA CO WA 120-B2
Rt#-241 HIGHWAY
BENTON CO WA 120-B2
SUNNYSIDE WA 120-B2
YAKIMA CO WA 120-B2
Rt#-241 MABTON-SUNNYSIDE RD
SATUS WA 120-B3
SUNNYSIDE WA 120-B3
YAKIMA CO WA 120-B3
Rt#-241 RESERVATION RD
SATUS WA 120-B3
Rt#-241 W RESERVATION RD
SATUS WA 120-B3
Rt#-241 WANETA RD
SUNNYSIDE WA 120-B2
YAKIMA CO WA 120-B2
Rt#-242 MCKENZIE HWY
DESCHUTES CO OR 211-C4
LANE CO OR 134-C2
LANE CO OR 211-A6
LINN CO OR 211-A6
SISTERS OR 211-C4
Rt#-243 HIGHWAY
GRANT CO WA 120-B1
Rt#-244 UKIAH-HILGARD HWY
UKIAH OR 129-B3
UMATILLA CO OR 129-B3
UNION CO OR 129-C3
UNION CO OR 130-A2
Rt#-245 DOOLEY MOUNTAIN HWY
BAKER CO OR 138-A1
Rt#-251 BOUNDARY HWY
NORTHPORT WA 106-B1
STEVENS CO WA 106-B1
Rt#-251 HIGHWAY
STEVENS CO WA 106-A1
Rt#-260 BLANTON RD
FRANKLIN CO WA 121-B1
Rt#-260 HAVLINA RD
FRANKLIN CO WA 121-B1
Rt#-260 HIGHWAY
ADAMS CO WA 121-C1
CONNELL WA 121-B1
FRANKLIN CO WA 121-C1
KAHLOTUS WA 121-C1
Rt#-260 MAIN ST
WASHTUCNA WA 121-C1
Rt#-261 HIGHWAY
ADAMS CO WA 113-C3
ADAMS CO WA 121-C1
COLUMBIA CO WA 122-A2
FRANKLIN CO WA 121-C1
FRANKLIN CO WA 122-A2
STARBUCK WA 122-A2
Rt#-261 MAIN ST
WASHTUCNA WA 121-C1
Rt#-261 PROVIDENCE RD
ADAMS CO WA 121-C1
Rt#-262 OSULLIVAN DAM RD
GRANT CO WA 121-A1
GRANT CO WA 242-B6
Rt#-262 ROAD A-SE
GRANT CO WA 120-C1
GRANT CO WA 242-A7

Rt#-263 HIGHWAY
SISKIYOU CO CA 150-A3
Rt#-263 LAKE OF THE WOODS HWY
SISKIYOU CO CA 149-C3
YREKA CA 149-C3
Rt#-263 N MAIN ST
YREKA CA 149-C3
Rt#-270 DAVIS WY
PULLMAN WA 249-A5
WHITMAN CO WA 249-A5
Rt#-270 HIGHWAY
MOSCOW ID 249-C5
PULLMAN WA 249-B5
WHITMAN CO WA 249-C5
Rt#-270 NE KAMIAKEN ST
PULLMAN WA 249-B5
Rt#-270 E MAIN ST
PULLMAN WA 249-B5
Rt#-270 SE OLSEN ST
PULLMAN WA 249-B5
Rt#-271 HIGHWAY
OAKESDALE WA 114-C3
WHITMAN CO WA 114-C3
Rt#-272 E CANYON ST
COLFAX WA 122-C1
WHITMAN CO WA 122-C1
Rt#-272 W CHURCH ST
PALOUSE WA 249-B1
WHITMAN CO WA 249-B1
Rt#-272 E ST
PALOUSE WA 249-C1
Rt#-272 N E ST
PALOUSE WA 249-C1
Rt#-272 HIGHWAY
COLFAX WA 122-C1
LATAH CO ID 249-C1
PALOUSE WA 249-C1
WHITMAN CO WA 122-C1
WHITMAN CO WA 249-B1
Rt#-272 E MAIN ST
PALOUSE WA 249-C1
Rt#-274 HIGHWAY
BENEWAH CO ID 115-A3
TEKOA WA 114-C3
WHITMAN CO WA 114-C3
WHITMAN CO WA 115-A3
Rt#-274 POPULAR ST
TEKOA WA 114-C3
Rt#-278 EMMA ST
ROCKFORD WA 114-C2
Rt#-278 E HOXIE RD
ROCKFORD WA 114-C2
SPOKANE CO WA 114-C2
Rt#-281 CENTRAL AV S
GRANT CO WA 112-B3
QUINCY WA 112-B3
Rt#-281 HIGHWAY
GRANT CO WA 112-B3
Rt#-281 ROAD 10-NW
GRANT CO WA 112-B3
Rt#-282 HIGHWAY
EPHRATA WA 112-C3
GRANT CO WA 112-C3
Rt#-283 HIGHWAY
GRANT CO WA 112-C3
Rt#-285 N CHELAN AV
WENATCHEE WA 238-D4
Rt#-285 S CHELAN AV
WENATCHEE WA 238-D4
WENATCHEE WA 239-A4
Rt#-285 HIGHWAY
EAST WENATCHEE WA 239-A4
SUNNYSLOPE WA 238-D3
WENATCHEE WA 238-D3
WENATCHEE WA 239-A4
WEST WENATCHEE WA 238-D3
Rt#-285 N MILLER ST
WENATCHEE WA 238-D4
Rt#-285 N MISSION ST
WENATCHEE WA 238-D4
Rt#-285 S MISSION ST
WENATCHEE WA 238-D4
WENATCHEE WA 239-A4
Rt#-285 PEACHEY ST
WENATCHEE WA 239-A4
Rt#-285 STEVENS ST
WENATCHEE WA 239-A4
Rt#-285 WENATCHEE AV
WENATCHEE WA 239-A4
Rt#-285 N WENATCHEE AV
WENATCHEE WA 238-D4
WEST WENATCHEE WA 238-D4
Rt#-285 S WENATCHEE AV
WENATCHEE WA 239-A4
Rt#-290 E TRENT AV
MILLWOOD WA 350-C5
SPOKANE WA 349-F7
SPOKANE CO WA 349-F7
SPOKANE CO WA 350-C6
Rt#-290 E TRENT RD
MILLWOOD WA 350-E5
OTIS ORCHARDS WA 351-C3
OTIS ORCHARDS WA 352-C7
SPOKANE CO WA 350-E5
SPOKANE CO WA 351-C3
SPOKANE CO WA 352-C7
TRENTWOOD WA 350-E5
TRENTWOOD WA 351-C3
Rt#-291 CORKSCREW CANYON RD
STEVENS CO WA 114-B1
STEVENS CO WA 246-A1
Rt#-291 W FRANCIS AV
SPOKANE WA 348-D1
SPOKANE WA 349-A1
TOWN AND COUNTRY WA 348-D1
TOWN AND COUNTRY WA 349-A1
Rt#-291 N NINE MILE RD
SPOKANE WA 246-A2
SPOKANE WA 346-A13
SPOKANE WA 348-C1
SPOKANE CO WA 246-A2
SPOKANE CO WA 346-A13
Rt#-292 HIGHWAY
SPRINGDALE WA 106-B3
STEVENS CO WA 106-B3
Rt#-292 NEVADA STATE ROUTE
HUMBOLDT CO NV 153-C3

Rt#-293 ANTELOPE HWY
JEFFERSON CO OR 135-C1
WASCO CO OR 127-C3
WASCO CO OR 135-C1
Rt#-293 KINGS RIVER RD
HUMBOLDT CO NV 154-A3
Rt#-293 LOWER ANTELOPE RD
ANTELOPE OR 127-C3
WASCO CO OR 127-C3
Rt#-293 SOUTH ST
ANTELOPE OR 127-C3
Rt#-300 HIGHWAY
MASON CO WA 173-D5
Rt#-300 NORTH SHORE RD
MASON CO WA 173-D6
Rt#-300 OLD BELFAIR HWY
MASON CO WA 173-D5
Rt#-302 ELGIN-CLIFTON RD
PIERCE CO WA 174-A7
Rt#-302 HIGHWAY
MASON CO WA 173-D6
Rt#-302 KEY PENINSULA HWY
PIERCE CO WA 174-A7
Rt#-302 PURDY DR
KITSAP CO WA 174-B6
PIERCE CO WA 174-B6
Rt#-302 ROCKY BAY PT
MASON CO WA 173-D7
MASON CO WA 174-A7
PIERCE CO WA 174-A7
Rt#-302 VICTOR CUT-OFF RD
MASON CO WA 173-D6
Rt#-303 NE BUCKLIN HILL RD
KITSAP CO WA 174-B1
Rt#-303 NW BUCKLIN HILL RD
KITSAP CO WA 174-B1
SILVERDALE WA 174-B1
Rt#-303 HIGHWAY
KITSAP CO WA 174-B1
KITSAP CO WA 270-J1
Rt#-303 WAAGA WY
KITSAP CO WA 174-B1
SILVERDALE WA 174-B1
Rt#-303 WARREN AV
BREMERTON WA 270-J10
Rt#-303 WHEATON WY
BREMERTON WA 270-J6
KITSAP CO WA 270-J6
Rt#-304 1ST ST
BREMERTON WA 270-J11
Rt#-304 4TH ST
BREMERTON WA 270-H11
Rt#-304 BURWELL PL
BREMERTON WA 270-G11
Rt#-304 BURWELL ST
BREMERTON WA 270-G11
Rt#-304 CALLOW AV N
BREMERTON WA 270-G10
Rt#-304 CALLOW AV S
BREMERTON WA 270-G12
Rt#-304 CAMBRIAN AV S
BREMERTON WA 270-F12
Rt#-304 FARRAGUT ST
BREMERTON WA 270-F12
Rt#-304 HIGHWAY
BREMERTON WA 270-F12
NAVY YARD CITY WA 270-F12
Rt#-304 WASHINGTON AV
BREMERTON WA 270-J11
Rt#-305 HIGHWAY
KITSAP CO WA 170-B6
KITSAP CO WA 174-C1
POULSBO WA 170-B6
SUQUAMISH WA 170-C7
WINSLOW WA 174-D1
Rt#-305 OLYMPIC WY SE
WINSLOW WA 174-D2
Rt#-307 BOND RD NE
KITSAP CO WA 170-C6
POULSBO WA 170-C6
Rt#-308 HIGHWAY
KITSAP CO WA 170-B7
Rt#-308 NW LUOTO RD
KITSAP CO WA 170-B7
Rt#-310 6TH ST
BREMERTON WA 270-G10
Rt#-310 KITSAP WY
BREMERTON WA 270-D10
Rt#-361 1ST AV
CULVER OR 208-B7
Rt#-361 CULVER HWY
CULVER OR 208-B7
JEFFERSON CO OR 208-B6
JEFFERSON CO OR 212-D1
MADRAS OR 208-B6
METOLIUS OR 208-B6
Rt#-361 SW D ST
MADRAS OR 208-C5
Rt#-361 JEFFERSON AV
JEFFERSON CO OR 208-B6
METOLIUS OR 208-B6
Rt#-372 CENTURY DRIVE HWY
BEND OR 332-A11
DESCHUTES CO OR 216-C4
DESCHUTES CO OR 217-B3
DESCHUTES CO OR 332-A11
Rt#-372 NW COLORADO AV
BEND OR 332-E8
Rt#-372 SW COLORADO AV
BEND OR 332-D9
Rt#-372 DIVISION ST
BEND OR 332-F8
Rt#-372 SE WILSON AV
BEND OR 332-F9
Rt#-380 HARDING RD
CROOK CO OR 213-D5
Rt#-380 PAULINA HWY
CROOK CO OR 135-C2
CROOK CO OR 136-A3
CROOK CO OR 213-D5
PRINEVILLE OR 213-D5
Rt#-395 HIGHWAY
BRITISH COLUMBIA 105-C1

STREET City State Page-Grid

Rt#-397 S 10TH AV
PASCO WA 343-F9
Rt#-397 E AINSWORTH AV
PASCO WA 343-G9
Rt#-397 W AINSWORTH AV
PASCO WA 343-G9
Rt#-397 BENTON-FRANKLN BRIDGE
KENNEWICK WA 343-E10
PASCO WA 343-F9
Rt#-397 CHEMICAL RD
BENTON CO WA 343-G12
FINLEY WA 121-A3
FINLEY WA 343-G12
KENNEWICK WA 343-F11
Rt#-397 N GUM ST
KENNEWICK WA 343-E10
Rt#-397 HIGHWAY
FINLEY WA 121-A3
Rt#-397 N OREGON AV
PASCO WA 343-G6
Rt#-397 S OREGON AV
FRANKLIN CO WA 343-H8
PASCO WA 343-H8
Rt#-401 HIGHWAY
PACIFIC CO WA 186-C5
Rt#-401 KNAPPTON FERRY RD
PACIFIC CO WA 186-C7
Rt#-403 EDEN VALLEY RD
WAHKIAKUM CO WA 117-A2
Rt#-403 HIGHWAY
WAHKIAKUM CO WA 117-A2
Rt#-407 ELOCHOMAN MAINLINE
WAHKIAKUM CO WA 117-B3
Rt#-407 HIGHWAY
WAHKIAKUM CO WA 117-B2
Rt#-407 SCHOONOVER RD
WAHKIAKUM CO WA 117-B2
Rt#-409 FRONT ST
CATHLAMET WA 117-B3
CLATSOP CO WA 117-B3
Rt#-409 HIGHWAY
CATHLAMET WA 117-B3
WAHKIAKUM CO WA 117-B3
Rt#-409 MAIN ST
CATHLAMET WA 117-B3
Rt#-409 PLYMPTON CREEK
CLATSOP CO WA 117-B3
Rt#-409 WESTPORT DOCK RD
CLATSOP CO WA 117-B3
Rt#-410 CHINOOK PASS HWY
KING CO WA 110-C3
PIERCE CO WA 110-C3
PIERCE CO WA 111-A3
Rt#-410 ENUMCLAW BUCKLEY RD
ENUMCLAW WA 110-C3
KING CO WA 110-C3
Rt#-410 S ENUMCLAW BUCKLEY RD
BUCKLEY WA 110-C3
BUCKLEY WA 182-D4
Rt#-410 ENUMCLAW CHNK PASS RD
KING CO WA 110-C3
Rt#-410 FRWY
PIERCE CO WA 182-C3
SUMNER WA 182-C3
Rt#-410 HIGHWAY
BONNEY LAKE WA 182-C4
BUCKLEY WA 110-C3
BUCKLEY WA 182-D4
KING CO WA 110-C3
PIERCE CO WA 110-C3
PIERCE CO WA 111-A3
PIERCE CO WA 119-A1
PIERCE CO WA 182-C3
SUMNER WA 182-C3
YAKIMA CO WA 119-B1
YAKIMA CO WA 240-A6
Rt#-410 MATHER MEMORIAL PKWY
PIERCE CO WA 119-A1
Rt#-410 NFD RD 7184
PIERCE CO WA 111-A3
Rt#-410 ROOSEVELT AV
ENUMCLAW WA 110-C3
Rt#-410 ROOSEVELT AV E
ENUMCLAW WA 110-C3
KING CO WA 110-C3
Rt#-410 SUMNER-BUCKLEY HWY
PIERCE CO WA 182-B3
SUMNER WA 182-B3
Rt#-411 1ST AV
KELSO WA 303-C9
LONGVIEW WA 303-C9
Rt#-411 1ST AV NW
KELSO WA 303-C7
Rt#-411 3RD AV
LONGVIEW WA 303-C9
Rt#-411 PEARDALE LN
LONGVIEW WA 303-C9
Rt#-411 WEST SIDE HWY
COWLITZ CO WA 187-C6
COWLITZ CO WA 189-C1
COWLITZ CO WA 303-D1
KELSO WA 303-C7
LEWIS CO WA 187-C6
LONGVIEW WA 303-C6
LONGVIEW HEIGHTS WA 303-C5
VADER WA 187-C6
Rt#-431 PACIFIC AV N
KELSO WA 303-D7
Rt#-431 PACIFIC HWY N
KELSO WA 303-E6
Rt#-432 3RD AV
LONGVIEW WA 303-B12
Rt#-432 HIGHWAY
COWLITZ CO WA 303-C12
KELSO WA 303-E13
LONGVIEW WA 303-C12
Rt#-432 INDUSTRIAL WY
COWLITZ CO WA 302-D8
LONGVIEW WA 302-D8
LONGVIEW WA 303-A12
Rt#-432 MOUNT SOLO RD
COWLITZ CO WA 302-C6
Rt#-432 OLD PACIFIC HWY
KELSO WA 303-F13
Rt#-432 TENNANT WY
COWLITZ CO WA 303-C12
LONGVIEW WA 303-B11
Rt#-432 WILLOW GROVE CONN
COWLITZ CO WA 302-A4
LONGVIEW WA 302-A4
WEST LONGVIEW WA 302-A4
Rt#-432 WILLOW GROVE RD
COWLITZ CO WA 302-A5
WEST LONGVIEW WA 302-A5
Rt#-433 OREGON WY
COLUMBIA CO OR 189-B4
COWLITZ CO WA 302-H13
LONGVIEW WA 302-J12
RAINIER OR 189-B4
RAINIER OR 302-H13
Rt#-500 NE 3RD AV
CAMAS WA 193-B7
Rt#-500 NE 3RD ST
CLARK CO WA 193-B6
Rt#-500 SE 6TH AV
CAMAS WA 193-B7
Rt#-500 NE 14TH AV
CAMAS WA 193-B7
Rt#-500 NE 44TH ST
CLARK CO WA 193-B6
Rt#-500 NE 54TH ST
CLARK CO WA 193-B6
Rt#-500 NE 58TH ST
CLARK CO WA 193-B5
Rt#-500 NE 232ND AV
CLARK CO WA 193-B5
Rt#-500 NE 237TH AV
CLARK CO WA 193-B6
Rt#-500 NE 238TH AV
CLARK CO WA 193-B6
Rt#-500 NE 242ND AV
CLARK CO WA 193-B6
Rt#-500 NE 267TH AV
CLARK CO WA 193-B6
Rt#-500 BRUNNER RD
CLARK CO WA 193-B6
Rt#-500 NE DALLAS ST
CAMAS WA 193-B7
Rt#-500 DRESSER RD
CLARK CO WA 193-B6
Rt#-500 SE EVERETT RD
CLARK CO WA 193-B6
Rt#-500 NE EVERETT ST
CAMAS WA 193-B7
CLARK CO WA 193-B7
Rt#-500 NE FOURTH PLAIN RD
CLARK CO WA 192-D5
CLARK CO WA 193-A5
VANCOUVER WA 192-D5
VANCOUVER WA 193-A5
Rt#-500 NE GARFIELD ST
CAMAS WA 193-B7
Rt#-500 HIGHWAY
CLARK WA 306-C2
CLARK WA 307-J1
CLARK CO WA 192-D5
VANCOUVER WA 192-D5
VANCOUVER WA 305-H2
VANCOUVER WA 306-E2
VANCOUVER WA 307-H1
Rt#-500 SE UNION ST
CAMAS WA 193-B7
Rt#-501 NW 269TH ST
CLARK CO WA 192-C2
RIDGEFIELD WA 192-C2
Rt#-501 E FOURTH PLAIN BLVD
VANCOUVER WA 305-G3
Rt#-501 W FOURTH PLAIN BLVD
VANCOUVER WA 304-E3
VANCOUVER WA 305-E3
Rt#-501 LOWER RIVER RD
CLARK CO WA 192-B5
CLARK WA 304-A1
VANCOUVER WA 192-B5
VANCOUVER WA 304-A1
Rt#-501 NW LOWER RIVER RD
CLARK CO WA 192-B5
VANCOUVER WA 192-B5
Rt#-501 PIONEER ST
CLARK CO WA 192-C2
KNAPP WA 192-B2
RIDGEFIELD WA 192-C2
Rt#-502 NE 10TH AV
CLARK CO WA 192-C3
Rt#-502 NE 219TH ST
CLARK CO WA 192-D3
Rt#-502 W MAIN ST
BATTLE GROUND WA 192-D3
BATTLE GROUND WA 193-A3
CLARK CO WA 192-D3
Rt#-503 GOERIG ST
WOODLAND WA 118-A3
WOODLAND WA 192-C1
Rt#-503 HIGHWAY
CLARK CO WA 118-A3
CLARK CO WA 190-A7
COWLITZ CO WA 118-A3
COWLITZ CO WA 190-A6
WOODLAND WA 192-C1
Rt#-503 LEWIS RIVER DR
COWLITZ CO WA 118-A3
COWLITZ CO WA 190-A6
WOODLAND WA 118-A3
Rt#-503 LEWIS RIVER RD
COWLITZ CO WA 190-A6
Rt#-504 HIGHWAY
COWLITZ CO WA 118-A2
SKAMANIA CO WA 118-B2
SKAMANIA CO WA 190-B1
Rt#-504 SPIRIT LAKE HWY
CASTLE ROCK WA 187-C7
COWLITZ CO WA 118-A2
COWLITZ CO WA 187-C7
Rt#-505 N 5TH ST
LEWIS CO WA 187-D4
TOLEDO WA 187-D4
Rt#-505 COWLITZ ST
LEWIS CO WA 187-D4
TOLEDO WA 187-D4
Rt#-505 HIGHWAY
COWLITZ CO WA 118-A2
LEWIS CO WA 118-A2
LEWIS CO WA 187-C3
TOLEDO WA 187-D4
WINLOCK WA 187-C3
Rt#-505 KERRON AV
WINLOCK WA 187-C3
Rt#-505 E WALNUT ST
WINLOCK WA 187-C3
Rt#-505 WINLOCK-TOLEDO RD
LEWIS CO WA 187-C3
Rt#-506 7TH ST
VADER WA 187-B5
Rt#-506 HIGHWAY
COWLITZ CO WA 187-B5
LEWIS CO WA 187-C4
VADER WA 187-C5
Rt#-507 ALDER ST
CENTRALIA WA 299-E4
Rt#-507 BINGHAMPTON ST
RAINIER WA 118-A1
THURSTON CO WA 118-A1
Rt#-507 BUCODA HWY
LEWIS CO WA 184-C5
Rt#-507 W CHERRY ST
CENTRALIA WA 299-E4
Rt#-507 D ST
TENINO WA 184-D3
Rt#-507 E DOWNING RD
CENTRALIA WA 184-C5
LEWIS CO WA 184-C5
Rt#-507 FRONT ST
BUCODA WA 184-D4
THURSTON CO WA 184-D4
Rt#-507 HIGHWAY
LEWIS CO WA 184-C5
THURSTON CO WA 118-A1
THURSTON CO WA 184-D3
Rt#-507 MCKENNA-YELM HWY
PIERCE CO WA 118-A1
THURSTON CO WA 118-A1
Rt#-507 MELLEN ST
CENTRALIA WA 299-D5
Rt#-507 N PEARL ST
CENTRALIA WA 184-C5
CENTRALIA WA 299-F1
LEWIS CO WA 184-C5
Rt#-507 S PEARL ST
CENTRALIA WA 299-F4
Rt#-507 RAINIER-YELM HWY
THURSTON CO WA 118-A1
YELM WA 118-A1
Rt#-507 E SIXTH ST
CENTRALIA WA 299-F2
Rt#-507 SIXTH ST
TENINO WA 184-D3
Rt#-507 SPANAWAY-MCKENNA HWY
PIERCE CO WA 118-A1
PIERCE CO WA 181-C7
ROY WA 181-C7
Rt#-507 SUMNER ST
BUCODA WA 184-D4
TENINO WA 184-D4
THURSTON CO WA 184-D4
Rt#-507 SUSSEX ST
TENINO WA 184-D3
THURSTON CO WA 184-D3
Rt#-507 THIRD ST
TENINO WA 184-D3
Rt#-507 N TOWER AV
CENTRALIA WA 299-F3
Rt#-507 S TOWER AV
CENTRALIA WA 299-F4
Rt#-507 YELM AV
THURSTON CO WA 118-A1
YELM WA 118-A1
Rt#-508 HIGHWAY
LEWIS CO WA 118-A2
LEWIS CO WA 187-C1
MORTON WA 118-B2
Rt#-508 MAIN AV
MORTON WA 118-B2
Rt#-508 MORTON-BEAR CANYON RD
LEWIS CO WA 118-B2
MORTON WA 118-B2
Rt#-508 NFD RD 92
LINCOLN CO MA 107-C1
Rt#-508 NFD RD 508
LINCOLN CO MA 107-C2
Rt#-509 1ST AV S
DES MOINES WA 175-A6
KING CO WA 175-A6
NORMANDY PARK WA 175-A6
Rt#-509 S 174TH ST
BURIEN WA 175-A5
KING CO WA 175-A5
Rt#-509 S 216TH PL
DES MOINES WA 175-A6
NORMANDY PARK WA 175-A6
Rt#-509 S 216TH ST
DES MOINES WA 175-A6
DES MOINES WA 290-A5
NORMANDY PARK WA 175-A6
NORMANDY PARK WA 290-A5
Rt#-509 AMBAUM BLVD
BURIEN WA 175-A5
BURIEN WA 288-A7
KING WA 288-A7
KING CO WA 175-A5
Rt#-509 SW DASH POINT RD
FEDERAL WAY WA 182-A1
PIERCE CO WA 182-A1
Rt#-509 DES MOINES MEM DR
BURIEN WA 288-A7
BURIEN WA 290-A1
KING WA 288-A7
KING WA 290-A1
SEATAC WA 290-A1
Rt#-509 FRWY
BURIEN WA 175-A5
BURIEN WA 288-A2
BURIEN WA 290-A1
KING WA 286-A5
KING WA 288-A2
SEATAC WA 288-A6
SEATAC WA 290-A1
SEATTLE WA 285-J1
SEATTLE WA 286-A5
TACOMA WA 182-A2
TACOMA WA 293-J6
Rt#-509 MARINE VIEW DR
DES MOINES WA 290-A7
PIERCE CO WA 181-D1
PIERCE CO WA 182-A1
TACOMA WA 181-D1
TACOMA WA 182-A1
Rt#-510 CLAIR CUT-OFF RD
THURSTON CO WA 181-A7
Rt#-510 HIGHWAY
THURSTON CO WA 181-A6
Rt#-510 MARVIN RD NE
LACEY WA 181-A6
Rt#-510 MARVIN RD SE
LACEY WA 181-A6
THURSTON CO WA 181-A6
Rt#-510 OLYMPIA-YELM HWY
THURSTON CO WA 118-A1
THURSTON CO WA 181-B7
YELM WA 118-A1
Rt#-510 PACIFIC AV SE
THURSTON CO WA 181-A6
Rt#-510 PACIFIC HWY SE
THURSTON CO WA 181-A6
Rt#-510 YELM AV
YELM WA 118-A1
Rt#-512 FRWY
LAKEWOOD WA 181-D4
PIERCE CO WA 181-D4
PIERCE CO WA 182-A4
PUYALLUP WA 182-A4
Rt#-513 NE 45TH ST
SEATTLE WA 274-D5
SEATTLE WA 275-E5
Rt#-513 MONTLAKE BLVD
SEATTLE WA 274-D6
SEATTLE WA 278-D1
Rt#-513 SAND POINT WY NE
SEATTLE WA 171-B7
SEATTLE WA 275-G1
Rt#-515 104TH AV SE
KENT WA 175-C7
KING CO WA 175-C7
Rt#-515 108TH AV SE
KING CO WA 175-C6
Rt#-515 BENSON RD SE
KING CO WA 175-C6
Rt#-515 S GRADY WY
RENTON WA 175-C5
Rt#-515 HIGHWAY
KING CO WA 175-C5
RENTON WA 175-C5
Rt#-515 MAIN AV S
RENTON WA 175-C5
Rt#-516 SE 256TH ST
KENT WA 175-C7
Rt#-516 CANYON DR SE
KENT WA 175-C7
Rt#-516 CENTRAL AV N
KENT WA 175-C7
Rt#-516 CENTRAL AV S
KENT WA 175-C7
Rt#-516 FRWY
KENT WA 290-D7
Rt#-516 KENT-DES MOINES RD
DES MOINES WA 290-B7
KENT WA 175-B7
KENT WA 290-B7
Rt#-516 KENT-DES MOINES RD S
KENT WA 175-B7
KENT WA 290-E7
KING CO WA 175-B7
Rt#-516 KENT KANGLEY RD
KENT WA 175-C7
KING CO WA 175-C7
KING CO WA 176-A7
Rt#-516 E SMITH ST
KENT WA 175-C7
Rt#-516 W WILLIS ST
KENT WA 175-C7
Rt#-518 FRWY
BURIEN WA 175-A5
BURIEN WA 288-B4
SEATAC WA 288-B4
TUKWILA WA 288-D5
TUKWILA WA 289-F4
Rt#-519 ALASKAN WY S
SEATTLE WA 277-J7
SEATTLE WA 278-A7
Rt#-519 S ROYAL BROUGHAM WY
SEATTLE WA 281-J1
SEATTLE WA 282-A1
Rt#-520 FRWY
BELLEVUE WA 175-D1
CLYDE HILL WA 175-D1
HUNTS POINT WA 175-D1
KING CO WA 175-D1
MEDINA WA 175-D1
MEDINA WA 279-E1
REDMOND WA 175-D1
SEATTLE WA 278-D1
SEATTLE WA 279-E1
YARROW POINT WA 175-D1
Rt#-522 BOTHELL WY NE
BOTHELL WA 171-C6
LAKE FOREST PARK WA 171-B6
Rt#-522 NE BOTHELL WY
BOTHELL WA 171-B6
KING CO WA 171-B6
LAKE FOREST PARK WA 171-B6
Rt#-522 FRWY
BOTHELL WA 171-C6
KING CO WA 171-C6
SNOHOMISH CO WA 171-C6
WOODINVILLE WA 171-C6
Rt#-522 HIGHWAY
MONROE WA 110-C1
SNOHOMISH CO WA 110-C1
SNOHOMISH CO WA 171-D5
Rt#-522 LAKE CITY WY NE
SEATTLE WA 171-B7
SEATTLE WA 274-C2
Rt#-522 WOODINVILLE DR
BOTHELL WA 171-C6
Rt#-523 N 145TH ST
SEATTLE WA 171-A7
SHORELINE WA 171-A7
Rt#-524 3RD AV N
EDMONDS WA 171-A5
Rt#-524 9TH AV N
EDMONDS WA 171-A5
Rt#-524 196TH ST SW
EDMONDS WA 171-B5
LYNNWOOD WA 171-B5
SNOHOMISH CO WA 171-B5
Rt#-524 CASPERS ST
EDMONDS WA 171-A5
Rt#-524 FILBERT RD
SNOHOMISH CO WA 171-B5
Rt#-524 MAIN ST
EDMONDS WA 171-A5
Rt#-524 MALTBY RD
SNOHOMISH CO WA 171-C5
Rt#-524 PARADISE LAKE RD
SNOHOMISH CO WA 171-D5
Rt#-524 PUGET DR
EDMONDS WA 171-A5
Rt#-524 YEW WY
SNOHOMISH CO WA 171-D5
Rt#-525 HIGHWAY
AULT FIELD WA 170-C1
ISLAND CO WA 167-C5
ISLAND CO WA 170-C1
ISLAND CO WA 171-A1
LANGLEY WA 171-A2
SNOHOMISH CO WA 171-B4
Rt#-525 MUKILTEO SPEEDWAY
MUKILTEO WA 171-B4
MUKILTEO WA 266-D3
MUKILTEO WA 267-E5
SNOHOMISH WA 267-E6
SNOHOMISH CO WA 171-B4
Rt#-526 84TH ST SW
MUKILTEO WA 266-E4
MUKILTEO WA 267-E4
Rt#-526 FRWY
EVERETT WA 267-F4
EVERETT WA 268-A4
MUKILTEO WA 267-F4
SNOHOMISH WA 267-F4
Rt#-527 19TH AV
EVERETT WA 171-C4
EVERETT WA 268-D6
Rt#-527 113TH PL SE
EVERETT WA 171-C4
Rt#-527 BOTHELL WY NE
BOTHELL WA 171-C6
Rt#-527 BOTHELL EVERETT HWY
BOTHELL WA 171-C4
EVERETT WA 171-C4
MILL CREEK WA 171-C4
SNOHOMISH CO WA 171-C4
Rt#-528 4TH ST
MARYSVILLE WA 171-C1
SNOHOMISH CO WA 171-C1
Rt#-528 64TH ST NE
MARYSVILLE WA 168-D7
MARYSVILLE WA 171-C1
SNOHOMISH CO WA 168-D7
SNOHOMISH CO WA 171-D1
Rt#-529 EVERETT AV
EVERETT WA 264-D3
EVERETT WA 265-E3
Rt#-529 HIGHWAY
MARYSVILLE WA 171-C1
SNOHOMISH CO WA 171-C1
Rt#-529 MAPLE ST
EVERETT WA 265-F4
Rt#-529 E MARINE VIEW DR
EVERETT WA 171-C1
Rt#-529 W MARINE VIEW DR
EVERETT WA 171-C1
EVERETT WA 264-D3
Rt#-529 PACIFIC AV
EVERETT WA 265-F4
Rt#-529 PACIFIC HWY
EVERETT WA 171-C1
MARYSVILLE WA 171-C1
SNOHOMISH CO WA 171-C1
Rt#-529 STATE AV
MARYSVILLE WA 171-C1
Rt#-530 DARRNGTN BNTTS STR RD
DARRINGTON WA 103-A3
SKAGIT CO WA 103-A3
SNOHOMISH CO WA 103-A3
Rt#-530 EMENS AV
DARRINGTON WA 103-A3
Rt#-530 HIGHWAY
ARLINGTON WA 168-D5
DARRINGTON WA 103-A3
SNOHOMISH CO WA 102-C3
SNOHOMISH CO WA 103-A3
SNOHOMISH CO WA 168-D4
Rt#-530 SAUK VALLEY RD
SKAGIT CO WA 103-A2
Rt#-530 SEEMANN ST
DARRINGTON WA 103-A3
Rt#-531 172ND ST NE
ARLINGTON WA 168-C6
SNOHOMISH CO WA 168-C6
Rt#-531 E LAKE GOODWIN RD
SNOHOMISH CO WA 168-B5
Rt#-531 LAKEWOOD RD
SNOHOMISH CO WA 168-B5
Rt#-532 268TH ST NW
ISLAND CO WA 167-D4
ISLAND CO WA 168-A4
SNOHOMISH CO WA 168-A4
STANWOOD WA 168-A4
Rt#-532 HIGHWAY
SNOHOMISH CO WA 168-C4
STANWOOD WA 168-B4
Rt#-534 HIGHWAY
SKAGIT CO WA 168-B2
Rt#-536 S 3RD ST
MOUNT VERNON WA 260-C12
Rt#-536 W DIVISION ST
MOUNT VERNON WA 260-B12
Rt#-536 KINCAID ST
MOUNT VERNON WA 260-C13
Rt#-536 MEMORIAL HWY
MOUNT VERNON WA 260-A11
SKAGIT CO WA 161-A7
SKAGIT CO WA 260-A11
Rt#-538 COLLEGE WY
MOUNT VERNON WA 260-D10
SKAGIT CO WA 161-C7
SKAGIT CO WA 260-H10
Rt#-539 GUIDE MERIDIAN RD
BELLINGHAM WA 158-D6
BELLINGHAM WA 258-C1
LYNDEN WA 158-D6
WHATCOM CO WA 158-D6
Rt#-539 MERIDIAN ST
BELLINGHAM WA 258-C2
Rt#-540 SLATER RD
BELLINGHAM WA 158-C6
FERNDALE WA 158-C6
WHATCOM CO WA 158-C6
Rt#-542 MOUNT BAKER
WHATCOM CO WA 103-A1
Rt#-542 MOUNT BAKER HWY
WHATCOM CO WA 102-B1
Rt#-542 E SUNSET DR
BELLINGHAM WA 258-G3
WHATCOM CO WA 102-B1
WHATCOM CO WA 258-G3
Rt#-543 HIGHWAY
BLAINE WA 158-B3
WHATCOM CO WA 158-B3
Rt#-544 COLUMBIA ST
NOOKSACK WA 102-B1
Rt#-544 EVERSON AV
EVERSON WA 102-B1
NOOKSACK WA 102-B1
Rt#-544 EVERSON GOSHEN RD
EVERSON WA 102-B1
WHATCOM CO WA 102-B1
Rt#-544 KALE ST
EVERSON WA 102-B1
Rt#-544 MAIN ST
NOOKSACK WA 102-B1
Rt#-544 E POLE RD
EVERSON WA 102-B1
WHATCOM CO WA 102-B1
WHATCOM CO WA 158-D5
Rt#-546 E BADGER RD
WHATCOM CO WA 102-B1
WHATCOM CO WA 158-D3
Rt#-547 E BADGER RD
WHATCOM CO WA 102-B1
Rt#-547 FRONT ST
SUMAS WA 102-B1
WHATCOM CO WA 102-B1
Rt#-547 GARRISON RD
WHATCOM CO WA 102-B1
Rt#-547 HALVERSTICK RD
SUMAS WA 102-B1
WHATCOM CO WA 102-B1
Rt#-547 KENDALL RD
WHATCOM CO WA 102-B1
Rt#-547 REESE HILL RD
WHATCOM CO WA 102-B1
Rt#-547 ROCK RD
WHATCOM CO WA 102-B1
Rt#-547 SUMAS RD
WHATCOM CO WA 102-B1
Rt#-548 BLAINE RD
BIRCH BAY WA 158-B4
BLAINE WA 158-B3
WHATCOM CO WA 158-B3
Rt#-548 GRANDVIEW RD
BIRCH BAY WA 158-B5
WHATCOM CO WA 158-B5
Rt#-599 FRWY
TUKWILA WA 286-D7
TUKWILA WA 287-E7
TUKWILA WA 289-E1
Rt#-702 MCKENNA TANWAX
PIERCE CO WA 118-A1
Rt#-706 MOUNTAIN HWY E
PIERCE CO WA 118-B1
PIERCE CO WA 185-A5
Rt#-730 COLUMBIA RIVER HWY
UMATILLA CO OR 121-A3
WALLA WALLA CO WA 121-A3
Rt#-730 HIGHWAY
WALLA WALLA CO WA 121-B3
Rt#-821 HIGHWAY
KITTITAS CO WA 241-B7
KITTITAS CO WA 243-B1
YAKIMA CO WA 243-C4
Rt#-821 THRALL RD
KITTITAS CO WA 241-B7
Rt#-823 S 1ST ST
SELAH WA 243-B5
YAKIMA CO WA 243-B5
Rt#-823 HARRISON RD
YAKIMA CO WA 243-B5
Rt#-823 HIGHWAY
YAKIMA CO WA 243-B6
Rt#-823 E NACHES AV
SELAH WA 243-B5
Rt#-823 SELAH RD
YAKIMA CO WA 243-B6
Rt#-823 WENAS AV
SELAH WA 243-B5
YAKIMA CO WA 243-B5
Rt#-900 S 2ND ST
RENTON WA 175-C5
Rt#-900 S 3RD ST
RENTON WA 175-C5
Rt#-900 17TH AV NW
ISSAQUAH WA 175-D3
Rt#-900 BRONSON WY N
RENTON WA 175-C5
Rt#-900 EMPIRE WY S
TUKWILA WA 287-E5
Rt#-900 HOUSER WY S
RENTON WA 175-C5

STREET City State Page-Grid

Rt#-900 MAIN AV S
RENTON WA 175-C5
Rt#-900 MLK JR WY
KING WA 287-E6
KING WA 289-G1
KING CO WA 175-C5
SEATTLE WA 287-E6
TUKWILA WA 287-E6
TUKWILA WA 289-G1
Rt#-900 MILL AV S
RENTON WA 175-C5
Rt#-900 NE PARK DR
RENTON WA 175-C4
Rt#-900 SE RENTON ISSAQUAH RD
KING CO WA 175-D4
RENTON WA 175-C4
Rt#-900 RENTON ISSAQUAH RD SE
ISSAQUAH WA 175-D4
KING CO WA 175-D4
Rt#-900 SUNSET BLVD
RENTON WA 175-C5
Rt#-900 NE SUNSET BLVD
RENTON WA 175-C4
Rt#-900 SW SUNSET BLVD
KING CO WA 175-C5
RENTON WA 175-C5
Rt#-902 W HALLETT RD
SPOKANE CO WA 246-A5
Rt#-902 HIGHWAY
MEDICAL LAKE WA 114-B2
SPOKANE CO WA 114-B2
SPOKANE CO WA 246-A5
Rt#-902 LEFEVRE ST
MEDICAL LAKE WA 114-B2
Rt#-902 MEDICAL LAKE RD
MEDICAL LAKE WA 114-B2
SPOKANE CO WA 114-B2
Rt#-902 S MEDICAL LK TYLER RD
MEDICAL LAKE WA 114-B2
Rt#-902 W SALNAVE RD
MEDICAL LAKE WA 114-B2
SPOKANE CO WA 114-B2
Rt#-903 2ND AV
KITTITAS CO WA 240-A1
Rt#-903 E FIRST ST
CLE ELUM WA 240-B2
Rt#-903 N FIRST ST
ROSLYN WA 240-A1
Rt#-903 S FIRST ST
ROSLYN WA 240-A1
Rt#-903 W FIRST ST
CLE ELUM WA 240-B2
Rt#-903 HIGHWAY
CLE ELUM WA 240-B2
KITTITAS CO WA 240-A1
ROSLYN WA 240-A1
Rt#-903 W NEVADA AV
ROSLYN WA 240-A1
Rt#-903 SALMON LA SAC RD
KITTITAS CO WA 111-B3
KITTITAS CO WA 240-A1
Rt#-903 W SECOND ST
CLE ELUM WA 240-B2
Rt#-903 SECOND ST W
CLE ELUM WA 240-B2
Rt#-903 N SEVENTH ST
ROSLYN WA 240-A1
Rt#-903 STAFFORD AV
CLE ELUM WA 240-B2
Rt#-904 COLUMBIA BASIN HWY
CHENEY WA 246-A7
SPOKANE CO WA 246-A7
Rt#-904 FIRST ST
CHENEY WA 246-A7
Rt#-904 W FIRST ST
CHENEY WA 246-A7
Rt#-904 HIGHWAY
CHENEY WA 246-A7
SPOKANE CO WA 114-B2
SPOKANE CO WA 246-A6
Rt#-906 HIGHWAY
KING CO WA 111-A2
KITTITAS CO WA 111-A2
Rt#-908 NE 85TH ST
KIRKLAND WA 175-C1
Rt#-908 CLEVELAND ST
REDMOND WA 175-D1
Rt#-908 NE REDMOND DR
REDMOND WA 175-C1
Rt#-908 NE REDMOND WY
REDMOND WA 175-C1
Rt#-970 HIGHWAY
KITTITAS CO WA 240-D1
Rt#-970 SUNSET HWY
KITTITAS CO WA 240-B2
Rt#-971 NAVARRE COULEE RD
CHELAN CO WA 236-B3
U.S.-2 1 RD SE
DOUGLAS CO WA 112-C2
U.S.-2 2 1/2 RD NW
DOUGLAS CO WA 236-C7
WATERVILLE WA 236-C7
U.S.-2 6TH ST
NEWPORT WA 106-C3
U.S.-2 12 RD NE
DOUGLAS CO WA 112-C2
U.S.-2 W 14TH AV
AIRWAY HEIGHTS WA 246-A4
SPOKANE CO WA 246-A4
U.S.-2 15TH ST NW
EAST WENATCHEE BENCH WA 239-A4
U.S.-2 ALBANY RD
BONNER CO ID 107-A3
PRIEST RIVER ID 107-A3
U.S.-2 E BROADWAY ST
REARDAN WA 114-A2
U.S.-2 W BROADWAY ST
REARDAN WA 114-A2
U.S.-2 N BROWNE ST
SPOKANE WA 349-A9
U.S.-2 S BROWNE ST
SPOKANE WA 349-A10
U.S.-2 S CENTRAL AV
WATERVILLE WA 236-C7
U.S.-2 N CHELAN AV
WATERVILLE WA 236-C7
U.S.-2 CROFT AV
GOLD BAR WA 110-C1
SNOHOMISH CO WA 110-C1
U.S.-2 N DIVISION ST
SPOKANE WA 346-J12
SPOKANE WA 347-A14
SPOKANE WA 349-A4
TOWN AND COUNTRY WA 346-J12
TOWN AND COUNTRY WA 347-A14
TOWN AND COUNTRY WA 349-A4
U.S.-2 S DIVISION ST
SPOKANE WA 349-A9
U.S.-2 FRWY
CASHMERE WA 238-C2
CHELAN CO WA 238-C2
DOUGLAS CO WA 239-A3
EAST WENATCHEE BENCH WA 238-C2
EAST WENATCHEE BENCH WA 239-A3
EVERETT WA 265-J4
SNOHOMISH WA 265-J4
SNOHOMISH CO WA 171-D2
SUNNYSLOPE WA 238-C2
U.S.-2 HIGHWAY
ALMIRA WA 237-D7
BONNER CO ID 106-C3
BONNER CO ID 107-A3
BONNER CO ID 244-A2
BOUNDARY CO ID 107-B1
CHELAN CO WA 111-C2
CHELAN CO WA 238-A1
COULEE CITY WA 113-A2
COUNTRY HOMES WA 347-B10
CRESTON WA 113-C1
DAVENPORT WA 114-A2
DOUGLAS CO WA 112-C2
DOUGLAS CO WA 113-A2
DOUGLAS CO WA 236-B6
DOUGLAS CO WA 239-A1
DOVER ID 107-A3
DOVER ID 244-A2
FAIRCHILD AFB WA 114-B2
FAIRWOOD WA 347-C7
GRANT CO WA 113-A2
LEAVENWORTH WA 238-A1
LINCOLN CO MT 107-C2
LINCOLN CO WA 113-C1
LINCOLN CO WA 114-A2
LINCOLN CO WA 237-D7
MOYIE SPRINGS ID 107-B1
NEWPORT WA 106-C3
OLDTOWN ID 106-C3
OLDTOWN ID 107-A3
PEND OREILLE CO WA 106-C3
SANDPOINT ID 244-A2
SPOKANE WA 346-J12
SPOKANE WA 347-A11
SPOKANE CO WA 106-C3
SPOKANE CO WA 114-C1
SPOKANE CO WA 246-A4
SPOKANE CO WA 347-F1
SPOKANE CO WA 348-A11
TROY MT 107-C2
WATERVILLE WA 236-C7
WILBUR WA 113-B1
U.S.-2 E MAIN AV
LINCOLN CO WA 113-B1
WILBUR WA 113-B1
U.S.-2 W MAIN AV
WILBUR WA 113-B1
U.S.-2 MISSOULA AV
LINCOLN CO MT 107-C2
TROY MT 107-C2
U.S.-2 E MISSOULA AV
TROY MT 107-C2
U.S.-2 MORGAN ST
DAVENPORT WA 114-A2
LINCOLN CO WA 114-A2
U.S.-2 N NEWPORT HWY
FAIRWOOD WA 347-C8
SPOKANE CO WA 347-E5
U.S.-2 PINE ST
SANDPOINT ID 244-A2
U.S.-2 E POPLAR ST
DOUGLAS CO WA 236-C7
WATERVILLE WA 236-C7
U.S.-2 N RUBY ST
SPOKANE WA 349-A6
U.S.-2 SAND HILL RD
BOUNDARY CO ID 107-B1
U.S.-2 W SPOKANE FALLS BLVD
SPOKANE WA 349-A9
U.S.-2 STEVENS PASS HWY
GOLD BAR WA 110-C1
KING CO WA 111-B1
MONROE WA 110-C1
SNOHOMISH WA 171-D3
SNOHOMISH CO WA 110-C1
SNOHOMISH CO WA 111-A1
SNOHOMISH CO WA 171-D3
SULTAN WA 110-C1
U.S.-2 NE STEVENS PASS HWY
KING CO WA 111-A1
SNOHOMISH CO WA 111-A1
U.S.-2 SUNSET FRWY
DOUGLAS CO WA 238-D3
EAST WENATCHEE BENCH WA 238-D3
SUNNYSLOPE WA 238-D3
U.S.-2 W SUNSET HWY
AIRWAY HEIGHTS WA 246-A4
SPOKANE CO WA 246-A4
SPOKANE CO WA 348-A11
U.S.-2 WALNUT ST
NEWPORT WA 106-C3
OLDTOWN ID 106-C3
U.S.-2 N WASHINGTON AV
NEWPORT WA 106-C3
U.S.-2 S WASHINGTON AV
NEWPORT WA 106-C3
U.S.-2 WATSON ST
CRESTON WA 113-C1
U.S.-11 HIGHWAY
CLEARWATER CO ID 123-C2
LEWIS CO ID 123-C2
U.S.-12 1ST ST
LEWISTON ID 250-B4
U.S.-12 5TH ST
LEWISTON ID 250-B4
U.S.-12 18TH ST
LEWISTON ID 250-C4
U.S.-12 183RD AV SW
ROCHESTER WA 184-A3
THURSTON CO WA 184-A3
U.S.-12 ARROW AV
NEZ PERCE CO ID 123-A2
U.S.-12 BRIDGE ST
CLARKSTON WA 250-B4
LEWISTON ID 250-B4
U.S.-12 COPPEI AV
WAITSBURG WA 122-A2
U.S.-12 D ST
LEWISTON ID 250-B4
U.S.-12 DIKE BYPS
LEWISTON ID 250-B4
U.S.-12 FRWY
CENTRAL PARK WA 178-C7
ELMA WA 179-A7
GRAYS HARBOR CO WA 178-B7
GRAYS HARBOR CO WA 179-A7
MONTESANO WA 178-D7
PASCO WA 343-H5
U.S.-12 HIGHWAY
ASOTIN CO WA 122-C2
ASOTIN CO WA 250-A4
BURBANK WA 121-A3
CLEARWATER CO ID 123-B2
COLUMBIA CO WA 122-A2
DAYTON WA 122-A2
ELMA WA 179-B7
FRANKLIN CO WA 121-A3
FRUITVALE WA 243-B6
GARFIELD CO WA 122-A2
GRAND MOUND WA 184-B4
GRAYS HARBOR CO WA 117-B1
GRAYS HARBOR CO WA 179-B7
GRAYS HARBOR CO WA 184-A3
IDAHO CO ID 123-C2
KAMIAH ID 123-C2
LEWIS CO ID 123-C2
LEWIS CO WA 118-C2
LEWIS CO WA 119-A1
LEWIS CO WA 185-D6
LEWIS CO WA 187-C2
LEWISTON ID 250-C4
MORTON WA 118-B2
MOSSYROCK WA 118-A2
NACHES WA 119-C1
NACHES WA 243-A4
NEZ PERCE CO ID 123-B2
NEZ PERCE CO ID 250-D3
OAKVILLE WA 117-B1
OROFINO ID 123-C2
PASCO WA 121-A3
PASCO WA 343-H5
POMEROY WA 122-B2
ROCHESTER WA 184-A3
THURSTON CO WA 184-A3
WAITSBURG WA 122-A2
WALLA WALLA WA 344-J7
WALLA WALLA WA 345-J4
WALLA WALLA CO WA 121-A3
WALLA WALLA CO WA 122-A2
WALLA WALLA CO WA 344-A9
WALLA WALLA CO WA 345-J3
WALLA WALLA WEST WA 344-F7
YAKIMA WA 243-B6
YAKIMA CO WA 119-C1
YAKIMA CO WA 243-A4
U.S.-12 INLAND EMPIRE HWY
ASOTIN CO WA 250-B4
WALLA WALLA CO WA 344-D7
WALLA WALLA WEST WA 344-D7
U.S.-12 MAIN ST
DAYTON WA 122-A2
LEWISTON ID 250-C4
U.S.-12 E MAIN ST
COLUMBIA CO WA 122-A2
DAYTON WA 122-A2
LEWISTON ID 250-C4
U.S.-12 W MAIN ST
DAYTON WA 122-A2
U.S.-12 NATIONAL PARK HWY
LEWIS CO WA 118-B2
MORTON WA 118-B2
U.S.-12 PINE ST
OAKVILLE WA 117-B1
U.S.-12 PRESTON AV
WAITSBURG WA 122-A2
U.S.-12 WISHKAH ST
ABERDEEN WA 178-B7
GRAYS HARBOR CO WA 178-B7
U.S.-20 2ND ST
BENTON CO OR 327-H9
CORVALLIS OR 327-H9
U.S.-20 NE 3RD ST
BEND OR 332-F4
U.S.-20 3RD ST W
CORVALLIS OR 327-G10
U.S.-20 4TH ST W
CORVALLIS OR 327-H9
U.S.-20 A ST E
VALE OR 139-A3
U.S.-20 A ST W
VALE OR 139-A3
U.S.-20 ALBANY-CORVALLIS HWY
ALBANY OR 207-B5
ALBANY OR 326-A6
BENTON CO OR 207-B5
BENTON CO OR 326-A6
BENTON CO OR 327-J8
CORVALLIS OR 207-B5
CORVALLIS OR 327-J8
U.S.-20 BROADWAY AV
ADA CO ID 253-D3
BOISE ID 253-D3
U.S.-20 N BROADWAY AV
BURNS OR 145-B1
U.S.-20 CAROLINA ST
LEBANON OR 133-C1
U.S.-20 CASCADE ST
DESCHUTES CO OR 211-D5
SISTERS OR 211-D5
U.S.-20 CENTRAL OREGON HWY
BEND OR 217-C2
BEND OR 332-G7
BURNS OR 145-A1
DESCHUTES CO OR 135-B3
DESCHUTES CO OR 143-C1
DESCHUTES CO OR 144-A1
DESCHUTES CO OR 217-C2
DESCHUTES CO OR 332-G7
HARNEY CO OR 138-A3
HARNEY CO OR 144-B1
HARNEY CO OR 145-A1
HARNEY CO OR 146-A1
HINES OR 145-A1
LAKE CO OR 144-A1
MALHEUR CO OR 138-C3
MALHEUR CO OR 139-A3
MALHEUR CO OR 146-A1
NYSSA OR 139-A3
VALE OR 138-C3
VALE OR 139-A3
U.S.-20 E CHINDEN BLVD
ADA CO ID 253-B2
BOISE ID 253-B2
EAGLE ID 253-B2
GARDEN CITY ID 253-C2
U.S.-20 W CHINDEN BLVD
ADA CO ID 147-C1
ADA CO ID 253-A2
U.S.-20 CORVALLIS-NEWPORT HWY
BENTON CO OR 133-A1
CORVALLIS OR 133-A1
CORVALLIS OR 327-E11
LINCOLN CO OR 133-A1
LINCOLN CO OR 206-D3
NEWPORT OR 206-B4
PHILOMATH OR 133-A1
TOLEDO OR 206-C4
U.S.-20 NW DESCHUTES PL
BEND OR 332-E6
U.S.-20 DIVISION ST
BEND OR 332-F6
U.S.-20 ELGIN AV
CANYON CO ID 147-B1
NOTUS ID 147-B1
U.S.-20 ELLSWORTH ST
ALBANY OR 326-C8
U.S.-20 FRANKLIN RD
CALDWELL ID 147-B1
CANYON CO ID 147-B1
U.S.-20 FRONT ST
BOISE ID 253-C2
U.S.-20 NE GREENWOOD AV
BEND OR 332-F7
U.S.-20 NW GREENWOOD AV
BEND OR 332-E7
U.S.-20 HIGHWAY
CANYON CO ID 139-A3
CANYON CO ID 147-B1
LINCOLN CO OR 206-C4
MALHEUR CO OR 139-A3
TOLEDO OR 206-C4
VALE OR 139-A3
U.S.-20 LYON ST
ALBANY OR 326-C8
U.S.-20 MAIN ST
BENTON CO OR 133-B1
LEBANON OR 133-C1
LINN CO OR 133-C1
MALHEUR CO OR 139-A3
NYSSA OR 139-A3
PHILOMATH OR 133-B1
SWEET HOME OR 133-C2
U.S.-20 MCKENZIE-BEND HWY
BEND OR 332-F1
DESCHUTES CO OR 211-D5
DESCHUTES CO OR 212-A6
DESCHUTES CO OR 217-B1
DESCHUTES CO OR 332-F1
U.S.-20 W MONROE ST
BURNS OR 145-B1
U.S.-20 E MYRTLE ST
BOISE ID 253-C3
U.S.-20 W MYRTLE ST
BOISE ID 253-C3
U.S.-20 OLIVE ST
NEWPORT OR 206-B4
U.S.-20 E OLIVE ST
NEWPORT OR 206-B4
U.S.-20 OREGON CENTRAL HWY
CANYON CO ID 139-A3
U.S.-20 PARK ST
LEBANON OR 133-C1
U.S.-20 PHILOMATH BLVD
BENTON CO OR 133-B1
BENTON CO OR 327-A12
CORVALLIS OR 133-B1
CORVALLIS OR 327-A12
U.S.-20 NE REVERE AV
BEND OR 332-E6
U.S.-20 SANTIAM HWY
ALBANY OR 326-F8
DESCHUTES CO OR 211-C3
JEFFERSON CO OR 211-A2
LINN CO OR 133-C1
LINN CO OR 134-A2
LINN CO OR 207-D5
LINN CO OR 211-A2
LINN CO OR 326-F8
SISTERS OR 211-C3
SWEET HOME OR 133-C2
SWEET HOME OR 134-A2
U.S.-20 THE DALLES-CALIF HWY
BEND OR 332-F3
DESCHUTES CO OR 332-G3
U.S.-20 VALE-WEST HWY
VALE OR 139-A3
U.S.-20 NW WALL ST
BEND OR 332-E6
U.S.-20 WASHINGTON ST E
VALE OR 139-A3
U.S.-20 WASHINGTON ST W
VALE OR 139-A3
U.S.-26 NW 4TH ST
MADRAS OR 208-C5
U.S.-26 SW 4TH ST
MADRAS OR 208-C5
U.S.-26 5TH ST
MADRAS OR 208-C5
U.S.-26 12TH ST N
MALHEUR CO OR 139-A3
VALE OR 139-A3
U.S.-26 SW CANYON RD
PORTLAND OR 312-C6
U.S.-26 FRANKLIN AV
DAYVILLE OR 136-C2
GRANT CO OR 136-C2
U.S.-26 FRONT ST
GRANT CO OR 137-B2
PRAIRIE CITY OR 137-B2
U.S.-26 JOHN DAY HWY
BAKER CO OR 137-C2
BAKER CO OR 138-A2
DAYVILLE OR 136-C1
GRANT CO OR 136-C1
GRANT CO OR 137-C2
JOHN DAY OR 137-C2
MALHEUR CO OR 138-B2
MALHEUR CO OR 139-A3
MOUNT VERNON OR 137-C2
UNITY OR 138-A2
VALE OR 139-A3
U.S.-26 MADRAS-PRINEVILLE HWY
CROOK CO OR 213-C3
JEFFERSON CO OR 213-C3
PRINEVILLE OR 213-C3
U.S.-26 SE MADRAS-PRINVLL HWY
JEFFERSON CO OR 208-C7
JEFFERSON CO OR 213-B2
U.S.-26 SW MADRAS-PRINVLL HWY
JEFFERSON CO OR 208-C6
U.S.-26 E MAIN ST
GRANT CO OR 137-B2
JOHN DAY OR 137-B2
U.S.-26 W MAIN ST
MOUNT VERNON OR 137-A2
U.S.-26 MOUNT HOOD HWY
CLACKAMAS CO OR 200-C3
CLACKAMAS CO OR 201-B4
CLACKAMAS CO OR 202-A6
GRESHAM OR 200-C3
MULTNOMAH CO OR 200-C3
SANDY OR 200-C3
U.S.-26 SE MOUNT HOOD HWY
GRESHAM OR 200-A2
MULTNOMAH CO OR 200-A2
PORTLAND OR 200-A2
U.S.-26 OCHOCO HWY
CROOK CO OR 135-C2
CROOK CO OR 136-A2
CROOK CO OR 213-D5
GRANT CO OR 136-B1
MITCHELL OR 136-B1
PRINEVILLE OR 213-D5
WHEELER CO OR 136-B1
U.S.-26 PIONEER BLVD
SANDY OR 200-C4
U.S.-26 E POWELL BLVD
GRESHAM OR 200-B2
U.S.-26 SE POWELL BLVD
GRESHAM OR 200-A2
PORTLAND OR 200-A2
PORTLAND OR 317-H1
PORTLAND OR 318-B2
PORTLAND OR 319-H2
U.S.-26 W POWELL BLVD
GRESHAM OR 200-A2
U.S.-26 PROCTOR BLVD
SANDY OR 200-C4
U.S.-26 SUNSET HWY
BEAVERTON OR 199-A1
CLATSOP CO OR 125-A1
CLATSOP CO WA 117-A3
CLATSOP CO WA 188-C7
COLUMBIA CO OR 125-A1
HILLSBORO OR 125-C1
HILLSBORO OR 192-A7
HILLSBORO OR 199-A1
MULTNOMAH OR 312-B7
MULTNOMAH CO OR 199-A1
NORTH PLAINS OR 125-C1
PORTLAND OR 199-A1
PORTLAND OR 312-B7
PORTLAND OR 316-B1
TILLAMOOK CO OR 125-A1
WASHINGTON CO OR 125-C1
WASHINGTON CO OR 192-A7
WASHINGTON CO OR 199-A1
U.S.-26 THE DALLES-CALIF HWY
JEFFERSON CO OR 208-C6
MADRAS OR 208-C5
U.S.-26 WARM SPRINGS HWY
CLACKAMAS CO OR 202-A6
JEFFERSON CO OR 135-A1
JEFFERSON CO OR 208-B3
MADRAS OR 208-B3
WARM SPRINGS OR 135-A1
WARM SPRINGS OR 208-A2
WASCO CO OR 126-C3
WASCO CO OR 127-A3
WASCO CO OR 135-A1
WASCO CO OR 202-A6
U.S.-30 10TH ST
BAKER CITY OR 138-B1
U.S.-30 11TH AV
NAMPA ID 147-B1
U.S.-30 11TH AV N
NAMPA ID 147-C1
U.S.-30 2ND ST S
NAMPA ID 147-B1
U.S.-30 3RD ST S
NAMPA ID 147-B1
U.S.-30 8TH ST
ASTORIA WA 300-C5
U.S.-30 ADAMS AV
LA GRANDE OR 130-A2
U.S.-30 AUBURN AV
BAKER CITY OR 138-B1
U.S.-30 BLAINE ST
CALDWELL ID 147-B1
U.S.-30 NW BRIDGE AV
PORTLAND OR 192-B7
U.S.-30 BRIDGE ST
BAKER CITY OR 138-B1
U.S.-30 BROADWAY ST
BAKER CITY OR 138-B1
U.S.-30 E B ST
RAINIER OR 189-C4
U.S.-30 W B ST
RAINIER OR 189-C4
U.S.-30 BUTTON BRIDGE RD
HOOD RIVER CO OR 195-D5
U.S.-30 CALDWELL BLVD
CANYON CO ID 147-B1
NAMPA ID 147-B1
U.S.-30 CASCADE AV
HOOD RIVER OR 195-C5
HOOD RIVER CO OR 195-C5
U.S.-30 CASCADE LOCKS HWY
CASCADE LOCKS OR 194-D6
HOOD RIVER CO OR 194-D6
U.S.-30 CENTENNIAL WY
CALDWELL ID 147-B1
U.S.-30 CLEVELAND BLVD
CALDWELL ID 147-B1
CANYON CO ID 147-B1
U.S.-30 NE COLUMBIA BLVD
PORTLAND OR 315-H1
U.S.-30 COLUMBIA RIVER HWY
ASTORIA WA 188-D1
ASTORIA WA 300-E5
CLATSKANIE OR 117-B3
CLATSOP CO WA 117-A3
CLATSOP CO WA 188-D1
COLUMBIA CITY OR 192-A3
COLUMBIA CO OR 117-B3
COLUMBIA CO OR 189-A4
COLUMBIA CO OR 192-A3
COLUMBIA CO OR 302-A14
RAINIER OR 189-A4
SAINT HELENS OR 192-A3
SCAPPOOSE OR 192-A3
U.S.-30 COMMERCIAL ST
ASTORIA WA 300-C5
U.S.-30 CO RD 900
PENDLETON OR 129-B1
UMATILLA CO OR 129-B1
U.S.-30 NW COURT AV
PENDLETON OR 129-B1
U.S.-30 SW COURT AV
PENDLETON OR 129-B1
U.S.-30 SE COURT AV
PENDLETON OR 129-B1
U.S.-30 SE DORION AV
PENDLETON OR 129-B1
U.S.-30 SW DORION AV
PENDLETON OR 129-B1
U.S.-30 ELM ST
BAKER CITY OR 138-B1
U.S.-30 FRONT ST
HOOD RIVER OR 195-D5
U.S.-30 GARRITY BLVD
CANYON CO ID 147-C1
NAMPA ID 147-C1
U.S.-30 E H AV
LA GRANDE OR 130-A2
U.S.-30 HIGHWAY
HOOD RIVER OR 195-D5
HOOD RIVER CO OR 195-C5
MALHEUR CO OR 139-A3
NEW PLYMOUTH ID 139-B3
PAYETTE CO ID 139-B3
U.S.-30 HUNTINGTON HWY
BAKER CO OR 138-C2
BAKER CO OR 139-A2
HUNTINGTON OR 138-C2
MALHEUR CO OR 139-A2
U.S.-30 IDAHO AV
ONTARIO OR 139-A3
U.S.-30 NE KILLINGSWORTH ST
PORTLAND OR 311-F7
U.S.-30 LA GRANDE-BAKER HWY
BAKER CITY OR 138-B1
BAKER CO OR 130-A3
BAKER CO OR 138-B1
HAINES OR 130-B3
LA GRANDE OR 130-A3
UNION CO OR 130-A3
U.S.-30 N LOMBARD ST
PORTLAND OR 192-B7
PORTLAND OR 308-B4
PORTLAND OR 309-E5
U.S.-30 NE LOMBARD ST
PORTLAND OR 309-G5
PORTLAND OR 310-B6
U.S.-30 MAIN ST
BAKER CITY OR 138-B1
U.S.-30 MARINE DR
ASTORIA WA 300-C5
U.S.-30 W MARINE DR
ASTORIA WA 300-B4
U.S.-30 MOSIER-THE DALLES HWY
MOSIER OR 196-A5
THE DALLES OR 196-A5
WASCO CO OR 196-A5
U.S.-30 OAK ST
HOOD RIVER OR 195-C5
U.S.-30 OLDS FRRY-ONTARIO HWY
MALHEUR CO OR 139-A3
ONTARIO OR 139-A3
U.S.-30 OREGON ST
MALHEUR CO OR 139-A3
ONTARIO OR 139-A3
U.S.-30 N OREGON ST
ONTARIO OR 139-A3
U.S.-30 PENDLETON HWY
UMATILLA CO OR 129-B1
U.S.-30 NW PENDLETON HWY
PENDLETON OR 129-B1
UMATILLA CO OR 129-B1
U.S.-30 N PHILADELPHIA AV
PORTLAND OR 192-B7

STREET City State Page-Grid

U.S.-30 PLYMOUTH AV
NEW PLYMOUTH ID 139-B3
U.S.-30 NE PORTLAND HWY
PORTLAND OR 310-D6
PORTLAND OR 311-E7
U.S.-30 NW SAINT HELENS RD
MULTNOMAH CO OR 192-A5
PORTLAND OR 192-A5
PORTLAND OR 199-B1
U.S.-30 NE SANDY BLVD
FAIRVIEW OR 200-A1
GRESHAM OR 200-A1
PORTLAND OR 200-A1
PORTLAND OR 315-J1
U.S.-30 SOUTHEAST AV
NEW PLYMOUTH ID 139-B3
PAYETTE CO ID 139-B3
U.S.-30 STATE AV
HOOD RIVER OR 195-D5
HOOD RIVER CO OR 195-D5
U.S.-30 WASHINGTON ST E
HUNTINGTON OR 138-C2
U.S.-30 WASHINGTON ST W
HUNTINGTON OR 138-C2
U.S.-30 WESTGATE AV
PENDLETON OR 129-B1
U.S.-30 NW YEON AV
PORTLAND OR 199-B1
PORTLAND OR 312-A1
U.S.-95 N 1ST AV
SANDPOINT ID 244-A2
U.S.-95 S 1ST AV
SANDPOINT ID 244-A2
U.S.-95 S 3RD ST
FRUITLAND ID 139-A3
U.S.-95 5TH AV
SANDPOINT ID 244-A2
U.S.-95 N 5TH AV
SANDPOINT ID 244-A2
U.S.-95 5TH ST
CANYON CO ID 147-A1
WILDER ID 147-A1
U.S.-95 7TH ST
WEISER ID 139-A2
U.S.-95 E 7TH ST
WEISER ID 139-A2
U.S.-95 S 7TH ST
PAYETTE ID 139-A3
U.S.-95 N 16TH ST
PAYETTE ID 139-A3
U.S.-95 S 16TH ST
PAYETTE ID 139-A3
U.S.-95 A
COTTONWOOD ID 123-C3
GRANGEVILLE ID 123-C3
IDAHO CO ID 123-B3
U.S.-95 CEDAR ST
SANDPOINT ID 244-A2
U.S.-95 CEMETERY RD
OWYHEE CO ID 147-B1
U.S.-95 CENTRAL BLVD
CAMBRIDGE ID 139-B1
WASHINGTON CO ID 139-B1
U.S.-95 CLARK ST
LEWIS CO ID 123-B2
WINCHESTER ID 123-B2
U.S.-95 E COEUR D'ALENE AV
BENEWAH CO ID 115-A3
TENSED ID 115-A3
U.S.-95 DARTMOUTH ST
ADAMS CO ID 139-C1
COUNCIL ID 139-C1
U.S.-95 W ELDER RD
KOOTENAI CO ID 247-D5
U.S.-95 F ST
WORLEY ID 115-A2
U.S.-95 E GROVE ST
CANYON CO ID 139-A3
PARMA ID 139-A3
U.S.-95 W GROVE ST
PARMA ID 139-A3
U.S.-95 HIGHWAY
ADAMS CO ID 131-C2
ADAMS CO ID 139-C1
ADAMS CO ID 251-A1
ATHOL ID 245-B2
BENEWAH CO ID 115-A2
BONNER CO ID 107-B2
BONNER CO ID 244-A1
BONNER CO ID 245-B1
BONNERS FERRY ID 107-B1
BOUNDARY CO ID 107-B1
CANYON CO ID 139-A3
CANYON CO ID 147-A1
COEUR D'ALENE ID 355-D2
COUNCIL ID 139-C1
CRAIGMONT ID 123-B2
CULDESAC ID 123-B2
FRUITLAND ID 139-A3
GRANGEVILLE ID 123-C3
HAYDEN ID 245-A5
HAYDEN ID 355-D1
HOMEDALE ID 147-A1
IDAHO CO ID 123-B3
IDAHO CO ID 131-C1
IDAHO CO ID 251-A1
KOOTENAI CO ID 115-A2
KOOTENAI CO ID 245-B1
KOOTENAI CO ID 247-D4
KOOTENAI CO ID 354-J13
KOOTENAI CO ID 355-D2
LAPWAI ID 123-A2
LATAH CO ID 115-A3
LATAH CO ID 249-D1
LATAH CO ID 250-C1
LEWIS CO ID 123-B2
LEWISTON ID 250-C4
MALHEUR CO OR 139-A2
MIDVALE ID 139-B1
MOSCOW ID 249-C5
NEZ PERCE CO ID 123-A2
NEZ PERCE CO ID 250-C1
OWYHEE CO ID 147-A1
PAYETTE ID 139-A3
PAYETTE CO ID 139-A2
PLUMMER ID 115-A2
PONDERAY ID 244-A1
RIGGINS ID 131-C2
SANDPOINT ID 244-A2
WASHINGTON CO ID 139-B1
WEISER ID 139-A2
WILDER ID 147-A1
WINCHESTER ID 123-B2
WORLEY ID 115-A2
U.S.-95 E IDAHO AV
HOMEDALE ID 147-A1
U.S.-95 W IDAHO ST
WEISER ID 139-A2
U.S.-95 IDAHO-OREGN-NVADA HWY
HUMBOLDT CO NV 154-B3
JORDAN VALLEY OR 147-A2
MALHEUR CO OR 146-C3
MALHEUR CO OR 147-A2
MALHEUR CO OR 154-B1
OWYHEE CO ID 147-A2
U.S.-95 ILLINOIS AV
COUNCIL ID 139-C1
U.S.-95 N JACKSON ST
MOSCOW ID 249-C5
U.S.-95 S JACKSON ST
MOSCOW ID 249-C5
U.S.-95 JOSEPH AV
WINCHESTER ID 123-B2
U.S.-95 LAUER CROSSING RD
IDAHO CO ID 123-B3
U.S.-95 LINCOLN WY
COEUR D'ALENE ID 355-D8
U.S.-95 LITTLE WEISER RD
ADAMS CO ID 139-B1
U.S.-95 MAIN ST
BONNERS FERRY ID 107-B2
FERDINAND ID 123-B3
HOMEDALE ID 147-A1
IDAHO CO ID 123-B3
U.S.-95 E MAIN ST
WEISER ID 139-A2
U.S.-95 N MAIN ST
LATAH CO ID 249-C4
MOSCOW ID 249-C5
U.S.-95 S MAIN ST
BONNERS FERRY ID 107-B2
MOSCOW ID 249-C5
U.S.-95 W MAIN ST
WEISER ID 139-A2
U.S.-95 MARX ST
IDAHO CO ID 131-C2
RIGGINS ID 131-C2
U.S.-95 MEADOW CREEK RD
IDAHO CO ID 123-B3
U.S.-95 MICHIGAN ST
COUNCIL ID 139-C1
U.S.-95 NORRIS AV
ADAMS CO ID 251-A4
NEW MEADOWS ID 251-A4
U.S.-95 PENNSYLVANIA AV
PAYETTE CO ID 139-A3
U.S.-95 S PENNSYLVANIA AV
FRUITLAND ID 139-A3
PAYETTE CO ID 139-A3
U.S.-95 PINE ST
SANDPOINT ID 244-A2
U.S.-95 PRAIRIE AV
CRAIGMONT ID 123-B2
U.S.-95 RAILROAD ST
MIDVALE ID 139-B1
U.S.-95 SALMON DR
IDAHO CO ID 131-C2
U.S.-95 STATE ST
WEISER ID 139-A2
U.S.-95 SUPERIOR ST
CAMBRIDGE ID 139-B1
SANDPOINT ID 244-A2
U.S.-95 S SUPERIOR ST
CAMBRIDGE ID 139-B1
U.S.-95 VIRGINIA ST
ADAMS CO ID 251-A4
NEW MEADOWS ID 251-A4
U.S.-95 S WASHINGTON ST
MOSCOW ID 249-C5
U.S.-95 WEISER SPUR
MALHEUR CO OR 139-A2
U.S.-95 WHITLEY DR
FRUITLAND ID 139-A3
U.S.-95 N WHITLEY DR
FRUITLAND ID 139-A3
PAYETTE CO ID 139-A3
U.S.-95 WILLIAM H BUNDY BLVD
LAPWAI ID 123-A2
NEZ PERCE CO ID 123-A2
U.S.-97 NE 3RD ST
BEND OR 332-F6
U.S.-97 SE 3RD ST
BEND OR 332-F9
U.S.-97 4TH ST
GRASS VALLEY OR 127-C2
SHANIKO OR 127-C3
WASCO CO OR 127-C3
U.S.-97 NW 5TH ST
REDMOND OR 212-D5
U.S.-97 SW 5TH ST
REDMOND OR 212-D5
U.S.-97 NW 6TH ST
REDMOND OR 212-D5
U.S.-97 SW 6TH ST
REDMOND OR 212-D5
U.S.-97 NW 10TH ST
TERREBONNE OR 212-D3
U.S.-97 CHELAN FALLS RD
CHELAN CO WA 236-D3
U.S.-97 DRY CREEK RD
KITTITAS CO WA 241-A4
SISKIYOU CO CA 150-B3
U.S.-97 EVERGREEN HWY
TOPPENISH WA 120-A2
YAKIMA CO WA 120-A2
U.S.-97 FAUST RD
KITTITAS CO WA 241-B5
U.S.-97 NE FRANKLIN AV
BEND OR 332-F7
U.S.-97 NW FRANKLIN AV
BEND OR 332-E7
U.S.-97 FRWY
EAST WENATCHEE BENCH WA 238-D3
SUNNYSLOPE WA 238-D3
U.S.-97 HIGHWAY
BREWSTER WA 104-B3
CHELAN CO WA 112-B1
CHELAN CO WA 236-D2
CHELAN CO WA 238-B1
DOUGLAS CO WA 236-D3
ELLENSBURG WA 241-B5
GOLDENDALE WA 127-C1
KITTITAS CO WA 111-C3
KITTITAS CO WA 238-B6
KITTITAS CO WA 240-D1
KITTITAS CO WA 241-A1
KLAMATH FALLS OR 338-C4
KLICKITAT CO WA 119-C3
KLICKITAT CO WA 127-C1
OKANOGAN WA 104-C3
OKANOGAN CO WA 104-C1
OKANOGAN CO WA 112-B1
OMAK WA 104-C2
OROVILLE WA 104-C1
PATEROS WA 104-B3
PATEROS WA 112-B1
RIVERSIDE WA 104-C2
SHERMAN CO OR 127-C1
SISKIYOU CO CA 150-C3
SUNNYSLOPE WA 238-D3
TONASKET WA 104-C2
TOPPENISH WA 120-A2
UNION GAP WA 120-A2
UNION GAP WA 243-C7
WAPATO WA 120-A2
YAKIMA CO WA 119-C3
YAKIMA CO WA 120-A2
U.S.-97 MAIN ST
MORO OR 127-C2
OKANOGAN CO WA 104-C1
OROVILLE WA 104-C1
UNION GAP WA 120-A2
UNION GAP WA 243-C7
WAPATO WA 120-A2
U.S.-97 E OLD TOWN RD
UNION GAP WA 243-C7
U.S.-97 SHERMAN HWY
GRASS VALLEY OR 127-C2
MORO OR 127-C2
SHANIKO OR 127-C2
SHERMAN CO OR 127-C1
WASCO CO OR 127-B3
U.S.-97 THE DALLES-CALIF HWY
BEND OR 332-D14
CHILOQUIN OR 231-D3
DESCHUTES CO OR 143-A1
DESCHUTES CO OR 212-C7
DESCHUTES CO OR 217-C1
DESCHUTES CO OR 332-D14
DESCHUTES RIVER WOODS OR 217-C1
DESCHUTES RIVER WOODS OR 332-D14
JEFFERSON CO OR 135-B1
JEFFERSON CO OR 208-C4
JEFFERSON CO OR 212-D3
KLAMATH CO OR 142-C3
KLAMATH CO OR 143-A1
KLAMATH CO OR 150-C1
KLAMATH CO OR 231-D3
KLAMATH CO OR 235-C1
KLAMATH CO OR 338-A1
KLAMATH FALLS OR 338-A1
MADRAS OR 208-C4
REDMOND OR 212-D3
TERREBONNE OR 212-D3
WASCO CO OR 127-B3
WASCO CO OR 135-B1
U.S.-97 WHITCOMB AV
OKANOGAN CO WA 104-C2
TONASKET WA 104-C2
U.S.-99E 2ND ST
HALSEY OR 210-B2
U.S.-99E 3RD ST
HARRISBURG OR 210-A5
U.S.-99E ALBANY-JCT CITY HWY
ALBANY OR 207-C7
ALBANY OR 326-C14
HALSEY OR 210-A4
HARRISBURG OR 210-A5
JUNCTION CITY OR 210-A5
LANE CO OR 210-A5
LINN CO OR 207-C7
LINN CO OR 210-A4
TANGENT OR 207-C7
U.S.-99E JEFFERSON HWY
LINN CO OR 207-D3
U.S.-99E PACIFIC BLVD
ALBANY OR 326-F8
LINN CO OR 326-F8
MILLERSBURG OR 326-F8
U.S.-101 1ST AV N
ILWACO WA 186-A6
PACIFIC CO WA 186-A6
U.S.-101 E 1ST ST
PORT ANGELES WA 261-F4
U.S.-101 2ND ST SE
BANDON OR 220-B6
U.S.-101 7TH ST
NEHALEM OR 191-B4
U.S.-101 SW 100TH ST
NEWPORT OR 206-A5
U.S.-101 N ALDER ST
ABERDEEN WA 178-B7
U.S.-101 S ALDER ST
ABERDEEN WA 178-B7
U.S.-101 N BROADWAY ST
COOS BAY OR 333-H9
U.S.-101 S BROADWAY ST
COOS BAY OR 333-H11
U.S.-101 CHETCO AV
BROOKINGS OR 232-C6
U.S.-101 W CURTIS ST
ABERDEEN WA 178-B7
U.S.-101 EVANS BLVD
COOS BAY OR 333-H11
U.S.-101 FIRST ST
COSMOPOLIS WA 178-B7
U.S.-101 E FIRST ST
COSMOPOLIS WA 117-A1
U.S.-101 FORKS AV N
FORKS WA 169-D1
U.S.-101 FORKS AV S
FORKS WA 169-D1
U.S.-101 FRWY
MASON CO WA 180-B5
OLYMPIA WA 296-E7
THURSTON CO WA 180-B5
THURSTON CO WA 296-B5
TUMWATER WA 296-E7
U.S.-101 S G ST
ABERDEEN WA 178-B7
U.S.-101 GARIBALDI AV
GARIBALDI OR 191-B7
TILLAMOOK CO OR 191-B7
U.S.-101 E HERON ST
ABERDEEN WA 178-B7
U.S.-101 W HERON ST
ABERDEEN WA 178-B7
U.S.-101 HIGHWAY
CLALLAM CO WA 109-C1
CLALLAM CO WA 162-D7
CLALLAM CO WA 163-B6
CLALLAM CO WA 164-A6
CLALLAM CO WA 165-A6
CLALLAM CO WA 169-C1
CLALLAM CO WA 262-B12
COSMOPOLIS WA 117-A1
CURRY CO OR 224-B7
FORKS WA 169-C1
GRAYS HARBOR CO WA 108-C2
GRAYS HARBOR CO WA 109-A2
GRAYS HARBOR CO WA 117-A1
GRAYS HARBOR CO WA 172-B3
GRAYS HARBOR CO WA 177-D2
GRAYS HARBOR CO WA 178-A1
HOQUIAM WA 178-A7
ILWACO WA 186-A6
JEFFERSON CO WA 108-C1
JEFFERSON CO WA 109-C1
JEFFERSON CO WA 169-D3
JEFFERSON CO WA 172-A1
JEFFERSON CO WA 173-D1
MASON CO WA 173-C2
MASON CO WA 180-A1
NEAH BAY WA 262-F11
PACIFIC CO WA 117-A1
PACIFIC CO WA 183-C6
PACIFIC CO WA 186-B1
PACIFIC CO WA 188-C1
RAYMOND WA 117-A1
SHELTON WA 180-A2
SOUTH BEND WA 117-A1
U.S.-101 H ST
NEHALEM OR 191-B4
U.S.-101 S H ST
ABERDEEN WA 178-B7
U.S.-101 L ST
CRESCENT CITY CA 148-B3
U.S.-101 LEVEE ST
HOQUIAM WA 178-A7
U.S.-101 LINCOLN ST
HOQUIAM WA 178-A7
U.S.-101 S LINCOLN ST
PORT ANGELES WA 261-E5
U.S.-101 MAIN AV
TILLAMOOK OR 197-B2
TILLAMOOK CO OR 197-B2
U.S.-101 W MARINE DR
ASTORIA WA 300-A5
U.S.-101 NEWPORT AV
BUNKER HILL OR 333-J12
COOS BAY OR 333-J12
U.S.-101 OCEAN AV
RAYMOND WA 117-A1
U.S.-101 OLYMPIC HWY
CLALLAM CO WA 164-A6
CLALLAM CO WA 165-B6
CLALLAM CO WA 166-C7
CLALLAM CO WA 261-A6
JEFFERSON CO WA 109-C1
JEFFERSON CO WA 166-C7
PORT ANGELES WA 261-A6
U.S.-101 OREGON ST
PORT ORFORD OR 224-A6
U.S.-101 OREGON COAST HWY
ASTORIA WA 188-C1
ASTORIA WA 300-A1
BANDON OR 220-C4
BAY CITY OR 191-B5
BAY CITY OR 197-B1
BROOKINGS OR 232-C5
BUNKER HILL OR 333-J12
CANNON BEACH OR 191-A2
CANNON BEACH WA 188-B7
CLATSOP CO OR 191-A2
CLATSOP CO WA 188-C1
CLATSOP CO WA 300-A1
CLATSOP CO WA 301-F14
COOS CO OR 218-B5
COOS CO OR 220-C4
COOS CO OR 224-B4
COOS CO OR 333-G2
CURRY CO OR 224-B4
CURRY CO OR 228-A1
CURRY CO OR 232-B2
DEPOE BAY OR 203-A7
DEPOE BAY OR 206-B3
DOUGLAS CO OR 214-A7
DOUGLAS CO OR 218-B2
DUNES CITY OR 214-B4
FLORENCE OR 214-B4
GARIBALDI OR 191-B5
GEARHART WA 301-H4
GOLD BEACH OR 228-A6
HARBOR OR 232-D6
LAKESIDE OR 218-B2
LANE CO OR 132-B2
LANE CO OR 209-A6
LANE CO OR 214-B4
LINCOLN BEACH OR 203-A7
LINCOLN CITY OR 203-B3
LINCOLN CO OR 203-B3
LINCOLN CO OR 206-B3
LINCOLN CO OR 209-A3
LINCOLN CO OR 328-D2
MANZANITA OR 191-B5
NEWPORT OR 206-B3
NORTH BEND OR 333-G2
PORT ORFORD OR 224-B6
REEDSPORT OR 218-B2
U.S.-101 OREGON COAST HWY
ROCKAWAY BEACH OR 191-B5
SEASIDE WA 188-B7
SEASIDE WA 301-H4
TILLAMOOK CO OR 191-B5
TILLAMOOK CO OR 197-B7
TILLAMOOK CO OR 197-C4
TILLAMOOK CO OR 203-B3
WALDPORT OR 328-D2
WARRENTON WA 188-B2
WHEELER OR 191-B5
YACHATS OR 209-A3
U.S.-101 PACIFIC AV
TILLAMOOK OR 197-B2
TILLAMOOK CO OR 197-B2
U.S.-101 PARK DR
GEARHART WA 301-H5
U.S.-101 N PARK ST
ABERDEEN WA 178-B7
U.S.-101 S PARK ST
ABERDEEN WA 178-B7
U.S.-101 PERRY AV
HOQUIAM WA 178-A7
U.S.-101 REDWOOD HWY
CRESCENT CITY CA 148-B3
DEL NORTE CO CA 148-B3
DEL NORTE CO CA 232-D7
U.S.-101 RIVERSIDE AV
HOQUIAM WA 178-A7
U.S.-101 RIVERSIDE DR
NEHALEM OR 191-B4
U.S.-101 ROBERT BUSH DR
PACIFIC CO WA 183-D6
SOUTH BEND WA 117-A1
SOUTH BEND WA 183-D6
U.S.-101 ROOSEVELT DR
SEASIDE WA 301-H7
U.S.-101 SEVENTH ST
HOQUIAM WA 178-A7
U.S.-101 SHERIDAN AV
NORTH BEND OR 333-G4
U.S.-101 SHERMAN AV
NORTH BEND OR 333-G5
U.S.-101 SIMPSON AV
ABERDEEN WA 178-B7
HOQUIAM WA 178-A7
U.S.-101 SIXTH ST
RAYMOND WA 117-A1
U.S.-101 SPRUCE ST E
ILWACO WA 186-A6
U.S.-101 STATE ST
NORTH BEND OR 333-G6
U.S.-101 SUMNER AV
HOQUIAM WA 178-A7
U.S.-101 SUMNER ST
ABERDEEN WA 178-B7
HOQUIAM WA 178-A7
U.S.-101 TREMONT ST
COOS BAY OR 333-G7
NORTH BEND OR 333-G7
U.S.-101 WARRENTON-ASTRIA HWY
CLATSOP CO WA 188-C2
CLATSOP CO WA 300-A10
WARRENTON WA 188-B2
U.S.-101 E WASHINGTON ST
CLALLAM CO WA 166-B7
NEAH BAY WA 262-E11
U.S.-101 W WASHINGTON ST
CLALLAM CO WA 165-D6
CLALLAM CO WA 166-A6
NEAH BAY WA 262-D11
U.S.-101 S WEST BLVD
ABERDEEN WA 178-B7
COSMOPOLIS WA 178-B7
U.S.-101 WINCHESTER AV
REEDSPORT OR 218-C1
U.S.-101 WISHKAH ST
ABERDEEN WA 178-B7
U.S.-101 E WISHKAH ST
ABERDEEN WA 178-B7
U.S.-101 W WISHKAH ST
ABERDEEN WA 178-B7
U.S.-195 BROADWAY ST
COLTON WA 250-A1
U.S.-195 HIGHWAY
COLFAX WA 122-C1
COLTON WA 250-A1
NEZ PERCE CO ID 250-B3
SPOKANE WA 246-B5
SPOKANE WA 348-F11
SPOKANE CO WA 114-C2
SPOKANE CO WA 246-C6
UNIONTOWN WA 250-B1
WHITMAN CO WA 114-C3
WHITMAN CO WA 122-C1
WHITMAN CO WA 249-A4
WHITMAN CO WA 250-A1
U.S.-195 INLAND ST
WHITMAN CO WA 114-C3
U.S.-195 S INLAND EMPIRE HWY
SPOKANE WA 246-C5
SPOKANE CO WA 246-C5
U.S.-195 E JAMES ST
COLFAX WA 122-C1
U.S.-195 N MAIN ST
COLFAX WA 122-C1
U.S.-195 S MAIN ST
COLFAX WA 122-C1
U.S.-197 DESCHUTES AV
MAUPIN OR 127-B3
U.S.-197 HIGHWAY
KLICKITAT CO WA 196-C6
U.S.-197 NORTH BANK RD
DEL NORTE CO CA 148-B3
U.S.-197 THE DALLES-CALIF HWY
DUFUR OR 127-B2
MAUPIN OR 127-B3
THE DALLES OR 196-D7
WASCO CO OR 127-B2
WASCO CO OR 196-D7
U.S.-199 N 6TH ST
GRANTS PASS OR 335-F8
U.S.-199 S 6TH ST
GRANTS PASS OR 335-E9
U.S.-199 NW 6TH ST
GRANTS PASS OR 335-F8
U.S.-199 NE 7TH ST
GRANTS PASS OR 335-F8
U.S.-199 SE 7TH ST
GRANTS PASS OR 335-E9
U.S.-199 CONGER RD
GRANTS PASS OR 335-E10
U.S.-199 F ST
GRANTS PASS OR 335-H9
JOSEPHINE CO OR 335-H9
U.S.-199 E F ST
GRANTS PASS OR 335-G9
U.S.-199 REDWOOD HWY
CAVE JUNCTION OR 233-B3
DEL NORTE CO CA 148-B3
DEL NORTE CO CA 233-A6
GRANTS PASS OR 335-F7
JOSEPHINE CO OR 149-A1
JOSEPHINE CO OR 229-A7
JOSEPHINE CO OR 233-B3
JOSEPHINE CO OR 335-A12
U.S.-199 NE REDWOOD HWY
GRANTS PASS OR 335-F7
U.S.-199 ROGUE RIVER HWY
GRANTS PASS OR 335-G11
U.S.-395 N 1ST ST
HERMISTON OR 129-A1
U.S.-395 W 5TH AV
COLVILLE WA 106-A2
U.S.-395 BARNES AV
SENECA OR 137-B3
U.S.-395 S CANYON BLVD
JOHN DAY OR 137-B2
U.S.-395 N DIVISION ST
COUNTRY HOMES WA 346-J11
COUNTRY HOMES WA 347-A8
FAIRWOOD WA 347-A8
SPOKANE WA 346-J11
TOWN AND COUNTRY WA 346-J11
U.S.-395 N ELY ST
KENNEWICK WA 342-J10
U.S.-395 S ELY ST
BENTON CO WA 342-J11
KENNEWICK WA 342-J11
U.S.-395 F ST N
LAKEVIEW OR 152-A2
U.S.-395 F ST S
LAKE CO OR 152-A2
LAKEVIEW OR 152-A2
U.S.-395 FREMONT HWY
LAKE CO OR 152-A2
LAKEVIEW OR 152-A2
MODOC CO CA 152-A3
U.S.-395 FRWY
BENTON CO WA 121-A3
HIGHLAND WA 121-A3
KENNEWICK WA 343-B9
LEWISTON OR 121-A3
PASCO WA 343-D5
UMATILLA CO OR 121-A3
WEST PASCO WA 343-C5
U.S.-395 G ST N
LAKEVIEW OR 152-A2
U.S.-395 HIGHWAY
ADAMS CO WA 113-C3
ADAMS CO WA 121-C1
BENTON CO WA 121-A3
COLVILLE WA 106-A2
CONNELL WA 121-B1
DEER PARK WA 114-B1
FAIRWOOD WA 347-A6
FERRY CO WA 105-C1
FERRY CO WA 106-A1
FRANKLIN CO WA 121-B1
FRANKLIN CO WA 343-F1
HIGHLAND WA 121-A3
KENNEWICK WA 121-A3
KENNEWICK WA 342-J10
KENNEWICK WA 343-B10
KETTLE FALLS WA 106-A2
MESA WA 121-B2
PASCO WA 121-A2
PASCO WA 343-G1
SPOKANE CO WA 114-B1
SPOKANE CO WA 346-J1
SPOKANE CO WA 347-A2
STEVENS CO WA 106-A2
STEVENS CO WA 114-B1
U.S.-395 JOHN DAY HWY
GRANT CO OR 137-A2
JOHN DAY OR 137-A2
MOUNT VERNON OR 137-A2
U.S.-395 JOHN DAY-BURNS HWY
CANYON CITY OR 137-B2
GRANT CO OR 137-B2
HARNEY CO OR 137-B3
HARNEY CO OR 145-B1
JOHN DAY OR 137-B2
SENECA OR 137-B3
U.S.-395 LAKEVIEW-BURNS HWY
HARNEY CO OR 144-C2
LAKE CO OR 144-B3
LAKE CO OR 152-A1
U.S.-395 E MAIN ST
MOUNT VERNON OR 137-A2
U.S.-395 N MAIN ST
COLVILLE WA 106-A2
U.S.-395 S MAIN ST
COLVILLE WA 106-A2
U.S.-395 W MAIN ST
GRANT CO OR 137-B2
JOHN DAY OR 137-B2
U.S.-395 MCNARY HWY
UMATILLA OR 129-A1
UMATILLA CO OR 129-A1
U.S.-395 MOUNTAIN BLVD
MOUNT VERNON OR 137-A2
U.S.-395 N PARK ST
CHEWELAH WA 106-B3
STEVENS CO WA 106-B3
U.S.-395 S PARK ST
CHEWELAH WA 106-B3
STEVENS CO WA 106-B3
U.S.-395 PENDLTN-JOHN DAY HWY
GRANT CO OR 129-B3
GRANT CO OR 137-A1
LONG CREEK OR 137-A1
MOUNT VERNON OR 137-A1

STREET City State Page-Grid

U.S.-395 PENDLTN-JOHN DAY HWY
PENDLETON OR 129-B2
PILOT ROCK OR 129-B2
UMATILLA CO OR 129-B2

U.S.-395 PIONEER MEM BRDG
KENNEWICK WA 343-B9
PASCO WA 343-B9

U.S.-395 UMATILLA-STANFLD HWY
HERMISTON OR 129-A1
STANFIELD OR 129-A1
UMATILLA OR 129-A1
UMATILLA CO OR 129-A1

U.S.-730 6TH ST
UMATILLA OR 129-A1
UMATILLA CO OR 129-A1

U.S.-730 COLUMBIA RIVER HWY
IRRIGON OR 128-C1
MORROW CO OR 128-C1
UMATILLA OR 129-A1
UMATILLA CO OR 128-C1
UMATILLA CO OR 129-A1

U.S.-730 MAIN AV E
IRRIGON OR 128-C1

AIRPORTS

FEATURE NAME	City State	Page-Grid
ALBANY MUNICIPAL AIRPORT	PRICE RD, LINN CO OR	326 - H7
ALKALI LAKE STATE AIRPORT	LAKEVIEW-BURNS HWY, LAKE CO OR	144 - B3
ANACORTES AIRPORT	OFF ANACOPPER RD, ANACORTES WA	259 - C4
ARLINGTON AIRPORT	59TH AV NE, ARLINGTON WA	168 - D5
ARLINGTON MUNICIPAL AIRPORT	AIRPORT RD, ARLINGTON OR	128 - A1
ASHLAND MUNICIPAL AIRPORT	DEAD INDIAN & MUN AIRPRT, ASHLAND OR	337 - J8
AUBURN MUNICIPAL AIRPORT	23RD ST NE & D ST NE, AUBURN WA	182 - C1
AURORA AIRPORT	AIRPORT RD, MARION CO OR	199 - B7
AVEY FIELD STATE AIRPORT	HWY 395, FERRY CO WA	105 - C1
BANDERA STATE AIRPORT	BANDERA, KING CO WA	111 - A2
BANDON STATE AIRPORT	OREGON COAST HWY, COOS CO OR	220 - B6
BEAVER MARSH STATE AIRPORT	THE DALLES-CALIFORNIA HWY, KLAMATH CO OR	142 - C2
BELLINGHAM INTERNATIONAL AIRPORT	W BAKERVIEW RD, WHATCOM CO WA	158 - D7
BEND MUNICIPAL AIRPORT	POWELL BUTTE HWY & MARKET RD, DESCHUTES CO	217 - D2
BLAINE MUNICIPAL AIRPORT	PIPELINE RD, BLAINE WA	158 - B3
BOEING FIELD INTERNATIONAL AIRPORT	AIRPORT WAY, SEATTLE WA	286 - C2
BOISE MUNICIPAL AIRPORT	W WRIGHT ST, BOISE ID	253 - D4
BOUNDARY BAY AIRPORT	OFF 72ND ST, DISTRICT OF DELTA BC	101 - C1
BOUNDARY COUNTY AIRPORT	HWY 2 & HWY 95, BOUNDARY CO ID	107 - B1
BROOKINGS STATE AIRPORT	OFF OREGON COAST HWY, CURRY CO OR	232 - C5
BURNS MUNICIPAL AIRPORT	AIRPORT RD, HARNEY CO OR	145 - B1
CAPE BLANCO STATE AIRPORT	AIRPORT RD, CURRY CO OR	224 - A4
CASCADE LOCKS-STEVENSON STATE AIRPORT	BONNEVILLE DAM, HOOD RIVER CO OR	194 - D6
CHEHALIS-CENTRALIA AIRPORT	NW LOUISIANA AV, CHEHALIS WA	299 - C9
CHELAN MUNICIPAL AIRPORT	APPLE ACRES RD & HWY 97, CHELAN CO WA	236 - D2
CHILOQUIN STATE AIRPORT	THE DALLES-CALIFORNIA HWY, CHILOQUIN OR	231 - D3
COEUR D'ALENE AIR TERMINAL	HAYDEN, KOOTENAI CO ID	245 - A5
COLVILLE MUNICIPAL AIRPORT	COLVILLE, COLVILLE WA	106 - A2
COMOX AIRPORT	HWY 19, BRITISH COLUMBIA	92 - B2
CONCRETE MUNICIPAL AIRPORT	OFF HWY 20, SKAGIT CO WA	102 - C2
CONDON STATE AIRPORT	JOHN DAY HWY, GILLIAM CO OR	128 - A2
CONNELL CITY AIRPORT	US HWY 395, FRANKLIN CO WA	121 - B1
CORVALLIS MUNICIPAL AIRPORT	AIRPORT AV & PACIFIC HWY W, BENTON CO OR	207 - A7
COTTAGE GROVE STATE AIRPORT	SEARS RD, LANE CO OR	215 - C7
COTTONWOOD MUNICIPAL AIRPORT	OFF HWY 95, IDAHO CO ID	123 - C3
COUNCIL MUNICIPAL AIRPORT	LITTLE WEISER RD, ADAMS CO ID	139 - C1
CRAIGMONT MUNICIPAL AIRPORT	COLD SPRINGS RD, CRAIGMONT ID	123 - B2
CRESCENT LAKE STATE AIRPORT	HWY 58, KLAMATH CO OR	142 - B1
CURLEW AIRPORT	CURLEW, FERRY CO WA	105 - B1
DAVIS AIRPORT	N SANTIAM HWY, LINN CO OR	134 - A1
DAVIS FIELD AIRPORT	SEQUIM, CLALLAM CO WA	262 - E8
DEER PARK MUNICIPAL AIRPORT	E DEER PARK-MILAN RD, DEER PARK WA	114 - B1
DONNELLY AIRPORT	MAIN ST & W ROSEBERRY RD, VALLEY CO ID	252 - D2
DUKE-S PRIVATE AIRPORT	SEQUIM, NEAH BAY WA	262 - F12
EASTON STATE AIRPORT	KACHESS LAKE, KITTITAS CO WA	111 - B3
ECKHART INTERNATIONAL AIRPORT	HWY 1, BOUNDARY CO ID	107 - B1
ELMA MUNICIPAL AIRPORT	WENZEL SLOUGH RD, GRAYS HARBOR CO WA	179 - B7
EMMETT MUNICIPAL AIRPORT	SOUTHSLOPE RD, GEM CO ID	139 - C3
ENTERPRISE MUNICIPAL AIRPORT	ANT FLAT RD, WALLOWA CO OR	130 - C2
ENUMCLAW AIRPORT	KING CO WA	110 - C3
EPHRATA MUNICIPAL AIRPORT	DIVISION AV & AIRPORT ST, EPHRATA WA	112 - C3
FAIRCHILD, WILLIAM R INTL AIRPORT	W LAURIDSEN BLVD, PORT ANGELES WA	165 - A6
FELTS FIELD MUNICIPAL AIRPORT	E RUTTER AV, SPOKANE WA	349 - J5
FERRY COUNTY AIRPORT	HWY 21, FERRY CO WA	105 - B2
FLORENCE MUNICIPAL AIRPORT	HWY 101 & 9TH ST, FLORENCE OR	214 - B3
FORKS MUNICIPAL AIRPORT	OFF HWY 101, FORKS WA	169 - C2
GOLD BEACH MUNICIPAL AIRPORT	AIRPORT WY, GOLD BEACH OR	228 - A6
GRAND COULEE DAM AIRPORT	HWY 155 & AIRPORT RD, GRANT CO WA	237 - B3
GRAND VIEW INTERNATIONAL AIRPORT	CARLSBORG RD, CLALLAM CO WA	166 - A6
GRANT COUNTY AIRPORT	RANDOLPH RD & TYNDALL RD, MOSES LAKE N WA	242 - C1
HAMPTON STATE AIRPORT	OFF CENTRAL OREGON HWY, DESCHUTES CO OR	144 - A1
HARBORD FIELD AIRPORT	SEQUIM, CLALLAM CO WA	262 - G6
HERMISTON MUNICIPAL AIRPORT	UMATILLA-STANFIELD HWY, HERMISTON OR	129 - A1
HOOD RIVER COUNTY AIRPORT	TUCKER RD, HOOD RIVER CO OR	195 - C6
IDAHO COUNTY AIRPORT	OFF HWY 95, IDAHO CO ID	123 - C3
INDEPENDENCE STATE AIRPORT	OFF HOFFMAN RD, POLK CO OR	204 - B7
IONE MUNICIPAL AIRPORT	IONE, PEND OREILLE CO WA	106 - B2
JEFFERSON COUNTY INTL AIRPORT	AIRPORT RD, JEFFERSON CO WA	263 - B12
JOHN DAY STATE AIRPORT	AIRPORT RD, GRANT CO OR	137 - B2
JOSEPHINE COUNTY AIRPORT	BROOKSIDE & MONUMENT, JOSEPHINE CO OR	229 - B4
JOSEPH STATE AIRPORT	RUSSEL LN, WALLOWA CO OR	130 - C2
KAMIAH MUNICIPAL AIRPORT	OFF HWY 12, IDAHO CO ID	123 - C3
KELSO MUNICIPAL AIRPORT	TALLEY AV, KELSO WA	303 - E12
KITSAP COUNTY AIRPORT	OFF HWY 3, KITSAP CO WA	174 - A4
KLAMATH FALLS INTL AIRPORT	ALTAMONT & JOE WRIGHT, KLAMATH FALLS OR	235 - C5
LA CENTER VIEW-AIR AIRPORT	ARIEL, CLARK CO WA	192 - D1
LA CROSSE AIRPORT	LA CROSSE AIRPORT RD, WHITMAN CO WA	122 - A1
LA GRANDE/UNION COUNTY AIRPORT	OFF PIERCE RD, UNION CO OR	130 - A2
LAKE BILLY CHINOOK STATE AIRPORT	SW JORDAN RD, JEFFERSON CO OR	208 - A7
LAKE COUNTY AIRPORT	OFF STOCK DRIVE RD, LAKE CO OR	152 - A2
LAKE WENATCHEE STATE AIRPORT	PLAIN, CHELAN CO WA	111 - C1
LANGLEY AIRPORT	56TH AV & 216TH ST, LANGLEY BC	158 - C1
LEBANON STATE AIRPORT	AIRPORT DR, LEBANON OR	133 - C1
LEWISTON AIRPORT	4TH ST & BURRELL AV, LEWISTON ID	250 - C5
LEXINGTON AIRPORT	AIRPORT RD, MORROW CO OR	128 - C2
LIND AIRPORT	US HWY 395, ADAMS CO WA	121 - C1
LYNDEN AIRPORT	OFF HWY 546, LYNDEN WA	102 - B1
MADRAS CITY-COUNTY AIRPORT	OFF WARM SPRINGS HWY, JEFFERSON CO OR	208 - B4
MAHLON SWEET MUNICIPAL AIRPORT	GREEN HILL RD, LANE CO OR	215 - A1
MCCALL AIRPORT	MISSION ST, MCCALL ID	251 - C5
MCDERMITT STATE AIRPORT	IDAHO-OREGON-NEVADA HWY, MALHEUR CO OR	154 - B2
MCKENZIE BRIDGE STATE AIRPORT	MCKENZIE HWY, LANE CO OR	134 - B2
MCMINNVILLE MUNICIPAL AIRPORT	SALMON RIVER HWY, MCMINNVILLE OR	198 - B7
METHOW VALLEY STATE AIRPORT	HWY 20, OKANOGAN CO WA	104 - A3
MILLICAN AIRPORT	CENTRAL OREGON HWY, DESCHUTES CO OR	135 - B3
MOSES LAKE MUNICIPAL AIRPORT	CHEROKEE RD & RD L-NE, MOSES LAKE WA	242 - D3
MULINO AIRPORT	MULINO RD, CLACKAMAS CO OR	199 - D7
MYRTLE CREEK MUNICIPAL AIRPORT	PACIFIC HWY & WEAVER RD, DOUGLAS CO OR	225 - C2
NAMPA MUNICIPAL AIRPORT	AIRPORT RD, NAMPA ID	147 - C1
NEHALEM BAY STATE AIRPORT	CAREY ST, TILLAMOOK CO OR	191 - B4
NEW MEADOWS AIRPORT	US HWY 95, ADAMS CO ID	251 - A4
NEWPORT MUNICIPAL AIRPORT	84TH ST, NEWPORT OR	206 - B5
NEZ PERCE MUNICIPAL AIRPORT	POWERLINE RD, LEWIS CO ID	123 - C2
NORTH BEND MUNICIPAL AIRPORT	AIRPORT AV, NORTH BEND OR	333 - E3
OAK HARBOR AIR PARK AIRPORT	OAK HARBOR, NEAH BAY WA	262 - C11
OAKRIDGE STATE AIRPORT	HWY 58, LANE CO OR	142 - A1
OCEAN SHORES MUNICIPAL AIRPORT	OCEAN SHORES BLVD, OCEAN SHORES WA	177 - B6
ODESSA MUNICIPAL AIRPORT	DUCK LAKE RD, LINCOLN CO WA	113 - B2
OLYMPIA AIRPORT	CAPITOL BLVD, TUMWATER WA	296 - G14
OLYMPIA MUNICIPAL AIRPORT	PACIFIC HWY, TUMWATER WA	184 - C1
ONTARIO MUNICIPAL AIRPORT	OLDS FERRY-ONTARIO HWY, ONTARIO OR	139 - A3
OROFINO MUNICIPAL AIRPORT	OFF HWY 12, CLEARWATER CO ID	123 - C2
OTHELLO MUNICIPAL AIRPORT	W BENCH RD, ADAMS CO WA	121 - A1
OWYHEE RESERVOIR STATE AIRPORT	DEADMAN GULCH RD, MALHEUR CO OR	146 - C1
PACIFIC CITY STATE AIRPORT	OFF BROOTEN RD, TILLAMOOK CO OR	197 - A7
PAINE FIELD SNOHOMISH CO AIRPORT	AIRPORT RD, SNOHOMISH WA	267 - G6
PARMA AIRPORT	SAND RD, CANYON CO ID	139 - A3
PAYETTE MUNICIPAL AIRPORT	IOWA AV N & AIRPORT RD, PAYETTE ID	139 - A2
PENDLETON MUNICIPAL AIRPORT	STAGE GULCH RD, PENDLETON OR	129 - B1
PIERCE COUNTY AIRPORT	MERIDIAN E, PIERCE CO WA	182 - B5
PINEHURST STATE AIRPORT	GREEN SPRINGS HWY, JACKSON CO OR	150 - A2
PITT MEADOWS AIRPORT	FORD RD & BAYNES RD, PITT MEADOWS BC	157 - B5
PORTLAND-HILLSBORO AIRPORT	NE CORNELL RD, HILLSBORO OR	198 - D1
PORTLAND INTERNATIONAL AIRPORT	7000 NE AIRPORT WY, PORTLAND OR	310 - A2
PORT OF ASTORIA AIRPORT	AIRPORT RD, WARRENTON WA	188 - B2
POWERS STATE AIRPORT	OFF COQUILLE RIVER RD, COOS CO OR	140 - B3
PRIEST RIVER MUNICIPAL AIRPORT	HWY 57, PRIEST RIVER ID	107 - A3
PRINEVILLE AIRPORT	OCHOCO HWY, CROOK CO OR	213 - C5
PULLMAN/MOSCOW REGIONAL AIRPORT	AIRPORT RD, WHITMAN CO WA	249 - B4
QUILLAYUTE STATE AIRPORT	QUILLAYUTE RD, CLALLAM CO WA	169 - B2
QUINCY MUNICIPAL AIRPORT	RD 9-NW & RD P-NW, GRANT CO WA	112 - B3
RANGER CREEK STATE AIRPORT	SUN TOP, PIERCE CO WA	111 - A3
REDLAND AIRPORT	S REDLAND RD, CLACKAMAS CO OR	200 - A5
REDMOND MUNICIPAL AIRPORT	SE AIRPORT WY, REDMOND OR	212 - D6
RENTON AIRPORT	N AIRPORT WY, RENTON WA	175 - C4
RICHLAND AIRPORT	TERMINAL DR, RICHLAND WA	340 - D11
RITZVILLE MUNICIPAL AIRPORT	VAN VLEET RD & WEBER RD, ADAMS CO WA	113 - C3
RIVER BEND AIRPORT	JAMESON LAKE SOUTH WEST, PEND OREILLE CO	106 - C2
ROBERTS YOUNG AIRPORT	MARINE DR, WHATCOM CO WA	101 - C1
ROGUE VALLEY INTL-MEDFORD AIRPORT	BIDDLE RD & AIRPORT RD, MEDFORD OR	336 - D5
ROME STATE AIRPORT	IDAHO-OREGON-NEVADA HWY, MALHEUR CO OR	146 - B3
ROSALIA MUNICIPAL AIRPORT	MALDEN RD, WHITMAN CO WA	114 - C3
ROSEBURG MUNICIPAL AIRPORT	AIRPORT RD & STEWART PKWY, ROSEBURG OR	334 - F2
SAINT MARIES MUNICIPAL AIRPORT	SAINT MARIES, BENEWAH CO ID	248 - C7
SANDERSON FIELD AIRPORT	HWY 101, MASON CO WA	180 - A2
SANDPOINT AIRPORT	N BOYER AV, SANDPOINT ID	244 - A1
SANDY RIVER AIRPORT	SHIPLEY RD, CLACKAMAS CO OR	200 - D4
SANTIAM JUNCTION STATE AIRPORT	SANTIAM HWY, LINN CO OR	134 - C2
SEASIDE STATE AIRPORT	AIRPORT RD, CLATSOP CO WA	301 - H5
SEATTLE TACOMA INTERNATIONAL AIRPORT	AIR CARGO RD S, SEATAC WA	290 - B1
SEKIU AIRPORT	HWY 112, CLALLAM CO WA	163 - A2
SHADY OAKS AIRPORT	HEIPLE RD, CLACKAMAS CO OR	200 - B5
SILETZ AIRPORT	SILETZ HWY, LINCOLN CO OR	206 - C2
SILETZ BAY STATE AIRPORT	OREGON COAST HWY, LINCOLN CO OR	203 - A6
SISKIYOU COUNTY AIRPORT	MULE HILL, SISKIYOU CO CA	150 - A3
SISTERS EAGLE AIR AIRPORT	CAMP POLK RD, DESCHUTES CO OR	211 - D4
SKAGIT REGIONAL BAY VIEW AIRPORT	HIGGINS AIRPORT WY, SKAGIT CO WA	161 - A6
SPOKANE INTERNATIONAL AIRPORT	W AIRPORT DR, SPOKANE CO WA	246 - A5
SUNNYSIDE MUNICIPAL AIRPORT	E EDISON AV, SUNNYSIDE WA	120 - B2
SUTHERLIN MUNICIPAL AIRPORT	COMSTOCK & ELKTON-SUTHERLIN, SUTHERLIN OR	221 - C1
TACOMA NARROWS AIRPORT	STONE DR NW, PIERCE CO WA	181 - C2
THE DALLES MUNICIPAL AIRPORT	DALLESPORT RD, KLICKITAT CO WA	196 - C7
TIETON STATE AIRPORT	TIETON BASIN, YAKIMA CO WA	119 - B2
TILLAMOOK AIRPORT	LONG PRAIRIE RD, TILLAMOOK CO OR	197 - C3
TOLEDO STATE AIRPORT	SOUTHBAY RD, LINCOLN CO OR	206 - C5
TRI-CITIES AIRPORT	GLADE, COLUMBIA POINT, PASCO WA	343 - E3
TROUTDALE AIRPORT	NE MARINE DR, TROUTDALE OR	200 - B1
TULE LAKE MUNICIPAL AIRPORT	OFF HWY 139, MODOC CO CA	151 - A3
TWISP MUNICIPAL AIRPORT	TWISP EAST, OKANOGAN CO WA	104 - A3
VALLEY VIEW AIRPORT	DUUS RD, CLACKAMAS CO OR	200 - C6
VANCOUVER INTERNATIONAL AIRPORT	GRANT MCCONACHIE WY, CITY OF RICHMOND BC	156 - B5
VASHON MUNICIPAL AIRPORT	OFF SW COVE RD, KING CO WA	174 - D5
VICTORIA INTERNATIONAL AIRPORT	HWY 17, DISTRICT OF NORTH SAANICH BC	159 - C2
VISTA FIELD AIRPORT	N KELLOGG ST, KENNEWICK WA	342 - D9
WAKONDA BEACH AIRPORT	SW WAKONDA BEACH RD, LINCOLN CO OR	328 - B10
WALLA WALLA CITY-COUNTY AIRPORT	MIDDLE WAITSBURG RD, WALLA WALLA CO WA	345 - F3
WALLOWA STATE AIRPORT	SHERROD RD, WALLOWA CO OR	130 - B2
WARDEN MUNICIPAL AIRPORT	RD 8-SE, WARDEN WA	121 - A1
WASCO STATE AIRPORT	WASCO-HEPPNER HWY, SHERMAN CO OR	127 - C2
WEISER MUNICIPAL AIRPORT	AIRPORT RD, WASHINGTON CO ID	139 - A2
WESTPORT AIRPORT	MONTESANO ST, WESTPORT WA	298 - J12
WILLAPA HARBOR MUNICIPAL AIRPORT	HWY 105, PACIFIC CO WA	117 - A1
WOODLAND STATE AIRPORT	WOODLAND, CLARK CO WA	192 - C1
YAKIMA MUNICIPAL AIRPORT	W WASHINGTON AV, YAKIMA WA	243 - B7

BEACHES & HARBORS

FEATURE NAME	City State	Page-Grid
ALKI BEACH PARK	ALKI AV SW, SEATTLE WA	276 - D7
ANTELOPE RESERVOIR	ANTELOPE CANAL RD, MALHEUR CO OR	147 - A3
BASS LAKE ACCESS	OFF HWY 1, BOUNDARY CO ID	107 - B1
BEAVER BAY SWIM AREA	BAYVIEW, KOOTENAI CO ID	245 - C1
BEULAH RESERVOIR	BEULAH RD, MALHEUR CO OR	138 - A3
BLACK CANYON RESERVOIR	OFF HWY 52, GEM CO ID	139 - C3
BONNER LAKE ACCESS AREA	OFF HWY 2, BOUNDARY CO ID	107 - C1
BRACKETTS LANDING BEACH	MAIN ST & RAILROAD AV N, EDMONDS WA	171 - A5
BROUGHTON BEACH	NE MARINE DR, PORTLAND OR	310 - C2
BROWNLEE RESERVOIR	SNAKE RIVER RD, BAKER CO OR	139 - A1
BULLY CREEK RESERVOIR	BULLY CREEK RD, MALHEUR CO OR	138 - C3
BUMPING LAKE	NFD RD 1800, YAKIMA CO WA	119 - A1
CALDWELL PONDS PUBLIC FISHING AREA	OFF ELGIN AV, CANYON CO ID	147 - B1
CALEDONIA BEACH	HYADA BLVD NE, PIERCE CO WA	181 - D1
CARKEEK PARK BEACH	NW CARKEEK PARK RD, SEATTLE WA	171 - A7

FEATURE NAME	City State	Page-Grid
CASCADE RESERVOIR	WEST MOUNTAIN RD, VALLEY CO ID	252 - D4
CHASE LAKE ACCESS AREA	EASTSIDE RD, BONNER CO ID	107 - A2
CLEAR LAKE RESERVOIR	CLEAR LAKE RD, MODOC CO CA	151 - B3
CLE ELUM LAKE	SALMON LA SAC RD, KITTITAS CO WA	111 - B3
COCOLALLA LAKE ACCESS AREA	OFF HWY 95, BONNER CO ID	244 - A5
COLD SPRINGS RESERVOIR	LOOP RD, UMATILLA CO OR	129 - A1
COLUMBIA BEACH	BURMA RD, WARRENTON WA	188 - B2
COTTAGE GROVE LAKE	COTTAGE GROVE RESERVOIR RD, LANE CO OR	219 - D2
CRANE CREEK RESERVOIR	CRANE CREEK RES RD, WASHINGTON CO ID	139 - B2
CRANE PRAIRIE RESERVOIR	LAVA LAKE RD, DESCHUTES CO OR	142 - C1
CRATER LAKE	OFF NATIONAL PARK HWY, KLAMATH CO OR	227 - C3
CRESCENT LAKE	CRESCENT LAKE HWY, KLAMATH CO OR	142 - B1
CRUMP LAKE	HOGBACK RD, LAKE CO OR	152 - B2
DAVIS LAKE	ODELL RD, DESCHUTES CO OR	142 - C1
DAWSON LAKE ACCESS AREA	OFF HWY 95, BOUNDARY CO ID	107 - B1
DEEP CREEK ACCESS AREA	OLD US HWY 2, BOUNDARY CO ID	107 - B2
DETROIT LAKE	N SANTIAM HWY, MARION CO OR	134 - B1
DEVILS LAKE	DEVILS LAKE RD, LINCOLN CO OR	203 - B4
DIAMOND LAKE	DIAMOND LAKE HWY, DOUGLAS CO OR	223 - C6
DREWS RESERVOIR	KLAMATH FALLS-LAKEVIEW HWY, LAKE CO OR	151 - C2
DUFF LANE POND PUBLIC FISHING AREA	DUFF LN & LINDEN RD, CANYON CO ID	147 - B1
EAST LAKE	NEWBERRY CRATER RD, DESCHUTES CO OR	143 - B1
EDMONDS MARINA BEACH	ADMIRAL WY, EDMONDS WA	171 - A5
ELK RIVER DAM PUBLIC FISHING AREA	ELK RIVER RD, CLEARWATER CO ID	123 - C1
FLAGSTAFF LAKE	FLAGSTAFF LAKE RD, LAKE CO OR	152 - B1
FOSTER LAKE	SANTIAM HWY, LINN CO OR	134 - A2
FREEMAN LAKE ACCESS AREA	NEWPORT, BONNER CO ID	106 - C3
GARFIELD BAY ACCESS AREA	GARFIELD BAY CTO, BONNER CO ID	244 - B3
GERBER RESERVOIR	GERBER RD, KLAMATH CO OR	151 - B2
GOOSE LAKE	FREMONT HWY, MODOC CO CA	152 - A3
GOOSE LAKE	GOOSE LAKE RD, ADAMS CO ID	251 - B2
GRANITE LAKE	OFF WARREN WAGON RD, VALLEY CO ID	251 - D1
GRANITE LAKE ACCESS	OFF GRANITE-KELSO RD, BONNER CO ID	107 - A3
GREEN PETER LAKE	QUARTZVILLE DR, LINN CO OR	134 - A2
HART LAKE	HART MOUNTAIN RD, LAKE CO OR	152 - B1
HAZARD LAKE	HAZARD LAKE RD, IDAHO CO ID	131 - C2
HELLS CANYON RESERVOIR	NFD RD 454, ADAMS CO ID	131 - B2
HILLS CREEK LAKE	RIGDON RD, LANE CO OR	142 - A1
JEWEL LAKE ACCESS AREA	JEWEL LAKE RD, BONNER CO ID	107 - A3
JUANITA BEACH PARK	9703 NE JUANITA DR, KIRKLAND WA	171 - C7
KELSO LAKE ACCESS	OFF GRANITE-KELSO RD, BONNER CO ID	107 - A3
LAKE ABERT	LAKEVIEW-BURNS HWY, LAKE CO OR	152 - A1
LAKE CHELAN	HWY 97 & HWY 150, CHELAN CO WA	236 - B2
LAKE LOWELL	RIVERSIDE RD, CANYON CO ID	147 - B1
LAKE OWYHEE	OWYHEE LAKE RD, MALHEUR CO OR	147 - A1
LAKE WENATCHEE	WHITE RIVER RD, CHELAN CO WA	111 - C1
LITTLE GRASSY RESERVOIR	THREE FORKS RD, MALHEUR CO OR	146 - C3
LITTLE PAYETTE LAKE	LICK CREEK RD, VALLEY CO ID	251 - D5
LOST VALLEY RESERVOIR	NFD RD 89, ADAMS CO ID	131 - B3
LUANA BEACH	SW LUANA BEACH RD, KING CO WA	175 - A6
MALHEUR LAKE	NARROWS-PRINCETON RD, HARNEY CO OR	145 - B2
MALHEUR RESERVOIR	WILLOW CREEK RD, MALHEUR CO OR	138 - B2
MANN CREEK RESERVOIR	JACKSON RD, WASHINGTON CO ID	139 - A2
MANN LAKE PUBLIC FISHING AREA	RESERVATION LINE RD, NEZ PERCE CO ID	250 - D5
MATTHEWS BEACH PARK	49TH AV NE & NE 93RD ST, SEATTLE WA	275 - F1
MCARTHUR LAKE ACCESS	OFF HWY 2, BOUNDARY CO ID	107 - B2
MCKAY RESERVOIR	SHAW-HOLMES RD, UMATILLA CO OR	129 - B1
MCKEES BEACH	FRANS DR & EVERGREEN WY, SNOHOMISH CO WA	168 - A6
MIRROR LAKE ACCESS	NFD RD 2233, BONNER CO ID	244 - B4
MISSION BEACH	MISSION BEACH RD, SNOHOMISH CO WA	171 - B1
MORTON SLOUGH ACCESS	DUFORT RD, BONNER CO ID	107 - A3
MOYIE RIVER ACCESS AREA	MOYIE RIVER RD, BOUNDARY CO ID	107 - C1
NAKETA BEACH	NAKETA BEACH RD, MUKILTEO WA	266 - D3
ODELL LAKE	WILLAMETTE HWY, KLAMATH CO OR	142 - B1
OLYMPIC BEACH	DAYTON ST & ADMIRAL WY, EDMONDS WA	171 - A5
OWENS BEACH	OWENS BEACH RD, TACOMA WA	181 - C1
OWYHEE LAKE	LESLIE GULCH RD, MALHEUR CO OR	146 - C1
PAULINA LAKE	NEWBERRY CRATER RD, DESCHUTES CO OR	143 - A1
PAYETTE LAKE	WARREN WAGON RD, VALLEY CO ID	251 - C4
PHILLIPS LAKE	WHITNEY HWY, BAKER CO OR	138 - A1
PRIEST LAKE MARINA	OFF HWY 57, BONNER CO ID	107 - A2
PRINEVILLE RESERVOIR	SALT CREEK RD, CROOK CO OR	135 - C3
PRITCHARD ISLAND BEACH	GRATTAN ST & 55TH AV S, SEATTLE WA	287 - G2
PUBLIC BOAT LAUNCH & FISHING AREA	SE 312TH ST, KING CO WA	110 - C3
RICHMOND BEACH PARK	RICHMOND BEACH DR NW, SHORELINE WA	171 - A6
ROSE LAKE ACCESS AREA	ROSE LAKE, KOOTENAI CO ID	248 - D2
SAINT MARIES RIVER ACCESS AREA	SAINT MARIES, BENEWAH CO ID	248 - D7
SHEPHERD LAKE ACCESS AREA	OFF TALACHE RD, BONNER CO ID	244 - A4
SILTCOOS LAKE	SILTCOOS STATION RD, LANE CO OR	214 - B5
SPIRIT LAKE	OFF NFD RD 99, SKAMANIA CO WA	190 - C1
SPRING VALLEY RES PUBLIC FISHING AREA	OFF HWY 8, LATAH CO ID	123 - A1
STAR LANE POND PUBLIC FISHING AREA	STAR LN, GEM CO ID	139 - B3
SUMMER LAKE	FREMONT HWY, LAKE CO OR	143 - C3
SWIFT CREEK RESERVOIR	NFD RD 91013, SKAMANIA CO WA	190 - C5
TAHKENITCH LAKE	OREGON COAST HWY, DOUGLAS CO OR	214 - A6
THOMPSON RESERVOIR	NFD RD 3142, LAKE CO OR	143 - B3
TILLICUM BEACH	TILLICUM BCH DR & KAREN WY, ISLAND CO WA	168 - A6
TOTEM BEACH	TOTEM BEACH RD, SNOHOMISH CO WA	168 - B7
UPPER COW LAKE	LOWER COW CREEK RD, MALHEUR CO OR	146 - C2
UPPER PAYETTE LAKE	WARREN WAGON RD, VALLEY CO ID	251 - D1
WALDO LAKE	HWY 58, LANE CO OR	142 - B1
WALLOWA LAKE	JOSEPH-WALLOWA LAKE HWY, WALLOWA CO OR	130 - C2
WARM BEACH	SOUNDVIEW DR & 188TH ST, SNOHOMISH CO WA	168 - A5
WARM SPRINGS RESERVOIR	WARM SPRINGS RD, HARNEY CO OR	146 - A1
WICKIUP RESERVOIR	WICKIUP RD, DESCHUTES CO OR	142 - C1
WINCHESTER LAKE PUBLIC FISHING AREA	OFF CAMAS RD, LEWIS CO ID	123 - B2
YALE LAKE	LEWIS RIVER RD, COWLITZ CO WA	190 - A6

BUILDINGS

FEATURE NAME	City State	Page-Grid
1ST INTERSTATE BANK TOWER	1300 SW 5TH AV, PORTLAND OR	313 - E7
COUCH MANSION	ELK PRAIRIE, CLACKAMAS CO OR	126 - A3
FAIRVIEW HOME PRIGG COTTAGE	AUMSVILLE HWY SE, SALEM OR	325 - F6
FOUNTAIN PLAZA	1414 SW 3RD AV, PORTLAND OR	313 - F7
HATFIELD MARINE SCIENCE CENTER	MARINE SCIENCE DR, NEWPORT OR	206 - B4
HEWLETT PACKARD	11311 E CHINDEN BLVD, BOISE ID	253 - B2
KOIN BUILDING	222 W COLUMBIA ST, PORTLAND OR	313 - F7
LEONA M SUNDQUIST MARINE LABORATORY	OFF OAKES AV, ANACORTES WA	259 - A3
LOOKOUT AT HARBOUR CENTRE TOWER THE	555 W HASTINGS ST, VANCOUVER BC	254 - H9
MANITO PARK GREENHOUSE	S PARK DR, SPOKANE WA	349 - A12
MEDICAL RESEARCH FOUNDATION OF OREGON	505 NW 185TH AV, HILLSBORO OR	199 - A1
MIKADO BUILDING	117 SW TAYLOR ST, PORTLAND OR	313 - F6
MINNEHAHA GRANGE	NE ST JOHNS RD & NE 52ND ST, CLARK CO WA	306 - A1
MULTNOMAH BUILDING	319 SW PINE ST, PORTLAND OR	313 - F5
NATL HIST OREGON TR INTERPRETIVE CTR	BAKER-COPPERFIELD HWY, BAKER CO OR	138 - B1
NEWPORT GEOPHYSICAL OBSERVATORY	LE CLERC RD, PEND OREILLE CO WA	106 - C3
NICHOLSON PAVILION	ELLENSBURG NORTH, ELLENSBURG WA	241 - B5
OLYMPIA BREWING COMPANY	CAPITOL BLVD & CUSTER ST, TUMWATER WA	296 - H9
PACWEST BANK TOWER	SW MADISON ST & SW 5TH AV, PORTLAND OR	313 - E6
PITTOCK BLOCK	921 SW WASHINGTON ST, PORTLAND OR	313 - E6
PORTLAND BUILDING	SW MAIN ST & SW 5TH AV, PORTLAND OR	313 - F6
PORTLAND PLAZA	SW CLAY ST & SW 5TH AV, PORTLAND OR	313 - E7
ROYAL BROUGHAM PAVILION	3RD AV W & W NICKERSON ST, SEATTLE WA	273 - G7
STANDARD INSURANCE BUILDING	900 SW 5TH AV, PORTLAND OR	313 - F6
US BANCORP TOWER	111 SW 5TH AV, PORTLAND OR	313 - F5
WALL ST BUILDING	COLBY AV & WALL ST, EVERETT WA	264 - D4

BUILDINGS - GOVERNMENTAL

FEATURE NAME	City State	Page-Grid
COUNTY/CITY BUILDING	S 11TH ST & S TACOMA AV, TACOMA WA	293 - G5
DEPARTMENT OF LICENSING	6402-C S YAKIMA AV, TACOMA WA	295 - G6
FAA/AFS OFFICE BUILDING	PORTLAND INTL AIRPORT, PORTLAND OR	311 - F5
FIRCREST STATE INSTITUTE	15230 15TH AV NE, SHORELINE WA	171 - B7
FIRE DEPARTMENT TRAINING CENTER	E RESERVE ST, VANCOUVER WA	305 - J4
GREEN WYATT FEDERAL BUILDING	1220 SW 3RD AV, PORTLAND OR	313 - F7
IDAHO STATE CAPITOL	W STATE ST, BOISE ID	253 - C2
NATIONAL OCEANIC & ATMOSPHERIC ADMIN	SAND POINT WY NE, SEATTLE WA	275 - H2
NIGHTHAWK CUSTOMS	LOOMIS-OROVILLE RD, OKANOGAN CO WA	104 - C1
OREGON DEPARTMENT OF TRANSPORTATION	NW 1ST AV & NW GLISAN ST, PORTLAND OR	313 - F5
OREGON STATE CAPITOL	COURT ST NE, SALEM OR	322 - J13
PARK ADMINISTRATION	3500 W ELMORE ST, SEATTLE WA	272 - C5
PIERCE COUNTY ANNEX	S 35TH ST, TACOMA WA	294 - E1
POLICE HEADQUARTERS	1120 SW 3RD AV, PORTLAND OR	313 - F6
PUBLIC SERVICE BUILDING	920 SW 6TH AV, PORTLAND OR	313 - E6
REMANN HALL JUVENILE COURT	6TH AV & SHIRLEY ST, TACOMA WA	292 - A5
STATE AND FEDERAL OFFICES	S 13TH ST & S TACOMA AV, TACOMA WA	293 - G6
STATE BUILDING	1400 SW 5TH AV, PORTLAND OR	313 - E7
STATE BUILDING	800 NE OREGON ST, PORTLAND OR	313 - H5
STATE DEPT OF SOCIAL HEALTH SERVICES	S 19TH ST & S SPRAGUE AV, TACOMA WA	293 - E7
US BANK BUILDING	309 SW 6TH AV, PORTLAND OR	313 - F6
US CUSTOMS POST	HWY 3, OKANOGAN CO WA	104 - C1
US CUSTOMS STATION	HWY 543, BLAINE WA	158 - B2
US CUSTOMS STATION	INTERSTATE 5, BLAINE WA	158 - B3
US DEPARTMENT OF ENERGY HANFORD SITE	BENTON CO WA	120 - C2
US DEPARTMENT OF ENERGY HANFORD SITE	BENTON CO WA	121 - A2
US DEPARTMENT OF ENERGY HANFORD SITE	BENTON CO WA	340 - B2
US DEPARTMENT OF ENERGY HANFORD SITE	FRANKLIN CO WA	121 - A2
US FEDERAL BUILDING	511 NW BROADWAY, PORTLAND OR	313 - F5
US WEATHER BUREAU STATION	OLD OREGON TRAIL HWY, UMATILLA CO OR	129 - C2
WASHINGTON CORRECTIONS CENTER	DAYTON-AIRPORT RD, MASON CO WA	179 - D2
WASHINGTON STATE CAPITOL	14TH AV, OLYMPIA WA	296 - G6
WASHINGTON STATE PENITENTIARY	N 13TH AV, WALLA WALLA WA	344 - H5

CAMPGROUNDS

FEATURE NAME	City State	Page-Grid
ABBOT CREEK CAMPGROUND	NFD RD 12, JEFFERSON CO OR	134 - C1
ABBOTT CREEK CAMPGROUND	ABBOTT BUTTE, JACKSON CO OR	226 - C4
ADAMS FORK CAMPGROUND	EAST CANYON RIDGE, SKAMANIA CO WA	118 - C2
ADELL CAMPGROUND	MILLER LAKE, KLAMATH CO OR	142 - B2
AHTANUM MEADOW CAMPGROUND	FOUNDATION RIDGE, YAKIMA CO WA	119 - B2
ALBENI COVE CAMPGROUND	ALBENI COVE RD, BONNER CO ID	106 - C3
ALDER CAMPGROUND	CONCONULLY WEST, OKANOGAN CO WA	104 - B2
ALDER SWAMP SHELTER	BULL OF THE WOODS, CLACKAMAS CO OR	126 - B3
ALDER THICKET CAMPGROUND	ROSE SPRINGS, GARFIELD CO WA	122 - B2
ALICE LAKE CAMPGROUND	HWY 99, BRITISH COLUMBIA	93 - C2
ALKALI CAMP	FISH MOUNTAIN, DOUGLAS CO OR	226 - D1
ALLAN SPRINGS CAMPGROUND	METOLIUS RIVER RD, JEFFERSON CO OR	134 - C1
ALLEN CREEK CAMPGROUND	OFF SCOTT CAMP RD, CROOK CO OR	136 - A2
ALLISON CREEK CAMPGROUND	NFD RD 1614, IDAHO CO ID	131 - C2
ALLISON LAKE CAMPGROUND	HWY 5A, BRITISH COLUMBIA	95 - C2
ALOUETTE CAMPGROUND	FERN CRES, MAPLE RIDGE BC	94 - B3
ALPINE CAMPGROUND	OFF NFD RD 9712, CHELAN CO WA	238 - C6
ALPINE CAMPGROUND	MOUNT HOOD SOUTH, CLACKAMAS CO OR	202 - A5
ALPINE MEADOWS CAMPGROUND	TRINITY, CHELAN CO WA	111 - C1
ALTA CAMPGROUND	DEVILS PEAK, KLAMATH CO OR	150 - B1
AMANITA CAMPGROUND	MOUNTAIN RD, VALLEY CO ID	252 - C2
AMERICAN CAMPSITE	CATTLE POINT RD, SAN JUAN CO WA	101 - C2
AMERICAN FORKS CAMPGROUND	OLD SCAB MOUNTAIN, YAKIMA CO WA	119 - B1
ANDREWS CREEK CAMPGROUND	COLEMAN PEAK, OKANOGAN CO WA	104 - A1
ANTELOPE CAMPGROUND	OFF HANCOCK RD, GEM CO ID	139 - C2
ANTHONY LAKES CAMPGROUND	ANTHONY LAKES RD, BAKER CO OR	130 - A3
ANTILON LAKE CAMPGROUND	GRADE CREEK RD & LONG JIM RES, CHELAN CO	112 - A1
ARCHIE KNOWLES CAMPGROUND	FLORENCE-EUGENE & MAPLETON RD, LANE CO OR	132 - C3
ASH SWALE SHELTER	LOST CREEK RD, LANE CO OR	133 - C3
ASPEN CAMPGROUND	BENHAM FALLS, DESCHUTES CO OR	217 - A4
ASPEN POINT CAMPGROUND	LAKE OF THE WOODS NORTH, KLAMATH CO OR	150 - B1
ASPERKAHA CAMPGROUND	HYATT RESERVOIR, JACKSON CO OR	150 - A2
ATKINSON FLAT CAMPGROUND	MOUNT DAVID, TRINITY, CHELAN CO WA	111 - C1
BADGER LAKE CAMPGROUND	BADGER LAKE, HOOD RIVER CO OR	202 - C6
BAGBY HOT SPRINGS CAMPGROUND	BAGBY HOT SPRINGS, CLACKAMAS CO OR	126 - B3
BAKER CREEK CAMPGROUND	LIBERTY, KITTITAS CO WA	111 - C3
BALD MOUNTAIN SHELTER	BULL RUN LAKE, HOOD RIVER CO OR	202 - A4
BALLARD CAMPGROUND	MCLEOD MOUNTAIN, OKANOGAN CO WA	104 - A2
BALLARD CAMPGROUND	ROBINSON MOUNTAIN, OKANOGAN CO WA	103 - C2
BAMBERTON PARK CAMPGROUND	TRANS CANADA HWY, BRITISH COLUMBIA	159 - A3
BARK SHANTY SHELTER	MOUNT WALKER, JEFFERSON CO WA	109 - C1

PNW

INDEX

FEATURE NAME	City State	Page-Grid
BARLOW CAMPGROUND	GOVERNMENT CAMP, CLACKAMAS CO OR	201 - D6
BARNHOUSE CAMPGROUND	BUCK POINT RD, WHEELER CO OR	136 - B2
BARTOO CAMPGROUND	PRIEST LAKE SW, BONNER CO ID	107 - A2
BATTLE CREEK SHELTER	OFF BREITENBUSH RD, MARION CO OR	134 - B1
BEACH CAMPGROUND	CASCADE LAKES HWY, DESCHUTES CO OR	216 - A4
BEAR CAMPGROUND	NFD RD 105, ADAMS CO ID	131 - B3
BEAR CANYON CAMPGROUND	OFF NFD RD 62, WALLOWA CO OR	130 - B1
BEAR CREEK CAMPGROUND	BONE MOUNTAIN, DOUGLAS CO OR	140 - C3
BEAR CREEK CAMPGROUND	DEADMANS HILL, CLALLAM CO WA	163 - B6
BEAR CREEK SHELTER	COPPER MOUNTAIN, WHATCOM CO WA	103 - A1
BEAR LAKE CAMPGROUND	TIETON BASIN, YAKIMA CO WA	119 - B1
BEAR SKULL SHELTER	JACK MOUNTAIN, WHATCOM CO WA	103 - B1
BEAR WALLOW CREEK CAMPGROUND	UKIAH-HILGARD HWY, UMATILLA CO OR	129 - B3
BEAR WALLOW SPRING CAMPGROUND	NFD RD 54, UMATILLA CO OR	129 - B2
BEAUTY CREEK CAMPGROUND	MOUNT COEUR D'ALENE, KOOTENAI CO ID	248 - B1
BEAVER BAY CAMPGROUND	COUGAR, COWLITZ CO WA	190 - B5
BEAVER CAMPGROUND	BLUE BUCK MOUNTAIN, OKANOGAN CO WA	104 - B2
BEAVER CAMPGROUND	STABLER, SKAMANIA CO WA	194 - C2
BEAVER DAM CAMPGROUND	BROWN MOUNTAIN, JACKSON CO OR	150 - A2
BEAVER LAKE CAMPGROUND	BODIE, OKANOGAN CO WA	105 - A1
BEAVER PASS SHELTER	MOUNT PROPHET, WHATCOM CO WA	103 - B1
BEAVER SHELTER	FISH CREEK DESERT, DOUGLAS CO OR	222 - D6
BEAVER SWAMP CAMPGROUND	BUCKEYE LAKE, DOUGLAS CO OR	222 - C7
BEDAL CAMPGROUND	BEDAL, SNOHOMISH CO WA	103 - A3
BEDROCK CAMPGROUND	BIG FALL CREEK RD, LANE CO OR	134 - A3
BEECH CREEK CAMPGROUND	PENDLETON-JOHN DAY HWY, GRANT CO OR	137 - A1
BEEHIVE SPRING CAMPGROUND	NFD RD 9712, CHELAN CO WA	238 - C6
BELL BAY CAMPGROUND	HARRISON, KOOTENAI CO ID	248 - A4
BENHAM FALLS CAMPGROUND	BENHAM FALLS, DESCHUTES CO OR	217 - A5
BESSEN CAMPGROUND	BENHAM FALLS, DESCHUTES CO OR	217 - A6
BESSIE SHELTER	RED BLANKET MOUNTAIN, JACKSON CO OR	227 - A7
BETH LAKE CAMPGROUND	BODIE, OKANOGAN CO WA	105 - A1
BEVERLY CAMPGROUND	MOUNT STUART, KITTITAS CO WA	111 - B2
BIG BEAR CAMPGROUND	PUMPKIN MOUNTAIN, WHATCOM CO WA	103 - B1
BIG BEN CAMPGROUND	IMNAHA CREEK, JACKSON CO OR	150 - A1
BIG CREEK CAMPGROUND	LAKE CHELAN, CHELAN CO WA	112 - A1
BIG CREEK CAMPGROUND	MARBLE CREEK, SHOSHONE CO ID	115 - C2
BIG CREEK CAMPGROUND	NFD RD 16, GRANT CO OR	137 - C2
BIG CREEK CAMPGROUND	SAWTOOTH RIDGE, LEWIS CO WA	118 - C1
BIG EDDY CAMPGROUND	AHSAHKA, CLEARWATER CO ID	123 - B2
BIG ELK CAMPGROUND	BIG ELK CREEK RD, LINCOLN CO OR	133 - A1
BIG FLAT SHELTER	OWL MOUNTAIN, JEFFERSON CO WA	109 - A1
BIG HANK CAMPGROUND	POND PEAK, SHOSHONE CO ID	115 - C1
BIG HILL CAMPGROUND	NFD RD 112, CHELAN CO WA	112 - A1
BIGHORN CAMPGROUND	RHODODENDRON, CLACKAMAS CO OR	201 - C6
BIG LAKE CAMPGROUND	OFF OLD SANTIAM WAGON RD, LINN CO OR	134 - C2
BIG MEADOWS CAMPGROUND	OFF SANTIAM HWY, LINN CO OR	134 - C2
BIG POOL CAMPGROUND	BIG FALL CREEK RD, LANE CO OR	134 - A3
BIG RIVER CAMPGROUND	ANNS BUTTE, DESCHUTES CO OR	216 - D7
BIG SLIDE CAMPGROUND	GOLDEN, JOSEPHINE CO OR	149 - A1
BIG SPRING CAMPGROUND	STENTZ SPRING, GARFIELD CO WA	122 - B3
BIG SPRINGS CAMPGROUND	OFF BUCK HOLLOW RD, CROOK CO OR	136 - B2
BIG SPRINGS CAMPGROUND	OFF SANTIAM HWY, MARION CO OR	134 - B1
BIG TREE CAMPGROUND	CHINA FLAT, COOS CO OR	140 - C3
BIG TWIN LAKES CAMPGROUND	TWIN LAKES MOUNTAIN, DOUGLAS CO OR	222 - B4
BIG WINDY CREEK CAMPGROUND	GOLDEN, JOSEPHINE CO OR	148 - C1
BINGHAM PRAIRIE CAMPGROUND	OPAL MOUNTAIN, CROOK CO OR	135 - C2
BINGHAMS SHELTER	DIAMOND PEAK, LANE CO OR	142 - B1
BIRD CREEK CAMPGROUND	GLENWOOD, YAKIMA CO WA	119 - A3
BLACKBERRY CAMPGROUND	ALSEA HWY, LINCOLN CO OR	209 - D2
BLACKHORSE CAMPGROUND	WALLOWA MOUNTAIN LP, WALLOWA CO OR	131 - A2
BLACK LAKE CAMPGROUND	HELLS CANYON RECREATION AREA, ADAMS CO ID	131 - B2
BLACK PINE CAMPGROUND	JACK RIDGE, CHELAN CO WA	111 - B2
BLACK PINE CAMPGROUND	WAHA, NEZ PERCE CO ID	123 - A3
BLACKPINE LAKE CAMPGROUND	HOODOO PEAK, OKANOGAN CO WA	104 - A3
BLAIR LAKE CAMPGROUND	OFF CANYON RD, LANE CO OR	134 - B3
BLUEBILL LAKE CAMPGROUND	EMPIRE, COOS CO OR	218 - A6
BLUE CREEK CAMPGROUND	SILVER FALLS, CHELAN CO WA	111 - C1
BLUE GROUSE CAMPSITE	WAHTUM LAKE, HOOD RIVER CO OR	194 - D7
BLUE JAY CAMPGROUND	GLENWOOD, YAKIMA CO WA	119 - A3
BLUE LAKE CREEK CAMPGROUND	BLUE LAKE, LEWIS CO WA	118 - C2
BOAT LANDING CAMPGROUND	BUMPING LAKE, YAKIMA CO WA	119 - A1
BOB CREEK SHELTER	BOB CREEK, JEFFERSON CO WA	109 - A1
BOGACHIEL SHELTER	INDIAN PASS, CLALLAM CO WA	108 - C1
BOGUS CREEK CAMPGROUND	MACE MOUNTAIN, DOUGLAS CO OR	141 - C2
BOLAN LAKE CAMPGROUND	BOLAN LAKE RD, JOSEPHINE CO OR	233 - D7
BOLT SHELTER	BURNT PEAK, SKAMANIA CO WA	118 - C3
BONA FIDA SHELTER	CHILCOOT MOUNTAIN, LANE CO OR	141 - C1
BONANZA CAMPGROUND	TIPTOP, CHELAN CO WA	238 - B5
BONAPARTE CAMPGROUND	MOUNT BONAPARTE, OKANOGAN CO WA	105 - A1
BONE SPRING CAMPGROUND	NORTH OF NFD RD 63, WALLOWA CO OR	130 - A1
BONNEY MEADOWS CAMPGROUND	BADGER LAKE, HOOD RIVER CO OR	202 - C6
BORDEAUX CAMPGROUND	LITTLEROCK, THURSTON CO WA	180 - A7
BOULDER CAVE CAMPGROUND	RT 412 & BOULDER CAVE, YAKIMA CO WA	119 - B1
BOULDER CREEK CAMPGROUND	DUMONT CREEK, DOUGLAS CO OR	141 - C2
BOULDER CREEK CAMPGROUND	MOUNT CARRIE, CLALLAM CO WA	109 - A1
BOULDER CREEK CAMPGROUND	WELKER PEAK, WHATCOM CO WA	102 - C2
BOULDER FLAT CAMPGROUND	ILLAHEE ROCK, DOUGLAS CO OR	222 - C3
BOULDER LAKE SHELTER	MOUNT CARRIE, CLALLAM CO WA	109 - A1
BOULDER PARK CAMPGROUND	NFD RD 7755, BAKER CO OR	130 - C3
BOULDER SHELTER	MOUNT DECEPTION, JEFFERSON CO WA	109 - C1
BOUNDARY CAMPGROUND	CHINA FLAT, COOS CO OR	140 - B3
BOUNDARY CAMPGROUND	END OF BEAR CREEK RD, WALLOWA CO OR	130 - B2
BOUNDARY CAMPGROUND	GRANGEVILLE EAST, IDAHO CO ID	123 - C3
BOUNDARY SPRINGS CAMPGROUND	CRESCENT, KLAMATH CO OR	142 - C2
BOZE SHELTER	TWIN LAKES MOUNTAIN, DOUGLAS CO OR	222 - B6
BRADBURY CAMPGROUND	BANGS MOUNTAIN, STEVENS CO WA	106 - A2
BRANDYWINE FALLS CAMPGROUND	HWY 99, WHISTLER BC	93 - C1
BREAKWATER CAMPGROUND	BUMBLEBEE PEAK, KOOTENAI CO ID	115 - B2
BREITENBUSH CAMPGROUND	BREITENBUSH RD, MARION CO OR	134 - B1
BRIDGE CAMPGROUND	BAYVIEW, KOOTENAI CO ID	245 - C1
BRIDGE CREEK CAMPGROUND	CASHMERE MOUNTAIN, CHELAN CO WA	111 - C2
BRIDGE CREEK CAMPGROUND	MCGREGOR MOUNTAIN, CHELAN CO WA	103 - C2
BRIGGS CREEK CAMPGROUND	GOLDEN, JOSEPHINE CO OR	148 - C1
BRIGGS VALLEY CAMPGROUND	GOLDEN, JOSEPHINE CO OR	149 - A1
BROWN CREEK CAMPGROUND	LIGHTNING PEAK, MASON CO WA	109 - B2
BROWNS CREEK CAMPGROUND	DAVIS MOUNTAIN, DESCHUTES CO OR	142 - C1
BROWNS LAKE CAMPGROUND	BROWNS LAKE, PEND OREILLE CO WA	106 - C2
BRUCES EDDY CAMPGROUND	AHSAHKA, CLEARWATER CO ID	123 - C2
BRUIN RUN CAMPGROUND	GOVERNMENT CAMP, CLACKAMAS CO OR	201 - D6
BRUSH LAKE CAMPGROUND	HALL MOUNTAIN, BOUNDARY CO ID	107 - B1
BRUSHY BAR CAMPGROUND	MARIAL, CURRY CO OR	148 - C1
BUCK CAMP	HAMAKER BUTTE, DOUGLAS CO OR	223 - A7
BUCK CREEK CAMPGROUND	HUCKLEBERRY MOUNTAIN, SNOHOMISH CO WA	103 - A3
BUCK CREEK CAMPGROUND	NFD RD 32, UMATILLA CO OR	130 - A1
BUCKEYE LAKE CAMPGROUND	BUCKEYE LAKE, DOUGLAS CO OR	226 - C1
BUCKHEAD MOUNTAIN CAMPGROUND	TWIN LAKES MOUNTAIN, DOUGLAS CO OR	222 - B6
BUCKHORN CAMPGROUND	BUCKHORN RD, WALLOWA CO OR	131 - A1
BUCK LAKE CAMPGROUND	LEWIS BUTTE, OKANOGAN CO WA	104 - A2
BUCKSKIN CREEK CAMPGROUND	SITDOWN MOUNTAIN, FERRY CO WA	105 - C2
BUCK SPRING CAMPGROUND	OFF SAWMILL CREEK RD, HARNEY CO OR	144 - C1
BULL BEND CAMPGROUND	WICKIUP DAM, DESCHUTES CO OR	142 - C1
BULL GAP CAMPGROUND	MOUNT ASHLAND, JACKSON CO OR	234 - C6
BULLY CREEK CAMPGROUND	HOPE BUTTE RD, MALHEUR CO OR	138 - C3
BUMBLEBEE CAMPGROUND	BUMBLEBEE PEAK, SHOSHONE CO ID	115 - B1
BUMPING DAM CAMPGROUND	BUMPING LAKE, YAKIMA CO WA	119 - A1
BUNCHGRASS MEADOWS SHELTER	PICKETT BUTTE, DOUGLAS CO OR	141 - C3
BUNKER HILL CAMPGROUND	LEMOLO LAKE, DOUGLAS CO OR	223 - C3
BUTLER BAR CAMPGROUND	FATHER MOUNTAIN, CURRY CO OR	224 - D6
CABIN CREEK CAMPGROUND	NFD RD 186, ADAMS CO ID	252 - B3
CABIN LAKE CAMPGROUND	NFD RD 18, LAKE CO OR	143 - B1
CALAWAH SHELTER	INDIAN PASS, CLALLAM CO WA	108 - C1
CAMAS CREEK CAMPGROUND	FISH CREEK DESERT, DOUGLAS CO OR	222 - C5
CAMPBELL LAKE CAMPGROUND	LEE THOMAS CROSSING, LAKE CO OR	151 - C1
CAMPBELL SHELTER	COLONEL BOB, GRAYS HARBOR CO WA	109 - A2
CAMPBELL TREE GROVE CAMPGROUND	COLONEL BOB, GRAYS HARBOR CO WA	109 - A2
CAMP BROWN FOREST PARK	ROARING CREEK, WASHINGTON CO OR	125 - B1
CAMP CREEK CAMPGROUND	GOVERNMENT CAMP, CLACKAMAS CO OR	201 - D6
CAMPGROUND	HWY 19, BRITISH COLUMBIA	92 - A2
CAMPGROUND	HWY 4, BRITISH COLUMBIA	92 - A3
CAMPGROUND	BRITISH COLUMBIA	92 - C3
CAMPGROUND	BRITISH COLUMBIA	93 - A2
CAMPGROUND	GAMBIER ISLAND, BRITISH COLUMBIA	93 - B2
CAMPGROUND	OFF HWY 101, BRITISH COLUMBIA	93 - B3
CAMPGROUND	OFF HWY 99, BRITISH COLUMBIA	93 - C1
CAMPGROUND	TRANS CANADA HWY, BRITISH COLUMBIA	93 - C2
CAMPGROUND	BRITISH COLUMBIA	94 - C2
CAMPGROUND	HWY 1, BRITISH COLUMBIA	95 - A3
CAMPGROUND	HWY 5, BRITISH COLUMBIA	95 - B1
CAMPGROUND	HWY 3, BRITISH COLUMBIA	95 - C3
CAMPGROUND	HIGHWAY 18, BRITISH COLUMBIA	100 - C1
CAMPGROUND	BRITISH COLUMBIA	100 - C2
CAMPGROUND	BRITISH COLUMBIA	101 - A2
CAMPGROUND	OFF HWY 3, BRITISH COLUMBIA	105 - B1
CAMPGROUND	TRANS CANADA HWY, BRITISH COLUMBIA	101 - A1
CAMPGROUND	CLACKAMAS CO OR	200 - B6
CAMPGROUND	KILBY RD, DISTRICT OF KENT BC	94 - C3
CAMPGROUND	BELL ST, DISTRICT OF MISSION BC	94 - B3
CAMPGROUND	MT SEYMOUR RD, DISTRICT OF NORTH VANCOUV	156 - D2
CAMPGROUND	MAPLE RIDGE BC	94 - B3
CAMPGROUND	SUNNYSIDE RD, MAPLE RIDGE BC	157 - A3
CAMPGROUND	HWY 99, WHISTLER BC	93 - C1
CAMPGROUND NUMBER ONE	DOG LAKE, LAKE CO OR	151 - C2
CAMPGROUND NUMBER TWO	DOG LAKE, LAKE CO OR	151 - C2
CAMP SEKANI	SPOKANE NE, SPOKANE CO WA	350 - A3
CANAL CREEK CAMPGROUND	OFF CANAL CREEK RD, LINCOLN CO OR	209 - C2
CANDLE CREEK CAMPGROUND	OFF METOLIUS RIVER RD, JEFFERSON CO OR	134 - C1
CANTON CREEK CAMPGROUND	STEAMBOAT, DOUGLAS CO OR	141 - C2
CANTON SHELTER	SCAREDMAN CREEK, DOUGLAS CO OR	141 - C2
CANTRALL-BUCKLEY CAMPGROUND	RUCH, JACKSON CO OR	149 - B2
CANYON CREEK CAMPGROUND	BANGS MOUNTAIN, FERRY CO WA	105 - C2
CANYON CREEK CAMPGROUND	CANYON CREEK RD, CROOK CO OR	136 - A2
CANYON CREEK CAMPGROUND	GLACIER, WHATCOM CO WA	102 - C1
CANYON CREEK CAMPGROUND	SIOUXON PEAK, SKAMANIA CO WA	193 - D1
CANYON CREEK CAMPGROUNDS	RANKIN RD, JEFFERSON CO OR	211 - C1
CANYON CREEK SHELTER	BOGACHIEL PEAK, CLALLAM CO WA	109 - A1
CANYON CREEK SHELTER	GAMMA PEAK, SNOHOMISH CO WA	103 - B3
CAPE PERPETUA CAMPGROUND	CUMMINS PEAK RD, LINCOLN CO OR	209 - A4
CARBERRY CAMPGROUND	CARBERRY CREEK, JACKSON CO OR	149 - B2
CARROL CAMPGROUND	OFF SUMMIT RD, WHEELER CO OR	136 - A2
CARTER LAKE CAMPGROUND	OREGON COAST HWY, DOUGLAS CO OR	214 - A5
CASCADE ISLAND CAMPGROUND	MARBLEMOUNT, SKAGIT CO WA	103 - A2
CASTLE ROCK CAMPGROUND	HEBO, TILLAMOOK CO OR	197 - C7
CASTLE ROCK CAMPGROUND	OFF JENCK RD, TILLAMOOK CO OR	197 - B7
CAT CREEK CAMPGROUND	GREEN MOUNTAIN, SKAMANIA CO WA	119 - A2
CAT ISLAND CAMPGROUND	HOZOMEEN MOUNTAIN, WHATCOM CO WA	103 - B1
CAVITT SHELTER	LANE MOUNTAIN, DOUGLAS CO OR	141 - B2
CAYUSE CAMPGROUND	DAVIS PEAK, KITTITAS CO WA	111 - B2
CCC CAMPGROUND	MARBLE CREEK, SHOSHONE CO ID	115 - C2
CEDAR CREEK CAMPGROUND	CLARKIA, SHOSHONE CO ID	115 - C3
CEDAR GROVE CAMPGROUND	BLEWETT, CHELAN CO WA	238 - A4
CEDAR SPRINGS CAMPGROUND	OLD SCAB MOUNTAIN, YAKIMA CO WA	119 - B1
CEDAR SWAMP CAMPSITE	WAHTUM LAKE TR, HOOD RIVER CO OR	195 - A6
CHAIN OF LAKES CAMPGROUND	GREEN MOUNTAIN, SKAMANIA CO WA	119 - A2
CHAMBERS LAKE CAMPGROUND	HAMILTON BUTTES, LEWIS CO WA	119 - A2
CHANCELLOR CAMPGROUND	SHULL MOUNTAIN, WHATCOM CO WA	103 - C2
CHARLTON LAKE SHELTER	THE TWINS, LANE CO OR	142 - B1
CHATTER CREEK CAMPGROUND	JACK RIDGE, CHELAN CO WA	111 - C2
CHEWUCH CAMPGROUND	DOE MOUNTAIN, OKANOGAN CO WA	104 - A2
CHIEF PAULINA CAMPGROUND	NEWBERRY CRATER RD, DESCHUTES CO OR	143 - A1
CHIMNEY ROCK CAMPGROUND	STEARNS BUTTE, CROOK CO OR	135 - C3

PNW

INDEX

FEATURE NAME	City State	Page-Grid
CHINA FLAT CAMPGROUND	CHINA FLAT, COOS CO OR	140 - B3
CHINA HAT CAMPGROUND	CHINA HAT RD, DESCHUTES CO OR	143 - B1
CHOCWICH CAMPGROUND	BEDAL, SNOHOMISH CO WA	103 - A3
CHOPAKA LAKE CAMPGROUND	NIGHTHAWK, OKANOGAN CO WA	104 - B1
CHURCH CREEK SHELTER	MOUNT TEBO, MASON CO WA	109 - B2
CINDER HILL CAMPGROUND	NEWBERRY CRATER RD, DESCHUTES CO OR	143 - B1
CITY CREEK SHELTER	REYNOLDS RIDGE, LANE CO OR	142 - A1
CLACKAMAS LAKE CAMPGROUND	MOUNT WILSON, CLACKAMAS CO OR	126 - C3
CLALLAM RIVER CAMPGROUND	ELLIS MOUNTAIN, CLALLAM CO WA	163 - B3
CLEAR CREEK CAMP	HAMAKER BUTTE, DOUGLAS CO OR	223 - A7
CLEAR CREEK CAMPGROUND	HELENA RIDGE, SNOHOMISH CO WA	103 - A3
CLEAR CREEK CAMPGROUND	POST POINT, WASCO CO OR	127 - A3
CLEAR LAKE CAMPGROUND	SPIRAL BUTTE, YAKIMA CO WA	119 - A2
CLEAR LAKE CAMPGROUND	WAPINITIA PASS, WASCO CO OR	126 - C3
CLEAR LAKE NORTH CAMPGROUND	SPIRAL BUTTE, YAKIMA CO WA	119 - A1
CLEAR LAKE SOUTH CAMPGROUND	SPIRAL BUTTE, YAKIMA CO WA	119 - B2
CLE ELUM RIVER CAMPGROUND	CLE ELUM LAKE, KITTITAS CO WA	111 - B3
CLIFF LAKE CAMPGROUND	BUCKEYE LAKE, DOUGLAS CO OR	226 - B2
CLIFF LAKE CAMPGROUND	DEVILS PEAK, KLAMATH CO OR	150 - B1
CLIFF LAKE SHELTER	THREE SISTERS WILDERNESS AREA, LANE CO OR	134 - C3
CLINE-CLARK CAMPGROUND	OAKRIDGE, LANE CO OR	142 - A1
CLINGER CAMPGROUND	DOG RIVER, HOOD RIVER CO OR	202 - C4
CLOUD CAP SADDLE CAMPGROUND	MOUNT HOOD NORTH, HOOD RIVER CO OR	202 - B4
CLOVERLEAF BEACH CAMPGROUND	INCHELIUM, STEVENS CO WA	106 - A3
COAL CREEK CAMPGROUND	CHINA FLAT, COOS CO OR	140 - C3
COAST CREEK SHELTER	SPRINGER MOUNTAIN, YAMHILL CO OR	125 - A2
CODWATER CAMPGROUND	TAFT MOUNTAIN, DOUGLAS CO OR	222 - A4
COHO CAMPGROUND	WYNOOCHEE LAKE, GRAYS HARBOR CO WA	109 - A2
COLD CREEK CAMPGROUND	DOLE, CLARK CO WA	193 - C4
COLDSPRING CAMPGROUND	HWY 3, BRITISH COLUMBIA	103 - C1
COLD SPRING CAMPGROUND	LONE BUTTE, SKAMANIA CO WA	118 - C3
COLD SPRINGS CAMPGROUND	MOUNT ADAMS EAST, YAKIMA CO WA	119 - A3
COLD SPRINGS CAMPGROUND	NFD RD 89, ADAMS CO ID	131 - C3
COLD SPRINGS CAMPGROUND	UNION PEAK, KLAMATH CO OR	227 - C5
COLONIAL CREEK CAMPGROUND	ROSS DAM, WHATCOM CO WA	103 - B2
COMMONWEALTH CAMPGROUND	SNOQUALMIE PASS, KING CO WA	111 - A2
COMPANY CREEK CAMPGROUND	STEHEKIN, CHELAN CO WA	103 - C3
CONTORTA POINT CAMPGROUND	COWHORN MOUNTAIN, KLAMATH CO OR	142 - B1
COPPER CREEK CAMPGROUND	EASTPORT, BOUNDARY CO ID	107 - C1
COPPERFIELD CAMPGROUND	ATHENA-HOLDMAN HWY, UMATILLA CO OR	129 - C1
COPPERFIELD CAMPGROUND	BAKER-COPPERFIELD HWY, BAKER CO OR	131 - A3
COPPER MINE BOTTOM CAMPGROUND	CHRISTMAS CREEK, JEFFERSON CO WA	108 - C1
CORRAL CREEK CAMPGROUND	GEARHART MOUNTAIN, LAKE CO OR	151 - C1
CORRAL CREEK CAMPGROUND	LAKE CHELAN, CHELAN CO WA	112 - A1
CORRIGAL SPRING CAMPGROUND	OFF BULL RUN TO BAKER RD, GRANT CO OR	137 - C1
COTTER CAMPGROUND	GRANGEVILLE EAST, IDAHO CO ID	123 - C3
COTTONWOOD CAMPGROUND	ANDERSON CREEK, JEFFERSON CO WA	169 - D5
COTTONWOOD CAMPGROUND	CONCONULLY WEST, OKANOGAN CO WA	104 - B2
COTTONWOOD CAMPGROUND	DEER RD, WHEELER CO OR	136 - B2
COTTONWOOD CAMPGROUND	OFF HWY 410, YAKIMA CO WA	240 - A7
COTTONWOOD MEADOW CAMPGROUND	COUGAR PEAK, LAKE CO OR	151 - C2
COUGAR CREEK CAMPGROUND	COUGAR PEAK, LAKE CO OR	151 - C2
COUGAR FLAT CAMPGROUND	OLD SCAB MOUNTAIN, YAKIMA CO WA	119 - B1
COUGAR ISLAND CAMPGROUND	PUMPKIN MOUNTAIN, WHATCOM CO WA	103 - B2
COUGAR ROCK CAMPGROUND	MOUNT RAINIER WEST, PIERCE CO WA	185 - B5
COUNCIL LAKE CAMPGROUND	EAST CANYON RIDGE, SKAMANIA CO WA	119 - A3
COVERDALE CAMPGROUND	UPPER MOUNTAIN RD, WALLOWA CO OR	131 - A3
COW CAMP CAMPGROUND	OFF LOOKOUT MOUNTAIN RD, DESCHUTES CO OR	216 - A7
COWICHAN RIVER CAMPGROUND	HWY 18, BRITISH COLUMBIA	101 - A1
COYOTE SPRING CAMPGROUND	BUCKHORN RD, WALLOWA CO OR	131 - A1
CRANE CREEK CAMPGROUND	OFF NFD RD 16, GRANT CO OR	137 - C2
CRANE PRAIRIE CAMPGROUND	S CENTURY RD, DESCHUTES CO OR	216 - B7
CRATER CREEK CAMPGROUND	HUNGRY MOUNTAIN, OKANOGAN CO WA	104 - A3
CRAWFISH LAKE CAMPGROUND	CRAWFISH LAKE, OKANOGAN CO WA	105 - A2
CRAWFISH SHELTER	FAIRVIEW PEAK, LANE CO OR	141 - C1
CRESCENT CREEK CAMPGROUNDS	ODELL BUTTE, KLAMATH CO OR	142 - C1
CRESCENT LAKE CAMPGROUND	BOUNDARY DAM, PEND OREILLE CO WA	106 - C1
CRIPPEN CAMPGROUND	BOWEN ISLAND, BRITISH COLUMBIA	93 - B3
CROWN ZELLERBACK CAMPGROUND	OREGON COAST HWY, DOUGLAS CO OR	214 - A6
CRYSTAL CREEK CAMPGROUND	PUGH MOUNTAIN, SNOHOMISH CO WA	103 - A3
CRYSTAL SPRINGS CAMPGROUND	STAMPEDE PASS, KITTITAS CO WA	111 - A3
CULTUS CREEK CAMPGROUND	LONE BUTTE, SKAMANIA CO WA	118 - C3
CULTUS LAKE CAMPGROUND	NFD RD 4635, DESCHUTES CO OR	216 - A7
CURLEW LAKE CAMPGROUND	REPUBLIC, FERRY CO WA	105 - B2
CURLY CREEK CAMPGROUND	BURNT PEAK, SKAMANIA CO WA	118 - C3
DAIRY CREEK CAMPGROUND	COLEMAN POINT, LAKE CO OR	151 - C1
DAIRY CREEK CAMPGROUND	LEE THOMAS CROSSING, LAKE CO OR	151 - C1
DAIRY POINT CAMPGROUND	COLEMAN POINT, LAKE CO OR	151 - C1
DAISY CAMPGROUND	DUNCAN RIDGE, OKANOGAN CO WA	104 - B1
DAM CAMPGROUND	ROCK CREEK RESERVOIR, WASCO CO OR	127 - A3
DANA YELVERTON SHELTER	OLD SNOWY MOUNTAIN, LEWIS CO WA	119 - A2
DAPHNE GROVE CAMPGROUND	ILLAHE, COOS CO OR	140 - B3
DASH POINT CAMPGROUND	5700 SW DASH POINT RD, FEDERAL WAY WA	182 - A1
DAVIS LAKE CAMPGROUND	BOYDS, FERRY CO WA	105 - C2
DEADHORSE CAMPGROUND	COLEMAN POINT, LAKE CO OR	151 - C1
DEAD HORSE LAKE CAMPGROUND	LEE THOMAS CROSSING, LAKE CO OR	151 - C1
DEARINGER CAMPGROUND	PRAIRIE MOUNTAIN, SKAGIT CO WA	103 - A3
DECEPTION CREEK CAMPGROUND	SCENIC, KING CO WA	111 - B1
DECEPTION FALLS CAMPGROUND	SCENIC, KING CO WA	111 - B2
DEEP CREEK CAMPGROUND	NAPLES, BOUNDARY CO ID	107 - B2
DEEP CREEK CAMPGROUND	NELSON RD, CROOK CO OR	136 - B2
DEEP CREEK CAMPGROUND	NFD RD 4015, LAKE CO OR	152 - A2
DEEP CREEK CAMPGROUND	PLAIN, CHELAN CO WA	111 - C1
DEER CREEK CAMPGROUND	OFF WHITNEY HWY, BAKER CO OR	138 - A1
DEER CREEK SUMMIT CAMPGROUND	MOUNT LEONA, FERRY CO WA	105 - C1
DEERHORN CAMPGROUND	UPPER MIDDLE FORK RD, GRANT CO OR	137 - C1
DEER LAKE SHELTER	BOGACHIEL PEAK, CLALLAM CO WA	109 - A1
DEER PARK CAMPGROUND	MAIDEN PEAK, CLALLAM CO WA	109 - B1
DEER POINT CAMPGROUND	LAKE CHELAN, CHELAN CO WA	112 - A1
DELP CREEK SHELTER	BIG FALL CREEK RD, LANE CO OR	134 - A3
DELTA CAMPGROUND	MCKENZIE RD, LANE CO OR	134 - B2
DEPRESSION LAKE CAMPGROUND	WELKER PEAK, WHATCOM CO WA	102 - C2
DE ROUX CAMPGROUND	MOUNT STUART, KITTITAS CO WA	111 - B2
DETILLION CAMPGROUND	MCCOY LAKE, LINCOLN CO WA	113 - C1
DEVILS ELBOW CAMPGROUND	POND PEAK, SHOSHONE CO ID	115 - C1
DEVILS FLAT CAMPGROUND	COW CREEK RD, DOUGLAS CO OR	141 - B3
DEVILS HALF ACRE MEADOW CAMPGROUND	BARLOW RD, HOOD RIVER CO OR	202 - B6
DEVILS MEADOW CAMPGROUND	GOVERNMENT CAMP, CLACKAMAS CO OR	201 - D5
DIAMOND LAKE CAMPGROUND	DIAMOND LAKE, DOUGLAS CO OR	223 - C6
DIAMOND LAKE TRAILER CAMP AREA	DIAMOND LAKE, DOUGLAS CO OR	223 - C6
DICKENSHEET CAMPGROUND	OUTLET BAY, BONNER CO ID	107 - A2
DICKEY CREEK CAMPGROUND	RED TOP MOUNTAIN, KITTITAS CO WA	111 - C3
DICK SPERRY CAMPGROUND	SILVERTON, SNOHOMISH CO WA	103 - A3
DIGIT POINT CAMPGROUND	MILLER LAKE, KLAMATH CO OR	142 - B2
DILLON FALLS CAMPGROUND	BENHAM FALLS, DESCHUTES CO OR	217 - A4
DIRT OVEN CAMPGROUND	SHORTY PEAK, BOUNDARY CO ID	107 - A1
DIRTYFACE CAMPGROUND	LAKE WENATCHEE, CHELAN CO WA	111 - C1
DIVIDE WELL CAMPGROUND	NFD RD 5320, UMATILLA CO OR	129 - A3
DIXIE CAMPGROUND	JOHN DAY-BURNS RD, GRANT CO OR	137 - C1
DOE CREEK CAMPGROUND	GOLDEN, JOSEPHINE CO OR	149 - A1
DOG LAKE CAMPGROUND	DOG LAKE, LAKE CO OR	151 - C2
DOG LAKE CAMPGROUND	SPIRAL BUTTE, YAKIMA CO WA	119 - A1
DOG PRAIRIE SHELTER	GARWOOD BUTTE, DOUGLAS CO OR	223 - B5
DOLLY VARDEN CAMPGOUND	MCGREGOR MOUNTAIN, CHELAN CO WA	103 - B3
DOLLY VARDEN CAMPGROUND	BIG FALL CREEK RD, LANE CO OR	134 - A3
DOLLY VISTA SHELTER	GAMMA PEAK, SNOHOMISH CO WA	103 - B3
DOMKE FALLS CAMPGROUND	LUCERNE, CHELAN CO WA	103 - C3
DOMKE LAKE CAMPGROUND	LUCERNE, CHELAN CO WA	103 - C3
DOSEWALLIPS CAMPGROUND	THE BROTHERS, JEFFERSON CO WA	109 - C1
DOSEWALLIPS STATE PARK CAMPGROUND	BRINNON, JEFFERSON CO WA	109 - C1
DOUGAN CREEK CAMPGROUND	BOBS MOUNTAIN, SKAMANIA CO WA	194 - A5
DOUGHERTY SPRING CAMPGROUND	BUCKHORN RD, WALLOWA CO OR	131 - A1
DOUGLAS FIR CAMPGROUND	GLACIER, WHATCOM CO WA	102 - C1
DOVE CREEK CAMPGROUND	OFF NFD RD 454, WALLOWA CO OR	131 - B3
DOVRE CAMPGROUND	TRASK MOUNTAIN, TILLAMOOK CO OR	125 - A2
DOWNEY CREEK CAMPGROUND	DOWNEY MOUNTAIN, SNOHOMISH CO WA	103 - B3
DREWS CREEK CAMPGROUND	FITZWATER POINT, LAKE CO OR	151 - C2
DRIFT CAMPGROUND	METOLIUS BENCH, JEFFERSON CO OR	135 - A1
DRIFT CREEK SHELTER	OFF RISLEY CREEK RD, LINCOLN CO OR	209 - C1
DRIFT FENCE CAMPGROUND	NFD RD 52, UMATILLA CO OR	129 - B3
DRIFTWOOD CAMPGROUND	OFF OREGON COAST HWY, LANE CO OR	214 - A5
DRIFTWOOD CAMPGROUND	THREE CREEKS LAKE RD, DESCHUTES CO OR	216 - C1
DRIFTWOOD II CAMPGROUND	OFF OREGON COAST HWY, LANE CO OR	214 - A5
DRY CREEK CAMPGROUND	CLE ELUM LAKE, KITTITAS CO WA	111 - B3
DRY CREEK CAMPGROUND	DRY CREEK RD, JEFFERSON CO OR	208 - B2
DRY CREEK CAMPGROUND	SUN TOP, PIERCE CO WA	111 - A3
DUCKABUSH SHELTER	MOUNT STEEL, JEFFERSON CO WA	109 - B2
DUCK LAKE CAMPGROUND	OFF DUCK CREEK RD, WALLOWA CO OR	131 - A3
DUNGENESS FORKS CAMPGROUND	MOUNT ZION, CLALLAM CO WA	109 - C1
DUNGENESS RECREATION AREA CAMPGROUND	WEST OF DUNGENESS, CLALLAM CO WA	166 - A5
DUTCH CREEK SHELTER	BULL OF THE WOODS, CLACKAMAS CO OR	126 - B3
EAGLE CREEK CAMPGROUND	BONNEVILLE DAM, NORTH BONNEVILLE WA	194 - C6
EAGLE CREEK FOREST CAMPGROUND	NFD RD 77, BAKER CO OR	130 - C3
EAGLE FORKS FOREST CAMPGROUND	EAGLE CREEK DR, BAKER CO OR	130 - C3
EAGLE ROCK CAMPGROUND	ILLAHEE ROCK, DOUGLAS CO OR	222 - B3
EARLY WINTERS CAMPGROUND	MAZAMA, OKANOGAN CO WA	104 - A2
EAST CARTER CAMPGROUND	OREGON COAST HWY, DOUGLAS CO OR	214 - A5
EAST DAVIS LAKE CAMPGROUND	HAMNER BUTTE, KLAMATH CO OR	142 - C1
EAST FORK SHELTER	COLONEL BOB, GRAYS HARBOR CO WA	109 - A2
EAST LAKE CAMPGROUND	NEWBERRY CRATER RD, DESCHUTES CO OR	143 - B1
EAST LEMOLO CAMPGROUND	LEMOLO LAKE, DOUGLAS CO OR	223 - C3
EASTSIDE CAMPGROUND	OFF HANCOCK RD, GEM CO ID	139 - C2
EAST SIDE BUCK CREEK CAMPGROUND	HUCKLEBERRY MOUNTAIN, SNOHOMISH CO WA	103 - A3
ECHO CAMPGROUND	SOUTH FORK RD, LANE CO OR	134 - B3
EDEN VALLEY CAMPGROUND	EDEN VALLEY, COOS CO OR	140 - C3
EDGEWATER CAMPGROUND	METALINE, PEND OREILLE CO WA	106 - B1
EEL CREEK CAMPGROUND	LAKESIDE, COOS CO OR	218 - B4
EIGHTMILE CAMPGROUND	CASHMERE MOUNTAIN, CHELAN CO WA	111 - C2
EIGHTMILE LAKE CAMPGROUND	CASHMERE MOUNTAIN, CHELAN CO WA	111 - C2
ELBOW LAKE CAMPGROUND	LA FLEUR LAKE, FERRY CO WA	105 - C2
ELBOW LAKE CAMPGROUND	OREGON COAST HWY, DOUGLAS CO OR	214 - A7
ELDORADO CAMPGROUND	E CAMP CREEK RD, BAKER CO OR	138 - A2
ELEPHANT ROCK CAMPGROUND	LUCERNE, CHELAN CO WA	103 - C3
ELK CAMPGROUND	NFD RD 32, UMATILLA CO OR	130 - A1
ELK CREEK CAMPGROUND	CHINA FLAT, COOS CO OR	140 - C3
ELK CREEK CAMPGROUND	NFD RD 16, GRANT CO OR	137 - C2
ELK FALLS CREEK CAMPGROUND	CHINA FLAT, COOS CO OR	140 - C3
ELK LAKE CAMPGROUND	CASCADE LAKES HWY, DESCHUTES CO OR	216 - A4
ELK LAKE CAMPGROUND	OFF BREITENBUSH RD, MARION CO OR	134 - B1
EMERALD CREEK CAMPGROUND	CLARKIA, SHOSHONE CO ID	115 - B3
EMIGRANT CAMPGROUND	EMIGRANT CREEK RD, HARNEY CO OR	137 - A3
EMILE SHELTER	TAFT MOUNTAIN, DOUGLAS CO OR	141 - C2
EMORY CREEK CAMPGROUND	HWY 1, BRITISH COLUMBIA	95 - A2
ENGLISH CAMPSITE	SAN JUAN CO WA	101 - C2
ENGLISHMAN FALLS CAMPGROUND	OFF HWY 19, BRITISH COLUMBIA	93 - A3
ENGLISHMAN RIVER FALLS CAMPGROUND	HWY 4, BRITISH COLUMBIA	92 - C3
ERICKSONS BAY CAMPGROUND	ALLENS BAY, CLALLAM CO WA	162 - B5
ERRIN CAMPGROUND	HOLLAND POINT, LANE CO OR	142 - A1
EVANS CAMPGROUND	MARCUS, STEVENS CO WA	106 - A2
EVERGREEN CAMPGROUND	UPPER MOUNTAIN RD, WALLOWA CO OR	131 - A3
EVERGREEN CAMPGROUND	US HWY 95, ADAMS CO ID	131 - C3
FAIRHOLM CAMPGROUND	OLYMPIC HWY, CLALLAM CO WA	164 - A6
FAIRVIEW CAMPGROUND	COLLIER BUTTE, CURRY CO OR	228 - D7
FAIRY SHELTER	STEAMBOAT, DOUGLAS CO OR	222 - A4
FALL CREEK CAMPGROUND	CAPITOL PEAK, THURSTON CO WA	184 - A1
FALL CREEK CAMPGROUND	MACE MOUNTAIN, DOUGLAS CO OR	141 - C2
FALL RIVER CAMPGROUND	PISTOL BUTTE, DESCHUTES CO OR	142 - C1
FALLS CREEK CAMPGROUND	DOE MOUNTAIN, OKANOGAN CO WA	104 - A2
FALLS VIEW CAMPGROUND	MOUNT TOWNSEND, JEFFERSON CO WA	109 - C1
FAN CREEK CAMPGROUND	TRASK MOUNTAIN, TILLAMOOK CO OR	125 - A2
FERRY LAKE CAMPGROUND	SWAN LAKE, FERRY CO WA	105 - B2

FEATURE NAME	City State	Page-Grid
FIFTEEN MILE CAMPGROUND	FLAG POINT, WASCO CO OR	202 - D5
FIFTEENMILE SHELTER	HUNGER MOUNTAIN, CLALLAM CO WA	108 - C1
FILLONGLEY CAMPGROUND	HWY 19, BRITISH COLUMBIA	92 - B2
FINNER CREEK CAMPGROUND	SCHAEFER LAKE, CHELAN CO WA	111 - C1
FINNEY CREEK SHELTER	FINNEY PEAK, SKAGIT CO WA	102 - C2
FISH CREEK CAMPGROUND	BEDFORD POINT, CLACKAMAS CO OR	126 - B3
FISH CREEK CAMPGROUND	FISH CREEK DESERT, DOUGLAS CO OR	222 - D5
FISH CREEK MEADOW CAMPGROUND	GOODWIN MEADOWS, IDAHO CO ID	123 - C3
FISH CREEK SHELTER	FISH MOUNTAIN, DOUGLAS CO OR	222 - D7
FISH CREEK SHELTER	LUCERNE, CHELAN CO WA	103 - C3
FISH LAKE CAMPGROUND	BUCKEYE LAKE, DOUGLAS CO OR	222 - C7
FISH LAKE CAMPGROUND	FISH LAKE RD, HARNEY CO OR	145 - C3
FISH LAKE CAMPGROUND	PEER-HOPE RD, BAKER CO OR	131 - A3
FISH LAKE CAMPGROUND	THE CRADLE, KITTITAS CO WA	111 - B2
FISH POND CAMPGROUND	PLAIN, CHELAN CO WA	111 - C1
FIVEMILE SHELTER	NFD RD 5087, LINCOLN CO OR	206 - C7
FLAPJACK SHELTER	HUNGER MOUNTAIN, CLALLAM CO WA	108 - C1
FLAT CAMPGROUND	LEWIS BUTTE, OKANOGAN CO WA	104 - A2
FLICK CREEK CAMPGROUND	SUN MOUNTAIN, CHELAN CO WA	103 - C3
FLODELLE CAMPGROUND	LAKE GILLETTE, STEVENS CO WA	106 - B2
FLUMET FLAT CAMPGROUND	SQUAW LAKES, JACKSON CO OR	149 - B2
FOGGY DEW CAMPGROUND	HUNGRY MOUNTAIN, OKANOGAN CO WA	104 - A3
FOPIAN CAMPGROUND	NFD RD 16, BAKER CO OR	137 - C2
FORLORN LAKES CAMPGROUND	GIFFORD PEAK, SKAMANIA CO WA	118 - C3
FOSS RIVER CAMPGROUND	SKYKOMISH, KING CO WA	111 - B2
FOSTER BAR CAMPGROUND	ILLAHE, CURRY CO OR	148 - B1
FOUR CORNERS CAMPGROUND	UKIAH-HILGARD HWY, UMATILLA CO OR	129 - C3
FOURMILE CAMPGROUND	CUMMINS PEAK RD, LINCOLN CO OR	209 - A4
FOURMILE LAKE CAMPGROUND	LAKE OF THE WOODS NORTH, KLAMATH CO OR	150 - B1
FOX CREEK CAMPGROUND	SILVER FALLS, CHELAN CO WA	111 - C1
FRANCIS CREEK CAMPSITE	KIMTA PEAK, JEFFERSON CO WA	109 - A2
FRAZIER CAMPGROUND	OFF NFD RD 58, GRANT CO OR	136 - C2
FRAZIER CAMPGROUND	UKIAH-HILGARD HWY, UMATILLA CO OR	129 - C3
FRAZIER FORK CAMPGROUND	HIGH ROCK, CLACKAMAS CO OR	126 - B3
FRAZIER TURNAROUND CAMPGROUND	HIGH ROCK, CLACKAMAS CO OR	126 - C3
FRED MCNEIL CAMPGROUND	BULL RUN LAKE, CLACKAMAS CO OR	201 - D4
FREEMAN CREEK CAMPGROUND	AHSAHKA, CLEARWATER CO ID	123 - B1
FRENCH BEACH CAMPGROUND	BRITISH COLUMBIA	101 - A2
FRENCH CREEK CAMPGROUND	CHIWAUKUM MOUNTAINS, CHELAN CO WA	111 - B2
FRENCH GULCH CAMPGROUND	SQUAW LAKES, JACKSON CO OR	149 - B2
FROG LAKE CAMPGROUND	WAPINITIA PASS, WASCO CO OR	202 - A7
GATE CREEK CAMPGROUND	MCLEOD MOUNTAIN, OKANOGAN CO WA	104 - A2
GATTON CREEK CAMPGROUND	LAKE QUINAULT EAST, GRAYS HARBOR CO WA	109 - A2
GERTRUDE SHELTER	BEARBONES MOUNTAIN, LANE CO OR	142 - A1
GLACIER VIEW CAMPGROUND	LAKE WENATCHEE, CHELAN CO WA	111 - C1
GODMAN CAMPGROUND	GODMAN SPRING, COLUMBIA CO WA	122 - B3
GOLD BASIN CAMPGROUND	MALLARDY RIDGE, SNOHOMISH CO WA	102 - C3
GOLD CREEK CAMPGROUND	FERN CRES, MAPLE RIDGE BC	94 - B3
GOLD CREEK SHELTER	MOUNT ZION, CLALLAM CO WA	109 - C1
GONE CREEK CAMPGROUND	TIMOTHY LAKE, CLACKAMAS CO OR	126 - C3
GOODELL CAMPGROUND	MOUNT TRIUMPH, WHATCOM CO WA	103 - B2
GOOSE CREEK CAMPGROUND	PLAIN, CHELAN CO WA	111 - C1
GOOSE LAKE CAMPGROUND	GIFFORD PEAK, SKAMANIA CO WA	118 - C3
GORDON BAY PROVINCIAL CAMPGROUND	BRITISH COLUMBIA	100 - C1
GORGE CAMPGROUND	MOUNT ZION, CLALLAM CO WA	109 - C1
GRAHAM HARBOR CAMPGROUND	BIG GOAT MOUNTAIN, CHELAN CO WA	104 - A3
GRANDE RONDE LAKE CAMPGROUND	ANTHONY LAKES RD, UNION CO OR	130 - A3
GRANDVIEW CAMPGROUND	OFF NFD RD 3120, UNION CO OR	130 - A2
GRASSHOPPER MEADOWS CAMPGROUND	MOUNT DAVID, CHELAN CO WA	111 - B1
GRASS LAKE CAMPGROUND	DEVILS PEAK, KLAMATH CO OR	150 - B1
GRASS LAKE CAMPGROUND NUMBER 2	DEVILS PEAK, KLAMATH CO OR	150 - B1
GRAVES CREEK CAMPGROUND	MOUNT HOQUIAM, JEFFERSON CO WA	109 - B2
GREEN CANYON CAMPGROUND	RHODODENDRON, CLACKAMAS CO OR	201 - C6
GREYBALL SHELTER	COPPER MOUNTAIN, WHATCOM CO WA	103 - A1
GREY CREEK CAMPGROUND	DARLAND MOUNTAIN, YAKIMA CO WA	119 - B2
GROUP CAMPGROUND	MOUNT TRIUMPH, WHATCOM CO WA	103 - A2
GROUSE CAMPGROUND	OLD GOOSE LAKE RD, ADAMS CO ID	251 - C2

FEATURE NAME	City State	Page-Grid
GROUSE CREEK CAMPGROUND	CHIKAMIN CREEK, CHELAN CO WA	111 - C1
GROUSE GAP SHELTER	MOUNT ASHLAND, JACKSON CO OR	234 - C6
GROUSE MOUNTAIN CAMPGROUND	NFD RD 5900, CHELAN CO WA	112 - A1
GULL POINT CAMPGROUND	DAVIS MOUNTAIN, DESCHUTES CO OR	142 - C1
HAAG COVE CAMPGROUND	BANGS MOUNTAIN, FERRY CO WA	105 - C2
HAGER LAKE SHELTER	PACKWOOD LAKE, LEWIS CO WA	119 - A2
HALFWAY FLAT CAMPGROUND	CLIFFDELL, YAKIMA CO WA	119 - B1
HALFWAY HOUSE CAMPSITE	KIMTA PEAK, JEFFERSON CO WA	109 - A2
HALFWAY SPRING CAMPGROUND	SILVER FALLS, CHELAN CO WA	111 - C1
HAMAKER CAMPGROUND	HAMAKER BUTTE, DOUGLAS CO OR	227 - A1
HAMBONE SPRINGS CAMPGROUND	HIGH ROCK, CLACKAMAS CO OR	126 - C3
HAMMA HAMMA CAMPGROUND	HAMMA HAMMA RD, MASON CO WA	173 - A2
HAMPTON CAMPGROUND	HWY 3, BRITISH COLUMBIA	103 - C1
HAMPTON CAMPGROUND	WILLAMETTE HWY, LANE CO OR	134 - A3
HAND LAKE SHELTER	MCKENZIE HWY, LANE CO OR	134 - C2
HANDY SPRING CAMPGROUND	NFD RD 5900, CHELAN CO WA	112 - A1
HANEY MEADOW CAMPGROUND	BLEWETT PASS, KITTITAS CO WA	238 - B6
HANGING TREE CAMPGROUND	NILE, YAKIMA CO WA	119 - B1
HANNEGAN CAMPGROUND	MOUNT SEFRIT, WHATCOM CO WA	103 - A1
HAPPY FOUR SHELTER	MOUNT TOM, JEFFERSON CO WA	109 - A1
HARRIS BEACH STATE PARK CAMPGROUND	BROOKINGS, BROOKINGS OR	232 - C5
HATCHERY CAMPGROUND	LUCERNE, CHELAN CO WA	103 - C3
HATCHERY RV CAMPGROUND	OHANAPECOSH HOT SPRINGS, LEWIS CO WA	185 - D7
HAUSE CREEK CAMPGROUND	TIETON BASIN, YAKIMA CO WA	119 - B1
HAYSTACK RESERVOIR CAMPGROUND	OPAL CITY, JEFFERSON CO OR	213 - A1
HAZARD CAMPGROUND	HAZARD LAKE RD, IDAHO CO ID	131 - C2
HEAD OF THE RIVER CAMPGROUND	FUEGO MOUNTAIN, KLAMATH CO OR	151 - A1
HEART LAKE SHELTER	MOUNT CARRIE, CLALLAM CO WA	109 - A1
HEART OF THE HILLS CAMPGROUND	HEART OF THE HILLS PKWY, CLALLAM CO WA	165 - B7
HEBO LAKE CAMPGROUND	HEBO, TILLAMOOK CO OR	197 - C6
HELLIWELL CAMPGROUND	BRITISH COLUMBIA	92 - B2
HEMLOCK LAKE CAMPGROUND	PELICAN BUTTE, KLAMATH CO OR	150 - B1
HEMLOCK LAKE CAMPGROUND	QUARTZ MOUNTAIN, DOUGLAS CO OR	222 - A5
HEMLOCK MEADOW CAMPGROUND	QUARTZ MOUNTAIN, DOUGLAS CO OR	222 - A5
HEMPLE CREEK CAMPGROUND	MALLARDY RIDGE, SNOHOMISH CO WA	102 - C3
HIDDEN CAMPGROUND	UPPER MOUNTAIN RD, WALLOWA CO OR	131 - A3
HIDDEN BEACH CAMPGROUND	MOON MOUNTAIN, FERRY CO WA	105 - C3
HIDEAWAY LAKE CAMPGROUND	MOUNT MITCHELL, CLACKAMAS CO OR	126 - B3
HIGH BRIDGE CAMPGROUND	MCGREGOR MOUNTAIN, CHELAN CO WA	103 - C3
HIGH ROCK CAMPGROUND	SAWTOOTH RIDGE, LEWIS CO WA	185 - A6
HIGH ROCK SPRING CAMPGROUND	HIGH ROCK, CLACKAMAS CO OR	126 - C3
HILL CAMPGROUND	BAYVIEW, KOOTENAI CO ID	245 - C1
HOH CAMPGROUND	OWL MOUNTAIN, JEFFERSON CO WA	109 - A1
HOH OX BOW CAMPGROUND	WINFIELD CREEK, JEFFERSON CO WA	108 - C1
HOLDEN CAMPGROUND	HOLDEN, CHELAN CO WA	103 - C3
HOLLYWOOD POINT CAMPGROUND	OFF HANCOCK RD, GEM CO ID	139 - C2
HOLMAN CAMPGROUND	PASAYTEN PEAK, OKANOGAN CO WA	103 - C1
HOMESTEAD CAMPGROUND	NEWMAN LAKE, SPOKANE CO WA	247 - B1
HOME SWEET HOME SHELTER	MOUNT STEEL, JEFFERSON CO WA	109 - B2
HONEYMOON CAMPGROUND	SWEETGRASS BUTTE, OKANOGAN CO WA	104 - A2
HONEYSUCKLE CAMPGROUND	SKITWISH PEAK, KOOTENAI CO ID	245 - D6
HOOD VIEW CAMPGROUND	TIMOTHY LAKE, CLACKAMAS CO OR	126 - C3
HOPS HILL CAMPGROUND	MONTE CRISTO, SNOHOMISH CO WA	111 - A1
HORNE LAKE CAVES CAMPGROUND	HWY 19, BRITISH COLUMBIA	92 - B3
HORSESHOE BEND CAMPGROUND	STEAMBOAT, DOUGLAS CO OR	222 - B3
HORSESHOE COVE CAMPGROUND	WELKER PEAK, WHATCOM CO WA	103 - A2
HOT SPRINGS CAMPGROUND	NEWBERRY CRATER RD, DESCHUTES CO OR	143 - B1
HOT SPRINGS CAMPGROUND	OFF BLM RD 61064, LAKE CO OR	152 - C1
HOUR CREEK CAMPGROUND	DAVIS PEAK, KITTITAS CO WA	111 - B2
HOZOMEEN CAMPGROUND	HOZOMEEN MOUNTAIN, WHATCOM CO WA	103 - B1
HUCKLEBERRY CAMPGROUND	OFF NFD RD 105, ADAMS CO ID	131 - B3
HUCKLEBERRY FLAT CAMPGROUND	MARBLE CREEK, SHOSHONE CO ID	115 - C2
HUCKLEBERRY LAKE CAMPGROUND	ABBOTT BUTTE, DOUGLAS CO OR	226 - B4
HUELSDONK CAMPGROUND	SPRUCE MOUNTAIN, JEFFERSON CO WA	108 - C1
HUMBUG CAMPGROUND	BREITENBUSH RD, MARION CO OR	134 - B1
HUMBUG MOUNTAIN CAMPGROUND	PORT ORFORD, CURRY CO OR	224 - B7
HUNTER CAMPGROUND	CASTLE ROCK RD, MALHEUR CO OR	138 - A3

FEATURE NAME	City State	Page-Grid
HURRYON CAMP	HAMAKER BUTTE, DOUGLAS CO OR	227 - A1
HYAK SHELTER	SLIDE PEAK, CLALLAM CO WA	109 - A1
HYATT LAKE CAMPGROUND	HYATT RESERVOIR, JACKSON CO OR	150 - A2
ICE CAVE CAMPGROUND	LITTLE HUCKLEBERRY MTN, SKAMANIA CO WA	118 - C3
ICE CREEK SHELTER	SASKA PEAK, CHELAN CO WA	103 - C3
IDA CREEK CAMPGROUND	CASHMERE MOUNTAIN, CHELAN CO WA	111 - C2
IDLEWILD CAMPGROUND	JOHN DAY-BURNS HWY, HARNEY CO OR	137 - B3
IKE KINSWA CAMPGROUND	MAYFIELD LAKE, LEWIS CO WA	118 - A2
ILLAHE CAMPGROUND	ILLAHE, CURRY CO OR	148 - B1
INDEPENDENCE CAMPGROUND	CATHEDRAL PEAK, SHOSHONE CO ID	115 - C1
INDIAN CREEK CAMPGROUND	GOLD BEACH, CURRY CO OR	228 - A5
INDIAN CREEK CAMPGROUND	PRIEST LAKE SE, BONNER CO ID	107 - A2
INDIAN CREEK CAMPGROUND	RIMROCK LAKE, YAKIMA CO WA	119 - B1
INDIAN CREEK SHELTER	COPPER MOUNTAIN, WHATCOM CO WA	103 - A1
INDIAN FLAT CAMPGROUND	OLD SCAB MOUNTAIN, YAKIMA CO WA	119 - B1
INDIAN HENRY CAMPGROUND	FISH CREEK MOUNTAIN, CLACKAMAS CO OR	126 - B3
INDIAN HOLE CAMPGROUND	MORTON, LEWIS CO WA	118 - A2
INDIAN SPRINGS CAMPGROUND	OFF NFD RD 16, GRANT CO OR	137 - B2
INDIAN SPRINGS CAMPGROUND	WAHTUM LAKE, HOOD RIVER CO OR	201 - D1
INDIGO LAKE CAMPGROUND	COWHORN MOUNTAIN, DOUGLAS CO OR	223 - D1
INLET CAMPGROUND	LEMOLO LAKE, DOUGLAS CO OR	223 - C3
IPSUT CREEK CAMPGROUND	MOWICH LAKE, PIERCE CO WA	185 - B1
IRISH AND TAYLOR CAMPGROUND	OFF CANYON RD, LANE CO OR	134 - B3
IRISHMANS CAMPGROUND	COX FLAT, LAKE CO OR	151 - C2
IRON CREEK CAMPGROUND	GREENHORN BUTTES, LEWIS CO WA	118 - C2
IRON GATE CAMPGROUND	HORSESHOE BASIN, OKANOGAN CO WA	104 - B1
ISLAND CAMPGROUND	KING MOUNTAIN, YAKIMA CO WA	119 - A3
ISLAND LAKE CAMPGROUND	PELICAN BUTTE, KLAMATH CO OR	150 - B1
ISLAND SHELTER	STEAMBOAT MOUNTAIN, SKAMANIA CO WA	118 - C3
JACK LAKE CAMPGROUND	OFF JACK LAKE RD, JEFFERSON CO OR	211 - A1
JACKMAN PARK CAMPGROUND	STEENS MOUNTAIN LOOP RD, HARNEY CO OR	153 - C1
JACKSON CREEK CAMPGROUND	WILLIAMSON RIVER RD, KLAMATH CO OR	143 - A3
JAMES CREEK SHELTER	THREE SISTERS WILDERNESS AREA, LANE CO OR	216 - A2
JINGLE POT CAMPSITE	OFF HWY 19, BRITISH COLUMBIA	93 - A3
JOAQUIN MILLER CAMPGROUND	JOHN DAY-BURNS HWY, HARNEY CO OR	137 - B3
JOEMMA BEACH CAMPGROUND	BAY RD KPS, PIERCE CO WA	180 - D3
JOHNNY CREEK CAMPGROUND	CASHMERE MOUNTAIN, CHELAN CO WA	111 - C2
JONES CREEK CAMPGROUND	LARCH MOUNTAIN, CLARK CO WA	193 - C5
JORDAN CREEK CAMPGROUND	JORDAN CREEK, SHOSHONE CO ID	115 - C1
JUBILEE LAKE CAMPGROUND	NFD RD 63, UNION CO OR	130 - A1
JULY CREEK CAMPGROUND	LAKE QUINAULT EAST, GRAYS HARBOR CO WA	109 - A2
JUNGLE CREEK CAMPSITE	MOUNT CLIFTY, KITTITAS CO WA	111 - B3
JUNIOR POINT CAMPGROUND	NFD RD 5900, CHELAN CO WA	112 - A1
JUSTRITE CAMPGROUND	NFD RD 9, WASHINGTON CO ID	139 - A1
KACHESS CAMPGROUND	KACHESS LAKE, KITTITAS CO WA	111 - A2
KALALOCH CAMPGROUND	OFF HIGHWAY 101, JEFFERSON CO WA	172 - A1
KAMLOOPS ISLAND CAMPGROUND	MARCUS, FERRY CO WA	106 - A2
KOA ASHLAND	5310 HWY 66, JACKSON CO OR	234 - D4
KOA ASTORIA/SEASIDE	1100 RIDGE RD, WARRENTON WA	188 - B1
KOA BANDON-PORT ORFORD	46612 HWY 101, CURRY CO OR	224 - B3
KOA BAY CENTER WILLAPA BAY	BAY CENTER RD, PACIFIC CO WA	183 - C7
KOA BURLINGTON	646 N GREEN RD, SKAGIT CO WA	161 - B5
KOA CAMPGROUND	298 OREGON AV, LANE CO OR	215 - C4
KOA CAMPGROUND	33775 OAKVILLE RD, LINN CO OR	207 - B6
KOA CAMPGROUND	HWY 20, OKANOGAN CO WA	104 - A3
KOA CASCADE LOCKS	STAR RTE BOX 660, CASCADE LOCKS OR	194 - D5
KOA CHEHALIS/HWY 12 EAST	118 US HWY 12, LEWIS CO WA	187 - D2
KOA COEUR D'ALENE	LANE, KOOTENAI CO ID	248 - C1
KOA COEUR D'ALENE NORTH HAYDEN LAKE	HAYDEN, KOOTENAI CO ID	245 - B4
KOA CRESCENT CITY	4241 HWY 101 N, DEL NORTE CO CA	148 - B3
KOA ELLENSBURG	OFF CANYON RD, KITTITAS CO WA	241 - B6
KOA ELLENSBURG	TEANAWAY BUTTE, KITTITAS CO WA	241 - B5
KOA GRANTS PASS/REDWOOD HWY	13370 REDWOOD HWY, JOSEPHINE CO OR	233 - B2
KOA GRANTS PASS/SUNNY VALLEY	140 OLD STAGE RD, JOSEPHINE CO OR	229 - B2
KOA ILWACO	HWY 101, ILWACO WA	186 - A6
KOA KLAMATH FALLS	3435 SHASTA WY, KLAMATH FALLS OR	338 - G9
KOA LEAVENWORTH/WENATCHEE	OFF HWY 2, CHELAN CO WA	238 - A1

FEATURE NAME	City State	Page-Grid
KOA LINCOLN CITY	5298 NE PARK LN, LINCOLN CO OR	203 - B4
KOA LYNDEN	E BADGER RD, LYNDEN WA	102 - B1
KOA MADRAS/CULVER	2435 JERICHO LN, JEFFERSON CO OR	212 - D1
KOA MEDFORD/GOLD HILL	BLACKWELL RD & HWY 234, JACKSON CO OR	230 - B6
KOA OREGON DUNES	4135 OREGON COAST HWY, COOS CO OR	218 - B5
KOA PORT ANGELES/SEQUIM	OBRIEN RD, CLALLAM CO WA	165 - D6
KOA SISTERS/BEND	67667 MCKENZIE-BEND HWY, DESCHUTES CO OR	212 - A5
KOA SPOKANE	3025 N BARKER RD, SPOKANE WA	351 - E5
KOA SWEET HOME/FOSTER LAKE	6191 SANTIAM HWY, LINN CO OR	134 - A2
KOA VANCOUVER	40TH AV & HWY 99A, DISTRICT OF SURREY BC	158 - A1
KOA VANTAGE	VANTAGE HWY, KITTITAS CO WA	120 - B1
KOA VICTORIA WEST	TRANS CANADA HWY, BRITISH COLUMBIA	159 - A5
KOA WALDPORT/ALSEA BAY	OREGON COAST HWY, LINCOLN CO OR	328 - C3
KOA YAKIMA	1500 KEYS RD, YAKIMA CO WA	243 - C7
KANASKAT-PALMER CAMPGROUND	KING CO WA	110 - C3
KANER FLAT CAMPGROUND	MOUNT CLIFTY, KITTITAS CO WA	111 - B3
KEENIG CAMPGROUND	JORDAN CREEK, TILLAMOOK CO OR	125 - A1
KELLER CREEK CAMPGROUND	YACHATS RIVER RD, LINCOLN CO OR	209 - B4
KELLOGG SILVER VALLEY CAMPGROUND	KOA BOX 949, SHOSHONE CO ID	115 - C2
KELSAY VALLEY TRAILHEAD CAMPGROUND	TOLO MOUNTAIN, DOUGLAS CO OR	223 - D3
KENTUCKY ALLEYNE CAMPGROUND	HWY 5A, BRITISH COLUMBIA	95 - C1
KERR CAMPGROUND	CONCONULLY WEST, OKANOGAN CO WA	104 - B2
KESTREL CAMPGROUND	BAYVIEW, KOOTENAI CO ID	245 - C1
KETTLE FALLS CAMPGROUND	KETTLE FALLS, STEVENS CO WA	106 - A2
KETTLE RIVER CAMPGROUND	MARCUS, FERRY CO WA	106 - A2
KIAHANIE CAMPGROUND	CANYON RD, LANE CO OR	134 - B3
KIAWANIS CAMPGROUND	NFD RD 9, WASHINGTON CO ID	139 - A1
KILLEN CREEK CAMPGROUND	GREEN MOUNTAIN, SKAMANIA CO WA	119 - A2
KIN BEACH CAMPGROUND	BRITISH COLUMBIA	92 - B2
KINGSLEY CAMPGROUND	KINGSLEY RD, HOOD RIVER CO OR	195 - B6
KINNIKINNICK CAMPGROUND	MOUNT HOOD NORTH, HOOD RIVER CO OR	202 - B3
KINZEL LAKE CAMPGROUND	GOVERNMENT CAMP, CLACKAMAS CO OR	201 - D7
KIRKLAND CAMPGROUND	E OF ENTRPRSE-LEWISTN HWY, WALLOWA CO OR	130 - C1
KIT PRICE CAMPGROUND	GRIZZLY MOUNTAIN, SHOSHONE CO ID	115 - C1
KLAHANIE CAMPGROUND	READE HILL, CLALLAM CO WA	169 - D1
KLAHOWA CAMPGROUND	SNIDER PEAK, CLALLAM CO WA	163 - C6
KLICKITAT SHELTER	RISLEY CREEK RD, LINCOLN CO OR	209 - D1
KLIPCHUCK CAMPGROUND	SILVER STAR MOUNTAIN, OKANOGAN CO WA	103 - C2
KLOOTCHIE CREEK CAMPGROUND	TILLAMOOK HEAD, CLATSOP CO OR	188 - B7
KNEBAL SPRING CAMPGROUND	FIVEMILE BUTTE, WASCO CO OR	202 - D3
KNUPPENBURG LAKE CAMPGROUND	WHITE PASS, LEWIS CO WA	119 - A2
KULSHAN CAMPGROUND	WELKER PEAK, WHATCOM CO WA	102 - C2
KUM BACK SHELTER	BURNT PEAK, SKAMANIA CO WA	118 - C3
LADD CREEK CAMPGROUND	BULL RUN LAKE, HOOD RIVER CO OR	202 - A3
LAFFERTY CAMPGROUND	NFD RD 2, ADAMS CO ID	131 - B3
LAGOON CAMPGROUND	OFF OREGON COAST HWY, LANE CO OR	214 - A5
LAKE CREEK CAMPGROUND	POE MOUNTAIN, CHELAN CO WA	111 - B1
LAKE CREEK CAMPGROUND	SILVER FALLS, CHELAN CO WA	111 - C1
LAKE ELLEN CAMPGROUND	BANGS MOUNTAIN, FERRY CO WA	105 - C2
LAKE FORK CAMPGROUND	NORTH PINE CREEK RD, BAKER CO OR	131 - A3
LAKE IN THE WOODS CAMPGROUND	QUARTZ MOUNTAIN, DOUGLAS CO OR	141 - C2
LAKE LEO CAMPGROUND	IONE, PEND OREILLE CO WA	106 - B2
LAKE LOVELY WATER REC AREA CAMPGROUND	LK LOVELY WATER REC AREA, BRITISH COLUMBIA	93 - B2
LAKE MARIE CAMPGROUND	WINCHESTER BAY, DOUGLAS CO OR	218 - C2
LAKE PLEASENT	24025 BOTHELL EVERETT HWY, BOTHELL WA	171 - C6
LAKE SELMAC CAMPGROUND	LAKESHORE DR, JOSEPHINE CO OR	233 - B2
LAKE THOMAS CAMPGROUND	LAKE GILLETTE, STEVENS CO WA	106 - B2
LAKEVIEW PARK CAMPGROUND	HIGHWAY 18, BRITISH COLUMBIA	100 - C1
LAKE WENATCHEE CAMPGROUND	LAKE WENATCHEE, CHELAN CO WA	111 - C1
LANE CREEK CAMPGROUND	UKIAH-HILGARD HWY, UMATILLA CO OR	129 - B3
LARCH LAKE CAMPGROUND	SASKA PEAK, CHELAN CO WA	103 - C3
LAST CHANCE CAMPGROUND	OLD GOOSE LAKE RD, ADAMS CO ID	251 - B3
LATGOWE COVE CAMPGROUND	SQUAW LAKES, JACKSON CO OR	149 - B2
LAVA CAMPGROUND	HAMNER BUTTE, KLAMATH CO OR	142 - C1
LAVA CAST FOREST CAMPGROUND	LAVA CAST FOREST, DESCHUTES CO OR	217 - C7
LAVA FLOW CAMPGROUND	HAMNER BUTTE, DESCHUTES CO OR	142 - C1
LAVA ISLAND CAMPGROUND	BENHAM FALLS, DESCHUTES CO OR	217 - B4
LAVA ISLAND SHELTER	BENHAM FALLS, DESCHUTES CO OR	217 - A4
LAVA ISLAND SHELTER (PREHISTORIC)	BENHAM FALLS, DESCHUTES CO OR	217 - B4
LAVA LAKE CAMPGROUND	LAVA LAKE RD, DESCHUTES CO OR	216 - B5
LA WIS WIS CAMPGROUND	OHANAPECOSH HOT SPRINGS, LEWIS CO WA	185 - D7
LEADER LAKE CAMPGROUND	MALOTT, OKANOGAN CO WA	104 - C3
LEE THOMAS CAMPGROUND	LEE THOMAS CROSSING, LAKE CO OR	151 - C1
LELAND LAKE CAMPGROUND	CENTER, JEFFERSON CO WA	109 - C1
LEMITI CAMPGROUND	PINHEAD BUTTES, CLACKAMAS CO OR	126 - C3
LEMOLO FALLS CAMPGROUND	LEMOLO LAKE, DOUGLAS CO OR	223 - B2
LEMOLO TWO FOREBAY CAMPGROUND	TOKETEE FALLS, DOUGLAS CO OR	222 - D3
LENA CREEK CAMPGROUND	NFD RD 25, MASON CO WA	173 - A2
LENA LAKE CAMPGROUND	MOUNT WASHINGTON, JEFFERSON CO WA	173 - A2
LEWIS CAMP	FISH MOUNTAIN, DOUGLAS CO OR	226 - D1
LEWIS RIVER CAMPGROUND	QUARTZ CREEK BUTTE, SKAMANIA CO WA	118 - C3
LICK CREEK CAMPGROUND	WALLOWA MOUNTAIN RD, WALLOWA CO OR	131 - A3
LIGHTING CREEK CAMPGROUND	HOZOMEEN MOUNTAIN, WHATCOM CO WA	103 - B1
LILLIAN SHELTER	HURRICANE HILL, CLALLAM CO WA	109 - B1
LILLIWAUP CREEK CAMPGROUND	NFD RD 24, MASON CO WA	173 - A4
LINDSAY CAMPGROUND	OLD SCAB MOUNTAIN, YAKIMA CO WA	119 - B1
LINNEY CREEK CAMPGROUND	WOLF PEAK, CLACKAMAS CO OR	201 - D7
LION ROCK SPRING CAMPGROUND	BLEWETT PASS, KITTITAS CO WA	241 - B1
LITTLE BADGER CAMPGROUND	FRIEND, WASCO CO OR	127 - A2
LITTLE BEAVER CAMPGROUND	HOZOMEEN MOUNTAIN, WHATCOM CO WA	103 - B1
LITTLE BLANKET SHELTER	OFF WINBERRY CREEK RD, LANE CO OR	134 - A3
LITTLE BOULDER CAMPGROUND	BOVILL, LATAH CO ID	123 - B1
LITTLE CHILLIWACK SHELTER	COPPER MOUNTAIN, WHATCOM CO WA	103 - A1
LITTLE CRANE CAMPGROUND	NFD RD 16, GRANT CO OR	137 - C2
LITTLE CRATER CAMPGROUND	NEWBERRY CRATER RD, DESCHUTES CO OR	143 - A1
LITTLE CRATER LAKE CAMPGROUND	WAPINITIA PASS, CLACKAMAS CO OR	126 - C3
LITTLE CULTUS CAMPGROUND	OFF LAVA LAKE RD, DESCHUTES CO OR	134 - C3
LITTLE DESCHUTES CAMPGROUND	ODELL BUTTE, KLAMATH CO OR	142 - C2
LITTLE FAN CREEK CAMPGROUND	BULL OF THE WOODS, CLACKAMAS CO OR	126 - B3
LITTLE FAWN CAMPGROUND	OFF CASCADE LAKES HWY, DESCHUTES CO OR	216 - A4
LITTLE FISH SHELTER	SKAGIT PEAK, WHATCOM CO WA	103 - B1
LITTLE GOOSE CAMPGROUND	SLEEPING BEAUTY, SKAMANIA CO WA	118 - C3
LITTLE LAVA LAKE CAMPGROUND	OFF LAVA LAKE RD, DESCHUTES CO OR	216 - B5
LITTLE NACHES CAMPGROUND	CLIFFDELL, YAKIMA CO WA	119 - B1
LITTLE QUALICUM FALL CAMPGROUND	HWY 4, BRITISH COLUMBIA	92 - B3
LITTLE REDWOOD CAMPGROUND	BOSLEY BUTTE, CURRY CO OR	148 - B2
LITTLE SODA SPRINGS CAMPGROUND	STABLER, SKAMANIA CO WA	194 - C2
LITTLE SUMMIT CAMPGROUND	OFF DEER RD, WHEELER CO OR	136 - B2
LOBSTER CREEK CAMPGROUND	QUOSATANA BUTTE, CURRY CO OR	228 - B4
LOCKABY CAMPGROUND	BEDFORD POINT, CLACKAMAS CO OR	126 - B3
LODGEPOLE CAMPGROUND	NORSE PEAK, YAKIMA CO WA	119 - A1
LODGEPOLE CAMPGROUND	OREGON COAST HWY, LANE CO OR	214 - A5
LOFTON RESERVOIR CAMPGROUND	QUARTZ VALLEY, LAKE CO OR	151 - C2
LONE FIR CAMPGROUND	WASHINGTON PASS, OKANOGAN CO WA	103 - C2
LONE PEAK CAMPGROUND	OFF NFD RD 5900, CHELAN CO WA	112 - A1
LONESOME COVE CAMPGROUND	RIMROCK LAKE, YAKIMA CO WA	119 - B2
LONESOME SPRING CAMPGROUND	OFF PETERSON CREEK RD, CROOK CO OR	136 - B2
LONE WOLF SHELTER	WESTFIR WEST, LANE CO OR	142 - A1
LONG CREEK CAMPGROUND	OFF NFD RD 16, BAKER CO OR	138 - A2
LONG LAKE CAMPGROUND	BALD KNOB, FERRY CO WA	105 - B2
LONGMILE MEADOWS CAMPGROUND	MOUNT CLIFTY, KITTITAS CO WA	111 - B3
LONGMIRE CAMPGROUND	WAHPENAYO PEAK, LEWIS CO WA	185 - B5
LONG RIDGE CAMPGROUND	QUAIL PRAIRIE MOUNTAIN, CURRY CO OR	148 - B2
LONG SWAMP CAMPGROUND	CORRAL BUTTE, OKANOGAN CO WA	104 - B1
LOOKOUT SPRINGS CAMPGROUND	THREE LYNX, CLACKAMAS CO OR	126 - B3
LOONEY SPRING CAMPGROUND	OFF JOHN DAY HWY, GRANT CO OR	137 - C2
LOST LAKE CAMPGROUND	BULL RUN LAKE, HOOD RIVER CO OR	201 - D2
LOST LAKE CAMPGROUND	MOUNT BONAPARTE, OKANOGAN CO WA	105 - A1
LOST LAKE CAMPGROUND	OREGON COAST HWY, DOUGLAS CO OR	214 - A6
LOST LAKE CAMPGROUND	SANTIAM HWY, LINN CO OR	134 - C2
LOST LAKE CAMPGROUND	TIETON BASIN, YAKIMA CO WA	119 - B1
LOST SPRINGS CAMPGROUND	POLAND BUTTE, YAKIMA CO WA	119 - B3
LOUP LOUP CAMPGROUND	LOUP LOUP SUMMIT, OKANOGAN CO WA	104 - B3
LOWER BOWMAN CAMPSITE	WHITE PINE BUTTES, KLICKITAT CO WA	119 - B3
LOWER BRIDGE CAMPGROUND	OFF METOLIUS RIVER RD, JEFFERSON CO OR	134 - C1
LOWER EIGHTMILE CAMPGROUND	FIVEMILE BUTTE, WASCO CO OR	202 - D3
LOWER FALLS CAMPGROUND	SPENCER BUTTE, SKAMANIA CO WA	118 - C3
LOWER TWIN CAMPGROUND	WAPINITIA PASS, WASCO CO OR	202 - B7
LUBY BAY CAMPGROUND	PRIEST LAKE SW, BONNER CO ID	107 - A2
LUCERNE CAMPGROUND	LUCERNE, CHELAN CO WA	103 - C3
LYNCH CREEK CAMPGROUND	OFF NFD RD 454, WALLOWA CO OR	131 - B2
LYRE RIVER CAMPGROUND	LYRE RIVER RD, CLALLAM CO WA	164 - B5
MACMILLAN CAMPGROUND	HWY 4, BRITISH COLUMBIA	92 - B3
MAGONE LAKE CAMPGROUND	OFF KEENEY FORKS RD, GRANT CO OR	137 - B1
MAIN EAGLE BRIDGE CAMPGROUND	NFD RD 77, BAKER CO OR	130 - C3
MAITLEN	METALINE FALLS, PEND OREILLE CO WA	106 - C1
MALLARD MARSH CAMPGROUND	OFF MUD LAKE RD, DESCHUTES CO OR	216 - A4
MAMMOTH SPRING CAMPGROUND	SOUTH FORK BURNT RIVER RD, BAKER CO OR	137 - C2
MANLY WHAM CAMPGROUND	STEHEKIN, CHELAN CO WA	103 - C3
MANSON LANDING CAMPGROUND	BRITISH COLUMBIA	92 - A1
MAPLE CREEK CAMPGROUND	TRINITY, CHELAN CO WA	111 - C1
MAPLE GROVE CAMPGROUND	WELKER PEAK, WHATCOM CO WA	103 - A2
MAPLE LEAF CAMPGROUND	PURCELL MOUNTAIN, LEWIS CO WA	118 - C2
MAPLE MOUNTAIN CENTENNIAL CAMPGROUND	TRANS CANADA HWY, BRITISH COLUMBIA	101 - B1
MAPLE RIDGE CAMPSITE	132ND AV & 236TH ST, MAPLE RIDGE BC	157 - D5
MARBLE CREEK CAMPGROUND	BIG DEVIL PEAK, SKAGIT CO WA	103 - B2
MARBLE CREEK CAMPGROUND	MARBLE MOUNTAIN, SHOSHONE CO ID	115 - C3
MARCUS ISLAND CAMPGROUND	MARCUS, STEVENS CO WA	106 - A2
MARGARET MCKENNY CAMPGROUND	LITTLEROCK, THURSTON CO WA	184 - A1
MARIEN CREEK CAMPGROUND	SILVERTON, SNOHOMISH CO WA	103 - A3
MARINE PARK AND CAMPGROUND	BONNEVILLE DAM, CASCADE LOCKS OR	194 - D6
MARION FORKS CAMPGROUND	N SANTIAM HWY, LINN CO OR	134 - C1
MARMES ROCK SHELTER	HWY 261, FRANKLIN CO WA	121 - C2
MARSTERS SPRING CAMPGROUND	MORGAN BUTTE, LAKE CO OR	151 - C1
MARYS PEAK CAMPGROUND	MARYS PEAK, BENTON CO OR	133 - A1
MASON DAM CAMPGROUND	WHITNEY HWY, BAKER CO OR	138 - A1
MAZAMA CAMPGROUND	UNION PEAK, KLAMATH CO OR	227 - C5
MAZAMA CREEK CAMPGROUND	OFF N SANTIAM HWY, LINN CO OR	134 - C1
MCBRIDE CAMPGROUND	EAGLE CREEK DR, BAKER CO OR	130 - C3
MCCORNICK CAMPGROUND	OFF HWY 71, ADAMS CO ID	131 - A3
MCCUBBINS GULCH CAMPGROUND	FOREMAN POINT, WASCO CO OR	127 - A3
MCCULLY FORKS CAMPGROUND	GRANITE HILL RD, BAKER CO OR	138 - A1
MCCURDY CAMPGROUND	OPHIR MOUNTAIN, CURRY CO OR	228 - D1
MCGRIBBLE CAMPGROUND	PORT ORFORD, CURRY CO OR	224 - C7
MCKENZIE BRIDGE CAMPGROUND	MCKENZIE HWY, LANE CO OR	134 - B2
MCNAUGHTON SPRING CAMPGROUND	STRAWBERRY RD, GRANT CO OR	137 - B2
MCQUDE CREEK SHELTER	OFF QUARTZVILLE DR, LINN CO OR	134 - B1
MEADOW CAMPGROUND	BENHAM FALLS, DESCHUTES CO OR	217 - B4
MEADOW CAMPGROUND	OFF NFD RD 9712, CHELAN CO WA	238 - C6
MEADOW CREEK CAMPGROUND	GOLDEN, JOSEPHINE CO OR	148 - C2
MEADOW CREEK CAMPGROUND	MEADOW CREEK, BOUNDARY CO ID	107 - C1
MEADOW CREEK CAMPGROUND	PLAIN, CHELAN CO WA	111 - C1
MEADOW CREEK SHELTER	LUCERNE, CHELAN CO WA	103 - C3
MEADOWS CAMPGROUND	SLATE PEAK, OKANOGAN CO WA	103 - C2
MEDITATION POINT CAMPGROUND	WOLF PEAK, CLACKAMAS CO OR	126 - C3
MEMORIAL CAMPGROUND	LEWIS BUTTE, OKANOGAN CO WA	104 - A2
MENEARS BEND CAMPGROUND	SANTIAM HWY, LINN CO OR	134 - A2
MERRILL LAKE CAMPGROUND	COUGAR, COWLITZ CO WA	190 - A4
MERRYS BAY CAMPGROUND	AHSAHKA, CLEARWATER CO ID	123 - C2
MIDDLE EEL CAMPGROUND	LAKESIDE, COOS CO OR	218 - B4
MIDDLE FORK CAMPGROUND	UPPER MIDDLE FORK RD, GRANT CO OR	137 - B1
MIDDLE WADDEL CAMPGROUND	LITTLEROCK, THURSTON CO WA	184 - A1
MILE CAMPGROUND	CASCADE LAKES HWY, DESCHUTES CO OR	216 - A6
MILL CREEK CAMPGROUND	PROSPECT NORTH, JACKSON CO OR	226 - C6
MILLER RIVER CAMPGROUND	GROTTO, KING CO WA	111 - A2
MILL POND CAMPGROUND	METALINE FALLS, PEND OREILLE CO WA	106 - B1
MILLPOND CAMPGROUND	OFF GRANT RD, JACKSON CO OR	230 - C7
MINA FALLS TRAILHEAD CAMPGROUND	LITTLEROCK, THURSTON CO WA	184 - B2
MINERAL CAMPGROUND	FAIRVIEW PEAK, LANE CO OR	141 - C1
MINERAL PARK CAMPGROUND	SONNY BOY LAKES, SKAGIT CO WA	103 - B2
MINERAL SPRINGS CAMPGROUND	LIBERTY, KITTITAS CO WA	111 - C3

FEATURE NAME	City State	Page-Grid
MINERS CREEK SHELTER	GAMMA PEAK, SNOHOMISH CO WA	103 - B3
MINK LAKE SHELTER	THREE SISTERS WILDERNESS AREA, LANE CO OR	134 - C3
MINNIE PETERSON CAMPGROUND	WINFIELD CREEK, JEFFERSON CO WA	108 - C1
MISERY SPRING CAMPGROUND	SADDLE BUTTE, GARFIELD CO WA	122 - B3
MITCHELL CREEK CAMPGROUND	LAKE CHELAN, CHELAN CO WA	112 - A1
MOKINS BAY CAMPGROUND	HAYDEN LAKE, KOOTENAI CO ID	245 - B5
MONA CAMPGROUND	OFF RABBIT CAMP RD, LANE CO OR	134 - B2
MONCK CAMPGROUND	HWY 5A, BRITISH COLUMBIA	95 - C1
MONEY CREEK CAMPGROUND	NE STEVENS PASS HWY, KING CO WA	111 - A1
MONTAGUE HARBOUR CAMPGROUND	BRITISH COLUMBIA	101 - B1
MONTE CRISTO CAMPGROUND	MONTE CRISTO, SNOHOMISH CO WA	111 - A1
MONTY CAMPGROUND	METOLIUS BENCH, JEFFERSON CO OR	135 - A1
MOON LAKE SHELTER	WARNER MOUNTAIN, LANE CO OR	142 - A1
MOORE POINT CAMPGROUND	LUCERNE, CHELAN CO WA	103 - C3
MORA CAMPGROUND	QUILLAYUTE PRAIRIE, CLALLAM CO WA	169 - A2
MORGAN CREEK CAMPGROUND	CLE ELUM LAKE, KITTITAS CO WA	111 - B3
MORRISON CREEK CAMPGROUND	MOUNT ADAMS WEST, YAKIMA CO WA	119 - A3
MORSE CREEK CAMPGROUND	NORSE PEAK, YAKIMA CO WA	119 - A1
MOSS CREEK CAMPGROUND	OKLAHOMA RD, SKAMANIA CO WA	195 - B3
MOSS SPRING CAMPGROUND	MILL CREEK RD, UNION CO OR	130 - B2
MOTTET CAMPGROUND	NORTH OF NFD RD 63, WALLOWA CO OR	130 - A1
MOUNT HEBO CAMPGROUND	NIAGARA CREEK, TILLAMOOK CO OR	197 - D7
MOUNT MOLLY CAMPGROUND	LITTLEROCK, THURSTON CO WA	184 - A1
MOUNT TOM SHELTER	OWL MOUNTAIN, JEFFERSON CO WA	109 - A1
MOWITCH CAMPGROUND	WHITNEY HWY, BAKER CO OR	138 - A1
MUD CREEK CAMPGROUND	OFF NFD RD 3615, LAKE CO OR	152 - A2
MUD LAKE CAMPGROUND	ANTHONY LAKES RD, BAKER CO OR	130 - A3
MUD SPRING CAMPGROUND	OFF RAGER RD, CROOK CO OR	136 - C2
MULE DEER CAMPGROUND	HWY 3, BRITISH COLUMBIA	103 - C1
MULKEY SHELTER	LAKE QUINAULT EAST, GRAYS HARBOR CO WA	109 - A2
MULLIGAN BAY CAMPGROUND	SQUAW LAKES, JACKSON CO OR	149 - B2
MURRAY CAMPGROUND	OFF NFD RD 16, GRANT CO OR	137 - C2
MURRIN PARK CAMPGROUND	TRANS CANADA HWY, SQUAMISH BC	93 - C2
MYERS CREEK CAMPGROUND	GOLDEN, JOSEPHINE CO OR	149 - A1
MYRTLE GROVE CAMPGROUND	CHINA FLAT, COOS CO OR	140 - C3
MYRTLEWOOD CAMPGROUND	POWERS, COOS CO OR	140 - C3
MYSTERY CAMPGROUND	MIDNIGHT MOUNTAIN, OKANOGAN CO WA	104 - A3
NACHES PASS CAMPSITE	MOUNT CLIFTY, KITTITAS CO WA	111 - B3
NANITCH CAMPGROUND	MOUNT HOOD SOUTH, CLACKAMAS CO OR	202 - A6
NASON CREEK CAMPGROUND	LAKE WENATCHEE, CHELAN CO WA	111 - C1
NASON CREEK CAMPGROUND	PLAIN, CHELAN CO WA	111 - C1
NAVIGATION CAMPGROUND	UPPER PRIEST LAKE, BONNER CO ID	107 - A1
NEAL SPRINGS CAMPGROUND	ABBOTT BUTTE, DOUGLAS CO OR	226 - B4
NEBY SHELTER	MOUNT TEBO, MASON CO WA	109 - B2
NETARTS BAY CAMPGROUND	WHISKEY CREEK RD, TILLAMOOK CO OR	197 - A4
NEWBERRY GROUP CAMPGROUND	NEWBERRY CRATER RD, DESCHUTES CO OR	143 - A1
NEWCASTLE ISLAND CAMPGROUND	OFF HWY 19, NANAIMO BC	93 - A3
NEWHALEM CAMPGROUND	MOUNT TRIUMPH, WHATCOM CO WA	103 - B2
NICE CAMPGROUND	DOE MOUNTAIN, OKANOGAN CO WA	104 - A2
NICKEL CREEK SHELTER	CHINOOK PASS, LEWIS CO WA	185 - D5
NICOLUM RIVER CAMPGROUND	HWY 3, BRITISH COLUMBIA	95 - A3
NIGHTHAWK CAMPGROUND	BAYVIEW, KOOTENAI CO ID	245 - C1
NINETEENMILE CAMPGROUND	TRINITY, CHELAN CO WA	111 - C1
NOISY CREEK CAMPGROUND	METALINE FALLS, PEND OREILLE CO WA	106 - C1
NO MAN SHELTER	SCAREDMAN CREEK, DOUGLAS CO OR	141 - C1
NO NAME LAKE CAMPGROUND	SKOOKUM CREEK, PEND OREILLE CO WA	106 - C3
NOOKSACK CAMPGROUND	BEARPAW MOUNTAIN, WHATCOM CO WA	102 - C1
NORDMAN CAMPGROUND	PRIEST LAKE NW, BONNER CO ID	107 - A2
NORTH COVE CAMPGROUND	NEWBERRY CRATER RD, DESCHUTES CO OR	143 - A1
NORTH COVE CAMPGROUND	PRIEST LAKE SW, BONNER CO ID	107 - A2
NORTH CREEK CAMPGROUND	CAPITOL PEAK, GRAYS HARBOR CO WA	117 - B1
NORTH CREEK CAMPGROUND	LEE THOMAS CROSSING, LAKE CO OR	151 - C1
NORTH CREEK CAMPGROUND	NFD RD 19, LINCOLN CO OR	203 - B6
NORTH DAVIS CREEK CAMPGROUND	DAVIS MOUNTAIN, DESCHUTES CO OR	142 - C1
NORTH EEL CAMPGROUND	LAKESIDE, COOS CO OR	218 - B3
NORTH FORK ANTHONY CAMPGROUND	END OF NORTH POWDER RIVER LN, BAKER CO OR	130 - A3
NORTH FORK CAMPGROUND	BUNCH LAKE, JEFFERSON CO WA	109 - A2
NORTH FORK CAMPGROUND	MOUNT MCLOUGHLIN, JACKSON CO OR	150 - A1
NORTH FORK CAMPGROUND	SILVER FALLS, CHELAN CO WA	111 - C1
NORTH FORK CAMPGROUND	SLATE CREEK RD, IDAHO CO ID	131 - C1
NORTH FORK CAMPGROUND	TOWER ROCK, LEWIS CO WA	118 - C2
NORTH FORK JOHN DAY CAMPGROUND	NFD RD 73 & NFD RD 52, GRANT CO OR	129 - C3
NORTH FORK MALHEUR CAMPGROUND	NFD RD 16, GRANT CO OR	137 - C2
NORTH FORK NINEMILE CAMPGROUND	DUNCAN RIDGE, OKANOGAN CO WA	104 - B1
NORTH FORK SIUSLAW CAMPGROUND	UPPER NORTH FORK RD, LANE CO OR	214 - D1
NORTH GORGE CAMPGROUND	BOSSBURG, STEVENS CO WA	106 - A1
NORTH PINE CAMPGROUND	NORTH PINE CREEK RD, BAKER CO OR	131 - A3
NORTH SKOOKUM CAMPGROUND	BROWNS LAKE, PEND OREILLE CO WA	106 - C2
NORTH TWIN LAKE CAMPGROUND	DAVIS MOUNTAIN, DESCHUTES CO OR	142 - C1
NORTH WALDO CAMPGROUND	WALDO MOUNTAIN, LANE CO OR	142 - B1
NORTH WICKIUP CAMPGROUND	DAVIS MOUNTAIN, DESCHUTES CO OR	142 - C1
NOTTINGHAM CAMPGROUND	BADGER LAKE, HOOD RIVER CO OR	202 - C5
OAK FORK CAMPGROUND	TIMOTHY LAKE, CLACKAMAS CO OR	126 - C3
OBSERVATION BERRYFIELD CAMPGROUND	BARE MOUNTAIN, SKAMANIA CO WA	190 - D7
OCHOCO DIVIDE CAMPGROUND	OCHOCO HWY, WHEELER CO OR	136 - A2
ODELL CREEK CAMPGROUND	ODELL LAKE, KLAMATH CO OR	142 - B1
ODESSA CAMPGROUND	PELICAN BAY, KLAMATH CO OR	231 - B6
OGDEN GROUP CAMPGROUND	PAULINA-EAST LAKE RD, DESCHUTES CO OR	143 - A1
OHANAPECOSH CAMPGROUND	OHANAPECOSH HOT SPRINGS, LEWIS CO WA	185 - D6
OKANOGAN INDIAN CAMPING GROUND	32ND AV, BRITISH COLUMBIA	104 - C1
OKEOVER ARM CAMPGROUND	HWY 101, BRITISH COLUMBIA	92 - B1
OKLAHOMA CAMPGROUND	OKLAHOMA RD, SKAMANIA CO WA	195 - B2
OLALLIE LAKE CAMPGROUND	GREEN MOUNTAIN, SKAMANIA CO WA	119 - A2
OLALLIE LAKE CAMPGROUND	OFF BIA RD 33, JEFFERSON CO OR	134 - C1
OLALLIE PENINSULA CAMPGROUND	OFF BIA RD 33, JEFFERSON CO OR	134 - C1
OLLOKOT CAMPGROUND	WALLOWA MOUNTAIN LP, WALLOWA CO OR	131 - A3
OPAL LAKE CAMPGROUND	COWHORN MOUNTAIN, DOUGLAS CO OR	223 - C1
OREGON CAMPGROUND	JOHN DAY-BURNS HWY, BAKER CO OR	137 - C1
ORIENTAL CREEK CAMPGROUND	NFD RD 5506, GRANT CO OR	129 - B3
ORIOLE CAMPGROUND	CONCONULLY WEST, OKANOGAN CO WA	104 - B2
OSPREY CAMPGROUND	PRIEST LAKE SW, BONNER CO ID	107 - A2
OTTER LAKE CAMPGROUND	HWY 5A, BRITISH COLUMBIA	95 - C2
OUTLET CAMPGROUND	OUTLET BAY, BONNER CO ID	107 - A2
OUTLET CREEK CAMPGROUND	OUTLET FALLS, KLICKITAT CO WA	119 - B3
OWL CREEK CAMPGROUND	PUGH MOUNTAIN, SNOHOMISH CO WA	103 - B3
OZETTE CAMPGROUND	OZETTE, CLALLAM CO WA	162 - B4
PACKARD CREEK CAMPGROUND	OAKRIDGE, LANE CO OR	142 - A1
PADDOCK CAMP	CAMPBELL RESERVOIR, KLAMATH CO OR	151 - B1
PALISADES CAMPGROUND	OHANAPECOSH HOT SPRINGS, LEWIS CO WA	185 - D7
PALMER LAKE CAMPGROUND	NIGHTHAWK, OKANOGAN CO WA	104 - C1
PANHANDLE CAMPGROUND	RUBY, PEND OREILLE CO WA	106 - C2
PANJAB CAMPGROUND	PANJAB CREEK, COLUMBIA CO WA	122 - B3
PANORAMA POINT CAMPGROUND	WELKER PEAK, WHATCOM CO WA	103 - A2
PANTHER CREEK CAMPGROUND	FATHER MOUNTAIN, CURRY CO OR	224 - D7
PANTHER CREEK CAMPGROUND	STABLER, SKAMANIA CO WA	194 - D3
PAPOOSE CAMPGROUND	SEVEN DEVILS RD, IDAHO CO ID	131 - C2
PARADISE CAMPGROUND	NFD RD 9, WASHINGTON CO ID	139 - A1
PARADISE CREEK CAMPGROUND	TERMINATION POINT, SKAMANIA CO WA	118 - C3
PARK CAMPGROUND	LIBERTY, KITTITAS CO WA	238 - A6
PARK CAMPGROUND	STOUT MOUNTAIN, MARION CO OR	205 - D7
PARK CREEK CAMPGROUND	GOODE MOUNTAIN, CHELAN CO WA	103 - B2
PARK CREEK CAMPGROUND	WELKER PEAK, WHATCOM CO WA	103 - A2
PASS CREEK SHELTER	SCAREDMAN CREEK, DOUGLAS CO OR	141 - C1
PATAHA CAMPGROUND	ROSE SPRINGS, GARFIELD CO WA	122 - B2
PAULINA CREEK CAMPGROUND	NEWBERRY CRATER RD, DESCHUTES CO OR	143 - A1
PAULINA LAKE CAMPGROUND	NEWBERRY CRATER RD, DESCHUTES CO OR	143 - A1
PEARSON CAMPGROUND	NFD RD 52, UMATILLA CO OR	129 - B3
PEBBLE FORD CAMPGROUND	FIVEMILE BUTTE, WASCO CO OR	202 - D4
PELTON CREEK SHELTER	BOB CREEK, JEFFERSON CO WA	109 - A1
PENINSULA CAMPGROUND	RIMROCK LAKE, YAKIMA CO WA	119 - B1
PENLAND LAKE CAMPGROUND	COAL MINE HILL & NFD RD 210, MORROW CO OR	129 - A3
PENROSE POINT CAMPGROUND	158TH AV KPS, PIERCE CO WA	181 - A2
PERRY CREEK CAMPGROUND	SILVERTON, SNOHOMISH CO WA	103 - A3
PERRY CREEK SHELTER	MOUNT SPICKARD, WHATCOM CO WA	103 - B1
PERRY SOUTH CAMPGROUND	FLY CREEK, JEFFERSON CO OR	135 - A1
PETERSON CAMPGROUND	BAYVIEW, KOOTENAI CO ID	245 - C1
PETERSON PRAIRIE CAMPGROUND	LITTLE HUCKLEBRRY MOUNTN, SKAMANIA CO WA	118 - C3
PETIT LAKE CAMPGROUND	ORWIG HUMP, PEND OREILLE CO WA	106 - C2
PHELPS CREEK CAMPGROUND	TRINITY, CHELAN CO WA	103 - C3
PHLOX POINT CAMPGROUND	MOUNT HOOD SOUTH, CLACKAMAS CO OR	202 - A5
PIERRE LAKE CAMPGROUND	LAURIER, STEVENS CO WA	105 - C1
PILCHUCK BRIDGE CAMPGROUND	MCMURRAY, SKAGIT CO WA	168 - D2
PINE CAMPGROUND	BLEWETT PASS, CHELAN CO WA	238 - B5
PINE CREEK CAMPGROUND	OFF PAULINA HWY, CROOK CO OR	136 - A3
PINE FLAT CAMPGROUND	NFD RD 5700, CHELAN CO WA	112 - A1
PINE MEADOWS CAMPGROUND	COTTAGE GROVE LAKE, LANE CO OR	219 - D2
PINE NEEDLE CAMPGROUND	OLD SCAB MOUNTAIN, YAKIMA CO WA	119 - B1
PINE POINT CAMPGROUND	TIMOTHY LAKE, CLACKAMAS CO OR	126 - C3
PINE TREE CAMPGROUND	SOUTH FORK RD, GRANT CO OR	136 - C2
PIONEER CAMPGROUND	EDEN VALLEY, COOS CO OR	140 - C3
PIONEER FORD CAMPGROUND	METOLIUS RIVER RD, JEFFERSON CO OR	134 - C1
PIRATES COVE MARINE CAMPGROUND	OFF SHORE ISLAND, BRITISH COLUMBIA	93 - A3
PLEASANT VALLEY CAMPGROUND	GOOSE PRAIRIE, YAKIMA CO WA	119 - A1
PLOWBOY CAMPGROUND	UPPER PRIEST LAKE, BONNER CO ID	107 - A1
POINT CAMPGROUND	CASCADE LAKES HWY, DESCHUTES CO OR	216 - A4
POISON CREEK CAMPGROUND	OSS PEAK, CHELAN CO WA	104 - A3
POISON CREEK CAMPGROUND	WEST MOUNTAIN RD, VALLEY CO ID	252 - D3
POLALLIE CAMPGROUND	DOG RIVER, HOOD RIVER CO OR	202 - C4
POLE BRIDGE CAMPGROUND	BROWN MOUNTAIN, JACKSON CO OR	150 - A2
POLE PATCH CAMPGROUND	FRENCH BUTTE, SKAMANIA CO WA	118 - C2
POOLE CREEK CAMPGROUND	LEMOLO LAKE, DOUGLAS CO OR	223 - B3
POPLAR FLAT CAMPGROUND	MIDNIGHT MOUNTAIN, OKANOGAN CO WA	104 - A2
PORCUPINE BAY CAMPGROUND	MCCOY LAKE, LINCOLN CO WA	113 - C1
PORCUPINE LAKE CAMPGROUND	CLARK FORK, BONNER CO ID	107 - C3
PORPOISE BAY CAMPGROUND	OFF HWY 101, BRITISH COLUMBIA	93 - A2
PORTEAU COVE CAMPGROUND	TRANS CANADA HWY, BRITISH COLUMBIA	93 - C2
POTLATCH STATE PARK CAMPGROUND	US 101, MASON CO WA	173 - A7
PRAIRIE CAMPGROUND	PAULINA-EAST LAKE RD, DESCHUTES CO OR	143 - A1
PRAIRIE SPRING CAMPGROUND	NFD RD 5212, CHELAN CO WA	112 - A2
PRIEST RIVER CAMPGROUND	PRIEST RIVER, BONNER CO ID	107 - A3
PRIMITIVE CAMPGROUND	COTTAGE GROVE LAKE, LANE CO OR	219 - D2
PRINCE CREEK CAMPGROUND	PRINCE CREEK, CHELAN CO WA	104 - A3
PRINEVILLE CAMP	HAMAKER BUTTE, DOUGLAS CO OR	223 - B7
PRINGLE FALLS CAMPGROUND	CRANE PRAIRIE RESERVOIR, DESCHUTES CO OR	142 - C1
PRIOR CENTENNIAL CAMPGROUND	BRITISH COLUMBIA	101 - C1
PURPLE POINT CAMPGROUND	STEHEKIN, CHELAN CO WA	103 - C3
QUARTZ CREEK BIG TREES CAMPGROUND	COWLITZ FALLS, LEWIS CO WA	118 - B2
QUINN RIVER CAMPGROUND	CRANE PRAIRIE RESERVOIR, DESCHUTES CO OR	142 - C1
QUOSATANA CAMPGROUND	QUOSATANA BUTTE, CURRY CO OR	228 - C4
RAINBOW CAMPGROUND	EMIGRANT CREEK RD, HARNEY CO OR	137 - A3
RAINBOW BAY CAMPGROUND	LAKE OF THE WOODS NORTH, KLAMATH CO OR	150 - B1
RAINBOW FALLS CAMPGROUND	STEHEKIN, CHELAN CO WA	103 - C3
RAINBOW POINT CAMPGROUND	MOUNTAIN RD, VALLEY CO ID	252 - C2
RAINBOW POINT CAMPGROUND	PUMPKIN MOUNTAIN, WHATCOM CO WA	103 - B1
RAINY HILL CAMPGROUND	MEDIMONT, KOOTENAI CO ID	248 - C4
RAMONA PARK CAMPGROUND	STORMY MOUNTAIN, CHELAN CO WA	236 - A1
RATHTREVOR BEACH CAMPGROUND	HWY 4, BRITISH COLUMBIA	92 - C3
RATTLESNAKE CAMPGROUND	ROBINSON MOUNTAIN, OKANOGAN CO WA	103 - C2
RAY COLE CAMPGROUND	CANYON CREEK RD, GRANT CO OR	137 - B2
RED BRIDGE CAMPGROUND	MALLARDY RIDGE, SNOHOMISH CO WA	103 - A3
RED LAKE CAMPGROUND	PELICAN BUTTE, KLAMATH CO OR	150 - B1
RED MOUNTAIN CAMPGROUND	CLE ELUM LAKE, KITTITAS CO WA	111 - B2
REEDER BAY CAMPGROUND	PRST LK NW, PRST LK SW, BONNER CO ID	107 - A2
REFRIGERATOR CAMPGROUND	LUCERNE, CHELAN CO WA	103 - C3
RESERVOIR CAMPGROUND	DAVIS MOUNTAIN, DESCHUTES CO OR	142 - C1
RESERVOIR CAMPGROUND	MOUNT HOOD NORTH, HOOD RIVER CO OR	202 - B3
REX CREEK SHELTER	LUCERNE, CHELAN CO WA	103 - C3
REYNOLDS SHELTER	REYNOLDS RIDGE, DOUGLAS CO OR	222 - C1
RHODODENDRON ISLAND CAMPGROUND	WALDO LAKE, LANE CO OR	142 - B1
RHODODENDRON RIDGE SHELTER	MOUNT LOWE, CLACKAMAS CO OR	126 - C3
RIVER CAMPGROUND	CRANE PRAIRIE RESERVOIR, DESCHUTES CO OR	142 - C1

FEATURE NAME / City State	Page-Grid
RIVER CAMPGROUND GRANDE RONDE RIVER RD, UNION CO OR	129 - C3
RIVER CAMPGROUND MOUNT ZION, CLALLAM CO WA	109 - C1
RIVER BAR CAMPGROUND MALLARDY RIDGE, SNOHOMISH CO WA	103 - A3
RIVER BAR CAMPGROUND OHANAPECOSH HOT SPRINGS, LEWIS CO WA	185 - D7
RIVERBEND CAMPGROUND SCHAEFER LAKE, CHELAN CO WA	111 - C1
RIVER BEND CAMPGROUND TIETON BASIN, YAKIMA CO WA	119 - B1
RIVER BRIDGE CAMPGROUND PROSPECT NORTH, JACKSON CO OR	226 - C5
RIVER EDGE CAMPGROUND ALSEA HWY, LINCOLN CO OR	209 - D2
RIVERS BEND CAMPGROUND ROBINSON MOUNTAIN, OKANOGAN CO WA	103 - C2
RIVERSIDE CAMPGROUND MOUNT HOWARD, CHELAN CO WA	111 - B1
RIVERSIDE CAMPGROUND N SANTIAM HWY, LINN CO OR	134 - C1
ROADS END CAMPGROUND GILBERT, OKANOGAN CO WA	103 - C2
ROARING RIVER CAMPGROUND SOUTH FORK RD, LANE CO OR	134 - B3
ROBERTS CREEK CAMPGROUND 101 HWY, BRITISH COLUMBIA	93 - B2
ROBINHOOD CAMPGROUND BADGER LAKE, HOOD RIVER CO OR	202 - C5
ROBINSON LAKE CAMPGROUND EASTPORT, BOUNDARY CO ID	107 - B1
ROCK CREEK CAMPGROUND BUCK MOUNTAIN, OKANOGAN CO WA	104 - B3
ROCK CREEK CAMPGROUND CRANE PRAIRIE RESERVOIR, DESCHUTES CO OR	142 - C1
ROCK CREEK CAMPGROUND DOLE, CLARK CO WA	193 - C4
ROCK CREEK CAMPGROUND ILLAHE, COOS CO OR	140 - B3
ROCK CREEK CAMPGROUND SCHAEFER LAKE, CHELAN CO WA	111 - C1
ROCK CREEK RESERVOIR CAMPGROUND ROCK CREEK RESERVOIR, WASCO CO OR	127 - A3
ROCK CREEK SHELTER SNOQUALMIE PASS, KING CO WA	111 - A2
ROCK ISLAND CAMPGROUND JACK RIDGE, CHELAN CO WA	111 - B2
ROCK LAKES CAMPGROUND BUCK MOUNTAIN, OKANOGAN CO WA	104 - B2
ROCK SPRINGS CAMPGROUND SILVIES-HOPPER RANCH RD, GRANT CO OR	137 - B3
ROCKY BEND CAMPGROUND SPRINGER MOUNTAIN, TILLAMOOK CO OR	125 - A2
ROCKY FORD CAMPGROUND ANTHONY LAKES RD, BAKER CO OR	130 - A3
ROCKY POINT CAMPGROUND PRIEST LAKE SW, BONNER CO ID	107 - A2
ROCKY POINT CAMPGROUND TWIN LAKES, FERRY CO WA	105 - C3
ROCKY TOP SHELTER OFF N SANTIAM HWY, MARION CO OR	134 - B1
ROLLING GROUNDS CAMP FISH CREEK DESERT, DOUGLAS CO OR	222 - D6
ROLLING RIFFLE CAMPGROUND RHODODENDRON, CLACKAMAS CO OR	201 - C7
ROSLAND CAMPGROUND BURGESS RD, DESCHUTES CO OR	143 - A1
ROUND LAKE CAMPGROUND MORTON, BONNER CO ID	107 - A3
ROUND LAKE CAMPGROUND MOUNT LOWE, MARION CO OR	126 - B3
ROUND SWAMP CAMPGROUND WICKIUP DAM, DESCHUTES CO OR	142 - C1
ROUTSON COUNTY PARK CAMPGROUND DOG RIVER, HOOD RIVER CO OR	202 - C3
RUCKLE PARK CAMPGROUND BRITISH COLUMBIA	101 - B1
RUFFED GROUSE CAMPGROUND SWEETGRASS BUTTE, OKANOGAN CO WA	104 - A2
RUJADA CAMPGROUND ROSE HILL, LANE CO OR	141 - C1
RUSSIAN CREEK CAMPGROUND GOLDEN, JOSEPHINE CO OR	149 - A1
SACAJAWEA CAMPGROUND NFD RD 4240, WALLOWA CO OR	131 - B2
SACANDAGA CAMPGROUND RIGDON POINT, LANE CO OR	142 - A1
SADDLE CAMPGROUND LONE BUTTE, SKAMANIA CO WA	118 - C3
SADDLE CAMPGROUND RUSTLER PEAK, JACKSON CO OR	150 - A1
SADDLE CREEK CAMPGROUND NFD RD 4240, WALLOWA CO OR	131 - B2
SADDLE DAM CAMPGROUND YALE DAM, COWLITZ CO WA	190 - A6
SAFETY HARBOR CAMPGROUND LAKE CHELAN, CHELAN CO WA	112 - A1
SAFETY HARBOR CREEK CAMPGROUND SOUTH NAVARRE PEAK, CHELAN CO WA	104 - A3
SAGE HEN CAMPGROUND OFF HANCOCK RD, GEM CO ID	139 - C2
SAINT MARYS LAKE CAMPGROUND NORTH END RD, BRITISH COLUMBIA	101 - B1
SALMON LA SAC CAMPGROUND DAVIS PEAK, KITTITAS CO WA	111 - B2
SALMON MEADOWS CAMPGROUND COXIT MOUNTAIN, OKANOGAN CO WA	104 - B2
SALT CREEK CAMPGROUND OFF CAMP HAYDEN RD, CLALLAM CO WA	164 - D5
SALT CREEK FALLS CAMPGROUND WILLAMETTE PASS, LANE CO OR	142 - B1
SALTERY BAY CAMPGROUND HWY 101, BRITISH COLUMBIA	92 - C1
SALTWATER CAMPGROUND MARINE VIEW DR S & S 259TH ST, KING CO WA	175 - A7
SAND BEACH CAMPGROUND GALLOWAY RD, TILLAMOOK CO OR	197 - A5
SANDHILL CAMPGROUND SANDHILL CROSSING, LAKE CO OR	151 - B1
SAND LAKE SHELTER WHITE PASS, YAKIMA CO WA	119 - A1
SAND PRAIRIE CAMPGROUND WARNER MOUNTAIN, LANE CO OR	142 - A1
SAND SPRING CAMPGROUND SAND SPRINGS RD, DESCHUTES CO OR	143 - C1
SAN JUAN CAMPGROUND BLANCA LAKE, SNOHOMISH CO WA	111 - A1
SAUK RIVER CAMPGROUND MONTE CRISTO, SNOHOMISH CO WA	111 - A1
SAWMILL FLATS CAMPGROUND CLIFFDELL, YAKIMA CO WA	119 - B1
SCATTER CREEK CAMPGROUND THE CRADLE, KITTITAS CO WA	111 - B2
SCHAEFER CREEK CAMPGROUND SCHAEFER LAKE, CHELAN CO WA	111 - C1
SCHNEIDER CAMPGROUND PRIEST LAKE SW, BONNER CO ID	107 - A2
SCHOONER CREEK CAMPGROUND S SCHOONER CREEK RD, LINCOLN CO OR	203 - B5
SCOTT CAMPGROUND BAYVIEW, KOOTENAI CO ID	245 - C1
SCOTT LAKE CAMPGROUND MCKENZIE HWY & NFD RD 260, LANE CO OR	134 - C2
SCOTTS CAMPGROUND SCOTTS CAMP RD, CROOK CO OR	136 - B2
SCOTTY CREEK CAMPGROUND BLEWETT, CHELAN CO WA	238 - A5
SEAL ROCK CAMPGROUND BRINNON, JEFFERSON CO WA	109 - C1
SECRET COVE CAMPGROUND OFF HWY 101, BRITISH COLUMBIA	93 - A2
SENATOR CREEK CAMPGROUND CATHEDRAL PEAK, SHOSHONE CO ID	115 - C1
SEQUIM BAY STATE PARK CAMPGROUND E WASHINGTON ST, CLALLAM CO WA	166 - C7
SEVEN-AND-A-HALF MILE CAMPSITE WAHTUM LAKE, HOOD RIVER CO OR	194 - D7
SEVEN-AND-A-HALF MILE CAMPSITE WAHTUM LAKE TR, HOOD RIVER CO OR	195 - A7
SEVEN DEVILS CAMPGROUND SEVEN DEVILS RD, IDAHO CO ID	131 - B2
SEVENMILE MARSH CAMPGROUND DEVILS PEAK, KLAMATH CO OR	231 - A1
SEVENMILE SHELTER MOUNT CARRIE, CLALLAM CO WA	109 - A1
SHADOW FALLS CAMPGROUND RED BUTTE, DOUGLAS CO OR	141 - C2
SHADOWY SAINT JOE CAMPGROUND SAINT JOE BALDY, BENEWAH CO ID	115 - B2
SHADY CAMPGROUND MCGREGOR MOUNTAIN, CHELAN CO WA	103 - C3
SHADY COVE CAMPGROUND OFF NFD RD 2207, MARION CO OR	134 - B1
SHADY PASS CAMPGROUND NFD RD 5900, CHELAN CO WA	112 - A1
SHANNON CREEK CAMPGROUND BACON PEAK, WHATCOM CO WA	103 - A2
SHANNON FALLS CAMPGROUND TRANS CANADA HWY, SQUAMISH BC	93 - C2
SHEEP BRIDGE CAMPGROUND DAVIS MOUNTAIN, DESCHUTES CO OR	142 - C1
SHERMAN CREEK CAMPGROUND BANGS MOUNTAIN, FERRY CO WA	106 - A2
SHERMAN PASS CAMPGROUND SHERMAN PEAK, FERRY CO WA	105 - C2
SHERMAN VALLEY CAMPGROUND CAPITOL PEAK, THURSTON CO WA	184 - A2
SHERWOOD CAMPGROUND DOG RIVER, HOOD RIVER CO OR	202 - C4
SHINING LAKE CAMPGROUND THREE LYNX, CLACKAMAS CO OR	126 - B3
SHUKSAN CAMPGROUND MOUNT LARRABEE, WHATCOM CO WA	102 - C1
SILESIA CREEK SHELTER MOUNT SEFRIT, WHATCOM CO WA	103 - A1
SILVER CAMPGROUND PRIEST LAKE SW, BONNER CO ID	107 - A2
SILVER CREEK CAMPGROUND RANDLE, LEWIS CO WA	118 - C2
SILVER CREEK MARSH CAMPGROUND BRIDGE CREEK RD, LAKE CO OR	143 - B3
SILVER CREEK SHELTER MOUNT ZION, CLALLAM CO WA	109 - C1
SILVER FALLS CAMPGROUND SILVER FALLS, CHELAN CO WA	111 - C1
SILVER FIR CAMPGROUND MOUNT LARRABEE, WHATCOM CO WA	102 - C1
SILVER SPRINGS CAMPGROUND WHITE RIVER PARK, PIERCE CO WA	111 - A3
SILVERTIP CAMPGROUND MONTE CRISTO, SNOHOMISH CO WA	111 - A1
SIMAX BEACH CAMPGROUNDS CRESCENT LAKE, KLAMATH CO OR	142 - C1
SISSONS CAMPGROUND GRIZZLY MOUNTAIN, SHOSHONE CO ID	115 - C1
SITKUM SHELTER INDIAN PASS, CLALLAM CO WA	108 - C1
SIXMILE SHELTER DOWNEY MOUNTAIN, SKAGIT CO WA	103 - B3
SKEELTER SHELTER WHITE PASS, LEWIS CO WA	119 - A2
SKIMMERHORN CAMPGROUND BUCKEYE LAKE, DOUGLAS CO OR	222 - C7
SKOOKUMCHUCK CAMPGROUND US HWY 95, IDAHO CO ID	131 - C1
SKOOKUM LAKE CAMPGROUND BAGBY HOT SPRINGS, CLACKAMAS CO OR	126 - B3
SLAUGHTER GULCH CAMPGROUND NFD RD 535, ADAMS CO ID	131 - C3
SLIDE CAMPGROUND ALSEA HWY, LINCOLN CO OR	209 - D2
SLIDE CREEK CAMPGROUND OFF SOUTH FORK RD, LANE CO OR	134 - B3
SLIDE CREEK CAMPGROUND STRAWBERRY RD, GRANT CO OR	137 - B2
SLIM CHANCE CAMPGROUND REYNOLDS RIDGE, LANE CO OR	142 - A1
SLOAN CREEK CAMPGROUND SLOAN PEAK, SNOHOMISH CO WA	111 - B1
SLOUGH CAMPGROUND BENHAM FALLS, DESCHUTES CO OR	217 - A5
SMELT BAY CAMPGROUND BRITISH COLUMBIA	92 - A1
SMITH LAKE CAMPGROUND RITZ, BOUNDARY CO ID	107 - B1
SMITH SPRINGS CAMPGROUND OLD FAIRVIEW, DOUGLAS CO OR	141 - C2
SMOKY CREEK CAMPGROUND SLEEPING BEAUTY, SKAMANIA CO WA	118 - C3
SNAG COVE CAMPGROUND MARCUS, STEVENS CO WA	106 - A2
SNOWBERRY CAMPGROUND BAYVIEW, KOOTENAI CO ID	245 - C1
SNOWBIRD SHELTER QUARTZ MOUNTAIN, DOUGLAS CO OR	222 - A5
SNUFF SHELTER ILLAHEE ROCK, DOUGLAS CO OR	222 - C4
SOCHOLIS CAMPGROUND SOCHOLIS CANYON, KLAMATH CO OR	150 - C1
SODA SPRING CAMPGROUND JUNGLE BUTTE, YAKIMA CO WA	119 - A3
SODA SPRINGS CAMPGROUND MOUNT HOWARD, CHELAN CO WA	111 - B1
SODA SPRINGS CAMPGROUND OFF SODA SPRINGS RD, KLICKITAT CO WA	196 - D1
SODA SPRINGS CAMPGROUND OLD SCAB MOUNTAIN, YAKIMA CO WA	119 - B1
SODA SPRINGS CAMPGROUND WHITE PASS, LEWIS CO WA	119 - A1
SOLEDUCK CAMPGROUND BOGACHIEL PEAK, CLALLAM CO WA	109 - A1
SOUTH CAMPGROUND LONE BUTTE, SKAMANIA CO WA	118 - C3
SOUTH CAMPGROUND MUD LAKE RD, DESCHUTES CO OR	216 - A4
SOUTH BEACH CAMPGROUND OFF HIGHWAY 101, JEFFERSON CO WA	172 - A2
SOUTH CREEK CAMPGROUND GILBERT, OKANOGAN CO WA	103 - C2
SOUTH EEL CREEK CAMPGROUND LAKESIDE, COOS CO OR	218 - B4
SOUTH FORK CAMP CREEK CAMPGROUND NFD RD 16, BAKER CO OR	138 - A2
SOUTH FORK CAMPGROUND DARLAND MOUNTAIN, YAKIMA CO WA	119 - B2
SOUTH FORK CAMPGROUND NFD RD 32, UMATILLA CO OR	130 - A1
SOUTH FORK CAMPGROUND RHODODENDRON, CLACKAMAS CO OR	201 - C6
SOUTH FORK CAMPGROUND SOUTH FORK BURNT RIVER RD, BAKER CO OR	138 - A2
SOUTH FORK HOH CAMPGROUND OWL MOUNTAIN, JEFFERSON CO WA	108 - C1
SOUTH FORK JUNCTION CAMPGROUND LOOMIS, OKANOGAN CO WA	104 - B1
SOUTH FORK SHELTER WINBERRY CREEK RD, LANE CO OR	134 - A3
SOUTH ISLAND CAMPGROUND PELICAN BUTTE, KLAMATH CO OR	150 - B1
SOUTH LAKE CAMPGROUND DEVILS PEAK, KLAMATH CO OR	150 - B1
SOUTH LAKE CAMPGROUND NIAGARA CREEK, YAMHILL CO OR	197 - D7
SOUTH NAVARRE CAMPGROUND SOUTH NAVARRE PEAK, CHELAN CO WA	104 - A3
SOUTH SKOOKUM LAKE CAMPGROUND BROWNS LAKE, PEND OREILLE CO WA	106 - C2
SOUTH TWIN LAKE CAMPGROUND DAVIS MOUNTAIN, DESCHUTES CO OR	142 - C1
SOUTH WALDO SHELTER WALDO LAKE, LANE CO OR	142 - B1
SOUTHWEST SHORE CAMPGROUND OFF WHITNEY HWY, BAKER CO OR	138 - A1
SPALDING MILL CAMPGROUND GOLDEN, JOSEPHINE CO OR	148 - C1
SPECTACLE LAKE CAMPGROUND ENTERPRISE, OKANOGAN CO WA	104 - C1
SPIDER LAKE CAMPGROUND HWY 19, BRITISH COLUMBIA	92 - B3
SPINREEL CAMPGROUND LAKESIDE, COOS CO OR	218 - B4
SPOOL CART CAMPGROUND GRANDE RONDE RIVER RD, UNION CO OR	129 - C3
SPORTA LAKE CAMPGROUND HWY 4, BRITISH COLUMBIA	92 - A3
SPRING BAR CAMPGROUND NFD RD 1614, IDAHO CO ID	131 - C2
SPRING CAMPGROUND NFD RD 9712, CHELAN CO WA	238 - C6
SPRING CREEK CAMPGROUND FLY CREEK, JEFFERSON CO OR	135 - A1
SPRING CREEK CAMPGROUND FORT KLAMATH, KLAMATH CO OR	231 - D2
SPRING CREEK CAMPGROUND GREEN MOUNTAIN, SKAMANIA CO WA	119 - A2
SPRING CREEK CAMPGROUND NFD RD 9, WASHINGTON CO ID	139 - A1
SPRING POINT CAMPGROUND LAKESHORE DR, BONNER CO ID	244 - A3
SPRUCE BAY CAMPGROUND GIBSON PASS RD, BRITISH COLUMBIA	103 - C1
SPRUCE BOTTOM SHELTER KLOOCHMAN ROCK, JEFFERSON CO WA	109 - A2
SPRUCE GROVE CAMPGROUND PYRAMID MOUNTAIN, CHELAN CO WA	111 - C1
SPRUCE SPRING CAMPGROUND STENTZ SPRING, GARFIELD CO WA	122 - B3
SQUAW LAKE CAMPGROUND ILLAHE, COOS CO OR	140 - C3
SQUAW LAKES CAMPGROUND SQUAW LAKES, JACKSON CO OR	149 - B2
SQUAW SPRING CAMPGROUND BONE SPRING, WALLOWA CO OR	122 - A3
STAGGER INN CAMPGROUND HELMER MOUNTAIN, PEND OREILLE CO WA	106 - C1
STAG SHELTER OFF HIGH PRAIRIE RD, LANE CO OR	134 - A3
STAIRCASE CAMPGROUND MOUNT SKOKOMISH, MASON CO WA	109 - B2
STAMP FALLS CAMPGROUND HWY 4, BRITISH COLUMBIA	92 - A3
STARR CAMPGROUND JOHN DAY-BURNS HWY, GRANT CO OR	137 - B2
STEAMBOAT FALLS CAMPGROUND BENJAMIN LAKE, DOUGLAS CO OR	222 - B2
STEAMBOAT LAKE CAMPGROUND STEAMBOAT MOUNTAIN, SKAMANIA CO WA	118 - C3
STEHEKIN CAMPGROUND STEHEKIN, CHELAN CO WA	103 - C3
STEVENS CREEK CAMPGROUND SOUTH FORK BURNT RIVER RD, BAKER CO OR	137 - C2
STILL CREEK CAMPGROUND MOUNT HOOD SOUTH, CLACKAMAS CO OR	202 - A6
STOCKADE SPRING CAMPGROUND ECKLER MOUNTAIN, COLUMBIA CO WA	122 - B3
STOUT CAMPGROUND GLENWOOD, YAKIMA CO WA	119 - A3
STRAWBERRY CAMPGROUND STRAWBERRY RD, GRANT CO OR	137 - C2
STRINGTOWN CAMPGROUND SQUAW LAKES, JACKSON CO OR	149 - B2
STUART CAMPGROUND LUCERNE, CHELAN CO WA	103 - C3
STUMP CAMPGROUND BLEWETT PASS, CHELAN CO WA	238 - B5
SUCKER CREEK SHELTER GOLDEN, JOSEPHINE CO OR	149 - A2
SUGAR CREEK CAMPGROUND RAGER RD, CROOK CO OR	136 - B2
SUGARLOAF CAMPGROUNDS CONCONULLY EAST, OKANOGAN CO WA	104 - C2
SUGAR PINE CAMPGROUND HYATT RESERVOIR, JACKSON CO OR	150 - A2
SUGARPINE SHELTER BUTLER BUTTE, DOUGLAS CO OR	226 - A4
SULLIVAN LAKE CAMPGROUND METALINE FALLS, PEND OREILLE CO WA	106 - C1
SULPHUR CREEK CAMPGROUND LIME MOUNTAIN, SNOHOMISH CO WA	103 - B3
SUMMIT CREEK CAMPGROUND OHANAPECOSH HOT SPRINGS, LEWIS CO WA	119 - A1

FEATURE NAME / City State	Page-Grid
SUMMIT LAKE CAMPGROUND EMIGRANT BUTTE, KLAMATH CO OR	142 - B1
SUMMIT LAKE CAMPGROUND TIMOTHY LAKE, CLACKAMAS CO OR	126 - C3
SUNRISE DAY USE AREA BAYVIEW, KOOTENAI CO ID	245 - C1
SUNSET CAMPGROUND GUMBOOT MOUNTAIN, SKAMANIA CO WA	193 - D3
SUNSET COVE CAMPGROUND ODELL LAKE, KLAMATH CO OR	142 - B1
SUNSET SHELTER TAFT MOUNTAIN, DOUGLAS CO OR	141 - C2
SUNSHINE CREEK CAMPGROUND FATHER MOUNTAIN, CURRY CO OR	228 - B1
SUNSHINE POINT CAMPGROUND SAWTOOTH RIDGE, LEWIS CO WA	185 - A6
SUTTON CREEK CAMPGROUND HWY 101 & SUTTON BEACH RD, LANE CO OR	214 - B1
SUTTON LAKE CAMPGROUND HWY 101 & SUTTON BEACH RD, LANE CO OR	214 - B1
SWAMPY LAKES SHELTER OFF CENTURY DRIVE HWY, DESCHUTES CO OR	216 - C3
SWAN LAKE CAMPGROUND SWAN LAKE, FERRY CO WA	105 - B2
SWAUK CAMPGROUND OFF HWY 97, KITTITAS CO WA	238 - A6
SWEAT CREEK CAMPGROUND WAUCONDA SUMMIT, OKANOGAN CO WA	105 - B2
SWEDE RIDGE SHELTER TUMALO FALLS, DESCHUTES CO OR	216 - D3
SWIFT FOREST CAMPGROUND CEDAR FLATS, SKAMANIA CO WA	190 - D5
TAHKENITCH CAMPGROUND OREGON COAST HWY, DOUGLAS CO OR	214 - A6
TALMAKS CAMPGROUND WINCHESTER EAST, LEWIS CO ID	123 - B3
TAMARACK CAMPGROUND NFD RD 77, BAKER CO OR	130 - C3
TAMARACK SPRING CAMPGROUND QUARTZ MOUNTAIN RD, KITTITAS CO WA	240 - B4
TAMARACK SPRING CAMPGROUND SOUTH FORK BURNT RIVER RD, BAKER CO OR	138 - A2
TANDY BAY CAMPGROUND COWHORN MOUNTAIN, KLAMATH CO OR	142 - B1
TANEUM CAMPGROUND TANEUM RD, KITTITAS CO WA	240 - C3
TARBELL CAMPGROUND DOLE, CLARK CO WA	193 - C3
TARGET MEADOWS CAMPGROUND OFF NFD RD 64, UMATILLA CO OR	130 - A1
TAYLOR ARM CAMPGROUND HWY 4, BRITISH COLUMBIA	92 - A3
TENMILE ISLAND CAMPGROUND PUMPKIN MOUNTAIN, WHATCOM CO WA	103 - B1
TENMILE SHELTER MOUNT PROPHET, WHATCOM CO WA	103 - B1
TENMILE SHELTER MOUNT TOWNSEND, JEFFERSON CO WA	109 - C1
TENMILE SHELTER OFF RISLEY CREEK RD, LINCOLN CO OR	209 - D1
TEPEE CAMPGROUND OREGON BUTTE, COLUMBIA CO WA	122 - B3
THESEUS CREEK CAMPGROUND LABYRINTH MOUNTAIN, CHELAN CO WA	111 - B1
THIELSEN VIEW CAMPGROUND DIAMOND LAKE, DOUGLAS CO OR	223 - C6
THIRTEENMILE CAMPGROUND THIRTEENMILE CREEK, FERRY CO WA	105 - B2
THIRTYMILE CAMPGROUND COLEMAN PEAK, OKANOGAN CO WA	104 - B1
THOMAS CREEK CAMPGROUND COX FLAT, LAKE CO OR	151 - C2
THOMPSON RESERVOIR CAMPGROUND BRIDGE CREEK RD, LAKE CO OR	143 - B3
THREE CREEK CAMPGROUND PYRAMID MOUNTAIN, CHELAN CO WA	111 - C1
THREE CREEK LAKE CAMPGROUND OFF THREE CREEKS LAKE RD, DESCHUTES CO OR	216 - C2
THREE CREEK MEADOW CAMPGROUND THREE CREEKS LAKE RD, DESCHUTES CO OR	216 - C1
THREE FORKS SHELTER TYLER PEAK, CLALLAM CO WA	109 - B1
THREEHORN CAMPGROUND RAGSDALE BUTTE, DOUGLAS CO OR	141 - C3
THREE LAKES CAMP GARWOOD BUTTE, DOUGLAS CO OR	223 - B7
THREEMILE SHELTER OFF RISLEY CREEK RD, LINCOLN CO OR	209 - C1
THREE PINES CAMPGROUND PRIEST LAKE SW, BONNER CO ID	107 - A2
THREE TREES CAMP (HISTORICAL) COLLIER BUTTE, CURRY CO OR	232 - D1
TIFFANY SPRING CAMPGROUND TIFFANY MOUNTAIN, OKANOGAN CO WA	104 - B2
TILLICUM CAMPGROUND LONE BUTTE, SKAMANIA CO WA	118 - C3
TILLICUM BEACH CAMPGROUND OFF OREGON COAST HWY, LINCOLN CO OR	328 - A13
TIMBERLINE CAMPGROUND MOUNT ADAMS EAST, YAKIMA CO WA	119 - A3
TIMBERLINE CAMPGROUND MOUNT SAINT HELENS, SKAMANIA CO WA	190 - C2
TIME AND A HALF CAMPGROUND GRANDE RONDE RIVER RD, UNION CO OR	129 - C3
TIMOTHY SPRING CAMPGROUND NORTH OF NFD RD 63, WALLOWA CO OR	130 - A1
TIMPANOGAS CAMPGROUND COWHORN MOUNTAIN, DOUGLAS CO OR	223 - C1
TIN CAN CAMPGROUND GOLDEN, JOSEPHINE CO OR	149 - A1
TODD LAKE CAMPGROUND OFF NFD RD 370, DESCHUTES CO OR	216 - B3
TOKETEE LAKE CAMPGROUND TOKETEE FALLS, DOUGLAS CO OR	222 - D3
TOLLBRIDGE CAMPGROUND NFD 10 & PENDLTN-JOHN DAY, UMATILLA CO OR	129 - B3
TOMBSTONE PRAIRIE CAMPGROUND SANTIAM HWY, LINN CO OR	134 - B2
TOWER ROCK CAMPGROUND TOWER ROCK, LEWIS CO WA	118 - C2
TRANQUIL COVE CAMPGROUND COWHORN MOUNTAIN, KLAMATH CO OR	142 - B1
TRAPPER SHELTER KIMTA PEAK, JEFFERSON CO WA	109 - A2
TRAPPER SHELTER SCAREDMAN CREEK, DOUGLAS CO OR	141 - C2
TREE PHONES CAMPGROUND PISCOE MEADOW, YAKIMA CO WA	119 - B2
TRIBUNE BAY CAMPGROUND BRITISH COLUMBIA	92 - B2
TRILLIUM LAKE CAMPGROUND MOUNT HOOD SOUTH, CLACKAMAS CO OR	202 - A6
TRONSEN CAMPGROUND BLEWETT PASS, CHELAN CO WA	238 - B6
TROUBLESOME CREEK CAMPGROUND MONTE CRISTO, SNOHOMISH CO WA	111 - A1
TROUGH CREEK CAMPGROUND NFD RD 55, UMATILLA CO OR	129 - B3
TROUT LAKE CAMPGROUND BANGS MOUNTAIN, FERRY CO WA	105 - C2
TROUT LAKE CAMPGROUND BIA RD 33, JEFFERSON CO OR	134 - C1
TROUT LAKE CAMPGROUND JACK RIDGE, CHELAN CO WA	111 - B2
TROUT LAKE CREEK CAMPGROUND TROUT LAKE, SKAMANIA CO WA	119 - A3
TUCANNON CAMPGROUND PANJAB CREEK, COLUMBIA CO WA	122 - B3
TUCQUALA MEADOW CAMPGROUND THE CRADLE, KITTITAS CO WA	111 - B2
TUMALO FALLS SHELTER TUMALO FALLS, DESCHUTES CO OR	216 - D3
TUMWATER CAMPGROUND MCGREGOR MOUNTAIN, CHELAN CO WA	103 - C3
TUMWATER CAMPGROUND WINTON, CHELAN CO WA	111 - C2
TUNNEL CREEK SHELTER MOUNT TOWNSEND, JEFFERSON CO WA	109 - C1
TURLO CAMPGROUND VERLOT, SNOHOMISH CO WA	102 - C3
TWELVE MILE SHELTER MOUNT CHRISTIE, JEFFERSON CO WA	109 - B1
TWENTYNINE PINES CAMPGROUND RED TOP MOUNTAIN, KITTITAS CO WA	111 - C3
TWENTYONE MILE CAMPGROUND THIRTEENMILE CREEK, FERRY CO WA	105 - B3
TWENTYONE MILE SHELTER SLIDE PEAK, CLALLAM CO WA	109 - A1
TWIN BRIDGES CAMPGROUND GOVERNMENT CAMP, CLACKAMAS CO OR	201 - D5
TWINBUCK SHELTER ACKER ROCK, DOUGLAS CO OR	226 - A1
TWIN FALLS CAMPGROUND STEAMBOAT MOUNTAIN, SKAMANIA CO WA	118 - C3
TWIN LAKES CAMPGROUND DUCK CREEK RD, WALLOWA CO OR	131 - A3
TWIN RIVERS CAMPGROUND GARDEN VALLEY, DOUGLAS CO OR	221 - B3
TWIN ROCKS SHELTER FAIRVIEW PEAK, LANE CO OR	141 - C1
TWIN SPRINGS CAMPGROUND OFF BUCK HOLLOW RD, CROOK CO OR	136 - B2
TWIN SPRINGS CAMPGROUND SOUTH FORK RD, LANE CO OR	134 - B3
TWO COLOR CAMPGROUND NFD RD 7755, BAKER CO OR	130 - C3
TWO PAN CAMPGROUND END OF LOSTINE RIVER RD, WALLOWA CO OR	130 - C2
TYE CANYON CAMPGROUND SCENIC, KING CO WA	111 - B2
TYEE CAMPGROUND OREGON COAST HWY, LANE CO OR	214 - A5
UMATILLA FORKS CAMPGROUND NFD RD 32, UMATILLA CO OR	130 - A1
UNION CREEK CAMPGROUND UNION CREEK, JACKSON CO OR	226 - C4
UNION CREEK CAMPGROUND WHITNEY HWY, BAKER CO OR	138 - A1
UPPER CAMPGROUND CASCADE LAKES HWY, DESCHUTES CO OR	216 - B6
UPPER ARM CAMPGROUND BREITENBUSH RD, MARION CO OR	134 - B1
UPPER BOWMAN CAMPSITE WHITE PINE BUTTES, KLICKITAT CO WA	119 - B3
UPPER CLEARWATER CAMPGROUND STEQUALEHO CREEK, JEFFERSON CO WA	108 - C1
UPPER END CAMPGROUND BIG FALL CREEK RD, LANE CO OR	134 - A3
UPPER PAYETTE CAMPGROUND W SIDE OF UPPER PAYETTE LK, VALLEY CO ID	251 - D1
UPPER PAYETTE LAKE CAMPGROUND W SIDE OF UPPER PAYETTE LK, VALLEY CO ID	251 - D1
UPPER SOUTH FORK CAMPGRND (ROGUE RIV) RUSTLER PEAK, JACKSON CO OR	150 - A1
VAN CREEK CAMPGROUND NFD RD 1614, IDAHO CO ID	131 - C2
VERLOT CAMPGROUND VERLOT, SNOHOMISH CO WA	102 - C3
VERMILLION BAR CAMPGROUND OFF NFD RD 454, WALLOWA CO OR	131 - B3
VIGNE CAMPGROUND CHESNIMNUS LN, WALLOWA CO OR	131 - A1
WAHTUM LAKE CAMPGROUND WAHTUM LAKE, HOOD RIVER CO OR	195 - A7
WALDRON CAMPGROUND BAYVIEW, KOOTENAI CO ID	245 - C1
WALLACE FALLS CAMPGROUND LEY RD, SNOHOMISH CO WA	110 - C1
WALTON LAKE CAMPGROUND HOWARD CREEK RD, CROOK CO OR	136 - A2
WALUPT LAKE CAMPGROUND WALUPT LAKE, LEWIS CO WA	119 - A2
WAMPUS CAMPGROUND WICKIUP DAM, DESCHUTES CO OR	142 - C1
WAR CREEK CAMPGROUND OVAL PEAK, OKANOGAN CO WA	104 - A3
WARD CAMPGROUND BAYVIEW, KOOTENAI CO ID	245 - C1
WARM SPRINGS CAMPGROUND NEWBERRY CRATER RD, DESCHUTES CO OR	143 - A1
WATKINS CAMPGROUND CARBERRY CREEK, JACKSON CO OR	149 - B2
WAXMYRTLE CAMPGROUND OFF OREGON COAST HWY, LANE CO OR	214 - A5
WEAVER POINT CAMPGROUND STEHEKIN, CHELAN CO WA	103 - C3
WEEPING ROCK CAMPGROUND ILLAHEE ROCK, DOUGLAS CO OR	222 - B3
WENBERG CAMPGROUND E LAKE GOODWIN RD, SNOHOMISH CO WA	168 - B6
WEST CULTUS LAKE CAMPGROUND OFF DEER LAKE RD, DESCHUTES CO OR	134 - C3
WEST DAVIS LAKE CAMPGROUND HAMNER BUTTE, KLAMATH CO OR	142 - C1
WEST EAGLE MEADOW CAMPGROUND NFD RD 77, UNION CO OR	130 - C3
WEST FORK CAMPGROUND GROTTO, KING CO WA	111 - A2
WESTVIEW SHELTER WILLAMETTE PASS, LANE CO OR	142 - B1
WETMORE CAMPGROUND JOHN DAY HWY, BAKER CO OR	138 - A1
WHISKEY CREEK CAMPGROUND GOLDEN, JOSEPHINE CO OR	149 - A1
WHISPERING FALLS CAMPGROUND N SANTIAM HWY, MARION CO OR	134 - B1
WHITE CHUCK CAMPGROUND WHITE CHUCK MOUNTAIN, SNOHOMISH CO WA	103 - A3
WHITE CREEK CAMPGROUND TAFT MOUNTAIN, DOUGLAS CO OR	141 - C2
WHITEHORSE FALLS CAMPGROUND GARWOOD BUTTE, DOUGLAS CO OR	223 - A4
WHITE PASS CAMPGROUND WHITE PASS, YAKIMA CO WA	119 - A1
WHITE PINE CAMPGROUND LAKE OF THE WOODS NORTH, KLAMATH CO OR	150 - B1
WHITE PINE CAMPGROUND LAKE WENATCHEE, CHELAN CO WA	111 - C1
WHITE RIVER CAMPGROUND SUNRISE, PIERCE CO WA	185 - D2
WHITE RIVER FALLS CAMPGROUND MOUNT DAVID, CHELAN CO WA	111 - B1
WHITE RIVER PARK CAMPGROUND MOUNT HOOD SOUTH, HOOD RIVER CO OR	202 - B6
WHITETAIL CAMPGROUND BAYVIEW, KOOTENAI CO ID	245 - C1
WHITEWATER CAMPGROUND N SANTIAM HWY, LINN CO OR	134 - B1
WICKIUP CAMPGROUND CANYON CREEK RD, GRANT CO OR	137 - B2
WICKIUP CAMPGROUND PINKHAM BUTTE, GARFIELD CO WA	122 - C3
WICKIUP BUTTE CAMPGROUND WICKIUP DAM, DESCHUTES CO OR	142 - C1
WICKIUP SHELTER RUSTLER PEAK, KLAMATH CO OR	150 - A1
WICKY CREEK SHELTER TROUT LAKE, SKAMANIA CO WA	119 - A3
WILDCAT CAMPGROUND GOLDEN, JOSEPHINE CO OR	149 - A1
WILDHORSE CAMPGROUND QUOSATANA BUTTE, CURRY CO OR	228 - D5
WILD ROSE CAMPGROUND TIETON BASIN, YAKIMA CO WA	119 - B1
WILDWOOD CAMPGROUND OFF SUMMIT RD, WHEELER CO OR	136 - A2
WILEY CAMP FISH MOUNTAIN, DOUGLAS CO OR	222 - D7
WILEY FLAT CAMPGROUND OFF PAULINA HWY, CROOK CO OR	136 - A3
WILLIAMS CREEK CAMPGROUND MACE MOUNTAIN, DOUGLAS CO OR	141 - C2
WILLIAMSON RIVER CAMPGROUND SOLOMAN BUTTE, KLAMATH CO OR	231 - D2
WILLOUGHBY CREEK CAMPGROUND WINFIELD CREEK, JEFFERSON CO WA	108 - C1
WILLOW CAMPGROUND CHEMULT, KLAMATH CO OR	142 - C2
WILLOW CREEK CAMPGROUND OFF NFD RD 4015, LAKE CO OR	152 - A2
WILLOW DAY USE AREA BAYVIEW, KOOTENAI CO ID	245 - C1
WILLOW POINT CAMPGROUND HYATT RESERVOIR, JACKSON CO OR	150 - A2
WILLOWS CAMPGROUND TIETON BASIN, YAKIMA CO WA	119 - B1
WILLOW VALLEY CAMPGROUND BRADY BUTTE, KLAMATH CO OR	151 - B3
WINBERRY CAMPGROUND WINBERRY CREEK RD, LANE CO OR	134 - A3
WINCHUCK CAMPGROUND FOURTH OF JULY CREEK, CURRY CO OR	148 - B2
WINDY POINT CAMPGROUND WEDDLE CANYON, YAKIMA CO WA	119 - B1
WINDY SADDLE CAMPGROUND SEVEN DEVILS RD, IDAHO CO ID	131 - B2
WINSTON CREEK CAMPGROUND HATCHET MOUNTAIN, LEWIS CO WA	118 - A2
WINTER COVE CAMPGROUND WINTER COVE RD, BRITISH COLUMBIA	101 - C1
WISH POOSH CAMPGROUND CLE ELUM LAKE, KITTITAS CO WA	111 - B3
WIZARD FALLS CAMPGROUND OFF METOLIUS RIVER RD, JEFFERSON CO OR	134 - C1
WOLF BAR CAMPSITE MOUNT HOQUIAM, JEFFERSON CO WA	109 - A2
WOLF CREEK CAMPGROUND BULL SPRING RD, CROOK CO OR	136 - B2
WOLF CREEK CAMPGROUND RED BUTTE, DOUGLAS CO OR	141 - C2
WOLF SHELTER GROUNDHOG MOUNTAIN, LANE CO OR	142 - A1
WOODLAND PARK CAMPGROUND WESTON-ELGIN HWY, UNION CO OR	130 - A1
WY'EAST CAMPSITE WAHTUM LAKE, HOOD RIVER CO OR	194 - D7
WYETH CAMPGROUND WYETH, HOOD RIVER CO OR	195 - A5
WYNOOCHEE FALLS CAMPGROUND WYNOOCHEE LAKE, GRAYS HARBOR CO WA	109 - B2
WYNOOCHEE SHELTER WYNOOCHEE LAKE, GRAYS HARBOR CO WA	109 - B2
YAHOO LAKE CAMPGROUND STEQUALEHO CREEK, JEFFERSON CO WA	108 - C1
YELLOWJACKET CAMPGROUND OFF HINES LOGGING RD, HARNEY CO OR	137 - A3
YELLOW PINE CAMPGROUND JOHN DAY HWY, BAKER CO OR	138 - A1
YEW TREE CAMPGROUND LITTLEROCK, THURSTON CO WA	184 - A1
YOUNG CREEK SHELTER MUD RIVER, CHELAN CO WA	112 - A1

COLLEGES & UNIVERSITIES

FEATURE NAME / City State	Page-Grid
BAKER COLLEGE LA GRANDE-BAKER HWY, BAKER CITY OR	138 - B1
BATES VOCATIONAL TECHNICAL COLLEGE S 12TH ST & YAKIMA AV, TACOMA WA	293 - G5
BATES VOCATIONAL TECHNICAL SCHOOL S 74TH ST & WAPATO ST, TACOMA WA	294 - E7
BELLEVUE COMMUNITY COLLEGE 3000 LANDERHOLM CIR SE, BELLEVUE WA	175 - C3
BIBLE COLLEGE IRENE ST, BOISE ID	253 - C2
BLUE MOUNTAIN COMMUNITY COLLEGE COLD SPRINGS HWY, PENDLETON OR	129 - B1
BOISE STATE UNIVERSITY OFF BROADWAY AV, BOISE ID	253 - C3
BRITISH COLUMBIA INST OF TECHNOLOGY WILLINGDON AV, DISTRICT OF BURNABY BC	156 - C5
CASCADE COLLEGE 9101 E BURNSIDE ST, PORTLAND OR	315 - G5
CENTRALIA COMMUNITY COLLEGE S WASHINGTON AV & LOCUST ST, CENTRALIA WA	299 - E4
CENTRAL OREGON COMMUNITY COLLEGE NW COLLEGE WY, BEND OR	332 - B5
CENTRAL WASHINGTON UNIVERSITY ELLENSBURG NORTH, ELLENSBURG WA	241 - B5
CLACKAMAS COMMUNITY COLLEGE 19600 MOLALLA AV, OREGON CITY OR	199 - D5
CLARK COMMUNITY COLLEGE 1800 E MCLOUGHLIN BLVD, VANCOUVER WA	305 - J4

PNW

INDEX

FEATURE NAME City State	Page-Grid
CLATSOP COMMUNITY COLLEGE JEROME AV, ASTORIA WA	300 - D5
CLOVER PARK TECHNICAL COLLEGE 45000 STEILACOOM BLVD SW, LAKEWOOD WA	181 - D4
COGSWELL, HENRY COLLEGE NORTH 10626 NE 37TH CIR, BELLEVUE WA	175 - C1
COLLEGE OF IDAHO S INDIANA AV & E LINDEN ST, CALDWELL ID	147 - B1
COLUMBIA BASIN COMMUNITY COLLEGE N 20TH AV, PASCO WA	343 - D4
CONCORDIA UNIVERSITY 2811 NE HOLMAN ST, PORTLAND OR	310 - A6
DOUGLAS COLLEGE 8TH ST, NEW WESTMINSTER BC	156 - D6
EASTERN OREGON COLLEGE OFF HWY 203, LA GRANDE OR	130 - A2
EASTERN WASHINGTON UNIVERSITY WASHINGTON ST, CHENEY WA	246 - A7
EDMONDS COMMUNITY COLLEGE 20000 68TH AV W, LYNNWOOD WA	171 - B5
EVERETT COMMUNITY COLLEGE 801 WETMORE AV, EVERETT WA	171 - C1
EVERGREEN STATE COLLEGE THE THE EVERGREEN COL PKWY, THURSTON CO WA	296 - A1
FORT WRIGHT COLLEGE N WRIGHT RD & OFFUT RD, SPOKANE WA	348 - D7
FRASER VALLEY COLLEGE YALE RD E, DISTRICT OF CHILLIWACK BC	94 - C3
GEORGE FOX COLLEGE 414 N MERIDIAN ST, NEWBERG OR	198 - D5
GONZAGA UNIVERSITY SCHOOL OF LAW E BOONE AV, SPOKANE WA	349 - B8
GRAYS HARBOR COLLEGE S BOONE ST, ABERDEEN WA	178 - B7
GREEN RIVER COMMUNITY COLLEGE 12401 SE 320TH ST, KING CO WA	182 - C1
HIGHLINE COMMUNITY COLLEGE S 240TH ST & PACIFIC HWY S, DES MOINES WA	175 - B7
KWANTIEN COLLEGE GLOVER RD & LANGLEY BYPS, LANGLEY BC	157 - C7
LAKE WASHINGTON TECHNICAL COLLEGE 11605 132ND AV NE, KIRKLAND WA	171 - C7
LANE COMMUNITY COLLEGE 101 & 35TH ST, FLORENCE OR	214 - B3
LANE COMMUNITY COLLEGE E 30TH AV, LANE CO OR	330 - G12
LANE COMMUNITY COLLEGE MADISON ST, EUGENE OR	329 - J5
LEWIS AND CLARK COLLEGE 9615 SW PALATINE HILL RD, PORTLAND OR	321 - F2
LEWIS-CLARK STATE COLLEGE 11TH AV, LEWISTON ID	250 - B4
LINFIELD COLLEGE LINFIELD AV, MCMINNVILLE OR	198 - A7
LINN-BENTON COMMUNITY COLLEGE PACIFIC BLVD & BELMONT AV, ALBANY OR	326 - B14
LOWER COLUMBIA JUNIOR COLLEGE MAPLE ST, LONGVIEW WA	303 - A8
LUTHERAN BIBLE INSTITUTE 4421 228TH AV SE, KING CO WA	176 - A3
MALASPINA COLLEGE 900 5TH ST, NANAIMO BC	93 - A3
MOUNT HOOD COMMUNITY COLLEGE 26000 SE STARK ST, GRESHAM OR	200 - B1
NORTH IDAHO COLLEGE COEUR D'ALENE, COEUR D'ALENE ID	355 - D11
NORTH SEATTLE COMMUNITY COLLEGE 9600 COLLEGE WY N, SEATTLE WA	171 - A7
NORTHWEST CHRISTIAN COLLEGE KINCAID ST, EUGENE OR	330 - B7
NORTHWEST COLLEGE 108TH AV NE & NE 53RD ST, KIRKLAND WA	175 - C1
NORTHWESTERN SCHOOL OF LAW SW TERWILLIGER BLVD, PORTLAND OR	321 - E1
NORTHWEST INDIAN COLLEGE KWINA RD, WHATCOM CO WA	158 - C7
NORTHWEST NAZARENE COLLEGE 12TH AV RD & LOCUST LN, CANYON CO ID	147 - B1
OLYMPIC COLLEGE BREMERTON WEST, BREMERTON WA	270 - J9
OREGON COLLEGE OF EDUCATION MISTLETOE RD, MONMOUTH OR	204 - A7
OREGON GRADUATE INST OF SCI & TECH 20000 NW WALKER RD, HILLSBORO OR	199 - A1
OREGON HEALTH SCIENCES UNIVERSITY 3181 SW SAM JACKSON PK RD, PORTLAND OR	316 - D1
OREGON INSTITUTE OF TECHNOLOGY 7726 SE HARMONY RD, CLACKAMAS CO OR	199 - D3
OREGON INSTITUTE OF TECHNOLOGY COLLEGE WY, KLAMATH FALLS OR	338 - C3
OREGON STATE UNIVERSITY CAMPUS WY, CORVALLIS OR	327 - E10
OREGON STATE UNIV AGRICULTURAL EXP STA OREGON-WASHINGTON HWY, UMATILLA CO OR	129 - C1
OREGON STATE UNIV EXPERIMENT FARM ELECTRIC RD, LINN CO OR	327 - J9
OREGON STATE UNIV MARINE SCIENCE CTR FERRY SLIP RD, NEWPORT OR	206 - B4
OREGON TECHNICAL INSTITUTE FORT KLAMATH RD, KLAMATH CO OR	338 - H3
PACIFIC UNIVERSITY 2043 COLLEGE WY, FOREST GROVE OR	198 - B1
PACIFIC LUTHERAN UNIVERSITY 121ST ST S & PARK AV S, PIERCE CO WA	181 - D4
PACIFIC NORTHWEST COLLEGE OF ART 1219 SW PARK AV, PORTLAND OR	313 - E6
PENINSULA COLLEGE (FORKS BRANCH) FORKS AV N, FORKS WA	169 - C1
PENINSULA JUNIOR COLLEGE PARK AV, PORT ANGELES WA	261 - G6
PIERCE COLLEGE 1601 39TH AV SE, PUYALLUP WA	182 - B4
PIERCE COLLEGE 9401 FARWEST DR, LAKEWOOD WA	181 - C4
PORTLAND COMMUNITY COLLEGE 12000 SW 49TH AV, PORTLAND OR	320 - A3
PORTLAND COM COLLEGE ROCK CREEK 17705 NW SPRINGVILLE RD, WASHINGTON CO OR	192 - A7
PORTLAND STATE UNIVERSITY 724 SW HARRISON ST, PORTLAND OR	312 - E7
REED COLLEGE 3203 SE WOODSTOCK BLVD, PORTLAND OR	318 - A4
RENTON TECHNICAL COLLEGE 3000 NE 4TH ST, RENTON WA	175 - C4
SAINT MARTINS COLLEGE MARTIN WY SE, LACEY WA	297 - G6
SEATTLE CENTRAL COMMUNITY COLLEGE 1701 BROADWAY, SEATTLE WA	278 - B4
SEATTLE PACIFIC UNIVERSITY 3307 3RD AV W, SEATTLE WA	273 - G7
SEATTLE UNIVERSITY BROADWAY & MADISON ST, SEATTLE WA	278 - B5
SHORELINE COMMUNITY COLLEGE 16101 GREENWOOD AV N, SHORELINE WA	171 - A6
SIMON FRASER UNIVERSITY UNIVERSITY DR, DISTRICT OF BURNABY BC	156 - D4
SKAGIT VALLEY JUNIOR COLLEGE N 9TH ST, MOUNT VERNON WA	260 - D12
SOUTHERN OREGON STATE COLLEGE SISKIYOU BLVD, ASHLAND OR	337 - F9
SOUTH SEATTLE COMMUNITY COLLEGE 6000 16TH AV, SEATTLE WA	281 - H7
SOUTHWESTERN OREGON COMM COLLEGE CAPE ARAGO HWY & FIR ST, COOS BAY OR	333 - D6
SPOKANE COMMUNITY COLLEGE E MISSION AV, SPOKANE WA	349 - F7
SPOKANE FALLS COMMUNITY COLLEGE SPOKANE NW, SPOKANE CO WA	348 - E7
TACOMA COMMUNITY COLLEGE 5900 62ND AV CT NW, TACOMA WA	181 - C2
TREASURE VALLEY COMMUNITY COLLEGE SW 4TH ST & SE 5TH AV, ONTARIO OR	139 - A3
TRINITY WESTERN UNIVERSITY TRNS CANADA & GLOVER, TNSHP OF LANGLEY BC	157 - C7
UMPQUA COMMUNITY COLLEGE OAKLAND-SHADY HWY & PAGE, DOUGLAS CO OR	221 - C3
UNIVERSITY OF BRITISH COLUMBIA UNIV BLVD, UNIVERSITY ENDOWMENT LAND BC	156 - A4
UNIVERSITY OF IDAHO HWY 95 & HWY 8, MOSCOW ID	249 - C5
UNIV OF IDAHO CLARK FORK FIELD CAMPUS OFF HWY 200, BONNER CO ID	107 - C3
UNIVERSITY OF OREGON UNIVERSITY ST, EUGENE OR	330 - B7
UNIVERSITY OF PORTLAND 5000 N WILLAMETTE BLVD, PORTLAND OR	308 - A6
UNIVERSITY OF PUGET SOUND 1500 N WARNER ST, TACOMA WA	292 - D4
UNIVERSITY OF VICTORIA MCKENZIE AVE, DISTRICT OF OAK BAY BC	257 - C4
UNIVERSITY OF WASHINGTON MONTLAKE BL NE, SEATTLE WA	274 - D6
UNIVERSITY OF WASHINGTON TACOMA 1103 A ST, TACOMA WA	293 - G6
WALLA WALLA COLLEGE N COLLEGE RD, COLLEGE PLACE WA	344 - E10
WALLA WALLA COMMUNITY COLLEGE APPLESIDE BLVD, VINELAND WA	250 - B4
WARNER PACIFIC COLLEGE 2219 SE 68TH AV, PORTLAND OR	318 - E1
WASHINGTON BAPTIST TEACHERS COLLEGE 2402 S 66TH ST, TACOMA WA	294 - E6
WASHINGTON STATE UNIVERSITY STADIUM WY, PULLMAN WA	249 - B5
WENATCHEE VALLEY COLLEGE HWY 215, OMAK WA	104 - C2
WENATCHEE VALLEY JUNIOR COLLEGE FIFTH ST, WENATCHEE WA	238 - D4
WESTERN BAPTIST COLLEGE DEER PARK DR SE, SALEM OR	325 - F7
WESTERN EVANGELICAL SEMINARY 12753 SW 68TH PKWY, TIGARD OR	199 - B3
WESTERN STATES CHIROPRACTIC COLLEGE 2900 NW 132ND AV, PORTLAND OR	200 - A1
WESTERN WASHINGTON UNIVERSITY HIGH ST, BELLINGHAM WA	258 - C8
WEST SEATTLE RESEARCH LABORATORY UNIV 21ST AV SW & SW GENESEE ST, SEATTLE WA	281 - G5
WHITMAN COLLEGE BOYER AV, WALLA WALLA WA	345 - B7
WHITWORTH COLLEGE N WHITWORTH DR, COUNTRY HOMES WA	346 - H10
WILLAMETTE UNIVERSITY STATE ST SE & 12TH ST SE, SALEM OR	322 - J13
YAKIMA VALLEY JUNIOR COLLEGE NOB HILL BLVD & S 16TH AV, YAKIMA WA	243 - B7

ENTERTAINMENT & SPORTS

FEATURE NAME City State	Page-Grid
4TH FAIRGROUNDS HWY 202 & WALLUSKI LOOP RD, CLATSOP CO WA	300 - G10
AUTZEN STADIUM CENTENNIAL BLVD, EUGENE OR	330 - C5
BAKER COUNTY FAIRGROUNDS HALFWAY-CORNUCOPIA HWY, BAKER CO OR	131 - A3
BENTON COUNTY FAIRGROUNDS 53RD ST & CAMPUS WY, BENTON CO OR	327 - B9
BENTON FRANKLIN FAIRGROUND S OAK ST, KENNEWICK WA	343 - F12
BREMERTON MEMORIAL STADIUM BREMERTON WEST, BREMERTON WA	270 - H9
BRITISH COLUMBIA PLACE STADIUM VANCOUVER BC	254 - G11
BUCKEROO RODEO GROUNDS SHIRLEY ST & N COLE AV, MOLALLA OR	126 - A3
CHENEY STADIUM S TYLER ST & FRWY 16, TACOMA WA	292 - B7
CIVIC STADIUM 1844 SW MORRISON ST, PORTLAND OR	312 - D5
CLACKAMAS COUNTY FAIRGROUNDS 694 NE 4TH AV, CANBY OR	199 - C6
CLALLAM COUNTY FAIRGROUND L ST & W LAURIDSEN BLVD, PORT ANGELES WA	261 - A4
CLARK COUNTY FAIRGROUNDS NE 179TH ST & NE 2ND AV, CLARK CO WA	192 - C4
CLOVERDALE FAIRGROUNDS 176TH ST & 60TH AV, DISTRICT OF SURREY BC	157 - B7
CROOK COUNTY FAIRGROUNDS CROOKED RIV HWY & LYNN BLVD, CROOK CO OR	213 - D5
CURRY COUNTY FAIRGROUNDS OREGON COAST HWY, GOLD BEACH OR	228 - A6
DAYTON & COLUMBIA CO FAIRGROUND OFF HWY 12, COLUMBIA CO WA	122 - A2
DESCHUTES COUNTY FAIRGROUNDS THE DALLES-CALIFORNIA HWY, REDMOND OR	212 - D5
DOUGLAS COUNTY FAIRGROUNDS FREAR ST, DOUGLAS CO OR	334 - E9
DREWSEY RODEO GROUND DREWSEY RD & OTIS VALLEY RD, HARNEY CO OR	137 - C3
EMERALD DOWNS EMERALD DOWNS DR & 29TH ST NW, AUBURN WA	182 - B1
EMPIRE STADIUM HASTINGS ST E, VANCOUVER BC	255 - E10
EUGENE SPEEDWAY W 11TH AV, EUGENE OR	329 - B7
EVERGREEN STATE FAIRGROUNDS HWY 2 & 179TH AV SE, SNOHOMISH CO WA	110 - C1
EXHIBITION GROUNDS AND REC DEPT ASHWELL & HODGINS, DIST OF CHILLIWACK BC	94 - C3
FAIRGROUNDS BRITISH COLUMBIA	101 - A1
FAIRGROUNDS 7TH AV, DISTRICT OF MISSION BC	94 - B3
FAIRGROUNDS 7TH AV, ELLENSBURG WA	241 - B6
GILLIAM COUNTY FAIRGROUNDS JOHN DAY HWY, GILLIAM CO OR	128 - A2
GM PLACE GEORGIA ST, VANCOUVER BC	254 - G10
GRANT COUNTY FAIRGROUNDS 3RD AV & ELM ST, JOHN DAY OR	137 - B2
GRANT COUNTY FAIRGROUNDS AIRWAY DR & VALLEY RD, GRANT CO WA	242 - C3
GRAYS HARBOR COUNTY FAIRGROUNDS FAIRGROUNDS RD, GRAYS HARBOR CO WA	179 - B7
HAMMOND STADIUM 207TH ST & RIVER RD W, MAPLE RIDGE BC	157 - C5
HARNEY COUNTY FAIRGROUNDS HOTCHKISS LN, HARNEY CO OR	145 - B1
HEHE MILL RODEO GROUND WARM SPRINGS HWY, WASCO CO OR	127 - A3
HUSKY STADIUM MONTLAKE BL NE, SEATTLE WA	274 - D7
HYDROPLANE RACE COURSE LAKE WASHINGTON, SEATTLE WA	283 - G3
INTERSTATE FAIRGROUNDS E BROADWAY AV & HAVANA ST, SPOKANE CO WA	349 - G8
JEFFERSON COUNTY FAIRGROUNDS SW FAIRGROUNDS AV, MADRAS OR	208 - B5
JOSEPH A ALBI MEMORIAL STADIUM N ASSEMBLY ST, SPOKANE WA	348 - C3
KEY ARENA 305 HARRISON ST, SEATTLE WA	277 - H4
KING COUNTY FAIRGROUNDS SE 456TH ST & 284TH AV SE, KING CO WA	110 - C3
KING COUNTY STADIUM/KINGDOME 201 S KING ST, SEATTLE WA	278 - A7
KLAMATH COUNTY FAIRGROUNDS CREST ST, ALTAMONT OR	338 - H10
KOOTENAI COUNTY FAIRGROUND COEUR D'ALENE, KOOTENAI CO ID	355 - E5
LAKE COUNTY FAIRGROUNDS ROBERTA AV, LAKE CO OR	152 - A2
LANE COUNTY FAIRGROUNDS 13TH AV, EUGENE OR	329 - H7
LINCOLN COUNTY FAIRGROUNDS 3RD ST, NEWPORT OR	206 - B4
LOGGERS RODEO GROUNDS ENUMCLAW BUCKLEY RD, BUCKLEY WA	110 - C3
MALHEUR COUNTY FAIRGROUNDS NW 8TH AV, ONTARIO OR	139 - A3
MARYMOOR PARK VELODROME NE MARYMOOR WY, KING CO WA	175 - D1
MCCULLOCH STADIUM HIGH ST SE & MISSION ST SE, SALEM OR	322 - H14
MEMORIAL COLISEUM 1401 N WHEELER AV, PORTLAND OR	313 - G4
MEMORIAL STADIUM BROADWAY & 38TH ST, EVERETT WA	264 - E5
MEYDENBAUER CENTER NE 6TH ST & 112TH AV NE, BELLEVUE WA	175 - C2
MORROW COUNTY FAIRGROUNDS HEPPNER HWY, MORROW CO OR	128 - C2
MULTNOMAH CO FAIRGROUNDS & EXPO CTR N MARINE DR & N FORCE AV, PORTLAND OR	308 - E1
MULTNOMAH GREYHOUND PARK NW FAIRVIEW & NE GLISAN, WOOD VILLAGE OR	200 - B1
OLYMPIC STADIUM SUMNER AV, HOQUIAM WA	178 - A7
OREGON CONVENTION CENTER 777 NE MARTIN LUTHER KING, PORTLAND OR	313 - G5
OREGON STATE FAIRGROUNDS SUNNYVIEW RD, SALEM OR	323 - B10
PACIFIC COLISEUM MCGILL ST & RENFREW ST, VANCOUVER BC	255 - E9
PAYETTE COUNTY FAIRGROUNDS IDAHO ST, PAYETTE CO ID	139 - B3
PLAYFAIR RACETRACK OFF E SPRAGUE AV, SPOKANE WA	349 - D8
POLK COUNTY FAIRGROUNDS PACIFIC HWY, POLK CO OR	204 - B6
PORTLAND INTERNATIONAL RACEWAY N VICTORY AV, PORTLAND OR	308 - D2
PORTLAND MEADOWS RACE TRACK N SCHMEER RD, PORTLAND OR	309 - F3
PORTLAND SPEEDWAY 9727 N M L KING JR BLVD, PORTLAND OR	309 - G3
RENTON MEMORIAL HS STADIUM N 4TH ST & LOGAN AV N, RENTON WA	175 - C5
ROSE GARDEN ARENA THE 1 CENTER COURT ST, PORTLAND OR	313 - G4
SAGE ACRES RACETRACK HOMEDALE RD & WAGNER RD, CANYON CO ID	147 - B1
SANDOWN RACEWAY HWY 17, DISTRICT OF NORTH SAANICH BC	159 - C2
SEATTLE CENTER STADIUM SEATTLE WA	277 - H4
SEATTLE INTERNATIONAL RACEWAY 148TH AV SE, KING CO WA	182 - C1
SEATTLE UNIVERSITY GYMNASIUM E JEFFERSON ST & 15TH AV, SEATTLE WA	278 - C6
SHERMAN COUNTY FAIRGROUNDS SHERMAN HWY & LONE ROCK RD, SHERMAN CO OR	127 - C2
SOUTHWEST WASHINGTON FAIRGROUNDS NATIONAL AV, LEWIS CO WA	299 - E7
STADIUM SCHUSTER PKWY, TACOMA WA	293 - G3
STADIUM/ARENA HIGHWAY 18, BRITISH COLUMBIA	100 - C1
STADIUM/ARENA HWY 3 GRAND FORKS, BRITISH COLUMBIA	105 - C1
TACOMA CONVENTION CENTER S 13TH ST & MARKET ST, TACOMA WA	293 - H6
TACOMA DOME E D ST, TACOMA WA	293 - J7
TACOMAS LANDMARK CONVENTION CENTER 47 SAINT HELENS AV, TACOMA WA	293 - G4
TILLAMOOK COUNTY FAIRGROUNDS TILLAMOOK, TILLAMOOK CO OR	197 - C2
TYGH VALLEY FAIRGROUNDS FAIRGROUND RD, WASCO CO OR	127 - B2
UMATILLA COUNTY FAIRGROUNDS W HIGHLAND AV, HERMISTON OR	129 - A1
UNDERSEA WORLD HWY 101, DEL NORTE CO CA	148 - B3
VETERANS MEMORIAL ARENA N LINCOLN ST, SPOKANE WA	348 - J8
VINCE GENNA STADIUM SE WILSON AV & SE 5TH ST, BEND OR	332 - F9
WALLA WALLA COUNTY FAIRGROUNDS W TIETAN ST, WALLA WALLA CO WA	345 - A9
WALLOWA COUNTY FAIRGROUNDS ENTERPRISE-LEWISTON HWY, ENTERPRISE OR	130 - C2
WASHINGTON COUNTY FAIRGROUNDS 872 NE 28TH AV, HILLSBORO OR	198 - D1
WASHINGTON ST CONVENTION & TRADE CTR 800 CONVENTION PL, SEATTLE WA	278 - A5
WESTERN IDAHO FAIRGROUND OFF GLENWOOD ST, ADA CO ID	253 - C2
WESTERN WASHINGTON FAIRGROUNDS MERIDIAN ST S & 9TH AV SW, PUYALLUP WA	182 - B4
WHEELER COUNTY FAIRGROUNDS JOHN DAY HWY, WHEELER CO OR	128 - A3

FEATURE NAME	City State	Page-Grid
WILD WAVES WATER PARK	36201 ENCHANTED PKWY S, KING CO WA	182 - B2
YAMHILL COUNTY FAIRGROUNDS	LAFAYETTE AV, MCMINNVILLE OR	198 - B7

GOLF COURSES

FEATURE NAME	City State	Page-Grid
18 PASTURES GOLF COURSE	WILSON ST, DISTRICT OF MISSION BC	94 - B3
AMERICAN LEGION MEM PK & GOLF COURSE	ALVERSON BLVD, EVERETT WA	171 - C1
ARDMORE GOLF COURSE	930 ARDMORE, DISTRICT OF NORTH SAANICH BC	159 - B3
ARROWHEAD GOLF CLUB	28301 S HIGHWAY 213, CLACKAMAS CO OR	199 - D7
AUBURN CENTER GOLF COURSE	CENTER ST NE, MARION CO OR	323 - G13
AUBURN REGIONAL GOLF COURSE	29630 GREEN RIVER RD, AUBURN WA	182 - C1
AWBREY GLEN GOLF COURSE	NW MOUNT WASHINTON DR, BEND OR	332 - A4
BALLINGER PARK MUNICIPAL GOLF COURSE	23000 LAKEVIEW DR, MOUNTLAKE TERRACE WA	171 - B6
BATTLE CREEK COUNTRY CLUB	SALEM OR	325 - A9
BATTLE CREEK GOLF COURSE	6006 MERIDIAN AV N, SNOHOMISH CO WA	168 - C7
BEACH GROVE GOLF CLUB	DISTRICT OF DELTA BC	101 - C1
BEAR CREEK COUNTRY CLUB	202ND AV NE, KING CO WA	171 - D7
BELLEVUE MUNICIPAL GOLF COURSE	5450 140TH AV NE, BELLEVUE WA	175 - D1
BEND GOLF COURSE	COUNTRY CLUB & HIGHLAND, DESCHUTES CO OR	332 - E13
BLENKINSOP VALLEY GOLF COURSE	BLENKINSOP RD, DISTRICT OF SAANICH BC	256 - J1
BOISE RANCH GOLF COURSE	E LAKE HAZEL RD, ADA CO ID	253 - B4
BROADMOOR GOLF CLUB	2340 BROADMOOR DR E, SEATTLE WA	278 - E2
BROADMOOR GOLF COURSE	3509 NE COLUMBIA BLVD, PORTLAND OR	310 - B5
BROKEN TOP GOLF COURSE	CAMPBELL DR, DESCHUTES CO OR	332 - A9
BROOKDALE GOLF CLUB	1802 BROOKDALE RD E, PIERCE CO WA	182 - A5
BURNABY MOUNTAIN GOLF COURSE	DISTRICT OF BURNABY BC	156 - D4
CANTERWOOD GOLF COURSE & COUNTRY CLUB	4026 CANTERWOOD DR NW, PIERCE CO WA	174 - B7
CAPILANO GOLF CLUB	STEVENS DR, DISTRICT OF WEST VANCOUVE BC	254 - G1
CARNATION GOLF COURSE	1810 W SNOQUALMIE RIVER RD NE, KING CO WA	176 - B2
CARNOUSTIE GOLF COURSE	DOMINION AV, PORT COQUITLAM BC	157 - B4
CASCADE GOLF COURSE	14303 436TH AV SE, KING CO WA	176 - C5
CEDARCREST GOLF COURSE	6810 84TH ST NE, MARYSVILLE WA	168 - D7
CEDAR HILL GOLF COURSE	1400 DERBY RD, DISTRICT OF SAANICH BC	256 - J4
CEDAR LINKS GOLF COURSE	FOOTHILL RD & CEDAR LINKS RD, MEDFORD OR	336 - H8
CEDARS GOLF CLUB	15001 NE 181ST ST, CLARK CO WA	193 - A4
CENTRALIA ELKS GOLF COURSE	MAGNOLIA ST & BYRD ST, CENTRALIA WA	299 - G4
CHARBONNEAU GOLF COURSE	CHARBONNEAU DR, WILSONVILLE OR	199 - B6
CHEAM GOLF COURSE	44610 LUCKAKCK, DISTRICT OF CHILLIWACK BC	94 - C3
CHILLIWACK GOLF COURSE	SUMAS CENTRAL, DISTRICT OF CHILLIWACK BC	94 - C3
CHRISTINA LAKE GOLF AND COUNTRY CLUB	HWY 3 & HWY 395, BRITISH COLUMBIA	105 - C1
CLASSIC COUNTRY CLUB	4908 208TH ST E, PIERCE CO WA	182 - A6
COLLEGE PLACE DRIVING RANGE	208TH ST SW, LYNNWOOD WA	171 - B5
COLUMBIA-EDGEWATER COUNTRY CLUB	2138 NE MARINE DR, PORTLAND OR	309 - J2
COLUMBIA GOLF COURSE	COLUMBIA DR SE, KENNEWICK WA	343 - B9
COLWOOD NATIONAL GOLF COURSE	7313 NE COLUMBIA BLVD, PORTLAND OR	311 - F5
CORDOVA BAY GOLF COURSE	CORDOVA BAY RD, DISTRICT OF SAANICH BC	159 - C5
CORVALLIS COUNTRY CLUB	COUNTRY CLUB DR, BENTON CO OR	327 - D12
CRESTVIEW HILLS GOLF COURSE	GREEN DR, WALDPORT OR	328 - D7
DELTA PUBLIC GOLF COURSE	DISTRICT OF DELTA BC	101 - C1
DESERT SPRINGS GOLF COURSE	LAKESHORE DR & 44TH AVE, BRITISH COLUMBIA	104 - C1
DOWNRIVER MUNICIPAL GOLF COURSE	W DOWNRIVER PARK DR, SPOKANE WA	348 - D6
EASTMORELAND GOLF COURSE	2425 SE BYBEE BLVD, PORTLAND OR	317 - J5
ECHO FALLS COUNTRY CLUB	20414 121ST AV SE, SNOHOMISH CO WA	171 - D5
EDGEWATER GOLF COURSE	FALLON DR, WEST RICHLAND WA	340 - A11
ELK RUN GOLF COURSE	228TH AV SE & SE 275TH PL, KING CO WA	175 - D7
ELKS-ALLENMORE GOLF CLUB	2125 S CEDAR ST, TACOMA WA	292 - D7
ELKS MEMORIAL GOLF COURSE	GRADE ST, KELSO WA	303 - D9
ENUMCLAW GOLF COURSE	45220 284TH AV SE, KING CO WA	110 - C3
ESMERALDA MUNICIPAL GOLF COURSE	N FREYA ST, SPOKANE WA	349 - F4
EVERETT GOLF & COUNTRY CLUB	1500 52ND ST SE, EVERETT WA	268 - D1
FAIRWAY VILLAGE GOLF COURSE	15509 SE FERNWOOD DR, CLARK CO WA	193 - A7
FAIRWOOD GOLF & COUNTRY CLUB	17070 140TH AV SE, KING CO WA	175 - C5
FIRCREST GOLF COURSE	6520 REGENTS BLVD, FIRCREST WA	181 - C3
FOREST HILLS GOLF COURSE	TONGUE & JOHNSON SCHOOL, WASHINGTON CO OR	198 - C2
FORT LANGLEY GOLF COURSE	9782 MCKINNON RD, TOWNSHIP OF LANGLEY BC	157 - C6
FORT LEWIS GOLF COURSE	STEILACOOM-DUPONT RD SW, PIERCE CO WA	181 - B5
FORT STEILACOOM GOLF COURSE	8202 ELWOOD DR SW, LAKEWOOD WA	181 - C4
FOSTER GOLF COURSE	13500 INTERURBAN AV S, TUKWILA WA	289 - G2
FRASERVIEW GOLF COURSE	VANCOUVER BC	156 - C5
FRONTIER GOLF COURSE	N HOLLY ST, CLACKAMAS CO OR	199 - C6
GEARHART GOLF COURSE	GEARHART LOOP & MARION, CLATSOP CO WA	301 - G3
GIG HARBOR GOLF & COUNTRY CLUB	6909 ARTONDALE DR NW, PIERCE CO WA	181 - B1
GLEN ACRES GOLF CLUB	1000 S 112TH ST, KING WA	286 - B6
GLENDALE GOLF & COUNTRY CLUB	13440 MAIN ST, BELLEVUE WA	175 - C2
GLENDOVEER GOLF COURSE & FITNESS TR	14015 NE GLISAN ST, PORTLAND OR	200 - A1
GLENEAGLE GOLF COURSE	7619 COUNTRY CLUB RD E, ARLINGTON WA	168 - D5
GLENEAGLES GOLF COURSE	DISTRICT OF WEST VANCOUVE BC	156 - A2
GLEN MEADOWS GOLF COURSE	1050 MCTAVISH, DIST OF NORTH SAANICH BC	159 - C3
GOLF CLUB AT NEWCASTLE	15401 SE NEWCASTLE COAL CK, NEWCASTLE WA	175 - D4
GOLF COURSE	OLD OWEN RD, SNOHOMISH CO WA	110 - C1
GORGE VALE GOLF COURSE	1005 CRAIGFLOWER, TOWN OF ESQUILMALT BC	256 - C6
GREEN ACRES GOLF COURSE	CITY OF RICHMOND BC	156 - C6
GREENLEA GOLF COURSE	26736 SE KELSO RD, CLACKAMAS CO OR	200 - B3
GREEN MEADOWS GOLF COURSE	NE 78TH ST & NE 72ND AV, CLARK CO WA	192 - D5
GRESHAM GOLF & COUNTRY CLUB	2155 NE DIVISION ST, GRESHAM OR	200 - B2
GUILDFORD GOLF COURSE	152ND ST, DISTRICT OF SURREY BC	157 - A7
HARBOUR POINTE GOLF CLUB	11817 HARBOUR POINTE BLVD, MUKILTEO WA	171 - B4
HAZELMERE GOLF COURSE	8TH AV, DISTRICT OF SURREY BC	158 - B2
HERON LAKES GOLF COURSE	N PORTLAND RD, PORTLAND OR	308 - C1
HIGH CEDARS GOLF & COUNTRY CLUB	14604 149TH STCT E, PIERCE CO WA	182 - B5
HIGHLANDS GOLF COURSE	1400 HIGHLANDS PKWY N, TACOMA WA	181 - C2
HILL GOLF CLUB	OTTER POINT RD, BRITISH COLUMBIA	101 - A2
HOLLIES GOLF COURSE	FRASER HWY & 192ND, DISTRICT OF SURREY BC	157 - B7
HOOD RIVER GOLF COURSE	COUNTRY CLUB RD, HOOD RIVER CO OR	195 - C6
HOPE GOLF COURSE	HWY 1, BRITISH COLUMBIA	95 - A3
HORSESHOE LAKE GOLF COURSE	15932 SIDNEY RD SW, KITSAP CO WA	174 - B6
HOUND HOLLOW GOLF CENTER	23010 ARATA RD, WOOD VILLAGE OR	200 - B1
INDIAN CANYON MUNICIPAL GOLF COURSE	S INDIAN CANYON DR, SPOKANE WA	348 - D10
INDIAN LAKES GOLF COURSE	OFF S COLE RD, ADA CO ID	253 - C4
INGLEWOOD COUNTRY CLUB	INGLEWOOD RD NE, KING CO WA	171 - B7
INTERBAY GOLF COURSE	W WHEELER ST & 15TH AV W, SEATTLE WA	277 - F1
JACKSON PARK GOLF COURSE	1000 NE 135TH ST, SEATTLE WA	171 - B7
JEFFERSON PARK GOLF COURSE	4101 BEACON AV S, SEATTLE WA	282 - C4
KAYAK POINT GOLF COURSE	156TH ST NW, SNOHOMISH CO WA	168 - B6
KENWANDA GOLF COURSE	14030 KENWANDA DR, SNOHOMISH CO WA	171 - D4
KING CITY GOLF COURSE	15355 SW ROYALTY PKWY, KING CITY OR	199 - B4
KINKORA GOLF COURSE	46050 HIGGINSON, DIST OF CHILLIWACK BC	94 - C3
LAKE CHELAN MUNICIPAL GOLF COURSE	HWY 150, CHELAN WA	236 - C3
LAKE OSWEGO MUNICIPAL GOLF COURSE	17525 SW STAFFORD RD, LAKE OSWEGO OR	199 - C4
LAKE SPANAWAY GOLF COURSE	15602 PACIFIC AV, PIERCE CO WA	181 - D5
LAKE WILDERNESS GOLF COURSE	25400 WITTE RD SE, KING CO WA	175 - D7
LANGARA GOLF COURSE	VANCOUVER BC	156 - B5
LANGLEY GOLF CENTER	216TH ST, TOWNSHIP OF LANGLEY BC	158 - C1
LEDGEVIEW GOLF COURSE	LOWER SUMAS MTN RD, DIST OF MATSQUI BC	102 - B1
LIBERTY LAKE GOLF COURSE	S LAKESIDE RD, LIBERTY LAKE WA	247 - B4
LINDEN GOLF & COUNTRY CLUB	2519 E MAIN AV, PUYALLUP WA	182 - B3
LIPOMA FIRS GOLF COURSE	18615 110TH AV E, PIERCE CO WA	182 - B6
LONGVIEW GOLF AND COUNTRY CLUB	PACIFIC WY, LONGVIEW WA	302 - J6
LYNNWOOD MUNICIPAL GOLF COURSE	20200 68TH AV W, LYNNWOOD WA	171 - B5
MADRONA LINKS GOLF COURSE	3604 22ND AV NW, PIERCE CO WA	181 - C1
MAPLE RIDGE GOLF COURSE	207TH ST & GOLF LN, MAPLE RIDGE BC	157 - C5
MAPLEWOOD GOLF COURSE	13020 RENTON-MAPLE VALLEY RD, RENTON WA	175 - C5
MARINE DRIVE GOLF COURSE	VANCOUVER BC	156 - B5
MAYFAIR LAKES GOLF COURSE	CITY OF RICHMOND BC	156 - C6
MCCALL GOLF COURSE	DAVIS ST & LICK CREEK RD, MCCALL ID	251 - D5
MCCLEERY GOLF COURSE	VANCOUVER BC	156 - B5
MEADOW GARDENS GOLF COURSE	19675 LOUGHEED HWY, PITT MEADOWS BC	157 - C5
MEADOWLANDS GOLF AND COUNTRY CLUB	47823 YALE RD, DISTRICT OF CHILLIWACK BC	94 - C3
MEADOW PARK GOLF COURSE	7108 LAKEWOOD DR W, UNIVERSITY PLACE WA	294 - A6
MEADWOOD GOLF COURSE	E VALLEYWAY AV, LIBERTY LAKE WA	247 - B4
MERIDIAN VALLEY GOLF & COUNTRY CLUB	24830 136TH AV SE, KING CO WA	175 - C7
MERIWETHER NATIONAL GOLF CLUB	SW ROOD BRIDGE RD, WASHINGTON CO OR	198 - D2
METCHOSIN GOLF COURSE	METCHOSIN RD, DISTRICT OF METCHOSIN BC	159 - A7
MICHELBROOK COUNTRY CLUB	1301 MICHELBROOK LN, MCMINNVILLE OR	198 - A7
MILL CREEK COUNTRY CLUB	15550 COUNTRY CLUB DR, MILL CREEK WA	171 - C4
MISSION GOLF COURSE	NELSON ST, DISTRICT OF MISSION BC	94 - B3
MOUNTAIN VIEW GOLF COURSE	27195 SE KELSO RD, CLACKAMAS CO OR	200 - B3
MOUNTAIN VIEW GOLF COURSE	340 SE ORCHARD DR, NORTH BEND WA	176 - C5
MOUNT DOUGLAS GOLF COURSE	BLENKINSOP RD, DISTRICT OF SAANICH BC	256 - J1
MOUNT SI GOLF COURSE	9010 BOALCH AV SE, SNOQUALMIE WA	176 - C4
MUNICIPAL GOLF COURSE	N 20TH AV, PASCO WA	343 - D4
MUSQUEAM GOLF CENTRE	VANCOUVER BC	156 - A5
MYLORA DRIVING RANGE	CITY OF RICHMOND BC	156 - B7
MYLORA GOLF COURSE	CITY OF RICHMOND BC	156 - B7
NEWLANDS GOLF COURSE	48TH AV, LANGLEY BC	158 - C1
NICO WYND GOLF CLUB	CRESCENT RD, DISTRICT OF SURREY BC	158 - A1
NILE TEMPLE GOLF COURSE	500 NE 205TH ST, MOUNTLAKE TERRACE WA	171 - B6
NISQUALLY VALLEY GOLF COURSE	RAINIER-YELM HWY & YELM, THURSTON CO WA	118 - A1
NORTH SHORE GOLF COURSE	1611 BROWNS POINT BLVD NE, TACOMA WA	182 - A2
OAKBROOK GOLF & COUNTRY CLUB	8102 ZIRCON DR SW, LAKEWOOD WA	181 - C3
OAK KNOLL GOLF COURSE	GREEN SPRINGS HWY & OAK KNOLL, ASHLAND OR	337 - J10
OAK KNOLL GOLF COURSE	WILLAMINA-SALEM HWY, POLK CO OR	204 - B5
OAKWAY GOLF COURSE	OAKWAY RD, EUGENE OR	330 - B3
OLYMPIC VIEW GOLF COURSE	643 LATORIA RD, CITY OF COLWOOD BC	159 - B7
ORCHARD HILLS GOLF COURSE	39TH ST, CLARK CO WA	193 - C7
OREGON CITY GOLF CLUB	20124 S BEAVERCREEK RD, CLACKAMAS CO OR	199 - D5
OREGON GOLF CLUB THE	25700 PETES MOUNTAIN RD, CLACKAMAS CO OR	199 - C5
ORENCO WOODS GOLF COURSE	22200 NE BIRCH ST, WASHINGTON CO OR	199 - A1
OSOYOOS GOLF AND COUNTRY CLUB	15TH ST, BRITISH COLUMBIA	104 - C1
OSWEGO LAKE COUNTRY CLUB	20 IRON MOUNTAIN BLVD, CLACKAMAS CO OR	320 - D5
OVERLAKE GOLF & COUNTRY CLUB	8000 NE 16TH ST, MEDINA WA	175 - C2
PEACE PORTAL GOLF COURSE	HWY 99, DISTRICT OF SURREY BC	158 - B2
PENINSULA GOLF COURSE	GOLF COURSE RD, PORT ANGELES WA	261 - H6
PINECREST GOLF COURSE	NW BLISS RD, CLARK CO WA	192 - C4
PITT MEADOWS GOLF COURSE	RIPPINGTON RD, PITT MEADOWS BC	157 - B5
PLEASANT VALLEY GOLF CLUB	12300 SE 162ND AV, CLACKAMAS CO OR	200 - A3
POINT GREY GOLF COURSE	VANCOUVER BC	156 - A5
POPPY ESTATES GOLF COURSE	FRASER HWY, TOWNSHIP OF LANGLEY BC	158 - D1
PORTLAND GOLF CLUB	5900 SW SCHOLLS FERRY, WASHINGTON CO OR	199 - B2
PORTLAND MEADOWS GOLF COURSE	901 N SCHMEER RD, PORTLAND OR	309 - F3
PROGRESS DOWNS GOLF COURSE	8200 SW SCHOLLS FERRY, WASHINGTON CO OR	199 - B3
PROSPECT LAKE GOLF COURSE	4633 PROSPECT LAKE, DIST OF SAANICH BC	159 - B5
PUMPKIN RIDGE GOLF COURSE	12930 OLD PUMPKN RDG RD, WASHINGTON CO OR	125 - C1
QUAIL VALLEY GOLF COURSE	12565 NW AERTS RD, WASHINGTON CO OR	125 - B1
QUILCHENA GOLF COURSE	CITY OF RICHMOND BC	156 - A6
RAINIER GOLF COURSE & COUNTRY CLUB	1856 S 112TH ST, KING WA	286 - C6
RANCH HILLS GOLF COURSE	RANCH HILLS RD, CLACKAMAS CO OR	199 - D7
REAMES COUNTRY CLUB	KLAMATH CO OR	338 - B13
RESORT AT THE MOUNTAIN GOLF COURSE	WELCHES RD & FAIRWAY AV, CLACKAMAS CO OR	201 - C5
RICHMOND GOLF AND COUNTRY CLUB	CITY OF RICHMOND BC	156 - B7
RIVERBEND GOLF COMPLEX	RUSSELL RD, KENT WA	175 - B7
RIVERGREENS GOLF COURSE	480 RIVER RD, GLADSTONE OR	199 - D4
RIVERS EDGE GOLF COURSE	THE DALLES-CALIFORNIA HWY, BEND OR	332 - D3
RIVERSIDE DRIVING RANGE	KING GEORGE HWY, DISTRICT OF SURREY BC	158 - A1
RIVERSIDE GOLF & COUNTRY CLUB	8105 NE 33RD DR, PORTLAND OR	310 - A4
RIVERWAY GOLF COURSE	DISTRICT OF BURNABY BC	156 - C6
RIVERWOOD GOLF COURSE	21050 RIVERWOOD RD, YAMHILL CO OR	198 - C7
ROCK CREEK COUNTRY CLUB	5100 NW NEAKAHNIE AV, WASHINGTON CO OR	192 - A7
ROGUE VALLEY COUNTRY CLUB	BLACK OAK & COUNTRY CLUB DR, MEDFORD OR	336 - G12
ROSEBURG MUNICIPAL GOLF COURSE	NW GARDEN VLY & NW DOGWOOD, ROSEBURG OR	334 - D5
ROSE CITY GOLF COURSE	2200 NE 70TH AV, PORTLAND OR	314 - E3
ROYAL COLWOOD GOLF AND COUNTRY CLUB	GOLDSTREAM AVE, CITY OF COLWOOD BC	159 - B6
ROYAL OAK GOLF COURSE	HWY 17, DISTRICT OF SAANICH BC	159 - C5
ROYAL OAKS COUNTRY CLUB	NE ROYAL OAK & NE 97TH AV, VANCOUVER WA	307 - G2
SAH-HAH-LEE GOLF COURSE	17104 SE 130TH AV, CLACKAMAS CO OR	200 - A4
SALEM GOLF CLUB	SALEM OR	324 - E2
SALISHAN GOLF LINKS	OREGON COAST HWY, LINCOLN CO OR	203 - A6
SANDELIE GOLF COURSE	28333 SW MOUNTAIN RD, CLACKAMAS CO OR	199 - C5
SAND POINT COUNTRY CLUB	8333 55TH AV NE, SEATTLE WA	275 - G2
SEATTLE GOLF AND COUNTRY CLUB	210 NW 145TH ST, SHORELINE WA	171 - A7
SEYMOUR GOLF AND COUNTRY CLUB	DISTRICT OF NORTH VANCOUV BC	156 - D3
SHAM-NA-PUM GOLF COURSE	RIVER POINT RD, RICHLAND WA	341 - H3
SHAUGHNESSY GOLF COURSE	UNIVERSITY ENDOWMENT LAND BC	156 - A5

PNW

INDEX

FEATURE NAME	City State	Page-Grid
SNOHOMISH GOLF COURSE	7806 147TH AV SE, SNOHOMISH CO WA	110 - C1
SPOKANE COUNTRY CLUB	N COUNTRY CLUB DR, FAIRWOOD WA	346 - E8
SPRING VALLEY GOLF COURSE	SAN JUAN, PORT TOWNSEND WA	263 - F4
SPRINGWATER GOLF COURSE	WALLENS RD, CLACKAMAS CO OR	200 - C7
SUMMERFIELD GOLF & COUNTRY CLUB	10650 SW SUMMERFIELD DR, KING CITY OR	199 - B3
SUMNER MEADOWS GOLF LINKS	14802 8TH ST E, SUMNER WA	182 - B3
SUNSET GROVE GOLF COURSE	41615 OSTERMAN RD, WASHINGTON CO OR	125 - B1
SUNSHINE HILLS GOLF COURSE	DISTRICT OF DELTA BC	156 - D7
SURREY DRIVING RANGE	133RD ST, DISTRICT OF SURREY BC	157 - A5
SURREY GOLF COURSE	7700 168TH ST, DISTRICT OF SURREY BC	157 - B7
TACOMA COUNTRY CLUB & GOLF CLUB	COUNTRY CLUB DR SW, LAKEWOOD WA	181 - C5
TALL CHIEF GOLF COURSE	1313 W SNOQUALMIE RIVER RD SE, KING CO WA	176 - B3
TALL TIMBERS GOLF COURSE	23523 56TH AV, TOWNSHIP OF LANGLEY BC	157 - D7
TAPPS ISLAND GOLF COURSE	20818 ISLAND PARK WY, PIERCE CO WA	182 - C3
TOP O SCOTT GOLF COURSE	12000 SE STEVENS RD, CLACKAMAS CO OR	199 - D3
TSAWWASSEN GOLF CLUB	DISTRICT OF DELTA BC	101 - C1
TUALATIN COUNTRY CLUB	SW TUALATIN RD, TUALATIN OR	199 - B4
TWIN LAKES GOLF COURSE	3583 SW 320TH ST, FEDERAL WAY WA	182 - A1
TYEE VALLEY GOLF COURSE	2401 S 192ND ST, SEATAC WA	290 - C2
UNIVERSITY GOLF COURSE	754 124TH ST S, PIERCE CO WA	181 - D4
UNIVERSITY GOLF COURSE	UNIVERSITY ENDOWMENT LAND BC	156 - A4
UPLANDS GOLF COURSE	CADBORO BAY RD, DISTRICT OF OAK BAY BC	257 - D5
VASHON GOLF COURSE	SW 248TH ST, KING CO WA	174 - D7
VETERANS HOSPITAL GOLF COURSE	VETERANS DR SW, PIERCE CO WA	181 - C4
VETERANS MEMORIAL GOLF COURSE	US HWY 12, WALLA WALLA WA	345 - A5
VICTORIA GOLF COURSE	1110 BEACH DR, DISTRICT OF OAK BAY BC	257 - D10
WALLA WALLA COUNTRY CLUB	COUNTRY CLUB RD, WALLA WALLA WA	344 - J11
WALTER E HALL REC AREA & GOLF COURSE	1226 W CASINO RD, EVERETT WA	267 - J5
WANDERMERE LAKE GOLF COURSE	HWY 395 & LTTLE SPOKANE DR, SPOKANE CO WA	347 - A5
WAVERLEY COUNTRY CLUB	1100 SE WAVERLY DR, CLACKAMAS CO OR	321 - H1
WAYNE GOLF COURSE	WAYNITA DR, BOTHELL WA	171 - C6
WELLINGTON HILLS GOLF COURSE	240TH ST SE & 71ST AV SE, SNOHOMISH CO WA	171 - D6
WENATCHEE GOLF COURSE	EASTMONT AV, EAST WENATCHEE BENCH WA	239 - A4
WEST SEATTLE GOLF COURSE & REC CTR	SW GENESEE ST, SEATTLE WA	281 - F5
WILDWOOD GOLF COURSE	21881 NW SAINT HELENS RD, MULTNOMAH CO OR	192 - A5
WILLAMETTE VALLEY COUNTRY CLUB	900 COUNTRY CLUB PL, CANBY OR	199 - C6
WILLOWS RUN GOLF COURSE	10442 WILLOWS RD, REDMOND WA	175 - D1

HOSPITALS

FEATURE NAME	City State	Page-Grid
ADVENTIST MEDICAL CENTER	10123 SE MARKET ST, PORTLAND OR	315 - H7
ALLENMORE HOSPITAL	S 19TH ST & S UNION AV, TACOMA WA	292 - D7
ASHLAND COMMUNITY HOSPITAL	MAPLE ST & CHESTNUT ST, ASHLAND OR	337 - B6
AUBURN GENERAL HOSPITAL	20 2ND ST NE, AUBURN WA	182 - B1
BAY AREA HOSPITAL	THOMPSON RD & N 16TH ST, COOS BAY OR	333 - F8
BONNER GENERAL HOSPITAL	US ROUTE 2, SANDPOINT ID	244 - A2
BOUNDARY COUNTY COMMUNITY HOSPITAL	OFF HWY 95, BOUNDARY CO ID	107 - B1
BURNABY GENERAL HOSPITAL	SMITH AV, DISTRICT OF BURNABY BC	156 - C5
CARE CENTER FOR CHILDREN	WILLNGDN & CANADA, DISTRICT OF BURNABY BC	255 - H14
CASCADE COMMUNITY HOSPITAL	BUSH ST & 2ND ST, CENTRAL POINT OR	230 - C7
CENTRALIA GENERAL HOSPITAL	COOKS HILL RD & WARD RD, CENTRALIA WA	299 - C4
CENTRAL OREGON DISTRICT HOSPITAL	N CANAL BLVD, REDMOND OR	212 - D5
CHILDRENS HOSPITAL	OAK ST, VANCOUVER BC	156 - B5
CHILDRENS HOSPITAL & MED CTR	4800 SAND PT WY NE, SEATTLE WA	275 - F5
CLATSOP COUNTY HOME	NEHALEM HWY, CLATSOP CO WA	300 - G10
COLUMBIA BASIN HOSPITAL	D ST SE & SOUTHEAST BL, EPHRATA WA	112 - C3
COLUMBIA DISTRICT HOSPITAL	PITTSBURG & COLUMBIA RIV, SAINT HELENS OR	192 - B1
COLUMBIA MEMORIAL HOSPITAL	22ND ST, ASTORIA WA	300 - E5
COMMUNITY MEMORIAL HOSPITAL	1450 BATTERSBY AV, ENUMCLAW WA	110 - C3
COQUILLE VALLEY HOSPITAL	5TH ST, COQUILLE OR	220 - D5
COUNTY HOSPITAL	29232 S ELLENSBURG AV, GOLD BEACH OR	228 - A6
COWLITZ GENERAL HOSPITAL	7TH AV, LONGVIEW WA	303 - B9
DAMMASCH STATE HOSPITAL	28801 SW 110TH AV, CLACKAMAS CO OR	199 - B5
DAYTON GENERAL HOSPITAL	OFF HWY 12, COLUMBIA CO WA	122 - A2
DEACONESS HOSPITAL	CHERRY ST & S OKANOGAN AV, WENATCHEE WA	238 - D4
DELTA HOSPITAL	DISTRICT OF DELTA BC	101 - C1
DOUGLAS COMMUNITY HOSPITAL	W HARVARD BLVD & W UMPQUA ST, ROSEBURG OR	334 - E7
EAGLE RIDGE HOSPITAL	IOCO RD & GUILDFORD WY, PORT MOODY BC	157 - A4
EASTERN OREGON STATE HOSPITAL	OLD OREGON TRAIL HWY, PENDLETON OR	129 - B1
EASTERN STATE HOSPITAL	OFF HWY 902, MEDICAL LAKE WA	114 - B2
EASTMORELAND GENERAL HOSPITAL	2900 SE STEELE ST, PORTLAND OR	318 - A4
EASTSIDE HOSPITAL, THE	2700 152ND AV NE, REDMOND WA	175 - D2
EDGECLIFF HOSPITAL	S PARK RD, SPOKANE CO WA	350 - B9
ELKS HOSPITAL	OFF RESERVE ST, ADA CO ID	253 - D2
EUGENE HOSPITAL	13TH AV, EUGENE OR	330 - A7
EVERGREEN HOSPITAL MED CTR	12040 NE 128TH ST, KIRKLAND WA	171 - C7
FAIRVIEW HOSPITAL	PRINGLE RD SE, SALEM OR	325 - A5
FORKS COMMUNITY HOSPITAL	BOGACHIEL WY, FORKS WA	169 - C2
GENERAL HOSPITAL	HOSPITAL RD, SEDRO-WOOLLEY WA	260 - J2
GEORGE DERBY HOSPITAL	CARIBOO RD, DISTRICT OF BURNABY BC	156 - D5
GOOD SAMARITAN HOSPITAL	SAMARITAN DR, CORVALLIS OR	327 - H5
GOOD SAMARITAN COMMUNITY HOSPITAL	407 14TH AV SE, PUYALLUP WA	182 - B4
GOOD SHEPHERD COMMUNITY HOSPITAL	OFF HWY 207, HERMISTON OR	129 - A1
GORGE ROAD HOSPITAL	GEORGE RD W, CITY OF VICTORIA BC	256 - E6
GRACE HOSPITAL	OAK ST, VANCOUVER BC	156 - B5
GRANDE RONDE HOSPITAL	OFF HWY 203, UNION CO OR	130 - A2
GRAYS HARBOR COMMUNITY HOSPITAL	CANNON ST, ABERDEEN WA	178 - A7
GRITMAN MEDICAL CENTER	HWY 95 & 6TH ST, MOSCOW ID	249 - C5
GROUP HEALTH CO-OP CENTRAL HOSPITAL	201 16TH AV E, SEATTLE WA	278 - C4
HAPPY ACRES MEMORIAL HOSPITAL	HWY 99W, YAMHILL CO OR	204 - B1
HARBORVIEW MEDICAL CENTER	325 9TH AV, SEATTLE WA	278 - B6
HARRISON MEMORIAL HOSPITAL	BREMERTON E & BREMERTON W, BREMERTON WA	270 - J8
HIGHLINE COMMUNITY HOSPITAL	16251 SYLVESTER RD SW, BURIEN WA	175 - A5
HIGHLINE COMM HOSPITAL SPECIALTY CENTER	12844 MILITARY RD S, TUKWILA WA	288 - D1
HOLY FAMILY HOSPITAL	VICTORIA DR, VANCOUVER BC	156 - C5
HOLY ROSARY HOSPITAL	NW 8TH AV & W IDAHO AV, ONTARIO OR	139 - A3
HOOD RIVER MEMORIAL HOSPITAL	12TH ST, HOOD RIVER OR	195 - D5
HOSPITAL	TRANS CANADA HWY, BRITISH COLUMBIA	93 - C2
HOSPITAL	HWY 5, BRITISH COLUMBIA	95 - C1
HOSPITAL	HWY 3, BRITISH COLUMBIA	95 - C3
HOSPITAL	BRITISH COLUMBIA	100 - A1
HOSPITAL	BRITISH COLUMBIA	101 - A1
HOSPITAL	BRITISH COLUMBIA	105 - C1
HOSPITAL	HWY 19, CAMPBELL RIVER BC	92 - A1
HOSPITAL	FAIRFIELD RD, CITY OF VICTORIA BC	257 - B10
HOSPITAL	CURTIS ST, DISTRICT OF BURNABY BC	156 - D4
HOSPITAL	HODGINS AV, DISTRICT OF CHILLIWACK BC	94 - C3
HOSPITAL	WILLIAM HEAD RD, DISTRICT OF METCHOSIN BC	165 - A1
HOSPITAL	HURD ST, DISTRICT OF MISSION BC	94 - B3
HOSPITAL	DUNCAN BC	101 - A1
HOSPITAL	W 1ST ST, PEND OREILLE CO WA	106 - C3
HOSPITAL	ROSSLAND, ROSSLAND BC	106 - A1
HOSPITAL	ADMIRALS RD, TOWN OF ESQUILMALT BC	256 - B7
HOSPITAL	COLVILLE RD, TOWN OF ESQUILMALT BC	256 - C7
JOSEPHINE GENERAL HOSPITAL	DIMMICK ST & A ST, GRANTS PASS OR	335 - E8
KADLEC HOSPITAL	STEVENS DR, RICHLAND WA	341 - F1
KAISER FOUNDATION HOSPITAL	10200 SE SUNNYSIDE RD, CLACKAMAS CO OR	199 - D3
KAISER FOUNDATION HOSPITAL - PORTLAND	5055 N GREELEY AV, PORTLAND OR	308 - D7
KEIZER MEMORIAL HOSPITAL	CAPE ARAGO HWY & UNION AV, NORTH BEND OR	333 - G4
KLICKITAT VALLEY HOSPITAL	S COLUMBUS AV, GOLDENDALE WA	127 - C1
KOOTENAI MEDICAL CENTER	COEUR D'ALENE, COEUR D'ALENE ID	355 - D8
LADNER PRIVATE HOSPITAL	DISTRICT OF DELTA BC	101 - C1
LAKE CHELAN COMMUNITY HOSPITAL	GIBSON ST & UNION VALLEY LOOP, CHELAN WA	236 - D3
LAKEVIEW HOSPITAL	OFF HWY 395, LAKE CO OR	152 - A2
LANGLY MEMORIAL HOSPITAL	52ND AV, TOWNSHIP OF LANGLEY BC	158 - C1
LANGMACK HOSPITAL	HALSEY-SWEET HOME HWY, LINN CO OR	133 - C2
LEBANON COMMUNITY HOSPITAL	SANTIAM HWY, LINN CO OR	133 - C1
LEGACY EMANUEL HOSPITAL & HEALTH CTR	2801 GANTENBEIN AV, PORTLAND OR	313 - G3
LEGACY GOOD SAMARITAN HOSPITAL	1015 NW 22ND AV, PORTLAND OR	312 - D4
LEGACY MERIDIAN PARK HOSPITAL	19300 SW 65TH AV, TUALATIN OR	199 - B4
LEGACY MOUNT HOOD MEDICAL CENTER	24800 SE STARK ST, GRESHAM OR	200 - B1
LINCOLN COUNTY HOSPITAL	OFF HWY 2, LINCOLN CO WA	114 - A2
LOWER UMPQUA HOSPITAL	RANCH RD, REEDSPORT OR	218 - C1
MADIGAN ARMY MEDICAL CENTER	BERKLEY JACKSON & MADIGAN, PIERCE CO WA	181 - C5
MALHEUR MEMORIAL HOSPITAL	OREGN CENTRL HWY & ALBRTA, MALHEUR CO OR	139 - A3
MAPLE RIDGE HOSPITAL	LOUGHEED HWY & LAITY ST, MAPLE RIDGE BC	157 - C5
MARK E REED MEMORIAL HOSPITAL	MOMMSEN RD, MCCLEARY WA	179 - D6
MARY BRIDGE CHILDRENS HOSPITAL	317 MARTIN LUTHER KING JR WY, TACOMA WA	293 - G4
MASON GENERAL HOSPITAL	13TH ST, SHELTON WA	180 - A2
MCKENZIE-WILLAMETTE HOSPITAL	MOHAWK BLVD & N G ST, SPRINGFIELD OR	331 - A6
MED CTR	2700 SALMON RIVER HWY, YAMHILL CO OR	198 - B7
MEMORIAL HOSPITAL	STADIUM WY, PULLMAN WA	249 - B5
MEMORIAL HOSPITAL	W 10TH AV & S ADAMS ST, RITZVILLE WA	113 - C3
MEMORIAL HOSPITAL	WINTER ST SE, SALEM OR	322 - H14
MERCY MEDICAL CENTER	E ROOSEVELT AV, NAMPA ID	147 - B1
MERCY MEDICAL CENTER	NW MEDICAL LP & NW STEWART, ROSEBURG OR	334 - D3
MID VALLEY HOSPITAL	HWY 20, OKANOGAN CO WA	104 - C3
MOUNTAIN VIEW HOSPITAL	NE B ST, MADRAS OR	208 - C5
MOUNT CARMEL HOSPITAL	COLVILLE, STEVENS CO WA	106 - A2
MSA GENERAL HOSPITAL	MCCALLUM RD, DISTRICT OF MATSQUI BC	102 - B1
NEEDHAM HOSPITAL	E VICTOR ST, BELLINGHAM WA	258 - C4
NEW HOPE CENTER HOSPITAL	FAIRVIEW AV & N COLE RD, BOISE ID	253 - C2
NORTHERN STATE HOSPITAL	OFF FRUITDALE RD, SKAGIT CO WA	161 - C5
NORTH IDAHO CANCER TREATMENT CENTER	COEUR D'ALENE, COEUR D'ALENE ID	355 - E9
NORTH IDAHO DAY SURGERY & LASER CENTER	COEUR D'ALENE, COEUR D'ALENE ID	355 - D8
NORTH IDAHO IMMEDIATE CARE CENTER	COEUR D'ALENE, COEUR D'ALENE ID	355 - D8
NORTH VALLEY HOSPITAL	TONASKET-HAVILLAH RD, OKANOGAN CO WA	104 - C2
NORTHVIEW HOSPITAL	NORTHVIEW ST & N COLE RD, BOISE ID	253 - C2
NORTHWEST HOSPITAL	1550 N 115TH ST, SEATTLE WA	171 - A7
OKANOGAN DOUGLAS COUNTY HOSPITAL	HWY 173, OKANOGAN CO WA	104 - B3
OLYMPIC MEMORIAL HOSPITAL	CAROLINE ST & LIBERTY ST, PORT ANGELES WA	261 - H5
OREGON HOSPITAL	MIDLAND & WASHINGTON BLVD, GRANTS PASS OR	335 - F6
OREGON STATE HOSPITAL	CENTER ST NE & PARK AV, SALEM OR	323 - C13
OVERLAKE HOSPITAL & MEDICAL CENTER	1035 116TH AV NE, BELLEVUE WA	175 - C2
PACIFIC GATEWAY HOSPITAL	1345 SE HARNEY ST, PORTLAND OR	317 - H7
PEACE ARCH HOSPITAL	16TH AV, CITY OF WHITE ROCK BC	158 - A2
PEARSON T B HOSPITAL	OAK ST, VANCOUVER BC	156 - B5
PENDLETON COMMUNITY MEMORIAL HOSPITAL	SW TUTUILLA CREEK RD, PENDLETON OR	129 - B1
PINE CREST HOSPITAL	COEUR D'ALENE, COEUR D'ALENE ID	355 - D8
PIONEER HOSPITAL	HEPPNER & WASCO-HEPPNER HWY, MORROW CO OR	128 - C2
PIONEER MEMORIAL HOSPITAL	MCKAY RD & LOPER AV, CROOK CO OR	213 - D4
PROVIDENCE HOSPITAL	CRATER LAKE AV & E MCANDREWS, MEDFORD OR	336 - E10
PROVIDENCE MEDICAL CENTER	500 17TH AV, SEATTLE WA	278 - C6
PROVIDENCE GENERAL MED CTR-COLBY AV	1321 COLBY AV, EVERETT WA	171 - C1
PROVIDENCE GENERAL MED CTR-PACIFIC AV	916 PACIFIC AV, EVERETT WA	264 - C4
PROVIDENCE MILWAUKIE HOSPITAL	10150 SE 32ND AV, MILWAUKIE OR	199 - D3
PROVIDENCE NEWBERG HOSPITAL	501 N VILLA RD, NEWBERG OR	198 - D5
PROVIDENCE PORTLAND MEDICAL CENTER	4805 NE GLISAN ST, PORTLAND OR	314 - C5
PROVIDENCE SAINT VINCENT MEDICAL CTR	9205 SW BARNES RD, WASHINGTON CO OR	199 - B1
PROVIDENCE SEASIDE HOSPITAL	WAHANNA RD, SEASIDE WA	301 - H9
PUGET SOUND HOSPITAL	215 S 36TH ST, TACOMA WA	295 - H2
PUGET SOUND HOSPITAL	BREMERTON WEST, BREMERTON WA	270 - F10
QUEEN ALEXANDRAS HOSPITAL	ARBUTUS RD, DISTRICT OF SAANICH BC	257 - E3
QUINCY VALLEY HOSPITAL	J ST SW & 7TH AV SW, QUINCY WA	112 - B3
RICHMOND GENERAL HOSPITAL	WESTMINSTER HWY, CITY OF RICHMOND BC	156 - B6
RIVER CREST HOSPITAL	16TH AV, LEWISTON ID	250 - B4
RIVERVIEW HOSPITAL	HWY 7, COQUITLAM BC	157 - A5
ROGUE VALLEY MEMORIAL HOSPITAL	E BARNETT RD & MURPHY RD, MEDFORD OR	336 - H13
ROSLYN & CLE ELUM HOSPITAL & CLINIC	OFF I-90, CLE ELUM WA	240 - B2
ROYAL COLUMBIAN HOSPITAL	COLUMBIAN ST, NEW WESTMINSTER BC	156 - D5
ROYAL JUBILEE HOSPITAL	FORT ST, CITY OF VICTORIA BC	257 - B8
SAANICH PENINSULA HOSPITAL	MT NEWTN CROSS RD, DIST OF CTL SAANICH BC	159 - C3
SACRED HEART GENERAL HOSPITAL	HILYARD ST, EUGENE OR	330 - B7
SAINT ALPHONSUS HOSPITAL	N CURTIS RD & EMERALD ST, BOISE ID	253 - C3
SAINT ANTHONY HOSPITAL	CRAWFORD ST & S MILLER ST, WENATCHEE WA	238 - D4
SAINT ANTHONY HOSPITAL	OREGON-WASHINGTON HWY, UMATILLA CO OR	129 - B1
SAINT CHARLES MEDICAL CENTER	MEDICAL CENTER DR, BEND OR	332 - J6
SAINT CLARE HOSPITAL	11315 BRIDGEPORT WY SW, LAKEWOOD WA	181 - D4
SAINT FRANCIS HOSPITAL	34515 9TH AV S, FEDERAL WAY WA	182 - A1
SAINT JOHNS HOSPITAL	DOUGLAS ST, LONGVIEW WA	303 - A10
SAINT JOHNS HOSPITAL	SHERIDAN ST, PORT TOWNSEND WA	263 - E6
SAINT JOSEPH HOSPITAL	16TH AV W, VANCOUVER BC	254 - J14
SAINT JOSEPH MEDICAL CENTER	1717 S J ST, TACOMA WA	293 - G6

FEATURE NAME	City State	Page-Grid
SAINT JOSEPHS HOSPITAL	CHEWELAH, CHEWELAH WA	106 - B3
SAINT JOSEPHS HOSPITAL	N F ST, ABERDEEN WA	178 - B7
SAINT JOSEPHS HOSPITAL	SQUALICUM PKWY, BELLINGHAM WA	258 - E3
SAINT LUKES HOSPITAL	GRANT ST, BELLINGHAM WA	258 - E7
SAINT LUKES HOSPITAL	RESERVE ST, BOISE ID	253 - D2
SAINT MARYS HOSPITAL	5TH AV S, WALLA WALLA WA	345 - A8
SAINT MARYS HOSPITAL	6TH ST, NEW WESTMINSTER BC	156 - D5
SAINT MARYS PRIORY	GOLDSTREAM AV, CITY OF COLWOOD BC	159 - B6
SAINT PAULS HOSPITAL	COMOX ST, VANCOUVER BC	254 - F10
SAINT PETERS HOSPITAL	5TH AV, OLYMPIA WA	296 - G5
SAINT VINCENTS HOSPITAL	CAMBIE ST, VANCOUVER BC	156 - B5
SALEM GENERAL HOSPITAL	MEDICAL CENTER DR, SALEM OR	323 - B13
SHAUGHNESSY HOSPITAL	CAMBIE ST, VANCOUVER BC	156 - B5
SHRINERS HOSPITAL FOR CHILDREN	3101 SW SAM JACKSON PARK RD, PORTLAND OR	316 - E1
SIMPSON HOSPITAL	GLOVER RD & 88TH, TOWNSHIP OF LANGLEY BC	157 - D6
SKAGIT VALLEY HOSPITAL	13TH ST, MOUNT VERNON WA	260 - D13
SKYLINE HOSPITAL	OFF HWY 141, KLICKITAT CO WA	195 - D5
SNOHOMISH COUNTY PUBLIC HOSPITAL	330 S STILLAGUAMISH AV, ARLINGTON WA	168 - D5
SNOQUALMIE VALLEY HOSPITAL	9050 384TH AV SE, KING CO WA	176 - C4
SNOQUALMIE VALLEY HOSPITAL	9575 MEADOWBROOK WY SE, SNOQUALMIE WA	176 - C4
SOUTHWEST WASHINGTON MEDICAL CENTER	400 NE MOTHER JOSEPH PL, VANCOUVER WA	307 - F5
SOUTHWEST WASH MED CTR (MEM CAMPUS)	3400 MAIN ST, VANCOUVER WA	305 - G2
SPOKANE VALLEY HOSPITAL	E MISSION AV, OPPORTUNITY WA	350 - H7
SQUAMISH HOSPITAL	TRANS CANADA HWY, SQUAMISH BC	93 - C2
STATE HOSPITAL NORTH	OFF HWY 12, CLEARWATER CO ID	123 - C2
STEVENS HOSPITAL	21601 76TH AV W, EDMONDS WA	171 - B5
SUNNY HILL CHILDRENS HOSPITAL	22ND AV, VANCOUVER BC	255 - D14
SURREY MEMORIAL HOSPITAL	9600 KING GEORGE, DISTRICT OF SURREY BC	157 - A6
SWEDISH MEDICAL CENTER	747 BROADWAY, SEATTLE WA	278 - B6
SWEDISH MEDICAL CENTER BALLARD	5300 TALLMAN AV NW, SEATTLE WA	273 - E4
TACOMA GENERAL HOSPITAL	315 MARTIN LUTHER KING JR WY, TACOMA WA	293 - F4
THE DALLES GENERAL HOSPITAL	E 19TH ST, WASCO CO OR	196 - C7
TILLAMOOK COUNTY GENERAL HOSPITAL	3RD ST & ASH AV, TILLAMOOK OR	197 - B2
TRI-COUNTY HOSPITAL	W CRAWFORD ST, DEER PARK WA	114 - B1
TRI-STATE MEMORIAL HOSPITAL	16TH AV, ASOTIN CO WA	250 - B4
TUALITY COMMUNITY HOSPITAL	335 SE 8TH AV, HILLSBORO OR	198 - D1
TUALITY FOREST GROVE HOSPITAL	1809 MAPLE ST, FOREST GROVE OR	198 - C1
UNIVERSITY HOSPITAL	3181 SW SAM JACKSON PARK RD, PORTLAND OR	316 - E1
UNIVERSITY HOSPITAL	WESTBROOK MALL, UNIV ENDOWMENT LANDS BC	156 - A4
UNIVERSITY OF WASHINGTON MED CTR	1959 NE PACIFIC ST, SEATTLE WA	274 - C7
VALLEY GENERAL HOSPITAL	14701 179TH AV SE, MONROE WA	110 - C1
VALLEY LANE HOSPITAL	MONROE ST, EUGENE OR	329 - J6
VALLEY MEDICAL CENTER	400 S 43RD ST, RENTON WA	175 - C5
VALLEY VIEW HOSPITAL	COLVILLE, STEVENS CO WA	106 - A2
VANCOUVER GENERAL HOSPITAL	12TH AV W, VANCOUVER BC	254 - F13
VETERANS HOSPITAL	BOISE SOUTH, BOISE ID	253 - D2
VETERANS HOSPITAL	N ASSEMBLY ST, SPOKANE WA	348 - D3
VETERANS ADMINISTRATION HOSPITAL	STEWART PARK DR, ROSEBURG OR	334 - D5
VETERANS ADMINISTRATION HOSPITAL	1601 E FOURTH PLAIN BLVD, VANCOUVER WA	305 - H4
VETERANS ADMINISTRATION HOSPITAL	W CHESTNUT ST, WALLA WALLA WA	344 - J9
VETERANS AFFAIRS MEDICAL CENTER	1660 S COLUMBIAN WY, SEATTLE WA	282 - C5
VETERANS AFFAIRS MEDICAL CENTER	3710 SW VETERANS HOSPITAL RD, PORTLAND OR	316 - E2
VETERANS AFFAIRS MEDICAL CENTER	3710 SW VETERANS HOSPITAL RD, PORTLAND OR	317 - E2
VETERANS AFFAIRS MEDICAL CENTER	VETERANS DR SW, PIERCE CO WA	181 - C4
VICTORIA GENERAL HOSPITAL	QUADRA ST, CITY OF VICTORIA BC	256 - H10
VICTORIA GENERAL HOSPITAL	VICTORIA GENERAL, TOWN OF VIEW ROYAL BC	256 - B3
VIRGINIA MASON MEDICAL CENTER	1100 9TH AV, SEATTLE WA	278 - A5
WESTERN WASHINGTON STATE HOSPITAL	9601 STEILACOOM BLVD SW, LAKEWOOD WA	181 - C4
WHIDBEY GENERAL HOSPITAL	MAIN ST N, COUPEVILLE WA	167 - B4
WHITMAN COMMUNITY HOSPITAL	ALMOTA RD, WHITMAN CO WA	122 - C1
WILLAMETTE FALLS HOSPITAL	1500 DIVISION ST, OREGON CITY OR	199 - D5
WOODLAND PARK HOSPITAL	10300 NE HANCOCK ST, PORTLAND OR	315 - J4

HOTELS & MOTELS

FEATURE NAME	City State	Page-Grid
ABENDBLUME PENSION	12570 RANGER RD, CHELAN CO WA	238 - A1
ABERDEEN MANSION INN B&B	807 N M ST, ABERDEEN WA	178 - B7
ADMIRAL MOTEL	257 BELLEVILLE ST, CITY OF VICTORIA BC	256 - F9
ADOBE MOTEL	1555 OREGON COAST HWY, LINCOLN CO OR	209 - A3
AERIE RESORT	TRANS CANADA HWY, BRITISH COLUMBIA	159 - A4
ALEXANDERS COUNTRY INN	37515 MOUNTAIN HWY E, PIERCE CO WA	118 - C1
ALEXIS HOTEL	1007 1ST AV, SEATTLE WA	278 - A6
ALL SEASONS RIVER INN B&B	ICICLE RD, CHELAN CO WA	238 - A2
ALPEN INN	405 W HWY 2, CHELAN CO WA	111 - C2
AMERITEL INN	7965 W EMERALD ST, BOISE ID	253 - C3
ANGELICAS MANSION B&B	1321 W 9TH AV, SPOKANE WA	348 - H10
ANN STARRETT MANSION	744 CLAY ST, PORT TOWNSEND WA	263 - H4
ARTISTS STUDIO LOFT B&B	16529 91ST AV SW, KING CO WA	174 - D5
ASHLEY INN	3430 OREGON COAST HWY, LINCOLN CITY OR	203 - A4
ATRIUM INN, THE	2889 HASTINGS ST E, VANCOUVER BC	255 - D10
BARN MOTOR INN	490 WINE COUNTRY RD, PROSSER WA	120 - C3
BAY CITY MOTOR INN	116 N SAMISH WY, BELLINGHAM WA	258 - E9
BAYERN ON THE RIVER	1505 ALPEN SEE STRASSE, LEAVENWORTH WA	238 - A1
BEACHWOOD B&B	671 BEACH DR, SEASIDE WA	301 - F9
BEAR CREEK LODGE	3492 HWY 55, CASCADE ID	252 - D5
BELLA VISTA RESORT MOTEL	6904 PONDEROSA DR, BRITISH COLUMBIA	104 - C1
BELLEVUE CLUB HOTEL	11200 SE 6TH, BELLEVUE WA	175 - C2
BELLEVUE HILTON INN	100 112TH AV NE, BELLEVUE WA	175 - C2
BENSON, THE	309 SW BROADWAY, PORTLAND OR	313 - F5
BEST WESTERN ABERCORN INN	9260 BRIDGEPORT RD, CITY OF RICHMOND BC	156 - B6
BEST WESTERN AIRPORT EXECUTEL	20717 INTERNATIONAL BLVD, SEATAC WA	290 - C4
BEST WESTERN AIRPORT MOTOR INN	2660 AIRPORT WY, BOISE ID	253 - C3
BEST WESTERN ALADDIN MOTOR INN	310 LONG AV, KELSO WA	303 - C7
BEST WESTERN ALADDIN MOTOR INN	900 CAPITOL WAY, OLYMPIA WA	296 - H5
BEST WESTERN BARON INN	19233 HWY 2, MONROE WA	110 - C1
BEST WESTERN BEACHFRONT INN	OFF OREGON COAST HWY, CURRY CO OR	232 - C6
BEST WESTERN BELLEVUE	11211 MAIN ST, BELLEVUE WA	175 - C2
BEST WESTERN BROOKINGS INN	1143 CHETCO AV, BROOKINGS OR	232 - C6
BEST WESTERN CAPILANO INN & SUITES	1634 CAPILANO, DIST OF NORTH VANCOUVER BC	254 - G4
BEST WESTERN CARLTON PLAZA HOTEL	642 JOHNSON ST, CITY OF VICTORIA BC	256 - G8
BEST WESTERN CASCADIA INN	2800 PACIFIC AV, EVERETT WA	265 - F4
BEST WESTERN CHATEAU GRANVILLE	1100 GRANVILLE ST, VANCOUVER BC	254 - F11
BEST WESTERN CHOICE LODGE	24415 RUSSELL RD, KENT WA	175 - B7
BEST WESTERN-COLISEUM	10 N WEIDLER ST, PORTLAND OR	313 - G4
BEST WESTERN COLUMBIA RIVER INN	735 WANAPA ST, HOOD RIVER CO OR	194 - D6
BEST WESTERN CONNIES MOTOR INN	323 W CEDAR ST, SANDPOINT ID	244 - A2
BEST WESTERN CONT PLAZA MOTEL	2500 AURORA AV N, SEATTLE WA	277 - J1
BEST WESTERN-CONVENTION CENTER	420 NE HOLLADAY ST, PORTLAND OR	313 - G4
BEST WESTERN COTTON TREE INN & CON	2300 MARKET ST, MOUNT VERNON WA	260 - C9
BEST WESTERN ELLENSBURG INN	1700 CANYON RD, KITTITAS CO WA	241 - B6
BEST WESTERN EMERALD MOTOR INN	2306 BEACON AVE, TOWN OF SIDNEY BC	159 - C2
BEST WESTERN EVERGREEN MTR INN	13700 AURORA AV N, SEATTLE WA	171 - B7
BEST WESTERN EXECUTIVE INN	200 TAYLOR AV N, SEATTLE WA	277 - J4
BEST WESTERN EXECUTIVE INN	5700 PACIFIC HWY E, FIFE WA	182 - A2
BEST WESTERN EXIBITION PARK	3475 E HASTINGS ST, VANCOUVER BC	255 - F10
BEST WESTERN FEDERAL WAY EXECUTEL	31611 20TH AV S, FEDERAL WAY WA	182 - B1
BEST WESTERN FERRYMANS INN	7901 NE 6TH AV, CLARK CO WA	192 - C5
BEST WESTERN FORTNITER MOTEL	4911 NE 82ND AV, PORTLAND OR	315 - F1
BEST WESTERN GRAND MANOR INN	925 NW GARFIELD AV, CORVALLIS OR	327 - G7
BEST WESTERN GREENTREE INN	1759 FRANKLIN BLVD, EUGENE OR	330 - C7
BEST WESTERN HALLMARK INN	3500 NE CORNELL RD, HILLSBORO OR	198 - D1
BEST WESTERN HALLMARK INN	3000 MARINA DR, MOSES LAKE WA	242 - C3
BEST WESTERN HALLMARK RESORT	744 SW ELIZABETH ST, NEWPORT OR	206 - B4
BEST WESTERN HARBOR PLAZA	5691 SR 20, ISLAND CO WA	160 - C7
BEST WESTERN HERITAGE INN	1405 SMITTYS BLVD, ADAMS CO WA	113 - C3
BEST WESTERN HERITAGE INN	151 E MCLEOD RD, BELLINGHAM WA	258 - D2
BEST WESTERN HERITAGE INN	4319 NW YEON AV, PORTLAND OR	312 - A1
BEST WESTERN HERITAGE INN	1905 N WENATCHEE AV, WEST WENATCHEE WA	238 - D4
BEST WESTERN HOOD RIVER INN	1108 E MARINA WY, HOOD RIVER OR	195 - D5
BEST WESTERN ICICLE INN	505 W HWY 2, CHELAN CO WA	111 - C2
BEST WESTERN INN	251 GOODFELLOW LN, MALHEUR CO OR	139 - A3
BEST WESTERN INN AT THE ROGUE	8959 ROGUE RIVER HWY, GRANTS PASS OR	335 - E10
BEST WESTERN INN-CHATEAU 290	17993 LOWER BOONES FERRY RD, TIGARD OR	199 - B4
BEST WESTERN INNER HARBOR	412 QUEBEC ST, CITY OF VICTORIA BC	256 - G9
BEST WESTERN INN OF THE BEACHCOMBER	OREGON COAST HWY, CURRY CO OR	228 - A7
BEST WESTERN INN-THE MEADOWS	1215 N HAYDEN MEADOWS DR, PORTLAND OR	309 - F3
BEST WESTERN KIRKLAND INN	12223 NE 116TH, KIRKLAND WA	171 - C7
BEST WESTERN LAKEWAY INN	714 LAKEWAY DR, BELLINGHAM WA	258 - E7
BEST WESTERN LAKEWOOD INN	6125 MOTOR AV SW, LAKEWOOD WA	181 - C4
BEST WESTERN LAKEWOOD MOTOR INN	6125 MOTOR AV SW, LAKEWOOD WA	181 - C4
BEST WESTERN LANDMARK HOTEL	4300 200TH ST SW, LYNNWOOD WA	171 - B5
BEST WESTERN LINCOLN SANDS	535 NW INLET AV, LINCOLN CITY OR	203 - A4
BEST WESTERN LISTEL ODOULS HOTEL	1300 ROBSON ST, VANCOUVER BC	254 - F9
BEST WESTERN LOYAL INN	2301 8TH AV, SEATTLE WA	277 - J4
BEST WESTERN MILL CREEK INN	3125 RYAN DR SE, SALEM OR	325 - C1
BEST WESTERN NEW KINGS INN	3658 MARKET ST NE, SALEM OR	323 - D11
BEST WESTERN NEW OREGON MOTEL	1655 FRANKLIN BLVD, EUGENE OR	330 - C7
BEST WESTERN NICOLA INN	4025 WALTERS ST, BRITISH COLUMBIA	95 - C1
BEST WESTERN NORTHPOINTE MINI-SUITE	9601 N NEWPORT HWY, SPOKANE WA	347 - A11
BEST WESTERN OCEAN VIEW RESORT	414 N PROM, SEASIDE WA	301 - F8
BEST WESTERN OF PRINEVILLE	1475 E 3RD ST, CROOK CO OR	213 - D5
BEST WESTERN OLYMPIC INN	2627 S 6TH ST, KLAMATH FALLS OR	338 - G9
BEST WESTERN OLYMPIC LODGE	140 DEL GUZZI DR, PORT ANGELES WA	261 - J6
BEST WESTERN PACIFIC HIGHWAY INN	4646 PORTLAND RD NE, SALEM OR	323 - D6
BEST WESTERN PARK PLAZA	9620 S HILL PARK PL, PUYALLUP WA	182 - B4
BEST WESTERN PONDEROSA LODGE	MCKENZIE HWY, DESCHUTES CO OR	211 - D5
BEST WESTERN PONY SOLDIER INN	1060 NE CLEVELAND AV, GRESHAM OR	200 - B2
BEST WESTERN PONY SOLDIER INN	9901 NE SANDY BLVD, PORTLAND OR	315 - H1
BEST WESTERN PONY SOLDIER MOTEL	1521 D ST NE, AUBURN WA	182 - C1
BEST WESTERN PONY SOLDIER MOTOR INN	1233 N CENTRAL AV, KENT WA	175 - C6
BEST WESTERN PONY SOLDIER MOTOR INN	2340 CRATER LAKE HWY, MEDFORD OR	336 - D8
BEST WESTERN PONY SOLDIER MOTOR INN	HWY 82, UNION CO OR	130 - A2
BEST WESTERN RAMA INN	4430 OREGON COAST HWY, LINCOLN CITY OR	203 - A5
BEST WESTERN RAMA INN	1019 S PROGRESS AV, MERIDIAN ID	253 - A3
BEST WESTERN RAMA INN	2630 SW 17TH PL, REDMOND OR	212 - D6
BEST WESTERN RICHMOND INN & CONV CENTER	7551 WESTMINSTER, CITY OF RICHMOND BC	156 - B6
BEST WESTERN RIO MIRADA MOTOR INN	1603 TERRACE HEIGHTS DR, YAKIMA WA	243 - C6
BEST WESTERN RIVERTREE INN	1257 BRIDGE ST, CLARKSTON WA	250 - B4
BEST WESTERN ROSE GARDEN	10 NE WEIDLER ST, PORTLAND OR	313 - G4
BEST WESTERN SAFARI MOTOR INN	1070 GROVE ST, BOISE ID	253 - C2
BEST WESTERN SALBASGEON INN	1400 HWY 101, REEDSPORT OR	218 - C1
BEST WESTERN SANDS	1755 DAVIE ST, VANCOUVER BC	254 - E9
BEST WESTERN SEQUIM BAY LODGE	268522 HIGHWAY 101, CLALLAM CO WA	109 - C1
BEST WESTERN SHERWOOD INN	15700 UPPER BOONES FERRY RD, TIGARD OR	199 - B3
BEST WESTERN SUNNYSIDE INN	12855 SE 97TH AV, CLACKAMAS CO OR	199 - D3
BEST WESTERN SUNRIDGE INN	OLD OREGON TRAIL HWY, BAKER CO OR	138 - B1
BEST WESTERN TACOMA INN	8726 S HOSMER ST, TACOMA WA	181 - D4
BEST WESTERN TEMPLINS RESORT HOTEL	414 E 1ST AV, POST FALLS ID	353 - H8
BEST WESTERN THUNDERBIRD INN	120 W 3RD AVE, SPOKANE WA	349 - A10
BEST WESTERN TRADE WINDS NORTH	3033 N DIVISION, SPOKANE WA	349 - A5
BEST WESTERN TULALIP INN	6128 33RD AV NE, SNOHOMISH CO WA	168 - C7
BEST WESTERN TUMWATER INN	5188 CAPITOL BLVD, TUMWATER WA	296 - G11
BEST WESTERN UNIVERSITY INN	1516 W PULLMAN RD, LATAH CO ID	249 - C5
BEST WESTERN VILLAGE GREEN	725 ROW RIVER RD, COTTAGE GROVE OR	215 - B7
BEST WESTERN VISTA INN	2645 AIRPORT WY, BOISE ID	253 - C3
BEST WESTERN WALLA WALLA SUITES INN	7 E OAK ST, WALLA WALLA WA	345 - A7
BEST WESTERN WILLAMETTE INN	30800 SW PARKWAY AV, WILSONVILLE OR	199 - B6
BIG TREE B&B	4840 FREMONT ST, SUDDEN VALLEY WA	161 - A1
BISHOP VICTORIAN GUEST SUITES	714 WASHINGTON ST, PORT TOWNSEND WA	263 - H4
BLACK BAR LODGE	OFF GALICE RD, JOSEPHINE CO OR	148 - C1
BLACKBIRD LODGE	305 8TH ST, LEAVENWORTH WA	238 - A1
BLUE HORIZON HOTEL	1225 ROBSON ST, VANCOUVER BC	254 - F9
BOAT YARD INN	200 WHARF ST, LANGLEY WA	171 - A1
BOISE PARK SUITE HOTEL	424 E PARK CENTER BLVD, BOISE ID	253 - D3
BOSCH GARTEN	9846 DYE RD, CHELAN CO WA	238 - A1
CANTERBURY INN	310 GORGE RD E, CITY OF VICTORIA BC	256 - F6
CANTERBURY INN	643 OCEAN SHORES BLVD, OCEAN SHORES WA	298 - B3
CASTLE ROCK LODGE	OFF THREE RIVERS HWY, TILLAMOOK CO OR	197 - C7
CASWELLS ON THE BAY	25204 SANDRIDGE RD, OCEAN PARK WA	186 - A3
CAVANAUGHS AT COLUMBIA CENTER	1101 N COLUMBIA CENTER BLVD, KENNEWICK WA	342 - C8
CAVANAUGHS AT YAKIMA CENTER	607 W YAKIMA AV, YAKIMA WA	243 - B6
CAVANAUGHS INN AT THE PARK	303 W NORTH RIVER DR, SPOKANE WA	348 - J8
CAVANAUGHS RIVER INN	700 N DIVISION ST, SPOKANE WA	349 - A8

FEATURE NAME / City State	Page-Grid
CEDARWOOD MOTEL 9522 LOCHSIDE DR, TOWN OF SIDNEY BC	159 - C2
CENTURY PLAZA HOTEL 1015 BARRARD ST, VANCOUVER BC	254 - F10
CHANTICLEER INN 120 GRESHAM ST, ASHLAND OR	337 - D8
CHANTICLEER INN B&B 1208 FRANKLIN ST, PORT TOWNSEND WA	263 - H4
CHATEAU VICTORIA 740 BURDETT AVE, CITY OF VICTORIA BC	256 - G9
CHATEAU WESTPORT 710 W HANCOCK AV, WESTPORT WA	298 - F14
CHEVY CHASE INN CHEVY CHASE RD, JEFFERSON CO WA	166 - D7
CHICK A DEE INN AT ILWACO 120 WILLIAMS ST, PACIFIC CO WA	186 - A6
CLARION HOTEL AIRPORT 6233 NE 78TH CT, PORTLAND OR	311 - F6
CLARION HOTEL GRAND PACIFIC 450 QUEBEC ST, CITY OF VICTORIA BC	256 - G9
CLARION INN AT TOTEM LAKE 12233 NE TOTEM LAKE WAY, KIRKLAND WA	171 - C7
CLEARWATER INN 5616 W CLEARWATER AV, KENNEWICK WA	342 - F10
CLOUD CAP INN MOUNT HOOD NORTH, HOOD RIVER CO OR	202 - B4
COAST BASTION INN, THE TRANS CANADA HWY, NANAIMO BC	93 - A3
COAST VANCOUVER AIRPORT HOTEL 1041 SW NARINE DR, VANCOUVER BC	156 - B5
COEUR D'ALENE INN CONF & ENT CENTER 524 E SHERMAN AV, COEUR D'ALENE ID	355 - F11
COEUR D'ALENE RESORT 115 S 2ND AV, COEUR D'ALENE ID	355 - E12
COIT HOUSE B&B 502 N 4TH ST, SANDPOINT ID	244 - A2
COLBURN DAY LODGE OFF HWY 95, BONNER CO ID	107 - A2
COLWELL MOTOR INN 501 W 1ST AV, ADAMS CO WA	113 - C3
COMFORT INN 2526 AIRPORT WY, BOISE ID	253 - C3
COMFORT INN 13207 NE 20TH AV, CLARK CO WA	192 - C5
COMFORT INN 280 W APPLEWAY AV, COEUR D'ALENE ID	355 - D8
COMFORT INN 7801 W QUINAULT AVE, KENNEWICK WA	342 - C9
COMFORT INN 2500 S 6TH ST, KLAMATH FALLS OR	338 - G9
COMFORT INN OFF OLD OREGON TRAIL HWY, LA GRANDE OR	130 - A2
COMFORT INN 1100 HILTON RD, MEDFORD OR	336 - D8
COMFORT INN 520 N 2ND ST, WALLA WALLA WA	345 - A7
COMFORT INN AT SEATAC 19333 PACIFIC HWY S, SEATAC WA	290 - D2
COMFORT INN FIFE/TACOMA 5 5601 PACIFIC HWY E, FIFE WA	182 - A2
COMFORT INN-LLOYD CENTER 431 NE MULTNOMAH ST, PORTLAND OR	313 - G4
COMFORT SUITES 12010 NE AIRPORT WY, PORTLAND OR	311 - J6
COMPASS ROSE 508 S MAIN ST, ISLAND CO WA	167 - B4
COONEY MANSION B&B 1705 FIFTH ST, COSMOPOLIS WA	178 - B7
COUNTRY WILLOWS INN 1313 CLAY ST, JACKSON CO OR	337 - G11
COUPEVILLE INN 200 COVELAND ST, COUPEVILLE WA	167 - B4
COURTYARD BY MARRIOTT 8500 SW NIMBUS AV, BEAVERTON OR	199 - B2
COURTYARD BY MARRIOTT 14615 NE 29TH PL, BELLEVUE WA	175 - C2
COURTYARD BY MARRIOTT 11550 NE AIRPORT, PORTLAND OR	193 - A7
COURTYARD BY MARRIOTT 15686 SW SEQUOIA PKWY, TIGARD OR	199 - B3
COURTYARD BY MARRIOTT 400 ANDOVER PARK W, TUKWILA WA	289 - G6
CRATER LAKE LODGE RIM DR, KLAMATH CO OR	227 - C4
CROWN PLAZA HOTEL 1113 6TH AV, SEATTLE WA	278 - A5
CYPRESS INN 9040 SE ADAMS ST, CLACKAMAS CO OR	199 - D3
CYPRESS INN KENT/SEA SOUTH 22218 84TH AV S, KENT WA	175 - C6
DAVENPORT HOTEL S POST ST & W 1ST AV, SPOKANE WA	348 - J9
DAYS INN 9717 SE SUNNYSIDE RD, CLACKAMAS CO OR	199 - D3
DAYS INN 125 E KELLOGG RD, MOUNT VERNON WA	260 - C10
DAYS INN BELLEVUE 3214 156TH AV SE, BELLEVUE WA	175 - D3
DAYS INN CENTER 1414 SW 6TH AV, PORTLAND OR	313 - F6
DAYS INN SEATAC AIRPORT 19015 INTERNATIONAL BLVD, SEATAC WA	290 - D2
DAYS INN STATE CAPITAL 120 COLLEGE ST SE, LACEY WA	297 - G5
DAYS INN TACOMA 6802 TACOMA MALL BLVD, TACOMA WA	295 - E6
DAYS INN TOWN CENTER 2205 7TH AV, SEATTLE WA	277 - J4
DELTA INN 9930 N WHITTAKER RD, PORTLAND OR	309 - F3
DELTA PACIFIC RESORT & CONF CENTER 10251 SAINT EDWARDS, CITY OF RICHMOND BC	156 - B6
DELTA VANCOUVER AIRPORT HOTEL 3500 CESSNA DR, CITY OF RICHMOND BC	156 - B6
DER RITTERHOF MOTOR INN 190 HWY 2, CHELAN CO WA	111 - C2
DESERT MOTOR INN 7702 MAIN ST, BRITISH COLUMBIA	104 - C1
DOUBLE TREE 18740 INTERNATIONAL BLVD, SEATAC WA	290 - D1
DOUBLETREE CLUB HOTEL AT PARK CTR 475 W PARK CENTER BLVD, BOISE ID	253 - D3
DOUBLETREE HOTEL AT THE QUAY 100 COLUMBIA ST, VANCOUVER WA	305 - F6
DOUBLETREE HOTEL COLUMBIA RIVER 1401 N HAYDEN ISLAND DR, PORTLAND OR	305 - F7
DOUBLETREE HOTEL/DOWNTOWN 310 SW LINCOLN ST, PORTLAND OR	313 - E7
DOUBLETREE HOTEL JANTZEN BEACH 909 N HAYDEN ISLAND DR, PORTLAND OR	305 - F7
DOUBLETREE HOTEL-LLOYD CENTER 1000 NE MULTNOMAH ST, PORTLAND OR	313 - H4
DOUBLETREE INN 205 STRANDER BLVD, TUKWILA WA	289 - G6
DOUBLETREE SUITES 16500 SOUTHCENTER PKWY, TUKWILA WA	289 - G6
DRIFTWOOD SHORES RESORT & CONF CTR 88416 1ST AV, LANE CO OR	214 - A2
D-SANDS CONDOMINIUM MOTEL 171 OREGON COAST HWY, LINCOLN CITY OR	203 - A5
DUFFY HOUSE B&B 685 ARGYLE AV, SAN JUAN CO WA	101 - C2
EAGLES NEST INN 3236 E SARATOGA RD, ISLAND CO WA	167 - D7
ECHO LODGE SURISE RD, WHATCOM CO WA	160 - B2
ECONO LODGE 801 E WASHINGTON ST, NEAH BAY WA	262 - F12
EDGEWATER BEACH B&B 26818 EDGEWATER BLVD, KITSAP CO WA	170 - B5
EDGEWATER INN 275 E JOHNSON AV, COOS BAY OR	333 - H11
EDGEWATER INN 2411 ALASKAN WY, SEATTLE WA	277 - H5
EGAN MEMORIAL LODGE OFF CENTURY DRIVE HWY, DESCHUTES CO OR	216 - B3
ELK LAKE LODGE CASCADE LAKES HWY, DESCHUTES CO OR	216 - A4
EMBASSY INN 520 MENZIES ST, CITY OF VICTORIA BC	256 - G10
EMBASSY SUITES 3225 158TH AV SE, BELLEVUE WA	175 - D3
EMBASSY SUITES 15920 W VALLEY HWY, TUKWILA WA	289 - H5
EMBASSY SUITES HOTEL-PORTLAND 9000 SW WASHINGTON SQ RD, TIGARD OR	199 - B3
EMPRESS HOTEL, THE 721 GOVERNMENT ST, CITY OF VICTORIA BC	256 - G9
ENZIAN MOTOR INN 590 HWY 2, CHELAN CO WA	111 - C2
EUGENE HILTON 66 E 6TH ST & OAK ST, EUGENE OR	330 - A6
EVERETT COMFORT INN 1602 SE EVERETT MALL WY, EVERETT WA	268 - D5
EXECUTIVE HOUSE HOTEL 777 DOUGLAS ST, CITY OF VICTORIA BC	256 - G9
EXECUTIVE INN HOTEL 7211 WESMINSTER HWY, CITY OF RICHMOND BC	156 - B6
FAIRFIELD INN 2303 N 4TH ST, COEUR D'ALENE ID	355 - E8
FAIRFIELD INN BY MARRIOTT 3300 S SHOSHONE ST, BOISE ID	253 - C4
FAIRFIELD INN BY MARRIOTT 7809 W QUINAULT AV, KENNEWICK WA	342 - C9
FAIRFIELD INN BY MARRIOTT 311 N RIVERPOINT BLVD, SPOKANE WA	349 - A9
FALL RIVER LODGE N TWIN LAKES RD, DESCHUTES CO OR	142 - C1
FAR VUE MOTEL 808 E SIMCOE DR, KLICKITAT CO WA	127 - C1
FIDALGO COUNTRY INN 1250 HWY 20, ANACORTES WA	259 - J6
FLAGSHIP INN 4320 KITSAP WY, BREMERTON WA	270 - E10
FOTHERINGHAM HOUSE 2128 W 2ND AV, SPOKANE WA	348 - G9
FOUR SEASONS HOTEL 791 W GEORGIA ST, VANCOUVER BC	254 - G10
FOUR SEASONS OLYMPIC HOTEL 411 UNIVERSITY ST, SEATTLE WA	278 - A5
FRIDAY HARBOR HOUSE 130 WEST ST, FRIDAY HARBOR WA	101 - C2
F W HASTINGS HOUSE OLD CONSULATE 313 WALKER ST, PORT TOWNSEND WA	263 - G5
GALICE RESORT MERLIN-GALICE & GALICE, JOSEPHINE CO OR	149 - A1
GARDEN ISLE GUEST COTTAGES 207 NW COVELAND ST, COUPEVILLE WA	167 - B4
GEORGIAN COURT HOTEL, THE 773 BEATTY ST, VANCOUVER BC	254 - F11
GLENCOVE HOTEL VAUGHN-GLENCOVE RD KPN, PIERCE CO WA	174 - A7
GOLD BEACH RESORT 29232 S ELLENSBURG AV, GOLD BEACH OR	228 - A6
GOVERNOR HOTEL 611 SW 10TH AV, PORTLAND OR	313 - E6
GREEN GABLES INN 850 BLANSHARD ST, CITY OF VICTORIA BC	256 - G9
GREEN GABLES INN 922 BONSELLA, WALLA WALLA WA	345 - B6
GREENWOOD INN 10700 SW ALLEN BLVD, BEAVERTON OR	199 - B2
GREGORYS MCFARLAND HOUSE B&B 601 FOSTER AV, COEUR D'ALENE ID	355 - F10
GREY GULL 651 OCEAN SHORES BLVD, OCEAN SHORES WA	298 - B3
GREYWOLF INN 395 KEELER RD, CLALLAM CO WA	262 - J14
HAMPTON INN 3985 BENNETT DR, BELLINGHAM WA	158 - D7
HAMPTON INN 3270 S SHOSHONE ST, BOISE ID	253 - C3
HAMPTON INN 15 NE BUTLER RD, DESCHUTES CO OR	217 - C2
HAMPTON INN 3039 NE 181ST AV, GRESHAM OR	200 - A1
HAMPTON INN SEATTLE SOUTHCENTER 7200 S 156TH ST, TUKWILA WA	289 - J5
HAMPTON SPOKANE 2010 S ASSEMBLY RD, SPOKANE CO WA	348 - D13
HARBORSIDE INN 330 BENEDICT ST, PORT TOWNSEND WA	263 - G5
HARBOUR COURT HWY 14, BRITISH COLUMBIA	101 - A2
HARBOUR TOWERS HOTEL 345 QUEBEC ST, CITY OF VICTORIA BC	256 - F9
HARMONY FALLS LODGE SPIRIT LAKE EAST, SKAMANIA CO WA	118 - B2
HARRIMAN LODGE WESTSIDE RD, KLAMATH CO OR	231 - A6
HARRISON HOT SPRINGS HOTEL 100 ESPLANADE AV, DISTRICT OF KENT BC	94 - C3
HEATHMAN HOTEL 1001 SW BROADWAY, PORTLAND OR	313 - E6
HELMS INN 600 DOUGLAS ST, CITY OF VICTORIA BC	256 - G10
HERON IN LA CONNER 117 MAPLE AV, SKAGIT CO WA	167 - D1
HOLIDAY INN 3300 VISTA AV, BOISE ID	253 - C3
HOLIDAY INN-AIRPORT 8439 NE COLUMBIA BLVD, PORTLAND OR	311 - G7
HOLIDAY INN CROWNE PLAZA 14811 KRUSE OAKS BLVD, LAKE OSWEGO OR	199 - B3
HOLIDAY INN EXPRESS 1100 PRICE RD SE, ALBANY OR	326 - H8
HOLIDAY INN EXPRESS 4220 W 27TH PL, BENTON CO WA	343 - B14
HOLIDAY INN EXPRESS 2613 S VISTA AV, BOISE ID	253 - C3
HOLIDAY INN EXPRESS 2209 E SHERMAN AV, COEUR D'ALENE ID	355 - H11
HOLIDAY INN EXPRESS 34827 PACIFIC HWY S, FEDERAL WAY WA	182 - B2
HOLIDAY INN EXPRESS 3501 PACIFIC HWY E, FIFE WA	182 - A2
HOLIDAY INN EXPRESS 2475 OREGON COAST HWY, FLORENCE OR	214 - B3
HOLIDAY INN EXPRESS 1745 E KITTLESON, GRANT CO WA	242 - D3
HOLIDAY INN EXPRESS 2323 NE 181ST AV, GRESHAM OR	200 - A1
HOLIDAY INN EXPRESS 1095 E WASHINGTON ST, NEAH BAY WA	262 - F11
HOLIDAY INN EXPRESS 1121 BAY ST, PORT ORCHARD WA	270 - J14
HOLIDAY INN EXPRESS 19801 NE 7TH, POULSBO WA	170 - B7
HOLIDAY INN EXPRESS 1190 SE BISHOP BLVD, PULLMAN WA	249 - B5
HOLIDAY INN EXPRESS 6311 33RD AV NE, SNOHOMISH CO WA	168 - C7
HOLIDAY INN EXPRESS 801 N DIVISION, SPOKANE WA	349 - A8
HOLIDAY INN EXPRESS 9107 NE VANCOUVER MALL DR, VANCOUVER WA	307 - G1
HOLIDAY INN EXPRESS AIRPORT 11938 NE AIRPORT WY, PORTLAND OR	193 - A7
HOLIDAY INN EXPRESS BELLINGHAM 4160 GUIDE MERIDIAN, BELLINGHAM WA	158 - D7
HOLIDAY INN EXPRESS GRANTS PASS 105 NE AGNESS AV, JOSEPHINE CO OR	335 - J10
HOLIDAY INN EXPRESS OF LONGVIEW 723 7TH AV, LONGVIEW WA	303 - A11
HOLIDAY INN EXPRESS WOODBURN 2887 NEWBERG HWY, WOODBURN OR	205 - B2
HOLIDAY INN HOTEL & CONF CTR 101 128TH ST SE, SNOHOMISH CO WA	171 - C4
HOLIDAY INN HOTEL AND SUITES 1110 HOWE ST, VANCOUVER BC	254 - F11
HOLIDAY INN ISSAQUAH 1801 12TH AV NW, ISSAQUAH WA	175 - D4
HOLIDAY INN OF YAKIMA 9 N 9TH ST, YAKIMA WA	243 - C6
HOLIDAY INN ONTARIO-OREGON 1249 TAPADERA AV, ONTARIO OR	139 - A3
HOLIDAY INN PORTLAND-DOWNTOWN 1021 NE GRAND AV, PORTLAND OR	313 - G4
HOLIDAY INN PORTLAND-SOUTH 25425 SW BOONES FERRY RD, WILSONVILLE OR	199 - B5
HOLIDAY INN SEATAC 17338 INTERNATIONAL BLVD, SEATAC WA	288 - D7
HOLIDAY INN SEATTLE-BOEING FIELD 11244 PACIFIC HWY S, TUKWILA WA	286 - D6
HOLIDAY INN SEATTLE-RENTON 800 RAINIER AV S, RENTON WA	175 - C5
HOLIDAY INN SELECT 2300 S EVERGREEN PARK DR SW, OLYMPIA WA	296 - F7
HOLIDAY INN VICTORIA 3020 BLANSHARD ST, CITY OF VICTORIA BC	256 - G6
HOLLAND HOUSE INN 595 MICHIGAN ST, CITY OF VICTORIA BC	256 - G10
HOLLY HILL HOUSE 611 POLK, PORT TOWNSEND WA	263 - H4
HOMECOURT ALL SUITE HOTEL 6329 S 212TH ST, KENT WA	291 - G5
HOTEL GABRIOLA ISLAND, BRITISH COLUMBIA	93 - A3
HOTEL HWY 19, BRITISH COLUMBIA	92 - A2
HOTEL OFF HWY 19, BRITISH COLUMBIA	92 - A2
HOTEL BRITISH COLUMBIA	100 - C2
HOTEL INTERNATIONAL 5621 196TH SW, LYNNWOOD WA	171 - B5
HOTEL MCCALL 1101 N 3RD ST, MCCALL ID	251 - C5
HOTEL-PENSION ANNA 926 COMMERCIAL ST, LEAVENWORTH WA	238 - A1
HOTEL PLANTER 715 S FIRST ST, LA CONNER WA	167 - D1
HOTEL RIO VISTA 285 RIVERSIDE AV, OKANOGAN CO WA	104 - A2
HOTEL VANCOUVER 900 W GEORGIA ST, VANCOUVER BC	254 - G10
HOTEL VINTAGE PARK 1100 5TH AV, SEATTLE WA	278 - A6
HOTEL VINTAGE PLAZA 422 SW BROADWAY, PORTLAND OR	313 - F6
HOWARD JOHNSON PLAZA HOTEL 3105 PINE ST, EVERETT WA	265 - F4
HOWARD JOHNSONS AIRPORT 7101 NW 82ND AV, PORTLAND OR	311 - F6
HYATT REGENCY BELLEVUE 900 BELLEVUE WAY NE, BELLEVUE WA	175 - C2
HYATT REGENCY VANCOUVER 655 BURRARD ST, VANCOUVER BC	254 - G10
ILLAHE LODGE OFF NFD RD 33, CURRY CO OR	148 - B1
IMPERIAL HOTEL 400 SW BROADWAY, PORTLAND OR	313 - F6
INN AMERICA 702 21ST ST, LEWISTON ID	250 - C4
INN AMERICA-A BUDGET MOTEL 2275 AIRPORT WY, BOISE ID	253 - C3
INN AT EAGLE CREST 1522 CLINE FALLS RD, DESCHUTES CO OR	212 - C5
INN AT FRIDAY HARBOR SUITES 680 SPRING ST, FRIDAY HARBOR WA	101 - C2
INN AT FRIDAY HARBOR, THE 410 SPRING ST, FRIDAY HARBOR WA	101 - C2
INN AT LANGLEY 400 FIRST ST, LANGLEY WA	171 - A1
INN AT PENN COVE 702 N MAIN ST, ISLAND CO WA	167 - B4
INN AT PRIEST LAKE 1 EAST SHORE RD, BONNER CO ID	107 - A2
INN AT SEMI-AH-MOO A WYNDHAM 9565 SEMIAHMOO PKWY, BLAINE WA	158 - B3
INN AT SNOHOMISH 323 2ND ST, SNOHOMISH WA	171 - D3
INN AT SOAP LAKE 226 E MAIN AV, GRANT CO WA	112 - C2
INN AT SPANISH HEAD 4009 OREGON COAST HWY, LINCOLN CITY OR	203 - A5
INN AT THE MARKET 86 PINE ST, SEATTLE WA	277 - J5
INN AT VIRGINIA MASON, THE 1006 SPRING ST, SEATTLE WA	278 - A5
INN OF THE 7TH MOUNTAIN 18575 CENTURY DRIVE HWY, DESCHUTES CO OR	217 - A4

FEATURE NAME	City State	Page-Grid
IVY CHAPEL INN B&B	164 D ST SW, GRANT CO WA	112 - C3
JACKSONVILLE INN	175 E CALIFORNIA ST, JACKSON CO OR	149 - B2
JAMES HOUSE, THE	1238 WASHINGTON ST, PORT TOWNSEND WA	263 - H5
J J SHAW HOUSE B&B INN	1411 W FRANKLIN ST, BOISE ID	253 - C2
JUAN DE FUCA COTTAGES	182 MARINE DR, CLALLAM CO WA	166 - A5
KENNEWICK SILVER CLOUD INN	7901 W QUINALT AV, KENNEWICK WA	342 - C9
KING OSCAR MOTEL	8820 S HOSMER ST, TACOMA WA	181 - D4
LA CONNER CHANNEL LODGE	205 N 1ST ST, LA CONNER WA	167 - D1
LA CONNER COUNTRY INN	107 S 2ND ST, LA CONNER WA	167 - D1
LANDMARK HOTEL AND CONFERENCE CENTRE	1400 ROBSON ST, VANCOUVER BC	254 - E9
LA QUINTA INN	10530 NE NORTHUP WY, KIRKLAND WA	175 - C2
LA QUINTA INN	1425 E 27TH ST, TACOMA WA	182 - A3
LA QUINTA INN SEATAC INTL	2824 S 188TH ST, SEATAC WA	290 - D2
LEAVENWORTH VILLAGE INN	1016 COMMERCIAL ST, LEAVENWORTH WA	238 - A1
LEWIS RIVER INN	1100 LEWIS RIVER RD, CLARK CO WA	192 - C1
LINDERHOF MOTOR INN	690 HWY 2, CHELAN CO WA	111 - C2
LOGANITA LODGE	W SHORE DR, WHATCOM CO WA	160 - B1
LONGMIRE HOTEL	NATIONAL PARK HWY, PIERCE CO WA	185 - B5
LONSDALE QUAY HOTEL	123 CARRIE CATES CT, NORTH VANCOUVER BC	255 - B7
LYTLE HOUSE BED & BREAKFAST	509 CHENAULT, HOQUIAM WA	178 - A7
MALLORY HOTEL	729 SW 15TH AV, PORTLAND OR	312 - E6
MANRESA CASTLE	7TH & SHERIDAN, PORT TOWNSEND WA	263 - E6
MARIAL LODGE	MARIAL, CURRY CO OR	140 - C3
MARIANNA STOLTZ HOUSE B & B	427 W INDIANA AV, SPOKANE WA	348 - H7
MARINA INN	3300 COMMERCIAL AV, ANACORTES WA	259 - H4
MARK 205 INN	221 NE CHKALOV DR, VANCOUVER WA	307 - J6
MARKS CREEK LODGE	OCHOCO HWY, CROOK CO OR	136 - A2
MARRIOTT RESIDENCE INN	16201 WEST VALLEY HWY, TUKWILA WA	289 - H5
MARRIOTT RESIDENCE INN SEATTLE E	14455 NE 29TH PL, BELLEVUE WA	175 - C2
MARY KAYS WHALEY MANSION	415 3RD ST, CHELAN CO WA	236 - D4
MAYFLOWER PARK HOTEL	405 OLIVE WY, SEATTLE WA	277 - J5
MEANY TOWER HOTEL	4507 BROOKLYN AV, SEATTLE WA	274 - C5
METROPOLITAN HOTEL	645 HAWE ST, VANCOUVER BC	254 - G10
MIDWAY INN	2909 WHEATON WY, BREMERTON WA	270 - J8
MILL VILLAGE MOTEL	210 CENTER ST E, EATONVILLE WA	118 - B1
MINAM LODGE	OFF MILL CREEK RD, WALLOWA CO OR	130 - B2
MONARCH HOTEL & CONFERENCE CENTER	12566 SE 93RD AV, CLACKAMAS CO OR	199 - D3
MONET	36 2ND ST, ASHLAND OR	337 - C8
MORICAL HOUSE GARDEN INN	668 N MAIN, ASHLAND OR	337 - C5
MOUNT ASHLAND INN	550 MOUNT ASHLAND SKI RD, JACKSON CO OR	234 - D6
MOUNT BAKER LODGE	MOUNT BAKER HWY, WHATCOM CO WA	103 - A1
MOUNT HOOD INN	111 NE AGNESS AV, JOSEPHINE CO OR	335 - J10
MOUNT VERNON	300 W COLLEGE WY, MOUNT VERNON WA	260 - C10
MOUNT VERNON TRAVELODGE	1910 FREEWAY DR, MOUNT VERNON WA	260 - B10
MR SANDMAN MOTEL	OFF OLD OREGON TRAIL HWY, UNION CO OR	130 - A2
NENDELS INN SEATTLE SOUTHCENTER	15901 W VALLEY RD, TUKWILA WA	289 - J5
NISQUALLY LODGE	31609 MOUNTAIN HWY E, PIERCE CO WA	118 - C1
NITES INN	1200 S RUBY ST, ELLENSBURG WA	241 - B6
NORTH GARDEN INN	1014 N GARDEN, BELLINGHAM WA	258 - D7
NOR WEST INN	45810 SE NORTH BEND WY, KING CO WA	176 - D5
NOTARAS LODGE	14 CANNA ST S, SOAP LAKE WA	112 - C2
OBERTAL MOTOR INN	922 COMMERCIAL ST, LEAVENWORTH WA	238 - A1
OCANADA HOUSE	1114 BARCLAY ST, VANCOUVER BC	254 - F10
OCCUSA MOTEL	370 W RIO VISTA, BURLINGTON WA	260 - C5
OCEAN POINTE RESORT HOTEL & SPA	45 SONGHEEDS ST, CITY OF VICTORIA BC	256 - G9
OLDE ENGLAND INN	429 LAMPSON ST, TOWN OF ESQUILMALT BC	256 - D9
OLD HONEY FARM COUNTRY INN	9050 384TH AV SE, KING CO WA	176 - C4
OLD MORRIS FARM B&B	105 W MORRIS RD, ISLAND CO WA	167 - C4
OWYHEE PLAZA HOTEL	1109 MAIN ST, BOISE ID	253 - C3
OXFORD SUITES	12226 N JANTZEN DR, PORTLAND OR	305 - F7
PACIFIC PALISADES HOTEL	1277 ROBSON ST, VANCOUVER BC	254 - F11
PACIFIC PLAZA HOTEL	400 SPRING ST, SEATTLE WA	278 - A6
PALACE HOTEL	1004 WATER ST, PORT TOWNSEND WA	263 - G5
PAN PACIFIC HOTEL VANCOUVER, THE	999 CANADA PL, VANCOUVER BC	254 - G9
PARADISE RANCH RESORT	MONUMNT DR & BRKSDE BLVD, JOSEPHINE CO OR	229 - B4
PARAMOUNT HOTEL, THE	724 PINE ST, SEATTLE WA	278 - A5
PARKHILL HOTEL	1160 DAVIE ST, VANCOUVER BC	254 - F10
PEAR TREE MOTEL	3730 FERN VALLEY RD, PHOENIX OR	234 - B2
PHOENIX INN-TIGARD	9575 SW LOCUST ST, TIGARD OR	199 - B3
PINE RIDGE INN	1200 CENTURY DRIVE HWY, DESCHUTES CO OR	217 - A4
PLAZA 500 HOTEL	500 W 12TH AVE, VANCOUVER BC	156 - B5
PLAZA PARK SUITES	1011 PIKE ST, SEATTLE WA	278 - A5
PLAZA SUITE HOTEL	409 S COLE RD, BOISE ID	253 - C3
POLYNESIAN CONDOMINIUM RESORT	615 OCEAN SHORES BLVD, OCEAN SHORES WA	298 - B3
PONY SOLDIER MOTOR INN	1716 MAIN ST, LEWISTON ID	250 - C4
PONY SOLDIER MOTOR INN	325 E MAIN ST, WALLA WALLA WA	345 - B7
POPLARS MOTEL	6404 67TH ST, BRITISH COLUMBIA	104 - C1
PORTLAND HILTON	921 SW 6TH AV, PORTLAND OR	313 - E6
PORTLAND INN, THE	1414 SW 6TH AV, PORTLAND OR	313 - E7
PORTLAND MARRIOTT HOTEL	1401 SW FRONT AV, PORTLAND OR	313 - F7
QUALITY INN	350 OLD HOPE PRINCETON, BRITISH COLUMBIA	95 - A3
QUALITY INN	7001 NE HIGHWAY 99, CLARK CO WA	192 - C4
QUALITY INN AIRPORT SUITES	2717 VISTA AV, BOISE ID	253 - C3
QUALITY INN BARON SUITES	100 E KELLOGG RD, WHATCOM CO WA	158 - D7
QUALITY INN BREMERTON	4303 KITSAP WY, BREMERTON WA	270 - E10
QUALITY INN CONF CENTER	700 PORT DR, CLARKSTON WA	250 - B4
QUALITY INN FLAGSHIP	2520 ASHLAND ST, ASHLAND OR	337 - G9
QUALITY INN HARBOUR VIEW	455 BELLEVILLE ST, CITY OF VICTORIA BC	256 - G9
QUALITY INN OAKWOOD	7919 N DIVISION ST, SPOKANE WA	347 - A13
QUALITY INN-PORTLAND AIRPORT	8247 NE SANDY BLVD, PORTLAND OR	315 - F1
QUALITY INN PRDS CRK MOTOR INN	1050 SE BISHOP BLVD, PULLMAN WA	249 - B5
QUALITY INN-SEATAC	17101 INTERNATIONAL BLVD, SEATAC WA	288 - D6
QUALITY INN THE DALLES	2114 W 6TH ST, THE DALLES OR	196 - C7
QUALITY INN VALLEY SUITES	8923 E MISSION AV, DISHMAN WA	350 - D7
QUALITY INN WADDLING DOG	2476 MOUNT NEWTN, DIST OF CNTL SAANICH BC	159 - C3
QUALITY INN-YAKIMA VALLEY	12 E VALLEY MALL BLVD, YAKIMA WA	243 - C7
QUALITY NEW REDMOND HOTEL	521 SW 6TH ST, REDMOND OR	212 - D5
QUEEN VICTORIA INN	655 DOUGLAS ST, CITY OF VICTORIA BC	256 - G9
RADISSON HOTEL	17001 INTERNATIONAL BLVD, SEATAC WA	288 - C6
RADISSON PRESIDENT HOTEL	8181 CAMBIE RD, CITY OF RICHMOND BC	156 - B6
RAINBOW LODGE	BAKER CREEK RD, YAMHILL CO OR	125 - B2
RAMADA HUNTINGDON MANOR	330 QUEBEC ST, CITY OF VICTORIA BC	256 - G9
RAMADA INN	9602 19TH AV SE, EVERETT WA	268 - D6
RAMADA INN	2611 E E ST, TACOMA WA	293 - J7
RAMADA INN BEAVERTON	13455 SW TUALATN VALLEY, WASHINGTON CO OR	199 - B2
RAMADA INN BELLINGHAM	215 SAMISH WAY, BELLINGHAM WA	258 - E8
RAMADA INN-PORTLAND AIRPORT	6221 NE 82ND AV, PORTLAND OR	311 - F6
RAMADA INN SEATTLE AT NORTHGATE	2140 N NORTHGATE WAY, SEATTLE WA	171 - B7
RAMADA INN SEATTLE DOWNTOWN	2200 5TH AV, SEATTLE WA	277 - J4
RAMADA PLAZA CONV SUITES	621 21ST ST, LEWISTON ID	250 - C4
RAVENSCROFT	533 QUINCY ST, PORT TOWNSEND WA	263 - H4
RED LION BAYSHORE INN	221 N LINCOLN ST, PORT ANGELES WA	261 - F4
RED LION HOTEL BELLEVUE	300 112TH AV SE, BELLEVUE WA	175 - C2
RED LION HOTEL-DOWNTOWNER	1800 FAIRVIEW AV, BOISE ID	253 - C2
RED LION HOTEL-JANZEN BEACH	909 N HAYDEN ISLAND DR, PORTLAND OR	192 - B6
RED LION HOTEL RIVERSIDE	2900 CHINDEN BLVD, BOISE ID	253 - C3
RED LION INN	3612 S 6TH ST, ALTAMONT OR	338 - H10
RED LION INN	1313 N BAYSHORE DR, COOS BAY OR	333 - H9
RED LION INN	205 COBURG RD, EUGENE OR	330 - B4
RED LION INN	510 KELSO DR, KELSO WA	303 - E7
RED LION INN	200 N RIVERSIDE AV, MEDFORD OR	336 - D11
RED LION INN	1255 N WENATCHEE AV, WENATCHEE WA	238 - D4
RED LION INN	818 N 1ST ST, YAKIMA WA	243 - B6
RED LION INN/BELLEVUE CENTER	818 112TH AV NE, BELLEVUE WA	175 - C2
RED LION INN-COLISEUM	1225 N THUNDERBIRD WY, PORTLAND OR	313 - F4
RED LION INN EUGENE-SPRINGFIELD	3280 GATEWAY RD, LANE CO OR	133 - A3
RED LION INN-HANFORD HOUSE	802 GEORGE WASHINGTON WY, RICHLAND WA	341 - G1
RED LION INN INDIAN HILLS	304 SE NYE AV, UMATILLA CO OR	129 - B1
RED LION INN-NORTH	1415 NE 3RD ST, BEND OR	332 - F6
RED LION INN-YAKIMA VALLEY	1507 N 1ST ST, YAKIMA WA	243 - B6
RED LION PASCO	2525 N 20TH AV, PASCO WA	343 - D5
RED LION SPOKANE VALLEY	1100 N SULLIVAN RD, SPOKANE WA	351 - C7
REDMOND INN	17601 NE REDMOND WY, REDMOND WA	175 - D1
RESIDENCE INN	15200 SW BANGY RD, CLACKAMAS CO OR	199 - B3
RESIDENCE INN BY MARRIOTT BELLEVUE	14455 NE 29TH PL, BELLEVUE WA	175 - C2
RESIDENCE INN BY MARRIOTT HILLSBORO	18855 NW TANASBOURNE DR, WASHINGTON CO OR	199 - A1
RESIDENCE INN BY MARRIOTT PORTLAND	1710 NE MULTNOMAH ST, PORTLAND OR	313 - J4
RESIDENCE INN BY MARRIOTT SEATTLE	11920 NE 195TH ST, BOTHELL WA	171 - C6
RESIDENCE INN BY MARRIOTT SEATTLE	800 FAIRVIEW AV N, SEATTLE WA	278 - A3
RESIDENCE INN BY MARRIOTT-SEATTLE NORTH	18200 ALDERWOOD MALL BLVD, LYNNWOOD WA	171 - B5
RESIDENCE INN-PORTLAND NORTH	8005 NE PARKWAY DR, VANCOUVER WA	307 - F1
RESORT AT THE MOUNTAIN, THE	68010 FAIRWAY AV, CLACKAMAS CO OR	201 - C5
RIDDLE LODGE	HELLS CANYON RECREATION AREA, IDAHO CO ID	131 - B1
RIDGEWAY B&B	1292 MCLEAN RD, SKAGIT CO WA	260 - B12
RIDPATH, THE - A WESTCOAST HOTEL	515 W SPRAGUE AVE, SPOKANE WA	348 - J9
RIVERBEND INN	4105 W RIVERBEND AV, POST FALLS ID	353 - C8
RIVERHOUSE MOTOR INN	3075 N HWY 97, BEND OR	332 - F4
RIVER INN SNOQUALMIE VALLEY	4548 TOLT RIVER RD, CARNATION WA	176 - B2
RIVERPLACE ALEXIS HOTEL	1510 SW HARBOR WY, PORTLAND OR	313 - F7
RIVERSIDE INN, THE	50 SW MORRISON ST, PORTLAND OR	313 - F6
RODEWAY INN	3710 MERIDIAN ST, BELLINGHAM WA	258 - C2
ROGUE REGENCY INN	2345 CRATER LAKE HWY, MEDFORD OR	336 - D8
ROMEO INN	295 IDAHO, ASHLAND OR	337 - D8
ROOSEVELT HOTEL	1531 7TH AV, SEATTLE WA	278 - A5
ROYAL COACHMAN INN	5805 PACIFIC HWY E, PIERCE CO WA	182 - A2
ROYAL SCOT INN	425 QUEBEC ST, CITY OF VICTORIA BC	256 - G10
RUN OF THE RIVER	9308 E LEAVENWORTH, CHELAN CO WA	238 - A1
SAFARI MOTOR INN	345 HWY 99W, MCMINNVILLE OR	198 - A7
SAHARA COURTYARD INN	6204 67TH ST, BRITISH COLUMBIA	104 - C1
SAINT HELENS LODGE	HWY 504, SKAMANIA CO WA	190 - C1
SALISH LODGE	6501 RAILROAD AV SE, SNOQUALMIE WA	176 - C4
SALISH LODGE, THE	37807 SE FALL CITY SNOQ, SNOQUALMIE WA	176 - C4
SCANDINAVIAN GARDENS INN B&B	1610 CALIFORNIA AV S, LONG BEACH WA	186 - A5
SCENIC LODGE	RATHDRUM, KOOTENAI CO ID	115 - A1
SCHNAUZER CROSSING	4421 LAKEWAY DR, WHATCOM CO WA	161 - A1
SEASONS MOTEL	MORTON RD & HWY 12, LEWIS CO WA	118 - B2
SEATAC AIRPORT TRAVELODGE	2900 S 192ND, SEATAC WA	290 - D2
SEATTLE AIRPORT HILTON	17620 INTERNATIONAL BLVD, SEATAC WA	288 - D7
SEATTLE HILTON	1301 6TH AV, SEATTLE WA	278 - A5
SEATTLE MARRIOTT SEATAC AIRPORT	3201 S 176TH ST, SEATAC WA	288 - D7
SEATTLE UNIVERSITY LODGE	SUN TOP, PIERCE CO WA	111 - A3
SEQUIM WEST INN	740 W WASHINGTON ST, NEAH BAY WA	262 - C11
SHELBURNE INN	4415 PACIFIC HWY, PACIFIC CO WA	186 - A6
SHERATON PORTLAND AIRPORT HOTEL	8235 NE AIRPORT WY, PORTLAND OR	311 - G4
SHERATON SEATTLE HOTEL & TOWERS	1400 6TH AV, SEATTLE WA	278 - A5
SHERATON TACOMA HOTEL	1320 BROADWAY PZ, TACOMA WA	293 - H5
SHILO INN	702 W APPLEWAY, COEUR D'ALENE ID	355 - D7
SHILO INN	1819 E KITTLESON, MOSES LAKE WA	242 - D3
SHILO INN	501 SITKA AV, NEWBERG OR	198 - D5
SHILO INN	923 E 3RD AV, SPOKANE WA	349 - B10
SHILO INN	7414 S HOSMER ST, TACOMA WA	295 - E7
SHILO INN	1609 E HARBOR DR, WARRENTON WA	188 - B2
SHILO INN BEAVERTON	9900 SW CANYON RD, WASHINGTON CO OR	199 - B2
SHILO INN CONFERENCE & FAMILY RESORT	707 OCEAN SHORES BLVD, OCEAN SHORES WA	298 - B3
SHILO INN-DOWNTOWN VANCOUVER	401 E 13TH ST, VANCOUVER WA	305 - G4
SHILO INN-HAZEL DELL	11506 NE 3RD ST, CLARK CO WA	192 - C5
SHILO INN PORTLAND SUITES HOTEL	11707 NE AIRPORT WY, PORTLAND OR	193 - A7
SHILO INN-RIVERSHORE	50 COMSTOCK ST, RICHLAND WA	341 - H3
SHILO INN SALEM SUITES	3304 MARKET ST NE, SALEM OR	323 - E12
SHILO INN-SEASIDE OCEANFRONT RESORT	30 N PROM, SEASIDE WA	301 - F8
SHILO INN SUITES-BOISE AIRPORT	4111 BROADWAY AV, BOISE ID	253 - C4
SHILO INN SUITES HOTEL	3105 O B RILEY RD, BEND OR	332 - F3
SHILO INN-TILLAMOOK	2515 N MAIN, TILLAMOOK CO OR	197 - C1
SHILO INN-WASHINGTON SQUARE	10830 SW GREENBURG RD, TIGARD OR	199 - B3
SHILO SUITES HOTEL	2500 ALMOND ST, KLAMATH FALLS OR	338 - C4
SILVER CLOUD INN	10621 NE 12TH ST, BELLEVUE WA	175 - C2
SILVER CLOUD INN	19332 36TH AV W, LYNNWOOD WA	171 - B5
SILVER CLOUD INN	2426 NW VAUGHN ST, PORTLAND OR	312 - C3
SILVER CLOUD INN AT KIRKLAND	12202 NE 124TH ST, KING CO WA	171 - C7
SILVER CLOUD INN AT LYNNWOOD	19332 36TH AV W, LYNNWOOD WA	171 - B5
SILVER CLOUD INN AT REDMOND	15304 NE 21ST ST, REDMOND WA	175 - D2

FEATURE NAME City State	Page-Grid
SILVER CLOUD INN AT RENTON 1850 MAPLE VALLEY RD, RENTON WA	175 - C5
SILVER CLOUD INN AT TUKWILA 13050 48TH AV S, TUKWILA WA	289 - F1
SILVERDALE HOTEL ON THE BAY 3073 NW BUCKLIN HILL RD, SILVERDALE WA	174 - B1
SIX AVENUE INN 2000 6TH AV N, SEATTLE WA	277 - J5
SORRENTO HOTEL 900 MADISON ST, SEATTLE WA	278 - A6
SPIRIT LAKE LODGE HWY 504, SKAMANIA CO WA	190 - C1
STATES INN 2039 W VALLEY RD, SAN JUAN CO WA	101 - C2
STAY N SAVE MOTOR INN 10551 SAINT EDWARDS DR, RICHMOND BC	156 - B6
STAY N SAVE MOTOR INN 3233 MAPLE ST, DISTRICT OF SAANICH BC	256 - G5
STEWARD LODGE 805 W FIRST ST, CLE ELUM WA	240 - B2
STOUFFER MADISON HOTEL 515 MADISON ST, SEATTLE WA	278 - A6
SUMMITT INN AT SNOQUALMIE PASS SR 906, KITTITAS CO WA	111 - A2
SUN COUNTRY INN 1700 N 1ST ST, YAKIMA WA	243 - B6
SUN MOUNTAIN LODGE PATTERSON LAKE RD, OKANOGAN CO WA	104 - A2
SUNRISE LODGE SUNRISE PARK RD, PIERCE CO WA	185 - D2
SUNSET INN TRAVEL APARMENTS 1111 BURNABY ST, VANCOUVER BC	254 - F10
SUPER 8 MOTEL LONG BEACH 500 OCEAN BEACH BLVD, LONG BEACH WA	186 - A5
SURREY INN 9850 KING GEORGE, DISTRICT OF SURREY BC	157 - A6
SUTTON PLACE HOTEL, THE 845 BURRARD ST, VANCOUVER BC	254 - G10
SWANS HOTEL 506 PANDORA AVE, CITY OF VICTORIA BC	256 - G8
SWAUK LODGE OFF HWY 97, KITTITAS CO WA	238 - A6
SWEETBRIER INN 7125 SW NYBERG RD, TUALATIN OR	199 - B4
TACOMA TRAVELODGE 8820 S HOSMER ST, TACOMA WA	181 - D4
THREE MEADOWS LODGE OFF VIEW POINT RD, CLEARWATER CO ID	123 - C1
THREE RIVERS INN 210 BALL ST, SEDRO-WOOLLEY WA	161 - C5
TIMBER LODGE MOTEL 301 W FIRST ST, CLE ELUM WA	240 - B2
TOLSTOJ SOKOL LODGE RICHARDSONS GAP RD, LINN CO OR	133 - C1
TOPPENISH INN MOTEL 515 S ELM ST, TOPPENISH WA	120 - A2
TRAVELODGE 101 N SAMISH WY, BELLINGHAM WA	258 - E8
TRAVELODGE BY THE SPACE NEEDLE 200 6TH AV N, SEATTLE WA	277 - J4
TRAVELODGE CENTRALIA 1049 ECKERSON RD, CENTRALIA WA	299 - D2
TRAVELODGE HOTEL 1441 NE 2ND AV, PORTLAND OR	313 - G4
TRAVELODGE SEATTLE NORTH 23825 HWY 99, EDMONDS WA	171 - A6
TRAVELODGE VANCOUVER NE HAZEL DELL AV, CLARK CO WA	192 - C5
TRAVELODGE VICTORIA 229 GORGE RD E, CITY OF VICTORIA BC	256 - F7
TRAVELODGE WENATCHEE 1004 N WENATCHEE AV, WENATCHEE WA	238 - D4
TROUT LODGE OFF HWY 12, YAKIMA CO WA	119 - B1
TUDOR INN B&B 1108 S OAK, PORT ANGELES WA	261 - E5
TU TU TUN LODGE 96550 NORTH BANK ROGUE, CURRY CO OR	228 - B4
TWICKENHAM HOUSE INN B&B 5023 LANGLEY RD, ISLAND CO WA	171 - A2
TYEE LODGE OCEANFRONT B&B 4905 NW FALL ST, NEWPORT OR	206 - B3
UNION CLUB OF BRITISH COLUMBIA 805 GORDON ST, CITY OF VICTORIA BC	256 - G9
UNIVERSITY INN 4140 ROOSEVELT WY NE, SEATTLE WA	274 - B6
UNIVERSITY PLAZA HOTEL 400 NE 45TH ST, SEATTLE WA	274 - B5
UNIVERSITY SILVER CLOUD INN 5036 25TH AV NE, SEATTLE WA	274 - D5
VALLEY RIVER INN 1000 VALLEY RIVER WY, EUGENE OR	329 - H3
VAL-U INN 9 14TH AV NW, AUBURN WA	182 - B1
VAL-U INN 805 LAKEWAY DR, BELLINGHAM WA	258 - E7
VAL U INN 22420 84TH AV S, KING CO WA	175 - B7
VAL-U INN 1900 CLACKAMETTE DR, OREGON CITY OR	199 - D4
VICTORIAN B&B 602 N MAIN ST, ISLAND CO WA	167 - B4
VICTORIA REGENT HOTEL, THE 1234 WHARF ST, CITY OF VICTORIA BC	256 - G9
VILLAGE INN MOTEL 229 COTTAGE AV, CHELAN CO WA	238 - C2
VILLA ISOLA B&B INN 5489 S COLES RD, ISLAND CO WA	171 - A1
WALL CENTRE GARDEN HOTEL 1088 BURRARD ST, VANCOUVER BC	254 - F10
WALLOWA LAKE LODGE JOSEPH-WALLOWA LAKE HWY, WALLOWA CO OR	130 - C2
WARWICK HOTEL 401 LENORA ST, SEATTLE WA	277 - J5
WATERFRONT CENTRE HOTEL 900 CANADA PLACE WAY, VANCOUVER BC	254 - G9
WAUMILLA LODGE OLYMPIC HOT SPRINGS RD, CLALLAM CO WA	109 - B1
WAVERLY PLACE B&B 709 W WAVERLY PL, SPOKANE WA	348 - J5
WAYSIDE MOTOR INN 11460 SW PACIFIC HWY, TIGARD OR	199 - B3
WEDGEWOOD HOTEL 845 HORNBY ST, VANCOUVER BC	254 - F10
WEINHARD HOTEL OFF HWY 12, COLUMBIA CO WA	122 - A2
WESTCOAST BELLEVUE HOTEL 625 116TH AV NE, BELLEVUE WA	175 - C2
WEST COAST VANCE HOTEL 620 STEWART ST, SEATTLE WA	278 - A5
WESTCOAT TYEE HOTEL 500 TYEE DR, TUMWATER WA	296 - G11
WESTERN INN 9920 S TACOMA, LAKEWOOD WA	181 - D4
WESTIN BAYSHORE, THE 1601 W GEORGIA ST, VANCOUVER BC	254 - F9
WESTIN HOTEL SEATTLE 1900 5TH AV, SEATTLE WA	277 - J5
WILLCOX HOUSE 2390 TEKIU RD NW, KITSAP CO WA	173 - C3
WINDMILL INN OF MEDFORD 1950 BIDDLE RD, MEDFORD OR	336 - D9
WINDMILLS ASHLAND HILLS INN 2525 ASHLAND ST, ASHLAND OR	337 - G9
WOODLANDER INN 1500 ATLANTIC ST, WOODLAND WA	189 - D7
WOODMARK HOTEL ON LAKE WASHINGTON 1200 CARILLON POINT, KIRKLAND WA	175 - C1
WOODS HOUSE BED & BREAKFAST INN 333 N MAIN ST, ASHLAND OR	337 - C6
WYNDHAM GARDEN HOTEL SEATAC 18118 INTERNATIONAL BLVD, SEATAC WA	290 - D1

MILITARY INSTALLATIONS

FEATURE NAME City State	Page-Grid
ARMORY S 11TH ST & S YAKIMA AV, TACOMA WA	293 - G5
ARMORY SOUTH SHORE BLVD, LAKE OSWEGO OR	320 - E7
BOARDMAN BOMBING RANGE BOMBING RANGE RD, MORROW CO OR	128 - C1
CAMP MCKEAN (US NAVY) OFF KITSAP LAKE RD, KITSAP CO WA	270 - A10
CAMP MURRAY WASHINGTON NATIONAL GUARD MILITIA DR, PIERCE CO WA	181 - C5
CAMP RILEA (OREGON NATIONAL GUARD) RIDGE LAKE DR, CLATSOP CO WA	188 - B2
CAMP SEVEN MILE MILITARY RESERVATION RIVERSIDE PARK DR, SPOKANE CO WA	348 - A1
CAMP WESLEY HARRIS NAVAL RESERVATION SEABECK HWY NW, KITSAP CO WA	174 - A2
CAMP WITHYCOMBE NATIONAL GUARD CLACKAMAS & SE INDUSTRL, CLACKAMAS CO OR	199 - D3
CANADIAN COAST GUARD DALLAS RD & SIMCOE ST, CTY OF VICTORIA BC	256 - E9
CANADIAN FORCES BASE ESQUIMALT ESQUIMALT RD & CANTEEN RD, ESQUIMALT BC	256 - A8
COOS HEAD US NAVAL FACILITY COOS CO OR	220 - C1
DEPARTMENT OF NATIONAL DEFENSE BEWDLEY & PETERS, TOWN ESQUILMALT BC	256 - D9
DEPARTMENT OF NATIONAL DEFENSE WILLIAM HEAD RD, DISTRICT OF METCHOSIN BC	165 - B1
FAIRCHILD AIR FORCE BASE HWY 2 & N RAMBO RD, FAIRCHILD A F B WA	114 - B2
FORT LAWTON MILITARY RESERVATION MAGNOLIA BLVD W & W EMERSN ST, SEATTLE WA	272 - A5
FORT LEWIS MILITARY RESERVATION STEILACOOM-DUPONT RD SW, PIERCE CO WA	181 - C4
GRAND ARMY ENCAMPMENT GROUNDS FARRAGUT AV, WESTPORT WA	298 - F14
GRAYS HARBOR COAST GUARD NYHUS ST & WILSON AV, WESTPORT WA	298 - H11
MCCHORD AIR FORCE BASE 112TH ST S, PIERCE CO WA	181 - D5
MILITARY RESERVATION CLARK CO WA	193 - B5
MILITARY RESERVATION FRONT ST, MUKILTEO WA	171 - B2
NATIONAL GUARD ARMORY IZEE RD TO BUSH RANCH RD, GRANT CO OR	198 - C1
NATIONAL GUARD ARMORY TAYLOR, FOREST GROVE OR	198 - D1
NATIONAL GUARD ARMORY NE CORNELL RD, HILLSBORO OR	198 - D5
NATIONAL GUARD ARMORY N HARRISON ST, NEWBERG OR	277 - F1
NATIONAL GUARD ARMORY W ARMORY WY, SEATTLE WA	278 - A3
NAVAL RES ARMORY VALLEY ST, SEATTLE WA	271 - G11
NAVAL RESERVATION BEACH DR E, MANCHESTER WA	264 - C1
NAVAL STATION EVERETT W MARINE VIEW DR & 18TH ST, EVERETT WA	310 - E5
PORTLAND AIR NATIONAL GUARD BASE 6801 NE CORNFOOT RD, PORTLAND OR	270 - G12
PUGET SOUND NAVAL SHIPYARD BREMERTON WA	165 - A1
ROCKY POINT NAVAL ESTABLISHMENT EAST SOOKE RD, DISTRICT OF METCHOSIN BC	191 - B7
TILLAMOOK BAY COAST GUARD STATION GARIBALDI AV, GARIBALDI OR	188 - D1
TONGUE POINT NAVAL BASE (HISTORICAL) OLD COLUMBIA RIVER HWY, CLATSOP CO WA	168 - C7
TULALIP MILITARY RESERVATION 116TH ST NE & 34TH AV NE, SNOHOMISH CO WA	128 - C1
UMATILLA ORDNANCE DEPOT OLD OREGON TRAIL HWY, MORROW CO OR	171 - B2
US COAST GUARD FRONT ST, MUKILTEO WA	172 - B7
US COAST GUARD RESERVATION OFF HIGHWAY 109, GRAYS HARBOR CO WA	298 - F12
US COAST GUARD RESERVATION ELIZABETH AV & OLYMPIC AV, WESTPORT WA	261 - G1
US COAST GUARD STATION EDIZ HOOK RD, PORT ANGELES WA	243 - D4
US MILITARY RESERVATION US 97 & FIRING CENTER RD, YAKIMA CO WA	270 - C7
US NAVAL RESERVATION OFF HWY 3, BREMERTON WA	177 - B2
US NAVAL RESERVATION OFF HWY 109, GRAYS HARBOR CO WA	170 - B1
US NAVAL RESERVATION OFF HWY 116, JEFFERSON CO WA	263 - J13
US NAVAL RESERVATION OFF HWY 116, JEFFERSON CO WA	170 - A7
US NAVAL RESERVATION OFF CLEAR CREEK RD NW, KITSAP CO WA	174 - B1
US NAVAL RESERVATION OFF CLEAR CREEK RD NW, KITSAP CO WA	167 - C3
US NAVAL RESERVATION OFF HWY 20, OAK HARBOR WA	186 - A6
US NAVAL RESERVATION FORT CANBY RD, PACIFIC CO WA	275 - H3
US NAVAL SUPPORT ACTIVITY SAND POINT WY NE, SEATTLE WA	175 - B7
WASHINGTON NATIONAL GUARD ARMORY 24410 MILITARY RD S, KENT WA	167 - B1
WHIDBEY ISLAND NAVAL AIR STATION OFF HWY 20, AULT FIELD WA	

MUSEUMS

FEATURE NAME City State	Page-Grid
ABERDEEN MUSEUM OF HISTORY 111 E 3RD ST, ABERDEEN WA	178 - B7
ALPHINSTONE PIONEER MUSEUM OFF HWY 101, BRITISH COLUMBIA	93 - B3
AMERICAN ADVERTISING MUSEUM 50 SW 2ND AV, PORTLAND OR	313 - F5
AMERICAN HOP MUSEUM 22 S B ST, TOPPENISH WA	120 - A2
ANACORTES MUSEUM 1305 8TH ST, ANACORTES WA	259 - H1
APE CAVE MUSEUM NFD RAINIER RD & RAINIER-YELM, SKMC WA	190 - B4
APPALOOSA HORSE CLUB AND MUSEUM OFF HWY 8, MOSCOW ID	249 - C5
ASOTIN MUSEUM OFF HWY 129, ASOTIN WA	250 - B6
BALDWIN HOTEL MUSEUM 31 MAIN ST, KLAMATH CO OR	235 - C5
BASQUE MUSEUM AND CULTURAL CENTER 611 GROVE ST, BOISE ID	253 - C3
BELLEVUE ART MUSEUM 301 BELLEVUE SQ, BELLEVUE WA	175 - C2
BENTON COUNTY HISTORICAL MUSEUM 1101 MAIN ST, BENTON CO OR	133 - B1
BENTON COUNTY HISTORICAL MUSEUM PATERSON RD, PROSSER WA	120 - C3
BERNABY VILLAGE MUSEUM CANADA WY, DISTRICT OF BURNABY BC	156 - D5
BLACK DIAMOND DEPOT MUSEUM RAILROAD AV & BAKER ST, BLACK DIAMOND WA	110 - C3
BLACK DIAMOND HISTORICAL MUSEUM BLACK DIAMOND WA	110 - C3
BLACKMAN HISTORY MUSEUM 118 AVE B, SNOHOMISH WA	171 - D3
BLEHYL LIBRARY AND POWELL MUSEUM GRANDVIEW, GRANDVIEW WA	120 - B3
BOISE ART MUSEUM 670 S JULIA DAVIS DR, BOISE ID	253 - C3
BREMERTON NAVAL MUSEUM 130 WASHINGTON AV, BREMERTON WA	270 - J10
BC FARM MACHINERY & AGRICULTURAL MUS 9131 KING ST, TOWNSHIP OF LANGLEY BC	157 - D6
BRITISH COLUMBIA HALL OF FAME RENFREW ST & HASTINGS ST E, VANCOUVER BC	255 - E10
BC SUGAR MUSEUM ROGER ST, VANCOUVER BC	255 - A10
BRITTANCOURT HOUSE MUSEUM RAINBOW RD, BRITISH COLUMBIA	101 - B1
BROUGHER MUSEUM GEORGE FOX COLLEGE, NEWBERG OR	198 - D5
BRUCE MEMORIAL MUSEUM OFF HWY 124, WALLA WALLA CO WA	122 - A3
BURKE MUSEUM 17TH AV NE & NE 45TH ST, SEATTLE WA	274 - C5
BUSH BARN HIGH ST SE, SALEM OR	322 - H14
BUSH HOUSE MUSEUM HIGH ST SE, SALEM OR	322 - H14
BUTTERFLY WORLD HWY 4, BRITISH COLUMBIA	92 - C3
CAMBRIDGE MUSEUM US 95 & RTE 71, WASHINGTON CO ID	139 - B1
CAMP 6 LOGGING MUSEUM FIVE MILE SCENIC DR, TACOMA WA	181 - C1
CANADIAN LACROSSE HALL OF FAME MCBRIDE BLVD, NEW WESTMINSTER BC	156 - D5
CENTRAL WASHINGTON AGRICULTURAL MUS 4508 MAIN ST, UNION GAP WA	243 - C7
CHENEY COWLES MUSEUM W RIVERSIDE AV, SPOKANE WA	348 - G9
CHILDRENS MUSEUM IZEE RD TO BUSH RANCH RD, GRANT CO OR	137 - A3
CHILDRENS MUSEUM PENDLETON-JOHN DAY HWY, GRANT CO OR	137 - A1
CHILDRENS MUSEUM OF TACOMA 925 COURT C, TACOMA WA	293 - H5
CHILDRENS MUSEUM, THE 305 HARRISON ST, SEATTLE WA	277 - H4
CHILLIWACK MUSEUM 45820 SPADINA AV, DIST OF CHILLIWACK BC	94 - C3
CLACKAMAS COUNTY HISTORY MUSEUM 211 TUMWATER DR, OREGON CITY OR	199 - D5
CLACKAMAS COUNTY MUSEUM 211 TUMWATER DR, OREGON CITY OR	199 - D5
CLALLAM COUNTY MUSEUM S LINCOLN ST, PORT ANGELES WA	261 - D5
CLARK COUNTY HISTORIAL MUSEUM 1511 MAIN ST, VANCOUVER WA	305 - G4
CLE ELUM TELEPHONE MUSEUM 221 E FIRST ST, CLE ELUM WA	240 - B2
CLYMER MUSEUM N PEARL ST, ELLENSBURG WA	241 - B6
COAST GUARD MUSEUM PIER 36, SEATTLE WA	281 - J1
COLLIER STATE PARK & LOGGING MUSEUM THE DALLES-CALIFORNIA HWY, KLAMATH CO OR	231 - D4
COLUMBIA COUNTY HISTORICAL MUSEUM 511 E BRIDGE ST, VERNONIA OR	125 - B1
COLUMBIA RIVER MARITIME MUSEUM 1792 MARINE DR, ASTORIA WA	300 - E4
COOS ART MUSEUM CURTIS AV & 4TH ST, COOS BAY OR	333 - H10
COOS COUNTY HISTORICAL SOCIETY MUSEUM SHERMAN AV, NORTH BEND OR	333 - G3
COTTAGE GROVE MUSEUM W MAIN ST, COTTAGE GROVE OR	215 - B7
COWLITZ COUNTY HISTORICAL MUSEUM 405 ALLEN ST, KELSO WA	303 - D8
CRAIG HERITAGE MUSEUM 1245 E ISLAND HWY, BRITISH COLUMBIA	92 - C3
CRATER ROCK MUSEUM ROGUE VALLEY HWY, JACKSON CO OR	230 - C7
DEL NORTE COUNTY HISTORICAL SOCIETY MUS OFF HWY 101, DEL NORTE CO CA	148 - B3
DEPOT MUSEUM 888 NE 4TH AV, CANBY OR	199 - C6
DOLLY WARES DOLL MUSEUM 101 & 35TH ST, FLORENCE OR	214 - B3
DOUGLAS COUNTY HISTORICAL MUSEUM 124 W WALNUT ST, DOUGLAS CO WA	236 - C7
DUPONT HISTORICAL MUSEUM 207 BARKSDALE AV, DUPONT WA	181 - B5
EAST BENTON HISTORICAL MUSEUM 205 KEEWAYDIN DR, KENNEWICK WA	343 - D12
EASTERN OREGON MUSEUM LA GRANDE-BAKER HWY, BAKER CO OR	130 - A3
EDMONDS HISTORICAL MUSEUM 118 5TH AV N, EDMONDS WA	171 - A5
EMILY CARR MUSEUM 207 GOVERNMENT ST, CITY OF VICTORIA BC	256 - G10
F ARNOLD POLSON PARK AND MUSEUM 1611 RIVERSIDE AV, HOQUIAM WA	178 - A7
FAVELL MUSEUM OF WESTERN ART 125 W MAIN ST, KLAMATH FALLS OR	338 - C8
FLAVEL HOUSE MUSEUM 441 EIGTH ST, ASTORIA WA	300 - C5
FOOTHILLS HISTORICAL MUSEUM N RIVER AV & N COTTAGE ST, BUCKLEY WA	110 - C3
FORKS TIMBER MUSEUM HWY 101 & RTE 110, CLALLAM CO WA	169 - D2

FEATURE NAME City State	Page-Grid
FORT DALLES MUSEUM W 13TH ST, THE DALLES OR	196 - C7
FORT LEWIS MILITARY MUSEUM I-5 FRWY, PIERCE CO WA	181 - B5
FORT SHERMAN MUSEUM ROSENBERRY DR, COEUR D'ALENE ID	355 - D11
FRANKLIN COUNTY HISTORICAL MUSEUM 305 N FOURTH AV, PASCO WA	343 - F7
GILBERT HOUSE CHILDRENS MUSEUM 116 MARION ST NE, SALEM OR	322 - H12
GRANT COUNTY HISTORICAL MUSEUM 742 N BASIN ST, GRANT CO WA	112 - C3
GRANTS PASS MUSEUM OF ART PARK ST & OAKVIEW DR, GRANTS PASS OR	335 - E10
HARNEY COUNTY HISTORICAL MUSEUM 18 W D ST, BURNS OR	145 - A1
HERITAGE MUSEUM 1618 EXCHANGE ST, ASTORIA WA	300 - D5
HIGH DESERT MUSEUM, THE DALLES-CALIFORNIA HWY, DESCHUTES CO OR	217 - B4
HOOD RIVER COUNTY HISTORIC MUSEUM INT 84 & HWY 35, HOOD RIVER OR	195 - D5
HOOVER-MINTHORN HOUSE MUSEUM 115 S RIVER ST, NEWBERG OR	198 - D5
H R MACMILLAN PLANETARIUM 100 CHESTNUT ST, VANCOUVER BC	254 - D11
IDAHO HISTORICAL MUSEUM 610 N JULIA DAVIS DR, BOISE ID	253 - C3
ILWACO HERITAGE MUSEUM 115 SE LAKE ST, ILWACO WA	186 - A6
ISLAND COUNTY HISTORICAL MUSEUM NE PARKER RD, COUPEVILLE WA	167 - B4
JACKSONVILLE MUS OF SOUTHERN OREGON HWY 238 & OLD STAGE RD, JACKSONVILLE OR	149 - B2
JENSEN ARCTIC MUSEUM 590 W CHURCH ST, MONMOUTH OR	204 - B7
JOSEPHINE COUNTY KERBYVILLE MUSEUM US 199 & KIRBY, JOSEPHINE CO OR	233 - B3
KARPELES MANUSCRIPT LIBRARY 407 S G ST, TACOMA WA	293 - G4
KILBY HISTORIC STORE AND FARM 215 KILBY RD, DISTRICT OF KENT BC	94 - C3
KITSAP COUNTY MUSEUM OFF SILVERDALE WY NW, SILVERDALE WA	174 - B1
KITTITAS COUNTY HISTORICAL MUSEUM E 3RD ST, ELLENSBURG WA	241 - B6
KLAMATH COUNTY MUSEUM 125 W MAIN ST, KLAMATH CO OR	235 - C5
LACEY MUSEUM 829 LACEY ST, LACEY WA	297 - H6
LAKE CHELAN MUSEUM HWY 150 & WOODIN AV, CHELAN WA	236 - D3
LANE COUNTY HISTORICAL MUSEUM 740 W 13TH AV, EUGENE OR	329 - H7
LANGLEY CENTENNIAL MUSEUM 9135 KING ST, TOWNSHIP OF LANGLEY BC	157 - D6
LEWIS COUNTY HISTORICAL MUSEUM 599 NW FRONT WAY, CHEHALIS WA	299 - D11
LINCOLN COUNTY HISTORICAL MUSEUM OFF HWY 2, DAVENPORT WA	114 - A2
LINN COUNTY HISTORICAL MUSEUM 101 PARK AV, BROWNSVILLE OR	210 - C2
LIVING ROCK MUSEUM, THE HALSEY-SWEET HOME HWY, LINN CO OR	210 - C2
LONGMIRE MUSEUM NATIONAL PARK HWY, PIERCE CO WA	185 - B5
LOPEZ HISTORICAL MUSEUM LOPEZ ISLAND, SAN JUAN CO WA	101 - C2
LUNA HOUSE MUSEUM OFF HWY 12, LEWISTON ID	250 - B4
LYNDEN PIONEER MUSEUM 217 W FRONT ST, LYNDEN WA	102 - B1
MARION COUNTY HISTORICAL MUSEUM 260 12TH ST SE, SALEM OR	322 - J13
MARITIME MUSEUM 28 BASTION SQ, CITY OF VICTORIA BC	256 - G9
MARYHILL MUSEUM LEWIS & CLARK HWY, KLICKITAT CO WA	127 - B1
MARYMOOR MUSEUM 6406 W LAKE SAMMAMISH PKWY, KING CO WA	175 - D1
MASON COUNTY MUSEUM W RAILROAD AV, SHELTON WA	180 - A3
MILWAUKIE HISTORICAL SOCIETY MUSEUM SE RR AV & SE ADAMS ST, MILWAUKIE OR	199 - D3
MINIATURE WORLD 721 GOVERNMENT ST, CITY OF VICTORIA BC	256 - G9
MINING MUSEUM TRANS CANADA HWY, BRITISH COLUMBIA	93 - C2
MISSION MUSEUM 33201 2ND AV, DISTRICT OF MISSION BC	94 - B3
MOLSON MUSEUM MOLSON RD, OKANOGAN CO WA	105 - A1
MOLSON SCHOOL MUSEUM OFF HWY 97, OKANOGAN CO WA	104 - C1
MUSEUM HWY 19, BRITISH COLUMBIA	92 - A2
MUSEUM OFF HWY 19, BRITISH COLUMBIA	92 - A2
MUSEUM OFF HWY 4, BRITISH COLUMBIA	92 - B3
MUSEUM HIGHWAY 18, BRITISH COLUMBIA	100 - C1
MUSEUM BRITISH COLUMBIA	100 - C2
MUSEUM BRITISH COLUMBIA	101 - A1
MUSEUM TRANS CANADA HWY, BRITISH COLUMBIA	101 - A2
MUSEUM TRUNK RD, DUNCAN BC	101 - A1
MUSEUM AT WARM SPRINGS, THE 2189 WARM SPRINGS HWY, WARM SPRINGS OR	208 - A2
MUSEUM OF ANTHROPOLOGY 6393 NW MARINE DR, UNIV ENDOWMENT LAND BC	156 - A4
MUSEUM OF FLIGHT 9404 E MARGINAL WY S, TUKWILA WA	286 - D4
MUSEUM OF HISTORY & INDUSTRY 2700 24TH AV E, SEATTLE WA	278 - D1
MUSEUM OF NORTH IDAHO 115 NORTHWEST BLVD, COEUR D'ALENE ID	355 - C8
M Y WILLIAMS GEOLOGICAL MUSEUM MARINE DR, UNIVERSITY ENDOWMENT LAND BC	156 - A4
NANAIMO MUSEUM TRANS CANADA HWY, NANAIMO BC	93 - A3
NAVAL UNDERSEA MUSEUM OFF HWY 308, KITSAP CO WA	170 - C7
NETHERLANDS CENTENNIAL CARILLON, THE BELLEVILLE & GOVERNMENT, VICTORIA BC	256 - G10
NORDIC HERITAGE MUSEUM 3014 NW 67TH ST, SEATTLE WA	272 - D3
NORTH CENTRAL WASHINGTON MUSEUM 127 S MISSION ST, WENATCHEE WA	239 - A4
NORTHERN PACIFIC RAILROAD MUSEUM 219 SIXTH ST, WALLACE ID	115 - C2

FEATURE NAME City State	Page-Grid
NORTH VANCOUVER MUSEUM & ARCHIVES 4TH ST, CITY OF NORTH VANCOUVER BC	255 - A5
OF SEA AND SHORE MUSEUM OFF HWY 104, KITSAP CO WA	170 - C4
OKANOGAN COUNTY HISTORICAL MUSEUM HWY 215, OKANOGAN WA	104 - C3
OLD AURORA COLONY MUSEUM NE 2ND ST & LIBERTY ST, AURORA OR	199 - B7
OLD HASTINGS MILL STORE MUSEUM 1575 ALMA RD, UNIV ENDOWMENT LANDS BC	254 - A11
OLD SHIP MUSEUM LAKE ST S, KIRKLAND WA	175 - C1
OREGON HISTORY CENTER 1200 SW PARK AV, PORTLAND OR	313 - E6
OREGON MARITIME CENTER & MUSEUM 113 SW FRONT AV, PORTLAND OR	313 - F6
OREGON MILITARY MUSEUM CAMP WITHYCOMBE, CLACKAMAS CO OR	199 - D3
OREGON MUSEUM OF SCIENCE & INDUSTRY 1945 SE WATER AV, PORTLAND OR	313 - G7
OREGON SPORTS HALL OF FAME 900 SW 4TH AV, PORTLAND OR	313 - F6
OREGON TRAIL REGIONAL MUSEUM OFF HWY 7, BAKER CITY OR	138 - B1
OSOYOOS MUSEUM PARK PL, BRITISH COLUMBIA	104 - C1
PACIFIC COUNTY HISTORICAL MUSEUM 1008 W ROBERT BUSH DR, PACIFIC CO WA	117 - A1
PACIFIC NORTHWEST MUSEUM OF HISTORY 1500 E MAIN ST, ASHLAND OR	337 - F7
PACIFIC SCIENCE CENTER 200 2ND AV N, SEATTLE WA	277 - H4
PACIFIC UNIVERSITY MUSEUM 2043 COLLEGE WY, YAMHILL CO OR	198 - B3
PEARSON AIR MUSEUM 1105 E 5TH ST, VANCOUVER WA	305 - H6
PIONEER FARM MUSEUM PIERCE CO WA	118 - B1
PIONEER MEMORIAL MUSEUM MOUNT ANGELES RD, PORT ANGELES WA	261 - F7
PITTOCK MANSION 3229 NW PITTOCK DR, PORTLAND OR	312 - B5
PORT GAMBLE HISTORIC MUSEUM OFF HWY 104, KITSAP CO WA	170 - C4
PORTLAND ART MUSEUM 1219 SW PARK ST, PORTLAND OR	313 - E6
PORTLAND CHILDRENS MUSEUM 3037 SW 2ND AV, PORTLAND OR	317 - E1
POWELL RIVER HISTORIC MUSEUM HWY 101, BRITISH COLUMBIA	92 - C1
PRESBY MUSEUM 127 W BROADWAY, GOLDENDALE WA	127 - C1
PREWITT ALLEN ARCHAELOGICAL MUSEUM DEER PARK DR SE, SALEM OR	325 - F6
PRINTING MUSEUM COOS BAY HWY, COOS BAY OR	333 - H9
RENTON HISTORICAL MUSEUM 235 MILL AV S, RENTON WA	175 - C5
RICHMOND CENTRE GALLERY MUS AND ARCH 7700 MINORU GATE, CITY OF RICHMOND BC	156 - B6
ROBERT NEWELL HOUSE MUSEUM CHAMPOEG RD, MARION CO OR	199 - A7
ROSLYN MUSEUM 203 PENNSYLVANIA AV, ROSLYN WA	240 - A1
ROYAL BRITISH COLUMBIA MUSEUM 675 BELLEVILLE ST, CITY OF VICTORIA BC	256 - G10
ROYAL LONDON WAX MUSEUM 470 BELLEVILLE ST, CITY OF VICTORIA BC	256 - G9
SAANICH HISTORICAL ARTIFACTS SOCIETY 7321 LOCHSIDE DR, DIST OF CNTL SAANICH BC	159 - C4
SAMSON V MARITIME MUSEUM MCBRIDE BLVD, NEW WESTMINSTER BC	156 - D5
SANDY HISTORICAL MUSEUM 39260 PIONEER BLVD, SANDY OR	200 - D4
SCHMIDT HOUSE MUSEUM 508 SW 5TH ST, GRANTS PASS OR	335 - E9
SCHMINCK MEMORIAL MUSEUM OFF HWY 395, LAKEVIEW OR	152 - A2
SCIENCE WORLD 1455 QUEBEC ST, VANCOUVER BC	254 - H11
SEALAND OF THE PUBLIC BEACH DR, DISTRICT OF OAK BAY BC	257 - D9
SEASIDE MUSEUM 570 NECANIUM DR, SEASIDE WA	301 - G8
SEATTLE ART MUSEUM 100 UNIVERSITY ST, SEATTLE WA	277 - J6
SEATTLE ASIAN ART MUSEUM 1400 E PROSPECT ST, SEATTLE WA	278 - C3
SEQUIM-DUNGENESS VALLEY MUSEUM 175 W CEDAR, NEAH BAY WA	262 - E11
SHAFER MUSEUM HWY 20, OKANOGAN CO WA	104 - A2
SHORELINE HISTORICAL MUSEUM 749 N 175TH ST, SHORELINE WA	171 - A6
SIDNEY ART GALLERY AND MUSEUM 202 SIDNEY AV, PORT ORCHARD WA	270 - H14
SIDNEY MUSEUM 2440 SIDNEY AVE, TOWN OF SIDNEY BC	159 - C2
SISKIYOU COUNTY MUSEUM GREENHORN DR, YREKA CA	149 - C3
SIUSLAW PIONEER MUSEUM OREGON COAST HWY, LANE CO OR	214 - B3
SKAGIT COUNTY HISTORICAL MUSEUM 501 S 4TH ST, LA CONNER WA	167 - D1
SNOHOMISH COUNTY MUSEUM 2817 ROCKEFELLER AV, EVERETT WA	264 - E3
SNOLQUAMIE VALLEY MUSEUM 320 S NORTH BEND, OREGON CITY OR	199 - D5
SNOQUALMIE VALLEY HISTORICAL MUSEUM 320 NORTH BEND BLVD S, NORTH BEND WA	176 - C5
SOOKE REGION MUSEUM HWY 14, BRITISH COLUMBIA	101 - A2
STAFF HOUSE MUSEUM 820 MC KINLEY AV, KELLOGG ID	115 - C2
STEILACOOM HISTORICAL MUSEUM 112 MAIN ST, STEILACOOM WA	181 - C4
STEVENS-CRAWFORD MUSEUM 603 6TH ST, OREGON CITY OR	199 - D5
STEVESTON MUSEUM MONCTON ST, CITY OF RICHMOND BC	156 - A7
SUNNYSIDE MUSEUM 704 S 4TH ST, SUNNYSIDE WA	120 - B2
SUQUAMISH MUSEUM 15838 SANDY HOOK RD, SUQUAMISH WA	170 - C7
SURREY CENTENNIAL MUSEUM 6022 176TH ST, DISTRICT OF SURREY BC	157 - B7
TACOMA ART MUSEUM PACIFIC AV & VILLARD ST, TACOMA WA	293 - H5
TENINO DEPOT MUSEUM 339 W PARK ST, TENINO WA	184 - D3
THREE RIVERS CHILDRENS MUSEUM 650 GEORGE WASHINGTON WY, RICHLAND WA	341 - G2
TILLAMOOK COUNTY PIONEER MUSEUM MAIN AV & 1ST ST, TILLAMOOK OR	197 - B2

FEATURE NAME City State	Page-Grid
TILLAMOOK NAVAL AIR STATION MUSEUM 6030 HANGAR RD, TILLAMOOK CO OR	197 - C3
TOPPENISH MUSEUM 1 S ELM ST, TOPPENISH WA	120 - A2
UMATILLA COUNTY HISTORICAL MUSEUM 108 SW FRAZER, PENDLETON OR	129 - B1
UNDERSEA GARDENS 490 BELLEVILLE ST, CITY OF VICTORIA BC	256 - F9
UNION COUNTY MUSEUM 311 S MAIN ST, NEWBERG OR	198 - D6
UPPERTOWN FIREFIGHTERS MUSEUM 30TH ST, ASTORIA WA	300 - E4
VANCOUVER ART GALLERY 750 HORNBY ST, VANCOUVER BC	254 - G10
VANCOUVER MUSEUM 1100 CHESTNUT ST, VANCOUVER BC	254 - E11
VANCOUVER MARITIME MUSEUM OGDEN AV, VANCOUVER BC	254 - D10
WAHKIAKUM COUNTY HISTORICAL MUSEUM 65 RIVER ST, WAHKIAKUM CO WA	117 - B3
WALLOWA COUNTY MUSEUM OFF WALLOWA LAKE HWY, WALLOWA CO OR	130 - B1
WANAPUM DAM AND HERITAGE CENTER HWY 243, GRANT CO WA	120 - B1
WASHINGTON COUNTY HISTORICAL MUSEUM 17677 NW SPRINGVILLE RD, WASHINGTON CO OR	192 - A7
WASHINGTON STATE CAPITOL MUSEUM 21ST ST, OLYMPIA WA	296 - H7
WASHINGTON STATE HISTORICAL SOCIETY 315 N STADIUM WY, TACOMA WA	293 - G3
WASHINGTON STATE HISTORY MUSEUM 1911 PACIFIC AV, TACOMA WA	293 - H6
WESTPORT MUSEUM 2201 WESTHAVEN DR, WESTPORT WA	298 - G10
WHALE MUSEUM 62 FIRST ST N, FRIDAY HARBOR WA	101 - C2
WHATCOM CHILDRENS MUSEUM 227 PROSPECT ST, BELLINGHAM WA	258 - C6
WHATCOM MUSEUM OF HISTORY 121 PROSPECT ST, BELLINGHAM WA	161 - A1
WHITE RIVER VALLEY MUSEUM 918 H ST SE, AUBURN WA	182 - C1
WHYEL, ROSALIE MUSEUM OF DOLL ART 1116 108TH AV NE, BELLEVUE WA	175 - C2
WILLAMETTE FALLS LOCKS MUSEUM MILL ST, WEST LINN OR	199 - D4
WILLIS CAREY HISTORICAL MUSEUM RIVERFRONT DR, CASHMERE WA	238 - C2
WONDER WORKS CHILDRENS MUSEUM 419 E 2ND ST, THE DALLES OR	196 - C7
WORLD KITE MUSEUM AND HALL OF FAME PACIFIC HWY, LONG BEACH WA	186 - A5
YAKIMA ELECTRIC RAILWAY MUSEUM 5TH AV AND WALNUT ST, YAKIMA WA	243 - B6
YAKIMA VALLEY MUSEUM 2105 TIETON DR, YAKIMA WA	243 - B6
YAMHILL COUNTY HISTORICAL MUSEUM 605 MARKET ST, LAFAYETTE OR	198 - B6

OPEN SPACE PRESERVES

FEATURE NAME City State	Page-Grid
ALPINE LAKES WILDERNESS CHELAN CO WA	111 - B2
BADGER CREEK WILDERNESS AREA WASCO CO OR	202 - D5
BEAVER MARSH NATURAL PRESERVE NE 98TH AV & NE 39TH ST, VANCOUVER WA	307 - G2
BIDDLE, HENRY J NATURE PRESERVE LEWIS & CLARK HWY, VANCOUVER WA	311 - J2
BLACK CANYON WILDERNESS OCHOCO NATIONAL FOREST, WHEELER CO OR	136 - C2
BOULDER CREEK WILDERNESS NORTH UMPQUA HWY, DOUGLAS CO OR	222 - C2
BOULDER RIVER WILDERNESS OFF HWY 530, SNOHOMISH CO WA	102 - C3
BRIDGE CREEK WILDERNESS OCHOCO NATIONAL FOREST, WHEELER CO OR	136 - A2
BULL OF THE WOODS WILDERNESS MARION CO OR	134 - B1
BULL RUN NATURAL AREA CLACKAMAS CO OR	201 - D3
BULL RUN RESERVE CLACKAMAS CO OR	201 - B2
COLUMBIA WILDERNESS COLUMBIA RIVER HWY, HOOD RIVER CO OR	194 - C7
COMMONAGE RESERVE HWY 5A, BRITISH COLUMBIA	95 - C1
CUMMINS CREEK WILDERNESS OREGON COAST HWY, LANE CO OR	209 - A5
DIAMOND PEAK WILDERNESS AREA KLAMATH CO OR	142 - B1
DRIFT CREEK WILDERNESS LINCOLN CO OR	206 - C7
EAGLE CAP WILDERNESS UNION CO OR	130 - B2
GLACIER PEAK WILDERNESS CHELAN CO WA	103 - B3
GOAT ROCKS WILDERNESS LEWIS CO WA	119 - A2
GRASSY KNOB WILDERNESS CURRY CO OR	224 - C5
HELLS CANYON WILDERNESS IDAHO CO ID	131 - B2
INNIS ARDEN RESERVE 14TH AV NW & NW 177TH ST, SHORELINE WA	171 - A6
JACKSON, HENRY M WILDERNESS CHELAN CO WA	111 - B1
JUNIPER DUNES WILDERNESS PASCO-KAHLOTUS RD, FRANKLIN CO WA	121 - B2
KALMIOPSIS WILDERNESS JOSEPHINE CO OR	148 - C2
LAKE CHELAN-SAWTOOTH WILDERNESS CHELAN CO WA	104 - A3
MARBLE MOUNTAIN WILDERNESS AREA OFF SCOTT RIVER RD, SISKIYOU CO CA	149 - B3
MENAGERIE WILDERNESS AREA LINN CO OR	134 - B2
MIDDLE SANTIAM WILDERNESS AREA LINN CO OR	134 - B1
MONUMENT ROCK WILDERNESS BAKER CO OR	137 - C2
MOUNT ADAMS WILDERNESS YAKIMA CO WA	119 - A3
MOUNTAIN LAKES WILDERNESS KLAMATH CO OR	231 - A7
MOUNT BAKER WILDERNESS OFF HWY 542, WHATCOM CO WA	102 - C1
MOUNT HOOD WILDERNESS AREA CLACKAMAS CO OR	201 - C5
MOUNT PASAYTEN WILDERNESS OKANOGAN CO WA	103 - C1
MOUNT THIELSEN WILDERNESS DOUGLAS CO OR	223 - D6
MOUNT WASHINGTON WILDERNESS AREA DESCHUTES CO OR	211 - A4

PNW

INDEX

FEATURE NAME	City State	Page-Grid
MOUNT WASHINGTON WILDERNESS AREA	LANE CO OR	134 - C2
NORSE PEAK WILDERNESS	PIERCE CO WA	111 - A3
NORTH FORK JOHN DAY WILDERNESS	UMATILLA CO OR	129 - C3
NORTH FORK UMATILLA WILDERNESS	WESTON-ELGIN HWY, UMATILLA CO OR	130 - A1
OCHOCO DIVIDE RESEARCH AREA	OCHOCO HWY, WHEELER CO OR	136 - A2
OREGON CASCADES RECREATION WILDERNESS	KLAMATH CO OR	142 - B2
PASAYTEN WILDERNESS	OKANOGAN CO WA	104 - A1
PATAHA RESEARCH NATURAL AREA	OFF PATAHA CREEK RD, GARFIELD CO WA	122 - C2
ROCK CREEK WILDERNESS	OREGON COAST HWY, LANE CO OR	209 - A6
ROGUE-UMPQUA DIVIDE WILDERNESS	DOUGLAS CO OR	222 - D7
SALMON HUCKLEBERRY WILDERNESS	CLACKAMAS CO OR	201 - B6
SALMO-PRIEST WILDERNESS	PEND OREILLE CO WA	106 - C1
SHELLFISH RESERVE	HAMMOND BAY RD, NANAIMO BC	93 - A3
SKY LAKES WILDERNESS	KLAMATH CO OR	150 - A1
STRAWBERRY MOUNTAIN WILDERNESS	GRANT CO OR	137 - B2
TABLE ROCK WILDERNESS	MIDDLEFORK RD, CLACKAMAS CO OR	126 - A3
THREE SISTERS WILDERNESS AREA	LANE CO OR	134 - B3
THREE SISTERS WILDERNESS AREA	LANE CO OR	216 - B2
WALDO LAKE WILDERNESS AREA	LANE CO OR	134 - B3
WASHINGTON STATE OYHUT GAME RANGE	OCEAN SHORES, OCEAN SHORES WA	298 - C6
WENAHA-TUCANNON WILDERNESS	WALLOWA CO OR	130 - B1
WILD ROGUE WILDERNESS	COOS CO OR	140 - C3
WORLD CENTER FOR BIRDS OF PREY	5666 W FLYING HAWK LN, ADA CO ID	253 - C4
PARKS & RECREATION		
8TH & I PARK	S 8TH ST & S I ST, TACOMA WA	293 - G5
132ND SQUARE PARK	NE 132ND ST & 132ND PL NE, KING CO WA	171 - C7
ABERNATHY GREEN	1726 WASHINGTON ST, OREGON CITY OR	199 - D4
ABRAMS PARK	DIVISION ST, RIDGEFIELD WA	192 - C2
ADAIR COUNTY PARK	RYALS AV, BENTON CO OR	207 - B4
ADAMS PARK	NW CORNELL RD, PORTLAND OR	312 - A5
ADAMS ACRES PARK	NW ROCK CREEK BLVD, WASHINGTON CO OR	192 - A7
ADELAIDE PARK	30619 16TH AV SW, FEDERAL WAY WA	182 - A1
ADMIRALTY PARK	PORT MOODY BC	156 - D3
AGATE BEACH COUNTY PARK	LOPEZ ISLAND, SAN JUAN CO WA	101 - C2
AGATE LAKE RECREATION AREA	E ANTELOPE RD, JACKSON CO OR	149 - C1
AGREN MEMORIAL PARK	THORSEN RD SW & SW BANK RD, KING CO WA	174 - D5
AGRICULTURAL PARK	SHAUGHNESSY & CHESTER, PORT COQUITLAM BC	157 - B4
AILSA PARK	AILSA AV, PORT MOODY BC	157 - A4
AINSWORTH STATE PARK	MULTNOMAH CO OR	194 - B7
AIRPORT PARK	34038 N HONEYMAN RD, COLUMBIA CO OR	192 - A3
AIRPORT PARK	ARMORY WY, MCMINNVILLE OR	198 - B7
AIRPORT PARK	DES MOINES MEM DR & S 176TH ST, BURIEN WA	288 - A7
ALBERTA PARK	NE KILLINGSWORTH ST, PORTLAND OR	309 - J7
ALBERT KELLY PARK	SW BOUNDARY ST, PORTLAND OR	316 - B3
ALBINA PARK	N FLINT AV & N RUSSELL ST, PORTLAND OR	313 - F3
ALDERBROOK PARK	SW 325TH PL & 13TH AV SW, FEDERAL WAY WA	182 - A1
ALDERDALE PARK	2700 SW 340TH PL, FEDERAL WAY WA	182 - A1
ALDERGROVE PARK	272ND ST, TOWNSHIP OF LANGLEY BC	102 - B1
ALDERGROVE LAKE REGIONAL PARK	HUNTINGDON RD, DISTRICT OF MATSQUI BC	102 - B1
ALDER LAKE PARK	MOUNTAIN HWY E, PIERCE CO WA	118 - B1
ALDERMAN PARK	KREDER RD RD, DAYTON OR	198 - C7
ALDERWOOD PARK	16TH AV, DISTRICT OF SURREY BC	158 - A2
ALDERWOOD PARK	33RD ST NE & 30TH ST NE, TACOMA WA	182 - A2
ALDERWOOD PARK	DISTRICT OF NORTH VANCOUV BC	254 - G5
ALDERWOOD STATE PARK	LANE CO OR	133 - A2
ALDRICH PARK	SALEM OR	323 - A14
ALEXANDER PARK	RIVERSIDE DR, LEWIS CO WA	299 - C13
ALEX HOPE PARK	88TH AV & 208TH ST, TOWNSHP OF LANGLEY BC	157 - C6
ALFRED A LOEB STATE PARK	NORTH BANK CHETCO RIVER RD, CURRY CO OR	232 - D5
ALGONA PARK	402 WARDE ST, ALGONA WA	182 - B2
ALKI PLAYGROUND	59TH AV SW & LANDER ST, SEATTLE WA	280 - C2
ALLCO PARK	ALOUETTE RD, MAPLE RIDGE BC	157 - D5
ALLENTOWN PEA PATCH PARK	S 124TH ST & 42ND AV S, TUKWILA WA	289 - E1
ALLEN YORK PARK	W TAPPS HWY & BONNEY LAKE, BONNEY LAKE WA	182 - C4
ALLING PARK	S SHERIDAN AV & S 61ST ST, TACOMA WA	295 - F5
ALMOND PARK	VANCOUVER BC	254 - A13
ALOHAWOOD PARK	SW 175TH & SW OAKWOOD, WASHINGTON CO OR	199 - A2
ALPENTAL SKI AREA	SNOQUALMIE PASS, STMPEDE PASS, KING CO WA	111 - A2
ALPINE PARK	DISTRICT OF NORTH VANCOUV BC	156 - C2
ALPINE PARK	S ALPINE ST & S 23RD AV, CORNELIUS OR	198 - C1
ALTA LAKE STATE PARK	ALTA LAKE RD, OKANOGAN CO WA	112 - B1
ALTAMONT BEACH PARK	DIST OF WEST VANCOUVER BC	156 - A3
AMBASSADOR PARK	AMBASSADOR AV, DISTRICT OF SAANICH BC	256 - H2
AMBLESIDE PARK	DIST OF WEST VANCOUVER BC	254 - D4
AMERICAN LAKE NORTH COUNTY PARK	VETERANS DR SW, LAKEWOOD WA	181 - C4
A M KENNEDY PARK	SW KENNEDY ST & SW 102ND AV, BEAVERTON OR	199 - B2
ANDERSON PARK	168TH AV NE & NE 79TH ST, REDMOND WA	175 - D1
ANDERSON PARK	21400 RUSSELL RD, KENT WA	291 - F5
ANDERSON, FRANCES PARK	7TH AV S & MAIN ST, EDMONDS WA	171 - A5
ANDERSON GREENBELT	S 259TH ST & 88TH AV S, KENT WA	175 - C7
ANDERSON HILL PARK	BEACH DR, DISTRICT OF OAK BAY BC	257 - D11
ANDERSON LAKE STATE PARK	OFF ANDERSON LAKE RD, JEFFERSON CO WA	170 - A1
ANGLE LAKE PARK	INTERNATIONAL BL & S 194TH ST, SEATAC WA	290 - D2
APOLLO RIDGE PARK	NW 173RD AV, BEAVERTON OR	199 - A1
APRIL HILL PARK	SW 59TH AV & SW LOGAN CT, PORTLAND OR	199 - B2
ARBOR LAKE PARK	124TH ST & 4TH AV S, KING WA	286 - A7
ARBOR LODGE PARK	N BRYANT ST & N GREELEY AV, PORTLAND OR	308 - D5
ARDENWALD PARK	SE ROSWELL ST, MILWAUKIE OR	318 - B7
ARDMORE PARK	NE 30TH ST & 168TH AV NE, BELLEVUE WA	175 - D2
ARGAY PARK	NE 141ST DR & NE FAILING ST, PORTLAND OR	200 - A1
ARLEDA PARK	SW 197TH AV, WASHINGTON CO OR	199 - A1
ARNADA PARK	E FOURTH PLAIN BL & F ST, VANCOUVER WA	305 - G3
ARNOLD PARK	HARRISON BLVD, CORVALLIS OR	327 - D8
ARNOLD PARK	NE ARNOLD RD, VANCOUVER WA	305 - J2
ARNOLD PARK	SW 182ND & SW VINCENT, WASHINGTON CO OR	199 - A2
ARTHUR JOHNSON PARK	NE UNION HILL & 196TH AV NE, REDMOND WA	175 - D1
ASBERY FIELD	7TH ST & ALDER AV, MARYSVILLE WA	168 - C7
ASPEN PARK	DOWNES RD, DISTRICT OF MATSQUI BC	102 - B1
ASPEN HIGHLANDS PARK	NE 24TH ST & SE 226TH AV, GRESHAM OR	200 - B1
ATFALATI PARK	6600 SW SAGERT ST, TUALATIN OR	199 - B4
ATHLETIC FIELD	13TH ST & ROCKEFELLER AV, EVERETT WA	171 - C1
ATHLETIC FIELD	BROADWAY & 24TH ST, EVERETT WA	265 - E3
ATKINSON PARK	1601 JACKSON ST, OREGON CITY OR	199 - D4
ATLANTIC CITY PARK	SEWARD PARK S & S HENDERSON, SEATTLE WA	287 - G3
AUBURNDALE PARK	108TH AV SE & SE 315TH PL, KING CO WA	182 - C1
AUBURN GAME FARM PARK	3030 R ST SE, AUBURN WA	182 - C2
AUBURN NARROWS PARK	AUBURN BLK DIAMND RD & RTE 18, KING CO WA	182 - C1
AUDUBON PARK	N MILTON ST, SPOKANE WA	348 - F5
AUTUMN RIDGE PARK	NW AUTUMN RIDGE DR, BEAVERTON OR	199 - A1
AVALON PARK	PACIFIC HWY WEST, WASHINGTON CO OR	199 - B4
AVERY PARK	AVERY PARK DR, CORVALLIS OR	327 - F11
AVONDALE PARK	AVONDALE ST, DISTRICT OF BURNABY BC	255 - G14
AZALEA PARK	NORTH BANK CHETCO RIVER RD, BROOKINGS OR	232 - C6
BACHELOR SKI LIFT	OFF CENTURY DRIVE HWY, DESCHUTES CO OR	216 - B4
BACKMAN COUNTY PARK	DARRINGTON CLEAR CREEK, SNOHOMISH CO WA	103 - A3
BADGER MOUNTAIN PARK	BRENTWOOD AV, RICHLAND WA	341 - G6
BAGLEY PARK	FALK RD & PLOMONDON ST, VANCOUVER WA	306 - B3
BAGLEY PARK	NE JACKSON ST & NE 2ND AV, HILLSBORO OR	198 - D1
BAKER PARK	PARK ST & PARKDALE DR, GRANTS PASS OR	335 - F10
BAKERVIEW PARK	16TH AV, DISTRICT OF SURREY BC	158 - A2
BALACLAVA PARK	VANCOUVER BC	156 - B5
BALD PEAK STATE PARK	BALD PEAK RD, YAMHILL CO OR	198 - C4
BALL PARK	MARION CO OR	323 - G14
BALLANTREE PARK	DISTRICT OF WEST VANCOUVE BC	156 - B2
BALLARD PARK	R ST SE & 37TH WY SE, AUBURN WA	182 - C2
BALLARD PLAYGROUND	NW 65TH ST & 14TH AV NW, SEATTLE WA	273 - F3
BALLINGER PARK	74TH AV W & 75TH PL W, MOUNTLAKE TERR WA	171 - B6
BALLINGER PARK	NE 200TH ST, KING CO WA	171 - B6
BALTIMORE PARK	N 47TH ST & SHIRLEY ST, TACOMA WA	181 - D1
BANDON STATE PARK	COOS CO OR	220 - A7
BANFIELD PARK	CRAIGFLOWER RD, CITY OF VICTORIA BC	256 - E7
BANNERWOOD BALLFIELD PARK	127TH PL SE, BELLEVUE WA	175 - C3
BARD PARK	22ND AV & KINGWOOD ST, FOREST GROVE OR	198 - C1
BARNARD PARK	ESQUIMALT RD, CITY OF VICTORIA BC	256 - E8
BARNES FIELD PARK	SW WALKER RD, WASHINGTON CO OR	199 - B1
BARNES STATE PARK	BARNES RD, COWLITZ CO WA	187 - C5
BARNET BEACH PARK	DISTRICT OF BURNABY BC	156 - D4
BAR-S PLAYGROUND	SW ADMIRAL WY & 65TH AV SW, SEATTLE WA	280 - B3
BARTON PARK	BARTON PARK RD, CLACKAMAS CO OR	200 - B4
BARVIEW STATE WAYSIDE	CAPE ARAGO HWY & WILSHRE BLVD, BARVIEW OR	220 - C1
BASEBALL PARK	E FAIRGROUND RD, SPOKANE CO WA	349 - G8
BASSETT POND PARK	18000 NE 165TH ST, KING CO WA	171 - D7
BASTENDORFF BEACH COUNTY PARK	CAPE ARAGO HWY, COOS CO OR	220 - B1
BATEMAN PARK	OFF HWY 11, DISTRICT OF MATSQUI BC	102 - B1
BATTERSBY FIELD	HALLECK ST, BELLINGHAM WA	258 - D6
BATTLE GROUND STATE PARK	NE 249TH ST, CLARK CO WA	193 - A3
BATTLE MOUNTAIN STATE PARK	PENDLETON-JOHN DAY HWY, UMATILLA CO OR	129 - B2
BAUMAN PARK	SW OLESON RD, WASHINGTON CO OR	199 - B2
BAYVIEW PLAYGROUND	W ARMOUR ST & 24TH AV W, SEATTLE WA	272 - E7
BEACHSIDE STATE PARK	LINCOLN CO OR	328 - A11
BEACON HILL PARK	DOUGLAS ST & DALLS ST, VICTORIA BC	256 - G11
BEACON HILL PARK	SW EMERALD ST, BEAVERTON OR	199 - A2
BEACON ROCK STATE PARK	SKAMANIA CO WA	194 - B5
BEACONSFIELD PARK	SLOCAN ST, VANCOUVER BC	255 - D14
BEAR CREEK PARK	AVONDALE WY NE & UNION HILL, REDMOND WA	175 - D1
BEAR CREEK PARK	KING GEORGE HWY & 88TH, DIST OF SURREY BC	157 - A6
BEAR CREEK PARK	SISKIYOU BLVD & HIGHLAND DR, MEDFORD OR	336 - F13
BEAR HILL REGIONAL PARK	BEAR HILL RD, DISTRICT OF SAANICH BC	159 - C4
BEAVER CREEK PROVINCIAL PARK	HWY 22A, BRITISH COLUMBIA	106 - B1
BEAVER LAKE PARK	24400 SE 24TH ST, KING CO WA	176 - A3
BEECH PARK	NE 129TH AV, PORTLAND OR	200 - A1
BEECHER PARK	EASTLAWN DR, DISTRICT OF BURNABY BC	156 - D4
BELCARRA PARK	BEDWELL BAY RD, MAPLE RIDGE BC	157 - A3
BELL PARK	OFF 16TH AV, DISTRICT OF SURREY BC	158 - A2
BELLA VISTA PARK	NW 1ST ST, GRESHAM OR	200 - A2
BELLA VISTA PARK	SE BELLA VISTA RD, CLARK CO WA	193 - A7
BELLEFIELDS NATURE PARK	BELLEVUE WY SE & 112TH AV SE, BELLEVUE WA	175 - C3
BELLEVUE HIGHLAND PARK	140TH AV NE & BELLEVUE REDM, BELLEVUE WA	175 - C2
BELL VIEW POINT	SAUVIE ISLAND, MULTNOMAH CO OR	192 - B6
BELVEDERE VIEWPOINT PARK	SW ADMIRAL WY & OLGA ST, SEATTLE WA	281 - F2
BENBOW PARK	DISTRICT OF WEST VANCOUVE BC	156 - A3
BEN HUR LAMPMAN STATE WAYSIDE	SAMS VALLEY HWY, JACKSON CO OR	230 - B6
BENN PARK	N I ST, ABERDEEN WA	178 - B7
BENSKI PARK	CARRIAGE WY & HUNTER WY, WEST LINN OR	199 - C4
BENSON STATE PARK	MULTNOMAH CO OR	194 - A7
BERKELEY PARK	SE 39TH AV & SE BYBEE BL, PORTLAND OR	318 - B5
BERRY PARK	OFF TRAN CANADA HWY, DIST OF ABBOTSFRD BC	102 - B1
BERRYDALE PARK	SE 92ND AV & SE TAYLOR ST, PORTLAND OR	315 - G7
BEULAH PARK	NE LINCOLN ST, ROSEBURG OR	334 - G6
BEULAN CITY PARK	3RD ST & HEMLOCK ST, YAMHILL OR	198 - B5
BEVERLY BEACH STATE PARK	LINCOLN CO OR	206 - B2
BICENTENNIAL PARK	222ND ST SW & 39TH AV W, MOUNTLKE TERR WA	171 - B5
BICENTENNIAL PARK	AUBURN WY S & 6TH ST SE, AUBURN WA	182 - C1
BICENTENNIAL PARK	CHRISTENSEN RD & STRANDER BL, TUKWILA WA	289 - H6
BICENTENNIAL PARK	NE PARKWOOD ST & NE 25TH AV, HILLSBORO OR	198 - D1
BIDDLEWOOD PARK	SE RIVERRIDGE DR, VANCOUVER WA	311 - J1
BIG BEND PARK	MALHEUR CO OR	147 - A1
BIG CREEK STATE PARK	LINCOLN CO OR	328 - A10
BIG FINN HILL PARK	JUANITA DR NE & NE 138TH ST, KING CO WA	171 - B7
BILLICK-DUNDEE SCHOOL PARK	HERBERT HOOVER HWY, DUNDEE OR	198 - C6
BILL REAMS EAST SAMMAMISH PARK	NE 16TH ST & 212TH AV NE, KING CO WA	175 - D2
BIRCH BAY STATE PARK	BIRCH BAY DR, BIRCH BAY WA	158 - B5
BIRCHLAND PARK	ELLIS DR & LABURNUM AV, PORT COQUITLAM BC	157 - B4
BIRCHWOOD PARK	FRASER AV & LARCH WY, PORT COQUITLAM BC	157 - B4
BITTER LAKE PARK	N 130TH ST & LINDEN AV N, SEATTLE WA	171 - A7
BLACK BAY PARK	POST FALLS ID	353 - J7
BLACKIE SPIT PARK	DISTRICT OF SURREY BC	101 - C1
BLACK RIVER RIPARIAN FOREST	MONSTER RD SW, RENTON WA	289 - J3
BLAINE, DENNY PARK	LAKE WASHINGTON & DENNY BLA, SEATTLE WA	279 - F4
BLAKE ISLAND STATE PARK	BLAKE ISLAND, KITSAP CO WA	174 - D4
BLENKIN MEMORIAL PARK	HWY 19, BRITISH COLUMBIA	92 - A1

FEATURE NAME	City State	Page-Grid
BLOEDE DONOVAN PARK	ELECTRIC AV, BELLINGHAM WA	258 - J6
BLOOMINGTON PARK	SE 100TH AV & SE STEELE ST, PORTLAND OR	319 - H4
BLUEGRASS DOWNS PARK	NW WOODMERE CT, BEAVERTON OR	199 - A1
BLUE LAKE COUNTY PARK	NE MARINE DR & NE 223RD AV, FAIRVIEW OR	200 - B1
BLUE MOUNTAIN PARK	BLUEMOUNTAIN ST, COQUITLAM BC	157 - A5
BLUERIDGE PARK	BERKLEY AV, DISTRICT OF NORTH VANCOUV BC	255 - J4
BLUEWOOD SKI AREA	N FORK TOUCHET RIVER RD, COLUMBIA CO WA	122 - B3
BLUFFS PARK	GEOGESON BAY RD, BRITISH COLUMBIA	101 - B1
BLUFFS PARK, THE	NW SOUTH DR, WASHINGTON CO OR	199 - B1
BLUNDELL PARK	CITY OF RICHMOND BC	156 - B6
BLYTH PARK	W RIVERSIDE DR, BOTHELL WA	171 - C6
BOBCAT PARK	236TH ST SW & 32ND AV W, BRIER WA	171 - B6
BOB HEIRMAN WILDLIFE PARK	CONNELLY RD, SNOHOMISH CO WA	171 - D4
BOB STRAUB STATE PARK	MCPHILLIPS RD, TILLAMOOK CO OR	197 - A7
BOGACHIEL STATE PARK	OFF HWY 101, CLALLAM CO WA	169 - D2
BOISE NATIONAL FOREST	GEM CO ID	139 - C2
BOLIVAR PARK	114TH AV, DISTRICT OF SURREY BC	157 - A5
BOLON ISLAND STATE PARK	DOUGLAS CO OR	218 - C1
BONNEVILLE FIELD BALL PARK	16TH ST NE, SNOHOMISH CO WA	110 - C1
BONNEVILLE STATE PARK	MULTNOMAH CO OR	194 - C6
BONNY SLOPE PARK	NW THOMPSON RD, WASHINGTON CO OR	199 - B1
BOONES FERRY PARK	TRUCHMAN ST & MAIN ST, WILSONVILLE OR	199 - B6
BOOTH PARK	LEBANON OR	133 - C1
BORDEN PLAYFIELD	W JAMES ST & 4TH AV N, KENT WA	175 - B7
BOREN PARK	15TH AV E, SEATTLE WA	278 - C2
BOTHELL LANDING	WOODINVILLE DR & 100TH AV NE, BOTHELL WA	171 - C6
BOTHWELL PARK	168TH ST & 96TH ST, DISTRICT OF SURREY BC	157 - B6
BOULEVARD PARK	GRAND BLVD, CITY OF NORTH VANCOUVER BC	255 - C5
BOULEVARD LANE PARK	SE 192ND ST & 124TH AV SE, KING CO WA	175 - C6
BOUNDARY BAY PARK	DISTRICT OF DELTA BC	101 - C1
BOUNDARY CREEK PROVINCIAL PARK	HWY 3, BRITISH COLUMBIA	105 - B1
BOUNDARY CREEK RAVINE PARK	DISTRICT OF BURNABY BC	156 - C5
BOVEE PARK	NE 16TH PL & 108TH AV NE, BELLEVUE WA	175 - C2
BOWERS ROCK STATE PARK	CHERRY LN, LINN CO OR	207 - B5
BOW LAKE PARK	50TH CT S & S 178TH ST, SEATAC WA	289 - F7
BOWL AND PITCHER PARK	AUBREY L WHITE PKWY, SPOKANE CO WA	348 - B4
BOYER PARK AND MARINA	ALMOTA FERRY RD, GARFIELD CO WA	122 - C1
BOY SCOUT PARK	S MAIN ST & DEPOT ST, BANKS OR	125 - B1
BRACKETTS LANDING PARK SOUTH	RAILROAD AV S & MAIN ST, EDMONDS WA	171 - A5
BRADLEY PARK	SALEM OR	324 - H3
BRAEFOOT PARK	MCKENZIE AVE, DISTRICT OF SAANICH BC	256 - J3
BRAEMAR PARK	VANCOUVER BC	156 - B5
BRANNAN PARK	26TH ST NE & M ST NE, AUBURN WA	182 - C1
BRANTFORD PARK	DISTRICT OF BURNABY BC	156 - D5
BRENTWOOD PARK	SE 62ND AV & SE COOPER ST, PORTLAND OR	318 - D5
BRENTWOOD PARK	SOUTHLAWN DR, DISTRICT OF BURNABY BC	255 - J12
BREWERS PARK	VANCOUVER BC	156 - C5
BRIDAL VEIL FALLS PROVINCIAL PARK	BRIDAL FALLS RD, BRITISH COLUMBIA	94 - C3
BRIDGEMAN PARK	KEITH RD, DISTRICT OF NORTH VANCOUV BC	255 - E6
BRIDGEVIEW PARK	114TH AV & 125A ST, DISTRICT OF SURREY BC	157 - A5
BRIDLE CREST TRAIL PARK	W LAKE SAMMAMISH PKWY, REDMOND WA	175 - D1
BRIDLE TRAILS STATE PARK	116TH AV NE & N 53RD ST, KING CO WA	175 - C1
BRIERWOOD PARK	28TH AV W & 211TH PL SW, BRIER WA	171 - B5
BRIGHT ANGEL PARK	TRANS CANADA HWY, BRITISH COLUMBIA	101 - A2
BRIGHTON PLAYGROUND	S JUNEAU ST & 39TH AV S, SEATTLE WA	283 - E7
BRINK, DAVID E PARK	55 LAKE ST S, KIRKLAND WA	175 - C1
BRISCO PARK	62ND AV S & S 190TH ST, KENT WA	291 - G2
BROAD VIEW PARK	CANADA WY, DISTRICT OF BURNABY BC	255 - G14
BROADWAY PARK	CORNWALL AV, BELLINGHAM WA	258 - D4
BRONSON CREEK PARK	NW CORNELL RD, BEAVERTON OR	199 - A1
BROOKE ST PARK	BROOKE ST, CITY OF VICTORIA BC	256 - J10
BROOKHAVEN PARK	SW MURRAY BLVD, BEAVERTON OR	199 - A2
BROOKLYN PARK	SE 10TH AV & SE HAIG ST, PORTLAND OR	317 - H2
BROOKLYN SCHOOL PARK	SE 15TH AV & SE BUSH ST, PORTLAND OR	317 - H2
BROOKMERE PARK	DISTRICT OF COQUITLAM BC	156 - D5
BROOKSBANK PARK	DRAYTON ST, DISTRICT OF NORTH VANCOUV BC	255 - E5
BROOKSIDE PARK	4100 PLOMONDON ST, VANCOUVER WA	306 - A3
BROOKS MEMORIAL STATE PARK	HWY 97, KLICKITAT CO WA	127 - C1
BROOKVIEW PARK	SW GLENBROOK RD, BEAVERTON OR	199 - A2
BROWN PARK	W HARVARD BLVD, ROSEBURG OR	334 - C7
BROWN ROAD PARK	240TH ST, TOWNSHIP OF LANGLEY BC	158 - D1
BROWNS FERRY PARK	5855 SW NYBERG LN, TUALATIN OR	199 - B4
BROWNS POINT LIGHTHOUSE PARK	201 TULALIP NE, PIERCE CO WA	181 - D1
BROWNS POINT PLAYFIELD	WAY ST & WANA-WANA PL, PIERCE CO WA	181 - D1
BRUCEPORT PARK	US 101, PACIFIC CO WA	183 - D6
BRUGGERS BOG PARK	NE BALLINGER WY & 22ND AV NE, KING CO WA	171 - B6
BRUNDAGE SKI AREA	BRUNDAGE RD, ADAMS CO ID	251 - C3
BRUSETH PARK	N CASCADES HWY & SAUK VLY, DARRINGTON WA	103 - A3
BRYANT PARK	40TH AV NE & NE 65TH ST, SEATTLE WA	275 - F3
BRYANT PARK	BRYANT WY & CALAPOOIA ST, ALBANY OR	326 - B7
BRYANT WOODS PARK	SW CHILDS & SW CANAL RD, LAKE OSWEGO OR	199 - C4
BRYN MAWR PARK	80TH AV S & S 118TH ST, KING CO WA	175 - C4
BUCKINHAM PARK	DISTRICT OF BURNABY BC	156 - D5
BUCK ISLAND PARK	SIMONS RD, MONROE WA	110 - C1
BUCKLEY PARK	OFF 200TH ST, LANGLEY BC	158 - C1
BUCKMAN FIELD	NE 12TH AV & NE GLISAN ST, PORTLAND OR	313 - H5
BUCKSKIN PARK	SW BUCKSKIN TER, BEAVERTON OR	199 - B3
BUENA VISTA OCEAN WAYSIDE STATE PARK	OREGON COAST HWY, CURRY CO OR	228 - A6
BUFORD RECREATIONAL AREA	FRANK PARISH RD, LANE CO OR	331 - C11
BULLARDS BEACH STATE PARK	PARK RD, BANDON OR	220 - B5
BULLEN PARK	ESQUIMALT RD, TOWN OF ESQUILMALT BC	256 - C8
BUNDY PARK	SE 141ST AV, PORTLAND OR	200 - A2
BUNNELL PARK	SE PARK & SE PINE, CLACKAMAS CO OR	321 - J6
BURIEN PARK	SW 146TH ST & 4TH AV SW, BURIEN WA	175 - A5
BURKE MOUNTAIN REGIONAL PARK	COAST MERIDIAN & HARPER RD, COQUITLAM BC	157 - B3
BURLINGAME PARK	SW 12TH AV & SW FALCON ST, PORTLAND OR	316 - D6
BURLINGTON GREEN PARK	W SMITH ST & RAILROSD AV N, KENT WA	175 - B7
BURNABY HEIGHTS PARK	TRINITY ST, DISTRICT OF BURNABY BC	255 - G9
BURNABY LAKE PARK	DISTRICT OF BURNABY BC	156 - D5
BURNABY MOUNTAIN PARK	DISTRICT OF BURNABY BC	156 - D4
BURNS PARK	BURNS ST & DELESTRE AV, COQUITLAM BC	157 - A5
BURNSIDE PARK	BUCK ST, WEST LINN OR	199 - D4
BURNSRIDGE PARK	SW 185TH AV, WASHINGTON CO OR	199 - A2
BURNT BRIDGE CREEK GREENWAY	E FOURTH PLAIN BLVD, VANCOUVER WA	306 - B4
BURNTWOOD PARK	SW HART RD, BEAVERTON OR	199 - A2
BURNTWOOD UPPER WEST PARK	SW IVY GLEN ST, BEAVERTON OR	199 - A2
BURNTWOOD WEST PARK	SW TIMBERLAND DR, BEAVERTON OR	199 - A2
BURQUITLAM PARK	DISTRICT OF COQUITLAM BC	156 - D4
BURRARD INLET MARINE PARK	DISTRICT OF BURNABY BC	156 - D4
BURRARD VIEW PARK	TRINITY ST, VANCOUVER BC	255 - D9
BURROWS LANDING PARK	SE 15TH ST & 96TH AV SE, BELLEVUE WA	175 - C2
BURTON ACRES PARK	SW HARBOR DR & SW BURTON DR, KING CO WA	174 - D7
BUSH PASTURE PARK	SALEM OR	322 - H14
BUSH PIONEER COUNTY PARK	PACIFIC CO WA	183 - C7
BUTCHART GARDENS	800 BENVENUTO AV, DIST OF CTRL SAANICH BC	159 - B4
BUTLER CREEK PARK	SW 27TH DR, GRESHAM OR	200 - A2
BUTTERFIELD PARK	MT NEWTON CROSS, DIST OF CTRL SAANICH BC	159 - C3
BUTTERFLY PARK	7720 SW MACADAM AV, PORTLAND OR	317 - F6
BUTTERNUT PARK	SW BUTTERNUT ST, WASHINGTON CO OR	199 - A2
BY-PASS SHELTERBELT	BY-PASS HWY, RICHLAND WA	340 - D14
BYRD PARK	S 92ND ST & S ALASKA ST, TACOMA WA	181 - D4
BYRNE CREEK RAVINE PARK	DISTRICT OF BURNABY BC	156 - D5
BYRON PARK	BYRON RD, DISTRICT OF NORTH VANCOUV BC	255 - J4
CADBORO GYRO PARK	CDBORO BAY & PNDNNIS, DIST OF SAANICH BC	257 - E4
CADY PARK	MAPLE AV & UNION AV, SNOHOMISH WA	171 - D3
CAFFERKY PARK	DISTRICT OF BURNABY BC	156 - D5
CAMANO ISLAND STATE PARK	W CAMANO DR, ISLAND CO WA	167 - D6
CAMASSIA CONSERVANCY PARK	WEST A ST, WEST LINN OR	199 - D4
CAMBELL PARK	MCMICHAEL & VERONIA, SAINT HELENS OR	192 - B2
CAMBIE PARK	VANCOUVER BC	156 - B5
CAMELOT PARK	40TH PL S & S 296TH ST, KING CO WA	182 - B1
CAMILLE PARK	SW MARJORIE LN, BEAVERTON OR	199 - B2
CAMPBELL RIVER REGIONAL PARK	4TH AV, TOWNSHIP OF LANGLEY BC	158 - C2
CAMP SEALTH RECREATION AREA	SE CAMP SEALTH RD, KING CO WA	174 - C7
CAMPUS PARK	CANYON DR SE & S 252ND ST, KENT WA	175 - C7
CAMRON PARK	ACADEMY DR SE & LEMON TREE LN, AUBURN WA	182 - C2
CANAL ACRES PARK	SW CANAL RD & SW CHILDS, LAKE OSWEGO OR	199 - C4
CANBY COMMUNITY PARK	BERG PKWY, CANBY OR	199 - C7
CANEMAH PARK	815 4TH AV, OREGON CITY OR	199 - D5
CANNON HILL PARK	W SHOSHONE PL, SPOKANE WA	348 - J12
CAPE ARGO STATE PARK	CAPE ARAGO HWY, COOS CO OR	220 - B2
CAPE BLANCO STATE PARK	CURRY CO OR	224 - A4
CAPE KIWANDA STATE PARK	MCPHILLIPS RD, TILLAMOOK CO OR	197 - A6
CAPE LOOKOUT STATE PARK	CAPE LOOKOUT RD, TILLAMOOK CO OR	197 - A3
CAPE MEARES STATE PARK	CAPE MEARES LOOP RD, TILLAMOOK CO OR	197 - A1
CAPE SEBASTIAN STATE PARK	OREGON COAST HWY, CURRY CO OR	228 - A7
CAPILANO RIVER REGIONAL PARK	DISTRICT OF NORTH VANCOUV BC	254 - G3
CAPITOL STATE FOREST	HWY 12, THURSTON CO WA	184 - A3
CAP SANTE PARK	W AV, ANACORTES WA	259 - J2
CARIBOO PARK	DISTRICT OF BURNABY BC	156 - D5
CARIBOO HILL PARK	DISTRICT OF BURNABY BC	156 - D5
CARKEEK PARK	NW CARKEEK PK & NW 116TH ST, SEATTLE WA	171 - A7
CARL G WASHBURNE MEMORIAL PARK	OREGON COAST HWY, LANE CO OR	209 - A6
CARMANAH PACIFIC PROVINCIAL PARK	BRITISH COLUMBIA	100 - B2
CARNARVON PARK	HENDERSON RD, DISTRICT OF OAK BAY BC	257 - C7
CARNARVON PARK	VANCOUVER BC	254 - B14
CAROLWOOD PARK	SW CAROLWOOD DR, BEAVERTON OR	199 - A2
CARTER PARK	COLUMBIA ST & W 33RD ST, VANCOUVER WA	305 - G3
CASCADE PARK	SE 11TH ST & SE 128TH AV, CLARK CO WA	193 - A6
CASCADE PARK	SE 164TH PL, KING CO WA	175 - C5
CASCADE EVERGREEN PARK	NE 9TH ST, CLARK CO WA	193 - A6
CASCADE HEAD EXPERIMENTAL FOREST	OREGON COAST HWY, TILLAMOOK CO OR	203 - B2
CASCADE VIEW PARK	88TH ST SE & 4TH PL, EVERETT WA	268 - C5
CASCADIA STATE PARK	LINN CO OR	134 - A2
CASEY STATE PARK	CRATER LAKE HWY, JACKSON CO OR	149 - C1
CATERPILLAR ISLAND RECREATION AREA	CATERPILLAR ISLAND, CLARK CO WA	192 - B5
CATES PARK	DISTRICT OF NORTH VANCOUV BC	156 - D4
CATHEDRAL PARK	BRITISH COLUMBIA	104 - A1
CATHEDRAL PARK	N EDISON ST & N PITTSBURG AV, PORTLAND OR	192 - B7
CATHERINE PARK	20TH ST NE & 130TH DR NE, LAKE STEVENS WA	110 - C1
CEDAR COTTAGE PARK	BROADWAY E, VANCOUVER BC	255 - A13
CEDAR DRIVE PARK	PRAIRIE AV, PORT COQUITLAM BC	157 - B4
CEDAR GROVE PARK	276TH AV SE & CEDAR RIVER, KING CO WA	176 - A7
CEDAR GROVE PARK	RENTON MAPLE VALLEY RD, KING CO WA	175 - D5
CEDAR HILLS PARK	SW CEDAR HILLS BLVD, WASHINGTON CO OR	199 - B2
CEDAR HILLS REC CENTER	SW CEDAR HILLS BL, WASHINGTON CO OR	199 - B1
CEDAR ISLAND PARK	ELMRAN AV & NIXON AV, WEST LINN OR	199 - D4
CEDAR LANES PARK	25TH ST SE & K ST SE, AUBURN WA	182 - C2
CEDAR MILL PARK	NW 102ND AV, WASHINGTON CO OR	199 - B1
CEDAROAK SCHOOL PARK	TRILLIUM WY & CEDAROAK DR, WEST LINN OR	199 - C4
CEDAR RIVER PARK	MAPLE VALLEY RD & I-405, RENTON WA	175 - C5
CEDAR RIVER PARK	RNTON MAPLE VLY RD & 161ST AV, KING CO WA	175 - D5
CEDAR RIVER NATURAL ZONE	ROYAL HILL DRIVE SE, RENTON WA	175 - C5
CEDAR RIVER REGIONAL PARK	RENTON MAPLE VALLEY RD, RENTON WA	175 - C5
CEDAR RIVER TRAIL	N RIVERSIDE DR & N 6TH ST, RENTON WA	175 - C5
CEDAR RIVER TRAIL PARK	276TH AV SE, KING CO WA	176 - A7
CEDARVALE PARK	MILL HILL RD, DISTRICT OF LANGFORD BC	159 - B6
CELILO PARK	OFF COLUMBIA RIVER HWY, WASCO CO OR	127 - B1
CE MASON WETLANDS PARK	SW SUNNYHILL LN, BEAVERTON OR	199 - B2
CENTENNIAL PARK	GLADWIN RD, CITY OF WHITE ROCK BC	158 - A2
CENTENNIAL PARK	GLADWIN RD, DISTRICT OF MATSQUI BC	102 - B1
CENTENNIAL PARK	GOLDSTREAM AV, DISTRICT OF LANGFORD BC	159 - B6
CENTENNIAL PARK	GRAND ST & 14TH AV, DIST OF MISSION BC	94 - B3
CENTENNIAL PARK	WALLACE DR, DIST OF CTRL SAANICH BC	159 - C4
CENTENNIAL VIEWPOINT PARK	MOUNTAIN VIEW DR, AUBURN WA	182 - B1
CENTER STREET PARK	SW FAIRFIELD & SW 121ST, WASHINGTON CO OR	199 - B2
CENTRAL PARK	DISTRICT OF BURNABY BC	156 - C5
CENTRAL PARK	HAWTHORNE & ROWLAND ST, PORT COQUITLAM BC	157 - B4
CENTRAL PARK	MADISON AV, CORVALLIS OR	327 - G10
CENTRAL PARK	QUADRA ST, CITY OF VICTORIA BC	256 - H8
CENTRAL PARK NORTH	E FOURTH PLAIN BLVD & T ST, VANCOUVER WA	305 - H3

PNW

INDEX

FEATURE NAME / City State	Page-Grid
CENTRAL PARK PITCH AND PUTT DISTRICT OF BURNABY BC	156 - C5
CENTURY PARK LEBANON OR	133 - C1
CENTURY PARK SE 35TH AV & EDISON ST, MILWAUKIE OR	199 - D3
CFV EXIBITION PARK MACLURE RD, DISTRICT OF MATSQUI BC	102 - B1
CHAMBERS CREEK PARK CHAMBERS CREEK RD W, LAKEWOOD WA	181 - C3
CHAMPOEG STATE PARK 8239 CHAMPOEG RD, MARION CO OR	198 - D6
CHANNING HEIGHTS PARK SW HYLAND WY, BEAVERTON OR	199 - B2
CHAPIN PARK 340 WARNER PARROTT RD, OREGON CITY OR	199 - D5
CHAPMAN SQUARE PARK SW MAIN ST & SW 4TH AV, PORTLAND OR	313 - F6
CHARLAIS PARK NW CHARLAIS ST, WASHINGTON CO OR	199 - A1
CHARLES RUMMEL PARK DISTRICT OF BURNABY BC	156 - D5
CHARLESTON PARK VANCOUVER BC	254 - F12
CHELSEA PARK SW 136TH ST & 8TH AV SW, BURIEN WA	175 - A5
CHEMAINUS RIVER PROVINCIAL PARK HWY 18, BRITISH COLUMBIA	101 - A1
CHERRY PARK SE 106TH AV & SE STEPHENS ST, PORTLAND OR	315 - J7
CHERRY PARK SE 106TH AV & SE STEPHENS ST, PORTLAND OR	319 - J1
CHERRY PARK SE STARK ST & NE 242ND DR, GRESHAM OR	200 - B1
CHERRY CREST PARK 3400 124TH AV NE, BELLEVUE WA	175 - C2
CHESTERFIELD BEACH PARK 100TH AV SE, BELLEVUE WA	175 - C3
CHETZEMOLKA PARK JACKSON ST, PORT TOWNSEND WA	263 - H3
CHIEF GARRY PARK E MISSION AV, SPOKANE WA	349 - E7
CHIEF KAMIAKIN COUNTY PARK OFF FUGATE RD, WHITMAN CO WA	249 - B2
CHIMNEY PARK 9360 N COLUMBIA BLVD, PORTLAND OR	192 - B7
CHINA CREEK PARK HWY 4, BRITISH COLUMBIA	92 - B3
CHINA LAKE PARK S 19TH ST & FRWY 16, TACOMA WA	292 - A6
CHINOOK LANDING MARINE PARK NE 223RD AV & NE MARINE DR, FAIRVIEW OR	200 - B1
CHIN TIMINI PARK TAYLOR AV, CORVALLIS OR	327 - F8
CHIP ROSS PARK KINGS BLVD, BENTON CO OR	327 - E3
CHISM BEACH PARK SE 15TH ST & 97TH PL SE, BELLEVUE WA	175 - C2
CHRISTENSEN GREENBELT PARK 70TH AV S & STRANDER BL, TUKWILA WA	289 - H6
CHRISTINA LAKE PROVINCIAL PARK HWY 3 & HWY 395, BRITISH COLUMBIA	105 - C1
CHRISTMAS HILL PARK RAINBOW ST, DISTRICT OF SAANICH BC	256 - F2
CHURCH CREEK PARK 72ND AV NW & 272ND ST NW, STANWOOD WA	168 - B4
CHURCH LAKE PARK CHURCH LAKE DR & 70TH ST, BONNEY LAKE WA	182 - C3
CITY PARK 4258 PARK AV, SAINT PAUL OR	198 - D7
CITY PARK COEUR D'ALENE ID	355 - E11
CITY PARK EDMONDS WY & PINE ST, EDMONDS WA	171 - A5
CITY PARK H ST NE & 4TH ST NE, AUBURN WA	182 - C1
CITY PARK N 31ST AV & N CLARK ST, CORNELIUS OR	198 - C1
CITY PARK NE MAIN ST & NE PARK AV, AURORA OR	199 - B7
CITY PARK NORTH LN & 123RD DR NE, LAKE STEVENS WA	171 - D1
CITY PARK OFF 208TH ST, LANGLEY BC	158 - C1
CITY PARK ROSS ST & MOLALLA AV, MOLALLA OR	126 - A3
CITY PARK SE ISSAQUAH FALL CITY RD, KING CO WA	176 - A3
CITY PARK SW WATSON AV & SW 4TH ST, BEAVERTON OR	199 - B2
CITY PARK W 2ND ST & ADAMS ST, MCMINNVILLE OR	198 - A7
CITY HALL PARK SW 174TH & 12TH PL SW, NORMANDY PARK WA	175 - A5
CITY PARK AT CRESCENT CREEK VERNHARDSON ST, GIG HARBOR WA	174 - C7
CIVIC CENTER PARK 194TH ST SW & 44TH AV W, LYNNWOOD WA	171 - B5
CIVIC CENTER PARK FOSTER AV, COQUITLAM BC	157 - A4
CIVIC CENTER PLAYFIELD 6TH AV N & EDMONDS ST, EDMONDS WA	171 - A5
CLACKAMETTE PARK 1955 CLACKAMETTE DR, OREGON CITY OR	199 - D4
CLAREMONT PARK CLAREMONT AVE, DISTRICT OF SAANICH BC	159 - C5
CLARK PARK 15TH AV, VANCOUVER BC	255 - B14
CLARK PARK 25TH ST & OAKES AV, EVERETT WA	264 - E3
CLARKE BEACH PARK 7700 E MERCER WY, MERCER ISLAND WA	175 - C4
CLARK ISLAND STATE MARINE PARK CLARK ISLAND, SAN JUAN CO WA	160 - B1
CLARK, JANE PLAYGROUND ORCHARD ST & N 39TH ST, TACOMA WA	292 - B1
CLARK LAKE PARK SE 240TH ST, KENT WA	175 - C7
CLARKS CREEK PARK 7TH AV SW, PUYALLUP WA	182 - B4
CLARK-WILSON PARK GERMANTOWN RD, PORTLAND OR	192 - B7
CLATSOP STATE FOREST CLATSOP CO WA	117 - A3
CLAYTON PARK 184TH ST & 72ND AV, DISTRICT OF SURREY BC	157 - B7
CLEARWATER PARK AND LANDING CLEARWATER LN, LANE CO OR	331 - E10
CLEONE PARK NE 213TH AV, FAIRVIEW OR	200 - B1
CLEVELAND PARK DIST OF NORTH VANCOUVER BC	156 - B2
CLEVELAND PARK TALBOT RD S & S 194TH ST, KING CO WA	175 - C6
CLIFF PARK W 12TH AV, SPOKANE WA	348 - J11
CLINE FALLS STATE PARK DESCHUTES CO OR	212 - C5
CLINTON PARK 1ST AV, VANCOUVER BC	255 - D12
CLINTON PARK SE 55TH AV & SE WOODWARD ST, PORTLAND OR	318 - D1
CLISE PARK ISLAND CREST & 84TH AV, MERCER ISLAND WA	175 - C3
CLOVERDALE PARK E Q ST & E 57TH ST, TACOMA WA	182 - A3
CLOVERLAND PARK 29TH ST, CORVALLIS OR	327 - F7
CLYDE BEACH PARK 94TH AV NE & NE LK WASINGTON, BELLEVUE WA	175 - C2
CLYDE HILL TOWN PARK 95TH AV NE, CLYDE HILL WA	175 - C2
COAL CREEK PARK COAL CREEK PKWY, BELLEVUE WA	175 - C4
COALFIELD PARK 164TH AV SE, KING CO WA	175 - D5
COCHRANE PARK RAINIER-YELM HWY & YELM AV, YELM WA	118 - A1
COE CIRCLE PARK NE 39TH AV & NE GLISAN ST, PORTLAND OR	314 - B5
COEUR D'ALENE PARK W 4TH AV & S CHESTNUT ST, SPOKANE WA	348 - G10
COEUR D'ALENE NATIONAL FOREST KOOTENAI CO ID	245 - B7
COLES BAY PARK INVERNSS & ADMORE, DIST OF N SAANICH BC	159 - B3
COLGATE PARK CREST VIEW DR W, UNIVERSITY PLACE WA	181 - C3
COLLEGE PARK E FOURTH PLAIN BLVD, VANCOUVER WA	306 - C3
COLLEGE PARK NW MARYHURST CT, WASHINGTON CO OR	192 - A7
COLLEGE PARK SIERRA VISTA ST, NEWBERG OR	198 - D5
COLLIER MEMORIAL STATE PARK THE DALLES-CALIFORNIA HWY, KLAMATH CO OR	231 - D2
COLMAN PARK LAKE WASHINGTON BLVD S, SEATTLE WA	282 - D2
COLUMBIA PARK 1900 SW CHERRY PARK RD, TROUTDALE OR	200 - B1
COLUMBIA PARK COLUMBIA DR SE, KENNEWICK WA	342 - H8
COLUMBIA PARK N LOMBARD ST & N DANA ST, PORTLAND OR	308 - C4
COLUMBIA PARK S ALASKA ST & RAINIER AV S, SEATTLE WA	282 - E5
COLUMBIA LANCASTER PARK MISSOULA AV & MONTANA LN, VANCOUVER WA	306 - D5
COLUMBIA RIVER GORGE NATL SCENIC AREA COLUMBIA RIVER HWY, HOOD RIVER CO OR	195 - B5
COLUMBIA VIEW PARK NE 169TH AV & NE HASSALO ST, GRESHAM OR	200 - A1
COLVILLE NATIONAL FOREST FERRY CO WA	105 - C1
COLWOOD CREEK PARK HWY 14, CITY OF COLWOOD BC	159 - B7
COMEFORD PARK STATE AV & 5TH ST, MARYSVILLE WA	168 - C7
COMMENCEMENT PARK MCCARVER ST & RUSTON WY, TACOMA WA	293 - E2
COMMODORE PARK W COMMODORE WY & 33RD AV W, SEATTLE WA	272 - D4
COMMONS PLAYFIELD W JAMES ST & 5TH AV N, KENT WA	175 - B7
COMMONWEALTH PARK SW HUNTINGTON AV, WASHINGTON CO OR	199 - B1
COMO LAKE PARK GATENSBURY RD, COQUITLAM BC	157 - A4
COMSTOCK PARK W 29TH AV, SPOKANE WA	348 - J13
CONE ISLANDS STATE PARK CONE ISLANDS, SKAGIT CO WA	160 - B4
CONFEDERATION PARK PENZANCE DR, DISTRICT OF BURNABY BC	255 - H9
CONGER PARK DALLES-CALIFORNIA HWY, KLAMATH FALLS OR	338 - B6
CONNAUGHT PARK VANCOUVER BC	254 - C13
COOK PARK SW 92ND AV, TIGARD OR	199 - B4
COOKS BUTTE PARK SW DELENKA LN, LAKE OSWEGO OR	199 - C4
COOPERIDGE PARK HWY 17, DIST OF CENTRAL SAANICH BC	159 - C4
COOPER MOUNTAIN PARK SW SUGAR PLUM LN, WASHINGTON CO OR	199 - A2
COOPER SPUR SKI AREA DOG RIVER, HOOD RIVER CO OR	202 - C4
COOS COUNTY FOREST COOS CO OR	220 - C3
COPELAND ISLANDS MARINE PARK BRITISH COLUMBIA	92 - B1
COPLEY MEMORIAL PARK CAREY RD, DISTRICT OF SAANICH BC	256 - E1
COQUITLAM RIVER PARK SHAUGHNESSY ST & LINCOLN AV, COQUITLAM BC	157 - B4
CORBETT SNO-PARK SANTIAM HWY, JEFFERSON CO OR	211 - A2
CORBIN PARK W WAVERLY PL, SPOKANE WA	348 - J5
CORMORANT PARK CORMORANT DR & CHAPMAN LP, STEILACOOM WA	181 - B4
COTTAGE LAKE PARK 18800 WOODINVILLE-DUVALL RD, KING CO WA	171 - D6
COTTONWOOD GROVE FRAGER RD, KENT WA	175 - B7
COUCH PARK NW 19TH AV & NW GLISAN ST, PORTLAND OR	312 - D5
COUGAR MOUNTAIN COMMUNITY PARK SE COUGAR MOUNTAIN WY, BELLEVUE WA	175 - D4
COUGAR MOUNTAIN REGIONAL WILDLAND PK LAKEMONT BLVD SE, KING CO WA	175 - D4
COULEE DAM NATIONAL RECREATION AREA FERRY CO WA	105 - C3
COULEE DAM NATIONAL RECREATION AREA OFF HWY 174, GRANT CO WA	237 - D3
COULEE DAM NATIONAL RECREATION AREA STEVENS CO WA	106 - A3
COULON, GENE MEMORIAL BEACH PARK LAKE WASHINGTON BL N, RENTON WA	175 - C4
COUNCIL CREST PARK SW COUNCIL CREST DR, PORTLAND OR	316 - B1
COUNTY PARK E WELLESLEY AV, TRENTWOOD WA	350 - H3
COUNTY PARK SE 118TH AV & SE RAYMOND ST, PORTLAND OR	200 - A2
COURTHOUSE SQUARE PARK MAIN ST & 3RD ST, DAYTON OR	198 - C7
COURTSIDE ESTATES PARK WIMBLEDON CIR S, WILSONVILLE OR	199 - B5
COVE PALISADES STATE PARK, THE JEFFERSON CO OR	208 - A6
COWEN PARK BROOKLYN AV & NE 62ND ST, SEATTLE WA	274 - C4
COWICHAN LAKE PROVINCIAL FOREST HWY 18, BRITISH COLUMBIA	100 - C1
CP PARK 1212 SW 28TH ST, TROUTDALE OR	200 - B1
CRABTREE PARK WORDEN HILL & KNUDSEN LN, YAMHILL CO OR	198 - C6
CRANBERRY LAKE PARK CRANBERRY LAKE RD, ANACORTES WA	259 - E3
CRATER LAKE NATIONAL PARK DOUGLAS CO OR	223 - C7
CRATER LAKE NATIONAL PARK KLAMATH CO OR	227 - B1
CRATER LAKE SKI BOWL MAKLAKS CRATER, DOUGLAS CO OR	141 - B3
CREEKSIDE PARK 272ND ST, TOWNSHIP OF LANGLEY BC	102 - B1
CRESCENT PARK 128TH ST, DISTRICT OF SURREY BC	158 - A2
CRESCENT HEIGHTS PARK NASSAU AV NE & 42ND ST NE, TACOMA WA	182 - A1
CRESCENT LAKE COUNTY PARK TALMO DR NW & CRESCENT LAKE DR, PIERCE CO	174 - C6
CRESTON PARK SE 43RD AV & SE POWELL BLVD, PORTLAND OR	318 - B2
CRESTVIEW PARK S 160TH ST, TUKWILA WA	289 - E5
CRESTWOOD PARK BALMORAL AV, COQUITLAM BC	157 - A4
CRESTWOOD PARK SE 31ST ST & 163RD PL SE, BELLEVUE WA	175 - D3
CRESTWOODS PARK 1818 6TH ST, KIRKLAND WA	175 - C1
CROMIE PARK DISTRICT OF DELTA BC	101 - C1
CROMWELL PARK N 179TH ST, SHORELINE WA	171 - B6
CROSS PARK E CLACKAMAS BLVD, GLADSTONE OR	199 - D4
CROSSLEY PARK OFF HWY 11, DISTRICT OF ABBOTSFORD BC	102 - B1
CROSSROADS PARK NE 8TH ST & 160TH AV NE, BELLEVUE WA	175 - D2
CROWELL COURT PARK SW BEAVER CT, WASHINGTON CO OR	199 - A1
CROWN PARK NE EVERETT ST, CAMAS WA	193 - B7
CROWN CONTINENTAL PARK NE 106TH ST & NE 9TH AV, CLARK CO WA	192 - C5
CROWN POINT STATE PARK COLUMBIA RIVER HWY, MULTNOMAH CO OR	200 - D1
CRYSTAL GARDEN 713 DOUGLAS ST, CITY OF VICTORIA BC	256 - G9
CRYSTAL SPRINGS PARK S 160TH ST & 51ST AV S, TUKWILA WA	289 - F5
CULLABY LAKE COUNTY PARK OREGON COAST, CLATSOP CO WA	188 - B3
CULTUS LAKE PROVINCIAL PARK CULTUS LAKE RD, BRITISH COLUMBIA	102 - C1
CUSTER PARK SW CAPITOL HILL RD, PORTLAND OR	316 - C5
CYPRESS FALLS PARK DIST OF WEST VANCOUVER BC	156 - A2
CYPRESS PROVINCIAL PARK DIST OF WEST VANCOUVER BC	156 - A1
DABNEY STATE PARK E HIST COLUMBIA RIV HWY, MULTNOMAH CO OR	200 - C2
DAHL PARK SE RIVER RD & W ARLINGTON, GLADSTONE OR	199 - D4
DAHL, WALDO PLAYGROUND 25TH AV NE, SEATTLE WA	274 - D2
DAIRY CREEK PARK SW 17TH AV, HILLSBORO OR	198 - D1
DALE WAY PARK 60TH AV W & DALE WY, LYNNWOOD WA	171 - B5
DAMELART PARK DAMELART WAY, DIST OF CTRL SAANICH BC	159 - B4
DANIELS CREEK PARK 18000 WOODINVILLE-DUVALL RD, KING CO WA	171 - D6
DARCY ISLAND MARINE PARK BRITISH COLUMBIA	159 - D4
DARNELL PARK AURORA AV & N 165TH ST, SHORELINE WA	171 - A6
DARRINGTON CITY PARK N CASCADES HWY & SAUK VLY, DARRINGTON WA	103 - A3
DASH POINT PARK WHITMAN ST, PIERCE CO WA	181 - D1
DASH POINT HIGHLANDS PARK SW 324TH PL & 53RD PL SW, FEDERAL WAY WA	182 - A1
DASH POINT STATE PARK 5700 SW DASH POINT RD, FEDERAL WAY WA	182 - A1
DAVID GREY PARK DISTRICT OF BURNABY BC	156 - C5
DAVID SPENCER PARK SHELBOURNE ST, CITY OF VICTORIA BC	257 - A7
DAVIDS WINDSOR PARK SW SHELDRAKE WY, BEAVERTON OR	199 - A3
DAVIS PARK 127TH ST & 27TH AV NE, SEATTLE WA	171 - B7
DAVIS PARK N MAIN AV, KNAPP WA	192 - B2
DAVIS PARK SE 194TH AV, GRESHAM OR	200 - A1
DAVIS LAKE PROVINCIAL PARK SYLVESTER RD, BRITISH COLUMBIA	94 - B3
DAWES HILL PARK DAWES HILLS RD, COQUITLAM BC	157 - A5
DAWSON PARK N WILLIAMS AV & N STANTON ST, PORTLAND OR	313 - G2
DAWSON PARK SLUGGETT RD, DIST OF CENTRAL SAANICH BC	159 - B4
DAWSON PLAYFIELD PORTLAND AV & 90TH ST E, PIERCE CO WA	182 - A4
DAYBREAK PARK DAYBREAK RD, CLARK CO WA	192 - D2
DEADMAN LAKE PROVINCIAL PARK HWY 97, BRITISH COLUMBIA	104 - C1
DEADMANS ISLAND STATE PARK CUTTS ISLAND, PIERCE CO WA	181 - B1
DEARBORN PARK S BRANDON ST & 29TH ST S, SEATTLE WA	282 - D6
DEAS ISLAND REGIONAL PARK DISTRICT OF DELTA BC	156 - C7
DECEPTION PASS STATE PARK OFF HWY 20, SKAGIT CO WA	259 - F13
DE COURSEY PARK 7TH AV SW, PUYALLUP WA	182 - A4
DEEP COVE PARK DISTRICT OF NORTH VANCOUV BC	156 - D3

FEATURE NAME / City State	Page-Grid
DEER CREEK PARK SE JACKSON & NE DIAMOND LAKE, ROSEBURG OR	334 - G7
DEERFIELD PARK NW WEST UNION RD, WASHINGTON CO OR	192 - A7
DEERFIELD II PARK NW SPRINGVILLE RD, WASHINGTON CO OR	192 - A7
DEER LAKE PARK DISTRICT OF BURNABY BC	156 - D5
DELAIR PARK LWR SUMAS MTN RD, DIST OF ABBOTSFORD BC	102 - B1
DELBROOK PARK DELBROOK AV, DISTRICT OF NORTH VANCOUV BC	255 - A2
DEL NORTE COAST REDWOODS STATE PARK REDWOOD HWY, DEL NORTE CO CA	148 - B3
DELONG PLAYGROUND S 12TH ST & MULLEN ST, TACOMA WA	292 - B6
DEL REY PARK SW DICKINSON ST & SW 57TH AV, PORTLAND OR	199 - B3
DELRIDGE PLAYFIELD DELRIDGE WY SW & SW GENESEE, SEATTLE WA	281 - F5
DELTA VIEW PARK DISTRICT OF SURREY BC	101 - C1
DEMENT PARK CHARMAN ST & JERSEY AV, OREGON CITY OR	199 - D5
DENHAM TILL PARK BIRCH RD, DISTRICT OF NORTH SAANICH BC	159 - B2
DENNISON PARK DISTRICT OF DELTA BC	101 - C1
DENNY PARK DENNY WY & DEXTER AV, SEATTLE WA	277 - J4
DENNY PARK HOLMES PT NE & NE 124TH ST, KING CO WA	171 - B7
DEPOT PARK E HIST COLUMBIA RIVER HWY, TROUTDALE OR	200 - B1
DEPOT PARK FRONT ST & NW ALDER PL, ISSAQUAH WA	176 - A4
DERBY REACH REGIONAL PARK ALLARD CR, TOWNSHIP OF LANGLEY BC	157 - C6
DESCHUTES NATIONAL FOREST DESCHUTES CO OR	211 - D4
DESCHUTES NATIONAL FOREST JEFFERSON CO OR	212 - A2
DESCHUTES NATIONAL FOREST KLAMATH CO OR	223 - D2
DESCHUTES RIVER STATE RECREATION AREA OFF CELILO-WASCO HWY, SHERMAN CO OR	127 - B1
DES MOINES BEACH PARK CLIFF AVE S, DES MOINES WA	290 - A5
DES MOINES CREEK PARK DES MOINES MEMORIAL DR S, DES MOINES WA	290 - A5
DES MOINES CREEK PARK S 204TH ST, SEATAC WA	290 - B4
DES MOINES FIELDHOUSE PARK S 219TH ST & 11TH AV S, DES MOINES WA	290 - A5
DES MOINES MEMORIAL PARK SR 509 & DES MOINES MEM, DES MOINES WA	290 - A5
DESOLATION SOUND PROVINCIAL MARINE PARK DESOLATION SOUND, BRITISH COLUMBIA	92 - B1
DETROIT LAKE STATE PARK MARION CO OR	134 - B1
DEVILS ELBOW PARK OREGON COAST HWY, LANE CO OR	209 - A7
DEVILS PUNCH BOWL STATE PARK LINCOLN CO OR	206 - A2
DEWITT PARK SW SUNSET BLVD & SW DEWITT, PORTLAND OR	316 - D4
DICKINSON COUNTY PARK SW ALFRED CT & SW 57TH PL, PORTLAND OR	199 - B3
DIEFENBAKER PARK DISTRICT OF DELTA BC	101 - C1
DIERICKX FIELD 800 RISLEY AV, GLADSTONE OR	199 - D4
DIONISIO POINT PROV PARK PORLIER PASS RD, BRITISH COLUMBIA	101 - B1
DISCOVERY PARK 36TH AV W & W EMERSON ST, SEATTLE WA	272 - B4
DISCOVERY ISLAND MARINE PARK OFFSHORE ISLAND, BRITISH COLUMBIA	257 - J10
DIXIE SKI BOWL JOHN DAY HWY, GRANT CO OR	137 - C1
DOCKTON PARK DOCKTON RD & SW 260TH ST, KING CO WA	174 - D7
DOE ISLAND STATE MARINE PARK OFF OLGA TO PT LAWRENCE, SAN JUAN CO WA	160 - A3
DOGWOOD PARK 20TH AV, DISTRICT OF SURREY BC	158 - A2
DOGWOOD PARK S 26TH AV & S GINGER ST, CORNELIUS OR	198 - C1
DOGWOOD PARK SE ADAMS ST & SE MAIN ST, MILWAUKIE OR	321 - J3
DORAN PARK KILMER PL, DISTRICT OF NORTH VANCOUV BC	255 - F1
DOUGLAS PARK VANCOUVER BC	254 - F14
DOUGLAS, DAVID PARK GARRISON RD, VANCOUVER WA	306 - E5
DOWNRIVER PARK W DOWNRIVER PARK DR, SPOKANE WA	348 - D5
DOWNTOWN PARK 100TH AV NE & NE 1ST ST, BELLEVUE WA	175 - C2
DRAKE PARK BEND OR	332 - D7
DRAPER PARK 29TH AV, ALBANY OR	326 - D11
DRAYCOTT PARK DRAYCOTT RD, DISTRICT OF NORTH VANCOUV BC	255 - F2
DR RIZAL PARK 12TH AV S & S JUDKINS ST, SEATTLE WA	282 - B1
DRUMBEG PARK GABRIOLA ISLAND, BRITISH COLUMBIA	93 - A3
DRUMHELLER SPRINGS W EUCLID AV, SPOKANE WA	348 - G5
DUBOIS PARK BLANDFORD DR, VANCOUVER WA	306 - B6
DUGALD MORRISON PARK DISTRICT OF DELTA BC	101 - C1
DULLENTY PARK NE 46TH ST & NE 144TH AV, CLARK CO WA	193 - A6
DUMAS BAY PARK 30844 44TH AV SW, FEDERAL WAY WA	182 - A1
DUNACH PARK MOUNT LEHMAN RD, DISTRICT OF MATSQUI BC	102 - B1
DUNDARAVE PARK DIST OF WEST VANCOUVER BC	254 - A3
DUNIWAY PARK SW 6TH AV & SW SHERIDAN ST, PORTLAND OR	317 - E1
DURHAM CITY PARK SW 82ND AV, DURHAM OR	199 - B4
DUTHIE UNION PARK DISTRICT OF BURNABY BC	156 - D4
DUVALL PARK CARNATION-DUVALL RD & 138TH, KING CO WA	110 - C1
DUWAMISH PARK 44TH AV S & 44TH PL S, TUKWILA WA	287 - E7
DUWAMISH RIVER PARK 10TH AV S & S KENYON ST, SEATTLE WA	286 - A2
DYKSTRA PARK 1533 22ND ST NE, AUBURN WA	182 - C1
EAGLE FERN PARK EAGLE FERN RD, CLACKAMAS CO OR	200 - C5
EAGLE ISLAND STATE PARK EAGLE ISLAND, PIERCE CO WA	181 - B3
EAGLE ISLAND STATE PARK OFF N LINDER RD, ADA CO ID	253 - A1
EAGLE RIDGE PARK GUILDFORD WY, COQUITLAM BC	157 - A4
EAGLES PARK ROSE ST, ROSEBURG OR	334 - F8
EARL BOYLES PARK SE BOISE ST, PORTLAND OR	319 - J3
EARLINGTON PARK THOMAS AV SW, RENTON WA	175 - C5
EASTBURN PARK DISTRICT OF BURNABY BC	156 - D5
EAST CLARK PARK SHIRLEY ST & PARK AV, MOLALLA OR	126 - A3
EAST DELTA PARK PACIFIC HWY WEST & N UNION, PORTLAND OR	309 - F2
EASTGATE PARK 14400 SE NEWPORT WY, KING CO WA	175 - C3
EAST GREEN RIVER PARK 5 SE GREEN VALLEY RD, KING CO WA	182 - C2
EAST HILL PARK SE 248TH ST & 109TH AV SE, KENT WA	175 - C7
EASTLAKE PARK DISTRICT OF BURNABY BC	156 - D5
EAST NORWAY HILL PARK 119TH AV NE & NE 154TH ST, KING CO WA	171 - C7
EASTON SNO-PARK KACHESS LAKE, KITTITAS CO WA	111 - B3
EASTRIDGE PARK 143RD AV SE, KENT WA	175 - C7
EAST SOOKE REGIONAL PARK EAST SOOKE RD, BRITISH COLUMBIA	164 - D1
EAST SPENCER BUTTE PARK RIDGELINE TR, LANE CO OR	215 - B3
EASTVIEW PARK RUFUS DR, CITY OF NORTH VANCOUVER BC	255 - E4
EASTWOOD PARK DOUGLAS AV NE, ROSEBURG OR	334 - J8
EATONVILLE PLAYFIELD WASHINGTON AV & CARTER ST, EATONVILLE WA	118 - B1
ECHO LAKE PARK N 200TH ST & ASHWORTH AV N, SHORELINE WA	171 - A6
ECHO VALLEY SKI AREA COOPER MOUNTAIN RD, CHELAN CO WA	236 - C1
ECOLA STATE PARK TILLAMOOK HEAD COVE RD, CLATSOP CO WA	301 - B12
ED BENEDICT PARK SE 99TH AV & SE POWELL BL, PORTLAND OR	319 - H3
EDGECLIFF PARK S PARK RD, SPOKANE CO WA	350 - B10
EDGEMONT PLAYFIELD 110TH AV E & 24TH ST E, EDGEWOOD WA	182 - B3
EDGEWATER PARK BEHRENS-MILLETT RD, SKAGIT CO WA	260 - A13
EDGEWATER PARK MUKILTEO BL, EVERETT WA	171 - B2
EDGEWOOD PARK EDGEWOOD DR, VANCOUVER WA	306 - A5
EDISON SNO-PARK EDISON ICE CAVE RD, DESCHUTES CO OR	216 - C5
EDITH MOULTON PARK 108TH AV NE & NE 137TH ST, KING CO WA	171 - C7
EDWARDS, MYRTLE PARK ALASKAN WY W, SEATTLE WA	277 - G4
EICHLER PARK SW FARMINGTON RD & ROSE LN, BEAVERTON OR	199 - B2
EIDON PARK DISTRICT OF NORTH VANCOUV BC	254 - H1
E J ROBERTS PARK NE 6TH ST & THRASHER AV NE, NORTH BEND WA	176 - C5
ELBOW LAKE PARK BALD HILL RD, THURSTON CO WA	118 - A1
ELEANOR PARK FRONT AV, ALBANY OR	326 - E8
ELGIN HERITAGE PARK CRESCENT RD, DISTRICT OF SURREY BC	158 - A1
ELIOT PARK 12TH ST, HOOD RIVER OR	195 - D5
ELIZABETH PARK WASHINGTON ST, BELLINGHAM WA	258 - C5
ELIZABETH MEADOWS PARK SW ALEXANDER ST, WASHINGTON CO OR	199 - A2
ELK-BEAVER LAKE REGIONAL PARK HWY 17, DISTRICT OF SAANICH BC	159 - C5
ELK FALLS PARK HWY 19, BRITISH COLUMBIA	92 - A1
ELLIOTT BAY PARK ALASKAN WY W, SEATTLE WA	277 - G3
ELLIOTT R CORBETT II MEM STATE PARK OFF SUTTLE LAKE LP, JEFFERSON CO OR	211 - A2
ELLIOTT STATE FOREST COOS CO OR	218 - C5
ELLMAKER STATE PARK CORVALLIS-NEWPORT HWY, LINCOLN CO OR	133 - A1
ELLSWORTH PARK SE 10TH ST & SE 105TH AV, VANCOUVER WA	307 - H7
EMERSON PARK 40TH ST W & WESTMOUNT DR, FIRCREST WA	181 - C3
EMIGRANT LAKE COUNTY RECREATION AREA OFF EMIGRANT CREEK RD, JACKSON CO OR	234 - D4
EMILY CARR PARK CAROLWOOD DR, DISTRICT OF SAANICH BC	159 - C5
ENATAI PARK 108TH AV SE & SE 25TH ST, BELLEVUE WA	175 - C3
ENATAI BEACH PARK 106TH AV SE, BELLEVUE WA	175 - C3
ENDOLYNE PARK SW 98TH ST & 49TH AV SW, SEATTLE WA	284 - D4
ENGLEWOOD PARK SW SPRINGWOOD DR, TIGARD OR	199 - B3
ENTIAT VALLEY SKI AREA ENTIAT RIVER RD, CHELAN CO WA	112 - A1
ENUMCLAW COUNTY PARK ENUMCLAW CHINOOK PASS RD, KING CO WA	110 - C3
ENUMCLAW SPORTSMAN PARK ENUMCLAW CHINOOK PASS RD, KING CO WA	110 - C3
ERNIE WINCH PARK DISTRICT OF BURNABY BC	156 - D5
ERROL HEIGHTS PARK SE 52ND AV & SE TENINO CT, PORTLAND OR	318 - C7
ESPERANCE PARK 80TH AV W & 222ND ST SW, SNOHOMISH CO WA	171 - B6
ESSEX PARK SE 79TH AV & SE CENTER ST, PORTLAND OR	319 - F3
ESTEBO PARK PRESTON RD SE & 324TH PL SE, KING CO WA	176 - B4
ESTHER SHORT PARK ESTHER ST & W 8TH ST, VANCOUVER WA	305 - F5
EVEREST PARK 500 8TH ST S, KIRKLAND WA	175 - C1
EVERETT PARK OFF HWY 11, DISTRICT OF ABBOTSFORD BC	102 - B1
EVERGREEN PARK 56TH AV W & 222ND ST SW, MOUNTLKE TERR WA	171 - B6
EVERGREEN PARK ROSSITER LN, VANCOUVER WA	306 - A4
EVERGREEN HIGH PARK NE 20TH CIR & NE 149TH AV, CLARK CO WA	193 - A6
EWING PARK W EWING ST & 3RD AV W, SEATTLE WA	273 - G6
EWING YOUNG HISTORICAL PARK S BLAINE ST & E 9TH ST, NEWBERG OR	198 - D6
EXHIBITION PARK HASTINGS ST E, VANCOUVER BC	255 - E10
FAIRFIELD HILL PARK FAIRFIELD RD, CITY OF VICTORIA BC	256 - J11
FAIRGROUNDS PARK FAIRGROUND AV & NE 219TH, BTTLE GROUND WA	193 - A3
FAIRHAVEN PARK CHUCKANUT DR, BELLINGHAM WA	258 - B11
FAIRMOUNT PARK FAIRMOUNT AV SW & ADMIRAL WY, SEATTLE WA	281 - E2
FAIRMOUNT PARK SALEM OR	324 - G1
FAIRMOUNT PLAYGROUND FAUNTLEROY WY SW & SW BRANDON, SEATTLE WA	281 - E6
FAIRWEATHER PARK EVERGREEN PT RD & NE 32ND ST, MEDINA WA	175 - C2
FAIRWOOD CAMELOT PARK N DIVISION ST, FAIRWOOD WA	347 - A8
FALAISE PARK WORTHINGTON DR, VANCOUVER BC	255 - E13
FALL CITY MEMORIAL PARK SE 42ND ST & 333RD AV SE, KING CO WA	176 - B3
FALL CITY RIVERFRONT PARK FALL CITY CARNATION RD SE, KING CO WA	176 - B3
FALLS PARK POST FALLS ID	353 - G7
FANNO CREEK PARK SW ASH AV, TIGARD OR	199 - B3
FANNO CREEK PARK SW BEL AIRE DR, BEAVERTON OR	199 - B2
FARMERS PARK SE 436TH ST & 228TH AV SE, KING CO WA	182 - D3
FARRAGUT PARK N FARRAGUT ST & N KERBY AV, PORTLAND OR	309 - G4
FARRAGUT STATE PARK KOOTENAI CO ID	245 - C1
FARRELL MARSH PARK BEECH ST, STEILACOOM WA	181 - C4
FARREL-MCWHIRTER PARK 192ND AV NE & NE 103RD ST, REDMOND WA	171 - D7
FATHER BLANCHET PARK BIRMINGHAM WY & LOUISIANA, VANCOUVER WA	306 - E6
FAUNTLEROY PARK SW BARTON ST & 40TH AV SW, SEATTLE WA	284 - D4
FERGUSON PARK FERGUSON PARK RD, SNOHOMISH WA	171 - D3
FERNHILL PARK NE 37TH AV & NE AINSWORTH ST, PORTLAND OR	310 - B6
FERN HILL PARK S 88TH ST & S FAWCETT AV, TACOMA WA	181 - D4
FERNWOOD PARK 233RD AV SE & SE 266TH ST, KING CO WA	176 - A7
FERRY PARK S 14TH ST & CUSHMAN AV, TACOMA WA	293 - F6
FIRCREST PARK ELECTRON & CONTRA COSTA AV, FIRCREST WA	292 - A7
FIRCREST PARK SALEM OR	324 - F4
FIREFIGHTERS MEMORIAL PARK 229TH PL SW, MOUNTLAKE TERRACE WA	171 - B6
FIREMANS PARK CLIFF AV & S 9TH ST, TACOMA WA	293 - H5
FIRGROVE PARK SW 130TH AV & SW 22ND ST, BEAVERTON OR	199 - B2
FIRGROVE PLAYFIELD 13918 MERIDIAN E, PIERCE CO WA	182 - B5
FIRLAND PARKWAY SE 72ND AV & SE FOSTER RD, PORTLAND OR	319 - E3
FIRST HILL PARK 72ND AV SE & SE 32ND ST, MERCER ISLAND WA	283 - J2
FIRST HILL PARK JEFFERSON & 8TH, SEATTLE WA	278 - B6
FISH CREEK RECREATION AREA IDAHO CO ID	131 - C1
FISHERMANS WHARF PARK ERIE ST, CITY OF VICTORIA BC	256 - F9
FISH HATCHERY PARK WETHERBEE & FSH HATCHERY, JOSEPHINE CO OR	229 - A7
FISHING HOLE PARK W MEEKER ST & KENT DES MOINES, KENT WA	175 - B7
FISHING RECREATION AREA SE 308TH ST & 190TH PL SE, KING CO WA	182 - D1
FIVE MILE LAKE COUNTY PARK MILITARY RD S & S 364TH ST, KING CO WA	182 - B2
FLAG ISLAND COUNTY PARK COLUMBIA RIVER, MULTNOMAH CO OR	200 - C1
FLAMING GEYSER PARK SE FLAMING GEYSER RD, KING CO WA	182 - D2
FLAMING GEYSER STATE PARK SE FLAMING GEYSER RD, KING CO WA	110 - C3
FLAVEL PARK SE LAMBERT ST & SE 75TH PL, PORTLAND OR	319 - E6
FLEETWOOD PARK 80TH AV & 160TH ST, DISTRICT OF SURREY BC	157 - B7
FLO WARE PARK S JACKSON ST & 29TH AV S, SEATTLE WA	278 - D7
FLOWING LAKE COUNTY PARK 48TH ST SE, SNOHOMISH CO WA	110 - C1
FLOYD LIGHT PARK SE 111TH AV & SE ALDER ST, PORTLAND OR	315 - J7
FOGARTY CREEK STATE PARK OREGON COAST HWY, LINCOLN CO OR	203 - A7
FOOTHILLS PARK 59TH ST NE, MARYSVILLE WA	171 - D1
FOOTHILLS PARK SW LAKEWOOD ST, WASHINGTON CO OR	199 - B1
FORBES CREEK PARK 11615 NE 106TH LN, KIRKLAND WA	175 - C1
FOREST PARK NW SAINT HELENS RD, PORTLAND OR	312 - A3
FOREST PARK PIGEON CREEK RD, EVERETT WA	264 - C6
FOREST & CEDAR PARK FOREST ST, BELLINGHAM WA	258 - C8
FOREST COUNTY PARK FARWEST DR, LAKEWOOD WA	181 - C4
FOREST CREST PARK 236TH ST SW & 49TH PL W, MOUNTLKE TERR WA	171 - B6

FEATURE NAME	City State	Page-Grid
FOREST GLEN PARK	DISTRICT OF BURNABY BC	156 - C5
FOREST GLEN PARK	GALES CREEK RD, FOREST GROVE OR	198 - B1
FOREST GLEN PARK	SE 63RD ST, BELLEVUE WA	175 - C3
FOREST GLEN PARK	SW HAYSTACK DR & SW 130TH, BEAVERTON OR	199 - B3
FOREST HILL PARK	SE 49TH ST & 134TH AV SE, BELLEVUE WA	175 - C3
FOREST HILLS PARK	SW BUTNER RD, WASHINGTON CO OR	199 - B1
FOREST HOME PARK	NW LOGAN ST, CAMAS WA	193 - B7
FOREST RIDGE PARK	NE PINECREEK ST & NE 17TH, VANCOUVER WA	307 - G4
FORSGREN COUNTY PARK	14TH AV W & 240TH ST SW, SNOHOMISH CO WA	171 - B6
FORT BORST PARK	HARRISON AV & CAVENESS DR, CENTRALIA WA	299 - C3
FORT CANBY STATE PARK	PACIFIC CO WA	186 - A7
FORT CASEY STATE PARK	S ENGLE RD, ISLAND CO WA	167 - B5
FORT COLUMBIA STATE PARK	PACIFIC CO WA	186 - B7
FORT DENT PARK	SOUTHCENTER BLVD, TUKWILA WA	289 - H3
FORT FLAGLER STATE PARK	FLAGLER RD, JEFFERSON CO WA	167 - B6
FORT LANGLEY MARINA PARK	GLOVER RD & RIVER, TWNSHP OF LANGLEY BC	157 - D6
FORT RODD HILL NATIONAL HISTORICAL PARK	OCEAN BLVD, CITY OF COLWOOD BC	159 - B7
FORT SIMCOE HISTORICAL STATE PARK	FORT SIMCO RD, YAKIMA CO WA	119 - C2
FORT STEILACOOM PARK	ANGLE LN SW, LAKEWOOD WA	181 - C4
FORT STEVENS STATE PARK	JETTY RD, WARRENTON WA	188 - B1
FORT WALLA WALLA CITY PARK	MYRA RD, WALLA WALLA WA	344 - H10
FORT WORDEN STATE PARK	FORT WORDEN WY, PORT TOWNSEND WA	263 - G1
FORTY NINE DEGREES NORTH SKI AREA	GODDARDS PEAK, STEVENS CO WA	106 - B3
FOSTER PARK	S 259TH ST & 74TH AV S, KENT WA	175 - B7
FOSTER, JOSEPH MEMORIAL PARK	S 139TH ST & 53RD AV S, TUKWILA WA	289 - F2
FOUR CORNERS COUNTY PARK	FOUR CORNERS OR	325 - E1
FOX CHASE PARK	11249 SW CHAMPEOG DR, WILSONVILLE OR	199 - B6
FOX, DOROTHY PARK	NW SIERRA ST & NW 23RD AV, CAMAS WA	193 - B7
FOX ISLAND PLAYFIELD	9TH AV FI & GWAY DR FI, PIERCE CO WA	181 - B2
FRANKLIN PARK	NW CHERRY ST & NW 56TH ST, VANCOUVER WA	192 - C5
FRANKLIN PARK	N WHITEHOUSE ST, SPOKANE WA	348 - J2
FRANKLIN PARK	S 12TH ST & PUGENT SOUND AV, TACOMA WA	292 - D6
FRASER RIVER PARK	DISTRICT OF BURNABY BC	156 - C6
FRASER RIVER HERITAGE PARK	LOUGHEED HWY, DISTRICT OF MISSION BC	94 - B3
FRAZER PARK	NE 52ND AV & NE HASSALO ST, PORTLAND OR	314 - C4
FREEMAN KING PARK	PROSPECT LAKE RD, DISTRICT OF SAANICH BC	159 - B6
FREEMONT PARK	CEDAR DR, COQUITLAM BC	157 - B4
FREEPONS PARK	HEMLOCK ST & BUCKNER ST, LAKE OSWEGO OR	321 - F7
FREEWAY PARK	6TH AV & SENECA ST, SEATTLE WA	278 - A5
FREEWAY PARK 3	5TH AV NE & NE 60TH ST, SEATTLE WA	274 - B4
FREEWAY LAKES COUNTY PARK	THREE LAKES RD, LINN CO OR	326 - H14
FREMONT CANAL PARK	N CANAL ST & PHINNEY AV, SEATTLE WA	273 - H6
FREMONT NATIONAL FOREST	KLAMATH CO OR	143 - A3
FREMONT NATIONAL FOREST	MALIN OR	151 - A3
FREMONT NATIONAL FOREST	MODOC CO CA	152 - A3
FREYRER PARK	FREYRER PARK RD & FAWN, CLACKAMAS CO OR	126 - A3
FRINK PARK	S FRINK PL, SEATTLE WA	278 - E7
FROGGERS CREEK RAVINE PARK	DISTRICT OF BURNABY BC	156 - C5
FRONTIER COUNTY PARK	21800 MERIDIAN AV E, PIERCE CO WA	182 - B6
FRUIT VALLEY PARK	FRUIT VALLEY RD, VANCOUVER WA	304 - D2
FRYELANDS PARK	FRYELANDS BLVD, MONROE WA	110 - C1
FUDPUCKER PARK	SPIRIT & CONSTITUTION, SNOHOMISH CO WA	168 - B6
FULMER FIELD	HARVEY RD NE & 5TH ST NE, AUBURN WA	182 - C1
FULTON PARK	SW BARBUR BL & SW MILES ST, PORTLAND OR	317 - E6
FURNBERG PARK	SE FURNBERG ST, MILWAUKIE OR	199 - D3
GABRIEL PARK	SW 45TH AV & SW VERMONT ST, PORTLAND OR	316 - A5
GABRIOLA ISLAND PARK	GABRIOLA ISLAND, BRITISH COLUMBIA	93 - A3
GADDIS PARK	NW HICKS ST, ROSEBURG OR	334 - E6
GALE-JOSEPH PARK	18TH AV, FOREST GROVE OR	198 - C1
GALENA PARK	TURNER AV & E GALENA ST, GRANITE FALLS WA	102 - C3
GALLOWAY PARK	GALLOWAY RD, CITY OF COLWOOD BC	159 - B7
GAME FARM WILDERNESS PARK	2401 STUCK RIVER DR, AUBURN WA	182 - C2
GAMMANS PARK	N BURRAGE AV & N GAMMANS PL, PORTLAND OR	308 - D5
GARDEN HOME PARK	SW ALDEN ST & SW 82ND, WASHINGTON CO OR	199 - B2
GARDEN HOME REC CENTER	SW OLESON RD, WASHINGTON CO OR	199 - B2
GARDNER PARK	MACLURE RD, DISTRICT OF MATSQUI BC	102 - B1
GARFIELD PARK	BOROUGH RD & N STADIUM WY, TACOMA WA	293 - F2
GARFIELD PARK	CLEVELAND AV, CORVALLIS OR	327 - G7
GARFIELD PLGD	WALNUT ST & 24TH ST, EVERETT WA	265 - F2
GARIBALDI PROVINCIAL PARK	OFF TRANS CANADA HWY, BRITISH COLUMBIA	93 - C1
GARRETT PARK	HILLCREST AV & PORTER ST, ENUMCLAW WA	110 - C3
GARRISON CREEK PARK	S 218TH ST & 98TH AV S, KENT WA	175 - C6
GARY GRANT SOOS CREEK PARK	SE LAKE YOUNGS WY, KING CO WA	175 - C6
GARY ISLAND COUNTY PARK	COLUMBIA RIVER, MULTNOMAH CO OR	200 - C1
GARY POINT PARK	CITY OF RICHMOND BC	156 - A7
GAS WORKS PARK	N NORTHLAKE WY & MERIDIAN AV, SEATTLE WA	274 - A7
GEARHART MOUNTAIN WILDERNESS	LAKE CO OR	151 - C1
GENEL PARK	SE CRESTVIEW DR, HILLSBORO OR	198 - D1
GEN ANDERSON PARK	BURDICK AV & E ARIZONA DR, VANCOUVER WA	306 - D6
GENERAL BROCK PARK	VANCOUVER BC	156 - C5
GENESSE PLAYGROUND	S GENESSE ST & 42ND AV S, SEATTLE WA	283 - F5
GEORGE PARK	N SENECA ST & N BURR AV, PORTLAND OR	192 - B7
GEORGE GREEN PARK	DISTRICT OF BURNABY BC	156 - D4
GEORGE HIMES PARK	SW TERWILLIGER BLVD, PORTLAND OR	316 - E4
GEORGE LEAF PARK	DISTRICT OF BURNABY BC	156 - D5
GEORGE ROGERS PARK	STATE ST & LADD ST, LAKE OSWEGO OR	321 - G7
GEORGE SMALLWOOD PARK	MASHELL AV, EATONVILLE WA	118 - B1
GEORGE T GERLINGER STATE EXPER FOREST	POLK CO OR	125 - A3
GEORGE W JOSEPH STATE PARK	HAINES RD, MULTNOMAH CO OR	200 - D1
GIBSON PARK	105 WILDWOOD BLVD SW, ISSAQUAH WA	176 - A4
GIFFORD PINCHOT NATIONAL FOREST	COWLITZ CO WA	190 - A2
GIFFORD PINCHOT NATIONAL FOREST	KLICKITAT CO WA	195 - C1
GIFFORD PINCHOT NATIONAL FOREST	LEWIS CO WA	185 - A6
GIFFORD PINCHOT NATIONAL FOREST	WIND RIVER RD, CLARK CO WA	193 - C4
GIFFORD PINCHOT NATIONAL FOREST	WIND RIVER RD, SKAMANIA CO WA	194 - A4
GILBERT CREEK PARK	HAWTHORNE AV & HILLCREST, GRANTS PASS OR	335 - E6
GILBERT HEIGHTS PARK	SE 130TH AV, PORTLAND OR	200 - A2
GILBERT PRIMARY PARK	SE 134TH AV & SE FOSTER RD, PORTLAND OR	200 - A2
GILMAN, BURKE PARK	SAND PT WY NE & NE 50TH ST, SEATTLE WA	275 - F5
GILMAN PLAYGROUND	NW 54TH ST & 11TH AV NW, SEATTLE WA	273 - F4
GINKO PETRIFIED FOREST STATE PARK	KITTITAS CO WA	120 - B1
GISSBERG TWIN LAKES COUNTY PARK	TWIN LAKES AV, SNOHOMISH CO WA	168 - C6
GLACIER VIEW PARK	N ANTONIE AV & CARTER ST, EATONVILLE WA	118 - B1
GLANFORD PARK	KENNETH ST, DISTRICT OF SAANICH BC	256 - F3
GLEN PARK	WESTWOOD ST & LINCOLN AV, COQUITLAM BC	157 - B4
GLENCO PARK	NE 24TH ST & ANACORTES AV NE, RENTON WA	175 - C4
GLENCOE PARK	GLENCOE DR, PORT MOODY BC	157 - A4
GLENCOE SWALE	NE LORIE DR, HILLSBORO OR	198 - D1
GLENFAIR PARK	NE 151ST AV & NE DAVIS CT, PORTLAND OR	200 - A1
GLENHAVEN PARK	NE 82ND AV & NE SISKIYOU ST, PORTLAND OR	315 - F3
GLENMORE PARK	DISTRICT OF WEST VANCOUVE BC	156 - B2
GLENMORRIE PARK	GLENMORRIE & PACIFIC HWY, LAKE OSWEGO OR	199 - C4
GLENN NELSON PARK	MILITARY RD S & S 268TH ST, KENT WA	175 - B7
GLENWOOD PARK	SE 87TH AV & SE CLAYBOURNE, PORTLAND OR	319 - G5
GOAT ISLAND PARK	WILAMETTE RIVER, WEST LINN OR	199 - D4
GODDARD PARK	100TH AV NE & NE 8TH ST, BELLEVUE WA	175 - C2
GOLDCREEK COUNTY PARK	148TH AV NE & NE 147TH PL, KING CO WA	171 - D7
GOLDEN & SILVER FALLS STATE PARK	EAST FORK GLENN CREEK RD, COOS CO OR	140 - C1
GOLDEN EARS PROVINCIAL PARK	FERN CRES, MAPLE RIDGE BC	157 - D2
GOLDEN GARDENS PARK	GOLDEN GARDENS DR NW, SEATTLE WA	272 - C1
GOLD HILL REGIONAL PARK	SAMS VALLEY HWY, GOLD HILL OR	230 - B6
GOLD LAKE SNO-PARK	WILLAMETTE PASS, LANE CO OR	142 - B1
GOLD NUGGET RECREATION AREA	SAMS VALLEY HWY, JACKSON CO OR	230 - B5
GOLDSMITH PARK	148TH AV NE, BELLEVUE WA	175 - C2
GOLDSMITH PARK	REDMOND RD, BELLEVUE WA	175 - D2
GOLDSTREAM PROVINCIAL PARK	TRANS CANADA HWY, DISTRICT OF LANGFORD BC	159 - A6
GONYEA COUNTY PARK	10TH AV S & 136TH ST CT S, PIERCE CO WA	181 - D5
GOODLOW MOUNTAIN NATURAL AREA	OFF GERBER RD, KLAMATH CO OR	151 - B2
GOOD NEIGHBOUR PARK	FOSTER AV & SCHOOLHOUSE ST, COQUITLAM BC	157 - A4
GOOSE LAKE RECREATION AREA	OFF FREMONT HWY, LAKE CO OR	152 - A3
GOOT PARK	SE YALE ST, CAMAS WA	193 - B7
GORDON BAY PROVINCIAL PARK	BRITISH COLUMBIA	100 - C1
GORE PARK	GREIG AV, DIST OF CENTRAL SAANICH BC	159 - B4
GORGE PARK	GORGE RD W, DISTRICT OF SAANICH BC	256 - E6
GOVERNMENT HOUSE GARDENS	1401 ROCKLAND AV, CITY OF VICTORIA BC	256 - J10
GOVERNOR PATTERSON MEMORIAL PARK	LINCOLN CO OR	328 - B6
GOVERNORS PARK	SW DAVENPORT ST, PORTLAND OR	316 - D1
GOVERNOR TOM MCCALL WATERFRONT PARK	SW FRONT AV, PORTLAND OR	317 - F1
GOWLLAND-TOD PROVINCIAL PARK	WILLIS POINT RD, BRITISH COLUMBIA	159 - A5
GRAHAM PARK	DISTRICT OF BURNABY BC	156 - D5
GRANADA PARK	SW BANY RD, WASHINGTON CO OR	199 - A2
GRAND AV PARK	16TH ST & GRAND AV, EVERETT WA	264 - D1
GRAND PRAIRIE PARK	WAVERLY DR, ALBANY OR	326 - F11
GRANDVIEW PARK	MILITARY RD S, SEATAC WA	290 - D6
GRANDVIEW FOREST PARK	GRAND VIEW ST & STANICH AV, GIG HARBOR WA	181 - C1
GRANT PARK	NE US GRANT PL & NE 33RD AV, PORTLAND OR	314 - A3
GRASS LAWN PARK	OLD REDMOND RD & 143RD CT NE, REDMOND WA	175 - C1
GRAUER PARK	DISTRICT OF DELTA BC	101 - C1
GRAY CREEK RAVINE PARK	DISTRICT OF BURNABY BC	156 - C5
GRAYLAND PARK	N MERIDIAN & 5TH AV NE, PUYALLUP WA	182 - B3
GREEN LAKE PARK	GREEN LAKE DR N, SEATTLE WA	273 - J3
GREENMOUNT PARK	OXFORD ST, PORT COQUITLAM BC	157 - B4
GREEN PARK PLAYGROUND	N DIVISION ST, WALLA WALLA WA	345 - C6
GREEN PARK PLAYGROUND	OFF PALOUSE COVE RD, WHITMAN CO WA	249 - C1
GREEN TIMBERS URBAN FOREST	FRASER HWY & 96TH, DISTRICT OF SURREY BC	157 - A6
GREENTREE PARK	GREENTREE CIR & CARTER PL, LAKE OSWEGO OR	199 - C4
GREEN TREE PARK	SE 216TH ST & 120TH AV SE, KING CO WA	175 - C6
GREENTREE VILLAGE PARK	DISTRICT OF BURNABY BC	156 - C5
GREENWAY PARK	SW HALL BLVD, BEAVERTON OR	199 - B3
GREENWOOD PARK	GRAND BLVD, CITY OF NORTH VANCOUVER BC	255 - C3
GRENADIER PARK	LANSKY RD, MASON CO WA	180 - D3
GRIFFIN PARK	ROGUE RIVER LOOP HWY, JOSEPHINE CO OR	229 - A5
GRIFFIN OAKS PARK	NE GRIFFIN OAKS ST, HILLSBORO OR	198 - D1
GRIFFITH PARK	SW GRIFFITH DR, BEAVERTON OR	199 - B2
GRIFFITHS-PRIDAY OCEAN STATE PARK	OFF HWY 109, GRAYS HARBOR CO WA	177 - B4
GRIMER PARK	CHERRY AV, DISTRICT OF MISSION BC	94 - B3
GRIMSTON PARK	NEW WESTMINSTER BC	156 - D6
GROSE, WILLIAM PARK	31ST AV, SEATTLE WA	278 - E4
GROTTO, THE	NE 85TH AV & NE SANDY BLVD, PORTLAND OR	315 - G2
GROUSEWOODS PARK	DISTRICT OF NORTH VANCOUV BC	156 - B2
GROVELAND PARK	DEERFORD RD, MERCER ISLAND WA	283 - J6
G S A PARK	15TH ST SW & C ST SW, AUBURN WA	182 - B1
GUILBY PARK	GUILBY ST & EDGAR AV, COQUITLAM BC	157 - A5
GUSTAFSON, CARL PARK	NASHVILLE WY & TENNESSEE LN, VANCOUVER WA	306 - E6
GUY W TALBOT STATE PARK	CROWN POINT HWY, MULTNOMAH CO OR	200 - D1
HALDON PARK	THOMSON PL, DIST OF CENTRAL SAANICH BC	159 - C3
HALE PASS RECREATION CENTER	36TH ST NW & 97TH AV NW, PIERCE CO WA	181 - B1
HALF DOLLAR PARK	120TH ST E & 94TH AV E, PIERCE CO WA	182 - B4
HALL PARK	NE 23RD ST, GRESHAM OR	200 - B1
HALLER LAKE PLAYGROUND	N 130TH ST & ASHWORTH AV N, SEATTLE WA	171 - B7
HAMBY PARK	NE JACKSON SCHOOL RD, HILLSBORO OR	198 - D1
HAMILTON PARK	RUSTON WY, TACOMA WA	292 - E1
HAMILTON PARK	SW 45TH AV & SW HAMILTON ST, PORTLAND OR	316 - A3
HAMILTON VIEW PARK	CALIFORNIA WY SW, SEATTLE WA	276 - E7
HAMLIN PARK	15TH AV NE & NE 165TH ST, SHORELINE WA	171 - B7
HAMLLIK PARK	ADDY ST & ADDY LP, WASHOUGAL WA	193 - C7
HAMMERLE PARK	HOLMES ST & LEWIS ST, WEST LINN OR	199 - D4
HAMPTON PARK	TILLICUM RD, DISTRICT OF SAANICH BC	256 - E5
HANCOCK PARK	NE 90TH AV & NE TILLAMOOK ST, PORTLAND OR	315 - G4
HANDY PARK	NW FAIRVIEW AV & CEDAR ST, FAIRVIEW OR	200 - B1
HAPPY VALLEY PARK	SE RIDGECREST RD, HAPPY VALLEY OR	200 - A3
HARBORVIEW PARK	MUKILTEO BL, EVERETT WA	264 - A7
HARBOUR VIEW PARK	DISTRICT OF BURNABY BC	156 - D4
HARLEMAN PARK	S HEATHER ST & S 10TH AV, CORNELIUS OR	198 - C1
HARMAN SWIM CTR & PARK	SW SCHOLLS FERRY RD, BEAVERTON OR	199 - B2
HARMON FIELD	N MARKET ST, SPOKANE WA	349 - D1
HARMON PLAYGROUND	S 80TH ST & S J ST, TACOMA WA	181 - D4
HARNEY PARK	E 13TH ST & MCLOUGHLIN BL, VANCOUVER WA	306 - A5
HARNEY PARK	SE 67TH AV & SE HARNEY ST, PORTLAND OR	318 - E7
HARPER PARK	HIGHLAND DR, COQUITLAM BC	157 - B4
HARRIS BEACH STATE PARK	OREGON COAST HWY, BROOKINGS OR	232 - C6

PNW

INDEX

FEATURE NAME	City State	Page-Grid
HARRISON PARK	SE 83RD AV & SE HARRISON ST, PORTLAND OR	319 - F1
HARRY SPRINKER RECREATION CENTER	MILITARY RD S & C ST S, PIERCE CO WA	181 - D5
HARRY TODD PARK	WOODLAND AV & N THORNE LN SW, LAKEWOOD WA	181 - C5
HARTKE PARK	556 HARTKE LP, OREGON CITY OR	199 - D5
HART MEADOWS PARK	SW RIGERT RD & SW 159TH PL, BEAVERTON OR	199 - A2
HARTWOOD HIGHLAND PARK	SW MURRAY BLVD, BEAVERTON OR	199 - A2
HARWOOD PARK	LAUREL ST, DISTRICT OF BURNABY BC	255 - J14
HASTINGS MILL PARK	UNIVERSITY ENDOWMENT LAND BC	254 - A11
HATCHERY PARK	AUBURN BLACK DIAMOND RD, KING CO WA	182 - C1
HATHAWAY PARK	25TH ST, WASHOUGAL WA	193 - C7
HAT ROCK STATE PARK	COLUMBIA RIVER HWY, UMATILLA CO OR	129 - A1
HATZIC PARK	DEWDNEY TRNK & DOUGLS, DIST OF MISSION BC	94 - B3
HAUGE HOMESTEAD PARK	SILVERLAKE RD & BOTHL EVRT HW, EVERETT WA	171 - C4
HAWTHORNE PARK	104TH AV & 148TH ST, DIST OF SURREY BC	157 - A6
HAWTHORNE PARK	DISTRICT OF DELTA BC	101 - C1
HAYNES POINT PROVINCIAL PARK	32ND ST, BRITISH COLUMBIA	104 - C1
HAYS PARK	N CRESTLINE ST, SPOKANE WA	349 - C4
HAZELDALE PARK	SW 196TH AV, WASHINGTON CO OR	199 - A2
HAZEL DELL PARK	NE 68TH ST, CLARK CO WA	192 - C5
HAZELNUT PARK	59TH AV S & S 147TH ST, TUKWILA WA	289 - G3
HAZEL SILLS PARK	WILLAMINA AV, FOREST GROVE OR	198 - B1
HAZEL VALLEY PARK	SW 126TH ST & 3RD AV SW, KING CO WA	175 - A5
HAZELWOOD PARK	920 LAURELWOOD DR, OREGON CITY OR	199 - D5
HAZELWOOD PARK	RIVERSIDE DR, ALBANY OR	326 - A9
HAZELWOOD PARK	SE 73RD PL & 121ST PL SE, NEWCASTLE WA	175 - C4
H B FULLER PARK	NW 139TH ST & NW 2ND AV, CLARK CO WA	192 - C4
HEALS RIFLE RANGE	WILLIS POINT RD, DISTRICT OF SAANICH BC	159 - B4
HEALY HEIGHTS PARK	SW COUNCIL CREST DR, PORTLAND OR	316 - C2
HEARTHWOOD PARK	NE HEARTHWOOD BLVD, CLARK CO WA	193 - A6
HEBB MEMORIAL PARK	HEBB PARK RD, CLACKAMAS CO OR	199 - C6
HEDDIE NOTZ PARK	7821 STRAWBERRY LN, CLACKAMAS CO OR	199 - D4
HEIDELBERG ATHLETIC FIELD	S 19TH ST & S TYLER ST, TACOMA WA	292 - B7
HEINIE HEUMANN PARK	TUALATIN ST & 15TH ST, SAINT HELENS OR	192 - B2
HELEN ALTHAUS PARK	SW 4TH ST, TROUTDALE OR	200 - B1
HELLS CANYON NATIONAL RECREATION AREA	ADAMS CO ID	131 - B1
HELLS GATE STATE PARK	SNAKE RIVER AV, NEZ PERCE CO ID	250 - B5
HELMCKEN PARK	HELMCKEN RD, TOWN OF VIEW ROYAL BC	256 - B4
HELMICK STATE PARK	HELMICK RD, POLK CO OR	207 - B2
HEMLOCK SKI AREA	MORRIS VALLEY RD, BRITISH COLUMBIA	94 - C3
HENDERSON PARK	CALAPOOIA ST, ALBANY OR	326 - C8
HENDERSON PARK	CEDAR HILL CROSS RD, DIST OF OAK BAY BC	257 - C5
HENDRICKS PARK	FAIRMOUNT BLVD, EUGENE OR	330 - D8
HERBERT HOOVER PARK	E 1ST ST & S RIVER ST, NEWBERG OR	198 - D5
HERBERTS POND PARK	MAIN ST & TILLER-TRAIL HWY, DOUGLAS CO OR	225 - C3
HERITAGE PARK	276TH ST NW, STANWOOD WA	168 - A4
HERITAGE PARK	MAPLE ST & NARROW ST, SUMNER WA	182 - B3
HERITAGE PARK	SE 2ND ST & E COLUMBIA AV, SCAPPOOSE OR	192 - A4
HERON PARK	VILLAGE GREEN & 155TH SE, MILL CREEK WA	171 - C4
HEYBURN STATE PARK	CEDAR ST, CHATCOLET ID	248 - B7
HIAWATHA PLAYGROUND	CALIFORNIA AV SW & LANDER ST, SEATTLE WA	280 - E2
HICKORY PARK	64TH ST NE & 67TH AV NE, MARYSVILLE WA	168 - D7
HIDDEN PARK	FRANKLIN ST & W 38TH ST, VANCOUVER WA	305 - F2
HIDDEN VALLEY SPORTS PARK	112TH AV NE, BELLEVUE WA	175 - C2
HIDEAWAY PARK	SW OLESON RD, WASHINGTON CO OR	199 - B2
HIGH BRIDGE PARK	W SUNSET BLVD, SPOKANE WA	348 - F10
HIGH DRIVE PARKWAY	S HIGH DR, SPOKANE WA	348 - H13
HIGHLAND PARK	BURCHAM ST, KELSO WA	303 - E7
HIGHLAND MEMORIAL PARK	76TH ST SW & 44TH AV W, EVERETT WA	267 - E3
HIGHLANDS PARK	11210 NE 102ND ST, KIRKLAND WA	175 - C1
HIGHLANDS PARK	HIGHLANDS BLVD SE, MILL CREEK WA	171 - C4
HIGHLANDS PARK	NE 7TH ST & EDMONDS AV NE, RENTON WA	175 - C4
HIGHPOINT PLAYGROUND	SW MYRTLE ST & 31ST AV SW, SEATTLE WA	281 - F7
HIGHROCK PARK	LAMPSON ST, TOWN OF ESQUILMALT BC	256 - D8
HIGH ROCKS PARK	82ND DR & COLUMBIA AV, GLADSTONE OR	199 - D4
HILDA PARK	DISTRICT OF BURNABY BC	156 - D5
HILGARD JUNCTION STATE PARK	OLD OREGON TR & UKIAH-HILGRD, UNION CO OR	130 - A2
HILL PARK	PARK AV, SNOHOMISH WA	171 - D3
HILLAIRE PARK	NE 6TH ST, BELLEVUE WA	175 - D2
HILLCREST PARK	E BLACKBURN RD, MOUNT VERNON WA	260 - D14
HILLENDALE PARK	19260 CLAIRMONT WY, OREGON CITY OR	199 - D5
HILLSBORO HS FIELD	NE DELSEY RD & NE GRANT ST, HILLSBORO OR	198 - D1
HILLSDALE PARK	SW 25TH AV & HILLSDALE HWY, PORTLAND OR	316 - C4
HILLSIDE PARK	AUBREY BUTTE RD & HILLS AV, BEND OR	332 - C6
HILLSIDE PARK	S GRANITE AV & UNION ST, GRANITE FALLS WA	102 - C3
HILLSIDE PARK	SEAFORTH WY, PORT MOODY BC	157 - A4
HILLSIDE CENTER PARK	NW ARIEL TER, PORTLAND OR	312 - B5
HILLTOP PARK	24TH AV S & S 128TH ST, KING WA	288 - C1
HILL TOWER PARK	19TH AV, MILTON WA	182 - B2
HILLWOOD PARK	NW 189TH ST & 3RD AV NW, SHORELINE WA	171 - A6
HING HAY PARK	MAYNARD AV S & KING ST, SEATTLE WA	278 - A7
HITEON PARK	SW BROCKMAN RD, BEAVERTON OR	199 - B3
HITEON MEADOWS PARK	SW CITATION DR, BEAVERTON OR	199 - B3
HITT MOUNTAIN SKI AREA	COW CAMP RD, WASHINGTON CO ID	139 - A1
H J ANDREWS EXPERIMENTAL FOREST	LANE CO OR	134 - A3
HOFFMAN PARK	19130 122 AV, PITT MEADOWS BC	157 - B5
HOLIDAY PARK	PERIMETER RD & HOLIDAY DR, PIERCE CO WA	181 - D5
HOLLADAY WEST PARK	NE 11TH AV & NE HOLLADAY ST, PORTLAND OR	313 - H4
HOLLAND PARK	OLD YALE RD, DISTRICT OF SURREY BC	157 - A6
HOLLY PARK	148TH ST & 107A AV, DISTRICT OF SURREY BC	157 - A6
HOLLYBROOK PARK	SW BIRDSDALE DR, GRESHAM OR	200 - A2
HOLLYWOOD PARK	FAIRFIELD RD, CITY OF VICTORIA BC	257 - A11
HOLMAN PARK	NW HOLMAN LN IN FOREST PARK, PORTLAND OR	312 - A3
HOLMES PARK	WHITE OAK DR, MEDFORD OR	336 - G13
HOMESTEAD FIELD	SE 40TH ST & 80TH AV SE, MERCER ISLAND WA	175 - C3
HONEYMOON BAY NATURE PARK	BRITISH COLUMBIA	100 - C1
HOODOO SKI BOWL SNO-PARK	OFF SANTIAM HWY, LINN CO OR	134 - C2
HOODSPORT TRAIL STATE PARK	HWY 119, MASON CO WA	173 - A6
HORIZON VIEW PARK	47TH NE & NE 201ST, LAKE FRST PARK WA	171 - B6
HORN CREEK PARK	MACLURE RD, DISTRICT OF MATSQUI BC	102 - B1
HORNER PARK	CEDAR HILL CROSS RD, DIST OF SAANICH BC	257 - B4
HORSESHOE BAY PARK	DISTRICT OF WEST VANCOUVE BC	156 - A2
HORSETHIEF LAKE STATE PARK	HWY 14, KLICKITAT CO WA	196 - D6
HORTH HILL REGIONAL PARK	TATLOW RD, DISTRICT OF NORTH SAANICH BC	159 - C2
HOUGEN PARK	OFF TRANS CAN HWY, DIST OF ABBOTSFORD BC	102 - B1
HOUGHTON BEACH PARK	5811 LAKE WASHINGTON BLVD NE, KIRKLAND WA	175 - C1
HOUGHTON NEIGHBORHOOD PARK	NE 47TH ST & 108TH AV NE, KIRKLAND WA	175 - C1
HOWARD AMON PARK	LEE BLVD, RICHLAND WA	341 - G1
HOWARD TIETAN PARK	E TIETAN ST, WALLA WALLA WA	345 - C10
HOWARTH PARK	OLYMPIC BLVD, EVERETT WA	264 - A6
HOWELL PARK	E HOWELL PL, SEATTLE WA	279 - F4
HOWELL TERRITORIAL PARK	SAUVIE ISLAND RD, MULTNOMAH CO OR	192 - B6
HOY CREEK PARK	JOHNSON ST & GUILDFORD WY, COQUITLAM BC	157 - A4
HUGH BOYD PARK	CITY OF RICHMOND BC	156 - A7
HUGHES PARK	OFF HUNTINGDON RD, DISTRICT OF MATSQUI BC	102 - B1
HUGHES PLAYGROUND	SW HOLDEN ST & 28TH AV SW, SEATTLE WA	285 - F2
HUGO RAY PARK	DISTRICT OF WEST VANCOUVE BC	254 - G3
HUG POINT STATE PARK	OREGON COAST HWY, CLATSOP CO OR	191 - A2
HULT PARK	RIDGELINE TR, EUGENE OR	330 - B14
HUMBOLDT NATIONAL FOREST	HUMBOLDT CO NV	154 - C3
HUMBOLDT NATIONAL FOREST	HUMBOLDT CO NV	155 - A3
HUMBUG MOUNTAIN STATE PARK	CURRY CO OR	224 - B7
HUME PARK	NEW WESTMINSTER BC	156 - D5
HUMMINGBIRD HILL PARK	SPRAGUE ST, EDMONDS WA	171 - A5
HUNTS POINT PARK	84TH AV NE & NE 30TH ST, HUNTS POINT WA	175 - C2
HURRICANE RIDGE SKI LODGE	HEART OF THE HILLS RD, CLALLAM CO WA	109 - B1
HUTT PARK	187TH ST SW, EDMONDS WA	171 - A5
HYACINTH PARK	INTERURBAN RD, DISTRICT OF SAANICH BC	256 - D2
HYLAND FOREST PARK	SW SEXTON MOUNTAIN DR, BEAVERTON OR	199 - B2
HYLEBOS STATE PARK	411 S 348TH ST, FEDERAL WAY WA	182 - A2
IBACH PARK	10455 SW IBACH ST, TUALATIN OR	199 - B4
IBACH NATURE PARK	ROSEPARK DR & PARKVIEW TER, WEST LINN OR	199 - C4
IDYLWOOD PARK	SAMMAMISH PKWY NE & NE 38TH ST, REDMND WA	175 - D2
ILLINOIS RIVER STATE PARK	REDWOOD HWY, JOSEPHINE CO OR	233 - A4
INDEX CITY PARK	AVENUE A & 5TH ST, INDEX WA	111 - A1
INDIAN CANYON PARK	S INDIAN CANYON DR, SPOKANE WA	348 - D10
INDIAN JOHN ISLAND	SANDY RIVER, MULTNOMAH CO OR	200 - C2
INDIAN MART PARK	OFF MERLIN-GALICE RD, JOSEPHINE CO OR	149 - A1
INDIAN SUMMER PARK	113TH ST NE & 183RD DR NE, SNOHOMSH CO WA	102 - C3
INDIAN TOM PARK	6TH ST NE & HENRY RD, AUBURN WA	182 - C1
INGLEMOOR COUNTY PARK	88TH AV NE & NE 157TH ST, KING CO WA	171 - C7
INLET PARK	MURRAY ST, PORT MOODY BC	157 - A4
INTEL ALOHA WETLANDS	SW ALEXANDER ST, WASHINGTON CO OR	199 - A2
INTERBAY ATHLETIC FIELD	2800 15TH AV NW, SEATTLE WA	273 - F7
INTERLAKEN PARK	E INTERLAKEN BL & DELMAR DR E, SEATTLE WA	278 - C1
INVERGARRY PARK	CURRIE DR, DISTRICT OF SURREY BC	157 - A6
IRON MOUNTAIN PARK	TWIN FIR RD & BROOKSDE RD, LAKE OSWEGO OR	320 - B6
IRVING PARK	MENZIES ST, CITY OF VICTORIA BC	256 - G10
IRVING PARK	NE 7TH AV & NE FREMONT ST, PORTLAND OR	313 - H2
IRVING PLAYGROUND	S 25TH ST & HOSMER ST, TACOMA WA	295 - E1
ISAAC EVANS PARK	29627 GREEN RIVER RD, AUBURN WA	182 - C1
ISLAND CREST PARK	IS CREST & SE 58TH, MERCER ISLAND WA	175 - C3
ISLAND VIEW PARK	HWY 17, DISTRICT OF CENTRAL SAANI BC	159 - C4
IVANHOE PARK	NORTHUP WY & 168TH AV NE, BELLEVUE WA	175 - D2
JACK PARK	SW BELL CT, TIGARD OR	199 - B3
JACK LONG PARK	58TH AV W & 222ND PL, MOUNTLKE TERRACE WA	171 - B5
JACK SHAW GARDENS	KINGFISHER DR, BRITISH COLUMBIA	104 - C1
JACKSON COUNTY EXPO PARK	PENINGER RD, JACKSON CO OR	336 - A4
JACKSON, HENRY M PARK	E MARINE VIEW DR & SUMMIT DR, EVERETT WA	265 - F1
JACOBS MEMORIAL PARK	6TH ST & WASHINGTON ST, OREGON CITY OR	199 - D5
JACOBYS SHORECREST COUNTY PARK	CRESTVIEW DR, MASON CO WA	180 - B3
JAGGY ROAD PARK	NE 72ND AV & NE 45TH ST, VANCOUVER WA	306 - D1
JAMES ISLAND STATE PARK	OFF DECATUR ISLAND, SAN JUAN CO WA	160 - A5
JAMES J LAWLESS PARK	GOETHALS DR, RICHLAND WA	341 - F2
JAMES KEOUGH PARK	N 167TH ST & CORLISS AV N, SHORELINE WA	171 - B6
JAQUITH PARK	COLLEGE ST & SIERRA VISTA ST, NEWBERG OR	198 - D5
JEFFERSON PARK	MALCOLM ST, WALLA WALLA WA	345 - A9
JEFFERSON PARK	N 9TH ST & MASON AV, TACOMA WA	292 - C5
JEFFERSON PARK	S BROADWAY & S 17TH ST, TACOMA WA	293 - H6
JENKINS CREEK PARK	SE 267TH ST, KING CO WA	175 - D7
JENKINS ESTATE PARK	SW FARMINGTON RD, WASHINGTON CO OR	199 - A2
JENKS PARK	W TAPPS DR & 191ST AV CT E, PIERCE CO WA	182 - C3
JENNE BUTTE PARK	SW BORDER WY, GRESHAM OR	200 - A2
JENNINGS PARK	64TH ST NE, MARYSVILLE WA	168 - C7
JERICHO BEACH PARK	UNIVERSITY ENDOWMENT LAND BC	156 - A4
JERRY MEEKER PARK	MARINE VIEW & LE-LOU-WA, PIERCE CO WA	181 - D1
JERSICH PARK & DOCK	HARBORVIEW DR, GIG HARBOR WA	181 - C1
JESSIE M HONEYMAN MEMORIAL STATE PARK	OREGON COAST HWY, LANE CO OR	214 - B4
JJ COLLINS MEMORIAL PARK	MULTNOMAH CHANNEL, COLUMBIA CO OR	192 - B3
JJ HILL PARK	BROADWAY & HEWITT AV, EVERETT WA	265 - E3
JOE BROWN PARK	OFF HWY 99, DISTRICT OF SURREY BC	158 - A1
JOE DANCER PARK	BROOKS ST, MCMINNVILLE OR	198 - B7
JOEMMA BEACH STATE PARK	BAY RD KPS, PIERCE CO WA	180 - D3
JOHNATHAN HARTMAN PARK	17100 NE 104TH ST, REDMOND WA	175 - D1
JOHN BALL PARK	KAUFMAN AV & W 23RD ST, VANCOUVER WA	305 - F3
JOHN DEAN PROVINCIAL PARK	DEAN PARK RD, DIST OF NORTH SAANICH BC	159 - B3
JOHN DOBSON PARK	SE FIRST ST & ADAMS AV, CHEHALIS WA	299 - E11
JOHN DYCK MEMORIAL PARK	OFF HUNTINGDON RD, DISTRICT OF MATSQUI BC	102 - B1
JOHN HENDRY PARK	VICTORIA DR S, VANCOUVER BC	255 - C13
JOHN LAWSON PARK	DIST OF WEST VANCOUVER BC	254 - C4
JOHN LUBY PARK	NE 128TH AV & NE BRAZEE ST, PORTLAND OR	200 - A1
JOHN MARTY PARK	NW CHARLAIS ST, WASHINGTON CO OR	199 - A1
JOHN MATTHEWS CREEK RAVINE PARK	DISTRICT OF BURNABY BC	156 - D5
JOHNSON CREEK PARK	SE 21ST AV & SE CLATSOP ST, PORTLAND OR	317 - J7
JOHNSTONE CREEK PROVINCIAL PARK	HWY 3, BRITISH COLUMBIA	105 - A1
JOHN STORVIK PLAYGROUND	32ND ST, ANACORTES WA	259 - G4
JOHNSWOOD PARK	N COLUMBIA BLVD, PORTLAND OR	192 - B7
JONES PARK	WELL AV S & CEDAR RIVER, RENTON WA	175 - C5
JORDAN BRIDGE COUNTY PARK	143RD AV NE & JORDAN RD, SNOHOMISH CO WA	102 - C3
JORGENSON PARK	NW 3RD AV & NW 70TH ST, CLARK CO WA	192 - C5
JOSEPH STEWART STATE PARK	CRATER LAKE HWY, JACKSON CO OR	149 - C1
J SMITH REDWOODS STATE PARK	REDWOOD HWY, DEL NORTE CO CA	148 - B3

FEATURE NAME	City State	Page-Grid
JUAN DE FUCA RECREATION CENTRE	OLD ISLAND HWY, CITY OF COLWOOD BC	159 - B6
JUANITA BAY PARK	98TH AV NE & NE 106TH ST, KIRKLAND WA	171 - C7
JUNIPER PARK	BEND OR	332 - F7
KACHESS SNO-PARK	STAMPEDE PASS, KITTITAS CO WA	111 - A3
KAIBARA PARK	W MEEKER ST & 1ST AV S, KENT WA	175 - B7
KAISER RIDGE PARK	NW 147TH AV, WASHINGTON CO OR	199 - A1
KANAKA CREEK REGIONAL PARK	256TH ST, MAPLE RIDGE BC	157 - D6
KANASKAT-PALMER STATE PARK	CUMBERLAND-KANASAT RD, KING CO WA	110 - C3
KANDLE PLAYGROUND	N 23RD ST & SHIRLEY ST, TACOMA WA	292 - A3
KANE ROAD PARK	NE KANE RD & NE 5TH ST, GRESHAM OR	200 - B2
KANIKSU NATIONAL FOREST	BONNER CO ID	106 - C2
KANIKSU NATIONAL FOREST	SANDERS CO MT	107 - C3
KASCH MEMORIAL PARK	100TH ST SW & 22ND AV W, EVERETT WA	267 - H5
KATHRYN C LEWIS PARK	23600 NE UNION HILL RD, KING CO WA	176 - A1
KAYAK POINT COUNTY PARK	140TH ST NE & MARINE DR, SNOHOMISH CO WA	168 - B6
KAYMAR RAVINE PARK	DISTRICT OF BURNABY BC	156 - C5
KEENEY PARK	NORTHUP WY, BELLEVUE WA	175 - D2
KEEWAYDIN PARK	PARK DR, KENNEWICK WA	343 - C11
KELLER PARK	SE 18TH AV & SE LARK ST, MILWAUKIE OR	321 - H4
KELLEY POINT PARK	KELLY POINT PARK RD, PORTLAND OR	192 - B6
KELLY BUTTE PARK	SE 103RD AV & SE CLINTON ST, PORTLAND OR	319 - H2
KELSEY CREEK PARK	SE 4TH PL & 130TH AV SE, BELLEVUE WA	175 - C2
KENILWORTH PARK	SE 34TH AV & SE HOLGATE BL, PORTLAND OR	318 - A3
KENNEDY PARK	DISTRICT OF SURREY BC	156 - D6
KENNYDALE BEACH PARK	N 36TH ST & LK WASHINGTON BL N, RENTON WA	175 - C4
KENNYDALE LIONS PARK	ABERDEEN AV NE & NE 24TH ST, RENTON WA	175 - C4
KENSINGTON PARK	DISTRICT OF BURNABY BC	156 - D4
KENSINGTON PITCH AND PUTT PARK	DISTRICT OF BURNABY BC	156 - D4
KENT COMMONS	W JAMES ST & 4TH AV N, KENT WA	175 - B7
KENTON PARK	N DELAWARE AV & N ARGYLE ST, PORTLAND OR	308 - E4
KERN PARK	SE 67TH AV & SE CENTER ST, PORTLAND OR	318 - E3
KERRY PARK	200 W PROSPECT ST, SEATTLE WA	277 - G3
KERRY PARK	OFF 184TH ST, DISTRICT OF SURREY BC	158 - B2
KESWICK PARK	DISTRICT OF BURNABY BC	156 - D5
KETTLE RIVER PROVINCIAL RECREATION PARK	HWY 33, BRITISH COLUMBIA	105 - A1
KEVANNA PARK	NE 47TH ST & NE 109TH AV, VANCOUVER WA	307 - H1
KIGGINS BOWL	MAIN ST & NW 44TH ST, VANCOUVER WA	305 - G1
KIKU PARK	1800 SE BEAVER CREEK LN, TROUTDALE OR	200 - B1
KILLARNEY PARK	VANCOUVER BC	156 - C5
KILLARNEY GLEN PARK	104TH AV SE & SE 19TH ST, BELLEVUE WA	175 - C3
KILMER PARK	DEMPSEY RD, DISTRICT OF NORTH VANCOUV BC	255 - F1
KILMER PARK	POOLEY AV, PORT COQUITLAM BC	157 - B5
KIMBALL, JACKSON F STATE PARK	SUN MOUNTAIN RD HWY, KLAMATH CO OR	142 - B3
KING COUNTY PARK	JONES AV NE, RENTON WA	175 - C4
KING SCHOOL PARK	NE GOING ST & NE 6TH AV, PORTLAND OR	313 - G1
KINGSCREST PARK	VANCOUVER BC	156 - C5
KINGSGATE PARK	NE 140TH ST & 116TH AV NE, KING CO WA	171 - C7
KINGSLEY PARK	NW SAINT HELENS RD, PORTLAND OR	192 - B7
KINNEAR PARK	W OLYMPIC PL & 7TH AV W, SEATTLE WA	277 - G3
KINSMEN GORGE PARK	CRAIGFLOWER RD, TOWN OF ESQUILMALT BC	256 - D6
KIRK PARK	NE 188TH DR & NE HASSALO ST, GRESHAM OR	200 - A1
KIRK, PETER PARK	202 3RD ST, KIRKLAND WA	175 - C1
KIRKSTONE PARK	KIRKSTONE RD, DIST OF NORTH VANCOUVER BC	255 - E3
KIRSTINE M BURGER PARK	FARRELLY ST, ENUMCLAW WA	110 - C3
KISBEY PARK	DISTRICT OF BURNABY BC	156 - D5
KITSILANO BEACH PARK	VANCOUVER BC	254 - C11
KIWANIS PARK	1405 10TH ST W, KIRKLAND WA	175 - C1
KIWANIS PARK	150 SW 162ND ST, BURIEN WA	175 - A5
KIWANIS PARK	1ST AV S & W CROW ST, KENT WA	175 - B7
KIWANIS PARK	36TH ST & ROCKEFELLER AV, EVERETT WA	264 - E5
KIWANIS PARK	98TH AV S, KENT WA	175 - C7
KIWANIS PARK	SE SECOND ST, COLLEGE PLACE WA	344 - F10
KIWANIS PARK	SW 4TH ST & SW 2ND AV, BATTLE GROUND WA	193 - A3
KIWANIS PARK	UNION AV NE, RENTON WA	175 - C4
KIWANIS BICENTENNIAL AIR PARK	RAINIER AV N & N AIRPORT WY, RENTON WA	175 - C5
KIWANIS MARINE PARK	THREE MILE LN & BROOKS ST, MCMINNVILLE OR	198 - A7
KLAHANIE PARK	DISTRICT OF W VANCOUVER BC	254 - F4
KLAHANIE PARK	SE 32ND ST, KING CO WA	176 - A3
KLAHAYA PARK	AVENUE B & 1ST ST, SNOHOMISH WA	171 - D3
KLAMATH NATIONAL FOREST	LAKE OF THE WOODS HWY, SISKIYOU CO CA	149 - A3
KLEE WYCK PARK	DISTRICT OF WEST VANCOUVE BC	254 - G3
KLOOTCHMAN PARK	DISTRICT OF WEST VANCOUVE BC	156 - A3
KNOCKAN HILL PARK	HELMCKEN RD, DISTRICT OF SAANICH BC	256 - C3
KNOTT STREET PARK	NE 117TH AV & NE KNOTT ST, PORTLAND OR	315 - J3
KOBE TERRACE PARK	S MAIN ST & 7TH AV S, SEATTLE WA	278 - B7
KOKSILAH RIVER PROVICIAL PARK	BRITISH COLUMBIA	101 - A2
KOLL CENTER WETLANDS PARK	SW CREEKSIDE PL, BEAVERTON OR	199 - B2
KONUKSON PARK	SEA POINT DR, DISTRICT OF SAANICH BC	257 - G5
KOOTENAI NATIONAL FOREST	BONNER CO ID	107 - C1
KOPACHUCK STATE PARK	ARTNDALE DR NW & 56TH ST NW, PIERCE CO WA	181 - B1
KUBOTA GARDENS	RENTON AV S & 55TH AV S, SEATTLE WA	287 - F5
LACAMAS PARK	SE CROWN RD, CLARK CO WA	193 - B7
LADDS CIR & SQUARES PARK	SE LADD CIR, PORTLAND OR	317 - H1
LADNER HARBOUR PARK	DISTRICT OF DELTA BC	156 - B7
LADNER LIONS PARK	DISTRICT OF DELTA BC	101 - C1
LAFARGE PARK	PIPELINE RD & GUILDFORD WY, COQUITLAM BC	157 - B4
LAFKY PARK	9655 SW SILETZ DR, TUALATIN OR	199 - B4
LAGOON PARK	NE REDMOND WY & 159TH PL NE, REDMOND WA	175 - D1
LAIRHILL PARK	SW BARBUR BLVD & SW WOODS ST, PORTLAND OR	317 - E1
LAKE BOREN PARK	SE 84TH WY, NEWCASTLE WA	175 - C4
LAKE BURIEN SCHOOL PARK	16TH AV SW & SW 148TH ST, BURIEN WA	175 - A5
LAKE CHELAN NATIONAL REC AREA	CHELAN CO WA	103 - C3
LAKE CITY PARK	LAKE CITY WY NE & NE 125TH ST, SEATTLE WA	171 - B7
LAKE CUSHMAN STATE PARK	LAKE CUSHMAN RD, MASON CO WA	109 - B2
LAKE EARL STATE PARK	LAKE EARL DR, DEL NORTE CO CA	148 - B3
LAKE FENWICK PARK	LAKE FENWICK RD, KENT WA	175 - B7
LAKE FRANCIS PARK	244TH AV SE & SE 200TH ST, KING CO WA	176 - A6
LAKE GENEVA PARK	MILITARY RD S & S 342ND ST, KING CO WA	182 - B1
LAKE GOODWIN COUNTY PARK	LAKEWOOD RD, SNOHOMISH CO WA	168 - B5
LAKE GROVE PARK	833 SW 308TH ST, FEDERAL WAY WA	182 - A1
LAKE GROVE PARK	LAKEVIEW BLVD, LAKE OSWEGO OR	320 - A7
LAKE HEIGHTS PARK	COAL CREEK PKWY & NEWPORT WY, BELLEVUE WA	175 - C3
LAKE HILLS PARK	SE PHANTOM WY & 164TH AV SE, BELLEVUE WA	175 - D2
LAKE HILLS COMMUNITY CENTER PLAYGROUND	159TH PL SE & SE 8TH ST, BELLEVUE WA	175 - D2
LAKE HILLS GREENBELT PARK	156TH AV SE & SE 16TH ST, BELLEVUE WA	175 - D3
LAKE JANE PARK	68TH ST E & 188TH AV E, BONNEY LAKE WA	182 - C3
LAKELAND COUNTY PARK	LAKELAND AV SW, LAKEWOOD WA	181 - C4
LAKELAND HILLS PARK	HIGHLAND DR SE, AUBURN WA	182 - C2
LAKE LOVELY WATER REC AREA	OFF TRANS CANADA HWY, BRITISH COLUMBIA	93 - C2
LAKE MERIDIAN PARK	148TH AV SE & KENT KANGLEY RD, KENT WA	175 - C7
LAKEMONT COMMUNITY PARK	LAKEMONT BL & VILLGE PARK DR, BELLEVUE WA	175 - D3
LAKE OF THE WOODS RECREATION AREA	KLAMATH CO OR	150 - B2
LAKE OWYHEE STATE PARK	OWYHEE LAKE RD, MALHEUR CO OR	147 - A1
LAKERIDGE PARK	HOLYOKE WY S, SEATTLE WA	287 - H6
LAKE ROESIGER COUNTY PARK	LAKE ROESIGER RD, SNOHOMISH CO WA	110 - C1
LAKE SAMMAMISH STATE PARK	NW SAMMAMISH RD & 17TH AV NW, KING CO WA	175 - D3
LAKE SAWYER PARK	SE 296TH ST, KING CO WA	182 - D1
LAKE SELMAC PARK	LAKESHORE DR, JOSEPHINE CO OR	233 - B2
LAKE STREET PARK	LAKE AV S & S 15TH ST, RENTON WA	175 - C5
LAKE SYLVIA STATE PARK	SYLVIA LAKE RD, MONTESANO WA	178 - D7
LAKE TAPPS NORTH PARK	198TH AV E & DIKE RD, PIERCE CO WA	182 - C3
LAKEVIEW PARK	DISTRICT OF BURNABY BC	156 - D5
LAKEVIEW PARK	LAKE WASHINGTON BL E, SEATTLE WA	279 - E4
LAKEVIEW PARK	SW 158TH ST & 6TH AV SW, BURIEN WA	175 - A5
LAKE WASHINGTON PARK	NE 124TH ST & 89TH PL NE, KING CO WA	171 - C7
LAKE WILDERNESS PARK	23601 SE 248TH ST, KING CO WA	176 - A7
LAKEWOLD GARDENS	12317 GRAVELLY LAKE DR SW, LAKEWOOD WA	181 - C4
LAKEWOOD PARK	SW 108TH ST & 8TH AV SW, KING WA	285 - H6
LAKEWOOD ACTIVE PARK	DOUGLAS DR SW & 104TH ST SW, LAKEWOOD WA	181 - D4
LAKEWOOD BAY PARK	STATE ST, LAKE OSWEGO OR	321 - F6
LAKEWOOD KIWANIS COUNTY PLAYFIELD	FAIRLAWN DR SW, LAKEWOOD WA	181 - C4
LAKE YOUNGS PARK	148TH AV SE & SE 192ND ST, KING CO WA	175 - C6
LAKOTA PARK	31334 SW DASH POINT RD, FEDERAL WAY WA	182 - A1
LAMBRICK PARK	TYNDALL AVE, DISTRICT OF SAANICH BC	257 - B2
LANDSBERG TRAIL HEAD PARK	276TH AV SE, KING CO WA	176 - A7
LANGLEY BAND PARK	GLOVER RD, TOWNSHIP OF LANGLEY BC	157 - D6
LANGUS RIVERFRONT PARK	SMITH ISLAND RD, EVERETT WA	265 - G1
LA PINE STATE RECREATION AREA	LA PINE STATE PARK RD, DESCHUTES CO OR	143 - A1
LARCHMONT PLAYGROUND	A ST & E 88TH ST, TACOMA WA	181 - D4
LARRABEE STATE PARK	HWY 11, WHATCOM CO WA	160 - D2
LARRY FROST PARK	PACIFIC AV & S 9TH ST, TACOMA WA	293 - H5
LATHROP PARK	LOWER RIVER RD, JOSEPHINE CO OR	229 - B6
LATIMER LAKE PARK	192ND ST, DISTRICT OF SURREY BC	158 - B2
LAURELHURST PARK	SE 39TH AV & SE STARK ST, PORTLAND OR	314 - A6
LAURELHURST PLAYFIELD	NE 45TH ST & 48TH AV NE, SEATTLE WA	275 - F6
LAUREL POINT PARK	KINGSTON ST, CITY OF VICTORIA BC	256 - F9
LAURELWOOD PARK	SE FOSTER RD & SE HOLGATE BL, PORTLAND OR	318 - D3
LAURELWOOD PARK	SE STEPHENS ST, ROSEBURG OR	334 - G7
LAURENTIAN PARK	LAURENTIAN CR, COQUITLAM BC	157 - A5
LAUSMANN STATE PARK	COLUMBIA RIVER HWY, HOOD RIVER CO OR	195 - B5
LAVA CAST FOREST	NWBERRY NATL VOLCNC MON, DESCHUTES CO OR	217 - C7
LAVA RIVER CAVES STATE PARK	THE DALLES-CALIF HWY, DESCHUTES CO OR	217 - B6
LAVIZZO PARK	MAIN ST, SEATTLE WA	278 - C7
LAWNDALE PARK	SW 176TH & SW WRIGHT, WASHINGTON CO OR	199 - A2
LAWTON PARK	WILLIAMS AV W & W EMERSON ST, SEATTLE WA	272 - D6
LAYRITZ PARK	MANN AVE, DISTRICT OF SAANICH BC	159 - C5
LAYTON PARK	E 6TH AV, KENNEWICK WA	343 - E11
LEACH PARK	K ST & E 28TH ST, VANCOUVER WA	305 - H3
LEACH BOTANICAL GARDEN	6704 SE 122ND DR, PORTLAND OR	200 - A2
LEADBETTER POINT STATE PARK	STACKPOLE RD, PACIFIC CO WA	183 - B7
LEAVITT PARK	E 11TH ST & S COLUMBIA ST, NEWBERG OR	198 - D6
LEDINGHAM PARK	DISTRICT OF BURNABY BC	156 - C5
LEE PARK	SALEM OR	323 - A14
LEE HILL PARK	SE 320TH ST & 124TH AV SE, KING CO WA	182 - C1
LEHIGH PARK	WAVERLY DR, ALBANY OR	326 - G9
LENTS PARK	SE 92ND AV & SE HOLGATE BL, PORTLAND OR	319 - G3
LESCHI PARK	LAKESIDE AV S, SEATTLE WA	279 - E7
LES GOVE MUSEUM PARK	9TH ST SE & H ST SE, AUBURN WA	182 - C1
LESSER PARK	SW HAINES RD & SW 57TH AV, MULTNMAH CO OR	194 - B7
LESSER PARK	SW HAINES RD & SW 57TH AV, PORTLAND OR	199 - B3
LEVDANSKY PARK	276TH AV SE & SE 224TH ST, KING CO WA	176 - A6
LEVERICH PARK	NE LEVERICH PARK WY, VANCOUVER WA	305 - H2
LEWELLYN PARK	1700 SE LEWELLYN AV, TROUTDALE OR	200 - B1
LEWIS AND CLARK STATE PARK	E HIST COLUMBIA RVR HWY, MULTNOMAH CO OR	200 - B1
LEWIS AND CLARK STATE PARK	JACKSON HWY, LEWIS CO WA	187 - D2
LEWISVILLE PARK	NE PARK DR, CLARK CO WA	193 - A2
LEXINGTON PARK	NW 216TH AV, WASHINGTON CO OR	199 - A1
LEYLAND PARK	DISTRICT OF WEST VANCOUVE BC	254 - E3
LIBERTY PARK	BRONSON WY N & HOUSER WY N, RENTON WA	175 - C5
LIBERTY PARK	E 4TH AV, SPOKANE WA	349 - C10
LIBRARY PARK	BOTHELL EVERETT HWY, MILL CREEK WA	171 - C4
LIBERTY LAKE PARK	S LIBERTY DR, SPOKANE CO WA	247 - B4
LICTON SPRINGS PARK	N 97TH ST & ASHWORTH AV N, SEATTLE WA	171 - A7
LID PARK	W MERCER WY & FRWY 90, MERCER ISLAND WA	283 - J1
LIDFORD PLAYFIELD	60TH ST E & 44TH AV E, PIERCE CO WA	182 - A3
LIESER CREST PARK	VIRGINIA LN, VANCOUVER WA	307 - E6
LIGHTHOUSE PARK	DISTRICT OF WEST VANCOUVE BC	156 - A3
LILLY K JOHNSON PARK	SW DIVISION ST, WASHINGTON CO OR	199 - A2
LIME BAY PARK	MILNE ST, CITY OF VICTORIA BC	256 - F8
LIME KILN POINT STATE PARK	WESTSIDE RD N, SAN JUAN CO WA	101 - C2
LINCOLN PARK	OFF HWY 543, BLAINE WA	158 - B3
LINCOLN PARK	MAIN ST, FOREST GROVE OR	198 - B1
LINCOLN PARK	LINCOLN ST, HOQUIAM WA	178 - A7
LINCOLN PARK	SE 138TH AV & SE MILL ST, PORTLAND OR	200 - A2
LINCOLN PARK	W LAURIDSEN BLVD, PORT ANGELES WA	261 - A4
LINCOLN PARK	FAUNTLEROY WY SW, SEATTLE WA	284 - D2
LINCOLN PARK	S THOMPSON AV & S 37TH ST, TACOMA WA	295 - G2
LINCOLN PARK	CRAWFORD ST & S MISSION ST, WENATCHEE WA	239 - A5
LINCOLN HEIGHTS PARK	S 37TH ST & IDAHO ST, TACOMA WA	294 - E2
LINDA HEIGHTS PARK	35TH AV S & S 248TH ST, KENT WA	175 - B7
LINDSEY CREEK STATE PARK	COLUMBIA RIVER HWY, HOOD RIVER CO OR	195 - A5

FEATURE NAME	City State	Page-Grid
LINNTON PARK	NW SAINT HELENS RD, PORTLAND OR	192 - B7
LINWOOD PARK	NE 193RD ST, KING CO WA	171 - B6
LIONS PARK	PARK DR & CASCADE DR, EVERETT WA	268 - D4
LIONS PARK	TACOMA CT, WALLA WALLA WA	345 - E6
LIONS WAY PARK	SHAUGHNESSY & LIONS WY, PORT COQUITLAM BC	157 - B4
LISABUELA PARK	LISABUELA RD, KING CO WA	174 - D6
LITHIA PARK	PIONEER AV, ASHLAND OR	337 - C9
LITTLE PEOPLE PARK	SW 5TH ST, BEAVERTON OR	199 - B2
LITTLE WOODROSE NATURE PARK	21000 SW BOONES FERRY RD, TUALATIN OR	199 - B4
LOBLEY PARK	DISTRICT OF BURNABY BC	156 - C5
LOCHDALE PARK	DISTRICT OF BURNABY BC	156 - D4
LOCHSIDE PARK	LOCHSIDE DR, DISTRICT OF SAANICH BC	159 - C5
LOCKS PARK	LOCKS RD, YAMHILL CO OR	198 - B7
LOGAN PARK	VIADUCT AVE W, DISTRICT OF SAANICH BC	159 - C5
LOGAN COUNTY PARK	LOCUST WY & S LOGAN RD, SNOHOMISH CO WA	171 - B5
LONE TREE HILL REGIONAL PARK	MUNNS RD, BRITISH COLUMBIA	159 - B5
LORD HILL REGIONAL PARK	127TH AV SE, SNOHOMISH CO WA	171 - D5
LOSS CREEK PROVINCIAL PARK	BRITISH COLUMBIA	100 - C2
LOST FOREST RESEARCH NATURAL AREA	OFF CHRISTMAS VLY-WAGONTIRE, LAKE CO OR	144 - A2
LOST PARK	NW 111TH AV, WASHINGTON CO OR	199 - B1
LOST PARK IV	NW 107TH AV, WASHINGTON CO OR	199 - B1
LOST LAKE PARK	SW 266TH LN, KING CO WA	174 - D7
LOUIS BLOCH PARK	NE JOY ST, CAMAS WA	193 - B7
LOUP LOUP SKI AREA	HWY 20, OKANOGAN CO WA	104 - B3
LOUTET PARK	TRANS CAN HWY, CITY OF NORTH VANCOUVER BC	255 - E5
LOUZON CREEK PARK	OFF HWY 11, DISTRICT OF ABBOTSFORD BC	102 - B1
LOVEJOY PARK	SW 4TH AV, PORTLAND OR	313 - E7
LOWELL PARK	20TH ST, BELLINGHAM WA	258 - C10
LOWELL PARK	JUNCTION AV, EVERETT WA	265 - E7
LOWER THREE CREEK SNO-PARK	THREE CREEKS LAKE RD, DESCHUTES CO OR	211 - C7
LOWMAN BEACH PARK	LINCOLN PKWY SW & BEACH DR SW, SEATTLE WA	284 - C1
LOWNSDALE SQUARE PARK	SW SALMON ST & SW 4TH AV, PORTLAND OR	313 - F6
LOYAL HEIGHTS PLAYFIELD	20TH AV NW & NW 75TH ST, SEATTLE WA	273 - E2
LOYALTY PARK	SUMNER AV & PARK ST, SUMNER WA	182 - B3
LUBBOCKS WOODS	DISTRICT OF BURNABY BC	156 - D5
LUNDEEN COUNTY PARK	VERNON RD, SNOHOMISH CO WA	171 - D1
LUTHER BURBANK PARK	84TH AV SE & N MERCR WY, MERCER ISLAND WA	175 - C3
LYNCHVIEW PARK	SE 167TH AV & SE MARKET ST, PORTLAND OR	200 - A1
LYNCHWOOD PARK	SE 170TH AV & SE HAIG ST, PORTLAND OR	200 - A2
LYNDHURST PARK	DISTRICT OF BURNABY BC	156 - D4
LYNN CANYON PARK	TRANS CANADA HWY, DIST OF N VANCOUVER BC	255 - G2
LYNNDALE PARK	190TH ST SW & 72ND AV W, LYNNWOOD WA	171 - B5
LYNN HEADWATERS REGIONAL PARK	BRITISH COLUMBIA	156 - C1
LYNN VALLEY PARK	MOUNTAIN HWY, DIST OF NORTH VANCOUVER BC	255 - E2
LYNNWOOD ATHLETIC COMPLEX	3003 184TH ST SW, LYNNWOOD WA	171 - B5
LYNNWOOD NEIGHBORHOOD PARK	44TH AV W & 186TH ST SW, LYNNWOOD WA	171 - B5
LYONS CITY PARK	SE LARCH AV, COLLEGE PLACE WA	344 - G11
LYONS FERRY STATE PARK	HWY 261, FRANKLIN CO WA	122 - A2
LYONS VIEW PARK	SPRAGUE RD & LYONS RD, CLACKAMAS CO OR	200 - A6
MACAULAY POINT PARK	LAMPSON ST, TOWN OF ESQUILMALT BC	256 - C9
MACDONALD PARK	NIAGARA ST, CITY OF VICTORIA BC	256 - F10
MACDONALD MEMORIAL PARK	NE 40TH ST & TOLT AV, KING CO WA	176 - B2
MACKIE PARK	DISTRICT OF DELTA BC	156 - D7
MACKIN PARK	BRUNETTE AV, COQUITLAM BC	157 - A5
MACLEAY PARK	NW CORNELL RD, PORTLAND OR	312 - A4
MADISON PARK	E MADISON ST & E HOWE ST, SEATTLE WA	279 - F2
MADRONA PARK	N GREELEY AV, PORTLAND OR	308 - D7
MADRONA PARK	LK WASHINGTON BL & MADRONA DR, SEATTLE WA	279 - F6
MAGGIES PARK	EVERETT AV & W MARINE VIEW DR, EVERETT WA	264 - D3
MAGNESS MEMORIAL TREE FARM	SW LADD HILL RD, CLACKAMAS CO OR	199 - A6
MAGNOLIA PARK	MAGNOLIA BLVD W, SEATTLE WA	276 - D2
MAGNUSON PARK	SAND POINT WY NE, SEATTLE WA	275 - J3
MAIN CITY PARK	S MAIN AV & E POWELL BLVD, GRESHAM OR	200 - B2
MALHEUR NATIONAL FOREST	GRANT CO OR	137 - B2
MALHEUR NATIONAL FOREST	HARNEY CO OR	145 - B1
MALTBY COMMUNITY PARK	206TH ST SE & BROADWY AV, SNOHOMISH CO WA	171 - D5
MALVERN PARK	DISTRICT OF BURNABY BC	156 - D5
MANCHESTER STATE PARK	BEACH DR E, KITSAP CO WA	271 - G9
MANITOBA PARK	MANITOBA AV & BONNEY ST, STEILACOOM WA	181 - C4
MANITO PARK	S PARK DR, SPOKANE WA	349 - A12
MANITOU PARK	S 66TH ST & GROVE ST, TACOMA WA	294 - B6
MANITOU COMMUNITY CENTER	4006 S 66TH ST, TACOMA WA	294 - A6
MANN CREEK STATE RECREATION AREA	MONROE CREEK & JACKSON, WASHINGTON CO ID	139 - A2
MANNING PROVINCIAL PARK	HWY 3, BRITISH COLUMBIA	95 - B3
MANORWOOD PARK	MANORWOOD DR & 37TH AV SE, PUYALLUP WA	182 - B4
MAPLE PARK	MAPLE RD & 41ST PL W, LYNNWOOD WA	171 - B5
MAPLE GROVE PARK	VANCOUVER BC	156 - B5
MAPLE RIDGE PARK	232ND ST & 132ND AV, MAPLE RIDGE BC	157 - D5
MAPLE STREET PARK	N MAPLE ST, CANBY OR	199 - C6
MAPLE VALLEY HEIGHTS PARK	188TH AV SE & SE 164TH ST, KING CO WA	175 - D5
MAPLEWOOD PARK	144TH AV SE & SE 138TH ST, KING CO WA	175 - C5
MAPLEWOOD PARK	RIVERSIDE DR, DIST OF NORTH VANCOUVER BC	255 - H7
MAPLEWOOD HEIGHTS PARK	168TH AV SE & SE 142ND ST, KING CO WA	175 - D5
MAPLEWOOD HILL PARK	88TH AV W & 197TH ST SW, EDMONDS WA	171 - A5
MAPLE WOOD PLAYGROUND	CORSON AV S & S SNOQUALMIE ST, SEATTLE WA	282 - B5
MAPLEWOOD ROADSIDE PARK	MAPLE VALLEY RD & SE 7TH ST, RENTON WA	175 - C5
MARIA C JACKSON STATE PARK	COOS CO OR	140 - C2
MARICARA PARK	SW 30TH AV & SW MARICARA ST, PORTLAND OR	320 - C2
MARINA PARK	25 LAKE AV W, KIRKLAND WA	175 - C1
MARINE PARK	RUSTON WY, TACOMA WA	292 - C1
MARINE PARK	SE MARINE PARK WY, VANCOUVER WA	306 - B7
MARINE PARK	W MARINE VIEW DR, EVERETT WA	171 - C1
MARINE DRIVE FORESHORE PARK	UNIVERSITY ENDOWMENT LAND BC	156 - A5
MARINE VIEW PARK	MARINE VIEW DR SW, NORMANDY PARK WA	175 - A6
MARITIME PARK	COLUMBIA RIVER HWY, ASTORIA WA	300 - D4
MARKET SQUARE PARK	RAILROAD ST & MONROE AV, ENUMCLAW WA	110 - C3
MARK TWAIN PARK	10625 132ND AV NE, KIRKLAND WA	175 - C1
MARQUAM NATURE PARK	8 MARQUAM HILL RD, PORTLAND OR	316 - D1
MARSHALL PARK	SW 18TH PL, PORTLAND OR	320 - D1
MARSHALL, GEN GEORGE E PARK	E MCLOUGHLIN BLVD, VANCOUVER WA	305 - H4
MARSH PARK	6605 LAKE WASHINGTON BLVD NE, KIRKLAND WA	175 - C1
MARTIN JOHNSON PARK	HARDING ST & LOWELL PL, ENUMCLAW WA	110 - C3
MARVISTA PARK	4TH AV SW, NORMANDY PARK WA	175 - A6
MARY PARK	DISTRICT OF BURNABY BC	156 - D5
MARYHILL STATE PARK	SHERMAN HWY, KLICKITAT CO WA	127 - C1
MARY MINERVA MCCROSKEY MEM STATE PARK	LATAH CO ID	115 - A3
MARYMOOR PARK	176TH AV NE & NE 65TH ST, KING CO WA	175 - D1
MARY S YOUNG STATE PARK	PACIFIC HWY, WEST LINN OR	199 - D4
MASKO PARK	S ORCHARD ST & RAMSDELL ST, FIRCREST WA	294 - A1
MASON HILL PARK	JOHNSON RD & NW MUNSN RD, MULTNOMAH CO OR	125 - C1
MATHESON LAKE REGIONAL PARK	MOUNT MATHESON RD, DIST OF METCHOSIN BC	165 - A1
MATIA ISLAND STATE PARK	MATIA ISLAND, SAN JUAN CO WA	160 - A1
MATILDA JACKSON STATE PARK	JACKSON HWY, LEWIS CO WA	187 - D2
MATSQUI PRAIRIE PARK	OFF HWY 11, DISTRICT OF MATSQUI BC	102 - B1
MATSQUI TRAIL REGIONAL PARK	RIVERSIDE ST, DISTRICT OF MATSQUI BC	94 - B3
MAUD WILLIAMSON STATE PARK	YAMHILL CO OR	204 - D2
MAURY ISLAND PARK	SW 244TH ST, KING CO WA	175 - A7
MAX PATTERSON MEMORIAL CITY PARK	E FAIRFIELD ST & CORNELL AV, GLADSTONE OR	199 - D4
MAY CREEK PARK	EDMONDS AV NE & NE 27TH ST, NEWCASTLE WA	175 - C4
MAYER STATE PARK	COLUMBIA RIVER HWY, WASCO CO OR	196 - C6
MAYFAIR PARK	3RD AV N, SEATTLE WA	277 - H1
MAYFAIR PLAYFIELD	136TH ST E & 13TH AV CT E, PIERCE CO WA	182 - A5
MAYNARD PARK	SINCLAIR & HOBBIS, DIST OF SAANICH BC	257 - E4
MAYS POND PARK	180TH ST SE, SNOHOMISH CO WA	171 - C5
MAY VALLEY COUNTY PARK	SE RENTON ISSAQUAH RD, KING CO WA	175 - D4
MAYWOOD PARK	DISTRICT OF BURNABY BC	156 - C5
MCBRIDE PARK	VANCOUVER BC	254 - A12
MCCARVER PLAYGROUND	S J ST & S 23RD ST, TACOMA WA	293 - G7
MCCLUGHAN PARK	208TH ST & 91A AV, TOWNSHIP OF LANGLEY BC	157 - C6
MCCOLLUM COUNTY PARK	DUMAS RD, SNOHOMISH CO WA	171 - C4
MCCORMICK PARK	N 165TH ST, SHORELINE WA	171 - B6
MCCORMICK PARK	NE 12TH ST, BELLEVUE WA	175 - C2
MCCORMICK PARK	OLD PORTLAND RD & S 18TH, SAINT HELENS OR	192 - B2
MCDONALD PROVINCIAL PARK	HWY 17, DISTRICT OF NORTH SAANICH BC	159 - C2
MCDONALD STATE FOREST	BENTON CO OR	327 - A1
MCDOWELL CREEK COUNTY PARK	LINN CO OR	134 - A2
MCEUEN FIELD	COEUR D'ALENE ID	355 - E12
MCFADDEN PARK	EVERGREEN DR & ADAMS AV, CHEHALIS WA	299 - F11
MCFARLAND PARK	CHINOOK AV & A ST, ENUMCLAW WA	110 - C3
MCGILL PARK	MCGILL ST, DISTRICT OF BURNABY BC	255 - H9
MCKECHNIE PARK	DISTRICT OF WEST VANCOUVE BC	156 - A3
MCKENNA PARK	N WALL AV & N PRINCETON ST, PORTLAND OR	308 - A4
MCKINLEY PARK	E MCKINLEY AV & E 43RD ST, TACOMA WA	295 - J1
MCKINLEY PARK	NW EBBERTS AV, HILLSBORO OR	198 - D1
MCKINLEY PARK	UPPER PARK ST, TACOMA WA	295 - J3
MCLEAN PARK	GRANT AV & YORK ST, PORT COQUITLAM BC	157 - B4
MCLEAN PARK	HOLLY ST & RIVER ST, WEST LINN OR	199 - D4
MCLEOD PARK	216TH ST, TOWNSHIP OF LANGLEY BC	157 - C7
MCLOUGHLIN PROMENADE PARK	MCLOUGHLIN BL, OREGON CITY OR	199 - D5
MCLOUGHLIN STATE PARK	MULTNOMAH CO OR	194 - B7
MCMICKEN HEIGHTS PARK	S 166TH ST & 40TH AV S, SEATAC WA	288 - E6
MCMILLAN PARK	GLOVER RD, TOWNSHIP OF LANGLEY BC	157 - C7
MCMILLAN PARK	OFF HWY 11, DISTRICT OF ABBOTSFORD BC	102 - B1
MCMILLAN PARK	SW 99TH AV & SW CYPRESS ST, BEAVERTON OR	199 - B2
MCNAIR PLACE PARK	DISTRICT OF NORTH VANCOUV BC	156 - C2
MCPHERSON PARK	DISTRICT OF BURNABY BC	156 - D5
MCSPADDEN PARK	VICTORIA DR S, VANCOUVER BC	255 - B12
MEADOW PARK	161ST AV NE & NE 108TH CT, REDMOND WA	175 - D1
MEADOWBROOK PARK	NE BURTON RD & NE 90TH AV, VANCOUVER WA	307 - F4
MEADOWBROOK PARK	SW 198TH & SW JAYLEE, WASHINGTON CO OR	199 - A2
MEADOWBROOK PLAYFIELD	30TH AV NE & RAVENNA AV NE, SEATTLE WA	171 - B7
MEADOWDALE PLAYFIELDS	16700 66TH AV W, LYNNWOOD WA	171 - B5
MEADOW HOMES PARK	E 18TH ST, VANCOUVER WA	306 - C4
MEADOWLAND PROVINCIAL PARK	HACK-BROWN RD, DISTRICT OF CHILLIWACK BC	94 - C3
MEADOWVALE BEACH COUNTY PARK	156TH ST SW & 70TH AV W, SNOHOMISH CO WA	171 - B4
MEDINA BEACH PARK	EVERGREEN POINT RD, MEDINA WA	279 - J5
MEDINA SOUTH PARK	NE 12TH ST & 80TH AV NE, MEDINA WA	175 - C2
MEE KWA MOOKS PARK	SW JACOBSEN RD & SW BEACH DR, SEATTLE WA	280 - C4
MEINIG MEMORIAL PARK	MEINIG AV, SANDY OR	200 - D4
MELDRUM BAR PARK	MELDRUM BAR PARK RD, GLADSTONE OR	199 - D4
MELILAH PARK	SW ARBORCREST CT, WASHINGTON CO OR	199 - A2
MEMALOOSE STATE PARK	COLUMBIA RIVER HWY, WASCO CO OR	196 - B5
MEMORIAL PARK	2ND AV SE, ISSAQUAH WA	176 - A4
MEMORIAL PARK	DISTRICT OF DELTA BC	101 - C1
MEMORIAL PARK	DISTRICT OF W VANCOUVER BC	254 - C3
MEMORIAL PARK	E 5TH ST & S BLAINE ST, NEWBERG OR	198 - D6
MEMORIAL PARK	SW WATSON AV & SW 7TH ST, BEAVERTON OR	199 - B2
MEMORIAL PARK SOUTH	VANCOUVER BC	156 - C5
MEMORIAL PARK WEST	VANCOUVER BC	156 - A5
MEMORY ISLAND PARK	SHAWNIGAN LAKE RD, BRITISH COLUMBIA	159 - A3
MERCERDALE PARK	SE 32ND ST & 78TH AV SE, MERCER ISLAND WA	175 - C3
MERCERDALE PLAYFIELD	SE 32ND ST, MERCER ISLAND WA	283 - J2
MERCER SLOUGH PARK	118TH AV SE, BELLEVUE WA	175 - C3
MERIDAN PARK	N 167TH ST & WLLNGFRD AV N, SHORELINE WA	171 - B6
MERIDIAN GLEN PARK	137TH AV SE, KENT WA	175 - C7
MERIDIAN PLAYGROUND	N 50TH ST & MERIDIAN AV N, SEATTLE WA	274 - A5
MERKLEY PARK	124TH AV, MAPLE RIDGE BC	157 - C5
MERRIFIELD PARK	NE 117TH AV & NE THOMPSON ST, PORTLAND OR	200 - A1
MERRITT ORCHARD PARK	SW WASHINGTON ST, WASHINGTON CO OR	199 - B1
MERRYFIELD PARK	CAMELOT ST, WILSONVILLE OR	199 - B5
METZGER COUNTY PARK	SW HALL BLVD, WASHINGTON CO OR	199 - B3
METZLER PARK	METZLER PARK RD, CLACKAMAS CO OR	200 - B7
METZLER-OGRADY PARK	SE GREEN VALLEY RD, KING CO WA	182 - D2
MEYDENBAUER PARK	NE LAKE WASHINGTON BL, BELLEVUE WA	175 - C2
MICELLI PARK	SE FLINT ST, ROSEBURG OR	334 - E8
MICHAEL PARK	DRAYTON ST, DISTRICT OF NORTH VANCOUV BC	255 - D5
MIDLAND PARK	SE MORRISON ST & SE 119TH AV, PORTLAND OR	200 - A1
MILL CREEK PARK	CANYON DR SE & 97TH PL S, KENT WA	175 - C7
MILL CREEK PARK	OFF RTE 101, COSMOPOLIS WA	117 - A1
MILL CREEK PARK	POLK CO OR	125 - B3
MILLER PARK	MILLER AV, COQUITLAM BC	157 - A4

FEATURE NAME	City State	Page-Grid
MILLERSYLVANIA STATE PARK	TILLEY RD SW, THURSTON CO WA	184 - C2
MILLET PARK	SW CHEHALIS AV, CHEHALIS WA	299 - D13
MILL HILL REGIONAL PARK	TRANS CANADA HWY, DISTRICT OF LANGFORD BC	159 - B6
MILLICOMA MYRTLE GROVE STATE PARK	COOS RIVER HWY, COOS CO OR	218 - D6
MILL PARK	SE 122ND AV & SE LINCOLN ST, PORTLAND OR	200 - A2
MILL POND PARK	KENNEDY AV SE, AUBURN WA	182 - C2
MILNER PARK	GLOVER RD & 216TH, TOWNSHIP OF LANGLEY BC	157 - C7
MILO MCIVER STATE PARK	SPRINGWATER RD, CLACKAMAS CO OR	200 - B6
MILWAUKEE PLAYFIELD	W SMITH ST & NADEN AV, KENT WA	175 - B7
MINGUS PARK	COMMERCIAL AV & N 10TH ST, COOS BAY OR	333 - G9
MINI PARK	200TH ST SW & 52ND PL W, LYNNWOOD WA	171 - B5
MINI PARK	NE BELLEVUE REDMOND RD, BELLEVUE WA	175 - C2
MINNEHAHA PARK	E LIBERTY AV, SPOKANE WA	349 - F5
MINNEKHADA REGIONAL PARK	QUARRY RD, COQUITLAM BC	157 - B4
MINNITTI PLAYGROUND	S PEARL ST & S 12TH ST, TACOMA WA	181 - C2
MINORU PARK	CITY OF RICHMOND BC	156 - B6
MINTO PARK	N SANTIAM HWY, MARION CO OR	134 - A1
MINTO-BROWNS ISLAND CITY PARK	SALEM OR	324 - E1
MIRACLE BEACH PARK	HWY 19, BRITISH COLUMBIA	92 - A1
MIRROR LAKE PARK	S 315TH ST & 10TH AV S, FEDERAL WAY WA	182 - B1
MISSION PARK	E MISSION AV, SPOKANE WA	349 - B7
MISSION RIDGE WINTER SPORTS AREA	OFF NFD RD 9712, CHELAN CO WA	238 - D7
MISSION SPORTS PARK	WREN ST, DISTRICT OF MISSION BC	94 - B3
MITCHELL PARK	NW 95TH AV, WASHINGTON CO OR	199 - B1
MITCHELL ROAD PARK	19000 MITCHELL RD, PITT MEADOWS BC	157 - B5
MODOC NATIONAL FOREST	MODOC CO CA	151 - B3
MOLALLA RIVER STATE PARK	NE 40TH AV, CLACKAMAS CO OR	199 - C6
MONTAGNE HARBOUR PROVINCIAL PARK	CLANTON RD, BRITISH COLUMBIA	101 - B1
MONTAVILLA PARK	NE 82ND AV & NE GLISAN ST, PORTLAND OR	315 - F5
MONTECITO PARK	DISTRICT OF BURNABY BC	156 - D4
MONTGOMERY PARK	HARDING ST & ELMONT AV, ENUMCLAW WA	110 - C3
MONTGOMERY PARK	MONTGOMERY ST, COQUITLAM BC	157 - A5
MONTLAKE PARK	E CALHOUN ST & 16TH AV E, SEATTLE WA	278 - C1
MOODY PARK	NEW WESTMINSTER BC	156 - D5
MOODYVILLE PARK	LOW LEVEL RD, CITY OF NORTH VANCOUVER BC	255 - C7
MOONSHADOW PARK	SW MAYO ST, WASHINGTON CO OR	199 - B2
MOORE PARK	LAKESHORE DR, KLAMATH FALLS OR	338 - B8
MOORLANDS PLAYFIELD	NE 155TH ST & 81ST AV NE, KING CO WA	171 - C7
MORAN STATE PARK	ORCAS TO OLGA RD, SAN JUAN CO WA	160 - A3
MORAN STATE PARK	SAN JUAN ISALND, SAN JUAN CO WA	101 - C2
MORNING SIDE PARK	NE 42ND PL & 95TH AV NE, YARROW POINT WA	175 - C1
MORNINGSIDE PARK	SALEM OR	324 - J4
MOSHIER PARK	S 156TH WY & 4TH AV S, BURIEN WA	288 - A4
MOSQUITO PARK	SKYLINE DR, DISTRICT OF N VANCOUVER BC	255 - A1
MOULTON FALLS PARK	NE LUCIA FALLS RD, CLARK CO WA	193 - B2
MOUNTAIN VIEW PARK	SMITH AV & GUILTNER ST, COQUITLAM BC	157 - A4
MOUNT ARROWSMITH PARK	HWY 4, BRITISH COLUMBIA	92 - B3
MOUNT BAKER PARK	LAKE WASHINGTON BLVD S, SEATTLE WA	283 - E2
MOUNT BAKER PARK	LAKE WASHINGTN S & S ALASKA, SEATTLE WA	283 - G5
MOUNT BAKER-SNOQUALMIE NATL FOREST	KING CO WA	176 - C7
MOUNT BAKER-SNOQUALMIE NATL FOREST	LEWIS CO WA	118 - A1
MOUNT BAKER-SNOQUALMIE NATL FOREST	OFF HWY 410, YAKIMA CO WA	240 - B7
MOUNT BAKER-SNOQUALMIE NATL FOREST	PIERCE CO WA	185 - A2
MOUNT BAKER-SNOQUALMIE NATL FOREST	SKAGIT CO WA	102 - C3
MOUNT BAKER-SNOQUALMIE NATL FOREST	SNOHOMISH CO WA	111 - A1
MOUNT BAKER-SNOQUALMIE NATL FOREST	SKI BOWL, WHATCOM CO WA	102 - C1
MOUNT DOUGLAS PARK	CORDOVA BAY RD, DISTRICT OF SAANICH BC	257 - A1
MOUNT ERIE PARK	ERIE MOUNTAIN DR, ANACORTES WA	259 - F9
MOUNT HOOD MEADOW SKI AREA	MOUNT HOOD HWY, HOOD RIVER CO OR	202 - B5
MOUNT HOOD NATIONAL FOREST	CLACKAMAS HWY, CLACKAMAS CO OR	201 - D6
MOUNT HOOD NATIONAL FOREST	CLACKAMAS HWY, HOOD RIVER CO OR	202 - A2
MOUNT HOOD NATIONAL FOREST	CLACKAMAS HWY, MULTNOMAH CO OR	194 - B7
MOUNT HOOD NATIONAL FOREST	JEFFERSON CO OR	134 - C1
MOUNT HOOD NATIONAL FOREST	LINN CO OR	211 - A1
MOUNT HOOD NATIONAL FOREST	MARION CO OR	134 - C1
MOUNT HOOD NATIONAL FOREST	WASCO CO OR	202 - D4
MOUNT MAXWELL PROV PARK	SEYMOUR RD, BRITISH COLUMBIA	101 - B1
MOUNT RAINIER NATIONAL PARK	LEWIS CO WA	185 - A1
MOUNT SCOTT PARK	SE 72ND AV & SE HAROLD ST, PORTLAND OR	319 - E4
MOUNT SEYMOUR PROVINCIAL PARK	BRITISH COLUMBIA	156 - D1
MOUNT SPOKANE STATE PARK	SPOKANE CO WA	114 - C1
MOUNT TABOR PARK	SE SALMON ST E OF 60TH, PORTLAND OR	314 - E7
MOUNT TABOR PARK	SE SALMON ST E OF 60TH, PORTLAND OR	318 - D1
MOUNT TOLMIE PARK	CEDAR HILL CROSS, DISTRICT OF SAANICH BC	257 - B4
MOUNT WORK REGIONAL PARK	WILLIS POINT RD, BRITISH COLUMBIA	159 - B5
MUKILTEO STATE PARK	FRONT ST, MUKILTEO WA	266 - D1
MUNDY PARK	2200 COMO LAKE AV, COQUITLAM BC	157 - A4
MUNRO, ED SEAHURST PARK	14TH AV SW & SW 136TH ST, BURIEN WA	175 - A5
MURDOCK PARK	SE ROY ST, SHERWOOD OR	199 - A4
MURDO FRAZER PARK	DISTRICT OF NORTH VANCOUV BC	254 - H3
MURRAYHILL OPEN SPACE PARK	SW OLD SCHOLLS FERRY RD, BEAVERTON OR	199 - A3
MYRTLE PARK	DISTRICT OF NORTH VANCOUV BC	156 - D3
NADEN PARK	NADEN AV, KENT WA	175 - B7
NAHEENO PARK	DISTRICT OF BURNABY BC	156 - D4
NANCY GREENE RECREATIONAL AREA	HWY 22 & HWY 3B, BRITISH COLUMBIA	106 - A1
NARAMORE FOUNTAIN PARK	6TH AV & SENECA ST, SEATTLE WA	278 - A6
NATURE TRAILS PARK	8TH SW & MARINE VIEW SW, NORMNDY PK WA	175 - A6
NE 12TH ST GREENBELT	NE 12TH ST & BELLEVUE WY NE, BELLEVUE WA	175 - C2
NEHALEM BAY STATE PARK	OFF CAREY ST, TILLAMOOK CO OR	191 - A5
NEILSON REGIONAL PARK	EDWARDS, DISTRICT OF MISSION BC	94 - B3
NELSON PARK	VANCOUVER BC	254 - F10
NELSON CANYON PARK	DISTRICT OF WEST VANCOUVE BC	156 - A2
NEPTUNE STATE PARK	OREGON COAST HWY, LANE CO OR	209 - A4
NE SAMMAMISH NEIGHBORHOOD PARK	SAHALEE WY NE & NE 36TH ST, KING CO WA	175 - D2
NE VASHON PARK	H L CUNLIFFE RD, KING CO WA	174 - D4
NEW BRIGHTON PARK	MCGILL ST, VANCOUVER BC	255 - E9
NEWCASTLE BEACH PARK	SE 50TH ST, BELLEVUE WA	175 - C3
NEWPORT HILLS PARK	SE 60TH ST & 120TH AV SE, BELLEVUE WA	175 - C3
NEW RIVER PARK	COOS CO OR	224 - B1
NEWTON PARK	132ND ST, DISTRICT OF SURREY BC	157 - A7
NEWTON ATHLETIC PARK	128TH ST, DISTRICT OF SURREY BC	157 - A7
NEZ PERCE NATIONAL FOREST	IDAHO CO ID	131 - B2
NEZ PERCE NATIONAL HISTORIC PARK	OFF US HWY 95, IDAHO CO ID	131 - C1
NICHOLAS ACRES PARK	SW 209TH AV, WASHINGTON CO OR	199 - A2
NIKE PARK	17200 NE 92ND ST, REDMOND WA	175 - D1
NOEL BOOTH PARK	36TH AV, TOWNSHIP OF LANGLEY BC	158 - C1
NOLTE STATE PARK	VEAZIE-CUMBERLAND RD, KING CO WA	110 - C3
NORGATE PARK	DISTRICT OF NORTH VANCOUV BC	254 - G4
NORMANDALE PARK	NE 57TH AV & NE HALSEY ST, PORTLAND OR	314 - D4
NORTH ACRES PARK	1ST AV NE & NE 130TH ST, SEATTLE WA	171 - B7
NORTH AUBURNDALE PARK	118TH AV SE, KING CO WA	182 - C1
NORTH BELLEVUE COMMUNITY PARK	NE 40TH ST & 148TH AV NE, BELLEVUE WA	175 - C2
NORTH CASCADES NATIONAL PARK	CHELAN CO WA	103 - B2
NORTH CITY PARK	NE 194TH ST & 10TH AV NE, SHORELINE WA	171 - B6
NORTH CLACKAMAS CENTRAL PARK	KELLOGG CREEK DR, MILWAUKIE OR	199 - D3
NORTHCREST PARK	8TH AV NE & NE 170TH ST, SHORELINE WA	171 - B6
NORTH DELTA PARK	DISTRICT OF DELTA BC	156 - D6
NORTHEAST TACOMA PLAYGROUND	29TH ST NE & 56TH AV NE, TACOMA WA	182 - A2
NORTHGATE PARK	N GENEVA AV & N FESSENDEN ST, PORTLAND OR	308 - A3
NORTH GREEN RIVER PARK	GREEN RIVER RD, AUBURN WA	175 - C7
NORTH GRESHAM PARK	SE 217TH AV & NW 25TH ST, GRESHAM OR	200 - B1
NORTH HIGHLANDS PARK	NE 16TH ST & KIRKLAND AV NE, RENTON WA	175 - C4
NORTH KIRKLAND COMMUNITY CENTER PARK	12421 103RD AV NE, KIRKLAND WA	171 - C7
NORTH MERIDIAN PARK	120TH AV SE & SE 231ST PL, KING CO WA	175 - C6
NORTH MYRTLE PARK	N MYRTLE CREEK RD, DOUGLAS CO OR	221 - D7
NORTH PARK BLOCKS	NW PARK AV & SW ANKENY ST, PORTLAND OR	313 - E5
NORTHPOINTE PARK	71ST AV NE & 71ST ST NE, MARYSVILLE WA	168 - D7
NORTH POWELLHURST PARK	SE 135TH AV & SE MAIN ST, PORTLAND OR	200 - A1
NORTHRIDGE PARK	KELLY VW LP & SW 189TH, WASHINGTON CO OR	199 - A2
NORTH ROSE HILL WOODLANDS PARK	NE 100TH ST & 124TH AV NE, KIRKLAND WA	175 - C1
NORTH SEATAC PARK	S 136TH ST & DES MOINES MEM DR, SEATAC WA	288 - B2
NORTH SEATTLE PARK	N NORTHGATE WY & N 107TH ST, SEATTLE WA	171 - A7
NORTH SHOREWOOD PARK	SW 102ND ST & 21ST AV SW, KING WA	285 - G5
NORTH TOWNE PARK	BELLEVUE WY NE, BELLEVUE WA	175 - C2
NORTH VIEW PARK	W MARINE VIEW DR, EVERETT WA	171 - C1
NORTHWEST COMMUNITY CENTER (PARK)	NE 24TH ST, BELLEVUE WA	175 - C2
NORWOOD VILLAGE NEIGHBORHOOD PARK	123RD PL SE & SE 24TH ST, BELLEVUE WA	175 - C3
NOTTINGHAM PARK	NOTTINGHAM RD, DISTRICT OF OAK BAY BC	257 - D7
NOWAK PARK	UPPER PRESTN RD & 312TH AV SE, KING CO WA	176 - B4
OAK PARK	VANCOUVER BC	156 - B5
OAKBROOK PARK	NE 99TH AV & NE 31ST ST, VANCOUVER WA	307 - H3
OAKLAND PLAYGROUND	S CENTER ST & S TYLER ST, TACOMA WA	294 - C1
OAKLANDS PARK	SHELBOURNE ST, CITY OF VICTORIA BC	257 - A7
OAKS PIONEER PARK	SE 7TH AV & SE SELLWOOD BLVD, PORTLAND OR	317 - G6
OBER PARK	17100 VASHON HWY SW, KING CO WA	174 - D5
OBRYANT PARK	SW WASHINGTON ST, PORTLAND OR	313 - E6
OCEAN CITY STATE PARK	OFF HWY 115, GRAYS HARBOR CO WA	177 - B6
OCEANVIEW PARK	ANNE CIR, CITY OF COLWOOD BC	159 - B7
OCHOCO LAKE STATE PARK	OCHOCO HWY, CROOK CO OR	135 - C2
OCHOCO NATIONAL FOREST	CROOK CO OR	213 - D1
OCHOCO NATIONAL FOREST	HARNEY CO OR	136 - C3
ODLIN COUNTY PARK	LOPEZ ISLAND, SAN JUAN CO WA	101 - C2
OGRADY PARK	SE GREEN VALLEY RD, KING CO WA	182 - D2
OHDE AVENUE PARK	OHDE AV & SLATER ST, KIRKLAND WA	175 - C1
OKANOGAN NATIONAL FOREST	OKANOGAN CO WA	104 - A2
OLD APPLE TREE PARK	COLUMBIA WY, VANCOUVER WA	305 - G6
OLD CANEMAH PARK	SOUTH END RD & SUNSET ST, OREGON CITY OR	199 - D5
OLD FORT TOWNSEND STATE PARK	OLD FORT TOWNSEND RD, JEFFERSON CO WA	263 - D10
OLD ORCHARD PARK	BENTLEY RD, PORT MOODY BC	157 - A4
OLD ORCHARD PARK	DISTRICT OF BURNABY BC	156 - C5
OLD TOWN PARK	N 30TH ST & CARR ST, TACOMA WA	293 - E2
OLD WAGON ROAD HISTORICAL AREA	COLUMBIA RIVER HWY, HOOD RIVER CO OR	195 - B5
OLGA MARINE STATE PARK	ORCAS TO OLGA RD, SAN JUAN CO WA	160 - A3
OLMSTEAD PLACE STATE PARK	KITTITAS CO WA	241 - C6
OLYMPIA WATERSHED TRAIL PARK	HENDERSON BLVD SE, OLYMPIA WA	297 - A7
OLYMPIC NATIONAL FOREST	CLALLAM CO WA	163 - B5
OLYMPIC NATIONAL FOREST	GRAYS HARBOR CO WA	172 - D3
OLYMPIC NATIONAL FOREST	JEFFERSON CO WA	173 - A1
OLYMPIC NATIONAL PARK	CLALLAM CO WA	261 - A14
OLYMPIC NATIONAL PARK	JEFFERSON CO WA	172 - C2
OLYMPIC NATIONAL PARK	MASON CO WA	109 - A1
OLYMPIC NATIONAL PARK	PORT ANGELES WA	261 - F9
OLYMPIC VIEW PARK	32ND AV SW & SW 329TH ST, FEDERAL WAY WA	182 - A1
OPPENLANDER ATHLETIC FIELDS	ROSEMONT RD, WEST LINN OR	199 - C4
OPTIMIST PLAYGROUND	HARMON ST & N 13TH ST, TACOMA WA	181 - C2
ORANGEGATE PARK	84TH ST E & 46TH AV E, PIERCE CO WA	182 - A4
ORCHARDS PARK	NE 58TH ST & NE 102ND AV, CLARK CO WA	307 - G1
OREGON PARK	NE 30TH AV & NE OREGON ST, PORTLAND OR	314 - A5
OREGON CASCADES RECREATION AREA	KLAMATH CO OR	223 - D1
OREGON DUNES NATIONAL RECREATION AREA	COOS CO OR	218 - B4
OREGON DUNES NATIONAL RECREATION AREA	DUNES CITY OR	214 - A3
OREGON ELECTRIC RIGHT OF WAY PARK	SW 86TH AV, WASHINGTON CO OR	199 - B2
OREGON STATE FOREST	DOUGLAS CO OR	225 - B6
OREILLY ACRES COUNTY PARK RESERVE	184TH AV NE, SNOHOMISH CO WA	102 - C3
OSWALD PARK	KIWANIS CEDAR HLL RD, CITY OF VICTORIA BC	256 - J6
OSWALD WEST STATE PARK	OREGON COAST HWY, TILLAMOOK CO OR	191 - A3
OSWEGO SWIM PARK	LAKEWOOD AV & RIDGEWAY RD, LAKE OSWEGO OR	321 - F7
OTHELLO PLAYGROUND	S OTHELLO ST & 45TH AV S, SEATTLE WA	287 - F1
OVERLOOK PARK	N OVERLOOK BL & N MELROSE DR, PORTLAND OR	313 - E2
OVERLOOK PARK	OLYMPIC VIEW DR, EDMONDS WA	171 - A5
OXBOW PARK	3010 SE OXBOW PKWY, MULTNOMAH CO OR	200 - C2
PACIFIC BEACH STATE PARK	OFF HWY 109, GRAYS HARBOR CO WA	177 - B2
PACIFIC CITY PARK	3RD AV SE, PACIFIC WA	182 - B2
PACIFIC RIM NATIONAL PARK	BRITISH COLUMBIA	100 - C2
PACIFIC SPIRIT REGIONAL PARK	UNIVERSITY ENDOWMENT LAND BC	156 - A4
PACIFIC WEST SKI AREA	SNOQUALMIE PASS, KITTITAS CO WA	111 - A2
PACKER JOHNS CABIN STATE PARK	HWY 55, ADAMS CO ID	251 - B4
PALISADES PARK	5039 SW DASH POINT RD, FEDERAL WAY WA	182 - A1
PALISADES PARK	N GOVERNMENT WY, SPOKANE CO WA	348 - D9
PALOMINO PARK	PALOMINO CT & PALOMINO WY, WEST LINN OR	199 - C4
PANDORA PARK	PANDORA ST, VANCOUVER BC	255 - C10

FEATURE NAME	City State	Page-Grid
PANORAMA POINT COUNTY PARK	EASTSIDE RD, HOOD RIVER CO OR	195 - D5
PANTHER CREEK EXPERIMENTAL FOREST	PANTHER CREEK RD, SKAMANIA CO WA	194 - D2
PARADISE POINT STATE PARK	CLARK CO WA	192 - C1
PARADISE RIDGE PARK	SW 220TH ST & 119TH AV SW, KING CO WA	174 - D6
PARAMOUNT PARK	NE 152ND ST & 10TH AV NE, SHORELINE WA	171 - B7
PARAMOUNT SCHOOL PARK	NE 155TH ST & 8TH AV NE, SHORELINE WA	171 - B7
PARK	102ND AV SE, KING CO WA	182 - C1
PARK	105A AV, DISTRICT OF SURREY BC	157 - A6
PARK	10730 MAIN ST, DONALD OR	199 - A7
PARK	10TH ST & MONROE ST, OREGON CITY OR	199 - D4
PARK	1111 PARK WY, MILTON WA	182 - B2
PARK	1200 5TH AV N, SEATTLE WA	277 - J2
PARK	124TH AV NE & NE 145TH ST, KING CO WA	171 - C7
PARK	128TH ST, DISTRICT OF SURREY BC	157 - A6
PARK	12TH AV NE & NE 66TH ST, SEATTLE WA	274 - C3
PARK	1339 GRIFFIN AV, ENUMCLAW WA	110 - C3
PARK	146TH AV SE & SE 18TH ST, BELLEVUE WA	175 - C3
PARK	156TH ST, DISTRICT OF SURREY BC	157 - A6
PARK	164TH AV SE & SE LAKE HOLM RD, KING CO WA	182 - D1
PARK	182ND AV E, PIERCE CO WA	182 - C2
PARK	18TH AV, VANCOUVER BC	255 - A14
PARK	192ND DR NE, SNOHOMISH CO WA	102 - C3
PARK	23RD AV, VANCOUVER BC	156 - C5
PARK	23RD AV, VANCOUVER BC	255 - A14
PARK	29TH AV S & S COLLEGE ST, SEATTLE WA	282 - D2
PARK	29TH AV SE, SNOHOMISH CO WA	171 - C4
PARK	34TH AV & E PINE ST, SEATTLE WA	278 - E5
PARK	3600 S HOLLY ST, SEATTLE WA	286 - E1
PARK	37TH ST, EVERETT WA	264 - D5
PARK	3RD ST & LINCOLN AV, MUKILTEO WA	266 - D1
PARK	3RD ST, CITY OF NORTH VANCOUVER BC	255 - B6
PARK	42ND AV S & S 122ND ST, TUKWILA WA	286 - E6
PARK	42ND AV S & S 122ND ST, TUKWILA WA	289 - E1
PARK	43RD AV E & E LYNN ST, SEATTLE WA	279 - F2
PARK	45TH AV NE & NE 86TH ST, SEATTLE WA	275 - F1
PARK	5550 LAKEMONT BLVD SE, BELLEVUE WA	175 - D3
PARK	5TH ST & N WASHINGTON AV, ARLINGTON WA	168 - D5
PARK	65TH AV NE, SEATTLE WA	275 - H4
PARK	67TH AV NE & 84TH ST NE, MARYSVILLE WA	168 - D7
PARK	7602 S CEDAR ST, TACOMA WA	294 - D7
PARK	78TH AV W & 240TH ST SW, EDMONDS WA	171 - B6
PARK	80TH AV, DISTRICT OF SURREY BC	157 - A7
PARK	84TH ST SE & E XAVIER WY, EVERETT WA	268 - C5
PARK	88TH AV NE, BOTHELL WA	171 - C6
PARK	89TH AV CT W, UNIVERSITY PLACE WA	181 - C3
PARK	8TH AV & FARM ST, CARBONADO WA	182 - D6
PARK	92A AV, DISTRICT OF SURREY BC	157 - A6
PARK	92ND ST SW & 49TH AV W, MUKILTEO WA	266 - E5
PARK	93RD ST E & 206TH AV E, BONNEY LAKE WA	182 - C4
PARK	ALAMEDA AV & 44TH ST W, FIRCREST WA	181 - C3
PARK	ALBANY OR	326 - B11
PARK	APPLEGATE TER, OREGON CITY OR	199 - D5
PARK	ASHLAND ST, ASHLAND OR	337 - G9
PARK	ASPEN ST, LAKE OSWEGO OR	199 - C4
PARK	BARCLAY HILLS DR, OREGON CITY OR	199 - D5
PARK	BARKSDALE AV & LOUVIERS AV, DUPONT WA	181 - B5
PARK	BARKSDALE AV & SANTA CRUZ ST, DUPONT WA	181 - B5
PARK	BARTLEY DR, ALBANY OR	326 - G12
PARK	BASSWOOD DR, EVERETT WA	264 - B7
PARK	BECKWITH AVE, DISTRICT OF SAANICH BC	256 - G1
PARK	BEDFORD RD, DISTRICT OF SAANICH BC	257 - G4
PARK	BELVIDERE AV SW & FAIRMNT AV, SEATTLE WA	281 - E2
PARK	BENTON CO OR	133 - B1
PARK	BENTON CO OR	327 - E6
PARK	BOCA RATAN DR & ANDREWS RD, CLACKAMAS OR	320 - E5
PARK	BOTHELL WY NE & REDER WY, BOTHELL WA	171 - C6
PARK	BOUNDARY DR E, DISTRICT OF SURREY BC	157 - A7
PARK	BOUNDARY RD, VANCOUVER BC	255 - F11
PARK	BRITISH COLUMBIA	107 - B1
PARK	BRITISH COLUMBIA	92 - B2
PARK	BRITISH COLUMBIA	93 - A3
PARK	BROOKSBANK AV, CITY OF NORTH VANCOUVER BC	255 - E7
PARK	CALISTOGA ST W & SKINNER WY SW, ORTING WA	182 - C5
PARK	CAMUS RD & 129TH AV CT, PIERCE CO WA	181 - A4
PARK	CASCADE DR & S ISLAND DR, BONNEY LAKE WA	182 - C3
PARK	CITY OF NORTH VANCOUVER BC	254 - J4
PARK	COLVILLE RD, TOWN OF ESQUILMALT BC	256 - C7
PARK	CONVENTION PL, SEATTLE WA	278 - A5
PARK	COOS CO OR	220 - C3
PARK	CORVALLIS OR	327 - H9
PARK	CROWN ST, DISTRICT OF N VANCOUVER BC	255 - E7
PARK	DEMPSEY RD, DISTRICT OF N VANCOUVER BC	255 - G1
PARK	DISTRICT OF N VANCOUVER BC	156 - D3
PARK	DISTRICT OF W VANCOUVER BC	254 - E4
PARK	DOCKTON RD SW, KING CO WA	174 - D6
PARK	DONCASTER DR, GLADSTONE OR	199 - D4
PARK	DOUGLAS CO OR	334 - A3
PARK	EARL AV NW, SEATTLE WA	171 - A7
PARK	EARL AV NW, SEATTLE WA	272 - E1
PARK	EDGECLIFF DR & CHANNON DR, NORMNDY PK WA	175 - A6
PARK	E HOWE ST & EVERETT AV E, SEATTLE WA	278 - C2
PARK	E JOHN ST & 15TH AV E, SEATTLE WA	278 - C4
PARK	FERN RD, DISTRICT OF N VANCOUVER BC	255 - F6
PARK	FERRY AV SW & CALIF AV SW, SEATTLE WA	280 - E1
PARK	GARDEN DR, VANCOUVER BC	255 - C12
PARK	GOLF DR & 14TH AV S, SEATTLE WA	282 - B1
PARK	GORDON HEAD RD, DISTRICT OF SAANICH BC	257 - C3
PARK	GRAHAM AV, SUMNER WA	182 - C3
PARK	GRANDVIEW DR, DISTRICT OF SAANICH BC	257 - D1
PARK	GIBSON BC	93 - B3
PARK	HARMAN WY S & CORRIN AV SE, ORTING WA	182 - C5
PARK	HARRISON ST & MINOR AV N, SEATTLE WA	278 - A4
PARK	HASTINGS ST E, VANCOUVER BC	255 - E10
PARK	HAWKS AV, VANCOUVER BC	254 - J10
PARK	HAWKS AV, VANCOUVER BC	255 - A11
PARK	HAWTHORNE DR, DISTRICT OF SAANICH BC	159 - D5
PARK	HIGH ST & LAUREL ST, BELLINGHAM WA	258 - D8
PARK	HILL DR, DISTRICT OF N VANCOUVER BC	255 - J4
PARK	HOMES AV, ASHLAND OR	337 - F9
PARK	HWY 101, BRITISH COLUMBIA	92 - C2
PARK	HWY 17, TOWN OF SIDNEY BC	159 - C2
PARK	HWY 19, BRITISH COLUMBIA	92 - C3
PARK	HWY 1, BRITISH COLUMBIA	95 - A3
PARK	HWY 202 & 224TH AV NE, KING CO WA	176 - A2
PARK	HWY 22 & HWY 3B, BRITISH COLUMBIA	106 - A1
PARK	HWY 3 & HWY 21, BRITISH COLUMBIA	105 - C1
PARK	HWY 3 & HWY 395, BRITISH COLUMBIA	105 - C1
PARK	HWY 33, BRITISH COLUMBIA	105 - A1
PARK	HWY 395, BRITISH COLUMBIA	105 - C1
PARK	HWY 3B, BRITISH COLUMBIA	106 - A1
PARK	HWY 3, BRITISH COLUMBIA	105 - B1
PARK	HWY 3, BRITISH COLUMBIA	95 - C3
PARK	HWY 4, BRITISH COLUMBIA	92 - B3
PARK	HWY 5A, BRITISH COLUMBIA	95 - C1
PARK	HWY 5, BRITISH COLUMBIA	95 - C1
PARK	HWY 8, BRITISH COLUMBIA	95 - C1
PARK	HWY 97 & 3A, BRITISH COLUMBIA	104 - C1
PARK	HWY 97, BRITISH COLUMBIA	104 - C1
PARK	HWY 99 & NE 119TH ST, CLARK CO WA	192 - C5
PARK	IDAHO CO ID	131 - C1
PARK	IOWA DR, AUBURN WA	182 - B1
PARK	IOWA ST, ASHLAND OR	337 - D8
PARK	IRIS AVE, DISTRICT OF SAANICH BC	256 - C3
PARK	JOHN ADAMS ST & 12TH ST, OREGON CITY OR	199 - D4
PARK	JONES AV, CITY OF NORTH VANCOUVER BC	255 - A4
PARK	JUANITA-WOODINVILLE WY NE, BOTHELL WA	171 - C6
PARK	LA CROSSE WA	122 - A1
PARK	LAKEVIEW & 228TH SW, MTLAKE TERRACE WA	171 - B6
PARK	LANSDOWNE RD, DISTRICT OF SAANICH BC	257 - B6
PARK	LAUREL DR & NILES AV, EVERETT WA	264 - C4
PARK	LILLOOET RD, DISTRICT OF N VANCOUVER BC	255 - G6
PARK	LINN CO OR	326 - H12
PARK	LLANFAIR CR, DIST OF CENTRAL SAANICH BC	159 - B4
PARK	LOCHSIDE DR, DISTRICT OF SAANICH BC	159 - C5
PARK	LONSDALE AV, CITY OF NORTH VANCOUVER BC	255 - B3
PARK	LOUGHEED HWY, PITT MEADOWS BC	157 - C5
PARK	LUCILLE PKWY NW, PIERCE CO WA	181 - C2
PARK	LUMLEY AV, MUKILTEO WA	266 - E2
PARK	LUMLEY AV, MUKILTEO WA	267 - E2
PARK	MADRONA DR & GRAND AV, SEATTLE WA	279 - E5
PARK	MADRONA DR, OREGON CITY OR	199 - C5
PARK	MAGNOLIA BLVD W, SEATTLE WA	272 - B7
PARK	MAGNOLIA BLVD W, SEATTLE WA	276 - B1
PARK	MAIN ST & WOODINVILLE-DUVALL R, DUVALL WA	110 - C1
PARK	MAIN ST, DISTRICT OF N VANCOUVER BC	255 - G7
PARK	MALTA AV, VANCOUVER BC	255 - F14
PARK	MCCALL ID	251 - C5
PARK	MCKENZIE & BORDEN, DIST OF SAANICH BC	256 - H3
PARK	METCHOSIN RD, CITY OF COLWOOD BC	159 - B7
PARK	MILDRED ST & SALMON BEACH ST, TACOMA WA	181 - C1
PARK	MINOR AV & UNIVERSITY ST, SEATTLE WA	278 - B5
PARK	MONTEITH ST, DISTRICT OF OAK BAY BC	257 - C8
PARK	MORSE AV, ALBANY OR	326 - B13
PARK	MOUNT SYMOUR PKWY, DIST OF N VANCOUVER BC	255 - J6
PARK	MT MCKINLEY DR SW, ISSAQUAH WA	175 - D4
PARK	MUNRO ST, TOWN OF ESQUILMALT BC	256 - D9
PARK	N 85TH ST & WALLINGFORD AV, SEATTLE WA	274 - A1
PARK	NANAIMO BC	93 - A3
PARK	NE 132ND ST & 120TH AV NE, KING CO WA	171 - C7
PARK	NE 140TH PL & 121ST AV NE, KING CO WA	171 - C7
PARK	NE 143RD ST & 128TH AV NE, KING CO WA	171 - C7
PARK	NE 145TH ST & 116TH PL NE, KING CO WA	171 - C7
PARK	NE 43RD ST & 9TH AV NE, SEATTLE WA	274 - B6
PARK	NE 5TH ST, CLARK CO WA	193 - A6
PARK	NE 6TH CIR, VANCOUVER WA	307 - G5
PARK	NE 75TH ST & NE BANNER PL, SEATTLE WA	274 - B2
PARK	NE CORNELL RD, HILLSBORO OR	198 - D1
PARK	NE HASSALO ST, PORTLAND OR	200 - A1
PARK	NE SALMON CREEK AV, CLARK CO WA	192 - D4
PARK	NEW WESTMINSTER BC	156 - D5
PARK	NORTH LAKE, FEDERAL WAY WA	182 - B1
PARK	NW 175TH ST & 8TH AV NW, SHORELINE WA	171 - A6
PARK	NW 92ND ST, SEATTLE WA	171 - A7
PARK	NW COMMERCIAL & NW 313TH, NORTH PLAINS OR	125 - C1
PARK	N WILLAMETTE BL & N WALL AV, PORTLAND OR	192 - B7
PARK	NW RICHMND BCH & 8TH AV NW, SHORELINE WA	171 - A6
PARK	OAK ST & 3RD ST, DAYTON OR	198 - C7
PARK	OCEAN SHORES WA	177 - B7
PARK	OFF DELTA AV, DISTRICT OF BURNABY BC	255 - J12
PARK	OFF HWY 3, BRITISH COLUMBIA	105 - A1
PARK	OFF MERLIN-GALICE RD, JOSEPHINE CO OR	149 - A1
PARK	OREGON PL & RUCKER AV, EVERETT WA	264 - D7
PARK	OSBORNE RD, DISTRICT OF N VANCOUVER BC	255 - B2
PARK	PALOUSE WA	249 - B1
PARK	PANDORA AVE, CITY OF VICTORIA BC	256 - H9
PARK	PARK DR & OLYMPIC DR, SHORELINE WA	171 - A6
PARK	PARK DR, STANWOOD WA	168 - B4
PARK	PARK ST, BLACK DIAMOND WA	110 - C3
PARK	PIERCE CO WA	118 - A1
PARK	PIONEER HWY & HEVLY RD, SNOHOMISH CO WA	168 - C5
PARK	POPLAR WY & 228TH ST SW, BRIER WA	171 - B6

PNW

INDEX

FEATURE NAME	City State	Page-Grid
PARK	PORTLAND OR	313 - H7
PARK	PRINCETON AV NE, SEATTLE WA	275 - F4
PARK	PROSPECT RD, DISTRICT OF N VANCOUVER BC	255 - B1
PARK	PT EDWARDS PL, WOODWAY WA	171 - A5
PARK	PULLMAN WA	249 - B5
PARK	REGENTS BLVD & ALTA VISTA PL, FIRCREST WA	294 - A1
PARK	RENFREW ST, VANCOUVER BC	255 - D10
PARK	RIGGINS ID	131 - C2
PARK	ROBERTS DR, BLACK DIAMOND WA	110 - C3
PARK	ROOSEVELT ST & SHORT ST, WILKESON WA	182 - D5
PARK	ROSEBURG OR	334 - E3
PARK	RUPERT ST, VANCOUVER BC	255 - E12
PARK	S 131ST ST & 42ND AV S, TUKWILA WA	288 - E1
PARK	SE 136TH ST & 144TH AV SE, KING CO WA	175 - D5
PARK	SE 170TH ST & 136TH PL SE, KING CO WA	175 - C5
PARK	SE 208TH ST & 124TH AV SE, KING CO WA	175 - C6
PARK	SE 6TH ST & MAPLEWOOD PL SE, RENTON WA	175 - C5
PARK	SECHELT DR, DISTRICT OF N VANCOUVER BC	255 - J4
PARK	SE HARRISON ST & SE 21ST AV, MILWAUKIE OR	321 - J3
PARK	SEOLA BEACH DR SW, SEATTLE WA	285 - F6
PARK	S GRANITE AV & GALENA ST, GRANITE FLLS WA	102 - C3
PARK	SILVER LAKE DR, EVERETT WA	171 - C4
PARK	S JACKSON ST & 3RD AV S, SEATTLE WA	278 - A7
PARK	S LANE ST & 7TH AV S, SEATTLE WA	278 - B7
PARK	S MAIN ST & OCCIDENTAL AV S, SEATTLE WA	278 - C6
PARK	S NORMAN ST, SEATTLE WA	278 - C7
PARK	S NORMAN ST, SEATTLE WA	282 - C1
PARK	SOUTH END RD & OAKTREE AV, OREGON CITY OR	199 - D5
PARK	SQUAMISH BC	93 - C2
PARK	STEILACOOM BLVD SW, LAKEWOOD WA	181 - C4
PARK	STURGUS AV S, SEATTLE WA	278 - C7
PARK	STURGUS AV S, SEATTLE WA	282 - C1
PARK	SW 3RD & TACOMA AV SW, SOUTH PRAIRIE WA	182 - D5
PARK	SW 5TH ST & SW ALGER AV, BEAVERTON OR	199 - B2
PARK	SW ATWTR LN & SW ATWTR RD, CLACKAMAS OR	320 - D5
PARK	SW DOGWD DR & SW MRLN AV, RIVERGROVE OR	199 - B4
PARK	SW ELSNER RD, WASHINGTON CO OR	199 - A4
PARK	SW KLAHANIE RD, KING CO WA	174 - D6
PARK	SW MAIN AV, BEAVERTON OR	199 - B2
PARK	SW NORMANDY TER, NORMANDY PARK WA	175 - A5
PARK	SW RIVERSIDE DR, MULTNOMAH CO OR	194 - B7
PARK	SW RIVERSIDE DR, MULTNOMAH OR	321 - H3
PARK	TAURUS ST, OCEAN SHORES WA	298 - C1
PARK	TULE LAKE RD & YAKMA AV S, PIERCE CO WA	181 - D4
PARK	UMATILLA CO OR	122 - A3
PARK	UNIVERSITY ENDOWMENT LAND BC	156 - A5
PARK	VANCOUVER BC	254 - J14
PARK	VICTORIA DR S, VANCOUVER BC	255 - B12
PARK	WALLACE DR, DIST OF CENTRAL SAANICH BC	159 - B4
PARK	WASHINGTON AV S & BRIDGE ST SW, ORTING WA	182 - C5
PARK	WHISTLER BC	93 - C1
PARK	WHITMAN CO WA	122 - B1
PARK	WHITMAN CO WA	249 - B3
PARK	W OLYMPIC PL & 1ST AV W, SEATTLE WA	277 - H3
PARK	WORTHINGTON DR, VANCOUVER BC	255 - F14
PARK	YACHATS, YACHATS OR	209 - A4
PARK	YESLER WY & 4TH AV, SEATTLE WA	278 - A6
PARK CREST PARK	DISTRICT OF BURNABY BC	156 - D4
PARKLANE PARK	SE MILLMAIN DR & SE MAIN ST, PORTLAND OR	200 - A1
PARK ORCHARD	110TH AV SE & SE 230TH ST, KING CO WA	175 - C6
PARK PLACE PARK	16180 FRONT ST, OREGON CITY OR	199 - D4
PARKSIDE PARK	S 244TH ST & 26TH PL S, DES MOINES WA	175 - B7
PARK VERDUN	DISTRICT OF W VANCOUVER BC	156 - A2
PARROTT CREEK PARK	BOOTH AV & SE STARMER ST, ROSEBURG OR	334 - F9
PARSONS GARDENS	8TH PL W & W HIGHLAND DR, SEATTLE WA	277 - G3
PAT PFEIFER PARK	NE 176TH AV & NE DAVIS ST, GRESHAM OR	200 - A1
PAT THOMPSON PARK	MT NWTN CRSS RD, DIST OF CNTRL SAANICH BC	159 - B3
PATTON SQUARE PARK	N INTERSTATE & N EMERSON, PORTLAND OR	309 - E7
PAULA JEAN PARK	SW JAY ST, WASHINGTON CO OR	199 - A1
PAUL BUNYAN RIFLE RANGE	STATE RTE 161 & 176TH ST E, PIERCE CO WA	182 - B5
PAUL DUNN STATE FOREST	TAMPICO RD, BENTON CO OR	207 - A4
PAYETTE LAKES SKI AREA	HWY 55 & ECKS FLAT RD, ADAMS CO ID	251 - B5
PAYETTE NATIONAL FOREST	ADAMS CO ID	251 - B2
PAYETTE NATIONAL FOREST	IDAHO CO ID	131 - C2
PAYETTE NATIONAL FOREST	VALLEY CO ID	251 - B2
PAYETTE NATIONAL FOREST	WASHINGTON CO ID	139 - B1
PEACE PARK	HWY 99, DISTRICT OF SURREY BC	158 - B3
PECK ATHLETIC FIELD	S SPRAGUE AV & S 15TH ST, TACOMA WA	293 - E6
PEDESTRIAN PARK	LOGAN AV S & N AIRPORT WY, RENTON WA	175 - C5
PEMBERTON PARK	FOUL BAY RD, CITY OF VICTORIA BC	257 - B10
PENDLETON PARK	SW IOWA ST & SW 55TH AV, PORTLAND OR	199 - B2
PEND OREILLE STATE PARK	PEND OREILLE CO WA	106 - C3
PENINSULA PARK	N ALBINA AV & N AINSWORTH ST, PORTLAND OR	309 - F6
PENINSULA JOINT USE PARK	46TH AV NW & ROSEDALE ST, GIG HARBOR WA	181 - C1
PENINSULA JOINT USE PARK	46TH AV NW & ROSEDALE ST, PIERCE CO WA	174 - C7
PENROSE POINT STATE PARK	158TH AV KPS, PIERCE CO WA	181 - A2
PEOPLES PARK	S L ST & S 10TH ST, TACOMA WA	293 - F5
PEOPLES COMMUNITY CENTER	M L KING JR WY & S 17TH ST, TACOMA WA	293 - G6
PEPPERTREE PARK	SW 126TH AV, WASHINGTON CO OR	199 - B1
PERIWINKLE PARK	ERMINE ST, ALBANY OR	326 - F10
PERKINS PARK	7TH ST & MARTIN ST, STEILACOOM WA	181 - C4
PETER KERR PARK	ELK ROCK ISLAND, MILWAUKIE OR	321 - H3
PETROVITSKY PARK	PETROVITSKY RD & SE 176TH PL, KING CO WA	175 - D6
PETTUS, TERRY PARK	E NEWTON ST & FAIRVIEW AV E, SEATTLE WA	278 - A2
PETTYGROVE PARK	SW HARRISON ST, PORTLAND OR	313 - F7
PHEASANT PARK	SW 185TH & SW PHEASNT, WASHINGTON CO OR	199 - A1
PHILLIP ARNOLD PARK	JONES AV S & S 7TH ST, RENTON WA	175 - C5
PHOENIX SKI HILL	OFF HWY 3, BRITISH COLUMBIA	105 - B1
PICCOLO PARK	SE 27TH AV & SE DIVISION ST, PORTLAND OR	317 - J1
PICNIC POINT PARK	PICNIC POINT RD, SNOHOMISH CO WA	171 - B4
PIDGEON PARK	CLACKAMAS & SE TONG, CLACKAMAS CO OR	200 - A4
PIER PARK	N SAINT JOHNS AV, PORTLAND OR	192 - B7
PIKES PEAK GREENBELT PARK	122ND AV NE & NE 39TH ST, BELLEVUE WA	175 - C2
PILCHUCK REC AREA	WOOD ST, SNOHOMISH WA	171 - D3
PILOT BUTTE STATE PARK	DESCHUTES CO OR	332 - H7
PINEBROOK PARK	SW PINEBROOK ST, TIGARD OR	199 - B3
PINEHURST PLAYGROUND	12100 12TH AV NE, SEATTLE WA	171 - B7
PINE LAKE PARK	SE 26TH ST & 228TH AV SE, KING CO WA	176 - A3
PINE MEADOW PARK	32ND AV SE & 157TH PL SE, MILL CREEK WA	171 - C4
PINE RIDGE PARK	85TH PL W & 207TH ST SW, EDMONDS WA	171 - A5
PINE STREET PARK	PINE ST & 6TH AV S, EDMONDS WA	171 - A5
PINE STREET SKI AREA	OFF BALDY MOUNTAIN RD, BONNER CO ID	107 - A3
PINE TREE PARK	114TH AV SE, KENT WA	175 - C7
PINEWAY PARK	RAMONA WY, ALBANY OR	326 - E12
PINNACLE PEAK PARK	276TH AV SE & SE 472ND ST, KING CO WA	110 - C3
PIONEER PARK	2ND ST SW & 4TH AV SW, PUYALLUP WA	182 - B4
PIONEER PARK	36TH AV W, LYNNWOOD WA	171 - B5
PIONEER PARK	BEND OR	332 - E6
PIONEER PARK	COMMERCIAL ST & MAIN ST, STEILACOOM WA	181 - C4
PIONEER PARK	CORVALLIS-NEWPORT HWY, CORVALLIS OR	327 - F11
PIONEER PARK	NW PIONEER & NW MEADOW, WASHINGTON CO OR	199 - A1
PIONEER PARK	SE 68TH ST & SE 70TH PL, MERCER ISLAND WA	175 - C4
PIONEER PARK	WHITMAN ST, WALLA WALLA WA	345 - C8
PIONEER SQUARE PARK	SW YAMHILL ST, PORTLAND OR	313 - E6
PIONEER SQUARE PARK	YESLER WY & 1ST AV, SEATTLE WA	278 - A6
PISTOL RIVER STATE PARK	OREGON COAST HWY, CURRY CO OR	232 - B2
PITTOCK ACRES PARK	NW PITTOCK DR, PORTLAND OR	312 - B5
PLATEAU PARK	DISTRICT OF W VANCOUVER BC	156 - A2
PLAYFAIR PARK	QUADRA ST, DISTRICT OF SAANICH BC	256 - H4
PLAYGROUND	12TH AV NE & NE 71ST ST, SEATTLE WA	274 - C3
PLAYGROUND	13TH AV S & S LUCILE ST, SEATTLE WA	282 - B6
PLAYGROUND	19TH AV E & E HARRISON ST, SEATTLE WA	278 - C4
PLAYGROUND	23RD AV & E JEFFERSON ST, SEATTLE WA	278 - D6
PLAYGROUND	2ND AV N & GALER ST, SEATTLE WA	277 - H2
PLAYGROUND	3RD AV N, SEATTLE WA	277 - H2
PLAYGROUND	50TH AV S & S FERDINAND ST, SEATTLE WA	283 - F5
PLAYGROUND	51ST AV S & S GRAHAM ST, SEATTLE WA	283 - F7
PLAYGROUND	8TH AV S & S SULLIVAN ST, SEATTLE WA	286 - A3
PLAYGROUND	BLAINE ST & 3RD AV W, SEATTLE WA	277 - G2
PLAYGROUND	E ALDER ST & 29TH AV, SEATTLE WA	278 - D6
PLAYGROUND	EASTLAKE AV & ROANOKE ST, SEATTLE WA	278 - B1
PLAYGROUND	E DENNY WY & MADRONA PL E, SEATTLE WA	279 - E4
PLAYGROUND	E PINE ST & 11TH AV E, SEATTLE WA	278 - B5
PLAYGROUND	E ROY ST & E FEDERAL AV, SEATTLE WA	278 - B3
PLAYGROUND	HARRINGTON AV NE & NE 16TH ST, RENTON WA	175 - C4
PLAYGROUND	HOWE ST & 2ND AV N, SEATTLE WA	277 - H2
PLAYGROUND	MARION ST & 34TH AV, SEATTLE WA	278 - E5
PLAYGROUND	N 41ST ST & FREMONT AV N, SEATTLE WA	273 - H6
PLAYGROUND	NE 50TH ST & 9TH AV NE, SEATTLE WA	274 - B5
PLAYGROUND	NW 43RD ST & BAKER AV NW, SEATTLE WA	273 - G5
PLAYGROUND	NW 60TH ST & 28TH AV NW, SEATTLE WA	272 - D3
PLAYGROUND	RAINIER AV S & S ALASKA ST, SEATTLE WA	282 - E5
PLAYGROUND	RAINIER AV S & S WINTHROP ST, SEATTLE WA	282 - D3
PLAYGROUND	ROOSEVELT WY NE & NE 82ND ST, SEATTLE WA	274 - C1
PLAYGROUND	S DAYTON AV & S MAIN ST, NEWBERG OR	198 - D6
PLAYGROUND	S GRAND ST & 14TH AV S, SEATTLE WA	282 - B1
PLAYGROUND	S GRAND ST & 23RD AV S, SEATTLE WA	282 - D1
PLAYGROUND	S HOMER ST & CORSON AV S, SEATTLE WA	282 - B6
PLAYGROUND	S NORFOLK ST & 59TH AV S, SEATTLE WA	287 - G5
PLAYGROUND	SW CLOVERDALE ST & SW 11TH AV, SEATTLE WA	285 - H3
PLAYGROUND	WALLINGFORD AV & N 43RD ST, SEATTLE WA	273 - J6
PLAYGROUND	WALLINGFORD AV & N 43RD ST, SEATTLE WA	274 - A6
PLAYGROUND	WARREN PL & 1ST AV N, SEATTLE WA	277 - H2
PLEASANT VALLEY PARK	NE 142ND ST, CLARK CO WA	192 - D4
POINT DEFIANCE PARK	N PARK AV, TACOMA WA	181 - C1
POMA SKI TOW	OFF CENTURY DRIVE HWY, DESCHUTES CO OR	216 - B4
PONDEROSA PARK	BEND OR	332 - H9
PONDEROSA STATE PARK	VALLEY CO ID	251 - D4
PONDER PARK	80TH AV, TOWNSHIP OF LANGLEY BC	157 - D7
POOL PARK	N VILLA RD & HAWORTH AV, NEWBERG OR	198 - D5
PORTAGE REGIONAL PARK	OLD ISLAND HIGHWAY, TOWN OF VIEW ROYAL BC	256 - A5
PORT COQUITLAM NATURE PARK	LNCOLN & COAST MERIDN, PORT COQUITLAM BC	157 - B4
PORTLAND AVENUE PARK	E 35TH ST & E PORTLAND AV, TACOMA WA	182 - A3
PORTLAND HEIGHTS PARK	SW PATTON RD, PORTLAND OR	316 - C1
PORTLAND WOMENS FORUM STATE PARK	E HIST COLUMBIA RVR HWY, MULTNOMAH CO OR	200 - D1
PORT OF BELLINGHAM MARINE PARK	HARRIS AV, BELLINGHAM WA	258 - A11
PORTSMOUTH PARK	N STANFORD AV & N DEPAUW ST, PORTLAND OR	308 - A4
POTHOLES STATE PARK	OSULLIVAN DAM RD, GRANT CO WA	242 - C6
POTLATCH STATE PARK	HWY 101, MASON CO WA	173 - A7
POWELL PARK	SE POWELL BLVD & SE 22ND AV, PORTLAND OR	317 - J2
POWELL BUTTE NATURE PARK	SE 162ND AV & W POWELL BL, PORTLAND OR	200 - A2
POWERHOUSE PARK	DISTRICT OF BURNABY BC	156 - D5
POWERS MARINE PARK	SW MACADAM AV, PORTLAND OR	317 - G7
PRATT PARK	18TH AV S & S MAIN ST, SEATTLE WA	278 - C7
PRESTON PARK	309TH PL SE, KING CO WA	176 - B4
PRESTON TRAILHEAD PARK	SE 87TH PL, KING CO WA	176 - B4
PRIEST POINT PARK	E BAY DR, OLYMPIA WA	296 - J1
PRINCESS PARK	PRINCESS AV, DISTRICT OF NORTH VANCOUV BC	255 - D2
PRINCESS MARGARET MARINE PARK	PORTLAND ISLAND, BRITISH COLUMBIA	159 - D1
PRINCE WALES PARK	VANCOUVER BC	156 - B5
PRINEVILLE RESERVOIR STATE PARK	JUNIPER CANYON RD, CROOK CO OR	135 - C3
PRINGLE FALLS EXPRMNTL FOREST ADDITION	DESCHUTES CO OR	216 - B7
PUBLIC FISHING REC AREA	W LAKE DESIRE DR & 174TH AV, KING CO WA	175 - D5
PUGET PARK	18TH AV SW, SEATTLE WA	281 - G5
PUGET PARK	PROCTOR ST & N 31ST ST, TACOMA WA	292 - C2
PUGET GARDENS PARK	N 36TH ST & N ALDER ST, TACOMA WA	292 - D1
PUGET SOUND PARK	1ST AV S, KING CO WA	175 - A5
PUGNETTI PARK	S 21ST ST & PACIFIC AV, TACOMA WA	293 - H7
PURDY SAND SPIT PARK	KEY PENINSULA HWY, PIERCE CO WA	174 - B7
QEMILIN PARK	POST FALLS ID	353 - G8
QUARNBERG PARK	E MILL PLAIN BL & U ST, VANCOUVER WA	305 - J5

FEATURE NAME	City State	Page-Grid
QUEEN ELIZABETH PARK	VANCOUVER BC	156 - B5
QUEENS PARK	NEW WESTMINSTER BC	156 - D5
QUICKS BOTTOM PARK	MARKHAM ST, DISTRICT OF SAANICH BC	159 - C5
QUILCHENA PARK	VANCOUVER BC	156 - B5
QUINTUS PARK	SW CENTER ST, ROSEBURG OR	334 - B6
RAFTER PARK	CEDAR RIVER, KING CO WA	176 - A6
RAILROAD PARK	1ST AV S & W TITUS ST, KENT WA	175 - B7
RAILROAD HISTORICAL PARK	MEDCO RD, MEDFORD OR	336 - C8
RAINBOW PARK	MCKENZIE AVE, DISTRICT OF SAANICH BC	256 - F3
RAINIER TRAIL PARK	244TH AV SE & HAMILTON PL, ENUMCLAW WA	110 - C3
RAINIERWOOD PARK	CHEROKEE BL & FOREST GRN BL, PUYALLUP WA	182 - B4
RALEIGH PARK	SW 78TH AV, WASHINGTON CO OR	199 - B2
RALEIGH SCHOLLS PARK	SW SCHOLLS FERRY RD, WASHINGTON CO OR	199 - B2
RALEIGHWOOD PARK	SW RALEIGHWOOD WY, WASHINGTON CO OR	199 - B2
RANCH PARK	DAYBREAK AV & SADDLE ST, COQUITLAM BC	157 - A4
RAPID RIVER RECREATION AREA	ADAMS CO ID	131 - B2
RATTLESNAKE RIDGE PARK	I-90 & RTE 202, KING CO WA	176 - C5
RAVENNA PARK	NE 62ND ST & 15TH AV NE, SEATTLE WA	274 - C4
RAVENSDALE PARK	KENT KANGLEY RD & 272ND AV SE, KING CO WA	176 - A7
RAY BENSON SNO-PARK	OFF SANTIAM HWY, LINN CO OR	211 - A3
REC AREA	118TH AV NE, KING CO WA	171 - C7
RECREATION AREA	SANDY SHORE DR SW, KING CO WA	174 - D7
RED BRIDGE STATE PARK	UKIAH-HILGARD HWY, UNION CO OR	129 - C2
RED FOX HILLS PARK #1	TIMBERLINE DR & FOX RUN, LAKE OSWEGO OR	320 - E4
RED FOX HILLS PARK #3	HIDEAWAY LN, LAKE OSWEGO OR	321 - E4
RED MOUNTAIN SKI AREA	HWY 3, BRITISH COLUMBIA	106 - A1
REDONDO PARK	REDONDO BEACH DR S, KING CO WA	175 - B7
RED SUNSET PARK	RED SUNSET DR, GRESHAM OR	200 - B1
REDWOOD PARK	16TH AV, DISTRICT OF SURREY BC	158 - B2
REDWOOD NATIONAL PARK	DEL NORTE CO CA	148 - C3
REESE PARK	OLD OWEN RD, SULTAN WA	110 - C1
REEVE PARK	REEVE ST & WILSON ST, PORT COQUITLAM BC	157 - B4
REGRADE PARK	3RD AV & BELL ST, SEATTLE WA	277 - J5
REID HARBOR STATE PARK	STUART ISLAND, SAN JUAN CO WA	101 - C2
RENE MEMORIAL PARK	DISTRICT OF BURNABY BC	156 - D5
RENFREW PARK	22ND AV, VANCOUVER BC	255 - D14
RENFREW RAVINE PARK	VANCOUVER BC	156 - C5
RENTON FISH & GAME CLUB REC AREA	SE 144TH ST, KING CO WA	175 - D5
RENTON PARK	130TH AV SE & SE 172ND ST, KING CO WA	175 - C5
RESERVOIR PARK	1501 3RD ST, KIRKLAND WA	175 - C1
RESERVOIR PARK	163RD PL NE & NE 95TH ST, REDMOND WA	175 - D1
RESERVOIR PARK	SW INGLEWOOD ST, WASHINGTON CO OR	199 - B2
REYNOLDS PARK	CEDAR HILL CROSS RD, DIST OF SAANICH BC	256 - J3
RHODY RIDGE COUNTY PARK	JOHN BAILEY & 3RD SE, SNOHOMISH CO WA	171 - C5
RICHMOND BEACH CENTER	NW 196TH ST & 21ST PL NW, SHORELINE WA	171 - A6
RICHMOND BEACH PARK	25TH AV NW & NW 191ST PL, SHORELINE WA	171 - A6
RICHMOND HIGHLANDS PARK	LINDEN AV N & N 167TH ST, SHORELINE WA	171 - A6
RICHMOND NATURE PARK	CITY OF RICHMOND BC	156 - B6
RIDGECREST PARK	NE 163RD ST, SHORELINE WA	171 - B7
RIDGECREST PARK	SW GREEN LN & SW ALPINE DR, BEAVERTON OR	199 - B2
RIDGEWOOD PARK	SW WILSHIRE ST, WASHINGTON CO OR	199 - B1
RIDGEWOOD VIEW PARK	SW WILLIAMS ST, WASHINGTON CO OR	199 - B2
RIGHT OF WAY PARK	30TH DR SE, SNOHOMISH CO WA	171 - C5
RIMROCK COUNTY PARK	129TH AV E, PIERCE CO WA	118 - B1
RISLEY PARK	SE SWAIN AV & SE RUBY DR, CLACKAMAS CO OR	321 - J7
RIVER PARK	LEBANON OR	133 - C1
RIVERCREST PARK	131 PARK DR, OREGON CITY OR	199 - D5
RIVER FRONT PARK	STEWART PARK DR, ROSEBURG OR	334 - E6
RIVER MEADOWS COUNTY PARK	JORDAN RD, SNOHOMISH CO WA	168 - D5
RIVER RUN PARK	RIVER RUN DR, LAKE OSWEGO OR	199 - C4
RIVERSIDE PARK	7TH ST & PARK ST, GRANTS PASS OR	335 - E10
RIVERSIDE PARK	HARRISON AV & LOWE ST, CENTRALIA WA	299 - D2
RIVERSIDE PARK	SE GRAND AV, PORTLAND OR	317 - G2
RIVERSIDE PARK	SE WATER & SE MANGAN, CLACKAMAS CO OR	199 - D4
RIVERSIDE PARK	SW OAK ST, ROSEBURG OR	334 - F7
RIVERSIDE COUNTY PARK	RIVERSIDE DR & 78TH ST E, PIERCE CO WA	182 - C4
RIVERSIDE STATE PARK	N AUBREY L WHITE PKWY, SPOKANE WA	346 - A14
RIVERSIDE STATE PARK	N AUBREY L WHITE PKWY, SPOKANE CO WA	348 - C5
RIVERVIEW PARK	MAPLE VALLEY RD & SE 5TH ST, RENTON WA	175 - C5
RIVER VIEW PARK	SE PARK ST & EUCLID AV SE, SNOQUALMIE WA	176 - C4
RIVERVIEW PARK	VANCOUVER BC	156 - B5
RIVERVIEW PLAYFIELD	12TH AV SW & SW WEBSTER ST, SEATTLE WA	285 - H1
RIVER VILLA PARK	SE BLUFF RD, CLACKAMAS CO OR	321 - H5
RIVERWAY WEST PARK	DISTRICT OF BURNABY BC	156 - C5
ROADSIDE PARK	LATAH CO ID	115 - A3
ROADSIDE PARK & VIEWPOINT	E LAKE SAMMAMISH PKWY SE, KING CO WA	175 - D2
ROANOKE PARK	ROANOKE ST & 10TH AV N, SEATTLE WA	278 - B1
ROANOKE PARK	W MERCR WY & ROANOKE WY, MERCER ISLAND WA	283 - J1
ROBERT BURNABY PARK	DISTRICT OF BURNABY BC	156 - D5
ROBERT F KENNEDY STATE PARK	BAY RD KPS, PIERCE CO WA	180 - D3
ROBERT J PORTER PARK	FAIRFIELD RD, CITY OF VICTORIA BC	256 - J10
ROBERT W SAWYER STATE PARK	BEND OR	332 - E3
ROBINSON POINT PARK	SW POINT ROBINSON RD, KING CO WA	175 - A7
ROBINSWOOD COMMUNITY PARK	153RD AV SE & SE 24TH ST, BELLEVUE WA	175 - D3
ROBSON PARK	100TH AV, DISTRICT OF SURREY BC	157 - A6
ROCHE COVE REGIONAL PARK	MOUNT MATHESON RD, BRITISH COLUMBIA	165 - A1
ROCHE POINT PARK	DISTRICT OF NORTH VANCOUV BC	156 - D3
ROCHESTER PARK	MAMARD AV, COQUITLAM BC	157 - A5
ROCK CREEK PARK	NW ROCK CREEK BLVD, WASHINGTON CO OR	199 - A1
ROCK CREEK LANDING PARK	NW ROCK CREEK BLVD, WASHINGTON CO OR	192 - A7
ROCK CREEK PROVINCIAL PARK	HWY 3, BRITISH COLUMBIA	105 - A1
ROCK ISLAND STATE PARK	HWY 28 & ROCK ISLAND GRADE, DOUGLAS CO WA	239 - C5
ROCK PRAIRIE COUNTY PARK	COQUILLE-FAIRVIEW RD, COOS CO OR	140 - B2
ROCKWOOD CENTRAL PARK	SE 178TH AV & SE MAIN ST, GRESHAM OR	200 - A1
ROCKY BUTTE STATE PARK	NE ROCKY BUTTE RD, PORTLAND OR	315 - H3
ROCKY POINT PARK	ESPLANADE, PORT MOODY BC	157 - A4
RODGERS PARK	3RD AV W & RAYE ST, SEATTLE WA	273 - G7
RODOLPH PARK	CNTRL SAANCH RD, DIST OF CNTRL SAANICH BC	159 - C4
ROEGNER PARK	ORAVETZ RD & MILL POND DR, AUBURN WA	182 - C2
ROEHR WATERFRONT PARK	OSWEGO POINTE DR, LAKE OSWEGO OR	321 - G6
ROGERS PARK	17TH AV & DOUGLAS ST, FOREST GROVE OR	198 - B1
ROGERS PLAYGROUND	E L ST & E 34TH ST, TACOMA WA	182 - A3
ROGUE RIVER NATIONAL FOREST	DOUGLAS CO OR	223 - A7
ROGUE RIVER NATIONAL FOREST	JACKSON CO OR	337 - F13
ROGUE RIVER NATIONAL FOREST	KLAMATH CO OR	150 - A1
ROLLEY LAKE PROVINCIAL PARK	BELL RD, DISTRICT OF MISSION BC	94 - B3
ROM KNOTT PARK	W SAANICH RD, DIST OF CENTRAL SAANICH BC	159 - B4
RONALD BOG PARK	N 175TH ST & MERIDIAN AV N, SHORELINE WA	171 - B6
RON MCLEAN PARK	DISTRICT OF BURNABY BC	156 - D5
ROOKE AND HIGGINS COUNTY PARK	COOS CO OR	218 - D7
ROOSEVELT FIELD	CAROLINA ST, BELLINGHAM WA	258 - G5
ROOSEVELT PLAYGROUND	ROOSEVELT AV & DIVISION ST, TACOMA WA	182 - A3
ROOSTER ROCK STATE PARK	COLUMBIA RIVER HWY, MULTNOMAH CO OR	200 - D1
ROSA ROAD PARK	SW ROSA RD, WASHINGTON CO OR	199 - A2
ROSE CITY PARK	NE 62ND AV & NE TILLAMOOK ST, PORTLAND OR	314 - D3
ROSEDALE COUNTY PLAYFIELD	86TH AV NW & ROSEDALE ST NW, PIERCE CO WA	181 - B1
ROSS LAKE NATIONAL RECREATION AREA	SKAGIT CO WA	103 - A2
ROSSMAN PARK	4TH ST & C AV, LAKE OSWEGO OR	321 - F5
ROTARY PARK	ALPINE ST SE & 27TH ST SE, AUBURN WA	182 - C2
ROTARY PARK	LOWELL-SNO RIVER RD, EVERETT WA	269 - F1
ROTARY PARK	SE 44TH ST & 89TH AV SE, MERCER ISLAND WA	175 - C3
ROUND LAKE STATE PARK	OFF DUFORT RD, BONNER CO ID	107 - A3
ROUTLEY PARK	WESTERN DR, PORT COQUITLAM BC	157 - B5
ROWLAND PARK	MARY HLL RD & WLSN AV, PORT COQUITLAM BC	157 - B4
ROXBURY PARK	SW ROXBURY AV, WASHINGTON CO OR	199 - B2
ROXHILL PARK	SW ROXBURY ST & 28TH AV SW, SEATTLE WA	285 - F4
ROYAL ATHLETIC PARK	COOK ST, CITY OF VICTORIA BC	256 - H8
ROYAL HEIGHTS PARK	DISTRICT OF SURREY BC	156 - D6
ROYAL KWANTIEN PARK	104TH AV & OLD YALE RD, DIST OF SURREY BC	157 - A6
ROYAL ROADS PARK	OCEAN BLVD, CITY OF COLWOOD BC	159 - B7
ROY CITY PARK	CEDAR ST & WARREN ST, ROY WA	181 - C7
ROY MORSE PARK	MORSE PARK WY, LONGVIEW WA	302 - C5
RUCKLE PROVINCIAL PARK	BEAVER POINT RD, BRITISH COLUMBIA	101 - B1
RUDD PARK	BOLESKINE RD, DISTRICT OF SAANICH BC	256 - F5
RUPERT PARK	1ST AV, VANCOUVER BC	255 - F12
RUSSELL ROAD PARK	RUSSELL RD, KENT WA	175 - B7
RUSSELL WOODS PARK	RUSSELL RD & S 228TH ST, KENT WA	291 - F7
RUTHTON PARK	COLUMBIA RIVER HWY, HOOD RIVER CO OR	195 - C5
RYALL PARK	NEW WESTMINSTER BC	156 - D6
SAANICHTON BAY PARK	ARDMORE DR, DIST OF CENTRAL SAANICH BC	159 - C3
SAANICHTON RESEARCH STATION	HWY 17, DISTRICT OF NORTH SAANICH BC	159 - C3
SAARINEN WAYSIDE PARK	20535 SW 86TH AV, TUALATIN OR	199 - B4
SABIN OCCUPATIONAL SKILL CENTER	SE JOHNSON RD, CLACKAMAS CO OR	199 - D3
SACAJAWEA PARK	NE 76TH AV & NE ALBERTA ST, PORTLAND OR	315 - F1
SACAJAWEA PARK	REDNDO WY & SW DSH PT RD, FEDERAL WAY WA	182 - B1
SACAJAWEA PLAYGROUND	1800 NE 94TH ST, SEATTLE WA	171 - B7
SACAJAWEA STATE PARK	US HWY 12, FRANKLIN CO WA	121 - A3
SADDLEBAG ISLAND STATE PARK	SADDLEBAG ISLAND, SKAGIT CO WA	160 - D5
SADDLE MOUNTAIN STATE PARK	CLATSOP CO WA	188 - D7
SAINT CLAIR PARK	SAINT CLAIR ST, BELLINGHAM WA	258 - H6
SAINT EDWARD STATE PARK	JUANITA DR NE & NE 145TH PL, KING CO WA	171 - B7
SAINT FRANCIS PARK	SE STARK ST, PORTLAND OR	313 - H6
SAINT HELENS PARK	E 13TH ST, VANCOUVER WA	306 - B5
SAINT JOE NATIONAL FOREST	BENEWAH CO ID	115 - B3
SAINT JOE NATIONAL FOREST	LATAH CO ID	123 - B1
SAINT JOE NATIONAL FOREST	SHOSHONE CO ID	115 - C3
SAINT JOHNS PARK	8427 N CENTRAL ST, PORTLAND OR	192 - B7
SALISHAN PLAYGROUND	E Q ST & E 39TH ST, TACOMA WA	182 - A3
SALISH PARK	YOUNG & CHEAM, DIST OF CHILLIWACK BC	94 - C3
SALIX PARK	SW 185TH AV & SW BASELNE RD, BEAVERTON OR	199 - A1
SALMON BAY PARK	NW CANOE PL & 19TH AV NW, SEATTLE WA	273 - E2
SALMON CREEK PARK	8TH AV SW & SW 118TH ST, KING WA	285 - H7
SALMON CREEK GREENWAY PARK	NE 117TH ST, CLARK CO WA	192 - C5
SALTAR PARK	1ST ST & CHAMPION, STEILACOOM WA	181 - B4
SALT CREEK RECREATION AREA	OFF CAMP HAYDEN RD, CLALLAM CO WA	164 - D5
SALTWATER STATE PARK	MARINE VIEW DR S & S 257TH ST, KING CO WA	175 - A7
SAM BROWN PARK	E DEVINE RD & IDAHO ST, VANCOUVER WA	306 - C5
SAM JACKSON PARK	SW TERWILLIGER BL, PORTLAND OR	317 - E1
SAMMAMISH RIVER PARK	LEARY WY NE, REDMOND WA	175 - D1
SAMMAMISH RIVER PARK	SAMMAMISH RIV & 102ND AV NE, BOTHELL WA	171 - C6
SAMMAMISH RIVER REGIONAL PARK	NE 116TH ST, KING CO WA	171 - D7
SAMMAMISH RIVER REGIONAL PARK	NE 116TH ST, REDMOND WA	175 - D1
SAMMAMISH RIVER REGIONAL PARK	NE 116TH ST, WOODINVILLE WA	171 - C6
SAMMAMISH RIVER REGIONAL PARK	NE 16TH ST & 150TH AV NE, REDMOND WA	171 - D7
SAMUEL H BOARDMAN STATE PARK	OREGON COAST HWY, CURRY CO OR	232 - B3
SANDEE PALISADES PARK	1206 SE LEWELLYN AV, TROUTDALE OR	200 - B1
SANDEL PLAYGROUND	92ND ST N & 1ST AV NW, SEATTLE WA	273 - H1
SAND STATION RECREATION AREA	COLUMBIA RIVER HWY, UMATILLA CO OR	129 - A1
SANDY COVE PARK	SE KING ST & FALLS AV SE, SNOQUALMIE WA	176 - C4
SANDY ISLAND PARK	BRITISH COLUMBIA	92 - B2
SANTANA COUNTY PARK	FOUR CORNERS OR	325 - F2
SANTIAM SNO-PARK	OFF SANTIAM HWY, LINN CO OR	211 - A2
SANTIAM STATE FOREST	LINN CO OR	134 - A1
SANTIAM STATE FOREST	S SAWTELL RD, CLACKAMAS CO OR	126 - A3
SAPPERTON PARK	NEW WESTMINSTER BC	156 - D5
SARDIS PARK	MANUEL RD, DISTRICT OF CHILLIWACK BC	94 - C3
SARITA PARK	DISTRICT OF NORTH VANCOUV BC	156 - C2
SASQUATCH PROVINCIAL PARK	ROCKWELL DR, DISTRICT OF KENT BC	94 - C3
SATHER PARK	FOSTER ST, PORT TOWNSEND WA	263 - G3
SAWYER PARK	SAWYER ST, TACOMA WA	295 - F2
SAXE POINT PARK	FRASER ST, TOWN OF ESQUILMALT BC	256 - B9
SAYRES, STAN MEMORIAL PARK	46TH AV S & LK WASHINGTN BL S, SEATTLE WA	283 - F3
SCENIC PARK	PENZANCE DR, DISTRICT OF BURNABY BC	255 - J9
SCENIC HILL PARK	S 257TH ST & WOODLAND WY S, KENT WA	175 - C7
SCHAFER STATE PARK	MASON CO WA	179 - A5
SCHEFFLER PARK	SW BERTHOLD ST, BEAVERTON OR	199 - B2
SCHMITZ PARK	SCHMITZ BLVD & ADMIRAL WY SW, SEATTLE WA	280 - C3
SCHMITZ, EMMA MEMORIAL OVERLOOK PARK	SW BEACH DR & SW OREGON ST, SEATTLE WA	280 - B5
SCHROEDER PARK	SCHROEDER LN, JOSEPHINE CO OR	335 - A9
SCHUEPBACH PARK	SW 160TH AV & SW VILLAGE LN, BEAVERTON OR	199 - A2
SCHWEITZER BASIN SKI AREA	OFF HWY 2, BONNER CO ID	107 - A2

FEATURE NAME	City State	Page-Grid
SCOGGINS VALLEY PARK	SCOGGINS VALLEY RD, WASHINGTON CO OR	198 - A2
SCOOTIE BROWN PARK	8TH ST NE & HENRY RD, AUBURN WA	182 - C1
SCOTT PARK	ROOSEVELT AV & COLE ST, ENUMCLAW WA	110 - C3
SCOTT PARK	SE HARRISON ST & SE 23RD AV, MILWAUKIE OR	321 - J2
SCRIBER CREEK PARK	CEDAR VLY RD & 200TH ST SW, LYNNWOOD WA	171 - B5
SCRIBER LAKE PARK	196TH ST SW & 56TH AV W, LYNNWOOD WA	171 - B5
SEACREST MARINA PARK	1800 HARBOR AV SW, SEATTLE WA	281 - F1
SEALAND OF THE PUBLIC	BEACH DR, DISTRICT OF OAK BAY BC	257 - D9
SEAQUEST STATE PARK	SPIRIT LAKE HWY, COWLITZ CO WA	187 - D7
SEATTLE TENNIS CLUB	MCGILVRA BLVD E & 39TH AV E, SEATTLE WA	279 - F3
SEAVIEW PARK	185TH ST SW & 82ND AV W, EDMONDS WA	171 - B5
SEAVIEW PARK	CECILE DR, PORT MOODY BC	157 - A4
SECOND NARROWS PARK	MONTROSE ST, DISTRICT OF BURNABY BC	255 - G9
SECRET PARK	W MERCR WY & SE 27TH ST, MERCER ISLAND WA	283 - J2
SECTION 36 PARK	NE 8TH ST, KING CO WA	176 - A2
SEDGEWICK PARK	WALFRED RD, DISTRICT OF LANGFORD BC	159 - B6
SEELEY LAKE COUNTY PARK	LAKEWOOD DR SW, LAKEWOOD WA	181 - D4
SEHOME HILL PARK	COLLEGE PKWY, BELLINGHAM WA	258 - D9
SEIBENTHALER PARK	16TH ST & BONNEY AV, SUMNER WA	182 - B3
SELLWOOD PARK	SE 7TH AV & SE MILLER ST, PORTLAND OR	317 - G6
SELLWOOD RIVERFRONT PARK	SE OAKS PARK WY, PORTLAND OR	317 - F6
SELVEY PARK	272ND ST, MAPLE RIDGE BC	94 - B3
SEMIAHMOO PARK	MARINE DR, DISTRICT OF SURREY BC	158 - A2
SEMINOLE PARK	SW BASELINE RD, WASHINGTON CO OR	199 - A1
SENECA FOUTS MEMORIAL STATE PARK	COLUMBIA RIVER HWY, HOOD RIVER CO OR	195 - C5
SEQUIM BAY STATE PARK	CLALLAM CO WA	166 - B7
SETTLEMIER PARK	WOODBURN OR	205 - B2
SEVEN DEVILS WAYSIDE PARK	SEVEN DEVILS RD, COOS CO OR	220 - B3
SEVEN OAKS PARK	SE 259TH PL & 118TH PL SE, KENT WA	175 - C7
SEWALLCREST PARK	SE 31ST AV & SE MARKET ST, PORTLAND OR	314 - A7
SEWARD PARK	S JUNEAU ST & WASHINGTON BL S, SEATTLE WA	283 - H6
SEXTON MOUNTAIN MEADOWS PARK	SW SEXTON MOUNTAIN DR, BEAVERTON OR	199 - A2
SEYLYNN PARK	MTN HWY, DISTRICT OF NORTH VANCOUV BC	255 - F6
SHADLE PARK	W WELLESLEY AV, SPOKANE WA	348 - G3
SHADOW CREEK PARK	SW GULL DR & SW MCKNGBRD WY, BEAVERTON OR	199 - A3
SHADYWOOD PARK	NE 24TH AV & NE LAURA ST, HILLSBORO OR	198 - D1
SHAMROCK PARK	SE ORCHARD DR, NORTH BEND WA	176 - C5
SHAUGHNESSY PARK	21ST ST SE, AUBURN WA	182 - C2
SHAW COUNTY PARK	SHAW ISLAND, SAN JUAN CO WA	101 - C2
SHAW ISLAND COUNTY PARK	SHAW ISLAND, SAN JUAN CO WA	101 - C2
SHAWNIGAN LAKE PARK	SHAWNIGAN LAKE RD, BRITISH COLUMBIA	159 - A2
SHENANDOAH PARK	18960 SHENANDOAH DR, OREGON CITY OR	199 - D5
SHEPPERDS DELL STATE PARK	CROWN POINT HWY, MULTNOMAH CO OR	201 - A1
SHEVLIN PARK	JACK PINE SPRING RD, DESCHUTES CO OR	217 - B2
SHIELD PARK	E UPRIVER DR, SPOKANE WA	349 - J4
SHIVELY PARK	WILLIAMSPORT RD, ASTORIA WA	300 - D6
SHORE ACRES STATE PARK	CAPE ARAGO HWY, COOS CO OR	220 - B2
SHORELINE CENTER PARK	1ST AV NE & NE 185TH ST, SHORELINE WA	171 - B6
SHOREVIEW PARK	NW 175TH ST & 3RD AV NW, SHORELINE WA	171 - A6
SHOREWOOD PARK	28TH AV SW, BURIEN WA	285 - F7
SHUTE PARK	SE MAPLE ST & SE 10TH AV, HILLSBORO OR	198 - D1
SIDNEY SPIT MARINE PARK	SIDNEY ISLAND, BRITISH COLUMBIA	159 - D3
SIERRA PARK	190TH ST SW, EDMONDS WA	171 - B5
SIERRA HEIGHTS PARK	SE 100TH ST & 128TH AV SE, KING CO WA	175 - C4
SILVERCREEK PARK	DEWDNEY TRUNK RD, DISTRICT OF MISSION BC	94 - B3
SILVER CREEK COUNTY PARK	180TH PL SE & 20TH DR SE, SNOHOMISH CO WA	171 - C5
SILVERDALE PARK	DONATELLI AV, DISTRICT OF MISSION BC	94 - B3
SILVER FALLS STATE PARK	MARION CO OR	205 - D7
SILVERHORN SKI AREA	MASONIA, SHOSHONE CO ID	115 - C2
SIMMONS PARK	74TH ST E & 183RD AV E, BONNEY LAKE WA	182 - C4
SIMON FRASER HILLS PARK	DISTRICT OF BURNABY BC	156 - D4
SIMPSON PARK	OREGON COAST HWY, NORTH BEND OR	333 - F2
SINGER CREEK PARK	130 LINN AV, OREGON CITY OR	199 - D5
SISKIYOU NATIONAL FOREST	COOS CO OR	140 - C3
SISKIYOU NATIONAL FOREST	CURRY CO OR	228 - C1
SISKIYOU NATIONAL FOREST	DEL NORTE CO CA	148 - C3
SISKIYOU NATIONAL FOREST	JOSEPHINE CO OR	233 - A7
SISTERS STATE PARK	DESCHUTES CO OR	211 - D5
SIUSLAW NATIONAL FOREST	BENTON CO OR	133 - A2
SIUSLAW NATIONAL FOREST	DOUGLAS CO OR	218 - D1
SIUSLAW NATIONAL FOREST	LANE CO OR	214 - A1
SIUSLAW NATIONAL FOREST	LINCOLN CO OR	328 - J2
SIUSLAW NATIONAL FOREST	TILLAMOOK CO OR	197 - C6
SI VIEW COUNTY PARK	SE ORCHRD DR & HEALEY AV S, NORTH BEND WA	176 - C5
SIX MILE SNOWPARK	PAULINA-EAST LAKE RD, DESCHUTES CO OR	143 - A1
SIX-PLEX BALLFIELDS	ENUMCLAW BUCKLEY RD, ENUMCLAW WA	110 - C3
SIX RIVERS NATIONAL FOREST	REDWOOD HWY, DEL NORTE CO CA	148 - C3
SIXTY ACRES PARK	NE 116TH ST & 150TH AV NE, REDMOND WA	171 - D7
SKAGIT VALLEY PROVINCIAL PARK	HWY 3, BRITISH COLUMBIA	95 - B3
SKI ACRES SKI AREA	SNOQUALMIE PASS, KITTITAS CO WA	111 - A2
SKI BOWL & MULTORPOR WINTR SPORTS AREA	MOUNT HOOD HWY, CLACKAMAS CO OR	202 - A6
SKIHIST PROVINCIAL PARK	HWY 1, BRITISH COLUMBIA	95 - A1
SKULL ISLAND STATE PARK	SKULL ISLAND, SAN JUAN CO WA	101 - C2
SKYKOMISH PARK	NE STEVENS PASS HWY, KING CO WA	111 - A1
SKYKOMISH RIVER CENTENNIAL PARK	SAMS ST, MONROE WA	110 - C1
SKYLINE RIDGE PARK	STONEHAVEN DR & TROON DR, WEST LINN OR	199 - C4
SKYLINERS PARK	SW COLORADO AV, DESCHUTES CO OR	332 - B9
SKYWAY PARK	S 120TH PL & 70TH AV S, KING WA	287 - J7
SMITH PARK	OFF HWY 20, OAK HARBOR WA	167 - B3
SMITH & BYBEE LAKES PARK	N COLUMBIA BLVD, PORTLAND OR	192 - B6
SMITH COVE PARK	W GALER ST & 23RD AV W, SEATTLE WA	276 - E2
SMITH RIVER NATIONAL REC AREA	REDWOOD HWY, DEL NORTE CO CA	148 - C2
SMITH ROCK STATE PARK	DESCHUTES CO OR	212 - D3
SNAKE LAKE PARK	1919 S TYLER ST, TACOMA WA	292 - C7
SNOHOMISH COUNTY PARK	OLYMPIC VIEW DR, EDMONDS WA	171 - A5
SNOHOMISH COUNTY NORTHCREEK PARK	183RD ST SE, SNOHOMISH CO WA	171 - C5
SNOQUALMIE SUMMIT SKI AREA	SNOQUALMIE PASS, KITTITAS CO WA	111 - A2
SNOW HAVEN SKI AREA	OFF HWY 13, IDAHO CO ID	123 - C3
SOMERSET MEADOWS PARK	NW PRK VIEW & NW ASHLND, WASHINGTON CO OR	199 - A1
SOMERSET WEST PARK	NW 185TH & NW PARK VIEW, WASHINGTON CO OR	199 - A1
SOOKE MOUNTAIN PROVINCIAL PARK	HWY 14, BRITISH COLUMBIA	101 - A2
SOUNDVIEW PLAYFIELD	NW 90TH ST & 15TH AV NW, SEATTLE WA	171 - A7
SOUTH PARK	DOUGLAS ST, CITY OF VICTORIA BC	256 - G10
SOUTH PARK	S TACOMA WY & S 50TH ST, TACOMA WA	294 - C4
SOUTH BEACH STATE PARK	NEWPORT OR	206 - A5
SOUTH BURNETT LINEAR PARK	BURNETT AV S & S 3RD ST, RENTON WA	175 - C5
SOUTH CLIFF PARK	UMATILLA WY & OREGON DR, VANCOUVER WA	306 - B5
SOUTHEAST PARK	SE SALQUIST RD, GRESHAM OR	200 - B2
SOUTH END RECREATION AREA	S TYLER ST & S 66TH ST, TACOMA WA	294 - B5
SOUTHERN HEIGHTS PARK	S 120TH ST & 14TH AV S, KING WA	286 - B7
SOUTHERN LITES PARK	SOUTHERN LITES DR, CLACKAMAS CO OR	200 - A3
SOUTHGATE PARK	40TH AV S, TUKWILA WA	289 - E2
SOUTH HILL PARK	86TH AV E & 144TH ST E, PIERCE CO WA	182 - B5
SOUTH KNOLL PARK	SE MAIN ST & MARSTERS AV, ROSEBURG OR	334 - F10
SOUTH LYNNWOOD NEIGHBORHOOD PARK	61ST AV W, LYNNWOOD WA	171 - B5
SOUTHMERE VILLAGE PARK	N BLUFF RD, DISTRICT OF SURREY BC	158 - A2
SOUTH PARK BLOCKS	SW PARK AV & SW JACKSON ST, PORTLAND OR	313 - E6
SOUTH PROSPECT LAKE PARK	PROSPECT LAKE RD, DISTRICT OF SAANICH BC	159 - B5
SOUTH SURREY ATHLETIC PARK	24TH AV, DISTRICT OF SURREY BC	158 - A2
SOUTH TALENT PARK	TALENT AV, TALENT OR	234 - C3
SOUTH VIEW PARK	W MARINE VIEW DR, EVERETT WA	171 - C1
SOUTH VILLAGE PARK	SALEM OR	324 - J4
SOUTHWEST PARK	W POWELL BLVD, GRESHAM OR	200 - A2
SOUTH WHIDBEY ISLAND STATE PARK	S SMUGGLERS COVE RD, ISLAND CO WA	167 - C7
SOUTHWOOD PARK	SW PAMELA ST, LAKE OSWEGO OR	199 - B3
SPANAWAY COUNTY PARK	MILITARY RD & BRESSMNN BL S, PIERCE CO WA	181 - D5
SPECTACLE LAKE PROVINCIAL PARK	WILLIS POINT RD, BRITISH COLUMBIA	159 - A4
SPENCER BUTTE PARK	RIDGELINE TR, LANE CO OR	329 - J14
SPENCER ISLAND PARK	4TH ST SE, SNOHOMISH WA	265 - J2
SPENCER SPIT STATE PARK	LOPEZ ISLAND, SAN JUAN CO WA	160 - A5
SPERLING PARK	DISTRICT OF BURNABY BC	156 - D4
SPHALLIE ILLAHEE PARK	ROSEPARK DR & LUPINE CT, WEST LINN OR	199 - C4
SPINNEY HOMESTEAD PARK	119TH PL NE, KIRKLAND WA	175 - C1
SPIRITBROOK PARK	151ST AV NE & NE 66TH ST, REDMOND WA	175 - D1
SPIRITRIDGE PARK	161ST AV SE & SE 33RD PL, BELLEVUE WA	175 - D3
SPORTS COMMUNITY PARK	SE PALMQUIST RD, GRESHAM OR	200 - B2
SPORTSMAN PARK	PACIFIC HWY & HIGHLND AV, JOSEPHINE CO OR	229 - B4
SPORTSMAN PARK	STEVENS PASS HWY, SULTAN WA	110 - C1
SPOUT SPRINGS SKI AREA	WESTON-ELGIN HWY, UNION CO OR	130 - A1
SPRING BEACH PARK	SW SPRING BEACH RD, KING CO WA	174 - C7
SPRINGBROOK GREENBELT	SW 43RD ST, KENT WA	291 - J1
SPRINGBROOK PARK	200TH ST SE, RENTON WA	175 - C6
SPRINGBROOK PARK	DIANE DR, LAKE OSWEGO OR	320 - B5
SPRING HILLS PARK	BELLEVUE WY NE, BELLEVUE WA	175 - C2
SPRING LAKE/LAKE DESIRE PARK	W SPRING LAKE DR, KING CO WA	175 - D6
SPRING MEADOW PARK	VITTORIA WY & PACIFIC HWY 99W, NEWBERG OR	198 - D5
SPRINGWATER TRAIL CORRIDOR	PORTLAND TO BORING, CLACKAMAS OR	319 - E7
SPRINGWATER TRAIL CORRIDOR	PORTLAND TO BORING, GRESHAM OR	200 - A2
SPRINGWATER TRAIL CORRIDOR	PORTLAND TO BORING, MILWAUKIE OR	199 - D3
SPRINGWATER TRAIL CORRIDOR	PORTLAND TO BORING, PORTLAND OR	319 - G6
SPRINGWOOD PARK	SE 276TH PL, KENT WA	175 - C7
SPRUCE PARK	21ST AV E & E FIR ST, SEATTLE WA	278 - C6
SPRUCE PARK	36TH AV W & 170TH ST SW, LYNNWOOD WA	171 - B5
SPYGLASS PARK	NW WEST UNION RD, WASHINGTON CO OR	199 - A1
SQUAK MOUNTAIN ST PARK NATURAL AREA	SQUAK MOUNTAIN RD, KING CO WA	175 - D4
SQUAK/TIGER MOUNTAIN CORRIDOR	ISSAQUAH HOBART RD & SE 113TH, KING CO WA	176 - A4
SQUAW BUTTE EXPERIMENT STATION	SQUAW BUTTE RD, HARNEY CO OR	144 - C1
SQUINT LAKE PARK	DISTRICT OF BURNABY BC	156 - D4
STADACONA PARK	BEGBIE ST, CITY OF VICTORIA BC	257 - A9
STAFFORD PARK	569 HOLMES LN, OREGON CITY OR	199 - D5
STAGLEAP PROVINCIAL PARK	HWY 3, BRITISH COLUMBIA	106 - C1
STAN HEDWALL PARK	INT 5 & RICE RD, CHEHALIS WA	299 - E14
STANLEY PARK	SE STANLEY AV & SE HARLW ST, MILWAUKIE OR	199 - D3
STANLEY PARK	VANCOUVER BC	254 - D6
STANLEY PLAYGROUND	S 19TH ST & HOSMER ST, TACOMA WA	293 - F6
STARKER PARK	45TH ST, CORVALLIS OR	327 - C12
STARKEY EXPERIMENTAL FOREST	OFF UKIAH-HILGARD HWY, UNION CO OR	129 - C2
STARR BOWL WINTER SPORTS AREA	JOHN DAY-BURNS HWY, GRANT CO OR	137 - A2
STARVATION CREEK STATE PARK	COLUMBIA RIVER HWY, HOOD RIVER CO OR	195 - B5
STEAMBOAT LANDING PARK	17TH ST & HWY 14, WASHOUGAL WA	193 - C7
STEELE PARK	248TH ST, TOWNSHIP OF LANGLEY BC	158 - D1
STEEL LAKE PARK	S 312TH ST & 28TH AV S, FEDERAL WAY WA	182 - B1
STEILACOOM LAKE COUNTY PARK	72ND AV SW & FOSTER ST SW, LAKEWOOD WA	181 - C4
STEINBRUECK, VICTOR PARK	LENORA ST & PIKE PL, SEATTLE WA	277 - H5
STELLA OLSON PARK	NW WASHINGTON ST, SHERWOOD OR	199 - A4
STEVENS PARK	CITY OF RICHMOND BC	156 - A7
STEWART GLEN BRNT BRDG CK GRNWY	NW BRNIE DR & NW LINCOLN AV, VANCOUVER WA	192 - C5
STEWART HEIGHTS PLAYFIELD	E 60TH ST & E B ST, TACOMA WA	295 - H5
STEWART PARK	STEWART ST, ROSEBURG OR	334 - D5
STEWART PARK	WISHKAH ST, ABERDEEN WA	178 - B7
STEWART PARK-FIR GROVE SECTION	W STEWART PARK DR, ROSEBURG OR	334 - D7
STOCKER PARK	OATFIELD RD, GLADSTONE OR	199 - D4
STONEMIST PARK	SW RIGERT & SW 170TH, WASHINGTON CO OR	199 - A2
STONERIDGE PARK	19489 SW 68TH AV, TUALATIN OR	199 - B4
STONEY CREEK PARK	DISTRICT OF BURNABY BC	156 - D4
STRATFORD PARK	DISTRICT OF BURNABY BC	156 - D4
STRATHAVEN PARK	DISTRICT OF NORTH VANCOUV BC	156 - D3
STRATHCONA PARK	HWY 19, BRITISH COLUMBIA	92 - A2
STRATHCONA PARK	VENABLES ST, VANCOUVER BC	255 - A11
STRATHCONA PROVINCIAL PARK	HWY 19, BRITISH COLUMBIA	92 - A2
STRIDE PARK	DISTRICT OF BURNABY BC	156 - D5
STUHR CENTER/HALL PARK	SW HALL BLVD, BEAVERTON OR	199 - B2
SUCCOR CREEK STATE RECREATION AREA	SUCCOR CREEK RD, MALHEUR CO OR	147 - A1
SUCIA ISLAND STATE PARK	SUCIA ISLAND, SAN JUAN CO WA	101 - C2
SULLIVAN PARK	152ND ST, DISTRICT OF SURREY BC	157 - A7
SULLIVAN PARK	N SULLIVAN RD, SPOKANE WA	351 - B6
SUMAS PARK	DISTRICT OF BURNABY BC	156 - D4
SUMAS MOUNTAIN PROVINCIAL PARK	TRANS CANADA HWY, BRITISH COLUMBIA	94 - B3
SUMMERCREST PARK	SW RIGERT RD, WASHINGTON CO OR	199 - A2
SUMMERLAKE PARK	SW GLACIER LILY CIR, TIGARD OR	199 - B3
SUMMERS, COLONEL PARK	SE TAYLOR ST & SE 20TH AV, PORTLAND OR	313 - J6

PNW

INDEX

FEATURE NAME	City State	Page-Grid
SUMMIT PARK	FINLAYSON ST, CITY OF VICTORIA BC	256 - H6
SUMMIT NORTH PARK	SE 63RD ST, BELLEVUE WA	175 - D3
SUMPTER PARK	SALEM OR	324 - G7
SUNBURST PARK	HUNTER WY, WEST LINN OR	199 - C4
SUNCREST PARK	DISTRICT OF BURNABY BC	156 - C5
SUNHEIGHTS PARK	SUNHEIGHTS DR, DISTRICT OF LANGFORD BC	159 - B7
SUN LAKES STATE PARK	HWY 17, GRANT CO WA	112 - C2
SUNNY HILLS PARK	14TH ST NW & R ST NW, AUBURN WA	182 - B1
SUNNYSIDE BEACH PARK	CHAMBERS CREEK RD, STEILACOOM WA	181 - C4
SUNNYSIDE SCHOOL PARK	SE 34TH AV & SE TAYLOR ST, PORTLAND OR	314 - A6
SUNRISE PARK	460 SW 21ST ST, TROUTDALE OR	200 - B1
SUNRISE PARK	HEYWOOD ST, CITY OF NORTH VANCOUVER BC	255 - E6
SUNRISE PARK	THURSTON ST, ALBANY OR	326 - D10
SUNRISE PARK	W LAKE SAMMAMISH PKWY SE, KING CO WA	175 - D3
SUNRISE BEACH COUNTY PARK	MOLLER DR NW, PIERCE CO WA	174 - C7
SUNSET PARK	BITTNER ST, WEST LINN OR	199 - D4
SUNSET PARK	MOUNT LEHMAN RD, DISTRICT OF MATSQUI BC	102 - B1
SUNSET PARK	NW TRAIL ST, WASHINGTON CO OR	199 - B1
SUNSET PARK	RESEARCH WY, CORVALLIS OR	327 - C12
SUNSET BAY STATE PARK	CAPE ARAGO HWY, COOS CO OR	220 - B1
SUNSET BEACH PARK	PACIFIC ST, VANCOUVER BC	254 - E10
SUNSET COUNTY PARK	E LAKE STEVENS & 3RD NE, SNOHOMISH CO WA	171 - D2
SUNSET COURT PARK	HARRINGTON PL NE, RENTON WA	175 - C4
SUNSET HIGHWAY STATE PARK	CLATSOP CO OR	125 - A1
SUNSET HILL VIEWPOINT PARK	NW 77TH ST & 34TH AV NW, SEATTLE WA	272 - D2
SUNSET RAVINE PARK	135TH AV SE, BELLEVUE WA	175 - C3
SUTHERLAND MEADOWS PARK	SW BASELINE RD, WASHINGTON CO OR	199 - A1
SWAMPY LAKES SNOWPARK	CENTURY DRIVE HWY, DESCHUTES CO OR	216 - D4
SWANSON PARK	PACIFIC BLVD & MONTGOMERY ST, ALBANY OR	326 - D8
SWAUK PASS SNO-PARK	BLEWETT PASS, KITTITAS CO WA	238 - B6
SWEETBRIAR PARK	3501 SE EVANS AV, TROUTDALE OR	200 - B1
SWENSSON PARK	OFF HWY 1A, DISTRICT OF MATSQUI BC	102 - B1
SWIFT SHORE PARK	OSTMAN RD, WEST LINN OR	199 - C5
TAKENA PARK	LAWNRIDGE ST, ALBANY OR	326 - B8
TALBOT HILL PARK	S 19TH ST & TALBOT RD S, RENTON WA	175 - C5
TALEISEN PARK	SW GLENN CT, BEAVERTON OR	199 - B2
TALISMAN PARK	1210 WILLIAMINA AV, FOREST GROVE OR	198 - B1
TAMARACK SKI AREA	OFF HWY 8, LATAH CO ID	123 - A1
TAM O SHANTER PARK	173RD AV NE, BELLEVUE WA	175 - D2
TAM O SHANTER PARK	TAM O SHANTER WY, KELSO WA	303 - E9
TANTULUS PARK	DISTRICT OF W VANCOUVER BC	156 - A2
TAPIOLA PARK	MARINE DR, ASTORIA WA	300 - B6
TARRYBROOKE PARK	S DOGWOOD ST & S 4TH AV, CORNELIUS OR	198 - C1
TASHKENT PARK	HARVARD AV E & E MERCER ST, SEATTLE WA	278 - B4
TATLOW PARK	VANCOUVER BC	254 - B11
TAYLOR PARK	1ST AV & PARK ST, DUVALL WA	110 - C1
TELOH CALAPOOIA PARK	PACIFIC BLVD & 53RD AV, ALBANY OR	326 - B13
TEMPLETON PARK	GARDEN DR, VANCOUVER BC	255 - C11
TEMPLIN BEACH PARK	LANE AV, ROSEBURG OR	334 - F7
TEN MILE SNOWPARK	PAULINA-EAST LAKE RD, DESCHUTES CO OR	143 - A1
TERMINAL PARK	12TH ST SE & C ST SE, AUBURN WA	182 - C1
TERRACE PARK	10333 NE 67TH ST, KIRKLAND WA	175 - C1
TERRACE CREEK PARK	52ND & 53RD AV W, MOUNTLAKE TERRACE WA	171 - B6
TERRACE RIDGE PARK	242ND ST SW, MOUNTLAKE TERRACE WA	171 - B6
TERRACE VIEW PARK	E 24TH AV, OPPORTUNITY WA	351 - A11
TERRAHUE PARK	METCHOSIN RD, CITY OF COLWOOD BC	159 - B7
TERRA LINDA PARK	NW 135TH AV, WASHINGTON CO OR	199 - B1
TERWILLIGER PARK	SW TERWILLIGER BLVD, PORTLAND OR	316 - D3
THETIS LAKE PARK	TRANS CANADA HWY, BRITISH COLUMBIA	159 - B6
THOM PARK	SE 9TH ST & SE SPRUCE CT, GRESHAM OR	200 - B2
THOMAS FRANCIS PARK	PROSPECT LAKE RD, DISTRICT OF SAANICH BC	256 - A1
THOMAS TEASDALE PARK	S 23RD ST & WILLIAMS AV S, RENTON WA	175 - C5
THOMPSON PARK	NE 138TH PL & NE THOMPSON ST, PORTLAND OR	200 - A1
THOMPSON PARK	TAYLOR ST & CNNGHT DR, PORT COQUITLAM BC	157 - B5
THORNTON A SULLIVAN PARK	SILVER LAKE RD, EVERETT WA	171 - C4
THORNTON CREEK PARK	10600 ROOSEVELT WY NE, SEATTLE WA	171 - B7
THREE FORKS PARK	42000 SE REINIG RD, KING CO WA	176 - C4
THUNDERBIRD PARK	DOUGLAS & BELLVLLE, CITY OF VICTORIA BC	256 - G10
TIBBETTS VALLEY PARK	SE NEWPORT WY & 12TH AV NW, ISSAQUAH WA	175 - D4
TIDEMAN JOHNSON PARK	SE 37TH AV & SE TENINO ST, PORTLAND OR	318 - B7
TIFFANY PARK	KIRKLAND AV SE, RENTON WA	175 - C5
TIGER MOUNTAIN STATE PARK	OFF I-90, KING CO WA	176 - A4
TIGER TREE PARK	NE 149TH AV & NE 85TH CIR, CLARK CO WA	193 - A5
TILLAMOOK STATE FOREST	TILLAMOOK CO OR	191 - D5
TILLAMOOK STATE FOREST	WASHINGTON CO OR	198 - A1
TILLICUM PARK	OFF HWY 101, FORKS WA	169 - D1
TILLICUM PARK	TRANS CANADA HWY, DISTRICT OF SAANICH BC	256 - D4
TIMBERHILL PARK	WALNUT BLVD, CORVALLIS OR	327 - E6
TIMBERLAKE PARK	LK SAMMSH PKWY & 182ND AV SE, KING CO WA	175 - D3
TIMBERLINE COVINGTON PARK	196TH AV SE, KING CO WA	182 - D1
TIMBER LINN MEMORIAL PARK	PRICE RD, ALBANY OR	326 - H7
TIPPERARY PARK	NEW WESTMINSTER BC	156 - D5
TITLOW BEACH PARK	6TH AV, TACOMA WA	181 - C2
TOLLBRIDGE PARK	CASCADE LOCKS OR	194 - D6
TOLL BRIDGE COUNTY PARK	HOOD RIVER CO OR	202 - C2
TOLMIE STATE PARK	SANDY POINT RD NE, THURSTON CO WA	181 - A5
TOMAHAWK SKI BOWL	LAKE OF THE WOODS HWY, KLAMATH CO OR	231 - A6
TONKIN PARK	WILLAMS AV S & S 4TH ST, RENTON WA	175 - C5
TOPAZ PARK	FINLAYSON ST, CITY OF VICTORIA BC	256 - H7
TOT LOTS	7408 S CEDAR ST, TACOMA WA	294 - D7
TOUCHET SNO-PARK	N FORK TOUCHET RIVER RD, COLUMBIA CO WA	122 - B3
TOU VELLE STATE PARK	AGATE RD & TOU VELLE RD, JACKSON CO OR	230 - C6
TOWN CENTER PARK	SW PARKWAY AV, WILSONVILLE OR	199 - B5
TOWN CENTRE PARK	MURRAY ST, PORT MOODY BC	157 - A4
TOWNSEND PARK	WOLFE & ASHWELL, DIST OF CHILLIWACK BC	94 - C3
TRACHSEL MEADOWS PARK	SW JOHNSON ST, WASHINGTON CO OR	199 - A2
TRACY OWEN STATION PARK	NE 175TH ST & 61ST AV NE, KING CO WA	171 - B6
TRAFALGAR PARK	KING GEORGE TERR, DISTRICT OF OAK BAY BC	257 - C12
TRANQUIL NATURE PARK	BROWN RD, WILSONVILLE OR	199 - B5
TRENTON PARK	N HAMLIN AV & N TRENTON ST, PORTLAND OR	308 - D3
TREVLAC PARK	PROSPECT LAKE RD, DISTRICT OF SAANICH BC	159 - C5
TRIANGLE PARK	OAK ST & 15TH AV, MILTON WA	182 - B2
TRILLIUM PARK	HARDY CRES, DISTRICT OF NORTH VANCOUV BC	255 - J5
TROUTDALE COMMUNITY PARK	E HIST COLUMBIA RIVER HWY, TROUTDALE OR	200 - B1
TRYON CREEK STATE PARK	SW TERWILLIGER BLVD, PORTLAND OR	321 - E3
TUALATIN COMMONS	7880 SW NYBERG ST, TUALATIN OR	199 - B4
TUALATIN COMMUNITY PARK	8515 SW TUALATIN RD, TUALATIN OR	199 - B4
TUALATIN HILLS NATURE PARK	SW 170TH AV, BEAVERTON OR	199 - A2
TUALATIN HILLS PARKS & REC DIST CTR	SW WALKER RD & NW 158TH AV, BEAVERTON OR	199 - A1
TUALATIN RIVER PARK	SW MICHAEL DR, WEST LINN OR	199 - C5
TUCANNON GAME RESERVE	COLUMBIA CO WA	122 - B2
TUKWILA PARK	65TH AV S & S 153RD ST, TUKWILA WA	289 - H4
TUMALO STATE PARK	DESCHUTES CO OR	217 - B1
TUNISON PARK	ALLEN ST, BENTON CO OR	327 - F12
TURNER CREEK PARK	SE CAMWAL DR, HILLSBORO OR	198 - D1
TURN ISLAND STATE PARK	TURN ISLAND, SAN JUAN CO WA	101 - C2
TURNKEY PARK	100TH AV SE & S 232ND ST, KENT WA	175 - C6
TUSCANY RIDGE PARK	84TH ST NE, MARYSVILLE WA	168 - D7
TWANOH STATE PARK	HWY 106, MASON CO WA	173 - C7
TWENTY FIVE MILE CREEK STATE PARK	SHADY PASS RD & HALE RD, CHELAN CO WA	112 - A1
TWIN CEDARS PARK	SW SHELTON ST, WASHINGTON CO OR	199 - A2
TWIN HARBORS BEACH STATE PARK	GRAYS HARBOR CO WA	183 - B2
TWIN PONDS PARK	N 155TH ST & CORLISS AV N, SHORELINE WA	171 - B7
TWIN RIVERS COUNTY PARK	TALCOTT ST & RT#-530, SNOHOMISH CO WA	168 - D5
TYNEHEAD REGIONAL PARK	176TH AV & 96TH AV, DISTRICT OF SURREY BC	157 - B6
UMATILLA NATIONAL FOREST	ASOTIN CO WA	122 - C3
UMATILLA NATIONAL FOREST	GRANT CO OR	129 - B7
UMATILLA NATIONAL FOREST	UNION CO OR	130 - A1
UMATILLA NATIONAL FOREST	WALLOWA CO OR	122 - B3
UMATILLA NATIONAL FOREST	WHEELER CO OR	128 - C3
UMPQUA PARK	FREAR ST, DOUGLAS CO OR	334 - E10
UMPQUA LIGHTHOUSE STATE PARK	DOUGLAS CO OR	218 - B3
UMPQUA NATIONAL FOREST	DOUGLAS CO OR	222 - B4
UMPQUA NATIONAL FOREST	LANE CO OR	133 - C3
UNDERHILL PLAYGROUND	E HARTSON AV, SPOKANE WA	349 - E10
UNION PARK	PRUNE ST & PLUM ST, MEDFORD OR	336 - B13
UNIVERSITY PARK	9009 N FOSS AV, PORTLAND OR	308 - C3
UNTHANK PARK	510 N SHAVER ST, PORTLAND OR	313 - F1
UPLANDS GREENBELT	FRAGER RD & S 226TH ST, KENT WA	291 - F6
UPLANDS PARK	LANSDOWNE RD, DISTRICT OF OAK BAY BC	257 - D7
UPPER BEAR CREEK	PARADISE LAKE RD, KING CO WA	171 - D6
UPPER PRIEST LAKE SCENIC AREA	OFF EAST SHORE RD, BONNER CO ID	107 - A1
UPPER THREE CREEK SNO-PARK	THREE CREEKS LAKE RD, DESCHUTES CO OR	211 - C7
VALE PARK	SW GLENEDEN DR, BEAVERTON OR	199 - A2
VALLEY MEMORIAL PARK	KING ST, CARNATION WA	176 - B2
VALLEY OF THE ROGUE STATE PARK	N RIVER RD & PACIFIC HWY, JACKSON CO OR	229 - D6
VALLEY RIDGE PARK	S 184TH ST & 48TH AV S, SEATAC WA	291 - F1
VAN AALST PARK	4TH ST & 13TH AV, KIRKLAND WA	175 - C1
VAN ASSELT PLAYGROUND	S MYRTLE PL & BEACON AV S, SEATTLE WA	286 - D1
VANCE PARK	SE 182ND AV & SE MAIN ST, GRESHAM OR	200 - A1
VANCOUVER PARK	NE FOURTH PLAIN BLVD, VANCOUVER WA	307 - F2
VANCOUVER LAKE PARK	HWY 501, CLARK CO WA	304 - A1
VAN DORENS LANDING PARK	RUSSELL RD, KENT WA	291 - F5
VAN FLEET PARK	FLINT AV & TOPEKA LN, VANCOUVER WA	306 - E5
VAN HORN PARK	FREEMAN RD & ROSE VLY DR, CENTRL POINT OR	230 - C7
VANIER PARK	CORNWALL AV, VANCOUVER BC	254 - E11
VANTREIGHT PARK	LEYNS RD, DISTRICT OF SAANICH BC	159 - D5
VASA PARK	W LAKE SAMMAMISH PKWY SE, KING CO WA	175 - D3
VASHON SPORTMENS CLUB	SINGER RD SW & SW CEMETERY RD, KING CO WA	174 - D6
VASSAULT PARK	N 37TH ST, TACOMA WA	181 - C2
VENDLA PARK	SW VENDLA PARK LN, WASHINGTON CO OR	199 - A2
VENTURA PARK	SE 115TH AV & SE STARK ST, PORTLAND OR	315 - J6
VERDE RIDGE PARK	73RD AV NE, MARYSVILLE WA	171 - D1
VETS MEMORIAL PARK	KLAMATH AV, KLAMATH FALLS OR	338 - D8
VETERANS MEMORIAL PARK	236TH & 58TH W, MOUNTLAKE TERRACE WA	171 - B6
VETERANS TRIANGLE PARK	ENUMCLAW BUCKLEY RD, ENUMCLAW WA	110 - C3
VICTIM ISLAND STATE PARK	VICTIM ISLAND, SAN JUAN CO WA	101 - C2
VICTORIA PARK	CHARLES ST, VANCOUVER BC	255 - B11
VICTORIA PARK	KEITH RD, CITY OF NORTH VANCOUVER BC	255 - B5
VICTORIA WEST PARK	WILSON ST, CITY OF VICTORIA BC	256 - F8
VICTORY PARK	NEW WESTMINSTER BC	156 - D5
VICTORY HEIGHTS PLAYGROUND	19TH AV NE & NE 106TH ST, SEATTLE WA	171 - B7
VIENTO STATE PARK	COLUMBIA RIVER HWY, HOOD RIVER CO OR	195 - B5
VIETNAM VETERANS MEMORIAL PARK	SW KNIGHT BLVD, PORTLAND OR	312 - B7
VIEWLYNN PARK	VIEWLYNN DR, DISTRICT OF NORTH VANCOUV BC	255 - F3
VIEWPOINT PARK	12TH AV S & S FOREST ST, SEATTLE WA	282 - B3
VIEWPOINT PARK	NE 24TH ST & 180TH AV NE, REDMOND WA	175 - D2
VIEWPOINT PARK	VASHON HWY SW, KING CO WA	174 - D7
VIEW RIDGE PLAYGROUND	NE 70TH ST & 45TH AV NE, SEATTLE WA	275 - F3
VIKING FIELD	5TH ST SW & 5TH AV SW, PUYALLUP WA	182 - B4
VILLAGE GREEN PARK	CONIFER BLVD, CORVALLIS OR	207 - B5
VINZENZ LAUSMANN STATE PARK	POST CANYON DR, HOOD RIVER CO OR	195 - C5
VIOLA OURSLER PARK	E MARINE VIEW DR & 9TH ST, EVERETT WA	171 - C1
VIRETTA PARK	EVERGREEN PL & 39TH AV E, SEATTLE WA	279 - F4
VIRGINIA MEISSNER SNOWPARK	CENTURY DRIVE HWY, DESCHUTES CO OR	216 - D4
VISTA BROOK PARK	SW BECKER & SW 86TH, WASHINGTON CO OR	199 - B2
VOLUNTEER PARK	1554 15TH AV E, SEATTLE WA	278 - B2
VOLUNTEER PARK	KEY PENINSULA HWY & 58TH ST, PIERCE CO WA	181 - A1
WAIT PARK	N GRANT ST & NW 4TH AV, CANBY OR	199 - C6
WALBRAN PARK	KING GEORGE TERR, DISTRICT OF OAK BAY BC	257 - B11
WALDO LAKE SNO-PARK	HWY 58, LANE CO OR	142 - B1
WALKER PARK	SALEM OR	323 - C13
WALKER FIELD PARK	SW WALKER & SW 121ST, WASHINGTON CO OR	199 - B2
WALLACE FALLS STATE PARK	SNOHOMISH CO WA	110 - C1
WALLACE PARK	NW 25TH AV & NW RALEIGH ST, PORTLAND OR	312 - C4
WALLACE SWAMP CREEK PARK	NE 195TH ST & 68TH AV NE, KING CO WA	171 - B6
WALLOWA LAKE STATE PARK	OFF JOSEPH-WALLOWA LK HWY, WALLOWA CO OR	130 - C2
WALLOWA-WHITMAN NATIONAL FOREST	BAKER CO OR	138 - A1
WALLOWA-WHITMAN NATIONAL FOREST	GRANT CO OR	137 - C1
WALLOWA-WHITMAN NATIONAL FOREST	IDAHO CO ID	123 - C3
WALLOWA-WHITMAN NATIONAL FOREST	UMATILLA CO OR	129 - B2

FEATURE NAME	City State	Page-Grid
WALLOWA-WHITMAN NATIONAL FOREST	UNION CO OR	130 - A3
WALLOWA-WHITMAN NATIONAL FOREST	WALLOWA CO OR	131 - A2
WALNUT PARK	WALNUT BLVD, CORVALLIS OR	327 - C6
WALNUT STREET PARK	SE WALNUT ST & SE 18TH AV, HILLSBORO OR	198 - D1
WALTER M HOLLERBACH PARK	90TH AV SE & SE 45TH ST, MERCER ISLAND WA	175 - C3
WALUGA PARK	DOUGLAS WY, LAKE OSWEGO OR	320 - A6
WANAPUM RECREATION AREA	KITTITAS CO WA	120 - B1
WANOGA SNOWMOBILE SNOWPARK	CENTURY DRIVE HWY, DESCHUTES CO OR	216 - D4
WAPATO LAKE PARK	WAPATO LAKE DR, TACOMA WA	295 - F6
WARD MEMORIAL STATE PARK	CANYON CO ID	147 - B1
WARNER CANYON SKI AREA	WARNER HWY, LAKE CO OR	152 - A2
WARNER LOAT PARK	DISTRICT OF BURNABY BC	156 - D5
WASHINGTON PARK	FILLMORE AV, CORVALLIS OR	327 - G9
WASHINGTON PARK	SUNSET AV, ANACORTES WA	259 - A4
WASHINGTON PARK	SW KINGSTON DR, PORTLAND OR	312 - B7
WASHINGTON PARK	WASHINGTON ST & S MILLER ST, WENATCHEE WA	238 - D4
WASHINGTON PARK	W CHERRY ST, WALLA WALLA WA	344 - J7
WASHINGTON PARK ARBORETUM	2300 ARBORETUM DR E, SEATTLE WA	278 - D2
WASHINGTON SCHOOL PARK	E 31ST & R ST, VANCOUVER WA	305 - J3
WATER PARK	N CLARK ST, CORNELIUS OR	198 - C1
WATER BOARD PARK	921 WATERBOARD PARK RD, OREGON CITY OR	199 - D5
WATERFRONT PARK	ALASKAN WY, SEATTLE WA	277 - J6
WATERFRONT PARK	COLUMBIA WY, VANCOUVER WA	305 - G6
WATERSHED PARK	4500 110TH AV NE, KIRKLAND WA	175 - C2
WATERSHED PARK	DISTRICT OF DELTA BC	156 - D7
WATER TOWER PARK	SE 40TH AV & SE HARVEY ST, MILWAUKIE OR	199 - D3
WATERWORKS PARK	E RESERVE ST, VANCOUVER WA	305 - J4
WAUCOMA PARK	OAK AV, HOOD RIVER OR	195 - D5
WAVERLY PARK	WAVERLY WY & MARKET ST, KIRKLAND WA	175 - C1
WAVERLY BEACH PARK	633 WAVERLY WY, KIRKLAND WA	175 - C1
WEAVER CREEK PROVINCIAL PARK	MORRIS VALLEY RD, BRITISH COLUMBIA	94 - C3
WEBER PARK	7000 SE HARMONY RD, MILWAUKIE OR	199 - D3
WEBSTER PARK	2ND ST & EUNICE ST, PORT ANGELES WA	261 - F5
WEEDIN PARK	1312 SE BEAVER CREEK LN, TROUTDALE OR	200 - B1
W E JOHNSON PARK	HALL RD, RICHLAND WA	340 - C14
WELCOME PARK	NE REDMOND WY & 140TH AV NE, REDMOND WA	175 - C1
WELDWOOD PARK	LEBANON OR	133 - C1
WELLINGTON PARK	NE 66TH AV & NE MASON ST, PORTLAND OR	314 - E1
WELLINGTON PARK	WELLINGTON & LINCOLN, PORT COQUITLAM BC	157 - B4
WENAHA-TUCANNON WILDERNESS AREA	COLUMBIA CO WA	122 - B3
WENATCHEE NATIONAL FOREST	CHELAN CO WA	238 - A3
WENATCHEE NATIONAL FOREST	KITTITAS CO WA	240 - A3
WENBERG STATE PARK	E LAKE GOODWIN RD, SNOHOMISH CO WA	168 - B6
WEOWNA BEACH COUNTY PARK	1400 168TH AV SE, BELLEVUE WA	175 - D3
WESBURN PARK	DISTRICT OF BURNABY BC	156 - C5
WEST BAY PARK	DISTRICT OF W VANCOUVER BC	156 - A3
WESTCREST PARK	SW CLOVERDALE ST, SEATTLE WA	285 - J3
WEST DELTA PARK	N VICTORY AV, PORTLAND OR	308 - D3
WEST FENWICK PARK	REITH RD & 38TH AV S, KENT WA	175 - B7
WESTHAVEN STATE PARK	HARBOR ST, WESTPORT WA	298 - E11
WESTHILL PARK	GLENAYRE DR, PORT MOODY BC	157 - A4
WESTHOLM PARK	ROGUE RIVER LP & HIGH, GRANTS PASS OR	335 - D9
WESTLAKE PARK	MELROSE ST, LAKE OSWEGO OR	320 - A5
WEST LANGLEY PARK	208TH ST & 93RD AV, TOWNSHP OF LANGLEY BC	157 - C6
WEST MAGNOLIA PLAYGROUND	34TH AV W, SEATTLE WA	276 - D1
WEST MILTON PARK	PORTER WY & KENT ST, MILTON WA	182 - B2
WEST MONTLAKE PARK	W PARK DR & E SHELBY ST, SEATTLE WA	274 - C7
WESTMORELAND PARK	SE MCLOUGHLIN BLVD, PORTLAND OR	317 - J6
WESTOVER PARK	DOVERCOURT RD, DISTRICT OF N VANCOUVER BC	255 - G2
WEST POWELLHURST PARK	SE DIVISION ST, PORTLAND OR	319 - J1
WESTRIDGE PARK	DISTRICT OF W VANCOUVER BC	156 - A3
WESTRIDGE PARK	WESTRIDGE DR, LAKE OSWEGO OR	199 - C4
WEST-SELLS PARK	FRANCIS ST, DISTRICT OF BURNABY BC	255 - G11
WEST SHAWNIGAN LAKE PARK	SHAWNIGAN LAKE RD, BRITISH COLUMBIA	159 - A2
WESTSIDE PARK	156TH AV NE, REDMOND WA	175 - D1
WEST SLOPE PARK	SW CANYON RD, WASHINGTON CO OR	199 - B2
WEST SYLVAN PARK	SW 81ST AV & SW W SLOPE DR, WASH CO OR	199 - B2
WEST WALUGA PARK	SW WALUGA DR & OAKRDGE RD, LAKE OSWEGO OR	199 - B3
WESTWOOD HIGHLANDS NEIGHBORHOOD PARK	HIGHLAND DR, BELLEVUE WA	175 - C3
WHATCOM FALLS PARK	SILVER BEACH RD, BELLINGHAM WA	258 - J6
WHIPPLE CREEK PARK	NW 31ST AV & NW 179TH ST, CLARK CO WA	192 - C4
WHISPERING WOODS PARK	SW 192ND & SW VISTA, WASHINGTON CO OR	199 - A1
WHITE CENTER PARK	15TH AV SW & SW 102ND ST, KING WA	285 - H5
WHITE CENTER HEIGHTS PARK	8TH AV SW & SW 102ND ST, KING WA	285 - H5
WHITE PASS SKI AREA	WHITE PASS, LEWIS CO WA	119 - A2
WHITE PASS X COUNTRY SKI AREA	WHITE PASS, YAKIMA CO WA	119 - A2
WHITE RIVER PARK	N RIVER AV, BUCKLEY WA	110 - C3
WHITNEY BRIDGE PARK	SE GREEN VALLEY RD, KING CO WA	182 - D2
WHITTIER PARK	CONTRA CSTA AV & ELM TREE LN, FIRCREST WA	294 - A1
WHYTECLIFF PARK	DISTRICT OF W VANCOUVER BC	156 - A2
WIARD PARK	WIARD ST, ALTAMONT OR	339 - A11
WICKENDON PARK	DISTRICT OF N VANCOUVER BC	156 - D3
WIGGUMS HOLLOW PARK	10TH ST & POPLAR ST, EVERETT WA	171 - C1
WILBURTON HILL PARK	128TH AV NE, BELLEVUE WA	175 - C2
WILCOX PARK	196TH ST SW, LYNNWOOD WA	171 - B5
WILDERNESS PARK	CLARK ST, WEST LINN OR	199 - D4
WILDHORSE PARK	SW WILDHORSE WY, BEAVERTON OR	199 - A3
WILD RIVER EXPERIMENTAL FOREST	SKAMANIA CO WA	194 - B2
WILDWOOD PARK	102ND AV SE & SE 3RD ST, BELLEVUE WA	175 - C2
WILDWOOD PARK	23RD AV S & S 300TH ST, FEDERAL WAY WA	182 - B1
WILDWOOD PARK	23RD AV SE & 9TH ST SE, PUYALLUP WA	182 - B4
WILDWOOD PARK	N DIVISION ST, WALLA WALLA WA	345 - C7
WILDWOOD MINI PARK	SW MAVERICK TER, BEAVERTON OR	199 - A2
WILKESON CREEK COUNTY PARK	JOHNS RD, PIERCE CO WA	182 - D5
WILLAMETTE PARK	12TH ST & VOLPP ST, WEST LINN OR	199 - C5
WILLAMETTE PARK	GOODNIGHT AV, CORVALLIS OR	327 - H13
WILLAMETTE PARK	SW MACADAM AV & SW NEVADA ST, PORTLAND OR	317 - F5
WILLAMETTE MISSION STATE PARK	MARION CO OR	204 - D3
WILLAMETTE MOORAGE PARK	SW MACADAM AV & SW MILES ST, PORTLAND OR	317 - F6
WILLAMETTE NATIONAL FOREST	DOUGLAS CO OR	223 - B1
WILLAMETTE NATIONAL FOREST	LANE CO OR	134 - B1
WILLAMETTE NATIONAL FOREST	LINN CO OR	211 - A3
WILLAMETTE NATIONAL FOREST	MARION CO OR	134 - B1
WILLAMETTE PASS SKI AREA	HWY 58, KLAMATH CO OR	142 - B1
WILLIAM F MCCORMIC PARK	NE STEPHENS ST, DUVALL WA	110 - C1
WILLIAM GRIFFIN PARK	QUEENS RD, DISTRICT OF N VANCOUVER BC	254 - J3
WILLIAM M TUGMAN STATE PARK	COOS CO OR	218 - C3
WILLIAMS PARK	64TH AV, TOWNSHIP OF LANGLEY BC	157 - D7
WILLIAM STEVENSON PARK	PEMBROKE ST, CITY OF VICTORIA BC	256 - J8
WILLIARD PARK	DISTRICT OF BURNABY BC	156 - D6
WILLINGDON HEIGHTS PARK	CARLTON AV, DISTRICT OF BURNABY BC	255 - G12
WILLIS STREET GREENBELT	4TH AV S & W WILLIS ST, KENT WA	175 - B7
WILLOUGHBY PARK	84TH AV, TOWNSHIP OF LANGLEY BC	157 - C7
WILLOW PARK	SW 144TH AV, BEAVERTON OR	199 - A2
WILLOW CREEK PARK	SW WILLOW CREEK DR, HILLSBORO OR	199 - A1
WILLOWS PARK	BEACH DR, DISTRICT OF OAK BAY BC	257 - D8
WILLSADA PARK	S SPRINGWATER RD, CLACKAMAS CO OR	200 - A4
WILMOT GATEWAY PARK	NE 175TH ST & 131ST AV NE, WOODINVILLE WA	171 - C6
WILSHIRE PARK	NE 33RD AV & NE SKIDMORE ST, PORTLAND OR	314 - A1
WILSONVILLE MEMORIAL PARK	WILSONVILLE RD, WILSONVILLE OR	199 - B6
WILSONVILLE MEMORIAL PARK EAST	ROSE LN & MONTGOMERY WY, WILSONVILLE OR	199 - B6
WILSONVILLE MEMORIAL PARK NORTH	WILSONVILLE RD, WILSONVILLE OR	199 - B6
WINDRIDGE PARK	LYTTON ST, DISTRICT OF N VANCOUVER BC	255 - J6
WINDSOR HILLS PARK	NE 4TH ST, RENTON WA	175 - C5
WINDSOR PARK	NEWPORT AVE, DISTRICT OF OAK BAY BC	257 - D9
WINDSOR PARK	PLYMOUTH DR, DISTRICT OF N VANCOUVER BC	255 - J6
WINDSOR VISTA PARK	NE 143RD ST, KING CO WA	171 - C7
WINEMA NATIONAL FOREST	KLAMATH CO OR	231 - D4
WINONA PARK	VANCOUVER BC	156 - B5
WINSKILL PARK	DISTRICT OF DELTA BC	101 - C1
WINTHROP PARK	SW 173RD AV, BEAVERTON OR	199 - A1
WINTLER PARK	CHELSEA AV, VANCOUVER WA	306 - D7
WITTYS LAGOON REGIONAL PARK	METCHOSIN RD, DISTRICT OF METCHOSIN BC	159 - B7
WM PENN PARK	100TH AV NE & NE 200TH ST, BOTHELL WA	171 - C6
WONDERLAND PARK	SW KING BLVD, BEAVERTON OR	199 - B2
WOODALE PARK	SW 23RD ST & SW LARSSON AV, TROUTDALE OR	200 - B1
WOODARD PARK	SW JOHNSON ST, TIGARD OR	199 - B3
WOODLAND PARK	GREEN LAKE DR N, SEATTLE WA	273 - H4
WOODLAND PARK	NE 117TH AV & NE KNOTT ST, PORTLAND OR	200 - A1
WOODLAWN PARK	NE 13TH AV & NE DEKUM ST, PORTLAND OR	309 - H5
WOODMONT PARK	WOODMONT BEACH RD S, KING CO WA	175 - B7
WOOD MOUNTAIN SKI PARK	HWY 19, BRITISH COLUMBIA	92 - A2
WOODRIDGE WATER TOWER PARK	SE 19TH ST & 125TH AV SE, BELLEVUE WA	175 - C3
WOODSIDE POND NATURE PARK	ALAMEDA W & 48TH W, UNIVERSITY PLACE WA	294 - A3
WOODS MEMORIAL PARK	SW 45TH DR & SW WOOD PKWY, PORTLAND OR	316 - A7
WOODSTOCK PARK	SE 47TH AV & SE STEELE ST, PORTLAND OR	318 - C4
WOOD VILLAGE CITY PARK	NE HALSEY ST, WOOD VILLAGE OR	200 - B1
WOOTON PARK	REDONDO WY, KING CO WA	175 - B7
WORMALD STATE PARK	CLARK CO WA	193 - C3
WORTMAN CITY PARK	MCDANIEL LN & ORCHARD AV, MCMINNVILLE OR	198 - B7
WREN PARK	SLVRHLL AV & MANZR ST, DIST OF MISSION BC	94 - B3
WRIGHT PARK	S 6TH AV & S I ST, TACOMA WA	293 - G4
WYATT COUNTY PARK	N DAVIES & CHAPEL HILL, SNOHOMISH CO WA	171 - D2
WYEAST PARK	1100 SE 136TH AV, CLARK CO WA	193 - A6
WYEAST JR HIGH PARK	SE 136TH AV, CLARK CO WA	193 - A7
WYGANT STATE PARK	COLUMBIA RIVER HWY, HOOD RIVER CO OR	195 - B5
YAKIMA SPORTSMAN STATE PARK	S KEYS RD, YAKIMA WA	243 - C7
ZIBA DIMMICK STATE PARK	HOOD RIVER CO OR	202 - C1

PERFORMING ARTS

FEATURE NAME	City State	Page-Grid
ARLENE SCHNITZER CONCERT HALL	1033 SW BROADWAY, PORTLAND OR	313 - E6
EVERETT PREFORMING ARTS CENTER	2710 WETMORE AV, EVERETT WA	264 - D3
HUGHES CULT ARTS CTR	YESLER WY & 17TH AV S, SEATTLE WA	278 - C7
HULT CENTER FOR THE PERFORMING ARTS	6TH AV, EUGENE OR	330 - B6
MCPHERSON PLAYHOUSE	DOUGLAS ST, CITY OF VICTORIA BC	256 - G8
OREGON SHAKESPEARE THEATRES	15 S PIONEER AV, ASHLAND OR	337 - C8
PANTAGES THEATER	901 S BROADWAY, TACOMA WA	293 - H5
PERFORMING ARTS CENTER	1111 SW BROADWAY, PORTLAND OR	313 - E6
QUEEN ELIZABETH THEATRE	649 CAMBIE ST, VANCOUVER BC	254 - G10
ROYAL THEATRE	805 BROUGHTON ST, CITY OF VICTORIA BC	256 - H9
TEMPLE THEATER	47 SAINT HELENS AV, TACOMA WA	293 - G4

POINTS OF INTEREST

FEATURE NAME	City State	Page-Grid
45 WINDMILL	OFF SOUTH FORK OWYHEE RIVER, OWYHEE CO ID	155 - B2
1980 CRATER	MOUNT SAINT HELENS, SKAMANIA CO WA	190 - C2
ALBRIGHT CAVE	OFF CONCONULLY RD, OKANOGAN CO WA	104 - C2
ALKI POINT LIGHTHOUSE	POINT PL SW, SEATTLE WA	280 - A3
ALSEA RIVER FISH HATCHERY	ALSEA HWY, BENTON CO OR	133 - A2
AMAZON POOL	HILYARD ST, EUGENE OR	330 - B9
APPLE COVE POINT LIGHT	EDMONDS WEST, KITSAP CO WA	170 - D5
ARAGO LIGHT	CHARLESTON, COOS CO OR	220 - B1
ARMSTEAD MEMORIAL	OSWALD WEST STATE PARK, TILLAMOOK CO OR	191 - A3
ARNOLD ICE CAVE	CHINA HAT RD, DESCHUTES CO OR	217 - D5
ASTORIA COLUMN	COXCOMB DR, ASTORIA WA	300 - E6
AUDUBON BIRD SANCTUARY	5151 NW CORNELL RD, MULTNOMAH CO OR	199 - B1
BARLOW CAVE	BUTLER MARKET & DICKEY, DESCHUTES CO OR	217 - D2
BATTERY POINT LIGHTHOUSE	OFF HWY 101, CRESCENT CITY CA	148 - B3
BATTLE POINT LIGHT	SUQUAMISH, KITSAP CO WA	174 - C1
BEAVER CREEK STATE FISH HATCHERY	BEAVER CREEK RD, WAHKIAKUM CO WA	117 - B3
BELLE ROCK LIGHT	LOPEZ PASS, SAN JUAN CO WA	160 - B5
BELLEVUE BOTANICAL GARDEN	12001 MAIN ST, BELLEVUE WA	175 - C2
BENJAMIN CAVES	OFF FRAZEE-FREDERICK RD, LAKE CO OR	144 - A1
BIG HOLE	FREMONT HWY, LAKE CO OR	143 - A2
BIG QUALICUM RIVER HATCHERY	HWY 19, BRITISH COLUMBIA	92 - B3
BLAKELY ROCK LIGHT	DUWAMISH, KITSAP CO WA	174 - D2
BLITZ-WEINHARD BREWERY	1137 W BURNSIDE ST, PORTLAND OR	313 - E5
BLOEDEL RESERVE	7571 NE DOLPHIN DR, KITSAP CO WA	170 - C7
BOCA CAVE	OFF N SANTIAM HWY, MARION CO OR	134 - C1
BOEING ASSEMBLY PLANT	75TH ST SW, EVERETT WA	267 - G3
BOGUS CREEK CAVE	OFF BOGUS RANCH RD, MALHEUR CO OR	146 - C3
BONANZA LEAD MILL	COLVILLE, STEVENS CO WA	106 - A2
BOULDER CAVE	CLIFFDELL, YAKIMA CO WA	119 - B1

FEATURE NAME	City State	Page-Grid
BOW FISH HATCHERY	CARSON (WA), HOOD RIVER CO OR	194 - D5
BOYD CAVE	CHINA HAT RD, DESCHUTES CO OR	217 - D5
BREMERTON YACHT CLUB	BREMERTON WEST, KITSAP CO WA	270 - F7
BRITISH COLUMBIA PLACE	PACIFIC BLVD N, VANCOUVER BC	254 - G11
BURNS CAVE	OFF TUB SPRINGS RD, MALHEUR CO OR	146 - B3
BURROWS ISLAND LIGHTHOUSE	DECEPTION PASS, SKAGIT CO WA	160 - B6
BUSH POINT LIGHT	FREELAND, ISLAND CO WA	170 - C1
CABINET GORGE HATCHERY	HWY 200, BONNER CO ID	107 - C3
CAMPBELL MILL	OFF FREMONT HWY, LAKE CO OR	152 - A1
CANNERY LIGHT	ROSBURG (WA), WAHKIAKUM CO WA	117 - A2
CAPE BLANCO LIGHTHOUSE	CAPE BLANCO, CURRY CO OR	224 - A4
CAPE DISAPPOINTMENT LIGHTHOUSE	CAPE DISAPPOINTMENT, PACIFIC CO WA	186 - A7
CAPE FLATTERY LIGHTHOUSE	CAPE FLATTERY, CLALLAM CO WA	100 - B2
CAPE MEARES LIGHTHOUSE	CAPE MEARES LOOP RD, TILLAMOOK CO OR	197 - A1
CAPILANO FISH HATCHERY	DISTRICT OF NORTH VANCOUV BC	156 - B2
CARNATION FARM	28901 NE CARNATION FARM RD, KING CO WA	176 - B1
CARSON NATIONAL FISH HATCHERY	STABLER, TERMINATION PT, SKAMANIA CO WA	194 - C2
CASCADE SALMON HATCHERY	BONNEVILLE DAM, MULTNOMAH CO OR	194 - C6
CASCADIA CAVE	OFF SANTIAM HWY, LINN CO OR	134 - A2
CATHEDRAL OF SAINT JOHN THE EVANGELIST	E 12TH AV & GRAND BLVD, SPOKANE WA	349 - A11
CATTLE POINT LIGHT	CATTLE POINT RD, SAN JUAN CO WA	101 - C2
CHARCOAL CAVE	CHINA HAT RD, DESCHUTES CO OR	217 - D6
CHARLES APPLEGATE HOUSE	DRAIN-YONCALLA & HALO, DOUGLAS CO OR	219 - B3
CHEESE CAVE	GULER MOUNTAIN, KLICKITAT CO WA	119 - A3
CHEHALIS HATCHERY	16250 MORRIS VALLEY RD, BRITISH COLUMBIA	94 - C3
CHELAN STATE FISH HATCHERY	HWY 150, CHELAN CO WA	236 - D3
CHENEY FLOUR MILL	OFF HWY 904, CHENEY WA	246 - A7
CHIEF JOSEPH MONUMENT	JOSEPH-WALLOWA LAKE HWY, WALLOWA CO OR	130 - C2
CHILEAN MEMORIAL MONUMENT	OLYMPIC NATIONAL PARK, CLALLAM CO WA	169 - A1
CHINATOWN	PENDER ST E, VANCOUVER BC	254 - H11
CHINOOK DIKE LIGHT	WARRENTON, CLATSOP CO WA	186 - B7
CHRISTMAS TREE CAVE	GULER MOUNTAIN, KLICKITAT CO WA	119 - A3
CIVIC AUDITORIUM	1500 SW 3RD AV, PORTLAND OR	313 - F7
CLARK FORK FISH HATCHERY	HWY 200, BONNER CO ID	107 - C3
COLE M RIVERS FISH HATCHERY	CRATER LAKE HWY, JACKSON CO OR	149 - C1
COLVOS ROCKS LIGHT	PORT LUDLOW, JEFFERSON CO WA	170 - B2
COOS RIVER FISH HATCHERY	SOUTH COOS RIVER RD, COOS CO OR	140 - C2
CORBIN HOUSE	S STEVENS ST, SPOKANE WA	348 - J10
COUGAR MOUNTAIN ZOOLOGICAL PARK	19525 SE 54TH ST, ISSAQUAH WA	175 - D3
COWLITZ TROUT HATCHERY	EDEN VALLEY, LEWIS CO WA	118 - A2
COYOTE TRAP CAVE	IRON MOUNTAIN RD, MALHEUR CO OR	146 - B3
CROSS RANCH	OFF JOHN DAY-BURNS HWY, HARNEY CO OR	137 - B3
CUMBERLAND MILL	OFF SILVER CITY RD, OWYHEE CO ID	147 - B3
CYPRESS ISLAND LIGHT	CYPRESS ISLAND, SKAGIT CO WA	160 - B4
DAM OBSERVATORY	OFF RIVERVIEW RD, JEFFERSON CO OR	208 - A6
DARK HOLE WIND CAVE	CHINA HAT RD, DESCHUTES CO OR	217 - D5
DAVIDSON ROCK LIGHT	LOPEZ PASS, SAN JUAN CO WA	160 - A7
DEADY CAVES	DEADY CROSSING RD, DOUGLAS CO OR	221 - C2
DEE WRIGHT OBSERVATORY	MCKENZIE HWY, DESCHUTES CO OR	211 - A5
DENZER BRIDGE	FIVE RIVERS & LOBSTR CREEK, LINCOLN CO OR	209 - D3
DEPOE BAY AQUARIUM	DAVENPORT AV, DEPOE BAY OR	206 - A1
DERRICK CAVE	NFD RD 2315 & NFD RD 700, LAKE CO OR	143 - C1
DE RUWE FARM	AYER RD, WALLA WALLA CO WA	121 - C2
DESTRUCTION ISLAND LIGHTHOUSE	DESTRUCTION ISLAND, JEFFERSON CO WA	169 - B7
DEVILS HOLE	MILLICAN RD, LAKE CO OR	143 - C1
DEVILS PUNCH BOWL	COW CREEK RD, DOUGLAS CO OR	141 - A3
DEVINE MONUMENT	JOHN DAY-BURNS HWY, HARNEY CO OR	145 - B1
DIAMOND LAKE INFORMATION CENTER	N UMPQUA HWY, DOUGLAS CO OR	223 - C6
DOFFLEMYER POINT LIGHTHOUSE	BOSTON HARBOR RD NE, THURSTON CO WA	180 - C4
DOUBLE BLUFF LIGHT	HANSVILLE, ISLAND CO WA	170 - C2
DR SUN SEN CLASSICAL CHINESE GARDENS	578 CARRAL ST, VANCOUVER BC	254 - H11
DUNGENESS LIGHTHOUSE	DUNGENESS BAY, CLALLAM CO WA	166 - B5
DWORSHAK DAM AND VISITOR CENTER	VIEW POINT RD, CLEARWATER CO ID	123 - C2
DWORSHAK NATIONAL FISH HATCHERY	VIEW POINT RD, CLEARWATER CO ID	123 - C2
EAGLE HATCHERY	OFF N LINDER RD, ADA CO ID	253 - A1
EAGLE CREEK NATIONAL FISH HATCHERY	34288 SE RAIBOW RD, CLACKAMAS CO OR	200 - D6
EDISON ICE CAVE	OFF EDISON ICE CAVE RD, DESCHUTES CO OR	216 - C5
ELK RIVER STATE FISH HATCHERY	ELK RIVER RD, CURRY CO OR	224 - B6
ELKS LODGE 174	1965 S UNION AV, TACOMA WA	292 - D7
ELLINGSON MILL	SOUTH FORK JOHN DAY RD, GRANT CO OR	136 - C2
ENCHANTED FOREST	8462 ENCHANTED WY, MARION CO OR	325 - B13
ENCHANTED PARKS	36201 ENCHANTED PKWY S, KING CO WA	182 - B2
ENGLISH SETTLEMENT	ELKHEAD RD & DRIVER VLY RD, DOUGLAS CO OR	219 - B6
ENTIAT FISH HATCHERY	ENTIAT RVR & ROARING CRK RD, CHELAN CO WA	112 - A2
FALL CREEK STATE FISH HATCHERY	FALL CREEK RD, LINCOLN CO OR	133 - A2
FINCH ARBORETUM	W WOODLAND BLVD, SPOKANE WA	348 - E12
FIRE BOAT STATION	RUSTON WY, TACOMA WA	292 - D1
FISH HATCHERY	HWY 19, BRITISH COLUMBIA	92 - A2
FISH HATCHERY	OFF LILLOOET RD, BRITISH COLUMBIA	156 - D1
FISH HATCHERY	316TH ST NE, SNOHOMISH CO WA	102 - C3
FISH HATCHERY	OFF LILLOOET RD, SQUAMISH BC	93 - C1
FOREST LEARNING CTR MOUNT SAINT HELENS	OFF RTE 504, COWLITZ CO WA	118 - B2
FORKS CREEK SALMON HATCHERY	RTE 6, PACIFIC CO WA	117 - A2
FORT ASTORIA	15TH ST, ASTORIA WA	300 - D5
FORT CLATSOP NATIONAL MEMORIAL	FORT CLATSOP RD, CLATSOP CO WA	188 - C3
FORT ROCK CAVE	FORT ROCK RD, LAKE CO OR	143 - B2
FORT ROCK STATE MONUMENT	OFF CABIN LAKE RD, LAKE CO OR	143 - B2
FORTYMILE CAVE	OFF IRON MOUNTAIN RD, MALHEUR CO OR	146 - B3
FOURMILE LIGHT	SPARROW PARK RD, DOUGLAS CO OR	214 - A7
FRONT RANGE LIGHT	CATHLAMET BAY, CLATSOP CO WA	188 - D1
GABLEHOUSE MILL	GULER MOUNTAIN, KLICKITAT CO WA	119 - A3
GEORGE ADAMS SALMON HATCHERY	HWY 101 & PURDY CUTOFF RD, MASON CO WA	180 - A1
GIBSON FARM	OFF HWY 112, CLALLAM CO WA	163 - D4
GOLDENDALE ASTRONOMICAL OBSERVATORY	PIPELINE RD, GOLDENDALE WA	127 - C1
GOLDENDALE TROUT HATCHERY	OFF FISH HATCHERY RD, KLICKITAT CO WA	127 - B1
GOODWIN TOMB	OFF CASTLE ROCK RD, MALHEUR CO OR	138 - A3
GORDON SOUTHAM MACMILLAN OBSERVATORY	1905 CHESTNUT ST, VANCOUVER BC	254 - D11
GRANGEVILLE HATCHERY	OFF HWY 95, IDAHO CO ID	123 - C3
GRAYS BAY LIGHT	GRAYS BAY, PACIFIC CO WA	186 - D7
GRAYS POINT LIGHT	KNAPPTON FERRY RD, PACIFIC CO WA	186 - D7
GRAYS RIVER STATE FISH HATCHERY	OFF RTE 4, PACIFIC CO WA	117 - A2
GREEN RIVER SALMON HATCHERY	SPIRIT LAKE HWY, COWLITZ CO WA	118 - A2
HALLS FERRY	OFF RIVER RD S, MARION CO OR	204 - C7
HIRAM M CHITTENDEN LOCKS	3015 NW 54TH ST, SEATTLE WA	272 - D4
H J MONUMENT	RABBIT CAMP RD, LANE CO OR	134 - B2
HOFFMAN COLUMBIA PLAZA	1300 SW 6TH AV, PORTLAND OR	313 - E6
HOOD CANAL LIGHT	QUILCENE, JEFFERSON CO WA	170 - A6
HOOD RIVER HATCHERY	PUNCH BOWL RD, HOOD RIVER CO OR	195 - B7
HORSE CAVE	OFF NEFF RD, DESCHUTES CO OR	217 - C2
HOYT ARBORETUM	4000 SW FAIRVIEW BLVD, PORTLAND OR	312 - B6
HUDSPETH MILL	OCHOCO HWY, WHEELER CO OR	136 - A1
ICE CAVE	FRAZEE-FREDERICK BUTTE RD, LAKE CO OR	143 - C2
ICE CAVES	LITTLE HUCKLEBERRY MTN, SKAMANIA CO WA	118 - C3
IDAHO BOTANICAL GARDEN	2355 OLD PENITENTIARY RD, BOISE ID	253 - D3
IDAHO STATE FISH HATCHERY	OFF HWY 200, BONNER CO ID	107 - C3
INDIAN CAVE	OFF NORTH UMPQUA HWY, DOUGLAS CO OR	222 - B3
INDIAN FORT	INDIAN FORT CREEK RD, MALHEUR CO OR	146 - C3
INTERNATIONAL ROSE TEST GARDENS	SW MARCONI AV, PORTLAND OR	312 - C6
IRON CREEK INFORMATION CENTER	GREENHORN BUTTES, LEWIS CO WA	118 - C2
ISLAND WINDMILL	OFF SIMNASHO RD, WASCO CO OR	127 - A3
ISSAQUAH STATE SALMON HATCHERY	125 W SUNSET WY, ISSAQUAH WA	176 - A4
JAPANESE GARDENS	SW KINGSTON DR, PORTLAND OR	312 - C6
JOBS GARDEN	NORTH UMPQUA HWY, DOUGLAS CO OR	141 - C2
JOHN DAY FOSSIL BEDS NATIONAL MONUMENT	SHANIKO-FOSSIL HWY, WHEELER CO OR	128 - A3
JOHN DAY FOSSIL BEDS NATIONAL MONUMENT	JOHN DAY HWY & OCHOCO HWY, GRANT CO OR	136 - C1
JOHN DAY FOSSIL BEDS NATIONAL MON (PHU)	BRIDGE CREEK RD, WHEELER CO OR	136 - A1
KALAMA FALLS SALMON HATCHERY	WOOLFORD CREEK, COWLITZ CO WA	118 - A3
KALA POINT LIGHTHOUSE	SAILVIEW DR, HADLOCK-IRONDALE WA	263 - G12
KELSO VOLCANO TOURIST INFO	105 MINOR RD, KELSO WA	303 - E6
KEMPER BREWERY	22381 FOSS RD NE, KITSAP CO WA	170 - B6
KLAMATH STATE FISH HATCHERY	CRATER LAKE HWY, KLAMATH CO OR	231 - C2
KLASKANINE FISH HATCHERY	NEHALEM HWY, CLATSOP CO WA	188 - D4
KLICKITAT STATE FISH HATCHERY	OUTLET FALLS, KLICKITAT CO WA	119 - B3
KUNA CAVE	OFF KUNA CAVE RD, ADA CO ID	253 - A7
LAKE ABERDEEN HATCHERY	LAKE ABERDEEN, GRAYS HARBOR CO WA	178 - C7
LAKEWOLD GARDENS	12317 GRAVELLY LAKE DR SW, LAKEWOOD WA	181 - C4
LANGSLET MONUMENT	WARNER HWY, LAKE CO OR	152 - C2
LATIMIER QUILT AND TEXTILE CENTER	2105 WILSON RIVER LP, TILLAMOOK CO OR	197 - C2
LAVA BEDS NATIONAL MONUMENT	SISKIYOU CO CA	150 - C3
LAVA BEDS NATIONAL MONUMENT	MODOC CO CA	151 - A3
LAVA CAVES	GIFFORD PEAK, SKAMANIA CO WA	118 - C3
LAVACICLE CAVE	SAND SPRINGS RD, DESCHUTES CO OR	143 - C1
LAVA LANDS VISITOR CENTER	NEWBRY NATL VOLCANC MON, DESCHUTES CO OR	217 - B5
LEACH BOTANICAL GARDEN	6704 SE 122 AV, PORTLAND OR	200 - A2
LEAVENWORTH NATIONAL FISH HATCHERY	LEAVENWORTH, CHELAN CO WA	238 - A1
LEO REEF LIGHT	BLAKELY ISLAND, SAN JUAN CO WA	160 - A4
LIGHTHOUSE	LINCOLN CO OR	206 - A3
LIGHTHOUSE	FRONT ST, MUKILTEO WA	171 - B2
LIGHTHOUSE	TANGLEWOOD ISLAND, PIERCE CO WA	181 - B2
LIGHTHOUSE	YOUNGS LANDING RD NW, PIERCE CO WA	181 - C1
LIGHTHOUSE	PORT ANGELES HARBOR, PORT ANGELES WA	261 - J1
LIGHTHOUSE	POINT DEFIANCE PARK, TACOMA WA	181 - C1
LIME KILN LIGHTHOUSE	WESTSIDE RD N, SAN JUAN CO WA	101 - C2
LINT SLOUGH FISH HATCHERY	OFF ALSEA HWY, WALDPORT OR	328 - E5
LITTLE WHITE SALMON NATL FISH HATCHERY	COOK UNDERWOOD RD, SKAMANIA CO WA	195 - B5
LOST BOY CAVE	CAPE MEARES LOOP RD, TILLAMOOK CO OR	197 - A2
LUCILE CAVES	US HWY 95, IDAHO CO ID	131 - C1
MAKAH NATIONAL SALMON HATCHERY	MAKAH BAY, CLALLAM CO WA	162 - B2
MALHEUR CAVE	MALHEUR CAVE RD, HARNEY CO OR	146 - A2
MAPLES, THE	OFF KOSYDAR RD, LINCOLN CO OR	206 - C1
MAPLEWOOD FARM	DOLLARTON HWY, DIST OF NORTH VANCOUVER BC	255 - H7
MARCH POINT LIGHT	ANACORTES NORTH, SKAGIT CO WA	160 - D5
MARINE SCIENCE CENTER	18743 FRONT ST NE, POULSBO WA	170 - B7
MARROWSTONE POINT LIGHTHOUSE	NORDLAND, JEFFERSON CO WA	167 - B6
MARTINS MILL	NORTH FORK BURNT RIVER RD, BAKER CO OR	138 - A1
MARYLHURST EDUCATIONAL CENTER	PACIFIC HWY, LAKE OSWEGO OR	199 - C4
MASONIC TEMPLE	1119 SW PARK AV, PORTLAND OR	313 - E6
MAYO	COCHRAN, WASHINGTON CO OR	125 - B1
MCALLISTER ROD GUN CLUB	NISQUALLY, THURSTON CO WA	181 - A5
MCKENZIE SALMON HATCHERY	OFF MCKENZIE HWY, LANE CO OR	134 - A3
MCKENZIE TROUT HATCHERY	MCKENZIE HWY, LANE CO OR	134 - A2
MCNARY DAM FISH LADDER	UMATILLA, UMATILLA CO OR	121 - A3
MEADOWDALE MARINE	16111 76TH PL W, EDMONDS WA	171 - B4
METRO WASHINGTON PARK ZOO	4001 SW CANYON CT, PORTLAND OR	312 - B7
MIDDLE WINDMILL	OFF SOUTH FORK OWYHEE RIVER, OWYHEE CO ID	155 - B2
MITCHELL MONUMENT	NFD RD 348, LAKE CO OR	151 - B1
MORRISON KNUDSEN NATURE CENTER	600 S WALNUT AV, BOISE ID	253 - D3
MOSSYROCK TROUT HATCHERY	MAYFIELD LAKE, LEWIS CO WA	118 - A2
MOUNT BAKER	MOUNT BAKER WILDERNESS, WHATCOM CO WA	102 - C2
MOUNT RAINIER	PIERCE CO WA	185 - B3
MOUNT SAINT HELENS CINEDOME	1239 MOUNT SAINT HELENS WY, COWLITZ CO WA	187 - C7
MOUNT SAINT HELENS VISITORS CENTER	JACKSON HWY, LEWIS CO WA	187 - D2
MOUNT SAINT HELENS NATL VOLCANIC MON	AMBOY, CLARK CO WA	118 - A3
MOUNT SAINT HELENS NATL VOLCANIC MON	COWLITZ CO WA	118 - B2
MOUNT SAINT HELENS NATL VOLCANIC MON	SKAMANIA CO WA	190 - B1
MOWICH CAVE	OFF N UMPQUA HWY, DOUGLAS CO OR	223 - A4
NAMPA HATCHERY	LOCUST LN, CANYON CO ID	147 - B1
NASELLE STATE SALMON HATCHERY	RTE 4, PACIFIC CO WA	186 - C5
NATURE CENTER AT SNAKE LAKE	1919 S TYLER ST, TACOMA WA	292 - B7
NEHALEM FISH HATCHERY	FOLEY PEAK, TILLAMOOK CO OR	191 - C5
NELSON MONUMENT	ARVID NELSON RD, CROOK CO OR	136 - A2
NEWBERRY NATIONAL VOLCANIC MONUMENT	DESCHUTES CO OR	217 - B5
NEW MARKET VILLAGE	50 SW 2ND AV, PORTLAND OR	313 - F5
NORTH HEAD LIGHTHOUSE	NORTH HEAD LIGHTHOUSE RD, PACIFIC CO WA	186 - A6
NORTHWEST TREK WILDLIFE PARK	11610 TREK DR E, PIERCE CO WA	118 - B1
OAKRIDGE FISH HATCHERY	SALMON CREEK RD, LANE CO OR	142 - A1
OBSERVATION TOWER	E PROSPECT ST & 14TH AV E, SEATTLE WA	278 - C3
OCEAN SHORES ENVIRONMENTAL CENTER	1013 CATALA AV SE, OCEAN SHORES WA	298 - F4
OLD PERPETUAL GEYSER	OFF HWY 395, LAKE CO OR	152 - A2
OREGON CAVES NATIONAL MONUMENT	OREGON CAVES HWY, JOSEPHINE CO OR	233 - D5
OREGON COAST AQUARIUM	2820 SE FERRY SLIP RD, NEWPORT OR	206 - B4

FEATURE NAME	City State	Page-Grid
OREGON COAST HISTORY CENTER	545 SW 9TH ST, NEWPORT OR	206 - B4
OREGONIAN BUILDING	1320 SW BROADWAY, PORTLAND OR	313 - E6
OREGON STATE FISH HATCHERY	RIVER RD, MARION CO OR	205 - A1
OREGON STATE FORESTRY HEADQUARTERS	NEHALEM HWY, CLATSOP CO WA	300 - G10
OREGON TR INTERP PK AT BLUE MTN CRSG	I-84 SOUTHEAST OF KAMELA, UNION CO OR	129 - C2
OREGON VORTEX & HOUSE OF MYSTERY, THE	SARDINE CREEK RD, JACKSON CO OR	230 - A5
OWYHEE RIVER CAVE	OFF TUB SPRINGS RD, MALHEUR CO OR	146 - B3
OX BOW SALMON HATCHERY	CARSON, CASCADE LOCKS OR	194 - D5
PACIFIC BIOLOGICAL STATION	HAMMOND BAY RD, NANAIMO BC	93 - A3
PAPOOSE CAVERN	SEVEN DEVILS RD, IDAHO CO ID	131 - B2
PARADISE GLACIER CAVES	STEVENS CANYON RD, PIERCE CO WA	185 - C4
PATOS LIGHT	SUCIA ISLAND, SAN JUAN CO WA	101 - C1
PEACE ARCH	USA/CANADA BORDER, BRITISH COLUMBIA	158 - B2
PENDLETON UNDERGROUND TOURS	37 SW EMIGRANT, UMATILLA CO OR	129 - B1
PETROGLYPHS	OFF HOPE PENINSULA RD, BONNER CO ID	244 - D4
PINE MOUNTAIN OBSERVATORY	W BASIN RD, DESCHUTES CO OR	143 - B1
POINT DEFIANCE ZOO & AQUARIUM	5400 N PEARL ST, TACOMA WA	181 - C1
POINT HANNON LIGHT	HANSVILLE, JEFFERSON CO WA	170 - C4
POINT HUDSON LIGHTHOUSE	HUDSON PL, PORT TOWNSEND WA	263 - J4
POINT MONROE LIGHT	SUQUAMISH, KITSAP CO WA	170 - D7
POINT NO POINT LIGHT	HANSVILLE, KITSAP CO WA	170 - D3
POINT PARTRIDGE LIGHTHOUSE	PORT TOWNSEND NORTH, ISLAND CO WA	167 - A4
POINT ROBERTS LIGHTHOUSE	MARINE DR, WHATCOM CO WA	101 - C1
POINT WILSON LIGHTHOUSE	PORT TOWNSEND NORTH, PORT TOWNSEND WA	167 - A5
POLE PASS LIGHT	SHAW ISLAND, SAN JUAN CO WA	101 - C2
POOR FARM	FIELDS-DENIO RD, HARNEY CO OR	153 - C2
PORTAGE, THE	MERCER LAKE, LANE CO OR	214 - B2
PORTLAND PUBLIC ASTRONOMY CENTER	9360 N COLUMBIA BLVD, PORTLAND OR	192 - B6
POWELLS BOOKS	1005 W BURNSIDE ST, PORTLAND OR	313 - E5
PREHISTORIC GARDENS	OFF HWY 101, CURRY CO OR	228 - B2
PYRAMID BREWERIES INC	110 W MARINE DR, KALAMA WA	189 - D6
RAINIER BREWERY	3100 AIRPORT WY S, SEATTLE WA	282 - A3
RAPID RIVER FISH HATCHERY	RAPID RIVER RD, IDAHO CO ID	131 - C2
RATTLESNAKE CAVE	IDAHO-OREGON-NEVADA HWY, MALHEUR CO OR	146 - C3
REAR ENTRANCE RANGE LIGHTHOUSE	CHINOOK, CLATSOP CO WA	186 - A7
REAR RANGE LIGHT	CATHLAMET BAY, CLATSOP CO WA	188 - D1
RED HOOK BREWERY	14300 NE 145TH ST, KING CO WA	171 - D7
REDMOND CAVE	SE AIRPORT WY, REDMOND OR	212 - D6
RENAISSANCE SQUARE	DISTRICT OF COQUITLAM BC	156 - D5
RHODODENDRON SPECIES BOTANICAL GARDEN	OFF HWY 18, FEDERAL WAY WA	182 - B1
RIPLEYS BELIEVE IT OR NOT	250 SW BAY BLVD, NEWPORT OR	206 - B4
ROARING RIVER STATE FISH HATCHERY	FISH HATCHERY DR, LINN CO OR	133 - C1
ROBERTS FARM	HUNT CLUB RD, GRAYS HARBOR CO WA	183 - B3
ROBERTSON FISH HATCHERY	HWY 4, BRITISH COLUMBIA	92 - A3
ROBINSON POINT LIGHTHOUSE	SW POINT ROBINSON RD, KING CO WA	175 - A7
ROCK CREEK FISH HATCHERY	ROCK CREEK RD, DOUGLAS CO OR	141 - C2
ROCK CREEK HIDEOUT	ALVORD AL, POLK CO OR	125 - A3
ROCKY POINT LIGHT	BRIX BAY, WAHKIAKUM CO WA	186 - D7
ROSS FARM	SPERRY, FRANKLIN CO WA	121 - C1
ROUND UP HALL OF FAME	INTERSTATE 84 & EXIT 207, UMATILLA CO OR	129 - B1
SACRAMENTO CAVES	OFF POLE CREEK RD, MALHEUR CO OR	155 - A1
SAINT MARYS FARM	OMAK LAKE RD, OKANOGAN CO WA	104 - C3
SAINT MARYS MISSION	NORTH END OMAK LAKE RD, OKANOGAN CO WA	104 - C3
SAND ISLAND DIKE LIGHT	CHINOOK, CLATSOP CO WA	186 - B7
SAND ISLAND DIKE MIDDLE LIGHT	CHINOOK, CLATSOP CO WA	186 - A7
SANDPOINT FISH HATCHERY	LAKESHORE DR, BONNER CO ID	244 - A3
SAWYERS CAVE	SANTIAM HWY, LINN CO OR	134 - B2
SEASIDE AQUARIUM	N PROM & 2ND AV, SEASIDE WA	301 - F8
SEATTLE AQUARIUM	PIER 59, SEATTLE WA	277 - J6
SEATTLE CENTER	W THOMAS ST & 5TH AV N, SEATTLE WA	277 - H4
SEATTLE SEAHAWKS HQ	NE 53RD ST & 112TH AV NE, KIRKLAND WA	175 - C1
SEATTLE YACHT CLUB	E SHELBY ST & W PARK DR, SEATTLE WA	274 - C7
SEYMOUR BOTANICAL CONSERVATORY	316 S G ST, TACOMA WA	293 - G4
SHELTON TROUT HATCHERY	SATSOP-CLOQUALLUM RD, MASON CO WA	179 - D1
SHERMAN CRATER	MOUNT BAKER, WHATCOM CO WA	102 - C2
SILCOX WARMING HUT	MOUNT HOOD SOUTH, CLACKAMAS CO OR	202 - A5
SILVER MOUNTAIN GONDOLA	610 BUNKER AV, KELLOGG ID	115 - C2
SIMPSON STATE SALMON HATCHERY	FISH HATCHERY RD, MASON CO WA	179 - B4
SINCLAIR ISLAND LIGHT	CYPRESS ISLAND, SKAGIT CO WA	160 - C3
SKELETON CAVE	CHINA HAT RD, DESCHUTES CO OR	217 - D5
SKIPANON WATERWAY LIGHTHOUSE	WARRENTON, WARRENTON WA	188 - B2
SKUNK BAY LIGHT	HANSVILLE, KITSAP CO WA	170 - C3
SKYLIGHT CAVE	OFF NFD RD 1028, DESCHUTES CO OR	211 - B4
SLIP POINT LIGHTHOUSE	SLIP POINT, CLALLAM CO WA	163 - B2
SMELTZER MILL	GULER MOUNTAIN, KLICKITAT CO WA	119 - A3
SMITH ISLAND LIGHTHOUSE	SMITH ISLAND, ISLAND CO WA	167 - A2
SMITH RIVER LIGHT	BUTLER CREEK RD, DOUGLAS CO OR	218 - D1
SNOWSHOE CAVE	OFF JUNIPER MOUNTAIN RD, OWYHEE CO ID	155 - B1
SOLEDUCK SALMON HATCHERY	LAKE PLEASANT, CLALLAM CO WA	163 - A6
SPACE NEEDLE	5TH AV N & THOMAS ST, SEATTLE WA	277 - H4
SPEELYAI STATE HATCHERY	1101 LEWIS RIVER RD, COWLITZ CO WA	190 - A6
SPLASHDOWN WATERSLIDE PARK	E MISSN AV & N BOWDSH RD, OPPORTUNITY WA	350 - F6
SPOKANE STATE FISH HATCHERY	W HATCHERY RD, SPOKANE CO WA	346 - C8
SPOKANE STATE GAME FARM	W STALEY RD, SPOKANE CO WA	114 - B1
STALEYS JUNCTION	BUXTON, WASHINGTON CO OR	125 - B1
STATE FISH HATCHERY	STEVENS PASS PK, SNOHOMISH CO WA	110 - C1
STATELINE WINDMILL	OFF STATE LINE RD, ELKO CO NV	155 - B2
STRASSEL	BUXTON, WASHINGTON CO OR	125 - B1
SUMMIT CRATER	MOUNT BAKER, WHATCOM CO WA	102 - C1
SUPPAH WINDMILL	OFF HOT SPRINGS RD, WASCO CO OR	127 - A3
SURVEYORS ICE CAVE	DAVILS HORN RD, DESCHUTES CO OR	143 - A1
SWEETWATER HATCHERY	ZAZA RD, NEZ PERCE CO ID	123 - A3
TACOMA YACHT CLUB	5401 N WATERFRONT DR, TACOMA WA	181 - D1
TACOMA YACHT CLUB	MANZANITA BEACH RD SW, KING CO WA	174 - D7
THOMAS CAIRN	OFF CAMP MORRISON DR, LINN CO OR	134 - A1
THREEMILE LIGHT	SPARROW PARK RD, DOUGLAS CO OR	214 - A7
THURMAN MILL	OFF E CHINDEN BLVD, ADA CO ID	253 - B2
TILLUSQUA FISH HATCHERY	KNAPPA, CLATSOP CO WA	117 - A3
TIRE TUBE CAVE	OFF IRON MOUNTAIN RD, MALHEUR CO OR	146 - B3
TONGUE POINT LIGHTHOUSE	ASTORIA, CLATSOP CO WA	188 - D1
TRASK HOUSE	TRASK RIVER RD, TILLAMOOK CO OR	125 - A2
TRASK RIVER REARING POND	SOUTH FORK RD, TILLAMOOK CO OR	125 - A2
TRASK RIVER STATE FISH HATCHERY	CHANCE RD, TILLAMOOK CO OR	197 - D2
TULANA FARMS	TOWNSHIP RD, KLAMATH CO OR	235 - B7
TURN POINT LIGHTHOUSE	STUART ISLAND, SAN JUAN CO WA	101 - C2
TURN ROCK LIGHT	SHAW ISLAND, SAN JUAN CO WA	101 - C2
UMPQUA DISCOVER CENTER	409 RIVERFRONT WY, REEDSPORT OR	218 - D1
UMPQUA LIGHTHOUSE	SALMON HARBOR DR, DOUGLAS CO OR	218 - B2
UNDERSEA GARDENS	250 SW BAY BLVD, NEWPORT OR	206 - B4
UNITED STATES FISH HATCHERY	MOUNT WALKER, JEFFERSON CO WA	109 - C1
VANCOUVER AQUARIUM	VANCOUVER BC	254 - F7
VAN DUSEN BOTANICAL GARDENS	VANCOUVER BC	156 - B5
VINCENT MASSEY AUDITORIUM	NEW WESTMINSTER BC	156 - D5
VOLUNTEER PARK CONSERVATORY	1300 E PROSPECT ST, SEATTLE WA	278 - B2
WALAN POINT LIGHTHOUSE	INDIAN ISLAND, JEFFERSON CO WA	263 - H10
WALK IN THE WILD ZOO	OFF N PINES RD, SPOKANE CO WA	350 - H5
WASCO LIGHT	COLUMBIA RIVER HWY, HOOD RIVER CO OR	195 - D5
WASHINGTON PARK ARBORETUM	2300 ARBORETUM DR E, SEATTLE WA	278 - E1
WASHOUGAL STATE SALMON HATCHERY	WASHOUGAL RIVER RD, SKAMANIA CO WA	194 - A6
WASP PASSAGE LIGHT	SHAW ISLAND, SAN JUAN CO WA	101 - C2
WAX WORKS, THE	250 SW BAY BLVD, NEWPORT OR	206 - B4
WEST LIGHT	CATHLAMET BAY, CLATSOP CO WA	188 - D1
WEST POINT LIGHT	SHILSHOLE BAY, KING CO WA	174 - D1
WEST POINT LIGHTHOUSE	SEATTLE WA	272 - A5
WHEATLAND FERRY	SE WHEATLAND RD, YAMHILL CO OR	204 - D3
WILBURTON HILL BOTANICAL GARDENS	MAIN ST & 124TH AV NE, BELLEVUE WA	175 - C2
WILLAMETTE FISH HATCHERY	OAKRIDGE, LANE CO OR	142 - A1
WILLARD NATIONAL FISH HATCHERY	WILLARD RD, SKAMANIA CO WA	195 - B4
WILSON CAVE	NELSON RD & DICKEY RD, DESCHUTES CO OR	217 - D2
WINTHROP NATIONAL FISH HATCHERY	OFF HWY 20, OKANOGAN CO WA	104 - A2
WIZARD FALLS STATE FISH HATCHERY	METOLIUS RIVER RD, JEFFERSON CO OR	134 - C1
WOODLAND PARK ZOO	5500 PHINNEY AV N, SEATTLE WA	273 - H4
WOOTEN STATE FISH HATCHERY	TUCANNON RD, COLUMBIA CO WA	122 - B2
WORLD FORESTRY CENTER	4033 SW CANYON CT, PORTLAND OR	312 - B7
WORLD TRADE CENTER	121 SW SALMON ST, PORTLAND OR	313 - F6
YAKIMA INDIAN RESERVATION HEADQUARTERS	TOPPENISH, YAKIMA CO WA	120 - A2
YAQUINA BAY LIGHTHOUSE	GOVERNMENT ST, NEWPORT OR	206 - A4
YMCA	SW TERWILLIGER BL, PORTLAND OR	317 - E1
YOUNGS BAY LIGHT	YOUNGS BAY, CLATSOP CO WA	300 - A8
YOUNGS BAY ENTRANCE LIGHT	WARRENTON, ASTORIA WA	188 - C1
YOUTH SERVICE CENTER	13TH AV & E REMINGTON CT, SEATTLE WA	278 - B6
YWCA	1111 SW 10TH AV, PORTLAND OR	312 - E6

POINTS OF INTEREST - HISTORIC

FEATURE NAME	City State	Page-Grid
ABERT RIM HISTORICAL MARKER	LAKEVIEW-BURNS HWY, LAKE CO OR	152 - A1
ADAIR AIR FORCE STATION (HISTORICAL)	RYALS AV, ADAIR VILLAGE OR	207 - B4
ANNE HATHAWAYS COTTAGE	429 LAMPSON ST, TOWN OF ESQUILMALT BC	256 - D9
BEELMAN HOUSE	STAGE RD S, JACKSON CO OR	234 - A1
BYBEE HOUSE	HOWELL PARK RD, MULTNOMAH CO OR	192 - B6
CASTLE ROCK EXHIBIT HALL	147 FRONT AV NW, CASTLE ROCK WA	187 - C7
COLUMBIA RIVER EXHIBITION	95 LEE BLVD, RICHLAND WA	341 - G2
CORNWALL HISTORICAL MARKER	PACIFIC HWY & GREEN VALLEY, DOUGLAS CO OR	219 - A7
CRAIGDARROCH CASTLE	1050 JOHN CRESCNT ST, CITY OF VICTORIA BC	256 - J9
CREEK STATE HISTORIC MONUMENT	IDAHO-OREGON-NEVADA HWY, MALHEUR CO OR	146 - B3
DAVID THOMPSON HISTORICAL MONUMENT	HWY 200, EAST HOPE ID	244 - D2
DEEPWOOD ESTATE	111 MISSION ST SE, SALEM OR	322 - H14
DENNY CREEK HISTORICAL MONUMENT	EAGLE RIDGE RD, KLAMATH CO OR	231 - C7
DORRIS RANCH LIVING HISTORY FARM	HARBOR DR, LANE CO OR	330 - H9
EDMONDS HISTORICAL GARDEN	118 N 5TH AV, EDMONDS WA	171 - A5
END OF THE OREGON TRAIL CENTER	1726 WASHINGTON ST, OREGON CITY OR	199 - D4
FORT HARNEY HISTORICAL MONUMENT	CENTRAL OREGON HWY, HARNEY CO OR	145 - B1
FORT LAMERICK (HISTORICAL)	KELSEY PEAK, CURRY CO OR	140 - C3
FORT NISQUALLY HISTORIC SITE	RTE 163, TACOMA WA	181 - C1
FORT RODD HILL NATIONAL HISTORIC SITE	HWY 1A, CITY OF COLWOOD BC	159 - B6
FORT SPOKANE	OFF HWY 25, LINCOLN CO WA	113 - C1
FORT VANCOUVER NATIONAL HISTORIC SITE	E EVERGREEN BLVD, VANCOUVER WA	305 - H5
GRAYS HARBOR HISTORICAL SEAPORT	813 E HERON ST, ABERDEEN WA	178 - B7
GREAT BASIN HISTORICAL MARKER	CENTRAL OREGON HWY, HARNEY CO OR	145 - C1
GULF OF GEORGIA CANNERY NATL HIST SITE	12138 4TH AVE, CITY OF RICHMOND BC	156 - B7
HELLS GATE	HWY 1, BRITISH COLUMBIA	95 - A2
HELMCKEN HOUSE	BELLEVILLE & GOVT, CITY OF VICTORIA BC	256 - G10
HERBFARM, THE	32804 ISSAQUAH-FALL CITY RD, KING CO WA	176 - B3
HISTORICAL FLIPPIN CASTLE	620 TICHENOR ST, CLATSKANIE OR	117 - B3
HISTORY CENTER	106 S CENTRAL AV, MEDFORD OR	336 - D12
HOQUIAMS CASTLE	515 CHENAULT AV, HOQUIAM WA	178 - A7
HOUSE OF MYRTLEWOOD	KRUSE AV & BROADWAY ST, COOS BAY OR	333 - H12
INDIAN CEREMONIAL GROUND	MISSION, UMATILLA CO OR	129 - C1
JESSIE APPLEGATE HISTORICAL MARKER	DRAIN-YONCALLA & BOSWELL, DOUGLAS CO OR	219 - B3
KELLER HISTORICAL PARK	700 N WYNNE ST, COLVILLE WA	106 - A2
MARITIME HERITAGE CENTER	1600 C ST, BELLINGHAM WA	258 - C6
MCCONNELL MANSION	110 S ADAMS ST, MOSCOW ID	249 - C5
MCLOUGHLIN HOUSE NATIONAL HISTORIC SITE	OREGON CITY OR	199 - D4
NEZ PERCE INDIAN WAR HISTORIC MONUMENT	OFF US HWY 95, IDAHO CO ID	131 - C1
OASIS WATERWORKS	6321 W CANAL DR, KENNEWICK WA	342 - D8
OLD CHURCH, THE	1422 SW 11TH AV, PORTLAND OR	312 - E6
OLD DOLE SMITH HOMESTEAD	OFF DEVINE RIDGE RD, HARNEY CO OR	137 - A3
OLD HUMBOLT DIGGINGS	JOHN DAY-BURNS HWY, CANYON CITY OR	137 - B2
OLD KELLY MILL	OFF SUMMIT RD, WHEELER CO OR	136 - A2
OLD OREGON TRAIL MONUMENT	OFF JOHN DAY CREEK, SHERMAN CO OR	128 - A1
OLD PONY EXPRESS STATION (RUINS)	WHITEHORSE RANCH RD, HARNEY CO OR	154 - A2
OLD SAINT PETERS LANDMARK	4TH ST & LIBERTY ST, THE DALLES OR	196 - C7
OLD SCOTCH CHURCH	30685 NW SCOTCH CHRCH, WASHINGTON CO OR	125 - C1
OREGON TRAIL MONUMENT	LA GRANDE-BAKER HWY, BAKER CO OR	138 - B1
OWENS MEMORIAL ROSE GARDEN	N JEFFERSON ST, EUGENE OR	329 - J5
PERKINS HOUSE NATIONAL HISTORIC PLACE	OFF HWY 26, COLFAX WA	122 - C1
PIONEER COURT HOUSE	555 SW YAMHILL ST, PORTLAND OR	313 - F6
PIONEER MONUMENT	OFF MOUNT GLEN RD, UNION CO OR	130 - A2
POINT ELLICE HOUSE	2616 PLEASANT ST, CITY OF VICTORIA BC	256 - F7
PRAIRIE DIGGINGS	CANYON CITY EAST RD, GRANT CO OR	137 - B2
SAINT ROCH NATIONAL HISTORIC SITE	CHESTNUT ST, VANCOUVER BC	254 - E11
SAN JUAN ISLAND NATIONAL HISTORIC PARK	SAN JUAN ISLAND, SAN JUAN CO WA	101 - C2
SEATTLE BIRTHPLACE MONUMENT	ALKI AV SW & 63RD AV SW, SEATTLE WA	280 - B2

FEATURE NAME	City State	Page-Grid
TREATY ROCK HISTORIC SITE	POST FALLS ID	353 - F6
TRIBAL CULTURAL CENTER	1515 LAFAYETTE ST, STEILACOOM WA	181 - C4
WEATHERFORD HISTORICAL MONUMENT	JOHN DAY & CEDAR SPRINGS, GILLIAM CO OR	128 - A1
WHITE BIRD BATTLEFIELD	US 95 NORTH OF COPPERVILLE, IDAHO CO ID	131 - C1
WHITMAN MISSION NATIONAL HISTORIC SITE	US HWY 12, WALLA WALLA CO WA	121 - C3
YOMAN FERRY LANDING	YOMAN RD & VILLA BEACH RD, PIERCE CO WA	181 - B4

SHOPPING MALLS

FEATURE NAME	City State	Page-Grid
ALDERWOOD MALL	184TH ST SW & 33RD AV W, LYNNWOOD WA	171 - B5
BEAVERTON MALL	3205 SW CEDAR HILLS BLVD, BEAVERTON OR	199 - B2
BELLEVUE SQUARE	NE 8TH ST & BELLEVUE WY, BELLEVUE WA	175 - C2
CLACKAMAS PROMENADE	I-205 & SE SUNNYSIDE RD, CLACKAMAS CO OR	199 - D3
CLACKAMAS TOWN CENTER	I-205 & SE SUNNYSIDE RD, CLACKAMAS CO OR	199 - D3
CROSSROADS	156TH AV NE & NE 8TH ST, BELLEVUE WA	175 - D2
EVERETT MALL	1402 SE EVERETT MALL WY, EVERETT WA	268 - C6
FACTORIA SQUARE MALL	128TH AV SE & SE 38TH ST, BELLEVUE WA	175 - C3
FOREST GROVE CENTER	2333 PACIFIC AV, FOREST GROVE OR	198 - B1
GRESHAM TOWN FAIR	400 NW EASTMAN PKWY, GRESHAM OR	200 - B2
JANTZEN BEACH CENTER	1700 JANTZEN BEACH CTR, PORTLAND OR	305 - E7
LAKEWOOD MALL	10509 GRAVELLY LAKE DR SW, LAKEWOOD WA	181 - C4
LLOYD CENTER	2201 LLOYD CTR, PORTLAND OR	313 - H4
MALL 205	9900 SE WASHINGTON ST, PORTLAND OR	315 - H7
MARYSVILLE TOWN CENTER MALL	4TH ST & STATE AV, MARYSVILLE WA	171 - C1
NORTHGATE MALL	NE NORTHGATE WY & 1ST AV NE, SEATTLE WA	171 - B7
OREGON CITY CENTER	SE MCLOUGHLN BL & MAIN ST, OREGON CITY OR	199 - D4
OVERLAKE FASHION PLAZA	148TH AV NE & NE 24TH ST, REDMOND WA	175 - D2
SEATAC MALL	S 320TH ST & PACIFIC HWY, FEDERAL WAY WA	182 - B1
SOUTHCENTER MALL	TUKWILA PWY & SOUTHCENTER PWY, TUKWILA WA	289 - G5
SOUTH HILL MALL	9TH ST SW & 39TH AV SW, PUYALLUP WA	182 - B4
SUNSET ESPLANADE, THE	TUALATIN VALLEY HWY, HILLSBORO OR	198 - D1
TACOMA MALL	S 47TH ST & TACOMA MALL BLVD, TACOMA WA	294 - D3
VANCOUVER MALL	8700 NE VANCOUVER MALL DR, VANCOUVER WA	307 - F1
VANCOUVER PLAZA	NE FOURTH PLAIN BLVD, VANCOUVER WA	307 - E2
WASHINGTON SQUARE CENTER	9585 SW WASHINGTON SQUARE RD, TIGARD OR	199 - B3
WESTWOOD TOWN CENTER	SW BARTON ST & 25TH AV SW, SEATTLE WA	285 - F3

TRANSPORTATION

FEATURE NAME	City State	Page-Grid
AMTRAK STATION	211 RAILROAD AV S, EDMONDS WA	171 - A5
AMTRAK STATION	S KING ST & 2ND AV S, SEATTLE WA	278 - A7
AMTRAK STATION	W 11TH ST & HILL ST, VANCOUVER WA	305 - E5
AMTRAK PASSENGER STATION	1001 PUYALLUP AV, TACOMA WA	293 - J7
AMTRAK PASSENGER STATION	2900 BOND ST, EVERETT WA	264 - C4
ANTOINE PLANTE FERRY SITE	E WELLESLEY AV, TRENTWOOD WA	350 - H3
BARBUR BLVD TRANSIT CENTER	PACIFIC HWY W & INTERSTATE 5, PORTLAND OR	320 - A1
BEAVERTON TRANSIT CENTER	SW 117TH AV, BEAVERTON OR	199 - B2
BNSF STATION	BOND ST, EVERETT WA	264 - C4
CEDAR HILLS TRANSIT CENTER	SW WILSHIRE & SW MARLOW, WASHINGTON CO OR	199 - B1
CIVIC STADIUM MAX STATION	SW 18TH AV & SW MORRISON ST, PORTLAND OR	312 - D5
CLACKAMAS TOWN CENTER TRANSIT CENTER	SE MONTEREY AV, CLACKAMAS CO OR	199 - D3
CONVENTION CENTER MAX STATION	NE 3RD AV & NE HOLLADAY ST, PORTLAND OR	313 - G4
CONVENTION PLACE STATION	PINE ST & 9TH AV, SEATTLE WA	278 - A5
EDMONDS FERRY TERMINAL	MAIN ST & RAILROAD AV N, EDMONDS WA	171 - A5
FAUNTLEROY FERRY TERMINAL	FAUNTLEROY WY SW, SEATTLE WA	284 - C3
GALLERIA MAX STATION	SW 10TH AV & MORRISON ST, PORTLAND OR	313 - E6
GATEWAY TRANSIT CENTER & MAX STATION	NE PACIFIC ST & NE 99TH AV, PORTLAND OR	315 - H5
GOOSE HOLLOW MAX STATION	SW JEFFERSON ST & SW 20TH AV, PORTLAND OR	312 - D6
GRESHAM CITY HALL MAX STATION	NW EASTMAN PKWY, GRESHAM OR	200 - B2
HOLLYWOOD TRANSIT CENTER & MAX STATION	NE HALSEY ST & NE 39TH AV, PORTLAND OR	314 - B4
INTERNATIONAL DISTRICT STATION	4TH AV S & 2ND AV EXT S, SEATTLE WA	278 - A7
KETRON ISLAND FERRY TERMINAL	MORRIS BLVD, PIERCE CO WA	181 - B4
KINGS HILL MAX STATION	SW 18TH AV & SW SALMON ST, PORTLAND OR	312 - D6
LIBRARY & 9TH AV MAX STATION	SW 10TH AV & SW YAMHILL ST, PORTLAND OR	313 - E6
LLOYD CENTER MAX STATION	NE 11TH AV & NE HOLLADAY ST, PORTLAND OR	313 - H4
LYONS FERRY	HWY 261, FRANKLIN CO WA	121 - C2
MALL MONORAIL TERMINAL	4TH AV & PINE ST, SEATTLE WA	277 - J5
MAX STATION	NE 102ND AV & E BURNSIDE ST, PORTLAND OR	315 - H6
MAX STATION	NE 148TH AV & E BURNSIDE ST, PORTLAND OR	200 - A1
MAX STATION	NE 162ND AV & SE BURNSIDE RD, GRESHAM OR	200 - A1
MAX STATION	NE 172ND AV & SE BURNSIDE RD, GRESHAM OR	200 - A1
MAX STATION	NE 60TH AV, PORTLAND OR	314 - D5
MAX STATION	NE 7TH AV & NE HOLLADAY ST, PORTLAND OR	313 - H4
MAX STATION	NE 82ND AV & NE HALSEY ST, PORTLAND OR	315 - F4
MAX STATION	SW 1ST AV & SW OAK ST, PORTLAND OR	313 - F6
MAX STATION	SW 3RD AV & SW MORRISON ST, PORTLAND OR	313 - F6
MAX STATION	SW 4TH ST & SW YAMHILL ST, PORTLAND OR	313 - F6
MAX STATION	SW 5TH AV & SW MORRISON ST, PORTLAND OR	313 - F6
MILWAUKIE TRANSIT CENTER	SE MAIN ST & SE JACKSON ST, MILWAUKIE OR	321 - J2
MUKILTEO FERRY TERMINAL	MUKILTEO SPEEDWAY, MUKILTEO WA	171 - B2
OLD TOWN/CHINATOWN MAX STATION	NW 1ST AV & NW DAVIS ST, PORTLAND OR	313 - F5
OREGON CITY TRANSIT CENTER	MAIN ST & 12TH ST, OREGON CITY OR	199 - D4
PIONEER SQUARE STATION	JAMES ST & 3RD AV, SEATTLE WA	278 - A6
PIONEER SQUARE MAX STATION NORTH	SW MORRISON ST & SW 6TH ST, PORTLAND OR	313 - F6
PIONEER SQUARE MAX STATION SOUTH	SW YAMHILL ST & SW 6TH ST, PORTLAND OR	313 - F6
POINT DEFIANCE FERRY TERMINAL	ROUTE 163 & N WATERFRONT DR, TACOMA WA	181 - D1
RAPID TRANSIT STATION	LAKE OSWEGO OR	321 - F6
ROSE QUARTER CENTER & MAX STATION	NE WHEELER AV & MULTNOMAH ST, PORTLAND OR	313 - G4
RUBY JUNCTION MAX STATION	SE 197TH AV & SE BURNSIDE RD, GRESHAM OR	200 - A1
SKIDMORE FOUNTAIN MAX STATION	N BURNSIDE ST & SW 1ST AV, PORTLAND OR	313 - F5
SOUTHWORTH FERRY TERMINAL	RTE 160, KITSAP CO WA	174 - D4
STATE FERRY TERMINAL	OAKES AV, ANACORTES WA	259 - B3
STEILACOOM FERRY TERMINAL	UNION AV & COMMERCIAL ST, STEILACOOM WA	181 - B4
TAHLEQUAH FERRY TERMINAL	VASHON HWY SW & TAHLEQUAH RD, KING CO WA	181 - D1
TIGARD TRANSIT CENTER	SW MAIN ST & SW COMMERCIAL ST, TIGARD OR	199 - B3
TRANSIT CENTER	930 COMMERCE ST, TACOMA WA	293 - H5
UNION STATION	800 NW 6TH AV, PORTLAND OR	313 - F4
UNIVERSITY STREET STATION	UNIVERSITY ST & 3RD AV, SEATTLE WA	278 - A5
VASHON FERRY TERMINAL	VASHON HWY SW & 103RD AV SW, KING CO WA	174 - D4
WASHINGTON PARK MAX STATION	SW KNIGHT BLVD, PORTLAND OR	312 - B7
WASHINGTON STATE PIER 52 FERRY TERMINAL	801 ALASKAN WY, SEATTLE WA	277 - J6
WESTLAKE STATION	5TH AV & PINE ST, SEATTLE WA	278 - A5
YAMHILL DISTRICT MAX STATION	SW YAMHILL ST & SW 1ST ST, PORTLAND OR	313 - F6

WINERIES

FEATURE NAME	City State	Page-Grid
ALPINE VINEYARDS	25904 GREEN PEAK RD, BENTON CO OR	133 - A2
AMITY VINEYARDS	18150 AMITY VINEYRDS RD SE, YAMHILL CO OR	204 - B2
ARGYLE WINERY	691 HWY 99W, YAMHILL CO OR	198 - D6
ASHLAND VINEYARDS	2775 E MAIN ST, JACKSON CO OR	337 - H8
AUTUMN WIND VINEYARD	15225 NE NORTH VALLEY RD, YAMHILL CO OR	198 - C4
BAINBRIDGE ISLAND VINEYARDS & WINERY	OFF FERNCLIFF AV NE, WINSLOW WA	174 - D2
BETHEL HEIGHTS VINEYARD	6060 BETHEL HEIGHTS, POLK CO OR	204 - C3
BRIDGEVIEW VINEYARD AND WINERY	4210 HOLLAND LOOP RD, JOSEPHINE CO OR	233 - B4
CHATEAU BENOIT WINERY	6580 MINERAL SPRINGS RD, YAMHILL CO OR	198 - B6
CHATEAU BIANCA WINERY	17485 WILLAMINA-SALEM HWY, POLK CO OR	204 - A5
CHATEAU STE MICHELLE WINERY	14111 NE 145TH ST, WOODINVILLE WA	171 - C7
COLUMBIA WINERY	14030 NE 145TH ST, WOODINVILLE WA	171 - C7
COOPER MOUNTAIN VINEYARDS	9480 SW GRABHORN RD, WASHINGTON CO OR	199 - A2
DUCK POND CELLARS	23145 HWY 99W, YAMHILL CO OR	198 - C6
DUNDEE WINE CO	691 HWY 99W, DUNDEE OR	198 - C6
EDGEFIELD WINERY	2126 NE HALSEY ST, TROUTDALE OR	200 - B1
ELK COVE VINEYARDS	27751 NW OLSON RD, KALAMA WA	189 - D5
ELK COVE VINEYARDS	27751 OLSON RD, YAMHILL CO OR	198 - B3
FOOTE - E B WINERY	9354 4TH AV S, KING WA	286 - A4
FORIS VINEYARD WINERY	654 KENDALL RD, JOSEPHINE CO OR	233 - C5
FRENCH CREEK CELLARS	17721 132ND AV NE, WOODINVILLE WA	171 - C6
HINMAN VINEYARDS	27012 BRIGGS HILL RD, LANE CO OR	133 - B3
HINZERLING WINERY	PROSSER WA	120 - B3
HONEYWOOD WINERY	1350 HINES ST SE, SALEM OR	324 - J1
HOOD RIVER VINEYARDS	4693 WESTWOOD DR, HOOD RIVER CO OR	195 - C5
HOODSPORT WINERY	23501 US 101, MASON CO WA	173 - A6
KNUDSEN ERATH WINERY	17000 NE KNUDSEN LN, YAMHILL CO OR	198 - C6
KRAMER VINEYARD	26830 OLSON RD, YAMHILL CO OR	198 - B3
LANGE WINERY	18380 NE BUENA VISTA DR, YAMHILL CO OR	198 - C5
LAUREL RIDGE WINERY	46350 NW DAVID HILL RD, WASHINGTON CO OR	125 - B1
MANFRED VIERTHALER WINERY	17136 STATE HWY 410, PIERCE CO WA	182 - C4
MONTINORE VINEYARDS	3663 SW DILLEY RD, WASHINGTON CO OR	198 - B2
MOUNT BAKER VINEYARDS	4298 MOUNT BAKER HWY, WHATCOM CO WA	102 - B1
OAK KNOLL WINERY	29700 SW BUCKHALTER RD, WASHINGTON CO OR	198 - D2
PAUL THOMAS WINERY	1717 136TH PL NE, BELLEVUE WA	175 - C2
PONZI VINEYARDS	14665 SW WINERY LN, WASHINGTON CO OR	199 - A3
REX HILL VINEYARDS	30835 HWY 99W, YAMHILL CO OR	198 - D5
SHAFER VINEYARD CELLARS	6200 NW GALES CRK RD, WASHNGTON CO OR	125 - B1
SILVER LAKE SPARKLING CELLARS	17721 132ND AV NE, WOODINVILLE WA	171 - C7
SILVER LAKE WINERY	17616 15TH AV SE, SNOHOMISH CO WA	171 - C5
SISKIYOU VINEYARDS	6220 OREGON CAVES HWY, JOSEPHINE CO OR	233 - C4
SNOQUALMIE WINERY	1000 WINERY RD, KING CO WA	176 - C4
SOKOL BLOSSER WINERY	5000 SOKOL BLOSSER LN, YAMHILL CO OR	198 - C6
STRINGERS WINERY	FREMONT HWY, MODOC CO CA	152 - A3
TUALATIN VINEYARDS	10850 NW SEAVEY RD, WASHINGTON CO OR	125 - B1
UMPQUA ESTATE WINERY	HUBBARD CREEK RD, DOUGLAS CO OR	221 - A1
WASSON BROTHERS WINERY	41901 MOUNT HOOD HWY, CLACKAMAS CO OR	200 - D4
WEISINGERS WINERY & TASTING ROOM	3150 SISKIYOU BLVD, ASHLAND OR	337 - E9

PNW

INDEX

NOTES

Notes

NOTES

WHAT IS THOMAS BROS. MAPS® EDUCATIONAL FOUNDATION?

'homas Bros. Maps Educational
undation was established in 1989
bring geography awareness to
dents during the early years of
ir education. We find that even
youngest child can discover
helpful connection with the
nmunity by using local maps as
eography tool.
chools, libraries, museums and
nmunity service groups all have
cess to Thomas Bros. Maps
ucational Foundation. Here a
alth of resources -- ranging from
as and instructional materials to
ailed lesson plans -- are available
enhance learning by making
ography come alive for children.
orkshops, sponsored by the
undation staff, instruct teachers
v to integrate geography with other
ciplines such as history, science,
guage arts, and math to create a
sitive classroom experience.
tside the school setting, the
undation works with organizations
d community service groups to
ganize innovative hands-on
ography activities for children.

> "Our Children:
> Their World
> Our Challenge:
> Their Future"

SPECIAL PROGRAMS

"GEOGRAPHY IS EVERYWHERE"

Available to schools, libraries and other groups on request, "Geography Is Everywhere" *is a curriculum driven newsletter for teachers. Regular features include geography ideas, lessons plans, reviews of geography products, a theme bibliography and hands-on geography activities.*

COMMUNITY MAP KITS

A child gazing at a globe, asks "Where do I live?" To help students understand their community, we created the "Community Map Kit". Each kit includes one large wall map, 35 smaller laminated maps and two copies of Thomas Bros. Maps Street Guides. The wall map and laminated maps are selected by the teacher to best fit classroom needs.

GEOGRAPHY RESOURCE CENTER

The Center, located at Thomas Bros. Maps headquarters in Irvine, CA, houses resource books, children's literature, geography games, educational toys, globes, maps and software. Come in and share ideas with the Foundation staff!! All products are available for review and may be borrowed.

THE FOUNDATION'S MISSION

The Thomas Bros. Maps Educational Foundation is a public non-profit organization dedicated to expanding students' horizons through the study of geography, ethnic, cultural, social and human values.

The Foundation provides geography programs, assistance and education through:

- *Researching, designing and producing resource materials for teaching geography.*
- *Showing the value of integrating geographic concepts into various aspects of teaching curricula.*
- *Facilitating the exchange of ideas and resources among teachers and education administrators by providing networking opportunities and sponsoring seminars and workshops.*
- *Establishing and administering scholarships to study cartography and other geography-related disciplines.*

THOMAS BROS. MAPS®
EDUCATIONAL FOUNDATION
17731 COWAN, IRVINE, CA 92714
714-863-1984 • FAX 714-757-1564 • 800-899-6277

PRODUCT INFORMATION LIST

THOMAS GUIDES®

CALIFORNIA

ITEM #	DESCRIPTION
3028	Alameda County
4028	Alameda / Contra Costa Counties
4037	Alameda / Santa Clara Counties
3065	Central Valley Cities (All urban areas from Stockton to Bakersfield)
3027	Contra Costa County
4027	Contra Costa / Solano Counties
4025	Golden Gate (Marin, San Francisco, San Mateo, and Santa Clara Counties)
3054	Los Angeles County
4054	Los Angeles / Orange Counties
4053	Los Angeles / Ventura Counties
3025	Marin County
3042	Monterey County - '95 Edition
3055	Orange County
4055	Orange / Los Angeles Counties
3056	Riverside County
4056	Riverside / Orange Counties
4058	Riverside / San Diego Counties
3023	Sacramento County including portions of Placer & El Dorado Counties
4024	Sacramento / Solano Counties
3051	San Bernardino County
4051	San Bernardino / Riverside Counties
3057	San Diego County
4057	San Diego / Orange Counties
3035	San Francisco County
4030	San Francisco / Alameda / Contra Costa Counties
4026	San Francisco / San Mateo Counties
3036	San Mateo County
3052	Santa Barbara and San Luis Obispo Counties
4052	Santa Barbara and San Luis Obispo / Ventura Counties
3037	Santa Clara County
4036	Santa Clara / San Mateo Counties
3022	Solano County including portions of Napa & Yolo Counties
3020	Sonoma County - '95 Edition
3053	Ventura County

ARIZONA - NEVADA - OREGON - WASHINGTON

943340	Clark County, NV ***(NEW)***
3072	Phoenix Metro Area, AZ
3099	Portland Metro Area including Vancouver, portions of Columbia and Clark Counties, WA; Multnoma, Clackamas, and portions of Washington and Yamhill Counties, OR
3090	King County, WA
4090	King / Pierce Counties, WA
4091	King / Pierce / Snohomish Counties, WA
3091	Pierce County, WA
3087	Snohomish County, WA

WASHINGTON, D.C. & VICINITY

3086	Anne Arundel County, MD
3085	Howard County, MD
3088	Loudoun County, VA
3087	Prince William County, VA

ROAD ATLAS & DRIVER'S GUIDES

3001	California Road Atlas & Driver's Guide
3003	Pacific Northwest Road Atlas & Driver's Guide ***(NEW)***

METROPOLITAN THOMAS GUIDES®

CALIFORNIA

3002	Metropolitan Bay Area including the metropolitan areas of Alameda, Contra Costa, Marin, San Francisco, San Mateo, and Santa Clara Counties
3007	Metropolitan Inland Empire - Portrait format ***(NEW)*** Including metropolitan areas of San Bernardino, Riverside, Eastern Los Angeles, and Northeastern Orange Counties

NEW METROPOLITAN BALTIMORE, MD

3006	Metropolitan Baltimore, MD

METROPOLITAN WASHINGTON, D.C. & VICINITY

3004	Metropolitan Washington DC including Montgomery and Prince George's Counties, MD
3080	Montgomery County & the Beltway
3081	Northern Virginia & the Beltway
3082	Prince George's County & the Beltway

ZIP CODE EDITION THOMAS GUIDES®

CALIFORNIA

4328	Alameda / Contra Costa Counties
3365	Central Valley Cities (All urban areas from Stockton to Bakersfield)
4325	Golden Gate (Marin, San Francisco, San Mateo, and Santa Clara Counties)
3354	Los Angeles County
4354	Los Angeles / Orange Counties
4353	Los Angeles / Ventura Counties
3355	Orange County

ZIP CODE EDITION THOMAS GUIDES® CONT...

CALIFORNIA

3323	Sacramento County including portions of Placer & El Dorado Counties
4351	San Bernardino / Riverside Counties
3357	San Diego County (NEW Portrait format)
4352	Santa Barbara and San Luis Obispo / Ventura Counties
3337	Santa Clara County

OREGON - WASHINGTON

3399	Portland Metro Area including Vancouver, portions of Columbia and Clark Counties, WA; Multnoma, Clackamas, and portions of Washington and Yamhill Counties, OR
4391	King / Pierce / Snohomish Counties

CENSUS TRACT EDITION THOMAS GUIDES®

Thomas Guides with a Census Tract Overlay are available for many areas of California, Oregon, and Washington. Call for more information.

WALL MAPS

CALIFORNIA

7072	Bay Area includes 6 Bay Area Counties
7272	Bay Area includes 6 Bay Area Counties (with ZIP Codes)
8055	Bay Area Arterial (not available with oak sticks)
8001	Bay Area Freeway & Artery
8091	California Wall Map
6211	East Bay (Alameda / Contra Costa Counties) (with ZIP Codes)
6071	Los Angeles County - Central
6072	Los Angeles County - South
7068	Los Angeles / Orange Counties
7268	Los Angeles / Orange Counties (with ZIP Codes)
7054	Northern Los Angeles County (Antelope Valley to Downtown)
7254	Northern Los Angeles County (with ZIP Codes)
6074	Orange County
6250	Sacramento County including Placerville (with ZIP Codes)
6075	San Bernardino / Riverside Counties (Inland Empire)
7076	San Bernardino / Riverside Counties (extended coverage)
7276	San Bernardino / Riverside Counties (extended coverage with ZIP Codes)
7080	San Diego County
6048	San Diego County - North
6049	San Diego County - South
6070	San Fernando Valley
6006	San Francisco
6206	San Francisco (with ZIP Codes)
6073	San Gabriel Valley
7266	Santa Barbara / Ventura Counties (with ZIP Codes)
8054	Southern California Arterial (not available with oak sticks)
8145	Southern California Freeway & Artery
8045	Southern California Freeway & Artery (with page overlay)
6208	Southern Peninsula and South Bay (with ZIP Codes)
8056	State of California Wall Map (not available with oak sticks)

ARIZONA - OREGON - WASHINGTON

6085	Phoenix and Vicinity
6299	Portland Metropolitan Area (with ZIP Codes)
6081	King County
6084	Pierce County
6083	Snohomish County
7290	King / Pierce / Snohomish Counties (with ZIP Codes)

METROPOLITAN WASHINGTON, D.C. AND BALTIMORE, MD

6010	Washington DC
6012	Northern Virginia
6013	Montgomery County
6014	Baltimore

GEOFINDER® FOR WINDOWS®

Professional Desktop Mapping software for Metro areas in California, Washington, Oregon, Washington D.C. and Baltimore, MD. Also available - GeoFinder California (full state coverage). Call for more information.

NEW THOMAS GUIDE *DIGITALEDITION*™ (CD-ROM)

The only mapping software with Thomas Guide quality. Available for Metro areas in California, Washington, Oregon, Washington D.C., and Baltimore, MD. Call for more information.

EXPRESS MAPS & EXPRESS WALL MAPS™

Affordable, high quality custom maps designed to your specifications. You select the coverage, choose black & white or full-color, optional ZIP & Census overlays. Lamination & mounting additional. Call for more information.

For more information, or to order, please contact Customer Service at 1-800-899-6277 or e-mail us at cust-serv@thomas.com or visit us at our web site at www.thomas.com

Our Secure On-line Store is Now Open!

Information subject to change without notice